Occupational Outlook Handbook

2012-13 Edition

W9-CAE-834

U.S. Department of Labor
U.S. Bureau of Labor Statistics

April 2012

Bulletin 2800

Suggested Citation: U.S. Bureau of Labor Statistics, U.S. Department of Labor, *Occupational Outlook Handbook, 2012-13 Edition*, http://www.bls.gov/ooh/

Copyright, 2012
by
Claitor's Publishing Division

Paperbound ISBN: 1-59804-650-0
Hardbound ISBN: 1-59804-651-9

Published and for sale by:
CLAITOR'S PUBLISHING DIVISION
P.O. Box 261333, Baton Rouge, LA 70826-1333
800-274-1403 (In LA 225-344-0476)
Fax: 225-344-0480
e mail: claitors@claitors.com
World Wide Web: *http://www.claitors.com*

*We acknowledge the input and assistance of the U.S. Department of Labor, since much of the following is extracted from their website at http://www.bls.gov/ooh

Acknowledgments and Important Note

Acknowledgments

The Bureau of Labor Statistics produced the *Occupational Outlook Handbook* under the general guidance and direction of Dixie Sommers, Assistant Commissioner for Occupational Statistics and Employment Projections, and Kristina J. Bartsch, Chief, Division of Occupational Outlook, Office of Occupational Statistics and Employment Projections. Roger J. Moncarz and Teresa L. Morisi, Managers of Occupational Outlook Studies, provided planning and day-to-day direction.

Supervisors overseeing the research and preparation of material were Alissa Emmel, Henry T. Kasper, T. Alan Lacey, and Michael Wolf. Occupational analysts who contributed material were Domingo Angeles, Adam Bibler, Lauren Csorny, Tamara Dillon, Christopher Harper, Stanislava Ilic-Godfrey, David Kay, Jonathan Kelinson, Erin Lane, William Lawhorn, Daniel Leffel, Rebecca Madden Sturges, Kevin M. McCarron, Alice Ramey, Michael J. Rieley, Emily Richards, Craig Stalzer, Megan Sweitzer, Patricia Tate, Colleen D. Teixeira Moffat, Jeffrey Wilkins, and Alan Zilberman. Other staff members who contributed material were Jeffrey Gruenert, James Hamilton, Drew Liming, C. Brett Lockard, Brian Roberts, and Elka Maria Torpey.

Kathleen Green and Drew Liming, Office of Occupational Statistics and Employment Projections, and Janice (Ginny) Redish provided editorial work. Editorial work also was provided by Brian I. Baker, Edith S. Baker, Monica R. Gabor, Charlotte M. Irby, Lawrence H. Leith, Carol Boyd Leon, Maureen Soyars, and James Titkemeyer, all of the Office of Publications and Special Studies, and Richard M. Devens, formerly of the Office of Publications and Special Studies, all under the supervision of Leslie Brown Joyner and Terry L. Schau, Branch Chiefs, Editorial Services. Data processing and technical support was provided by C. Brett Lockard, Brian Roberts, D. Terkanian, and Dalton B. Terrell, under the supervision of Michael Wolf. Technical and computer programming support was provided by David Brumage, Daniel Murphy, Bakul Patel, Jerie Refugia, Dinara Sagatova, Roopa Sengupta, Connie Sielaff, Reginald Simmons, and Jo-Ann Yu, all of the Office of Technology and Survey Processing, under the supervision of Amrit Kohli, Divsion Chief, Enterprise Web Systems. Design and usability support was provided by Jean Fox, Brandon Kopp, and William Mockovak, all of the Office of Survey Methods Research. The cover art was designed by Keith Tapscott, Office of Publications and Special Studies.

The majority of photographs used in the *Handbook* are stock photographs; however, the Bureau of Labor Statistics wishes to express its appreciation to the organizations who contributed photographs. Situations portrayed in the photographs may not be free of every possible safety or health hazard. Depiction of a company or trade name in no way constitutes endorsement by the Department of Labor.

Important Note

Many trade associations, professional societies, unions, industrial organizations, and government agencies provide career information that is valuable to counselors and jobseekers. For the convenience of *Handbook* users, some of these organizations and their Internet addresses are listed at the end of each occupational profile. Although these references were carefully compiled, the Bureau of Labor Statistics has neither the authority nor the facilities for investigating the organizations or the information or publications that may be sent in response to a request. As a result, the Bureau cannot guarantee the accuracy of such information and the listing of an organization does not constitute in any way an endorsement or recommendation by the Bureau, either of the organization and its activities or of the information it may supply. Each organization has sole responsibility for whatever information it may issue.

The *Handbook* describes the job outlook over a projected 10-year period for occupations across the nation; consequently, short-term labor market fluctuations and regional differences in job outlook generally are not discussed. Similarly, the *Handbook* provides a general, composite description of jobs and cannot be expected to reflect work situations in specific establishments or localities. The *Handbook*, therefore, is not intended, and should never be used, for any legal purpose. For example, the *Handbook* should not be used as a guide for determining wages, hours of work, the right of a particular union to represent workers, appropriate bargaining units, or formal job evaluation systems. Nor should earnings data in the *Handbook* be used to compute future loss of earnings in adjudication proceedings involving work injuries or accidental deaths.

The Bureau of Labor Statistics has no role in establishing educational, licensing, or practicing standards for any occupation; any such standards are established by national accrediting organizations and are merely reported by BLS in the *Handbook*. The education information provided by the *Handbook* pertains to the typical requirements for entry into that occupation and does not describe the education and training of those individuals already employed in the occupation. In addition, education requirements for occupations may change over time and often vary by employer or state. Therefore, the information in the *Handbook* should not be used to determine if an applicant is qualified to enter a specific job in an occupation.

All text, charts, and tables are in the public domain, and, with appropriate credit, may be reproduced without permission. Most photographs and illustrations are protected by copyright. Comments about the contents of this publication and suggestions for improving it are welcome. Address all comments to Chief, Division of Occupational Outlook, Office of Occupational Statistics and Employment Projections, Bureau of Labor Statistics, U.S. Department of Labor, 2 Massachusetts Ave. NE, Room 2135, Washington, DC 20212. Phone: **(202) 691-5700**. FAX: **(202) 691-5745**. Email: Contact us . Additional information is available on the Home Page (http://www.bls.gov/ooh/home.htm). Information in the *Handbook* is available to sensory-impaired individuals upon request. Voice phone: **(202) 691-5200**; Federal Relay Service:

Contents

Overview of the 2010–20 Projections

Total employment is expected to increase by 20.5 million jobs from 2010 to 2020, with 88 percent of detailed occupations projected to experience employment growth. Industries and occupations related to health care, personal care and social assistance, and construction are projected to have the fastest job growth between 2010 and 2020. Jobs requiring a master's degree are expected to grow the fastest, while those requiring a high school diploma will experience the slowest growth over the 2010–20 timeframe. Slower population growth and a decreasing overall labor force participation rate are expected to lead to slower civilian labor force growth.

Job openings result from the relationship that exists among the population, the labor force, and the demand for goods and services. The population restricts the size of the labor force, which consists of working individuals and those looking for work. The size and productivity of the labor force limits the quantity of goods and services that can be produced. In addition, changes in the demand for goods and services influence which industries expand or contract. Industries respond by hiring the workers necessary to produce goods and provide services. However, improvements in technology and productivity, changes in which occupations perform certain tasks, and changes in the supply of workers all affect which occupations will be employed by those industries. Examining past and present changes in these relationships in order to project future shifts is the foundation of the Employment Projections program of the Bureau of Labor Statistics (BLS, the Bureau). This page presents highlights of BLS population, labor force, and occupational and industry employment projections for 2010–2020. For more information, visit the Employment Projections program.

The Bureau introduced a new education and training classification system with the 2010–2020 projections. The existing system was revised to show the different dimensions of education and training, rather than combining them into one category. The system also was revised to allow for educational distinctions between occupations that typically require a high school diploma and occupations that do not. The new system consists of three categories of information that BLS analysts have assigned to each detailed occupation: typical education needed for entry into the occupation, work experience in a related occupation, and typical on-the-job training needed to attain competency in the occupation.

Population

Shifts in the size and composition of the population can influence the U.S. economy. Several factors, including slower population growth, an aging population, and increasing diversity, are expected to affect the population over the coming decade. The U.S. civilian noninstitutional population, including individuals ages 16 and older, is expected to increase by 25.2 million from 2010 to 2020 (Chart 1). The projected growth rate of 10.6 percent is less than both the 12.4-percent growth rate experienced over the 1990–2000 period and the 11.9-percent rate posted for the 2000-10 period. As in the past few decades, population growth will vary by age group, race, and ethnicity. Minorities and immigrants are expected to constitute a larger share of the U.S. population in 2020. The Asian and Hispanic origin populations are projected to continue to grow much faster than other racial and ethnic groups, with the number of Asians growing at a rate of 34 percent and Hispanics, 37 percent.

As the population continues to age, older groups of Americans are expected to have more rapid growth than younger groups. The 16- to- 24 age group is anticipated to experience little population change, with a growth rate of 0.3 percent during 2010–20, while the population ages 25 to 34 is projected to grow 10.5 percent over same timeframe. Meanwhile, the 45- to- 54 age group is expected to shrink by 7.6 percent, reflecting the slower birthrate following the baby boom generation. As the baby boomers continue to age, the 55 - and - older population is projected to increase by 29.1 percent, more than any other age group.

Labor force

Like the population, the labor force is growing more slowly, becoming older and more diverse. The labor force is composed of all persons 16 years and older in the civilian noninstitutional population who either are employed or are unemployed but available and looking for work. The civilian labor force is projected to reach 164.4 million by 2020, an increase of 6.8 percent.

The U.S. workforce is projected to become more diverse by 2020. Among racial groups, Whites are expected to make up a decreasing share of the labor force while Blacks, Asians, and all

Chart 1. Numeric change in the population and labor force

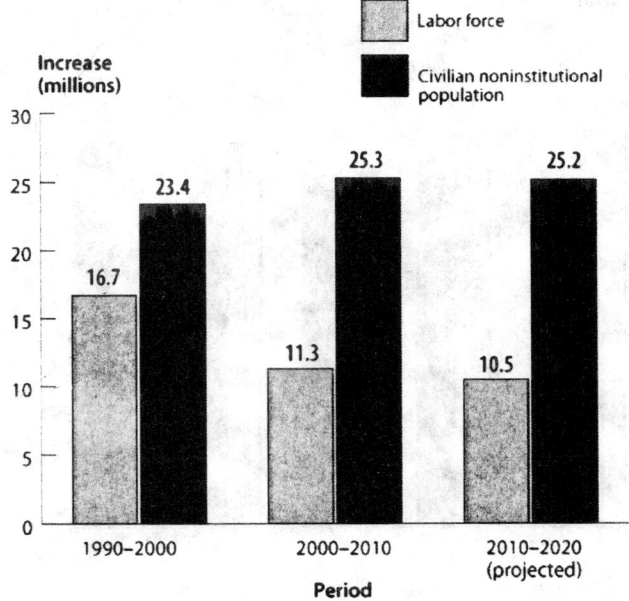

Source: BLS Division of Industry Employment Projections

Chart 2. Percent of labor force, by race and ethnic origin

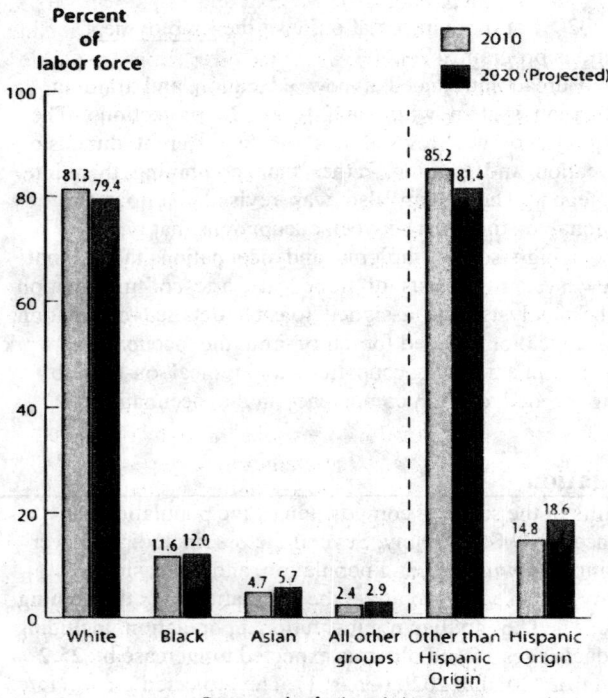

Note: The four race groups add to the total labor force. The two ethnic origin groups also add to the total labor force. Hispanics may be of any race.

Source: BLS Division of Industry Employment Projections

other groups will increase their share (Chart 2). Among ethnic groups, persons of Hispanic origin are projected to increase their share of the labor force from 14.8 percent to 18.6 percent.

The number of women in the labor force will grow at a slightly faster rate than the number of men. The male labor force is projected to grow by 6.3 percent from 2010 to 2020, compared with 7.4 percent for the female labor force.

The share of the youth labor force, workers ages 16 to 24, is expected to decrease from 13.6 percent in 2010 to 11.2 percent in 2020. The primary working - age group, those between 25 and 54 years old, is projected to decline from 66.9 percent of the labor force in 2010 to 63.7 percent in 2020. The share of workers ages 55 years and older, by contrast, are anticipated to leap from 19.5 percent to 25.2 percent of the labor force during the same period (Chart 3).

Employment

Total employment is expected to increase by 14 percent from 2010 to 2020, following a 2-percent decline in 2000–10. However, the 20.5 million jobs expected to be added by 2020 will not be evenly distributed across major industry and occupational groups. Changes in consumer demand, improvements in technology, and many other factors will contribute to the continually changing employment structure of the U.S. economy.

The next two sections examine projected employment change within industries and occupations. The industry

perspective is discussed in terms of wage and salary employment. The exception is employment in agriculture, which includes the self-employed and unpaid family workers in addition to wage and salary workers. The occupational profile is viewed in terms of total employment, including wage and salary workers, the self-employed, and unpaid family workers.

Employment change by industry

The analysis underlying BLS employment projections uses currently available information to focus on long-term structural changes in the economy. The 2010– 20 projections assume a full-employment economy in 2020. Because of the unpredictability of the business cycle over a 10-year period, the Bureau assumes that the economy will be at full employment in 2020 (the projection year). The December 2007–June 2009 recession had a large impact on U.S. employment, with some industries more affected than others. In many industries, employment had not recovered to prerecessionary levels by 2010. This fact, coupled with the assumed return to full employment, caused the projections to assume faster growth rates and more numerous openings than might have been expected in many industries and their occupations had the recession not occurred.

Goods-producing industries. Overall employment in these industries is expected to increase by 1.7 million new jobs, driven largely by rapid growth in construction. However, projected growth among the remaining goods-producing industries is expected to be slow or negative (Chart 4).

Agriculture, forestry, fishing, and hunting. Overall employment in agriculture, forestry, fishing, and hunting is expected to decrease by 4 percent. Employment is projected to

Chart 3. Percent of labor force, by age group

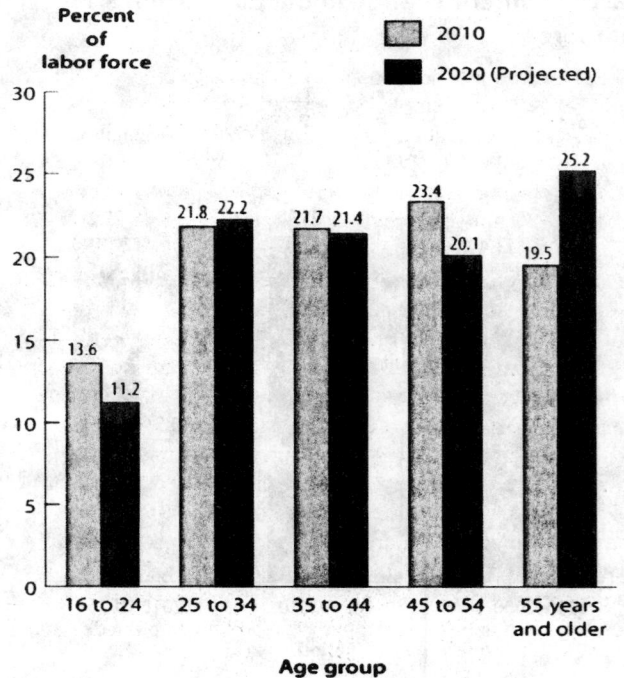

Source: BLS Division of Industry Employment Projections

Chart 4. Numeric change in wage and salary employment in goods-producing industries, 2010–20 (projected)

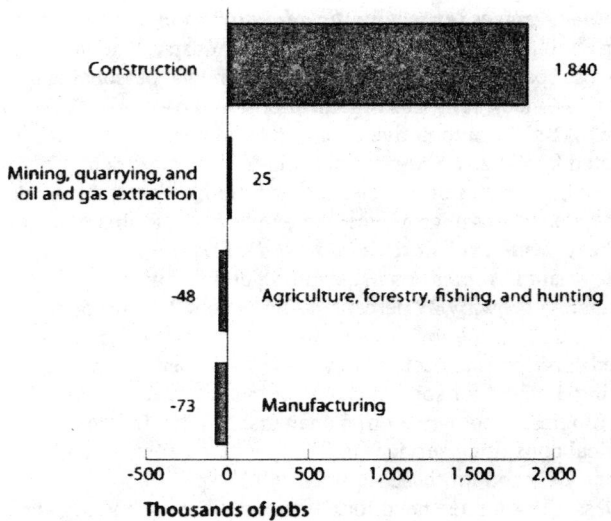

Source: BLS National Employment Matrix

continue to decline because of rising costs of production, more consolidation, and increases in productivity. Within this sector, the only industry that is expected to add jobs is logging, which is anticipated to grow by 6 percent. However, this growth rate corresponds to an increase of only 2,800 new jobs, because logging accounts for such a small share of the sector as a whole.

Construction. Employment in construction is expected to rise 33 percent by 2020, adding about 1.8 million jobs. All areas of construction are projected to contribute to the rapid job growth. The construction industry was hit hard by the recession, losing 2.2 million jobs from 2006 to 2010. Despite the fast projected growth rate, employment in the industry is not expected to recover to its prerecession level by 2020.

Manufacturing. Although output of manufactured goods is anticipated continue to increase, overall employment in this sector is projected to decline by 1 percent as productivity gains, automation, and international competition reduce the demand for labor in most manufacturing industries. The decline continues a trend witnessed during the recession, when the industry shed 2.6 million jobs from 2006 to 2010. Employment in computer and electronic product manufacturing is expected to decline by 14 percent over the decade, representing a loss of 156,800 jobs. Similarly, employment in machinery manufacturing, apparel manufacturing, and chemical manufacturing is expected to decline. However, employment in other manufacturing industries is projected to increase. For example, employment in fabricated metal product manufacturing is expected to grow by 12 percent, creating 151,600 new jobs. Other industries expected to add jobs are plastics and rubber products manufacturing and wood product manufacturing.

Mining, quarrying, and oil and gas extraction. Employment in mining, quarrying, and oil and gas extraction is projected to increase by 4 percent over the 2010–20 decade. Oil and gas

extraction and nonmetallic mineral mining and quarrying are expected to account for nearly all of the job growth in this industry, with growth rates of 15 percent and 14 percent, respectively. Coal and metal ore mining are expected to decline as support activities for mining is projected to experience little or no growth. Declining employment in these industries is attributable mainly to technology gains that boost worker productivity.

Service-providing industries. The employment shift in the U.S. economy away from goods-producing in favor of service-providing industries is expected to continue. Service-providing industries are anticipated to generate nearly 18 million new wage and salary jobs. As with goods-producing industries, growth among service-providing industries will vary (Chart 5).

Accommodation and food services. Employment in accommodation and food services is projected to grow by 9 percent, adding about 1 million new jobs through 2020. Job growth is expected to be concentrated in food services and drinking places, reflecting an increase in the population and the desire of timeconscious individuals to eat out.

Administrative and support and waste management and remediation services. Employment in this sector is expected to grow by 21 percent by 2020. Many new jobs will be created in employment services, an industry that is anticipated to account for 40 percent of all new jobs in the sector. Projected growth stems from the strong need for seasonal and temporary workers and for human resources services. The fastest growth in the industry is anticipated to be in waste collection, expected to grow 35 percent by 2020 through population growth and the privatization of waste collection services.

Arts, entertainment, and recreation. The arts, entertainment, and recreation industry is expected to grow by 18 percent through 2020. Most of the growth will be in the amusement,

Chart 5. Numeric change in wage and salary employment in service-providing industries, 2010–20 (projected)

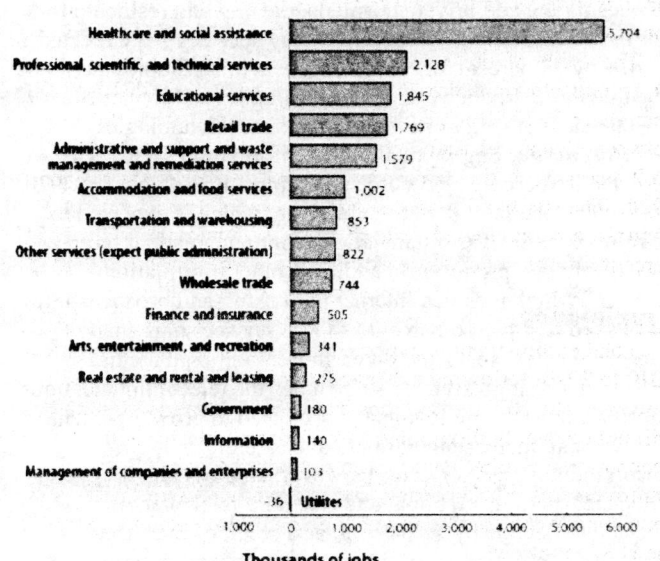

Source: BLS National Employment Matrix

gambling, and recreation sector. Job growth will stem from public participation in arts, entertainment, and recreation activities—reflecting increasing incomes, leisure time, and awareness of the health benefits of physical fitness.

Educational services. Employment in public and private educational services is anticipated to grow by 14 percent, adding about 1.8 million new jobs through 2020. Rising student enrollments at all levels of education are expected to create demand for educational services.

Finance and insurance. The finance and insurance industry is projected to increase by 9 percent from 2010 to 2020, resulting in 505,100 new jobs. Many of these jobs will stem from a recovery of the jobs lost during the recession. Employment in securities, commodity contracts, and other financial investments and related activities is expected to expand 25 percent by 2020. Growth will be driven by the wide range of financial assets available for trade, the number of baby boomers reaching retirement age and therefore seeking advice on retirement options, and the globalization of securities markets. Employment in credit intermediation and related activities, an industry that includes banks, is projected to grow by about 3 percent. Employment in insurance carriers and related activities is expected to grow by 9 percent, adding 194,800 new jobs by 2020. Growth will stem from both the needs of an increasing population and new insurance products on the market.

Government. Between 2010 and 2020, government employment, excluding employment in public education and hospitals, is expected to increase by 2 percent. Growth in government employment will be dampened by budgetary constraints and the outsourcing of government jobs to the private sector. Federal government employment, including jobs in the Postal Service, is expected to decline by 13 percent, as officials work to reduce the budget deficits and curb government spending. State and local governments, excluding education and hospitals, are anticipated to grow by 7 percent.

Healthcare and social assistance. The healthcare and social assistance industry is projected to create about 28 percent of all new jobs created in the U.S. economy. This industry—which includes public and private hospitals, nursing and residential care facilities, and individual and family services—is expected to grow by 33 percent, or 5.7 million new jobs. Employment growth will be driven by an aging population and longer life expectancies, as well as new treatments and technologies.

Information. Employment in the information sector is projected to increase by 5 percent, adding 140,300 jobs by 2020. The sector contains software publishing, which is expected to grow by 35 percent as organizations continue to adopt the newest software products. In addition, other information services," which includes Internet publishing and broadcasting, is expected to grow 16 percent as these services gain market share from newspapers and other, more traditional media.

The information sector also includes the telecommunications industry, in which employment is projected to grow 8 percent because of an increase in wireless and satellite telecommunications services. However, employment in newspaper, periodical, book, and directory publishers is expected to decline by 12 percent, as a result of increased efficiency in production, declining newspaper revenues, competition from Web publishers, and a trend toward using more freelance workers.

Management of companies and enterprises. Management of companies and enterprises is projected to grow relatively slowly, by 6 percent, as companies focus on reorganization to increase efficiency.

Other services (except public administration). Employment is expected to grow by 14 percent in this industry. The industry includes repair and maintenance establishments, personal and laundry services, religious organizations, and private households. The automotive repair and maintenance industry is expected to add 237,500 new jobs and have a 30 percent growth rate. As the number of vehicles on the road increases, the need for maintenance will grow, driving employment in this industry.

Professional, scientific, and technical services. Employment in professional, scientific, and technical services is projected to grow by 29 percent, adding about 2.1 million new jobs by 2020. Employment in computer systems design and related services is expected to increase by 47 percent, driven by growing demand for sophisticated computer network and mobile technologies. Employment in management, scientific, and technical consulting services is anticipated to expand, at 58 percent. Demand for these services will be spurred by businesses' continued need for advice on planning and logistics, the implementation of new technologies, and compliance with workplace safety, environmental, and employment regulations. Combined, the two industries—computer systems design and related services and management, scientific, and technical consulting services—will account for more than half of all new jobs in professional, scientific, and technical services.

Real estate and rental and leasing. The real estate and rental and leasing industry is expected to grow by 14 percent through 2020, a rate that will recover many of the jobs lost during the housing downturn. Growth will be due to increased demand for housing as the housing market recovers and the population continues to expand. Activities related to real estate, which includes the offices of property managers and real estate appraisers, is expected to add the most jobs within this industry over the 2010–20 period.

Retail trade. Employment in retail trade is expected to increase by 12 percent, adding approximately 1.8 million new jobs from 2010 to 2020. This growth reflects an increasing population and a projected rise in personal consumption over the next decade.

Transportation and warehousing. Employment in transportation and warehousing is expected to increase by 20 percent during 2010–20, adding about 853,000 jobs to the industry total. Truck transportation is anticipated to grow by 24 percent, and the warehousing and storage sector is projected to grow by 26 percent. Demand for truck transportation and warehousing services will expand as global trade grows and more goods are transported into and around the country.

Utilities. Overall employment in utilities is projected to decrease by 6 percent through 2020. Despite increased output, employment in electric power generation, transmission, and distribution is expected to decline because of improved technology that will increase worker productivity. However, employment in the water, sewage, and other systems industry is anticipated to increase 26 percent by 2020. As the population continues to grow, more water treatment facilities are being built, driving growth in this industry.

Wholesale trade. The number of workers in wholesale trade

Chart 6. Percent change in total employment, by occupational group, 2010–20 (projected)

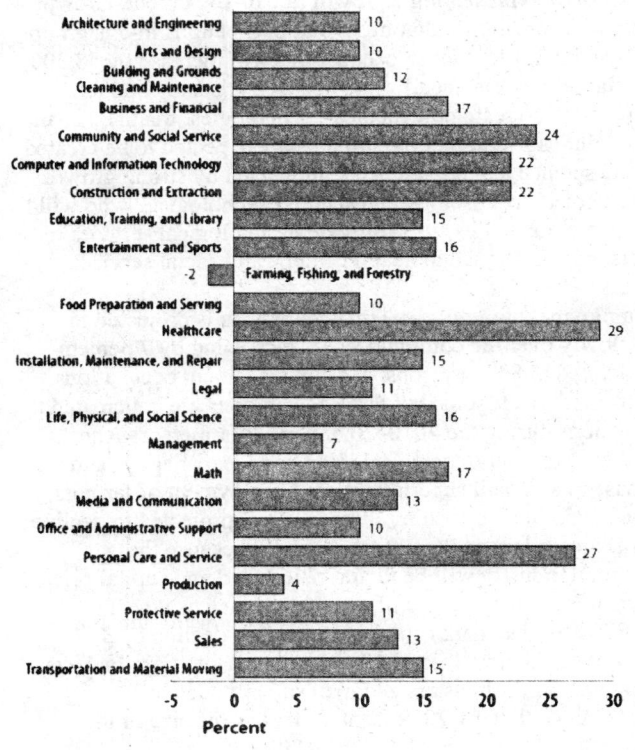

Occupational group	Percent
Architecture and Engineering	10
Arts and Design	10
Building and Grounds Cleaning and Maintenance	12
Business and Financial	17
Community and Social Service	24
Computer and Information Technology	22
Construction and Extraction	22
Education, Training, and Library	15
Entertainment and Sports	16
Farming, Fishing, and Forestry	-2
Food Preparation and Serving	10
Healthcare	29
Installation, Maintenance, and Repair	15
Legal	11
Life, Physical, and Social Science	16
Management	7
Math	17
Media and Communication	13
Office and Administrative Support	10
Personal Care and Service	27
Production	4
Protective Service	11
Sales	13
Transportation and Material Moving	15

Source: BLS Division of Occupational Outlook

is projected to increase by 14 percent over the next decade, adding about 744,100 jobs. Wholesale electronic markets and agents and brokers are expected to see the most growth in the industry, adding 342,100 new jobs.

Employment change by occupation

Demand for occupations is affected by industry growth or decline, among other factors, including productivity increases and changes in business practices. Job growth is projected to vary among major occupational groups (Chart 6).

Architecture and engineering occupations are projected to add roughly 252,800 jobs, representing a growth rate of 10 percent. Much of the growth in this group will be due to recovery from the recession, with 149,800 jobs having been lost from 2006 to 2010. Growth among engineering occupations, especially civil engineers, is expected to be high, with the occupation adding 51,100 positions. As the nation's infrastructure ages, a greater emphasis will be placed on maintaining existing structures as well as designing and implementing new roads, water systems, and pollution control systems.

Employment in *arts and design* occupations is projected to grow by 10 percent from 2010 to 2020, resulting in almost 76,100 new jobs. Nearly half of this growth is expected to occur among graphic designers. As more advertising is conducted over the Internet, a medium that generally includes many graphics, and as businesses increasingly seek professional design services, a greater number of graphic designers will be needed.

Employment in *building and grounds cleaning and maintenance* occupations is expected to grow by almost 664,000 jobs over the next decade, representing a growth rate of 12 percent. Part of the employment growth will be due to recovering some of the 246,100 jobs lost to the recession. As businesses continue to value the appearance of their surrounding grounds, and as households increasingly rely on contract workers to maintain their yards, grounds maintenance workers will see rapid employment growth. In addition, more building cleaning workers will be needed to maintain an increasing number of facilities, especially those related to health care.

Employment in *business and financial operations* occupations is projected to grow by 17 percent, resulting in 1.2 million new jobs. Some of these jobs make up for jobs lost during the recession. In addition, increasing financial regulations and the need for greater accountability and more oversight will drive demand for accountants and auditors, adding roughly 190,700 jobs to that occupation from 2010 to 2020. Further, as companies look for ways to control costs, demand will grow for management analysts, an occupation that is expected to add 157,200 jobs. Together, these two occupations are anticipated to account for 30 percent of new business and financial operations jobs.

Employment in *community and social services* occupations is projected to increase by 24 percent, representing roughly 582,300 jobs. As health insurance providers increasingly cover mental and behavioral health treatment, and as of the population of elderly people grows, the elderly will seek more and more social services and demand for these workers will rise.

Computer and information technology occupations are projected to grow by 22 percent, adding 758,800 new jobs from 2010 to 2020. Demand for workers in these occupations will be driven by the continuing need for businesses, government agencies, and other organizations to adopt and utilize the latest technologies. Workers in these occupations will be needed to develop software, increase cybersecurity, and update existing network infrastructure.

Construction and extraction workers build new residential and commercial buildings, roads, bridges, and other structures, and work in mines, quarries, and oil and gas fields. Employment of these workers is expected to grow 22 percent, adding about 1.4 million new jobs over the 2010–20 period. Construction trades and related workers, such as carpenters, painters, and plumbers, will account for about 1.1 million of these jobs. Gains will be widespread throughout this group, with construction laborers, carpenters, and electricians experiencing significant increases in employment. Job growth will result from increased construction of homes and office buildings, as well as from remodeling projects and the repair and replacement of the nation's infrastructure.

Most of these occupations are concentrated in the construction industry, which is projected to grow quickly, adding more than 1.8 million new jobs between 2010 and 2020. However, a large proportion of the projected gains reflect the recovery of nearly 2 million construction and extraction jobs lost to the 2007–09 recession, so employment is not expected to return to its prerecession level by 2020.

Education, training, and library occupations are anticipated to add more than 1.4 million jobs, representing a growth rate of more than 15 percent. As the school-age population increases, demand for elementary and middle school teachers and for teacher assistants will rise. In addition, more students are seeking higher education to meet their career goals, increasing demand for postsecondary teachers.

Entertainment and sports occupations will grow by 16 percent, resulting in 128,900 new jobs by 2020. Increasing demand for coaches and scouts will account for more than half of employment growth in this group of occupations.

Farming, fishing, and forestry workers cultivate plants and breed and raise livestock. Employment in these occupations is projected to decline by about 2 percent, with 19,400 jobs lost by 2020. Productivity increases in agriculture will be a prime cause of the decline, offsetting small gains among forest, conservation, and logging workers.

Employment in *food preparation and serving* occupations is projected to increase by roughly 1.1 million jobs from 2010 to 2020, reflecting a growth rate of 10 percent. Some of the growth will be the result of recovering jobs lost just prior to, during, and just after the recession—202,100 from 2006 to 2010. Growth will stem from time-conscious consumers patronizing fast-food establishments and full-service restaurants. Thirty-nine percent of this growth is expected to occur among fast-food and counter workers as customers continue to rely on low-price food options.

Employment among *healthcare* occupations is expected to increase by 29 percent. This growth, resulting in a projected 3.5 million new jobs, will be driven by increasing demand for healthcare services. As the number of elderly individuals continues to grow, and as new developments allow for the treatment of more medical conditions, more healthcare professionals will be needed. Within this group, two occupations are expected to add a substantial number of jobs: registered nurses, with some 711,900 new jobs; and home health aides, with roughly 706,300 new jobs. Much of the growth in this pair of occupations will be the result of increased demand for healthcare services as the expanding elderly population requires more care.

Workers in *installation, maintenance, and repair* occupations install new equipment and maintain and repair existing equipment. These occupations are projected to add 800,200 jobs by 2020, growing by 15 percent. Job growth will be widespread among the occupations in the group, because workers in these occupations are integral to the maintenance and development of buildings, communication structures, transportation systems, and other types of infrastructure. Demand will increase as customers opt to make repairs rather than buy new items. However, nearly half of the job growth will be due to economic recovery, given that these occupations lost 454,700 jobs between 2006 and 2010. Jobs in this occupational group are closely tied to the housing market, and as it recovers, demand for installation, maintenance, and repair workers will increase.

Legal occupations will increase by about 131,000, representing a growth rate of 11 percent. Lawyers will account for 73,600 of these new jobs. This growth reflects continued demand for legal services from government, individuals, and businesses alike. Paralegals and legal assistants are expected to account for 46,900 new jobs as legal establishments attempt to reduce costs by assigning these workers more tasks that were once performed by lawyers.

Employment in *life, physical, and social science* occupations is projected to increase by nearly 190,800 jobs from 2010 to 2020, representing a growth rate of 16 percent. Growth will be widespread throughout several occupations in this group. Employment in life science occupations will increase by 58,300, driven largely by the need for medical scientists to conduct research and to create new medical technologies, treatments, and pharmaceuticals. Another 56,500 jobs are expected to be created in social science and related occupations, led by strong growth among clinical, counseling, and school psychologists, who will be in greater demand as they provide psychological services in schools, hospitals, mental health centers, and social services agencies.

Employment in *management* occupations is projected to grow slowly over the coming decade, increasing by 7 percent and adding 615,800 new jobs. Most management occupations are expected to add jobs, but three occupations are anticipated to cut positions during the 2010–2020 period: farmers, ranchers, and other agricultural managers, food service managers, and postmasters and mail superintendents Employment of farmers, ranchers, and other agricultural managers is projected to decline by 8 percent, a loss of 96,100 jobs, chiefly because the agricultural industry will be facing rising land and capital prices and declining sales of some of its outputs, such as wheat and corn. Food service managers are expected to decline by 3 percent, resulting in a loss of 10,600 jobs. Due to tight budgets, employment of postmasters and mail superintendents is projected to decline by 28 percent, however, the size of the occupation will result in the loss of 6,800 jobs.

Employment in *math* occupations is expected to grow by 17 percent, adding 19,500 jobs by 2020. About half of these positions, 9,400, will be occupied by operations research analysts. Demand for these workers will increase as technology advances and companies need analysts to help them turn data into valuable information that can be used by managers to make better decisions in all aspects of their business.

Media and communications occupations are projected to experience employment growth of 13 percent, adding 106,100 jobs, led by rapid growth among public relations specialists. The growth of social media will result in the need for more workers to maintain an organization's public image. Interpreters and translators are also expected to add a significant number of jobs by 2020 as demand for these workers grows because of both a large increase in the number of non–English-speaking people in the United States and continued globalization.

Office and administrative support workers perform the day-to-day activities of an office, such as preparing and filing documents, dealing with the public, and distributing information. Employment in these occupations is expected to grow by 10 percent, adding 2.3 million new jobs by 2020. Most job gains in these occupations represent recovery from the recession: the occupational group lost 1.7 million jobs from 2006 to 2010. General office clerks, who are needed to carry out a variety of daily tasks in the workplace, will add 489,500 new jobs, the largest number of new jobs among all office and administrative support workers. Customer service representatives also are projected to experience employment growth, adding 338,400 new jobs as businesses increasingly emphasize building customer relationships in an effort to differentiate themselves from competitors. In addition, large gains in employment are expected for bookkeeping, accounting, and auditing clerks, as well as among receptionists and information clerks.

Employment in *personal care and service* occupations is anticipated to grow by 27 percent over the next decade, adding more than 1.3 million jobs. As consumers become more concerned with health, beauty, and fitness, the number of cosmetic and health spas will rise, causing an increase in demand for workers in this group. The personal care and service group contains a wide variety of occupations; however, two of them—personal care aides and childcare workers— will account for nearly two-thirds of the group's new jobs. Personal and home care aides will experience increased demand as a growing number of elderly people require assistance with daily tasks. Childcare workers will add jobs as the population of children continues to grow and emphasis is increasingly placed on the importance of early childhood education, resulting in more formal preschool programs. These programs will increase demand for both childcare workers and preschool teachers.

Production workers are employed mainly in manufacturing, where they assemble goods and operate plants. Production occupations are expected to grow by just 4 percent, adding 356,800 jobs by 2020. These new jobs represent less than 20 percent of the 2.1 million jobs lost by this group from 2006 to 2010. Textile, apparel, and furnishing workers are projected to lose 65,500 jobs by 2020 as improvements in productivity reduce the need for these workers, and as a growing number of jobs in the occupation are offshored, demand for production workers will decline. However, some production jobs will still be created over the next decade, mostly in metal and plastic working and in assembling and fabricating.

Protective service occupations are expected to add about 364,500 jobs, reflecting an 11-percent growth rate. More than half of the job growth in this group will occur among security guards. Demand for these workers will stem from business and other organizations that have concerns about crime and vandalism. In addition, demand for law enforcement workers will increase as the nation seeks to maintain the safety of its growing population.

Sales workers solicit goods and services for businesses and consumers. Sales and related occupations are expected to add 1.9 million new jobs by 2020, offsetting the 1.1 million jobs lost in these occupations from 2006 to 2010. As organizations offer a wider array of products and devote an increasing share of their resources to customer service, many new retail sales workers will be needed. More than half of the job growth in this group will occur in retail sales establishments.

Transportation and material moving workers transport people and materials by land, sea, or air. Employment of these workers is anticipated to increase by 15 percent, accounting for 1.3 million new jobs, nearly restoring employment to prerecession levels. These occupations lost 1.3 million jobs from 2006 to 2010. As the economy grows over the 2010–20 period and the demand for goods increases, truck drivers will be needed to transport those goods to businesses, consumers, and others. In addition, employment of laborers and hand, freight, stock and material movers will increase as these workers increasingly are needed to work in more warehouses because of an expected rise in consumer spending.

Employment Change by Detailed Occupation

Occupational growth can be considered in two ways: by the rate of growth and by the number of new jobs created by growth. Some occupations both have a fast growth rate and create a large number of new jobs. However, an occupation that employs few workers may experience rapid growth, but the resulting number of new jobs may be small. For example, a small occupation that employs just 1,000 workers and is projected to grow 50 percent over a 10-year period will add only 500 jobs. By contrast, a large occupation that employs 1.5 million workers may experience only 10 percent growth, but will add 150,000 jobs. As a result, to get a complete picture of employment growth, both measures must be considered.

Occupations with the fastest growth. Of the 20 fastest growing occupations in the economy (Table 1), several are related to healthcare. Employment in healthcare-related occupations is expected to continue to grow rapidly, in large part because of an aging population that will require more medical care. In addition, some healthcare occupations will be in greater demand for other reasons. As healthcare costs continue to rise, work is increasingly being delegated to lower paid workers in order to cut costs. For example, tasks that were previously performed by doctors, nurses, dentists, or other healthcare professionals increasingly are being performed by physician assistants, medical assistants, and physical therapist aides. Furthermore, patients increasingly are seeking home care as an alternative to costly stays in hospitals or residential care facilities, causing a significant increase in demand for home health aides. Although not classified as healthcare workers, personal and home care aides are being affected by this demand for home care as well.

Six of the fastest growing detailed occupations are in the construction and extraction occupational group. Helpers of brickmasons, blockmasons, stonemasons, and tile and marble setters and helpers of carpenters are projected to be the fourth- and fifth-fastest growing occupations, respectively. As the economy recovers from the 2007-09 recession, demand for these workers will increase as population growth contributes to the need for schools, hospitals, apartment buildings, and other structures. In addition, these helpers are needed to repair existing buildings, roads, and bridges. Also among the fastest growing occupations are reinforcing iron and rebar workers; helpers of pipelayers, plumbers, pipefitters, and steamfitters; glaziers; and brickmasons and blockmasons. Combined, these occupations are projected to add 132,900 jobs by 2020; however, most of these occupations will not reach the level of employment that they experienced prior to the recession.

Two business and financial operations occupations are included in the top 20 fastest growing occupations. By 2020, meeting, convention, and event planners and market research analysts and marketing specialists are expected to increase their employment by 44 percent and 41 percent, respectively. Demand for these workers will stem from the growing importance of meetings and conventions as businesses and other organizations become increasingly international. In addition, employment growth will be driven by an increased use of data and market research across all industries in order to understand the needs and wants of customers and measure the effectiveness of marketing and business strategies.

Table 1. Occupations with the fastest growth, projected 2010-20

Matrix Code	Occupation	Percent Change	Number of new jobs added	Wages (May 2010 median)	Entry-level Education	Related Work Experience	On-the-job Training
39-9021	Personal Care Aides	70	607,000	$19,640	Less than high school	None	Short-term on-the-job training
31-1011	Home Health Aides	69	706,300	20,560	Less than high school	None	Short-term on-the-job training
17-2031	Biomedical Engineers	62	9,700	81,540	Bachelor's degree	None	None
47-3011	Helpers--Brickmasons, Blockmasons, Stonemasons, and Tile and Marble Setters	60	17,600	27,780	Less than high school	None	Short-term on-the-job training
47-3012	Helpers--Carpenters	56	25,900	25,760	Less than high school	None	Short-term on-the-job training
29-2056	Veterinary Technologists and Technicians	52	41,700	29,710	Associate's degree	None	None
47-2171	Reinforcing Iron and Rebar Workers	49	9,300	38,430	High school diploma or equivalent	None	Apprenticeship
31-2021	Physical Therapist Assistants	46	30,800	49,690	Associate's degree	None	None
47-3015	Helpers--Pipelayers, Plumbers, Pipefitters, and Steamfitters	45	26,300	26,740	High school diploma or equivalent	None	Short-term on-the-job training
13-1121	Meeting, Convention, and Event Planners	44	31,300	45,260	Bachelor's degree	Less than 1 year	None
29-2032	Diagnostic Medical Sonographers	44	23,400	64,380	Associate's degree	None	None
31-2011	Occupational Therapy Assistants	43	12,300	51,010	Associate's degree	None	None
31-2022	Physical Therapist Aides	43	20,300	23,680	High school diploma or equivalent	None	Moderate-term on-the-job training
47-2121	Glaziers	42	17,700	36,640	High school diploma or equivalent	None	Apprenticeship
27-3091	Interpreters and Translators	42	24,600	43,300	Bachelor's degree	None	Long-term on-the-job training
43-6013	Medical Secretaries	41	210,200	30,530	High school diploma or equivalent	None	Moderate-term on-the-job training
13-1161	Market Research Analysts and Marketing Specialists	41	116,600	60,570	Bachelor's degree	None	None
21-1013	Marriage and Family Therapists	41	14,800	45,720	Master's degree	None	Internship/ residency
47-2021	Brickmasons and Blockmasons	41	36,100	46,930	High school diploma or equivalent	None	Apprenticeship
29-1123	Physical Therapists	39	77,400	76,310	Doctoral or professional degree	None	None

SOURCE: BLS Occupational Employment Statistics and Division of Occupational Outlook

Biomedical engineers are projected to be the third-fastest growing occupation in the economy. However, because of its small size, this occupation is projected to add only about 9,700 jobs. Biomedical engineers will be needed as the general population increasingly emphasizes health issues and demand for the medical devices and equipment designed by these workers rises. For example, the aging of the baby-boom generation will increase demand for biomedical devices and procedures, such as hip and knee replacements.

Of the 20 fastest growing occupations, half are in the associate degree or higher category. Nine of these occupations pay at least $10,000 more than the national annual median wage, which was $33,840 in May 2010. In fact, two of the occupations paid at least twice the national median in May 2010.

Occupations with the largest numerical growth. The 20 occupations projected to have the most new jobs are expected to account for more than onethird of all new jobs—7.4 million combined—over the 2010–20 period (Table 2). The occupations with the largest numerical increases cover a wider range of occupational categories than do those occupations with the

Table 2. Occupations with the largest numeric growth, projected 2010-20

Matrix Code	Occupation	Number of new jobs added	Percent change	Wages (May 2010 median)	Entry-Level Education	Related Work Experience	On-the-job Training
29-1111	Registered Nurses	711,900	26	$64,690	Associate's degree	None	None
41-2031	Retail Salespersons	706,800	17	20,670	Less than high school	None	Short-term on-the-job training
31-1011	Home Health Aides	706,300	69	20,560	Less than high school	None	Short-term on-the-job training
39-9021	Personal Care Aides	607,000	70	19,640	Less than high school	None	Short-term on-the-job training
43-9061	Office Clerks, General	489,500	17	26,610	High school diploma or equivalent	None	Short-term on-the-job training
35-3021	Combined Food Preparation and Serving Workers, Including Fast Food	398,000	15	17,950	Less than high school	None	Short-term on-the-job training
43-4051	Customer Service Representatives	338,400	15	30,460	High school diploma or equivalent	None	Short-term on-the-job training
53-3032	Heavy and Tractor-Trailer Truck Drivers	330,100	21	37,770	High school diploma or equivalent	1 to 5 years	Short-term on-the-job training
53-7062	Laborers and Freight, Stock, and Material Movers, Hand	319,100	15	23,460	Less than high school	None	Short-term on-the-job training
25-1000	Postsecondary Teachers	305,700	17	62,050	Doctoral or professional degree	None	None
31-1012	Nursing Aides, Orderlies, and Attendants	302,000	20	24,010	Postsecondary non-degree award	None	None
39-9011	Childcare Workers	262,000	20	19,300	High school diploma or equivalent	None	Short-term on-the-job training
43-3031	Bookkeeping, Accounting, and Auditing Clerks	259,000	14	34,030	High school diploma or equivalent	None	Moderate-term on-the-job training
41-2011	Cashiers	250,200	7	18,500	Less than high school	None	Short-term on-the-job training
25-2021	Elementary School Teachers, Except Special Education	248,800	17	51,660	Bachelor's degree	None	Internship/ residency
43-4171	Receptionists and Information Clerks	248,500	24	25,240	High school diploma or equivalent	None	Short-term on-the-job training
37-2011	Janitors and Cleaners, Except Maids and Housekeeping Cleaners	246,400	11	22,210	Less than high school	None	Short-term on-the-job training
37-3011	Landscaping and Groundskeeping Workers	240,800	21	23,400	Less than high school	None	Short-term on-the-job training
41-4012	Sales Representatives, Wholesale and Manufacturing, Except Technical and Scientific Products	223,400	16	52,440	High school diploma or equivalent	None	Moderate-term on-the-job training
47-2061	Construction Laborers	212,400	21	29,280	Less than high school	None	Short-term on-the-job training

SOURCE: BLS Occupational Employment Statistics and Division of Occupational Outlook

fastest growth rates. Healthcare occupations will account for some of these increases in employment, as will occupations in sales, office and administrative support, education, building and groundskeeping, personal care, and transportation.

Of the 20 occupations with the largest growth, one-fifth are in the office and administrative support services group. Together, these four occupations — bookkeeping, accounting and auditing clerks, customer service representatives, general office clerks, and receptionists and information clerks, are expected to grow by 1.3 million jobs, accounting for about 18 percent of job growth among the 20 occupations with the largest growth. Only 2 out of the 20 fastest growing occupations — home health aides and personal care aides — also are projected to be among the 20 occupations with the largest numerical increases in employment.

The education categories and wages of the occupations with the largest numbers of new jobs are considerably different than those of the fastest growing occupations. Only three of these occupations are in the associate's degree or higher category. Fourteen of the 20 occupations with the largest numbers of new jobs paid less than the national median wage of $33,840 in May 2010.

Declining occupations. Declining occupational employment stems from falling industry employment, technological advances, changes in business practices, and other factors. Almost all of the occupations that are projected to decline the fastest fall into two occupational groups. Eleven of the twenty fastest declining occupations are in the production occupational group; examples are shoe machine operators and tenders and fabric and apparel patternmakers, declining by 53 percent and 36 percent, respectively. Together, the 11 production occupations

are projected to shed 77,300 jobs by 2020.

Seven of the twenty occupations that are projected to decline the fastest are in the office and administrative support staff occupational group. The seven occupations are expected to contribute to a loss of 143,300 jobs over the coming decade (Table 3). Included among these fastest declining office and administrative support jobs are several postal service occupations. Postal service mail sorters, processors, and processing machine operators, the fastest declining office and administrative support occupation, are expected to decline by 49 percent. Both production occupations and office and administrative support occupations are adversely affected by increasing factory automation or the implementation of office technology, reducing the need for workers in those occupations. The difference between the office and administrative support occupations that are expected to experience the largest declines and those which are expected to see the largest increases is the extent to which job functions can be easily automated or performed by other workers. For instance, the duties of receptionists and customer service representatives involve a great deal of personal interaction, so automating their jobs is difficult or not desirable, whereas the duties of some file clerks, operators, and data entry workers can be automated or performed by other workers, such as administrative assistants.

Although farmers, ranchers, and other agricultural managers are not among the fastest declining occupations, their employment is projected to drop by 96,100, the most of any occupation.

Only three of the occupations with the fastest percent decline are in a category that indicates workers have any postsecondary education. Thirteen of these occupations paid less than the national median wage of $33,840 in May 2010.

Employment change by education category

The Bureau has introduced a new education and training classification system that consists of three categories of information: 1) Typical education needed for entry, 2) Work experience in a related occupation, and 3) Typical on-the-job training needed to obtain competency in the occupation. Growth for each education and training category is calculated by adding the growth across all occupations in the category. As a result, there is some variation in the growth rates among categories.

Occupations that require some postsecondary education are expected to experience slightly higher rates of growth than those which require high school diploma or less. Occupations in the master's degree category are projected to grow the fastest, about 22 percent; occupations in the bachelor's and associate's degree categories are anticipated to grow by about 17 percent and 18 percent, respectively, and occupations in the doctoral or professional degree category are expected to grow by about 20 percent. In contrast, occupations in the high school category are expected to grow by just 12 percent, while occupations in the less than high school diploma or equivalent category are projected to grow by 14 percent (Chart 7).

Chart 7. Percent change in employment, by education category, 2010–20 (projected)

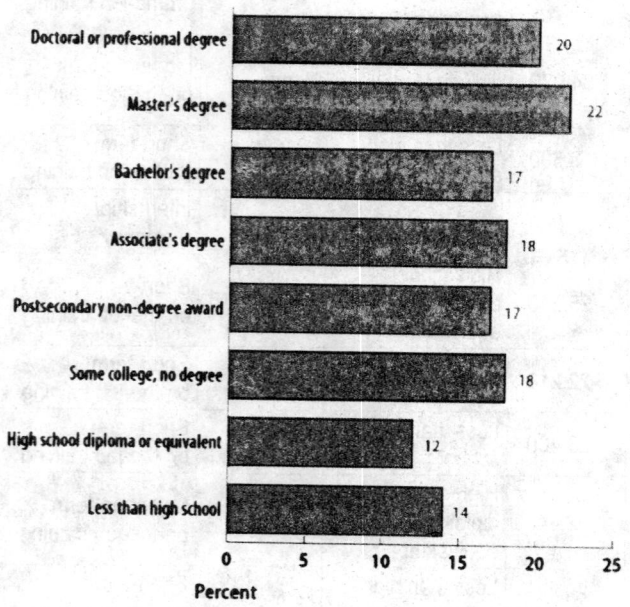

Source: BLS Division of Occupational Outlook

Table 3. Occupations with the fastest decline, projected 2010-20

Matrix Code	Occupations	Percent Change	Number of new jobs added	Wages (May 2010 median)	Entry-level Education	Related Work Experience	On-the-job Training
51-6042	Shoe Machine Operators and Tenders	-53	-1,700	$26,280	High school diploma or equivalent	None	Short-term on-the-job training
43-5053	Postal Service Mail Sorters, Processors, and Processing Machine Operators	-49	-68,900	53,080	High school diploma or equivalent	None	Short-term on-the-job training
43-5051	Postal Service Clerks	-48	-31,600	53,100	High school diploma or equivalent	None	Short-term on-the-job training
51-6092	Fabric and Apparel Patternmakers	-36	-2,100	38,970	High school diploma or equivalent	None	Moderate-term on-the-job training
11-9131	Postmasters and Mail Superintendents	-28	-6,800	60,300	High school diploma or equivalent	1 to 5 years	Moderate-term on-the-job training
51-6031	Sewing Machine Operators	-26	-42,100	20,600	Less than high school	None	Short-term on-the-job training
43-2011	Switchboard Operators, Including Answering Service	-23	-33,200	24,920	High school diploma or equivalent	None	Short-term on-the-job training
51-6062	Textile Cutting Machine Setters, Operators, and Tenders	-22	-3,300	23,490	High school diploma or equivalent	None	Moderate-term on-the-job training
51-6063	Textile Knitting and Weaving Machine Setters, Operators, and Tenders	-18	-4,100	25,870	High school diploma or equivalent	None	Moderate-term on-the-job training
51-9141	Semiconductor Processors	-18	-3,800	33,130	Associate's degree	None	Moderate-term on-the-job training
43-2021	Telephone Operators	-17	-3,100	31,970	High school diploma or equivalent	None	Short-term on-the-job training
51-2021	Coil Winders, Tapers, and Finishers	-16	-2,400	28,650	High school diploma or equivalent	None	Short-term on-the-job training
51-5111	Prepress Technicians and Workers	-16	-8,100	36,280	Postsecondary non-degree award	None	None
43-9031	Desktop Publishers	-15	-3,300	36,610	Associate's degree	None	Short-term on-the-job training
51-6061	Textile Bleaching and Dyeing Machine Operators and Tenders	-15	-2,100	22,970	High school diploma or equivalent	None	Short-term on-the-job training
51-6041	Shoe and Leather Workers and Repairers	-14	-1,400	23,000	High school diploma or equivalent	None	Moderate-term on-the-job training
51-8093	Petroleum Pump System Operators, Refinery Operators, and Gaugers	-14	-6,200	60,040	High school diploma or equivalent	None	Long-term on-the-job training
43-3041	Gaming Cage Workers	-13	-2,000	25,690	High school diploma or equivalent	None	Short-term on-the-job training
41-2012	Gaming Change Persons and Booth Cashiers	-12	-2,400	23,170	High school diploma or equivalent	None	Short-term on-the-job training
43-4021	Correspondence Clerks	-12	-1,200	33,410	High school diploma or equivalent	None	Short-term on-the-job training

SOURCE: BLS Occupational Employment Statistics and Division of Occupational Outlook

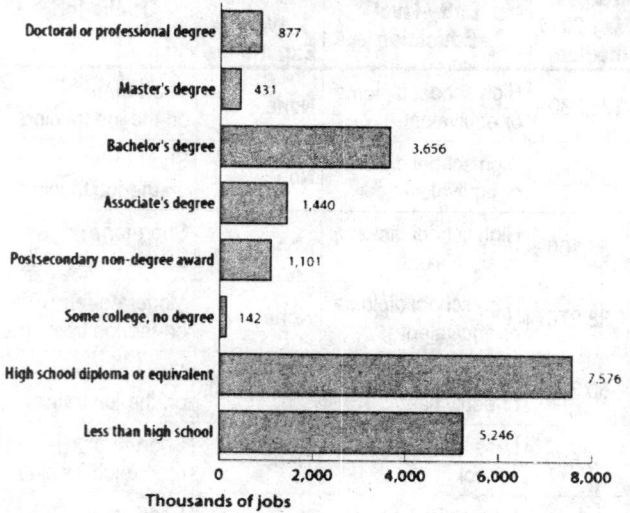

Chart 8. New jobs, by education category, 2010–20 (projected)

Education category	Thousands of jobs
Doctoral or professional degree	877
Master's degree	431
Bachelor's degree	3,656
Associate's degree	1,440
Postsecondary non-degree award	1,101
Some college, no degree	142
High school diploma or equivalent	7,576
Less than high school	5,246

Source: BLS Division of Occupational Outlook

Nevertheless, because many of the occupations require a high school diploma or less, they will account for the majority—63 percent—of new jobs between 2010 and 2020 (Chart 8).

Total job openings

Job openings stem from both employment growth and replacement needs (Chart 9). Replacement needs arise as workers leave occupations. Some workers transfer to other occupations, while others retire, return to school, or leave the labor force to assume household responsibilities. Replacement needs are projected to account for 63 percent of the approximately 54.8 million job openings between 2010 and 2020. Thus, even occupations that are projected to experience slower-than-average growth or to decline in employment will still have openings that are due to replacement needs. Office and administrative support occupations are projected to have the largest number of total job openings, 7.4 million, and 69 percent of those openings will be due to replacement needs. Generally, replacement needs are greatest in the largest occupations and in those with relatively low pay or limited training requirements. As a result, sales occupations and food preparation and serving workers are expected to generate a large number of jobs due to replacement needs. Sales occupations are expected to have 6.5 million job openings, 71 percent of which will be due to replacement needs, while food preparation and serving workers are expected to have 5.1 million job openings, 79 percent of which will be due to replacement needs. In contrast, healthcare occupations are projected to have 5.6 million job openings, but only 39 percent will be due to replacement needs. Most new healthcare jobs are expected to be due to job growth.

Farming, fishing, and forestry occupations should offer job opportunities despite overall declines in employment. These occupations will lose 19,400 jobs but are expected to provide 290,800 total job openings. Job openings will be due solely to the replacement needs of a workforce characterized by high levels of retirement and job turnover.

Education and training classification system

The BLS education and training classification system consists of three categories of information that BLS analysts have assigned to each detailed occupation in the 2010–2020 National Employment Matrix. The categories are 1) typical education needed for entry, 2) commonly required work experience in a related occupation, and 3) typical on-the-job training needed to obtain competency in the occupation. Each category and its related choice selections are defined below. This education and training system replaces the one used for the 2008–2018 projections cycle.

Typical education needed for entry

This category best describes the typical level of education that most workers need to enter the occupation. Occupations are assigned one of the following eight education levels:

Doctoral or professional degree. Completion of a doctoral degree (Ph.D.) usually requires at least 3 years of full-time academic work beyond a bachelor's degree. Completion of a professional degree usually requires at least 3 years of full-time academic study beyond a bachelor's degree. Examples of occupations for which a professional degree is the typical form of entry-level education include lawyers, physicians and surgeons, and dentists.

Master's degree. Completion of this degree usually requires 1 or 2 years of full-time academic study beyond a bachelor's degree. Examples of occupations in this category include statisticians, physician assistants, and educational, vocational, and school counselors.

Bachelor's degree. Completion of this degree generally requires at least 4 years, but not more than 5 years, of full-time academic study beyond high school. Examples of occupations in this category include budget analysts, dietitians, and civil engineers.

Associate's degree. Completion of this degree usually requires at least 2 years but not more than 4 years of full-time academic study beyond high school. Examples of occupations in this category include mechanical drafters, respiratory therapists, and dental hygienists.

Postsecondary non-degree award. These programs lead to a certificate or other award, but not a degree. The certificate is awarded by the educational institution and is the result of completing formal postsecondary schooling. Certification, which is issued by a professional organization or certifying body, is not included here. Some postsecondary non-degree award programs last only a few weeks, while others may last 1 to 2 years. Examples of occupations in this category include nursing aides, emergency medical technicians (EMTs) and paramedics, and hairstylists.

Some college, no degree. This category signifies the achievement of a high school diploma or equivalent plus the completion of one or more postsecondary courses that did not result in a degree or award. Examples of occupations in this category are actors and computer support specialists.

High school diploma or equivalent. This category signifies the completion of high school or an equivalent program

Chart 9. Number of jobs due to growth and replacement needs, by occupational group, 2010–20 (projected)

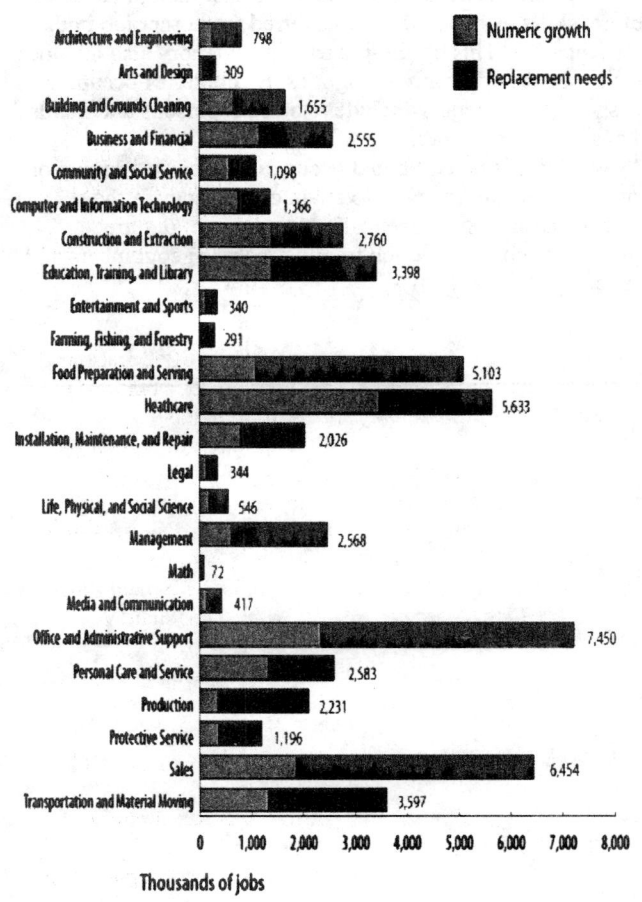

Legend: Numeric growth, Replacement needs

Occupational group	Value
Architecture and Engineering	798
Arts and Design	309
Building and Grounds Cleaning	1,655
Business and Financial	2,555
Community and Social Service	1,098
Computer and Information Technology	1,366
Construction and Extraction	2,760
Education, Training, and Library	3,398
Entertainment and Sports	340
Farming, Fishing, and Forestry	291
Food Preparation and Serving	5,103
Healthcare	5,633
Installation, Maintenance, and Repair	2,026
Legal	344
Life, Physical, and Social Science	546
Management	2,568
Math	72
Media and Communication	417
Office and Administrative Support	7,450
Personal Care and Service	2,583
Production	2,231
Protective Service	1,196
Sales	6,454
Transportation and Material Moving	3,597

Thousands of jobs

Source: BLS Division of Occupational Outlook

resulting in the award of a high school diploma or an equivalent, such as the General Educational Development (GED) credential. Examples of occupations in this category include social and human service assistants and pharmacy technicians.

Less than high school. This category signifies the completion of any level of primary or secondary education that did not result in the award of a high school diploma or equivalent. Examples of occupations in this category include janitors and cleaners, cashiers, and carpet installers.

Work experience in a related occupation

For some occupations, work experience in a related occupation may be a typical method of entry. The majority of occupations in this category are first-line supervisors or managers of service, sales, and production occupations. Although work experience in a related occupation is beneficial for all occupations, this metric is meant to capture work experience that is commonly considered necessary by employers, or is a commonly accepted substitute for other, more formal types of training or education. Occupations are assigned one of the following four categories that deal with length of time spent gaining related work experience:

More than 5 years. This is assigned to occupations if more than 5 years of work experience in a related occupation is typically needed for entry. Examples include construction managers and computer and information systems managers.

1 to 5 years. To enter occupations in this category, workers typically need 1-5 years of work experience in a related occupation. Examples include marketing managers and database administrators.

Less than 1 year. Examples of occupations that typically need less than 1 year of work experience in a related occupation include restaurant cooks and industrial truck and tractor operators.

None. No work experience in a related occupation is typically needed. Examples are audiologists and actuaries.

Typical on-the-job training needed to attain competency in the occupation

This category encompasses any additional training or preparation that is typically needed, once employed in an occupation, to attain competency in the skills needed in that occupation. Training is occupation-specific rather than job-specific; skills learned can be transferred to another job in the same occupation. Occupations are assigned one of the following six training categories:

Internship/residency. An internship or residency is training that involves preparation in a field such as medicine or teaching, generally under supervision in a professional setting, such as a hospital or classroom. This type of training may occur before one is employed. Completion of an internship or residency program is commonly required for state licensure or certification in fields including medicine, counseling, architecture, and teaching. This category does not include internships that are suggested for advancement. Examples of occupations in the internship/residency category include physicians and surgeons and marriage and family therapists.

Apprenticeship. An apprenticeship is a formal relationship between a worker and sponsor that consists of a combination of on-the-job training and related occupation-specific technical instruction in which the worker learns the practical and theoretical aspects of an occupation. Apprenticeship programs are sponsored by individual employers, joint employer-and-labor groups, and employer associations. The typical apprenticeship program provides at least 144 hours of occupation-specific technical instruction and 2,000 hours of on-the-job training per year over a 3-to-5 year period. Examples of occupations in the apprenticeship category include electricians and structural iron and steel workers.

Long-term on-the-job training. More than 12 months of on-the-job training or, alternatively, combined work experience and formal classroom instruction, are needed for workers to develop the skills to attain competency. Training is occupation specific rather than job specific; therefore, skills learned can be transferred to another job in the same occupation. This on-the-job training category also includes employer-sponsored training programs. Such programs include those offered by fire and police academies and schools for air traffic controllers and flight attendants. In other occupations—nuclear power reactor operators, for example—trainees take formal courses, often provided at the jobsite, to prepare for the required licensing exams. This category excludes apprenticeships. Examples of occupations in the long-term on-the-job training category include opticians and automotive service technicians and mechanics.

Moderate-term on-the-job training. Skills needed for a worker to attain competency in an occupation that can be acquired during 1 to 12 months of combined on-the-job experience and informal training. Training is occupation-specific rather than job-specific; therefore, skills learned can be transferred to another job in the same occupation. This on-the-job training category also includes employer-sponsored training programs. Examples of occupations in the moderate-term category include school bus drivers and advertising sales agents.

Short-term on-the-job training. Skills needed for a worker to attain competency in an occupation that can be acquired during 1 month or less of on-thejob experience and informal training. Training is occupation-specific rather than job specific; therefore, skills learned can be transferred to another job in the same occupation. This on-the-job training category also includes employer sponsored training programs. Examples of occupations in the short-term category include retail salespersons and maids and housekeeping cleaners.

None. There is no additional occupation-specific training or preparation typically required to attain competency in the occupation. Examples of occupations that do not require occupation-specific on-the-job training include geographers and pharmacists.

Fastest Growing Occupations

Fastest growing occupations: 20 occupations with the highest percent change of employment between 2010-20.

OCCUPATION	GROWTH RATE, 2010-20	2010 MEDIAN PAY
Personal Care Aides	70%	$19,640 per year.
Home Health Aides	69%	$20,560 per year.
Biomedical Engineers	62%	$81,540 per year.
Helpers--Brickmasons, Blockmasons, Stonemasons, and Tile and Marble Setters	60%	$27,780 per year.
Helpers--Carpenters	56%	$25,760 per year.
Veterinary Technologists and Technicians	52%	$29,710 per year.
Reinforcing Iron and Rebar Workers	49%	$38,430 per year.
Physical Therapist Assistants	46%	$49,690 per year.
Helpers--Pipelayers, Plumbers, Pipefitters, and Steamfitters	45%	$26,740 per year.
Meeting, Convention, and Event Planners	44%	$45,260 per year.
Diagnostic Medical Sonographers	44%	$64,380 per year.
Occupational Therapy Assistants	43%	$51,010 per year.
Physical Therapist Aides	43%	$23,680 per year.
Glaziers	42%	$36,640 per year.
Interpreters and Translators	42%	$43,300 per year.
Medical Secretaries	41%	$30,530 per year.
Market Research Analysts and Marketing Specialists	41%	$60,570 per year.
Marriage and Family Therapists	41%	$45,720 per year.
Brickmasons and Blockmasons	41%	$46,930 per year.
Physical Therapists	39%	$76,310 per year.

Highest Paying Occupations

Highest paying occupations: 20 occupations with the highest median annual pay in 2010.

OCCUPATION	2010 MEDIAN PAY
Oral and Maxillofacial Surgeons	This wage is equal to or greater than $166,400 per year.
Physicians and Surgeons	This wage is equal to or greater than $166,400 per year.
Orthodontists	This wage is equal to or greater than $166,400 per year.
Chief Executives	$165,080 per year.
Dentists, All Other Specialists	$161,020 per year.
Dentists, General	$141,040 per year.
Judges, Magistrate Judges, and Magistrates	$119,270 per year.
Architectural and Engineering Managers	$119,260 per year.
Prosthodontists	$118,400 per year.
Podiatrists	$118,030 per year.
Natural Sciences Managers	$116,020 per year.
Computer and Information Systems Managers	$115,780 per year.
Petroleum Engineers	$114,080 per year.
Marketing Managers	$112,800 per year.
Lawyers	$112,760 per year.
Pharmacists	$111,570 per year.
Air Traffic Controllers	$108,040 per year.
Political Scientists	$107,420 per year.
Physicists	$106,370 per year.
Financial Managers	$103,910 per year.

Most New Jobs

Most new jobs: 20 occupations with the highest projected numeric change in employment.

OCCUPATION	NUMBER OF NEW JOBS (PROJECTED), 2010-20	2010 MEDIAN PAY
Registered Nurses	711,900	$64,690 per year.
Retail Salespersons	706,800	$20,670 per year.
Home Health Aides	706,300	$20,560 per year.
Personal Care Aides	607,000	$19,640 per year.
Office Clerks, General	489,500	$26,610 per year.
Combined Food Preparation and Serving Workers, Including Fast Food	398,000	$17,950 per year.
Customer Service Representatives	338,400	$30,460 per year.
Heavy and Tractor-Trailer Truck Drivers	330,100	$37,770 per year.
Laborers and Freight, Stock, and Material Movers, Hand	319,100	$23,460 per year.
Postsecondary Teachers	305,700	$62,050 per year.
Nursing Aides, Orderlies, and Attendants	302,000	$24,010 per year.
Childcare Workers	262,000	$19,300 per year.
Bookkeeping, Accounting, and Auditing Clerks	259,000	$34,030 per year.
Cashiers	250,200	$18,500 per year.
Elementary School Teachers, Except Special Education	248,800	$51,660 per year.
Receptionists and Information Clerks	248,500	$25,240 per year.
Janitors and Cleaners, Except Maids and Housekeeping Cleaners	246,400	$22,210 per year.
Landscaping and Groundskeeping Workers	240,800	$23,400 per year.
Sales Representatives, Wholesale and Manufacturing, Except Technical and Scientific Products	223,400	$52,440 per year.
Construction Laborers	212,400	$29,280 per year.

Sources of Career Information

This section identifies some major sources of information on careers. These sources are meant to be used in addition to those listed at the "Contacts for More Info" tab for each profile.

How to use this information best. The sources mentioned in this section offer different types of information. For example, people you know may provide highly specific information because they have knowledge of you, your abilities and interests, and your qualifications. Other sources, such as those found in the state sources listed, provide information on occupations in each state. Gathering information from a wide range of sources is the best way to determine what occupations may be appropriate for you and in what geographic regions these occupations are found. The sources of information discussed in this section are not exhaustive, and other sources could prove equally valuable in your career search.

Like any major decision, selecting a career involves a lot of fact finding. Fortunately, some of the best informational resources are easily accessible. You should assess career guidance materials carefully. Information that seems out of date or glamorizes an occupation—overstates its earnings or exaggerates the demand for workers, for example—should be evaluated with skepticism. Gathering as much information as possible will help you make a more informed decision.

DISCLAIMER:

LINKS TO NON-BLS INTERNET SITES ARE PROVIDED FOR YOUR CONVENIENCE AND DO NOT CONSTITUTE AN ENDORSEMENT.

People you know. One of the best resources can be your friends and family. They may answer some questions about a particular occupation or put you in touch with someone who has some experience in the field. This personal networking can be invaluable in evaluating an occupation or an employer. People you know will be able to tell you about their specific duties and training, as well as what they did or did not like about a job. People who have worked in an occupation locally also may be able to give you a recommendation and get you in touch with specific employers.

Employers. These are the primary source of information on specific jobs. Employers may post lists of job openings and application requirements, including the exact training and experience required, starting wages and benefits, and advancement opportunities and career paths.

Informational interviews. People already working in a particular field often are willing to speak with people interested in joining their field. An informational interview will allow you to get good information from experts in a specific career without the pressure of undergoing a job interview. These interviews allow you to determine how a certain career may appeal to you while helping you build a network of personal contacts.

Professional societies, trade groups, and labor unions. These sources have information on an occupation or various related occupations with which they are associated or that they actively represent. This information may cover training requirements and earnings, and may provide listings of local employers. These sources may train members or potential members themselves, or they may be able to put you in contact with organizations or individuals who perform such training.

Each occupational profile in the **Handbook** concludes with a "Contact for More Info" section, which lists organizations that may be contacted for additional information.

Guidance counselors and career counselors. Counselors can help you make choices about which careers might suit you best. They can help you establish which occupations fit your skills by testing your aptitude for various types of work and determining your strengths and interests. Counselors can help you evaluate your options and search for a job in your field or help you select a new field altogether. They also can help you determine which educational or training institutions best fit your goals and then assist you in finding ways to finance your education or training. Some counselors offer other services, such as interview coaching, résumé building, and help in filling out various forms. Counselors in secondary schools and postsecondary institutions may arrange guest speakers, field trips, or job fairs.

You can find guidance and career counselors at:
- High school guidance offices
- College career planning and placement offices
- Placement offices in private vocational or technical schools and institutions
- Vocational rehabilitation agencies
- Counseling services offered by community organizations
- Private counseling agencies and private practices
- State employment service offices

When using a private counselor, check to see that the counselor is experienced. One way to do so is to ask people who have used the counselor's services in the past. The National Board of Certified Counselors is an institution that accredits career counselors. To verify the credentials of a career counselor and to find a career counselor in your area, visit www.nbcc.org/.

Postsecondary institutions. Colleges, universities, and other postsecondary institutions typically put a lot of effort into helping place their graduates in good jobs, because the success of their graduates reflects the quality of their institution and may affect the institution's ability to attract new students. Postsecondary institutions commonly have career centers with information on different careers, listings of related jobs, and alumni contacts in various professions. Career centers frequently employ career counselors who generally provide their services only to their students and alumni. Career centers can help you build your résumé, find internships and co-ops—which can lead to full-time positions—and tailor your course selection or program to make you a more marketable job applicant.

Local libraries. Libraries can be a valuable source of information. Because most areas have libraries, they can be a convenient place to look for information. Also, many libraries provide access to the Internet and email.

Libraries may have information on job openings, locally and nationally; potential contacts within occupations or industries; colleges and financial aid; vocational training; individual businesses or careers; and writing résumés. Libraries frequently have subscriptions to various trade magazines that can provide information on occupations and industries. Your local library also may have video materials. These sources often have references to organizations that can provide additional information about training and employment opportunities.

If you need help getting started or finding a resource, ask your librarian for assistance.

Internet resources. A wide variety of career information is easily accessible on the Internet. Online resources include job listings, résumé posting services, and information on job fairs, training, and local wages. Many of the resources listed elsewhere in this section have Internet sites that include valuable information on potential careers. No single source contains all information on an occupation, field, or employer, therefore, you will likely need to use a variety of sources.

When using Internet resources, be sure that the organization is a credible, established source of information on the particular occupation you are interested in. Individual companies may include job listings on their websites, as well as information about required credentials, wages and benefits, and the job's location. Contact information, such as whom to call or where to send a résumé, is usually included.

Some sources exist primarily as a Web service. These sources often have information on specific jobs and can greatly aid in the job-hunting process. Some commercial sites offer Web services, as do federal, state, and some local governments. CareerOneStop, a joint program sponsored by the U.S. Department of Labor and the states as well as local agencies, provides these services free of charge.

Online Sources from the Department of Labor. A major resource in the U.S. Department of Labor's Labor Market Information System is the CareerOneStop site. This site includes links to the following sources:

- State job banks allow you to search job openings listed with state employment agencies.
- America's Career InfoNet provides data on employment growth and wages by occupation; the knowledge, skills, and abilities required by an occupation; and links to employers.
- America's Service Locator is a comprehensive database of career centers and information on unemployment benefits, job training, and educational opportunities.
- O*net Online provides occupational information, including descriptors on hundreds of occupations.

For more information on specific occupations, you can also visit the Department of Labor's Bureau of Labor Statistics (BLS). BLS publishes a wide range of labor market information, from regional wages for specific occupations to statistics on national, state, and area employment. For more information, see the section on occupational wage data.

For information on training, workers' rights, and job listings, visit the Employment and Training Administration website.

The Occupational Outlook Quarterly (OOQ) is a career magazine published by the Bureau of Labor Statistics of the U.S. Department of Labor. The magazine includes many articles about finding, applying for, and choosing jobs. See, for example, the following OOQ articles:

- "Job search in the age of the Internet: Six job seekers in search of employers," online at http://www.bls.gov/opub/ooq/2003/summer/art01.pdf

- "Focused Jobseeking: A measured approach to looking for work," online at http://www.bls.gov/opub/ooq/2011/spring/art01.pdf
- "Résumés, applications, and cover letters," online at http://www.bls.gov/opub/ooq/2009/summer/art03.pdf
- "Informational interviewing: Get the inside scoop on careers," online at http://www.bls.gov/opub/ooq/2010/summer/art03.pdf
- "Getting back to work: Returning to the labor force after an absence," online at http://www.bls.gov/opub/ooq/2004/winter/art03.pdf

Organizations for specific groups. Some organizations provide information designed to help specific groups of people. Consult directories in your library's reference center or in a career guidance office for information on additional organizations associated with specific groups.

Workers with disabilities:

Information on employment opportunities, transportation, and other considerations for people with a wide variety of disabilities is available from the following sources:
- National Organization on Disability, 5 East 86th Street, New York, NY 10028. Telephone: (646) 505-1191
- Job Accommodation Network (JAN), Telephone: (800) 526-7234 TTY: (877) 781-9403
- A comprehensive federal Web site of disability-related resources, accessible at http://www.disability.gov

Workers with vision problems:

Information on the free national reference and referral service for the blind can be obtained by contacting National Federation of the Blind, 200 East Wells Street, Baltimore, MD 21230. Telephone: (410) 659-9314

Older workers:

- National Council on Aging, 1901 L St. NW., 4th Floor., Washington, DC 20036. Telephone: (202) 479-1200
- National Caucus and Center on Black Aged, Inc., 1220 L St. NW., Suite 800, Washington, DC 20005. Telephone: (202) 637-8400

Veterans:

Contact the nearest regional office of the U.S. Department of Labor's Veterans Employment and Training Service or Credentialing Opportunities Online (COOL), which explains how military personnel can meet civilian certification and license requirements related to their Military Occupational Specialty (MOS).

Women:

- Department of Labor, Women's Bureau, Telephone: (800) 827-5335

Federal laws, executive orders, and selected federal grant programs bar employment discrimination based on race, color, religion, sex, national origin, age, and handicap. Information on how to file a charge of discrimination is available from U.S. Equal Employment Opportunity Commission offices around the country. Their addresses and telephone numbers are listed in telephone directories under U.S. Government, EEOC. Telephone: (800) 669-4000 TTY: (800) 669-6820

Office of Personnel Management. Information on obtaining civilian positions within the federal government is available from the U.S. Office of Personnel Management through USAJobs.gov, the federal government's official employment information system.

Military. The military employs people in, and has information on, hundreds of occupations. Information is available on tuition assistance programs, which provide money for school and other educational debt repayments. Information on military service can be provided by your local recruiting office, or visit the **Handbook** profile on military careers. You can also find more information on careers in the military at Today's Military.

State Sources

State Sources. Most States have career information delivery systems (CIDS), which may be found in secondary and post-secondary institutions, as well as libraries, job training sites, vocational-technical schools, and employment offices. A wide range of information is provided, from employment opportunities to unemployment insurance claims.

Whereas the *Handbook* provides information for occupations on a national level, each State has detailed information on occupations and labor markets within their respective jurisdictions. State occupational projections are available at: **http://www.projectionscentral.com**

Alabama
Labor Market Information Division, Alabama Department of Industrial Relations, 649 Monroe St., Room 422, Montgomery, AL 36131.
Telephone: (334) 242-8859.
Internet: **http://dir.alabama.gov**

Alaska
Research and Analysis Section, Department of Labor and Workforce Development, P.O. Box 25501, Juneau, AK 99802-5501.
Telephone: (907) 465-4500.
Internet: **http://almis.labor.state.ak.us**

Arizona
Arizona Department of Economic Security, P.O. Box 6123 SC 733A, Phoenix, AZ 85005-6123.
Telephone: (602) 542-5984.
Internet: **https://www.azdes.gov**

Arkansas
Labor Market Information, Department of Workforce Services, #2 Capital Mall, Little Rock, AR 72201.
Telephone: (501) 682-3198.
Internet: **http://www.discoverarkansas.net**

California
State of California Employment Development Department, Labor Market Information Division, P.O. Box 826880, Sacramento, CA 94280-0001.
Telephone: (916) 262-2162.
Internet: **http://www.labormarketinfo.edd.ca.gov**

Colorado
Labor Market Information, Colorado Department of Labor and Employment, 633 17th St., Suite 600, Denver, CO 80202-3660.
Telephone: (303) 318-8850.
Internet: **http://lmigateway.coworkforce.com**

Connecticut
Office of Research, Connecticut Department of Labor, 200 Folly Brook Blvd., Wethersfield, CT 06109-1114.
Telephone: (860) 263-6275.
Internet: **http://www.ctdol.state.ct.us/lmi**

Delaware
Office of Occupational and Labor Market Information, Department of Labor, 19 West Lea Blvd., Wilmington, DE 19802.
Telephone: (302) 761-8069.
Internet: **http://www.delawareworks.com/oolmi/**

District of Columbia
DC Department of Employment Services, 64 New York Ave. NE., Suite 3000, Washington, D.C. 20002.
Telephone: (202) 724-7000.
Internet: **http://www.does.dc.gov/does**

Florida
Labor Market Statistics, Agency for Workforce Innovation, 107E. Madison St., MSC 110 - Caldwell Building, Tallahassee, FL 32399-4111.
Telephone: (850) 245-7105.
Internet: **http://www.labormarketinfo.com**

Georgia
Workforce Information and Analysis, Room 300, Department of Labor, 223 Courtland St., CWC Building, Atlanta, GA 30303.
Telephone: (404) 232-3875.
Internet: **http://www.dol.state.ga.us/em/get_labor_market_information.htm**

Guam
Guam Department of Labor, 504 D St., Tiyan, Guam 96910.
Telephone: (671) 475-0101.
Internet: **http://guamdol.net**

Hawaii
Research and Statistics Office, Department of Labor and Industrial Relations, 830 Punchbowl St., Room 304, Honolulu, HI 96813.
Telephone: (808) 586-9013.
Internet: **http://www.hiwi.org**

Idaho
Research and Analysis Bureau, Department of Commerce and Labor, 317 West Main St., Boise, ID 83735-0670.
Telephone: (208) 332-3570.
Internet: http://lmi.idaho.gov

Illinois
Illinois Department of Employment Security, Economic Information and Analysis Division, 33 S. State St., 9th Floor, Chicago, IL 60603.
Telephone: (312) 793-6521.
Internet: **http://lmi.ides.state.il.us**

Indiana
Research and Analysis—Indiana Workforce Development, Indiana Government Center South, 10 North Senate Ave., Indianapolis, IN 46204.
Telephone: (800) 891-6499.
Internet: **http://www.in.gov/dwd**

Iowa
Policy and Information Division, Iowa Workforce Development, 1000 East Grand Ave., Des Moines, IA 50319-0209.
Telephone: (515) 281-5387.
Internet: **http://www.iowaworkforce.org/lmi**

Kansas

Kansas Department of Labor, Labor Market Information Services, 401 SW Topeka Blvd., Topeka, KS 66603-3182.
Telephone: (785) 296-5000.
Internet: **http://laborstats.dol.ks.gov**

Kentucky

Research and Statistics Branch, Office of Employment and Training, 275 East Main St., Frankfort, KY 40621.
Telephone: (502) 564-7976.
Internet: **http://www.workforcekentucky.ky.gov**

Louisiana

Research and Statistics Division, Department of Labor, 1001 North 23rd St., Baton Rouge, LA 70802-3338.
Telephone: (225) 342-3111.
Internet: **http://www.laworks.net**

Maine

Labor Market Information Services Division, Maine Department of Labor, 45 Commerce Dr., State House Station 118, Augusta, ME 04330.
Telephone: (207) 623-7900.
Internet: **http://maine.gov/labor/lmis**

Maryland

Maryland Department of Labor Licensing and Regulation, Office of Labor Market Analysis and Information, 1100 N. Eutaw, Baltimore, MD 21201.
Telephone: (410) 767-2250.
Internet: **http://www.dllr.state.md.us/lmi/index.shtml**

Massachusetts

Executive Office of Labor and Workforce Development, Division of Career Services, 19 Staniford St., Boston, MA 02114.
Telephone: (617) 626-5300.
Internet: **http://www.detma.org/LMIdataprog.htm**

Michigan

Bureau of Labor Market Information and Strategic Initiatives, Department of Labor and Economic Growth, 3032 West Grand Blvd., Suite 9-100, Detroit, MI 48202.
Telephone: (313) 456-3100.
Internet: **http://www.milmi.org**

Minnesota

Department of Employment and Economic Development, Labor Market Information Office, 1st National Bank Building, 332 Minnesota St., Suite E200, St. Paul, MN 55101-1351.
Telephone: (888) 234-1114.
Internet: **http://www.deed.state.mn.us/lmi**

Mississippi

Labor Market Information Division, Mississippi Department of Employment Security, 1235 Echelon Pkwy., P.O. Box 1699, Jackson, MS 39215.
Telephone: (601) 321-6000.
Internet: **http://mdes.ms.gov**

Missouri

Missouri Economic Research and Information Center, P.O. Box 3150, Jefferson City, MO 65102-3150.
Telephone: (866) 225-8113.
Internet: **http://www.missourieconomy.org**

Montana

Research and Analysis Bureau, P.O. Box 1728, Helena, MT 59624.
Telephone: (800) 541-3904.
Internet: **http://www.ourfactsyourfuture.org**

Nebraska

Nebraska Workforce Development—Labor Market Information, Nebraska Department of Labor, 550 South 16th St., P.O. Box 94600, Lincoln, NE 68509.
Telephone: (402) 471-2600.
Internet:**www.dol.nebraska.gov/nwd/center.cfm?PRICAT=3&SUBCAT=4Z0**

Nevada

Research and Analysis, Department of Employment Training and Rehabilitation, 500 East Third St., Carson City, NV 89713.
Telephone: (775) 684-0450.
Internet: **http://www.nevadaworkforce.com**

New Hampshire

Economic and Labor Market Information Bureau, New Hampshire Employment Security, 32 South Main St., Concord, NH 03301-4857.
Telephone: (603) 228-4124.
Internet: **http://www.nh.gov/nhes/elmi**

New Jersey

Division of Labor Market and Demographic Research, Department of Labor and Workforce Development, P.O. Box 388, Trenton, NJ 08625-0388.
Telephone: (609) 984-2593.
Internet: **http://www.wnjpin.net**

New Mexico

New Mexico Department of Labor , Economic Research and Analysis, 401 Broadway NE., Albuquerque, NM 87102.
Telephone: (505) 222- 4683.
Internet: **http://www.dws.state.nm.us/dws-lmi.html**

New York

Research and Statistics, New York State Department of Labor, W. Averell Harriman State Office Campus, Building 12, Albany, NY 12240.
Telephone: (518) 457-9000.
Internet: **http://www.labor.state.ny.us**

North Carolina

Labor Market Information Division, Employment Security Commission, 700 Wade Ave., Raleigh, NC 27605.
Telephone: (919)733-2936.
Internet: **http://www.ncesc.com**

North Dakota

Labor Market Information Manager, Job Service North Dakota, 1000 East Divide Ave., Bismarck, ND 58506.
Telephone: (800) 732-9787.
Internet: **http://www.ndworkforceintelligence.com**

Ohio

Bureau of Labor Market Information, Ohio Department of Job and Family Services, 420 East 5th Ave., Columbus, OH 43219.
Telephone: (614) 752-9494.
Internet: **http://ohiolmi.com**

Oklahoma

Labor Market Information, Oklahoma Employment Security Commission, P.O. Box 52003., Oklahoma City, OK 73152.
Telephone: (405) 557-7172.
Internet: **http://www.ok.gov/oesc_web/Services/Find_Labor_Market_Statistics/index.html**

Oregon

Oregon Employment Department, Research Division, 875 Union St. NE., Salem, OR 97311.
Telephone: (503) 947-1200.
Internet: **http://www.qualityinfo.org/olmisj/OlmisZine**

Pennsylvania

Center for Workforce Information & Analysis, Pennsylvania Department of Labor and Industry, 220 Labor and Industry Building, Seventh and Forster Sts., Harrisburg, PA 17121.
Telephone: (877) 493-3282.
Internet: **http://www.paworkstats.state.pa.us**

Puerto Rico

Department of Work and Human Resources, Ave. Muñoz Rivera 505, Hato Rey, PR 00918.
Telephone: (787) 754-5353.
Internet: **http://www.dtrh.gobierno.pr**

Rhode Island

Labor Market Information, Rhode Island Department of Labor and Training, 1511 Pontiac Ave., Cranston, RI 02920.
Telephone: (401) 462-8740.
Internet: **http://www.dlt.ri.gov/lmi**

South Carolina

Labor Market Information Department, South Carolina Employment Security Commission, 631 Hampton St., Columbia, SC 29202.
Telephone: (803) 737-2660.
Internet: **http://www.sces.org/lmi/index.asp**

South Dakota

Labor Market Information Center, Department of Labor, P.O. Box 4730, Aberdeen, SD 57402-4730.
Telephone: (605) 626-2314.
Internet: **http://dol.sd.gov/lmic**

Tennessee

Research and Statistics Division, Department of Labor and Workforce Development, 220 French Landing Dr., Nashville, TN 37245.
Telephone: (615) 741-1729.
Internet: **http://www.state.tn.us/labor-wfd/lmi.htm**

Texas

Labor Market Information, Texas Workforce Commission, 9001 North IH-35, Suite 103A, Austin, TX 75753.
Telephone: (866) 938-4444.
Internet: **http://www.tracer2.com**

Utah

Director of Workforce Information, Utah Department of Workforce Services, P.O. Box 45249, Salt Lake City, UT 84145-0249.
Telephone: (801) 526-9675.
Internet: **http://jobs.utah.gov/opencms/wi**

Vermont

Economic and Labor Market Information, Vermont Department of Labor, P.O. Box 488, Montpelier, VT 05601-0488.
Telephone: (802) 828-4000.
Internet: **http://www.vtlmi.info**

Virgin Islands

Bureau of Labor Statistics, Department of Labor, 53A & 54AB Kronprindsens Gade, St Thomas, VI 00803-2608.
Telephone: (340) 776-3700.
Internet: **http://www.vidol.gov**

Virginia

Virginia Employment Commission, P.O. Box 1358, Richmond, VA 23218-1358.
Telephone: (800) 828-1140.
Internet: **http://www.vec.virginia.gov/vecportal/index.cfm**

Washington

Labor Market and Economic Analysis, Washington Employment Security Department, P.O. Box 9046, Olympia, WA 98507-9046.
Telephone: (360) 438-4833.
Internet: **http://www.workforceexplorer.com**

West Virginia

Workforce West Virginia, Research, Information and Analysis Division, 112 California Ave., Charleston, WV 25303-0112.
Telephone: (304) 558-2660.
Internet: **http://workforcewv.org/lmi**

Wisconsin

Bureau of Workforce Information, Department of Workforce Development, P.O. Box 7944, Madison, WI 53707-7944.
Telephone: (608) 266-7034.
Internet: **http://worknet.wisconsin.gov/worknet**

Wyoming

Research and Planning, Wyoming Department of Employment, 246 S. Center St., Casper, WY 82602.
Telephone: (307) 473-3807.
Internet: **http://doe.state.wy.us/lmi**

Sources of Education, Training, and Financial Aid

Education can present opportunities for those looking to start a new career or change specialty within their current occupation. This section outlines some major sources of education and training required to enter many occupations, as well as some ways to finance that education or training.

For information on the specific training and educational requirements for a particular occupation, and what training is typically provided by an employer, consult the "Training, Other Qualifications, and Advancement" section of the appropriate Handbook statement.

Sources of Education and Training

Four-year colleges and universities. These institutions provide detailed information on theory and practice for a wide variety of subjects. Colleges and universities can provide students with the knowledge and background necessary to be successful in many fields. They also can help to place students in cooperative education programs (often called "co-ops") or internships. Co-ops and internships are short-term jobs with firms related to a student's field of study that lead to college credit. In co-ops and internships, students learn the specifics of a job while making valuable contacts that can lead to a permanent position.

For more information on colleges and universities, go to your local library, consult your high school guidance counselor, or contact individual colleges. Also check with your State's higher education agency. A list of these agencies is available on the Internet: http://www.ed.gov/erod.

Junior and community colleges. Junior and community colleges offer a variety of programs that lead to associate degrees and training certificates. Community colleges tend to be less expensive than 4-year colleges and universities. They usually are more willing to accommodate part-time students than colleges and universities, and their programs are more tailored to the needs of local employers. Many community colleges have an open admissions policy, and they often offer weekend and night classes. Community colleges often form partnerships with local businesses that allow students to gain job-specific training. Many students may not be able to enroll in a college or university because of their academic record, limited finances, or distance from such an institution, so they attend junior or community colleges to earn credits that can be applied toward a degree at a 4-year college. Junior and community colleges also are noted for their extensive role in continuing and adult education.

For more information on junior and community colleges, go to your local library, consult your high school guidance counselor, or contact individual schools. Also check with your State's higher education agency. A list of these agencies is available on the Internet: http://www.ed.gov/erod.

Online colleges and universities. Online colleges and universities cover most of the same material as their traditional classroom counterparts, but they offer classes over the Internet. Offering classes on the Internet provides a great deal of flexibility to students, allowing many who work, travel frequently, or lack the ability or means to attend a traditional university to earn a degree from an accredited institution.

A prospective student should talk to a guidance counselor or advisor before deciding to enroll in an online college or university. Additionally, the prospective student should check the college or university's accreditation with the U.S. Department of Education. This can be done online at: http://ope.ed.gov/ accreditation.

Vocational and trade schools. These institutions train people in specific trades. They offer courses designed to provide handson experience. Vocational and trade schools tend to concentrate on trades, services, and other types of skilled work.

Vocational and trade schools frequently engage students in real-world projects, allowing them to apply field methods while learning theory in classrooms. Graduates of vocational and trade schools have an advantage over informally trained or selftrained jobseekers because graduates have an independent organization certifying that they have the knowledge, skills, and abilities necessary to perform the duties of a particular occupation. These schools also help students to acquire any license or other credentials needed to enter the job market.

For more information on vocational and trade schools, go to your local library, consult your high school guidance counselor, or contact individual schools. Also check with your State's director of vocational-technical education. A list of State directors of vocational-technical education is available on the Internet: http://www.ed.gov/erod.

Apprenticeships. An apprenticeship provides work experience as well as education and training for people entering certain occupations. Apprenticeships are offered by sponsors, who employ and train the apprentice. The apprentice follows a training course under close supervision and receives some formal education to learn the theory related to the job.

Apprenticeships, which generally last between 1 and 4 years, are a way for inexperienced people to become skilled workers. Some apprenticeships allow the apprentice to earn an associate degree. An Apprenticeship Completion Certificate is granted to those completing programs. This certificate is administered by federally approved State agencies.

For more information on apprenticeships and for assistance finding a program, go to the Office of Apprenticeship Training, Employer, and Labor Services on the Internet: http://www. doleta.gov/atels_bat.

Professional societies, trade associations, and labor unions. These groups are made up of people with common interests, usually in related occupations or industries. The groups frequently are able to provide training, access to training through their affiliates, or information on acceptable sources of training for their field. If licensing or certification is required, they also may be able to assist you in meeting those requirements.

For a listing of professional societies, trade associations, and labor unions related to an occupation, check the "Sources of Additional Information" section at the end of that occupational statement in the Handbook.

Employers. Many employers provide on-the-job training, which can range from spending a few minutes watching another employee demonstrate a task to participating in formal training programs that may last for several months. In some jobs, employees may continually undergo training to stay up to date with new developments and technologies or to add new skills.

Military. The United States Armed Forces trains and employs people in more than 4,100 different occupations. For more information, see the Handbook statement on "Job Opportunities in The Armed Forces." For detailed answers to specific questions, contact your local recruiting office. Valuable resources also are available on the Internet: http://www.todaysmilitary.com.

Sources of Financial Aid

Many people fund their education or training through financial aid or tuition assistance programs. Federal student aid comes in three forms: grants, work-study programs, and loans. All Federal student aid applicants must first fill out a Free Application for Federal Student Aid (FAFSA), which provides a Student Aid Report (SAR) and eligibility rating. Forms must be submitted to desired institutions of study, which determine the amount of aid you will receive.

For information on applying for Federal financial aid, visit the FAFSA Internet site: http://www.fafsa.ed.gov.

A U.S. Department of Education publication describing Federal financial aid programs, called Funding Education Beyond High School: The Guide to Federal Student Aid, is available at http://www.studentaid.ed.gov/students/publications/student_guide/index.html.

Information on Federal programs is available from http://www.studentaid.ed.gov and www.students.gov.

Information on State programs is available from your State's higher education agency. A list of these agencies is available at http://www.ed.gov/erod.

Grants. A grant is money that is given to students or the institution they are attending to pay for the student's education or training and any associated expenses. Grants are usually given on the basis of financial need. Grants are considered gifts and are not paid back. Federal grants are almost exclusively for undergraduate students. They include Pell Grants, which can be worth up to $5,350 annually. The maximum amount given out can change each year, however. Federal Supplemental Educational Opportunity Grants (FSEOG) can be worth up to $4,000 annually. Priority for FSEOG awards is given to those who have also received the Pell Grant and have exceptional financial need.

Additional information on grants is available on the Internet: http://www.studentaid.ed.gov. Information also is available from your State Higher Education agency. A list of these agencies is available at http://www.ed.gov/erod.

Federal Work-Study program. The Federal Work-Study program is offered at most institutions and consists of Federal sponsorship of a student who works part time at the institution he or she is attending. The money a student earns through this program goes directly toward the cost of attending the institution. There are no set minimum or maximum amounts for this type of aid, although, on average, a student can expect to earn about $2,000 per school year.

For additional information on work-study opportunities offered, check with individual institutions. General information on the Federal Work-Study program is available at http://studentaid.ed.gov/PORTALSWebApp/students/english/campusaid.jsp.

Scholarships. A scholarship is a sum of money donated to a student to help pay for his or her education or training and any associated costs. Scholarships can range from small amounts up to the full cost of schooling. They are based on financial need, academic merit, athletic ability, or a wide variety of other criteria set by the organizations that provide the scholarships. Frequently, students must meet minimum academic requirements to be considered for a scholarship. Other qualifying requirements—such as intended major field of study, heritage, or group membership—may be added by the organization providing the scholarship.

Scholarships are provided by a wide variety of institutions, including educational institutions, State and local governments, private associations, social groups, and individuals. There are no federally awarded scholarships based on academic merit. Most large scholarships are awarded to students by the institution they plan to attend. Students who have received State scholarships and plan to attend a school in another State should check with their State to see if the scholarship can be transferred.

Information on scholarships is typically available from high school guidance counselors and local libraries. Additional scholarship information is available from State higher education agencies. A list of these agencies is available at http:// www.ed.gov/erod. The College Board has information on available scholarships at http://www.collegeboard.com/pay.

Student loans. Many institutions, both public and private, provide low-interest loans to students and their parents or guardians. The Federal Government also provides several types of student loans based on the applicant's level of financial need. The amount of money a student can receive in loans varies by the distributing institution and depends on whether the student is claimed by a parent or guardian as a dependent. Since the process of applying for a loan may take several

months, it is a good idea to start applying for Federal student loans well in advance.

The available Federal loan programs can accommodate prospective undergraduate, graduate, vocational, and disabled students. Federal loans can be distributed through the school that the student is attending, from the Federal Government directly, or from a third-party private lender or bank. Perkins loans are distributed through the school the student is attending. Loans coming from the Federal Government directly from the William D. Ford Federal Direct Loan Program are dispersed by the Department of Education. Third-party loans through a private lender or bank are from the Federal Family Education Loan (FFEL) program. For all federally funded loans, payments are made to the institution that originally dispersed the funds.

For those with financial need, Federal Perkins loans and both Direct and FFEL-subsidized Stafford loans are available. Perkins loans have no minimum amount; they are capped at $5,500 per year for undergraduates. Students should visit the Department of Education's Web site (http://www.studentaid.ed.gov/PORTALSWebApp/students/english/fafsa.jsp) to learn about the current level of aid available because it will vary by year and a student's status (married, single, dependent, or independent). Subsidized Stafford loans vary in size and can increase as a student completes more years of undergraduate, graduate, or professional education. Interest rates for both loans will be gradually decreasing until 2012. Information on specific interest rates is available through the school's financial aid officer or the Department of Education's Web site. Individuals who receive Perkins loans are not responsible for starting to repay the loan until they have been out of school for 9 months. Those with subsidized Stafford loans must begin payments within 6 to 9 months of leaving school but are not charged monthly interest while in school.

For those who do not demonstrate financial need, Direct and FFEL-unsubsidized Stafford Loans and Federal Parent Loans for Students (PLUS) are available. Unsubsidized Stafford loans vary in value and are capped at the cost of attendance. With Federal unsubsidized Stafford Loans, interest payments start almost immediately and can be paid monthly or accrued until the completion of studies. The latter option results in a larger total loan cost but may be more convenient for some students. With PLUS loans, the parent must pay interest and principal payments while the student is enrolled in school and must continue payments after completion. Check with your lender for available repayment schedules. Students usually have 10 years to repay Perkins loans and from 10 to 30 years for unsubsidized Stafford loans.

Subsidized and unsubsidized Stafford loans are only available to students who are enrolled in an academic program at least half time. As with any loan, be sure to investigate different lenders, and understand what your loan contract requires of you before agreeing to any loan. Check with established financial institutions to compare the terms of available private student loans. Comparisons of the various types of loans are available on the Internet: http://www.studentaid.ed.gov/students/publications/student_guide/index.html. The College Board has information on available loans at http://www.collegeboard.com/pay.

Employer tuition support programs. Some employers offer tuition assistance programs as part of their employee benefits package. The terms of these programs depend on the firm and can vary by the type and amount of training subsidized, as well as by eligibility requirements. Consult your human resources department for information on tuition support programs offered by your employer.

Military tuition support programs. The United States Armed Forces offer various tuition assistance and loan repayment programs for military personnel. See the Handbook statement on "Job Opportunities in the Armed Forces" for more information, or go to http://www.todaysmilitary.com/benefits/tuition-support.

Finding and Applying for Jobs and Evaluating Offers

Finding—and getting—the job you want can be a challenging process, but knowing more about job search methods and application techniques can increase your chances of success. And knowing how to judge the job offers you receive makes it more likely that you will end up with the best possible job.

Where to learn about job openings

Personal contacts
School career planning and placement offices
Employers
Classified ads
   —National and local newspapers
   —Professional journals
   —Trade magazines
Internet resources
Professional associations
Labor unions
State employment service offices
Federal Government
Community agencies
Private employment agencies and career consultants
Internships

Job search methods

Finding a job can take months of time and effort. But you can speed the process by using many methods to find job openings. Data from the Bureau of Labor Statistics suggest that people who use many job search methods find jobs faster than people who use only one or two.

In the box above, some sources of job openings are listed. Those sources are described more fully below.

Personal contacts. Many jobs are never advertised. People get them by talking to friends, family, neighbors, acquaintances, teachers, former coworkers, and others who know of an opening. Be sure to tell people that you are looking for a job because the people you know may be some of the most effective resources for your search. To develop new contacts, join student, community, or professional organizations.

School career planning and placement offices. High school and college placement services help their students and alumni find jobs. Some invite recruiters to use their facilities for interviews or career fairs. They also may have lists of open jobs. Most also offer career counseling, career testing, and job search advice. Some have career resource libraries; host workshops on job search strategy, resume writing, letter writing, and effective interviewing; critique drafts of resumes; conduct mock interviews; and sponsor job fairs.

Employers. Directly contacting employers is one of the most successful means of job hunting. Through library and Internet research, develop a list of potential employers in your desired career field. Then call these employers and check their Web sites for job openings. Web sites and business directories can tell you how to apply for a position or whom to contact. Even if no open positions are posted, do not hesitate to contact the employer: You never know when a job might become available. Consider asking for an informational interview with people working in the career you want to learn more about. Ask them how they got started, what they like and dislike about the work, what type of qualifications are necessary for the job, and what type of personality succeeds in that position. In addition to giving you career information, they may be able to put you in contact with other employers who may be hiring, and they can keep you in mind if a position opens up.

Classified ads. The "Help Wanted" ads in newspapers and the Internet list numerous jobs, and many people find work by responding to these ads. But when using classified ads, keep the following in mind:

- Follow all leads to find a job; do not rely solely on the classifieds.
- Answer ads promptly, because openings may be filled quickly, even before the ad stops appearing in the paper.
- Read the ads every day, particularly the Sunday edition, which usually includes the most listings.
- Keep a record of all ads to which you have responded, including the specific skills, educational background, and personal qualifications required for the position. You may want to follow up on your initial inquiry.

Internet resources. The Internet includes many job hunting Web sites with job listings. Some job boards provide National listings of all kinds; others are local. Some relate to a specific type of work; others are general. To find good prospects, begin with an Internet search using keywords related to the job you want. Also look for the Web sites of related professional associations.

Also consider checking Internet forums, also called message boards. These are online discussion groups where anyone may post and read messages. Use forums specific to your profession or to career-related topics to post questions or messages and to read about the job searches or career experiences of other people. Although these message boards may seem helpful, carefully evaluate all advice before acting; it can be difficult to determine the reliability of information posted on message boards.

In online job databases, remember that job listings may be posted by field or discipline, so begin your search using keywords. Many Web sites allow job seekers to post their resumes online for free.

Professional associations. Many professions have associations that offer employment information, including career planning, educational programs, job listings, and job placement. Information can be obtained directly from most professional associations through the Internet, by telephone, or by mail. Associations usually require that you be a member to use these services.

Labor unions. Labor unions provide various employment services to members and potential members, including apprenticeship programs that teach a specific trade or skill. Contact the appropriate labor union or State apprenticeship council for more information.

State employment service offices. The State employment service, sometimes called the Job Service, operates in coordination with the U.S. Department of Labor's Employment and Training Administration. Local offices, found nationwide, help job seekers to find jobs and help employers to find qualified workers at no cost to either. To find the office nearest you, look in the State government telephone listings under "Job Service" or "Employment."

Job matching and referral. At the State employment service office, an interviewer will determine if you are "job ready" or if you need help from counseling and testing services to assess your occupational aptitudes and interests and to help you choose and prepare for a career. After you are job ready, you may examine available job listings and select openings that interest you. A staff member can then describe the job openings in detail and arrange for interviews with prospective employers.

Services for special groups. By law, veterans are entitled to priority job placement at State employment service centers. If you are a veteran, a veterans' employment representative can inform you of available assistance and help you to deal with problems.

State employment service offices also refer people to opportunities available under the Workforce Investment Act (WIA) of 1998. Educational and career services and referrals are provided to employers and job seekers, including adults, dislocated workers, and youth. These programs help to prepare people to participate in the State's workforce, increase their employment and earnings potential, improve their educational and occupational skills, and reduce their dependency on welfare.

Federal Government. Information on obtaining a position with the Federal Government is available from the U.S. Office of Personnel Management (OPM) through USAJOBS, the Federal Government's official employment information system. This resource for locating and applying for job opportunities can be accessed through the Internet at **http://www.usajobs.gov** or through an interactive voice response telephone system at (703) 724-1850, (866) 204-2858, or TDD (978) 461-8404. These numbers are not all toll free, and telephone charges may result.

Community agencies. Many nonprofit organizations, including religious institutions and vocational rehabilitation agencies, offer counseling, career development, and job placement services, generally targeted to a particular group, such as women, youths, minorities, ex-offenders, or older workers.

Private employment agencies and career consultants. Private agencies can save you time and they will contact employers who otherwise might be difficult to locate. Such agencies may be called recruiters, head hunters, or employment placement agencies. These agencies may charge for their services. Most operate on a commission basis, charging a percentage of the first-year salary paid to a successful applicant. You or the hiring company will pay the fee. Find out the exact cost and who is responsible for paying associated fees before using the service. When determining if the service is worth the cost, consider any guarantees that the agency offers.

Internships. Many people find jobs with business and organizations with whom they have interned or volunteered. Look for internships and volunteer opportunities on job boards, school career centers, and company and association Web sites, but also check community service organizations and volunteer opportunity databases. Some internships and long-term volunteer positions come with stipends and all provide experience and the chance to meet employers and other good networking contacts.

Applying for a job

After you have found some jobs that interest you, the next step is to apply for them. Many potential employers require complete resumes or application forms and cover letters. Later, you will probably need to go on interviews to meet with employers face to face.

Resumes and application forms. Resumes and application forms give employers written evidence of your qualifications and skills. The goal of these documents is to prove—as clearly and directly as possible—how your qualifications match the job's requirements. Do this by highlighting the experience, accomplishments, education, and skills that most closely fit the job you want.

Gathering information. Resumes and application forms both include the same information. As a first step, gather the following facts:

- Contact information, including your name, mailing address, e-mail address (if you have one you check often), and telephone number.
- Type of work or specific job you are seeking or a qualifications summary, which describes your best skills and experience in just a few lines.
- Education, including school name and its city and State, months and years of attendance, highest grade completed or diploma or degree awarded, and major subject or subjects studied. Also consider listing courses and awards that might be relevant to the position. Include a grade point average if you think it would help in getting the job.
- Experience, paid and volunteer. For each job, include the job title, name and location of employer, and dates of employment. Briefly describe your job duties and major accomplishments. In a resume, use phrases instead of sentences to describe your work; write, for example, "Supervised 10 children" instead of writing "I supervised 10 children."
- Special skills. You might list computer skills, proficiency in foreign languages, achievements, or membership in organizations in a separate section.
- References. Be ready to provide references if requested. Good references could be former employers, coworkers, or teachers or anyone else who can describe your abilities and job-related traits. You will be asked to provide contact information for the people you choose.

Professional associations. Many professions have associations that offer employment information, including career planning, educational programs, job listings, and job placement. Information can be obtained directly from most professional associations through the Internet, by telephone, or by mail. Associations usually require that you be a member to use these services.

Labor unions. Labor unions provide various employment services to members and potential members, including apprenticeship programs that teach a specific trade or skill. Contact the appropriate labor union or State apprenticeship council for more information.

State employment service offices. The State employment service, sometimes called the Job Service, operates in coordination with the U.S. Department of Labor's Employment and Training Administration. Local offices, found nationwide, help job seekers to find jobs and help employers to find qualified workers at no cost to either. To find the office nearest you, look in the State government telephone listings under "Job Service" or "Employment."

Job matching and referral. At the State employment service office, an interviewer will determine if you are "job ready" or if you need help from counseling and testing services to assess your occupational aptitudes and interests and to help you choose and prepare for a career. After you are job ready, you may examine available job listings and select openings that interest you. A staff member can then describe the job openings in detail and arrange for interviews with prospective employers.

Services for special groups. By law, veterans are entitled to priority job placement at State employment service centers. If you are a veteran, a veterans' employment representative can inform you of available assistance and help you to deal with problems.

State employment service offices also refer people to opportunities available under the Workforce Investment Act (WIA) of 1998. Educational and career services and referrals are provided to employers and job seekers, including adults, dislocated workers, and youth. These programs help to prepare people to participate in the State's workforce, increase their employment and earnings potential, improve their educational and occupational skills, and reduce their dependency on welfare.

Federal Government. Information on obtaining a position with the Federal Government is available from the U.S. Office of Personnel Management (OPM) through USAJOBS, the Federal Government's official employment information system. This resource for locating and applying for job opportunities can be accessed through the Internet at **http://www.usajobs.gov** or through an interactive voice response telephone system at (703) 724-1850, (866) 204-2858, or TDD (978) 461-8404. These numbers are not all toll free, and telephone charges may result.

Community agencies. Many nonprofit organizations, including religious institutions and vocational rehabilitation agencies, offer counseling, career development, and job placement services, generally targeted to a particular group, such as women, youths, minorities, ex-offenders, or older workers.

Private employment agencies and career consultants. Private agencies can save you time and they will contact employers who otherwise might be difficult to locate. Such agencies may be called recruiters, head hunters, or employment placement agencies. These agencies may charge for their services. Most operate on a commission basis, charging a percentage of the first-year salary paid to a successful applicant. You or the hiring company will pay the fee. Find out the exact cost and who is responsible for paying associated fees before using the service. When determining if the service is worth the cost, consider any guarantees that the agency offers.

Internships. Many people find jobs with business and organizations with whom they have interned or volunteered. Look for internships and volunteer opportunities on job boards, school career centers, and company and association Web sites, but also check community service organizations and volunteer opportunity databases. Some internships and long-term volunteer positions come with stipends and all provide experience and the chance to meet employers and other good networking contacts.

Applying for a job

After you have found some jobs that interest you, the next step is to apply for them. Many potential employers require complete resumes or application forms and cover letters. Later, you will probably need to go on interviews to meet with employers face to face.

Resumes and application forms. Resumes and application forms give employers written evidence of your qualifications and skills. The goal of these documents is to prove—as clearly and directly as possible—how your qualifications match the job's requirements. Do this by highlighting the experience, accomplishments, education, and skills that most closely fit the job you want.

Gathering information. Resumes and application forms both include the same information. As a first step, gather the following facts:

- Contact information, including your name, mailing address, e-mail address (if you have one you check often), and telephone number.
- Type of work or specific job you are seeking or a qualifications summary, which describes your best skills and experience in just a few lines.
- Education, including school name and its city and State, months and years of attendance, highest grade completed or diploma or degree awarded, and major subject or subjects studied. Also consider listing courses and awards that might be relevant to the position. Include a grade point average if you think it would help in getting the job.
- Experience, paid and volunteer. For each job, include the job title, name and location of employer, and dates of employment. Briefly describe your job duties and major accomplishments. In a resume, use phrases instead of sentences to describe your work; write, for example, "Supervised 10 children" instead of writing "I supervised 10 children."
- Special skills. You might list computer skills, proficiency in foreign languages, achievements, or membership in organizations in a separate section.
- References. Be ready to provide references if requested. Good references could be former employers, coworkers, or teachers or anyone else who can describe your abilities and job-related traits. You will be asked to provide contact information for the people you choose.

Evaluating a job offer

Once you receive a job offer, you must decide if you want the job. Fortunately, most organizations will give you a few days to accept or reject an offer.

There are many issues to consider when assessing a job offer. Will the organization be a good place to work? Will the job be interesting? Are there opportunities for advancement? Is the salary fair? Does the employer offer good benefits? Now is the time to ask the potential employer about these issues—and to do some checking on your own.

The organization. Background information on an organization can help you to decide whether it is a good place for you to work. Factors to consider include the organization's business or activity, financial condition, age, size, and location.

You generally can get background information on an organization, particularly a large organization, on its Web site or by telephoning its public relations office. A public company's annual report to the stockholders tells about its corporate philosophy, history, products or services, goals, and financial status. Most government agencies can furnish reports that describe their programs and missions. Press releases, company newsletters or magazines, and recruitment brochures also can be useful. Ask the organization for any other items that might interest a prospective employee. If possible, speak to current or former employees of the organization.

Background information on the organization may be available at your public or school library. If you cannot get an annual report, check the library for reference directories that may provide basic facts about the company, such as earnings, products and services, and number of employees. Some directories widely available in libraries either in print or as online databases include:

- *Dun & Bradstreet's Million Dollar Directory*
- *Standard and Poor's Register of Corporations*
- *Mergent's Industry Review* (formerly *Moody's Industrial Manual*)
- *Thomas Register of American Manufacturers*
- *Ward's Business Directory*

Stories about an organization in magazines and newspapers can tell a great deal about its successes, failures, and plans for the future. You can identify articles on a company by looking under its name in periodical or computerized indexes in libraries, or by using one of the Internet's search engines. However, it probably will not be useful to look back more than 2 or 3 years.

The library also may have government publications that present projections of growth for the industry in which the organization is classified. Long-term projections of employment and output for detailed industries, covering the entire U.S. economy, are developed by the Bureau of Labor Statistics and revised every 2 years. (See the *Career Guide to Industries*, online at http://www.bls.gov/oco/cg.) Trade magazines also may include articles on the trends for specific industries.

Career centers at colleges and universities often have information on employers that is not available in libraries. Ask a career center representative how to find out about a particular organization.

During your research consider the following questions:

Does the organization's business or activity match your own interests and beliefs?

It is easier to apply yourself to the work if you are enthusiastic about what the organization does.

How will the size of the organization affect you?

Large firms generally offer a greater variety of training programs and career paths, more managerial levels for advancement, and better employee benefits than do small firms. Large employers also may have more advanced technologies. However, many jobs in large firms tend to be highly specialized.

Jobs in small firms may offer broader authority and responsibility, a closer working relationship with top management, and a chance to clearly see your contribution to the success of the organization.

Should you work for a relatively new organization or one that is well established?

New businesses have a high failure rate, but for many people, the excitement of helping to create a company and the potential for sharing in its success more than offset the risk of job loss. However, it may be just as exciting and rewarding to work for a young firm that already has a foothold on success.

The job. Even if everything else about the job is attractive, you will be unhappy if you dislike the day-to-day work. Determining in advance whether you will like the work may be difficult. However, the more you find out about the job before accepting or rejecting the offer, the more likely you are to make the right choice. Consider the following questions:

Where is the job located?

If the job is in another section of the country, you need to consider the cost of living, the availability of housing and transportation, and the quality of educational and recreational facilities in that section of the country. Even if the job location is in your area, you should consider the time and expense of commuting.

Does the work match your interests and make good use of your skills?

The duties and responsibilities of the job should be explained in enough detail to answer this question.

How important is the job to the company or organization?

An explanation of where you fit in the organization and how you are supposed to contribute to its overall goals should give you an idea of the job's importance.

What will the hours be?

Most jobs involve regular hours—for example, 40 hours a week, during the day, Monday through Friday. Other jobs require night, weekend, or holiday work. In addition, some jobs routinely require overtime to meet deadlines or sales or production goals, or to better serve customers. Consider the effect that the work hours will have on your personal life.

How long do most people who enter this job stay with the company?

High turnover can mean dissatisfaction with the nature of the work or something else about the job.

Opportunities offered by employers. A good job offers you opportunities to learn new skills, increase your earnings, and rise to positions of greater authority, responsibility, and prestige. A lack of opportunities can dampen interest in the work and result in frustration and boredom.

Some companies develop training plans for their employees. What valuable new skills does the company plan to teach you?

The employer should give you some idea of promotion possibilities within the organization. What is the next step on the career ladder? If you have to wait for a job to become vacant before you can be promoted, how long does this usually take? When opportunities for advancement do arise, will you compete with applicants from outside the company? Can you apply for jobs for which you qualify elsewhere within the organization, or is mobility within the firm limited?

Salaries and benefits. When an employer makes a job offer, information about earnings and benefits are usually included. You will want to research to determine if the offer is fair. If you choose to negotiate for higher pay and better benefits, objective research will help you strengthen your case.

You may have to go to several sources for information. One of the best places to start is the information from the Bureau of Labor Statistics. Data on earnings by detailed occupation from the Occupational Employment Statistics (OES) Survey are available from:

➤ Bureau of Labor Statistics, Office of Occupational Statistics and Employment Projections, 2 Massachusetts Ave. NE., Room 2135, Washington, DC 20212-0001. Telephone: (202) 691-6569. Internet: http://www.bls.gov/OES.

Data from the Bureau's National Compensation Survey are available from:

➤ Bureau of Labor Statistics, Office of Compensation Levels and Trends, 2 Massachusetts Ave. NE., Room 4175, Washington, DC 20212-0001. Telephone: (202) 691-6199. Internet: http://www.bls.gov/eci.

You should also look for additional information, specifically tailored to your job offer and circumstances. Try to find family, friends, or acquaintances who recently were hired in similar jobs. Ask your teachers and the staff in placement offices about starting pay for graduates with your qualifications. Help-wanted ads in newspapers sometimes give salary ranges for similar positions. Check the library or your school's career center for salary surveys such as those conducted by the National Association of Colleges and Employers or various professional associations.

If you are considering the salary and benefits for a job in another geographic area, make allowances for differences in the cost of living, which may be significantly higher in a large metropolitan area than in a smaller city, town, or rural area.

You also should learn the organization's policy regarding overtime. Depending on the job, you may or may not be exempt from laws requiring the employer to compensate you for overtime. Find out how many hours you will be expected to work each week and whether you receive overtime pay or compensatory time off for working more than the specified number of hours in a week.

Also take into account that the starting salary is just that—the start. Your salary should be reviewed on a regular basis; many organizations do it every year. How much can you expect to earn after 1, 2, or 3 or more years? An employer may be unable to be specific about the amount of pay if it includes commissions and bonuses.

Benefits also can add a lot to your base pay, but they vary widely. Find out exactly what the benefit package includes and how much of the cost you must bear.

For more information

To learn more about finding and applying for jobs, visit your local library and career center. You can find career centers that are part of the U.S. Department of Labor One-Stop Career system by calling toll free (877) 348-0502 or visiting their Web site at http://www.careeronestop.org.

The *Occupational Outlook Quarterly*, a career magazine published by the Bureau of Labor Statistics, is one of the resources available at many libraries and career centers. The magazine includes many articles about finding, applying for, and choosing jobs. See, for example:

➤ "Career myths and how to debunk them," online at http://www.bls.gov/opub/ooq/2005/fall/art01.pdf.

➤ "Getting back to work: Returning to the labor force after an absence," online at http://www.bls.gov/opub/ooq/2004/winter/art03.pdf.

➤ "Job search in the age of the Internet: Six job seekers in search of employers," online at http://www.bls.gov/opub/ooq/2003/summer/art01.pdf.

➤ "Internships: Previewing a profession," online at http://www.bls.gov/opub/ooq/2006/summer/art02.pdf.

➤ "Resumes, applications, and cover letters," online at http://www.bls.gov/opub/ooq/2009/summer/art03.pdf.

Occupational Information Included in the OOH

The Occupational Outlook Handbook (OOH) is a career guidance resource offering information on the hundreds of occupations that provide the overwhelming majority of jobs in the United States. Each occupational profile discusses what workers in that occupation do, their work environment, the typical education and training needed to enter the occupation, pay, and the job outlook for the occupation. Each profile is in a standard format that makes it easy to compare occupations.

This page describes the content found in each occupational profile.

Sections of Occupational Profiles

- Quick Facts
- What They Do
- Work Environment
- How to Become One
- Pay
- Job Outlook
- Similar Occupations

Contacts for More Information

Quick Facts

All profiles have a "Quick Facts" table that gives information on the following topics:

2010 Median Pay: The wage at which half of the workers in the occupation earned more than that amount and half earned less. Median wage data are from the BLS Occupational Employment Statistics survey.

Entry-Level Education: Typical level of education that most workers need to enter the occupation.

Work Experience in a Related Occupation: Work experience that is commonly considered necessary by employers or is a commonly accepted substitute for more formal types of training or education.

On-the-job Training: Postemployment training necessary to attain competency in the skills needed in the occupation.

Number of Jobs, 2010: The employment, or size, of this occupation in 2010, the base year of the 2010-20 employment projections.

Job Outlook, 2010-20: The projected rate of change in employment for the 10-year timeframe between 2010 and 2020. The average growth rate for all occupations is 14.3 percent.

Employment Change, 2010-20: The projected numeric change in employment for this occupation between 2010 and 2020.

The summary section briefly describes all of the sections included in each occupational profile. In addition, a link is given to the Occupational Information Network (O*NET) system. State employment service offices use O*NET to classify applicants and job openings. For each occupation, O*NET lists descriptors, including common tasks, necessary knowledge and skills, and frequently used technology.

What They Do

This section describes the main work of people in the occupation.

All occupations have a list of duties or typical tasks performed by these workers. The list includes daily responsibilities, such as answering phone calls and taking a patient's medical history.

This section also may describe the equipment, tools, software, or other items that are typically used by people in the occupation. For example, medical records and health information technicians frequently use electronic health records to document a patient's medical information. This section also may describe those with whom workers in the occupation interact, such as clients, patients, and coworkers.

Some profiles discuss specific specialties, job titles, or types of occupations within a given occupation. This subsection includes a brief explanation of each specialty's job duties and how specialties differ from one another. For example, the profile on dentists lists several specialties, including orthodontists, oral and maxillofacial surgeons, and pediatric dentists.

Work Environment

This section describes an occupation's working conditions, including the workplace, expected level of physical activity, and typical hours.

The section typically begins by noting the employment size of the occupation in 2010 and often includes a table of the industries or settings that employed the most workers in an occupation that year. The workplace is described, and whether employees work in a safe work environment (such as an office) or a hazardous one (such as a commercial fishing boat) is discussed. If the workplace is hazardous, the section lists the type of equipment an employee must wear, such as a lab coat or protective goggles. In addition to information on the general work environment, the section also notes whether employees are expected to travel, and, if so, for how long.

The section includes information on the typical schedule for workers in an occupation, noting whether the majority of workers are employed full time or part time. Full-time workers typically work 35 or more hours in a week, whereas part-time employees work less than 35 hours. For some occupations, the profile might also include the time of a day an employee is expected to work and for how long. Nurses, for example, may work all hours of the day and on weekends, because medical facilities are open around the clock. Information on occupations, such as farmers, that have seasonal employment also can be found in this section.

How to Become One

This section describes the typical paths to entry into, and advancement in, an occupation. All profiles have subsections on education and on important qualities of workers in the occupation. Optional subsections include information on training, work experience, licenses, certification, and advancement.

Education

This subsection describes the education that most workers typically need to enter an occupation. Some occupations require no formal education, whereas others may require, for example, a doctoral degree or Ph.D. In some occupations, such as computer support specialist, workers have varying educational backgrounds. In these cases, the profile will discuss all of the typical paths of entry into the occupation.

This subsection also may include information on what subjects, majors, or minors people study in preparation for the occupation. Typical courses that may aid a student in preparing for an occupation may be listed. For example, high school students interested in applying to respiratory therapy programs should take courses in health, biology, mathematics, chemistry, and physics.

Work experience

This subsection describes whether employers require work experience in a related occupation. For example, some managers, such as architectural and engineering managers, typically have previous work experience as an architect or engineer.

Training

This subsection describes the typical on-the-job training necessary to attain competency in an occupation. Information is included on any practical or classroom training that workers receive after being hired. For example, firefighters must complete training at a fire academy or a similar program before they are considered prepared to combat fires.

In these profiles, apprenticeships and internship or residency programs are considered on-the-job training. For example, the profile on physicians and surgeons includes information on residency programs.

Licenses

This subsection describes whether licensing is typically needed for an occupation and, if so, how workers can become licensed.

Licenses are issued by states to signify that the person has met specific legal requirements to practice that occupation. To become licensed, workers usually need to pass an examination and comply with eligibility requirements, such as possessing a minimum level of education, work experience, or training, or completing an internship, a residency, or a formal apprenticeship. States have their own regulatory boards that set standards for practicing a licensed occupation, so rules and eligibility may vary from state to state, even for the same occupation.

Certification

This subsection describes whether workers in an occupation are typically certified and, if so, how they can become certified.

Some occupations have certification either as a requirement or as a nonrequired opportunity. As an example of the latter, fitness trainers and instructors are encouraged, not required, to become certified before entering the occupation, and employers will often allow a trainer or instructor to become certified after being hired.

Certification requires demonstrated competency in a skill or a set of skills and is commonly earned by passing an examination or having a certain amount and type of work experience or training. For some certification programs, the candidate must have a certain level of education before becoming eligible for certification.

This subsection explains any prerequisites to certification and how a person would complete certification (by passing an exam, performing a certain type of work, receiving certain training or education, etc). If states require workers to be certified before they can be licensed, that information also is noted here.

Certification should not be confused with certificates from an educational institution. A certificate awarded by a postsecondary educational institution is considered to be a postsecondary nondegree award and would be discussed in the subsection on education.

Important qualities

This subsection describes important characteristics of workers in the occupation and includes an explanation of why those characteristics are useful.

The qualities include areas of skills, aptitudes, and personal characteristics. For example, an emergency medical technician or paramedic must be physically strong, and a medical laboratory technologist or technician relies on technical skills to complete laboratory work.

Advancement

This subsection describes the possible advancement opportunities for workers in the occupation.

Opportunities for advancement can come from within the occupation, such as a promotion to a supervisory or managerial level; advancement into another occupation, such as moving from a computer support specialist to a network and computer systems administrator; or becoming self-employed, such as a dentist opening up his or her own practice.

The section often explains the requirements for advancement, such as certification or additional formal education.

Pay

This section discusses the wages of workers in the occupation.

For each occupation, pay varies by experience, responsibility, performance, tenure, and geographic area. Almost all occupations discussed in the OOH use median wage data from the Occupational Employment Statistics (OES) survey, which provides data on wage and salary workers. The median wage is the wage at which half of the workers in an occupation earned more and half earned less. This section might also include wages earned by workers in selected industries—those in which most of an occupation's workers are employed. The wage data by industry are also from the OES survey.

For all occupations for which OES survey data are used, the profile includes median wages and the wages earned by the top 10 percent and bottom 10 percent of workers in the occupation. The wage data are accompanied by a chart comparing the median wage of workers in the occupation to the median wage of workers across all occupations.

Unless otherwise noted, the source of pay data for occupations in the OOH is the Bureau of Labor Statistics. Some occupational profiles may cite wage data from sources other than the BLS. For example, wage data on physicians and surgeons is provided by the Medical Group Management Association.

Work schedule information, also found in the "Work Environment" section, is provided again here, and, if notable, this section might include the percentage of an occupation's workers who are members of a union.

Job Outlook

This section describes how employment will grow or decline between 2010 and 2020. Growth rates are from the 2010–20 occupational projections from the National Employment Matrix. In addition to presenting projections data, the outlook section cites major factors affecting the growth or decline of employment. Some common factors in employment growth or decline are industry growth or decline, technological change, fluctuating demand for a product or service, demographic change, or changes in business practices.

The outlook section sometimes also includes a "job prospects" subsection, which provides a qualitative measure of job competition.

Similar Occupations

This section links to other occupational profiles with similar job duties or required skills.

Contacts for More Information

This section includes external links to associations, organizations, and other institutions that may provide readers with additional information.

Key phrases in the OOH

The following tables explain how to interpret the key phrases used to describe projected changes in employment:

Changing employment between 2010 and 2020	
If the statement reads:	**Employment is projected to:**
Grow much faster than average	increase 29 percent or more
Grow faster than average	increase 20 to 28 percent
Grow about as fast as average	increase 10 to 19 percent
Grow more slowly than average	increase 3 to 9 percent
Little or no change	decrease 2 percent to increase 2 percent
Decline slowly or moderately	decrease 3 to 9 percent
Decline rapidly	decrease 10 percent or more

Occupational Coverage

Architecture and Engineering Occupations

Aerospace Engineering and Operations Technicians

QUICK FACTS: AEROSPACE ENGINEERING AND OPERATIONS TECHNICIANS	
2010 Median Pay	$58,080 per year $27.93 per hour
Entry-Level Education	Associate's degree
Work Experience in a Related Occupation	None
On-the-job Training	None
Number of Jobs, 2010	8,700
Job Outlook, 2010-20	-2% (Little or no change)
Employment Change, 2010-20	-100

What Aerospace Engineering and Operations Technicians Do

Aerospace engineering and operations technicians operate and maintain equipment used in testing new aircraft and spacecraft. Increasingly, their job requires programming and running computer simulations that test new designs. Their work is critical in preventing the failure of key parts of new aircraft, spacecraft, or missiles. They also help in quality assurance, testing, and operation of high-technology equipment used in producing aircraft and the systems that go into the aircraft.

Duties

Aerospace engineering and operations technicians typically do the following:

- Make sure that test procedures go smoothly and safely
- Operate and calibrate computer systems to comply with test requirements
- Record data from test parts and assemblies
- Meet with aerospace engineers to discuss details and implications of test procedures
- Build and maintain test facilities for aircraft systems
- Make and install parts and systems to be tested
- Install instruments in aircraft and spacecraft

- Monitor and assure quality in producing systems that go into the aircraft

New aircraft designs undergo years of testing before they are put into service because the failure of key parts during flight can be fatal. As part of the job, technicians often calibrate test equipment, such as wind tunnels, and determine causes of equipment malfunctions. They also may program and run computer simulations that test new designs.

Work Environment

Aerospace engineering and operations technicians held about 8,700 jobs in 2010. They usually work full time in laboratories, offices, and manufacturing or industrial plants. Many are exposed to hazards from equipment or from toxic materials, but incidents are rare as long as proper procedures are followed.

Industries that employed the largest numbers of aerospace engineering and operations technicians in 2010 were as follows:

Aerospace products and parts manufacturing	34%
Navigational, measuring, electromedical, and control instruments manufacturing	20
Architectural, engineering, and related services	14
Scheduled air transportation	5
Colleges, universities, and professional schools; state, local, and private	5

Aerospace engineering and operations technicians are physically active in constructing the designs that aerospace engineers develop. Consequently, these technicians often work directly in manufacturing or industrial plants, where they help to assemble aircraft, missiles, and spacecraft away from an office environment.

How to Become an Aerospace Engineering or Operations Technician

An associate's degree is becoming increasingly desired by employers of aerospace engineering and operations technicians, although vocational programs that grant certificates or diplomas also offer good preparation. Some aerospace engineering and operations technicians work on projects that are related to national defense and thus require security clearances. U.S. citizenship may be required for certain types and levels of clearances.

Aerospace engineering and operations technicians work to make sure that testing goes smoothly.

Education

High school students interested in becoming an aerospace engineering and operations technician should take classes in math, science, and, if available, drafting. Courses that help students develop skills working with their hands also are valuable, because these technicians build what aerospace engineers design. Employers also want these technicians to have a basic understanding of computers and programs to model or simulate products.

Vocational-technical schools include postsecondary public institutions that emphasize training needed by local employers. Students who complete these programs typically receive a diploma or certificate. Community colleges offer programs similar to those in technical institutes but include more theory-based and liberal arts coursework and programs. Community colleges typically award an associate's degree.

The Technology Accreditation Commission of ABET (formerly the Accreditation Board for Engineering and Technology), accredits programs that include at least college algebra, trigonometry, and basic science courses.

Many vocational and community college programs offer cooperative programs, with work experience built into the curriculum.

Important Qualities

Communication skills. Aerospace engineering and operations technicians receive instructions from aerospace engineers. Consequently, they must be able to understand and follow the instructions, as well as communicate any problems to their supervisors.

Critical-thinking skills. Aerospace engineering and operations technicians must be able to help aerospace engineers figure out why a particular design does not work as planned. They must be able to evaluate system capabilities, identify problems, formulate the right question, and then to find the right answer.

Detail oriented. Aerospace engineering and operations technicians make and keep precise measurements needed by aerospace engineers. Consequently, they must make correct measurements and keep accurate records.

Interpersonal skills. Aerospace engineering and operations technicians must be able to take instruction and offer advice. An ability to work well with supervising engineers, other technicians, and mechanics is critical as technicians increasingly interact with people from other divisions, businesses, and governments.

Math skills. Aerospace engineering and operations technicians use the principals of mathematics for analysis, design, and troubleshooting in their work.

Technical skills. Aerospace engineering and operations technicians must be able to help aerospace engineers by building what the engineers design and helping with the processes and directions required to move from design to production. They must have both the hands-on skills of mechanics and some technical knowledge of aerospace engineering.

Certification

Although certification is not required, skills-based certification programs help students prepare for certification offered by the Federal Aviation Administration (FAA). Certification may be beneficial because it shows employers that a technician can carry out the theoretical designs of aerospace engineers, and companies and the FAA seek to ensure the highest standards for the safety of the aircraft.

Pay

Aerospace Engineering and Operations Technicians Median annual wages, May 2010	
Aerospace Engineering and Operations Technicians	$58,080
Engineering Technicians, Except Drafters	$51,930
Total, All Occupations	$33,840

Note: All Occupations includes all occupations in the U.S. Economy.
Source: U.S. Bureau of Labor Statistics, Occupational Employment Statistics

The median annual wage of aerospace engineering and operations technicians was $58,080 in May 2010. The median wage is the wage at which half the workers in an occupation earned more than that amount and half earned less. The lowest 10 percent earned less than $34,590, and the top 10 percent earned more than $87,860.

Median annual wages in the industries employing the largest numbers of aerospace engineering and operations technicians in May 2010 were as follows:

Scheduled air transportation	$70,790
Aerospace products and parts manufacturing	59,230
Colleges, universities, and professional schools; state, local, and private	57,900
Architectural, engineering, and related services	57,220
Navigational, measuring, electromedical, and control instruments manufacturing	56,540

Job Outlook

Aerospace Engineering and Operations Technicians Percent change in employment, projected 2010-20	
Total, All Occupations	14%
Engineering Technicians, Except Drafters	5%
Aerospace Engineering and Operations Technicians	-2%

Note: All Occupations includes all occupations in the U.S. Economy.
Source: U.S. Bureau of Labor Statistics, Employment Projections program

Employment of aerospace engineering and operations technicians is expected to experience little or no change from 2010 to 2020. Aerospace engineering and operations technicians work on many projects that are related to national defense and require security clearances. These restrictions will help to keep jobs in the United States. In addition, aircraft are being redesigned to cut down on noise pollution and to raise fuel efficiency, increasing demand for research and development.

Although aerospace engineering and operations technicians are employed in several industries, most of their work is involved in national defense-related projects or in designing civilian aircraft. Research and development projects, ranging from unmanned aerial vehicles to new air transport concepts, will create demand for aerospace engineering and operations technicians.

Those who work on engines or propulsion will be increasingly needed as design and production emphasis shifts to rebuilding existing aircraft so that they give off less noise while using less fuel. Domestically, as space flight shifts to the civil market from government agencies, there will be a shift in hiring away from government agencies and to emerging civil space companies.

However, aerospace engineering and operations technicians also are working on improving productivity through the use of automation and robotics, and increased productivity will likely reduce low-end production employment in this occupation. Another factor that may slow growth in the occupation is the continuing adoption of computational fluid dynamics (CFD) software. This technology has lowered testing costs because companies no longer need to spend as much to test by traditional methods, typically performed by aerospace engineering and operations technicians. Thus, aerospace engineering and operations technicians will see a shift in work toward more high-end technology tasks.

Job Prospects

Despite the factors driving down overall employment in this occupation, job openings should be available for aerospace engineering and operations technicians. They usually retire at a younger age than aerospace engineers, and indications are that the proportion of those eligible to retire will be rising substantially over the next few years.

Employment projections data for aerospace engineering and operations technicians, 2010-20

Occupational Title	SOC Code	Employment, 2010	Projected Employment, 2020	Change, 2010-20	
				Percent	Numeric
Aerospace Engineering and Operations Technicians	17-3021	8,700	8,500	-2	-100
SOURCE: U.S. Bureau of Labor Statistics, Employment Projections program					

Similar Occupations

This table shows a list of occupations with job duties that are similar to those of aerospace engineering and operations technicians.

Occupation	Job Duties	Entry-Level Education	Median Annual Pay, May 2010
Aerospace Engineers	Aerospace engineers design aircraft, spacecraft, satellites, and missiles. In addition, they test prototypes to make sure that they function according to design.	Bachelor's degree	$97,480
Electro-mechanical Technicians	Electro-mechanical technicians combine knowledge of mechanical technology with knowledge of electrical and electronic circuits. They install, troubleshoot, repair, and upgrade electronic and computer-controlled mechanical systems, such as robotic assembly machines.	Associate's degree	$49,550
Industrial Engineering Technicians	Industrial engineering technicians plan ways to effectively use personnel, materials, and machines in factories, stores, hospitals, repair shops, and offices. As assistants to industrial engineers, they help prepare machinery and equipment layouts, plan workflows, conduct statistical production studies, and analyze production costs.	Associate's degree	$48,210
Mechanical Engineering Technicians	Mechanical engineering technicians help mechanical engineers design, develop, test, and manufacture industrial machinery, consumer products, and other equipment. They may make sketches and rough layouts, record and analyze data, make calculations and estimates, and report their findings.	Associate's degree	$50,110
Drafters	Drafters use software to convert the designs of engineers and architects into technical drawings and plans. Workers in production and construction use these plans to build everything from microchips to skyscrapers.	Associate's degree	$47,880

Contacts for More Information

For more information about accredited programs, visit ABET

For more information about careers in engineering, visit Technology Student Association

For more information about certification, visit SpaceTEC, Federal Aviation Administration

Suggested citation:

Bureau of Labor Statistics, U.S. Department of Labor, Occupational Outlook Handbook, 2012-13 Edition, Aerospace Engineering and Operations Technicians, on the Internet at http://www.bls.gov/ooh/architecture-and-engineering/aerospace-engineering-and-operations-technicians.htm .

Aerospace Engineers

QUICK FACTS: AEROSPACE ENGINEERS	
2010 Median Pay	$97,480 per year $46.86 per hour
Entry-Level Education	Bachelor's degree
Work Experience in a Related Occupation	None
On-the-job Training	None
Number of Jobs, 2010	81,000
Job Outlook, 2010-20	5% (Slower than average)
Employment Change, 2010-20	4,000

Aerospace engineers study the necessary physics for designing aircraft that will fly.

What Aerospace Engineers Do

Aerospace engineers design aircraft, spacecraft, satellites, and missiles. In addition, they test prototypes to make sure that they function according to design.

Duties

Aerospace engineers typically do the following:

- Direct and coordinate the design, manufacture, and testing of aircraft and aerospace products
- Assess proposals for projects to determine if they are technically and financially feasible
- Determine if proposed projects will result in safe aircraft and parts
- Evaluate designs to see that the products meet engineering principles, customer requirements, and environmental challenges
- Develop acceptance criteria for design methods, quality standards, sustainment after delivery, and completion dates
- Ensure that projects meet quality standards
- Inspect malfunctioning or damaged products to identify sources of problems and possible solutions

Aerospace engineers may develop new technologies for use in aviation, defense systems, and spacecraft. They often specialize in areas such as aerodynamic fluid flow; structural design; guidance, navigation, and control; instrumentation and communication; robotics; or propulsion and combustion.

Aerospace engineers can specialize in designing different types of

aerospace products, such as commercial and military airplanes and helicopters; remotely piloted aircraft and rotorcraft; spacecraft, including launch vehicles and satellites; and military missiles and rockets.

Aerospace engineers often become experts in one or more related fields: aerodynamics, thermodynamics, celestial mechanics, flight mechanics, propulsion, acoustics, and guidance and control systems.

Aerospace engineers typically are specialized in one of two types of engineering, aeronautical engineering or astronautical engineering:

Aeronautical engineers work with aircraft. They are involved primarily in designing aircraft and propulsion systems and in studying the aerodynamic performance of aircraft and construction materials. They work with the theory, technology, and practice of flight within the earth's atmosphere.

Astronautical engineers work with the science and technology of spacecraft and how they perform inside and outside the earth's atmosphere.

Aeronautical and astronautical engineers face different environmental and operational issues in designing aircraft and spacecraft. However, the two fields overlap a great deal because they both depend on the basic principles of physics.

Work Environment

Aerospace engineers held about 81,000 jobs in 2010. They are employed in industries whose workers design or build aircraft, missiles, systems for national defense, or spacecraft. Aerospace engineers are employed primarily in analysis and design, manufacturing, industries that perform research and development, and the federal government.

Aerospace product and parts manufacturing	35%
Architectural, engineering, and related services	15
Scientific research and development services	14
Federal government	13
Navigational, measuring, electromedical, and control instruments manufacturing	8

Aerospace engineers now spend more of their time in an office than they have in the past, because modern aircraft design requires the use of sophisticated computer equipment and software design tools, modeling, and simulations for tests, evaluation, and training.

Aerospace engineers typically work full time. Engineers who direct projects must often work extra hours to monitor progress, to ensure that the design meets requirements, to determine how to measure aircraft performance, to see that production meets design standards, and to ensure that deadlines are met.

How to Become an Aerospace Engineer

Aerospace engineers must have a bachelor's degree in aerospace engineering or some other field of engineering or science related to aerospace systems. Some aerospace engineers work on projects that are related to national defense and thus require security clearances. U.S. citizenship may be required for certain types and levels of clearances.

Education

Entry-level aerospace engineers usually need a bachelor's degree. High school students interested in studying aerospace engineering should take courses in chemistry, physics, and mathematics, including algebra, trigonometry, and calculus.

Bachelor's degree programs are designed to take 4 years and include classroom, laboratory, and field studies in subjects such as general engineering principles, propulsion, stability and control, structures, mechanics, and aerodynamics, which is the study of how air interacts with moving objects.

Some colleges and universities offer cooperative programs, in partnership with industry, that give students practical experience while they complete their education. Cooperative programs and internships allow students to get valuable experience and to finance part of their education.

At some universities, a student can enroll in a 5-year program that leads to both a bachelor's degree and master's degree upon completion. A graduate degree will allow an engineer to work as an instructor at a university or to do research and development. Programs in aerospace engineering are accredited by ABET (formerly the Accreditation Board for Engineering and Technology).

Important Qualities

Analytical skills. Aerospace engineers must be able to identify design elements that may not be meeting requirements in particular operating environments and then formulate alternatives to improve their performance.

Business skills. Much of the work done by aerospace engineers involves meeting federal government standards. Meeting these standards often requires knowledge of standard business practices, as well as knowledge of commercial law.

Critical-thinking skills. Aerospace engineers must be able to translate a set of issues into requirements and to figure out why a particular design does not work. They must be able to ask the right question and then to find an acceptable answer.

Math skills. Aerospace engineers use the principals of calculus, trigonometry, and other advanced topics in mathematics for analysis, design, and troubleshooting in their work.

Teamwork. Aerospace engineers must work with other professionals involved in designing and building aircraft, spacecraft, and their components. They must be able to communicate well, divide work into manageable tasks, and work with others toward a common goal.

Writing skills. Aerospace engineers work with many other professionals, often other kinds of engineers. They must be able to write papers that explain their designs clearly to these professionals. They must also create documentation for future reference.

Licenses

Aerospace engineers are not required to be licensed at the entry level. More experienced aerospace engineers, who have more responsibility, must be licensed as professional engineers (PE). Licensure generally requires the following:

- A degree from an engineering program accredited by ABET
- A passing score on the Fundamentals of Engineering (FE) exam
- Relevant work experience
- A passing score on the Professional Engineering (PE) exam

The initial Fundamentals of Engineering (FE) exam can be taken right after graduating with a bachelor's degree. Engineers who pass this exam commonly are called engineers in training (EITs) or engineer interns (EIs). After acquiring suitable work experience, EITs can take the second exam, called the Principles and Practice of Engineering exam.

Several states require engineers to take continuing education courses to keep their licenses. Most states recognize licenses from other states, as long as the other states' licensing requirements meet or exceed their own licensing requirements.

Advancement

Eventually, aerospace engineers may advance to become technical specialists or to supervise a team of engineers and technicians. Some may even become engineering managers or move into executive positions, such as program managers. However, preparation for assuming a managerial position usually requires serving an apprenticeship under a more experienced aerospace engineer. For more information, see the profile on architectural and engineering managers

Pay

Aerospace Engineers
Median annual wages, May 2010

Aerospace Engineers	$97,480
Engineers	$83,340
Total, All Occupations	$33,840

Note: All Occupations includes all occupations in the U.S. Economy.
Source: U.S. Bureau of Labor Statistics, Occupational Employment Statistics

The median annual wage of aerospace engineers was $97,480 in May 2010. The median wage is the wage at which half of the workers in an occupation earned more than that amount and half earned less. The lowest 10 percent earned less than $60,620, and the top 10 percent earned more than $143,360.

Median annual wages in the industries employing the largest numbers of aerospace engineers in May 2010 were as follows:

Federal government	$111,370
Scientific research and development services	105,470
Navigational, measuring, electromedical, and control instruments manufacturing	101,760
Architectural, engineering, and related services	95,220
Aerospace product and parts manufacturing	88,340

A compensation study by Aviation Week found that average annual pay among all aerospace engineers ranges from $61,379 at the entry level to $145,832 for the most senior aerospace engineers in 2010. Mid-career aerospace engineers made an average of $88,342 in 2010.

Aerospace engineers typically work full time. Engineers who direct projects must often work extra hours to monitor progress, to ensure that the design meets requirements, to determine how to measure aircraft performance, to see that production meets design standards, and to ensure that deadlines are met.

Job Outlook

Aerospace Engineers
Percent change in employment, projected 2010-20

Total, All Occupations	14%
Engineers	11%
Aerospace Engineers	

5%

Note: All Occupations includes all occupations in the U.S. Economy.
Source: U.S. Bureau of Labor Statistics, Employment Projections program

Employment of aerospace engineers is expected to grow 5 percent from 2010 to 2020, slower than the average for all occupations. Some aerospace engineers work on projects that are related to national defense and thus require security clearances. These restrictions will help to keep jobs in the United States. In addition, aircraft are being redesigned to cut down on noise pollution and to raise fuel efficiency, increasing demand for research and development. However, growth will be tempered since many of these engineers are employed in manufacturing industries that are projected to grow slowly or decline.

Most of their work involves national defense-related projects or designing civilian aircraft. Research and development projects, such as those related to improving the safety, efficiency, and environmental soundness of aircraft, should create demand for aerospace engineers.

Aerospace engineers who work on engines or propulsion will be needed as the emphasis in design and production shifts to rebuilding existing aircraft so that they are less noisy and use less fuel.

In addition, as governments refocus their space efforts, new companies are emerging to provide access to space outside of standard space agencies. Their efforts will include low orbit and beyond earth orbit capabilities for human and robotic space travel.

Job Prospects

Aerospace engineers who know how to use collaborative engineering tools and processes and who know about modeling, simulation and robotics should have good opportunities. Opportunities also should be favorable for those trained in Computational Fluid Dynamics software, which has enabled companies to test designs in a digital environment, thereby lowering testing costs.

Employment projections data for aerospace engineers, 2010-20

Occupational Title	SOC Code	Employment, 2010	Projected Employment, 2020	Change, 2010-20 Percent	Numeric
Aerospace Engineers	17-2011	81,000	85,000	5	4,000
SOURCE: U.S. Bureau of Labor Statistics, Employment Projections program					

Similar Occupations

This table shows a list of occupations with job duties that are similar to those of aerospace engineers.

Occupation	Job Duties	Entry-Level Education	Median Annual Pay, May 2010
Aerospace Engineering and Operations Technicians	Aerospace engineering and operations technicians operate and maintain equipment used in developing, testing, and producing new aircraft and spacecraft. Increasingly, they use computer-based modeling and simulation tools and processes in this work.	Associate's degree	$58,080
Architectural and Engineering Managers	Architectural and engineering managers plan, coordinate, and direct activities in architecture and engineering, including research and development in these fields.	Bachelor's degree	$119,260
Computer Hardware Engineers	Computer hardware engineers research, design, develop, and test computer equipment such as chips, circuit boards, or routers. By solving complex problems in computer hardware, these engineers create rapid advances in computer technology.	Bachelor's degree	$98,810
Electrical and Electronic Engineering Technicians	Electrical and electronic engineering technicians help engineers design and develop computers, communications equipment, medical monitoring devices, navigational equipment, and other electrical and electronic equipment. They often work in product evaluation and testing, using measuring and diagnostic devices to adjust, test, and repair equipment.	Associate's degree	$56,040
Electrical and Electronics Engineers	Electrical engineers design, develop, test, and supervise the manufacturing of electrical equipment such as electric motors, radar and navigation systems, communications systems, and power generation equipment. Electronics engineers design and develop electronic equipment, such as broadcast and communications systems€"from portable music players to global positioning systems (GPS).	Bachelor's degree	$87,180
Industrial Engineers	Industrial engineers find ways to eliminate wastefulness in production processes. They devise efficient ways to use workers, machines, materials, information, and energy to make a product or provide a service.	Bachelor's degree	$76,100
Materials Engineers	Materials engineers develop, process, and test materials used to create a range of products, from computer chips and aircraft wings to golf clubs and snow skis. They also help select materials and develop new ways to use materials.	Bachelor's degree	$83,120
Mechanical Engineers	Mechanical engineering is one of the broadest engineering disciplines. Mechanical engineers design, develop, build, and test mechanical devices, including tools, engines, and machines.	Bachelor's degree	$78,160

Contacts for More Information

For information about general engineering education and career resources, visit American Society for Engineering Education

Technology Student Association

For more information about licensure as an aerospace engineer, visit National Council of Examiners for Engineering and Surveying

National Society of Professional Engineers

For information about accredited engineering programs, visit ABET

For information about licensure and current developments in the aeronautics, visit American Institute of Aeronautics and Astronautics

Suggested citation:

Bureau of Labor Statistics, U.S. Department of Labor, Occupational Outlook Handbook, 2012-13 Edition, Aerospace Engineers, on the Internet at http://www.bls.gov/ooh/architecture-and-engineering/aerospace-engineers.htm.

Agricultural Engineers

QUICK FACTS: AGRICULTURAL ENGINEERS	
2010 Median Pay	$71,090 per year $34.18 per hour
Entry-Level Education	Bachelor's degree
Work Experience in a Related Occupation	None
On-the-job Training	None
Number of Jobs, 2010	2,700
Job Outlook, 2010-20	9% (Slower than average)
Employment Change, 2010-20	200

What Agricultural Engineers Do

Agricultural engineers€"also known as biological and agricultural engineers€"work on a variety of activities. These activities range from aquaculture (raising food, such as fish, that thrive in water) to land farming to forestry; from developing biofuels to improving conservation; from planning animal environments to finding better ways to process food.

Duties

Agricultural engineers typically do the following:

- Design agricultural machinery components and equipment, using computer-aided design (CAD) technology
- Test agricultural machinery and equipment to ensure that they perform adequately
- Design food-processing plants and supervise manufacturing operations
- Plan and direct construction of rural electric-power distribution systems
- Design structures to store and process crops
- Design housing and environments to maximize animals' comfort, health, and productivity
- Provide advice on water quality and issues related to managing pollution, controlling rivers, and protecting and using other water resources
- Design and supervise environmental and land reclamation projects in agriculture and related industries
- Discuss plans with clients, contractors, consultants, and other engineers so that the plans can be evaluated and any necessary changes made

Agricultural engineers apply technological advances to farming. For example, they design farming equipment that uses the Global Positioning System. They help agronomists create biological applications for developing crops with new, sturdier traits. And they help with pollution control at larger farms and with water resource matters. These engineers are also heavily involved in efforts to produce new forms of biomass, including algae, for power generation.

Some engineers specialize in areas such as power systems and machinery design, structural and environmental engineering, and food and bioprocess engineering. Agricultural engineers often work in research and development, production, sales, or management.

Work Environment

Agricultural engineers held about 2,700 jobs in 2010.

As shown below, 17 percent of agricultural engineers worked in the federal government in 2010:

Architectural, engineering, and related services	17%
Federal government, excluding postal service	17
Agriculture, construction, and mining machinery manufacturing	12
Food manufacturing	11
Educational services; state, local, and private	7

Agricultural engineers spend time at a variety of worksites, both indoors and out, traveling to agricultural settings to see that equipment and machinery are functioning according to both the manufacturers' instructions and federal and state regulations. They may work onsite when they supervise environmental reclamation or water resource management projects.

Other worksites where they are employed include research and development laboratories, classrooms, and offices.

Work Schedules

Agricultural engineers typically work full time. And because of the nature of agricultural projects, they must sometimes work overtime.

In addition, the supervisory duties of agricultural engineers mean that they often must be present for problems that may come up in manufacturing operations or rural construction projects.

Weather also has a role in their work schedule. Some outdoor projects for environmental reclamation or pollution management need favorable weather; and, therefore, agricultural engineers may work long hours to take advantage of good weather.

Agricultural engineers often have to observe the results of their work where the crops are actually grown.

How to Become an Agricultural Engineer

Agricultural engineers must have a bachelor's degree, preferably in agricultural engineering or biological engineering. Employers also value practical experience, so cooperative-education engineering programs at universities are valuable as well.

Education

Students who are interested in studying agricultural engineering will benefit from taking high school courses in mathematics, such as algebra, trigonometry, and calculus; and science, such as biology, chemistry, and physics.

Entry-level jobs in agricultural engineering require a bachelor's degree. Bachelor's degree programs typically are 4-year programs that include classroom, laboratory, and field studies in areas such as science, mathematics, and engineering principles. Most colleges and universities offer cooperative programs that allow students to gain practical experience while completing their education.

ABET (formerly the Accreditation Board for Engineering and Technology) accredits programs in agricultural engineering.

Important Qualities

Listening skills. Agricultural engineers must listen to and seek out information from clients, workers, and other professionals working on a project. Furthermore, they must be able to address the concerns of those who will be using the systems and solutions they design.

Math skills. Agricultural engineers use the principals of calculus, trigonometry, and other advanced topics in mathematics for analysis, design, and troubleshooting in their work.

Problem-solving skills. Agricultural engineers work on problems affecting many different aspects of agricultural production, from problems requiring the design of safer equipment for food processing to water erosion and control problems. To solve these problems, agricultural engineers must be able to apply general principles of engineering to new circumstances.

Systems analysis. Because agricultural engineers sometimes design systems that are part of a larger agricultural or environmental system, they must be able to propose solutions that interact well with other workers, machinery and equipment, and the environment.

Teamwork. Agricultural engineers must be able to work with others in designing solutions involving biological, mechanical, or environmental dimensions. They must be able to work with, and accept feedback from, people from a variety of backgrounds such as agronomy, animal sciences, genetics, and horticulture.

Licenses

Agricultural engineers who offer their services directly to the public must have a license. Licensed engineers are called professional engineers (PEs). Licensure generally requires
- A degree from an ABET-accredited engineering program
- A passing score on the Fundamentals of Engineering (FE) exam
- Relevant work experience, typically at least 4 years
- A passing score on the Professional Engineering (PE) exam

The initial Fundamentals of Engineering (FE) exam can be taken after earning a bachelor's degree. Engineers who pass this exam commonly are called engineers in training (EITs) or engineer interns (EIs). After getting suitable work experience, EITs and EIs can take the second exam, called the Principles and Practice of Engineering.

Several states require continuing education for engineers to keep their license. Most states recognize licensure from other states, if the licensing state's requirements meet or exceed their own licensure requirements.

Advancement

Beginning engineers usually work under the supervision of experienced engineers. As they gain knowledge and experience, beginning engineers move to more difficult projects with greater independence to develop designs, solve problems, and make decisions.

Eventually, agricultural engineers may advance to supervise a team of engineers and technicians. Some become engineering managers or move into other managerial positions or sales work.

Agricultural engineers who go into sales use their engineering background to discuss a product's technical aspects with potential buyers and help in product planning, installation, and use. For more information, see the profile on sales engineers .

Pay

Agricultural Engineers
Median annual wages, May 2010

Engineers	$83,340
Agricultural Engineers	$71,090
Total, All Occupations	$33,840

Note: All Occupations includes all occupations in the U.S. Economy.
Source: U.S. Bureau of Labor Statistics, Occupational Employment Statistics

The median annual wage of agricultural engineers was $71,090 in May 2010. The median wage is the wage at which half the workers in an occupation earned more than that amount and half earned less. The lowest 10 percent earned less than $42,210, and the top 10 percent earned more than $115,150.

Median annual wages in the industries employing the largest numbers of agricultural engineers in May 2010 were as follows:

Architectural, engineering, and related services	$78,940
Food manufacturing	77,670
Federal government, excluding postal service	74,770
Agriculture, construction, and mining machinery manufacturing	63,310
Educational services; state, local, and private	52,450

Agricultural engineers' work schedules differ from that of most other engineers. Their work must often be done when weather permits, and they must take full advantage of good weather to fulfill their clients' needs as quickly as possible.

Job Outlook

Agricultural Engineers
  Percent change in employment, projected 2010-20

Total, All Occupations	14%
Engineers	11%
Agricultural Engineers	9%

Note: All Occupations includes all occupations in the U.S. Economy.
Source: U.S. Bureau of Labor Statistics, Employment Projections program

  Employment of agricultural engineers is expected to grow 9 percent between 2010 and 2020, slower than the average for all occupations.
  Agricultural engineers are pursuing new areas related to agriculture, such as high-tech applications to agricultural products, water resource management, and alternative energies. However, activity related to designing new machinery and equipment in agriculture also is expected to continue to create employment opportunities.
  Demand is also expected to come from United States firms that market their farm technology products to farmers internationally.

Employment projections data for agricultural engineers, 2010-20

Occupational Title	SOC Code	Employment, 2010	Projected Employment, 2020	Change, 2010-20 Percent	Numeric
Agricultural Engineers	17-2021	2,700	2,900	9	200
SOURCE: U.S. Bureau of Labor Statistics, Employment Projections program					

Similar Occupations

  This table shows a list of occupations with job duties that are similar to those of agricultural engineers.

Occupation	Job Duties	Entry-Level Education	Median Annual Pay, May 2010
Agricultural and Food Science Technicians	Under the supervision of scientists, agricultural and food science technicians measure and analyze the quality of food and agricultural products.	Associate's degree	$32,760
Agricultural and Food Scientists	Agricultural and food scientists work to ensure agricultural productivity and food safety.	See How to Become One	$58,450
Biological Technicians	Biological technicians help biological and medical scientists conduct laboratory tests and experiments.	Bachelor's degree	$39,020
Hydrologists	Hydrologists study water and the water cycle. They use their expertise to solve problems in the areas of water quality or availability.	Master's degree	$75,690
Farmers, Ranchers, and Other Agricultural Managers	Farmers, ranchers, and other agricultural managers run establishments that produce crops, livestock, and dairy products.	High school diploma or equivalent	$60,750
Civil Engineers	Civil engineers design and supervise large construction projects, including roads, buildings, airports, tunnels, dams, bridges, and systems for water supply and sewage treatment.	Bachelor's degree	$77,560
Environmental Engineers	Environmental engineers use the principles of engineering, soil science, biology, and chemistry to develop solutions to environmental problems. They are involved in efforts to improve recycling, waste disposal, public health, and control of water and air pollution.	Bachelor's degree	$78,740
Industrial Engineers	Industrial engineers find ways to eliminate wastefulness in production processes. They devise efficient ways to use workers, machines, materials, information, and energy to make a product or provide a service.	Bachelor's degree	$76,100

Landscape Architects	Landscape architects plan and design land areas for parks, recreational facilities, highways, airports, and other properties. Projects include subdivisions and commercial, industrial, and residential sites.	Bachelor's degree	$62,090
Mechanical Engineers	Mechanical engineering is one of the broadest engineering disciplines. Mechanical engineers design, develop, build, and test mechanical devices, including tools, engines, and machines.	Bachelor's degree	$78,160

Contacts for More Information

For more information about agricultural engineers, visit American Society of Agricultural and Biological Engineers

For information about general engineering education and career resources, visit American Society for Engineering Education Technology Student Association

For more information about licensure as an agricultural engineer, visit National Council of Examiners for Engineering and Surveying, National Society of Professional Engineers

For information about accredited engineering programs, visit ABET

Suggested citation:

Bureau of Labor Statistics, U.S. Department of Labor, Occupational Outlook Handbook, 2012-13 Edition, Agricultural Engineers, on the Internet at http://www.bls.gov/ooh/architecture-and-engineering/agricultural-engineers.htm

Architects

Quick Facts: Architects	
2010 Median Pay	$72,550 per year $34.88 per hour
Entry-Level Education	Bachelor's degree
Work Experience in a Related Occupation	None
On-the-job Training	Internship/residency
Number of Jobs, 2010	113,700
Job Outlook, 2010-20	24% (Faster than average)
Employment Change, 2010-20	27,900

What Architects Do

Architects plan and design buildings and other structures.

Duties

Architects typically do the following:

- Seek new work by marketing and giving presentations
- Consult with clients to determine requirements for structures
- Estimate materials, equipment, costs, and construction time
- Prepare, design, and structure specifications
- Direct workers who prepare drawings and documents
- Prepare scaled drawings of the project
- Prepare contract documents for building contractors
- Manage construction contracts
- Visit worksites to ensure that construction adheres to architectural plans

People need places to live, work, play, learn, worship, meet, govern, shop, and eat. Architects are responsible for designing these places, whether they are private or public; indoors or outdoors; or rooms, buildings, or complexes.

Architects discuss with clients the objectives, requirements, and budget of a project. In some cases, architects provide various predesign services, such as feasibility and environmental impact studies, site selection, cost analyses and land-use studies, and design requirements. For example, architects may determine a building's space requirements by researching its number and types of potential users.

After discussing and agreeing on the initial proposal, architects develop final construction plans that show the building's appearance and details for its construction. Accompanying these plans are drawings of the structural system; air-conditioning, heating, and ventilating systems; electrical systems; communications systems; plumbing; and, possibly, site and landscape plans.

In developing designs, architects must follow building codes, zoning laws, fire regulations, and other ordinances, such as those requiring easy access by people who are disabled.

Computer-aided design and drafting (CADD) and building information modeling (BIM) technology have replaced traditional drafting paper and pencil as the most common methods for creating designs and construction drawings.

Architects also may help clients get construction bids, select contractors, and negotiate construction contracts.

As construction proceeds, architects may visit building sites to ensure that contractors follow the design, keep to the schedule, use the specified materials, and meet work-quality standards. The job is not complete until all construction is finished, required tests are conducted, and construction costs are paid.

Architects often work with workers in related professions. For more information on these occupations, see the profiles on civil engineers , urban and regional planners , interior designers , and landscape architects .

Architects use CADD during the design process.

Work Environment

Architects held about 113,700 jobs in 2010, of which 65 percent were employed in the architectural, engineering, and related services industry. About 24 percent were self-employed.

Architects spend most of their time in offices, where they consult with clients, develop reports and drawings, and work with other architects and engineers. However, they often visit construction sites to review the progress of projects.

Work Schedules

Nearly all architects work full time. Many work more than 50 hours per week. Working evenings and weekends is often necessary to meet deadlines.

How to Become an Architect

There are three main steps in becoming a licensed architect: completing a professional degree in architecture, gaining work experience through an internship, and passing the Architect Registration Exam.

Education

In most states, architects must hold a professional degree in architecture from one of the 123 schools of architecture accredited by the National Architectural Accrediting Board (NAAB). However, state architectural registration boards set their own standards, so, in a few states, graduation from a nonaccredited program may meet the educational requirement for licensing.

Most architects earn their professional degree through a 5-year Bachelor of Architecture degree program, intended for students with no previous architectural training. Others earn a master's degree which can take 1 to 5 years to complete, depending on the extent of one's previous training in architecture.

The choice of degree depends on preference and educational background. Although the 5-year bachelor of architecture offers the most direct route to the professional degree, courses are specialized. A typical program includes courses in architectural history and theory, building design with an emphasis on computer-aided design and drafting (CADD), structures, technology, construction methods, professional practice, math, physical sciences, and liberal arts. Central to most architectural programs is the design studio, where students apply the skills and concepts learned in the classroom to create drawings and three-dimensional models of their designs.

Many schools of architecture also offer postprofessional degrees for those who already have a bachelor's or master's degree in architecture or other areas. Although graduate education beyond the professional degree is not required for practicing architects, it may be useful for research, teaching, and certain specialties.

Training

All state architectural registration boards require architecture graduates to complete a training period€"usually at least 3 years€"before they may sit for the licensing exam. Most new graduates complete their training period by working as interns at architectural firms. Some states allow a portion of the training to occur in the offices of related professionals, such as engineers and general contractors. Architecture students who complete internships while still in school can count some of that time toward the 3-year training period.

Interns in architectural firms may help design part of a project. They may help prepare architectural documents and drawings, build models, and prepare construction drawings on CADD. Interns also may research building codes and write specifications for building materials, installation criteria, the quality of finishes, and other related details.

Licenses

All states and the District of Columbia require architects to be licensed. Licensing requirements include a professional degree in architecture, a period of practical training or internship, and a passing score on all parts of the Architect Registration Examination.

Most states also require some form of continuing education to keep a license, and some additional states are expected to adopt mandatory

continuing education. Requirements vary by state but usually involve additional education through workshops, formal university classes, conferences, self-study courses, or other sources.

Certification

A growing number of architects voluntarily seek certification by the National Council of Architectural Registration Boards (NCARB). Certification can make it easier to become licensed across states. In fact, it is the primary requirement for reciprocity of licensing among state boards that are NCARB members. In 2011, approximately one-third of all licensed architects had this certification.

Important Qualities

Analytical skills. Architects must understand the content of designs and the context in which they were created. For example, architects must understand the locations of mechanical systems and how those systems affect building operations.

Communication skills. Architects share their ideas, both orally and in writing, with clients, other architects, and workers who help prepare drawings. Many also give presentations to explain their designs.

Creativity. Architects create the overall look of buildings. Designs should be both pleasing to the eye and functional.

Critical-thinking skills. When designing a building, architects must be able to provide solutions to unanticipated challenges. These solutions often involve looking at the challenge from all perspectives.

Organizational skills. Architects often manage contracts. Therefore, they must keep records related to the details of a project, including total cost, materials used, and progress.

Technical skills. Architects use computer-aided design and drafting (CADD) programs to create plans as part of integrated building information modeling (BIM).

Visualization skills. Architects must be able to "see" how the parts of a structure relate to each other. They also must be able to visualize how the overall building will look once completed.

Pay

Architects	
Median annual wages, May 2010	
Architects, Except Landscape and Naval	$72,550
Architects, Surveyors, and Cartographers	$64,820
Total, All Occupations	$33,840

Note: All Occupations includes all occupations in the U.S. Economy.
Source: U.S. Bureau of Labor Statistics, Occupational Employment Statistics

The median annual wage of architects was $72,550 in May 2010. The median wage is the wage at which half the workers in an occupation earned more than that amount and half earned less. The lowest 10 percent earned less than $42,860, and the top 10 percent earned more than $119,500.

Earnings of partners in established architectural firms may fluctuate because of changing business conditions. Some architects have difficulty establishing their own practice and may go through a period when their expenses are greater than their income, requiring substantial financial resources.

Many firms pay tuition and fees toward continuing education requirements for their employees.

Nearly all architects work full time. Many work more than 50 hours per week. Working evenings and weekends is often necessary to meet deadlines.

Job Outlook

Architects

Percent change in employment, projected 2010-20

Architects, Except Landscape and Naval	24%
Architects, Surveyors, and Cartographers	24%
Total, All Occupations	14%

Note: All Occupations includes all occupations in the U.S. Economy.
Source: U.S. Bureau of Labor Statistics, Employment Projections program

Employment of architects is projected to grow 24 percent from 2010 to 2020, faster than the average for all occupations.

Current demographic trends will result in a greater need for architects. As campus buildings age, many school districts and universities will build new facilities or renovate existing ones. The population of sunbelt states continues to grow, and residents there will need new places to live and work. As the population continues to live longer and baby boomers retire, there will be a need for more healthcare facilities, nursing homes, and retirement communities.

There should be demand for architects with knowledge of green design, also called sustainable design. Sustainable design emphasizes the efficient use of resources, such as energy and water conservation; waste and pollution reduction; and environmentally friendly design, specifications, and materials. Rising energy costs and increased concern about the environment have led to many new buildings being built green.

During the construction boom, some architecture firms outsourced the drafting of construction documents and basic design for large-scale commercial and residential projects to architecture firms overseas. Recently, however, this trend of outsourcing overseas has slowed considerably.

Job Prospects

With a growing number of students graduating with architectural degrees, applicants will experience competition for jobs. Competition for jobs will be especially strong at the most prestigious architectural firms. Although those who have completed internships will have an advantage, the best job opportunities will be for candidates who can distinguish themselves with their creativity.

Employment of architects is strongly tied to the activity of the construction industry. Therefore, these workers, especially the self-employed, may experience periods of unemployment when the overall level of construction falls.

Employment projections data for architects, 2010-20

Occupational Title	SOC Code	Employment, 2010	Projected Employment, 2020	Change, 2010-20 Percent	Numeric
Architects, Except Landscape and Naval	17-1011	113,700	141,600	24	27,900

SOURCE: U.S. Bureau of Labor Statistics, Employment Projections program

Similar Occupations

This table shows a list of occupations with job duties that are similar to those of architects.

Occupation	Job Duties	Entry-Level Education	Median Annual Pay, May 2010
Construction Managers	Construction managers plan, coordinate, budget, and supervise construction projects from early development to completion.	Associate's degree	$83,860
Civil Engineers	Civil engineers design and supervise large construction projects, including roads, buildings, airports, tunnels, dams, bridges, and systems for water supply and sewage treatment.	Bachelor's degree	$77,560
Landscape Architects	Landscape architects plan and design land areas for parks, recreational facilities, highways, airports, and other properties. Projects include subdivisions and commercial, industrial, and residential sites.	Bachelor's degree	$62,090
Graphic Designers	Graphic designers create visual concepts, by hand or using computer software, to communicate ideas that inspire, inform, or captivate consumers. They help to make an organization recognizable by selecting color, images, or logo designs that represent a particular idea or identity to be used in advertising and promotions.	Bachelor's degree	$43,500
Industrial Designers	Industrial designers develop the concepts for manufactured products, such as cars, home appliances, and toys. They combine art, business, and engineering to make products that people use every day.	Bachelor's degree	$58,230
Interior Designers	Interior designers make interior spaces functional, safe, and beautiful for almost every type of building: offices, homes, airport terminals, shopping malls, and restaurants. They select and specify colors, finishes, fabrics, furniture, flooring and wallcoverings, lighting, and other materials to create useful and stylish interiors for buildings.	Bachelor's degree	$46,280
Urban and Regional Planners	Urban and regional planners develop plans and programs for the use of land. They use planning to create communities, accommodate growth, or revitalize physical facilities in towns, cities, counties, and metropolitan areas.	Master's degree	$63,040

Contacts for More Information

For information about careers in architecture, visit The American Institute of Architects, ARCHcareers, National Architectural Accrediting Board, National Council of Architectural Registration Boards

Suggested citation:

Bureau of Labor Statistics, U.S. Department of Labor, Occupational Outlook Handbook, 2012-13 Edition, Architects, on the Internet at http://www.bls.gov/ooh/architecture-and-engineering/architects.htm .

Cartographers and Photogrammetrists

Quick Facts: Cartographers and Photogrammetrists	
2010 Median Pay	$54,510 per year $26.21 per hour
Entry-Level Education	Bachelor's degree
Work Experience in a Related Occupation	None
On-the-job Training	None
Number of Jobs, 2010	13,800
Job Outlook, 2010-20	22% (Faster than average)
Employment Change, 2010-20	3,100

What Cartographers and Photogrammetrists Do

Cartographers and photogrammetrists measure, analyze, and interpret geographic information to create maps and charts for political, cultural, educational, and other purposes.

Cartographers are general mapmakers who compile data from multiple sources and then use principles of cartographic design to make maps. Photogrammetrists are specialized mapmakers who use aerial photographs, satellite images, and light-imaging detection and ranging technology (LIDAR) to build 3-D models of the Earth's surface and its features for purposes of creating maps.

Duties

Cartographers typically do the following:

- Collect and analyze geographic data, such as population density, demographic characteristics, and annual precipitation patterns

- Examine and compile data from ground surveys, reports, aerial photographs, and satellite images to prepare thematic maps

- Prepare thematic maps in digital or graphic form for social, environmental, political, business, educational, and design purposes

- Revise existing maps and charts to make corrections, adjustments, and updates

Photogrammetrists typically do the following:

- Plan aerial surveys to ensure proper coverage of the area in question

- Collect and analyze spatial data such as latitude, longitude, elevation, and distance

- Develop base maps that make it possible to produce useful cartographic output using a geographic information system (GIS)

Cartographers and photogrammetrists use information from geodetic surveys and remote sensing systems, including aerial cameras, satellites, and technologies such as light-imaging detection and ranging (LIDAR).

LIDAR uses lasers attached to planes and other equipment to digitally map the topography of the Earth. LIDAR is often more accurate than traditional surveying methods and also can be used to collect other forms of data, such as the location and density of forest canopies. Data from LIDAR are used to provide spatial information to specialists in water resource engineering, geology, seismology, forestry, construction, and other fields.

A cartographic professional who creates maps using geographic information system (GIS) technology is known as a **geographic information specialist.** A GIS is typically used to assemble, integrate,

analyze, and display spatial information in a digital format. Maps created with GIS technology link spatial graphic features with non-graphic information. These maps are useful for providing support for decisions involving environmental studies, geology, engineering, land-use planning, and business marketing.

Work Environment

Cartographers and photogrammetrists held about 13,800 jobs in 2010.

As shown in the tabulation below, about one half of cartographers and photogrammetrists worked in architectural and engineering services firms and for local government agencies in 2010.

Architectural, engineering, and related services	28%
Local government, excluding education and hospitals	22
Self-employed workers	14
Management, scientific, and technical consulting services	6
Federal government, excluding postal service	5

Cartographers and photogrammetrists spend much of their time in offices using computers with large monitors, so they can easily study and extract information from aerial photographs and other sources. However, certain jobs require extensive fieldwork to acquire data and verify results.

Cartographers typically do fieldwork to collect and verify data used in creating maps. Photogrammetrists do fieldwork to plan ground control for an aerial survey and to validate interpretations.

How to Become a Cartographer or Photogrammetrist

A bachelor's degree in cartography, geography, geomatics, or a related field is the most common path of entry into this occupation. (Geomatics combines the science, engineering, mathematics, and art of collecting and managing geographically referenced information.) Some states require cartographers and photogrammetrists to be licensed as surveyors, and some states have specific licenses for photogrammetrists.

Education

High school students interested in becoming a cartographer or photogrammetrist should take courses in algebra, geometry, trigonometry, drafting, mechanical drawing, and computer science.

Cartographers and photogrammetrists usually have a bachelor's degree in cartography, geography, geomatics, surveying, engineering, forestry, computer science, or a physical science. However, some come into this occupation after working as surveying and mapping technicians. For more information, see the profile on surveying and mapping technicians .

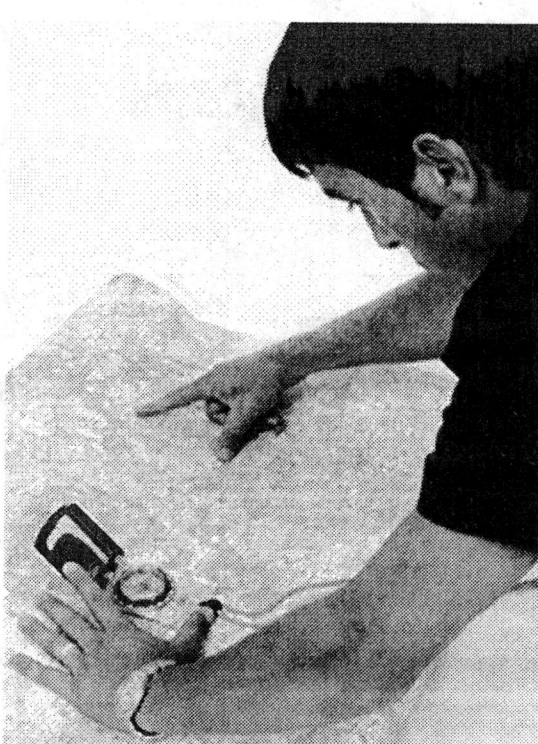

Cartographers and photogrammetrists are employed at firms in architectural and engineering services, and also in local and federal government agencies.

With the development of GIS technology, cartographers and photogrammetrists need more education and stronger technical skills€"including more experience with computers€"than they did in the past.

Cartographers must also be adept at Web-based mapping technologies including newer modes of compiling data that incorporate the positioning capabilities of mobile phones and in-car navigation systems.

Photogrammetrists also must be adept at remote sensing, image processing, and using the software necessary for these activities.

Important Qualities

Critical-thinking skills. Cartographers work from existing maps, surveys, and other records. To do so, they must be able to determine thematic and positional accuracy of each feature being mapped.

Decision-making skills. Both cartographers and photogrammetrists must make decisions about the accuracy and reliability of the final map. In addition, they must decide what further information they need to meet the client's needs.

Detail oriented. Cartographers must focus on details when including features needed on a final map. Photogrammetrists must pay close attention to detail when interpreting aerial photographs and remotely sensed data.

Problem-solving skills. Cartographers and photogrammetrists must be able to identify and resolve issues with the tools available to them.

Licenses

Licensing requirements for cartographers and photogrammetrists vary by state. A number of states require cartographers and photogrammetrists to be licensed as surveyors, and some states have specific licenses for photogrammetrists.

Although licensing requirements vary in those states requiring licensure, in general, licensing requires formal education and passing a test.

Certification

Cartographers and photogrammetrists may also receive certification from the American Society for Photogrammetry and Remote Sensing (ASPRS) based on experience, education, and passing an exam.

Pay

Cartographers and Photogrammetrists Median annual wages, May 2010	
Architects, Surveyors, and Cartographers	$64,820
Cartographers and Photogrammetrists	$54,510
Total, All Occupations	$33,840

Note: All Occupations includes all occupations in the U.S. Economy.
Source: U.S. Bureau of Labor Statistics, Occupational Employment Statistics

The median annual wage of cartographers and photogrammetrists was $54,510 in May 2010. The median wage is the wage at which half the workers in an occupation earned more than that amount and half earned less. The lowest 10 percent earned less than $33,260 and the top 10 percent earned more than $92,730.

Median annual wages in industries employing the largest numbers of cartographers and photogrammetrists in 2010 were as follows:

Federal government, excluding postal service	$82,570
Management, scientific, and technical consulting services	64,620
Local government, excluding education and hospitals	53,650
Architectural, engineering, and related services	52,180

Job Outlook

Cartographers and Photogrammetrists Percent change in employment, projected 2010-20	
Architects, Surveyors, and Cartographers	24%
Cartographers and Photogrammetrists	22%
Total, All Occupations	14%

Note: All Occupations includes all occupations in the U.S. Economy.
Source: U.S. Bureau of Labor Statistics, Employment Projections program

Employment of cartographers and photogrammetrists is expected to grow 22 percent from 2010 to 2020, faster than the average for all occupations.

Increasing use of maps for national security and local government planning will fuel most of the growth. Cartographers and photogrammetrists will be needed to ensure the reliability and accuracy of maps produced and updated.

Cartographers are also being asked to incorporate into the maps they make the data gathered from social media and Internet technologies.

In addition to openings from growth, job openings will arise from the need to replace workers who retire or leave the occupation. Many cartographers are approaching retirement age.

Cartographers primarily will be needed to visualize spatial information and design the final presentation of information for clients.

Job Prospects

Photogrammetrists should have excellent opportunities, because of the limited number of college graduates receiving degrees in this field.Employment projections data for cartographers and photogrammetrists, 2010-20

Employment projections data for cartographers and photogrammetrists, 2010-20

Occupational Title	SOC Code	Employment, 2010	Projected Employment, 2020	Change, 2010-20	
				Percent	Numberic
Cartographers and Photogrammetrists	17-1021	13,800	16,900	22	3,100
SOURCE: U.S. Bureau of Labor Statistics, Employment Projections program					

Similar Occupations

This table shows a list of occupations with job duties that are similar to those of cartographers and photogrammetrists.

Occupation	Job Duties	Entry-Level Education	Median Annual Pay, May 2010
Civil Engineers	Civil engineers design and supervise large construction projects, including roads, buildings, airports, tunnels, dams, bridges, and systems for water supply and sewage treatment.	Bachelor's degree	$77,560
Environmental Scientists and Specialists	Environmental scientists and specialists use their knowledge of the natural sciences to protect the environment. They identify problems and find solutions that minimize hazards to the health of the environment and the population.	Bachelor's degree	$61,700
Geographers	Geographers study the earth and its land, features, and inhabitants. They also examine phenomena such as political or cultural structures as they relate to geography. They study the physical or human geographic characteristics or both of a region, ranging in scale from local to global.	Bachelor's degree	$72,800
Landscape Architects	Landscape architects plan and design land areas for parks, recreational facilities, highways, airports, and other properties. Projects include subdivisions and commercial, industrial, and residential sites.	Bachelor's degree	$62,090
Surveying and Mapping Technicians	Surveying and mapping technicians assist surveyors and cartographers in collecting data and making maps of the earth's surface. Surveying technicians visit sites to take measurements of the land. Mapping technicians use geographic data to create maps.	High school diploma or equivalent	$37,900
Surveyors	Surveyors establish official land, airspace, and water boundaries. Surveyors work with civil engineers, landscape architects, and urban and regional planners to develop comprehensive design documents.	Bachelor's degree	$54,880
Urban and Regional Planners	Urban and regional planners develop plans and programs for the use of land. They use planning to create communities, accommodate growth, or revitalize physical facilities in towns, cities, counties, and metropolitan areas.	Master's degree	$63,040

Contacts for More Information

For more information about cartographers and photogrammetrists, visit American Congress on Surveying & Mapping, Cartography and Geographic Information Society.

For career information about photogrammetrists, photogrammetric technicians, remote sensing scientists, and image-based cartographers or geographic information system specialists, visit American Society for Photogrammetry and Remote Sensing.

For information about careers in remote sensing, photogrammetry, surveying, GIS analysis, and other geography-related disciplines, visit Association of American Geographers

Suggested citation:

Bureau of Labor Statistics, U.S. Department of Labor, Occupational Outlook Handbook, 2012-13 Edition, Cartographers and Photogrammetrists, on the Internet at http://www.bls.gov/ooh/architecture-and-engineering/cartographers-and-photogrammetrists.htm .

Chemical Engineers

Quick Facts: Chemical Engineers	
2010 Median Pay	$90,300 per year $43.42 per hour
Entry-Level Education	Bachelor's degree
Work Experience in a Related Occupation	None
On-the-job Training	None
Number of Jobs, 2010	30,200
Job Outlook, 2010-20	6% (Slower than average)
Employment Change, 2010-20	1,800

Chemical engineers draw on their knowledge of chemistry to design manufacturing of chemical goods on a large scale.

What Chemical Engineers Do

Chemical engineers apply the principles of chemistry, biology, and physics to solve problems involving the production or use of chemicals, fuel, drugs, food, and many other products. They design processes and equipment for large-scale manufacturing, plan and test methods of manufacturing products and treating byproducts, and supervise production.

Duties

Chemical engineers typically do the following:

- Develop safety procedures for those working with potentially dangerous chemicals
- Troubleshoot problems with manufacturing processes
- Evaluate equipment and processes to ensure compliance with safety and environmental regulations
- Conduct research to develop new and improved manufacturing processes
- Design and plan the layout of equipment
- Do tests and monitor performance of processes throughout production
- Estimate production costs for management
- Develop processes to separate components of liquids or gases or to generate electrical currents using controlled chemical processes

Chemical engineers apply principles of physics, biology, mathematics, mechanical and electrical engineering, and chemistry. Some specialize in a particular process, such as oxidation (burning chemicals to make other chemicals) or polymerization (making plastics). Others specialize in a particular field, such as nanomaterials (making extremely small substances), or in developing specific products.

Chemical engineers also work in a variety of industries other than chemical manufacturing. They work in producing energy, electronics, food, clothing, and paper. They work in health care, biotechnology, and business services.

Chemical engineers must be aware of all aspects in the manufacturing of chemicals, drugs, or other products. They must also understand how the manufacturing process affects the environment and the safety of workers and consumers.

Work Environment

Chemical engineers held about 30,200 jobs in 2010.

Chemical engineers work mostly in offices or laboratories. They may spend time at industrial plants, refineries, and other locations, where they monitor or direct operations or solve onsite problems. Some engineers travel extensively to plants or worksites both in the United States and abroad.

The industries employing the largest numbers of chemical engineers in 2010 were as follows:

Architectural, engineering, and related services	16%
Scientific research and development services	12
Basic chemical manufacturing	12
Resin, synthetic rubber, and artificial synthetic fibers and filaments manufacturing	7
Pharmaceutical and medicine manufacturing	5

Nearly all chemical engineers work full time.

How to Become a Chemical Engineer

Chemical engineers must have a bachelor's degree in chemical engineering, now sometimes known as a bachelor's degree in chemical and biomolecular engineering. Employers also value practical experience, so cooperative engineering programs, in which students earn college credit for structured job experience, are valuable as well. Having a Professional Engineer license may increase chances for employment.

Education

High school students interested in studying chemical engineering will benefit from taking science courses, such as chemistry, physics, biology. They also should take mathematics, including algebra, trigonometry, and calculus.

Entry-level chemical engineering jobs require a bachelor's degree. Programs usually take 4 years to complete and include classroom, laboratory, and field studies.

At some universities, a student can opt to enroll in a 5-year program that leads to both a bachelor's degree and a master's degree. A graduate degree allows an engineer to work as an instructor at some universities or in research and development.

Some colleges and universities offer cooperative programs where students gain practical experience while completing their education. Cooperative programs combine classroom study with practical work, permitting students to gain experience and to finance part of their education.

Programs in chemical engineering, which are also called chemical and biomolecular engineering, should be accredited by ABET (formerly the Accreditation Board for Engineering and Technology). ABET-accredited include courses in chemistry, physics, and biology. These programs also include applying the sciences to the design, analysis, and control of chemical, physical, and biological processes.

Important Qualities

Analytical skills. Chemical engineers must be able to figure out why a particular design does not work as planned. They must be able to ask the right question and then find an answer that works.

Deductive-reasoning skills. Chemical engineers learn the broad concepts of chemical engineering, but their work requires them to apply those concepts to specific production problems.

Interpersonal skills. Chemical engineers must develop good working relationships with people in production because their role is to put scientific principles into practice in manufacturing industries.

Math skills. Chemical engineers use the principals of calculus and other advanced topics in mathematics for analysis, design, and troubleshooting in their work.

Problem sensitivity. Chemical engineers must be able to anticipate and identify problems to prevent losses for their employers, safeguard workers' health, and prevent environmental damage.

Problem-solving skills. In designing equipment and processes for manufacturing, these engineers strive to solve several problems at once, including such issues as workers' safety and problems related to manufacturing and environmental protection.

Teamwork. Chemical engineers must be able to work with professionals who design other systems and with the technicians and mechanics who put the designs into practice.

Licenses

Licensure for chemical engineers is not as common as it is for other engineering occupations, but it is encouraged. Chemical engineers who become licensed carry the designation of professional engineers (PEs). Licensure generally requires the following:

- A degree from an engineering program accredited by ABET
- A passing score on the Fundamentals of Engineering (FE) exam
- Relevant work experience
- A passing score on the Professional Engineering (PE) exam

The initial Fundamentals of Engineering (FE) exam can be taken right after graduation. Engineers who pass this exam commonly are called engineers in training (EITs) or engineer interns (EIs). After they get work experience, EITs can take the second exam, called the Principles and Practice of Engineering exam.

Several states require engineers to take continuing education to keep their license. Most states recognize licensure from other states, if the licensing state's requirements meet or exceed their own licensure requirements.

Advancement

Entry-level engineers usually work under the supervision of experienced engineers. In large companies, new engineers may also receive formal training in classrooms or seminars. As beginning engineers gain knowledge and experience, they move to more difficult projects with greater independence to develop designs, solve problems, and make decisions.

Eventually, chemical engineers may advance to supervise a team of engineers and technicians. Some may become engineering managers. However, preparing for management positions usually requires working under the guidance of a more experienced chemical engineer.

For sales work, an engineering background enables chemical engineers to discuss a product's technical aspects and assist in product planning and use. For more information, see the profile on sales engineers.

Pay

Chemical Engineers
Median annual wages, May 2010

Chemical Engineers	$90,300
Engineers	$83,340
Total, All Occupations	$33,840

Note: All Occupations includes all occupations in the U.S. Economy.
Source: U.S. Bureau of Labor Statistics, Occupational Employment Statistics

The median annual wage of chemical engineers was $90,300 in May 2010. The median wage is the wage at which half the workers in an occupation earned more than that amount and half earned less. The lowest 10 percent earned less than $56,520, and the top 10 percent earned more than $139,670.

Median annual wages in the industries employing the largest numbers of chemical engineers in May 2010 were as follows:

Scientific research and development services	$94,640
Basic chemical manufacturing	92,590
Architectural, engineering, and related services	91,010
Pharmaceutical and medicine manufacturing	90,490
Resin, synthetic rubber, and artificial synthetic fibers and filaments manufacturing	84,940

Nearly all chemical engineers work full time.

Job Outlook

Chemical Engineers
Percent change in employment, projected 2010-20

Total, All Occupations	14%
Engineers	11%
Chemical Engineers	6%

Note: All Occupations includes all occupations in the U.S. Economy.
Source: U.S. Bureau of Labor Statistics, Employment Projections program

Employment of chemical engineers is expected to grow 6 percent from 2010 to 2020, slower than the average for all occupations. Demand for chemical engineers' services depends largely on demand for the products of various manufacturing industries. Employment will be sustained by the ability of these engineers to stay on the forefront of new, emerging technologies.

Many chemical engineers work in industries that have output sought by many manufacturing firms. Therefore, employment is tied to the state of overall manufacturing in the United States.

However, chemical engineering is also migrating into new fields, such as nanotechnology, alternative energies, and biotechnology, which will likely increase demand for engineering services in many manufacturing industries.

Job Prospects

Chemical engineers should have favorable job prospects as many workers in the occupation reach retirement age from 2010 to 2020.

Employment projections data for chemical engineers, 2010–20

Occupational Title	SOC Code	Employment, 2010	Projected Employment, 2020	Change, 2010-20 Percent Numeric	
Chemical Engineers	17-2041	30,200	32,000	6	1,800
SOURCE: U.S. Bureau of Labor Statistics, Employment Projections program					

Similar Occupations

This table shows a list of occupations with job duties that are similar to those of chemical engineers.

Occupation	Job Duties	Entry-Level Education	Median Annual Pay, May 2010
Architectural and Engineering Managers	Architectural and engineering managers plan, coordinate, and direct activities in architecture and engineering, including research and development in these fields.	Bachelor's degree	$119,260
Biomedical Engineers	Biomedical engineers analyze and design solutions to problems in biology and medicine, with the goal of improving the quality and effectiveness of patient care.	Bachelor's degree	$81,540
Chemists and Materials Scientists	Chemists and materials scientists study the structures, compositions, reactions, and other properties of substances. They use their knowledge to develop new and improved products, processes, and materials.	Bachelor's degree	$69,790
Nuclear Engineers	Nuclear engineers research and develop the processes, instruments, and systems used to get benefits from nuclear energy and radiation. Many of these engineers find industrial and medical uses for radioactive materials€"for example, in equipment used in medical diagnosis and treatment.	Bachelor's degree	$99,920

Contacts for More Information

For more information on becoming a chemical engineer, visit American Institute of Chemical Engineers.

For information about general engineering education and career resources, visit American Society for Engineering Education

Technology Student Association.

For more information about licensure as a chemical engineer, visit National Council of Examiners for Engineering and Surveying, National Society of Professional Engineers.

For information about accredited engineering programs, visit ABET

Suggested citation:

Bureau of Labor Statistics, U.S. Department of Labor, Occupational Outlook Handbook, 2012-13 Edition, Chemical Engineers, on the Internet at http://www.bls.gov/ooh/architecture-and-engineering/chemical-engineers.htm .

Civil Engineering Technicians

Quick Facts: Civil Engineering Technicians	
2010 Median Pay	$46,290 per year $22.26 per hour
Entry-Level Education	Associate's degree
Work Experience in a Related Occupation	None
On-the-job Training	None
Number of Jobs, 2010	79,000
Job Outlook, 2010-20	12% (About as fast as average)
Employment Change, 2010-20	9,400

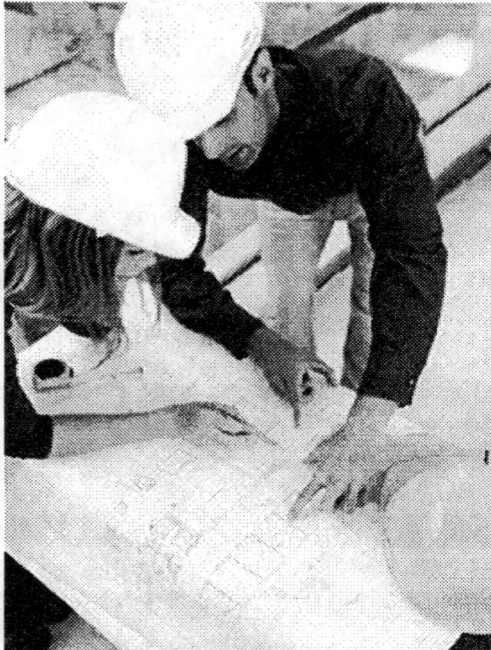

Civil engineering technicians confer with project supervisors to determine details of a project.

What Civil Engineering Technicians Do

Civil engineering technicians help civil engineers plan and design the construction of highways, bridges, utilities, and other major infrastructure projects. They also help with commercial, residential, and land development.

Duties

Civil engineering technicians typically do the following:
- Read and review project blueprints to determine dimensions of structures
- Confer with their supervisors about preparing plans and evaluating field conditions
- Inspect project sites and evaluate contractors' work to detect problems with a design
- Help to ensure that projects conform to design specifications and applicable codes
- Develop plans and estimate costs for installing systems and operating facilities
- Prepare reports and document project activities and data

Civil engineering technicians must work under the direction of a licensed

civil engineer. For more information, see the profile on civil engineers .

Civil engineering technicians generally help civil engineers, often doing many of the same tasks as the engineers. However, because they are not licensed, civil engineering technicians cannot approve designs or supervise the overall project.

These technicians sometimes estimate construction costs and specify the materials to be used. Other times, they prepare drawings or survey land. Civil engineering technicians may also set up and monitor various instruments for studies of traffic conditions.

Work Environment Civil

Civil engineering technicians held about 79,000 jobs in 2010.

Civil engineering technicians work in offices where they help civil engineers plan and design projects. They work primarily in architectural and engineering industries, and in federal, state, and local governments:

Architectural, engineering, and related services	44%
State government, excluding education and hospitals	29
Local government, excluding education and hospitals	18

Civil engineering technicians sometimes visit the job site where a construction project is taking place to test materials or inspect the project. They do this to help ensure that the designs approved by the licensed civil engineer are being carried out correctly.

How to Become a Civil Engineering Technician

Although not always required, an associate's degree in civil engineering technology is preferred for civil engineering technicians. It is best to seek programs that ABET (formerly the Accreditation Board for Engineering and Technology) has certified.

Education and Training

Prospective civil engineering technicians should take as many high school science and math courses as possible to prepare for programs in engineering technology after high school.

Employers generally want engineering technicians to have an associate's degree from an ABET-accredited program, although the degree is not always required. Engineering technology programs are also available at technical or vocational schools that award a postgraduate certificate or diploma.

Courses at technical or vocational schools may include engineering, design, and computer software. To complete an associate's degree in civil engineering technology, students also usually need to take other courses in liberal arts and the sciences.

Workers with less formal engineering technology training need to learn some skills on the job.

In contrast to civil engineering technicians, civil engineering technologists need a bachelor's degree in civil engineering technology to master and apply high-level principles of civil engineering in their work.

Important Qualities

Critical-thinking skills. Civil engineering technicians, as assistants to civil engineers, must help the engineers spot problems to avoid wasting time, effort, and funds.

Math skills. Civil engineering technicians use mathematics for analysis, design, and troubleshooting in their work.

Monitoring skills. Civil engineering technicians sometimes have to go to job sites and assess a project for the engineer. Therefore, they must know what to look for and how best to report back to the engineer overseeing the project.

Prioritizing skills. Pressures from deadlines mean that technicians must quickly see which types of information are most important.

Problem-solving skills. Like civil engineers, civil engineering technicians help design projects to solve a particular problem. Technicians must be able to understand and work with all the related systems involved in building a project.

Reading skills. Civil engineering technicians carry out plans and designs for projects that a civil engineer has approved. They must be able to understand all the reports about these designs.

Writing skills. Civil engineering technicians are often asked to relay their findings in writing. The reports must be well organized and clearly written.

Certification

Certification is not needed to enter this occupation, but it can help technicians advance their careers. The National Institute for Certification in Engineering Technologies (NICET) is one of the primary organizations overseeing certification for civil engineering technicians.

Certification as a technician requires an exam and documentation, including a work history, recommendations, and, for most programs, supervisor verification of specific experience.

Certification as a technologist requires a bachelor's degree in engineering technology. There is no additional exam for basic engineering technologist certification, but documentation, including a work history and endorsements, is required for advanced levels.

NICET requires technicians and technologists to update their skills and knowledge through a recertification process that encourages continuing professional development.

Advancement

Civil engineering technicians can advance in their careers by learning to design systems for a variety of projects, such as storm sewers and sanitary systems. It is also useful for civil engineering technicians to become proficient at reading graphic plans of proposed utility projects, called profiles.

Pay

Civil Engineering Technicians
Median annual wages, May 2010

Engineering Technicians, Except Drafters	$51,930
Civil Engineering Technicians	$46,290
Total, All Occupations	$33,840

Note: All Occupations includes all occupations in the U.S. Economy.
Source: U.S. Bureau of Labor Statistics, Occupational Employment Statistics

The median annual wage of civil engineering technicians was $46,290 in May 2010. The median wage is the wage at which half the workers in an occupation earned more than that amount and half earned less. The lowest 10 percent earned less than $29,060, and the top 10 percent earned more than $70,450.

Median annual wages in industries employing the largest numbers of civil engineering technicians in May 2010 were as follows:

Local government, excluding education and hospitals	$53,100
Architectural, engineering, and related services	45,630
State government, excluding education and hospitals	42,320

Job Outlook

Civil Engineering Technicians
Percent change in employment, projected 2010-20

Total, All Occupations	14%
Civil Engineering Technicians	12%
Engineering Technicians, Except Drafters	5%

Note: All Occupations includes all occupations in the U.S. Economy.
Source: U.S. Bureau of Labor Statistics, Employment Projections program

Employment of civil engineering technicians is expected to grow 12 percent from 2010 to 2020, about as fast as the average for all occupations.

The need to maintain and repair the country's infrastructure continues to increase: bridges need rebuilding, roads need maintaining, and levees and dams need upgrading. Moreover, a growing population means that water systems must be maintained to reduce or eliminate loss of drinkable water. Additionally, more waste treatment plants will be needed to help clean the nation's waterways. Civil engineers must plan, design, and oversee this work, and civil engineering technicians will be needed to help the engineers.

State and local governments will likely continue to face fiscal challenges over the decade, restricting their ability to fund all the projects that need attention. Eventually, however, infrastructure repairs and replacements will have to be made.

Job Prospects

Civil engineering technicians learn to use design software that civil engineers typically do not. Thus, those who master it, keep their skills current, and stay abreast of the latest software will likely improve their chances for employment.

Employment projections data for civil engineering technicians, 2010-20

Occupational Title	SOC Code	Employment, 2010	Projected Employment, 2020	Change, 2010-20 Percent	Numeric
Civil Engineering Technicians	17-3022	79,000	88,500	12	9,400

SOURCE: U.S. Bureau of Labor Statistics, Employment Projections program

Similar Occupations

This table shows a list of occupations with job duties that are similar to those of civil engineering technicians.

Occupation	Job Duties	Entry-Level Education	Median Annual Pay, May 2010
Civil Engineers	Civil engineers design and supervise large construction projects, including roads, buildings, airports, tunnels, dams, bridges, and systems for water supply and sewage treatment.	Bachelor's degree	$77,560
Drafters	Drafters use software to convert the designs of engineers and architects into technical drawings and plans. Workers in production and construction use these plans to build everything from microchips to skyscrapers.	Associate's degree	$47,880
Surveying and Mapping Technicians	Surveying and mapping technicians assist surveyors and cartographers in collecting data and making maps of the earth's surface. Surveying technicians visit sites to take measurements of the land. Mapping technicians use geographic data to create maps.	High school diploma or equivalent	$37,900
Surveyors	Surveyors establish official land, airspace, and water boundaries. Surveyors work with civil engineers, landscape architects, and urban and regional planners to develop comprehensive design documents.	Bachelor's degree	$54,880

Contacts for More Information

For more information about civil engineering technicians, visit Pathways to Technology

For more information about accredited programs, visit ABET

For more information about certification, visit American Society of Certified Engineering Technicians, National Institute for Certification in Engineering Technologies

Suggested citation:

Bureau of Labor Statistics, U.S. Department of Labor, Occupational Outlook Handbook, 2012-13 Edition, Civil Engineering Technicians, on the Internet at http://www.bls.gov/ooh/architecture-and-engineering/civil-engineering-technicians.htm .

Civil Engineers

Quick Facts: Civil Engineers	
2010 Median Pay	$77,560 per year $37.29 per hour
Entry-Level Education	Bachelor's degree
Work Experience in a Related Occupation	None
On-the-job Training	None
Number of Jobs, 2010	262,800
Job Outlook, 2010-20	19% (About as fast as average)
Employment Change, 2010-20	51,100

What Civil Engineers Do

Civil engineers design and supervise large construction projects, including roads, buildings, airports, tunnels, dams, bridges, and systems for water supply and sewage treatment.

Duties

Civil engineers typically do the following:

- Analyze survey reports, maps, and other data to plan projects
- Consider construction costs, government regulations, potential environmental hazards, and other factors in planning stages
- Test soils to determine the adequacy and strength of foundations
- Test building materials, such as concrete, asphalt, or steel, for use in particular projects
- Provide cost estimates for materials, equipment, or labor to determine a project's economic feasibility
- Use design software to plan and design transportation systems, hydraulic systems, and structures in line with industry and government standards
- Oversee, or participate in, surveying to establish reference points, grades, and elevations to guide construction

- Present their findings to the public on topics such as bid proposals, environmental impact statements, or property descriptions

Many civil engineers hold supervisory or administrative positions ranging from supervisor of a construction site to city engineer. Others work in design, construction, research, and teaching. They work with others on projects and may be assisted by civil engineering technicians and technologists.

The federal government employs about 12,100 civil engineers to do many of the same things done in private industry, except that the federally employed civil engineers may also inspect projects to be sure that they comply with regulations.

Civil engineers work on complex projects, so they usually specialize in one of several areas.

Geotechnical engineers work to make sure that foundations are solid. They focus on how structures built by civil engineers, such as buildings and tunnels, interact with the earth (including soil and rock). Additionally, they design and plan for slopes, retaining walls, and tunnels.

Structural engineers design and assess major projects, such as bridges or dams, to ensure their strength and durability.

Transportation engineers plan and design everyday systems, such as streets and highways, but they also plan larger projects, such as airports, ports, and harbors.

Civil engineers design major transportation projects.

Work Environment

Civil engineers held about 262,800 jobs in 2010. Civil engineers generally work indoors in offices. However, they sometimes spend time outdoors at construction sites so they can monitor operations or solve problems at the site. Occasionally, civil engineers travel abroad to work on large engineering projects in other countries.

Nearly all civil engineers work full time. However, many civil engineers work on projects that are under contractual deadlines. Engineers overseeing these projects often work longer hours to make sure that deadlines are met.

Industries employing the largest number of civil engineers in 2010 were as follows:

Architectural, engineering, and related services	48%
State government	13
Local government	11
Nonresidential building construction	5
Federal government	5

How to Become a Civil Engineer

Civil engineers need a bachelor's degree. They typically need a graduate degree for promotion to managerial positions. Civil engineers who sell their own services publicly must be licensed in all states and the District of Columbia.

Education

Civil engineers must first complete a bachelor's degree in civil engineering or one of its specialties. The degree should be from a program approved by ABET (formerly the Accreditation Board for Engineering and Technology). A program accredited by ABET is needed in order to gain licensure, which is required to work as a professional engineer (PE).

Programs in civil engineering typically take 4 years to complete and include coursework in mathematics, statistics, engineering mechanics and systems, and fluid dynamics, among other courses, depending on the specialty. Courses include a mix of traditional classroom learning and laboratory and field work.

About one of every five civil engineers has a master's degree. Further education after the bachelor's degree is helpful in getting a job as a manager. A civil engineer needs both a license and experience to become a manager.

Licenses

Civil engineers who sell their own services publicly must be licensed in all states and the District of Columbia. A license is required to exercise direct control of a project and to supervise other civil engineers, civil engineering technologists, and civil engineering technicians. A degree from an ABET-accredited engineering program is generally required to obtain a license.

Early in the licensing process, a civil engineer also must take and pass the Fundamentals of Engineering Examination. After passing this exam and meeting a particular state's requirements, an engineer then becomes a Civil Engineering (CE) Intern or an Engineer-in-Training. Afterward, depending on the state, civil engineers must have a minimum of experience, pass more exams, and satisfy other requirements to qualify as a CE Professional.

Important Qualities

Complex problem-solving skills. Civil engineers work at the highest level of design and plan large infrastructure projects, such as airports and roadways, which requires solving complex problems.

Decision-making skills. Civil engineers must determine the feasibility of plans, especially regarding financial costs and safety concerns. Urban and regional planners often look to civil engineers for advice on these issues.

Leadership skills. Civil engineers are ultimately responsible for the infrastructure project's design and implementation. Therefore, they must be able to lead surveyors, construction managers, civil engineering technicians, and others to implement the plan.

Math skills. Civil engineers use the principals of calculus, trigonometry, and other advanced topics in mathematics for analysis, design, and troubleshooting in their work.

Project management. Only licensed civil engineers can sign the plans for infrastructure projects. This makes it imperative that civil engineers be able to monitor and evaluate the work at the job site as a project progresses.

Writing skills. Civil engineers must be able to communicate with other professionals, such as architects, landscape architects, and urban and regional planners. This means that civil engineers must be able to write clear reports that people without an engineering background can follow.

Pay

Civil Engineers
Median annual wages, May 2010

Engineers	$83,340
Civil Engineers	$77,560
Total, All Occupations	$33,840

Note: All Occupations includes all occupations in the U.S. Economy.
Source: U.S. Bureau of Labor Statistics, Occupational Employment Statistics

The median annual wage of civil engineers was $77,560 in May 2010. The median wage is the wage at which half of the workers in an occupation earned more than that amount and half earned less. The lowest 10 percent earned less than $50,560, and the top 10 percent earned more than $119,320.

Median annual wages in the industries employing the largest numbers of civil engineers in May 2010 were as follows:

Federal government	$89,450
Local government	80,250
Architectural, engineering, and related services	76,620
Nonresidential building construction	76,120
State government	74,300

Nearly all civil engineers work full time. However, many civil engineers work on projects that are under contractual deadlines. Engineers overseeing these projects often work longer hours to make sure that deadlines are met.

Job Outlook

Civil Engineers

Percent change in employment, projected 2010-20

Civil Engineers	19%
Total, All Occupations	14%
Engineers	11%

Note: All Occupations includes all occupations in the U.S. Economy.
Source: U.S. Bureau of Labor Statistics, Employment Projections program

Employment of civil engineers is expected to grow 19 percent from 2010 to 2020, about as fast as the average for all occupations. As infrastructure continues to age, civil engineers will be needed to manage projects to rebuild bridges, repair roads, and upgrade levees and dams.

Moreover, a growing population means that water systems must be maintained to reduce or eliminate leaks of drinkable water. Additionally, more waste treatment plants will be needed to help clean the nation's waterways. Civil engineers play a key part in all of this work.

States will continue to face financial challenges and may have difficulty funding all the projects that need attention. Additionally, private investors are unlikely to lend financing for maintenance and repair work. However, whether or not there is federal funding, the repairs and replacements to the infrastructure will have to be made, creating demand for civil engineers.

Employment projections data for civil engineers, 2010-20

Occupational Title	SOC Code	Employment, 2010	Projected Employment, 2020	Change, 2010-20 Percent	Numeric
Civil Engineers	17-2051	262,800	313,900	19	51,100
SOURCE: U.S. Bureau of Labor Statistics, Employment Projections program					

Similar Occupations

This table shows a list of occupations with job duties that are similar to those of civil engineers.

Occupation	Job Duties	Entry-Level Education	Median Annual Pay, May 2010
Architects	Architects plan and design buildings and other structures.	Bachelor's degree	$72,550
Civil Engineering Technicians	Civil engineering technicians help civil engineers plan and design the construction of highways, bridges, utilities, and other major infrastructure projects. They also help with commercial, residential, and land development. Civil engineering technicians work under the direction of a licensed civil engineer.	Associate's degree	$46,290
Construction Managers	Construction managers plan, coordinate, budget, and supervise construction projects from early development to completion.	Associate's degree	$83,860
Landscape Architects	Landscape architects plan and design land areas for parks, recreational facilities, highways, airports, and other properties. Projects include subdivisions and commercial, industrial, and residential sites.	Bachelor's degree	$62,090
Surveyors	Surveyors establish official land, airspace, and water boundaries. Surveyors work with civil engineers, landscape architects, and urban and regional planners to develop comprehensive design documents.	Bachelor's degree	$54,880
Urban and Regional Planners	Urban and regional planners develop plans and programs for the use of land. They use planning to create communities, accommodate growth, or revitalize physical facilities in towns, cities, counties, and metropolitan areas.	Master's degree	$63,040

Contacts for More Information

For information about general engineering education and career resources, visit American Society for Engineering Education, Technology Student Association

For more information about licensure as a civil engineer, visit National Council of Examiners for Engineering and Surveying, National Society of Professional Engineers

For information about accredited engineering programs, visit ABET

For more information about civil engineers, visit American Society of Civil Engineers

Suggested citation:

Bureau of Labor Statistics, U.S. Department of Labor, Occupational Outlook Handbook, 2012-13 Edition, Civil Engineers, on the Internet at http://www.bls.gov/ooh/architecture-and-engineering/civil-engineers.htm .

Computer Hardware Engineers

Quick Facts: Computer Hardware Engineers	
2010 Median Pay	$98,810 per year $47.50 per hour
Entry-Level Education	Bachelor's degree
Work Experience in a Related Occupation	None
On-the-job Training	None
Number of Jobs, 2010	70,000
Job Outlook, 2010-20	9% (Slower than average)
Employment Change, 2010-20	6,300

What Computer Hardware Engineers Do

Computer hardware engineers research, design, develop, and test computer equipment such as chips, circuit boards, or routers. By solving complex problems in computer hardware, these engineers create rapid advances in computer technology.

Duties

Computer hardware engineers typically do the following:

- Design new computer hardware, creating blueprints of computer equipment to be built
- Test the completed models of the computer hardware they design
- Analyze the test results and modify the design as needed
- Update existing computer equipment so that it will work with new software
- Oversee the manufacturing process for computer hardware

Computer hardware engineers ensure that computer hardware components work together with the latest software developments. Therefore, hardware engineers sometimes work with software developers . For example, computer hardware engineers give developers of mobile applications information about what kind of software a cell phone can run.

Work Environment

Computer hardware engineers usually work in research laboratories that build and test various types of computer models. Most work in high-tech manufacturing firms. Some work in computer systems design firms, research and development firms, or for the federal government. Most work in research laboratories that build and test various types of computer models. More than

These engineers help create large server farms which are used to store huge amounts of data.

95 percent of computer hardware engineers work in metropolitan areas.

Computer hardware engineers held about 70,000 jobs in 2010. The following table shows the industries that employ the largest number of computer hardware engineers:

Computer and electronic product manufacturing	35%
Computer systems design and related services	19
Scientific research and development services	11
Federal government	7

Work Schedules

Most computer hardware engineers work full time. However, over a quarter work more than 40 hours per week.

How to Become a Computer Hardware Engineer

Having a bachelor's degree from an accredited school is the best way to become a computer hardware engineer.

Education

Most entry-level computer hardware engineers have a bachelor's degree in computer engineering, although a degree in electrical engineering generally is acceptable. A computer engineering major is similar to electrical engineering but with some computer science courses added to the curriculum.

Many engineering programs are accredited by ABET (formerly the Accreditation Board for Engineering and Technology). Some employers prefer students from an accredited program. To prepare for a major in computer or electrical engineering, students should have a solid background in math and science.

Because hardware engineers commonly work with computer software systems, a background in computer programming usually is needed. This background may be obtained through computer science courses. Some school programs offer co-ops or internships that can provide job experience.

Some large firms or specialized jobs require a master's degree in computer engineering. Some experienced engineers obtain a master's degree in business administration. All engineers must continue their learning over the course of their careers to keep up with rapid advances in technology.

Important Qualities

Analytical skills. Computer hardware engineers analyze complex equipment to determine the best way to improve it.

Creativity. Computer hardware engineers design new types of information technology devices.

Critical-thinking skills. These engineers use logic and reasoning to clarify goals, examine assumptions, and identify the strengths and weaknesses of alternative solutions to problems.

Problem-solving skills. Computer hardware engineers identify complex problems in computer hardware, develop and evaluate possible solutions, and figure out the best way to implement them.

Speaking skills. Engineers often work on teams and must be able to communicate with other types of engineers as well as with non-technical team members.

Pay

Computer Hardware Engineers
Median annual wages, May 2010

Computer Hardware Engineers	$98,810
Engineers	$83,340
Total, All Occupations	$33,840

Note: All Occupations includes all occupations in the U.S. Economy.
Source: U.S. Bureau of Labor Statistics, Occupational Employment Statistics

The median annual wage of computer hardware engineers was $98,810 in May 2010. The median wage is the wage at which half the workers in an occupation earned more than that amount and half earned less. The lowest 10 percent earned less than $61,360, and the top 10 percent earned more than $147,890.

The following table shows the median annual wages of computer hardware engineers in the occupation's top employing industries:

Federal government	$102,950
Computer and electronic product manufacturing	101,320
Computer systems design and related services	98,860
Scientific research and development services	92,080

Most computer hardware engineers work full time. However, over a quarter work more than 40 hours per week.

Job Outlook

Computer Hardware Engineers
Percent change in employment, projected 2010-20

Total, All Occupations	14%
Engineers	11%
Computer Hardware Engineers	9%

Note: All Occupations includes all occupations in the U.S. Economy.
Source: U.S. Bureau of Labor Statistics, Employment Projections program

Employment of computer hardware engineers is expected to increase 9 percent from 2010 to 2020, slower than the average for all occupations. A limited number of engineers will be needed to meet the demand for new computer hardware because more of the innovation in computers now takes place with software than with hardware. Although foreign competition in computer equipment will negatively affect the growth of this occupation, this will be partially offset by the development of computer chips that are embedded in other electronics such as household appliances, medical devices, or automobiles.

Most job growth is expected to occur in computer consulting firms as manufacturers increasingly contract out the design of hardware. This will allow hardware engineers to work more closely with software developers when designing computer products.

Job Prospects

Job applicants with a computer engineering degree from an ABET-accredited program will have better chances of finding a job. Engineers who have a higher-level degree and knowledge or experience with computer software will have the best job prospects.

Employment projections data for computer hardware engineers, 2010-20

Occupational Title	SOC Code	Employment, 2010	Projected Employment, 2020	Change, 2010-20	
				Percent	Numeric
Computer Hardware Engineers	17-2061	70,000	76,300	9	6,300
SOURCE: U.S. Bureau of Labor Statistics, Employment Projections program					

Similar Occupations

This table shows a list of occupations with job duties that are similar to those of computer hardware engineers.

Occupation	Job Duties	Entry-Level Education	Median Annual Pay, May 2010
Aerospace Engineers	Aerospace engineers design aircraft, spacecraft, satellites, and missiles. In addition, they test prototypes to make sure that they function according to design.	Bachelor's degree	$97,480
Computer and Information Research Scientists	Computer and information research scientists invent and design new technology and find new uses for existing technology. They study and solve complex problems in computing for business, science, medicine, and other uses.	Doctoral or professional degree	$100,660
Computer and Information Systems Managers	Computer and information systems managers, often called information technology managers (IT managers or IT project managers), plan, coordinate, and direct computer-related activities in an organization. They help determine the information technology goals of an organization and are responsible for implementing the appropriate computer systems to meet those goals.	Bachelor's degree	$115,780
Computer Programmers	Computer programmers write code to create software programs. They turn the program designs created by software developers and engineers into instructions that a computer can follow.	Bachelor's degree	$71,380
Electrical and Electronics Engineers	Electrical engineers design, develop, test, and supervise the manufacturing of electrical equipment such as electric motors, radar and navigation systems, communications systems, and power generation equipment.Electronics engineers design and develop electronic equipment, such as broadcast and communications systems€"from portable music players to global positioning systems (GPS).	Bachelor's degree	$87,180
Mathematicians	Mathematicians use high-level mathematics and technology to develop new mathematical principles, understand relationships between existing principles, and solve real-world problems.	Master's degree	$99,380

Mechanical Engineers	Mechanical engineering is one of the broadest engineering disciplines. Mechanical engineers design, develop, build, and test mechanical devices, including tools, engines, and machines.	Bachelor's degree	$78,160
Software Developers	Software developers are the creative minds behind computer programs. Some develop the applications that allow people to do specific tasks on a computer or other device. Others develop the underlying systems that run the devices or control networks.	Bachelor's degree	$90,530

Contacts for More Information

For more information about computer hardware engineers, visit
Association for Computing Machinery
Institute of Electrical and Electronics Engineers Computer Society
For more information about ABET-accredited college and university programs in applied science, computing, engineering, and technology, visit
ABET

Suggested citation:

Bureau of Labor Statistics, U.S. Department of Labor, Occupational Outlook Handbook, 2012-13 Edition, Computer Hardware Engineers, on the Internet at
http://www.bls.gov/ooh/architecture-and-engineering/computer-hardware-engineers.htm .

Drafters

Quick Facts: Drafters	
2010 Median Pay	$47,880 per year $23.02 per hour
Entry-Level Education	Associate's degree
Work Experience in a Related Occupation	None
On-the-job Training	None
Number of Jobs, 2010	205,100
Job Outlook, 2010-20	6% (Slower than average)
Employment Change, 2010-20	11,400

What Drafters Do

Drafters use software to convert the designs of engineers and architects into technical drawings and plans. Workers in production and construction use these plans to build everything from microchips to skyscrapers.

Duties

Drafters typically do the following:

- Design and prepare plans for using computer-aided design and drafting (CADD) software
- Produce effective product designs by using their understanding of engineering and manufacturing techniques
- Add structural details to architectural plans from their knowledge of building techniques

Drafters prepare technical drawings and plans.

- Prepare multiple versions of designs for review by engineers and architects
- Specify dimensions, materials, and procedures for new building projects or products
- Work under the supervision of engineers or architects

Many drafters are referred to as CADD operators. With CADD systems, drafters create and store drawings electronically so that they can be viewed, printed, or programmed directly into automated manufacturing systems. New software systems, such as building information modeling (BIM) and product data management (PDM), are coming into use. Through three-dimensional rendering, BIM software allows designers and engineers to see how elements in their projects work together. PDM software helps users track and control data, such as technical specifications, related to projects. Just as BIM is changing the work of architectural drafters as well as engineers and designers, PDM is changing the work of mechanical drafters. These software systems allow drafting and design work to be done at the same time as the work done by other professionals involved in the project.

There are several kinds of drafters, and the most common types of drafters are the following:

Aeronautical drafters prepare engineering drawings that show detailed plans and specifications used in manufacturing aircraft, missiles, and related parts.

Architectural drafters draw architectural and structural features of buildings for new construction projects. These workers may specialize in a type of building, such as residential or commercial. They may also specialize in materials, such as steel, wood, and reinforced concrete.

Civil drafters prepare topographical maps used in major construction or civil engineering projects, such as highways, bridges, and flood-control projects.

Electrical drafters prepare wiring diagrams that other workers use to install and repair electrical equipment and wiring in powerplants, electrical distribution systems, and buildings.

Electronics drafters produce wiring diagrams, assembly diagrams for circuit boards, and layout drawings used in manufacturing, installing, and repairing electronic devices and components.

Mechanical drafters prepare layouts that show details for a wide variety of machinery and mechanical devices. These layouts indicate dimensions, fastening methods, and other requirements needed for assembly.

Process piping or pipeline drafters prepare plans used in the layout, construction, and operation of oil and gas fields, refineries, chemical plants, and process piping systems.

Work Environment

Drafters held about 205,100 jobs in 2010. They work in engineering and drafting service firms, architectural and landscape architectural firms, and various manufacturing industries. The industries employing the largest numbers of drafters in 2010 were as follows:

Architectural, engineering, and related services	50%
Construction	7
Machinery manufacturing	6
Fabricated metal product manufacturing	5
Transportation equipment manufacturing	5

Like other workers who primarily use computers to do their work, drafters usually work indoors and full time, although overtime is not uncommon.

How to Become a Drafter

Drafters usually need some postsecondary training, such as an associate's degree, to enter the occupation.

Education

Employers prefer applicants who have completed training in drafting, typically an associate's degree from a technical institute or community college. Drafters who specialize in architecture may need a higher degree, such as a bachelor's degree. Training differs somewhat within the drafting specialties, but the basics, such as mathematics, are similar. To prepare for this training, high school courses in mathematics, science, computer technology, design, computer graphics, and, where available, drafting, are useful.

Technical institutes offer focused technical training in topics such as design fundamentals, sketching, and CADD software. They award certificates or diplomas, and programs vary considerably in length and in the types of courses offered. Many technical institutes also offer associate's degree programs.

Community colleges offer programs similar to those in technical institutes but typically include more classes in drafting theory and often require general education classes. Courses taken at community colleges are more likely to be accepted for credit at colleges or universities. After completing an associate's degree program, graduates may get jobs as drafters or continue their education in a related field at a 4-year college. Most 4-year colleges do not offer training in drafting, but they do offer classes in engineering, architecture, and mathematics that are useful for obtaining a job as a drafter.

Technical training in the military also can be applied in civilian drafting jobs. Some additional training may be necessary, depending on the technical area or military specialty.

Important Qualities

Critical-thinking skills. Drafters help the architects and engineers they work for by spotting problems with plans and designs.

Detail oriented. Drafters must pay attention to details so that the plans they are helping to build are technically accurate to all detailed specifications.

Interpersonal skills. Drafters must work closely with architects, engineers, and other designers to make sure that final plans are accurate. This requires the ability to take advice and constructive criticism, as well as to offer it.

Technical skills. Drafters in all specialties must be able to use computer software, such as CADD, and to work with database tools, such as BIM.

Time-management skills. Drafters often work under deadlines. They must be able to produce their output according to set schedules and so must plan their time well.

Certification

The American Design Drafting Association (ADDA) offers a certification program for drafters. Although employers usually do not require drafters to be certified, certification shows drafters' knowledge and an understanding of nationally recognized practices. The test does not cover software, which is specific to CADD or graphic production

Pay

Drafters

Median annual wages, May 2010

Drafters, Engineering Technicians, and Mapping Technicians	$49,600
Drafters	$47,880
Total, All Occupations	$33,840

Note: All Occupations includes all occupations in the U.S. Economy.
Source: U.S. Bureau of Labor Statistics, Occupational Employment Statistics

The median annual wage of drafters was $47,880 in May 2010. The median wage is the wage at which half the workers in an occupation earned more than that amount and half earned less. The lowest 10 percent earned less than $30,950, and the top 10 percent earned more than $74,820.

The median wages for detailed drafting occupations in May 2010 were as follows:

- $53,020 for architectural and civil drafters
- $48,810 for mechanical drafters
- $46,430 for electrical and electronics drafters
- $45,100 for drafters, all other

Job Outlook

Drafters

Percent change in employment, projected 2010-20

Total, All Occupations	14%
Drafters, Engineering Technicians, and Mapping Technicians	6%
Drafters	6%

Note: All Occupations includes all occupations in the U.S. Economy.
Source: U.S. Bureau of Labor Statistics, Employment Projections program

Overall, employment of all drafters is expected to grow 6 percent from 2010 to 2020, slower than the average for all occupations. However, growth will vary by specialty.

Work from construction projects will likely continue to create demand for architectural and civil drafters, and because this work should be kept in the United States, employment is expected to grow by 3 percent, slower than average growth. Because new technology reduces costs, architectural and civil drafters who can master new software programs, such as BIM and PDM, also should find opportunities in various industries

Employment of mechanical drafters is expected to experience about as fast as average growth, and electronic and electrical drafters is expected to experience slower than average growth from 2010 to 2020. Most of these workers are employed in declining or slow-growing manufacturing industries, offering few opportunities for growth from industry expansion. Demand for mechanical and electrical and electronic drafters is expected to be notably high in engineering and drafting service firms because of more complex problems associated with new products and manufacturing processes.

CADD systems that are easier to use and more powerful than current systems will allow other technical professionals to perform many tasks previously done only by drafters. This development should curb demand for all specialties. Also, some drafting work may be sent to other countries at lower wages.

Job Prospects

New software, such as PDM and BIM, will require drafters to work in collaboration with other professionals on projects, whether constructing a new building or manufacturing a new product. This new software, however, requires that someone build and maintain large databases. Workers with knowledge of drafting and of the software will be needed to oversee these databases.

Many drafting jobs are in construction and manufacturing, so they are subject to the ups and downs of those industries. Demand for particular drafting specialties varies across the country because jobs depend on the needs of local industries.

Employment projections data for drafters, 2010-20

Occupational Title	SOC Code	Employment, 2010	Projected Employment, 2020	Change, 2010-20	
				Percent	Numeric
Drafters	17-3010	205,100	216,500	6	11,400
Architectural and Civil Drafters	17-3011	92,700	95,700	3	3,000
Electrical and Electronics Drafters	17-3012	29,200	30,800	5	1,600
Mechanical Drafters	17-3013	67,400	74,900	11	7,500
Drafters, All Other	17-3019	15,800	15,200	-4	-600

SOURCE: U.S. Bureau of Labor Statistics, Employment Projections program

Similar Occupations

This table shows a list of occupations with job duties that are similar to those of drafters.

Occupation	Job Duties	Entry-Level Education	Median Annual Pay, May 2010
Architects	Architects plan and design buildings and other structures.	Bachelor's degree	$72,550
Cartographers and Photogrammetrists	Cartographers and photogrammetrists measure, analyze, and interpret geographic information to create maps and charts for political, cultural, educational, and other purposes. Cartographers are general mapmakers, and photogrammetrists are specialized mapmakers who use aerial photographs to create maps.	Bachelor's degree	$54,510
Electrical and Electronic Engineering Technicians	Electrical and electronic engineering technicians help engineers design and develop computers, communications equipment, medical monitoring devices, navigational equipment, and other electrical and electronic equipment. They often work in product evaluation and testing, using measuring and diagnostic devices to adjust, test, and repair equipment.	Associate's degree	$56,040
Electrical and Electronics Engineers	Electrical engineers design, develop, test, and supervise the manufacturing of electrical equipment such as electric motors, radar and navigation systems, communications systems, and power generation equipment.Electronics engineers design and develop electronic equipment, such as broadcast and communications systems€"from portable music players to global positioning systems (GPS).	Bachelor's degree	$87,180
Electrical and Electronics Installers and Repairers	Electrical and electronics installers and repairers install, repair, or replace a variety of electrical equipment in telecommunications, transportation, utilities, and other industries.	Postsecondary non-degree award	$49,170
Electro-mechanical Technicians	Electro-mechanical technicians combine knowledge of mechanical technology with knowledge of electrical and electronic circuits. They install, troubleshoot, repair, and upgrade electronic and computer-controlled mechanical systems, such as robotic assembly machines.	Associate's degree	$49,550
Industrial Designers	Industrial designers develop the concepts for manufactured products, such as cars, home appliances, and toys. They combine art, business, and engineering to make products that people use every day.	Bachelor's degree	$58,230
Landscape Architects	Landscape architects plan and design land areas for parks, recreational facilities, highways, airports, and other properties. Projects include subdivisions and commercial, industrial, and residential sites.	Bachelor's degree	$62,090
Mechanical Engineering Technicians	Mechanical engineering technicians help mechanical engineers design, develop, test, and manufacture industrial machinery, consumer products, and other equipment. They may make sketches and rough layouts, record and analyze data, make calculations and estimates, and report their findings.	Associate's degree	$50,110
Mechanical Engineers	Mechanical engineering is one of the broadest engineering disciplines. Mechanical engineers design, develop, build, and test mechanical devices, including tools, engines, and machines.	Bachelor's degree	$78,160

Surveying and Mapping Technicians	Surveying and mapping technicians assist surveyors and cartographers in collecting data and making maps of the earth's surface. Surveying technicians visit sites to take measurements of the land. Mapping technicians use geographic data to create maps.	High school diploma or equivalent	$37,900
Surveyors	Surveyors establish official land, airspace, and water boundaries. Surveyors work with civil engineers, landscape architects, and urban and regional planners to develop comprehensive design documents.	Bachelor's degree	$54,880

Contacts for More Information

For more information on schools offering programs in drafting and related fields, visit

Accrediting Commission of Career Schools and Colleges
For more information on certification, visit
American Design Drafting Association

Suggested citation:

Bureau of Labor Statistics, U.S. Department of Labor, Occupational Outlook Handbook, 2012-13 Edition, Drafters, on the Internet at http://www.bls.gov/ooh/architecture-and-engineering/drafters.htm .

Electrical and Electronics Engineers

Quick Facts: Electrical and Electronics Engineers	
2010 Median Pay	$87,180 per year $41.92 per hour
Entry-Level Education	Bachelor's degree
Work Experience in a Related Occupation	None
On-the-job Training	None
Number of Jobs, 2010	294,000
Job Outlook, 2010-20	6% (Slower than average)
Employment Change, 2010-20	17,600

What Electrical and Electronics Engineers Do

Electrical engineers design, develop, test, and supervise the manufacturing of electrical equipment such as electric motors, radar and navigation systems, communications systems, or power generation equipment. Electrical engineers also design the electrical systems of automobiles and aircraft.

Electronics engineers design and develop electronic equipment such as broadcast and communications systems, from portable music players to global positioning systems (GPS). Many also work in areas closely related to computer hardware.

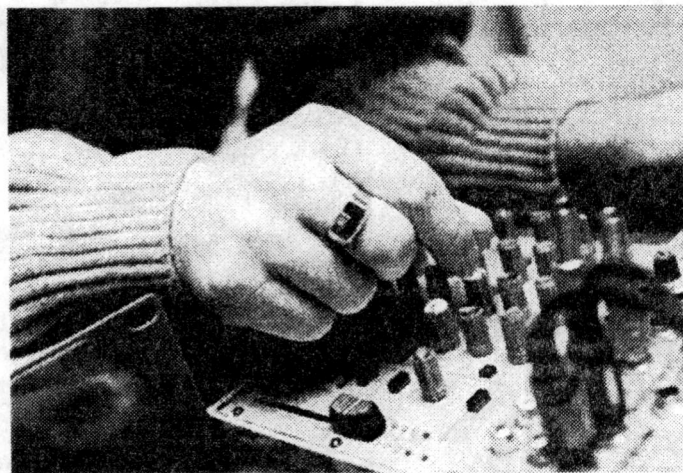

Electronics engineers analyze the requirements and costs of electrical systems.

Duties

Electrical engineers typically do the following:
- Design new ways to use electrical power to develop or improve products
- Do detailed calculations to compute manufacturing, construction, and installation standards and specifications
- Direct manufacturing, installing, and testing to ensure that the product as built meets specifications and codes
- Investigate complaints from customers or the public, evaluate problems, and recommend solutions
- Work with project managers on production efforts to ensure projects are completed satisfactorily, on time, and within budget

Electronics engineers typically do the following:
- Design electronic components, software, products, or systems for commercial, industrial, medical, military, or scientific applications
- Analyze electrical system requirements, capacity, cost, and customer needs and then develop a system plan
- Develop maintenance and testing procedures for electronic components and equipment
- Evaluate systems and recommend repair or design modifications
- Inspect electronic equipment, instruments, and systems to make sure they meet safety standards and applicable regulations
- Plan and develop applications and modifications for electronic properties used in parts and systems to improve technical performance

Electronics engineers who work for the federal government research, develop, and evaluate electronic devices used in diverse technologies, such as aviation, computing, transportation, and manufacturing. They work on federal electronic devices and systems, including satellites, flight systems, radar and sonar systems, and communications systems.

The work of electrical engineers and electronics engineers is often similar. Both use engineering and design software and equipment to do engineering tasks. Both types of engineers must also work with other engineers to discuss existing products and possibilities for engineering projects.

Engineers whose work is related exclusively to computer hardware are considered computer hardware engineers. For more information about this occupation, see the profile on computer hardware engineers .

Work Environment

Electrical and electronics engineers held about 294,000 jobs in 2010.

Electrical and electronics engineers worked primarily in engineering services firms, electric power generation, manufacturing, and research and development in 2010:

Architectural, engineering, and related services	22%
Navigational, measuring, electromedical, and control instruments manufacturing	10
Electric power generation, transmission and distribution	10
Semiconductor and other electronic component manufacturing	7
Scientific research and development services	5

Electronics engineers work mostly for the federal government, semiconductor manufacturing, and telecommunications companies. Industries employing the largest number of electronics engineers in 2010 were as follows:

Federal government, excluding postal service	14%
Wired telecommunications carriers	11
Semiconductor and other electronic component manufacturing	11
Architectural, engineering, and related services	8
Navigational, measuring, electromedical, and control instruments manufacturing	8

Electrical and electronics engineers generally work indoors in offices. However, they may visit sites to observe a problem or a piece of complex equipment.

Most of these engineers work full time, and overtime is not uncommon.

How to Become an Electrical or Electronics Engineer

Electrical and electronics engineers must have a bachelor's degree. Employers also value practical experience, so graduates of cooperative engineering programs, in which students earn academic credit for structured work experience, are valuable as well. Having a Professional Engineer license may improve an engineer's chances for employment.

Education

High school students interested in studying electrical or electronics engineering benefit from taking courses in physics and mathematics€"algebra, trigonometry, and calculus. Courses in drafting are also helpful, as these engineers are often required to prepare technical drawings.

Entry-level jobs in electrical or electronics engineering generally require a bachelor's degree. Programs typically last 4 years and include classroom, laboratory, and field studies. Courses include digital systems design, differential equations, and electrical circuit theory. Programs in electrical engineering should be accredited by ABET (formerly the Accreditation Board for Engineering and Technology).

Some colleges and universities offer cooperative programs in which students gain practical experience while completing their education. Cooperative programs combine classroom study with practical work.

At some universities, students can enroll in a 5-year program that leads to both a bachelor's degree and a master's degree. A graduate degree allows an engineer to work as an instructor at some universities, or in research and development.

Electrical and electronic engineers are mostly employed in industries conducting research and development or engineering service firms.

Important Qualities

Active learning. Electrical and electronics engineers have to apply knowledge learned in school to new tasks in every project they undertake. In addition, continuing education is important for them so that they can keep up with changes in technology.

Communication skills. Electrical and electronics engineers work closely with other engineers and technicians. They must be able to clearly explain their designs and reasoning and to relay instructions during product development and production. They may also need to explain complex issues to customers who have little or no technical expertise.

Detail oriented. Electrical and electronics engineers design and develop complex electrical systems and electronic components and products. They must keep track of multiple design elements and technical characteristics during these processes.

Math skills. Electrical and electronics engineers use the principals of calculus and other advanced topics in mathematics for analysis, design, and troubleshooting in their work.

Teamwork. Electrical and electronics engineers must work with others during production to ensure that their plans are being correctly applied. This includes monitoring technicians to see that plans are being implemented properly and devising remedies to problems as they come up.

Licenses

Licensure for electrical and electronics engineers is not as common as it is for other engineering occupations, but it is encouraged for those working in companies that have contracts with the government at all levels. Engineers who become licensed are designated professional engineers (PEs). Licensure generally requires the following:

- A degree from an engineering program accredited by the ABET
- A passing score on the Fundamentals of Engineering (FE) exam
- Relevant work experience
- A passing score on the Professional Engineering (PE) exam

The initial Fundamentals of Engineering (FE) exam can be taken right after graduation from a college or university. Engineers who pass this exam commonly are called engineers in training (EITs) or engineer interns (EIs). After getting work experience, EITs can take the second exam, called the Principles and Practice of Engineering exam.

Several states require engineers to take continuing education to keep their license. Most states recognize licensure from other states if the licensing state's requirements meet or exceed their own licensure requirements.

Advancement

Engineers may advance to supervise a team of engineers and technicians. Some may move into management positions, such as engineering managers or program managers. Preparation for managerial positions usually requires working under the guidance of a more experienced engineer.

For sales work, an engineering background enables engineers to discuss a product's technical aspects and assist in product planning and use. For more information, see the profile on sales engineers .

Pay

Electrical and Electronics Engineers
Median annual wages, May 2010

Electronics Engineers, Except Computer	$90,170
Electrical and Electronics Engineers	$87,180
Electrical Engineers	$84,540
Total, All Occupations	$33,840

Note: All Occupations includes all occupations in the U.S. Economy.
Source: U.S. Bureau of Labor Statistics, Occupational Employment Statistics

The median annual wage of electrical engineers was $84,540 in May 2010. The median wage is the wage at which half of the workers in an occupation earned more than that amount and half earned less. The lowest 10 percent earned less than $54,030, and the top 10 percent earned more than $128,610.

The median annual wage of electronics engineers was $90,170 in May 2010. The lowest 10 percent earned less than $57,860, and the top 10 percent earned more than $135,080.

Median annual wages in the industries employing the largest numbers of electrical engineers in May 2010 were as follows:

Semiconductor and other electronic component manufacturing	$92,070
Scientific research and development services	90,790
Navigational, measuring, electromedical, and control instruments manufacturing	89,590
Electric power generation, transmission and distribution	83,960
Architectural, engineering, and related services	83,750

Median annual wages in the industries employing the largest numbers of electronics engineers, except computer, in May 2010 were as follows:

Federal government, excluding postal service	$104,310
Semiconductor and other electronic component manufacturing	93,610
Architectural, engineering, and related services	89,360
Navigational, measuring, electromedical, and control instruments manufacturing	88,690
Wired telecommunications carriers	81,380

Most of these engineers work full time, and overtime is not uncommon.

Job Outlook

Electrical and Electronics Engineers
Percent change in employment, projected 2010-20

Total, All Occupations	14%
Electrical Engineers	7%
Electrical and Electronics Engineers	6%
Electronics Engineers, Except Computer	5%

Note: All Occupations includes all occupations in the U.S. Economy.
Source: U.S. Bureau of Labor Statistics, Employment Projections program

Employment of electrical and electronics engineers is expected to grow 6 percent from 2010 to 2020, slower than the average for all occupations. Job growth is expected because of electrical and electronics engineers' versatility in developing and applying emerging technologies. On the other hand, employment growth will be tempered by the slow growth or decline of most manufacturing sectors in which they are employed.

Growth for electrical and electronics engineers will largely occur in engineering services firms, as more companies are expected to cut costs by contracting engineering services rather than directly employing engineers. These engineers will also experience job growth in computer systems design and wireless telecommunications as these industries continue to implement more powerful portable computing devices.

The rapid pace of technological innovation and development will likely drive demand for electrical and electronics engineers in research and development, where their expertise will be needed to develop distribution systems related to new technologies.

Employment projections data for electrical and electronics engineers, 2010-20

Occupational Title	SOC Code	Employment, 2010	Projected Employment, 2020	Change, 2010-20	
				Percent	Numeric
Electrical and Electronics Engineers	17-2070	294,000	311,600	6	17,600
Electrical Engineers	17-2071	154,000	164,700	7	10,700
Electronics Engineers, Except Computer	17-2072	140,000	146,900	5	6,800

SOURCE: U.S. Bureau of Labor Statistics, Employment Projections program

Similar Occupations

This table shows a list of occupations with job duties that are similar to those of electrical and electronics engineers.

Occupation	Job Duties	Entry-Level Education	Median Annual Pay, May 2010
Aerospace Engineers	Aerospace engineers design aircraft, spacecraft, satellites, and missiles. In addition, they test prototypes to make sure that they function according to design.	Bachelor's degree	$97,480
Architectural and Engineering Managers	Architectural and engineering managers plan, coordinate, and direct activities in architecture and engineering, including research and development in these fields.	Bachelor's degree	$119,260
Biomedical Engineers	Biomedical engineers analyze and design solutions to problems in biology and medicine, with the goal of improving the quality and effectiveness of patient care.	Bachelor's degree	$81,540
Computer Hardware Engineers	Computer hardware engineers research, design, develop, and test computer equipment such as chips, circuit boards, or routers. By solving complex problems in computer hardware, these engineers create rapid advances in computer technology.	Bachelor's degree	$98,810
Electrical and Electronic Engineering Technicians	Electrical and electronic engineering technicians help engineers design and develop computers, communications equipment, medical monitoring devices, navigational equipment, and other electrical and electronic equipment. They often work in product evaluation and testing, using measuring and diagnostic devices to adjust, test, and repair equipment.	Associate's degree	$56,040
Electrical and Electronics Installers and Repairers	Electrical and electronics installers and repairers install, repair, or replace a variety of electrical equipment in telecommunications, transportation, utilities, and other industries.	Postsecondary non-degree award	$49,170
Electricians	Electricians install and maintain electrical systems in homes, businesses, and factories.	High school diploma or equivalent	$48,250
Electro-mechanical Technicians	Electro-mechanical technicians combine knowledge of mechanical technology with knowledge of electrical and electronic circuits. They install, troubleshoot, repair, and upgrade electronic and computer-controlled mechanical systems, such as robotic assembly machines.	Associate's degree	$49,550
Sales Engineers	Sales engineers sell complex scientific and technological products or services to businesses. They must have extensive knowledge of the products' parts and functions and must understand the scientific processes that make these products work.	Bachelor's degree	$87,390

Contacts for More Information

For information about general engineering education and career resources, visit American Society for Engineering Education, Technology Student Association

For more information about licensure as an electrical or electronics engineer, visit National Council of Examiners for Engineering and Surveying, National Society of Professional Engineers

For information about accredited engineering programs, visit ABET

Suggested citation:

Bureau of Labor Statistics, U.S. Department of Labor, Occupational Outlook Handbook, 2012-13 Edition, Electrical and Electronics Engineers, on the Internet at http://www.bls.gov/ooh/architecture-and-engineering/electrical-and-electronics -engineers.htm .

Electro-mechanical Technicians

Quick Facts: Electro-mechanical Technicians	
2010 Median Pay	$49,550 per year $23.82 per hour
Entry-Level Education	Associate's degree
Work Experience in a Related Occupation	None
On-the-job Training	None
Number of Jobs, 2010	16,400
Job Outlook, 2010-20	1% (Little or no change)
Employment Change, 2010-20	100

What Electro-mechanical Technicians Do

Electro-mechanical technicians combine knowledge of mechanical technology with knowledge of electrical and electronic circuits. They install, troubleshoot, repair, and upgrade electronic and computer-controlled mechanical systems, such as robotic assembly machines.

Duties

Electro-mechanical technicians typically do the following:
- Read blueprints, schematics, and diagrams to determine the method and sequence of assembly of a part, machine, or piece of equipment
- Verify dimensions of parts, using precision measuring instruments, to ensure that specifications are met
- Operate metalworking machines to make housings, fittings, and fixtures
- Repair and calibrate hydraulic and pneumatic assemblies
- Test the performance of electro-mechanical assemblies, using test instruments
- Install electronic parts and hardware, using soldering equipment and handtools

Electro-mechanical technicians sometimes test and operate machines in factories and other worksites. They also analyze and record test results, and prepare written documentation to describe the tests they did and what the test results were.

Work Environment

Electro-mechanical technicians held about 16,400 jobs in 2010. Electro-mechanical technicians work closely with electrical and

Electro-mechanical technicians install, repair, upgrade, and test electronic and computer-controlled mechanical systems.

mechanical engineers. They work primarily in manufacturing, utilities, and research and development. Their job tasks involve both engineering theory and assembly line production work. Consequently, they often work both at production sites and in offices.

In 2010, electro-mechanical technicians were mostly employed in the following industries:

Navigational, measuring, electromedical, and control instruments manufacturing	11%
Semiconductor and other electronic component manufacturing	10
Architectural, engineering, and related services	10
Communications equipment manufacturing	8
Scientific research and development services	7

Because their job involves manual work with many machines and types of equipment, electro-mechanical technicians are sometimes exposed to hazards from equipment or toxic materials. However, incidents are rare as long as they follow proper procedures.

How to Become an Electro-mechanical Technician

Electro-mechanical technicians typically need either an associate's degree or a postsecondary certificate.

Education

Associate's degree programs for electro-mechanical technicians usually take 2 years and are offered at vocational€'technical schools and community colleges. Vocational€'technical schools include postsecondary public institutions that serve local students and emphasize training needed by local employers. Community colleges offer programs similar to those in technical institutes but may include more theory-based and liberal arts coursework.

Most associate's degree programs that are accredited by ABET (formerly the Accreditation Board for Engineering and Technology) include at least college algebra and trigonometry as well as basic science courses. ABET-accredited programs offer training in engineering technology specialties.

In community college programs, prospective electro-mechanical technicians can concentrate in fields such as the following:
- Electro-mechanics
- Industrial maintenance
- Computer-integrated manufacturing

There are also bachelor's degree programs in electrical engineering technology and mechanical engineering technology, although most technicians earn an associate's degree. Graduates of bachelor's degree programs work as electrical engineering technologists and mechanical engineering technologists, rather than as technicians. Earning an associate's degree in electronic engineering technology eases entry into a bachelor's degree program.

Important Qualities

Detail oriented. Electro-mechanical technicians must make and keep the precise, accurate measurements that mechanical engineers need.

Information ordering skills. To carry out engineers' designs, inspect designs for quality control, and assemble prototypes, technicians must be able to read instructions and to follow a logical sequence or a specific set of rules.

Interpersonal skills. Electro-mechanical technicians must be able to take instruction and offer advice when needed. In addition, they often need to coordinate their work with that of others.

Manual dexterity. Electro-mechanical engineering technicians in particular must be able to use handtools and soldering irons on small circuitry and electronic parts to create detailed electronic components by hand.

Math skills. Electro-mechanical engineering technicians use mathematics for analysis, design, and troubleshooting in their work.

Mechanical skills. Electro-mechanical technicians must be able to apply the theory and instructions of engineers by creating or building new components for industrial machinery or equipment. They must be adept at operating machinery, including drill presses, grinders, and engine lathes.

Writing skills. These technicians must write reports on onsite construction, the results of testing, or problems they find when carrying out designs. Their writing must be clear and well organized so that the engineers they work with can understand the reports.

Pay

Electro-mechanical Technicians

Median annual wages, May 2010

Engineering Technicians, Except Drafters	$51,930
Electro-Mechanical Technicians	$49,550
Total, All Occupations	$33,840

Note: All Occupations includes all occupations in the U.S. Economy.
Source: U.S. Bureau of Labor Statistics, Occupational Employment Statistics

The median annual wage of electro-mechanical technicians was $49,550 in May 2010. The median wage is the wage at which half the workers in an occupation earned more than that amount and half earned less. The lowest 10 percent earned less than $31,310, and the top 10 percent earned more than $73,490.

Median annual wages in the industries employing the largest numbers of electro-mechanical technicians in May 2010 were as follows:

Scientific research and development services	$57,720
Architectural, engineering, and related services	51,590
Semiconductor and other electronic component manufacturing	45,680
Navigational, measuring, electromedical, and control instruments manufacturing	44,950
Communications equipment manufacturing	40,670

Job Outlook

Electro-mechanical Technicians

Percent change in employment, projected 2010-20

Total, All Occupations	14%
Engineering Technicians, Except Drafters	5%
Electro-Mechanical Technicians	1%

Note: All Occupations includes all occupations in the U.S. Economy.
Source: U.S. Bureau of Labor Statistics, Employment Projections program

Employment of electro-mechanical technicians is expected to grow 1 percent from 2010 to 2020, resulting in little or no change for this occupation. Many of these technicians are employed in manufacturing industries that are projected to decline.

Electro-mechanical technicians are generalists in technology, and their broad skill set will help sustain demand for their services.

As demand increases for engineers to design and build new equipment in various fields, employment of electro-mechanical technicians should also increase.

In the oil and gas industry, for example, engineers are studying drilling in the Arctic Ocean. Electro-mechanical technicians will be needed to help engineers manipulate underwater robotics in these operations.

Job Prospects

Job prospects are likely to be best for electro-mechanical technicians who train in a field known as mechatronics, which provides an understanding of four key systems:
- Mechanical systems
- Electronic systems
- Control systems
- Computer systems

Mechatronics training has two advantages for electro-mechanical technicians. First, it is multidisciplinary, which gives technicians more versatile training that is applicable across a broad range of fields. Second, it allows a technician to contribute to a product in its entirety, from concept and design to delivery.

Employment projections data for electro-mechanical technicians, 2010-20

Occupational Title	SOC Code	Employment, 2010	Projected Employment, 2020	Change, 2010-20	
				Percent	Numeric
Electro-Mechanical Technicians	17-3024	16,400	16,500	1	100
SOURCE: U.S. Bureau of Labor Statistics, Employment Projections program					

Similar Occupations

This table shows a list of occupations with job duties that are similar to those of electro-mechanical technicians.

Occupation	Job Duties	Entry-Level Education	Median Annual Pay, May 2010
Drafters	Drafters use software to convert the designs of engineers and architects into technical drawings and plans. Workers in production and construction use these plans to build everything from microchips to skyscrapers.	Associate's degree	$47,880
Electrical and Electronic Engineering Technicians	Electrical and electronic engineering technicians help engineers design and develop computers, communications equipment, medical monitoring devices, navigational equipment, and other electrical and electronic equipment. They often work in product evaluation and testing, using measuring and diagnostic devices to adjust, test, and repair equipment.	Associate's degree	$56,040

Electrical and Electronics Engineers	Electrical engineers design, develop, test, and supervise the manufacturing of electrical equipment such as electric motors, radar and navigation systems, communications systems, and power generation equipment.Electronics engineers design and develop electronic equipment, such as broadcast and communications systems€from portable music players to global positioning systems (GPS).	Bachelor's degree	$87,180
Electrical and Electronics Installers and Repairers	Electrical and electronics installers and repairers install, repair, or replace a variety of electrical equipment in telecommunications, transportation, utilities, and other industries.	Postsecondary non-degree award	$49,170
Machinists and Tool and Die Makers	Machinists and tool and die makers set up and operate a variety of computer-controlled or mechanically-controlled machine tools to produce precision metal parts, instruments, and tools.	High school diploma or equivalent	$39,910
Mechanical Engineering Technicians	Mechanical engineering technicians help mechanical engineers design, develop, test, and manufacture industrial machinery, consumer products, and other equipment. They may make sketches and rough layouts, record and analyze data, make calculations and estimates, and report their findings.	Associate's degree	$50,110
Mechanical Engineers	Mechanical engineering is one of the broadest engineering disciplines. Mechanical engineers design, develop, build, and test mechanical devices, including tools, engines, and machines.	Bachelor's degree	$78,160

Contacts for More Information

For information about general engineering education and career resources, visit American Society for Engineering Education, IEEE, Technology Student Association

For information on accredited programs, visit ABET

Suggested citation:

Bureau of Labor Statistics, U.S. Department of Labor, Occupational Outlook Handbook, 2012-13 Edition, Electro-mechanical Technicians, on the Internet at http://www.bls.gov/ooh/architecture-and-engineering/electro-mechanical-technicians.htm .

Environmental Engineering Technicians

Quick Facts: Environmental Engineering Technicians	
2010 Median Pay	$43,390 per year $20.86 per hour
Entry-Level Education	Associate's degree
Work Experience in a Related Occupation	None
On-the-job Training	None
Number of Jobs, 2010	18,800
Job Outlook, 2010-20	24% (Faster than average)
Employment Change, 2010-20	4,600

What Environmental Engineering Technicians Do

Environmental engineering technicians engineering technicians carry out the plans that environmental engineers develop.

Duties

Environmental engineering technicians typically do the following:

- Set up, test, operate, and modify equipment for preventing or cleaning up environmental pollution
- Maintain project records and computer program files
- Conduct pollution surveys, collecting and analyzing samples such as air and ground water
- Perform indoor and outdoor environmental quality work
- Work to mitigate sources of environmental pollution
- Review technical documents to ensure completeness and conformance to requirements
- Review work plans to schedule activities
- Arrange for the disposal of lead, asbestos, and other hazardous materials

In laboratories, environmental engineering technicians record observations, test results, and document photographs. To keep the laboratory supplied, they also may get product information, identify vendors and suppliers, and order materials and equipment.

Environmental engineering technicians also help environmental engineers develop devices for cleaning up environmental pollution. They also inspect facilities for compliance with the regulations that govern substances such as asbestos, lead, and wastewater.

Work Environment

Environment engineering technicians held about 18,800 jobs in 2010. The following industries employed the most environmental engineering technicians in 2010:

Management, scientific, and technical consulting services	16%
Local government, excluding education and hospitals	11
Waste management and remediation services	10
Testing laboratories	9
State government, excluding education and hospitals	6

Environment engineering technicians typically work indoors, usually in laboratories, and often have regular working hours. They also work outdoors, sometimes in remote locations.

Because environmental engineering technicians help in environmental cleanup, they can be exposed to hazards from equipment, chemicals, or other toxic materials. For this reason, they must follow proper safety procedures, such as wearing hazmat suits and sometimes respirators, even in warm weather. When they work in wet areas, environmental engineering technicians wear heavy rubber boots to keep their legs and feet dry.

Nearly all environmental engineering technicians work full time. However, they must sometimes work irregular hours to monitor operations.

How to Become an Environmental Engineering Technician

Although environmental engineering technicians do not necessarily need an associate's degree, employers prefer candidates who have one.

Education

Prospective engineering technicians should take as many high school science and math courses as possible to prepare for programs in engineering technology after high school.

Environmental engineering technicians typically have an associate's degree in environmental engineering technology or engineering technology. Vocational€'technical schools include postsecondary public institutions that serve local students and emphasize training needed by local employers. Community colleges offer programs similar to those in technical institutes but include more theory-based and liberal arts coursework. Associate's degree programs generally include courses in mathematics, chemistry, solid and hazardous waste, and environmental biology, among others.

Programs are accredited by ABET (formerly the Accreditation Board for Engineering and Technology). Some environmental engineering technicians enter the occupation with a bachelor's degree in the natural sciences, such as biology and chemistry.

Important Qualities

Listening skills. Environmental engineering technicians must be able to listen carefully to the instructions that the engineers give them.

Monitoring skills. Environmental engineering technicians are the eyes and ears of the environmental engineers and must assume responsibility for properly evaluating situations onsite.

Problem sensitivity. These technicians must be able to recognize problems so that the environmental engineers are informed as quickly as possible.

Reading-comprehension skills. Environmental engineering technicians must be able to read and understand legal and technical documents to ensure that regulatory requirements are being met.

Teamwork. Environmental engineering technicians work under engineers and as part of a team with other technicians. They must be able to communicate and work well with both supervisors and peers.

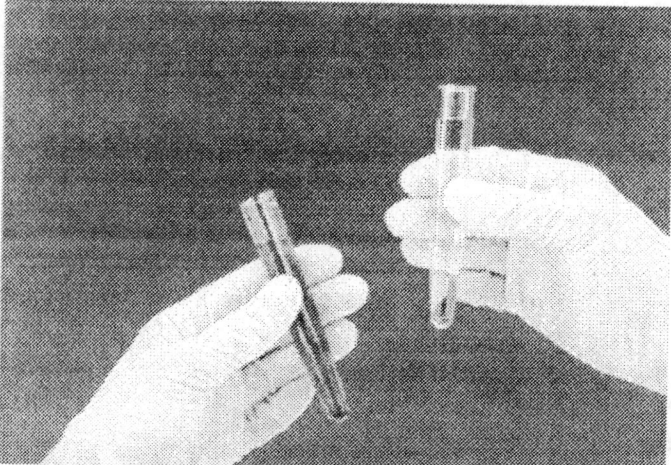

Environmental engineering technicians collect water samples.

Advancement

Environmental engineering technicians usually begin work as trainees in entry-level positions supervised by an environmental engineer or a more experienced technician. As they gain experience, technicians take on more responsibility and carry out assignments under general supervision. Some eventually become supervisors.

Technicians who have a bachelor's degree often are able to advance to engineering positions.

Pay

Environmental Engineering Technicians Median annual wages, May 2010	
Engineering Technicians, Except Drafters	$51,930
Environmental Engineering Technicians	$43,390
Total, All Occupations	$33,840

Note: All Occupations includes all occupations in the U.S. Economy.
Source: U.S. Bureau of Labor Statistics, Occupational Employment Statistics

The median annual wage of environmental engineering technicians was $43,390 in May 2010. The median wage is the wage at which half the workers in an occupation earned more than that amount and half earned less. The lowest 10 percent earned less than $28,000, and the top 10 percent earned more than $72,020.

Median annual wages in the industries employing the largest numbers of environmental engineering technicians in May 2010 were the following:

Local government, excluding education and hospitals	$49,350
State government, excluding education and hospitals	46,100
Waste management and remediation services	40,120
Testing laboratories	39,590
Management, scientific, and technical consulting services	38,600

Nearly all environmental engineering technicians work full time and typically have regular hours. However, they must sometimes work irregular hours to monitor operations.

Job Outlook

Environmental Engineering Technicians Percent change in employment, projected 2010-20	
Environmental Engineering Technicians	.24%
Total, All Occupations	14%
Engineering Technicians, Except Drafters	5%

Note: All Occupations includes all occupations in the U.S. Economy.
Source: U.S. Bureau of Labor Statistics, Employment Projections program

Employment of environmental engineering technicians is projected to grow 24 percent from 2010 to 2020, faster than the average for all occupations.

Employment in this occupation is typically tied to projects created by environmental engineers. State and local governments are expected to focus efforts and resources on efficient water use and wastewater treatment, which will support the demand for environmental engineering technicians.

The increasing call to clean up contaminated sites, as mandated by Congress and directed by the Environmental Protection Agency, is expected to help sustain demand for these technicians' services. In addition, wastewater treatment is becoming a larger concern in areas of the country where new methods of drilling for shale gas require the use and disposal of large volumes of water. Environmental engineering technicians will continue to be needed to help utilities and water treatment plants comply with new federal or state environmental regulations.

Employment projections data for environmental engineering technicians, 2010–20

Occupational Title	SOC Code	Employment, 2010	Projected Employment, 2020	Change, 2010-20	
				Percent	Numeric
Environmental Engineering Technicians	17-3025	18,800	23,300	24	4,600

SOURCE: U.S. Bureau of Labor Statistics, Employment Projections program

Similar Occupations

This table shows a list of occupations with job duties that are similar to those of environmental engineering technicians.

Occupation	Job Duties	Entry-Level Education	Median Annual Pay, May 2010
Environmental Engineers	Environmental engineers use the principles of engineering, soil science, biology, and chemistry to develop solutions to environmental problems. They are involved in efforts to improve recycling, waste disposal, public health, and control of water and air pollution.	Bachelor's degree	$78,740
Environmental Science and Protection Technicians	Environmental science and protection technicians do laboratory and field tests to monitor the environment and investigate sources of pollution, including those affecting health. Many work under the supervision of environmental scientists and specialists, who direct their work and evaluate their results.	Associate's degree	$41,380
Environmental Scientists and Specialists	Environmental scientists and specialists use their knowledge of the natural sciences to protect the environment. They identify problems and find solutions that minimize hazards to the health of the environment and the population.	Bachelor's degree	$61,700
Hazardous Materials Removal Workers	Hazardous materials (hazmat) removal workers identify and dispose of asbestos, radioactive and nuclear waste, arsenic, lead, and other hazardous materials. They also clean up materials that are flammable, corrosive, reactive, or toxic.	High school diploma or equivalent	$37,600

Contacts for More Information

For more information about accredited programs, visit ABET

For more information about general engineering education and career resources, visit Technology Student Association

Suggested citation:

Bureau of Labor Statistics, U.S. Department of Labor, Occupational Outlook Handbook, 2012-13 Edition, Environmental Engineering Technicians, on the Internet at http://www.bls.gov/ooh/architecture-and-engineering/environmental-engineering-technicians.htm .

Environmental Engineers

Quick Facts: Environmental Engineers	
2010 Median Pay	$78,740 per year $37.86 per hour
Entry-Level Education	Bachelor's degree
Work Experience in a Related Occupation	None
On-the-job Training	None
Number of Jobs, 2010	51,400
Job Outlook, 2010-20	22% (Faster than average)
Employment Change, 2010-20	11,300

What Environmental Engineers Do

Environmental engineers use the principles of engineering, soil science, biology, and chemistry to develop solutions to environmental problems. They are involved in efforts to improve recycling, waste disposal, public health, and control of water and air pollution. They also address global issues, such as safe drinking water, climate change, and sustainability.

Duties

Environmental engineers typically do the following:
- Prepare, review, and update environmental investigation reports
- Design projects leading to environmental protection, such as water reclamation facilities, air pollution control systems, and operations that convert waste to energy
- Obtain, update, and maintain plans, permits, and standard operating procedures
- Provide technical support for environmental remediation projects and legal actions
- Analyze scientific data and do quality-control checks
- Monitor progress of environmental improvement programs
- Inspect industrial and municipal facilities and programs to ensure compliance with environmental regulations
- Advise corporations and government agencies about procedures for cleaning up contaminated sites

Environmental engineers conduct hazardous-waste management studies in which they evaluate the significance of the hazard and advise on treating and containing it. They also design municipal water supply and industrial wastewater treatment systems and research the environmental impact of proposed construction projects. Environmental engineers in government develop regulations to prevent mishaps.

Some environmental engineers study ways to minimize the effects of acid rain, global warming, automobile emissions, and ozone depletion. They also collaborate with environmental scientists, planners, hazardous waste technicians, engineers, and other specialists, such as experts in law and business, to address environmental problems and sustainability. For more information, see the job profiles on environmental scientists and specialists, hazardous materials removal workers, lawyers, and urban and regional planners.

Work Environment

Environmental engineers held about 51,400 jobs in 2010. They work in a variety of settings because of the nature of the tasks they do:
- When they are working with other engineers and urban and regional planners, environmental engineers are likely to be in offices.
- When they are working with business people and lawyers, they are likely to be at seminars where they present information and answer questions.
- And when they work with hazardous waste technicians and environmental scientists, they work at specific sites outdoors.

Nearly one out of three environmental engineers worked in federal, state, or local governments in 2010:

Architectural, engineering, and related services	28%
Management, scientific, and technical consulting services	19
State government, excluding education and hospitals	15
Federal government, excluding postal service	8
Local government, excluding education and hospitals	8

Work Schedules

Most environmental engineers work full time. Those who manage projects often work more than 40 hours per week to monitor the project's progress and recommend corrective action when needed. This is necessary to make sure that deadlines are met and to ensure that the project is built according to specification.

How to Become an Environmental Engineer

Environmental engineers must have a bachelor's degree in environmental engineering or a related field, such as civil, chemical, or mechanical engineering. Employers also value practical experience. Therefore, cooperative engineering programs, in which college credit is awarded for structured job experience, are valuable as well. Getting a license improves the chances for employment.

Education

Students interested in studying environmental engineering should take high school courses in chemistry, biology, physics, and mathematics,

Environmental engineers design systems for managing and cleaning municipal water supplies.

including algebra, trigonometry, and calculus.

Entry-level environmental engineering jobs require a bachelor's degree. Bachelor's degree programs typically last 4 years and include classroom, laboratory, and field studies. Some colleges and universities offer cooperative programs where students gain practical experience while completing their education.

At some colleges and universities, a student can enroll in a 5-year program that leads to both a bachelor's and a master's degree. A graduate degree allows an engineer to work as an instructor at some colleges and universities or to do research and development.

Many engineering programs are accredited by ABET (formerly the Accreditation Board for Engineering and Technology). Some employers prefer to hire candidates who have graduated from an accredited program. A degree from an ABET-accredited program is usually necessary to become a licensed professional engineer.

Important Qualities

Communication skills. Environmental engineers must be able to write clearly so others without their specific training understand their plans, proposals, specifications, findings, and other documents.

Problem-solving skills. When designing facilities and processes for treating wastewater and other pollution, environmental engineers strive to solve several issues at once, from workers' safety to environmental protection. They must be able to identify and anticipate problems to prevent losses for their employers, safeguard workers' health, and mitigate environmental damage.

Reading-comprehension skills. Environmental engineers often work with business people, lawyers, and other professionals outside their field. They often are required to read and understand documents that are outside their scope of training.

Systems analysis. Environmental engineers sometimes have to design systems that will be part of larger ones. They must be able to foresee how the proposed designs will interact with other components in the process, including the workers, machinery, equipment, or the environment.

Teamwork. Environmental engineers must be able to work with others toward a common goal. They usually work with engineers and scientists who design other systems and with the technicians and mechanics who put the designs into practice.

Licenses

Environmental engineers are encouraged to obtain a professional engineer (PE) license. Licensure generally requires the following:
- A degree from an engineering program accredited by ABET
- A passing score on the Fundamentals of Engineering (FE) exam
- Relevant work experience
- A passing score on the Professional Engineering (PE) exam

The initial Fundamentals of Engineering (FE) exam can be taken after graduation. Engineers who pass this exam are commonly called engineers in training (EITs) or engineer interns (EIs). After getting suitable work experience, EITs can take the second exam, called the Principles and Practice of Engineering.

Several states require continuing education for engineers to keep their license. Most states recognize licensure from other states, if the licensing state's requirements meet or exceed their own requirements.

Certification

After licensing, environmental engineers can earn certification known as Board Certified from the American Academy of Environmental Engineers. This certification is similar to that for physicians and shows that an environmental engineer has expertise in one or more areas of specialization.

Advancement

As beginning engineers gain knowledge and experience, they move on to more difficult projects, and they have greater independence to develop designs, solve problems, and make decisions. Eventually, environmental engineers may advance to become technical specialists or to supervise a team of engineers and technicians.

Some may even become engineering managers or move into executive positions, such as program managers. However, before assuming a managerial position, an engineer usually works under the supervision of a more experienced engineer.

Pay

Environmental Engineers
Median annual wages, May 2010

Engineers	$83,340
Environmental Engineers	$78,740
Total, All Occupations	$33,840

Note: All Occupations includes all occupations in the U.S. Economy.
Source: U.S. Bureau of Labor Statistics, Occupational Employment Statistics

The median annual wage of environmental engineers was $78,740 in May 2010. The median wage is the wage at which half the workers in an occupation earned more than that amount and half earned less. The lowest 10 percent earned less than $48,980, and the top 10 percent earned more than $119,060.

Median annual wages in the industries employing the largest numbers of environmental engineers in May 2010 were the following:

Federal government, excluding postal service	$100,270
Architectural, engineering, and related services	78,450
Local government, excluding education and hospitals	75,280
Management, scientific, and technical consulting services	74,940
State government, excluding education and hospitals	69,050

Most environmental engineers work full time. Those who manage projects often work more than 40 hours per week.

Job Outlook

Environmental Engineers
Percent change in employment, projected 2010-20

Environmental Engineers	22%
Total, All Occupations	14%
Engineers	11%

Note: All Occupations includes all occupations in the U.S. Economy.
Source: U.S. Bureau of Labor Statistics, Employment Projections program

Employment of environmental engineers is projected to grow 22 percent from 2010 to 2020, faster than the average for all occupations.

State and local governments' concerns about water are leading to efforts to increase the efficiency of water use. This focus differs from that of wastewater treatment, for which this occupation is traditionally known.

The requirement by the federal government to clean up contaminated sites is expected to help sustain demand for these engineers' services. Additionally, wastewater treatment is becoming a larger concern in areas of the country where new methods of drilling for shale gas require the use and disposal of massive volumes of water. Environmental engineers will continue to be needed to help utilities and water treatment plants comply with any new federal or state environmental regulations.

All levels of government must comply with environmental regulations, especially federal. Because of this, employment of environmental engineers within the government sector as a whole should remain relatively stable through the year 2020.

Employment projections data for environmental engineers, 2010–20

Occupational Title	SOC Code	Employment, 2010	Projected Employment, 2020	Change, 2010-20 Percent	Numeric
Environmental Engineers	17-2081	51,400	62,700	22	11,300
SOURCE: U.S. Bureau of Labor Statistics, Employment Projections program					

Similar Occupations

This table shows a list of occupations with job duties that are similar to those of environmental engineers.

Occupation	Job Duties	Entry-Level Education	Median Annual Pay, May 2010
Environmental Engineering Technicians	Environmental engineering technicians carry out the plans that environmental engineers develop. They test, operate, and, if necessary, modify equipment for preventing or cleaning up environmental pollution. They may collect samples for testing, or they may work to mitigate sources of environmental pollution.	Associate's degree	$43,390
Environmental Scientists and Specialists	Environmental scientists and specialists use their knowledge of the natural sciences to protect the environment. They identify problems and find solutions that minimize hazards to the health of the environment and the population.	Bachelor's degree	$61,700
Hydrologists	Hydrologists study water and the water cycle. They use their expertise to solve problems in the areas of water quality or availability.	Master's degree	$75,690
Natural Sciences Managers	Natural sciences managers supervise the work of scientists, including chemists, physicists, and biologists. They direct research and development projects and coordinate activities such as testing, quality control, and production.	Bachelor's degree	$116,020

Contacts for More Information

For more information about environmental engineers, visit American Academy of Environmental Engineers

For more information about education for engineers, visit American Society for Engineering Education

For more information about accredited engineering programs, visit ABET

For more information about the Professional Engineer license, visit National Council of Examiners for Engineering and Surveying, National Society of Professional Engineers

Suggested citation:

Bureau of Labor Statistics, U.S. Department of Labor, Occupational Outlook Handbook, 2012-13 Edition, Environmental Engineers, on the Internet at http://www.bls.gov/ooh/architecture-and-engineering/environmental-engineers.htm .

Health and Safety Engineers

Quick Facts: Health and Safety Engineers	
2010 Median Pay	$75,430 per year $36.26 per hour
Entry-Level Education	Bachelor's degree
Work Experience in a Related Occupation	None
On-the-job Training	None
Number of Jobs, 2010	23,700
Job Outlook, 2010-20	13% (About as fast as average)
Employment Change, 2010-20	3,100

What Health and Safety Engineers Do

Health and safety engineers develop procedures and design systems to keep people from getting sick or injured and to keep property from being damaged. They combine a knowledge of health or safety and of systems engineering to make sure that chemicals, machinery, software, furniture, and other products are not going to cause harm to people or buildings.

Duties

Health and safety engineers typically do the following:

- Review plans and specifications for new machinery or equipment to make sure it meets safety requirements
- Inspect facilities, machinery, and safety equipment to identify and correct potential hazards
- Evaluate the effectiveness of various industrial control mechanisms
- Ensure that a building or product complies with health and safety regulations, especially after an inspection that required changes
- Install safety devices on machinery or direct the installation of these devices
- Review employee safety programs and recommend improvements

Health and safety in the workplace is a major concern of health and safety engineers.

- Maintain and apply their knowledge of current policies, regulations, and industrial processes

Health and safety engineers also investigate industrial accidents, injuries, or occupational diseases to determine their causes and to see whether they could have been or can be prevented. They interview employers and employees to learn about work environments and incidents leading up to accidents or injuries. They also evaluate the corrections that were made to remedy violations found during health inspections.

Health and safety engineers are also active in two related fields: industrial hygiene and occupational hygiene.

In industrial hygiene, they focus on the effects of chemical, physical, and biological agents. They recognize, evaluate, and control these agents to keep people from getting sick or injured. For example, they might anticipate that a particular manufacturing process will give off a potentially harmful chemical and recommend either a change to the process or a way to contain and control the chemical.

In occupational hygiene, health and safety engineers investigate the environment in which people work and use science and engineering to recommend changes to keep workers from being exposed to sickness or injuries. They help employers and employees understand the risks and improve working conditions and working practices. For example, they might observe that the noise level in a factory is likely to cause short-term and long-term harm to workers and recommend ways to reduce the noise level through changes to the building or by having workers wear strong headphones.

Health and safety engineering is a broad field covering many activities. The following are specific types of health and safety engineers:

Aerospace safety engineers work on missiles, radars, and satellites to make sure that they function safely as designed.

Fire prevention and protection engineers design fire prevention systems for all kinds of buildings. They often work for architects during the design phase of new buildings or renovations. They must be licensed, and they must keep up with changes in fire codes and regulations.

Product safety engineers investigate the causes of accidents or injuries that might have resulted from the use or misuse of a product. They propose solutions to reduce or eliminate any safety issues associated with products. They also participate in the design phase of new products to prevent injuries, illnesses, or property damage that could occur with the use of the product.

Systems safety engineers work in many fields, including aerospace, and are moving into new fields, such as software safety, medical safety, and environmental safety. These engineers take a systemic approach to identify hazards in these new fields so that accidents and injuries can be avoided.

For information on health and safety engineers who work in mines, see the profile on mining and geological engineers.

Work Environment

Health and safety engineers held about 23,700 jobs in 2010.

Health and safety engineers typically work in offices. However, they also must spend time at worksites when necessary, which sometimes requires travel. Most health and safety engineers work full time.

The industries employing the largest numbers of health and safety engineers in May 2010 were as follows:

Nonresidential building construction	9%
Management, scientific, and technical consulting services	8
Architectural, engineering, and related services	7
Local government, excluding education and hospitals	7
State government, excluding education and hospitals	6

How to Become a Health and Safety Engineer

Health and safety engineers must have a bachelor's degree, typically in electrical, chemical, mechanical, industrial, or some other engineering discipline. Employers value practical experience, so cooperative-education engineering programs at universities are valuable as well.

Education

High school students interested in becoming a health and safety engineer will benefit from taking high school courses in mathematics, such as algebra, trigonometry, and calculus; and science, such as biology, chemistry, and physics.

Entry-level jobs as a health and safety engineer require a bachelor's degree. Bachelor's degree programs typically are 4-year programs and include classroom, laboratory, and field studies in applied engineering. In addition to programs in mechanical, electrical, and industrial engineering, programs in systems engineering and fire protection engineering are offered at some colleges and universities. Students interested in becoming a health and safety engineer should seek out coursework in occupational safety and health, industrial hygiene, ergonomics, or environmental safety.

Students interested in entering the relatively new field of software safety engineering may pursue a degree in computer science.

Most colleges and universities offer cooperative programs, which allow students to gain practical experience while completing their education.

A few colleges and universities offer 5-year accelerated programs that lead to both a bachelor's and a master's degree. A master's degree allows engineers to enter the occupation at a higher level, where they can develop and implement safety systems.

ABET (formerly the Accreditation Board for Engineering and Technology) accredits programs in engineering.

Important Qualities

Creativity. Health and safety engineers are asked to produce designs showing potential problems and remedies for them. They must be creative to work with unique situations with each project.

Deductive reasoning. Health and safety engineers must be able to interpret federal and state regulations and understand the goals of those regulations so that they can propose proper designs for specific work environments.

Problem sensitivity. Health and safety engineers must identify potential hazards and problems before they cause material damage or become a threat to peoples' health. Thus, these engineers must be able to sense hazards to humans and property wherever they may arise in the workplace or, for consumer products, in the home.

Problem-solving skills. In designing solutions for entire organizational operations, health and safety engineers must take into account processes from more than one system at the same time. In addition, they must try to anticipate a range of human reactions to the changes they recommend.

Systems analysis. Health and safety engineers must observe and learn how operations currently function so that they can identify risks to people and property. This type of observation and learning requires the ability to think in terms of overall processes within an organization. Health and safety engineers can then recommend systemic changes to minimize risks.

Licenses

Only a few states require health and safety engineers to be licensed. Licensure is generally advised for those opting for a career in systems safety engineering.

Licensed engineers are called professional engineers (PEs). Licensure generally requires the following:

- A degree from an ABET-accredited engineering program
- A passing score on the Fundamentals of Engineering (FE) exam
- Relevant work experience, typically at least 4 years
- A passing score on the Professional Engineering (PE) exam

The initial Fundamentals of Engineering (FE) exam can be taken after graduation from college. Engineers who pass this exam are commonly called engineers in training (EITs) or engineer interns (EIs). After getting suitable work experience, EITs and EIs can take the second exam, called the Principles and Practice of Engineering.

Several states require continuing education for engineers to keep their license. Most states recognize licensure from other states, if the licensing state's requirements meet or exceed their own licensure requirements.

Certification

Health and safety engineers typically have professional certification. Most earn either the Certified Safety Professional (CSP) certification, awarded by the Board of Certified Safety Professionals , or the Certified Industrial Hygienist (CIH) certification, awarded by the American Board of Industrial Hygiene . Certification is generally needed to advance into management positions.

Advancement

New health and safety engineers usually work under the supervision of experienced engineers. To move to more difficult projects with greater independence, a graduate degree is generally required. This advanced degree allows an engineer to develop and implement safety programs. Certification as a safety professional or as an industrial hygienist is generally required for entry into management positions.

Pay

Health and Safety Engineers
Median annual wages, May 2010

Engineers	$83,340
Health and Safety Engineers, Except Mining Safety Engineers and Inspectors	$75,430
Total, All Occupations	$33,840

Note: All Occupations includes all occupations in the U.S. Economy.
Source: U.S. Bureau of Labor Statistics, Occupational Employment Statistics

The median annual wage of health and safety engineers was $75,430 in May 2010. The median wage is the wage at which half the workers in an occupation earned more than that amount and half earned less. The lowest 10 percent earned less than $45,530 and the top 10 percent earned more than $114,470.

Median annual wages in the industries employing the largest numbers of health and safety engineers in May 2010 were as follows:

State government, excluding education and hospitals	$82,760
Local government, excluding education and hospitals	81,130
Architectural, engineering, and related services	75,300
Management, scientific, and technical consulting services	73,520
Nonresidential building construction	68,360

Most health and safety engineers work full time.

Job Outlook

Health and Safety Engineers
   Percent change in employment, projected 2010-20

Total, All Occupations	14%
Health and Safety Engineers, Except Mining Safety Engineers and Inspectors	13%
Engineers	11%

Note: All Occupations includes all occupations in the U.S. Economy.
Source: U.S. Bureau of Labor Statistics, Employment Projections program

Employment of health and safety engineers is expected to grow 13 percent from 2010 to 2020, about as fast as the average for all occupations.

Health and safety engineers have long been employed in manufacturing industries to cut costs, save lives, and produce safe consumer products.

They are also now applying the same principles in new areas, such as health care, in which recent studies have documented the high costs of accidents in hospitals. Health and safety engineers can help prevent accidents as biomedical engineers develop advances in their field. Accident prevention is likely to become increasingly important for the healthcare industry as a way of cutting costs.

Another major factor likely to drive employment is the emerging field of software safety engineering. Software must work exactly as intended, especially when it controls, for example, elevators or automobiles, where a glitch in the software could cause serious injury to people and damage to equipment. The number of machines and mechanical devices controlled by software is expected to continue to grow, and the need to apply the principles of systems safety engineering to this software is expected to grow as well.

Employment projections data for health and safety engineers, 2010-20

Occupational Title	SOC Code	Employment, 2010	Projected Employment, 2020	Change, 2010-20 Percent	Numeric
Health and Safety Engineers, Except Mining Safety Engineers and Inspectors	17-2111	23,700	26,800	13	3,100
SOURCE: U.S. Bureau of Labor Statistics, Employment Projections program					

Similar Occupations

This table shows a list of occupations with job duties that are similar to those of health and safety engineers.

Occupation	Job Duties	Entry-Level Education	Median Annual Pay, May 2010
Construction and Building Inspectors	Construction and building inspectors ensure that new construction, changes, or repairs comply with local and national building codes and ordinances, zoning regulations, and contract specifications.	High school diploma or equivalent	$52,360
Industrial Engineers	Industrial engineers find ways to eliminate wastefulness in production processes. They devise efficient ways to use workers, machines, materials, information, and energy to make a product or provide a service.	Bachelor's degree	$76,100
Mining and Geological Engineers	Mining and geological engineers design mines for the safe and efficient removal of minerals, such as coal and metals, for manufacturing and utilities.	Bachelor's degree	$82,870
Occupational Health and Safety Specialists	Occupational health and safety specialists analyze many types of work environments and work procedures. Specialists inspect workplaces for adherence to regulations on safety, health, and the environment. They also design programs to prevent disease or injury to workers and damage to the environment.	Bachelor's degree	$64,660
Occupational Health and Safety Technicians	Occupational health and safety technicians collect data on the safety and health conditions of the workplace. Technicians work with occupational health and safety specialists in conducting tests and measuring hazards to help prevent harm to workers, property, the environment, and the general public.	High school diploma or equivalent	$45,330

Contacts for More Information

For information about general engineering education and career resources, visit American Society for Engineering Education, Technology Student Association

For more information about accredited engineering programs, visit ABET, American Society of Safety Engineers

For more information about the Professional Engineer license, visit National Council of Examiners for Engineering and Surveying, National Society of Professional Engineers

For information about protecting worker health, visit American Industrial Hygiene Association

For information about certification, visit American Board of Industrial Hygiene, Board of Certified Safety Professionals

Suggested citation:

Bureau of Labor Statistics, U.S. Department of Labor, Occupational Outlook Handbook, 2012-13 Edition, Health and Safety Engineers, on the Internet at
http://www.bls.gov/ooh/architecture-and-engineering/health-and-safety-engineers.htm .

Industrial Engineering Technicians

Quick Facts: Industrial Engineering Technicians	
2010 Median Pay	$48,210 per year $23.18 per hour
Entry-Level Education	Associate's degree
Work Experience in a Related Occupation	None
On-the-job Training	None
Number of Jobs, 2010	62,500
Job Outlook, 2010-20	4% (Slower than average)
Employment Change, 2010-20	2,600

What Industrial Engineering Technicians Do

Industrial engineering technicians plan ways to effectively use personnel, materials, and machines in factories, stores, health care organizations, repair shops, and offices. As assistants to industrial engineers, they help prepare machinery and equipment layouts, plan workflows, conduct statistical production studies, and analyze production costs.

Duties

Industrial engineering technicians typically do the following:

- Suggest revisions for methods of operation, material handling, or equipment layout
- Interpret engineering drawings, schematic diagrams, and formulas
- Confer with management or engineering staff to determine quality and reliability standards
- Suggest changes to production standards for achieving the best quality within the limits of equipment capacity
- Help plan work assignments, taking into account worker performance, machine capacity, and production schedules
- Prepare charts, graphs, and diagrams to illustrate workflow, routing, floor

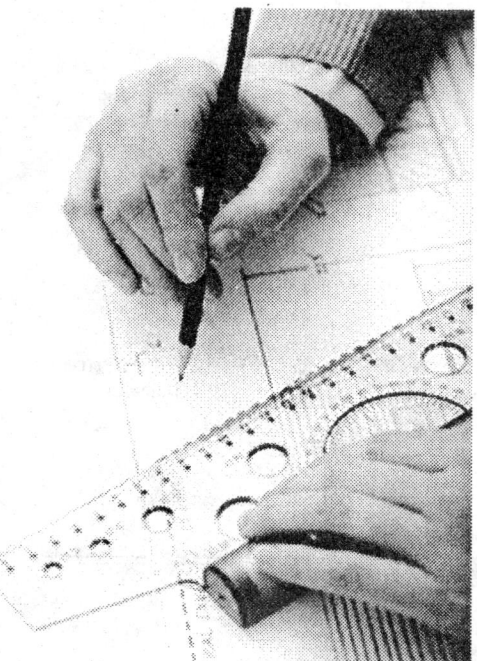

Industrial engineering technicians help to prepare layouts for machinery, equipment, and workflow.

layouts, how materials are handled and how machines are used

Industrial engineering technicians study the time and steps workers take to do a task (called "time and motion" studies). To set reasonable production rates, they consider how workers are doing operations such as maintenance, production, and service.

They also observe workers to make sure that the equipment is being used and maintained according to quality assurance standards. They then evaluate the resulting data to point out or justify changes to the operations or the standards to improve quality and efficiency.

Industrial engineering technicians generally work in teams under the supervision of industrial engineers.

Work Environment

Industrial engineering technicians held 62,500 jobs in 2010. They work in various industries and businesses to coordinate activities that ensure the quality of final products or services.

The following industries employed the largest numbers of industrial engineering technicians in 2010:

Semiconductor and other electronic component manufacturing	9%
Aerospace product and parts manufacturing	7
Navigational, measuring, electromedical, and control instruments manufacturing	6
Motor vehicle parts manufacturing	6
Plastics product manufacturing	4

Industrial engineers usually ask industrial engineering technicians to help carry out certain studies and make specific observations. Consequently, these technicians are often at the physical setting where the product is being manufactured or where the services are being delivered.

Industrial engineering technicians usually work standard schedules. Most work full time.

How to Become an Industrial Engineering Technician

Industrial engineering technicians typically need an associate's degree or postsecondary certificate. Associate's degree programs are typically offered by community colleges and technical institutes, and certificate programs are offered at vocational and technical schools.

Education

High school students interested in becoming industrial engineering technicians should take courses in math, science, and drafting, where available. Courses that help students develop computer skills are helpful when they later need to learn computer-aided design/computer-aided manufacturing software, known as CAD/CAM.

After high school, students interested in becoming industrial engineering technicians can continue at a vocational-technical school or at a community college or technical institute.

Vocational-technical schools include postsecondary public institutions that serve local students and emphasize training needed by local employers. These programs generally award a certificate.

Community colleges offer programs similar to those in technical institutes, but there are more theory-based liberal arts courses in community colleges. Students who complete the program earn an associate's degree.

ABET (formerly the Accreditation Board for Engineering and Technology) accredits engineering programs.

Generally, prospective industrial engineering technicians should major in applied science, industrial technology, or industrial engineering technology.

Important Qualities

Analytical skills. Industrial engineering technicians must be able to help industrial engineers figure out how a system should work and how changes in conditions, operations, and the environment will affect outcomes.

Detail oriented. Industrial engineering technicians must gather and record measurements and observations needed by industrial engineers.

Communication skills. Industrial engineering technicians follow instructions from industrial engineers. They must be able to clearly understand and follow instructions, and communicate problems to their supervisors.

Critical-thinking skills. Industrial engineering technicians must be able to help industrial engineers figure out why a certain process or operation is not working as well as it might. They must ask the right questions to identify and correct weaknesses.

Math skills. Industrial engineering technicians use the principals of mathematics for analysis, design, and troubleshooting in their work.

Observation skills. These technicians spend much of their time evaluating the performance of other people or organizations to make suggestions for improvements or corrective action. They must gather and record information without interfering with workers in their environments.

Pay

Industrial Engineering Technicians
  Median annual wages, May 2010

Engineering Technicians, Except Drafters	$51,930
Industrial Engineering Technicians	$48,210
Total, All Occupations	$33,840

Note: All Occupations includes all occupations in the U.S. Economy.
Source: U.S. Bureau of Labor Statistics, Occupational Employment Statistics

The median annual wage of industrial engineering technicians was $48,210 in May 2010. The median wage is the wage at which half the

workers in an occupation earned more than that amount and half earned less. The lowest 10 percent earned less than $31,560, and the top 10 percent earned more than $73,440.

Median annual wages in the industries employing the largest numbers of industrial engineering technicians in May 2010 were the following:

Aerospace product and parts manufacturing	$58,410
Semiconductor and other electronic component manufacturing	48,280
Navigational, measuring, electromedical, and control instruments manufacturing	47,790
Motor vehicle parts manufacturing	46,370
Plastics product manufacturing	44,380

Industrial engineering technicians usually work standard schedules. Most work full time.

Job Outlook

Industrial Engineering Technicians
  Percent change in employment, projected 2010-20

Total, All Occupations	14%
Engineering Technicians, Except Drafters	5%
Industrial Engineering Technicians	4%

Note: All Occupations includes all occupations in the U.S. Economy.
Source: U.S. Bureau of Labor Statistics, Employment Projections program

Employment of industrial engineering technicians is expected to grow 4 percent between 2010 and 2020, slower than the average for all occupations.

Industrial engineering is versatile because of its wide applicability in many industries. The growing emphasis on cost control through increasing efficiency is expected to sustain demand for industrial engineering technicians' services in most industries, including nonprofits.

Like industrial engineers, industrial engineering technicians work in a wide range of industries, including major manufacturing industries, health care, consulting and engineering services, and research and development. This is because one focus of industrial engineering is reducing internal costs, which is valuable to even the fastest growing industries.

Industrial engineering technicians' versatility allows them to be useful to a variety of businesses, governments, and nonprofits. They work in supply chain management to help businesses minimize inventory costs, in quality assurance to help businesses keep their customers satisfied, and in the growing field of project management to control costs and maximize efficiencies.

Employment projections data for industrial engineering technicians, 2010-20

Occupational Title	SOC Code	Employment, 2010	Projected Employment, 2020	Change, 2010-20 Percent	Numeric
Industrial Engineering Technicians	17-3026	62,500	65,100	4	2,600

SOURCE: U.S. Bureau of Labor Statistics, Employment Projections program

Similar Occupations

This table shows a list of occupations with job duties that are similar to those of industrial engineering technicians.

Occupation	Job Duties	Entry-Level Education	Median Annual Pay, May 2010
Cost Estimators	Cost estimators collect and analyze data to estimate the time, money, resources, and labor required for product manufacturing, construction projects, or services. Some specialize in a particular industry or product type.	Bachelor's degree	$57,860

Health and Safety Engineers	Health and safety engineers develop procedures and design systems to keep people from getting sick or injured and to keep property from being damaged. They combine knowledge of health or safety and of systems engineering to make sure that chemicals, machinery, software, furniture, and other products are not going to cause harm to people or buildings.	Bachelor's degree	$75,430
Industrial Engineers	Industrial engineers find ways to eliminate wastefulness in production processes. They devise efficient ways to use workers, machines, materials, information, and energy to make a product or provide a service.	Bachelor's degree	$76,100
Logisticians	Logisticians analyze and coordinate an organization's supply chain€"the system that moves a product from supplier to consumer. They manage the entire life cycle of a product, which includes how a product is acquired, distributed, allocated, and delivered.	Bachelor's degree	$70,800
Quality Control Inspectors	Quality control inspectors examine products and materials for defects or deviations from manufacturers' or industry specifications.	High school diploma or equivalent	$33,030

Contacts for More Information

For more information about accredited programs, visit ABET

For more information about industrial engineering, visit Institute of Industrial Engineers

For information on general engineering education and career resources, visit American Society for Engineering Education, Technology Student Association

Suggested citation:

Bureau of Labor Statistics, U.S. Department of Labor, Occupational Outlook Handbook, 2012-13 Edition, Industrial Engineering Technicians, on the Internet at http://www.bls.gov/ooh/architecture-and-engineering/industrial-engineering-technicians.htm.

Industrial Engineers

Quick Facts: Industrial Engineers	
2010 Median Pay	$76,100 per year $36.59 per hour
Entry-Level Education	Bachelor's degree
Work Experience in a Related Occupation	None
On-the-job Training	None
Number of Jobs, 2010	203,900
Job Outlook, 2010-20	6% (Slower than average)
Employment Change, 2010-20	13,100

What Industrial Engineers Do

Industrial engineers find ways to eliminate wastefulness in production processes. They devise efficient ways to use workers, machines, materials, information, and energy to make a product or provide a service.

Duties

Industrial engineers typically do the following:

- Review production schedules, engineering specifications, process flows, and other information to understand manufacturing and service methods and activities

- Figure out how to manufacture parts or products or deliver services with maximum efficiency

- Develop management control systems to make financial planning and cost analysis more efficient

- Enact quality control procedures to resolve production problems or minimize costs

- Work with customers and management to develop standards for design and production

- Design control systems to coordinate activities and production planning to ensure that products meet quality standards

- Confer with clients about product specifications, vendors about purchases, management personnel about manufacturing capabilities, and staff about the status of projects

Industrial engineers apply their skills to many different situations from manufacturing to business administration. For example, they design systems for

- moving heavy parts within manufacturing plants
- getting goods from a company to customers, including finding the most profitable places to locate manufacturing or processing plants
- evaluating how well people do their jobs
- paying workers

In all these different projects, industrial engineers focus on how get the work done most efficiently, balancing many factors€"such as time, number of workers needed, actions workers need to take, achieving the end with no errors, technology that is available, workers' safety, environmental concerns, and cost.

To find ways to reduce waste and improve performance, industrial engineers first study product requirements carefully. Then they use mathematical methods and models to design manufacturing and information systems to meet those requirements most efficiently.

Work Environment

Industrial engineers held about 203,900 jobs in 2010. Depending on their tasks, industrial engineers work both in offices and in the settings they are trying to improve. For example, when observing problems, they may watch workers on a factory floor or staff in a hospital. When solving problems, they may be in an office at a computer looking at data that they or others have collected. Industrial engineers work on teams with other professionals and production staff. Industrial engineers may need to travel to observe processes and make assessments in various work settings. Most industrial engineers work full time.

Industrial engineers develop job evaluation programs, amongst other duties.

The following industries employed the largest numbers of industrial engineers in 2010:

Aerospace product and parts manufacturing	8%
Architectural, engineering, and related services	6
Navigational, measuring, electromedical, and control instruments manufacturing	6
Motor vehicle parts manufacturing	5
Semiconductor and other electronic component manufacturing	5

How to Become an Industrial Engineer

Industrial engineers must have a bachelor's degree in industrial engineering. Employers also value experience, so cooperative-education engineering programs at universities are also valuable.

Education

Entry-level industrial engineering jobs require a bachelor's degree. Students interested in studying industrial engineering should take high school courses in mathematics, such as algebra, trigonometry, and calculus; computer science; and sciences such as chemistry and physics.

Bachelor's degree programs typically are 4-year programs and include lectures in classrooms and practice in laboratories. Courses include statistics, production systems planning, and manufacturing systems design, among others. Many colleges and universities offer cooperative-education programs in which students gain practical experience while completing their education.

Some colleges and universities offer 5-year degree programs that lead to a bachelor's and master's degree upon completion. A graduate degree will allow an engineer to work as a professor at a university or to engage in research and development. Some 5-year or even 6-year cooperative-education plans combine classroom study with practical work, permitting students to gain experience and to finance part of their education.

Programs in industrial engineering are accredited by ABET (formerly the Accreditation Board for Engineering and Technology).

Important Qualities

Critical-thinking skills. Industrial engineers create new systems to solve problems related to waste and inefficiency. Solving these problems requires logic and reasoning to identify strengths and weaknesses of alternative solutions, conclusions, or approaches to the problems.

Listening skills. These engineers often operate in teams, but they must also solicit feedback from customers, vendors, and production staff. They must listen to customers and clients to fully grasp ideas and problems the first time.

Math skills. Industrial engineers use the principals of calculus, trigonometry, and other advanced topics in mathematics for analysis, design, and troubleshooting in their work.

Problem-solving skills. In designing facilities for manufacturing and processes for providing services, these engineers deal with several issues at once, from workers' safety to quality assurance.

Speaking skills. Industrial engineers sometimes have to explain their instructions to production staff or technicians before they can make written instructions available. Being able to explain concepts clearly and quickly is crucial to preventing costly mistakes and loss of time.

Teamwork. Industrial engineers must be able to work with other professionals to serve as a bridge between the technical and business sides of an organization. This requires being able to work with people from a wide variety of backgrounds.

Writing skills. Industrial engineers must create documentation for other professionals or for future reference. The documentation must be coherent and explain their thinking clearly so that others can understand the information.

Licenses

Licensure for industrial engineers is not as common as it is for other engineering occupations, but it is encouraged for those working in companies that have government contracts. Industrial engineers who become licensed carry the designation of professional engineer (PE). Licensure generally requires the following:

- A degree from an engineering program accredited by ABET
- A passing score on the Fundamentals of Engineering (FE) exam
- Relevant work experience
- A passing score on the Professional Engineering (PE) exam

The initial FE exam can be taken right after graduating. Engineers who pass this exam commonly are called engineers in training (EITs) or engineer interns (EIs). After getting suitable work experience, EITs can take the second exam, called the Principles and Practice of Engineering exam.

Several states require engineers to take continuing education to keep their licenses. Most states recognize licenses from other states, as long as that the other state's licensing requirements meet or exceed their own licensing requirements.

Advancement

Beginning industrial engineers usually work under the supervision of experienced engineers. In large companies, new engineers also may receive formal training in classes or seminars. As beginning engineers gain knowledge and experience, they move to more difficult projects with greater independence to develop designs, solve problems, and make decisions.

Eventually, industrial engineers may advance to become technical specialists, such as quality engineers or facility planners. In that role, they supervise a team of engineers and technicians. Many industrial engineers move into management positions because the work they do is closely related to the work of managers. For more information, see the profile on architectural and engineering managers .

Pay

Industrial Engineers
   Median annual wages, May 2010

Engineers	$83,340
Industrial Engineers	$76,100
Total, All Occupations	$33,840

Note: All Occupations includes all occupations in the U.S. Economy.
Source: U.S. Bureau of Labor Statistics, Occupational Employment Statistics

The median annual wage of industrial engineers was $76,100 in May 2010. The median wage is the wage at which half of the workers in an occupation earned more than that amount and half earned less. The lowest 10 percent earned less than $49,700, and the top 10 percent earned more than $112,830.

Median annual wages in the industries employing the largest numbers of industrial engineers in May 2010 were as follows:

Semiconductor and other electronic component manufacturing	$83,620
Navigational, measuring, electromedical, and control instruments manufacturing	81,850
Architectural, engineering, and related services	80,990
Aerospace product and parts manufacturing	80,940
Motor vehicle parts manufacturing	72,840

Job Outlook

Industrial Engineers
   Percent change in employment, projected 2010-20

Total, All Occupations	14%
Engineers	11%
Industrial Engineers	6%

Note: All Occupations includes all occupations in the U.S. Economy.
Source: U.S. Bureau of Labor Statistics, Employment Projections program

Employment of industrial engineers is expected to grow 6 percent from 2010 to 2020, slower than the average for all occupations. This occupation is versatile both in the nature of the work it does and in the industries in which its expertise can be put to use. In addition, because industrial engineers' work can help with cost control by increasing efficiency, these engineers are attractive to employers in most industries, including nonprofits.

Because they are not as specialized as other engineers, industrial engineers are employed in a wide range of industries, including major manufacturing industries, hospitals, consulting and engineering services, and research and development firms. This versatility arises from the fact that these engineers' expertise focuses on reducing internal costs, making their work valuable even for the fastest growing industries. However, growth will be tempered since many are employed in manufacturing industries that are projected to be declining or slow growing.

Their versatility allows industrial engineers to engage in activities that are useful to a variety of businesses, governments, and nonprofits. Industrial engineers engage in supply chain management to help businesses minimize inventory costs, in quality assurance to help businesses keep their customer bases satisfied, and in the growing field of project management as industries across the economy seek to control costs and maximize efficiencies.

Employment projections data for industrial engineers, 2010-20

Occupational Title	SOC Code	Employment, 2010	Projected Employment, 2020	Change, 2010-20	
				Percent	Numeric
Industrial Engineers	17-2112	203,900	217,000	6	13,100
SOURCE: U.S. Bureau of Labor Statistics, Employment Projections program					

Similar Occupations

This table shows a list of occupations with job duties that are similar to those of industrial engineers.

Occupation	Job Duties	Entry-Level Education	Median Annual Pay, May 2010
Architectural and Engineering Managers	Architectural and engineering managers plan, coordinate, and direct activities in architecture and engineering, including research and development in these fields.	Bachelor's degree	$119,260
Cost Estimators	Cost estimators collect and analyze data to estimate the time, money, resources, and labor required for product manufacturing, construction projects, or services. Some specialize in a particular industry or product type.	Bachelor's degree	$57,860
Health and Safety Engineers	Health and safety engineers develop procedures and design systems to keep people from getting sick or injured and to keep property from being damaged. They combine knowledge of health or safety and of systems engineering to make sure that chemicals, machinery, software, furniture, and other products are not going to cause harm to people or buildings.	Bachelor's degree	$75,430
Industrial Engineering Technicians	Industrial engineering technicians plan ways to effectively use personnel, materials, and machines in factories, stores, hospitals, repair shops, and offices. As assistants to industrial engineers, they help prepare machinery and equipment layouts, plan workflows, conduct statistical production studies, and analyze production costs.	Associate's degree	$48,210
Industrial Production Managers	Industrial production managers oversee the daily operations of manufacturing and related plants. They coordinate, plan, and direct the activities used to create a wide range of goods, such as cars, computer equipment, or paper products.	Bachelor's degree	$87,160

Logisticians	Logisticians analyze and coordinate an organization's supply chain€the system that moves a product from supplier to consumer. They manage the entire life cycle of a product, which includes how a product is acquired, distributed, allocated, and delivered.	Bachelor's degree	$70,800
Management Analysts	Management analysts, often called management consultants, propose ways to improve an organization's efficiency. They advise managers on how to make organizations more profitable through reduced costs and increased revenues.	Bachelor's degree	$78,160
Materials Engineers	Materials engineers develop, process, and test materials used to create a range of products, from computer chips and aircraft wings to golf clubs and snow skis. They also help select materials and develop new ways to use materials.	Bachelor's degree	$83,120
Quality Control Inspectors	Quality control inspectors examine products and materials for defects or deviations from manufacturers' or industry specifications.	High school diploma or equivalent	$33,030

Contacts for More Information

For information about general engineering education and career resources, visit American Society for Engineering Education, Technology Student Association

For more information about licensure as an industrial engineer, visit National Council of Examiners for Engineering and Surveying, National Society of Professional Engineers

For information about accredited engineering programs, visit ABET

For more information about industrial engineers visit Institute of Industrial Engineers

Suggested citation:

Bureau of Labor Statistics, U.S. Department of Labor, Occupational Outlook Handbook, 2012-13 Edition, Industrial Engineers, on the Internet at http://www.bls.gov/ooh/architecture-and-engineering/industrial-engineers.htm

Landscape Architects

Quick Facts: Landscape Architects	
2010 Median Pay	$62,090 per year $29.85 per hour
Entry-Level Education	Bachelor's degree
Work Experience in a Related Occupation	None
On-the-job Training	Internship/residency
Number of Jobs, 2010	21,600
Job Outlook, 2010-20	16% (About as fast as average)
Employment Change, 2010-20	3,500

What Landscape Architects Do

Landscape architects plan and design land areas for parks, recreational facilities, highways, airports, and other properties. Projects may include subdivisions and commercial, industrial, and residential sites.

Landscape architects create graphic representations of plans.

Duties

Landscape architects typically do the following:
- Confer with clients, engineers, and building architects to understand a project
- Prepare site plans, specifications, and cost estimates
- Coordinate the arrangement of existing and proposed land features and structures
- Prepare graphic representations and drawings of proposed plans and designs
- Analyze environmental reports and data on land conditions, such as drainage
- Inspect landscape work to ensure that it adheres to original plans
- Approve the quality of work that others do
- Seek new work through marketing or by giving presentations

People enjoy attractively designed gardens, public parks, playgrounds, residential areas, college campuses, and golf courses. Landscape architects design these areas so that they are not only functional but also beautiful and harmonious with the natural environment.

Landscape architects plan the locations of buildings, roads, and walkways. They also plan where to plant flowers, shrubs, and trees. Landscape architects design and plan the restoration of natural places disturbed by humans, such as wetlands, stream corridors, and mined areas.

Many landscape architects specialize in a particular area, such as beautifying or otherwise improving streets and highways, waterfronts, parks and playgrounds, or shopping centers.

Increasingly, landscape architects are working in environmental remediation, such as preserving and restoring wetlands or managing storm-water runoff in new developments. They are also increasingly playing a role in preserving and restoring historic landscapes.

Landscape architects who work for government agencies do design sites and landscapes for government buildings, parks, and other public lands, as well as plan for landscapes and recreation areas in national parks and forests.

In addition, they prepare environmental impact statements and studies on environmental issues, such as planning for use of public lands.

Work Environment

Landscape architects held about 21,600 jobs in 2010, of which 47 percent were employed in the architectural, engineering, and related services industry. About 24 percent were self-employed.

Landscape architects spend most of their time in offices, creating plans and designs, preparing models and cost estimates, doing research, and attending meetings with clients and other professionals involved in designing or planning a project. They spend the rest of their work time at jobsites.

Work Schedules

Most work full time, and many work more than 50 hours per week. Working evenings and weekends is often necessary to meet deadlines.

How to Become a Landscape Architect

Every state requires landscape architects to be licensed. Requirements vary among states, but usually include a degree in landscape architecture from an accredited school, work experience, and a passing score on the Landscape Architect Registration Exam.

Education

A bachelor's or master's degree in landscape architecture usually is necessary for entry into the profession. In 2011, 68 colleges and universities offered undergraduate or graduate programs in landscape architecture that were accredited by the Landscape Architecture Accreditation Board, part of the American Society of Landscape Architects.

There are two undergraduate landscape architect professional degrees: a Bachelor of Landscape Architecture (BLA) and a Bachelor of Science in Landscape Architecture (BSLA). These programs usually require 4 or 5 years of study.

Those who hold an undergraduate degree in a field other than landscape architecture can enroll in a Master of Landscape Architecture (MLA) graduate degree program, which typically takes 3 years of full-time study. Those who hold undergraduate degrees in landscape architecture can earn their MLA in 2 years.

Common courses include surveying, landscape design and construction, landscape ecology, site design, and urban and regional planning. Other courses include history of landscape architecture, plant and soil science, geology, professional practice, and general management.

The design studio is a key component of any curriculum. Whenever possible, students are assigned real projects, providing them with valuable hands-on experience. While working on these projects, students become proficient in the use of computer-aided design (CAD), model building, geographic information systems (GISs), and video simulation.

Many employers recommend that prospective landscape architects complete an internship with a landscape architecture firm during their formal educational studies. Interns can improve their technical skills and gain an understanding of the day-to-day operations of the business, including how to win clients, generate fees, and work within a budget.

Training

New hires are called apprentices or intern landscape architects until they become licensed. Although duties vary with the type and size of the employing firm, all interns must work under the supervision of a licensed landscape architect. In addition, all drawings and specifications must be signed and sealed by the licensed landscape architect.

Licenses and Certification

Landscape architects who work outside of the federal government need a license. As of 2010, all 50 states required landscape architects to be licensed. Licensing is based on the Landscape Architect Registration Examination (L.A.R.E.), which is sponsored by the Council of Landscape Architectural Registration Boards. Candidates can take the L.A.R.E. at different times of the year in two parts€"three multiple-choice sections and two graphic response sections.

Applicants who want to take the exam usually need a degree from an accredited school and 1 to 4 years of work experience under the supervision of a licensed landscape architect, although standards vary by state. For those without an accredited landscape architecture degree, most states provide alternative paths to qualify to take the L.A.R.E., usually requiring more work experience.

Currently, 13 states require landscape architects to pass a state exam, in addition to the L.A.R.E., to satisfy registration requirements. State exams focus on laws, environmental regulations, plants, soils, climate, and other characteristics unique to the state.

Because requirements for licensure vary, landscape architects may find it difficult to transfer their registration from one state to another. Common requirements include graduating from an accredited program, serving 3 years of internship under the supervision of a registered landscape architect, and passing the L.A.R.E. By meeting national requirements, a landscape architect also can obtain certification from the Council of Landscape Architectural Registration Boards. That certification can be useful in getting one state to accept a license from another state.

Landscape architects who work for the federal government do not have to be licensed. For federal government jobs, landscape architects should have a bachelor's or master's degree in landscape architecture.

Important Qualities

Analytical skills. Landscape architects need to understand the content of designs. When designing a building's drainage system, for example, landscape architects need to understand how the building's location and surrounding land affect each other.

Communication skills. Landscape architects share their ideas, both orally and in writing, with clients, other architects, and workers who help prepare drawings. Many landscape architects also give presentations to explain their designs.

Creativity. Landscape architects create the overall look of gardens, parks, and other outdoor areas. Designs should be both pleasing to the eye and functional.

Critical-thinking skills. When designing outdoor spaces, landscape architects must be able to provide solutions to unanticipated challenges. These solutions often involve looking at the challenge from all perspectives.

Technical skills. Landscape architects use CAD programs to create plans. Some also must use GISs for their designs.

Visualization skills. Landscape architects must be able to imagine how the overall outdoor space will look once complete.

Pay

Landscape Architects
Median annual wages, May 2010

Architects, Surveyors, and Cartographers	$64,820
Landscape Architects	$62,090
Total, All Occupations	$33,840

Note: All Occupations includes all occupations in the U.S. Economy.
Source: U.S. Bureau of Labor Statistics, Occupational Employment Statistics

The median annual wage of landscape architects was $62,090 in May 2010. The median wage is the wage at which half the workers in an occupation earned more than that amount and half earned less. The lowest 10 percent earned less than $36,880, and the top 10 percent earned more than $101,530.

Most work full time, and many work more than 50 hours per week. Working evenings and weekends is often necessary to meet deadlines.

Job Outlook

Landscape Architects

Percent change in employment, projected 2010-20

Architects, Surveyors, and Cartographers	24%
Landscape Architects	16%
Total, All Occupations	14%

Note: All Occupations includes all occupations in the U.S. Economy.
Source: U.S. Bureau of Labor Statistics, Employment Projections program

Employment of landscape architects is projected to grow 16 percent from 2010 to 2020, about as fast as the average for all occupations.

Planning and development of new construction and redevelopment of existing buildings will drive employment growth. With land costs rising and the public's desire for more beautiful and functional spaces, the importance of good site planning and landscape design is expected to grow.

In addition, environmental concerns and increased demand for sustainably designed construction projects will spur demand for the services of landscape architects. For example, landscape architects are involved in the design of green roofs, which are covered with some form of vegetation and can significantly reduce air and water pollution and the costs of heating and cooling a building. Landscape architects also will be needed to design plans to manage storm-water runoff while conserving water resources and avoiding polluting waterways.

Job Prospects

Good job opportunities are expected overall. However, competition for jobs in the largest and most prestigious landscape architecture firms should be strong.

Many employers prefer to hire entry-level landscape architects who have internship experience, which significantly reduces the amount of on-the-job training required.

Job opportunities will be best for landscape architects who develop strong technical and communication skills and an in-depth knowledge of environmental codes and regulations. Those with additional training or experience in urban planning increase their job opportunities for employment in landscape architecture firms that specialize in site planning, as well as in landscape design.

Employment projections data for landscape architects, 2010-20

Occupational Title	SOC Code	Employment, 2010	Projected Employment, 2020	Change, 2010-20	
				Percent	Numeric
Landscape Architects	17-1012	21,600	25,100	16	3,500
SOURCE: U.S. Bureau of Labor Statistics, Employment Projections program					

Similar Occupations

This table shows a list of occupations with job duties that are similar to those of landscape architects.

Occupation	Job Duties	Entry-Level Education	Median Annual Pay, May 2010
Architects	Architects plan and design buildings and other structures.	Bachelor's degree	$72,550
Cartographers and Photogrammetrists	Cartographers and photogrammetrists measure, analyze, and interpret geographic information to create maps and charts for political, cultural, educational, and other purposes. Cartographers are general mapmakers, and photogrammetrists are specialized mapmakers who use aerial photographs to create maps.	Bachelor's degree	$54,510
Civil Engineers	Civil engineers design and supervise large construction projects, including roads, buildings, airports, tunnels, dams, bridges, and systems for water supply and sewage treatment.	Bachelor's degree	$77,560
Surveying and Mapping Technicians	Surveying and mapping technicians assist surveyors and cartographers in collecting data and making maps of the earth's surface. Surveying technicians visit sites to take measurements of the land. Mapping technicians use geographic data to create maps.	High school diploma or equivalent	$37,900
Surveyors	Surveyors establish official land, airspace, and water boundaries. Surveyors work with civil engineers, landscape architects, and urban and regional planners to develop comprehensive design documents.	Bachelor's degree	$54,880
Geoscientists	Geoscientists study the physical aspects of the Earth, such as its composition, structure, and processes, to learn about its past, present, and future.	Bachelor's degree	$82,500
Urban and Regional Planners	Urban and regional planners develop plans and programs for the use of land. They use planning to create communities, accommodate growth, or revitalize physical facilities in towns, cities, counties, and metropolitan areas.	Master's degree	$63,040
Hydrologists	Hydrologists study water and the water cycle. They use their expertise to solve problems in the areas of water quality or availability.	Master's degree	$75,690
Environmental Scientists and Specialists	Environmental scientists and specialists use their knowledge of the natural sciences to protect the environment. They identify problems and find solutions that minimize hazards to the health of the environment and the population.	Bachelor's degree	$61,700
Construction Managers	Construction managers plan, coordinate, budget, and supervise construction projects from early development to completion.	Associate's degree	$83,860

Contacts for More Information

For additional information, including a list of colleges and universities offering accredited programs in landscape architecture, visit American Society of Landscape Architects

For general information on registration or licensing requirements, visit Council of Landscape Architectural Registration Boards

Suggested citation:

Bureau of Labor Statistics, U.S. Department of Labor, Occupational Outlook Handbook, 2012-13 Edition, Landscape Architects, on the Internet at http://www.bls.gov/ooh/architecture-and-engineering/landscape-architects.htm

Marine Engineers and Naval Architects

Quick Facts: Marine Engineers and Naval Architects	
2010 Median Pay	$79,920 per year $38.42 per hour
Entry-Level Education	Bachelor's degree
Work Experience in a Related Occupation	None
On-the-job Training	None
Number of Jobs, 2010	5,900
Job Outlook, 2010-20	17% (About as fast as average)
Employment Change, 2010-20	1,000

What Marine Engineers and Naval Architects Do

Marine engineers and naval architects design, build, and maintain ships from aircraft carriers to submarines, from sailboats to tankers. Marine engineers work on the mechanical systems, such as propulsion and steering. Naval architects work on the basic design, including the form and stability of hulls.

Duties

Marine engineers typically do the following:

- Prepare system layouts and detailed drawings and schematics
- Inspect marine equipment and machinery to draw up work requests and job specifications
- Conduct environmental, operational, or performance tests on marine machinery and equipment
- Design and oversee testing, installation, and repair of marine apparatus and equipment
- Investigate and observe tests on machinery and equipment for compliance with standards

Marine engineers and naval architects design and supervise the construction of ships.

- Coordinate activities with regulatory bodies to ensure that repairs and alterations are done safely and at minimal cost
- Prepare technical reports for use by engineers, managers, or sales personnel
- Prepare cost estimates, schedules for design and construction, and contract specifications
- Maintain contact with contractors to be sure the work is being done correctly, on schedule, and within budget

The people who operate or supervise the operation of the machinery on a ship are sometimes called marine engineers, or, more frequently, ship engineers. Their work differs from that of the marine engineers in this profile. For more information on ship engineers, see the profile on water transportation occupations.

Marine engineers are increasingly putting their knowledge to work in power generation. Companies that formerly concentrated on other activities, such as papermaking, are now increasing their efforts to produce and sell electricity back to the power grid. These engineers' skills are also useful in the oil and gas industry, including offshore drilling operations.

Naval architects typically do the following:

- Study design proposals and specifications to establish basic characteristics of a ship, such as size, weight, and speed
- Develop sectional and waterline curves of the hull to establish the center of gravity, ideal hull form, and data on buoyancy and stability
- Design entire ship hulls and superstructures, following safety standards
- Design the layout of ships' interiors, including passenger compartments, cargo space, ladder wells, and elevators
- Confer with marine engineers to set up the layout of boiler room equipment, heating and ventilation systems, refrigeration equipment, and propulsion machinery
- Lead teams from a variety of specialties to oversee building and testing prototypes
- Evaluate how the ship does during trials both at the dock and at sea and change the design as needed to make sure the ship meets national and international standards.

Work Environment

Marine engineers and naval architects held 5,900 jobs in 2010. They typically work in offices, where they have access to computer software and other tools necessary for analyzing projects and designing solutions. Sometimes, they must go to sea on the ships to test them or maintain them.

Those working on power generation projects, such as offshore wind turbines or tidal power, work along the coast€"both offshore and on land. They also sometimes work on oil rigs where they oversee repair or maintenance of systems that they may have designed.

Industries employing the greatest numbers of marine engineers and naval architects in 2010 were the following:

Architectural, engineering, and related services	47%
Federal government, excluding postal service	17
Ship and boat building	10
Other professional, scientific, and technical services	6
Deep sea, coastal, and great lakes water transportation	4

How to Become a Marine Engineer or Naval Architect

Marine engineers and naval architects must have a bachelor's degree in marine engineering, naval architecture, or marine systems engineering. Employers also value practical experience, so cooperative engineering programs, which provide college credit for structured job experience, are valuable.

Education

Entry-level jobs in marine engineering and naval architecture require a bachelor's degree. Students interested in preparing for this occupation benefit from taking high school courses in mathematics, such as algebra, trigonometry, and calculus; and science, such as chemistry and physics. For aspiring naval architects, drafting courses are helpful.

Programs that lead to a bachelor's degree in engineering typically include courses in calculus, physics, and computer-aided design. Courses specific to marine engineering and naval architecture include fluid mechanics, ship hull strength, and mechanics of materials.

Programs in marine engineering, naval architecture, and marine systems engineering are accredited by ABET (formerly the Accreditation Board for Engineering and Technology).

Important Qualities

Communication skills. Marine engineers and naval architects must be able to give clear instructions and explain complex concepts when leading teams of professionals on projects.

Interpersonal skills. Marine engineers and naval architects meet with clients to analyze their needs for ship systems. Engineers must be able to discuss progress with clients to keep redesign options open before the project is too far along.

Math skills. Marine engineers and naval architects use the principals of calculus, trigonometry, and other advanced topics in mathematics for analysis, design, and troubleshooting in their work.

Problem-solving skills. Marine engineers must design several systems for ships that work well together. Naval architects and marine engineers are expected to solve problems for their clients. They must draw on their knowledge and experience to make effective decisions.

Teamwork. Naval architects often lead teams of diverse professionals to create a feasible design, and they must effectively use the skills that each person brings to the design process.

Licenses

Along with graduating from a bachelor's degree program, marine engineers and naval architects usually take an exam for a mariner's license from the U.S. Coast Guard. The first stage of the license is known as the 3rd Assistant License. With experience and further testing, a marine engineer may get a 2nd and then 1st Assistant License. The highest level of licensure is known as Chief Assistant. Higher grades of licensing are usually accompanied by higher pay and more responsibilities.

Advancement

Beginning marine engineers usually work under the supervision of experienced engineers. In larger companies, new engineers may also receive formal training in classrooms or seminars. As beginning engineers gain knowledge and experience, they move on to more difficult projects where they have greater independence to develop designs, solve problems, and make decisions.

Eventually, marine engineers may advance to become technical specialists or to supervise a team of engineers and technicians. Some may even become engineering managers or move into other managerial positions or sales work. In sales, an engineering background enables them to discuss technical aspects of certain kinds of engineering projects. Such knowledge is also useful in assisting clients in project planning, installation, and use.

Pay

Marine Engineers and Naval Architects
Median annual wages, May 2010

Engineers	$83,340
Marine Engineers and Naval Architects	$79,920
Total, All Occupations	$33,840

Note: All Occupations includes all occupations in the U.S. Economy.
Source: U.S. Bureau of Labor Statistics, Occupational Employment Statistics

The median annual wage of marine engineers and naval architects was $79,920 in May 2010. The median wage is the wage at which half of the workers in an occupation earned more than that amount and half earned less. The lowest 10 percent earned less than $43,200, and the top 10 percent earned more than $144,350.

Median annual wages in the industries employing the largest numbers of marine engineers and naval architects in May 2010 were the following:

Federal government, excluding postal service	$100,750
Deep sea, coastal, and great lakes water transportation	88,930
Architectural, engineering, and related services	77,670
Other professional, scientific, and technical services	68,460
Ship and boat building	65,860

Job Outlook

Marine Engineers and Naval Architects
Percent change in employment, projected 2010-20

Marine Engineers and Naval Architects	17%
Total, All Occupations	14%
Engineers	11%

Note: All Occupations includes all occupations in the U.S. Economy.
Source: U.S. Bureau of Labor Statistics, Employment Projections program

Employment of marine engineers and naval architects is expected to grow 17 percent from 2010 to 2020, about as fast as the average for all occupations. The need to design ships and systems to transport energy products, such as liquefied natural gas, across the globe will help to spur employment growth for this occupation. Employment of marine engineers and naval architects also will be supported by the need to modify existing ships and their systems because of new emissions and pollution regulations on cargo shipping.

Marine engineers design and maintain offshore oil rigs. These workers are expected to be in demand as more companies seek and drill for oil and gas deposits in the ocean floor.

Additionally, the increase in international overseas transportation of liquefied natural gas is expected to lead to demand for marine engineers to work on ship crews, though sometimes on ships sailing under foreign flags. The adoption of new and alternative energy sources, such as offshore wind turbines and tidal power generators, will also drive demand for marine engineer and naval architects.

Demand for naval architects will likely come from the need to update fleets to meet new federal requirements for double-hulled ships for transporting oil and gas. In addition, the skills of naval architects may further be required to help design offshore rigs that drill in more inhospitable climates.

Demand for marine engineers and naval architects will also come from the desire to have cargo ships that pollute less. The technology to do this is becoming more cost-effective and the United States and other countries are focusing more on reducing pollution.

Employment projections data for marine engineers and naval architects, 2010-20

Occupational Title	SOC Code	Employment, 2010	Projected Employment, 2020	Change, 2010-20 Percent	Numeric
Marine Engineers and Naval Architects	17-2121	5,900	7,000	17	1,000
SOURCE: U.S. Bureau of Labor Statistics, Employment Projections program					

Similar Occupations

This table shows a list of occupations with job duties that are similar to those of marine engineers and naval architects.

Occupation	Job Duties	Entry-Level Education	Median Annual Pay, May 2010
Aerospace Engineers	Aerospace engineers design aircraft, spacecraft, satellites, and missiles. In addition, they test prototypes to make sure that they function according to design.	Bachelor's degree	$97,480
Drafters	Drafters use software to convert the designs of engineers and architects into technical drawings and plans. Workers in production and construction use these plans to build everything from microchips to skyscrapers.	Associate's degree	$47,880
Mechanical Engineers	Mechanical engineering is one of the broadest engineering disciplines. Mechanical engineers design, develop, build, and test mechanical devices, including tools, engines, and machines.	Bachelor's degree	$78,160
Petroleum Engineers	Petroleum engineers design and develop methods for extracting oil and gas from deposits below the earth's surface. Petroleum engineers also find new ways to extract oil and gas from older wells.	Bachelor's degree	$114,080

Contacts for More Information

For information about general engineering education and career resources, visit American Society for Engineering Education, Technology Student Association

For information about accredited engineering programs, visit ABET

Suggested citation:

Bureau of Labor Statistics, U.S. Department of Labor, Occupational Outlook Handbook, 2012-13 Edition, Marine Engineers and Naval Architects, on the Internet at http://www.bls.gov/ooh/architecture-and-engineering/marine-engineers-and-naval-architects.htm.

Materials Engineers

Quick Facts: Materials Engineers	
2010 Median Pay	$83,120 per year $39.96 per hour
Entry-Level Education	Bachelor's degree
Work Experience in a Related Occupation	None
On-the-job Training	None
Number of Jobs, 2010	22,300
Job Outlook, 2010-20	9% (Slower than average)
Employment Change, 2010-20	1,900

What Materials Engineers Do

Materials engineers develop, process, and test materials used to create a range of products, from computer chips and aircraft wings to golf clubs and snow skis. They work with metals, ceramics, semiconductors, plastics, composites, and other substances to create new materials that meet certain mechanical, electrical, and chemical requirements. They also develop new ways to use materials.

Duties

Materials engineers typically do the following:

- Monitor how materials perform and evaluate how they deteriorate
- Determine causes of product failure and develop solutions
- Supervise the work of technologists, technicians, and other engineers and scientists
- Design and direct the testing of processing procedures
- Evaluate technical specifications and economic factors relating to the design objectives of processes or products
- Prepare proposals and budgets, analyze labor costs, write reports, and do other managerial tasks
- Plan and evaluate new projects, consulting with others as necessary

Materials engineers create and study materials at an atomic level. They use computers to replicate the characteristics of materials and their components. They solve problems in a number of engineering fields, such as mechanical, chemical, electrical, civil, nuclear, and aerospace engineering.

Materials engineers may specialize in understanding specific types of

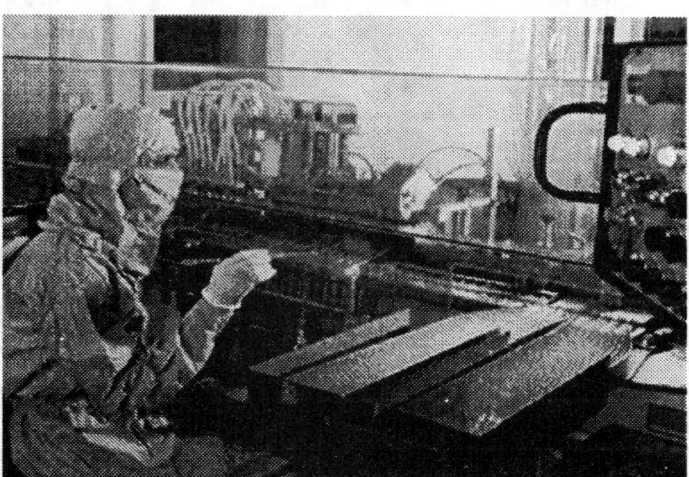

Materials engineers work with metals, ceramics, and plastics to create new materials.

materials. The following are types of materials engineers:

Ceramic engineers develop ceramic materials and the processes for making them into useful products, from high-temperature rocket nozzles to glass for LCD flat-panel displays.

Composites engineers work in developing materials with special, engineered properties for applications in aircraft, automobiles, and related products.

Metallurgical engineers specialize in metals, such as steel and aluminum, usually in alloyed form with additions of other elements to provide specific properties.

Plastics engineers work in developing and testing new plastics, known as polymers, for new applications.

Semiconductor processing engineers apply materials science and engineering principles to develop new microelectronic materials for computing and related applications.

Work Environment

Materials engineers held about 22,300 jobs in 2010. They often work in offices where they have access to computer-aided design (CAD) programs. Others work in supervisory roles either in the factory or in research and development laboratories.

Industries employing the largest numbers of materials engineers in 2010 were as follows:

Aerospace product and parts manufacturing	17%
Architectural, engineering, and related services	10
Semiconductor and other electronic component manufacturing	8
Navigational, measuring, electromedical, and control instruments manufacturing	7
Federal government	7

Most materials engineers work full time.

How to Become a Materials Engineer

Materials engineers typically have a bachelor's degree in materials science or engineering or a related field. Employers also value practical experience. Therefore, cooperative engineering programs, which provide college credit for structured job experience, are valuable as well.

Education

Students interested in studying materials engineering should take high school courses in mathematics, such as algebra, trigonometry, and calculus; and science, such as biology, chemistry, and physics.

Entry-level jobs as a materials engineer require a bachelor's degree.

Bachelor's degree programs typically last 4 years and include classroom and laboratory work focusing on engineering principles. Many colleges and universities offer cooperative programs in which students gain practical experience while earning college credits.

Some colleges and universities offer a 5-year program leading to both a bachelor's and master's degree. A graduate degree allows an engineer to work as an instructor at some colleges and universities or to do research and development. Some 5- or 6-year cooperative plans combine classroom study with practical work, allowing students to gain experience and to finance part of their education.

Many engineering programs are accredited by ABET (formerly the Accreditation Board for Engineering and Technology). Some employers prefer to hire candidates who have graduated from an accredited program. A degree from an ABET-accredited program is usually necessary to become a licensed professional engineer.

Important Qualities

Communication skills. In supervising technicians, technologists, and other engineers, materials engineers must be able to state concepts and directions clearly. When speaking with managers at high-level meetings, these engineers also must be able to communicate engineering concepts to people who do not have an engineering background.

Math skills. Materials engineers use the principals of calculus and other advanced topics in mathematics for analysis, design, and troubleshooting in their work.

Operations analysis. Materials engineers often work on projects related to other fields of engineering. They must be able to determine how materials will be used in a wide of conditions and how the materials must be structured to withstand the requirements of those conditions.

Problem-solving skills. Materials engineers must understand the relationship between the structure of materials and their properties and means of processing, and how these factors affect the product. They must also figure out why a product failed, design a solution, and then conduct tests to make sure the product does not fail again. This involves being able to identify root causes when many factors could be at fault.

Teamwork. Materials engineers must be able to work with scientists and engineers from other backgrounds. They must be able to present and defend a perspective while also accepting other specialists' input and feedback.

Writing skills. Materials engineers must write plans and reports clearly so that people without a materials engineering background understand the concepts.

Licenses

Some states license materials engineers; requirements vary by state. Licensed engineers are called professional engineers (PEs). Licensure generally has the following requirements:

- A degree from an ABET-accredited engineering program

- A passing score on the Fundamentals of Engineering (FE) exam

- Relevant work experience

- A passing score on the Professional Engineering (PE) exam

The initial Fundamentals of Engineering (FE) exam can be taken after graduation from college. Engineers who pass this exam are commonly called engineers in training (EITs) or engineer interns (EIs). After acquiring suitable work experience, EITs and EIs can take the second exam, called the Principles and Practice of Engineering.

Several states require continuing education for engineers to keep their license. Most states recognize licensure from other states, if the licensing state's requirements meet or exceed their own requirements.

Certification

Certification in the field of metallography is available through the Materials Information Society, ASM International . This certification is designed to supplement college courses in materials engineering or materials science.

Additional graduate work in fields directly related to metallurgy and materials' properties, such as corrosion or failure analysis, is available through ASM International.

Advancement

Beginning materials engineers usually work under the supervision of experienced engineers. In large companies, new engineers may receive formal training in classrooms or seminars. As engineers gain knowledge and experience, they move on to more difficult projects where they have greater independence to develop designs, solve problems, and make decisions.

Eventually, materials engineers may advance to become technical specialists or to supervise a team of engineers and technicians. Many become engineering managers or move into other managerial positions or sales work. An engineering background is useful in sales because it enables sales engineers to discuss a product's technical aspects and assist in product planning, installation, and use. For more information, see the profile on sales engineers .

Pay

Materials Engineers
Median annual wages, May 2010

Engineers	$83,340
Materials Engineers	$83,120
Total, All Occupations	$33,840

Note: All Occupations includes all occupations in the U.S. Economy.
Source: U.S. Bureau of Labor Statistics, Occupational Employment Statistics

The median annual wage of materials engineers was $83,120 in May 2010. The median wage is the wage at which half the workers in an occupation earned more than that amount and half earned less. The lowest 10 percent earned less than $51,680, and the top 10 percent earned more than $126,800.

Median annual wages in the industries employing the largest numbers of materials engineers in May 2010 were as follows:

Federal government	$110,590
Aerospace product and parts manufacturing	91,920
Navigational, measuring, electromedical, and control instruments manufacturing	87,660
Semiconductor and other electronic component manufacturing	86,380
Architectural, engineering, and related services	75,470

Most materials engineers work full time.

Job Outlook

Materials Engineers
Percent change in employment, projected 2010-20

Total, All Occupations	14%
Engineers	11%
Materials Engineers	9%

Note: All Occupations includes all occupations in the U.S. Economy.
Source: U.S. Bureau of Labor Statistics, Employment Projections program

Employment of materials engineers is expected to grow 9 percent from 2010 to 2020, slower than the average for all occupations.

Materials engineers will be needed to design uses for new materials both in traditional industries, such as aerospace manufacturing, and in industries focused on new medical or scientific products.

Materials engineers are in demand in growing fields such as nanotechnology and biomedical engineering. They find new uses for these technologies, which can help to address problems with consumer products, industrial processes, and medical needs. Because the work of materials engineers is closely connected to organizations' research and development, firms will likely seek to draw upon the skills of materials engineers to stay at the forefront of their respective industries.

Materials engineers work in many other fields as well, including thermal sprays. Thermal sprays are insulating coats of materials such as metal alloys, ceramics, and plastics, and they are widely accepted in reducing energy use. Thus, these engineers may find a growing role in weatherization efforts for institutions and companies seeking to cut energy costs.

Job Prospects

Despite the relatively lower projected growth rate for this occupation, there should be favorable job prospects as materials engineers are needed to fill positions as more experienced materials engineers get promoted or retire.

Employment projections data for materials engineers, 2010-20

Occupational Title	SOC Code	Employment, 2010	Projected Employment, 2020	Change, 2010-20 Percent	Numeric
Materials Engineers	17-2131	22,300	24,200	9	1,900
SOURCE: U.S. Bureau of Labor Statistics, Employment Projections program					

Similar Occupations

This table shows a list of occupations with job duties that are similar to those of materials engineers.

Occupation	Job Duties	Entry-Level Education	Median Annual Pay, May 2010
Aerospace Engineers	Aerospace engineers design aircraft, spacecraft, satellites, and missiles. In addition, they test prototypes to make sure that they function according to design.	Bachelor's degree	$97,480
Architectural and Engineering Managers	Architectural and engineering managers plan, coordinate, and direct activities in architecture and engineering, including research and development in these fields.	Bachelor's degree	$119,260
Biomedical Engineers	Biomedical engineers analyze and design solutions to problems in biology and medicine, with the goal of improving the quality and effectiveness of patient care.	Bachelor's degree	$81,540
Chemical Engineers	Chemical engineers apply the principles of chemistry, biology, and physics to solve problems. These problems involve the production or use of chemicals, fuel, drugs, food, and many other products. They design processes and equipment for large-scale safe and sustainable manufacturing, plan and test methods of manufacturing products and treating byproducts, and supervise production.	Bachelor's degree	$90,300
Chemists and Materials Scientists	Chemists and materials scientists study the structures, compositions, reactions, and other properties of substances. They use their knowledge to develop new and improved products, processes, and materials.	Bachelor's degree	$69,790
Electrical and Electronics Engineers	Electrical engineers design, develop, test, and supervise the manufacturing of electrical equipment such as electric motors, radar and navigation systems, communications systems, and power generation equipment. Electronics engineers design and develop electronic equipment, such as broadcast and communications systemsfrom portable music players to global positioning systems (GPS).	Bachelor's degree	$87,180
Mechanical Engineers	Mechanical engineering is one of the broadest engineering disciplines. Mechanical engineers design, develop, build, and test mechanical devices, including tools, engines, and machines.	Bachelor's degree	$78,160
Physicists and Astronomers	Physicists and astronomers study the fundamental nature of the universe, ranging from the vastness of space to the smallest of subatomic particles. They develop new technologies, methods, and theories based on the results of their research that deepen our understanding of how things work and contribute to innovative, real-world applications.	Doctoral or professional degree	$105,430
Sales Engineers	Sales engineers sell complex scientific and technological products or services to businesses. They must have extensive knowledge of the products' parts and functions and must understand the scientific processes that make these products work.	Bachelor's degree	$87,390

Contacts for More Information

For information about general engineering education and career resources, visit American Society for Engineering Education

Technology Student Association

For more information about licensure as a materials engineer, visit National Council of Examiners for Engineering and Surveying, National Society of Professional Engineers

For information about accredited engineering programs, visit ABET

For more information about certification, visit ASM: The Materials Information Society

Suggested citation:

Bureau of Labor Statistics, U.S. Department of Labor, Occupational Outlook Handbook, 2012-13 Edition, Materials Engineers, on the Internet at http://www.bls.gov/ooh/architecture-and-engineering/materials-engineers.htm

Mechanical Engineering Technicians

Quick Facts: Mechanical Engineering Technicians	
2010 Median Pay	$50,110 per year $24.09 per hour
Entry-Level Education	Associate's degree
Work Experience in a Related Occupation	None
On-the-job Training	None
Number of Jobs, 2010	44,900
Job Outlook, 2010-20	4% (Slower than average)
Employment Change, 2010-20	1,800

What Mechanical Engineering Technicians Do

Mechanical engineering technicians help mechanical engineers design, develop, test, and manufacture industrial machinery, consumer products, and other equipment. They may make sketches and rough layouts, record and analyze data, make calculations and estimates, and report their findings.

Duties

Mechanical engineering technicians typically do the following:

- Evaluate drawing designs for new or changed tools by measuring dimensions on the drawing and comparing them with the original specifications
- Prepare layouts and drawings of parts to be made and the process for putting them together
- Discuss changes with coworkers€"for example, in the design of the part, in the way it will be made and put together, and in the techniques and process they will use
- Review instructions and blueprints for the project to ensure the test specifications, procedures, and objectives
- Plan, make, and put together new or changed mechanical parts for products, such as industrial machinery or equipment
- Set up and conduct tests of complete units and of parts as they would really be used, as a way to investigate proposals for improving equipment performance
- Record test procedures and results, numerical and graphical data, and recommendations for changes in product or test methods
- Analyze test results in regarding design specifications and test objectives

Mechanical engineering technicians also estimate labor costs, equipment

Mechanical engineering technicians plan the assembly process to be used in industrial settings.

life, and plant space. Some test and inspect machines and equipment or work with engineers to eliminate production problems. They may assist in testing products by, for example, setting up instrumentation for vehicle crash tests.

Work Environment

Mechanical engineering technicians held about 44,900 jobs in 2010. They work closely with mechanical engineers and are employed primarily in traditional manufacturing settings and in research and development laboratories. Most mechanical engineering technicians work full-time.

Industries employing the largest numbers of mechanical engineering technicians in 2010 were as follows:

Research and development in the physical, engineering, and life sciences	8%
Testing laboratories	5
Motor vehicle parts manufacturing	4
Navigational, measuring, electromedical, and control instruments manufacturing	4
Aerospace product and parts manufacturing	4

Some mechanical engineering technicians may be exposed to hazards from equipment, chemicals, or toxic materials, but injuries are rare as long as proper procedures are followed.

How to Become a Mechanical Engineering Technician

Most employers prefer to hire someone with an associate's degree or other postsecondary training in mechanical engineering technology. Prospective engineering technicians should take as many science and math courses as possible while in high school.

Education

Prospective mechanical engineering technicians usually take courses in fluid mechanics, thermodynamics, and mechanical design in a program leading to an associate's degree. The Technology Accreditation Commission of ABET (formerly the Accreditation Board for Engineering and Technology) accredits programs that include at least college algebra, trigonometry, and basic science courses. Associate's degree programs are in the following types of institutions:

- Vocational-technical schools, which include postsecondary public institutions that serve local students and emphasize training needed by local employers.
- Community colleges, which offer programs similar to those in technical institutes but include more theory-based and liberal arts coursework.

There are also programs in mechanical engineering technology that lead to a bachelor's degree, although most technicians graduate from associate's degree programs. Those who complete a bachelor's degree work as mechanical engineering technologists, rather than as technicians. In some cases, they are considered applied mechanical engineers because they put current mechanical engineering concepts to immediate use. Completing an associate's degree in mechanical engineering technology opens the way to studying for a bachelor's degree.

Important Qualities

Communication skills. Mechanical engineering technicians follow instructions from mechanical engineers or mechanical engineering technologists. They must be able to clearly understand and follow instructions or, if they do not understand, to ask their supervisors to explain.

Creativity. Mechanical engineering technicians help to bring plans and designs to life.

Detail oriented. Mechanical engineering technicians must make precise measurements and keep accurate records for mechanical engineers.

Interpersonal skills. Mechanical engineering technicians must be able to take instructions and offer advice when it is needed.

Math skills. Mechanical engineering technicians use mathematics for analysis, design, and troubleshooting in their work.

Mechanical skills. Mechanical engineering technicians must apply theory and instructions from engineers by making new components for industrial machinery or equipment. They need to be able to operate machinery such as drill presses, grinders, and engine lathes.

Technical skills. Mechanical engineering technicians must be able to help engineers keep production machinery running and use equipment to record important data.

Pay

Mechanical Engineering Technicians
Median annual wages, May 2010

Engineering Technicians, Except Drafters	$51,930
Mechanical Engineering Technicians	$50,110
Total, All Occupations	$33,840

Note: All Occupations includes all occupations in the U.S. Economy.
Source: U.S. Bureau of Labor Statistics, Occupational Employment Statistics

The median annual wage of mechanical engineering technicians was $50,110 in May 2010. The median wage is the wage at which half of the workers in an occupation earned more than that amount and half earned less. The lowest 10 percent earned less than $31,940, and the top 10 percent earned more than $73,980.

Most technicians work full time.

Job Outlook

Mechanical Engineering Technicians
Percent change in employment, projected 2010-20

Total, All Occupations	14%
Engineering Technicians, Except Drafters	5%
Mechanical Engineering Technicians	4%

Note: All Occupations includes all occupations in the U.S. Economy.
Source: U.S. Bureau of Labor Statistics, Employment Projections program

Employment of mechanical engineering technicians is expected to increase by 4 percent from 2010 to 2020, slower than the average for all occupations. Employment in this occupation depends on the overall state of manufacturing, which is expected to decline. Mechanical engineering technicians also work for firms in engineering services and in research and development, both of which contract services from manufacturing and other industries. Contracting for this work allows firms to hire these services at a lower cost than employing technicians in-house. Employment of mechanical engineering technicians will not change at the same rate in every industry.

The two expanding fields in which mechanical engineering technicians may find broader opportunities in the future are remanufacturing and alternative energies.

- Remanufacturing, the art of restoring nonworking products to working condition, is becoming increasingly important because it can reduce waste disposal costs for counties and cities. Remanufacturing is likely to be confined to domestic activity, because transportation costs to remanufacture abroad would make these products less competitive compared with newly manufactured products.

- Products from alternative energy sources, such as wind power and solar power, should be in demand because of a drive to cut energy costs. Demand for mechanical engineering technicians is expected as mechanical engineers move into these alternative energies and need help implementing designs and plans.

Job Prospects

Mastering new technology and software will likely become more important for this occupation. Those who stay aware of the latest developments should have the best job prospects.

Employment projections data for mechanical engineering technicians, 2010-20

Occupational Title	SOC Code	Employment, 2010	Projected Employment, 2020	Change, 2010-20 Percent	Numeric
Mechanical Engineering Technicians	17-3027	44,900	46,700	4	1,800
SOURCE: U.S. Bureau of Labor Statistics, Employment Projections program					

Similar Occupations

This table shows a list of occupations with job duties that are similar to those of mechanical engineering technicians.

Occupation	Job Duties	Entry-Level Education	Median Annual Pay, May 2010
Drafters	Drafters use software to convert the designs of engineers and architects into technical drawings and plans. Workers in production and construction use these plans to build everything from microchips to skyscrapers.	Associate's degree	$47,880
Environmental Engineering Technicians	Environmental engineering technicians carry out the plans that environmental engineers develop. They test, operate, and, if necessary, modify equipment for preventing or cleaning up environmental pollution. They may collect samples for testing, or they may work to mitigate sources of environmental pollution.	Associate's degree	$43,390

Industrial Engineering Technicians	Industrial engineering technicians plan ways to effectively use personnel, materials, and machines in factories, stores, hospitals, repair shops, and offices. As assistants to industrial engineers, they help prepare machinery and equipment layouts, plan workflows, conduct statistical production studies, and analyze production costs.	Associate's degree	$48,210
Machinists and Tool and Die Makers	Machinists and tool and die makers set up and operate a variety of computer-controlled or mechanically-controlled machine tools to produce precision metal parts, instruments, and tools.	High school diploma or equivalent	$39,910

Contacts for More Information

For more information on general engineering education and career resources, visit Technology Student Association

For information about accredited programs, visit ABET

Suggested citation:

Bureau of Labor Statistics, U.S. Department of Labor, Occupational Outlook Handbook, 2012-13 Edition, Mechanical Engineering Technicians, on the Internet at http://www.bls.gov/ooh/architecture-and-engineering/mechanical-engineering-technicians.htm .

Mechanical Engineers

Quick Facts: Mechanical Engineers	
2010 Median Pay	$78,160 per year $37.58 per hour
Entry-Level Education	Bachelor's degree
Work Experience in a Related Occupation	None
On-the-job Training	None
Number of Jobs, 2010	243,200
Job Outlook, 2010-20	9% (Slower than average)
Employment Change, 2010-20	21,300

What Mechanical Engineers Do

Mechanical engineering is one of the broadest engineering disciplines. Mechanical engineers research, design, develop, build, and test mechanical devices, including tools, engines, and machines.

Duties

Mechanical engineers typically do the following:
- Analyze problems to see how a mechanical device might help solve the problem
- Design or redesign mechanical devices, creating blueprints so the device can be built
- Develop a prototype of the device and test the prototype
- Analyze the test results and change the design as needed
- Oversee the manufacturing process for the device

Mechanical engineers use many types of tools, engines, and machines. Examples include the following:
- Power-producing machines such as electric generators, internal combustion engines, and steam and gas turbines
- Power-using machines, such as refrigeration and air-conditioning
- Industrial production equipment, including robots used in manufacturing
- Other machines inside buildings, such as elevators and escalators
- Machine tools and tools for other engineers
- Material-handling systems, such as conveyor systems and automated transfer stations

Like other engineers, mechanical engineers use computers extensively. Computers help mechanical engineers to do the following:
- Produce and analyze designs
- Simulate and test how a machine is likely to work
- Generate specifications for parts
- Monitor the quality of products
- Control manufacturing and production

Work Environment

Mechanical engineers are the second-largest engineering occupation, holding about 243,200 jobs in 2010. They work mostly in engineering services, research and development, manufacturing industries, and the federal government.

Architectural, engineering, and related services	21%
Research and development in the physical, engineering, and life sciences	6
Navigational, measuring, electromedical, and control instruments manufacturing	5
Aerospace product and parts manufacturing	5
Federal government, excluding postal service	5

The rest are employed in general-purpose machinery manufacturing, automotive parts manufacturing, management of other companies, and testing laboratories.

Mechanical engineers generally work in professional office settings. They may occasionally visit worksites where a problem or piece of equipment needs their personal attention.

Most mechanical engineers work full time, with some working as many as 60 hours or more per week.

How to Become a Mechanical Engineer

Mechanical engineers need a bachelor's degree. A graduate degree is typically needed to be hired or promoted into managerial positions. Mechanical engineers who sell services publicly must be licensed in all states and the District of Columbia.

Mechanical engineers develop and build mechanical devices for use in industrial processes.

Education

Nearly all entry-level mechanical engineering jobs require a bachelor's degree in mechanical engineering.

Mechanical engineering degree programs usually include courses in mathematics and life and physical sciences, as well as engineering and design courses. The programs typically last 4 years, but many students take between 4 and 5 years to earn a degree. A mechanical engineering degree program may emphasize internships and co-ops to prepare students for work in industry. Theory is often another main focus, in order to prepare students for graduate-level work.

A few engineering schools allow students who spend 3 years in a liberal arts college studying pre-engineering subjects and 2 years in an engineering school studying core subjects to receive a bachelor's degree from each school.

Some colleges and universities offer 5-year programs that allow students to obtain both a bachelor's and a master's degree. Some 5- or even 6-year cooperative plans combine classroom study with practical work, enabling students to gain valuable experience and earn money to finance part of their education.

Many engineering programs are accredited by ABET (formerly the Accreditation Board for Engineering and Technology). Some employers prefer students from an accredited program. A degree from an ABET accredited program is usually necessary to become a licensed professional engineer.

Important Qualities

Creativity. Because mechanical engineers convert scientific concepts into real-world applications, they design and build sometimes complex or unique pieces of equipment and machinery. A creative mind is essential for this kind of work.

Listening skills. Mechanical engineers often work on projects with other engineers and professionals, such as architects. They must listen to and analyze different approaches to the task at hand.

Math skills. Mechanical engineers use the principals of calculus, trigonometry, and other advanced topics in mathematics for analysis, design, and troubleshooting in their work.

Mechanical skills. A background in mechanics, such as experience gained through a co-op in college or work as a mechanic, helps mechanical engineers develop skills that are useful in solving real-world problems. Such a background allows engineers to visualize basic engineering concepts and mechanical processes more easily. Also important is an ability to learn and use new tools and equipment.

Problem-solving skills. Mechanical engineers take scientific discoveries and seek to make them into products that would be useful to people, companies, and governments.

Licenses

All 50 states and the District of Columbia require licensure for engineers who offer their services directly to the public. Licensed mechanical engineers are designated as professional engineers (PEs). The PE license generally requires a degree from an engineering program accredited by ABET, Inc., 4 years of relevant work experience, and passing a state exam.

Recent graduates can start the licensing process by taking the exam in two stages. They can take the Fundamentals of Engineering (FE) exam right after graduation. Engineers who pass this exam commonly are called engineers in training (EITs) or engineer interns (EIs). After gaining experience, EITs can take a second exam, called the Principles and Practice of Engineering exam, for full licensure as a PE.

Several states require continuing education to renew the license every year. Most states recognize licensure from other states, as long as the way that the initial license was obtained meets or exceeds the recognizing state's own licensure requirements.

Certification

Professional organizations, such as the American Society of Mechanical Engineers, offer a variety of certification programs for engineers to demonstrate competency in specific fields of mechanical engineering.

Advancement

Graduate training is essential for engineering faculty positions in higher education, as well as for some research-and-development programs. Many experienced mechanical engineers get graduate degrees in engineering or business administration to learn new technology and broaden their education. Many become administrators or managers after obtaining a graduate degree.

Pay

Mechanical Engineers
Median annual wages, May 2010

Engineers	$83,340
Mechanical Engineers	$78,160
Total, All Occupations	$33,840

Note: All Occupations includes all occupations in the U.S. Economy.
Source: U.S. Bureau of Labor Statistics, Occupational Employment Statistics

The median annual wage of mechanical engineers was $78,160 in May 2010. The median wage is the wage at which half the workers in an occupation earned more than that amount and half earned less. The lowest 10 percent earned less than $50,550, and the top 10 percent earned more than $119,480.

The median annual wages in selected industries employing mechanical engineers in May 2010 were as follows:

Federal government, excluding postal service	$91,910
Research and development in the physical, engineering, and life sciences	88,190
Aerospace product and parts manufacturing	83,870
Navigational, measuring, electromedical, and control instruments manufacturing	83,310
Architectural, engineering, and related services	82,210

Most mechanical engineers work full time, with some working as many as 60 hours or more per week.

Job Outlook

Mechanical Engineers

Percent change in employment, projected 2010-20

Total, All Occupations	14%
Engineers	11%
Mechanical Engineers	9%

Note: All Occupations includes all occupations in the U.S. Economy.
Source: U.S. Bureau of Labor Statistics, Employment Projections program

Employment of mechanical engineers is expected to grow 9 percent from 2010 to 2020, slower than the average for all occupations. Job prospects may be best for those who stay abreast of the most recent advances in technology. Mechanical engineers can work in many industries and on many types of projects. As a result, their growth rate will differ by the industries that employ them.

Mechanical engineers should experience demand in architectural, engineering, and related services as companies continue to hire temporary engineering services as a cost-cutting measure rather than keeping engineers on staff. Mechanical engineers will also be involved in various manufacturing industries€"specifically, transportation equipment and machinery manufacturing. They will be needed to design the next generation of vehicles and vehicle systems, such as hybrid-electric cars and clean diesel automobiles. Machinery will continue to be in demand as machines replace more expensive human labor in various industries. This phenomenon in turn should drive demand for mechanical engineers who design industrial machinery.

Mechanical engineers often work on the newest industrial pursuits. The fields of alternative energies, remanufacturing, and nanotechnology may offer new directions for occupational growth.

Alternative energy sources, such as solar panels, have become popular forms of clean energy, and mechanical engineers are instrumental in their design and manufacture.

Remanufacturing€"rebuilding goods for use in a second life€"holds promise because it reduces the cost of waste disposal for local governments. Training in remanufacturing may become common in mechanical engineering at colleges and universities.

Nanotechnology, which involves manipulating matter at the tiniest levels, may affect employment for mechanical engineers because they will be needed to design production projects based on this technology. Nanotechnology will be useful in areas such as designing more powerful computer chips.

Job Prospects

Although prospects for mechanical engineers overall are expected to be good, they will be best for those with training in the latest software tools, such as Advanced Visualization Process (AVP). AVP allows engineers and designers to take a project from the conceptual phase directly to a finished product, eliminating the need for prototypes.

Employment projections data for mechanical engineers, 2010-20

Occupational Title	SOC Code	Employment, 2010	Projected Employment, 2020	Change, 2010-20 Percent	Numeric
Mechanical Engineers	17-2141	243,200	264,600	9	21,300
SOURCE: U.S. Bureau of Labor Statistics, Employment Projections program					

Similar Occupations

This table shows a list of occupations with job duties that are similar to those of mechanical engineers.

Occupation	Job Duties	Entry-Level Education	Median Annual Pay, May 2010
Architectural and Engineering Managers	Architectural and engineering managers plan, coordinate, and direct activities in architecture and engineering, including research and development in these fields.	Bachelor's degree	$119,260
Drafters	Drafters use software to convert the designs of engineers and architects into technical drawings and plans. Workers in production and construction use these plans to build everything from microchips to skyscrapers.	Associate's degree	$47,880
Materials Engineers	Materials engineers develop, process, and test materials used to create a range of products, from computer chips and aircraft wings to golf clubs and snow skis. They also help select materials and develop new ways to use materials.	Bachelor's degree	$83,120
Mathematicians	Mathematicians use high-level mathematics and technology to develop new mathematical principles, understand relationships between existing principles, and solve real-world problems.	Master's degree	$99,380
Mechanical Engineering Technicians	Mechanical engineering technicians help mechanical engineers design, develop, test, and manufacture industrial machinery, consumer products, and other equipment. They may make sketches and rough layouts, record and analyze data, make calculations and estimates, and report their findings.	Associate's degree	$50,110
Natural Sciences Managers	Natural sciences managers supervise the work of scientists, including chemists, physicists, and biologists. They direct research and development projects and coordinate activities such as testing, quality control, and production.	Bachelor's degree	$116,020
Petroleum Engineers	Petroleum engineers design and develop methods for extracting oil and gas from deposits below the earth's surface. Petroleum engineers also find new ways to extract oil and gas from older wells.	Bachelor's degree	$114,080
Physicists and Astronomers	Physicists and astronomers study the fundamental nature of the universe, ranging from the vastness of space to the smallest of subatomic particles. They develop new technologies, methods, and theories based on the results of their research that deepen our understanding of how things work and contribute to innovative, real-world applications.	Doctoral or professional degree	$105,430

Sales Engineers	Sales engineers sell complex scientific and technological products or services to businesses. They must have extensive knowledge of the products' parts and functions and must understand the scientific processes that make these products work.	Bachelor's degree	$87,390

Contacts for More Information

For information about general engineering education and mechanical engineering career resources, visit American Society of Mechanical Engineers, American Society for Engineering Education, Technology Student Association

For more information about licensure as a mechanical engineer, visit National Council of Examiners for Engineering and Surveying, National Society of Professional Engineers

For information about accredited engineering programs, visit ABET

Suggested citation:

Bureau of Labor Statistics, U.S. Department of Labor, Occupational Outlook Handbook, 2012-13 Edition, Mechanical Engineers, on the Internet at http://www.bls.gov/ooh/architecture-and-engineering/mechanical-engineers.htm

Mining and Geological Engineers

Quick Facts: Mining and Geological Engineers	
2010 Median Pay	$82,870 per year $39.84 per hour
Entry-Level Education	Bachelor's degree
Work Experience in a Related Occupation	None
On-the-job Training	None
Number of Jobs, 2010	6,400
Job Outlook, 2010-20	10% (About as fast as average)
Employment Change, 2010-20	600

What Mining and Geological Engineers Do

Mining and geological engineers design mines for the safe and efficient removal of minerals, such as coal and metals, for manufacturing and utilities.

Duties

Mining and geological engineers typically do the following:

Mining and geological engineers prepare technical reports for miners, engineers, and managers.

- Design open-pit and underground mines
- Supervise the construction of mine shafts and tunnels in underground operations
- Devise methods for transporting minerals to processing plants
- Prepare technical reports for miners, engineers, and managers
- Monitor production rates to assess the effectiveness of operations
- Provide solutions to problems related to land reclamation, water and air pollution, and sustainability
- Ensure that mines are operated in safe and environmentally sound ways

Mining engineers often specialize in one particular mineral or metal, such as coal or gold. They typically design and develop mines and determine the best way to extract metal or minerals to get the most out of deposits.

Some mining engineers work with geologists and metallurgical engineers to find and evaluate new ore deposits. Other mining engineers develop new equipment or direct mineral-processing operations to separate minerals from dirt, rock, and other materials.

Geological engineers use methods grounded in their knowledge of geology to search for mineral deposits and evaluate possible sites. Once a site is identified, they plan how the metals or minerals will be extracted in efficient and environmentally sound ways.

Mining safety engineers draw on their knowledge about mine design and best practices to ensure workers' safety and to ensure compliance with state and federal safety regulations. They inspect mines' walls and roofs, monitor the air quality, and examine mining equipment for possible hazards.

Engineers who hold a master's or a doctoral degree frequently teach engineering at colleges and universities. For more information, see the profile on postsecondary teachers .

Work Environment

Mining and geological engineers held about 6,400 jobs in 2010. They work at mining operations in remote locations. However, some work in sand-and-gravel operations that are located near larger cities. More experienced engineers can get jobs in offices of mining firms or consulting companies, which are generally in large urban areas.

The industries that employed the largest number of mining and geological engineers in 2010 were as follows:

Architectural, engineering, and related services	28%
Metal ore mining	14
Coal mining	13
Oil and gas extraction	7
Nonmetallic mineral mining and quarrying	5

Nearly all mining and geological engineers worked full time in 2010.

How to Become a Mining or Geological Engineer

A bachelor's degree from an accredited engineering program is required to become a mining or geological engineer, including a mining safety engineer. However, to work as a credentialed professional engineer requires licensure. Requirements for licensure vary by state but generally require passing two exams.

Education

Students interested in entering mining engineering programs should take courses in mathematics and science in high school.

Relatively few schools offer mining engineering programs. Typical bachelor's degree programs in mining engineering include courses in geology, physics, thermodynamics, mine design and safety, and mathematics. They involve extensive laboratory and field work as well as traditional classroom study.

Programs in mining and geological engineering are accredited by ABET (formerly the Accreditation Board for Engineering and Technology). ABET accreditation is based on a program's faculty, curriculum, facilities, and other factors.

Master's degree programs in mining and geological engineering typically are 2-year programs and include coursework in specialized subjects such as mineral resource development and mining regulations. Some programs require a written thesis for graduation.

Important Qualities

Decision-making skills. Mining and geological engineers do work that can affect not only companies' profits but miners' lives. The ability to anticipate problems and deal with them immediately is crucial.

Logical-thinking skills. In planning mines' operations, mineral processing, and environmental reclamation, these engineers have to be able to put work plans into a coherent, logical sequence.

Math skills. Mining and geological engineers use the principals of calculus, trigonometry, and other advanced topics in mathematics for analysis, design, and troubleshooting in their work.

Problem-solving skills. Mining and geological engineers must explore for mines, plan the operations of mines, work out the mineral processing, and design environmental reclamation projects. These are all complex projects requiring an ability to identify goals and build plans to reach the goals while solving problems along the way.

Systems analysis. These engineers must consider the wider implications of their immediate work to plan for environmental reclamation, for example. They must be able to consider several competing, but interconnected, issues at the same time.

Writing skills. Other workers, including miners, must read what these engineers write. Therefore, they must be able to write clearly so that others can easily understand their thoughts and plans.

Licenses

In every state, engineers who offer their services directly to the public must be licensed in that state. The National Council of Examiners for Engineering and Surveying (NCEES) administers two exams for licensure for this occupation. The first covers the fundamentals of engineering (FE), the second the principles and practices of engineering (PPE). The FE exam can be taken upon graduation. Engineers who pass this exam are commonly called engineers in training (EITs) or engineer interns (EIs). After 4 years of relevant work experience, EITs can take the PPE exam.

Licensed engineers are called professional engineers (PEs). Generally, licensure requires the following:

- A degree from an ABET-accredited engineering program
- 4 years of relevant work experience
- Successful completion of a state examination

In several states, engineers must take continuing education credits to keep their licenses. Most states recognize licenses from other states, provided that licensure requirements in the other states meet or exceed the first state's own requirements.

Advancement

Beginning engineering graduates usually work under the supervision of experienced engineers. In large companies, engineers starting out also may receive formal classroom or seminar-type training. As new engineers gain knowledge and experience, they are assigned more difficult projects with greater independence to develop designs, solve problems, and make decisions.

Engineers may advance to become technical specialists or to supervise a staff or team of engineers and technicians. Some eventually become engineering managers or enter other managerial or sales jobs. In sales, an engineering background enables them to discuss a product's technical aspects and assist in product planning, installation, and use.

Pay

Mining and Geological Engineers
Median annual wages, May 2010

Engineers	$83,340
Mining and Geological Engineers, Including Mining Safety Engineers	$82,870
Total, All Occupations	$33,840

Note: All Occupations includes all occupations in the U.S. Economy.
Source: U.S. Bureau of Labor Statistics, Occupational Employment Statistics

The median annual wage of mining and geological engineers, including mining safety engineers, was $82,870 in May 2010. The median wage is the wage at which half the workers in an occupation earned more than that amount and half earned less. The lowest 10 percent earned less than $48,950, and the top 10 percent earned more than $129,700.

Median annual wages in the industries employing the largest numbers of these engineers in May 2010 were as follows:

Oil and gas extraction	$98,430
Architectural, engineering, and related services	83,090
Metal ore mining	81,790
Coal mining	78,170
Nonmetallic mineral mining and quarrying	75,750

Job Outlook

Mining and Geological Engineers
Percent change in employment, projected 2010-20

Total, All Occupations	14%
Engineers	11%
Mining and Geological Engineers, Including Mining Safety Engineers	10%

Note: All Occupations includes all occupations in the U.S. Economy.
Source: U.S. Bureau of Labor Statistics, Employment Projections program

Employment of mining and geological engineers is expected to grow 10 percent from 2010 to 2020, about as fast as the average for all occupations. This does not mean that the expected growth of the occupation will be large in terms of the number of new positions overall, because the occupation is relatively small.

Employment growth for mining and geological engineers will be driven by demand for mining operations. Some growth may come from recent changes in federal policy concerning access to coal deposits on federal lands in some western states. Because this coal is low in sulfur content, it is in demand globally. The feasibility studies and proposals needed to gain access to these and other mineral deposits will push demand for these engineers.

Additionally, other countries may restrict exports of certain minerals known as €œrare earths,€• which are used in the manufacture of many high-tech products. This should help spur exploration and further development of mines in the United States that yield these minerals.

Employment growth also will be driven by demand for engineering services. As companies look for ways to cut costs, they are expected to contract more engineering services rather than employ engineers directly.

Job Prospects

Job prospects should be favorable for those entering the occupation, because many of these engineers will be reaching retirement age by 2020. In addition, the education and licensing required to enter this occupation will limit the supply of engineers competing for these positions. Lastly, mining and extraction companies are expected to seek the skills of mining safety engineers. Engineers who specialize in this area should enjoy favorable prospects.

Employment projections data for mining and geological engineers, 2010-20

Occupational Title	SOC Code	Employment, 2010	Projected Employment, 2020	Change, 2010-20 Percent	Numeric
Mining and Geological Engineers, Including Mining Safety Engineers	17-2151	6,400	7,000	10	600
SOURCE: U.S. Bureau of Labor Statistics, Employment Projections program					

Similar Occupations

This table shows a list of occupations with job duties that are similar to those of mining and geological engineers.

Occupation	Job Duties	Entry-Level Education	Median Annual Pay, May 2010
Architectural and Engineering Managers	Architectural and engineering managers plan, coordinate, and direct activities in architecture and engineering, including research and development in these fields.	Bachelor's degree	$119,260
Civil Engineers	Civil engineers design and supervise large construction projects, including roads, buildings, airports, tunnels, dams, bridges, and systems for water supply and sewage treatment.	Bachelor's degree	$77,560
Environmental Scientists and Specialists	Environmental scientists and specialists use their knowledge of the natural sciences to protect the environment. They identify problems and find solutions that minimize hazards to the health of the environment and the population.	Bachelor's degree	$61,700
Geoscientists	Geoscientists study the physical aspects of the Earth, such as its composition, structure, and processes, to learn about its past, present, and future.	Bachelor's degree	$82,500
Hydrologists	Hydrologists study water and the water cycle. They use their expertise to solve problems in the areas of water quality or availability.	Master's degree	$75,690
Mechanical Engineers	Mechanical engineering is one of the broadest engineering disciplines. Mechanical engineers design, develop, build, and test mechanical devices, including tools, engines, and machines.	Bachelor's degree	$78,160
Natural Sciences Managers	Natural sciences managers supervise the work of scientists, including chemists, physicists, and biologists. They direct research and development projects and coordinate activities such as testing, quality control, and production.	Bachelor's degree	$116,020
Petroleum Engineers	Petroleum engineers design and develop methods for extracting oil and gas from deposits below the earth's surface. Petroleum engineers also find new ways to extract oil and gas from older wells.	Bachelor's degree	$114,080
Sales Engineers	Sales engineers sell complex scientific and technological products or services to businesses. They must have extensive knowledge of the products' parts and functions and must understand the scientific processes that make these products work.	Bachelor's degree	$87,390

Contacts for More Information

For information about general engineering education and career resources, visit American Society for Engineering Education, Technology Student Association

For more information about licensure as a mining or geological engineer, visit National Council of Examiners for Engineering and Surveying, National Society of Professional Engineers

For information about accredited engineering programs, visit ABET

For more information about mining and geological engineers, visit Society for Mining, Metallurgy, and Exploration

Suggested citation:

Bureau of Labor Statistics, U.S. Department of Labor, Occupational Outlook Handbook, 2012-13 Edition, Mining and Geological Engineers, on the Internet at http://www.bls.gov/ooh/architecture-and-engineering/mining-and-geological-engineers.htm .

Nuclear Engineers

Quick Facts: Nuclear Engineers	
2010 Median Pay	$99,920 per year $48.04 per hour
Entry-Level Education	Bachelor's degree
Work Experience in a Related Occupation	None
On-the-job Training	None
Number of Jobs, 2010	19,100
Job Outlook, 2010-20	10% (About as fast as average)
Employment Change, 2010-20	2,000

What Nuclear Engineers Do

Nuclear engineers research and develop the processes, instruments, and systems used to derive benefits from nuclear energy and radiation. Many of these engineers find industrial and medical uses for radioactive materials€"for example, in equipment used in medical diagnosis and treatment. Many others specialize in the development of nuclear power sources for ships or spacecraft.

Duties

Nuclear engineers typically do the following:
- Design or develop nuclear equipment, such as reactor cores, radiation shielding, or associated instrumentation
- Monitor nuclear facility operations to identify any design, construction, or operation practices that violate safety regulations and laws
- Examine nuclear accidents and gather data that can be used to design preventive measures
- Write operational instructions to be used in nuclear plant operation or in handling and disposing of nuclear waste
- Direct operating or maintenance activities of operational nuclear powerplants to ensure that they meet safety standards
- Perform experiments to test whether methods of using nuclear material, reclaiming nuclear fuel, or disposing of nuclear waste are acceptable
- Take corrective actions or order plant shutdowns in emergencies

Nuclear engineers are also on the forefront of developing uses of nuclear material for medical imaging devices, such as positron emission tomography (PET) scanners. They also may develop or design cyclotrons, which produce a high-energy beam that the healthcare industry uses to treat cancerous tumors.

A principal job of nuclear engineers is to design and operate nuclear power plants.

Work Environment

Nuclear engineers held about 19,100 jobs in 2010 and typically work in offices. However, their work setting varies with the industry in which they are employed. For example, those employed in power generation and supply work in powerplants.

The industries employing the largest number of nuclear engineers in 2010 were as follows:

Electric power generation, transmission and distribution	35%
Federal government, excluding postal service	16
Management, scientific, and technical consulting services	14
Architectural, engineering, and related services	12
Scientific research and development services	7

Most nuclear engineers work full time. Overtime is common.

How to Become a Nuclear Engineer

Nuclear engineers must have a bachelor's degree in nuclear engineering. Employers also value experience, so cooperative-education engineering programs at universities are also valuable.

Education

Entry-level nuclear engineering jobs require a bachelor's degree. Students interested in studying nuclear engineering should take high school courses in mathematics, such as algebra, trigonometry, and calculus; and science, such as biology, chemistry, and physics.

Bachelor's degree programs typically are 4-year programs and encompass classroom, laboratory, and field studies in areas that include mathematics and engineering principles. Most colleges and universities offer cooperative-education programs in which students gain experience while completing their education.

Some universities offer 5-year programs leading to both a bachelor's and a master's degree. A graduate degree allows an engineer to work as an instructor at a university or engage in research and development. Some 5-year or even 6-year cooperative-education plans combine classroom study with work, permitting students to gain experience and to finance part of their education.

Programs in nuclear engineering are accredited by ABET (formerly the Accreditation Board for Engineering and Technology).

Important Qualities

Analytical-thinking skills. Nuclear engineers must be able to identify design elements to help build facilities and equipment that produce material needed by various industries.

Detail oriented. Nuclear engineers supervise the operation of nuclear facilities. They must pay close attentions to what is happening at all times, and ensure that operations comply with all regulations and laws pertaining to the safety of workers and the environment.

Logical-thinking skills. Nuclear engineers design complex systems. Therefore, they must be able to order information logically and clearly so that others can follow their written information and instructions.

Math skills. Nuclear engineers use the principals of calculus, trigonometry, and other advanced topics in mathematics for analysis, design, and troubleshooting in their work.

Teamwork. Nuclear engineers work with mechanical engineers and electrical engineers and therefore must be able to incorporate systems designed by these other engineers into their own designs.

Additionally, because of the potential hazard posed by nuclear materials and by accidents at facilities, nuclear engineers must be able to anticipate problems before they occur and suggest remedies.

Licenses

Nuclear engineers who work for nuclear powerplants are not required to be licensed. However, they are eligible to seek licensure as professional engineers. Those who become licensed carry the designation of professional engineer (PE). Licensure is recommended and generally requires the following:

- A degree from an engineering program accredited by ABET
- A passing score on the Fundamentals of Engineering (FE) exam
- Relevant work experience
- A passing score on the Professional Engineering (PE) exam

The initial Fundamentals of Engineering (FE) exam can be taken right after graduating. Engineers who pass this exam commonly are called engineers in training (EITs) or engineer interns (EIs). After getting work experience, EITs can take the second exam, called the Principles and Practice of Engineering exam.

Several states require engineers to take continuing education to keep their license. Most states recognize licenses from other states, as long as that the other state's licensing requirements meet or exceed their own licensing requirements.

Advancement

Beginning engineering graduates usually work under the supervision of experienced engineers. In large companies, new engineers may receive formal training in classrooms or seminars. As beginning engineers gain knowledge and experience, they move to more difficult projects with greater independence to develop designs, solve problems, and make decisions.

Eventually, nuclear engineers may advance to become technical specialists or to supervise a team of engineers and technicians. Some may become engineering managers or move into managerial positions or sales work. For more information, see the profile on architectural and engineering managers.

Nuclear engineers have the background needed to become medical physicists, who work in the relatively new field of nuclear medicine. A master's degree is necessary for a worker to enter this field.

Pay

Nuclear Engineers
Median annual wages, May 2010

Nuclear Engineers	$99,920
Engineers	$83,340
Total, All Occupations	$33,840

Note: All Occupations includes all occupations in the U.S. Economy.
Source: U.S. Bureau of Labor Statistics, Occupational Employment Statistics

The median annual wage of nuclear engineers was $99,920 in May 2010. The median wage is the wage at which half of the workers in an occupation earned more than that amount and half earned less. The lowest 10 percent earned less than $67,250, and the top 10 percent earned more than $142,290.

Median annual wages in the industries employing the largest numbers of nuclear engineers in May 2010 were as follows:

Management, scientific, and technical consulting services	$113,460
Scientific research and development services	105,170
Architectural, engineering, and related services	103,710
Electric power generation, transmission and distribution	98,330
Federal government, excluding postal service	91,420

Most nuclear engineers work full time. Overtime is common.

Job Outlook

Nuclear Engineers
Percent change in employment, projected 2010-20

Total, All Occupations	14%
Engineers	11%
Nuclear Engineers	10%

Note: All Occupations includes all occupations in the U.S. Economy.
Source: U.S. Bureau of Labor Statistics, Employment Projections program

Employment of nuclear engineers is expected to grow 10 percent from 2010 to 2020, about as fast as the average for all occupations. Employment trends in power generation may be favorable because of the likely need to upgrade safety systems at powerplants. These engineers also will find work in creating designs for powerplants to be built abroad and in the growing field of nuclear medicine.

Utilities that own or build nuclear powerplants have traditionally employed the greatest number of nuclear engineers. Potential new guidelines from the Nuclear Regulatory Commission (NRC) may affect that employment. Recent events might cause the NRC to issue guidelines for upgrading safety protocols at nuclear utility plants. Those upgrades may spur employment. However, the upgrades also could raise the cost of building new nuclear powerplants, and that might limit new plant construction.

Still, nuclear engineers will be hired to design and help build nuclear powerplants outside the United States.

Developments in nuclear medicine and diagnostic imaging also are expected to drive demand for nuclear engineers. These engineers will be needed to help build and operate cyclotrons, which produce a high-energy beam that the healthcare industry uses to treat cancerous tumors.

Job Prospects

Job prospects are expected to be relatively favorable for this occupation because many in the aging workforce will retire. The small number of nuclear engineering graduates is likely to be in rough balance with the number of job openings. In addition, training in new fields, such as nuclear medicine, should help to improve a person's chances of finding a job.

Employment projections data for nuclear engineers, 2010-20

Occupational Title	SOC Code	Employment, 2010	Projected Employment, 2020	Change, 2010-20 Percent	Numeric
Nuclear Engineers	17-2161	19,100	21,100	10	2,000

SOURCE: U.S. Bureau of Labor Statistics, Employment Projections program

Similar Occupations

This table shows a list of occupations with job duties that are similar to those of nuclear engineers.

Occupation	Job Duties	Entry-Level Education	Median Annual Pay, May 2010
Civil Engineers	Civil engineers design and supervise large construction projects, including roads, buildings, airports, tunnels, dams, bridges, and systems for water supply and sewage treatment.	Bachelor's degree	$77,560
Electrical and Electronics Engineers	Electrical engineers design, develop, test, and supervise the manufacturing of electrical equipment such as electric motors, radar and navigation systems, communications systems, and power generation equipment.Electronics engineers design and develop electronic equipment, such as broadcast and communications systems€"from portable music players to global positioning systems (GPS).	Bachelor's degree	$87,180
Electrical and Electronic Engineering Technicians	Electrical and electronic engineering technicians help engineers design and develop computers, communications equipment, medical monitoring devices, navigational equipment, and other electrical and electronic equipment. They often work in product evaluation and testing, using measuring and diagnostic devices to adjust, test, and repair equipment.	Associate's degree	$56,040
Health and Safety Engineers	Health and safety engineers develop procedures and design systems to keep people from getting sick or injured and to keep property from being damaged. They combine knowledge of health or safety and of systems engineering to make sure that chemicals, machinery, software, furniture, and other products are not going to cause harm to people or buildings.	Bachelor's degree	$75,430
Mechanical Engineers	Mechanical engineering is one of the broadest engineering disciplines. Mechanical engineers design, develop, build, and test mechanical devices, including tools, engines, and machines.	Bachelor's degree	$78,160
Physicists and Astronomers	Physicists and astronomers study the fundamental nature of the universe, ranging from the vastness of space to the smallest of subatomic particles. They develop new technologies, methods, and theories based on the results of their research that deepen our understanding of how things work and contribute to innovative, real-world applications.	Doctoral or professional degree	$105,430

Contacts for More Information

For information about general engineering education and career resources, visit American Society for Engineering Education, Technology Student Association

For more information about licensure as a nuclear engineer, visit National Council of Examiners for Engineering and Surveying, National Society of Professional Engineers

For information about accredited engineering programs, visit ABET

Suggested citation:

Bureau of Labor Statistics, U.S. Department of Labor, Occupational Outlook Handbook, 2012-13 Edition, Nuclear Engineers, on the Internet at http://www.bls.gov/ooh/architecture-and-engineering/nuclear-engineers.htm .

Petroleum Engineers

Quick Facts: Petroleum Engineers	
2010 Median Pay	$114,080 per year $54.85 per hour
Entry-Level Education	Bachelor's degree
Work Experience in a Related Occupation	None
On-the-job Training None	
Number of Jobs, 2010	30,200
Job Outlook, 2010-20	17% (About as fast as average)
Employment Change, 2010-20	5,100

What Petroleum Engineers Do

Petroleum engineers design and develop methods for extracting oil and gas from deposits below the earth's surface. Petroleum engineers also find new ways to extract oil and gas from older wells.

Duties

Petroleum engineers typically do the following:

- Design equipment to extract oil and gas in the most profitable way
- Develop ways to inject water, chemicals, gases, or steam into an oil reserve to force out more of the oil
- Develop plans to drill in oil and gas fields, and then to recover the oil and gas
- Make sure that wells, well testing, and well surveys are completed and evaluated
- Use computer-controlled drilling or fracturing to connect a larger area of an oil and gas deposit to a single well
- Make sure that oil field equipment is installed, operated, and maintained properly

Oil and gas deposits, or reservoirs, are located deep in rock formations underground. These reservoirs can only be accessed by drilling wells, either on land or at sea from off-shore oil rigs.

Once oil and gas are discovered, petroleum engineers work with geologists and other specialists to understand the geologic formation of the rock containing the reservoir. They then determine drilling methods, design and implement the drilling equipment, and monitor operations.

The best techniques currently being used recover only a portion of the oil and gas in a reservoir, so petroleum engineers also research and develop new

Petroleum engineers help find oil and gas for the country's energy needs.

ways to recover the oil and gas. This helps to lower the cost of drilling and production.

Work Environment

Petroleum engineers held about 30,200 jobs in 2010.

Petroleum engineers generally work in offices or in research laboratories. However, they must also spend time at drilling sites, often for long periods of time. This means they must travel, sometimes with little notice.

Industries employing the largest numbers of petroleum engineers in 2010 were as follows:

Oil and gas extraction	45%
Support activities for mining	15
Petroleum and coal products manufacturing	7

Petroleum engineers work around the world; and, in fact, the best employment opportunities may include some work in other countries.

Work Schedules

Petroleum engineers typically work full time. Many work as many as 50 or 60 hours per week when traveling to and from drilling sites to help in their operation or respond to problems as they arise. When they are at a drilling site, it is common for these engineers to work in a rotation: on duty for 84 hours and then off duty for 84 hours.

How to Become a Petroleum Engineer

Petroleum engineers must have a bachelor's degree in engineering, preferably in petroleum engineering. Employers also value work experience, so cooperative engineering programs, in which students earn academic credit for structured job experience, are valuable as well.

Education

Students interested in studying petroleum engineering will benefit from taking high school courses in mathematics, such as algebra, trigonometry, and calculus; and science, such as biology, chemistry, and physics.

Entry-level petroleum engineering jobs require a bachelor's degree. Bachelor's degree programs typically take 4 years and include classroom, laboratory, and field studies in areas such as engineering principles, geology, and thermodynamics. Most colleges and universities offer cooperative programs in which students gain practical experience while completing their education.

Some colleges and universities offer a 5-year program that leads to both a bachelor's degree and a master's degree. A graduate degree allows an engineer to work as an instructor at some universities or in research and development. Some 5-year or even 6-year cooperative plans combine coursework with practical work, permitting students to gain experience and to finance part of their education.

ABET (formerly the Accreditation Board for Engineering and

Technology) accredits programs in petroleum engineering.

Important Qualities

Analytical skills. Petroleum engineers must be able to assess complex plans for drilling and anticipate possible flaws or complications before the company commits money and people to carry out the plans.

Creativity. Petroleum engineers must come up with new ways to extract oil and gas because each new drill site presents challenges. They must know how to ask the necessary questions to find possible deposits of oil and gas.

Math skills. Petroleum engineers use the principals of calculus and other advanced topics in mathematics for analysis, design, and troubleshooting in their work.

Problem-solving skills. Identifying problems in drilling plans is critical for petroleum engineers because drilling operations can be costly. They must be careful not to overlook any possibilities that something unwanted may happen.

Teamwork. Petroleum engineers must be able to work with people from a wide variety of backgrounds, including other oil and gas workers who will carry out the engineers' drilling plans.

Licenses

All 50 states and the District of Columbia require petroleum engineers to have a license if they offer their services directly to the public. Licensed engineers are called professional engineers (PEs). Licensure generally has the following requirements:

- A degree from an ABET-accredited engineering program
- A passing score on the Fundamentals of Engineering (FE) exam
- Relevant work experience, a minimum of 4 years
- A passing score on the Professional Engineering (PE) exam

The initial Fundamentals of Engineering (FE) exam can be taken after earning a bachelor's degree. Engineers who pass this exam commonly are called engineers in training (EITs) or engineer interns (EIs). After getting suitable work experience, EITs and EIs can take the second exam, called the Principles and Practice of Engineering.

Several states require continuing education for engineers to keep their license. Most states recognize licensure from other states if the licensing state's requirements meet or exceed their own licensure requirements.

Certification

The Society of Petroleum Engineers offers certification. To be certified, petroleum engineers must be members of the Society, pass an exam, and meet other qualifications.

Advancement

Entry-level engineers usually work under the supervision of experienced engineers. In large companies, new engineers may also receive formal training. As beginning engineers gain knowledge and experience, they move to more difficult projects with greater independence to develop designs, solve problems, and make decisions.

Eventually, petroleum engineers may advance to supervise a team of engineers and technicians. Some become engineering managers or move into other managerial positions or sales work.

Petroleum engineers who go into sales use their engineering background to discuss a product's technical aspects with potential buyers and help in product planning, installation, and use. For more information, see the profile on sales engineers.

Pay

Petroleum Engineers
Median annual wages, May 2010

Petroleum Engineers	$114,080
Engineers	$83,340
Total, All Occupations	$33,840

Note: All Occupations includes all occupations in the U.S. Economy.
Source: U.S. Bureau of Labor Statistics, Occupational Employment Statistics

The median annual wage for petroleum engineers was $114,080 in May 2010. The median wage is the wage at which half the workers in an occupation earned more than that amount and half earned less. The lowest 10 percent earned less than $63,480, and the top 10 percent earned more than $166,400.

Median annual wages in the industries employing the largest numbers of petroleum engineers in May 2010 were as follows:

Oil and gas extraction	$123,410
Petroleum and coal products manufacturing	113,930
Support activities for mining	94,080

The Society of Petroleum Engineers reports that the median base pay in 2010 was $130,800, which was an increase of about 5 percent from their reported median in 2009.

Petroleum engineers typically work full time. Many work as many as 50 or 60 hours per week when traveling to and from drilling sites to help in their operation or respond to problems as they arise. When they are at a drilling site, it is common for these engineers to work in a rotation: on duty for 84 hours and then off duty for 84 hours.

Job Outlook

Petroleum Engineers
Percent change in employment, projected 2010-20

Petroleum Engineers	17%
Total, All Occupations	14%
Engineers	11%

Note: All Occupations includes all occupations in the U.S. Economy.
Source: U.S. Bureau of Labor Statistics, Employment Projections program

Employment of petroleum engineers is expected to grow 17 percent from 2010 to 2020, about as fast as the average for all occupations. Oil prices will be a major determinant of employment growth, as higher prices lead to increasing complexity of oil companies' operations. Additionally, job prospects should be highly favorable because many engineers are expected to retire.

Because oil and gas extraction is the largest industry employing petroleum engineers, any effects of rising oil prices will likely be noticed here first. Higher prices can cause oil and gas companies to drill in deeper waters and in less hospitable places and return to existing wells to try new extraction methods. This means that oil drilling operations will likely become more complex and will require more engineers to work on each drilling operation.

Demand for petroleum engineers in support activities for mining should also be strong, as oil and gas companies find it convenient and cost-effective to seek their services on an as-needed basis. This is partly because petroleum engineering is one of the higher paying occupations in the economy. Experienced petroleum engineers also may start their own companies and provide services to larger oil and gas companies.

Job Prospects

Job prospects are expected to be highly favorable because of projected growth and because many petroleum engineers retire or leave the occupation for other reasons.

Employment projections data for petroleum engineers, 2010–20

Occupational Title	SOC Code	Employment, 2010	Projected Employment, 2020	Change, 2010-20 Percent	Numeric
Petroleum Engineers	17-2171	30,200	35,300	17	5,100

SOURCE: U.S. Bureau of Labor Statistics, Employment Projections program

Similar Occupations

This table shows a list of occupations with job duties that are similar to those of petroleum engineers.

Occupation	Job Duties	Entry-Level Education	Median Annual Pay, May 2010
Aerospace Engineers	Aerospace engineers design aircraft, spacecraft, satellites, and missiles. In addition, they test prototypes to make sure that they function according to design.	Bachelor's degree	$97,480
Architectural and Engineering Managers	Architectural and engineering managers plan, coordinate, and direct activities in architecture and engineering, including research and development in these fields.	Bachelor's degree	$119,260
Chemists and Materials Scientists	Chemists and materials scientists study the structures, compositions, reactions, and other properties of substances. They use their knowledge to develop new and improved products, processes, and materials.	Bachelor's degree	$69,790
Geoscientists	Geoscientists study the physical aspects of the Earth, such as its composition, structure, and processes, to learn about its past, present, and future.	Bachelor's degree	$82,500
Industrial Engineering Technicians	Industrial engineering technicians plan ways to effectively use personnel, materials, and machines in factories, stores, hospitals, repair shops, and offices. As assistants to industrial engineers, they help prepare machinery and equipment layouts, plan workflows, conduct statistical production studies, and analyze production costs.	Associate's degree	$48,210
Industrial Engineers	Industrial engineers find ways to eliminate wastefulness in production processes. They devise efficient ways to use workers, machines, materials, information, and energy to make a product or provide a service.	Bachelor's degree	$76,100
Materials Engineers	Materials engineers develop, process, and test materials used to create a range of products, from computer chips and aircraft wings to golf clubs and snow skis. They also help select materials and develop new ways to use materials.	Bachelor's degree	$83,120
Mechanical Engineering Technicians	Mechanical engineering technicians help mechanical engineers design, develop, test, and manufacture industrial machinery, consumer products, and other equipment. They may make sketches and rough layouts, record and analyze data, make calculations and estimates, and report their findings.	Associate's degree	$50,110
Mechanical Engineers	Mechanical engineering is one of the broadest engineering disciplines. Mechanical engineers design, develop, build, and test mechanical devices, including tools, engines, and machines.	Bachelor's degree	$78,160
Sales Engineers	Sales engineers sell complex scientific and technological products or services to businesses. They must have extensive knowledge of the products' parts and functions and must understand the scientific processes that make these products work.	Bachelor's degree	$87,390

Contacts for More Information

For more information about engineers, visit Technology Student Association

For information about accredited engineering programs, visit ABET

For information about the Professional Engineer license, visit National Council of Examiners for Engineering and Surveying, National Society of Professional Engineers

For information about certification, visit Society of Petroleum Engineers

Suggested citation:

Bureau of Labor Statistics, U.S. Department of Labor, Occupational Outlook Handbook, 2012-13 Edition, Petroleum Engineers, on the Internet at http://www.bls.gov/ooh/architecture-and-engineering/petroleum-engineers.htm

Surveying and Mapping Technicians

Quick Facts: Surveying and Mapping Technicians	
2010 Median Pay	$37,900 per year $18.22 per hour
Entry-Level Education	High school diploma or equivalent
Work Experience in a Related Occupation	None
On-the-job Training	Moderate-term on-the-job training
Number of Jobs, 2010	56,900
Job Outlook, 2010-20	16% (About as fast as average)
Employment Change, 2010-20	9,000

What Surveying and Mapping Technicians Do

Surveying and mapping technicians assist surveyors, cartographers, and photogrammetrists. Together, they collect data and make maps of the earth's surface. Surveying technicians visit sites to take measurements of the land. Mapping technicians use geographic data to create maps.

Duties

Surveying technicians typically do the following:

- Operate surveying instruments, such as electronic distance-measuring equipment, to collect data on a location
- Visit sites to record survey measurements and other descriptive data
- Search for previous survey points, such as old stone markers
- Set out stakes and marks to conduct the survey, and then retrieve them
- Enter the data from surveying instruments into computers, either in the field or in an office

Surveying technicians assist surveyors in the field on teams, known as survey parties. Then, in the office, they help to process the data collected in the field. A typical survey party consists of a party chief and one or more surveying technicians and helpers. The party chief, either a surveyor or a senior surveying technician, leads day-to-day work activities.

Mapping technicians typically do the following:

- Select needed information from relevant databases to create maps
- Produce maps showing boundaries, water locations, elevation, and other features of the terrain
- Update maps to ensure accuracy
- Assist photogrammetrists by laying out aerial photographs in sequence to identify areas not captured by aerial photography

Surveying technicians assist surveyors in taking accurate measurements outdoors.

Mapping technicians help cartographers and photogrammetrists produce and upgrade maps. They do this work on computers, combining data from different sources.

Geographic information specialists are mapping specialists who use geographic information system (GIS) technology to assemble, integrate, and display data about a particular location in a digital format. They also use GIS technology to compile information from a variety of sources.

Work Environment

As shown in the tabulation below, most surveying and mapping technicians were employed in agricultural and engineering services in 2010:

Architectural, engineering, and related services	59%
Local government, excluding education and hospitals	15
Self-employed workers	5
Electric power generation, transmission and distribution	3
Federal government, excluding postal service	3

Most surveying and mapping technicians work for firms that provide engineering, surveying, and mapping services on a contract basis. State and local governments also employ these workers in highway and planning departments.

Surveying technicians work outside extensively and can be exposed to all types of weather. They often stand for long periods, walk considerable distances, and may have to climb hills with heavy packs of instruments and other equipment. Traveling is sometimes part of the job, and surveying technicians may commute long distances, stay away from home overnight, or temporarily relocate near a survey site.

Mapping technicians work primarily indoors on computers. However, mapping technicians must sometimes conduct research by using resources such as survey maps and legal documents to verify property lines and to obtain information needed for mapping. This task may require traveling to storage sites housing these legal documents, such as county courthouses or lawyers' offices.

Work Schedules

Surveying and mapping technicians typically work full time but may have longer hours during the summer, when weather and light conditions are most suitable for fieldwork. Construction-related work may be limited during times of harsh weather.

How to Become a Surveying or Mapping Technician

Surveying technicians usually need only a high school diploma. However, mapping technicians often need formal education after high school to study advances in technology such as GIS.

Education

Surveying technicians generally need a high school diploma, but some have postsecondary training in survey technology. Postsecondary training is more common among mapping technicians. An associate's degree or bachelor's degree in a relevant field, such as geomatics, is beneficial for these workers.

High school students interested in working as a surveying or mapping technician should take courses in algebra, geometry, trigonometry, drafting, mechanical drawing, and computer science. Knowledge of these subjects will help in finding a job and in advancing.

Important Qualities

Decision-making skills. As assistants to surveyors and cartographers, surveying technicians must be able to exercise some independent judgment in the field because they may be working away from team members and need to meet tight deadlines.

Listening skills. Surveying technicians work outdoors and must communicate with party chiefs and other team members across distances. Following spoken instructions from the party chief is crucial for saving time and preventing errors.

Stamina. Surveying technicians usually work outdoors, often in rugged terrain. Physical fitness is necessary to carry equipment and to stand most of the day.

Teamwork. Survey and mapmaking technicians work as part of a team, so they must be able to work well with other people.

Technical skills. Surveying and mapping technicians need to operate specialized equipment. They must be precise and accurate in their work.

Troubleshooting skills. Surveying and mapping technicians must be able to identify and fix problems with their equipment. Also, because party chiefs rely on them, they must note potential problems with the day's work plan.

Training

Surveying technicians learn their job duties under the supervision of a surveyor or a surveying party chief. Initially, surveying technicians handle simple tasks, such as placing markers on land and entering data into computers. With experience, they help to decide where and how to measure the land. Eventually, technicians can get an apprenticeship or an associate's degree so that they can develop skills based on math, drafting, and technical drawing.

Certification

Certification is becoming more common because of the growing need to make sure that data are of sufficient quality to be useful to other professionals. The American Society for Photogrammetry and Remote Sensing (ASPRS) offers certification for photogrammetric technologists, remote-sensing technologists, and geographic information system/land information system (GIS/LIS) technologists. The National Society of Professional Surveyors offers the Certified Survey Technician credential.

Advancement

With experience and formal training in surveying, surveying technicians may advance to senior survey technician, then to party chief. Depending on state licensing requirements, they can become licensed surveyors.

Pay

Surveying and Mapping Technicians
Median annual wages, May 2010

Drafters, Engineering Technicians, and Mapping Technicians	$49,600
Surveying and Mapping Technicians	$37,900
Total, All Occupations	$33,840

Note: All Occupations includes all occupations in the U.S. Economy.
Source: U.S. Bureau of Labor Statistics, Occupational Employment Statistics

The median annual wage of surveying and mapping technicians was $37,900 in May 2010. The median wage is the wage at which half the workers in an occupation earned more than that amount and half earned less. The lowest 10 percent earned less than $23,450, and the top 10 percent earned more than $60,870. Approximately 18 percent belonged to a union.

Surveying and mapping technicians typically work regular schedules but may have longer hours during the summer, when weather and light conditions are most suitable for fieldwork. Construction-related work may be limited during times of harsh weather.

Job Outlook

Surveying and Mapping Technicians
Percent change in employment, projected 2010-20

Surveying and Mapping Technicians	16%
Total, All Occupations	14%
Drafters, Engineering Technicians, and Mapping Technicians	6%

Note: All Occupations includes all occupations in the U.S. Economy.
Source: U.S. Bureau of Labor Statistics, Employment Projections program

Employment of surveying and mapping technicians is expected to grow 16 percent from 2010 to 2020, about as fast as the average for all occupations. Recent advancements in mapping technology have led to new uses for maps and a need for more of the data used to build maps. As a result, surveying and mapping technicians should have more work.

The digital revolution in mapmaking has created a need to harmonize property maps made the traditional way, with maps based on data fed into a GIS. Owners of private property will need to hire surveyors and surveying technicians to gather data in the field.

Cities, towns, and counties are finding that the data gathered by surveying and mapping technicians are crucial in implementing systems integration, the process of putting onto one map all the information about wires, pipes, and other underground infrastructure. That way, a city, town, or county can upgrade the entire infrastructure a street at the same time, resulting in savings for the local government.

The prevalence of smart phones and other mobile devices with Global Positioning System (GPS) technology has greatly increased the use of maps for finding businesses and other destinations. Surveying and mapping technicians will be needed to provide the data for these maps and to ensure that they are accurate.

Employment projections data for surveying and mapping technicians, 2010–20

Occupational Title	SOC Code	Employment, 2010	Projected Employment, 2020	Change, 2010-20 Percent	Numeric
Surveying and Mapping Technicians	17-3031	56,900	66,000	16	9,000

SOURCE: U.S. Bureau of Labor Statistics, Employment Projections program

Similar Occupations

This table shows a list of occupations with job duties that are similar to those of surveying and mapping technicians.

Occupation	Job Duties	Entry-Level Education	Median Annual Pay, May 2010
Cartographers and Photogrammetrists	Cartographers and photogrammetrists measure, analyze, and interpret geographic information to create maps and charts for political, cultural, educational, and other purposes. Cartographers are general mapmakers, and photogrammetrists are specialized mapmakers who use aerial photographs to create maps.	Bachelor's degree	$54,510
Drafters	Drafters use software to convert the designs of engineers and architects into technical drawings and plans. Workers in production and construction use these plans to build everything from microchips to skyscrapers.	Associate's degree	$47,880
Surveyors	Surveyors establish official land, airspace, and water boundaries. Surveyors work with civil engineers, landscape architects, and urban and regional planners to develop comprehensive design documents.	Bachelor's degree	$54,880

Contacts for More Information

For more information about surveying technicians, visit American Congress on Surveying and Mapping

For information about career opportunities, licensure requirements, and the surveying technician certification program, visit National Society of Professional Surveyors

For more information about photogrammetric technicians and geographic information system specialists, visit American Society for Photogrammetry and Remote Sensing

Suggested citation:

Bureau of Labor Statistics, U.S. Department of Labor, Occupational Outlook Handbook, 2012-13 Edition, Surveying and Mapping Technicians, on the Internet at http://www.bls.gov/ooh/architecture-and-engineering/surveying-and-mapping-technicians.htm .

Surveyors

Quick Facts: Surveyors	
2010 Median Pay	$54,880 per year $26.39 per hour
Entry-Level Education	Bachelor's degree
Work Experience in a Related Occupation	None
On-the-job Training	None
Number of Jobs, 2010	51,200
Job Outlook, 2010-20	25% (Faster than average)
Employment Change, 2010-20	13,000

What Surveyors Do

Surveyors establish land, airspace, and water boundaries. They measure the Earth's surface to collect data that are used to draw maps, determine the shape and contour of parcels of land, and set property lines and boundaries. They also define airspace for airports and measure construction and mining sites. Surveyors work with civil engineers, landscape architects, and urban and regional planners to develop comprehensive design documents.

Duties

Surveyors typically do the following:

- Measure distances, directions, and angles between points on, above, and below the Earth's surface
- Select known reference points and then determine the exact location of important features in the survey area using special equipment
- Establish official land and water boundaries
- Research land records and other sources of information affecting properties
- Look for evidence of previous boundaries to determine where boundary lines are
- Travel to locations to measure distances and directions between points
- Record the results of surveying and verify the accuracy of data
- Prepare plots, maps, and reports
- Work with cartographers (mapmakers), architects, construction managers, and others
- Present findings to clients, government agencies, and others
- Write descriptions of land for deeds, leases, and other legal documents
- Provide expert testimony in court regarding their work or that of other surveyors

Surveyors guide construction and development projects and provide information needed for the buying and selling of property. In construction, surveyors determine the precise location of roads or buildings and proper depths for foundations and roads. Whenever property is bought or sold, it needs to be surveyed for legal purposes.

In their work, surveyors use the Global Positioning System (GPS), a system of satellites that locates reference points with a high degree of precision. Surveyors interpret and verify the GPS results. They gather the data that is fed into a Geographic Information System (GIS), which is then used to

Surveyors map out boundaries for reasons having to do with law, property, and construction.

create detailed maps.

Surveyors take measurements in the field with a crew, a group that typically consists of a licensed surveyor and trained survey technicians. The person in charge of the crew (called the party chief) may be either a surveyor or a senior surveying technician. The party chief leads day-to-day work activities. For more information, see the profile on surveying and mapping technicians .

Some surveyors work in specialty fields to survey particular characteristics of the Earth. Examples include the following:

Geodetic surveyors use high-accuracy techniques, including satellite observations, to measure large areas of the Earth's surface.

Geophysical prospecting surveyors mark sites for subsurface exploration, usually to look for petroleum.

Marine or hydrographic surveyors survey harbors, rivers, and other bodies of water to determine shorelines, the topography of the bottom, water depth, and other features.

Work Environment

Surveyors held about 51,200 jobs in 2010. Most worked for private surveying or engineering firms. Some worked for state and local governments:

Architectural, engineering, and related services	65%
Self-employed workers	14
Local government, excluding education and hospitals	6
Heavy and civil engineering construction	4
State government, excluding education and hospitals	4

Surveying involves both field work and indoor work. Field work involves working outdoors, standing for long periods, and walking considerable distances. Surveyors sometimes climb hills with heavy packs of instruments and other equipment. When working outside, they are exposed to all types of weather, and they may need to stop outdoor work in bad weather.

Surveyors also do many tasks indoors, including researching land records, analyzing field survey data, mapping, presenting information to regulatory agencies, and providing expert testimony in courts of law.

Traveling is sometimes part of the job, and surveyors may commute long distances or stay at project locations for a period of time.

Work Schedules

Surveyors usually work full time. They may work longer hours during the summer, when warm weather and long hours of daylight are most suitable for field work.

How to Become a Surveyor

Surveyors typically need a bachelor's degree. They must be licensed before they can provide surveying services to the public and certify legal documents.

Education

Surveyors typically need a bachelor's degree.

About 26 colleges and universities offer a relevant bachelor's degree program, such as surveying technology. A degree in a closely related field, such as civil engineering or forestry, is often acceptable as well.

Some states require the degree to be from a school accredited by ABET (formerly the Accreditation Board for Engineering and Technology). Most states also have a continuing education requirement.

Licenses

Surveyors who are not licensed can work as survey technicians, but they must work under the supervision of licensed surveyors. For more information, see the profile on surveying and mapping technicians .

All 50 states and the District of Columbia require surveyors to be licensed before they can certify legal documents showing property lines or determine proper markings on construction projects. Licensure requires a number of years of experience working under the direction of a licensed surveyor. It usually takes about 4 years of work experience for a candidate with a bachelor's degree to earn a license.

The process for getting a license varies by state, but the National Council of Examiners for Engineering and Surveying has a generalized process of four steps:

- Complete the level of education required in your state.
- Pass the Fundamentals of Surveying (FS) exam.
- Gain sufficient work experience under a licensed surveyor.
- Pass the Principles and Practice of Surveying (PS) exam.

Important Qualities

Communication skills. On the job, surveyors have to give team members clear instructions. After the work in the field is done, surveyors must be able to explain the job's progress to developers, lawyers, financiers, or government authorities.

Detail oriented. Surveyors must work with precision and accuracy because mistakes can be costly.

Interpersonal skills. Surveying is a cooperative operation, so surveyors must be able to work well on a team.

Listening skills. Surveyors receive instructions from designers, such as architects, and they must listen carefully. They also depend on others on their team and must allow team members to respond as needed. They are often required to interview land owners about land boundaries and then interpret this information to resolve land boundary issues.

Physical stamina. Surveyors traditionally work outdoors and often in rugged terrain. They must have the ability to stand on their feet for many hours and over many weeks.

Problem-solving skills. Surveyors must figure out discrepancies between documents showing property lines and current conditions on the land. If there have been changes in previous years, they must figure out why the changes occurred so that property lines can be reestablished.

Time-management skills. Surveyors must be able to plan not only their time on the job but also that of their team members. This is critical when there are pressing deadlines or while working outside during winter months when daylight hours are short.

Visualization skills. Surveyors must be able to envision objects, distances and sizes.

Pay

Surveyors
Median annual wages, May 2010

Architects, Surveyors, and Cartographers	$64,820
Surveyors	$54,880
Total, All Occupations	$33,840

Note: All Occupations includes all occupations in the U.S. Economy.
Source: U.S. Bureau of Labor Statistics, Occupational Employment Statistics

The median annual wage of surveyors was $54,880 in May 2010. The median wage is the wage at which half the workers in an occupation earned more than that amount and half earned less. The lowest 10 percent earned less than $30,800, and the top 10 percent earned more than $89,930.

Median annual wages for surveyors in selected industries in May 2010 were the following:

State government, excluding education and hospitals	$71,020
Local government, excluding education and hospitals	60,930
Construction of buildings	56,970
Architectural, engineering, and related services	53,360
Heavy and civil engineering construction	52,060

Surveyors usually work full time. They may work longer hours during the summer, when warm weather and long hours of daylight are most suitable for field work.

Job Outlook

Surveyors
Percent change in employment, projected 2010-20

Surveyors	25%
Architects, Surveyors, and Cartographers	24%
Total, All Occupations	14%

Note: All Occupations includes all occupations in the U.S. Economy.
Source: U.S. Bureau of Labor Statistics, Employment Projections program

Employment of surveyors is expected to grow 25 percent from 2010 to 2020, faster than the average for all occupations. Growth will result from increased construction related to improving infrastructure.

The demand for traditional surveying services is closely tied to construction activity and opportunities will vary by year and geographic region, depending on local economic conditions. When real estate sales and construction slow down, surveyors may face greater competition for jobs. However, because surveyors can work on many different types of projects, they may have steadier work than others when construction slows.

An increasing number of firms are interested in geographic information and its applications. For example, a Geographic Information System (GIS) can be used to create maps and information for emergency planning, security, marketing, urban planning, natural resource exploration, construction, and other applications. Surveyors will still be needed for legal reasons to verify the accuracy of the data and information gathered for input into a GIS.

Job Prospects

Although surveyors have traditionally relied on construction projects for many of their opportunities, increased demand for geographic data should mean better opportunities for professionals who are involved in developing and using GIS technology and digital mapmaking. Other opportunities should result from the many surveyors who are expected to retire or permanently leave the occupation for other reasons.

Employment projections data for surveyors, 2010-20

Occupational Title	SOC Code	Employment, 2010	Projected Employment, 2020	Change, 2010-20 Percent	Numeric
Surveyors	17-1022	51,200	64,200	25	13,000

SOURCE: U.S. Bureau of Labor Statistics, Employment Projections program

Similar Occupations

This table shows a list of occupations with job duties that are similar to those of surveyors.

Occupation	Job Duties	Entry-Level Education	Median Annual Pay, May 2010
Architects	Architects plan and design buildings and other structures.	Bachelor's degree	$72,550
Cartographers and Photogrammetrists	Cartographers and photogrammetrists measure, analyze, and interpret geographic information to create maps and charts for political, cultural, educational, and other purposes. Cartographers are general mapmakers, and photogrammetrists are specialized mapmakers who use aerial photographs to create maps.	Bachelor's degree	$54,510
Civil Engineers	Civil engineers design and supervise large construction projects, including roads, buildings, airports, tunnels, dams, bridges, and systems for water supply and sewage treatment.	Bachelor's degree	$77,560
Landscape Architects	Landscape architects plan and design land areas for parks, recreational facilities, highways, airports, and other properties. Projects include subdivisions and commercial, industrial, and residential sites.	Bachelor's degree	$62,090
Surveying and Mapping Technicians	Surveying and mapping technicians assist surveyors and cartographers in collecting data and making maps of the earth's surface. Surveying technicians visit sites to take measurements of the land. Mapping technicians use geographic data to create maps.	High school diploma or equivalent	$37,900

Urban and Regional Planners	Urban and regional planners develop plans and programs for the use of land. They use planning to create communities, accommodate growth, or revitalize physical facilities in towns, cities, counties, and metropolitan areas.	Master's degree	$63,040

Contacts for More Information

For more information about surveyors, visit American Congress on Surveying and Mapping

For information about career opportunities and licensure requirements, visit National Society of Professional Surveyors, National Council of Examiners for Engineering and Surveying

For information about a career as a geodetic surveyor, visit American Association for Geodetic Surveying

Suggested citation:

Bureau of Labor Statistics, U.S. Department of Labor, Occupational Outlook Handbook, 2012-13 Edition, Surveyors, on the Internet at http://www.bls.gov/ooh/architecture-and-engineering/surveyors.htm .

Arts and Design Occupations

Art Directors

Quick Facts: Art Directors	
2010 Median Pay	$80,630 per year $38.77 per hour
Entry-Level Education	Bachelor's degree
Work Experience in a Related Occupation	1 to 5 years
On-the-job Training	None
Number of Jobs, 2010	73,900
Job Outlook, 2010-20	9% (Slower than average)
Employment Change, 2010-20	6,700

What Art Directors Do

Art directors are responsible for the visual style and images in magazines, newspapers, product packaging, and movie and television productions. They create the overall design and direct others who develop artwork or layouts.

Duties

Art directors typically do the following:
- Determine how best to represent a concept visually
- Determine which photographs, art, or other design elements to use
- Develop the overall look or style of a publication, an advertising campaign, or a theater, television, or film set
- Supervise design staff
- Review and approve designs, artwork, photography, and graphics developed by staff members
- Talk to clients to develop an artistic approach and style
- Coordinate activities with other artistic or creative departments
- Develop detailed budgets and timelines
- Present designs to clients for approval

Art directors typically oversee the work of other designers and

Art directors determine which photographs, art, or other design elements to use.

artists who produce images for television, film, live performances, advertisements, or video games. They determine the overall style or tone desired for each project and articulate their vision to artists who submit images, such as illustrations, graphics, photographs, charts and graphs, or stage and movie sets.

Art directors work with art and design staffs in advertising agencies, public relations firms, and book, magazine, or newspaper publishers to create designs and layouts. They also work with producers and directors of theater, television, or movie productions to oversee set designs. Their work requires them to understand the design elements of projects, inspire other creative workers, and keep projects on budget and on time. Sometimes, they are responsible for developing the budgets and timelines.

Art directors work in a variety of industries, and the type of work they do varies somewhat with the industry. However, almost all art directors set the overall artistic style and visual image to be created for each project, and oversee a staff of designers, artists, photographers, writers, or editors who are responsible for creating the individual works that collectively make up a completed product.

The following are some specifics of what art directors do in different industries:

In publishing, art directors typically oversee the page layout of newspapers and magazines. They also choose the cover art for books and periodicals. Often, this work includes Web publications.

In advertising and public relations, art directors ensure that their clients' desired message and image is conveyed to consumers. Art directors are responsible for the overall visual aspects of an advertising or media campaign and may coordinate the work of other artistic or design staff, such as graphic designers.

In movie production, art directors collaborate with directors to determine what sets will be needed for the film and what style or look the sets should have. They hire and supervise a staff of assistant art directors or set designers to complete designs.

Work Environment

Art directors held about 73,900 jobs in May 2010. About 12 percent of art directors work for advertising and public relations firms. Others work for newspaper and magazine publishers, specialized design services firms, and the motion picture and video industries.

The following table shows the industries that employed the most art directors in 2010:

Advertising, public relations, and related services	12%
Newspaper, periodical, book, and directory publishers	6
Specialized design services	3
Motion picture and video industries	3

About 59 percent of art directors are self-employed.

Work Schedules

Most art directors work full time.

How to Become an Art Director

Art directors need at least a bachelor's degree in an art or design subject and previous work experience. Depending on the industry, they may have worked as graphic designers, illustrators, copyeditors, or photographers, or in another art or design occupation, before becoming art directors.

Education

Many art directors start out as graphic, industrial, or set designers or in another art occupation, such as fine artists or photographers. They gain the appropriate education for that occupation, usually earning a Bachelor of Arts or Bachelor of Fine Arts degree. For more information, see the profiles for graphic designers , craft and fine artists , or photographers .

To supplement their work experience in those occupations and show their ability to take on a more creative or a more managerial role, some complete a Master of Fine Arts (MFA) degree or a Master of Business Administration (MBA) degree.

Work Experience

Art directors often work for 3 to 5 years in another occupation before being selected for positions as art directors. Depending upon the industry, they may work as graphic designers, illustrators, copyeditors, photographers, or in another art or design occupation, before becoming art directors.

For many artists, including art directors, developing a portfolio—a collection of an artist's work that demonstrates his or her styles and abilities—is essential. Managers, clients, and others look at an artist's portfolio when they are deciding whether to hire the person or contract for his or her work.

Important Qualities

Communication skills. Art directors must be able to listen to and speak with staff and clients to ensure that they understand employees' ideas and clients' desires for advertisements, publications, or movie sets.

Creativity. Art directors must be able to come up with interesting and innovative ideas to develop advertising campaigns, set designs, or layout options.

Leadership skills. Art directors must be able to organize, direct, and motivate other artists. They need to articulate their visions to artists and oversee their production.

Time management skills. Balancing competing priorities and multiple projects while meeting strict deadlines is critical for art directors.

Pay

Art Directors
Median annual wages, May 2010

Art Directors	$80,630
Arts, Design, Entertainment, Sports, and Media Occupations	$42,870
Total, All Occupations	$33,840

Note: All Occupations includes all occupations in the U.S. Economy.
Source: U.S. Bureau of Labor Statistics, Occupational Employment Statistics

The median annual wage for art directors was $80,630 in May 2010. The median wage is the wage at which half the workers in an occupation earned more than that amount and half earned less. The lowest 10 percent earned less than $42,840, and the top 10 percent earned more than $163,430. In May 2010, the wages of art directors in the industries employing the most art directors were as follows:

Motion picture and video industries	$108,860
Specialized design services	85,130
Advertising, public relations, and related services	82,770
Newspaper, periodical, book, and directory publishers	67,630

Most art directors work full time.

Job Outlook

Art Directors
Percent change in employment, projected 2010-20

Total, All Occupations	14%
Arts, Design, Entertainment, Sports, and Media Occupations	13%
Art Directors	9%

Note: All Occupations includes all occupations in the U.S. Economy.
Source: U.S. Bureau of Labor Statistics, Employment Projections program

Employment of art directors is expected to increase 9 percent from 2010 to 2020, slower than the average for all occupations. Art directors will continue to be needed to oversee the work of graphic designers, illustrators, photographers, and others engaged in artwork or layout design.

Employment of art directors is expected to experience little to no change in the publishing industry from 2010 to 2020. Although job opportunities may decline as traditional print publications lose ground to other media forms, new opportunities are expected to arise as the number of electronic magazines and Internet-based publications grows. Rather than focusing on the print layout of photographs and text, art directors for newspapers and magazines will design Web pages that incorporate a variety of photographs, illustrations, graphic designs, and text images.

The most new jobs are expected in the advertising, public relations, and related services and specialized design services industries. Advertising, public relations, and related services is expected to add 2,600 art director jobs from 2010 to 2020. Specialized design services is projected to add 700 art director jobs over the same period.

From 2010 to 2020, of the numeric change of art directors in the industries employing the most art directors is projected to be as follows:

Advertising, public relations, and related services	2,600
Specialized design services	700
Motion picture and video industries	300
Newspaper, periodical, book, and directory publishers	-100

Job Prospects

Strong competition for jobs is expected as many talented designers and artists seek to move into these positions.

Employment projections data for art directors, 2010-20

Occupational Title	SOC Code	Employment, 2010	Projected Employment, 2020	Change, 2010-20	
				Percent	Numeric
Art Directors	27-1011	73,900	80,600	9	6,700

SOURCE: U.S. Bureau of Labor Statistics, Employment Projections program

Similar Occupations

This table shows a list of occupations with job duties that are similar to those of art directors.

Occupation	Job Duties	Entry-Level Education	Median Annual Pay, May 2010
Craft and Fine Artists	Craft and fine artists use a variety of materials and techniques to create art for sale and exhibition. Craft artists create handmade objects, such as pottery, glassware, textiles, or other objects that are designed to be functional. Fine artists, including painters, sculptors, and illustrators, create original works of art for their aesthetic value, rather than a functional one.	High school diploma or equivalent	$43,470
Fashion Designers	Fashion designers create original clothing, accessories, and footwear. They sketch designs, select fabrics and patterns, and give instructions on how to make the products they designed.	High school diploma or equivalent	$64,530
Graphic Designers	Graphic designers create visual concepts, by hand or using computer software, to communicate ideas that inspire, inform, or captivate consumers. They help to make an organization recognizable by selecting color, images, or logo designs that represent a particular idea or identity to be used in advertising and promotions.	Bachelor's degree	$43,500
Industrial Designers	Industrial designers develop the concepts for manufactured products, such as cars, home appliances, and toys. They combine art, business, and engineering to make products that people use every day.	Bachelor's degree	$58,230
Multimedia Artists and Animators	Multimedia artists and animators create animation and visual effects for television, movies, video games, and other media. They create two- and three-dimensional models and animation.	Bachelor's degree	$58,510
Photographers	Photographers use their technical expertise, creativity, and composition skills to produce and preserve images that visually tell a story or record an event.	High school diploma or equivalent	$29,130
Set and Exhibit Designers	Set designers create sets for movie, television, theater, and other productions. They analyze scripts or other research documents to determine how many sets will be needed and how each set can best support the story. Exhibit designers create spaces to display products, art, or artifacts.	Bachelor's degree	$46,680

Contacts for More Information

For more information about art directors in advertising, public relations, or publishing, visit Art Directors Club

For more information about art directors in film and television, visit Art Directors Guild

Suggested citation:

Bureau of Labor Statistics, U.S. Department of Labor, Occupational Outlook Handbook, 2012-13 Edition, Art Directors, on the Internet at http://www.bls.gov/ooh/arts-and-design/art-directors.htm.

Craft and Fine Artists

Quick Facts: Craft and Fine Artists	
2010 Median Pay	$43,470 per year $20.90 per hour
Entry-Level Education	High school diploma or equivalent
Work Experience in a Related Occupation	None
On-the-job Training	Long-term on-the-job training
Number of Jobs, 2010	56,900
Job Outlook, 2010-20	5% (Slower than average)
Employment Change, 2010-20	3,100

What Craft and Fine Artists Do

Craft and fine artists use a variety of materials and techniques to create art for sale and exhibition. Craft artists create handmade objects, such as pottery, glassware, textiles or other objects that are designed to be functional. Fine artists, including painters, sculptors, and illustrators, create original works of art for their aesthetic value, rather than a functional one.

Duties

Craft and fine artists typically do the following:

- Use techniques such as knitting, weaving, glass blowing, painting, drawing, or sculpting
- Develop creative ideas or new methods for making art
- Create sketches, templates, or models to guide their work
- Select which materials to use on the basis of color, texture, strength, and other qualities
- Process materials, often by shaping, joining, or cutting
- Use visual elements, such as composition, color, space, and perspective, to produce desired artistic effects
- Develop portfolios highlighting their artistic styles and abilities to show to gallery owners and others interested in their work

Artists create objects that are beautiful or thought-provoking. They often strive to communicate ideas or feelings through their art.

Craft artists make a wide variety of objects, mostly by hand, to sell in their own studios, online, in stores, or at arts-and-crafts shows. Some craft artists display their works in galleries and museums.

Craft and fine artists use a variety of materials and techniques to create art for sale and exhibition.

Craft artists work with many different materials, including ceramics, glass, textiles, wood, metal, and paper, to create unique pieces of art, such as pottery, quilts, stained glass, furniture, jewelry, and clothing. Many craft artists also use fine-art techniques—for example, painting, sketching, and printing—to add finishing touches to their products.

Fine artists typically display their work in museums, commercial or non-profit art galleries, corporate collections, and private homes. Some of their artwork may be commissioned (requested by a client), but most is sold by the artist or through private art galleries or dealers. The gallery and the artist decide in advance how much of the sale proceeds each will keep.

Some craft and fine artists spend much time and effort selling their artwork to potential customers or clients and building a reputation. However, only the most successful artists are able to support themselves solely through the sale of their works. Many artists have at least one other job to support their craft or art careers.

Some artists work in museums or art galleries as arts directors or as curators, planning and setting up exhibits. Others teach craft or art classes or conduct workshops in schools or in their own studios. For more information on workers who teach art classes, see the profiles on kindergarten and elementary school teachers , middle school teachers , high school teachers , postsecondary teachers , and self-enrichment teachers.

Craft and fine artists specialize in one or more types of art. The following are examples of types of craft and fine artists:

Cartoonists draw political, advertising, comic, and sports cartoons. Some cartoonists work with others who create the idea or story and write captions. Some create plots and write captions themselves. Most cartoonists have comic, critical, or dramatic talents in addition to drawing skills.

Ceramic artists shape, form, and mold artworks out of clay, often using a potter's wheel and other tools. They glaze and fire pieces in kilns, which are special furnaces that dry and harden the clay.

Fiber artists use fabric, yarn, or other natural and synthetic fibers to weave, knit, crochet, or sew textile art. They may use a loom to weave fabric, needles to knit or crochet yarn, or a sewing machine to join pieces of fabric for quilts or other handicrafts.

Fine art painters paint landscapes, portraits, and other subjects in a variety of styles, ranging from realistic to abstract. They may use one or more media, such as watercolors, oil paints, or acrylics.

Furniture makers cut, sand, join, and finish wood and other materials to make handcrafted furniture. For more information about other workers who assemble wood furniture, see the profile on woodworkers .

Glass artists process glass in a variety of ways—such as by blowing, shaping, or joining it—to create artistic pieces. Specific processes used include glassblowing, lampworking, and stained glass. These workers also decorate glass objects, such as by etching or painting.

Illustrators create pictures for books, magazines, and other publications, and for commercial products, such as textiles, wrapping paper, stationery, greeting cards, and calendars. Increasingly, illustrators use computers in their work. They might draw in pen and pencil and then scan the image into a computer to be colored in, or use a special pen to draw images directly onto the computer.

Sketch artists, a particular type of illustrator, often create likenesses of subjects with pencil, charcoal, or pastels. Sketches are used by law enforcement agencies to help identify suspects, by the news media to show courtroom scenes, and by individual customers for their own enjoyment.

Jewelry artists use metals, stones, beads, and other materials to make objects for personal adornment, such as earrings or bracelets. For more information about other workers who create jewelry, see the profile on jewelers and precious stone and metal workers .

Medical and scientific illustrators combine drawing skills with knowledge of biology or other sciences. Medical illustrators work with computers or with pen and paper to create images of human anatomy and surgical procedures, as well as three-dimensional models and animations. Scientific illustrators draw animal and plant life, atomic and molecular structures, and geologic and planetary formations. These illustrations are used in medical and scientific publications and in audiovisual presentations for teaching purposes. Some medical and scientific illustrators work for lawyers, producing exhibits for court cases.

Printmakers create images on a silk screen, woodblock, lithography stone, metal etching plate, or other type of matrix. The matrix is then inked and transferred to a piece of paper using a printing press or hand press to create the final work of art. Workers who do photoengraving are called printing workers. For more information, see the profile on printing workers .

Sculptors design three-dimensional works of art, either by molding and joining materials such as clay, glass, plastic, or metal, or by cutting and carving forms from a block of plaster, wood, or stone. Some sculptors combine various materials to create mixed-media installations. For example, some incorporate light, sound, and motion into their works.

Work Environment

Craft and fine artists held about 56,900 jobs in 2010.

Most craft and fine artists are self-employed, while others are employed in various private sector industries and by government.

Craft artists, for example, might work for companies that manufacture glass or clay products, or for museums, historical sites, or similar institutions. Fine artists are often employed by newspaper, periodical, book, and directory publishers; colleges and universities; and software publishers. Other types of artists and related workers work for the federal government, motion picture and video production companies, and advertising and public relations firms.

Craft and fine artists commonly work in the following industries :

Performing arts, spectator sports, and related industries	10%
Federal government	8
Motion picture and video industries	5
Manufacturing	4
Educational services; state, local, and private	3

Many artists work in fine art or commercial art studios located in office buildings, warehouses, or lofts. Others work in private studios in their homes. Some artists share studio space, where they also may exhibit their work.

Studios are usually well-lighted and ventilated. However, artists may be exposed to fumes from glue, paint, ink, and other materials.

They may also have to deal with dust or other residue from filings, splattered paint, or spilled cleaners and other fluids.

Work Schedules

Part-time and variable work schedules are common for artists. Many also hold another job in addition to their work as an artist. During busy periods, artists may work overtime to meet deadlines. Self-employed artists can set their own hours.

How to Become a Craft or Fine Artist

Formal schooling is not required for craft and fine artists. However, many artists take classes or earn a bachelor's or master's degree in fine arts, which can improve their skills and job prospects.

Education

Formal schooling is rarely required for craft and fine artists. However, it is difficult to gain adequate artistic skills without some formal education in the fine arts.

Most craft and fine artists have at least a high school diploma. High school classes, such as those in art, shop, or home economics, can teach prospective artists some of the basic skills they will need, such as drawing, woodworking, or sewing.

Many artists pursue postsecondary education and take classes or earn degrees that can improve their skills and job prospects. Many colleges and universities offer bachelor's and master's degrees in fine arts. In addition to studio art and art history, courses may also include core subjects, such as English, social science, and natural science.

Independent schools of art and design also offer postsecondary training, which can lead to a certificate in an art-related specialty or to an associate's, bachelor's, or master's degree in fine arts.

In 2011, the National Association of Schools of Art and Design accredited approximately 300 postsecondary institutions with programs in art and design. Most of these schools award a degree in art.

Medical illustrators must have both a demonstrated artistic ability and a detailed knowledge of living organisms, surgical and medical procedures, and human and animal anatomy. They usually need a bachelor's degree combining art and premedical courses. However, most medical illustrators also choose to get a master's degree in medical illustration. Four accredited schools offer this degree in the United States.

Education gives artists an opportunity to develop a portfolio—a collection of an artist's work that demonstrates his or her styles and abilities. Portfolios are essential because art directors, clients, and others look at an artist's portfolio when deciding whether to hire the individual or buy his or her work.

Those who want to teach fine arts at public elementary or secondary schools usually must have a teaching certificate in addition to a bachelor's degree. An advanced degree in fine arts or arts administration is usually necessary for management or administrative positions in government or in foundations, or for teaching in colleges and universities. For more information on workers who teach art classes, see the profiles on kindergarten and elementary school teachers , middle school teachers , high school teachers , postsecondary teachers , and self-enrichment teachers .

Training

Craft and fine artists improve their skills through practice and repetition. They can train in several ways other than, or in addition to, attending formal schooling.

Some craft and fine artists learn on the job from more experienced artists. Others attend non-credit classes or workshops or take private lessons, which may be offered in artists' studios or at community colleges, art centers, galleries, museums, or other art-related institutions.

Still other craft and fine artists work closely with another artist on either a formal or informal basis. Formal arrangements may include internships or apprenticeship programs.

Advancement

Artists hired by firms often start with relatively routine work. While doing this work, however, they may observe other artists and practice their own skills.

Craft and fine artists advance professionally as their work circulates and as they establish a reputation for a particular style. Many of the most successful artists continually develop new ideas, and their work often evolves over time.

Many artists do freelance work while continuing to hold a full-time job until they are established as professional artists. Others freelance part time while still in school to develop experience and to build a portfolio of published work.

Freelance artists try to develop a set of clients who regularly contract for work. Some freelance artists are widely recognized for their skill in specialties such as cartooning or children's book illustration. These artists may earn high incomes and can choose the type of work they do.

Important Qualities

Artistic ability. Craft and fine artists create artwork and other objects that are visually appealing or thought-provoking. This usually requires significant skill in one or more art forms.

Creativity. Artists must have active imaginations to develop new and original ideas for their work.

Customer-service skills. Craft and fine artists, especially those who sell their work themselves, must be good at dealing with customers and potential buyers.

Interpersonal skills. Artists often must interact with many people, including co-workers, gallery owners, and the public.

Manual dexterity. Most artists work with their hands and must be good at manipulating tools and materials to create their art.

Sales and marketing skills. Craft and fine artists must promote themselves and their art to build a reputation and to sell what they have made. They often study the market for their crafts or artwork to increase their understanding of what potential customers might want.

Pay

Craft and Fine Artists
Median hourly wages, May 2010

Artists and Related Workers, All Other	$28.29
Fine Artists, Including Painters, Sculptors, and Illustrators	$21.56
Craft and Fine Artists	$20.90
Total, All Occupations	$16.27
Craft Artists	$12.95

Note: All Occupations includes all occupations in the U.S. Economy.
Source: U.S. Bureau of Labor Statistics, Occupational Employment Statistics

The median hourly wage of craft and fine artists was $20.90 in May 2010. The median wage is the wage at which half the workers in an occupation earned more than that amount and half earned less. The lowest 10 percent earned less than $9.10, and the top 10 percent earned more than $44.04.

The median hourly wages for craft and fine artists occupations in May 2010 were the following:
- $28.29 for all other artists and related workers
- $21.56 for fine artists, including painters, sculptors, and illustrators
- $12.95 for craft artists

Earnings for self-employed artists vary widely. Some charge only a nominal fee while they gain experience and build a reputation for their

work. Others, such as well-established freelance fine artists and illustrators, can earn more than salaried artists. Many, however, find it difficult to rely solely on income earned from selling paintings or other works of art.

Part-time and variable work schedules are common for artists. Many also hold another job in addition to their work as an artist. During busy periods, artists may work overtime to meet deadlines. Self-employed artists can set their own hours.

Job Outlook

Craft and Fine Artists
Percent change in employment, projected 2010-20

Total, All Occupations	14%
Fine Artists, Including Painters, Sculptors, and Illustrators	8%
Craft Artists	7%
Craft and Fine Artists	5%
Artists and Related Workers, All Other	1%

Note: All Occupations includes all occupations in the U.S. Economy.
Source: U.S. Bureau of Labor Statistics, Employment Projections program

Employment of craft and fine artists is projected to grow by 5 percent from 2010 to 2020, slower than the average for all occupations.

Employment growth of artists depends in large part on the overall state of the economy, because purchases of art are usually optional. During good economic times, more people and businesses are interested in buying artwork; during economic downturns, they buy less.

Although there is always a demand for art by collectors and museums, the employment of artists is also impacted by the level of charitable giving to the arts—which has been decreasing in recent years.

In addition, job growth for craft artists may be limited by the sale of inexpensive, mass-produced items designed to look like handmade American crafts. However, consumers' continued interest in locally-made products will likely offset some of these employment losses.

Demand for illustrators who work on a computer will increase as media companies use more detailed images and backgrounds in their designs. Illustrators and cartoonists who work in publishing may see job opportunities decline as traditional print publications lose ground to other media forms. However, new opportunities are expected to arise as the number of electronic magazines and Internet-based publications grows.

Job Prospects

Competition for jobs as craft and fine artists is expected to be strong because there are more qualified candidates than available jobs. Only the most successful craft and fine artists receive major commissions for their work.

Despite the competition, studios, galleries, and individual clients are always on the lookout for artists who display outstanding talent, creativity, and style. Talented individuals who have developed a mastery of artistic techniques and skills will have the best job prospects.

Competition among artists for the privilege of being shown in galleries is expected to remain intense, as will competition for grants from funders such as private foundations, state and local arts councils, and the National Endowment for the Arts. Because of their reliance on grants, and because the demand for artwork is dependent on consumers having extra income to spend, many of these artists will find that their income changes with the overall economy.

Employment projections data for craft and fine artists, 2010-20

Occupational Title	SOC Code	Employment, 2010	Projected Employment, 2020	Change, 2010-20	
				Percent	Numeric
Craft and Fine Artists	—	56,900	59,900	5	3,100
Craft Artists	27-1012	11,800	12,700	7	900
Fine Artists, Including Painters, Sculptors, and Illustrators	27-1013	25,700	27,700	8	2,000
Artists and Related Workers, All Other	27-1019	19,300	19,500	1	200

SOURCE: U.S. Bureau of Labor Statistics, Employment Projections program

Similar Occupations

This table shows a list of occupations with job duties that are similar to those of craft and fine artists.

Occupation	Job Duties	Entry-Level Education	Median Annual Pay, May 2010
Archivists	Archivists appraise, edit, and maintain permanent records and historically valuable documents. Many perform research on archival material.	Bachelor's degree	$45,200
Art Directors	Art directors are responsible for the visual style and images in magazines, newspapers, product packaging, and movie and television productions. They create the overall design and direct others who develop artwork or layouts.	Bachelor's degree	$80,630
Curators, Museum Technicians, and Conservators	Curators oversee collections, such as artwork and historic items, and may conduct public service activities for an institution. Museum technicians and conservators prepare and restore objects and documents in museum collections and exhibits.	See How to Become One	$42,310
Fashion Designers	Fashion designers create original clothing, accessories, and footwear. They sketch designs, select fabrics and patterns, and give instructions on how to make the products they designed.	High school diploma or equivalent	$64,530
Graphic Designers	Graphic designers create visual concepts, by hand or using computer software, to communicate ideas that inspire, inform, or captivate consumers. They help to make an organization recognizable by selecting color, images, or logo designs that represent a particular idea or identity to be used in advertising and promotions.	Bachelor's degree	$43,500
Industrial Designers	Industrial designers develop the concepts for manufactured products, such as cars, home appliances, and toys. They combine art, business, and engineering to make products that people use every day.	Bachelor's degree	$58,230
Jewelers and Precious Stone and Metal Workers	Jewelers and precious stone and metal workers design, manufacture, and sell jewelry. They also adjust, repair, and appraise gems and jewelry.	High school diploma or equivalent	$35,170
Multimedia Artists and Animators	Multimedia artists and animators create animation and visual effects for television, movies, video games, and other media. They create two- and three-dimensional models and animation.	Bachelor's degree	$58,510
Photographers	Photographers use their technical expertise, creativity, and composition skills to produce and preserve images that visually tell a story or record an event.	High school diploma or equivalent	$29,130
Self-enrichment Teachers	Self-enrichment teachers instruct in a variety of subjects that students take for fun or self-improvement, such as music and foreign languages. These classes generally do not lead to a degree or certification, and students take them voluntarily to learn new skills or gain understanding of a subject.	High school diploma or equivalent	$36,340
Woodworkers	Woodworkers build a variety of products, such as cabinets and furniture, using wood.	High school diploma or equivalent	$28,010

Contacts for More Information

For more about art and design and a list of accredited college-level programs, visit National Association of Schools of Art and Design

For more information on careers in the craft arts and for a list of schools and workshops, visit American Craft Council Library

For more information on careers in the arts, visit New York Foundation for the Arts

For more information on careers in illustration, visit Society of Illustrators

For more information on careers in medical illustration, visit Association of Medical Illustrators

For information on grant-funding programs and other local resources for artists, contact your state arts agency. A list of these agencies is available from the National Assembly of State Arts Agencies .

Suggested citation:

Bureau of Labor Statistics, U.S. Department of Labor, Occupational Outlook Handbook, 2012-13 Edition, Craft and Fine Artists, on the Internet at http://www.bls.gov/ooh/arts-and-design/craft-and-fine-artists.htm.

Fashion Designers

Quick Facts: Fashion Designers	
2010 Median Pay	$64,530 per year $31.02 per hour
Entry-Level Education	High school diploma or equivalent
Work Experience in a Related Occupation	None
On-the-job Training	Long-term on-the-job training
Number of Jobs, 2010	21,500
Job Outlook, 2010-20	0% (Little or no change)
Employment Change, 2010-20	0

What Fashion Designers Do

Fashion designers create original clothing, accessories, and footwear. They sketch designs, select fabrics and patterns, and give instructions on how to make the products they designed.

Duties

Fashion designers typically do the following:
- Study fashion trends and anticipate designs that will appeal to consumers
- Decide on a theme for a collection
- Sketch designs of clothing, footwear, and accessories
- Use computer-aided design programs (CAD) to create designs
- Visit manufacturers or trade shows to get fabric samples
- Select fabrics, embellishments, colors, or style for each garment or accessory
- Work with other designers or team members to create a prototype design
- Present design ideas to the creative director or showcase them in fashion or trade shows
- Market designs to clothing retailers or directly to consumers

Fashion designers sketch designs of clothing, footwear, and accessories.

- Oversee the final production of their designs

Larger apparel companies typically employ a team of designers headed by a creative designer. Some fashion designers specialize in clothing, footwear, or accessory design, but others create designs in all three fashion categories.

For some fashion designers, the first step in creating a new design is researching current fashion and making predictions of future trends, using trend reports published by fashion industry trade groups. Other fashion designers create collections from inspirations they get from their regular surroundings, from the cultures they have experienced and places they have visited, or from various art media that inspire them.

After they have an initial idea, fashion designers try out various fabrics and produce a prototype, often with less expensive material than will be used in the final product. They work with models to see how the design will look and adjust the designs as needed.

Although most designers first sketch their designs by hand, many now put their sketches online with computer-aided design (CAD) programs. CAD allows designers to see their work on virtual models. They can try out different colors, design, and shapes while making adjustments more easily than they can when working with real fabric on real people.

The designers produce samples with the actual materials that will be used in manufacturing. Samples that get good responses from editors or trade and fashion shows are then manufactured and sold to consumers.

Although the design process may vary by specialty, in general, it takes 6 months from initial design concept to final production, when either the spring or fall collection is released. Some companies may release new designs as frequently as every month, in addition to releases during the spring and fall.

The Internet and e-commerce allow fashion designers to offer their products outside of the traditional brick-and-mortar stores. Instead, they can ship directly to the consumer, without having to invest in a physical place to showcase their products lines.

The following are examples of types of fashion designers:

Clothing designers create and help produce men's, women's, and children's apparel, including casual wear, suits, sportswear, evening wear, outerwear, maternity, and intimate apparel.

Footwear designers create and help produce different styles of shoes and boots. As new materials become available, such as lightweight synthetic materials used in shoe soles, footwear designers produce new designs that combine comfort, form, and function.

Accessory designers design and produce items such as handbags, suitcases, belts, scarves, hats, hosiery, and eyewear.

Costume designers are responsible for designing costumes for the performing arts and for motion picture and television productions. They research the styles worn during the period in which the performance takes place, or they work with directors to select and create appropriate attire. They also must stay within the costume budget for the particular production.

Work Environment

Fashion designers held about 21,500 jobs in 2010. Fashion designers work in wholesale or manufacturing establishments, apparel companies, retailers, theater or dance companies, and design firms.

More fashion designers work for wholesalers or manufacturers than for any other industry. The lines of apparel and accessories of these wholesalers and manufacturers are sold to retailers or other marketers for distribution to individual stores, catalog companies, or online retailers. In many cases, these designers are €œin-house designers.€ Although the brands may be familiar to many consumers, the individual designers are largely unknown.

Thirty percent of fashion designers are self-employed. Some fashion designers own companies that bear their names. They typically design high-fashion garments and one-of-a-kind apparel on an individualized or custom basis. Self-employed fashion designers who are able to set up their own independent clothing lines often already have experience and a strong understanding of the industry.

The following table shows the industries that employed the most fashion designers in 2010:

Apparel, piece goods, and notions merchant wholesalers	29%
Apparel manufacturing	14
Management of companies and enterprises	7
Specialized design services	4
Performing arts, spectator sports, and related industries	2

Most designers travel several times a year to trade and fashion shows to learn about the latest fashion trends. Designers also sometimes travel to other countries to meet suppliers of materials and manufacturers who produce the final products.

Fashion designers are usually found in large cities, such as New York or Los Angeles. In May 2010, almost 75 percent of all salaried fashion designers worked in New York and California.

Work Schedules

Most fashion designers work full time; however, some work part time. Occasionally, fashion designers work long hours to meet production deadlines or prepare for fashion shows. Designers who freelance generally work under a contract and tend to work longer hours and adjust their workday to their clients' schedules and deadlines.

How to Become a Fashion Designer

Formal education is not required. However, most fashion designers entering the industry have some formal education where they learn design skills, such as how to use computer-aided design (CAD) technology. Employers usually seek applicants with creativity, as well as a good technical understanding of the production process for clothing, accessories, or footwear.

Education

Although formal education is not required for fashion designers, many take classes or earn a 2-year or 4-year degree in a related field, such as fashion merchandising, that can improve their knowledge of textiles and fabrics.

For many artists, including fashion designers, developing a portfolio—a collection of design ideas that demonstrates their styles and abilities—is essential because employers rely heavily on a designer's portfolio in deciding whether to hire the individual. For employers, it is an opportunity to gauge talent and creativity. Students studying fashion design often have opportunities to enter their designs in student or amateur contests, helping them to develop their portfolios.

The National Association of Schools of Art and Design accredits approximately 300 postsecondary institutions with programs in art and design, and many of these schools award degrees in fashion design. Many schools require students to have completed basic art and design courses before they enter a program. Applicants usually have to submit sketches and other examples of their artistic ability.

Training

Fashion designers often gain their initial experience in the fashion industry through internships or by working as an assistant designer. Internships provide aspiring fashion designers an opportunity to experience the design process, building their knowledge of textiles, colors, and how the industry works.

Advancement

Beginning fashion designers usually start out as patternmakers or sketching assistants to more experienced designers before advancing to higher level positions. Experienced designers may advance to chief designer, design department head, creative director, or another supervisory position in which they oversee certain fashion lines or brands by a company.

Some experienced designers may start their own design company or sell their designs in their own retail stores. A few of the most successful designers work for high-fashion design houses that offer personalized design services to their clients.

Important Qualities

Artistic ability. Fashion designers sketch their initial design ideas, which are used later to create prototypes. Consequently, designers must be able to express their vision for the design through illustration.

Communication skills. Fashion designers often work in teams throughout the design process and therefore must be effective in communicating with their team members. For example, they may need to give instructions to sewers regarding how the garment should be constructed.

Computer skills. Fashion designers use technology to design. They must be able to use computer-aided design (CAD) programs and be familiar with graphics editing software.

Creativity. Fashion designers work with a variety of fabrics, shapes, and colors. Their ideas must be unique, functional, and stylish.

Decision-making skills. Because they often work in teams, fashion designers are exposed to many ideas. They must be able to decide which ideas to incorporate into their designs.

Detail-oriented. Fashion designers must have a good eye for small differences in color and other details that can make a design successful.

Pay

Fashion Designers
Median annual wages, May 2010

Fashion Designers	$64,530
Arts, Design, Entertainment, Sports, and Media Occupations	$42,870
Total, All Occupations	$33,840

Note: All Occupations includes all occupations in the U.S. Economy.
Source: U.S. Bureau of Labor Statistics, Occupational Employment Statistics

The median annual wage of fashion designers was $64,530 in May 2010. The median wage is the wage at which half the workers in an occupation earned more than that amount and half earned less. The lowest 10 percent earned less than $32,500, and the top 10 percent earned more than $130,890.

Earnings in this occupation can vary widely based on experience, employer, and reputation. Starting salaries in fashion design tend be very low. Salaried fashion designers usually earn higher and more stable incomes than self-employed, freelance designers. However, a few of the most successful self-employed fashion designers earn many times the salary of the highest paid salaried designers. In May 2010, the wages of fashion designers in the industries employing most of the occupation were as follows:

Management of companies and enterprises	$70,660
Apparel manufacturing	65,790
Apparel, piece goods, and notions merchant wholesalers	63,750
Specialized design services	60,900
Performing arts, spectator sports, and related industries	44,130

Most fashion designers work full time; however, some work part time. Occasionally, fashion designers work long hours to meet production deadlines or prepare for fashion shows. Designers who freelance generally work under a contract and tend to work longer hours and adjust their workday to their clients' schedules and deadlines.

Job Outlook

Fashion Designers
Percent change in employment, projected 2010-20

Total, All Occupations	14%
Arts, Design, Entertainment, Sports, and Media Occupations	13%
Fashion Designers	0%

Note: All Occupations includes all occupations in the U.S. Economy.
Source: U.S. Bureau of Labor Statistics, Employment Projections program

Employment of fashion designers is expected to experience little to no change from 2010 to 2020.

Some growth is projected for this occupation in specialized design firms and for self-employed fashion designers. Clothing and accessories designers will be needed to design comfortable and more affordable items for the mass market and everyday wear. In addition, as new clothing technology is developed, fashion designers will be needed to create garments using new fabrics, such as moisture-wicking fabrics.

However, fashion designers in the apparel manufacturing industry are expected to face declining employment, which should prevent overall employment from increasing.

From 2010 to 2020, employment growth of fashion designers in the industries employing most of these workers is expected to be as follows:

Specialized design services	40%
Performing arts, spectator sports, and related industries	14
Management of companies and enterprises	3
Apparel, piece goods, and notions merchant wholesalers	0
Apparel manufacturing	-58

Job Prospects

Strong competition for jobs is expected because of the large number of people who seek employment as fashion designers and the relatively few positions available.

Those with formal education in fashion design, with excellent portfolios, and with industry experience will have the best job prospects.

In addition, it may be necessary for some fashion designers to relocate. Employment opportunities for fashion designers are highly concentrated in New York and California. In May 2010, almost 75 percent of all salaried fashion designers worked in these two states.

Employment projections data for fashion designers, 2010-20

Occupational Title	SOC Code	Employment, 2010	Projected Employment, 2020	Change, 2010-20 Percent	Numeric
Fashion Designers	27-1022	21,500	21,500	0	0

SOURCE: U.S. Bureau of Labor Statistics, Employment Projections program

Similar Occupations

This table shows a list of occupations with job duties that are similar to those of fashion designers.

Occupation	Job Duties	Entry-Level Education	Median Annual Pay, May 2010
Art Directors	Art directors are responsible for the visual style and images in magazines, newspapers, product packaging, and movie and television productions. They create the overall design and direct others who develop artwork or layouts.	Bachelor's degree	$80,630
Demonstrators and Product Promoters	Demonstrators and product promoters create public interest in products, such as cosmetics, housewares, and food. They encourage people and stores to buy their products by showing the products to prospective customers and answering questions.	High school diploma or equivalent	$23,110
Floral Designers	Floral designers, also called florists, cut and arrange live, dried, or silk flowers and greenery to make decorative displays. They also help customers select flowers, containers, ribbons, and other accessories.	High school diploma or equivalent	$23,610
Graphic Designers	Graphic designers create visual concepts, by hand or using computer software, to communicate ideas that inspire, inform, or captivate consumers. They help to make an organization recognizable by selecting color, images, or logo designs that represent a particular idea or identity to be used in advertising and promotions.	Bachelor's degree	$43,500
Industrial Designers	Industrial designers develop the concepts for manufactured products, such as cars, home appliances, and toys. They combine art, business, and engineering to make products that people use every day.	Bachelor's degree	$58,230

Jewelers and Precious Stone and Metal Workers	Jewelers and precious stone and metal workers design, manufacture, and sell jewelry. They also adjust, repair, and appraise gems and jewelry.	High school diploma or equivalent	$35,170
Models	Models pose for artists, photographers, or customers to help advertise a variety of products, including clothing, cosmetics, food, and appliances.	Less than high school	$32,920
Purchasing Managers, Buyers, and Purchasing Agents	Purchasing managers, buyers, and purchasing agents buy products for organizations to use or resell. They evaluate suppliers, negotiate contracts, and review product quality.	See How to Become One	$58,360
Sewers and Tailors	Sewers and tailors sew, join, reinforce, or finish clothing or other items. They may create new pieces of clothing from patterns and designs or alter existing garments to fit customers better.	Less than high school	$25,850

Contacts for More Information

For more information about careers in fashion design, visit Council of Fashion Designers of America

For more information about educational programs in fashion design, visit National Association of Schools of Art and Design

Suggested citation:

Bureau of Labor Statistics, U.S. Department of Labor, Occupational Outlook Handbook, 2012-13 Edition, Fashion Designers, on the Internet at http://www.bls.gov/ooh/arts-and-design/fashion-designers.htm.

Floral Designers

Quick Facts: Floral Designers	
2010 Median Pay	$23,610 per year $11.35 per hour
Entry-Level Education	High school diploma or equivalent
Work Experience in a Related Occupation	None
On-the-job Training	Short-term on-the-job training
Number of Jobs, 2010	66,500
Job Outlook, 2010-20	-9% (Decline moderately)
Employment Change, 2010-20	-6,200

What Floral Designers Do

Floral designers, also called florists, cut and arrange live, dried, or silk flowers and greenery to make decorative displays. They also help customers select flowers, containers, ribbons, and other accessories.

Duties

Floral designers typically do the following:

- Grow or order flowers from wholesalers to ensure an adequate supply to meet customers' needs
- Determine the type of arrangement desired, the occasion, and the date, time, and location that each arrangement is needed
- Recommend flowers and greenery for each arrangement
- Consider the customer's budget when making recommendations
- Design floral displays that evoke a particular sentiment or style
- Answer telephones, take orders, wrap arrangements

Floral designers may create a single arrangement for a special occasion or design floral displays for rooms and open spaces for large scale functions, such as weddings, funerals, and banquets. They use their sense of artistry and knowledge of different types of flowers to choose the appropriate flowers for each occasion. They need to know what flowers are in season and when they will be available.

Floral designers must know the color varieties of each flower and the average size of each type of flower. They might calculate the number of flowers that will fit into a particular vase, or how many rose petals are needed to cover a carpet.

Floral designers also need to know the properties of each flower. Some flowers, like carnations, can last for many hours outside of water. Other flowers are more delicate and wilt more quickly. Some plants are poisonous for certain types of animals. For example, lilies are toxic for cats.

Floral designers use all their knowledge to recommend flowers and designs to customers. After the customer selects the flowers, the designer arranges them in a visually appealing display.

Although more complex displays must be ordered in advance, designers will often create smaller bouquets or arrangements while customers wait. When they are responsible for floral arrangements for an occasion, such as a wedding or banquet, floral designers usually set up the floral decorations just before the event.

Floral designers also give customers instructions on how to care for flowers, including the ideal temperature and how often the water should be changed. For cut flowers, floral designers will often provide flower food for the customer to take home.

When not serving customers, floral designers order new flowers from suppliers. They process newly arrived flowers by stripping leaves that would be below the waterline. They cut new flowers, mix flower food solutions, fill floral containers with the food solutions, and sanitize workspaces. They keep most flowers in cool display cases so the flowers stay fresh and live longer.

Some designers may have long-term agreements with hotels and restaurants or the owners of office buildings and private homes to replace old flowers with new flower arrangements on a recurring schedule—usually daily, weekly, or monthly—to keep areas looking fresh and appealing. Some work with interior designers in creating these displays. For more information, see the profile on interior designers.

Floral designers who are self-employed or own their shop must also do business tasks. Some hire and supervise staff. They must keep track of income, expenses, and taxes——or hire others to help with those tasks.

Work Environment

Floral designers held 66,500 jobs in 2010. Most floral designers work in retail businesses: 46 percent work in floral shops and 11 percent work in grocery stores. As such, floral designers can expect walk-in business and telephone calls from customers seeking advice and placing orders, as well as orders transmitted electronically from other florists and from consumers ordering from websites.

The following table shows the industries that employed the most floral designers in 2010:

Florists	46%
Grocery stores	11
Merchant wholesalers, nondurable goods	2
Other general merchandise stores	2

Although designers often work in well-lighted, comfortable surroundings, room temperatures tend to be a little cooler than office or retail spaces because temperatures are set low to help keep the flowers fresh.

During certain times of the year, such as holidays, floral designers are predictably busier than at other times. Because live flowers are perishable, most orders cannot be completed too far in advance. Therefore, designers often work longer hours just before and during holidays.

About 31 percent of floral designers are self-employed.

Work Schedules

Most floral designers work full time, although their hours may differ depending on the location of the particular store. However, many part-time or seasonal opportunities can be found, particularly around holidays, such as Christmas, Valentine's Day, and Mother's Day.

Independent shops in downtown areas or business districts are typically open during business hours. Floral departments inside grocery stores or other stores in suburban locations or shopping malls may remain open longer.

How to Become a Floral Designer

Most floral designers have a high school diploma or the equivalent

Most floral designers learn their skills on the job over the course of a few months.

and learn their skills on the job over the course of a few months.

Training

Those training to become floral designers typically get hands-on experience working with an experienced floral designer. They may start by preparing simple flower arrangements and practicing the basics of tying bows and ribbons, cutting stems to appropriate lengths, and learning about the proper handling and care of flowers. They also learn about the different types of flowers, their growing properties and how to use them in more complex floral designs.

Education

Many programs in floral design and floriculture are available through private floral schools, vocational schools, and community colleges. Most offer a certificate or diploma. Some community colleges and universities offer an associate's or bachelor's degree in floral design.

Classes in flower and plant identification, floral design concepts, advertising, and other business courses, plus experience working in a greenhouse are part of many certificate or diploma programs. In addition to traditional academic classes, many courses are available online or through state and national floral design associations.

Certification

The American Institute of Floral Designers offers a Certified Floral Designer certification. Although certification in floral design is voluntary, it indicates a measure of achievement and expertise.

Work Experience

Many floral designers gain their initial experience working as cashiers or delivery people in retail floral stores.

Advancement

Advancement in the floral field is limited. Taking formal design training can help people who are interested in opening their own business or becoming a chief floral designer or supervisor.

Important Qualities

Artistic ability. Designers use their sense of style to develop aesthetically pleasing designs.

Creativity. Floral designers must use their artistic abilities and knowledge of design to develop appropriate designs for different occasions. They must also be open to new ideas as trends in floral design change quickly.

Customer service skills. Floral designers spend a substantial part of their day interacting with customers and suppliers. They must be able to understand what a customer is looking for, explain options, and ensure high-quality flowers and service.

Organizational skills. Floral designers need to be well organized to keep the business operating smoothly and ensure that orders are completed on time.

Pay

Floral Designers
Median annual wages, May 2010

Arts, Design, Entertainment, Sports, and Media Occupations	$42,870
Total, All Occupations	$33,840
Floral Designers	$23,610

Note: All Occupations includes all occupations in the U.S. Economy.
Source: U.S. Bureau of Labor Statistics, Occupational Employment Statistics

The median annual wage of floral designers was $23,610 in May 2010. The median wage is the wage at which half the workers in an occupation earned more than that amount, and half earned less. The lowest 10 percent earned less than $16,940 and the top 10 percent earned more than $35,840.

In May 2010, the wages of floral designers in the industries employing most of the occupation were as follows:

Grocery stores	$25,240
Merchant wholesalers, nondurable goods	23,300
Florists	23,270
Other general merchandise stores	21,670

Most floral designers work full time, although their hours may differ depending on the location of the particular store. However, many part-time or seasonal opportunities can be found, particularly around holidays, such as Christmas, Valentine's Day, and Mother's Day.

Independent shops in downtown areas or business districts are typically open during business hours. Floral departments inside grocery stores or other stores in suburban locations or shopping malls may remain open longer.

Job Outlook

Floral Designers

Percent change in employment, projected 2010-20

Total, All Occupations	14%
Arts, Design, Entertainment, Sports, and Media Occupations	13%
Floral Designers	-9%

Note: All Occupations includes all occupations in the U.S. Economy.
Source: U.S. Bureau of Labor Statistics, Employment Projections program

Employment of floral designers is expected to decline by 9 percent from 2010 to 2020. The need for floral designers is expected to decline as people buy fewer elaborate floral decorations.

Floral designers are largely concentrated in florist shops, where overall employment is expected to decline. Customers are purchasing fewer elaborate floral decorations from such shops, and increasingly buying loose cut fresh flowers from grocery stores and general merchandise stores. As a result, employment of floral designers is expected to decline 29 percent in florist shops and increase 8 percent in grocery stores.

Employment projections data for floral designers, 2010-20

Occupational Title	SOC Code	Employment, 2010	Projected Employment, 2020	Change, 2010-20 Percent	Change, 2010-20 Numeric
Floral Designers	27-1023	66,500	60,300	-9	-6,200
SOURCE: U.S. Bureau of Labor Statistics, Employment Projections program					

Similar Occupations

This table shows a list of occupations with job duties that are similar to those of floral designers.

Occupation	Job Duties	Entry-Level Education	Median Annual Pay, May 2010
Art Directors	Art directors are responsible for the visual style and images in magazines, newspapers, product packaging, and movie and television productions. They create the overall design and direct others who develop artwork or layouts.	Bachelor's degree	$80,630
Craft and Fine Artists	Craft and fine artists use a variety of materials and techniques to create art for sale and exhibition. Craft artists create handmade objects, such as pottery, glassware, textiles, or other objects that are designed to be functional. Fine artists, including painters, sculptors, and illustrators, create original works of art for their aesthetic value, rather than a functional one.	High school diploma or equivalent	$43,470
Meeting, Convention, and Event Planners	Meeting, convention, and event planners coordinate all aspects of professional meetings and events. They choose meeting locations, arrange transportation, and coordinate other details.	Bachelor's degree	$45,260
Fashion Designers	Fashion designers create original clothing, accessories, and footwear. They sketch designs, select fabrics and patterns, and give instructions on how to make the products they designed.	High school diploma or equivalent	$64,530
Graphic Designers	Graphic designers create visual concepts, by hand or using computer software, to communicate ideas that inspire, inform, or captivate consumers. They help to make an organization recognizable by selecting color, images, or logo designs that represent a particular idea or identity to be used in advertising and promotions.	Bachelor's degree	$43,500
Industrial Designers	Industrial designers develop the concepts for manufactured products, such as cars, home appliances, and toys. They combine art, business, and engineering to make products that people use every day.	Bachelor's degree	$58,230
Interior Designers	Interior designers make interior spaces functional, safe, and beautiful for almost every type of building: offices, homes, airport terminals, shopping malls, and restaurants. They select and specify colors, finishes, fabrics, furniture, flooring and wallcoverings, lighting, and other materials to create useful and stylish interiors for buildings.	Bachelor's degree	$46,280

Contacts for More Information

For more information about becoming a Certified Floral Designer, visit American Institute of Floral Designers

For more information about careers in floral design, visit Society of American Florists

Suggested citation:

Bureau of Labor Statistics, U.S. Department of Labor, Occupational Outlook Handbook, 2012-13 Edition, Floral Designers, on the Internet at http://www.bls.gov/ooh/arts-and-design/floral-designers.htm.

Graphic Designers

Quick Facts: Graphic Designers	
2010 Median Pay	$43,500 per year $20.92 per hour
Entry-Level Education	Bachelor's degree
Work Experience in a Related Occupation	None
On-the-job Training	None
Number of Jobs, 2010	279,200
Job Outlook, 2010-20	13% (About as fast as average)
Employment Change, 2010-20	37,300

What Graphic Designers Do

Graphic designers create visual concepts, by hand or using computer software, to communicate ideas that inspire, inform, or captivate consumers. They help to make an organization recognizable by selecting color, images, or logo designs that represent a particular idea or identity to be used in advertising and promotions.

Duties

Graphic designers typically do the following:
- Meet with clients or the art director to determine the scope of a project
- Advise clients on strategies to reach a particular audience
- Determine the message the design should portray
- Create images that identify a product or convey a message
- Develop graphics and visual or audio images for product illustrations, logos, and websites
- Create designs either by hand or using computer software packages
- Select colors, images, text style, and layout
- Present the design to clients or the art director
- Incorporate changes recommended by the clients into the final design
- Review designs for errors before printing or publishing them

Graphic designers combine art and technology to communicate ideas through images and the layout of web screens and printed pages. They may use a variety of design elements to achieve artistic or decorative effects. They develop the overall layout and production design for advertisements, brochures, magazines, and corporate reports.

Graphic designers work with both text and images. They often select the type, font, size, color, and line length of headlines, headings, and text. Graphic designers also decide how images and text will go together on a page or screen, including how much space each will have. When using text in layouts, graphic designers collaborate closely with writers who choose the words and decide whether the words will be put into paragraphs, lists, or tables.

Graphic design is becoming increasingly important in the sales and marketing of products. Therefore, graphic designers, also referred to as graphic artists or communication designers, often work closely with people in advertising and promotions, public relations, and marketing.

Frequently, designers specialize in a particular category or type of client. For example, some create credits for motion pictures, while others work with print media and create signs or posters.

Graphic designers also need to keep up to date with the latest software and computer technologies to remain competitive.

Some individuals with a background in graphic designers teach in design schools, colleges, and universities. For more information, see the profile on postsecondary teachers .

Work Environment

Graphic designers held about 279,200 jobs in 2010. Graphic designers are most commonly employed in the following industries:

Specialized design services	9%
Newspaper, periodical, book, and directory publishers	9
Advertising, public relations, and related services	8
Printing and related support activities	6
Computer systems design and related services	3

Graphic designers generally work in studios where they have access to drafting tables, computers, and the software necessary to create their designs. Although many graphic designers work independently, those who work for specialized graphic design firms

Graphic designers generally work in a studio where they have access to drafting tables and computers.

often work as part of a design team. Some designers telecommute. Many graphic designers collaborate with colleagues on projects or work with clients located around the world.

Work Schedules

Most graphic designers work full time, but schedules can vary depending on workload and deadlines.

In 2010, about 29 percent of graphic designers were self-employed. Graphic designers who are self-employed may need to adjust their workday to meet with clients in the evenings or on weekends. In addition, they may spend some of their time looking for new projects or competing with other designers for contracts.

How to Become a Graphic Designer

A bachelor's degree in graphic design or a related field is usually required for jobs in this field. Candidates should demonstrate their creativity and originality through a professional portfolio that features their best designs.

Education

A bachelor's degree in graphic design or a related field is usually required. However, those with a bachelor's degree in another field may pursue technical training in graphic design to meet most hiring qualifications.

The National Association of Schools of Art and Design accredits about 300 postsecondary colleges, universities, and independent institutes with programs in art and design. Most schools include studio art, principles of design, computerized design, commercial graphics production, printing techniques, and website design. In addition, students should consider courses in writing, marketing, and business, all of which are useful in helping designers work effectively on project teams.

Many programs provide students with the opportunity to build a professional portfolio of their designs. This means collecting examples of their designs from classroom projects, internships, or other experiences. Students can use these examples of their work to demonstrate their design skills when applying for jobs and bidding on projects. A good portfolio often is the deciding factor in getting a job.

Students interested in graphic design programs should take basic art and design courses in high school, if the courses are available. Many bachelor's degree programs require students to have had a year of basic art and design courses before being admitted to a formal degree program. Some schools require applicants to submit sketches and other examples of their artistic ability.

Graphic designers must keep up with new and updated computer graphics and design software, either on their own or through formal software training programs.

Advancement

Beginning graphic designers usually need 1 to 3 years of work experience before they can advance to higher positions. Experienced graphic designers may advance to chief designer, art or creative director, or other supervisory positions.

Important Qualities

Artistic ability. Graphic designers must be able to create designs that are artistically interesting and appealing to clients and consumers. They produce rough illustrations of design ideas, either by hand sketching or by using a computer program.

Communication skills. Graphic designers must communicate with clients, customers, and other designers to ensure that their designs accurately reflect the desired message and effectively express information.

Computer skills. Most graphic designers use specialized graphic design software to prepare their designs.

Creativity. Graphic designers must be able to think of new approaches to communicating ideas to consumers. They develop unique designs that convey a recognizable meaning on behalf of their clients.

Teamwork. Graphic designers often work on projects with other graphic designers and marketers, business analysts, writers, and programmers. They must collaborate to produce successful websites, publications, and other products.

Time-management skills. Graphic designers often work on multiple projects at the same time, each with a different deadline.

Pay

Graphic Designers
Median annual wages, May 2010

Graphic Designers	$43,500
Arts, Design, Entertainment, Sports, and Media Occupations	$42,870
Total, All Occupations	$33,840

Note: All Occupations includes all occupations in the U.S. Economy.
Source: U.S. Bureau of Labor Statistics, Occupational Employment Statistics

The median annual wage of graphic designers was $43,500 in May 2010. The median wage is the wage at which half the workers in an occupation earned more than that amount and half earned less. The lowest 10 percent earned less than $26,200, and the top 10 percent earned more than $76,910.

Most graphic designers work full time, but schedules can vary depending on workload and deadlines.

In 2010, about 29 percent of graphic designers were self-employed. Graphic designers who are self-employed may need to adjust their workday to meet with clients in the evenings or on weekends. In addition, they may spend some of their time looking for new projects or competing with other designers for contracts.

Job Outlook

Graphic Designers
Percent change in employment, projected 2010-20

Total, All Occupations	14%
Graphic Designers	13%
Arts, Design, Entertainment, Sports, and Media Occupations	13%

Note: All Occupations includes all occupations in the U.S. Economy.
Source: U.S. Bureau of Labor Statistics, Employment Projections program

Employment of graphic designers is expected to increase by 13 percent from 2010 to 2020, about as fast as the average for all occupations.

Employment of graphic designers in printing and publishing is expected to increase by 2 percent and decline by 4 percent respectively, during the projection period. However, as shown in the table below, employment for graphic designers in computer systems design and related services is expected to grow by 61 percent over the same period.

Computer systems design and related services	61%
Specialized design services	27
Advertising, public relations, and related services	17
Printing and related support activities	2
Publishing industries (except Internet)	-4

With the increased use of the Internet, designers will be needed to create designs and images for portable devices, websites, electronic publications, and video entertainment media.

Graphic designers will take on increasingly important roles in the marketing of products. For example, graphic designers working in advertising or for computer design firms may influence the design of websites and publications. Designers will work with advertising and marketing staff to create graphics for websites, mobile phones, and other technology.

Job Prospects

Graphic designers are expected to face competition for available positions. Many talented individuals are attracted to careers as graphic designers. Prospects will be best for job applicants with website design and other interactive media experience.

Employment projections data for graphic designers, 2010-20

Occupational Title	SOC Code	Employment, 2010	Projected Employment, 2020	Change, 2010-20 Percent	Change, 2010-20 Numeric
Graphic Designers	27-1024	279,200	316,500	13	37,300

SOURCE: U.S. Bureau of Labor Statistics, Employment Projections program

Similar Occupations

This table shows a list of occupations with job duties that are similar to those of graphic designers.

Occupation	Job Duties	Entry-Level Education	Median Annual Pay, May 2010
Advertising, Promotions, and Marketing Managers	Advertising, promotions, and marketing managers plan programs to generate interest in a product or service. They work with art directors, sales agents, and financial staff members.	Bachelor's degree	$108,260
Art Directors	Art directors are responsible for the visual style and images in magazines, newspapers, product packaging, and movie and television productions. They create the overall design and direct others who develop artwork or layouts.	Bachelor's degree	$80,630
Craft and Fine Artists	Craft and fine artists use a variety of materials and techniques to create art for sale and exhibition. Craft artists create handmade objects, such as pottery, glassware, textiles, or other objects that are designed to be functional. Fine artists, including painters, sculptors, and illustrators, create original works of art for their aesthetic value, rather than a functional one.	High school diploma or equivalent	$43,470
Desktop Publishers	Desktop publishers use computer software to design page layouts for newspapers, books, brochures, and other items that will be printed or put online. They collect the text, graphics, and other materials they will need and then format them into a finished product.	Associate's degree	$36,610
Drafters	Drafters use software to convert the designs of engineers and architects into technical drawings and plans. Workers in production and construction use these plans to build everything from microchips to skyscrapers.	Associate's degree	$47,880
Industrial Designers	Industrial designers develop the concepts for manufactured products, such as cars, home appliances, and toys. They combine art, business, and engineering to make products that people use every day.	Bachelor's degree	$58,230
Information Security Analysts, Web Developers, and Computer Network Architects	Information security analysts, web developers, and computer network architects all use information technology (IT) to advance their organization's goals. Security analysts ensure a firm's information stays safe from cyberattacks. Web developers create websites to help firms have a public face. Computer network architects create the internal networks all workers within organizations use.	Bachelor's degree	$75,660
Multimedia Artists and Animators	Multimedia artists and animators create animation and visual effects for television, movies, video games, and other media. They create two- and three-dimensional models and animation.	Bachelor's degree	$58,510
Printing Workers	Printing workers produce print material in three stages: prepress, press, and binding and finishing. They review specifications, identify and fix problems with printing equipment, and assemble pages.	See How to Become One	$33,150
Technical Writers	Technical writers, also called technical communicators, produce instruction manuals and other supporting documents to communicate complex and technical information more easily. They also develop, gather, and disseminate technical information among customers, designers, and manufacturers.	Bachelor's degree	$63,280

Contacts for More Information

For general career information about graphic design, visit The Professional Association for Design

Graphic Artists Guild

For general information about art and design and a list of accredited college-level programs, visit National Association of Schools of Art and Design

Suggested citation:

Bureau of Labor Statistics, U.S. Department of Labor, Occupational Outlook Handbook, 2012-13 Edition, Graphic Designers, on the Internet at http://www.bls.gov/ooh/arts-and-design/graphic-designers.htm.

Industrial Designers

Quick Facts: Industrial Designers	
2010 Median Pay	$58,230 per year $27.99 per hour
Entry-Level Education	Bachelor's degree
Work Experience in a Related Occupation	None
On-the-job Training	None
Number of Jobs, 2010	40,800
Job Outlook, 2010-20	10% (About as fast as average)
Employment Change, 2010-20	4,300

What Industrial Designers Do

Industrial designers develop the concepts for manufactured products, such as cars, home appliances, and toys. They combine art, business, and engineering to make products that people use every day. Industrial designers focus on the user experience in creating style and function for a particular gadget or appliance.

Duties

Industrial designers typically do the following:

- Research who will use the product and the various ways it might be used
- Sketch out ideas or create blueprints
- Use computer software to develop virtual models of different designs
- Examine materials and production costs to determine manufacturing requirements

Industrial designers work primarily in offices, but they may travel to the places where the products are manufactured.

- Work with other specialists to evaluate whether their design concepts will fill the need at a reasonable cost
- Evaluate product safety, appearance, and function to determine if a design is practical
- Present designs and demonstrate prototypes to clients for approval

Industrial designers generally focus on a particular product category. For example, some design medical equipment, while others work on consumer electronics products, such as computers or smart phones. Other designers develop ideas for new bicycles, furniture, housewares, or snowboards.

They imagine how consumers might use a product and test different designs with consumers to see how each design looks and works. Industrial designers often work with engineers, production experts, and marketing specialists to find out if their designs are feasible and to apply their colleagues' professional expertise to their designs. For example, industrial designers may work with marketing specialists to develop plans to market new product designs to consumers.

Computers are a major tool for industrial designers. They use computer-aided design software (CAD) to sketch ideas because computers make it easy to make changes and show alternatives. If they work for manufacturers, they may also use computer-aided industrial design software (CAID) to create specific machine-readable instructions that tell other machines exactly how to build the product.

Work Environment

Industrial designers held about 40,800 jobs in 2010. Work spaces for industrial designers often include drafting tables for sketching designs, meeting rooms with whiteboards for brainstorming with colleagues, and computers and other office equipment for preparing designs and communicating with clients. Although industrial designers work primarily in offices, they may travel to testing facilities, design centers, client's exhibit sites, users' homes or workplaces, and places where the product is manufactured.

Although they design manufactured products, only about 29 percent of industrial designers are employed directly by manufacturers.

The following industries employed the most industrial designers in 2010:

Manufacturing	29%
Architectural, engineering, and related services	8
Specialized design services	7
Wholesale trade	6
Retail trade	3

Work Schedules

Most industrial designers work full time, especially if they are employed by manufacturers, large corporations, or design firms.

Many industrial designers are self-employed or work for firms that hire them out to other organizations that need industrial design services. In these cases, industrial designers frequently adjust their workday to meet with clients in the evenings or on weekends. In addition, they may spend some of their time looking for new projects or competing with other designers for contracts.

How to Become an Industrial Designer

A bachelor's degree is usually required for most entry-level industrial design jobs. It is also important for industrial designers to have a professional portfolio with examples of their best design projects.

Education

A bachelor's degree in industrial design, architecture, or engineering is usually required for entry-level industrial design jobs. Most design programs include the courses that industrial designers need in design: sketching, computer-aided design and drafting (CADD), industrial materials and processes, and manufacturing methods.

The National Association of Schools of Art and Design accredits approximately 300 postsecondary colleges, universities, and independent institutes with programs in art and design. Many schools require successful completion of some basic art and design courses before entry into a bachelor's degree program. Applicants also may need to submit sketches and other examples of their artistic ability.

Many programs provide students with the opportunity to build a professional portfolio of their designs by collecting examples of their designs from classroom projects, internships, or other experiences. Students can use these examples of their work to demonstrate their design skills when applying for jobs and bidding on contracts for work.

An increasing number of designers are also getting a Master of Business Administration (MBA) to gain business skills. Business skills help designers understand how to fit their designs into a firm's overall business plan.

Work Experience

Industrial designers typically demonstrate their knowledge and skill by promoting their best designs from previous projects. Work experience is another way to build a good reputation and establish expertise in an industrial design specialty.

Advancement

Experienced designers in large firms may advance to chief designer, design department head, or other supervisory positions. Some designers become teachers in design schools or in colleges and universities. Many teachers continue to consult privately or operate small design studios in addition to teaching. Some experienced designers open their own design firms.

Important Qualities

Creativity. Industrial designers must be innovative. They imagine new designs and new uses for their products.

Critical-thinking skills. They use logic or reasoning skills to study the market for new products and participate in planning new products.

Interpersonal skills. Industrial designers must communicate well to develop cooperative working relationships with colleagues and customers.

Problem-solving skills. They identify complex design problems, such as the need, size, cost, and anticipate production issues, then develop alternatives, evaluate options, and implement solutions.

Technical skills. Industrial designers must understand the technical aspects of how products work, at least for the types of products that they design.

Pay

Industrial Designers
Median annual wages, May 2010

Commercial and Industrial Designers	$58,230
Arts, Design, Entertainment, Sports, and Media Occupations	$42,870
Total, All Occupations	$33,840

Note: All Occupations includes all occupations in the U.S. Economy.
Source: U.S. Bureau of Labor Statistics, Occupational Employment Statistics

The median annual wage of industrial designers was $58,230 in May 2010. The median wage is the wage at which half the workers in an occupation earned more than that amount and half earned less. The lowest 10 percent earned less than $33,190, and the top 10 percent earned more than $94,270.

As shown in the tabulation below, median annual wages for industrial designers in the manufacturing industry was $55,520 in May 2010, lower than the median annual wage for the occupation in general.

Architectural, engineering, and related services	$68,790
Specialized design services	56,300
Manufacturing	55,520
Wholesale trade	55,170
Retail trade	45,090

Most industrial designers work full time, especially if they are employed by manufacturers, large corporations, or design firms.

Many industrial designers are self-employed or work for firms that hire them out to other organizations that need industrial design services. In these cases, industrial designers frequently adjust their workday to meet with clients in the evenings or on weekends. In addition, they may spend some of their time looking for new projects or competing with other designers for contracts.

Job Outlook

Industrial Designers
Percent change in employment, projected 2010-20

Total, All Occupations	14%
Arts, Design, Entertainment, Sports, and Media Occupations	13%
Commercial and Industrial Designers	10%

Note: All Occupations includes all occupations in the U.S. Economy.
Source: U.S. Bureau of Labor Statistics, Employment Projections program

Employment of industrial designers is expected to grow by 10 percent from 2010 to 2020, about as fast as the average for all occupations. Increasing consumer demand for new products and new product styles should increase demand for industrial designers. However, growth will be slower for contract design firms because smaller manufacturers are usually cautious about committing new resources for product development.

Employment of industrial designers who design precision

instruments and medical equipment is likely to grow more rapidly. Both areas require a high degree of technical ability and design sophistication. Products in these areas also require detailed specifications and precise equipment manufacturing because of the delicate uses of the finished product.

Job Prospects

Prospects are best for job applicants with a strong background in computer-aided design (CAD) and computer-aided industrial design (CAID).

Employment projections data for industrial designers, 2010-20

Occupational Title	SOC Code	Employment, 2010	Projected Employment, 2020	Change, 2010-20	
				Percent	Numeric
Commercial and Industrial Designers	27-1021	40,800	45,100	10	4,300
SOURCE: U.S. Bureau of Labor Statistics, Employment Projections program					

Similar Occupations

This table shows a list of occupations with job duties that are similar to those of industrial designers.

Occupation	Job Duties	Entry-Level Education	Median Annual Pay, May 2010
Architects	Architects plan and design buildings and other structures.	Bachelor's degree	$72,550
Computer Programmers	Computer programmers write code to create software programs. They turn the program designs created by software developers and engineers into instructions that a computer can follow.	Bachelor's degree	$71,380
Desktop Publishers	Desktop publishers use computer software to design page layouts for newspapers, books, brochures, and other items that will be printed or put online. They collect the text, graphics, and other materials they will need and then format them into a finished product.	Associate's degree	$36,610
Drafters	Drafters use software to convert the designs of engineers and architects into technical drawings and plans. Workers in production and construction use these plans to build everything from microchips to skyscrapers.	Associate's degree	$47,880
Graphic Designers	Graphic designers create visual concepts, by hand or using computer software, to communicate ideas that inspire, inform, or captivate consumers. They help to make an organization recognizable by selecting color, images, or logo designs that represent a particular idea or identity to be used in advertising and promotions.	Bachelor's degree	$43,500
Industrial Engineers	Industrial engineers find ways to eliminate wastefulness in production processes. They devise efficient ways to use workers, machines, materials, information, and energy to make a product or provide a service.	Bachelor's degree	$76,100
Interior Designers	Interior designers make interior spaces functional, safe, and beautiful for almost every type of building: offices, homes, airport terminals, shopping malls, and restaurants. They select and specify colors, finishes, fabrics, furniture, flooring and wallcoverings, lighting, and other materials to create useful and stylish interiors for buildings.	Bachelor's degree	$46,280
Software Developers	Software developers are the creative minds behind computer programs. Some develop the applications that allow people to do specific tasks on a computer or other device. Others develop the underlying systems that run the devices or control networks.	Bachelor's degree	$90,530

Contacts for More Information

For more information about industrial designers, visit Industrial Designers Society of America

For more information about accredited college-level programs in art and design, visit National Association of Schools of Art and Design

Suggested citation:

Bureau of Labor Statistics, U.S. Department of Labor, Occupational Outlook Handbook, 2012-13 Edition, Industrial Designers, on the Internet at http://www.bls.gov/ooh/arts-and-design/industrial-designers.htm.

Interior Designers

Quick Facts: Interior Designers	
2010 Median Pay	$46,280 per year $22.25 per hour
Entry-Level Education	Bachelor's degree
Work Experience in a Related Occupation	None
On-the-job Training	None
Number of Jobs, 2010	56,500
Job Outlook, 2010-20	19% (About as fast as average)
Employment Change, 2010-20	10,900

What Interior Designers Do

Interior designers make interior spaces functional, safe, and beautiful for almost every type of building: offices, homes, airport terminals, shopping malls, and restaurants. They select and specify colors, finishes, fabrics, furniture, flooring and wallcoverings, lighting, and other materials to create useful and stylish interiors for buildings.

Duties

Interior designers typically do the following:
- Determine the client's goals and requirements of the project
- Consider how the space will be used and how people will move through the space
- Sketch preliminary design plans
- Specify materials and furnishings, such as lighting, furniture, wallcoverings, flooring, equipment, and artwork
- Prepare final plans using computer applications
- Create a timeline for the interior design project and estimate project costs
- Oversee installing the design elements
- Visit after the project to ensure that the client is satisfied
- Search for and bid on new projects

Interior designers work closely with architects, structural engineers, and builders to determine how interior spaces will look and be furnished. Interior designers may read blueprints and must be aware of building codes and inspection regulations.

Although some sketches or drawings may be freehand, most interior designers use computer-aided design (CAD) software for the majority of their drawings.

Interior designers make interior spaces functional, safe, and beautiful for almost every type of building.

Many designers specialize in particular types of buildings (homes, hospitals, or hotels), specific rooms (bathrooms or kitchens), or specific styles (early American or French Renaissance). Some designers work for home furnishings stores, providing design services to help customers choose materials and furnishings.

Some interior designers produce designs, plans, and drawings for construction and installation. This may include floor plans, lighting plans, or plans needed for building permits. Interior designers may draft the preliminary design into documents that could be as simple as sketches or as inclusive as construction documents, with schedules and attachments.

The following are examples of types of interior designers.

Sustainable designers use strategies to improve energy and water efficiencies and indoor air quality, and they specify environmentally preferable products such as bamboo or cork for floors. They may obtain certification in Leadership in Energy and Environmental Design (LEED) from the U.S. Green Building Council. Such certification indicates that a building or its interior space was designed with the use of sustainable concepts.

Universal designers renovate spaces to make them more accessible. Often, these designs are used to renovate spaces for elderly people or people with special needs; however, universal designs can benefit anyone. For example, an entry with no steps may be necessary for someone in a wheelchair, but it is also helpful for someone pushing a baby stroller.

Kitchen and bath designers specialize in kitchens and bathrooms and have expert knowledge of the variety of cabinets, fixtures, appliances, plumbing, and electrical solutions for these rooms.

Lighting designers focus on the effect of lighting for home, office, or public spaces. For example, lighting designers may work on stage productions, in gallery or museum spaces, or in health care facilities to find appropriate light fixtures and lighting effects for each space.

Closet designers design closet space for homes to maximize storage and increase orderliness. They work with both fixed structures and stand-alone storage systems.

Work Environment

Interior designers held about 56,500 jobs in 2010. Most interior designers work in clean, comfortable offices. About 30 percent of interior designers were self-employed, and some of these designers worked from home. Technology has changed the way many designers work. For example, rather than using drafting tables, interior designers now use complex software to create 2-D or 3-D images on the computer.

As shown in the following tabulation, about 27 percent of interior designers worked in the specialized design services industry. About 14 percent of interior designers worked in the architectural, engineering, and related services industry. About 4 percent of interior designers are employed in the construction industry, but many others are heavily dependent on the industry to generate new construction or renovation projects for them to work on. Another 8 percent worked in the furniture and home furnishings stores industry.

Specialized design services	27%
Architectural, engineering, and related service	14
Furniture and home furnishings stores	8
Building material and supplies dealers	4
Construction	4

Work Schedules

Most interior designers work full time. They may need to adjust their workday to suit their clients' schedules and deadlines, meeting with clients during evening and weekend hours when necessary. Interior designers also travel to the clients' design sites.

How to Become an Interior Designer

Interior designers need a bachelor's degree plus training in interior design.

Education

A bachelor's degree is usually required, as are classes in interior design, drawing, and computer-aided design (CAD). A bachelor's degree in any field is acceptable, and interior design programs are available at the associate's, bachelor's, and master's degree levels.

The National Association of Schools of Art and Design accredits about 300 postsecondary colleges, universities, and independent institutes with programs in art and design. The Council for Interior Design Accreditation accredits more than 150 professional-level (bachelor's or master's degrees) interior design programs.

The National Kitchen and Bath Association accredits kitchen and bath design specialty programs (certificate, associate's, and bachelor's degree level) in 46 colleges and universities.

Applicants may be required to submit sketches and other examples of their artistic ability for admission to interior design programs.

Licenses

Licensure requirements vary by state. Many states have laws that restrict the use of the title €œinterior designer.€ For example, in these states, both licensed and unlicensed designers may do interior design work. But only those who pass their state-approved exam, most commonly the National Council for Interior Design Qualification (NCIDQ) exam, may call themselves registered interior designers.

The NCIDQ exam is the nationally recognized exam required for licensure. (California requires a different exam, administered by the California Council for Interior Design Certification.) Qualification to take the exam include a combination of education and experience. Typically, applicants have at least a bachelor's degree in interior design plus 2 years of experience.

Certification

Voluntary certification in an interior design specialty, such as kitchens and baths, allows interior designers to demonstrate their expertise in a particular area of interior design. Interior designers often specialize to distinguish the type of design work they do and to promote their expertise. Certifications usually are available through professional or trade associations and are independent from the NCIDQ licensing examination.

Important Qualities

Artistic ability. Interior designers use their sense of style to develop designs that look great and are aesthetically pleasing.

Creativity. Interior designers need to be imaginative in selecting furnishings and fabrics and in creating spaces that serve the client's needs and fit the client's lifestyle.

Detail oriented. Interior designers need to be precise in measuring interior spaces and making drawings so that furniture and furnishings will fit correctly and create the appropriate environment.

Interpersonal skills. Interior designers need to be able to communicate effectively with clients and others. Much of their time is spent soliciting new work and new clients and collaborating with other designers, engineers, and general building contractors on ongoing projects.

Problem-solving skills. Interior designers must address challenges such as construction delays or the high cost or sudden unavailability of selected materials while keeping the project on time and within budget.

Visualization. Interior designers need a strong sense of proportion and visual awareness to understand how pieces of a design will fit together to create the intended interior environment.

Pay

Interior Designers
Median annual wages, May 2010

Interior Designers	$46,280
Arts, Design, Entertainment, Sports, and Media Occupations	$42,870
Total, All Occupations	$33,840

Note: All Occupations includes all occupations in the U.S. Economy.
Source: U.S. Bureau of Labor Statistics, Occupational Employment Statistics

The median annual wage of interior designers was $46,280 in May 2010. The median wage is the wage at which half the workers in an occupation earned more than that amount and half earned less. The lowest 10 percent earned less than $26,380, and the top 10 percent earned more than $84,900.

As shown in the tabulation below, median annual wage for interior designers in architectural, engineering, and related services was $51,990 in May 2010, the highest among those industries employing much of the occupation.

Architectural, engineering, and related services	$51,990
Specialized design services	45,280
Construction	44,350
Furniture and home furnishings stores	40,320
Building material and supplies dealers	38,720

Most interior designers work full time. They may need to adjust their workday to suit their clients' schedules and deadlines, meeting with clients during evening and weekend hours when necessary. Interior designers also travel to the clients' design sites.

Job Outlook

Interior Designers
Percent change in employment, projected 2010-20

Interior Designers	19%
Total, All Occupations	14%
Arts, Design, Entertainment, Sports, and Media Occupations	13%

Note: All Occupations includes all occupations in the U.S. Economy.
Source: U.S. Bureau of Labor Statistics, Employment Projections program

Employment of interior designers is expected to grow by 19 percent from 2010 to 2020, about as fast as the average for all occupations. Designers will be needed to respond to consumer expectations that the interiors of homes and offices meet certain conditions, such as being environmentally friendly or more easily accessible.

Although the number of home remodeling projects that use interior designers is related to economic conditions, remodeling of large public spaces and facilities, such as hospitals, hotels, and schools, is often funded as part of a long-term project. Companies typically budget money over many years so that they can afford remodeling efforts when necessary, regardless of economic conditions. In addition, as part of creating their corporate image, more companies are expected to take advantage of opportunities to use new furnishing and design concepts to make their interior space easily identifiable.

Employment for interior designers in specialized design firms is expected to grow by 27 percent from 2010 to 2020. As interior designers focus on increasingly specialized design areas, there will be a greater need for them to collaborate with other designers and in other design-related fields.

Job Prospects

Job prospects should be better in higher income areas, because wealthier clients are more likely to engage in remodeling or renovating their homes.

Interior designers who specialize, such as those who design kitchens, may benefit by becoming an expert in their particular area. By specializing in a unique area of design, interior designers can use their knowledge of products to better fulfill customer requests.

Employment projections data for interior designers, 2010-20

Occupational Title	SOC Code	Employment, 2010	Projected Employment, 2020	Change, 2010-20 Percent	Change, 2010-20 Numeric
Interior Designers	27-1025	56,500	67,400	19	10,900 .
SOURCE: U.S. Bureau of Labor Statistics, Employment Projections program					

Similar Occupations

This table shows a list of occupations with job duties that are similar to those of interior designers.

Occupation	Job Duties	Entry-Level Education	Median Annual Pay, May 2010
Architects	Architects plan and design buildings and other structures.	Bachelor's degree	$72,550
Art Directors	Art directors are responsible for the visual style and images in magazines, newspapers, product packaging, and movie and television productions. They create the overall design and direct others who develop artwork or layouts.	Bachelor's degree	$80,630
Craft and Fine Artists	Craft and fine artists use a variety of materials and techniques to create art for sale and exhibition. Craft artists create handmade objects, such as pottery, glassware, textiles, or other objects that are designed to be functional. Fine artists, including painters, sculptors, and illustrators, create original works of art for their aesthetic value, rather than a functional one.	High school diploma or equivalent	$43,470
Fashion Designers	Fashion designers create original clothing, accessories, and footwear. They sketch designs, select fabrics and patterns, and give instructions on how to make the products they designed.	High school diploma or equivalent	$64,530
Floral Designers	Floral designers, also called florists, cut and arrange live, dried, or silk flowers and greenery to make decorative displays. They also help customers select flowers, containers, ribbons, and other accessories.	High school diploma or equivalent	$23,610
Industrial Designers	Industrial designers develop the concepts for manufactured products, such as cars, home appliances, and toys. They combine art, business, and engineering to make products that people use every day.	Bachelor's degree	$58,230
Landscape Architects	Landscape architects plan and design land areas for parks, recreational facilities, highways, airports, and other properties. Projects include subdivisions and commercial, industrial, and residential sites.	Bachelor's degree	$62,090

Contacts for More Information

For more information about interior designers, visit American Society of Interior Designers, International Interior Design Association

For more information on accredited college degree programs in interior design, visit National Association of Schools of Art and Design, Council for Interior Design Accreditation

For more information on the national licensure qualifying exam, visit National Council for Interior Design Qualification

For more information on accredited kitchen and bath specialty programs in colleges and universities and voluntary certification

programs in residential kitchen and bath design, visit National Kitchen & Bath Association

Suggested citation:

Bureau of Labor Statistics, U.S. Department of Labor, Occupational Outlook Handbook, 2012-13 Edition, Interior Designers, on the Internet at http://www.bls.gov/ooh/arts-and-design/interior-designers.htm.

Multimedia Artists and Animators

Quick Facts: Multimedia Artists and Animators	
2010 Median Pay	$58,510 per year $28.13 per hour
Entry-Level Education	Bachelor's degree
Work Experience in a Related Occupation	None
On-the-job Training	Moderate-term on-the-job training
Number of Jobs, 2010	66,500
Job Outlook, 2010-20	8% (Slower than average)
Employment Change, 2010-20	5,500

What Multimedia Artists and Animators Do

Multimedia artists and animators create animation and visual effects for television, movies, video games, and other forms of media. They create two- and three-dimensional models and animation.

Duties

Multimedia artists and animators typically do the following:

- Create graphics and animation using computer programs and illustration
- Work with a team of animators and artists to create a movie, game, or visual effect
- Research upcoming projects to help create a realistic design or animation
- Develop storyboards that map out key scenes in the animation
- Edit animation and effects based on feedback from directors, head animators, game designers, or clients
- Meet with clients, head animators, games designers, and directors to review deadlines and development timelines

Multimedia artists and animators often work in a specific medium. Some focus on creating animated movies or video games. Others create visual effects for movies and television shows. Visual effects, also called computer generated images or CGI, include creating animation from images of actors performing or designing scenery or backgrounds for locations.

Artists and animators can further specialize within these fields. Within animated movies and video games, artists often specialize in

Multimedia artists and animators often work in a specific form of media, such as animated movies, video games, or visual effects.

characters or scenery and background design. Video game artists may focus on level design: creating the look, feel, and layout for the levels of a video game.

Animators work in teams to develop a movie, visual effect, or electronic game. Each animator works on a portion of the project, and then they put the pieces together to create one cohesive animation.

Some multimedia artists and animators create their work primarily using computer software or by writing their own computer code. Many animation companies have their own computer animation software that artists must learn to use.

Other artists and animators prefer to work by drawing and painting by hand and then translating that work into computer programs. Some multimedia artists use storyboards, which look like a comic strip, to help visualize the final product during the design process.

Work Environment

Multimedia artists and animators held 66,500 jobs in 2010. In 2010, 59 percent of workers were self-employed. They often work from home. Some work for motion picture or video game studios. They frequently work in offices.

In 2010, the industries employing the most multimedia artists were as follows:

Motion picture and video industries	11%
Software publishers	5
Computer systems design and related services	5
Advertising, public relations, and related services	5

Work Schedules

Multimedia artists and animators often work long hours; it is not unusual for them to work 50-hour weeks. When deadlines are approaching, they may work nights and weekends.

How to Become a Multimedia Artist or Animator

Many multimedia artists and animators pursue a bachelor's degree in computer graphics, art, or a related field to develop a good portfolio of work and learn the strong technical skills that many employers prefer.

Education

Employers typically do not require a degree, but they look for workers who have a good portfolio of work and strong technical skills. However, many multimedia artists and animators have a bachelor's degree in fine art, computer graphics, animation, or a related field. Programs in computer graphics often include courses in computer science, such as programming, and in graphics.

Bachelor's degree programs in art include courses in painting, drawing, and sculpture. Degrees in animation often require classes in drawing, animation, and film. Some schools have specialized degrees in topics such as interactive media or game design.

Training

Some animation studios have their own software and computer applications that they use to create films. They give workers on-the-job training to use this software. Animators may be hired for a probationary period while they prove that they have the skills and talent to become a permanent employee.

Important Qualities

Artistic talent. Animators and artists should have artistic ability and a good understanding of color, texture, and light. However, they may be able to compensate for a lack of artistic ability with better technical skills.

Computer skills. Many multimedia artists and animators do most of their work using computer programs or writing programming code. However, those with artistic talent may be able to find work without strong computer skills.

Creativity. Artists and animators must be able to think creatively to develop original ideas and make their ideas come to life.

People skills. Multimedia artists and animators need to work as part of a team and respond well to criticism and feedback.

Physical stamina. The hours required by most studio and game design companies are long, particularly when there are tight deadlines. Artists and animators need to be able to keep up with the long hours and challenging work.

Pay

Multimedia Artists and Animators
  Median annual wages, May 2010

Multimedia Artists and Animators	$58,510
Art and Design Workers	$41,490
Total, All Occupations	$33,840

Note: All Occupations includes all occupations in the U.S. Economy.
Source: U.S. Bureau of Labor Statistics, Occupational Employment Statistics

The median annual wage of multimedia artists and animators was $58,510 in May 2010. The median wage is the wage at which half the workers in an occupation earned more than that amount and half earned less. The lowest 10 percent earned less than $33,840, and the top 10 percent earned more than $99,830.

In May 2010, annual median wages of multimedia artists and animators in the industries employing the most multimedia artists and animators were as follows:

Motion picture and video industries	$66,190
Software publishers	65,290
Computer systems design and related services	56,000
Advertising, public relations, and related services	55,890

Multimedia artists and animators often work long hours; it is not unusual for them to work 50-hour weeks. When deadlines are approaching, they may work nights and weekends.

Job Outlook

Multimedia Artists and Animators
  Percent change in employment, projected 2010-20

Total, All Occupations	14%
Art and Design Workers	10%
Multimedia Artists and Animators	8%

Note: All Occupations includes all occupations in the U.S. Economy.
Source: U.S. Bureau of Labor Statistics, Employment Projections program

Employment of multimedia artists and animators is expected to grow by 8 percent from 2010 to 2020, slower than the average for all occupations. Expected growth will be due to increased demand for animation and visual effects in video games, movies, and television. However, it will be slowed by companies hiring animators who work oversees.

Consumers will continue to demand more realistic video games, movie and television special effects, and three-dimensional movies. Video game studios will require additional multimedia artists and animators to meet this increased demand.

In addition, an increased demand for computer graphics for mobile devices, such as smart phones, will lead to more job opportunities. Multimedia artists will be needed to create animation for games and applications for mobile devices.

However, growth will likely be limited because some animation work is being sent to other countries. Studios can often save money on animation by using lower-paid workers outside of the United States.

From 2010 to 2020, employment growth of multimedia artists and animators in the industries employing the most multimedia artists and animators is expected to be as follows:

Software publishers	49%
Computer systems design and related services	43
Advertising, public relations, and related services	17
Motion picture and video industries	-5

Job Prospects

Despite job growth, there will be competition for job openings because many people are interested in entering the occupation. Opportunities should be best for those who have artistic talent or who are highly skilled in creating computer graphics.

Employment projections data for multimedia artists and animators, 2010-20

Occupational Title	SOC Code	Employment, 2010	Projected Employment, 2020	Change, 2010-20	
				Percent	Numeric
Multimedia Artists and Animators	27-1014	66,500	72,000	8	5,500
SOURCE: U.S. Bureau of Labor Statistics, Employment Projections program					

Similar Occupations

This table shows a list of occupations with job duties that are similar to those of multimedia artists and animators.

Occupation	Job Duties	Entry-Level Education	Median Annual Pay, May 2010
Art Directors	Art directors are responsible for the visual style and images in magazines, newspapers, product packaging, and movie and television productions. They create the overall design and direct others who develop artwork or layouts.	Bachelor's degree	$80,630
Computer Programmers	Computer programmers write code to create software programs. They turn the program designs created by software developers and engineers into instructions that a computer can follow.	Bachelor's degree	$71,380
Craft and Fine Artists	Craft and fine artists use a variety of materials and techniques to create art for sale and exhibition. Craft artists create handmade objects, such as pottery, glassware, textiles, or other objects that are designed to be functional. Fine artists, including painters, sculptors, and illustrators, create original works of art for their aesthetic value, rather than a functional one.	High school diploma or equivalent	$43,470
Graphic Designers	Graphic designers create visual concepts, by hand or using computer software, to communicate ideas that inspire, inform, or captivate consumers. They help to make an organization recognizable by selecting color, images, or logo designs that represent a particular idea or identity to be used in advertising and promotions.	Bachelor's degree	$43,500
Information Security Analysts, Web Developers, and Computer Network Architects	Information security analysts, web developers, and computer network architects all use information technology (IT) to advance their organization's goals. Security analysts ensure a firm's information stays safe from cyberattacks. Web developers create websites to help firms have a public face. Computer network architects create the internal networks all workers within organizations use.	Bachelor's degree	$75,660

Contacts for More Information

For more information about careers in video game design, read the Occupational Outlook Quarterly article titled €œ Work for Play: Careers in Video Game Development .

For information accredited schools of art and design, visit National Association of Schools of Art and Design

Suggested citation:

Bureau of Labor Statistics, U.S. Department of Labor, Occupational Outlook Handbook, 2012-13 Edition, Multimedia Artists and Animators, on the Internet at http://www.bls.gov/ooh/arts-and-design/multimedia-artists-and-animators.htm.

Set and Exhibit Designers

Quick Facts: Set and Exhibit Designers	
2010 Median Pay	$46,680 per year $22.44 per hour
Entry-Level Education	Bachelor's degree
Work Experience in a Related Occupation	None
On-the-job Training	None
Number of Jobs, 2010	11,700
Job Outlook, 2010-20	10% (About as fast as average)
Employment Change, 2010-20	1,200

What Set and Exhibit Designers Do

Set designers create sets for movie, television, theater, and other productions. They analyze scripts or other research documents to determine how many sets will be needed and how each set can best support the story.

Exhibit designers create spaces to display products, art, or artifacts.

Duties

Set and exhibit designers typically do the following:

- Develop set or exhibit designs based on their evaluation of scripts or of artifacts to be exhibited, budgets, and location
- Collaborate with directors, curators, clients, other designers, and production staff on specific design features
- Consult with producers, curators, and clients to identify the intended audience and determine what set or exhibit characteristics may appeal to them
- Prepare hand-drawn sketches or use Computer Aided Design (CAD) programs to create electronic drawings and diagrams to show what the finished sets or exhibits will look like
- Prepare budgets for all necessary sets or exhibits
- Create sets and exhibit spaces that help to tell a story

Set and exhibit designers create a space to communicate a particular message to an audience. In film, theater, or television, set or scenic designers communicate the author's or director's ideas to the audience through the look and feel of scenery, furniture, and props.

Set and exhibit designers take into account such things as the size of the space, lighting, and the intended audience.

They must take into account the scene's historical period, time of day, location, season, and other aspects of the story. In addition, set designers help the audience gain a better sense of the physical space in which the action takes place.

Exhibit designers must take into account the lighting, size of the space, message, and intended audience when they design exhibits. Lighting is essential because it can make a space more appealing or draw visitors' attention to something specific.

Increasingly, museum and trade show exhibits are becoming interactive and integrate multimedia effects, such as video and sound, into the experience. Exhibits are no longer just a few posters or paintings on the wall; they have become three-dimensional experiences.

Exhibit designers are responsible for developing a concept and then seeing the design project through to the opening of the exhibit.

Set and exhibit designers may work on traveling shows and exhibits, such as concert tours, theatrical road shows, and traveling museum exhibits. Often, these sets must be easily erected and dismantled for transport to new venues and must be flexible to accommodate performing or exhibit spaces of different sizes.

Many set and exhibit designers eventually specialize in designing sets for a particular purpose. Most, however, start out learning a common set of skills and taking a variety of set and exhibit design jobs while building their credentials, expertise, and personal style.

The following are examples of types of set and exhibit designers:

Live theatrical performance set designers work on stage sets for theater, ballet, opera, or other live performances. They collaborate with directors to ensure that the set enhances the story and is appropriate for the space and size of the production.

Television or movie set designers design sets for television programs or motion pictures. Filming may take place either on location or on a production set, and set designers are responsible for any background that appears on camera.

Television studio set designers create set designs for in-studio programs, such as news and sports broadcasts, talk shows, and interviews. Their designs take into account the desired brightness of studio lights, any permanent background images, and the ability to display other visual images, such as images shown through television monitors or screen projections.

Trade show or convention exhibit designers work on designs for exhibiting or demonstrating products at trade shows and conventions. They are responsible for making maximum use of the available space and attracting visitors with a visually pleasing display.

Exhibit designers work with curators, artists, and museum directors to design sets that display art or artifacts for museum exhibits. Exhibit designers must be able to tell a story through exhibit pieces while allowing visitors to walk through the exhibit area easily.

Work Environment

Set and exhibit designers held about 11,700 jobs in 2010. About 30 percent are self-employed. Set and exhibit designers were employed in the following industries in 2010:

Motion picture and video industries	13%
Performing arts companies	10
Museums, historical sites, and similar institutions	10
Professional, scientific, and technical services	7
Promoters of events, and agents and managers	5

Many designers move from one short-term full-time job to another, working for a series of employers rather than only one employer. As a result, set and exhibit designers may work in multiple industries throughout their career.

Work on a major motion picture may last a year. Work on a scripted television show may provide several months' employment while the show is in production.

Many theaters employ resident designers on a year-round basis to create sets for live stage productions and performances of ballets and concerts. However, they increasingly are hiring designers on a contract basis for individual productions.

Designers who work on an individual short-term project generally are paid a negotiated fee for their work. Those under contract for a longer time, such as designers who are needed for film and television production work, receive periodic paychecks, typically weekly, through the end of each project, which could be a single motion picture or a season of a television show.

Exhibit designers may be employed by museums or work on a contract basis. Typically, museums that display large objects requiring some expertise and museums that regularly host rotating exhibits employ their own exhibit designers.

Smaller galleries with less frequent exhibit turnover may have only an occasional need to hire an exhibit designer. They usually work with self-employed exhibit designers on a contract basis.

Most set designers who work for movie, television, and theater productions are members of the International Alliance of Theatrical and Stage Employees (IATSE), which includes distinct unions representing different workers in their respective fields.

Exhibit designers do not have to be members of any union, but many are IATSE members.

Work Schedules

Set and exhibit designers usually work full time, but their hours often are flexible. They may work evenings or weekends to oversee the installation of a set or exhibit. Similarly, work schedules could become hectic under the pressure of deadlines or when last-minute changes to designs need to be made.

How to Become a Set or Exhibit Designer

Set and exhibit designers often need a bachelor's degree in set design, scenic design, or theater.

Education

Although most set and exhibit designers are trained in scenic design programs, a few are trained as actors first. Academic programs train students to research the history, period, and story of a production.

Classes teach drawing, painting, model building, hand drafting and computer-aided drawing. Many programs give students the opportunity to build a professional portfolio—a collection of designs from classroom projects, internships, or other experiences. Students can use these examples of their work to show their design skills when they apply for jobs.

The National Association of Schools of Art and Design accredits about 300 postsecondary institutions with programs in art and design. The National Association of Schools of Theatre accredits more than 150 programs in theater arts.

Important Qualities

Computer skills. Set and exhibit designers do much of their design work on computers with specialty design software, such as Computer Aided Design (CAD) programs. They must be comfortable using computers.

Creativity. Set and exhibit designers must be able to interpret scripts and use their artistic abilities to conceive a set or exhibit that will help tell a story.

Problem-solving skills. Set and exhibit designers must find ways to carry out an author's, director's, or curator's vision for a set or exhibit while ensuring that construction of the finished set or exhibit can be completed on time and within budget.

Teamwork. Because a great deal of their work is collaborative, set and exhibit designers need to be able to communicate easily and effectively with directors, curators, the craftspeople who build the set or exhibit, and other designers.

Pay

Set and Exhibit Designers
Median annual wages, May 2010

Set and Exhibit Designers	$46,680
Arts, Design, Entertainment, Sports, and Media Occupations	$42,870
Total, All Occupations	$33,840

Note: All Occupations includes all occupations in the U.S. Economy.
Source: U.S. Bureau of Labor Statistics, Occupational Employment Statistics

The median annual wage of set and exhibit designers was $46,680 in May 2010. The median wage is the wage at which half the workers in an occupation earned more than that amount and half earned less. The lowest 10 percent earned less than $25,580, and the top 10 percent earned more than $84,180.

Set and exhibit designers usually work full time, but their hours often are flexible. They may work evenings or weekends to oversee the installation of a set or exhibit. Similarly, work schedules could become hectic when under the pressure of deadlines or when last-minute changes to designs need to be made.

Job Outlook

Set and Exhibit Designers
Percent change in employment, projected 2010-20

Total, All Occupations	14%
Arts, Design, Entertainment, Sports, and Media Occupations	13%
Set and Exhibit Designers	10%

Note: All Occupations includes all occupations in the U.S. Economy.
Source: U.S. Bureau of Labor Statistics, Employment Projections program

Employment of set and exhibit designers is expected to grow by 10 percent from 2010 to 2020, about as fast as the average for all occupations.

Employment of set and exhibit designers who work primarily on designing museum exhibit space is expected to grow by 17 percent. As the number of private museums and of museums that specialize in a narrow topic area grows, the number of designers who are permanent employees of these museums also will grow.

Some set and exhibit designers serve as resident designers for theater, dance, and opera companies that produce shows year round.

However, many companies prefer to contract out their set designs to self-employed or freelance designers on a show-by-show basis. This trend is expected to increase, in part because some producers find it more economical to contract for design work than to employ designers full time. As a result, employment of set and exhibit designers in specialized design firms is expected to grow by 27 percent from 2010 to 2020.

Employment projections data for set and exhibit designers, 2010-20

Occupational Title	SOC Code	Employment, 2010	Projected Employment, 2020	Change, 2010-20 Percent	Numeric
Set and Exhibit Designers	27-1027	11,700	12,800	10	1,200
SOURCE: U.S. Bureau of Labor Statistics, Employment Projections program					

Similar Occupations

This table shows a list of occupations with job duties that are similar to those of set and exhibit designers.

Occupation	Job Duties	Entry-Level Education	Median Annual Pay, May 2010
Architects	Architects plan and design buildings and other structures.	Bachelor's degree	$72,550
Art Directors	Art directors are responsible for the visual style and images in magazines, newspapers, product packaging, and movie and television productions. They create the overall design and direct others who develop artwork or layouts.	Bachelor's degree	$80,630
Craft and Fine Artists	Craft and fine artists use a variety of materials and techniques to create art for sale and exhibition. Craft artists create handmade objects, such as pottery, glassware, textiles, or other objects that are designed to be functional. Fine artists, including painters, sculptors, and illustrators, create original works of art for their aesthetic value, rather than a functional one.	High school diploma or equivalent	$43,470
Fashion Designers	Fashion designers create original clothing, accessories, and footwear. They sketch designs, select fabrics and patterns, and give instructions on how to make the products they designed.	High school diploma or equivalent	$64,530
Graphic Designers	Graphic designers create visual concepts, by hand or using computer software, to communicate ideas that inspire, inform, or captivate consumers. They help to make an organization recognizable by selecting color, images, or logo designs that represent a particular idea or identity to be used in advertising and promotions.	Bachelor's degree	$43,500
Industrial Designers	Industrial designers develop the concepts for manufactured products, such as cars, home appliances, and toys. They combine art, business, and engineering to make products that people use every day.	Bachelor's degree	$58,230
Interior Designers	Interior designers make interior spaces functional, safe, and beautiful for almost every type of building: offices, homes, airport terminals, shopping malls, and restaurants. They select and specify colors, finishes, fabrics, furniture, flooring and wallcoverings, lighting, and other materials to create useful and stylish interiors for buildings.	Bachelor's degree	$46,280
Landscape Architects	Landscape architects plan and design land areas for parks, recreational facilities, highways, airports, and other properties. Projects include subdivisions and commercial, industrial, and residential sites.	Bachelor's degree	$62,090
Multimedia Artists and Animators	Multimedia artists and animators create animation and visual effects for television, movies, video games, and other media. They create two- and three-dimensional models and animation.	Bachelor's degree	$58,510

Contacts for More Information

For more information about scenic design, visit United Scenic Artists, International Alliance of Theatrical and Stage Employees (IATSE) Local 829

For more information about set and exhibit design, visit Art Directors Guild, IATSE Local 800

For more information on accredited college degree programs in set design, visit National Association of Schools of Art and Design, National Association of Schools of Theatre

Suggested citation:

Bureau of Labor Statistics, U.S. Department of Labor, Occupational Outlook Handbook, 2012-13 Edition, Set and Exhibit Designers, on the Internet at http://www.bls.gov/ooh/arts-and-design/set-and-exhibit-designers.htm.

Building and Grounds Cleaning Occupations

Grounds Maintenance Workers

Quick Facts: Grounds Maintenance Workers	
2010 Median Pay	$23,740 per year $11.41 per hour
Entry-Level Education	See How to Become One
Work Experience in a Related Occupation	None
On-the-job Training	See How to Become One
Number of Jobs, 2010	1,249,700
Job Outlook, 2010-20	20% (Faster than average)
Employment Change, 2010-20	254,600

What Grounds Maintenance Workers Do

Grounds maintenance workers provide a pleasant outdoor environment by ensuring that the grounds of houses, businesses, and parks are attractive, orderly, and healthy.

Duties

Grounds maintenance workers typically do the following:
- Mow, edge, and fertilize lawns
- Weed and mulch landscapes
- Trim hedges, shrubs, and small trees
- Remove dead, damaged, or unwanted trees
- Plant flowers, trees, and shrubs
- Water lawns, landscapes, and gardens

Grounds maintenance workers do a variety of tasks to achieve a pleasant and functional outdoor environment. They also care for indoor gardens and plantings in commercial and public facilities, such as malls, hotels, and botanical gardens.

The following are types of grounds maintenance workers:

Landscaping workers create new outdoor spaces or upgrade existing ones by planting trees, flowers, and shrubs. They also trim, fertilize, mulch, and water plants. Some grade and install lawns or construct hardscapes such as walkways, patios, and decks. Others help install lighting or sprinkler systems. Landscaping workers work in a variety of residential and commercial settings, such as homes, apartment buildings, office buildings, shopping malls, and hotels and motels.

Groundskeeping workers, also called **groundskeepers**, maintain existing grounds. They care for plants and trees, rake and mulch leaves, and clear snow from walkways. They work on athletic fields, golf courses, cemeteries, university campuses, and parks, as well as in many of the same settings as landscaping workers. They also see to the proper upkeep and repair of sidewalks, parking lots, groundskeeping equipment, fountains, fences, planters, and benches.

Groundskeeping workers who care for athletic fields keep natural and artificial turf in top condition, mark out boundaries, and paint turf with team logos and names before events. They mow, water, fertilize, and aerate the fields regularly. They must make sure that the underlying soil on fields with natural turf has the required composition to allow proper drainage and to support the grasses used on the field. In sports venues, they vacuum and disinfect synthetic turf after its use to prevent the growth of harmful bacteria, and they remove the turf and replace the cushioning pad periodically.

Groundskeepers in parks and recreation facilities care for lawns, trees, and shrubs; maintain playgrounds; clean buildings; and keep parking lots, picnic areas, and other public spaces free of litter. They also may erect and dismantle snow fences, and maintain swimming pools. These workers inspect buildings and equipment, make needed repairs, and keep everything freshly painted.

Some groundskeepers specialize in caring for cemeteries and memorial gardens. They dig graves to specified depths, generally using a backhoe. They mow grass regularly, apply fertilizers and other chemicals, prune shrubs and trees, plant flowers, and remove debris from graves.

Greenskeepers maintain golf courses. Their work is similar to that of groundskeepers, but they also periodically relocate holes on putting greens and maintain benches and tee markers along the course. In addition, greenskeepers keep canopies, benches, and tee markers repaired and freshly painted.

Pesticide handlers, sprayers, and applicators apply herbicides, fungicides, or insecticides on plants or the soil to prevent or control weeds, insects, and diseases. Those who work for chemical lawn or tree service firms are more specialized, inspecting lawns for problems and applying fertilizers, pesticides, and other chemicals to stimulate growth and prevent or control weeds, diseases, or insect infestations.

Tree trimmers and pruners, also called **arborists**, cut away dead or excess branches from trees or shrubs to clear utility lines, roads, and sidewalks. Although many workers strive to improve the appearance and health of trees and plants, some specialize in diagnosing and treating tree diseases. Others specialize in pruning, trimming, and shaping ornamental trees and shrubs. Tree trimmers and pruners use chainsaws, chippers, and stump grinders while on the job. When trimming near power lines, they usually work on truck-mounted lifts and use power pruners.

Work Environment

Grounds maintenance workers held about 1.2 million jobs in 2010.

Grounds maintenance workers mow, edge, and fertilize lawns.

The industries that employed the most grounds maintenance workers in 2010 were as follows:

Services to buildings and dwellings	37%
Other amusement and recreation industries	8
Local government, excluding education and hospitals	7
Junior colleges, colleges, universities, and professional schools	2

Employment in the detailed occupations that make up grounds maintenance workers was distributed as follows:

Landscaping and groundskeeping workers	1,151,500
Tree trimmers and pruners	50,600
Pesticide handlers, sprayers, and applicators, vegetation	29,500
Grounds maintenance workers, all other	18,200

Grounds maintenance work is done outdoors in all kinds of weather. The work can be repetitive and physically demanding, requiring frequent bending, lifting, and shoveling.

Injuries

Full-time grounds maintenance workers experience a rate of injury and illness that is much higher than the national average. Workers who use chemicals, such as pesticides or fertilizers, or dangerous equipment, including lawnmowers and chain saws, must take precautions. Workers who use motorized equipment must protect their hearing.

Work Schedules

Many grounds maintenance jobs are seasonal. Jobs are most common in the spring, summer, and fall, when planting, mowing, and trimming are necessary.

How to Become a Grounds Maintenance Worker

Most grounds maintenance workers need no formal education and are trained on the job. Most states require licensing for workers who apply pesticides.

Education

Although most grounds maintenance jobs have no education requirements, some employers may require formal education in areas such as landscape design, horticulture, or arboriculture.

Licenses

Most states require workers who apply pesticides to be licensed. Getting a license usually involves passing a test on the proper use and disposal of insecticides, herbicides, and fungicides.

Certification

The Professional Landcare Network offers seven certifications in landscaping and grounds maintenance for workers at various experience levels.

The Tree Care Industry Association offers certification for tree care safety professionals.

The International Society of Arboriculture offers four certifications for workers at various experience levels.

Advancement

Grounds maintenance workers who have good communication skills may become crew leaders or advance into other supervisory positions. Becoming a manager or a landscape contractor may require some formal education and several years of experience. Some workers use their experience to start their own businesses.

Training

A short period of on-the-job training is usually enough to teach new hires the skills they need, which often include how to plant and maintain areas and how to use mowers, trimmers, leaf blowers, small tractors, and other equipment. Large institutional employers such as golf courses, university campuses, or municipalities may supplement on-the-job training with coursework in horticulture or small-engine repair.

Important Qualities

Self-motivated. Because they often work with little supervision, grounds maintenance workers must be able to do their job independently.

Stamina. Grounds maintenance workers must be capable of doing physically strenuous labor for long hours, occasionally in extreme heat or cold.

Pay

Grounds Maintenance Workers
  Median hourly wages, May 2010

Total, All Occupations	$16.27
Grounds Maintenance Workers	$11.41
Building and Grounds Cleaning and Maintenance Occupations	$10.81

Note: All Occupations includes all occupations in the U.S. Economy.
Source: U.S. Bureau of Labor Statistics, Occupational Employment Statistics

The median hourly wage of grounds maintenance workers was $11.41 in May 2010. The median wage is the wage at which half the workers in an occupation earned more than that amount and half earned less. The lowest 10 percent earned less than $8.19, and the top 10 percent earned more than $18.27.

Median hourly wages for grounds maintenance occupations in May 2010 were the following:

- $14.64 for tree trimmers and pruners
- $14.37 for pesticide handlers, sprayers, and applicators, vegetation
- $11.25 for landscaping and groundskeeping workers
- $11.61 for grounds maintenance workers, all other

Many grounds maintenance jobs are seasonal. Jobs are most common in the spring, summer, and fall, when planting, mowing, and trimming are necessary.

Job Outlook

Grounds Maintenance Workers
  Percent change in employment, projected 2010-20

Grounds Maintenance Workers	20%
Total, All Occupations	14%
Building and Grounds Cleaning and Maintenance Occupations	12%

Note: All Occupations includes all occupations in the U.S. Economy.
Source: U.S. Bureau of Labor Statistics, Employment Projections program

Employment of grounds maintenance workers is projected to grow 20 percent from 2010 to 2020, faster than the average for all occupations.

More workers will be needed to keep up with increasing demand for lawn care and landscaping services from large institutions, including universities and corporate headquarters. Many aging or busy homeowners also will require lawn care services to help maintain their yards.

Employment of tree trimmers and pruners is expected to grow 18 percent, about as fast as the average for all occupations. Many municipalities are planting more trees in urban areas, likely increasing the demand for these workers.

Job Prospects

Overall job opportunities are expected to be very good. Job opportunities will come both from faster than average employment growth and from the need to replace workers who leave the occupation.

Job opportunities should be best in areas with temperate climates, where landscaping services are required year round.

Employment projections data for grounds maintenance workers, 2010-20

Occupational Title	SOC Code	Employment, 2010	Projected Employment, 2020	Change, 2010-20 Percent	Change, 2010-20 Numeric
Grounds Maintenance Workers	—	1,249,700	1,504,300	20	254,600
Landscaping and Groundskeeping Workers	37-3011	1,151,500	1,392,300	21	240,800
Pesticide Handlers, Sprayers, and Applicators, Vegetation	37-3012	29,500	32,500	10	3,000
Tree Trimmers and Pruners	37-3013	50,600	59,700	18	9,100
Grounds Maintenance Workers, All Other	37-3019	18,200	19,900	9	1,700

SOURCE: U.S. Bureau of Labor Statistics, Employment Projections program

Similar Occupations

This table shows a list of occupations with job duties that are similar to those of grounds maintenance workers.

Occupation	Job Duties	Entry-Level Education	Median Annual Pay, May 2010
Agricultural Workers	Agricultural workers maintain the quality of farms, crops, and livestock by operating machinery and doing physical labor under the supervision of agricultural managers.	See How to Become One	$18,970
Farmers, Ranchers, and Other Agricultural Managers	Farmers, ranchers, and other agricultural managers run establishments that produce crops, livestock, and dairy products.	High school diploma or equivalent	$60,750
Forest and Conservation Workers	Forest and conservation workers measure and improve the quality of forests. Under the supervision of foresters and forest and conservation technicians, they help to develop, maintain, and protect forests.	High school diploma or equivalent	$23,900
Landscape Architects	Landscape architects plan and design land areas for parks, recreational facilities, highways, airports, and other properties. Projects include subdivisions and commercial, industrial, and residential sites.	Bachelor's degree	$62,090
Logging Workers	Logging workers harvest thousands of acres of forests each year. The timber they harvest provides the raw material for countless consumer and industrial products.	High school diploma or equivalent	$32,870

Contacts for More Information

For more information about tree trimmers and pruners, including certification, visit International Society of Arboriculture

Tree Care Industry Association, For information about landscaping and groundskeeping workers, visit Professional Grounds Management Society Professional Landcare Network

For information about becoming a licensed pesticide applicator, contact your state's Department of Agriculture or Department of Environmental Protection or Conservation.

Suggested citation:

Bureau of Labor Statistics, U.S. Department of Labor, Occupational Outlook Handbook, 2012-13 Edition, Grounds Maintenance Workers, on the Internet at http://www.bls.gov/ooh/building-and-grounds-cleaning/grounds-maintenance-workers.htm .

Janitors and Building Cleaners

Quick Facts: Janitors and Building Cleaners	
2010 Median Pay	$22,210 per year $10.68 per hour
Entry-Level Education	Less than high school
Work Experience in a Related Occupation	None
On-the-job Training	Short-term on-the-job training
Number of Jobs, 2010	2,310,400
Job Outlook, 2010-20	11% (About as fast as average)
Employment Change, 2010-20	246,400

What Janitors and Building Cleaners Do

Janitors and building cleaners keep many types of buildings clean, orderly, and in good condition.

Duties

Janitors and building cleaners typically do the following:

- Gather and empty trash and trash bins
- Clean building floors by sweeping, mopping, or vacuuming them
- Clean bathrooms and stock them with soap, toilet paper, and other supplies
- Keep buildings secure by locking doors
- Clean spills and other hazards using sponges and squeegees
- Wash windows, walls, and glass

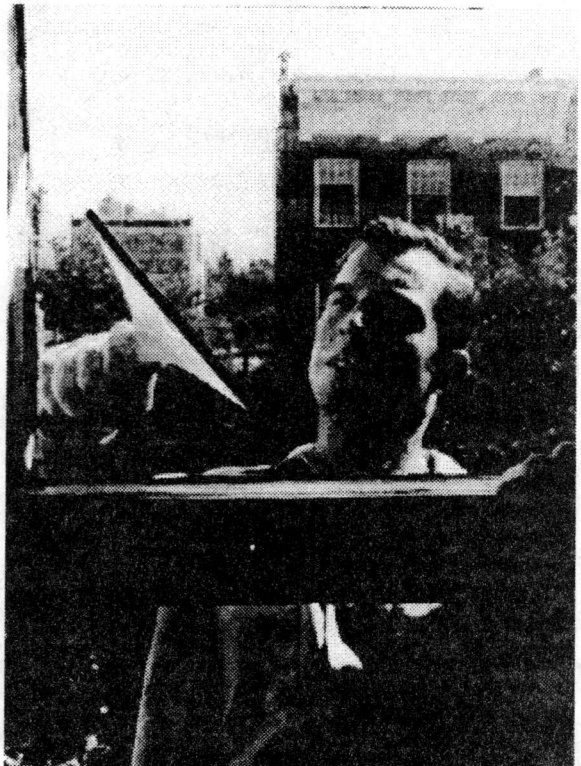

Janitors and building cleaners wash windows, walls, and glass.

- Order cleaning supplies
- Make minor repairs to the building, such as changing light bulbs
- Notify managers when the building needs major repairs

Janitors and building cleaning workers keep office buildings, schools, hospitals, retail stores, hotels, and other places clean, sanitary, and in good condition. Some do only cleaning, while others have a wide range of duties.

In addition to keeping the inside of buildings clean and orderly, some janitors and building cleaners work outdoors, mowing lawns, sweeping walkways, or shoveling snow. Some janitors also monitor the heating and cooling system, ensuring that it functions properly.

Janitors and building cleaners use many tools and equipment. Simple cleaning tools may include mops, brooms, rakes, and shovels. Other tools may include snowblowers and floor buffers.

Some janitors may be responsible for repairing small problems with electricity or plumbing, such as leaky faucets.

Work Environment

Janitors and building cleaning workers held about 2.3 million jobs in 2010. About 32 percent were employed in the services to buildings and dwellings industry, and another 14 percent were employed in elementary and secondary schools. The remainder was employed throughout other industries.

Most janitors and building cleaners work indoors, but some work outdoors part of the time, sweeping walkways, mowing lawns, or shoveling snow. They spend most of the day standing, sometimes moving or lifting heavy supplies or equipment. As a result, the work may be strenuous on the back, arms, and legs. And some tasks, such as cleaning bathrooms and trash rooms, can be dirty and unpleasant.

Injuries

Janitors and building cleaners have one of the highest work-related injury rates. Workers may suffer cuts, bruises, and burns from machines, tools, and chemicals.

Work Schedules

Most janitors and building cleaners work full time, but a significant number work part time. Because office buildings are usually cleaned while they are empty, many cleaning workers work evening hours. Janitors in schools, however, usually work during the day. When there is a need for 24-hour maintenance, janitors may work in shifts. This is particularly true of hospitals and hotels.

How to Become a Janitor or Building Cleaner

Most janitors and building cleaning workers learn on the job. They do not need formal education.

Education and Training

Most janitors and building cleaners learn on the job. Beginners typically work with a more experienced janitor or cleaner, learning how to use and maintain machines, such as wet-and-dry vacuums and floor buffers and polishers. They may also learn on the job how to repair minor problems with the electricity or plumbing.

Janitors and building cleaners should be able to do simple arithmetic and follow instructions. High school shop courses are generally helpful for jobs involving repair work.

Certification

Although not required, certification is available through the Building Service Contractors Association International and the International Sanitary Supply Association . Certification demonstrates competence and may make applicants more appealing to employers.

Important Qualities

Interpersonal skills. Janitors and building cleaners must get along well with other cleaners, the people who live or work in the buildings they clean, and their supervisors.

Mechanical skills. Janitors and building cleaners should understand general building operations. They should be able to make routine repairs, such as changing light bulbs and repairing leaky faucets.

Physical strength. Janitors and building cleaners should be able to lift and move cleaning materials and heavy equipment. Cases of liquid cleaner are often very heavy, so workers should be able to lift them without injuring their back.

Stamina. Janitors and building cleaners should be able to spend most of their time on their feet—lifting or moving supplies or equipment and tools—without tiring.

Pay

Janitors and Building Cleaners
Median hourly wages, May 2010

Total, All Occupations	$16.27
Building and Grounds Cleaning and Maintenance Occupations	$10.81
Janitors and Cleaners, Except Maids and Housekeeping Cleaners	$10.68

Note: All Occupations includes all occupations in the U.S. Economy.
Source: U.S. Bureau of Labor Statistics, Occupational Employment Statistics

The median hourly wage for janitors and building cleaners was $10.68 in May 2010. The median wage is the wage at which half the workers in an occupation earned more than the amount and half earned less. The lowest 10 percent earned less than $7.86 per hour, and the top 10 percent earned more than $17.88 per hour.

In May 2010, the median hourly wages in industries employing some of the largest numbers of janitors and building cleaners were as follows:

Local government	$13.14
Elementary and secondary schools	13.04
Colleges, universities, and professional schools	12.37
General medical and surgical hospitals	11.76
Services to buildings and dwellings	9.48

Most janitors and building cleaners work full time. Because office buildings are usually cleaned while they are empty, many cleaning workers work evening hours. When there is a need for 24-hour maintenance, janitors may work in shifts. This is particularly true of hospitals and hotels.

Job Outlook

Janitors and Building Cleaners
Percent change in employment, projected 2010-20

Total, All Occupations	14%
Building and Grounds Cleaning and Maintenance Occupations	12%
Janitors and Cleaners, Except Maids and Housekeeping Cleaners	11%

Note: All Occupations includes all occupations in the U.S. Economy.
Source: U.S. Bureau of Labor Statistics, Employment Projections program

Employment of janitors and building cleaners is expected to grow 11 percent from 2010 to 2020, about as fast as the average for all occupations. Many new jobs are expected in facilities related to health care, as this industry is expected to grow rapidly. In addition, as more companies outsource their cleaning services, janitorial contractors are likely to benefit and experience demand. However, employment growth is expected to be tempered as fewer new buildings are built over the projections decade.

Job Prospects

Job prospects are expected to be favorable. Those with experience should have the best job opportunities. Most job openings will come from the need to replace many workers who leave or retire from this very large occupation.

Employment projections data for janitors and building cleaners, 2010-20

Occupational Title	SOC Code	Employment, 2010	Projected Employment, 2020	Change, 2010-20	
				Percent	Numeric
Janitors and Cleaners, Except Maids and Housekeeping Cleaners	37-2011	2,310,400	2,556,800	11	246,400
SOURCE: U.S. Bureau of Labor Statistics, Employment Projections program					

Similar Occupations

This table shows a list of occupations with job duties that are similar to those of janitors and building cleaners.

Occupation	Job Duties	Entry-Level Education	Median Annual Pay, May 2010
Grounds Maintenance Workers	Grounds maintenance workers provide a pleasant outdoor environment by ensuring that the grounds of houses, businesses, and parks are attractive, orderly, and healthy.	See How to Become One	$23,740
Maids and Housekeeping Cleaners	Maids and housekeeping cleaners do general cleaning tasks, including making beds and vacuuming halls, in private homes and commercial establishments.	Less than high school	$19,300

Contacts for More Information

For more information about janitors and building cleaners, visit
Building Service Contractors Association International
Association of Residential Cleaning Services International
International Sanitary Supply Association
Information about janitorial and building cleaning jobs is available from state employment service offices.

Suggested citation:

Bureau of Labor Statistics, U.S. Department of Labor, Occupational Outlook Handbook, 2012-13 Edition, Janitors and Building Cleaners, on the Internet at http://www.bls.gov/ooh/building-and-grounds-cleaning/janitors-and-building-cleaners.htm .

Maids and Housekeeping Cleaners

Quick Facts: Maids and Housekeeping Cleaners	
2010 Median Pay	$19,300 per year $9.28 per hour
Entry-Level Education	Less than high school
Work Experience in a Related Occupation	None
On-the-job Training	Short-term on-the-job training
Number of Jobs, 2010	1,427,300
Job Outlook, 2010-20	8% (Slower than average)
Employment Change, 2010-20	111,600

What Maids and Housekeeping Cleaners Do

Maids and housekeeping cleaners perform general cleaning tasks, including making beds and vacuuming halls, in private homes and commercial establishments.

Duties

Maids and housekeeping cleaners typically do the following:
- Clean rooms, hallways, and other living or work areas
- Change sheets and towels; make beds; wash, fold, and iron clothes
- Empty wastebaskets and take trash to disposal areas
- Replenish supplies, such as soap and toilet paper
- Dust and polish furniture and equipment
- Sweep, wax, or polish floors using brooms, mops, or other floor-cleaning equipment
- Vacuum rugs, carpets, and upholstered furniture
- Clean or polish windows, walls, and woodwork
- Lift and move lightweight objects and equipment

Maids and housekeeping cleaners do light cleaning tasks in homes and commercial establishments, such as hotels, restaurants, hospitals, and nursing homes.

In addition to keeping these places clean and neat, maids who work in private homes also may prepare meals, polish silver, and clean ovens, refrigerators, and sometimes windows. Some also shop for groceries, pick up and drop off dry cleaning, and do other errands.

Those who work in hotels, hospitals, and other commercial establishments are responsible for cleaning and maintaining the premises. They may also share other duties. For example, housekeeping cleaners in hotels may deliver ironing boards, cribs, and rollaway beds to guests' rooms. In hospitals, workers may have to wash bed frames and disinfect and sanitize equipment with germicides.

Work Environment

Maids and housekeeping cleaners held about 1.4 million jobs in 2010. About 12 percent were self-employed.

Most maids and housekeeping cleaners work full time. Although most cleaners work indoors in a hotel, restaurant, hospital, or nursing home, many maids who work for individuals or families may have to run errands outside the home. The work can be physically demanding.

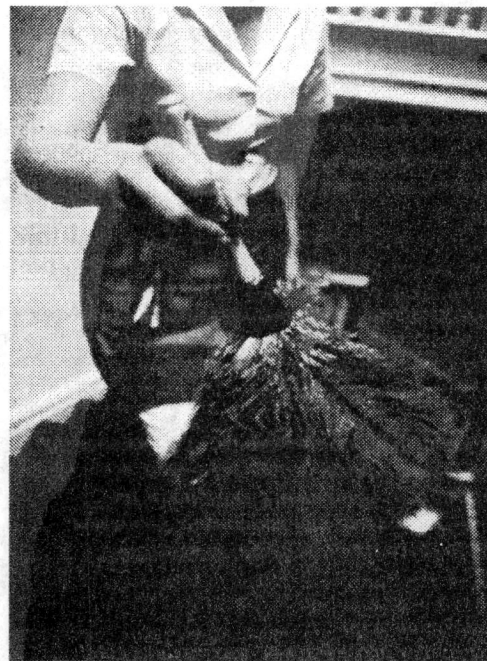

Maids and housekeeping cleaners dust and polish furniture and woodwork.

The following industries employed the most maids and housekeeping cleaners in 2010:

Traveler accommodation, including hotels and motels	29%
Private households	25
Nursing and residential care facilities	9
Hospitals; state, local, and private	8
Services to buildings and dwellings	6

Injuries

Maids and housekeeping cleaners spend most of their day on their feet, sometimes lifting or pushing heavy furniture. Many tasks, such as dusting or sweeping, require constant bending, stooping, and stretching. Lifting today's heavier mattresses at nicer hotels to change the linens can cause back injuries and sprains. As a result, these workers have a rate of injury and illness that is much higher than the national average.

Work Schedules

Most maids and housekeeping cleaners work full time. Part-time maids and cleaners often work weekends and evenings, particularly those who work at hotels and hospitals.

How to Become a Maid or Housekeeping Cleaner

Most maids and housekeeping cleaners are trained on the job.

Education and Training

There are no formal training or education requirements. Most maids and housekeeping cleaners are trained on the job. Entry-level maids and housekeeping cleaners typically work alongside a more experienced cleaner and gain more responsibilities and more difficult work as they become experienced.

Important Qualities

Detail oriented. Because maids and housekeeping cleaners are responsible for cleaning rooms, they must pay close attention to detail. For example, household maids need to be thorough when polishing silver.

Interpersonal skills. Maids and housekeeping cleaners who work in private homes must get along well with the people who hire them. Those who work in hotels, hospitals, office buildings, and other places also often come into contact with people whose spaces they are cleaning. They must be polite and friendly.

Stamina. Maids and housekeeping cleaners must be able to spend the day on their feet, scrubbing, bending, and stretching, without getting overly tired.

Pay

Maids and Housekeeping Cleaners
Median annual wages, May 2010

Total, All Occupations	$33,840
Building and Grounds Cleaning and Maintenance Occupations	$22,490
Maids and Housekeeping Cleaners	$19,300

Note: All Occupations includes all occupations in the U.S. Economy.
Source: U.S. Bureau of Labor Statistics, Occupational Employment Statistics

The median annual wage of maids and housekeeping cleaners was $19,300 in May 2010. The median wage is the wage at which half the workers in an occupation earned more than that amount and half earned less. The lowest 10 percent earned less than $15,980, and the top 10 percent earned more than $29,510.

The following are median annual wages for maids and housekeeping cleaners in select industries:

General medical and surgical hospitals	$22,090
Community care facilities for the elderly	19,850
Nursing care facilities	19,330
Services to buildings and dwellings	19,070
Traveler accommodation	18,750

Most maids and housekeeping cleaners work full time. Part-time maids and cleaners often work weekends and evenings, particularly those who work at hotels and hospitals.

Job Outlook

Maids and Housekeeping Cleaners
Percent change in employment, projected 2010-20

Total, All Occupations	14%
Building and Grounds Cleaning and Maintenance Occupations	12%
Maids and Housekeeping Cleaners	8%

Note: All Occupations includes all occupations in the U.S. Economy.
Source: U.S. Bureau of Labor Statistics, Employment Projections program

Employment of maids and housekeeping cleaners is expected to grow 8 percent from 2010 to 2020, slower than the average for all occupations. Some new jobs are expected in hotels as demand for accommodations increases. Companies that supply cleaning services on a contract basis will also experience some growth, as more of this work is being contracted out.

Job Prospects

Despite slow employment growth, job opportunities are expected to be good overall and more favorable for those who have some experience. Some job openings will result from the need to replace workers who leave the occupation.

Employment projections data for maids and housekeeping cleaners, 2010-20

Occupational Title	SOC Code	Employment, 2010	Projected Employment, 2020	Change, 2010-20 Percent	Change, 2010-20 Numeric
Maids and Housekeeping Cleaners	37-2012	1,427,300	1,538,900	8	111,600
SOURCE: U.S. Bureau of Labor Statistics, Employment Projections program					

Similar Occupations

This table shows a list of occupations with job duties that are similar to those of maids and housekeeping cleaners.

Occupation	Job Duties	Entry-Level Education	Median Annual Pay, May 2010
Janitors and Building Cleaners	Janitors and building cleaners keep many types of buildings clean, orderly, and in good condition.	Less than high school	$22,210

Contacts for More Information

For more information about certification for maids and housekeeping cleaners, visit Building Service Contractors Association International

International Executive Housekeepers Association

Suggested citation:

Bureau of Labor Statistics, U.S. Department of Labor, Occupational Outlook Handbook, 2012-13 Edition, Maids and Housekeeping Cleaners, on the Internet at http://www.bls.gov/ooh/building-and-grounds-cleaning/maids-and-housekeeping-cleaners.htm .

Pest Control Workers

Quick Facts: Pest Control Workers	
2010 Median Pay	$30,340 per year $14.59 per hour
Entry-Level Education	High school diploma or equivalent
Work Experience in a Related Occupation	None
On-the-job Training	Moderate-term on-the-job training
Number of Jobs, 2010	68,400
Job Outlook, 2010-20	26% (Faster than average)
Employment Change, 2010-20	17,900

What Pest Control Workers Do

Pest control workers control, manage, or remove unwanted creatures, such as roaches, rats, ants, termites, and bedbugs, that infest buildings and surrounding areas.

Duties

Pest control workers typically do the following:
- Inspect buildings and premises for signs of pests or infestation
- Determine the type of treatment needed to eliminate pests
- Measure the dimensions of the area needing treatment
- Estimate the cost of their services
- Set bait and traps to remove or kill pests
- Spray or dust pesticides into rooms
- Design and carry out pest management plans
- Drive trucks equipped with power spraying equipment
- Create barriers to prevent pests from entering a building

Unwanted pests that infest buildings or surrounding areas can pose serious risks to the health and safety of occupants. Pest control workers control, manage, or remove these creatures from homes, apartments, offices, and other structures to protect people and to maintain buildings' structural integrity.

To design and carry out integrated pest management (IPM) plans, pest control workers must know the identity and biology of a wide

Pest control workers inspect a building and its premises for signs of pests.

range of pests. They must also know the best ways to control or remove the pests.

Pest control workers' position titles and job duties often vary by state. The following are types of pest control workers:

Pest control technicians identify potential pest problems, conduct inspections, and design control strategies. They work directly with customers and, as entry-level workers, use only a limited range of pesticides.

Applicators use a wide range of pesticides and may specialize in a particular area of pest control:

- **Termite control technicians** use chemicals and modify structures to eliminate termites and prevent future infestations. Some also repair structural damage caused by termites and build barriers to separate pests from their source of food.
- **Fumigators** use poisonous gases, called fumigants, to treat serious infestations. Fumigators seal infested buildings before using hoses to fill the structure with fumigants. Warning signs are posted to keep people from going into fumigated buildings, and fumigators monitor buildings closely to detect and stop leaks.

Work Environment

Pest control workers held about 68,400 jobs in 2010. About 87 percent worked in the services to buildings and dwellings industry.

Pest control workers must travel to clients' sites. They work both indoors and outdoors, in all types of weather. To inspect sites and treat them, workers must often kneel, bend, and crawl in tight spaces.

When working with pesticides, pest control workers must wear protective gear, including respirators, gloves, and goggles.

Work Schedules

Most pest control workers are employed full time. Working evenings and weekends is common.

Injuries

Pest control chemicals are toxic and can be harmful when not used properly. Although workers are trained and licensed for pesticide use and wear protective equipment, they still experience injuries and illnesses more frequently than workers in many other occupations.

How to Become a Pest Control Worker

State laws require pest control workers to be licensed. Most workers need a high school diploma and receive on-the-job training, which usually lasts less than 3 months.

Many pest control companies require that employees have good driving records.

Education and Training

A high school diploma or the equivalent is the minimum qualification for the majority of pest control jobs.

Most pest control workers begin as technicians, receiving both formal technical instruction and on-the-job training from employers. They often study specialties such as rodent control, termite control, fumigation, and ornamental and turf control. Technicians also must complete general training in pesticide use and safety. Pest control training can usually be completed in less than 3 months.

After completing the required training, workers are qualified to provide supervised pest control services. Because pest control methods change, workers often attend continuing education classes, which are frequently provided by product manufacturers.

Licenses

Pest control workers must be licensed. Licensure requirements vary by state, but workers usually must complete training and pass an exam. Some states have additional requirements, such as having a high school diploma or GED, completing an apprenticeship, and passing a

background check. States may have more requirements for applicators.

Advancement

Pest control workers typically advance as they gain experience. Applicators with several years of experience often become supervisors. Some experienced workers start their own pest management company.

Important Qualities

Bookkeeping skills. Pest control workers must keep accurate records of the hours they work, chemicals they use, and bills they collect. Self-employed workers need these skills to run their businesses.

Customer-service skills. Pest control workers must be friendly and polite when they interact with customers at the customers' homes or businesses.

Detail oriented. Because pest control workers sometimes apply toxic chemicals, they must follow instructions carefully to prevent harm to residents, pets, the environment, and themselves.

Physical Strength. Pest control workers often must spend hours on their feet, frequently crouching, kneeling, and crawling. Applicators, in particular, also must wear heavy protective gear.

Stamina. Pest control workers must be able to withstand uncomfortable conditions, such as heat when they climb into attics in the summertime and cold when they slide into crawl spaces during winter.

Pay

Pest Control Workers
Median annual wages, May 2010

Total, All Occupations	$33,840
Pest Control Workers	$30,340
Building and Grounds Cleaning and Maintenance Occupations	$22,490

Note: All Occupations includes all occupations in the U.S. Economy.
Source: U.S. Bureau of Labor Statistics, Occupational Employment Statistics

The median annual wage of pest control workers was $30,340 in May 2010. The median wage is the wage at which half of the workers in an occupation earned more than that amount and half earned less. The lowest 10 percent earned less than $20,340, and the top 10 percent earned more than $46,930.

In May 2010, median annual wages in industries employing the largest numbers of pest control workers were as follows:

Federal executive branch	$55,890
Local government	45,720
Elementary and secondary schools	39,530
Services to buildings and dwellings	37,580
Employment services	36,260

Most pest control workers are employed full time. Working evenings and weekends is common.

Job Outlook

Pest Control Workers
Percent change in employment, projected 2010-20

Pest Control Workers	26%
Total, All Occupations	14%
Building and Grounds Cleaning and Maintenance Occupations	12%

Note: All Occupations includes all occupations in the U.S. Economy.
Source: U.S. Bureau of Labor Statistics, Employment Projections program

Employment of pest control workers is expected to grow 26 percent from 2010 to 2020, faster than the average for all occupations. Employment is projected to increase as more people use professional pest control services rather than trying to control pests themselves. Environmental and health concerns also will result in more people hiring professionals.

Population growth, particularly in the South, where pests are more common, should result in more buildings that will require additional pest management.

Job Prospects

Job opportunities are expected to be very good. The limited number of people seeking work in pest control, expected job growth, and the need to replace workers who leave this occupation should result in many job openings.

Employment projections data for pest control workers, 2010-20

Occupational Title	SOC Code	Employment, 2010	Projected Employment, 2020	Change, 2010-20	
				Percent	Numeric
Pest Control Workers	37-2021	68,400	86,200	26	17,900
SOURCE: U.S. Bureau of Labor Statistics, Employment Projections program					

Similar Occupations

This table shows a list of occupations with job duties that are similar to those of pest control workers.

Occupation	Job Duties	Entry-Level Education	Median Annual Pay, May 2010
Construction Laborers and Helpers	Construction laborers and helpers do many basic tasks that require physical labor on construction sites.	See How to Become One	$28,410
Grounds Maintenance Workers	Grounds maintenance workers provide a pleasant outdoor environment by ensuring that the grounds of houses, businesses, and parks are attractive, orderly, and healthy.	See How to Become One	$23,740
Janitors and Building Cleaners	Janitors and building cleaners keep many types of buildings clean, orderly, and in good condition.	Less than high school	$22,210

Contacts for More Information

For information about state licensing requirements, contact the local office of the U.S. Department of Agriculture or the state's environmental protection (or conservation) agency. For more information on pest control careers, visit National Pest Management Association

Suggested citation:

Bureau of Labor Statistics, U.S. Department of Labor, Occupational Outlook Handbook, 2012-13 Edition, Pest Control Workers, on the Internet at http://www.bls.gov/ooh/building-and-grounds-cleaning/pest-control-workers.htm.

Accountants and Auditors

Quick Facts: Accountants and Auditors	
2010 Median Pay	$61,690 per year $29.66 per hour
Entry-Level Education	Bachelor's degree
Work Experience in a Related Occupation	None
On-the-job Training	None
Number of Jobs, 2010	1,216,900
Job Outlook, 2010-20	16% (About as fast as average)
Employment Change, 2010-20	190,700

What Accountants and Auditors Do

Accountants and auditors prepare and examine financial records. They ensure that financial records are accurate and that taxes are paid properly and on time. Accountants and auditors assess financial operations and work to help ensure that organizations run efficiently.

Duties

Accountants and auditors typically do the following:

- Examine financial statements to be sure that they are accurate and comply with laws and regulations
- Compute taxes owed, prepare tax returns, and ensure that taxes are paid properly and on time
- Inspect account books and accounting systems for efficiency and use of accepted accounting procedures
- Organize and maintain financial records
- Assess financial operations and make best-practices recommendations to management
- Suggest ways to reduce costs, enhance revenues, and improve profits

In addition to examining and preparing financial documentation, accountants and auditors must explain their findings. This includes face-to-face meetings with organization managers and individual clients, and preparing written reports.

Many accountants and auditors specialize, depending on the particular organization that they work for.Some organizations specialize in assurance services (improving the quality or context of information for decision makers) or risk management (determining the

Accountants and auditors examine financial statements for accuracy and conformance with laws.

probability of a misstatement on financial documentation). Other organizations specialize in specific industries, such as healthcare.

Some workers with a background in accounting and auditing teach in colleges and universities. For more information, see the profile on postsecondary teachers .

The four main types of accountants and auditors are the following:

Public accountants do a broad range of accounting, auditing, tax, and consulting tasks. Their clients include corporations, governments, and individuals.

They work with financial documents that clients are required by law to disclose. These include tax forms and balance sheet statements that corporations must provide potential investors. For example, some public accountants concentrate on tax matters, advising corporations about the tax advantages of certain business decisions or preparing individual income tax returns.

External auditors review clients' financial statements and inform investors and authorities that the statements have been correctly prepared and reported.

Public accountants, many of whom are Certified Public Accountants (CPAs), generally have their own businesses or work for public accounting firms.

Some public accountants specialize in forensic accounting, investigating financial crimes, such as securities fraud and embezzlement, bankruptcies and contract disputes, and other complex and possibly criminal financial transactions. Forensic accountants combine their knowledge of accounting and finance with law and investigative techniques to determine if an activity is illegal. Many forensic accountants work closely with law enforcement personnel and lawyers during investigations and often appear as expert witnesses during trials.

Management accountants, also called cost, managerial, industrial, corporate, or private accountants, record and analyze the financial information of the organizations for which they work. The information that management accountants prepare is intended for internal use by business managers, not by the general public.

They often work on budgeting and performance evaluation. They may also help organizations plan the cost of doing business. Some may work with financial managers on asset management, which involves planning and selecting financial investments such as stocks, bonds, and real estate.

Government accountants maintain and examine the records of government agencies and audit private businesses and individuals whose activities are subject to government regulations or taxation. Accountants employed by federal, state, and local governments ensure that revenues are received and spent in accordance with laws and regulations.

Internal auditors check for mismanagement of an organization's funds. They identify ways to improve the processes for finding and eliminating waste and fraud. The practice of internal auditing is not regulated, but the Institute of Internal Auditors (IIA) provides generally accepted standards.

Information technology auditors are internal auditors who review controls for their organization's computer systems, to ensure that the financial data comes from a reliable source.

Work Environment

Accountants and auditors held about 1.2 million jobs in 2010.

Most accountants and auditors work in offices, although some work from home. Auditors may travel to their clients' places of business.

The following industries employed the most accountants and auditors in 2010:

Accounting, tax preparation, bookkeeping, and payroll services	24%
Finance and insurance	8
State and local government, excluding education and hospitals	7
Manufacturing	6
Management of companies and enterprises	6

Work Schedules

Most accountants and auditors work full time. In 2010, one in five worked more than 40 hours per week. Longer hours are typical at certain times of the year, such as at the end of the budget year or during tax season.

How to Become an Accountant or Auditor

Most accountants and auditors need at least a bachelor's degree in accounting or a related field. Certification within a specific field of accounting improves job prospects. For example, many accountants become Certified Public Accountants (CPAs).

Education

Most accountant and auditor positions require at least a bachelor's degree in accounting or a related field. Some employers prefer to hire applicants who have a master's degree, either in accounting or in business administration with a concentration in accounting.

A few universities and colleges offer specialized programs, such as a bachelor's degree in internal auditing. In some cases, graduates of community colleges, as well as bookkeepers and accounting clerks who meet the education and experience requirements set by their employers, get junior accounting positions and advance to accountant positions by showing their accounting skills on the job.

Work experience is important for getting a job, and most states require experience before an accountant can apply for a CPA license. Many colleges help students gain practical experience through summer or part-time internships with public accounting or business firms.

Licenses

Every accountant filing a report with the Securities and Exchange Commission (SEC) is required by law to be a Certified Public Accountant (CPA). Many other accountants choose to become a CPA to enhance their job prospects or to gain clients.

CPAs are licensed by their state's Board of Accountancy. Becoming a CPA requires passing a national exam and meeting other state requirements.

As of 2012, 46 states and the District of Columbia required CPA candidates to complete 150 semester hours of college coursework, which is 30 hours more than the usual 4-year bachelor's degree. Many schools offer a 5-year combined bachelor's and master's degree to meet the 150-hour requirement, but a master's degree is not required.

A few states allow a number of years of public accounting experience to substitute for a college degree.

All states use the four-part Uniform CPA Examination from the American Institute of Certified Public Accountants. Candidates do not have to pass all four parts at once, but most states require that they pass all four parts within 18 months of passing their first part.

Almost all states require CPAs to take continuing education to keep their license.

Certification

Certification provides an advantage in the job market because it shows professional competence in a specialized field of accounting and auditing. Accountants and auditors seek certifications from a variety of professional societies. Some of the most common certifications are listed below:

The Institute of Management Accountants offers the Certified Management Accountant (CMA). Applicants must have worked at least 2 years in management accounting, pass a four-part exam, agree to meet continuing education requirements, and comply with standards of professional conduct.

The Institute of Internal Auditors (IIA) offers the Certified Internal Auditor (CIA) to graduates from accredited colleges and universities who have worked for 2 years as internal auditors and have passed a four-part exam. The IIA also offers the Certified in Control Self-Assessment (CCSA), Certified Government Auditing Professional (CGAP), and Certified Financial Services Auditor (CFSA) to those who pass the exams and meet both educational and experience requirements.

ISACA offers the Certified Information Systems Auditor (CISA) to candidates who pass an exam and have 5 years of experience auditing information systems. Information systems experience, financial or operational auditing experience, or related college credit hours can be substituted for up to 2 years of experience in information systems auditing, control, or security.

For accountants with a CPA, the American Institute of CPAs (AICPA) offers the option to receive any or all of the Accredited in Business Valuation (ABV), Certified Information Technology Professional (CITP), or Personal Financial Specialist (PFS) certifications. The business valuation certification requires a written exam and completion of at least 10 business valuation projects that demonstrate a candidate's experience and competence. The technology certification requires the achievement of a set number of points awarded for business technology experience and education. Candidates for the personal financial specialist certification also must achieve a certain numbers of points based on experience and education, pass a written exam, and submit references.

Advancement

Some top executives have a background in accounting, internal auditing, or finance. For more information, see the profile on top executives .

Beginning public accountants often advance to positions with more responsibility in 1 or 2 years and to senior positions within another few years. Those who excel may become supervisors, managers, or partners; open their own public accounting firm; or transfer to executive positions in management accounting or internal auditing in private firms.

Management accountants often start as cost accountants, junior internal auditors, or trainees for other accounting positions. As they rise through the organization, they may advance to accounting manager, chief cost accountant, budget director, or manager of internal auditing. Some become controllers, treasurers, financial vice presidents, chief financial officers, or corporation presidents.

Public accountants, management accountants, and internal auditors can move from one aspect of accounting and auditing to another. Public accountants often move into management accounting or internal auditing. Management accountants may become internal auditors, and internal auditors may become management accountants. However, it is less common for management accountants or internal auditors to move into public accounting.

Important Qualities

Analytical skills. Accountants and auditors must be able to identify issues in documentation and suggest solutions. For example, public accountants use analytical skills in their work to minimize tax liability, and internal auditors do so when identifying fraudulent use of funds.

Communication skills. Accountants and auditors must be able to listen carefully to facts and concerns from clients, managers, and others. They must also be able to discuss the results of their work in both meetings and written reports.

Detail oriented. Accountants and auditors must pay attention to detail when compiling and examining documentation.

Math skills. Accountants must be able to analyze, compare, and interpret facts and figures, although complex math skills are not necessary.

Organizational skills. Strong organizational skills are important for accountants and auditors who often work with a range of financial documents for a variety of clients.

Pay

Accountants and Auditors
Median annual wages, May 2010

Accountants and Auditors	$61,690
Business and Financial Operations Occupations	$60,670
Total, All Occupations	$33,840

Note: All Occupations includes all occupations in the U.S. Economy.
Source: U.S. Bureau of Labor Statistics, Occupational Employment Statistics

The median annual wage of accountants and auditors was $61,690 in May 2010. The median wage is the wage at which half the workers in an occupation earned more than that amount and half earned less. The lowest 10 percent earned less than $38,940 and the top 10

percent earned more than $106,880.

Most accountants and auditors work full time. In 2010, one in five worked more than 40 hours per week. Longer hours are typical at certain times of the year, such as at the end of the budget year or during tax season.

Job Outlook

Accountants and Auditors
Percent change in employment, projected 2010-20

Business and Financial Operations Occupations	17%
Accountants and Auditors	16%
Total, All Occupations	14%

Note: All Occupations includes all occupations in the U.S. Economy.
Source: U.S. Bureau of Labor Statistics, Employment Projections program

Employment of accountants and auditors is expected to grow 16 percent from 2010 to 2020, about as fast as the average for all occupations. There has been an increased focus on accounting in response to corporate scandals and recent financial crises. Stricter laws and regulations, particularly in the financial sector, will likely increase the demand for accounting services as organizations seek to comply with new standards. Additionally, tighter lending standards are expected to increase the importance of audits, as this is a key way for organizations to demonstrate their creditworthiness.

The continued globalization of business should lead to more demand for accounting expertise and services related to international trade and international mergers and acquisitions.

Job Prospects

Accountants and auditors who have earned professional recognition, especially as a Certified Public Accountants (CPA), should have the best prospects. Job applicants who have a master's degree in accounting or a master's degree in business with a concentration in accounting also may have an advantage.

However, competition should be strong for jobs with the most prestigious accounting and business firms.

Employment projections data for accountants and auditors, 2010-20

Occupational Title	SOC Code	Employment, 2010	Projected Employment, 2020	Change, 2010-20	
				Percent	Numeric
Accountants and Auditors	13-2011	1,216,900	1,407,600	16	190,700
SOURCE: U.S. Bureau of Labor Statistics, Employment Projections program					

Similar Occupations

This table shows a list of occupations with job duties that are similar to those of accountants and auditors.

Occupation	Job Duties	Entry-Level Education	Median Annual Pay, May 2010
Bookkeeping, Accounting, and Auditing Clerks	Bookkeeping, accounting, and auditing clerks produce financial records for organizations. They record financial transactions, update statements, and check financial records for accuracy.	High school diploma or equivalent	$34,030
Budget Analysts	Budget analysts help public and private institutions organize their finances. They prepare budget reports and monitor institutional spending.	Bachelor's degree	$68,200
Cost Estimators	Cost estimators collect and analyze data to estimate the time, money, resources, and labor required for product manufacturing, construction projects, or services. Some specialize in a particular industry or product type.	Bachelor's degree	$57,860
Financial Analysts	Financial analysts provide guidance to businesses and individuals making investment decisions. They assess the performance of stocks, bonds, and other types of investments.	Bachelor's degree	$74,350

Financial Examiners	Financial examiners ensure compliance with laws governing financial institutions and transactions. They review balance sheets, evaluate the risk level of loans, and assess bank management.	Bachelor's degree	$74,940
Financial Managers	Financial managers are responsible for the financial health of an organization. They produce financial reports, direct investment activities, and develop strategies and plans for the long-term financial goals of their organization.	Bachelor's degree	$103,910
Management Analysts	Management analysts, often called management consultants, propose ways to improve an organization's efficiency. They advise managers on how to make organizations more profitable through reduced costs and increased revenues.	Bachelor's degree	$78,160
Personal Financial Advisors	Personal financial advisors give financial advice to people. They help with investments, taxes, and insurance decisions.	Bachelor's degree	$64,750
Postsecondary Teachers	Postsecondary teachers instruct students in a wide variety of academic and vocational subjects beyond the high school level. They also conduct research and publish scholarly papers and books.	Doctoral or professional degree	$62,050
Tax Examiners and Collectors, and Revenue Agents	Tax examiners and collectors, and revenue agents ensure that governments get their tax money from businesses and citizens. They review tax returns, conduct audits, identify taxes owed, and collect overdue tax payments.	Bachelor's degree	$49,360
Top Executives	Top executives devise strategies and policies to ensure that an organization meets its goals. They plan, direct, and coordinate operational activities of companies and public or private-sector organizations.	See How to Become One	$101,250

Contacts for More Information

For more information about accredited accounting programs, visit AACSB International—Association to Advance Collegiate Schools of Business

For more information about management accounting and the CMA designation, visit Institute of Management Accountants

For more information about internal auditing and the CIA designation, visit The Institute of Internal Auditors

For more information about information systems auditing and the CISA designation, visit ISACA

Suggested citation:

Bureau of Labor Statistics, U.S. Department of Labor, Occupational Outlook Handbook, 2012-13 Edition, Accountants and Auditors, on the Internet at http://www.bls.gov/ooh/business-and-financial/accountants-and-auditors.htm.

Appraisers and Assessors of Real Estate

Quick Facts: Appraisers and Assessors of Real Estate	
2010 Median Pay	$48,500 per year $23.32 per hour
Entry-Level Education	High school diploma or equivalent
Work Experience in a Related Occupation	None
On-the-job Training	Apprenticeship
Number of Jobs, 2010	77,800
Job Outlook, 2010-20	7% (Slower than average)
Employment Change, 2010-20	5,800

What Appraisers and Assessors of Real Estate Do

Appraisers and assessors of real estate estimate the value of real property—land and the buildings on that land— before it is sold, mortgaged, taxed, insured, or developed.

Duties

Appraisers and assessors of real estate typically do the following:

- Verify legal descriptions of real estate properties in public records
- Inspect new and existing properties, noting unique characteristics
- Photograph the interior and exterior of properties
- Use "comparables," or similar nearby properties, to help determine value
- Prepare written reports on the property value
- Prepare and maintain current data on each real estate property

Appraisers and assessors work in localities that they are familiar with so that they know any environmental or other concerns that may affect the property's value.

Appraisers typically value one property at a time, and they often specialize in a certain type of real estate. For example,

- **Commercial appraisers** specialize in property used commercially, such as office buildings, stores, and hotels.
- **Residential appraisers** focus on appraising property in which people live, such as duplexes and condominiums, and appraise only those that house one to four families.

When estimating a property's value, appraisers note unique characteristics of the property and surrounding area, such as a noisy highway nearby. They also consider the condition of a building's foundation and roof or any renovations that may have been done. In addition to photographing the outside of the building to document its condition, appraisers might also photograph a certain room or feature. After visiting the property, the appraiser estimates the value of the property by considering things such as comparable home sales, lease records, location, view, previous appraisals, and income potential. During the entire process, appraisers meticulously record their research, observations, and methods used in calculating the property's value.

Assessors mostly work for local governments and value properties for property tax assessments. Unlike appraisers, who generally focus on one property at a time, assessors often value an entire neighborhood of homes at once by using mass appraisal techniques and computer-assisted mass appraisal systems.

Assessors must be up-to-date on tax assessment procedures. Taxpayers sometimes challenge the assessment because they feel they are being charged too much for property tax. Assessors must be able to defend the accuracy of their property assessments, either to the owner directly or at a public hearing.

Assessors also keep a database of every property in their jurisdiction, identifying the property owner, assessment history, and size of the property, as well as property maps detailing the property distribution of the jurisdiction.

Work Environment

Appraisers and assessors of real estate held about 77,800 jobs in 2010. The following industries employed the most appraisers and assessors of real estate in 2010:

Activities related to real estate	34%
Local government	33
State government	4
Nondepository credit intermediation	2
Depository credit intermediation	2

Although appraisers and assessors of real estate work in offices, they spend a large part of their day in the field, conducting site visits. Time spent in the field versus in the office depends on the specialty. Residential appraisers tend to spend less time on office work than commercial appraisers, who might spend up to several weeks analyzing information and writing reports on one property. Appraisers who work for banks and mortgage companies generally spend most of their time inside the office, making site visits when necessary.

Work Schedules

Appraisers and assessors of real estate typically work full time during regular business hours. However, self-employed appraisers, often called "independent fee appraisers," usually work more than a

Appraisers and assessors of real estate inspect new and existing properties.

standard 40-hour workweek, including writing reports during evenings and on weekends.

How to Become an Appraiser or Assessor of Real Estate

The requirements to become a fully qualified appraiser or assessor are complex and vary by state and, sometimes, by the value or type of property. In general, most appraisers of residential real property must have at least an associate's degree, while appraisers of commercial real property must have at least a bachelor's degree. In some localities, appraisers may qualify with a high school diploma. Employers generally require these candidates to take basic appraisal courses, complete on-the-job training through an apprenticeship, and work enough hours to meet the requirements for appraisal licenses or certificates. In addition, both appraisers and assessors must be licensed or certified, but requirements vary by state. Check with your state's licensing board for specific requirements.

Education and Training

Although requirements vary by state, appraisers of residential real property usually must have at least an associate's degree, and appraisers of commercial property usually must have at least a bachelor's degree. In practice, however, most have a bachelor's degree. Courses in subjects such as economics, finance, mathematics, computer science, English, and business or real estate law can be very useful for prospective appraisers and assessors.

For assessors, most states set education and experience requirements that an assessor must meet to practice. A few states have no statewide requirements; instead, each locality sets the standards. In some localities, candidates may qualify with a high school diploma. Employers generally require these candidates to take basic appraisal courses, complete on-the-job training through an apprenticeship, and work enough hours to meet the requirements for appraisal licenses or certificates.

Licenses and Certification

Federal law requires that most appraisers have state certification. There is no such federal requirement for assessors, although some states require certification.

Appraisers generally value one property at a time, while assessors value many at once, but both occupations use similar methods and techniques. As a result, assessors and appraisers tend to take the same courses for certification. In addition to passing a statewide examination, candidates must usually complete a set number of on-the-job hours.

The level of certification determines what type of property a person may appraise. The two federally required certifications are:
- Certified Residential Real Property Appraiser
- Certified General Real Property Appraiser

Being a Certified Residential Real Property Appraiser is the minimum requirement to appraise a residential property with a loan amount over $250,000 or any other type of property even if the loan amount is less than $250,000. To get this certification requires:
- an associate's degree or 21 units of continuing education
- 200 hours of appraiser-specific classroom training
- 2,500 hours of work experience over at least 2 years

Being a Certified General Real Property Appraiser permits a person to appraise any property of any type and any value. To get this certification requires:
- a bachelor's degree or 30 units of continuing education
- 300 hours of appraiser-specific classroom training
- 3,000 hours of work experience over at least 2½ years

Most states offer a third certification: the Licensed Residential Real Property Appraiser. With this certification, appraisers may appraise noncomplex one-to-four unit residences with a value of less than

$1,000,000 and complex one-to-four unit residences with a value of less than $250,000. To get this certification requires:
- 150 qualifying education hours
- 2,000 hours of on-the-job training over at least 1 year

For all of these certifications, candidates must:
- have 15 hours of classroom instruction on the Uniform Standards of Professional Appraisal Practice
- pass an exam

In most states, people who are working on the requirements for licenses or certification as an appraiser are considered to be trainees. Training programs vary by state, but they usually require candidates to take at least 75 hours of specified appraiser education before applying for a job as a trainee.

Unlike appraisers, assessors have no federal requirement for certification. In states that mandate certification for assessors, the requirements are usually similar to those for appraisers. Some states also have more than one level of certification.

For those states that do not require certificates for assessors, the hiring office usually requires the candidate to take basic appraisal courses, complete on-the-job training, and work enough hours to meet the requirements for appraisal licenses or certificates. Many assessors also have a state appraisal license.

Assessors tend to start working in an assessor's office that provides on-the-job training; smaller municipalities are often unable to provide this experience. An alternate source of experience for aspiring assessors is through a revaluation firm.

Both appraisers and assessors must take continuing education to keep the license or certification. Requirements vary by state.

Important Qualities

Analytical skills. Appraisers and assessors of real estate use many sources of data when valuing real estate. As a result, they must carefully research and analyze all data before producing a final written report.

Customer-service skills. Because appraisers must regularly interact with clients, being polite and friendly is important. In addition, these characteristics may help expand future business opportunities.

Organizational skills. To successfully accomplish all the tasks related to appraising and assessing a property, appraisers and assessors of real estate need good organizational skills.

Problem-solving skills. Appraisers and assessors of real estate may encounter unexpected problems when appraising or assessing a property's value. The ability to develop and apply an alternative solution is crucial to successfully completing the report on time.

Time-management skills. Appraisers and assessors of real estate often work under time constraints, sometimes appraising many properties in a single day. As a result, managing time and meeting deadlines are important.

Pay

Appraisers and Assessors of Real Estate	
Median annual wages, May 2010	
Business and Financial Operations Occupations	$60,670
Appraisers and Assessors of Real Estate	$48,500
Total, All Occupations	$33,840

Note: All Occupations includes all occupations in the U.S. Economy.
Source: U.S. Bureau of Labor Statistics, Occupational Employment Statistics

The median annual wage of appraisers and assessors of real estate was $48,500 in May 2010. The median wage is the wage at which half the workers in an occupation earned more than that amount and half earned less. The lowest 10 percent earned less than $25,920, and the top 10 percent earned more than $90,650.

In May 2010, median annual wages in industries employing the largest numbers of appraisers and assessors were as follows:

Nondepository credit intermediation	$62,050
Depository credit iintermediation	58,350
State government	52,260
Activities related to real estate	49,000
Local government	45,370

Appraisers and assessors of real estate typically work full time during regular business hours. However, self-employed appraisers, often called "independent fee appraisers," usually work more than a standard 40-hour workweek, including spending their evenings and weekends writing reports.

Earnings for independent-fee appraisers can vary significantly because they are paid fees on the basis of each appraisal.

Job Outlook

Appraisers and Assessors of Real Estate

Percent change in employment, projected 2010-20

Business and Financial Operations Occupations	17%
Total, All Occupations	14%
Appraisers and Assessors of Real Estate	7%

Note: All Occupations includes all occupations in the U.S. Economy.
Source: U.S. Bureau of Labor Statistics. Employment Projections program

Employment of appraisers and assessors of real estate is expected to grow 7 percent from 2010 to 2020, slower than the average for all occupations. Demand for appraisal services is strongly tied to the real estate market, which can fluctuate in the short term. Over the long term, employment growth will be driven by economic expansion and population increases—factors that generate demand for real property. However, employment is projected to be held down by productivity increases brought about by the increased use of mobile technologies, which allow workers to appraise and assess more properties. The increased use of automated valuation models to appraise property for mortgages might also shift work from appraisers.

Job Prospects

Overall job opportunities are expected to be highly competitive. Employment opportunities should be best in areas with active real estate markets. Although opportunities for established certified appraisers are expected to be available in these areas, the cyclical nature of the real estate market will directly affect the number of jobs for appraisers, especially those who appraise residential properties. In times of recession, fewer people buy or sell real estate, decreasing the demand for appraisers. As a result, job opportunities should be best for appraisers who are able to switch specialties and appraise different types of properties.

Employment projections data for appraisers and assessors of real estate, 2010-20

Occupational Title	SOC Code	Employment, 2010	Projected Employment, 2020	Change, 2010-20	
				Percent	Numeric
Appraisers and Assessors of Real Estate	13-2021	77,800	83,500	7	5,800
SOURCE: U.S. Bureau of Labor Statistics, Employment Projections program					

Similar Occupations

This table shows a list of occupations with job duties that are similar to those of appraisers and assessors of real estate.

Occupation	Job Duties	Entry-Level Education	Median Annual Pay, May 2010
Claims Adjusters, Appraisers, Examiners, and Investigators	Claims adjusters, appraisers, examiners, and investigators evaluate insurance claims. They decide whether an insurance company must pay a claim, and if so, how much.	See How to Become One	$58,460
Construction and Building Inspectors	Construction and building inspectors ensure that new construction, changes, or repairs comply with local and national building codes and ordinances, zoning regulations, and contract specifications.	High school diploma or equivalent	$52,360
Real Estate Brokers and Sales Agents	Real estate brokers and sales agents help clients buy, sell, and rent properties. Brokers and agents do the same type of work, but brokers are licensed to manage their own real estate businesses. Sales agents must work with a broker.	High school diploma or equivalent	$42,680

Contacts for More Information

For more information about appraisers of real estate, visit American Society of Appraisers Appraisal Institute

For more information about assessors of real estate, visit International Association of Assessing Officers

For more information about licensure requirements for appraisers and assessors of real estate, visit Appraisal Foundation

Suggested citation:

Bureau of Labor Statistics, U.S. Department of Labor, Occupational Outlook Handbook, 2012-13 Edition, Appraisers and Assessors of Real Estate, on the Internet at http://www.bls.gov/ooh/business-and-financial/appraisers-and-assessors-of-real-estate.htm .

Budget Analysts

Quick Facts: Budget Analysts	
2010 Median Pay	$68,200 per year $32.79 per hour
Entry-Level Education	Bachelor's degree
Work Experience in a Related Occupation	None
On-the-job Training	None
Number of Jobs, 2010	62,100
Job Outlook, 2010-20	10% (About as fast as average)
Employment Change, 2010-20	6,500

What Budget Analysts Do

Budget analysts help public and private institutions organize their finances. They prepare budget reports and monitor institutional spending.

Duties

Budget analysts typically do the following:

- Work with program and project managers to develop the organization's budget
- Review managers' budget proposals for completeness, accuracy, and compliance with laws and other regulations
- Combine all the program and department budgets together into a consolidated organizational budget and review all funding requests for merit
- Explain their recommendations for funding requests to others in the organization, legislators, and the public
- Help the chief operation officer, agency head, or other top managers analyze the proposed plan and find alternatives if the projected results are unsatisfactory
- Monitor organizational spending to ensure that it is within budget
- Inform program managers of the status and availability of funds
- Estimate future financial needs

Budget analysts advise various institutions—including governments, universities, and businesses—on how to organize their finances. They prepare annual and special reports and evaluate budget proposals. They analyze data to determine the costs and benefits of various programs and recommend funding levels based on their

Budget analysts prepare budget reports and monitor spending.

findings. Although elected officials (in government) or top executives (in a private company) usually make the final decision on an organization's budget, they rely on the work of budget analysts to prepare the information for that decision. For more information about elected officials and top executives, see the profiles on legislators and top executives .

Sometimes, budget analysts use cost-benefit analyses to review financial requests, assess program tradeoffs, and explore alternative funding methods. Budget analysts also may examine past budgets and research economic and financial developments that affect the organization's income and expenditures. Budget analysts may recommend program spending cuts or redistributing extra funds.

Throughout the year, budget analysts oversee spending to ensure compliance with the budget and determine whether changes to funding levels are needed for certain programs. Analysts also evaluate programs to determine whether they are producing the desired results.

In addition to providing technical analysis, budget analysts must effectively communicate their recommendations to officials within the organization. For example, if there is a difference between the approved budget and actual spending, budget analysts may write a report explaining the variations and recommend changes to reconcile the differences.

Budget analysts working in government attend committee hearings to explain their recommendations to legislators. Occasionally, budget analysts may evaluate how well a program is doing, provide policy analysis, and draft budget-related legislation.

Work Environment

Budget analysts held 62,100 jobs in 2010. They worked in a variety of settings, including government agencies, universities, and companies. Although budget analysts usually work in offices, some may travel to get budget details firsthand or to verify funding allocations. The following industries employed the most budget analysts in 2010:

Federal government, excluding postal service	21%
Educational services; state, local, and private	14
State government, excluding education and hospitals	12
Local government, excluding education and hospitals	11
Manufacturing	10

Budget analysts spend most of their time working independently, compiling and analyzing data and preparing budget proposals. In nonprofit and government organizations, analysts try to find the most efficient way to distribute funds and other resources among various departments and programs. In private firms, a budget analyst's main responsibility is to review the budget and seek new ways to improve efficiency and increase profits.

Work Schedules

Most budget analysts work full time, and overtime is sometimes required during final reviews of budgets. The pressures of deadlines and tight work schedules can be stressful.

How to Become a Budget Analyst

A bachelor's degree is typically required, although some employers prefer candidates with a master's degree.

Education

Employers generally require budget analysts to have at least a bachelor's degree. However, some employers may require candidates to have a master's degree. Because developing a budget requires strong numerical and analytical skills, courses in statistics or accounting are helpful. For the federal government, a bachelor's degree in any field is enough for an entry-level budget analyst position. State and local governments have varying requirements but usually require a bachelor's degree in one of many areas, such as accounting, finance, business, public administration, economics, statistics, political science, or sociology.

Sometimes, budget-related or finance-related work experience can be substituted for formal education.

Training

In some organizations, budget analysts learn the job by working through one complete budget cycle. During the cycle, which typically lasts 1 year, analysts become familiar with the steps involved in the budgeting process. Many budget analysts also take professional development classes throughout their careers.

Certification

Government budget analysts may earn the Certified Government Financial Manager credential from the Association of Government Accountants . To earn this certification, candidates must have a minimum of a bachelor's degree, 24 credit hours of study in financial management, 2 years of professional-level experience in governmental financial management, and pass a series of exams. To keep the certification, budget analysts must take 80 hours of continuing education every 2 years.

Advancement

Entry-level budget analysts begin with limited responsibilities, but advancement is common. As analysts gain experience, they have the opportunity to advance to intermediate and senior budget analyst positions.

Important Qualities

Analytical skills. Budget analysts must be able to process a variety of information, evaluate costs and benefits, and solve complex problems.

Communication skills. Budget analysts need strong communication skills because they often have to explain and defend their analyses and recommendations in meetings and legislative committee hearings.

Detail oriented. Creating an efficient budget requires careful analysis of each budget item.

Math skills. Most budget analysts need math skills and should be able to use certain software, including spreadsheets, database functions, and financial analysis programs.

Writing skills. Budget analysts must present technical information in writing that is understandable for the intended audience.

Pay

Budget Analysts
Median annual wages, May 2010

Budget Analysts	$68,200
Business and Financial Operations Occupations	$60,670
Total, All Occupations	$33,840

Note: All Occupations includes all occupations in the U.S. Economy.
Source: U.S. Bureau of Labor Statistics. Occupational Employment Statistics

The median annual wage of budget analysts was $68,200 in May 2010. The median wage is the wage at which half the workers in an occupation earned more than that amount and half earned less. The lowest 10 percent earned less than $44,860, and the top 10 percent earned more than $101,660.

Most budget analysts work full time, and overtime is sometimes required during final reviews of budgets.

Job Outlook

Budget Analysts
Percent change in employment, projected 2010-20

Business and Financial Operations Occupations	17%
Total, All Occupations	14%
Budget Analysts	10%

Note: All Occupations includes all occupations in the U.S. Economy.
Source: U.S. Bureau of Labor Statistics. Employment Projections program

Employment of budget analysts is expected to grow 10 percent from 2010 to 2020, about as fast as the average for all occupations. Budget analysis is getting more complex as more types of data and statistical techniques become available. The greater complexity of the job and its expanding job duties are expected to create a need for more budget analysts.

Efficient use of public funds is increasingly expected. During periods of budget cutbacks, the expertise of budget analysts remains in high demand, meaning employment remains more stable in comparison with other public employees. Therefore, some employment growth from 2010 to 2020 is likely, but it also will likely be tempered by limited government spending.

Employment projections data for budget analysts, 2010-20

Occupational Title	SOC Code	Employment, 2010	Projected Employment, 2020	Change, 2010-20	
				Percent	Numeric
Budget Analysts	13-2031	62,100	68,500	10	6,500
SOURCE: U.S. Bureau of Labor Statistics, Employment Projections program					

Similar Occupations

This table shows a list of occupations with job duties that are similar to those of budget analysts.

Occupation	Job Duties	Entry-Level Education	Median Annual Pay, May 2010
Accountants and Auditors	Accountants and auditors prepare and examine financial records. They ensure that financial records are accurate and that taxes are paid properly and on time. Accountants and auditors assess financial operations and work to help ensure that organizations run efficiently.	Bachelor's degree	$61,690
Cost Estimators	Cost estimators collect and analyze data to estimate the time, money, resources, and labor required for product manufacturing, construction projects, or services. Some specialize in a particular industry or product type.	Bachelor's degree	$57,860
Economists	Economists study the production and distribution of resources, goods, and services.	Bachelor's degree	$89,450
Financial Analysts	Financial analysts provide guidance to businesses and individuals making investment decisions. They assess the performance of stocks, bonds, and other types of investments.	Bachelor's degree	$74,350
Financial Managers	Financial managers are responsible for the financial health of an organization. They produce financial reports, direct investment activities, and develop strategies and plans for the long-term financial goals of their organization.	Bachelor's degree	$103,910
Management Analysts	Management analysts, often called management consultants, propose ways to improve an organization's efficiency. They advise managers on how to make organizations more profitable through reduced costs and increased revenues.	Bachelor's degree	$78,160
Tax Examiners and Collectors, and Revenue Agents	Tax examiners and collectors, and revenue agents ensure that governments get their tax money from businesses and citizens. They review tax returns, conduct audits, identify taxes owed, and collect overdue tax payments.	Bachelor's degree	$49,360

Contacts for More Information

For information about becoming a state budget analyst, visit National Association of State Budget Officers

For information about the Government Financial Manager certification, visit Association of Government Accountants

Suggested citation:

Bureau of Labor Statistics, U.S. Department of Labor, Occupational Outlook Handbook, 2012-13 Edition, Budget Analysts, on the Internet at
http://www.bls.gov/ooh/business-and-financial/budget-analysts.htm .

Claims Adjusters, Appraisers, Examiners, and Investigators

Quick Facts: Claims Adjusters, Appraisers, Examiners, and Investigators	
2010 Median Pay	$58,460 per year $28.11 per hour
Entry-Level Education	See How to Become One
Work Experience in a Related Occupation	None
On-the-job Training	See How to Become One
Number of Jobs, 2010	290,700
Job Outlook, 2010-20	3% (Slower than average)
Employment Change, 2010-20	7,500

What Claims Adjusters, Appraisers, Examiners, and Investigators Do

Claims adjusters, appraisers, examiners, and investigators evaluate insurance claims. They decide whether an insurance company must pay a claim, and if so, how much.

Duties

Claims adjusters, appraisers, examiners, and investigators typically do the following:

- Investigate, evaluate, and settle insurance claims
- Determine whether the insurance policy covers the loss claimed
- Decide the appropriate amount the insurance company should pay
- Ensure that claims are not fraudulent
- Contact claimants' doctors or employers to get additional information on questionable claims
- Confer with legal counsel on claims when needed
- Keep claims files, such as records of settled claims and an inventory of claims requiring detailed analysis
- Negotiate settlements
- Authorize payments

What insurance adjusters, examiners, and investigators do varies by the type of insurance company they work for. They must know a lot about what their company insures. For example, workers in property

Claims adjusters inspect property damage to determine how much the company should pay for the loss.

and casualty insurance must know housing and construction costs to properly evaluate damage from floods or fires. Workers in health insurance must be able to determine which types of treatments are medically necessary and which are questionable.

Some claims adjusters work as self-employed public adjusters.

Often, they are hired by claimants who prefer not to rely on the insurance company's adjuster. The goal of adjusters working for insurance companies is to save as much money for the company as possible. The goal of a public adjuster working for a claimant is to get the highest possible amount paid to the claimant.

Sometimes, self-employed adjusters are hired by insurance companies in place of hiring adjusters as regular employees. In this case, the self-employed adjusters work in the interest of the insurance company.

Adjusters inspect property damage to determine how much the insurance company should pay for the loss. The property they inspect could be a home, a business, or an automobile.

They interview the claimant and witnesses, inspect the property, and do additional research, such as look at police reports. Adjusters may consult with other workers, such as accountants, architects, construction workers, engineers, lawyers, and physicians, who can offer a more expert evaluation of a claim.

They gather information—including photographs and statements, either written or recorded audio or video—and put it in a report that claims examiners use to evaluate the claim. When the examiner approves policyholder's claim, the claims adjuster negotiates with the claimant and settles the claim.

If the claimant contests the outcome of the claim or the settlement, adjusters work with attorneys and expert witnesses to defend the insurer's position.

Appraisers estimate the cost or value of an insured item. Most appraisers who work for insurance companies and independent adjusting firms are auto damage appraisers. They inspect damaged vehicles after an accident and estimate the cost of repairs. This information then goes to the adjuster, who puts the estimated cost of repairs into the settlement.

Claims examiners review claims after they are submitted to ensure that proper guidelines have been followed by claimants and adjusters. They may assist adjusters with complicated claims or when, for example, a natural disaster occurs and the volume of claims increases.

Most claims examiners work for life or health insurance companies. Examiners who work for health insurance companies review health-related claims to see whether the costs are reasonable, given the diagnosis. After they review the claim, they authorize appropriate payment, deny the claim, or refer the claim to an investigator.

Examiners who work for life insurance companies review the

causes of death and pay particular attention to accidents, because most life insurance companies pay additional benefits if a death is accidental. Examiners also may review new applications for life insurance policies to make sure the applicants have no serious illnesses that would make them a high risk to insure.

Insurance investigators handle claims in which the company suspects fraudulent or criminal activity such as arson, staged accidents, or unnecessary medical treatments. The severity of insurance fraud cases varies, from claimants overstating vehicle damage to complicated fraud rings. Investigators often do surveillance work. For example, in the case of a fraudulent workers' compensation claim, an investigator may covertly watch the claimant to see if he or she does activities that would be ruled out by injuries stated in the claim.

Work Environment

Claims adjusters, appraisers, examiners, and investigators held 290,700 jobs in 2010. Their work environments vary. Claims adjusters and examiners spend time in offices reviewing documents and conducting research, in addition to working outside when examining damaged property. Appraisers and investigators work outside more often, inspecting damaged buildings and automobiles and conducting surveillance.

Workers who inspect damaged buildings must be wary of potential hazards, such as collapsed roofs and floors, as well as weakened structures.

Claims adjusters, appraisers, examiners, and investigators worked in the following industries in 2010:

Direct insurance (except life, health, and medical) carriers	32%
Federal government, excluding postal service	18
Other insurance related activities	17
State and local government, excluding education and hospitals	4
Management of companies and enterprises	2

Work Schedules

Most claims adjusters, appraisers, examiners, and investigators work full time. However, their work schedules vary.

In contrast, adjusters often must arrange their work schedules to accommodate evening and weekend appointments with clients. This sometimes results in adjusters working irregular schedules, especially when they have a lot of claims to review.

Auto damage appraisers typically work regular hours and rarely work on the weekends, although they often spend much of their time at automotive body shops estimating vehicle damage costs.

Insurance investigators often work irregular schedules because of the need to conduct surveillance and contact people who are not available during normal working hours. Early morning, evening, and weekend work is common.

How to Become a Claims Adjuster, Appraiser, Examiner, or Investigator

A high school diploma or equivalent is typically the minimum requirement to work as an adjuster, appraiser, examiner, or investigator.

Education

A high school diploma or equivalent is typically the minimum requirement to work as an adjuster, appraiser, examiner, or investigator. However, employers sometimes prefer to hire applicants

who have a bachelor's degree or some insurance-related work experience or vocational training. Auto damage appraisers typically have a 2-year postsecondary award or experience working in an auto repair shop, identifying and estimating the cost of automotive repair.

Different backgrounds or college coursework are best for different types of work in this occupation. For example, a business or an accounting background might be best for someone to specialize in claims of financial loss due to strikes, equipment breakdowns, or merchandise damage. College training in architecture or engineering is helpful for adjusting industrial claims, such as those involving damage from fires or other accidents. A legal background is beneficial to someone handling workers' compensation and product liability cases. A medical background is useful for examiners working on medical and life insurance claims.

Although auto damage appraisers are not required to have a college education, most companies prefer to hire people who have formal training, experience, or knowledge and technical skills to identify and estimate the cost of automotive repair. Many vocational colleges offer 2-year programs in auto body repair and teach students how to estimate the costs to repair damaged vehicles.

For investigator jobs, a high school diploma or equivalent is the typical education requirement. Most insurance companies prefer to hire people trained as law enforcement officers, private investigators, claims adjusters, or examiners because these workers have good interviewing and interrogation skills.

Training

At the beginning of their careers, claims adjusters, appraisers, examiners, and investigators work on small claims, under the supervision of an experienced worker. As they learn more about claims investigation and settlement, they are assigned larger, more complex claims.

Auto damage appraisers typically get on-the-job training, which may last several months. This training usually involves working under supervision of a more experienced appraiser while estimating damage costs until the employer decides the trainee is ready to do estimates on his or her own.

Licenses

Licensing requirements for claims adjusters, appraisers, examiners, and investigators vary by state. Some states have few requirements, and others require either completing pre-licensing education, a satisfactory score on a licensing exam, or both.

In some states, claims adjusters employed by insurance companies can work under the company license and need not become licensed themselves.

Public adjusters may need to meet separate or additional requirements.

Some states that require licensing also require a certain number of continuing education credits per year to renew the license. Federal and state laws and court decisions affect how claims must be handled and what insurance policies can and must cover. Examiners working on life and health claims must stay up-to-date on new medical procedures and prescription drugs. Examiners working on auto claims must be familiar with new car models and repair techniques. Workers can fulfill their continuing education requirements by attending classes or workshops, by writing articles for claims publications, or by giving lectures and presentations.

Important Qualities

Analytical skills. Adjusters and examiners must evaluate whether the insurance company is obligated to pay a claim and determine the amount to pay. Adjusters must carefully consider various pieces of information to reach a decision.

Communication skills. Claims adjusters and investigators must get information from a wide range of people, including claimants, witnesses, and medical experts. They must know the right questions to ask to gather the information they need.

Interpersonal skills. Adjustors, examiners, and investigators often meet with claimants and others who may be upset by the situation that requires a claim or by the settlement the company is offering. These workers must be understanding and yet firm with their company's policies.

Math skills. Appraisers must be able to calculate property damage.

Pay

Claims Adjusters, Appraisers, Examiners, and Investigators
Median annual wages, May 2010

Claims Adjusters, Examiners, and Investigators	$58,620
Claims Adjusters, Appraisers, Examiners, and Investigators	$58,460
Insurance Appraisers, Auto Damage	$56,230
Total, All Occupations	$33,840

Note: All Occupations includes all occupations in the U.S. Economy.
Source: U.S. Bureau of Labor Statistics. Occupational Employment Statistics

The median annual wage of claims adjusters, examiners, and investigators was $58,620 in May 2010. The median wage is the wage at which half of the workers in an occupation earned more than that amount and half earned less. The lowest 10 percent earned less than $35,710, and the top 10 percent earned more than $88,320.

The median annual wage of insurance appraisers of auto damage was $56,230 in May 2010. The lowest 10 percent earned less than $39,550, and the top 10 percent earned more than $78,950.

Most claims adjusters, appraisers, examiners, and investigators work full time. However, their work schedules vary.

In contrast, adjusters often must arrange their work schedules to accommodate evening and weekend appointments with clients. This sometimes results in adjusters working irregular schedules, especially when they have a lot of claims to review.

Auto damage appraisers typically work regular hours and rarely work on the weekends, although they often spend much of their time at automotive body shops estimating vehicle damage costs.

Insurance investigators often work irregular schedules because of the need to conduct surveillance and contact people who are not available during normal working hours. Early morning, evening, and weekend work is common.

Job Outlook

Claims Adjusters, Appraisers, Examiners, and Investigators
Percent change in employment, projected 2010-20

Total, All Occupations	14%
Claims Adjusters, Appraisers, Examiners, and Investigators	3%
Claims Adjusters, Examiners, and Investigators	3%
Insurance Appraisers, Auto Damage	-8%

Note: All Occupations includes all occupations in the U.S. Economy.
Source: U.S. Bureau of Labor Statistics. Employment Projections program

Employment of claims adjusters, examiners, and investigators is expected to grow 3 percent from 2010 to 2020, slower than the average for all occupations.

Employment growth should stem primarily from the growth of the health insurance industry. Federal legislation mandating individual coverage may increase the number of health insurance customers, including high-risk individuals who are more likely to file claims. This is expected to increase the demand for claims adjusters to determine which treatments are approved and how much the company will pay.

In addition, rising medical costs may result in a greater need for claims examiners to carefully review a growing number of medical claims. An increase in the number of claims being made by a growing elderly population should also spur demand for health insurance claims adjusters and examiners.

Demand for claims adjusters in property and casualty insurance is influenced by the total number of natural disasters, such as floods and fires. According to data from the Federal Emergency Management Agency, the number of natural disasters has increased in recent years. If this trend continues, claims adjusters in this field may see strong employment growth.

Despite these factors, employment in the largest employers of claims adjusters, examiners and investigators—direct insurance (except life, health, and medical) carriers and the federal government—is projected to decline, which will result in slow overall employment growth.

Employment of auto damage appraisers is expected to decline 8 percent from 2010 to 2020. As automobiles become safer, the number of traffic accidents is expected to decline. This will result in decreased demand for the services of auto damage appraisers.

Job Prospects

Job opportunities for claims adjusters and examiners should be best in the health insurance industry as the number of health insurance customers expands. Additionally, prospects for claims adjusters in property and casualty insurance will likely be best in areas susceptible to natural disasters. These areas include the Gulf Coast, which can have a large number of hurricanes, and the West Coast, which is vulnerable to wildfires.

Employment projections data for claims adjusters, appraisers, examiners, and investigators, 2010-20

Occupational Title	SOC Code	Employment, 2010	Projected Employment, 2020	Change, 2010-20 Percent	Numeric
Claims Adjusters, Appraisers, Examiners, and Investigators	13-1030	290,700	298,200	3	7,500
Claims Adjusters, Examiners, and Investigators	13-1031	280,100	288,400	3	8,300
Insurance Appraisers, Auto Damage	13-1032	10,600	9,800	-8	-800

SOURCE: U.S. Bureau of Labor Statistics, Employment Projections program

Similar Occupations

This table shows a list of occupations with job duties that are similar to those of claims adjusters, appraisers, examiners, and investigators.

Occupation	Job Duties	Entry-Level Education	Median Annual Pay, May 2010
Appraisers and Assessors of Real Estate	Appraisers and assessors of real estate estimate the value of real property—land and the buildings on that land— before it is sold, mortgaged, taxed, insured, or developed.	High school diploma or equivalent	$48,500
Automotive Body and Glass Repairers	Automotive body and glass repairers restore, refinish, and replace vehicle bodies and frames, windshields, and window glass.	High school diploma or equivalent	$37,580
Automotive Service Technicians and Mechanics	Automotive service technicians and mechanics, often called service technicians or service techs, inspect, maintain, and repair cars and light trucks.	High school diploma or equivalent	$35,790
Construction and Building Inspectors	Construction and building inspectors ensure that new construction, changes, or repairs comply with local and national building codes and ordinances, zoning regulations, and contract specifications.	High school diploma or equivalent	$52,360
Cost Estimators	Cost estimators collect and analyze data to estimate the time, money, resources, and labor required for product manufacturing, construction projects, or services. Some specialize in a particular industry or product type.	Bachelor's degree	$57,860
Fire Inspectors and Investigators	Fire inspectors visit and inspect buildings and other structures, such as sports arenas and shopping malls, to search for fire hazards and to ensure that federal, state, and local fire codes are met. They also test and inspect fire protection and fire extinguishing equipment to ensure that it works. Fire investigators determine the origin and cause of fires by searching the surrounding scene and collecting evidence.	High school diploma or equivalent	$52,230

Contacts for More Information

For more information about insurance, visit American Institute for Chartered Property Casualty Underwriters and the Insurance Institute of America ,International Claim Association, National Association of Public Insurance Adjusters

Suggested citation:

Bureau of Labor Statistics, U.S. Department of Labor, Occupational Outlook Handbook, 2012-13 Edition, Claims Adjusters, Appraisers, Examiners, and Investigators, on the Internet at http://www.bls.gov/ooh/business-and-financial/claims-adjusters-appraisers-examiners-and-investigators.htm .

Cost Estimators

Quick Facts: Cost Estimators	
2010 Median Pay	$57,860 per year $27.82 per hour
Entry-Level Education	Bachelor's degree
Work Experience in a Related Occupation	None
On-the-job Training	None
Number of Jobs, 2010	185,400
Job Outlook, 2010-20	36% (Much faster than average)
Employment Change, 2010-20	67,500

What Cost Estimators Do

Cost estimators collect and analyze data to estimate the time, money, resources, and labor required for product manufacturing, construction projects, or services. Some specialize in a particular industry or product type.

Duties

Cost estimators typically do the following:

- Consult with industry experts to discuss estimates and resolve issues
- Identify and quantify cost factors, such as production time and raw material, equipment, and labor expenses
- Travel to job sites to gather information on materials needed, labor requirements, and other factors
- Read blueprints and technical documents to prepare estimates
- Collaborate with engineers, architects, owners, and contractors on estimates
- Use sophisticated computer software to calculate estimates
- Evaluate a product's cost effectiveness or profitability
- Recommend ways to make a product more cost effective or profitable
- Prepare estimates for clients and other business managers
- Develop project plans for the duration of the project

Accurately predicting the cost, size, and duration of future construction and manufacturing projects is vital to the survival of any business. Cost estimators' calculations give managers or investors this information.

When making calculations, estimators analyze many inputs to determine how much time, money, and labor a project needs, or how profitable it will be. These estimates have to take many factors into account, including allowances for wasted material, bad weather, shipping delays, and other factors that can increase costs and lower profitability.

Cost estimators use sophisticated computer software, including database, simulation, and complex mathematical programs. Cost estimators often use a computer database with information on the costs of other similar projects.

General contractors usually hire cost estimators for specific parts of a large construction project, such as estimating the electrical work or the excavation phase. In such cases, the estimator calculates the cost of the construction phase for which the contractor is responsible, rather than calculating the cost of the entire project. The general contractor usually also has a cost estimator who calculates the total project cost by analyzing the bids that the subcontractors' cost estimators prepared.

Some estimators are hired by manufacturers to analyze certain products or processes.

The following are the two primary types of cost estimators:

Construction cost estimators estimate construction work. More than half of all cost estimators work in the construction industry. They may, for example, estimate the total cost of building a bridge or a highway. They may identify direct costs, such as raw materials and labor requirements, and set a timeline for the project. Although many work directly for construction firms, some work for contractors, architects, and engineering firms.

Manufacturing cost estimators calculate the costs of developing, producing, or redesigning a company's goods and services. For example, a cost estimator working for a home appliance manufacturer may determine whether a new type of dishwasher will be profitable to manufacture.

Some manufacturing cost estimators work in software development. Many high-technology products require a considerable amount of computer programming, and the costs of software development are difficult to calculate.

Two other groups also sometimes do cost estimating in their jobs. Operations research, production control, cost, and price analysts who work for government agencies may do significant amounts of cost estimating in the course of their usual duties. Construction managers also may spend considerable time estimating costs. For more information, see the profiles on operations research analysts and construction managers.

Estimators often collaborate with engineers and architects.

Work Environment

Cost estimators held about 185,400 jobs in 2010. The industries that employed the most cost estimators in 2010 were as follows:

Specialty trade contractors	36%
Construction of buildings	16
Manufacturing	15
Heavy and civil engineering construction	6
Repair and maintenance	6

While cost estimators generally work in offices, they often visit factory floors or construction sites. Depending on the industry, this may involve frequent travel.

Cost estimators often work under pressure and experience stress because of the need to meet deadlines. Inaccurate estimates can cause a firm to lose a bid or to lose money on a job that otherwise could have been profitable.

Work Schedules

Cost estimators usually work full time. However, overtime is common, especially when deadlines need to be met.

How to Become a Cost Estimator

A bachelor's degree and related work experience are increasingly important for becoming a cost estimator. However, some highly experienced construction workers with analytical abilities may qualify without a bachelor's degree.

Education and Training

A growing number of employers prefer candidates that have a bachelor's degree. A strong background in mathematics is essential.

Construction cost estimators generally need a bachelor's degree in an industry-related field, such as construction management or building science. Those interested in estimating manufacturing costs typically need a bachelor's degree in engineering, physical sciences, mathematics, or statistics. Some employers prefer candidates with backgrounds in business-related disciplines, such as accounting, finance, business, or economics.

Newly hired estimators often learn the industry by working alongside a more experienced cost estimator. This on-the-job training may last anywhere from several months to a few years, depending on the employer. Each company has its own way of handling estimates, and cost estimators have to learn their employers' ways of estimating costs.

Work Experience

It is important to gain relevant work experience in an industry before becoming a cost estimator. For example, construction cost estimators should have work experience in the construction industry. People interested in cost estimating can get experience through internships, cooperative education programs, or industry-related jobs.

Certification

Voluntary certification can show competence and experience in the field. In some instances, employers may require professional certification before hiring. The American Society of Professional Estimators , the Association for the Advancement of Cost Estimating International (also known as AACE International), and the Society of Cost Estimating and Analysis each offer a variety of certifications.

To become certified, estimators generally must have at least two years of estimating experience and must pass a written exam. In addition, some certification requirements may include publishing at least one article or paper in the field.

Important Qualities

Analytical skills. Accurately evaluating detailed specifications is crucial to a cost estimator's success. For example, a cost estimator must determine how to minimize costs without sacrificing quality.

Critical-thinking skills. Cost estimators must identify the strengths and weaknesses of potential strategies, especially when considering profitability. Information critical to a product's cost is not always straightforward, so estimators must devise creative ways to assess it.

Detail oriented. Cost estimators must pay attention to small details because they may have a large impact on a product's overall cost.

Speaking skills. Cost estimators must have good speaking skills because they often discuss complex product information with other industry specialists. They must also present and defend their estimates and recommendations in a clear and convincing way.

Technical skills. Detailed knowledge of industry processes, materials, and costs are vital to estimators. In addition, they should be able to use sophisticated computer programs to calculate equations and handle large databases.

Time-management skills. Because cost estimators often work on fixed deadlines, they must plan their work in advance and do their tasks efficiently and accurately.

Writing skills. Cost estimators must be able to write detailed reports. Often, these reports determine whether or not contracts are awarded or products are manufactured.

Pay

Cost Estimators
Median annual wages, May 2010

Business Operations Specialists	$60,660
Cost Estimators	$57,860
Total, All Occupations	$33,840

Note: All Occupations includes all occupations in the U.S. Economy.
Source: U.S. Bureau of Labor Statistics, Occupational Employment Statistics

The median annual wage of cost estimators was $57,860 in May 2010. The median wage is the wage at which half the workers in an occupation earned more than that amount and half earned less. The lowest 10 percent earned less than $34,100, and the top 10 percent earned more than $95,620.

Median annual wages in the industries employing the largest numbers of cost estimators in 2010 were as follows:

Heavy and civil engineering construction	$64,730
Construction of buildings	60,490
Specialty trade contractors	58,660
Manufacturing	54,260
Repair and maintenance	50,300

Cost estimators usually work full time. However, overtime is common, especially when deadlines need to be met.

Job Outlook

Cost Estimators
Percent change in employment, projected 2010-20

Cost Estimators	36%
Business Operations Specialists	18%
Total, All Occupations	14%

Note: All Occupations includes all occupations in the U.S. Economy.
Source: U.S. Bureau of Labor Statistics, Employment Projections program

Employment of cost estimators is expected to grow 36 percent from 2010 to 2020, much faster than the average for all occupations.

Demand for cost estimators is expected to remain strong as companies look for more accurate cost projections and products and services that are more cost-effective.

Growth of the construction industry will create the majority of new jobs. In particular, construction and repair of the national infrastructure, including roads, bridges, airports, and subway systems, will drive demand for qualified estimators.

Job Prospects

Job prospects are expected to be good overall. Jobseekers with a bachelor's degree and related work experience will have the best job opportunities as employers increasingly seek cost estimators with that background.

In manufacturing, those with a strong background in mathematics, statistics, engineering, or accounting, and knowledge of cost estimation software, should have the best prospects.

In construction, those with knowledge of Building Information Modeling (BIM) software are likely to have the best job prospects. Jobs of cost estimators working in construction, like those of many other trades in the construction industry, are sensitive to changing economic conditions. During economic downturns, there are frequent layoffs. During boom times, however, there may be shortages of workers.

Employment projections data for cost estimators, 2010-20

Occupational Title	SOC Code	Employment, 2010	Projected Employment, 2020	Change, 2010-20	
				Percent	Numeric
Cost Estimators	13-1051	185,400	252,900	36	67,500
SOURCE: U.S. Bureau of Labor Statistics, Employment Projections program					

Similar Occupations

This table shows a list of occupations with job duties that are similar to those of cost estimators.

Occupation	Job Duties	Entry-Level Education	Median Annual Pay, May 2010
Accountants and Auditors	Accountants and auditors prepare and examine financial records. They ensure that financial records are accurate and that taxes are paid properly and on time. Accountants and auditors assess financial operations and work to help ensure that organizations run efficiently.	Bachelor's degree	$61,690
Budget Analysts	Budget analysts help public and private institutions organize their finances. They prepare budget reports and monitor institutional spending.	Bachelor's degree	$68,200
Claims Adjusters, Appraisers, Examiners, and Investigators	Claims adjusters, appraisers, examiners, and investigators evaluate insurance claims. They decide whether an insurance company must pay a claim, and if so, how much.	See How to Become One	$58,460
Construction Managers	Construction managers plan, coordinate, budget, and supervise construction projects from early development to completion.	Associate's degree	$83,860
Financial Analysts	Financial analysts provide guidance to businesses and individuals making investment decisions. They assess the performance of stocks, bonds, and other types of investments.	Bachelor's degree	$74,350
Financial Managers	Financial managers are responsible for the financial health of an organization. They produce financial reports, direct investment activities, and develop strategies and plans for the long-term financial goals of their organization.	Bachelor's degree	$103,910
Industrial Production Managers	Industrial production managers oversee the daily operations of manufacturing and related plants. They coordinate, plan, and direct the activities used to create a wide range of goods, such as cars, computer equipment, or paper products.	Bachelor's degree	$87,160

Contacts for More Information

For more information about cost estimators, visit Association for the Advancement of Cost Estimating International

American Society of Professional Estimators, Society of Cost Estimating and Analysis

Suggested citation:

Bureau of Labor Statistics, U.S. Department of Labor, Occupational Outlook Handbook, 2012-13 Edition, Cost Estimators, on the Internet at http://www.bls.gov/ooh/business-and-financial/cost-estimators.htm .

Financial Analysts

Quick Facts: Financial Analysts	
2010 Median Pay	$74,350 per year $35.75 per hour
Entry-Level Education	Bachelor's degree
Work Experience in a Related Occupation	None
On-the-job Training	None
Number of Jobs, 2010	236,000
Job Outlook, 2010-20	23% (Faster than average)
Employment Change, 2010-20	54,200

What Financial Analysts Do

Financial analysts provide guidance to businesses and individuals making investment decisions. They assess the performance of stocks, bonds, and other types of investments.

Duties

Financial analysts typically do the following:

- Recommend individual investments and collections of investments, which are known as portfolios
- Evaluate current and historical data
- Study economic and business trends
- Study a company's financial statements and analyze commodity prices, sales, costs, expenses, and tax rates to determine a company's value by projecting the company's future earnings
- Meet with company officials to gain better insight into the company's prospects and management
- Prepare written reports
- Meet with investors to explain recommendations

Financial analysts evaluate investment opportunities. They work in banks, pension funds, mutual funds, securities firms, insurance companies, and other businesses. They are also called securities analysts and investment analysts.

Financial analysts can be divided into two categories: buy side analysts and sell side analysts.

- Buy side analysts develop investment strategies for companies that have a lot of money to invest. These companies, called institutional investors, include mutual funds, hedge funds, insurance companies, independent money managers, and nonprofit organizations with large endowments, such as some universities.
- Sell side analysts advise financial services sales agents who sell stocks, bonds, and other investments.

Some analysts work for the business media and are impartial, falling into neither the buy side nor the sell side.

Financial analysts generally focus on trends affecting a specific industry, geographical region, or type of product. For example, an analyst may focus on a subject area such as the energy industry, a world region such as Eastern Europe, or the foreign exchange market. They must understand how new regulations, policies, and political and economic trends may affect investments.

Investing is become more global, and some financial analysts specialize in a particular country or region. Companies want those financial analysts to understand the language, culture, business environment, and political conditions in the country or region that they cover.

The following are examples of types of financial analysts:

Portfolio managers supervise a team of analysts and select the mix of products, industries, and regions for their company's investment portfolio. These managers not only are responsible for the overall portfolio but also are expected to explain investment decisions and strategies in meetings with investors.

Fund managers work exclusively with hedge funds or mutual funds. Both fund and portfolio managers frequently make split-second buy or sell decisions in reaction to quickly changing market conditions.

Ratings analysts evaluate the ability of companies or governments to pay their debts, including bonds. On the basis of their evaluation, a management team rates the risk of a company or government not being able to repay its bonds.

Risk analysts evaluate the risk in investment decisions and determine how to manage unpredictability and limit potential losses. This job is carried out by making investment decisions such as selecting dissimilar stocks or having a combination of stocks, bonds, and mutual funds in a portfolio.

Work Environment

Financial analysts held about 236,000 jobs in 2010. They work primarily in offices. Most work full time, and many work more than 40 hours per week. They travel frequently to visit companies or potential investors, and face deadline pressure. Much of their research must be done after office hours because their days are filled with telephone calls and meetings.

Many financial analysts work at large financial institutions based in New York City or other major financial centers. In 2010, about 46 percent of financial analysts worked in finance and insurance industries. They worked primarily for security and commodity brokerages, banks and credit institutions, and insurance carriers. Others worked throughout private industry and for government.

Financial analysts work in banks, pension funds, and insurance companies.

The following industries employed the most financial analysts in 2010:

Other financial investment activities	14%
Management of companies and enterprises	11
Securities and commodity contracts intermediation and brokerage	8
Depository credit intermediation	8
Insurance carriers	8

Work Schedules

Financial analysts often work more than 40 hours a week. In fact, almost one-third of full-time analysts usually work between 50 and 70 hours a week.

How to Become a Financial Analyst

Financial analysts typically must have a bachelor's degree, but a master's degree is required for advanced positions.

Education

Many positions require a bachelor's degree in a related field, such as accounting, business administration, economics, finance, or statistics. Employers often require a master's in business administration (MBA) or a master's degree in finance. Knowledge of options pricing, bond valuation, and risk management are important.

Licenses

The Financial Industry Regulatory Authority (FINRA) is the main licensing organization for the securities industry. It requires licenses for many financial analyst positions. Most of the licenses require sponsorship by an employer, so companies do not expect individuals to have these licenses before starting a job.

Certification

Certification is often recommended by employers and can improve the chances for advancement. An example is the Chartered Financial Analyst certification from the CFA Institute, which financial analysts can get if they have a bachelor's degree, 4 years of experience, and pass three exams. Financial analysts can also become certified in their field of specialty.

Advancement

Financial analysts typically start by specializing in a specific investment field. As they gain experience, they can become portfolio managers, who supervise a team of analysts and select the mix of investments for the company's portfolio. They can also become fund managers, who manage large investment portfolios for individual investors. A master's degree in finance or business administration can improve an analyst's chances of advancing to one of these positions.

Important Qualities

Analytical skills. Financial analysts must process a range of information in finding profitable investments.

Communication skills. Financial analysts must explain their recommendations to clients in clear language that clients can easily understand.

Decision-making skills. Financial analysts must provide a recommendation to buy, hold, or sell a security. Fund managers must make split-second trading decisions.

Detail oriented. Financial analysts must pay attention to details when reviewing possible investments as small facts may have large implications for the health of an investment.

Math skills. Financial analysts use mathematical skills when estimating the value of financial securities.

Technical skills. Financial analysts must be adept at using software packages to analyze financial data, see trends, create portfolios, and make forecasts.

To be successful, financial analysts must be motivated to seek out obscure information that may be important to the investment. Many work independently and must have self-confidence in their judgment.

Pay

Financial Analysts
Median annual wages, May 2010

Financial Analysts	$74,350
Business and Financial Operations Occupations	$60,670
Total, All Occupations	$33,840

Note: All Occupations includes all occupations in the U.S. Economy.
Source: U.S. Bureau of Labor Statistics. Occupational Employment Statistics

The median annual wage of financial analysts was $74,350 in May 2010. The median wage is the wage at which half the workers in an occupation earned more than that amount and half earned less. The lowest 10 percent earned less than $44,490, and the top 10 percent earned more than $141,700.

Financial analysts often work more than 40 hours a week. In fact, almost one-third of full-time analysts usually work between 50 and 70 hours a week.

Job Outlook

Financial Analysts
Percent change in employment, projected 2010-20

Financial Analysts	23%
Business and Financial Operations Occupations	17%
Total, All Occupations	14%

Note: All Occupations includes all occupations in the U.S. Economy.
Source: U.S. Bureau of Labor Statistics. Employment Projections program

Employment of financial analysts is expected to grow 23 percent from 2010 to 2020, faster than the average for all occupations. A growing range of financial products and the need for in-depth knowledge of geographic regions are expected to lead to strong employment growth.

Investment portfolios are becoming more complex, and there are more financial products available for trade. In addition, emerging markets throughout the world are providing new investment opportunities, which require expertise in geographic regions where those markets are.

Regulatory reform enacted in 2010 should allow the financial industry to grow at a similar pace as in previous decades. Restrictions on trading by banks may shift employment of financial analysts from investment banks to hedge funds and private equity groups.

Job Prospects

Despite employment growth, competition is expected for these high-paying jobs. Growth in financial services should create new positions, but there are still far more people who would like to enter the occupation than there are jobs in the occupation. Having certifications and a graduate degree can significantly improve an applicant's prospects.

Employment projections data for financial analysts, 2010-20

Occupational Title	SOC Code	Employment, 2010	Projected Employment, 2020	Change, 2010-20	
				Percent	Numeric
Financial Analysts	13-2051	236,000	290,200	23	54,200

SOURCE: U.S. Bureau of Labor Statistics, Employment Projections program

Similar Occupations

This table shows a list of occupations with job duties that are similar to those of financial analysts.

Occupation	Job Duties	Entry-Level Education	Median Annual Pay, May 2010
Budget Analysts	Budget analysts help public and private institutions organize their finances. They prepare budget reports and monitor institutional spending.	Bachelor's degree	$68,200
Financial Managers	Financial managers are responsible for the financial health of an organization. They produce financial reports, direct investment activities, and develop strategies and plans for the long-term financial goals of their organization.	Bachelor's degree	$103,910
Insurance Underwriters	Insurance underwriters decide whether to provide insurance and under what terms. They evaluate insurance applications and determine coverage amounts and premiums.	Bachelor's degree	$59,290
Personal Financial Advisors	Personal financial advisors give financial advice to people. They help with investments, taxes, and insurance decisions.	Bachelor's degree	$64,750
Securities, Commodities, and Financial Services Sales Agents	Securities, commodities, and financial services sales agents connect buyers and sellers in financial markets. They sell securities to individuals, advise companies in search of investors, and conduct trades.	Bachelor's degree	$70,190

Contacts for More Information

For more information about licensure for financial analysts, visit Financial Industry Regulatory Authority (FINRA), Securities Industry and Financial Markets Association

For more information on training and certification, visit American Academy of Financial Management, CFA Institute

Suggested citation:

Bureau of Labor Statistics, U.S. Department of Labor, Occupational Outlook Handbook, 2012-13 Edition, Financial Analysts, on the Internet at http://www.bls.gov/ooh/business-and-financial/financial-analysts.htm .

Financial Examiners

Quick Facts: Financial Examiners	
2010 Median Pay	$74,940 per year $36.03 per hour
Entry-Level Education	Bachelor's degree
Work Experience in a Related Occupation	None
On-the-job Training	Moderate-term on-the-job training
Number of Jobs, 2010	29,300
Job Outlook, 2010-20	27% (Faster than average)
Employment Change, 2010-20	7,900

What Financial Examiners Do

Financial examiners ensure compliance with laws governing financial institutions and transactions. They review balance sheets, evaluate the risk level of loans, and assess bank management.

Duties

Financial examiners typically do the following:
- Monitor the financial condition of banks and other financial institutions
- Review balance sheets, operating income and expense accounts, and loan documentation to confirm institution assets and liabilities
- Prepare reports that detail an institution's safety and soundness
- Examine the minutes of meetings of managers and directors
- Recommend solutions to questionable financial conditions
- Train other examiners in the financial examination process
- Review and analyze new regulations and policies to determine their impact on the organization
- Establish guidelines for procedures and policies that comply with new and revised regulations

Financial examiners typically work in one of two main areas: risk scoping or consumer compliance.

Those working in risk scoping evaluate the health of financial institutions. Their role is to ensure that banks and other financial institutions offer safe loans and that they have enough cash on hand to handle unexpected losses. These procedures help ensure that the financial system as a whole remains stable. These examiners also evaluate the performance of bank managers.

Financial examiners working in consumer compliance monitor

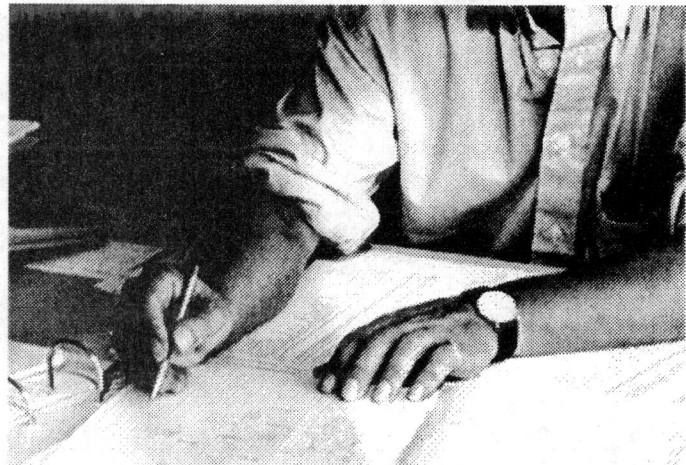

Financial examiners working in consumer compliance monitor lending activity to ensure that borrowers are treated fairly.

lending activity to ensure that borrowers are treated fairly. They ensure that banks extend loans that borrowers are likely to be able to pay back. They help borrowers avoid "predatory loans"—loans that may generate profit for banks through high interest payments but may be costly to borrowers and damage their credit scores. Examiners also ensure that banks do not discriminate against borrowers based on ethnicity or other characteristics.

Work Environment

Financial examiners typically work in offices. They occasionally may have to travel to inspect a bank onsite.

Financial examiners held 29,300 jobs in 2010. The following industries employed the most financial examiners in 2010:

Finance and insurance	47%
Federal government, excluding postal service	24
State government, excluding education and hospitals	15
Management of companies and enterprises	5

Work Schedules

Most financial examiners worked full time in 2010.

How to Become a Financial Examiner

Financial examiners typically must have a bachelor's degree that includes some coursework in accounting. Entry-level examiners are trained on the job by senior examiners.

Education

Specific requirements for financial examiners vary between federal and state governments. However, all financial examiners typically need a bachelor's degree that includes some coursework in accounting, finance, economics, or a related field. Examiners working for the Federal Deposit Insurance Corporation (FDIC) must have at least six semester hours in accounting.

Training

Once hired, financial examiners receive some on-the-job training. Entry-level workers begin under the supervision of senior examiners and learn their basic job duties and the agency's policies and procedures. This period typically takes between 1 month and 1 year.

Advancement

After a few years of experience, financial examiners can advance to a senior examiner position. Requirements for these positions vary by employer but often require a master's degree in accounting or business or becoming a Certified Public Accountant (CPA).

Important Qualities

Analytical skills. Financial examiners need strong analytical skills to evaluate how well bank managers are handling risk and whether the bank's individual loans are safe.

Detail oriented. Financial examiners must pay close attention to details when reviewing a bank's balance sheet to identify risky assets.

Math skills. Financial examiners need good basic math skills to monitor a bank's balance sheet and see if the bank's available cash is dangerously low.

Writing skills. Financial examiners regularly write reports on the safety and soundness of financial institutions. They must be able to explain technical information clearly.

Pay

Financial Examiners

Median annual wages, May 2010

Financial Examiners	$74,940
Business and Financial Operations Occupations	$60,670
Total, All Occupations	$33,840

Note: All Occupations includes all occupations in the U.S. Economy.
Source: U.S. Bureau of Labor Statistics, Occupational Employment Statistics

The median annual wage of financial examiners was $74,940 in May 2010. The median wage is the wage at which half the workers in an occupation earned more than that amount and half earned less. The lowest 10 percent earned less than $43,170, and the top 10 percent earned more than $134,820.

Most financial examiners worked full time in 2010.

Job Outlook

Financial Examiners

Percent change in employment, projected 2010-20

Financial Examiners	27%
Business and Financial Operations Occupations	17%
Total, All Occupations	14%

Note: All Occupations includes all occupations in the U.S. Economy.
Source: U.S. Bureau of Labor Statistics, Employment Projections program

Employment of financial examiners is projected to grow 27 percent from 2010 to 2020, faster than the average for all occupations. Implementation of new financial regulations is expected to create a need for more examiners.

For example, some large financial institutions that were not previously subject to Federal Deposit Insurance Corporation (FDIC) regulation have now been placed under that agency's supervision. More examiners will be needed to monitor these institutions' available cash levels and risky trading activity.

In addition, the creation of the Consumer Financial Protection Bureau (CFPB) will require more financial examiners working on consumer compliance. This agency's mission is to provide more oversight to the mortgage-lending process and prevent the types of abuses that contributed to the recent subprime crisis and housing crash.

However, hiring increases will be restricted by overall decreases in federal government spending and employment. Overall employment in the federal government is expected to decline, but employment of financial examiners in the federal government is expected to grow.

Employment projections data for financial examiners, 2010-20

Occupational Title	SOC Code	Employment, 2010	Projected Employment, 2020	Change, 2010-20 Percent	Numeri
Financial Examiners	13-2061	29,300	37,200	27	7,900
SOURCE: U.S. Bureau of Labor Statistics, Employment Projections program					

Similar Occupations

This table shows a list of occupations with job duties that are similar to those of financial examiners.

Occupation	Job Duties	Entry-Level Education	Median Annual Pay, May 2010
Accountants and Auditors	Accountants and auditors prepare and examine financial records. They ensure that financial records are accurate and that taxes are paid properly and on time. Accountants and auditors assess financial operations and work to help ensure that organizations run efficiently.	Bachelor's degree	$61,690
Budget Analysts	Budget analysts help public and private institutions organize their finances. They prepare budget reports and monitor institutional spending.	Bachelor's degree	$68,200
Financial Analysts	Financial analysts provide guidance to businesses and individuals making investment decisions. They assess the performance of stocks, bonds, and other types of investments.	Bachelor's degree	$74,350
Loan Officers	Loan officers evaluate, authorize, or recommend approval of loan applications for people and businesses.	High school diploma or equivalent	$56,490
Tax Examiners and Collectors, and Revenue Agents	Tax examiners and collectors, and revenue agents ensure that governments get their tax money from businesses and citizens. They review tax returns, conduct audits, identify taxes owed, and collect overdue tax payments.	Bachelor's degree	$49,360

Contacts for More Information

For more information about financial examiners, visit Federal Deposit Insurance Corporation

Suggested citation:

Bureau of Labor Statistics, U.S. Department of Labor, Occupational Outlook Handbook, 2012-13 Edition, Financial Examiners, on the Internet at http://www.bls.gov/ooh/business-and-financial/financial-examiners.htm.

Human Resources Specialists

Quick Facts: Human Resources Specialists	
2010 Median Pay	$52,690 per year $25.33 per hour
Entry-Level Education	Bachelor's degree
Work Experience in a Related Occupation	None
On-the-job Training	None
Number of Jobs, 2010	442,200
Job Outlook, 2010-20	21% (Faster than average)
Employment Change, 2010-20	90,700

What Human Resources Specialists Do

Human resources specialists recruit, screen, interview, and place workers. They also may handle human resources work in a variety of other areas, such as employee relations, payroll and benefits, and training.

Duties

Human resources specialists typically do the following:

- Consult with employers to identify employment needs and preferred qualifications
- Interview applicants about their experience, education, training, and skills
- Contact references and perform background checks on job applicants
- Inform applicants about job details, such as duties, benefits, and working conditions
- Hire or refer qualified candidates for employers
- Conduct or help with new employee orientation
- Keep employment records and process paperwork

Many specialists are trained in all human resources disciplines and do tasks throughout all areas of the department. In addition to recruiting and placing workers, these specialists help guide employees through all human resources procedures and answer questions about policies. They often administer benefits, process payroll, and handle any associated questions or problems. They also ensure that all human resources functions comply with federal, state, and local regulations.

The following are types of human resources specialists:

Recruitment specialists may distribute information at job fairs.

Employment interviewers work in an employment office and interview potential applicants for job openings. They then refer suitable candidates to employers for consideration.

Human resources generalists handle all aspects of human resources work. They may have duties in all areas of human resources including recruitment, employee relations, payroll and benefits, training, and administration of human resources policies, procedures, and programs.

Labor relations specialists interpret and administer a labor contract, regarding issues such as wages and salaries, employee welfare, healthcare, pensions, and union and management practices. They also handle grievance procedures, which are a formal process through which employees can make complaints.

Placement specialists match employers with qualified jobseekers. They search for candidates who have the skills, education, and work experience needed for jobs, and they try to place those candidates with employers. They also may help set up interviews.

Recruitment specialists, sometimes known as **personnel recruiters**, find, screen, and interview applicants for job openings in an organization. They search for job applicants by posting job listings, attending job fairs, and visiting college campuses. They also may test applicants, contact references, and extend job offers.

Work Environment

Human resources specialists held about 442,200 jobs in 2010 and are employed in nearly every industry. About 17 percent worked in the employment services industry, which includes employment placement agencies, temporary help services, and professional employer organizations. Because hiring needs may vary throughout the year, many organizations contract recruitment and placement work to outside human resources firms rather than keep permanent human resources specialists on staff.

Human resources specialists generally work in offices. Some, particularly recruitment specialists, travel extensively to attend job fairs, visit college campuses, and meet with applicants. Most work full time.

How to Become a Human Resources Specialist

Most positions require that applicants have a bachelor's degree. However, the level of education and experience required to become a human resources specialist varies by position and employer.

Education and Work Experience

Most positions require a bachelor's degree. When hiring a human resources generalist, for example, most employers prefer applicants who have a bachelor's degree in human resources, business, or a related field.

Although candidates with a high school diploma may qualify for some interviewing and recruiting positions, employers usually require several years of related work experience as a substitute for education.

Some positions, particularly human resources generalists, may require work experience. Candidates often gain experience as human resources assistants, in customer service positions, or in other related jobs.

Certification

Many professional associations that specialize in human resources offer courses intended to enhance the skills of their members, and some offer certification programs. Although certification is usually voluntary, some employers may prefer or require it. Human resources generalists, in particular, can benefit from certification, because it shows knowledge and competence across all human resources areas.

Important Qualities

Decision-making skills. Human resources specialists use decision-making skills when reviewing candidates' qualifications and in recruiting and selecting them for job openings.

Detail oriented. Human resources specialists must be detail oriented when evaluating applicants' qualifications, performing background checks, and maintaining employment records.

Interpersonal skills. Interpersonal skills are essential for human resources specialists. When recruiting and interviewing candidates, they continually interact with new people and must be able to converse and connect with people from varied backgrounds.

Listening skills. Listening skills are essential for human resources specialists. When interviewing job applicants, for example, they must pay careful attention to candidates' responses, understand the points they are making, and ask relevant follow-up questions.

Speaking skills. Human resources specialists need strong speaking skills to be effective at their job. They often give presentations and must be able to clearly convey information about their organizations and jobs within them. Recruiters also must persuade top candidates to consider their organization.

Pay

Human Resources Specialists
Median annual wages, May 2010

Business Operations Specialists	$60,660
Human Resources Specialists	$52,690
Total, All Occupations	$33,840

Note: All Occupations includes all occupations in the U.S. Economy.
Source: U.S. Bureau of Labor Statistics, Occupational Employment Statistics

The median annual wage of human resources specialists was $52,690 in May 2010. The median wage is the wage at which half the workers in an occupation earned more than that amount and half earned less. The lowest 10 percent earned less than $29,050, and the top 10 percent earned more than $93,260.

Median annual wages in the industries employing the largest numbers of human resources specialists in May 2010 were:

Federal government, excluding postal service	$77,370
Management of companies and enterprises	58,220
Religious, grantmaking, civic, professional, and similar organizations	48,660
State government, excluding education and hospitals	44,810
Employment services	43,770

Many human resources specialists, particularly recruiters, travel extensively to attend job fairs, visit college campuses, and meet with applicants. Most work full time.

Job Outlook

Human Resources Specialists
Percent change in employment, projected 2010-20

Human Resources Specialists	21%
Business Operations Specialists	18%
Total, All Occupations	14%

Note: All Occupations includes all occupations in the U.S. Economy.
Source: U.S. Bureau of Labor Statistics, Employment Projections program

Employment of human resources specialists is expected to grow 21 percent from 2010 to 2020, faster than the average for all occupations.

Specifically, employment will increase 55 percent in the employment services industry. About 17 percent of human resources specialists work in this industry, which includes employment placement agencies, temporary help services, and professional employer organizations. Organizations will continue to outsource human resources functions to professional employer organizations—companies that provide human resources services to client businesses. Additionally, rather than having recruiters and interviewers on staff, these businesses will contract preliminary staffing work to employment placement and temporary staffing agencies as needed.

In other industries, employment growth largely depends on the growth of individual firms. As firms grow, they will expand their human resources departments to continue to provide the same level of services and functions. Companies will need human resources specialists to find replacements for workers leaving the workforce, and companies are increasingly emphasizing the importance of finding and keeping quality employees. In addition, organizations will likely need more human resources generalists to handle increasingly complex employment laws and health care coverage options.

Employment growth of human resources specialists, however, may be tempered as companies better use available technologies. Rather than sending recruiters to colleges and job fairs, for example, some employers increasingly have their entire recruiting and application process online. In addition, some of the tasks of generalists can be automated or made more efficient using Human Resources Information Systems—software that allows workers to quickly manage, process, or update human resource information.

Job Prospects

Overall job opportunities for human resources specialists are expected to be favorable. Opportunities should be best in the employment services industry, as companies continue to outsource portions of their human resources functions to other firms.

Candidates with a bachelor's degree and related work experience should have the best job prospects. Human resources generalists, in particular, also may benefit from having knowledge of human resources programs, employment laws, and human resources information systems.

Employment projections data for human resources specialists, 2010-20

Occupational Title	SOC Code	Employment, 2010	Projected Employment, 2020	Change, 2010-20	
				Percent	Numeric
Human Resources, Training, and Labor Relations Specialists, All Other	13-1078	442,200	532,900	21	90,700
SOURCE: U.S. Bureau of Labor Statistics, Employment Projections program					

Similar Occupations

This table shows a list of occupations with job duties that are similar to those of human resources specialists.

Occupation	Job Duties	Entry-Level Education	Median Annual Pay, May 2010
Insurance Sales Agents	Insurance sales agents help insurance companies generate new business by contacting potential customers and selling one or more types of insurance. An agent explains various insurance policies and helps clients choose plans that suit them.	High school diploma or equivalent	$46,770
Compensation and Benefits Managers	Compensation managers plan, direct, and coordinate how and how much an organization pays its employees. Benefits managers do the same for retirement plans, health insurance, and other benefits an organization offers its employees.	Bachelor's degree	$89,270
Human Resources Managers	Human resources managers plan, direct, and coordinate the administrative functions of an organization. They oversee the recruiting, interviewing, and hiring of new staff; consult with top executives on strategic planning; and serve as a link between an organization's management and its employees.	Bachelor's degree	$99,180
Training and Development Managers	Training and development managers plan, direct, and coordinate programs to enhance the knowledge and skills of an organization's employees. They also oversee a staff of training and development specialists.	Bachelor's degree	$89,170
Public Relations Managers and Specialists	Public relations managers and specialists create and maintain a favorable public image for their employer or client. They write material for media releases, plan and direct public relations programs, and raise funds for their organizations.	Bachelor's degree	$57,550
Tax Examiners and Collectors, and Revenue Agents	Tax examiners and collectors, and revenue agents ensure that governments get their tax money from businesses and citizens. They review tax returns, conduct audits, identify taxes owed, and collect overdue tax payments.	Bachelor's degree	$49.360
Social and Human Service Assistants	Social and human service assistants help people get through difficult times or get additional support. They help other workers, such as social workers, and they help clients find benefits or community services.	High school diploma or equivalent	$28,200
Customer Service Representatives	Customer service representatives interact with customers on behalf of an organization. They provide information about products and services and respond to customer complaints. Some also take orders and process returns.	High school diploma or equivalent	$30,460

Contacts for More Information

For more information about human resources careers and certification, visit Society for Human Resources Management

Suggested citation:

Bureau of Labor Statistics, U.S. Department of Labor, Occupational Outlook Handbook, 2012-13 Edition, Human Resources Specialists, on the Internet at http://www.bls.gov/ooh/business-and-financial/human-resources-specialists.htm .

Insurance Underwriters

Quick Facts: Insurance Underwriters	
2010 Median Pay	$59,290 per year $28.51 per hour
Entry-Level Education	Bachelor's degree
Work Experience in a Related Occupation	None
On-the-job Training	Moderate-term on-the-job training
Number of Jobs, 2010	101,800
Job Outlook, 2010-20	6% (Slower than average)
Employment Change, 2010-20	6,000

What Insurance Underwriters Do

Insurance underwriters decide whether to provide insurance and under what terms. They evaluate insurance applications and determine coverage amounts and premiums.

Duties

Insurance underwriters typically do the following:
- Analyze information in insurance applications
- Determine the risk of insuring a client
- Screen applicants on the basis of set criteria
- Evaluate recommendations from underwriting software
- Decide whether to offer insurance
- Determine appropriate premiums and amounts of coverage
- Write policies to cover potential loss

Underwriters are the main link between an insurance company and an insurance agent. Insurance underwriters use computer software programs to determine whether to approve an applicant. They take specific information about a client and enter it into a program. The program then provides recommendations on coverage and premiums. Underwriters evaluate these recommendations and, using predetermined criteria, decide whether to approve or reject the application. If a decision is difficult, they may consult additional sources, such as medical documents and credit scores.

Insurance underwriters must achieve a balance between risky and cautious decisions. If underwriters allow too much risk, the insurance company will pay out too many claims. But if they don't approve enough applications, the company will not make enough money from premiums.

Most insurance underwriters specialize in one of four broad fields: life, health, mortgage, and property and casualty. Although job duties are similar, the criteria used by underwriters vary. For example, for someone seeking life insurance, underwriters consider age and financial history. For someone applying for car insurance (a form of property and casualty insurance), underwriters consider the person's driving record.

Within the broad field of property and casualty, underwriters may specialize even further into commercial (business insurance) or personal insurance. They may also specialize by the type of policy, such as insuring automobiles, boats (marine insurance), or homes (homeowners' insurance).

Work Environment

Insurance underwriters held about 101,800 jobs in 2010. They work indoors in a comfortable office setting. Some property and casualty underwriters may visit properties to assess them in person. The following industries employed the most insurance underwriters in 2010:

Insurance carriers	70%
Agencies, brokerages, and other insurance related activities	19
Credit intermediation and related activities	4
Management of companies and enterprises	2

Work Schedules

Most underwriters work full time.

How to Become an Insurance Underwriter

Employers prefer to hire candidates who have a bachelor's degree. However, insurance-related work experience and strong computer skills may be enough. Certification is necessary for advancement to senior underwriter and underwriter manager positions.

Education

Most firms prefer to hire applicants who have a bachelor's degree. Courses in business, finance, economics, and mathematics are particularly helpful.

Insurance underwriters use computer software programs to determine whether an applicant should be approved.

Training

Beginning underwriters usually work as trainees under the supervision of senior underwriters. Trainees work on basic applications and learn the most common risk factors. As they gain experience, they become responsible for more complex applications and work independently.

Certification

Employers often expect underwriters to get certification through coursework. These courses are important for keeping current with new insurance policies and adjusting to new technology and changes in state and federal regulations. Certification is often necessary for advancement to senior underwriter and underwriter management positions. Many certification options are available.

For beginning underwriters, the Insurance Institute of America offers a training program. The Institute also offers two special designations, an Associate in Commercial Underwriting (AU) and an Associate in Personal Insurance (API). To earn either the AU or API designation, underwriters complete a series of courses and exams that generally take 1 to 2 years.

The American College also offers an introductory course in basic insurance concepts: The Life Underwriter Training Council Fellow (LUTCF). They also offer a Chartered Life Underwriter (CLU) and Registered Health Underwriter (RHU) designation.

For underwriters with at least three years of insurance experience, the American Institute for Chartered Property Casualty Underwriters offers the Chartered Property and Casualty Underwriter designation (CPCU).

Important Qualities

Analytical skills. Underwriters must be able to evaluate information and solve complex problems.

Decision-making skills. Underwriters must have the ability to consider the costs and benefits of various decisions and to choose the appropriate one.

Detail oriented. Underwriters must pay attention to detail, because each individual item on an insurance application can affect the coverage decision.

Interpersonal skills. Underwriters need good communication and interpersonal skills because much of their work involves dealing with other people, such as insurance agents.

Technical skills. Underwriters must be comfortable working with computers and making mathematical calculations.

Pay

Insurance Underwriters
Median annual wages, May 2010

Business and Financial Operations Occupations	$60,670
Insurance Underwriters	$59,290
Total, All Occupations	$33,840

Note: All Occupations includes all occupations in the U.S. Economy.
Source: U.S. Bureau of Labor Statistics, Occupational Employment Statistics

The median annual wage of insurance underwriters was $59,290 in May 2010. The median wage is the wage at which half the workers in an occupation earned more than that amount and half earned less. The lowest 10 percent earned less than $36,700, and the top 10 percent earned more than $102,540.

Most underwriters work full time.

Job Outlook

Insurance Underwriters
Percent change in employment, projected 2010-20

Business and Financial Operations Occupations	17%
Total, All Occupations	14%
Insurance Underwriters	6%

Note: All Occupations includes all occupations in the U.S. Economy.
Source: U.S. Bureau of Labor Statistics, Employment Projections program

Employment of underwriters is expected to increase 6 percent from 2010 to 2020, slower than the average for all occupations. New types of automated underwriting software allow workers to process applications more quickly than before, reducing the need for underwriters. However, there still will be a need for underwriters to evaluate automated recommendations.

Among underwriter specialties, underwriters working in health insurance are projected to have faster employment growth. Federal healthcare reform will require more individuals to purchase health insurance, leading to an increase in applications. In addition, as the population ages, there will likely be increased demand for long-term care insurance.

Job Prospects

The need to replace workers who retire or transfer to another occupation should create many additional job openings. Job opportunities should be best for those with a background in finance, and strong computer and communication skills.

Employment projections data for insurance underwriters, 2010-20

Occupational Title	SOC Code	Employment, 2010	Projected Employment, 2020	Change, 2010-20	
				Percent	Numeric
Insurance Underwriters	13-2053	101,800	107,700	6	6,000
SOURCE: U.S. Bureau of Labor Statistics, Employment Projections program					

Similar Occupations

This table shows a list of occupations with job duties that are similar to those of insurance underwriters.

Occupation	Job Duties	Entry-Level Education	Median Annual Pay, May 2010
Actuaries	Actuaries analyze the financial costs of risk and uncertainty. They use mathematics, statistics, and financial theory to assess the risk that an event will occur and to help businesses and clients develop policies that minimize the cost of that risk.	Bachelor's degree	$87,650

Budget Analysts	Budget analysts help public and private institutions organize their finances. They prepare budget reports and monitor institutional spending.	Bachelor's degree	$68,200
Claims Adjusters, Appraisers, Examiners, and Investigators	Claims adjusters, appraisers, examiners, and investigators evaluate insurance claims. They decide whether an insurance company must pay a claim, and if so, how much.	See How to Become One	$58,460
Cost Estimators	Cost estimators collect and analyze data to estimate the time, money, resources, and labor required for product manufacturing, construction projects, or services. Some specialize in a particular industry or product type.	Bachelor's degree	$57,860
Insurance Sales Agents	Insurance sales agents help insurance companies generate new business by contacting potential customers and selling one or more types of insurance. An agent explains various insurance policies and helps clients choose plans that suit them.	High school diploma or equivalent	$46,770
Loan Officers	Loan officers evaluate, authorize, or recommend approval of loan applications for people and businesses.	High school diploma or equivalent	$56,490

Contacts for More Information

For more information about property and casualty insurance, visit Insurance Information Institute

For more information about certifications, visit American Institute for Chartered Property and Casualty Underwriters and Insurance Institute of America, CPCU Society, The American College

Suggested citation:

Bureau of Labor Statistics, U.S. Department of Labor, Occupational Outlook Handbook, 2012-13 Edition, Insurance Underwriters, on the Internet at http://www.bls.gov/ooh/business-and-financial/insurance-underwriters.htm .

Loan Officers

Quick Facts: Loan Officers	
2010 Median Pay	$56,490 per year $27.16 per hour
Entry-Level Education	High school diploma or equivalent
Work Experience in a Related Occupation	None
On-the-job Training	Moderate-term on-the-job training
Number of Jobs, 2010	289,400
Job Outlook, 2010-20	14% (About as fast as average)
Employment Change, 2010-20	41,000

What Loan Officers Do

Loan officers evaluate, authorize, or recommend approval of loan applications for people and businesses.

Duties

Loan officers typically do the following:

- Contact companies or people to ask if they need a loan
- Meet with loan applicants to gather personal information and answer questions
- Explain different types of loans and the terms of each one to applicants
- Obtain and verify financial information, such as the applicant's credit rating and income level
- Analyze and evaluate the applicant's finances to decide if the applicant should get the loan
- Approve loan applications or refer them to management for a decision

Loan officers use a process called underwriting to assess whether applicants qualify for loans. After collecting and verifying all the required financial documents, the loan officer evaluates this information to determine the applicant's loan needs and ability to pay back the loan. Some firms underwrite loans manually, calculating the applicant's financial status by following a certain formula or set of guidelines. Other firms use underwriting software, which analyze applications almost instantly. More often, firms use underwriting software to produce a recommendation, while relying on loan officers to consider any additional information to make a final decision.

The work of loan officers has sizeable customer service and sales components. Loan officers often answer questions and guide customers through the application process. In addition, many loan officers must market the products and services of their lending institution and actively solicit new business.

The following are common types of loan officers:

Commercial loan officers specialize in loans to businesses. Businesses often use loans to start companies, buy supplies, and upgrade or expand operations. Commercial loans are often larger and more complicated than other types of loans. Because companies have such complex financial situations and statements, commercial loans usually require human judgment in addition to the analysis by underwriting software. Furthermore, some commercial loans are so large that a single bank will not provide the entire amount requested. In such cases, loan officers may have to work with multiple banks to put together a package of loans.

Consumer loan officers specialize in loans to people. Consumers take out loans for many reasons, such as buying a car or paying for college tuition. For some simple consumer loans, the underwriting process is fully automated. However, the loan officer is still needed to

Loan officers may approve loans.

guide applicants through the process and to handle cases with unusual circumstances. Some institutions—usually small banks and credit unions—do not use underwriting software and instead rely on loan officers to complete the underwriting process manually.

Mortgage loan officers specialize in loans used to buy real estate (property and buildings), which are called mortgage loans. Mortgage loan officers work on loans for both residential and commercial properties. Often, mortgage loan officers must seek out clients, which requires developing relationships with real estate companies and other sources that can refer prospective applicants.

Within these three fields, some loan officers specialize in a particular part of the loan process:

Loan collection officers contact borrowers who fail to make their loan payments on time. They work with borrowers to help them find a way to keep paying off the loan. If the borrower continues to miss payments, loan officers start the process of taking away what the borrower used to secure the loan (the collateral)—often a home or car—and selling it to repay the loan.

Loan underwriters specialize in evaluating whether a client is credit worthy. They do this by collecting, verifying, and evaluating the client's financial information provided on their loan applications. They may use loan underwriting software, or they may perform the process manually.

Work Environment

Loan officers held about 289,400 jobs in 2010, about 86 percent of which were in the credit intermediation and related activities industry. This includes commercial banks, credit unions, mortgage companies, and other financial institutions.

Loan officers who specialize in consumer loans usually work in offices. Mortgage and commercial loan officers often work outside the office and meet with clients at their homes or businesses.

Work Schedules

Most loan officers work full time. Some loan officers who work on commission choose to take on additional clients and therefore must work longer hours than those who have fewer clients.

How to Become a Loan Officer

Most loan officers need a high school diploma and receive on-the-job training. Commercial loan officers, however, generally need a bachelor's degree in finance, business, economics, or a related field. Mortgage loan officers must be licensed.

Education

Loan officers need at least a high school diploma. Some positions, particularly commercial loan officers, require a bachelor's degree in finance, business, economics, or a related field. Because commercial loan officers analyze the finances of businesses applying for credit, they need to understand general business accounting, including how to read financial statements.

Training

Loan officers usually learn their work through on-the-job training. This may be a combination of formal, company-sponsored training, and informal training during the few first months on the job. Those who use underwriting software often take classes to learn the company's software programs.

Licenses

Mortgage loan officers must have a <u>Mortgage Loan Originator</u> (MLO) license. To become licensed, mortgage loan officers must complete at least 20 hours of coursework, pass an exam, and submit to background and credit checks. Licenses must be renewed annually, and individual states may have additional requirements.

Certification

Several banking associations and schools offer courses or certifications for loan officers. The <u>American Bankers Association</u> and the <u>Mortgage Bankers Association</u> both offer certification and training programs for loan officers. Although not required, certification shows dedication and expertise and thus may enhance a candidate's employment opportunities.

Work Experience

Many employers prefer candidates who have work experience in lending, banking, sales, or customer service. For those without a bachelor's degree, work experience in a related field can be particularly useful.

Important Qualities

Decision-making skills. Decision-making skills are important for loan officers, who must assess an applicant's financial information and decide whether to award a loan.

Initiative. Loan officers need to have initiative when seeking out clients. They often act as salespeople, promoting their lending institution and contacting firms to determine their loan needs.

Interpersonal skills. Because loan officers work with people, they must be able to guide customers through the application process and answer their questions.

Pay

Loan Officers
Median annual wages, May 2010

Business Operations Specialists	$60,660
Loan Officers	$56,490
Total, All Occupations	$33,840

Note: All Occupations includes all occupations in the U.S. Economy.
Source: U.S. Bureau of Labor Statistics, Occupational Employment Statistics

The median annual wage of loan officers was $56,490 in May 2010. The median wage is the wage at which half the workers in that occupation earned more than that amount and half earned less. The lowest 10 percent earned less than $30,930, and the top 10 percent earned more than $112,370.

The form of compensation varies widely by employer. Some loan officers are paid a flat salary; others are paid on commission. Those on commission usually are paid a base salary plus a commission for the loans they originate. Loan officers also may receive extra commission or bonuses based on the number of loans they originate or how well the loans do.

Most loan officers work full time. Some loan officers who work on commission choose to take on additional clients, which requires that they work longer hours.

Job Outlook

Loan Officers

Percent change in employment, projected 2010-20

Business Operations Specialists	18%
Total, All Occupations	14%
Loan Officers	14%

Note: All Occupations includes all occupations in the U.S. Economy.
Source: U.S. Bureau of Labor Statistics. Employment Projections program

Employment of loan officers is expected to grow 14 percent from 2010 to 2020, as fast as the average for all occupations. The need for loan officers fluctuates with the economy, generally increasing in times of economic growth, low interest rates, and population growth—all of which create demand for loans.

After a period of decreased lending resulting from the recent recession, banks and other lending institutions are granting an increasing number of loans to people and businesses. Because lending activity is sensitive to fluctuations in the economy, consumer and mortgage loans are expected to increase as the economy recovers. Similarly, many businesses postponed borrowing funds for maintenance, improvement, and expansion during the recession, so commercial loans should increase as businesses are more willing to borrow and banks are more willing to lend.

However, growth in the number of jobs is expected to be tempered by the expanded use of loan underwriting software, which has made the loan application process much faster than in the past. Some loan applications can be completed online and underwritten automatically, allowing loan officers to process more applications in a much shorter period of time. This factor may limit the number of new loan officers needed in the future, despite an increasing number of loan applications.

Job Prospects

Prospects for loan officers should improve over the coming decade as lending activity rebounds from the recent recession. Job opportunities should be good for those with a college degree and lending, banking, or sales experience. In addition, some firms require loan officers to find their own clients, so candidates with established contacts and a referral network should have the best job opportunities.

Employment projections data for loan officers, 2010-20

Occupational Title	SOC Code	Employment, 2010	Projected Employment, 2020	Change, 2010-20 Percent	Change, 2010-20 Numeric
Loan Officers	13-2072	289,400	330,400	14	41,000
SOURCE: U.S. Bureau of Labor Statistics, Employment Projections program					

Similar Occupations

This table shows a list of occupations with job duties that are similar to those of loan officers.

Occupation	Job Duties	Entry-Level Education	Median Annual Pay, May 2010
Financial Analysts	Financial analysts provide guidance to businesses and individuals making investment decisions. They assess the performance of stocks, bonds, and other types of investments.	Bachelor's degree	$74,350
Financial Examiners	Financial examiners ensure compliance with laws governing financial institutions and transactions. They review balance sheets, evaluate the risk level of loans, and assess bank management.	Bachelor's degree	$74,940
Insurance Underwriters	Insurance underwriters decide whether to provide insurance and under what terms. They evaluate insurance applications and determine coverage amounts and premiums.	Bachelor's degree	$59,290
Personal Financial Advisors	Personal financial advisors give financial advice to people. They help with investments, taxes, and insurance decisions.	Bachelor's degree	$64,750
Tax Examiners and Collectors, and Revenue Agents	Tax examiners and collectors, and revenue agents ensure that governments get their tax money from businesses and citizens. They review tax returns, conduct audits, identify taxes owed, and collect overdue tax payments.	Bachelor's degree	$49,360
Insurance Sales Agents	Insurance sales agents help insurance companies generate new business by contacting potential customers and selling one or more types of insurance. An agent explains various insurance policies and helps clients choose plans that suit them.	High school diploma or equivalent	$46,770

Securities, Commodities, and Financial Services Sales Agents	Securities, commodities, and financial services sales agents connect buyers and sellers in financial markets. They sell securities to individuals, advise companies in search of investors, and conduct trades.	Bachelor's degree	$70,190
Real Estate Brokers and Sales Agents	Real estate brokers and sales agents help clients buy, sell, and rent properties. Brokers and agents do the same type of work, but brokers are licensed to manage their own real estate businesses. Sales agents must work with a broker.	High school diploma or equivalent	$42,680

Contacts for More Information

For more information about certification and training for loan officers, visit American Bankers Association

For more information about a career as a mortgage loan officer, visit Mortgage Bankers Association

For more information about licensing for mortgage loan officers, visit Nationwide Mortgage Licensing System & Registry Resource Center

State bankers' associations have specific information about job opportunities in their state. Also, individual banks can supply information about job openings and the activities, responsibilities, and preferred qualifications of their loan officers.

Suggested citation:

Bureau of Labor Statistics, U.S. Department of Labor, Occupational Outlook Handbook, 2012-13 Edition, Loan Officers, on the Internet at http://www.bls.gov/ooh/business-and-financial/loan-officers.htm .

Logisticians

Quick Facts: Logisticians	
2010 Median Pay	$70,800 per year $34.04 per hour
Entry-Level Education	Bachelor's degree
Work Experience in a Related Occupation	1 to 5 years
On-the-job Training	None
Number of Jobs, 2010	108,900
Job Outlook, 2010-20	26% (Faster than average)
Employment Change, 2010-20	27,800

What Logisticians Do

Logisticians analyze and coordinate an organization's supply chain—the system that moves a product from supplier to consumer. They manage the entire life cycle of a product, which includes how a product is acquired, distributed, allocated, and delivered.

Duties

Logisticians typically do the following:

- Develop business relationships with suppliers and customers
- Work to understand customers' needs and how to meet them
- Direct the allocation of materials, supplies, and finished products
- Design strategies to minimize the cost or time required to move goods
- Review the success of logistical functions and identify areas for improvement
- Present performance data to management
- Propose improvements to management and customers
- Stay current on advances in logistics technology and incorporate new technologies into procedures

Logisticians oversee activities including purchasing, shipping and transportation, inventory, warehousing, and delivery. They may direct the movement of a range of goods, people, or supplies, from common consumer goods to military supplies.

Logisticians use sophisticated software systems to plan and track the movement of goods. They operate software programs specifically tailored to manage logistical functions, such as procurement, inventory management, and other supply chain planning and management systems.

Work Environment

Logisticians held about 108,900 jobs in 2010 and work in nearly

Logisticians direct the acquisition, distribution, and delivery functions of an organization.

every industry. The federal government employed the largest number of logisticians, many of whom were civilians doing logistical work for the military. Some logisticians work in the logistical department of a company, and others work for firms that specialize in logistical work, such as a freight shipping company. In 2010, the industries employing the largest number of logisticians were as follows:

Federal government	28%
Manufacturing	22
Professional, scientific, and technical services	16
Management of companies and enterprises	9
Wholesale trade	6

The job can be stressful because logistical work is fast-paced. Logisticians must ensure that operations stay on schedule, and they must work quickly to solve any problems that arise. Some logisticians travel frequently to visit a company's manufacturing plants or distribution centers.

Work Schedules

Most logisticians work full time during regular business hours. When dealing with delivery problems or other logistical issues, they may work overtime to ensure that operations stay on schedule.

How to Become a Logistician

Although an associate's degree is sufficient for many logistician jobs, candidates increasingly need a bachelor's degree to advance beyond entry-level positions.

Education

Logisticians can qualify for positions with an associate's degree in business or engineering or by taking courses on logistics. However, as logistics becomes increasingly complex, more companies prefer to hire workers who have at least a bachelor's degree. Many logisticians have a bachelor's or master's degree in business, finance, industrial engineering, or supply chain management.

Certification

Logisticians may get certification through the American Society of Transportation and Logistics (ASTL) or the International Society of Logistics (SOLE). The certification offered by each organization typically requires a combination of education, experience, and passing an exam. Although it is not required, certification can demonstrate professional competence and a broad knowledge of logistics.

Work Experience

Logisticians typically need work experience in a field related to logistics or business. Because military operations require a large amount of logistical work, some logisticians gain work experience while serving in the military. Some firms allow applicants to substitute several years of work experience for a degree.

Important Qualities

Communication skills. Logisticians need strong communication skills to collaborate with colleagues and do business with suppliers and customers.

Critical-thinking skills. Logisticians must develop, adjust, and successfully carry out logistical plans, and they often must find ways to cut costs and improve efficiency.

Organizational skills. Logisticians must be able to do several tasks at one time, keep detailed records, and manage several projects at once in a fast-paced workplace.

Problem-solving skills. Logisticians must handle unforeseen circumstances, such as delivery problems, and adjust plans as needed to resolve the issues.

Pay

Logisticians
Median annual wages, May 2010

Logisticians	$70,800
Business Operations Specialists	$60,660
Total, All Occupations	$33,840

Note: All Occupations includes all occupations in the U.S. Economy.
Source: U.S. Bureau of Labor Statistics, Occupational Employment Statistics

The median annual wage of logisticians was $70,800 in May 2010. The median wage is the wage at which half the workers in an occupation earned more than that amount and half earned less. The lowest 10 percent earned less than $43,530, and the top 10 percent earned more than $108,080.

Median annual wages in the industries employing the largest numbers of logisticians in May 2010 were as follows:

Federal executive branch	$77,980
Manufacturing	69,570
Professional, scientific, and technical services	68,830
Management of companies and enterprises	68,550
Wholesale trade	65,630

Most logisticians work full time during regular business hours. When dealing with delivery problems or other logistical issues, they may work overtime to ensure that operations stay on schedule.

Job Outlook

Logisticians
Percent change in employment, projected 2010-20

Logisticians	26%
Business Operations Specialists	18%
Total, All Occupations	14%

Note: All Occupations includes all occupations in the U.S. Economy.
Source: U.S. Bureau of Labor Statistics, Employment Projections program

Employment of logisticians is expected to grow 26 percent from 2010 to 2020, faster than the average for all occupations. Employment growth will be driven by the important role logistics play in an increasingly global economy.

Companies rely on logisticians to manage the movement of their products and supplies, which allows the company to compete in a highly globalized market. The performance of a company's logistical and supply chain process is an important factor in a company's profitability. Supply and distribution systems have become increasingly complex to maximize efficiency while minimizing cost. Therefore, employment is expected to grow rapidly as companies need logisticians to move products efficiently, solve problems, and identify areas for improvement.

Governments and the military also rely on logisticians. Planning for and moving military supplies and personnel require an enormous amount of logistical work. Employment of logisticians in government and contracting firms will continue to grow to meet the needs of the military.

Job Prospects

Job prospects should be good for those with a bachelor's degree in supply chain management, industrial engineering, business, or a related field. Prospects should be best for those with a college degree and work experience related to logistics, particularly previous experience using logistical software or doing logistical work for the military.

Employment projections data for logisticians, 2010-20

Occupational Title	SOC Code	Employment, 2010	Projected Employment, 2020	Change, 2010-20 Percent	Change, 2010-20 Numeric
Logisticians	13-1081	108,900	136,700	26	27,800
SOURCE: U.S. Bureau of Labor Statistics, Employment Projections program					

Similar Occupations

This table shows a list of occupations with job duties that are similar to those of logisticians.

Occupation	Job Duties	Entry-Level Education	Median Annual Pay, May 2010
Cost Estimators	Cost estimators collect and analyze data to estimate the time, money, resources, and labor required for product manufacturing, construction projects, or services. Some specialize in a particular industry or product type.	Bachelor's degree	$57,860
Industrial Production Managers	Industrial production managers oversee the daily operations of manufacturing and related plants. They coordinate, plan, and direct the activities used to create a wide range of goods, such as cars, computer equipment, or paper products.	Bachelor's degree	$87,160
Quality Control Inspectors	Quality control inspectors examine products and materials for defects or deviations from manufacturers' or industry specifications.	High school diploma or equivalent	$33,030
Industrial Engineering Technicians	Industrial engineering technicians plan ways to effectively use personnel, materials, and machines in factories, stores, hospitals, repair shops, and offices. As assistants to industrial engineers, they help prepare machinery and equipment layouts, plan workflows, conduct statistical production studies, and analyze production costs.	Associate's degree	$48,210
Industrial Engineers	Industrial engineers find ways to eliminate wastefulness in production processes. They devise efficient ways to use workers, machines, materials, information, and energy to make a product or provide a service.	Bachelor's degree	$76,100
Management Analysts	Management analysts, often called management consultants, propose ways to improve an organization's efficiency. They advise managers on how to make organizations more profitable through reduced costs and increased revenues.	Bachelor's degree	$78,160
Operations Research Analysts	Operations research analysts use advanced methods of analysis to help organizations solve problems and make better decisions.	Bachelor's degree	$70,960

Contacts for More Information

For more information about logisticians, including certification, visit American Society of Transportation and Logistics, International Society of Logistics

Suggested citation:

Bureau of Labor Statistics, U.S. Department of Labor, Occupational Outlook Handbook, 2012-13 Edition, Logisticians, on the Internet at http://www.bls.gov/ooh/business-and-financial/logisticians.htm .

Management Analysts

Quick Facts: Management Analysts	
2010 Median Pay	$78,160 per year $37.58 per hour
Entry-Level Education	Bachelor's degree
Work Experience in a Related Occupation	1 to 5 years
On-the-job Training	None
Number of Jobs, 2010	718,800
Job Outlook, 2010-20	22% (Faster than average)
Employment Change, 2010-20	157,200

What Management Analysts Do

Management analysts, often called management consultants, propose ways to improve an organization's efficiency. They advise managers on how to make organizations more profitable through reduced costs and increased revenues.

Duties

Management analysts typically do the following:

- Gather and organize information about the problem to be solved or the procedure to be improved
- Interview personnel and conduct on-site observations to determine the methods, equipment, and personnel that will be needed
- Analyze financial and other data, including revenue, expenditure, and employment reports, including, sometimes, building and using sophisticated mathematical models
- Develop solutions or alternative practices
- Recommend new systems, procedures, or organizational changes
- Make recommendations to management through presentations or written reports
- Confer with managers to ensure that the changes are working

Although some management analysts work for the organization that they are analyzing, most work as consultants on a contractual basis.

Whether they are self-employed or part of a large consulting

Although some management analysts work for the company that they are analyzing, most work as consultants on a contractual basis.

company, the work of a management analyst may vary from project to project. Some projects require a team of consultants, each specializing in one area. In other projects, consultants work independently with the client organization's managers.

Management analysts often specialize in certain areas, such as inventory management or reorganizing corporate structures to eliminate duplicate and nonessential jobs. Some consultants specialize in a specific industry, such as healthcare or telecommunications. In government, management analysts usually specialize by type of agency.

Organizations hire consultants to develop strategies for entering and remaining competitive in the electronic marketplace.

Management analysts who work on contract may write proposals and bid for jobs. Typically, an organization that needs the help of a management analyst solicits proposals from a number of consultants and consulting companies that specialize in the needed work. Those who want the work must then submit a proposal by the deadline that explains how they will do the work, who will do the work, why they are the best consultants to do the work, what the schedule will be, and how much it will cost. The organization that needs the consultants then selects the proposal that best meets its needs and budget.

Work Environment

Management analysts held 718,800 jobs in 2010. They usually divide their time between their offices and the client's site. Because they must spend a significant amount of time with clients, analysts travel frequently. Analysts may experience stress when trying to meet a client's demands, often on a tight schedule.

In 2010, about 23 percent of management analysts were self-employed. Self-employed analysts can decide how much, when, and where to work. However, self-employed analysts often are under more pressure than those who are wage and salary employees, because their livelihood depends on their ability to maintain and expand their client base.

Management analysts worked in the following industries in 2010:

Management, scientific, and technical consulting services	20%
Finance and insurance	9
Federal government, excluding postal service	8
State and local government, excluding education and hospitals	6
Computer systems design and related services	5

Work Schedules

Analysts work under tight deadlines, which often require working long hours. In 2010, nearly one-third worked more than 40 hours per week.

How to Become a Management Analyst

Most management analysts have at least a bachelor's degree. The Certified Management Consultant (CMC) designation may improve job prospects.

Education

A bachelor's degree is the typical entry-level requirement for management analysts. However, some employers prefer to hire candidates who have a master's degree in business administration (MBA). In 2010, 28 percent of management analysts had a master's degree.

Few colleges and universities offer formal programs in management consulting. However, many fields of study provide a suitable education because of the range of areas that management analysts address. Common fields of study include business, management, accounting, marketing, economics, statistics, computer and information science, and engineering.

Analysts also routinely attend conferences to stay up to date on current developments in their field.

Certification

The Institute of Management Consultants USA, Inc. (IMC USA) offers the Certified Management Consultant (CMC) designation to those who meet minimum levels of education and experience, submit client reviews, and pass an interview and exam covering the IMC USA's Code of Ethics. Management consultants with a CMC designation must be recertified every 3 years. Management analysts are not required to get certification, but it may give jobseekers a competitive advantage.

Work Experience

Many analysts enter the occupation with years of work experience. Organizations that specialize in certain fields try to hire candidates who have experience in those areas. Typical work backgrounds include management, human resources, and information technology.

Advancement

As consultants gain experience, they often take on more responsibility. At the senior level, consultants may supervise teams working on more complex projects and become more involved in seeking out new business. Those with exceptional skills may eventually become partners in their consulting organization and focus on attracting new clients and bringing in revenue. Senior consultants who leave their consulting company often move to senior management positions at non-consulting organizations.

Important Qualities

Analytical skills. Management analysts must be able to interpret a wide range of information and use their findings to make proposals.

Communication skills. Management analysts must be able to communicate clearly and precisely in both writing and speaking. Successful analysts also need good listening skills to understand the organization's problems and propose appropriate solutions.

Interpersonal skills. Management analysts must work with managers and other employees of the organizations where they provide consulting services. They should work as a team toward achieving the organization's goals.

Problem-solving skills. Management analysts must be able to think creatively to solve clients' problems. Although some aspects of different clients' problems may be similar, each situation is likely to present unique challenges for the analyst to solve.

Self-confidence. Management analysts work under fairly high pressure. They should be confident and self-motivated when working with clients.

Time-management skills. Management analysts often work under tight deadlines and must use their time efficiently to complete projects on time.

Pay

Management Analysts
Median annual wages, May 2010

Management Analysts	$78,160
Business and Financial Operations Occupations	$60,670
Total, All Occupations	$33,840

Note: All Occupations includes all occupations in the U.S. Economy.
Source: U.S. Bureau of Labor Statistics, Occupational Employment Statistics

The median annual wage of management analysts was $78,160 in May 2010. The median wage is the wage at which half the workers in an occupation earned more than that amount and half earned less. The lowest 10 percent earned less than $43,900, and the top 10 percent earned more than $138,790.

Analysts work under tight deadlines, which often require working long hours. In 2010, nearly one-third worked more than 40 hours per week.

Job Outlook

Management Analysts
Percent change in employment, projected 2010-20

Management Analysts	22%
Business and Financial Operations Occupations	17%
Total, All Occupations	14%

Note: All Occupations includes all occupations in the U.S. Economy.
Source: U.S. Bureau of Labor Statistics, Employment Projections program

Employment of management analysts is expected to grow 22 percent from 2010 to 2020, faster than that average for all occupations. Demand for consulting services is expected to grow as organizations seek ways to improve efficiency and control costs. As markets become more competitive, firms will need to use resources more efficiently.

Growth will be particularly strong in smaller consulting companies that specialize in specific industries or types of business function. In addition, more management analysts will continue to be needed in the public sector, as federal, state, and local government agencies seek to reduce spending and improve efficiency.

Growth of international business will also contribute to an expected increase in demand for management analysts. As U.S. organizations expand their business abroad, many will hire management analysts to help them form the right strategy for entering the foreign market.

Many firms are also expected to hire information and other technology consultants who specialize in areas such as lowering energy consumption or implementing "green" initiatives.

Job Prospects

Jobseekers may face strong competition for management analyst positions because the high earning potential in this occupation makes it attractive to many jobseekers. Job opportunities are expected to be best for those who have a graduate degree or a certification, specialized expertise, and a talent for salesmanship and public relations.

Employment projections data for management analysts, 2010-20

Occupational Title	SOC Code	Employment, 2010	Projected Employment, 2020	Change, 2010-20	
				Percent	Numeric
Management Analysts	13-1111	718,800	876,000	22	157,200
SOURCE: U.S. Bureau of Labor Statistics, Employment Projections program					

Similar Occupations

This table shows a list of occupations with job duties that are similar to those of management analysts.

Occupation	Job Duties	Entry-Level Education	Median Annual Pay, May 2010
Accountants and Auditors	Accountants and auditors prepare and examine financial records. They ensure that financial records are accurate and that taxes are paid properly and on time. Accountants and auditors assess financial operations and work to help ensure that organizations run efficiently.	Bachelor's degree	$61,690
Budget Analysts	Budget analysts help public and private institutions organize their finances. They prepare budget reports and monitor institutional spending.	Bachelor's degree	$68,200
Cost Estimators	Cost estimators collect and analyze data to estimate the time, money, resources, and labor required for product manufacturing, construction projects, or services. Some specialize in a particular industry or product type.	Bachelor's degree	$57,860
Financial Analysts	Financial analysts provide guidance to businesses and individuals making investment decisions. They assess the performance of stocks, bonds, and other types of investments.	Bachelor's degree	$74,350
Market Research Analysts	Market research analysts study market conditions in local, regional, or national areas to examine potential sales of a product or service. They help companies understand what products people want, who will buy them, and at what price.	Bachelor's degree	$60,570
Administrative Services Managers	Administrative services managers plan, direct, and coordinate supportive services of an organization. Their specific responsibilities vary by the type of organization and may include keeping records, distributing mail, and planning and maintaining facilities.	High school diploma or equivalent	$77,890
Financial Managers	Financial managers are responsible for the financial health of an organization. They produce financial reports, direct investment activities, and develop strategies and plans for the long-term financial goals of their organization.	Bachelor's degree	$103,910
Top Executives	Top executives devise strategies and policies to ensure that an organization meets its goals. They plan, direct, and coordinate operational activities of companies and public or private-sector organizations.	See How to Become One	$101,250
Economists	Economists study the production and distribution of resources, goods, and services.	Bachelor's degree	$89,450
Survey Researchers	Survey researchers design or conduct surveys and analyze survey data. Many groups use surveys to collect factual data, such as employment and salary information, or to ask questions that help them understand people's opinions, attitudes, beliefs, or desires.	Bachelor's degree	$36,050
Operations Research Analysts	Operations research analysts use advanced methods of analysis to help organizations solve problems and make better decisions.	Bachelor's degree	$70,960

Contacts for More Information

For more information about management consulting, visit
American Academy of Financial Management
  Association of Management Consulting Firms
For more information about the Certified Management Consultant designation, visit **Institute of Management Consultants**

Suggested citation:

Market Research Analysts

Quick Facts: Market Research Analysts	
2010 Median Pay	$60,570 per year $29.12 per hour
Entry-Level Education	Bachelor's degree
Work Experience in a Related Occupation	None
On-the-job Training	None
Number of Jobs, 2010	282,700
Job Outlook, 2010-20	41% (Much faster than average)
Employment Change, 2010-20	116,600

What Market Research Analysts Do

Market research analysts study market conditions in local, regional, or national areas to examine potential sales of a product or service. They help companies understand what products people want, who will buy them, and at what price.

Duties

Market research analysts typically do the following:
- Monitor and forecast marketing and sales trends
- Measure the effectiveness of marketing programs and strategies
- Devise and evaluate methods for collecting data, such as surveys, questionnaires, or opinion polls
- Gather data about consumers, competitors, and market conditions
- Analyze data using statistical software
- Convert complex data and findings into understandable tables, graphs, and written reports
- Prepare reports and present results to clients or management

Market research analysts perform research and gather data to help a company market its products or services. They gather data on consumer demographics, preferences, needs, and buying habits. They collect data and information using a variety of methods, such as interviews, questionnaires, focus groups, market analysis surveys, public opinion polls, and literature reviews.

Analysts help determine a company's position in the marketplace by researching their competitors and analyzing their prices, sales, and marketing methods. Using this information, they may determine potential markets, product demand, and pricing. Their knowledge of

the targeted consumer enables them to develop advertising brochures and commercials, sales plans, and product promotions.

Market research analysts evaluate data using statistical techniques and software. They must interpret what the data means for their client, and they may forecast future trends. They often make charts, graphs, or other visual aids to present the results of their research.

Workers who design and conduct surveys are known as survey researchers. For more information, see the profile on survey researchers .

Some market research analysts may become professors or teachers. For more information, see the profile on postsecondary teachers . As an instructor in a junior or community college, a market research analyst may need only a master's degree, but a Ph.D. is usually required to teach in a college or university.

Work Environment

Market research analysts held about 282,700 jobs in 2010. Because most industries use market research, these analysts are employed throughout the economy.

The following industries employed the most market research analysts in 2010:

Professional, scientific, and technical services	29%
Finance and insurance	11
Information	8
Wholesale trade	8
Management of companies and enterprises	8

Some market research analysts work for the company that hires them to do research. Some work for consulting firms that do market research for many clients. A small percentage—about 5 percent—are self-employed. Those who hold full-time jobs in government, business, or teaching also may consult on a part-time basis.

Market research analysts generally work alone at a computer, collecting and analyzing marketing data and preparing reports. Some, however, work directly with the public to collect information and data.

Work Schedules

Market research analysts generally work full time during regular business hours. Some, however, work under pressure of deadlines and tight schedules, which may require longer hours.

How to Become a Market Research Analyst

Market research analysts need strong math and analytical skills. Most market research analysts need at least a bachelor's degree, and top research positions often require a master's degree.

Market research analysts gather and analyze data on consumers and competitors.

Education

Market research analysts need a bachelor's degree in market research or a related field. Many have degrees in fields such as statistics, math, or computer science. Others have a background in business administration, one of the social sciences, or communications. Courses in statistics, research methods, and marketing are essential for these workers; courses in communications and social sciences—such as economics, psychology, and sociology—are also important.

Many market research analyst jobs require a master's degree. Several schools offer graduate programs in marketing research, but many analysts complete degrees in other fields, such as statistics, marketing, or a Master of Business Administration (MBA). A master's degree is often required for leadership positions or positions that perform more technical research.

Work Experience

Most market research analysts benefit from internships or work experience in business, marketing, or sales. Experience in other positions that require analyzing data, writing reports, or surveying or collecting data can also be helpful in finding a market research position.

Certification

The Marketing Research Association offers the Professional Researcher Certification (PRC) for market research analysts. Certification is voluntary, but analysts may pursue certification to demonstrate a level of professional competency. Candidates qualify based on experience and knowledge; they must pass an exam, be a member of a professional organization, and have at least 3 years working in opinion and marketing research. To keep their certification valid, market research analysts must take continuing education courses and apply for renewal every 2 years.

Important Qualities

Analytical skills. Market research analysts must be able to understand large amounts of data and information.

Communication skills. Market research analysts need strong communication skills when gathering information and interpreting and presenting results to clients.

Critical-thinking skills. Market research analysts must assess all available information and use it to determine what marketing strategy would work best for a company.

Detail oriented. Market research analysts must be detail oriented because they often do precise data analysis.

Pay

Market Research Analysts
Median annual wages, May 2010

Business Operations Specialists	$60,660
Market Research Analysts	$60,570
Total, All Occupations	$33,840

Note: All Occupations includes all occupations in the U.S. Economy.
Source: U.S. Bureau of Labor Statistics. Occupational Employment Statistics

The median annual wage of market research analysts was $60,570 in May 2010. The median wage is the wage at which half the workers in an occupation earned more than that amount and half earned less.The lowest 10 percent earned less than $33,350, and the top 10 percent earned more than $111,440.

Median annual wages in the industries employing the largest numbers of market research analysts in May 2010 were:

Information	$70,970
Management of companies and enterprises	65,750
Wholesale trade	61,710
Finance and insurance	61,320
Professional, scientific, and technical services	61,250

Market research analysts generally work full time during regular business hours. Some, however, work under pressure of deadlines and tight schedules, which may require longer hours.

Job Outlook

Market Research Analysts
Percent change in employment, projected 2010-20

Market Research Analysts	41%
Business Operations Specialists	18%
Total, All Occupations	14%

Note: All Occupations includes all occupations in the U.S. Economy.
Source: U.S. Bureau of Labor Statistics. Employment Projections program

Employment of market research analysts is expected to grow 41 percent from 2010 to 2020, much faster than the average for all occupations. Employment growth will be driven by an increased use of data and market research across all industries in order to understand the needs and wants of customers and measure the effectiveness of marketing and business strategies.

Companies increasingly use research on consumer behavior to develop improved marketing strategies. By doing so, companies are better able to market directly to their target population. In addition, market research provides companies and organizations with an opportunity to cut costs.

Market research also lets companies monitor customer satisfaction and gather feedback about how to improve products or services, allowing them to build an advantage over their competitors. They may use research to decide the location of stores, placement of products, and services offered. As more companies use research to develop marketing strategies, competing companies will need to engage in similar market research.

Organizations such as research firms, social and civic organizations, colleges and universities, and government agencies will also increasingly use market research to ensure that program resources are being used effectively. For example, they may use research to show whether a particular social program reaches its target population or whether a transportation system meets the population's needs.

Job Prospects

Overall job prospects for market research analysts are expected to be good. Rapid employment growth in most industries means good job opportunities should be available throughout the economy.

Because many positions require a master's degree, those with a bachelor's degree are expected to face strong competition for jobs. Those with a strong background in statistical and data analysis or related work experience will have better job opportunities.

Prospects should be best for jobseekers with a master's degree in market research, marketing, statistics, or business administration. Analysts may find more opportunities in consulting and market research firms, as companies without established marketing or research departments often find it easier to hire a person outside the organization to perform market research services.

Employment projections data for market research analysts, 2010-20

Occupational Title	SOC Code	Employment, 2010	Projected Employment, 2020	Change, 2010-20	
				Percent	Numeric
Market Research Analysts and Marketing Specialists	13-1161	282,700	399,300	41	116,600
SOURCE: U.S. Bureau of Labor Statistics, Employment Projections program					

Similar Occupations

This table shows a list of occupations with job duties that are similar to those of market research analysts.

Occupation	Job Duties	Entry-Level Education	Median Annual Pay, May 2010
Cost Estimators	Cost estimators collect and analyze data to estimate the time, money, resources, and labor required for product manufacturing, construction projects, or services. Some specialize in a particular industry or product type.	Bachelor's degree	$57,860
Advertising, Promotions, and Marketing Managers	Advertising, promotions, and marketing managers plan programs to generate interest in a product or service. They work with art directors, sales agents, and financial staff members.	Bachelor's degree	$108,260
Public Relations Managers and Specialists	Public relations managers and specialists create and maintain a favorable public image for their employer or client. They write material for media releases, plan and direct public relations programs, and raise funds for their organizations.	Bachelor's degree	$57,550
Operations Research Analysts	Operations research analysts use advanced methods of analysis to help organizations solve problems and make better decisions.	Bachelor's degree	$70,960
Statisticians	Statisticians use mathematical techniques to analyze and interpret data and draw conclusions.	Master's degree	$72,830
Economists	Economists study the production and distribution of resources, goods, and services.	Bachelor's degree	$89,450
Survey Researchers	Survey researchers design or conduct surveys and analyze survey data. Many groups use surveys to collect factual data, such as employment and salary information, or to ask questions that help them understand people's opinions, attitudes, beliefs, or desires.	Bachelor's degree	$36,050

Contacts for More Information

For more information about market research analysts, visit Council of American Survey Research Organizations
Marketing Research Association

Suggested citation:

Bureau of Labor Statistics, U.S. Department of Labor, Occupational Outlook Handbook, 2012-13 Edition, Market Research Analysts, on the Internet at http://www.bls.gov/ooh/business-and-financial/market-research-analysts.htm .

Meeting, Convention, and Event Planners

Quick Facts: Meeting, Convention, and Event Planners	
2010 Median Pay	$45,260 per year $21.76 per hour
Entry-Level Education	Bachelor's degree
Work Experience in a Related Occupation	Less than 1 year
On-the-job Training	None
Number of Jobs, 2010	71,600
Job Outlook, 2010-20	44% (Much faster than average)
Employment Change, 2010-20	31,300

What Meeting, Convention, and Event Planners Do

Meeting, convention, and event planners coordinate all aspects of professional meetings and events. They choose meeting locations, arrange transportation, and coordinate other details.

Duties

Meeting, convention, and event planners typically do the following:

- Meet with clients to understand the purpose of the meeting or event
- Plan the scope of the event, including time, location, program, and cost
- Solicit bids from places and service providers (for example, florists or photographers)
- Work with the client to choose where to hold the event and whom to contract with for services
- Inspect places to ensure they meet the client's requirements
- Coordinate event services such as rooms, transportation, and food service
- Confer with on-site staff to coordinate details
- Monitor event activities to ensure the client and event attendees are satisfied
- Review event bills and approve payment

Whether it is a wedding, educational conference, or business convention, meetings and events bring people together for a common purpose. Meeting, convention, and event planners work to ensure that this purpose is achieved seamlessly.

They coordinate every detail of events, from beginning to end. Before a meeting, for example, planners will meet with clients to estimate attendance and determine the meeting's purpose. During the meeting, they handle meeting logistics such as registering guests and setting up audio/visual equipment for speakers. After the meeting, they survey attendees to find out what topics interested them the most.

Meeting, convention, and event planners also search for potential meeting sites, such as hotels and convention centers. They consider the lodging and services that the facility can provide, how easy it will be for people to get there, and the attractions that the surrounding area has to offer. More recently, planners also consider whether an online meeting can achieve the same objectives as a face-to-face meeting.

Once a location is selected, planners arrange meeting space and support services. For example, they negotiate contracts with suppliers to provide meals for attendees and coordinate plans with on-site staff. They organize speakers, entertainment, and activities. They also oversee the finances of meetings and conventions. On the day of the event, planners may register attendees, coordinate transportation, and make sure meeting rooms are set up properly.

The following are types of meeting, convention, and event planners:

Association planners organize annual conferences and trade shows for professional associations. Because member attendance is often voluntary, marketing the meeting's value is an important aspect of their work.

Corporate planners organize business meetings, usually under tight deadlines.

Government meeting planners organize meetings for government officials and agencies. Being familiar with government regulations, such as procedures for buying materials and booking hotels, is vital to their work.

Convention service managers help organize major events as employees of hotels and convention centers. They act as liaisons between the meeting facility and the planners who work for associations, businesses, or governments. They present food service options to outside planners, coordinate special requests, and suggest hotel services, depending on the planner's budget.

Event planners arrange the details of a variety of events, including weddings and large parties.

Digital technology is increasingly popular among meeting planners.

Work Environment

Meeting, convention, and event planners spend most of their time in offices. During meetings and events, they usually work on-site at hotels or convention centers. They travel regularly to attend events they organize and to visit prospective meeting sites, sometimes in exotic locations around the world. Planners regularly collaborate with clients, hospitality workers, and meeting attendees.

The work of meeting, convention, and event planners can be fast-paced and demanding. Planners oversee many aspects of the event at the same time, face numerous deadlines, and orchestrate the activities of several different groups of people.

In 2010, meeting, convention, and event planners held about 71,600 jobs. Most worked for private companies, and about 9 percent were self-employed. Industries employing the largest numbers of meeting, convention, and event planners were as follows:

Business, professional, labor and political organizations	13%
Hotels and motels	10
Other support services, including trade show organizers	9
Colleges, universities and professional schools	6
Grantmaking and giving services	3

Work Schedules

Most meeting, convention, and event planners work full time. In addition, many are required to work long, irregular hours in the time leading up to a major event. During meetings or conventions, planners may work very long days, starting early in the morning and working late into the evening. Sometimes, they must work on weekends.

How to Become a Meeting, Convention, or Event Planner

Applicants should have at least a bachelor's degree and some work experience related to planning.

Education

Many employers prefer applicants who have a bachelor's degree and related work experience in hotels or planning. The proportion of planners with a bachelor's degree is increasing because work responsibilities are becoming more complex and because there are more college degree programs. If an applicant's degree is not related to hospitality management, employers are likely to require at least 1 to 2 years of related work experience.

Meeting, convention, and event planners come from a variety of academic disciplines. Some related undergraduate majors include marketing, public relations, communications, business, and hospitality management. Planners who have studied hospitality management may start out with greater responsibilities than those from other academic disciplines. College students may also gain experience through an internship or by planning meetings for a university club. In addition, some colleges offer continuing education courses in meeting and event planning.

Work Experience

Some event planners enter the profession by gaining experience in a related occupation, such as a catering coordinator. For example, catering coordinators may begin planning smaller events, including weddings. As they gain experience and establish their reputation, they may start their own wedding planning business.

Once hired, planners learn many skills through experience. Entry-level planners generally begin by performing small tasks under the supervision of senior meeting professionals. Those who start at small organizations have the opportunity to learn more quickly because they must take on a larger variety of tasks.

Advancement

To advance in their careers, planners should volunteer to take on more responsibility and find better ways of doing their job. The most important factors in advancement are demonstrated skill, determination, and respect from peers. Because formal education is also increasingly important, those with limited experience may enhance their standing by enrolling in event planning courses offered by universities or professional associations.

As meeting, convention, and event planners establish themselves, they are given greater responsibility. This may mean taking on a wider range of duties or moving to another planning specialty to gain more experience. For example, a talented planner may be promoted from conference coordinator, with responsibility for meeting logistics, to program coordinator, with responsibility for speakers and event programming. The next step up may be to meeting manager, with responsibility for supervising all parts of the meeting. Entry-level planners tend to focus on meeting logistics, such as registering guests and setting up audio/visual equipment, while experienced planners manage interpersonal tasks, such as client relations and contract negotiations. With significant experience, meeting, convention, and event planners can become independent consultants or executive directors of associations.

Certification

The Convention Industry Council offers the Certified Meeting Professional (CMP) credential, a voluntary certification for meeting and convention planners. Although the CMP is not required, it is widely recognized in the industry and may help in career advancement. To qualify, candidates must have a minimum of 3 years of meeting management experience, recent employment in a meeting management job, and proof of continuing education credits. Those who qualify must then pass an exam that covers topics such as adult learning, financial management, facilities and services, logistics, and meeting programs.

The Society of Government Meeting Professionals (SGMP) offers the Certified Government Meeting Professional (CGMP) credential for meeting planners who work for, or contract with, federal, state, or local government. This certification is not required to work as a government meeting planner; however, it may be helpful for those who want to show that they know government buying policies and travel regulations. To qualify, candidates must have worked as a meeting planner for at least 1 year and have been a member of SGMP for 6 months. To become a certified planner, members must take a 3-day course and pass an exam.

Important Qualities

Communication skills. Meeting, convention, and event planners communicate with clients, suppliers, and event staff. They must have excellent written and oral communication skills and be able to convey the needs of their clients effectively.

Composure. Planners often work in a fast-paced environment and must be able to think on their feet and remain calm under pressure.

Computer skills. Planners must be familiar with computers, database software, budgets, and online social media.

Customer-service skills. Planners must understand their clients' needs. They must act professionally in a variety of situations, know how to keep an audience engaged, and help participants network with peers.

Interpersonal skills. Planners must be good at establishing and maintaining positive relationships with clients and suppliers. They should also be able to help event participants network with peers.

Negotiation skills. Planners must be able to negotiate service contracts that get the best prices for their clients.

Organizational skills. To provide high quality meetings, planners must be detail-oriented, good at multitasking, and able to meet tight deadlines. Many meetings are planned more than a year in advance, so long-term thinking ability is vital.

Problem-solving skills. When problems arise, planners must be able to come up with creative solutions that satisfy clients.

Pay

Meeting, Convention, and Event Planners
Median annual wages, May 2010

Business and Financial Operations Occupations	$60,670
Meeting, Convention, and Event Planners	$45,260
Total, All Occupations	$33,840

Note: All Occupations includes all occupations in the U.S. Economy.
Source: U.S. Bureau of Labor Statistics, Occupational Employment Statistics

The median annual wage of meeting, convention, and event planners was $45,260 in May 2010. The median wage is the wage at which half the workers in an occupation earned more than that amount and half earned less. The lowest 10 percent earned less than $27,090, and the top 10 percent earned more than $76,840.

In May 2010, median annual wages in industries employing the largest numbers of meeting, convention, and event planners were as follows:

Business, professional, labor and political organizations	$49,730
Grantmaking and giving services	49,330
Other support services, including trade show organizers	45,560
Colleges, universities and professional schools	44,360
Hotels and motels	43,030

Most meeting, convention, and event planners work full time. In addition, many are required to work long, irregular hours in the time leading up to a major event. During meetings or conventions, planners may work very long days, starting early in the morning and working late into the evening. Sometimes, they must work on weekends.

Job Outlook

Meeting, Convention, and Event Planners
Percent change in employment, projected 2010-20

Meeting, Convention, and Event Planners	44%
Business and Financial Operations Occupations	17%
Total, All Occupations	14%

Note: All Occupations includes all occupations in the U.S. Economy.
Source: U.S. Bureau of Labor Statistics, Employment Projections program

Employment of meeting, convention, and event planners is expected to grow 44 percent from 2010 to 2020, much faster than the average for all occupations. As businesses and organizations become increasingly international, meetings and conventions are expected to become even more important. For many of these organizations, meetings are the only time they can bring their members together. Despite the spread of online communication, face-to-face interaction is irreplaceable. In addition, industries and businesses increasingly recognize the value of hiring professional meeting planners who can deliver top-notch meetings at the best available price.

Job Prospects

In addition to rapid employment growth, many job openings are expected to arise from the need to replace workers who leave the occupation. However, job seekers can expect strong competition because the occupation usually attracts more applicants than job openings.

Job opportunities should be best for people with a bachelor's degree in hospitality management. A Certified Meeting Planner (CMP) credential is also viewed favorably by potential employers. Those who have experience with virtual meeting software and social media outlets also should have an advantage in the job search.

Job opportunities for corporate planners go up and down with the economy. When the economy is poor, companies often cut budgets for meetings. Planners who get laid off during a recession often go to work as private contractors until they can get a full-time job again.

Planners who work for the healthcare industry are least likely to experience cutbacks during a recession because attendance at medical meetings is often required for healthcare professionals to maintain their license.

Event planners can also expect strong competition for jobs. Those with related work experience should have the best job opportunities.

Employment projections data for meeting, convention, and event planners, 2010-20

Occupational Title	SOC Code	Employment, 2010	Projected Employment, 2020	Change, 2010-20 Percent	Numeric
Meeting, Convention, and Event Planners	13-1121	71,600	102,900	44	31,300

SOURCE: U.S. Bureau of Labor Statistics, Employment Projections program

Similar Occupations

This table shows a list of occupations with job duties that are similar to those of meeting, convention, and event planners.

Occupation	Job Duties	Entry-Level Education	Median Annual Pay, May 2010
Administrative Services Managers	Administrative services managers plan, direct, and coordinate supportive services of an organization. Their specific responsibilities vary by the type of organization and may include keeping records, distributing mail, and planning and maintaining facilities.	High school diploma or equivalent	$77,890
Food Service Managers	Food service managers are responsible for the daily operations of restaurants and other establishments that prepare and serve food and beverages to customers. Managers ensure that customers are satisfied with their dining experience.	High school diploma or equivalent	$48,130

Lodging Managers	Lodging managers make sure that guests on vacation or business travel have a pleasant experience, while also ensuring that an establishment is run efficiently and profitably.	High school diploma or equivalent	$46,880
Public Relations Managers and Specialists	Public relations managers and specialists create and maintain a favorable public image for their employer or client. They write material for media releases, plan and direct public relations programs, and raise funds for their organizations.	Bachelor's degree	$57,550
Travel Agents	Travel agents sell transportation, lodging, and admission to entertainment activities to individuals and groups who are planning trips. They offer advice on destinations, plan trip itineraries, and make travel arrangements for clients.	High school diploma or equivalent	$31,870

Contacts for More Information

For more information about meeting, convention, and event planners, including information about certification and industry trends, visit Convention Industry Council, Society of Government Meeting Professionals, Professional Convention Management Association, Meeting Professionals International

Suggested citation:

Bureau of Labor Statistics, U.S. Department of Labor, Occupational Outlook Handbook, 2012-13 Edition, Meeting, Convention, and Event Planners, on the Internet at http://www.bls.gov/ooh/business-and-financial/meeting-convention-and-event-planners.htm .

Personal Financial Advisors

Quick Facts: Personal Financial Advisors	
2010 Median Pay	$64,750 per year $31.13 per hour
Entry-Level Education	Bachelor's degree
Work Experience in a Related Occupation	None
On-the-job Training	None
Number of Jobs, 2010	206,800
Job Outlook, 2010-20	32% (Much faster than average)
Employment Change, 2010-20	66,400

What Personal Financial Advisors Do

Personal financial advisors give financial advice to people. They help with investments, taxes, and insurance decisions.

Duties

Personal financial advisors typically do the following:

- Meet with clients in person to discuss their financial goals
- Explain the types of financial services they provide
- Educate clients and answer questions about investment options and potential risks
- Recommend investments to clients or select investments on their behalf
- Help clients plan for specific circumstances, such as education expenses or retirement
- Monitor clients' accounts and determine if changes are needed to improve account performance or accommodate life changes, such as getting married or having children
- Research investment opportunities

Personal financial advisors assess the financial needs of individuals and help them with investments (such as stocks and bonds), tax laws, and insurance decisions. Advisors help clients plan for short-term and long-term goals, such as education expenses and retirement. They recommend investments to match the clients' goals. They invest clients' money based on the clients' decisions.

Many also provide tax advice or sell insurance.

Although most planners offer advice on a wide range of topics, some specialize in areas such as retirement or risk management (evaluating how willing the investor is to take chances, and adjusting investments accordingly).

Many personal financial advisors spend a lot of time marketing their services, and they meet potential clients by giving seminars or through business and social networking. Networking is the process of meeting and exchanging information with people, or groups of people, who have similar interests.

After they have invested funds for a client, they, as well as the client, get regular reports of the investments. They monitor the client's investments and usually meet with each client at least once a year to update the client on potential investments and to adjust the financial plan because of the client's changed circumstances or because investment options have changed.

Many personal financial advisors are licensed to directly buy and sell financial products, such as stocks, bonds, annuities, and insurance.

Personal financial advisors meet with clients to discuss their financial goals.

Depending on the agreement they have with their clients, personal financial advisors may have the clients' permission to make decisions about buying and selling stocks and bonds.

Private bankers or **wealth managers** are personal financial advisors who work for people who have a lot of money to invest. These clients are similar to institutional investors (commonly companies or organizations), and they approach investing differently from the general public. Private bankers manage a collection of investments, called a portfolio, for these clients by using the resources of the bank, including teams of financial analysts, accountants, and other professionals. For more information on the duties of these other financial workers, see the profiles on financial analysts and accountants and auditors .

Work Environment

Personal financial advisors held about 206,800 jobs in 2010.

The following industries employed the most personal financial advisors in 2010:

Other financial investment activities	26%
Monetary authorities, credit intermediation, and related activities	19
Securities and commodity contracts intermediation and brokerage	19
Insurance carriers and related activities	3
Professional, scientific, and technical services	3

Personal financial advisors typically work in offices. Almost one-fourth of personal financial advisors are self-employed. Many also travel to attend conferences or teach finance classes in the evening to bring in more clients.

Work Schedules

Most personal financial advisors work full time, and 24 percent work more than 50 hours per week. They often go to meetings on evenings and weekends to meet with existing clients or to try to bring in new ones.

How to Become a Personal Financial Advisor

Personal financial advisors typically need a bachelor's degree. A master's degree and certification can improve chances for advancement in the occupation.

Education

Personal financial advisors typically need a bachelor's degree. Although employers usually do not require a specific field of study for personal financial advisors, a degree in finance, economics, accounting, business, mathematics, or law is good preparation for this occupation. Courses in investments, taxes, estate planning, and risk management are also helpful. Programs in financial planning are becoming more available in colleges and universities.

Licenses

Personal financial advisors who directly buy or sell stocks, bonds, insurance policies, or specific investment advice need a combination of licenses that varies based upon the products they sell. In addition to those licenses, smaller firms that manage clients' investments must be registered with state regulators, and larger firms must be registered with the Securities and Exchange Commission . Personal financial advisors who choose to sell insurance need licenses issued by state boards. State licensing board information and requirements for registered investment advisors are available from the North American Securities Administrators Association .

Certification

Certifications can enhance a personal financial advisor's reputation and can help bring in new clients. The Certified Financial Planner Board of Standards offers the Certified Financial Planner (CFP). For this certification, advisors must have a bachelor's degree, at least 3 years of relevant work experience, pass an exam, and agree to adhere to a code of ethics. The exam covers the financial planning process, insurance and risk management, employee benefits planning, taxes and retirement planning, investment and real estate planning, debt management, planning liability, emergency fund reserves, and statistical modeling.

Advancement

A master's degree in an area such as finance or business administration can improve a personal financial advisor's chances of moving into a management position and attracting new clients.

Important Qualities

Analytical skills. In determining an investment portfolio for a client, personal financial advisors must be able to take into account a range of information, including economic trends, regulatory changes, and the client's comfort with risky decisions.

Interpersonal skills. A major part of a personal financial advisor's job is making clients feel comfortable. They must establish trust with clients and respond well to their questions and concerns.

Math skills. Personal financial advisors should be good at mathematics because they constantly work with numbers. They determine the amount invested, how that amount has grown or shrunk over time, and how a portfolio is distributed among different investments.

Selling skills. To expand their base of clients, personal financial advisors must be convincing and persistent in selling their services.

Speaking skills. Personal financial advisors interact with clients every day. They must explain complex financial concepts in understandable language.

Pay

Personal Financial Advisors
Median annual wages, May 2010

Personal Financial Advisors	$64,750
Business and Financial Operations Occupations	$60,670
Total, All Occupations	$33,840

Note: All Occupations includes all occupations in the U.S. Economy.
Source: U.S. Bureau of Labor Statistics, Occupational Employment Statistics

The median annual wage of personal financial advisors was $64,750 in May 2010. The median wage is the wage at which half the workers in an occupation earned more than that amount and half earned less. The lowest 10 percent earned less than $32,660, and the top 10 percent earned more than $166,400.

Wages of self-employed advisors are not included in the earnings reported here.

Personal financial advisors who work for financial services firms are often paid a salary plus bonuses. Bonuses are not included in the wage data here.

Advisors who work for financial investment firms or planning firms or who are self-employed typically earn their money by charging a percentage of the clients' assets that they manage. They may also earn money by charging an hourly fee or by getting fees on stock and insurance purchases. In addition to their fees, advisors generally get commissions for financial products that they sell.

Most personal financial advisors work full time, and 24 percent work more than 50 hours per week. They often go to meetings on evenings and weekends to meet with existing clients or to try to bring in new ones.

Job Outlook

Personal Financial Advisors

Percent change in employment, projected 2010-20

Personal Financial Advisors	32%
Business and Financial Operations Occupations	17%
Total, All Occupations	14%

Note: All Occupations includes all occupations in the U.S. Economy.
Source: U.S. Bureau of Labor Statistics, Employment Projections program

Employment of personal financial advisors is projected to grow 32 percent from 2010 to 2020, much faster than the average for all occupations.

The primary driver of growth will be the aging population. As large numbers of baby boomers approach retirement, they will seek planning advice from personal financial advisors.

Decreased funds for corporate and state pensions also are expected to contribute to the trend of hiring personal financial advisors. Private corporations and state and local governments are facing shortfalls in their pension funds, which may lead to benefit reductions. This will require more financial planning from individuals and increase the demand for personal financial advisors.

Job Prospects

Personal financial advisors are expected to face competition as the combination of relatively high wages and few formal educational requirements attracts many applicants for each opening.

Employment projections data for personal financial advisors, 2010-20

Occupational Title	SOC Code	Employment, 2010	Projected Employment, 2020	Change, 2010-20 Percent	Change, 2010-20 Numeric
Personal Financial Advisors	13-2052	206,800	273,200	32	66,400

SOURCE: U.S. Bureau of Labor Statistics, Employment Projections program

Similar Occupations

This table shows a list of occupations with job duties that are similar to those of personal financial advisors.

Occupation	Job Duties	Entry-Level Education	Median Annual Pay, May 2010
Budget Analysts	Budget analysts help public and private institutions organize their finances. They prepare budget reports and monitor institutional spending.	Bachelor's degree	$68,200
Financial Analysts	Financial analysts provide guidance to businesses and individuals making investment decisions. They assess the performance of stocks, bonds, and other types of investments.	Bachelor's degree	$74,350
Financial Managers	Financial managers are responsible for the financial health of an organization. They produce financial reports, direct investment activities, and develop strategies and plans for the long-term financial goals of their organization.	Bachelor's degree	$103,910
Insurance Sales Agents	Insurance sales agents help insurance companies generate new business by contacting potential customers and selling one or more types of insurance. An agent explains various insurance policies and helps clients choose plans that suit them.	High school diploma or equivalent	$46,770
Insurance Underwriters	Insurance underwriters decide whether to provide insurance and under what terms. They evaluate insurance applications and determine coverage amounts and premiums.	Bachelor's degree	$59,290
Real Estate Brokers and Sales Agents	Real estate brokers and sales agents help clients buy, sell, and rent properties. Brokers and agents do the same type of work, but brokers are licensed to manage their own real estate businesses. Sales agents must work with a broker.	High school diploma or equivalent	$42,680
Securities, Commodities, and Financial Services Sales Agents	Securities, commodities, and financial services sales agents connect buyers and sellers in financial markets. They sell securities to individuals, advise companies in search of investors, and conduct trades.	Bachelor's degree	$70,190

Contacts for More Information

For more information about personal financial advisors, visit American Academy of Financial Management

For more information about regulation and licensure of personal financial advisors, visit Financial Industry Regulatory Authority (FINRA), Securities Industry and Financial Markets Association, North American Securities Administrator Association, Securities and Exchange Commission (SEC), Certified Financial Planner Board of Standards

Suggested citation:

Bureau of Labor Statistics, U.S. Department of Labor, Occupational Outlook Handbook, 2012-13 Edition, Personal Financial Advisors, on the Internet at http://www.bls.gov/ooh/business-and-financial/personal-financial-advisors.htm .

Purchasing Managers, Buyers, and Purchasing Agents

Quick Facts: Purchasing Managers, Buyers, and Purchasing Agents	
2010 Median Pay	$58,360 per year $28.06 per hour
Entry-Level Education	See How to Become One
Work Experience in a Related Occupation	See How to Become One
On-the-job Training	See How to Become One
Number of Jobs, 2010	487,200
Job Outlook, 2010-20	7% (Slower than average)
Employment Change, 2010-20	31,700

What Purchasing Managers, Buyers, and Purchasing Agents Do

Purchasing managers, buyers, and purchasing agents buy products for organizations to use or resell. They evaluate suppliers, negotiate contracts, and review product quality.

Duties

Purchasing managers, buyers, and purchasing agents typically do the following:

- Evaluate suppliers based on price, quality, and delivery speed
- Interview vendors and visit suppliers' plants and distribution centers to examine and learn about products, services, and prices
- Attend meetings, trade shows, and conferences to learn about new industry trends and make contacts with suppliers
- Analyze price proposals, financial reports, and other information to determine reasonable prices
- Negotiate contracts on behalf of their organization
- Work out policies with suppliers, such as when products will be delivered
- Meet with staff and vendors to discuss defective or unacceptable goods or services and determine corrective action
- Evaluate and monitor contracts to be sure that vendors and supplies comply with the terms and conditions of the contract and to

Purchasing agents and buyers consider price, quality, availability, reliability, and technical support when choosing suppliers and merchandise.

determine need for changes
- Maintain and review records of items bought, costs, deliveries, product performance, and inventories

Purchasing managers, buyers, and purchasing agents buy farm products, durable and nondurable goods, and services for organizations and institutions. They try to get the best deal for their organization—the highest quality goods and services at the lowest cost. They do this by studying sales records and inventory levels of current stock, identifying foreign and domestic suppliers, and keeping up to date with changes affecting both the supply of, and demand for, products and materials.

Purchasing agents and buyers consider price, quality, availability, reliability, and technical support when choosing suppliers and merchandise. To be effective, purchasing agents and buyers must have a working technical knowledge of the goods or services to be bought.

Evaluating suppliers is one of the most critical functions of a purchasing manager, buyer, or purchasing agent. Many organizations now run on a lean manufacturing schedule and use just-in-time inventories, so any delays in the supply chain can shut down production and potentially cost the organization customers.

Purchasing managers, buyers, and purchasing agents use many resources to find out all they can about potential suppliers. They attend meetings, trade shows, and conferences to learn about new industry trends and make contacts with suppliers.

They often interview prospective suppliers and visit their plants and distribution centers to assess their capabilities. For example, they may discuss the design of products with design engineers, quality concerns with production supervisors, or shipping issues with managers in the receiving department.

They must make certain that the supplier can deliver the desired goods or services on time, in the correct quantities, and without sacrificing quality. Once they have gathered information on suppliers, they sign contracts with suppliers who meet the organization's needs, and they place orders.

Buyers who purchase items to resell to customers largely determine which products their organization will sell. They need to be able to predict what will appeal to their customers. If they are wrong, they could jeopardize the profits and reputation of their organization.

The following are examples of types of purchasing managers, buyers, and purchasing agents:

Wholesale and retail buyers purchase goods for resale to consumers. Examples of these goods are clothing and electronics. Purchasing specialists who buy finished goods for resale are commonly known as buyers or merchandise managers. Buyers who work for large organizations usually specialize in one or two lines of merchandise (for example, men's clothing or women's shoes or children's toys). Buyers who work for small stores may be responsible for buying everything the store sells.

Purchasing agents and buyers of farm products buy agricultural products for further processing or resale. Examples of these products include grain, cotton, and tobacco.

Purchasing agents, except wholesale, retail, and farm products buy items for the operation of an organization. Examples of these items include paper, pens, and industrial equipment.

Purchasing managers plan and coordinate the work of buyers and purchasing agents, and they usually handle more complicated purchases. Those employed by government agencies or manufacturing firms usually are called purchasing directors, managers, or agents; sometimes they are known as contract specialists. Some purchasing managers, called contract or supply managers, specialize in negotiating and supervising contracts for supplies.

Work Environment

Purchasing managers, buyers, and purchasing agents held about 487,200 jobs in 2010.

The following industries employed the most purchasing managers in 2010:

Manufacturing	34%
Management of companies and enterprises	14
Wholesale trade	12
Federal government	6

The following industries employed the most buyers and purchasing agents, farm products in 2010:

Merchant wholesalers, nondurable goods	35%
Manufacturing	15
Retail trade	8
Management of companies and enterprises	6
Wholesale electronic markets and agents and brokers	4

The following industries employed the most wholesale and retail buyers, except farm products in 2010:

Retail trade	28%
Merchant wholesalers, durable goods	18
Management of companies and enterprises	14
Merchant wholesalers, nondurable goods	13
Wholesale electronic markets and agents and brokers	6

The following industries employed the most purchasing agents, except wholesale, retail, and farm products in 2010:

Manufacturing	32%
Federal government	14
Professional, scientific, and technical services	8
Wholesale trade	6

Most purchasing managers, buyers, and purchasing agents work in comfortable offices. Travel is sometimes necessary, and purchasers for global organizations may need to travel outside the United States.

Work Schedules

Most purchasing managers and agents work full time. Overtime is common in this occupation. In 2010, about 30 percent of purchasing managers and 20 percent of buyers and purchasing agents worked more than 40 hours per week.

How to Become a Purchasing Manager, Buyer, or Purchasing Agent

Buyers and purchasing agents need a high school diploma and on-the-job training. Purchasing managers need a bachelor's degree and work experience as a buyer or purchasing agent.

Education

Educational requirements usually vary with the size of the organization. A high school diploma is enough at many organizations for entry into the purchasing agent occupation, although large stores and distributors may prefer applicants who have completed a bachelor's degree program and have taken some business or accounting classes. Many manufacturing firms put an even greater emphasis on formal training, preferring applicants who have a bachelor's or master's degree in engineering, business, economics, or one of the applied sciences.

Purchasing managers usually have at least a bachelor's degree and some work experience in the field. A master's degree may be required for advancement to some top-level purchasing manager jobs.

Training

Buyers and purchasing agents typically get on-the-job training for more than 1 year. During this time, they learn how to perform their basic duties, including monitoring inventory levels and negotiating with suppliers.

Certification

There are several recognized credentials for purchasing agents and purchasing managers. These certifications involve oral or written exams and have education and work experience requirements.

The Certified Professional in Supply Management (CPSM) credential covers a wide scope of duties that purchasing professionals do. The exam requires applicants to have a bachelor's degree and 3 years of supply management experience.

The American Purchasing Society offers two certifications: the Certified Purchasing Professional (CPP) and Certified Professional Purchasing Manager (CPPM). These certifications require at least 3 years of purchasing-related experience or a combination of education and experience.

The Association for Operations Management (APICS) offers the Certified Supply Chain Professional (CSCP) credential.

The National Institute of Governmental Purchasing offers workers in federal, state, and local government, two certifications: Certified Professional Public Buyer (CPPB) and Certified Public Purchasing Officer (CPPO).

Work Experience

Purchasing managers typically must have at least 5 years of experience as a buyer or purchasing agent. At the top levels, purchasing manager duties may overlap with other management functions, such as production, planning, logistics, and marketing.

Advancement

An experienced purchasing agent or buyer may become an assistant purchasing manager before advancing to purchasing manager, supply manager, or director of materials management.

Important Qualities

Analytical skills. When evaluating suppliers, purchasing managers and agents must analyze their options and choose a supplier with the best combination of price and quality.

Decision-making skills. Purchasing managers and agents must have the ability to make informed and timely decisions in choosing products that will sell.

Math skills. Purchasing managers and agents must possess basic math skills. They must be able to compare prices from different suppliers to ensure that their organization is getting the best deal.

Negotiating skills. Purchasing managers and agents often must negotiate the terms of a contract with a supplier. Interpersonal skills and self-confidence, in addition to knowledge of the product, can help lead to successful negotiation.

Pay

Purchasing Managers, Buyers, and Purchasing Agents
Median annual wages, May 2010

Purchasing Managers, Buyers, and Purchasing Agents	$58,360
Total, All Occupations	$33,840

Note: All Occupations includes all occupations in the U.S. Economy.
Source: U.S. Bureau of Labor Statistics, Occupational Employment Statistics

The median annual wage of purchasing managers, buyers, and purchasing agents was $58,360 in May 2010. The median wage is the wage at which half the workers in an occupation earned more than that amount and half earned less. The lowest 10 percent earned less than $34,110, and the top 10 percent earned more than $105,610.

The median wages of purchasing managers, buyers, and purchasing agent occupations in May 2010 were as follows:

- $95,070 for purchasing managers
- $56,580 for purchasing agents, except wholesale, retail, and farm products
- $54,220 for buyers and purchasing agents, farm products
- $49,650 for wholesale and retail buyers, except farm products

Most purchasing managers and agents work full time. Overtime is common in this occupation. In 2010, about 30 percent of purchasing managers and 20 percent of buyers and purchasing agents worked more than 40 hours per week.

Job Outlook

Purchasing Managers, Buyers, and Purchasing Agents
Percent change in employment, projected 2010-20

Total, All Occupations	14%
Purchasing Managers, Buyers, and Purchasing Agents	7%

Note: All Occupations includes all occupations in the U.S. Economy.
Source: U.S. Bureau of Labor Statistics, Employment Projections program

Employment of purchasing managers, buyers, and purchasing agents is expected to increase 7 percent from 2010 to 2020, slower than the average for all occupations.

These workers will be needed to buy goods and services for business operations or for resale to customers. Growth will vary based on the type of purchasing agent or manager and the specific industry.

Employment of wholesale and retail buyers, except farm products, is expected to grow 9 percent from 2010 to 2020, slower than the average for all occupations. Growth will be driven largely by the performance of the wholesale and retail industries.

Employment of purchasing agents, farm products, is expected to grow 5 percent from 2010 to 2020, slower than the average for all occupations. Slower growth in the agricultural industry has led to slow growth in this occupation, and the trend is expected to continue.

Employment of purchasing agents, except wholesale, retail, and farm products, is expected to grow 5 percent from 2010 to 2020, slower than the average for all occupations. Continued employment decreases in manufacturing, as well as decreases in federal government, which includes defense purchasing, are expected. However, growth is expected for this occupation in healthcare and computer systems design and related services firms.

Employment of purchasing managers is expected to grow 7 percent from 2010 to 2020, slower than the average for all occupations. The trends affecting growth for agents and buyers will also affect purchasing managers, although there should still be a need for purchasing managers to plan and direct buying activities for organizations and to supervise purchasing agents and buyers.

Employment projections data for purchasing managers, buyers, and purchasing agents, 2010-20

Occupational Title	SOC Code	Employment, 2010	Projected Employment, 2020	Change, 2010-20 Percent	Change, 2010-20 Numeric
Purchasing Managers, Buyers, and Purchasing Agents	—	487,200	518,900	7	31,700
Purchasing Managers	11-3061	68,000	72,900	7	4,900
Buyers and Purchasing Agents, Farm Products	13-1021	13,000	13,700	5	700
Wholesale and Retail Buyers, Except Farm Products	13-1022	122,000	133,000	9	11,000
Purchasing Agents, Except Wholesale, Retail, and Farm Products	13-1023	284,200	299,300	5	15,100

SOURCE: U.S. Bureau of Labor Statistics, Employment Projections program

Similar Occupations

This table shows a list of occupations with job duties that are similar to those of purchasing managers, buyers, and purchasing agents.

Occupation	Job Duties	Entry-Level Education	Median Annual Pay, May 2010
Advertising, Promotions, and Marketing Managers	Advertising, promotions, and marketing managers plan programs to generate interest in a product or service. They work with art directors, sales agents, and financial staff members.	Bachelor's degree	$108,260
Bookkeeping, Accounting, and Auditing Clerks	Bookkeeping, accounting, and auditing clerks produce financial records for organizations. They record financial transactions, update statements, and check financial records for accuracy.	High school diploma or equivalent	$34,030

Financial Clerks	Financial clerks do administrative work for banking, insurance, and other companies. They keep records, help customers, and carry out financial transactions.	High school diploma or equivalent	$33,710
Food Service Managers	Food service managers are responsible for the daily operations of restaurants and other establishments that prepare and serve food and beverages to customers. Managers ensure that customers are satisfied with their dining experience.	High school diploma or equivalent	$48,130
Lodging Managers	Lodging managers make sure that guests on vacation or business travel have a pleasant experience, while also ensuring that an establishment is run efficiently and profitably.	High school diploma or equivalent	$46,880
Logisticians	Logisticians analyze and coordinate an organization's supply chain—the system that moves a product from supplier to consumer. They manage the entire life cycle of a product, which includes how a product is acquired, distributed, allocated, and delivered.	Bachelor's degree	$70,800
Wholesale and Manufacturing Sales Representatives	Wholesale and manufacturing sales representatives sell goods for wholesalers or manufacturers to businesses, government agencies, and other organizations. They contact customers, explain product features, answer any questions that their customers may have, and negotiate prices.	See How to Become One	$56,620

Contacts for More Information

For more information about purchasing managers, including education, training, employment, and certification, visit American Purchasing Society, Association for Operations Management (APICS), Institute for Supply Management, National Institute of Governmental Purchasing

Suggested citation:

Bureau of Labor Statistics, U.S. Department of Labor, Occupational Outlook Handbook, 2012-13 Edition, Purchasing Managers, Buyers, and Purchasing Agents, on the Internet at http://www.bls.gov/ooh/business-and-financial/purchasing-managers-buyers-and-purchasing-agents.htm .

Tax Examiners and Collectors, and Revenue Agents

Quick Facts: Tax Examiners and Collectors, and Revenue Agents	
2010 Median Pay	$49,360 per year $23.73 per hour
Entry-Level Education	Bachelor's degree
Work Experience in a Related Occupation	None
On-the-job Training	Moderate-term on-the-job training
Number of Jobs, 2010	74,500
Job Outlook, 2010-20	7% (Slower than average)
Employment Change, 2010-20	5,500

What Tax Examiners and Collectors, and Revenue Agents Do

Tax examiners and collectors, and revenue agents ensure that governments get their tax money from businesses and citizens. They review tax returns, conduct audits, identify taxes owed, and collect overdue tax payments.

Duties

Tax examiners and collectors, and revenue agents typically do the following:

- Review filed tax returns to determine whether tax credits and deductions claimed are allowed by law
- Contact taxpayers by mail or telephone to address problems and to request supporting documentation
- Conduct field audits and investigations of income tax returns to verify information or to update tax liabilities
- Evaluate financial information, using their familiarity with accounting procedures and knowledge of changes to tax laws and regulations
- Keep records on each case they deal with, including contacts, telephone numbers, and actions taken
- Notify taxpayers of any overpayment or underpayment, and either issue a refund or request further payment

Tax examiners and collectors, and revenue agents are responsible for ensuring that individuals and businesses pay the taxes they owe. They ensure that tax returns are filed properly, and they follow up with taxpayers whose returns are questionable or who owe more than they have paid.

Different levels of government collect different types of taxes. The federal government deals primarily with personal and business income taxes. State governments collect income and sales taxes. Local governments collect sales and property taxes.

Because many states assess individual income taxes based on the taxpayer's reported federal adjusted gross income, tax examiners working for the federal government report to the states any adjustments or corrections they make. State tax examiners then determine whether the adjustments affect how much the taxpayer owes the state.

Tax examiners, collectors, and revenue agents have different duties and responsibilities:

Tax examiners usually deal with the simplest tax returns—those filed by individual taxpayers with few deductions and those filed by small businesses. At the entry level, many tax examiners do clerical

Tax examiners and collectors, and revenue agents are responsible for ensuring that individuals and businesses pay the taxes they owe.

tasks, such as reviewing tax returns and entering them into a computer system for processing. If there is a problem, tax examiners may contact the taxpayer to try to resolve it.

Much of a tax examiner's job involves making sure that tax credits and deductions claimed by taxpayers are lawful. If a taxpayer owes additional taxes, tax examiners adjust the total amount by assessing fees, interest, and penalties and then notify the taxpayer of the total amount owed.

Revenue agents specialize in tax-related accounting for the U.S. Internal Revenue Service (IRS) and for equivalent agencies in state and local governments. Like tax examiners, they review returns for accuracy. However, revenue agents handle complicated tax returns of businesses and large corporations.

Many experienced revenue agents specialize in specific areas. For example, they may focus exclusively on multinational businesses. Regardless of their specialty, revenue agents must keep up to date with changes in the lengthy and complex tax laws and regulations.

Collectors, also called revenue officers in the IRS, deal with overdue accounts. The process of collecting an overdue payment starts with the revenue agent or tax examiner sending a report to the taxpayer. If the taxpayer makes no effort to pay, the case is assigned to a collector.

When a collector takes a case, he or she first sends the taxpayer a notice. The collector then works with the taxpayer to settle the debt. Settlement may involve setting up a plan in which the amount owed is paid back in small amounts over time.

Collectors verify assertions that delinquent taxpayers cannot pay their taxes. They investigate these claims by researching information on mortgages or financial statements and by locating items of value through third parties, such as neighbors or local departments of motor vehicles. Ultimately, collectors must decide whether the IRS should take a lien—a claim on an asset such as a bank account, real estate, or an automobile—to settle a debt. Collectors also have the authority to garnish wages—that is, take a portion of earned wages—to collect taxes owed.

Work Environment

Tax examiners and collectors, and revenue agents held about 74,500 jobs in 2010.

Tax examiners and collectors, and revenue agents work for federal, state, and local governments. Many work primarily in an office; others spend most of their time conducting field audits by visiting taxpayers in their home or business. Some agents may be permanently stationed

in offices of large corporations that have complicated tax structures, such as those that do business internationally.

The distribution of tax examiners and collectors and revenue agents across federal, state, and local government in 2010 was as follows:

Federal government, excluding postal service	49%
State government, excluding education and hospitals	32
Local government, excluding education and hospitals	19

Work Schedules

Tax examiners and collectors, and revenue agents generally work full time, although some overtime might be needed during tax season.

How to Become a Tax Examiner or Collector, or Revenue Agent

Many tax examiners and collectors, and revenue agents have a bachelor's degree. Field of study and work experience requirements vary by level of government.

Education

Tax examiners need a bachelor's degree in accounting or a related discipline or a combination of relevant education and experience in accounting, auditing, or tax compliance work. Tax examiner candidates at the Internal Revenue Service (IRS) must have a bachelor's degree or 1 year of full-time specialized experience, which could include work in accounting, bookkeeping, or tax analysis.

Revenue agents need a bachelor's degree in accounting, business administration, economics, or a related discipline, or a combination of relevant education and full-time business administration, accounting, or auditing work. Revenue agents with the IRS must have either a bachelor's degree or 30 semester hours of accounting coursework, along with specialized experience. Specialized experience includes work in accounting, bookkeeping, or tax analysis.

Collectors usually must have some combination of relevant college education and experience. The experience may be in collections, management, customer service, or tax compliance, or as a loan officer or credit manager. A bachelor's degree is required for employment as a collector with the IRS. No additional experience is required, and experience may not be substituted for the degree. Degrees in business, finance, accounting, and criminal justice are good backgrounds.

At the state and local level, a bachelor's degree is not always required, although related work experience is desired.

Training

After they are hired, tax examiners get some formal training, which can last up to a year. In addition, tax examiners keep current with changes in the tax code and enforcement procedures.

Entry-level collectors get both formal training and on-the-job training under an instructor's guidance before working independently. Also, collectors are encouraged to continue their professional education by attending meetings to exchange information about how modifications to tax laws affect collection methods.

Work Experience

Work experience may serve as a qualification for employment in place of education for these workers, particularly at the state and local levels. Employers may hire tax examiners and revenue agents who have previous work experience in accounting, bookkeeping, or tax analysis. Employers also may hire collectors who have work experience in related areas, such as collections, customer service, or credit checking.

Advancement

Advancement potential in federal, state, and local agencies varies for tax examiners, revenue agents, and collectors. Tax examiners working on individual returns have the opportunity to advance to a revenue agent positions, working on more complex business returns. Advancement to a position supervising other examiners and revenue agents also is possible but generally requires previous experience in a supervisory or managerial position. Collectors who demonstrate leadership skills and a thorough knowledge of tax collection activities may advance to supervisory or managerial collector positions.

Important Qualities

Analytical skills. Tax examiners and revenue agents must be able to find questionable credits and deductions. Ultimately, they must be able to determine, on further review of financial documentation, if the credits or deductions are lawful.

Detail oriented. Tax examiners and revenue agents verify the accuracy of each entry on the tax returns they review. Therefore, it is crucial that they pay attention to detail.

Interpersonal skills. Collectors must be comfortable dealing with people, including speaking with them during confrontational situations. When pursuing overdue accounts, they should be firm and composed.

Organizational skills. Tax examiners and revenue agents often work with multiple returns and a variety of financial documentation. Keeping the various pieces of information organized is essential.

Pay

Tax Examiners and Collectors, and Revenue Agents
Median annual wages, May 2010

Business and Financial Operations Occupations	$60,670
Tax Examiners and Collectors, and Revenue Agents	$49,360
Total, All Occupations	$33,840

Note: All Occupations includes all occupations in the U.S. Economy.
Source: U.S. Bureau of Labor Statistics, Occupational Employment Statistics

The median annual wage of tax examiners and collectors, and revenue agents was $49,360 in May 2010. The median wage is the wage at which half the workers in an occupation earned more than that amount and half earned less. The lowest 10 percent earned less than $29,540 and the top 10 percent earned more than $92,250.

The table below shows the May 2010 median annual wage for tax examiners and collectors, and revenue agents in federal, state and local government.

Federal government	$55,270
State government	46,830
Local government	38,890

Tax examiners, collectors, and revenue agents generally work full time, although some overtime might be needed during tax season.

Job Outlook

Tax Examiners and Collectors, and Revenue Agents
Percent change in employment, projected 2010-20

Business and Financial Operations Occupations	17%
Total, All Occupations	14%
Tax Examiners and Collectors, and Revenue Agents	7%

Note: All Occupations includes all occupations in the U.S. Economy.
Source: U.S. Bureau of Labor Statistics, Employment Projections program

Employment of tax examiners and collectors, and revenue agents is expected to grow 7 percent from 2010 to 2020, slower than the average for all occupations. Historically, employment of these workers has increased with the overall economy, with growth in the number of businesses and individuals filing tax returns creating a need for more workers in tax enforcement.

In addition, demand for tax enforcement is expected to increase, particularly at the federal level. When government budgets are tight, these workers are more likely than other government employees to be kept on the job, because stronger tax enforcement and collection increases government budgets.

Accordingly, employment of these workers should increase, even if overall government spending and employment are reduced.

Governments also are expected to hire third-party collectors to work on special cases—for example, those that cross state lines. These collectors should work together with those employed directly by governments, not replace them.

Employment projections data for tax examiners and collectors, and revenue agents, 2010-20

Occupational Title	SOC Code	Employment, 2010	Projected Employment, 2020	Change, 2010-20 Percent	Numeric
Tax Examiners and Collectors, and Revenue Agents	13-2081	74,500	80,000	7	5,500
SOURCE: U.S. Bureau of Labor Statistics, Employment Projections program					

Similar Occupations

This table shows a list of occupations with job duties that are similar to those of tax examiners and collectors, and revenue agents.

Occupation	Job Duties	Entry-Level Education	Median Annual Pay, May 2010
Accountants and Auditors	Accountants and auditors prepare and examine financial records. They ensure that financial records are accurate and that taxes are paid properly and on time. Accountants and auditors assess financial operations and work to help ensure that organizations run efficiently.	Bachelor's degree	$61,690
Budget Analysts	Budget analysts help public and private institutions organize their finances. They prepare budget reports and monitor institutional spending.	Bachelor's degree	$68,200
Cost Estimators	Cost estimators collect and analyze data to estimate the time, money, resources, and labor required for product manufacturing, construction projects, or services. Some specialize in a particular industry or product type.	Bachelor's degree	$57,860
Financial Analysts	Financial analysts provide guidance to businesses and individuals making investment decisions. They assess the performance of stocks, bonds, and other types of investments.	Bachelor's degree	$74,350
Financial Managers	Financial managers are responsible for the financial health of an organization. They produce financial reports, direct investment activities, and develop strategies and plans for the long-term financial goals of their organization.	Bachelor's degree	$103,910
Loan Officers	Loan officers evaluate, authorize, or recommend approval of loan applications for people and businesses.	High school diploma or equivalent	$56,490
Personal Financial Advisors	Personal financial advisors give financial advice to people. They help with investments, taxes, and insurance decisions.	Bachelor's degree	$64,750

Contacts for More Information

For information about tax examiner and collector, and revenue agent careers at the Internal Revenue Service (IRS), visit Internal Revenue Service

Suggested citation:

Bureau of Labor Statistics, U.S. Department of Labor, Occupational Outlook Handbook, 2012-13 Edition, Tax Examiners and Collectors, and Revenue Agents, on the Internet at http://www.bls.gov/ooh/business-and-financial/tax-examiners-and-collectors-and-revenue-agents.htm .

Community and Social Service Occupations

Health Educators

Quick Facts: Health Educators	
2010 Median Pay	$45,830 per year $22.03 per hour
Entry-Level Education	Bachelor's degree
Work Experience in a Related Occupation	None
On-the-job Training	None
Number of Jobs, 2010	63,400
Job Outlook, 2010-20	37% (Much faster than average)
Employment Change, 2010-20	23,200

What Health Educators Do

Health educators teach people about behaviors that promote wellness. They develop programs and materials to encourage people to make healthy decisions.

Duties

Health educators typically do the following:

- Assess the needs of the people they serve
- Develop programs and events to teach people about health topics
- Create and distribute health-related posters, pamphlets, and other educational materials
- Evaluate the effectiveness of programs and materials
- Help people find health services or information
- Supervise staff who implement health education programs
- Collect and analyze data to learn about their audience and improve programs
- Advocate for improved health resources and policies

The duties of health educators vary based on where they work. Most work in health care facilities, colleges, public health departments, nonprofits, and private businesses. Health educators who teach health classes in middle and high schools are considered teachers. For more information, see the profiles on middle school teachers and high school

Health educators use a variety of methods to present information, such as video, pamphlets, and group discussions.

teachers .

In **health care facilities**, health educators often work one-on-one with patients and their families. They teach patients about their diagnoses and about necessary treatments or procedures. They direct people to outside resources, such as support groups and home health agencies. Health educators in health care facilities also help organize health screenings, such as blood pressure checks, and health classes on topics such as correctly installing a car seat. They also train medical staff to interact better with patients. For example, they may teach doctors how to explain complicated procedures to patients in simple language.

In **colleges**, health educators create programs and materials on topics that affect young adults, such as smoking and alcohol use. They may train students to be peer educators and lead programs on their own.

In **public health departments**, health educators administer public health campaigns on topics such as proper nutrition. They develop materials to be used by other public health officials. During emergencies, they provide safety information to the public and the media. They help health-related nonprofits obtain funding and other resources. Some health educators work with other professionals to create public policies that support healthy behaviors. Some participate in statewide and local committees on topics such as aging.

In **nonprofits** (including community health organizations), health educators create programs and materials about health issues for the community that their organization serves. Many nonprofits focus on a particular disease or audience, so health educators in these organizations limit programs to that specific topic or audience. In addition, health educators may lobby policymakers to pass laws to improve public health.

In **private businesses**, health educators identify common health problems among employees and create programs to improve health. They work with management to develop incentives for employees to adopt healthy behaviors, such as losing weight. Health educators recommend changes to the workplace, such as creating smoke-free areas, to improve employee health.

Work Environment

Health educators held about 63,400 jobs in 2010. Health educators work in a variety of settings, including hospitals, non-profit organizations, government, doctors' offices, private business, and colleges.

Although most health educators work in an office, they may spend a lot of time away from the office to carry out programs or attend meetings.

The following industries employed the most health educators in 2010:

Health care	37%
Government	21
Religious, grantmaking, civic, professional, and similar organizations	15
Social assistance	12
Educational services; state, local, and private	9

Work Schedules

Most health educators work full time. They may need to work nights and weekends to attend programs or meetings.

How to Become a Health Educator

A bachelor's degree is required for entry-level positions. Some employers may require the Certified Health Education Specialist (CHES) credential.

Education

Entry-level positions require a bachelor's degree in health education or health promotion. These programs teach students theories and methods of health education and help students gain the knowledge and skills to develop health education materials and programs. Most programs include an internship. Courses in psychology, human development, and a foreign language can be attractive to employers.

Some positions, such as those in the federal government or in state public health agencies, require a master's degree. Graduate programs are commonly called community health education, school health education, public health education, or health promotion. Entering a master's degree program requires a bachelor's degree, but a variety of undergraduate majors are acceptable.

Certification

Some employers hire only health educators who are Certified Health Education Specialists (CHES). CHES is a certification offered by the National Commission for Health Education Credentialing, Inc Certification is awarded after the candidate passes a test on the basic responsibilities of health educators. The exam is aimed at entry-level health educators who have completed a bachelor's degree or are within 3 months of completion. To maintain their certification, health educators must complete 75 hours of continuing education every 5 years.

Important Qualities

Analytical skills. Health educators analyze data and other information to evaluate programs and to determine the needs of the people they serve.

Instructional skills. Health educators should be good at teaching and public speaking so that they can lead programs and teach classes.

People skills. Health educators interact with many people. They must be good listeners and be culturally sensitive to respond to the needs of the people they serve.

Problem-solving skills. Health educators need to think creatively about how to improve the health of their audience through health education programs. In addition, they need to solve problems that arise in planning programs.

Writing skills. Health educators develop written materials to convey health-related information. They also write proposals to develop programs and apply for funding.

Pay

Health Educators

Median annual wages, May 2010	
Health Educators	$45,830
Community and Social Service Occupations	$39,280
Total, All Occupations	$33,840

Note: All Occupations includes all occupations in the U.S. Economy.
Source: U.S. Bureau of Labor Statistics, Occupational Employment Statistics

The median annual wage of health educators was $45,830 in May 2010. The median wage is the wage at which half the workers in an occupation earned more than that amount and half earned less. The lowest 10 percent earned less than $26,730, and the top 10 percent earned more than $81,430.

In 2010, the wages of the industries employing the most health educators were as follows:

Hospitals; state, local, and private	$58,440
Government	48,900
Ambulatory health care services	41,210
Religious, grantmaking, civic, professional, and similar organizations	40,430
Social assistance	34,850

Most health educators work full time. They may need to work nights and weekends to attend programs or meetings.

Job Outlook

Health Educators

Percent change in employment, projected 2010-20	
Health Educators	37%
Community and Social Service Occupations	24%
Total, All Occupations	14%

Note: All Occupations includes all occupations in the U.S. Economy.
Source: U.S. Bureau of Labor Statistics, Employment Projections program

Employment of health educators is expected to grow by 37 percent from 2010 to 2020, much faster than the average for all occupations. Growth will be driven by efforts to reduce healthcare costs by teaching people about healthy habits and behaviors.

As healthcare costs continue to rise, insurance companies, employers, and governments are trying to find ways to curb costs. One way is to employ health educators, who teach people how to live healthy lives and avoid costly diseases. Lifestyle changes can reduce the likelihood of contracting a number of illnesses, such as lung cancer, HIV, heart disease, and skin cancer. Health educators help people understand how what they do affects their health.

For many illnesses, such as breast cancer and testicular cancer, finding the disease early greatly increases the likelihood that treatment will be successful. Therefore, it is important for people to know how to find possible problems on their own. The need to provide the public with this kind of information is expected to result in an increased demand for health educators.

Projected growth for the industries employing the most health educators is as follows:

Religious, grantmaking, civic, professional, and similar organizations	60%
Social assistance	60
Health care	38
Educational services; state, local, and private	36
Government	9

Employment projections data for health educators, 2010-20

Occupational Title	SOC Code	Employment, 2010	Projected Employment, 2020	Change, 2010-20 Percent	Numeric
Health Educators	21-1091	63,400	86,600	37	23,200
SOURCE: U.S. Bureau of Labor Statistics, Employment Projections program					

Similar Occupations

This table shows a list of occupations with job duties that are similar to those of health educators.

Occupation	Job Duties	Entry-Level Education	Median Annual Pay, May 2010
Dietitians and Nutritionists	Dietitians and nutritionists are experts in food and nutrition. They advise people on what to eat in order to lead a healthy lifestyle or achieve a specific health-related goal.	Bachelor's degree	$53,250
High School Teachers	High school teachers help prepare students for life after graduation. They teach academic lessons and various skills that students will need to attend college and to enter the job market.	Bachelor's degree	$53,230
Mental Health Counselors and Marriage and Family Therapists	Mental health counselors and marriage and family therapists help people manage or overcome mental and emotional disorders and problems with their family and relationships. They listen to clients and ask questions to help the clients understand their problems and develop strategies to improve their lives.	Master's degree	$39,710
Middle School Teachers	Middle school teachers educate students, most of whom are in sixth through eighth grades. They help students build on the fundamentals they learned in elementary school and prepare them for the more difficult lessons they will learn in high school.	Bachelor's degree	$51,960
School and Career Counselors	School counselors help students develop social skills and succeed in school. Career counselors assist people with the process of making career decisions by helping them choose a career or educational program.	Master's degree	$53,380
Social and Human Service Assistants	Social and human service assistants help people get through difficult times or get additional support. They help other workers, such as social workers, and they help clients find benefits or community services.	High school diploma or equivalent	$28,200
Social Workers	There are two main types of social workers: direct-service social workers, who help people solve and cope with problems in their everyday lives, and clinical social workers, who diagnose and treat mental, behavioral, and emotional issues.	See How to Become One	$42,480
Substance Abuse and Behavioral Disorder Counselors	Substance abuse and behavioral disorder counselors advise people who have alcoholism or other types of addiction, eating disorders, or other behavioral problems. They provide treatment and support to help the client recover from addiction or modify problem behaviors.	High school diploma or equivalent	$38,120

Contacts for More Information

For more information about health educators, visit American Association for Health Education, Society for Public Health Education
For more information about the Certified Health Education Specialist (CHES) credential, visit National Commission for Health Education Credentialing, Inc

Suggested citation:

Bureau of Labor Statistics, U.S. Department of Labor, Occupational Outlook Handbook, 2012-13 Edition, Health Educators, on the Internet at http://www.bls.gov/ooh/community-and-social-service/health-educators.htm .

Mental Health Counselors and Marriage and Family Therapists

Quick Facts: Mental Health Counselors and Marriage and Family Therapists	
2010 Median Pay	$39,710 per year $19.09 per hour
Entry-Level Education	Master's degree
Work Experience in a Related Occupation	None
On-the-job Training	Internship/residency
Number of Jobs, 2010	156,300
Job Outlook, 2010-20	37% (Much faster than average)
Employment Change, 2010-20	58,500

What Mental Health Counselors and Marriage and Family Therapists Do

Mental health counselors and marriage and family therapists help people manage or overcome mental and emotional disorders and problems with their family and relationships. They listen to clients and ask questions to help the clients understand their problems and develop strategies to improve their lives.

Duties

Mental health counselors and marriage and family therapists typically do the following:

- Diagnose and treat mental and emotional disorders, such as anxiety and depression
- Encourage clients to discuss their emotions and experiences
- Help clients process their reactions and adjust to changes in their life, such as divorce or layoffs
- Guide clients through the process of making decisions about their future
- Help clients develop strategies and skills to change their behavior or cope with difficult situations
- Coordinate treatment with other professionals, such as psychiatrists and social workers
- Refer clients to other resources or services in the community, such as support groups or inpatient treatment facilities

Many mental health counselors and marriage and family therapists work in private practice.

Mental health counselors and marriage and family therapists use a variety of techniques and tools to help their clients. Many apply cognitive behavioral therapy, a goal-oriented approach that helps clients understand harmful thoughts, feelings, and beliefs and replace them with positive, life-enhancing ones. Furthermore, cognitive behavioral therapy teaches clients to eliminate unwanted or damaging behaviors and replace them with more productive ones.

Some disorders can be overcome, but others need to be managed. In these cases, mental health counselors and marriage and family therapists help the client develop strategies and skills to minimize the effects of their disorders or illnesses.

Some mental health counselors and marriage and family therapists work in private practice. They must spend time marketing their practice to prospective clients and working with insurance companies and clients to get payment for their services.

Mental health counselors provide treatment to individuals, families, couples, and groups. Some work with specific populations, such as the elderly, college students, or children. Mental health counselors deal with a variety of issues, including anxiety, depression, grief, low self-esteem, stress, and suicidal impulses. They also help with mental and emotional health issues, and relationship problems.

Marriage and family therapists work with individuals, couples, and families. Unlike other types of mental health professionals, they bring a family-centered perspective to treatment, even when treating individuals. They evaluate family roles and development to understand how clients' families affect their mental health. They treat the clients' relationships, not just the clients themselves. They address issues such as low self-esteem, stress, addiction and substance abuse.

Work Environment

In 2010, mental health counselors held about 120,300 jobs, and marriage and family therapists held about 36,000 jobs.

Mental health counselors and marriage and family therapists work in variety of settings, such as mental health centers, substance abuse treatment centers, hospitals, and colleges. They also work in private practice and in employee assistance programs (EAPs), which are mental health programs that some employers provide to help employees deal with personal problems.

The following table shows the industries with the highest percentages of mental health counselors in 2010:

Individual and family services	18%
Outpatient mental health and substance abuse centers	16
Hospitals; state, local, and private	12
State and local government, excluding education and hospitals	11
Residential mental health and substance abuse facilities	10

The following table shows the industries with the highest percentages of marriage and family therapists in 2010:

Individual and family services	27%
State and local government, excluding education and hospitals	22
Outpatient mental health and substance abuse centers	11
Offices of mental health practitioners (except physicians)	6
Nursing and residential care facilities	4

Dealing every day with the array of problems that clients bring may be stressful.

Work Schedules

Mental health counselors and marriage and family therapists generally work full time. Because counseling sessions are scheduled to accommodate clients who may have job or family responsibilities, some counselors and therapists work evenings and weekends.

How to Become a Mental Health Counselor or Marriage and Family Therapist

All states require both mental health counselors and marriage and family therapists to have a master's degree and a license to practice.

Education

A master's degree in counseling or marriage and family therapy is required. A bachelor's degree in most fields is acceptable to enter a master's-level program.

Counseling programs prepare students to recognize symptoms of mental and emotional disorders and to use effective counseling strategies. Marriage and family therapy programs teach students about how marriages, families, and relationships function and how they affect mental and emotional disorders. Both programs typically require a period of supervised experience, such as an internship.

Licenses

Mental health counselors must be licensed. Licensure requires a master's degree and 2,000 to 4,000 hours of supervised clinical experience. In addition, counselors must pass a state-recognized exam and complete annual continuing education classes. Contact information for state regulating boards is available through the National Board for Certified Counselors .

Marriage and family therapists must be licensed. Licensure requires a master's degree and 2 years of supervised clinical experience. Like counselors, marriage and family therapists must pass a state-recognized exam and complete annual continuing education classes. Contact information for state regulating boards is available through the Association of Marital and Family Therapy Regulatory Boards .

Important Qualities

Compassion. Counselors and therapists often work with people who are dealing with stressful and difficult situations, so they must be compassionate and empathize with their clients.

Listening skills. Good listening skills are essential for mental health counselors and marriage and family therapists, both of whom need to give their full attention to their clients to understand their problems and values.

Organizational skills. Good organizational skills are especially important for counselors and therapists in private practice, who must keep track of payments and work with insurance companies.

People skills. Being able to work with different types of people is

essential for counselors and therapists, who spend most of their time working directly with clients or other professionals and must be able to encourage good relationships.

Speaking skills. Mental health counselors and marriage and family therapists need to be able to communicate with clients effectively. They must express ideas and information in a way that clients can easily understand.

Pay

Mental Health Counselors and Marriage and Family Therapists
Median annual wages, May 2010

Marriage and Family Therapists	$45,720
Mental Health Counselors and Marriage and Family Therapists	$39,710
Mental Health Counselors	$38,150
Total, All Occupations	$33,840

Note: All Occupations includes all occupations in the U.S. Economy.
Source: U.S. Bureau of Labor Statistics, Occupational Employment Statistics

The median annual wage of mental health counselors was $38,150 in May 2010. The median wage is the wage at which half the workers in an occupation earned more than that amount and half earned less. The lowest 10 percent earned less than $24,180, and the top 10 percent earned more than $63,630.

In May 2010, wages for mental health counselors in the industries employing the most mental health counselors were as follows:

Local government	$46,590
Hospitals	41,930
Outpatient mental health and substance abuse centers	38,840
Individual and family services	37,700
Residential mental health and substance abuse facilities	30,260

The median annual wage of marriage and family therapists was $45,720 in May 2010. The lowest 10 percent earned less than $23,870, and the top 10 percent earned more than $72,280.

In May 2010, wages for marriage and family therapists in the industries employing the most marriage and family therapists were as follows:

State government	$56,320
Local government	54,340
Outpatient mental health and substance abuse centers	47,480
Offices of mental health practitioners (except physicians)	46,800
Individual and family services	42,150

Mental health counselors and marriage and family therapists generally work full time. Because counseling sessions are scheduled to accommodate clients who may have job or family responsibilities, some counselors and therapists work evenings and weekends.

Job Outlook

Mental Health Counselors and Marriage and Family Therapists
Percent change in employment, projected 2010-20

Marriage and Family Therapists	41%
Mental Health Counselors and Marriage and Family Therapists	37%
Mental Health Counselors	36%
Total, All Occupations	14%

Note: All Occupations includes all occupations in the U.S. Economy.
Source: U.S. Bureau of Labor Statistics, Employment Projections program

Employment of mental health counselors and marriage and family therapists is expected to grow by 37 percent from 2010 to 2020, much faster than the average for all occupations. Employment of mental health counselors is expected to grow by 36 percent from 2010 to 2020, much faster than the average for all occupations. Employment of marriage and family therapists is expected to grow by 41 percent over the same period, much faster than the average for all occupations.

Insurance companies increasingly provide for reimbursement of counselors and marriage and family therapists as a less costly alternative to psychiatrists and psychologists. People seeking mental health treatment are more likely to see a mental health counselor or a marriage and family therapist over other providers.

Furthermore, more people are expected to seek treatment for problems with mental and emotional problems than in earlier decades. As the population grows, the number of individuals entering therapy is expected to increase as well. This trend will cause a continued demand for counselors in mental health centers, hospitals, and colleges.

From 2010 to 2020, employment growth of mental health counselors in industries employing the most mental health counselors is expected to be as follows:

Individual and family services	50%
Residential mental health and substance abuse facilities	44
Outpatient mental health and substance abuse centers	34
Hospitals; state, local, and private	17
State and local government, excluding education and hospitals	12

From 2010 to 2020, employment growth for marriage and family therapists in industries employing the most marriage and family therapists is expected to be as follows:

Offices of mental health practitioners (except physicians)	96%
Individual and family services	51
Nursing and residential care facilities	46
Outpatient mental health and substance abuse centers	34
State and local government, excluding education and hospitals	12

Employment projections data for mental health counselors and marriage and family therapists, 2010-20

Occupational Title	SOC Code	Employment, 2010	Projected Employment, 2020	Change, 2010-20	
				Percent	Numeric
Mental Health Counselors and Marriage and Family Therapists	—	156,300	214,800	37	58,500
Marriage and Family Therapists	21-1013	36,000	50,800	41	14,800
Mental Health Counselors	21-1014	120,300	163,900	36	43,600
SOURCE: U.S. Bureau of Labor Statistics, Employment Projections program.					

Similar Occupations

This table shows a list of occupations with job duties that are similar to those of mental health counselors and marriage and family therapists.

Occupation	Job Duties	Entry-Level Education	Median Annual Pay, May 2010
Physicians and Surgeons	Physicians and surgeons diagnose and treat injuries and illnesses in patients. Physicians examine patients, take medical histories, prescribe medications, and order, perform, and interpret diagnostic tests. Surgeons operate on patients to treat injuries, such as broken bones; diseases, such as cancerous tumors; and deformities, such as cleft palates.	Doctoral or professional degree	This wage is equal to or greater than $166,400 per year.
Psychologists	Psychologists study mental processes and human behavior by observing, interpreting, and recording how people and other animals relate to one another and the environment.	See How to Become One	$68,640
Rehabilitation Counselors	Rehabilitation counselors help people with emotional and physical disabilities live independently. They help their clients overcome personal, social, and professional effects of disabilities as they relate to employment or independent living.	Master's degree	$32,350
School and Career Counselors	School counselors help students develop social skills and succeed in school. Career counselors assist people with the process of making career decisions by helping them choose a career or educational program.	Master's degree	$53,380
Social and Community Service Managers	Social and community service managers coordinate and supervise social service programs and community organizations. They direct and lead staff who provide services to the public.	Bachelor's degree	$57,950
Social and Human Service Assistants	Social and human service assistants help people get through difficult times or get additional support. They help other workers, such as social workers, and they help clients find benefits or community services.	High school diploma or equivalent	$28,200

Social Workers	There are two main types of social workers: direct-service social workers, who help people solve and cope with problems in their everyday lives, and clinical social workers, who diagnose and treat mental, behavioral, and emotional issues.	See How to Become One	$42,480
Substance Abuse and Behavioral Disorder Counselors	Substance abuse and behavioral disorder counselors advise people who have alcoholism or other types of addiction, eating disorders, or other behavioral problems. They provide treatment and support to help the client recover from addiction or modify problem behaviors.	High school diploma or equivalent	$38,120

Contacts for More Information

For more information about mental health counselors, visit American Mental Health Counselors Association

For more information about marriage and family therapists, visit American Association for Marriage and Family Therapy

For general information about counseling and for information about counseling specialties, visit American Counseling Association

For information about contacting state regulating boards, visit National Board for Certified Counselors

Suggested citation:

Bureau of Labor Statistics, U.S. Department of Labor, Occupational Outlook Handbook, 2012-13 Edition, Mental Health Counselors and Marriage and Family Therapists, on the Internet at http://www.bls.gov/ooh/community-and-social-service/mental-health-counselors-and-marriage-and-family-therapists.htm .

Probation Officers and Correctional Treatment Specialists

Quick Facts: Probation Officers and Correctional Treatment Specialists	
2010 Median Pay	$47,200 per year $22.69 per hour
Entry-Level Education	Bachelor's degree
Work Experience in a Related Occupation	None
On-the-job Training	Short-term on-the-job training
Number of Jobs, 2010	93,200
Job Outlook, 2010-20	18% (About as fast as average)
Employment Change, 2010-20	17,100

What Probation Officers and Correctional Treatment Specialists Do

Many people who are convicted of crimes are placed on probation, instead of being sent to prison. People who have served time in prison are often released on parole. During probation and parole—and while they are in prison—offenders must stay out of trouble and meet other requirements. Probation officers and correctional treatment specialists work with and monitor offenders to prevent them from committing new crimes.

Duties

Probation officers and correctional treatment specialists typically do the following:

- Evaluate offenders to determine the best course of treatment
- Provide offenders with resources to aid in rehabilitation
- Discuss treatment options with offenders
- Arrange treatment programs
- Supervise offenders and monitor their progress
- Conduct meetings with offenders as well as their family and friends
- Write reports on the progress of offenders

Probation officers and correctional treatment specialists work with offenders who are given probation instead of jail time, who are still in prison, or who have been released from prison. The following are types of probation officers and correctional treatment specialists:

Probation officers, who are called **community supervision officers** in some states, supervise people who have been placed on probation. They work to ensure that the offender is not a danger to the community and to help in their rehabilitation. Probation officers write reports that detail each offender's treatment plans and their progress since they were put on probation. Most probation officers work with

Correctional treatment specialists counsel offenders and create rehabilitation plans for them to follow when they are no longer in prison.

either adults or juveniles. Only in small, mostly rural, jurisdictions do probation officers counsel both adults and juveniles.

Pretrial services officers investigate an offender's background to determine if that offender can be safely allowed back into the community before his or her trial date. They must assess the risk and make a recommendation to a judge who decides on the appropriate sentencing or bond amount. When offenders are allowed back into the community, pretrial officers supervise them to make sure that they stay with the terms of their release and appear at their trials.

Parole officers work with people who have been released from jail and are serving parole to help them re-enter society. Parole officers monitor post-release offenders and provide them with various resources, such as substance abuse counseling or job training, to aid in their rehabilitation. By doing so, the officers try to change the offenders' behavior and thus reduce the risk of that person committing another crime and having to return to jail or prison.

Both probation and parole officers supervise offenders though personal contact with the offenders and their families. Probation and patrol officers require regularly scheduled contact with offenders by telephone or through office visits, and they may also check on offenders at their homes or places of work. Probation and parole officers also oversee drug testing and electronic monitoring of offenders. In some states, officers do the jobs of both probation and parole officers.

Correctional treatment specialists, who also may be known as **case managers** or **correctional counselors**, counsel offenders and develop rehabilitation plans for them to follow when they are no longer in prison or on parole. They may evaluate inmates using questionnaires and psychological tests. They also work with inmates, probation officers, and staff of other agencies to develop parole and release plans. For example, they may plan education and training programs to improve offenders' job skills.

Correctional treatment specialists write case reports that cover the inmate's history and the likelihood that he or she will commit another crime. When their clients are eligible for release, the case reports are given to the appropriate parole board. The specialist may help set up counseling for the offenders and their families, find substance-abuse or mental health treatment options, aid in job placement, and find housing.

Correctional treatment specialists also explain the terms and conditions of the prisoner's release, write reports, and keep detailed written accounts of each offender's progress. Specialists who work in parole and probation agencies have many of the same duties as their counterparts in correctional institutions.

The number of cases a probation officer or correctional treatment specialist handles at one time depends on the needs of offenders and the risks associated with each individual. Higher risk offenders usually command more of the officer's time and resources. Caseload size also varies by agency.

Technological advancements—such as improved tests for screening drug use, electronic devices to monitor clients, and kiosks that allow clients to check in remotely—help probation officers and correctional treatment specialists supervise and counsel offenders.

Work Environment

Probation officers and correctional treatment specialists held about 93,200 jobs in 2010. They work with criminal offenders, some of whom may be dangerous. While supervising offenders, they may interact with others, such as family members and friends of their clients, who may be upset or difficult to work with. Workers may be assigned to fieldwork in high-crime areas or in institutions where there is a risk of violence or communicable disease.

In 2010, nearly all probation officers and correctional treatment specialists worked for either state or local governments:

State government, excluding education and hospitals	56%
Local government, excluding education and hospitals	41
Social assistance	2
Nursing and residential care facilities	1

Probation officers and correctional treatment specialists must meet many court-imposed deadlines, which contributes to heavy workloads and extensive paperwork. Many officers travel to do home and employment checks and property searches, especially in rural areas. Because of the hostile environments probation officers may encounter, some must carry a firearm or other weapon for protection.

All of these factors, as well as the frustration some officers and specialists feel in dealing with offenders who violate the terms of their release, contribute to a stressful work environment. Although the high stress levels can make the job difficult at times, this work also can be rewarding. Many officers and specialists receive personal satisfaction from counseling members of their community and helping them become productive citizens.

Work Schedules

Although many officers and specialists work full time, the demands of the job often lead to their working much longer hours. For example, many agencies rotate an on-call officer position. When these workers are on-call, they must respond to any issues with offenders or law enforcement 24 hours a day. Extensive travel and paperwork can also contribute to their having to work longer hours.

How to Become a Probation Officer or Correctional Treatment Specialist

Qualifications vary by agency, but a bachelor's degree is usually required. Most employers require candidates to pass oral, written, and psychological exams.

Important Qualities

Communication skills. Probation officers and correctional treatment specialists must be able to effectively interact and communicate with a wide range of people.

Critical-thinking skills. Probation officers and correctional treatment specialists must be able to assess the needs of individual offenders before determining the best resources for helping them.

Decision-making skills. Probation officers and correctional treatment specialists must consider the relative costs and benefits of potential actions and be able to choose appropriately.

Emotional stability. Probation officers and correctional treatment specialists must cope with hostile or otherwise upsetting situations, as well as with other stresses on the job.

Organizational skills. Probation officers and correctional treatment specialists must be able to manage multiple case files at one time.

Writing skills. Probation officers and correctional treatment specialists interpret training materials and write detailed reports on a regular basis.

Education and Training

A bachelor's degree in social work, criminal justice, psychology, or a related field is usually required. Some employers require a master's degree in a related field for candidates who do not have previous related work experience.

Although job requirements may vary, related work may include work in probation, pretrial services, parole, corrections, criminal investigations, substance abuse treatment, social work, or counseling. Work in any of these fields is typically considered a plus in the hiring process.

Most probation officers and correctional treatment specialists must complete a training program sponsored by their state government or the federal government, after which they may have to pass a certification test. In addition, they may be required to work as trainees or on a probationary period for up to 1 year before being offered a permanent position.

Some probation officers go on to specialize in a certain type of casework. For example, an officer may work only with domestic violence offenders or deal only with substance-abuse cases. Officers receive training specific to the group that they are working with so that they are better prepared to help that type of offender.

Most agencies require applicants to be at least 21 years old and, for federal employment, not older than 37 years of age. In addition, most departments require candidates to have a record free of felony convictions and to submit to drug testing. A valid driver's license is often required.

Advancement

Advancement to supervisory positions is primarily based on experience and performance. A graduate degree, such as a master's degree in criminal justice, social work, or psychology, may be helpful or required for advancement.

Pay

Probation Officers and Correctional Treatment Specialists
    Median annual wages, May 2010
    Probation Officers and Correctional Treatment Specialists $47,200
    Counselors, Social Workers, and Other Social Service Spec... $39,250
    Total, All Occupations $33,840

Note: All Occupations includes all occupations in the U.S. Economy.
Source: U.S. Bureau of Labor Statistics, Occupational Employment Statistics

The median annual wage of probation officers and correctional treatment specialists was $47,200 in May 2010. The median wage is the wage at which half of the workers in an occupation earned more than that amount and half earned less. The lowest 10 percent earned less than $30,920, and the top 10 percent earned more than $80,750.

Although many officers and specialists work full time, the demands of the job often lead to their working much longer hours. For example, many agencies rotate an on-call officer position. When these workers are on-call, they must respond to any issues with offenders or law enforcement 24 hours a day. Extensive travel and paperwork can also contribute to their having to work longer hours.

Job Outlook

Probation Officers and Correctional Treatment Specialists
    Percent change in employment, projected 2010-20
    Counselors, Social Workers, and Other Social Service Specialists 28%
    Probation Officers and Correctional Treatment Specialists 18%
    Total, All Occupations 14%

Note: All Occupations includes all occupations in the U.S. Economy.
Source: U.S. Bureau of Labor Statistics, Employment Projections program

Employment of probation officers and correctional treatment specialists is expected to grow by 18 percent from 2010 to 2020, about as fast as average for all occupations. Continued growth in the demand for probation and parole services will lead to new openings for officers.

Mandatory sentencing guidelines in the 1980s and 1990s called for longer sentences and reduced parole for some offenses, resulting in an increase in the prison population. However, these guidelines are being reconsidered at both the federal and state levels due to budgetary constraints, court decisions, prison overcrowding, and doubts about the guidelines' effectiveness.

As guidelines are reduced or repealed, judges have more flexibility in sentencing offenders for each case. For offenders who are deemed to be a lower risk, this may result in less prison time, more community-based corrections, or some combination of the two.

As alternative forms of punishment, such as probation, become more widely used, the demand for probation and parole officers will grow. There also will be a need for parole and probation officers to supervise the large number of people who are now in prison when they are released.

Employment growth depends primarily on the amount of government funding for corrections, especially how much there is for probation and parole systems. Although community supervision is far less expensive than keeping offenders in prison, a change in political and social trends toward more imprisonment and away from community supervision could result in reduced employment opportunities.

Job Prospects

In addition to openings resulting from growth, many openings will be created by the need to replace large numbers of these workers expected to retire in the coming years. This occupation is not attractive to some potential entrants because of relatively low earnings, heavy workloads, and high stress. For these reasons, job opportunities should be excellent for those who qualify.

Employment projections data for probation officers and correctional treatment specialists, 2010-20

Occupational Title	SOC Code	Employment, 2010	Projected Employment, 2020	Change, 2010-20	
				Percent	Numeric
Probation Officers and Correctional Treatment Specialists	21-1092	93,200	110,400	18	17,100
SOURCE: U.S. Bureau of Labor Statistics, Employment Projections program					

Similar Occupations

This table shows a list of occupations with job duties that are similar to those of probation officers and correctional treatment specialists.

Occupation	Job Duties	Entry-Level Education	Median Annual Pay, May 2010
Correctional Officers	Correctional officers are responsible for overseeing individuals who have been arrested and are awaiting trial or who have been sentenced to serve time in a jail, reformatory, or prison.	High school diploma or equivalent	$39,020

Police and Detectives	Police officers protect lives and property. Detectives and criminal investigators, who sometimes are called agents or special agents, gather facts and collect evidence of possible crimes. Law enforcement officers' duties depend on the size and type of their organizations.	High school diploma or equivalent	$55,010
Social and Human Service Assistants	Social and human service assistants help people get through difficult times or get additional support. They help other workers, such as social workers, and they help clients find benefits or community services.	High school diploma or equivalent	$28,200
Social Workers	There are two main types of social workers: direct-service social workers, who help people solve and cope with problems in their everyday lives, and clinical social workers, who diagnose and treat mental, behavioral, and emotional issues.	See How to Become One	$42,480
Substance Abuse and Behavioral Disorder Counselors	Substance abuse and behavioral disorder counselors advise people who have alcoholism or other types of addiction, eating disorders, or other behavioral problems. They provide treatment and support to help the client recover from addiction or modify problem behaviors.	High school diploma or equivalent	$38,120

Contacts for More Information

For more information about probation officers and correctional treatment specialists, visit American Probation and Parole Association

For information about criminal justice job opportunities in your area, contact the departments of corrections, criminal justice, or probation for individual states.

Suggested citation:

Bureau of Labor Statistics, U.S. Department of Labor, Occupational Outlook Handbook, 2012-13 Edition, Probation Officers and Correctional Treatment Specialists, on the Internet at http://www.bls.gov/ooh/community-and-social-service/probation-officers-and-correctional-treatment-specialists.htm .

Rehabilitation Counselors

Quick Facts: Rehabilitation Counselors	
2010 Median Pay	$32,350 per year $15.55 per hour
Entry-Level Education	Master's degree
Work Experience in a Related Occupation	None
On-the-job Training	None
Number of Jobs, 2010	129,800
Job Outlook, 2010-20	28% (Faster than average)
Employment Change, 2010-20	36,600

What Rehabilitation Counselors Do

Rehabilitation counselors help people with emotional and physical disabilities live independently. They work with clients to overcome personal, social, and professional effects of disabilities as they relate to employment or independent living.

Duties

Rehabilitation counselors typically do the following:

- Provide individual and group counseling to help clients adjust to their disability
- Evaluate clients' abilities, interests, experience, skills, health, and education
- Develop a treatment plan in consultation with other professionals, such as doctors, mental health counselors, and psychologists
- Create treatment plans based on clients' values, strengths, limitations, and goals
- Arrange for clients to get service, such as medical care or career training
- Help employers understand the needs and abilities of disabled people
- Assist clients in creating strategies to develop their strengths and overcome their limitations

- Locate resources, such as wheelchairs or computer programs, that help clients live and work more independently
- Monitor clients' progress and adjust the treatment plan as necessary
- Advocate for the rights of people with disabilities to live in the community and work in the job of their choice

Rehabilitation counselors help people with physical, mental, emotional, or social disabilities at various stages in their lives. Some work with students to develop strategies to live with their disability and to move from school to work. Others help veterans cope with the mental or physical effects of their military service. Still others help elderly people adapt to disabilities developed later in life due to illness or injury. Because rehabilitation counselors deal with employment issues, they typically work with older students and adults rather than young children.

Some rehabilitation counselors work in private practice. These counselors must spend time marketing their practice to prospective clients and working with insurance companies and clients to get paid for their services.

Work Environment

Rehabilitation counselors held about 129,800 jobs in 2010.

They work in a variety of settings, such as colleges, elementary and secondary schools, prisons, and independent-living facilities. They

Some rehabilitation counselors help elderly people with health problems adjust to their new limitations.

also work in private practice and in state, private, and nonprofit rehabilitation agencies.

The following industries employed the most rehabilitation counselors in 2010:

Vocational rehabilitation services	30%
Nursing and residential care facilities	15
State government, excluding education and hospitals	15
Individual and family services	14
Local government, excluding education and hospitals	6

Work Schedules

Most rehabilitation counselors work full time.

How to Become a Rehabilitation Counselor

Most often, rehabilitation counselors must have a master's degree in rehabilitation counseling or a related field. Some positions require certification or a license.

Education

Most employers require a master's degree in rehabilitation counseling or a related field. Most master's programs in rehabilitation counseling accept a bachelor's degree in almost any field to enter. These programs focus on evaluating clients' needs, formulating and implementing job placement strategies, and providing mental health counseling. They typically require a period of supervised experience, such as an internship.

Some employers hire workers with a bachelor's degree in rehabilitation and disability studies. Generally, these workers cannot offer the full range of services that a rehabilitation counselor with a master's degree can provide. Bachelor's degree programs teach students about issues that people with disabilities face and about the process of providing rehabilitation services.

Licenses

Some employers prefer to hire licensed rehabilitation counselors, but a license may not be necessary in many settings. However, it is required to work in private practice. Licensure requires a master's degree and 2,000 to 3,000 hours of supervised clinical experience. In addition, counselors must pass a state-recognized exam and complete annual continuing education credits. Contact information for state regulating boards is available through the National Board of Certified Counselors .

Certification

Some employers prefer rehabilitation counselors who are Certified Rehabilitation Counselors (CRC). Applicants must meet advanced education, work experience, and clinical supervision requirements, and pass a test. Once certified, counselors must complete continuing education requirements. For more information, contact the Commission on Rehabilitation Counselor Certification .

Important Qualities

Compassion. Counselors often work with people who are dealing with stressful and difficult situations, so they must be compassionate and empathize with their clients.

Listening skills. Good listening skills are essential for rehabilitation counselors, who need to give their full attention to clients in order to understand their problems, concerns, and values.

Patience. To help people learn new skills and strategies, rehabilitation counselors must have patience as clients struggle to learn about and address the impact of their disabilities.

People skills. Being able to work with different types of people is essential for rehabilitation counselors, who spend most of their time working directly with clients, families, employers, or other professionals. They must be able to develop a good working relationship.

Speaking skills. Rehabilitation counselors need to be able to communicate with clients effectively, expressing ideas and information in a way that is easily understood.

Pay

Rehabilitation Counselors	
Median annual wages, May 2010	
Community and Social Service Occupations	$39,280
Total, All Occupations	$33,840
Rehabilitation Counselors	$32,350

Note: All Occupations includes all occupations in the U.S. Economy.
Source: U.S. Bureau of Labor Statistics, Occupational Employment Statistics

The median annual wage of rehabilitation counselors was $32,350 in May 2010. The median wage is the wage at which half the workers in an occupation earned more than that amount and half earned less. The lowest 10 percent earned less than $20,770 and the top 10 percent earned more than $56,720.

In May 2010, the median annual wages of rehabilitation counselors in the top employing industries were as follows:

State government, excluding education and hospitals	$42,930
Local government, excluding education and hospitals	38,790
Individual and family services	30,310
Vocational rehabilitation services	29,100
Nursing and residential care facilities	28,110

Most rehabilitation counselors work full time.

Job Outlook

Rehabilitation Counselors
Percent change in employment, projected 2010-20

Rehabilitation Counselors	28%
Community and Social Service Occupations	24%
Total, All Occupations	14%

Note: All Occupations includes all occupations in the U.S. Economy.
Source: U.S. Bureau of Labor Statistics, Employment Projections program

Employment of rehabilitation counselors is expected to grow by 28 percent from 2010 to 2020, faster than the average for all occupations. Demand for rehabilitation counselors is expected to grow with the increase in the elderly population and with the continued rehabilitation needs of other groups, such as veterans and people with disabilities.

Older adults are more likely than other age groups to become disabled or injured. They will need to learn to adapt to their disabilities and learn strategies to live independently. As a result, they will require the services of rehabilitation counselors. As the size of this population grows, so will the need for rehabilitation counselors.

In addition, there will be a continued need for rehabilitation counselors to work with veterans who were disabled during their military service. They will also be needed to work with other groups, such as people who have learning disabilities, autism spectrum disorders, or substance abuse problems.

From 2010 to 2020, expected employment growth of rehabilitation counselors in the top employing industries is as follows:

Individual and family services	67%
Vocational rehabilitation services	30
Nursing and residential care facilities	24
Local government, excluding education and hospitals	9
State government, excluding education and hospitals	4

Employment projections data for rehabilitation counselors, 2010-20

Occupational Title	SOC Code	Employment, 2010	Projected Employment, 2020	Change, 2010-20 Percent	Change, 2010-20 Numeric
Rehabilitation Counselors	21-1015	129,800	166,400	28	36,600

SOURCE: U.S. Bureau of Labor Statistics, Employment Projections program

Similar Occupations

This table shows a list of occupations with job duties that are similar to those of rehabilitation counselors.

Occupation	Job Duties	Entry-Level Education	Median Annual Pay, May 2010
Mental Health Counselors and Marriage and Family Therapists	Mental health counselors and marriage and family therapists help people manage or overcome mental and emotional disorders and problems with their family and relationships. They listen to clients and ask questions to help the clients understand their problems and develop strategies to improve their lives.	Master's degree	$39,710
Occupational Therapists	Occupational therapists treat patients with injuries, illnesses, or disabilities through the therapeutic use of everyday activities. They help these patients develop, recover, and improve the skills needed for daily living and working.	Master's degree	$72,320
Occupational Therapy Assistants and Aides	Occupational therapy assistants and aides work under the direction of occupational therapists in treating patients with injuries, illnesses, or disabilities through the therapeutic use of everyday activities. They help these patients develop, recover, and improve the skills needed for daily living and working.	See How to Become One	$47,490
Psychologists	Psychologists study mental processes and human behavior by observing, interpreting, and recording how people and other animals relate to one another and the environment.	See How to Become One	$68,640
School and Career Counselors	School counselors help students develop social skills and succeed in school. Career counselors assist people with the process of making career decisions by helping them choose a career or educational program.	Master's degree	$53,380
Social and Human Service Assistants	Social and human service assistants help people get through difficult times or get additional support. They help other workers, such as social workers, and they help clients find benefits or community services.	High school diploma or equivalent	$28,200
Special Education Teachers	Special education teachers work with students who have a wide range of learning, mental, emotional and physical disabilities. With students who have mild or moderate disabilities, they ensure that lessons and teaching strategies are modified to meet the students' needs. With students who have severe disabilities, they teach the students independent living skills and basic literacy, communication, and math.	Bachelor's degree	$53,220
Substance Abuse and Behavioral Disorder Counselors	Substance abuse and behavioral disorder counselors advise people who have alcoholism or other types of addiction, eating disorders, or other behavioral problems. They provide treatment and support to help the client recover from addiction or modify problem behaviors.	High school diploma or equivalent	$38,120

Contacts for More Information

For more information about counseling and information about counseling specialties, visit American Counseling Association

For more information about the Certified Rehabilitation Counselors certification, visit Commission on Rehabilitation Counselor Certification

For contact information for state regulating boards, visit National Board for Certified Counselors

Suggested citation:

Bureau of Labor Statistics, U.S. Department of Labor, Occupational Outlook Handbook, 2012-13 Edition, Rehabilitation Counselors, on the Internet at http://www.bls.gov/ooh/community-and-social-service/rehabilitation-counselors.htm .

School and Career Counselors

Quick Facts: School and Career Counselors	
2010 Median Pay	$53,380 per year $25.67 per hour
Entry-Level Education	Master's degree
Work Experience in a Related Occupation	None
On-the-job Training	None
Number of Jobs, 2010	281,400
Job Outlook, 2010-20	19% (About as fast as average)
Employment Change, 2010-20	53,400

What School and Career Counselors Do

School counselors help students develop social skills and succeed in school. Career counselors assist people with the process of making career decisions by helping them choose a career or educational program.

Duties

School counselors typically do the following:
- Help students understand and overcome social or behavioral problems through individual and group counseling
- Provide individual and small group counseling based on student needs
- Work with students to develop skills such as organization, time management, and effective study habits
- Help students set realistic academic and career goals and develop a plan to achieve them
- Evaluate students' abilities and interests through aptitude assessments and interviews
- Develop strategies with teachers, administrators, and parents to help students succeed
- Teach classes on topics such as bullying, drug abuse, and planning for college or careers after graduation
- Identify and report possible cases of neglect or abuse
- Refer students and parents to resources outside the school for additional support

The specific duties of school counselors vary with the ages of the students they work with.

Elementary school counselors focus on helping students develop skills they need to be successful in their social and academic lives, such as decision-making and study skills. They also help teachers and administrators identify possible behavioral or developmental problems. They observe children in the classroom and at play activities and confer with teachers and parents about children's strengths, problems, and special needs. They work with teachers and administrators to be sure the curriculum addresses the development needs of students as well as students' academic needs.

Middle school counselors work with students and parents to develop career and academic goals and to create a plan for students to achieve them. They help students develop the skills and strategies necessary to succeed academically and socially.

High school counselors advise students making academic and career plans. Many help students with personal problems that interfere with their education. They help students choose classes and plan for their lives after graduation. Counselors provide information about choosing and applying for colleges or training programs and for financial aid or apprenticeships. They help students develop job search skills, such as writing rÃ©sumÃ©s and interviewing.

Career counselors typically do the following:
- Use aptitude and achievement assessments to help clients evaluate their interests, skills, and abilities
- Evaluate clients' background, education, and training to help them develop realistic goals
- Guide clients through making decisions about their careers, such as choosing a new profession or the type of degree to pursue
- Help clients learn job search skills, such as interviewing and

Career counselors assist people with the process of making career decisions.

networking
- Assist clients in locating or applying for jobs by teaching them strategies to find openings and how to write a rÃ©sumÃ©
- Advise clients on how to resolve problems in the workplace, such as conflicts with bosses or coworkers
- Help clients select and apply for educational programs to obtain the necessary degrees, credentials, or skills

Career counselors work with clients at various stages in their careers. Some work with college students to help choose a college major. They also help students determine what jobs they are qualified for with their degrees. With people who have already entered the workforce, counselors provide advice about entering a new profession or develop plans to improve their client's current career. Some career counselors work in outplacement firms and assist laid-off workers to transition into a new job or career. Others work in corporate career centers to assist employees in making decisions about their career path within the company.

Some career counselors work in private practice. These counselors must spend time marketing their practice to prospective clients and working with clients to receive payments for their services.

Work Environment

School and career counselors held about 281,400 jobs in 2010. The industries employing the most school and career counselors in 2010 were as follows:

Elementary and secondary schools; state, local, and private	47%
Colleges, universities, and professional schools; state, local, and private	19
Junior colleges; state, local, and private	8
Vocational rehabilitation services	6

School counselors work in private and public schools. They often have private offices so that they can have confidential conversations with students. Career counselors work in colleges, businesses, prisons, and state government career centers such as Career One-Stops .

Work Schedules

Both school and career counselors generally work full time. Some school counselors have summers off when school is not in session.

How to Become a School or Career Counselor

All school counselors must be credentialed, which most often requires a master's degree. Many employers prefer that career counselors have a master's degree. Those who work in private practice generally must be licensed.

Education

In most states, school counselors must have a master's degree in school counseling or a related field. Programs in school counseling teach students about fostering academic development, conducting group and individual counseling, and working with parents, teachers, and other school staff. These programs often require students to gain experience through an internship or practicum.

Most employers prefer that career counselors have a master's degree in counseling with a focus on career development. Career counseling programs prepare students to teach career development techniques and assess clients' skills and interests. Many programs require students to have a period of supervised experience, such as an internship.

Licenses

School counselors must have a state-issued credential to practice. This credential can be called a certification, a license, or an

endorsement, depending on the state. Most states require a criminal background check as part of the credentialing process. Information about requirements for each state is available from the American School Counselors Association.

Although some employers prefer to hire licensed career counselors, a license is not required in many settings. Career counselors in private practice, however, generally must be licensed. Licensure requires a master's degree and 2,000 to 3,000 hours of supervised clinical experience. In addition, counselors must pass a state-recognized exam and complete annual continuing education credits. Contact information for state regulating boards is available from the National Board for Certified Counselors.

Important Qualities

Compassion. Counselors often work with people who are dealing with stressful and difficult situations, so they must be compassionate and empathize with their clients and students.

Listening skills. Good listening skills are essential for school and career counselors. They need to give their full attention to their students and clients to understand their problems and values.

People skills. Being able to work with different types of people is essential for counselors. They spend most of their time working directly with clients and students or other professionals and need good working relationships.

Speaking skills. School and career counselors must communicate effectively with clients and students. They should express ideas and information in a way that their clients understand easily.

Pay

School and Career Counselors
Median annual wages, May 2010

Educational, Guidance, School, and Vocational Counselors	$53,380
Community and Social Service Occupations	$39,280
Total, All Occupations	$33,840

Note: All Occupations includes all occupations in the U.S. Economy.
Source: U.S. Bureau of Labor Statistics, Occupational Employment Statistics

The median annual wage of school and career counselors was $53,380 in May 2010. The median wage is the wage at which half the workers in an occupation earned more than that amount and half earned less. The bottom 10 percent earned less than $31,630, and the top 10 percent earned more than $86,250.

In May 2010, the median annual wages in the industries employing the most school and career counselors were as follows:

Elementary and secondary schools; state, local, and private	$60,000
Junior colleges; state, local, and private	51,050
Colleges, universities, and professional schools; state, local, and private	44,610
Vocational rehabilitation services	35,210

School and career counselors generally work full time. Some school counselors have summers off when school is not in session.

Job Outlook

School and Career Counselors
Percent change in employment, projected 2010-20

Community and Social Service Occupations	24%
Educational, Guidance, School, and Vocational Counselors	19%
Total, All Occupations	14%

Note: All Occupations includes all occupations in the U.S. Economy.
Source: U.S. Bureau of Labor Statistics, Employment Projections program

Employment of school and career counselors is expected to grow by 19 percent from 2010 to 2020, about as fast as the average for all occupations. Growth is expected due to increasing student enrollments in schools.

Rising student enrollments in elementary, middle, and high schools are expected to increase demand for school counselors. As enrollments grow, schools will require more counselors to respond to the needs of their students. Employment of school and career counselors in elementary and secondary schools is expected to grow by 8 percent from 2010 to 2020.

Employment of career counselors also is expected to increase because of rising enrollments in colleges and universities. As the college-age population grows, colleges will need to hire additional counselors to meet the demand for career counseling services from their students. Employment of school and career counselors in colleges, universities and professional schools is expected to grow by 34 percent from 2010 to 2020.In addition, demand for career counselors is expected to continue in vocational rehabilitation organizations and in private practice.Employment of school and career counselors in vocational rehabilitation services is expected to grow by 30 percent from 2010 to 2020.

Employment projections data for school and career counselors, 2010-20

Occupational Title	SOC Code	Employment, 2010	Projected Employment, 2020	Change, 2010-20	
				Percent	Numeric
Educational, Guidance, School, and Vocational Counselors	21-1012	281,400	334,800	19	53,400
SOURCE: U.S. Bureau of Labor Statistics, Employment Projections program					

Similar Occupations

This table shows a list of occupations with job duties that are similar to those of school and career counselors.

Occupation	Job Duties	Entry-Level Education	Median Annual Pay, May 2010
High School Teachers	High school teachers help prepare students for life after graduation. They teach academic lessons and various skills that students will need to attend college and to enter the job market.	Bachelor's degree	$53,230
Human Resources Specialists	Human resources specialists recruit, screen, interview, and place workers. They also may handle human resources work in a variety of other areas, such as employee relations, payroll and benefits, and training.	Bachelor's degree	$52,690
Kindergarten and Elementary School Teachers	Kindergarten and elementary school teachers prepare younger students for future schooling by teaching them the basics of subjects such as math and reading.	Bachelor's degree	$51,380
Mental Health Counselors and Marriage and Family Therapists	Mental health counselors and marriage and family therapists help people manage or overcome mental and emotional disorders and problems with their family and relationships. They listen to clients and ask questions to help the clients understand their problems and develop strategies to improve their lives.	Master's degree	$39,710
Middle School Teachers	Middle school teachers educate students, most of whom are in sixth through eighth grades. They help students build on the fundamentals they learned in elementary school and prepare them for the more difficult lessons they will learn in high school.	Bachelor's degree	$51,960
Psychologists	Psychologists study mental processes and human behavior by observing, interpreting, and recording how people and other animals relate to one another and the environment.	See How to Become One	$68,640
Rehabilitation Counselors	Rehabilitation counselors help people with emotional and physical disabilities live independently. They help their clients overcome personal, social, and professional effects of disabilities as they relate to employment or independent living.	Master's degree	$32,350
Social and Community Service Managers	Social and community service managers coordinate and supervise social service programs and community organizations. They direct and lead staff who provide services to the public.	Bachelor's degree	$57,950
Social and Human Service Assistants	Social and human service assistants help people get through difficult times or get additional support. They help other workers, such as social workers, and they help clients find benefits or community services.	High school diploma or equivalent	$28,200
Social Workers	There are two main types of social workers: direct-service social workers, who help people solve and cope with problems in their everyday lives, and clinical social workers, who diagnose and treat mental, behavioral, and emotional issues.	See How to Become One	$42,480

Substance Abuse and Behavioral Disorder Counselors	Substance abuse and behavioral disorder counselors advise people who have alcoholism or other types of addiction, eating disorders, or other behavioral problems. They provide treatment and support to help the client recover from addiction or modify problem behaviors.	High school diploma or equivalent	$38,120

Contacts for More Information

For more information about counseling and information about counseling specialties, visit American Counseling Association

For more information about school counselors, visit American School Counselors Association

For more information about career counselors, visit National Career Developers Association

For more information about state credentialing, visit National Board for Certified Counselors

Suggested citation:

Bureau of Labor Statistics, U.S. Department of Labor, Occupational Outlook Handbook, 2012-13 Edition, School and Career Counselors, on the Internet at http://www.bls.gov/ooh/community-and-social-service/school-and-career-counselors.htm .

Social and Human Service Assistants

Quick Facts: Social and Human Service Assistants	
2010 Median Pay	$28,200 per year $13.56 per hour
Entry-Level Education	High school diploma or equivalent
Work Experience in a Related Occupation	None
On-the-job Training	Short-term on-the-job training
Number of Jobs, 2010	384,200
Job Outlook, 2010-20	28% (Faster than average)
Employment Change, 2010-20	106,000

What Social and Human Service Assistants Do

Social and human service assistants help people get through difficult times or get additional support. They help other workers, such as social workers, and they help clients find benefits or community services.

Duties

Social and human service assistants typically do the following:
- Work under the direction of social workers, psychologists, or others who have more education or experience
- Help determine what type of help their clients need
- Work with clients and other professionals, such as social workers, to develop a treatment plan
- Help clients get help with daily activities, such as eating and bathing
- Coordinate services provided to clients by their or other organizations
- Research services available to their clients in their communities
- Determine clients' eligibility for services such as food stamps and Medicaid
- Help clients complete paperwork to apply for assistance programs
- Monitor clients to ensure services are provided appropriately

Social and human service assistants have many job titles, including case work aide, clinical social work aide, family service assistant, social work assistant, addictions counselor assistant, and human service worker. They serve diverse populations with a range of problems. Their work varies, depending on the clients they serve.

With **children and families,** social and human service assistants ensure that children live in safe homes. They help parents get the resources, such as food stamps or childcare, they need to care for their children.

With the **elderly,** workers help clients stay in their own homes and under their own care whenever possible. They coordinate meal deliveries or find personal care aides to help older people with day-to-day needs, such as doing errands or bathing. In some cases, human service workers look for residential care facilities, such as nursing homes.

For **people with disabilities,** social and human service assistants help find rehabilitation services that aid their clients. They may work with employers to adapt positions to make them accessible to people with disabilities. Some workers find personal care services to help clients with daily living activities, such as bathing or making meals.

For **people with addictions,** human service assistants find rehabilitation centers that meet their clients' needs. They also find support groups or twelve-step programs. They work with people who are dependent on alcohol, drugs, gambling, or other substances or behaviors.

With **veterans,** assistants help people discharged from the military adjust to civilian life. They help with practical needs, such as finding housing and applying skills gained in the military to civilian jobs. They also help with navigating the overwhelming number of services available to veterans.

For **people with mental illnesses,** social and human service assistants help clients find resources to cope with their illness. They find self-help and support groups to provide their clients with an assistance network. In addition, they help those with more severe mental illnesses care for themselves by finding personal care services or group housing.

With **immigrants,** workers help clients adjust to living in a new country. They help clients locate jobs and housing. They also may help clients find programs that teach English, or they may find legal assistance to help immigrants get their paperwork in order.

With **former prison inmates,** human service assistants help clients re-enter society by finding job training or placement programs. Human

Social and human service assistants help the elderly to stay in their own homes and under their own care whenever possible.

service assistants help former inmates find housing and connect with programs that help them make a new life for themselves.

With **homeless people,** assistants help clients meet their basic needs. They find temporary or permanent housing. They find places, such as soup kitchens, that provide meals. Human service assistants also help homeless people find facilities for other problems they may have, such as joblessness.

Work Environment

Social and human service assistants held about 384,200 jobs in 2010. They work for nonprofit organizations, private for-profit social service agencies, and state and local government. They may work in offices, clinics, hospitals, group homes, and shelters. Some travel around their communities to see clients.

In 2010, the following industries employed the most social and human service assistants:

Individual and family services	21%
Nursing and residential care facilities	16
Community and vocational rehabilitation services	13
State government, excluding education and hospitals	12
Local government, excluding education and hospitals	12

Work Schedules

Most social and human service assistants work full time. Some work nights and weekends.

How to Become a Social and Human Service Assistant

The minimum requirement is a high school diploma or equivalent, but some employers prefer to hire workers who have additional education or experience. Without additional education, advancement opportunities are limited.

Education

A high school diploma is the minimum requirement, but some employers prefer to hire workers who have relevant work experience or education beyond high school. Certificates or associate's degrees in subjects such as human services, gerontology (working with older adults), or a social or behavioral science are common for workers entering this occupation. Some jobs may require a bachelor's or master's degree in human services or a related field, such as counseling, rehabilitation, or social work.

Human services degree programs train students to observe and interview patients, carry out treatment plans, and handle crises. These programs train students to work with people in difficult situations. Many programs include fieldwork to give students hands-on experience.

The level of education that social and human service assistants have completed often determines the responsibilities they are given. Those with a high school diploma are likely to do lower level work, such as helping clients fill out paperwork. However, assistants with some college education may coordinate program activities or manage a group home.

Training

Many social and human service assistants, particularly those without any postsecondary education, undergo a period of on-the-job training. Training prepares assistants to work with clients from a wide variety of backgrounds and respond to crisis situations.

Advancement

For social and human service assistants, additional education is almost always necessary for advancement. In general, advancement to case management or social work jobs requires a bachelor's or master's degree in human services, counseling, rehabilitation, social work, or a related field.

Important Qualities

Communication skills. Social and human service assistants talk with clients about the challenges in their lives and assist them in getting help. They must be able listen to their clients and to communicate their needs to organizations that can help.

Compassion. Social and human service assistants often work with people who are in stressful and difficult situations. To develop strong relationships, they must have compassion and empathy for their clients.

Organizational skills. Social and human service assistants often must do lots of paperwork and work with many different clients. They must be organized to ensure paperwork is filed properly and clients are getting the help they need.

People skills. Social and human service assistants must make their clients feel comfortable discussing sensitive issues. Assistants also need to build relationships with other service providers to help them learn about all of the resources that are available in their communities.

Problem-solving skills. Assistants help clients find solutions to their problems. They must be able to listen carefully to their client's needs and offer multiple solutions.

Time-management skills. Social and human service assistants often work with many clients. They must learn to manage their time effectively to ensure that their clients are getting the attention they need.

Some employers require a criminal background check. In some settings, workers need a valid driver's license.

Pay

Social and Human Service Assistants

Median hourly wages, May 2010	
Community and Social Service Occupations	$18.89
Total, All Occupations	$16.27
Social and Human Service Assistants	$13.56

Note: All Occupations includes all occupations in the U.S. Economy.
Source: U.S. Bureau of Labor Statistics, Occupational Employment Statistics

The median hourly wage of social and human service assistants was $13.56 in May 2010. The median wage is the wage at which half the workers in an occupation earned more than that amount and half earned less. The lowest 10 percent earned less than $9.03, and the top 10 percent earned more than $21.59.

In May 2010, the median hourly wages of social and human service assistants in industries employing the largest numbers of these workers were as follows:

State government, excluding education and hospitals	$16.27
Local government, excluding education and hospitals	15.94
Individual and family services	13.10
Nursing and residential care facilities	11.72

Most social and human service assistants work full time. Some work nights and weekends.

Job Outlook

Social and Human Service Assistants

Percent change in employment, projected 2010-20	
Social and Human Service Assistants	28%
Community and Social Service Occupations	24%
Total, All Occupations	14%

Note: All Occupations includes all occupations in the U.S. Economy.
Source: U.S. Bureau of Labor Statistics, Employment Projections program

Employment of social and human service assistants is expected to grow by 28 percent from 2010 to 2020, faster than the average for all occupations. Growth will be due to an increase in the elderly population and a rising demand for health care and social services.

Much of the growth will be due to the needs of an aging population. An increase in number of older adults will cause growth in demand for social services. The elderly population often needs services such as adult day care and meal delivery. Social and human service assistants, who help find and provide these services, will be needed to meet this increased demand.

In addition, growth is expected as more people seek treatment for their addictions and more drug offenders are sent to treatment programs rather than to jail. The result will be an increase in demand for social and human service assistants who work in treatment programs or work with people with addictions.

There also will be a continued demand for child and family social and human service assistants. They will be needed to help workers investigate child abuse cases, as well as to place children in foster care and with adoptive families.

Employment of social and human service assistants in the industries employing the largest number of these workers is expected to grow as follows from 2010 to 2020:

Individual and family services	57%
Community and vocational rehabilitation services	31
Nursing and residential care facilities	24
Local government, excluding education and hospitals	9
State government, excluding education and hospitals	4

Job Prospects

Low pay and heavy workloads cause many workers to leave this occupation, which creates good opportunities for new workers entering the field.

Employment projections data for social and human service assistants, 2010-20

Occupational Title	SOC Code	Employment, 2010	Projected Employment, 2020	Change, 2010-20	
				Percent	Numeric
Social and Human Service Assistants	21-1093	384,200	490,200	28	106,000

SOURCE: U.S. Bureau of Labor Statistics, Employment Projections program

Similar Occupations

This table shows a list of occupations with job duties that are similar to those of social and human service assistants.

Occupation	Job Duties	Entry-Level Education	Median Annual Pay, May 2010
Childcare Workers	Childcare workers care for children when parents and other family members are unavailable. They care for children's basic needs, such as bathing and feeding. In addition, some help children prepare for kindergarten, and many help older children with homework.	High school diploma or equivalent	$19,300
Health Educators	Health educators teach people about behaviors that promote wellness. They develop programs and materials to encourage people to make healthy decisions.	Bachelor's degree	$45,830

Home Health and Personal Care Aides	Home health and personal care aides help people who are disabled, chronically ill, or cognitively impaired. They also help older adults who may need assistance. They help with activities such as bathing and dressing, and they provide services such as light housekeeping. In some states, home health aides may be able to give a client medication or check the client's vital signs under the direction of a nurse or other healthcare practitioner.	Less than high school	$20,170
Mental Health Counselors and Marriage and Family Therapists	Mental health counselors and marriage and family therapists help people manage or overcome mental and emotional disorders and problems with their family and relationships. They listen to clients and ask questions to help the clients understand their problems and develop strategies to improve their lives.	Master's degree	$39,710
Probation Officers and Correctional Treatment Specialists	Probation officers and correctional treatment specialists work with and monitor offenders to prevent them from committing new crimes.	Bachelor's degree	$47,200
Rehabilitation Counselors	Rehabilitation counselors help people with emotional and physical disabilities live independently. They help their clients overcome personal, social, and professional effects of disabilities as they relate to employment or independent living.	Master's degree	$32,350
School and Career Counselors	School counselors help students develop social skills and succeed in school. Career counselors assist people with the process of making career decisions by helping them choose a career or educational program.	Master's degree	$53,380
Social and Community Service Managers	Social and community service managers coordinate and supervise social service programs and community organizations. They direct and lead staff who provide services to the public.	Bachelor's degree	$57,950
Social Workers	There are two main types of social workers: direct-service social workers, who help people solve and cope with problems in their everyday lives, and clinical social workers, who diagnose and treat mental, behavioral, and emotional issues.	See How to Become One	$42,480
Substance Abuse and Behavioral Disorder Counselors	Substance abuse and behavioral disorder counselors advise people who have alcoholism or other types of addiction, eating disorders, or other behavioral problems. They provide treatment and support to help the client recover from addiction or modify problem behaviors.	High school diploma or equivalent	$38,120

Contacts for More Information

For more information about careers in human services, visit National Organization for Human Services

Suggested citation:

Bureau of Labor Statistics, U.S. Department of Labor, Occupational Outlook Handbook, 2012-13 Edition, Social and Human Service Assistants, on the Internet at http://www.bls.gov/ooh/community-and-social-service/social-and-human-service-assistants.htm .

Social Workers

Quick Facts: Social Workers	
2010 Median Pay	$42,480 per year $20.42 per hour
Entry-Level Education	See How to Become One
Work Experience in a Related Occupation	None
On-the-job Training	None
Number of Jobs, 2010	650,500
Job Outlook, 2010-20	25% (Faster than average)
Employment Change, 2010-20	161,200

What Social Workers Do

There are two main types of social workers: direct-service social workers who help people solve and cope with problems in their everyday lives, and clinical social workers, who diagnose and treat mental, behavioral, and emotional issues.

Duties

Direct-service social workers typically do the following:
- Identify people who need help
- Assess clients' needs, situations, strengths, and support networks to determine their goals
- Develop plans to improve their clients' well-being
- Help clients adjust to changes and challenges in their lives, such as illness, divorce, or unemployment
- Research and refer clients to community resources, such as food stamps, child care, and healthcare
- Help clients work with government agencies to apply for and receive benefits such as Medicare
- Respond to crisis situations, such as natural disasters or child abuse
- Advocate for and help clients get resources that would improve their well-being
- Follow up with clients to ensure that their situations have improved
- Evaluate services provided to ensure that they are effective

Social workers help people cope with challenges in every stage of their lives. They help with a wide range of situations, such as adopting a child or being diagnosed with a terminal illness. Social workers work with many populations, including children, people with disabilities, and people with addictions.

Clinical social workers, also called licensed clinical social workers, typically do the following:
- Diagnose and treat mental, behavioral, and emotional disorders, including anxiety and depression
- Provide individual, group, family, and couples therapy
- Assess clients' histories, backgrounds, and situations to understand their needs, as well as their strengths and weaknesses
- Develop a treatment plan with the client, doctors, and other healthcare professionals
- Encourage clients to discuss their emotions and experiences to develop a better understanding of themselves and their relationships
- Help clients adjust to changes in their life, such as a divorce or being laid-off
- Work with clients to develop strategies to change behavior or cope with difficult situations
- Refer clients to other resources or services, such as support groups or other mental health professionals
- Evaluate their clients' progress and, if necessary, adjust the treatment plan

Many clinical social workers work in private practice. Some work in a group practice with other social workers or mental health professionals. Others work alone in a solo practice. In private practice, clinical social workers often do administrative and recordkeeping tasks. Among these tasks is working with clients and insurance companies to receive payment for their services. In addition, social workers market their practice to bring in new clients and to network with other professionals who may recommend them.

Direct-service social workers and clinical social workers often focus on a particular population or work environment. The following are some types of workers in this occupation:

Child and family social workers protect vulnerable children and help families in need of assistance. They help parents find services, such as child care, or apply for benefits, such as food stamps. They intervene when children are in danger of neglect or abuse. Some help arrange adoptions, locate foster families, or work to get families back together. Clinical social workers provide mental health care to help

Child and family social workers protect vulnerable children and support families in need of assistance.

children and families cope with changes in their lives, such as divorce or other family problems.

School social workers work with teachers, parents, and school administrators to develop plans and strategies to improve students' academic performance and social development. Students and their families are often referred to social workers to deal with problems such as aggressive behavior, bullying, or frequent absences from school.

Healthcare social workers help patients understand their diagnosis and make the necessary adjustments to their lifestyle, housing, or healthcare. They provide information on services, such as home health care or support groups, to help patients manage their illness or disease. Social workers help doctors and other healthcare professionals understand the effects diseases and illnesses have on patients' mental and emotional health.

Some healthcare social workers specialize in gerontological social work or hospice and palliative care social work.

- **Gerontological social workers** help senior citizens and their families. They help clients find services such as programs that provide older adults with meals or with home health care. In some cases, they provide information about assisted living facilities or nursing homes or work with older adults in those settings. They help clients and their families make plans for possible health complications or where clients will live if they can no longer care for themselves.
- **Hospice and palliative care social workers** help patients adjust to serious, chronic, or terminal illnesses. Palliative care focuses on relieving or preventing pain and other symptoms associated with serious illness. Hospice is a type of palliative care for people who are dying. Social workers in this setting provide and find services, such as support groups or grief counselors, to help patients and their families cope with the illness or disease.

Mental health and substance abuse social workers help clients with mental illnesses or addictions. They provide information on services, such as support groups or 12-step programs, to help clients cope with their illness.

Work Environment

Social workers held 650,500 jobs in 2010. They work in the following settings:
- Hospitals and clinics
- Nursing homes
- Community mental health clinics
- Private practices
- State and local governments
- Schools
- Colleges and universities
- Substance abuse clinics
- Military bases and hospitals

Although most social workers work in an office, they may spend a lot of time away from the office visiting clients. School social workers may be assigned to multiple schools and travel around the school district to see students. Understaffing and large case loads may make the work stressful.

In 2010, the industries employing the most child, family and school social workers were as follows:

Individual and family services	21%
State government, excluding education and hospitals	21
Local government, excluding education and hospitals	19
Elementary and secondary schools; state, local, and private	12
Health care	9

In 2010, the industries employing the most healthcare social workers were as follows:

Hospitals; state, local, and private	31%
Nursing and residential care facilities	13
Individual and family services	11
Home health care services	10
Local government, excluding education and hospitals	6

In 2010, the industries employing the most mental health substance abuse social workers were as follows:

Outpatient mental health and substance abuse centers	17%
Individual and family services	16
Hospitals; state, local, and private	14
Local government, excluding education and hospitals	10
Psychiatric and substance abuse hospitals; state, local, and private	8

Work Schedules

Social workers generally work full time. They may sometimes work evenings and weekends to see clients or attend meetings.

How to Become a Social Worker

A bachelor's degree is required for most direct-service social work positions, but some positions and settings require a master's degree. Clinical social workers must have a master's degree. Licensure varies by state. Clinical social workers must be licensed.

Education

A bachelor's degree in social work (BSW) is the most common requirement for entry-level positions. However, some employers may hire workers who have a bachelor's degree in a related field, such as psychology or sociology.

BSW programs prepare students for direct-service positions such as caseworker or mental health assistant. These programs teach students about diverse populations, human behavior, and social welfare policy. All programs require students to complete supervised fieldwork or an internship.

Some positions, including those in schools and in healthcare, frequently require a master's degree in social work (MSW). All clinical social workers must have an MSW.

MSWs generally take 2 years to complete. Some programs allow those with a BSW to earn their MSW in 1 year. MSW programs prepare students for work in their chosen specialty and develop the skills to do clinical assessments, manage a large number of clients, and take on supervisory duties. All programs require students to complete supervised fieldwork or an internship.

A BSW is not required to enter MSW programs. In fact, a degree in almost any major is acceptable. However, coursework in psychology, sociology, economics, and political science are recommended.

Licenses

Licensure varies by state. All states have some type of licensure or certification requirement. All states require clinical social workers to be licensed. However, some states provide exemptions for clinical social workers who work in government agencies.

Becoming a licensed clinical social worker usually requires a master's degree in social work and 2 years or 3,000 hours of supervised clinical experience after graduation. After completing their supervised experience, clinical social workers must pass an exam to be licensed.

Although most states also have licenses for nonclinical social workers, these licenses are often optional. For more information about licensure by state, contact the Association of Social Work Boards.

Important Qualities

Compassion. Social workers often work with people who are in stressful and difficult situations. To develop strong relationships, they must have compassion and empathy for their clients.

Listening skills. Clients talk to social workers about challenges in their lives. To effectively help, social workers must listen to and understand their clients' needs.

Organizational skills. Helping and managing multiple clients, often assisting with their paperwork or documenting their treatment, requires good organizational skills.

People skills. Being able to work with different groups of people is essential for social workers. They need strong people skills to foster healthy and productive relationships with their clients and colleagues.

Problem-solving skills. Social workers need to develop practical and innovative solutions to their clients' problems.

Time-management skills. Social workers often have many clients. They must manage their time well to provide adequate service to all of their clients.

Pay

Social Workers
Median annual wages, May 2010

Social Workers	$42,480
Counselors, Social Workers, and Other Social Service Spec	$39,250
Total, All Occupations	$33,840

Note: All Occupations includes all occupations in the U.S. Economy.
Source: U.S. Bureau of Labor Statistics, Occupational Employment Statistics

The median annual wage of social workers was $42,480 in May 2010. The median wage is the wage at which half the workers in an occupation earned more than that amount and half earned less. The lowest 10 percent earned less than $26,710 and the top 10 percent earned more than $70,390.

The median annual wages of social workers in May 2010 were the following:

- $47,230 for healthcare social workers
- $40,210 for child, family, and schools social workers
- $38,600 for mental health and substance abuse social workers
- $51,500 for all other social workers

In May 2010, the median annual wages of child, family and school social workers in the industries employing the most of these workers were as follows:

Elementary and secondary schools	$54,260
Local government, excluding education and hospitals	47,130
State government, excluding education and hospitals	39,750
Individual and family services	35,120

In May 2010, the median annual wages of healthcare social workers in the industries employing the most of these workers were as follows:

Hospitals	$53,400
Home health care services	48,530
Local government, excluding education and hospitals	44,810
Nursing and residential care facilities	41,860
Individual and family services	39,310

In May 2010, the median annual wages of mental health and substance abuse social workers in the industries employing the most of these workers were as follows:

Hospitals	$48,010
Psychiatric and substance abuse hospitals	47,710
Local government	45,210
Outpatient mental health and substance abuse centers	36,780
Individual and family services	36,740

Social workers generally work full time. They may sometimes work evenings and weekends to see clients or attend meetings.

Job Outlook

Social Workers
Percent change in employment, projected 2010-20

Counselors, Social Workers, and Other Social Service Specialists	26%
Social Workers	25%
Total, All Occupations	14%

Note: All Occupations includes all occupations in the U.S. Economy.
Source: U.S. Bureau of Labor Statistics, Employment Projections program

Employment of social workers is expected to grow by 25 percent from 2010 to 2020, faster than the average for all occupations. Growth will be due to an increase in demand for health care and social services but will vary by specialty.

Employment of child, family, and school social workers is expected to grow by 20 percent from 2010 to 2020, faster than the average for all occupations. Demand for child and family social workers should continue to grow because they will be needed to investigate child abuse cases and to place children in foster care and with adoptive families. However, growth in this occupation may be limited by budget constraints at all levels of government. In schools, more social workers will be needed to respond to rising student enrollments. The availability of federal, state, and local funding will be a major factor in determining the actual employment growth in schools.

Employment of healthcare social workers is expected to grow by 34 percent, much faster than the average for all occupations. As baby boomers age, they and their families will require help from social workers to find care, which will increase demand for healthcare social workers.

Employment of mental health and substance abuse social workers is expected to grow by 31 percent, much faster than the average for all occupations. Growth is expected as more people seek treatment for mental illness and addiction. In addition, drug offenders are increasingly being sent to treatment programs rather than to jail. As a result, use of substance abuse treatment programs is expected to grow, increasing demand for mental health and substance abuse social workers.

Employment projections data for social workers, 2010-20

Occupational Title	SOC Code	Employment, 2010	Projected Employment, 2020	Change, 2010-20	
				Percent	Numeric
Social Workers	21-1020	650,500	811,700	25	161,200
Child, Family, and School Social Workers	21-1021	295,700	353,900	20	58,200
Healthcare Social Workers	21-1022	152,700	203,900	34	51,200
Mental Health and Substance Abuse Social Workers	21-1023	126,100	165,600	31	39,500
Social Workers, All Other	21-1029	76,000	88,300	16	12,300
SOURCE: U.S. Bureau of Labor Statistics, Employment Projections program					

Similar Occupations

This table shows a list of occupations with job duties that are similar to those of social workers.

Occupation	Job Duties	Entry-Level Education	Median Annual Pay, May 2010
Health Educators	Health educators teach people about behaviors that promote wellness. They develop programs and materials to encourage people to make healthy decisions.	Bachelor's degree	$45,830
Mental Health Counselors and Marriage and Family Therapists	Mental health counselors and marriage and family therapists help people manage or overcome mental and emotional disorders and problems with their family and relationships. They listen to clients and ask questions to help the clients understand their problems and develop strategies to improve their lives.	Master's degree	$39,710
Probation Officers and Correctional Treatment Specialists	Probation officers and correctional treatment specialists work with and monitor offenders to prevent them from committing new crimes.	Bachelor's degree	$47,200
Psychologists	Psychologists study mental processes and human behavior by observing, interpreting, and recording how people and other animals relate to one another and the environment.	See How to Become One	$68,640
Rehabilitation Counselors	Rehabilitation counselors help people with emotional and physical disabilities live independently. They help their clients overcome personal, social, and professional effects of disabilities as they relate to employment or independent living.	Master's degree	$32,350
School and Career Counselors	School counselors help students develop social skills and succeed in school. Career counselors assist people with the process of making career decisions by helping them choose a career or educational program.	Master's degree	$53,380
Social and Community Service Managers	Social and community service managers coordinate and supervise social service programs and community organizations. They direct and lead staff who provide services to the public.	Bachelor's degree	$57,950
Social and Human Service Assistants	Social and human service assistants help people get through difficult times or get additional support. They help other workers, such as social workers, and they help clients find benefits or community services.	High school diploma or equivalent	$28,200
Substance Abuse and Behavioral Disorder Counselors	Substance abuse and behavioral disorder counselors advise people who have alcoholism or other types of addiction, eating disorders, or other behavioral problems. They provide treatment and support to help the client recover from addiction or modify problem behaviors.	High school diploma or equivalent	$38,120

Contacts for More Information

For more information about social workers and clinical social workers, visit National Association of Social Workers

Center for Clinical Social Work , For more information about licensure requirements, visit Association of Social Work Boards

Suggested citation:

Bureau of Labor Statistics, U.S. Department of Labor, Occupational Outlook Handbook, 2012-13 Edition, Social Workers, on the Internet at http://www.bls.gov/ooh/community-and-social-service/social-workers.htm .

Substance Abuse and Behavioral Disorder Counselors

Quick Facts: Substance Abuse and Behavioral Disorder Counselors	
2010 Median Pay	$38,120 per year $18.33 per hour
Entry-Level Education	High school diploma or equivalent
Work Experience in a Related Occupation	None
On-the-job Training	Moderate-term on-the-job training
Number of Jobs, 2010	85,500
Job Outlook, 2010-20	27% (Faster than average)
Employment Change, 2010-20	23,400

What Substance Abuse and Behavioral Disorder Counselors Do

Substance abuse and behavioral disorder counselors advise people who have alcoholism or other types of addiction, eating disorders, or other behavioral problems. They provide treatment and support to help the client recover from addiction or modify problem behaviors.

Duties

Substance abuse and behavioral disorder counselors typically do the following:

- Evaluate clients' mental and physical health, addiction or problem behavior, and openness to treatment
- Help clients develop treatment goals and plans
- Review and recommend treatment options with clients and their families
- Help clients develop skills and behaviors necessary to recover from their addiction or modify their behavior
- Work with clients to identify behaviors or situations that interfere with their recovery

Substance abuse and behavioral disorder counselors help the client recover from addiction by providing treatment and support.

- Teach families about addiction or behavior disorders and help them develop strategies to cope with those problems
- Refer clients to other resources or services, such as job placement services and support groups
- Develop and conduct outreach programs to help people learn about addictions and destructive behavior how to avoid them

Substance abuse and behavioral disorder counselors, also called addiction counselors, work with clients both one-on-one and in group sessions. Many incorporate the principles of 12-step programs, such as Alcoholics Anonymous, to guide their practice. They teach clients how to cope with stress and life's problems in ways that help them recover. Furthermore, they help clients rebuild professional relationships and, if necessary, reestablish their career. They also help clients improve their personal relationships and find ways to discuss their addiction or other problem with family and friends.

Many addiction counselors work with other health and mental health professionals, such as psychiatrists, social workers, doctors, and nurses. Some work in facilities that employ many types of healthcare and mental health professionals. In these settings, treatment professionals work in teams to develop treatment plans and coordinate care for patients. For more information, see the profiles on social workers , physicians and surgeons , and registered nurses .

Some counselors work with clients who have been ordered by a judge to receive treatment for addiction. Others work with specific populations, such as teenagers, veterans, or people with disabilities. Some specialize in crisis intervention; these counselors step in when someone is endangering their life or the lives of others. Other counselors specialize in noncrisis interventions, which encourage a person with addictions or other problems to get help. Noncrisis interventions often are performed at the request of friends and family.

Some substance abuse and behavioral disorder counselors work in private practice, where they work alone or with a group of counselors or other professionals. These counselors manage their practice as a business. This includes working with clients and insurance companies to receive payment for their services. In addition, they market their practice to bring in new clients.

Work Environment

Substance abuse and behavioral disorder counselors held about 85,500 jobs in 2010. The industries employing the most substance abuse and behavioral disorder counselors in 2010 were as follows:

Outpatient mental health and substance abuse centers	18%
Residential mental health and substance abuse facilities	16
Individual and family services	14
State and local government, excluding education and hospitals	12
Hospitals; state, local, and private	11

Substance abuse and behavioral disorder counselors work in a wide variety of settings, including mental health centers, prisons, probation or parole agencies, and juvenile detention facilities. They also work in halfway houses, detox centers, or in employee assistance programs (EAPs). EAPs are mental health programs provided by some companies to help employees deal with personal problems.

Some addiction counselors work in residential treatment centers, where clients live in the facility for a fixed period of time. Others work with clients in outpatient treatment centers. Some counselors work in private practice, where they may work alone or with a group of counselors or other professionals.

Although rewarding, the work of substance abuse and behavioral disorder counselors is often stressful. Many counselors have to deal with large workloads. They do not always have enough resources to meet the demand for their services. Also, they may have to intervene in crisis situations or work with agitated clients, which can be tense.

Work Schedules

Most substance abuse and behavioral disorder counselors work full time. In some settings, such as inpatient facilities, they may need to work evenings, nights, or weekends.

How to Become a Substance Abuse or Behavioral Disorder Counselor

Educational requirements range from a high school diploma to a master's degree, depending on the setting, type of work, state regulations, and level of responsibility.

Education

Requirements range from a high school diploma and certification to a master's degree. However, workers with more education are able to provide more services to their clients, such as private one-on-one counseling sessions, and they require less supervision than those with less education. Those interested should research their state's educational requirements.

Licenses and Certification

Substance abuse and behavioral disorder counselors in private practice must be licensed. Being licensed to work in this setting requires a master's degree and 2,000 to 3,000 hours of supervised clinical experience. In addition, counselors must pass a state-recognized exam and complete continuing education every year. Contact information for your state's regulating board can be found through the National Board for Certified Counselors .

The licensure or certification criteria for substance abuse and behavioral disorder counselors outside of private practice vary from state to state. For example, not all states require a specific degree, but many require applicants to pass an exam. Contact information for your state's licensing board can found through the Addiction Technology Transfer Center.

Training

Workers with less education, such as a high school diploma, may be required to go through a period of on-the-job training. Training prepares counselors how to respond to a crisis situation, and interact with families and people with addictions.

Important Qualities

Compassion. Counselors often work with people who are dealing with stressful and difficult situations, so they must be compassionate

and empathize with their clients.

Listening skills. Good listening skills are essential for substance abuse and behavioral disorder counselors. They need to give their full attention to a client to be able to understand that client's problems and values.

Patience. Substance abuse and behavioral disorder counselors must be able to remain calm when working with all types of clients, including those who may be distressed or angry.

People skills. Counselors must be able to work with different types of people. They spend most of their time working directly with clients or other professionals and must be able to develop and nurture good relationships.

Speaking skills. Substance abuse and behavioral disorder counselors need to be able to communicate with clients effectively. They must express ideas and information in a way that their clients easily understand.

Pay

Substance Abuse and Behavioral Disorder Counselors
Median annual wages, May 2010

Community and Social Service Occupations	$39,280
Substance Abuse and Behavioral Disorder Counselors	$38,120
Total, All Occupations	$33,840

Note: All Occupations includes all occupations in the U.S. Economy.
Source: U.S. Bureau of Labor Statistics, Occupational Employment Statistics

The median annual wage of substance abuse and behavioral disorder counselors was $38,120 in May 2010. The median wage is the wage at which half the workers in an occupation earned more than that amount and half earned less. The lowest 10 percent earned less than $24,690 and the top 10 percent earned more than $60,400.

In 2010, the median annual wages for substance abuse and behavioral disorder counselors in the industries employing the most substance abuse and behavioral disorder counselors were as follows:

Hospitals; state, local, and private	$45,160
Local government	44,280
Individual and family services	37,020
Outpatient mental health and substance abuse centers	35,670
Residential mental health and substance abuse facilities	33,570

Most substance abuse and behavioral disorder counselors work full time. In some settings, such as inpatient facilities, they may need to work evenings, nights, or weekends.

Job Outlook

Substance Abuse and Behavioral Disorder Counselors
Percent change in employment, projected 2010-20

Substance Abuse and Behavioral Disorder Counselors	27%
Community and Social Service Occupations	24%
Total, All Occupations	14%

Note: All Occupations includes all occupations in the U.S. Economy.
Source: U.S. Bureau of Labor Statistics, Employment Projections program

Employment of substance abuse and behavioral disorder counselors is expected to grow by 27 percent from 2010 to 2020, faster than the average for all occupations. Growth is expected as more people seek treatment for their addictions or other behaviors and drug offenders are increasingly sentenced to treatment rather than jail time.

In recent years, the criminal justice system has recognized that people committing crimes related to drugs are less likely to offend again if they get treatment for addiction. As a result, sentences for drug offenders often include treatment programs. This practice is expected to increase the use of substance abuse treatment programs and the demand for addiction counselors.

Also, over the projections period, more people are expected to seek treatment for problems with addiction or other problems. As the population grows, the number of individuals entering therapy is expected to increase as well. This is expected to cause a continued demand for counselors in mental health centers, halfway houses, and detox centers.

Employment of substance abuse and behavioral disorder counselors in residential mental health and substance abuse facilities is expected to grow by 44 percent from 2010 to 2020. As more individuals seek treatment, there will be an increase in demand for counseling services in residential facilities.

Employment growth from 2010 to 2020 for the industries employing the most substance abuse and behavioral disorder counselors is as follows:

Individual and family services	49%
Residential mental health and substance abuse facilities	44
Hospitals; state, local, and private	17
Outpatient mental health and substance abuse centers	16
State and local government, excluding education and hospitals	7

Job Prospects

Job prospects are excellent for substance abuse and behavioral disorder counselors, particularly for those with specialized training or education. Employers often have difficulty recruiting workers with the proper educational requirements and experience in working with addiction. In addition, many workers leave the field after a few years and need to be replaced. As result, those interested in entering this field should find favorable prospects.

Employment projections data for substance abuse and behavioral disorder counselors, 2010-20

Occupational Title	SOC Code	Employment, 2010	Projected Employment, 2020	Change, 2010-20	
				Percent	Numeric
Substance Abuse and Behavioral Disorder Counselors	21-1011	85,500	108,900	27	23,400

SOURCE: U.S. Bureau of Labor Statistics, Employment Projections program

Similar Occupations

This table shows a list of occupations with job duties that are similar to those of substance abuse and behavioral disorder counselors.

Occupation	Job Duties	Entry-Level Education	Median Annual Pay, May 2010
Mental Health Counselors and Marriage and Family Therapists	Mental health counselors and marriage and family therapists help people manage or overcome mental and emotional disorders and problems with their family and relationships. They listen to clients and ask questions to help the clients understand their problems and develop strategies to improve their lives.	Master's degree	$39,710
Psychologists	Psychologists study mental processes and human behavior by observing, interpreting, and recording how people and other animals relate to one another and the environment.	See How to Become One	$68,640
Rehabilitation Counselors	Rehabilitation counselors help people with emotional and physical disabilities live independently. They help their clients overcome personal, social, and professional effects of disabilities as they relate to employment or independent living.	Master's degree	$32,350
School and Career Counselors	School counselors help students develop social skills and succeed in school. Career counselors assist people with the process of making career decisions by helping them choose a career or educational program.	Master's degree	$53,380
Social and Community Service Managers	Social and community service managers coordinate and supervise social service programs and community organizations. They direct and lead staff who provide services to the public.	Bachelor's degree	$57,950
Social and Human Service Assistants	Social and human service assistants help people get through difficult times or get additional support. They help other workers, such as social workers, and they help clients find benefits or community services.	High school diploma or equivalent	$28,200
Social Workers	There are two main types of social workers: direct-service social workers, who help people solve and cope with problems in their everyday lives, and clinical social workers, who diagnose and treat mental, behavioral, and emotional issues.	See How to Become One	$42,480

Contacts for More Information

For more information about addiction counselors, visit Addiction Technology Transfer Center Network

For more information about counseling and counseling specialties, visit American Counseling Association

For contact information for State regulating boards, visit National Board for Certified Counselors

Suggested citation:

Bureau of Labor Statistics, U.S. Department of Labor, Occupational Outlook Handbook, 2012-13 Edition, Substance Abuse and Behavioral Disorder Counselors, on the Internet at http://www.bls.gov/ooh/community-and-social-service/substance-abuse-and-behavioral-disorder-counselors.htm.

Computer and Information Technology Occupations

Computer and Information Research Scientists

Quick Facts: Computer and Information Research Scientists	
2010 Median Pay	$100,660 per year $48.39 per hour
Entry-Level Education	Doctoral or professional degree
Work Experience in a Related Occupation	None
On-the-job Training	None
Number of Jobs, 2010	28,200
Job Outlook, 2010-20	19% (About as fast as average)
Employment Change, 2010-20	5,300

What Computer and Information Research Scientists Do

Computer and information research scientists invent and design new technology and find new uses for existing technology. They study and solve complex problems in computing for business, science, medicine, and other uses.

Duties

Computer and information research scientists typically do the following:

- Explore fundamental issues in computation and develop theories and models to address those issues
- Help scientists and engineers solve complex computing problems
- Invent new computing languages, tools, and methods to improve the way in which people work with computers
- Develop and improve the software systems that form the basis of the modern computing experience
- Design experiments to test the operation of these software systems
- Analyze the results of their experiments
- Publish their findings in academic journals

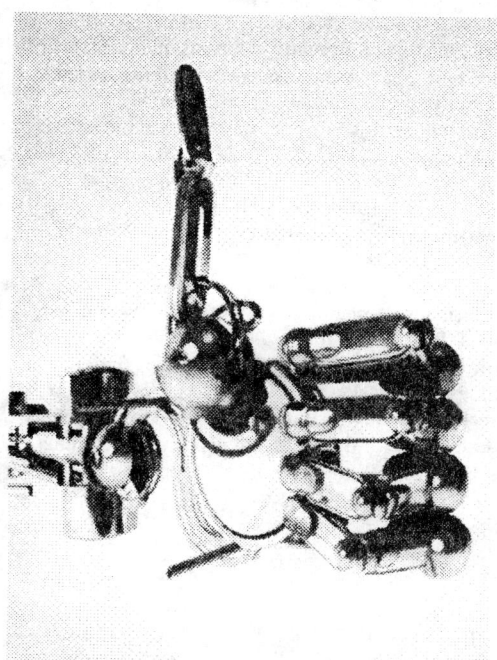

Some computer scientists create programs to control robots.

Computer and information research scientists create and improve computer algorithms, which are sets of instructions that tell a computer what to do. Some computer tasks are very difficult and require complex algorithms. Computer and information research scientists try to simplify these instructions to make the computer system as efficient as possible. These algorithms become the foundation for advancements in many types of technology, such as machine learning systems and cloud computing.

Computer and information research scientists' work often leads to advancement and increased efficiency in many areas, such as better networking technology, faster computing speeds, and improved information security. In general, computer and information research scientists work on a more theoretical level than other computer professionals.

Many people with a computer and information research science background become professors and teachers. For more information on computer science professors, see the profile on postsecondary teachers. In general, researchers in an academic setting focus on computer theory, although those working for businesses or scientific organizations usually focus on projects that have the possibility of producing profits.

Some computer scientists collaborate with electrical engineers, computer hardware engineers, and other specialists to work on multidisciplinary projects. The following are examples of some specialties for computer and information research scientists:

Hardware. Computer and information research scientists who study hardware architecture discover new ways to process and send information. They design computer chips and processors using new materials and technology to make chips and processors work faster and to give them more computing power.

Robotics. Some computer and information research scientists study how to improve robots. Robotics explores how a machine can interact with the physical world as effectively as humans and other living creatures. Computer and information research scientists create the programs that control the robots. They work closely with engineers who focus on the hardware design of robots. Together, these workers test how well the robots do the tasks they were created to do €" such as assemble cars and collect data on other planets.

Software. Computer and information research scientists write the software that controls the electronic components in cars and other advanced machines. The embedded software written by computer scientists is complex and requires a high degree of accuracy because of the consequences of failure of the electronic components within such products, such as a car's braking system or an ultrasound machine.

Work Environment

Computer and information research scientists held about 28,200 jobs in 2010. Most computer and information research scientists work for computer systems design and related services firms, scientific research and development companies, or the federal government. Some also work for software companies.

The following industries employed the most computer and information research scientists in 2010:

Federal government	24%
Computer systems design and related services	23
Scientific research and development services	13
Educational services; state, local, and private	9
Software publishers	5

Work Schedules

Most computer and information research scientists work full time. Those working on independent research may have flexibility in their work schedules.

How to Become a Computer and Information Research Scientist

A Ph.D. in computer science or a related subject is required for most computer and information research scientist jobs. In the federal government, a bachelor's degree may be sufficient for some jobs.

Education

Most computer and information research scientists need a Ph.D. in computer science or a related subject, such as computer engineering. A Ph.D. usually requires 4 to 5 years of study after the bachelor's degree, usually in a computer-related field such as computer science or information systems. Students spend the first two years in a Ph.D. program taking a range of computer science classes. They then choose a specialty and spend the remaining years doing research within that specialty.

For some computer scientist positions in the federal government, a bachelor's degree in computer science is sufficient. For computer scientists seeking employment in a specialized field, such as finance or biology, knowledge of that field, along with the computer science degree, may be helpful in attaining a job.

Important Qualities

Advanced math skills. Advanced math and other technical topics are critical in computing.

Analytical skills. Computer and information research scientists must be organized in their thinking and analyze the results of their research to formulate conclusions.

Communication skills. Computer and information research scientists must communicate well with programmers and managers, as well as be able to clearly explain their conclusions to people who may have no technical background. They often write for academic journals and similar publications.

Critical-thinking skills. Computer and information research scientists work on many complex problems.

Detail oriented. Computer and information research scientists must pay close attention to their work because a small error can cause an entire project to fail.

Ingenuity. Computer and information research scientists must continually come up with innovative ways to solve problems, particularly when their ideas do not initially work as they had hoped.

Logical thinking. Computer algorithms rely on logic. Computer and information research scientists must have an aptitude for reasoning.

Pay

Computer and Information Research Scientists
Median annual wages, May 2010

Computer and Information Research Scientists	$100,660
Computer Occupations	$73,710
Total, All Occupations	$33,840

Note: All Occupations includes all occupations in the U.S. Economy.
Source: U.S. Bureau of Labor Statistics, Occupational Employment Statistics

The median annual wage of computer and information research scientists was $100,660 in May 2010. The median wage is the wage at which half the workers in an occupation earned more than that amount and half earned less. The lowest 10 percent earned less than $57,630, and the top 10 percent earned more than $153,120.

Most computer and information research scientists work full time. Those working on independent research may have flexibility in their work schedules.

Job Outlook

Computer and Information Research Scientists
Percent change in employment, projected 2010-20

Computer Occupations	22%
Computer and Information Research Scientists	19%
Total, All Occupations	14%

Note: All Occupations includes all occupations in the U.S. Economy.
Source: U.S. Bureau of Labor Statistics, Employment Projections program

Employment of computer and information research scientists is expected to grow by 19 percent from 2010 to 2020, about as fast as the average for all occupations. Computer scientists will be needed to develop the software that controls increasingly complicated electronics. These electronic components, called embedded systems, are in many products, from cars to machines that are used for performing some healthcare procedures remotely. A growing emphasis on cyber security also should lead to new jobs, as computer scientists will be needed to identify innovative ways to prevent attacks or track hackers.

In addition, growth will be driven by an increase in cloud computing systems, which allow users to store files, get software, and use other information technology (IT) services over the Internet. Computer scientists will be needed to design the infrastructure to enable widespread adoption of cloud computing.

Job Prospects

Computer and information research scientists are likely to enjoy excellent job prospects. There are a limited number of Ph.D. graduates each year. As a result, many companies report difficulties finding a sufficient supply of these highly skilled workers.

For applicants seeking employment in a specialized field, such as finance or biology, knowledge of that field, along with the computer science degree, may be helpful in attaining a job.

Employment projections data for computer and information research scientists, 2010-20

Occupational Title	SOC Code	Employment, 2010	Projected Employment, 2020	Change, 2010-20	
				Percent	Numeric
Computer and Information Research Scientists	15-1111	28,200	33,500	19	5,300
SOURCE: U.S. Bureau of Labor Statistics, Employment Projections program					

Similar Occupations

This table shows a list of occupations with job duties that are similar to those of computer and information research scientists.

Occupation	Job Duties	Entry-Level Education	Median Annual Pay, May 2010
Computer and Information Systems Managers	Computer and information systems managers, often called information technology managers (IT managers or IT project managers), plan, coordinate, and direct computer-related activities in an organization. They help determine the information technology goals of an organization and are responsible for implementing the appropriate computer systems to meet those goals.	Bachelor's degree	$115,780
Computer Hardware Engineers	Computer hardware engineers research, design, develop, and test computer equipment such as chips, circuit boards, or routers. By solving complex problems in computer hardware, these engineers create rapid advances in computer technology.	Bachelor's degree	$98,810
Computer Programmers	Computer programmers write code to create software programs. They turn the program designs created by software developers and engineers into instructions that a computer can follow.	Bachelor's degree	$71,380
Database Administrators	Database administrators use software to store and organize data, such as financial information and customer shipping records. They make sure that data are available to users and are secure from unauthorized access.	Bachelor's degree	$73,490
Postsecondary Teachers	Postsecondary teachers instruct students in a wide variety of academic and vocational subjects beyond the high school level. They also conduct research and publish scholarly papers and books.	Doctoral or professional degree	$62,050
Software Developers	Software developers are the creative minds behind computer programs. Some develop the applications that allow people to do specific tasks on a computer or other device. Others develop the underlying systems that run the devices or control networks.	Bachelor's degree	$90,530

Contacts for More Information

For more information about computer and information research scientists, visit Association for Computing Machinery (ACM)

Institute of Electrical and Electronics Engineers Computer Society

For more information about IT education, visit National Workforce Center for Emerging Technologies

For information about opportunities for women pursing IT careers, visit National Center for Women and Information Technology

Suggested citation:

Bureau of Labor Statistics, U.S. Department of Labor, Occupational Outlook Handbook, 2012-13 Edition, Computer and Information Research Scientists, on the Internet at http://www.bls.gov/ooh/computer-and-information-technology/computer-and-information-research-scientists.htm.

Computer Programmers

Quick Facts: Computer Programmers	
2010 Median Pay	$71,380 per year $34.32 per hour
Entry-Level Education	Bachelor's degree
Work Experience in a Related Occupation	None
On-the-job Training	None
Number of Jobs, 2010	363,100
Job Outlook, 2010-20	12% (About as fast as average)
Employment Change, 2010-20	43,700

What Computer Programmers Do

Computer programmers write code to create software programs. They turn the program designs created by software developers and engineers into instructions that a computer can follow. Programmers must debug the programs—that is, test them to ensure that they produce the expected results. If a program does not work correctly, they check the code for mistakes and fix them.

Duties

Computer programmers typically do the following:

- Write programs in a variety of computer languages, such as C++ and Java
- Update and expand existing programs
- Debug programs by testing for and fixing errors
- Build and use computer-assisted software engineering (CASE) tools to automate the writing of some code
- Use code libraries, which are collections of independent lines of code, to simplify the writing

Programmers work closely with software developers and, in some businesses, their work overlaps. When this happens, programmers can do the work typical of developers, such as designing the program. This entails initially planning the software, creating models and flowcharts detailing how the code is to be written, and designing an application or system interface. For more information, see the profile on software developers.

Some programs are relatively simple and usually take a few days to

Programmers write instructions that a computer can follow, allowing it to perform specific tasks.

write, such as mobile applications for cell phones. Other programs, like computer operating systems, are more complex and can take a year or more to complete.

Software-as-a-service (SaaS), which consists of applications provided through the Internet, is a growing field. Although programmers typically need to rewrite their programs to work on different systems platforms such as Windows or OS X, applications created using SaaS work on all platforms. That is why programmers writing for software-as-a-service applications may not have to update as much code as other programmers and can instead spend more time writing new programs.

Work Environment

Computer programmers usually work in offices, most commonly in the computer systems design and related services industry and information service industry.Computer programmers held about 363,100 jobs in 2010, and were concentrated in the following industries in 2010:

Computer systems design and related services	32%
Information	12
Finance and insurance	7
Administrative and support services	6
Government	5

Programmers normally work alone, but sometimes work with other computer specialists on large projects. Because writing codes can be done anywhere, many programmers telecommute. About 25 percent work in California, New York, and Texas.

Work Schedules

Most computer programmers work full time.

How to Become a Computer Programmer

Most computer programmers have a bachelor's degree; however, some employers hire workers with an associate's degree. Most programmers specialize in a few programming languages.

Education

Most computer programmers have a bachelor's degree; however, some employers hire workers who have an associate's degree. Most programmers get a degree in computer science or a related subject. Programmers who work in specific fields, such as healthcare or accounting, may take classes in that field in addition to their degree in computer programming. In addition, employers value experience, which many students get through internships.

Most programmers learn only a few computer languages while in school. However, a computer science degree also gives students the skills needed to learn new computer languages easily. During their classes, students receive hands-on experience writing code, debugging programs, and many other tasks that they will do on the job.

To keep up with changing technology, computer programmers may take continuing education and professional development seminars to learn new programming languages or about upgrades to programming languages they already know.

Certification

Certification is a way to demonstrate a level of competence and may provide a jobseeker with a competitive advantage. Certification programs, generally available through product vendors or software firms, offer programmers a way to become certified in specific programming languages or for vendor-specific programming products. Some companies may require their computer programmers to be certified in the products they use.

Advancement

Programmers who have general business experience may become computer systems analysts. Programmers with specialized knowledge of, and experience with, a language or operating system may become computer software developers. They also may be promoted to managerial positions.For more information, see the profiles on computer systems analysts , software developers , and computer and information systems managers.

Important Qualities

Analytical skills. Computer programmers must understand complex instructions in order to create computer code.

Concentration. Programmers must be able to work at a computer, writing lines of code for long periods of time.

Detail oriented. Computer programmers must closely examine the code they write because a small mistake can affect the entire computer program.

Troubleshooting skills. An important part of a programmer's job is to check the program for errors and fix any they find.

Pay

Computer Programmers
Median annual wages, May 2010

Computer Occupations	$73,710
Computer Programmers	$71,380
Total, All Occupations	$33,840

Note: All Occupations includes all occupations in the U.S. Economy.
Source: U.S. Bureau of Labor Statistics, Occupational Employment Statistics

The median annual wage of computer programmers was $71,380 in May 2010. The median wage is the wage at which half the workers in an occupation earned more than that amount and half earned less. The lowest 10 percent earned less than $40,820, and the top 10 percent earned more than $114,180.

Most computer programmers work full time.

Job Outlook

Computer Programmers
Percent change in employment, projected 2010-20

Computer Occupations	22%
Total, All Occupations	14%
Computer Programmers	12%

Note: All Occupations includes all occupations in the U.S. Economy.
Source: U.S. Bureau of Labor Statistics, Employment Projections program

Employment of computer programmers is expected to increase by 12 percent from 2010 to 2020, about as fast as the average for all occupations. Since computer programming can be done from anywhere in the world, companies often hire programmers in countries where wages are lower. This ongoing trend will limit growth for computer programmers in the United States. However, companies may continue to hire computer programmers in low cost areas within the United States.

Most computer programmers work in computer system design and related services, an industry which is expected to grow as a result of an increasing demand for new computer software. This includes software offered over the Internet, which should lower costs for firms and allow for more customization for users. In addition, new applications will have to be developed for mobile technology and the healthcare industry. An increase in computer systems that are built into electronics and into other non-computer products should result in some job growth for computer programmers and software developers.

Job Prospects

Job prospects will be best for programmers who have a bachelor's degree or higher and knowledge of a variety of programming languages. Keeping up to date with the newest programming tools will also improve prospects.

As employers increasingly contract with outside firms to do programming jobs, more opportunities are expected to arise for experienced programmers who have expertise in a specific area to work as consultants.

Employment projections data for computer programmers, 2010-20

Occupational Title	SOC Code	Employment, 2010	Projected Employment, 2020	Change, 2010-20 Percent	Numeric
Computer Programmers	15-1131	363,100	406,800	12	43,700
SOURCE: U.S. Bureau of Labor Statistics, Employment Projections program					

Similar Occupations

This table shows a list of occupations with job duties that are similar to those of computer programmers.

Occupation	Job Duties	Entry-Level Education	Median Annual Pay, May 2010
Computer and Information Systems Managers	Computer and information systems managers, often called information technology managers (IT managers or IT project managers), plan, coordinate, and direct computer-related activities in an organization. They help determine the information technology goals of an organization and are responsible for implementing the appropriate computer systems to meet those goals.	Bachelor's degree	$115,780
Computer Hardware Engineers	Computer hardware engineers research, design, develop, and test computer equipment such as chips, circuit boards, or routers. By solving complex problems in computer hardware, these engineers create rapid advances in computer technology.	Bachelor's degree	$98,810
Computer Support Specialists	Computer support specialists provide help and advice to people and organizations using computer software or equipment. Some, called technical support specialists, support information technology (IT) employees within their organization. Others, called help-desk technicians, assist non-IT users who are having computer problems.	Some college, no degree	$46,260
Computer Systems Analysts	Computer systems analysts study an organization's current computer systems and procedures and make recommendations to management to help the organization operate more efficiently and effectively. They bring business and information technology (IT) together by understanding the needs and limitations of both.	Bachelor's degree	$77,740
Database Administrators	Database administrators use software to store and organize data, such as financial information and customer shipping records. They make sure that data are available to users and are secure from unauthorized access.	Bachelor's degree	$73,490
Information Security Analysts, Web Developers, and Computer Network Architects	Information security analysts, web developers, and computer network architects all use information technology (IT) to advance their organization's goals. Security analysts ensure a firm's information stays safe from cyberattacks. Web developers create websites to help firms have a public face. Computer network architects create the internal networks all workers within organizations use.	Bachelor's degree	$75,660
Network and Computer Systems Administrators	Network and computer systems administrators are responsible for the day-to-day operation of an organization's computer networks. They organize, install, and support an organization's computer systems, including local area networks (LANs), wide area networks (WANs), network segments, intranets, and other data communication systems.	Bachelor's degree	$69,160
Software Developers	Software developers are the creative minds behind computer programs. Some develop the applications that allow people to do specific tasks on a computer or other device. Others develop the underlying systems that run the devices or control networks.	Bachelor's degree	$90,530

Contacts for More Information

For more information about computer programmers, visit Association for Computing Machinery, Institute of Electrical and Electronics Engineers Computer Society

For information about IT education, visit National Workforce Center for Emerging Technologies

For information about opportunities for women pursuing IT careers, visit National Center for Women and Information Technology

Suggested citation:

Bureau of Labor Statistics, U.S. Department of Labor, Occupational Outlook Handbook, 2012-13 Edition, Computer Programmers, on the Internet at http://www.bls.gov/ooh/computer-and-information-technology/computer-programmers.htm.

Computer Support Specialists

Quick Facts: Computer Support Specialists	
2010 Median Pay	$46,260 per year $22.24 per hour
Entry-Level Education	Some college, no degree
Work Experience in a Related Occupation	None
On-the-job Training	Moderate-term on-the-job training
Number of Jobs, 2010	607,100
Job Outlook, 2010-20	18% (About as fast as average)
Employment Change, 2010-20	110,000

What Computer Support Specialists Do

Computer support specialists provide help and advice to people and organizations using computer software or equipment. Some, called technical support specialists, support information technology (IT) employees within their organization. Others, called help-desk technicians, assist non-IT users who are having computer problems.

Duties

Technical support specialists typically do the following:
- Test and evaluate existing network systems
- Perform regular maintenance to ensure that networks operate correctly
- Troubleshoot local area networks (LANs), wide area networks (WANs), and Internet systems

Technical support specialists, also called computer network support specialists, usually work in their organization's IT department. They help IT staff analyze, troubleshoot, and evaluate computer network problems. They play an important role in the daily upkeep of their organization's networks by finding solutions to problems as they occur. Solving an IT problem in a timely manner is important because organizations depend on their computer systems. Technical support specialists may provide assistance to the organization's computer users through phone, email, or in-person visits. They often work under network and computer systems administrators, who handle more complex tasks. For more information, see the profile on network and computer systems administrators.

Help-desk technicians provide assistance to computer users.

Help-desk technicians typically do the following:
- Pay attention to customers when they describe their computer problems
- Ask customers questions to properly diagnose the problem
- Walk customers through the problem-solving steps
- Set up or repair computer equipment and related devices
- Train users to use new computer hardware or software, including printing, installation, word processing, and email
- Give information to others in the organization about what gives customers the most trouble and other concerns customers have

Help-desk technicians, also called computer user support specialists, usually provide technical help to non-IT computer users. They respond to phone and email requests for help. Sometimes they make site visits so that they can solve a problem in person.

Help-desk technicians may solve a range of problems that vary with the industry and the particular firm. Some technicians work for large software companies and for support service firms and must give instructions to business customers on how to use complex programs. Others work in call centers answering simpler questions from consumers. Some technicians work for organizations and help non-IT workers with their computer problems.

Work Environment

Computer support specialists held about 607,100 jobs in 2010. They work in many different industries, including information technology (IT), education, finance, health care, and telecommunication. Many help-desk technicians work for outside support service firms on a contract basis and provide help to a range of businesses and consumers.

In 2010, the industries employing the most computer support specialist were as follows:

Computer systems design and related services	18%
Educational services; state, local, and private	13
Information	11
Finance and insurance	7
Wholesale trade	7

Faster computer networks are making it possible for some support specialists, particularly help-desk technicians, to work from a home office. However, specialized help-desk technicians may have to travel to a client's location to solve a problem.

Work Schedules

Most computer support specialists have full-time work schedules; however, many do not work typical 9-to-5 jobs. Because computer support is important for businesses, support specialists must be available 24 hours a day. As a result, many support specialists must work nights or weekends.

How to Become a Computer Support Specialist

Because of the wide range of skills for different computer support jobs, there are many paths into the occupation. A bachelor's degree is required for some computer support specialist positions, but an associate's degree or postsecondary classes may be enough for others. After being hired, many workers enter a training program that lasts for several months.

Education

Training requirements for computer support specialists vary, but many employers prefer to hire applicants who have a bachelor's degree. More technical positions are likely to require a degree in a field such as computer science, engineering, or information science, but for others the applicant's field of study is less important. Some lower level help-desk jobs or call-center jobs require some computer knowledge, but not necessarily a postsecondary degree.

Training

Computer support specialists usually get on-the-job training after they are hired. For many workers, this training lasts for about 3 months. The training period may be longer for more complex jobs.

To keep up with changes in technology, many computer support specialists continue their training throughout their careers.

Advancement

Entry-level support specialists often work on simple problems. Over time, they may advance to positions that handle questions on complex software or equipment. Many of these workers advance to other IT positions, such as network and computer systems administrators or software developers. Some become managers in the computer support services department. For more information, see the profiles on network and computer systems administrators and software developers.

Important Qualities

Interpersonal skills. Computer support specialists must be patient and sympathetic. They must often help people who are frustrated with the software or hardware they are trying to use.

Listening skills. Support workers must be able to understand the problem that their customer is describing and know when to ask questions to clarify the situation.

Problem-solving skills. Support workers must identify both simple and complex computer problems, analyze them, and provide a proper solution.

Speaking skills. Support workers must describe the solution to a computer problem in a way that a nontechnical person can understand.

Writing skills. Strong writing skills are useful for preparing instructions and email responses for employees and customers.

Pay

Computer Support Specialists
Median annual wages, May 2010

Computer Occupations	$73,710
Computer Support Specialists	$46,260
Total, All Occupations	$33,840

Note: All Occupations includes all occupations in the U.S. Economy.
Source: U.S. Bureau of Labor Statistics, Occupational Employment Statistics

The median annual wage of computer support specialists was $46,260 in May 2010. The median wage is the wage at which half the workers in an occupation earned more than the amount and half earned less. The lowest 10 percent earned less than $28,300, and the top 10 percent earned more than $76,970.

Most computer support specialists have full-time work schedules; however, many do not work typical 9-to-5 jobs. Because computer support is important for businesses, support specialists must be available 24 hours a day. As a result, many support specialists must work nights or weekends.

Job Outlook

Computer Support Specialists
Percent change in employment, projected 2010-20

Computer Occupations	22%
Computer Support Specialists	18%
Total, All Occupations	14%

Note: All Occupations includes all occupations in the U.S. Economy.
Source: U.S. Bureau of Labor Statistics, Employment Projections program

Employment of computer support specialists is expected to grow 18 percent from 2010 to 2020, about as fast as the average for all occupations. More support services will be needed as organizations upgrade their computer equipment and software. Computer support staff will be needed to respond to the installation and repair requirements of increasingly complex computer equipment and software.

Employment growth should also be strong in healthcare industries. This field is expected to greatly increase its use of information technology (IT), and support services will be crucial to keep everything running properly.

Some lower level tech support jobs, commonly found in call centers, may be sent to countries that have lower wage rates. However, a recent trend to move jobs to lower cost regions of the United States may offset some loss of jobs to other countries.

Job Prospects

Job prospects should be favorable. There are usually clear advancement possibilities for this occupation, creating new job openings. Applicants with a bachelor's degree and a strong technical background should have the best job opportunities.

Employment projections data for computer support specialists, 2010-20

Occupational Title	SOC Code	Employment, 2010	Projected Employment, 2020	Change, 2010-20 Percent	Numeric
Computer Support Specialists	15-1150	607,100	717,100	18	110,000
SOURCE: U.S. Bureau of Labor Statistics, Employment Projections program					

Similar Occupations

This table shows a list of occupations with job duties that are similar to those of computer support specialists.

Occupation	Job Duties	Entry-Level Education	Median Annual Pay, May 2010
Computer and Information Systems Managers	Computer and information systems managers, often called information technology managers (IT managers or IT project managers), plan, coordinate, and direct computer-related activities in an organization. They help determine the information technology goals of an organization and are responsible for implementing the appropriate computer systems to meet those goals.	Bachelor's degree	$115,780
Customer Service Representatives	Customer service representatives interact with customers on behalf of an organization. They provide information about products and services and respond to customer complaints. Some also take orders and process returns.	High school diploma or equivalent	$30,460
Computer Programmers	Computer programmers write code to create software programs. They turn the program designs created by software developers and engineers into instructions that a computer can follow.	Bachelor's degree	$71,380
Computer Systems Analysts	Computer systems analysts study an organization's current computer systems and procedures and make recommendations to management to help the organization operate more efficiently and effectively. They bring business and information technology (IT) together by understanding the needs and limitations of both.	Bachelor's degree	$77,740
Database Administrators	Database administrators use software to store and organize data, such as financial information and customer shipping records. They make sure that data are available to users and are secure from unauthorized access.	Bachelor's degree	$73,490
Information Security Analysts, Web Developers, and Computer Network Architects	Information security analysts, web developers, and computer network architects all use information technology (IT) to advance their organization's goals. Security analysts ensure a firm's information stays safe from cyberattacks. Web developers create websites to help firms have a public face. Computer network architects create the internal networks all workers within organizations use.	Bachelor's degree	$75,660
Network and Computer Systems Administrators	Network and computer systems administrators are responsible for the day-to-day operation of an organization's computer networks. They organize, install, and support an organization's computer systems, including local area networks (LANs), wide area networks (WANs), network segments, intranets, and other data communication systems.	Bachelor's degree	$69,160
Software Developers	Software developers are the creative minds behind computer programs. Some develop the applications that allow people to do specific tasks on a computer or other device. Others develop the underlying systems that run the devices or control networks.	Bachelor's degree	$90,530

Contacts for More Information

For more information about computer support specialists, visit Technical Services Industry Association, Help Desk Institute (HDI)

For more information about computer careers, visit Association for Computing Machinery, Institute of Electrical and Electronics Engineers Computer Society, Computing Research Association

For more information about IT education, visit National Workforce Center for Emerging Technologies

For information about opportunities for women pursing IT careers, visit National Center for Women and Information Technology

Suggested citation:

Bureau of Labor Statistics, U.S. Department of Labor, Occupational Outlook Handbook, 2012-13 Edition, Computer Support Specialists, on the Internet at http://www.bls.gov/ooh/computer-and-information-technology/computer-support-specialists.htm.

Computer Systems Analysts

Quick Facts: Computer Systems Analysts	
2010 Median Pay	$77,740 per year $37.38 per hour
Entry-Level Education	Bachelor's degree
Work Experience in a Related Occupation	None
On-the-job Training	None
Number of Jobs, 2010	544,400
Job Outlook, 2010-20	22% (Faster than average)
Employment Change, 2010-20	120,400

What Computer Systems Analysts Do

Computer systems analysts study an organization's current computer systems and procedures and make recommendations to management to help the organization operate more efficiently and effectively. They bring business and information technology (IT) together by understanding the needs and limitations of both.

Duties

Computer systems analysts typically do the following:

- Consult with managers to determine the role of the IT system in an organization
- Research emerging technologies to decide if installing them can increase the organization's efficiency and effectiveness
- Prepare an analysis of costs and benefits so that management can decide if computer upgrades are financially worthwhile
- Devise ways to make existing computer systems meet new needs
- Design and develop new systems by choosing and configuring hardware and software

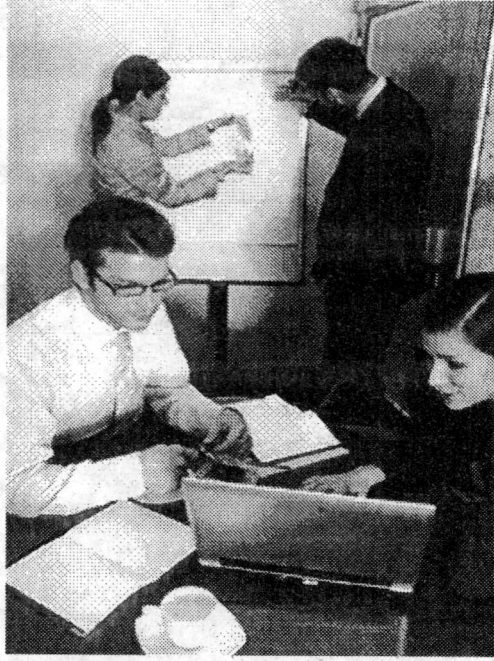

Analysts create diagrams to help programmers and architects build computer systems.

- Oversee installing and configuring the new system to customize it for the organization
- Do tests to ensure that the systems work as expected
- Train the system's end users and write instruction manuals, when required

Analysts use a variety of techniques to design computer systems such as data-modeling systems, which create rules for the computer to follow when presenting data, thereby allowing analysts to make faster decisions. They also do information engineering, designing and setting up information systems to improve efficiency and communication.

Because analysts work closely with an organization's business leaders, they help the IT team understand how its computer systems can best serve the organization.

Analysts determine requirements for how much memory and speed the computer system needs, as well as other necessary features. They prepare flowcharts or diagrams for programmers or engineers to use when building the system. Analysts also work with these people to solve problems that arise after the initial system is set up.

Most systems analysts specialize in certain types of computer systems that are specific to the organization they work with. For example, an analyst might work predominantly with financial computer systems or engineering systems.

In some cases, analysts who supervise the initial installation or upgrade of IT systems from start to finish may be called IT project managers. They monitor a project's progress to ensure that deadlines, standards, and cost targets are met. IT project managers who plan and direct an organization's IT department or IT policies are included in the profile on computer and information systems managers. For more information, see the profile on computer and information systems managers.

The following are examples of types of computer system analysts.

Systems analysts specialize in developing new systems or fine-tuning existing ones to meet an organization's needs.

Systems designers or systems architects specialize in helping organizations choose a specific type of hardware and software system. They develop long-term goals for the computer systems and a plan to reach those goals. They work with management to ensure that systems are set up to best serve the organization's mission.

Software quality assurance (QA) analysts do in-depth testing of the systems they design. They run tests and diagnose problems to make sure that certain requirements are met. QA analysts write reports to management recommending ways to improve the system.

Programmer analysts design and update their system's software and create applications tailored to their organization's needs. They do more coding and debugging the code than other types of analysts, although they still work extensively with management to determine what business needs the applications are meant to address. Other occupations that do programming are computer programmers and software developers. For more information, see the profiles on computer programmers and software developers.

Work Environment

Computer system analysts held 544,400 jobs in 2010.

Although 1 in 4 are employed by computer systems design firms, systems analysts work in many different industries. The industries employing the most systems analysts in 2010 are shown in the following table.

Computer systems design and related services	25%
Finance and insurance	14
Information	8
Management of companies and enterprises	7
Government	7

Computer systems analysts work directly for an organization, or they work as consultants. Consultants can be self-employed or work for an information technology firm. Although technological advances have made telecommuting more common, many consultants still need to travel to see their clients. The length of an assignment can vary with the complexity of the job.

Work Schedules

Most systems analysts work full time. Many work more than 40 hours per week.

How to Become a Computer Systems Analyst

A bachelor's degree in a computer or information science field is common, although not always a requirement. Some firms hire analysts with business or liberal arts degrees who know how to write computer programs.

Education

Most computer systems analysts have a bachelor's degree in a computer-related field. Because computer systems analysts are also heavily involved in the business side of a company, it may be helpful to take business courses or major in management information systems (MIS).

Some employers prefer applicants who have a Master of Business Administration (MBA) with a concentration in information systems. For more technically complex jobs, a master's degree in computer science may be more appropriate.

Although many analysts have technical degrees, such a degree is not always a requirement. Many systems analysts have liberal arts degrees and have gained programming or technical expertise elsewhere.

Some analysts have an associate's degree and experience in a related occupation.

Many systems analysts continue to take classes throughout their careers so that they can learn about new and innovative technologies and keep their skills competitive. Technological advances come so rapidly in the computer field that continual study is necessary to remain competitive.

Systems analysts must also understand the business field they are working in. For example, a hospital may want an analyst with a background or coursework in health management. An analyst working for a bank may need to understand finance.

Advancement

With experience, systems analysts can advance to project manager and lead a team of analysts. Some can eventually become information

technology (IT) directors or chief technology officers. For more information, see the profile on computer and information systems managers.

Important Qualities

Analytical skills. Analysts must interpret complex information from various sources and be able to decide the best way to move forward on a project. They must also be able to predict how changes may affect the project.

Communication skills. Analysts work as a go-between with management and the IT department and must be able to explain complex issues in a way that both will understand.

Creativity. Because analysts are tasked with finding innovative solutions to computer problems, an ability to "think outside the box" is important.

Teamwork. The projects that computer systems analysts work on usually require them to collaborate and coordinate with others.

Pay

Computer Systems Analysts
Median annual wages, May 2010

Computer Systems Analysts	$77,740
Computer Occupations	$73,710
Total, All Occupations	$33,840

Note: All Occupations includes all occupations in the U.S. Economy.
Source: U.S. Bureau of Labor Statistics, Occupational Employment Statistics

The median annual wage of computer systems analysts was $77,740 in May 2010. The median wage is the wage at which half the workers in an occupation earned more than that amount and half earned less. The lowest 10 percent earned less than $48,360, and the top 10 percent earned more than $119,070.

Pay varies by work setting. Some examples of industries that employ many computer systems analysts and the annual median wages those workers received in May 2010 are shown in the following table.

Computer systems design and related services	$ 80,830
Information	79,540
Management of companies and enterprises	78,650
Finance and insurance	77,890
Government	70,430

Most systems analysts work full time. Many work more than 40 hours per week.

Job Outlook

Computer Systems Analysts
Percent change in employment, projected 2010-20

Computer Systems Analysts	22%
Computer Occupations	22%
Total, All Occupations	14%

Note: All Occupations includes all occupations in the U.S. Economy.
Source: U.S. Bureau of Labor Statistics, Employment Projections program

Employment of computer systems analysts is expected to grow 22 percent from 2010 to 2020, faster than the average of all occupations.

As organizations across the economy increase their reliance on information technology (IT), workers in this occupation will be hired to design and install new computer systems. Growth in wireless and mobile networks will create a need for new systems that work well with these networks.

Additional job growth is expected in healthcare fields. A large increase is expected in electronic medical records, e-prescribing, and other forms of healthcare IT, and analysts will be needed to design computer systems to accommodate the increase.

There is also expected to be an increase in the number of systems analysts working at IT consulting firms. These analysts, who will be hired by organizations in a variety of industries to design computer systems, will move on to another business when they are finished. As more small and medium-size firms demand advanced systems, this practice is expected to grow. Systems analysts are expected to grow 43 percent in the computer systems design and related services industry.

Job Prospects

Job applicants with a background in business may have better prospects because this occupation often requires knowledge of an organization's business needs. An understanding of the specific field an analyst is working in is also helpful. For example, a hospital may desire an analyst with a background or coursework in health management.

Employment projections data for computer systems analysts, 2010-20

Occupational Title	SOC Code	Employment, 2010	Projected Employment, 2020	Change, 2010-20	
				Percent	Numeric
Computer Systems Analysts	15-1121	544,400	664,800	22	120,400
SOURCE: U.S. Bureau of Labor Statistics, Employment Projections program					

Similar Occupations

This table shows a list of occupations with job duties that are similar to those of computer systems analysts.

Occupation	Job Duties	Entry-Level Education	Median Annual Pay, May 2010
Actuaries	Actuaries analyze the financial costs of risk and uncertainty. They use mathematics, statistics, and financial theory to assess the risk that an event will occur and to help businesses and clients develop policies that minimize the cost of that risk.	Bachelor's degree	$87,650
Computer and Information Research Scientists	Computer and information research scientists invent and design new technology and find new uses for existing technology. They study and solve complex problems in computing for business, science, medicine, and other uses.	Doctoral or professional degree	$100,660
Computer and Information Systems Managers	Computer and information systems managers, often called information technology managers (IT managers or IT project managers), plan, coordinate, and direct computer-related activities in an organization. They help determine the information technology goals of an organization and are responsible for implementing the appropriate computer systems to meet those goals.	Bachelor's degree	$115,780
Computer Programmers	Computer programmers write code to create software programs. They turn the program designs created by software developers and engineers into instructions that a computer can follow.	Bachelor's degree	$71,380
Database Administrators	Database administrators use software to store and organize data, such as financial information and customer shipping records. They make sure that data are available to users and are secure from unauthorized access.	Bachelor's degree	$73,490
Information Security Analysts, Web Developers, and Computer Network Architects	Information security analysts, web developers, and computer network architects all use information technology (IT) to advance their organization's goals. Security analysts ensure a firm's information stays safe from cyberattacks. Web developers create websites to help firms have a public face. Computer network architects create the internal networks all workers within organizations use.	Bachelor's degree	$75,660
Management Analysts	Management analysts, often called management consultants, propose ways to improve an organization's efficiency. They advise managers on how to make organizations more profitable through reduced costs and increased revenues.	Bachelor's degree	$78,160
Network and Computer Systems Administrators	Network and computer systems administrators are responsible for the day-to-day operation of an organization's computer networks. They organize, install, and support an organization's computer systems, including local area networks (LANs), wide area networks (WANs), network segments, intranets, and other data communication systems.	Bachelor's degree	$69,160
Operations Research Analysts	Operations research analysts use advanced methods of analysis to help organizations solve problems and make better decisions.	Bachelor's degree	$70,960

Software Developers	Software developers are the creative minds behind computer programs. Some develop the applications that allow people to do specific tasks on a computer or other device. Others develop the underlying systems that run the devices or control networks.	Bachelor's degree	$90,530

Contacts for More Information

For more information about computer systems analysts, visit Association for Computing Machinery, Institute of Electrical and Electronics Engineers Computer Society, Computing Research Association

For more information about education in information technology, visit National Workforce Center for Emerging Technologies

For information about opportunities for women pursuing IT careers, visit National Center for Women and Information Technology

Suggested citation:

Bureau of Labor Statistics, U.S. Department of Labor, Occupational Outlook Handbook, 2012-13 Edition, Computer Systems Analysts, on the Internet at http://www.bls.gov/ooh/computer-and-information-technology/computer-systems-analysts.htm.

Database Administrators

Quick Facts: Database Administrators	
2010 Median Pay	$73,490 per year $35.33 per hour
Entry-Level Education	Bachelor's degree
Work Experience in a Related Occupation	1 to 5 years
On-the-job Training	None
Number of Jobs, 2010	110,800
Job Outlook, 2010-20	31% (Much faster than average)
Employment Change, 2010-20	33,900

What Database Administrators Do

Database administrators use software to store and organize data, such as financial information and customer shipping records. They make sure that data are available to users and are secure from unauthorized access.

Duties

Database administrators typically do the following:
- Identify user needs to create and administer databases
- Ensure that the database operates efficiently and without error
- Make and test modifications to the database structure when needed

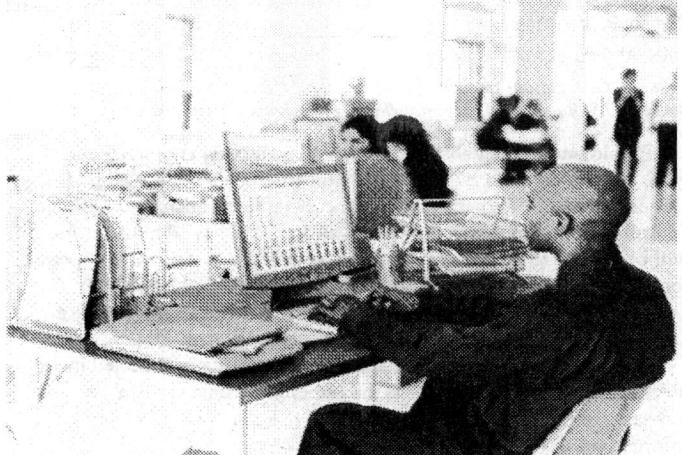

Database administrators ensure databases run efficiently.

- Maintain the database and update permissions
- Merge old databases into new ones
- Backup and restore data to prevent data loss

Database administrators, often called DBAs, make sure that data analysts can easily use the database to find the information they need and that the system performs as it should. DBAs sometimes work with an organization's management to understand the company's data needs and to plan the goals of the database. Database administrators often plan security measures, making sure that data are secure from unauthorized access. Many databases contain personal or financial information, making security important. Database administrators are responsible for backing up systems in case of a power outage or other disaster. They also ensure the integrity of the database, guaranteeing that the data stored in it come from reliable sources.

Many database administrators are general-purpose DBAs and have all these duties. However, some DBAs specialize in certain tasks that vary with the organization and its needs. Two common specialties are as follows:

System DBAs are responsible for the physical and technical aspects of a database, such as installing upgrades and patches to fix program bugs. They typically have a background in system architecture and ensure that the database in a firm's computer systems works properly.

Application DBAs support a database that has been designed for a specific application or a set of applications, such as customer service software. Using complex programming languages, they may write or debug programs and must be able to manage the aspects of the applications that work with the database. They also do all the tasks of a general DBA, but only for their particular application.

Work Environment

Database administrators (DBAs) held about 110,800 jobs in 2010, and were employed in many types of industries. The largest number work for computer systems design and related services firms, such as Internet service providers and data-processing firms. Other DBAs are employed by firms with large databases, such as insurance companies and banks, both of which keep track of vast amounts of personal and financial data for their clients. Some DBAs administer databases for retail companies that keep track of their buyers' credit card and shipping information; others work for healthcare firms and manage patients' medical records.

The following industries employed the most database administrators in 2010:

Computer systems design and related services	15%
Finance and insurance	13
Information	10
Educational services; state, local, and private	9
Government	7

Work Schedules

Almost all database administrators work full time and about 25 percent work more than 40 hours per week.

How to Become a Database Administrator

Database administrators (DBAs) usually have a bachelor's degree in an information- or computer- related subject. Before becoming an administrator, these workers typically get experience in a related field.

Education

Most database administrators have a bachelor's degree in management information systems (MIS) or a computer-related field. Firms with large databases may prefer applicants who have a Master of Business Administration (MBA) with a concentration in information systems. An MBA typically requires 2 years of schooling after the undergraduate level.

Database administrators need an understanding of database languages, the most common of which is SQL. Most database systems use some variation of SQL, and a DBA will need to become familiar with whichever language the firm uses.

Certification

Certification is a way to demonstrate competence and may provide a jobseeker with a competitive advantage. Certification programs are generally offered by product vendors or software firms. Some companies may require their database administrators to be certified in the product they use.

Work Experience

Most database administrators do not begin their careers in that occupation. Many first work as database developers or data analysts. A database developer is a type of software developer who specializes in creating databases. The job of a data analyst is to interpret the information stored in a database in a way the firm can use. Depending on their specialty, data analysts can have different job titles, including financial analyst, market research analyst, and operations research analyst. After mastering these fields, they may become a database administrator. For more information, see the profiles on software developers , financial analysts , market research analysts , and operations research analysts.

Important Qualities

Analytical skills. DBAs must be able to monitor a database system's performance to determine when action is needed. They must be able to evaluate complex information that comes from a variety of sources.

Communication skills. Most database administrators work on teams and must be able to communicate effectively with developers, managers, and other workers.

Detail oriented. Working with databases requires an understanding of complex systems, in which a minor error can cause major problems. For example, mixing up customers' credit card information can cause someone to be charged for a purchase he or she didn't make.

Logical thinking. Database administrators use software to make sense of information and to arrange and organize it into meaningful patterns. The information is then stored in the databases that these workers administer, test, and maintain.

Problem-solving skills. When problems with a database arise, administrators must be able to diagnose and correct them.

Pay

Database Administrators
Median annual wages, May 2010

Computer Occupations	$73,710
Database Administrators	$73,490
Total, All Occupations	$33,840

Note: All Occupations includes all occupations in the U.S. Economy.
Source: U.S. Bureau of Labor Statistics, Occupational Employment Statistics

The median annual wage of database administrators (DBAs) was $73,490 in May 2010. The median wage is the wage at which half the workers in an occupation earned more than that amount and half earned less. The lowest 10 percent earned less than $41,570, and the top 10 percent earned more than $115,660.

The wages for DBAs vary with the industry in which they work:

Computer systems design and related services	$82,820
Finance and insurance	81,640
Federal, state, and local government	69,320
Health care and social assistance	65,380
Educational services	62,580

Almost all database administrators work full time, and about 25 percent work more than 40 hours per week.

Job Outlook

Database Administrators
Percent change in employment, projected 2010-20

Database Administrators	31%
Computer Occupations	22%
Total, All Occupations	14%

Note: All Occupations includes all occupations in the U.S. Economy.
Source: U.S. Bureau of Labor Statistics, Employment Projections program

Employment of database administrators (DBAs) is projected to grow 31 percent from 2010 to 2020, much faster than the average for all occupations. Rapid growth in data collection by businesses will contribute to the growth of this occupation. Database administrators will be needed to organize and present data in a way that makes it easy for analysts and other stakeholders to understand. Additional job growth will occur as database security needs grow and as DBAs are called on to implement information security measures.

Employment growth for database administrators is expected in healthcare industries because, as the use of electronic medical records increases, more databases will be needed to keep track of patient information.

Job Prospects

Job prospects should be favorable. Database administrators are in high demand, and firms sometimes have difficulty finding qualified workers. Applicants who have experience with new technology should have the best prospects.

Employment projections data for database administrators, 2010-20

Occupational Title	SOC Code	Employment, 2010	Projected Employment, 2020	Change, 2010-20	
				Percent	Numeric
Database Administrators	15-1141	110,800	144,800	31	33,900
SOURCE: U.S. Bureau of Labor Statistics, Employment Projections program					

Similar Occupations

This table shows a list of occupations with job duties that are similar to those of database administrators.

Occupation	Job Duties	Entry-Level Education	Median Annual Pay, May 2010
Computer and Information Systems Managers	Computer and information systems managers, often called information technology managers (IT managers or IT project managers), plan, coordinate, and direct computer-related activities in an organization. They help determine the information technology goals of an organization and are responsible for implementing the appropriate computer systems to meet those goals.	Bachelor's degree	$115,780
Computer Programmers	Computer programmers write code to create software programs. They turn the program designs created by software developers and engineers into instructions that a computer can follow.	Bachelor's degree	$71,380
Computer Support Specialists	Computer support specialists provide help and advice to people and organizations using computer software or equipment. Some, called technical support specialists, support information technology (IT) employees within their organization. Others, called help-desk technicians, assist non-IT users who are having computer problems.	Some college, no degree	$46,260
Computer Systems Analysts	Computer systems analysts study an organization's current computer systems and procedures and make recommendations to management to help the organization operate more efficiently and effectively. They bring business and information technology (IT) together by understanding the needs and limitations of both.	Bachelor's degree	$77,740
Information Security Analysts, Web Developers, and Computer Network Architects	Information security analysts, web developers, and computer network architects all use information technology (IT) to advance their organization's goals. Security analysts ensure a firm's information stays safe from cyberattacks. Web developers create websites to help firms have a public face. Computer network architects create the internal networks all workers within organizations use.	Bachelor's degree	$75,660
Network and Computer Systems Administrators	Network and computer systems administrators are responsible for the day-to-day operation of an organization's computer networks. They organize, install, and support an organization's computer systems, including local area networks (LANs), wide area networks (WANs), network segments, intranets, and other data communication systems.	Bachelor's degree	$69,160
Operations Research Analysts	Operations research analysts use advanced methods of analysis to help organizations solve problems and make better decisions.	Bachelor's degree	$70,960
Software Developers	Software developers are the creative minds behind computer programs. Some develop the applications that allow people to do specific tasks on a computer or other device. Others develop the underlying systems that run the devices or control networks.	Bachelor's degree	$90,530
Statisticians	Statisticians use mathematical techniques to analyze and interpret data and draw conclusions.	Master's degree	$72,830

Contacts for More Information

For more information about database administrators, visit Association for Computing Machinery, Institute of Electrical and Electronics Engineers Computer Society, Computing Research Association

For information about an education in information technology (IT), visit National Workforce Center for Emerging Technologies

For information regarding opportunities for women pursuing IT careers, visit National Center for Women and Information Technology

Suggested citation:

Bureau of Labor Statistics, U.S. Department of Labor, Occupational Outlook Handbook, 2012-13 Edition, Database Administrators, on the Internet at http://www.bls.gov/ooh/computer-and-information-technology/database-administrators.htm.

Information Security Analysts, Web Developers, and Computer Network Architects

Quick Facts: Information Security Analysts, Web Developers, and Computer Network Architects	
2010 Median Pay	$75,660 per year $36.37 per hour
Entry-Level Education	Bachelor's degree
Work Experience in a Related Occupation	1 to 5 years
On-the-job Training	None
Number of Jobs, 2010	302,300
Job Outlook, 2010-20	22% (Faster than average)
Employment Change, 2010-20	65,700

What Information Security Analysts, Web Developers, and Computer Network Architects Do

Information security analysts, web developers, and computer network architects all use information technology (IT) to advance their organization's goals. Security analysts ensure a firm's information stays safe from cyberattacks. Web developers create websites to help firms have a public face. Computer network architects create the internal networks all workers within organizations use.

Duties

Information security analysts plan and carry out security measures to protect an organization's computer networks and systems. Their responsibilities are continually expanding as the number of cyberattacks increase.

Information security analysts typically do the following:

Network architects design LANs, WANs, and intranets.

- Research the latest information technology security trends
- Monitor their organization's networks for security breaches and investigate a violation when one occurs
- Help plan and carry out an organization's way of handling security
- Develop security standards and best practices for their organization
- Install and use software, such as firewalls and data encryption programs, to protect sensitive information
- Recommend security enhancements to management or senior IT staff
- Help computer users when they need to install or learn about new security products and procedures

Information security analysts must continually adapt to stay a step ahead of cyberattackers. They must stay up to date on the latest methods attackers are using to infiltrate computer systems and on IT security. Analysts need to research new security technology to decide what will most effectively protect their organization. This may involve attending cybersecurity conferences to hear firsthand accounts of other professionals who have experienced new types of attacks.

IT security analysts create their organization's disaster recovery plan, a procedure that IT employees follow in case of emergency. The plan lets an organization's IT department continue functioning. It includes preventative measures such as regularly copying and transferring data to an offsite location. It also involves plans to restore proper IT functioning after a disaster. Analysts continually test the steps in their recovery plans.

Because information security is important, analysts usually report directly to upper management. Many information security analysts work with an organization's Chief Technology Officer (CTO) to design security or disaster recovery systems. For more information on chief technology officers, see the profile on computer and information systems managers.

Computer network architects, or **network engineers**, design and build data communication networks, including local area networks (LANs), wide area networks (WANs), and intranets. These networks range from a small connection between two offices to a multinational series of globally distributed communications systems. Network architects must have thorough knowledge of an organization's business plan to design a network that can help the organization achieve its goals.

Computer network architects typically do the following:
- Create a plan and layout for a data communication network
- Present the plan to management and explain why it is in the organization's best interest to pursue it
- Decide what hardware, such as routers or adaptors, and software, such as network drivers, will be needed to support the network
- Determine how cables will be laid out in the building and where other hardware will go
- Research new technology to determine what would best support their organization in the future
- Consider information security when designing a network

Architects often work with their organization's Chief Technology Officer (CTO) to predict the highest need for new networks. They spend most of their time planning these new networks. Some network architects work in the field, supervising engineers and workers who build the networks an architect has designed. Network architects are often experienced staff and have 5 to 10 years of experience working in network administration or with other IT systems.

Web developers design and create websites. They are responsible for the look of the site. They are also responsible for the site's technical aspects, such as performance and capacity, which are measures of a website's speed and how much traffic the site can handle. They also may create content for the site.

Web developers typically do the following:
- Meet with their clients or management to discuss the needs of the website and the expected needs of the website's audience and plan how it should look
- Create and debug applications for a website
- Write code for the site, using programming languages such as HTML or XML
- Work with other team members to determine what information the site will contain
- Work with graphics and other designers to determine the website's layout
- Integrate graphics, audio, and video into the website
- Monitor website traffic

When creating a website, developers have to make their client's vision a reality. They work with clients to determine what sites should be used for, including ecommerce, news, or gaming. The developer has to decide which applications and designs will fit the site best.

The following are some types of web developers:

Web architects or programmers are responsible for the overall technical construction of the website. They create the basic framework of the site and ensure that it works as expected. Web architects also establish procedures for allowing others to add new pages to the website and meet with management to discuss major changes to the site.

Web designers are responsible for how a website looks. They create the site's layout and integrate graphics; applications, such as a retail checkout tool; and other content into the site. They also write web-design programs in a variety of computer languages, such as HTML or JavaScript.

Webmasters maintain websites and keep them updated. They ensure that websites operate correctly and test for errors such as broken links. Many webmasters respond to user comments as well.

Work Environment

Information security analysts, web developers, and computer network architects held about 302,300 jobs in 2010. The following table shows the industries that employed the most information security analysts, web developers and computer network architects in 2010:

Computer systems design and related services	18%
Telecommunications	8
Finance and insurance	7
Management of companies and enterprises	5

About 17 percent of information security analysts, web developers, and computer network architects were self-employed in 2010.

Work Schedules

Most information security analysts, web developers, and computer network architects work full time. Information security analysts sometimes have to be on call outside of normal business hours in case of an emergency at their organization.

How to Become an Information Security Analyst, Web Developer, or Computer Network Architect

Most information security analysts, web developers, and computer network architects have a bachelor's degree in a computer-related field. Information security analysts and computer network architects usually need experience in a related occupation, and additional knowledge of web programming languages can help web developers.

Education

Information security analysts usually need at least a bachelor's degree in computer science, programming, or a related field. As information security continues to develop as a career field, many schools are responding with information security programs to prepare students for the job. These programs may become a common path for entry into the occupation.

Employers of information security analysts sometimes prefer applicants who have a Master of Business Administration (MBA) in information systems. Programs offering the MBA in information systems generally require 2 years of study beyond the undergraduate level and include both business and computer-related courses.

Computer network architects usually need at least a bachelor's degree in computer science, information systems, engineering, or a related field. Employers of network architects sometimes prefer applicants to have a Master of Business Administration (MBA) in information systems. These programs generally require 2 years of study beyond the undergraduate level and include both business and computer-related courses.

Educational requirements for web developers vary with the setting they work in and the type of work they do. Requirements range from a high school diploma to a bachelor's degree. An associate's degree may be sufficient for webmasters who do not do a lot of programming.

However, for web architect or other, more technical, developer positions, some employers prefer workers who have at least a bachelor's degree in computer science, programming, or a related field.

Web developers need to have a thorough understanding of HTML. Many employers also want developers to understand other languages, such as JavaScript or SQL, as well as have some knowledge of multimedia publishing tools, such as Flash. Throughout their career, web developers must keep up to date on new tools and computer languages.

Some employers prefer web developers who have both a computer degree and have taken classes in graphic design, especially when hiring developers who will be heavily involved in the website's visual appearance.

Work Experience

Information security analysts generally need to have previous experience in a related occupation. Many employers look for people who have already worked in fields related to the one in which they are hiring. For example, if the job opening is in database security, they may look for a database administrator. If they are hiring in systems security, a computer systems analyst may be an ideal candidate.

Network architects generally need to have previous experience in a related occupation. They usually have at least 5 to 10 years of experience working in network administration or with other information technology (IT) systems.

Important Qualities

Analytical skills. Information security analysts must carefully examine computer systems and networks to determine if they have been compromised. Computer network architects have to examine data networks and decide how to best connect the networks based on the needs and resources of the organization.

Concentration. Web developers must sit at a computer and write detailed code for long periods.

Creativity. Web developers are often involved in designing the appearance of a website and must make sure that it looks innovative and up to date.

Customer-service skills. Webmasters have to respond politely and correctly to user questions and requests.

Detail oriented. Because cyberattacks can be difficult to detect, information security analysts pay careful attention to their computer systems and watch for minor changes in performance. Computer network architects create comprehensive plans of the networks they are creating with precise information describing how the network parts will work together. When web developers write in HTML, a minor error could cause an entire webpage to stop working.

Ingenuity. Information security analysts try to outthink cybercriminals and invent new ways to protect their organization's computer systems and networks.

Leadership skills. Many computer network architects direct teams of engineers who build the networks they have designed.

Organization skills. Computer network architects who work for large firms must coordinate many different types of communication networks and make sure they work well together.

Problem-solving skills. Information security analysts uncover and fix flaws in computer systems and networks.

Teamwork. Workers in all three of these occupations must be able to work with different types of employees to accomplish their goals.

Pay

Information Security Analysts, Web Developers, and Computer Network Architects
Median annual wages, May 2010

Information Security Analysts, Web Developers, and Network Architects	$75,660
Computer Occupations	$73,710
Total, All Occupations	$33,840

Note: All Occupations includes all occupations in the U.S. Economy.
Source: U.S. Bureau of Labor Statistics, Occupational Employment Statistics

The median annual wage of information security analysts, web developers, and computer network architects was $75,660 in May 2010. The median wage is the wage at which half the workers in an occupation earned more than that amount and half earned less. The lowest 10 percent earned less than $43,190, and the top 10 percent earned more than $119,940.

A survey by Robert Half Technology estimated the salary of data

security analysts to be between $89,000 and $121,500 in 2012 and a systems or network security administrator's wages to be between $85,000 and $117,750.

The same survey estimated that a network architect makes between $95,500 and $137,000 in 2012.

Web developers make between $61,250 and $99,250 in 2012 according to Robert Half Technology.

Most information security analysts, web developers, and computer network architects work full time. Information security analysts sometimes have to be on call outside of normal business hours in case of an emergency at their organization.

Job Outlook

Information Security Analysts, Web Developers, and Computer Network Architects
Percent change in employment, projected 2010-20

Information Security Analysts, Web Developers, and Network Architects	22%
Computer Occupations	22%
Total, All Occupations	14%

Note: All Occupations includes all occupations in the U.S. Economy.
Source: U.S. Bureau of Labor Statistics, Employment Projections program

Employment of information security analysts, web developers, and computer network architects is projected to grow 22 percent from 2010 to 2020, faster than the average for all occupations.

Demand for information security analysts is expected to be very high. Cyberattacks have grown in frequency and sophistication over the last few years, and many organizations are behind in their ability to detect these attacks. Analysts will be needed to come up with innovative ways to prevent hackers from stealing critical information or creating havoc on computer networks.

The federal government is expected to greatly increase its hiring of information security analysts to protect the nation's critical information technology (IT) systems. In addition, as the healthcare industry expands its use of electronic medical records, ensuring patients' privacy and protecting personal data are becoming more important. More information security analysts are likely to be needed to create the safeguards that will satisfy patients' concerns.

Demand for computer network architects will increase as firms continue to expand their use of wireless and mobile networks. This occupation will be needed to design and build these new networks, as well as upgrade existing ones. In addition, the expansion of healthcare information technology will cause an increase in the use of networking technology in that industry, and more computer network architects will be employed there.

Adoption of cloud computing, which allows users to access storage, software, and other computer services over the Internet, is likely to cause a decrease in the demand for computer network architects. Organizations will no longer have to design and build networks in-house; instead, this will be done by firms that provide cloud services. However, because architects at cloud providers can work on more than one organization's network, these providers will not have to employ as many architects as individual organizations to do the same amount of work, thereby reducing the overall need for network architects.

Employment of web developers is expected to grow as ecommerce continues to grow. Online purchasing is expected to continue to grow faster than the overall retail industry. As retail firms expand their online offerings, demand for web developers will increase.

Because websites can be built from anywhere in the world, some web developer jobs may be moved to countries with lower wages, lessening U.S. job growth. However, this practice may decline because of a growing trend of firms hiring workers in low-cost areas of the U.S. instead of in foreign countries.

Job Prospects

Prospects for information security analysts should be good. Information security analysts with related work experience will have the best opportunities. For example, an applicant with experience as a database administrator would have better prospects in database security than someone without that experience.

Prospects for computer network architects should be favorable, as many companies report difficulty finding network architects due to the considerable amount of education and work experience required for these highly skilled positions.

Web developers' job prospects should also be favorable. Those with knowledge of multiple programming languages and digital multimedia tools, such as Flash and Photoshop, will have the best opportunities.

Employment projections data for information security analysts, web developers, and computer network architects, 2010-20

Occupational Title	SOC Code	Employment, 2010	Projected Employment, 2020	Change, 2010-20	
				Percent	Numeric
Information Security Analysts, Web Developers, and Computer Network Architects	15-1179	302,300	367,900	22	65,700
SOURCE: U.S. Bureau of Labor Statistics, Employment Projections program					

Similar Occupations

This table shows a list of occupations with job duties that are similar to those of information security analysts, web developers, and computer network architects.

Occupation	Job Duties	Entry-Level Education	Median Annual Pay, May 2010
Computer and Information Research Scientists	Computer and information research scientists invent and design new technology and find new uses for existing technology. They study and solve complex problems in computing for business, science, medicine, and other uses.	Doctoral or professional degree	$100,660
Computer and Information Systems Managers	Computer and information systems managers, often called information technology managers (IT managers or IT project managers), plan, coordinate, and direct computer-related activities in an organization. They help determine the information technology goals of an organization and are responsible for implementing the appropriate computer systems to meet those goals.	Bachelor's degree	$115,780
Computer Hardware Engineers	Computer hardware engineers research, design, develop, and test computer equipment such as chips, circuit boards, or routers. By solving complex problems in computer hardware, these engineers create rapid advances in computer technology.	Bachelor's degree	$98,810
Computer Programmers	Computer programmers write code to create software programs. They turn the program designs created by software developers and engineers into instructions that a computer can follow.	Bachelor's degree	$71,380
Computer Support Specialists	Computer support specialists provide help and advice to people and organizations using computer software or equipment. Some, called technical support specialists, support information technology (IT) employees within their organization. Others, called help-desk technicians, assist non-IT users who are having computer problems.	Some college, no degree	$46,260
Computer Systems Analysts	Computer systems analysts study an organization's current computer systems and procedures and make recommendations to management to help the organization operate more efficiently and effectively. They bring business and information technology (IT) together by understanding the needs and limitations of both.	Bachelor's degree	$77,740
Database Administrators	Database administrators use software to store and organize data, such as financial information and customer shipping records. They make sure that data are available to users and are secure from unauthorized access.	Bachelor's degree	$73,490
Graphic Designers	Graphic designers create visual concepts, by hand or using computer software, to communicate ideas that inspire, inform, or captivate consumers. They help to make an organization recognizable by selecting color, images, or logo designs that represent a particular idea or identity to be used in advertising and promotions.	Bachelor's degree	$43,500
Network and Computer Systems Administrators	Network and computer systems administrators are responsible for the day-to-day operation of an organization's computer networks. They organize, install, and support an organization's computer systems, including local area networks (LANs), wide area networks (WANs), network segments, intranets, and other data communication systems.	Bachelor's degree	$69,160

Software Developers	Software developers are the creative minds behind computer programs. Some develop the applications that allow people to do specific tasks on a computer or other device. Others develop the underlying systems that run the devices or control networks.	Bachelor's degree	$90,530
Technical Writers	Technical writers, also called technical communicators, produce instruction manuals and other supporting documents to communicate complex and technical information more easily. They also develop, gather, and disseminate technical information among customers, designers, and manufacturers.	Bachelor's degree	$63,280

Contacts for More Information

For more information about computer careers, visit Association for Computing Machinery, Institute of Electrical and Electronics Engineers Computer Society, Computer Research Association

For more information about an education in information technology (IT), visit National Workforce Center for Emerging Technologies

For information about opportunities for women pursuing IT careers, visit National Center for Women and Information Technology

Suggested citation:

Bureau of Labor Statistics, U.S. Department of Labor, Occupational Outlook Handbook, 2012-13 Edition, Information Security Analysts, Web Developers, and Computer Network Architects, on the Internet at http://www.bls.gov/ooh/computer-and-information-technology/informa tion-security-analysts-web-developers-and-computer-network-architect s.htm.

Network and Computer Systems Administrators

Quick Facts: Network and Computer Systems Administrators	
2010 Median Pay	$69,160 per year $33.25 per hour
Entry-Level Education	Bachelor's degree
Work Experience in a Related Occupation	None
On-the-job Training	None
Number of Jobs, 2010	347,200
Job Outlook, 2010-20	28% (Faster than average)
Employment Change, 2010-20	96,600

What Network and Computer Systems Administrators Do

Computer networks are critical parts of almost every organization. Network and computer systems administrators are responsible for the day-to-day operation of these networks. They organize, install, and support an organization's computer systems, including local area networks (LANs), wide area networks (WANs), network segments, intranets, and other data communication systems.

Duties

Network and computer systems administrators typically do the following:

- Determine what the organization needs in a network and computer system before it is set up
- Install all network hardware and software and make needed upgrades and repairs
- Maintain network and computer system security and ensure that all systems are operating correctly
- Collect data to evaluate the network's or system's performance and help make the system work better and faster
- Train users on the proper use of hardware and software when necessary
- Solve problems quickly when a user or an automated monitoring system lets them know about a problem

Administrators manage an organization's servers. They ensure that email and data storage networks work properly. They also make sure that employees' workstations are working efficiently and stay connected to the central computer network. Some administrators manage telecommunication networks at their organization.

In some cases, administrators help network architects who design and analyze network models. They also participate in decisions about buying future hardware or software to upgrade the organization's network. Some administrators provide technical support to computer users, and they may supervise computer support specialists who help users with computer problems.

Work Environment

Network and computer systems administrators held about 347,200 jobs in 2010. They work with the physical computer networks of a variety of organizations and therefore are employed in many industries, including educational institutions, hospitals, banks, large corporations, and government agencies. Many also work for information technology (IT) firms.

Selected industries that employ network and computer systems administrators are as follows:

Computer systems design and related services	14%
Educational services; state, local, and private	12
Finance and insurance	10
Manufacturing	7
Telecommunications	6

Network and computer systems administrators work with many other types of workers. They often interact with network architects and

Administrators fix computer server problems.

IT management but also regularly work with an organization's non-IT staff. For more information, see the profiles on <u>information security analysts, web developers, and computer network architects</u> and <u>computer and information systems managers</u>.

Work Schedules

In 2010, over 90 percent of network and computer systems administrators worked full time. Most organizations depend on their computer networks, so many administrators must work overtime to ensure that the networks are operating properly. Administrators may have to be at work outside of normal business hours to resolve problems.

How to Become a Network and Computer Systems Administrator

Network and computer systems administrators must often have a bachelor's degree, although some positions require an associate's degree or professional certification along with related work experience.

Education

A bachelor's degree in fields related to computer or information science is most common. However, because administrators work with computer hardware and equipment, a degree in computer engineering or electrical engineering usually is acceptable as well. These programs usually include classes in computer programming, networking, or systems design.

Some positions require an associate's degree or a postsecondary certificate in a computer field with related work experience.

Because network technology is continually changing, administrators need to keep up with the latest developments. Many continue to take courses throughout their careers. Some businesses require that an administrator get a master's degree.

Certification

Certification is a way to show a level of competence and may provide a jobseeker with a competitive advantage. Certification

programs are generally offered by product vendors or software firms. Companies may require their network and computer systems administrators to be certified in the product they use. Some of the most common certifications are offered from Microsoft, Red Hat, and Cisco.

Important Qualities

Analytical skills. Administrators need analytical skills to evaluate network and system performance and determine how changes in the environment will affect it.

Communication skills. Administrators work with many other types of workers and have to be able to describe problems and their solutions to them.

Computer skills. Administrators oversee the connections of many different types of computer equipment and must ensure that they all work together properly.

Multi-tasking skills. Administrators may have to work on many problems and tasks at the same time.

Problem-solving skills. Administrators must be able to quickly resolve problems with computer networks when they occur.

Pay

Network and Computer Systems Administrators
Median annual wages, May 2010

Computer Occupations	$73,710
Network and Computer Systems Administrators	$69,160
Total, All Occupations	$33,840

Note: All Occupations includes all occupations in the U.S. Economy.
Source: U.S. Bureau of Labor Statistics, Occupational Employment Statistics

The median annual wage of network and computer systems administrators was $69,160 in May 2010. The median wage is the wage at which half the workers in an occupation earned more than that amount and half earned less. The lowest 10 percent earned less than $42,400, and the top 10 percent earned more than $108,090.

Network and computer systems administrators are employed in many different industries, and pay varies by industry. The following table shows the median annual wages of these workers in some industries in which they are employed:

Computer systems design and related services	$74,230
Finance and insurance	72,660
Manufacturing	67,870
Health care and social assistance	64,560
Educational services; state, local, and private	59,230

In 2010, over 90 percent of network and computer systems administrators worked full time. Most organizations depend on their computer networks, so many administrators work overtime to ensure that the networks are operating properly. Administrators may have to be at work outside of normal business hours to resolve problems.

Job Outlook

Network and Computer Systems Administrators
Percent change in employment, projected 2010-20

Network and Computer Systems Administrators	28%
Computer Occupations	22%
Total, All Occupations	14%

Note: All Occupations includes all occupations in the U.S. Economy.
Source: U.S. Bureau of Labor Statistics, Employment Projections program

Employment of network and computer systems administrators is expected to grow 28 percent from 2010 to 2020, faster than the average for all occupations. Demand for these workers is high and should continue to grow as firms invest in newer, faster technology and mobile networks. In addition, information security concerns are increasing for many businesses as managers realize that their current security measures are not enough to combat growing threats. More administrators with proper training will be needed to reinforce network and system security.

Growth is expected in healthcare industries as their use of information technology increases. More administrators will be required to manage the growing systems and networks found at hospitals and other healthcare institutions.

Job Prospects

Job opportunities should be favorable for this occupation. Prospects should be best for applicants who have a bachelor's degree in computer science and who are up to date on the latest technology.

Employment projections data for network and computer systems administrators, 2010-20

Occupational Title	SOC Code	Employment, 2010	Projected Employment, 2020	Change, 2010-20	
				Percent	Numeric
Network and Computer Systems Administrators	15-1142	347,200	443,800	28	96,600

SOURCE: U.S. Bureau of Labor Statistics, Employment Projections program

Similar Occupations

This table shows a list of occupations with job duties that are similar to those of network and computer systems administrators.

Occupation	Job Duties	Entry-Level Education	Median Annual Pay, May 2010
Computer and Information Systems Managers	Computer and information systems managers, often called information technology managers (IT managers or IT project managers), plan, coordinate, and direct computer-related activities in an organization. They help determine the information technology goals of an organization and are responsible for implementing the appropriate computer systems to meet those goals.	Bachelor's degree	$115,780
Computer Hardware Engineers	Computer hardware engineers research, design, develop, and test computer equipment such as chips, circuit boards, or routers. By solving complex problems in computer hardware, these engineers create rapid advances in computer technology.	Bachelor's degree	$98,810
Computer Programmers	Computer programmers write code to create software programs. They turn the program designs created by software developers and engineers into instructions that a computer can follow.	Bachelor's degree	$71,380
Computer Support Specialists	Computer support specialists provide help and advice to people and organizations using computer software or equipment. Some, called technical support specialists, support information technology (IT) employees within their organization. Others, called help-desk technicians, assist non-IT users who are having computer problems.	Some college, no degree	$46,260
Computer Systems Analysts	Computer systems analysts study an organization's current computer systems and procedures and make recommendations to management to help the organization operate more efficiently and effectively. They bring business and information technology (IT) together by understanding the needs and limitations of both.	Bachelor's degree	$77,740
Database Administrators	Database administrators use software to store and organize data, such as financial information and customer shipping records. They make sure that data are available to users and are secure from unauthorized access.	Bachelor's degree	$73,490
Electrical and Electronics Engineers	Electrical engineers design, develop, test, and supervise the manufacturing of electrical equipment such as electric motors, radar and navigation systems, communications systems, and power generation equipment.Electronics engineers design and develop electronic equipment, such as broadcast and communications systems—from portable music players to global positioning systems (GPS).	Bachelor's degree	$87,180
Information Security Analysts, Web Developers, and Computer Network Architects	Information security analysts, web developers, and computer network architects all use information technology (IT) to advance their organization's goals. Security analysts ensure a firm's information stays safe from cyberattacks. Web developers create websites to help firms have a public face. Computer network architects create the internal networks all workers within organizations use.	Bachelor's degree	$75,660
Software Developers	Software developers are the creative minds behind computer programs. Some develop the applications that allow people to do specific tasks on a computer or other device. Others develop the underlying systems that run the devices or control networks.	Bachelor's degree	$90,530

Contacts for More Information

For more information about computer careers, visit Association for Computing Machinery, Institute of Electrical and Electronics Engineers Computer Society

For more information about IT education, visit National Workforce Center for Emerging Technologies

For more information about opportunities for women pursing IT careers, visit National Center for Women and Information Technology

Software Developers

Quick Facts: Software Developers	
2010 Median Pay	$90,530 per year $43.52 per hour
Entry-Level Education	Bachelor's degree
Work Experience in a Related Occupation	None
On-the-job Training	None
Number of Jobs, 2010	913,100
Job Outlook, 2010-20	30% (Much faster than average)
Employment Change, 2010-20	270,900

What Software Developers Do

Software developers are the creative minds behind computer programs. Some develop the applications that allow people to do specific tasks on a computer or other device. Others develop the underlying systems that run the devices or control networks.

Duties

Software developers typically do the following:

- Analyze users' needs, then design, test, and develop software to meet those needs
- Recommend software upgrades for customers' existing programs and systems
- Design each piece of the application or system and plan how the pieces will work together
- Create flowcharts and other models that instruct programmers how to write the software's code

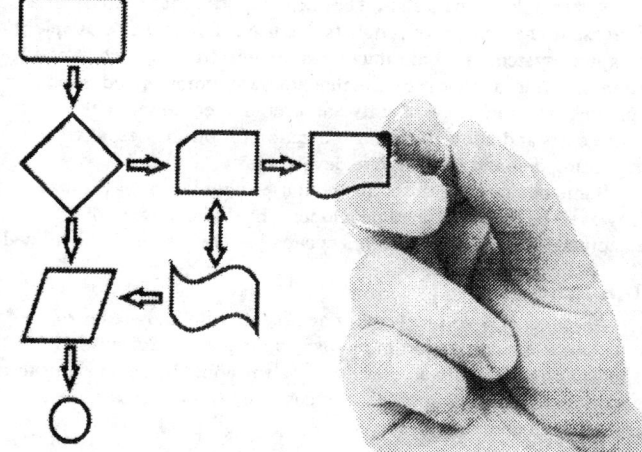

Developers create flow charts that help programmers write computer code.

- Ensure that the software continues to function normally through software maintenance and testing
- Document every aspect of the application or system as a reference for future maintenance and upgrades
- Collaborate with other computer specialists to create optimum software

Software developers are in charge of the entire development process for a software program. They begin by understanding how the customer plans to use the software. They design the program and then give instructions to programmers, who write computer code and test it. If the program does not work as expected or people find it to difficult to use, software developers go back to the design process to fix the problems or improve the program. After the program is released to the customer, a developer may perform upgrades and maintenance.

Developers usually work closely with computer programmers. However, in some companies, developers write code themselves instead of giving instructions to programmers. For more information, see the profile on computer programmers.

Developers who supervise a software project from the planning stages through implementation sometimes are called IT (information technology) project managers. These workers monitor the project's progress to ensure that it meets deadlines, standards, and cost targets. IT project managers who plan and direct an organization's IT department or IT policies are included in the profile on computer and information systems managers. For more information, see the profile on computer and information systems managers.

The following are types of software developers:

Applications software developers design computer applications, such as word processors and games, for consumers. They may create custom software for a specific customer or commercial software to be sold to the general public. Some applications software developers create complex databases for organizations. They also create programs that people use over the Internet and within a company's intranet.

Systems software developers create the systems that keep computers functioning properly. These could be operating systems that are part of computers the general public buys or systems built specifically for an organization. Often, systems software developers also build the system's interface, which is what allows users to interact with the computer. Systems software developers create the operating systems that control most of the consumer electronics in use today, including those in phones or cars.

Work Environment

Software developers held 913,100 jobs in 2010.

Many software developers work for computer systems design and related services firms or software publishers. Some work in computer and electronic product manufacturing industries. Some developers telecommute (work away from the office).

The following table shows the industries where software developers are most commonly employed.

Computer systems design and related services	32%
Computer and electronic product manufacturing	10
Finance and insurance	8
Software publishers	7

Work Schedules

Most software developers work full time, and long hours are common. Nearly one-fourth worked more than 40 hours per week in 2010.

How to Become a Software Developer

Software developers usually have a bachelor's degree in computer science and strong computer-programming skills.

Education

Software developers usually have a bachelor's degree, typically in computer science, software engineering, or a related field. A degree in mathematics is also acceptable. Computer science degree programs are the most common, because they tend to cover a broad range of topics. Students should focus on classes related to building software in order to better prepare themselves for work in the occupation. For some positions, employers may prefer a master's degree.

Although writing code is not their first priority, developers must have a strong background in computer programming. They usually gain this experience in school. Throughout their career, developers must keep up to date on new tools and computer languages.

Software developers also need skills related to the industry in which they work. Developers working in a bank, for example, should have knowledge of finance so that they can understand a bank's computing needs.

Important Qualities

Analytical skills. Developers must analyze users' needs and then design software to meet those needs.

Communication skills. Developers must be able to give clear instructions to others working on a project.

Creativity. Developers are the creative minds behind a new piece of computer software.

Customer-service skills. Some developers must be able to explain to their customers how the software works and answer any questions that arise.

Detail oriented. Developers often work on many parts of an application or system at the same time and must be able to concentrate and pay attention to detail.

Problem-solving skills. Because developers are in charge of the software from beginning to end, they must be able to solve problems that arise throughout the design process.

Teamwork. Software developers must be able to work well with others, who contribute to designing, developing, and programming

successful software.

Technical skills. Developers must understand computer capabilities and languages in order to design an effective piece of software.

Pay

Software Developers
Median annual wages, May 2010

Software Developers, Systems Software	$94,180
Software Developers	$90,530
Software Developers, Applications	$87,790
Total, All Occupations	$33,840

Note: All Occupations includes all occupations in the U.S. Economy.
Source: U.S. Bureau of Labor Statistics, Occupational Employment Statistics

The median annual wage of applications developers was $87,790 in May 2010. The median wage is the wage at which half the workers in an occupation earned more than the amount and half earned less. The lowest 10 percent earned less than $54,360, and the top 10 percent earned more than $133,110. The median annual wage of systems developers was $94,180 in May 2010. The lowest 10 percent earned less than $61,040, and the top 10 percent earned more than $143,330.

Most software developers work full time, and long hours are common. Nearly one-fourth worked more than 40 hours per week in 2010.

Job Outlook

Software Developers
Percent change in employment, projected 2010-20

Software Developers, Systems Software	32%
Software Developers	30%
Software Developers, Applications	28%
Total, All Occupations	14%

Note: All Occupations includes all occupations in the U.S. Economy.
Source: U.S. Bureau of Labor Statistics, Employment Projections program

Employment of software developers is projected to grow 30 percent from 2010 to 2020, much faster than the average for all occupations. Employment of applications developers is projected to grow 28 percent, and employment of systems developers is projected to grow 32 percent.

The main reason for the rapid growth is a large increase in the demand for computer software. Mobile technology requires new applications. Also, the healthcare industry is greatly increasing its use of computer systems and applications. Finally, concerns over cybersecurity should result in more investment in security software to protect computer networks and electronic infrastructure.

Systems developers should see new opportunities because of an increase in the number of products that use software. For example, computer systems are built into consumer electronics, such as cell phones, and into other products that are now computerized, such as appliances. An increase in software offered over the Internet should lower costs and allow more customization for businesses, also increasing demand for software developers.

Some outsourcing to foreign countries with lower wages may occur. However, because software developers should be close to their customers, the offshoring of this occupation is expected to be limited.

Job Prospects

Job prospects will be best for applicants with knowledge of the most up-to-date programming tools and languages. Consulting opportunities for software developers also should be good as businesses seek help to manage, upgrade, and customize their increasingly complicated computer systems.

Employment projections data for software developers, 2010-20

Occupational Title	SOC Code	Employment, 2010	Projected Employment, 2020	Change, 2010-20	
				Percent	Numeric
Software Developers	—	913,100	1,184,000	30	270,900
Software Developers, Applications	15-1132	520,800	664,500	28	143,800
Software Developers, Systems Software	15-1133	392,300	519,400	32	127,200
SOURCE: U.S. Bureau of Labor Statistics, Employment Projections program					

Similar Occupations

This table shows a list of occupations with job duties that are similar to those of software developers.

Occupation	Job Duties	Entry-Level Education	Median Annual Pay, May 2010
Computer and Information Research Scientists	Computer and information research scientists invent and design new technology and find new uses for existing technology. They study and solve complex problems in computing for business, science, medicine, and other uses.	Doctoral or professional degree	$100,660
Computer and Information Systems Managers	Computer and information systems managers, often called information technology managers (IT managers or IT project managers), plan, coordinate, and direct computer-related activities in an organization. They help determine the information technology goals of an organization and are responsible for implementing the appropriate computer systems to meet those goals.	Bachelor's degree	$115,780
Computer Hardware Engineers	Computer hardware engineers research, design, develop, and test computer equipment such as chips, circuit boards, or routers. By solving complex problems in computer hardware, these engineers create rapid advances in computer technology.	Bachelor's degree	$98,810
Computer Programmers	Computer programmers write code to create software programs. They turn the program designs created by software developers and engineers into instructions that a computer can follow.	Bachelor's degree	$71,380
Computer Support Specialists	Computer support specialists provide help and advice to people and organizations using computer software or equipment. Some, called technical support specialists, support information technology (IT) employees within their organization. Others, called help-desk technicians, assist non-IT users who are having computer problems.	Some college, no degree	$46,260
Computer Systems Analysts	Computer systems analysts study an organization's current computer systems and procedures and make recommendations to management to help the organization operate more efficiently and effectively. They bring business and information technology (IT) together by understanding the needs and limitations of both.	Bachelor's degree	$77,740
Database Administrators	Database administrators use software to store and organize data, such as financial information and customer shipping records. They make sure that data are available to users and are secure from unauthorized access.	Bachelor's degree	$73,490
Information Security Analysts, Web Developers, and Computer Network Architects	Information security analysts, web developers, and computer network architects all use information technology (IT) to advance their organization's goals. Security analysts ensure a firm's information stays safe from cyberattacks. Web developers create websites to help firms have a public face. Computer network architects create the internal networks all workers within organizations use.	Bachelor's degree	$75,660
Mathematicians	Mathematicians use high-level mathematics and technology to develop new mathematical principles, understand relationships between existing principles, and solve real-world problems.	Master's degree	$99,380

Contacts for More Information

For more information about software developers, visit Association for Computing Machinery, Institute of Electrical and Electronics Engineers Computer Society ,Computing Research Association

For more information about an IT education, visitNational Workforce Center for Emerging Technologies

For more information about opportunities for women pursuing IT careers, visit National Center for Women and Information Technology

Suggested citation:

Bureau of Labor Statistics, U.S. Department of Labor, Occupational Outlook Handbook, 2012-13 Edition, Software Developers, on the Internet at http://www.bls.gov/ooh/computer-and-information-technology/software-developers.htm.

Boilermakers

Quick Facts: Boilermakers	
2010 Median Pay	$54,640 per year $26.27 per hour
Entry-Level Education	High school diploma or equivalent
Work Experience in a Related Occupation	None
On-the-job Training	Apprenticeship
Number of Jobs, 2010	19,800
Job Outlook, 2010-20	21% (Faster than average)
Employment Change, 2010-20	4,200

What Boilermakers Do

Boilermakers assemble, install, and repair boilers, closed vats, and other large vessels or containers that hold liquids and gases.

Duties

Boilermakers typically do the following:

- Use blueprints to determine locations, positions, or dimensions of parts
- Install small premade boilers into buildings and manufacturing facilities
- Lay out prefabricated parts of larger boilers before assembling them
- Assemble boiler tanks, often using robotic or automatic welders
- Test and inspect boiler systems for leaks or defects
- Clean vats using scrapers, wire brushes, and cleaning solvents
- Replace or repair broken valves, pipes, or joints, using hand and power tools, gas torches, and welding equipment

Boilers, tanks, and vats are used in many buildings, factories, and ships. Boilers heat water or other fluids under extreme pressure to generate electric power and to provide heat. Large tanks and vats are used to store and process chemicals, oil, beer, and hundreds of other products.

Boilers are made out of steel, iron, copper, or stainless steel. Manufacturers are increasingly automating the production of boilers to improve the quality of these vessels. However, boilermakers still use many tools in making or repairing boilers. For example, they use hand and power tools or flame cutting torches to cut pieces for a boiler. To bend the pieces into shape and accurately line them up, boilermakers

Boilermakers often weld.

use plumb bobs, levels, wedges, and turnbuckles.

If the plate sections are very large, large cranes lift the parts into place. Once they have the parts lined up, they use metalworking machinery and other tools to remove irregular edges so the parts fit together properly. They join the parts by bolting, welding, or riveting them together.

In addition to installing and maintaining boilers and other vessels, boilermakers help erect and repair air pollution equipment, blast furnaces, water treatment plants, storage and process tanks, and smokestacks. Boilermakers also install refractory brick and other heat-resistant materials in fireboxes or pressure vessels. Some install and maintain the huge pipes used in dams to send water to and from hydroelectric power generation turbines.

Because boilers last a long time—sometimes 50 years or more—boilermakers must regularly maintain them and upgrade parts. They frequently inspect fittings, feed pumps, safety and check valves, water and pressure gauges, and boiler controls.

Work Environment

Boilermakers held about 19,800 jobs in 2010. Industries employing the most boilermakers in 2010 were as follows:

Nonresidential building construction	24%
Building equipment contractors	23
Utility system construction	11
Boiler, tank, and shipping container manufacturing	7

Boilermakers perform physically demanding and dangerous work. They often work outdoors in all types of weather, including extreme heat and cold.

Dams, boilers, storage tanks, and pressure vessels are usually large. Therefore, boilermakers often work at great heights. When working on a dam, for example, they may be hundreds of feet above the ground.

Boilermakers also work in cramped quarters inside boilers, vats, or tanks that are often dark, damp, and poorly ventilated.

Injuries

Although boilermakers often use dangerous equipment, they have lower rates of injuries and illnesses than many other construction occupations. Common injuries include burns from acetylene torches, cuts from power grinders, muscle strains from lifting heavy parts and tools, and falls from ladders or large vessels.

To reduce the chance of injury, boilermakers often wear hardhats, harnesses, protective clothing, earplugs, and safety glasses. In addition, when working inside enclosed spaces, boilermakers often need to wear a respirator.

Work Schedules

Nearly all boilermakers work full time and may experience extended periods of overtime when equipment is shut down for maintenance. Overtime work also may be necessary to meet construction or production deadlines.

In contrast, because most field construction and repair work is contract work, there may be periods of unemployment when a contract is complete.

Many boilermakers must travel to worksites and live away from home for long stretches of time.

How to Become a Boilermaker

Most boilermakers learn their trade through a formal apprenticeship program. Candidates are more likely to get into training programs if they already have welding experience and certification.

Apprenticeship

Most boilermakers learn their trade through a 4- or 5-year apprenticeship. Each year, apprentices must have at least 144 hours of related technical training and 2,000 hours of paid on-the-job training.

On the job, apprentices learn to use the tools and equipment of the trade. Those who already have welding experience complete training sooner than those without it.

In the technical training, apprentices learn about metals and installation techniques, as well as basic mathematics, blueprint reading and sketching, general construction techniques, safety practices, and first aid.

When they finish the apprenticeship program, boilermakers are considered to be journey workers, who perform tasks with guidance from more experienced workers.

A few groups, including unions and contractor associations, sponsor apprenticeship programs. The basic qualifications to enter an apprenticeship program are as follows:

● Minimum age of 18
● High school education or equivalent
● Physically able to do the work

In addition to satisfying these qualifications, candidates with certification or documented welding experience have priority over applicants without experience.

Education

A high school diploma or GED is generally required. High school courses in math and welding are considered to be useful.

Important Qualities

Physical strength. Workers must be strong enough to move heavy vat components into place.

Stamina. Workers must have high endurance because they spend many hours on their feet while lifting heavy boiler components.

Unafraid of confined spaces. Because workers often work inside boilers and vats, they cannot be claustrophobic.

Unafraid of heights. Some boilermakers must work at great heights. While installing water storage tanks, for example, workers may need to weld tanks several stories above the ground.

Pay

Boilermakers
Median annual wages, May 2010

Boilermakers	$54,640
Construction Trades Workers	$38,240
Total, All Occupations	$33,840

Note: All Occupations includes all occupations in the U.S. Economy.
Source: U.S. Bureau of Labor Statistics, Occupational Employment Statistics

The median annual wage of boilermakers was $54,640 in May 2010. The median wage is the wage at which half the workers in an occupation earned more than that amount and half earned less. The lowest 10 percent earned less than $30,410, and the top 10 percent earned more than $80,830.

Apprentices usually start between 30 percent and 50 percent of the rate paid to fully trained boilermakers. They receive pay increases as they become more skilled.

Nearly all boilermakers work full time and may experience extended periods of overtime when equipment is shut down for maintenance. Overtime work also may be necessary to meet construction or production deadlines.

In contrast, because most field construction and repair work is contract work, there may be periods of unemployment when a contract is complete. Many boilermakers must travel to worksites and live away from home for long stretches of time.

Boilermakers have a higher rate of union membership than many other construction occupations. Although there is no single union that covers all boilermakers, the largest organizer of these workers is the International Brotherhood of Boilermakers, Iron Ship Builders, Blacksmiths, Forgers, and Helpers.

Job Outlook

Boilermakers
Percent change in employment, projected 2010-20

Construction Trades Workers	23%
Boilermakers	21%
Total, All Occupations	14%

Note: All Occupations includes all occupations in the U.S. Economy.
Source: U.S. Bureau of Labor Statistics, Employment Projections program

Employment of boilermakers is projected to grow 21 percent from 2010 to 2020, faster than the average for all occupations.

Employment growth reflects the need to maintain and upgrade, rather than replace, the many boilers that are getting older. Employment growth will also result as a growing population demands more electric power. Although boilers typically last more than 50 years, the need to replace parts, such as boiler tubes, heating elements, and ductwork, is an ongoing process that will continue to spur demand for boilermakers.

To meet requirements of the Clean Air Act, utility companies also will need to continue upgrading their boiler and scrubbing systems. The installation of new boilers and pressure vessels, air pollution equipment, water treatment plants, storage and process tanks, electric static precipitators, and stacks and liners will further drive employment growth of boilermakers, although to a lesser extent than repairs will.

Job Prospects

Overall job prospects should be favorable because the work of a boilermaker remains hazardous and physically demanding, leading some qualified applicants to seek other types of work. Although employment growth will generate some job openings, the majority of positions will arise from the need to replace the large number of boilermakers expected to retire in the coming decade.

People who have welding training or a welding certificate should have the best opportunities to be selected for boilermaker apprenticeship programs.

As with many other construction workers, employment of boilermakers is sensitive to fluctuations of the economy. On the one hand, workers may experience periods of unemployment when the overall level of construction falls. On the other hand, shortages of workers may occur in some areas during peak periods of building activity.

However, maintenance and repair of boilers must continue even during economic downturns, so boilermaker mechanics in manufacturing and other industries generally have more stable employment than those in construction.

Employment projections data for oilermakers, 2010-20

Occupational Title	SOC Code	Employment, 2010	Projected Employment, 2020	Change, 2010-20	
				Percent	Numeric
Boilermakers	47-2011	19,800	24,000	21	4,200
SOURCE: U.S. Bureau of Labor Statistics, Employment Projections program					

Similar Occupations

This table shows a list of occupations with job duties that are similar to those of boilermakers.

Occupation	Job Duties	Entry-Level Education	Median Annual Pay, May 2010
Assemblers and Fabricators	Assemblers and fabricators assemble both finished products and the parts that go into them. They use tools, machines, and their hands to make engines, computers, aircraft, toys, electronic devices, and more.	High school diploma or equivalent	$28,360
Stationary Engineers and Boiler Operators	Stationary engineers and boiler operators control stationary engines, boilers, or other mechanical equipment to provide utilities for buildings or for industrial purposes.	High school diploma or equivalent	$52,140
Welders, Cutters, Solderers, and Brazers	Welders, cutters, solderers, and brazers weld or join metal parts. They also fill holes, indentions, or seams of metal products, using hand-held welding equipment.	High school diploma or equivalent	$35,450
Machinists and Tool and Die Makers	Machinists and tool and die makers set up and operate a variety of computer-controlled or mechanically-controlled machine tools to produce precision metal parts, instruments, and tools.	High school diploma or equivalent	$39,910
Industrial Machinery Mechanics and Maintenance Workers	Industrial machinery mechanics and maintenance workers maintain and repair factory equipment and other industrial machinery, such as conveying systems, production machinery, and packaging equipment.	High school diploma or equivalent	$44,160
Millwrights	Millwrights install, dismantle, repair, reassemble, and move machinery in factories, power plants, and construction sites.	High school diploma or equivalent	$48,360
Plumbers, Pipefitters, and Steamfitters	Plumbers, pipefitters, and steamfitters install and repair pipes that carry water, steam, air, or other liquids or gases to and in businesses, homes, and factories.	High school diploma or equivalent	$46,660
Sheet Metal Workers	Sheet metal workers fabricate or install products that are made from thin metal sheets, such as ducts used for heating and air-conditioning.	High school diploma or equivalent	$41,710

Contacts for More Information

For information about apprenticeships or job opportunities as a boilermaker, contact local boiler construction contractors, a local chapter of the International Brotherhood of Boilermakers, Iron Ship Builders, Blacksmiths, Forgers, and Helpers, a local joint union-management apprenticeship committee, or the nearest office of your state employment service or apprenticeship agency. Apprenticeship information is available from the U.S. Department of Labor's toll free help line, 1 (877) 872-5627, or Employment and Training Administration.

For apprenticeship information, visit International Brotherhood of Boilermakers, Iron Ship Builders, Blacksmiths, Forgers, and Helpers
For certification information, visit American Welding Society

Suggested citation:

Bureau of Labor Statistics, U.S. Department of Labor, Occupational Outlook Handbook, 2012-13 Edition, Boilermakers, on the Internet at http://www.bls.gov/ooh/construction-and-extraction/boilermakers.htm.

Brickmasons, Blockmasons, and Stonemasons

Quick Facts: Brickmasons, Blockmasons, and Stonemasons	
2010 Median Pay	$45,410 per year $21.83 per hour
Entry-Level Education	High school diploma or equivalent
Work Experience in a Related Occupation	None
On-the-job Training	Apprenticeship
Number of Jobs, 2010	104,800
Job Outlook, 2010-20	40% (Much faster than average)
Employment Change, 2010-20	41,800

What Brickmasons, Blockmasons, and Stonemasons Do

Brickmasons, blockmasons, and stonemasons (or, simply, masons) use bricks, concrete blocks, and natural stones to build fences, walkways, walls, and other structures.

Duties

Masons typically do the following:

- Read blueprints or drawings to calculate materials needed
- Lay out patterns or foundations, using a straightedge
- Break or cut bricks, stones, or blocks to their appropriate size
- Mix mortar or grout and spread it onto a slab or foundation
- Lay bricks, blocks, or stones according to plans
- Clean excess mortar with trowels and other handtools
- Construct corners with a corner pole or by building a corner pyramid
- Ensure that a structure is perfectly vertical and horizontal, using a plumb bob and level
- Clean and polish surfaces with hand or power tools
- Fill expansion and contraction joints with the appropriate caulking materials

The following are common types of masons:

Brickmasons and **blockmasons**—who often are called **bricklayers**—build and repair walls, floors, partitions, fireplaces, chimneys, and other structures with brick, precast masonry panels, concrete block, and other masonry materials.

Pointing, cleaning, and caulking workers repair brickwork, particularly on older structures on which mortar has come loose. Special care must be taken not to damage the structural integrity or the existing bricks.

Refractory masons are brickmasons who specialize in installing firebrick and refractory tile in high-temperature boilers, furnaces, cupolas, ladles, and soaking pits in industrial establishments. Most of these workers are employed in steel mills, where molten materials flow on refractory beds from furnaces to rolling machines. They also are employed at oil refineries, glass furnaces, incinerators, and other locations with manufacturing processes that require high temperatures.

Stonemasons build stone walls, as well as set stone exteriors and floors. They work with two types of stone: natural-cut stone, such as marble, granite, and limestone; and artificial stone, made from concrete, marble chips, or other masonry materials. Using a special hammer or a diamond-blade saw, workers cut stone to make various shapes and sizes. Some stonemasons specialize in setting marble, which is similar to setting large pieces of stone.

Work Environment

Masons held about 104,800 jobs in 2010, of which 48 percent were employed in the masonry contractors industry. About 29 percent of masons were self-employed. Many self-employed contractors work on small jobs, such as patios, walkways, and fireplaces. Although most masons work in residential construction, nonresidential construction is growing in importance because most nonresidential buildings are now built with walls made of some combination of concrete block, brick veneer, stone, granite, marble, tile, and glass.

As in many other construction occupations, the work is physically demanding. Masons must often lift heavy materials and stand, kneel, and bend for long stretches of time.

They usually work outdoors, and poor weather conditions may reduce work activity.

Injuries

Overall, masons experience a rate of injury and illness that is much higher than the national average. Stonemasons experience a higher rate of injury and illness than brickmasons and blockmasons. Muscle strains from lifting heavy materials are the most common injuries. Other

Blockmasons often use a level.

hazards include injuries from tools and falls from scaffolds.

Work Schedules

Although most masons work full time, some work longer hours to meet construction deadlines. Because they primarily work outdoors, they may have to stop work in extreme cold or rainy weather. However, new processes and materials are allowing masons to work in a greater variety of weather conditions than in the past.

About 29 percent of masons were self-employed in 2010. Self-employed workers may be able to set their own schedule.

How to Become a Brickmason, Blockmason, or Stonemason

Although most masons learn through a formal apprenticeship, some learn informally on the job. Others learn through 1- or 2-year mason programs at technical colleges.

Apprenticeship

A 3- to 4-year apprenticeship is how most masons learn the occupation. For each year of the program, apprentices must complete at least 144 hours of related technical instruction and 2,000 hours of paid on-the-job training. Apprentices learn construction basics such as how to read blueprints, mathematics, building code requirements, and safety and first-aid practices.

In the coming years, the focus of apprenticeships is likely to change from time served to demonstrated competence. This may result in apprenticeships of shorter duration.

After completing an apprenticeship program, masons are considered journey workers and are able to do tasks on their own.

Several groups, including unions and contractor associations, sponsor apprenticeship programs. The basic qualifications for entering an apprenticeship program are as follows:

● . Minimum age of 18
● High school education or equivalent
● Physically able to do the work

Some contractors have their own training programs for masons. Although workers may enter apprenticeships directly, some masons start out as <u>construction helpers</u>.

Education

Many technical colleges offer 1-year programs in basic masonry. These programs operate both independently and in conjunction with formal training. The credits earned as part of an apprenticeship program usually count toward an associate's degree. Some people take courses before being hired, and some take them later as part of on-the-job training.

For someone interested in becoming a mason, high school courses in English, math, mechanical drawing, and shop are useful.

Important Qualities

Creativity. Stonemasons must be able to shape stones into a finished structure that is functional and looks attractive.

Dexterity. Workers must be able to apply smooth, even layers of mortar, set bricks, and remove any excess, before the mortar hardens.

Math skills. Knowledge of math—including measurement, volume, and mixing proportions—is important in this trade.

Physical strength. Workers must be strong enough to lift blocks that sometimes weigh more than 40 pounds. They must also carry heavy tools, equipment, and other materials, such as bags of mortar and grout.

Stamina. Brickmasons must keep a steady pace while setting bricks all day. Although no individual brick is extremely heavy, the constant lifting can be tiring.

Pay

Brickmasons, Blockmasons, and Stonemasons
Median annual wages, May 2010

Brickmasons and Blockmasons	$46,930
Construction Trades Workers	$38,240
Stonemasons	$37,180
Total, All Occupations	$33,840

Note: All Occupations includes all occupations in the U.S. Economy.
Source: U.S. Bureau of Labor Statistics, Occupational Employment Statistics

The median annual wage of brickmasons, blockmasons, and stonemasons was $45,410 in May 2010. The median wage is the wage at which half the workers in an occupation earned more than that amount and half earned less.

The median annual wage for brickmasons and blockmasons was $46,930 in May 2010. The lowest 10 percent earned less than $28,790, and the top 10 percent earned more than $78,630.

The median annual wage for stonemasons was $37,180 in May 2010. The lowest 10 percent earned less than $23,560, and the top 10 percent earned more than $61,370.

The starting pay for apprentices is usually between 30 percent and 50 percent of what fully trained workers make. They get pay increases as they gain more skill.

Although most masons work full time, some work longer hours to meet construction deadlines.

About 29 percent of masons were self-employed in 2010. Self-employed workers may be able to set their own schedule.

Job Outlook

Brickmasons, Blockmasons, and Stonemasons
Percent change in employment, projected 2010-20

Brickmasons and Blockmasons	41%
Stonemasons	36%
Construction Trades Workers	23%
Total, All Occupations	14%

Note: All Occupations includes all occupations in the U.S. Economy.
Source: U.S. Bureau of Labor Statistics, Employment Projections program

Overall employment of masons is projected to grow 40 percent from 2010 to 2020, much faster than the average for all occupations.

Population growth will create a need for schools, hospitals, apartment buildings, and other structures. However, construction of these buildings may be delayed as states and local governments face budget shortfalls.

Also stimulating demand for workers will be the need to restore a growing number of old brick buildings. Although expensive, brick and stone exteriors should remain popular, reflecting a preference for low-maintenance, durable exterior materials.

Building code requirements in hurricane-prone areas also will increase the demand for durable homes that use brick, block, or stone.

Job Prospects

Overall job prospects should improve over the coming decade as construction activity rebounds from the recent recession. As with many other construction workers, employment is sensitive to the fluctuations of the economy. On the one hand, workers may experience periods of unemployment when the overall level of construction falls. On the other hand, shortages of workers may occur in some areas during peak periods of building activity.

The masonry workforce is growing older, and a large number of masons are expected to retire over the next decade, which will create many job openings.

Highly skilled masons with a good job history and work experience in construction should have the best job opportunities.

Employment projections data for rickmasons, blockmasons, and stonemasons, 2010-20

Occupational Title	SOC Code	Employment, 2010	Projected Employment, 2020	Change, 2010-20 Percent	Change, 2010-20 Numeric
Brickmasons, Blockmasons, and Stonemasons	—	104,800	146,700	40	41,800
Brickmasons and Blockmasons	47-2021	89,200	125,300	41	36,100
Stonemasons	47-2022	15,600	21,400	36	5,700

SOURCE: U.S. Bureau of Labor Statistics, Employment Projections program

Similar Occupations

This table shows a list of occupations with job duties that are similar to those of brickmasons, blockmasons, and stonemasons.

Occupation	Job Duties	Entry-Level Education	Median Annual Pay, May 2010
Carpenters	Carpenters construct and repair building frameworks and structures—such as stairways, doorframes, partitions, and rafters—made from wood and other materials. They also may install kitchen cabinets, siding, and drywall.	High school diploma or equivalent	$39,530
Cement Masons and Terrazzo Workers	Cement masons pour, smooth, and finish concrete floors, sidewalks, roads, and curbs. Using a cement mixture, terrazzo workers create durable and decorative surfaces for floors and stairways.	See How to Become One	$35,530
Construction Laborers and Helpers	Construction laborers and helpers do many basic tasks that require physical labor on construction sites.	See How to Become One	$28,410
Drywall and Ceiling Tile Installers, and Tapers	Drywall and ceiling tile installers hang wallboards to walls and ceilings inside buildings. Tapers prepare the wallboards for painting, using tape and other materials. Many workers do both installing and taping.	Less than high school	$38,290
Insulation Workers	Insulation workers install and replace the materials used to insulate buildings and their mechanical systems to help control and maintain temperature.	See How to Become One	$35,110
Plasterers and Stucco Masons	Plasterers and stucco masons apply coats of plaster or stucco to walls, ceilings, or partitions for functional and decorative purposes. Some workers apply ornamental plaster.	Less than high school	$37,210
Tile and Marble Setters	Tile and marble setters apply hard tile, marble, and wood tiles to walls, floors, and other surfaces.	Less than high school	$38,110

Contacts for More Information

For details about apprenticeships or other work opportunities for brickmasons, blockmasons, and stonemasons, contact the offices of the state employment service, the state apprenticeship agency, local contractors or firms that employ masons, or local union–management apprenticeship committees. Information on apprenticeships is available from the U.S. Department of Labor's toll-free help line, 1 (877) 872-5627, or Employment and Training Administration.

For information about training for brickmasons, blockmasons, and stonemasons, visit Mason Contractors Association of America, National Association of Home Builders

For information about training, including obtaining a credential in green construction, visit International Masonry Institute, National Center for Construction Education and Research

For general information about the work of bricklayers, visit Associated General Contractors of America

Suggested citation:

Bureau of Labor Statistics, U.S. Department of Labor, Occupational Outlook Handbook, 2012-13 Edition, Brickmasons, Blockmasons, and Stonemasons, on the Internet at http://www.bls.gov/ooh/construction-and-extraction/brickmasons-block masons-and-stonemasons.htm.

Carpenters

Quick Facts: Carpenters	
2010 Median Pay	$39,530 per year $19.00 per hour
Entry-Level Education	High school diploma or equivalent
Work Experience in a Related Occupation	None
On-the-job Training	Apprenticeship
Number of Jobs, 2010	1,001,700
Job Outlook, 2010-20	20% (Faster than average)
Employment Change, 2010-20	196,000

What Carpenters Do

Carpenters construct and repair building frameworks and structures—such as stairways, doorframes, partitions, and rafters—made from wood and other materials. They also may install kitchen cabinets, siding, and drywall.

Duties

Carpenters typically do the following:

- Follow blueprints and building plans to meet the needs of clients
- Install structures and fixtures, such as windows and molding
- Measure, cut, or shape wood, plastic, fiberglass, drywall, and other materials
- Construct building frameworks, including wall studs, floor joists, and doorframes
- Help put up, level, and install building framework with the aid of large pulleys and cranes
- Inspect and replace damaged framework or other structures and fixtures

Carpenters work with many different types of tools.

- Instruct and direct laborers and other construction trade helpers

Carpenters are one of the most versatile construction occupations, with workers usually doing a variety of tasks. For example, some carpenters insulate office buildings; others install drywall or kitchen cabinets in homes. Those who help construct large buildings or bridges often make the wooden concrete forms for cement footings or pillars. Some carpenters build braces and scaffolding for buildings.

Carpenters use many different hand and power tools to cut and shape wood, plastic, fiberglass, or drywall. They commonly use handtools, including squares, levels, and chisels, as well as many power tools, such as sanders, circular saws, and nail guns. Carpenters put materials together with nails, screws, staples, and adhesives, and do a final check of their work to ensure accuracy. They use a tape measure on every project because proper measuring increases productivity, reduces waste, and ensures that the pieces being cut are the proper size.

The following are types of carpenters:

Residential carpenters typically specialize in new-home, townhome, and condominium building and remodeling. As part of a single job, they might build and set forms for footings, walls and slabs, and frame and finish exterior walls, roofs, and decks. They frame interior walls, build stairs, and install drywall, crown molding, doors, and kitchen cabinets. Highly-skilled carpenters may also tile floors and lay wood floors and carpet. Fully-trained construction carpenters are easily able to switch from new-home building to remodeling.

Commercial carpenters typically remodel and help build commercial office buildings, hospitals, hotels, schools, and shopping malls. Some specialize in working with light gauge and load-bearing steel framing for interior partitions, exterior framing, and curtain wall construction. Others specialize in working with concrete forming systems and finishing interior and exterior walls, partitions, and ceilings. Highly skilled carpenters can usually do many of the same tasks as residential carpenters.

Industrial carpenters typically work in civil and industrial settings where they put up scaffolding and build and set forms for pouring concrete. Some industrial carpenters build tunnel bracing or partitions in underground passageways and mines to control the circulation of air to worksites. Others build concrete forms for tunnels, bridges, dams, power plants, or sewer construction projects.

Work Environment

Carpenters held about 1 million jobs in 2010; about 39 percent were self-employed. Most carpenters work in the construction industry, where they account for the largest share of the building trades occupations.

Residential building construction	17%
Nonresidential building construction	12
Building finishing contractors	9
Foundation, structure, and building exterior contractors	7

Because carpenters are involved in many types of construction, from building highways and bridges to installing kitchen cabinets, they may work both indoors and out.

Carpenters may work in cramped spaces, and constant lifting, standing, and kneeling can be tiring. Those who work outdoors are subject to variable weather conditions.

Injuries

Carpenters experience a higher than average rate of injuries and illnesses. Injuries may include muscle strains from lifting heavy materials, falls from ladders, and cuts from sharp objects and tools.

Work Schedules

Nearly all carpenters work full time, which may include working evenings and weekends. Overtime is common in order to meet deadlines.

About 39 percent of carpenters were self-employed in 2010. Self-employed workers may be able to set their own schedule.

How to Become a Carpenter

Although most carpenters learn their trade through a formal apprenticeship, some learn on the job, starting as a helper.

Apprenticeship

Most carpenters learn their trade through a 3- or 4-year apprenticeship. For each year of the program, apprentices must complete at least 144 hours of paid technical training and 2,000 hours of paid on-the-job training. In the technical training, apprentices learn carpentry basics, blueprint reading, mathematics, building code requirements, and safety and first-aid practices. They also may receive specialized training in concrete, rigging, scaffold building, fall protection, confined workspaces, and Occupational Safety and Health Administration (OSHA) 10- and 30-hour safety courses.

After finishing an apprenticeship, carpenters are considered to be journey workers and may do tasks on their own.

Several groups, including unions and contractor associations, sponsor apprenticeship programs. The basic qualifications for a person to enter an apprenticeship program are as follows:

- Minimum age of 18
- High school education or equivalent
- Physically able to do the work
- U.S. citizen or proof of legal residency
- Pass substance abuse screening

Some contractors have their own carpenter training program. Although many workers enter apprenticeships directly, some start out as helpers.

Education

Some 2-year technical schools offer carpentry degrees that are affiliated with unions and contractor organizations. Credits earned as part of an apprenticeship program usually count toward an associate's degree.

Advancement

Because they are exposed to the entire construction process, carpenters usually have more opportunities than other construction workers to become general construction supervisors or independent contractors. For those who would like to advance, it is increasingly important to be able to communicate in both English and Spanish to relay instructions to workers.

Important Qualities

Detail oriented. Carpenters do many tasks that are important in the overall building process. Making precise measurements, for example, may reduce air gaps between windows and frames, limiting any leaks around the window.

Manual dexterity. Carpenters use many handtools and need eye-hand coordination to avoid injury. Striking the head of a nail, for example, is crucial to not damaging wood.

Math skills. Carpenters use basic math skills every day. They need to be able to calculate volume and measure materials to be cut.

Physical strength. Many of the tools and materials that carpenters use are heavy. For example, plywood sheets can weigh 50 to 100 pounds.

Problem-solving skills. Because all construction jobs vary, carpenters must adjust project plans accordingly. For example, they may have to use wedges to level cabinets in homes that have settled and are slightly sloping.

Stamina. Carpenters need physical endurance. They often must lift tools and wood while standing, climbing, bending, or kneeling for long periods.

Pay

Carpenters
Median annual wages, May 2010

Carpenters	$39,530
Construction Trades Workers	$38,240
Total, All Occupations	$33,840

Note: All Occupations includes all occupations in the U.S. Economy.
Source: U.S. Bureau of Labor Statistics, Occupational Employment Statistics

The median annual wage of carpenters was $39,530 in May 2010. The median wage is the wage at which half the workers in an occupation earned more than that amount and half earned less. The lowest 10 percent earned less than $24,650, and the top 10 percent earned more than $71,660.

The starting pay for apprentices usually is between 30 percent and 50 percent of what fully trained carpenters make. As they gain more skill, they receive pay increases.

Nearly all carpenters work full time, which may include working evenings and weekends. Overtime is common in order to meet deadlines.

About 39 percent of carpenters were self-employed in 2010. Self-employed workers may be able to set their own schedule.

About 16 percent of carpenters are union members. Although there is no single union, the largest organizer for carpenters is the United Brotherhood of Carpenters and Joiners of America.

Job Outlook

Carpenters
Percent change in employment, projected 2010-20

Construction Trades Workers	23%
Carpenters	20%
Total, All Occupations	14%

Note: All Occupations includes all occupations in the U.S. Economy.
Source: U.S. Bureau of Labor Statistics, Employment Projections program

Employment of carpenters is projected to grow 20 percent from 2010 to 2020, faster than the average for all occupations. Population growth should result in new-home construction—the largest segment employing carpenters—which will stimulate the need for many new workers. Demand for carpenters is expected to be driven by home remodeling needs as well.

The need to repair and replace roads and bridges also will spur some employment growth for carpenters. Much of this growth, however, depends on spending by federal and state governments as they attempt to upgrade existing infrastructure.

Construction of factories and powerplants also may result in some new jobs.

Offsetting growth, however, will be the increasing use of modular and prefabricated components. Roof assemblies, walls, stairs, and complete bathrooms are just a few of the prefabricated components that can be manufactured in a separate plant and then assembled onsite by carpenters. The prefabricated components replace the most labor intensive and time consuming onsite building activities.

Job Prospects

Overall job prospects for carpenters should improve over the coming decade as construction activity rebounds from the recent recession.

The number of openings is expected to vary by geographic area. Because construction activity parallels the movement of people and businesses, areas of the country with the largest population increases will require the most carpenters.

Employment of carpenters, like that of many other construction workers, is sensitive to fluctuations in the economy. On the one hand, workers in these trades may experience periods of unemployment when the overall level of construction falls. On the other hand, peak periods of building activity may produce shortages of carpenters. Experienced carpenters should have the best job opportunities.

Employment projections data for carpenters, 2010-20

Occupational Title	SOC Code	Employment, 2010	Projected Employment, 2020	Change, 2010-20	
				Percent	Numeric
Carpenters	47-2031	1,001,700	1,197,600	20	196,000
SOURCE: U.S. Bureau of Labor Statistics, Employment Projections program					

Similar Occupations

This table shows a list of occupations with job duties that are similar to those of carpenters.

Occupation	Job Duties	Entry-Level Education	Median Annual Pay, May 2010
Carpet Installers	Carpet installers lay carpet in homes, offices, restaurants, and many other types of buildings.	Less than high school	$36,090
Cement Masons and Terrazzo Workers	Cement masons pour, smooth, and finish concrete floors, sidewalks, roads, and curbs. Using a cement mixture, terrazzo workers create durable and decorative surfaces for floors and stairways.	See How to Become One	$35,530
Construction Laborers and Helpers	Construction laborers and helpers do many basic tasks that require physical labor on construction sites.	See How to Become One	$28,410
Drywall and Ceiling Tile Installers, and Tapers	Drywall and ceiling tile installers hang wallboards to walls and ceilings inside buildings. Tapers prepare the wallboards for painting, using tape and other materials. Many workers do both installing and taping.	Less than high school	$38,290
Insulation Workers	Insulation workers install and replace the materials used to insulate buildings and their mechanical systems to help control and maintain temperature.	See How to Become One	$35,110
Tile and Marble Setters	Tile and marble setters apply hard tile, marble, and wood tiles to walls, floors, and other surfaces.	Less than high school	$38,110
Millwrights	Millwrights install, dismantle, repair, reassemble, and move machinery in factories, power plants, and construction sites.	High school diploma or equivalent	$48,360

Contacts for More Information

For details about apprenticeships or other work opportunities in this trade, contact the offices of the state employment service, the state apprenticeship agency, local contractors or firms that employ carpenters, or local union-management carpenter apprenticeship committees. Apprenticeship information is available from the U.S. Department of Labor's toll-free help line, 1 (877) 872-5627, and Employment and Training Administration.

For more information about carpenters, including training opportunities, visit Associated Builders and Contractors, Inc., Associated General Contractors of America, Inc. ,National Center for Construction Education and Research, National Association of Home Builders

United Brotherhood of Carpenters and Joiners of America, Carpenters Training Fund

Suggested citation:

Bureau of Labor Statistics, U.S. Department of Labor, Occupational Outlook Handbook, 2012-13 Edition, Carpenters, on the Internet at http://www.bls.gov/ooh/construction-and-extraction/carpenters.htm.

Carpet Installers

Quick Facts: Carpet Installers	
2010 Median Pay	$36,090 per year $17.35 per hour
Entry-Level Education	Less than high school
Work Experience in a Related Occupation	None
On-the-job Training	Short-term on-the-job training
Number of Jobs, 2010	47,500
Job Outlook, 2010-20	10% (About as fast as average)
Employment Change, 2010-20	4,900

What Carpet Installers Do

Carpet installers lay carpet in homes, offices, restaurants, and many other types of buildings.

Duties

Carpet installers typically do the following:

- Remove old carpet or flooring to prepare surfaces for laying new carpet
- Inspect the condition of the surface to be covered
- Fix any problems that could show through the carpet or cause uneven wear
- Measure the area to be carpeted
- Plan the layout of carpeting to get the best appearance and least wear
- Install a padded cushion underneath the carpet
- Roll out, measure, mark, and cut the carpet
- Fit the carpet so that it lays evenly and snugly
- Tack, glue, or staple carpeting to hold it in place
- Finish the edges so that the carpet looks neat

Carpet installers lay carpet in many types of new and old buildings, including homes, offices, restaurants, and museums. Although installing carpet in newly constructed buildings requires minimal preparation, those who replace existing carpet must first remove old flooring, including any padding, glue, tacks, or staples. In some cases, carpet installers lay carpet over existing tile or hardwood.

Carpet steamers are rolled across seams to blend carpet yarn.

Carpet installers work with special tools, including a "knee kicker" to position the carpet and a power stretcher to pull the carpet snugly against walls. When they have to join seams of carpet (for example, in large rooms), they use special heat-activated tape. In commercial installations, they may glue the carpet to the floor or to padding that they have glued to the floor. On steps, they may use staples to hold the carpet in place. They also use carpet knives, carpet shears (scissors), hammers, power sanders, and other tools.

Work Environment

Carpet installers held about 47,500 jobs in 2010. About 30 percent were employed in the building finishing contractors industry, and 17 percent were employed in the home furnishing stores industry. About 48 percent were self-employed.

By the time workers install carpets, most of the construction has been completed and the work area is relatively clean and uncluttered.

Carpet installers spend a lot of time kneeling and bending. They also need to lift and pull heavy carpet. Because installations are often done in less than a day, carpet installers may travel to more than one worksite.

Injuries

Although their work is not as dangerous as that of some other construction trades, carpet installers still experience a high rate of injuries and illnesses compared with most other occupations. The most common injuries are cuts from knives and muscle strains from lifting carpet. Some installers also get burns from heat guns used to join carpet.

Work Schedules

Most carpet installers work full time. In commercial settings, carpet installers may work nights or evenings to avoid disturbing regular business operations.

About 48 percent of carpet installers were self-employed in 2010. Self-employed workers may have the ability to set their own schedule.

How to Become a Carpet Installer

The vast majority of carpet installers learn their trade on the job.

Training

Most carpet installers learn by helping more experienced workers and gradually getting more duties. Employers provide this training on the job. New carpet installers start by helping to move carpet, after which they progress to cutting and trimming carpet. Some workers learn to install carpet while working in another construction occupation, such as carpentry or construction labor.

Education

Although there is no formal educational requirement for carpet installers, high school courses in basic math are considered helpful.

Important Qualities

Customer-service skills. Working with customers in their homes is common. Therefore, carpet installers must be considerate of the homeowners' property while quickly completing tasks.

Math skills. Carpet installers use basic math skills on every job. Besides measuring the area to be carpeted, installers must calculate the amount of carpet needed to cover the floor.

Physical strength. Carpet installers must be strong enough to carry heavy rolls of carpet. They also should be able to lift the rolls to move them into position.

Stamina. Carpet installers must have endurance because they spend many hours on their feet. Also, when cutting carpet, installers need to be on their knees to easily reach the edge that must be trimmed.

Pay

Carpet Installers
Median annual wages, May 2010

Construction Trades Workers	$38,240
Carpet Installers	$36,090
Total, All Occupations	$33,840

Note: All Occupations includes all occupations in the U.S. Economy.
Source: U.S. Bureau of Labor Statistics, Occupational Employment Statistics

The median annual wage of carpet installers was $36,090 in May 2010. The median wage is the wage at which half the workers in an occupation earned more than that amount and half earned less. The lowest 10 percent earned less than $21,130, and the top 10 percent earned more than $67,760.

Most carpet installers work full time. In commercial settings,

carpet installers may work nights or evenings to avoid disturbing regular business operations.

About 48 percent of carpet installers were self-employed in 2010. Self-employed workers may have the ability to set their own schedule.

Job Outlook

Carpet Installers
Percent change in employment, projected 2010-20

Construction Trades Workers	23%
Total, All Occupations	14%
Carpet Installers	10%

Note: All Occupations includes all occupations in the U.S. Economy.
Source: U.S. Bureau of Labor Statistics, Employment Projections program

Employment of carpet installers is projected to grow 10 percent from 2010 to 2020, about as fast as the average for all other occupations. Carpet is the most commonly used floor covering in the United States, and the need to replace carpet is the major source of demand for installers. In addition to wearing out, older carpet is replaced when people and businesses want to update their floor coverings.

Competition with other floor coverings, especially tile and hardwood, should offset some of the demand for workers. Residential investors and homeowners are expected to continue to choose these alternatives to carpet because of their durability and low maintenance, and because many owners perceive that hardwood and tile add greater value to their homes.

Job Prospects

Job prospects for carpet installers depend, in part, on the amount of new construction taking place in the economy. As construction activity rebounds over the projection decade, job opportunities for carpet installers should improve. In addition to job growth, many job openings will result from the need to replace workers who leave this occupation.

Employment projections data for carpet installers, 2010-20

Occupational Title	SOC Code	Employment, 2010	Projected Employment, 2020	Change, 2010-20	
				Percent	Numeric
Carpet Installers	47-2041	47,500	52,400	10	4,900
SOURCE: U.S. Bureau of Labor Statistics, Employment Projections program					

Similar Occupations

This table shows a list of occupations with job duties that are similar to those of carpet installers.

Occupation	Job Duties	Entry-Level Education	Median Annual Pay, May 2010
Carpenters	Carpenters construct and repair building frameworks and structures—such as stairways, doorframes, partitions, and rafters—made from wood and other materials. They also may install kitchen cabinets, siding, and drywall.	High school diploma or equivalent	$39,530
Construction Laborers and Helpers	Construction laborers and helpers do many basic tasks that require physical labor on construction sites.	See How to Become One	$28,410
Drywall and Ceiling Tile Installers, and Tapers	Drywall and ceiling tile installers hang wallboards to walls and ceilings inside buildings. Tapers prepare the wallboards for painting, using tape and other materials. Many workers do both installing and taping.	Less than high school	$38,290
Painters, Construction and Maintenance	Painters apply paint, stain, and coatings to walls, buildings, bridges, and other structures.	Less than high school	$34,280

Roofers	Roofers repair and install the roofs of buildings using a variety of materials, including shingles, asphalt, and metal.	Less than high school	$34,220
Tile and Marble Setters	Tile and marble setters apply hard tile, marble, and wood tiles to walls, floors, and other surfaces.	Less than high school	$38,110

Contacts for More Information

For more information about training for carpet installers, visit Finishing Trades Institute International

Suggested citation:

Bureau of Labor Statistics, U.S. Department of Labor, Occupational Outlook Handbook, 2012-13 Edition, Carpet Installers, on the Internet at http://www.bls.gov/ooh /construction-and-extraction/carpet-installers.htm.

Cement Masons and Terrazzo Workers

Quick Facts: Cement Masons and Terrazzo Workers	
2010 Median Pay	$35,530 per year $17.08 per hour
Entry-Level Education	See How to Become One
Work Experience in a Related Occupation	None
On-the-job Training	See How to Become One
Number of Jobs, 2010	148,400
Job Outlook, 2010-20	34% (Much faster than average)
Employment Change, 2010-20	50,700

What Cement Masons and Terrazzo Workers Do

Cement masons pour, smooth, and finish concrete floors, sidewalks, roads, and curbs. Using a cement mixture, terrazzo workers create durable and decorative surfaces for floors and stairways.

Duties

Cement masons typically do the following:

- Set the forms that hold concrete in place
- Install reinforcing rebar or mesh wire to strengthen the concrete
- Signal truck drivers to facilitate the pouring of concrete
- Spread, level, and smooth concrete, using a trowel, float, or screed
- Mold expansion joints and edges
- Monitor curing (hardening) to ensure a durable, smooth, and uniform finish
- Apply sealants or waterproofing to protect concrete

Terrazzo workers typically do the following (in addition to what cement masons do):

- Measure ingredients for terrazzo
- Blend a marble chip mixture that may have colors in it
- Grind and polish surfaces for a smooth, lustrous look

Concrete is one of the most common and durable materials used in construction. Once set, concrete—a mixture of cement, sand, gravel, and water—becomes the foundation for everything from decorative patios and floors to huge dams or miles of roadways.

The following are types of cement masons and terrazzo workers:

Cement masons and **concrete finishers** place and finish concrete. They may color concrete surfaces, expose aggregate (small stones) in walls and sidewalks, or make concrete beams, columns, and panels.

Throughout the process of pouring, leveling, and finishing concrete, cement masons must monitor how the wind, heat, or cold affects the curing of the concrete. They must have a thorough knowledge of the characteristics of concrete so that, by using sight and touch, they can determine what is happening to the concrete and take measures to prevent defects.

Terrazzo workers and **finishers** create decorative walkways, floors, patios, and panels. Although much of the preliminary work in pouring, leveling, and finishing concrete is similar to that of cement masons, terrazzo workers create more decorative finishes by blending a fine marble chip into the cement, which is often colored. Once the terrazzo is thoroughly set, workers correct any depressions or imperfections with a grinder to create a smooth, uniform finish.

Work Environment

Concrete masons and terrazzo workers held about 148,400 jobs in 2010. About 87 percent were employed in the construction industry, mostly in the specialty trade contractors industry.

Concrete and terrazzo work is fast paced and strenuous. Because most of the work is done at floor level, workers often must bend and kneel. The work, either indoors or outdoors, may be in areas that are muddy, dusty, or dirty.

Injuries

Cement masons experience lower rates of injuries and illnesses than terrazzo workers. However, both group of workers may experience chemical burns from uncured concrete, falls from scaffolding, and cuts from tools. To avoid injuries, many workers wear protective gear, including kneepads and water-repellent boots.

Work Schedules

Most cement masons and terrazzo workers are employed full time. About 6 percent are self-employed, many of whom have the ability to set their own schedule.

Because many jobs are outdoors, work generally stops in wet or cold weather. Hours may vary for other reasons, such as construction deadlines or coordination with other work activities.

How to Become a Cement Mason or Terrazzo Worker

Although most cement masons and terrazzo workers learn informally on the job, some learn their trade through a formal apprenticeship.

Training

Most on-the-job training programs consist of informal instruction in which experienced workers teach helpers to use the tools, equipment, machines, and materials of the trade. Trainees begin with

A precast concrete wall section is lifted into place.

tasks such as edging, jointing, and using a straightedge on freshly placed concrete. As training progresses, assignments become more complex and trainees can usually do finishing work more quickly.

Some cement masons and terrazzo workers learn their trade through a 3-year apprenticeship. Each year, apprentices must have at least 144 hours of technical instruction and 2,000 hours of paid on-the-job training. Apprentices learn construction basics such as blueprint reading, mathematics, building code requirements, and safety and first-aid practices.

After completing an apprenticeship program, cement masons and terrazzo workers are considered to be journey workers, qualifying them to do tasks on their own.

Several groups, including unions and contractor associations, sponsor apprenticeship programs. The basic qualifications for entering an apprenticeship program are

- Minimum age of 18
- High school education or equivalent
- Physically able to do the work

Some contractors have their own cement masonry or terrazzo training programs. Although workers may enter apprenticeships directly, many start out as helpers or construction laborers. For more information, see the profile on construction laborers.

Education

While there are no specific education requirements for cement masons and concrete finishers, terrazzo workers must usually have a high school diploma. High school courses in math, mechanical drawing, and blueprint reading are considered to helpful.

Important Qualities

Color vision. Terrazzo workers must determine small color variances when setting terrazzo patterns. Because these patterns often include many different colors, terrazzo workers must be able to distinguish between colors for the best looking finish.

Physical strength. Cement masons and terrazzo workers must be able to lift and carry heavy materials. For example, the forms into which concrete is poured are often large and heavy.

Stamina. Cement masons and terrazzo workers must be able to spend a lot of time kneeling, bending, and reaching.

Pay

Cement Masons and Terrazzo Workers
Median annual wages, May 2010

Terrazzo Workers and Finishers	$38,720
Construction Trades Workers	$38,240
Cement Masons and Concrete Finishers	$35,450
Total, All Occupations	$33,840

Note: All Occupations includes all occupations in the U.S. Economy.
Source: U.S. Bureau of Labor Statistics, Occupational Employment Statistics

The median annual wage of cement masons and terrazzo workers was $35,530 in May 2010. The median wage is the wage at which half the workers in an occupation earned more than that amount and half earned less.

The median annual wage of cement masons was $35,450 in May 2010. The lowest 10 percent earned less than $23,130, and the top 10 percent earned more than $63,400.

The median annual wage of terrazzo workers was $38,720 in May 2010. The lowest 10 percent earned less than $24,190, and the top 10 percent earned more than $63,650.

The starting pay for apprentices usually is between 30 percent and 50 percent of what fully trained workers make. Apprentices receive pay increases as they gain more skill.

Most cement masons and terrazzo workers are employed full time. About 6 percent are self-employed, many of whom have the ability to set their own schedule. Because many jobs are outdoors, work generally stops in wet or cold weather. Hours may vary for other reasons, such as construction deadlines or coordination with other work activities.

Job Outlook

Cement Masons and Terrazzo Workers
Percent change in employment, projected 2010-20

Cement Masons and Concrete Finishers	35%
Construction Trades Workers	23%
Terrazzo Workers and Finishers	15%
Total, All Occupations	14%

Note: All Occupations includes all occupations in the U.S. Economy.
Source: U.S. Bureau of Labor Statistics, Employment Projections program

Overall employment of cement masons and terrazzo workers is projected to grow 34 percent from 2010 to 2020, much faster than the average for all occupations. Although employment growth will vary by specialty, both specialties' growth will depend on the number of heavy construction and civil construction projects, including roads, bridges, and buildings.

Employment of cement masons is projected to grow 35 percent, much faster than the average for all occupations. More cement masons will be needed to build new highways, bridges, factories, and residential structures to meet the demands of a growing population.

In addition, cement masons will be needed to repair and renovate existing highways and bridges and other aging structures.

The use of concrete for buildings is increasing because its strength is an important asset in areas prone to severe weather. For example, residential construction projects in Florida are using more concrete as building requirements change in reaction to the increased frequency and intensity of hurricanes. The use of concrete is likely to expand into other hurricane-prone areas as the durability of the Florida homes becomes more established.

Employment of terrazzo workers is projected to grow 15 percent, about as fast as the average for all occupations. Terrazzo is a durable and attractive flooring option that is often used in schools, government buildings, and hospitals. The construction and renovation of such buildings will spur demand for these workers.

Job Prospects

Job opportunities for cement masons and terrazzo workers are expected to be good, particularly for those with more experience and skills. During peak construction periods, employers report difficulty in finding workers with the right skills, because many qualified jobseekers often prefer work that is less strenuous and has more comfortable working conditions.

Applicants who take masonry-related courses at technical schools will have the best job opportunities.

As with many other construction workers, employment of cement masons and terrazzo workers is sensitive to the fluctuations of the economy. On the one hand, workers may experience periods of unemployment when the overall level of construction falls. On the other hand, shortages of workers may occur in some areas during peak periods of building activity.

Employment projections data for cement masons and terrazzo workers, 2010-20

Occupational Title	SOC Code	Employment, 2010	Projected Employment, 2020	Change, 2010-20	
				Percent	Numeric
Cement Masons and Terrazzo Workers	—	148,400	199,100	34	50,700
Cement Masons and Concrete Finishers	47-2051	144,700	194,800	35	50,100
Terrazzo Workers and Finishers	47-2053	3,700	4,300	15	600
SOURCE: U.S. Bureau of Labor Statistics, Employment Projections program					

Similar Occupations

This table shows a list of occupations with job duties that are similar to those of cement masons and terrazzo workers.

Occupation	Job Duties	Entry-Level Education	Median Annual Pay, May 2010
Brickmasons, Blockmasons, and Stonemasons	Brickmasons, blockmasons, and stonemasons (or, simply, masons) use bricks, concrete blocks, and natural stones to build fences, walkways, walls, and other structures.	High school diploma or equivalent	$45,410
Drywall and Ceiling Tile Installers, and Tapers	Drywall and ceiling tile installers hang wallboards to walls and ceilings inside buildings. Tapers prepare the wallboards for painting, using tape and other materials. Many workers do both installing and taping.	Less than high school	$38,290
Plasterers and Stucco Masons	Plasterers and stucco masons apply coats of plaster or stucco to walls, ceilings, or partitions for functional and decorative purposes. Some workers apply ornamental plaster.	Less than high school	$37,210
Construction Laborers and Helpers	Construction laborers and helpers do many basic tasks that require physical labor on construction sites.	See How to Become One	$28,410
Tile and Marble Setters	Tile and marble setters apply hard tile, marble, and wood tiles to walls, floors, and other surfaces.	Less than high school	$38,110

Contacts for More Information

For information about apprenticeships or job opportunities as a cement mason or terrazzo worker, contact local cement or terrazzo contractors, a local joint union–management apprenticeship committee, or the nearest office of your state employment service or apprenticeship agency. Apprenticeship information is available from the U.S. Department of Labor's toll-free help line, 1 (877) 872-5627, or Employment and Training Administration.

For general information about cement masons and terrazzo workers, visit Associated Builders and Contractors, Associated General Contractors of America, International Masonry Institute, National Center for Construction Education and Research ,The National Terrazzo and Mosaic Association , Operative Plasterers' and Cement Masons' International Association

For more information about careers and training as a mason, visit Mason Contractors Association of America

Suggested citation:

Bureau of Labor Statistics, U.S. Department of Labor, Occupational Outlook Handbook, 2012-13 Edition, Cement Masons and Terrazzo Workers, on the Internet at http://www.bls.gov/ooh/ construction-and-extraction/cement-mason-and-terrazzo-workers.htm.

Construction and Building Inspectors

Quick Facts: Construction and Building Inspectors	
2010 Median Pay	$52,360 per year $25.18 per hour
Entry-Level Education	High school diploma or equivalent
Work Experience in a Related Occupation	More than 5 years
On-the-job Training	Moderate-term on-the-job training
Number of Jobs, 2010	102,400
Job Outlook, 2010-20	18% (About as fast as average)
Employment Change, 2010-20	18,400

What Construction and Building Inspectors Do

Construction and building inspectors ensure that new construction, changes, or repairs comply with local and national building codes and ordinances, zoning regulations, and contract specifications.

Duties

Construction and building inspectors typically do the following:

- Review and approve plans that meet building codes, local ordinances, and zoning regulations
- Inspect and monitor construction sites to ensure overall compliance
- Use survey instruments, metering devices, and test equipment to perform inspections
- Monitor installation of plumbing, electrical, and other systems to ensure that the building meets codes
- Verify level, alignment, and elevation of structures and fixtures to ensure building compliance
- Issue violation notices and stop-work orders until building is compliant
- Keep daily logs, including photographs taken during inspection

Construction and building inspectors examine buildings, highways and streets, sewer and water systems, dams, bridges, and other structures. They also inspect electrical; heating, ventilation, air-conditioning, and refrigeration (HVACR); and plumbing systems. Although no two inspections are alike, inspectors do an initial check during the first phase of construction and follow-up inspections throughout the construction project. When the project is finished, they do a final, comprehensive inspection.

The following are types of construction and building inspectors:

Building inspectors check the structural quality and general safety of buildings. Some specialize in structural steel or reinforced-concrete structures, for example.

Electrical inspectors examine the installed electrical systems to ensure they function properly and comply with electrical codes and standards. The inspectors visit worksites to inspect new and existing sound and security systems, wiring, lighting, motors, and generating equipment. They also inspect the installed electrical wiring for HVACR systems and appliances.

Elevator inspectors examine lifting and conveying devices, such as elevators, escalators, moving sidewalks, lifts and hoists, inclined railways, ski lifts, and amusement rides.

Home inspectors typically inspect newly built or previously owned homes, condominiums, townhomes, and other dwellings. Prospective home buyers often hire home inspectors to check and report on a home's structure and overall condition. Sometimes, homeowners hire a home inspector to evaluate their home's condition before placing it on the market.

In addition to examining structural quality, home inspectors examine all home systems and features, including roofing, exterior walls, attached garage or carport, foundation, interior, plumbing, electrical, and HVACR systems. They look for and report violations of building codes, but they do not have the power to enforce compliance with the codes.

Mechanical inspectors examine the installation of HVACR systems and equipment to ensure that they are installed and function properly. They also may inspect commercial kitchen equipment, gas-fired appliances, and boilers.

Plan examiners determine whether the plans for a building or other structure comply with building codes. They also determine whether the structure is suited to the engineering and environmental demands of the building site.

Plumbing inspectors examine the installation of potable water, waste, and vent piping systems to ensure the safety and health of the drinking water system, piping for industrial uses, and the sanitary disposal of waste.

Public works inspectors ensure that federal, state, and local government water and sewer systems, highways, streets, bridges, and dam construction conform to detailed contract specifications. Workers inspect excavation and fill operations, the placement of forms for concrete, concrete mixing and pouring, asphalt paving, and grading

Home inspectors inform potential homebuyers of a home's deficiencies.

operations. Public works inspectors may specialize in highways, structural steel, reinforced concrete, or ditches. Others specialize in dredging operations required for bridges and dams or for harbors.

Specification inspectors ensure that work is performed according to design specifications. Specification inspectors represent the owner's interests, not those of the general public. Insurance companies and financial institutions also may use their services.

A primary concern of building inspectors is fire prevention safety. For more information, see the profile on fire inspectors and investigators.

Work Environment

Construction and building inspectors held about 102,400 jobs in 2010. About 51 percent of inspectors were employed in government, most of which were in local government. An additional 25 percent were employed in the architectural, engineering, and related services industry. About 11 percent were self-employed.

Although construction and building inspectors spend most of their time inspecting construction worksites, they also spend time in a field office reviewing blueprints, writing reports, and scheduling inspections.

Some inspectors may have to climb ladders or crawl in tight spaces.

Inspectors typically work alone. However, several inspectors may be assigned to large, complex projects, particularly because inspectors usually specialize in different areas of construction.

Work Schedules

Most construction and building inspectors work full time during regular business hours. However, some may work additional hours during periods of heavy construction activity. Also, if an accident occurs at a construction site, inspectors must respond immediately and may work additional hours to complete their report. Nongovernment inspectors—especially those who are self-employed—may have to work evenings and weekends.

How to Become a Construction or Building Inspector

Most employers require construction and building inspectors to have at least a high school diploma and considerable knowledge of construction trades. Construction and building inspectors typically learn informally on the job. Many states and local jurisdictions require some type of license or certification.

Training

Training requirements vary by type of inspector, state, and local jurisdictions. In general, construction and building inspectors receive much of their training on the job, although they must learn building codes and standards on their own. Working with an experienced inspector, they learn about inspection techniques; codes, ordinances, and regulations; contract specifications; and recordkeeping and reporting duties. Supervised onsite inspections also may be a part of the training.

Education

Most employers require workers to have at least a high school diploma, even for workers who have considerable experience.

Employers also seek candidates who have studied engineering or architecture or who have a certificate or an associate's degree that includes completion of courses in building inspection, home inspection, construction technology, and drafting. Many community colleges offer programs in building inspection technology. Courses in blueprint reading, algebra, geometry, shop, and English also are useful.

A growing number of construction and building inspectors are entering the occupation with a bachelor's degree, which often can substitute for experience.

Licenses and Certification

Many states and local jurisdictions require some type of license or certification. Typical requirements for licensure or certification include experience; minimum education, such as a high school diploma; and passing a state-approved exam.

Some states have individual licensing programs for construction and building inspectors. Others may require certification by associations such as the International Code Council, International Association of Plumbing and Mechanical Officials, International Association of Electrical Inspectors, and National Fire Protection Association.

Similarly, most states require home inspectors to follow defined trade practices or get a state-issued license or certification. Currently, 35 states have regulations affecting home inspectors. Requirements for a home inspector license or certification vary by state but may include having a minimum level of education, having a set amount of experience with inspections, purchasing liability insurance of a certain amount, and passing an exam. The exam is often based on American Society of Home Inspectors and National Association of Home Inspectors exams. Most inspectors must renew their license every few years and take continuing education courses.

Inspectors must have a valid driver's license because they must travel to inspection sites.

Work Experience

Because inspectors must possess the right mix of technical knowledge, experience, and education, employers prefer applicants who have both formal training and experience. For example, many inspectors previously worked as carpenters, electricians, or plumbers. Home inspectors combine knowledge of multiple specialties, so many of them come into the occupation having a combination of certifications and previous experience in various construction trades.

Important Qualities

Communication skills. Home inspectors must have good communication skills to be able to explain any problems they find and to help people understand what is needed to fix the problems.

Craft experience. Although not required, having experience in a related construction occupation provides inspectors with the necessary background that may help them with the certification process.

Detail oriented. Inspectors must thoroughly examine many different construction activities, often at the same time. Therefore, inspectors must pay close attention to detail so as to not overlook any items that need to be inspected.

Mechanical knowledge. Inspectors use a variety of testing equipment as they check complex systems. In addition to using such equipment, they must also have detailed knowledge of how the systems operate.

Pay

Construction and Building Inspectors
Median annual wages, May 2010

Construction and Building Inspectors	$52,360
Other Construction and Related Workers	$38,820
Total, All Occupations	$33,840

Note: All Occupations includes all occupations in the U.S. Economy.
Source: U.S. Bureau of Labor Statistics, Occupational Employment Statistics

The median annual wage of construction and building inspectors was $52,360 in May 2010. The median wage is the wage at which half the workers in an occupation earned more than that amount and half earned less. The lowest 10 percent earned less than $31,970, and the top 10 percent earned more than $81,050.

Most inspectors work full time during regular business hours. However, some may work additional hours during periods of heavy construction activity. Also, if an accident occurs at a construction site, inspectors must respond immediately and may work additional hours to complete their report. Nongovernment inspectors—especially those who are self-employed—may have to work evenings and weekends. About 11 percent of construction and building inspectors were self-employed in 2010, which is similar to other construction occupations.

Job Outlook

Construction and Building Inspectors

Percent change in employment, projected 2010-20

Construction and Building Inspectors	18%
Other Construction and Related Workers	15%
Total, All Occupations	14%

Note: All Occupations includes all occupations in the U.S. Economy.
Source: U.S. Bureau of Labor Statistics, Employment Projections program

Employment of construction and building inspectors is expected to grow 18 percent from 2010 to 2020, about as fast as the average for all occupations. Concern for public safety and a desire to improve the quality of construction should continue to increase demand for inspectors. Employment growth is expected to be strongest in government and in firms specializing in architectural, engineering, and related services.

Concerns about natural and manmade disasters are increasing the need for qualified inspectors. New niche fields, including green and sustainable design, may require additional inspectors.

Although employment of home inspectors should continue to grow, some states are increasingly limiting entry into the field to those with experience or to those who are certified.

Job Prospects

Construction and building inspectors who are certified and can do a variety of inspections should have the best job opportunities. Inspectors with construction-related work experience or training in engineering, architecture, construction technology, or related fields will likely also have better job prospects. In addition, inspectors with thorough knowledge of construction practices and skills, such as reading and evaluating blueprints and plans, should have better job opportunities.

Larger jurisdictions usually hire specialized inspectors with knowledge in a particular area of construction, such as electrical or plumbing. Conversely, for budgetary reasons, smaller jurisdictions typically prefer to hire combination inspectors with broad knowledge of multiple disciplines.

Until recently, inspectors were thought to be less affected by the ups and downs of construction activity. Significant staff cuts in some areas, however, should result in strong competition for available jobs. Those who are self-employed, such as home inspectors, are more likely to be affected by economic downturns or fluctuations in the real estate market.

Employment projections data for construction and building inspectors, 2010-20

Occupational Title	SOC Code	Employment, 2010	Projected Employment, 2020	Change, 2010-20	
				Percent	Numeric
Construction and Building Inspectors	47-4011	102,400	120,800	18	18,400
SOURCE: U.S. Bureau of Labor Statistics, Employment Projections program					

Similar Occupations

This table shows a list of occupations with job duties that are similar to those of construction and building inspectors.

Occupation	Job Duties	Entry-Level Education	Median Annual Pay, May 2010
Carpenters	Carpenters construct and repair building frameworks and structures—such as stairways, doorframes, partitions, and rafters—made from wood and other materials. They also may install kitchen cabinets, siding, and drywall.	High school diploma or equivalent	$39,530
Electricians	Electricians install and maintain electrical systems in homes, businesses, and factories.	High school diploma or equivalent	$48,250
Plumbers, Pipefitters, and Steamfitters	Plumbers, pipefitters, and steamfitters install and repair pipes that carry water, steam, air, or other liquids or gases to and in businesses, homes, and factories.	High school diploma or equivalent	$46,660
Architects	Architects plan and design buildings and other structures.	Bachelor's degree	$72,550
Cartographers and Photogrammetrists	Cartographers and photogrammetrists measure, analyze, and interpret geographic information to create maps and charts for political, cultural, educational, and other purposes. Cartographers are general mapmakers, and photogrammetrists are specialized mapmakers who use aerial photographs to create maps.	Bachelor's degree	$54,510
Electrical and Electronic Engineering Technicians	Electrical and electronic engineering technicians help engineers design and develop computers, communications equipment, medical monitoring devices, navigational equipment, and other electrical and electronic equipment. They often work in product evaluation and testing, using measuring and diagnostic devices to adjust, test, and repair equipment.	Associate's degree	$56,040

Civil Engineers	Civil engineers design and supervise large construction projects, including roads, buildings, airports, tunnels, dams, bridges, and systems for water supply and sewage treatment.	Bachelor's degree	$77,560
Electrical and Electronics Engineers	Electrical engineers design, develop, test, and supervise the manufacturing of electrical equipment such as electric motors, radar and navigation systems, communications systems, and power generation equipment. Electronics engineers design and develop electronic equipment, such as broadcast and communications systems—from portable music players to global positioning systems (GPS).	Bachelor's degree	$87,180
Surveying and Mapping Technicians	Surveying and mapping technicians assist surveyors and cartographers in collecting data and making maps of the earth's surface. Surveying technicians visit sites to take measurements of the land. Mapping technicians use geographic data to create maps.	High school diploma or equivalent	$37,900
Surveyors	Surveyors establish official land, airspace, and water boundaries. Surveyors work with civil engineers, landscape architects, and urban and regional planners to develop comprehensive design documents.	Bachelor's degree	$54,880
Surveying and Mapping Technicians	Surveying and mapping technicians assist surveyors and cartographers in collecting data and making maps of the earth's surface. Surveying technicians visit sites to take measurements of the land. Mapping technicians use geographic data to create maps.	High school diploma or equivalent	$37,900
Construction Managers	Construction managers plan, coordinate, budget, and supervise construction projects from early development to completion.	Associate's degree	$83,860
Cost Estimators	Cost estimators collect and analyze data to estimate the time, money, resources, and labor required for product manufacturing, construction projects, or services. Some specialize in a particular industry or product type.	Bachelor's degree	$57,860
Appraisers and Assessors of Real Estate	Appraisers and assessors of real estate estimate the value of real property—land and the buildings on that land— before it is sold, mortgaged, taxed, insured, or developed.	High school diploma or equivalent	$48,500

Contacts for More Information

For more information about building codes, certification, and a career as a construction or building inspector, visit

International Code Council, National Fire Protection Association

For more information about construction inspectors, visit Association of Construction Inspectors

For more information about electrical inspectors, visit International Association of Electrical Inspectors

For more information about elevator inspectors, visit National Association of Elevator Safety Authorities International

For more information about education and training for mechanical and plumbing inspectors, visit International Association of Plumbing and Mechanical Officials

For information about becoming a home inspector, visit American Society of Home Inspectors, National Association of Home Inspectors, Inc.

Suggested citation:

Bureau of Labor Statistics, U.S. Department of Labor, Occupational Outlook Handbook, 2012-13 Edition, Construction and Building Inspectors, on the Internet at http://www.bls.gov/ooh/construction-and-extraction/construction-and-building-inspectors.htm.

Construction Equipment Operators

Quick Facts: Construction Equipment Operators	
2010 Median Pay	$39,460 per year $18.97 per hour
Entry-Level Education	High school diploma or equivalent
Work Experience in a Related Occupation	None
On-the-job Training	Moderate-term on-the-job training
Number of Jobs, 2010	404,900
Job Outlook, 2010-20	23% (Faster than average)
Employment Change, 2010-20	94,800

What Construction Equipment Operators Do

Construction equipment operators drive, maneuver, or control the heavy machinery used to construct roads, bridges, buildings, and other structures.

Duties

Construction equipment operators typically do the following:
- Check to make sure that equipment functions properly
- Clean, maintain, and make basic repairs to equipment
- Report malfunctions to supervisors
- Move levers, push pedals, or turn valves to activate power equipment
- Drive and maneuver equipment
- Coordinate machine actions with crew members in response to hand or audio signals
- Ensure that safety standards are met

Construction equipment operators use machinery to move construction materials, earth, and other heavy materials at construction sites and mines. They operate equipment that clears and grades land to prepare it for construction of roads, bridges, and buildings, as well as airport runways, power generation facilities, dams, levees, and other structures.

The following are types of construction equipment operators:

Operating engineers and other construction equipment operators work with one or several types of power construction equipment. They may operate excavation and loading machines equipped with scoops, shovels, or buckets that dig sand, gravel, earth, or similar materials. In addition to operating the familiar bulldozer, they operate trench excavators, road graders, and similar equipment. Sometimes, they may drive and control industrial trucks or tractors equipped with forklifts or booms for lifting materials. They also may operate and maintain air compressors, pumps, and other power equipment at construction sites.

Paving and surfacing equipment operators control the machines that spread and level asphalt or spread and smooth concrete for roadways or other structures. Paving and surfacing equipment operators may specialize further:
- **Asphalt spreader operators** turn valves to regulate the temperature of asphalt and the flow of asphalt onto the roadbed. They must ensure that the machine distributes the paving material evenly, and they also must ensure that there is a constant flow of asphalt into the hopper.
- **Concrete paving machine operators** control levers and turn handwheels to move attachments that spread, vibrate, and level wet concrete. They must watch the surface of the concrete carefully to identify low spots into which workers must add concrete.
- **Tamping equipment operators** use machines that compact earth and other fill materials for roadbeds or other construction sites. They also may operate machines with interchangeable hammers to cut or break up old pavement and drive guardrail posts into the ground.

Piledriver operators use large machines mounted on skids, barges, or cranes to hammer piles into the ground. Piles are long, heavy beams of wood or steel driven into the ground to support retaining walls, bridges, piers, or building foundations. Some piledriver operators work on offshore oil rigs.

Some workers operate cranes to move construction materials. For more information on these workers, see the profile on material moving machine operators.

Work Environment

Construction equipment operators held about 404,900 jobs in 2010. About 4 percent were self-employed. The following industries employed the most workers:

State and local government, excluding education and hospitals	21%
Highway, street, and bridge construction	14
Utility system construction	10
Other specialty trade contractors	22

Construction equipment operators work in nearly every type of climate and weather condition. Workers often get dirty, greasy, muddy, or dusty. Some operators work in remote locations on large construction projects, such as highways and dams, or in factories or mines.

Pile drivers commonly drive piles for a variety of purposes.

Injuries

Operating engineers and other construction equipment operators have a higher rate of injuries and illnesses than other occupations. However, accidents generally can be avoided by observing proper operating procedures and safety practices, but some repetitive stress injuries do occur. In addition, bulldozers, scrapers, and especially piledrivers, are noisy and shake or jolt the operator.

Work Schedules

Operators may have irregular hours because work on some construction projects continues around the clock or must be done late at night. Cold or rain can stop some types of construction. Nearly all operators work full time.

How to Become a Construction Equipment Operator

Many workers learn equipment operation through a formal apprenticeship, while others learn informally on the job, in the military, or by attending private trade schools.

Training

Many operators learn their trade through a 3- or 4-year apprenticeship. For each year of the program, apprentices must have at least 144 hours of technical instruction and 2,000 hours of paid on-the-job training. On the job, apprentices learn to maintain equipment, operate machinery, and use special technology, such as global positioning system (GPS) units. In the classroom, apprentices are taught map reading, operating procedures for special equipment, safety practices, and first aid. Because apprentices learn to operate a wider variety of machines than do other beginners, they usually have better job opportunities.

After completing an apprenticeship program, apprentices are considered journey workers, doing tasks with less guidance.

A few groups, including unions and contractor associations, sponsor apprenticeship programs. The basic qualifications for entering an apprenticeship program are as follows:
- Minimum age of 18
- High school education or equivalent
- Physically able to do the work

Other workers may start by operating light equipment under the guidance of an experienced operator. Later, they may operate heavier equipment, such as bulldozers. Technologically advanced construction equipment with computerized controls and improved hydraulics and electronics requires greater skill to operate. Operators of such equipment may need more training and some understanding of electronics.

Education

Private vocational schools offer programs in certain types of construction equipment operation. Finishing one of these programs may help someone get a job. However, people considering this kind of training should check the school's reputation among employers in the area and find out if the school offers the opportunity to work on actual machines in realistic situations.

A lot of information can be learned through instruction; to become a skilled construction equipment operator, however, a worker needs to physically do the various tasks. Many training facilities incorporate sophisticated simulators into their training, allowing beginners to familiarize themselves with the equipment in a controlled environment.

A high school diploma or equivalent is usually required. High school courses in English, math, and shop are useful. A course in auto mechanics is helpful because these workers may do maintenance on their machines.

Licenses

Construction equipment operators often need a commercial driver's license to haul their equipment to various jobsites. State rules about commercial driver's licenses vary.

A few states have special operator's licenses for operators of backhoes, loaders, and bulldozers.

Piledriver operators may need to have a crane operator certification or license. Because some states classify piledrivers as cranes, 18 states currently require piledriver operators to have a crane license. In addition, the cities of Chicago, New Orleans, New York, Omaha, Philadelphia, and Washington, DC, require special crane licensure.

Advancement

Some construction equipment operators choose to teach in training facilities. Other operators start their own contracting businesses, although doing so may be difficult because of high equipment startup costs.

Important Qualities

Eye–hand–foot coordination. Workers should have steady hands and feet to guide and control heavy machinery precisely, sometimes in tight spaces.

Mechanical skills. Because workers must often do basic maintenance on the equipment they operate, they should have good mechanical skills.

Unafraid of heights. A few equipment operators must work at great heights. For example, piledriver operators may need to service the pulleys that are located on the roof of a building.

Pay

Construction Equipment Operators
Median annual wages, May 2010

Pile-Driver Operators	$47,860
Operating Engineers and Other Construction Equipment Operators	$40,400
Construction Trades Workers	$38,240
Paving, Surfacing, and Tamping Equipment Operators	$34,150
Total, All Occupations	$33,840

Note: All Occupations includes all occupations in the U.S. Economy.
Source: U.S. Bureau of Labor Statistics, Occupational Employment Statistics

The median annual wage of construction equipment operators was $39,460 in May 2010. The median wage is the wage at which half the workers in an occupation earned more than that amount and half earned less.

The median wages for construction equipment operators in May 2010 were as follows:
- $34,150 for paving, surfacing, and tamping equipment operators
- $47,860 for pile-driver operators
- $40,400 for operating engineers and other construction equipment operators

Operators may have irregular hours because work on some construction projects continues around the clock or must be done late at night. Cold and rain may stop construction work. Nearly all construction equipment operators work full time.

The starting pay for apprentices is usually between 40 percent and 60 percent of what fully trained operators make. They get pay increases as they become more skilled.

Construction equipment operators have a high rate of union membership. Although no single union covers all operators, the largest organizer of these workers is the International Union of Operating Engineers.

Job Outlook

Construction Equipment Operators

Percent change in employment, projected 2010-20

Pile-Driver Operators	36%
Operating Engineers and Other Construction Equipment Operators	23%
Construction Trades Workers	23%
Paving, Surfacing, and Tamping Equipment Operators	22%
Total, All Occupations	14%

Note: All Occupations includes all occupations in the U.S. Economy.
Source: U.S. Bureau of Labor Statistics, Employment Projections program

Overall employment of construction equipment operators is expected to grow 23 percent from 2010 to 2020, faster than the average for all occupations. The likelihood of increased spending on infrastructure to improve roads, bridges, water and sewer systems, and the electric power grid, all of which are in great need of repair across the country, is expected to result in numerous jobs. In addition, population growth increases the need for construction projects such as new roads and sewer lines, which also is expected to generate some jobs. However, without the extra spending on infrastructure by the federal government, employment may be flat as states and localities struggle with reduced taxes and budget shortfalls to pay for road and other improvements.

Job Prospects

Workers with the ability to operate multiple types of equipment should have the best job opportunities.

As with many other construction workers, employment of construction equipment operators is sensitive to fluctuations of the economy. Workers may experience periods of unemployment when the overall level of construction falls. However, shortages of workers may occur in some areas during peak periods of building activity.

Employment opportunities should be best in metropolitan areas, where most large commercial and multifamily buildings are constructed, and in states that are undertaking large transportation-related projects.

In addition, the need to replace workers who leave the occupation should result in some job opportunities.

Employment projections data for construction equipment operators, 2010-20

Occupational Title	SOC Code	Employment, 2010	Projected Employment, 2020	Change, 2010-20 Percent	Change, 2010-20 Numeric
Construction Equipment Operators	—	404,900	499,600	23	94,800
Paving, Surfacing, and Tamping Equipment Operators	47-2071	51,600	63,000	22	11,400
Pile-Driver Operators	47-2072	4,100	5,600	36	1,500
Operating Engineers and Other Construction Equipment Operators	47-2073	349,100	431,000	23	81,900
SOURCE: U.S. Bureau of Labor Statistics, Employment Projections program					

Similar Occupations

This table shows a list of occupations with job duties that are similar to those of construction equipment operators.

Occupation	Job Duties	Entry-Level Education	Median Annual Pay, May 2010
Material Moving Machine Operators	Material moving machine operators use machinery to transport various objects. Some operators move construction materials around building sites or earth around a mine. Others move goods around a warehouse or onto and off of container ships.	Less than high school	$30,800
Heavy and Tractor-trailer Truck Drivers	Heavy and tractor-trailer truck drivers transport goods from one location to another. Most tractor-trailer drivers are long-haul drivers and operate trucks with a capacity of at least 26,001 pounds per gross vehicle weight (GVW). They deliver goods over intercity routes, sometimes spanning several states.	High school diploma or equivalent	$37,770

Contacts for More Information

For information about apprenticeships or job opportunities as a construction equipment operator, contact local cement or highway construction contractors, a local joint union–management apprenticeship committee, or the nearest office of your state employment service or apprenticeship agency. Information on apprenticeships is available from the U.S. Department of Labor's toll-free help line, 1 (877) 872-5627, or Employment and Training Administration.

For more information on construction equipment operators, visit Associated General Contractors of America, National Center for Construction Education and Research, Pile Driving Contractors Association

For information on training of construction equipment operators, visit International Union of Operating Engineers

For information about crane and derrick operator certification and licensure, visit National Commission for the Certification of Crane Operators

Suggested citation:

Bureau of Labor Statistics, U.S. Department of Labor, Occupational Outlook Handbook, 2012-13 Edition, Construction Equipment Operators, on the Internet at http://www.bls.gov/ooh/construction-and-extraction/construction-equipment-operators.htm.

Construction Laborers and Helpers

Quick Facts: Construction Laborers and Helpers	
2010 Median Pay	$28,410 per year $13.66 per hour
Entry-Level Education	See How to Become One
Work Experience in a Related Occupation	None
On-the-job Training	Short-term on-the-job training
Number of Jobs, 2010	1,250,200
Job Outlook, 2010-20	25% (Faster than average)
Employment Change, 2010-20	314,200

What Construction Laborers and Helpers Do

Construction laborers and helpers do many basic tasks that require physical labor on construction sites.

Duties

Construction laborers and helpers typically do the following:

- Clean and prepare construction sites by removing debris and possible hazards
- Load or unload building materials to be used in construction
- Build or take apart bracing, barricades, forms (molds that determine the shape of concrete), scaffolding, and temporary structures
- Dig trenches, backfill holes, or compact earth to prepare for construction
- Operate or tend equipment and machines used in construction, such as concrete mixers
- Help other craftworkers with their duties
- Follow construction plans and instructions from the people they are working for

Construction laborers and helpers work on almost all construction sites, doing a wide range of tasks from the very easy to the extremely difficult and hazardous. Although many of the tasks they do require some training and experience, most jobs usually require little skill and can be learned quickly.

The following are occupational specialties:

Construction laborers do a variety of construction-related activities during all phases of construction. Although most laborers are generalists—such as those who install barricades, cones, and markers to control traffic patterns—many others specialize. For example, those who operate the machines and equipment that lay concrete or asphalt on roads are more likely to specialize in those areas.

Most construction laborers work in the following areas:

- Building homes and businesses
- Tearing down buildings
- Removing hazardous materials
- Building highways and roads
- Digging tunnels and mine shafts

Construction laborers use a variety of tools and equipment. Some tools are simple, such as brooms and shovels; other equipment is more sophisticated, such as pavement breakers, jackhammers, earth tampers, and surveying equipment.

With special training, laborers may help transport and use explosives or run hydraulic boring machines to dig out tunnels. They may learn to use laser beam equipment to place pipes and use computers to control robotic pipe cutters. They may become certified to remove asbestos, lead, or chemicals.

Helpers assist construction craftworkers, such as electricians and carpenters, with a variety of basic tasks. They may carry tools and materials or help set up equipment. For example, many helpers work with cement masons to move and set forms. Many other helpers assist with taking apart equipment, cleaning up sites, and disposing of waste, as well as helping with any other needs of craftworkers.

Many construction trades have helpers who assist craftworkers. The following are examples of trades that have associated helpers:

- Brickmasons, blockmasons, stonemasons, and tile and marble setters
- Carpenters
- Electricians
- Painters, paperhangers, plasterers, and stucco masons
- Pipelayers, plumbers, pipefitters, and steamfitters
- Roofers

Work Environment

Construction laborers held about 1 million jobs in 2010, of which 59 percent were employed in the construction industry. About 23 percent of construction laborers were self-employed. The employment levels of the construction helper specialties were as follows:

Electrician helpers	73,500
Pipelayer, plumber, pipefitter, and steamfitter helpers	57,900
Carpenter helpers	46,500
Brickmason, blockmason, stonemason, and tile and marble setter helpers	29,400
Roofer helpers	12,700
Painter, paperhanger, plasterer, and stucco mason helpers	11,900
All other helpers	19,600

Most construction laborers and helpers do physically demanding work. Some work at great heights or outdoors in all weather conditions. Some may be required to work in tunnels. They must use earplugs around loud equipment and wear gloves, safety glasses, and other protective gear.

Injuries

Construction laborers have one of the highest rates of on-the-job injuries and illnesses compared to the national average. Workers may experience cuts from materials and tools, falls from ladders and scaffolding, and burns from chemicals or equipment. Some jobs expose workers to harmful materials, fumes, odors, or dangerous machinery. Workers also may face muscle fatigue and injuries related to lifting and carrying heavy materials. Although they face similar hazards, construction helpers generally experience a rate of injury and illness that is close to the national average.

Work Schedules

Like many construction workers, most laborers and helpers work full time. Although they may have to stop because of bad weather, they commonly work overtime to meet deadlines. Laborers and helpers on highway and bridge projects may need to work overnight, a time during which traffic is least disrupted. In some parts of the country, construction laborers and helpers may work only during certain seasons.

About 23 percent of construction laborers were self-employed. Self-employed workers may be able to set their own schedule. In contrast, very few helpers were self-employed.

How to Become a Construction Laborer or Helper

Most construction laborers and helpers learn their trade through short-term on-the-job training.

Although there are no formal educational requirements, high school classes in English, mathematics, blueprint reading, welding, and shop can be helpful.

Training

Most construction laborers and helpers learn through short-term on-the-job training after being hired by a construction contractor or a temporary-help employment agency. Workers typically gain experience by doing jobs under the guidance of experienced workers.

Although the majority of workers learn informally, some opt for formal apprenticeship programs. Programs generally include 2 to 4 years of technical instruction and on-the-job training. In the first 200 hours, workers learn basic construction skills, such as how to read blueprints, the correct use of tools and equipment, and safety and health procedures. The remainder of the curriculum consists of specialized skills training in three of the largest segments of the construction industry: building construction, heavy and highway construction, and environmental remediation such as lead or asbestos removal.

Several groups, including unions and contractor associations, sponsor apprenticeship programs. The basic qualification for entering an apprenticeship program is being age 18 or older. A high school diploma or its equivalent is preferred but not required.

Education

Although there are no formal educational requirements, some workers may choose or be required to attend a trade or vocational school, association training class, or community college to get further trade-related training.

Licenses

Laborers who remove hazardous material (hazmat) must have a federal hazmat license. For more information, see the profile on hazardous materials removal workers.

Certification

Depending on the work they do, laborers may need specific certifications. Certification helps workers prove that they have the knowledge to perform more complex tasks.

The following are examples of areas which my require certification:

- Asbestos
- Energy Auditor
- Lead
- Operators Qualification for Pipeline
- OSHA 10 and/or 30 Hour Construction Safety Certification
- Radiological Worker
- Rough Terrain Forklift Operation

- Scaffold User and Builder
- Signalperson Qualification
- Weatherization Technician Installer and Supervisor
- Welder
- Workzone Safety Technician, Flagger and Supervisor

Advancement

Through experience and training, construction laborers can advance into positions that involve more complex activities. For example, laborers may earn certifications in welding, scaffold erecting, or concrete finishing and then spend more time performing activities that require the specialized knowledge.

Through training and experience, helpers can move into construction craft occupations. For example, a bricklayer's helper may have a chance to set bricks on the job and later join the contractor's apprenticeship program.

Important Qualities

Color vision. Laborers and helpers may need to be able to distinguish colors to do their job. For example, an electrician's helper must be able to distinguish different colors of wire to help the lead electrician.

Math skills. Laborers and some helpers need to perform basic math calculations to do their job. They often help with measuring on jobsites and may be part of a surveying crew.

Physical strength. Laborers and helpers often must lift heavy materials or equipment. For example, cement mason helpers must move cinder blocks, which weigh more than 40 pounds each.

Stamina. Laborers and helpers must have endurance to perform strenuous tasks throughout the day. Highway laborers, for example, spend hours on their feet—often in hot temperatures—with few breaks.

Technical skills. Laborers frequently are required to operate heavy equipment, such as driving a forklift.

Pay

Construction Laborers and Helpers
Median annual wages, May 2010

Construction Trades Workers	$38,240
Total, All Occupations	$33,840
Construction Laborers	$29,280
Helpers, Construction Trades	$26,360

Note: All Occupations includes all occupations in the U.S. Economy.
Source: U.S. Bureau of Labor Statistics, Occupational Employment Statistics

The median annual wage of construction laborers and helpers was $28,410 in May 2010. The median wage is the wage at which half the workers in an occupation earned more than that amount and half earned less.

The median wages for construction laborers and helpers in May 2010 were the following:

- $27,780 for brickmason, blockmason, stonemason, and tile and marble setter helpers
- $25,760 for carpenter helpers
- $29,280 for construction laborers
- $27,220 for electrician helpers
- $23,290 for painter, paperhanger, plasterer, and stucco mason helpers
- $26,740 for pipelayer, plumber, pipefitter, and steamfitter helpers
- $23,320 for roofer helpers
- $25,200 for all other construction helpers

The starting pay for apprentices is usually between 30 percent and 60 percent what fully trained laborers make. They get pay increases as they become more skilled.

About 10 percent of construction laborers are members of a union. The largest organizer of laborers is the Laborers' International Union of North America.

Like many construction workers, most construction laborers and helpers work full time. Although they may need to stop because of bad weather, they commonly work overtime to meet deadlines. Laborers and helpers on highway and bridge projects may need to work overnight, a time during which traffic is least disrupted.

Job Outlook

Construction Laborers and Helpers

Percent change in employment, projected 2010-20

Helpers, Construction Trades	40%
Construction Trades Workers	23%
Construction Laborers	21%
Total, All Occupations	14%

Note: All Occupations includes all occupations in the U.S. Economy.
Source: U.S. Bureau of Labor Statistics, Employment Projections program

Employment of construction laborers is expected to grow 21 percent from 2010 to 2020, faster than the average for all occupations. Laborers work in all fields of construction, and demand for laborers will mirror the level of overall construction activity. Repairing and replacing the nation's infrastructure, such as roads, bridges, and water lines, should result in steady demand for laborers.

Although employment growth of specific types of helpers is expected to vary (see table below), demand for helpers will be driven by the construction of schools, office buildings, factories, and powerplants. Population growth also is expected to result in new-home construction, which will stimulate the need for many additional helpers. Remodeling needs will also result in some new jobs.

However, demand for helpers is also affected by economic downturns. In the slowdown in construction since the 2007-09 recession, the number of jobs for helpers decreased faster than jobs for the workers they help. Contractors kept their more experienced workers and had them do tasks that helpers would normally do. As construction returns to normal levels, helpers will be needed to do their standard tasks again.

Job Prospects

Construction laborers with the most skills should have the best job opportunities. Opportunities also will vary by occupation; for example, carpenters' helpers should have the best job prospects, while painters', paperhangers', plasterers', and stucco masons' helpers will likely find fewer job openings. Prospective employees with military service often have better opportunities when applying for a job.

Employment of construction laborers and helpers is especially sensitive to the fluctuations of the economy. On the one hand, workers in these trades may experience periods of unemployment when the overall level of construction falls. On the other hand, shortages of these workers may occur in some areas during peak periods of building activity.

Employment projections data for construction laborers and helpers, 2010-20

Occupational Title	SOC Code	Employment, 2010	Projected Employment, 2020	Change, 2010-20	
				Percent	Numeric
Construction Laborers and Helpers	—	1,250,200	1,564,400	25	314,200
Construction Laborers	47-2061	998,800	1,211,200	21	212,400
Helpers–Brickmasons, Blockmasons, Stonemasons, and Tile and Marble Setters	47-3011	29,400	47,000	60	17,600
Helpers–Carpenters	47-3012	46,500	72,400	56	25,900
Helpers–Electricians	47-3013	73,500	96,000	31	22,500
Helpers–Painters, Paperhangers, Plasterers, and Stucco Masons	47-3014	11,900	14,500	22	2,600
Helpers–Pipelayers, Plumbers, Pipefitters, and Steamfitters	47-3015	57,900	84,200	45	26,300
Helpers–Roofers	47-3016	12,700	13,900	10	1,200
Helpers, Construction Trades, All Other	47-3019	19,600	25,200	29	5,600
SOURCE: U.S. Bureau of Labor Statistics, Employment Projections program					

Similar Occupations

This table shows a list of occupations with job duties that are similar to those of construction laborers and helpers.

Occupation	Job Duties	Entry-Level Education	Median Annual Pay, May 2010
Brickmasons, Blockmasons, and Stonemasons	Brickmasons, blockmasons, and stonemasons (or, simply, masons) use bricks, concrete blocks, and natural stones to build fences, walkways, walls, and other structures.	High school diploma or equivalent	$45,410
Carpenters	Carpenters construct and repair building frameworks and structures—such as stairways, doorframes, partitions, and rafters—made from wood and other materials. They also may install kitchen cabinets, siding, and drywall.	High school diploma or equivalent	$39,530

Electricians	Electricians install and maintain electrical systems in homes, businesses, and factories.	High school diploma or equivalent	$48,250
Hazardous Materials Removal Workers	Hazardous materials (hazmat) removal workers identify and dispose of asbestos, radioactive and nuclear waste, arsenic, lead, and other hazardous materials. They also clean up materials that are flammable, corrosive, reactive, or toxic.	High school diploma or equivalent	$37,600
Painters, Construction and Maintenance	Painters apply paint, stain, and coatings to walls, buildings, bridges, and other structures.	Less than high school	$34,280
Plasterers and Stucco Masons	Plasterers and stucco masons apply coats of plaster or stucco to walls, ceilings, or partitions for functional and decorative purposes. Some workers apply ornamental plaster.	Less than high school	$37,210
Plumbers, Pipefitters, and Steamfitters	Plumbers, pipefitters, and steamfitters install and repair pipes that carry water, steam, air, or other liquids or gases to and in businesses, homes, and factories.	High school diploma or equivalent	$46,660
Material Moving Machine Operators	Material moving machine operators use machinery to transport various objects. Some operators move construction materials around building sites or earth around a mine. Others move goods around a warehouse or onto and off of container ships.	Less than high school	$30,800
Grounds Maintenance Workers	Grounds maintenance workers provide a pleasant outdoor environment by ensuring that the grounds of houses, businesses, and parks are attractive, orderly, and healthy.	See How to Become One	$23,740

Contacts for More Information

For details about apprenticeships or other work opportunities for construction laborers and helpers, contact the offices of the state employment service, the state apprenticeship agency, local construction contractors or firms that employ laborers, or local union–management apprenticeship committees. Apprenticeship information is available from the U.S. Department of Labor's toll-free help line, 1 (877) 872-5627, or Employment and Training Administration.

For information about education programs for laborers, visit Laborers' International Union of North America, National Center for Construction Education and Research

Suggested citation:

Bureau of Labor Statistics, U.S. Department of Labor, Occupational Outlook Handbook, 2012-13 Edition, Construction Laborers and Helpers, on the Internet at http://www.bls.gov/ooh/construction-and-extraction/construction-laborers-and-helpers.htm.

Drywall and Ceiling Tile Installers, and Tapers

Quick Facts: Drywall and Ceiling Tile Installers, and Tapers	
2010 Median Pay	$38,290 per year $18.41 per hour
Entry-Level Education	Less than high school
Work Experience in a Related Occupation	None
On-the-job Training	Moderate-term on-the-job training
Number of Jobs, 2010	129,600
Job Outlook, 2010-20	29% (Much faster than average)
Employment Change, 2010-20	37,300

What Drywall and Ceiling Tile Installers, and Tapers Do

Drywall and ceiling tile installers hang wallboards to walls and ceilings inside buildings. Tapers prepare the wallboards for painting, using tape and other materials. Many workers do both installing and taping.

Duties

Drywall installers typically do the following:
- Review design plans to minimize the number of cuts and waste of wallboard
- Measure the location of electrical outlets, plumbing, windows, and vents
- Cut drywall to the right size, using utility knives and power saws
- Fasten drywall panels to interior wall studs, using nails or screws
- Trim and smooth rough edges so boards join evenly

Ceiling tile installers typically do the following:
- Measure according to blueprints or drawings
- Nail or screw supports
- Put tiles or sheets of shock-absorbing materials on ceilings
- Keep the tile in place with cement adhesive, nails, or screws

Tapers typically do the following:
- Prepare wall surface (wallboard) by patching nail holes
- Apply tape and use sealing compound to cover joints between wallboards
- Apply additional coats of sealing compound to create an even surface
- Sand all joints and holes to a smooth, seamless finish

Installers are also called **framers** or **hangers**. Tapers are also called **finishers**. Ceiling tile installers are sometimes called **acoustical carpenters** because they work with tiles that block sound.

Once wallboards are hung, workers use increasingly wider trowels to spread multiple coats of spackle over cracks, indentations, and any remaining imperfections. Some workers may use a mechanical applicator, a tool that spreads sealing compound on the wall joint while dispensing and setting tape at the same time.

To work on ceilings, drywall and ceiling tile installers and tapers may use mechanical lifts or stand on stilts, ladders, or scaffolds.

Work Environment

Drywall and ceiling tile installers and tapers held about 129,600 jobs in 2010, of which 59 percent were employed in the drywall and insulation contractors industry. About 27 percent were self-employed.

Drywall and ceiling tile installers and tapers work indoors. As in many other construction trades, the work is physically demanding. Workers spend most of the day standing, bending, or stretching, and they often must lift and maneuver heavy, oversized wallboards. To work on ceilings, drywall and ceiling tile installers and tapers may have to stand on stilts, ladders, or scaffolds.

The work can be dusty and dirty, irritating the skin, eyes, and lungs, so workers must wear protective masks, goggles, and gloves.

Injuries

Drywall and ceiling tile installers have a rate of injuries and illnesses that is higher than the average for all occupations. Tapers have an average rate of injuries and illnesses. Common injuries include falls from ladders or stilts, cuts from sharp tools, and muscle strains from lifting heavy materials.

Work Schedules

Most drywall and ceiling tile installers and tapers work full time.

About 27 percent of drywall and ceiling tile installers and tapers were self-employed. Self-employed workers may be able to set their own schedule.

How to Become a Drywall and Ceiling Tile Installer, or Taper

Although most drywall and ceiling tile installers and tapers learn their trade informally on the job, a few learn through a formal apprenticeship.

Training

Most drywall and ceiling tile installers and tapers learn their trade informally by helping more experienced workers and gradually being given more duties. They start by carrying materials, lifting, and

Drywallers work with many different types of tools.

cleaning up. They learn to use the tools of the trade. Then they learn to measure, cut, and install or apply materials. Employers usually give some on-the-job training that may last from 1 to 12 months.

A few drywall and ceiling tile installers and tapers learn their trade through a 3- or 4-year apprenticeship. For each year of the program, apprentices must have at least 144 hours of related technical work and 2,000 hours of paid on-the-job training. During training, apprentices learn construction basics related to blueprint reading, mathematics, building code requirements, and safety and first-aid practices.

After completing an apprenticeship program, drywall and ceiling tile installers and tapers are considered journey workers and may perform duties on their own.

A few groups, including unions and contractor associations, sponsor apprenticeship programs. The basic qualifications for entering an apprenticeship program are as follows:
- Minimum age of 18
- High school education or equivalent
- Physically able to perform the work

Education

Although there are no formal education requirements to become a drywall and ceiling tile installer and taper, high school math and general shop courses are considered useful.

Important Qualities

Math skills. Drywall and ceiling tile installers and tapers use basic math skills on every job. For example, they must be able to estimate the quantity of materials needed and accurately measure for cutting panels.

Physical strength. Standard drywall sheets can weigh 50 to 100 pounds. Also, drywall and ceiling tile installers often must lift heavy pieces of material over their heads to put on the ceiling.

Stamina. Because drywall and ceiling tile installers constantly lift and move heavy materials into place, they should have excellent physical stamina.

Pay

Drywall and Ceiling Tile Installers, and Tapers
Median annual wages, May 2010

Tapers	$45,490
Construction Trades Workers	$38,240
Drywall and Ceiling Tile Installers	$37,320
Total, All Occupations	$33,840

Note: All Occupations includes all occupations in the U.S. Economy.
Source: U.S. Bureau of Labor Statistics, Occupational Employment Statistics

The median annual wage of drywall and ceiling tile installers and tapers was $38,290 in May 2010. The median wage is the wage at which half the workers in an occupation earned more than that amount

and half earned less.

The median annual wage of drywall and ceiling tile installers was $37,320 in May 2010. The lowest 10 percent earned less than $24,470, and the top 10 percent earned more than $68,660.

The median annual wage of tapers was $45,490 in May 2010. The lowest 10 percent earned less than $27,480, and the top 10 percent earned more than $77,380.

The starting wage for apprentices is usually between 30 percent and 50 percent of what fully trained drywall and ceiling tile installers and tapers make. As they gain more skill, they receive pay increases.

Most drywall and ceiling tile installers and tapers work full time.

About 27 percent of drywall and ceiling tile installers and tapers were self-employed. Self-employed workers may be able to set their own schedule.

Job Outlook

Drywall and Ceiling Tile Installers, and Tapers
Percent change in employment, projected 2010-20

Tapers	35%
Drywall and Ceiling Tile Installers	28%
Construction Trades Workers	23%
Total, All Occupations	14%

Note: All Occupations includes all occupations in the U.S. Economy.
Source: U.S. Bureau of Labor Statistics, Employment Projections program

Employment of drywall and ceiling tile installers and tapers is projected to grow 29 percent from 2010 to 2020, much faster than the average for all other occupations. Drywall is, and will continue to be, the most common interior wall covering in nearly every building. As a result, new residential and commercial building construction will drive demand for workers. Home improvement and remodeling projects also are expected to create jobs because existing homes and other buildings are getting old and need repair.

Job Prospects

Job prospects for drywall and ceiling tile installers and tapers should improve over the coming decade as construction activity rebounds from the recent recession. As with many other construction workers, employment of these workers is sensitive to the fluctuations of the economy. On the one hand, they may experience periods of unemployment when the overall level of construction falls. On the other hand, shortages of workers may occur in some areas during peak periods of building activity.

Skilled drywall and ceiling tile installers and tapers with good work history and experience in the construction industry should have the best job opportunities.

Employment projections data for drywall and ceiling tile installers, and tapers, 2010-20

Occupational Title	SOC Code	Employment, 2010	Projected Employment, 2020	Change, 2010-20	
				Percent	Numeric
Percent	Numeric				
Drywall Installers, Ceiling Tile Installers, and Tapers	—	129,600	166,900	29	37,300
Drywall and Ceiling Tile Installers	47-2081	106,700	136,000	28	29,400
Tapers	47-2082	22,900	30,900	35	8,000
SOURCE: U.S. Bureau of Labor Statistics, Employment Projections program					

Similar Occupations

This table shows a list of occupations with job duties that are similar to those of drywall and ceiling tile installers, and tapers.

Occupation	Job Duties	Entry-Level Education	Median Annual Pay, May 2010
Brickmasons, Blockmasons, and Stonemasons	Brickmasons, blockmasons, and stonemasons (or, simply, masons) use bricks, concrete blocks, and natural stones to build fences, walkways, walls, and other structures.	High school diploma or equivalent	$45,410
Carpenters	Carpenters construct and repair building frameworks and structures—such as stairways, doorframes, partitions, and rafters—made from wood and other materials. They also may install kitchen cabinets, siding, and drywall.	High school diploma or equivalent	$39,530
Carpet Installers	Carpet installers lay carpet in homes, offices, restaurants, and many other types of buildings.	Less than high school	$36,090
Construction Laborers and Helpers	Construction laborers and helpers do many basic tasks that require physical labor on construction sites.	See How to Become One	$28,410
Insulation Workers	Insulation workers install and replace the materials used to insulate buildings and their mechanical systems to help control and maintain temperature.	See How to Become One	$35,110
Painters, Construction and Maintenance	Painters apply paint, stain, and coatings to walls, buildings, bridges, and other structures.	Less than high school	$34,280
Plasterers and Stucco Masons	Plasterers and stucco masons apply coats of plaster or stucco to walls, ceilings, or partitions for functional and decorative purposes. Some workers apply ornamental plaster.	Less than high school	$37,210
Tile and Marble Setters	Tile and marble setters apply hard tile, marble, and wood tiles to walls, floors, and other surfaces.	Less than high school	$38,110

Contacts for More Information

For details about apprenticeships or other work opportunities in this trade, contact the offices of the state employment service, the state apprenticeship agency, local contractors or firms that employ drywall installers, ceiling tile installers, and tapers, or local union-management finishing trade apprenticeship committees. Apprenticeship information is available from the U.S. Department of Labor's toll-free help line, 1 (877) 872-5627, or Employment and Training Administration.

For more information about drywall and ceiling tile installers and tapers, visit Associated Builders and Contractors ,Association of the Wall and Ceiling Industry ,Finishing Trades Institute

Suggested citation:

Bureau of Labor Statistics, U.S. Department of Labor, Occupational Outlook Handbook, 2012-13 Edition, Drywall and Ceiling Tile Installers, and Tapers, on the Internet at http://www.bls.gov/ooh/construction-and-extraction/drywall-and-ceiling -tile-installers-and-tapers.htm.

Electricians

Quick Facts: Electricians	
2010 Median Pay	$48,250 per year $23.20 per hour
Entry-Level Education	High school diploma or equivalent
Work Experience in a Related Occupation	None
On-the-job Training	Apprenticeship
Number of Jobs, 2010	577,000
Job Outlook, 2010-20	23% (Faster than average)
Employment Change, 2010-20	133,700

What Electricians Do

Electricians install and maintain electrical systems in homes, businesses, and factories.

Duties

Electricians typically do the following:
- Read blueprints or technical diagrams before doing work
- Install and maintain wiring and lighting systems
- Inspect electrical components, such as transformers and circuit breakers
- Identify electrical problems with a variety of testing devices
- Repair or replace wiring, equipment, or fixtures using hand tools and power tools
- Follow state and local building regulations based on the National Electric Code
- Direct and train workers to install, maintain, or repair electrical wiring or equipment

Almost every building has an electrical system that is installed during construction and maintained after that. Electricians do both the installing and maintaining of electrical systems.

Installing electrical systems is less complicated than maintaining older equipment. This is because it is easier to get to electrical wiring during construction. Maintaining older equipment, however, involves identifying problems and repairing malfunctioning equipment that is

Electricians often cap wires before installing an outlet.

sometimes difficult to reach. Electricians doing maintenance work may need to fix or replace outlets, circuit breakers, motors, or robotic control systems.

Electricians read blueprints, which are technical diagrams of electrical systems that show the location of circuits, outlets, and other equipment. They use different types of hand and power tools, such as pipe benders, to run and protect wiring. Other commonly used hand and power tools include screwdrivers, wire strippers, drills, and saws. While troubleshooting, electricians also may use ammeters, voltmeters, and multimeters to find problems and ensure that components are working properly.

Many electricians work independently, but sometimes they collaborate with others. For example, experienced electricians may work with building engineers and architects to help design electrical systems in new construction. Some electricians also may consult with other construction specialists, such as elevator installers and heating and air conditioning workers, to help install or maintain electrical or power systems. At larger companies, electricians are more likely to work as part of a crew; they may direct helpers and apprentices to complete jobs.

The following are examples of occupational specialties:

Inside electricians maintain and repair large motors, equipment, and control systems in businesses and factories. They use their knowledge of electrical systems to help these facilities run safely and efficiently. Some also install the wiring for businesses and factories that are being built. To minimize equipment failure, inside electricians often perform scheduled maintenance.

Residential electricians install wiring and troubleshoot electrical problems in peoples' homes. Those who work in new-home construction install outlets and provide access to power where needed. Those who work in maintenance and remodeling repair and replace faulty equipment. For example, if a circuit breaker is tripped, electricians determine the reason and fix it.

Work Environment

Electricians held about 577,000 jobs in 2010, of which 62 percent were employed in the electrical contractors and other wiring installation contractors industry. About 10 percent of electricians were self-employed.

Electricians work indoors and out, in homes, businesses, factories, and construction sites. They occasionally work in cramped spaces. Constant lifting, standing, and kneeling can be tiring. Those who work in factories are often subject to noisy machinery. Some may need to travel long distances to get to jobsites.

Injuries

Electricians have a higher-than-average injury and illness rate. The most common risks are electrical shocks and burns, but electricians also risk cuts, falls, and other common construction-related injuries. As a result, they must follow safety guidelines and wear protective clothing and safety glasses to reduce these risks.

Work Schedules

Almost all electricians work full time, which may include evenings and weekends. During scheduled maintenance, inside electricians can expect to work overtime. Overtime is also common on construction worksites, where meeting deadlines is critical.

About 10 percent of electricians were self-employed in 2010. Self-employed workers may have the ability to set their own schedule.

How to Become an Electrician

Although most electricians learn through a formal apprenticeship, some start out by attending a technical school. Most states require licensure.

Apprenticeship

Most electricians learn their trade in a 4-year apprenticeship. For each year of the program, apprentices must complete at least 144 hours of technical training and 2,000 hours of paid on-the-job training. In the classroom, apprentices learn electrical theory, blueprint reading, mathematics, electrical code requirements, and safety and first-aid practices. They also may receive specialized training related to soldering, communications, fire alarm systems, and elevators. Because of this comprehensive training, those who complete apprenticeship programs qualify to do both construction and maintenance work.

After completing an apprenticeship program, electricians are considered to be journey workers and may perform duties on their own.

Several groups, including unions and contractor associations, sponsor apprenticeship programs. The basic qualifications to enter an apprenticeship program are as follows:
- Minimum age of 18
- High school education or equivalent
- One year of algebra
- Qualifying score on an aptitude test
- Drug free

Some electrical contractors have their own training program. Although most workers enter apprenticeships directly, some start out as helpers.

Education

Some electricians start out by attending a technical school. Many technical schools offer programs related to safety and basic electrical information. Graduates usually receive credit toward their 4-year apprenticeship.

Electricians may be required to take continuing education courses. These courses usually involve instruction related to safety practices, changes to the electrical code, and training from manufacturers in specific products.

Licenses

Most states require licensure. Requirements vary by state. Contact your state's licensing agency for more information.

Important Qualities

Color vision. Electricians need good color vision because workers frequently must identify electrical wires by color.

Critical-thinking skills. Electricians perform tests and use the results to diagnose problems. For example, when an outlet is not working, they may use a multimeter to check the voltage, amperage, or resistance to determine the best course of action.

Customer-service skills. Electricians work with people on a regular basis. As a result, they should be friendly and be able to address customers' questions.

Managerial skills. Some electricians must be able to direct others' work as well as plan work schedules. Often, this work includes

preparing estimates and other administrative tasks.

Troubleshooting skills. Electricians find, diagnose, and repair problems. For example, if a motor stops working, they perform tests to determine the cause of its failure and then, depending on the results, fix or replace the motor.

Pay

Electricians

Median annual wages, May 2010

Electricians	$48,250
Construction Trades Workers	$38,240
Total, All Occupations	$33,840

Note: All Occupations includes all occupations in the U.S. Economy.
Source: U.S. Bureau of Labor Statistics, Occupational Employment Statistics

The median annual wage of electricians was $48,250 in May 2010. The median wage is the wage at which half the workers in an occupation earned more than that amount and half earned less. The lowest 10 percent earned less than $29,400, and the top 10 percent earned more than $80,890.

The starting pay for apprentices usually is between 30 percent and 50 percent of what fully trained electricians make, receiving pay increases as they gain more skill.

About one-third of electricians are union members. Although there is no single union, the largest organizer for electricians is the International Brotherhood of Electrical Workers.

Almost all electricians work full time, which may include evenings and weekends. During scheduled maintenance, inside electricians can expect to work overtime. Overtime is also common on construction worksites, where meeting deadlines is critical.

About 10 percent of electricians were self-employed in 2010. Self-employed workers may have the ability to set their own schedule.

Job Outlook

Electricians

Percent change in employment, projected 2010-20

Electricians	23%
Construction Trades Workers	23%
Total, All Occupations	14%

Note: All Occupations includes all occupations in the U.S. Economy.
Source: U.S. Bureau of Labor Statistics, Employment Projections program

Employment of electricians is expected to grow 23 percent from 2010 to 2020, faster than the average for all occupations. Homes and businesses need more wiring than ever before, and electricians will be needed to install the necessary components. Overall growth of the construction industry and maintenance of older equipment in manufacturing plants also will require more electricians.

Alternative power generation, such as solar and wind, is an emerging field that should require more electricians for installation. Furthermore, electricians will be needed to link these alternative power sources to homes and power grids. Employment growth stemming from these sources, however, is largely dependent on government policy.

With greater efficiency and reliability of newer manufacturing plants, demand for electricians in manufacturing should be offset by the closing of old facilities.

Job Prospects

Employment of electricians fluctuates with the overall economy. On the one hand, there is great demand for electricians during peak periods of building and manufacturing. On the other hand, workers may experience periods of unemployment when the overall level of construction falls. Inside electricians in factories tend to have the most stable employment.

Electricians with the widest variety of skills should have the best job opportunities.

Employment projections data for electricians, 2010-20

Occupational Title	SOC Code	Employment, 2010	Projected Employment, 2020	Change, 2010-20 Percent	Numeric
Electricians	47-2111	577,000	710,600	23	133,700
SOURCE: U.S. Bureau of Labor Statistics, Employment Projections program					

Similar Occupations

This table shows a list of occupations with job duties that are similar to those of electricians.

Occupation	Job Duties	Entry-Level Education	Median Annual Pay, May 2010
Computer, ATM, and Office Machine Repairers	Computer, ATM, and office machine repairers install, fix, and maintain many of the machines that businesses, households, and other consumers use.	Postsecondary non-degree award	$37,280
Construction Laborers and Helpers	Construction laborers and helpers do many basic tasks that require physical labor on construction sites.	See How to Become One	$28,410
Drafters	Drafters use software to convert the designs of engineers and architects into technical drawings and plans. Workers in production and construction use these plans to build everything from microchips to skyscrapers.	Associate's degree	$47,880
Electrical and Electronic Engineering Technicians	Electrical and electronic engineering technicians help engineers design and develop computers, communications equipment, medical monitoring devices, navigational equipment, and other electrical and electronic equipment. They often work in product evaluation and testing, using measuring and diagnostic devices to adjust, test, and repair equipment.	Associate's degree	$56,040
Electrical and Electronics Installers and Repairers	Electrical and electronics installers and repairers install, repair, or replace a variety of electrical equipment in telecommunications, transportation, utilities, and other industries.	Postsecondary non-degree award	$49,170
Elevator Installers and Repairers	Elevator installers and repairers install, fix, and maintain elevators, escalators, moving walkways, and other lifts.	High school diploma or equivalent	$70,910
Heating, Air Conditioning, and Refrigeration Mechanics and Installers	Heating, air conditioning, and refrigeration mechanics and installers—often referred to as HVACR technicians—work on heating, ventilation, cooling, and refrigeration systems that control the air quality in many types of buildings.	Postsecondary non-degree award	$42,530
Home Entertainment Equipment Installers and Repairers	Home entertainment equipment installers and repairers set up and fix household audio and video equipment, such as televisions, stereo components, and home theater systems.	Postsecondary non-degree award	$32,940
Line Installers and Repairers	Line installers and repairers install or repair electrical power systems and telecommunications cables, including fiber optics.	High school diploma or equivalent	$54,290

Contacts for More Information

For details about apprenticeships or other work opportunities in this trade, contact the offices of the state employment service, the state apprenticeship agency, local electrical contractors or firms that employ maintenance electricians, or local union-management electrician apprenticeship committees. Apprenticeship information is available from the U.S. Department of Labor's toll-free help line, 1 (877) 872-5627, and Employment and Training Administration.

For information about union apprenticeship and training programs for electricians, visit

The International Brotherhood of Electrical Workers and National Electrical Contractors Association's National Joint Apprenticeship Training Committee

For information about independent apprenticeship and training programs, visit Associated Builders and Contractors, Inc., Independent Electrical Contractors, Inc. , National Association of Home Builders, National Center for Construction Education and Research

Suggested citation:

Bureau of Labor Statistics, U.S. Department of Labor, Occupational Outlook Handbook, 2012-13 Edition, Electricians, on the Internet at http://www.bls.gov/ooh/construction-and-extraction/electricians.htm.

Elevator Installers and Repairers

Quick Facts: Elevator Installers and Repairers	
2010 Median Pay	$70,910 per year $34.09 per hour
Entry-Level Education	High school diploma or equivalent
Work Experience in a Related Occupation	None
On-the-job Training	Apprenticeship
Number of Jobs, 2010	19,900
Job Outlook, 2010-20	11% (About as fast as average)
Employment Change, 2010-20	2,300

What Elevator Installers and Repairers Do

Elevator installers and repairers install, fix, and maintain elevators, escalators, moving walkways, and other lifts.

Duties

Elevator installers and repairers typically do the following:

- Read blueprints to determine the equipment needed for installation or repair
- Install or repair elevator doors, steel frames and cables, motors, and control systems
- Locate malfunctions in brakes, motors, switches, and control systems
- Connect electrical wiring to control panels and electric motors
- Use test equipment, such as ammeters and voltmeters, to diagnose problems
- Adjust counterweights, door mechanisms, and safety controls
- Test newly installed equipment to ensure that it meets specifications
- Comply with safety regulations and building codes
- Keep service records of all maintenance and repair tasks

Elevator installers and repairers, also called **elevator constructors** or **elevator mechanics**, assemble, install, and replace elevators, escalators, chairlifts, moving walkways, and similar equipment in buildings. When the equipment is in service, they maintain and repair it.

Elevator installers and repairers usually specialize in installation, maintenance, or repair work. Maintenance and repair workers generally

Mechanics check many parts, including the rails of an escalator.

need greater knowledge of electronics, hydraulics, and electricity than do installers because a large part of maintenance and repair work is troubleshooting. In fact, most elevators today have computerized control systems, resulting in more complex systems and troubleshooting than in the past.

After an elevator is operating correctly, elevator installers and repairers must regularly maintain and service it to keep the elevator working. They generally do preventive maintenance, such as oiling and greasing moving parts, replacing worn parts, and adjusting equipment for optimal performance. They also troubleshoot and may be called to do emergency repairs. Unlike most elevator installers, people who specialize in elevator maintenance typically service many of the same elevators on multiple occasions over time.

A service crew usually handles major repairs—for example, replacing cables, elevator doors, or machine bearings. These tasks may require the use of cutting torches or rigging equipment—tools that an elevator repairer would not normally carry. Service crews also do major modernization and alteration work, such as replacing electrical motors, hydraulic pumps, and control panels.

The following are types of elevator installers and repairers:

Adjusters specialize in fine-tuning all the equipment after installation. They ensure that an elevator operates according to specifications and stops correctly at each floor within a specified time. Adjusters need a thorough knowledge of electronics, electricity, and computers to ensure that newly installed elevators operate properly.

Assistant mechanics have completed a 4-year apprenticeship program. Even after they are fully trained, assistant mechanics start with easier tasks and are assigned more difficult tasks, such as wiring and adjusting counterweights, as they gain work experience.

Work Environment

Elevator installers and repairers held about 19,900 jobs in 2010, of which 92 percent were employed in the building equipment contractors industry. In contrast to other construction trades, few elevator installers and repairers are self-employed.

Elevator installers and repairers must regularly lift and carry heavy equipment and parts. Although installation and major repairs require mechanics to work in teams, workers often work alone when troubleshooting small problems.

Because most of their work is indoors, elevator installers and repairers lose less work time due to bad weather than workers in many other construction occupations.

Injuries

Elevator installers and repairers have a rate of injury and illness that is slightly higher than the national average. Potential risks include injuries due to falls from ladders and scaffolding, burns or other injuries due to electrical shocks from control systems, and muscle strains from lifting and carrying equipment. As a result, workers must wear protective equipment such as hardhats, harnesses, and safety glasses.

Work Schedules

Almost all elevator installers and repairers work full time. They may need to work overtime when emergency repairs need to be made or construction deadlines need to be met. Some workers are on call 24 hours a day.

How to Become an Elevator Installer and Repairer

Nearly all elevator installers and repairers learn through a formal apprenticeship. A few states require licensure.

Apprenticeship

Elevator installers and repairers learn their trade through a 4-year apprenticeship. For each year of the program, apprentices must have at least 144 hours of related technical instruction and 2,000 hours of paid on-the-job training. During training, apprentices learn blueprint reading, electrical and electronic theory, mathematics, applied physics, and safety.

Unions and individual contractors offer apprenticeship programs. The basic qualifications for workers to enter an apprenticeship program are the following:

- Minimum age of 18
- High school diploma or equivalent
- Physically able to do the job
- Pass basic math, reading, and mechanical aptitude test

Education

A high school diploma or equivalent is required. High school classes in math, mechanical drawing, and shop may help applicants compete for apprenticeship openings.

Licenses

Several states require elevator installers and repairers to be licensed. To get a license, applicants must pass an exam about electrical systems. Check with your state's individual licensing agencies for specific requirements.

Certification

Some associations offer certification for workers. Although not required, certification can show competence and proficiency in the field. The National Association of Elevator Contractors offers two certification programs for elevator installers and repairers:

- Certified Elevator Technician
- Certified Accessibility and Private Residence Lift Technician

Advancement

Ongoing training is important for elevator installers and repairers to keep up with technological developments. Union elevator installers and repairers typically get training throughout their careers. This training improves a worker's chances of keeping their jobs and getting promoted. Some installers may get additional training in specialized areas and advance to be a mechanic-in-charge, adjustor, supervisor, or elevator inspector.

Important Qualities

Detail oriented. Elevator installers must keep accurate records of their service schedules. These records are used to schedule future maintenance times, which often help reduce breakdowns.

Mechanical skills. Elevator installers use a variety of power tools and handtools to install and repair lifts. Escalators, for example, run on tracks that must be installed using wrenches and screwdrivers.

Physical strength. Elevator installers must often lift heavy equipment and parts, including escalator steps, conduit, and metal

tracks. Some apprentices must be able to lift 100 pounds to participate in a program.

Stamina. Elevators installers must be able to do hard work for long periods without getting overly tired.

Troubleshooting skills. Elevator installers and repairers must diagnose and repair problems. When an escalator stops moving, for example, mechanics must determine why it stopped and make the necessary repairs.

Pay

Elevator Installers and Repairers
Median annual wages, May 2010

Elevator Installers and Repairers	$70,910
Other Construction and Related Workers	$38,820
Total, All Occupations	$33,840

Note: All Occupations includes all occupations in the U.S. Economy.
Source: U.S. Bureau of Labor Statistics, Occupational Employment Statistics

The median annual wage for elevator installers and repairers was $70,910 in May 2010. The median wage is the wage at which half the workers in an occupation earned more than that amount and half earned less. The lowest 10 percent earned less than $39,060, and the top 10 percent earned more than $101,390.

The starting pay for apprentices is usually between 30 percent and 50 percent of what fully trained elevator installers and repairers make. They get pay increases as they become more skilled.

Assistant mechanics, by union contract, get 80 percent of the rate paid to journey elevator installers and repairers.

Nearly all elevator installers and repairers work full time, which may include evenings and weekends. They often are required to be on call to handle emergencies. Overtime is common on construction sites because deadlines must be met.

Many elevator installers and repairers are members of a union. Although no single union covers all elevator installers and repairers, the largest organizer of these workers is the International Union of Elevator Constructors.

Job Outlook

Elevator Installers and Repairers
Percent change in employment, projected 2010-20

Other Construction and Related Workers	15%
Total, All Occupations	14%
Elevator Installers and Repairers	11%

Note: All Occupations includes all occupations in the U.S. Economy.
Source: U.S. Bureau of Labor Statistics, Employment Projections program

Employment of elevator installers and repairers is expected to grow 11 percent from 2010 to 2020, about as fast as the average for all occupations. Demand for workers will depend on growth in nonresidential construction, such as office buildings and stores that have elevators and escalators. This sector of the construction industry is expected to grow rapidly during the projections decade as the economy rebounds from the recent recession.

In addition, the need to continually maintain, update, and repair old equipment; provide access to the disabled; and install increasingly sophisticated equipment and controls should add to the demand for elevator installers and repairers.

Another factor causing an increase in demand for elevator installers and repairers is a growing number of elderly people who require stair lifts and elevators for easier access in their homes.

Job Prospects

Overall job opportunities should be excellent because the dangerous and physically challenging aspects of the work reduce the number of qualified applicants. Job prospects for entry-level workers should be best for those who have postsecondary education in electronics or who have experience in the military.

Elevators, escalators, lifts, moving walkways, and related equipment need to keep working year-round, so employment of

elevator repairers is less affected by economic downturns and seasonality than employment in other construction occupations.

Employment projections data for elevator installers and repairers, 2010-20

Occupational Title	SOC Code	Employment, 2010	Projected Employment, 2020	Change, 2010-20	
				Percent	Numeric
Elevator Installers and Repairers	47-4021	19,900	22,200	11	2,300
SOURCE: U.S. Bureau of Labor Statistics, Employment Projections program					

Similar Occupations

This table shows a list of occupations with job duties that are similar to those of elevator installers and repairers.

Occupation	Job Duties	Entry-Level Education	Median Annual Pay, May 2010
Boilermakers	Boilermakers assemble, install, and repair boilers, closed vats, and other large vessels or containers that hold liquids and gases.	High school diploma or equivalent	$54,640
Electricians	Electricians install and maintain electrical systems in homes, businesses, and factories.	High school diploma or equivalent	$48,250
Sheet Metal Workers	Sheet metal workers fabricate or install products that are made from thin metal sheets, such as ducts used for heating and air-conditioning.	High school diploma or equivalent	$41,710
Structural Iron and Steel Workers	Structural iron and steel workers install iron or steel beams, girders, and columns to form buildings, bridges, and other structures. They are often referred to as ironworkers.	High school diploma or equivalent	$44,540
Electrical and Electronics Installers and Repairers	Electrical and electronics installers and repairers install, repair, or replace a variety of electrical equipment in telecommunications, transportation, utilities, and other industries.	Postsecondary non-degree award	$49,170
Industrial Machinery Mechanics and Maintenance Workers	Industrial machinery mechanics and maintenance workers maintain and repair factory equipment and other industrial machinery, such as conveying systems, production machinery, and packaging equipment.	High school diploma or equivalent	$44,160
Millwrights	Millwrights install, dismantle, repair, reassemble, and move machinery in factories, power plants, and construction sites.	High school diploma or equivalent	$48,360

Contacts for More Information

For information about apprenticeships or job opportunities as an elevator mechanic, contact local elevator contractors, a local chapter of the International Union of Elevator Constructors, a local joint union-management apprenticeship committee, or the nearest office of your state employment service or apprenticeship agency. Apprenticeship information is available from the U.S. Department of Labor's toll-free help line, 1 (877) 872-5627, or Employment and Training Administration.

For more information about elevator installers and repairers, visit International Union of Elevator Constructors

For more information about the Certified Elevator Technician program or the Certified Accessibility and Private Residence Lift Technician program, visit National Association of Elevator Contractors

Suggested citation:

Bureau of Labor Statistics, U.S. Department of Labor, Occupational Outlook Handbook, 2012-13 Edition, Elevator Installers and Repairers, on the Internet at http://www.bls.gov/ooh/construction-and-extraction/elevator-installers-and-repairers.htm.

Glaziers

Quick Facts: Glaziers	
2010 Median Pay	$36,640 per year $17.61 per hour
Entry-Level Education	High school diploma or equivalent
Work Experience in a Related Occupation	None
On-the-job Training	Apprenticeship
Number of Jobs, 2010	41,900
Job Outlook, 2010-20	42% (Much faster than average)
Employment Change, 2010-20	17,700

What Glaziers Do

Glaziers install glass in windows, skylights, storefronts, and display cases to create distinctive designs or reduce the need for artificial lighting.

Duties

Glaziers typically do the following:

- Follow blueprints or specifications for size, color, type, and thickness of glass to be used
- Remove any old or broken glass before installing replacement glass
- Cut glass to the specified size and shape
- Make or install sashes or moldings for glass installation
- Fasten glass into sashes or frames with clips, moldings, or other types of fasteners
- Add weather seal or putty around pane edges to seal joints

Glass has many uses in modern life. For example, insulated and specially treated glass keeps in warm or cool air and controls sound and condensation. Tempered and laminated glass makes doors and windows more secure. The creative use of large windows, glass doors, skylights, and sunroom additions makes buildings bright, airy, and inviting. Glaziers specialize in installing these different glass products.

In homes, glaziers install or replace windows, mirrors, shower doors, and bathtub enclosures. They fit glass for tabletops and display cases. On commercial interior projects, glaziers install items such as heavy, often etched, decorative room dividers or security windows. Glazing projects also may involve replacing storefront windows for supermarkets, auto dealerships, banks, and so on.

Workers who replace and repair glass in motor vehicles are not covered in this profile. For more information, see the profile on automotive body and glass repairers.

For most large scale construction jobs, glass is precut and mounted into frames at a factory or a contractor's shop. The finished glass arrives at the jobsite ready for glaziers to position and secure into place. Using cranes or hoists with suction cups, workers lift large, heavy pieces of glass for installation. In cases where the glass is not secure inside the frame, glaziers may attach steel and aluminum sashes or frames to the building, and then secure the glass with clips, moldings, or other types of fasteners.

A few glaziers work with plastics, granite, marble, and other materials used as glass substitutes. Some work with films or laminates that improve the durability or safety of the glass.

Work Environment

Glaziers held about 41,900 jobs in 2010, of which 62 percent were employed in the foundation, structure, and building exterior contractors industry. Another 15 percent were employed in the building material and supplies dealers industry. About 5 percent of glaziers were self-employed.

As in many other construction trades, the work is physically demanding. Glaziers spend most of the day standing, bending, or stretching, and workers often have to lift and maneuver heavy, cumbersome materials, such as large glass plates.

Injuries

Glaziers experience one of the highest rates of injuries and illnesses. Typical injuries include cuts from tools and glass, and falls from ladders and scaffolding.

Work Schedules

Most glaziers work full time. About 5 percent of glaziers were self-employed in 2010; self-employed workers are often able to set their own schedule.

How to Become a Glazier

Although some glaziers learn their trade through a formal apprenticeship, most learn informally on the job.

Training

On the job, trainees often start with basic tasks such as carrying glass and cleaning up debris in glass shops. By working with experienced glaziers, trainees eventually acquire the skills of a fully qualified glazier. After several months, trainees start making their first cuts on discarded glass. Later, they may begin cutting glass and helping experienced workers on simple installation jobs.

Suction handles are used to pick up and maneuver glass.

Apprenticeship

Some glaziers learn their trade through a 3-year apprenticeship. Each year, apprentices must have at least 144 hours of related technical training and 2,000 hours of paid on-the-job training. On the job, they learn to use the tools and equipment of the trade; handle, measure, cut, and install glass and metal framing; cut and fit moldings; and install and balance glass doors. Technical training includes instruction in glass and installation techniques as well as basic mathematics, blueprint reading and sketching, general construction techniques, safety practices, and first aid.

After completing an apprenticeship program, glaziers are considered to be journey workers who may do tasks on their own.

A few groups sponsor apprenticeship programs, including several union and contractor associations. The basic qualifications to enter an apprenticeship program are as follows:
- Minimum age of 18
- High school education or equivalent
- Physically able to perform the work

Education

Although there are no formal educational requirements to become a glazier, high school math courses are considered useful.

Licenses

Connecticut is the only state that requires licensure for glaziers. Licensure requirements include passing a test, completing an apprenticeship, and a combination of education and experience.

Certifications

The National Glass Association offers a series of written exams that certify an individual's competency to perform glazier work as a Certified Glass Installer Technician.

Important Qualities

Balance. To minimize the risk of falling, glaziers need a good sense of balance while working on ladders and scaffolding.

Hand-eye coordination. Glass must be precisely cut. As a result, a steady hand is needed to achieve a cut of the correct size and shape.

Physical strength. Glaziers must often lift heavy pieces of glass for hanging. Physical strength, therefore, is important in their work.

Pay

Glaziers

Median annual wages, May 2010

Construction Trades Workers	$38,240
Glaziers	$36,640
Total, All Occupations	$33,840

Note: All Occupations includes all occupations in the U.S. Economy.
Source: U.S. Bureau of Labor Statistics, Occupational Employment Statistics

The median annual wage of glaziers was $36,640 in May 2010.

The median wage is the wage at which half the workers in an occupation earned more than that amount and half earned less. The lowest 10 percent earned less than $22,760, and the top 10 percent earned more than $66,810.

The starting pay for apprentices usually is between 30 percent and 50 percent of what fully trained glaziers make, receiving pay increases as they gain more skill.

Most glaziers work full time. About 5 percent of glaziers were self-employed in 2010; self-employed workers are often able to set their own schedule.

Job Outlook

Glaziers

Percent change in employment, projected 2010-20

Glaziers	42%
Construction Trades Workers	23%
Total, All Occupations	14%

Note: All Occupations includes all occupations in the U.S. Economy.
Source: U.S. Bureau of Labor Statistics, Employment Projections program

Employment of glaziers is projected to grow 42 percent from 2010 to 2020, much faster than the average for all occupations. Employment growth is expected as commercial construction increasingly uses glass exteriors. As glass manufacturers continue to improve the energy efficiency of glass windows, architects are designing more buildings with glass exteriors, especially in the South.

In addition, the continuing need to modernize and repair existing structures, including many homes, often involves installing new windows. Demand for specialized safety glass and coated glass with protective laminates is also growing due to a greater need for security and the need for structures, particularly many commercial and government buildings, to withstand high winds associated with storms.

Nonetheless, the availability of prefabricated windows that carpenters and general contractors can install is expected to limit overall employment growth of glaziers.

Job Prospects

Good job opportunities are expected as many openings should arise from the need to replace glaziers who leave the occupation. Because employers prefer workers who do many different tasks, glaziers with a wide range of skills will have the best job opportunities. In addition, workers with military service are viewed favorably during initial hiring.

Like many other construction workers, employment of glaziers is sensitive to the fluctuations of the economy. On the one hand, glaziers may experience periods of unemployment when the overall level of construction falls. On the other hand, shortages of workers may occur in some areas during peak periods of building activity. Employment opportunities should be best in the South and in metropolitan areas, where most glazing contractors and glass shops are located.

Employment projections data for glaziers, 2010-20

Occupational Title	SOC Code	Employment, 2010	Projected Employment, 2020	Change, 2010-20	
				Percent	Numeric
Glaziers	47-2121	41,900	59,600	42	17,700
SOURCE: U.S. Bureau of Labor Statistics, Employment Projections program					

Similar Occupations

This table shows a list of occupations with job duties that are similar to those of glaziers.

Occupation	Job Duties	Entry-Level Education	Median Annual Pay, May 2010
Brickmasons, Blockmasons, and Stonemasons	Brickmasons, blockmasons, and stonemasons (or, simply, masons) use bricks, concrete blocks, and natural stones to build fences, walkways, walls, and other structures.	High school diploma or equivalent	$45,410
Carpenters	Carpenters construct and repair building frameworks and structures—such as stairways, doorframes, partitions, and rafters—made from wood and other materials. They also may install kitchen cabinets, siding, and drywall.	High school diploma or equivalent	$39,530
Construction Laborers and Helpers	Construction laborers and helpers do many basic tasks that require physical labor on construction sites.	See How to Become One	$28,410
Sheet Metal Workers	Sheet metal workers fabricate or install products that are made from thin metal sheets, such as ducts used for heating and air-conditioning.	High school diploma or equivalent	$41,710
Tile and Marble Setters	Tile and marble setters apply hard tile, marble, and wood tiles to walls, floors, and other surfaces.	Less than high school	$38,110
Automotive Body and Glass Repairers	Automotive body and glass repairers restore, refinish, and replace vehicle bodies and frames, windshields, and window glass.	High school diploma or equivalent	$37,580

Contacts for More Information

For details about apprenticeships or other work opportunities in this trade, contact the offices of the state employment service, the state apprenticeship agency, local contractors or firms that employ glaziers, or local union-management finishing trade apprenticeship committees. Apprenticeship information is available from the U.S. Department of Labor's toll free help line: 1 (877) 872-5627 or Employment and Training Administration.

For more information about glaziers, visit Associated Builders and Contractors, Finishing Trades Institute, International Union of Painters and Allied Trades, National Glass Association

Suggested citation:

Bureau of Labor Statistics, U.S. Department of Labor, Occupational Outlook Handbook, 2012-13 Edition, Glaziers, on the Internet at http://www.bls.gov/ooh/construction-and-extraction/glaziers.htm.

Hazardous Materials Removal Workers

Quick Facts: Hazardous Materials Removal Workers	
2010 Median Pay	$37,600 per year $18.08 per hour
Entry-Level Education	High school diploma or equivalent
Work Experience in a Related Occupation	None
On-the-job Training	Moderate-term on-the-job training
Number of Jobs, 2010	38,100
Job Outlook, 2010-20	23% (Faster than average)
Employment Change, 2010-20	8,800

What Hazardous Materials Removal Workers Do

Hazardous materials (hazmat) removal workers identify and dispose of asbestos, radioactive and nuclear waste, arsenic, lead, and other hazardous materials. They also clean up materials that are flammable, corrosive, reactive, or toxic.

Duties

Hazmat removal workers typically do the following:

- Comply with safety procedures and federal laws regarding waste disposal
- Construct scaffolding or build containment areas before cleaning up
- Remove or clean up hazardous materials that are found or spilled
- Clean contaminated equipment for reuse
- Operate equipment that removes and stores waste materials
- Keep records of cleanup activities

Hazmat removal workers clean up materials that are harmful to people and the environment. The work they do depends on the substances they are cleaning. Removing lead and asbestos is different from cleaning up radiation contamination and toxic spills. Differences also can relate to why these workers have been called in to clean a site. For example, cleaning up a fuel spill from a train derailment is more urgent than removing lead paint from a bridge.

The following are types of hazmat removal workers:

Asbestos abatement workers and **lead abatement workers** remove asbestos and lead from buildings that are going to be fixed up

Hazmat removal workers contain liquid spills with absorbents.

or taken down. Most of this work is in older buildings that were originally built with asbestos insulation and lead-based paints—both of which are now banned from being used in newer buildings and must be removed from older ones.

Until the 1970s, asbestos was often used in buildings for fireproofing, insulation, and other uses. However, asbestos particles can cause deadly lung diseases. Similarly, until the 1970s, lead was commonly used in paint, pipes, and plumbing fixtures. Inhaling lead dust or ingesting chips of lead-based paint can cause serious health problems, though, especially in children.

Lead abatement workers use chemicals and may need to know how to operate sandblasters, high-pressure water sprayers, and other common tools.

Decommissioning and decontamination workers remove and treat radioactive materials generated by nuclear facilities and powerplants. They break down contaminated items such as "gloveboxes," which are used to process radioactive materials. When a facility is being closed or decommissioned (taken out of service), these workers clean the facility and decontaminate it from radioactive materials.

Decontamination technicians do tasks similar to those of janitors and cleaners, but the items and areas they clean are radioactive. Some of these jobs are now being done by robots controlled by people away from the contamination site. Increasingly, many of these remote devices automatically monitor and survey floors and walls for contamination.

Emergency and disaster response workers must work quickly to clean up hazardous materials after train and trucking accidents. Immediate, thorough cleanups help to control and prevent more damage to accident or disaster sites.

Radiation-protection technicians use radiation survey meters and other remote devices to locate and assess the hazard associated with radiated materials, operate high-pressure cleaning equipment for decontamination, and package radioactive materials for moving or disposing.

Treatment, storage, and disposal workers transport and prepare materials for treatment, storage, or disposal. To ensure proper treatment of materials, workers must follow laws enforced by the U.S. Environmental Protection Agency (EPA) or the U.S. Occupational Safety and Health Administration (OSHA). At incinerator facilities, treatment, storage, and disposal workers move materials from the customer or service center to the incinerator. At landfills, they organize and track the location of items in the landfill and may help change the state of a material from liquid to solid to prepare it to be stored. These workers typically operate heavy machinery, such as forklifts, earthmoving machinery, and large trucks and rigs.

Mold remediation makes up a small segment of hazardous materials removal work. Although mold is present in almost all structures and is not usually defined as a hazardous material, some mold—especially the types that cause allergic reactions—can infest a building to such a degree that extensive efforts must be taken to remove it safely.

Work Environment

Hazardous materials (hazmat) removal workers held about 38,100 jobs in 2010, of which 78 percent were employed in the waste management and remediation services industry.

Hazmat removal workers have different working conditions, depending on their area of expertise.

Asbestos and lead abatement workers usually work in office buildings, schools, or historic buildings that are being fixed up. Frequently, completing projects requires night and weekend work to avoid interfering with normal business activity.

Treatment, storage, and disposal workers are usually employed at facilities such as landfills, incinerators, and industrial furnaces. These facilities often are located in remote areas, so workers may have to commute long distances to their jobs.

Decommissioning and decontamination workers, decontamination technicians, and radiation protection technicians work at nuclear facilities and electric powerplants. These hazmat removal workers must deal with the stress of handling radioactive materials.

Injuries

Hazmat removal workers function in a highly structured environment to minimize the danger they face. This concern for safety keeps occupational injuries below the national average. Each phase of an operation is planned in advance, and workers are trained to deal with hazardous situations. Crews and supervisors take every safety measure to ensure that the worksite is safe.

No matter the material being cleaned, hazmat workers must often stand for long periods.

To reduce their exposure to harmful materials, workers often wear coveralls, gloves, shoe covers, safety glasses, or goggles. Some must wear fully enclosed protective suits for several hours at a time; these suits may be hot and uncomfortable and may cause the workers who wear them to experience claustrophobia (fear of enclosed spaces). In extremely toxic cleanups, hazmat workers are required to wear respirators to protect themselves from airborne particles or noxious gases. Lead abatement workers wear a personal air monitor that measures the amount of lead to which the worker has been exposed.

Work Schedules

Although most hazmat removal workers are employed full time, overtime and shift work are common, especially for emergency and disaster response workers. Hazmat removal workers may be required to travel outside their normal working areas to respond to emergency cleanups, which sometimes take several days or weeks to complete. During a cleanup, workers may be away from home for the entire time. Hazmat removal workers who work at nuclear facilities are busiest during refueling and may experience unemployment during other times.

How to Become a Hazardous Materials Removal Worker

Hazardous materials (hazmat) removal workers learn on the job. They take at least 40 hours of mandatory Occupational Safety and Health Administration (OSHA) training. There are no formal educational requirements beyond a high school diploma.

Licenses

To become an emergency and disaster response worker or a treatment, storage, and disposal worker, candidates must have a federal license that OSHA requires. Employers are responsible for ensuring that employees complete a formal 40-hour training program, given either in house or in OSHA-approved training centers. The program covers health hazards, personal protective equipment and clothing, site safety, recognizing and identifying hazards, and decontamination.

Training

Workers who treat asbestos and lead, the most common contaminants, must complete an employer-sponsored training program that meets OSHA standards. Employer-sponsored training is usually given in-house, and the employer is responsible for covering all technical and safety subjects outlined by OSHA.

In some cases, workers may discover one hazardous material while dealing with another. If workers are not licensed to handle the newly discovered material, they cannot continue to work with it. Many experienced workers opt to take courses in additional types of hazardous material removal to avoid this situation.

Training is most extensive for decommissioning and decontamination workers employed at nuclear facilities. In addition to getting a license through the standard 40-hour training course in hazardous waste removal, workers must take courses dealing with regulations about nuclear materials and radiation safety as mandated by the Nuclear Regulatory Commission.

These courses add up to about 3 months of training, although most are not taken consecutively. Many agencies, organizations, and companies nationwide provide training programs that are approved by the U.S. Environmental Protection Agency, the U.S. Department of Energy, and other regulatory agencies. To keep their license, workers in all fields must take continuing education courses each year.

OSHA does not regulate mold removal, but each state does.

Education

There is no formal education requirement, but most hazardous materials removal workers entering the occupation have a high school diploma. High school math courses are helpful, as are general vocational technical education courses. Additionally, there are several associate's degree programs related to radiation protection.

Work Experience

To work at some nuclear facilities, workers must have 2 years of related work experience. Experience in the U.S. Navy and internships related to associate's degree programs often count, as does experience working as a janitor at a nuclear facility.

For other workers in this occupation, a background in construction is helpful because much of the work is done in buildings.

Important Qualities

Detail oriented. Hazmat removal workers must follow safety procedures closely and keep records of their work. For example, workers must track the amount and type of waste disposed, equipment used, and number of containers stored.

Math skills. Workers must be able to do basic mathematical conversions and calculations when mixing solutions that neutralize contaminants.

Mechanical skills. Depending on the size and type of the cleanup, hazmat removal workers may use sandblasters, power washers, or earthmovers to clean contaminated sites.

Stamina. The work that hazmat crews do can be strenuous. Hazmat removal workers stand and scrub equipment for hours at a time to remove toxic materials.

Teamwork. Most workers in this occupation work in crews. Because the work is highly structured, with each crew member assigned a particular task, ability to work with others and take instruction is important.

Troubleshooting skills. Hazmat removal workers must be able to quickly diagnose the contents of a spill or leak and choose the proper method for cleaning up. For example, when a chemical tanker overturns, workers must find out what was spilled, decide if evacuation is needed, and clean up the site.

Pay

Hazardous Materials Removal Workers
   Median annual wages, May 2010

Other Construction and Related Workers	$38,820
Hazardous Materials Removal Workers	$37,600
Total, All Occupations	$33,840

Note: All Occupations includes all occupations in the U.S. Economy.
Source: U.S. Bureau of Labor Statistics, Occupational Employment Statistics

The median annual wage of hazardous materials (hazmat) removal workers was $37,600 in May 2010. The median wage is the wage at which half the workers in an occupation earned more than that amount and half earned less. The lowest 10 percent earned less than $24,720, and the top 10 percent earned more than $63,800.

Although most hazmat removal workers are employed full time, overtime and shift work are common, especially for emergency and disaster response workers. Hazmat removal workers may be required to travel outside their normal working areas to respond to emergency cleanups, which sometimes take several days or weeks to complete. During a cleanup, workers may be away from home for the entire time. Hazmat removal workers who work at nuclear facilities are busiest during refueling and may experience unemployment during other times.

Some hazmat removal workers are union members. The Laborers' International Union of North America is one of the largest organizers of these workers.

Job Outlook

Hazardous Materials Removal Workers
   Percent change in employment, projected 2010-20

Hazardous Materials Removal Workers	23%
Other Construction and Related Workers	15%
Total, All Occupations	14%

Note: All Occupations includes all occupations in the U.S. Economy.
Source: U.S. Bureau of Labor Statistics, Employment Projections program

Employment of hazardous materials (hazmat) removal workers is expected to grow 23 percent from 2010 to 2020, faster than the average for all occupations. The need for decontamination technicians, radiation safety technicians, and decommissioning workers in response to increased pressure for cleaner electric generation facilities is expected to drive employment growth.

In addition, numerous abandoned hazardous material sites (Superfund) recognized by the Environmental Protection Agency still require cleanup. However, employment growth will be determined largely by federal funding.

With a declining number of structures containing asbestos and lead, demand for workers who remove these materials is expected to be somewhat limited. However, regulations for asbestos and lead removal have become stricter, and the need to remove these materials from many federal and historic buildings should continue.

Mold remediation is a small specialty and is unlikely to produce a significant number of jobs.

Job Prospects

Many job openings are expected for hazmat removal workers because of the need to replace workers who leave the occupation. Job opportunities for radiation safety technicians and decontamination workers should be good as new workers replace those who retire or leave the occupation for other reasons. Additional job openings may result for remediation workers as new facilities open in the coming decade.

Lead and asbestos workers will likely have limited job opportunities at specialty remediation companies as the restoration of federal buildings and historic structures continues at a slower pace than in the past. Also, hazmat removal workers should continue to face competition from construction laborers and insulation workers to do these cleanups.

The best employment opportunities for mold remediation workers should be in the Southeast and parts of the Northeast and Northwest, where mold tends to thrive.

Applicants who have experience working with reactors in the U.S. Navy have better opportunities when they apply for hazmat removal work at nuclear facilities.

Employment projections data for hazardous materials removal workers, 2010-20

Occupational Title	SOC Code	Employment, 2010	Projected Employment, 2020	Change, 2010-20 Percent	Change, 2010-20 Numeric
Hazardous Materials Removal Workers	47-4041	38,100	46,900	23	8,800
SOURCE: U.S. Bureau of Labor Statistics, Employment Projections program					

Similar Occupations

This table shows a list of occupations with job duties that are similar to those of hazardous materials removal workers.

Occupation	Job Duties	Entry-Level Education	Median Annual Pay, May 2010
Construction Laborers and Helpers	Construction laborers and helpers do many basic tasks that require physical labor on construction sites.	See How to Become One	$28,410
Insulation Workers	Insulation workers install and replace the materials used to insulate buildings and their mechanical systems to help control and maintain temperature.	See How to Become One	$35,110
Painters, Construction and Maintenance	Painters apply paint, stain, and coatings to walls, buildings, bridges, and other structures.	Less than high school	$34,280
Firefighters	Firefighters protect the public by responding to fires and other emergencies. They are frequently the first emergency personnel on the scene of an accident.	Postsecondary non-degree award	$45,250

Police and Detectives	Police officers protect lives and property. Detectives and criminal investigators, who sometimes are called agents or special agents, gather facts and collect evidence of possible crimes. Law enforcement officers' duties depend on the size and type of their organizations.	High school diploma or equivalent	$55,010
Water and Wastewater Treatment Plant and System Operators	Water and wastewater treatment plant and system operators manage a system of machines, often through the use of control boards, to transfer or treat water or wastewater.	High school diploma or equivalent	$40,770
Power Plant Operators, Distributors, and Dispatchers	Power plant operators, distributors, and dispatchers control the systems that generate and distribute electric power.	High school diploma or equivalent	$65,360

Contacts for More Information

For more information about hazardous materials removal workers in the construction industry, including information on training, visit Laborers' International Union of North America

For more information about working in the nuclear industry, visit Nuclear Energy Institute

Suggested citation:

Bureau of Labor Statistics, U.S. Department of Labor, Occupational Outlook Handbook, 2012-13 Edition, Hazardous Materials Removal Workers, on the Internet at http://www.bls.gov/ooh/construction-and-extraction/hazardous-materials-removal-workers.htm.

Insulation Workers

Quick Facts: Insulation Workers	
2010 Median Pay	$35,110 per year $16.88 per hour
Entry-Level Education	See How to Become One
Work Experience in a Related Occupation	None
On-the-job Training	See How to Become One
Number of Jobs, 2010	51,400
Job Outlook, 2010-20	28% (Faster than average)
Employment Change, 2010-20	14,400

What Insulation Workers Do

Insulation workers install and replace the materials used to insulate buildings and their mechanical systems to help control and maintain temperature. Workers are often referred to as insulators.

Duties

Insulation workers typically do the following:
- Remove old insulation and dispose of it properly
- Read blueprints and specifications to determine job requirements
- Determine the amounts and types of insulation needed
- Measure and cut insulation to fit into walls and around pipes
- Fasten insulation in place with staples, tape, or screws
- Use compressors to spray insulation into some spaces
- Install plastic barriers to protect insulation from moisture
- Follow safety guidelines

Properly insulated buildings save energy by keeping heat in during the winter and out in the summer. Insulated vats, vessels, boilers, steam pipes, and hot-water pipes also prevent the wasteful loss of heat or cold and prevent burns. Insulation also helps reduce noise that passes through walls and ceilings.

When renovating old buildings, insulators often must remove the old insulation. In the past, asbestos—now known to cause cancer—was used extensively to insulate walls, ceilings, pipes, and industrial equipment. Because of this danger, specially trained workers are required to remove asbestos before insulation workers can install the new insulating materials. For more information, see the profile on hazardous materials removal workers.

Insulation workers use common hand tools, such as knives and scissors. They also may use a variety of power tools including power saws to cut insulating materials, welders to secure clamps, and staple guns to fasten insulation to walls. Some insulators use compressors to spray insulation onto walls.

Workers sometimes wrap a cover of aluminum, sheet metal, or vapor barrier (plastic sheeting) over the insulation. Doing so protects the insulation by keeping moisture out.

The following are examples of insulation workers:

Floor, ceiling, and wall insulators install insulation in attics, floors, and behind walls in homes and other buildings. Most of these workers unroll, cut, fit, and staple batts of fiberglass insulation between wall studs and ceiling joists. Some workers, however, spray foam insulation with a compressor hose into the space being filled.

Mechanical insulators apply insulation to pipes or ductwork in businesses, factories, and many other types of buildings. When insulating a steam pipe, for example, the temperature, thickness, and diameter of the pipe are all factors that determine the type of insulation to be used.

Work Environment

Insulators held about 51,400 jobs in 2010. Employment was about split between mechanical insulators and floor, ceiling, and wall insulators. Only 4 percent of all insulators were self-employed. Most

Mechanical insulators often insulate components.

floor, ceiling, and wall insulators were employed in the drywall and insulation contractors industry. Mechanical insulators were concentrated in the specialty trade contractor industry, as shown in the following table:

Drywall and insulation contractors	25%
Plumbing, heating, and air-conditioning contractors	19
Other building equipment contractors	37

Insulation workers generally work indoors in residential and industrial settings. They spend most of their workday standing, bending, or kneeling, often in confined spaces.

Those who insulate gas and oil pipelines may have to stop work due to rain or cold weather.

Injuries

Floor, ceiling, and wall insulators have one of the highest rates of injury and illness. In contrast, mechanical insulators have a very low rate of injury and illness. Falls from ladders and cuts from knives are common hazards. Also, small particles from insulation materials, especially when sprayed, can irritate the eyes, skin, and lungs. To protect themselves, they keep the work area well ventilated. They also wear protective suits, masks, and they may wear respirators.

Mechanical insulators may get burns from the pipes they insulate.

How to Become an Insulation Worker

Most floor, ceiling, and wall insulation workers learn their trade informally on the job. Most mechanical insulators complete a formal apprenticeship program.

Apprenticeship

Most mechanical insulation workers learn their trade through a 4-year apprenticeship. Some apprenticeships may last up to 5 years, depending on the program. For each year of the program, apprentices must have at least 1,700 to 2,000 hours of paid on-the-job training and a minimum of 144 hours of related technical instruction. The technical portion includes learning about insulation and installation techniques as well as basic mathematics, how to read and draw blueprints, general construction techniques, safety practices, and first aid.

Unions and individual businesses offer apprenticeship programs. Although most workers enter apprenticeships directly, some start out as helpers first. The basic qualifications to enter an apprenticeship

program are as follows:
- Being 18 years old
- High school diploma or equivalent
- Physically able to do the work

Education

There are no formal education requirements for floor, ceiling, and wall insulation workers. Mechanical insulation workers should have a high school diploma. High school courses in English, math, woodworking, mechanical drawing, algebra, and general science are considered helpful for all insulation workers.

Certification

Insulation workers who remove and handle asbestos must be certified by the U.S. Environmental Protection Agency.

Insulation contractor organizations offer voluntary certification to help workers prove their skills and knowledge of residential and industrial insulation.

The National Insulation Association also offers a certification for mechanical insulators in doing an energy appraisal to determine if and how insulation can benefit industrial customers.

Important Qualities

Dexterity. Insulation workers must be able to work in confined spaces while maintaining coordination and control of tools and materials. Also, insulators often must reach above their heads to fit and fasten insulation into place.

Mechanical skills. Insulation workers use a variety of hand and power tools to install insulation. Those who apply foam insulation, for example, must be able to operate a compressor and sprayer to spread the foam onto walls or across attics.

Stamina. Because insulators spend most of the day standing, stretching, and bending, workers should be able to stay physically active without getting tired.

Pay

Insulation Workers
Median annual wages, May 2010

Construction Trades Workers	$38,240
Insulation Workers, Mechanical	$37,650
Total, All Occupations	$33,840
Insulation Workers, Floor, Ceiling, and Wall	$31,830

Note: All Occupations includes all occupations in the U.S. Economy.
Source: U.S. Bureau of Labor Statistics, Occupational Employment Statistics

The median annual wage of insulation workers was $35,110 in May 2010. The median wage is the wage at which half the workers in an occupation earned more than that amount and half earned less. The lowest 10 percent earned less than $22,390, and the top 10 percent earned more than $67,360.

The median annual wage of floor, ceiling, and wall insulation workers was $31,830 in May 2010. The lowest 10 percent earned less than $20,360, and the top 10 percent earned more than $60,990.

The median annual wage of mechanical insulation workers was $37,650 in May 2010. The lowest 10 percent earned less than $25,030, and the top 10 percent earned more than $70,470.

The starting pay for apprentices is usually between 30 percent and 50 percent of what fully trained insulators make. They get pay increases as they gain more skills.

Mechanical insulation workers are more likely to be union members. The International Association of Heat and Frost Insulators and Allied Workers is the largest organizer of mechanical insulation workers.

Job Outlook

Insulation Workers

Percent change in employment, projected 2010-20

Insulation Workers, Mechanical	32%
Insulation Workers, Floor, Ceiling, and Wall	23%
Construction Trades Workers	23%
Total, All Occupations	14%

Note: All Occupations includes all occupations in the U.S. Economy.
Source: U.S. Bureau of Labor Statistics, Employment Projections program

Overall employment of insulation workers is expected to grow 28 percent from 2010 to 2020, faster than the average for all occupations. Growth rates, however, will vary by occupational specialty.

Employment of floor, ceiling, and wall insulators is expected to grow 23 percent from 2010 to 2020, faster than the average for all occupations. Modest increases in home building will spur employment growth over the coming decade. Insulation will continue to be added into existing buildings to save energy.

Employment of mechanical insulation workers is expected to grow 32 percent from 2010 to 2020, much faster than the average for all occupations, spurred by the need to make existing buildings more energy efficient. In the past, mechanical insulation has been reduced or cut from building plans as a cost-saving method, but energy analyses show that improved insulation provides a greater return on investment. The anticipated construction of new powerplants, big users of insulated pipes and equipment, should also result in greater employment demand.

Job Prospects

Floor, ceiling, and wall insulators are expected to face competition for openings as they often compete for jobs with other construction workers. Openings will, nonetheless, continue to arise because the irritating nature of many insulation materials, combined with the often difficult working conditions, causes many residential insulation workers to leave the occupation each year.

Mechanical insulation workers with formal training should have the best job opportunities.

Insulation workers in the construction industry may experience periods of unemployment because of the short duration of many construction projects and the cyclical nature of construction activity. Workers employed to do industrial plant maintenance generally have more stable employment because maintenance and repair must be done continually.

Employment projections data for insulation workers, 2010-20

Occupational Title	SOC Code	Employment, 2010	Projected Employment, 2020	Change, 2010-20	
				Percent	Numeric
Insulation Workers	—	51,400	65,800	28	14,400
Insulation Workers, Floor, Ceiling, and Wall	47-2131	23,200	28,600	23	5,400
Insulation Workers, Mechanical	47-2132	28,300	37,300	32	9,000
SOURCE: U.S. Bureau of Labor Statistics, Employment Projections program					

Similar Occupations

This table shows a list of occupations with job duties that are similar to those of insulation workers.

Occupation	Job Duties	Entry-Level Education	Median Annual Pay, May 2010
Carpenters	Carpenters construct and repair building frameworks and structures—such as stairways, doorframes, partitions, and rafters—made from wood and other materials. They also may install kitchen cabinets, siding, and drywall.	High school diploma or equivalent	$39,530
Carpet Installers	Carpet installers lay carpet in homes, offices, restaurants, and many other types of buildings.	Less than high school	$36,090
Construction Laborers and Helpers	Construction laborers and helpers do many basic tasks that require physical labor on construction sites.	See How to Become One	$28,410
Drywall and Ceiling Tile Installers, and Tapers	Drywall and ceiling tile installers hang wallboards to walls and ceilings inside buildings. Tapers prepare the wallboards for painting, using tape and other materials. Many workers do both installing and taping.	Less than high school	$38,290
Plasterers and Stucco Masons	Plasterers and stucco masons apply coats of plaster or stucco to walls, ceilings, or partitions for functional and decorative purposes. Some workers apply ornamental plaster.	Less than high school	$37,210
Roofers	Roofers repair and install the roofs of buildings using a variety of materials, including shingles, asphalt, and metal.	Less than high school	$34,220
Sheet Metal Workers	Sheet metal workers fabricate or install products that are made from thin metal sheets, such as ducts used for heating and air-conditioning.	High school diploma or equivalent	$41,710

Oil and Gas Workers

Quick Facts: Oil and Gas Workers	
2010 Median Pay	$37,640 per year $18.09 per hour
Entry-Level Education	Less than high school
Work Experience in a Related Occupation	None
On-the-job Training	See How to Become One
Number of Jobs, 2010	134,800
Job Outlook, 2010-20	8% (Slower than average)
Employment Change, 2010-20	11,200

What Oil and Gas Workers Do

Oil and gas workers carry out the plans for drilling that petroleum engineers have designed. Drilling workers operate the equipment that drills the well through the soil and rock formation, and they prepare the well for use. Service workers then finish preparing the well and assemble the equipment that removes the oil or gas from the well.

Duties

Oil and gas workers include roustabouts, derrick operators, service unit operators, and rotary drill operators.

Roustabouts typically do the following:

- Clean equipment and keep the work area orderly and free of debris
- Use electronic detectors and make visual inspections in flow lines to locate leaks
- Use truck winches and motorized lifts to move pipes to and from trucks or move the pipes by hand
- Dismantle and repair oil field machinery, boilers, and steam engine parts
- Guide cranes that move loads
- Attach lifting slings to loads moved by cranes or by other special equipment, such as gin-pole trucks

Derrick operators typically do the following:

- Inspect derricks, or order their inspection, before they are raised or lowered
- Make sure the drilling fluid continues to flow correctly
- Repair pumps and other equipment related to the drilling fluid system
- Ensure that rig pumps and other drilling systems are working properly
- Use harnesses and platform climbing devices to position and align derrick elements
- Supervise crew members and help train them
- Guide lengths of pipe into and out of elevators
- Help maintain other rig equipment

Service unit operators typically do the following:

- Maintain wells by removing tubes or rods from the hole that is drilled into the ground
- Observe load variations on gauges, pumps, and pressure indicators
- Inspect engines, rotary chains, and other equipment to detect faulty operations or unusual equipment conditions
- Drive truck-mounted units to well sites
- Install pressure-control devices onto wellheads
- Thread cables through derrick pulleys
- Operate pumps that circulate water, oil, or other fluids through wells to remove sand or other materials obstructing the free flow of oil
- Operate controls that raise derricks or level rigs

Rotary drill operators, also known as drillers, typically do the following:

- Oversee maintenance of the drill rig and implementation of the well plan
- Train crews and introduce procedures to make operations safe andeffective
- Observe pressure gauges and move throttles and levers, both to control the speed of rotary tables and to regulate the pressure of tools at the bottoms of drill holes
- Observe gauges that monitor well flow to prevent an overflow
- Keep records of footage drilled, locations and the nature of layers drilled, materials and drilling tools used, services performed, and time required
- Start and examine pump operations to ensure circulation and consistency of drilling fluids or mud in wells
- Use special tools to locate and recover lost or broken bits, casings, and drill pipes from wells

Rotary drilling crews do most of the work in oil fields. Most workers involved in gas processing are known as operators.

Additional occupations on drilling crews are as follows:

Engine operators are in charge of engines that provide the power for well site operations. They also do general maintenance of the engines and keep the rig equipment lubricated.

Pumpers operate and maintain the equipment that regulates the flow of oil out of the well.

Gas treaters oversee automatic treating units that remove water and other impurities from natural gas.

Gas-pumping-station operators tend compressors that raise the pressure of gas to send it through pipelines.

Gas-compressor operators often assist gas treaters and

Oil and gas workers repair oil field machinery.

gas-pumping-station operators.

Work Environment

Oil and gas workers held about 134,800 jobs in 2010. Oil and gas sites generally operate year round regardless of weather conditions.

Oil and gas workers are employed mainly in oil and gas extraction and in firms offering support for mining. Oil and gas sites can be on land, in inland waters, or at sea (offshore). During hazardous weather, such as a hurricane, coastal land rigs and offshore production and drilling facilities may have to be evacuated.

The industries employing the largest numbers of oil and gas workers in 2010 were the following:

Support activities for mining	77%
Oil and gas extraction	15
Heavy and civil engineering construction	2

Injuries

Derrick operators and rotary drill operators experience higher-than-average rates of nonfatal injuries. Constant care must be taken to minimize incidents and maximize safety in a work environment where secure footing is often a concern. Proper use of personal protective equipment, such as hard hats, minimizes risks on job sites. An additional danger is the constant, loud noise from the drilling machinery. This noise makes communication difficult, so it is important for workers to follow safety instructions from supervisors and other experienced co-workers.

Work Schedules

Most oil and gas workers work full time, but they often have to work overtime. Oil and gas drilling rigs usually operate 24 hours a day, 7 days a week.

Workers on land drilling rigs typically work 8- or 12-hour shifts.While some land drilling rig personnel work 7 days a week without days off until the well is complete, most work 7 or 14 days on and then equal days off. The remote location of offshore oil rigs requires some workers to live onsite for weeks at a time, frequently working 12-hour shifts, followed by an extended leave period onshore. As a result, part-time opportunities are rare.

How to Become an Oil and Gas Worker

Workers in oil and gas occupations usually must be at least 18 years old, be in good physical condition, and pass a drug test. A high school diploma is not necessarily required but is preferred by some employers.

Education

The typical level of education required for entry into oil and gas occupations is less than a high school diploma.However, some employers prefer to hire graduates of high school vocational programs in which students learn such skills as basic mechanics, welding, and heavy equipment operations.

Important Qualities

Depth perception. The skill required to move large and heavy pieces of equipment or machinery also requires depth perception. The safety of other workers may depend on it as well.

Detail oriented. Oil and gas workers use equipment that must be carefully watched. Engineers need the information collected by monitoring gauges to judge the effectiveness of drilling operations.

Eye-hand coordination. These workers need an ability to move large pieces of machinery or equipment into exact placement.

Interpersonal skills. These workers operate in teams, so listening to and interacting with other team members and to supervisors is important.

Physical strength. Oil and gas workers must have the strength to move heavy equipment, materials, and machinery.

Training

There are few formal education requirements for oil and gas workers. However, they need a lot of job training and experience before they can do most tasks or advance to more skilled positions.

Most workers start as helpers to experienced workers and learn skills on the job. However, formal training is becoming more important as more technologically advanced machinery and methods are increasingly used.

Advancement

As workers gain more experience, they can move up to higher paying jobs that require greater skill. For example, a roustabout may become a rotary helper and advance to derrick operator and then driller. A similar progression is available to service workers as well.

Because of the extreme environment and critical nature of the work, offshore oil crews generally are more experienced than land crews. For work on an offshore rig, many companies hire only workers who are already experienced in oilfield operations. As a result, workers who have gained experience as part of a land crew might advance to offshore operations. Positions are usually filled on the basis of seniority and ability.

Pay

Oil and Gas Workers

Median annual wages, May 2010

Extraction Workers	$39,040
Oil and Gas Workers	$37,640
Total, All Occupations	$33,840

Note: All Occupations includes all occupations in the U.S. Economy.
Source: U.S. Bureau of Labor Statistics, Occupational Employment Statistics

The median annual wage of oil and gas workers was $37,640 in May 2010. The median wage is the wage at which half the workers in an occupation earned more than that amount and half earned less.The lowest 10 percent earned less than $24,440, and the top 10 percent earned more than $64,260.

The median wages foroil and gas worker occupations in May2010 were the following:

- $51,980 for rotary drill operators
- $43,470 for derrick operators
- $38,920 for service unit operators
- $31,770 for roustabouts

Job Outlook

Oil and Gas Workers

Percent change in employment, projected 2010-20

Total, All Occupations	14%
Oil and Gas Workers	8%
Extraction Workers	7%

Note: All Occupations includes all occupations in the U.S. Economy.
Source: U.S. Bureau of Labor Statistics, Employment Projections program

Employment of oil and gas workers is expected to increase by 8 percent from 2010 to 2020, slower than the average for all occupations. Demand for oil and gas workers will depend on the demand for the products and services of two industries in particular: oil and gas extraction and support for mining activities.

Because of higher prices for resources, oil and gas companies are more likely to drill in deeper waters and harsher environments than in the past. These complex operations require more workers. Higher prices will also encourage oil and gas companies to return to existing wells to try new extraction methods, thereby increasing demand for oil and gas workers. Also, changes in policy could expand exploration and drilling for oil and natural gas in currently protected areas, potentially boosting employment.

However, new production technologies are expected to dampen overall demand for oil and gas workers. New drilling and extraction techniques allow more efficient production from a reduced number of drill sites, and that may reduce employment growth in these occupations.

Employment projections data for oil and gas workers, 2010-20

Occupational Title	SOC Code	Employment, 2010	Projected Employment, 2020	Change, 2010-20	
				Percent	Numeric
Oil and Gas Workers	—	134,800	146,000	8	11,200
Derrick Operators, Oil and Gas	47-5011	18,900	20,700	9	1,800
Rotary Drill Operators, Oil and Gas	47-5012	22,500	24,100	7	1,600
Service Unit Operators, Oil, Gas, and Mining	47-5013	40,700	44,200	9	3,500
Roustabouts, Oil and Gas	47-5071	52,700	57,100	8	4,400
SOURCE: U.S. Bureau of Labor Statistics, Employment Projections program					

Similar Occupations

This table shows a list of occupations with job duties that are similar to those of oil and gas workers.

Occupation	Job Duties	Entry-Level Education	Median Annual Pay, May 2010
Construction Laborers and Helpers	Construction laborers and helpers do many basic tasks that require physical labor on construction sites.	See How to Become One	$28,410
Industrial Machinery Mechanics and Maintenance Workers	Industrial machinery mechanics and maintenance workers maintain and repair factory equipment and other industrial machinery, such as conveying systems, production machinery, and packaging equipment.	High school diploma or equivalent	$44,160
Plumbers, Pipefitters, and Steamfitters	Plumbers, pipefitters, and steamfitters install and repair pipes that carry water, steam, air, or other liquids or gases to and in businesses, homes, and factories.	High school diploma or equivalent	$46,660
Reinforcing Iron and Rebar Workers	Reinforcing iron and rebar workers install mesh, steel bars (rebar), or cables to reinforce concrete.	High school diploma or equivalent	$38,430
Stationary Engineers and Boiler Operators	Stationary engineers and boiler operators control stationary engines, boilers, or other mechanical equipment to provide utilities for buildings or for industrial purposes.	High school diploma or equivalent	$52,140
Structural Iron and Steel Workers	Structural iron and steel workers install iron or steel beams, girders, and columns to form buildings, bridges, and other structures. They are often referred to as ironworkers.	High school diploma or equivalent	$44,540

Contacts for More Information

For more information about oil and gas workers, visit International Association of Drilling Contractors Association of Energy Service Companies American Petroleum Institute

Suggested citation:

Bureau of Labor Statistics, U.S. Department of Labor, Occupational Outlook Handbook, 2012-13 Edition, Oil and Gas Workers, on the Internet at http://www.bls.gov/ooh/construction-and-extraction/oil-and-gas-workers.htm.

Painters, Construction and Maintenance

Quick Facts: Painters, Construction and Maintenance	
2010 Median Pay	$34,280 per year $16.48 per hour
Entry-Level Education	Less than high school
Work Experience in a Related Occupation	None
On-the-job Training	Moderate-term on-the-job training
Number of Jobs, 2010	390,500
Job Outlook, 2010-20	18% (About as fast as average)
Employment Change, 2010-20	72,100

What Painters, Construction and Maintenance Do

Painters apply paint, stain, and coatings to walls, buildings, bridges, and other structures.

Duties

Painters typically do the following:

- Cover floors and furniture with drop-cloths and tarps to protect surfaces
- Remove fixtures such as pictures, door knobs, or electric switch covers
- Put up scaffolding and set up ladders
- Fill holes and cracks with caulk, putty, plaster, or other compounds
- Prepare surfaces by scraping, wire brushing, or sanding to a smooth finish
- Calculate the area to be painted and the amount of paint needed
- Apply primers or sealers so the paint will adhere
- Choose and mix paints and stains to reach desired color and appearance
- Apply paint or other finishes using hand brushes, rollers, or sprayers

Applying paint to interior walls makes surfaces attractive and vibrant. In addition, paints and other sealers protect exterior surfaces from erosion caused by exposure to the weather.

Because there are several ways to apply paint, workers must be able to choose the proper tool for each job, such as the correct roller, power sprayer, and the right size brush. Choosing the right tool typically depends on the surface to be covered and the characteristics of the finish.

A few painters—mainly industrial—must use special safety equipment. For example, painting in confined spaces such as the inside of a large storage tank, requires workers to wear self-contained suits to avoid inhaling toxic fumes. When painting bridges, tall buildings, or oil rigs, painters may work from scaffolding, bosun's chairs, and harnesses to reach work areas.

The following are examples of types of painters:

Construction painters apply paints, stains, and coatings to interior and exterior walls, new buildings, and other structural surfaces.

Maintenance painters remove old finishes and apply paints, stains, and coatings later in a structure's life. Some painters specialize in painting or coating industrial structures, such as bridges and oil rigs, to prevent corrosion.

Artisan painters specialize in creating distinct finishes by using one of many decorative techniques. One technique is adding glaze for added depth and texture. Other common techniques may include sponging, distressing, rag-rolling, color blocking, and faux finishes.

Painting and coating workers apply materials to manufactured products, such as furniture, toys and pottery, as well as transportation equipment including trucks, buses, boats, and airplanes. For more information about these painters, see the profile on painting and coating workers.

Work Environment

Painters held about 390,500 jobs in 2010, of which 29 percent were employed in the painting and wall covering contractors industry. About 53 percent were self-employed.

Because painters apply finishes to a wide variety of structures—from bridges to the interiors and exteriors of buildings—they may work both indoors and out. Painting requires a lot of climbing, bending, kneeling, and stretching. Industrial painters typically work outdoors in dry, warm weather. Those who paint bridges or building infrastructure may be exposed to extreme heights and uncomfortable positions; some painters work suspended with ropes or cables.

Injuries

Painters have a rate of injury and illness that is among the highest of all occupations. Falls from ladders, muscle strains from lifting, and exposure to irritants such as plaster dust are common risks.

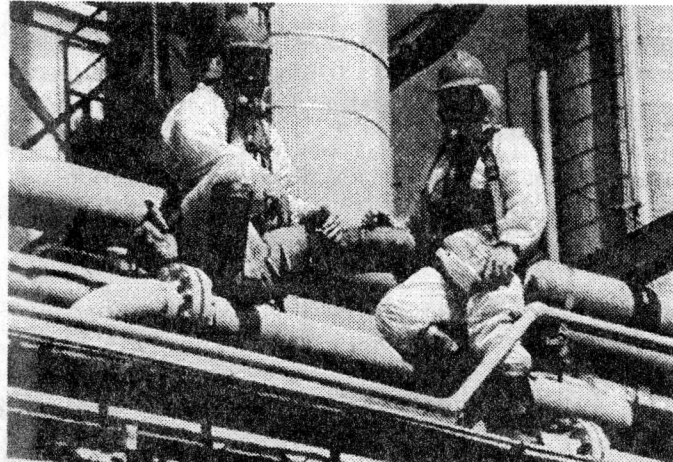

Painters sometimes wear self-contained suits for protection from fumes.

Work Schedules

Most painters work full time. About 53 percent of painters were self-employed in 2010. Self-employed workers may be able to set their own schedule. Those who paint bridges, buildings, and other structures outside are not able to work when it rains.

How to Become a Painter, Construction or Maintenance

Although most painters learn their trade informally on the job, some learn through a formal apprenticeship.

Training

Some painters learn their trade through a 3- or 4-year apprenticeship, although a few local unions have additional time requirements. For each year of the program, apprentices must have at least 144 hours of technical instruction and 2,000 hours of paid on-the-job training. Through technical instruction, apprentices learn how colors go together; how to use and care for tools and equipment, to prepare surfaces, mix and match paint, and read blueprints; application techniques; characteristics of different finishes; wood finishing; and safety practices.

After completing an apprenticeship program, painters are considered journey workers and may do tasks on their own.

Unions and contractors sponsor apprenticeship programs. The basic qualifications to enter an apprenticeship program are as follows:

- Minimum age of 18
- High school diploma or equivalent
- Physically able to do the work

Although the vast majority of workers learn their trade informally on the job or through a formal apprenticeship, some contractors offer their own training program.

Education

There is no formal educational requirement, but high school courses in English, math, shop, and blueprint reading can be useful. Also, some 2-year technical schools offer courses connected to union and contractor organization apprenticeships. Credits earned as part of an apprenticeship program usually count toward an associate's degree.

Certification

Those interested in industrial painting can earn several certifications from the National Association of Corrosion Engineers. The most common one for construction painters is called Protective Coating Specialist. Courses range from 1 day to several weeks, depending on the certification program and specialty. Applicants must also meet requirements for work experience.

Important Qualities

Color recognition. Painters must be able to identify and differentiate between subtle differences in paint color.

Customer-service skills. Workers who paint the inside and outside of residential homes often interact with clients. They must communicate with the client, listen to what the client wants, and select colors and application techniques that satisfy the client.

Detail oriented. Painters must be precise when creating or painting edges because minor flaws can be noticeable.

Stamina. Painters should be able to stay physically active for many hours, as they spend most of the day standing with their arms often raised above their head.

Pay

Painters, Construction and Maintenance
Median annual wages, May 2010

Construction Trades Workers	$38,240
Painters, Construction and Maintenance	$34,280
Total, All Occupations	$33,840

Note: All Occupations includes all occupations in the U.S. Economy.
Source: U.S. Bureau of Labor Statistics, Occupational Employment Statistics

The median annual wage of construction and maintenance painters was $34,280 in May 2010. The median wage is the wage at which half the workers in an occupation earned more than that amount and half earned less. The lowest 10 percent earned less than $22,450, and the top 10 percent earned more than $58,480.

The starting pay for apprentices is usually between 30 percent and 50 percent of what fully trained painters make. They get pay increases as they gain more skill.

Most painters work full time. About 53 percent of painters were self-employed in 2010. Self-employed workers may be able to set their own schedule. Those who paint bridges, buildings, and other structures outside are not able to work when it rains.

Job Outlook

Painters, Construction and Maintenance
Percent change in employment, projected 2010-20

Construction Trades Workers	23%
Painters, Construction and Maintenance	18%
Total, All Occupations	14%

Note: All Occupations includes all occupations in the U.S. Economy.
Source: U.S. Bureau of Labor Statistics, Employment Projections program

Employment of painters is expected to grow 18 percent from 2010 to 2020, about as fast as the average for all occupations. The relatively short life of paint on homes as well as changing trends in color and application will continue to support demand for painters. Investors who sell properties or rent them out will also require painters' services. Nonetheless, the ability of many homeowners to do the work themselves will somewhat temper employment growth.

Growing demand for industrial painting will be driven by the need to prevent corrosion and deterioration of the many industrial structures by painting or coating them. Applying a protective coating to the inside of a steel tank, for example, can add years to its life expectancy.

Job Prospects

Overall job prospects should be good because of the need to replace workers who leave the occupation. There are no formal training requirements for entry into these jobs, so many people with limited skills work as painters for a relatively short time and then move on to other types of work with higher pay or better working conditions.

Job opportunities for industrial painters should be excellent as the positions available should be greater than the pool of qualified individuals to fill them. Although industrial structures that require painting are located throughout the nation, the best employment opportunities should be in the Gulf Coast region, where strong demand and the largest concentration of workers exist.

New painters and those with little experience should expect some periods of unemployment. In addition, many construction painting projects last only a short time. Employment of painters, like that of many other construction workers, is also sensitive to fluctuations in the economy. On the one hand, painters may experience periods of unemployment when the overall level of construction falls. On the other hand, peak periods of building activity may produce shortages of painters.

Employment projections data for painters, construction and maintenance, 2010-20

Occupational Title	SOC Code	Employment, 2010	Projected Employment, 2020	Change, 2010-20	
				Percent	Numeric
Painters, Construction and Maintenance	47-2141	390,500	462,700	18	72,100
SOURCE: U.S. Bureau of Labor Statistics, Employment Projections program					

Similar Occupations

This table shows a list of occupations with job duties that are similar to those of painters, construction and maintenance.

Occupation	Job Duties	Entry-Level Education	Median Annual Pay, May 2010
Carpenters	Carpenters construct and repair building frameworks and structures—such as stairways, doorframes, partitions, and rafters—made from wood and other materials. They also may install kitchen cabinets, siding, and drywall.	High school diploma or equivalent	$39,530
Carpet Installers	Carpet installers lay carpet in homes, offices, restaurants, and many other types of buildings.	Less than high school	$36,090
Construction Laborers and Helpers	Construction laborers and helpers do many basic tasks that require physical labor on construction sites.	See How to Become One	$28,410
Plasterers and Stucco Masons	Plasterers and stucco masons apply coats of plaster or stucco to walls, ceilings, or partitions for functional and decorative purposes. Some workers apply ornamental plaster.	Less than high school	$37,210
Painting and Coating Workers	Painting and coating workers paint and coat a wide range of products, including cars, jewelry, lacquer, and candy.	High school diploma or equivalent	$31,170

Contacts for More Information

For details about apprenticeships or other work opportunities for painters, contact the offices of the state employment service, the state apprenticeship agency, local contractors or firms that employ painters, or local union-management painter apprenticeship committees. Apprenticeship information is available from the U.S. Department of Labor's toll free help line, 1 (877) 872-5627 or Employment and Training Administration.

For more information about painters, including training opportunities, visit Associated Builders and Contractors ,International Union of Painters and Allied Trades ,National Center for Construction Education and Research Painting and Decorating Contractors of America

For general information about the work of industrial painters and opportunities for training and certification as a protective coating specialist, visit

NACE International

Suggested citation:

Bureau of Labor Statistics, U.S. Department of Labor, Occupational Outlook Handbook, 2012-13 Edition, Painters, Construction and Maintenance, on the Internet at http://www.bls.gov/ooh/construction-and-extraction/painters-construction-and-maintenance.htm.

Plasterers and Stucco Masons

Quick Facts: Plasterers and Stucco Masons	
2010 Median Pay	$37,210 per year $17.89 per hour
Entry-Level Education	Less than high school
Work Experience in a Related Occupation	None
On-the-job Training	Long-term on-the-job training
Number of Jobs, 2010	27,900
Job Outlook, 2010-20	17% (About as fast as average)
Employment Change, 2010-20	4,800

What Plasterers and Stucco Masons Do

Plasterers and stucco masons apply coats of plaster or stucco to walls, ceilings, or partitions for functional and decorative purposes. Some workers apply ornamental plaster.

Duties

Plasterers and stucco masons typically do the following:

- Clean and prepare surfaces
- Nail a wire mesh to the surface to ensure the plaster or stucco stays in place
- Mix plaster and stucco to desired consistency
- Apply two or three coats of plaster or stucco using trowels, brushes, or spray guns
- Rough the undercoat surface with a scratcher so the finish coat will stick
- Create decorative textures using brushes, trowels, sand, or stones
- Apply sealants or waxes to protect the finish and allow for easy cleaning

Plasterers apply coats of plaster to interior walls and ceilings to form fire-resistant and relatively soundproof surfaces. Using trowels, workers spread plaster on solid surfaces, such as concrete block, or supportive wire mesh called lath. They also may apply plaster over drywall to create smooth or textured scratch-resistant finishes. Using molds and a variety of troweling techniques, some plasterers make decorative and ornamental designs, which require special skills and creativity.

Plasterers may also install prefabricated exterior insulation systems over existing walls—for good insulation and interesting architectural effects—and cast ornamental designs in plaster.

Stucco masons usually apply stucco—a mixture of cement, lime, and sand—on building exteriors over wire lath, concrete, or masonry. Stucco masons also may apply other durable plasters, such as polymer-based acrylic finishes, to exterior surfaces. Stucco masons may also embed marble or gravel chips into the finish coat to achieve a pebble-like, decorative finish.

In addition, when required, stucco masons apply insulation to the exterior of new and old buildings. They cover the outer wall with rigid foam insulation board and reinforcing mesh, and then trowel on a base coat.

Work Environment

Plasterers and stucco masons held about 27,900 jobs in 2010. The vast majority were employed in the specialty trade contractors industry. About 53 percent were employed in the drywall and insulation contractors industry, while 15 percent were employed in the masonry contractors industry. An additional 11 percent were self-employed.

Like many other construction trades, the work of plasterers and stucco masons is physically demanding. They spend most of the day on their feet, either standing, bending, or stretching.

Plasterers must hold plaster in one hand using a hawk—a square board with a handle on the bottom—while troweling with the other hand, and the plaster can be heavy.

Plasterers and stucco masons may also work on ladders or scaffolding, occasionally up high. The work can often be dusty and dirty, which can irritate the skin, eyes, and lungs. Workers usually wear protective masks, goggles, and gloves to reduce the effects of these problems.

Injuries

Although the work is not inherently dangerous, plasterers and stucco masons experience a rate of injury and illness that is higher than the national average. Muscle strain from lifting heavy plaster and stucco is the most common injury, and workers sometimes fall from ladders or scaffolds.

Work Schedules

Most plasterers and stucco masons work full time; others work part time or have variable schedules. Because stucco masons work outdoors, they may have to stop work in bad weather. About 11 percent of plasterers and stucco masons were self-employed in 2010.

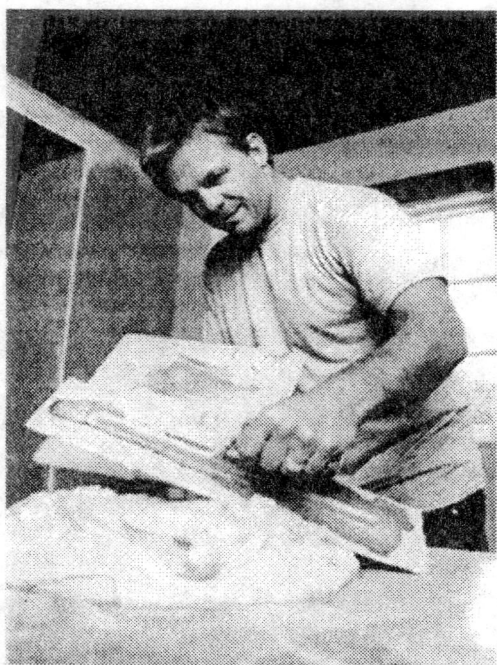

Plasterers use "hawks" to hold plaster.

Self-employed workers may be able to set their own schedule.

How to Become a Plasterer or Stucco Mason

Although most plasterers and stucco masons learn informally on the job, a few learn their trade through a formal apprenticeship.

Training

Most plasterers and stucco masons learn through long-term on-the-job training after being hired. Workers typically gain experience by doing jobs under the guidance of experienced workers. For example, they learn how to mix and apply coats of plaster or stucco.

A few plasterers and stucco masons learn through 3- or 4-year apprenticeships. For each year of a program, apprentices must have at least 144 hours of related technical instruction and 2,000 hours of paid on-the-job training. Apprentices learn construction basics such as blueprint reading, mathematics, building code requirements, safety, and first-aid practices.

After completing an apprenticeship program, plasterers and stucco masons are considered journey workers who may perform tasks on their own.

Several groups sponsor apprenticeship programs, including unions and contractor associations. The basic qualifications for entering an apprenticeship program are as follows:

- Minimum age of 18
- High school diploma or equivalent
- Physically able to do the work

Some contractors have their own plasterer and stucco mason training programs. While some workers enter apprenticeships directly, many begin as helpers.

Education

Although there are no formal educational requirements, taking high school courses in math, shop, mechanical drawing, and blueprint reading is considered to be helpful.

Certification

Some organizations related to masonry trades offer training and certification intended to enhance the skills of their members. For example, the International Union of Bricklayers and Allied Craftworkers' International Masonry Institute offers certifications in several areas of specialization, including one for plastering. Candidates who complete a 12-week certification program become a "journey level plasterer" by passing a competency-based exam. Experienced candidates can become a "Certified Instructor for Journeyworkers and Apprentices in the Trowel Trades."

Important Qualities

Creativity/Artistic ability. Interior plasterers who apply decorative and ornamental finishes should have a degree of artistic ability so they can make designs or match decorations.

Hand-eye coordination. Workers need to be able to apply smooth, even coats of plaster. Plasterers transfer plaster from hawks to trowels and then spread it on the wall.

Physical strength. Workers need to be strong enough to hold a hawk—a square board with a handle on the bottom—loaded with plaster in one hand while troweling with the other.

Stamina. Because workers apply plaster and stucco from floor to ceiling, they must have enough endurance to spend many hours on their feet while bending and reaching.

Pay

Plasterers and Stucco Masons
Median annual wages, May 2010

Construction Trades Workers	$38,240
Plasterers and Stucco Masons	$37,210
Total, All Occupations	$33,840

Note: All Occupations includes all occupations in the U.S. Economy.
Source: U.S. Bureau of Labor Statistics, Occupational Employment Statistics

The median annual wage of plasterers and stucco masons was $37,210 in May 2010. The median wage is the wage at which half the workers in an occupation earned more than that amount and half earned less. The lowest 10 percent earned less than $24,880, and the top 10 percent earned more than $66,500.

The starting pay for apprentices is usually between 30 percent and 50 percent of what fully trained workers make. They get pay increases as they gain more skills.

Most plasterers and stucco masons work full time; the rest work part time or have variable schedules.

Job Outlook

Plasterers and Stucco Masons
Percent change in employment, projected 2010-20

Construction Trades Workers	23%
Plasterers and Stucco Masons	17%
Total, All Occupations	14%

Note: All Occupations includes all occupations in the U.S. Economy.
Source: U.S. Bureau of Labor Statistics, Employment Projections program

Employment of plasterers and stucco masons is projected to grow 17 percent from 2010 to 2020, about as fast as the average for all occupations. But because plasterers and stucco masons are part of a niche market, overall employment growth will be somewhat limited. In addition, the growing use of less costly and easy-to-install alternatives, such as drywall, will likely slow employment growth of plasterers.

At the same time, the need to fireproof refineries and powerplants should result in some demand for plasterers. Stucco masons will experience employment growth that results from demand for polymer-based exterior insulating finishes, which are gaining popularity, particularly in the South and Southwest regions of the country.

Job Prospects

Overall job prospects should improve over the coming decade as construction activity rebounds from the recent recession. Like many other construction workers, employment of plasterers and stucco masons is particularly sensitive to fluctuations in the economy, and workers in this trade can expect periods of unemployment when the overall level of construction falls. However, shortages of workers may occur in some areas during peak periods of building activity.

Highly skilled workers with good job histories and work experience in construction should have the best opportunities. Stucco masons will have the best job opportunities in parts of the country where stucco homes and other buildings are popular, such as the South and some Southwestern states. Plasterers will have better job opportunities in areas where powerplants and oil refineries are being built or refurbished.

Employment projections data for plasterers and stucco masons, 2010-20

Occupational Title	SOC Code	Employment, 2010	Projected Employment, 2020	Change, 2010-20	
				Percent	Numeric
Plasterers and Stucco Masons	47-2161	27,900	32,700	17	4,800
SOURCE: U.S. Bureau of Labor Statistics, Employment Projections program					

Similar Occupations

This table shows a list of occupations with job duties that are similar to those of plasterers and stucco masons.

Occupation	Job Duties	Entry-Level Education	Median Annual Pay, May 2010
Brickmasons, Blockmasons, and Stonemasons	Brickmasons, blockmasons, and stonemasons (or, simply, masons) use bricks, concrete blocks, and natural stones to build fences, walkways, walls, and other structures.	High school diploma or equivalent	$45,410
Carpenters	Carpenters construct and repair building frameworks and structures—such as stairways, doorframes, partitions, and rafters—made from wood and other materials. They also may install kitchen cabinets, siding, and drywall.	High school diploma or equivalent	$39,530
Carpet Installers	Carpet installers lay carpet in homes, offices, restaurants, and many other types of buildings.	Less than high school	$36,090
Cement Masons and Terrazzo Workers	Cement masons pour, smooth, and finish concrete floors, sidewalks, roads, and curbs. Using a cement mixture, terrazzo workers create durable and decorative surfaces for floors and stairways.	See How to Become One	$35,530
Drywall and Ceiling Tile Installers, and Tapers	Drywall and ceiling tile installers hang wallboards to walls and ceilings inside buildings. Tapers prepare the wallboards for painting, using tape and other materials. Many workers do both installing and taping.	Less than high school	$38,290
Insulation Workers	Insulation workers install and replace the materials used to insulate buildings and their mechanical systems to help control and maintain temperature.	See How to Become One	$35,110
Tile and Marble Setters	Tile and marble setters apply hard tile, marble, and wood tiles to walls, floors, and other surfaces.	Less than high school	$38,110
Construction Laborers and Helpers	Construction laborers and helpers do many basic tasks that require physical labor on construction sites.	See How to Become One	$28,410

Contacts for More Information

For details about apprenticeships or other work opportunities for plasterers and stucco masons, contact the offices of the state employment service, the state apprenticeship agency, local contractors or firms that employ plasterers and stucco masons, or local union-management apprenticeship committees. Apprenticeship information is available from the U.S. Department of Labor's toll free help line, 1 (877) 872-5627, or Employment and Training Administration.

For information about plasterers and stucco masons, visit Association of the Wall and Ceiling Industry ,Operative Plasterers' and Cement Masons' International Association International Masonry Institute ,International Union of Bricklayers and Allied Craftworkers

Suggested citation:

Bureau of Labor Statistics, U.S. Department of Labor, Occupational Outlook Handbook, 2012-13 Edition, Plasterers and Stucco Masons, on the Internet at http://www.bls.gov/ooh/construction-and-extraction/plasterers-and-stucco-masons.htm.

Plumbers, Pipefitters, and Steamfitters

Quick Facts: Plumbers, Pipefitters, and Steamfitters	
2010 Median Pay	$46,660 per year $22.43 per hour
Entry-Level Education	High school diploma or equivalent
Work Experience in a Related Occupation	None
On-the-job Training	Apprenticeship
Number of Jobs, 2010	419,900
Job Outlook, 2010-20	26% (Faster than average)
Employment Change, 2010-20	107,600

What Plumbers, Pipefitters, and Steamfitters Do

Plumbers, pipefitters, and steamfitters install and repair pipes that carry water, steam, air, or other liquids or gases to and in businesses, homes, and factories.

Duties

Plumbers, pipefitters, and steamfitters typically do the following:

- Install pipes and fixtures
- Study blueprints and follow state and local building codes
- Determine the amount of material and type of equipment needed
- Inspect and test installed pipe systems and pipelines
- Troubleshoot and repair systems that are not working
- Replace worn parts

Although plumbers, pipefitters, and steamfitters are three distinct specialties, their duties are often similar. For example, they all install pipes and fittings that carry water, steam, air, or other liquids or gases. They connect pipes, determine the necessary materials for a job, and perform pressure tests to ensure a pipe system is airtight and watertight.

Plumbers, pipefitters, and steamfitters install, maintain, and repair

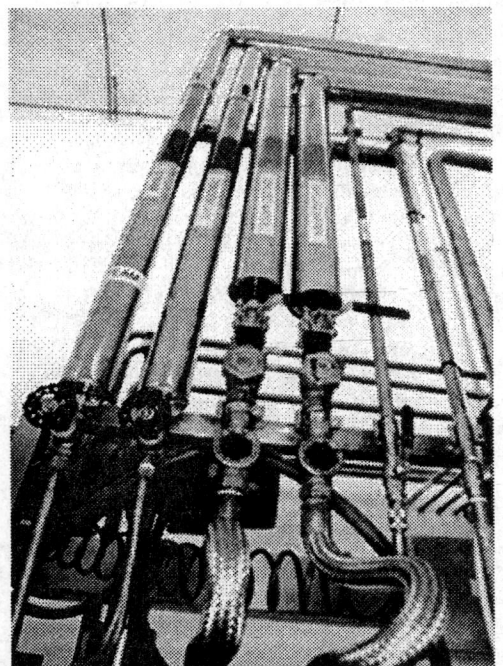

Pipefitters install a variety of pipes to move liquids and gasses.

many different types of pipe systems. Some of these systems carry water, dispose of waste, supply gas to ovens, or heat and cool buildings. Other systems, such as those in power plants, carry the steam that powers huge turbines. Pipes also are used in manufacturing plants to move acids, gases, and waste byproducts through the production process.

Master plumbers on construction jobs may be involved with developing blueprints that show where all the pipes and fixtures will go. Their input helps ensure that a structure's plumbing meets building codes, stays within budget, and works well with the location of other features, such as electric wires.

Plumbers and fitters may use many different materials and construction techniques, depending on the type of project. Residential water systems, for example, use copper, steel, and plastic pipe that one or two plumbers can install. Power-plant water systems, by contrast, are made of large steel pipes that usually take a crew of pipefitters to install. Some workers install stainless steel pipes on dairy farms and in factories, mainly to prevent contamination.

Plumbers and fitters sometimes cut holes in walls, ceilings, and floors. With some pipe systems, workers may hang steel supports from ceiling joists to hold the pipe in place. Because pipes are seldom manufactured to the exact size or length, plumbers and fitters measure and then cut and bend lengths of pipe as needed. Their tools include saws, pipe cutters, and pipe-bending machines.

They then connect the pipes, using methods that vary by type of pipe. For example, copper pipe is joined with solder, but steel pipe is often screwed together.

In addition to installation and repair work, journey- and master-level plumbers, pipefitters, and steamfitters often direct apprentices and helpers.

Following are examples of occupational specialties:

Plumbers install and repair water, drainage, and gas pipes in homes, businesses, and factories. They install and repair large water lines, such as those that supply water to buildings, and smaller ones, including ones that supply water to refrigerators. Plumbers also install plumbing fixtures—bathtubs, showers, sinks, and toilets—and appliances such as dishwashers, garbage disposals, and water heaters. They also fix plumbing problems. For example, when a pipe is clogged or leaking, plumbers remove the clog or replace the pipe. Some plumbers maintain septic systems, the large, underground holding tanks that collect waste from houses not connected to a city or county's sewer system.

Pipefitters install and maintain pipes that carry chemicals, acids, and gases. These pipes are mostly in manufacturing, commercial, and industrial settings. They often install and repair pipe systems in power plants, as well as heating and cooling systems in large office buildings. Some pipefitters specialize:

- **Gasfitters** install pipes that provide clean oxygen to patients in hospitals.

- **Sprinklerfitters** install and repair fire sprinkler systems in businesses, factories, and residential buildings.
- **Steamfitters** install pipe systems that move steam under high pressure. Most steamfitters work at campus and natural gas power plants where heat and electricity is generated, but others work in factories that use high-temperature steam pipes.
-

Work Environment

Plumbers, pipefitters, and steamfitters held about 419,900 jobs in 2010, of which 57 percent were employed in the plumbing, heating, and air-conditioning contractors industry. About 14 percent of plumbers, pipefitters, and steamfitters were self-employed.

Plumbers, pipefitters, and steamfitters work in factories, homes, businesses, and wherever else there are pipes or septic systems.

Plumbers and fitters often must lift heavy materials, climb ladders, and work in tight spaces. Some plumbers travel to a variety of work sites every day. Some plumbers and fitters may have to work outdoors, even in bad weather.

Injuries

Plumbers, pipefitters, and steamfitters have a higher-than-average risk of injury and illness. Cuts from sharp tools, burns from hot pipes and soldering equipment, and falls from ladders are common injuries.

Work Schedules

Most plumbers, pipefitters, and steamfitters work full time, including nights and weekends. They are often on call to handle emergencies, and overtime is common on construction sites to meet completion deadlines. About 14 percent of plumbers, pipefitters, and steamfitters were self-employed in 2010. Although self-employed plumbers can set their own schedules, they are also more likely to deal with after-hours emergencies.

How to Become a Plumber, Pipefitter, or Steamfitter

Most plumbers, pipefitters, and steamfitters learn on the job through an apprenticeship. Some start out by attending a technical school. Most states and localities require plumbers to have a license.

Apprenticeship

A 4- or 5-year apprenticeship is how most plumbers, pipefitters, and steamfitters learn their trade. Each year, apprentices must have at least 1,700 to 2,000 hours of paid on-the-job training and a minimum of 246 hours of related technical education. Apprentices learn safety, local plumbing codes and regulations, and how to read blueprints. They also study mathematics, applied physics, and chemistry. They become familiar with different types of piping systems and plumbing tasks.

After completing an apprenticeship program, plumbers, pipefitters, and steamfitters are considered to be a journey worker, which qualifies them to perform duties on their own.

Apprenticeship programs are offered by unions and businesses. Although most workers enter apprenticeships directly, some start out as helpers. To enter an apprenticeship program, a trainee must meet these requirements:

- Be at least 18 years old
- Have a high school diploma or equivalent
- Pass a basic math test
- Pass a drug test
- Know how to use computers

Education

Technical schools offer courses on pipe system design, safety, and tool use. They also offer welding courses that are considered necessary by some pipefitter and steamfitter apprenticeship training programs.

Licenses

Most states and localities require plumbers to be licensed. Although licensing requirements vary, most states and localities require workers to have 2 to 5 years of experience and to pass an exam that tests their knowledge of the trade and of local plumbing codes before they are permitted to work independently. Several states require a special license to work on gas lines. A few states require pipefitters to be licensed. Getting a license requires a test, experience, or both. Check with the state licensing board.

Important Qualities

Customer service skills. Plumbers work with customers on a regular basis, so they should be polite and courteous.

Managerial skills. Plumbers, pipefitters, and steamfitters —especially those who own their own business—must be able to direct workers, bid on jobs, and plan work schedules. They may have to provide training and choose the right number of workers for a job.

Mechanical skills. Plumbers, pipefitters, and steamfitters use a variety of tools to assemble and repair pipe systems. Choosing the right tool and successfully installing, repairing, or maintaining a system is crucial to their work.

Physical strength. Plumbers, pipefitters, and steamfitters must be strong enough to lift and move heavy pipe.

Troubleshooting skills. Plumbers, pipefitters, and steamfitters find, diagnose, and repair problems. For example, plumbers must be able to perform pressure tests to pinpoint the location of a leak.

Pay

Plumbers, Pipefitters, and Steamfitters
Median annual wages, May 2010

Plumbers, Pipefitters, and Steamfitters	$46,660
Construction Trades Workers	$38,240
Total, All Occupations	$33,840

Note: All Occupations includes all occupations in the U.S. Economy.
Source: U.S. Bureau of Labor Statistics, Occupational Employment Statistics

The median annual wage of plumbers, pipefitters, and steamfitters was $46,660 in May 2010. The median wage is the wage at which half the workers in an occupation earned more than that amount and half earned less. The lowest 10 percent earned less than $27,580, and the top 10 percent earned more than $79,920.

The starting pay for apprentices usually is between 30 percent and 50 percent of the rate paid to fully trained plumbers, pipefitters, and steamfitters. They receive pay increases as they become more skilled.

A higher-than-average number of plumbers, pipefitters, and steamfitters are union members. The largest organizer of these workers is the United Association of Journeymen and Apprentices of the Plumbing and Pipefitting Industry of the United States and Canada.

Plumbers, pipefitters, and steamfitters work full time, including nights and weekends. They are often on call to handle emergencies, and overtime is common on construction sites to meet completion deadlines. About 14 percent of plumbers, pipefitters, and steamfitters were self-employed in 2010. Although self-employed plumbers can set their own schedules, they are also more likely to deal with after-hours emergencies.

Job Outlook

Plumbers, Pipefitters, and Steamfitters
Percent change in employment, projected 2010-20

Plumbers, Pipefitters, and Steamfitters	26%
Construction Trades Workers	23%
Total, All Occupations	14%

Note: All Occupations includes all occupations in the U.S. Economy.
Source: U.S. Bureau of Labor Statistics, Employment Projections program

Employment of plumbers, pipefitters, and steamfitters is projected to grow 26 percent from 2010 to 2020, faster than the average for all occupations. Demand for plumbers is expected to come from new building construction and stricter water efficiency standards for plumbing systems, such as low-flow toilets and showerheads.

The construction of new power plants and factories should spur demand for pipefitters and steamfitters. Beginning in 2011, employment of sprinklerfitters and plumbers is expected to increase as states adopt a change to the International Residential Code that requires new single- and double-family homes to have fire sprinkler systems.

Job Prospects

Job opportunities are expected to be good as some employers continue to report difficulty finding qualified professionals. In addition, many workers are expected to retire over the next 10 years, which will result in more job openings. Workers with welding experience may have the best opportunities.

Like that of many other types of construction work, employment of plumbers, pipefitters, and steamfitters is sensitive to fluctuations of the economy. On the one hand, workers may experience periods of unemployment when the overall level of construction falls. On the other hand, shortages of workers may occur in some areas during peak periods of building activity.

However, maintenance and repair of plumbing and pipe systems must continue even during economic downturns, so plumbers and fitters outside of construction, especially those in manufacturing, tend to have more stable employment.

Employment projections data for plumbers, ipefitters, and steamfitters, 2010-20

Occupational Title	SOC Code	Employment, 2010	Projected Employment, 2020	Change, 2010-20 Percent	Numeric
Plumbers, Pipefitters, and Steamfitters	47-2152	419,900	527,500	26	107,600
SOURCE: U.S. Bureau of Labor Statistics, Employment Projections program					

Similar Occupations

This table shows a list of occupations with job duties that are similar to those of plumbers, pipefitters, and steamfitters.

Occupation	Job Duties	Entry-Level Education	Median Annual Pay, May 2010
Stationary Engineers and Boiler Operators	Stationary engineers and boiler operators control stationary engines, boilers, or other mechanical equipment to provide utilities for buildings or for industrial purposes.	High school diploma or equivalent	$52,140
Millwrights	Millwrights install, dismantle, repair, reassemble, and move machinery in factories, power plants, and construction sites.	High school diploma or equivalent	$48,360
Industrial Machinery Mechanics and Maintenance Workers	Industrial machinery mechanics and maintenance workers maintain and repair factory equipment and other industrial machinery, such as conveying systems, production machinery, and packaging equipment.	High school diploma or equivalent	$44,160
Heating, Air Conditioning, and Refrigeration Mechanics and Installers	Heating, air conditioning, and refrigeration mechanics and installers—often referred to as HVACR technicians—work on heating, ventilation, cooling, and refrigeration systems that control the air quality in many types of buildings.	Postsecondary non-degree award	$42,530
Construction Managers	Construction managers plan, coordinate, budget, and supervise construction projects from early development to completion.	Associate's degree	$83,860
Construction and Building Inspectors	Construction and building inspectors ensure that new construction, changes, or repairs comply with local and national building codes and ordinances, zoning regulations, and contract specifications.	High school diploma or equivalent	$52,360
Construction Laborers and Helpers	Construction laborers and helpers do many basic tasks that require physical labor on construction sites.	See How to Become One	$28,410
Electricians	Electricians install and maintain electrical systems in homes, businesses, and factories.	High school diploma or equivalent	$48,250
Boilermakers	Boilermakers assemble, install, and repair boilers, closed vats, and other large vessels or containers that hold liquids and gases.	High school diploma or equivalent	$54,640

Contacts for More Information

For details about apprenticeship or other opportunities in this trade, contact the offices of the state employment service, the state apprenticeship agency, local plumbing, heating and cooling contractors or firms that employ fitters, or local union-management apprenticeship committees. Apprenticeship information is available from the U.S. Department of Labor's toll-free help line: 1 (877) 872-5627; or Employment and Training Administration.

For more information about apprenticeships for plumbers, pipefitters, and steamfitters, visit United Association

For more information about plumbers and pipefitters, visit Mechanical Contractors Association of America ,National Center for Construction Education and Research ,Plumbing-Heating-Cooling Contractors Association

For general information about sprinklerfitters, visit American Fire Sprinkler Association ,National Fire Sprinkler Association, Inc.

Suggested citation:
Bureau of Labor Statistics, U.S. Department of Labor, Occupational Outlook Handbook, 2012-13 Edition, Plumbers, Pipefitters, and Steamfitters, on the Internet at http://www.bls.gov/ooh/construction-and-extraction/plumbers-pipefitters-and-steamfitters.htm.

Reinforcing Iron and Rebar Workers

Quick Facts: Reinforcing Iron and Rebar Workers	
2010 Median Pay	$38,430 per year $18.48 per hour
Entry-Level Education	High school diploma or equivalent
Work Experience in a Related Occupation	None
On-the-job Training	Apprenticeship
Number of Jobs, 2010	19,100
Job Outlook, 2010-20	49% (Much faster than average)
Employment Change, 2010-20	9,300

What Reinforcing Iron and Rebar Workers Do

Reinforcing iron and rebar workers install wire mesh, steel bars (rebar), or cables to reinforce concrete.

Duties

Reinforcing iron and rebar workers typically do the following:
- Use blueprints, sketches, or other instructions for installation
- Determine quantities, sizes, shapes, and locations of reinforcing rods
- Cut mesh and rebar with metal shears, hacksaws, or acetylene torches
- Bend rebar or weld it together to match design specifications
- Position and secure steel bars, rods, cables, or mesh in concrete forms
- Install cables (post-tensioning systems)
- Place blocks under rebar to hold the bars off the deck when reinforcing floors
- Fasten rods together by tying wire around them with pliers
- Bend or place caps on exposed rebar to make it less hazardous

Concrete is often used in construction. To reinforce the concrete, reinforcing iron and rebar workers use one of three different materials:
- Rebar is used to reinforce concrete that forms highways, buildings, bridges, and other structures. These workers are often called **rodbusters** because they work with rods of rebar.
- Cable is used to reinforce concrete by a technique called post-tensioning. Post-tensioning allows designers to create larger open areas in a building because supports can be placed further apart. As a result, post-tensioning is commonly used for parking garages and arenas.
- Welded wire fabric is also used to reinforce concrete. Workers put the wire fabric into position using hooked rods.

Work Environment

Reinforcing iron and rebar workers held about 19,100 jobs in 2010. Workers were concentrated in three industries:

Foundation, structure, and building exterior contractors	63%
Nonresidential building construction	17
Highway, street, and bridge construction	9

Installing rebar is physically demanding because workers spend a lot of their time moving, bending, and stooping. Workers must be able to carry, bend, cut, and connect rebar at a rapid pace to keep projects on schedule.

Injuries

Reinforcing iron and rebar workers experience a rate of injury and illness that is higher than most other occupations. Hazards include falls from ladders and scaffolds, cuts from sharp metal, and burns from equipment.

Work Schedules

Nearly all reinforcing iron and rebar workers work full time. Because they are reinforcing concrete, weather conditions that affect the curing time of concrete can impact work schedules.

In contrast to other construction trades, few reinforcing iron and rebar workers are self-employment.

How to Become a Reinforcing Iron and Rebar

Workers must align rebar to match specifications.

Worker

Although most reinforcing iron and rebar workers learn their trade informally on the job, some get their training through a formal apprenticeship program. A high school diploma is generally required for becoming a reinforcing iron and rebar worker.

Training

On the job, trainees start by carrying rebar and setting it in place as directed by a foreman or supervisor. With experienced workers guiding them, trainees eventually acquire the skills of a fully qualified reinforcing iron and rebar worker.

Apprenticeship

Some reinforcing iron and rebar workers learn their trade through a 3- or 4- year apprenticeship. For each year of the program, apprentices must have at least 144 hours of related technical training and 1,400 to 2,000 hours of paid on-the-job training. Nearly all apprenticeship programs teach both reinforcing and structural ironworking, but a few programs focus exclusively on reinforcing and rebar work.

On the job, apprentices learn to use the tools and equipment of the trade; handle, measure, cut, and lay rebar; and construct metal frameworks. In technical instruction, they are taught about reinforcing metals and installation techniques, as well as basic mathematics, how to read and draw blueprints, general construction techniques, safety practices, and first aid.

After completing an apprenticeship program, they are considered journey workers who may do tasks on their own.

A few groups, including unions and contractor associations, sponsor apprenticeship programs. The basic qualifications for entering an apprenticeship program are as follows:

- Minimum age of 18
- High school diploma or equivalent
- Physically able to do the work

Education

A high school diploma is generally required for becoming a reinforcing iron and rebar worker. High school courses in math, shop, and blueprint reading are useful. Training in post-tensioning systems also is helpful.

Important Qualities

Hand-eye coordination. Workers must be able to quickly tie rebar together. An experienced worker can tie rebar together in seconds and move on to the next spot, while a beginner may take much longer.

Physical strength. Workers must be strong enough to carry heavy bundles of rebar. Although individual rebar only weighs 5 to 10 pounds, the weight quickly adds up when they are bundled.

Stamina. Workers must have endurance because they spend many hours on their feet. Also, workers must bend over frequently to easily reach the rebar, especially when tying flat-surface reinforcement.

Pay

Reinforcing Iron and Rebar Workers
Median annual wages, May 2010

Reinforcing Iron and Rebar Workers	$38,430
Construction Trades Workers	$38,240
Total, All Occupations	$33,840

Note: All Occupations includes all occupations in the U.S. Economy.
Source: U.S. Bureau of Labor Statistics, Occupational Employment Statistics

The median annual wage of reinforcing iron and rebar workers was $38,430 in May 2010. The median wage is the wage at which half the workers in an occupation earned more than that amount and half earned less. The lowest 10 percent earned less than $24,280, and the top 10 percent earned more than $74,210.

The starting pay for apprentices is usually between 50 percent and 60 percent of what fully trained reinforcing iron and rebar workers make. They get pay increases as they become more skilled.

Nearly all reinforcing iron and rebar workers work full time. Because they are reinforcing concrete, weather conditions that affect the curing time of concrete can impact work schedules.

In contrast to other construction trades, few reinforcing iron and rebar workers are self-employed.

Reinforcing iron and rebar workers have a rate of union membership that is higher than the national average. Although there is no single union that covers all reinforcing iron and rebar workers, the largest organizer of these workers is the International Association of Bridge, Structural, Ornamental, and Reinforcing Iron Workers.

Job Outlook

Reinforcing Iron and Rebar Workers
Percent change in employment, projected 2010-20

Reinforcing Iron and Rebar Workers	49%
Construction Trades Workers	23%
Total, All Occupations	14%

Note: All Occupations includes all occupations in the U.S. Economy.
Source: U.S. Bureau of Labor Statistics, Employment Projections program

Employment of reinforcing iron and rebar workers is projected to grow 49 percent from 2010 to 2020, much faster than the average for all occupations. However, because it is a small occupation, the fast employment growth will result in only 9,300 new jobs over the 10-year period.

The need to rehabilitate, maintain, and replace a growing number of older buildings, powerplants, highways, and bridges is expected to drive employment growth. State and federal legislatures will likely continue funding road construction and related infrastructure projects, which will result in new jobs over the projections decade.

Job Prospects

Rapid employment growth should result in good job opportunities. Because employers prefer workers who can do a variety of tasks, reinforcing iron and rebar workers with additional skills, such as welding, should have the best job opportunities. Those with prior military service are also viewed favorably during initial hiring.

Like employment of many other construction workers, employment of reinforcing iron and rebar workers is sensitive to fluctuations in the economy. Workers may experience periods of unemployment when the overall level of construction falls. However, shortages of workers may occur in some areas during peak periods of building activity.

Employment opportunities should be greatest in metropolitan areas, where most large commercial and multifamily buildings are constructed.

Employment projections data for reinforcing iron and ebar workers, 2010-20

Occupational Title	SOC Code	Employment, 2010	Projected Employment, 2020	Change, 2010-20	
				Percent	Numeric
Reinforcing Iron and Rebar Workers	47-2171	19,100	28,400	49	9,300
SOURCE: U.S. Bureau of Labor Statistics, Employment Projections program					

Similar Occupations

This table shows a list of occupations with job duties that are similar to those of reinforcing iron and rebar workers.

Occupation	Job Duties	Entry-Level Education	Median Annual Pay, May 2010
Boilermakers	Boilermakers assemble, install, and repair boilers, closed vats, and other large vessels or containers that hold liquids and gases.	High school diploma or equivalent	$54,640
Carpenters	Carpenters construct and repair building frameworks and structures—such as stairways, doorframes, partitions, and rafters—made from wood and other materials. They also may install kitchen cabinets, siding, and drywall.	High school diploma or equivalent	$39,530
Cement Masons and Terrazzo Workers	Cement masons pour, smooth, and finish concrete floors, sidewalks, roads, and curbs. Using a cement mixture, terrazzo workers create durable and decorative surfaces for floors and stairways.	See How to Become One	$35,530
Construction Laborers and Helpers	Construction laborers and helpers do many basic tasks that require physical labor on construction sites.	See How to Become One	$28,410
Structural Iron and Steel Workers	Structural iron and steel workers install iron or steel beams, girders, and columns to form buildings, bridges, and other structures. They are often referred to as ironworkers.	High school diploma or equivalent	$44,540
Assemblers and Fabricators	Assemblers and fabricators assemble both finished products and the parts that go into them. They use tools, machines, and their hands to make engines, computers, aircraft, toys, electronic devices, and more.	High school diploma or equivalent	$28,360
Welders, Cutters, Solderers, and Brazers	Welders, cutters, solderers, and brazers weld or join metal parts. They also fill holes, indentions, or seams of metal products, using hand-held welding equipment.	High school diploma or equivalent	$35,450

Contacts for More Information

For information about apprenticeships or job opportunities as a reinforcing iron and rebar worker, contact local cement or highway construction contractors, a local joint union-management apprenticeship committee, or the nearest office of your state employment service or apprenticeship agency. Apprenticeship information is available from the U.S. Department of Labor's toll free help line, 1 (877) 872-5627, or Employment and Training Administration.

For apprenticeship information, visit International Association of Bridge, Structural, Ornamental and Reinforcing Iron Workers

Suggested citation:

Bureau of Labor Statistics, U.S. Department of Labor, Occupational Outlook Handbook, 2012-13 Edition, Reinforcing Iron and Rebar Workers, on the Internet at http://www.bls.gov/ooh/construction-and-extraction/reinforcing-iron-and-rebar-workers.htm.

Roofers

Quick Facts: Roofers	
2010 Median Pay	$34,220 per year $16.45 per hour
Entry-Level Education	Less than high school
Work Experience in a Related Occupation	None
On-the-job Training	Moderate-term on-the-job training
Number of Jobs, 2010	136,700
Job Outlook, 2010-20	18% (About as fast as average)
Employment Change, 2010-20	24,400

What Roofers Do

Roofers repair and install the roofs of buildings using a variety of materials, including shingles, asphalt, and metal.

Duties

Roofers typically do the following:

- Inspect problem roofs to determine the best way to repair them
- Measure roof to calculate the quantities of materials needed
- Replace damaged or rotting joists or plywood
- Install vapor barriers or layers of insulation
- Install shingles, asphalt, metal, or other materials to make the roof watertight
- Align roofing materials with edges of the roof
- Cut roofing materials to fit angles formed by walls, vents, or intersecting roof surfaces
- Cover exposed nail or screw heads with roofing cement or caulk to prevent leakage

Roofers commonly apply asphalt shingles.

Properly installed roofs keep water from leaking into buildings and damaging the interior, equipment, or furnishings. There are two basic types of roofs, low-slope and steep-slope:

- Low-slope: About two-thirds of all roofs are low-slope. Most commercial, industrial, and apartment buildings have low-slope roofs. Low-slope roofs rise 4 inches or less per horizontal foot and are installed in layers.

  — For low-slope roofs, roofers typically use several layers of roofing materials or felt membranes stuck together with hot bitumen (a tar-like substance). They glaze the top layer to make a smooth surface or embed gravel in the hot bitumen to make a rough surface.
  — An increasing number of low-slope roofs are covered with a single-ply membrane of waterproof rubber or thermoplastic compounds.

- Steep-slope: Most of the remaining roofs are steep-slope. Most single-family houses have steep-slope roofs. Steep-slope roofs rise more than 4 inches per horizontal foot.

  — For steep-slope roofs, roofers typically use asphalt shingles, which often cost less than other coverings. On steep-slope roofs, some roofers also install tile, solar shingles, fiberglass shingles, metal shingles, or shakes (rough wooden shingles).
  — To apply shingles, roofers first lay, cut, and tack 3-foot strips of roofing over the entire roof. Then, starting from the bottom edge, they nail overlapping rows of shingles to the roof.

A small but increasing number of buildings now have "green" roofs that incorporate landscape roofing systems. A landscape roofing system typically begins with a single or multiple waterproof layers. After that layer is proven to be leak free, roofers put a root barrier over it, and, finally, layers of soil, in which vegetation is planted. Roofers must ensure that the roof is watertight and can endure the weight and water needs of the plants.

Work Environment

Roofers held about 136,700 jobs in 2010, of which 67 percent were employed in the roofing contractors industry. About 27 percent were self-employed.

Roofing work is strenuous and tiring. It often involves heavy lifting, as well as climbing, bending, and kneeling. Roofers work outdoors in all types of weather, particularly when making repairs. However, they rarely work when it rains or when it is very cold because snow-covered or icy roofs are especially dangerous. Although some roofers work alone, many work as part of a crew.

Injuries

Roofers have one of the highest rates of injuries and illnesses of all occupations. Workers may slip or fall from scaffolds, ladders, or roofs. They may get burns from hot bitumen. However, proper safety precautions can prevent most accidents. Roofs can also become extremely hot during the summer, which can cause heat-related illnesses.

Work Schedules

Like many construction workers, most roofers work full time. In northern states, roofing work is limited during the winter months. During the summer, roofers may work overtime to complete jobs quickly, especially before rainfall. About 27 percent of roofers were self-employed in 2010. Self-employed workers may be able to set their own schedules.

How to Become a Roofer

There are no specific educational requirements for roofers. Although most roofers learn informally on the job, some learn their trade through a formal apprenticeship program.

Training

Most on-the-job training programs consist of informal instruction in which experienced workers teach new workers how to use roofing tools, equipment, machines, and materials. Trainees begin with tasks such as carrying equipment and material and erecting scaffolds and hoists. Within 2 or 3 months, they are taught to measure, cut, and fit roofing materials and, later, to lay asphalt or fiberglass shingles. Because some roofing materials, such as solar tiles, are used infrequently, it can take several years to get experience working on all types of roofing. As training progresses, assignments become more complex, and trainees can usually do finishing work within a short time.

Some roofers learn through a 3-year apprenticeship. For each year of the program, apprentices must have at least 144 hours of related technical training and 2,000 hours of paid on-the-job training. Apprentices learn construction basics, such as blueprint reading, mathematics, building code requirements, and safety and first-aid practices.

After completing an apprenticeship program, roofers are considered journey workers who can do tasks on their own.

Several groups sponsor apprenticeship programs, including unions and contractor associations. The basic qualifications to enter an apprenticeship program are as follows:

- Minimum age of 18
- High school diploma or equivalent
- Physically able to do the work

Education

Although there are no formal educational requirements for roofers, high school courses in math, shop, mechanical drawing, and blueprint reading are helpful.

Important Qualities

Balance. Roofing is often done on steep slopes at significant heights. As a result, workers should have excellent balance to avoid falling.

Physical strength. Roofers often lift and carry heavy materials. Some roofers, for example, must carry bundles of shingles that weigh 70 pounds or more.

Stamina. Roofers must have endurance to perform strenuous duties throughout the day. They may spend hours on their feet, bending and stooping—often in hot temperatures—with few breaks.

Unafraid of heights. Because work is often done at significant heights, roofers must not fear working far above the ground.

Pay

Roofers

Median annual wages, May 2010

Construction Trades Workers	$38,240
Roofers	$34,220
Total, All Occupations	$33,840

Note: All Occupations includes all occupations in the U.S. Economy.
Source: U.S. Bureau of Labor Statistics, Occupational Employment Statistics

The median annual wage of roofers was $34,220 in May 2010. The median wage is the wage at which half the workers in an occupation earned more than that amount, and half earned less. The lowest 10 percent earned less than $22,030, and the top 10 percent earned more than $60,610.

The starting pay for apprentices is usually between 30 percent and 50 percent of what fully trained workers make. They get pay increases as they gain more skill.

Like many construction workers, most roofers work full time. In northern states, roofing work is limited during the winter months. During the summer, roofers may work overtime to complete jobs quickly, especially before rainfall. About 27 percent of roofers were self-employed in 2010. Self-employed workers may be able to set their own schedules.

About 6 percent of roofers are members of a union. The largest organizer of roofers is the United Union of Roofers, Waterproofers and Allied Workers.

Job Outlook

Roofers

Percent change in employment, projected 2010-20

Construction Trades Workers	23%
Roofers	18%
Total, All Occupations	14%

Note: All Occupations includes all occupations in the U.S. Economy.
Source: U.S. Bureau of Labor Statistics, Employment Projections program

Employment of roofers is expected to grow 18 percent from 2010 to 2020, about as fast as the average for all occupations.

Roofs deteriorate more quickly than most other parts of buildings and, as a result, they need to be repaired or replaced more often. In fact, results of a National Roofing Contractors Association survey indicate that about three-fourths of all roofing work is for repair and replacement.

Areas of the country that commonly have severe storms have a greater need for workers to repair and replace storm-damaged roofs. In addition to repair and replacement work, the need to install roofs on new buildings should result in some job growth.

However, more roofing work is now being done by other construction workers, and that may slow job growth for traditional roofing contractors.

Job Prospects

Job opportunities for roofers will occur primarily because of the need to replace workers who leave the occupation. The proportion of roofers who leave the occupation each year is higher than in most construction trades—roofing work is hot, strenuous, and dirty, and a considerable number of workers treat roofing as a temporary job until they find other work. Some roofers leave the occupation to go into other construction trades. Jobs are generally easier to find during spring and summer.

Like many other construction occupations, employment of roofers is somewhat sensitive to fluctuations in the economy. Workers may experience periods of unemployment when the overall level of construction falls. However, shortages of workers may occur in some areas during peak periods of building activity. Demand for roofers is less vulnerable to downturns than demand for other construction trades because much roofing work consists of repair and reroofing, in addition to new construction.

Employment projections data for roofers, 2010-20

Occupational Title	SOC Code	Employment, 2010	Projected Employment, 2020	Change, 2010-20	
				Percent	Numeric
Roofers	47-2181	136,700	161,100	18	24,400
SOURCE: U.S. Bureau of Labor Statistics, Employment Projections program					

Similar Occupations

This table shows a list of occupations with job duties that are similar to those of roofers.

Occupation	Job Duties	Entry-Level Education	Median Annual Pay, May 2010
Carpenters	Carpenters construct and repair building frameworks and structures—such as stairways, doorframes, partitions, and rafters—made from wood and other materials. They also may install kitchen cabinets, siding, and drywall.	High school diploma or equivalent	$39,530
Carpet Installers	Carpet installers lay carpet in homes, offices, restaurants, and many other types of buildings.	Less than high school	$36,090
Cement Masons and Terrazzo Workers	Cement masons pour, smooth, and finish concrete floors, sidewalks, roads, and curbs. Using a cement mixture, terrazzo workers create durable and decorative surfaces for floors and stairways.	See How to Become One	$35,530
Drywall and Ceiling Tile Installers, and Tapers	Drywall and ceiling tile installers hang wallboards to walls and ceilings inside buildings. Tapers prepare the wallboards for painting, using tape and other materials. Many workers do both installing and taping.	Less than high school	$38,290
Sheet Metal Workers	Sheet metal workers fabricate or install products that are made from thin metal sheets, such as ducts used for heating and air-conditioning.	High school diploma or equivalent	$41,710
Tile and Marble Setters	Tile and marble setters apply hard tile, marble, and wood tiles to walls, floors, and other surfaces.	Less than high school	$38,110
Construction Laborers and Helpers	Construction laborers and helpers do many basic tasks that require physical labor on construction sites.	See How to Become One	$28,410

Contacts for More Information

For details about apprenticeships or other work opportunities for roofers, contact the offices of the state employment service, the state apprenticeship agency, local contractors or firms that employ roofers, or local union-management apprenticeship committees. Apprenticeship information is available from the U.S. Department of Labor's toll free help line, 1 (877) 872-5627, or Employment and Training Administration.

For information about the work of roofers, visit National Roofing Contractors Association ,United Union of Roofers, Waterproofers and Allied Workers

Suggested citation:

Bureau of Labor Statistics, U.S. Department of Labor, Occupational Outlook Handbook, 2012-13 Edition, Roofers, on the Internet at http://www.bls.gov/ooh/construction-and-extraction/roofers.htm.

Sheet Metal Workers

Quick Facts: Sheet Metal Workers	
2010 Median Pay	$41,710 per year $20.05 per hour
Entry-Level Education	High school diploma or equivalent
Work Experience in a Related Occupation	None
On-the-job Training	Apprenticeship
Number of Jobs, 2010	136,100
Job Outlook, 2010-20	18% (About as fast as average)
Employment Change, 2010-20	23,900

What Sheet Metal Workers Do

Sheet metal workers fabricate or install products that are made from thin metal sheets, such as ducts used for heating and air-conditioning.

Duties

Sheet metal workers typically do the following:

- Select types of sheet metal or nonmetallic material
- Measure and mark dimensions and reference lines on metal sheets
- Drill holes in metal, for screws, bolts, and rivets
- Install metal sheets with supportive frameworks
- Fabricate or alter parts at construction sites
- Maneuver large parts to be installed, and anchor the parts
- Fasten seams or joints by welding, bolting, riveting, or soldering

Sheet metal workers make, install, and maintain thin sheet metal products. Although sheet metal is used to make many products, such as rain gutters, outdoor signs, and siding, it is most commonly used to make ducts for heating and air-conditioning.

Sheet metal workers study plans and specifications to determine the kind and quantity of materials they will need. Using computer-controlled saws, lasers, shears, and presses, they measure, cut, bend, and fasten pieces of sheet metal.

In shops without computerized equipment, sheet metal workers make the required calculations and use tapes and rulers to lay out the work. Then, they cut or stamp the parts with machine tools.

In manufacturing plants, sheet metal workers program and operate computerized metalworking equipment. For example, they may make sheet metal parts for aircraft or industrial equipment. Sheet metal

Sheet metal workers sometimes install roofs.

workers in those jobs may be responsible for programming the computer control systems of the equipment they operate.

Before assembling pieces, sheet metal workers check each part for accuracy. If necessary, they use hand, rotary, or squaring shears and hacksaws to finish pieces.

After inspecting the metal pieces, workers fasten seams and joints with welds, bolts, rivets, solder, or other connecting devices. Then they take the parts constructed in the shop and assemble the pieces further as they install them.

Most fabrication work is done in shops with some final assembly done on the job. Some jobs are done completely at the jobsite. When installing a metal roof, for example, sheet metal workers usually measure and cut the roofing panels onsite.

In addition to installing sheet metal, some workers install fiberglass and plastic board.

In some shops and factories, sheet metal workers care for and maintain the equipment they use.

Sheet metal workers do both construction-related work and the mass production of sheet metal products in manufacturing. Sheet metal workers are often separated into four specialties: fabrication, installation, maintenance, and testing and balancing. The following describes these types of sheet metal workers:

Fabrication sheet metal workers, sometimes called **precision sheet metal workers**, make ducts, gutters, and other metal products. Most work in shops and factories, operating tools and equipment. Although some of the fabrication techniques used in large-scale manufacturing are similar to those used in smaller shops, the work may be highly automated and repetitive. Many fabrication shops have automated machinery, and workers use computer-aided drafting (CAD) and building information modeling (BIM) systems to make products.

Installation sheet metal workers install heating, ventilation, and air-conditioning (HVAC) ducts. They also install other sheet metal products, such as metal roofs, siding, or gutters. They work on new construction and on renovation projects.

Maintenance sheet metal workers repair and clean ventilation systems so the systems use less energy. Workers remove dust and moisture and fix leaks or breaks in the sheet metal that makes up the ductwork.

Testing and balancing sheet metal specialists ensure that HVAC systems heat and cool rooms properly. They ensure that hot and cold air is transferred through sheet metal ducts efficiently. For more information on workers who install or repair HVAC systems, see the profile on heating, air conditioning, and refrigeration mechanics and installers.

Work Environment

Sheet metal workers held about 136,100 jobs in 2010. About 62 percent worked in the construction industry and 25 percent worked in manufacturing.

Sheet metal fabricators usually work in small shops and manufacturing plants that are well-ventilated. They must often lift heavy materials and stand for long periods.

Workers who install sheet metal at construction sites or inside buildings must bend, climb, and squat, sometimes in close quarters or in awkward positions.

Sheet metal installers who work outdoors are exposed to all kinds of weather.

Injuries

Sheet metal workers have one of the highest rates of injuries and illnesses of all occupations. Common injuries include cuts from sharp metal, burns from soldering or welding, and falls from ladders or scaffolds.

Some sheet metal workers work around high-speed machines, which can be dangerous. Because of these hazards, they often must wear safety glasses and must not wear jewelry or loose-fitting clothing that could easily be caught in a machine.

To avoid repetitive-type injuries, sheet metal workers may work at a variety of different production stations.

Work Schedules

Nearly all sheet metal workers are employed full time.

How to Become a Sheet Metal Worker

Although most sheet metal workers learn their trade through formal apprenticeships, some learn informally on the job or in technical colleges. Formal apprenticeships are more likely in construction.

Training

Most sheet metal workers learn their trade through 4- or 5-year apprenticeships. Each year, apprentices must have at least 1,700 to 2,000 hours of paid on-the-job training and a minimum of 246 hours of related technical instruction. Apprentices learn construction basics such as blueprint reading, mathematics, building code requirements, and safety and first-aid practices.

After completing an apprenticeship program, sheet metal workers are considered to be journey workers, qualifying them to do tasks on their own.

Apprenticeship programs are offered by unions and businesses. The basic qualifications for entering an apprenticeship program are reaching the age of 18 and having a high school diploma or the equivalent.

Although most workers enter apprenticeships directly after finishing high school or getting their GED, some start out as with a job as helper before entering an apprenticeship.

Education

Those interested in becoming a sheet metal worker should take high school classes in English, algebra, geometry, physics, mechanical drawing and blueprint reading, and general shop.

Many technical colleges have programs that teach welding and metalworking. These programs help provide the basic knowledge that many sheet metal workers need to do their job.

Some manufacturers work through local technical schools to develop training programs specific to their factories.

Certification

Although not required, sheet metal workers can obtain certifications for several of the tasks that they perform. For example, some sheet metal workers gain certification in welding from the American Welding Society. In addition, the Sheet Metal Institute offers certification in building information modeling, welding, testing and balancing, and other related skills.

Important Qualities

Computer skills. Designing and cutting sheet metal often requires the use of computer-aided drafting (CAD) programs and building information modeling (BIM) systems.

Customer-service skills. Because many sheet metal workers install ducts in customers' homes, workers should be polite and courteous.

Manual dexterity. Sheet metal workers need good eye–hand coordination to make precise cuts and bends in metal pieces.

Mechanical skills. Sheet metal workers use saws, lasers, shears, and presses to do their job. As a result, they should have good mechanical skills.

Physical strength. Sheet metal workers must be able to lift and move ductwork that is often heavy and cumbersome.

Spatial relationships. Ductwork for heating and air-conditioning is often large and bulky. Workers must be able to visualize and install large pieces of ductwork within small spaces.

Pay

Sheet Metal Workers
Median annual wages, May 2010

Sheet Metal Workers	$41,710
Construction Trades Workers	$38,240
Total, All Occupations	$33,840

Note: All Occupations includes all occupations in the U.S. Economy.
Source: U.S. Bureau of Labor Statistics, Occupational Employment Statistics

The median annual wage of sheet metal workers was $41,710 in May 2010. The median wage is the wage at which half the workers in an occupation earned more than that amount and half earned less. The lowest 10 percent earned less than $24,990, and the top 10 percent earned more than $73,980.

The starting pay for apprentices usually is between 30 percent and 50 percent of what fully trained sheet metal workers make. As they gain more skill, their pay increases.

Nearly all sheet metal workers are employed full time. Those who work in manufacturing are more likely to participate in profit sharing, work overtime, and receive output incentives to supplement their basic wages.

About 36 percent of sheet metal workers are members of a union. Although there is no single union, the largest organizer for sheet metal workers is the Sheet Metal Workers International Association.

Job Outlook

Sheet Metal Workers
Percent change in employment, projected 2010-20

Construction Trades Workers	23%
Sheet Metal Workers	18%
Total, All Occupations	14%

Note: All Occupations includes all occupations in the U.S. Economy.
Source: U.S. Bureau of Labor Statistics, Employment Projections program

Employment of sheet metal workers is expected to grow 18 percent from 2010 to 2020, about as fast as the average for all occupations.

Employment growth reflects more industrial, commercial, and residential structures expected to be built over the coming decade. It also reflects the need to install energy-efficient air-conditioning, heating, and ventilation systems in older buildings and to renovate and maintain these systems.

Sheet metal workers in manufacturing are expected to experience faster-than-average employment growth as small amounts of work that used to be done in other countries returns to the United States.

Job Prospects

Job opportunities should be particularly good for sheet metal workers who complete apprenticeship training or who are certified welders.

Some manufacturing companies report having difficulty finding qualified applicants. Workers who have programming skills, possess multiple welding skills, and show commitment to their work will have the best job opportunities.

Employment of sheet metal workers, like that of many other construction workers, is sensitive to fluctuations in the economy. On the one hand, workers in these trades may experience periods of unemployment when the overall level of construction falls. On the other hand, peak periods of building activity may produce shortages of sheet metal workers.

Employment projections data for sheet metal workers, 2010-20

Occupational Title	SOC Code	Employment, 2010	Projected Employment, 2020	Change, 2010-20 Percent	Change, 2010-20 Numeric
Sheet Metal Workers	47-2211	136,100	160,000	18	23,900

SOURCE: U.S. Bureau of Labor Statistics, Employment Projections program

Similar Occupations

This table shows a list of occupations with job duties that are similar to those of sheet metal workers.

Occupation	Job Duties	Entry-Level Education	Median Annual Pay, May 2010
Glaziers	Glaziers install glass in windows, skylights, storefronts, and display cases to create distinctive designs or reduce the need for artificial lighting.	High school diploma or equivalent	$36,640
Heating, Air Conditioning, and Refrigeration Mechanics and Installers	Heating, air conditioning, and refrigeration mechanics and installers—often referred to as HVACR technicians—work on heating, ventilation, cooling, and refrigeration systems that control the air quality in many types of buildings.	Postsecondary non-degree award	$42,530
Assemblers and Fabricators	Assemblers and fabricators assemble both finished products and the parts that go into them. They use tools, machines, and their hands to make engines, computers, aircraft, toys, electronic devices, and more.	High school diploma or equivalent	$28,360
Machinists and Tool and Die Makers	Machinists and tool and die makers set up and operate a variety of computer-controlled or mechanically-controlled machine tools to produce precision metal parts, instruments, and tools.	High school diploma or equivalent	$39,910
Metal and Plastic Machine Workers	Metal and plastic machine workers set up and operate machines that cut, shape, and form metal and plastic materials or pieces.	High school diploma or equivalent	$31,910

Contacts for More Information

For more information about apprenticeships or other work opportunities, contact local sheet metal contractors or heating, refrigeration, and air-conditioning contractors; a local of the Sheet Metal Workers International Association; a local of the Sheet Metal and Air-Conditioning Contractors National Association; a local joint union–management apprenticeship committee; or the nearest office of your state employment service or apprenticeship agency. Apprenticeship information is available from the U.S. Department of Labor's toll-free help line, 1 (877) 872-5627, and Employment and Training Administration.

For general information about sheet metal workers, visit Fabricators and Manufacturers Association, International ,International Training Institute for the Sheet Metal and Air Conditioning Industry ,National Center for Construction Education and Research ,Sheet Metal and Air Conditioning Contractors' National Association ,Sheet Metal Workers International Association

For certification information, visit American Welding Society ,Sheet Metal Institute

Suggested citation:

Bureau of Labor Statistics, U.S. Department of Labor, Occupational Outlook Handbook, 2012-13 Edition, Sheet Metal Workers, on the Internet at http://www.bls.gov/ooh/construction-and-extraction/sheet-metal-workers.htm.

Structural Iron and Steel Workers

Quick Facts: Structural Iron and Steel Workers	
2010 Median Pay	$44,540 per year $21.42 per hour
Entry-Level Education	High school diploma or equivalent
Work Experience in a Related Occupation	None
On-the-job Training	Apprenticeship
Number of Jobs, 2010	59,800
Job Outlook, 2010-20	22% (Faster than average)
Employment Change, 2010-20	13,100

What Structural Iron and Steel Workers Do

Structural iron and steel workers install iron or steel beams, girders, and columns to form buildings, bridges, and other structures. They are often referred to as ironworkers.

Duties

Ironworkers typically do the following:
- Unload and stack prefabricated steel so that it can be lifted easily with slings
- Use a crane to lift steel beams, girders, and columns into place
- Stand on beams or girders to help position steel pieces that are being lifted
- Signal crane operators for positioning of the structural steel
- Align beams and girders into position
- Verify vertical and horizontal alignment of the structural steel
- Connect columns, beams, and girders with bolts or by welding them into place
- Use metal shears, torches, and welding equipment to cut, bend, and weld the steel

Iron and steel are important parts of buildings, bridges, and other structures. Even though the primary metal involved in this work is steel, these workers often are known as **ironworkers** or **erectors**.

When building tall structures such as a skyscraper, ironworkers erect steel frames and assemble the cranes and derricks that move structural steel, reinforcing bars, buckets of concrete, lumber, and other materials and equipment around the construction site. Once this job has been completed, workers begin to connect steel columns, beams, and girders according to blueprints and instructions from construction

Ironworkers must adjust the position of beams.

supervisors.

As they work, they use a variety of tools. They use rope (called a tag line) to guide the steel while it is being lifted; they use spud wrenches (long wrenches with a pointed handle) to put the steel in place; and they use driftpins or the handle of the spud wrench to line up the holes in the steel with the holes in the framework. To check the alignment, they may use plumb bobs, laser equipment, or levels.

Structural steel generally comes to the construction site ready to be put up—cut to the proper size, with holes drilled for bolts and numbered for assembly.

Some ironworkers make structural metal in fabricating shops, which are usually located away from the construction site. For more information, see the profile on assemblers and fabricators.

Work Environment

Structural iron and steel workers held about 59,800 jobs in 2010. About 85 percent were employed in the construction industry, and only 4 percent were self-employed. The following industries employed the most workers:

Foundation, structure, and building exterior contractors	43%
Nonresidential building construction	20
Heavy and civil engineering construction	10

Ironworkers perform physically demanding and dangerous work. They usually work outside in all types of weather, and some must work at great heights. As a result, workers must wear safety devices, such as harnesses, to reduce the risk of falling.

Injuries

Ironworkers have one of the highest rates of injuries of all occupations. In fact, ironworkers experience several work-related deaths each year due to falls. In addition to falls, workers may experience cuts from sharp metal edges and equipment, as well as muscle strains and other injuries from moving and guiding structural steel.

Work Schedules

Most ironworkers work for a wage or salary for an employer; only 4 percent were self-employed in 2010.

Nearly all ironworkers work full time. Those who work at great heights do not work during wet, icy, or extremely windy conditions.

How to Become a Structural Iron and Steel Worker

Although most structural iron and steel workers learn through a formal apprenticeship, some learn informally on the job. Certifications in welding and rigging can be useful.

Apprenticeship

Most ironworkers learn their trade through a 3- or 4-year apprenticeship. For each year of the program, apprentices must have at least 144 hours of related technical training and 2,000 hours of paid on-the-job training. Nearly all apprenticeship programs teach both reinforcing and structural ironworking. On the job, apprentices learn to use the tools and equipment of the trade; handle, measure, cut, and lay rebar; and construct metal frameworks. In technical training, they are taught techniques for reinforcing and installing metals, as well as basic mathematics, blueprint reading and sketching, general construction techniques, safety practices, and first aid.

After completing an apprenticeship program, they are considered journey workers who do tasks with less guidance.

A few groups, including unions and contractor associations, sponsor apprenticeship programs. The basic qualifications required for entering an apprenticeship program are as follows:

- Minimum age of 18
- High school diploma or equivalent
- Physical ability to perform the work

Certification

Many ironworkers become welders certified by the American Welding Society. Certifications in welding and rigging may increase a worker's usefulness on the jobsite.

Education

A high school diploma is generally required. High school courses in math, shop, blueprint reading, and welding are useful.

Important Qualities

Balance. Because workers often walk on narrow beams, a good sense of balance is important to keep them from falling while doing their job. They also need excellent eyesight and depth perception to work safely at great heights.

Physical strength. Ironworkers must be strong enough to guide heavy beams into place and tighten bolts.

Stamina. Ironworkers must have endurance because they spend many hours on their feet while connecting heavy and often cumbersome beams.

Unafraid of heights. Some ironworkers must not be afraid to work at great heights. For example, as they erect skyscrapers, workers must walk on narrow beams at great heights while connecting beams and girders.

Pay

Structural Iron and Steel Workers
Median annual wages, May 2010

Structural Iron and Steel Workers	$44,540
Construction Trades Workers	$38,240
Total, All Occupations	$33,840

Note: All Occupations includes all occupations in the U.S. Economy.
Source: U.S. Bureau of Labor Statistics, Occupational Employment Statistics

The median annual wage of structural iron and steel workers was $44,540 in May 2010. The median wage is the wage at which half the workers in an occupation earned more than that amount and half earned less. The lowest 10 percent earned less than $26,330, and the top 10 percent earned more than $80,030.

The starting pay for apprentices is usually between 30 percent and 50 percent of what fully trained ironworkers make. They get pay increases as they become more skilled.

Most ironworkers work for a wage or salary for an employer; only 4 percent were self-employed in 2010.

Nearly all ironworkers work full time. Those who work at great heights do not work during wet, icy, or extremely windy conditions.

Ironworkers have a higher rate of union membership than many other construction occupations. Although there is no single union that covers all ironworkers, the largest organizer of these workers is the International Association of Bridge, Structural, Ornamental and Reinforcing Iron Workers.

Job Outlook

Structural Iron and Steel Workers
Percent change in employment, projected 2010-20

Construction Trades Workers	23%
Structural Iron and Steel Workers	22%
Total, All Occupations	14%

Note: All Occupations includes all occupations in the U.S. Economy.
Source: U.S. Bureau of Labor Statistics, Employment Projections program

Employment of ironworkers is projected to grow 22 percent from 2010 to 2020, faster than the average for all occupations. The need to rehabilitate, maintain, or replace a growing number of older highways and bridges is expected to drive employment growth, particularly because state and federal legislatures will likely continue funding these infrastructure projects.

In addition, steel is an important part of commercial and industrial buildings. The construction of these structures should create additional demand for ironworkers.

Job Prospects

Those who are certified in welding and rigging should have the best job opportunities. Those with prior military service are also viewed favorably during initial hiring.

As with many other construction workers, employment of ironworkers is sensitive to the fluctuations of the economy. On the one hand, workers may experience periods of unemployment when the overall level of construction falls. On the other hand, shortages of workers may occur in some areas during peak periods of building activity. Employment opportunities should be best in metropolitan areas, where most large commercial and industrial buildings are constructed.

Employment projections data for structural iron and steel workers, 2010-20

Occupational Title	SOC Code	Employment, 2010	Projected Employment, 2020	Change, 2010-20 Percent	Change, 2010-20 Numeric
Structural Iron and Steel Workers	47-2221	59,800	72,900	22	13,100
SOURCE: U.S. Bureau of Labor Statistics, Employment Projections program					

Similar Occupations

This table shows a list of occupations with job duties that are similar to those of structural iron and steel workers.

Occupation	Job Duties	Entry-Level Education	Median Annual Pay, May 2010
Boilermakers	Boilermakers assemble, install, and repair boilers, closed vats, and other large vessels or containers that hold liquids and gases.	High school diploma or equivalent	$54,640
Carpenters	Carpenters construct and repair building frameworks and structures—such as stairways, doorframes, partitions, and rafters—made from wood and other materials. They also may install kitchen cabinets, siding, and drywall.	High school diploma or equivalent	$39,530
Cement Masons and Terrazzo Workers	Cement masons pour, smooth, and finish concrete floors, sidewalks, roads, and curbs. Using a cement mixture, terrazzo workers create durable and decorative surfaces for floors and stairways.	See How to Become One	$35,530
Construction Laborers and Helpers	Construction laborers and helpers do many basic tasks that require physical labor on construction sites.	See How to Become One	$28,410
Reinforcing Iron and Rebar Workers	Reinforcing iron and rebar workers install mesh, steel bars (rebar), or cables to reinforce concrete.	High school diploma or equivalent	$38,430
Assemblers and Fabricators	Assemblers and fabricators assemble both finished products and the parts that go into them. They use tools, machines, and their hands to make engines, computers, aircraft, toys, electronic devices, and more.	High school diploma or equivalent	$28,360
Welders, Cutters, Solderers, and Brazers	Welders, cutters, solderers, and brazers weld or join metal parts. They also fill holes, indentions, or seams of metal products, using hand-held welding equipment.	High school diploma or equivalent	$35,450

Contacts for More Information

For information about apprenticeships or job opportunities as a structural iron and steel worker, contact local structural iron and steel construction contractors, a local joint union–management apprenticeship committee, or the nearest office of your state employment service or apprenticeship agency. Apprenticeship information is available from the U.S. Department of Labor's toll-free help line, 1 (877) 872-5627, or Employment and Training Administration.

For apprenticeship information, visit International Association of Bridge, Structural, Ornamental and Reinforcing Iron Workers

For more information about ironworkers, visit Associated Builders and Contractors ,Associated General Contractors of America

Suggested citation:

Bureau of Labor Statistics, U.S. Department of Labor, Occupational Outlook Handbook, 2012-13 Edition, Structural Iron and Steel Workers, on the Internet at http://www.bls.gov/ooh/construction-and-extraction/structural-iron-and-steel-workers.htm.

Tile and Marble Setters

Quick Facts: Tile and Marble Setters	
2010 Median Pay	$38,110 per year $18.32 per hour
Entry-Level Education	Less than high school
Work Experience in a Related Occupation	None
On-the-job Training	Long-term on-the-job training
Number of Jobs, 2010	58,700
Job Outlook, 2010-20	25% (Faster than average)
Employment Change, 2010-20	14,900

What Tile and Marble Setters Do

Tile and marble setters apply hard tile, marble, and wood tiles to walls, floors, and other surfaces.

Duties

Tile and marble setters typically do the following:

- Clean and level the surface to be tiled
- Measure and cut tile and marble
- Arrange tiles according to the design plans
- Prepare and apply mortar or other adhesives
- Install tile and marble in the planned area
- Apply grout with a rubber trowel
- Wipe off excess grout and apply necessary finishes, such as sealants

Tile installers, tilesetters, and **marble setters** install materials on a variety of surfaces, such as floors, walls, ceilings, countertops, patios, and roof decks. Because tile and marble must be set on smooth, even surfaces, installers often must level the surface to be tiled with a layer of mortar or plywood. If the area to be tiled is unstable, workers must nail a support of metal mesh or tile backer board to create a stable surface.

To cut tiles, workers use power wet saws, tile scribes, or hand-held tile cutters to create even edges. They use trowels of different sizes to spread mortar or a sticky paste, called mastic, evenly on the surface to be tiled. To minimize imperfections and keep rows straight and even, they put spacers between tiles. The spacers keep tiles the same distance from each other until the mortar is dry. After the mortar dries and the tiles are set, they apply grout between tiles using a rubber trowel

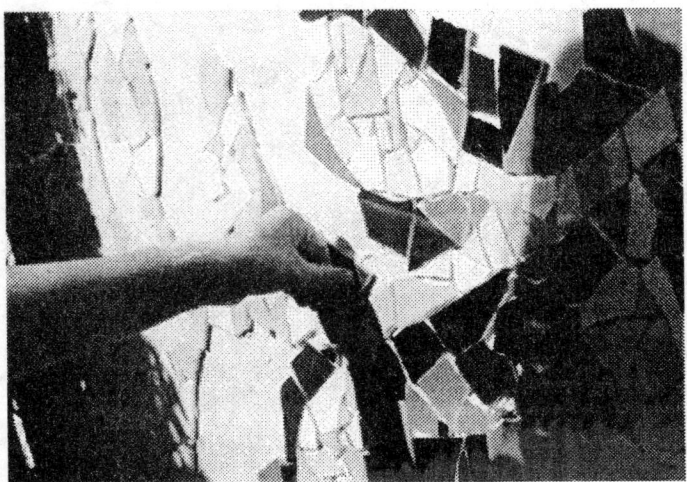

Some tilesetters create intricate designs.

(called a float).

Marble setters may cut marble to a specified size with a power wet saw. After putting the marble in place, marble setters polish the marble to a high luster, using power or hand sanders.

Work Environment Tile grout is used to fill in the space between tiles.

Tile and marble setters held about 58,700 jobs in 2010, of which 38 percent were employed in the building finishing contractors industry. About 48 percent of tile and marble setters were self-employed.

Tile and marble are usually installed after most of the construction has been completed, so the work area for installers is typically clean and uncluttered. Still, mortar, adhesives, or grout may be sticky and messy.

Installing tile and marble is labor intensive, with workers spending much of their time reaching, bending, and kneeling. As a result, workers must wear kneepads for protection. Tile and marble installers must also wear safety goggles when using grinders, saws, and sanders.

Injuries

Although the occupation is not as dangerous as some other construction trades, tile setters still experience a high rate of injuries and illnesses. Workers are subject to cuts from tools or materials, falls from ladders, and strained muscles from lifting heavy boxes of tile and marble.

Work Schedules

Most tile and marble setters work full time. In commercial settings, tilesetters may work evenings and weekends, often for higher wages, to avoid disturbing regular business operations.

About 48 percent of tile and marble setters were self-employed in 2010. Self-employed workers may have the ability to set their own schedule.

How to Become a Tile and Marble Setter These workers may grout tile in a shower.

Although some tile and marble setters learn their trade through a formal apprenticeship, many learn informally on the job, starting as a helper.

Training

Some tile and marble setters learn their trade through a 2- to 4-year apprenticeship. For each year of the program, apprentices must complete at least 144 hours of related technical training and 2,000 hours of paid on-the-job training. Tile and marble setters may begin with 12-week pre-apprenticeship training at a training center to learn construction basics. Construction basics include mathematics, building code requirements, safety and first-aid practices, and reading blueprints.

After completing an apprenticeship program, tile and marble setters are considered to be journey workers and may perform duties on their own.

Several groups, including unions and contractor associations, sponsor apprenticeship programs. The basic qualifications for entering an apprenticeship program are as follows:

- Minimum age of 18
- High school education or equivalent
- Physically able to perform the work

Some contractors have their own training programs for tile and marble setters. Although workers may enter apprenticeships directly, many first start out as helpers.

Education

Some 2-year technical schools offer courses that are affiliated with unions and contractor organizations. The credits earned as part of an apprenticeship program usually count toward an associate's degree.

Important Qualities

Color vision. Setting tile patterns involves determining small color variations. Because tile patterns often include many different colors, tilesetters must be able to distinguish between colors and patterns for the best looking finish.

Customer-service skills. Working in customers' homes is common. Therefore, tile and marble setters must be courteous and considerate of a customers' property while completing tasks.

Detail oriented. Some tile arrangements can be highly detailed and artistic, so workers must ensure that the patterns are properly and accurately arranged.

Math skills. Basic math skills are used on every job. Besides measuring the area to be tiled, installers must calculate the number of tiles needed to cover an area.

Physical strength. Some marble setters need to be strong enough to carry and lift heavy marble countertops into position.

Stamina. Tile and marble setters must have the endurance to spend many hours on their feet. When setting tile or marble, installers also may be on their knees for hours at a time.

Pay

Tile and Marble Setters
Median annual wages, May 2010

Construction Trades Workers	$38,240
Tile and Marble Setters	$38,110
Total, All Occupations	$33,840

Note: All Occupations includes all occupations in the U.S. Economy.
Source: U.S. Bureau of Labor Statistics, Occupational Employment Statistics

The median annual wage of tile and marble setters was $38,110 in May 2010. The median wage is the wage at which half of the workers in an occupation earned more than that amount and half earned less. The lowest 10 percent earned less than $21,730, and the top 10 percent earned more than $68,980.

The starting pay for apprentices usually is between 30 percent and 50 percent of what fully trained tile and marble setters make. As they gain more skill, they receive pay increases.

Most tile and marble setters work full time. In commercial settings, tilesetters may work evenings and weekends, often for higher wages, to avoid disturbing regular business operations.

About 48 percent of tile and marble setters were self-employed in 2010. Self-employed workers may have the ability to set their own schedule.

Job Outlook

Tile and Marble Setters
Percent change in employment, projected 2010-20

Tile and Marble Setters	25%
Construction Trades Workers	23%
Total, All Occupations	14%

Note: All Occupations includes all occupations in the U.S. Economy.
Source: U.S. Bureau of Labor Statistics, Employment Projections program

Employment of tile and marble setters is projected to grow 25 percent from 2010 to 2020, faster than the average for all occupations. Population growth and business growth, coupled with the increasing popularity of tile and marble, will be the major source of demand for tile and marble setters. Tile and natural stone are used heavily in shopping malls, hospitals, schools, and restaurants, as well as other commercial and government buildings, and this trend is expected to continue. Tiles, including those made of glass, mosaic, and other high-end tiles and marble, are also becoming more popular, particularly in new and remodeled homes.

Job Prospects

Overall job prospects should improve over the coming decade as construction activity rebounds from the recent recession. As with many other construction workers, employment of tile and marble setters is sensitive to the fluctuations of the economy. On the one hand, workers may experience periods of unemployment when the overall level of construction falls. On the other hand, shortages of workers may occur in some areas during peak periods of building activity.

Highly skilled workers with a good job history and work experience in construction will have the best opportunities.

Employment projections data for tile and marble setters, 2010-20

Occupational Title	SOC Code	Employment, 2010	Projected Employment, 2020	Change, 2010-20	
				Percent	Numeric
Tile and Marble Setters	47-2044	58,700	73,700	25	14,900
SOURCE: U.S. Bureau of Labor Statistics, Employment Projections program					

Similar Occupations

This table shows a list of occupations with job duties that are similar to those of tile and marble setters.

Occupation	Job Duties	Entry-Level Education	Median Annual Pay, May 2010
Carpenters	Carpenters construct and repair building frameworks and structures—such as stairways, doorframes, partitions, and rafters—made from wood and other materials. They also may install kitchen cabinets, siding, and drywall.	High school diploma or equivalent	$39,530

Carpet Installers	Carpet installers lay carpet in homes, offices, restaurants, and many other types of buildings.	Less than high school	$36,090
Construction Laborers and Helpers	Construction laborers and helpers do many basic tasks that require physical labor on construction sites.	See How to Become One	$28,410
Drywall and Ceiling Tile Installers, and Tapers	Drywall and ceiling tile installers hang wallboards to walls and ceilings inside buildings. Tapers prepare the wallboards for painting, using tape and other materials. Many workers do both installing and taping.	Less than high school	$38,290
Painters, Construction and Maintenance	Painters apply paint, stain, and coatings to walls, buildings, bridges, and other structures.	Less than high school	$34,280
Roofers	Roofers repair and install the roofs of buildings using a variety of materials, including shingles, asphalt, and metal.	Less than high school	$34,220

Contacts for More Information

For details about apprenticeships or other work opportunities in this trade, contact the offices of the state employment service, the state apprenticeship agency, local contractors or firms that employ tile and marble setters, or local union-management tile-and-marble-setting apprenticeship committees. Apprenticeship information is available from the U.S. Department of Labor's toll-free help line, 1 (877) 872-5627, and Employment and Training Administration.

For more information about tile installers and finishers, visit National Association of Home Builders

For more information about tilesetting and tile training, visit National Tile Contractors Association, Finishing Trades Institute International

Suggested citation:

Bureau of Labor Statistics, U.S. Department of Labor, Occupational Outlook Handbook, 2012-13 Edition, Tile and Marble Setters, on the Internet at http://www.bls.gov/ooh/construction-and-extraction/tile-and-marble-setters.htm.

Education, Training, and Library Occupations

Adult Literacy and GED Teachers

Quick Facts: Adult Literacy and GED Teachers	
2010 Median Pay	$46,530 per year $22.37 per hour
Entry-Level Education	Bachelor's degree
Work Experience in a Related Occupation	None
On-the-job Training	Internship/residency
Number of Jobs, 2010	86,900
Job Outlook, 2010-20	15% (About as fast as average)
Employment Change, 2010-20	12,700

What Adult Literacy and GED Teachers Do

Adult literacy and General Education Development (GED) teachers instruct adults and youths who are out of school in basic skills, such as reading, writing, and speaking English. They also help students earn their GED or high school diploma.

Duties

Adult literacy and GED teachers typically do the following:
- Evaluate students' strengths and weaknesses
- Plan and teach lessons to help students gain the knowledge and skills they need to meet their goals, such as learning English or getting their GED
- Emphasize skills that will help students find jobs, such as learning English words and phrases used in the workplace
- Work with each student to challenge him or her and overcome the student's weaknesses
- Assess students for possible learning disabilities
- Monitor students' progress toward their goals
- Help students develop study skills
- Connect students to other resources in their community, such as mental health services or job placement services

Before students enter these education programs, their educational level and skills are assessed. Sometimes the teachers do this assessment, but in many cases another staff member does it.

In many programs, the teacher then works with other staff members to use information from the assessment and information about the student's goals to develop an individualized educational program

Adult literacy and GED teachers need to use different teaching strategies to meet their students' needs.

(IEP).

Teachers must formally evaluate their students periodically to determine their progress and potential to go on to the next level. However, they informally evaluate their students' progress continually.

Adult literacy and GED teachers often have students of various levels in their classes. As a result, teachers need to use teaching strategies and methods that meet all of their students' needs. In addition, teachers focus on helping students develop skills they need in the workplace. For example, they may teach students how to read a contract or how to estimate the cost of materials needed to remodel a kitchen. Teachers may work with students in classes or tutor them one-on-one.

There are three basic types of education that adult literacy and GED teachers provide:

Adult basic education classes teach students the basics of reading, writing, and math. Students often enter these classes at or below an eighth-grade level in these subjects. Students generally are 16 years and older and need to gain proficiency in these skills to improve their job situation.

GED and adult secondary education classes prepare students to take the test to earn their GED. Sometimes these classes help students finish the credits necessary for them to earn a high school diploma. Some programs are combined with career preparation programs so that students can earn their GED or high school diploma and a career-related credential at the same time.

Passing the GED means passing five tests: reading, writing, mathematics, science, and social studies. In addition, GED and adult secondary teachers help their students improve their skills in communicating, critical thinking, and problem solving—skills they will need for further education and successful careers.

English as a Second Language (ESL) classes teach students to read, write, and speak English. These classes are sometimes also called English for speakers of other languages (ESOL). People in these classes are recent immigrants to the United States and others whose native language is not English.

ESL teachers often focus on helping their students with practical vocabulary for jobs and daily living. They may also focus on preparing their students to take the citizenship exam.

In one class, an ESL teacher may have students from many different countries and cultures. Because the ESL teacher and the students may not share a common native language, ESL teachers must be creative in fostering communication in the classroom to achieve their education goals.

Work Environment

Adult literacy and GED teachers held about 86,900 jobs in 2010.

Adult literacy and General Education Development (GED) teachers are often employed by community colleges, community-based organizations, and public schools. Some work in prisons.

The following industries employed the most adult literacy and GED teachers in 2010:

Elementary and secondary schools; state, local, and private	27%
Junior colleges; state, local, and private	23
Other educational services; state, local, and private	13
State and local government, excluding education and hospitals	6

Students in adult literacy and GED programs attend classes by choice. As a result, they are often highly motivated, which can make teaching them rewarding and satisfying.

Work Schedules

Classes are held at times when students are not at work, so many teachers work in the mornings and evenings.

How to Become an Adult Literacy or GED Teacher

Most adult literacy and General Education Development (GED) teachers must have at least a bachelor's degree and a teaching certification.

Education

Most states require adult literacy and GED teachers to have at least a bachelor's degree in education, but some employers prefer to hire those with a master's degree.

Master's degrees in adult education prepare prospective teachers to use effective teaching strategies for adult learners, to work with students from various backgrounds, and to develop adult education programs. Some programs allow these prospective teachers to specialize in adult basic education, secondary education, or English as a second language (ESL).

Some colleges and universities offer master's degrees or graduate certificates in teaching adult education or English for speakers of other languages (ESOL). Programs help prospective teachers learn how to teach adults, work with learners from a variety of cultures, and how to teach adults with learning disabilities.

Programs in English as a second language not only help these prospective teachers understand how adults learn languages but also prepare them to teach communication skills. Prospective ESL teachers should take courses or training in linguistics and theories of how people learn second languages. Knowledge of a second language is not necessary to teach ESL, but it is helpful to understand what students are going through.

Many adult literacy and GED teachers take professional development classes to ensure that they keep up with the latest research in teaching adults and improve their teaching skills.

Licenses

Many states require adult literacy and GED teachers to have a teaching certificate to work in government-run programs. Some states have certificates specifically for adult education. Other states require teachers to have a certificate in elementary or secondary education. To get a license, adult literacy and GED teachers typically need a bachelor's degree and must have passed an approved teacher-training program.

Work Experience

Employers typically prefer workers who have some teaching experience, which they can get through teaching children or adults.

Important Qualities

Communication skills. Teachers must collaborate with other

teachers and program administrators. In addition, they talk to students about their progress and goals.

Cultural sensitivity. Adult literacy and GED teachers must be able to work with students from a variety of cultural, educational, and economic backgrounds. They must be understanding and respectful of their students' backgrounds and be familiar with their concerns.

Instructional skills. Adult literacy and GED teachers need to be able to explain concepts in terms that students can understand. In addition, they need to be able to alter their teaching methods to meet the needs of each student they teach and find ways to keep students engaged in learning.

Patience. Working with students of different abilities and backgrounds can be difficult. Teachers must be with patient when students struggle with material.

Pay

Adult Literacy and GED Teachers
Median annual wages, May 2010

Adult Basic and Secondary Education and Literacy Teacherss	$46,530
Education, Training, and Library Occupations	$45,690
Total, All Occupations	$33,840

Note: All Occupations includes all occupations in the U.S. Economy.
Source: U.S. Bureau of Labor Statistics, Occupational Employment Statistics

The median annual wage of adult literacy and General Education Development (GED) teachers, also known as adult basic and secondary education and literacy teachers and instructors, was $46,530 in May 2010. The median wage is the wage at which half the workers in an occupation earned more than that amount and half earned less. The lowest 10 percent earned less than $27,090, and the top 10 percent earned more than $83,580.

Classes are held at times when students are not at work, so many teachers work in the mornings and evenings.

Job Outlook

Adult Literacy and GED Teachers
Percent change in employment, projected 2010-20

Education, Training, and Library Occupations	15%
Adult Basic and Secondary Education and Literacy Teachers	15%
Total, All Occupations	14%

Note: All Occupations includes all occupations in the U.S. Economy.
Source: U.S. Bureau of Labor Statistics, Employment Projections program

Employment of adult literacy and General Education Development (GED) teachers, also known as adult basic and secondary education and literacy teachers and instructors, is expected to grow by 15 percent from 2010 to 2020, about as fast as the average for all occupations. Growth is expected from continued immigration to the United States and demand for adult education programs.

From 2010 to 2020, the number of Americans who need adult education is expected to continue to increase. Many adults leave high school before getting their high school diploma and seek their diploma or GED through an adult education program.

In addition, traditional schooling does not give some adults the literacy or other skills they need to find employment. These students often seek to improve their skills in adult education programs later in life. Adult literacy and GED teachers will be needed to instruct them and run adult education programs.

Furthermore, immigration is expected to continue to grow from 2010 to 2020. Some immigrants do not speak English and will want to improve their communications skills to find jobs in the United States. Adult literacy teachers who teach classes in English as a second language will be needed to help these students gain the required skills.

Employment projections data for adult literacy and GED teachers, 2010-20

Occupational Title	SOC Code	Employment, 2010	Projected Employment, 2020	Change, 2010-20	
				Percent	Numeric
Adult Basic and Secondary Education and Literacy Teachers and Instructors	25-3011	86,900	99,600	15	12,700
SOURCE: U.S. Bureau of Labor Statistics, Employment Projections program					

Similar Occupations

This table shows a list of occupations with job duties that are similar to those of adult literacy and GED teachers.

Occupation	Job Duties	Entry-Level Education	Median Annual Pay, May 2010
Career and Technical Education Teachers	Career and technical education teachers help students in middle school and high school develop career-related and technical skills. They help students explore or prepare to enter a particular occupation, such as one in auto repair, healthcare, business, or the culinary arts.	Bachelor's degree	$53,920
High School Teachers	High school teachers help prepare students for life after graduation. They teach academic lessons and various skills that students will need to attend college and to enter the job market.	Bachelor's degree	$53,230
Instructional Coordinators	Instructional coordinators oversee school districts' curriculums and teaching standards. They work with teachers and school administrators to implement new teaching techniques to improve the quality of education.	Master's degree	$58,830
Kindergarten and Elementary School Teachers	Kindergarten and elementary school teachers prepare younger students for future schooling by teaching them the basics of subjects such as math and reading.	Bachelor's degree	$51,380
Librarians	Librarians help people find information from many sources. They maintain library collections and do other work as needed to keep the library running.	Master's degree	$54,500
Middle School Teachers	Middle school teachers educate students, most of whom are in sixth through eighth grades. They help students build on the fundamentals they learned in elementary school and prepare them for the more difficult lessons they will learn in high school.	Bachelor's degree	$51,960
Postsecondary Teachers	Postsecondary teachers instruct students in a wide variety of academic and vocational subjects beyond the high school level. They also conduct research and publish scholarly papers and books.	Doctoral or professional degree	$62,050
School and Career Counselors	School counselors help students develop social skills and succeed in school. Career counselors assist people with the process of making career decisions by helping them choose a career or educational program.	Master's degree	$53,380
Social Workers	There are two main types of social workers: direct-service social workers, who help people solve and cope with problems in their everyday lives, and clinical social workers, who diagnose and treat mental, behavioral, and emotional issues.	See How to Become One	$42,480
Special Education Teachers	Special education teachers work with students who have a wide range of learning, mental, emotional and physical disabilities. With students who have mild or moderate disabilities, they ensure that lessons and teaching strategies are modified to meet the students' needs. With students who have severe disabilities, they teach the students independent living skills and basic literacy, communication, and math.	Bachelor's degree	$53,220
Teacher Assistants	Teacher assistants work under a teacher's supervision to give students additional attention and instruction.	High school diploma or equivalent	$23,220

Contacts for More Information

For more information about adult education in your state, visit U.S. Department of Education

For more information about teaching English as a second language, visit Center for Applied Linguistics

Suggested citation:

Bureau of Labor Statistics, U.S. Department of Labor, Occupational Outlook Handbook, 2012-13 Edition, Adult Literacy and GED Teachers, on the Internet at http://www.bls.gov/ooh/education-training-and-library/adult-literacy-and-ged-teachers.htm .

Archivists

Quick Facts: Archivists	
2010 Median Pay	$45,200 per year $21.73 per hour
Entry-Level Education	Bachelor's degree
Work Experience in a Related Occupation	None
On-the-job Training	None
Number of Jobs, 2010	6,100
Job Outlook, 2010-20	12% (About as fast as average)
Employment Change, 2010-20	700

What Archivists Do

Archivists appraise, edit, and maintain permanent records and historically valuable documents. Many perform research on archival material.

Duties

Archivists typically do the following:

- Create and maintain accessible computer archives and databases
- Organize and classify archival records to make it easy to find materials
- Authenticate and appraise historical documents and archival materials
- Provide reference services and help for users
- Direct workers who help arrange, exhibit, and maintain collections
- Safeguard records by copying to film, videotape, disk, or computer formats
- Preserve and maintain documents and objects
- Set and administer policy guidelines concerning public access to materials
- Locate new materials and direct their acquisition and display

Archivists often convert text to digital format.

Archivists preserve many documents and records for their importance, potential value, or historical significance. Most archivists coordinate educational and public outreach programs, such as tours, workshops, lectures, and classes. Some work with the boards of institutions to administer plans and policies. In addition, archivists may research topics or items relevant to their collections.

Some archivists specialize in an area of history, such as colonial history, so they can more accurately determine which records in that area should be kept and should become part of the archives. Archivists also may work with specialized forms of records, such as manuscripts, electronic records, websites, photographs, maps, motion pictures, or sound recordings.

Archivists usually use computers to generate and maintain archival records. Professional standards for handling electronic archival records are still evolving. However, computer capabilities will continue to expand and more records will be stored and exhibited electronically, providing both increased access and better protection for archived documents.

Archives technicians help archivists organize, maintain, and provide access to historical documentary materials.

Work Environment

Archivists held about 6,100 jobs in 2010. The following industries employed the most archivists in 2010:

Colleges, universities, and professional schools; state, local, and private	23%
State and local government, excluding education and hospitals	18
Museums, historical sites, and similar institutions	16
Other information services	9
Federal government, excluding postal service	8

Archivists work in museums, government, colleges and universities, corporations, and other institutions that require experts to preserve important records. Although most archivists provide reference assistance and educational services to clients, some do research or process records, reducing the occasion to work with others.

Work Schedules

Archivists in government agencies and corporations generally work full time during regular business hours. Those who manage historical record archives may only work part time.

How to Become an Archivist

Archivists must usually have a bachelor's degree in history or library science, although some employers require an advanced degree and related work experience. People often gain experience by working or volunteering in archives.

Education

Although archivists may enter the profession with a variety of undergraduate degrees, including history and library science, most employers prefer a graduate degree in history, library science, archival science, or records management.

Many colleges and universities offer courses or practical training in archival techniques in history, library science, and other similar programs. A few institutions offer master's degrees in archival studies.

Some positions may require knowledge of the discipline related to a collection, such as computer science, business, or medicine. Some institutions are developing special computer and information systems training to prepare students to manage digital records.

Many archives offer volunteer or internship opportunities where students can gain experience.

Certification

The Academy of Certified Archivists offers voluntary certification for archivists. Archivists with at least a master's degree and a year of appropriate archival experience can obtain the Certified Archivist credential by passing a written exam. They must renew their certification periodically by retaking the exam or fulfilling continuing education credits. At this time, only few employers require or prefer certification.

Advancement

Continuing education is available through meetings, conferences, and workshops sponsored by archival, historical, and museum associations. Some larger organizations, such as the National Archives and Records Administration in Washington, DC, offer training in-house.

Many archives, especially those maintained by one archivist, are very small and have limited opportunities for promotion. Archivists typically advance by transferring to a larger archive that has supervisory positions. A doctorate in history, library science, or a related field may be needed for some advanced positions, such as director of a state archive.

Important Qualities

Analytical skills. Because not all documents are easy to decipher, archivists need good analytical skills to determine a document's importance or historical significance.

Computer skills. Archivists should have good computer skills because they use and develop complex databases related to the materials they store and access.

Customer-service skills. Archivists work with the general public on a regular basis. They must be courteous and friendly and be able to help users find materials.

Organizational skills. Archivists must store and easily retrieve any records or documents. They also develop logical systems of storage for the public to use.

Pay

Archivists
Median annual wages, May 2010

Archivists	$45,200
Librarians, Curators, and Archivists	$43,170
Total, All Occupations	$33,840

Note: All Occupations includes all occupations in the U.S. Economy.
Source: U.S. Bureau of Labor Statistics, Occupational Employment Statistics

The median annual wage of archivists was $45,200 in May 2010. The median wage is the wage at which half the workers in an occupation earned more than that amount and half earned less. The lowest 10 percent earned less than $25,480 and the top 10 percent earned more than $80,650.

The median annual wage of archivists in the federal government was $77,990 in May 2010.

Archivists in government agencies and corporations generally work full time during regular business hours. Those who manage historical record archives may only work part time.

Job Outlook

Archivists
Percent change in employment, projected 2010-20

Total, All Occupations	14%
Archivists	12%
Librarians, Curators, and Archivists	8%

Note: All Occupations includes all occupations in the U.S. Economy.
Source: U.S. Bureau of Labor Statistics, Employment Projections program

Employment of archivists is projected to grow 12 percent from 2010 to 2020, about as fast as the average for all occupations.

Jobs for archivists are expected to increase as public and private organizations require organization of, and access to, increasing volumes of records and information. The growing use of electronic records will cause demand for archivists who specialize in electronic records and records management to grow more rapidly than demand for archivists who specialize in older media formats.

Job Prospects

Workers seeking jobs as archivists are likely to face strong competition because qualified applicants generally outnumber job openings. Graduates with highly specialized training, such as master's degrees in both library science and history, with a concentration in archives or records management, extensive computer skills, and volunteer experience, should have the best job opportunities. Job opportunities for those who manage electronic records are expected to be better than for those who specialize in older media formats.

Archives can be subject to cuts in funding during recessions or periods of budget tightening, reducing demand for archivists. Although the number of archivists who move to other occupations is relatively low, the need to replace workers who retire will create some job openings.

Employment projections data for archivists, 2010-20

Occupational Title	SOC Code	Employment, 2010	Projected Employment, 2020	Change, 2010-20	
				Percent	Numeric
Archivists	25-4011	6,100	6,800	12	700
SOURCE: U.S. Bureau of Labor Statistics, Employment Projections program					

Similar Occupations

This table shows a list of occupations with job duties that are similar to those of archivists.

Occupation	Job Duties	Entry-Level Education	Median Annual Pay, May 2010
Anthropologists and Archeologists	Anthropologists and archeologists study the origin, development, and behavior of human beings, past and present. They examine the cultures, languages, archeological remains, and physical characteristics of people in various parts of the world.	Master's degree	$54,230
Historians	Historians research, analyze, interpret, and present the past by studying a variety of historical documents and sources.	Master's degree	$53,520
Craft and Fine Artists	Craft and fine artists use a variety of materials and techniques to create art for sale and exhibition. Craft artists create handmade objects, such as pottery, glassware, textiles, or other objects that are designed to be functional. Fine artists, including painters, sculptors, and illustrators, create original works of art for their aesthetic value, rather than a functional one.	High school diploma or equivalent	$43,470
Curators, Museum Technicians, and Conservators	Curators oversee collections, such as artwork and historic items, and may conduct public service activities for an institution. Museum technicians and conservators prepare and restore objects and documents in museum collections and exhibits.	See How to Become One	$42,310
Librarians	Librarians help people find information from many sources. They maintain library collections and do other work as needed to keep the library running.	Master's degree	$54,500

Contacts for More Information

For information on archivists and on schools offering courses in archival studies, visit Society of American Archivists

For information about archivists and archivist certification, visit Academy of Certified Archivists

For information about government archivists, visit Council of State Archivists ,National Association of Government Archives & Records Administrators

For information on job openings as an archivist with the federal government, visit USAJobs

Suggested citation:

Bureau of Labor Statistics, U.S. Department of Labor, Occupational Outlook Handbook, 2012-13 Edition, Archivists, on the Internet at http://www.bls.gov/ooh/education-training-and-library/archivists.htm .

Career and Technical Education Teachers

Quick Facts: Career and Technical Education Teachers	
2010 Median Pay	$53,920 per year
Entry-Level Education	Bachelor's degree
Work Experience in a Related Occupation	1 to 5 years
On-the-job Training	Internship/residency
Number of Jobs, 2010	103,000
Job Outlook, 2010-20	2% (Little or no change)
Employment Change, 2010-20	2,300

What Career and Technical Education Teachers Do

Career and technical education teachers help students in middle school and high school develop career-related and technical skills. They help students explore or prepare to enter a particular occupation, such as one in auto repair, healthcare, business, or the culinary arts.

Duties

Career and technical education teachers typically do the following:

- Plan lessons in the subject they teach, such as information technology (IT) or automotive repair

- Teach students how to apply information learned in academic classes, such as math and chemistry

- Develop relationships with businesses to ensure that students develop the skills employers seek and to coordinate internships and apprenticeships

- Coordinate their curriculum with local community colleges

- Assess students to evaluate their abilities, strengths, and weaknesses

- Grade students' assignments to monitor their progress

- Communicate with parents about their student's progress

- Develop and enforce classroom rules

Career and technical education teachers assign students hands on tasks so that they can gain experience.

- Advise student organizations related to career fields

Career and technical education teachers use a variety of methods to help students learn and develop skills.

They teach students the theories and techniques of their field and the laws and regulations that affect that industry. They demonstrate tasks, techniques, and tools used in the field.

They also assign hands-on tasks, such as styling hair on mannequins and replacing brakes on cars, to help students develop skills. Students typically practice these tasks in laboratories in the school.

In addition, teachers use work-based experiences to help students apply what they have learned in the classroom to real-world settings. Some students use class time to work at a business that is willing to let them learn on the job; the business then provides feedback about the student's performance to the teacher. In some schools, students run businesses that are owned by the school, such as a school store, to apply their knowledge and skills in a nonclassroom setting.

Some career and technical education teachers teach in traditional schools. These teachers may be part of a career academy, where they work closely with academic colleagues to create a career-themed school within a school. Others teach in regional career and technical education centers that serve students from many districts. Some teach in a career and technical education high school, where students are in workshops and laboratories for most of the school day.

What career and technical education teachers do depends on their particular field. The following are examples of types of career and technical education teachers:

In **agricultural science**, students learn a variety of subjects related to the science and business of agriculture. Classes may cover topics such as agricultural production; agriculture-related business; veterinary science; and plant, animal, and food systems. Teachers in this field may have students plant and care for crops or tend to animals to apply what they have learned in the classroom.

Career and technical education teachers in **family and consumer science** teach students about nutrition, culinary art, sewing, and child development. Students in these settings may run early childhood education classes with teacher supervision, manufacture and market clothing, or create menus and cook for a school function.

In **health-related occupations**, students learn the skills necessary to work as technicians or assistants, such as nursing or dental assistants, in health care. Teachers in this field may have students practice their skills by measuring blood pressure and administering blood sugar tests on other staff in the school. Some programs allow students to receive the certifications necessary to enter the field.

Business and marketing students learn the skills needed to run a business or make sales. They learn the basics of financial management and marketing. Career and technical education teachers in this field may guide students as they develop and establish a business. Many programs operate school-based enterprises in which students operate real businesses that are open to the public.

Career and technical education teachers in **trade and industry** specialize in an occupation such as in automotive technology, cosmetology, heating and air-conditioning repair, electrical wiring, or computer networking and computer repair. Teachers use laboratory work to allow students to learn through a hands-on approach.

Career and technical education teachers in **technology** instruct students in general education subjects, such as math and science, through the hands-on application of technology. For example, they may have students build a robot to learn about physics, computer science, and math. These programs are often a precursor to engineering degrees.

Work Environment

In 2010, career and technical education teachers held 103,000 jobs. Most career and technical education teachers work in public and private schools.

Work Schedules

Career and technical education teachers generally work school hours, between 8 a.m. and 3 p.m. They often spend time in the evenings and on weekends grading assignments, preparing lessons, or advising student organizations. They may meet with parents, students, and other teachers before and after school.

Many career and technical education teachers work the traditional 10-month school year, with a 2-month break during the summer. Some teachers teach summer programs. Teachers in districts with a year-round schedule typically work 8 weeks in a row, are on break for 1 week, and have a 5-week midwinter break.

How to Become a Career or Technical Education Teacher

Public school teachers must have a state-issued certification or license. Requirements for certification vary by state. However, most states require the completion of a teacher preparation **program** and at least a bachelor's degree or extensive work experience.

Education

There are a variety of ways that someone can become licensed to teach as a career and technical education teacher.

Some teachers get a bachelor's degree from a teacher preparation program in which they major in a content area, such as agriculture, and take classes in education and child psychology.

Other career and technical education teachers have a bachelor's degree in the field they teach, such as engineering, computer science, or business.

Some teachers have a high school diploma and significant work experience in the field they teach, such as automotive mechanics or culinary arts. Teachers without training in education must enroll in an alternative certification program to receive the teacher training they need to get a state teacher's license.

Work Experience

Most states require career and technical education teachers to have work experience in the field they want to teach. As a result, many teachers spend time working before moving into teaching. For prospective teachers whose highest level of education is a high school diploma, extensive experience is typically required.

Licenses and Certification

All states require teachers in public schools to be licensed, or, as it is frequently referred to, certified. Those who teach in private schools are not required to be licensed.

Requirements for certification vary by state. However, most states require completing a teacher preparation program and at least a bachelor's degree or work experience in the field. Teacher preparation programs include supervised experience in teaching, which is typically gained through student teaching.

Some states require a minimum grade point average. States typically require candidates to pass a general teaching certification test, as well as a test of their knowledge in the subject they will teach. For certification requirements in your state, contact the U.S. Department of Education .

Teachers often must take annual professional development classes to keep their license. Most states require teachers to pass a background check, and some states require teachers to complete a master's degree after receiving their certification.

All states offer an alternative route to certification for people who already have a bachelor's degree or work experience in their field but lack the education courses required for certification.

Some alternative certification programs allow candidates to begin teaching immediately, under the supervision of an experienced teacher. These programs cover teaching methods and child development. When they finish the program, candidates are awarded full certification.

Other programs require students to take classes in education before teaching.

Students may be awarded a master's degree after completing either of these programs. For information about alternative certification programs, contact the National Center for Alternative Certification .

Advancement

Experienced teachers can advance to become mentors or lead teachers, working with less experienced teachers to help them improve their teaching skills.

With additional education or certification, teachers may become school counselors, school librarians, or instructional coordinators. Some become assistant principals or principals, positions that generally require additional training in education administration or leadership. For more information, see the profiles on school and career counselors , librarians , instructional coordinators , and elementary, middle, and high school principals .

After gaining enough experience, some career and technical education teachers instruct at community colleges. For more information, see the profile on postsecondary teachers .

Important Qualities

Communication skills. Career and technical education teachers must collaborate with other teachers and members of the community. In addition, they need to discuss students' needs with parents and administrators.

Creativity. Teachers must be able to develop interesting lesson plans to keep students' attention and to teach students who learn in different ways.

Instructional skills. Career and technical education teachers need to be able to explain difficult concepts in terms that students understand. They help students develop skills through a variety of teaching techniques.

Organizational skills. Teachers in middle school and high school have many students in different classes throughout the day. They must be able to organize their materials and their time well.

Patience. Working with students of different abilities and backgrounds can be difficult. Teachers must be patient with students who struggle with material.

Pay

Career and Technical Education Teachers
Median annual wages, May 2010

Career/Technical Education Teachers, Secondary School	$54,310
Career and Technical Education Teachers	$53,920
Career/Technical Education Teachers, Middle School	$51,470
Total, All Occupations	$33,840

Note: All Occupations includes all occupations in the U.S. Economy.
Source: U.S. Bureau of Labor Statistics, Occupational Employment Statistics

The median annual wage of middle school career and technical education teachers was $51,470 in May 2010. The median wage is the wage at which half the workers in an occupation earned more than that amount and half earned less. The lowest 10 percent earned less than $34,860, and the top 10 percent earned more than $78,160.

The median annual wage of high school career and technical education teachers was $54,310 in May 2010. The lowest 10 percent earned less than $36,300, and the top 10 percent earned more than $80,050.

Career and technical education teachers generally work school hours, between 8 a.m. and 3 p.m. They often spend time in the evenings and on weekends grading assignments, preparing lessons, or advising student organizations. They may meet with parents, students, and other teachers before and after school.

Many career and technical education teachers work the traditional 10-month school year, with a 2-month break during the summer. Some teachers teach summer programs. Teachers in districts with a year-round schedule typically work 8 weeks in a row, are on break for 1 week, and have a 5-week midwinter break.

Job Outlook

Career and Technical Education Teachers
Percent change in employment, projected 2010-20

Total, All Occupations	14%
Career/Technical Education Teachers, Middle School	9%
Career and Technical Education Teachers	2%
Career/Technical Education Teachers, Secondary School	1%

Note: All Occupations includes all occupations in the U.S. Economy.
Source: U.S. Bureau of Labor Statistics, Employment Projections program

Overall employment of career and technical education teachers is projected to experience little or no change from 2010 to 2020.

High school career and technical education teachers are expected to have employment growth of 1 percent, which is little or no change.

Employment of middle school career and technical education teachers is expected to grow by 9 percent, slower than the average for all occupations.

Employment growth will be due to rising school enrollments, which increase demand for these workers. However, growth will likely be limited by an increased focus on traditional academic subjects.

From 2010 to 2020, overall student enrollments in middle and secondary schools—a key factor in the demand for teachers—are expected to rise more slowly than in the past as children of the baby-boom generation leave the school system. Projected enrollments will vary by region. Rapidly growing states in the South and West will likely experience the largest enrollment increases. Enrollments in the Midwest are expected to hold relatively steady, and those in the Northeast are projected to decline.

Employment projections data for career and technical education teachers, 2010-20

Occupational Title	SOC Code	Employment, 2010	Projected Employment, 2020	Change, 2010-20	
				Percent	Numeric
Career and Technical Education Teachers	—	103,000	105,300	2	2,300
Career/Technical Education Teachers, Middle School	25-2023	14,400	15,700	9	1,300
Career/Technical Education Teachers, Secondary School	25-2032	88,600	89,600	1	1,000
SOURCE: U.S. Bureau of Labor Statistics, Employment Projections program					

Similar Occupations

This table shows a list of occupations with job duties that are similar to those of career and technical education teachers.

Occupation	Job Duties	Entry-Level Education	Median Annual Pay, May 2010
Elementary, Middle, and High School Principals	Elementary, middle, and high school principals lead teachers and other members of school staff. They manage the day-to-day operations of elementary, middle, and high schools. They set goals and objectives and evaluate their school's progress toward meeting them.	Master's degree	$86,970
High School Teachers	High school teachers help prepare students for life after graduation. They teach academic lessons and various skills that students will need to attend college and to enter the job market.	Bachelor's degree	$53,230
Instructional Coordinators	Instructional coordinators oversee school districts' curriculums and teaching standards. They work with teachers and school administrators to implement new teaching techniques to improve the quality of education.	Master's degree	$58,830
Librarians	Librarians help people find information from many sources. They maintain library collections and do other work as needed to keep the library running.	Master's degree	$54,500

Middle School Teachers	Middle school teachers educate students, most of whom are in sixth through eighth grades. They help students build on the fundamentals they learned in elementary school and prepare them for the more difficult lessons they will learn in high school.	Bachelor's degree	$51,960
Postsecondary Teachers	Postsecondary teachers instruct students in a wide variety of academic and vocational subjects beyond the high school level. They also conduct research and publish scholarly papers and books.	Doctoral or professional degree	$62,050
School and Career Counselors	School counselors help students develop social skills and succeed in school. Career counselors assist people with the process of making career decisions by helping them choose a career or educational program.	Master's degree	$53,380
Social Workers	There are two main types of social workers: direct-service social workers, who help people solve and cope with problems in their everyday lives, and clinical social workers, who diagnose and treat mental, behavioral, and emotional issues.	See How to Become One	$42,480
Special Education Teachers	Special education teachers work with students who have a wide range of learning, mental, emotional and physical disabilities. With students who have mild or moderate disabilities, they ensure that lessons and teaching strategies are modified to meet the students' needs. With students who have severe disabilities, they teach the students independent living skills and basic literacy, communication, and math.	Bachelor's degree	$53,220
Teacher Assistants	Teacher assistants work under a teacher's supervision to give students additional attention and instruction.	High school diploma or equivalent	$23,220

Contacts for More Information

For more information about career and technical education teachers, visit Association for Career and Technical Education

For information about teaching and becoming a teacher, visit U.S. Department of Education

For information about alternative certification programs, visit National Center for Alternative Certification

Suggested citation:

Bureau of Labor Statistics, U.S. Department of Labor, Occupational Outlook Handbook, 2012-13 Edition, Career and Technical Education Teachers, on the Internet at http://www.bls.gov/ooh/education-training-and-library/career-and-technical-education-teachers.htm .

Curators, Museum Technicians, and Conservators

Quick Facts: Curators, Museum Technicians, and Conservators	
2010 Median Pay	$42,310 per year $20.34 per hour
Entry-Level Education	See How to Become One
Work Experience in a Related Occupation	None
On-the-job Training	None
Number of Jobs, 2010	23,800
Job Outlook, 2010-20	16% (About as fast as average)
Employment Change, 2010-20	3,800

What Curators, Museum Technicians, and Conservators Do

Curators oversee collections, such as artwork and historic items, and may conduct public service activities for an institution. Museum technicians and conservators prepare and restore objects and documents in museum collections and exhibits.

Duties

Curators, museum technicians, and conservators typically do the following:

- Acquire, store, and exhibit collections
- Select the theme and design of exhibits
- Develop or set up exhibit materials
- Design, organize, or conduct tours and workshops for the public
- Attend meetings and civic events to promote the institution

- Clean objects using cleansers, solvents, and soap solutions
- Direct and supervise curatorial, technical, and student staff
- Plan and conduct special research projects

Many objects and documents are important or historically significant. Curators, museum technicians, and conservators preserve and organize the display of these materials.

The following are occupational specialties:

Curators manage museums, zoos, aquariums, botanical gardens, nature centers, and historic sites. The **museum director** often is a curator. Curators direct the acquisition, storage, and exhibit of collections, including negotiating and authorizing the purchase, sale, exchange, or loan of collections. They also may authenticate, evaluate, and categorize the specimens in a collection.

Curators often oversee and help conduct the institution's research

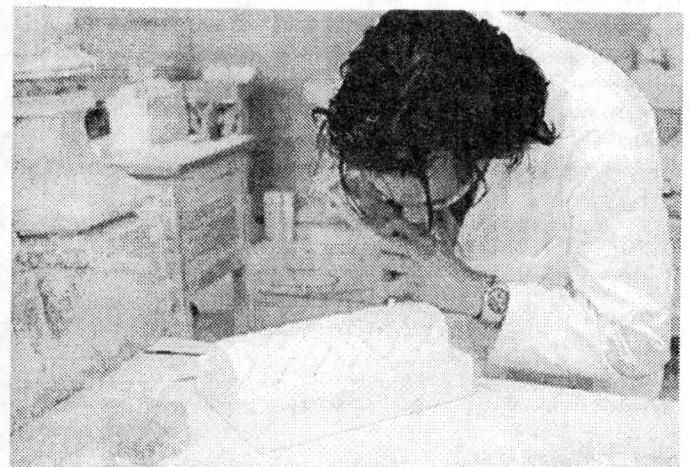

Museum technicians often prepare materials for display.

Museums, historical sites, and similar institutions	41%
Federal government	15
Colleges, universities, and professional schools; state, local, and private	14
State and local government, excluding education and hospitals	14

projects and related educational programs.

Today, an increasing part of a curator's duties involves fundraising and promotion, which may include writing and reviewing grant proposals, journal articles, and publicity materials. In addition, many curators attend meetings, conventions, and civic events.

Most curators specialize in a particular field, such as botany, art, or history. Those who work in large institutions may be highly specialized. A large natural history museum, for example, might employ separate curators for its collections of birds, fishes, insects, and mammals.

Some curators take care of their collections, some do research related to items in the collection, and others do administrative tasks. In small institutions with only one or a few curators, one curator may be responsible for a number of tasks, from taking care of collections to directing the affairs of the museum.

Museum technicians, commonly known as **registrars**, help curators by preparing and taking care of museum items. Registrars also may answer questions from the public and help curators and outside scholars use the collections.

Conservators manage, preserve, treat, and document works of art, artifacts, and specimens—work that may require substantial historical, scientific, and archaeological research. Conservators document their findings and treat items to minimize their deterioration or to restore them to their original state.

Conservators usually specialize in a particular material or group of objects, such as documents and books, paintings, decorative arts, textiles, metals, or architectural material. They use x rays, chemical testing, microscopes, special lights, and other laboratory equipment and techniques to examine objects, determine their condition, and decide on the best way to preserve them.

In addition to their conservation work, conservators participate in outreach programs, research topics in their specialty, and write articles for scholarly journals. They may be employed by a museum or other institution that has objects needing conservation, or they may be self-employed and have several clients.

Work Environment

Curators, museum technicians, and conservators held about 23,800 jobs in 2010. The following industries employed the most curators, museum technicians, and conservators in 2010:

Because most curators work at museums, zoos, aquariums, botanical gardens, nature centers, and historical sites, their working conditions vary. Some spend their time working with the public, providing reference assistance and educational services. Some curators conduct research or process records, which reduces the opportunity to work with others.

Those who restore and set up exhibits or work with bulky, heavy record containers may lift objects, climb, or stretch.

Museum technicians generally work in museums. When helping to prepare exhibits, they may need to lift heavy objects, climb ladders and scaffolding, or reach and stretch to put items in place.

Conservators work in conservation laboratories. The size of the objects in the collection with which they are working determines the amount of effort involved in lifting, reaching, and moving objects.

Work Schedules

Curators in large institutions may travel extensively to evaluate potential additions to the collection, organize exhibits, and conduct research. However, for curators in small institutions, travel may be rare.

Most curators, museum technicians, and conservators work full time.

How to Become a Curator, Museum Technician, or Conservator

Although some curator jobs require only a bachelor's degree, many employers require curators to have related work experience or a master's degree. Museum technicians must have a bachelor's degree; conservators generally need a master's degree.

Education

Curators. Most museums require curators to have a master's degree in an appropriate discipline of the museum's specialty—art, history, or archaeology—or in museum studies. Some employers prefer that curators have a doctoral degree, particularly for positions in natural history or science museums. Earning two graduate degrees—in museum studies (museology) and a specialized subject—may give candidates an advantage in a competitive job market.

In small museums, curator positions may be available to people with a bachelor's degree. Because curators, particularly those in small museums, may have administrative and managerial responsibilities, courses in business administration, public relations, marketing, and fundraising are recommended. For some positions, applicants need to have completed an internship of full-time museum work, as well as courses in museum practices.

Museum technicians (registrars). Registrars usually need a bachelor's degree related to the museum's specialty, training in museum studies, or previous experience working in museums, particularly in designing exhibits. Relatively few schools grant a bachelor's degree in museum studies; more common are undergraduate minors or tracks of study that are part of an undergraduate degree in a related field, such as art history, history, or archaeology.

Students interested in further study might get a master's degree in museum studies, offered in colleges and universities throughout the country. However, many employers feel that, although a degree in museum studies is helpful, a thorough knowledge of the museum's specialty and museum work experience are more important.

Conservators. When hiring conservators, employers look for a master's degree in conservation or in a closely related field, together with substantial experience. Only a few graduate programs in museum conservation techniques are offered in the United States. Competition for entry to these programs is keen. To qualify, a student must have a background in chemistry, archaeology, studio art, and art history, as well as work experience. For some programs, knowledge of a foreign language also is helpful. Completing a conservation apprenticeship or internship as an undergraduate can enhance admission prospects. Graduate programs last 2 to 4 years, the latter years of which include internship training.

Advancement

In large museums, curators may advance through several levels of responsibility, eventually becoming museum directors. Curators often start in smaller local and regional establishments at the beginning of their careers. As they gain experience, they may get the opportunity to work in larger facilities. The top museum positions are highly sought after and competitive. Individual research and publications are important for advancement in larger institutions.

Important Qualities

Analytical skills. Curators, registrars, and conservators need excellent analytical skills to figure out the origin, history, and importance of many of the objects they work with.

Critical-thinking skills. Many artifacts need to be restored, maintained, and then classified. Curators must be able to determine the origins and authenticity of the objects that they are adding to their collections.

Customer-service skills. Curators who work at museums, zoos, and historical sites often work directly with the general public. Therefore, they must be able to describe, in detail, the collections to nontechnical visitors.

Organizational skills. Museums have many collections. Curators need to display these collections logically.

Stamina. Curators in zoos, botanical gardens, and other outdoor museums and historic sites often walk great distances.

Technical skills. Many historical objects need to be analyzed and preserved. Conservators must use the appropriate chemicals and techniques to preserve the different objects they deal with, such as documents, paintings, fabrics, and pottery, to prevent further deterioration.

Pay

Curators, Museum Technicians, and Conservators
Median annual wages, May 2010

Curators	$48,450
Curators, Museum Technicians, and Conservators	$42,310
Museum Technicians and Conservators	$37,310
Total, All Occupations	$33,840

Note: All Occupations includes all occupations in the U.S. Economy.
Source: U.S. Bureau of Labor Statistics, Occupational Employment Statistics

The median annual wage of curators and museum technicians was $42,310 in May 2010. The median wage is the wage at which half the workers in an occupation earned more than that amount and half earned less.

The median annual wage of curators was $48,450 in May 2010. The lowest 10 percent earned less than $27,640, and the top 10 percent earned more than $86,450.

The median annual wage of museum technicians and conservators was $37,310 in May 2010. The lowest 10 percent earned less than $24,440, and the top 10 percent earned more than $68,250.

In May 2010, the median annual wage of curators in the federal government was $75,600, and the median annual wage of museum technicians and conservators in the federal government was $38,790.

Curators in large institutions may travel extensively to evaluate potential additions to the collection, organize exhibits, and conduct research. However, for curators in small institutions, travel may be rare.

Most curators, museum technicians, and conservators work full time.

Job Outlook

Curators, Museum Technicians, and Conservators
Percent change in employment, projected 2010-20

Curators	25%
Curators, Museum Technicians, and Conservators	16%
Total, All Occupations	14%
Museum Technicians and Conservators	7%

Note: All Occupations includes all occupations in the U.S. Economy.
Source: U.S. Bureau of Labor Statistics, Employment Projections program

Overall employment of curators, museum technicians, and conservators is projected to grow 16 percent from 2010 to 2020, about as fast as the average for all occupations. Employment growth will vary be specialty.

Employment of curators is projected to grow 25 percent, faster than the average for all occupations. Employment of museum technicians and conservators is projected to grow 7 percent, slower than the average for all occupations. Public interest in science, art, history, and technology will continue to spur demand for curators, museum technicians, and conservators.

Because museum attendance is expected to rise over the coming decade, many museums should remain financially healthy and are expected to schedule additional building and renovation projects.

Job Prospects

Curator jobs are attractive to many people, and many applicants have the necessary training and knowledge. Combined with the relatively few job openings, candidates are likely to face very strong competition for jobs.

To gain marketable experience, candidates may have to work part time, as an intern, or even as a volunteer assistant curator or research associate after completing their formal education. Substantial work experience in collection management, research, exhibit design, or restoration, as well as database management skills, will be necessary for permanent status. Familiarity and skills related to mobile technology will be viewed favorably by hiring officials.

Museum technicians and conservators also can expect strong competition when applying for jobs. Competition is stiff for the limited number of openings in conservation graduate programs, and applicants need a technical background. Conservator program graduates with knowledge of a foreign language and a willingness to relocate should have better job opportunities.

Museums and other cultural institutions can have funding cut during recessions or periods of budget tightening, reducing demand for these workers. Although the number of curators who move to other occupations is relatively low, the need to replace workers who retire or leave the occupation will create some job openings. However, workers in these occupations tend to work beyond the typical retirement age of workers in other occupations.

Employment projections data for curators, museum technicians, and conservators, 2010-20

Occupational Title	SOC Code	Employment, 2010	Projected Employment, 2020	Change, 2010-20	
				Percent	Numeric
Curators, Museum Technicians, and Conservators	—	23,800	27,600	16	3,800
Curators	25-4012	12,000	14,900	25	3,000
Museum Technicians and Conservators	25-4013	11,900	12,700	7	800
SOURCE: U.S. Bureau of Labor Statistics, Employment Projections program					

Similar Occupations

This table shows a list of occupations with job duties that are similar to those of curators, museum technicians, and conservators.

Occupation	Job Duties	Entry-Level Education	Median Annual Pay, May 2010
Archivists	Archivists appraise, edit, and maintain permanent records and historically valuable documents. Many perform research on archival material.	Bachelor's degree	$45,200
Librarians	Librarians help people find information from many sources. They maintain library collections and do other work as needed to keep the library running.	Master's degree	$54,500
Craft and Fine Artists	Craft and fine artists use a variety of materials and techniques to create art for sale and exhibition. Craft artists create handmade objects, such as pottery, glassware, textiles, or other objects that are designed to be functional. Fine artists, including painters, sculptors, and illustrators, create original works of art for their aesthetic value, rather than a functional one.	High school diploma or equivalent	$43,470
Anthropologists and Archeologists	Anthropologists and archeologists study the origin, development, and behavior of human beings, past and present. They examine the cultures, languages, archeological remains, and physical characteristics of people in various parts of the world.	Master's degree	$54,230
Historians	Historians research, analyze, interpret, and present the past by studying a variety of historical documents and sources.	Master's degree	$53,520

Contacts for More Information

For more information about museum careers, including schools offering courses in museum studies for curators and museum technicians, visit American Association of Museums

For more information about careers and education programs in conservation and preservation for conservators, visit American Institute for Conservation of Historic and Artistic Works

Information about how to get a job as a curator or museum technician with the federal government is available from the Office of Personnel Management through USAJOBS, the federal government's official employment information system.

Suggested citation:

Bureau of Labor Statistics, U.S. Department of Labor, Occupational Outlook Handbook, 2012-13 Edition, Curators, Museum Technicians, and Conservators, on the Internet at http://www.bls.gov/ooh/education-training-and-library/curators-and-museum-technicians.htm .

High School Teachers

Quick Facts: High School Teachers	
2010 Median Pay	$53,230 per year
Entry-Level Education	Bachelor's degree
Work Experience in a Related Occupation	None
On-the-job Training	Internship/residency
Number of Jobs, 2010	1,037,600
Job Outlook, 2010-20	7% (Slower than average)
Employment Change, 2010-20	71,900

What High School Teachers Do

High school teachers help prepare students for life after graduation. They teach academic lessons and various skills that students will need to attend college and to enter the job market.

Duties

High school teachers typically do the following:

- Plan lessons in the subjects they teach, such as biology or history
- Assess students to evaluate their abilities, strengths, and weaknesses
- Teach students as an entire class or in small groups
- Grade students' assignments to monitor progress
- Communicate with parents about students' progress
- Work with individual students to challenge them, to improve their abilities, and to work on their weaknesses
- Prepare students for standardized tests required by the state
- Develop and enforce classroom rules
- Supervise students outside of the classroom—for example, at lunchtime or during detention

High school teachers generally teach students from the 9th through 12th grades. They usually teach one or two of the subjects or classes a student has throughout the day. For example, they may teach government and history.

In one class, high school teachers may work with students from different grades because, in many schools, students are divided into classes based on their abilities, not only their age. For example, a high school teacher of Spanish may have students from 9th through 12th grades in first-year Spanish and also have students from 9th to 12th

grades in advanced Spanish—depending on how much language instruction the students have had.

High school teachers see several different classes of students throughout the day. They may teach the same material—for example, world history—to more than one class if the school has many students taking that subject.

Some teachers instruct special classes, such as art, music, and physical education. For more information, see the profile on career and technical education teachers .

Teachers use time during the day, when they do not have classes, to plan lessons, grade assignments, and meet with other teachers and staff.

In some schools, there are English as a second language (ESL) or English for speakers of other languages (ESOL) teachers who work exclusively with students who are learning English. These students are often referred to as English language learners (ELLs). These teachers work with students individually or in groups to help them improve their English skills and to help students with assignments for other classes.

Students with learning disabilities and emotional or behavioral disorders often are taught in traditional classes. Therefore, high school teachers may work with special education teachers to adapt lessons to these students' needs and to monitor the students' progress. For more information, see the profile on special education teachers .

Some teachers maintain websites to communicate with parents about students' assignments, upcoming events, and grades. For students, teachers may create websites or discussion boards to present information and to expand a lesson taught in class.

Some high school teachers coach sports and advise student clubs and other groups, activities which frequently happen before or after school.

Work Environment

High school teachers held about 1 million jobs in 2010.

Most high school teachers work in either public or private schools. Some teach in public magnet and charter schools. Others teach in private religious or secular schools.

Most states have tenure laws, which mean that after a certain number of years of teaching satisfactorily (the probationary period), teachers have some job security.

Seeing students develop new skills and gain an appreciation for knowledge and learning can be very rewarding. However, teaching may be stressful. Some schools have large classes and lack important teaching tools, such as computers and up-to-date textbooks. Most teachers are held accountable for their students' performance on standardized tests, which can be frustrating. Occasionally, teachers must cope with unmotivated or disrespectful students.

In 2010, a large number of high school teachers belonged to unions—mainly the American Federation of Teachers and the National Education Association .

High school teachers generally specialize in a subject, such as English, math, or science.

Work Schedules

High school teachers generally work school hours, which vary somewhat. However, they often spend time in the evenings and on weekends grading papers and preparing lessons. In addition, they may meet with parents, students, and other teachers before and after school. Plus, teachers who coach sports or advise clubs generally do so before or after school.

Many work the traditional 10-month school year with a 2-month break during the summer. Although most do not teach during the summer, some teach in summer programs. Teachers in districts with a year-round schedule typically work 8 weeks in a row, are on break for 1 week, and have a 5-week midwinter break.

How to Become a High School Teacher

High school teachers must have a bachelor's degree. In addition, public school teachers must have a state-issued certification or license. For information about teacher preparation programs and certification requirements in your state, contact the U.S. Department of Education .

Education

All states require public high school teachers to have at least a bachelor's degree. Most states require high school teachers to have majored in a content area, such as chemistry or history. While majoring in a content area, future teachers typically enroll in their higher education's teacher preparation program and take classes in education and child psychology, as well.

Teacher preparation—or teacher education—programs instruct how to present information to students and how to work with students of varying abilities and backgrounds. Programs typically include fieldwork, such as student teaching.

Some states require high school teachers to earn a master's degree after earning their teaching certification.

Teachers in private schools do not need to meet state requirements. However, private schools typically seek high school teachers who have a bachelor's degree and a major in a content area.

Licenses and Certification

All states require teachers in public schools to be licensed, which is frequently referred to as a certification. Those who teach in private schools are not required to be licensed.

High school teachers typically are awarded a secondary or high school certification. This allows them to teach the 7th through the 12th grades.

Requirements for certification vary by state. However, all states require at least a bachelor's degree. States also require completing a teacher preparation program and supervised experience in teaching, typically gained through student teaching. Some states require a minimum grade point average.

States typically require candidates to pass a general teaching certification test, as well as a test that demonstrates their knowledge in the subject they will teach.

Often, teachers are required to complete annual professional development classes to keep their license. Most states require teachers to pass a background check, and some states require teachers to complete a master's degree after receiving their certification.

All states offer an alternative route to certification for people who already have a bachelor's degree but lack the education courses required for certification. Some alternative certification programs allow candidates to begin teaching immediately under the supervision of an experienced teacher. These programs cover teaching methods and child development. After they complete the program, candidates are awarded full certification.

Other programs require students to take classes in education before they can teach. Students may be awarded a master's degree after

completing either type of programs. For more information about alternative certification programs, contact the National Center for Alternative Certification.

Advancement

Experienced teachers can advance to be mentors or lead teachers. In these positions, they often work with less-experienced teachers to help them improve their teaching skills.

With additional education or certification, teachers may become school counselors, school librarians, or instructional coordinators. Some become assistant principals or principals. Becoming a principal usually requires additional instruction in education administration or leadership. For more information, see the profiles on school and career counselors , librarians , instructional coordinators , and elementary, middle, and high school principals .

Important Qualities

Communication skills. Teachers must collaborate with other teachers and special education teachers. In addition, teachers need to discuss students' needs with parents and administrators.

Instructional skills. High school teachers need to explain difficult concepts in terms students can understand. In addition, they must be able to engage students in learning and adapt lessons to each student's needs.

Patience. Working with students of different abilities and backgrounds can be difficult. High school teachers must be patient when students struggle with material.

Pay

High School Teachers
Median annual wages, May 2010

Secondary School Teachers, Except Special and Career/Technical Education	$53,230
Education, Training, and Library Occupations	$45,690
Total, All Occupations	$33,840

Note: All Occupations includes all occupations in the U.S. Economy.
Source: U.S. Bureau of Labor Statistics, Occupational Employment Statistics

The median annual wage of high school teachers was $53,230 in May 2010. The median wage is the wage at which half the workers in an occupation earned more than that amount and half earned less. The lowest 10 percent earned less than $35,020, and the top 10 percent earned more than $83,230.

High school teachers generally work school hours, which vary somewhat. However, they often spend time in the evenings and on weekends grading papers and preparing lessons. In addition, they may meet with parents, students, and other teachers before and after school. Plus, teachers who coach sports or advise clubs generally do so before or after school.

Many work the traditional 10-month school year, with a 2-month break during the summer. Although most do not teach during the summer, some teach in summer programs. Teachers in districts with a year-round schedule typically work 8 weeks in a row, are on break for 1 week, and have a 5-week midwinter break.

Job Outlook

High School Teachers
Percent change in employment, projected 2010-20

Education, Training, and Library Occupations	15%
Total, All Occupations	14%
Secondary School Teachers, Except Special and Career/Technical Education	7%

Note: All Occupations includes all occupations in the U.S. Economy.
Source: U.S. Bureau of Labor Statistics, Employment Projections program

Employment of high school teachers is expected to grow by 7 percent from 2010 to 2020, slower than the average for all occupations.

Overall growth is expected because of declines in student-to-teacher ratios and increases in enrollment. However, employment growth will vary by region.

From 2010 to 2020, the student-to-teacher ratio is expected to decline. The student-to teacher-ratio is the number of students for each teacher in school. When this ratio declines, each teacher is responsible for fewer students, so more teachers are required to instruct the same number of students. The expected decline in the student-to-teacher ratio will increase demand for high school teachers.

Over the projections period, the number of students in high schools is expected to increase, and the number of classes needed to accommodate these students will also rise. As a result, more teachers will be required to teach these additional classes of high school students.

However, enrollment growth in high school is expected to be slower than enrollment growth in other grades. Therefore, employment of high school teachers is expected to grow more slowly than that of other education occupations.

Although overall student enrollment is expected to grow, there will be variation by region. Enrollment is expected to grow fastest in the South and West. In the Midwest, enrollment is expected to hold steady, but the Northeast is projected to have declines. As a result, employment growth for high school teachers is expected to be faster in the South and West than in the Midwest and Northeast.

Despite expected increases in enrollment, however, employment growth for public high school teachers will depend on state and local government budgets. When state and local governments experience budget deficits, school boards may lay off employees, including teachers. As a result, employment growth of high school teachers may be reduced by state and local government budget deficits.

Job Prospects

From 2010 to 2020, a significant number of older teachers is expected to reach retirement age. These retirements will create job openings for new teachers.

In addition to overall openings, many schools report having difficulty filling teaching positions for certain subjects, including math, science (especially chemistry and physics), English as a second language, and special education. As a result, teachers with education or certifications to teach these specialties should have better job prospects. For more information about high school special education teachers, see the profile on special education teachers .

There is significant variation by region of the country and school setting. Opportunities should be better in the South and West, which are expected to experience rapid enrollment growth. Furthermore, opportunities should be better in urban and rural school districts than in suburban school districts.

Employment projections data for high school teachers, 2010-20

Occupational Title	SOC Code	Employment, 2010	Projected Employment, 2020	Change, 2010-20	
				Percent	Numeric
Secondary School Teachers, Except Special and Career/Technical Education	25-2031	1,037,600	1,109,500	7	71,900
SOURCE: U.S. Bureau of Labor Statistics, Employment Projections program					

Similar Occupations

This table shows a list of occupations with job duties that are similar to those of high school teachers.

Occupation	Job Duties	Entry-Level Education	Median Annual Pay, May 2010
Career and Technical Education Teachers	Career and technical education teachers help students in middle school and high school develop career-related and technical skills. They help students explore or prepare to enter a particular occupation, such as one in auto repair, healthcare, business, or the culinary arts.	Bachelor's degree	$53,920
Childcare Workers	Childcare workers care for children when parents and other family members are unavailable. They care for children's basic needs, such as bathing and feeding. In addition, some help children prepare for kindergarten, and many help older children with homework.	High school diploma or equivalent	$19,300
Elementary, Middle, and High School Principals	Elementary, middle, and high school principals lead teachers and other members of school staff. They manage the day-to-day operations of elementary, middle, and high schools. They set goals and objectives and evaluate their school's progress toward meeting them.	Master's degree	$86,970
Instructional Coordinators	Instructional coordinators oversee school districts' curriculums and teaching standards. They work with teachers and school administrators to implement new teaching techniques to improve the quality of education.	Master's degree	$58,830
Kindergarten and Elementary School Teachers	Kindergarten and elementary school teachers prepare younger students for future schooling by teaching them the basics of subjects such as math and reading.	Bachelor's degree	$51,380
Librarians	Librarians help people find information from many sources. They maintain library collections and do other work as needed to keep the library running.	Master's degree	$54,500
Middle School Teachers	Middle school teachers educate students, most of whom are in sixth through eighth grades. They help students build on the fundamentals they learned in elementary school and prepare them for the more difficult lessons they will learn in high school.	Bachelor's degree	$51,960

Postsecondary Teachers	Postsecondary teachers instruct students in a wide variety of academic and vocational subjects beyond the high school level. They also conduct research and publish scholarly papers and books.	Doctoral or professional degree	$62,050
Preschool Teachers	Preschool teachers educate and care for children, usually ages 3 to 5, who have not yet entered kindergarten. They explain reading, writing, science, and other subjects in a way that young children can understand.	Associate's degree	$25,700
School and Career Counselors	School counselors help students develop social skills and succeed in school. Career counselors assist people with the process of making career decisions by helping them choose a career or educational program.	Master's degree	$53,380
Social Workers	There are two main types of social workers: direct-service social workers, who help people solve and cope with problems in their everyday lives, and clinical social workers, who diagnose and treat mental, behavioral, and emotional issues.	See How to Become One	$42,480
Special Education Teachers	Special education teachers work with students who have a wide range of learning, mental, emotional and physical disabilities. With students who have mild or moderate disabilities, they ensure that lessons and teaching strategies are modified to meet the students' needs. With students who have severe disabilities, they teach the students independent living skills and basic literacy, communication, and math.	Bachelor's degree	$53,220
Teacher Assistants	Teacher assistants work under a teacher's supervision to give students additional attention and instruction.	High school diploma or equivalent	$23,220

Contacts for More Information

For more information about teaching and becoming a teacher, visit U.S. Department of Education ,American Federation of Teachers ,National Education Association

For more information about teacher preparation programs, visit National Council for Accreditation of Teacher Education ,Teacher Education Accreditation Council

For more information about alternative certification programs, visit National Center for Alternative Certification

Suggested citation:

Bureau of Labor Statistics, U.S. Department of Labor, Occupational Outlook Handbook, 2012-13 Edition, High School Teachers, on the Internet at http://www.bls.gov/ooh/education-training-and-library/high-school-teachers.htm .

Instructional Coordinators

Quick Facts: Instructional Coordinators	
2010 Median Pay	$58,830 per year $28.28 per hour
Entry-Level Education	Master's degree
Work Experience in a Related Occupation	More than 5 years
On-the-job Training	None
Number of Jobs, 2010	139,700
Job Outlook, 2010-20	20% (Faster than average)
Employment Change, 2010-20	27,300

What Instructional Coordinators Do

Instructional coordinators oversee school districts' curriculums and teaching standards. They work with teachers and school administrators to implement new teaching techniques to improve the quality of education.

Duties

Instructional coordinators typically do the following:

- Oversee the development of the school system's curriculum
- Arrange for professional development opportunities for teachers
- Evaluate the effectiveness of both the curriculum and teaching methods by analyzing student test data

Instructional coordinators assist teachers in adopting new strategies and techniques to instruct students.

- Ensure that schools in their district are meeting local, state, and federal regulations and standards
- Review and choose textbooks and other educational materials, such as computer programs
- Stay up to date with teaching techniques and help teachers adopt new strategies
- Help teachers understand and use new technologies in their classes
- Develop procedures to ensure that teachers are properly implementing the curriculum
- Train teachers and other instructional staff in new content or programs
- Mentor or coach teachers who need help improving their skills

Instructional coordinators assess the effectiveness of the district's curriculum and teaching techniques. They make changes to the curriculum and adopt new teaching strategies and techniques to improve students' test scores and outcomes.

For example, when a state or school district introduces new standards for what students must learn in specific grades, instructional coordinators explain the new standards to teachers and help them develop ways to teach so students learn what the standards cover.

Instructional coordinators are also known as curriculum specialists, instructional coaches, or assistant superintendents of instruction. In some school districts, they specialize in particular grade levels, such as elementary or high school, or specific subjects, such as language arts or math. Other instructional coordinators focus on special education, English as a second language, or gifted-and-talented programs.

Coordinators generally travel to schools in their district to work with school administrators and teachers, teach professional development classes, and monitor the implementation of the curriculum.

Work Environment

Instructional coordinators held 139,700 jobs in 2010. They work in public and private schools. Coordinators generally have an office in the headquarters of their school district, but they also spend a lot of time traveling to schools within the district.

In 2010, the industries employing the most instructional coordinators were as follows:

Elementary and secondary schools; state, local, and private	38%
Colleges, universities, and professional schools; state, local, and private	16
State and local government	8
Educational support services; state, local, and private	6
Junior colleges; state, local, and private	6

Work Schedules

Instructional coordinators generally work year-round and do not have summer breaks, as do workers in some other education occupations. Coordinators may need to meet with teachers and other administrators before and after school.

How to Become an Instructional Coordinator

Most school districts require instructional coordinators to have at least a master's degree. In addition, they often require them to be licensed teachers or licensed school administrators.

Education

School districts generally require instructional coordinators to have at least a master's degree in curriculum and instruction or in a related field. Some instructional coordinators have a master's degree in the content field they plan to specialize in, such as math or history.

Master's programs in curriculum and instruction teach students about curriculum design, instructional theory, and collecting and analyzing data. To enter these master's programs, students usually need a bachelor's degree from a teacher education program or in a related field.

Licenses

Instructional coordinators in public schools are generally required to be licensed. Most school districts require a teaching license; some require an education administrator license. For information about teaching licenses, see the profile on high school teachers . For information about education administrator licenses, see the profile on elementary, middle, and high school principals .

Work Experience

Most school districts require instructional coordinators to have experience working as a teacher or as a principal or other school administrator. For some positions, they may require experience teaching a specific subject or grade level.

Important Qualities

Analytical skills. Instructional coordinators review data on students and use the information to adjust the curriculum and teaching strategies.

Communication skills. Instructional coordinators need to explain changes in the curriculum and teaching standards to teachers and school administrators. To do so, they need good communication skills.

Decision-making skills. Instructional coordinators decide on aspects of education that have profound implications for what teachers do and what students learn. They must use good judgment in choosing textbooks and choosing classroom instruction techniques.

Instructional skills. Instructional coordinators need to be able to train teachers on the newest teaching techniques and tools.

People skills. Working with teachers and other administrators is an important part of instructional coordinators' jobs. They need to be able to establish and maintain good working relationships with their colleagues.

Pay

Instructional Coordinators
Median annual wages, May 2010

Instructional Coordinators	$58,830
Total, All Occupations	$33,840
Other Education, Training, and Library Occupations	$24,800

Note: All Occupations includes all occupations in the U.S. Economy.
Source: U.S. Bureau of Labor Statistics, Occupational Employment Statistics

The median annual wage of instructional coordinators was $58,830 in May 2010. The median wage is the wage at which half the workers in an occupation earned more than that amount and half earned less. The lowest 10 percent earned less than $33,490, and the top 10 percent earned more than $93,080.

In May 2010, wages in the industries employing the most instructional coordinators were as follows:

Elementary and secondary schools; state, local, and private	$65,210
Educational support services; state, local, and private	59,230
Junior colleges; state, local, and private	54,490
Colleges, universities, and professional schools; state, local, and private	52,350

Instructional coordinators generally work year-round and do not have summer breaks, as do workers in some other education occupations. Coordinators may need to meet with teachers and other administrators before and after school.

Job Outlook

Instructional Coordinators
Percent change in employment, projected 2010-20

Instructional Coordinators	20%
Other Education, Training, and Library Occupations	15%
Total, All Occupations	14%

Note: All Occupations includes all occupations in the U.S. Economy.
Source: U.S. Bureau of Labor Statistics, Employment Projections program

Employment of instructional coordinators is expected to grow by 20 percent from 2010 to 2020, faster than the average for all occupations. Employment growth is anticipated as schools increasingly focus on improving teachers' effectiveness.

Many school districts and states are increasingly working to improve teacher effectiveness by focusing on the teacher's role in improving students' learning and test scores. In addition, there is an increased emphasis on holding teachers accountable for student outcomes. Some states and school districts are using students' outcomes and test scores to evaluate teachers.

As more schools move toward these techniques, instructional coordinators will be needed to help teachers who are not meeting expectations. Coordinators will work to improve these teachers' skills by offering them professional development, mentoring, and coaching. As schools seek to provide additional training to teachers, demand for instructional coordinators is expected to grow.

However, employment growth for instructional coordinators will depend on state and local government budgets. When state and local governments have budget deficits, they may lay off employees, including instructional coordinators. As a result, employment growth may be tempered.

Employment projections data for instructional coordinators, 2010-20

Occupational Title	SOC Code	Employment, 2010	Projected Employment, 2020	Change, 2010-20	
				Percent	Numeric
Instructional Coordinators	25-9031	139,700	166,900	20	27,300

SOURCE: U.S. Bureau of Labor Statistics, Employment Projections program

Similar Occupations

This table shows a list of occupations with job duties that are similar to those of instructional coordinators.

Occupation	Job Duties	Entry-Level Education	Median Annual Pay, May 2010
Elementary, Middle, and High School Principals	Elementary, middle, and high school principals lead teachers and other members of school staff. They manage the day-to-day operations of elementary, middle, and high schools. They set goals and objectives and evaluate their school's progress toward meeting them.	Master's degree	$86,970
High School Teachers	High school teachers help prepare students for life after graduation. They teach academic lessons and various skills that students will need to attend college and to enter the job market.	Bachelor's degree	$53,230
Kindergarten and Elementary School Teachers	Kindergarten and elementary school teachers prepare younger students for future schooling by teaching them the basics of subjects such as math and reading.	Bachelor's degree	$51,380
Librarians	Librarians help people find information from many sources. They maintain library collections and do other work as needed to keep the library running.	Master's degree	$54,500
Middle School Teachers	Middle school teachers educate students, most of whom are in sixth through eighth grades. They help students build on the fundamentals they learned in elementary school and prepare them for the more difficult lessons they will learn in high school.	Bachelor's degree	$51,960
Postsecondary Teachers	Postsecondary teachers instruct students in a wide variety of academic and vocational subjects beyond the high school level. They also conduct research and publish scholarly papers and books.	Doctoral or professional degree	$62,050
Preschool Teachers	Preschool teachers educate and care for children, usually ages 3 to 5, who have not yet entered kindergarten. They explain reading, writing, science, and other subjects in a way that young children can understand.	Associate's degree	$25,700
School and Career Counselors	School counselors help students develop social skills and succeed in school. Career counselors assist people with the process of making career decisions by helping them choose a career or educational program.	Master's degree	$53,380
Social Workers	There are two main types of social workers: direct-service social workers, who help people solve and cope with problems in their everyday lives, and clinical social workers, who diagnose and treat mental, behavioral, and emotional issues.	See How to Become One	$42,480
Special Education Teachers	Special education teachers work with students who have a wide range of learning, mental, emotional and physical disabilities. With students who have mild or moderate disabilities, they ensure that lessons and teaching strategies are modified to meet the students' needs. With students who have severe disabilities, they teach the students independent living skills and basic literacy, communication, and math.	Bachelor's degree	$53,220
Teacher Assistants	Teacher assistants work under a teacher's supervision to give students additional attention and instruction.	High school diploma or equivalent	$23,220

Contacts for More Information

For more information about instructional coordinators, visit
Learning Forward

Suggested citation:

Bureau of Labor Statistics, U.S. Department of Labor, Occupational Outlook Handbook, 2012-13 Edition, Instructional Coordinators, on the Internet at http://www.bls.gov/ooh/education-training-and-library/instructional-coordinators.htm .

Kindergarten and Elementary School Teachers

Quick Facts: Kindergarten and Elementary School Teachers	
2010 Median Pay	$51,380 per year
Entry-Level Education	Bachelor's degree
Work Experience in a Related Occupation	None
On-the-job Training	Internship/residency
Number of Jobs, 2010	1,655,800
Job Outlook, 2010-20	17% (About as fast as average)
Employment Change, 2010-20	281,500

What Kindergarten and Elementary School Teachers Do

Kindergarten and elementary school teachers prepare younger students for future schooling by teaching them the basics of subjects such as math and reading.

Duties

Kindergarten and elementary school teachers typically do the following:

- Plan lessons that teach students subjects, such as reading and math, and skills, such as study skills and social skills
- Assess students to evaluate their abilities, strengths, and weaknesses
- Teach students as an entire class or in small groups the lessons they have planned
- Grade students' assignments to monitor their progress
- Communicate with parents about their child's progress
- Work with individual students to challenge them and overcome their weaknesses
- Prepare students for standardized tests required by the state
- Develop and enforce classroom rules to teach children proper behavior
- Supervise children outside of the classroom—for example, at lunchtime or during recess

Kindergarten and elementary school teachers act as facilitators or coaches to help students learn and apply important concepts. Many teachers use a hands-on approach, including props, to help students

Kindergarten and elementary school teachers use a variety of tools, such as computers, to present information to students.

understand abstract concepts, solve problems, and develop critical thinking skills.

For example, they may show students how to do a science experiment and then have the students do the experiment. They may have students work together to learn how to collaborate to solve problems.

Kindergarten and elementary school teachers generally teach kindergarten through fourth or fifth grade. However, in some schools elementary school teachers may teach sixth, seventh, and eighth grade.

Kindergarten and elementary school teachers most often teach students many subjects, such as reading, science, and social studies, which students learn throughout the day.

Some teachers, particularly those who teach young students, may teach a multilevel class that includes children who would traditionally be in different grades. They may have the same group of students for several years.

Kindergarten and elementary school students spend most of their day in one classroom. Teachers may escort students to assemblies; to classes taught by other teachers, such as art or music; or to recess. While students are away from the classroom, teachers plan lessons, grade assignments, or meet with other teachers and staff.

In some schools with older students, teachers work in teams. These teachers often specialize in teaching one of two pairs of specialties, either English and social studies or math and science. Generally, students spend half their time with one teacher and half their time with the other.

Some kindergarten and elementary school teachers teach special classes, such as art, music, and physical education.

Some schools employ teachers of English as a second language (ESL) or English for speakers of other languages (ESOL). Both of these types of teachers work exclusively with students who are learning English, often referred to as English language learners (ELLs). The teachers work with students individually or in groups to help them improve their English skills and to help them with assignments they got in other classes.

Students with learning disabilities or emotional or behavioral disorders are often taught in traditional classes. Teachers work with special education teachers to adapt lessons to these students' needs and monitor the students' progress. In some cases, kindergarten and elementary school teachers may co-teach lessons with special education teachers. For more information, see the profile on special education teachers.

Some teachers maintain websites to communicate with parents about students' assignments, upcoming events, and grades. For students in higher grades, teachers may create websites or discussion boards to present information or to expand on a lesson taught in class.

Work Environment

Kindergarten and elementary school teachers held about 1.7 million jobs in 2010.

Kindergarten and elementary school teachers work in public and private schools. Some private early childhood education programs have preschool classes in addition to kindergarten.

Most states have tenure laws, which mean that after a certain number of years of teaching satisfactorily (the probationary period), teachers have some job security.

Seeing students develop new skills and learn information can be rewarding. At the same time, however, teaching also may be stressful. Some schools have large classes and lack important teaching tools, such as computers and up-to-date textbooks. Most teachers are held accountable for their students' performances on standardized tests, which can be frustrating.

In 2010, a large number of kindergarten and elementary school teachers belonged to unions—mainly the American Federation of Teachers and the National Education Association .

Work Schedules

Kindergarten and elementary school teachers generally work school hours when students are present. They may meet with parents, students, and other teachers before and after school. They often spend time in the evenings and on weekends grading papers and preparing lessons.

Many kindergarten and elementary school teachers work the traditional 10-month school year, with a 2-month break during the summer. Some teachers may teach summer programs. Teachers in districts with a year-round schedule typically work 8 weeks in a row, are on break for 1 week, and have a 5-week midwinter break.

How to Become a Kindergarten or Elementary School Teacher

Kindergarten and elementary school teachers must have a bachelor's degree. In addition, public school teachers must have a state-issued certification or license. For information about teacher preparation programs and certification requirements in your state, contact the U.S. Department of Education.

Education

All states require public kindergarten and elementary school teachers to have at least a bachelor's degree in elementary education. Some states also require kindergarten and elementary school teachers to major in a content area, such as math or science. Those who major in a content area typically enroll in their university's teacher preparation program and also take classes in education and child psychology.

In teacher education programs, future teachers learn how to present information to young students and how to work with young students of varying abilities and backgrounds. Programs typically include fieldwork, such as student teaching.

Some states require kindergarten and elementary school teachers to earn a master's degree after receiving their teaching certification.

Teachers in private schools do not need to meet state requirements. However, private schools typically seek kindergarten and elementary school teachers who have a bachelor's degree in elementary education.

Licenses and certification

All states require teachers in public schools to be licensed. A license is frequently referred to as a certification. Those who teach in private schools are generally not required to be licensed.

Kindergarten and elementary school teachers are typically certified to teach early childhood grades, which are usually preschool through third grade, or elementary school grades, which are usually first through sixth grades or first through eighth grades.

Requirements for certification vary by state. However, all states require at least a bachelor's degree. They also require completing a teacher preparation program and supervised experience in teaching, typically gained through student teaching. Some states require a

minimum grade point average. States often require candidates to pass a general teaching certification test, as well as a test that demonstrates their knowledge of the subject they will teach. Although kindergarten and elementary school teachers typically do not teach only a single subject, they may still be required to pass a content area test to earn their certification.

Teachers are frequently required to complete annual professional development classes to keep their license. Most states require teachers to pass a background check. Some states require teachers to complete a master's degree after receiving their certification.

All states offer an alternative route to certification for people who already have a bachelor's degree but lack the education courses required for certification.

Some alternative certification programs allow candidates to begin teaching immediately after graduation, under the supervision of an experienced teacher. These programs cover teaching methods and child development. After they complete the program, candidates are awarded full certification.

Other programs require students to take classes in education before they can teach. Students may be awarded a master's degree after completing either of these programs. For information about alternative certification programs, contact the National Center for Alternative Certification.

Advancement

Experienced teachers can advance to be mentors or lead teachers. These teachers often work with less experienced teachers to help them improve their teaching skills.

With additional education or certification, teachers may become school counselors, school librarians, or instructional coordinators. Some become assistant principals or principals, both of which generally require additional education in education administration or leadership. For more information, see the profiles on school and career counselors , librarians , instructional coordinators , and elementary, middle, and high school principals .

Important Qualities

Communication skills. Teachers must collaborate with teacher assistants and special education teachers. In addition, they need to discuss students' needs with parents and administrators.

Creativity. Kindergarten and elementary school teachers must plan lessons that engage young students, adapting the lessons to every student's learning style.

Instructional skills. Kindergarten and elementary school teachers need to be able to explain difficult concepts in terms that young students can understand. In addition, they must be able to get students engaged in learning and adapt their lessons to each student's needs.

Patience. Working with students of different abilities and backgrounds can be difficult. Kindergarten and elementary school teachers must respond be patient when students struggle with material.

Pay

Kindergarten and Elementary School Teachers Median annual wages, May 2010	
Elementary School Teachers, Except Special Education	$51,660
Kindergarten and Elementary School Teachers	$51,380
Kindergarten Teachers, Except Special Education	$48,800
Total, All Occupations	$33,840

Note: All Occupations includes all occupations in the U.S. Economy.
Source: U.S. Bureau of Labor Statistics, Occupational Employment Statistics

The median annual wage of kindergarten teachers was $48,800 in May 2010. The median wage is the wage at which half the workers in an occupation earned more than that amount and half earned less. The lowest 10 percent earned less than $31,720, and the top 10 percent earned more than $76,490.

The median annual wage of elementary school teachers was $51,660. The lowest 10 percent earned less than $34,390, and the top 10 percent earned more than $80,140.

Kindergarten and elementary school teachers generally work school hours when students are present. They may meet with parents, students, and other teachers before and after school. They often spend time in the evenings and on weekends grading papers and preparing lessons.

Many kindergarten and elementary school teachers work the traditional 10-month school year, with a 2-month break during the summer. Some teachers may teach summer programs. Teachers in districts with a year-round schedule typically work 8 weeks in a row, are on break for 1 week, and have a 5-week midwinter break.

Job Outlook

Kindergarten and Elementary School Teachers
Percent change in employment, projected 2010-20

Kindergarten Teachers, Except Special Education	18%
Elementary School Teachers, Except Special Education	17%
Kindergarten and Elementary School Teachers	17%
Total, All Occupations	14%

Note: All Occupations includes all occupations in the U.S. Economy.
Source: U.S. Bureau of Labor Statistics, Employment Projections program

Employment of kindergarten and elementary school teachers is expected to grow by 17 percent from 2010 to 2020, about as fast as the average for all occupations. Growth is expected because of both declines in student–teacher ratios and increases in enrollment. However, employment growth will vary by region.

From 2010 to 2020, the student–teacher ratio is expected to decline. This ratio is the number of students for each teacher in the school. A decline in the ratio means that each teacher is responsible for fewer students, and, consequently, more teachers are needed to teach the same number of students.

In addition, the number of students in kindergarten and elementary schools is expected to increase over the coming decade, and the number of classes needed to accommodate these students will also rise. As a result, more teachers will be required to teach these additional classes of kindergarten and elementary school students.

Although overall student enrollment is expected to grow, there will be some variation by region. Enrollment is expected to grow fastest in the South and West. In the Midwest, enrollment is expected to hold steady, and the Northeast is projected to have declines. As a result, employment growth for kindergarten and elementary school teachers is expected to be faster in the South and West than in the Midwest and Northeast.

However, despite expected increases in enrollment, employment growth for kindergarten and elementary school teachers will depend on state and local government budgets. When state and local governments experience budget deficits, they may lay off employees, including teachers. As a result, employment growth of kindergarten and elementary school teachers may be somewhat reduced by state and local government budget deficits.

Job Prospects

A significant number of older teachers is expected to reach retirement age from 2010 to 2020. Their retirement will create job openings for new teachers. However, many areas of the country have a surplus of teachers who are trained to teach kindergarten and elementary school, making it more difficult for new teachers to find jobs.

Teachers of English as a second language (ESL) and special education teachers are in short supply. Kindergarten and elementary school teachers with education or certifications to teach these specialties should have better job opportunities. For more information about kindergarten and elementary school special education teachers, see the profile on special education teachers .

Opportunities will vary by region and school setting. Job prospects should be better in the South and West, which are expected to have rapid enrollment growth. Furthermore, opportunities will be better in urban and rural school districts than in suburban school districts.

Employment projections data for kindergarten and elementary school teachers, 2010-20

Occupational Title	SOC Code	Employment, 2010	Projected Employment, 2020	Change, 2010-20 Percent	Change, 2010-20 Numeric
Kindergarten and Elementary School Teachers	—	1,655,800	1,937,200	17	281,500
Kindergarten Teachers, Except Special Education	25-2012	179,200	211,900	18	32,700
Elementary School Teachers, Except Special Education	25-2021	1,476,500	1,725,300	17	248,800
SOURCE: U.S. Bureau of Labor Statistics, Employment Projections program					

Similar Occupations

This table shows a list of occupations with job duties that are similar to those of kindergarten and elementary school teachers.

Occupation	Job Duties	Entry-Level Education	Median Annual Pay, May 2010
Career and Technical Education Teachers	Career and technical education teachers help students in middle school and high school develop career-related and technical skills. They help students explore or prepare to enter a particular occupation, such as one in auto repair, healthcare, business, or the culinary arts.	Bachelor's degree	$53,920
Childcare Workers	Childcare workers care for children when parents and other family members are unavailable. They care for children's basic needs, such as bathing and feeding. In addition, some help children prepare for kindergarten, and many help older children with homework.	High school diploma or equivalent	$19,300

Elementary, Middle, and High School Principals	Elementary, middle, and high school principals lead teachers and other members of school staff. They manage the day-to-day operations of elementary, middle, and high schools. They set goals and objectives and evaluate their school's progress toward meeting them.	Master's degree	$86,970
High School Teachers	High school teachers help prepare students for life after graduation. They teach academic lessons and various skills that students will need to attend college and to enter the job market.	Bachelor's degree	$53,230
Instructional Coordinators	Instructional coordinators oversee school districts' curriculums and teaching standards. They work with teachers and school administrators to implement new teaching techniques to improve the quality of education.	Master's degree	$58,830
Librarians	Librarians help people find information from many sources. They maintain library collections and do other work as needed to keep the library running.	Master's degree	$54,500
Middle School Teachers	Middle school teachers educate students, most of whom are in sixth through eighth grades. They help students build on the fundamentals they learned in elementary school and prepare them for the more difficult lessons they will learn in high school.	Bachelor's degree	$51,960
Postsecondary Teachers	Postsecondary teachers instruct students in a wide variety of academic and vocational subjects beyond the high school level. They also conduct research and publish scholarly papers and books.	Doctoral or professional degree	$62,050
Preschool Teachers	Preschool teachers educate and care for children, usually ages 3 to 5, who have not yet entered kindergarten. They explain reading, writing, science, and other subjects in a way that young children can understand.	Associate's degree	$25,700
School and Career Counselors	School counselors help students develop social skills and succeed in school. Career counselors assist people with the process of making career decisions by helping them choose a career or educational program.	Master's degree	$53,380
Social Workers	There are two main types of social workers: direct-service social workers, who help people solve and cope with problems in their everyday lives, and clinical social workers, who diagnose and treat mental, behavioral, and emotional issues.	See How to Become One	$42,480
Special Education Teachers	Special education teachers work with students who have a wide range of learning, mental, emotional and physical disabilities. With students who have mild or moderate disabilities, they ensure that lessons and teaching strategies are modified to meet the students' needs. With students who have severe disabilities, they teach the students independent living skills and basic literacy, communication, and math.	Bachelor's degree	$53,220
Teacher Assistants	Teacher assistants work under a teacher's supervision to give students additional attention and instruction.	High school diploma or equivalent	$23,220

Contacts for More Information

For more information about teaching and becoming a teacher, visit U.S. Department of Education ,American Federation of Teachers ,National Education Association

For more information about teacher preparation programs, visit National Council for Accreditation of Teacher Education ,Teacher Education Accreditation Council

For more information about alternative certification programs, visit National Center for Alternative Certification

Suggested citation:

Bureau of Labor Statistics, U.S. Department of Labor, Occupational Outlook Handbook, 2012-13 Edition, Kindergarten and Elementary School Teachers, on the Internet at http://www.bls.gov/ooh/education-training-and-library/kindergarten-and-elementary-school-teachers.htm .

Librarians

Quick Facts: Librarians	
2010 Median Pay	$54,500 per year $26.20 per hour
Entry-Level Education	Master's degree
Work Experience in a Related Occupation	None
On-the-job Training	None
Number of Jobs, 2010	156,100
Job Outlook, 2010-20	7% (Slower than average)
Employment Change, 2010-20	10,800

What Librarians Do

Librarians help people find information from many sources. Most librarians, such as those in public and academic libraries, maintain library collections and do other work as needed to keep the library running.

Duties

Librarians typically do the following:

- Help library patrons find the information they need
- Organize library materials so they are easy to find
- Plan programs for different groups, such as storytelling for young children
- Develop and index databases of library materials
- Read book reviews, publishers' announcements, and catalogs to see what is available
- Choose new books, audio books, videos, and other materials for the library
- Research and buy new computers and other equipment as needed for the library
- Train and direct library technicians, assistants, and other support staff
- Prepare library budgets

In small libraries, librarians are often responsible for many or all aspects of library operations. They may manage a staff of library assistants and technicians. In larger libraries, librarians usually focus

Librarians plan outreach programs targeted toward different groups, such as story time for children.

on a specific area, such as user services, technical services, or administrative services.

Librarians working in user services help patrons find the information they need. They listen to what patrons are looking for and help them research the subject using both electronic and print resources. User services librarians also teach patrons how to use library resources to find information on their own. This may include familiarizing patrons with catalogs of print materials, helping them access and search digital libraries, or educating them on Internet search techniques.

Technical services librarians get, prepare, and classify library materials. They organize materials to make it easy for patrons to find information. These librarians are less likely to work directly with the public.

Librarians in administrative services manage libraries. They hire and supervise staff, prepare budgets, and negotiate contracts for library materials and equipment. Some conduct public relations or fundraising for the library.

Librarians who work in different settings sometimes have different job duties. The following are examples of types of librarians:

School librarians, sometimes called school media specialists, work in elementary, middle, and high school libraries and teach students how to use library resources. They also help teachers develop lesson plans and find materials for classroom instruction.

Special librarians work in settings other than school or public libraries. They are sometimes called information professionals. Law firms, hospitals, businesses, museums, government agencies, and many other groups have their own libraries with special librarians. The main purpose of these libraries and information centers is to serve the information needs of the organization that houses the library. Therefore, special librarians collect and organize materials focused on those subjects. The following are examples of special librarians:

- **Government librarians** provide research services and access to information for government staff and the public.
- **Law librarians** help lawyers, law students, judges, and law clerks locate and organize legal resources.
- **Medical librarians** help health professionals, patients, and researchers find health and science information. They may provide information about new clinical trials and medical treatments and procedures, teach medical students how to locate medical information, or answer consumers' health questions.

Work Environment

Librarians held about 156,100 jobs in 2010. About 60 percent were employed by public and private educational institutions. Another 28 percent were employed by local government.

Librarians work indoors. Some have private offices, but those in smaller libraries may share work space with others.

The following industries employed the most librarians in 2010:

Elementary and secondary schools; local	35%
Local government, excluding education and hospitals	28
Colleges, universities, and professional schools; state, local, and private	17
Elementary and secondary schools; private	4
Junior colleges; state, local, and private	3

Work Schedules

Most librarians work full time, although opportunities exist for part-time work. In 2010, 26 percent of librarians worked part time. Public and academic librarians often work on weekends and evenings and may work on some holidays. School librarians usually have the same work and vacation schedules as teachers, including summers off. Librarians in special libraries, such as law or corporate libraries, typically work normal business hours but may need to work longer hours to help meet deadlines.

How to Become a Librarian

Most librarians need a master's degree in library science. Some positions have additional requirements, such as a teaching certificate or a degree in another field.

Education

A bachelor's degree is needed to enter a graduate program in library science, but any undergraduate major is accepted. Colleges and universities have different names for their library science programs. They are often called Master's in Library Science (MLS) programs but sometimes have other names, such as Master of Information Studies or Master of Library and Information Studies. Many colleges offer library science programs, but, as of 2011, only 56 programs in the United States were accredited by the American Library Association. A degree from an accredited program may lead to better job opportunities.

A master's degree in library science usually takes 1 to 2 years to complete. The coursework usually covers selecting and processing library materials, organizing information, research methods and strategies, online reference systems, and Internet search methods.

Librarians working in a special library, such as a law or corporate library, usually supplement a master's degree in library science with knowledge of their specialized field. They may earn a master's or professional degree or a Ph.D. in that subject.

Licenses and Certification

Most states require certification or licensure for librarians in public schools. This often includes being certified as a teacher in that state. Many states also require certification for librarians in public libraries. Requirements vary by state.Contact your state's licensing board for specific requirements.

Important Qualities

Active learning. New information, technology, and resources constantly change the details of what librarians do. They must be able and willing to continually update their knowledge on these changes to be effective at their jobs in the varying circumstances.

Communication skills. Librarians need to be strong communicators. They need to be able to understand other people's written and spoken thoughts and to respond clearly.

Computer skills. Librarians use computers to help patrons research topics. They also use computers to classify resources, create databases, and perform administrative duties.

Interpersonal skills. Librarians must be able to work both as part of a team and with the public or with researchers.

Problem-solving skills. Librarians conduct and assist with research. This requires being able to identify a problem, figure out where to find information, and draw conclusions based on the information found.

Reading comprehension. All librarians must be excellent readers. Those working in special libraries continually read the latest literature in their field of specialization.

Pay

Librarians
Median annual wages, May 2010

Librarians	$54,500
Education, Training, and Library Occupations	$45,690
Total, All Occupations	$33,840

Note: All Occupations includes all occupations in the U.S. Economy.
Source: U.S. Bureau of Labor Statistics, Occupational Employment Statistics

The median annual wage of librarians was $54,500 in May 2010. The median wage is the wage at which half of the workers in an occupation earned more than that amount and half earned less. The lowest 10 percent earned less than $33,590, and the top 10 percent earned more than $83,510.

Most librarians work full time, although opportunities exist for part-time work. In 2010, 26 percent of librarians worked part time. Public and academic librarians often work on weekends and evenings and may work on some holidays. School librarians usually have the same work and vacation schedules as teachers, including summers off. Librarians in special libraries, such as law or corporate libraries, typically work normal business hours but may need to work longer hours to help meet deadlines.

Job Outlook

Librarians
Percent change in employment, projected 2010-20

Education, Training, and Library Occupations	15%
Total, All Occupations	14%
Librarians	7%

Note: All Occupations includes all occupations in the U.S. Economy.
Source: U.S. Bureau of Labor Statistics, Employment Projections program

Employment of librarians is expected to grow by 7 percent from 2010 to 2020, slower than the average for all occupations.

There will continue to be a need for librarians to manage libraries and staff and help patrons find information. As electronic resources become more common, patrons and support staff will be more comfortable using them, so fewer librarians will be needed for assistance. However, the increased availability of electronic information is also expected to increase the demand for librarians in research and special libraries, where they will be needed to help sort through the large amount of available information.

Budget limitations, especially in local government and educational services, may slow demand for librarians. Some libraries may close, reduce the size of their staff, or focus on hiring library technicians and assistants, who can fulfill some librarian duties at a lower cost.

Job Prospects

Jobseekers may face strong competition for jobs, especially early in the decade, as many people with master's degrees in library science compete for a limited number of available positions. Later in the decade, prospects should be better as older library workers retire and population growth generates openings.

Even though people with a master's in library science may have trouble finding a job as a librarian, their research and analytical skills are valuable for jobs in a variety of other fields, such as market researchers or computer and information systems managers.

Employment projections data for librarians, 2010-20

Occupational Title	SOC Code	Employment, 2010	Projected Employment, 2020	Change, 2010-20	
				Percent	Numeric
Librarians	25-4021	156,100	166,900	7	10,800
SOURCE: U.S. Bureau of Labor Statistics, Employment Projections program					

Similar Occupations

This table shows a list of occupations with job duties that are similar to those of librarians.

Occupation	Job Duties	Entry-Level Education	Median Annual Pay, May 2010
Adult Literacy and GED Teachers	Adult literacy and General Education Development (GED) teachers instruct adults and youths who are out of school in basic skills, such as reading, writing, and speaking English. They also help students earn their GED or high school diploma.	Bachelor's degree	$46,530
Archivists	Archivists appraise, edit, and maintain permanent records and historically valuable documents. Many perform research on archival material.	Bachelor's degree	$45,200
Curators, Museum Technicians, and Conservators	Curators oversee collections, such as artwork and historic items, and may conduct public service activities for an institution. Museum technicians and conservators prepare and restore objects and documents in museum collections and exhibits.	See How to Become One	$42,310
High School Teachers	High school teachers help prepare students for life after graduation. They teach academic lessons and various skills that students will need to attend college and to enter the job market.	Bachelor's degree	$53,230
Kindergarten and Elementary School Teachers	Kindergarten and elementary school teachers prepare younger students for future schooling by teaching them the basics of subjects such as math and reading.	Bachelor's degree	$51,380
Library Technicians and Assistants	Library technicians and assistants help librarians acquire, prepare, and organize materials. They also do other tasks that are needed to run a library.	See How to Become One	$26,330
Middle School Teachers	Middle school teachers educate students, most of whom are in sixth through eighth grades. They help students build on the fundamentals they learned in elementary school and prepare them for the more difficult lessons they will learn in high school.	Bachelor's degree	$51,960

Contacts for More Information

For more information about librarians, including accredited library education programs, visit American Library Association

For information about medical librarians, visit Medical Library Association

For information about law librarians, visit American Association of Law Libraries

For information about many different types of special librarians, visit Special Libraries Association

Suggested citation:

Bureau of Labor Statistics, U.S. Department of Labor, Occupational Outlook Handbook, 2012-13 Edition, Librarians, on the Internet at http://www.bls.gov/ooh/education-training-and-library/librarians.htm .

Library Technicians and Assistants

Quick Facts: Library Technicians and Assistants	
2010 Median Pay	$26,330 per year $12.66 per hour
Entry-Level Education	See How to Become One
Work Experience in a Related Occupation	None
On-the-job Training	See How to Become One
Number of Jobs, 2010	231,500
Job Outlook, 2010-20	10% (About as fast as average)
Employment Change, 2010-20	22,100

What Library Technicians and Assistants Do

Library technicians and assistants help librarians acquire, prepare, and organize materials. They also do other tasks that are needed to run a library.

Duties

Library technicians and assistants typically do the following:

- Loan library materials to patrons and collect returned materials
- Sort and reshelve returned books, periodicals, and other materials
- Organize and maintain library materials
- Handle interlibrary loans
- Register new patrons and issue library cards
- Answer patrons' questions and help them find library resources
- Maintain computer databases used to locate library materials
- Help plan and participate in special programs, such as used-book sales and outreach programs

Library technicians and assistants are usually supervised by a librarian. Library technicians may have more responsibilities than library assistants, such as administering library programs and overseeing lower-level staff.

Library technicians and assistants in smaller libraries have a broad range of duties. In larger libraries, they tend to specialize in a particular area. The list that follows gives examples of types of library technicians and assistants, based either on the type of library they work in or the type of work they do:

Library technicians and assistants loan library materials to patrons and collect returned materials.

School library technicians and assistants work in school libraries. They teach students how to find and use library resources, and they help teachers develop curriculum materials.

Special library technicians and assistants work in libraries in government agencies, corporations, law firms, and medical centers. They search library resources, compile bibliographies, and provide information on subjects of interest to the organization.

Braille-and-talking-books clerks help library patrons who have vision problems. They review patrons' lists of desired reading material, and locate large-type, Braille, or audiobook versions of the materials to give to patrons.

Bookmobile library technicians and assistants operate bookmobiles, which are trucks that are loaded with books. Bookmobiles travel to locations such as shopping centers, schools, and nursing homes to provide library materials in a more convenient manner. Library technicians and assistants drive the bookmobiles to each location and interact with patrons, answering questions, collecting returns, and checking out materials.

Work Environment

Library technicians and assistants held about 231,500 jobs in 2010. As shown below, about 53 percent worked for local governments in 2010.

State and local government, excluding education and hospitals	53%
Elementary and secondary schools; local	16
Colleges, universities, and professional schools; private	9
Colleges, universities, and professional schools; state	9
Junior colleges; state, local, and private	3

Except for those who work in bookmobiles, library technicians and assistants generally work indoors. They spend much of their time at desks or computer terminals. Most also spend time in the library stacks while cataloguing or reshelving books, a task that may require bending or stretching to reach the shelves.

Work Schedules

About 63 percent of clerical library assistants worked part time in 2010.

Library technicians and assistants in school libraries work during regular school hours.

Those in public or college libraries work weekends, evenings, and some holidays.

In corporate libraries, library technicians and assistants work normal business hours but may be asked to work overtime.

The schedule of library technicians and assistants who work in bookmobiles is dependent on the locations they serve.

How to Become a Library Technician or Assistant

Library technicians and assistants have varying levels of education. Some have only high school diplomas, while others have specialized postsecondary degrees. Library technicians are more likely to have to have formal education beyond high school.

Education

Most libraries prefer to hire library technicians who have a postsecondary certificate or an associate's degree. However, some smaller libraries might hire prospective technicians with only a high school diploma.

Courses required for an associate's degree or a certificate in library technology include acquisitions, cataloguing, circulation, and automated library systems.

Usually, library technicians who work in public schools must meet the same requirements as teacher assistants. For more information, see the profile on teacher assistants .

No formal education is required for library assistants. Most libraries prefer to hire assistants who have earned a high school diploma or General Educational Development (GED) certificate, but some will hire high school students.

Advancement

Library technicians and assistants can advance as they assume additional responsibilities in other areas of the library. Some eventually become supervisors and oversee daily library operations. To become a librarian, technicians and assistants need to earn a master's degree in library science.

Important Qualities

Computer skills. Library technicians and assistants use computers to help patrons research topics. Library technicians and assistants also use computers to maintain the library's database of collections.

Customer-service skills. Library technicians and assistants interact with and help library patrons. They must be friendly, polite, and willing to help.

Information-ordering skills. Library technicians and assistants must be able to understand the organizational systems that their library uses so that they can correctly classify and find materials.

Pay

Library Technicians and Assistants
Median hourly wages, May 2010

Total, All Occupations	$16.27
Library Technicians	$14.36
Library Technicians and Assistants	$12.66
Library Assistants, Clerical	$11.12

Note: All Occupations includes all occupations in the U.S. Economy.
Source: U.S. Bureau of Labor Statistics, Occupational Employment Statistics

The median hourly wage of library technicians was $14.36 in May 2010. The median wage is the wage at which half the workers in an occupation earned more than that amount and half earned less. The lowest 10 percent earned less than $8.64, and the top 10 percent earned more than $22.59.

The median hourly wage of clerical library assistants was $11.12 in May 2010. The lowest 10 percent earned less than $7.95, and the top 10 percent earned more than $17.98.

About 63 percent of clerical library assistants worked part time in 2010. Library technicians and assistants in school libraries work during regular school hours. Those in public or college libraries might work weekends, evenings, and some holidays. In corporate libraries, library technicians and assistants work normal business hours but may be asked to work overtime. The schedule of library technicians and assistants who work in bookmobiles is dependent on the locations they serve.

Job Outlook

Library Technicians and Assistants
Percent change in employment, projected 2010-20

Total, All Occupations	14%
Library Technicians and Assistants	10%
Library Assistants, Clerical	10%
Library Technicians	9%

Note: All Occupations includes all occupations in the U.S. Economy.
Source: U.S. Bureau of Labor Statistics, Employment Projections program

Employment of library technicians is expected to grow 9 percent from 2010 to 2020, slower than the average for all occupations.

Employment of library assistants is expected to grow 10 percent from 2010 to 2020, about as fast as the average for all occupations.

Electronic information systems have simplified some tasks, allowing them to be performed by technicians and assistants, rather than librarians. Library technicians and assistants earn less than librarians; so as more libraries face budget issues, technicians and assistants will be increasingly used as a lower cost method of providing library services.

Employment projections data for library technicians and assistants, 2010-20

Occupational Title	SOC Code	Employment, 2010	Projected Employment, 2020	Change, 2010-20	
				Percent	Numeric
Library Technicians	25-4031	115,400	125,600	9	10,200

SOURCE: U.S. Bureau of Labor Statistics, Employment Projections program

Similar Occupations

This table shows a list of occupations with job duties that are similar to those of library technicians and assistants.

Occupation	Job Duties	Entry-Level Education	Median Annual Pay, May 2010
Librarians	Librarians help people find information from many sources. They maintain library collections and do other work as needed to keep the library running.	Master's degree	$54,500
Medical Records and Health Information Technicians	Medical records and health information technicians organize and manage health information data by ensuring its quality, accuracy, accessibility, and security in both paper and electronic systems. They use various classification systems to code and categorize patient information for reimbursement purposes, for databases and registries, and to maintain patients' medical and treatment histories.	Postsecondary non-degree award	$32,350
Receptionists	Receptionists perform various administrative tasks, including answering telephones and giving information to the public and customers.	High school diploma or equivalent	$25,240
Teacher Assistants	Teacher assistants work under a teacher's supervision to give students additional attention and instruction.	High school diploma or equivalent	$23,220

Contacts for More Information

For general career information about library technicians and assistants, visit American Library Association

Suggested citation:

Bureau of Labor Statistics, U.S. Department of Labor, Occupational Outlook Handbook, 2012-13 Edition, Library Technicians and Assistants, on the Internet at http://www.bls.gov/ooh/education-training-and-library/library-technicians-and-assistants.htm .

Middle School Teachers

Quick Facts: Middle School Teachers	
2010 Median Pay	$51,960 per year
Entry-Level Education	Bachelor's degree
Work Experience in a Related Occupation	None
On-the-job Training	Internship/residency
Number of Jobs, 2010	641,700
Job Outlook, 2010-20	17% (About as fast as average)
Employment Change, 2010-20	108,300

What Middle School Teachers Do

Middle school teachers educate students, most of whom are in sixth through eighth grade. They help students build on the fundamentals they learned in elementary school and prepare them for the more difficult lessons they will learn in high school.

Duties

Middle school teachers typically do the following:

- Plan lessons that teach students subjects such as biology and history
- Assess students to evaluate their abilities, strengths, and weaknesses
- Teach students as an entire class or in small groups the lessons they have planned
- Grade students' assignments to monitor their progress
- Communicate with parents about their child's progress
- Work with individual students to challenge them and overcome their weaknesses
- Prepare students for standardized tests required by the state
- Develop and enforce classroom rules
- Supervise students outside of the classroom—for example, at lunchtime or during detention

Middle school teachers generally teach students from sixth to eighth grades. However, in some school districts, they may teach students as early as fourth grade or as late as ninth grade.

In many schools, middle school teachers are responsible for only some of the subjects their students learn throughout the day. For example, one teacher may be responsible for teaching English and social studies while another is responsible for teaching math and science.

Some middle school instructors teach special classes, such as art, music, or physical education.

Often, students change classrooms several times a day to attend lessons in different subjects. As a result, middle school teachers in these schools see several different classes of students throughout the day.

In some schools, middle school teachers teach all the subjects for one class of students the entire day.

In either type of school, teachers use time during the day when they do not have classes to plan lessons, grade assignments, or meet with other teachers and staff.

Some middle school teachers work in teams that teach the same group of students. These teachers meet to discuss students' progress and to plan future lessons.

In some schools, teachers of English as a second language (ESL) or English for speakers of other languages (ESOL) work exclusively with students who are learning English. These students are often referred to

Some middle school teachers specialize in teaching a particular subject, such as science or math.

as English language learners (ELLs.) ESL and ESOL teachers work with students individually or in groups to help them improve their English skills and to help the students with assignments for their other classes.

Middle school teachers also work with special education teachers to adapt lessons to the needs of students with learning disabilities and emotional or behavioral disorders who are taught in traditional classes and to monitor these students' progress. In some cases, middle school teachers may co-teach lessons with special education teachers. For more information, see the profile on special education teachers .

Some teachers maintain websites to communicate with parents about their students' assignments, upcoming events, and grades. For students, teachers may create websites or discussion boards to present information or to expand a lesson taught in class.

Some middle school teachers coach sports teams and advise student clubs and groups, whose practices and meetings frequently take place before or after school.

Work Environment

Middle school teachers held about 641,700 jobs in 2010.

The majority of middle school teachers work in public and private schools.

Most states have tenure laws, which mean that after a certain number of years of teaching satisfactorily (the probationary period), teachers have some job security.

Seeing students develop new skills and gain an appreciation for knowledge and learning can be very rewarding. However, teaching may be stressful. Some schools have large classes and lack important teaching tools, such as computers and up-to-date textbooks. Most teachers are held accountable for their students' performance on standardized tests, which can be frustrating. Occasionally, teachers must cope with unmotivated or disrespectful students.

In 2010, a large number of middle school teachers belonged to unions—mainly the American Federation of Teachers and the National Education Association.

Work Schedules

Middle school teachers generally work school hours when students are present. They may meet with parents, students, and other teachers before and after school. Teachers who coach sports or advise clubs generally do so before or after school. Teachers often spend time in the evenings and on weekends grading papers and preparing lessons.

Many work the traditional 10-month school year, with a 2-month break during the summer. Some teachers teach summer programs. Teachers in districts with a year-round schedule typically work 8 weeks in a row, are on break for 1 week, and have a 5-week midwinter break.

How to Become a Middle School Teacher

Middle school teachers must have a bachelor's degree. In addition, public school teachers must have a state-issued certification or license.

For information about teacher preparation programs and certification requirements in your state, contact the U.S. Department of Education .

Education

All states require public middle school teachers to have at least a bachelor's degree. Many states require middle school teachers to major in a content area, such as math or science. Other states require middle school teachers to major in elementary education. Those who major in a content area typically enroll in their university's teacher preparation program and take classes in education and child psychology.

Teacher education programs teach prospective middle school teachers how to present information to students and how to work with students of varying abilities and backgrounds. Programs typically include fieldwork, such as student teaching.

Some states require middle school teachers to earn a master's degree after receiving their teaching certification.

Teachers in private schools do not need to meet state requirements. However, private schools typically seek middle school teachers who have a bachelor's degree and a major in elementary education or a content area.

Licenses and Certification

All states require teachers in public schools to be licensed, or certified, as it is frequently referred to. Those who teach in private schools are not usually required to be licensed.

Certification of middle school teachers varies considerably from state to state. In some states, they are certified to teach elementary school grades, which are typically first through 6th grades or first through 8th grades. In other states, they are certified to teach middle school grades, which include 6th through 8th grades. Still other states provide middle school teachers with a secondary school or high school certification, which often includes 7th through 12th grades.

Requirements for certification also vary by state. However, all states require at least a bachelor's degree. They also require completing a teacher preparation program and supervised experience in teaching, which is typically gained through student teaching. Some states require a minimum grade point average.

States typically require candidates to pass a general teaching certification test, as well as a test that demonstrates their knowledge of the subject they will teach.

Teachers are often required to complete annual professional development classes to keep their license. Most states require teachers to pass a background check, and some states require teachers to complete a master's degree after receiving their certification.

All states offer an alternative route to certification for people who already have a bachelor's degree but lack the education courses required for certification. Some alternative certification programs allow candidates to begin teaching immediately after graduation, under the supervision of an experienced teacher. These programs cover teaching methods and child development. After they complete the program, candidates are awarded full certification.

Other programs require students to take classes in education before they can teach. Students may be awarded a master's degree after completing either of these programs. For more information about alternative certification programs, contact the National Center for Alternative Certification .

Advancement

Experienced teachers can advance to become mentors or lead teachers. In these positions, they often work with less experienced teachers to help them improve their teaching skills.

With additional education or certification, teachers may become school counselors, school librarians, or instructional coordinators. Some become assistant principals or principals, both of which generally require additional education in education administration or leadership. For more information, see the profiles on school and career counselors , librarians , instructional coordinators , and elementary, middle, and high school principals .

Important Qualities

Communication skills. Teachers must collaborate with other teachers and special education teachers. In addition, they need to discuss students' needs with parents and administrators.

Instructional skills. Middle school teachers need to be able to explain difficult concepts in terms that students can understand. In addition, they need to be able to get students engaged in learning and adapt lessons to each student's needs.

Patience. Working with students of different abilities and backgrounds can be difficult. Middle school teachers must be patient when students struggle with material.

Pay

Middle School Teachers

Median annual wages, May 2010

Middle School Teachers, Except Special and Career/Technical	$51,960
Education, Training, and Library Occupations	$45,690
Total, All Occupations	$33,840

Note: All Occupations includes all occupations in the U.S. Economy.
Source: U.S. Bureau of Labor Statistics, Occupational Employment Statistics

The median annual wage of middle school teachers was $51,960 in May 2010. The median wage is the wage at which half the workers in an occupation earned more than that amount and half earned less. The lowest 10 percent earned less than $34,990, and the top 10 percent earned more than $80,940.

Middle school teachers generally work school hours when students are present. They often spend time in the evenings and on weekends grading papers and preparing lessons. They may meet with parents, students, and other teachers before and after school. Teachers who coach sports or advise clubs generally do so before or after school.

Many work the traditional 10-month school year, with a 2-month break during the summer. Some teachers teach summer programs. Teachers in districts with a year-round schedule typically work 8 weeks in a row, are on break for 1 week, and have a 5-week midwinter break.

Job Outlook

Middle School Teachers

Percent change in employment, projected 2010-20

Middle School Teachers, Except Special and Career/Technical Education	17%
Education, Training, and Library Occupations	15%
Total, All Occupations	14%

Note: All Occupations includes all occupations in the U.S. Economy.
Source: U.S. Bureau of Labor Statistics, Employment Projections program

Employment of middle school teachers is expected to grow by 17 percent from 2010 to 2020, about as fast as the average for all occupations. Growth is expected because of both declines in student–teacher ratios and increases in enrollment. However, employment growth will vary by region.

From 2010 to 2020, the student–teacher ratio is expected to decline. This ratio is the number of students for each teacher in the school. A decline in the ratio means that each teacher is responsible for fewer students, and, consequently, more teachers are needed to teach the same number of students.

In addition, the number of students in middle schools is expected to increase over the coming decade, and the number of classes needed to accommodate these students will also rise. As a result, more teachers will be required to teach the additional classes of middle school students.

Although overall student enrollment is expected to grow, there will be some variation by region. Enrollment is expected to grow fastest in the South and West. In the Midwest, enrollment is projected to hold steady; the Northeast is projected to have declines. As a result, employment growth for middle school teachers is expected to be greater in the South and West than in the Midwest and Northeast.

Despite expected increases in enrollment, employment growth for middle school teachers will depend on state and local government budgets. When state and local governments experience budget deficits, they may lay off employees, including teachers. As a result, employment growth of middle school teachers may be somewhat reduced by state and local government budget difficulties.

Job Prospects

From 2010 to 2020, a significant number of older teachers is expected to reach retirement age. Their retirement will create job openings for new teachers. The short supply of teachers of English as a Second Language (ESL) and special education teachers will further result in job opportunities.

Middle school teachers with education or certifications to teach these specialties should have better job opportunities. For more information on middle school special education teachers, see the profile on special education teachers .

Supply and demand for middle school teachers are roughly in balance, meaning that there are about as many jobs as there are applicants. However, there is wide variation by region. Some regions of the country, such as the Northwest, are experiencing a surplus of teachers. Other regions, such as the Southeast, are experiencing a shortage. Furthermore, opportunities should be better in urban and rural school districts than in suburban school districts.

Employment projections data for middle school teachers, 2010-20

Occupational Title	SOC Code	Employment, 2010	Projected Employment, 2020	Change, 2010-20	
				Percent	Numeric
Middle School Teachers, Except Special and Career/Technical Education	25-2022	641,700	750,000	17	108,300
SOURCE: U.S. Bureau of Labor Statistics, Employment Projections program					

Similar Occupations

This table shows a list of occupations with job duties that are similar to those of middle school teachers.

Occupation	Job Duties	Entry-Level Education	Median Annual Pay, May 2010
Elementary, Middle, and High School Principals	Elementary, middle, and high school principals lead teachers and other members of school staff. They manage the day-to-day operations of elementary, middle, and high schools. They set goals and objectives and evaluate their school's progress toward meeting them.	Master's degree	$86,970
Career and Technical Education Teachers	Career and technical education teachers help students in middle school and high school develop career-related and technical skills. They help students explore or prepare to enter a particular occupation, such as one in auto repair, healthcare, business, or the culinary arts.	Bachelor's degree	$53,920
Childcare Workers	Childcare workers care for children when parents and other family members are unavailable. They care for children's basic needs, such as bathing and feeding. In addition, some help children prepare for kindergarten, and many help older children with homework.	High school diploma or equivalent	$19,300
High School Teachers	High school teachers help prepare students for life after graduation. They teach academic lessons and various skills that students will need to attend college and to enter the job market.	Bachelor's degree	$53,230
Instructional Coordinators	Instructional coordinators oversee school districts' curriculums and teaching standards. They work with teachers and school administrators to implement new teaching techniques to improve the quality of education.	Master's degree	$58,830
Kindergarten and Elementary School Teachers	Kindergarten and elementary school teachers prepare younger students for future schooling by teaching them the basics of subjects such as math and reading.	Bachelor's degree	$51,380
Librarians	Librarians help people find information from many sources. They maintain library collections and do other work as needed to keep the library running.	Master's degree	$54,500
Postsecondary Teachers	Postsecondary teachers instruct students in a wide variety of academic and vocational subjects beyond the high school level. They also conduct research and publish scholarly papers and books.	Doctoral or professional degree	$62,050
Preschool Teachers	Preschool teachers educate and care for children, usually ages 3 to 5, who have not yet entered kindergarten. They explain reading, writing, science, and other subjects in a way that young children can understand.	Associate's degree	$25,700
School and Career Counselors	School counselors help students develop social skills and succeed in school. Career counselors assist people with the process of making career decisions by helping them choose a career or educational program.	Master's degree	$53,380
Social Workers	There are two main types of social workers: direct-service social workers, who help people solve and cope with problems in their everyday lives, and clinical social workers, who diagnose and treat mental, behavioral, and emotional issues.	See How to Become One	$42,480
Special Education Teachers	Special education teachers work with students who have a wide range of learning, mental, emotional and physical disabilities. With students who have mild or moderate disabilities, they ensure that lessons and teaching strategies are modified to meet the students' needs. With students who have severe disabilities, they teach the students independent living skills and basic literacy, communication, and math.	Bachelor's degree	$53,220
Teacher Assistants	Teacher assistants work under a teacher's supervision to give students additional attention and instruction.	High school diploma or equivalent	$23,220

Contacts for More Information

For more information about teaching and becoming a teacher, visit U.S. Department of Education ,American Federation of Teachers , National Education Association

For more information about teacher preparation programs, visit National Council for Accreditation of Teacher Education , Teacher Education Accreditation Council

For more information about alternative certification programs, visit National Center for Alternative Certification

Suggested citation:

Bureau of Labor Statistics, U.S. Department of Labor, Occupational Outlook Handbook, 2012-13 Edition, Middle School Teachers, on the Internet at http://www.bls.gov/ooh/education-training-and-library/middle-school-teachers.htm .

Postsecondary Teachers

Quick Facts: Postsecondary Teachers	
2010 Median Pay	$62,050 per year
Entry-Level Education	Doctoral or professional degree
Work Experience in a Related Occupation	None
On-the-job Training	None
Number of Jobs, 2010	1,756,000
Job Outlook, 2010-20	17% (About as fast as average)
Employment Change, 2010-20	305,700

What Postsecondary Teachers Do

Postsecondary teachers instruct students in a wide variety of academic and vocational subjects beyond the high school level. They also conduct research and publish scholarly papers and books.

Duties

Postsecondary teachers typically do the following:

- Teach courses on a wide variety of subjects, such as chemistry, culinary arts, and nursing
- Work with students who are studying for a degree or a certificate or certification or are taking classes to improve their knowledge or career skills
- Develop a curriculum for their course and ensure that it meets college and department standards
- Plan lessons and assignments
- Assess students' progress by grading papers and tests
- Advise students about which classes to take and how to achieve their goals
- Stay informed about changes and innovations in their field
- Conduct research and experiments to advance knowledge in their field
- Supervise graduate students who are working toward doctoral degrees
- Publish original research and analysis in books and academic journals
- Serve on academic and administrative committees that review and recommend policies, make budget decisions, or advise on hiring and promotions within their department

Professors may teach a wide variety of subjects, such as English, math, and nursing.

Professors and other postsecondary teachers specialize in any of a wide variety of subjects and fields. Some teach academic subjects, such as English or philosophy. Others focus on career-related subjects, such as law, nursing, or culinary arts.

Postsecondary teachers work for different types of institutions, and their job duties vary with the kind of organization they work for.

Some postsecondary teachers are professors who work for large universities. In this setting, they often spend a large portion of their time conducting research and experiments and applying for grants to fund their research. Frequently, they spend less time teaching. Classes may be taught by graduate teaching assistants, who are supervised by a professor.

At colleges and universities, professors (together called the "faculty" of the school) are organized into departments based on the subject matter of their specialty, such as English, physics, Spanish, or music. They may teach one or more courses within that department, such as a mathematics professor teaching calculus, statistics, and a graduate seminar in a very specific area of mathematics.

Professors may teach large classes of several hundred students (usually with the help of several graduate teaching assistants), small classes of about 40 to 50 students, seminars with just a few students, or laboratories where students practice the subject matter. They may work with an increasingly varied student population as more part-time, older, and culturally diverse students are coming to postsecondary schools.

Professors keep up with developments in their field by reading scholarly articles, talking with colleagues, and participating in professional conferences. To gain tenure (a guarantee that a professor cannot be fired without just cause), they must do research, such as experiments, document analysis, or critical reviews, and publish their findings.

Other postsecondary teachers work in smaller colleges and universities or in community colleges. Postsecondary teachers in this setting often spend more time teaching classes and working with students. They may spend some time conducting research, but are not given as much time to devote to it.

Some postsecondary teachers work for online universities or teach online classes. They use websites to present lessons and information and to assign and accept students' work. They communicate with students by email and by phone and may never meet their students in person.

The amount of time postsecondary teachers spend teaching, serving on committees, and doing research also varies with their position in the university. Full-time professors, particularly those who have tenure, often are expected to spend more time on their research. They also may be expected to serve on more college and university committees. Part-time professors, often known as **adjunct professors**, spend most of their time teaching students.

Graduate teaching assistants, often referred to as **graduate TAs**, assist faculty by teaching or assisting with classes, while earning a graduate degree as a student. Some teaching assistants have full responsibility for teaching a course. Others help faculty members by grading papers, monitoring exams and quizzes, holding help sessions for students and conducting laboratory sessions. Graduate teaching assistants may work one-on-one with a faculty member, or, in large classes, they may be one of several assistants.

Work Environment

Postsecondary teachers held about 1.8 million jobs in 2010.

In 2010, 70 percent of postsecondary teachers worked for colleges, universities and professional schools and 22 percent worked for junior colleges.

Many postsecondary teachers find their jobs rewarding because they are surrounded by others who enjoy their subject. The opportunity to share their expertise with others also is appealing to many.

However, some postsecondary teachers must find a balance between teaching students and doing research and publishing their findings. This can be stressful, especially for beginning teachers seeking advancement in 4-year research universities.

Like college and university instructors, graduate teaching assistants usually have flexibility in their work schedules, but they also must devote time to their own academic coursework and studies. Work may be stressful, particularly when assistants have full responsibility for teaching a class.

Work Schedules

Classes are generally held during the day. Some are held on nights and weekends to accommodate students who have jobs or family obligations.

Many postsecondary teachers do not teach classes in the summer, but they use that time to conduct research or to travel. Other postsecondary teachers teach summer courses.

Postsecondary teachers' schedules are generally flexible. Postsecondary teachers need to be on campus to teach classes and keep office hours. Otherwise, they are free to set their schedule and decide when and where they will prepare for class and will grade assignments.

About 29 percent of postsecondary teachers worked part time in 2010. Some postsecondary teachers work part time at several colleges or universities.

Most graduate teaching assistants work part time while also studying for their degree. The number of hours they work may vary, depending on the institution and their particular assistantship.

How to Become a Postsecondary Teacher

Educational requirements vary with the subject taught and the type of educational institution. Most commonly, postsecondary teachers must have a Ph.D. However, a master's degree may be enough for some postsecondary teachers at community colleges. In technical and trade schools, work experience may be important for getting a postsecondary teaching job.

Education

Postsecondary teachers who work for 4-year colleges and universities are most often required to have a doctoral degree in their field. However, some schools may hire those who have a master's degree or those who are doctoral degree candidates for some specialties, such as fine arts, or for some part-time positions.

Doctoral programs generally take 6 years of full-time study after the completion of a bachelor's degree program. Included in the 6 years is time spent completing a master's degree and then writing a doctoral dissertation, which is a paper presenting original research in the student's field of study. Candidates usually specialize in a subfield, such as organic chemistry or European history.

Two-year colleges or career and technical schools also may hire those with a master's degree. However, in some fields, there are more applicants than available positions. In these situations, institutions can be more selective, and they frequently choose applicants who have a Ph.D. over those with a master's degree.

Postsecondary teachers who teach career and technical education courses, such as culinary arts or cosmetology, may not be required to have graduate-level education. Instead, schools may seek workers who have experience or certification in the field they wish to teach.

Work Experience

Some institutions prefer to hire professors who have teaching experience.

Some prospective professors gain experience by working as graduate teaching assistants—students who are enrolled in a graduate program and teach classes in the institution where they are enrolled.

Other postsecondary teachers gain experience by working in other professions and have full-time jobs in other settings, such as government agencies, private businesses, or nonprofit organizations.

Advancement

For postsecondary teachers, a major goal in the traditional academic career is attaining tenure—a guarantee that a professor cannot be fired without just cause. Tenure can take up to 7 years of moving up the ranks in tenure-track positions. The ranks are assistant professor, associate professor, and professor.

Tenure is granted through a review of the candidate's research, contribution to the institution, and their teaching. However, institutions are relying more heavily on limited-term contracts and part-time faculty, so tenure positions and positions on a "tenure track" are declining.

Some tenured professors advance to administrative positions, such as dean, or president. For information on deans and other administrative positions, see the profile on postsecondary education administrators . For more information about college and university presidents, see the profile on top executives .

Important Qualities

Communication skills. Postsecondary teachers need to write papers, give lectures, and serve on committees. To do so, they need good communication skills.

Critical-thinking skills. To challenge established theories and beliefs, conduct original research, and design experiments, postsecondary teachers need good critical-thinking skills.

Instructional skills. Postsecondary teachers need to be able to present information in a way that students will understand. They need to adapt to the different learning styles of their students and teach students who have little or no experience with the subject.

Writing skills. Most professors publish original research and analysis. Consequently, they need to be skilled writers.

Pay

Postsecondary Teachers
Median annual wages, May 2010

Postsecondary Teachers	$62,050
Education, Training, and Library Occupations	$45,690
Total, All Occupations	$33,840

Note: All Occupations includes all occupations in the U.S. Economy.
Source: U.S. Bureau of Labor Statistics, Occupational Employment Statistics

The median annual wage of postsecondary teachers was $62,050 in May 2010. The median wage is the wage at which half the workers in an occupation earned more than that amount and half earned less. The lowest 10 percent earned less than $30,720, and the top 10 percent earned more than $130,510.

Classes are generally held during the day. Some are held on nights and weekends to accommodate students who have jobs or family obligations. Many postsecondary teachers do not teach classes in the summer, but they use that time to conduct research or to travel. Other postsecondary teachers teach summer courses.

Postsecondary teachers' schedules are generally flexible. Postsecondary teachers need to be on campus to teach classes and keep office hours. Otherwise they are free to set their schedule and decide when and where they will prepare for class and will grade assignments.

About 29 percent of postsecondary teachers worked part time in 2010. Some postsecondary teachers work part time at several colleges or universities.

Most graduate teaching assistants work part time while also studying for their degree. The number of hours they work may vary, depending on the institution and their particular assistantship.

Job Outlook

Postsecondary Teachers
Percent change in employment, projected 2010-20

Postsecondary Teachers	17%
Education, Training, and Library Occupations	15%
Total, All Occupations	14%

Note: All Occupations includes all occupations in the U.S. Economy.
Source: U.S. Bureau of Labor Statistics, Employment Projections program

Employment of postsecondary teachers is expected to grow by 17 percent from 2010 to 2020, about as fast as the average for all occupations. Growth is expected as enrollments at postsecondary institutions continue to rise.

The number of people attending postsecondary institutions is expected to grow from 2010 to 2020. These students will seek higher education to gain the additional education and skills they need to meet their career goals. As more people enter colleges and universities, more postsecondary teachers will be needed to serve these additional students.

Employment is expected to grow fastest in for-profit institutions, which have experienced rapid enrollment growth over the past decade. This trend is expected to continue from 2010 to 2020.

However, despite expected increases in enrollment, employment growth in public colleges and universities will depend on state and local government budgets. When state and local governments have budget deficits, they may lay off employees. As a result, employment growth may be somewhat dampened by state and local government budget deficits.

Job Prospects

Colleges and universities are moving away from tenure-track positions and toward adjunct and part-time positions. As a result, there is a lot of competition for tenure-track positions. Still, opportunities should be available for part-time or adjunct professors.

In addition, a number of postsecondary teachers are expected to retire, creating opportunities for new people entering the field.

Some specialties, such as nursing and engineering, will likely experience better job prospects than others, such as those in the humanities.

Employment projections data for ostsecondary teachers, 2010-20

Occupational Title	SOC Code	Employment, 2010	Projected Employment, 2020	Change, 2010-20 Percent	Change, 2010-20 Numeric
Postsecondary Teachers	25-1000	1,756,000	2,061,700	17	305,700
SOURCE: U.S. Bureau of Labor Statistics, Employment Projections program					

Similar Occupations

This table shows a list of occupations with job duties that are similar to those of postsecondary teachers.

Occupation	Job Duties	Entry-Level Education	Median Annual Pay, May 2010
Anthropologists and Archeologists	Anthropologists and archeologists study the origin, development, and behavior of human beings, past and present. They examine the cultures, languages, archeological remains, and physical characteristics of people in various parts of the world.	Master's degree	$54,230
Biochemists and Biophysicists	Biochemists and biophysicists study the chemical and physical principles of living things and of biological processes such as cell development, growth, and heredity.	Doctoral or professional degree	$79,390
Chemists and Materials Scientists	Chemists and materials scientists study the structures, compositions, reactions, and other properties of substances. They use their knowledge to develop new and improved products, processes, and materials.	Bachelor's degree	$69,790
Career and Technical Education Teachers	Career and technical education teachers help students in middle school and high school develop career-related and technical skills. They help students explore or prepare to enter a particular occupation, such as one in auto repair, healthcare, business, or the culinary arts.	Bachelor's degree	$53,920
Economists	Economists study the production and distribution of resources, goods, and services.	Bachelor's degree	$89,450
Geographers	Geographers study the earth and its land, features, and inhabitants. They also examine phenomena such as political or cultural structures as they relate to geography. They study the physical or human geographic characteristics or both of a region, ranging in scale from local to global.	Bachelor's degree	$72,800
Historians	Historians research, analyze, interpret, and present the past by studying a variety of historical documents and sources.	Master's degree	$53,520

Microbiologists	Microbiologists study the growth, development, and other characteristics of microscopic organisms such as bacteria, algae, and fungi.	Bachelor's degree	$65,920
Political Scientists	Political scientists study the origin, development, and operation of political systems. They research political ideas and analyze the structure and operation of governments, policies, political trends, and related issues.	Master's degree	$107,420
Postsecondary Education Administrators	Postsecondary education administrators oversee student services, academics, and research at colleges and universities. Their job duties vary depending on the area of the college they manage, such as admissions, student life, or the office of the registrar.	Master's degree	$83,710
Sociologists	Sociologists study society and social behavior by examining the groups, cultures, organizations, social institutions, and processes that people develop.	Master's degree	$72,360
Zoologists and Wildlife Biologists	Zoologists and wildlife biologists study the characteristics and habitats of animals and wildlife.	Bachelor's degree	$57,430

Contacts for More Information

For more information about postsecondary teachers, visit Council of Graduate Schools , Association for Career and Technical Education

Suggested citation:

Bureau of Labor Statistics, U.S. Department of Labor, Occupational Outlook Handbook, 2012-13 Edition, Postsecondary Teachers, on the Internet at http://www.bls.gov/ooh/education-training-and-library/postsecondary-teachers.htm .

Preschool Teachers

Quick Facts: Preschool Teachers	
2010 Median Pay	$25,700 per year $12.35 per hour
Entry-Level Education	Associate's degree
Work Experience in a Related Occupation	None
On-the-job Training	None
Number of Jobs, 2010	456,800
Job Outlook, 2010-20	25% (Faster than average)
Employment Change, 2010-20	113,600

What Preschool Teachers Do

Preschool teachers educate and care for children, usually ages 3 to 5, who have not yet entered kindergarten. They explain reading, writing, science, and other subjects in a way that young children can understand.

Preschool teachers use play to teach children about the world.

Duties

Preschool teachers typically do the following:

- Prepare children for kindergarten by introducing concepts they will explore further in kindergarten and elementary school
- Work with children in groups or one on one, depending on the needs of children and the subject matter
- Plan and carry out a curriculum that targets different areas of child development, such as language, motor, and social skills
- Organize activities so children can learn about the world, explore interests, and develop talents
- Develop schedules and routines to ensure children have enough physical activity, rest, and playtime
- Watch for signs of emotional or developmental problems in children and bring problems to the attention of parents
- Keep records of the students' progress, routines, and interests, and keep parents informed about their child's development

Preschool teachers use play to teach children about the world. For example, they use storytelling and rhyming games to teach language and vocabulary. They may help improve children's social skills by having them work together to build a neighborhood in a sandbox or teach science and math by having children count when building with blocks.

Preschool teachers work with children from different ethnic, racial, and religious backgrounds. Teachers may include multicultural topics in their lessons to teach children about people of different backgrounds and cultures.

Work Environment

Preschool teachers held about 456,800 jobs in 2010. The following industries employed the most preschool teachers in 2010:

Child day care services	58%
Religious, grantmaking, civic, professional, and similar organizations	17
Elementary and secondary schools; state, local, and private	15

Many preschool teachers work in in formal childcare centers that have preschool classrooms. Others work in public and private schools. Still others work for charitable or religious organizations that have preschool programs or Head Start programs. Head Start programs receive federal funding for disadvantaged children between the ages of 3 and 5.

Seeing children develop new skills and gain an appreciation of knowledge and learning can be very rewarding. However, it can also be tiring to work with young, active children all day.

Work Schedules

Preschool teachers generally work during school hours, typically 9 a.m. to 3 p.m. Many work the traditional 10-month school year, which includes a 2-month break during the summer. Some preschool teachers may teach in summer programs. Teachers in districts with a year-round schedule typically work 8 weeks in a row, then have a break for 1 week, and have a 5-week midwinter break. Those working in day care settings often work the whole year.

How to Become a Preschool Teacher

Education and training requirements vary based on settings and state regulations. They range from a high school diploma and certification to a college degree.

Education

In childcare centers, preschool teachers generally are required to have a least a high school diploma and a certification in early childhood education. However, employers may prefer to hire workers with at least some postsecondary education in early childhood education.

Preschool teachers in Head Start programs must have at least an associate's degree. However, by 2013, at least 50 percent of preschool teachers in Head Start programs nationwide must have a bachelor's degree in early childhood education or a related field. As a result, Head Start programs may prefer to hire workers with a bachelor's degree. Those with a degree in a related field must have experience teaching preschool-age children.

In public schools, preschool teachers are generally required to have at least a bachelor's degree in early childhood education or a related field. Bachelor's degree programs teach students about children's development, strategies to teach young children, and how to observe and document children's progress.

Certification

Some states and employers require preschool teachers to have a nationally recognized certification such as the Child Development Associate (CDA) offered by the Council for Professional Recognition.

Requirements to earn the CDA include a high school diploma, experience in the field, and coursework. For more information about the CDA, contact the Council for Professional Recognition .

Some states recognize the Child Care Professional (CCP) designation offered by the National Child Care Association. Requirements to earn the CCP include a high school diploma, experience in the field, and continuing education courses. For more information about the CCP, contact the National Child Care Association.

Work Experience

Some states require preschool teachers to have some work experience in a childcare setting. The amount of experience necessary varies by state. Preschool teachers often start out as childcare workers or teacher assistants. For more information, see the profiles on childcare workers or teacher assistants .

Licenses

Many states require childcare centers to be licensed. To meet licensure requirements, their staff must pass a background check, have a record of immunizations, and meet a minimum training requirement.

In public schools, preschool teachers must be licensed to teach early childhood education, which covers preschool through third grade. Requirements vary by state, but they generally require a bachelor's degree and passing an exam to demonstrate competency. Most states require teachers to complete continuing education credits to maintain their license.

Advancement

Preschool teachers can work their way up from assistant teacher to teacher to lead teacher (who may be responsible for the instruction of several classes) to director of the preschool. For more information, see the profile on preschool and childcare center directors . Those with a bachelor's degree frequently are qualified to teach kindergarten through grade 3, in addition to preschool. Teaching positions at these higher grades typically pay more.

Important Qualities

Communication skills. Preschool teachers need good communication skills to tell parents and colleagues about students' progress. They need good writing and speaking skills to convey this information effectively.

Creativity. Preschool teachers must plan lessons that engage young students. In addition, they need to adapt their lessons to suit different learning styles.

Instructional skills. Preschool teachers need to be organized and able to explain difficult concepts in terms young children can understand.

Patience. Working with children can be frustrating, and preschool teachers should be able to respond calmly to overwhelming and difficult situations.

People skills. Preschool teachers must understand children's emotional needs and be able to develop good relationships with parents, children, and colleagues.

Pay

Preschool Teachers
Median annual wages, May 2010

Education, Training, and Library Occupations	$45,690
Total, All Occupations	$33,840
Preschool Teachers, Except Special Education	$25,700

Note: All Occupations includes all occupations in the U.S. Economy.
Source: U.S. Bureau of Labor Statistics, Occupational Employment Statistics

The median annual wage of preschool teachers was $25,700 in May 2010. The median wage is the wage at which half the workers in an occupation earned more than that amount and half earned less. The lowest 10 percent earned less than $17,200, and the top 10 percent earned more than $46,830.

In 2010, the median annual wages of industries employing the most preschool teachers were as follows:

Elementary and secondary schools	$39,470
Religious, grantmaking, civic, professional, and similar organizations	25,200
Child day care services	23,520

Preschool teachers generally work during school hours, typically 9 a.m. to 3 p.m. Many work the traditional 10-month school year, which includes a 2-month break during the summer. Some preschool teachers may teach in summer programs. Teachers in districts with a year-round schedule typically work 8 weeks in a row, are on break for 1 week, and have a 5-week midwinter break. Those working in day care settings often work the whole year.

Job Outlook

Preschool Teachers

Percent change in employment, projected 2010-20

Preschool Teachers, Except Special Education	25%
Education, Training, and Library Occupations	15%
Total, All Occupations	14%

Note: All Occupations includes all occupations in the U.S. Economy.

Source: U.S. Bureau of Labor Statistics, Employment Projections program

Employment of preschool teachers is expected to grow by 25 percent from 2010 to 2020, faster than the average for all occupations.

It is widely accepted that early childhood education is important for a child's intellectual and social development. As a result, there has been increasing demand for preschool programs, which is expected to create demand for preschool teachers.

In addition, the population of children ages 3 to 5 is expected to increase. Because children between these ages are typically enrolled in preschool, increases to that population will increase the demand for preschool teachers.

The following are the growth rates from 2010 to 2020 for the industries employing the most preschool teachers:

Child day care services	30%
Religious, grantmaking, civic, professional, and similar organizations	17
Elementary and secondary schools; state, local, and private	12

Job Prospects

Workers who have postsecondary education, particularly those with a bachelor's degree, should have better job prospects than those with less education. In addition, workers with the Child Development Associate (CDA) or Child Care Professional (CCP) credential should have better prospects than those without these certifications.

Employment projections data for preschool teachers, 2010-20

Occupational Title	SOC Code	Employment, 2010	Projected Employment, 2020	Change, 2010-20	
				Percent	Numeric
Preschool Teachers, Except Special Education	25-2011	456,800	570,400	25	113,600
SOURCE: U.S. Bureau of Labor Statistics, Employment Projections program					

Similar Occupations

This table shows a list of occupations with job duties that are similar to those of preschool teachers.

Occupation	Job Duties	Entry-Level Education	Median Annual Pay, May 2010
Childcare Workers	Childcare workers care for children when parents and other family members are unavailable. They care for children's basic needs, such as bathing and feeding. In addition, some help children prepare for kindergarten, and many help older children with homework.	High school diploma or equivalent	$19,300
High School Teachers	High school teachers help prepare students for life after graduation. They teach academic lessons and various skills that students will need to attend college and to enter the job market.	Bachelor's degree	$53,230
Kindergarten and Elementary School Teachers	Kindergarten and elementary school teachers prepare younger students for future schooling by teaching them the basics of subjects such as math and reading.	Bachelor's degree	$51,380
Middle School Teachers	Middle school teachers educate students, most of whom are in sixth through eighth grades. They help students build on the fundamentals they learned in elementary school and prepare them for the more difficult lessons they will learn in high school.	Bachelor's degree	$51,960
Preschool and Childcare Center Directors	Preschool and childcare center directors are responsible for all aspects of their program. They direct and lead staff, oversee daily activities, and prepare plans and budgets.	Bachelor's degree	$42,960

Special Education Teachers	Special education teachers work with students who have a wide range of learning, mental, emotional and physical disabilities. With students who have mild or moderate disabilities, they ensure that lessons and teaching strategies are modified to meet the students' needs. With students who have severe disabilities, they teach the students independent living skills and basic literacy, communication, and math.	Bachelor's degree	$53,220
Teacher Assistants	Teacher assistants work under a teacher's supervision to give students additional attention and instruction.	High school diploma or equivalent	$23,220

Contacts for More Information

For more information about early childhood education, visit National Association for the Education of Young Children

For more information about professional credentials, visit Council for Professional Recognition , National Child Care Association

Suggested citation:

Bureau of Labor Statistics, U.S. Department of Labor, Occupational Outlook Handbook, 2012-13 Edition, Preschool Teachers, on the Internet at http://www.bls.gov/ooh/education-training-and-library/preschool-teachers.htm .

Self-enrichment Teachers

Quick Facts: Self-enrichment Teachers	
2010 Median Pay	$36,340 per year $17.47 per hour
Entry-Level Education	High school diploma or equivalent
Work Experience in a Related Occupation	1 to 5 years
On-the-job Training	None
Number of Jobs, 2010	252,800
Job Outlook, 2010-20	21% (Faster than average)
Employment Change, 2010-20	52,800

What Self-enrichment Teachers Do

Self-enrichment teachers instruct in a variety of subjects that students take for fun or self-improvement, such as music and foreign languages. These classes generally do not lead to a degree or certification, and students take them voluntarily to learn new skills or gain understanding of a subject.

Duties

Self-enrichment teachers generally provide instruction in formal education programs, such as adult education programs, or they teach classes or lessons on their own as a private instructor.

Some self-enrichment teachers teach classes intended solely for recreation, such as scuba diving.

Self-enrichment teachers in formal education programs typically do the following:
- Create and teach lessons
- Propose new classes to program directors or their supervisor
- Determine class goals and objectives and develop a curriculum to meet those goals
- Evaluate the course and make any necessary improvements or changes
- Help advertise and promote classes

In formal education programs, self-enrichment teachers instruct students in a variety of subjects. Some teach academic subjects, such as literature, foreign languages, and history. Others teach classes that provide students with useful life skills, such as cooking, personal finance, and time management.

Self-enrichment teachers also teach classes intended solely for recreation, such as photography, pottery, and painting. Some teach classes offered through religious institutions, such as marriage preparation for couples or religious education for children.

Most self-enrichment classes are relatively informal. Some classes, such as pottery or sewing, may be largely hands-on. The instructor may demonstrate techniques and then observe and correct students as they try to do the activity themselves. Other classes, such as financial planning or religious studies, may include lectures or rely more heavily on group discussions.

Self-enrichment classes may last 1 or 2 days or several weeks. These brief classes may be introductory and generally focus on one topic. For example, a cooking class might focus on making bread. Others, such as language classes, last longer and help students progress with increasing levels of difficulty. Some self-enrichment classes introduce children and youth to activities such as drama. They may be designed to last from 1 week to several months.

Private self-enrichment teachers typically do the following:
- Advertise their services to find new students

- Locate a space to give lessons, which in some cases may be in the teacher's home
- Schedule lessons
- Teach students one-on-one or in small groups
- Determine rates and keep financial records

Private self-enrichment teachers often teach lessons in piano, guitar, singing, or other instruments. The instructor might work with the student for only 1 or 2 hours per week and then tell the student what to practice between lessons. Many instructors work with the same students each week for years.

All self-enrichment teachers must prepare lessons. The amount of time needed to prepare varies, depending on the subject and the length of the course.

Work Environment

Self-enrichment teachers held about 252,800 jobs in 2010.

About 14 percent of self-enrichment teachers are self-employed. Others work for community educational programs, religious organizations, or elementary and secondary schools.

The work setting varies, depending on the type of class being taught. Some teachers, such as horseback riding instructors or sailing instructors, spend most of their time outdoors. Others, such as citizenship instructors, may work in a classroom.

Work Schedules

It is common for self-enrichment teachers to have a full-time job in another occupation, but some have several part-time teaching assignments.

Many classes for adults are held in the evenings and on weekends to accommodate students who have jobs or family responsibilities. Classes for children are usually held after school or on weekends.

How to Become a Self-enrichment Teacher

There are no formal education requirements, but employers generally require self-enrichment teachers to have experience in the subject they teach. Some employers prefer workers who have teaching experience.

Education

In general, there are few educational or training requirements for self-enrichment teachers beyond having expert knowledge of the chosen subject. However, self-enrichment teachers may be required to have formal training in disciplines where educational programs are available, such as music or foreign languages.

Work Experience

Self-enrichment teachers generally need to have some experience in the field in which they teach. For example, a pottery teacher should have some experience in designing and making pottery. They can get this experience through formal work experience, but they can also get it through volunteer work or personal hobbies. Formal education programs may prefer to hire workers who have some teaching experience.

Important Qualities

Instructional skills. Self-enrichment teachers need to be able to present new information and demonstrate skills to students who sometimes have little experience or knowledge of the topic.

Organizational skills. Self-enrichment teachers, particularly those who are self-employed, need to be well-organized. They usually keep their own financial records, track their own income, and file taxes.

Patience. Working with students of different skill levels can be difficult, so self-enrichment teachers need to be patient when students have trouble understanding or mastering a skill.

Pay

Self-enrichment Teachers
Median hourly wages, May 2010

Education, Training, and Library Occupations	$21.97
Self-Enrichment Education Teachers	$17.47
Total, All Occupations	$16.27

Note: All Occupations includes all occupations in the U.S. Economy.
Source: U.S. Bureau of Labor Statistics, Occupational Employment Statistics

The median hourly wage of self-enrichment teachers was $17.47 in May 2010. The median wage is the wage at which half the workers in an occupation earned more than that amount and half earned less. The lowest 10 percent earned less than $9.03 and the top 10 percent earned more than $33.92.

It is common for teachers to have a full-time job in another occupation, but some have several part-time teaching assignments. Part-time instructors are usually paid for each class that they teach and receive few benefits.

Many classes for adults are held in the evenings and on weekends to accommodate students with jobs or family responsibilities. Classes for children are usually held after school or on weekends.

Job Outlook

Self-enrichment Teachers
Percent change in employment, projected 2010-20

Self-Enrichment Education Teachers	21%
Education, Training, and Library Occupations	15%
Total, All Occupations	14%

Note: All Occupations includes all occupations in the U.S. Economy.
Source: U.S. Bureau of Labor Statistics, Employment Projections program

Employment of the self-enrichment teachers is expected to grow by 21 percent from 2010 to 2020, faster than the average for all occupations. Growth is expected as more people want to learn new hobbies and gain marketable skills.

From 2010 to 2020, adults and children are expected to continue seeking new hobbies and pastimes and will take classes to learn these skills. Self-enrichment teachers will be needed to teach these classes.

In addition, more people will seek to gain skills to make themselves more attractive to prospective employers. Some self-enrichment teachers offer instruction in foreign languages, computer programming, public speaking, and many other subjects that help workers gain marketable skills. People are increasingly taking courses to improve their job skills, which will create more demand for self-enrichment teachers.

Employment projections data for self-enrichment teachers, 2010-20

Occupational Title	SOC Code	Employment, 2010	Projected Employment, 2020	Change, 2010-20	
				Percent	Numeric
Self-Enrichment Education Teachers	25-3021	252,800	305,600	21	52,800
SOURCE: U.S. Bureau of Labor Statistics, Employment Projections program					

Similar Occupations

This table shows a list of occupations with job duties that are similar to those of self-enrichment teachers.

Occupation	Job Duties	Entry-Level Education	Median Annual Pay, May 2010
Athletes and Sports Competitors	Athletes and sports competitors participate in organized, officiated sports events to entertain spectators.	High school diploma or equivalent	$43,740
Coaches and Scouts	Coaches teach amateur and professional athletes the skills they need to succeed at their sport. Scouts look for new players, evaluating athletes' strengths and weaknesses as possible recruits. Many coaches also scout out new talent.	High school diploma or equivalent	$28,340
Craft and Fine Artists	Craft and fine artists use a variety of materials and techniques to create art for sale and exhibition. Craft artists create handmade objects, such as pottery, glassware, textiles, or other objects that are designed to be functional. Fine artists, including painters, sculptors, and illustrators, create original works of art for their aesthetic value, rather than a functional one.	High school diploma or equivalent	$43,470
Dancers and Choreographers	Dancers and choreographers use movements to express ideas and stories in performances. There are many types of dance, such as ballet, modern dance, tap, and jazz.	High school diploma or equivalent	The annual wage is not available.
High School Teachers	High school teachers help prepare students for life after graduation. They teach academic lessons and various skills that students will need to attend college and to enter the job market.	Bachelor's degree	$53,230
Kindergarten and Elementary School Teachers	Kindergarten and elementary school teachers prepare younger students for future schooling by teaching them the basics of subjects such as math and reading.	Bachelor's degree	$51,380
Middle School Teachers	Middle school teachers educate students, most of whom are in sixth through eighth grades. They help students build on the fundamentals they learned in elementary school and prepare them for the more difficult lessons they will learn in high school.	Bachelor's degree	$51,960
Multimedia Artists and Animators	Multimedia artists and animators create animation and visual effects for television, movies, video games, and other media. They create two- and three-dimensional models and animation.	Bachelor's degree	$58,510
Musicians and Singers	Musicians and singers play instruments or sing for live audiences and in recording studios. They perform in a variety of styles, such as classical, jazz, opera, rap, or rock.	High school diploma or equivalent	The annual wage is not available.
Recreation Workers	Recreation workers design and lead leisure activities for groups in volunteer agencies or recreation facilities, such as playgrounds, parks, camps and senior centers. They may lead activities in areas such as arts and crafts, sports, games, music, and camping.	Bachelor's degree	$22,260

Contacts for More Information

The Handbook does not have contacts for more information for this occupation.

Suggested citation:

Bureau of Labor Statistics, U.S. Department of Labor, Occupational Outlook Handbook, 2012-13 Edition, Self-enrichment Teachers, on the Internet at http://www.bls.gov/ooh/education-training-and-library/self-enrichment-teachers.htm .

Special Education Teachers

Quick Facts: Special Education Teachers	
2010 Median Pay	$53,220 per year
Entry-Level Education	Bachelor's degree
Work Experience in a Related Occupation	None
On-the-job Training	Internship/residency
Number of Jobs, 2010	459,600
Job Outlook, 2010-20	17% (About as fast as average)
Employment Change, 2010-20	77,400

What Special Education Teachers Do

Special education teachers work with students who have a wide range of learning, mental, emotional, and physical disabilities. With students who have mild or moderate disabilities, they ensure that lessons and teaching strategies are modified to meet the students' needs. With students who have severe disabilities, they teach the students independent living skills and basic literacy, communication, and math.

Duties

Special education teachers typically do the following:

- Assess students' knowledge and skills to determine their strengths and needs
- Adapt, and collaborate with teachers to adapt, lessons to meet the needs of special education students
- Help develop Individualized Education Programs (IEPs), which outline the services and accommodations each student will receive
- Develop transition plans that outline services to help students as they graduate or move to a new school
- Ensure that students are receiving the services outlined in their IEPs
- Update IEPs throughout the school year to reflect students'

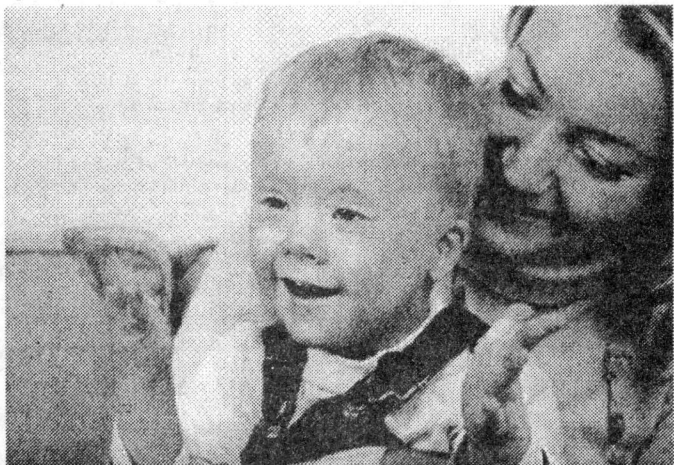

With students with mild or moderate disabilities, special education teachers ensure that lessons and teaching strategies are modified to meet students' needs and with students with severe disabilities, they teach students independent living skills and basic literacy, communication, and math.

progress and goals

- Meet with parents, teachers, counselors, and administrators to discuss students' progress
- Work with teacher assistants to ensure that they have the skills and information necessary to work with special education students
- Ensure that schools comply with requirements of the Individuals with Disabilities Education Act (IDEA)

Special education services are offered in a variety of ways.

Some special education teachers work exclusively in special education classes that include only students who have IEPs. In this setting, special education teachers plan and present lessons and adapt the lessons to meet each of the students' needs.

In settings with more inclusive models of special education, in which the students receiving special education services attend general education classes, special education teachers may spend a portion of the day teaching classes together with general education teachers. The special education teachers help present the information in a manner that is more easily understood by special education students.

They also serve as consultants to general education teachers to help them adapt lessons that will meet the needs of the special education students in their classes. Special education teachers may have students who visit them throughout the day to get extra help with particular subjects or lessons.

A team that includes special and general education teachers, counselors, parents, and, in some cases, the students themselves develop the individualized educational programs (IEPs). IEPs outline which services each special education student will receive, such as sessions with the school psychologist or counselor and class periods or times when the student will receive individual attention from special education teachers.

IEPs also may list services such as community mental health services, mentoring, and tutoring, which other organizations in the community provide. Special education teachers are responsible for ensuring that the students receive the services outlined in their IEPs.

Special education teachers work with students who have a wide variety of mental, emotional, physical, and learning disabilities. Some students need assistance only in a few subject areas, such as reading and math. Other students need help understanding how they learn and adapting study skills and strategies that best meet their needs.

Some special education teachers work with students who have physical and sensory disabilities, such as blindness and deafness, or with students who are wheelchair-bound. They also work with students who have autism spectrum disorders and with students who have emotional disorders, such as anxiety and depression.

Special education teachers work with infants to high school students. Students who have severe disabilities may work with a special education teacher until they turn 21 years old.

Special education teachers working with young children try to intervene as early as possible. Early intervention in the development of language, speech and social and motor skills allows children the best opportunity to improve in those areas.

With older students who have more severe disabilities, special education teachers help the students develop the skills necessary to live independently and find a job, such as balancing a checkbook and managing their time.

Work Environment

Special education teachers held about 459,600 jobs in 2010.

Special education teachers work in public and private schools. Some teach in public magnet and charter schools. Others teach in private religious and secular schools. Some work with young children in childcare centers.

A few special education teachers work in residential facilities where special education students live or tutor students who must stay at home or in the hospital. Some special education teachers who work with infants and toddlers go to the child's home and work together with the child's parents, teaching the parents how to help the child develop skills.

Helping special education students can be highly rewarding. It can also be quite stressful—emotionally demanding and physically draining.

Work Schedules

Special education teachers generally work school hours when students are present. They may meet with parents, students, and other teachers before and after school. In the evenings and on weekends, they often spend time grading papers, completing paperwork, and preparing lessons.

Many work the traditional 10-month school year, with a 2-month break during the summer. Some teachers may teach during summer programs. Teachers in districts with a year-round schedule typically work 8 weeks in a row, are on break for 1 week, and have a 5-week midwinter break.

How to Become a Special Education Teacher

Public school teachers are required to have a least a bachelor's degree and a state-issued certification or license. Private schools typically require teachers to have a bachelor's degree. Teachers in private schools are not required to be licensed or certified, but private schools may prefer to hire teachers who have a license. For information about teacher preparation programs and certification requirements in your state, contact the U.S. Department of Education.

Education

All states require public special education teachers to have at least a bachelor's degree. Some of these teachers major in elementary education or a content area, such as math or chemistry, and minor in special education. Others get a degree specifically in special education.

In a program leading to a bachelor's degree in special education, prospective teachers learn about the different types of disabilities and how to present information so that special education students will understand. These programs typically include fieldwork, such as student teaching. Some states require special education teachers to earn a master's degree in special education after earning their teaching certification.

Teachers in private schools do not need to meet state requirements. However, private schools typically seek teachers who have at least a bachelor's degree in special education.

Licenses

All states require teachers in public schools to be licensed. A license is frequently referred to as a certification. Those who teach in private schools are not required to be licensed.

Requirements for certification vary by state. However, all states require at least a bachelor's degree. They also require completing a teacher preparation program and supervised experience in teaching, which is typically gained through student teaching. Some states require a minimum grade point average.

Many states offer general special education licenses that allow teachers to work with students across a variety of disability categories. Others license different specialties within special education.

Teachers are often required to complete annual professional development classes to keep their license. Most states require teachers to pass a background check. Some states require teachers to complete a master's degree after receiving their certification.

Some states allow special education teachers to transfer their licenses from another state. However, some states require even an experienced teacher to pass their own licensing requirements.

All states offer an alternative route to certification for people who already have a bachelor's degree but lack the education courses required for certification. Some alternative certification programs allow candidates to begin teaching immediately, under the close supervision of an experienced teacher.

These alternative programs cover teaching methods and child development. When they finish the program, candidates are awarded full certification. Other programs require students to take classes in education before they can start to teach. Students may be awarded a master's degree after completing either type of program. For more information about alternative certification programs, contact the National Center for Alternative Certification.

Advancement

Experienced teachers can advance to become mentor or lead teachers. Mentors and lead teachers often work with less experienced teachers to help them improve their teaching skills.

With additional education or certification, teachers may become school counselors, school librarians, or instructional coordinators. Some become assistant principals or principals. Both positions generally require additional degrees in education administration or leadership. For more information, see the profiles on school and career counselors , librarians , instructional coordinators and elementary, middle, and high school principals .

Important Qualities

Communication skills. Special education teachers must collaborate with teacher assistants and general education teachers. In addition, they must discuss students' needs with parents and administrators.

Creativity. Special education teachers need to think creatively to develop new ways to present information in a manner that meets the learning styles of the students they serve.

Critical-thinking skills. Special education teachers review and analyze data about students' progress, strengths, and weaknesses and use that information to develop strategies to help students learn.

Instructional skills. Special education teachers need to be able to explain difficult concepts in terms that students with learning disabilities can understand. In addition, they need to be able to get students engaged in learning and help other teachers adapt their content to special education students' needs.

Patience. Working with students of different abilities and backgrounds can be difficult. Special education teachers must be patient when students struggle with material.

People skills. Special education teachers must work with general education teachers, school counselors, administrators, and parents to develop Individualized Education Plans that are in the students' best interests. Managing the priorities of these different groups can be difficult, so special education teachers need to be able to build good working relationships.

Pay

Special Education Teachers
Median annual wages, May 2010

Special Education Teachers, Secondary School	$54,810
Special Education Teachers, Middle School	$53,440
Special Education Teachers	$53,220
Special Education Teachers, Preschool, Kindergarten, Elementary	$52,250
Total, All Occupations	$33,840

Note: All Occupations includes all occupations in the U.S. Economy.
Source: U.S. Bureau of Labor Statistics, Occupational Employment Statistics

The median annual wage of special education teachers was $53,220 in May 2010. The median wage is the wage at which half the workers in an occupation earned more than that amount and half earned less. The lowest 10 percent earned less than $35,580, and the top 10 percent earned more than $83,410.

The median annual wages for special education teachers by grade level in May 2010 were as follows:
- $54,810 for high school special education teachers
- $53,440 for middle school special education teachers
- $52,250 for preschool, kindergarten and elementary school special education teachers

Special education teachers generally work school hours when students are present. They may meet with parents, students, and other teachers before and after school. In the evenings and on weekends, they often spend time grading papers, completing paperwork, and preparing lessons.

Many work the traditional 10-month school year, with a 2-month break during the summer. Some teachers may teach during summer programs. Teachers in districts with a year-round schedule typically work 8 weeks in a row, are on break for 1 week, and have a 5-week midwinter break.

Job Outlook

Special Education Teachers
Percent change in employment, projected 2010-20

Special Education Teachers, Preschool, Kindergarten, Elementary	21%
Special Education Teachers, Middle School	20%
Special Education Teachers	17%
Total, All Occupations	14%
Special Education Teachers, Secondary School	7%

Note: All Occupations includes all occupations in the U.S. Economy.
Source: U.S. Bureau of Labor Statistics, Employment Projections program

Employment of special education teachers is expected to grow by 17 percent from 2010 to 2020, about as fast as the average for all occupations. Growth is expected because of increasing enrollment and continued demand for special education services.

From 2010 to 2020, overall enrollment is expected to grow in elementary and secondary schools, increasing the number of students receiving special education services. However, enrollment growth will not be equal across all grades.

Enrollment of special education students in kindergarten, elementary, and middle school grades is expected to grow faster than that in high school grades. As a result, employment of preschool, kindergarten, and elementary school special education teachers is expected to grow 21 percent from 2010 to 2020, faster than the average for all occupations, employment of middle school special education teachers is expected to grow 20 percent from 2010 to 2020, faster than the average for all occupations, and employment of high school special education teachers is expected to grow by 7 percent from 2010 to 2020, slower than the average for all occupations.

Along with enrollment growth, continued demand for special education services is expected.

Children with special needs are being identified earlier, increasing the need for special education teachers for young children. Early identification is important because early intervention is essential in educating children who have special needs.

Laws emphasizing training and employment for people with disabilities are expected to lead to some job growth for special education teachers, as are new higher standards for high school graduation. More parents are expected to seek special services for children who have difficulty meeting the higher standards required of students.

Students will need the services of special education teachers to adapt lessons to their different learning styles and needs. Furthermore, general education teachers will need the help of special education teachers to learn how to present information to students who have learning disabilities.

Although overall student enrollment is expected to grow, there will be some variation by region. Enrollment is expected to grow fastest in the South and West. In the Midwest, enrollment is expected to hold steady, and the Northeast is projected to have declines. As a result, employment growth for special education teachers is expected to be faster in the South and West than in the Midwest and Northeast.

However, despite expected increases in enrollment, employment growth for special education teachers will depend on state and local government budgets. When state and local governments experience budget deficits, they may lay off employees, including teachers. As a result, employment growth of special education teachers may be somewhat reduced by state and local government budget deficits.

Job Prospects

From 2010 to 2020, a significant number of older special education teachers are expected to reach retirement age. Their retirement will create job openings for new teachers.

In addition, many schools, particularly those in urban and rural areas, have difficulties recruiting and keeping special education teachers. As a result, special education teachers should have little difficulty finding employment.

Job opportunities may be better in certain specialties, such as early childhood intervention or working with students who have multiple disabilities, severe disabilities, or autism spectrum disorders.

Employment projections data for special education teachers, 2010-20

Occupational Title	SOC Code	Employment, 2010	Projected Employment, 2020	Change, 2010-20	
				Percent	Numeric
Special Education Teachers	—	459,600	537,000	17	77,400
Special Education Teachers, Preschool, Kindergarten, and Elementary School	25-2041	222,800	270,200	21	47,400
Special Education Teachers, Middle School	25-2053	98,100	117,900	20	19,900
Special Education Teachers, Secondary School	25-2054	138,700	148,800	7	10,100

SOURCE: U.S. Bureau of Labor Statistics, Employment Projections program

Similar Occupations

This table shows a list of occupations with job duties that are similar to those of special education teachers.

Occupation	Job Duties	Entry-Level Education	Median Annual Pay, May 2010
Audiologists	Audiologists diagnose and treat a patient's hearing and balance problems using advanced technology and procedures.	Doctoral or professional degree	$66,660
Career and Technical Education Teachers	Career and technical education teachers help students in middle school and high school develop career-related and technical skills. They help students explore or prepare to enter a particular occupation, such as one in auto repair, healthcare, business, or the culinary arts.	Bachelor's degree	$53,920
Childcare Workers	Childcare workers care for children when parents and other family members are unavailable. They care for children's basic needs, such as bathing and feeding. In addition, some help children prepare for kindergarten, and many help older children with homework.	High school diploma or equivalent	$19,300
Elementary, Middle, and High School Principals	Elementary, middle, and high school principals lead teachers and other members of school staff. They manage the day-to-day operations of elementary, middle, and high schools. They set goals and objectives and evaluate their school's progress toward meeting them.	Master's degree	$86,970
High School Teachers	High school teachers help prepare students for life after graduation. They teach academic lessons and various skills that students will need to attend college and to enter the job market.	Bachelor's degree	$53,230
Instructional Coordinators	Instructional coordinators oversee school districts' curriculums and teaching standards. They work with teachers and school administrators to implement new teaching techniques to improve the quality of education.	Master's degree	$58,830
Kindergarten and Elementary School Teachers	Kindergarten and elementary school teachers prepare younger students for future schooling by teaching them the basics of subjects such as math and reading.	Bachelor's degree	$51,380
Middle School Teachers	Middle school teachers educate students, most of whom are in sixth through eighth grades. They help students build on the fundamentals they learned in elementary school and prepare them for the more difficult lessons they will learn in high school.	Bachelor's degree	$51,960
Occupational Therapists	Occupational therapists treat patients with injuries, illnesses, or disabilities through the therapeutic use of everyday activities. They help these patients develop, recover, and improve the skills needed for daily living and working.	Master's degree	$72,320
Preschool Teachers	Preschool teachers educate and care for children, usually ages 3 to 5, who have not yet entered kindergarten. They explain reading, writing, science, and other subjects in a way that young children can understand.	Associate's degree	$25,700
Recreational Therapists	Recreational therapists plan, direct, and coordinate recreation programs for people with disabilities or illnesses. They use a variety of techniques, including arts and crafts, drama, music, dance, sports, games, and field trips. These programs help maintain or improve a client's physical and emotional well-being.	Bachelor's degree	$39,410
School and Career Counselors	School counselors help students develop social skills and succeed in school. Career counselors assist people with the process of making career decisions by helping them choose a career or educational program.	Master's degree	$53,380
Social Workers	There are two main types of social workers: direct-service social workers, who help people solve and cope with problems in their everyday lives, and clinical social workers, who diagnose and treat mental, behavioral, and emotional issues.	See How to Become One	$42,480
Teacher Assistants	Teacher assistants work under a teacher's supervision to give students additional attention and instruction.	High school diploma or equivalent	$23,220

Contacts for More Information

For more information about special education teachers, visit Council for Exceptional Children , Personnel Improvement Center

For more information about teaching and becoming a teacher, visit U.S. Department of Education , American Federation of Teachers , National Education Association

For more information about alternative certification programs, visit National Center for Alternative Certification

Suggested citation:

Bureau of Labor Statistics, U.S. Department of Labor, Occupational Outlook Handbook, 2012-13 Edition, Special Education Teachers, on the Internet at http://www.bls.gov/ooh/education-training-and-library/special-education-teachers.htm .

Teacher Assistants

Quick Facts: Teacher Assistants	
2010 Median Pay	$23,220 per year
Entry-Level Education	High school diploma or equivalent
Work Experience in a Related Occupation	None
On-the-job Training	Short-term on-the-job training
Number of Jobs, 2010	1,288,300
Job Outlook, 2010-20	15% (About as fast as average)
Employment Change, 2010-20	191,100

What Teacher Assistants Do

Teacher assistants work under a teacher's supervision to give students additional attention and instruction.

Duties

Teacher assistants typically do the following:

- Reinforce lessons presented by teachers by reviewing material with students one-on-one or in small groups
- Enforce school and class rules to help teach students proper behavior
- Help teachers with recordkeeping, such as tracking attendance and calculating grades
- Help teachers prepare for lessons by getting materials ready or setting up equipment, such as computers
- Supervise students in class, between classes, during lunch and recess, and on field trips

Teacher assistants are also called teacher aides, instructional aides, paraprofessionals, and paraeducators.

Generally, teachers introduce new material to students, and teacher assistants help reinforce the lessons by working with individual students or small groups of students. For example, they may help students learn research skills by helping them find information for reports.

Teacher assistants sometimes help teachers by grading tests and checking homework.

Teachers may seek feedback from assistants to monitor students' progress. Some teachers and teacher assistants meet regularly to discuss lesson plans and student development.

Some teacher assistants work exclusively with special education students who attend traditional classes.

Some teacher assistants work only with special education students. These students often are mainstreamed (attend regular classes), and teacher assistants help them understand the material and adapt the information to their learning style.

With students who have more severe disabilities, assistants may work with them both in regular classes and in separate classes. Teacher assistants may help these students with basic needs, such as feeding or personal hygiene. With young adults, they may help students with disabilities learn skills necessary for them to find a job after graduation.

Some teacher assistants work in specific locations in the school. For example, some work in computer laboratories, teaching students how to use computers and helping them use software. Others work as recess or lunchroom attendants, supervising students during these times of the day.

Although most teacher assistants work in elementary, middle, and high schools, others work in preschools and other childcare centers. Often, one or two assistants work with a lead teacher to give the individual attention that young children need. They help with educational activities. They also supervise the children at play and help with feeding and other basic care.

Work Environment

Teacher assistants held 1.3 million jobs in 2010. They work in both private and public elementary, middle, and high schools. They also work in preschools, childcare centers, community centers, and for religious organizations.

In 2010, 76 percent of teacher assistants were employed by elementary and secondary schools and 9 percent were employed by child day care services.

Teacher assistants may spend some time outside, when students are at recess or getting on and off the bus. Those who work with special education students may need to lift them.

Work Schedules

About 37 percent of teacher assistants work part time. Some ride the bus with students before and after school. Many do not work during the summer, but some work in year-round schools or help teachers in summer school.

How to Become a Teacher Assistant

Educational requirements, which vary by school district and position, range from a high school diploma to an associate's degree.

Education

Some districts require applicants to have a high school diploma; others require at least 2 years of college or an associate's degree. Teacher assistants in schools that have Title 1 programs (a federal program for schools with a large proportion of students from low-income households) must have at least a 2-year degree, or 2 years of college, or pass a state or local assessment.

Associate's degree programs for teacher assistants prepare the participants to develop educational materials, observe students, and understand the role of teachers in the classroom.

Most states require passing a skills-based test for instructional aides who work with special needs students.

Training

Schools may provide training for teacher assistants to acquaint them with the school district and school policies. Unions or professional associations may offer additional training. Teacher assistants must familiarize themselves with the material their students are covering in class. Doing so may require reviewing the topics with teachers to ensure that the assistants understand and can properly explain the information to students.

Important Qualities

Communication skills. Teacher assistants need to discuss students' progress with teachers, so they need to be able to communicate well.

Instructional skills. To reinforce lessons, teacher assistants must explain information to students in a way that meets each student's learning style.

Patience. Working with students of different abilities and backgrounds can be difficult. Teacher assistants must be patient with students who struggle with material.

People skills. Teacher assistants interact with a variety of people, including teachers, students, parents, and administrators. They need to develop good working relationships with the people they work with.

Pay

Teacher Assistants
Median annual wages, May 2010

Education, Training, and Library Occupations	$45,690
Total, All Occupations	$33,840
Teacher Assistants	$23,220

Note: All Occupations includes all occupations in the U.S. Economy.
Source: U.S. Bureau of Labor Statistics, Occupational Employment Statistics

The median annual wage of teacher assistants was $23,220 in May 2010. The median wage is the wage at which half the workers in an occupation earned more than that amount and half earned less. The lowest 10 percent earned less than $16,510, and the top 10 percent earned more than $36,130.

About 37 percent of teacher assistants work part time. Some ride the bus with students before and after school. Many do not work during the summer, but some work in year-round schools or assist teachers in summer school.

Job Outlook

Teacher Assistants
Percent change in employment, projected 2010-20

Teacher Assistants	15%
Education, Training, and Library Occupations	15%
Total, All Occupations	14%

Note: All Occupations includes all occupations in the U.S. Economy.
Source: U.S. Bureau of Labor Statistics, Employment Projections program

Employment of teacher assistants is expected to grow by 15 percent from 2010 to 2020, about as fast as the average for all occupations. Growth is expected to result from increases in student enrollment, continued demand for special education services, and increases in childcare and preschool enrollment.

Student enrollment in public and private elementary and secondary schools is expected to increase from 2010 to 2020. Because teacher assistants work directly with students, the increase in the number of students will spur demand for teacher assistants. In addition, there will be continued demand for special education services and, in turn, demand for teacher assistants who work with these students.

Furthermore, enrollment is expected to increase in childcare services and preschool programs, both of which employ teacher assistants. Increases in enrollment will increase demand for teacher assistants in these settings.

Job Prospects

In addition to job openings from employment growth, numerous openings will arise as assistants leave the job and must be replaced. Because this occupation requires limited formal education and has low pay, many workers transfer to other occupations or leave the labor force because of family responsibilities, to return to school, or for other reasons.

Job opportunities for teach assistants vary significantly by geography. Opportunities should be better in the South and West, which are expected to have rapid increases in enrollment, and in urban schools, which often have difficulty recruiting and keeping teacher assistants.

Employment projectons data for teacher assistants, 2010-20

Occupational Title	SOC Code	Employment, 2010	Projected Employment, 2020	Change, 2010-20	
				Percent	Numeric
Teacher Assistants	25-9041	1,288,300	1,479,300	15	191,100
SOURCE: U.S. Bureau of Labor Statistics, Employment Projections program					

Similar Occupations

This table shows a list of occupations with job duties that are similar to those of teacher assistants.

Occupation	Job Duties	Entry-Level Education	Median Annual Pay, May 2010
Career and Technical Education Teachers	Career and technical education teachers help students in middle school and high school develop career-related and technical skills. They help students explore or prepare to enter a particular occupation, such as one in auto repair, healthcare, business, or the culinary arts.	Bachelor's degree	$53,920

Childcare Workers	Childcare workers care for children when parents and other family members are unavailable. They care for children's basic needs, such as bathing and feeding. In addition, some help children prepare for kindergarten, and many help older children with homework.	High school diploma or equivalent	$19,300
High School Teachers	High school teachers help prepare students for life after graduation. They teach academic lessons and various skills that students will need to attend college and to enter the job market.	Bachelor's degree	$53,230
Kindergarten and Elementary School Teachers	Kindergarten and elementary school teachers prepare younger students for future schooling by teaching them the basics of subjects such as math and reading.	Bachelor's degree	$51,380
Library Technicians and Assistants	Library technicians and assistants help librarians acquire, prepare, and organize materials. They also do other tasks that are needed to run a library.	See How to Become One	$26,330
Middle School Teachers	Middle school teachers educate students, most of whom are in sixth through eighth grades. They help students build on the fundamentals they learned in elementary school and prepare them for the more difficult lessons they will learn in high school.	Bachelor's degree	$51,960
Occupational Therapy Assistants and Aides	Occupational therapy assistants and aides work under the direction of occupational therapists in treating patients with injuries, illnesses, or disabilities through the therapeutic use of everyday activities. They help these patients develop, recover, and improve the skills needed for daily living and working.	See How to Become One	$47,490
Preschool Teachers	Preschool teachers educate and care for children, usually ages 3 to 5, who have not yet entered kindergarten. They explain reading, writing, science, and other subjects in a way that young children can understand.	Associate's degree	$25,700
Special Education Teachers	Special education teachers work with students who have a wide range of learning, mental, emotional and physical disabilities. With students who have mild or moderate disabilities, they ensure that lessons and teaching strategies are modified to meet the students' needs. With students who have severe disabilities, they teach the students independent living skills and basic literacy, communication, and math.	Bachelor's degree	$53,220

Contacts for More Information

For more information about teacher assistants, visit National Education Association , American Federation of Teachers ,National Resource Center for Paraprofessionals

Suggested citation:

Bureau of Labor Statistics, U.S. Department of Labor, Occupational Outlook Handbook, 2012-13 Edition, Teacher Assistants, on the Internet at http://www.bls.gov/ooh/education-training-and-library/teacher-assistants.htm .

Entertainment and Sports Occupations

Actors

Quick Facts: Actors	
2010 Median Pay	$17.44 per hour
Entry-Level Education	Some college, no degree
Work Experience in a Related Occupation	None
On-the-job Training	Long-term on-the-job training
Number of Jobs, 2010	66,500
Job Outlook, 2010-20	4% (Slower than average)
Employment Change, 2010-20	2,600

What Actors Do

Actors express ideas and portray characters in theater, film, television, and other performing arts media. They also work at theme parks or for other live events. They interpret a writer's script to entertain or inform an audience.

Duties

Actors typically do the following:
- Read scripts and meet with agents and other professionals before accepting a role
- Audition in front of directors and producers
- Research their character's personal traits and circumstances to better portray them to an audience
- Memorize and rehearse their lines with other actors
- Discuss their role with the director and other actors to improve the overall performance of the show
- Perform the role, following the director's directions

Most actors struggle to find steady work, and few achieve recognition as stars. Some work as "extras," actors who appear on screen with no lines to deliver. Some do voiceover or narration work for animated features, audiobooks, or other electronic media.

In some stage or film productions, actors sing, dance, or play a musical instrument. For some roles, an actor must learn a new skill, such as horseback riding or stage fighting.

Most actors have long periods of unemployment between roles and often hold other jobs to make a living. Some actors teach acting classes in high schools, university drama departments, or community programs as a second job. For more information on workers who teach acting classes, see the profiles on self-enrichment teachers , high school

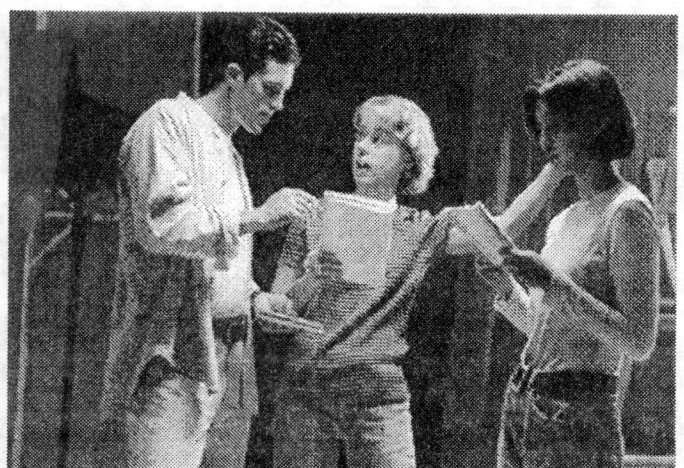

Actors spend a lot of time rehearsing their lines.

teachers , and postsecondary teachers .

Work Environment

Actors held about 66,500 jobs in 2010. Most work under pressure and are often under stress about finding their next job. Work assignments are usually short, ranging from 1 day to a few months, and actors often hold another job to make a living.

On location (where a movie is being made), and sometimes in a studio, they may need to perform in unpleasant conditions, such as bad weather or while wearing an uncomfortable costume.

Work Schedules

Work hours for actors are long and irregular. Evening, weekend, and holiday work is common. Few actors work full time, and many have variable schedules. Those who work in theater may travel with a touring show across the country. Actors in movies may also travel to work on location.

How to Become an Actor

Many actors enhance their skills through formal dramatic training. Especially in theater, many actors have a bachelor's degree, although it is not required. Actors usually learn some of their skills on the job; therefore, long-term training is common.

Education

Although some people succeed in acting without getting a formal education, most actors acquire some formal training through an acting conservatory or a university drama or theater arts program. Students can take college classes in drama or filmmaking to prepare for a career as an actor. Classes in dance or music may help as well. Actors who do not get a college degree may take acting or film classes to learn their craft. Community colleges, acting conservatories, and private film schools offer these classes. Many community theaters also have education programs. A bachelor's of arts degree in theater is becoming more common among stage actors.

Training

It takes many years of practice to develop the skills needed to be successful, and actors never truly finish training. They work to improve their acting skills throughout their career. Many actors continue to train through workshops or mentoring by a drama coach.

Every role is different, and an actor may need to learn something new each time. For example, a role may require learning how to sing or dance, or an actor may have to learn a foreign accent or how to play an instrument or a sport.

Many aspiring actors participate in high school, college, and local community plays. In television and film, actors usually start out in smaller roles or independent movies and work their way up to bigger productions.

Advancement

As an actor's reputation grows, he or she may work on bigger projects or in more prestigious venues. Some actors become producers or directors. For more information, see the profile on producers and directors .

Important Qualities

Creativity. Actors interpret their characters' feelings and motives to portray the characters in the most believable way.

Memorization skills. Actors memorize many lines before filming begins or a show opens. Television actors often appear on camera and have little time to memorize scripts, which can be revised frequently or written moments before filming.

Persistence. Actors may audition for many roles before getting a job. They must be able to take rejection and keep going.

Physical stamina. Actors should be in good enough physical condition to endure heat from stage or studio lights and the weight of heavy costumes. They may work long hours, including more than one performance a day, and they must do so without getting overly tired.

Reading skills. When looking for a new role, actors read many scripts and must be able to interpret how a writer has described their character.

Speaking skills. Actors, particularly stage actors, must be able to say their lines clearly, project their voice, and pronounce words so that the audience understands them.

In addition to these qualities, actors usually must be physically coordinated to perform predetermined, sometimes complex movements with other actors to complete a scene.

Pay

Actors

Median hourly wages, May 2010

Entertainers and Performers, Sports and Related Workers	$17.93
Actors	$17.44
Total, All Occupations	$16.27

Note: All Occupations includes all occupations in the U.S. Economy.
Source: U.S. Bureau of Labor Statistics, Occupational Employment Statistics

The median hourly wage of actors was $17.44 in May 2010. The median wage is the wage at which half the workers in an occupation earned more than that amount and half earned less. The lowest 10 percent earned less than $8.58, and the top 10 percent earned more than $64.04 in May 2010.

Work hours for actors are long and irregular. Evening, weekend, and holiday work is common. Few actors work full time, and many have variable schedules. Those who work in theater may travel with a touring show across the country. Actors in movies may also travel to work on location.

Job Outlook

Actors

Percent change in employment, projected 2010-20

Entertainers and Performers, Sports and Related Workers	16%
Total, All Occupations	14%
Actors	4%

Note: All Occupations includes all occupations in the U.S. Economy.
Source: U.S. Bureau of Labor Statistics, Employment Projections program

Employment of actors is projected to grow 4 percent from 2010 to 2020, slower than the average for all occupations. Job growth in the motion picture industry will stem from continued strong demand for new movies and television shows. However, employment is not expected to keep pace with that demand.

Production companies are experimenting with new content delivery methods, such as mobile and online television, which may lead to more work for actors in the future. However, these delivery methods are still in their early stages, and it remains to be seen how successful they will be.

Actors who work in performing arts companies are expected to see slower job growth than those in film. Many small and medium-size theaters have difficulty getting funding. As a result, the number of performances is expected to decline. Large theaters, with their more stable sources of funding, should provide more opportunities.

Job Prospects

Actors face intense competition for jobs. Most roles, no matter how minor, have many actors auditioning for them. For stage roles, actors with a bachelor's degree in theater will have a better chance than those without one.

Employment projections data for actors, 2010-20

Occupational Title	SOC Code	Employment, 2010	Projected Employment, 2020	Change, 2010-20 Percent	Change, 2010-20 Numeric
Actors	27-2011	66,500	69,100	4	2,600

SOURCE: U.S. Bureau of Labor Statistics, Employment Projections program

Similar Occupations

This table shows a list of occupations with job duties that are similar to those of actors.

Occupation	Job Duties	Entry-Level Education	Median Annual Pay, May 2010
Dancers and Choreographers	Dancers and choreographers use movements to express ideas and stories in performances. There are many types of dance, such as ballet, modern dance, tap, and jazz.	High school diploma or equivalent	The annual wage is not available.
Film and Video Editors and Camera Operators	Film and video editors and camera operators record images that entertain or inform an audience. Camera operators capture a wide range of material for TV shows, motion pictures, music videos, documentaries, or news and sporting events. Editors construct the final productions from the many different images camera operators capture. They collaborate with producers and directors to create the final production.	Bachelor's degree	$45,490

High School Teachers	High school teachers help prepare students for life after graduation. They teach academic lessons and various skills that students will need to attend college and to enter the job market.	Bachelor's degree	$53,230
Multimedia Artists and Animators	Multimedia artists and animators create animation and visual effects for television, movies, video games, and other media. They create two- and three-dimensional models and animation.	Bachelor's degree	$58,510
Musicians and Singers	Musicians and singers play instruments or sing for live audiences and in recording studios. They perform in a variety of styles, such as classical, jazz, opera, rap, or rock.	High school diploma or equivalent	The annual wage is not available.
Producers and Directors	Producers and directors are in charge of creating motion pictures, television shows, live theater, and other performing arts productions. They interpret a writer's script to entertain or inform an audience.	Bachelor's degree	$68,440
Postsecondary Teachers	Postsecondary teachers instruct students in a wide variety of academic and vocational subjects beyond the high school level. They also conduct research and publish scholarly papers and books.	Doctoral or professional degree	$62,050
Announcers	Announcers present music, news, and sports and may provide commentary or interview guests about these topics or other important events. Some act as a master of ceremonies (emcee) or disc jockey (DJ) at weddings, parties, or clubs.	See How to Become One	$27,010
Self-enrichment Teachers	Self-enrichment teachers instruct in a variety of subjects that students take for fun or self-improvement, such as music and foreign languages. These classes generally do not lead to a degree or certification, and students take them voluntarily to learn new skills or gain understanding of a subject.	High school diploma or equivalent	$36,340
Set and Exhibit Designers	Set designers create sets for movie, television, theater, and other productions. They analyze scripts or other research documents to determine how many sets will be needed and how each set can best support the story. Exhibit designers create spaces to display products, art, or artifacts.	Bachelor's degree	$46,680

Contacts for More Information

For more information about actors, visit Screen Actors Guild , Actors Equity , National Endowment for the Arts

Suggested citation:

Bureau of Labor Statistics, U.S. Department of Labor, Occupational Outlook Handbook, 2012-13 Edition, Actors, on the Internet at http://www.bls.gov/ooh/entertainment-and-sports/actors.htm

Athletes and Sports Competitors

Quick Facts: Athletes and Sports Competitors	
2010 Median Pay	$43,740 per year
Entry-Level Education	High school diploma or equivalent
Work Experience in a Related Occupation	None
On-the-job Training	Long-term on-the-job training
Number of Jobs, 2010	16,500
Job Outlook, 2010-20	22% (Faster than average)
Employment Change, 2010-20	3,600

What Athletes and Sports Competitors Do

Athletes and sports competitors participate in organized, officiated sports events to entertain spectators.

Duties

Athletes and sports competitors typically do the following:

- Attend scheduled practices and training sessions to develop their skills
- Exercise and practice under the direction of coaches, sports instructors, or athletic trainers
- Keep the equipment they use in their sport in good condition
- Stay in the best physical condition by training and following special diets
- Take instructions from coaches and other sports staff regarding strategy and tactics
- Play or compete in their sport, obeying the rules of the sport
- Assess how they did after each event, identifying their strengths and weaknesses

Few people who dream of becoming a paid professional athlete beat the odds and make a full-time living from professional athletics. And when they do, professional athletes often have short careers with little job security.

When playing a game, athletes and sports competitors must understand the game strategies while obeying the rules and regulations of the sport. The events in which athletes compete include team sports, such as baseball, softball, hockey, and soccer, and individual sports,

Athletes and sports competitors participate in officiated sports events to entertain spectators.

such as golf, tennis, swimming, and skiing. The level of play varies greatly, where sometimes the best from around the world compete in events broadcast on international television.

Being an athlete involves more than competing in athletic events. Athletes spend many hours each day practicing skills and improving teamwork under the guidance of a coach or a sports instructor. They view videotapes to critique their own performances and techniques and to learn their opponents' tendencies and weaknesses so as to gain a competitive advantage.

Some athletes work regularly with strength trainers to gain muscle and stamina and to prevent injury. Many athletes push their bodies to the limit during both practice and play, so career-ending injury is always a risk; even minor injuries may put a player at risk of replacement.

Because competition at all levels is extremely intense and job security is always in question, many athletes train throughout the year to maintain excellent form and technique and peak physical condition. Very little downtime from the sport exists at the professional level.

Work Environment

Athletes and sports competitors held about 16,500 jobs in 2010. More than half were employed in the spectator sports industry.

Athletes and sports competitors who participate in competitions that are held outdoors may be exposed to all weather conditions of the season in which they play their sport. Additionally, they must travel to sporting events, which may include long bus rides or, in some cases, international air travel.

The following industries employed the most athletes and sports competitors in 2010:

Spectator sports	56%
Other amusement and recreation industries	16
Colleges, universities, and professional schools;state, local, and private	2
Promoters of performing arts, sports, and similar event	1

Work Schedules

Athletes and sports competitors often work irregular hours, including evenings, weekends, and holidays. They usually work more than 40 hours a week for several months during the sports season, if not most of the year.

Injuries

Athletes who play a contact sport—such as football or hockey—are highly susceptible to injuries. Because of this, many sports competitors wear pads, gloves, goggles, helmets, and other protective gear to safeguard against injury.

How to Become an Athlete or Sports Competitor

Athletes and sports competitors must have immense knowledge of their sport, which they usually get through years of experience at lower levels. A high school diploma is usually required.

Education and Training

Most athletes develop their skills by playing the sport at some level. Regardless of the level, they must have extensive knowledge of the way the sport is played, especially its rules, regulations, and strategies. They often learn by playing the sport in school or at a recreation center, with the help of instructors or coaches, or in a camp that teaches the fundamentals of the sport.

Athletes get their training in several ways. For most team sports, athletes gain experience by competing in high school and collegiate athletics or on club teams. Other athletes learn their sport by taking private or group lessons, such as in gymnastics or tennis.

Licenses and Certification

Some sports and localities require athletes and sports competitors to be licensed or certified to practice. For example, in drag racing, drivers need to graduate from approved schools to be licensed to compete in the various drag racing series. The governing body of the sport may revoke licenses and suspend players who do not meet the required performance, education, or training. In addition, athletes may have their licenses or certification suspended for inappropriate activity.

Advancement

For most athletes, turning professional is the biggest advancement. They often begin to compete immediately, although some may spend more time on the bench (as a reserve) to gain experience. In some sports, such as baseball, athletes may begin their professional career on a minor league team before moving up to the major leagues. Professional athletes generally advance in their sport by winning and achieving accolades, and in turn they earn a higher salary.

Important Qualities

Athleticism. Nearly all athletes and sports competitors must possess superior athletic ability to be able to compete successfully against opponents.

Concentration. Athletes and sports competitors must be extremely focused when competing. The difference between winning and losing can often be a result of a momentary lapse in concentration.

Decision-making skills. Athletes and sports competitors often must make split-second decisions. Football quarterbacks, for example, usually only have seconds to decide whether to pass the football or run with it.

Desire and dedication. Athletes and sports competitors must practice regularly to develop their skills and improve or maintain their physical conditioning. It often takes years to become successful, so athletes must be dedicated to their sport.

Hand-eye coordination. For many sports, including tennis and baseball, the need to gauge and strike a fast-moving ball is highly dependent on the athlete's hand-eye coordination.

Stamina. Endurance can benefit athletes and sports competitors, particularly in long-lasting sports competitions, such as marathons.

Teamwork. Because many athletes compete in a team sport, such as hockey or soccer, the ability to cooperate with teammates and work together as a cohesive unit is essential for success.

Many professional athletes are required to pass drug tests.

Pay

Athletes and Sports Competitors
Median annual wages, May 2010

Athletes and Sports Competitors	$43,740
Entertainers and Performers, Sports and Related Workers	$37,290
Total, All Occupations	$33,840

Note: All Occupations includes all occupations in the U.S. Economy.
Source: U.S. Bureau of Labor Statistics, Occupational Employment Statistics

The median annual wage of athletes and sports competitors was $43,740 in May 2010. The median wage is the wage at which half the workers in an occupation earned more than that amount, and half earned less. The lowest 10 percent earned less than $17,120, and the top 10 percent earned more than $166,400.

In May 2010, median annual wages in industries employing the largest numbers of athletes and sports competitors were as follows:

Promoters of performing arts, sports, and similar events	$51,000
Spectator sports	49,430
Colleges, universities, and professional schools	43,060
Other amusement and recreation industries	38,890

Athletes and sports competitors often work irregular hours, including evenings, weekends, and holidays. They usually work more than 40 hours a week several months during the sports season, if not most of the year.

Job Outlook

Athletes and Sports Competitors
Percent change in employment, projected 2010-20

Athletes and Sports Competitors	22%
Entertainers and Performers, Sports and Related Workers	16%
Total, All Occupations	14%

Note: All Occupations includes all occupations in the U.S. Economy.
Source: U.S. Bureau of Labor Statistics, Employment Projections program

Employment of athletes and sports competitors is expected to grow 22 percent from 2010 to 2020, faster than the average for all occupations. The continuing expansion of nontraditional or new professional and semiprofessional sports, including local and regional teams and leagues, is expected to spur demand for athletes and sports competitors.

Job Prospects

Competition for professional athlete jobs will continue to be extremely intense, with progressively more favorable opportunities in lower levels of competition. In major sports, such as basketball and football, only about 1 in 5,000 high school athletes become professionals in these sports.

The expansion of nontraditional sports may create some additional job opportunities. Most professional athletes' careers last only a few years because of debilitating injuries. Therefore, yearly replacement needs for these jobs is high, creating some job opportunities.

However, the talented young men and women who dream of becoming sports superstars greatly outnumber the number of openings.

Employment projections data for athletes and sports competitors, 2010-20

Occupational Title	SOC Code	Employment, 2010	Projected Employment, 2020	Change, 2010-20 Percent	Numeric
Athletes and Sports Competitors	27-2021	16,500	20,100	22	3,600
SOURCE: U.S. Bureau of Labor Statistics, Employment Projections program					

Similar Occupations

This table shows a list of occupations with job duties that are similar to those of athletes and sports competitors.

Occupation	Job Duties	Entry-Level Education	Median Annual Pay, May 2010
Coaches and Scouts	Coaches teach amateur and professional athletes the skills they need to succeed at their sport. Scouts look for new players, evaluating athletes' strengths and weaknesses as possible recruits. Many coaches also scout out new talent.	High school diploma or equivalent	$28,340
Fitness Trainers and Instructors	Fitness trainers and instructors lead, instruct, and motivate individuals or groups in exercise activities, including cardiovascular exercise (exercises for the heart and blood system), strength training, and stretching. They work with people of all ages and skill levels.	High school diploma or equivalent	$31,090
Recreation Workers	Recreation workers design and lead leisure activities for groups in volunteer agencies or recreation facilities, such as playgrounds, parks, camps and senior centers. They may lead activities in areas such as arts and crafts, sports, games, music, and camping.	Bachelor's degree	$22,260
Umpires, Referees, and Other Sports Officials	Umpires, referees, and other sports officials preside over competitive athletic or sporting events. They detect infractions and decide penalties according to the rules of the game.	High school diploma or equivalent	$22,840

Contacts for More Information

For more information about team and individual sports, visit National Collegiate Athletic Association , National Council of Youth Sports

National Federation of State High School Associations

For more information related to individual sports, refer to the organization that represents the sport.

Suggested citation:

Bureau of Labor Statistics, U.S. Department of Labor, Occupational Outlook Handbook, 2012-13 Edition, Athletes and Sports Competitors, on the Internet at http://www.bls.gov/ooh/entertainment-and-sports/athletes-and-sports-competitors.htm .

Coaches and Scouts

Quick Facts: Coaches and Scouts	
2010 Median Pay	$28,340 per year
Entry-Level Education	High school diploma or equivalent
Work Experience in a Related Occupation	None
On-the-job Training	Long-term on-the-job training
Number of Jobs, 2010	242,900
Job Outlook, 2010-20	29% (Much faster than average)
Employment Change, 2010-20	71,400

What Coaches and Scouts Do

Coaches teach amateur and professional athletes the skills they need to succeed at their sport. Scouts look for new players, evaluating athletes' strengths and weaknesses as possible recruits. Many coaches also scout out new talent.

Duties

Coaches typically do the following:

- Plan, organize, and conduct practice sessions
- Analyze the strengths and weaknesses of individual athletes and opposing teams
- Plan strategies and choose team members for each game
- Provide direction, encouragement, and motivation to prepare athletes for games
- Call plays and make decisions about strategy and player substitutions during games
- Plan and direct physical conditioning programs that enable athletes to achieve maximum performance
- Instruct athletes on proper techniques, game strategies, sportsmanship, and the rules of the sport
- Keep records of athletes' and opponents' performance
- Identify and recruit potential athletes; arrange for and offer incentives to prospective players

Scouts typically do the following:

Coaches and scouts instruct amateur and professional athletes, teaching them the fundamental skills of sports.

- Read newspapers and other news sources to find athletes to consider
- Attend games, view videotapes of the athletes' performances, and study statistics about the athletes to determine talent and potential
- Talk to the athlete's coach to see if the athlete has what it takes to be successful
- Report to the coach, manager, or owner of the team for which he or she is scouting
- Arrange for and offer incentives to prospective players

The following are examples of occupational specialties:

Coaches teach professional and amateur athletes the fundamental skills of individual and team sports. They hold training and practice sessions to improve the athletes' form, technique, skills, and stamina. Along with refining athletes' individual skills, coaches also are responsible for instilling in their players the importance of good sportsmanship, a competitive spirit, and teamwork.

Many coaches evaluate their opponents to determine game strategies and to establish specific plays to practice. During competition, coaches may call specific plays intended to surprise or overpower the opponent, and they may substitute players for optimum team chemistry and success.

Many high school coaches are primarily teachers of academic subjects who supplement their income by coaching part time. For more information, see the profile on high school teachers .

Coaches who work with athletes in individual sports are often called sports instructors rather than coaches.

Sports instructors teach professional and nonprofessional athletes individually. They instruct and train athletes in sports such as bowling, tennis, and golf. Because of the diversity of individual sports, instructors usually specialize in a single activity, such as weightlifting, scuba diving, or karate. Like coaches, sports instructors also hold daily practice sessions, assign specific drills, correct athletes' techniques, and devise a competitive game strategy.

Coaches and sports instructors sometimes differ in their approaches to athletes because of the focus of their work. For example, coaches manage the team during a game to optimize its chance for victory, while sports instructors often are not permitted to instruct their athletes during competition. Sports instructors spend more of their time with athletes working one-on-one, which permits them to design customized training programs for each individual.

Scouts evaluate the skills of both amateur and professional athletes. The scout acts as a sports intelligence agent, primarily seeking out top athletic candidates for the team he or she represents. At the professional level, scouts typically work for scouting organizations or as self-employed scouts. At the college level, the head scout often is an assistant coach, although freelance scouts may help colleges by reporting to coaches about exceptional players. They often seek talent by reading newspapers, contacting coaches and alumni, attending games, and studying videotapes of prospects' performances.

Work Environment

Coaches and scouts held about 242,900 jobs in 2010. About 19 percent were self-employed.

The following industries employed the most coaches and scouts in 2010:

Elementary and secondary schools	22%
Colleges, universities, and professional school	18
Other schools and instruction	15
Fitness and recreational sports centers	8
Civic and social organizations	3

Coaches and scouts who work outdoors may be exposed to all weather conditions of the season. Additionally, they often must travel to sporting events, usually taking long bus rides and, in some cases, flying internationally. This is particularly true for those in professional sports.

Coaches and scouts often work irregular hours, including evenings, weekends, and holidays. They usually work more than 40 hours a week for several months during the sports season, if not most of the year. Some high school coaches in educational institutions work part time, and they often coach more than one sport.

How to Become a Coach or Scout

Coaches and scouts must have immense knowledge of the game, which they usually get through their own experiences playing the sport at some level. Although some jobs require a bachelor's degree, some entry-level coaching positions require only experience as an athlete or competitor in the sport. Scouting jobs often require experience playing a sport at the college or professional level, which makes it possible to locate young talent.

Education and Training

Although there is no specific education requirement, head coaches at public secondary schools and sports instructors at all levels usually must have a bachelor's degree.

For high school coaching and sports instructor jobs, schools usually prefer, and are sometimes required, to hire teachers to take on these part-time jobs. If no suitable teacher is found, schools hire a qualified candidate from outside the school.

College coaches must usually have abachelor's degree. Degree programs specifically related to coaching include exercise and sports science, physiology, kinesiology, nutrition and fitness, physical education, and sports medicine. Some entry-level positions for coaches or instructors require only experience from participating in the sport or activity.

Scouting jobs often require experience playing a sport at the college or professional level. This familiarity makes it possible to spot young players who have exceptional athletic ability and skills.

Most scouts begin working as part-time talent spotters in a particular area or region.

Certification

Some sports and localities require coaches to be certified to practice. For example, most public high school coaches need to meet state requirements for certification to become a head coach. Certification, however, may not be required for coaching and sports instructor jobs in private schools. College coaches may be required to be certified. Certification often requires coaches to be a minimum age (at least 18 years old) and certified in cardiopulmonary resuscitation (CPR). Participation in a clinic, camp, or school is also usually required for certification.

For those interested in becoming scuba, tennis, golf, karate, or an instructor in another individual sport, certification is highly desirable and may be required. There are many certifying organizations specific to the various sports, and their requirements vary.

Part-time workers and those in smaller facilities are less likely to need formal education or training and may not need certification.

Advancement

Many coaches begin their careers as assistant coaches to gain the knowledge and experience needed to become a head coach. Large schools and colleges that compete at the highest levels require a head coach with substantial experience at another school or as an assistant coach. To reach the ranks of professional coaches, someone usually needs years of coaching experience and a winning record in the lower ranks or experience as an athlete in that sport.

Important Qualities

Communication skills. Because coaches instruct, organize, and motivate athletes, they must have excellent communication skills. They must effectively communicate proper techniques, strategies, and rules of the sport so every player on a team understands.

Decision-making skills. Coaches must choose the appropriate players to use at a given position at a given time during a game and find a strategy that yields the best chance for winning. Coaches and scouts also must be very selective when recruiting players from lower levels of athletics.

Dedication. Coaches must practice daily and direct their team and individual athletes to develop their skills and improve their physical conditioning. Coaches must, therefore, be dedicated to their sport, as it often takes years to become successful.

Interpersonal skills. Being able to relate to athletes may help coaches and scouts to foster positive relationships with their current players and to recruit potential players.

Leadership skills. Coaches must demonstrate good leadership skills to get the most out of athletes. They also must be able to motivate, develop, and direct young athletes.

Resourcefulness. Coaches must use talent on a team that will result in the best chances for winning. For example, a coach may change players during the game to meet the defensive needs of a team.

Pay

Coaches and Scouts
Median annual wages, May 2010

Total, All Occupations	$33,840
Athletes, Coaches, Umpires, and Related Workers	$28,390
Coaches and Scouts	$28,340

Note: All Occupations includes all occupations in the U.S. Economy.
Source: U.S. Bureau of Labor Statistics, Occupational Employment Statistics

The median annual wage of coaches and scouts was $28,340 in May 2010. The median wage is the wage at which half the workers in an occupation earned more than that amount, and half earned less. The lowest 10 percent earned less than $16,380, and the top 10 percent earned more than $63,720.

In May 2010, median annual wages in industries employing the largest numbers of coaches and scouts were as follows:

Colleges, universities, and professional schools	$39,750
Fitness and recreational sports centers	28,850
Other schools and instruction	25,150
Elementary and secondary schools	22,670
Civic and social organizations	21,150

Coaches and scouts often work irregular hours, including evenings, weekends, and holidays. They usually work more than 40 hours a week for several months during the sports season, if not most of the year. Some high school coaches in educational institutions work part time, and they often coach more than one sport.

Job Outlook

Coaches and Scouts

Percent change in employment, projected 2010-20

Coaches and Scouts	29%
Athletes, Coaches, Umpires, and Related Workers	28%
Total, All Occupations	14%

Note: All Occupations includes all occupations in the U.S. Economy.
Source: U.S. Bureau of Labor Statistics, Employment Projections program

Employment of coaches and scouts is expected to grow 29 percent from 2010 to 2020, much faster than the average for all occupations. A larger overall population will continue to participate in organized sports for entertainment, recreation, and physical conditioning, boosting demand for coaches and sports instructors.

Job growth also will be driven by the increasing number of retirees who are expected to participate more in leisure activities such as swimming, golf, and tennis. These retirees may require instruction.

Population growth is expected to lead to more schools, and more schools should result in more jobs for coaches and instructors. However, funding for athletic programs often is cut first when budgets become tight. Still, the popularity of team sports often enables shortfalls to be offset with help from fundraisers, booster clubs, and parents.

In colleges, most of the expansion is expected to be in women's sports.

Job Prospects

Those who have a degree or are state-certified to teach academic subjects should have the best prospects for getting coaching and instructor jobs at high schools. The need to replace the many high school coaches who change occupations or leave the labor force also will provide some jobs.

Coaches in girls' and women's sports may have better job opportunities and face less competition for positions.

Strong competition is expected for higher paying jobs at the college level and will be even greater for jobs in professional sports. Competition should also be strong for paying jobs as scouts, particularly for professional teams, because there are few available jobs.

Employment projections data for coaches and scouts, 2010-20

Occupational Title	SOC Code	Employment, 2010	Projected Employment, 2020	Change, 2010-20	
				Percent	Numeric
Coaches and Scouts	27-2022	242,900	314,300	29	71,400
SOURCE: U.S. Bureau of Labor Statistics, Employment Projections program					

Similar Occupations

This table shows a list of occupations with job duties that are similar to those of coaches and scouts.

Occupation	Job Duties	Entry-Level Education	Median Annual Pay, May 2010
Athletes and Sports Competitors	Athletes and sports competitors participate in organized, officiated sports events to entertain spectators.	High school diploma or equivalent	$43,740
Dietitians and Nutritionists	Dietitians and nutritionists are experts in food and nutrition. They advise people on what to eat in order to lead a healthy lifestyle or achieve a specific health-related goal.	Bachelor's degree	$53,250
Fitness Trainers and Instructors	Fitness trainers and instructors lead, instruct, and motivate individuals or groups in exercise activities, including cardiovascular exercise (exercises for the heart and blood system), strength training, and stretching. They work with people of all ages and skill levels.	High school diploma or equivalent	$31,090
High School Teachers	High school teachers help prepare students for life after graduation. They teach academic lessons and various skills that students will need to attend college and to enter the job market.	Bachelor's degree	$53,230
Kindergarten and Elementary School Teachers	Kindergarten and elementary school teachers prepare younger students for future schooling by teaching them the basics of subjects such as math and reading.	Bachelor's degree	$51,380
Middle School Teachers	Middle school teachers educate students, most of whom are in sixth through eighth grades. They help students build on the fundamentals they learned in elementary school and prepare them for the more difficult lessons they will learn in high school.	Bachelor's degree	$51,960
Postsecondary Teachers	Postsecondary teachers instruct students in a wide variety of academic and vocational subjects beyond the high school level. They also conduct research and publish scholarly papers and books.	Doctoral or professional degree	$62,050

Umpires, Referees, and Other Sports Officials	Umpires, referees, and other sports officials preside over competitive athletic or sporting events. They detect infractions and decide penalties according to the rules of the game.	High school diploma or equivalent	$22,840

Contacts for More Information

For more information about coaching and scouting for team and individual sports, visit American Football Coaches Association , National Association of Basketball Coaches , National Collegiate Scouting Association , Women's Basketball Coaches Association

Suggested citation:

Bureau of Labor Statistics, U.S. Department of Labor, Occupational Outlook Handbook, 2012-13 Edition, Coaches and Scouts, on the Internet at http://www.bls.gov/ooh/entertainment-and-sports/coaches-and-scouts.htm .

Dancers and Choreographers

Quick Facts: Dancers and Choreographers	
2010 Median Pay	$15.97 per hour
Entry-Level Education	High school diploma or equivalent
Work Experience in a Related Occupation	See How to Become One
On-the-job Training	Long-term on-the-job training
Number of Jobs, 2010	25,600
Job Outlook, 2010-20	18% (About as fast as average)
Employment Change, 2010-20	4,600

What Dancers and Choreographers Do

Dancers and choreographers use movements to express ideas and stories in performance. There are many types of dance, such as ballet, modern dance, tap, and jazz.

Duties

Dancers typically do the following:
- Audition for a part in a show or for a job with a dance company
- Learn complex dance movements that entertain an audience
- Spend several hours each day in rehearsals to prepare for their performance
- Study new and emerging types of dance
- Work closely with instructors or other dancers to interpret or modify choreography

There are many different types of dance, such as ballet (shown here), modern, tap, or jazz.

- Attend promotional events, such as photography sessions, for the production in which they are appearing

Dancers spend years learning dances and perfecting their skills. They normally perform as part of a group in a variety of settings, including ballet, musical theater, and modern dance companies. Many perform on TV or in music videos, where they also may sing or act. Many dancers perform in shows at casinos, theme parks, or on cruise ships.

Choreographers typically do the following:
- Audition dancers for a role in a show or with a dance company
- Choose the music that will accompany their dance routine
- Assist with costume design, lighting, and other artistic aspects of a show
- Teach complex dance movements that entertain an audience
- Study new and emerging types of dance to design more creative dance routines
- Help with the administrative duties of a dance company, such as budgeting

Choreographers create original dances and develop new interpretations of existing dances. They work in theaters, dance companies, or movie studios. During rehearsals, they typically demonstrate dance moves to instruct dancers in the proper technique. Some choreographers work with performers other than dancers. For example, the complex martial arts scenes in movies are arranged by choreographers who specialize in martial arts.

Some people with dance backgrounds become dance teachers. For more information, see the profiles on self-enrichment teachers and postsecondary teachers .

Work Environment

Dancers and choreographers held about 25,600 jobs in 2010. About 10 percent were self-employed.

About 40 percent of dancers work in performing arts companies, and about 78 percent of choreographers work in other schools and instruction, which include dance and fine arts schools.

Many dance companies tour for part of the year, and dancers and choreographers in those companies travel for months at a time.

Injuries

Dance takes a toll on a person's body, giving dancers one of the highest rates of nonfatal on-the-job injuries. Many dancers stop performing by their late thirties because of the physical demands dancing makes on the body. Nonperforming dancers may continue to work as a choreographer, director, or dance teacher. For more information on dance teachers, see the profiles on self-enrichment teachers and postsecondary teachers .

Work Schedules

Dancers' schedules vary, depending on where they work. Some spend most of the day in rehearsals and have performances at night, giving them long workdays. Some work part time at casinos, on cruise ships, or at theme parks. Although choreographers who work in dance schools may have a standard workweek when they are instructing students, they spend many hours on their own coming up with new dance routines.

How to Become a Dancer or Choreographer

Education and training requirements vary with the type of dancer; however, all dancers need many years of formal training. Nearly all choreographers began their careers as dancers.

Training

Many dancers begin training when they are very young and continue to learn throughout their careers. Ballet dancers begin training the earliest, usually between the ages of 5 and 8 for girls and a few years later for boys. Their training becomes more serious as they enter their teens, and most ballet dancers begin their professional careers by the time they are 18.

Leading dance companies sometimes have summer training programs from which they select candidates for admission to their regular full-time training programs.

Modern dancers normally begin formal training while they are in high school. They attend after-school dance programs and summer training programs to prepare for their career or for a college dance program.

Education

Many colleges and universities offer a bachelor's or master's degree in dance, typically through departments of theater or fine arts. The National Association of Schools of Dance accredits more than 70 dance programs. Most focus on modern dance but also include courses in jazz, ballet, hip hop, and other forms. Most entrants into college dance programs have previous formal training.

Even though it is not required, many dancers choose to earn a degree in an unrelated field to prepare for a career after dance, because dance careers are usually brief. Teaching dance in college, high school, or elementary school requires a college degree. Some dance studios or conservatories prefer instructors who have a degree, but may accept performance experience instead.

Work Experience

Nearly all choreographers began their careers as dancers. While working as a dancer, they study different types of dance and learn how to choreograph routines.

Advancement

Some dancers take on more responsibility by becoming a dance captain in musical theater or a ballet master/ballet mistress in concert dance companies, by leading rehearsals, or by working with less-experienced dancers when the choreographer is not at practice. Eventually, some dancers become choreographers.

Dancers and choreographers also may advance to become producers or directors. For more information, see the profile on producers and directors .

Important Qualities

Balance. Successful dancers must have excellent balance so they can move their bodies without falling or losing their sense of rhythm.

Creativity. Dancers need artistic ability and creativity to express ideas through movement. Choreographers also must have artistic ability and innovative ideas to create new and interesting dance routines.

Leadership skills. Choreographers must be able to direct a group of dancers to perform the routines that they have created.

Persistence. Dancers must commit to years of intense practice. They need to be able to accept rejection after an audition and continue to practice for a future role. Choreographers must keep studying and creating new works even if some of their routines are not successful.

Physical stamina. Dancers are often physically active for long periods, so they must be able to work for many hours without getting tired.

Teamwork. Most dance routines involve a group, so dancers must be able to work together to be successful.

In addition, dancers must be agile, flexible, coordinated, and musical.

Pay

Dancers and Choreographers
Median hourly wages, May 2010

Choreographers	$18.11
Total, All Occupations	$16.27
Dancers and Choreographers	$15.97
Dancers	$13.16

Note: All Occupations includes all occupations in the U.S. Economy.
Source: U.S. Bureau of Labor Statistics, Occupational Employment Statistics

The median hourly wage of dancers was $13.16 in May 2010. The median wage is the wage at which half the workers in an occupation earned more than that amount and half earned less. The lowest 10 percent earned less than $7.79, and the top 10 percent earned more than $30.43.

The median hourly wage of choreographers was $18.11 in May 2010. The lowest 10 percent earned less than $8.93, and the top 10 percent earned more than $34.22.

Dancers' schedules vary, depending on where they work. Some spend most of the day in rehearsals and have performances at night, giving them long workdays. Some work part time at casinos, on cruise ships, or at theme parks. Although choreographers who work in dance schools may have a standard workweek when they are instructing students, they spend many hours on their own coming up with new dance routines.

Job Outlook

Dancers and Choreographers
Percent change in employment, projected 2010-20

Choreographers	24%
Dancers and Choreographers	18%
Total, All Occupations	14%
Dancers	11%

Note: All Occupations includes all occupations in the U.S. Economy.
Source: U.S. Bureau of Labor Statistics, Employment Projections program

Employment of dancers is projected to grow 11 percent from 2010 to 2020, about as fast as the average for all occupations. Dance companies are not expected to add many jobs over the decade.

Generally, when one company disappears, a new one replaces it without any growth in the total number of companies.

On the one hand, a long-term trend in which the public appears to be losing interest in traditional dance also is slowing down the growth of dance companies. On the other hand, a growing interest in dance in pop culture may provide opportunities in fields outside of dance companies, such as on TV or in movies, casinos, or theme parks.

Employment of choreographers is projected to grow 24 percent from 2010 to 2020, faster than the average for all occupations. The growing interest in dance in pop culture is expected to lead more people to enroll in dance schools, and growing enrollment should create more jobs for choreographers. In addition, the number of dance schools is growing faster than the number of employees of dance schools. Because they are needed at all schools, choreographers may experience faster employment growth than other employees at dance schools.

Job Prospects

Dancers and choreographers face intense competition and the number of applicants is expected to vastly exceed the number of job openings.

Dancers who attend schools or conservatories associated with a dance company may have a better chance of finding work at that company. In addition, many choreographers recruit dancers from nationally accredited college programs.

Employment projections data for dancers and choreographers, 2010-20

Occupational Title	SOC Code	Employment, 2010	Projected Employment, 2020	Change, 2010-20	
				Percent	Numeric
Dancers and Choreographers	—	25,600	30,200	18	4,600
Dancers	27-2031	12,400	13,700	11	1,400
Choreographers	27-2032	13,200	16,400	24	3,200
SOURCE: U.S. Bureau of Labor Statistics, Employment Projections program					

Similar Occupations

This table shows a list of occupations with job duties that are similar to those of dancers and choreographers.

Occupation	Job Duties	Entry-Level Education	Median Annual Pay, May 2010
Actors	Actors express ideas and portray characters in theater, film, television, and other performing arts media. They also work at theme parks or for other live events. They interpret a writer's script to entertain or inform an audience.	Some college, no degree	The annual wage is not available.
Art Directors	Art directors are responsible for the visual style and images in magazines, newspapers, product packaging, and movie and television productions. They create the overall design and direct others who develop artwork or layouts.	Bachelor's degree	$80,630
Music Directors and Composers	Music directors (also called conductors) lead orchestras and other musical groups during performances and recording sessions. Composers write and arrange original music in a variety of musical styles.	Bachelor's degree	$45,970
Musicians and Singers	Musicians and singers play instruments or sing for live audiences and in recording studios. They perform in a variety of styles, such as classical, jazz, opera, rap, or rock.	High school diploma or equivalent	The annual wage is not available.
Postsecondary Teachers	Postsecondary teachers instruct students in a wide variety of academic and vocational subjects beyond the high school level. They also conduct research and publish scholarly papers and books.	Doctoral or professional degree	$62,050
Producers and Directors	Producers and directors are in charge of creating motion pictures, television shows, live theater, and other performing arts productions. They interpret a writer's script to entertain or inform an audience.	Bachelor's degree	$68,440
Self-enrichment Teachers	Self-enrichment teachers instruct in a variety of subjects that students take for fun or self-improvement, such as music and foreign languages. These classes generally do not lead to a degree or certification, and students take them voluntarily to learn new skills or gain understanding of a subject.	High school diploma or equivalent	$36,340
Set and Exhibit Designers	Set designers create sets for movie, television, theater, and other productions. They analyze scripts or other research documents to determine how many sets will be needed and how each set can best support the story. Exhibit designers create spaces to display products, art, or artifacts.	Bachelor's degree	$46,680

Contacts for More Information

For more information about dancers and choreographers, visit Dance USA ,Stage Director and Choreographer Society ,National Endowment for the Arts ,National Association of Schools of Dance

Suggested citation:

Bureau of Labor Statistics, U.S. Department of Labor, Occupational Outlook Handbook, 2012-13 Edition, Dancers and Choreographers, on the Internet at http://www.bls.gov/ooh/entertainment-and-sports/dancers-and-choreographers.htm.

Music Directors and Composers

Quick Facts: Music Directors and Composers	
2010 Median Pay	$45,970 per year $22.10 per hour
Entry-Level Education	Bachelor's degree
Work Experience in a Related Occupation	1 to 5 years
On-the-job Training	None
Number of Jobs, 2010	93,200
Job Outlook, 2010-20	10% (About as fast as average)
Employment Change, 2010-20	9,600

What Music Directors and Composers Do

Music directors (also called conductors) lead orchestras and other musical groups during performances and recording sessions. Composers write and arrange original music in a variety of musical styles.

Duties

Music directors typically do the following:

- Select musical arrangements and compositions to be performed for live audiences or recordings
- Prepare for performances by reviewing and interpreting musical scores
- Direct rehearsals to prepare for performances and recordings
- Choose guest performers and soloists
- Audition new performers or assist section leaders with auditions
- Practice conducting to improve technique
- Meet with potential donors and attend fundraisers

Music directors lead orchestras and other musical groups. They ensure that the musicians play with one coherent sound, balancing the timing, rhythm, and volume. Working with a variety of orchestras and musical groups, they give feedback to musicians and section leaders so that they can achieve the sound and style they want for the piece.

Music directors may conduct youth orchestras or orchestras at colleges and universities. Some work with orchestras that accompany dance and opera companies.

Composers typically do the following:

- Write original music that orchestras, bands, and other musical groups perform
- Arrange existing music into new compositions
- Write lyrics for music or work with a lyricist
- Meet with companies, orchestras, or other musical groups that are interested in commissioning a piece of music
- Study and listen to music of various styles for inspiration
- Work with musicians to record their music

Composers write music for a variety of musical groups and users. Some work in a particular style of music, such as classical, jazz, or rock. They also may write for musicals, operas, or other types of theatrical productions.

Some composers write scores for movies or television; others write jingles for commercials. Many songwriters focus on composing music for popular audiences. Some composers are hired by music publishers and producers to write music for bands and groups that are under contract with the company.

Some composers use instruments to help them as they write music. Others use software that allows them to hear a piece without musicians.

For more information about careers in music, see the profile on musicians and singers. Some music directors and composers work as self-enrichment teachers, giving private music lessons to children and adults. Others work as music teachers in elementary, middle, or high schools. For more information, see the profiles on self-enrichment teachers , kindergarten and elementary school teachers , middle school teachers and high school teachers .

Work Environment

Music directors and composers held about 93,200 jobs in 2010. About 38 percent of music directors and composers are self-employed.

Jobs for music directors and composers are found all over the country. However, many jobs are located in cities in which entertainment and recording activities are concentrated, such as New York, Los Angeles, and Chicago.

Music directors often work for religious organizations, frequently as choir directors. They also work in concert halls and recording studios. Music directors may spend a lot of time traveling to different performances.

Composers can work in offices, recording studios, or their own homes.

Work Schedules

Rehearsals and recording sessions are commonly held during business hours, but performances take place most often on nights and weekends. Because music writing is done primarily independently, composers may be able to set their own schedules.

How to Become a Music Director or Composer

Educational and training requirements for music directors and composers vary. A conductor for a symphony orchestra typically needs a master's degree, but a choir director may need a bachelor's degree. There are no educational requirements for those interested in writing popular music.

Education

A degree in music theory, music composition, or conducting is generally preferred for those who want to work as a conductor or classical composer. To enter these programs, applicants are typically required to submit recordings or audition in person or both.

These programs teach students about music history and styles, as well as composing and conducting techniques. Information on degree programs is available from the National Association of Schools of Music.

A bachelor's degree is typically required for those who want to work as a choir director.

There are no specific educational requirements for those interested in writing popular music. These composers usually find employment by submitting recordings of their compositions to bands, singers, and music and movie studios. They may seek representation by an agent, who helps them find employment and performance opportunities.

Music directors, also called conductors, lead orchestras and other musical groups during performances and recording sessions.

Work Experience

Music directors and composers typically begin their musical training as a child, learning to play an instrument or sing.

Music directors and composers who are interested in classical music may seek additional training through music camps and fellowships. These programs provide participants with classes, lessons, and performance opportunities.

Important Qualities

Discipline. Talent is not enough for most music directors and composers to find employment in this field. They must constantly practice and seek to improve their technique and style.

Musical talent. To become a music director or composer, one must have the talent to play, write, and conduct music.

People skills. Music directors and composers need to work with agents, musicians, and recording studios. Being friendly, respectful, open to criticism as well as praise, and enjoying being with others can help music directors and composers work well with a variety of people.

Perseverance. Attending auditions and submitting compositions can be frustrating because it may take many different auditions and submissions to find a job. Music directors and composers need determination and perseverance to continue attending auditions and

submitting work after receiving many rejections.

Pay

Music Directors and Composers Median annual wages, May 2010	
Music Directors and Composers	$45,970
Arts, Design, Entertainment, Sports, and Media Occupations	$42,870
Total, All Occupations	$33,840

Note: All Occupations includes all occupations in the U.S. Economy.
Source: U.S. Bureau of Labor Statistics, Occupational Employment Statistics

The median annual wage of music directors and composers was $45,970 in May 2010. The median wage is the wage at which half the workers in an occupation earned more than that amount and half earned less. The lowest 10 percent earned less than $21,720, and the top 10 percent earned more than $85,020.

Rehearsals and recording sessions are commonly held during business hours, but performances take place most often on nights and weekends. Because music writing is done primarily independently, composers may be able to set their own schedules.

Job Outlook

Music Directors and Composers Percent change in employment, projected 2010-20	
Total, All Occupations	14%
Arts, Design, Entertainment, Sports, and Media Occupations	13%
Music Directors and Composers	10%

Note: All Occupations includes all occupations in the U.S. Economy.
Source: U.S. Bureau of Labor Statistics, Employment Projections program

Employment of music directors and composers is expected to grow by 10 percent from 2010 to 2020, about as fast as the average for all occupations. Growth is expected from increases in demand for musical performances.

From 2010 to 2020, the number of people attending musical performances, such as symphonies and concerts, and theatrical performances, such as ballets and musical theater, is expected to increase. More music directors will be needed to lead orchestras for concerts and musical theater performances and to accompany ballet troupes and opera companies.

In addition, there will likely be an increased need for composers to write original music and arrange known works for performance. Composers are also expected to be needed to write film scores and music for television and commercials.

However, growth is expected to be limited, because orchestras, opera companies, and other musical groups have difficulty getting funds. Some music groups are nonprofit organizations that rely on donations and corporate sponsorships, in addition to ticket sales, to fund their work. During economic downturns, these organizations may have difficulty finding enough money to cover their expenses.

Job Prospects

Despite expected growth, strong competition for jobs is anticipated because of the large number of people who are interested in entering this field. In particular, there will be considerable competition for full-time positions. Those with exceptional musical talent and abilities should have the best opportunities. Many music directors and composers experience periods of unemployment or work in another occupation and attend auditions or write music outside of working hours.

Employment projections data for music directors and composers, 2010-20

Occupational Title	SOC Code	Employment, 2010	Projected Employment, 2020	Change, 2010-20 Percent	Numeric
Music Directors and Composers	27-2041	93,200	102,800	10	9,600

SOURCE: U.S. Bureau of Labor Statistics, Employment Projections program

Similar Occupations

This table shows a list of occupations with job duties that are similar to those of music directors and composers.

Occupation	Job Duties	Entry-Level Education	Median Annual Pay, May 2010
Actors	Actors express ideas and portray characters in theater, film, television, and other performing arts media. They also work at theme parks or for other live events. They interpret a writer's script to entertain or inform an audience.	Some college, no degree	The annual wage is not available.
Dancers and Choreographers	Dancers and choreographers use movements to express ideas and stories in performances. There are many types of dance, such as ballet, modern dance, tap, and jazz.	High school diploma or equivalent	The annual wage is not available.
High School Teachers	High school teachers help prepare students for life after graduation. They teach academic lessons and various skills that students will need to attend college and to enter the job market.	Bachelor's degree	$53,230
Kindergarten and Elementary School Teachers	Kindergarten and elementary school teachers prepare younger students for future schooling by teaching them the basics of subjects such as math and reading.	Bachelor's degree	$51,380
Middle School Teachers	Middle school teachers educate students, most of whom are in sixth through eighth grades. They help students build on the fundamentals they learned in elementary school and prepare them for the more difficult lessons they will learn in high school.	Bachelor's degree	$51,960
Musicians and Singers	Musicians and singers play instruments or sing for live audiences and in recording studios. They perform in a variety of styles, such as classical, jazz, opera, rap, or rock.	High school diploma or equivalent	The annual wage is not available.
Producers and Directors	Producers and directors are in charge of creating motion pictures, television shows, live theater, and other performing arts productions. They interpret a writer's script to entertain or inform an audience.	Bachelor's degree	$68,440
Postsecondary Teachers	Postsecondary teachers instruct students in a wide variety of academic and vocational subjects beyond the high school level. They also conduct research and publish scholarly papers and books.	Doctoral or professional degree	$62,050
Self-enrichment Teachers	Self-enrichment teachers instruct in a variety of subjects that students take for fun or self-improvement, such as music and foreign languages. These classes generally do not lead to a degree or certification, and students take them voluntarily to learn new skills or gain understanding of a subject.	High school diploma or equivalent	$36,340
Writers and Authors	Writers and authors develop original written content for advertisements, books, magazines, movie and television scripts, songs, and online publications.	Bachelor's degree	$55,420

Contacts for More Information

For information about music degree programs, visit National Association of Schools of Music

Suggested citation:

Bureau of Labor Statistics, U.S. Department of Labor, Occupational Outlook Handbook, 2012-13 Edition, Music Directors and Composers, on the Internet at http://www.bls.gov/ooh/entertainment-and-sports/music-directors-and-composers.htm .

Musicians and Singers

Quick Facts: Musicians and Singers	
2010 Median Pay	$22.39 per hour
Entry-Level Education	High school diploma or equivalent
Work Experience in a Related Occupation	None
On-the-job Training	Long-term on-the-job training
Number of Jobs, 2010	176,200
Job Outlook, 2010-20	10% (About as fast as average)
Employment Change, 2010-20	17,900

What Musicians and Singers Do

Musicians and singers play instruments or sing for live audiences and in recording studios. They perform in a variety of styles, such as classical, jazz, opera, rap, or rock.

Duties

Musicians and singers typically do the following:
- Perform music for live audiences and recordings
- Audition for positions in orchestras, choruses, bands, and other music groups
- Practice playing instruments or singing to improve their technique
- Rehearse to prepare for performances
- Find locations for performances or concerts
- Travel, sometimes great distances, to performance venues
- Promote their careers by doing photo shoots and interviews or maintaining a website or social media presence

Musicians play one or more instruments. To make themselves more marketable, many musicians become proficient in multiple musical instruments or styles.

Musicians play in bands, orchestras, or small groups. Those in bands may play at weddings, private parties, clubs, or bars while they try to build enough fans to get a recording contract or representation by an agent. Some musicians work as a part of a large group of musicians who must work and practice together, such as an orchestra. A few musicians become section leaders, who may be responsible for assigning parts to other musicians or leading rehearsals.

Others musicians are session musicians, who specialize in playing

Musicians and singers play instruments or sing for live audiences and in recording studios in a variety of styles, such as classical, jazz, or rock.

backup for a singer or band leader during recording sessions and live performances.

Singers perform vocal music in a variety of styles. Some specialize in a particular vocal style, such as opera or jazz; others perform in a variety of musical genres. Singers, particularly those who specialize in opera or classical music, may perform in different languages, such as French or Italian. Opera singers act out a story by singing instead of saying the dialogue.

Some singers become background singers, providing vocals to harmonize or support the lead singer.

In some cases, musicians and singers write their own music to record and perform. For more information about careers in songwriting, see the profile on music directors and composers .

Musicians and singers who give private music lessons to children and adults are classified as self-enrichment teachers. For more information, see the profile on self-enrichment teachers .

Others with a background in music may teach music in public schools, but they typically need a bachelor's degree and a teaching license. See the profiles on kindergarten and elementary school teachers , middle school teachers , and high school teachers .

Work Environment

Musicians and singers held about 176,200 jobs in 2010. They often perform in settings such as concert halls, arenas, and clubs. They often work in religious organizations and performing arts companies. In 2010, 43 percent of musicians and singers were self-employed.

They may spend a lot of time traveling between performances. Some spend time in recording studios. There are many jobs in cities that have a high concentration of entertainment and recording activities, such as New York, Los Angeles, Chicago, and Nashville.

Musicians and singers who give recitals or perform in nightclubs travel frequently and may tour nationally or internationally.

However, many musicians and singers find only part-time or intermittent work and have long periods of unemployment between jobs. The stress of constantly looking for work leads many to accept permanent full-time jobs in other occupations while working part time as a musician or singer.

In 2010, the industries employing the most musicians and singers were as follows:

Religious, grantmaking, civic, professional, and similar organizations	37%
Performing arts companies	14
Educational services; state, local, and private	2

Work Schedules

Rehearsals and recording sessions are commonly held during business hours, but live performances are most often at night and on weekends.

How to Become a Musician or Singer

Educational and training requirements for musicians and singers vary. There are no formal education requirements for those interested in performing popular music, but those interested in performing classical and opera typically need at least a bachelor's degree.

Education

To work as a classical musician or singer, a bachelor's degree in music theory or music performance is generally required. To be accepted into one of these programs, applicants are typically required to submit recordings or audition in person—and sometimes must do both.

For some schools, applicants must first be admitted to the college and then prepare a separate application for the music program. Undergraduate music programs teach students about music history and styles and teach methods for improving their instrumental and vocal technique and musical expression.

Some musicians and singers choose to continue their education by pursuing a master's degree in fine arts or music.

Musicians interested in performing popular music typically find jobs by attending auditions or arranging for their own performances. They may seek representation by an agent who will help them find jobs and performance opportunities.

Training

Musicians and singers need extensive and prolonged training and practice to acquire the skills and knowledge necessary to interpret music at a professional level. They typically begin singing or learning to play an instrument by taking lessons and classes when they are children. In addition, they must practice often to develop their talent and technique.

Musicians and singers interested in classical music may seek additional training through music camps and fellowships. These programs provide participants with classes, lessons, and performance opportunities. Sometimes these programs are associated with professional orchestras and may lead to a permanent spot in that orchestra.

Advancement

As with other occupations in which people perform, advancement for musicians and singers means becoming better known, finding work more easily, and earning more money for each performance. Successful musicians and singers often rely on agents or managers to find them jobs, negotiate contracts, and develop their careers.

Important Qualities

Discipline. Talent is not enough for most musicians and singers to find employment in this field. They must constantly practice and seek to improve their technique, style, and performances.

Musical talent. Professional musicians or singers must have superior musical abilities.

People skills. Musicians and singers need to work well with a variety of people, such as agents, music producers, conductors, and other musicians. Good people skills are helpful in building good working relationships.

Perseverance. Auditioning for jobs can be a frustrating process because it may take many different auditions to get hired. Musicians and singers need determination and perseverance to continue to audition after receiving many rejections.

Physical stamina. Musicians and singers who play in concerts or in nightclubs and those who tour must be able to endure frequent travel and irregular performance schedules.

Pay

Musicians and Singers
Median hourly wages, May 2010

Musicians and Singers	$22.39
Arts, Design, Entertainment, Sports, and Media Occupations	$20.61
Total, All Occupations	$16.27

Note: All Occupations includes all occupations in the U.S. Economy.
Source: U.S. Bureau of Labor Statistics, Occupational Employment Statistics

The median hourly wage of musicians and singers was $22.39 in May 2010. The median wage is the wage at which half the workers in an occupation earned more than that amount and half earned less. The lowest 10 percent earned less than $8.50, and the top 10 percent earned more than $60.02.

In May 2010, median hourly wages in the industries employing the most musicians and singers were as follows:

Performing arts companies	$24.91
Educational services; state, local, and private	19.78
Religious, grantmaking, civic, professional, and similar organizations	14.95

Rehearsals and recording sessions are commonly held during business hours, but live performances are most often at night and on weekends.

Job Outlook

Musicians and Singers
Percent change in employment, projected 2010-20

Total, All Occupations	14%
Arts, Design, Entertainment, Sports, and Media Occupations	13%
Musicians and Singers	10%

Note: All Occupations includes all occupations in the U.S. Economy.
Source: U.S. Bureau of Labor Statistics, Employment Projections program

Employment of musicians and singers is expected to grow by 10 percent from 2010 to 2020, about as fast as the average for all occupations. Expected growth will be due to increases in demand for musical performances.

The number of people attending musical performances, such as orchestra, opera, and rock concerts, is expected to increase from 2010 to 2020. As a result, more musicians and singers will be needed to play at these performances.

There will be additional demand for musicians to serve as session musicians and backup artists for recordings and to go on tour. Singers will be needed to sing backup and to make recordings for commercials, films, and television.

However, growth will likely be limited as orchestras, opera companies, and other musical groups have difficulty getting funding. Some musicians and singers work for nonprofit organizations that rely on donations and corporate sponsorships in addition to ticket sales to fund their work. During economic downturns, these organizations may have trouble finding enough funding to cover their expenses.

Job Prospects

Despite expected growth, there should be strong competition for jobs because of the large number of workers who are interested in becoming musicians and singers. In particular, there will likely be considerable competition for full-time positions.

Musicians and singers with exceptional musical talent should have the best opportunities.

Many musicians and singers experience periods of unemployment.

Employment projections data for musicians and singers, 2010-20

Occupational Title	SOC Code	Employment, 2010	Projected Employment, 2020	Change, 2010-20	
				Percent	Numeric
Musicians and Singers	27-2042	176,200	194,100	10	17,900
SOURCE: U.S. Bureau of Labor Statistics, Employment Projections program					

Similar Occupations

This table shows a list of occupations with job duties that are similar to those of musicians and singers.

Occupation	Job Duties	Entry-Level Education	Median Annual Pay, May 2010
Actors	Actors express ideas and portray characters in theater, film, television, and other performing arts media. They also work at theme parks or for other live events. They interpret a writer's script to entertain or inform an audience.	Some college, no degree	The annual wage is not available.
Dancers and Choreographers	Dancers and choreographers use movements to express ideas and stories in performances. There are many types of dance, such as ballet, modern dance, tap, and jazz.	High school diploma or equivalent	The annual wage is not available.
High School Teachers	High school teachers help prepare students for life after graduation. They teach academic lessons and various skills that students will need to attend college and to enter the job market.	Bachelor's degree	$53,230
Kindergarten and Elementary School Teachers	Kindergarten and elementary school teachers prepare younger students for future schooling by teaching them the basics of subjects such as math and reading.	Bachelor's degree	$51,380
Middle School Teachers	Middle school teachers educate students, most of whom are in sixth through eighth grades. They help students build on the fundamentals they learned in elementary school and prepare them for the more difficult lessons they will learn in high school.	Bachelor's degree	$51,960
Music Directors and Composers	Music directors (also called conductors) lead orchestras and other musical groups during performances and recording sessions. Composers write and arrange original music in a variety of musical styles.	Bachelor's degree	$45,970
Postsecondary Teachers	Postsecondary teachers instruct students in a wide variety of academic and vocational subjects beyond the high school level. They also conduct research and publish scholarly papers and books.	Doctoral or professional degree	$62,050
Producers and Directors	Producers and directors are in charge of creating motion pictures, television shows, live theater, and other performing arts productions. They interpret a writer's script to entertain or inform an audience.	Bachelor's degree	$68,440
Self-enrichment Teachers	Self-enrichment teachers instruct in a variety of subjects that students take for fun or self-improvement, such as music and foreign languages. These classes generally do not lead to a degree or certification, and students take them voluntarily to learn new skills or gain understanding of a subject.	High school diploma or equivalent	$36,340

Contacts for More Information

For more information about music degree programs, visit National Association of Schools of Music

Suggested citation:

Bureau of Labor Statistics, U.S. Department of Labor, Occupational Outlook Handbook, 2012-13 Edition, Musicians and Singers, on the Internet at http://www.bls.gov/ooh/entertainment-and-sports/musicians-and-singers.htm .

Producers and Directors

Quick Facts: Producers and Directors	
2010 Median Pay	$68,440 per year $32.90 per hour
Entry-Level Education	Bachelor's degree
Work Experience in a Related Occupation	1 to 5 years
On-the-job Training	None
Number of Jobs, 2010	122,500
Job Outlook, 2010-20	11% (About as fast as average)
Employment Change, 2010-20	13,500

What Producers and Directors Do

Producers and directors are in charge of creating motion pictures, television shows, live theater, and other performing arts productions. They interpret a writer's script to entertain or inform an audience.

Duties

Producers and directors typically do the following:
- Select scripts
- Audition and select cast members and the film or stage crew
- Approve the design and financial aspects of a production
- Ensure that a project stays on schedule and within budget
- Approve new developments in the production

Large productions often have associate, assistant, and line producers who share responsibilities. For example, on a large movie set an executive producer is in charge of the entire production, and a line producer runs the day-to-day operations. A TV show may employ several assistant producers, whom the head or executive producer gives certain duties, such as supervising the costume and makeup team.

Similarly, large productions usually employ several assistant

Producers and directors work from behind the camera in motion pictures and television.

directors, who help the director with tasks such as making set changes or notifying the performers when it is their time to go onstage. The specific responsibilities of assistant producers or directors vary with the size and type of production they work on.

Producers make the business and financial decisions for a motion picture, TV show, or stage production. They raise money for the project and hire the director and crew. The crew may include set and costume designers, a musical director, a choreographer, and other workers. Some producers may assist in the selection of cast members. Producers set the budget and approve any major changes to the project. They make sure that the film or show is completed on time, and they are responsible for the way the finished project turns out.

Directors are responsible for the creative decisions of a production. They select cast members, conduct rehearsals, and direct the work of the cast and crew. During rehearsal, they work with the actors to help them portray their characters better.

Directors work with designers to build a project's set. During a film's postproduction phase, they work closely with film editors to make sure that the final product comes out the way the producer and director want.

Although directors are in charge of the creative aspects of a show, they ultimately answer to the executive producer.

Work Environment

Producers and directors work under a lot of pressure, and most are under constant stress to find their next job. Work assignments are usually short, ranging from 1 day to a few months. Producers and directors may have long periods of unemployment. They often hold another job to make a living. They sometimes must work in unpleasant conditions, such as bad weather.

Producers and directors held about 122,500 jobs in 2010.

About 29 percent of producers and directors are self-employed; the remainder most commonly worked in the following industries in 2010:

Motion picture and video industries	23%
Radio and television broadcasting	16
Performing arts, spectator sports, and related industries	7
Cable and other subscription programming	4

Work Schedules

Work hours for producers and directors are long and irregular. Evening, weekend, and holiday work is common. Very few producers and directors work a standard 40-hour workweek, and many have variable schedules. Those who work in theater may travel with a touring show across the country, while those in film may work on location (a site away from the studio where all or part of the filming occurs).

How to Become a Producer or Director

Most producers and directors have a bachelor's degree and several years of work experience in a related occupation, such as an actor or writer.

Education

Producers and directors usually earn a bachelor's degree. There are no formal training programs for producers or film directors, but some major in writing, acting, journalism, or communication while in college. Some producers earn a degree in business, arts management, or nonprofit management.

Many stage directors complete a degree in theater, and some go on to receive a Master of Fine Arts (MFA) degree. Classes may include directing, playwriting, and set design, as well as some acting classes. The National Association of Schools of Theater accredits more than 150 programs in theater arts.

Work Experience

Producers and directors usually have several years of work experience in a related occupation. Many directors begin as actors, writers, film editors, or choreographers, and over the years they learn about directing. Many begin as assistants to successful directors on a film set. For more information, see the profiles on actors , writers and authors , film and video editors and camera operators , or dancers and choreographers .

In nonprofit theaters, most aspiring directors begin as assistant directors, a position that is usually treated as an unpaid internship.

Producers might start out working in a theatrical management office, as a business manager, or as an assistant or another low-profile job in a TV or movie studio. Some were directors or worked in another role behind the scenes of a show or movie.

Advancement

As a producer's or director's reputation grows, he or she may work on bigger and more expensive projects.

Important Qualities

Communication skills. Producers and directors must coordinate the work of many different people to finish a production on time and within budget.

Creativity. Because a script can be interpreted in different ways, directors must decide how they want to interpret it and then how to physically represent the script's ideas.

Leadership skills. A director instructs actors and helps them portray their characters in a believable manner.

Management skills. Producers must find and hire the best director and crew for the production and make sure that all involved do their jobs effectively and efficiently.

Pay

Producers and Directors
Median annual wages, May 2010

Producers and Directors	$68,440
Entertainers and Performers, Sports and Related Workers	$37,290
Total, All Occupations	$33,840

Note: All Occupations includes all occupations in the U.S. Economy.
Source: U.S. Bureau of Labor Statistics, Occupational Employment Statistics

The median annual wage of producers and directors was $68,440 in May 2010. The median wage is the wage at which half the workers in an occupation earned more than that amount and half earned less. The lowest 10 percent earned less than $32,140, and the top 10 percent earned more than $166,400 in May 2010.

Some producer's and director's income is earned as a percentage of ticket sales. A few of the most successful producers and directors have extraordinarily high earnings, but most do not.

Median annual wages in the industries employing the largest numbers of producers and directors in May 2010 were as follows:

Motion picture and video industries	$ 92,820
Cable and other subscription programming	81,290
Radio and television broadcasting	54,120
Performing arts, spectator sports, and related industries	51,960

Work hours for producers and directors are long and irregular. Evening, weekend, and holiday work is common. Very few producers and directors work a standard 40-hour workweek, and many have variable schedules. Those who work in theater may travel with a touring show across the country, while those in film may work on location (a site away from the studio where all or part of the filming occurs).

Job Outlook

Producers and Directors
Percent change in employment, projected 2010-20

Entertainers and Performers, Sports and Related Workers	16%
Total, All Occupations	14%
Producers and Directors	11%

Note: All Occupations includes all occupations in the U.S. Economy.
Source: U.S. Bureau of Labor Statistics, Employment Projections program

Employment of producers and directors is projected to grow 11 percent from 2010 to 2020, about as fast as the average for all occupations.

Job growth in the motion picture and video industry is expected to stem from strong demand from the public for more movies and television shows, as well as an increased demand from foreign audiences for U.S.-produced films. In addition, production companies are experimenting with new content delivery methods, such as mobile and online TV, which may lead to more work for producers and directors in the future. However, these delivery methods are still in their early stages, and their potential for success is not yet known.

Employment of self-employed producers and directors is expected to grow 16 percent, faster than that of those in the motion picture industry, as the number of independent films grow.

In broadcasting, some producer and director jobs may be lost as radio stations continue to consolidate; however, this loss will be slowed by the public's increased desire for local programming in both TV and radio.

Producers and directors who work in small and medium-sized theaters may see slower job growth because many of those theaters have difficulty finding funding as the number of performances decline. Large theaters, which usually have more stable sources of funding, should provide more opportunities.

Job Prospects

Producers and directors face intense competition for jobs because there are many more people who want to work in this field than there are jobs available. In film, directors who have experience on movies sets should have the best job prospects. Producers who have good business skills will likely have the best prospects.

Employment projections data for producers and directors, 2010-20

Occupational Title	SOC Code	Employment, 2010	Projected Employment, 2020	Change, 2010-20	
				Percent	Numeric
Producers and Directors	27-2012	122,500	136,000	11	13,500
SOURCE: U.S. Bureau of Labor Statistics, Employment Projections program					

Similar Occupations

This table shows a list of occupations with job duties that are similar to those of producers and directors.

Occupation	Job Duties	Entry-Level Education	Median Annual Pay, May 2010
Actors	Actors express ideas and portray characters in theater, film, television, and other performing arts media. They also work at theme parks or for other live events. They interpret a writer's script to entertain or inform an audience.	Some college, no degree	The annual wage is not available.
Dancers and Choreographers	Dancers and choreographers use movements to express ideas and stories in performances. There are many types of dance, such as ballet, modern dance, tap, and jazz.	High school diploma or equivalent	The annual wage is not available.
Musicians and Singers	Musicians and singers play instruments or sing for live audiences and in recording studios. They perform in a variety of styles, such as classical, jazz, opera, rap, or rock.	High school diploma or equivalent	The annual wage is not available.
Film and Video Editors and Camera Operators	Film and video editors and camera operators record images that entertain or inform an audience. Camera operators capture a wide range of material for TV shows, motion pictures, music videos, documentaries, or news and sporting events. Editors construct the final productions from the many different images camera operators capture. They collaborate with producers and directors to create the final production.	Bachelor's degree	$45,490
Announcers	Announcers present music, news, and sports and may provide commentary or interview guests about these topics or other important events. Some act as a master of ceremonies (emcee) or disc jockey (DJ) at weddings, parties, or clubs.	See How to Become One	$27,010
Writers and Authors	Writers and authors develop original written content for advertisements, books, magazines, movie and television scripts, songs, and online publications.	Bachelor's degree	$55,420
Art Directors	Art directors are responsible for the visual style and images in magazines, newspapers, product packaging, and movie and television productions. They create the overall design and direct others who develop artwork or layouts.	Bachelor's degree	$80,630
Multimedia Artists and Animators	Multimedia artists and animators create animation and visual effects for television, movies, video games, and other media. They create two- and three-dimensional models and animation.	Bachelor's degree	$58,510
Set and Exhibit Designers	Set designers create sets for movie, television, theater, and other productions. They analyze scripts or other research documents to determine how many sets will be needed and how each set can best support the story. Exhibit designers create spaces to display products, art, or artifacts.	Bachelor's degree	$46,680
Top Executives	Top executives devise strategies and policies to ensure that an organization meets its goals. They plan, direct, and coordinate operational activities of companies and public or private-sector organizations.	See How to Become One	$101,250

Contacts for More Information

For more information about producers and directors, visit Directors Guild of America, Stage Directors and Choreographers Society,

National Endowment for the Arts, National Association of Schools of Theater

Suggested citation:

Bureau of Labor Statistics, U.S. Department of Labor, Occupational Outlook Handbook, 2012-13 Edition, Producers and Directors, on the Internet at http://www.bls.gov/ooh/entertainment-and-sports/producers-and-directors.htm .

Umpires, Referees, and Other Sports Officials

Quick Facts: Umpires, Referees, and Other Sports Officials	
2010 Median Pay	$22,840 per year
Entry-Level Education	High school diploma or equivalent
Work Experience in a Related Occupation	None
On-the-job Training	Long-term on-the-job training
Number of Jobs, 2010	19,500
Job Outlook, 2010-20	20% (Faster than average)
Employment Change, 2010-20	3,900

What Umpires, Referees, and Other Sports Officials Do

Umpires, referees, and other sports officials preside over competitive athletic or sporting events. They detect infractions and decide penalties according to the rules of the game.

Duties

Umpires, referees, and other sports officials typically do the following:

- Officiate sporting events, games, and competitions
- Judge performances in sporting competitions to determine a winner
- Inspect sports equipment and examine all participants to ensure safety
- Keep track of event times, starting or stopping play when necessary
- Signal participants and other officials when infractions occur or to regulate play or competition
- Settle claims of infractions or complaints by participants
- Enforce the rules of the game and assess penalties when necessary

In officiating at sporting events, umpires, referees, and sports officials anticipate play and put themselves where they can best see the action, assess the situation, and determine any violations of the rules.

Some sports officials, such as boxing referees, may work independently. Others, such as umpires, work in groups.

Regardless of the sport, the job is highly stressful because officials often must make split-second decisions, sometimes resulting in strong disagreement expressed by opposing team players, coaches, and spectators.

Umpires, referees, and other sports officials preside over competitive athletic or sporting events.

Work Environment Umpires

Umpires, referees, and other sports officials held about 19,500 jobs in 2010. About 19 percent were self-employed. Umpires, referees, and other sports officials work indoors and out, in all types of weather. Some workers must travel on long bus rides to sporting events. Others, especially officials in professional sports, travel by air.

Because sports officials must observe play and often make split-second decisions, the work can be filled with pressure. In some instances, strong disagreements may take place between officials, on the one hand, and competitors and coaches, on the other, resulting in additional stress.

The following industries employed the most umpires, referees, and other sports officials in 2010:

Local government, excluding education and hospitals	29%
Spectator sports	13
Other amusement and recreation industries	12
Elementary and secondary schools; state, local, and private	11
Civic, social, professional, and similar organizations	10

Work Schedules

Umpires, referees, and sports officials often work irregular hours, including evenings, weekends, and holidays. Those who officiate sports in schools typically work part time.

How to Become an Umpire, Referee, or Other Sports Official

Education and training requirements for umpires, referees, and other sports officials vary by the level and type of sport. In all sports, these jobs require immense knowledge of the game, which they usually get from years of experience at lower levels. Some officiating jobs require vocational training.

Education and Training

Each sport has its own requirements for umpires, referees, and other sports officials; some require these officials to pass a test of their knowledge of the sport. Umpires, referees, and other sports officials often begin their careers with a high school diploma and gain needed experience by volunteering to officiate at community and recreational league competitions.

Certification

To officiate at high school athletic events, umpires, referees, and other officials must register with the state agency that oversees high school athletics and must pass an exam on the rules of the particular game. For college refereeing, candidates must be certified by an officiating school and be evaluated during a probationary period. Some larger college sports conferences require officials to have certification and other qualifications, such as maintaining a residence in or near the conference boundaries, along with several years of experience officiating at high school, community college, or other college conference games.

Advancement

For most umpires, referees, and other sports officials, reaching professional ranks is the biggest advancement. In some sports, such as baseball, umpires may begin their professional career officiating in the minor leagues before moving up to the major leagues.

Standards for umpires and other officials become more stringent as the level of competition advances. Attendance at a local or state academy may be a requirement for refereeing a school baseball game. Those seeking to officiate at minor or major league games must attend a professional umpire training school. To advance to umpiring in Major League Baseball, umpires usually need 7 to 10 years of experience in various minor leagues before being considered for major league jobs.

Important Qualities

Communication skills. Umpires, referees, and other sports officials must have good communication skills because they instruct athletes and settle disputes between competing players. Some sports officials also must communicate violations and infractions to opposing team players, coaches, and spectators.

Decision-making skills. Umpires, referees, and other sports officials must observe play, assess various situations, and often make split-second decisions.

Good vision. Umpires, referees, and other sports officials must have good vision to view infractions and determine any violations during play. In some sports, such as diving or gymnastics, sports officials must also be able to clearly observe an athlete's form for imperfections.

Stamina. Because many umpires, referees, and sports officials are required to stand, walk, run, or squat for long periods, having stamina is important.

Teamwork. Because many umpires, referees, and sports officials work in teams, the ability to cooperate and come to a mutual decision is essential.

Pay

Umpires, Referees, and Other Sports Officials
Median annual wages, May 2010

Total, All Occupations	$33,840
Athletes, Coaches, Umpires, and Related Workers	$28,390
Umpires, Referees, and Other Sports Officials	$22,840

Note: All Occupations includes all occupations in the U.S. Economy.
Source: U.S. Bureau of Labor Statistics, Occupational Employment Statistics

The median annual wage of umpires, referees, and other sports officials was $22,840 in May 2010. The median wage is the wage at which half the workers in an occupation earned more than that amount

and half earned less. The lowest 10 percent earned less than $16,310, and the top 10 percent earned more than $50,350.

In May 2010, median annual wages in industries employing the largest numbers of umpires, referees, and other sports officials were as follows:

Elementary and secondary schools	$29,170
Local government	23,770
Spectator sports	21,550
Civic and social organizations	19,590
Other amusement and recreation industries	19,500

Umpires, referees, and sports officials often work irregular hours, including evenings, weekends, and holidays. Those who officiate sports in schools typically work part time.

Job Outlook

Umpires, Referees, and Other Sports Officials
Percent change in employment, projected 2010-20

Athletes, Coaches, Umpires, and Related Workers	28%
Umpires, Referees, and Other Sports Officials	20%
Total, All Occupations	14%

Note: All Occupations includes all occupations in the U.S. Economy.
Source: U.S. Bureau of Labor Statistics, Employment Projections program

Employment of umpires, referees, and other sports officials is expected to increase 20 percent from 2010 to 2020, faster than the average for all occupations. A larger overall population that will continue to participate in organized sports for entertainment, recreation, and physical conditioning is expected to boost demand for umpires, referees, and sports officials.

Population growth is expected to lead to more schools, and more schools should result in more jobs for sports officials. However, funding for athletic programs often is cut first when budgets become tight. Still, the popularity of interscholastic sports often enables shortfalls to be offset with assistance from fundraisers, booster clubs, and parents.

In colleges, most of the expansion is expected to be in women's sports.

Job Prospects

Overall job prospects for umpires, referees, and sports officials are expected to be good. Job opportunities should be best for people seeking part-time umpire, referee, and other sports official jobs at the high school level.

Officials in women's sports may have better job opportunities and face less competition for positions. Competition is expected for higher-paying jobs at the college level and will be even greater for jobs in professional sports.

Employment projections data for umpires, referees, and other sports officials, 2010-20

Occupational Title	SOC Code	Employment, 2010	Projected Employment, 2020	Change, 2010-20	
				Percent	Numeric
Umpires, Referees, and Other Sports Officials	27-2023	19,500	23,400	20	3,900
SOURCE: U.S. Bureau of Labor Statistics, Employment Projections program					

Similar Occupations

This table shows a list of occupations with job duties that are similar to those of umpires, referees, and other sports officials.

Occupation	Job Duties	Entry-Level Education	Median Annual Pay, May 2010
Athletes and Sports Competitors	Athletes and sports competitors participate in organized, officiated sports events to entertain spectators.	High school diploma or equivalent	$43,740
Coaches and Scouts	Coaches teach amateur and professional athletes the skills they need to succeed at their sport. Scouts look for new players, evaluating athletes' strengths and weaknesses as possible recruits. Many coaches also scout out new talent.	High school diploma or equivalent	$28,340

Contacts for More Information

For more information about umpires, referees, and other sports officials, visit National Association of Sports Officials

Suggested citation:

Bureau of Labor Statistics, U.S. Department of Labor, Occupational Outlook Handbook, 2012-13 Edition, Umpires, Referees, and Other Sports Officials, on the Internet at http://www.bls.gov/ooh/entertainment-and-sports/umpires-referees-and-other-sports-officials.htm.

Farming, Fishing, and Forestry Occupations

Agricultural Workers

Quick Facts: Agricultural Workers	
2010 Median Pay	$18,970 per year $9.12 per hour
Entry-Level Education	See How to Become One
Work Experience in a Related Occupation	See How to Become One
On-the-job Training	Short-term on-the-job training
Number of Jobs, 2010	757,900
Job Outlook, 2010-20	-3% (Decline moderately)
Employment Change, 2010-20	-20,000

What Agricultural Workers Do

Agricultural workers maintain the quality of farms, crops, and livestock by operating machinery and doing physical labor under the supervision of agricultural managers.

Duties

Agricultural workers typically do the following:
- Harvest and inspect crops by hand
- Irrigate farm soil and maintain ditches or pipes and pumps
- Direct and monitor the activities of work crews as they plant, weed, or harvest
- Operate and service farm machinery
- Spray fertilizer or pesticide solutions to control insects, fungi, and weeds
- Move shrubs, plants, and trees with wheelbarrows or tractors
- Feed livestock and clean and disinfect their pens, cages, yards, and hutches

Agricultural workers maintain the quality of farms, crops, and livestock by operating machinery and performing physical labor under the supervision of agricultural managers.

- Examine animals to detect symptoms of illness or injury
- Use brands, tags, or tattoos to mark livestock to identify ownership and grade
- Herd livestock to pastures for grazing or to scales, trucks, or other enclosures
- Administer vaccines to protect animals from diseases

The following are types of agricultural workers:

Crop, nursery, and greenhouse farmworkers and laborers do numerous tasks related to growing and harvesting grains, fruits, vegetables, nuts, and other crops. They plant and seed, prune, irrigate, harvest, and pack and load crops for shipment.

Farmworkers also apply pesticides, herbicides, and fertilizers to crops. They repair fences and some farm equipment.

Nursery and greenhouse workers prepare land or greenhouse beds for growing horticultural products, such as trees, plants, flowers, and sod. They also plant, water, prune, weed, and spray the plants. They may cut, roll, and stack sod; stake trees; tie, wrap, and pack plants to fill orders; and dig up or move field-grown shrubs and trees.

Farm and ranch animal farmworkers care for live animals, including cattle, sheep, pigs, goats, horses, poultry, finfish, or shellfish. These animals are usually raised to supply meat, fur, skins, feathers, eggs, milk, or honey.

These farmworkers may feed, herd, brand, weigh, and load animals. They also keep records on animals; examine animals to detect diseases and injuries; and administer medications, vaccinations, or insecticides.

Many workers clean and maintain animal housing areas every day. On dairy farms, animal farmworkers operate milking machines.

Agricultural equipment operators use a variety of farm equipment to plow, sow seeds, and maintain and harvest crops. They may use tractors, fertilizer spreaders, balers, combines, threshers, and trucks. These workers also operate machines to harvest and treat crops, such as conveyor belts, loading machines, separators, cleaners, and dryers. Workers may make adjustments and minor repairs to equipment.

Animal breeders use their knowledge of genetics and animal science to select and breed animals that will produce offspring with desired traits and characteristics. For example, they breed chickens that lay more eggs, pigs that produce leaner meat, and sheep with more desirable wool. Other animal breeders breed and raise cats, dogs, and other household pets.

To know which animals to breed and when to breed them, animal breeders keep detailed records. Breeders note animals' health, size and weight, and the amount and quality of the product they produce. Animal breeders also track the traits of animals' offspring.

Some animal breeders work as consultants for farmers, but others breed and raise their own animals for sale or future breeding. Breeders fix and clean animals' shelters, feed and water animals, and oversee animals' health.

Work Environment

Agricultural workers held about 757,900 jobs in 2010.

They usually work outdoors in all kinds of weather. Animal breeders may travel from farm to farm to consult with farmers, ranchers, and managers about their livestock. For more information, see the profile on farmers, ranchers, and agricultural managers .

Agricultural workers' work can be difficult. To harvest fruits and vegetables by hand, workers frequently bend and crouch. They also lift and carry crops and tools. Workers may have limited access to drinking water and bathrooms while working in fields.

Agricultural workers risk exposure to pesticides sprayed on crops or plants. However, exposure can be minimal if safety procedures are followed. Tractors and other farm machinery can cause serious injury, so workers must be constantly alert. Agricultural workers who work directly with animals risk being bitten or kicked.

Some agricultural workers, also called migrant farmworkers, move from location to location as crops ripen. Their unsettled lifestyles and periods of unemployment between jobs can cause stress.

Work Schedules

Many agricultural workers have seasonal work schedules. Seasonal workers are typically expected to work longer hours during planting or harvesting times or when animals must be sheltered and fed.

How to Become an Agricultural Worker

Agricultural workers typically receive on-the-job training. Many do not need a high school diploma before they begin working, but employers require animal breeders to have either more work experience and training or a college degree.

Education and Training

Most agricultural workers do not need a high school diploma. Instead, they usually get up to a year of on-the-job training, depending on their responsibilities. In addition to on-the-job training, some animal breeders have a bachelor's degree in animal science and genetics.

Work Experience

Animal breeders typically have several years of experience in a related occupation.

Important Qualities

Listening skills. Agricultural workers need to work well with others. Because they take instructions from farmers and other agricultural managers, effective listening is critical.

Manual dexterity. Agricultural workers need excellent hand-eye coordination to harvest crops and operate farm machinery.

Physical stamina. Agricultural workers need to be able to perform laborious tasks repeatedly.

Physical strength. Agricultural workers must be strong enough to lift heavy objects, including tools and crops.

Technical skills. Agricultural workers must be able to competently operate complex farm machinery. They also occasionally do routine maintenance on the machinery.

Advancement

Agricultural workers may advance to crew leader or other supervisory positions. The ability to speak both English and Spanish is helpful for agricultural supervisors.

Some agricultural workers aspire to become farmers, ranchers, and agricultural managers or to own their own farms and ranches. Knowledge of produce may provide an excellent background for becoming a purchasing agent and buyer of farm products. Those who earn a college degree in agricultural science could become agricultural and food scientists. For more information, see the profiles on farmers, ranchers, and agricultural managers and agricultural and food scientists.

Pay

Agricultural Workers

Median annual wages, May 2010

Total, All Occupations	$33,840
Animal Breeders	$31,340
Agricultural Workers	$18,970
Miscellaneous Agricultural Workers	$18,960

Note: All Occupations includes all occupations in the U.S. Economy.
Source: U.S. Bureau of Labor Statistics, Occupational Employment Statistics

The median annual wage of agricultural workers was $18,970 in May 2010. The median wage is the wage at which half the workers in an occupation earned more than that amount and half earned less. The lowest 10 percent earned less than $16,810, and the top 10 percent earned more than $29,740.

Many agricultural workers have seasonal work schedules. Seasonal workers are typically expected to work longer hours.

Job Outlook

Agricultural Workers

Percent change in employment, projected 2010-20

Total, All Occupations	14%
Agricultural Workers	-3%
Miscellaneous Agricultural Workers	-3%
Animal Breeders	-8%

Note: All Occupations includes all occupations in the U.S. Economy.
Source: U.S. Bureau of Labor Statistics, Employment Projections program

Employment of agricultural workers is expected to decline by about three percent between 2010 and 2020. However, agricultural workers should have good job prospects overall.

Employment for agricultural workers is expected to decline slightly because of the large concentration of farmworkers and laborers in crop production, which is expected to decrease.

Despite increasing international demand for food and meat, fewer agricultural workers may be needed as agricultural and livestock establishments continue to consolidate.

Technological advancements in farm equipment raises output per farm worker, which could also affect employment for agricultural workers.

In addition, the agriculture industry is expected to face increased competition from foreign countries, particularly Central America and China, because of trade agreements with those regions.

Pending federal legislation also may reduce demand for agricultural workers.

Nursery and greenhouse workers might experience some job growth, if the demand for landscaping plants continues.

Job Prospects

Opportunities should be good because workers regularly leave these jobs, which pay relatively low wages and have relatively high physical demands. This is especially true for agricultural equipment operators and crop, greenhouse, and nursery farmworkers.

Those who work with animals tend to have a more settled lifestyle, because the work does not require them to follow crops for harvest. The average age of agricultural workers is rising, which may lead to further job turnover.

About a quarter of all crop workers are in Arizona, California, Colorado, Texas, and New Mexico. California, Florida, and Oregon have the most nursery workers.

Employment projections data for agricultural workers, 2010-20

Occupational Title	SOC Code	Employment, 2010	Projected Employment, 2020	Change, 2010-20 Percent	Numeric
Agricultural Workers	—	757,900	738,000	-3	-20,000
Animal Breeders	45-2021	11,500	10,700	-8	-900
Miscellaneous Agricultural Workers	45-2090	746,400	727,300	-3	-19,100

SOURCE: U.S. Bureau of Labor Statistics, Employment Projections program

Similar Occupations

This table shows a list of occupations with job duties that are similar to those of agricultural workers.

Occupation	Job Duties	Entry-Level Education	Median Annual Pay, May 2010
Agricultural and Food Science Technicians	Under the supervision of scientists, agricultural and food science technicians measure and analyze the quality of food and agricultural products.	Associate's degree	$32,760
Animal Care and Service Workers	Animal care and service workers care for the needs of animals. They feed, water, groom, bathe, and exercise pets and other nonfarm animals. Job tasks vary by position and place of work.	See How to Become One	$19,780
Farmers, Ranchers, and Other Agricultural Managers	Farmers, ranchers, and other agricultural managers run establishments that produce crops, livestock, and dairy products.	High school diploma or equivalent	$60,750
Forest and Conservation Workers	Forest and conservation workers measure and improve the quality of forests. Under the supervision of foresters and forest and conservation technicians, they help to develop, maintain, and protect forests.	High school diploma or equivalent	$23,900
Grounds Maintenance Workers	Grounds maintenance workers provide a pleasant outdoor environment by ensuring that the grounds of houses, businesses, and parks are attractive, orderly, and healthy.	See How to Become One	$23,740

Contacts for More Information

For more information on agricultural workers, visit The National Agricultural Workers Survey

For more information about agriculture policy and farm advocacy, visit Center for Rural Affairs

For more information about the Beginner Farmer and Rancher Competitive Grants Program, visit National Institute of Food and Agriculture

For more general information about farming in the United States, visit Farm Service Agency

Suggested citation:

Bureau of Labor Statistics, U.S. Department of Labor, Occupational Outlook Handbook, 2012-13 Edition, Agricultural Workers, on the Internet at http://www.bls.gov/ooh/farming-fishing-and-forestry/agricultural-workers.htm .

Fishers and Related Fishing Workers

Quick Facts: Fishers and Related Fishing Workers	
2010 Median Pay	$25,590 per year $12.30 per hour
Entry-Level Education	Less than high school
Work Experience in a Related Occupation	None
On-the-job Training	Moderate-term on-the-job training
Number of Jobs, 2010	32,000
Job Outlook, 2010-20	-6% (Decline moderately)
Employment Change, 2010-20	-2,000

What Fishers and Related Fishing Workers Do

Fishers and related fishing workers catch and trap various types of marine life. The fish they catch are for human food, animal feed, bait, and other uses.

Duties

Fishers and related fishing workers typically do the following:
- Locate fish using fish-finding equipment
- Direct fishing operations and supervise crew
- Steer vessels and operate navigational instruments
- Maintain engines, fishing gear, and other onboard equipment by doing minor repairs
- Sort, pack, and store catch in holds with salt and ice
- Measure fish to ensure they comply with legal size
- Return undesirable or illegal catches to the water
- Guide nets, traps, and lines onto vessels by hand or using hoisting equipment
- Signal other workers to move, hoist, and position loads

To plot the ship's course, fishing boat captains use compasses, charts, and electronic navigational equipment, including global positioning systems (GPS). They also use radar and sonar to avoid obstacles above and below the water and to find fish.

Some fishers work in deep water on large fishing boats that are equipped for long stays at sea. Some process the fish they catch on board and prepare them for sale.

Other fishers work in shallow water on small boats that often have a crew of only one or two members. They might put nets across the

Fishers and fishing workers catch and trap various types of marine life

mouths of rivers or inlets or pots and traps for fish or shellfish, such as lobsters and crabs, or use dredges to gather other shellfish, such as oysters and scallops.

A small portion of commercial fishing requires diving with diving suits or scuba gear. These divers use spears to catch fish and nets to gather shellfish, sea urchins, abalone, and sponges.

Some fishers harvest marine vegetation rather than fish. They use rakes and hoes to gather Irish moss and kelp.

Although most fishers work in commercial fishing, some in this occupation use their expertise in sport or recreational fishing.

Aquaculture—raising and harvesting fish and other aquatic life under controlled conditions in ponds or confined bodies of water—is a different occupation. For more information, see the profile for farmers, ranchers, and agricultural managers.

The following are examples of types of fishers and related fishing workers:

The **fishing boat captain** plans and oversees the fishing operation, fish to be sought, location of the best fishing grounds, method of capture, duration of the trip, and sale of the catch. Captains direct the fishing operation and record daily activities in the ship's log. Increasingly, they use the Internet to bypass processors and sell fish directly to consumers, grocery stores, and restaurants.

Fishers that specialize in catching certain species include **crabbers** and **lobster catchers**.

Work Environment

Fishers and related fishing workers held about 32,000 jobs in 2010. Fifty-eight percent of fishers and fishing-related workers are self-employed. Fishing operations are conducted under various environmental conditions, depending on the region, body of water, and kinds of fish sought. Storms, fog, and wind may hamper fishing vessels or cause them to suspend fishing operations and return to port.

Although fishing gear has improved and operations have become more mechanized, netting and processing fish are strenuous activities. Newer vessels have improved living quarters and amenities, such as television and shower stalls, but crews still experience the aggravations of confined quarters and the absence of family.

Injuries

Fishers and related fishing workers often work under hazardous conditions, and transportation to a hospital or doctor often is not readily available when injuries do occur. The crew must guard against the danger of injury from malfunctioning fishing gear, entanglement in fishing nets and gear, slippery decks, ice formation, or large waves washing over the deck. Malfunctioning navigation or communication equipment may lead to collisions or shipwrecks.

Work Schedules

Fishers and related fishing workers endure strenuous outdoor work and long hours. Commercial fishing trips may require a stay of weeks or months away from the home port. Lookout watches are a regular responsibility, and crewmembers stand watch at prearranged times of the day or night.

Many fishers are seasonal workers, and those jobs are usually filled by students and by people from other occupations, such as teachers. For example, salmon season in Alaska makes employment of fishers in that state more than double in the summer.

How to Become a Fisher or Related Fishing Worker

Fishers and related fishing workers usually learn on the job. No formal education is required.

Training

Most fishers learn on the job. They start by finding work through family or friends, or simply by walking around the docks and asking for employment. Some larger trawlers and processing ships are run by larger companies, in which new workers can apply through the companies' human resources department. Operators of large commercial fishing vessels must complete a Coast Guard-approved training course.

Education

Formal education is not required to be a fisher. However, by enrolling in 2-year vocational-technical programs offered by some high schools, fishers can improve their chances of getting a job. In addition, some community colleges and universities offer fishery technology and related programs that include courses in seamanship, vessel operations, marine safety, navigation, vessel repair, and fishing gear technology. Secondary and postsecondary programs are typically near coastal areas and include hands-on experience.

Experienced fishers may find short-term workshops especially useful. These workshops generally are offered through postsecondary institutions and provide a good working knowledge of electronic equipment used in navigation and communication.

Important Qualities

Analytical skills. Fishers and related fishing workers must measure the quality of their catch, which requires precision and accuracy.

Critical-thinking skills. Fishers and related fishing workers reach conclusions through sound reasoning and judgment. They determine how to improve the catch and must react appropriately to weather conditions.

Listening skills. Fishers and related fishing workers need to work well with others—they take instructions from captains and others—so effective listening is critical.

Machine operation skills. Fishers and related fishing workers must be able to operate complex fishing machinery competently and occasionally do routine maintenance.

Physical fitness. Fishers and related fishing workers must have hand dexterity, physical strength, and coordination to perform difficult tasks repeatedly.

Physical stamina. Fishers and related fishing workers must be able to work long hours, often in strenuous conditions.

Licenses

. Captains of fishing boats must be licensed.

Crewmembers on certain fish-processing vessels may need a merchant mariner's document. The U.S. Coast Guard issues these documents and licenses to people who meet the specific health, physical, and academic requirements.

States set licensing requirements for boats operating in state waters, defined as inland waters and waters within 3 miles of the coast.

Fishers need a permit to fish in almost any water. Permits are distributed by states for state waters and by regional fishing councils for federal waters. The permits specify the fishing season, the type and amount of fish that may be caught, as well as sometimes the type of permissible fishing gear.

Advancement

Experienced, reliable fishing boat deckhands can become boatswains, then second mates, first mates, and, finally, captains. Those who are interested in ship engineering may get experience with maintaining and repairing ship engines to become licensed chief engineers on large commercial boats. That requires meeting the Coast Guard's licensing requirements. For more information, see the profile for water transportation occupations .

Almost all captains are self-employed, and most eventually own, or partially own, one or more fishing boats.

Pay

Fishers and Related Fishing Workers
Median annual wages, May 2010

Total, All Occupations	$33,840
Fishers and Related Fishing Workers	$25,590
Farming, Fishing, and Forestry Occupations	$19,630

Note: All Occupations includes all occupations in the U.S. Economy.
Source: U.S. Bureau of Labor Statistics, Occupational Employment Statistics

The median annual wage of fishers and related fishing workers was $25,590 in May 2010. The median wage is the wage at which half the workers in an occupation earned more than that amount and half earned less. The lowest 10 percent earned less than $17,300, and the top 10 percent earned more than $40,200.

Fishers and related fishing workers endure strenuous outdoor work and long hours. Commercial fishing trips may require a stay of weeks or months away from the home port. Lookout watches are a regular responsibility, and crewmembers stand watch at prearranged times of the day or night.

Many fishers are seasonal workers, and those jobs are usually filled by students and by people from other occupations, such as teachers. For example, salmon season in Alaska makes employment of fishers in that state more than double in the summer.

Job Outlook

Fishers and Related Fishing Workers
Percent change in employment, projected 2010-20

Total, All Occupations	14%
Farming, Fishing, and Forestry Occupations	-2%
Fishers and Related Fishing Workers	-6%

Note: All Occupations includes all occupations in the U.S. Economy.
Source: U.S. Bureau of Labor Statistics, Employment Projections program

Employment of fishers and related fishing workers is expected to decline moderately (by 6 percent) from 2010 to 2020.

Fishers and related fishing workers depend on the natural ability of fish stocks to replenish themselves through growth and reproduction. They also depend on governmental regulation to promote replenishment of fisheries. Because the use of sophisticated equipment has raised the efficiency of finding fish stocks, the need for setting limits to catches also has risen. Additionally, improvements in fishing gear and highly automated floating processors have increased fish hauls.

Fisheries councils issue various restrictions to prevent overharvesting and to allow stocks of fish and shellfish to replenish naturally. Fishing councils are shifting to an individual quota system that tends to reduce employment. Nonetheless, such a system benefits workers who remain in the industry because it lengthens the fishing seasons and steadies employment.

Rising seafood imports and increasing competition from farm-raised fish are adversely affecting fishing income and also are causing some fishers to leave the industry. However, because competition from farm-raised and imported seafood tends to be concentrated in specific species, some regions are more affected than others.

Governmental efforts to replenish stocks are having some positive results, which should increase fish stocks in the future. Efforts by private fishers' associations on the West Coast to increase government monitoring of fisheries may help prevent the type of decline in fish stocks found in waters off the East Coast. Nevertheless, pollution is now recognized as a new factor affecting the reproduction of fish, and it may take many years to improve that situation.

Job Prospects

Most job openings will result from the need to replace fishers and related fishing workers who leave the occupation because of the strenuous and hazardous nature of the job and the lack of a steady year-round income. The best prospects should be with large fishing operations; opportunities with small independent fishers are expected to be limited.

Employment projections data for fishers and related fishing workers, 2010-20

Occupational Title	SOC Code	Employment, 2010	Projected Employment, 2020	Change, 2010-20	
				Percent	Numeric
Fishers and Related Fishing Workers	45-3011	32,000	30,000	-6	-2,000
SOURCE: U.S. Bureau of Labor Statistics, Employment Projections program					

Similar Occupations

This table shows a list of occupations with job duties that are similar to those of fishers and related fishing workers.

Occupation	Job Duties	Entry-Level Education	Median Annual Pay, May 2010
Food Processing Occupations	Food processing occupations include butchers and meat cutters; meat, poultry, and fish cutters and trimmers; and operators and tenders of roasting, baking, and drying machinery. These workers cut, trim, or otherwise process food items, such as meat, or nonfood items, such as tobacco, for retail sale.	Less than high school	$23,950
Water Transportation Occupations	Workers in water transportation occupations operate and maintain ships that take cargo and people over water. These ships travel to and from foreign ports across the ocean, to domestic ports along the coasts, across the Great Lakes, and along the country's many inland waterways.	See How to Become One	$46,610

Contacts for More Information

For more information about licensing of fishing boat captains and about requirements for merchant mariner documentation, visit National Maritime Center, Coast Guard Headquarters

Suggested citation:

Bureau of Labor Statistics, U.S. Department of Labor, Occupational Outlook Handbook, 2012-13 Edition, Fishers and Related Fishing Workers, on the Internet at http://www.bls.gov/ooh/farming-fishing-and-forestry/fishers-and-related-fishing-workers.htm.

Forest and Conservation Workers

Quick Facts: Forest and Conservation Workers	
2010 Median Pay	$23,900 per year $11.49 per hour
Entry-Level Education	High school diploma or equivalent
Work Experience in a Related Occupation	None
On-the-job Training	Moderate-term on-the-job training
Number of Jobs, 2010	13,700
Job Outlook, 2010-20	1% (Little or no change)
Employment Change, 2010-20	100

What Forest and Conservation Workers Do

Forest and conservation workers measure and improve the quality of forests. Under the supervision of foresters and forest and conservation technicians, they help to develop, maintain, and protect forests.

Duties

Forest and conservation workers typically do the following:
- Plant seedlings to reforest land
- Clear away brush and debris from camping trails, roadsides, and camping areas
- Count trees during tree-measuring efforts
- Select or cut trees according to markings, sizes, types, or grades
- Spray trees with insecticides and fungicides to kill insects and protect the trees from disease
- Identify and remove diseased or undesirable trees
- Inject vegetation with insecticides and herbicides
- Help prevent and suppress forest fires
- Check equipment to ensure that it is operating properly

Forest and conservation workers are often supervised by foresters and forest and conservation technicians, who direct their work and evaluate their progress.

They do basic tasks to maintain and improve forest quality, such as planting seedlings or removing diseased trees. To plant seedlings, they use digging and planting tools. To cut trees, they use handsaws or power saws.

Forest and conservation workers may perform fire suppression activities under the supervision of foresters and forest and conservation technicians.

Some forest workers work on tree farms, where they plant, cultivate, and harvest many different kinds of trees. Their duties vary with the type of farm and may include planting seedlings, spraying to control weed growth and insects, and harvesting trees.

Some forest and conservation workers work in forest nurseries, where they sort through tree seedlings, discarding those that don't meet standards. Others use hand tools or their hands to gather woodland products, such as decorative greens, tree cones, bark, moss, and other wild plant life. Some may tap trees to make syrup or chemicals.

Forest and conservation workers who are employed by or under contract with state and local governments may clear brush and debris from trails, roadsides, and camping areas. They may clean kitchens and rest rooms at recreational facilities and campgrounds.

Workers with a fire protection background also help to prevent fires. For example, they may construct firebreaks, which are gaps in vegetation that can help slow down or stop the progress of a fire. They also may work with technicians to study how quickly fires spread and how successful fire suppression activities were. For example, workers help count how many trees will be affected by a fire. They also sometimes respond to forest emergencies.

Work Environment

Forest and conservation workers held about 13,700 jobs in 2010. Industries that employed the largest numbers of forest and conservation workers in 2010, were as follows:

State government, excluding education and hospitals	30%
Forestry and logging	18
Local government, excluding education and hospitals	14
Sawmills and wood preservation	2

Forest and conversation workers typically work for state and local governments or on privately owned forest lands. Those employed by forest management services may work for the federal government on a contract basis.

Forest and conservation workers' jobs are concentrated in the West and Southeast, where there are many national and private forests and parks.

Forest and conversation workers typically work outdoors, sometimes in remote locations and in all types of weather. However, the increased use of machines has reduced some of the discomfort of working in bad weather and has made tasks much safer. Workers also use proper safety measures and equipment, such as hardhats, protective eyewear, and safety clothing.

Most of these jobs are physically demanding. Forest and conservation workers may have to walk long distances through densely wooded areas.

Work Schedules

Most forest and conservation workers are employed full time and have a routine work schedule. Seasonal employees may be expected to work longer hours and at night. Responding to an emergency may require workers to work longer hours and at any time of day.

How to Become a Forest and Conservation Worker

Forest and conservation workers typically need a high school diploma before they begin working. Most workers get on-the-job training.

Education and Training

Forest and conservation workers typically need a high school diploma before they begin working. Entry-level forest and conservation workers generally get on-the-job training as they help more experienced workers. They do routine labor-intensive tasks, such as planting or thinning trees.

When the opportunity arises, they learn from experienced technicians and foresters who do more complex tasks, such as gathering data.

Training programs for forest and conservation workers also are common in many states. These programs, which typically take place in the field, encourage the health and productivity of the nation's forests through programs such as the Sustainable Forest Initiative .

Some vocational and technical schools and community colleges offer courses leading to a two-year technical degree in forest management technology, wildlife management, conservation, and forest harvesting. Programs that include field trips to watch and participate in forestry activities provide a particularly good background.

Important Qualities

Communication skills. Forest and conservation workers must effectively convey information to technicians and other workers.

Decision-making skills. Forest and conservation workers must make quick, intelligent decisions when hazards arise.

Detail oriented. Forest and conservation workers must watch gauges, dials, or other indicators to determine whether equipment and tools are working properly.

Listening skills. Forest and conservation workers must give full attention to what their superiors are saying. They must understand the instructions they are given before performing tasks.

Physical stamina. Forest and conservation workers must plant trees and perform a variety of repeated physical tasks. They must also be able to walk long distances through densely wooded areas.

Advancement

To advance their careers and become forest and conservation technicians or foresters, forest and conservation workers usually need an associate's or bachelor's degree in forestry or a related field. For more information, see the profiles on forest and conservation technicians and conservation scientists and foresters .

Pay

Forest and Conservation Workers
Median annual wages, May 2010

Total, All Occupations	$33,840
Forest and Conservation Workers	$23,900
Farming, Fishing, and Forestry Occupations	$19,630

Note: All Occupations includes all occupations in the U.S. Economy.
Source: U.S. Bureau of Labor Statistics, Occupational Employment Statistics

The median annual wage of forest and conservation workers was $23,900 in May 2010. The median wage is the wage at which half the workers in an occupation earned more than that amount and half earned less. The lowest 10 percent earned less than $16,730, and the top 10 percent earned more than $44,780.

Median annual wages in the industries employing the largest number of forestry and conservation workers in May 2010 were as follows:

Forestry and logging	$29,870
Local government, excluding education and hospitals	27,410
Sawmills and wood preservation	23,990
State government, excluding education and hospitals	20,880

Most forest and conservation workers are employed full time and have a routine work schedule. Seasonal employees may be expected to work longer hours and at night. Responding to an emergency may require workers to work longer hours and at any time of day.

Job Outlook

Forest and Conservation Workers
Percent change in employment, projected 2010-20

Total, All Occupations	14%
Forest and Conservation Workers	1%
Farming, Fishing, and Forestry Occupations	-2%

Note: All Occupations includes all occupations in the U.S. Economy.
Source: U.S. Bureau of Labor Statistics, Employment Projections program

Employment of forest and conservation workers is expected to experience little or no change, growing 1 percent from 2010 to 2020. Heightened demand for American timber and wood pellets will help increase demand for forest and conservation workers.

Jobs in private forests will grow with the increasing demand for timber and pellets, but ongoing fiscal crises will likely lessen the number of available positions in state and local governments. Wildfires caused by unpredictable climate conditions may increase the fire suppression activities of forest and conservation workers.

Most employment growth for forest and conservation technicians will be in federally owned forest lands. Recent developments in western forests may result in the conversion of unused roads into forest land, thus creating some new jobs. In addition, increasing pressure on the Forest Service (part of the U.S. Department of Agriculture) to undertake major road repair may result in higher levels of employment.

Employment projections data for forest and conservation workers, 2010-20

Occupational Title	SOC Code	Employment, 2010	Projected Employment, 2020	Change, 2010-20	
				Percent	Numeric
Forest and Conservation Workers	45-4011	13,700	13,900	1	100
SOURCE: U.S. Bureau of Labor Statistics, Employment Projections program					

Similar Occupations

This table shows a list of occupations with job duties that are similar to those of forest and conservation workers.

Occupation	Job Duties	Entry-Level Education	Median Annual Pay, May 2010
Agricultural Workers	Agricultural workers maintain the quality of farms, crops, and livestock by operating machinery and doing physical labor under the supervision of agricultural managers.	See How to Become One	$18,970
Conservation Scientists and Foresters	Conservation scientists and foresters manage overall land quality of forests, parks, rangelands, and other natural resources.	Bachelor's degree	$57,420
Firefighters	Firefighters protect the public by responding to fires and other emergencies. They are frequently the first emergency personnel on the scene of an accident.	Postsecondary non-degree award	$45,250
Forest and Conservation Technicians	Forest and conservation technicians measure and improve the quality of forests, rangeland, and other natural areas.	Associate's degree	$33,390
Grounds Maintenance Workers	Grounds maintenance workers provide a pleasant outdoor environment by ensuring that the grounds of houses, businesses, and parks are attractive, orderly, and healthy.	See How to Become One	$23,740
Logging Workers	Logging workers harvest thousands of acres of forests each year. The timber they harvest provides the raw material for countless consumer and industrial products.	High school diploma or equivalent	$32,870

Contacts for More Information

For information about forestry careers and schools offering education in forestry, visit Society of American Foresters

For information about careers in forestry—particularly conservation forestry and land management, visit Forest Guild

Suggested citation:

Bureau of Labor Statistics, U.S. Department of Labor, Occupational Outlook Handbook, 2012-13 Edition, Forest and Conservation Workers, on the Internet at http://www.bls.gov/ooh/farming-fishing-and-forestry/forest-and-conservation-workers.htm.

Logging Workers

Quick Facts: Logging Workers	
2010 Median Pay	$32,870 per year $15.80 per hour
Entry-Level Education	High school diploma or equivalent
Work Experience in a Related Occupation	None
On-the-job Training	Moderate-term on-the-job training
Number of Jobs, 2010	53,200
Job Outlook, 2010-20	4% (Slower than average)
Employment Change, 2010-20	2,300

What Logging Workers Do

Logging workers harvest thousands of acres of forests each year. The timber they harvest provides the raw material for countless consumer and industrial products.

Duties

Logging workers typically do the following:

- Cut down trees with hand-held power chain saws or mobile felling machines
- Fasten chains around logs to be dragged by tractors
- Drag logs to the landing or deck area
- Separate logs by species and type of wood and load them onto trucks
- Drive and maneuver tractors and tree harvesters to shear trees and cut logs into desired lengths
- Drive tractors to build or repair logging roads
- Grade logs according to characteristics such as knot size and straightness

Logging workers harvest thousands of acres of forests each year.

- Inspect equipment for safety before using it and do necessary basic maintenance tasks
- Calculate total board feet, cordage, or other wood measurement units, using conversion tables

Timber-cutting and logging are done by a logging crew. The following are some types of logging workers:

Fallers cut down trees with hand-held power chain saws or mobile felling machines.

Buckers trim the tops and branches of felled trees and buck (cut) the logs into specific lengths.

Choke setters fasten chokers (steel cables or chains) around logs to be skidded (dragged) by tractors or forwarded by the cable-yarding system to the landing or deck area, where the logs are separated by species and type of product, such as pulpwood, saw logs, or veneer logs, and loaded onto trucks.

Rigging slingers and chasers set up and dismantle the cables and guy wires of the yarding system.

Log sorters, markers, movers, and chippers sort, mark, and move logs, based on species, size, and ownership, and tend machines that chip up logs.

Logging equipment operators use tree harvesters to fell trees, shear tree limbs off, and cut trees into desired lengths. They drive tractors and operate self-propelled machines called skidders or forwarders, which drag or transport logs to a loading area.

Log graders and scalers inspect logs for defects and measure the logs to determine their volume. They estimate the value of logs or pulpwood. These workers often use hand-held data collection devices to enter data about trees. The data are later downloaded to a computer.

A typical crew might consist of

- one or two tree fallers or one logging equipment operator with a tree harvester to cut down trees
- one bucker to cut logs
- two logging equipment operators with tractors to drag cut trees to the loading deck
- one logging equipment operator to load the logs onto trucks.

Work Environment

Logging workers held about 53,200 jobs in 2010.

Logging is physically demanding and can be hazardous. Workers spend all their time outdoors, sometimes in poor weather and often in isolated areas. The increased use of enclosed machines has decreased some of the discomforts caused by bad weather and has generally made logging much safer.

Workers in some sparsely populated western states and northern Maine commute long distances between their homes and logging sites.

A few logging camps in Alaska and Maine house workers in bunkhouses. In the more densely populated eastern and southern states, commuting distances are shorter.

Injuries

Most logging work involves lifting, climbing, and other strenuous activities, although machinery has eliminated some heavy labor. Falling branches, vines, and rough terrain are constant hazards, as are dangers associated with felling trees and handling logs.

Workers must use hearing protection while logging. They must also be careful and use proper safety measures and equipment, such as hardhats, safety clothing, and boots.

How to Become a Logging Worker

Most logging workers have a high school diploma. They get on-the-job training to become familiar with forest environments and to learn how to operate logging machinery.

Training

Many states have training programs for loggers. Although specific coursework may vary by state, most programs usually include technical instruction or field training in a number of areas, including best management practices, environmental compliance, and reforestation.

Safety training is a vital part of logging workers' instruction. Many state forestry or logging associations provide training sessions for tree fallers, whose jobs require more skill and experience than other logging positions. Sessions may take place in the field, where trainees have the opportunity to practice various felling techniques.

Logging companies and trade associations also offer training programs for workers who operate large, expensive machinery and equipment. Often, a representative of the equipment manufacturer spends several days in the field, teaching loggers how to operate newly purchased machinery.

Important Qualities

Decision-making skills. Logging workers must make quick, intelligent decisions when hazards arise.

Detail oriented. Logging workers must watch gauges, dials, and other indicators to determine whether equipment and tools are working properly.

Listening skills. Logging workers must give full attention to what their superiors are saying. They must understand the instructions they are given before performing tasks.

Physical stamina. Logging workers need to be able to perform laborious tasks repeatedly.

Physical strength. Logging workers must be able to handle heavy equipment.

Education

A high school diploma is enough for most logging workers. Some vocational and technical schools and community colleges offer courses leading to a two-year technical degree in forest harvesting. This degree may help workers get a job. Courses may include field trips to observe or participate in logging activities.

A few community colleges offer training for equipment operators.

Pay

Logging Workers
Median annual wages, May 2010

Total, All Occupations	$33,840
Logging Workers	$32,870
Farming, Fishing, and Forestry Occupations	$19,630

Note: All Occupations includes all occupations in the U.S. Economy.
Source: U.S. Bureau of Labor Statistics, Occupational Employment Statistics

The median annual wage of logging workers was $32,870 in May 2010. The median wage is the wage at which half the workers in an occupation earned than that amount and half earned less. The lowest 10 percent earned less than $21,660, and the top 10 percent earned more than $49,370.

The median annual wages of logging worker occupations in May 2010 were as follows:
- $34,470 for fallers
- $32,430 for log graders and scalers
- $32,390 for logging equipment operators
- $34,560 for all other logging workers

Job Outlook

Logging Workers
Percent change in employment, projected 2010-20

Total, All Occupations	14%
Logging Workers	4%
Farming, Fishing, and Forestry Occupations	-2%

Note: All Occupations includes all occupations in the U.S. Economy.
Source: U.S. Bureau of Labor Statistics, Employment Projections program

Employment of logging workers is expected to increase by 4 percent between 2010 and 2020, slower than the average for all occupations. Logging workers should have good job prospects overall.

New policies allowing some access to federal timberland may result in some logging jobs. Federal legislation designed to prevent destructive wildfires by proactively thinning susceptible forests may result in additional jobs.

Foreign and domestic demand for wood products, such as wood pellets, is expected to lead to some employment growth.

Nonetheless, domestic timber producers continue to face increasing competition from foreign producers, which can harvest at a lower cost.

The logging industry will continue to consolidate to reduce costs, an approach that may offset the creation of new jobs.

Increased mechanization of logging operations and improvements in logging equipment will continue to depress demand for many timber-cutting and logging workers who work by hand.

Overall employment should decline as more labor-saving equipment is used. Employment of machinery and equipment operators will be less affected and should rise as logging companies switch away from tree felling by hand.

Job Prospects

Despite slower-than-average employment growth, job opportunities should be good because of the need to replace workers who leave the occupation for other jobs that are less physically demanding.

Employment of logging workers can be unsteady because changes in the level of construction, particularly residential construction, can cause short-term slowdowns in logging activities.

In addition, logging operations must be relocated when all of the timber in a particular area has been harvested. During prolonged periods of inactivity, some workers may stay on the job to maintain or repair logging machinery and equipment while others are laid off or forced to find jobs elsewhere.

Employment projections data for logging workers, 2010-20

Occupational Title	SOC Code	Employment, 2010	Projected Employment, 2020	Change, 2010-20 Percent	Change, 2010-20 Numeric
Logging Workers	45-4020	53,200	55,500	4	2,300
Fallers	45-4021	9,600	9,900	3	300
Logging Equipment Operators	45-4022	35,100	36,400	4	1,300
Log Graders and Scalers	45-4023	3,800	4,300	13	500
Logging Workers, All Other	45-4029	4,800	4,900	3	100
SOURCE: U.S. Bureau of Labor Statistics, Employment Projections program					

Similar Occupations

This table shows a list of occupations with job duties that are similar to those of logging workers.

Occupation	Job Duties	Entry-Level Education	Median Annual Pay, May 2010
Conservation Scientists and Foresters	Conservation scientists and foresters manage overall land quality of forests, parks, rangelands, and other natural resources.	Bachelor's degree	$57,420
Construction Equipment Operators	Construction equipment operators drive, maneuver, or control the heavy machinery used to construct roads, bridges, buildings, and other structures.	High school diploma or equivalent	$39,460
Forest and Conservation Technicians	Forest and conservation technicians measure and improve the quality of forests, rangeland, and other natural areas.	Associate's degree	$33,390
Forest and Conservation Workers	Forest and conservation workers measure and improve the quality of forests. Under the supervision of foresters and forest and conservation technicians, they help to develop, maintain, and protect forests.	High school diploma or equivalent	$23,900

Contacts for More Information

For information about timber-cutting and logging careers and about secondary and postsecondary programs offering training for logging occupations, visit Forest Resources Association, Inc.

Suggested citation:

Bureau of Labor Statistics, U.S. Department of Labor, Occupational Outlook Handbook, 2012-13 Edition, Logging Workers, on the Internet at http://www.bls.gov/ooh/farming-fishing-and-forestry/logging-workers.htm.

Food Preparation and Serving Occupations

Bartenders

Quick Facts: Bartenders	
2010 Median Pay	$18,680 per year $8.98 per hour
Entry-Level Education	Less than high school
Work Experience in a Related Occupation	None
On-the-job Training	Short-term on-the-job training
Number of Jobs, 2010	503,200
Job Outlook, 2010-20	9% (Slower than average)
Employment Change, 2010-20	45,500

What Bartenders Do

Bartenders mix and serve drinks to customers directly or through wait staff.

Duties

Bartenders typically do the following:

- Greet customers, inform them about daily specials, and give them menus
- Take drink orders from customers
- Pour wine and serve draft or bottled beer and other alcoholic or nonalcoholic drinks
- Mix drinks according to recipes
- Check identification of customers to ensure they are of legal drinking age
- Clean bars, tables, and work areas
- Operate cash registers, collect payments from customers, and return change
- Manage bar operation and order and maintain liquor and bar supplies

Bartenders fill drink orders either directly from patrons at the bar or through waiters and waitresses who place drink orders for dining room customers. Bartenders must know a wide range of drink recipes and be able to mix drinks accurately, quickly, and without waste.

Bartenders also are responsible for checking the identification of customers seated at the bar to ensure they meet the minimum age requirement to buy alcohol and tobacco products.

Some establishments, especially busy establishments with many customers, use equipment that automatically measures, pours, and mixes drinks at the push of a button. Bartenders who use this equipment, however, still must work quickly to handle a large quantity of drink orders and be familiar with the ingredients for special drink requests.

Bartenders in some establishments also may use carbonated beverage dispensers, cocktail shakers or accessories, commercial strainers, mist or trigger sprayers, and ice shaver machines.

In addition to mixing and serving drinks, bartenders stock and prepare garnishes for drinks and maintain an adequate supply of ice, glasses, and other bar supplies. They also may wash glassware and utensils, and serve food to customers who eat at the bar. Bartenders are usually responsible for ordering and maintaining an inventory of liquor, mixers, and other bar supplies.

Work Environment

Bartenders held about 503,200 jobs in 2010. The industries that employed the most bartenders in 2010 were as follows:

Full-service restaurants	39%
Drinking places (alcoholic beverages)	30
Civic, social, professional, and similar organizations	9
Traveler accommodation, including hotels and motels	7
Other amusement and recreation industries	5

Bartenders work at restaurants, bars, clubs, hotels, and other food service establishments.

During busy hours, they are under pressure to serve customers quickly and efficiently, while ensuring that no alcohol is served to minors or overly intoxicated customers.

Bartenders perform repetitive tasks, and sometimes they lift heavy kegs of beer and cases of liquor. In addition, the work can be stressful because they often deal with heavily intoxicated customers to whom they must deny service.

Many bartenders work full time, and they often must work late evenings, weekends, and holidays. About 40 percent work part time.

How to Become a Bartender

Many bartenders are promoted from other jobs at the food service establishments in which they work and receive short-term on-the-job training. However, those who wish to work at more upscale establishments usually need previous work experience or vocational training.

Although most states require workers who serve alcoholic beverages to be at least 18 years old, many employers prefer to hire people who are 25 or older.

There are no specific education requirements.

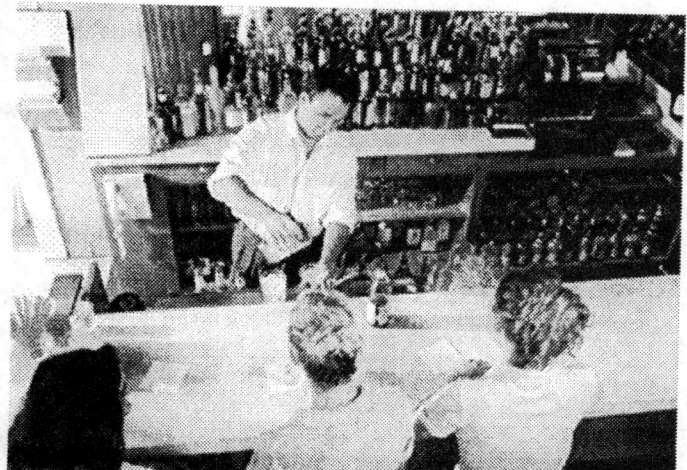

Bartenders mix and serve drinks to customers at a bar.

Training

Most bartenders receive short-term on-the-job training, usually lasting a few weeks, under the guidance of a more experienced bartender. Training programs focus on basic customer service, teamwork, and food safety procedures. Programs also provide an opportunity to discuss proper ways to handle unruly customers and unpleasant situations.

Some employers teach new workers using self-study programs, online programs, audiovisual presentations, or instructional booklets that explain service skills. Such programs communicate the philosophy of the establishment, help new bartenders build personal rapports with other staff, and instill a desire to work as a team.

Work Experience

Some bartenders qualify through work-related experience. They may start as bartender helpers and progress into full-fledged bartenders as they learn basic mixing procedures and recipes. New workers often learn by working with a more experienced bartender.

Education

Some bartenders acquire their skills through formal training, either by attending a school for bartending or a vocational and technical school with bartending classes. These programs often include instruction on state and local laws and regulations, cocktail recipes, proper attire and conduct, and stocking a bar. The lengths of programs vary, but most courses last a few weeks. Some schools help their graduates find jobs.

Advancement

Advancement for bartenders is usually limited to finding a job in a busier or more expensive restaurant or bar where prospects of earning tips are better. Some bartenders advance to supervisory jobs, such as dining room supervisor, maitre d', assistant manager, or restaurant general manager. A few bartenders open their own bar.

Important Qualities

Customer-service skills. Because establishments that serve alcohol rely on retaining old and attracting new customers, bartenders should have good customer service skills to ensure repeat business.

Decision-making skills. Because of the legal issues that come with serving alcohol, bartenders must make good decisions at all times. For example, they should be able to detect intoxicated customers and deny service to those customers.

People skills. Bartenders should be friendly, tactful, and attentive when dealing with customers. For example, they should be able to tell a joke and laugh with a customer to build rapport.

Stamina. Bartenders work on their feet for long periods of time. Many lift heavy cases of liquor, beer, or other bar supplies.

Teamwork. Bartenders often fill drink orders for waiters and waitresses who are serving dining room customers. As a result, bartenders must work well with their colleagues to ensure that customers receive prompt service.

Pay

Bartenders
Median hourly wages, May 2010

Total, All Occupations	$16.27
Bartenders	$8.98
Food and Beverage Serving Workers	$8.75

Note: All Occupations includes all occupations in the U.S. Economy.
Source: U.S. Bureau of Labor Statistics, Occupational Employment Statistics

The median hourly wage (including tips) of bartenders was $8.98 in May 2010. The median wage is the wage at which half the workers in an occupation earned more than that amount and half earned less. The lowest 10 percent earned less than $7.60 per hour, and the top 10 percent earned more than $15.14 per hour.

Bartenders' earnings often come from a combination of hourly wages and customers' tips. Earnings vary greatly, depending on the type of establishment. For example, in many full-service restaurants, tips are higher than wages.

Many entry-level or inexperienced workers earn the federal minimum wage. However, many others earn more per hour because they work in states that set minimum wages higher than the federal minimum.

Many bartenders work full time, and they must often work late evenings, weekends, and holidays. About 40 percent work part time.

Job Outlook

Bartenders
Percent change in employment, projected 2010-20

Total, All Occupations	14%
Food and Beverage Serving Workers	12%
Bartenders	9%

Note: All Occupations includes all occupations in the U.S. Economy.
Source: U.S. Bureau of Labor Statistics, Employment Projections program

Employment of bartenders is expected to grow 9 percent from 2010 to 2020, slower than the average for all occupations.

As people continue to dine out and drink at a variety of food and drinking places, many new bars, taverns, and restaurants are expected to open to meet demand. However, the growing popularity of take-out food and the growing number and variety of places that offer self-service or carryout options, including many full-service restaurants, will limit employment growth.

Job Prospects

Job opportunities are expected to be good because of the need to replace workers who leave the occupation. Strong competition is expected for bartending jobs in popular restaurants and fine-dining establishments, where potential earnings from tips are greatest. Those who have graduated from bartending school and those with previous work experience and excellent customer-service skills will have the best job prospects.

Employment projections data for bartenders, 2010-20

Occupational Title	SOC Code	Employment, 2010	Projected Employment, 2020	Change, 2010-20	
				Percent	Numeric
Bartenders	35-3011	503,200	548,700	9	45,500

SOURCE: U.S. Bureau of Labor Statistics, Employment Projections program

Similar Occupations

This table shows a list of occupations with job duties that are similar to those of bartenders.

Occupation	Job Duties	Entry-Level Education	Median Annual Pay, May 2010
Cashiers	Cashiers handle payments from customers purchasing goods and services.	Less than high school	$18,500
Flight Attendants	Flight attendants provide personal services to ensure the safety and comfort of airline passengers.	High school diploma or equivalent	$37,740
Food and Beverage Serving and Related Workers	Food and beverage serving and related workers perform a variety of customer service, food preparation, and cleaning duties in full-service restaurants, casual dining eateries, and other eating and drinking places.	Less than high school	$18,130
Food Preparation Workers	Food preparation workers perform many routine tasks under the guidance of cooks or food supervisors. They prepare cold foods, slice meat, peel and cut vegetables, brew coffee or tea, and do many other tasks.	Less than high school	$19,100
Waiters and Waitresses	Waiters and waitresses take orders and serve food and beverages to customers in dining establishments.	Less than high school	$18,330

Contacts for More Information

For more information on becoming a bartender, visit National Restaurant Association

Suggested citation:

Bureau of Labor Statistics, U.S. Department of Labor, Occupational Outlook Handbook, 2012-13 Edition, Bartenders, on the Internet at http://www.bls.gov/ooh/food-preparation-and-serving/bartenders.htm .

Chefs and Head Cooks

Quick Facts: Chefs and Head Cooks	
2010 Median Pay	$40,630 per year $19.53 per hour
Entry-Level Education	High school diploma or equivalent
Work Experience in a Related Occupation	1 to 5 years
On-the-job Training	None
Number of Jobs, 2010	100,600
Job Outlook, 2010-20	-1% (Little or no change)
Employment Change, 2010-20	-800

What Chefs and Head Cooks Do

Chefs and head cooks oversee the daily food preparation at restaurants or other places where food is served. They direct kitchen staff and handle any food-related concerns.

Duties

Chefs and head cooks typically do the following:

- Check freshness of food and ingredients
- Supervise and coordinate activities of cooks and other food preparation workers
- Develop recipes and determine how to present the food
- Plan menus and ensure uniform serving sizes and quality of meals
- Inspect supplies, equipment, and work areas for cleanliness and functionality
- Hire, train, and supervise cooks and other food preparation workers
- Order and maintain inventory of food and supplies needed to ensure efficient operations
- Monitor sanitation practices and ensure that kitchen safety standards are followed

Chefs use a variety of kitchen and cooking equipment, including step-in coolers, high-quality knives, meat slicers, and grinders. They also have access to large quantities of meats, spices, and produce. Some chefs use scheduling and purchasing software to help them in their administrative duties.

Chefs might also be a restaurant's owner. Some may be busy with kitchen and office work and not have time to interact with diners.

The following are types of chefs and head cooks:

Executive chefs, head cooks, and chefs de cuisine are primarily responsible for overseeing the operation of a kitchen. They coordinate the work of sous chefs and other cooks, who prepare most of the meals. Executive chefs also have many duties beyond the kitchen. They design the menu, review food and beverage purchases, and often train employees. Some executive chefs are primarily occupied by administrative tasks and spend little time in the kitchen.

Sous chefs are a kitchen's second-in-command. They supervise the restaurant's cooks, do some meal preparation tasks, and report results to the head chefs. In the absence of the head chef, sous chefs run the kitchen.

Chefs oversee the daily operation of a restaurant.

Personal chefs plan and prepare meals in private homes. They also may order groceries and supplies, serve meals, and wash dishes and utensils. Personal chefs are often self-employed or employed by a private cooking company, preparing food for a variety of customers.

Private household chefs typically work full time for one client, such as a corporate executive, university president, or diplomat, who regularly entertains as part of his or her official duties.

Work Environment

Chefs and head cooks held about 100,600 jobs in 2010. Industries employing the most chefs and head cooks in 2010 were as follows:

Full-service restaurants	46%
Traveler accommodation, including hotels and motels	11
Special food services	9
Other amusement and recreation industries	6
Limited-service eating places	5

Chefs work in restaurants, hotels, private households, and other food service facilities, all of which must be kept clean and sanitary. Kitchens are usually hot, crowded, and filled with potential dangers. Hazards may include slips, falls, cuts, and burns, but these injuries are seldom serious. Chefs and head cooks usually must stand for long periods of time and work in a fast-paced environment.

Work Schedules

Most chefs and head cooks work full time, including early mornings, late evenings, weekends, and holidays. Many executive chefs regularly work 12-hour days because they oversee the delivery of food supplies early in the day and use the afternoon to plan the menu and prepare any special items for dishes.

How to Become a Chef or Head Cook

Most chefs acquire their skills through work experience. Many others, however, receive formal training at a community college, technical school, culinary arts school, or a 2-year or 4-year college. A few learn through apprenticeship programs or in the armed forces.

Work Experience

Most chefs and head cooks start working in kitchens in other positions, such as line cooks or dishwashers, learning cooking skills from the chefs they work for. Many spend years working in kitchens before learning enough to get promoted to chef or head cook positions.

Education

A growing number of chefs and head cooks receive formal training at community colleges, technical schools, culinary arts schools, and 2-year or 4-year institutions. Students in culinary programs spend most of their time in kitchens practicing their cooking skills. These programs cover all aspects of kitchen work, including menu planning, food sanitation procedures, and purchasing and inventory methods. Most formal training programs also require students to get experience in a commercial kitchen through an internship, apprenticeship, or out-placement program.

Apprenticeship

Formal apprenticeship programs sponsored by professional culinary institutes, industry associations, and trade unions in coordination with the U.S. Department of Labor , also are common. Apprenticeship programs generally last about 2 years and combine classroom training and work experience. The American Culinary Federation accredits more than 200 formal academic training programs at post-secondary schools and sponsors apprenticeships around the country.

Training

Some chefs and head cooks train in mentorship programs, where they work under the direction of experienced chefs. Executive chefs, head cooks, and sous chefs who work in fine-dining restaurants have many years of training and experience.

Some chefs receive formal training through the armed forces or from individual hotel or restaurant chains.

Certification

Although not required, certification can show competence and lead to advancement and higher paying positions. The American Culinary Federation certifies pastry professionals, personal chefs, and culinary educators in addition to various levels of chefs. Certification standards are based primarily on work-related experience and formal training. The minimum work experience for certification can range from 6 months to 5 years, depending on the level of certification.

Important Qualities

Business skills. Executive chefs must understand the business of restaurant work. They should be skilled at administrative tasks, such as accounting and personnel management, and be able to manage a restaurant efficiently and profitably.

Creativity. Chefs and head cooks need creativity to develop and prepare interesting and innovative recipes. They must be able to use different ingredients and create appealing dishes for their customers.

Leadership skills. Chefs and head cooks must have the ability to motivate kitchen staff and develop constructive and cooperative working relationships with them. Because the pace in the kitchen can be hectic during peak dining hours, chefs must be able to communicate their orders clearly and effectively.

Manual dexterity. All chefs and head cooks need excellent manual dexterity, including proper knife techniques for cutting, chopping, and dicing.

Sense of taste and smell. All chefs and head cooks must have a keen sense of taste and smell in order to inspect food and design meals that will be to customers' liking.

Time-management skills. Chefs and head cooks need to be able to efficiently manage their time and the time of kitchen staff. They must have menus ready when kitchen staff start preparing meals. And when customers are waiting for food, they must keep the kitchen running efficiently.

Pay

Chefs and Head Cooks
Median annual wages, May 2010

Chefs and Head Cooks	$40,630
Total, All Occupations	$33,840
Supervisors of Food Preparation and Serving Workers	$30,370

Note: All Occupations includes all occupations in the U.S. Economy.
Source: U.S. Bureau of Labor Statistics, Occupational Employment Statistics

The median annual wage of chefs and head cooks was $40,630 in May 2010. The median wage is the wage at which half the workers in an occupation earned more than that amount and half earned less. The lowest 10 percent earned less than $23,260, and the top 10 percent earned more than $70,960.

The median annual wages in the industries employing the largest numbers of chefs and head cooks in 2010 were as follows:

Traveler accommodation, including hotels and motels	$47,350
Other amusement and recreation industries	47,340
Special food services	42,380
Full-service restaurants	38,520
Limited-service eating places	27,840

The level of pay for chefs and head cooks varies greatly by region and employer. Pay is usually highest in upscale restaurants and hotels, where many executive chefs are employed, as well as in major metropolitan and resort areas.

Most chefs and head cooks work full time, and they often work early mornings, late evenings, weekends, and holidays. Many executive chefs regularly work 12-hour days because they oversee the delivery of food products early in the day and use the afternoon to plan the menu and prepare any special items for dishes.

Job Outlook

Chefs and Head Cooks
Percent change in employment, projected 2010-20

Total, All Occupations	14%
Supervisors of Food Preparation and Serving Workers	9%
Chefs and Head Cooks	-1%

Note: All Occupations includes all occupations in the U.S. Economy.
Source: U.S. Bureau of Labor Statistics, Employment Projections program

Employment of chefs and head cooks is projected to experience little or no change from 2010 to 2020. Population and income growth is expected to result in greater demand for more high-quality dishes at a variety of dining venues, including many up-scale establishments. However, employment growth will be tempered as many restaurants, in an effort to lower costs, use lower-level cooks to perform the work normally done by chefs and head cooks.

Job Prospects

Job opportunities will be best for chefs and head cooks with several years of work experience. The majority of job openings will stem from the need to replace workers who leave the occupation. The fast pace, long hours, and high energy levels required for these jobs often lead to a high rate of turnover.

There will be strong competition for jobs at upscale restaurants, hotels, and casinos, which tend to pay more. Workers with a combination of business skills, previous work experience, and creativity will have the best job prospects.

Employment projections data for chefs and head cooks, 2010-20

Occupational Title	SOC Code	Employment, 2010	Projected Employment, 2020	Change, 2010-20 Percent	Change, 2010-20 Numeric
Chefs and Head Cooks	35-1011	100,600	99,800	-1	-800
SOURCE: U.S. Bureau of Labor Statistics, Employment Projections program					

Similar Occupations

This table shows a list of occupations with job duties that are similar to those of chefs and head cooks.

Occupation	Job Duties	Entry-Level Education	Median Annual Pay, May 2010
Bakers	Bakers mix and bake ingredients according to recipes to make a variety of breads, pastries, and other baked goods.	Less than high school	$23,450
Cooks	Cooks prepare, season, and cook a wide range of foods, such as soups, salads, entrees, and desserts.	See How to Become One	$20,260
Food and Beverage Serving and Related Workers	Food and beverage serving and related workers perform a variety of customer service, food preparation, and cleaning duties in full-service restaurants, casual dining eateries, and other eating and drinking places.	Less than high school	$18,130
Food Preparation Workers	Food preparation workers perform many routine tasks under the guidance of cooks or food supervisors. They prepare cold foods, slice meat, peel and cut vegetables, brew coffee or tea, and do many other tasks.	Less than high school	$19,100
Food Service Managers	Food service managers are responsible for the daily operations of restaurants and other establishments that prepare and serve food and beverages to customers. Managers ensure that customers are satisfied with their dining experience.	High school diploma or equivalent	$48,130

Contacts for More Information

For career information about chefs, including a directory of 2-year and 4-year colleges that offer courses or training programs, visit National Restaurant Association , American Culinary Federation ,For information about becoming a personal or private chef, visit American Personal & Private Chefs Association

Suggested citation:

Bureau of Labor Statistics, U.S. Department of Labor, Occupational Outlook Handbook, 2012-13 Edition, Chefs and Head Cooks, on the Internet at http://www.bls.gov/ooh/food-preparation-and-serving/chefs-and-head-cooks.htm .

Cooks

Quick Facts: Cooks	
2010 Median Pay	$20,260 per year $9.74 per hour
Entry-Level Education	See How to Become One
Work Experience in a Related Occupation	See How to Become One
On-the-job Training	See How to Become One
Number of Jobs, 2010	2,050,800
Job Outlook, 2010-20	8% (Slower than average)
Employment Change, 2010-20	161,800

What Cooks Do

Cooks prepare, season, and cook a wide range of foods, such as soups, salads, entrees, and desserts.

Duties

Cooks typically do the following:
- Check freshness of food and ingredients before cooking
- Weigh, measure, and mix ingredients according to recipes
- Bake, roast, grill, broil, or fry meats, fish, vegetables, and other foods
- Boil and steam meats, fish, vegetables, and other foods

Cooks season and prepare a wide range of food.

- Garnish, arrange, and serve food
- Clean work areas, equipment, utensils, dishes, and silverware
- Cook, hold, and store food or food ingredients

Large restaurants and food service establishments tend to have varied menus and large kitchen staffs. Teams of restaurant cooks, sometimes called **assistant** or **line cooks**, work at assigned stations equipped with the necessary types of stoves, grills, pans, and ingredients.

Job titles often reflect the principal ingredient cooks prepare or the type of cooking they do—**vegetable cook, fry cook**, or **grill cook**, for example. Cooks usually work under the direction or supervision of chefs, head cooks, or food service managers. For more information on these occupations, see the profiles on chefs and head cooks and food service managers .

Depending on the type of eating place, cooks use a variety of kitchen equipment, including broilers, grills, slicers, grinders, and blenders.

The responsibilities of cooks vary depending on where they work, the size of the facility, and the complexity and level of service offered.

The following are types of cooks:

Institution and cafeteria cooks work in the kitchens of schools, cafeterias, businesses, hospitals, and other institutions. For each meal, they prepare a large quantity of a limited number of entrees, vegetables, and desserts, according to preset menus. Because meals generally are prepared in advance, cooks seldom prepare special orders.

Restaurant cooks usually prepare a wide selection of dishes and cook most orders individually. Some restaurant cooks may order supplies, set menu prices, and plan the daily menu.

Short-order cooks prepare foods in restaurants and coffee shops that emphasize fast service and quick food preparation. They usually prepare sandwiches, fry eggs, and cook french fries, often working on several orders at the same time.

Fast-food cooks prepare a limited selection of menu items in fast-food restaurants. They cook and package food, such as hamburgers and fried chicken, to be kept warm until served. For more information on workers who prepare and serve items in fast-food restaurants, see the profile on food preparation workers and food and beverage serving and related workers .

Private household cooks plan and prepare meals in private homes, according to the client's tastes and dietary needs. They order groceries and supplies, clean the kitchen, and wash dishes and utensils. They also may cater parties, holiday meals, luncheons, and other social events. Most private household chefs typically work for one full-time client.

Work Environment

Cooks held about 2.1 million jobs in 2010. The industries that employed the most cooks in 2010 were as follows:

Full-service restaurants	41%
Limited-service eating places	27
Health care and social assistance	8
Elementary and secondary schools	6

Cooks work in restaurants, schools, hospitals, hotels, and other places where food is served. Some work in private homes.

Kitchens are usually hot, crowded, and filled with potential dangers. Cooks usually must stand for a long period of time and work under pressure in a fast-paced environment.

Injuries

Although the work is generally not dangerous, hazards include slips, falls, cuts from sharp knives, and burns from hot ovens.

Work Schedules

Most cooks work full time but many work part time. Work shifts can include early mornings, late evenings, weekends, and holidays. Schedules for cooks in school cafeterias and some institutional cafeterias usually are more regular. Cooks working in schools may work only during the school year, usually for 9 or 10 months. Similarly, resort establishments offer seasonal employment only.

How to Become a Cook

Short-term on-the-job training and work-related experience are the most common ways to become a cook. Although no formal education is required, some restaurant cooks and private household cooks attend cooking schools. Others attend vocational or apprenticeship programs.

Training

Most cooks obtain their skills through short-term on-the-job training, usually lasting a few weeks. Training usually starts with learning kitchen basics and workplace safety and continues with food handling and cooking procedures.

Professional culinary institutes, industry associations, and trade unions sponsor formal apprenticeship programs for cooks, in coordination with the U.S. Department of Labor. Typical apprenticeships last 2 years and combine technical training and work experience. The American Culinary Federation accredits more than 200 formal academic training programs and sponsors apprenticeship programs around the country.

Some hotels, restaurants, and the Armed Forces have their own training and job-placement programs.

Work Experience

Many cooks obtain their skills through work-related experience. They typically start as a kitchen helper or food preparation worker and progress into a cooking position. Some learn by working under the guidance of a more experienced cook.

Education

Independent and vocational cooking schools, professional culinary institutes, and college degree programs also provide training for aspiring cooks. Programs generally last from a few months to 2 years or more. Many offer training in advanced cooking techniques, international cuisines, and cooking styles.

Advancement

The American Culinary Federation certifies chefs and culinarians in different skill levels. For cooks seeking certification and advancement to higher level chef positions, certification can show accomplishment and lead to higher paying positions.

Advancement opportunities for cooks often depend on training, work experience, and the ability to do more sophisticated tasks. Those who demonstrate an eagerness to learn new cooking skills and who accept greater responsibility may advance and be asked to train or supervise kitchen staff who have fewer skills.

Some may become head cooks, chefs, or food preparation and serving supervisors.

Important Qualities

Comprehension. Cooks must be able to understand customers' orders and to read recipes to prepare dishes correctly.

Customer-service skills. Restaurant and short-order cooks must be able to deal with customer complaints and special requests.

Manual dexterity. Cooks should have excellent hand-eye coordination. For example, they need to know the proper knife techniques for cutting, chopping, and dicing.

Sense of taste and smell. All cooks must have a keen sense of taste and smell to prepare food that customers enjoy.

Stamina. The work of a cook can be physically tiring. They must spend a lot of time standing, cooking food over hot stoves, and cleaning work areas.

Teamwork. Cooks often prepare only part of a dish. They must coordinate with other cooks and food workers.

Pay

Cooks

Median hourly wages, May 2010

Total, All Occupations	$16.27
Cooks	$9.74
Cooks and Food Preparation Workers	$9.53

Note: All Occupations includes all occupations in the U.S. Economy.
Source: U.S. Bureau of Labor Statistics, Occupational Employment Statistics

The median hourly wage of cooks was $9.74 in May 2010. The median wage is the wage at which half the workers in an occupation earned more than that amount and half earned less. The lowest 10 percent earned less than $7.73 per hour, and the top 10 percent earned more than $14.67 per hour.

Median hourly wages for cook occupations in May 2010 were as follows:

- $12.29 for cooks, private household
- $10.93 for cooks, institution and cafeteria
- $10.65 for cooks, restaurant
- $9.42 for cooks, short order
- $8.70 for cooks, fast food
- $10.93 for cooks, all other

Earnings of cooks vary greatly by region and type of employer. Earnings usually are highest in fine dining restaurants and luxury hotels, which are often found in major metropolitan and resort areas.

Most cooks work full time but many work part time. Work shifts can include early mornings, late evenings, weekends, and holidays. Schedules for cooks in school cafeterias and some institutional cafeterias usually are more regular. Cooks working in schools may work only during the school year, usually for 9 or 10 months. Similarly, resort establishments offer seasonal employment only.

Job Outlook

Cooks

Percent change in employment, projected 2010-20

Total, All Occupations	14%
Cooks and Food Preparation Workers	9%
Cooks	8%

Note: All Occupations includes all occupations in the U.S. Economy.
Source: U.S. Bureau of Labor Statistics, Employment Projections program

Overall employment of cooks is projected to grow 8 percent from 2010 to 2020, slower than the average for all occupations. Individual growth rates will vary by specialty.

People continue to eat out, buy take-out meals, or have food delivered. In response, more restaurants will open, and nontraditional food-service operations, such as those found inside grocery stores, will serve more prepared food dishes, spurring demand for cooks.

Employment growth for cooks will also increase as, in an effort to lower costs, many full-service restaurants will hire lower level cooks instead of chefs and head cooks.

Job Prospects

Overall job opportunities are expected to be good as a combination of employment growth and current workers leaving the occupation leads to a large number of job openings. Cooks with formal training will have the best job prospects.

Candidates who demonstrate eagerness and are able to do more refined tasks will have the best job opportunities at restaurant chains, upscale restaurants, and hotels. Nonetheless, those seeking full-time jobs at upscale restaurants and hotels are likely to face competition, as the number of job applicants often exceeds the number of job openings.

Employment projections data for cooks, 2010-20

Occupational Title	SOC Code	Employment, 2010	Projected Employment, 2020	Change, 2010-20 Percent	Change, 2010-20 Numeric
Cooks	35-2010	2,050,800	2,212,600	8	161,800
Cooks, Fast Food	35-2011	530,400	511,400	-4	-19,100
Cooks, Institution and Cafeteria	35-2012	405,300	455,100	12	49,800
Cooks, Private Household	35-2013	3,600	4,100	14	500
Cooks, Restaurant	35-2014	915,400	1,033,200	13	117,800
Cooks, Short Order	35-2015	174,200	183,600	5	9,400
Cooks, All Other	35-2019	21,900	25,200	15	3,300

SOURCE: U.S. Bureau of Labor Statistics, Employment Projections program

Similar Occupations

This table shows a list of occupations with job duties that are similar to those of cooks.

Occupation	Job Duties	Entry-Level Education	Median Annual Pay, May 2010
Bakers	Bakers mix and bake ingredients according to recipes to make a variety of breads, pastries, and other baked goods.	Less than high school	$23,450
Chefs and Head Cooks	Chefs and head cooks oversee the daily food preparation at restaurants or other places where food is served. They direct kitchen staff and handle any food-related concerns.	High school diploma or equivalent	$40,630
Food and Beverage Serving and Related Workers	Food and beverage serving and related workers perform a variety of customer service, food preparation, and cleaning duties in full-service restaurants, casual dining eateries, and other eating and drinking places.	Less than high school	$18,130
Food Preparation Workers	Food preparation workers perform many routine tasks under the guidance of cooks or food supervisors. They prepare cold foods, slice meat, peel and cut vegetables, brew coffee or tea, and do many other tasks.	Less than high school	$19,100
Food Service Managers	Food service managers are responsible for the daily operations of restaurants and other establishments that prepare and serve food and beverages to customers. Managers ensure that customers are satisfied with their dining experience.	High school diploma or equivalent	$48,130

Contacts for More Information

For information about culinary apprenticeship programs registered with the U.S. Department of Labor, contact the local office of your state employment service agency, check the Employment and Training Administration website, or call the toll-free helpline, 1 (877) 872-5627.

For more information about cooking careers, visit National Restaurant Association ,American Culinary Federation

Suggested citation:

Bureau of Labor Statistics, U.S. Department of Labor, Occupational Outlook Handbook, 2012-13 Edition, Cooks, on the Internet at http://www.bls.gov/ooh/food-preparation-and-serving/cooks.htm .

Food and Beverage Serving and Related Workers

Quick Facts: Food and Beverage Serving and Related Workers	
2010 Median Pay	$18,130 per year $8.72 per hour
Entry-Level Education	Less than high school
Work Experience in a Related Occupation	None
On-the-job Training	See How to Become One
Number of Jobs, 2010	4,110,400
Job Outlook, 2010-20	12% (About as fast as average)
Employment Change, 2010-20	491,600

What Food and Beverage Serving and Related Workers Do

Food and beverage serving and related workers perform a variety of customer service, food preparation, and cleaning duties in full-service restaurants, casual dining eateries, and other eating and drinking places.

Duties

Food and beverage serving and related workers typically do the following:

- Prepare and clean assigned work areas
- Replenish and stock service stations, cabinets, and tables
- Serve food and drinks to customers from behind a counter
- Greet customers, escort them to their seats, and hand them menus
- Answer customers' questions about menu items and specials
- Clean tables and dining areas
- Set tables for new customers

Food and beverage serving and related workers are the front line of customer service in full-service restaurants, casual dining eateries, and other food service establishments. Depending on the establishment, they might take customers' food and drink orders and prepare and serve food and beverages. Most work as part of a team, helping coworkers to improve workflow and customer service.

The job titles of food and beverage serving and related workers vary depending on where they work and what they do. The following are types of food and beverage serving and related workers:

Combined food preparation and serving workers, including

Food and beverage workers are employed by restaurants and eateries.

fast food, are employed primarily by fast-food restaurants. They take food and beverage orders, retrieve items when ready, fill drink cups, and accept payment. They also may heat food items and assemble salads and sandwiches.

Counter attendants take orders and serve food over a counter in snack bars, cafeterias, movie theaters, and coffee shops. They fill cups with coffee, soda, and other beverages, and may prepare fountain specialties, such as milkshakes and ice cream sundaes. Counter attendants take carryout orders from diners and wrap or place items in containers. They clean counters, write itemized bills, and sometimes accept payment.

Food servers, nonrestaurant, serve food to patrons outside of a restaurant environment. Many deliver room service meals in hotels or meals to hospital rooms. Some act as carhops, bringing orders to parked cars.

Dining room and cafeteria attendants and bartender helpers—sometimes collectively referred to as bus staff—help waiters, waitresses, and bartenders by cleaning and setting tables, removing dirty dishes, and keeping serving areas stocked with supplies. They also may help waiters and waitresses by bringing meals out of the kitchen, distributing dishes to diners, filling water glasses, and delivering condiments. **Cafeteria attendants** stock serving tables with food trays, dishes, and silverware. They may carry trays to dining tables for patrons. **Bartender helpers** keep bar equipment clean and glasses washed.

Hosts and hostesses welcome customers and keep reservation and waiting lists. They may direct customers to coatrooms, restrooms, or to a waiting area until their table is ready. Hosts and hostesses assign guests to tables suitable for the size of their group, escort patrons to their seats, and provide menus. They also take reservations, arrange parties, and help with other requests.

Work Environment

Food and beverage serving and related workers held about 4.1 million jobs in 2010.

The industries that employed the most workers in 2010 were as follows:

Limited-service eating places	55%
Full-service restaurants	16
Special food services	4
Elementary and secondary schools	4
Grocery stores	3

Food and beverage serving and related workers are on their feet most of the time and often carry heavy trays of food, dishes, and glassware. During busy dining periods, they are under pressure to serve customers quickly and efficiently.

Injuries

Although the work is generally safe, injuries from slips, cuts, and burns can result from hurrying or mishandling sharp tools.

Work Schedules

In 2010, about half of all food and beverage serving and related workers worked part time. Food service and drinking establishments typically have long dining hours and offer flexible and varied work opportunities. Many workers work evenings, weekends, and holidays.

Additionally, long business hours allow for flexible schedules that appeal to many teenagers, who can gain work experience. Compared to all other occupations, a much larger proportion of food and beverage serving and related workers were 16 to 19 years old in 2010.

How to Become a Food and Beverage Serving or Related Worker

Most food and beverage service jobs are entry level and do not require a high school diploma. The majority of workers receive short-term on-the-job training.

Training

All new employees receive some training from their employer. They typically learn basic customer service, kitchen safety, and safe food-handling procedures and sanitation.

Some employers, particularly those in fast-food restaurants, teach new workers using self-study programs, online programs, audiovisual presentations, or instructional booklets that explain food preparation and service skills. But most food and beverage serving and related workers pick up their skills by watching and working with more experienced workers.

Some full-service restaurants also provide new dining room employees with classroom training that alternates with periods of on-the-job work experience. These training programs communicate the operating philosophy of the restaurant, help new employees establish a personal rapport with other staff, teach formal serving techniques, and instill a desire to work as a team.

Advancement

Advancement opportunities are often limited to those who remain on the job for a long period of time. After gaining experience, some dining room and cafeteria attendants and bartender helpers may advance into jobs as a waiter, waitress, or bartender.

Important Qualities

Customer-service skills. Food service establishments rely on good food and customer service to keep customers and succeed in a competitive industry. As a result, workers should be courteous and be able to quickly attend to customers' requests.

Stamina. Food and beverage serving and related workers must be able to spend much of their work time standing, carrying heavy trays, cleaning work areas, and attending to customers' needs.

Teamwork. Food serving places can often be fast-paced and hectic during peak dining hours. Food and beverage serving and related workers must be able to work well as a team to ensure that customers feel welcomed and receive prompt service.

Pay

Food and Beverage Serving and Related Workers
Median hourly wages, May 2010

Total, All Occupations	$16.27
Food Preparation and Serving Related Occupations	$9.02
Food and Beverage Serving and Related Workers	$8.72

Note: All Occupations includes all occupations in the U.S. Economy.
Source: U.S. Bureau of Labor Statistics, Occupational Employment Statistics

The median hourly wage for food and beverage serving and related workers was $8.72 in May 2010. The median wage is the wage at which half the workers in an occupation earned more than that amount and half earned less. The lowest 10 percent earned less than $7.54 per hour, and the top 10 percent earned more than $11.62 per hour.

Median hourly wages for food and beverage serving and related workers in May 2010 were as follows:

- $9.34 for food servers, nonrestaurant
- $8.87 for hosts and hostesses, restaurant, lounge, and coffee shop
- $8.83 for counter attendants, cafeteria, food concession, and coffeeshop
- $8.75 for dining room and cafeteria attendants and bartender helpers
- $8.63 for combined food preparation and serving workers, including fast food
- $9.61 for food preparation and serving related workers, all other

Some food and beverage serving workers receive customer tips. In some restaurants, workers contribute all or a portion of their tips to a tip pool, which is distributed among qualifying workers. Tip pools allow workers who do not usually receive tips directly from customers, such as dining room attendants, to be part of a team and to share in the rewards for good service.

Although some workers in this occupation earn tips, the majority get their earnings from hourly wages. Many entry-level or inexperienced workers earn the federal minimum wage ($7.25 per hour as of July 24, 2009). However, many others earn more per hour because they work in states that set minimum wages higher than the federal minimum.

Also, various exceptions to the minimum wage apply under specific circumstances to disabled workers, full-time students, youths under age 20 in their first 90 days of employment, tipped employees, and student learners. Tipped employees are those who customarily and regularly receive more than $30 a month in tips. According to the Fair Labor Standards Act, the employer may consider tips as part of wages, but the employer must pay at least $2.13 an hour in direct wages.

In 2010, about half of all food and beverage serving and related workers worked part time. Food service and drinking establishments typically have long dining hours and offer flexible and varied work opportunities. Many workers work evenings, weekends, and holidays.

Job Outlook

Food and Beverage Serving and Related Workers
Percent change in employment, projected 2010-20

Total, All Occupations	14%
Food and Beverage Serving and Related Workers	12%
Food Preparation and Serving Related Occupations	10%

Note: All Occupations includes all occupations in the U.S. Economy.
Source: U.S. Bureau of Labor Statistics, Employment Projections program

Overall employment of food and beverage serving and related workers is projected to grow 12 percent from 2010 to 2020, about as fast as the average for all occupations. Employment growth will vary by specialty.

Nonrestaurant servers, such as those who deliver food trays in hotels, hospitals, residential care facilities, and at catered events, are expected to have about as fast as average employment growth. Combined food preparation and serving workers, which includes fast-food workers, will also have about as fast as average employment growth. Because these workers are essential to the operation of a food-serving establishment, they will continue to be in demand.

Employment growth of dining room and cafeteria attendants, counter attendants, and hosts and hostesses is expected to be slower than the average. Despite slower than average employment growth, these workers will still be needed to perform important duties at food-serving establishments as a growing population continues to eat outside of the home.

Job Prospects

Job opportunities for food and beverage serving and related workers are expected to be excellent, because of the large number of workers who need to be replaced.

Workers with related work experience and excellent customer-service skills should have the best job opportunities at upscale restaurants. Still, those seeking positions at these establishments may face competition, as potential earnings from tips are greatest, so the number of job applicants often exceeds the number of job openings.

Employment projections data for food and beverage serving and related workers, 2010-20

Occupational Title	SOC Code	Employment, 2010	Projected Employment, 2020	Change, 2010-20	
				Percent	Numeric
Food and Beverage Serving and Related Workers	—	4,110,400	4,602,000	12	491,600
Combined Food Preparation and Serving Workers, Including Fast Food	35-3021	2,682,100	3,080,100	15	398,000
Counter Attendants, Cafeteria, Food Concession, and Coffee Shop	35-3022	445,500	472,900	6	27,400
Food Servers, Nonrestaurant	35-3041	208,900	246,500	18	37,600
Dining Room and Cafeteria Attendants and Bartender Helpers	35-9011	397,000	414,700	4	17,700
Hosts and Hostesses, Restaurant, Lounge, and Coffee Shop	35-9031	330,500	344,100	4	13,600
Food Preparation and Serving Related Workers, All Other	35-9099	46,400	43,700	-6	-2,700

SOURCE: U.S. Bureau of Labor Statistics, Employment Projections program

Similar Occupations

This table shows a list of occupations with job duties that are similar to those of food and beverage serving and related workers.

Occupation	Job Duties	Entry-Level Education	Median Annual Pay, May 2010
Bartenders	Bartenders mix and serve drinks to customers directly or through wait staff.	Less than high school	$18,680
Cashiers	Cashiers handle payments from customers purchasing goods and services.	Less than high school	$18,500
Cooks	Cooks prepare, season, and cook a wide range of foods, such as soups, salads, entrees, and desserts.	See How to Become One	$20,260
Food Preparation Workers	Food preparation workers perform many routine tasks under the guidance of cooks or food supervisors. They prepare cold foods, slice meat, peel and cut vegetables, brew coffee or tea, and do many other tasks.	Less than high school	$19,100
Waiters and Waitresses	Waiters and waitresses take orders and serve food and beverages to customers in dining establishments.	Less than high school	$18,330

Contacts for More Information

For more information on food and beverage serving careers, visit National Restaurant Association

Suggested citation:

Bureau of Labor Statistics, U.S. Department of Labor, Occupational Outlook Handbook, 2012-13 Edition, Food and Beverage Serving and Related Workers, on the Internet at http://www.bls.gov/ooh/food-preparation-and-serving/food-and-beverage-serving-and-related-workers.htm .

Food Preparation Workers

Quick Facts: Food Preparation Workers	
2010 Median Pay	$19,100 per year $9.18 per hour
Entry-Level Education	Less than high school
Work Experience in a Related Occupation	None
On-the-job Training	Short-term on-the-job training
Number of Jobs, 2010	813,700
Job Outlook, 2010-20	10% (About as fast as average)
Employment Change, 2010-20	84,100

What Food Preparation Workers Do

Food preparation workers perform many routine tasks under the guidance of cooks or food supervisors. They prepare cold foods, slice meat, peel and cut vegetables, brew coffee or tea, and do many other tasks.

Duties

Food preparation workers typically do the following:

- Clean and sanitize work areas, equipment, utensils, and dishes
- Weigh or measure ingredients, such as meat and cheeses
- Prepare fresh condiments, including lettuce, tomatoes, and onions
- Cut and grind meats, poultry, and seafood to prepare for cooking
- Mix ingredients for salads
- Store food in designated containers and storage areas to prevent spoilage
- Take and record temperatures of food and food storage areas
- Place food trays over food warmers for immediate service

Food preparation workers perform routine, repetitive tasks under the direction of cooks or food supervisors. To help cooks and other kitchen staff, they prepare ingredients for complex dishes by slicing

Food preparation workers cut fresh ingredients.

and dicing vegetables and by making salads and cold items.

Although most help prepare food, some are also responsible for retrieving cooking utensils, pots, and pans, or for cleaning and storing other kitchen equipment. Other common duties include keeping salad bars and buffet tables stocked and clean.

Those who work at hotels or full-service restaurants often use soda machines, coffee makers, and espresso and cappuccino machines to prepare beverages for customers. In fast food restaurants, food preparation workers may take customer orders and process payments using cash registers.

In some kitchens, food preparation workers use a variety of commercial kitchen equipment, such as commercial dishwashers, blenders, slicers, grinders, and ovens.

Work Environment

Food preparation workers held about 813,700 jobs in 2010.

The industries that employed the most food preparation workers in 2010 were as follows:

Full-service restaurants	25%
Limited-service eating places	21
Grocery stores	14
Nursing and residential care facilities	7
Elementary and secondary schools; local	7

Food preparation workers are employed in restaurants, hotels, and other places where food is served, such as grocery stores, schools, hospitals, and cafeterias.

The work is often strenuous and tiring. Food preparation workers may stand or walk for hours at a time while cleaning or preparing ingredients. Some may be required to lift and carry heavy pots or unload heavy food supplies.

Depending on the type of establishment where they work and the type of food items they handle, they may have to wear protective gloves, hairnets, or aprons.

Work Schedules

About 53 percent of food preparation workers worked part time. Because many food service establishments are open for many hours a day, food preparation workers often must work early mornings, late evenings, weekends, or holidays. Those who work in school cafeterias have more regular hours and may work only during the school year, which is usually 9 or 10 months. Similarly, resorts usually offer seasonal employment only.

Injuries

Although injuries and illnesses are seldom serious in this occupation, hazards may include slips, falls, cuts, and burns from hot ovens. As a result, food preparation workers experience a rate of injuries and illnesses that is higher than the average for all occupations.

How to Become a Food Preparation Worker

Short-term on-the-job training is the most common way to learn the skills necessary for food preparation workers. No formal education or previous work experience is required.

Training

Most food preparation workers obtain their skills through short-term on-the-job training, which often lasts several weeks. Many start as kitchen helpers and progress into food preparation positions as they learn basic knife skills. Training generally starts with basic sanitation and workplace safety regulations and continues with instructions on how to handle, prepare, and cook food.

Advancement

Advancement opportunities for food preparation workers depend on their training, work experience, and ability to do more refined tasks. Many food preparation workers move into assistant or line cook positions as they learn basic cooking techniques.

Important Qualities

Listening skills. To help cooks, food preparation workers must be able to understand specific orders and follow directions.

Manual dexterity. Because food preparation workers chop vegetables, cut meat, and do other tasks with sharp knives, they must have good hand control.

Stamina. Food preparation workers must be able to spend most of their work time on their feet as they prepare foods, clean work areas, or lift heavy pots from the stove.

Teamwork. The fast-paced environment in kitchens can be hectic and stressful, especially during peak dining hours. Food preparation workers must be able to work well as part of a team to ensure that dishes are prepared properly, quickly, and efficiently.

Pay

Food Preparation Workers
Median hourly wages, May 2010

Total, All Occupations	$16.27
Food Preparation Workers	$9.18
Food Preparation and Serving Related Occupations	$9.02

Note: All Occupations includes all occupations in the U.S. Economy.
Source: U.S. Bureau of Labor Statistics, Occupational Employment Statistics

The median hourly wage of food preparation workers was $9.18 in May 2010. The median wage is the wage at which half the workers in an occupation earned more than that amount and half earned less. The lowest 10 percent earned less than $7.65 per hour, and the top 10 percent earned more than $13.68 per hour.

Pay for food preparation workers varies by region and employer. Pay is usually highest for workers in elementary and secondary schools, and in major metropolitan and resort areas.

About 53 percent of food preparation workers worked part time. Because many food service establishments are open for many hours each day, food preparation workers often must work early mornings, late evenings, weekends, or holidays. Those who work in school cafeterias have more regular hours and may work only during the school year, which is usually 9 or 10 months. Similarly, resorts usually offer seasonal employment only.

Job Outlook

Food Preparation Workers
Percent change in employment, projected 2010-20

Total, All Occupations	14%
Food Preparation and Serving Related Occupations	10%
Food Preparation Workers	10%

Note: All Occupations includes all occupations in the U.S. Economy.
Source: U.S. Bureau of Labor Statistics, Employment Projections program

Employment of food preparation workers is expected to grow 10 percent from 2010 to 2020, about as fast as the average for all occupations.

People will continue to eat out and take carry-out meals home. In response, more restaurants will open and nontraditional food service operations, such as those found inside grocery stores, will serve more prepared food dishes. In addition, because preparing fresh and made-from-scratch meals is labor intensive, many chefs at upscale restaurants will require the help of food preparation workers.

However, a growing number of fast-food restaurants and school and hospital cafeterias are customizing their food orders from wholesalers and distributors in an effort to lower costs. As more food service establishments use these cost-saving strategies, the need for food preparation workers to wash, portion, and season ingredients should be diminished.

Job Prospects

Job opportunities for food preparation workers are expected to be good because of the need to replace the large number of workers who leave the occupation each year. Because many of these jobs are part time and pay relatively low wages, turnover in the occupation is fairly high.

Those with related work experience should have the best job opportunities at large or upscale restaurants. However, individuals seeking full-time positions at these kinds of restaurants may face stiff competition, as the number of job applicants usually is greater than the number of job openings.

Employment projections data for food preparation workers, 2010-20

Occupational Title	SOC Code	Employment, 2010	Projected Employment, 2020	Change, 2010-20	
				Percent	Numeric
Food Preparation Workers	35-2021	813,700	897,900	10	84,100
SOURCE: U.S. Bureau of Labor Statistics, Employment Projections program					

Similar Occupations

This table shows a list of occupations with job duties that are similar to those of food preparation workers.

Occupation	Job Duties	Entry-Level Education	Median Annual Pay, May 2010
Bakers	Bakers mix and bake ingredients according to recipes to make a variety of breads, pastries, and other baked goods.	Less than high school	$23,450
Slaughterers and Meat Packers	Slaughterers and meat packers kill and clean animals, divide carcasses into manageable sections, and grind or otherwise prepare and pack products, such as boxed beef, for shipping to distribution centers.	Less than high school	$23,380
Chefs and Head Cooks	Chefs and head cooks oversee the daily food preparation at restaurants or other places where food is served. They direct kitchen staff and handle any food-related concerns.	High school diploma or equivalent	$40,630
Cooks	Cooks prepare, season, and cook a wide range of foods, such as soups, salads, entrees, and desserts.	See How to Become One	$20,260
Food and Beverage Serving and Related Workers	Food and beverage serving and related workers perform a variety of customer service, food preparation, and cleaning duties in full-service restaurants, casual dining eateries, and other eating and drinking places.	Less than high school	$18,130

Contacts for More Information

For more information about job opportunities, contact local employers and local offices of the state employment service.

For information on becoming a food preparation worker, visit National Restaurant Association

Suggested citation:

Bureau of Labor Statistics, U.S. Department of Labor, Occupational Outlook Handbook, 2012-13 Edition, Food Preparation Workers, on the Internet at http://www.bls.gov/ooh/food-preparation-and-serving/food-preparation-workers.htm .

Waiters and Waitresses

Quick Facts: Waiters and Waitresses	
2010 Median Pay	$18,330 per year $8.81 per hour
Entry-Level Education	Less than high school
Work Experience in a Related Occupation	None
On-the-job Training	Short-term on-the-job training
Number of Jobs, 2010	2,260,300
Job Outlook, 2010-20	9% (Slower than average)
Employment Change, 2010-20	195,900

What Waiters and Waitresses Do

Waiters and waitresses take orders and serve food and beverages to customers in dining establishments.

Duties

Waiters and waitresses typically do the following:

- Greet customers, present menus, and explain daily specials to customers
- Answer questions related to menu items and make recommendations
- Take food and beverage orders from customers
- Relay food and beverage orders to the kitchen staff
- Prepare drinks and food garnishes
- Carry trays of food or drinks from the kitchen to the dining tables
- Remove dirty dishes and glasses and clean tables after customers finish meals
- Prepare itemized checks and hand them to customers and sometimes take payment
- Clean and set up dining areas, refill condiments, roll silverware, and stock service areas

Waiters and waitresses, also called servers, are responsible for ensuring that customers have a satisfying dining experience. The specific duties of servers vary considerably with the establishment in which they work.

In casual-dining restaurants that offer routine, straightforward fare, such as salads, soups, and sandwiches, servers are expected to provide fast, efficient, and courteous service. In fine-dining restaurants, where more complicated meals are prepared and are often served over several courses, waiters and waitresses provide more formal service. They emphasize personal, attentive treatment at a more leisurely pace.

Waiters and waitresses may meet with managers and chefs before each shift to discuss the menu and any new items or specials, review ingredients for potential food allergies, or talk about any food safety concerns. They also discuss coordination between the kitchen and the dining room and review any customer service issues from the previous

Waiters and waitresses take food and beverage orders from customers.

day or shift.

In addition, waiters and waitresses usually check the identification of patrons to ensure that they meet the minimum age requirement for the purchase of alcohol.

Work Environment

Waiters and waitresses held about 2.3 million jobs in 2010. Approximately three-fourths of them worked in full-service restaurants.

Waiters and waitresses are on their feet most of the time and often carry heavy trays of food, dishes, and glassware. During busy dining periods, they are under pressure to serve customers quickly and efficiently. Although the work is relatively safe, rushed servers can suffer injuries from slips.

Work Schedules

The majority of waiters and waitress work part time, and many work early mornings, late evenings, weekends, and holidays. This is especially true for those who work in full-service restaurants, which employ 76 percent of all waiters and waitresses.

Those who work in resorts are normally employed by the resort for only a few months each year.

How to Become a Waiter or Waitress

Most waiter and waitress jobs are at the entry level, and workers learn through short-term on-the-job training. No formal education or previous work experience is required to enter the occupation.

Most states require workers who serve alcoholic beverages to be at least 18 years of age, but some states require servers to be older. Waiters and waitresses who serve alcohol need to be familiar with state and local laws concerning the sale of alcoholic beverages.

Training

Although most employers prefer to hire high school graduates, many entrants to these jobs are in their late teens or early twenties and have less than a high school education. Waiter and waitress jobs are a major source of part-time employment for high school and college students, multiple jobholders, and those seeking supplemental incomes.

All new employees receive some training from their employer. For example, workers learn procedures for handling food safely and sanitation practices.

Some full-service restaurants also provide new dining room employees with some form of classroom training that alternates with periods of on-the-job work experience. These training programs

communicate the operating philosophy of the restaurant, help new servers establish a personal rapport with other staff, teach formal serving techniques, and instill a desire to work as a team. They also provide an opportunity to discuss customer service situations and the proper ways to handle unpleasant circumstances or unruly patrons.

Some waiters and waitresses can acquire more skills by attending relevant classes offered by public or private vocational schools, restaurant associations, or large restaurant chains. Although some of these schools help their graduates find jobs, employers are more likely to hire and promote employees on the basis of their people skills and personal qualities than on the basis of their education.

Important Qualities

Communication skills. Waiters and waitresses must listen carefully to customers' specific requests, ask any questions, and correctly relay the information they get from the customers to the kitchen staff, so that orders are prepared to the customers' satisfaction.

Customer and personal-service skills. Waiters and waitresses spend most of their work time serving customers. They should be friendly and polite and be able to develop a natural rapport with customers.

Good memory. Waiters and waitresses must keep customers' orders straight. They also should be able to recall the faces, names, and food and drink preferences of frequent customers.

People skills. Waiters and waitresses must be courteous, tactful, and attentive as they deal with customers in all circumstances. For example, they must show that they understand customers' complaints and that they are able to resolve any issues that arise.

Physical stamina. Waiters and waitresses must be able to spend hours on their feet carrying heavy trays, dishes, and glassware.

Team oriented. Because busy dining hours can be hectic and fast paced, workers must be able to work well as a team to ensure that customers feel welcome and receive prompt service.

Well-groomed and neat appearance. Because waiters and waitresses are the front line of customer service in food service and drinking establishments, a neat appearance is often important.

Pay

Waiters and Waitresses
Median hourly wages, May 2010

Total, All Occupations	$16.27
Food Preparation and Serving Related Occupations	$9.02
Waiters and Waitresses	$8.81

Note: All Occupations includes all occupations in the U.S. Economy.
Source: U.S. Bureau of Labor Statistics, Occupational Employment Statistics

The median hourly wage (including tips) of waiters and waitresses was $8.81 in May 2010. The median wage is the wage at which half the workers in an occupation earned more than that amount and half earned less. The lowest 10 percent earned less than $7.54, and the top 10 percent earned more than $14.41.

Many waiters and waitresses get their earnings from a combination of hourly wages and customer tips. Earnings vary greatly with the type of establishment and region. For example, tips are generally much higher in upscale restaurants in major metropolitan areas and resorts.

Many entry-level or inexperienced workers earn the federal minimum wage. However, many others earn more per hour because they work in states that set minimum wages higher than the federal minimum.

Also, various exceptions to the minimum wage apply under specific circumstances to disabled workers, full-time students, youths under age 20 in their first 90 days of employment, tipped employees, and student learners. Tipped employees are those who customarily and regularly receive more than $30 a month in tips. According to the <u>Fair Labor Standards Act</u>, the employer may consider tips as part of wages, but the employer must pay at least $2.13 an hour in direct wages.

The majority of waiters and waitress work part time, and many work early mornings, late evenings, weekends, and holidays. This is especially true for those who work in full-service restaurants, which employ 76 percent of all waiters and waitresses.

Those who work in resorts are normally employed by the resort for only a few months each year.

Many employers provide free meals and furnish uniforms, but some may deduct from wages the cost, or fair value, of any meals or lodging provided. Waiters and waitresses who work full time often receive typical benefits, but part-time workers usually do not.

Job Outlook

Waiters and Waitresses

Percent change in employment, projected 2010-20

Total, All Occupations	14%
Food Preparation and Serving Related Occupations	10%
Waiters and Waitresses	9%

Note: All Occupations includes all occupations in the U.S. Economy.
Source: U.S. Bureau of Labor Statistics, Employment Projections program

Employment of waiters and waitresses is expected to grow 9

percent from 2010 to 2020, slower than the average for all occupations. Employment is expected to increase as the population expands and people continue to eat at restaurants.

However, employment will grow more slowly than in the past as people change their dining habits. The increasing popularity of takeout food and the growing number and variety of places that offer self-service or carryout options will slow the employment growth of waiters and waitresses.

In addition, technology-driven payment systems should moderate employment growth of waiters and waitresses in limited-service eating places.

Job Prospects

Job opportunities for waiters and waitresses are expected to be very good, primarily because of the large number of workers who leave the occupation.

Candidates with previous work experience and excellent customer service skills will have the best job opportunities in fine-dining and upscale restaurants. Still, they will likely face strong competition at these establishments, as potential earnings from tips are greatest and the number of job applicants far exceeds the number of job openings.

Employment projections data for waiters and waitresses, 2010-20

Occupational Title	SOC Code	Employment, 2010	Projected Employment, 2020	Change, 2010-20	
				Percent	Numeric
Waiters and Waitresses	35-3031	2,260,300	2,456,200	9	195,900
SOURCE: U.S. Bureau of Labor Statistics, Employment Projections program					

Similar Occupations

This table shows a list of occupations with job duties that are similar to those of waiters and waitresses.

Occupation	Job Duties	Entry-Level Education	Median Annual Pay, May 2010
Bartenders	Bartenders mix and serve drinks to customers directly or through wait staff.	Less than high school	$18,680
Cashiers	Cashiers handle payments from customers purchasing goods and services.	Less than high school	$18,500
Food and Beverage Serving and Related Workers	Food and beverage serving and related workers perform a variety of customer service, food preparation, and cleaning duties in full-service restaurants, casual dining eateries, and other eating and drinking places.	Less than high school	$18,130
Flight Attendants	Flight attendants provide personal services to ensure the safety and comfort of airline passengers.	High school diploma or equivalent	$37,740
Retail Sales Workers	Retail sales workers include both those who sell retail merchandise, such as clothing, furniture, and automobiles, (called retail salespersons) and those who sell spare and replacement parts and equipment, especiallycar parts, (called parts salespersons). Both groups help customers find the products they want and process customers' payments.	Less than high school	$20,990

Contacts for More Information

For more information on careers as a waiter or waitress, visit National Restaurant Association

Suggested citation:

Bureau of Labor Statistics, U.S. Department of Labor, Occupational Outlook Handbook, 2012-13 Edition, Waiters and Waitresses, on the Internet at http://www.bls.gov/ooh/food-preparation-and-serving/waiters-and-waitresses.htm .

Healthcare Occupations

Athletic Trainers

Quick Facts: Athletic Trainers	
2010 Median Pay	$41,600 per year
Entry-Level Education	Bachelor's degree
Work Experience in a Related Occupation	None
On-the-job Training	None
Number of Jobs, 2010	18,200
Job Outlook, 2010-20	30% (Much faster than average)
Employment Change, 2010-20	5,500

What Athletic Trainers Do

Athletic trainers specialize in preventing, diagnosing, and treating muscle and bone injuries and illnesses. They work with people of all ages and all skill levels, from young children to soldiers and professional athletes. They work under the direction of a physician, as well as other healthcare providers.

Duties

Athletic trainers typically do the following:

- Apply protective or injury-preventive devices such as tape, bandages, and braces
- Recognize and evaluate injuries
- Provide first aid or emergency care
- Develop and carry out rehabilitation programs for injured athletes
- Plan and implement comprehensive programs to prevent injury and illness from athletics
- Do administrative tasks, such as keeping records and writing reports on injuries and treatment programs

Athletic trainers are usually one of the first healthcare providers on the scene when injuries occur. Athletic trainers work under the direction of a licensed physician and with other healthcare providers. They often discuss specific injuries and treatment options or evaluate and treat patients as directed by a physician. Some athletic trainers meet with a team physician or consulting physician regularly. An athletic trainer's administrative responsibilities may include regular meetings with an athletic director or other administrative officer to deal with budgets, purchasing, policy implementation, and other business-related issues.

Athletic trainers should not be confused with fitness trainers and instructors, including personal trainers. For more information , see the profile on fitness trainers and instructors.

Work Environment

Athletic trainers held about 18,200 jobs in 2010.

Many athletic trainers work in educational facilities, such as secondary schools and colleges. Others may work in physicians' offices or for professional sports teams. Some athletic trainers work in rehabilitation and therapy clinics, in the military, or with performing artists. They may spend much of their time working outdoors on sports fields in all types of weather.

The following industries employed a majority of athletic trainers in 2010:

Colleges, universities, and professional schools; state, local, and private	27%
Fitness and recreational sports centers	11
Elementary and secondary schools; state, local, and private	9
Offices of physicians	6
Spectator sports	4

Athletic trainers who work with teams during sporting events may work evenings or weekends and travel often.

How to Become an Athletic Trainer

Athletic trainers need at least a bachelor's degree, although both bachelor's and master's degrees are common. In most states, athletic trainers need a license or certification; requirements vary by state.

Education

For most jobs, athletic trainers need a bachelor's degree in athletic training from an accredited college or university; however, master's degrees are also common. The Commission on Accreditation of Athletic Training Education (CAATE) accredits most programs. All programs have both classroom and clinical components. Courses include science and health-related courses, such as anatomy, physiology, nutrition, and biomechanics.

Athletic trainers may need a higher degree to be eligible for some positions, especially trainers in colleges and universities, or to increase their advancement opportunities.

High school students interested in athletic trainer programs should take courses in anatomy, physiology, and physics.

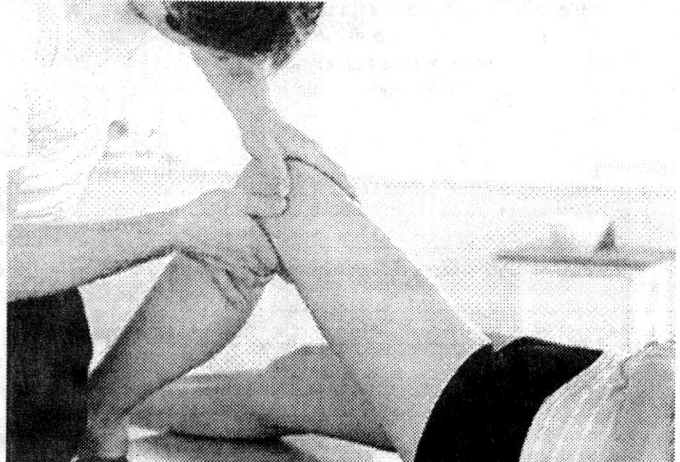

Athletic trainers help prevent and treat injuries for people of all ages.

Important Qualities

Applied knowledge. Athletic trainers need to be able to retain a wide range of medical knowledge. They must evaluate patients' symptoms, consult with other healthcare professionals, and recommend and administer appropriate treatments.

Decision-making skills. Athletic trainers must be able to make quick de—cisions that could affect the health or career of their clients.

Detail oriented. Athletic trainers must be able to record detailed, accurate progress and ensure that patients are receiving the appropriate treatments.

Interpersonal skills. Athletic trainers must have strong interpersonal skills and be able to manage sometimes stressful situations. They must be able to communicate well with others, including physicians, athletes, coaches, and parents.

Certification

Nearly all states require athletic trainers to be certified. The independent Board of Certification, Inc. (BOC) offers the standard certification examination that most states use for licensure. Certification requires completing the BOC exam, adhering to the BOC Standards of Practice and Disciplinary Process, and taking continuing education courses. Athletic trainers must graduate from a CAATE-accredited program before taking the BOC exam.

Licenses

In most states, athletic trainers must be licensed; requirements vary by state.Requirements in most states include graduating from an accredited athletic training program and passing the BOC exam or a separate state exam. For specific information on requirements, contact the local state regulatory agency.

In school settings, athletic trainers may take on some teaching responsibilities and may need a teaching certificate or license.

Advancement

Assistant athletic trainers may become head athletic trainers, ath—letic directors, or physician, hospital, or clinic practice adminis—trators, where they assume a management role. Some athletic trainers move into sales and marketing positions, using their expertise to sell medical and athletic equipment.

Pay

Athletic Trainers

Median annual wages, May 2010

Other Healthcare Practitioners and Technical Occupations	$51,850
Athletic Trainers	$41,600
Total, All Occupations	$33,840

Note: All Occupations includes all occupations in the U.S. Economy.
Source: U.S. Bureau of Labor Statistics, Occupational Employment Statistics

The median annual wage of athletic trainers was $41,600 in May 2010.The median wage is the wage at which half the workers in an occupation earned more than that amount and half earned less. The lowest 10 percent earned less than $25,750, and the top 10 percent earned more than $64,390.

Because some work with teams during sporting events, they might be required to work evenings or weekends and travel often.

Job Outlook

Athletic Trainers

Percent change in employment, projected 2010-20

Athletic Trainers	30%
Other Healthcare Practitioners and Technical Occupations	16%
Total, All Occupations	14%

Note: All Occupations includes all occupations in the U.S. Economy.
Source: U.S. Bureau of Labor Statistics, Employment Projections program

Employment of athletic trainers is expected to grow by 30 percent from 2010 to 2020, much faster than the average for all occupations. However, because it is a small occupation, the fast growth will result in only about 5,500 new jobs over the 10-year period. As people become more aware of sports-related injuries at a young age, demand for athletic trainers is expected to increase, most significantly in schools and youth leagues.

New research reveals that the effects of concussions are particularly severe and long lasting in child athletes. Although concussions are dangerous to athletes at any age, children's brains are still developing and are at risk for permanent complications, such as fatal brain swelling and learning disabilities. Parents and coaches are becoming educated about these greater risks through community health efforts. Because athletic trainers are usually on site with athletes and are often the first line of defense when injuries occur, the demand for trainers should continue to increase.

Additionally, advances in injury prevention and detection and more sophisticated treatments are projected to increase the demand for athletic trainers. Growth in an increasingly active middle-aged and elderly population will likely lead to an increased incidence of athletic-related injuries, such as sprains. Sports programs at all ages and for all experience levels will continue to create demand for athletic trainers.

Insurance and workers' compensation costs have become a concern for many employers and insurance companies, especially in areas where employees are often injured on the job. For example, military bases hire athletic trainers to help train military personnel in how to properly lift items or to create training programs aimed at keeping injury rates down. More insurance companies are recognizing athletic trainers as healthcare providers and are reimbursing the cost of an athletic trainer's services.

Employment projections data for athletic trainers, 2010-20

Occupational Title	SOC Code	Employment, 2010	Projected Employment, 2020	Change, 2010-20	
				Percent	Numeric
Athletic Trainers	29-9091	18,200	23,700	30	5,500
SOURCE: U.S. Bureau of Labor Statistics, Employment Projections program					

Similar Occupations

This table shows a list of occupations with job duties that are similar to those of athletic trainers.

Occupation	Job Duties	Entry-Level Education	Median Annual Pay, May 2010
Chiropractors	Chiropractors treat patients with health problems of the musculoskeletal system, which is made up of bones, muscles, ligaments, and tendons. They use spinal manipulation and other techniques to treat patients' ailments, such as back or neck pain.	Doctoral or professional degree	$67,200
EMTs and Paramedics	Emergency medical technicians (EMTs) and paramedics care for the sick or injured in emergency medical settings. People's lives often depend on their quick reaction and competent care. EMTs and paramedics respond to emergency calls, performing medical services and transporting patients to medical facilities.	Postsecondary non-degree award	$30,360
Licensed Practical and Licensed Vocational Nurses	Licensed practical and licensed vocational nurses (known as LPNs or LVNs, depending on the state in which they work) provide basic nursing care. They work under the direction of registered nurses and doctors.	Postsecondary non-degree award	$40,380
Massage Therapists	Massage therapists treat clients by using touch to manipulate the soft-tissue muscles of the body. With their touch, therapists relieve pain, rehabilitate injuries, reduce stress, increase relaxation, and aid in the general wellness of clients.	Postsecondary non-degree award	$34,900
Occupational Therapists	Occupational therapists treat patients with injuries, illnesses, or disabilities through the therapeutic use of everyday activities. They help these patients develop, recover, and improve the skills needed for daily living and working.	Master's degree	$72,320
Physical Therapists	Physical therapists help people who have injuries or illnesses improve their movement and manage their pain. They are often an important part of rehabilitation and treatment of patients with chronic conditions or injuries.	Doctoral or professional degree	$76,310
Physician Assistants	Physician assistants, also known as PAs, practice medicine under the direction of physicians and surgeons. They are formally trained to examine patients, diagnose injuries and illnesses, and provide treatment.	Master's degree	$86,410
Physicians and Surgeons	Physicians and surgeons diagnose and treat injuries and illnesses in patients. Physicians examine patients, take medical histories, prescribe medications, and order, perform, and interpret diagnostic tests. Surgeons operate on patients to treat injuries, such as broken bones; diseases, such as cancerous tumors; and deformities, such as cleft palates.	Doctoral or professional degree	This wage is equal to or greater than $166,400 per year.
Podiatrists	Podiatrists provide medical and surgical care for people suffering foot, ankle, and lower leg problems. They diagnose illnesses, treat injuries, and perform surgery.	Doctoral or professional degree	$118,030
Recreational Therapists	Recreational therapists plan, direct, and coordinate recreation programs for people with disabilities or illnesses. They use a variety of techniques, including arts and crafts, drama, music, dance, sports, games, and field trips. These programs help maintain or improve a client's physical and emotional well-being.	Bachelor's degree	$39,410
Registered Nurses	Registered nurses (RNs) provide and coordinate patient care, educate patients and the public about various health conditions, and provide advice and emotional support to patients and their family members.	Associate's degree	$64,690
Respiratory Therapists	Respiratory therapists care for patients who have trouble breathing; for example, from a chronic respiratory disease, such as asthma or emphysema. They also provide emergency care to patients suffering from heart attacks, stroke, drowning, or shock.	Associate's degree	$54,280

Contacts for More Information

For more information about athletic trainers, visit National Athletic Trainers' Association

For more information about certification and state regulatory requirements, visit Board of Certification, Inc.

Suggested citation:

Bureau of Labor Statistics, U.S. Department of Labor, Occupational Outlook Handbook, 2012-13 Edition, Athletic Trainers, on the Internet at http://www.bls.gov/ooh/healthcare/athletic-trainers.htm .

Audiologists

Quick Facts: Audiologists	
2010 Median Pay	$66,660 per year $32.05 per hour
Entry-Level Education	Doctoral or professional degree
Work Experience in a Related Occupation	None
On-the-job Training	None
Number of Jobs, 2010	13,000
Job Outlook, 2010-20	37% (Much faster than average)
Employment Change, 2010-20	4,800

What Audiologists Do

Audiologists diagnose and treat a patient's hearing and balance problems using advanced technology and procedures.

Duties

Audiologists typically do the following:

- Examine patients who have hearing, balance, or related ear problems
- Assess the results of the examination and diagnose problems
- Determine and administer treatment
- Fit and dispense hearing aids
- Counsel patients and their families on ways to listen and communicate, such as by lip reading or through sign language
- See patients regularly to check on hearing and balance and to continue or change the treatment plan
- Keep records on the progress of patients
- Conduct research related to the causes and treatment of hearing and balance disorders

Audiologists use audiometers, computers, and other devices to test patients' hearing ability and balance, determine the extent of hearing damage, and identify the underlying cause. Audiologists measure the volume at which a person begins to hear sounds and the person's ability to distinguish between sounds. Also, before determining treatment options, they evaluate psychological information to measure the impact of hearing loss on a patient. Treatment options vary and may include

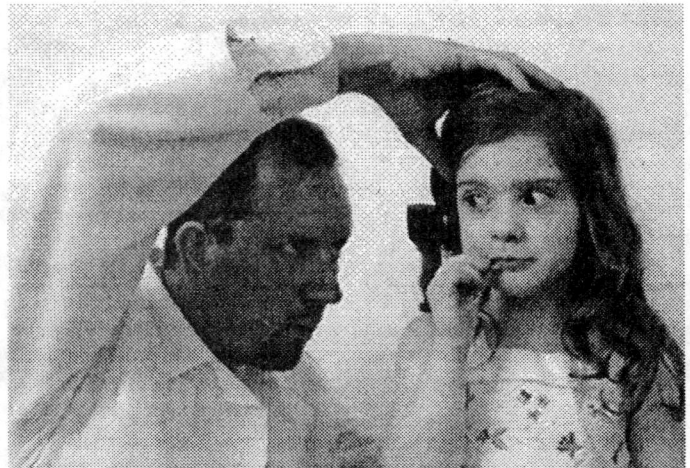

Audiologists examine patients who have hearing, balance, or related ear problems.

cleaning wax out of ear canals, fitting and checking hearing aids, or fitting and programming the patient with cochlear implants to improve hearing. (Cochlear implants are tiny devices that are placed under the skin near the ear in an operation. Cochlear implants deliver electrical impulses directly to the auditory nerve in the brain so a person with certain types of deafness can hear.) Audiologists also counsel patients on other ways to cope with profound hearing loss, such as by learning to lip read or use American Sign Language.

Some audiologists specialize in working with the elderly or with children. Others design products to help protect the hearing of workers on the job. Audiologists who are self-employed build a client base, hire employees, keep records, order equipment and supplies, and do other tasks related to running a business.

Work Environment disorders.

Most audiologists work in healthcare facilities, such as hospitals, physicians' offices, and audiology clinics. Some work in schools. Although not physically demanding, the job requires attention to detail, intense concentration and critical thinking.

Work Schedules

Most audiologists work full time. Some may work weekends and evenings to meet patients' needs. Those who work on a contract basis may spend a lot of time traveling between facilities. For example, an audiologist who is contracted by a school system might have to travel between different school buildings to provide services.

How to Become an Audiologist

New audiologists must earn a doctoral degree to enter the practice. All audiologists must be licensed; requirements vary by state.

Education

The doctoral degree in audiology (Au.D.) is a graduate program typically lasting 4 years. A bachelor's degree in any field is needed to enter one of these doctoral programs.

Graduate coursework in audiology includes anatomy, physiology, physics, genetics, normal and abnormal communication development, diagnosis and treatment, pharmacology, and ethics. Graduate programs also include supervised clinical practice. Graduation from a program accredited by the Council on Academic Accreditation is required to get a license in some states.

Licenses and Certification

Audiologists must be licensed in all states; requirements vary by state. For specific requirements, contact your state's licensing board for audiologists.

Audiologists can earn the Certificate of Clinical Competence in Audiology (CCC-A), offered by the American Speech-Language-Hearing Association. They also may be credentialed through the American Board of Audiology . Although it is not required, certification may satisfy some or all of the requirements for licensure and may be required by some employers.

Important Qualities

Compassion. Audiologists work with people who are having problems with hearing or balance. They must be supportive of patients and their families.

Communication skills. Audiologists need to communicate test results, diagnoses, and proposed treatments so that patients clearly understand the situation and options. They also may need to work with other healthcare providers and education specialists regarding patient care.

Critical-thinking skills. Audiologists must concentrate when testing a patient's hearing and be able to analyze each patient's situation to offer the best treatment. They must also be open to providing alternatives plans when patients do not respond to initial treatment.

Patience. Audiologists must work with patients who may need a lot of time and special attention.

Problem-solving skills. Audiologists must figure out the causes of problems with hearing and balance and the appropriate treatment to address them.

Pay

Audiologists
Median annual wages, May 2010

Health Diagnosing and Treating Practitioners	$71,490
Audiologists	$66,660
Total, All Occupations	$33,840

Note: All Occupations includes all occupations in the U.S. Economy.
Source: U.S. Bureau of Labor Statistics, Occupational Employment Statistics

The median annual wage of audiologists was $66,660 in May 2010. The median wage is the wage at which half the workers in an occupation earned more than that amount and half earned less. The lowest 10 percent earned less than $42,590, and the top 10 percent earned more than $102,210.

Most audiologists work full time. Some may work weekends and evenings to meet patients' needs. Those who work on a contract basis may spend a lot of time traveling between facilities.

Job Outlook

Audiologists
Percent change in employment, projected 2010-20

Audiologists	37%
Health Diagnosing and Treating Practitioners	26%
Total, All Occupations	14%

Note: All Occupations includes all occupations in the U.S. Economy.
Source: U.S. Bureau of Labor Statistics, Employment Projections program

Employment of audiologists is expected to grow by 37 percent from 2010 to 2020, much faster than the average for all occupations. However, because it is a small occupation, the fast growth will result in only about 4,800 new jobs over the 10-year period. Hearing loss increases as people age, so an aging population is likely to increase demand for audiologists. The early identification and diagnosis of hearing disorders in infants also will spur employment growth. Advances in hearing aid design, such as the reduction of feedback and a smaller size, may make the devices more appealing as a means to minimize hearing loss, leading to more demand for the audiologists who provide hearing aids.

Job Prospects

Job prospects are expected to be favorable for audiologists with a doctoral degree. Demand may be greater in areas with large numbers of retirees, so audiologists who are willing to relocate may have the best job prospects.

Employment projections data for audiologists, 2010-20

Occupational Title	SOC Code	Employment, 2010	Projected Employment, 2020	Change, 2010-20 Percent	Numeric
Audiologists	29-1181	13,000	17,800	37	4,800

SOURCE: U.S. Bureau of Labor Statistics, Employment Projections program

Similar Occupations

This table shows a list of occupations with job duties that are similar to those of audiologists.

Occupation	Job Duties	Entry-Level Education	Median Annual Pay, May 2010
Occupational Therapists	Occupational therapists treat patients with injuries, illnesses, or disabilities through the therapeutic use of everyday activities. They help these patients develop, recover, and improve the skills needed for daily living and working.	Master's degree	$72,320
Optometrists	Optometrists perform eye exams to check for vision problems and diseases. They prescribe eyeglasses or contact lenses as needed.	Doctoral or professional degree	$94,990

Physical Therapists	Physical therapists help people who have injuries or illnesses improve their movement and manage their pain. They are often an important part of rehabilitation and treatment of patients with chronic conditions or injuries.	Doctoral or professional degree	$76,310
Psychologists	Psychologists study mental processes and human behavior by observing, interpreting, and recording how people and other animals relate to one another and the environment.	See How to Become One	$68,640
Speech-Language Pathologists	Speech-language pathologists diagnose and treat communication and swallowing disorders in patients.	Master's degree	$66,920

Contacts for More Information

For information on the specific licensing requirements of your state, contact that state's licensing board.

For more information about audiologists, including requirements for certification and state licensure, visit American Speech-Language-Hearing Association ,American Board of Audiology

For information on doctoral programs in audiology, visit American Speech-Language-Hearing Association

Suggested citation:

Bureau of Labor Statistics, U.S. Department of Labor, Occupational Outlook Handbook, 2012-13 Edition, Audiologists, on the Internet at http://www.bls.gov/ooh/healthcare/audiologists.htm .

Cardiovascular Technologists and Technicians and Vascular Technologists

Quick Facts: Cardiovascular Technologists and Technicians and Vascular Technologists	
2010 Median Pay	$49,410 per year $23.75 per hour
Entry-Level Education	Associate's degree
Work Experience in a Related Occupation	None
On-the-job Training	None
Number of Jobs, 2010	49,400
Job Outlook, 2010-20	29% (Much faster than average)
Employment Change, 2010-20	14,500

What Cardiovascular Technologists and Technicians and Vascular Technologists Do

Cardiovascular technologists and technicians and vascular technologists use imaging technology to help physicians diagnose cardiac (heart) and peripheral vascular (blood vessel) ailments in patients. They also help physicians treat problems with cardiac and vascular systems, such as blood clots.

Duties

Cardiovascular technologists and technicians and vascular technologists typically do the following:

- Prepare patients for procedures by taking their medical history and answering their questions
- Prepare and maintain imaging equipment
- Perform noninvasive procedures, such as taking ultrasound images
- Analyze the images to check for quality and to ensure adequate coverage of the area being diagnosed
- Recognize the difference between normal and abnormal images
- Discuss image results with the physician
- Help physicians during invasive procedures, such as inserting catheters (small tubes)
- Record findings and track patient records

Technologists and technicians do or help do tests that can be either invasive or noninvasive. An invasive procedure requires inserting probes or other instruments into a patient's body, and a noninvasive procedure does not.

Cardiology technologists monitor patients' heart rates and help diagnose and treat problems with patients' hearts. The procedures can be invasive (such as inserting catheters) or noninvasive (such as using ultrasound equipment to take images of the heart).

Cardiac catheterization involves helping a physician thread a catheter through a patient's artery to the heart. The procedure determines whether a blockage exists in the blood vessels that supply the heart muscle or helps to diagnose other problems. Some of these procedures may involve balloon angioplasty, which can be used to treat blockages of blood vessels or heart valves without the need for heart surgery.

Technologists prepare patients for these procedures by shaving and cleansing the area where the catheter will be inserted and administering topical anesthesia. During the procedure, they monitor the patient's blood pressure and heart rate. Some cardiology technologists also prepare and monitor patients during open-heart surgery and during the insertion of pacemakers and stents that open blockages in arteries to the heart and other major blood vessels.

Vascular technologists (Vascular sonographers) help physicians diagnose disorders affecting blood flow. Vascular technologists listen to the blood flow in the arteries and veins to check for abnormalities. They do noninvasive procedures using ultrasound instruments to record information, such as blood flow in veins, blood pressure, and oxygen saturation. Many of these tests are done during or immediately after

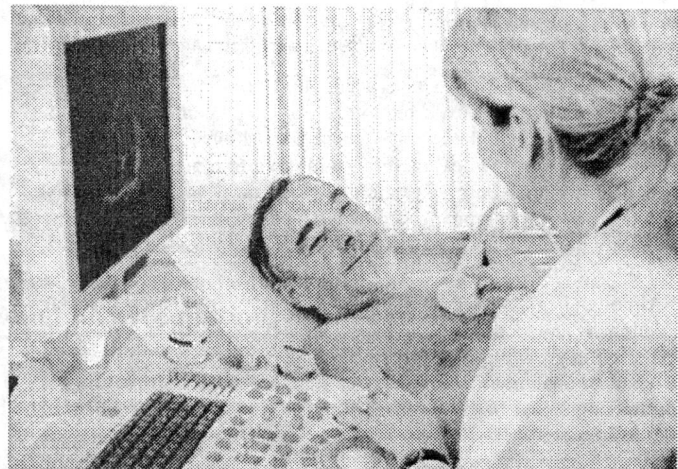

Cardiovascular and vascular technologists assist physicians in diagnosing and treating cardiac (heart) and peripheral vascular (blood vessel) systems in patients.

surgery.

Cardiac sonographers (Echocardiographers) use ultrasound to examine the heart's chambers, valves, and vessels. They use ultrasound instruments to create images called echocardiograms or electrocardiograms (EKGs). The echocardiogram may be done while the patient is either resting or physically active.

To test a patient at rest, EKGs monitor the heart's performance through electrodes attached to a patient's chest, arms, and legs while the patient is lying on a table.

To test a physically active patient, the cardiac sonographer uses a Holter monitor or runs a stress test. The technologist puts electrodes on the patient's chest and attaches a portable EKG monitor to the patient's belt. The Holter monitor records normal activity for 24 or more hours, and the technologist then removes the tape from the monitor, places the monitor in a scanner, checks its quality, and prints the image for later analysis by a physician. For a stress test, the patient walks on a treadmill and the technologist gradually increases the speed to observe the effect of increased exertion.

Cardiovascular technicians work closely with cardiovascular technologists. Technicians who specialize in EKG testing are known as cardiographic or electrocardiogram (EKG) technicians.

Technologists and technicians often work closely with diagnostic medical sonographers. For more information, see the profile on diagnostic medical sonographers .

Work Environment

Cardiovascular technologists and technicians and vascular technologists held about 49,400 jobs in 2010. They typically work in healthcare facilities, which must be sanitary. In 2010, more than 75 percent worked in state, local, and private hospitals; others primarily worked in physician's offices, medical and diagnostic laboratories, and outpatient care centers.

Technologists and technicians are on their feet for long periods and may need to lift or turn patients who have a disability.

Work Schedules

Because technologists and technicians are sometimes needed to help when physicians diagnose and treat patients in emergencies, some work evenings, weekends, or overnight.

How to Become a Cardiovascular Technologist or Technician or Vascular Technologist

There are several ways to become a cardiovascular technologist or technician or vascular technologist. Although some technologists and technicians are trained on the job, the most common path is formal education that leads to an associate's degree. Many employers also require professional certification.

Education

High school students who are interested in cardiovascular and vascular technology should take courses in anatomy, physiology, and mathematics.

Most cardiovascular technologists and technicians and vascular technologists get an associate's degree by completing a 2-year community college program. However, some 4-year programs that lead to bachelor's degree are available at colleges and universities.

Programs include coursework in either invasive or noninvasive cardiovascular or vascular technology. Most programs also include a clinical component in which students earn credit while working under a more experienced technologist in a hospital, physician's office, or imaging laboratory.

One-year certificate programs are also available from community colleges. Certificate programs are often helpful to those who have already received education or training in related healthcare jobs.

Some technologists graduate with an associate's or bachelor's degree in radiologic technology or nursing and then are trained on the job. Employers prefer candidates who have a degree or certificate from an accredited institute or hospital program.

Cardiovascular technicians who work as electrocardiogram (EKG) technicians are typically trained on the job by their employer. These programs usually take 4 to 6 weeks to complete. One-year certification programs are also available from community colleges and may substitute for on-the-job training.

Certification

Although certification is not required to enter the occupation, employers prefer to hire certified technologists or technicians. Certification is considered the standard by professionals and the ultrasound community. Many insurance providers, including Medicare, pay for procedures only if a certified technologist or technician did the work.

Cardiovascular technologists and technicians and vascular technologists earn various certifications, depending on their clinical focus. To take the certification exam, technologists and technicians usually must complete an accredited education program. In most cases, technologists and technicians must take continuing education to keep their certification. Cardiovascular technologists and technicians and vascular technologists can be certified in several areas.

Important Qualities

Detail oriented. Cardiovascular technologists and technicians and vascular technologists must follow exact instructions from physicians.

Interpersonal skills. Cardiovascular technologists and technicians and vascular technologists must work closely with patients. Sometimes patients are in extreme pain or under mental stress, and the technologist or technician must get patients to cooperate to do the procedures.

Physical stamina. Cardiovascular technologists and technicians and vascular technologists work on their feet for long periods and must be able to lift and move patients who need help.

Technical skills. Cardiovascular technologists and technicians and vascular technologists must understand how to operate complex machinery to provide useful diagnostic information to physicians and other healthcare workers.

Pay

Cardiovascular Technologists and Technicians and Vascular Technologists
Median annual wages, May 2010

Cardiovascular Technologists and Technicians	$49,410
Health Technologists and Technicians	$39,340
Total, All Occupations	$33,840

Note: All Occupations includes all occupations in the U.S. Economy.
Source: U.S. Bureau of Labor Statistics, Occupational Employment Statistics

The median annual wage of cardiovascular technologists and technicians and vascular technologists was $49,410 in May 2010. The median wage is the wage at which half the workers in an occupation earned more than that amount and half earned less. The lowest 10 percent earned less than $26,610, and the top 10 percent earned more than $77,020.

Because technologists and technicians are sometimes needed to help when physicians diagnose and treat patients in emergencies, some work evenings, weekends, or overnight.

Job Outlook

Cardiovascular Technologists and Technicians and Vascular Technologists
Percent change in employment, projected 2010-20

Cardiovascular Technologists and Technicians	29%
Health Technologists and Technicians	26%
Total, All Occupations	

Note: All Occupations includes all occupations in the U.S. Economy.
Source: U.S. Bureau of Labor Statistics, Employment Projections program

Employment of cardiovascular technologists and technicians and vascular technologists is expected to grow by 29 percent from 2010 to 2020, much faster than the average for all occupations. As imaging technology evolves, medical facilities will use it to replace more invasive, costly procedures. Technological advances and less expensive equipment now allow more procedures to be done outside of hospitals. Third-party payers encourage the use of these noninvasive measures over invasive ones.

Although hospitals remain the primary employer of cardiovascular technologists and technicians and vascular technologists, employment is expected to grow more rapidly in physicians' offices and in medical and diagnostic laboratories. Employment in these healthcare settings is expected to increase because of a shift toward outpatient care whenever possible.

As the large baby-boom population ages and people remain active later in life, the need to diagnose medical conditions—such as blood clots and tumors—with imaging technology will likely increase. Cardiovascular technologists and technicians and vascular technologists will continue to be needed to use and maintain the equipment needed for diagnosis and treatment.

Job prospects

Job prospects should be best for those who have multiple professional credentials and are trained to do a wide range of procedures. Technologists or technicians who are willing to move or to work irregular hours also should have better opportunities.

Employment projections data for cardiovascular technologists and technicians and vascular technologists, 2010-20

Occupational Title	SOC Code	Employment, 2010	Projected Employment, 2020	Change, 2010-20	
				Percent	Numeric
Cardiovascular Technologists and Technicians	29-2031	49,400	63,900	29	14,500
SOURCE: U.S. Bureau of Labor Statistics, Employment Projections program					

Similar Occupations

This table shows a list of occupations with job duties that are similar to those of cardiovascular technologists and technicians and vascular technologists.

Occupation	Job Duties	Entry-Level Education	Median Annual Pay, May 2010
Diagnostic Medical Sonographers	Diagnostic medical sonographers use special imaging equipment that directs sound waves into a patient's body (in a procedure commonly known as an ultrasound, sonogram, or echocardiogram) to assess and diagnose various medical conditions.	Associate's degree	$64,380
Nuclear Medicine Technologists	Nuclear medicine technologists use a scanner to create images of various areas of a patient's body. They prepare radioactive drugs and administer them to patients undergoing the scans. The radioactive drugs cause abnormal areas of the body to appear different from normal areas in the images.	Associate's degree	$68,560
Radiologic Technologists	Radiologic technologists perform diagnostic imaging examinations, such as x rays, on patients.	Associate's degree	$54,340
Radiation Therapists	Radiation therapists treat cancer and other diseases in patients by giving radiation treatments.	Associate's degree	$74,980
Respiratory Therapists	Respiratory therapists care for patients who have trouble breathing; for example, from a chronic respiratory disease, such as asthma or emphysema. They also provide emergency care to patients suffering from heart attacks, stroke, drowning, or shock.	Associate's degree	$54,280

Contacts for More Information

For more information about cardiovascular technologists and technicians, visit Alliance of Cardiovascular Professionals

For a list of accredited programs in cardiovascular or vascular technology, visit Commission on Accreditation of Allied Health Education Programs , Society for Vascular Ultrasound

For information about registration and certification, visit Cardiovascular Credentialing International ,American Registry for Diagnostic Medical Sonography

Suggested citation:

Bureau of Labor Statistics, U.S. Department of Labor, Occupational Outlook Handbook, 2012-13 Edition, Cardiovascular Technologists and Technicians and Vascular Technologists, on the Internet at http://www.bls.gov/ooh/healthcare/cardiovascular-technologists-and-tec hnicians.htm .

Chiropractors

Quick Facts: Chiropractors	
2010 Median Pay	$67,200 per year $32.31 per hour
Entry-Level Education	Doctoral or professional degree
Work Experience in a Related Occupation	None
On-the-job Training	None
Number of Jobs, 2010	52,600
Job Outlook, 2010-20	28% (Faster than average)
Employment Change, 2010-20	14,900

What Chiropractors Do

Chiropractors treat patients with health problems of the musculoskeletal system, which is made up of bones, muscles, ligaments, and tendons. They use spinal manipulation and other techniques to treat patients' ailments, such as back or neck pain.

Duties

Chiropractors typically do the following:

- Assess a patient's medical condition by reviewing his or her medical history, listening to the patient's concerns, and performing a physical examination
- Analyze the patient's posture and spine
- Provide musculoskeletal therapy, which involves adjusting a patient's spinal column and other joints by hand
- Conduct additional diagnostic tests, including evaluating a patient's

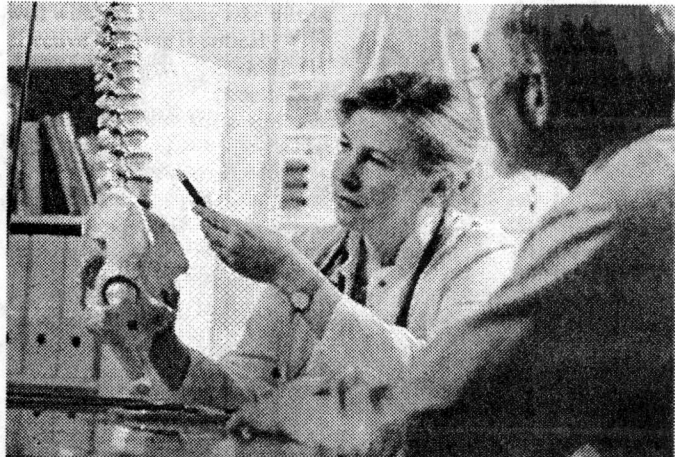

Chiropractors counsel patients on musculoskeletal problems and overall health issues.

posture or taking x rays
- Provide additional treatments, such as applying heat or cold to a patient's injured areas
- Advise patients on health and lifestyle issues, such as exercise and sleep habits
- Refer patients to other medical specialists if needed

Chiropractors focus on patients' overall health. Many believe that misalignments of the spinal joints interfere with a person's nervous system and can result in lower resistance to disease and many different conditions of diminished health.

Some chiropractors use additional procedures, such as acupuncture, massage therapy, and ultrasound. They also may apply supports, such as straps, tape, braces, or shoe inserts, to treat patients and alleviate pain.

In addition to operating a general chiropractic practice, some chiropractors specialize in sports injuries, neurology, orthopedics, pediatrics, nutrition, internal disorders, or diagnostic imaging.

Many chiropractors are solo or group practitioners who also have the administrative responsibilities of running a practice. In larger offices, chiropractors delegate these tasks to office managers and chiropractic assistants. Chiropractors in private practice are responsible for developing a patient base, hiring employees, and keeping records.

Work Environment

Chiropractors held about 52,600 jobs in 2010. Most chiropractors work in a solo or group practice. Many are self-employed, meaning that they own or are partners in owning their practice. A small number work in hospitals or physicians' offices.

Chiropractors typically work in office settings that are clean and comfortable. They might be on their feet for long periods when treating patients.

Work Schedules

Although most chiropractors work full time, 21 percent worked part time in 2010. About 1 out of 4 chiropractors worked 50 hours or more per week. Chiropractors may work in the evenings to accommodate working patients. Self-employed chiropractors set their own hours.

How to Become a Chiropractor

Becoming a chiropractor requires earning a Doctor of Chiropractic (D.C.) degree and getting a state license. Doctor of Chiropractic programs take 4 years to complete and require 3 years of previous undergraduate college education for admission.

Education

Prospective chiropractors are required to have a Doctor of Chiropractic (D.C.) degree, a postgraduate professional degree that takes 4 years to complete. Admission to D.C. programs requires at least 90 semester hours of undergraduate education, with courses in the liberal arts and laboratory sciences, such as physics, chemistry, and biology. Although not required, many students earn a bachelor's degree before going on to a chiropractic program. Chiropractors also may gain master's degrees in related areas, such as nutrition or sports rehabilitation.

Chiropractic education consists of classroom work in anatomy, physiology, biology, and similar subjects. This work is completed during the first 2 years of a D.C. program. Chiropractic students then get supervised clinical experience, in which they train in spinal manipulation and diagnosis. Following graduation, some chiropractors complete residencies to get additional training in specialty areas, such as chiropractic radiology or pediatrics.

The Council on Chiropractic Education has accredited 15 programs to award D.C. degrees.

Licenses

All states and the District of Columbia require chiropractors to be licensed. Although specific requirements vary by state, all jurisdictions require the completion of an accredited Doctor of Chiropractic (D.C.) program.

All jurisdictions also require passing exams, either their own specific exams or those administered by the National Board of Chiropractic Examiners or both. These exams include written tests and, usually, a practical evaluation. States usually require continuing education to keep the license. Check with your state's board of chiropractic examiners or health department for more specific information on licensure.

Important Qualities

Detail oriented. Chiropractors must be observant and pay attention to details to make proper diagnoses and avoid mistakes that might harm patients.

Dexterity. Because they use their hands to perform spinal manipulation, chiropractors should be skilled and coordinated to perform the necessary therapy effectively.

Empathy. Chiropractors are often treating people who are in pain. They must be sympathetic to their patients' needs.

Interpersonal skills. Chiropractors must be personable to keep clients coming to them. Also, because chiropractors frequently touch patients in performing therapy, they should be able to able to put their patients at ease.

Pay

Chiropractors
Median annual wages, May 2010

Health Diagnosing and Treating Practitioners	$71,490
Chiropractors	$67,200
Total, All Occupations	$33,840

Note: All Occupations includes all occupations in the U.S. Economy.
Source: U.S. Bureau of Labor Statistics, Occupational Employment Statistics

The median annual wage of chiropractors was $67,200 in May 2010. The median wage is the wage at which half the workers in an occupation earned more than that amount and half earned less. The lowest 10 percent earned less than $32,270, and the top 10 percent earned more than $143,670.

Chiropractors tend to earn significantly less early in their careers and then earn more as they build a client base and become owners of or partners in a practice. According to a survey conducted by Chiropractic Economics magazine, the average salary for chiropractors was $87,538 in 2010.

Although most chiropractors work full time, 21 percent worked part time in 2010. About 1 out of 4 chiropractors worked 50 or more hours per week. Chiropractors may stay open in the evenings to accommodate working patients. Self-employed chiropractors set their own hours.

Job Outlook

Chiropractors
Percent change in employment, projected 2010-20

Chiropractors	28%
Health Diagnosing and Treating Practitioners	26%
Total, All Occupations	14%

Note: All Occupations includes all occupations in the U.S. Economy.
Source: U.S. Bureau of Labor Statistics, Employment Projections program

Employment of chiropractors is expected to increase by 28 percent from 2010 to 2020, faster than the average for all occupations.

People across all age groups are increasingly seeking chiropractic care, because most chiropractors treat patients without performing surgery or prescribing drugs. Chiropractic treatment of the back, neck, limbs, and joints has become more accepted as a result of research and changing attitudes about alternative healthcare.

The aging of the large baby-boom generation will lead to new opportunities for chiropractors, because older adults are more likely to experience musculoskeletal and joint problems.

Demand for chiropractic treatment is related to the ability of patients to pay, either directly or through health insurance. Although more insurance plans now cover chiropractic services, the extent of such coverage varies among plans. Chiropractors must educate communities about the benefits of chiropractic care to establish a successful practice.

Employment projections data for chiropractors, 2010-20

Occupational Title	SOC Code	Employment, 2010	Projected Employment, 2020	Change, 2010-20	
				Percent	Numeric
Chiropractors	29-1011	52,600	67,400	28	14,900
SOURCE: U.S. Bureau of Labor Statistics, Employment Projections program					

Similar Occupations

This table shows a list of occupations with job duties that are similar to those of chiropractors.

Occupation	Job Duties	Entry-Level Education	Median Annual Pay, May 2010
Podiatrists	Podiatrists provide medical and surgical care for people suffering foot, ankle, and lower leg problems. They diagnose illnesses, treat injuries, and perform surgery.	Doctoral or professional degree	$118,030
Physicians and Surgeons	Physicians and surgeons diagnose and treat injuries and illnesses in patients. Physicians examine patients, take medical histories, prescribe medications, and order, perform, and interpret diagnostic tests. Surgeons operate on patients to treat injuries, such as broken bones; diseases, such as cancerous tumors; and deformities, such as cleft palates.	Doctoral or professional degree	This wage is equal to or greater than $166,400 per year.
Physical Therapists	Physical therapists help people who have injuries or illnesses improve their movement and manage their pain. They are often an important part of rehabilitation and treatment of patients with chronic conditions or injuries.	Doctoral or professional degree	$76,310
Occupational Therapists	Occupational therapists treat patients with injuries, illnesses, or disabilities through the therapeutic use of everyday activities. They help these patients develop, recover, and improve the skills needed for daily living and working.	Master's degree	$72,320
Massage Therapists	Massage therapists treat clients by using touch to manipulate the soft-tissue muscles of the body. With their touch, therapists relieve pain, rehabilitate injuries, reduce stress, increase relaxation, and aid in the general wellness of clients.	Postsecondary non-degree award	$34,900
Athletic Trainers	Athletic trainers specialize in preventing, diagnosing, and treating muscle and bone injuries and illnesses. They work with people of all ages and all skill levels, from young children to soldiers and professional athletes.	Bachelor's degree	$41,600

Contacts for More Information

For information on a career as a chiropractor, visit American Chiropractic Association

For a list of chiropractic programs and institutions, as well as for general information on chiropractic education, visit Association of Chiropractic Colleges

For information on state education and licensure requirements, visit Federation of Chiropractic Licensing Boards

Suggested citation:

Bureau of Labor Statistics, U.S. Department of Labor, Occupational Outlook Handbook, 2012-13 Edition, Chiropractors, on the Internet at http://www.bls.gov/ooh/healthcare/chiropractors.htm .

Dental Assistants

Quick Facts: Dental Assistants	
2010 Median Pay	$33,470 per year $16.09 per hour
Entry-Level Education	Postsecondary non-degree award
Work Experience in a Related Occupation	None
On-the-job Training	None
Number of Jobs, 2010	297,200
Job Outlook, 2010-20	31% (Much faster than average)
Employment Change, 2010-20	91,600

What Dental Assistants Do

Dental assistants have many tasks, ranging from patient care to record keeping, in a dental office. Their duties vary by state and by the dentists' offices where they work.

Duties

Dental assistants typically do the following:

- Work with patients to make them comfortable in the dental chair and to prepare them for treatments and procedures
- Sterilize dental instruments
- Prepare the work area for patient treatment by setting out instruments and materials
- Help dentists by handing them instruments during procedures
- Keep patients' mouths dry by using suction hoses or other equipment
- Instruct patients in proper dental hygiene
- Process x rays and do lab tasks under the direction of a dentist
- Keep records of dental treatments

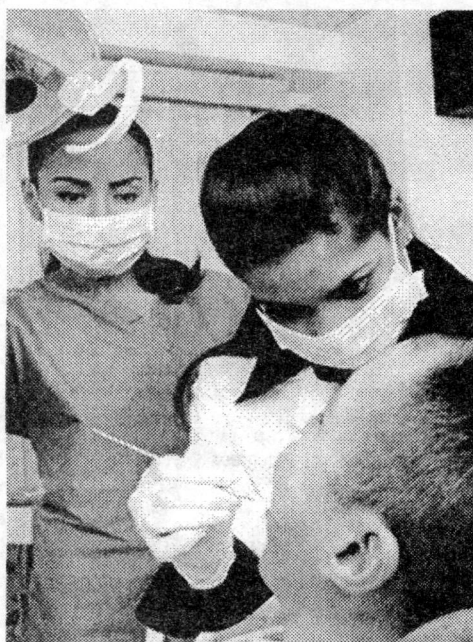

Dental assistants work closely with dentists.

- Schedule patient appointments
- Work with patients on billing and payment

Assistants who do lab tasks, such as making casts of a patient's teeth, work under the direction of a dentist. They might prepare materials for a cast of teeth or create temporary crowns.

All dental assistants do tasks such as helping dentists with procedures and keeping patient records, but there are four regulated tasks that assistants may also be able to do, depending on the state where they work.

- Coronal polishing
- Sealant application
- Fluoride application
- Topical anesthetics application

Coronal polishing, which means removing soft deposits such as plaque, gives teeth a cleaner appearance. In sealant application, dental assistants paint a thin, plastic substance over teeth that seals out food particles and acid-producing bacteria to keep teeth from developing cavities. Fluoride application, in which fluoride is put directly on the teeth, is another anti-cavity measure. For topical anesthetics application, some dental assistants may be qualified to apply topical anesthetic to an area of the patient's mouth, temporarily numbing the area.

Not all states allow dental assistants to do these tasks. Each state regulates the scope of practice for dental assistants and may require them to take specific exams or meet other requirements before allowing them to do these procedures.

Work Environment

Dental assistants held about 297,200 jobs in 2010. Almost all dental assistants work in dentists' offices. Dental assistants work under the supervision of dentists and may work closely with dental hygienists in their day-to-day activities. For more information, see the profiles on dentists and dental hygienists .

Dental assistants wear safety glasses, surgical masks, protective clothing, and gloves to protect themselves and patients from infectious diseases. They must also follow safety procedures to minimize risks associated with x-ray machines.

Work Schedules

Most dental assistants work full time. However, almost 2 in 5 assistants worked part time in 2010. Some work evenings or weekends, depending on the hours of operation at the office where they work.

How to Become a Dental Assistant

There are several possible paths to becoming a dental assistant. Some states require assistants to graduate from an accredited program and possibly pass a state exam. In other states, there are no formal educational requirements. Most states regulate what dental assistants may do, but that varies by state.

Education

High school students interested in a career as a dental assistant should take courses in biology, chemistry, and anatomy. Some states require assistants to graduate from an accredited program and pass a state exam. Most programs take about 1 year to complete and lead to a certificate or diploma and are offered by community colleges. Two-year programs, also offered in community colleges, are less common and lead to an associate's degree. The Commission on Dental Accreditation (CODA), part of the American Dental Association , approved more than 285 dental-assisting training programs in 2011.

Accredited programs include classroom and laboratory work in which students learn about teeth, gums, jaws, and other areas that dentists work on and the instruments that dentists use. These programs also include supervised, practical experience.

In other states, there are no formal educational requirements to become an entry-level dental assistant. Contact your state board of dentistry for specific requirements.

Training

On-the-job training often is required regardless of what educational path a dental assistant takes. Dentists have their own ways of doing things, and their assistants may need time to become comfortable working with them.

Dental assistants who do not get formal education learn their duties through on-the-job training. The dentist or other dental assistants in the office teach the new assistant dental terminology, the names of the instruments, how to do daily tasks, how to interact with patients, and other activities necessary to help keep the dental office running smoothly.

Although some job duties are easy to learn, others may take a few months before new dental assistants are knowledgeable about and comfortable doing all their tasks without help.

Certification

Some states require dental assistants to be certified; requirements vary by state. To get certification, dental assistants must pass the Certified Dental Assistant (CDA) exam from the Dental Assisting National Board (DANB). To take the exam, dental assistants must have graduated from an accredited program or have graduated high school and completed the required amount of on-the-job training. Applicants must also have current certification in CPR (cardiopulmonary resuscitation).

Licenses

Some states require that dental assistants be licensed or register with DANB to complete regulated tasks, such as coronal polishing, in a dentist's office; requirements vary by state. Contact your state board of dentistry for specific requirements.

Important Qualities

Detail oriented—. Dental assistants must follow specific rules and protocols to help dentists treat a patient. Assistants must be aware of what practices they are allowed to do in the state where they work.

Interpersonal skills. Dental assistants must work closely with dentists and patients. Sometimes patients are in extreme pain or mental stress, and the assistant must be sensitive to their emotions.

Listening skills. Dental assistants must have good listening skills. They need to follow directions from a dentist or dental hygienist so they can help treat patients and do tasks such as taking an x ray.

Organizational skills. Dental assistants must have excellent organizational skills. They should have the correct tools in place for a dentist or dental hygienist to use when treating a patient.

Pay

Dental Assistants

Median annual wages, May 2010

Total, All Occupations	$33,840
Dental Assistants	$33,470
Healthcare Support Occupations	$24,760

Note: All Occupations includes all occupations in the U.S. Economy.
Source: U.S. Bureau of Labor Statistics, Occupational Employment Statistics

The median annual wage of dental assistants was $33,470 in May 2010. The median wage is the wage at which half the workers in an occupation earned more than that amount and half earned less. The lowest 10 percent earned less than $22,680, and the top 10 percent earned more than $47,090.

Most dental assistants work full time. However, almost 2 in 5 assistants worked part time in 2010. Some work evenings or weekends, depending on the hours of operation at the office where they work.

Job Outlook

Dental Assistants

Percent change in employment, projected 2010-20

Healthcare Support Occupations	34%
Dental Assistants	31%
Total, All Occupations	14%

Note: All Occupations includes all occupations in the U.S. Economy.
Source: U.S. Bureau of Labor Statistics, Employment Projections program

Employment of dental assistants is expected to grow by 31 percent from 2010 to 2020, much faster than the average for all occupations. Ongoing research linking oral health and general health will likely continue to increase the demand for preventive dental services. Dentists will continue to hire more dental assistants to complete routine tasks, allowing the dentist to see more patients in their practice and spend their time on more complex procedures. As dental practices grow, more dental assistants will be needed.

As the large baby-boom population ages, and as people keep more of their original teeth than did previous generations, the need to maintain and treat teeth will continue to increase the need for dental assistants.

Employment projections data for dental assistants, 2010-20

Occupational Title	SOC Code	Employment, 2010	Projected Employment, 2020	Change, 2010-20 Percent	Change, 2010-20 Numeric
Dental Assistants	31-9091	297,200	388,900	31	91,600
SOURCE: U.S. Bureau of Labor Statistics, Employment Projections program					

Similar Occupations

This table shows a list of occupations with job duties that are similar to those of dental assistants.

Occupation	Job Duties	Entry-Level Education	Median Annual Pay, May 2010
Medical Assistants	Medical assistants complete administrative and clinical tasks in the offices of physicians, podiatrists, chiropractors, and other health practitioners. Their duties vary with the location, specialty, and size of the practice.	High school diploma or equivalent	$28,860
Occupational Therapy Assistants and Aides	Occupational therapy assistants and aides work under the direction of occupational therapists in treating patients with injuries, illnesses, or disabilities through the therapeutic use of everyday activities. They help these patients develop, recover, and improve the skills needed for daily living and working.	See How to Become One	$47,490
Physical Therapist Assistants and Aides	Physical therapist assistants and physical therapist aides work under the direction of physical therapists. They help patients who are recovering from injuries, illnesses, and surgeries regain movement and manage pain.	See How to Become One	$37,710
Surgical Technologists	Surgical technologists, also called operating room technicians, assist in surgical operations. They prepare operating rooms, arrange equipment, and help doctors and nurses during surgeries.	Postsecondary non-degree award	$39,920
Pharmacy Technicians	Pharmacy technicians help licensed pharmacists dispense prescription medication.	High school diploma or equivalent	$28,400

Contacts for More Information

For more information about becoming a dental assistant and for a list of accredited dental assistant programs, visit Commission on Dental Accreditation, American Dental Association

For more information about becoming a Certified Dental Assistant and for a list of state boards of dentistry, visit Dental Assisting National Board

Suggested citation:

Bureau of Labor Statistics, U.S. Department of Labor, Occupational Outlook Handbook, 2012-13 Edition, Dental Assistants, on the Internet at http://www.bls.gov/ooh/healthcare/dental-assistants.htm .

Dental Hygienists

Quick Facts: Dental Hygienists	
2010 Median Pay	$68,250 per year $32.81 per hour
Entry-Level Education	Associate's degree
Work Experience in a Related Occupation	None
On-the-job Training	None
Number of Jobs, 2010	181,800
Job Outlook, 2010-20	38% (Much faster than average)
Employment Change, 2010-20	68,500

What Dental Hygienists Do

Dental hygienists clean teeth, examine patients for signs of oral diseases such as gingivitis, and provide other preventative dental care. They also educate patients on ways to improve and maintain good oral health.

Duties

Dental hygienists typically do the following:

- Remove tartar, stains, and plaque from teeth
- Apply sealants and fluorides to help protect teeth
- Take and develop dental x rays
- Keep track of patient care and treatment plans
- Teach patients oral hygiene, such as how to brush and floss correctly

Dental hygienists use many types of tools to do their job. They clean and polish teeth with both hand and powered tools, as well as ultrasonic devices. In some cases, they remove stains with an air polishing device, which sprays a combination of air, water, and baking soda. They polish teeth with a powered tool that works like an automatic toothbrush. Hygienists use x-ray machines to take pictures to check for tooth or jaw problems.

Dental hygienists help patients develop and keep good oral health. For example, they may explain the relationship between diet and oral health. They also may give advice to patients on how to select toothbrushes and other oral-care devices.

Other tasks hygienists may perform vary by state. Some states allow hygienists to place and carve filling materials, temporary fillings, and periodontal dressings.

Work Environment

Dental hygienists held about 181,800 jobs in 2010. Almost all dental hygienists work in dentists' offices, which are clean and well-lit. They work closely with dentists and dental assistants. For more information, see the profiles on dentists and dental assistants .

Dental hygienists wear safety glasses, surgical masks, and gloves to protect themselves and patients from infectious diseases. When taking x rays they follow strict procedures to protect themselves and patients. They may spend long periods of time bending over to work on patients.

Work Schedules

Flexible scheduling is a distinctive feature of this job. More than one half of dental hygienists work part time. Dentists often hire hygienists to work only a few days a week, so some hygienists work for more than one dentist. About 38 percent of hygienists worked full time in 2010.

How to Become a Dental Hygienist

Dental hygienists typically need an associate's degree in dental hygiene. Every state requires dental hygienists to be licensed; requirements vary by state.

Education

Dental hygienists typically need an associate's degree in dental hygiene to enter the occupation. Certificates, bachelor's degrees, and master's degrees in dental hygiene are also available but are less common among dental hygienists. Private dental offices usually require a minimum of an associate's degree or certificate in dental hygiene. A bachelor's or master's degree is usually required for research, teaching, or clinical practice in public or school health programs.

High school students interested in becoming dental hygienists should take courses in biology, chemistry, and mathematics. Some dental hygiene programs also require applicants to have completed at least one year of college. Specific entrance requirements vary from one school to another.

Most schools offer laboratory, clinical, and classroom instruction. Hygienists study anatomy, physiology, nutrition, radiography, and periodontology, which is the study of gum disease.

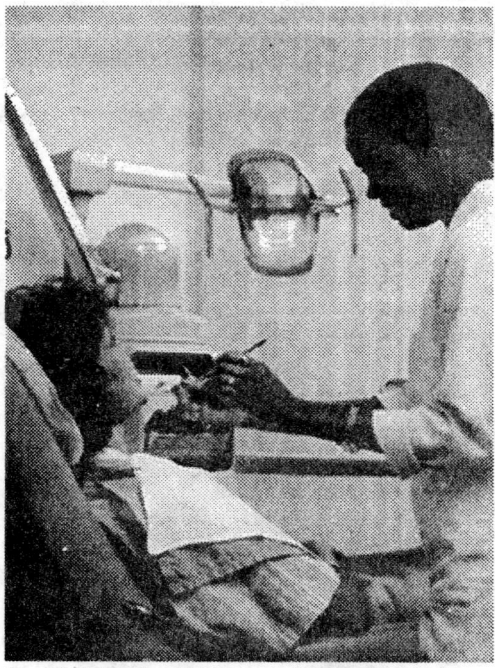

Dental hygienists examine patients' teeth and gums and record the presence of diseases or abnormalities.

Important Qualities

Compassion. Sometimes patients are in extreme pain or mental stress, and the hygienist must be sensitive to their emotions.

Detail oriented. Dental hygienist must follow specific rules and protocols to help diagnose and treat a patient. In rare cases, dental hygienists work without the direct supervision of a dentist.

Dexterity. Dental hygienists must be good at working with their hands. They generally work in tight quarters on a small part of the body using very precise tools.

Interpersonal skills. Dental hygienists must work closely with dentists and patients.

Stamina. Dental hygienists should be comfortable performing physical tasks, such as bending over patients for a long time.

Technical skills. Dental hygienists must understand how to operate complex machinery, including x-ray machines and powered instruments.

Licenses

Every state requires dental hygienists to be licensed; requirements vary by state. In most states, licensure requires a degree from an accredited dental hygiene program and passing written and practical examinations. For specific application requirements, contact your state's medical or health board.

Pay

Dental Hygienists
Median annual wages, May 2010

Dental Hygienists	$68,250
Health Technologists and Technicians	$39,340
Total, All Occupations	$33,840

Note: All Occupations includes all occupations in the U.S. Economy.
Source: U.S. Bureau of Labor Statistics, Occupational Employment Statistics

The median annual wage of dental hygienists was $68,250 in May 2010. The median wage is the wage at which half the workers in an occupation earned more than that amount and half earned less. The lowest 10 percent earned less than $45,000, and the top 10 percent earned more than $93,820.

Pay for dental hygienists may be for each hour worked, each day

worked, on a regular yearly salary, or on commission. Some dental hygienists also get benefits, such as vacation, sick leave, and contributions to their retirement fund. However, benefits vary by employer and may be available only to full-time workers.

Most dental hygienists work part time. About 38 percent of hygienists worked full time in 2010.

Job Outlook

Dental Hygienists
Percent change in employment, projected 2010-20

Dental Hygienists	38%
Health Technologists and Technicians	26%
Total, All Occupations	14%

Note: All Occupations includes all occupations in the U.S. Economy.
Source: U.S. Bureau of Labor Statistics, Employment Projections program

Employment of dental hygienists is expected to grow by 38 percent from 2010 to 2020, much faster than the average for all occupations. Ongoing research linking oral health and general health will continue to spur the demand for preventative dental services, which dental hygienists often provide. New and increasingly accurate technologies to help diagnose oral health problems are also expected to increase demand. For example, new tests use saliva samples that a hygienist takes to spot early signs of oral cancer.

As their practices expand, dentists will hire more hygienists to perform routine dental care, allowing the dentist to see more patients. Also, as the large baby boomer population ages and people keep more of their original teeth than previous generations, the need to maintain and treat these teeth will continue to drive the need for hygienists' services.

Job Prospects

Demand for dental services follows the trends in the economy because the patient or private insurance companies pay for these services. As a result, during slow times in the economy, demand for dental services may decrease. During such times, dental hygienists may have difficulty finding employment or, if they are currently employed, they might work fewer hours.

Employment projections data for dental hygienists, 2010-20

Occupational Title	SOC Code	Employment, 2010	Projected Employment, 2020	Change, 2010-20 Percent	Change, 2010-20 Numeric
Dental Hygienists	29-2021	181,800	250,300	38	68,500
SOURCE: U.S. Bureau of Labor Statistics, Employment Projections program					

Similar Occupations

This table shows a list of occupations with job duties that are similar to those of dental hygienists.

Occupation	Job Duties	Entry-Level Education	Median Annual Pay, May 2010
Dental Assistants	Dental assistants have many tasks, ranging from patient care to record keeping, in a dental office. Their duties vary by state and by the dentists' offices where they work.	Postsecondary non-degree award	$33,470
Medical Assistants	Medical assistants complete administrative and clinical tasks in the offices of physicians, podiatrists, chiropractors, and other health practitioners. Their duties vary with the location, specialty, and size of the practice.	High school diploma or equivalent	$28,860
Occupational Therapy Assistants and Aides	Occupational therapy assistants and aides work under the direction of occupational therapists in treating patients with injuries, illnesses, or disabilities through the therapeutic use of everyday activities. They help these patients develop, recover, and improve the skills needed for daily living and working.	See How to Become One	$47,490

Physical Therapist Assistants and Aides	Physical therapist assistants and physical therapist aides work under the direction of physical therapists. They help patients who are recovering from injuries, illnesses, and surgeries regain movement and manage pain.	See How to Become One	$37,710
Physician Assistants	Physician assistants, also known as PAs, practice medicine under the direction of physicians and surgeons. They are formally trained to examine patients, diagnose injuries and illnesses, and provide treatment.	Master's degree	$86,410
Registered Nurses	Registered nurses (RNs) provide and coordinate patient care, educate patients and the public about various health conditions, and provide advice and emotional support to patients and their family members.	Associate's degree	$64,690
Radiation Therapists	Radiation therapists treat cancer and other diseases in patients by giving radiation treatments.	Associate's degree	$74,980

Contacts for More Information

For information about dental hygienists, including educational requirements, and about available accredited programs, visit American Dental Hygienists' Association

For information about accredited programs and educational requirements, visit Commission on Dental Accreditation, American Dental Association

The State Board of Dental Examiners in each state can give information on licensing requirements.

Suggested citation:

Bureau of Labor Statistics, U.S. Department of Labor, Occupational Outlook Handbook, 2012-13 Edition, Dental Hygienists, on the Internet at http://www.bls.gov/ooh/healthcare/dental-hygienists.htm .

Dentists

Quick Facts: Dentists	
2010 Median Pay	$146,920 per year $70.64 per hour
Entry-Level Education	Doctoral or professional degree
Work Experience in a Related Occupation	None
On-the-job Training	Internship/residency
Number of Jobs, 2010	155,700
Job Outlook, 2010-20	21% (Faster than average)
Employment Change, 2010-20	32,200

What Dentists Do

Dentists diagnose and treat problems with a patient's teeth, gums, and related parts of the mouth. They provide advice and instruction on taking care of teeth and gums and on diet choices that affect oral health.

Duties

Dentists typically do the following:

- Remove decay from teeth and fill cavities
- Repair cracked or fractured teeth and remove teeth
- Straighten teeth to correct bite issues
- Place sealants or whitening agents on teeth
- Give anesthetics to keep patients from feeling pain during procedures
- Write prescriptions for antibiotics or other medications
- Examine x rays of teeth, gums, the jaw, and nearby areas for problems
- Make models and measurements for dental appliances, such as dentures, to fit patients
- Teach patients about diet, flossing, use of fluoride, and other aspects of dental care

Dentists use a variety of equipment, including x-ray machines, drills, mouth mirrors, probes, forceps, brushes, and scalpels. They also use lasers, digital scanners, and other computer technologies.

Dentists in private practice also oversee a variety of administrative tasks, including bookkeeping and buying equipment and supplies. They employ and supervise dental hygienists, dental assistants, dental laboratory technicians, and receptionists. For more information, see the profiles on dental hygienists , dental assistants , dental laboratory technicians , or receptionists .

Most dentists are general practitioners and handle a variety of dental needs. Other dentists practice in one of nine specialty areas:

Dental public health specialists promote good dental health and the prevention of dental diseases in specific communities.

Endodontists perform root-canal therapy, by which they remove the nerves and blood supply from injured or infected teeth.

Oral and maxillofacial radiologists diagnose diseases in the head and neck through the use of imaging technologies.

Oral and maxillofacial surgeons operate on the mouth, jaws, teeth, gums, neck, and head, including procedures such as surgically repairing a cleft lip and palate or removing impacted teeth.

Oral pathologists diagnose oral diseases, such as oral cancer or oral lesions (bumps or ulcers in the mouth).

Orthodontists straighten teeth by applying pressure to the teeth with braces or other appliances.

Pediatric dentists focus on dentistry for children and special-needs

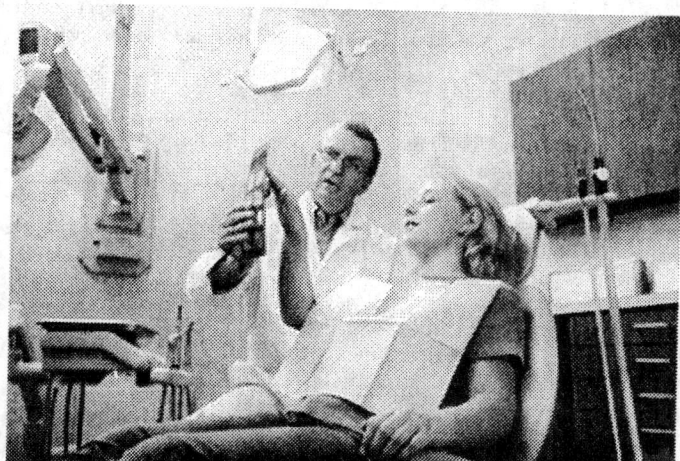

Dentists diagnose and treat problem with teeth and tissues in the mouth, along with giving advice and administering care to help prevent future problems.

patients.

Periodontists treat the gums and bone supporting the teeth.

Prosthodontists replace missing teeth with permanent fixtures, such as crowns and bridges, or with removable fixtures such as dentures.

Work Environment

Dentists held about 155,700 jobs in 2010. Some dentists own their own businesses and work alone or with a small staff. Other dentists have partners in their practice, and a few work for more established dentists as associate dentists.

Dentists usually work in offices. They wear masks, gloves, and safety glasses to protect themselves and their patients from infectious diseases.

Most dentists work full time. Some work evenings and weekends to meet their patients' needs. The number of hours worked varies greatly among dentists. It is common for dentists to continue in part-time practice well beyond the usual retirement age.

How to Become a Dentist

Dentists must be licensed in all states; requirements vary by state. To qualify for a license in most states, applicants must graduate from an accredited dental school and pass written and practical exams.

Education and Training

High school students who want to become dentists should take courses in chemistry, physics, biology, anatomy, and mathematics.

Most dental students need at least a bachelor's degree before entering dental school; requirements vary by school. All dental schools require applicants to have completed certain required science courses, such as biology and chemistry. Majoring in a science, such as biology, might increase the chances of being accepted, but no specific major is required to enter most dental programs.

College undergraduates who plan on applying to dental school must usually take the Dental Acceptance Test (DAT) during their junior year. Admission to dental school can be competitive. Dental schools use these tests, along with other factors such as grade point average and recommendations, to admit students into their programs.

Dental schools require students to take classes such as local anesthesia, anatomy, periodontology (the study of oral disease and

health), and radiology. All dental schools include practice where students work with patients in a clinical setting under the supervision of a licensed dentist.

All nine dental specialties require dentists to complete additional training before practicing that specialty. They must usually take a 1- or 2-year residency in a program related to their specialty.

Dentists who want to teach or research full time usually spend an additional 2 to 5 years in advanced dental training. Many practicing dentists also teach part time, including supervising students in dental school clinics. For more information, see the profile on <u>postsecondary teachers</u>.

Licenses

Dentists must be licensed in all states; requirements vary by state. In most states, a license requires a degree from an accredited dental school and passing a written and practical exam.

In addition, a dentist who wants to practice in one of the nine specialties that all states recognize must have a license in that specialty. This usually requires 2 to 4 years of additional education after dental school and, in some cases, the completion of a special state exam. A postgraduate residency term also may be required, usually lasting up to 2 years.

Important Qualities

Communication skills. Dentists must have excellent communication skills. They must be able to communicate effectively with patients, dental hygienists, dental assistants, and receptionists.

Detail oriented. Dentists must be detail oriented so patients receive appropriate treatments and medications. They must also pay attention to space, shape, and color. For example, they may need to closely match a false tooth with a patient's other teeth.

Dexterity. Dentists must be good at working with their hands. They work with tools in a limited area.

Leadership skills. Most dentists work in their own practice. This requires them to manage and lead a staff.

Organizational skills. Strong organizational skills, including keeping accurate records of patient care, are critical in both medical and business settings.

Patience. Dentists may work for long periods of time with patients who need special attention. Children and patients with a fear of dental work may require a lot of patience.

Problem-solving skills. Dentists need strong problem-solving skills. They must evaluate patients' symptoms and choose the appropriate treatments.

Stamina. Dentists should be comfortable performing physical tasks, such as bending over patients for long periods.

Pay

Dentists

Median annual wages, May 2010

Dentists	$146,920
Health Diagnosing and Treating Practitioners	$71,490
Total, All Occupations	$33,840

Note: All Occupations includes all occupations in the U.S. Economy.
Source: U.S. Bureau of Labor Statistics, Occupational Employment Statistics

The median annual wage of dentists was $146,920 in May 2010. The median wage is the wage at which half the workers in an occupation earned more than that amount and half earned less. The lowest 10 percent earned less than $71,210, and the top 10 percent earned $166,400 or more. Earnings vary according to number of years in practice, location, hours worked, and specialty.

The median annual wages of dentist occupations in May 2010 were the following:

- Equal to or greater than $166,400 for oral and maxillofacial surgeons
- Equal to or greater than $166,400 for orthodontists
- $161,020 for dentists, all other specialists
- $141,040 for general dentists
- $118,400 for prosthodontists

Most dentists work full time. Some work evenings and weekends to meet their patients' needs.

Job Outlook

Dentists

Percent change in employment, projected 2010-20

Health Diagnosing and Treating Practitioners	26%
Dentists	21%
Total, All Occupations	14%

Note: All Occupations includes all occupations in the U.S. Economy.
Source: U.S. Bureau of Labor Statistics, Employment Projections program

Employment of dentists is expected to grow by 21 percent from 2010 to 2020, faster than the average for all occupations.

Many members of the baby-boom generation will need complicated dental work. In addition, because each generation is more likely to keep their teeth than past generations, more dental care will be needed in the years to come. Dentists will continue to see an increase in public demand for their services as studies continue to link oral health to overall health.

Employment of dentists is not expected to keep pace with the increased demand for dental services. There are still areas of the country where patients have little access to dental care. Whether patients seek care is largely dependent on their insurance coverage. People with new or expanded dental insurance coverage will be more likely to visit a dentist than in the past. Cosmetic dental services, such as teeth-whitening treatments, will become increasingly popular. This trend is expected to continue as new technologies allow for less invasive, faster procedures.

Dentists are likely to hire more hygienists and dental assistants to handle routine services. Productivity increases from new technology should allow dentists to reduce the time needed to see each patient. These factors allow the dentist to see more patients when their practices expand.

Dentists will continue to provide care and instruction aimed at promoting good oral hygiene, rather than just providing treatments such as fillings.

Employment projections data for dentists, 2010-20

Occupational Title	SOC Code	Employment, 2010	Projected Employment, 2020	Change, 2010-20	
				Percent	Numeric
Dentists	29-1020	155,700	187,900	21	32,200
Dentists, General	29-1021	130,700	158,300	21	27,600
Oral and Maxillofacial Surgeons	29-1022	8,000	9,700	21	1,700
Orthodontists	29-1023	8,300	10,100	21	1,800
Prosthodontists	29-1024	1,000	1,200	21	200
Dentists, All Other Specialists	29-1029	7,800	8,700	12	900

SOURCE: U.S. Bureau of Labor Statistics, Employment Projections program

Similar Occupations

This table shows a list of occupations with job duties that are similar to those of dentists.

Occupation	Job Duties	Entry-Level Education	Median Annual Pay, May 2010
Chiropractors	Chiropractors treat patients with health problems of the musculoskeletal system, which is made up of bones, muscles, ligaments, and tendons. They use spinal manipulation and other techniques to treat patients' ailments, such as back or neck pain.	Doctoral or professional degree	$67,200
Optometrists	Optometrists perform eye exams to check for vision problems and diseases. They prescribe eyeglasses or contact lenses as needed.	Doctoral or professional degree	$94,990
Physicians and Surgeons	Physicians and surgeons diagnose and treat injuries and illnesses in patients. Physicians examine patients, take medical histories, prescribe medications, and order, perform, and interpret diagnostic tests. Surgeons operate on patients to treat injuries, such as broken bones; diseases, such as cancerous tumors; and deformities, such as cleft palates.	Doctoral or professional degree	This wage is equal to or greater than $166,400 per year.
Podiatrists	Podiatrists provide medical and surgical care for people suffering foot, ankle, and lower leg problems. They diagnose illnesses, treat injuries, and perform surgery.	Doctoral or professional degree	$118,030
Veterinarians	Veterinarians care for the health of animals. They diagnose, treat, or research medical conditions and diseases of pets, livestock, and animals in zoos, racetracks, and laboratories.	Doctoral or professional degree	$82,040

Contacts for More Information

For more information about dentists, including accredited dental schools and state boards of dental examiners, visit American Dental Association, Commission on Dental Accreditation

For information on admission to dental schools, visit American Dental Education Association

For more information on general dentistry or on a specific dental specialty, visit Academy of General Dentistry ,American Association of Orthodontists , American Association of Oral and Maxillofacial Surgeons , American Academy of Pediatric Dentistry , American Academy of Periodontology , American College of Prosthodontists , American Association of Endodontists , American Academy of Oral and Maxillofacial Radiology , American Association of Public Health Dentistry

Suggested citation:

Bureau of Labor Statistics, U.S. Department of Labor, Occupational Outlook Handbook, 2012-13 Edition, Dentists, on the Internet at http://www.bls.gov/ooh/healthcare/dentists.htm .

Diagnostic Medical Sonographers

Quick Facts: Diagnostic Medical Sonographers	
2010 Median Pay	$64,380 per year $30.95 per hour
Entry-Level Education	Associate's degree
Work Experience in a Related Occupation	None
On-the-job Training	None
Number of Jobs, 2010	53,700
Job Outlook, 2010-20	44% (Much faster than average)
Employment Change, 2010-20	23,400

What Diagnostic Medical Sonographers Do

Diagnostic medical sonographers use special imaging equipment that directs sound waves into a patient's body (in a procedure commonly known as an ultrasound, sonogram, or echocardiogram) to assess and diagnose various medical conditions.

Duties

Diagnostic medical sonographers typically do the following:
- Prepare patients for procedures by taking a patient's history and answering any questions about the procedure
- Prepare and maintain imaging equipment
- Apply a gel to aid the sound waves' ability to show the inside of the body
- Operate equipment to get diagnostic images of areas in the patient's body
- Analyze the images to check for quality and adequate coverage of the area needed for diagnosis
- Recognize the difference between normal and abnormal images
- Analyze images to provide preliminary findings for physicians
- Record findings and keep track of patients' records

Diagnostic ultrasound uses high-frequency sound waves to produce images of the inside of the body. The sonographer presses an instrument called an ultrasound transducer to the parts of the patient's body that are being examined. The transducer emits pulses of sound that bounce back, causing echoes. The echoes are then sent to the ultrasound machine, which processes them and displays them as images.

Diagnostic medical sonographers specialize in different parts of the body. The following are examples of specific types of sonographers:

Abdominal sonographers specialize in imaging a patient's abdominal cavity and nearby organs, such as the kidney, liver, gallbladder, pancreas, or spleen.

Breast sonographers specialize in imaging a patient's breast tissues. Sonography aids mammography in the detection of breast cancer. Breast sonography is also used to track tumors in breast cancer patients.

Musculoskeletal sonographers specialize in imaging muscles, ligaments, tendons, and joints.

Neurosonographers specialize in imaging a patient's nervous system, including the brain.

Obstetric and gynecologic sonographers specialize in imaging the female reproductive system. Many pregnant women receive ultrasounds to track the baby's growth and health.

Cardiovascular and vascular technologists use sonography to assist

Diagnostic medical sonographers use sound waves to perform diagnostic imaging examinations on patients.

physicians in diagnosing problems with a patient's heart, arteries and veins. For more information, see the profile on cardiovascular technologists and technicians and vascular technologists .

Work Environment

Diagnostic medical sonographers held about 53,700 jobs in 2010 and work in healthcare facilities. About 61 percent worked in hospitals in 2010, others worked in areas such as physician's offices and medical and diagnostic laboratories:

Hospitals; state, local, and private	61%
Offices of physicians	24
Medical and diagnostic laboratories	9
Outpatient care centers	2

Diagnostic medical sonographers do most of their work at diagnostic imaging machines in dimly lit rooms, but they may also perform procedures at patients' bedsides. Sonographers may be on their feet for long periods and may need to lift or turn patients who are disabled.

Work Schedules

Most diagnostic medical sonographers work full time. Because imaging is sometimes needed in emergencies, sonographers sometimes work evenings, weekends, or overnight.

How to Become a Diagnostic Medical Sonographer

Diagnostic medical sonographers need formal education, such as an associate's degree or a postsecondary certificate. Many employers also require professional certification.

Education

Colleges and universities offer both associate's and bachelor's degree programs in sonography. One-year certificate programs also are available, although these are usually useful only to those who are already employed in related healthcare jobs, such as nursing. Employers prefer a degree or certificate from an accredited institute or hospital program. The accredited programs usually follow a specific course of study and include clinical training. These programs also include courses in medical terminology and interpreting sonographic images. Most programs are divided into the specialized fields that correspond to the relevant certification exams, such as abdominal sonography or breast sonography.

Some sonographers graduate with a degree in radiologic technology or nursing and then receive on-the-job training by their employer. High school students who are interested in diagnostic medical sonography should take courses in anatomy, physiology, and mathematics.

Licenses and Certification

Most employers prefer to hire sonographers who have professional certification. A sonographer can get certification by graduating from an accredited program and passing an exam. Most exams relate to the specialty that the sonographer is most interested in—for example, an exam to be become certified in abdominal sonography. A few states require diagnostic medical sonographers to be licensed. Typically, professional certification is required for licensure; other requirements vary by state. Sonographers must take continuing education to keep their certification current.

Important Qualities

Detail oriented. Diagnostic medical sonographers must follow precise instructions to obtain the images needed to diagnose and treat the patient. They also must pay attention to the screen while scanning a patient's body because the cues that contrast healthy areas with unhealthy ones may be subtle.

Hand-eye coordination. To get quality images, diagnostic medical sonographers must be able to move equipment on the patient's body in response to what they see on the screen.

Interpersonal skills. Diagnostic medical sonographers must work closely with patients. Sometimes patients are in extreme pain or mental stress, and the sonographer must get cooperation from the patient to create usable images.

Stamina. Diagnostic medical sonographers work on their feet for long periods and must be able to lift and move patients who need assistance.

Technical skills. Diagnostic medical sonographers must understand how to operate complex machinery and computerized instruments.

Pay

Diagnostic Medical Sonographers
Median annual wages, May 2010

Health Diagnosing and Treating Practitioners	$71,490
Diagnostic Medical Sonographers	$64,380
Total, All Occupations	$33,840

Note: All Occupations includes all occupations in the U.S. Economy.
Source: U.S. Bureau of Labor Statistics, Occupational Employment Statistics

The median annual wage of diagnostic medical sonographers was $64,380 in May 2010. The median wage is the wage at which half the workers in an occupation earned more than that amount and half earned less. The lowest 10 percent earned less than $44,900, and the top 10 percent earned more than $88,490.

As shown below, the median annual wage of diagnostic medical sonographers in hospitals was $64,440 in May 2010:

Outpatient care centers	$69,740
Offices of physicians	64,560
Hospitals; State, local, and private	64,440
Medical and diagnostic laboratories	62,290

Most diagnostic medical sonographers work full time. Because imaging is sometimes needed in emergencies, sonographers sometime work evenings, weekends, or overnight.

Job Outlook

Diagnostic Medical Sonographers
Percent change in employment, projected 2010-20

Diagnostic Medical Sonographers	44%
Health Diagnosing and Treating Practitioners	26%
Total, All Occupations	14%

Note: All Occupations includes all occupations in the U.S. Economy.
Source: U.S. Bureau of Labor Statistics, Employment Projections program

Employment of diagnostic medical sonographers is expected to grow by 44 percent from 2010 to 2020, much faster than the average for all occupations. As ultrasound imaging technology evolves, it will be used by medical facilities as a substitute for procedures that are costly, invasive, or expose patients to radiation. The use of sonography will continue to increase as patients, when given the option, choose to avoid exposure to radiation or undergo invasive procedures. Although hospitals remain the main employer of diagnostic medical sonographers, employment is expected to grow more rapidly in physicians' offices and in medical and diagnostic laboratories. Employment in these healthcare settings is expected to increase because of the shift toward outpatient care whenever possible. Outpatient care is encouraged by third-party payers as a cost-saving measure and is made possible by technological advances, such as less expensive ultrasound equipment, which allow for more procedures to be done outside of hospitals.

As the large baby-boom population ages and remains active later in life, the need to diagnose medical conditions, such as blood clots and tumors, with imaging technology should increase. Diagnostic medical sonographers will be needed to use and maintain the imaging equipment.

Job Prospects

Sonographers who are certified in more than one specialty are expected to have better job opportunities.

Employment projections data for diagnostic medical sonographers, 2010-20

Occupational Title	SOC Code	Employment, 2010	Projected Employment, 2020	Change, 2010-20	
Percent	Numeric			Percent	Numeric
Diagnostic Medical Sonographers	29-2032	53,700	77,100	44	23,400
SOURCE: U.S. Bureau of Labor Statistics, Employment Projections program					

Similar Occupations

This table shows a list of occupations with job duties that are similar to those of diagnostic medical sonographers.

Occupation	Job Duties	Entry-Level Education	Median Annual Pay, May 2010
Cardiovascular Technologists and Technicians and Vascular Technologists	Cardiovascular technologists and technicians and vascular technologists use imaging technology to help physicians diagnose cardiac (heart) and peripheral vascular (blood vessel) ailments in patients. They also help physicians treat problems with cardiac and vascular systems, such as blood clots.	Associate's degree	$49,410
Medical and Clinical Laboratory Technologists and Technicians	Medical laboratory technologists (also known as medical laboratory scientists) and medical laboratory technicians collect samples and perform tests to analyze body fluids, tissue, and other substances.	See How to Become One	$46,680
Nuclear Medicine Technologists	Nuclear medicine technologists use a scanner to create images of various areas of a patient's body. They prepare radioactive drugs and administer them to patients undergoing the scans. The radioactive drugs cause abnormal areas of the body to appear different from normal areas in the images.	Associate's degree	$68,560
Radiologic Technologists	Radiologic technologists perform diagnostic imaging examinations, such as x rays, on patients.	Associate's degree	$54,340

Contacts for More Information

For more information about diagnostic medical sonographers, visit Society of Diagnostic Medical Sonography

For more information on becoming a registered diagnostic medical sonographer, visit American Registry for Diagnostic Medical Sonography

For information on certification as a diagnostic medical sonographer, visit The American Registry of Radiologic Technologists

For more information on the use of ultrasound in medicine and accredited practices, visit American Institute of Ultrasound in Medicine

For a current list of accredited education programs in diagnostic medical sonography, visit Joint Review Committee on Education in Diagnostic Medical Sonography , Commission on Accreditation of Allied Health Education Programs

Suggested citation:

Bureau of Labor Statistics, U.S. Department of Labor, Occupational Outlook Handbook, 2012-13 Edition, Diagnostic Medical Sonographers, on the Internet at http://www.bls.gov/ooh/healthcare/diagnostic-medical-sonographers.htm .

Dietitians and Nutritionists

Quick Facts: Dietitians and Nutritionists	
2010 Median Pay	$53,250 per year $25.60 per hour
Entry-Level Education	Bachelor's degree
Work Experience in a Related Occupation	None
On-the-job Training	Internship/residency
Number of Jobs, 2010	64,400
Job Outlook, 2010-20	20% (Faster than average)
Employment Change, 2010-20	12,700

What Dietitians and Nutritionists Do

Dietitians and nutritionists are experts in food and nutrition. They advise people on what to eat in order to lead a healthy lifestyle or achieve a specific health-related goal.

Duties

Dietitians and nutritionists typically do the following:

- Explain nutrition issues
- Assess patients' and clients' health needs and diet
- Develop meal plans, taking both cost and clients' preferences into account
- Evaluate the effects of meal plans and change the plans as needed
- Promote better nutrition by giving talks to groups about diet, nutrition, and the relationship between good eating habits and preventing or managing specific diseases
- Keep up with the latest nutritional science research

Some dietitians and nutritionists provide customized information for specific individuals. For example, a dietitian or nutritionist might teach a patient with high blood pressure how to use less salt when preparing meals. Others work with groups of people who have similar needs. A dietitian or nutritionist might, for example, plan a diet with reduced fat and sugar to help overweight people lose weight.

Although all dietitians and nutritionists do similar tasks, there are several specialties within the occupations. The following are examples of types of dietitians and nutritionists:

Clinical dietitians provide medical nutrition therapy. They work in hospitals, long-term care facilities, and other institutions. They create

Dietitians and nutritionists are experts in food.

both individualized and group nutritional programs based on the health needs of patients or residents. Clinical dietitians may further specialize, such as working only with patients with kidney diseases. They may work with other healthcare professionals.

Management dietitians plan meal programs. They work in food service settings such as cafeterias, hospitals, and food corporations. They may be responsible for buying food and for carrying out other business-related tasks. Management dietitians may oversee kitchen staff or other dietitians.

Community dietitians educate the public on topics related to food and nutrition. They often work with specific groups of people, such as pregnant women. They work in public health clinics, government and non-profit agencies, health maintenance organizations (HMOs), and other settings.

Work Environment

Dietitians and nutritionists held about 64,400 jobs in 2010.

As shown below, nearly one-third of dietitians and nutritionists worked in hospitals in 2010:

Hospitals; state, local, and private	32%
Self-employed workers	15
Nursing care facilities	8
Outpatient care centers	6
Offices of physicians	4

Dietitians and nutritionists work in hospitals, cafeterias, nursing homes, and schools. Some dietitians and nutritionists are self-employed and maintain their own practice. They work as consultants, providing advice to individual clients, or they work for healthcare establishments on a contract basis.

Work Schedules

Most dietitians and nutritionists work full time, although about 20 percent work part time. Self-employed, consultant dietitians have more flexibility in setting their schedules.

How to Become a Dietitian or Nutritionist

Most dietitians and nutritionists have earned a bachelor's degree and receive supervised training through an internship or as a part of their coursework. Also, many states require dietitians and nutritionists to be licensed.

Education

Most dietitians and nutritionists have earned a bachelor's degree in dietetics, foods and nutrition, food service systems management, or a related area. Programs include courses in nutrition, physiology, chemistry, and biology.

Training

Dietitians and nutritionists typically participate in several hundred hours of supervised training, usually in the form of an internship following graduation from college. However, some programs in dietetics include this training as part of the coursework.

Many dietitians and nutritionists have advanced degrees.

Licenses and Certification

Most states require licensure of dietitians and nutritionists. Other states require only state registration or certification, and a few have no state regulations.

Most states have enacted state licensure or certification for dietitians or nutritionists or both. The requirements for state licensure and state certification include having a bachelor's degree in food and nutrition or a related area, supervised practice, and passing an exam.

One way to become licensed is to earn the Registered Dietitian (RD) credential. While the RD is not always required, the qualifications necessary to become an RD are parallel to the qualifications necessary to become a licensed dietitian in all states that require a license. Many employers prefer or require the RD, which is administered by the Commission on Dietetic Registration , the credentialing agency for the Academy of Nutrition and Dietetics.

The requirements for the RD credential are similar, but not identical to the licensing requirements in many states. The RD requires dietitians to complete education and supervised practice programs. These programs are accredited by the Accreditation Council for Education in Nutrition and Dietetics (ACEND). In order to maintain the RD credential, Registered Dietitians must complete continuing professional education courses.

Important Qualities

Analytical skills. Dietitians must keep up to date with the latest nutrition research. They should be able to interpret scientific studies and translate nutrition science into practical eating advice.

Organizational skills. Because there are many aspects to the work of dietitians and nutritionists, they should have the ability to stay organized. Management dietitians, for example, must consider both the nutritional needs of their customers and the costs of meals.

People skills. Dietitians and nutritionists must listen carefully to understand clients' goals and concerns. They also have to be emphatic to help clients confront and overcome dietary struggles.

Speaking skills. Dietitians and nutritionists must explain complicated topics in a way that people with less technical knowledge understand. For example, a clinical dietitian must be able to clearly tell clients about what to eat and why eating the recommended foods is important.

Pay

Dietitians and Nutritionists
Median annual wages, May 2010

Health Diagnosing and Treating Practitioners	$71,490
Dietitians and Nutritionists	$53,250
Total, All Occupations	$33,840

Note: All Occupations includes all occupations in the U.S. Economy.
Source: U.S. Bureau of Labor Statistics, Occupational Employment Statistics

The median annual wage of dietitians and nutritionists was $53,250 in May 2010. The median annual wage is the wage at which half the workers in an occupation earned more than that amount and half earned less. The lowest 10 percent earned less than $33,330, and the top 10 percent earned more than $75,480.

Most dietitians and nutritionists work full time, although about 20 percent work part time. Self-employed, consultant dietitians have more flexibility in setting their schedules.

Job Outlook

Dietitians and Nutritionists
Percent change in employment, projected 2010-20

Health Diagnosing and Treating Practitioners	26%
Dietitians and Nutritionists	20%
Total, All Occupations	14%

Note: All Occupations includes all occupations in the U.S. Economy.
Source: U.S. Bureau of Labor Statistics, Employment Projections program

Employment of dietitians and nutritionists is expected to increase 20 percent from 2010 to 2020, faster than average for all occupations.

In recent years, there has been increased interest in the role of food in promoting health and wellness, particularly as a part of preventative healthcare in medical settings. The importance of diet in preventing and treating illnesses such as diabetes and heart disease is now well known. More dietitians and nutritionists will be needed to provide care for people with these conditions.

An aging population also will increase the need for dietitians and nutritionists in nursing homes.

Employment projections data for dietitians and nutritionists, 2010-20

Occupational Title	SOC Code	Employment, 2010	Projected Employment, 2020	Change, 2010-20	
				Percent	Numeric
Dietitians and Nutritionists	29-1031	64,400	77,100	20	12,700
SOURCE: U.S. Bureau of Labor Statistics, Employment Projections program					

Similar Occupations

This table shows a list of occupations with job duties that are similar to those of dietitians and nutritionists.

Occupation	Job Duties	Entry-Level Education	Median Annual Pay, May 2010
Health Educators	Health educators teach people about behaviors that promote wellness. They develop programs and materials to encourage people to make healthy decisions.	Bachelor's degree	$45,830

Contacts for More Information

For a list of academic programs, scholarships, and other information about dietitians, visit Academy of Nutrition and Dietetics

For information on the Registered Dietitian (RD) exam and other specialty credentials, visit Commission on Dietetic Registration

Suggested citation:

Bureau of Labor Statistics, U.S. Department of Labor, Occupational Outlook Handbook, 2012-13 Edition, Dietitians and Nutritionists, on the Internet at http://www.bls.gov/ooh/healthcare/dietitians-and-nutritionists.htm .

EMTs and Paramedics

Quick Facts: EMTs and Paramedics	
2010 Median Pay	$30,360 per year $14.60 per hour
Entry-Level Education	Postsecondary non-degree award
Work Experience in a Related Occupation	None
On-the-job Training	None
Number of Jobs, 2010	226,500
Job Outlook, 2010-20	33% (Much faster than average)
Employment Change, 2010-20	75,400

What EMTs and Paramedics Do

Emergency medical technicians (EMTs) and paramedics care for the sick or injured in emergency medical settings. People's lives often depend on their quick reaction and competent care. EMTs and paramedics respond to emergency calls, performing medical services and transporting patients to medical facilities.

A 911 operator sends EMTs and paramedics to the scene of an emergency, where they often work with police and firefighters. For more information, see the profiles on police and detectives and firefighters.

Duties

EMTs and paramedics typically do the following:

- Respond to 911 calls for emergency medical assistance, such as cardiopulmonary resuscitation (CPR) or bandaging a wound
- Assess a patient's condition and determine a course of treatment
- Follow guidelines that they learned in training and that they receive from physicians who oversee their work

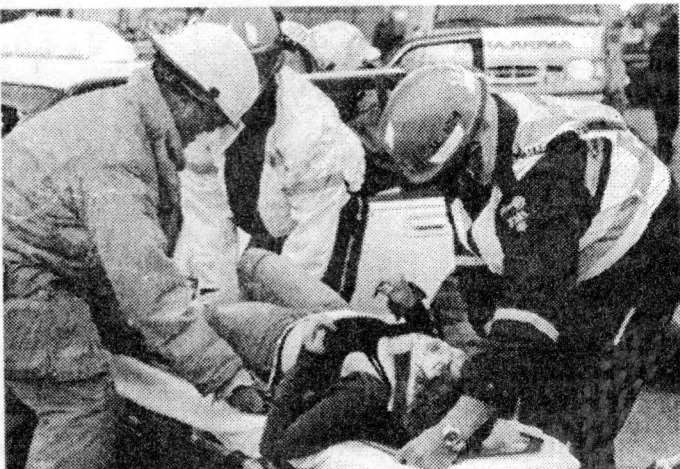

In emergencies, EMTs and paramedics are dispatched by a 911 operator to the scene, where they often work with police and firefighters.

- Use backboards and restraints to keep patients still and safe in an ambulance for transport
- Help transfer patients to the emergency department of a healthcare facility and report their observations and treatment to the staff
- Create a patient care report; documenting the medical care they gave the patient
- Replace used supplies and check or clean equipment after use

When taking a patient to the hospital, one EMT or paramedic may drive the ambulance while another monitors the patient's vital signs and gives additional care. Some paramedics work as part of a helicopter's flight crew to transport critically ill or injured patients to a hospital.

EMTs and paramedics also take patients from one medical facility to another. Some patients may need to be transferred to a hospital that specializes in treating their injury or illness or to a facility that provides long-term care, such as a nursing home.

If a patient has a contagious disease, EMTs and paramedics decontaminate the interior of the ambulance and may need to report these cases to the proper authorities.

The specific responsibilities of EMTs and paramedics depend on their level of training and the state they work in. The National Registry of Emergency Medical Technicians (NREMT) provides national certification of EMTs and paramedics at four levels: EMT-Basic, EMT-Intermediate (which has two levels, respectively called 1985 and 1999), and Paramedic. Some states, however, have their own certification programs and use different titles.

An **EMT-Basic**, also known as an EMT, cares for patients at the scene and while taking patients by ambulance to a hospital. An EMT-Basic has the emergency skills to assess a patient's condition and manage respiratory, cardiac, and trauma emergencies.

An **EMT-Intermediate (1985 or 1999)**, also known as Advanced EMT, has completed the training required at the EMT-Basic level, as well as training for more advanced skills, such as the use of intravenous fluids and some medications.

Paramedics provide more extensive prehospital care than do EMTs. In addition to carrying out the procedures that EMTs use, paramedics can give medications orally and intravenously, interpret electrocardiograms (EKGs)—used to monitor heart function—and use other monitors and complex equipment.

The specific tasks or procedures EMTs and paramedics are allowed to perform at any level vary by state.

Work Environment

Emergency medical technicians (EMTs) and paramedics held about 226,500 jobs in 2010. They work both indoors and outdoors, in all types of weather. Their work is physically strenuous and can be stressful, sometimes involving life-or-death situations and patients who are suffering. Most career EMTs and paramedics work in metropolitan areas. Volunteer EMTs and paramedics are more common in small cities, towns, and rural areas. These individuals volunteer for fire departments, providers of emergency medical services, or hospitals and may respond to only a few calls per month.

As shown below, almost half of paid EMTs and paramedics worked as employees of ambulance services in 2010. Others worked in hospitals or local government:

Ambulance services	48%
Local government, excluding education and hospitals	29
Hospitals; state, local, and private	17

In 2010, about 22 percent of EMTs and paramedics belonged to a union or were covered by a union contract.

Injuries

EMTs and paramedics experience a much larger than average number of work-related injuries or illnesses. They are required to do considerable kneeling, bending, and lifting while caring for and moving patients. They may be exposed to contagious diseases, such as hepatitis B and AIDS. Sometimes they can be injured by mentally unstable or combative patients. These risks can be reduced by following proper safety procedures, such as waiting for police to clear an area in violent situations or wearing gloves while working with a patient.

Work Schedules

Most EMTs and paramedics work full time. About one-third worked more than full time in 2010. Because EMTs and paramedics must be available to work in emergencies, they may work overnight and on weekends. Some EMTs and paramedics are volunteers and have varied work schedules.

How to Become an EMT or Paramedic

All emergency medical technicians (EMTs) and paramedics must complete a formal training program. All states require EMTs and paramedics to be licensed; requirements vary by state.

Education and Training

Both a high school diploma or equivalent and cardiopulmonary resuscitation (CPR) certification are prerequisites for most formal education and training programs. High school students interested in entering these occupations should take courses in anatomy and physiology. Formal training is offered by technical institutes, community colleges, and facilities that specialize in emergency care training.

At the EMT-Basic level, training includes instruction in assessing patients' conditions, dealing with trauma and cardiac emergencies, clearing obstructed airways, using field equipment, and handling emergencies. Formal courses include about 100 hours of specialized training. Some training may be required in a hospital or ambulance setting.

The EMT-Intermediate 1985 or EMT-Intermediate 1999 level, also known as the Advanced EMT level, typically requires 1,000 hours of training based on the scope of practice. At this level, people must complete the training required at the EMT level, as well as more advanced training, such as training in the use of complex airway devices, intravenous fluids, and some medications.

Paramedics have the most advanced level of training. They must complete EMT-level and Advanced EMT training, as well as training in advanced medical skills. Community colleges and technical schools may offer this training, in which graduates may receive an associate's degree. Paramedic programs require about 1,300 hours of training and may take up to 2 years. Their broader scope of practice may include stitching wounds or administering IV medications.

Separate training and licensure is required to drive an ambulance. Although some emergency medical services hire separate drivers, most EMTs and paramedics take a course requiring about 8 hours of training before they can drive an ambulance.

Licenses and Certification

The National Registry of Emergency Medical Technicians (NREMT) certifies EMTs and paramedics. All levels of NREMT certification require completing a certified training or education program and passing the national exam. The national exam has both a written part and a practical part.

All states require EMTs and paramedics to be licensed; requirements vary by state. In most states, an individual who has NREMT certification qualifies for licensure; in some, passing an equivalent state exam is required. Typically to apply for a license, an applicant must be over the age of 18. Many states require background checks and may decide not to give a license to an applicant who has a criminal history.

Important Qualities

Compassion. EMTs and paramedics must provide emotional support to patients in an emergency, especially patients who are in life-threatening situations or extreme mental distress.

Interpersonal skills. EMTs and paramedics almost always work on teams and must be able to coordinate their activities closely with others in stressful situations.

Listening skills. EMTs and paramedics need to listen to patients to determine the extent of their injuries or illnesses.

Physical strength. EMTs and paramedics need to be physically fit. Their job requires a lot of bending, lifting, and kneeling.

Problem-solving skills. EMTs and paramedics need strong problem-solving skills. They must evaluate patients' symptoms and administer the appropriate treatments.

Speaking skills. EMTs and paramedics need to be able to comfort and explain procedures to the patient, give orders, and relay information to others.

Pay

EMTs and Paramedics
Median annual wages, May 2010

Health Technologists and Technicians	$39,340
Total, All Occupations	$33,840
Emergency Medical Technicians and Paramedics	$30,360

Note: All Occupations includes all occupations in the U.S. Economy.
Source: U.S. Bureau of Labor Statistics, Occupational Employment Statistics

The median annual wage of emergency medical technicians (EMTs) and paramedics was $30,360 in May 2010. The median wage is the wage at which half the workers in an occupation earned more than that amount and half earned less. The lowest 10 percent earned less than $19,710, and the top 10 percent earned more than $51,370.

Most EMTs and paramedics work full time. About one-third worked more than full time in 2010. Because EMTs and paramedics must be available to work in emergencies, they may work overnight and on weekends. Some EMTs and paramedics are volunteers and have varied work schedules.

Job Outlook

EMTs and Paramedics
Percent change in employment, projected 2010-20

Emergency Medical Technicians and Paramedics	33%
Health Technologists and Technicians	26%
Total, All Occupations	14%

Note: All Occupations includes all occupations in the U.S. Economy.
Source: U.S. Bureau of Labor Statistics, Employment Projections program

Employment of emergency medical technicians (EMTs) and paramedics is expected to grow by 33 percent from 2010 to 2020, much faster than the average for all occupations. Emergencies such as car crashes, natural disasters, and violence will continue to create demand for EMTs and paramedics. There will also continue to be demand for part-time, volunteer EMTs and paramedics in rural areas and smaller metropolitan areas.

Growth in the middle-aged and elderly population will lead to an increase in the number of age-related health emergencies, such as heart attacks or strokes. This, in turn, will lead to an increase in the demand for EMTs and paramedic services. An increase in specialized medical facilities will require more EMTs and paramedics to transfer patients with specific conditions to these facilities for treatment.

In recent years, companies that build ambulances have started to update and redesign their interiors to keep EMTs, paramedics, and patients safer during transport. These companies are hiring EMTs and paramedics as consultants to learn their ideas about such updates and designs.

Employment projections data for EMTs and paramedics, 2010-20

Occupational Title	SOC Code	Employment, 2010	Projected Employment, 2020	Change, 2010-20 Percent	Change, 2010-20 Numeric
Emergency Medical Technicians and Paramedics	29-2041	226,500	301,900	33	75,400
SOURCE: U.S. Bureau of Labor Statistics, Employment Projections program					

Similar Occupations

This table shows a list of occupations with job duties that are similar to those of EMTs and paramedics.

Occupation	Job Duties	Entry-Level Education	Median Annual Pay, May 2010
Firefighters	Firefighters protect the public by responding to fires and other emergencies. They are frequently the first emergency personnel on the scene of an accident.	Postsecondary non-degree award	$45,250
Police and Detectives	Police officers protect lives and property. Detectives and criminal investigators, who sometimes are called agents or special agents, gather facts and collect evidence of possible crimes. Law enforcement officers' duties depend on the size and type of their organizations.	High school diploma or equivalent	$55,010
Air Traffic Controllers	Air traffic controllers coordinate the movement of air traffic to ensure that planes stay safe distances apart.	Associate's degree	$108,040
Physician Assistants	Physician assistants, also known as PAs, practice medicine under the direction of physicians and surgeons. They are formally trained to examine patients, diagnose injuries and illnesses, and provide treatment.	Master's degree	$86,410
Registered Nurses	Registered nurses (RNs) provide and coordinate patient care, educate patients and the public about various health conditions, and provide advice and emotional support to patients and their family members.	Associate's degree	$64,690

Contacts for More Information

For more information about emergency medical technicians and paramedics, visit National Association of Emergency Medical Technicians

National Highway Traffic Safety Administration, Office of Emergency Medical Services , National Registry of Emergency Medical Technicians

Suggested citation:

Bureau of Labor Statistics, U.S. Department of Labor, Occupational Outlook Handbook, 2012-13 Edition, EMTs and Paramedics, on the Internet at http://www.bls.gov/ooh/healthcare/emts-and-paramedics.htm .

Home Health and Personal Care Aides

Quick Facts: Home Health and Personal Care Aides	
2010 Median Pay	$20,170 per year $9.70 per hour
Entry-Level Education	Less than high school
Work Experience in a Related Occupation	None
On-the-job Training	Short-term on-the-job training
Number of Jobs, 2010	1,878,700
Job Outlook, 2010-20	70% (Much faster than average)
Employment Change, 2010-20	1,313,200

What Home Health and Personal Care Aides Do

Home health and personal care aides help people who are disabled, chronically ill, or cognitively impaired. They also help older adults who may need assistance. They help with activities such as bathing and dressing, and they provide services such as light housekeeping. In some states, home health aides may be able to give a client medication or check the client's vital signs under the direction of a nurse or other healthcare practitioner.

Duties

Home health and personal care aides typically do the following:

- Help clients in their daily personal tasks, such as bathing or dressing
- Do light housekeeping, such as laundry, washing dishes, and vacuuming in a client's home
- Organize a client's schedule and plan appointments
- Arrange transportation to doctors' offices or for other kinds of outings
- Shop for groceries and prepare meals
- Provide companionship

Aides often keep track of when a client's prescriptions need to be filled or when the client has his or her next doctor's appointment. Aides may prepare leisure activities, including exercise, to keep their clients active and healthy. They may go for walks with their clients or play games with them. In some states, home health aides may be able to provide some medical services. Aides may be expected to complete unpleasant tasks such as emptying a client's bedpan or changing soiled bed linens.

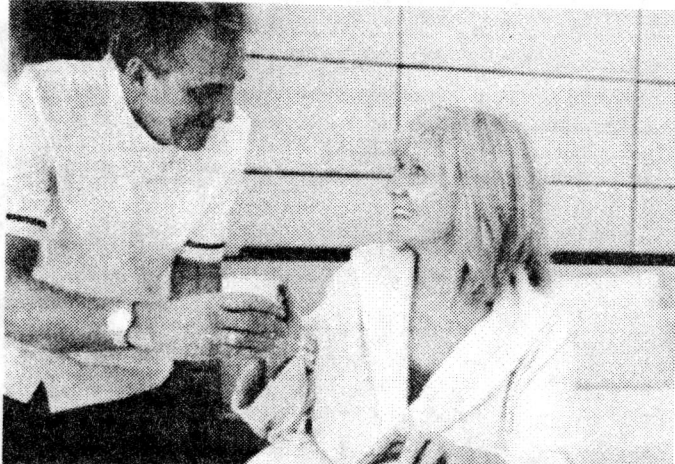

Home health and personal care aides help people in their own homes or in residential facilities.

Some aides are hired directly by the client or the client's family. In these situations, the client or the client's family supervises the aide and gives the aide tasks to do.

Home health aides, unlike personal care aides, typically work for certified home health or hospice agencies that receive government funding and therefore must comply with regulations. They work under the direct supervision of a medical professional, usually a nurse. These aides keep records of services performed and of the client's condition and progress. They report changes in the client's condition to the supervisor or case manager. Aides also work with therapists and other medical staff.

Home health aides may provide some basic health-related services, such as checking clients' pulse, temperature, and respiration rate. They also may help with simple prescribed exercises and with giving medications. Occasionally, they change simple dressings, give massages, care for skin, or help with braces and artificial limbs. With special training, experienced home health aides also may help with medical equipment such as ventilators, which help clients breathe.

Personal care aides—also called homemakers, caregivers, companions, and personal attendants—provide clients with companionship and help with daily tasks in a client's home. They are often hired in addition to other medical health workers, such as hospice workers, who may visit a client's home. Personal care aides do not provide any type of medical service.

Direct support professionals work with people who have developmental or intellectual disabilities. They may help create a behavior plan, provide employment support, and teach self-care skills, such as doing laundry or cooking meals. They may also provide other personal assistance services.

Work Environment

Home health and personal care aides held about 1.9 million jobs in 2010. They work in a variety of settings. Most work in a client's home; others work in small group homes or larger care communities. Some aides go to the same home every day or week for months or even years. Some visit four or five clients on the same day. Others work only with one client all day. This may involve working with other aides in shifts so the client always has an aide. They may help people in hospices and day services programs and may also help people with disabilities go to work and stay engaged in their communities.

The following industries employed the largest numbers of home health aides in 2010:

Home health care services	34%
Residential mental retardation facilities	16
Services for the elderly and persons with disabilities	14
Community care facilities for the elderly	14
Nursing care facilities	4

The following industries employed the largest numbers of personal care aides in 2010:

Services for the elderly and persons with disabilities	33%
Home health care services	26
Private households	10
Self-employed workers	7
Vocational rehabilitation services	5

Injuries

Home health and personal care aides had a higher-than-average number of work-related injuries and illnesses in 2010. Work as an aide can be physically and emotionally demanding. Aides must guard against back injury because they may have to move clients into and out of bed or help them to stand or walk.

In addition, aides may frequently work with clients who have cognitive impairments or mental health issues and who may display difficult or violent behaviors. Aides may also face hazards from minor infections and exposure to communicable diseases, but can avoid infections by following proper procedures.

How to Become a Home Health or Personal Care Aide

There are no formal education requirements for home health and personal care aides, but most aides have a high school diploma. Home health aides working in certified home health or hospice agencies must get formal training and pass a standardized test.

Education and Training

Although a high school diploma or equivalent is not generally required, most aides have one before entering the occupation. They usually are trained on the job by nurses, other aides, or supervisors.

Aides may be trained in housekeeping tasks, such as cooking for clients who have special dietary needs. They learn basic safety techniques, including how to respond in an emergency.

A competency evaluation may be required to ensure that the aide can perform some required tasks. Clients have their own preferences and aides may need time to become comfortable working with them.

In some states, the only requirement for employment is on-the-job training, which employers generally provide. Other states require formal training, which is available from community colleges, vocational schools, elder care programs, and home health care agencies. In addition, states may conduct background checks on prospective aides.

Without additional training, advancement in this occupation is limited.

Important Qualities

Detail oriented—. Home health and personal care aides must follow specific rules and protocols to help take care of clients.

Interpersonal skills. Home health and personal care aides must work closely with their clients. Sometimes, clients are in extreme pain or mental stress, and aides must be sensitive to their emotions. Aides must be cheerful, compassionate, and emotionally stable. They must enjoy helping people.

Physical stamina. Home health and personal care aides should be comfortable performing physical tasks. They might need to lift or turn clients who have a disability.

Time management skills. Clients and their families rely on home health and personal care aides. Therefore, it is important that aides stick to the agreed-upon schedule and arrive when they are expected.

Certification

Home health aides who work for agencies that receive reimbursement from Medicare or Medicaid must get a minimum level of training and pass a competency evaluation or receive state certification. Training includes learning about personal hygiene, reading and recording vital signs, infection control, and basic nutrition. Aides may take a competency exam to become certified without taking any training. These are the minimum requirements by law; additional requirements for certification vary by state.

Aides can be certified by the National Association for Home Care & Hospice (NAHC). Although certification is not always required, employers prefer to hire certified aides. Certification requires 75 hours of training, observation and documentation of 17 skills demonstrating competency, and passing a written exam.

Pay

Home Health and Personal Care Aides
Median annual wages, May 2010

Total, All Occupations	$33,840
Healthcare Support Occupations	$24,760
Home Health Aides	$20,560
Other Personal Care and Service Workers	$20,420
Personal Care Aides	$19,640

Note: All Occupations includes all occupations in the U.S. Economy.
Source: U.S. Bureau of Labor Statistics, Occupational Employment Statistics

The median annual wage of home health aides was $20,560 in May 2010. The median wage is the wage at which half the workers in an occupation earned more than that amount and half earned less. The lowest 10 percent earned less than $16,300, and the top 10 percent earned more than $29,390.

The median annual wage of personal care aides was $19,640 in May 2010. The lowest 10 percent earned less than $15,970, and the top 10 percent earned more than $25,900.

Job Outlook

Home Health and Personal Care Aides
Percent change in employment, projected 2010-20

Personal Care Aides	70%
Home Health Aides	69%
Other Personal Care and Service Workers	35%
Healthcare Support Occupations	34%
Total, All Occupations	14%

Note: All Occupations includes all occupations in the U.S. Economy.
Source: U.S. Bureau of Labor Statistics, Employment Projections program

Employment of home health aides is expected to grow by 69 percent from 2010 to 2020, much faster than the average for all occupations. Employment of personal care aides is expected to grow by 70 percent from 2010 to 2020, much faster than the average for all occupations.

As the baby-boom population ages and the elderly population grows, the demand for home health and personal care aides to provide assistance and companionship will continue to increase. Older clients often have health problems and need some help with daily activities.

Elderly and disabled clients increasingly rely on home care as a less expensive alternative to nursing homes or hospitals. Clients who need help with everyday tasks and household chores, rather than medical care, can reduce their medical expenses by returning to their homes.

Another reason for home care is that most clients prefer to be cared for in their homes, where they are most comfortable. Studies have found that home treatment is often more effective than care in a nursing home or hospital.

Job Prospects

Job prospects for both home health aides and personal care aides are excellent. These occupations are large and expected to grow very quickly, thus adding many jobs. In addition, the low pay and high emotional demands cause many workers to leave these occupations, and they will have to be replaced.

Employment projections data for home health and personal care aides, 2010-20

Occupational Title	SOC Code	Employment, 2010	Projected Employment, 2020	Change, 2010-20	
				Percent	Numeric
Home Health and Personal Care Aides	—	1,878,700	3,191,900	70	1,313,200
Home Health Aides	31-1011	1,017,700	1,723,900	69	706,300
Personal Care Aides	39-9021	861,000	1,468,000	70	607,000

SOURCE: U.S. Bureau of Labor Statistics, Employment Projections program

Similar Occupations

This table shows a list of occupations with job duties that are similar to those of home health and personal care aides.

Occupation	Job Duties	Entry-Level Education	Median Annual Pay, May 2010
Childcare Workers	Childcare workers care for children when parents and other family members are unavailable. They care for children's basic needs, such as bathing and feeding. In addition, some help children prepare for kindergarten, and many help older children with homework.	High school diploma or equivalent	$19,300
Licensed Practical and Licensed Vocational Nurses	Licensed practical and licensed vocational nurses (known as LPNs or LVNs, depending on the state in which they work) provide basic nursing care. They work under the direction of registered nurses and doctors.	Postsecondary non-degree award	$40,380
Medical Assistants	Medical assistants complete administrative and clinical tasks in the offices of physicians, podiatrists, chiropractors, and other health practitioners. Their duties vary with the location, specialty, and size of the practice.	High school diploma or equivalent	$28,860
Nursing Aides, Orderlies, and Attendants	Nursing aides, orderlies, and attendants help provide basic care for patients in hospitals and residents of long-term care facilities, such as nursing homes.	Postsecondary non-degree award	$24,010
Registered Nurses	Registered nurses (RNs) provide and coordinate patient care, educate patients and the public about various health conditions, and provide advice and emotional support to patients and their family members.	Associate's degree	$64,690
Occupational Therapy Assistants and Aides	Occupational therapy assistants and aides work under the direction of occupational therapists in treating patients with injuries, illnesses, or disabilities through the therapeutic use of everyday activities. They help these patients develop, recover, and improve the skills needed for daily living and working.	See How to Become One	$47,490
Physical Therapist Assistants and Aides	Physical therapist assistants and physical therapist aides work under the direction of physical therapists. They help patients who are recovering from injuries, illnesses, and surgeries regain movement and manage pain.	See How to Become One	$37,710
Radiation Therapists	Radiation therapists treat cancer and other diseases in patients by giving radiation treatments.	Associate's degree	$74,980
Social and Human Service Assistants	Social and human service assistants help people get through difficult times or get additional support. They help other workers, such as social workers, and they help clients find benefits or community services.	High school diploma or equivalent	$28,200

Contacts for More Information

For information about voluntary credentials for personal care aides, visit National Association for Home Care & Hospice

Suggested citation:

Bureau of Labor Statistics, U.S. Department of Labor, Occupational Outlook Handbook, 2012-13 Edition, Home Health and Personal Care Aides, on the Internet at http://www.bls.gov/ooh/healthcare/home-health-and-personal-care-aides.htm .

Licensed Practical and Licensed Vocational Nurses

Quick Facts: Licensed Practical and Licensed Vocational Nurses	
2010 Median Pay	$40,380 per year $19.42 per hour
Entry-Level Education	Postsecondary non-degree award
Work Experience in a Related Occupation	None
On-the-job Training	None
Number of Jobs, 2010	752,300
Job Outlook, 2010-20	22% (Faster than average)
Employment Change, 2010-20	168,500

What Licensed Practical and Licensed Vocational Nurses Do

Licensed practical and licensed vocational nurses (known as LPNs or LVNs, depending on the state in which they work) provide basic medical care. They work under the direction of registered nurses and doctors.

Duties

Licensed practical and licensed vocational nurses typically do the following:

- Monitor patients' health—for example, by checking their blood pressure
- Administer basic nursing care, including changing bandages and inserting catheters
- Provide for the basic comfort of patients, such as helping them bathe or dress
- Discuss health care with patients and listen to their concerns
- Report patients' status to registered nurses and doctors
- Keep records on patients' health

Duties of LPNs and LVNs vary, depending on their work setting, For example, they may teach family members how to care for a relative; help to deliver, care for, and feed infants; collect samples for testing and do routine laboratory tests; or feed patients who need help eating.

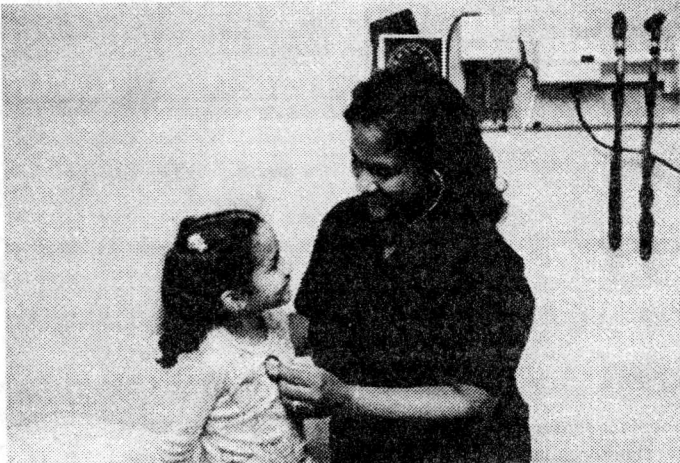

Licensed practical and vocational nurses use stethoscopes to listen to patients' hearts.

Because medical care is regulated, LPNs and LVNs may be limited to doing certain tasks, depending on their state. In some states, for example, LPNs with proper training can give medication or start intravenous (IV) drips, while in other states they cannot. State regulations govern the extent to which LPNs and LVNs must be directly supervised; for example, an LPN may provide certain forms of care only with instructions from a registered nurse.

Experienced licensed practical and licensed vocational nurses oversee and direct other LPNs or LVNs and unlicensed medical staff.

Work Environment

Licensed practical and licensed vocational nurses held about 752,300 jobs in 2010. As shown below, only 12 percent of licensed practical and licensed vocational nurses worked in physicians' offices in 2010:

Nursing care facilities	29%
General medical and surgical hospitals; private	15
Offices of physicians	12
Home health care services	9
Community care facilities for the elderly	5

Licensed practical and licensed vocational nurses work in settings such as nursing homes and extended care facilities, hospitals, physicians' offices, and private homes. LPNs and LVNs often wear scrubs, a type of medical clothing that usually consists of a V-neck shirt and drawstring pants.

Nurses must often be on their feet for much of the day and may have to help lift patients who have trouble moving in bed, standing, or walking. These duties can be stressful, as can dealing with ill and injured people.

Work Schedules

Three-fourths of licensed practical and licensed vocational nurses worked full time in 2010. The rest worked part time or on variable schedules. Many LPNs and LVNs work nights, weekends, and holidays because medical care takes place at all hours. They may be required to work shifts of longer than 8 hours.

How to Become a Licensed Practical or Licensed Vocational Nurse

Becoming a licensed practical or licensed vocational nurse requires completing an approved educational program. LPNs and LVNs must also have a license.

Education

LPNs and LVNs must complete an accredited program, which takes about 1 year. These programs are commonly in technical schools and community colleges. They may occasionally be in high schools and hospitals as well. Practical nursing programs combine classroom learning in subjects such as nursing, biology, and pharmacology, with supervised clinical experience. These programs give certificates in practical nursing. Contact your state's board of nursing for a list of approved programs.

Licenses

After getting a certificate, prospective LPNs or LVNs can take the National Council Licensure Examination, or NCLEX-PN. They must pass the exam to get a license and work as an LPN or LVN in all states.

Important Qualities

Compassion. Licensed practical and licensed vocational nurses must be empathetic and caring toward the people they serve.

Detail oriented. LPNs and LVNs need to be responsible and detail-oriented because they must make sure that patients get the correct treatment at the right time.

Interpersonal skills. Interacting with patients and healthcare specialists is a big part of their jobs, so LPNs and LVNs need good interpersonal skills.

Patience. Dealing with sick and injured people is often stressful. LPNs and LVNs should be patient so they can cope with stress that can come from providing healthcare to these patients.

Speaking skills. It is important that LPNs and LVNs be able to communicate effectively. For example, they might need to relay a patient's current condition to a registered nurse.

Stamina. LPNs and LVNs should be comfortable performing physical tasks, such as bending over patients for a long time.

Advancement

With experience, licensed practical and licensed vocational nurses can advance to supervisory positions. Some LPNs and LVNs advance to other medical occupations, such as registered nurses, by getting more education through LPN to RN (registered nurse) education programs. For more information, see the profile on registered nurses .

Pay

Licensed Practical and Licensed Vocational Nurses
    Median annual wages, May 2010

Licensed Practical and Licensed Vocational Nurses	$40,380
Health Technologists and Technicians	$39,340
Total, All Occupations	$33,840

Note: All Occupations includes all occupations in the U.S. Economy.
Source: U.S. Bureau of Labor Statistics, Occupational Employment Statistics

The median annual wage of licensed practical and licensed vocational nurses was $40,380 in May 2010. The median wage is the wage at which half the workers in an occupation earned more than that amount and half earned less. The lowest 10 percent earned less than $29,680, and the top 10 percent earned more than $56,010.

Three-fourths of licensed practical and licensed vocational nurses worked full time in 2010. The rest worked part time or on variable schedules. Many LPNs and LVNs work nights, weekends, and holidays because medical care takes place at all hours. They may be required to work shifts of longer than 8 hours.

Job Outlook

Licensed Practical and Licensed Vocational Nurses
    Percent change in employment, projected 2010-20

Health Technologists and Technicians	26%
Licensed Practical and Licensed Vocational Nurses	22%
Total, All Occupations	14%

Note: All Occupations includes all occupations in the U.S. Economy.
Source: U.S. Bureau of Labor Statistics, Employment Projections program

Employment of licensed practical and licensed vocational nurses is expected to grow 22 percent from 2010 to 2020, faster than the average for all occupations. As the U.S. population ages, the overall need for healthcare is expected to increase. This trend will lead to increased employment of LPNs and LVNs in hospitals, physicians' offices, and other healthcare settings. LPNs and LVNs also will be needed in residential care facilities such as nursing homes and assisted-living centers. Many procedures that once could be done only in hospitals are now being done outside of hospitals, creating demand in other settings, such as outpatient care centers.

Job Prospects

A large number of licensed practical and licensed vocational nurses are expected to retire over the coming decade. Job prospects should, therefore, be excellent for licensed and experienced LPNs and LVNs.

Employment projections data for licensed practical and licensed vocational nurses, 2010-20

Occupational Title	SOC Code	Employment, 2010	Projected Employment, 2020	Change, 2010-20 Percent	Change, 2010-20 Numeric
Licensed Practical and Licensed Vocational Nurses	29-2061	752,300	920,800	22	168,500
SOURCE: U.S. Bureau of Labor Statistics, Employment Projections program					

Similar Occupations

This table shows a list of occupations with job duties that are similar to those of licensed practical and licensed vocational nurses.

Occupation	Job Duties	Entry-Level Education	Median Annual Pay, May 2010
Occupational Therapists	Occupational therapists treat patients with injuries, illnesses, or disabilities through the therapeutic use of everyday activities. They help these patients develop, recover, and improve the skills needed for daily living and working.	Master's degree	$72,320
Occupational Therapy Assistants and Aides	Occupational therapy assistants and aides work under the direction of occupational therapists in treating patients with injuries, illnesses, or disabilities through the therapeutic use of everyday activities. They help these patients develop, recover, and improve the skills needed for daily living and working.	See How to Become One	$47,490
Optometrists	Optometrists perform eye exams to check for vision problems and diseases. They prescribe eyeglasses or contact lenses as needed.	Doctoral or professional degree	$94,990
Physical Therapist Assistants and Aides	Physical therapist assistants and physical therapist aides work under the direction of physical therapists. They help patients who are recovering from injuries, illnesses, and surgeries regain movement and manage pain.	See How to Become One	$37,710
Physician Assistants	Physician assistants, also known as PAs, practice medicine under the direction of physicians and surgeons. They are formally trained to examine patients, diagnose injuries and illnesses, and provide treatment.	Master's degree	$86,410
Physicians and Surgeons	Physicians and surgeons diagnose and treat injuries and illnesses in patients. Physicians examine patients, take medical histories, prescribe medications, and order, perform, and interpret diagnostic tests. Surgeons operate on patients to treat injuries, such as broken bones; diseases, such as cancerous tumors; and deformities, such as cleft palates.	Doctoral or professional degree	This wage is equal to or greater than $166,400 per year.
Podiatrists	Podiatrists provide medical and surgical care for people suffering foot, ankle, and lower leg problems. They diagnose illnesses, treat injuries, and perform surgery.	Doctoral or professional degree	$118,030
Psychiatric Technicians and Aides	Psychiatric technicians and aides care for people who have mental illness and developmental disabilities. The two occupations are related, but technicians typically provide therapeutic care, and aides help patients in their daily activities and ensure a safe, clean environment.	See How to Become One	$26,880
Registered Nurses	Registered nurses (RNs) provide and coordinate patient care, educate patients and the public about various health conditions, and provide advice and emotional support to patients and their family members.	Associate's degree	$64,690
Surgical Technologists	Surgical technologists, also called operating room technicians, assist in surgical operations. They prepare operating rooms, arrange equipment, and help doctors and nurses during surgeries.	Postsecondary non-degree award	$39,920
Physical Therapists	Physical therapists help people who have injuries or illnesses improve their movement and manage their pain. They are often an important part of rehabilitation and treatment of patients with chronic conditions or injuries.	Doctoral or professional degree	$76,310
Nursing Aides, Orderlies, and Attendants	Nursing aides, orderlies, and attendants help provide basic care for patients in hospitals and residents of long-term care facilities, such as nursing homes.	Postsecondary non-degree award	$24,010

Contacts for More Information

For more information about licensed practical or licensed vocational nurses, visit National Association for Practical Nurse Education and Service

National Federation of Licensed Practical Nurses , National League for Nursing

Suggested citation:

Bureau of Labor Statistics, U.S. Department of Labor, Occupational Outlook Handbook, 2012-13 Edition, Licensed Practical and Licensed Vocational Nurses, on the Internet at http://www.bls.gov/ooh/healthcare/licensed-practical-and-licensed-vocational-nurses.htm .

Massage Therapists

Quick Facts: Massage Therapists	
2010 Median Pay	$34,900 per year $16.78 per hour
Entry-Level Education	Postsecondary non-degree award
Work Experience in a Related Occupation	None
On-the-job Training	None
Number of Jobs, 2010	153,700
Job Outlook, 2010-20	20% (Faster than average)
Employment Change, 2010-20	30,900

What Massage Therapists Do

Massage therapists treat clients by using touch to manipulate the soft-tissue muscles of the body. With their touch, therapists relieve pain, rehabilitate injuries, reduce stress, increase relaxation, and aid in the general wellness of clients.

Duties

Massage therapists typically do the following:

- Talk with clients about symptoms, medical history, and desired results
- Evaluate clients to locate painful or tense areas of the body
- Manipulate muscles or other soft tissues of the body
- Provide clients with guidance on how to improve posture, stretching, strengthening, and overall relaxation

Massage therapists use their hands, fingers, forearms, elbows, and sometimes feet to knead muscles and soft tissue of the body to treat injuries and to promote general wellness. A massage can be as short as 5–10 minutes or could last more than an hour.

Therapists also may use lotions and oils, massage tables or chairs, and medical heat lamps when treating a client. Massage therapists may

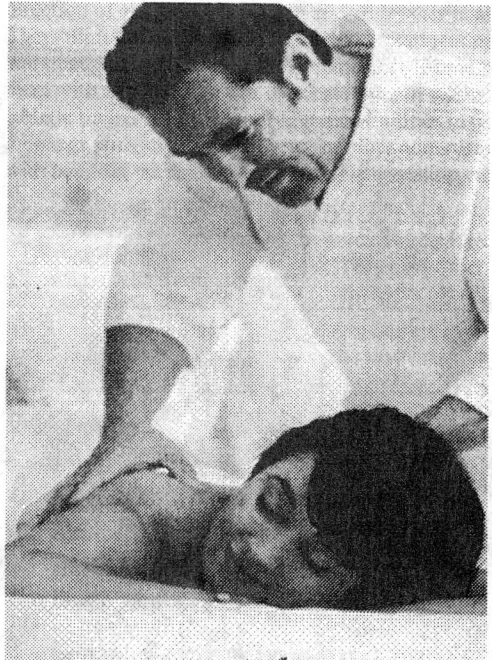

Massage therapists use touch to manipulate a client's muscles.

offer clients information about additional relaxation techniques to practice between sessions.

Massage therapists can specialize in many different types of massage, called modalities.Swedish massage, deep-tissue massage, and sports massage are just a few of the many modalities of massage therapy.Most massage therapists specialize in several modalities, which require different techniques.

Usually, the type of massage given depends on the client's needs and physical condition. For example, therapists may use a special technique for elderly clients that they would not use for athletes. Some forms of massage are given solely to one type of client; for example, prenatal massage is given to pregnant women.

Work Environment

Massage therapists held about 153,700 jobs in 2010. The majority of massage therapists were self-employed in 2010. Others worked mainly in personal care services and various healthcare industries.

As shown below, the majority of massage therapists were self-employed in 2010:

Self-employed workers	60%
Personal care services	18
Offices of chiropractors	5
Traveler accommodation, including hotels and motels	4
Fitness and recreational sports centers	2

Massage therapists work in an array of settings, both private and public, such as private offices, spas, hospitals, fitness centers, and shopping malls. Some massage therapists also travel to clients' homes or offices to give a massage. Most massage therapists, especially those who are self-employed, provide their own table or chair, sheets, pillows, and body lotions or oils.

A massage therapist's working conditions depend heavily on the location and what the client wants. For example, a massage meant to help rehabilitate an injury may be conducted in a well-lit setting with several other clients receiving treatment in the same room. But when giving a massage to help clients relax, massage therapists generally work in dimly lit settings and use candles, incense, and calm, soothing music.

Because massage is physically demanding, massage therapists can injure themselves if they do not use the proper techniques. Repetitive-motion problems and fatigue from standing for extended periods are most common.

Therapists can limit these risks by using good techniques, spacing sessions properly, exercising and, in many cases, receiving a massage themselves regularly.

Work Schedules

Many massage therapists work part time; only about 1 out of 4 worked full time in 2010.

Because therapists work by appointment in most cases, their schedules and the number of hours worked each week vary considerably. In addition to hours giving massages, therapists may also spend time recording patient notes, marketing, booking clients, washing linens, and other general business tasks.

How to Become a Massage Therapist

Massage therapists typically complete a postsecondary education program that can require 500 hours or more of study and experience, although standards and requirements vary greatly by state and locality. Most states regulate massage therapy and require massage therapists to have a license or certificate.

Important Qualities

Communication skills. Massage therapists need to listen carefully to clients to understand what they want to achieve through massage appointments.

Decision-making skills. Massage therapists must evaluate each client's needs and recommend the best treatment based on that person's needs.

Empathy. Massage therapists must give clients a positive experience, which requires building trust between therapist and client. Making clients feel comfortable is necessary for therapists to expand their client base.

Physical stamina. Massage therapists may give several treatments during a work day and have to stay on their feet throughout massage appointments.

Physical strength and dexterity. Massage therapists must be strong and able to exert pressure through a variety of movements of the arms and hands when manipulating a client's muscles.

Education

Training standards and requirements for massage therapists vary greatly by state and locality. Education programs are typically found in private or public postsecondary institutions and can require 500 hours or more of study to complete.

A high school diploma or equivalent degree is usually required for admission. Massage therapy programs generally cover subjects such as anatomy; physiology, which is the study of organs and tissues; kinesiology, which is the study of motion and body mechanics; business management; ethics; and the hands-on practice of massage techniques.

Training programs may concentrate on certain modalities, or specialties, of massage. Several programs also offer job placement and continuing education. Both full-time and part-time programs are available.

Licenses and Certification

In 2011, 43 states and the District of Columbia regulated massage therapy. Although not all states license massage therapy, they may have regulations at the local level.

In states with massage therapy regulations, workers must get either a license or certification after graduating from an accredited training program and before practicing massage. Passing an exam is usually required for licensure.

The exam may be solely a state exam or one of two nationally

recognized tests: the Massage and Bodywork Licensing Examination (MBLEx) and the National Certification Examination for Therapeutic Massage & Bodywork (NCETMB). Massage therapy licensure boards decide which certifications and tests to accept on a state-by-state basis.

Those wishing to practice massage therapy should look into legal requirements for the state and locality in which they intend to practice. A fee and periodic license renewal also may be required.

Pay

Massage Therapists
Median annual wages, May 2010

Massage Therapists	$34,900
Total, All Occupations	$33,840
Healthcare Support Occupations	$24,760

Note: All Occupations includes all occupations in the U.S. Economy.
Source: U.S. Bureau of Labor Statistics, Occupational Employment Statistics

The median annual wage of massage therapists was $34,900 in May 2010. The median wage is the wage at which half the workers in an occupation earned more than that amount and half earned less. The lowest 10 percent earned less than $17,970, and the top 10 percent earned more than $69,000.

Most massage therapists earn a combination of wages and tips.

Many massage therapists work part time; only about 1 out of 4 worked full time in 2010. Because therapists work by appointment in most cases, their schedules and the number of hours worked each week vary considerably. In addition to hours giving massages, therapists may also spend time recording patient notes, marketing, booking clients, washing linens, and other general business tasks.

Job Outlook

Massage Therapists
Percent change in employment, projected 2010-20

Healthcare Support Occupations	34%
Massage Therapists	20%
Total, All Occupations	14%

Note: All Occupations includes all occupations in the U.S. Economy.
Source: U.S. Bureau of Labor Statistics, Employment Projections program

Employment of massage therapists is expected to grow by 20 percent from 2010 to 2020, faster than the average for all occupations. Continued growth in the demand for massage services will lead to new openings for massage therapists.

The number of spas, which employ a large number of therapists, has increased in recent years. The number of massage clinic franchises has also been increasing, many of which offer more affordable massages than those at spas and resorts, making them available to a wider range of customers.

In addition, as an increasing number of states adopt licensing requirements and standards for therapists, the practice of massage is likely to be respected and accepted by more people as a way to treat pain and to improve overall wellness.

Massage also offers specific benefits to particular groups of people, whose continued demand for massage services will lead to overall growth for the occupation. For example, as workplaces try to distinguish themselves as employee-friendly, providing professional in-office, seated massages for employees is becoming a popular on-the-job benefit.

Older people in nursing homes or assisted-living facilities also are finding benefits from massage, such as increased energy levels and reduced health problems. Demand for massage therapy should grow among older age groups because they increasingly are enjoying longer, more active lives.

Job Prospects

In states that regulate massage therapy, opportunities should be available to those who complete formal training programs and pass a professionally recognized exam. However, new massage therapists should expect to work only part time in spas, hotels, hospitals, physical therapy centers, and other businesses until they can build their own client base.

Because referrals are a very important source of work for massage therapists, networking will increase the number of job opportunities. Joining a professional association also can help build strong contacts and further increase the likelihood of steady work.

Employment projections data for massage therapists, 2010-20

Occupational Title	SOC Code	Employment, 2010	Projected Employment, 2020	Change, 2010-20 Percent	Change, 2010-20 Numeric
Massage Therapists	31-9011	153,700	184,600	20	30,900
SOURCE: U.S. Bureau of Labor Statistics, Employment Projections program					

Similar Occupations

This table shows a list of occupations with job duties that are similar to those of massage therapists.

Occupation	Job Duties	Entry-Level Education	Median Annual Pay, May 2010
Athletic Trainers	Athletic trainers specialize in preventing, diagnosing, and treating muscle and bone injuries and illnesses. They work with people of all ages and all skill levels, from young children to soldiers and professional athletes.	Bachelor's degree	$41,600
Chiropractors	Chiropractors treat patients with health problems of the musculoskeletal system, which is made up of bones, muscles, ligaments, and tendons. They use spinal manipulation and other techniques to treat patients' ailments, such as back or neck pain.	Doctoral or professional degree	$67,200
Physical Therapist Assistants and Aides	Physical therapist assistants and physical therapist aides work under the direction of physical therapists. They help patients who are recovering from injuries, illnesses, and surgeries regain movement and manage pain.	See How to Become One	$37,710
Physical Therapists	Physical therapists help people who have injuries or illnesses improve their movement and manage their pain. They are often an important part of rehabilitation and treatment of patients with chronic conditions or injuries.	Doctoral or professional degree	$76,310

Contacts for More Information

For more information about careers in massage therapy, visit Associated Bodywork & Massage Professionals ,American Massage Therapy Association

For a directory of schools providing accredited massage therapy training programs, visit Accrediting Commission of Career Schools and Colleges

Commission on Massage Therapy Accreditation

For more information on national testing and national certification, visit Federation of State Massage Therapy Boards ,National Certification Board for Therapeutic Massage & Bodywork

Suggested citation:

Bureau of Labor Statistics, U.S. Department of Labor, Occupational Outlook Handbook, 2012-13 Edition, Massage Therapists, on the Internet at http://www.bls.gov/ooh/healthcare/massage-therapists.htm .

Medical and Clinical Laboratory Technologists and Technicians

Quick Facts: Medical and Clinical Laboratory Technologists and Technicians	
2010 Median Pay	$46,680 per year $22.44 per hour
Entry-Level Education	See How to Become One
Work Experience in a Related Occupation	None
On-the-job Training	None
Number of Jobs, 2010	330,600
Job Outlook, 2010-20	13% (About as fast as average)
Employment Change, 2010-20	42,900

What Medical and Clinical Laboratory Technologists and Technicians Do

Medical laboratory technologists (also known as medical laboratory scientists) and medical laboratory technicians collect samples and perform the tests to analyze body fluids, tissue, and other substances.

Duties

Medical laboratory technologists and medical laboratory technicians have different job responsibilities: technologists perform more complex tests and procedures than do technicians, and they typically supervise technicians. Medical laboratory technologists typically do the following:

- Analyze body fluids such as blood, urine, and tissue samples to determine normal or abnormal findings
- Collect and study blood samples for use in transfusions by identifying the number of cells, the cell morphology or the blood group, blood type, and compatibility with other blood types
- Operate sophisticated laboratory equipment such as microscopes and cell counters
- Use automated equipment and computerized instruments capable of performing a number of tests at the same time
- Log data from medical tests and enter results into a patient's medical record
- Discuss results and findings of laboratory tests and procedures with physicians

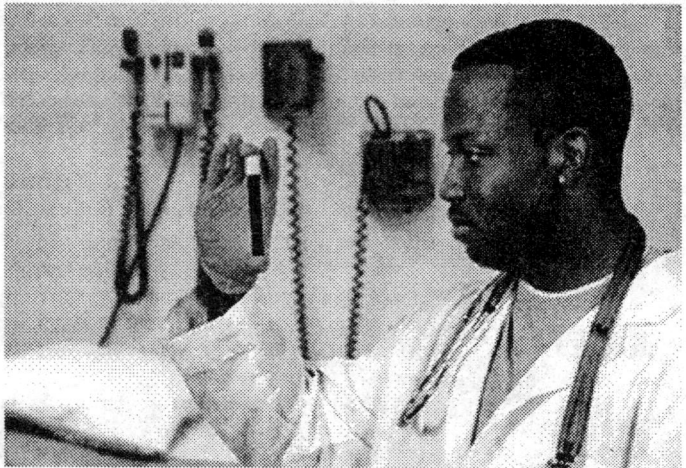

Clinical laboratory personnel examine and test body fluids and cells.

- Supervise or train medical laboratory technicians

Medical laboratory technicians usually work under the supervision of medical laboratory technologists or laboratory managers. Both technicians and technologists perform tests and procedures that physicians or other healthcare personnel order. However, technologists perform more complex tests and laboratory procedures than technicians do. For example, technologists may prepare specimens and operate automated analyzers or perform manual tests that are based on detailed instructions.

Technologists in small laboratories perform many types of tests; in large laboratories, they generally specialize. The following are examples of types of specialized medical laboratory technologists:

Blood bank technologists, or **immunohematology technologists,** collect blood, classify it by type, and prepare blood and its components for transfusions.

Clinical chemistry technologists prepare specimens and analyze the chemical and hormonal contents of body fluids.

Cytotechnologists prepare slides of body cells and examine these cells with a microscope for abnormalities that may signal the beginning of a cancerous growth.

Immunology technologists examine elements of the human immune system and its response to foreign bodies.

Microbiology technologists examine and identify bacteria and other microorganisms.

Molecular biology technologists perform complex protein and nucleic acid tests on cell samples.

Like technologists, medical laboratory technicians may work in several areas of the laboratory or specialize in one particular area.

Phlebotomists collect blood samples.

Histotechnicians cut and stain tissue specimens for pathologists, doctors who study cause and development of diseases at a microscopic level.

Work Environment

Fifty-two percent of medical laboratory technologists and technicians were employed in hospitals in 2010. Most others worked in doctors' offices or diagnostic laboratories:

Hospitals; state, local, and private	52%
Medical and diagnostic laboratories	16
Offices of physicians	10
Federal government	3

Technologists and technicians can be on their feet for long periods collecting samples, and they may need to lift or turn disabled patients.

Laboratories are usually clean and well lit. However, some of the materials they use may produce fumes.

Medical laboratory personnel are trained to work with infectious specimens. When they follow proper methods to control infection and sterilize equipment, few hazards exist. They usually wear protective masks, gloves, and goggles for their safety and protection.

Work Schedules

Most medical laboratory technologists and technicians work full time. Technologists and technicians who work in facilities that operate around the clock, such as hospitals and some independent laboratories, may work evening, weekend, or overnight hours.

How to Become a Medical and Clinical Laboratory Technologist or Technician

Medical laboratory technologists typically need a bachelor's degree. Technicians usually need an associate's degree or a postsecondary certificate. Some states require technologists and technicians to be licensed.

Education

High school students who are interested in pursuing a career in the medical laboratory sciences should take courses in chemistry, biology, and mathematics.

Universities and hospitals offer medical technology programs. An entry-level job for technologists usually requires a bachelor's degree in medical technology or life sciences.

A bachelor's degree in medical laboratory technology includes courses in chemistry, biology, microbiology, mathematics, and statistics, as well as courses on clinical laboratory skills, management, and education. This degree is sometimes known as a medical laboratory scientist program.

The courses may be offered through a hospital-based program that students attend during their senior year of college. College graduates who major in other sciences and meet a program's prerequisites, such as having completed required courses in biology and chemistry, may also apply to a medical laboratory science program.

Prospective medical laboratory technicians must complete an associate's degree program that includes science and clinical laboratory science courses. Often, 1-year certificate programs are available from hospitals for those who already have a degree in a related field, such as nursing. The Armed Forces and vocational or technical schools may also offer certificate programs for medical laboratory technicians. The technician coursework addresses the theoretical and practical aspects of each of the major laboratory disciplines, but the courses are not as in-depth as those that technologists take.

Licenses

Some states require laboratory personnel to be licensed or registered. To be licensed, a technologist often needs a bachelor's degree and must pass an exam. However, requirements vary by state and specialty. For specific requirements, contact your state's department of health or board of occupational licensing.

Certification

Certification of medical laboratory technologists and technicians is required for licensure in some states and by some individual employers. Although certification is not required to enter the occupation in all cases, employers typically prefer to hire certified technologists and technicians. Medical laboratory technologists and technicians can obtain a general certification as a medical laboratory technologist or technician, or a certification in a specialty, such as

phlebotomy or medical biology. Most credentials require that technologists complete an accredited education program to qualify to sit for an examination. Continuing education is required in most cases to maintain certification.

Important Qualities

Compassion. Medical laboratory technologists and technicians need to be empathetic while completing challenging tasks. They work closely with patients who may be in extreme pain or emotional stress and whose cooperation they must be able to get.

Detail oriented—. Medical laboratory technologists and technicians must follow exact instructions from physicians in order to perform the correct tests or procedures.

Dexterity. Medical laboratory technologists and technicians require skill while working with their hands. They work closely with needles and precise laboratory instruments and must be able to handle these tools effectively.

Stamina. Medical laboratory technologists and technicians may work on their feet for long periods while collecting samples. They may need to lift or turn disabled patients to collect samples for testing.

Technical skills. Medical laboratory technologists and technicians must understand how to operate complex machinery.

Pay

Medical and Clinical Laboratory Technologists and Technicians
Median annual wages, May 2010

Health Diagnosing and Treating Practitioners	$71,490
Medical and Clinical Laboratory Technologists	$56,130
Medical and Clinical Laboratory Technicians	$36,280
Total, All Occupations	$33,840

Note: All Occupations includes all occupations in the U.S. Economy.
Source: U.S. Bureau of Labor Statistics, Occupational Employment Statistics

The median annual wage of medical laboratory technologists was $56,130 in May 2010. The median wage is the wage at which half the workers in an occupation earned more than that amount and half earned less. The lowest 10 percent earned more than $38,810, and the highest 10 percent earned more than $76,780.

The median annual wages in selected industries employing medical laboratory technologists were as follows:

Federal government	$62,880
Hospitals; state, local, and private	56,470
Medical and diagnostic laboratories	55,930
Offices of physicians	52,250

The median annual wage of medical laboratory technicians was $36,280 in May 2010. The lowest 10 percent earned more than $24,210, and the highest 10 percent earned more than $56,040.

The median annual wages in selected industries employing medical laboratory technicians were as follows:

Federal government	$40,180
Hospitals; state, local, and private	37,130
Offices of physicians	35,790
Medical and diagnostic laboratories	34,280

According to the American Society for Clinical Pathology, the median hourly wages of staff clinical laboratory technologists and technicians in various specialties and in different types of laboratories in 2010 were as follows:

Specialty	Hospital	Private Clinic	Physician's Office	Reference Lab	Total
Medical Laboratory Scientist/Medical Technologist	$28.62	$27.36	$25.26	$30.56	$28.64
Medical Laboratory Technician	$21.02	$18.84	$18.94	$21.62	$20.66
Phlebotomy Technician	$13.50	$15.90	$13.00	$20.16	$14.52
Histotechnologist	$28.66	$25.00	$29.14	$30.10	$28.94
Histotechnician	$24.16	$23.74	$27.82	$26.62	$24.78
Cytotechnologist	$31.02	$33.10	$39.00	$31.34	$31.14

Most medical laboratory technologists and technicians work full time. Technologists and technicians who work in facilities that operate around the clock, such as hospitals and some independent laboratories, may work evening, weekend, or overnight hours.

Job Outlook

Medical and Clinical Laboratory Technologists and Technicians
Percent change in employment, projected 2010-20

Health Diagnosing and Treating Practitioners	26%
Medical and Clinical Laboratory Technicians	15%
Total, All Occupations	14%
Medical and Clinical Laboratory Technologists	11%

Note: All Occupations includes all occupations in the U.S. Economy.
Source: U.S. Bureau of Labor Statistics, Employment Projections program

Employment of medical laboratory technologists is expected to grow by 11 percent between 2010 and 2020, about as fast as the average for all occupations. Employment of medical laboratory technicians is expected to grow by 15 percent between 2010 and 2020, about as fast as the average for all occupations. An increase in the aging population will lead to a greater need to diagnose medical conditions, such as cancer or type 2 diabetes, through laboratory procedures. Medical laboratory technologists and technicians will be needed to use and maintain the equipment needed for diagnosis and treatment.

Employment projections data for medical and clinical laboratory technologists and technicians, 2010-20

Occupational Title	SOC Code	Employment, 2010	Projected Employment, 2020	Change, 2010-20 Percent	Numeric
Clinical Laboratory Technologists and Technicians	29-2010	330,600	373,500	13	42,900
Medical and Clinical Laboratory Technologists	29-2011	169,400	188,600	11	19,200
Medical and Clinical Laboratory Technicians	29-2012	161,200	184,900	15	23,800
SOURCE: U.S. Bureau of Labor Statistics, Employment Projections program					

Similar Occupations

This table shows a list of occupations with job duties that are similar to those of medical and clinical laboratory technologists and technicians.

Occupation	Job Duties	Entry-Level Education	Median Annual Pay, May 2010
Veterinary Technologists and Technicians	Veterinary technologists and technicians perform medical tests under the supervision of a licensed veterinarian to treat or to help veterinarians diagnose the illnesses and injuries of animals.	Associate's degree	$29,710
Biological Technicians	Biological technicians help biological and medical scientists conduct laboratory tests and experiments.	Bachelor's degree	$39,020
Chemical Technicians	Chemical technicians use special instruments and techniques to help chemists and chemical engineers in researching, developing, and producing chemical products and processes.	Associate's degree	$42,040
Chemists and Materials Scientists	Chemists and materials scientists study the structures, compositions, reactions, and other properties of substances. They use their knowledge to develop new and improved products, processes, and materials.	Bachelor's degree	$69,790

Contacts for More Information

For more information about medical laboratory technologists and technicians, visit American Society for Clinical Laboratory Science , American Society of Cytopathology , Clinical Laboratory Management Association

For a list of accredited and approved educational programs for medical laboratory personnel, visit National Accrediting Agency for Clinical Laboratory Sciences

. For information on certification, visit American Association of Bioanalysts, Board of Registry , American Medical Technologists , American Society for Clinical Pathology , National Credentialing Agency for Laboratory Personnel

Suggested citation:

Bureau of Labor Statistics, U.S. Department of Labor, Occupational Outlook Handbook, 2012-13 Edition, Medical and Clinical Laboratory Technologists and Technicians, on the Internet at http://www.bls.gov/ooh/healthcare/medical-and-clinical-laboratory-technologists-and-technicians.htm .

Medical Assistants

Quick Facts: Medical Assistants	
2010 Median Pay	$28,860 per year / $13.87 per hour
Entry-Level Education	High school diploma or equivalent
Work Experience in a Related Occupation	None
On-the-job Training	Moderate-term on-the-job training
Number of Jobs, 2010	527,600
Job Outlook, 2010-20	31% (Much faster than average)
Employment Change, 2010-20	162,900

What Medical Assistants Do

Medical assistants complete administrative and clinical tasks in the offices of physicians, podiatrists, chiropractors, and other health practitioners. Their duties vary with the location, specialty, and size of the practice.

Duties

Medical assistants typically do the following:
- Take patient history and measure vital signs
- Help the physician with patient examinations
- Give patient injections as directed by the physician
- Schedule patient appointments

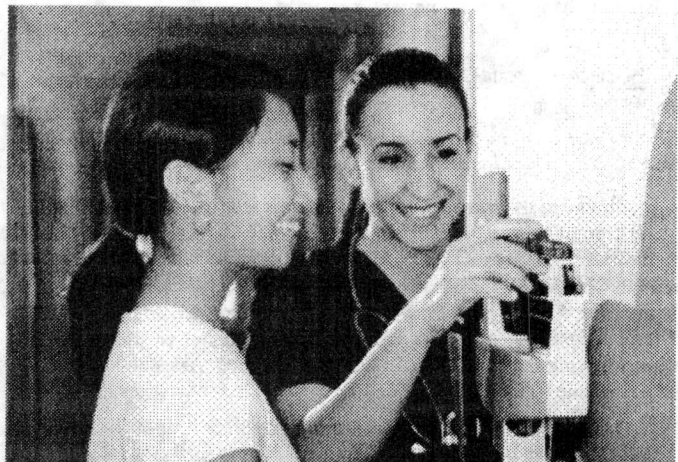

Medical assistants usually do many different kinds of tasks, handling both administrative and clinical duties.

- Prepare blood for laboratory tests

Electronic health records (EHRs) are changing medical assistants' jobs. More and more physicians are adopting EHRs, moving all their patient information online. Assistants need to learn the EHR software that their office uses.

Medical assistants take and record patients' personal information. They must be able to keep that information confidential and discuss it only with other medical personnel who are involved in treating the patient.

Medical assistants should not be confused with physician assistants, who examine, diagnose, and treat patients under a physician's supervision. For more information, see the profile on physician assistants .

In larger practices or hospitals, medical assistants may specialize in either administrative or clinical work.

Administrative medical assistants often fill out insurance forms or code patients' medical information. Some assistants buy and store supplies and equipment for the office.

Clinical medical assistants have different duties, depending on the state where they work. They may do basic laboratory tests, dispose of contaminated supplies, and sterilize medical instruments. They might have additional responsibilities, such as instructing patients about medication or special diets, preparing patients for x rays, removing stitches, drawing blood, or changing dressings.

Some medical assistants specialize in a specific type of medical office.

Ophthalmic medical assistants and optometric assistants help ophthalmologists and optometrists, respectively, provide eye care. They show patients how to insert, remove, and care for contact lenses. Ophthalmic medical assistants also may help an ophthalmologist in surgery.

Podiatric medical assistants work closely with podiatrists (foot doctors). They may make castings of feet, expose and develop x rays, and help podiatrists in surgery.

Work Environment

Medical assistants held about 527,600 jobs in 2010. Most of these assistants work in physicians' offices and other healthcare facilities. In 2010, more than half of all medical assistants worked in physicians' offices.

Work Schedules

Most medical assistants work full time. Some work evenings or weekends to cover shifts in medical facilities that are always open.

How to Become a Medical Assistant

In most states, there are no formal educational requirements for becoming a medical assistant. Most have at least a high school diploma. Many assistants learn through on-the-job training.

Education

High school students interested in a career as a medical assistant should take courses in biology, chemistry, and anatomy.

Medical assistants typically have a high school diploma or equivalent. There are no formal educational requirements for becoming a medical assistant in most states. However, some medical assistants graduate from formal education programs, and employers may prefer such training. Programs are available from community colleges, vocational schools, technical schools, or universities and take about 1 year to complete. These programs usually lead to a certificate or diploma. Some community and junior colleges offer 2-year programs that lead to an associate's degree. All programs have classroom and laboratory portions that include lessons in anatomy and medical terminology.

Some states may require assistants to graduate from an accredited program or pass an exam or both to do advanced tasks, such as taking x rays and giving injections.

Training

Through on-the-job training, a physician or another medical assistant in the office may teach the new assistant medical terminology, the names of the instruments, how to do daily tasks, how to interact with patients, and other tasks that help keep the office running smoothly. An assistant also learns how to code both paper and electronic health records and how to record patient information. It can take several months for an assistant to complete training, depending on the facility.

Certification

Medical assistants are not required to be certified. However, employers prefer to hire certified assistants.

Several organizations offer certification. Some require the assistant to pass an exam, and others require graduation from an accredited program. In most cases, an applicant must be at least 18 years old before applying for certification.

The National Commission for Certifying Agencies, part of the Institute for Credentialing Excellence , accredits four certifications for medical assistants:

- Certified Medical Assistant (CMA) from the American Association of Medical Assistants (AAMA)
- Registered Medical Assistant (RMA) from the American Medical Technologists
- National Certified Medical Assistant (NCMA) from the National Center for Competency Testing
- Certified Clinical Medical Assistant (CCMA) from the National Healthcareer Association

To be eligible for the CMA Certification Examination, an assistant must have completed a postsecondary medical assisting program accredited by either the Commission on Accreditation of Allied Health Education Programs (CAAHEP) or the Accrediting Bureau of Health Education Schools (ABHES) and passed the certification exam. For the other three certifications, no formal education is required to take the certification exam.

Important Qualities

Analytical skills. Medical assistants must be able to understand and follow medical charts and diagnoses. They may be required to code a patient's medical records for billing purposes.

Detail oriented. Medical assistants must be precise when taking vital signs or recording patient information. Physicians and insurance companies rely on accurate records.

Interpersonal skills. Medical assistants need to be able to discuss patient information with other medical personnel, such as a physician. They often interact with patients who may be in pain or in distress, so they need to be able to act in a calm and professional manner.

Technical skills. Medical assistants should be able to use basic clinical instruments so they can take a patient's vital signs, such as heart rate or blood pressure.

Pay

Medical Assistants
Median annual wages, May 2010

Total, All Occupations	$33,840
Other Healthcare Support Occupations	$29,790
Medical Assistants	$28,860

Note: All Occupations includes all occupations in the U.S. Economy.
Source: U.S. Bureau of Labor Statistics, Occupational Employment Statistics

The median annual wage of medical assistants was $28,860 in May 2010. The median wage is the wage at which half the workers in an occupation earned more than that amount and half earned less. The lowest 10 percent earned less than $20,810, and the top 10 percent earned more than $40,190.

Most medical assistants work full time. Some work evenings or weekends to cover shifts in medical facilities that are always open.

Job Outlook

Medical Assistants
Percent change in employment, projected 2010-20

Medical Assistants	31%
Other Healthcare Support Occupations	25%
Total, All Occupations	14%

Note: All Occupations includes all occupations in the U.S. Economy.
Source: U.S. Bureau of Labor Statistics, Employment Projections program

Employment of medical assistants is expected to grow by 31 percent from 2010 to 2020, much faster than the average for all occupations. The growth of the aging baby-boom population will continue to spur demand for preventive medical services, which are often provided by physicians. As their practices expand, physicians will hire more assistants to perform routine administrative and clinical duties, allowing the physicians to see more patients. Assistants will likely continue to be used in place of more expensive workers, such as nurses, to reduce costs.

In addition, an increasing number of group practices, clinics, and other healthcare facilities need support workers, particularly medical assistants, to do both administrative and clinical duties. Medical assistants work mostly in primary care, a steadily growing sector of the healthcare industry.

Additional demand also is expected as a result of new and changing tasks for medical assistants as part of the medical team. As more and more physicians' practices switch to electronic health records (EHRs), medical assistants' job responsibilities will continue to change. Assistants will need to become familiar with EHR computer software, including maintaining EHR security and analyzing electronic data, to improve healthcare information.

Employment projections data for medical assistants, 2010-20

Occupational Title	SOC Code	Employment, 2010	Projected Employment, 2020	Change, 2010-20	
Percent	Numeric				
Medical Assistants	31-9092	527,600	690,400	31	162,900
SOURCE: U.S. Bureau of Labor Statistics, Employment Projections program					

Similar Occupations

This table shows a list of occupations with job duties that are similar to those of medical assistants.

Occupation	Job Duties	Entry-Level Education	Median Annual Pay, May 2010
Dental Assistants	Dental assistants have many tasks, ranging from patient care to record keeping, in a dental office. Their duties vary by state and by the dentists' offices where they work.	Postsecondary non-degree award	$33,470
Dental Hygienists	Dental hygienists clean teeth, examine patients for oral diseases such as gingivitis, and provide other preventative dental care. They also educate patients on ways to improve and maintain good oral health.	Associate's degree	$68,250
Licensed Practical and Licensed Vocational Nurses	Licensed practical and licensed vocational nurses (known as LPNs or LVNs, depending on the state in which they work) provide basic nursing care. They work under the direction of registered nurses and doctors.	Postsecondary non-degree award	$40,380
Nursing Aides, Orderlies, and Attendants	Nursing aides, orderlies, and attendants help provide basic care for patients in hospitals and residents of long-term care facilities, such as nursing homes.	Postsecondary non-degree award	$24,010
Medical Records and Health Information Technicians	Medical records and health information technicians organize and manage health information data by ensuring its quality, accuracy, accessibility, and security in both paper and electronic systems. They use various classification systems to code and categorize patient information for reimbursement purposes, for databases and registries, and to maintain patients' medical and treatment histories.	Postsecondary non-degree award	$32,350
Pharmacy Technicians	Pharmacy technicians help licensed pharmacists dispense prescription medication.	High school diploma or equivalent	$28,400
Psychiatric Technicians and Aides	Psychiatric technicians and aides care for people who have mental illness and developmental disabilities. The two occupations are related, but technicians typically provide therapeutic care, and aides help patients in their daily activities and ensure a safe, clean environment.	See How to Become One	$26,880
Occupational Therapy Assistants and Aides	Occupational therapy assistants and aides work under the direction of occupational therapists in treating patients with injuries, illnesses, or disabilities through the therapeutic use of everyday activities. They help these patients develop, recover, and improve the skills needed for daily living and working.	See How to Become One	$47,490
Physical Therapist Assistants and Aides	Physical therapist assistants and physical therapist aides work under the direction of physical therapists. They help patients who are recovering from injuries, illnesses, and surgeries regain movement and manage pain.	See How to Become One	$37,710

Contacts for More Information

For more information about becoming a medical assistant, including information on certification, visit American Association of Medical Assistants , American Medical Technologists , National Center for Competency Testing , National Healthcareer Association , Institute for Credentialing Excellence , American Optometric Association , American Society of Podiatric Medical Assistants ,Joint Commission on Allied Health Personnel in Ophthalmology

For lists of accredited educational programs in medical assisting, visit Commission on Accreditation of Allied Health Education Programs ,Accrediting Bureau of Health Education School

Suggested citation:

Bureau of Labor Statistics, U.S. Department of Labor, Occupational Outlook Handbook, 2012-13 Edition, Medical Assistants, on the Internet at http://www.bls.gov/ooh/healthcare/medical-assistants.htm .

Medical Records and Health Information Technicians

Quick Facts: Medical Records and Health Information Technicians	
2010 Median Pay	$32,350 per year $15.55 per hour
Entry-Level Education	Postsecondary non-degree award
Work Experience in a Related Occupation	None
On-the-job Training	None
Number of Jobs, 2010	179,500
Job Outlook, 2010-20	21% (Faster than average)
Employment Change, 2010-20	37,700

What Medical Records and Health Information Technicians Do

Medical records and health information technicians organize and manage health information data by ensuring its quality, accuracy, accessibility, and security in both paper and electronic systems. They use various classification systems to code and categorize patient information for insurance reimbursement purposes, for databases and registries, and to maintain patients' medical and treatment histories.

Duties

All technicians document patients' health information, including the medical history, symptoms, examination and test results, treatments, and other information about healthcare provider services. Medical records and health information technicians' duties vary with the size of the facility in which they work.

Medical records and health information technicians typically do the following:

- Review patient records for timeliness, completeness, accuracy, and appropriateness of health data
- Organize and maintain data for clinical databases and registries
- Track patient outcomes for quality assessment
- Use classification software to assign clinical codes for reimbursement and data analysis

Medical records and health information technicians need to be able to discuss patient information and discrepancies with other professionals such as physicians and insurance personnel.

- Electronically record data for collection, storage, analysis, retrieval, and reporting
- Protect patients' health information for confidentiality, authorized access for treatment, and data security

Although medical records and health information technicians do not provide direct patient care, they work regularly with physicians and other healthcare professionals. They meet with these workers to clarify diagnoses or to get additional information to make sure that records are complete and accurate.

The increasing use of electronic health records (EHRs) will continue to change the job responsibilities of medical records and health information technicians. Technicians will need to be familiar with, or be able to learn, EHR computer software, follow EHR security and privacy practices, and analyze electronic data to improve healthcare information as more healthcare providers and hospitals adopt EHR systems.

Medical records and health information technicians can specialize in many aspects of health information. Most work as medical coders, sometimes called coding specialists, or as cancer registrars.

Medical coders typically do the following:

- Review patient information for preexisting conditions such as diabetes
- Retrieve patient records for medical personnel
- Work as a liaison between the health clinician and billing offices

Cancer registrars typically do the following:

- Review patient records and pathology reports for completeness and accuracy
- Assign classification codes to represent the diagnosis and treatment of cancers and benign tumors
- Conduct annual followups to track treatment, survival, and recovery
- Analyze and compile cancer patient information for research purposes
- Maintain facility, regional, and national databases of cancer patients

Work Environment

Medical records and health information technicians held about 179,500 jobs in 2010. Most medical records and health information technicians worked in hospitals or physicians' offices. Some worked for the government. Technicians typically work at desks or in offices and may spend many hours in front of computer monitors.

The industries that employed the most medical records and health information technicians in 2010 were as follows:

Hospitals; state, local, and private	39%
Offices of physicians	23
Nursing care facilities	7
Home health care services	3

Work Schedules

Most medical records and health information technicians work full time. In healthcare facilities that are open 24 hours a day, technicians may work evening or overnight shifts. About 15 percent of technicians worked part time in 2010.

How to Become a Medical Records or Health Information Technician

Medical records and health information technicians typically need a postsecondary certificate to enter the occupation, although they may have an associate's degree. Many employers also require professional certification.

Education

Postsecondary certificate and associate's degree programs in health information technology typically include courses in medical terminology, anatomy and physiology, health data requirements and standards, classification and coding systems, healthcare reimbursement methods, healthcare statistics, and computer systems. Applicants to health information technology programs increase their chances of admission by taking high school courses in health, computer science, math, and biology.

Certification

Most employers prefer to hire medical records and health information technicians who have professional certification. A medical records and health information technician can get certification from several organizations. Some organizations base certification on passing an exam. Others require graduation from an accredited program. Once certified, technicians typically must renew their certification regularly and take continuing education courses. Certifications include Registered Health Information Technician (RHIT) and Certified Tumor Registrar (CTR), among others. Many coding certifications require coding experience in a work setting. Some states require cancer registrars to have certification; requirements vary by state.

Important Qualities

Analytical skills. Medical records and health information technicians must be able to understand and follow medical records and diagnoses, and then decide how best to code them in a patient's medical records.

Detail oriented. Medical records and health information technicians must be pay attention to details to be accurate when recording and coding patient information.

Interpersonal skills. Medical records and health information technicians need to be able to discuss patient information, discrepancies, and data requirements with other professionals such as physicians and finance personnel.

Technical skills. Medical records and health information technicians must be able to use coding and classification software and the EHR system that their healthcare organization or physician practice has adopted.

Pay

Medical Records and Health Information Technicians
Median annual wages, May 2010

Health Technologists and Technicians	$39,340
Total, All Occupations	$33,840
Medical Records and Health Information Technicians	$32,350

Note: All Occupations includes all occupations in the U.S. Economy.
Source: U.S. Bureau of Labor Statistics, Occupational Employment Statistics

The median annual wage of medical records and health information technicians was $32,350 in May 2010. The median wage is the wage at which half the workers in an occupation earned more than that amount and half earned less. The lowest 10 percent earned less than $21,240, and the top 10 percent earned more than $53,430.

Most medical records and health information technicians work full time. Some work evenings or weekends to cover shifts in medical facilities that remain open 24 hours a day.

Job Outlook

Medical Records and Health Information Technicians
Percent change in employment, projected 2010-20

Health Technologists and Technicians	26%
Medical Records and Health Information Technicians	21%
Total, All Occupations	14%

Note: All Occupations includes all occupations in the U.S. Economy.
Source: U.S. Bureau of Labor Statistics, Employment Projections program

Employment of medical records and health information technicians is expected to increase by 21 percent from 2010 to 2020, faster than the average for all occupations. The demand for health services is expected to increase as the population ages. An aging population will need more medical tests, treatments, and procedures. This will also mean more claims for reimbursement from private and public insurance. Additional records, coupled with widespread use of electronic health records by all types of healthcare providers, should lead to an increased need for technicians to organize and manage the associated information in all areas of the healthcare industry.

Cancer registrars are expected to continue to be in high demand. As the population ages, there will likely be more types of special purpose registries because many more types of illnesses are detected and treated later in life.

Job Prospects

Prospects will be best for those with a certification in health information. As EHR systems continue to become more common, technicians with computer skills will be needed to use them.

Employment projections data for medical records and health information technicians, 2010-20

Occupational Title	SOC Code	Employment, 2010	Projected Employment, 2020	Change, 2010-20	
				Percent	Numeric
Medical Records and Health Information Technicians	29-2071	179,500	217,300	21	37,700
SOURCE: U.S. Bureau of Labor Statistics, Employment Projections program					

Similar Occupations

This table shows a list of occupations with job duties that are similar to those of medical records and health information technicians.

Occupation	Job Duties	Entry-Level Education	Median Annual Pay, May 2010
Medical Transcriptionists	Medical transcriptionists listen to voice recordings that physicians and other health professionals make and convert them into written reports. They interpret medical terminology and abbreviations in preparing patients' medical histories, discharge summaries, and other documents.	Postsecondary non-degree award	$32,900
Medical and Health Services Managers	Medical and health services managers, also called healthcare executives or healthcare administrators, plan, direct, and coordinate medical and health services. They might manage an entire facility, specialize in managing a specific clinical area or department, or manage a medical practice for a group of physicians.	Bachelor's degree	$84,270

Contacts for More Information

For more information about medical records and health information technicians, including details about certification, visit American Health Information Management Association ,American Academy of Professional Coders ,The Professional Association of Healthcare Coding Specialists ,National Cancer Registrars Association

For a list of accredited training programs, visit Commission on Accreditation for Health Informatics and Information Management

Suggested citation:

Bureau of Labor Statistics, U.S. Department of Labor, Occupational Outlook Handbook, 2012-13 Edition, Medical Records and Health Information Technicians, on the Internet at http://www.bls.gov/ooh/healthcare/medical-records-and-health-information-technicians.htm .

Medical Transcriptionists

Quick Facts: Medical Transcriptionists	
2010 Median Pay	$32,900 per year $15.82 per hour
Entry-Level Education	Postsecondary non-degree award
Work Experience in a Related Occupation	None
On-the-job Training	None
Number of Jobs, 2010	95,100
Job Outlook, 2010-20	6% (Slower than average)
Employment Change, 2010-20	5,600

What Medical Transcriptionists Do

Medical transcriptionists listen to voice recordings that physicians and other health professionals make and convert them into written reports. They interpret medical terminology and abbreviations in preparing patients' medical histories, discharge summaries, and other documents. The documents they produce become part of a patient's permanent file.

Duties

Medical transcriptionists typically do the following:

- Listen to the recorded dictation of a doctor or other health professional
- Transcribe the dictation into diagnostic test results, operative reports, referral letters, and other documents
- Edit drafts prepared by speech recognition software, making sure that the transcription is correct and has a consistent style
- Translate medical abbreviations or jargon into the appropriate long form
- Recognize inconsistencies within a report and follow up with the healthcare provider to ensure accuracy
- Submit written reports for physicians to approve
- Follow patient confidentiality guidelines and legal documentation requirements

Medical transcriptionists use audio playback equipment, often including a headset and foot pedal—to control the recording playback speed—that are connected to their computer. They use word-processing and other specialized software, as well as medical reference materials as needed.

To do their work, medical transcriptionists must become familiar with medical words, anatomy and physiology, diagnostic procedures, pharmacology, and treatment assessments. Their ability to understand and correctly transcribe what the health professional has said is critical to reducing the chance that patients will get ineffective or even harmful treatments. They are part of the team that ensures high-quality patient care.

Medical transcriptionists who work in doctors' offices may have other duties, such as answering phones or greeting patients.

Work Environment

Medical transcriptionist held about 95,100 jobs in 2010. Most medical transcriptionists work for hospitals or in physicians' offices. Some work for companies that provide transcription services to healthcare establishments, and others are self-employed.

Transcriptionists must understand medical terminology, anatomy and physiology, diagnostic procedures, and treatment assessment.

The following industries employed the majority of medical transcriptionists in 2010:

Hospitals; state, local, and private	35%
Offices of physicians	22
Business support services	15
Outpatient care centers	2
Medical and diagnostic laboratories	2

Many transcriptionists work from home offices, receiving dictation and submitting drafts electronically.

Work Schedules

Most medical transcriptionists work full time. Medical transcriptionists who work from home may work outside typical business hours or have some flexibility in determining their schedules.

How to Become a Medical Transcriptionist

Medical transcriptionists typically need postsecondary training. Prospective medical transcriptionists must have an understanding both of grammar and of word-processing software.

Education

Employers prefer to hire transcriptionists who have completed postsecondary training in medical transcription, which is offered by many vocational schools, community colleges, and distance-learning programs.

A 1-year certificate program or 2-year associate's degree normally includes coursework in anatomy, medical terminology, legal issues relating to healthcare documentation, and English grammar and punctuation. Many of these programs include supervised on-the-job experience. Some transcriptionists, especially those already familiar with medical terminology from previous experience as a nurse or medical secretary, become proficient through refresher courses and training.

Medical transcription programs do not have to be accredited, but transcriptionists who want to get certification may first need to complete an accredited program.

Certification

Although certification is not required, some medical transcriptionists choose to become certified. The Association for Healthcare Documentation Integrity offers two certifications: Registered Medical Transcriptionist (RMT) and Certified Medical Transcriptionist (CMT).

The RMT certification is for recent graduates with less than 2 years of experience and who work in a single specialty environment, such as a clinic or a doctor's office.

The CMT credential is for transcriptionists who handle dictation in several medical specialties.

Both certifications require passing an exam and periodic retesting or continuing education.

Important Qualities

Computer skills. Medical transcriptionists must be comfortable using computers and word-processing software, because those tools are an essential part of their jobs.

Detail oriented. Transcriptionists must focus on details to write reports correctly and spot any inaccuracies and inconsistencies in finished drafts.

Time-management skills. Because dictation must be done quickly, medical transcriptionists must be comfortable working under short deadlines.

Writing skills. Medical transcriptionists need a good understanding of the English language and grammar.

Pay

Medical Transcriptionists
Median annual wages, May 2010

Total, All Occupations	$33,840
Medical Transcriptionists	$32,900
Other Healthcare Support Occupations	$29,790

Note: All Occupations includes all occupations in the U.S. Economy.
Source: U.S. Bureau of Labor Statistics, Occupational Employment Statistics

The median annual wage of medical transcriptionists was $32,900 in May 2010. The median annual wage is the wage at which half the workers in an occupation earned more than that amount and half earned less. The lowest 10 percent earned less than $21,960, and the top 10 percent earned more than $46,220.

Median annual wages in the industries employing the largest numbers of medical transcriptionists in 2010 were the following:

Medical and diagnostic laboratories	$35,690
Hospitals; state, local, and private	34,370
Outpatient care centers	33,530
Offices of physicians	32,640
Business support services	27,910

Some medical transcriptionists may be paid based on the volume of transcription they produce. Others are paid an hourly rate or an annual salary.

Job Outlook

Medical Transcriptionists
Percent change in employment, projected 2010-20

Other Healthcare Support Occupations	25%
Total, All Occupations	14%
Medical Transcriptionists	6%

Note: All Occupations includes all occupations in the U.S. Economy.
Source: U.S. Bureau of Labor Statistics, Employment Projections program

Employment of medical transcriptionists is expected to grow 6 percent from 2010 to 2020, slower than the average for all occupations. The volume of healthcare services is expected to continue to increase, resulting in a growing number of medical tests and procedures, all of which will require transcription.

At the same time, technological advances in recent years have changed the way medical transcription is done. In the past, medical transcriptionists would listen to an entire dictation to produce a transcribed report. Today, many medical documents are prepared with the use of back-end speech recognition technology, in which specialized software automatically prepares an initial draft of a report. The transcriptionist then reviews the draft for accuracy, listening to the original recording as needed. Such technological advances are expected to continue, making the individual transcriptionist far more productive and limiting employment growth overall.

As healthcare providers seek to cut costs, some have hired transcription services in other countries. However, concerns about patient confidentiality and data security suggest a continued need for transcriptionists within the United States.

Employment projections data for medical transcriptionists, 2010-20

Occupational Title	SOC Code	Employment, 2010	Projected Employment, 2020	Change, 2010-20 Percent	Change, 2010-20 Numeric
Medical Transcriptionists	31-9094	95,100	100,700	6	5,600
SOURCE: U.S. Bureau of Labor Statistics, Employment Projections program					

Similar Occupations

This table shows a list of occupations with job duties that are similar to those of medical transcriptionists.

Occupation	Job Duties	Entry-Level Education	Median Annual Pay, May 2010
Court Reporters	Court reporters attend legal proceedings and public speaking events to create word-for-word transcriptions. Some court reporters provide captioning for television and at public events.	Postsecondary non-degree award	$47,700
Medical Assistants	Medical assistants complete administrative and clinical tasks in the offices of physicians, podiatrists, chiropractors, and other health practitioners. Their duties vary with the location, specialty, and size of the practice.	High school diploma or equivalent	$28,860
Medical Records and Health Information Technicians	Medical records and health information technicians organize and manage health information data by ensuring its quality, accuracy, accessibility, and security in both paper and electronic systems. They use various classification systems to code and categorize patient information for reimbursement purposes, for databases and registries, and to maintain patients' medical and treatment histories.	Postsecondary non-degree award	$32,350
Receptionists	Receptionists perform various administrative tasks, including answering telephones and giving information to the public and customers.	High school diploma or equivalent	$25,240
Secretaries and Administrative Assistants	Secretaries and administrative assistants perform routine clerical and organizational tasks. They organize files, draft messages, schedule appointments, and support other staff.	High school diploma or equivalent	$34,660

Contacts for More Information

For more information about medical transcriptionists and for a list of accredited medical transcription programs, visit Association for Healthcare Documentation Integrity

Suggested citation:

Bureau of Labor Statistics, U.S. Department of Labor, Occupational Outlook Handbook, 2012-13 Edition, Medical Transcriptionists, on the Internet at http://www.bls.gov/ooh/healthcare/medical-transcriptionists.htm .

Nuclear Medicine Technologists

Quick Facts: Nuclear Medicine Technologists	
2010 Median Pay	$68,560 per year $32.96 per hour
Entry-Level Education	Associate's degree
Work Experience in a Related Occupation	None
On-the-job Training	None
Number of Jobs, 2010	21,900
Job Outlook, 2010-20	19% (About as fast as average)
Employment Change, 2010-20	4,100

What Nuclear Medicine Technologists Do

Nuclear medicine technologists use a scanner to create images of various areas of a patient's body. They prepare radioactive drugs and administer them to patients undergoing the scans. The radioactive drugs cause abnormal areas of the body to appear different from normal areas in the images.

Duties

Nuclear medicine technologists typically do the following:

- Explain imaging procedures to the patient and answer questions
- Follow safety procedures to protect the patient and themselves from excessive radiation exposure
- Examine machines to make sure that they are safe and working properly
- Prepare radioactive drugs and administer them to the patient
- Monitor the patient to check for unusual reactions to drugs
- Operate equipment that creates images of areas in the body, such as images of organs
- Keep detailed records of procedures

Radioactive drugs, known as radiopharmaceuticals, give off radiation, allowing special scanners to monitor tissue and organ functions. Abnormal areas show higher-than-expected or lower-than-expected concentrations of radioactivity. Physicians then interpret the images to help diagnose the patient's condition. For example, tumors can be seen in organs during a scan because of their concentration of the radioactive drugs.

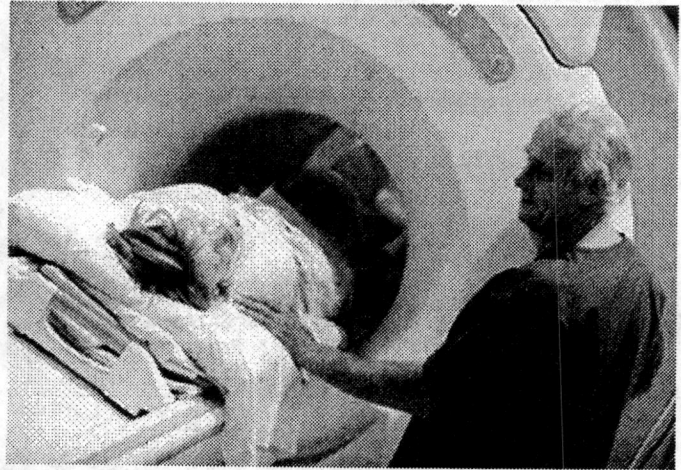

Nuclear medicine technologists work in various healthcare facilities.

Work Environment

Nuclear medicine technologists held about 21,900 jobs in 2010. Technologists are on their feet for long periods and may need to lift or turn patients who are disabled.

As shown in the following tabulation, most nuclear medicine technologists worked in hospitals in 2010:

Hospitals; state, local, and private	63%
Offices of physicians	25
Medical and diagnostic laboratories	6
Outpatient care centers	2

Although radiation hazards exist in this occupation, they are minimized by the use of gloves and other shielding devices. Nuclear medicine technologists wear badges that measure radiation levels in the radiation area. Instruments monitor their radiation exposure and detailed records are kept on how much radiation they get over their lifetime. When preparing radioactive drugs, technologists use safety standards to keep the chance of radiation exposure low for patients, other healthcare workers, and themselves.

Like other healthcare workers, nuclear medicine technologists may be exposed to infectious diseases.

Work Schedules

Because imaging is sometimes needed in emergencies, some nuclear medicine technologists work evenings, weekends, or on call.

How to Become a Nuclear Medicine Technologist

Nuclear medicine technologists typically need an associate's degree in nuclear medicine technology. Formal education programs in nuclear medicine technology or a related healthcare field lead to a certificate, an associate's degree, or a bachelor's degree. Technologists must be licensed in some states; requirements vary by state.

Education

Nuclear medicine technologists typically need an associate's degree in nuclear medicine technology; there are also bachelor's degree programs. Some technologists become qualified by completing an associate's or a bachelor's degree program in a related health field, such as radiologic technology or nursing, and then completing a 12-month certificate program in nuclear medicine technology. Generally, certificate programs are offered in hospitals; associate's degrees in community colleges, and bachelor's degrees in 4-year colleges and universities.

Nuclear medicine technology programs include clinical experience—practice under the supervision of a certified nuclear medicine technologist and a physician who specializes in nuclear medicine. In addition, these programs often include courses in human anatomy and physiology, physics, chemistry, radioactive drugs, and computer science.

Licenses and Certification

Nuclear medicine technologists must be licensed in some states; requirements vary by state. For specifics, contact your state's health board.

Some nuclear medicine technologists get certification. Although certification is not required for a license, it fulfills most of the requirements for state licensure on its own.

Without certification, most states require testing and have other requirements to get a license. Some employers require national certification, regardless of state regulations. Certification usually involves completing required coursework and having the necessary hours of clinical experience, as well as graduating from an accredited nuclear medicine technology program.

Certified nuclear medicine technologists must also take continuing education to keep their certification. Frequent innovations and technology changes in the field of nuclear medicine make continuing education necessary.

In addition to receiving general certification, technologists can get specialty certifications that show their proficiency in specific procedures or on certain equipment. A technologist can earn a certification in positron emission tomography (PET), nuclear cardiology (NCT), magnetic resonance imaging (MRI), or computed tomography (CT).

PET uses a machine that creates a three-dimensional image of a part of the body, such as the brain. NCT uses radioactive drugs to obtain images of the heart. Patients exercise during the imaging while the technologist creates images of the heart and blood flow. MRI uses a magnetic field to create images of an area of the body. CT uses computers to show the layers of x-ray images taken of a patient in a three-dimensional view. Each field requires the technologist to have a high level of knowledge about the specific procedures and technologies involved. The Nuclear Medicine Technology Certification Board (NMTCB) offers NCT and PET certification exams. The American Registry of Radiologic Technologists (ARRT) offers the CT and MRI certification exams.

Important Qualities

Compassion. To get the images needed for a diagnosis, nuclear medicine technologists must be able to reassure and calm patients who are under physical and emotional stress.

Detail oriented. Nuclear medicine technologists must follow exact instructions to make sure that the correct dosage is given and that the patient is not overexposed to radiation.

Interpersonal skills. Nuclear medicine technologists interact with patients and often work as part of a team. They must be able to follow instructions from a supervising physician.

Science, math, and technical skills. Nuclear medicine technologists must understand anatomy, physiology, and other sciences and be able to calculate accurate dosages. They also work with computers and large pieces of technological equipment and must be comfortable operating them.

Strength and stamina. Nuclear medicine technologists must stand for long periods and be able to lift and move patients who need help.

Pay

Nuclear Medicine Technologists
Median annual wages, May 2010

Nuclear Medicine Technologists	$68,560
Health Technologists and Technicians	$39,340
Total, All Occupations	$33,840

Note: All Occupations includes all occupations in the U.S. Economy.
Source: U.S. Bureau of Labor Statistics, Occupational Employment Statistics

The median annual wage of nuclear medicine technologists was $68,560 in May 2010. The median wage is the wage at which half the workers in an occupation earned more than that amount and half earned less. The lowest 10 percent earned less than $49,130, and the top 10 percent earned more than $91,970.

Because imaging is sometimes needed in emergencies, some nuclear medicine technologists work evenings, weekends, or on call.

Job Outlook

Nuclear Medicine Technologists
Percent change in employment, projected 2010-20

Health Technologists and Technicians	26%
Nuclear Medicine Technologists	19%
Total, All Occupations	14%

Note: All Occupations includes all occupations in the U.S. Economy.
Source: U.S. Bureau of Labor Statistics, Employment Projections program

Employment of nuclear medicine technologists is expected to grow by 19 percent from 2010 to 2020, about as fast as the average for all occupations. However, because it is a small occupation, the growth will result in only about 4,100 new jobs over the 10-year period.

Nuclear medicine technologists work mostly with adult patients, although procedures may be performed on children. A larger aging population should lead to the need to diagnose and treat medical conditions that require imaging, such as heart disease. Nuclear medicine technologists will be needed to administer radioactive drugs and maintain the imaging equipment required for diagnosis.

Overall employment growth is expected to be driven by rapidly growing industries, including physicians' offices and diagnostic laboratories, which employed about 31 percent of nuclear medicine technologists in 2010.

Job Prospects

Nuclear medicine technologists can improve their job prospects by getting a specialty certification. A technologist can earn a certification in positron emission tomography (PET), nuclear cardiology (NCT), magnetic resonance imaging (MRI), or computed tomography (CT). The Nuclear Medicine Technology Certification Board (NMTCB) offers NCT and PET certification exams. The American Registry of Radiologic Technologists (ARRT) offers the CT and MRI certification exams.

Employment projections data for nuclear medicine technologists, 2010-20

Occupational Title	SOC Code	Employment, 2010	Projected Employment, 2020	Change, 2010-20	
				Percent	Numeric
Nuclear Medicine Technologists	29-2033	21,900	26,100	19	4,100
SOURCE: U.S. Bureau of Labor Statistics, Employment Projections program					

Similar Occupations

This table shows a list of occupations with job duties that are similar to those of nuclear medicine technologists.

Occupation	Job Duties	Entry-Level Education	Median Annual Pay, May 2010
Cardiovascular Technologists and Technicians and Vascular Technologists	Cardiovascular technologists and technicians and vascular technologists use imaging technology to help physicians diagnose cardiac (heart) and peripheral vascular (blood vessel) ailments in patients. They also help physicians treat problems with cardiac and vascular systems, such as blood clots.	Associate's degree	$49,410
Diagnostic Medical Sonographers	Diagnostic medical sonographers use special imaging equipment that directs sound waves into a patient's body (in a procedure commonly known as an ultrasound, sonogram, or echocardiogram) to assess and diagnose various medical conditions.	Associate's degree	$64,380
Radiologic Technologists	Radiologic technologists perform diagnostic imaging examinations, such as x rays, on patients.	Associate's degree	$54,340
Medical and Clinical Laboratory Technologists and Technicians	Medical laboratory technologists (also known as medical laboratory scientists) and medical laboratory technicians collect samples and perform tests to analyze body fluids, tissue, and other substances.	See How to Become One	$46,680
Radiation Therapists	Radiation therapists treat cancer and other diseases in patients by giving radiation treatments.	Associate's degree	$74,980

Contacts for More Information

For more information about nuclear medicine technologists, visit Society of Nuclear Medicine

For a list of accredited programs in nuclear medicine technology, visit Joint Review Committee on Educational Programs in Nuclear Medicine Technology

For more information about certification for nuclear medicine technologists, visit Nuclear Medicine Technology Certification Board, American Registry of Radiologic Technologists

Suggested citation:

Bureau of Labor Statistics, U.S. Department of Labor, Occupational Outlook Handbook, 2012-13 Edition, Nuclear Medicine Technologists, on the Internet at http://www.bls.gov/ooh/healthcare/nuclear-medicine-technologists.htm .

Nursing Aides, Orderlies, and Attendants

Quick Facts: Nursing Aides, Orderlies, and Attendants	
2010 Median Pay	$24,010 per year $11.54 per hour
Entry-Level Education	Postsecondary non-degree award
Work Experience in a Related Occupation	None
On-the-job Training	None
Number of Jobs, 2010	1,505,300
Job Outlook, 2010-20	20% (Faster than average)
Employment Change, 2010-20	302,000

What Nursing Aides, Orderlies, and Attendants Do

Nursing aides, orderlies, and attendants help provide basic care for patients in hospitals and residents of long-term care facilities, such as nursing homes.

Duties

Nursing aides, sometimes called nursing attendants or nursing assistants, provide basic care and help with basic living activities. They typically do the following:

- Clean and bathe patients or residents
- Help patients use the toilet and dress
- Turn, reposition, and transfer patients between beds and wheelchairs
- Listen to and record patients' health concerns and report that information to nurses
- Measure patients' vital signs, such as blood pressure and temperature

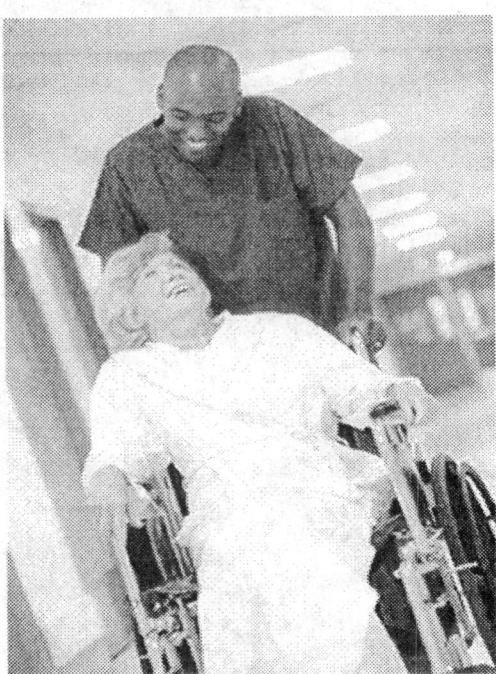

Nursing aides, orderlies, and attendants help transport patients in hospitals or residents of nursing homes.

- Serve meals and help patients eat

Some nursing aides and attendants may also dispense medication, depending on their training level and the state in which they work.

In nursing homes, aides and attendants are often the principal caregivers. They have more contact with residents than other members of the staff. Because some residents stay in a nursing home for months or years, aides and attendants may develop close, caring relationships with their patients.

Orderlies may do some of the same tasks as nursing aides and attendants, although they do not usually provide healthcare services. They typically do the following:

- Transport patients, such as taking a hospital patient to an operating room
- Clean equipment and facilities

Nursing aides, orderlies, and attendants work as part of a healthcare team under the supervision of licensed practical or vocational nurses or registered nurses.

Work Environment

Nursing aides, orderlies, and attendants held about 1,505,300 jobs in 2010. The majority of nursing aides, orderlies, and attendants work in nursing and residential care facilities. Others are employed in hospitals, home care, and hospices.

As shown below, more than half of all nursing aides, orderlies, and attendants worked in nursing and residential care facilities in 2010:

Nursing and residential care facilities	55%
Hospitals; state, local, and private	28
Home health care services	3
Self-employed workers	2
Employment services	2

The work of nursing aides, orderlies, and attendants is strenuous. They spend much of their time on their feet as they take care of many patients or residents. They may also have to do unpleasant tasks, such as emptying bedpans and changing soiled sheets.

They wear uniforms to protect their clothing and to promote cleanliness.

Injuries

Because they frequently lift people and do other physically demanding tasks, on-the-job injuries are more common for nursing aides, orderlies, and attendants than for most other occupations. They should be trained in how to properly lift and move patients, which can reduce the risk of injury.

Work Schedules

Most nursing aides, orderlies, and attendants work full time.

Because nursing homes and hospitals provide care at all hours, nursing aides, orderlies, and attendants may need to work nights, weekends, and holidays.

How to Become a Nursing Aide, Orderly, or Attendant

Nursing aides and attendants typically need a postsecondary certificate or award. Orderlies generally have at least a high school diploma. Nursing aides must pass their state's competency exam.

Education and Training

Nursing aides and attendants must earn a postsecondary certificate or award, in which they learn the basic principles of nursing and complete supervised clinical work. These programs are found in community colleges, vocational and technical schools, and in hospitals and nursing homes. Some high schools offer nursing aide programs.

Orderlies typically have at least a high school diploma. Orderlies who are not involved in patient care may be trained on the job.

Certification

When they finish their state-required education, nursing aides and attendants take a competency exam. Passing this exam allows them to use state-specific titles. In some states, a nursing aide or attendant is called a Certified Nursing Assistant (CNA), but titles vary from state to state.

Nursing aides and attendants who have passed the exam are placed on a state registry. In many states, nursing aides and attendants must be on the state registry to work in a nursing home.

Some states have other requirements as well, such as continuing education and a criminal background check. Check with your state's board of nursing or health, for more information.

In some states, nursing aides and attendants can get additional credentials beyond a CNA, such as becoming a Certified Medication Assistant (CMA). As a CMA, they can give medications.

Important Qualities

Compassion. Nursing aides, orderlies, and attendants provide care for the sick, injured, and elderly. Doing so requires a compassionate and empathetic attitude.

Patience. The routine tasks of cleaning, feeding, and bathing patients or residents can be stressful. Nursing aides, orderlies, and attendants must be patient to provide quality care.

Speaking skills. Nursing aides, orderlies, and attendants must be able to communicate effectively to address patients' or residents' concerns. They also need to relay patients' statuses to other healthcare workers.

Pay

Nursing Aides, Orderlies, and Attendants
Median annual wages, May 2010

Total, All Occupations	$33,840
Healthcare Support Occupations	$24,760
Nursing Aides, Orderlies, and Attendants	$24,010

Note: All Occupations includes all occupations in the U.S. Economy.
Source: U.S. Bureau of Labor Statistics, Occupational Employment Statistics

The median annual wage for nursing aides, orderlies, and attendants was $24,010 in May 2010. The median wage is the wage at which half the workers in an occupation earned more than that amount and half earned less. The lowest 10 percent earned less than $17,790, and the top 10 percent earned more than $34,580.

Most nursing aides, orderlies, and attendants work full time. Because nursing homes and hospitals provide care at all hours, nursing aides and orderlies may need to work nights, weekends, and holidays.

Job Outlook

Nursing Aides, Orderlies, and Attendants
Percent change in employment, projected 2010-20

Healthcare Support Occupations	34%
Nursing Aides, Orderlies, and Attendants	20%
Total, All Occupations	14%

Note: All Occupations includes all occupations in the U.S. Economy.
Source: U.S. Bureau of Labor Statistics, Employment Projections program

Employment of nursing aides, orderlies, and attendants is expected to grow by 20 percent from 2010 to 2020, faster than the average for all occupations.

Because of the growing elderly population, many nursing aides, orderlies, and attendants will be needed in long-term care facilities, such as nursing homes. Growth in the demand for healthcare services should lead to increased opportunities for nursing aides, orderlies, and attendants in other industries as well, such as hospitals and clinics.

Demand for nursing aides, orderlies, and attendants may be constrained, however, by the fact that many nursing homes rely on government funding, which tends to increase slower than the cost of patient care.

Job Prospects

Job prospects for nursing aides, orderlies, and attendants with formal training should be excellent, particularly in long-term care facilities. Because of the emotional and physical demands of this occupation, many nursing aides, orderlies, and attendants choose to leave the profession to get more training or another job. This creates opportunities for jobseekers who want to become nursing aides.

Employment projections data for nursing aides, orderlies, and attendants, 2010-20

Occupational Title	SOC Code	Employment, 2010	Projected Employment, 2020	Change, 2010-20	
				Percent	Numeric
Nursing Aides, Orderlies, and Attendants	31-1012	1,505,300	1,807,200	20	302,000
SOURCE: U.S. Bureau of Labor Statistics, Employment Projections program					

Similar Occupations

This table shows a list of occupations with job duties that are similar to those of nursing aides, orderlies, and attendants.

Occupation	Job Duties	Entry-Level Education	Median Annual Pay, May 2010
Home Health and Personal Care Aides	Home health and personal care aides help people who are disabled, chronically ill, or cognitively impaired. They also help older adults who may need assistance. They help with activities such as bathing and dressing, and they provide services such as light housekeeping. In some states, home health aides may be able to give a client medication or check the client's vital signs under the direction of a nurse or other healthcare practitioner.	Less than high school	$20,170
Licensed Practical and Licensed Vocational Nurses	Licensed practical and licensed vocational nurses (known as LPNs or LVNs, depending on the state in which they work) provide basic nursing care. They work under the direction of registered nurses and doctors.	Postsecondary non-degree award	$40,380
Medical Assistants	Medical assistants complete administrative and clinical tasks in the offices of physicians, podiatrists, chiropractors, and other health practitioners. Their duties vary with the location, specialty, and size of the practice.	High school diploma or equivalent	$28,860
Occupational Therapy Assistants and Aides	Occupational therapy assistants and aides work under the direction of occupational therapists in treating patients with injuries, illnesses, or disabilities through the therapeutic use of everyday activities. They help these patients develop, recover, and improve the skills needed for daily living and working.	See How to Become One	$47,490
Psychiatric Technicians and Aides	Psychiatric technicians and aides care for people who have mental illness and developmental disabilities. The two occupations are related, but technicians typically provide therapeutic care, and aides help patients in their daily activities and ensure a safe, clean environment.	See How to Become One	$26,880
Physical Therapist Assistants and Aides	Physical therapist assistants and physical therapist aides work under the direction of physical therapists. They help patients who are recovering from injuries, illnesses, and surgeries regain movement and manage pain.	See How to Become One	$37,710
Registered Nurses	Registered nurses (RNs) provide and coordinate patient care, educate patients and the public about various health conditions, and provide advice and emotional support to patients and their family members.	Associate's degree	$64,690

Contacts for More Information

For more information on nursing aides, orderlies, and attendants, visit National Association of Health Care Assistants , National Network of Career Nursing Assistants

Suggested citation:

Bureau of Labor Statistics, U.S. Department of Labor, Occupational Outlook Handbook, 2012-13 Edition, Nursing Aides, Orderlies, and Attendants, on the Internet at http://www.bls.gov/ooh/healthcare/nursing-assistants.htm .

Occupational Health and Safety Specialists

Quick Facts: Occupational Health and Safety Specialists	
2010 Median Pay	$64,660 per year $31.09 per hour
Entry-Level Education	Bachelor's degree
Work Experience in a Related Occupation	None
On-the-job Training	Moderate-term on-the-job training
Number of Jobs, 2010	58,700
Job Outlook, 2010-20	9% (Slower than average)
Employment Change, 2010-20	5,000

What Occupational Health and Safety Specialists Do

Occupational health and safety specialists analyze many types of work environments and work procedures. Specialists inspect workplaces for adherence to regulations on safety, health, and the environment. They also design programs to prevent disease or injury to workers and damage to the environment.

Duties

Occupational health and safety specialists typically do the following:

- Identify chemical, physical, radiological, and biological hazards in the workplace
- Collect samples of potentially toxic materials for analysis
- Inspect and evaluate workplace environments, equipment, and practices to ensure that safety standards and government regulations are being followed
- Recommend measures to help protect workers from potentially hazardous work conditions
- Investigate accidents to identify their causes and to determine how they might be prevented in the future

Occupational health and safety specialists, also known as occupational safety and health inspectors, examine lighting, equipment, ventilation, and other conditions that could affect employee health, safety, comfort, and performance. Workers usually are more alert and productive in environments that have specific levels of lighting or temperature.

Specialists seek to increase worker productivity by reducing absenteeism and equipment downtime. They also seek to save money by lowering insurance premiums and workers' compensation payments and by preventing government fines. Some specialists develop and conduct employee safety and training programs. These programs cover a range of topics, such as how to use safety equipment correctly and how to respond in an emergency.

Specialists work to prevent harm not only to workers but also to property, the environment, and the public by inspecting workplaces for chemical, radiological, and biological hazards. Specialists who work for governments conduct safety inspections and can impose fines.

Occupational health and safety specialists work with engineers and physicians to control or fix potentially hazardous conditions or equipment. They also work closely with occupational health and safety technicians to collect and analyze data in the workplace. For more information, see the profile on occupational health and safety technicians .

The tasks of occupational health and safety specialists vary by industry, workplace, and types of hazards affecting employees.

Environmental protection officers evaluate and coordinate storing and handling hazardous waste, cleaning up contaminated soil or water, and other activities that affect the environment.

Ergonomists consider the design of industrial, office, and other equipment to maximize workers' comfort, safety, and productivity.

Health physicists work in locations that use radiation and radioactive material, helping to protect people and the environment from hazardous radiation exposure.

Industrial hygienists identify workplace health hazards, such as lead, asbestos, noise, pesticides, and communicable diseases.

Loss prevention specialists work for insurance companies. They inspect the facilities that are insured and suggest improvements to prevent losses.

Work Environment

Occupational health and safety specialists held about 58,700 jobs in 2010. They work in a variety of settings, such as offices, factories, and mines. Their jobs often involve considerable fieldwork and travel.

Thirty eight percent of occupational health and safety specialists worked for federal, state, and local governments in 2010. In the federal government, specialists are employed by various agencies, including the Occupational Safety and Health Administration (OSHA) of the U.S. Department of Labor. Most large government agencies employ specialists to protect agency employees. In addition to working for governments, occupational safety and health specialists worked in management, scientific, and technical consulting services; education services; hospitals; and chemical manufacturing.

Occupational health and safety specialists may be exposed to strenuous, dangerous, or stressful conditions. Specialists use gloves,

Occupational health and safety specialists examine lighting, equipment, ventilation, and other conditions that could affect employee health, comfort, or performance.

helmets, and other safety equipment to minimize injury.

Work Schedules

Most occupational health and safety specialists work full time. Some specialists may work weekends or irregular hours in emergencies.

How to Become an Occupational Health and Safety Specialist

Occupational health and safety specialists typically need a bachelor's degree. Specialists are trained in the specific laws or inspection procedures through a combination of classroom and on-the-job training.

Education

High school students interested in becoming occupational health and safety specialists should take courses in English, mathematics, chemistry, biology, and physics.

Occupational health and safety specialists typically need a bachelor's degree in occupational health, safety, or a related scientific or technical field, such as engineering, biology, or chemistry. For some positions, a master's degree is required in industrial hygiene, health physics, or a related subject.

Typical courses include radiation science, hazardous material management and control, risk communications, and respiratory protection. These courses may vary, depending on the specialty in which a student wants to work. For example, courses in health physics focus on topics that differ from those in industrial hygiene.

Work experience is often important in this occupation. Internships are not required, but employers often prefer to hire candidates who have had one.

Training

Although occupational health and safety specialists learn standard laws and procedures in their formal education, they also need a moderate amount of on-the-job training for specific work environments. For example, all workplaces must meet a certain standard for air quality. However, a specialist who will inspect offices needs different training than a specialist concentrating on factories.

Important Qualities

Communication skills. Occupational health and safety specialists must be able to communicate safety instructions and concerns to employees and managers. They need to be able to work with technicians to collect and test samples of possible hazards, such as dust or vapors, in the workplace.

Detail oriented. Occupational health and safety specialists must pay attention to details. They need to recognize and adhere to specific safety standards and government regulations.

Physical stamina. Occupational health and safety specialists must be able to stand on their feet for long periods and be able to travel regularly. Some specialists work in environments that can be uncomfortable, such as tunnels or mines.

Problem-solving skills. Occupational health and safety specialists must be able to solve problems. They need to be able to find solutions to unsafe working conditions and environmental concerns in the workplace.

Technical skills. Occupational health and safety specialists must be able to use advanced technology. They often work with complex testing equipment.

Certification

Although certification is voluntary, many employers encourage it. Certification is available through several organizations, depending on the field in which the specialists work. Specialists must have graduated from an accredited educational program and have work experience to be eligible to take most certification exams. To keep their certification, specialists are usually required to complete periodic continuing education.

Pay

Occupational Health and Safety Specialists Median annual wages, May 2010	
Occupational Health and Safety Specialists	$64,660
Other Healthcare Practitioners and Technical Occupations	$51,850
Total, All Occupations	$33,840

Note: All Occupations includes all occupations in the U.S. Economy.
Source: U.S. Bureau of Labor Statistics, Occupational Employment Statistics

The median annual wage of occupational health and safety specialists was $64,660 in May 2010. The median wage is the wage at which half the workers in an occupation earned more than that amount and half earned less. The lowest 10 percent earned less than $38,780, and the top 10 percent earned more than $94,180.

Most occupational health and safety specialists work full time. Some specialists may work weekends or irregular hours in emergencies.

Job Outlook

Occupational Health and Safety Specialists Percent change in employment, projected 2010-20	
Other Healthcare Practitioners and Technical Occupations	16%
Total, All Occupations	14%
Occupational Health and Safety Specialists	9%

Note: All Occupations includes all occupations in the U.S. Economy.
Source: U.S. Bureau of Labor Statistics, Employment Projections program

Employment of occupational health and safety specialists is expected to grow by 9 percent from 2010 to 2020, slower than the average for all occupations. New environmental regulations and laws will require specialists to create and enforce procedures in the workplace.

The increased adoption of nuclear power as a source of energy may be a major factor for job growth for specialists in that field. These specialists will be needed to create and carry out programs to maintain the safety of both the workers and the environment.

Insurance and workers' compensation costs have become a concern for many employers and insurance companies, especially with an aging population remaining in the workforce longer. Older workers usually have a greater proportion of workers' compensation claims. Also, as the workforce ages, employers will have to provide more illness- and injury-related benefits, including sick leave. In addition, job growth should be good for those specializing in loss prevention.

Employment projections data for occupational health and safety specialists, 2010-20

Occupational Title	SOC Code	Employment, 2010	Projected Employment, 2020	Change, 2010-20	
				Percent	Numeric
Occupational Health and Safety Specialists	29-9011	58,700	63,700	9	5,000
SOURCE: U.S. Bureau of Labor Statistics, Employment Projections program					

Similar Occupations

This table shows a list of occupations with job duties that are similar to those of occupational health and safety specialists.

Occupation	Job Duties	Entry-Level Education	Median Annual Pay, May 2010
Construction and Building Inspectors	Construction and building inspectors ensure that new construction, changes, or repairs comply with local and national building codes and ordinances, zoning regulations, and contract specifications.	High school diploma or equivalent	$52,360
Fire Inspectors and Investigators	Fire inspectors visit and inspect buildings and other structures, such as sports arenas and shopping malls, to search for fire hazards and to ensure that federal, state, and local fire codes are met. They also test and inspect fire protection and fire extinguishing equipment to ensure that it works. Fire investigators determine the origin and cause of fires by searching the surrounding scene and collecting evidence.	High school diploma or equivalent	$52,230
Health and Safety Engineers	Health and safety engineers develop procedures and design systems to keep people from getting sick or injured and to keep property from being damaged. They combine knowledge of health or safety and of systems engineering to make sure that chemicals, machinery, software, furniture, and other products are not going to cause harm to people or buildings.	Bachelor's degree	$75,430
Occupational Health and Safety Technicians	Occupational health and safety technicians collect data on the safety and health conditions of the workplace. Technicians work with occupational health and safety specialists in conducting tests and measuring hazards to help prevent harm to workers, property, the environment, and the general public.	High school diploma or equivalent	$45,330
Environmental Scientists and Specialists	Environmental scientists and specialists use their knowledge of the natural sciences to protect the environment. They identify problems and find solutions that minimize hazards to the health of the environment and the population.	Bachelor's degree	$61,700

Contacts for More Information

For more information about industrial hygienists, visit American Industrial Hygiene Association

For more information about credentialing in industrial hygiene, visit American Board of Industrial Hygiene

For more information about occupations in safety, a list of safety and related academic programs, and credentialing, visit Board of Certified Safety Professionals

For more information about health physicists, visit Health Physics Society

For more information about occupational health and safety, visit U.S. Department of Health and Human Services, Centers for Disease Control and Prevention , U.S. Department of Labor, Occupational Safety & Health Administration

For job vacancies within the federal government, visit USAJOBS

Suggested citation:

Bureau of Labor Statistics, U.S. Department of Labor, Occupational Outlook Handbook, 2012-13 Edition, Occupational Health and Safety Specialists, on the Internet at http://www.bls.gov/ooh/healthcare/occupational-health-and-safety-specialists.htm .

Occupational Health and Safety Technicians

Quick Facts: Occupational Health and Safety Technicians	
2010 Median Pay	$45,330 per year $21.79 per hour
Entry-Level Education	High school diploma or equivalent
Work Experience in a Related Occupation	None
On-the-job Training	Moderate-term on-the-job training
Number of Jobs, 2010	10,600
Job Outlook, 2010-20	13% (About as fast as average)
Employment Change, 2010-20	1,400

What Occupational Health and Safety Technicians Do

Occupational health and safety technicians collect data on the safety and health conditions of the workplace. Technicians work with occupational health and safety specialists in conducting tests and measuring hazards to help prevent harm to workers, property, the environment, and the general public. For more information, see the profile on occupational health and safety specialists .

Duties

Occupational health and safety technicians typically do the following:

- Inspect, test, and evaluate workplace environments, equipment, and practices to ensure they follow safety standards and government regulations
- Collect samples of potentially toxic materials for analysis by occupational health and safety specialists
- Work with occupational health and safety specialists to control and fix hazardous and potentially hazardous conditions or equipment
- Carry out and evaluate programs on workplace safety and health
- Demonstrate the correct use of safety equipment
- Investigate accidents to identify why they happened and how they might be prevented in the future

Occupational health and safety technicians work with occupational health and safety specialists to prevent harm to workers, property, the environment, and the general public.

Technicians conduct tests and collect samples and measurements as part of workplace inspections. For example, they may collect and handle samples of dust, mold, gases, vapors, or other potentially hazardous materials. They conduct both routine inspections and special inspections that a specialist orders. For more information about specialists, see the profile on occupational health and safety specialists.

Technicians may examine and test machinery and equipment such as scaffolding and lifting devices to be sure that they meet appropriate safety regulations. They may check that workers are using protective gear, such as masks and hardhats, as regulations say they must.

Technicians also check that hazardous materials are stored correctly. They test and identify work areas for potential health and safety hazards.

In addition to making workers safer, technicians work with specialists to increase worker productivity by reducing the number of worker absences and equipment downtime. They save companies money by lowering insurance premiums and worker compensation payments and by preventing government fines.

Technicians' duties vary based on where they are employed. For example, a technician may test the levels of biohazard at a waste processing plant or may inspect the lighting and ventilation in an office setting. Both of these inspections are focused on maintaining the health of the workers and the environment.

The responsibilities of occupational health and safety technicians vary by industry, workplace, and types of hazards affecting employees. The following are examples of types of occupational health and safety technicians:

Environmental protection technicians evaluate and coordinate the storage and handling of hazardous waste, the cleanup of contaminated soil or water, evaluation of air pollution, or other activities that affect the environment.

Health physics technicians work in places that use radiation and radioactive material. Their goal is to protect people and the environment from hazardous radiation exposure.

Industrial hygiene technicians examine the workplace for health hazards, such as exposure to lead, asbestos, pesticides, or contagious diseases.

Mine examiners inspect mines for proper air flow and health hazards such as the buildup of methane or other harmful gases.

Work Environment

Occupational health and safety technicians held about 10,600 jobs in 2010. They work in a variety of settings, including offices, factories, and mines. Their jobs often involve considerable fieldwork and travel.

As shown below, about 23 percent of technicians worked for state or local governments in 2010:

State and local government, excluding education and hospitals	23%
Hospitals; state, local, and private	9
Mining, quarrying, and oil and gas extraction	6
Management, scientific, and technical consulting services	6
Waste management and remediation services	5

Other employers of occupational health and safety technicians were hospitals; mining, quarrying, and oil and gas extraction; management, scientific and technical consulting services; and waste management and remediation services. Most private companies either employ their own occupational health and safety workers or contract with firms that provide such services.

Occupational health and safety technicians may be exposed to strenuous, dangerous, or stressful conditions. Injuries are minimized by the use of gloves, helmets, and other safety equipment.

Work Schedules

Some occupational health and safety technicians may work weekends or irregular hours in emergency situations.

How to Become an Occupational Health and Safety Technician

Occupational health and safety technicians can enter the occupation through two main paths. The most common path is through on-the-job training. However, others enter with formal education, such as an associate degree or certificate. Technicians are trained in the specific laws or inspection procedures through a combination of classroom and on-the-job training.

Training

It is common for technicians to enter the occupation through a combination of related work experience and training. These technicians typically take on health and safety tasks at the company where they are employed at the time. For example, an employee may volunteer to complete annual workstation inspections for an office where they already work. They usually receive on-the-job training along with some formal education on how to conduct the correct tests or recognize common problems.

Education

High school students interested in the occupation should complete courses in English, mathematics, chemistry, biology, and physics.

Some technicians attend community college or vocational school and earn an associate's degree or certificate. These programs typically include courses in respiratory protection, hazard communication, and material handling and storage procedures. Some or all courses may be taken online, depending on the program.

Occupational health and safety technicians may train in more than one area of interest. Although technicians with formal education learn standard laws and procedures while in school, a moderate amount of on-the-job training is required for specific work environments.

Occupational health and safety technicians can become specialists by earning a bachelor's or advanced degree.

Certification

Certification is not required to become an occupational health and safety technician; however, many employers encourage it. The Board of Certified Safety Professionals (BCSP) offers certification at the technician level.

To apply for any certification, technicians must either have formal education in health and safety resulting in a degree or certificate, or at least 3 years of on-the-job experience in occupational health or safety. All applicants must pass a standardized health and safety exam.

There are three common certifications for technicians:

Construction Health and Safety Technician Certification (CHST) requires the applicant to have specific education or experience in construction safety. These technicians protect workers on construction sites from injury or illness.

Occupational Health and Safety Technologist Certification (OHST) certification is designed for workers who do occupational health and safety tasks full-time or part-time as part of their job duties.

Safety Trained Supervisor (STS) certification is geared toward first-line supervisors or managers. These workers are not safety practitioners but take on the certification in addition to their other job duties.

Important Qualities

Communication skills. Occupational health and safety technicians must be able to work with specialists to collect and test samples of possible hazards, such as dust or vapors, in the workplace.

Detail oriented—. Occupational health and safety technicians must be able to understand and adhere to specific safety standards and government regulations.

Problem-solving skills. Occupational health and safety technicians must be able to use their skills to find solutions to unsafe working conditions and environmental concerns in the workplace.

Stamina. Occupational health and safety technicians must be able to stay on their feet for long periods of time and to travel on a regular basis.

Technical skills. Occupational health and safety technicians often work with computers and complex testing equipment.

Pay

Occupational Health and Safety Technicians
Median annual wages, May 2010

Other Healthcare Practitioners and Technical Occupations	$51,850
Occupational Health and Safety Technicians	$45,330
Total, All Occupations	$33,840

Note: All Occupations includes all occupations in the U.S. Economy.
Source: U.S. Bureau of Labor Statistics, Occupational Employment Statistics

The median annual wage of occupational health and safety technicians was $45,330 in May 2010. The median wage is the wage at which half the workers in an occupation earned more than that amount and half earned less. The lowest 10 percent earned less than $27,580, and the top 10 percent earned more than $72,220.

Some occupational health and safety technicians may work weekends or irregular hours in emergency situations.

Job Outlook

Occupational Health and Safety Technicians
Percent change in employment, projected 2010-20

Other Healthcare Practitioners and Technical Occupations	16%
Total, All Occupations	14%
Occupational Health and Safety Technicians	13%

Note: All Occupations includes all occupations in the U.S. Economy.
Source: U.S. Bureau of Labor Statistics, Employment Projections program

Employment of occupational health and safety technicians is expected to grow by 13 percent from 2010 to 2020, about as fast as the average for all occupations. New environmental regulations and laws will require new or revised procedures in the workplace. The increased adoption of nuclear power as a source of energy is expected to be a major factor for job growth in that field as new regulations and precautions need to be enforced. These technicians will be needed to collect and test the data to maintain the safety of both the workers and the environment.

Insurance and worker's compensation costs have become a concern for many employers and insurance companies, especially with an aging population remaining in the workforce longer. Older workers usually have a greater incidence of workers' compensation claims. Occupational health and safety technicians will be needed to work with specialists in maintaining safety for all workers.

Although most occupational health and safety technicians work under the supervision of specialists, technicians can complete many routine tasks with little or no supervision. As a result, to contain costs, some employers operate with more technicians and fewer specialists. For more information, see the profile on occupational health and safety specialists.

Job Prospects

Occupational health and safety technicians with a wide breadth of knowledge in more than one area of health and safety along with general business functions will have the best prospects.

Employment projections data for occupational health and safety technicians, 2010-20

Occupational Title	SOC Code	Employment, 2010	Projected Employment, 2020	Change, 2010-20 Percent	Change, 2010-20 Numeric
Occupational Health and Safety Technicians	29-9012	10,600	12,000	13	1,400

SOURCE: U.S. Bureau of Labor Statistics, Employment Projections program

Similar Occupations

This table shows a list of occupations with job duties that are similar to those of occupational health and safety technicians.

Occupation	Job Duties	Entry-Level Education	Median Annual Pay, May 2010
Construction and Building Inspectors	Construction and building inspectors ensure that new construction, changes, or repairs comply with local and national building codes and ordinances, zoning regulations, and contract specifications.	High school diploma or equivalent	$52,360
Fire Inspectors and Investigators	Fire inspectors visit and inspect buildings and other structures, such as sports arenas and shopping malls, to search for fire hazards and to ensure that federal, state, and local fire codes are met. They also test and inspect fire protection and fire extinguishing equipment to ensure that it works. Fire investigators determine the origin and cause of fires by searching the surrounding scene and collecting evidence.	High school diploma or equivalent	$52,230
Environmental Science and Protection Technicians	Environmental science and protection technicians do laboratory and field tests to monitor the environment and investigate sources of pollution, including those affecting health. Many work under the supervision of environmental scientists and specialists, who direct their work and evaluate their results.	Associate's degree	$41,380
Occupational Health and Safety Specialists	Occupational health and safety specialists analyze many types of work environments and work procedures. Specialists inspect workplaces for adherence to regulations on safety, health, and the environment. They also design programs to prevent disease or injury to workers and damage to the environment.	Bachelor's degree	$64,660

Contacts for More Information

For more information about occupational health and safety technicians, visit U.S. Department of Health and Human Services, Center for Disease Control and Prevention , U.S. Department of Labor, Occupational Safety & Health Administration

For information on industrial hygiene, visit American Industrial Hygiene Association

For information on health physics, visit Health Physics Society

For more information on careers in safety and a list of safety and related academic programs, visit Board of Certified Safety Professionals

Information about jobs in federal, state, and local governments and in private industry is available from state employment service offices.

Occupational Therapists

Quick Facts: Occupational Therapists	
2010 Median Pay	$72,320 per year $34.77 per hour
Entry-Level Education	Master's degree
Work Experience in a Related Occupation	None
On-the-job Training	None
Number of Jobs, 2010	108,800
Job Outlook, 2010-20	33% (Much faster than average)
Employment Change, 2010-20	36,400

What Occupational Therapists Do

Occupational therapists treat patients with injuries, illnesses, or disabilities through the therapeutic use of everyday activities. They help these patients develop, recover, and improve the skills needed for daily living and working.

Duties

Occupational therapists typically do the following:

- Observe patients doing tasks, ask the patient questions, and review the patient's medical history
- Use the observations, answers, and medical history to evaluate the patient's condition and needs
- Establish a treatment plan for patients, laying out the types of activities and specific goals to be accomplished
- Help people with various disabilities with different tasks, such as helping an older person with poor memory use a computer, or leading an autistic child in play activities
- Demonstrate exercises that can help relieve pain for people with chronic conditions, such as joint stretches for arthritis sufferers

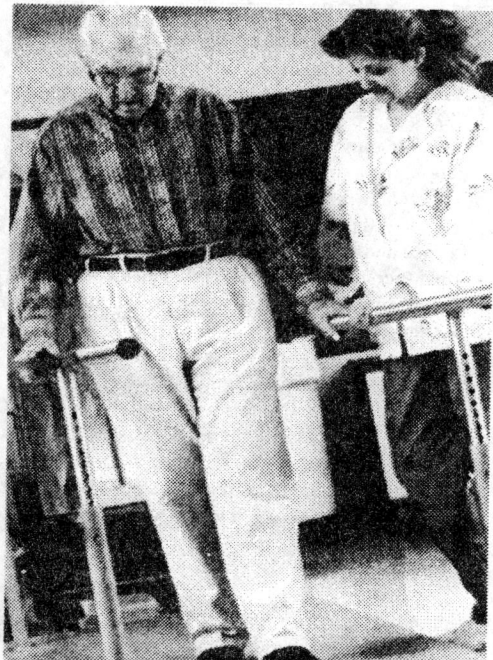

Occupational therapists can help the elderly cope with arthritis and other ailments.

- Evaluate a patient's home or workplace and identify how it can be better suited to the patient's health needs
- Educate a patient's family and employer about how to accommodate and care for the patient
- Recommend special equipment, such as wheelchairs and eating aids, and instruct patients how to use that equipment
- Assess and record patients' activities and progress for evaluating clients, for billing, and for reporting to physicians and other healthcare providers

Patients with permanent disabilities, such as cerebral palsy, often need help performing daily tasks. Therapists show patients how to use appropriate adaptive equipment, such as leg or knee braces, wheelchairs, and eating aids. Patients can function independently and control their living environment by using these devices.

Some occupational therapists work in educational settings with children one on one or in small groups. They evaluate disabled children's abilities, modify classroom equipment to accommodate certain disabilities, and help children participate in school activities.

Some therapists provide early intervention therapy to infants and toddlers who have, or are at risk of having, developmental delays.

Therapists who work with the elderly help their patients lead more independent and active lives. They asses the patient's abilities and environment and make recommendations, such as using adaptive equipment or identifying and removing potential fall hazards in the home.

In some cases, occupational therapists help patients create functional work environments. They evaluate the work space, plan work activities, and meet with the patient's employer to collaborate on changes to the patient's work environment or schedule.

Occupational therapists also may work in mental health settings where they help patients who suffer from developmental disabilities, mental illness, or emotional problems. They help these patients cope with and engage in daily life by teaching skills such as time management, budgeting, using public transportation, and doing household chores. Additionally, therapists may work with individuals who have problems with drug abuse, alcoholism, depression, or suffer from other disorders.

Some occupational therapists—such as those employed in hospitals or physicians' offices—work as part of a healthcare team, along with doctors, registered nurses, and other types of therapists. They also may oversee the work of occupational therapy assistants and aides. For more information, see the profile on occupational therapy assistants and aides .

Work Environment

Occupational therapists held about 108,800 jobs in 2010. Forty-eight percent of occupational therapists worked in offices of physical, occupational and speech therapists, and audiologist or hospitals. Others worked in schools, nursing homes, and home health services in 2010:

Hospitals; state, local, and private	27%
Offices of physical, occupational and speech therapists, and audiologists	21
Nursing care facilities	9
Home health care services	7
Individual and family services	3

Therapists spend a lot of time on their feet working with patients. They also may be required to lift and move patients or heavy equipment. Many work in multiple facilities and have to travel from one job to another.

Work Schedules

Most occupational therapists worked full time in 2010. About 30 percent worked part time. They may work nights or weekends, as needed, to accommodate patients' schedules.

How to Become an Occupational Therapist

Occupational therapists need a master's degree from an accredited occupational therapy program. Occupational therapists must also be licensed.

Education

Most occupational therapists enter the occupation with a master's degree in occupational therapy. A small number of programs offer doctoral degrees in occupational therapy.

Admission to occupational therapy programs generally requires a bachelor's degree and specific coursework, including biology and physiology. Many programs also require applicants to have volunteered or worked in an occupational therapy setting.

Master's programs generally take 2 years to complete; doctoral programs take longer. Some schools offer a dual degree program in which the student earns a bachelor's degree and a master's degree in 5 years. Part-time programs that offer courses on nights and weekends are also available. Both master's and doctoral programs require several months of supervised fieldwork, in which prospective occupational therapists gain real-world experience.

Important Qualities

Communication skills. Occupational therapists have to be able to explain clearly what they want their patients to do.

Compassion. Occupational therapists are usually drawn to the profession by a desire to help people and improve the daily lives of others.

Interpersonal skills. Because occupational therapists spend their time teaching and explaining therapies to patients, they should inspire trust and respect from their clients.

Listening skills. Occupational therapists must be able to listen attentively to what their patients tell them.

Patience. Dealing with injuries, illnesses, and disabilities is frustrating for many people. Occupational therapists should be patient in order to provide quality care from the people they serve.

Writing skills. Occupational therapists must be able to explain clearly to others on the patient's medical team what they are doing and how it is going.

Licenses and Certification

Certification is voluntary, but many occupational therapists choose to become certified. They must pass the National Board for Certification of Occupational Therapists (NBCOT) exam to become certified. Certification allows therapists to use the title of Occupational Therapist Registered (OTR). They must also take continuing education classes to maintain certification.

All states require occupational therapists to be licensed. Licensure requires a degree from an accredited educational program and passing the NBCOT certification exam. Other requirements, such as continuing education and fees, vary by state.

Pay

Occupational Therapists
Median annual wages, May 2010

Occupational Therapists	$72,320
Health Diagnosing and Treating Practitioners	$71,490
Total, All Occupations	$33,840

Note: All Occupations includes all occupations in the U.S. Economy.
Source: U.S. Bureau of Labor Statistics, Occupational Employment Statistics

The median annual wage of occupational therapists was $72,320 in May 2010. The median wage is the wage at which half the workers in an occupation earned more than that amount and half earned less. The lowest 10 percent earned less than $48,920, and the top 10 percent more than $102,520. Median annual wages in selected industries employing occupational therapists in May 2010 were:

Home health care services	$79,570
Nursing care facilities	78,410
Offices of physical, occupational and speech therapists, and audiologists	73,770
Hospitals; state, local, and private	72,450
Individual and family services	64,520

Most occupational therapists worked full time in 2010. About 30 percent worked part time. They may work nights or weekends, as needed, to accommodate patients' schedules.

Job Outlook

Occupational Therapists
Percent change in employment, projected 2010-20

Occupational Therapists	33%
Health Diagnosing and Treating Practitioners	26%
Total, All Occupations	14%

Note: All Occupations includes all occupations in the U.S. Economy.
Source: U.S. Bureau of Labor Statistics, Employment Projections program

Employment of occupational therapists is expected to increase 33 percent from 2010 to 2020, much faster than the average for all occupations. Occupational therapy will continue to be an important part of treatment for people with various illnesses and disabilities, such as Alzheimer's disease, cerebral palsy, autism, or the loss of a limb.

The need for occupational therapists will increase as the large baby-boom population ages and people remain active later in life. Specifically, occupational therapists help senior citizens maintain their independence by recommending home modifications and strategies that make daily activities easier.

Occupational therapists also play a large role in the treatment of many conditions commonly associated with aging, such as osteoarthritis and Parkinson's disease. Patients will continue to seek noninvasive outpatient treatment for long-term disabilities and illnesses, either in their homes or in residential care environments. In addition, medical advances now enable more patients with critical problems to survive—patients who ultimately may need extensive therapy.

Job Prospects

Job opportunities should be good for licensed occupational therapists in all setting, particularly in acute hospital, rehabilitation, and orthopedic settings because the elderly receive most of their treatment in these settings. Occupational therapists with specialized knowledge in a treatment area also will have increased job prospects.

Employment projections data for occupational therapists, 2010-20

Occupational Title	SOC Code	Employment, 2010	Projected Employment, 2020	Change, 2010-20	
				Percent	Numeric
Occupational Therapists	29-1122	108,800	145,200	33	36,400
SOURCE: U.S. Bureau of Labor Statistics, Employment Projections program					

Similar Occupations

This table shows a list of occupations with job duties that are similar to those of occupational therapists.

Occupation	Job Duties	Entry-Level Education	Median Annual Pay, May 2010
Athletic Trainers	Athletic trainers specialize in preventing, diagnosing, and treating muscle and bone injuries and illnesses. They work with people of all ages and all skill levels, from young children to soldiers and professional athletes.	Bachelor's degree	$41,600
Occupational Therapy Assistants and Aides	Occupational therapy assistants and aides work under the direction of occupational therapists in treating patients with injuries, illnesses, or disabilities through the therapeutic use of everyday activities. They help these patients develop, recover, and improve the skills needed for daily living and working.	See How to Become One	$47,490
Physical Therapists	Physical therapists help people who have injuries or illnesses improve their movement and manage their pain. They are often an important part of rehabilitation and treatment of patients with chronic conditions or injuries.	Doctoral or professional degree	$76,310
Recreational Therapists	Recreational therapists plan, direct, and coordinate recreation programs for people with disabilities or illnesses. They use a variety of techniques, including arts and crafts, drama, music, dance, sports, games, and field trips. These programs help maintain or improve a client's physical and emotional well-being.	Bachelor's degree	$39,410
Respiratory Therapists	Respiratory therapists care for patients who have trouble breathing; for example, from a chronic respiratory disease, such as asthma or emphysema. They also provide emergency care to patients suffering from heart attacks, stroke, drowning, or shock.	Associate's degree	$54,280

Contacts for More Information

For more information about occupational therapists, visit American Occupational Therapy Association

For information regarding the requirements to practice as an occupational therapist in schools, contact the appropriate occupational therapy regulatory agency for your state.

Suggested citation:

Bureau of Labor Statistics, U.S. Department of Labor, Occupational Outlook Handbook, 2012-13 Edition, Occupational Therapists, on the Internet at http://www.bls.gov/ooh/healthcare/occupational-therapists.htm .

Occupational Therapy Assistants and Aides

Quick Facts: Occupational Therapy Assistants and Aides	
2010 Median Pay	$47,490 per year $22.83 per hour
Entry-Level Education	See How to Become One
Work Experience in a Related Occupation	None
On-the-job Training	See How to Become One
Number of Jobs, 2010	36,000
Job Outlook, 2010-20	41% (Much faster than average)
Employment Change, 2010-20	14,800

What Occupational Therapy Assistants and Aides Do

Occupational therapy assistants and aides work under the direction of occupational therapists in treating patients with injuries, illnesses, or disabilities through the therapeutic use of everyday activities. They help these patients develop, recover, and improve the skills needed for daily living and working. For more information, see the profile on occupational therapists .

Occupational therapy assistants are typically more directly involved in giving therapy. Occupational therapy aides typically do support activities.

Duties

Occupational therapy assistants typically do the following:

- Help patients do therapeutic activities, such as specific stretches and other exercises
- Work with children who have development disabilities, leading them in play activities that promote coordination

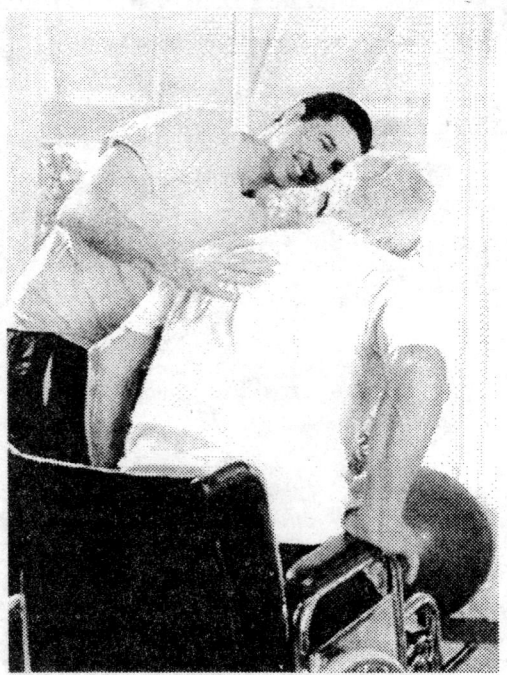

Occupational therapy assistants help transport patients to therapy areas and set up equipment.

- Teach patients how to use special equipment; for example, showing a patient with Parkinson's disease how to use devices that make eating easier
- Record patients' progress, report to occupational therapists, and do other administrative tasks

Occupational therapy aides typically do the following:

- Help clients with billing and insurance forms
- Prepare treatment areas, such as setting up therapy equipment
- Do clerical tasks, including scheduling appointments and answering telephones
- Help patients move to and from treatment areas

Occupational therapy assistants collaborate with occupational therapists to develop a treatment plan for each patient. Then, the occupational therapy assistant carries out the plan with the patient. Activities in the plans range from teaching the proper way to move from a bed into a wheelchair to the best way to stretch and limber one's muscles.

For example, an occupational therapy assistant might work with injured workers to help them get back into the work force by teaching them how to work around lost motor skills. An occupational therapy assistant might work with people with learning disabilities to teach them skills that let them be more independent.

Assistants monitor activities to make sure patients are doing them correctly. They also encourage the patients. They record the patient's progress so the therapist can change the treatment plan if the patient is not getting the desired results.

Occupational therapy aides typically prepare materials and assemble equipment used during treatment. Aides fill out insurance forms and other paperwork and are responsible for a range of clerical tasks, such as scheduling appointments and answering the telephone.

Work Environment

Occupational therapy assistants held about 28,500 jobs in 2010. Occupational therapy aides held about 7,500 jobs in 2010.

As shown below, only 15 percent of occupational therapy assistants worked in general hospitals in 2010:

Offices of physical, occupational and speech therapists, and audiologists	33%
Nursing care facilities	19
General medical and surgical hospitals; state, local, and private	15
Elementary and secondary schools; state, local, and private	7
Home health care services	5

As shown below, nearly one out of four occupational therapy aides worked in offices of physical, occupational and speech therapists, and audiologists in 2010:

Offices of physical, occupational and speech therapists, and audiologists	23%
General medical and surgical hospitals; state, local, and private	18
Nursing care facilities	18
Specialty (except psychiatric and substance abuse) hospitals; state, local, and private	10
Elementary and secondary schools; state, local, and private	6

Occupational therapy assistants and aides work primarily in occupational therapists' offices and hospitals. They also work in nursing care facilities and for home health agencies.

Occupational therapy assistants and aides spend much of their time on their feet setting up equipment and, in the case of assistants, working with patients. Constant kneeling and stooping are part of the job, as is the need to sometimes lift patients.

Work Schedules

Most occupational therapy assistants and aides work full time. Occupational therapy assistants and aides may work during evenings or on weekends to match patients' schedules.

How to Become an Occupational Therapy Assistant or Aide

An associate's degree is required to become an occupational therapy assistant. They must also be licensed in most states. Occupational therapy aides typically have a high school diploma or equivalent.

Education

People interested in becoming an occupational therapy assistant should take high school courses in biology and health. They can also increase their chances of getting into a community college or technical school program by doing volunteer work in a healthcare setting, such as a nursing care facility, an occupational therapist's office, or a physical therapist's office.

Occupational therapy assistants generally have an associate's degree. Occupational therapy assistant programs are commonly found in community colleges and technical schools. These programs generally require two years of full-time study. They include classroom instruction in subjects such as psychology, biology, and pediatric health. Occupational therapy assistants also complete clinical fieldwork as part of their education to gain hands-on work experience.

To be licensed, occupational therapy assistants must graduate from an accredited program. In 2010, there were about 300 programs for occupational therapy assistants that the Accreditation Council for Occupational Therapy Education (ACOTE) had accredited.

Occupational therapy aides typically have a high school diploma or equivalent. They are trained on the job. This training can last from several weeks to a few months and includes classroom and practical training where the aide works under the direct supervision of more experienced assistants or aides.

Important Qualities

Compassion. Occupational therapy assistants and aides frequently work with patients who struggle with many of life's basic activities. As a result, they should be compassionate and caring and have the ability to encourage others.

Detail oriented. Occupational therapy assistants and aides must be able to quickly and accurately follow the instructions, both written and spoken, of an occupational therapist.

Interpersonal skills. Assistants and aides spend much of their time interacting with patients. They should be friendly and courteous, and they should be able to communicate with patients to the extent of their ability and training.

Physical strength. Assistants and aides need to have a moderate degree of strength because of the physical exertion required to assist patients. Constant kneeling, stooping, and standing for long periods also are part of the job.

Licenses

Most states require occupational therapy assistants to be licensed. Licensure usually requires completing an accredited occupational therapy assistant education program and passing an exam. Some states have additional requirements, such as continuing education.

Occupational therapy aides are not required to be licensed.

Certification

Occupational therapy assistants who have completed an accredited program can become certified by passing an exam offered by the National Board for Certification in Occupational Therapy. Certification is voluntary and allows assistants to use the title "Certified Occupational Therapy Assistant" (COTA).

Advancement

Some occupational therapy assistants and aides advance by taking additional education to become occupational therapists. A small number of occupational therapist "bridge" education programs are designed for qualifying occupational therapy assistants to advance to therapists.

Pay

Occupational Therapy Assistants and Aides
Median annual wages, May 2010

Occupational Therapy Assistants	$51,010
Occupational Therapy Assistants and Aides	$47,490
Total, All Occupations	$33,840
Occupational Therapy Aides	$27,430

Note: All Occupations includes all occupations in the U.S. Economy.
Source: U.S. Bureau of Labor Statistics, Occupational Employment Statistics

The median annual wage of occupational therapy assistants was $51,010 in May 2010. The median wage is the wage at which half the workers in an occupation earned more than that amount and half earned less. The lowest 10 percent earned less than $33,110 and the top 10 percent earned more than $70,790.

The median annual wage of occupational therapy aides was $27,430 in May 2010. The lowest 10 percent earned less than $17,440, and the top 10 percent earned more than $52,750.

Median annual wages in the industries employing the largest numbers of occupational therapy assistants in May 2010 were as follows:

Home health care services	$54,950
Nursing care facilities	54,460
Offices of physical, occupational and speech therapists, and audiologists	53,910
General medical and surgical hospitals; state, local, and private	46,620
Elementary and secondary schools; state, local, and private	42,700

Median annual wages in the industries employing the largest numbers of occupational therapy aides in May 2010 were as follows:

Specialty (except psychiatric and substance abuse) hospitals; state, local, and private	$51,260
Nursing care facilities	29,940
General medical and surgical hospitals; state, local, and private	27,810
Offices of physical, occupational and speech therapists, and audiologists	26,850
Elementary and secondary schools; state, local, and private	26,030

Most occupational therapy assistants and aides work full time. Occupational therapy assistants and aides may work during evenings or on weekends to match patients' schedules.

Job Outlook

Occupational Therapy Assistants and Aides
Percent change in employment, projected 2010-20

Occupational Therapy Assistants	43%
Occupational Therapy Assistants and Aides	41%
Occupational Therapy Aides	33%
Total, All Occupations	14%

Note: All Occupations includes all occupations in the U.S. Economy.
Source: U.S. Bureau of Labor Statistics, Employment Projections program

Employment of occupational therapy assistants is expected to increase 43 percent from 2010 to 2020, much faster than the average for all occupations. Employment of occupational therapy aides is expected to increase 33 percent from 2010 to 2020, much faster than the average for all occupations.

Demand for occupational therapy is expected to rise significantly over the coming decade in response to the health needs of the aging baby-boom generation and a growing elderly population. Older adults are especially prone to conditions such as arthritis that affect their everyday activities. Occupational therapy assistants and aides will be needed to assist occupational therapists in caring for these people. Occupational therapy will also continue to be used for treating children and young adults with developmental disabilities like autism.

Demand for occupational therapy assistants is also expected to come from occupational therapists employing more assistants to reduce the cost of occupational therapy services. After the therapist has evaluated a patient and designed a treatment plan, the occupational therapy assistant can provide many aspects of the treatment that the therapist prescribed.

Job Prospects

Occupational therapy assistants and aides with experience working in an occupational therapy office or other healthcare setting should have the best job opportunities. In addition to overall employment growth, job openings will also result from the need to replace occupational therapy assistants and aides who leave the occupation.

Employment projections data for occupational therapy assistants and aides, 2010-20

Occupational Title	SOC Code	Employment, 2010	Projected Employment, 2020	Change, 2010-20 Percent	Change, 2010-20 Numeric
Occupational Therapy Assistants and Aides	—	36,000	50,800	41	14,800
Occupational Therapy Assistants	31-2011	28,500	40,800	43	12,300
Occupational Therapy Aides	31-2012	7,500	9,900	33	2,500
SOURCE: U.S. Bureau of Labor Statistics, Employment Projections program					

Similar Occupations

This table shows a list of occupations with job duties that are similar to those of occupational therapy assistants and aides.

Occupation	Job Duties	Entry-Level Education	Median Annual Pay, May 2010
Dental Assistants	Dental assistants have many tasks, ranging from patient care to record keeping, in a dental office. Their duties vary by state and by the dentists' offices where they work.	Postsecondary non-degree award	$33,470
Medical Assistants	Medical assistants complete administrative and clinical tasks in the offices of physicians, podiatrists, chiropractors, and other health practitioners. Their duties vary with the location, specialty, and size of the practice.	High school diploma or equivalent	$28,860
Occupational Therapists	Occupational therapists treat patients with injuries, illnesses, or disabilities through the therapeutic use of everyday activities. They help these patients develop, recover, and improve the skills needed for daily living and working.	Master's degree	$72,320
Pharmacy Technicians	Pharmacy technicians help licensed pharmacists dispense prescription medication.	High school diploma or equivalent	$28,400
Physical Therapist Assistants and Aides	Physical therapist assistants and physical therapist aides work under the direction of physical therapists. They help patients who are recovering from injuries, illnesses, and surgeries regain movement and manage pain.	See How to Become One	$37,710

Contacts for More Information

For more information about occupational therapy assistants or aides, visit American Occupational Therapy Association
National Board for Certification in Occupational Therapy

Suggested citation:

Bureau of Labor Statistics, U.S. Department of Labor, Occupational Outlook Handbook, 2012-13 Edition, Occupational Therapy Assistants and Aides, on the Internet at http://www.bls.gov/ooh/healthcare/occupational-therapy-assistants-and-aides.htm .

Opticians, Dispensing

Quick Facts: Dispensing Opticians	
2010 Median Pay	$32,940 per year $15.84 per hour
Entry-Level Education	High school diploma or equivalent
Work Experience in a Related Occupation	None
On-the-job Training	Long-term on-the-job training
Number of Jobs, 2010	62,600
Job Outlook, 2010-20	29% (Much faster than average)
Employment Change, 2010-20	18,100

What Dispensing Opticians Do

Dispensing opticians help fit eyeglasses and contact lenses, following prescriptions from ophthalmologists and optometrists. They also help customers decide which eyeglass frames or type of contact lenses to buy.

Duties

Opticians typically do the following:

- Receive customers' prescriptions, which ophthalmologists and optometrists have written, for eyeglasses or contact lenses
- Take measurements of customers' eyes, such as the width or thickness of their corneas
- Help customers choose eyeglass frames and lens treatments, such as tints or nonreflective coatings, based on their vision needs and style preferences
- Create work orders for ophthalmic laboratory technicians, providing information about the lenses needed
- Make adjustments to finished eyeglasses to ensure a good fit
- Repair or refit broken eyeglass frames
- Educate customers about eyewear—for example, showing them how to care for their contact lenses
- Do business tasks, such as maintaining sales records, keeping track of customers' prescriptions, and ordering inventory

Opticians who work in small shops or prepare custom orders may grind lenses and insert them into frames themselves, tasks usually performed by ophthalmic laboratory technicians. For more information, see the profile on ophthalmic laboratory technicians .

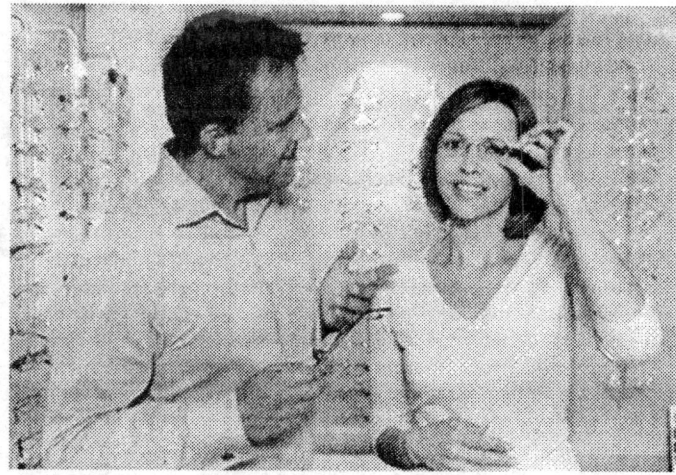

Opticians advise customers on styles of eyewear that suit their needs.

Work Environment

Dispensing opticians held about 62,600 jobs in 2010. The industries employing the largest numbers of dispensing opticians in 2010 were as follows:

Offices of optometrists	41%
Health and personal care stores	33
Offices of physicians	12
Other general merchandise stores	6
Department stores	2

Some opticians work in stores that sell glasses, contact lenses, and other optical goods. These stores may be stand-alone businesses or parts of larger retail establishments, such as department stores.

Other opticians work as part of a group optometry or medical practice, where optometrists and ophthalmologists provide eye-related medical care to patients. For more information, see the profiles on optometrists and on physicians and surgeons .

Work Schedules

Opticians who work in larger retail establishments, such as department stores, may have to work evenings and weekends. Most opticians work full time, although part-time opportunities also are available.

How to Become a Dispensing Optician

Opticians typically have a high school diploma or equivalent and some form of on-the-job training. Licensure also is required in some states.

Education and Training

Most opticians have at least a high school diploma. Opticians typically learn job skills through formal on-the-job programs. This training includes technical instruction in which, for example, new opticians measure a customer's eyes or adjust frames under the supervision of an experienced optician. Trainees also learn sales and office management practices.

A number of community colleges and technical schools offer formal education in opticianry. Some award an associate's degree, which takes two years. Others offer a certificate, which takes one year. As of 2010, the Commission on Opticianry Accreditation accredited 21 associate's degree programs in 14 states.

Coursework includes classes in optics, eye physiology, and business management, among others. Also, students do supervised clinical work that gives them hands-on experience working as opticians and learning optical mathematics, optical physics, and the use of precision measuring instruments. Some programs have distance-learning options.

Courses in physics, basic anatomy, algebra, and trigonometry are particularly valuable.

Licenses

Twenty-three states require opticians to be licensed. Licensure usually requires completing formal education through an approved program or completing an apprenticeship. In addition to being licensed, states require opticians to pass one or more of the following (depending on the state): a state written exam, a state practical exam, or certification exams, described in the certification section.

In most states, opticians must renew their licenses periodically, and they must take continuing education.

Certification

Opticians may choose to become certified in eyeglass dispensing or contact lens dispensing or both. Certification requires passing exams from the American Board of Opticianry (ABO) and National Contact Lens Examiners (NCLE) . Nearly all state licensing boards use the ABO and NCLE exams as the basis for state licensing.

Important Qualities

Communication skills. Opticians must be able to listen closely to what customers want. They must be able to explain options and instructions for care in ways that customers understand.

Customer service skills. Because most opticians work in stores, they must answer questions and know about the products they sell. They interact with customers on a very personal level, fitting eyeglasses or contact lenses. To succeed, they must be friendly, courteous, patient, and helpful to customers.

Management skills. Opticians are often responsible for the business aspects of running an optical store. They should be comfortable making decisions and have some knowledge of sales and inventory management.

Manual dexterity. Opticians frequently use special tools to make final adjustments and repairs to eyeglasses. They must have good hand-eye coordination to do that work quickly and accurately.

Pay

Dispensing Opticians
Median annual wages, May 2010

Healthcare Practitioners and Technical Occupations	$58,490
Total, All Occupations	$33,840
Opticians, Dispensing	$32,940

Note: All Occupations includes all occupations in the U.S. Economy.
Source: U.S. Bureau of Labor Statistics, Occupational Employment Statistics

The median annual wage of opticians was $32,940 in May 2010. The median wage is the wage at which half the workers in an occupation earned more than that amount and half earned less. The lowest 10 percent earned less than $21,070, and the top 10 percent earned more than $50,780.

Median annual wages in the industries employing the largest number of dispensing opticians in May 2010 were as follows:

Other general merchandise stores	$36,280
Health and personal care stores	35,470
Offices of physicians	33,980
Offices of optometrists	30,370
Department stores	29,660

Opticians employed in department stores or other retail settings may be required to work evenings and weekends. Most opticians work full time, although part-time opportunities also are available.

Job Outlook

Dispensing Opticians
Percent change in employment, projected 2010-20

Opticians, Dispensing	29%
Healthcare Practitioners and Technical Occupations	26%
Total, All Occupations	14%

Note: All Occupations includes all occupations in the U.S. Economy.
Source: U.S. Bureau of Labor Statistics, Employment Projections program

Employment of opticians is expected to grow by 29 percent from 2010 to 2020, much faster than the average for all occupations.

An aging population is anticipated to lead to greater demand for eye care services. People usually have eye problems in greater frequency when they reach middle age, so the need for opticians is expected to grow with the increase in the number of older people.

Awareness of the importance of eye exams is increasing across all age groups. Also, fashion influences demand for frames and contact lenses.

In addition, more opticians are finding employment in group medical practices. Optometrists and ophthalmologists are increasingly offering glasses and contact lenses to their patients as a way to expand their businesses, leading to a greater need for opticians in those settings.

However, employment growth is expected to be constrained by increases in productivity that will allow a given number of opticians to serve more customers.

Employment projections data for dispensing opticians, 2010-20

Occupational Title	SOC Code	Employment, 2010	Projected Employment, 2020	Change, 2010-20	
				Percent	Numerice
Opticians, Dispensing	29-2081	62,600	80,700	29	18,100
SOURCE: U.S. Bureau of Labor Statistics, Employment Projections program					

Similar Occupations

This table shows a list of occupations with job duties that are similar to those of dispensing opticians.

Occupation	Job Duties	Entry-Level Education	Median Annual Pay, May 2010
Jewelers and Precious Stone and Metal Workers	Jewelers and precious stone and metal workers design, manufacture, and sell jewelry. They also adjust, repair, and appraise gems and jewelry.	High school diploma or equivalent	$35,170
Ophthalmic Laboratory Technicians	Ophthalmic laboratory technicians make prescription eyeglasses and contact lenses. They are also commonly known as manufacturing opticians, optical mechanics, or optical goods workers.	High school diploma or equivalent	$27,970
Optometrists	Optometrists perform eye exams to check for vision problems and diseases. They prescribe eyeglasses or contact lenses as needed.	Doctoral or professional degree	$94,990
Orthotists and Prosthetists	Orthotists and prosthetists, also called O&P professionals, design medical support devices and measure and fit patients for them. These devices include artificial limbs (arms, hands, legs, and feet), braces, and other medical or surgical devices.	Master's degree	$65,060

Contacts for More Information

For more information about dispensing opticians, including voluntary certification for opticians and a list of state licensing boards for opticians, visit American Board of Opticianry and National Contact Lens Examiners

For a list of associate's degree programs accredited by the Commission on Opticianry Accreditation, visit National Federation of Opticianry Schools

For more information about optician education, visit National Academy of Opticianry

Suggested citation:

Bureau of Labor Statistics, U.S. Department of Labor, Occupational Outlook Handbook, 2012-13 Edition, Opticians, Dispensing, on the Internet at http://www.bls.gov/ooh/healthcare/opticians-dispensing.htm .

Optometrists

Quick Facts: Optometrists	
2010 Median Pay	$94,990 per year $45.67 per hour
Entry-Level Education	Doctoral or professional degree
Work Experience in a Related Occupation	None
On-the-job Training	None
Number of Jobs, 2010	34,200
Job Outlook, 2010-20	33% (Much faster than average)
Employment Change, 2010-20	11,300

What Optometrists Do

Optometrists perform eye exams to check for vision problems and diseases. They prescribe eyeglasses or contact lenses as needed.

Duties

Optometrists typically do the following:

- Perform vision tests to check for sight problems, such as nearsightedness or farsightedness
- Check for eye diseases, such as glaucoma
- Prescribe eyeglasses, contact lenses, and medications
- Provide other treatments, such as vision therapy or low-vision rehabilitation
- Provide pre- and postoperative care to patients undergoing eye surgery—for example, examining a patient's eyes the day after surgery
- Promote eye health by counseling patients, including explaining how to clean and wear contact lenses

Some optometrists spend much of their time providing specialized care, particularly if they are working in a group practice with other optometrists or doctors. For example, some optometrists mostly treat patients with only partial or no sight, a condition known as low vision. Others may focus on pre- or postoperative care if they work in a facility that does many eye surgeries. Optometrists may also teach or do research in optometry colleges or work as consultants in the eye care industry. Those who teach are classified as postsecondary school teachers. For more information, see the profile on postsecondary teachers .

Many optometrists own their practice and may spend more time on general business activities such as hiring employees and ordering supplies. Optometrists should not be confused with ophthalmologists and with dispensing opticians. Ophthalmologists are physicians who perform eye surgery and treat eye disease in addition to examining eyes and prescribing eyeglasses and contact lenses. Dispensing opticians fit and adjust eyeglasses and in some states fill contact lens prescriptions that an optometrist or ophthalmologist has written. For more information, see the profile on dispensing opticians .

Work Environment

Optometrists held about 34,200 jobs in 2010. About half of optometrists work in stand-alone offices of optometry. Optometrists may also work in doctors' offices, retail stores, outpatient clinics, and hospitals. Some optometrists are self-employed.

As shown in the following tabulation, 50 percent of optometrists were employed in offices of optometrists in 2010:

Offices of optometrists	50%
Self-employed workers	22
Offices of physicians	13
Health and personal care stores	8
Outpatient care centers	2

Work Schedules

Most optometrists work full time. Some work evenings and weekends to suit patients' needs.

How to Become an Optometrist

Optometrists must complete a Doctor of Optometry program and get a state license. Doctor of Optometry programs take 4 years to complete after earning an undergraduate degree.

Education

Optometrists need a Doctor of Optometry (O.D.) degree. In 2011, there were 20 accredited Doctor of Optometry programs in the United States, one of which was in Puerto Rico. Applicants to O.D. programs must have completed at least 3 years of postsecondary education, including coursework in biology, chemistry, physics, English, and mathematics. In practice, most students get a bachelor's degree before enrolling in a Doctor of Optometry program. Applicants must also take the Optometry Admission Test (OAT) to apply to O.D. programs.

Doctor of Optometry programs take 4 years to complete. They combine classroom learning and supervised clinical experience.

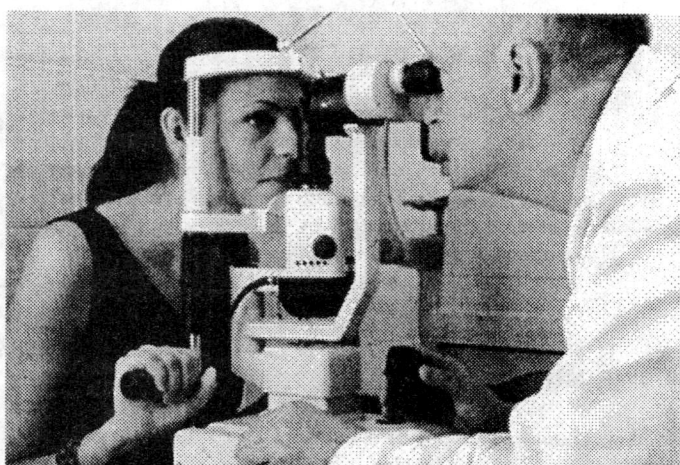

Optometrists use an instrument called a phoropter to check patients' vision and determine their need for corrective lenses.

Coursework includes anatomy, physiology, biochemistry, optics and visual science, and the diagnosis and treatment of diseases and disorders of the visual system. After finishing the O.D., some optometrists do a 1-year residency program to get advanced clinical training in a specialty. Specialty areas for residency programs include family practice, primary eye care, pediatric or geriatric optometry, vision therapy and rehabilitation, cornea and contact lenses, refractive and ocular surgery, low vision rehabilitation, ocular disease, and community health optometry.

Licenses

All states require optometrists to be licensed. To get a license, a prospective optometrist must have an O.D. from an accredited optometry school and must complete all sections of the National Boards in Optometry. Some states require an additional exam. Many states require optometrists to take continuing education and renew their license periodically.

Important Qualities

Decision-making skills. Optometrists must be able to evaluate the results of a variety of optical tests and decide on the best course of treatment for a patient.

Interpersonal skills. Because they spend much of their time examining patients, optometrists must be able to ensure that their patients are at ease.

Speaking skills. Optometrists must be able to clearly explain eye-care instructions to their patients, as well as answer patients' questions.

Pay

Optometrists
Median annual wages, May 2010

Optometrists	$94,990
Health Diagnosing and Treating Practitioners	$71,490
Total, All Occupations	$33,840

Note: All Occupations includes all occupations in the U.S. Economy.
Source: U.S. Bureau of Labor Statistics, Occupational Employment Statistics

The median annual wage of optometrists was $94,990 in May 2010. The median wage is the wage at which half the workers in an occupation earned more than that amount and half earned less. The lowest 10 percent earned less than $49,630, and the top 10 percent earned $166,400 or more.

Most optometrists work full time. Some work evenings and weekends to suit patients' needs.

Job Outlook

Optometrists
Percent change in employment, projected 2010-20

Optometrists	33%
Health Diagnosing and Treating Practitioners	26%
Total, All Occupations	14%

Note: All Occupations includes all occupations in the U.S. Economy.
Source: U.S. Bureau of Labor Statistics, Employment Projections program

Employment of optometrists is expected to grow by 33 percent from 2010 to 2020, much faster than the average for all occupations. However, because it is a small occupation, the fast growth will result in only about 11,300 new jobs over the 10-year period. Because vision problems tend to occur more frequently later in life, more optometrists will be needed to meet the health needs of an aging population. Also, the number of people with chronic diseases, such as diabetes, has increased in recent years. These diseases frequently cause vision problems and require treatment from optometrists. In addition, an increasing number of insurance plans, including Medicare and Medicaid, provide some vision or eye-care insurance coverage.

Job Prospects

Because the number of optometrists is limited by the number of accredited optometry schools, licensed optometrists should expect good job prospects. Admission to Doctor of Optometry programs is competitive, however, as it is for professional degree programs in other fields. In addition, a large number of currently practicing optometrists is expected to retire over the coming decade, creating opportunities for new optometrists.

Employment projections data for optometrists, 2010-20

Occupational Title	SOC Code	Employment, 2010	Projected Employment, 2020	Change, 2010-20 Percent	Change, 2010-20 Numeric
Optometrists	29-1041	34,200	45,500	33	11,300
SOURCE: U.S. Bureau of Labor Statistics, Employment Projections program					

Similar Occupations

This table shows a list of occupations with job duties that are similar to those of optometrists.

Occupation	Job Duties	Entry-Level Education	Median Annual Pay, May 2010
Dentists	Dentists diagnose and treat problems with a patient's teeth, gums, and other parts of the mouth. They provide advice and instruction on taking care of teeth and gums and on diet choices that affect oral health.	Doctoral or professional degree	$146,920
Opticians, Dispensing	Dispensing opticians help fit eyeglasses and contact lenses, following prescriptions from ophthalmologists and optometrists. They also help customers decide which eyeglass frames or type of contact lenses to buy.	High school diploma or equivalent	$32,940
Physicians and Surgeons	Physicians and surgeons diagnose and treat injuries and illnesses in patients. Physicians examine patients, take medical histories, prescribe medications, and order, perform, and interpret diagnostic tests. Surgeons operate on patients to treat injuries, such as broken bones; diseases, such as cancerous tumors; and deformities, such as cleft palates.	Doctoral or professional degree	This wage is equal to or greater than $166,400 per year.

Podiatrists	Podiatrists provide medical and surgical care for people suffering foot, ankle, and lower leg problems. They diagnose illnesses, treat injuries, and perform surgery.	Doctoral or professional degree	$118,030
Veterinarians	Veterinarians care for the health of animals. They diagnose, treat, or research medical conditions and diseases of pets, livestock, and animals in zoos, racetracks, and laboratories.	Doctoral or professional degree	$82,040

Contacts for More Information

For more information about optometrists, including a list of accredited optometric institutions of education, visit Association of Schools and Colleges of Optometry

For more information about optometry, visit American Optometric Association

The board of optometry in each state can supply information on licensing requirements. For information on specific admission requirements and sources of financial aid, contact the admissions officers of individual optometry schools.

Suggested citation:

Bureau of Labor Statistics, U.S. Department of Labor, Occupational Outlook Handbook, 2012-13 Edition, Optometrists, on the Internet at http://www.bls.gov/ooh/healthcare/optometrists.htm .

Orthotists and Prosthetists

Quick Facts: Orthotists and Prosthetists	
2010 Median Pay	$65,060 per year $31.28 per hour
Entry-Level Education	Master's degree
Work Experience in a Related Occupation	None
On-the-Job Training	None
Number of Jobs, 2010	6,300
Job Outlook, 2010-20	12% (About as fast as average)
Employment Change, 2010-20	800

What Orthotists and Prosthetists Do

Orthotists and prosthetists, also called O&P professionals, design medical supportive devices and measure and fit patients for them. These devices include artificial limbs (arms, hands, legs, and feet), braces, and other medical or surgical devices.

Duties

Orthotists and prosthetists typically do the following:

- Evaluate and interview patients to determine their needs
- Measure patients to design and fit medical devices
- Design orthopedic and prosthetic devices based on physicians' prescriptions
- Take a mold of the part of the body that will be fitted with a brace or artificial limb
- Select materials to be used for the orthotic or prosthetic device
- Fit, test, and adjust devices on patients
- Instruct patients in how to use and care for their devices
- Repair or update prosthetic and orthotic devices
- Document care in patients' records

O&P professionals may work in both orthotics and prosthetics, or they may choose to specialize in one. Orthotists are specifically trained to work with medical supportive devices, such as braces and inserts. Prosthetists are specifically trained to work with prostheses, such as artificial limbs and other body parts.

Some O&P professionals may construct devices for their patients. Others supervise the construction of the orthotic or prosthetic devices

by medical appliance technicians. For more information, see the profile on medical appliance technicians .

Work Environment

Orthotists and prosthetists held about 6,300 jobs in 2010. Most work in offices, where they meet with patients and then design orthotic and prosthetic devices. They can work in small, private offices or in larger facilities, and they sometimes work in the shops where the orthotics and prosthetics are made.

The following industries employed the largest numbers of orthotists and prosthetists in 2010:

Medical equipment and supplies manufacturing	34%
Health and personal care stores	19
Offices of physicians	12
Hospitals; state, local, and private	10
Federal government, excluding postal service	9

O&P professionals who create orthotics and prosthetics may be exposed to health or safety hazards when handling certain materials, but there is little risk of injury if workers follow proper procedures, such as wearing goggles, gloves, and masks.

How to Become an Orthotist and Prosthetist

Orthotists and prosthetists need at least a master's degree and certification before entering the field. Both orthotists and prosthetists must complete a 1-year residency before they can be certified.

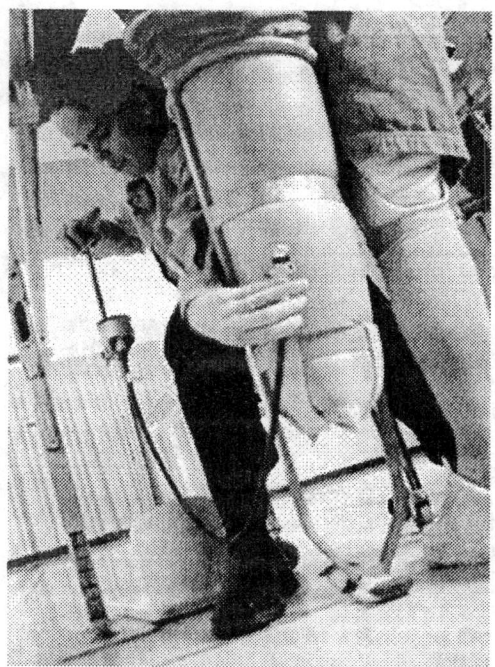

O&P professionals can work on both orthotics and prosthetics or may choose to specialize in one or the other.

Education

All orthotists and prosthetists must complete a master's degree in orthotics and prosthetics. These programs include courses such as upper and lower extremity orthotics and prosthetics, spinal orthotics, and plastics and other materials.

All graduate degree programs have a clinical component in which the student works under the direction of an O&P professional. Most programs require at least 500 hours of clinical experience, split equally between orthotics and prosthetics.

Master's programs usually take 2 years to complete. Prospective students can have a bachelor's degree in any discipline if they have fulfilled prerequisite courses in science and mathematics; requirements vary by program.

Certification and Training

Most O&P professionals become certified by passing the exam administered by the American Board for Certification in Orthotics, Prosthetics and Pedorthics (ABC). To qualify for the exam, an O&P professional must have completed a master's program in orthotics and prosthetics. Applicants must also have a 1-year formal residency in orthotics or prosthetics before sitting for the exam. Professionals who want to be certified in both orthotics and prosthetics need to complete a year of residency for each specialty and pass both sets of exams.

Important Qualities

Communication skills. Orthotists and prosthetists must have excellent communication skills. They must be able to communicate effectively with the technicians who often create the medical devices. They also must be able to explain to patients how to use and care for the devices.

Detail oriented. Orthotists and prosthetists must be precise when recording measurements to ensure that devices are designed and fit properly.

Dexterity. Orthotists and prosthetists must be good at working with their hands. They may design orthotics or prosthetics with intricate mechanical parts.

Leadership skills. Orthotists and prosthetists who work in their own offices must be effective leaders. They must be able to manage a staff of other professionals in their office.

Organizational skills. Some orthotists and prosthetists own their practice or work in private offices. Strong organizational skills, including good recordkeeping, are critical in both medical and business settings.

Patience. Orthotists and prosthetists may work for long periods with patients who need special attention.

Physical stamina. Orthotists and prosthetists should be comfortable performing physical tasks, such and working with shop equipment and hand tools. They may spend a lot of time bending over or crouching to examine or measure patients.

Problem-solving skills. Orthotists and prosthetists must evaluate their patients' situations and often look for creative solutions to their rehabilitation needs.

Pay

Orthotists and Prosthetists
Median annual wages, May 2010

Orthotists and Prosthetists	$65,060
Health Technologists and Technicians	$39,340
Total, All Occupations	$33,840

Note: All Occupations includes all occupations in the U.S. Economy.
Source: U.S. Bureau of Labor Statistics, Occupational Employment Statistics

The median annual wage of orthotists and prosthetists was $65,060 in May 2010. The median wage is the wage at which half the workers in an occupation earned more than that amount and half earned less. The lowest 10 percent earned less than $33,690, and the top 10 percent earned more than $106,800.

The wages of orthotists and prosthetists vary substantially by the industries they work in. The following tabulation shows the median annual wages of orthotists and prosthetists in specific industries in 2010:

Medical equipment and supplies manufacturing	$71,070
Health and personal care stores	68,240
Federal government, excluding postal service	67,110
Offices of physicians	57,660
Hospitals; state, local, and private	49,430

Job Outlook

Orthotists and Prosthetists
Percent change in employment, projected 2010-20

Health Technologists and Technicians	26%
Total, All Occupations	14%
Orthotists and Prosthetists	12%

Note: All Occupations includes all occupations in the U.S. Economy.
Source: U.S. Bureau of Labor Statistics, Employment Projections program

Employment of orthotists and prosthetists is expected to grow by 12 percent from 2010 to 2020, about as fast as the average for all occupations.

The aging baby-boom population will create a need for prosthetists because the two leading causes of limb loss, diabetes and cardiovascular disease, occur more frequently as people age. In addition, advances in technology may spur demand for prostheses that allow for more natural movement. The demand for orthotic devices, such as braces and orthopedic footwear, will likely increase because older people tend to need these support devices.

Employment projections data for orthotists and prosthetists, 2010-20

Occupational Title	SOC Code	Employment, 2010	Projected Employment, 2020	Change, 2010-20 Percent	Numeric
Orthotists and Prosthetists	29-2091	6,300	7,000	12	800
SOURCE: U.S. Bureau of Labor Statistics, Employment Projections program					

Similar Occupations

This table shows a list of occupations with job duties that are similar to those of orthotists and prosthetists.

Occupation	Job Duties	Entry-Level Education	Median Annual Pay, May 2010
Physical Therapists	Physical therapists help people who have injuries or illnesses improve their movement and manage their pain. They are often an important part of rehabilitation and treatment of patients with chronic conditions or injuries.	Doctoral or professional degree	$76,310
Physicians and Surgeons	Physicians and surgeons diagnose and treat injuries and illnesses in patients. Physicians examine patients, take medical histories, prescribe medications, and order, perform, and interpret diagnostic tests. Surgeons operate on patients to treat injuries, such as broken bones; diseases, such as cancerous tumors; and deformities, such as cleft palates.	Doctoral or professional degree	This wage is equal to or greater than $166,400 per year.
Respiratory Therapists	Respiratory therapists care for patients who have trouble breathing; for example, from a chronic respiratory disease, such as asthma or emphysema. They also provide emergency care to patients suffering from heart attacks, stroke, drowning, or shock.	Associate's degree	$54,280
Medical Appliance Technicians	Medical appliance technicians construct, fit, and repair medical supportive devices, including prosthetic limbs, arch supports, facial parts, and foot and leg braces.	High school diploma or equivalent	$35,670

Contacts for More Information

For more information about orthotists and prosthetists, visit American Academy of Orthotists & Prosthetists

For a list of accredited programs for orthotists and prosthetists, visit National Commission on Orthotic & Prosthetic Education

For information about certification for orthotists and prosthetists, visit American Board for Certification in Orthotics, Prosthetics & Pedorthics

Suggested citation:

Bureau of Labor Statistics, U.S. Department of Labor, Occupational Outlook Handbook, 2012-13 Edition, Orthotists and Prosthetists, on the Internet at http://www.bls.gov/ooh/healthcare/orthotists-and-prosthetists.htm .

Pharmacists

Quick Facts: Pharmacists	
2010 Median Pay	$111,570 per year $53.64 per hour
Entry-Level Education	Doctoral or professional degree
Work Experience in a Related Occupation	None
On-the-job Training	None
Number of Jobs, 2010	274,900
Job Outlook, 2010-20	25% (Faster than average)
Employment Change, 2010-20	69,700

What Pharmacists Do

Pharmacists dispense prescription medications to patients and offer advice on their safe use.

Duties

Pharmacists typically do the following:

- Fill prescriptions, verifying instructions from physicians on the proper amounts of medication to give to patients
- Check whether the prescription will interact negatively with other drugs that a patient is taking or conditions the patient has
- Instruct patients on how and when to take a prescribed medicine
- Advise patients on potential side effects they may experience from taking the medicine
- Advise patients about general health topics, such as diet, exercise, and managing stress, and on other issues, such as what equipment or supplies would be best for a health problem
- Complete insurance forms and work with insurance companies to be sure that patients get the medicines they need
- Oversee the work of pharmacy technicians and pharmacists in training (interns)
- Keep records and do other administrative tasks
- Teach other healthcare practitioners about proper medication therapies for patients

Some pharmacists who own their store or manage a chain pharmacy spend more time on business activities, such as inventory

Pharmacists answer customers' questions and explain the safe use of medications.

management. Pharmacists also take continuing education throughout their career to keep up with the latest advances in pharmacological science.

Pharmacists who work in universities or for pharmaceutical manufacturers are involved in researching and testing new medications.

With most drugs, pharmacists use standard dosages from pharmaceutical companies. However, some pharmacists create customized medications by mixing ingredients themselves, a process known as compounding.

Although most pharmacists work in retail stores, some work in specialized fields. The following are examples of types of pharmacists who work in settings outside of retail:

Clinical pharmacists work in hospitals and other healthcare settings. They spend little time dispensing prescriptions. Instead, they are involved in direct patient care. For example, they may go on rounds with a doctor and recommend medications to give to patients. They also counsel patients on how and when to take medications and monitor patients' health.

Consultant pharmacists advise healthcare facilities or insurance providers on how to make pharmacy services more efficient. They also may give advice directly to patients, such as helping seniors manage their prescriptions.

Some pharmacists work full time or part time as college professors. For more information, see the profile on <u>postsecondary teachers</u> .

Work Environment

Pharmacists held about 274,900 jobs in 2010. The following industries employed the largest number of pharmacists in 2010:

Pharmacies and drug stores	43%
Hospitals; state, local, and private	23
Grocery stores	8
Department stores	6
Other general merchandise stores	5

Pharmacists work in pharmacies, including those in grocery and drug stores. They also work in hospitals and clinics. In most settings, they spend much of the workday on their feet.

Work Schedules

Most pharmacists work full time, although about 21 percent worked part time in 2010. Because many pharmacies are open at all hours, some pharmacists work nights and weekends.

How to Become a Pharmacist

Pharmacists must pay attention to detail, ensuring the accuracy of the prescriptions they fill.

Pharmacists must have a Doctor of Pharmacy (Pharm.D.) degree from an accredited school. They also must be licensed, which requires passing two exams.

Education

All Doctor of Pharmacy programs require applicants to have taken postsecondary courses such as chemistry, biology, and anatomy. Applicants need at least 2 to 3 years of undergraduate study; for some programs, applicants must have a bachelor's degree. For most programs, applicants also must take the Pharmacy College Admissions Test (PCAT).

Pharm.D. programs usually take 4 years to finish, although some programs offer a 3-year option. A Pharm.D. program includes courses in pharmacology and medical ethics, as well as supervised work experiences in different settings, such as hospitals and retail pharmacies.

Pharmacists seeking an advanced pharmacy position, such as a clinical pharmacy or research job, complete a 1- to 2-year residency following their Pharm. D. Some pharmacists who own their own store may choose to get a master's degree in business administration (MBA). Others may get a degree in public health.

Licenses

All states license pharmacists. After they finish the Pharm. D., prospective pharmacists must pass two exams to get a license. One of the exams is in pharmacy skills and knowledge. The other is in pharmacy law in the state giving the pharmacy license.

Important Qualities

Analytical skills. Pharmacists must provide safe medications efficiently. To do this, they must be able to evaluate a customer's needs, evaluate the prescriber's orders, and have extensive knowledge about the effects and appropriate circumstances for giving out a specific medication.

Communication skills. Pharmacists frequently offer advice to customers. They might need to explain how to take a medicine, for example, and what its side effects are. They also need to offer clear direction to pharmacy technicians and interns.

Detail oriented. Pharmacists are responsible for ensuring the accuracy of the prescriptions they fill, because improper use of medication can pose serious health risks.

Managerial skills. Pharmacists—particularly those who run a retail pharmacy— must have good managerial skills, including managing inventory and overseeing a staff.

Pay

Pharmacists
Median annual wages, May 2010

Pharmacists	$111,570
Health Diagnosing and Treating Practitioners	$71,490
Total, All Occupations	$33,840

Note: All Occupations includes all occupations in the U.S. Economy.
Source: U.S. Bureau of Labor Statistics, Occupational Employment Statistics

The median wage of pharmacists was $111,570 in May 2010. The median wage is the wage at which half the workers in an occupation earned more than that amount and half earned less. The lowest 10 percent earned less than $82,090, and the top 10 percent earned more than $138,620.

Most pharmacists work full time, although about 21 percent worked part time in 2010. Because pharmacies are often open at all hours, some pharmacists work nights and weekends.

Job Outlook

Pharmacists
Percent change in employment, projected 2010-20

Health Diagnosing and Treating Practitioners	26%
Pharmacists	25%
Total, All Occupations	14%

Note: All Occupations includes all occupations in the U.S. Economy.
Source: U.S. Bureau of Labor Statistics, Employment Projections program

Employment of pharmacists is expected to increase by 25 percent from 2010 to 2020, faster than the average for all occupations. Several factors are likely to contribute to this increase. Scientific advances will lead to new drug products. More people may get insurance coverage for medications. The number of older people is growing, and older people use more prescription medicines than younger people. As healthcare continues to become more complex and as more people take multiple medications, more pharmacists will be needed to counsel patients on how to use their medications safely.

Demand is also likely to increase for pharmacists in physicians' offices, outpatient care centers, and nursing homes.

Job Prospects

Because a significant number of pharmacists are expected to retire in the coming decade, new pharmacists should expect good job prospects.

Employment projections data for pharmacists, 2010-20

Occupational Title	SOC Code	Employment, 2010	Projected Employment, 2020	Change, 2010-20 Percent	Numeric
Pharmacists	29-1051	274,900	344,600	25	69,700
SOURCE: U.S. Bureau of Labor Statistics, Employment Projections program					

Similar Occupations

This table shows a list of occupations with job duties that are similar to those of pharmacists.

Occupation	Job Duties	Entry-Level Education	Median Annual Pay, May 2010
Biochemists and Biophysicists	Biochemists and biophysicists study the chemical and physical principles of living things and of biological processes such as cell development, growth, and heredity.	Doctoral or professional degree	$79,390

Medical Scientists	Medical scientists conduct research aimed at improving overall human health. They often use clinical trials and other investigative methods to reach their findings.	Doctoral or professional degree	$76,700
Pharmacy Technicians	Pharmacy technicians help licensed pharmacists dispense prescription medication.	High school diploma or equivalent	$28,400
Physicians and Surgeons	Physicians and surgeons diagnose and treat injuries and illnesses in patients. Physicians examine patients, take medical histories, prescribe medications, and order, perform, and interpret diagnostic tests. Surgeons operate on patients to treat injuries, such as broken bones; diseases, such as cancerous tumors; and deformities, such as cleft palates.	Doctoral or professional degree	This wage is equal to or greater than $166,400 per year.
Registered Nurses	Registered nurses (RNs) provide and coordinate patient care, educate patients and the public about various health conditions, and provide advice and emotional support to patients and their family members.	Associate's degree	$64,690

Contacts for More Information

For more information about pharmacists, visit American Society of Health-System Pharmacists , National Association of Chain Drug Stores American Pharmacists Association

For information on pharmacy as a career, preprofessional and professional requirements, programs offered by colleges of pharmacy, and student financial aid, visit American Association of Colleges of Pharmacy

Suggested citation:

Bureau of Labor Statistics, U.S. Department of Labor, Occupational Outlook Handbook, 2012-13 Edition, Pharmacists, on the Internet at http://www.bls.gov/ooh/healthcare/pharmacists.htm .

Pharmacy Technicians

Quick Facts: Pharmacy Technicians	
2010 Median Pay	$28,400 per year $13.65 per hour
Entry-Level Education	High school diploma or equivalent
Work Experience in a Related Occupation	None
On-the-Job Training	Moderate-term on-the-job training
Number of Jobs, 2010	334,400
Job Outlook, 2010-20	32% (Much faster than average)
Employment Change, 2010-20	108,300

What Pharmacy Technicians Do

Pharmacy technicians help licensed pharmacists dispense prescription medication. They work in retail pharmacies and hospitals.

Duties

Pharmacy technicians typically do the following:

- Take from customers or health professionals the information needed to fill a prescription
- Count tablets and measure amounts of other medication for prescriptions
- Compound or mix medications, such as preparing ointments
- Package and label prescriptions
- Accept payment for prescriptions and process insurance claims
- Do routine pharmacy tasks, such as answering phone calls from customers

Pharmacy technicians work under the supervision of pharmacists, who must review all prescriptions before they are given to patients. If a customer's question is about the medication or health matters, the pharmacy technician arranges for the customer to speak with the pharmacist.

Pharmacy technicians working in hospitals and other medical facilities prepare a greater variety of medications, such as intravenous medications. They may make rounds in the hospital, giving medications to patients.

Work Environment

Pharmacy technicians held about 334,400 jobs in 2010. They worked primarily in pharmacies, including those found in grocery and drug stores, and in hospitals. Pharmacy technicians spend most of the workday on their feet.

As shown in the following tabulation, more than half of pharmacy technicians were employed in pharmacies and drug stores in 2010.

Pharmacies and drug stores	54%
Hospitals; state, local, and private	18
Grocery stores	7
Other general merchandise stores	7
Department stores	5

Work Schedules

Pharmacies may be open at all hours. Therefore, pharmacy technicians may have to work nights or weekends. Although most pharmacy technicians work full time, many work part time.

Pharmacy technicians field customers' phone calls and perform other administrative duties in pharmacies.

How to Become a Pharmacy Technician

Becoming a pharmacy technician usually requires earning a high school diploma or the equivalent. Other requirements vary by state, with some states requiring passing an exam or completing a formal training program.

Education and Training

Many pharmacy technicians learn how to perform their duties through on-the-job training. Others attend postsecondary education programs in pharmacy technology at vocational schools or community colleges, which award certificates. These programs typically last 1 year or less and cover a variety of subjects, such as arithmetic used in pharmacies, recordkeeping, ways of dispensing medications, and pharmacy law and ethics. Technicians also learn the names, actions, uses, and doses of medications. Many training programs include internships, in which students get hands-on experience in a pharmacy.

Licenses and Certification

Most states regulate pharmacy technicians in some way. Consult your state's Board of Pharmacy for its particular regulations. Requirements for pharmacy technicians typically include some or all of the following:
- High school diploma or GED
- Criminal background check
- Formal training program
- Exam
- Fees
- Continuing education

Some states and employers require pharmacy technicians to have certification. Even where it is not required, certification may make it easier to get a job. Many employers will pay for their pharmacy technicians to take the certification exam.

Two organizations offer certification: The Pharmacy Technician Certification Board (PTCB) and the National Healthcareer Association (NHA).

Important Qualities

Customer service skills. Pharmacy technicians spend much of their time interacting with customers, so being helpful and polite are required of pharmacy technicians in a retail setting.

Detail oriented. Serious health problems can result from mistakes in filling prescriptions. Although the pharmacist is responsible for ensuring the safety of all medications dispensed, pharmacy technicians should be detail oriented so complications are avoided.

Organizational skills. Working as a pharmacy technician involves balancing a variety of responsibilities. Pharmacy technicians need good organizational skills to complete the work delegated by pharmacists while satisfying customers or patients.

Pay

Pharmacy Technicians
Median annual wages, May 2010

Health Technologists and Technicians	$39,340
Total, All Occupations	$33,840
Pharmacy Technicians	$28,400

Note: All Occupations includes all occupations in the U.S. Economy.
Source: U.S. Bureau of Labor Statistics, Occupational Employment Statistics

The median annual wage of pharmacy technicians was $28,400 in May 2010. The median wage is the wage at which half the workers in an occupation earned more than that amount and half earned less. The lowest 10 percent earned less than $19,840, and the top 10 percent earned more than $40,710.

As shown in the tabulation below, median annual wages for pharmacy technicians in hospitals were $32,400 in May 2010, highest among those industries employing much of the occupation:

Hospitals; state, local, and private	$32,400
Grocery stores	28,720
Pharmacies and drug stores	27,160
Department stores	25,780
Other general merchandise stores	25,330

Pharmacies may be open at all hours. Therefore, pharmacy technicians may have to work nights or weekends. Although most pharmacy technicians work full time, many work part time.

Job Outlook

Pharmacy Technicians
Percent change in employment, projected 2010-20

Pharmacy Technicians	32%
Health Technologists and Technicians	26%
Total, All Occupations	14%

Note: All Occupations includes all occupations in the U.S. Economy.
Source: U.S. Bureau of Labor Statistics, Employment Projections program

Employment of pharmacy technicians is expected to grow by 32 percent from 2010 to 2020, much faster than the average for all occupations. As a result of advances in pharmaceutical research, more prescription medications are being used to fight diseases. Also, the number of older people is growing, and older people use more prescription drugs than younger people.

Job Prospects

Job prospects should be excellent for pharmacy technicians, particularly those with formal training and those with experience in retail settings.

Employment projections data for pharmacy technicians, 2010-20

Occupational Title	SOC Code	Employment, 2010	Projected Employment, 2020	Change, 2010-20	
				Percent	Numeric
Pharmacy Technicians	29-2052	334,400	442,600	32	108,300
SOURCE: U.S. Bureau of Labor Statistics, Employment Projections program					

Similar Occupations

This table shows a list of occupations with job duties that are similar to those of pharmacy technicians.

Occupation	Job Duties	Entry-Level Education	Median Annual Pay, May 2010
Dental Assistants	Dental assistants have many tasks, ranging from patient care to record keeping, in a dental office. Their duties vary by state and by the dentists' offices where they work.	Postsecondary non-degree award	$33,470
Medical Assistants	Medical assistants complete administrative and clinical tasks in the offices of physicians, podiatrists, chiropractors, and other health practitioners. Their duties vary with the location, specialty, and size of the practice.	High school diploma or equivalent	$28,860
Medical Records and Health Information Technicians	Medical records and health information technicians organize and manage health information data by ensuring its quality, accuracy, accessibility, and security in both paper and electronic systems. They use various classification systems to code and categorize patient information for reimbursement purposes, for databases and registries, and to maintain patients' medical and treatment histories.	Postsecondary non-degree award	$32,350
Medical Transcriptionists	Medical transcriptionists listen to voice recordings that physicians and other health professionals make and convert them into written reports. They interpret medical terminology and abbreviations in preparing patients' medical histories, discharge summaries, and other documents.	Postsecondary non-degree award	$32,900
Pharmacists	Pharmacists dispense prescription medications to patients and offer advice on their safe use.	Doctoral or professional degree	$111,570

Contacts for More Information

For information on becoming a pharmacy technician, visit National Pharmacy Technician Association

Suggested citation:

Bureau of Labor Statistics, U.S. Department of Labor, Occupational Outlook Handbook, 2012-13 Edition, Pharmacy Technicians, on the Internet at http://www.bls.gov/ooh/healthcare/pharmacy-technicians.htm .

Physical Therapist Assistants and Aides

Quick Facts: Physical Therapist Assistants and Aides	
2010 Median Pay	$37,710 per year $18.13 per hour
Entry-Level Education	See How to Become One
Work Experience in a Related Occupation	None
On-the-job Training	See How to Become One
Number of Jobs, 2010	114,400
Job Outlook, 2010-20	45% (Much faster than average)
Employment Change, 2010-20	51,100

What Physical Therapist Assistants and Aides Do

Both physical therapist assistants and physical therapist aides work under the direction of physical therapists. They help patients who are recovering from injuries, illnesses, and surgery regain movement and manage pain. Physical therapist assistants are involved in the direct care of patients. Physical therapist aides often do tasks that are indirectly related to patient care, such as cleaning and setting up the treatment area, moving patients, and clerical tasks.

Duties

Physical therapist assistants typically do the following:

- Observe patients before and during therapy, noting their status and reporting to a physical therapist
- Help patients do specific exercises
- Use a variety of techniques, such as massage and stretching, to treat patients

Physical therapist assistants and physical therapist aides help patients recovering from injuries, illnesses, and surgery regain movement and manage pain.

- Use devices and equipment, such as walkers, to help patients
- Educate a patient and family members about what to do after treatment

Physical therapist aides typically do the following:

- Clean treatment areas and set up therapy equipment
- Help patients move to or from a therapy area
- Do clerical tasks, such as answering phones or helping patients with insurance paperwork

Physical therapist assistants help physical therapists provide care to patients. Under the direction and supervision of physical therapists, they give therapy through exercise; therapeutic methods, such as electrical stimulation, mechanical traction, and ultrasound; massage; and gait and balance training. Physical therapist assistants record patients' responses to treatment and report the results of each treatment to the physical therapist.

Physical therapist aides help make therapy sessions productive, under the direct supervision of a physical therapist or physical therapist assistant. They usually are responsible for keeping the treatment area clean and organized and for preparing for each patient's therapy. They also help patients who need assistance moving to or from a treatment area.

In states where physical therapist assistants must be licensed, aides are not licensed and so cannot do tasks involving direct patient care. The duties of aides include some clerical tasks, such as ordering depleted supplies and filling out insurance forms and other paperwork.

Work Environment

Physical therapist assistants held about 67,400 jobs in 2010. Physical therapist aides held about 47,000 jobs in 2010.

As shown below, more than half of all physical therapist assistants worked in ambulatory health care services in 2010:

Ambulatory health care services	55%
Hospitals; state, local, and private	28
Nursing and residential care facilities	12

As shown below, almost 25 percent of physical therapist aides worked in hospitals in 2010:

Ambulatory health care services	61%
Hospitals; state, local, and private	24
Nursing and residential care facilities	9

Physical therapist assistants and aides are frequently on their feet and moving as they set up equipment and help and treat patients.

Work Schedules

Most physical therapist assistants and aides work full time. About one in four worked part time in 2010. Many physical therapy offices and clinics have evening and weekend hours to match patients' personal schedules.

How to Become a Physical Therapist Assistant or Aide

·Most states require physical therapist assistants to have an associate's degree from an accredited physical therapist program. Physical therapist aides usually have a high school diploma and get on-the-job training.

Education

Most states require physical therapist assistants to have an associate's degree from an accredited physical therapist program. In 2011, there were 280 associate's degree programs for physical therapist assistants accredited by the Commission on Accreditation in Physical Therapy Education .

Programs are divided into academic coursework and clinical experience. Academic courses include algebra, English, anatomy and physiology, and psychology. Clinical work includes certifications in cardiopulmonary resuscitation (CPR) and other first aid and hands-on experience in treatment centers. Many physical therapist assistants and aides continue their formal education to qualify for jobs in administration, management, and education.

Physical therapist aides typically have a high school diploma or equivalent. They commonly get clinical experience through on-the-job training. This training can last from a few weeks to several months.

Important Qualities

Compassion. Physical therapy is an important part of the recovery process for people who have been through surgeries, illnesses, and injuries. Physical therapist assistants and aides should enjoy helping people.

Detail oriented. Like other healthcare professionals, physical therapist assistants and aides should be organized and have a keen eye for detail. They must keep accurate records and follow written instructions carefully to ensure quality care.

Dexterity. Physical therapist assistants should be comfortable using their hands to provide manual therapy and therapeutic exercises. Aides should also be comfortable working with their hands to set up equipment and prepare treatment areas.

Interpersonal skills. Both physical therapist assistants and aides spend much of their time interacting with clients. They should be courteous and friendly.

Physical stamina. Physical therapist assistants and aides are frequently on their feet and moving as they work with their patients. They must often kneel, stoop, bend, and stand for long periods. They should enjoy physical activity.

Licenses

Most states require physical therapist assistants to be licensed. Licensure typically requires graduation from an accredited physical therapist assistant program and passing the Physical National Physical Therapy Exam. Some states require additional state-administered exams. In some states, physical therapist assistants also need to take continuing education courses. Check with your state licensing board .

Physical therapist aides are not required to be licensed.

Pay

Physical Therapist Assistants and Aides
Median annual wages, May 2010

Physical Therapist Assistants	$49,690
Physical Therapist Assistants and Aides	$37,710
Total, All Occupations	$33,840
Physical Therapist Aides	$23,680

Note: All Occupations includes all occupations in the U.S. Economy.
Source: U.S. Bureau of Labor Statistics, Occupational Employment Statistics

The median annual wage of physical therapist assistants was $49,690 in May 2010. The median annual wage is the wage at which half the workers in an occupation earned more than that amount and half earned less. The lowest 10 percent earned less than $31,070, and the top 10 percent earned more than $68,820.

The median annual wage of physical therapist aides was $23,680 in May 2010. The lowest 10 percent earned less than $17,270, and the top 10 percent earned more than $34,670.

Most physical therapist assistants and aides work full time. About one in four worked part time in 2010. Many physical therapy offices and clinics have evening and weekend hours to match patients' personal schedules.

Job Outlook

Physical Therapist Assistants and Aides
Percent change in employment, projected 2010-20

Physical Therapist Assistants	46%
Physical Therapist Assistants and Aides	45%
Physical Therapist Aides	43%
Total, All Occupations	14%

Note: All Occupations includes all occupations in the U.S. Economy.
Source: U.S. Bureau of Labor Statistics, Employment Projections program

Employment of physical therapist assistants is expected to increase 46 percent from 2010 to 2020, much faster than the average for all occupations.

Employment of physical therapist aides is expected to increase 43 percent from 2010 to 2020, much faster than the average for all occupations.

Employment of physical therapist assistants is projected to grow faster than that of aides, as assistants deliver therapy services directly.

Demand for physical therapy services is expected to increase in response to the health needs of an aging population, particularly the large baby-boom generation. This group is staying more active later in life than previous generations.

However, baby boomers also are entering the prime age for heart attacks and strokes, increasing the demand for cardiac and physical rehabilitation. Older people are particularly vulnerable to chronic and debilitating conditions that require therapeutic services. These patients often need additional help in their treatment, making the roles of assistants and aides vital.

Medical and technological developments should permit an increased percentage of trauma victims and newborns with birth defects to survive, creating added demand for therapy and rehabilitative services.

Physical therapists are expected to increasingly use assistants and aides to reduce the cost of physical therapy services. Once the physical therapist has evaluated a patient and designed a treatment plan, the physical therapist assistant can provide many parts of the treatment, as directed by the therapist.

In addition, changes to restrictions on reimbursements for physical therapy services by third-party payers will increase patient access to services and increase demand.

Job Prospects

Opportunities for physical therapist assistants are expected to be very good. With help from physical therapist assistants, physical therapists can manage more patients.

However, physical therapy aides may face keen competition from the large pool of qualified people.

Job opportunities should be particularly good in acute hospital, skilled nursing, and orthopedic settings, where the elderly are most often treated. Job prospects should be especially favorable in rural areas, as many physical therapists cluster in highly populated urban and suburban areas.

Employment projections data for physical therapist assistants and aides, 2010-20

Occupational Title	SOC Code	Employment, 2010	Projected Employment, 2020	Change, 2010-20	
				Percent	Numeric
Physical Therapist Assistants and Aides	31-2020	114,400	165,500	45	51,100
Physical Therapist Assistants	31-2021	67,400	98,200	46	30,800
Physical Therapist Aides	31-2022	47,000	67,300	43	20,300
SOURCE: U.S. Bureau of Labor Statistics, Employment Projections program					

Similar Occupations

This table shows a list of occupations with job duties that are similar to those of physical therapist assistants and aides.

Occupation	Job Duties	Entry-Level Education	Median Annual Pay, May 2010
Dental Assistants	Dental assistants have many tasks, ranging from patient care to record keeping, in a dental office. Their duties vary by state and by the dentists' offices where they work.	Postsecondary non-degree award	$33,470
Medical Assistants	Medical assistants complete administrative and clinical tasks in the offices of physicians, podiatrists, chiropractors, and other health practitioners. Their duties vary with the location, specialty, and size of the practice.	High school diploma or equivalent	$28,860
Nursing Aides, Orderlies, and Attendants	Nursing aides, orderlies, and attendants help provide basic care for patients in hospitals and residents of long-term care facilities, such as nursing homes.	Postsecondary non-degree award	$24,010
Occupational Health and Safety Technicians	Occupational health and safety technicians collect data on the safety and health conditions of the workplace. Technicians work with occupational health and safety specialists in conducting tests and measuring hazards to help prevent harm to workers, property, the environment, and the general public.	High school diploma or equivalent	$45,330
Pharmacy Technicians	Pharmacy technicians help licensed pharmacists dispense prescription medication.	High school diploma or equivalent	$28,400
Physical Therapists	Physical therapists help people who have injuries or illnesses improve their movement and manage their pain. They are often an important part of rehabilitation and treatment of patients with chronic conditions or injuries.	Doctoral or professional degree	$76,310
Psychiatric Technicians and Aides	Psychiatric technicians and aides care for people who have mental illness and developmental disabilities. The two occupations are related, but technicians typically provide therapeutic care, and aides help patients in their daily activities and ensure a safe, clean environment.	See How to Become One	$26,880

Contacts for More Information

For more information about physical therapist assistants, including a list of schools offering accredited programs, visit American Physical Therapy Association , Federation of State Boards of Physical Therapy

Suggested citation:

Bureau of Labor Statistics, U.S. Department of Labor, Occupational Outlook Handbook, 2012-13 Edition, Physical Therapist Assistants and Aides, on the Internet at http://www.bls.gov/ooh/healthcare/physical-therapist-assistants-and-aides.htm .

Physical Therapists

Quick Facts: Physical Therapists	
2010 Median Pay	$76,310 per year $36.69 per hour
Entry-Level Education	Doctoral or professional degree
Work Experience in a Related Occupation	None
On-the-job Training	None
Number of Jobs, 2010	198,600
Job Outlook, 2010-20	39% (Much faster than average)
Employment Change, 2010-20	77,400

What Physical Therapists Do

Physical therapists, sometimes referred to as PTs, help people who have injuries or illnesses improve their movement and manage their pain. They are often an important part of rehabilitation and treatment of patients with chronic conditions or injuries.

Duties

Physical therapists typically do the following:

- Diagnose patients' dysfunctional movements by watching them stand or walk and by listening to their concerns, among other methods
- Set up a plan for their patients, outlining the patient's goals and the planned treatments
- Use exercises, stretching maneuvers, hands-on therapy, and equipment to ease patients' pain and to help them increase their ability to move

Physical therapists help people with injuries or disabilities build and maintain mobility.

- Evaluate a patient's progress, modifying a treatment plan and trying new treatments as needed
- Educate patients and their families about what to expect during recovery from injury and illness and how best to cope with what happens

Physical therapists provide care to people of all ages who have functional problems resulting from back and neck injuries; sprains, strains, and fractures; arthritis; amputations; stroke; birth conditions, such as cerebral palsy; injuries related to work and sports; and other conditions.

Physical therapists are trained to use a variety of different techniques—sometimes called modalities—to care for their patients. These techniques include applying heat and cold, hands-on stimulation or massage, and using assistive and adaptive devices and equipment.

The work of physical therapists varies with the type of patients they serve. For example, a patient suffering from loss of mobility due to Parkinson's disease needs different care than an athlete recovering from an injury. Some physical therapists specialize in one type of care, such as pediatrics (treating children) or sports physical therapy.

Physical therapists work as part of a healthcare team, overseeing the work of physical therapist assistants and aides and consulting with physicians and surgeons and other specialists. Physical therapists also work at preventing loss of mobility by developing fitness- and wellness-oriented programs to encourage healthier and more active lifestyles. For more information, see the profiles on physical therapist assistants and aides and physicians and surgeons .

Work Environment

Physical therapists held about 198,600 jobs in 2010. Physical therapists typically work in private offices and clinics, hospitals, and nursing homes. They spend much of their time on their feet, being active. Some physical therapists are self-employed, meaning that they own or are partners in owning their practice.

As shown below, most physical therapists worked in offices of health practitioners or hospitals in 2010:

Offices of health practitioners	37%
Hospitals; state, local, and private	28
Home health care services	10
Self-employed workers	7
Nursing and residential care facilities	7

Work Schedules

Most physical therapists work full time. About 29 percent worked part time in 2010.

How to Become a Physical Therapist

Physical therapists typically need a doctoral degree in physical therapy. All states require physical therapists to be licensed.

Education

Physical therapists are required to have a postgraduate professional degree. Physical therapy programs usually award a Doctor of Physical Therapy (DPT) degree, although a small number award a Master of Physical Therapy (MPT) degree. Doctoral programs typically last 3 years; MPT programs require 2 to 3 years of study. Most programs, either DPT or MPT, require a bachelor's degree for admission, and many require specific prerequisites, such as anatomy, physiology, biology, and chemistry.

Physical therapy programs often include courses in biomechanics, anatomy, physiology, neuroscience, and pharmacology. Physical therapy students also complete clinical rotations, enabling them to gain supervised work experience in areas such as acute care and orthopedic care.

Physical therapists may apply to and complete residency programs after graduation. Residencies last 9 months to 3 years and provide additional training and experience in advanced or specialty areas of care.

Important Qualities

Compassion. Physical therapists are often drawn to the profession in part by a desire to help people. They work with people who are in pain and must have empathy to help their patients.

Detail oriented.— Like other healthcare providers, physical therapists should have strong analytic and observational skills to diagnose a patient's problem, evaluate treatments, and provide safe, effective care.

Dexterity. Physical therapists should be comfortable using their hands to provide manual therapy and therapeutic exercises.

Interpersonal skills. Because physical therapists spend their time interacting with patients, they should enjoy working with people. They must be able to explain treatment programs, educate their patients, and listen to the patients' concerns to provide effective therapy.

Physical stamina. Physical therapists spend much of their time on their feet, moving as they work with their patients. They should enjoy physical activity.

Licenses

All states require physical therapists to be licensed. Licensing requirements vary by state but typically include passing the National Physical Therapy Examination or a similar state-administered exam. A number of states require continuing education for physical therapists to keep their license.

Certification

After gaining work experience, some physical therapists choose to become board certified in a particular clinical specialty, such as pediatrics or sports physical therapy. Board certification requires passing an exam.

Pay

Physical Therapists
Median annual wages, May 2010

Physical Therapists	$76,310
Health Diagnosing and Treating Practitioners	$71,490
Total, All Occupations	$33,840

Note: All Occupations includes all occupations in the U.S. Economy.
Source: U.S. Bureau of Labor Statistics, Occupational Employment Statistics

The median annual wage of physical therapists was $76,310 in May 2010. The median annual wage is the wage at which half the workers in an occupation earned more than that amount and half earned less. The lowest 10 percent earned less than $53,620, and the top 10 percent earned more than $107,920.

Physical therapists who own their own practice or who are partners in owning their practice must provide their own benefits and those of their employees.

Most physical therapists work full time. About 29 percent worked part time in 2010.

Job Outlook

Physical Therapists
Percent change in employment, projected 2010-20

Physical Therapists	39%
Health Diagnosing and Treating Practitioners	26%
Total, All Occupations	14%

Note: All Occupations includes all occupations in the U.S. Economy.
Source: U.S. Bureau of Labor Statistics, Employment Projections program

Employment of physical therapists is expected to increase 39 percent from 2010 to 2020, much faster than the average for all occupations.

Demand for physical therapy services will come, in large part, from the aging baby boomers, who are staying active later in life than previous generations did. Older persons are more likely to suffer heart attacks, strokes, and mobility-related injuries that require physical therapy for rehabilitation.

Advances in medical technology have increased the use of outpatient surgery to treat a variety of injuries and illnesses. Physical therapists will continue to play an important role in helping these patients recover more quickly from surgery.

Medical and technological developments also are expected to permit a greater percentage of trauma victims and newborns with birth defects to survive, creating additional demand for rehabilitative care. In addition, the incidence of chronic diseases, such as diabetes, has increased in recent years, and more physical therapists will be needed to help patients manage the effects of these diseases.

Job Prospects

Job opportunities will likely be good for licensed physical therapists in all settings. Job opportunities should be particularly good in acute hospital, skilled nursing, and orthopedic settings, where the elderly are most often treated. Job prospects should be especially favorable in rural areas because many physical therapists live in highly populated urban and suburban areas.

Employment projections data for physical therapists, 2010-20

Occupational Title	SOC Code	Employment, 2010	Projected Employment, 2020	Change, 2010-20 Percent	Change, 2010-20 Numeric
Physical Therapists	29-1123	198,600	276,000	39	77,400
SOURCE: U.S. Bureau of Labor Statistics, Employment Projections program					

Similar Occupations

This table shows a list of occupations with job duties that are similar to those of physical therapists.

Occupation	Job Duties	Entry-Level Education	Median Annual Pay, May 2010
Audiologists	Audiologists diagnose and treat a patient's hearing and balance problems using advanced technology and procedures.	Doctoral or professional degree	$66,660
Chiropractors	Chiropractors treat patients with health problems of the musculoskeletal system, which is made up of bones, muscles, ligaments, and tendons. They use spinal manipulation and other techniques to treat patients' ailments, such as back or neck pain.	Doctoral or professional degree	$67,200
Occupational Therapists	Occupational therapists treat patients with injuries, illnesses, or disabilities through the therapeutic use of everyday activities. They help these patients develop, recover, and improve the skills needed for daily living and working.	Master's degree	$72,320
Recreational Therapists	Recreational therapists plan, direct, and coordinate recreation programs for people with disabilities or illnesses. They use a variety of techniques, including arts and crafts, drama, music, dance, sports, games, and field trips. These programs help maintain or improve a client's physical and emotional well-being.	Bachelor's degree	$39,410
Speech-Language Pathologists	Speech-language pathologists diagnose and treat communication and swallowing disorders in patients.	Master's degree	$66,920

Contacts for More Information

For more information about physical therapists and a list of accredited educational programs in physical therapy, visit American Physical Therapy Association

Suggested citation:

Bureau of Labor Statistics, U.S. Department of Labor, Occupational Outlook Handbook, 2012-13 Edition, Physical Therapists, on the Internet at http://www.bls.gov/ooh/healthcare/physical-therapists.htm .

Physician Assistants

Quick Facts: Physician Assistants	
2010 Median Pay	$86,410 per year $41.54 per hour
Entry-Level Education	Master's degree
Work Experience in a Related Occupation	None
On-the-job Training	None
Number of Jobs, 2010	83,600
Job Outlook, 2010-20	30% (Much faster than average)
Employment Change, 2010-20	24,700

What Physician Assistants Do

Physician assistants, also known as PAs, practice medicine under the direction and supervision of physicians and surgeons. They are formally trained to examine patients, diagnose injuries and illnesses, and provide treatment.

Duties

Physician assistants typically do the following:

- Work under the supervision of a physician or surgeon
- Review patients' medical histories
- Do physical exams to check patients' health
- Order and interpret diagnostic tests, such as x rays or blood tests
- Make preliminary diagnoses concerning a patient's injury or illness
- Provide treatment, such as setting broken bones and giving immunizations
- Counsel patients and their families; for example, answering questions about how to care for a child with asthma

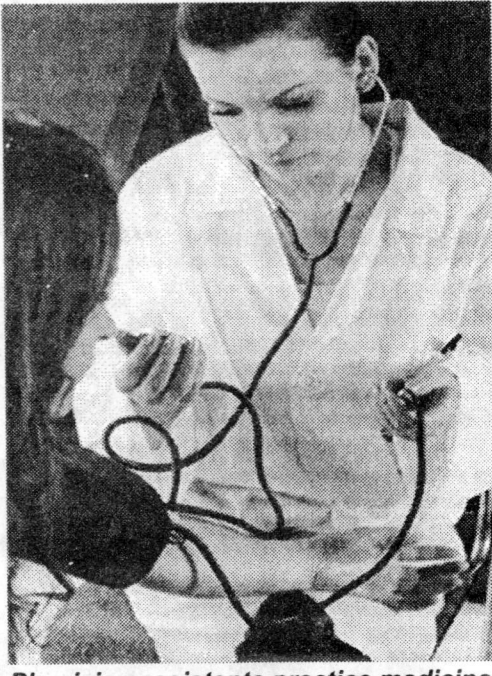

Physician assistants practice medicine under the supervision of physicians and surgeons.

- Prescribe medicine, when needed
- Record a patient's progress
- Complete insurance paperwork

Physician assistants are different from medical assistants. Medical assistants do routine clinical and clerical tasks; they do not practice medicine. For more information, see the profile on medical assistants .

A physician assistant's specific duties and the extent to which he or she must be supervised by physicians and surgeons differ from state to state.

Physician assistants work in all areas of medicine, including primary care and family medicine, emergency medicine, and psychiatry. The work of physician assistants depends in large part on their specialty and what their supervising physician needs them to do. For more information, see the profile on physicians and surgeons .

For example, a physician assistant working in surgery may close incisions and provide care before and after the operation. A physician assistant working in pediatrics may examine a child or give routine vaccinations.

In rural areas and inner cities, physician assistants may be the primary care providers at clinics where a physician is present only 1 or 2 days per week. In these locations, physician assistants confer with the physician and other healthcare workers as needed and as required by law.

Some physician assistants make house calls or visit nursing homes to treat patients, reporting back to the physician afterward.

Some physician assistants supervise medical technicians and medical assistants.

Work Environment

Physician assistants held about 83,600 jobs in 2010.

As shown below, most physician assistants worked in physicians' offices or hospitals in 2010:

Offices of physicians	54%
Hospitals; state, local, and private	24
Outpatient care centers	9
Government	4
Colleges, universities, and professional schools; state, local, and private	3

Physician assistants spend much of their time on their feet, making rounds and evaluating patients. Physician assistants who work in operating rooms often stand for extended periods.

Work Schedules

Most physician assistants work full time. About 13 percent reported working 50 hours or more per week in 2010. In hospitals, physician assistants may work nights, weekends, or holidays. They may also be on call, meaning they must be ready to respond to a work request with little notice.

How to Become a Physician Assistant

Physician assistants typically need a master's degree. Most applicants to master's programs already have a bachelor's degree and some work experience. Then, they must complete an accredited educational program for physician assistants. That usually takes at least 2 years of full-time study and typically leads to a master's degree. All states require physician assistants to be licensed.

Education

Most applicants to physician assistant education programs already have a bachelor's degree and some healthcare-related work experience. However, admissions requirements vary from program to program.

Many assistants already have experience as registered nurses, emergency medical technicians (EMTs), or paramedics before they apply to a physician assistant program. For more information, see the profiles on registered nurses and EMTs and paramedics .

Physician assistant education programs usually take at least 2 years of full-time study. In 2011, the Accreditation Review Commission on Education for the Physician Assistant accredited 165 education programs. Most of these accredited programs offer a master's degree. Others offer a bachelor's degree, and a very few award an associate's degree or graduate certificate.

These physician assistant programs are at schools of allied health, academic health centers, medical schools, and 4-year colleges. A few are part of the military or are found at community colleges or hospitals.

Physician assistant education includes classroom and laboratory instruction in subjects such as pathology, human anatomy, physiology, clinical medicine, physical diagnosis, and medical ethics. The programs also include supervised clinical training in several areas, including family medicine, internal medicine, emergency medicine, and pediatrics. Many accredited programs have clinical teaching affiliations with medical schools.

Sometimes, students serve in one or more of these areas under the supervision of a physician who is looking to hire a physician assistant. In this way, the rotation may lead to permanent employment.

Important Qualities

Compassion. Many physician assistants are drawn to the profession by a desire to help people. They should enjoy helping others.

Detail oriented. Physician assistants should be focused and observant to properly evaluate patients and follow doctor's orders.

Emotional stability. —Physician assistants, particularly those working in surgery or emergency medicine, should be able to work well under pressure. They must remain calm in stressful situations to provide quality care.

Licenses

All states and the District of Columbia require physician assistants to be licensed. To become licensed, they must pass the Physician Assistant National Certifying Examination from the National Commission on Certification of Physician Assistants (NCCPA). After they pass the exam, they may use the credential "Physician Assistant-Certified."

Physician assistants must take continuing education to keep their license. Every 6 years, they must pass a recertification exam or complete an alternative program combining learning experience and a take-home exam.

Advancement

Some physician assistants pursue additional education in a specialty. Postgraduate educational programs are available in areas such as internal medicine, rural primary care, and occupational medicine. To enter one of these programs, a physician assistant must be a graduate of an accredited program and be certified by the NCCPA.

As they get greater clinical knowledge and experience, physician assistants can earn new responsibilities and higher wages. However, by the very nature of the profession, clinically practicing physician assistants always are supervised by physicians. For more information, see the profile on physicians and surgeons .

Pay

Physician Assistants
Median annual wages, May 2010

Physician Assistants	$86,410
Health Diagnosing and Treating Practitioners	$71,490
Total, All Occupations	$33,840

Note: All Occupations includes all occupations in the U.S. Economy.
Source: U.S. Bureau of Labor Statistics, Occupational Employment Statistics

The median annual wage of physician assistants was $86,410 in May 2010. The median annual wage is the wage at which half the workers in an occupation earned more than that amount and half earned less. The lowest 10 percent earned less than $57,450, and the top 10 percent earned more than $117,720.

Median annual wages in the industries employing the largest numbers of physician assistants in May 2010 were as follows:

Hospitals; state, local, and private	$89,500
Outpatient care centers	88,160
Offices of physicians	85,340
Government	85,170
Colleges, universities, and professional schools; state, local, and private	80,810

Most physician assistants work full time. In hospitals, physician assistants may work nights, weekends, or holidays. They may also be on call, meaning they must be ready to respond to a work request with little notice.

Job Outlook

Physician Assistants
Percent change in employment, projected 2010-20

Physician Assistants	30%
Health Diagnosing and Treating Practitioners	26%
Total, All Occupations	14%

Note: All Occupations includes all occupations in the U.S. Economy.
Source: U.S. Bureau of Labor Statistics, Employment Projections program

Employment of physician assistants is expected to increase 30 percent from 2010 to 2020, much faster than the average for all occupations.

As more physicians enter specialty areas of medicine, there will be a greater need for primary healthcare providers, such as physician assistants. Because physician assistants are more cost-effective than physicians, they are expected to have an increasing role in giving routine care.

Physician assistants also will be needed because the population in general is growing. More people means more need for healthcare specialists.

In addition, employment growth is expected because the large baby-boom generation is getting older. As they age, baby boomers will be increasingly susceptible to ailments and conditions such as heart attack, stroke, and diabetes. Physician assistants are expected to have an increasing role in keeping these people healthy and caring for them when they get ill.

Healthcare providers are also expected to use more physician assistants in new ways as states continue to allow assistants to do more procedures.

Job Prospects

Good job prospects are expected. This should be particularly true for physician assistants working in rural and medically underserved areas, as well as physician assistants working in primary care.

Employment projections data for physician assistants, 2010-20

Occupational Title	SOC Code	Employment, 2010	Projected Employment, 2020	Change, 2010-20 Percent	Change, 2010-20 Numeric
Physician Assistants	29-1071	83,600	108,300	30	24,700

SOURCE: U.S. Bureau of Labor Statistics, Employment Projections program

Similar Occupations

This table shows a list of occupations with job duties that are similar to those of physician assistants.

Occupation	Job Duties	Entry-Level Education	Median Annual Pay, May 2010
Audiologists	Audiologists diagnose and treat a patient's hearing and balance problems using advanced technology and procedures.	Doctoral or professional degree	$66,660
EMTs and Paramedics	Emergency medical technicians (EMTs) and paramedics care for the sick or injured in emergency medical settings. People's lives often depend on their quick reaction and competent care. EMTs and paramedics respond to emergency calls, performing medical services and transporting patients to medical facilities.	Postsecondary non-degree award	$30,360
Occupational Therapists	Occupational therapists treat patients with injuries, illnesses, or disabilities through the therapeutic use of everyday activities. They help these patients develop, recover, and improve the skills needed for daily living and working.	Master's degree	$72,320
Physical Therapists	Physical therapists help people who have injuries or illnesses improve their movement and manage their pain. They are often an important part of rehabilitation and treatment of patients with chronic conditions or injuries.	Doctoral or professional degree	$76,310
Physicians and Surgeons	Physicians and surgeons diagnose and treat injuries and illnesses in patients. Physicians examine patients, take medical histories, prescribe medications, and order, perform, and interpret diagnostic tests. Surgeons operate on patients to treat injuries, such as broken bones; diseases, such as cancerous tumors; and deformities, such as cleft palates.	Doctoral or professional degree	This wage is equal to or greater than $166,400 per year.
Registered Nurses	Registered nurses (RNs) provide and coordinate patient care, educate patients and the public about various health conditions, and provide advice and emotional support to patients and their family members.	Associate's degree	$64,690
Speech-Language Pathologists	Speech-language pathologists diagnose and treat communication and swallowing disorders in patients.	Master's degree	$66,920

Contacts for More Information

For more information on physician assistants, including a list of accredited programs, visit American Academy of Physician Assistants

For a list of accredited physician assistant programs, visit Physician Assistant Education Association

Suggested citation:

Bureau of Labor Statistics, U.S. Department of Labor, Occupational Outlook Handbook, 2012-13 Edition, Physician Assistants, on the Internet at http://www.bls.gov/ooh/healthcare/physician-assistants.htm .

Physicians and Surgeons

Quick Facts: Physicians and Surgeons	
2010 Median Pay	This wage is equal to or greater than $166,400 per year or $80.00 per hour.
Entry-Level Education	Doctoral or professional degree
Work Experience in a Related Occupation	None
On-the-job Training	Internship/residency
Number of Jobs, 2010	691,000
Job Outlook, 2010-20	24% (Faster than average)
Employment Change, 2010-20	168,300

What Physicians and Surgeons Do

Physicians and surgeons diagnose and treat injuries or illnesses. Physicians examine patients, take medical histories, prescribe medications, and order, perform, and interpret diagnostic tests. They often counsel patients on diet, hygiene, and preventive health care. Surgeons operate on patients to treat injuries, such as broken bones; diseases, such as cancerous tumors; and deformities, such as cleft palates.

There are two types of physicians: M.D. (Medical Doctor) and D.O. (Doctor of Osteopathic Medicine). Both types of physicians use the same methods of treatment, including drugs and surgery, but D.O.s place additional emphasis on the body's musculoskeletal system, preventive medicine, and holistic (whole person) patient care.

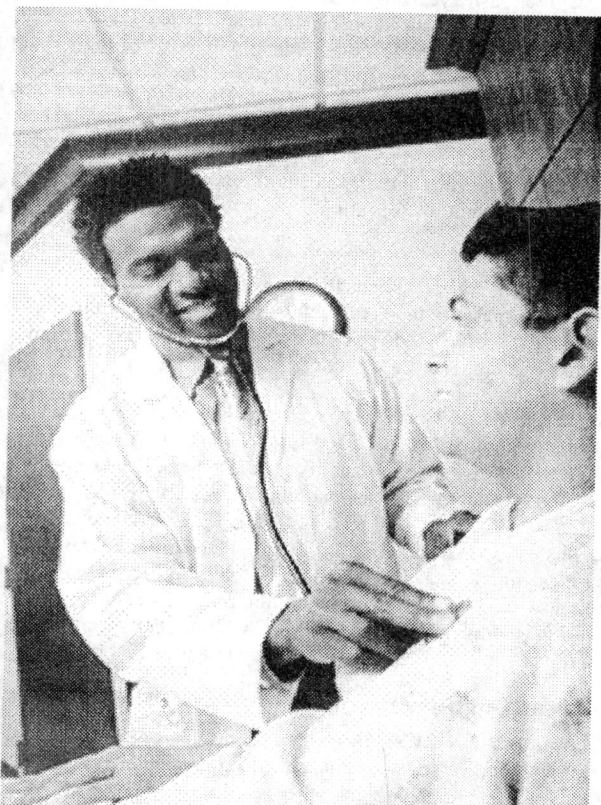

Physicians examine patients, obtain medical histories, and order, perform, and interpret diagnostic tests.

Duties

Physicians and surgeons typically do the following:

- Take a patient's medical history
- Update charts and patient information to show current findings
- Order tests for nurses or other healthcare staff to do
- Review test results to identify any abnormal findings
- Recommend and design a plan of treatment
- Answer concerns or questions that patients have about their health and well-being
- Help patients take care of their health by discussing topics such as proper nutrition and hygiene

In addition, surgeons operate on patients to treat injuries, diseases, or deformities.

Physicians and surgeons work in one or more of several specialties. The following are some of the many types of physicians and surgeons:

Anesthesiologists focus on the care of surgical patients and pain relief. They administer the drugs (anesthetics) that reduce or eliminate the sensation of pain during an operation or other medical procedure. During surgery, they are responsible for adjusting the amount of anesthetic as needed and monitoring the patient's heart rate, body temperature, blood pressure, and breathing. They also work outside of the operating room, providing pain relief in the intensive care unit, during labor and delivery, and for those who suffer from chronic pain. Anesthesiologists work with other physicians and surgeons to decide on treatments and procedures before, during, and after surgery.

Family and general physicians assess and treat a range of conditions that occur in everyday life. These conditions include anything from sinus and respiratory infections to broken bones. Family and general physicians typically have a base of regular, long-term patients. These doctors sometimes refer patients with more serious conditions to specialists or other healthcare facilities for additional care.

General internists diagnose and provide nonsurgical treatment for a range of problems that affect internal organ systems such as the stomach, kidneys, liver, and digestive tract. Internists use a variety of diagnostic techniques to treat patients through medication or hospitalization. They may refer patients to other specialists when more complex care is required. They work mostly with adult patients.

General pediatricians provide care for infants, children, teenagers, and young adults. They specialize in diagnosing and treating problems specific to younger people. Most pediatricians treat day-to-day illnesses, minor injuries, and infectious diseases and administer vaccinations. Some pediatricians specialize in pediatric surgery or serious medical conditions that commonly affect younger patients, such as autoimmune disorders or serious chronic ailments.

Obstetricians and gynecologists (OB/GYNs) provide care related to pregnancy and the female reproductive system. OB/GYNs specialize in childbirth. They treat and counsel women throughout their pregnancy, and they deliver babies. They also diagnose and treat health issues specific to women, such as breast cancer, cervical cancer, hormonal disorders, and symptoms related to menopause.

Psychiatrists are primary mental health physicians. They diagnose and treat mental illnesses through a combination of personal counseling (psychotherapy), psychoanalysis, hospitalization, and medication. Psychotherapy involves regular discussions with patients about their problems. The psychiatrist helps them find solutions through changes in their behavioral patterns, exploring their past experiences, or group and family therapy sessions. Psychoanalysis involves long-term psychotherapy and counseling for patients. Psychiatrists may prescribe medications to correct chemical imbalances that cause some mental illnesses.

Surgeons specialize in treating injury, disease, and deformity through operations. Using a variety of instruments, and with patients under anesthesia, a surgeon corrects physical deformities, repairs bone and tissue after injuries, or performs preventive surgeries on patients. Although a large number perform general surgery, many surgeons choose to specialize in a specific area. Specialties include orthopedic surgery (the treatment of the musculoskeletal system), neurological surgery (treatment of the brain and nervous system), cardiovascular surgery, and plastic or reconstructive surgery. Like other physicians, surgeons also examine patients, perform and interpret diagnostic tests, and counsel patients on preventive healthcare. Some specialist physicians also perform surgery.

D.O.s are most likely to be primary care physicians, although they can be found in all specialties. About 60 percent of D.O.s specialize in primary care areas such as family medicine, internal medicine, OB/GYN, and pediatrics.

Among physicians and surgeons who work in a number of other medical and surgical specialists and subspecialties are allergists (specialists in diagnosing and treating hay fever and other allergies), cardiologists (heart specialists), dermatologists (skin specialists), gastroenterologists, (specialists in the digestive system), pathologists (who study body tissue to see if it is normal), radiologists (who review and interpret x-ray pictures and deliver radiation treatments for cancer and other illnesses), and many others.

Physicians work daily with other healthcare staff, such as nurses, other physicians, and medical assistants. For more information, see the profiles on registered nurses and medical assistants .

Work Environment

Physicians and surgeons held about 691,000 jobs in 2010. Many physicians work in private offices or clinics, often helped by a small staff of nurses and administrative personnel.

Increasingly, physicians work in group practices, health care organizations, or hospitals where they share a large number of patients with other doctors. The group setting gives doctors backup coverage, allows them more time off, and lets them coordinate care for their patients, but it gives them less independence than solo practitioners have.

Surgeons and anesthesiologists usually work in sterile environments while performing surgery and may stand for long periods.

Work Schedules

Many physicians and surgeons work long, irregular, and overnight hours. Physicians and surgeons may travel between their offices and hospitals to care for their patients. While on call, a physician may need to address a patient's concerns over the phone or make an emergency visit to a hospital or nursing home.

How to Become a Physician or Surgeon

Physicians and surgeons have demanding education and training requirements. Almost all physicians complete at least 4 years of undergraduate school, 4 years of medical school, and 3 to 8 years in internship and residency programs, depending on their specialty.

Education

Most applicants to medical school have at least a bachelor's degree, and many have advanced degrees. While a specific major is not required, all students must complete undergraduate work in biology, chemistry, physics, mathematics, and English. Students also take courses in the humanities and social sciences. Some students volunteer at local hospitals or clinics to gain experience in a healthcare setting.

Medical schools are highly competitive. Most applicants must submit transcripts, scores from the Medical College Admission Test (MCAT), and letters of recommendation. Schools also consider an applicant's personality, leadership qualities, and participation in extracurricular activities. Most schools require applicants to interview with members of the admissions committee.

A few medical schools offer combined undergraduate and medical school programs that last 6 or 7 years.

Students spend most of the first 2 years of medical school in laboratories and classrooms, taking courses such as anatomy, biochemistry, pharmacology, psychology, medical ethics, and the laws governing medicine. They also gain practical skills, learning to take medical histories, examine patients, and diagnose illnesses.

During their last 2 years, medical students work with patients under the supervision of experienced physicians in hospitals and clinics. Through rotations in internal medicine, family practice, obstetrics and gynecology, pediatrics, psychiatry, and surgery, they gain experience in diagnosing and treating illnesses in a variety of areas.

Physician education is very expensive. According to the Association of American Medical Colleges , 88 percent of public medical school graduates and 85 percent of private medical school graduates were in debt for educational expenses in 2010.

Training

After medical school, almost all graduates enter a residency program in the specialty they are interested in. A residency usually takes place in a hospital and varies in duration, usually lasting from 3 to 8 years, depending on the specialty.

Licenses

All states require physicians and surgeons to be licensed; requirements vary by state. To qualify for a license, candidates must graduate from an accredited medical school, complete residency training in their specialty, and pass written and practical exams.

All physicians and surgeons must pass a standardized national licensure examination. M.D.s take the U.S. Medical Licensing Examination (USMLE). D.O.s take the Comprehensive Osteopathic Medical Licensing Examination (COMLEX-USA). For specific state information about licensing, contact your state's medical board.

Important Qualities

Communication skills. Physicians and surgeons need to be excellent communicators. They must be able to communicate effectively with their patients and other healthcare support staff.

Detail oriented. Physicians and surgeons must ensure that patients are receiving appropriate treatment and medications. They must also monitor and record various pieces of information related to patient care.

Dexterity. Physicians and surgeons must be good at working with their hands. They work with very precise and sometimes sharp tools, and mistakes can have serious consequences.

Empathy. Physicians and surgeons deal with patients who are sick or injured. Some patients have long-term medical problems. Physicians and surgeons must be able to treat patients and their families with compassion and understanding.

Leadership skills. Physicians who work in their own practice need to be effective leaders. They must be able to manage a staff of other professionals to run their practice.

Organizational skills. Some physicians own their own practice. Strong organizational skills, including good recordkeeping, are critical in both medical and business settings.

Patience. Physicians and surgeons may work for long periods with patients who need special attention. Children and patients with a fear of medical treatment may require more patience.

Physical stamina. Physicians and surgeons should be comfortable performing physical tasks, such as lifting or turning disabled patients. Surgeons may spend a great deal of time bending over patients during surgery.

Problem-solving skills. Physicians and surgeons need to evaluate patients' symptoms and administer the appropriate treatments. They often need to do this quickly in order to save a patient's life.

Certification

Certification is not required for physicians and surgeons; however, it may increase their employment opportunities. M.D.s and D.O.s seeking board certification in a specialty may spend up to 7 years in residency training; the length of time varies by specialty. An examination after residency is required for certification by the American Board of Medical Specialties (ABMS) or the American Osteopathic Association (AOA).

Pay

Physicians and Surgeons
Median annual wages, May 2010

Physicians and Surgeons This wage is	equal to or greater than $166,400
Health Diagnosing and Treating Practitioners	$71,490
Total, All Occupations	$33,840

Note: All Occupations includes all occupations in the U.S. Economy.
Source: U.S. Bureau of Labor Statistics, Occupational Employment Statistics

Wages of physicians and surgeons are among the highest of all occupations. According to the Medical Group Management Association's Physician Compensation and Production Survey, median total compensation for physicians varied by their type of practice. In 2010, physicians practicing primary care received total median annual compensation of $202,392, and physicians practicing in medical specialties received total median annual compensation of $356,885.

Median annual compensations for selected specialties in 2010, as reported by the Medical Group Management Association, were as follows:

Anesthesiology	$407,292
General surgery	343,958
Obstetrics/gynecology	281,190
Internal medicine	205,379
Psychiatry	200,694
Pediatrics/adolecent medicine	192,148
Family practice (without obstetrics)	189,402

Earnings vary with the physician's or surgeon's number of years in practice, geographic region of practice, hours worked, skill, personality, and professional reputation.

Job Outlook

Physicians and Surgeons
Percent change in employment, projected 2010-20

Health Diagnosing and Treating Practitioners	26%
Physicians and Surgeons	24%
Total, All Occupations	14%

Note: All Occupations includes all occupations in the U.S. Economy.
Source: U.S. Bureau of Labor Statistics, Employment Projections program

Employment of physicians and surgeons is expected to grow by 24 percent from 2010 to 2020, faster than the average for all occupations. Job growth will occur because of the continued expansion of healthcare-related industries. The growing and aging population is expected to drive overall growth in the demand for physician services as consumers continue to seek high levels of care that uses the latest technologies, diagnostic tests, and therapies. Many medical schools are increasing their enrollments based on perceived higher demand for physicians.

Although the demand for physicians and surgeons should continue, some factors will likely reduce growth. New technologies will allow physicians to treat more patients in the same amount of time, thereby reducing the number of physicians who would be needed to complete the same tasks. Physician assistants and nurse practitioners (a type of registered nurse) can do many of the routine duties of physicians and may increasingly be used to reduce costs at hospitals and outpatient care facilities. For more information, see the profiles on physician assistants and registered nurses.

Furthermore, demand for physicians' services is sensitive to changes in healthcare reimbursement policies. Consumers may demand fewer physician services if changes to health coverage result in higher out-of-pocket costs for them.

Job Prospects

Job prospects should be good for physicians who are willing to practice in rural and low-income areas, because these areas tend to have difficulty attracting physicians. Job prospects also should be good for physicians in specialties dealing with health issues that largely affect aging baby boomers. For example, physicians specializing in cardiology and radiology will be needed because the risks for heart disease and cancer increase as people age.

Employment projections data for physicians and surgeons, 2010-20

Occupational Title	SOC Code	Employment, 2010	Projected Employment, 2020	Change, 2010-20	
				Percent	Numeric
Physicians and Surgeons	29-1060	691,000	859,300	24	168,300
SOURCE: U.S. Bureau of Labor Statistics, Employment Projections program					

Similar Occupations

This table shows a list of occupations with job duties that are similar to those of physicians and surgeons.

Occupation	Job Duties	Entry-Level Education	Median Annual Pay, May 2010
Chiropractors	Chiropractors treat patients with health problems of the musculoskeletal system, which is made up of bones, muscles, ligaments, and tendons. They use spinal manipulation and other techniques to treat patients' ailments, such as back or neck pain.	Doctoral or professional degree	$67,200
Optometrists	Optometrists perform eye exams to check for vision problems and diseases. They prescribe eyeglasses or contact lenses as needed.	Doctoral or professional degree	$94,990
Physician Assistants	Physician assistants, also known as PAs, practice medicine under the direction of physicians and surgeons. They are formally trained to examine patients, diagnose injuries and illnesses, and provide treatment.	Master's degree	$86,410
Podiatrists	Podiatrists provide medical and surgical care for people suffering foot, ankle, and lower leg problems. They diagnose illnesses, treat injuries, and perform surgery.	Doctoral or professional degree	$118,030
Registered Nurses	Registered nurses (RNs) provide and coordinate patient care, educate patients and the public about various health conditions, and provide advice and emotional support to patients and their family members.	Associate's degree	$64,690
Dentists	Dentists diagnose and treat problems with a patient's teeth, gums, and other parts of the mouth. They provide advice and instruction on taking care of teeth and gums and on diet choices that affect oral health.	Doctoral or professional degree	$146,920
Veterinarians	Veterinarians care for the health of animals. They diagnose, treat, or research medical conditions and diseases of pets, livestock, and animals in zoos, racetracks, and laboratories.	Doctoral or professional degree	$82,040

Contacts for More Information

For more information about physicians and surgeons, visit American Medical Association , American Osteopathic Association

For information about various medical specialties, visit American Academy of Family Physicians , American Board of Medical Specialties ,American Congress of Obstetricians and Gynecologists ,American College of Surgeons

For a list of medical schools and residency programs, as well as for general information on premedical education, financial aid, and medicine as a career, visit Association of American Medical Colleges , American Association of Colleges of Osteopathic Medicine

For information about licensing, visit Federation of State Medical Boards

Suggested citation:

Bureau of Labor Statistics, U.S. Department of Labor, Occupational Outlook Handbook, 2012-13 Edition, Physicians and Surgeons, on the Internet at http://www.bls.gov/ooh/healthcare/physicians-and-surgeons.htm .

Podiatrists

Quick Facts: Podiatrists	
2010 Median Pay	$118,030 per year $56.75 per hour
Entry-Level Education	Doctoral or professional degree
Work Experience in a Related Occupation	None
On-the-job Training	Internship/residency
Number of Jobs, 2010	12,900
Job Outlook, 2010-20	20% (Faster than average)
Employment Change, 2010-20	2,600

What Podiatrists Do

Podiatrists provide medical and surgical care for people suffering foot, ankle, and lower leg problems. They diagnose illnesses, treat injuries, and perform surgery. For example, podiatrists treat calluses, ingrown toenails, heel spurs, and arch problems. They also treat foot and leg problems associated with diabetes and other diseases; they may set fractures.

Duties

Podiatrists typically do the following:
- Listen to a patient's concerns about their feet, ankles, or lower legs
- Diagnose foot, ankle, and lower-leg problems, through physical exams, x rays, medical laboratory tests, and other methods
- Provide treatment for foot, ankle, and lower-leg ailments, such as prescribing special shoe inserts (orthotics) to improve a patient's mobility
- Perform foot and ankle surgeries, such as removing bone spurs
- Offer advice and instruction on foot and ankle care
- Prescribe medications
- Refer patients to physicians or specialists if they detect larger health problems, such as diabetes
- Read journals and attend conferences to keep up with advances in podiatric medicine

Podiatrists who own their practice may also spend time on business related activities, such as hiring employees and managing inventory.

The following are examples of types of podiatrists:

Podiatric sports medicine focuses on treating and preventing foot and ankle injuries commonly encountered by athletes.

Pediatric care podiatrists provide treatment to children with foot and lower-leg health problems.

Advanced surgical podiatrists spend most of their time performing advanced surgeries, such as foot and ankle reconstruction.

Work Environment

Most podiatrists work in offices of podiatry, either on their own or with other podiatrists. Some work in hospitals. Others work in group practices with other physicians or specialists. Many podiatrists are self-employed; they own or are partners in their medical practice. Podiatrists also work in health maintenance organizations (HMO's), the U.S. Department of Veterans Affairs, the military, and academic health science centers and universities.

As shown in the following tabulation, 51 percent of podiatrists were employed in the office of other health practitioners, including podiatry offices, in 2010.

Offices of other health practitioners	51%
Self-employed workers	26
Offices of physicians	10
Federal government, excluding postal service	6
General medical and surgical hospitals; private	4

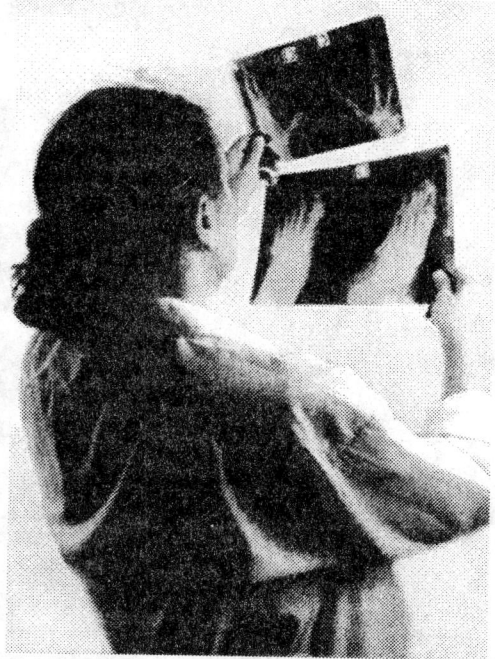

Podiatrists use x rays to diagnose foot and ankle problems.

Work Schedules

Most podiatrists work full time. Podiatrists' offices may be open in the evenings to accommodate patients. In hospitals, podiatrists may have to work occasional nights or weekends or may be on call.

How to Become a Podiatrist

Becoming a podiatrist requires completing an undergraduate college education, a 4-year postgraduate degree, and a 3-year medical and surgical residency. Podiatrists also must be licensed.

Education

Podiatrists must have a Doctor of Podiatric Medicine (DPM) degree, which is a 4-year degree after earning a bachelor's degree. Admission to podiatric medicine programs requires at least 3 years of undergraduate education, including specific courses in laboratory sciences such as biology, chemistry, and physics, as well as general coursework in subjects such as English. In practice, nearly all prospective podiatrists have earned a bachelor's degree before attending a school of podiatry. Admission to DPM programs usually also requires taking the Medical College Admission Test (MCAT). In 2011, there were nine colleges of podiatric medicine in the United States.

Courses for a Doctor of Podiatric Medicine degree are similar to those for other medical degrees. They include anatomy, pharmacology, and disease pathology, among other subjects. Also, during their last 2 years, podiatric medical students must complete clinical rotations, where they gain supervised experience in hospital settings, in specialties such as general surgery and emergency medicine. After earning a DPM, podiatrists must apply to and complete residency programs, which last 3 years. They may do additional training beyond 3 years in specific fellowship areas. Residencies allow for additional training in a clinical setting.

Important Qualities

Critical-thinking skills. Podiatrists must have a sharp, analytical mind to correctly diagnose a patient and determine the best course of treatment.

Detail oriented. To provide safe, effective healthcare, a podiatrist should be detail oriented. For example, a podiatrist must pay attention to a patient's medical history as well as current condition when diagnosing a problem and deciding on a treatment.

Interpersonal skills. Because podiatrists spend much of their time interacting with patients, they should be able to listen well and communicate effectively. For example, they should be able to tell a patient who is slated to undergo surgery what to expect and calm his or her fears.

Licenses

Podiatrists must be licensed in every state. Licensure usually requires passing a state exam (written or oral) and paying a fee. In most states, podiatrists also must have completed a residency program to be licensed. Licenses must typically be renewed periodically, and podiatrists must take continuing medical education.

Certification

Many podiatrists choose to become board certified, either in podiatric surgery or in orthopedics and primary care podiatry. The American Board of Podiatric Surgery is the certifying agency in podiatric surgery, and the American Board of Podiatric Orthopedics and Primary Podiatric Medicine is the certifying agency in orthopedics and primary care podiatry. Certification requires a combination of work experience and passing scores on exams.

Pay

Podiatrists
Median annual wages, May 2010

Podiatrists	$118,030
Health Diagnosing and Treating Practitioners	$71,490
Total, All Occupations	$33,840

Note: All Occupations includes all occupations in the U.S. Economy.
Source: U.S. Bureau of Labor Statistics, Occupational Employment Statistics

The median annual wage of podiatrists was $118,030 in May 2010. The median annual wage is the wage at which half the workers in an occupation earned more than that amount and half earned less. The lowest 10 percent earned less than $50,150, and the top 10 percent earned more than $166,400.

Self-employed podiatrists may earn more than salaried doctors, but they are also responsible for the costs of running a business, such as providing benefits for themselves and employees.

Most podiatrists work full time. Podiatrists' offices may be open in the evenings to accommodate patients.

Job Outlook

Podiatrists
Percent change in employment, projected 2010-20

Health Diagnosing and Treating Practitioners	26%
Podiatrists	20%
Total, All Occupations	14%

Note: All Occupations includes all occupations in the U.S. Economy.
Source: U.S. Bureau of Labor Statistics, Employment Projections program

Employment of podiatrists is expected to increase 20 percent from 2010 to 2020, faster than the average for all occupations. As the U.S. population both ages and increases, the number of people expected to have mobility and foot-related problems will rise. More podiatrists will be needed to provide this care. In addition, podiatrists are increasingly working in group practices along with other healthcare professionals. Continued growth in the use of outpatient surgery also will create new opportunities for podiatrists, as all podiatrists complete 3 years of standardized hospital-based residency training.

Job Prospects

Job prospects for trained podiatrists should be good, given that there are a limited number of colleges of podiatry. In addition, the retirement of currently practicing podiatrists in the coming years is expected to increase the number of job openings for podiatrists.

Employment projections data for podiatrists, 2010-20

Occupational Title	SOC Code	Employment, 2010	Projected Employment, 2020	Change, 2010-20	
				Percent	Numeric
Podiatrists	29-1081	12,900	15,500	20	2,600
SOURCE: U.S. Bureau of Labor Statistics, Employment Projections program					

Similar Occupations

This table shows a list of occupations with job duties that are similar to those of podiatrists.

Occupation	Job Duties	Entry-Level Education	Median Annual Pay, May 2010
Chiropractors	Chiropractors treat patients with health problems of the musculoskeletal system, which is made up of bones, muscles, ligaments, and tendons. They use spinal manipulation and other techniques to treat patients' ailments, such as back or neck pain.	Doctoral or professional degree	$67,200

Occupational Therapists	Occupational therapists treat patients with injuries, illnesses, or disabilities through the therapeutic use of everyday activities. They help these patients develop, recover, and improve the skills needed for daily living and working.	Master's degree	$72,320
Optometrists	Optometrists perform eye exams to check for vision problems and diseases. They prescribe eyeglasses or contact lenses as needed.	Doctoral or professional degree	$94,990
Orthotists and Prosthetists	Orthotists and prosthetists, also called O&P professionals, design medical support devices and measure and fit patients for them. These devices include artificial limbs (arms, hands, legs, and feet), braces, and other medical or surgical devices.	Master's degree	$65,060
Physical Therapists	Physical therapists help people who have injuries or illnesses improve their movement and manage their pain. They are often an important part of rehabilitation and treatment of patients with chronic conditions or injuries.	Doctoral or professional degree	$76,310
Physicians and Surgeons	Physicians and surgeons diagnose and treat injuries and illnesses in patients. Physicians examine patients, take medical histories, prescribe medications, and order, perform, and interpret diagnostic tests. Surgeons operate on patients to treat injuries, such as broken bones; diseases, such as cancerous tumors; and deformities, such as cleft palates.	Doctoral or professional degree	This wage is equal to or greater than $166,400 per year.

Contacts for More Information

For more information about podiatrists, visit American Podiatric Medical Association

For information on colleges of podiatric medicine and their entrance requirements, curricula, and student financial aid, visit American Association of Colleges of Podiatric Medicine

Suggested citation:

Bureau of Labor Statistics, U.S. Department of Labor, Occupational Outlook Handbook, 2012-13 Edition, Podiatrists, on the Internet at http://www.bls.gov/ooh/healthcare/podiatrists.htm .

Psychiatric Technicians and Aides

Quick Facts: Psychiatric Technicians and Aides	
2010 Median Pay	$26,880 per year $12.92 per hour
Entry-Level Education	See How to Become One
Work Experience in a Related Occupation	None
On-the-job Training	Short-term on-the-job training
Number of Jobs, 2010	142,500
Job Outlook, 2010-20	15% (About as fast as average)
Employment Change, 2010-20	21,800

What Psychiatric Technicians and Aides Do

Psychiatric technicians and aides care for people who have mental illness and developmental disabilities. The two occupations are related, but technicians typically provide therapeutic care, and aides help patients in their daily activities and ensure a safe, clean environment.

Duties

Psychiatric technicians typically do the following:
- Observe patients' behavior, listen to their concerns, and record their condition
- Lead patients in therapeutic and recreational activities
- Give medications and other treatments, following instructions from doctors and other medical professionals
- Help with admitting and discharging patients
- Monitor patients' vital signs, such as their blood pressure
- Help patients with activities of daily living, including eating and bathing
- Restrain patients who may become physically violent

Psychiatric aides typically do the following:
- Monitoring patients' behavior and location in a mental healthcare facility
- Help patients with their daily living activities, such as bathing or dressing
- Serve meals and help patients eat
- Help keep facilities clean by doing tasks such as changing bed linens
- Interact with patients, leading them in educational or therapeutic activities
- Participate in group activities, such as playing sports or going on field trips
- Help transport patients within a hospital or residential care facility
- Restrain patients who may become physically violent

Many psychiatric technicians and aides work with patients who are severely developmentally disabled and need intensive care. Others work with patients undergoing rehabilitation for drug and alcohol addiction. Their work varies depending on the types of patients they work with.

Psychiatric technicians and aides work as part of a medical team, under the direction of physicians and alongside other healthcare professionals, including psychiatrists, psychologists, psychiatric nurses, social workers, and therapists. Because they have such close contact with patients, psychiatric technicians and aides can have a great deal of influence on patients' outlook and treatment.

Psychiatric technicians and aides work in psychiatric hospitals, residential mental health facilities, and related healthcare settings, like drug or alcohol treatment centers.

Work Environment

Psychiatric technicians held about 74,900 jobs in 2010. Psychiatric aides held about 67,700 jobs in 2010.

As shown below, about 39 percent of psychiatric technicians were employed by psychiatric and substance abuse hospitals in 2010:

Psychiatric and substance abuse hospitals; state, local, and private	39%
General medical and surgical hospitals; state, local, and private	11
Residential mental retardation, mental health and substance abuse facilities	6
Outpatient care centers	2

As shown below, about 24 percent of psychiatric aides were employed in residential mental retardation, mental health and substance abuse facilities in 2010:

Psychiatric and substance abuse hospitals; state, local, and private	36%
Residential mental retardation, mental health and substance abuse facilities	24
General medical and surgical hospitals; state, local, and private	7
Individual, family, community, and vocational rehabilitation services	3

Psychiatric technicians and aides work in psychiatric hospitals, residential mental health facilities, and related healthcare settings, such as drug or alcohol treatment centers. They may spend much of their shift on their feet.

Some of the work that psychiatric aides do may be unpleasant. They may care for patients whose illnesses make them disoriented, uncooperative, or violent.

Injuries

Because their work requires many physically demanding tasks, such as lifting patients, psychiatric technicians and aides have high rates of on-the-job injury.

Work Schedules

Psychiatric technicians and aides may work full time or part time. Because hospitals and residential facilities are open at all hours, many psychiatric aides work nights, weekends, and holidays.

How to Become a Psychiatric Technician or Aide

Psychiatric technicians typically need postsecondary education, and aides need at least a high school diploma. Technicians and aides get on-the-job training before they can start working without direct supervision.

Education

Psychiatric technicians typically enter the occupation with a postsecondary certificate. Programs in psychiatric or mental health technology are commonly offered by community colleges and technical schools.

Psychiatric technician programs include courses in biology, psychology, and counseling. The programs also may include supervised work experience or cooperative programs, in which students gain academic credit for structured work experience.

Programs for psychiatric technicians range in length from one semester to two years, and they may award a certificate or an associate's degree.

Psychiatric aides typically need a high school diploma or equivalent. Postsecondary courses in psychology or mental health technology may be helpful.

Training

Psychiatric technicians and aides typically must participate in on-the-job training before they can work without direct supervision. This training may last for a few weeks or for several months.

Training may include gaining hands-on experience while working under the supervision of an experienced technician or aide. Technicians and aides may also attend workshops, lectures, or in-service training.

Important Qualities

Compassion. Because psychiatric technicians and aides spend much of their time interacting with patients, they should be caring and want to help people.

Interpersonal skills. Psychiatric technicians and aides often provide ongoing care for patients, so they should be able to develop a rapport with patients to evaluate their condition and provide treatment.

Patience. Working with the mentally ill can be emotionally challenging. Psychiatric technicians and aides must be able to stay calm and be helpful.

Physical stamina. Psychiatric technicians and aides must be able to lift and move patients and heavy objects. They must also be able to spend much of their time on their feet.

Licenses

In 2011, four states—Arkansas, California, Colorado, and Kansas—required licensure of psychiatric technicians. Although specific requirements vary, states usually require psychiatric technicians to complete an accredited education program, pass an exam, and pay a fee to be licensed.

Psychiatric aides are not required to be licensed.

For psychiatric technicians and aides working in states that do not offer licensure, a national certification program is available from the American Association of Psychiatric Technicians .

Pay

Psychiatric Technicians and Aides
Median annual wages, May 2010

Total, All Occupations	$33,840
Psychiatric Technicians	$28,710
Psychiatric Technicians and Aides	$26,880
Psychiatric Aides	$24,950

Note: All Occupations includes all occupations in the U.S. Economy.
Source: U.S. Bureau of Labor Statistics, Occupational Employment Statistics

The median annual wage of psychiatric technicians was $28,710 in May 2010. The median wage is the wage at which half the workers in an occupation earned more than that amount and half earned less. The lowest 10 percent earned less than $18,420, and the top 10 percent earned more than $50,430.

The median annual wage of psychiatric aides was $24,950 in May 2010. The lowest 10 percent earned less than $17,270, and the top 10 percent earned more than $40,070.

Median annual wages in the industries employing the largest numbers of psychiatric technicians in May 2010 were as follows:

General medical and surgical hospitals; state, local, and private	$30,930
Psychiatric and substance abuse hospitals; state, local, and private	29,500
Outpatient care centers	23,820
Residential mental retardation, mental health and substance abuse facilities	23,360

Median annual wages in the industries employing the largest numbers of psychiatric aides in May 2010 were as follows:

Psychiatric and substance abuse hospitals; state, local, and private	$28,120
General medical and surgical hospitals; state, local, and private	26,970
Residential mental retardation, mental health and substance abuse facilities	22,380
Individual, family, community, and vocational rehabilitation services	21,390

Psychiatric technicians and aides may work full time or part time. Because hospitals and residential facilities are open at all hours, many psychiatric aides work nights, weekends, and holidays.

Job Outlook

Psychiatric Technicians and Aides
Percent change in employment, projected 2010-20

Psychiatric Technicians	15%
Psychiatric Aides	15%
Psychiatric Technicians and Aides	15%
Total, All Occupations	14%

Note: All Occupations includes all occupations in the U.S. Economy.
Source: U.S. Bureau of Labor Statistics, Employment Projections program

Employment of psychiatric technicians is expected to increase 15 percent from 2010 to 2020, about as fast as the average for all occupations. Employment of psychiatric aides is expected to increase 15 percent from 2010 to 2020, about as fast as the average for all occupations.

As the nation's population ages and people live longer, there is likely to be an increase in the number of people with cognitive mental diseases, such as Alzheimer's disease. Demand for psychiatric technicians and aides in residential facilities are expected to rise as a result.

More psychiatric technicians and aides will also be needed in residential treatment facilities for people with developmental disabilities, mental illness, and substance abuse problems. There is a long-term trend toward treating psychiatric patients outside of hospitals, because it is more cost-effective and allows patients greater independence. Also, an increasing number of mentally disabled adults who were cared for by their parents will need help as their parents become too old to provide that care.

In addition, an aging prison population has increased the need for psychiatric technicians and aides working in correctional facilities.

Employment projections data for psychiatric technicians and aides, 2010-20

Occupational Title	SOC Code	Employment, 2010	Projected Employment, 2020	Change, 2010-20 Percent	Numeric
Psychiatric Technicians and Aides	—	142,500	164,400	15	21,800
Psychiatric Technicians	29-2053	74,900	86,400	15	11,600
Psychiatric Aides	31-1013	67,700	77,900	15	10,200

SOURCE: U.S. Bureau of Labor Statistics, Employment Projections program

Similar Occupations

This table shows a list of occupations with job duties that are similar to those of psychiatric technicians and aides.

Occupation	Job Duties	Entry-Level Education	Median Annual Pay, May 2010
Childcare Workers	Childcare workers care for children when parents and other family members are unavailable. They care for children's basic needs, such as bathing and feeding. In addition, some help children prepare for kindergarten, and many help older children with homework.	High school diploma or equivalent	$19,300

Home Health and Personal Care Aides	Home health and personal care aides help people who are disabled, chronically ill, or cognitively impaired. They also help older adults who may need assistance. They help with activities such as bathing and dressing, and they provide services such as light housekeeping. In some states, home health aides may be able to give a client medication or check the client's vital signs under the direction of a nurse or other healthcare practitioner.	Less than high school	$20,170
Licensed Practical and Licensed Vocational Nurses	Licensed practical and licensed vocational nurses (known as LPNs or LVNs, depending on the state in which they work) provide basic nursing care. They work under the direction of registered nurses and doctors.	Postsecondary non-degree award	$40,380
Medical Assistants	Medical assistants complete administrative and clinical tasks in the offices of physicians, podiatrists, chiropractors, and other health practitioners. Their duties vary with the location, specialty, and size of the practice.	High school diploma or equivalent	$28,860
Nursing Aides, Orderlies, and Attendants	Nursing aides, orderlies, and attendants help provide basic care for patients in hospitals and residents of long-term care facilities, such as nursing homes.	Postsecondary non-degree award	$24,010
Occupational Therapy Assistants and Aides	Occupational therapy assistants and aides work under the direction of occupational therapists in treating patients with injuries, illnesses, or disabilities through the therapeutic use of everyday activities. They help these patients develop, recover, and improve the skills needed for daily living and working.	See How to Become One	$47,490
Social and Human Service Assistants	Social and human service assistants help people get through difficult times or get additional support. They help other workers, such as social workers, and they help clients find benefits or community services.	High school diploma or equivalent	$28,200
Registered Nurses	Registered nurses (RNs) provide and coordinate patient care, educate patients and the public about various health conditions, and provide advice and emotional support to patients and their family members.	Associate's degree	$64,690

Contacts for More Information

For more information about psychiatric technicians and aides, visit American Association of Psychiatric Technicians .

Suggested citation:

Bureau of Labor Statistics, U.S. Department of Labor, Occupational Outlook Handbook, 2012-13 Edition, Psychiatric Technicians and Aides, on the Internet at http://www.bls.gov/ooh/healthcare/psychiatric-technicians-and-aides.htm.

Radiation Therapists

Quick Facts: Radiation Therapists	
2010 Median Pay	$74,980 per year $36.05 per hour
Entry-Level Education	Associate's degree
Work Experience in a Related Occupation	None
On-the-job Training	None
Number of Jobs, 2010	16,900
Job Outlook, 2010-20	20% (Faster than average)
Employment Change, 2010-20	3,400

What Radiation Therapists Do

Radiation therapists treat cancer and other diseases in patients by giving radiation treatments.

Duties

Radiation therapists typically do the following:

- Examine machines to make sure they are safe and work properly
- Explain treatment plans to the patient and answer questions about treatment
- Follow safety procedures to protect the patient and themselves from overexposure
- X-ray the patient to determine the exact location of the area requiring treatment
- Check the computer programs to make sure that they will give the correct dose of radiation to the correct area of the patient's body
- Operate the equipment to treat the patient with radiation
- Monitor the patient to check for unusual reactions to the treatment

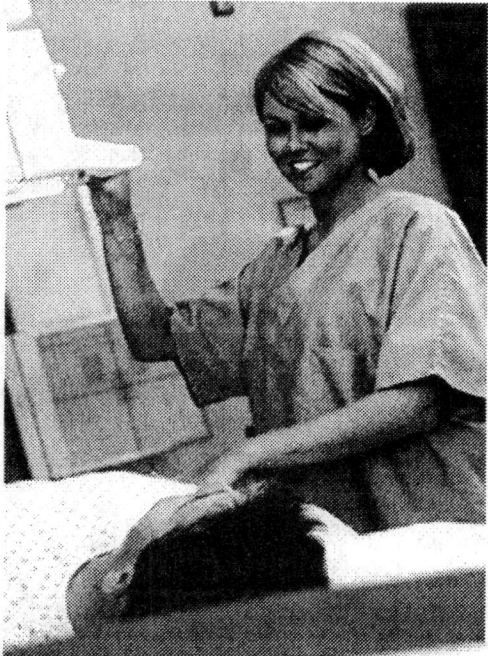

Radiation therapists treat cancer and other diseases in patients by administering radiation treatments.

- Keep detailed records of treatment

Most radiation therapy uses machines called linear accelerators. These machines direct high-energy x-rays at specific cancer cells in a patient's body, shrinking or removing them.

Radiation therapists are part of the oncology team that treats patients with cancer. They often work with the following specialists:

- Radiation oncologists, physicians who specialize in radiation therapy
- Oncology nurses, nurses who specialize in patients with cancer
- Radiation physicists, physicists who calibrate linear accelerators
- Dosimetrists, workers who calculate the correct dose of radiation to use in the treatment

Work Environment

Radiation therapists work in healthcare facilities or cancer treatment centers. Radiation therapists are on their feet for long periods and may need to lift or turn disabled patients. Because they work with radiation and radioactive material, radiation therapists must follow safety procedures to make sure that they are not exposed to a potentially harmful amount of radiation. This restriction usually means standing in a different room while the patient undergoes radiation procedures.

Work Schedules

Most radiation therapists work full time. Because radiation therapy procedures are usually planned in advance, radiation therapists keep a regular work schedule.

How to Become a Radiation Therapist

Radiation therapists need to complete formal education programs. Most programs lead to a bachelor's degree or associate's degree in radiation therapy. Radiation therapists must be licensed in most states; requirements vary by state.

Education

Although candidates may qualify by completing a 12-month certificate program, employers usually prefer to hire applicants who have an associate's or a bachelor's degree in radiation therapy.

Radiation therapy programs include courses in radiation therapy procedures and the scientific theories behind them. In addition, these programs often include courses in human anatomy and physiology, physics, algebra, computer science, and research methodology.

Licenses and Certification

In most states, radiation therapists must have a license. Requirements vary by state. To be licensed, radiation therapists must usually graduate from an accredited radiation therapy program and be certified by the American Registry of Radiologic Technologists (ARRT). To become ARRT certified, an applicant must complete an accredited radiation therapy program, adhere to ARRT ethical standards, and pass the ARRT certification exam. The exam covers radiation protection and quality assurance, clinical concepts in radiation oncology, treatment planning, treatment delivery, and patient care and education.

Important Qualities

Detail oriented. Radiation therapists must follow exact instructions and input exact measurements to make sure the patient is neither underexposed nor overexposed to the radiation.

Interpersonal skills. Radiation therapists work closely with patients. Because radiation therapists see their patients on a recurring basis, it is important that they be comfortable interacting with people who may be going through difficult physical and emotional stress.

Science and mathematical skills. Radiation therapists must understand anatomy, physiology, and other sciences. They may also need to mix the right dose of chemicals used in imaging procedures.

Stamina. Radiation therapists must be able to be on their feet for long periods and be able to lift and move patients who need assistance.

Technical skills. Radiation therapists work with computers and large pieces of technological equipment, so they must be comfortable operating those devices.

Advancement

Experienced radiation therapists may advance to manage radiation therapy programs in treatment centers or other healthcare facilities. Managers generally continue to treat patients while taking on management responsibilities. Other advancement opportunities include teaching, technical sales, and research. With additional training and certification, therapists also can become dosimetrists.

Pay

Radiation Therapists
Median annual wages, May 2010

Radiation Therapists	$74,980
Health Diagnosing and Treating Practitioners	$71,490
Total, All Occupations	$33,840

Note: All Occupations includes all occupations in the U.S. Economy.
Source: U.S. Bureau of Labor Statistics, Occupational Employment Statistics

The median annual wage of radiation therapists was $74,980 in May 2010. The median wage is the wage at which half the workers in an occupation earned more than that amount and half earned less. The lowest 10 percent earned less than $50,950, and the top 10 percent earned more than $110,550.

Most radiation therapists work full time. Because radiation therapy procedures are usually planned in advance, radiation therapists keep a regular work schedule.

Job Outlook

Radiation Therapists
Percent change in employment, projected 2010-20

Health Diagnosing and Treating Practitioners	26%
Radiation Therapists	20%
Total, All Occupations	14%

Note: All Occupations includes all occupations in the U.S. Economy.
Source: U.S. Bureau of Labor Statistics, Employment Projections program

Employment of radiation therapists is expected to grow by 20 percent between 2010 and 2020, faster than the average for all occupations. However, because it is a small occupation, the fast growth will result in only about 3,400 new jobs over the 10-year period.

The risk of cancer increases as people age, so an aging population will increase demand for radiation therapists. Early diagnosis and the development of more sophisticated treatment techniques will also increase employment.

Employment projections data for radiation therapists, 2010-20

Occupational Title	SOC Code	Employment, 2010	Projected Employment, 2020	Change, 2010-20	
				Percent	Numeric
Radiation Therapists	29-1124	16,900	20,300	20	3,400

SOURCE: U.S. Bureau of Labor Statistics, Employment Projections program

Similar Occupations

This table shows a list of occupations with job duties that are similar to those of radiation therapists.

Occupation	Job Duties	Entry-Level Education	Median Annual Pay, May 2010
Cardiovascular Technologists and Technicians and Vascular Technologists	Cardiovascular technologists and technicians and vascular technologists use imaging technology to help physicians diagnose cardiac (heart) and peripheral vascular (blood vessel) ailments in patients. They also help physicians treat problems with cardiac and vascular systems, such as blood clots.	Associate's degree	$49,410
Dental Hygienists	Dental hygienists clean teeth, examine patients for oral diseases such as gingivitis, and provide other preventative dental care. They also educate patients on ways to improve and maintain good oral health.	Associate's degree	$68,250
Diagnostic Medical Sonographers	Diagnostic medical sonographers use special imaging equipment that directs sound waves into a patient's body (in a procedure commonly known as an ultrasound, sonogram, or echocardiogram) to assess and diagnose various medical conditions.	Associate's degree	$64,380

Nuclear Medicine Technologists	Nuclear medicine technologists use a scanner to create images of various areas of a patient's body. They prepare radioactive drugs and administer them to patients undergoing the scans. The radioactive drugs cause abnormal areas of the body to appear different from normal areas in the images.	Associate's degree	$68,560
Nursing Aides, Orderlies, and Attendants	Nursing aides, orderlies, and attendants help provide basic care for patients in hospitals and residents of long-term care facilities, such as nursing homes.	Postsecondary non-degree award	$24,010
Physical Therapist Assistants and Aides	Physical therapist assistants and physical therapist aides work under the direction of physical therapists. They help patients who are recovering from injuries, illnesses, and surgeries regain movement and manage pain.	See How to Become One	$37,710
Radiologic Technologists	Radiologic technologists perform diagnostic imaging examinations, such as x rays, on patients.	Associate's degree	$54,340
Registered Nurses	Registered nurses (RNs) provide and coordinate patient care, educate patients and the public about various health conditions, and provide advice and emotional support to patients and their family members.	Associate's degree	$64,690

Contacts for More Information

For information about radiation therapists, visit The American Registry of Radiologic Technologists , American Society of Radiologic Technologists

Suggested citation:

Bureau of Labor Statistics, U.S. Department of Labor, Occupational Outlook Handbook, 2012-13 Edition, Radiation Therapists, on the Internet at http://www.bls.gov/ooh/healthcare/radiation-therapists.htm .

Radiologic Technologists

Quick Facts: Radiologic Technologists	
2010 Median Pay	$54,340 per year $26.13 per hour
Entry-Level Education	Associate's degree
Work Experience in a Related Occupation	None
On-the-job Training	None
Number of Jobs, 2010	219,900
Job Outlook, 2010-20	28% (Faster than average)
Employment Change, 2010-20	61,000

What Radiologic Technologists Do

Radiologic technologists perform diagnostic imaging examinations, such as x rays, on patients.

Duties

Radiologic technologists typically do the following:

- Adjust and maintain imaging equipment
- Precisely follow orders from physicians on what areas of the body to image
- Prepare patients for procedures, including taking a medical history and answering questions about the procedure
- Protect the patient by shielding exposed areas that do not need to be imaged
- Position the patient and the equipment in the location needed to get the correct image
- Operate the computerized equipment to take the images
- Work with radiologists reading the images to determine whether other images need to be taken
- Keep detailed patient records

Healthcare professionals use many types of diagnostic equipment to diagnose patients. Radiologic technologists specialize in x-ray, computed tomography (CT), and magnetic resonance imaging (MRI) equipment. They may be called CT technicians or MRI technicians, depending on the equipment they work with. Radiologic technologists might also specialize in mammography. Mammographers use low-dose x-ray systems to produce images of the breast. Technologists may be certified in multiple specialties.

Healthcare professionals who specialize in other diagnostic equipment include nuclear medicine technologists, diagnostic medical sonographers, cardiovascular technologists and technicians, and vascular technologists. For more information, see the profiles on nuclear medicine technologists , diagnostic medical sonographers , and cardiovascular technologists and technicians and vascular technologists .

Some radiologic technologists prepare a mixture for the patient to drink that allows soft tissue to be seen on the images that the radiologist reviews.

Work Environment

Radiologic technologists held about 219,900 jobs in 2010. Radiologic technologists work in healthcare facilities. Like other healthcare workers,radiologic technologists may be exposed to infectious diseases. Technologists are often on their feet for long periods and may need to lift or turn patients who are disabled.

The following industries employed a majority of radiologic technologists in 2010:

Hospitals; state, local, and private	61%
Offices of physicians	21
Medical and diagnostic laboratories	9
Outpatient care centers	3
Federal government	2

Although radiation hazards exist in this occupation, they are minimized by the use of protective lead aprons, gloves, and other shielding devices, and by instruments that monitor exposure to radiation. Radiologic technologists wear badges measuring radiation levels in the radiation area, and detailed records are kept on their cumulative lifetime dose.

Work Schedules

Most radiologic technologists work full time. Because imaging is needed in emergency situations, some radiologic technologists work evenings, weekends, or on call.

How to Become a Radiologic Technologist

An associate's degree is the most common educational path for radiologic technologists. Technologists must be licensed or certified in most states; requirements vary by state.

Education

There are formal training programs in radiography that lead to a certificate, an associate's degree, or a bachelor's degree. Associate's degree programs are the most common. Certificate programs typically last 6 to 12 months. Typical programs include both classroom training and clinical training. Coursework includes anatomy, pathology, patient care, radiation physics and protection, and image evaluation.

The Joint Review Committee on Education in Radiologic Technology (JRCERT) accredits educational and training programs in radiography. Completing an accredited program is required for licensure in some states.

High school students who are interested in radiologic technology should take courses that focus on science and math. Suggested courses include anatomy, biology, chemistry, physiology, mathematics, and physics.

Licenses and Certification

Radiologic technologists must be licensed or certified in most states; requirements vary by state. To be licensed in most states, radiologic technologists must have graduated from an accredited program and must pass a certification exam from the state or from The American Registry of Radiologic Technologist (ARRT). For specific state requirements, contact your state's health board. To keep their certification, radiologic technologists must meet continuing education requirements.

Important Qualities

Detail oriented. Radiologic technologists must follow exact instructions to get the images needed to diagnose and treat the patient.

Interpersonal skills. Radiologic technologists must work closely with patients. Patients may be in extreme pain or mental stress and the technologist must get cooperation from the patient to make usable images.

Science and mathematical skills. Radiologic technologists must understand anatomy, physiology, and other sciences. They may also need to mix the right dose of chemicals used in imaging procedures.

Stamina. Radiologic technologists often work on their feet for long

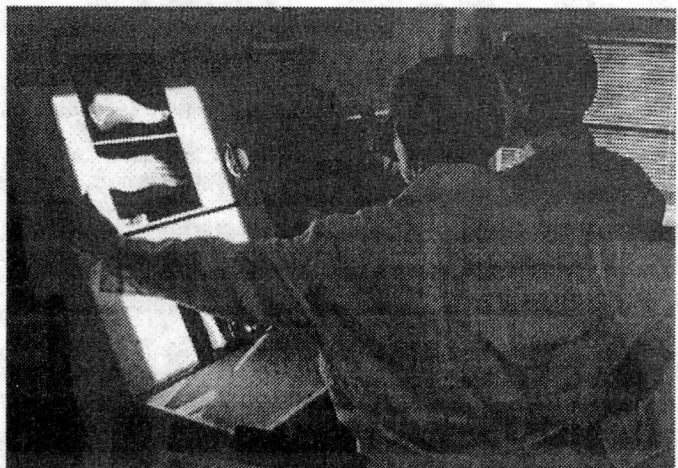

Radiologic technologists work with radiologists to determine if other scans or images need to be taken.

periods and must be able to lift and move patients who need assistance.

Technical skills. Radiologic technologists must understand how to operate complex machinery.

Pay

Radiologic Technologists
Median annual wages, May 2010

Radiologic Technologists and Technicians	$54,340
Health Technologists and Technicians	$39,340
Total, All Occupations	$33,840

Note: All Occupations includes all occupations in the U.S. Economy.
Source: U.S. Bureau of Labor Statistics, Occupational Employment Statistics

The median annual wage of radiologic technologists was $54,340 in May 2010. The median wage is the wage at which half the workers in an occupation earned more than that amount and half earned less. The lowest 10 percent earned less than $36,510 and the highest 10 percent earned more than $76,850.

Most radiologic technologists work full time. Because imaging is needed in emergencies, some radiologic technologists work evenings, weekends, or on call.

Job Outlook

Radiologic Technologists
Percent change in employment, projected 2010-20

Radiologic Technologists and Technicians	28%
Health Technologists and Technicians	26%
Total, All Occupations	14%

Note: All Occupations includes all occupations in the U.S. Economy.
Source: U.S. Bureau of Labor Statistics, Employment Projections program

Employment of radiologic technologists is expected to grow by 28 percent between 2010 and 2020, faster than the average for all occupations.

An increasing aging population will have more medical conditions, such as breaks and fractures caused by osteoporosis, which require imaging to diagnose and treat. Radiologic technologists will be needed to maintain and use the diagnostic equipment.

Although hospitals will remain the main employer of radiologic technologists, a number of new jobs will be in physicians' offices and in imaging centers. Employment in these healthcare settings is expected to increase because of the shift toward outpatient care whenever possible. Outpatient care is encouraged by third-party payers as a cost-saving measure and is made possible by technological advances, such as less expensive equipment, which allow for more procedures to be done outside of hospitals.

Job Prospects

Radiologic technologists with multiple certifications will have the best job prospects.

Employment projections data for radiologic technologists, 2010-20

Occupational Title	SOC Code	Employment, 2010	Projected Employment, 2020	Change, 2010-20	
				Percent	Numeric
Radiologic Technologists and Technicians	29-2037	219,900	281,000	28	61,000
SOURCE: U.S. Bureau of Labor Statistics, Employment Projections program					

Similar Occupations

This table shows a list of occupations with job duties that are similar to those of radiologic technologists.

Occupation	Job Duties	Entry-Level Education	Median Annual Pay, May 2010
Cardiovascular Technologists and Technicians and Vascular Technologists	Cardiovascular technologists and technicians and vascular technologists use imaging technology to help physicians diagnose cardiac (heart) and peripheral vascular (blood vessel) ailments in patients. They also help physicians treat problems with cardiac and vascular systems, such as blood clots.	Associate's degree	$49,410
Diagnostic Medical Sonographers	Diagnostic medical sonographers use special imaging equipment that directs sound waves into a patient's body (in a procedure commonly known as an ultrasound, sonogram, or echocardiogram) to assess and diagnose various medical conditions.	Associate's degree	$64,380
Nuclear Medicine Technologists	Nuclear medicine technologists use a scanner to create images of various areas of a patient's body. They prepare radioactive drugs and administer them to patients undergoing the scans. The radioactive drugs cause abnormal areas of the body to appear different from normal areas in the images.	Associate's degree	$68,560
Radiation Therapists	Radiation therapists treat cancer and other diseases in patients by giving radiation treatments.	Associate's degree	$74,980

Contacts for More Information

For information about radiologic technology, visit American Society of Radiologic Technologists , Joint Review Committee on Education in Radiologic Technology , The American Registry of Radiologic Technologists

Suggested citation:

Bureau of Labor Statistics, U.S. Department of Labor, Occupational Outlook Handbook, 2012-13 Edition, Radiologic Technologists, on the Internet at http://www.bls.gov/ooh/healthcare/radiologic-technologists.htm .

Recreational Therapists

Quick Facts: Recreational Therapists	
2010 Median Pay	$39,410 per year $18.95 per hour
Entry-Level Education	Bachelor's degree
Work Experience in a Related Occupation	None
On-the-job Training	None
Number of Jobs, 2010	22,400
Job Outlook, 2010-20	17% (About as fast as average)
Employment Change, 2010-20	3,800

What Recreational Therapists Do

Recreational therapists plan, direct, and coordinate recreation programs for people with disabilities or illnesses. They use a variety of techniques, including arts and crafts, drama, music, dance, sports, games, and field trips. These activities help maintain or improve a client's physical and emotional well-being.

Duties

Recreational therapists typically do the following:

- Assess clients' needs through observations, medical records, standardized tests, and talking with medical staff, clients' families, and the clients
- Work with other healthcare professionals to form treatment plans
- Create programs that meet clients' needs and interests
- Plan and carry out interventions to prevent harm to a client
- Engage clients in activities, such as games, drama, and field trips
- Help clients learn social skills needed to become or remain independent

Recreational therapists provide treatment services and recreational activities for individuals with disabilities or illnesses.

- Explain to clients ways to cope with anxiety or depression
- Record and analyze a client's progress

Recreational therapists help people reduce depression, stress, and anxiety; recover basic physical and mental abilities; build confidence; and socialize effectively. They help people with disabilities integrate into the community by teaching them how to use community resources and recreational activities.

Recreational therapists use activities, such as arts and crafts, dance and movement, or sports, to help their clients. For example, people who are paralyzed on one side may need therapists to teach them to recover basic motor skills, such as picking up a cup with their functional side.

Therapists may help people with disabilities by teaching them how to use community resources, such as public transportation or parks.

They may also provide interventions to clients who need help developing new coping skills. For example, they might encourage clients who have limited social skills to play games with others.

Recreational therapists work in places such as substance abuse centers, rehabilitation centers, assisted living facilities, special education departments, and parks and recreation departments.

Therapists who work in hospitals and rehabilitation centers may work with physicians, nurses, psychologists, social workers, physical therapists, and occupational therapists. For more information, see the profiles on physicians and surgeons , registered nurses , psychologists , social workers , physical therapists , and occupational therapists .

Recreational therapists are different from recreation workers, who organize recreational activities primarily for enjoyment. For more information, see the profile on recreation workers .

Work Environment

Recreational therapists held about 22,400 jobs in 2010. The following industries employed the largest number of recreational therapists in 2010:

Nursing care facilities	22%
General medical and surgical hospitals; state, local, and private	17
Psychiatric and substance abuse hospitals; state, local, and private	12
Community care facilities for the elderly	6
Individual, family, community, and vocational rehabilitation services	6

Recreational therapists work in a variety of settings and may arrange to have activities both indoors and outdoors. Therapists often work in hospitals or nursing and residential care facilities. They may work in places such as substance abuse centers, rehabilitation centers, special education departments, and parks and recreation departments.

They may use offices for planning or other administrative activities, such as client assessment, but may travel when working with clients. Therapists and their clients commonly go to fields and parks for sports and other outdoor activities.

Work Schedules

Some recreational therapists work evenings and weekends to meet the needs of their clients.

How to Become a Recreational Therapist

Recreational therapists typically need a bachelor's degree. Most employers require therapists to be certified by the National Council for Therapeutic Recreation Certification (NCTRC).

Education

Most recreational therapists need a bachelor's degree in therapeutic recreation or a related field. Though less common, associate's, master's, or doctoral degrees are also available.

Therapeutic recreation programs include courses in assessment, human anatomy, medical and psychiatric terminology, characteristics of illnesses and disabilities, and the use of assistive devices and technology. Bachelor's degree programs usually include an internship.

Certification and Licenses

Most employers prefer to hire certified recreational therapists. Hospitals and other clinical settings often require certification by the NCTRC. The council offers the Certified Therapeutic Recreation Specialist (CTRS) credential to candidates who pass a written certification exam and complete a supervised internship of at least 480 hours.

NCTRC also offers specialty certification in five areas of practice: geriatrics, behavioral health, physical medicine/rehabilitation, developmental disabilities, or community inclusion services. Although therapists typically need at least a bachelor's degree in recreational therapy, in some cases therapists may qualify for certification with an alternate combination of education, training, and experience.

Some states require recreational therapists to be licensed; requirements vary by state. As of 2010, only Oklahoma, North Carolina, Utah, and New Hampshire required recreational therapists to hold a license. For specific requirements, contact the state's medical board.

Important Qualities

Compassion. Recreational therapists should be kind, gentle, and sympathetic when providing support to clients and their families. They may deal with clients who are in a great deal of pain or under severe emotional stress.

Critical-thinking skills. Recreational therapists should be able to quickly think of adaptations to activities when a client's therapy plan requires adjustment.

Leadership skills. Recreational therapists must be organized and able to plan, development and implement intervention programs in an effective manner.

Listening skills. Recreational therapists must listen to a client's problems and concerns. They can then determine the course of treatment or therapy program appropriate for that client.

Patience. Recreational therapists may work with clients who need more time and special attention than other clients.

Speaking skills. Recreational therapists need to communicate well with their clients. They need to be able to give directions during activities or instruct a client on healthy coping techniques.

Pay

Recreational Therapists
Median annual wages, May 2010

Health Diagnosing and Treating Practitioners	$71,490
Recreational Therapists	$39,410
Total, All Occupations	$33,840

Note: All Occupations includes all occupations in the U.S. Economy.
Source: U.S. Bureau of Labor Statistics, Occupational Employment Statistics

The median annual wage of recreational therapists was $39,410 in May 2010. The median wage is the wage at which half the workers in an occupation earned more than that amount and half earned less. The lowest 10 percent earned less than $24,640, and the top 10 percent earned more than $62,670.

Some recreational therapists work evenings and weekends to meet the needs of their clients.

Job Outlook

Recreational Therapists
Percent change in employment, projected 2010-20

Health Diagnosing and Treating Practitioners	26%
Recreational Therapists	17%
Total, All Occupations	14%

Note: All Occupations includes all occupations in the U.S. Economy.
Source: U.S. Bureau of Labor Statistics, Employment Projections program

Employment of recreational therapists is expected to grow by 17 percent from 2010 to 2020, about as fast as the average for all occupations.

As the large baby-boom generation ages, they will need recreational therapists to help treat age-related injuries and illnesses, such as strokes. As people age, their declines in general physical ability, and sometimes mental ability, may also be treated with recreational therapy.

Legislation requiring federally-funded services for disabled students will continue to shape the need for recreational therapists in education settings.

Additionally, third party payers will continue to use therapists' services as a way to cut costs in patients' recoveries from injuries or illnesses, moving treatment to outpatient settings rather than more costly hospital settings.

Job prospects

Job prospects will be best for recreational therapists with both a bachelor's degree and certification. Therapists who specialize in working with the elderly or who earn certification in geriatric therapy may have the best job prospects. Nursing and residential care facilities employ almost a third of recreational therapists. As the percentage of older adults continues to grow, employment in nursing and residential care facilities industry will grow as a whole, increasing the need for these workers.

Employment projections data for recreational therapists, 2010-20

Occupational Title	SOC Code	Employment, 2010	Projected Employment, 2020	Change, 2010-20	
				Percent	Numeric
Recreational Therapists	29-1125	22,400	26,300	17	3,800
SOURCE: U.S. Bureau of Labor Statistics, Employment Projections program					

Similar Occupations

This table shows a list of occupations with job duties that are similar to those of recreational therapists.

Occupation	Job Duties	Entry-Level Education	Median Annual Pay, May 2010
Occupational Therapists	Occupational therapists treat patients with injuries, illnesses, or disabilities through the therapeutic use of everyday activities. They help these patients develop, recover, and improve the skills needed for daily living and working.	Master's degree	$72,320
Physical Therapists	Physical therapists help people who have injuries or illnesses improve their movement and manage their pain. They are often an important part of rehabilitation and treatment of patients with chronic conditions or injuries.	Doctoral or professional degree	$76,310
Speech-Language Pathologists	Speech-language pathologists diagnose and treat communication and swallowing disorders in patients.	Master's degree	$66,920
Rehabilitation Counselors	Rehabilitation counselors help people with emotional and physical disabilities live independently. They help their clients overcome personal, social, and professional effects of disabilities as they relate to employment or independent living.	Master's degree	$32,350
School and Career Counselors	School counselors help students develop social skills and succeed in school. Career counselors assist people with the process of making career decisions by helping them choose a career or educational program.	Master's degree	$53,380
Special Education Teachers	Special education teachers work with students who have a wide range of learning, mental, emotional and physical disabilities. With students who have mild or moderate disabilities, they ensure that lessons and teaching strategies are modified to meet the students' needs. With students who have severe disabilities, they teach the students independent living skills and basic literacy, communication, and math.	Bachelor's degree	$53,220

Contacts for More Information

For information and materials on careers and academic programs in recreational therapy, visit American Therapeutic Recreation Association

For information on certification, visit National Council for Therapeutic Recreation Certification

Suggested citation:

Bureau of Labor Statistics, U.S. Department of Labor, Occupational Outlook Handbook, 2012-13 Edition, Recreational Therapists, on the Internet at http://www.bls.gov/ooh/healthcare/recreational-therapists.htm .

Registered Nurses

Quick Facts: Registered Nurses	
2010 Median Pay	$64,690 per year $31.10 per hour
Entry-Level Education	Associate's degree
Work Experience in a Related Occupation	None
On-the-job Training	None
Number of Jobs, 2010	2,737,400
Job Outlook, 2010-20	26% (Faster than average)
Employment Change, 2010-20	711,900

What Registered Nurses Do

Registered nurses (RNs) provide and coordinate patient care, educate patients and the public about various health conditions, and provide advice and emotional support to patients and their family members.

Duties

Registered nurses typically do the following:

- Record patients' medical histories and symptoms
- Give patients medicines and treatments
- Set up plans for patients' care or contribute to existing plans
- Observe patients and record the observations
- Consult with doctors and other healthcare professionals
- Operate and monitor medical equipment
- Help perform diagnostic tests and analyze results
- Teach patients and their families how to manage their illnesses or injuries
- Explain what to do at home after treatment

Some registered nurses oversee licensed practical nurses, nursing aides, and home care aides. For more information, see the profiles on licensed practical and licensed vocational nurses ; nursing aides, orderlies, and attendants ; and home health and personal care aides .

Registered nurses sometimes work to promote general health by educating the public on warning signs and symptoms of disease. They might also run general health screenings or immunization clinics, blood drives, or other outreach programs.

Most registered nurses work as part of a team with physicians and other healthcare specialists.

Some nurses have jobs in which they do not work directly with patients, but they must still have an active registered nurse license. For example, they may work as nurse educators, healthcare consultants, public policy advisors, researchers, hospital administrators, salespeople for pharmaceutical and medical supply companies, or as medical writers and editors.

Registered nurses' duties and titles often depend on where they work and the patients they work with. They can focus on the following specialties:

- A specific health condition, such as a diabetes management nurse who helps patients with diabetes or an oncology nurse who helps cancer patients
- A specific part of the body, such as a dermatology nurse working with patients who have skin problems
- A specific group of people, such as a geriatric nurse who works with the elderly or a pediatric nurse who works with children and teens
- A specific workplace, such as an emergency or trauma nurse who works in a hospital or stand-alone emergency department or a school nurse working in an elementary, middle, or high school rather than in a hospital or doctor's office.

Some registered nurses combine one or more of these specialties. For example, a pediatric oncology nurse works with children and teens who have cancer.

Many possibilities for specializing exist. The following list includes just a few other examples of ways that some registered nurses specialize:

Addiction nurses care for patients who need help to overcome addictions to alcohol, drugs, tobacco, and other substances.

Cardiovascular nurses treat patients with heart disease and people who have had heart surgery.

Critical care nurses work in intensive care units in hospitals, providing care to patients with serious, complex, and acute illnesses and injuries that need very close monitoring and treatment.

Genetics nurses provide screening, counseling, and treatment of patients with genetic disorders, such as cystic fibrosis and Huntington's disease.

Neonatology nurses take care of newborn babies.

Nephrology nurses treat patients who have kidney-related health issues that are attributable to diabetes, high blood pressure, substance abuse, or other causes.

Rehabilitation nurses care for patients with temporary or permanent disabilities.

Advanced practice registered nurses may provide primary and specialty care, and, in most states, they may prescribe medicines. All

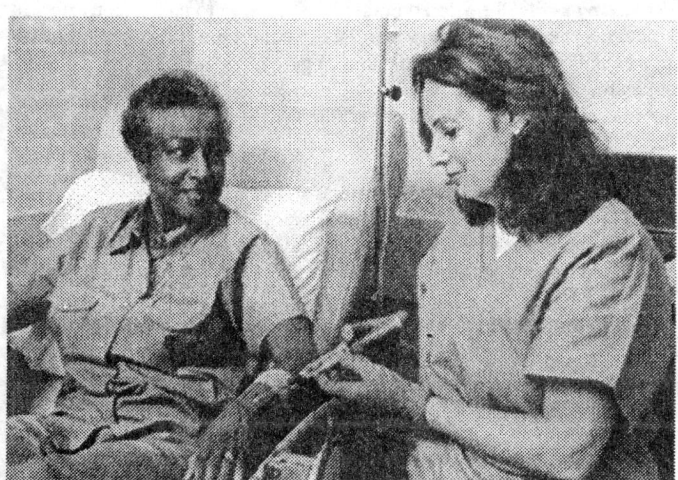

Nurses may provide medications to patients, including intravenous (IV) drugs.

states specifically define requirements for registered nurses in these four advanced practice roles:

- **Clinical nurse specialists** provide direct patient care and expert consultations in one of many nursing specialties, such as psychiatric-mental health.
- **Nurse anesthetists** provide anesthesia and related care before and after surgical, therapeutic, diagnostic, and obstetrical procedures. They also provide pain management and emergency services.
- **Nurse-midwives** provide care to women, including gynecological exams, family planning advice, prenatal care, assistance in labor and delivery, and care of newborns.
- **Nurse practitioners** serve as primary and specialty care providers, providing a blend of nursing and primary care services to patients and families.

Work Environment

As the largest healthcare occupation, registered nurses held about 2.7 million jobs in 2010. The industries that employed the most registered nurses in 2010 were as follows:

General medical and surgical hospitals; private	48%
Offices of physicians	8
General medical and surgical hospitals; local	6
Home health care services	5
Nursing care facilities	5

The remainder worked mainly in government agencies, administrative and support services, and educational services.

Most registered nurses work in well-lit, comfortable healthcare facilities. Home health and public health nurses travel to patients' homes, schools, community centers, and other sites.

Some registered nurses work in correctional facilities, schools, summer camps, and nurses often work with the military. Some move frequently, traveling in the United States and throughout the world to help care for patients in places where there are not enough healthcare workers.

Injuries

Registered nurses may spend a lot of time walking, bending, stretching, and standing. They are vulnerable to back injuries because they must often lift and move patients. The work of registered nurses may put them in close contact with people who have infectious diseases, and they often come in contact with potentially harmful and hazardous drugs and other substances. Therefore, registered nurses must follow strict, standardized guidelines to guard against diseases and other dangers, such as radiation, accidental needle sticks, or the chemicals they use to sterilize instruments.

Work Schedules

Because patients in hospitals and nursing care facilities need round-the-clock care, nurses in these settings usually work in rotating shifts, covering all 24 hours. They may work nights, weekends, and holidays. They may also be on call.

Nurses who work in offices, schools, and other places that do not provide 24-hour care are more likely to work regular business hours. In 2010, about 20 percent of registered nurses worked part time.

How to Become a Registered Nurse

Registered nurses usually take one of three education paths: a bachelor's of science degree in nursing (BSN), an associate's degree in nursing (ADN), or a diploma from an approved nursing program. Registered nurses must also be licensed.

Education

In all nursing education programs, students take courses in nursing, anatomy, physiology, microbiology, chemistry, nutrition, psychology and other social and behavioral sciences, as well as in liberal arts. BSN programs typically take four years to complete; ADN and diploma programs usually take two to three years to complete.

All programs also include supervised clinical experience in hospital departments such as pediatrics, psychiatry, maternity, and surgery. A number of programs include clinical experience in extended and long-term care facilities, public health departments, home health agencies, or ambulatory (walk-in) clinics.

Bachelor's degree programs usually include more training in the physical and social sciences, communication, leadership, and critical thinking, which is becoming more important as nursing practice becomes more complex. They also offer more clinical experience in nonhospital settings. A bachelor's degree or higher is often necessary for administrative positions, research, consulting, and teaching.

Generally, licensed graduates of any of the three types of education programs (bachelor's, associate's, or diploma) qualify for entry-level positions as a staff nurse.

Many registered nurses with an ADN or diploma find an entry-level position and then take advantage of tuition reimbursement benefits to work toward a BSN by completing an RN-to-BSN program. There are also master's degree programs in nursing, combined bachelor's and master's programs, and programs for those who wish to enter the nursing profession but hold a bachelor's degree in another field.

Important Qualities

Critical-thinking skills. Registered nurses must be able to assess changes in the health state of patients, including when to take corrective action and when to make referrals.

Compassion. Registered nurses should be caring and sympathetic, characteristics that are valuable when treating patients.

Detail oriented. Registered nurses must be responsible and detail oriented because they must make sure that patients get the correct treatments and medicines at the right time.

Emotional stability. Registered nurses need emotional stability to cope with human suffering, emergencies, and other stresses.

Organizational skills. Nurses often work with multiple patients with various health needs, and organizational skills are critical to ensure the patient is given proper care.

Patience. Registered nurses should be patient so they can provide quality care under stressful or hectic circumstances.

Speaking skills. Registered nurses must be able to talk effectively with patients to correctly assess their health conditions. Nurses need to clearly explain how to take medication or give other instructions. They must be able to work in teams with other health professionals and communicate the patients' needs.

Licenses

In all states, the District of Columbia, and U.S. territories, registered nurses must have a nursing license.

To become licensed, nurses must graduate from an approved nursing program and pass the National Council Licensure Examination, or NCLEX-RN.

Other requirements for licensing vary by state. Each state's board of nursing can give details. (For more on the NCLEX-RN examination and a list of state boards of nursing visit the National Council of State Boards of Nursing .)

Certification

Nurses may become credentialed through professional associations in specialties such as ambulatory care, gerontology, and pediatrics, among others. Although certification is usually voluntary, it demonstrates adherence to a higher standard, and some employers may require it. Certification is required for all registered nurses serving in any of the four advanced practice registered nurse roles.

Advancement

Most registered nurses begin as staff nurses in hospitals or community health settings. With experience, good performance, and continuous education they can move to other settings or be promoted to positions with more responsibility.

In management, nurses can advance from assistant unit manager or head nurse to more senior-level administrative roles, such as assistant director, director, vice president, or chief of nursing. Increasingly, management-level nursing positions require a graduate degree in nursing or health services administration. Administrative positions require leadership, communication and negotiation skills, and good judgment.

Some RNs choose to become advanced practice registered nurses (APRNs). APRNs work independently or in collaboration with physicians. They may provide primary care, and, in most states, they may prescribe medications. APRNs require at least a master's degree. Each state's board of nursing can provide the specific regulations regarding APRNs.

Some nurses move into the business side of healthcare. Their nursing expertise and experience on a healthcare team equip them to manage ambulatory, acute, home-based, and chronic care businesses.

Employers—including hospitals, insurance companies, pharmaceutical manufacturers, and managed care organizations, among others—need registered nurses for jobs in health planning and development, marketing, consulting, policy development, and quality assurance.

Other nurses work as postsecondary teachers in colleges and universities. For more information, see the profile on postsecondary teachers .

Pay

Registered Nurses
Median annual wages, May 2010

Health Diagnosing and Treating Practitioners	$71,490
Registered Nurses	$64,690
Total, All Occupations	$33,840

Note: All Occupations includes all occupations in the U.S. Economy.
Source: U.S. Bureau of Labor Statistics, Occupational Employment Statistics

The median annual wage of registered nurses was $64,690 in May 2010. The median wage is the wage at which half of the workers in an occupation earned more than that amount and half earned less. The lowest 10 percent earned less than $44,190 and the top 10 percent earned more than $95,130.

As shown in the tabulation below, median annual wages for registered nurses in private general medical and surgical hospitals were $66,650 in May 2010, highest among those industries employing much of the occupation.

General medical and surgical hospitals; private	$66,650
Offices of physicians	62,880
General medical and surgical hospitals; local	62,690
Home health care services	60,690
Nursing care facilities	58,180

Many employers offer flexible work schedules, child care, educational benefits, and bonuses. About 19 percent of registered nurses are union members or covered by a union contract.

Because patients in hospitals and nursing care facilities need round-the-clock care, nurses in these settings usually work in rotating shifts, covering all 24 hours. They may work nights, weekends, and holidays. They may also be on call, which means they are on duty and must be available to work on short notice.

Nurses who work in offices, schools, and other places that do not provide 24-hour care are more likely to work regular business hours.

In 2010, about 20 percent of registered nurses worked part time.

Job Outlook

Registered Nurses
Percent change in employment, projected 2010-20

Health Diagnosing and Treating Practitioners	26%
Registered Nurses	26%
Total, All Occupations	14%

Note: All Occupations includes all occupations in the U.S. Economy.
Source: U.S. Bureau of Labor Statistics, Employment Projections program

Employment of registered nurses is expected to grow 26 percent from 2010 to 2020, faster than the average for all occupations. Growth will occur primarily because of technological advancements, permitting a greater number of health problems to be treated; an increased emphasis on preventive care; and the large, aging baby boomer population who will demand more healthcare services as they live longer and more active lives than previous generations. Faster than average growth is expected in traditional hospital settings, as well as in non-hospital settings, such as physician's offices and home healthcare services.

Growth is expected to be much faster than average in outpatient care centers, where patients do not stay overnight, such as those that provide same-day chemotherapy, rehabilitation, and surgery. Also, an increased number of procedures, as well as more sophisticated procedures once done only in hospitals, are being done in physicians' offices.

The financial pressure on hospitals to discharge patients as soon as possible should mean more people admitted to extended and long-term care facilities and more need for home healthcare. As the baby boomers grow older, there will be greater demand for home healthcare.

In addition, because many older people want to be treated at home or in residential care facilities, registered nurses will be in demand in those settings. Job growth is also expected in facilities that provide long-term rehabilitation for stroke and head injury patients, as well as facilities that treat people with Alzheimer's disease (memory loss, dementia).

Job Prospects

Overall, job opportunities for registered nurses are expected to be excellent. Employers in some parts of the country and in some employment settings report difficulty in attracting and keeping enough registered nurses.

Job opportunities should be excellent, even in hospitals, because of the relatively high turnover of hospital nurses. To attract and keep qualified nurses, hospitals may offer signing bonuses, family-friendly work schedules, or subsidized training.

In physicians' offices and outpatient care centers, registered nurses may face greater competition for positions because these jobs generally offer regular working hours and provide more comfortable working conditions than hospitals.

Generally, registered nurses with at least a bachelor's degree in nursing (BSN) will have better job prospects than those without one.

In addition, all four advanced practice registered nurses—clinical nurse specialists, nurse anesthetists, nurse-midwives, and nurse practitioners—will be in high demand, particularly in medically underserved areas such as inner cities and rural areas.

Employment projections data for registered nurses, 2010-20

Occupational Title	SOC Code	Employment, 2010	Projected Employment, 2020	Change, 2010-20	
				Percent	Numeric
Registered Nurses	29-1111	2,737,400	3,449,300	26	711,900
SOURCE: U.S. Bureau of Labor Statistics, Employment Projections program					

Similar Occupations

This table shows a list of occupations with job duties that are similar to those of registered nurses.

Occupation	Job Duties	Entry-Level Education	Median Annual Pay, May 2010
Dental Hygienists	Dental hygienists clean teeth, examine patients for oral diseases such as gingivitis, and provide other preventative dental care. They also educate patients on ways to improve and maintain good oral health.	Associate's degree	$68,250
Diagnostic Medical Sonographers	Diagnostic medical sonographers use special imaging equipment that directs sound waves into a patient's body (in a procedure commonly known as an ultrasound, sonogram, or echocardiogram) to assess and diagnose various medical conditions.	Associate's degree	$64,380
EMTs and Paramedics	Emergency medical technicians (EMTs) and paramedics care for the sick or injured in emergency medical settings. People's lives often depend on their quick reaction and competent care. EMTs and paramedics respond to emergency calls, performing medical services and transporting patients to medical facilities.	Postsecondary non-degree award	$30,360
Licensed Practical and Licensed Vocational Nurses	Licensed practical and licensed vocational nurses (known as LPNs or LVNs, depending on the state in which they work) provide basic nursing care. They work under the direction of registered nurses and doctors.	Postsecondary non-degree award	$40,380
Physician Assistants	Physician assistants, also known as PAs, practice medicine under the direction of physicians and surgeons. They are formally trained to examine patients, diagnose injuries and illnesses, and provide treatment.	Master's degree	$86,410

Contacts for More Information

For more information about registered nurses, including credentialing, visit American Nurses Association

For more information about nursing education and being a registered nurse, visit National League for Nursing ,Registered Nurse RN

For information about undergraduate and graduate nursing education, nursing career options, and financial aid, visit American Association of Colleges of Nursing

For information about the National Council Licensure Examination (NCLEX-RN) and a list of individual state boards of nursing, visit National Council of State Boards of Nursing

For information about clinical nurse specialists, including a list of accredited programs, visit National Association of Clinical Nurse Specialists

For information about nurse anesthetists, including a list of accredited programs, visit American Association of Nurse Anesthetists

For information about nurse-midwives, including a list of accredited programs, visit American College of Nurse-Midwives

For information about nurse practitioners, including a list of accredited programs, visit American Academy of Nurse Practitioners

Suggested citation:

Respiratory Therapists

Quick Facts: Respiratory Therapists	
2010 Median Pay	$54,280 per year $26.10 per hour
Entry-Level Education	Associate's degree
Work Experience in a Related Occupation	None
On-the-job Training	None
Number of Jobs, 2010	112,700
Job Outlook, 2010-20	28% (Faster than average)
Employment Change, 2010-20	31,200

What Respiratory Therapists Do

Respiratory therapists care for patients who have trouble breathing; for example, from a chronic respiratory disease, such as asthma or emphysema. Their patients range from premature infants with undeveloped lungs to elderly patients who have diseased lungs. They also provide emergency care to patients suffering from heart attacks, drowning, or shock.

Duties

Respiratory therapists typically do the following:
- Interview and examine patients with breathing or cardiopulmonary disorders
- Consult with physicians to develop patient treatment plans
- Perform diagnostic tests such as measuring lung capacity
- Treat patients, using a variety of methods, including chest physiotherapy and aerosol medications
- Monitor and record the progress of treatment
- Supervise respiratory therapy technicians during tests and evaluate the findings of the tests
- Teach patients how to use treatments

Respiratory therapists use various tests to evaluate patients. For example, therapists test lung capacity by having patients breathe into an instrument that measures the volume and flow of oxygen when they inhale and exhale. Respiratory therapists may also take blood samples and use a blood gas analyzer to test the oxygen and carbon dioxide levels present.

Respiratory therapists perform chest physiotherapy on patients to

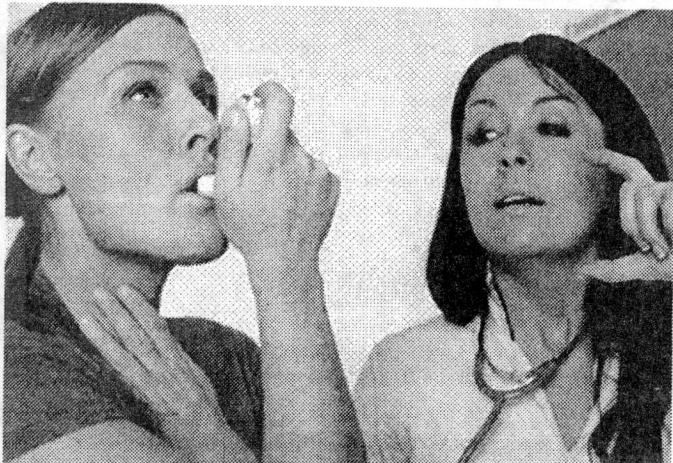

Respiratory therapists teach patients how to use treatments such as inhalers to help improve their breathing.

remove mucus from their lungs and make it easier for them to breathe. Removing mucus is necessary for patients suffering from lung diseases, such as cystic fibrosis, and involves the therapist vibrating the patient's rib cage, often by tapping the patient's chest and encouraging him or her to cough.

Respiratory therapists may connect patients who cannot breathe on their own to ventilators to deliver oxygen to the lungs. Therapists insert a tube in the patient's windpipe (trachea), and connect the tube to ventilator equipment. They set and monitor the equipment to ensure that the patient is receiving the correct amount of oxygen at the correct rate.

Respiratory therapists who work in home care teach patients and their families to use ventilators and other life-support systems in their homes. During these visits, they may inspect and clean equipment, check the home for environmental hazards, and ensure that patients know how to use their medications. Therapists also make emergency home visits when necessary.

In some hospitals, respiratory therapists are involved in related areas, such as counseling people on how to stop smoking and diagnosing breathing problems for people with sleep apnea.

Work Environment

Respiratory therapists held about 112,700 jobs in 2010. Most respiratory therapists work in hospitals. Others may work in nursing care facilities or travel to patients' homes. Respiratory therapists are on their feet for long periods and may need to lift or turn disabled patients.

Like other healthcare workers, respiratory therapists may be exposed to infectious diseases.

Work Schedules

Most respiratory therapists work full time. Because they may work in medical facilities such as hospitals that are always open, some may work evening, night, or weekend hours.

How to Become a Respiratory Therapist

Respiratory therapists need an associate's or bachelor's degree. Respiratory therapists are licensed in all states except Alaska; requirements vary by state.

Education

Respiratory therapists need at least an associate's degree, but employers look favorably on applicants who have more education. Many colleges and universities, vocational-technical institutes, and the Armed Forces offer training. Most programs award an associate's or bachelor's degree.

All programs have clinical components that allow therapists to earn course credit and gain supervised, practical experience treating patients.

Respiratory therapy programs include courses in human anatomy and physiology, chemistry, physics, microbiology, pharmacology, and mathematics. Other courses deal with therapeutic and diagnostic procedures and tests, equipment, patient assessment, and cardiopulmonary resuscitation (CPR).

High school students interested in applying to respiratory therapy programs should take courses in health, biology, mathematics, chemistry, and physics.

Licenses

Respiratory therapists are licensed in all states except Alaska, although requirements vary by state. Licensure requirements in most states include completing a state or professional certification exam. For specific state requirements, contact your state's health board.

Certification

Many employers prefer to hire respiratory therapists who have certification. Certification is not always required, but it is widely respected throughout the occupation. Certification usually requires graduating from an accredited program and passing a certification exam and is often required in order to get a state license.

The National Board for Respiratory Care (NBRC) is the main certifying body for respiratory therapists. The Board offers two levels of certification: the Certified Respiratory Therapist (CRT) and the Registered Respiratory Therapist (RRT).

The first-level certification available from NBRC for respiratory therapists is the CRT certification. Applicants must have earned an associate's degree from an accredited respiratory therapy program, or completed the equivalent coursework in a bachelor's degree program, and pass an exam.

The second-level certification available from NBRC is the RRT certification. Applicants must have a CRT certification, meet other education or experience requirements, and pass an exam.

Important Qualities

Compassion. Respiratory therapists should be able to provide emotional support to patients undergoing treatment and be sympathetic to their needs.

Detail oriented. Respiratory therapists must be detail oriented to ensure that patients are receiving the appropriate treatments and medications in a timely manner. They must also monitor and record various pieces of information related to patient care.

Interpersonal skills. Respiratory therapists interact with patients and often work as part of a team. They must be able to follow instructions from a supervising physician.

Patience. Respiratory therapists may work for long periods with patients who need special attention.

Problem-solving skills. Respiratory therapists need strong problem-solving skills. They must evaluate patients' symptoms, consult with other healthcare professionals, and recommend and administer the appropriate treatments.

Science and mathematical skills. Respiratory therapists must understand anatomy, physiology, and other sciences and be able to calculate the right dose of a patient's medicine.

Pay

Respiratory Therapists
Median annual wages, May 2010

Health Diagnosing and Treating Practitioners	$71,490
Respiratory Therapists	$54,280
Total, All Occupations	$33,840

Note: All Occupations includes all occupations in the U.S. Economy.
Source: U.S. Bureau of Labor Statistics, Occupational Employment Statistics

The median annual wage of respiratory therapists was $54,280 in May 2010. The median wage is the wage at which half the workers in an occupation earned more than that amount and half earned less. The lowest 10 percent earned less than $39,990, and the top 10 percent more than $73,410.

As shown in the tabulation below, the median annual wage for respiratory therapists varies between the industries they are employed in.

Nursing care facilities	$57,450
Home health care services	55,960
Hospitals; state, local, and private	54,210
Offices of physicians	52,500

Most respiratory therapists work full time. Because they may work in medical facilities such as hospitals that are always open, some work evening, night, or weekend hours.

Job Outlook

Respiratory Therapists
Percent change in employment, projected 2010-20

Respiratory Therapists	28%
Health Diagnosing and Treating Practitioners	26%
Total, All Occupations	14%

Note: All Occupations includes all occupations in the U.S. Economy.
Source: U.S. Bureau of Labor Statistics, Employment Projections program

Employment of respiratory therapists is expected to grow by 28 percent from 2010 to 2020, faster than the average for all occupations. Growth in the middle-aged and elderly population will lead to an increased incidence of respiratory conditions such as emphysema, chronic bronchitis, and pneumonia, respiratory disorders that permanently damage the lungs or restrict lung function. These factors will lead to an increased demand for respiratory therapy services and treatments, mostly in hospitals and nursing homes. In addition, advances in preventing and detecting disease, improved medications, and more sophisticated treatments will increase the demand for respiratory therapists. Other conditions affecting the general population, such as smoking, air pollution, and respiratory emergencies, will continue to create demand for respiratory therapists.

Job Prospects

Respiratory therapists with certification or a bachelor's degree will have the best job prospects.

Employment projections data for respiratory therapists, 2010-20

Occupational Title	SOC Code	Employment, 2010	Projected Employment, 2020	Change, 2010-20	
				Percent	Numeric
Respiratory Therapists	29-1126	112,700	143,900	28	31,200
SOURCE: U.S. Bureau of Labor Statistics, Employment Projections program					

Similar Occupations

This table shows a list of occupations with job duties that are similar to those of respiratory therapists.

Occupation	Job Duties	Entry-Level Education	Median Annual Pay, May 2010
Athletic Trainers	Athletic trainers specialize in preventing, diagnosing, and treating muscle and bone injuries and illnesses. They work with people of all ages and all skill levels, from young children to soldiers and professional athletes.	Bachelor's degree	$41,600
Occupational Therapists	Occupational therapists treat patients with injuries, illnesses, or disabilities through the therapeutic use of everyday activities. They help these patients develop, recover, and improve the skills needed for daily living and working.	Master's degree	$72,320
Physical Therapists	Physical therapists help people who have injuries or illnesses improve their movement and manage their pain. They are often an important part of rehabilitation and treatment of patients with chronic conditions or injuries.	Doctoral or professional degree	$76,310
Radiation Therapists	Radiation therapists treat cancer and other diseases in patients by giving radiation treatments.	Associate's degree	$74,980
Registered Nurses	Registered nurses (RNs) provide and coordinate patient care, educate patients and the public about various health conditions, and provide advice and emotional support to patients and their family members.	Associate's degree	$64,690

Contacts for More Information

For more information about respiratory therapists, visit American Association for Respiratory Care

For a list of accredited educational programs for respiratory care practitioners, visit Commission on Accreditation for Respiratory Care

For a list of state licensing agencies, as well as information on gaining credentials in respiratory care, visit National Board for Respiratory Care, Inc.

Suggested citation:

Bureau of Labor Statistics, U.S. Department of Labor, Occupational Outlook Handbook, 2012-13 Edition, Respiratory Therapists, on the Internet at http://www.bls.gov/ooh/healthcare/respiratory-therapists.htm .

Speech-Language Pathologists

Quick Facts: Speech-Language Pathologists	
2010 Median Pay	$66,920 per year $32.17 per hour
Entry-Level Education	Master's degree
Work Experience in a Related Occupation	None
On-the-job Training	None
Number of Jobs, 2010	123,200
Job Outlook, 2010-20	23% (Faster than average)
Employment Change, 2010-20	28,800

What Speech-Language Pathologists Do

Speech-language pathologists, sometimes called speech therapists, assess, diagnose, treat, and help to prevent communication and swallowing disorders in patients. Speech, language, and swallowing disorders result from a variety of causes such as a stroke, brain injury, hearing loss, developmental delay, a cleft palate, cerebral palsy, or emotional problems.

Duties

When diagnosing patients, speech-language pathologists typically do the following:

- Communicate with patients to evaluate their levels of speech or language difficulty
- Determine the extent of communication problems by having a patient complete basic reading and vocalizing tasks or by giving standardized tests
- Identify treatment options
- Create and carry out an individualized treatment plan

When treating patients, speech-language pathologists typically do the following:

- Teach patients how to make sounds and improve their voices
- Teach alternative communication methods, such as sign language, to patients with little or no speech capability

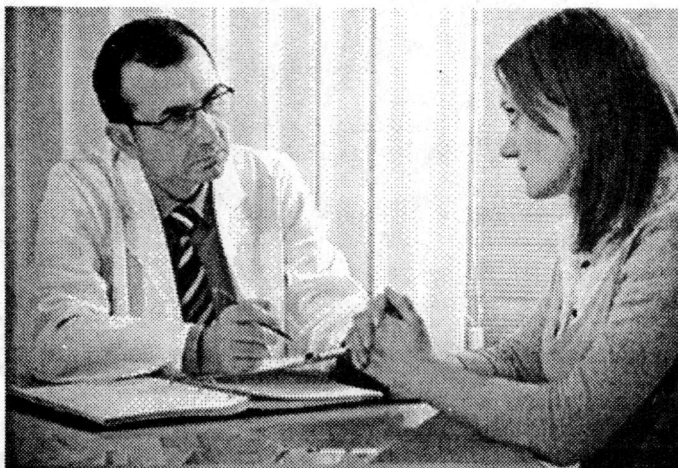

Speech-language pathologists diagnose and treat a variety of speech, language, and swallowing disorders in patients.

- Work with patients to increase their ability to read and write correctly
- Work with patients to develop and strengthen the muscles used to swallow
- Counsel patients and families on how to cope with communication disorders

Speech-language pathologists work with patients who have problems with speech, such as being unable to speak at all or speaking with difficulty, or with rhythm and fluency, such as stuttering. They may work with those who are unable to understand language or with people who have voice disorders, such as inappropriate pitch or a harsh voice.

Speech-language pathologists must also do various administrative tasks, including keeping good records. They record their initial patient evaluations and diagnoses, treatment progress, any changes in a patient's condition or treatment plan, and, eventually, their final evaluation when the patient finishes the therapy.

Some speech-language pathologists specialize in working with specific age groups, such as children or the elderly. Others focus on treatment programs for specific communication or swallowing problems, such as those resulting from strokes or cleft palate.

In medical facilities, speech-language pathologists work with physicians, social workers, psychologists, and other therapists. For more information, see the profiles on physicians and surgeons , social workers , and psychologists . In schools, they work with teachers, special educators, other school personnel, and parents to develop and carry out individual or group programs, provide counseling, and support classroom activities. For more information, see the profiles on preschool , kindergarten and elementary school , middle school , high school , and special education teachers .

Work Environment

Speech-language pathologists held about 123,200 jobs in 2010. Almost half of all speech-language pathologists work in schools. Most others work in healthcare facilities. Some work in patients' homes.

The following industries employed the majority of speech-language pathologists in 2010:

Elementary and secondary schools; state, local, and private	44%
Offices of physical, occupational and speech therapists, and audiologists	15
Hospitals; state, local, and private	13
Nursing care facilities	4
Home health care services	3

Work Schedules

Most speech-language pathologists work full time. Those who work on a contract basis may spend a lot of time traveling between facilities.

How to Become a Speech-Language Pathologist

Speech-language pathologists typically need at least a master's degree. They must be licensed in most states; requirements vary by state.

Education

The standard level of education for speech-language pathologists is a master's degree. Although master's programs do not specify a particular undergraduate degree for admission, certain courses must be taken before entering the program. Required courses vary by institution. Graduate programs often include courses in age-specific speech disorders, alternative communication methods, and swallowing disorders. These programs also include supervised clinical practice in addition to coursework.

The Council on Academic Accreditation (CAA), part of the American Speech-Language-Hearing Association , accredits education programs in speech-language pathology. In 2010, the CAA accredited 253 master's degree programs in speech-language pathology.

Licenses

Speech-language pathologists must be licensed in almost all states. A license requires at least a master's degree and supervised clinical experience. Some states require graduation from an accredited program to get a license. For specific requirements, contact your state's medical or health licensure board.

Certification

Speech-language pathologists can earn the Certificate of Clinical Competence in Speech-Language Pathology (CCC-SLP) offered by the American Speech-Language-Hearing Association . Certification satisfies some or all of the requirements for licensure and may be required by some employers.

Important Qualities

Compassion. Speech-language pathologists work with people who are often frustrated by their difficulties. Speech-language pathologists must be able to support emotionally demanding patients and their families.

Critical-thinking skills. Speech-language pathologists must be able to adjust their treatment plans as needed, finding alternative ways to help their patients.

Detail oriented. The work of speech-language pathologists requires intense concentration to listen to what patients are able to say and to help them improve their speech.

Listening skills. Speech-language pathologists must listen to a patient's symptoms and problems to decide on a course of treatment.

Patience. Speech-language pathologists may work with people who need more time and attention.

Speaking skills. Speech-language pathologists need to communicate test results, diagnoses, and proposed treatments in a way that patients and their families can understand.

Pay

Speech-Language Pathologists
Median annual wages, May 2010

Health Diagnosing and Treating Practitioners	$71,490
Speech-Language Pathologists	$66,920
Total, All Occupations	$33,840

Note: All Occupations includes all occupations in the U.S. Economy.
Source: U.S. Bureau of Labor Statistics, Occupational Employment Statistics

The median annual wage of speech-language pathologists was $66,920 in May 2010. The median wage is the wage at which half the workers in an occupation earned more than that amount and half earned less. The lowest 10 percent earned less than $42,970, and the top 10 percent more than $103,630.

Most speech-language pathologists work full time. Those who work on a contract basis may spend considerable time traveling between facilities to treat patients.

Job Outlook

Speech-Language Pathologists
Percent change in employment, projected 2010-20

Health Diagnosing and Treating Practitioners	26%
Speech-Language Pathologists	23%
Total, All Occupations	14%

Note: All Occupations includes all occupations in the U.S. Economy.
Source: U.S. Bureau of Labor Statistics, Employment Projections program

Employment of speech-language pathologists is expected to grow by 23 percent from 2010 to 2020, faster than the average for all occupations.

As the large baby-boom population grows older, there will be more instances of health conditions that cause speech or language impairments, such as strokes and hearing loss. These increases are expected to add to the number of speech and language disorders in the population and require more speech-language pathologists to treat these patients.

Increased awareness of speech and language disorders, such as stuttering, in younger children should also lead to a need for more speech-language pathologists who specialize in treating that age group.

In addition, medical advances are improving the survival rate of premature infants and victims of trauma and strokes, many of whom need help from speech-language pathologists.

Employment projections data for speech-language pathologists, 2010-20

Occupational Title	SOC Code	Employment, 2010	Projected Employment, 2020	Change, 2010-20	
				Percent	Numeric
Speech-Language Pathologists	29-1127	123,200	152,000	23	28,800
SOURCE: U.S. Bureau of Labor Statistics, Employment Projections program					

Similar Occupations

This table shows a list of occupations with job duties that are similar to those of speech-language pathologists.

Occupation	Job Duties	Entry-Level Education	Median Annual Pay, May 2010
Occupational Therapists	Occupational therapists treat patients with injuries, illnesses, or disabilities through the therapeutic use of everyday activities. They help these patients develop, recover, and improve the skills needed for daily living and working.	Master's degree	$72,320
Physical Therapists	Physical therapists help people who have injuries or illnesses improve their movement and manage their pain. They are often an important part of rehabilitation and treatment of patients with chronic conditions or injuries.	Doctoral or professional degree	$76,310
Recreational Therapists	Recreational therapists plan, direct, and coordinate recreation programs for people with disabilities or illnesses. They use a variety of techniques, including arts and crafts, drama, music, dance, sports, games, and field trips. These programs help maintain or improve a client's physical and emotional well-being.	Bachelor's degree	$39,410
Audiologists	Audiologists diagnose and treat a patient's hearing and balance problems using advanced technology and procedures.	Doctoral or professional degree	$66,660
Psychologists	Psychologists study mental processes and human behavior by observing, interpreting, and recording how people and other animals relate to one another and the environment.	See How to Become One	$68,640

Contacts for More Information

For more information about speech-language pathologists, a description of the CCC-SLP credential, and a listing of accredited graduate programs in speech-language pathology, visit American Speech-Language-Hearing Association

State licensing boards have information about licensure requirements. State departments of education can provide information about certification requirements for those who want to work in public schools.

Suggested citation:

Bureau of Labor Statistics, U.S. Department of Labor, Occupational Outlook Handbook, 2012-13 Edition, Speech-Language Pathologists, on the Internet at http://www.bls.gov/ooh/healthcare/speech-language-pathologists.htm .

Surgical Technologists

Quick Facts: Surgical Technologists	
2010 Median Pay	$39,920 per year $19.19 per hour
Entry-Level Education	Postsecondary non-degree award
Work Experience in a Related Occupation	None
On-the-job Training	None
Number of Jobs, 2010	93,600
Job Outlook, 2010-20	19% (About as fast as average)
Employment Change, 2010-20	17,700

What Surgical Technologists Do

Surgical technologists, also called operating room technicians, assist in surgical operations. They prepare operating rooms, arrange equipment, and help doctors and nurses during surgeries.

Duties

Surgical technologists typically do the following:

- Prepare operating rooms for surgery
- Sterilize equipment and make sure that there are adequate supplies for surgery
- Prepare patients for surgery, such as washing and disinfecting incision sites
- Help surgeons and nurses during surgery by passing them instruments and other sterile supplies

Surgical technologists work as members of a healthcare team alongside physicians and surgeons, registered nurses, and other healthcare workers. For more information, see the profiles on physicians and surgeons or registered nurses .

Before an operation, surgical technologists prepare the operating room by setting up surgical instruments and equipment. They also prepare patients for surgery by washing and disinfecting incision sites, positioning patients on the operating table, and covering patients with sterile drapes. Surgical technologists prepare sterile solutions used in surgery and check that all surgical equipment is working properly. They help the surgical team put on sterile gowns and gloves.

During an operation, surgical technologists pass instruments and supplies to surgeons and first assistants. Technologists also may prepare, care for, and dispose of specimens taken for laboratory analysis. In addition, they apply dressings. After an operation, surgical technologists may help transfer patients to recovery rooms and may clean and restock operating rooms.

Work Environment

Surgical technologists held about 93,600 jobs in 2010. The industries employing the largest number of surgical technologists in 2010 were as follows:

General medical and surgical hospitals; state, local, and private	69%
Offices of physicians	12
Outpatient care centers	8
Offices of dentists	4

Most surgical technologists work in hospitals. Some work in outpatient surgery centers or in offices of physicians or dentists who perform outpatient surgery. Surgical technologists wear scrubs (special sterile clothing) while they are in the operating room. They are typically on their feet and work next to others. At times, they may be exposed to communicable diseases and unpleasant sights, odors, and materials.

Work Schedules

Most surgical technologists work full time. Surgical technologists employed in hospitals may work or be on call during nights, weekends, and holidays. They may be required to work shifts lasting longer than eight hours.

How to Become a Surgical Technologist

Surgical technologists typically need a postsecondary certificate or associate's degree. Certification also can help a surgical technologist find a position. A small number of states regulate surgical technologists.

Education

People interested in surgical technology should take high school courses in health, biology, chemistry, and mathematics.

Surgical technologists typically need some type of postsecondary education. Accredited programs in surgical technology are in many

Surgical technologists assist doctors in the operating room.

community colleges and vocational schools. Programs range in length from several months to two years, and they grant a certificate or associate's degree. Admission typically requires a high school diploma or equivalent.

Surgical technology education includes courses in anatomy, biology, medical terminology, and other topics. Students also work in supervised clinical settings to gain hands-on skills as technologists. In addition, technologists are trained in the care and safety of patients, sterilization techniques, and preventing and controlling infections.

In 2010, accredited training programs were recognized by the Commission on Accreditation of Allied Health Education Programs (CAAHEP).

Important Qualities

Detail oriented. Surgical technologists must pay close attention to their work at all times. For example, they need to provide the correct sterile equipment for surgeons and nurses during an operation.

Dexterity. Surgical technologists should be comfortable working with their hands. They must be able to provide the needed equipment quickly.

Stamina. Surgical technologists should be comfortable standing for an extended period.

Stress-management skills. Working in an operating room can be stressful. Surgical technologists should be able to work well under pressure while providing a high level of care.

Certification

Certification can help a surgical technologist find a position. Surgical technologists earn certification through one of two credentialing organizations. Certification through the National Board of Surgical Technology and Surgical Assisting allows the use of the title "Certified Surgical Technologist." Certification through the National Center for Competency Testing allows the use of the title "Tech in Surgery-Certified." Certification typically requires completing an accredited formal education program, passing an exam, and undergoing continuing education.

The National Healthcare Association (NHA) also offers the Certified Operating Room and Surgical Technician (CORST) certification. Candidates can complete an accredited training program, or have one year of experience working in the field. After passing the exam, individuals may use the designation Certified Operating Room Surgical Technician (CORST). This certification must be renewed every two years through either continuing education or reexamination. Additional information can be found on the CORST information page .

A small number of states and the District of Columbia have regulations governing the work of surgical technologists. In these jurisdictions, surgical technologists must have graduated from an accredited education program and received certification.

Advancement

With experience and additional education, surgical technologists can advance to become surgical assistants. Surgical technologists also occasionally advance to other healthcare occupations, such as physician assistants or registered nurses. For more information, see the profiles on physician assistants and registered nurses .

Pay

Surgical Technologists
Median annual wages, May 2010

Surgical Technologists	$39,920
Health Technologists and Technicians	$39,340
Total, All Occupations	$33,840

Note: All Occupations includes all occupations in the U.S. Economy.
Source: U.S. Bureau of Labor Statistics, Occupational Employment Statistics

The median annual wage of surgical technologists was $39,920 in May 2010. The median annual wage is the wage at which half the workers in an occupation earned more than that amount and half earned less. The lowest 10 percent earned less than $28,100, and the top 10 percent earned more than $57,330.

Median annual wages in the industries employing the largest number of surgical technologists in May 2010 were as follows:

Outpatient care centers	$41,210
Offices of physicians	41,030
General medical and surgical hospitals; state, local, and private	39,600
Offices of dentists	36,480

Most surgical technologists work full time. Surgical technologists employed in hospitals may work or be on call during nights, weekends, and holidays. They may be required to work shifts lasting longer than 8 hours.

Job Outlook

Surgical Technologists
Percent change in employment, projected 2010-20

Health Technologists and Technicians	26%
Surgical Technologists	19%
Total, All Occupations	14%

Note: All Occupations includes all occupations in the U.S. Economy.
Source: U.S. Bureau of Labor Statistics, Employment Projections program

Employment of surgical technologists is expected to increase 19 percent from 2010 to 2020, about as fast as the average for all occupations.

Advances in medical technology have made surgery safer, and more operations are being done to treat a variety of illnesses and injuries. The aging of the large number of baby boomers also is expected to increase the need for surgical technologists because older people usually require more operations, including joint replacements and heart-related procedures. Hospitals will continue to be the primary employer of surgical technologists, reducing costs by employing technologists, instead of higher paid registered nurses, in operating rooms.

Job Prospects

Job prospects should be best for surgical technologists who have completed an accredited education program and who maintain their professional certification.

Employment projections data for surgical technologists, 2010-20

Occupational Title	SOC Code	Employment, 2010	Projected Employment, 2020	Change, 2010-20 Percent	Change, 2010-20 Numeric
Percent	Numeric				
Surgical Technologists	29-2055	93,600	111,300	19	17,700

SOURCE: U.S. Bureau of Labor Statistics, Employment Projections program

Similar Occupations

This table shows a list of occupations with job duties that are similar to those of surgical technologists.

Occupation	Job Duties	Entry-Level Education	Median Annual Pay, May 2010
Dental Hygienists	Dental hygienists clean teeth, examine patients for oral diseases such as gingivitis, and provide other preventative dental care. They also educate patients on ways to improve and maintain good oral health.	Associate's degree	$68,250
Licensed Practical and Licensed Vocational Nurses	Licensed practical and licensed vocational nurses (known as LPNs or LVNs, depending on the state in which they work) provide basic nursing care. They work under the direction of registered nurses and doctors.	Postsecondary non-degree award	$40,380
Medical and Clinical Laboratory Technologists and Technicians	Medical laboratory technologists (also known as medical laboratory scientists) and medical laboratory technicians collect samples and perform tests to analyze body fluids, tissue, and other substances.	See How to Become One	$46,680
Medical Assistants	Medical assistants complete administrative and clinical tasks in the offices of physicians, podiatrists, chiropractors, and other health practitioners. Their duties vary with the location, specialty, and size of the practice.	High school diploma or equivalent	$28,860

Contacts for More Information

For more information about surgical technologists, including a list of accredited programs, visit Association of Surgical Technologists , Commission on Accreditation of Allied Health Education Programs

For information about becoming a Certified Surgical Technologist, visit National Board of Surgical Technology and Surgical Assisting

For information about becoming a Tech in Surgery-Certified, visit National Center for Competency Testing

Suggested citation:

Bureau of Labor Statistics, U.S. Department of Labor, Occupational Outlook Handbook, 2012-13 Edition, Surgical Technologists, on the Internet at http://www.bls.gov/ooh/healthcare/surgical-technologists.htm .

Veterinarians

Quick Facts: Veterinarians	
2010 Median Pay	$82,040 per year $39.44 per hour
Entry-Level Education	Doctoral or professional degree
Work Experience in a Related Occupation	None
On-the-job Training	None
Number of Jobs, 2010	61,400
Job Outlook, 2010-20	36% (Much faster than average)
Employment Change, 2010-20	22,000

What Veterinarians Do

Veterinarians care for the health of animals. They diagnose, treat, or research medical conditions and diseases of pets, livestock, and animals in zoos, racetracks, and laboratories.

Duties

Veterinarians typically do the following:

- Examine animals to diagnose their health problems
- Treat and dress wounds
- Perform surgery on animals
- Test for and vaccinate against diseases
- Operate medical equipment such as x-ray machines
- Advise animal owners about general care, medical conditions, and treatments
- Prescribe medication
- Euthanize animals

Veterinarians in private clinical practices treat the injuries and illnesses of pets and farm animals with a variety of medical equipment, including surgical tools and x-ray machines. They provide treatment for animals that is similar to what a doctor would do to treat humans.

The following are common types of veterinarians:

Companion animal veterinarians treat pets and generally work in private clinics. According to the American Veterinary Medical Association, 77 percent of veterinarians who work in private clinical practice treat pets. They most often care for cats and dogs, but also treat other pets, such as birds, ferrets, and rabbits. These veterinarians

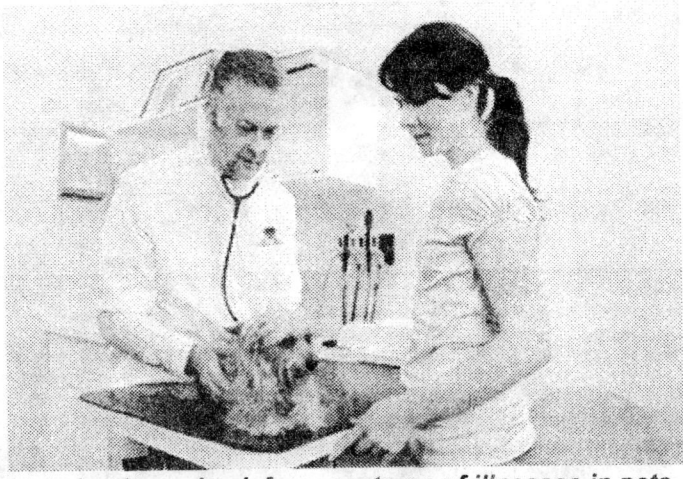

Veterinarians check for symptoms of illnesses in pets.

diagnose animal health problems, consult with owners of animals, and carry out medical procedures, such as vaccinations and setting fractures.

Equine veterinarians work with horses. About 6 percent of private practice veterinarians treat horses.

Food animal veterinarians work with farm animals such as pigs, cattle, and sheep. About 8 percent of private practice veterinarians treat food animals. They spend much of their time at farms and ranches treating illnesses and injuries and testing for and vaccinating against disease. They also may advise owners or managers about feeding, housing, and general health practices.

Food safety and inspection veterinarians inspect livestock and animal products and enforce government food safety regulations. They may inspect livestock, checking the animals for E. coli and other transmittable diseases. They check for food purity and sanitation by inspecting food products, animals and carcasses, and slaughtering and processing plants. Others may work along the country's borders in food safety and security, ensuring abundant and safe food supplies.

Research veterinarians work in laboratories, conducting clinical research on human and animal health problems. These veterinarians may perform tests on animals to identify the effects of drug therapies, or they may test new surgical techniques. They may also research how to prevent, control, or eliminate food- and animal-borne illnesses and diseases.

Some veterinarians teach at colleges and universities. For more information, see the profile on postsecondary teachers .

Work Environment

Veterinarians held about 61,400 jobs in 2010, of which 81 percent were in the veterinary services industry. Others held positions at colleges or universities; in private industry, such as medical or research laboratories; or in federal, state, or local government. About 9 percent were self-employed.

Although most veterinarians work in private clinics, others travel to farms, work outdoors, or work in laboratories.

Veterinarians who treat horses or food animals must travel between their offices and farms or ranches. They work outdoors in all kinds of weather and may have to perform surgery, often under unsanitary conditions.

Veterinarians who work in food safety and inspection must travel to farms, slaughterhouses, and food-processing plants.

Veterinarians who conduct research work primarily in offices and laboratories and spend much of their time dealing with people rather than animals.

Veterinarians' work can sometimes be emotionally stressful as they deal with sick animals and the animals' anxious owners. Also, the workplace can be noisy as the animals make noise when sick or being handled.

When working with animals that are frightened or in pain,

veterinarians risk being bitten, kicked, or scratched.

Work Schedules

Veterinarians often work long hours. Some work nights or weekends, and they may have to respond to emergencies outside of scheduled work hours. About 1 in 4 veterinarians worked more than 50 hours per week in 2010.

How to Become a Veterinarian

Veterinarians must have a Doctor of Veterinary Medicine degree and a state license.

Education

Veterinarians must complete a Doctor of Veterinary Medicine (D.V.M. or V.M.D.) degree at an accredited college of veterinary medicine. There are currently 28 colleges with accredited programs. A veterinary medicine program generally takes 4 years to complete and includes classroom, laboratory, and clinical components.

Although not required, most applicants to veterinary school have a bachelor's degree. Veterinary medical colleges typically require applicants to have taken many science classes, including biology, chemistry, anatomy, physiology, zoology, microbiology, and animal science. Some programs also require math and humanities or social science courses.

Admission to veterinary programs is competitive, and less than half of all applicants were accepted in 2010.

In veterinary medicine programs, students take courses on normal animal anatomy and physiology, as well as disease prevention, diagnosis, and treatment. Most programs include 3 years of classroom, laboratory, and clinical work. Students typically spend the final year of the 4-year program doing clinical rotations in a veterinary medical center or hospital. In veterinary schools today, increasingly, courses also include general business management and career development classes to help new veterinarians learn how to effectively run a practice.

Licenses

All states and the District of Columbia require veterinarians to have a license. Licensing requirements vary by state, but all states require prospective veterinarians to complete an accredited veterinary program and to pass the North American Veterinary Licensing Exam .

Most states require not only the national exam but also have a state exam that covers state laws and regulations. Few states accept licenses from other states, so veterinarians who want to be licensed in a new state must usually take that state's exam.

Training

Although graduates of a veterinary program can begin practicing once they receive their license, many veterinarians pursue further education and training. Some new veterinary graduates enter 1-year internship programs to gain experience. Internships can be valuable experience for veterinarians who apply for competitive or better paying positions or in preparation for a certification program.

Certification

The American Veterinary Medical Association offers certification in 40 different specialties, such as surgery, microbiology, and internal medicine. Although certification is not required for veterinarians, it can show exceptional skill or expertise in a particular field. To sit for the certification exam, veterinarians must have a certain number of years of experience in the field, complete additional education, or complete a residency program, typically lasting 3 to 4 years. Requirements vary by specialty.

Work Experience

When deciding whom to admit, some veterinary medical colleges weigh experience heavily. Formal experience, such as work with veterinarians or scientists in clinics, agribusiness, research, or some area of health science, is particularly advantageous. Less formal experience, such as working with animals on a farm, at a stable, or in an animal shelter, can also be helpful.

Important Qualities

Compassion. Veterinarians must be compassionate when working with animals and their owners. They must treat animals with kindness and must be sensitive when dealing with the owners of sick pets.

Decision-making skills. Veterinarians must decide the correct method for treating the injuries and illnesses of animals. Deciding between euthanizing and treating a sick animal, for instance, can be very difficult.

Interpersonal skills. Strong communication skills are essential for veterinarians, who must be able to explain treatment options to animal owners and give instructions to their staff.

Management skills. Management skills are important for those veterinarians who are in charge of running private clinics or laboratories. In these settings, they are responsible for providing direction, delegating work, and overseeing daily operations.

Manual dexterity. Manual dexterity is important for veterinarians because they must control their hand movements and be precise when treating injuries and performing surgery.

Problem-solving skills. Veterinarians need strong problem-solving skills because they must figure out what is ailing animals. Those who test animals to determine the effects of drug therapies also need excellent diagnostic skills.

Pay

Veterinarians

Median annual wages, May 2010

Veterinarians	$82,040
Health Diagnosing and Treating Practitioners	$71,490
Total, All Occupations	$33,840

Note: All Occupations includes all occupations in the U.S. Economy.
Source: U.S. Bureau of Labor Statistics, Occupational Employment Statistics

The median annual wage of veterinarians was $82,040 in May 2010. The median wage is the wage at which half the workers in an occupation earned more than that amount and half earned less. The lowest 10 percent earned less than $49,910, and the top 10 percent earned more than $145,230.

According to a survey by the American Veterinary Medical Association, average starting salaries for veterinary medical college graduates in 2011 in different private specialties were as follows:

Food animal exclusive	$71,096
Companion animal exclusive	69,789
Companion animal predominant	69,654
Food animal predominant	67,338
Mixed animal	62,655
Equine	43,405

The average annual wage for veterinarians in the federal government was $88,340 in May 2010.

Veterinarians often work long hours. Some work nights or weekends, and they may have to respond to emergencies outside of scheduled work hours. About 1 in 4 veterinarians worked more than 50 hours per week in 2010.

Job Outlook

Veterinarians

Percent change in employment, projected 2010-20

Veterinarians	36%
Health Diagnosing and Treating Practitioners	26%
Total, All Occupations	14%

Note: All Occupations includes all occupations in the U.S. Economy.
Source: U.S. Bureau of Labor Statistics, Employment Projections program

Employment of veterinarians is expected to grow 36 percent from 2010 to 2020, much faster than the average for all occupations.

The need for veterinarians will increase to keep up with the demands of a growing pet population. Many people consider their pets to be a part of their family and are willing to pay more for pet care than owners have in the past. Also, veterinary medicine has advanced considerably, and many of the veterinary services offered today are comparable to health care for humans, including cancer treatments and kidney transplants.

There also will be employment growth in fields related to food and animal safety, disease control, and public health. As the population grows, more veterinarians will be needed to inspect the food supply and ensure animal and human health.

Job Prospects

Overall job opportunities for veterinarians are expected to be good. Although veterinary medicine is growing quickly, there are only 28 accredited veterinary programs in the United States, which produce a limited number of graduates—about 2,500—each year. However, most veterinary graduates are attracted to companion animal care, so job opportunities in that field will be fewer than in other areas.

Job opportunities in large animal practice, public health, and government should be best. Although jobs in farm animal care are not growing as quickly as those in companion animal care, opportunities will be better because fewer veterinarians compete to work with large animals. There also will be excellent job opportunities for government veterinarians in food safety, animal health, and public health.

Employment projections data for veterinarians, 2010-20

Occupational Title	SOC Code	Employment, 2010	Projected Employment, 2020	Change, 2010-20 Percent	Change, 2010-20 Numeric
Veterinarians	29-1131	61,400	83,400	36	22,000
SOURCE: U.S. Bureau of Labor Statistics, Employment Projections program					

Similar Occupations

This table shows a list of occupations with job duties that are similar to those of veterinarians.

Occupation	Job Duties	Entry-Level Education	Median Annual Pay, May 2010
Physicians and Surgeons	Physicians and surgeons diagnose and treat injuries and illnesses in patients. Physicians examine patients, take medical histories, prescribe medications, and order, perform, and interpret diagnostic tests. Surgeons operate on patients to treat injuries, such as broken bones; diseases, such as cancerous tumors; and deformities, such as cleft palates.	Doctoral or professional degree	This wage is equal to or greater than $166,400 per year.
Veterinary Assistants and Laboratory Animal Caretakers	Veterinary assistants and laboratory animal caretakers look after nonfarm animals in laboratories, animal hospitals, and clinics. They care for the well-being of animals by doing routine tasks under the supervision of veterinarians, scientists, or veterinary technologists or technicians.	High school diploma or equivalent	$22,040
Veterinary Technologists and Technicians	Veterinary technologists and technicians perform medical tests under the supervision of a licensed veterinarian to treat or to help veterinarians diagnose the illnesses and injuries of animals.	Associate's degree	$29,710
Medical Scientists	Medical scientists conduct research aimed at improving overall human health. They often use clinical trials and other investigative methods to reach their findings.	Doctoral or professional degree	$76,700
Zoologists and Wildlife Biologists	Zoologists and wildlife biologists study the characteristics and habitats of animals and wildlife.	Bachelor's degree	$57,430
Animal Care and Service Workers	Animal care and service workers care for the needs of animals. They feed, water, groom, bathe, and exercise pets and other nonfarm animals. Job tasks vary by position and place of work.	See How to Become One	$19,780
Agricultural and Food Scientists	Agricultural and food scientists work to ensure agricultural productivity and food safety.	See How to Become One	$58,450

Contacts for More Information

For more information on careers in veterinary medicine, a list of U.S. schools and colleges of veterinary medicine, and information on accreditation policies, visit American Veterinary Medical Association

For more information on veterinary education, visit Association of American Veterinary Medical Colleges

For information on veterinarian positions with the federal government, visit USAJOBS

Suggested citation:

Bureau of Labor Statistics, U.S. Department of Labor, Occupational Outlook Handbook, 2012-13 Edition, Veterinarians, on the Internet at http://www.bls.gov/ooh/healthcare/veterinarians.htm .

Veterinary Assistants and Laboratory Animal Caretakers

Quick Facts: Veterinary Assistants and Laboratory Animal Caretakers	
2010 Median Pay	$22,040 per year $10.60 per hour
Entry-Level Education	High school diploma or equivalent
Work Experience in a Related Occupation	None
On-the-job Training	Short-term on-the-job training
Number of Jobs, 2010	73,200
Job Outlook, 2010-20	14% (About as fast as average)
Employment Change, 2010-20	10,400

What Veterinary Assistants and Laboratory Animal Caretakers Do

Veterinary assistants and laboratory animal caretakers look after nonfarm animals in laboratories, animal hospitals, and clinics. They care for the well-being of animals by doing routine tasks under the supervision of veterinarians, scientists, or veterinary technologists or technicians.

Duties

Veterinary assistants and laboratory animal caretakers typically do the following:

- Monitor and care for animals after surgery
- Maintain and sterilize surgical instruments and equipment
- Clean and disinfect cages, kennels, and examining and operating rooms
- Help provide emergency first aid to sick or injured animals
- Give medication or immunizations that veterinarians prescribe
- Do routine laboratory tests, such as taking x rays
- Feed and bathe animals
- Collect samples such as blood, urine, or tissue for testing

Veterinary assistants and laboratory animal caretakers do many daily tasks, such as feeding, weighing, and taking the temperature of animals. Other routine duties may include giving medication, cleaning cages, or providing nursing care before and after surgery or other medical procedures.

Veterinary assistants and laboratory animal caretakers play a large role in helping veterinarians and scientists with surgery and other procedures. They may prepare equipment and pass surgical instruments and materials to veterinarians during surgery. They may also move animals and hold or restrain them during testing and other procedures.

Veterinary assistants work mainly in clinics and animal hospitals, helping veterinarians or veterinary technicians and technologists treat the injuries and illnesses of animals.

Laboratory animal caretakers work in laboratories under the supervision of a veterinarian, scientist, veterinary technician, or veterinary technologist. Their daily tasks include feeding animals, cleaning kennels, and monitoring the general well-being of laboratory animals.

Work Environment

In 2010, about 84 percent of veterinary assistants and laboratory animal caretakers were employed in the veterinary services industry, which includes private clinics and animal hospitals. Most of the others were employed in laboratories, colleges and universities, and research facilities.

Although the majority of veterinary assistants work in clinics and animal hospitals, others may work outside. Laboratory animal caretakers tend to animals indoors in laboratories and research facilities.

The work of veterinary assistants and laboratory animal caretakers may be physically or emotionally demanding. They may witness abused animals or may need to help euthanize sick, injured, or unwanted animals.

Injuries

Veterinary assistants and laboratory animal caretakers experience a work-related injury and illness rate that is much higher than that of most occupations. When working with scared or aggressive animals, they may be bitten, scratched, or kicked. A worker may be injured while holding, bathing, or restraining an animal.

Work Schedules

Many clinics and laboratories must be staffed 24 hours a day, so veterinary assistants and laboratory animal caretakers may be required to work nights, weekends, or holidays.

How to Become a Veterinary Assistant or Laboratory Animal Caretaker

Most veterinary assistants and laboratory animal caretakers have a high school diploma and learn on the job. Experience working with animals can be useful.

Education

There is no formal education requirement for becoming a veterinary assistant or laboratory animal caretaker, but most entering the occupation have a high school diploma or its equivalent.

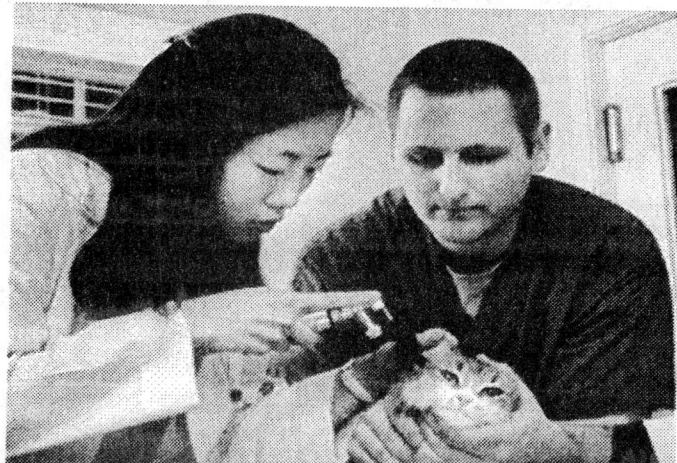

Veterinary assistants may hold or restrain animals during procedures.

Training

Most veterinary assistants and laboratory animal caretakers are trained on the job, but some employers prefer candidates who already have experience working with animals.

Certifications

For laboratory animal caretakers seeking work in a research facility, the American Association for Laboratory Animal Science (AALAS) offers three levels of certification: assistant laboratory animal technician (ALAT), laboratory animal technician (LAT), and laboratory animal technologist (LATG). Although certification is not mandatory, it allows workers at each level to demonstrate competency in animal husbandry, health and welfare, or facility administration and management. To become certified, candidates must have work experience in a laboratory animal facility and pass the AALAS exam.

Important Qualities

Compassion. Veterinary assistants and laboratory animal caretakers must treat animals with kindness and be compassionate to both the animals and their owners.

Detail oriented. These workers must follow strict instructions. For example, workers must be precise when sterilizing surgical equipment, monitoring animals, and giving medication.

Dexterity. Veterinary assistants and laboratory animal caretakers must handle animals and use medical instruments and laboratory equipment with care.

Physical strength. Veterinary assistants and laboratory animal caretakers must be able to handle, move, and restrain animals.

Pay

Veterinary Assistants and Laboratory Animal Caretakers
Median annual wages, May 2010

Total, All Occupations	$33,840
Healthcare Support Occupations	$24,760
Veterinary Assistants and Laboratory Animal Caretakers	$22,040

Note: All Occupations includes all occupations in the U.S. Economy.
Source: U.S. Bureau of Labor Statistics, Occupational Employment Statistics

The median annual wage of veterinary assistants and laboratory animal caretakers was $22,040 in May 2010. The median wage is the wage at which half the workers in an occupation earned more than that amount and half earned less. The lowest 10 percent earned less than $16,490, and the top 10 percent earned more than $33,780.

Veterinary assistants and laboratory animal caretakers working in research positions often earn more than those in clinics and animal hospitals. Median annual wages in the industries employing the largest numbers of veterinary assistants and laboratory animal caretakers in May 2010 were as follows:

Scientific research and development services	$31,810
Colleges, universities, and professional schools	30,660
Veterinary services	21,380

Many clinics and laboratories must be staffed 24 hours a day, so veterinary assistants and laboratory animal caretakers may be required to work nights, weekends, or holidays.

Job Outlook

Veterinary Assistants and Laboratory Animal Caretakers
Percent change in employment, projected 2010-20

Healthcare Support Occupations	34%
Total, All Occupations	14%
Veterinary Assistants and Laboratory Animal Caretakers	14%

Note: All Occupations includes all occupations in the U.S. Economy.
Source: U.S. Bureau of Labor Statistics, Employment Projections program

Employment of veterinary assistants and laboratory animal caretakers is expected to grow 14 percent from 2010 to 2020, as fast as the average for all occupations.

Employment of veterinary assistants and laboratory animal caretakers is concentrated in veterinary services, an industry that is expected to grow very quickly during the projection decade. Fast industry growth will be spurred by a growing pet population and advancements in veterinary medicine. Although veterinary assistants and laboratory animal caretakers will be needed to assist veterinarians and other veterinary care staff, some veterinary practices are expected to increasingly replace veterinary assistants with higher skilled veterinary technicians and technologists, thus slowing the demand for veterinary assistants.

Continued support for public health, food and animal safety, and national disease control programs, as well as biomedical research on human health problems, is expected to contribute to demand for laboratory animal caretakers.

Job Prospects

Overall job opportunities for veterinary assistants and laboratory animal caretakers are expected to be excellent. Although some establishments are replacing veterinary assistant positions with higher skilled veterinary technicians and technologists, growth of the pet care industry means that the number of veterinary assistant positions should continue to increase. Furthermore, veterinary assistants experience a high rate of turnover, so many positions will be available through workers leaving the occupation.

Employment projections data for veterinary assistants and laboratory animal caretakers, 2010-20

Occupational Title	SOC Code	Employment, 2010	Projected Employment, 2020	Change, 2010-20 Percent	Change, 2010-20 Numeric
Veterinary Assistants and Laboratory Animal Caretakers	31-9096	73,200	83,600	14	10,400
SOURCE: U.S. Bureau of Labor Statistics, Employment Projections program					

Similar Occupations

This table shows a list of occupations with job duties that are similar to those of veterinary assistants and laboratory animal caretakers.

Occupation	Job Duties	Entry-Level Education	Median Annual Pay, May 2010
Dental Hygienists	Dental hygienists clean teeth, examine patients for oral diseases such as gingivitis, and provide other preventative dental care. They also educate patients on ways to improve and maintain good oral health.	Associate's degree	$68,250

Dental Assistants	Dental assistants have many tasks, ranging from patient care to record keeping, in a dental office. Their duties vary by state and by the dentists' offices where they work.	Postsecondary non-degree award	$33,470
Nursing Aides, Orderlies, and Attendants	Nursing aides, orderlies, and attendants help provide basic care for patients in hospitals and residents of long-term care facilities, such as nursing homes.	Postsecondary non-degree award	$24,010
Surgical Technologists	Surgical technologists, also called operating room technicians, assist in surgical operations. They prepare operating rooms, arrange equipment, and help doctors and nurses during surgeries.	Postsecondary non-degree award	$39,920
Veterinarians	Veterinarians care for the health of animals. They diagnose, treat, or research medical conditions and diseases of pets, livestock, and animals in zoos, racetracks, and laboratories.	Doctoral or professional degree	$82,040
Veterinary Technologists and Technicians	Veterinary technologists and technicians perform medical tests under the supervision of a licensed veterinarian to treat or to help veterinarians diagnose the illnesses and injuries of animals.	Associate's degree	$29,710
Animal Care and Service Workers	Animal care and service workers care for the needs of animals. They feed, water, groom, bathe, and exercise pets and other nonfarm animals. Job tasks vary by position and place of work.	See How to Become One	$19,780

Contacts for More Information

For more information about certification as a laboratory animal caretaker, visit American Association for Laboratory Animal Science

Suggested citation:

Bureau of Labor Statistics, U.S. Department of Labor, Occupational Outlook Handbook, 2012-13 Edition, Veterinary Assistants and Laboratory Animal Caretakers, on the Internet at http://www.bls.gov/ooh/healthcare/veterinary-assistants-and-laboratory-animal-caretakers.htm .

Veterinary Technologists and Technicians

Quick Facts: Veterinary Technologists and Technicians	
2010 Median Pay	$29,710 per year $14.28 per hour
Entry-Level Education	Associate's degree
Work Experience in a Related Occupation	None
On-the-job Training	None
Number of Jobs, 2010	80,200
Job Outlook, 2010-20	52% (Much faster than average)
Employment Change, 2010-20	41,700

What Veterinary Technologists and Technicians Do

Veterinary technologists and technicians perform medical tests under the supervision of a licensed veterinarian to treat or to help veterinarians diagnose the illnesses and injuries of animals.

Duties

Veterinary technologists and technicians typically do the following:

- Observe the behavior and condition of animals
- Provide nursing care or emergency first aid to recovering or injured animals
- Administer anesthesia to animals and monitor their responses
- Collect laboratory samples, such as blood, urine, or tissue, for testing
- Perform laboratory tests, such as urinalyses and blood counts
- Take and develop x rays
- Prepare animals and instruments for surgery
- Administer medications, vaccines, and treatments prescribed by a veterinarian
- Collect and record patients' case histories

To provide superior animal care, veterinarians rely on the skills of veterinary technologists and technicians, who do many of the same tasks for a veterinarian that nurses would for a doctor. Despite differences in formal education and training, veterinary technologists

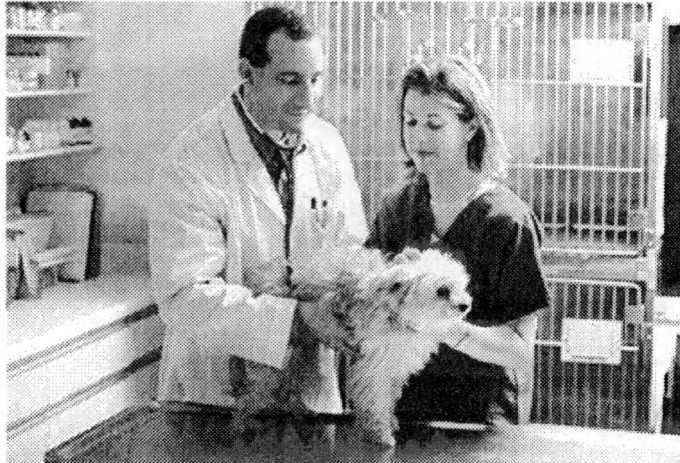

Veterinary technicians work under the supervision of a veterinarian.

and technicians carry out many similar tasks.

Many veterinary technologists and technicians work in private clinics, animal hospitals, and veterinary testing laboratories. They conduct a variety of clinical and laboratory procedures, including postoperative care, dental care, and specialized nursing care.

Veterinary technologists and technicians who work in research-related jobs do similar work. For example, they are responsible for making sure that animals are handled carefully and humanely. They commonly help veterinarians or scientists on research projects in areas such as biomedical research, disaster preparedness, and food safety.

Veterinary technologists and technicians most often work with small-animal practitioners who care for cats and dogs, but they may also do a variety of tasks with mice, rats, sheep, pigs, cattle, and birds.

Veterinary technologists and technicians can specialize in a particular discipline. Specialties include dental technology, anesthesia, emergency and critical care, and zoological medicine.

The differences between technologists and technicians are the following:

Veterinary technologists usually have a 4-year bachelor's degree in veterinary technology. Although some technologists work in private clinical practices, many work in more advanced research-related jobs, usually under the guidance of a scientist and sometimes a veterinarian. Working primarily in a laboratory setting, they may administer medications; prepare tissue samples for examination; or record information on an animal's genealogy, weight, diet, food intake, and signs of pain.

Veterinary technicians usually have a 2-year associate's degree in a veterinary technology program. Most work in private clinical practices under the guidance of a licensed veterinarian. Technicians may perform laboratory tests, such as a urinalysis, and help veterinarians conduct a variety of other diagnostic tests. Although some of their work is done in a laboratory setting, many technicians also talk with animal owners. They explain, for example, a pet's condition or how to administer medication prescribed by a veterinarian.

Work Environment

Veterinary technologists and technicians held about 80,200 jobs in 2010, 91 percent of which were in the veterinary services industry.

Veterinary technologists and technicians typically work in private clinics, laboratories, and animal hospitals. Some work in boarding kennels, animal shelters, rescue leagues, and zoos.

Their jobs may be physically or emotionally demanding. For example, they may witness abused animals or may need to help euthanize sick, injured, or unwanted animals.

Injuries

Veterinary technologists and technicians experience a rate of injuries and illnesses that is much higher than the national average. When working with scared or aggressive animals, they may be bitten, scratched, or kicked. Injuries may happen while the technologist or technician is holding, cleaning, or restraining an animal.

Work Schedules

Many clinics and laboratories must be staffed 24 hours a day, so veterinary technologists and technicians may have to work evenings, weekends, or holidays.

How to Become a Veterinary Technologist or Technician

There are primarily two levels of education and training for entry into this occupation: a 4-year program for veterinary technologists and a 2-year program for veterinary technicians. Typically, both technologists and technicians must take a credentialing exam and must become registered, licensed, or certified, depending on the state.

Education

Veterinary technologists and technicians must complete a postsecondary program in veterinary technology. In 2011, there were 191 veterinary technology programs accredited by the American Veterinary Medical Association (AVMA). Most of these programs offer a 2-year associate's degree for veterinary technicians. Twenty-one colleges offer a 4-year bachelor's degree in veterinary technology. Nine schools offer distance learning.

People interested in becoming a veterinary technologist or technician should take high school classes in biology, other sciences, and math.

Licenses and Certification

Although each state regulates veterinary technologists and technicians differently, most candidates must take a credentialing exam. Most states require the Veterinary Technician National Examination . Depending on the state, candidates must become certified, licensed, or registered to practice.

For technologists seeking work in a research facility, the American Association for Laboratory Animal Science (AALAS) offers three levels of certification: assistant laboratory animal technician (ALAT), laboratory animal technician (LAT), and laboratory animal technologist (LATG). Although certification is not mandatory, workers at each level can show competency in animal husbandry, health and welfare, and facility administration and management to prospective employers. To become certified, candidates must have work experience in a laboratory animal facility and pass the AALAS examination.

Important Qualities

Compassion. Veterinary technologists and technicians must treat animals with kindness and must be sensitive when dealing with the owners of sick pets.

Detail oriented. Veterinary technologists and technicians must pay attention to details and be precise when recording information, doing diagnostic tests, and administering medication. They must monitor the behavior and condition of animals and be able to recognize any problems that arise.

Interpersonal skills. Veterinary technologists and technicians spend a substantial amount of their time communicating with supervisors, animal owners, and other staff. In addition, a growing number of technicians counsel pet owners on animal behavior and nutrition.

Manual dexterity. Dexterity is important for veterinary technologists and technicians because they must handle animals, medical instruments, and laboratory equipment with care. They also do intricate tasks, such as dental work, giving anesthesia, and taking x rays, which require a steady hand.

Pay

Veterinary Technologists and Technicians
Median annual wages, May 2010

Health Technologists and Technicians	$39,340
Total, All Occupations	$33,840
Veterinary Technologists and Technicians	$29,710

Note: All Occupations includes all occupations in the U.S. Economy.
Source: U.S. Bureau of Labor Statistics, Occupational Employment Statistics

The median annual wage of veterinary technologists and technicians was $29,710 in May 2010. The median wage is the wage at which half the workers in an occupation earned more than that amount and half earned less. The lowest 10 percent earned less than $20,500, and the top 10 percent earned more than $44,030.

Veterinary technologists and technicians working in research positions often earn more than those in other fields. Median annual wages in the industries employing the largest numbers of veterinary technologists and technicians in May 2010 were as follows:

Colleges, universities, and professional schools; state, local, and private	$36,450
Scientific research and development services	36,200
Veterinary services	29,290

Many clinics and laboratories must be staffed 24 hours a day, so veterinary technologists and technicians may have to work evenings, weekends, or holidays.

Job Outlook

Veterinary Technologists and Technicians
Percent change in employment, projected 2010-20

Veterinary Technologists and Technicians	52%
Health Technologists and Technicians	26%
Total, All Occupations	14%

Note: All Occupations includes all occupations in the U.S. Economy.
Source: U.S. Bureau of Labor Statistics, Employment Projections program

Employment of veterinary technologists and technicians is expected to grow 52 percent from 2010 to 2020, much faster than the average for all occupations.

A growing pet population will require more veterinary technologists and technicians. In addition, many people consider their pets to be part of their family and are willing to pay more for pet care than in the past. Also, veterinary medicine has advanced considerably, and many of the veterinary services offered today are now comparable to health services for humans.

As veterinarians perform more specialized tasks, clinics and animal hospitals are increasingly using veterinary technologists and technicians to provide more general care and to do more laboratory work. Furthermore, as the number of veterinary services grows, veterinarians will continue to prefer higher skilled veterinary technologists and technicians over veterinary assistants for more complex work.

Continued support for public health, food and animal safety, and national disease control programs, as well as biomedical research on human health problems, also will contribute to demand for veterinary technologists.

Job Prospects

Overall job opportunities for veterinary technologists and technicians are expected to be excellent, particularly in rural areas. The number of veterinary technology programs has been growing, but rapid employment growth means that the number of positions available will continue to outpace the number of new graduates. Workers leaving the occupation will also result in job openings.

Employment projections data for veterinary technologists and technicians, 2010-20

Occupational Title	SOC Code	Employment, 2010	Projected Employment, 2020	Change, 2010-20 Percent	Change, 2010-20 Numeric
Veterinary Technologists and Technicians	29-2056	80,200	121,900	52	41,700

SOURCE: U.S. Bureau of Labor Statistics, Employment Projections program

Similar Occupations

This table shows a list of occupations with job duties that are similar to those of veterinary technologists and technicians.

Occupation	Job Duties	Entry-Level Education	Median Annual Pay, May 2010
Animal Care and Service Workers	Animal care and service workers care for the needs of animals. They feed, water, groom, bathe, and exercise pets and other nonfarm animals. Job tasks vary by position and place of work.	See How to Become One	$19,780
Medical and Clinical Laboratory Technologists and Technicians	Medical laboratory technologists (also known as medical laboratory scientists) and medical laboratory technicians collect samples and perform tests to analyze body fluids, tissue, and other substances.	See How to Become One	$46,680
Radiologic Technologists	Radiologic technologists perform diagnostic imaging examinations, such as x rays, on patients.	Associate's degree	$54,340
Surgical Technologists	Surgical technologists, also called operating room technicians, assist in surgical operations. They prepare operating rooms, arrange equipment, and help doctors and nurses during surgeries.	Postsecondary non-degree award	$39,920
Veterinarians	Veterinarians care for the health of animals. They diagnose, treat, or research medical conditions and diseases of pets, livestock, and animals in zoos, racetracks, and laboratories.	Doctoral or professional degree	$82,040
Veterinary Assistants and Laboratory Animal Caretakers	Veterinary assistants and laboratory animal caretakers look after nonfarm animals in laboratories, animal hospitals, and clinics. They care for the well-being of animals by doing routine tasks under the supervision of veterinarians, scientists, or veterinary technologists or technicians.	High school diploma or equivalent	$22,040

Contacts for More Information

For information on careers in veterinary medicine and a listing of AVMA-accredited veterinary technology programs, visit American Veterinary Medical Association

For more information on becoming a veterinary technician or technologist, visit National Association of Veterinary Technicians in America

For information on certification as a laboratory animal technician or technologist, visit American Association for Laboratory Animal Science

For information on the Veterinary Technician National Examination, visit: American Association of Veterinary State Boards

Suggested citation:

Bureau of Labor Statistics, U.S. Department of Labor, Occupational Outlook Handbook, 2012-13 Edition, Veterinary Technologists and Technicians, on the Internet at http://www.bls.gov/ooh/healthcare/veterinary-technologists-and-technicians.htm .

Installation, Maintenance, and Repair Occupations

Aircraft and Avionics Equipment Mechanics and Technicians

Quick Facts: Aircraft and Avionics Equipment Mechanics and Technicians	
2010 Median Pay	$53,220 per year $25.59 per hour
Entry-Level Education	Postsecondary non-degree award
Work Experience in a Related Occupation	None
On-the-job Training	None
Number of Jobs, 2010	142,300
Job Outlook, 2010-20	6% (Slower than average)
Employment Change, 2010-20	9,100

What Aircraft and Avionics Equipment Mechanics and Technicians Do

Aircraft and avionics equipment mechanics and technicians repair and perform scheduled maintenance on airplanes and helicopters. They also inspect airplanes and helicopters as required by the Federal Aviation Administration (FAA).

Duties

Aircraft mechanics typically do the following:

- Examine aircraft frames and parts for defects
- Diagnose mechanical or electrical problems
- Measure parts for wear, using precision instruments
- Read maintenance manuals to identify methods of repair
- Repair wings, brakes, electrical systems, and other aircraft components
- Replace defective parts, using handtools
- Test aircraft parts with gauges and other diagnostic equipment
- Inspect completed work to ensure that it meets performance standards
- Keep records of maintenance and repair work

Avionics technicians typically do the following:

- Test electronic instruments, using circuit testers, oscilloscopes, and voltmeters
- Interpret flight test data to diagnose malfunctions and performance problems
- Assemble components, such as electrical controls and junction boxes
- Install instrument panels, using handtools, power tools, and soldering irons
- Repair or replace malfunctioning components
- Keep records of maintenance and repair work

Today's airplanes are highly complex machines that require reliable parts and service to fly safely. To keep an airplane in peak operating condition, aircraft and avionics equipment mechanics and technicians do scheduled maintenance, make repairs, and complete inspections.

Some mechanics work on many different types of aircraft, such as jets, propeller-driven airplanes, and helicopters. Others specialize in one section of a particular type of aircraft, such as the engine, hydraulics, or electrical system of a jet. In small, independent repair shops, mechanics usually inspect and repair many different types of aircraft.

Most mechanics who work on civilian aircraft have the FAA's Airframe and Powerplant (A&P) certificate. Mechanics who have this certificate are authorized to work on any part of the aircraft, except electronic flight instruments. Maintaining a plane's electronic flight instruments is the job of avionics technicians.

The following are types of aircraft and avionics equipment mechanics and technicians:

Maintenance mechanics specialize in preventive maintenance and inspect aircraft. Every aircraft must be inspected regularly. The schedule for inspection may be based on hours flown, days since the last inspection, trips flown, or a combination of these factors.

Maintenance mechanics inspect aircraft engines, landing gear, instruments, brakes, air conditioning systems, and other parts. They use precision instruments to measure wear and replace worn out parts.

They inspect a plane's exterior and repair metal sheets. They may use x rays and magnetic inspection equipment to check for cracks that can't be seen. They check for corrosion, distortion, and cracks in the aircraft's main body, wings, and tail.

In planes equipped with aircraft monitoring systems, mechanics can gather valuable diagnostic information from electronic consoles. After completing all repairs, mechanics must test the equipment to ensure that it works properly. Mechanics also must keep records of all maintenance that they do on an aircraft.

Repair mechanics specialize in repair work rather than inspection. They find and fix problems that pilots describe. For example, during a preflight check, a pilot may discover that the aircraft's fuel gauge is not working. Mechanics must figure out the problem and replace any defective electrical parts. They must work as fast as safety permits so that the aircraft can be put back into service quickly.

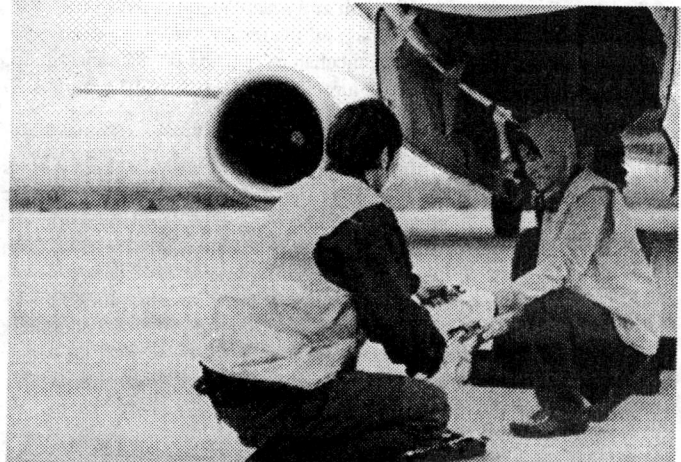

Airplane mechanics ensure that a plane's operating system is in safe working order.

519

Avionic technicians repair and maintain a plane's electronic systems, such as radio communications, radar systems, and flight instruments. As the use of automated technology increases, more time is spent maintaining a plane's computer systems. Technicians are often needed to analyze and solve complex electronic problems.

Work Environment

Aircraft mechanics and avionic technicians held about 142,300 jobs in 2010. Approximately 87 percent were mechanics and the rest were avionic technicians. The majority worked for private companies and about 15 percent worked for the federal government.

Employment of aircraft mechanics and avionic technicians is concentrated in a small number of industries. In 2010, the following industries employed the largest numbers of aircraft mechanics:

Scheduled air transportation	26%
Support activities for air transportation (including airports)	23
Aerospace products and parts manufacturing	16
Federal government, excluding postal service	16
Nonscheduled air transportation	4

In 2010, the following industries employed the largest numbers of avionics technicians:

Aerospace products and parts manufacturing	31%
Support activities for air transportation (including airports)	26
Federal government, excluding postal service	12
Scheduled air transportation	11
Navigational, measuring, electromedical, and control instruments manufacturing	4

Approximately 28 percent of mechanics and technicians belong to unions, including the Aircraft Mechanics Fraternal Association.

Mechanics and technicians work in hangars, in repair stations, or on airfields. They must often meet strict deadlines to maintain flight schedules. At the same time, they must maintain safety standards, and doing both can cause stress.

Most mechanics and technicians work near major airports. Airline mechanics often work outside, on the airfield, while repair and corporate mechanics work in climate-controlled shops. Civilian mechanics employed by the U.S. Armed Forces work on military installations.

Injuries

Mechanics often lift heavy objects, handle dangerous chemicals, or operate large power tools. They frequently stand, lie, or kneel in awkward positions and work on scaffolds or ladders. Noise and vibrations are common when engines are being tested, so ear protection is necessary.

Because airline mechanics work outside, they must often endure hot and cold temperatures. Although their work is not inherently dangerous, aircraft mechanics and service technicians experience rates of injuries and illnesses that are higher than the average across all occupations.

Work Schedules

Mechanics and technicians usually work full time on rotating 8-hour shifts. Overtime and weekend work is common. Day shifts are usually reserved for mechanics with the most seniority.

How to Become an Aircraft and Avionics Equipment Mechanic or Technician

Aircraft mechanics and avionic technicians must be certified by the Federal Aviation Administration (FAA). Most mechanics learn their trade at an FAA-Approved Aviation Maintenance Technician School.

Education and Training

Most mechanics and technicians learn their trade at an FAA-Approved Aviation Maintenance Technician School. Coursework normally lasts 18 to 24 months and provides training with the tools and equipment used on the job.

About one-third of these schools award 2- or 4-year degrees in avionics, aviation technology, or aviation maintenance management. Increasingly, employers are looking more favorably on those with a bachelor's degree.

Aircraft trade schools are placing more emphasis on technologies being used in new airplanes, such as turbine engines, composite materials, and aviation electronics. These technical advances require mechanics to have stronger backgrounds in composite materials and electronics.

Courses in mathematics, physics, chemical engineering, electronics, computer science, and mechanical drawing are helpful because they teach the principles involved in operating an airplane. Mechanics often need this knowledge to figure out what is wrong and how to fix it.

Courses that develop writing, communication, and management skills are important for mechanics who want to move into senior positions.

Certification

The FAA requires that aircraft maintenance be done by certified mechanics or under the supervision of a supervised mechanic. The FAA offers separate certifications for airframe mechanics and engine mechanics, but most airlines prefer to hire mechanics with a combined Airframe and Powerplant (A&P) certificate.

To qualify, mechanics must be at least 18 years of age, be fluent in English, and have 30 months of experience working on airframes and engines. However, completion of a program at an FAA-Approved Aviation Maintenance Technician School can substitute for the experience requirement.

In addition to having experience or formal training, applicants must pass written, oral, and practical exams that demonstrate required skills. Candidates take the written tests on a computer at one of many designated testing facilities around the world. An FAA Designated Mechanic Examiner gives the oral and practical tests. To get the certification, candidates must pass all the tests within two years.

To keep their certification, mechanics must by do an inspection or repair every 90 days and attend a refresher course every 24 months. To fulfill this requirement, mechanics often take classes from their employer or an airplane manufacturer.

The FAA allows certified airframe mechanics to work on avionics equipment. Although there is no avionic-specific certification, avionic technicians must have the required training and tools. Many avionics technicians gain the necessary experience from military training, from a technical school, or by working for an avionics manufacturer. Avionics technicians who work on communications equipment must have a restricted radio-telephone operator license from the Federal Communications Commission (FCC).

Advancement

As aircraft mechanics gain experience, they may advance to lead mechanic, lead inspector, or shop supervisor. Opportunities are best for those who have an aircraft inspector's authorization. To get an inspector's authorization, a mechanic must have held an A&P certificate for at least 3 years, with 24 months of hands-on experience.

In addition, as a bachelor's degree has become increasingly important for career advancement, some mechanics continue their education.

Mechanics with broad experience in maintenance and repair might become inspectors with the FAA.

With additional business and management training, some may open their own maintenance facility.

Traditionally, mechanics have advanced from general aviation jobs to airline jobs. Because salaries are similar between general aviation and airline companies, however, mechanics also should consider the work environment as they search for jobs. Although airline jobs come with standby travel perks, these mechanics often have to work outside, whereas mechanics at corporations or repair shops often work in climate-controlled buildings.

Important Qualities

Agility. Mechanics should be able to climb on airplanes, balance, and reach with no fear of heights.

Detail oriented. Mechanics should be able to adjust airplane parts to exact specifications. For example, mechanics often use precision tools to tighten wheel bolts to an exact tension.

Manual dexterity. Mechanics should be able to precisely coordinate the movement of their fingers and hands to grasp, manipulate, or assemble parts.

Technical skills. Mechanics should be able to interpret engine noises, gauges, dials, and other technical instruments to determine whether a plane's mechanical systems are working properly.

Troubleshooting skills. Mechanics should be able to diagnose complex problems and evaluate options to correct those problems.

Pay

Aircraft and Avionics Equipment Mechanics and Technicians
Median annual wages, May 2010

Aircraft Mechanics and Service Technicians	$53,420
Aircraft and Avionics Equipment Mechanics and Technicians	$53,220
Avionics Technicians	$52,320
Total, All Occupations	$33,840

Note: All Occupations includes all occupations in the U.S. Economy.
Source: U.S. Bureau of Labor Statistics, Occupational Employment Statistics

The median annual wage of aircraft mechanics was $53,420 in May 2010. The median wage is the wage at which half the workers in an occupation earned more than that amount and half earned less. The lowest 10 percent of aircraft mechanics earned less than $33,630, and the top 10 percent earned more than $72,250.

In May 2010, median annual wages in industries employing the largest numbers of aircraft mechanics were as follows:

Scheduled air transportation	$56,850
Federal executive branch	54,990
Aerospace products and parts manufacturing	54,970
Nonscheduled air transportation	51,540
Support activities for air transportation (including airports)	45,160

The median annual wage of avionics technicians was $52,320 in May 2010. The lowest 10 percent of avionics technicians earned less than $36,810, and the top 10 percent earned more than $67,560.

In May 2010, median annual wages in industries employing the largest numbers of avionics technicians were as follows:

Scheduled air transportation	$56,550
Aerospace products and parts manufacturing	54,050
Federal executive branch	53,140
Navigational, measuring, electromedical, and control instruments manufacturing	51,120
Support activities for air transportation (including airports)	46,160

Mechanics and technicians usually work full time on rotating 8-hour shifts. Overtime and weekend work is often required. Day shifts are usually reserved for mechanics with the most seniority. Mechanics typically receive health and retirement benefits as part of their compensation package.

Job Outlook

Aircraft and Avionics Equipment Mechanics and Technicians
Percent change in employment, projected 2010-20

Total, All Occupations	14%
Avionics Technicians	7%
Aircraft Mechanics and Service Technicians	6%
Aircraft and Avionics Equipment Mechanics and Technicians	6%

Note: All Occupations includes all occupations in the U.S. Economy.
Source: U.S. Bureau of Labor Statistics, Employment Projections program

Employment of aircraft mechanics and avionics technicians is projected to grow 6 percent from 2010 to 2020, slower than the average for all occupations.

Modest employment growth is expected as air travel gradually increases over the coming decade. However, as airlines increasingly outsource maintenance work to other countries, employment growth is expected to be limited.

Job Prospects

Job prospects should be best for mechanics and technicians who hold an Airframe and Powerplant (A&P) certificate and a bachelor's degree in aircraft maintenance. Job prospects also will be better for those who keep up with technical advances in aircraft electronics and composite materials.

Job opportunities may arise from the need to replace mechanics who leave the workforce. Over the next decade, many aircraft mechanics are expected to retire. As older mechanics retire and younger mechanics advance, entry-level positions may open up.

However, if airlines continue to send maintenance work to other countries, competition for new jobs will remain strong.

Employment projections data for aircraft and avionics equipment mechanics and technicians, 2010-20

Occupational Title	SOC Code	Employment, 2010	Projected Employment, 2020	Change, 2010-20	
				Percent	Numeric
Aircraft and Avionics Equipment Mechanics and Technicians	—	142,300	151,500	6	9,100
Avionics Technicians	49-2091	18,600	19,800	7	1,300
Aircraft Mechanics and Service Technicians	49-3011	123,800	131,600	6	7,800
SOURCE: U.S. Bureau of Labor Statistics, Employment Projections program					

Similar Occupations

This table shows a list of occupations with job duties that are similar to those of aircraft and avionics equipment mechanics and technicians.

Occupation	Job Duties	Entry-Level Education	Median Annual Pay, May 2010
Automotive Service Technicians and Mechanics	Automotive service technicians and mechanics, often called service technicians or service techs, inspect, maintain, and repair cars and light trucks.	High school diploma or equivalent	$35,790
Automotive Body and Glass Repairers	Automotive body and glass repairers restore, refinish, and replace vehicle bodies and frames, windshields, and window glass.	High school diploma or equivalent	$37,580
Electrical and Electronics Installers and Repairers	Electrical and electronics installers and repairers install, repair, or replace a variety of electrical equipment in telecommunications, transportation, utilities, and other industries.	Postsecondary non-degree award	$49,170
Electricians	Electricians install and maintain electrical systems in homes, businesses, and factories.	High school diploma or equivalent	$48,250
Electro-mechanical Technicians	Electro-mechanical technicians combine knowledge of mechanical technology with knowledge of electrical and electronic circuits. They install, troubleshoot, repair, and upgrade electronic and computer-controlled mechanical systems, such as robotic assembly machines.	Associate's degree	$49,550
Heavy Vehicle and Mobile Equipment Service Technicians	Heavy vehicle and mobile equipment service technicians inspect, maintain, and repair vehicles and machinery used in construction, farming, rail transportation, and other industries.	High school diploma or equivalent	$42,630

Contacts for More Information

For more information about aircraft and avionics equipment mechanics and technicians, visit Federal Aviation Administration

Professional Aviation Maintenance Association , Aviation Maintenance magazine , Aircraft Mechanics Fraternal Association

For additional career information about aircraft mechanics and avionics technicians, see the Occupational Outlook Quarterly article " Sky-high careers: jobs related to airlines ."

For more information about job opportunities, contact an airline company personnel manager, browse the classified section of aviation trade magazines, or contact employers at local airports.

Suggested citation:

Bureau of Labor Statistics, U.S. Department of Labor, Occupational Outlook Handbook, 2012-13 Edition, Aircraft and Avionics Equipment Mechanics and Technicians, on the Internet at http://www.bls.gov/ooh/installation-maintenance-and-repair/aircraft-and-avionics-equipment-mechanics-and-technicians.htm .

Automotive Body and Glass Repairers

Quick Facts: Automotive Body and Glass Repairers	
2010 Median Pay	$37,580 per year $18.07 per hour
Entry-Level Education	High school diploma or equivalent
Work Experience in a Related Occupation	None
On-the-job Training	Moderate-term on-the-job training
Number of Jobs, 2010	170,900
Job Outlook, 2010-20	19% (About as fast as average)
Employment Change, 2010-20	32,700

What Automotive Body and Glass Repairers Do

Automotive body and glass repairers restore, refinish, and replace vehicle bodies and frames, windshields, and window glass.

Duties

Automotive body and glass repairers typically do the following:

- Review damage reports, prepare cost estimates, and plan work
- Remove damaged body parts, including bumpers, fenders, hoods, grilles, and trim
- Realign car frames and chassis to repair structural damage
- Hammer out or patch dents, dimples, and other minor body damage
- Fit, attach, and weld replacement parts into place
- Install and weatherproof windows and windshields
- Grind, sand, buff, and prime refurbished and repaired surfaces

Automotive body and glass repairers restore and replace automobile frames.

- Apply new finish to restored body parts

Automotive body and glass repairers can repair most damage from everyday vehicle collisions and make vehicles look and drive like new. Damage may be minor, such as replacing a cracked windshield, or major, such as replacing an entire door panel.

Repair technicians use many tools for their work. To remove damaged parts, such as bumpers and door panels, they use pneumatic tools, metal-cutting guns, and plasma cutters. For major structural repairs, such as aligning the body, they often use heavy-duty hydraulic jacks and hammers. For some work, they use common handtools, such as metal files, pliers, wrenches, hammers, and screwdrivers.

In some cases, repair technicians do an entire job by themselves. In other cases, especially in large shops, they use an assembly line approach in which they work as a team with each repair technician specializing.

Although repair technicians sometimes prime and paint repaired parts, automotive painters generally perform these tasks. For more information, see the profile on painting and coating workers .

The following are occupational specialties:

Automotive body and related repairers, or **collision repair technicians**, straighten metal panels, remove dents, and replace parts that cannot be fixed. Although they repair all types of vehicles, most work primarily on cars, sport utility vehicles, and small trucks.

Automotive glass installers and repairers remove and replace broken, cracked, or pitted windshields and window glass. They also weatherproof newly installed windows and windshields with chemical treatments.

Work Environment

Automotive body and glass repairers held about 170,900 jobs in 2010. About 61 percent worked in automotive repair shops, 16 percent worked for automobile dealers, and another 16 percent were self-employed.

Repair technicians work indoors in body shops, which are often noisy. Most shops are well ventilated to disperse dust and paint fumes. Repair technicians sometimes work in awkward and cramped positions, and their work can be physically demanding.

Injuries

Repair technicians have a rate of injuries and illnesses that is much higher than the average for all occupations. Although technicians commonly suffer minor injuries, such as cuts, burns, and scrapes, when they follow safety procedures, they can usually avoid serious accidents.

Work Schedules

Most repair technicians work full time. When shops have to complete a backlog of work, overtime is common, which often includes repair technicians working evenings and weekends.

How to Become an Automotive Body or Glass Repairer

Most employers prefer to hire repair technicians who have completed a formal training program in automotive body repair or refinishing. Still, many new repair technicians begin work without formal training. Industry certification is increasingly important.

Education and Training

High school, trade and technical school, and community college programs in collision repair combine hands-on practice and classroom instruction. Topics usually include electronics, physics, and mathematics, which provide a strong educational foundation for a career as a repair technician. Although not required, postsecondary education often provides the best preparation.

Trade and technical school programs typically award certificates after 6 months to 1 year of study. Some community colleges offer 2-year programs in collision repair. Many of these schools also offer certificates for individual courses, so students can take classes part time or as needed.

New workers typically begin their on-the-job training by helping an experienced repair technician with basic tasks. As they gain experience, they move on to more complex work. Some workers may become trained in as little as a 1 year, but generally, workers may need 3-4 years of hands-on training to become fully qualified repair technicians.

Basic automotive glass installation and repair can be learned in as little as 6 months, but becoming fully qualified can take up to 1 year.

Formally educated workers often require significantly less on-the-job training and typically advance to independent work more quickly than those who do not have the same level of training.

To keep up with rapidly changing automotive technology, repair technicians need to continue their education and training throughout their careers. Repair technicians are expected to develop their skills by reading technical manuals and by attending classes and seminars. Many employers regularly send workers to advanced training programs.

Certification

Although not required, certification is recommended because it shows competence and usually brings higher pay. In some instances, however, it is required for advancement beyond entry-level work.

Certification from the National Institute for Automotive Service Excellence is a standard credential for repair technicians. Many repair technicians get further certification through the Inter-Industry Conference on Auto Collision Repair.

In addition, many vehicle and paint manufacturers have product certification programs that train repair technicians in specific technologies and repair methods.

Important Qualities

Critical-thinking skills. Repair technicians must be able to evaluate vehicle damage and determine necessary repair strategies for each vehicle they work on. In some cases, they must decide if a vehicle is "totaled," or too damaged to justify the cost of repair.

Customer-service skills. Repair technicians must discuss auto body and glass problems, along with options to fix them, with customers. Because self-employed workers depend on repeat clients for business, they must be courteous, good listeners, and ready to answer customers' questions.

Detail oriented. Repair technicians must pay close attention to detail.Restoring a damaged auto body to its original state requires workers to have a keen eye for even the smallest imperfection.

Dexterity. Many repair technicians' tasks, such as removing door panels, hammering out dents, and using handtools to install parts, require a steady hand and good hand–eye coordination.

Technical skills. Repair technicians must know which diagnostic, hydraulic, pneumatic, and other power equipment and tools are appropriate for certain procedures and repairs. They must be skilled with techniques and methods necessary to repair modern automobiles.

Pay

Automotive Body and Glass Repairers
Median annual wages, May 2010

Automotive Body and Related Repairers	$38,130
Automotive Body and Glass Repairers	$37,580
Total, All Occupations	$33,840
Automotive Glass Installers and Repairers	$33,160

Note: All Occupations includes all occupations in the U.S. Economy.
Source: U.S. Bureau of Labor Statistics, Occupational Employment Statistics

The median annual wage of automotive body and related repairers was $38,130 in May 2010. The median wage is the wage at which half the workers in an occupation earned more than that amount and half earned less. The lowest 10 percent earned less than $22,990, and the top 10 percent earned more than $64,320.

The median annual wage of automotive glass installers and repairers was $33,160 in May 2010. The lowest 10 percent earned less than $20,660, and the top 10 percent earned more than $49,960.

The majority of repair shops and auto dealers pay repair technicians on an incentive basis. In addition to receiving a guaranteed base salary, employers pay workers a set amount for completing various tasks. Their earnings depend on both the amount of work assigned and how fast they complete it.

Trainees typically earn between 30 percent and 60 percent of skilled workers' pay. They are paid by the hour until they are competent enough to be paid on an incentive basis.

Although they vary by employer, benefits such as paid leave, health insurance, and retirement assistance are becoming more common.

Most repair technicians work full time. When shops have to complete a backlog of work, overtime is common, which often includes repair technicians working evenings and weekends.

Job Outlook

Automotive Body and Glass Repairers
Percent change in employment, projected 2010-20

Automotive Glass Installers and Repairers	25%
Automotive Body and Glass Repairers	19%
Automotive Body and Related Repairers	18%
Total, All Occupations	14%

Note: All Occupations includes all occupations in the U.S. Economy.
Source: U.S. Bureau of Labor Statistics, Employment Projections program

Employment of automotive body and glass repairers is expected to grow 19 percent from 2010 to 2020, about as fast as the average for all occupations.

The growing number of vehicles in use should increase overall demand for collision repair services during the next decade. However, overall job growth will be limited because new repair technology allows fewer workers to do more work.

In addition, advances in automotive technology have increased the prices of new and replacement parts. This increases the likelihood that a damaged car is declared "totaled"—where repairing the car costs more than its overall value. This scenario will also likely reduce demand for repair work.

Job Prospects

Job opportunities should be very good for jobseekers with industry certification and formal training in automotive body repair and refinishing and in collision repair. Furthermore, demand for qualified workers with knowledge of specific technologies, materials, and makes and models of cars should create new job opportunities. Those without any training or experience will face strong competition for jobs.

The need to replace experienced repair technicians who retire, change occupations, or stop working for other reasons also will provide some job opportunities.

Employment projections data for automotive body and glass repairers, 2010-20

Occupational Title	SOC Code	Employment, 2010	Projected Employment, 2020	Change, 2010-20 Percent	Change, 2010-20 Numeric
Automotive Body and Glass Repairers	—	170,900	203,600	19	32,700
Automotive Body and Related Repairers	49-3021	152,900	181,100	18	28,200
Automotive Glass Installers and Repairers	49-3022	18,100	22,600	25	4,500
SOURCE: U.S. Bureau of Labor Statistics, Employment Projections program					

Similar Occupations

This table shows a list of occupations with job duties that are similar to those of automotive body and glass repairers.

Occupation	Job Duties	Entry-Level Education	Median Annual Pay, May 2010
Automotive Service Technicians and Mechanics	Automotive service technicians and mechanics, often called service technicians or service techs, inspect, maintain, and repair cars and light trucks.	High school diploma or equivalent	$35,790
Diesel Service Technicians and Mechanics	Diesel service technicians and mechanics inspect, repair, or overhaul buses, trucks, and anything else with a diesel engine.	High school diploma or equivalent	$40,850
Glaziers	Glaziers install glass in windows, skylights, storefronts, and display cases to create distinctive designs or reduce the need for artificial lighting.	High school diploma or equivalent	$36,640
Heavy Vehicle and Mobile Equipment Service Technicians	Heavy vehicle and mobile equipment service technicians inspect, maintain, and repair vehicles and machinery used in construction, farming, rail transportation, and other industries.	High school diploma or equivalent	$42,630
Painting and Coating Workers	Painting and coating workers paint and coat a wide range of products, including cars, jewelry, lacquer, and candy.	High school diploma or equivalent	$31,170

Contacts for More Information

For information about careers in automotive body and glass repair, visit Accrediting Commission of Career Schools and Colleges , Auto Careers Today , Automotive Service Association ,Inter-Industry Conference on Auto Collision Repair ,National Automotive Technicians Education Foundation ,National Glass Association ,National Institute for Automotive Service Excellence ,Society of Collision Repair Specialists

Suggested citation:

Bureau of Labor Statistics, U.S. Department of Labor, Occupational Outlook Handbook, 2012-13 Edition, Automotive Body and Glass Repairers, on the Internet at http://www.bls.gov/ooh/installation-maintenance-and-repair/automotive-body-and-glass-repairers.htm .

Automotive Service Technicians and Mechanics

Quick Facts: Automotive Service Technicians and Mechanics	
2010 Median Pay	$35,790 per year $17.21 per hour
Entry-Level Education	High school diploma or equivalent
Work Experience in a Related Occupation	None
On-the-job Training	Long-term on-the-job training
Number of Jobs, 2010	723,400
Job Outlook, 2010-20	17% (About as fast as average)
Employment Change, 2010-20	124,800

What Automotive Service Technicians and Mechanics Do

Automotive service technicians and mechanics, often called service technicians or service techs, inspect, maintain, and repair cars and light trucks.

Duties

Automotive service technicians and mechanics typically do the following:

- Test parts and systems to ensure that they are working properly
- Identify mechanical problems, often by using computerized diagnostic equipment
- Follow checklists to ensure that all critical parts are examined
- Test and lubricate the vehicle's engine and other major components
- Perform basic care and maintenance, including oil changes, tuneups, and tire rotations
- Repair or replace worn parts, such as brake pads and wheel bearings
- Disassemble and reassemble parts
- Use testing equipment to ensure that repairs and maintenance are effective
- Explain to clients their automotive problems and the repairs done on their vehicles

Service technicians work on traditional mechanical components, such as engines, transmissions, belts, and hoses. However, they must also be familiar with a growing number of electronic systems. Braking, transmission, and steering systems, for example, are controlled primarily by computers and electronic components.

Other integrated electronic systems, such as accident-avoidance sensors, are becoming common as well. In addition, a growing number of technicians are required to work on vehicles that run on alternative fuels, such as ethanol and electricity.

Service technicians use many different tools, including computerized diagnostic tools and power tools such as pneumatic wrenches, lathes, welding torches, and jacks and hoists. These tools usually are owned by their employers.

Service technicians also use many common handtools, such as pliers, wrenches, and screwdrivers, which generally are their own. In fact, experienced workers often have thousands of dollars invested in their personal tool collection.

Service technicians sometimes specialize in a particular type of repair that may be subject to specific regulations or procedures. For instance, those focused on air-conditioning system repairs must follow federal and state regulations governing the handling, recycling, and disposal of refrigerants.

In some shops, technicians may specialize. The following are types of service technicians:

Automotive air-conditioning repairers install and repair air conditioners and service parts, such as compressors, condensers, and controls. They are trained in government regulations related to their work.

Brake repairers adjust brakes, replace brake linings and pads, and make other repairs on brake systems. Some technicians specialize in both brake and front-end work.

Front-end mechanics align and balance wheels and repair steering mechanisms and suspension systems. They frequently use special alignment equipment and wheel-balancing machines.

Transmission technicians and rebuilders work on gear trains, couplings, hydraulic pumps, and other parts of transmissions. Extensive knowledge of computer controls, the ability to diagnose electrical and hydraulic problems, and other specialized skills are needed to work on these complex components.

Tune-up technicians adjust ignition timing and valves and adjust or replace spark plugs and other parts to ensure efficient engine performance. They often use electronic testing equipment to isolate and adjust malfunctions in fuel, ignition, and emissions control systems.

For information about technicians who work on large trucks and buses, see the profile on diesel service technicians and mechanics .

For information about technicians who work on farm equipment, construction vehicles, and rail cars, see the profile on heavy vehicle and mobile equipment service technicians .

For information about technicians who repair and service

Automotive service technicians and mechanics repair cars and light trucks.

motorcycles, motorboats, and small all-terrain vehicles, see the profile on small engine mechanics .

Work Environment

Automotive service technician and mechanics held about 723,400 jobs in 2010. Most worked full time for private companies, and about 18 percent were self-employed.

Industries employing the most automotive service technicians and mechanics in 2010 were as follows:

Automotive repair and maintenance	31%
Automobile dealers	26
Automotive parts, accessories and tire stores	8
Local government, excluding education and hospitals	3

Most service technicians work in well-ventilated and well-lit repair shops. Although many problems can be identified and fixed with computers, technicians frequently work with greasy parts and tools, sometimes in uncomfortable positions.

Work Schedules

Most service technicians work full time, and many work evenings or weekends. Overtime is common.

Injuries

Automotive service technicians and mechanics have a rate of injuries and illnesses that is higher than the national average. Service technicians must often lift heavy parts and tools. As a result, minor workplace injuries, such as small cuts and bruises, are common. However, the work is not generally dangerous if workers follow safety procedures and practices.

How to Become an Automotive Service Technician or Mechanic

Because automotive technology is becoming increasingly sophisticated, employers prefer service technicians who have completed a formal training program in a postsecondary institution. Industry certification is usually required once the person is employed.

Education

High school courses in automotive repair, electronics, computers, mathematics, and English provide a good background for prospective service technicians. However, high school graduates often need further training to become fully qualified.

Completing a vocational or other postsecondary training program in automotive service technology is considered the best preparation for entry-level positions. Programs usually last 6 months to a year and provide intensive career preparation through classroom instruction and hands-on practice. Short-term certificate programs in a particular skill are also available.

Some service technicians get a 2-year associate's degree.Courses usually include basic mathematics, computers, electronics, and automotive repair. Some programs have recently added classes in customer service, English, and other necessary skills.

Various automobile manufacturers and dealers sponsor 2-year associate's degree programs. Students in these programs typically spend alternating periods attending classes full time and working full time in service shops under the guidance of an experienced technician.

Training

Most service technicians must complete on-the-job training, often as part of a formal education program.

Depending on a new service technician's educational background, it typically takes 2 to 5 years of experience to become a fully qualified service technician. It then takes an additional 1 to 2 years of experience

for service technicians to become familiar with all types of repairs.

New workers generally start as trainee technicians, technicians' helpers, or lubrication workers and gradually acquire and practice their skills by working with experienced mechanics and technicians.

Licenses

The U.S. Environmental Protection Agency (EPA) requires all technicians who buy or work with refrigerants to be licensed in proper refrigerant handling. Formal test preparation is not required, but many trade schools, unions, and employer associations offer training programs designed for the EPA exam.

Certification

Certification from the National Institute for Automotive Service Excellence is the standard credential for service technicians. Certification demonstrates competence and usually brings higher pay. Many employers require their service technicians to become certified.

Certification is available in eight different areas, including: automatic transmission/transaxle, brakes, electrical/electronic systems, engine performance, engine repair, heating and air conditioning, manual drive train and axles, and suspension and steering.

For each area, technicians must have at least 2 years of experience (or relevant schooling and 1 year of experience) and pass an exam. To become a Master Automobile Technician, technicians must pass all 8 exams.

Important Qualities

Customer-service skills. Service technicians must discuss automotive problems—along with options to fix them—with their customers. Because self-employed workers depend on repeat clients for business, they must be courteous, good listeners, and ready to answer customers' questions.

Detail oriented. Mechanical and electronic malfunctions are often due to misalignments or other easy-to-miss reasons. Service mechanics must, therefore, account for such details when inspecting or repairing engines and components.

Dexterity. Many tasks that service technicians do, such as disassembling engine parts, connecting or attaching components, and using handtools, require a steady hand and good hand–eye coordination.

Mechanical skills. Service technicians must be familiar with engine components and systems and know how they interact with each other. They must often take apart major parts for repairs and be able to put them back together properly.

Technical skills. Service technicians use sophisticated diagnostic equipment on engines, systems, and components. They must be familiar with electronic control systems and the appropriate tools needed to fix and maintain them.

Troubleshooting skills. Service technicians must be able to identify and fix problems in increasingly complicated mechanical and electronic systems.

Pay

Automotive Service Technicians and Mechanics
Median annual wages, May 2010

Installation, Maintenance, and Repair Occupations	$40,120
Automotive Service Technicians and Mechanics	$35,790
Total, All Occupations	$33,840

Note: All Occupations includes all occupations in the U.S. Economy.
Source: U.S. Bureau of Labor Statistics, Occupational Employment Statistics

The median annual wage of automotive service technicians and mechanics was $35,790 in May 2010. The median wage is the wage at which half the workers in an occupation earned more than that amount and half earned less. The lowest 10 percent earned less than $20,200, and the top 10 percent earned more than $59,590.

In May 2010, median annual wages in industries employing the largest numbers of automotive service technicians and mechanics were as follows:

Local government	$44,340
Automobile dealers	40,650
Automotive repair and maintenance	33,010
Automotive parts, accessories, and tire stores	31,160

Many experienced technicians working for automobile dealers and independent repair shops receive a commission related to the labor cost charged to the customer. Under this system, weekly earnings depend on the amount of work completed in addition to a guaranteed minimum salary.

Most service technicians work full time, and many work evenings or weekends. Overtime is common.

Job Outlook

Automotive Service Technicians and Mechanics
Percent change in employment, projected 2010-20

Automotive Service Technicians and Mechanics	17%
Installation, Maintenance, and Repair Occupations	15%
Total, All Occupations	14%

Note: All Occupations includes all occupations in the U.S. Economy.
Source: U.S. Bureau of Labor Statistics, Employment Projections program

Employment of automotive service technicians and mechanics is expected to grow 17 percent from 2010 to 2020, about as fast as the average for all occupations.

As the number of vehicles in use continues to grow, more entry-level service technicians will be needed to do basic maintenance and repair, such as brake pad replacements and oil changes. The increasing lifespan of late-model cars and light trucks will further increase demand for qualified workers.

However, continuing consolidation in the automotive industry may lessen the need for new mechanics.

Job Prospects

Job opportunities for qualified applicants should be very good as some employers report difficulty finding workers with the right skills and education. Jobseekers who have completed formal postsecondary training programs—especially candidates with training in advanced automotive technology, such as hybrid fuel or computer systems—should enjoy the best job prospects.

Those without formal automotive training are likely to face strong competition for entry-level jobs.

The majority of job openings will be in automobile dealerships and independent repair shops, where most service technicians currently work.

Employment projections data for automotive service technicians and mechanics, 2010-20

Occupational Title	SOC Code	Employment, 2010	Projected Employment, 2020	Change, 2010-20	
				Percent	Numeric
Automotive Service Technicians and Mechanics	49-3023	723,400	848,200	17	124,800
SOURCE: U.S. Bureau of Labor Statistics, Employment Projections program					

Similar Occupations

This table shows a list of occupations with job duties that are similar to those of automotive service technicians and mechanics.

Occupation	Job Duties	Entry-Level Education	Median Annual Pay, May 2010
Automotive Body and Glass Repairers	Automotive body and glass repairers restore, refinish, and replace vehicle bodies and frames, windshields, and window glass.	High school diploma or equivalent	$37,580
Diesel Service Technicians and Mechanics	Diesel service technicians and mechanics inspect, repair, or overhaul buses, trucks, and anything else with a diesel engine.	High school diploma or equivalent	$40,850
Heavy Vehicle and Mobile Equipment Service Technicians	Heavy vehicle and mobile equipment service technicians inspect, maintain, and repair vehicles and machinery used in construction, farming, rail transportation, and other industries.	High school diploma or equivalent	$42,630
Small Engine Mechanics	Small engine mechanics inspect, service, and repair motorized power equipment. Mechanics often specialize in one type of equipment, such as motorcycles, motorboats, or outdoor power equipment.	High school diploma or equivalent	$31,790

Contacts for More Information

For more details about work opportunities, contact local automobile dealers and repair shops or local offices of the state employment service. The state employment service also may have information about training programs.

For information about careers, education, and training programs, visit Automotive Youth Educational Systems ,National Institute for Automotive Service Excellence ,Auto Careers Today ,Auto Career Development Center ,National Automotive Technicians Education Foundation , Accrediting Commission of Career Schools and Colleges

Suggested citation:

Bureau of Labor Statistics, U.S. Department of Labor, Occupational Outlook Handbook, 2012-13 Edition, Automotive Service Technicians and Mechanics, on the Internet at http://www.bls.gov/ooh/installation-maintenance-and-repair/automotive-service-technicians-and-mechanics.htm .

Computer, ATM, and Office Machine Repairers

Quick Facts: Computer, ATM, and Office Machine Repairers	
2010 Median Pay	$37,280 per year $17.92 per hour
Entry-Level Education	Postsecondary non-degree award
Work Experience in a Related Occupation	None
On-the-job Training	None
Number of Jobs, 2010	146,200
Job Outlook, 2010-20	7% (Slower than average)
Employment Change, 2010-20	9,500

What Computer, ATM, and Office Machine Repairers Do

Computer, ATM, and office machine repairers install, fix, and maintain many of the machines that businesses, households, and other consumers use.

Duties

Computer, ATM, and office machine repairers typically do the following:

- Travel to customers' locations in response to service requests
- Communicate with customers to determine the source of a problem
- Do administrative tasks, such as completing work order forms
- Use a variety of tools, such as a multimeter, to help diagnose the problem
- Install large equipment, such as mainframe computers and ATMs
- Explain the basic functions of machines and equipment to customers
- Replace malfunctioning machine parts, such as video cards in desktop computers or keypads on ATM machines
- Provide preventative maintenance, such as cleaning the internal parts of machines
- Test newly installed systems to make sure they work properly

In most cases, machines do not break down entirely. Often just one broken part can keep a machine from working properly. Repairers

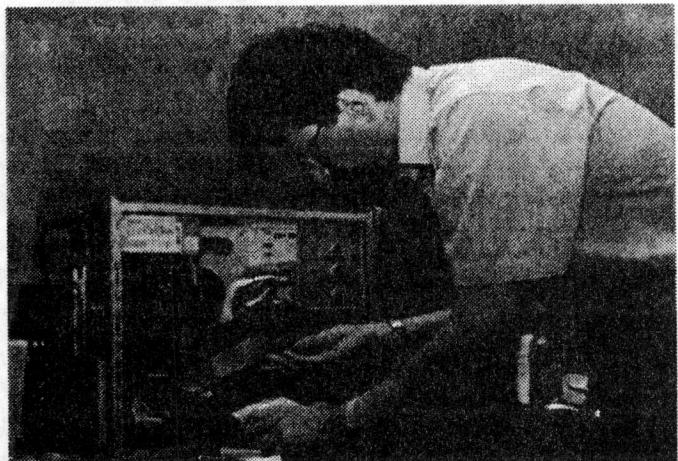

Computer repairers replace malfunctioning components within machines, such as a hard drive in a desktop computer.

often fix machines by replacing these parts and other defective equipment because it is often less expensive than replacing the entire machine.

Although the work of computer, ATM, and office machine repairers is very similar, the exact tasks differ depending on the type of equipment. For example, computer repairers often must replace desktop parts, such as a motherboard, because of hardware failure. ATM repairers may replace a worn magnetic head on a card reader to allow an ATM to recognize customers' bank cards. Office machine repairers replace parts of office machines that break down from general wear and tear, such as the printheads of inkjet printers.

Some repairers have assigned areas where they do preventive maintenance on a regular basis.

Computer repairers service and repair computer parts, network connections, and computer equipment, such as an external hard drive or computer monitor. Computer repairers must be familiar with various operating systems and commonly used software packages. Some work from repair shops, while others travel to customers' locations.

ATM repairers install and repair automated teller machines and, increasingly, electronic kiosks. They often work with a network of ATMs and travel to ATM locations when they are alerted to a malfunction.

Office machine repairers fix machinery at customers' workplaces because these machines are often large and stationary, such as office printers or copiers. Office machines often need preventive maintenance, such as cleaning, or replacement of commonly used parts as they break down from general wear and tear.

Work Environment

Computer, ATM, and office machine repairers held about 146,200 jobs in 2010. They mostly worked for private businesses, but about 24 percent were self-employed.

Computer and office machine repairers work in air-conditioned and well-ventilated offices because computers and office machines are sensitive to extreme temperatures and humidity.

ATM repairers work in various environments depending on the location of an ATM. Some ATMs are outdoors, while others are indoors, such as in lobbies of buildings.

Some repairers, often called field technicians, work on-site and have to travel to various locations to install, maintain, or repair a customer's equipment. Other repairers, often called bench technicians, work in repair shops. In smaller companies, repairers may work both in repair shops and at customers' locations.

In the course of repairs, repairers often must lift equipment and work in a variety of postures, although it is not usually strenuous.

Work Schedules

Most computer, ATM, and office machine repairers work full time, although some are employed as part-time workers. Some occasionally work evenings, weekends, and holidays to maintain machines that may break down.

How to Become a Computer, ATM, or Office Machine Repairer

Some workers enter this field with a high school diploma. However, knowledge of electronics is required, so these workers commonly have a postsecondary degree or certificate. Strong communication and customer service skills are important because computer, ATM, and office machine repairers often interact with customers to figure out what needs to be repaired.

Education

Employers often prefer workers who have training in electronics from the military or a vocational school. Workers who study basic electronics at a vocational school typically learn about circuits and transistors. They are also taught how to troubleshoot major issues, which means discovering which part is causing a machine to malfunction. A basic understanding of mechanical equipment is also important because many of the parts that fail in office machines and ATMs, such as paper loaders, are mechanical.

Training

Repairers typically know electronics when they are hired. However, because the tools they use vary by specialty, repairers usually get some company-specific training on the job to become familiar with diagnostic tools, such as proprietary software. As new tools and technology become available, repairers will typically attend classes that teach how to use and apply these tools.

In some cases, entry-level repairers with limited knowledge and experience will get on-the-job training from more experienced mentors. Newly hired repairers may work on problems that are less complex, such as doing preventive maintenance on machines. However, with experience, they can advance to positions where they maintain more sophisticated systems.

Certification

Various organizations offer certification for computer, ATM, and office machine repairers. For example, the Electronics Technicians Association International (ETA) offers more than 80 certification programs in numerous electronics specialties for varying levels of competence.

To become certified, applicants must meet several prerequisites and pass a comprehensive written or online exam. Certifications show a level of competency, and they can make an applicant more attractive to employers or increase an employee's opportunity for advancement.

Advancement

Over time, repairers become experts in their specialty and may train entry-level repairers. They may also move into management positions where they supervise other repairers.

Important Qualities

Analytical skills. Repairers often face problems with no standard solution. They must use logic, reasoning, and their experience to evaluate different possible solutions.

Communication skills. Repairers must be able to communicate effectively with customers because they work closely with customers to understand the problems with a machine.

Information technology (IT) skills. Repairers work with a number of advanced diagnostic tools and techniques, such as the ability to

access a computer remotely. They must be able to use technology to test various processes and evaluate results.

Manual dexterity. Repairers must be able to make precise, coordinated movements with their fingers or hands to grasp, manipulate, or assemble objects.

Troubleshooting skills. Workers find, diagnose, and repair problems. They devise methods to run tests to determine the cause of problems. They solve the problem to repair the equipment.

Pay

Computer, ATM, and Office Machine Repairers Median annual wages, May 2010	
Installation, Maintenance, and Repair Occupations	$40,120
Computer, ATM, and Office Machine Repairers	$37,280
Total, All Occupations	$33,840

Note: All Occupations includes all occupations in the U.S. Economy.
Source: U.S. Bureau of Labor Statistics, Occupational Employment Statistics

The median annual wage of computer, ATM, and office machine repairers was $37,280 in May 2010. The median wage is the wage at which half the workers in an occupation earned more than that amount and half earned less. The lowest 10 percent earned less than $22,600, and the top 10 percent earned more than $58,620.

Most computer, ATM, and office machine repairers work full time, although some are employed as part-time workers. Some occasionally work evenings, weekends, and holidays to maintain machines that may break down.

Job Outlook

Computer, ATM, and Office Machine Repairers Percent change in employment, projected 2010-20	
Installation, Maintenance, and Repair Occupations	15%
Total, All Occupations	14%
Computer, ATM, and Office Machine Repairers	7%

Note: All Occupations includes all occupations in the U.S. Economy.
Source: U.S. Bureau of Labor Statistics, Employment Projections program

Employment of computer, ATM, and office machine repairers is expected to grow 7 percent from 2010 to 2020, slower than the average for all occupations.

Computer repairers will see a continued demand for their services as computer parts need replacing or organizations need hardware upgrades. As companies modernize and use new technology in their day-to-day operations, computer repairers will continue to see employment opportunities.

Office and machine repairers will also continue to see demand for their services as office equipment continues to break down and need preventive maintenance.

However, increasing use of electronic banking is causing a decline in the demand for new ATMs, which may result in a decreased need for ATM repairers.

Job Prospects

Workers with experience, education from a trade school, and some certification often will have the best opportunities. Employers also prefer to hire workers whose military service has provided them with relevant training and experience. ATM repairers with training in the security of ATM networks have the best job prospects.

Employment projections data for computer, ATM, and office machine repairers, 2010-20

Occupational Title	SOC Code	Employment, 2010	Projected Employment, 2020	Change, 2010-20	
				Percent	Numeric
Computer, Automated Teller, and Office Machine Repairers	49-2011	146,200	155,800	7	9,500
SOURCE: U.S. Bureau of Labor Statistics, Employment Projections program					

Similar Occupations

This table shows a list of occupations with job duties that are similar to those of computer, ATM, and office machine repairers.

Occupation	Job Duties	Entry-Level Education	Median Annual Pay, May 2010
Broadcast and Sound Engineering Technicians	Broadcast and sound engineering technicians set up, operate, and maintain the electrical equipment for radio and television broadcasts, concerts, sound recordings, and movies and in office and school buildings.	See How to Become One	$39,870
Electrical and Electronics Installers and Repairers	Electrical and electronics installers and repairers install, repair, or replace a variety of electrical equipment in telecommunications, transportation, utilities, and other industries.	Postsecondary non-degree award	$49,170
Electricians	Electricians install and maintain electrical systems in homes, businesses, and factories.	High school diploma or equivalent	$48,250
General Maintenance and Repair Workers	General maintenance and repair workers maintain and repair machines, mechanical equipment, and buildings. They work on plumbing, electrical, and air-conditioning and heating systems.	High school diploma or equivalent	$34,730
Home Appliance Repairers	Home appliance repairers install and repair household appliances, such as refrigerators, microwaves, and washer and dryers.	High school diploma or equivalent	$34,730
Home Entertainment Equipment Installers and Repairers	Home entertainment equipment installers and repairers set up and fix household audio and video equipment, such as televisions, stereo components, and home theater systems.	Postsecondary non-degree award	$32,940
Telecommunications Equipment Installers and Repairers Except Line Installers	Telecommunications equipment installers and repairers, also known as telecom technicians, set up and maintain devices or equipment that carry communications signals, connect to telephone lines, or access the Internet.	Postsecondary non-degree award	$54,710

Contacts for More Information

For more information about careers in computer repair, visit Association of Computer Repair Business Owners

For more information on electronic careers and certification, visit Electronics Technician Association International

Suggested citation:

Bureau of Labor Statistics, U.S. Department of Labor, Occupational Outlook Handbook, 2012-13 Edition, Computer, ATM, and Office Machine Repairers, on the Internet at http://www.bls.gov/ooh/installation-maintenance-and-repair/computer-atm-and-office-machine-repairers.htm .

Diesel Service Technicians and Mechanics

Quick Facts: Diesel Service Technicians and Mechanics	
2010 Median Pay	$40,850 per year $19.64 per hour
Entry-Level Education	High school diploma or equivalent
Work Experience in a Related Occupation	None
On-the-job Training	Long-term on-the-job training
Number of Jobs, 2010	242,200
Job Outlook, 2010-20	15% (About as fast as average)
Employment Change, 2010-20	35,200

What Diesel Service Technicians and Mechanics Do

Diesel service technicians and mechanics inspect, repair, or overhaul buses, trucks, and anything else with a diesel engine.

Duties

Diesel service technicians and mechanics typically do the following:

- Follow a checklist of inspection procedures
- Test drive vehicles to diagnose malfunctions
- Read and interpret diagnostic test results, often by using dials, gauges, and other computer equipment
- Raise trucks, buses, and heavy parts or equipment by using hydraulic jacks or hoists
- Inspect brake systems, steering mechanisms, transmissions, engines, and other parts of vehicles

- Do routine maintenance, such as changing oil, checking batteries, and lubricating equipment and parts
- Adjust and align wheels, tighten bolts and screws, and attach system components
- Repair or replace malfunctioning components, parts, and other mechanical or electrical equipment
- Disassemble and reassemble equipment and parts
- Test drive vehicles to ensure that they run smoothly

Because of their efficiency and durability, diesel engines have become the standard in powering our nation's trucks and buses. Other heavy vehicles and mobile equipment, including bulldozers and cranes, also are powered by diesel engines, as are many commercial boats, passenger vehicles, pickups, and other work trucks. Diesel service technicians who service and repair these engines are commonly known as diesel mechanics.

Diesel mechanics handle many kinds of repairs. They may work on a vehicle's electrical system, make major engine repairs, or retrofit engines with emission control systems to comply with pollution regulations.

Diesel engine maintenance is becoming increasingly complex as engines and other components use more electronic systems to control their operation. For example, fuel injection and engine timing systems rely heavily on microprocessors to maximize fuel efficiency. In most shops, workers often use hand-held or laptop computers to diagnose problems and adjust engine functions.

In addition to computerized diagnostic equipment, diesel mechanics use a variety of power and machine tools, such as pneumatic wrenches, lathes, grinding machines, and welding equipment. Handtools, including pliers, wrenches, and screwdrivers, are also commonly used.

Employers typically provide expensive power tools and computerized equipment, but workers generally acquire their own hand tools over time.

For information on technicians and mechanics who work primarily on automobiles, see the profile on automotive service technicians and mechanics .

For information on technicians and mechanics who work primarily on farm equipment, construction vehicles, and rail cars, see the profile on heavy vehicle and mobile equipment service technicians .

For information on technicians and mechanics who primarily work on motorboats, motorcycles, and small all-terrain vehicles, see the profile on small engine mechanics .

Diesel service technicians and mechanics repair diesel engine vehicles, such as buses and trucks.

Work Environment

Diesel service technicians and mechanics held about 242,200 jobs in 2010. The majority worked for private companies, but about 11 percent worked for government. About 18 percent belonged to a union.

In 2010, industries employing the largest numbers of diesel service technicians and mechanics were as follows:

General freight trucking	12%
Local government, excluding education and hospitals	9
Automotive repair and maintenance	8
Motor vehicle and parts wholesalers	7
Specialized freight trucking	5

Diesel mechanics usually work in well-ventilated and sometimes noisy repair shops. Occasionally, they repair vehicles on roadsides or at worksites.

Work Schedules

Most diesel mechanics work full time. Overtime is common as many repair shops extend their service hours during evenings and weekends. In addition, some truck and bus repair shops provide 24-hour maintenance and repair services.

Injuries

Diesel service technicians and mechanics have a rate of injuries and illnesses that is much higher than the national average. Diesel mechanics often lift heavy parts and tools, handle greasy or dirty equipment, and work in uncomfortable positions. Although cuts or burns are common, the work is generally not hazardous when workers follow basic safety precautions.

How to Become a Diesel Service Technician or Mechanic

Many diesel mechanics learn informally on the job, but employers increasingly prefer applicants who have completed postsecondary training programs in diesel engine repair. Although not required, industry certification is important for diesel mechanics.

Education

Most employers require a high school diploma or equivalent. High school or postsecondary courses in automotive repair, electronics, and mathematics provide a strong educational background for a career as a diesel mechanic.

Many employers look for workers with postsecondary training in diesel engine repair. A large number of community colleges and trade and vocational schools offer programs in diesel engine repair. These programs usually last 6 months to 2 years and may lead to a certificate of completion or an associate's degree.

Programs mix classroom instruction with hands-on training, including the basics of diesel technology, repair techniques and equipment, and practical exercises. Students also learn how to interpret technical manuals and electronic diagnostic reports.

Graduates usually advance to journey-worker status, where they may then work with minimal supervision.

Training

Some diesel mechanics begin working without postsecondary education and are trained on the job. Trainees are assigned basic tasks, such as cleaning parts, checking fuel and oil levels, and driving vehicles in and out of the shop.

After they learn routine maintenance and repair tasks and demonstrate competence, trainees move on to more complicated jobs. This process can last from 3 to 4 years, at which point a trainee is usually considered a journey-level diesel mechanic.

Over the course of their careers, diesel mechanics must learn new techniques and equipment. Employers often send experienced mechanics to special training classes conducted by manufacturers and vendors to learn about the latest diesel technology.

Certification

Certification from the National Institute for Automotive Service Excellence (ASE) is the recognized industry credential for diesel and other automotive service technicians and mechanics. Although not required, this certification shows a diesel mechanic's competence, experience, and value to potential employers and clients.

Diesel mechanics may be certified in specific repair areas, such as drive trains, electronic systems, or preventative maintenance and inspection. To earn certification, mechanics must have 2 years' work experience and pass one or more ASE exams. To remain certified, diesel mechanics must pass the test again every 5 years.

Licenses

Some diesel mechanics may be required to have a commercial driver's license if their job duties include test driving buses or large trucks.

Important Qualities

Customer-service skills. Diesel mechanics frequently talk to their customers about automotive problems and work that they have planned, started, or completed. They must be courteous, good listeners, and ready to answer customers' questions.

Dexterity. Mechanics need a steady hand and good hand-and-eye coordination for many tasks, such as disassembling engine parts, connecting or attaching components, or using hand tools.

Mechanical skills. Diesel mechanics must be familiar with parts and components of engines, transmissions, braking mechanisms, and other complex systems. They must also be able to disassemble, work on, and reassemble parts and machinery.

Technical skills. Modern diesel engines rely heavily on electronic systems to function. Diesel mechanics must be familiar with how the electronic systems operate and with the tools needed to work on them.

Troubleshooting skills. Diesel mechanics must be able to identify mechanical and electronic problems, make repairs, and offer a proper maintenance strategy.

Pay

Diesel Service Technicians and Mechanics
Median annual wages, May 2010

Diesel Service Technicians and Mechanics	$40,850
Installation, Maintenance, and Repair Occupations	$40,120
Total, All Occupations	$33,840

Note: All Occupations includes all occupations in the U.S. Economy.
Source: U.S. Bureau of Labor Statistics, Occupational Employment Statistics

The median annual wage of diesel service technicians and mechanics was $40,850 in May 2010. The median wage is the wage at which half the workers in an occupation earned more than that amount and half earned less. The lowest 10 percent earned less than $26,550, and the top 10 percent earned more than $60,830.

In May 2010, median annual wages in industries employing the largest numbers of diesel service technicians and mechanics were as follows:

Local government	$48,070
Motor vehicle and parts wholesalers	41,070
Automotive repair and maintenance	38,320
General freight trucking	38,010
Specialized freight trucking	36,110

Many diesel mechanics, especially those employed by truck fleet dealers and repair shops, receive a commission in addition to their base salary.

Most diesel mechanics work full time. Overtime is common as many repair shops extend their service hours during evenings and weekends. In addition, some truck and bus repair shops provide 24-hour maintenance and repair services.

Job Outlook

Diesel Service Technicians and Mechanics

Percent change in employment, projected 2010-20

Diesel Service Technicians and Mechanics	15%
Installation, Maintenance, and Repair Occupations	15%
Total, All Occupations	14%

Note: All Occupations includes all occupations in the U.S. Economy.
Source: U.S. Bureau of Labor Statistics, Employment Projections program

Employment of diesel mechanics is expected to grow 15 percent from 2010 to 2020, about as fast as the average for all occupations.

As more freight is shipped across the country, additional diesel-powered trucks will be needed. As a result, diesel mechanics will be needed to maintain and repair the nation's truck fleet. Demand for new workers in the freight trucking and automotive repair and maintenance industries is expected to drive overall diesel mechanic job growth.

Some older vehicles will need to be retrofitted and modernized to comply with environmental regulations, creating additional jobs for diesel mechanics.

Overall employment growth, however, may be dampened due to increasing durability of new truck and bus diesel engines. Continuing advances in repair technology, including computerized diagnostic equipment, also will result in fewer mechanics doing the same amount of work, further reducing demand for mechanics.

Job Prospects

Job opportunities should be good for those who have completed formal postsecondary education and have strong technical skills, as employers sometimes report difficulty finding qualified workers.

Workers without formal training often require more supervision and on-the-job instruction than others—an expensive and time-consuming process for employers. Because of this, untrained candidates will face strong competition for jobs.

Employment projections data for diesel service technicians and mechanics, 2010-20

Occupational Title	SOC Code	Employment, 2010	Projected Employment, 2020	Change, 2010-20 Percent	Change, 2010-20 Numeric
Bus and Truck Mechanics and Diesel Engine Specialists	49-3031	242,200	277,400	15	35,200

SOURCE: U.S. Bureau of Labor Statistics, Employment Projections program

Similar Occupations

This table shows a list of occupations with job duties that are similar to those of diesel service technicians and mechanics.

Occupation	Job Duties	Entry-Level Education	Median Annual Pay, May 2010
Aircraft and Avionics Equipment Mechanics and Technicians	Aircraft and avionics equipment mechanics and technicians repair and perform scheduled maintenance on airplanes and helicopters. They also inspect airplanes and helicopters as required by the Federal Aviation Administration (FAA).	Postsecondary non-degree award	$53,220
Automotive Body and Glass Repairers	Automotive body and glass repairers restore, refinish, and replace vehicle bodies and frames, windshields, and window glass.	High school diploma or equivalent	$37,580
Automotive Service Technicians and Mechanics	Automotive service technicians and mechanics, often called service technicians or service techs, inspect, maintain, and repair cars and light trucks.	High school diploma or equivalent	$35,790
Heavy Vehicle and Mobile Equipment Service Technicians	Heavy vehicle and mobile equipment service technicians inspect, maintain, and repair vehicles and machinery used in construction, farming, rail transportation, and other industries.	High school diploma or equivalent	$42,630
Small Engine Mechanics	Small engine mechanics inspect, service, and repair motorized power equipment. Mechanics often specialize in one type of equipment, such as motorcycles, motorboats, or outdoor power equipment.	High school diploma or equivalent	$31,790

Contacts for More Information

For general information about careers, education, or certification, visit Association of Diesel Specialists , National Institute for Automotive Service Excellence ,National Automotive Technicians Education Foundation

Suggested citation:

Bureau of Labor Statistics, U.S. Department of Labor, Occupational Outlook Handbook, 2012-13 Edition, Diesel Service Technicians and Mechanics, on the Internet at http://www.bls.gov/ooh/installation-maintenance-and-repair/diesel-service-technicians-and-mechanics.htm .

Electrical and Electronics Installers and Repairers

Quick Facts: Electrical and Electronics Installers and Repairers	
2010 Median Pay	$49,170 per year $23.64 per hour
Entry-Level Education	Postsecondary non-degree award
Work Experience in a Related Occupation	None
On-the-job Training	See How to Become One
Number of Jobs, 2010	141,100
Job Outlook, 2010-20	3% (Slower than average)
Employment Change, 2010-20	3,600

What Electrical and Electronics Installers and Repairers Do

Electrical and electronics installers and repairers install, repair, or replace a variety of electrical equipment in telecommunications, transportation, utilities, and other industries.

Duties

Electrical and electronics installers and repairers typically do the following:

- Prepare cost estimates for clients
- Refer to service guides, schematics, and manufacturer specifications
- Repair or replace defective parts, such as motors, fuses, or gaskets
- Reassemble and test equipment after repairs
- Maintain records of parts used, labor time, and final charges

Electrical and electronics installers and repairers work on complex pieces of electronic equipment.

Automated electronic control systems are becoming increasingly complex. As a result, repairers use software programs and testing

An electronics repairer must determine problems with equipment by troubleshooting.

equipment to diagnose malfunctions. Among their diagnostic tools are multimeters—which measure voltage, current, and resistance—and advanced multimeters, which measure the capacitance, inductance, and current gain of transistors.

Repairers also use signal generators, which provide test signals, and oscilloscopes, which display signals graphically. In addition, repairers use handtools such as pliers, screwdrivers, soldering irons, and wrenches to replace faulty parts and adjust equipment.

Commercial and industrial equipment electrical and electronics repairers repair, test, adjust, or install electronic equipment, such as industrial controls, transmitters, and antennas.

Electrical and electronics installers and repairers of transportation equipment install, adjust, or maintain mobile communication equipment, including sound, sonar, security, navigation, and surveillance systems on trains, watercraft, or other vehicles.

Powerhouse, substation, and relay electrical and electronics repairers inspect, test, maintain, or repair electrical equipment used in generating stations, substations, and inservice relays. These workers may be known as powerhouse electricians, relay technicians, or power transformer repairers.

Electric motor, power tool, and related repairers—such as armature winders, generator mechanics, and electric golf cart repairers—specialize in installing, maintaining, and repairing electric motors, wiring, or switches.

Electronic equipment installers and repairers of motor vehicles install, diagnose, and repair sound, security, and navigation equipment in motor vehicles. Motor vehicle installers and repairers work with an increasingly complex range of electronic equipment, including DVD players, navigation systems, and passive and active security systems.

Electrical and electronic installers and repairers may specialize, according to how and where they work:

Field technicians often travel to factories or other locations to repair equipment. When equipment breaks down, field technicians go to a customer's site to repair the equipment. Because repairing components is a complex activity, workers on the factory floor usually remove and replace defective units, such as circuit boards, instead of fixing them. Defective units are discarded or returned to the manufacturer or a specialized shop for repair.

Bench technicians work in repair shops in factories and service centers, fixing components that cannot be repaired on the factory floor. These workers also locate and repair circuit defects, such as poorly soldered joints, blown fuses, or malfunctioning transistors.

Work Environment

Electrical and electronics installers and repairers held about 141,100 jobs in 2010. Employment in the detailed occupations that make up this group was distributed as follows:

Electrical and electronics repairers, commercial and industrial equipment	69,100
Electrical and electronics repairers, powerhouse, substation, and relay	23,400
Electric motor, power tool, and related repairers	19,800
Electronic equipment installers and repairers, motor vehicles	16,000
Electrical and electronics installers and repairers, transportation equipment	12,700

Many electrical and electronics installers and repairers work on factory floors, where they are subject to noise, dirt, and heat. Bench technicians work primarily in repair shops, which are quiet and well lit. Motor vehicle electronic equipment installers and repairers normally work in repair shops.

Injuries

Electric motor, power tools, and related repairers and electrical and electronics installers and repairers of transportation equipment have a higher rate of work-related injuries and illnesses than the average for all other occupations.

Installers and repairers may have to lift heavy equipment and work in awkward positions. Workers must follow safety guidelines and wear protective goggles and hardhats. When working on ladders or on elevated equipment, repairers must wear harnesses to avoid falls.

Before repairing a piece of machinery, these workers must follow procedures to ensure that others cannot start the equipment during the repair process. They also must take precautions against electric shock by locking off power to the unit under repair.

Work Schedules

Nearly all electrical and electronics installers and repairers work full time.

How to Become an Electrical or Electronics Installer and Repairer

Most electrical and electronics installers and repairers obtain specialized training at a technical college. Gaining voluntary certification is common and can be useful for getting a job.

Education

Electrical and electronics installers and repairers have to understand electrical equipment and electronics to get a job.

Employers often prefer to hire applicants who have an associate's degree from a community college or technical school, but having a high school diploma may be enough for some jobs. Entry-level repairers may begin by working with experienced technicians, who provide technical guidance, and work independently after developing their skills.

Certification

Various organizations offer certification. For example, the Electronics Technicians Association International (ETA) offers more than 50 certification programs in numerous electronics specialties for various levels of competence. The International Society of Certified Electronics Technicians also offers certification for several levels of competence. The organization focuses on a broad range of topics, including basic electronics, electronic systems, and appliance service. To become certified, applicants must meet prerequisites and pass a comprehensive exam.

Important Qualities

Color vision. Workers need to identify the color-coded components that are often used in electronic equipment.

Communication skills. Field technicians work closely with customers, so they must listen to understand customers' problems and explain solutions in a simple, clear manner.

Technical skills. Workers use a variety of tools to install or repair equipment.

Troubleshooting skills. Electrical equipment and systems often involve intricate parts. Workers must be able to identify malfunctions and make the necessary repairs.

Pay

Electrical and Electronics Installers and Repairers
Median annual wages, May 2010

Electrical and Electronics Installers and Repairers	$49,170
Electrical and Electronic Equipment Mechanics, Installers, and Repairers	$46,130
Total, All Occupations	$33,840

Note: All Occupations includes all occupations in the U.S. Economy.
Source: U.S. Bureau of Labor Statistics, Occupational Employment Statistics

The median annual wage of electrical and electronics installers and repairers was $49,170 in May 2010. The median wage is the wage at which half the workers in an occupation earned more than that amount and half earned less. The lowest 10 percent earned less than $26,480, and the top 10 percent earned more than $73,420.

Median annual wages for electrical and electronics installers and repairers in May 2010 were the following:
- $65,230 for electrical and electronics repairers, powerhouse, substation, and relay
- $51,820 for electrical and electronics repairers, commercial and industrial equipment
- $48,410 for electrical and electronics installers and repairers, transportation equipment
- $36,170 for electric motor, power tool, and related repairers
- $28,450 for electronic equipment installers and repairers, motor vehicles

Nearly all electrical and electronics installers and repairers work full time.

Job Outlook

Electrical and Electronics Installers and Repairers
Percent change in employment, projected 2010-20

Total, All Occupations	14%
Electrical and Electronic Equipment Mechanics, Installers, and Repairers	12%
Electrical and Electronics Installers and Repairers	3%

Note: All Occupations includes all occupations in the U.S. Economy.
Source: U.S. Bureau of Labor Statistics, Employment Projections program

Overall employment of electrical and electronics installers and repairers is expected to grow 3 percent from 2010 to 2020, slower than the average for all occupations.

Projected employment change for specific groups of workers within this occupation is as follows:
- Electrical and electronics installers and repairers of commercial and industrial equipment: little or no change. As competition increases, businesses strive to lower costs by increasing and improving automation. This equipment needs service and repair, and generally increases the demand for electrical workers, but improved reliability of equipment is expected to temper employment growth.
- Motor vehicle electronic equipment installers and repairers: 3 percent growth. As motor vehicle manufacturers install more and better sound, security, entertainment, and navigation systems in new vehicles, and as newer electronic systems require progressively less maintenance, employment growth for aftermarket electronic equipment installers will be limited.
- Electric motor, power tool, and related repairers: 5 percent growth. Retrofitting electrical generators in public buildings to reduce

emissions and energy consumption will spur some employment growth. However, improvements in electrical and electronic equipment design, as well as the increased use of disposable tool parts, should limit employment growth.

- Electrical and electronic installers and repairers of transportation equipment: little or no change. Declining employment in the rail transportation industry will dampen growth in this occupational specialty even as other transportation systems need additional workers.
- Powerhouse, substation, and relay electrical and electronics installers and repairers: 5 percent growth. Although privatization in utilities industries should improve productivity and hinder employment growth, the installation of newer, energy-efficient green technologies will spur some demand for employment.

Job Prospects

Overall job opportunities should be best for applicants who have an associate's degree in electronics, certification, or related experience. In addition to employment growth, the need to replace workers who transfer to other occupations or leave the labor force will result in some job openings.

Employment projections data for electrical and electronics installers and repairers, 2010-20

Occupational Title	SOC Code	Employment, 2010	Projected Employment, 2020	Change, 2010-20	
				Percent	Numeric
Electrical and Electronics Installers and Repairers	—	141,100	144,700	3	3,600
Electric Motor, Power Tool, and Related Repairers	49-2092	19,800	20,800	5	1,000
Electrical and Electronics Installers and Repairers, Transportation Equipment	49-2093	12,700	13,000	2	300
Electrical and Electronics Repairers, Commercial and Industrial Equipment	49-2094	69,100	69,900	1	800
Electrical and Electronics Repairers, Powerhouse, Substation, and Relay	49-2095	23,400	24,600	5	1,100
Electronic Equipment Installers and Repairers, Motor Vehicles	49-2096	16,000	16,400	3	400
SOURCE: U.S. Bureau of Labor Statistics, Employment Projections program					

Similar Occupations

This table shows a list of occupations with job duties that are similar to those of electrical and electronics installers and repairers.

Occupation	Job Duties	Entry-Level Education	Median Annual Pay, May 2010
Electricians	Electricians install and maintain electrical systems in homes, businesses, and factories.	High school diploma or equivalent	$48,250
Aircraft and Avionics Equipment Mechanics and Technicians	Aircraft and avionics equipment mechanics and technicians repair and perform scheduled maintenance on airplanes and helicopters. They also inspect airplanes and helicopters as required by the Federal Aviation Administration (FAA).	Postsecondary non-degree award	$53,220
Computer, ATM, and Office Machine Repairers	Computer, ATM, and office machine repairers install, fix, and maintain many of the machines that businesses, households, and other consumers use.	Postsecondary non-degree award	$37,280
Home Entertainment Equipment Installers and Repairers	Home entertainment equipment installers and repairers set up and fix household audio and video equipment, such as televisions, stereo components, and home theater systems.	Postsecondary non-degree award	$32,940
Telecommunications Equipment Installers and Repairers Except Line Installers	Telecommunications equipment installers and repairers, also known as telecom technicians, set up and maintain devices or equipment that carry communications signals, connect to telephone lines, or access the Internet.	Postsecondary non-degree award	$54,710
Elevator Installers and Repairers	Elevator installers and repairers install, fix, and maintain elevators, escalators, moving walkways, and other lifts.	High school diploma or equivalent	$70,910
General Maintenance and Repair Workers	General maintenance and repair workers maintain and repair machines, mechanical equipment, and buildings. They work on plumbing, electrical, and air-conditioning and heating systems.	High school diploma or equivalent	$34,730

Broadcast and Sound Engineering Technicians	Broadcast and sound engineering technicians set up, operate, and maintain the electrical equipment for radio and television broadcasts, concerts, sound recordings, and movies and in office and school buildings.	See How to Become One	$39,870

Contacts for More Information

For information about electric motor, power tool, and related repairers, including careers and certification, visit   Electronics Technicians Association International ,International Society of Certified Electronics Technicians

Suggested citation:

Bureau of Labor Statistics, U.S. Department of Labor, Occupational Outlook Handbook, 2012-13 Edition, Electrical and Electronics Installers and Repairers, on the Internet at http://www.bls.gov/ooh/installation-maintenance-and-repair/electrical-and-electronics-installers-and-repairers.htm .

General Maintenance and Repair Workers

Quick Facts: General Maintenance and Repair Workers	
2010 Median Pay	$34,730 per year $16.70 per hour
Entry-Level Education	High school diploma or equivalent
Work Experience in a Related Occupation	None
On-the-job Training	Moderate-term on-the-job training
Number of Jobs, 2010	1,289,000
Job Outlook, 2010-20	11% (About as fast as average)
Employment Change, 2010-20	142,000

What General Maintenance and Repair Workers Do

General maintenance and repair workers maintain and repair machines, mechanical equipment, and buildings. They work on plumbing, electrical, and air-conditioning and heating systems.

General maintenance and repair workers use tools to fix appliances and equipment.

Duties

General maintenance and repair workers typically do the following:

- Maintain and repair machines, mechanical equipment, and buildings
- Troubleshoot and fix faulty electrical switches
- Inspect and diagnose problems and figure out the best way to correct them, frequently checking blueprints, repair manuals, and parts catalogs
- Do routine preventive maintenance to ensure that machines continue to run smoothly
- Assemble and set up machinery or equipment
- Plan repair work using blueprints or diagrams
- Do general cleaning and upkeep of buildings and properties
- Order supplies from catalogs and storerooms
- Meet with clients to estimate repairs and costs
- Keep detailed records of their work

General maintenance and repair workers are hired for maintenance and repair tasks that are not complex enough to need the specialized training of a licensed tradesperson, such as a plumber or electrician.

They are also responsible for recognizing when a job is above their skill level and needs the skills of a tradesperson. For more information about other trade occupations, see the profiles on electricians ; carpenters ; heating, air-conditioning, and refrigeration mechanics and installers ; and plumbers, pipefitters, and steamfitters .

Workers may fix plaster or drywall. They may fix or paint roofs, windows, doors, floors, woodwork, and other parts of buildings.

They also maintain and repair specialized equipment and machinery in cafeterias, laundries, hospitals, stores, offices, and factories.

They get supplies and repair parts from distributors or storerooms to fix problems. They use common hand and power tools such as screwdrivers, saws, drills, wrenches, and hammers to fix, replace, or repair equipment and parts of buildings.

Work Environment

General maintenance and repair workers held about 1.3 million jobs in 2010. The following industries employed the most general maintenance and repair workers in 2010:

Real estate and rental and leasing	19%
Manufacturing	15
Government	12
Educational services; state, local, and private	8
Health care and social assistance	8

General maintenance and repair workers often carry out many different tasks in a single day, at any number of locations. They may work inside a single building, such as a hotel or hospital, or be responsible for the maintenance of many buildings, such as those in an apartment complex or college campus.

General maintenance and repair workers may have to stand for long periods or lift heavy objects. These workers may work in uncomfortably hot or cold environments, in uncomfortable and cramped positions, or on ladders. The work involves a lot of walking, climbing, and reaching.

Injuries

Some tasks put workers at risk of electrical shock, burns, falls, cuts, and bruises. Full-time general maintenance workers experienced a work-related injury and illness rate that was much higher than the national average for all full-time workers.

Work Schedules

Most general maintenance workers work full time. Some work evening, night, or weekend shifts or are on call for emergency repairs.

How to Become a General Maintenance and Repair Worker

Jobs in this field typically do not require any formal education beyond high school. General maintenance and repair workers often learn their skills on the job. They start by doing simple tasks and watching and learning from skilled maintenance workers.

Education

Many maintenance and repair workers may learn some basic skills in high school shop or technical educations classes, postsecondary trade or vocational schools, or community colleges.

Courses in mechanical drawing, electricity, woodworking, blueprint reading, science, mathematics, and computers are useful. Maintenance and repair workers often do work that involves electrical, plumbing, heating, and air-conditioning systems or painting and roofing tasks. Workers need a good working knowledge of many repair and maintenance tasks.

Practical training, available at many adult education centers and community colleges, is another option for workers to learn tasks such as drywall repair and basic plumbing.

Training

General maintenance and repair workers usually start by watching and learning from skilled maintenance workers. They begin by doing simple tasks, such as fixing leaky faucets and replacing light bulbs. They go on to more difficult tasks, such as overhauling machinery or building walls.

Some learn their skills by working as helpers to other types of repair or construction workers, including machinery repairers, carpenters, or electricians.

Because a growing number of new buildings rely on computers to control their systems, general maintenance and repair workers may need to know basic computer skills, such as how to log onto a central computer system and navigate through a series of menus. Companies that install computer-controlled equipment usually give on-site training for general maintenance and repair workers.

Certification

General maintenance and repair workers can show their competency by attaining voluntary certification. The Society for Maintenance and Reliability Professionals (SMRP) offers the Certified Maintenance and Reliability Professional (CMRP) designation to those who successfully complete the program and pass an exam. Certification can help applicants find jobs and provide them with better advancement opportunities.

Licensing

Licensing requirements vary by state and locality. For more complex tasks, workers may need to be licensed in a particular specialty, such as electrical or plumbing work.

Advancement

Some maintenance and repair workers decide to train in one specific craft and become craft workers, such as electricians , heating and air-conditioning mechanics , or plumbers . Within small organizations, promotion opportunities may be limited.

Important Qualities

Computer skills. Many new buildings have automated controls. Workers must be able to navigate a centralized computer system to adjust and monitor the controls.

Customer-service skills. Workers interact with customers on a regular basis. They need to be friendly and able to address customers' questions.

Dexterity. Many technician tasks, such as repairing small devices, connecting or attaching components, and using handtools, require a steady hand and good hand-eye coordination.

Troubleshooting skills. Workers find, diagnose, and repair problems. They do tests to figure out the cause of problems before fixing equipment.

Pay

General Maintenance and Repair Workers
Median annual wages, May 2010

Other Installation, Maintenance, and Repair Occupations	$38,010
Maintenance and Repair Workers, General	$34,730
Total, All Occupations	$33,840

Note: All Occupations includes all occupations in the U.S. Economy.
Source: U.S. Bureau of Labor Statistics, Occupational Employment Statistics

The median annual wage of general maintenance and repair workers was $34,730 in May 2010. The median wage is the wage at which half the workers in an occupation earned more than that amount and half earned less. The lowest 10 percent earned less than $20,800, and the top 10 percent earned more than $56,090.

Most general maintenance workers work full time. Some work evening, night, or weekend shifts or are on call for emergency repairs.

Job Outlook

General Maintenance and Repair Workers
Percent change in employment, projected 2010-20

Other Installation, Maintenance, and Repair Occupations	15%
Total, All Occupations	14%
Maintenance and Repair Workers, General	11%

Note: All Occupations includes all occupations in the U.S. Economy.
Source: U.S. Bureau of Labor Statistics, Employment Projections program

Employment of general maintenance and repair workers is expected to grow 11 percent from 2010 to 2020, about as fast as the average for all occupations.

Because many general maintenance and repair workers work in industries related to real estate, employment opportunities may be sensitive to fluctuations in the economy. Some workers may experience periods of unemployment when the overall level of construction and real estate development falls. However, maintenance and repairs continue during economic downturns, and may even increase as people opt to repair rather than replace equipment.

Employment growth of general maintenance and repair workers may be negatively affected by the use of building management systems. These systems control and monitor the building's mechanical and electrical equipment, such as ventilation and lighting. For example, these systems can identify a broken ventilation fan or turn off lights automatically after a set amount of time. Building management systems make it easier to detect problems and automatically schedule repairs, partially reducing the need for general maintenance and repair workers.

Job Prospects

There should be many job openings for general maintenance and repair workers, due to growth and the need to replace workers who leave the occupation. Many job openings are expected as experienced workers retire. Those with experience in repair- or maintenance-related fields should continue to have the best job prospects.

Employment projections data for general maintenance and repair workers, 2010-20

Occupational Title	SOC Code	Employment, 2010	Projected Employment, 2020	Change, 2010-20 Percent	Change, 2010-20 Numeric
Maintenance and Repair Workers, General	49-9071	1,289,000	1,431,000	11	142,000
SOURCE: U.S. Bureau of Labor Statistics, Employment Projections program					

Similar Occupations

This table shows a list of occupations with job duties that are similar to those of general maintenance and repair workers.

Occupation	Job Duties	Entry-Level Education	Median Annual Pay, May 2010
Boilermakers	Boilermakers assemble, install, and repair boilers, closed vats, and other large vessels or containers that hold liquids and gases.	High school diploma or equivalent	$54,640
Carpenters	Carpenters construct and repair building frameworks and structures—such as stairways, doorframes, partitions, and rafters—made from wood and other materials. They also may install kitchen cabinets, siding, and drywall.	High school diploma or equivalent	$39,530
Electricians	Electricians install and maintain electrical systems in homes, businesses, and factories.	High school diploma or equivalent	$48,250
Heating, Air Conditioning, and Refrigeration Mechanics and Installers	Heating, air conditioning, and refrigeration mechanics and installers—often referred to as HVACR technicians—work on heating, ventilation, cooling, and refrigeration systems that control the air quality in many types of buildings.	Postsecondary non-degree award	$42,530
Plumbers, Pipefitters, and Steamfitters	Plumbers, pipefitters, and steamfitters install and repair pipes that carry water, steam, air, or other liquids or gases to and in businesses, homes, and factories.	High school diploma or equivalent	$46,660
Electrical and Electronics Installers and Repairers	Electrical and electronics installers and repairers install, repair, or replace a variety of electrical equipment in telecommunications, transportation, utilities, and other industries.	Postsecondary non-degree award	$49,170
Home Entertainment Equipment Installers and Repairers	Home entertainment equipment installers and repairers set up and fix household audio and video equipment, such as televisions, stereo components, and home theater systems.	Postsecondary non-degree award	$32,940

Contacts for More Information

For more information on the Certified Materials & Resources Professional (CMRP) designation, visit The Society for Maintenance and Reliability Professionals

Suggested citation:

Bureau of Labor Statistics, U.S. Department of Labor, Occupational Outlook Handbook, 2012-13 Edition, General Maintenance and Repair Workers, on the Internet at http://www.bls.gov/ooh/installation-maintenance-and-repair/general-maintenance-and-repair-workers.htm .

Heating, Air Conditioning, and Refrigeration Mechanics and Installers

Quick Facts: Heating, Air Conditioning, and Refrigeration Mechanics and Installers	
2010 Median Pay	$42,530 per year $20.45 per hour
Entry-Level Education	Postsecondary non-degree award
Work Experience in a Related Occupation	None
On-the-job Training	Long-term on-the-job training
Number of Jobs, 2010	267,800
Job Outlook, 2010-20	34% (Much faster than average)
Employment Change, 2010-20	90,300

What Heating, Air Conditioning, and Refrigeration Mechanics and Installers Do

Heating, air conditioning, and refrigeration mechanics and installers—often referred to as HVACR technicians—work on heating, ventilation, cooling, and refrigeration systems that control the air quality in many types of buildings.

Duties

Heating, air conditioning, and refrigeration mechanics and installers typically do the following:

- Travel to worksites
- Follow blueprints or other design specifications to install or repair HVACR systems
- Connect systems to fuel and water supply lines, air ducts, and other components
- Install electrical wiring and controls and test for proper operation
- Inspect and maintain customers' HVACR systems
- Test individual components to determine necessary repairs
- Repair or replace worn or defective parts

Heating and air-conditioning systems control the temperature, humidity, and overall air quality in homes, businesses, and other buildings. By providing a climate controlled environment, refrigeration systems make it possible to store and transport food, medicine, and other perishable items.

HVACR technicians repair heating, cooling, and refrigeration systems.

Although trained to do all three, HVACR technicians sometimes work strictly with heating, air-conditioning, or refrigeration systems. They also may specialize in certain types of HVACR equipment, such as water-based heating systems, solar panels, or commercial refrigeration.

Depending on the task, HVACR technicians use many different tools. For example, they often use screwdrivers, wrenches, pipe cutters and other basic handtools when installing systems. To test or install complex system components, technicians may use more sophisticated tools, such as carbon monoxide testers, voltmeters, combustion analyzers, and acetylene torches.

When working on air-conditioning and refrigeration systems, technicians must follow government regulations regarding the conservation, recovery, and recycling of refrigerants. This often entails proper handling and disposal of fluids.

Some HVACR technicians sell service contracts to their clients, providing regular maintenance of heating and cooling systems.

Other craft workers sometimes help install or repair cooling and heating systems. For example, on a large air-conditioning installation job, especially one in which workers are covered by union contracts, ductwork might be done by sheet metal workers and duct installers, or electrical work by electricians. In addition, home appliance repairers usually service window air conditioners and household refrigerators. For more information on these occupations, see the profiles on sheet metal workers , electricians , or home appliance repairers .

Work Environment

Heating, air conditioning, and refrigeration mechanics and installers held about 267,800 jobs in 2010. The majority worked full time for private companies. About 16 percent were self-employed.

Industries employing the most heating, air conditioning, and refrigeration mechanics and installers were as follows:

Building equipment contractors	55%
Direct selling establishments	4
Hardware, plumbing, and heating equipment wholesalers	3
Commercial and industrial machinery and equipment repair	3

HVACR technicians mostly work in residential homes, schools, stores, hospitals, office buildings, or factories. Some technicians are assigned to specific job sites at the beginning of each day. Others travel to several different locations making service calls.

Technicians generally work indoors, but some may have to work on outdoor heat pumps, for example, even in bad weather. They often work in awkward or cramped spaces, and some work in buildings that are uncomfortable because the air-conditioning or heating system is broken.

Work Schedules

The majority of HVACR technicians work full time, with occasional evening or weekend shifts. During peak heating and cooling seasons, they often work overtime or irregular hours. Although the majority of technicians work for construction contractors, about 16 percent are self-employed workers who have the ability to set their own schedules.

Technicians who service both heating and air-conditioning equipment generally have stable employment throughout the year, particularly as a growing number of manufacturers and contractors now provide or even require year-round service contracts.

About 1 in 6 HVACR technicians are union members.

Injuries

HVACR technicians have a rate of injuries and illnesses that is higher than the average for all occupations. Potential hazards include electrical shock, burns, muscle strains, and other injuries from handling heavy equipment.

Appropriate safety equipment is necessary when handling refrigerants because contact can cause skin damage, frostbite, or blindness. When working in tight spaces, inhalation of refrigerants is also a risk.

How to Become a Heating, Air Conditioning, or Refrigeration Mechanic and Installer

Because HVACR systems are increasingly complex, employers generally prefer applicants with technical training or those who have completed a formal apprenticeship. Some states and localities require technicians to be licensed.

Education

A growing number of HVACR technicians receive training from technical and trade schools or community colleges that offer programs in heating, air-conditioning, and refrigeration. These programs generally last 6 months to 2 years and can lead to a certificate or an associate's degree.

High school students interested in becoming HVACR technicians should take courses in shop, math, and physics. Some knowledge of plumbing or electrical work and a basic understanding of electronics can be helpful.

Training

Other HVACR technicians learn their trade on the job, although this is becoming much less common. Informally trained technicians usually begin by assisting experienced technicians with basic tasks, such as insulating refrigerant lines or cleaning furnaces. In time, they move on to more difficult tasks, including cutting and soldering pipes or checking electrical circuits.

Many technicians receive their training through a formal apprenticeship. Applicants for apprenticeships must have a high school diploma or general equivalency degree (GED). Math and reading skills are essential.

Apprenticeship programs normally last 3 to 5 years, and combine paid on-the-job training with technical instruction. Over the course of the apprenticeship, technicians become familiar with subjects such as safety practices, blueprint reading, and how to use tools.

After completing an apprenticeship program, technicians are considered skilled trades workers and capable of working alone.

Several groups, including unions and contractor associations, sponsor apprenticeship programs.

Apprenticeship programs frequently are run by joint committees representing local chapters of various organizations, including

- Air-Conditioning Contractors of America

- Mechanical Contractors Association of America
- Plumbing-Heating-Cooling Contractors Association
- Sheet Metal Workers' International Association
- Plumbing and Pipefitting Industry of the United States and Canada
- Associated Builders and Contractors
- National Association of Home Builders

Licenses

Some states and localities require HVACR technicians to be licensed. Although specific licensure requirements vary, all candidates must pass an exam.

In addition, the U.S. Environmental Protection Agency (EPA) requires all technicians who buy or work with refrigerants to be certified in proper refrigerant handling. To become certified, technicians must pass a written exam specific to 1 of 3 specializations: Type I—servicing small appliances; Type II—high-pressure refrigerants; Type III—low-pressure refrigerants.

Many trade schools, unions, and employer associations offer training programs designed for the EPA exam.

Certification

Throughout the training process, HVACR technicians may take several different tests that measure their skills. Technicians with relevant coursework and less than 2 years of experience may take the "entry-level" certification exams. These exams test basic competency in residential heating and cooling, light commercial heating and cooling, and commercial refrigeration. Technicians can take the exams at technical and trade schools.

HVACR technicians who have at least 1 year of installation experience and 2 years of maintenance and repair experience can take a number of specialized exams. These exams certify their competency in working with specific types of equipment, such as oil-burning furnaces or compressed-refrigerant cooling systems.

Many organizations offer certifying exams. For example, the Air-Conditioning, Heating, and Refrigeration Institute offers the Industry Competency Exam. HVAC Excellence offers a Secondary Employment Ready Exam, a Secondary Heat exam, and a Heat Plus exam. The National Occupational Competency Testing Institute offers a secondary exam. The Refrigeration Service Engineers Society offers two levels of certification.

Certifications can be helpful because they show that the technician has specific competencies. Some employers actively seek out industry-certified HVACR technicians.

Important Qualities

Customer-service skills. Technicians often work in customers' homes or business offices, so it is crucial that they be friendly, polite, and punctual. HVACR repair technicians must sometimes deal with unhappy customers whose heating or air condition is not working.

Detail oriented. Technicians must be able to find problems and make precise repairs or adjustments. They must pay attention to details when installing or repairing equipment to make sure it works properly.

Dexterity. Technicians use many handtools and must have good hand-eye coordination to avoid injury.

Mechanical skills. HVACR technicians install and work on complicated climate-control systems. Workers must understand the components and be able to properly assemble and disassemble them.

Physical strength. Workers may have to lift and support heavy equipment and components, often without help.

Time-management skills. HVACR technicians often have a set number of daily maintenance calls. They should be able to keep a schedule and complete all necessary repairs or tasks.

Troubleshooting skills. Heating, air-conditioning, and

refrigeration systems involve many intricate parts. To repair malfunctioning systems, technicians must be able to identify problems, often with sophisticated diagnostic equipment.

Pay

Heating, Air Conditioning, and Refrigeration Mechanics and Installers

Median annual wages, May 2010

Heating, Air Conditioning, and Refrigeration Mechanics and Installers	$42,530
Installation, Maintenance, and Repair Occupations	$40,120
Total, All Occupations	$33,840

Note: All Occupations includes all occupations in the U.S. Economy.
Source: U.S. Bureau of Labor Statistics, Occupational Employment Statistics

The median annual wage of heating, air conditioning, and refrigeration mechanics and installers was $42,530 in May 2010. The median wage is the wage at which half the workers in an occupation earned more than that amount and half earned less. The lowest 10 percent earned less than $26,490, and the top 10 percent earned more than $66,930.

In May 2010, median annual wages in industries employing the most heating, air conditioning, and refrigeration mechanics and installers were as follows:

Hardware, plumbing, and heating equipment wholesalers	$46,540
Direct selling establishments	44,210
Commercial and industrial machinery and equipment repair	43,460
Building equipment contractors	40,630

Apprentices usually earn about half of the wage paid to experienced workers. As they gain experience and improve their skills, they receive periodic raises until they reach the wage of experienced workers.

About 1 in 6 HVACR technicians are union members.

The majority of HVACR technicians work full time, with occasional evening or weekend shifts. During peak heating and cooling seasons, they often work overtime or irregular hours. Although the majority of technicians work for construction contractors, about 16 percent are self-employed workers who have the ability to set their own schedules.

Job Outlook

Heating, Air Conditioning, and Refrigeration Mechanics and Installers

Percent change in employment, projected 2010-20

Heating, Air Conditioning, and Refrigeration Mechanics and Installers	34%
Installation, Maintenance, and Repair Occupations	15%
Total, All Occupations	14%

Note: All Occupations includes all occupations in the U.S. Economy.
Source: U.S. Bureau of Labor Statistics, Employment Projections program

Employment of heating, air conditioning, and refrigeration mechanics and installers is expected to grow 34 percent from 2010 to 2020, much faster than the average for all occupations. Commercial and residential building construction will drive employment growth as the construction industry continues to recover from the 2007-09 recession. The growing number of sophisticated climate-control systems is also expected to increase demand for qualified HVACR technicians.

Climate-control systems generally need replacement after 10 to 15 years. A large number of recently constructed homes and commercial buildings will need replacement climate-control systems by 2020, spurring demand for technicians.

The growing emphasis on energy efficiency and pollution reduction will require more HVACR technicians as climate-control systems are retrofitted, upgraded, or replaced entirely. Regulations prohibiting the discharge and production of older types of refrigerant pollutants also will result in the need to modify or replace many existing air conditioning systems.

Job Prospects

Job opportunities for HVACR technicians are expected to be excellent, particularly for those who have completed training at an accredited technical school or through a formal apprenticeship. Candidates familiar with computers and electronics will have the best job opportunities as employers continue to have trouble finding qualified technicians to work on complex new systems.

Technicians who specialize in installation work may experience periods of unemployment when the level of new construction activity declines. Maintenance and repair work, however, usually remains relatively stable. Businesses and homeowners depend on their climate-control or refrigeration systems and must keep them in good working order, regardless of economic conditions.

Employment projections data for heating, air conditioning, and refrigeration mechanics and installers, 2010-20

Occupational Title	SOC Code	Employment, 2010	Projected Employment, 2020	Change, 2010-20	
				Percent	Numeric
Heating, Air Conditioning, and Refrigeration Mechanics and Installers	49-9021	267,800	358,100	34	90,300
SOURCE: U.S. Bureau of Labor Statistics, Employment Projections program					

Similar Occupations

This table shows a list of occupations with job duties that are similar to those of heating, air conditioning, and refrigeration mechanics and installers.

Occupation	Job Duties	Entry-Level Education	Median Annual Pay, May 2010
Boilermakers	Boilermakers assemble, install, and repair boilers, closed vats, and other large vessels or containers that hold liquids and gases.	High school diploma or equivalent	$54,640
Electricians	Electricians install and maintain electrical systems in homes, businesses, and factories.	High school diploma or equivalent	$48,250

Home Appliance Repairers	Home appliance repairers install and repair household appliances, such as refrigerators, microwaves, and washer and dryers.	High school diploma or equivalent	$34,730
Plumbers, Pipefitters, and Steamfitters	Plumbers, pipefitters, and steamfitters install and repair pipes that carry water, steam, air, or other liquids or gases to and in businesses, homes, and factories.	High school diploma or equivalent	$46,660
Sheet Metal Workers	Sheet metal workers fabricate or install products that are made from thin metal sheets, such as ducts used for heating and air-conditioning.	High school diploma or equivalent	$41,710

Contacts for More Information

For details about apprenticeships or other work opportunities, contact the offices of the state employment service, the state apprenticeship agency, local contractors, or local union-management HVACR apprenticeship committees. Apprenticeship information is available from the U.S. Department of Labor toll free help line: 1 (877) 872-5627, or visit: http://www.doleta.gov/OA/eta_default.cfm .

For information about career opportunities, training, and certification, visit Air Conditioning Contractors of America, Air-Conditioning, Heating, and Refrigeration Institute ,Associated Builders and Contractors ,Carbon Monoxide Safety Association , Green Mechanical Council , Home Builders Institute , HVAC Excellence ,Mechanical Contractors Association of America , National Center for Construction Education and Research , National Occupational Competency Testing Institute , North American Technician Excellence , Plumbing-Heating-Cooling Contractors Association ,Radiant Panel Association , Refrigeration Service Engineers Society ,Sheet Metal and Air Conditioning Contractors' National Association ,United Association

Suggested citation:

Bureau of Labor Statistics, U.S. Department of Labor, Occupational Outlook Handbook, 2012-13 Edition, Heating, Air Conditioning, and Refrigeration Mechanics and Installers, on the Internet at http://www.bls.gov/ooh/installation-maintenance-and-repair/heating-air-conditioning-and-refrigeration-mechanics-and-installers.htm .

Heavy Vehicle and Mobile Equipment Service Technicians

Quick Facts: Heavy Vehicle and Mobile Equipment Service Technicians	
2010 Median Pay	$42,630 per year $20.50 per hour
Entry-Level Education	High school diploma or equivalent
Work Experience in a Related Occupation	None
On-the-job Training	Long-term on-the-job training
Number of Jobs, 2010	179,200
Job Outlook, 2010-20	16% (About as fast as average)
Employment Change, 2010-20	28,200

What Heavy Vehicle and Mobile Equipment Service Technicians Do

Heavy vehicle and mobile equipment service technicians inspect, maintain, and repair vehicles and machinery used in construction, farming, rail transportation, and other industries.

Duties

Heavy vehicle and mobile equipment service technicians typically do the following:

- Read and understand operating manuals, blueprints, and drawings
- Perform scheduled maintenance, such as cleaning and lubricating parts
- Diagnose and identify malfunctions, using computerized tools and equipment
- Inspect, repair, and replace defective or worn parts, such as bearings, pistons, and gears
- Overhaul and test major components, such as engines, hydraulics, and electrical systems
- Disassemble and reassemble heavy equipment and components
- Travel to worksites to repair large equipment, such as cranes

Heavy vehicles and mobile equipment are critical to many industrial activities, including construction and railroad transportation. Various types of equipment, such as farm machinery, cranes, and bulldozers, are used to move materials, till land, lift beams, and dig earth to pave the way for development and construction.

Heavy vehicle and mobile equipment service technicians repair and maintain engines, hydraulic systems, transmissions, and electrical systems of agricultural, industrial, construction, and rail equipment. They ensure the performance and safety of fuel lines, brakes, transmissions, and other systems.

With many types of equipment and mechanical and electrical systems, service technicians use diagnostic computers to identify problems and make adjustments or repairs. Although the use of computerized testing equipment, such as tachometers and dynamometers, is common, technicians also use many different power and machine tools, including pneumatic wrenches, lathes, and welding

Heavy vehicle and mobile equipment service technicians repair vehicles such as tractors and trains.

equipment.

Service technicians also use many different handtools, such as screwdrivers, pliers, and wrenches, to work on small parts and in hard-to-reach areas. They generally purchase these tools over the course of their careers, often investing thousands of dollars in their collections.

After locating malfunctions, service technicians repair, replace, and recalibrate components such as hydraulic pumps or spark plugs. This may involve disassembling and reassembling major equipment or making adjustments through an onboard computer program.

The following are types of heavy vehicle and mobile equipment service technicians:

Farm equipment mechanics service and repair farm equipment, such as tractors and harvesters. They also work on smaller consumer-grade lawn and garden tractors. Most mechanics work for dealer repair shops, where farmers increasingly send their equipment for maintenance.

Mobile heavy equipment mechanics repair and maintain construction and surface mining equipment, such as bulldozers, cranes, graders, and excavators. Many work for equipment wholesale and distribution shops and large construction and mining companies. Those working for the federal government may work on tanks and other military equipment.

Rail car repairers specialize in servicing railroad locomotives, subway cars, and other rolling stock. They usually work for railroad, public and private transit companies, and rail car manufacturers.

For information about technicians and mechanics who work primarily on automobiles, see the profile on automotive service technicians and mechanics .

For information about technicians who work primarily on large trucks and buses, see the profile on diesel service technicians and mechanics .

For information about technicians and mechanics who primarily work on motorboats, motorcycles and small all-terrain vehicles, see the profile on small engine mechanics .

Work Environment

Heavy vehicle and mobile equipment service technicians held about 179,200 jobs in 2010. Most technicians worked for private companies, but about 7 percent worked for state and local government. About 25 percent of technicians are members of a union. Industries employing the largest numbers of heavy vehicle and mobile equipment service technicians in 2010 were as follows:

Merchant wholesalers, durable goods	29%
Rail transportation	7
Heavy and civil engineering construction	6
Mining (except oil and gas)	5
Rental and leasing services	5

Service technicians usually work indoors in noisy repair shops. They often lift heavy parts and tools, handle greasy and dirty equipment, and stand or lie in awkward positions.

It is often too expensive to transport heavy or mobile equipment to a repair shop. As a result, some service technicians travel to worksites to make repairs, often driving long distances. Generally, more experienced service technicians specialize in field service. They drive trucks that are specially equipped with replacement parts and tools. These workers spend considerable time outdoors.

Work Schedules

Most service technicians work full time, and many work evenings or weekends. Overtime is common.

Farm equipment mechanics' work varies by time of the year. During busy planting and harvesting seasons, for example, mechanics often work six or seven 12-hour days per week. In slow winter months, however, they may work less than full time.

Injuries

Service technicians have a rate of injuries and illnesses that is higher than the national average. Although cuts, burns, and bruises are common, serious accidents can be avoided by following basic safety precautions.

How to Become a Heavy Vehicle or Mobile Equipment Service Technician

Employers increasingly prefer to hire repair technicians who have completed formal postsecondary training programs. The majority of workers, however, still learn informally on the job.

Education and Training

High school or postsecondary courses in automobile repair, mathematics, and computers provide a strong foundation for a service technician's career.

Post-secondary programs and degrees in diesel technology or heavy equipment mechanics provide the most comprehensive training for new service technicians. Offered by vocational schools and community colleges, these programs cover the basics of diagnostic techniques, electronics, and other related subjects.

Most programs last 1 to 2 years and lead to certificates of completion. Other programs, which lead to associate's degrees, generally take 2 years to complete.

Education significantly reduces the amount of on-the-job training new service technicians need.

Entry-level workers with no formal background in heavy vehicle repair often receive a few months of on-the-job training before they begin doing routine service tasks and minor repairs. Trainees advance to more complex work as they show competence, and usually become fully qualified after 3 to 4 years of work.

Many employers send new technicians to training sessions conducted by equipment manufacturers. Training sessions may focus on particular components and technologies or types of equipment. Sessions generally last 1 week.

Certification

Some manufacturers offer certification in specific repair methods or equipment. Although not required, certification can demonstrate a mechanic's competence and usually brings higher pay.

Important Qualities

Dexterity. Many tasks, such as disassembling engine parts, connecting or attaching components, and using handtools, require a steady hand and good hand-eye coordination.

Mechanical skills. Service technicians must be familiar with engine components and systems and know how they interact with each other. They must often disassemble major parts for repairs and be able to reassemble them.

Physical strength. Service technicians must lift and move heavy equipment, tools, and parts without risking injury or fatigue.

Technical skills. Service technicians use sophisticated diagnostic equipment on engines, systems, and components. They must also be familiar with electronic control systems and the appropriate tools needed to fix and maintain them.

Troubleshooting skills. As heavy and mobile equipment become more complex, malfunctions become more difficult to identify. Service technicians must be able to find solutions to problems that are not immediately apparent.

Pay

Heavy Vehicle and Mobile Equipment Service Technicians
Median annual wages, May 2010

Rail Car Repairers	$47,410
Mobile Heavy Equipment Mechanics, Except Engines	$44,830
Heavy Vehicle and Mobile Equipment Service Technicians	$42,630
Total, All Occupations	$33,840
Farm Equipment Mechanics and Service Technicians	$33,640

Note: All Occupations includes all occupations in the U.S. Economy.
Source: U.S. Bureau of Labor Statistics, Occupational Employment Statistics

The median annual wage of heavy vehicle and mobile equipment service technicians was $42,630 in May 2010. The median wage is the wage at which half the workers in an occupation earned more than that amount and half earned less. The lowest 10 percent earned less than $27,140, and the top 10 percent earned more than $62,630.

In May 2010, median annual wages for heavy vehicle and mobile equipment service technician occupations were as follows:
- $47,410 for rail car repairers
- $44,830 for mobile heavy equipment mechanics
- $33,640 for farm equipment mechanic and service technicians

Most service technicians work full time, and many work evenings or weekends. Overtime is common.

Farm equipment mechanics' work varies by time of the year. During busy planting and harvesting seasons, for example, mechanics often work six or seven 12-hour days per week. In slow winter months, however, they may work less than full time.

About 25 percent of service technicians are members of unions. Members may enjoy job benefits, in addition to what employers provide.

Job Outlook

Heavy Vehicle and Mobile Equipment Service Technicians
Percent change in employment, projected 2010-20

Rail Car Repairers	17%
Mobile Heavy Equipment Mechanics, Except Engines	16%
Heavy Vehicle and Mobile Equipment Service Technicians	16%
Total, All Occupations	14%
Farm Equipment Mechanics and Service Technicians	13%

Note: All Occupations includes all occupations in the U.S. Economy.
Source: U.S. Bureau of Labor Statistics, Employment Projections program

Overall employment of heavy vehicle and mobile equipment service technicians is projected to grow 16 percent from 2010 to 2020, about as fast as the average for all occupations.

As the stock of heavy vehicles and mobile equipment continues to increase, more service technicians will be needed to maintain them. In particular, demand for heavy equipment used in construction, mining, and energy exploration will result in employment growth for service technicians. Growth rates will vary by specialty.

Employment of farm equipment mechanic and service technicians is projected to grow 13 percent, about as fast as the average for all occupations. Demand for farm equipment repairers will be primarily driven by the need for agricultural products to feed a growing population. Demand for other products, such as biofuels, will also increase repairer employment.

Employment of mobile heavy equipment mechanics is projected to grow 16 percent, about as fast as the average for all occupations. Employment growth of mobile heavy equipment mechanics will be spurred by increased construction activity. Population and business growth will result in the construction of more houses, office buildings, roads, bridges, and other structures.

Employment of rail car repairers is projected to grow 17 percent, about as fast as the average for all occupations. Rail car repairers will be needed to accommodate the continued expansion of railways for freight shipping and transportation.

Job Prospects

Most job opportunities will come from the need to replace workers who retire or leave the occupation. Those with certificates from vocational schools or 2-year degrees from community colleges should have very good job opportunities as employers strongly prefer these candidates. Those without formal training will have difficulty finding jobs.

The majority of job openings are expected to be in sectors that sell, rent, or lease heavy vehicles and mobile equipment, where a large proportion of service technicians are employed.

The construction and mining industries, which use large numbers of heavy equipment, are sensitive to fluctuations in the economy. As a result, job opportunities for service technicians in these sectors will vary with overall economic conditions.

Job opportunities for farm equipment mechanics are seasonal, and are, generally, best during warmer months.

Employment projections data for heavy vehicle and mobile equipment service technicians, 2010-20

Occupational Title	SOC Code	Employment, 2010	Projected Employment, 2020	Change, 2010-20	
				Percent	Numeric
Heavy Vehicle and Mobile Equipment Service Technicians	—	179,200	207,500	16	28,200
Farm Equipment Mechanics and Service Technicians	49-3041	32,900	37,300	13	4,400
Mobile Heavy Equipment Mechanics, Except Engines	49-3042	124,600	144,800	16	20,200
Rail Car Repairers	49-3043	21,700	25,400	17	3,700
SOURCE: U.S. Bureau of Labor Statistics, Employment Projections program					

Similar Occupations

This table shows a list of occupations with job duties that are similar to those of heavy vehicle and mobile equipment service technicians.

Occupation	Job Duties	Entry-Level Education	Median Annual Pay, May 2010
Aircraft and Avionics Equipment Mechanics and Technicians	Aircraft and avionics equipment mechanics and technicians repair and perform scheduled maintenance on airplanes and helicopters. They also inspect airplanes and helicopters as required by the Federal Aviation Administration (FAA).	Postsecondary non-degree award	$53,220
Automotive Service Technicians and Mechanics	Automotive service technicians and mechanics, often called service technicians or service techs, inspect, maintain, and repair cars and light trucks.	High school diploma or equivalent	$35,790
Diesel Service Technicians and Mechanics	Diesel service technicians and mechanics inspect, repair, or overhaul buses, trucks, and anything else with a diesel engine.	High school diploma or equivalent	$40,850
Industrial Machinery Mechanics and Maintenance Workers	Industrial machinery mechanics and maintenance workers maintain and repair factory equipment and other industrial machinery, such as conveying systems, production machinery, and packaging equipment.	High school diploma or equivalent	$44,160
Millwrights	Millwrights install, dismantle, repair, reassemble, and move machinery in factories, power plants, and construction sites.	High school diploma or equivalent	$48,360
Small Engine Mechanics	Small engine mechanics inspect, service, and repair motorized power equipment. Mechanics often specialize in one type of equipment, such as motorcycles, motorboats, or outdoor power equipment.	High school diploma or equivalent	$31,790

Contacts for More Information

For more details about job openings for heavy vehicle and mobile equipment service technicians and mechanics, consult local heavy and mobile equipment dealers and distributors, construction contractors, and government agencies. Local offices of the state employment service may also have information on job openings and training programs.

For general information about careers and training programs, visit Associated Equipment Distributors , National Automotive Technicians Education Foundation , National Institute for Automotive Service Excellence

Suggested citation:

Bureau of Labor Statistics, U.S. Department of Labor, Occupational Outlook Handbook, 2012-13 Edition, Heavy Vehicle and Mobile Equipment Service Technicians, on the Internet at http://www.bls.gov/ooh/installation-maintenance-and-repair/heavy-vehicle-and-mobile-equipment-service-technicians.htm .

Home Appliance Repairers

Quick Facts: Home Appliance Repairers	
2010 Median Pay	$34,730 per year $16.70 per hour
Entry-Level Education	High school diploma or equivalent
Work Experience in a Related Occupation	None
On-the-job Training	Moderate-term on-the-job training
Number of Jobs, 2010	47,700
Job Outlook, 2010-20	7% (Slower than average)
Employment Change, 2010-20	3,100

What Home Appliance Repairers Do

Home appliance repairers install and repair household appliances, such as refrigerators, microwaves, and washer and dryers.

Duties

Home appliance repairers typically do the following:

- Travel to customers' homes
- Install home appliances
- Connect major appliances to water, gas, or electrical lines
- Inspect equipment that is not working
- Estimate repair or replacement costs
- Repair or replace broken parts
- Instruct customers on how to use appliances
- Bill and collect payment from customers

Home appliance repairers, often called home appliance repair technicians, usually travel to customers' homes to do their work. They use many basic handtools, including screwdrivers, wrenches, and pliers, to determine the cause of unusual noises, leaks, or excessive

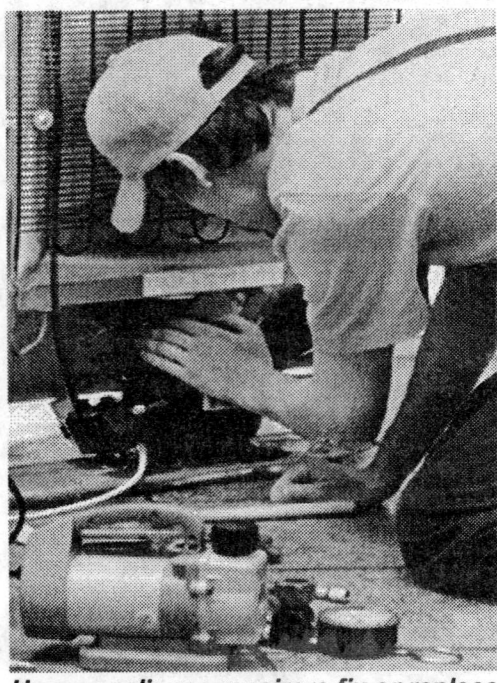

Home appliance repairers fix or replace broken parts.

vibration. Some use more specialized tools, such as ammeters, voltmeters, and wattmeters, to check for electrical problems. After identifying problems, workers repair or replace defective belts, motors, heating elements, switches, gears, or other items. They also may tighten, align, clean, and lubricate parts as necessary.

Most technicians explain to clients how to use a new appliance. If necessary, they may show clients how to use different functions of a newly repaired appliance.

Technicians also keep records of bills, payments, parts used, and hours worked. If an appliance is under warranty, a technician may need to contact the appliance's manufacturer to be paid for the work they did.

When working on refrigerators and window air-conditioners, repairers are required by law to conserve, recover, and recycle chlorofluorocarbon (CFC) and hydrofluorocarbon (HCFC) refrigerants used in cooling systems. Federal regulations also require that home appliance repair technicians document the capture and disposal of refrigerants. For more information, see the profile on heating, air conditioning, and refrigeration mechanics and installers .

Work Environment

Home appliance repairers held about 47,700 jobs in 2010. The industries that employed the most home appliance repairers in 2010 were as follows:

Personal and household goods repair and maintenance	23%
Electronics and appliance stores	22
Wholesale trade	3
Utilities	3

Because work typically is done on site at customers' homes, driving to appointments or making emergency calls is common. Some home appliance repairers work in service center repair shops, which can be noisy.

Technicians often work in small, cramped spaces, and must sometimes move or pick up heavy appliances. They also occasionally work near exposed electric or gas lines. However, as long as they are careful and follow basic safety precautions, their work is not dangerous.

Work Schedules

Most home appliance repairers work full time, and some have evening or weekend shifts. Sometimes they must stay on call in case of emergencies. Approximately one-third of home appliance repairers are self-employed.

Many technicians are busiest during summer months when window air conditioning units are in heavy use.

How to Become a Home Appliance Repairer

Most home appliance repair technicians are trained on the job. A growing number of employers, however, prefer to hire workers who have completed technical or vocational training.

Education and Training

Most home appliance repairers learn their skills on the job by working with experienced technicians. Some companies and appliance manufacturers provide further training through seminars, demonstrations, or coursework.

Introductory training in basic electricity or electronics may last several months to a few years, depending on the employer or specialty. Manufacturers also may require technicians to receive training to become authorized for warranty work.

Although on-the-job training is the most common method of training, employers generally prefer to hire workers who have attended high school or, increasingly, postsecondary vocational or technical programs in electronics or appliance repair. These programs can help reduce the amount of on-the-job training for entry-level workers.

Nearly all technicians must take continuing education courses to sharpen their skills and to be able to repair the newest appliance models.

Licenses

The U.S. Environmental Protection Agency (EPA) requires all technicians who buy or work with refrigerants to be licensed in the proper handling of refrigerants. Although formal test preparation is not required, many trade schools, unions, and employer associations offer training programs designed for the EPA exam.

A driver's license and a clean driving record also may be required because some home appliance repairers must drive to customers' homes to service their appliances.

Certification

Home appliance repairers may show their competence by earning voluntary certification. For example, they may get the National Appliance Service Technician Certification (NASTeC) from the International Society of Certified Electronics Technicians by passing an exam that tests their skills in diagnosing, repairing, and maintaining home appliances.

The Professional Service Association (PSA) offers a similar certification program based on skill competencies that the industry developed and updates annually. By passing the PSA exam, home appliance repairers can use the title, Master Certified Appliance Professional (MCAP).

These certifications can be helpful when looking for employment, and some employers actively seek out certified home appliance repairers.

Important Qualities

Bookkeeping skills. Home appliance repairers must be able to keep accurate records of hours worked, parts used, and bills collected. This is especially true for self-employed technicians.

Communication skills. Home appliance repairers need to explain complicated mechanical processes to people who have little or no technical knowledge.

Customer-service skills. Most home appliance repairers work in customers' homes, so it is important that they are friendly and polite.

Dexterity. Home appliance repairers need a steady hand and good hand-eye coordination for many of their tasks, such as repairing small devices, connecting or attaching components, and using handtools.

Technical skills. Home appliance repairers use sophisticated diagnostic equipment when working on complex appliances. They must be familiar with both appliances' internal parts and the appropriate tools needed to install or fix them.

Troubleshooting skills. As appliances become more intricate, malfunctions become more difficult to identify. Home appliance repairers must be able to find and solve problems that may not be immediately apparent.

Pay

Home Appliance Repairers
Median annual wages, May 2010

Other Installation, Maintenance, and Repair Occupations	$38,010
Home Appliance Repairers	$34,730
Total, All Occupations	$33,840

Note: All Occupations includes all occupations in the U.S. Economy.
Source: U.S. Bureau of Labor Statistics, Occupational Employment Statistics

The median annual wage of home appliance repairers was $34,730 in May 2010. The median wage is the wage at which half the workers in an occupation earned more than that amount and half earned less. The lowest 10 percent earned less than $20,400, and the highest 10 percent earned more than $56,500.

The median annual wages in the industries employing the largest numbers of home appliance repairers in May 2010 were as follows:

Utilities	$58,840
Wholesale trade	38,490
Personal and household goods repair and maintenance	36,200
Electronics and appliance stores	31,740

Earnings vary by skill level, specialization, and the type of equipment being worked on. Many technicians earn a commission along with their salary, making more money as they complete more jobs per day.

Most home appliance repairers work full time, and some have evening or weekend shifts. Sometimes they must stay on call in case of emergencies. Approximately one-third of home appliance repairers are self-employed.

Many home appliance repairers are busiest during summer months when window air conditioning units are in heavy use.

Job Outlook

Home Appliance Repairers
Percent change in employment, projected 2010-20

Other Installation, Maintenance, and Repair Occupations	15%
Total, All Occupations	14%
Home Appliance Repairers	7%

Note: All Occupations includes all occupations in the U.S. Economy.
Source: U.S. Bureau of Labor Statistics, Employment Projections program

Employment of home appliance repairers is expected to grow 7 percent from 2010 to 2020, slower than the average for all occupations.

Demand for workers will be driven by an increasing number of appliances being used in homes. The decision to repair an appliance often depends on the price to replace the appliance versus the cost to repair it. So although higher-priced appliances are more likely to be repaired, small and cheaper appliances are increasingly being discarded. With sales of high-end appliances growing, demand for major appliance repairers will be strong in the coming decade, but weaker for those who specialize in small, portable appliances.

Job Prospects

Despite slower than average employment growth, job opportunities for home appliance repairers should be very good because of job openings created by workers who retire or leave the occupation for other reasons. A lack of qualified workers in the field will also lead to good job prospects.

Technicians with vocational training in appliance and electronics repair will have better job prospects than those who do not.

Job opportunities at personal and household goods and repair shops should be very good as large electronics retail stores continue to outsource their repair work.

Employment projections data for home appliance repairers, 2010-20

Occupational Title	SOC Code	Employment, 2010	Projected Employment, 2020	Change, 2010-20	
				Percent	Numeric
Home Appliance Repairers	49-9031	47,700	50,800	7	3,100
SOURCE: U.S. Bureau of Labor Statistics, Employment Projections program					

Similar Occupations

This table shows a list of occupations with job duties that are similar to those of home appliance repairers.

Occupation	Job Duties	Entry-Level Education	Median Annual Pay, May 2010
Electrical and Electronics Installers and Repairers	Electrical and electronics installers and repairers install, repair, or replace a variety of electrical equipment in telecommunications, transportation, utilities, and other industries.	Postsecondary non-degree award	$49,170
Heating, Air Conditioning, and Refrigeration Mechanics and Installers	Heating, air conditioning, and refrigeration mechanics and installers—often referred to as HVACR technicians—work on heating, ventilation, cooling, and refrigeration systems that control the air quality in many types of buildings.	Postsecondary non-degree award	$42,530
Home Entertainment Equipment Installers and Repairers	Home entertainment equipment installers and repairers set up and fix household audio and video equipment, such as televisions, stereo components, and home theater systems.	Postsecondary non-degree award	$32,940
Small Engine Mechanics	Small engine mechanics inspect, service, and repair motorized power equipment. Mechanics often specialize in one type of equipment, such as motorcycles, motorboats, or outdoor power equipment.	High school diploma or equivalent	$31,790

Contacts for More Information

For more information on home appliance repair technicians, visit United Servicers Association

For more information on the Certified Appliance Professional program, visit Professional Service Association

For more information on the National Appliance Service Technician Certification program, visit International Society of Certified Electronics Technicians

For more information on the U.S. Environmental Protection Agency's technician certification, visit U.S. Environmental Protection Agency

Suggested citation:

Bureau of Labor Statistics, U.S. Department of Labor, Occupational Outlook Handbook, 2012-13 Edition, Home Appliance Repairers, on the Internet at http://www.bls.gov/ooh/installation-maintenance-and-repair/home-appliance-repairers.htm .

Home Entertainment Equipment Installers and Repairers

Quick Facts: Home Entertainment Equipment Installers and Repairers	
2010 Median Pay	$32,940 per year $15.84 per hour
Entry-Level Education	Postsecondary non-degree award
Work Experience in a Related Occupation	None
On-the-job Training	None
Number of Jobs, 2010	36,800
Job Outlook, 2010-20	14% (About as fast as average)
Employment Change, 2010-20	5,100

What Home Entertainment Equipment Installers and Repairers Do

Home entertainment equipment installers and repairers set up and fix household audio and video equipment, such as televisions, stereo components, and home theater systems.

Duties

Home entertainment equipment installers and repairers typically do the following:

- Install electronic equipment and devices, such as televisions and speaker systems
- Inspect malfunctioning equipment and devices
- Read and interpret electronic circuit diagrams, specifications, and service manuals
- Take apart equipment and repair or replace loose, worn, or defective parts and wiring
- Calibrate, tune, or adjust equipment and instruments to specified performance levels
- Test equipment and parts after installing or repairing them
- Make service calls to customers' homes or bring equipment or parts to shops for major repairs
- Teach customers the safe and proper use of audio and video equipment

Home entertainment equipment installers and repairers, also called service technicians install, troubleshoot, and fine-tune sound and picture quality, ensuring that a client's home entertainment system works at its peak capability.

Home entertainment equipment installers set up and fix household audio and video equipment.

They work on many types of equipment, including customer's televisions, stereos, satellite dishes, and surround-sound systems. They may specialize in one or many kinds of products.

When working on small portable equipment, such as DVD players and video cameras, technicians generally work in central repair shops. When repairing less mobile equipment, such as big-screen televisions, however, they must travel to the customer's location. If the job is overly complex, technicians may take the equipment back to the shop for further work.

Service technicians' work involves many different tools. For example, they may use basic handtools, such as screwdrivers, hammers, and wrenches, to disassemble and reassemble components.

They may also use more sophisticated diagnostic tools, including multimeters, voltmeters, oscilloscopes, and digital storage scopes, to identify electronic malfunctions, such as short circuits and failed capacitors. Because of the growing complexity of home entertainment systems, service technicians frequently consult schematics and manufacturers' specifications for instructions on how to repair certain problems.

Most service technicians keep records of bills, payments, parts used, and hours worked. Technicians also show customers how to use new equipment or explain the repairs they made.

Work Environment

Home entertainment equipment installers and repairers held about 36,800 jobs in 2010. Nearly half of these service technicians worked for electronics sales stores and repair shops. About 17 percent were self-employed.

In 2010, the industries employing the largest numbers of home entertainment equipment installers and repairers were as follows:

Electronics and appliance stores	36%
Building equipment contractors	15
Electronic and precision equipment repair and maintenance	14
Wired telecommunications carriers	4

Although most service technicians work in electronics repair shops, many spend significant time traveling to customers' homes. Some may be required to work in awkward positions and carry heavy equipment.

Injuries

Home entertainment equipment installers and repairers have a rate of injuries and illnesses that is higher than the national average. Home entertainment equipment often carries high voltage, even when turned off. To avoid burns and electric shock, service technicians must disconnect the power before working on this equipment. When service technicians take basic safety precautions, their work is safe.

Work Schedules

Most service technicians work full time, and many work evenings or weekends, including overtime.

How to Become a Home Entertainment Equipment Installer or Repairer

Although employers prefer to hire applicants who have completed postsecondary training courses, many service technicians train informally on the job. Industry certification is becoming increasingly important.

Education and Training

Many service technicians become qualified through informal on-the-job training, working closely with experienced technicians. Trainees receive from a few weeks to a few months of guidance and often learn the basics of electronics diagnostics and repair before beginning to work independently.

Although informal on-the-job training remains common, employers generally prefer to hire workers who have attended postsecondary vocational, technical, or associate's degree programs in electronics repair. These programs, which include hands-on and theoretical training in digital consumer electronics, often help reduce the amount of training new workers need.

Service technicians must stay familiar with rapidly changing technologies. Employers frequently require technicians to attend training sessions and read manuals and reports on new products to keep their knowledge and skills up to date.

Certification

Employers increasingly expect service technicians to be certified because certification shows competence. Technicians who gain employment through on-the-job training are often later required by their employer to become certified.

Various organizations offer certification in several different specializations and technologies. The Electronics Technicians Association International , for example, offers specialty credentials, including the Residential Electronics Systems Integrator certification. Also, the International Society of Certified Electronics Technicians offers certification in multimedia and electronic systems. To become certified, service technicians must meet several prerequisites and pass a comprehensive exam.

Important Qualities

Customer-service skills. Because many service technicians work in customers' homes, they must be friendly and polite. Also, they must often clearly explain how to operate home entertainment equipment to people with little or no technical knowledge.

Dexterity. Many service tasks, such as repairing small devices, connecting or attaching parts, and using handtools, require a steady hand and good hand–eye coordination.

Recordkeeping skills. Service technicians must keep accurate records of the number of hours worked, parts used, and bills collected. This is especially important for self-employed service technicians.

Technical skills. Service technicians often use sophisticated diagnostic equipment when working on complex electronic equipment. They must, therefore, be familiar with the components' internal parts and be able to choose the appropriate tools.

Troubleshooting skills. As home entertainment equipment becomes more intricate, malfunctions become more difficult to identify. As a result, service technicians must be able to find and solve problems that are not immediately apparent.

In addition to the above qualities, service technicians must have excellent vision and a keen sense of sound to fine-tune the products they install or repair.

Pay

Home Entertainment Equipment Installers and Repairers
Median annual wages, May 2010

Installation, Maintenance, and Repair Occupations	$40,120
Total, All Occupations	$33,840
Electronic Home Entertainment Equipment Installers and Repairers	$32,940

Note: All Occupations includes all occupations in the U.S. Economy.
Source: U.S. Bureau of Labor Statistics, Occupational Employment Statistics

The median annual wage of home entertainment equipment installers and repairers was $32,940 in May 2010. The median wage is the wage at which half the workers in an occupation earned more than that amount and half earned less. The lowest 10 percent earned less than $20,650, and the top 10 percent earned more than $53,500.

In May 2010, median annual wages in industries employing the largest numbers of home entertainment equipment installers and repairers were as follows:

Wired telecommunications carriers	$35,420
Building equipment contractors	34,950
Electronic and precision equipment repair and maintenance	33,390
Electronics and appliance stores	30,690

Most service technicians work full time, and many work evenings or weekends, including overtime.

Earnings vary by skill level, specialization, and the type of equipment being worked on. Some service technicians earn a commission in addition to their salary, making more money as they complete more jobs each day.

Job Outlook

Home Entertainment Equipment Installers and Repairers
Percent change in employment, projected 2010-20

Installation, Maintenance, and Repair Occupations	15%
Electronic Home Entertainment Equipment Installers and Repairers	14%
Total, All Occupations	14%

Note: All Occupations includes all occupations in the U.S. Economy.
Source: U.S. Bureau of Labor Statistics, Employment Projections program

Employment of home entertainment equipment installers and repairers is expected to grow 14 percent from 2010 to 2020, as fast as the average for all occupations.

Consumer demand for sophisticated home entertainment products, such as high-definition televisions, surround-sound systems, and other high-end home theater equipment, will increase demand for workers to install and service these systems. Home entertainment systems continue to grow in popularity, and consumers' desire for state-of-the-art sound and picture quality will further increase demand for workers.

The need for repairers, however, should be somewhat limited because technological advances have lowered prices and increased the durability of home entertainment equipment, including televisions and DVD players. When a malfunction occurs, consumers often find that replacing equipment is cheaper than repairing it, reducing the need for repairers.

Job Prospects

Certified applicants with good customer service skills and a background in electronics repair should have the best job opportunities. Noncertified applicants will likely face competition for jobs.

The majority of job openings will come from the need to replace workers who retire or leave the occupation. It is also likely that a majority of job openings will occur in electronics and appliance stores and repair shops, because these types of stores employ about one-third of all service technicians.

Employment projections data for home entertainment equipment installers and repairers, 2010-20

Occupational Title	SOC Code	Employment, 2010	Projected Employment, 2020	Change, 2010-20	
				Percent	Numeric
Electronic Home Entertainment Equipment Installers and Repairers	49-2097	36,800	41,900	14	5,100

SOURCE: U.S. Bureau of Labor Statistics, Employment Projections program

Similar Occupations

This table shows a list of occupations with job duties that are similar to those of home entertainment equipment installers and repairers.

Occupation	Job Duties	Entry-Level Education	Median Annual Pay, May 2010
Computer, ATM, and Office Machine Repairers	Computer, ATM, and office machine repairers install, fix, and maintain many of the machines that businesses, households, and other consumers use.	Postsecondary non-degree award	$37,280
Electrical and Electronics Installers and Repairers	Electrical and electronics installers and repairers install, repair, or replace a variety of electrical equipment in telecommunications, transportation, utilities, and other industries.	Postsecondary non-degree award	$49,170
Electricians	Electricians install and maintain electrical systems in homes, businesses, and factories.	High school diploma or equivalent	$48,250
General Maintenance and Repair Workers	General maintenance and repair workers maintain and repair machines, mechanical equipment, and buildings. They work on plumbing, electrical, and air-conditioning and heating systems.	High school diploma or equivalent	$34,730
Home Appliance Repairers	Home appliance repairers install and repair household appliances, such as refrigerators, microwaves, and washer and dryers.	High school diploma or equivalent	$34,730
Telecommunications Equipment Installers and Repairers Except Line Installers	Telecommunications equipment installers and repairers, also known as telecom technicians, set up and maintain devices or equipment that carry communications signals, connect to telephone lines, or access the Internet.	Postsecondary non-degree award	$54,710

Contacts for More Information

For information on home entertainment equipment installer and repairer careers and certification, visit Electronics Technicians Association International , International Society of Certified Electronics Technicians

Suggested citation:

Bureau of Labor Statistics, U.S. Department of Labor, Occupational Outlook Handbook, 2012-13 Edition, Home Entertainment Equipment Installers and Repairers, on the Internet at http://www.bls.gov/ooh/installation-maintenance-and-repair/home-entertainment-equipment-installers-and-repairers.htm .

Industrial Machinery Mechanics and Maintenance Workers

Quick Facts: Industrial Machinery Mechanics and Maintenance Workers	
2010 Median Pay	$44,160 per year $21.23 per hour
Entry-Level Education	High school diploma or equivalent
Work Experience in a Related Occupation	None
On-the-job Training	See How to Become One
Number of Jobs, 2010	357,000
Job Outlook, 2010-20	19% (About as fast as average)
Employment Change, 2010-20	66,400

What Industrial Machinery Mechanics and Maintenance Workers Do

Industrial machinery mechanics and maintenance workers maintain and repair factory equipment and other industrial machinery, such as conveying systems, production machinery, and packaging equipment.

Duties

Industrial machinery mechanics typically do the following:

- Read technical manuals to understand equipment and controls
- Disassemble machinery and equipment when there is a problem
- Repair or replace broken or malfunctioning components
- Perform tests to make sure that the machine is running smoothly
- Adjust and calibrate equipment and machinery

Machinery maintenance workers typically do the following:

- Detect minor problems by performing basic diagnostic tests
- Clean and lubricate equipment or machinery
- Check the performance of machinery
- Test damaged machine parts to determine whether major repairs are needed

Industrial machinery mechanics and maintenance workers repair manufacturing equipment.

- Adjust equipment and reset or calibrate sensors and controls

Industrial machinery mechanics and machinery maintenance workers maintain and repair complex machines, such as an automobile assembly line's conveyor belts, robotic welding arms, and hydraulic lifts.

The following are the two types of industrial machinery mechanics and machinery maintenance workers:

Industrial machinery mechanics, also called **industrial machinery repairers** or **maintenance machinists**, keep machines in good working order. To do this, they must be able to detect and correct errors before they become larger problems.

Machinery mechanics use technical manuals, their understanding of industrial equipment, and careful observation to discover the cause of a problem. For example, after hearing a vibration from a machine, a mechanic must decide whether it is due to worn belts, weak motor bearings, or some other problem. Mechanics often need years of training and experience to diagnose all problems fully. They also use computerized diagnostic systems and vibration analysis techniques to help figure out the source of problems.

After diagnosing a problem, the industrial machinery mechanic may take the equipment apart to repair or replace the necessary parts. Increasingly, mechanics are expected to have the electrical, electronics, and computer programming skills to repair sophisticated equipment on their own. Once a repair is made, mechanics test a machine to make sure that it is running smoothly. Industrial machinery mechanics might also do preventive maintenance.

In addition to handtools, mechanics commonly use lathes, grinders, or drill presses. Many are also required to weld.

Machinery maintenance workers do basic maintenance and repairs on machines. They are responsible for cleaning and lubricating machinery, performing basic diagnostic tests, checking performance, and testing damaged machine parts to determine whether major repairs are necessary.

Maintenance workers must follow machine specifications and adhere to maintenance schedules. They perform minor repairs, generally leaving major repairs to machinery mechanics.

All maintenance workers use a variety of tools to do repairs and preventive maintenance. For example, they may use a screwdriver or socket wrenches to adjust a motor's alignment. They may use a hoist to lift a heavy printing press off the ground.

Work Environment

Industrial machinery mechanics and maintenance workers held about 357,000 jobs in 2010. Most worked in factories, powerplants, or at construction sites.

Work Schedules

Most industrial machinery mechanics and maintenance workers are employed full time during regular business hours. However, mechanics may be on call or assigned to work nights or weekends. Overtime is common, particularly for mechanics.

Injuries

Industrial machinery mechanics and maintenance workers suffer common injuries, such as cuts, bruises, and strains. They also may work in awkward positions, including on top of ladders or in cramped conditions under large machinery.

To avoid injuries, they must follow safety precautions and use protective equipment, such as hardhats, safety glasses, steel-tipped shoes, and hearing protectors. Even so, industrial machinery mechanics and maintenance workers experience rates of injuries and illnesses that are much higher than those for all other occupations.

How to Become an Industrial Machinery Mechanics and Maintenance Worker

Industrial machinery mechanics usually need a year or more of formal education and training after high school. Machinery maintenance workers typically need a high school diploma and receive on-the-job training that lasts a few months to a year.

Education and Training

Employers of industrial machinery mechanics and maintenance workers generally require them to have earned at least a high school diploma or a General Educational Development (GED) certificate. However, employers increasingly prefer to hire workers with some training in industrial technology. Employers also prefer to hire workers who have taken high school or postsecondary courses in mechanical drawing, mathematics, blueprint reading, computer programming, or electronics.

Industrial machinery mechanics usually need a year or more of formal education and training after high school to learn the necessary mechanical and technical skills. Although mechanics used to specialize in one area, such as hydraulics or electronics, many factories now require every mechanic to understand electricity, electronics, hydraulics, and computer programming.

Some mechanics complete a 2-year associate's degree program in industrial maintenance. Others may start as helpers or in other factory jobs and learn the skills of the trade informally or by taking courses offered through their employer.

Employers may offer onsite technical training or send workers to local technical schools while they also receive on-the-job training. Classroom instruction focuses on subjects such as shop mathematics, blueprint reading, welding, electronics, and computer training. In addition to technical instruction, mechanics train on the specific machines that they will repair. They can get this training on the job, through dealers' or manufacturers' representatives, or in a classroom.

Machinery maintenance workers typically receive on-the-job training that lasts a few months to a year. They learn how to perform routine tasks, such as setting up, cleaning, lubricating, and starting machinery. This training may be offered by experienced workers, professional trainers, or representatives of equipment manufacturers.

Important Qualities

Manual dexterity. When handling very small parts, workers must have a steady hand and good hand–eye coordination.

Mechanical skills. Industrial machinery and maintenance workers must be able to reassemble large, complex machines back together after finishing a repair.

Problem-solving skills. Workers must be able to inspect damaged parts of large machinery and figure out why the machinery is not working.

Technical skills. Industrial machinery mechanics and maintenance workers use sophisticated diagnostic equipment to figure out why machines are not working.

Troubleshooting skills. Industrial machinery and maintenance workers must observe and properly diagnose and fix problems that a machine may be having.

Pay

Industrial Machinery Mechanics and Maintenance Workers
Median annual wages, May 2010

Industrial Machinery Mechanics	$45,420
Industrial Machinery Mechanics and Maintenance Workers	$44,160
Maintenance Workers, Machinery	$38,460
Total, All Occupations	$33,840

Note: All Occupations includes all occupations in the U.S. Economy.
Source: U.S. Bureau of Labor Statistics, Occupational Employment Statistics

The median annual wage of industrial machinery mechanics was $45,420 in May 2010. The median wage is the wage at which half the workers in an occupation earned more than that amount and half earned less. The lowest 10 percent earned less than $29,880, and the top 10 percent earned more than $68,130.

The median annual wage of machinery maintenance workers was $38,460 in May 2010. The lowest 10 percent earned less than $23,440, and the top 10 percent earned more than $59,640.

Most industrial machinery mechanics and maintenance workers are employed full time during regular business hours. However, mechanics may be on call or assigned to work nights or weekends. Overtime is common, particularly for mechanics.

Job Outlook

Industrial Machinery Mechanics and Maintenance Workers
Percent change in employment, projected 2010-20

Industrial Machinery Mechanics	22%
Industrial Machinery Mechanics and Maintenance Workers	19%
Total, All Occupations	14%
Maintenance Workers, Machinery	6%

Note: All Occupations includes all occupations in the U.S. Economy.
Source: U.S. Bureau of Labor Statistics, Employment Projections program

Employment of industrial machinery mechanics and maintenance workers is expected to grow 19 percent from 2010 to 2020, about as fast as the average for all occupations. Employment growth will vary by specialty.

Employment of industrial machinery mechanics is projected to grow 22 percent from 2010 to 2020, faster than the average for all occupations. Increased adoption of sophisticated manufacturing machinery will require more highly skilled mechanics to keep the machines in good working order.

Employment of machinery maintenance workers is projected to grow 6 percent from 2010 to 2020, slower than the average for all occupations. Increased automation, including the use of many new computer-controlled machines in factories and manufacturing plants, should result in less demand for lower-skilled maintenance workers.

Job Prospects

Applicants with a broad range of skills in machine repair should have good job prospects overall. The need to replace the many older workers who are expected to retire, as well as those who leave the occupation for other reasons, should result in numerous job openings. Some employers have reported difficulty in recruiting young workers with the necessary skills.

Mechanics are not as affected by changes in production levels as are other manufacturing workers because mechanics often are kept during production downtime to complete overhauls to major equipment and to keep expensive machinery in working order.

Employment projections data for industrial machinery mechanics and maintenance workers, 2010-20

Occupational Title	SOC Code	Employment, 2010	Projected Employment, 2020	Change, 2010-20 Percent	Change, 2010-20 Numeric
Industrial Machinery Mechanics and Maintenance Workers	—	357,000	423,400	19	66,400
Industrial Machinery Mechanics	49-9041	287,100	349,000	22	61,900
Maintenance Workers, Machinery	49-9043	69,900	74,400	6	4,500

SOURCE: U.S. Bureau of Labor Statistics, Employment Projections program

Similar Occupations

This table shows a list of occupations with job duties that are similar to those of industrial machinery mechanics and maintenance workers.

Occupation	Job Duties	Entry-Level Education	Median Annual Pay, May 2010
Electrical and Electronics Engineers	Electrical engineers design, develop, test, and supervise the manufacturing of electrical equipment such as electric motors, radar and navigation systems, communications systems, and power generation equipment. Electronics engineers design and develop electronic equipment, such as broadcast and communications systems—from portable music players to global positioning systems (GPS).	Bachelor's degree	$87,180
Electricians	Electricians install and maintain electrical systems in homes, businesses, and factories.	High school diploma or equivalent	$48,250
General Maintenance and Repair Workers	General maintenance and repair workers maintain and repair machines, mechanical equipment, and buildings. They work on plumbing, electrical, and air-conditioning and heating systems.	High school diploma or equivalent	$34,730
Machinists and Tool and Die Makers	Machinists and tool and die makers set up and operate a variety of computer-controlled or mechanically-controlled machine tools to produce precision metal parts, instruments, and tools.	High school diploma or equivalent	$39,910
Millwrights	Millwrights install, dismantle, repair, reassemble, and move machinery in factories, power plants, and construction sites.	High school diploma or equivalent	$48,360
Plumbers, Pipefitters, and Steamfitters	Plumbers, pipefitters, and steamfitters install and repair pipes that carry water, steam, air, or other liquids or gases to and in businesses, homes, and factories.	High school diploma or equivalent	$46,660
Welders, Cutters, Solderers, and Brazers	Welders, cutters, solderers, and brazers weld or join metal parts. They also fill holes, indentions, or seams of metal products, using hand-held welding equipment.	High school diploma or equivalent	$35,450

Contacts for More Information

For information about industrial machinery mechanics and maintenance workers, visit The International Maintenance Institute , Society for Maintenance and Reliability Professionals , The Association for Maintenance Professionals APICS, The Association for Operations Management , National Association of Manufacturers

For further information on apprenticeship programs, write to the Apprenticeship Council of your state's labor department or to local firms that employ machinery mechanics and repairers. You can also find information about registered apprenticeships, together with links to state apprenticeship programs, on the U.S. Department of Labor website: Employment and Training Administration . Apprenticeship information is available as well from the U.S. Department of Labor toll-free help line: (877) 872-5627.

Suggested citation:

Bureau of Labor Statistics, U.S. Department of Labor, Occupational Outlook Handbook, 2012-13 Edition, Industrial Machinery Mechanics and Maintenance Workers, on the Internet at http://www.bls.gov/ooh/installation-maintenance-and-repair/industrial-machinery-mechanics-and-maintenance-workers.htm .

Line Installers and Repairers

Quick Facts: Line Installers and Repairers	
2010 Median Pay	$54,290 per year $26.10 per hour
Entry-Level Education	High school diploma or equivalent
Work Experience in a Related Occupation	None
On-the-job Training	Long-term on-the-job training
Number of Jobs, 2010	269,100
Job Outlook, 2010-20	13% (About as fast as average)
Employment Change, 2010-20	36,200

What Line Installers and Repairers Do

Line installers and repairers install or repair electrical power systems and telecommunications cables, including fiber optics.

Duties

Electrical power-line installers and repairers typically do the following:

- Drive work vehicles to job sites
- Install, maintain, or repair the power lines that move and distribute electricity
- Identify defective devices, circuit breakers, fuses, voltage regulators, transformers, and switches
- Inspect and test power lines and auxiliary equipment
- String power lines between poles, towers, and buildings
- Climb poles and transmission towers and use truck-mounted buckets to get to equipment
- Operate power equipment when installing and repairing poles, towers, and lines
- Follow safety standards and procedures

Telecommunications line installers and repairers typically do the following:

- Drive work vehicles to job sites
- Install, maintain, or repair telecommunications equipment
- Inspect or test lines or cables
- Lay underground cable, including fiber optic lines, directly in trenches
- Operate power equipment when installing and repairing poles, towers, and lines
- Set up service for customers

Every time you turn on your lights, call someone on the phone, watch cable television, or access the Internet, you are connecting to complex networks of physical power lines and cables that provide you with electricity and connect you with the outside world. Line installers and repairers, also known as line workers or linemen, are the people who install and maintain these networks.

Line installers and repairers typically specialize, and the areas in which they specialize depend on the network and industry in which they work:

Electrical power-line installers and repairers install and maintain the power grid—the network of power lines that moves electricity from generating plants to customers. They routinely work with high-voltage electricity, which requires extreme caution. This can range from hundreds of thousands of volts for the long-distance transmission lines that make up the power grid to less than 10,000 volts for distribution lines that supply electricity to homes and businesses.

Line workers who maintain the interstate power grid work in crews that travel to work locations throughout a large region to take care of transmission lines and towers. Workers employed by local utilities work mainly with lower voltage distribution lines, maintaining equipment such as transformers, voltage regulators, and switches. They may also work on traffic lights and street lights.

Telecommunications line installers and repairers install and maintain the lines and cables used by local and long-distance telephone services, cable television, the Internet, and other communications networks. These services use different types of cables, including fiber-optic cables. Unlike metallic cables that carry electricity, fiber-optic cables are made of glass or plastic and transmit signals using light. Working with fiber optics requires special skills, such as the ability to splice and finish off optical cables. Additionally, workers test and troubleshoot cables and networking equipment.

Because these systems are so complicated, many line workers also specialize by duty:

Line installers install new cable. They may work for construction contractors, utilities, or telecommunications companies. They generally start a new job by digging underground trenches or putting up utility poles and towers to carry the wires and cables. They use a variety of construction equipment, including digger derricks, which are trucks equipped with augers and cranes used to dig holes in the ground and set poles in place. Line installers also use trenchers, cable plows, and directional bore machines, which are used to cut openings in the earth to lay underground cables. Once the poles, towers, tunnels, or trenches are ready, line installers string cable along poles and towers or through tunnels and trenches.

Line repairers are employed by utilities and telecommunications

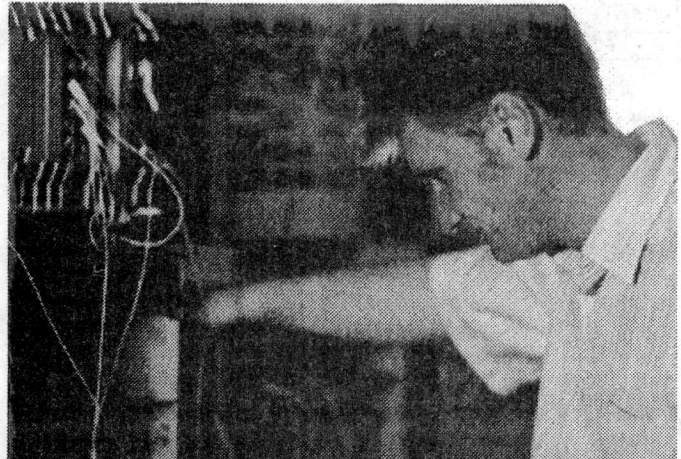

Line installers and repairers install and fix cables and wires, including fiber optic.

companies that maintain existing power and telecommunications lines. Maintenance needs may be identified in a variety of ways, including remote monitoring equipment, inspections by airplane or helicopter, and customer reports of service outages. Line repairers often must replace aging or outdated equipment, so many of these workers have installation duties in addition to their repair duties.

When a problem is reported, line repairers must identify the cause and fix it. This usually involves testing equipment and replacing it as necessary. To work on poles, line installers usually use bucket trucks to raise themselves to the top of the structure, although all line workers must be adept at climbing poles and towers when necessary. Workers use special safety equipment to keep them from falling when climbing utility poles and towers.

Storms and other natural disasters can cause extensive damage to networks of power lines. When a connection goes out, line repairers must work quickly to restore service to customers.

Work Environment

Line installers and repairers held about 269,100 jobs in 2010. About 34 percent worked in the telecommunications industry and 28 percent worked in the construction industry.

The following industries employed the most line installers and repairers in 2010:

Wired telecommunications carriers	30%
Utility system construction	17
Building equipment contractors	10
Local government, excluding education and hospitals	5
Cable and other subscription programming	5

The work of line installers and repairers can be physically demanding. Line installers must be comfortable working at great heights and in confined spaces. Despite the help of bucket trucks, all line workers must be able to climb utility poles and transmission towers and balance while working on them. Their work often requires that they drive utility vehicles, travel long distances, and work outdoors in poor weather.

They often must work under challenging weather conditions, including in snow, wind, rain, and extreme heat and cold, to keep electricity flowing.

Injuries

Line workers encounter serious hazards on their jobs and must follow safety procedures to minimize danger. They wear safety equipment when entering underground manholes, for example, and test for the presence of gas before going underground.

Electric power-line workers have hazardous jobs. A worker can be electrocuted if he or she comes in contact with a live cable on a high-voltage power line. When workers must work with live wires, they use electrically insulated protective devices and tools to minimize their risk. Power lines are typically higher than telephone and cable television lines, increasing the risk of severe injury from a fall. To prevent injuries, line installers use fall-protection equipment when working on poles or towers. Safety procedures and training have significantly reduced the danger for line workers. However, the occupation is still among the most dangerous. Both telecommunications and electrical line workers have a rate of injuries and illnesses that is much higher than the national average.

Work Schedules

Although most work full time during regular business hours, some line installers may work irregular hours on evenings and weekends. In emergencies or after storms and other disasters, these workers may have to work long hours for several days in a row.

How to Become a Line Installer or Repairer

To become proficient, most line installers and repairers require long-term on-the-job training and some technical instruction. Formal apprenticeships are common.

Education and Training

Most companies require line installers and repairers to have a high school diploma or equivalent. Employers look for people with basic knowledge of algebra and trigonometry and good reading skills. Technical knowledge of electricity or electronics obtained through military service, vocational programs, or community colleges is helpful.

Many community colleges offer programs in telecommunications, electronics, or electricity. Some programs work with local companies to offer 1-year certificates that emphasize hands-on field work. More advanced 2-year associate's degree programs provide students with a broad knowledge of the technology used in telecommunications and electrical utilities. These programs offer courses in electricity, electronics, fiber optics, and microwave transmission.

Line installers and repairers get most of their training on the job. Electrical line installers and repairers often must complete formal apprenticeships or other employer training programs. These programs, which can last up to 5 years, combine on-the-job training with technical instruction and are sometimes administered jointly by the employer and the union representing the workers. Safety regulations define the training and educational requirements for apprentice electrical line installers, but licensure is not required.

Line installers and repairers working for telephone and cable television companies receive several years of on-the-job training. They also may attend training or get technical instruction from equipment manufacturers, schools, unions, or industry training organizations.

Certification

Although it is not mandatory, certification for line installers and repairers is available from several associations. For example, the National Joint Apprenticeship and Training Committee offers certification for line installers and repairers in several specialty areas.

The Fiber Optic Association also offers certification programs specifically in fiber optics: the FOA Certification presents three levels of fiber optic certification for telecommunications line installers and repairers.

Advancement

Entry-level line workers generally begin with classroom training and an apprenticeship. Their on-the-job training begins with basic tasks, such as ground work and tree trimming. As they learn additional skills from more experienced workers, they may advance to stringing cable and doing service installations. In time, they advance to more sophisticated maintenance and repair positions in which they are responsible for increasingly large portions of the network.

After 3 to 5 years of working, qualified line workers reach the journey level. A journey-level line worker is no longer considered an apprentice and can do most tasks without supervision. Journey-level line workers may also qualify for positions at other companies. Workers with many years of experience may become first-line supervisors or may become trainers.

Important Qualities

Color vision. Workers who handle electrical wires and cables must be able to distinguish colors because the wires and cables are often color coded.

Mechanical skills. Line installers and repairers must have the knowledge and skills to repair or replace complex electrical and telecommunications lines and equipment.

Physical strength. Line installers and repairers must be strong enough to lift heavy tools, cables, and equipment on a regular basis.

Stamina. Line installers and repairers often must climb poles and work at great heights with heavy tools and equipment. Therefore, these workers must be able to be physically active for long periods without tiring.

Teamwork. Because workers often rely on their fellow crew members for their safety, teamwork is critical.

Technical skills. Line installers use sophisticated diagnostic equipment on circuit breakers, switches, and transformers. They must be familiar with electrical systems and the appropriate tools needed to fix and maintain them.

Troubleshooting skills. Line installers and repairers must be able to diagnose problems in increasingly complex electrical systems and telecommunication lines.

Workers who drive company vehicles usually need a commercial driver's license.

Pay

Line Installers and Repairers
Median annual wages, May 2010

Line Installers and Repairers	$54,290
Installation, Maintenance, and Repair Occupations	$40,120
Total, All Occupations	$33,840

Note: All Occupations includes all occupations in the U.S. Economy.
Source: U.S. Bureau of Labor Statistics, Occupational Employment Statistics

The median annual wage of electrical power-line installers and repairers was $58,030 in May 2010. The median wage is the wage at which half the workers in an occupation earned more than that amount and half earned less. The lowest 10 percent earned less than $33,680, and the top 10 percent earned more than $82,450.

In May 2010, median annual wages in industries employing the largest numbers of electrical power-line installers and repairers were as follows:

Natural gas distribution	$81,710
Electric power generation, transmission and distribution	61,540
Local government	56,250
Building equipment contractors	52,190
Utility system construction	49,620

The median annual wage of telecommunications line installers and repairers was $50,850 in May 2010. The lowest 10 percent earned less than $26,910, and the top 10 percent earned more than $73,320.

In May 2010, median annual wages in industries employing the largest numbers of telecommunications line installers and repairers were as follows:

Other telecommunications	$62,490
Wired telecommunications carriers	57,540
Cable and other subscription programming	43,360
Building equipment contractors	39,890
Utility system construction	36,770

Job Outlook

Line Installers and Repairers
Percent change in employment, projected 2010-20

Installation, Maintenance, and Repair Occupations	15%
Total, All Occupations	14%
Line Installers and Repairers	13%

Note: All Occupations includes all occupations in the U.S. Economy.
Source: U.S. Bureau of Labor Statistics, Employment Projections program

Overall employment of line installers and repairers is expected to grow 13 percent from 2010 to 2020, about as fast as the average for all occupations.

Employment of telecommunications line installers and repairers is projected to grow 14 percent from 2010 to 2020, as fast as the average for all occupations. As the population grows, installers will continue to be needed to provide new telephone, cable, and Internet services for new construction. In addition, the growth of the Internet will require more long-distance fiber-optic lines, including interstate and undersea cables.

Employment of electrical power-line installers and repairers is expected to grow 13 percent from 2010 to 2020, about as fast as the average for all occupations. As with telecommunications line installers and repairers, employment growth will be largely due to the growing population and expansion of cities. With each new housing development or office park, new lines are installed and will require maintenance. In addition, the interstate power grid will continue to grow in complexity to ensure reliability.

Job Prospects

Good job opportunities are expected overall. Highly skilled workers with apprenticeship training or a 2-year associate's degree in telecommunications, electronics, or electricity should have the best job opportunities.

Employment opportunities should be particularly good for electrical power-line installers and repairers, as many workers in this field are expected to retire.

Because of layoffs in the 1990s, more of the electrical power industry is near retirement age than in most industries. This is of special concern for electrical line workers who must be in good physical shape and cannot necessarily put off retirement.

Employment projections data for line installers and repairers, 2010-20

Occupational Title	SOC Code	Employment, 2010	Projected Employment, 2020	Change, 2010-20 Percent	Change, 2010-20 Numeric
Line Installers and Repairers	—	269,100	305,300	13	36,200
Electrical Power-Line Installers and Repairers	49-9051	108,400	122,800	13	14,400
Telecommunications Line Installers and Repairers	49-9052	160,600	182,500	14	21,900
SOURCE: U.S. Bureau of Labor Statistics, Employment Projections program					

Similar Occupations

This table shows a list of occupations with job duties that are similar to those of line installers and repairers.

Occupation	Job Duties	Entry-Level Education	Median Annual Pay, May 2010
Electrical and Electronics Engineers	Electrical engineers design, develop, test, and supervise the manufacturing of electrical equipment such as electric motors, radar and navigation systems, communications systems, and power generation equipment. Electronics engineers design and develop electronic equipment, such as broadcast and communications systems—from portable music players to global positioning systems (GPS).	Bachelor's degree	$87,180
Electricians	Electricians install and maintain electrical systems in homes, businesses, and factories.	High school diploma or equivalent	$48,250
Power Plant Operators, Distributors, and Dispatchers	Power plant operators, distributors, and dispatchers control the systems that generate and distribute electric power.	High school diploma or equivalent	$65,360
Telecommunications Equipment Installers and Repairers Except Line Installers	Telecommunications equipment installers and repairers, also known as telecom technicians, set up and maintain devices or equipment that carry communications signals, connect to telephone lines, or access the Internet.	Postsecondary non-degree award	$54,710

Contacts for More Information

For information about apprenticeships or job opportunities for line installers and repairers, contact local elevator contractors, a local chapter of the International Brotherhood of Electrical Workers, a local joint union-management apprenticeship committee, or the nearest office of your state employment service or apprenticeship agency. Apprenticeship information is available from the U.S. Department of Labor's toll-free help line, 1 (877) 872-5627 or Employment and Training Administration.

For more information about line installers and repairers, visit American Public Power Association , Center for Energy Workforce Development ,International Brotherhood of Electrical Workers ,Telecommunications Industry Association Headquarters

For information about certification, visit Fiber Optic Association ,National Joint Apprenticeship and Training Committee

Suggested citation:

Bureau of Labor Statistics, U.S. Department of Labor, Occupational Outlook Handbook, 2012-13 Edition, Line Installers and Repairers, on the Internet at http://www.bls.gov/ooh/installation-maintenance-and-repair/line-installers-and-repairers.htm .

Medical Equipment Repairers

Quick Facts: Medical Equipment Repairers	
2010 Median Pay	$44,490 per year $21.39 per hour
Entry-Level Education	Associate's degree
Work Experience in a Related Occupation	None
On-the-job Training	Moderate-term on-the-job training
Number of Jobs, 2010	37,900
Job Outlook, 2010-20	31% (Much faster than average)
Employment Change, 2010-20	11,900

What Medical Equipment Repairers Do

Medical equipment repairers install, maintain, and repair patient care equipment.

Duties

Medical equipment repairers typically do the following:

- Test and calibrate parts and equipment
- Repair and replace parts
- Perform preventive maintenance and service
- Keep records of maintenance and repairs
- Review technical manuals and regularly attend training sessions
- Explain and demonstrate correct operation of medical equipment

Medical equipment repairers, also known as **biomedical equipment technicians** (BMET), repair a wide variety of electronic, electromechanical, and hydraulic equipment used in hospitals and health practitioners' offices. They may work on patient monitors, defibrillators, medical imaging equipment (X rays, CAT scanners, and ultrasound equipment), voice-controlled operating tables, and electric wheelchairs, as well as on sophisticated medical equipment that dentists and eye doctors use.

If a machine has problems or is not functioning to its potential, the repairer may have to adjust the mechanical or hydraulic parts, or adjust the software to bring electronic equipment back into calibration. To do their work, medical equipment repairers use a variety of tools. They may use hand tools, such as screwdrivers, wrenches, and soldering irons. They may use electronic tools, such as multimeters (an electronic

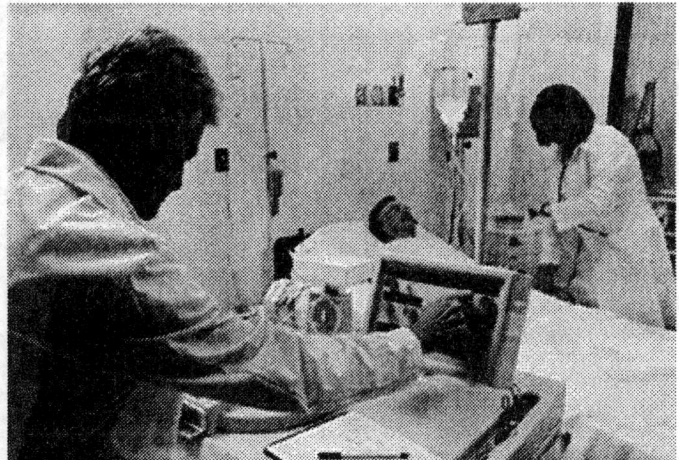

Medical equipment repairers adjust and repair medical equipment.

measuring device that combines several measures) and computers. Many of the pieces of equipment that they maintain and repair use specialized software, and repairers use that software to adjust the machines.

Many doctors, particularly specialty practitioners, rely on complex medical devices to run tests and diagnose patients, and they must be confident that the readings are accurate. Therefore, medical equipment repairers sometimes do routine scheduled maintenance to ensure that all equipment is in good working order.

In a hospital setting, medical equipment repairers must be comfortable working around patients because repairs occasionally must take place while equipment is being used. When this is the case, the repairer must take great care to ensure that repairs do not disturb patients.

Although some medical equipment repairers are trained to fix a variety of equipment, others specialize in repairing one or a small number of machines. For less complicated equipment, such as electric hospital beds, workers make repairs as needed.

Work Environment

Medical equipment repairers held about 37,900 jobs in 2010. About 13 percent were self-employed.

The following industries employed the most medical equipment repairers in 2010:

Professional and commercial equipment and supplies merchant wholesalers	28%
Hospitals; state, local, and private	16
Electronic and precision equipment repair and maintenance	14
Ambulatory health care services	7
Health and personal care stores	6

Medical equipment repairers work for wholesale suppliers and at hospitals, electronic repair and maintenance shops, and health and personal care stores. Because repairing vital medical equipment is urgent, the work can sometimes be stressful.

Medical equipment repairers who work as contractors often have to travel—sometimes long distances—to do needed repairs. Medical equipment repairers often must work in a patient environment, which has the potential to expose them to diseases and other health risks.

Work Schedules

Although medical equipment repairers usually work during the day, they are sometimes expected to be on call, including nights and weekends. Most work full time, but some repairers have variable schedules.

How to Become a Medical Equipment Repairer

Employers generally prefer candidates who have an associate's degree in biomedical technology or engineering. Depending on the area of specialization, and especially for advancement, repairers may need a bachelor's degree.

Education and Training

Education requirements for medical equipment repairers vary, depending on a worker's experience and area of specialization. However, the most common education is an associate's degree in biomedical equipment technology or engineering. Those who repair less-complicated equipment, such as hospital beds and electric wheelchairs, may learn entirely through on-the-job training. Others, particularly those who work on more sophisticated equipment, such as CAT scanners and defibrillators, may need a bachelor's degree.

New workers generally start by watching and helping experienced repairers for 3 to 6 months, learning about one piece of equipment at a time. Gradually, new workers begin working more independently while still under supervision.

Each piece of equipment is different, so medical equipment repairers must learn each one separately. In some cases, this requires studying a machine's technical specifications and manual. Medical device manufacturers also may provide technical training.

Medical equipment technology is rapidly evolving, and new devices are frequently introduced. Repairers must continually update their skills and knowledge of new technologies and equipment through seminars and self-study.

Certification

Certification is optional, but it allows medical equipment repairers to show that they have a level of competency that can make them more attractive to employers. It can also increase a repairer's opportunities for advancement. Most employers, particularly in hospitals, often pay for their in-house medical repairers to become certified.

Some associations offer certification for medical equipment repairers. For example, the Association for the Advancement of Medical Instrumentation (AAMI) offers certification in three specialty areas—Certified Biomedical Equipment Technician (CBET), Certified Radiology Equipment Specialists (CRES), and Certified Laboratory Equipment Specialist (CLEB).

Important Qualities

Dexterity. Many tasks, such as taking apart mechanical parts, connecting or attaching parts, and using handtools, require a steady hand and good hand-eye coordination.

Mechanical skills. Medical equipment repairers must be familiar with medical components and systems and how they interact. Often, repairers must take apart major parts for fixing and be able to put them back together when the work is complete.

Stamina. Standing, crouching, and bending in awkward positions are common when making repairs to equipment. Therefore, workers must be able to be physically active for long periods without tiring.

Technical skills. Technicians use sophisticated diagnostic equipment when working on complex medical equipment. They must be familiar with both the equipments' internal parts and the appropriate tools needed to fix them.

Time-management skills. Because repairing vital medical equipment is urgent, workers must make good use of their time and do repairs quickly.

Troubleshooting skills. As medical equipment becomes more intricate, problems become more difficult to identify. Therefore, repairers must be able to find and solve problems that are not immediately apparent.

Pay

Medical Equipment Repairers
Median annual wages, May 2010

Medical Equipment Repairers	$44,490
Other Installation, Maintenance, and Repair Occupations	$38,010
Total, All Occupations	$33,840

Note: All Occupations includes all occupations in the U.S. Economy.
Source: U.S. Bureau of Labor Statistics, Occupational Employment Statistics

The median annual wage of medical equipment repairers was $44,490 in May 2010. The median wage is the wage at which half the workers in an occupation earned more than that amount and half earned less. The lowest 10 percent earned less than $26,040, and the top 10 percent earned more than $70,260.

In May 2010, median annual wages in industries employing the largest numbers of medical equipment repairers were as follows:

General medical and surgical hospitals	$48,740
Professional and commercial equipment and supplies merchant wholesalers	45,280
Electronic and precision equipment repair and maintenance	43,600
Health and personal care stores	33,830
Consumer goods rental	32,300

Although medical equipment repairers usually work during the day, they are sometimes expected to be on call, including nights and weekends. Most work full time, but many workers have variable schedules.

Job Outlook

Medical Equipment Repairers
Percent change in employment, projected 2010-20

Medical Equipment Repairers	31%
Other Installation, Maintenance, and Repair Occupations	15%
Total, All Occupations	14%

Note: All Occupations includes all occupations in the U.S. Economy.
Source: U.S. Bureau of Labor Statistics, Employment Projections program

Employment of medical equipment repairers is expected to grow 31 percent from 2010 to 2020, much faster than the average for all occupations. Employment growth will stem from both greater demand for healthcare services and the increasing types and complexity of the equipment these workers maintain and repair.

A major factor in the greater demand for healthcare services is the aging population. As people age, they usually need more medical care. With the expected increase in the number of older adults and with people living longer, health professionals are prescribing more medical tests that use new, complex equipment.

Changes in technology are bringing hospitals and health professionals more types of equipment and more complex equipment. Medical equipment repairers will be needed to maintain and repair CAT scans, electrocardiograms, magnetic resonance imaging, ultrasounds, x-ray machines, and other new technology. They also will be needed to maintain and repair the sophisticated machines that private practitioners and technicians use to diagnose and treat problems with eyes, teeth, and other parts of the body. And they will still be needed to maintain and repair less complex health equipment, such as electric beds and wheelchairs.

Job Prospects

A combination of rapid employment growth and the need to replace workers leaving the occupation will likely result in excellent job opportunities from 2010 to 2020. Candidates who have an associate's degree in biomedical equipment technology or engineering should have the best job prospects. Job opportunities should be even better for those who are willing to relocate, because often there are relatively few qualified applicants in rural areas.

Employment projections data for medical equipment repairers, 2010-20

Occupational Title	SOC Code	Employment, 2010	Projected Employment, 2020	Change, 2010-20	
				Percent	Numeric
Medical Equipment Repairers	49-9062	37,900	49,900	31	11,900
SOURCE: U.S. Bureau of Labor Statistics, Employment Projections program					

Similar Occupations

This table shows a list of occupations with job duties that are similar to those of medical equipment repairers.

Occupation	Job Duties	Entry-Level Education	Median Annual Pay, May 2010
Computer, ATM, and Office Machine Repairers	Computer, ATM, and office machine repairers install, fix, and maintain many of the machines that businesses, households, and other consumers use.	Postsecondary non-degree award	$37,280
Medical and Clinical Laboratory Technologists and Technicians	Medical laboratory technologists (also known as medical laboratory scientists) and medical laboratory technicians collect samples and perform tests to analyze body fluids, tissue, and other substances.	See How to Become One	$46,680

Contacts for More Information

For more information about medical equipment repairers, including a listing of schools offering related programs of study and information about certification, visit Association for the Advancement of Medical Instrumentation

Suggested citation:

Bureau of Labor Statistics, U.S. Department of Labor, Occupational Outlook Handbook, 2012-13 Edition, Medical Equipment Repairers, on the Internet at http://www.bls.gov/ooh/installation-maintenance-and-repair/medical-equipment-repairers.htm .

Millwrights

Quick Facts: Millwrights	
2010 Median Pay	$48,360 per year $23.25 per hour
Entry-Level Education	High school diploma or equivalent
Work Experience in a Related Occupation	None
On-the-job Training	Long-term on-the-job training
Number of Jobs, 2010	36,500
Job Outlook, 2010-20	-5% (Decline moderately)
Employment Change, 2010-20	-1,800

What Millwrights Do

Millwrights install, dismantle, repair, reassemble, and move machinery in factories, power plants, and construction sites.

Duties

Millwrights typically do the following:

- Read highly technical instructions and blueprints on machinery
- Install or repair machinery and equipment
- Adjust and align moving parts
- Replace defective parts of machinery as needed
- Take apart existing machinery to clear floor space for new machinery
- Move machinery and equipment

Millwrights are highly skilled workers. Putting together a machine can take a few days or several weeks. Millwrights need to have a good understanding of how the machine works so that they can repair it when it breaks down. Repair includes replacing, as needed, worn or defective parts of the machinery.

Millwrights also may be involved in taking apart existing machines, a common situation when a manufacturing plant needs to

Millwrights install, dismantle, or move machinery in factories, powerplants, and construction sites.

clear floor space for new machinery. Breaking down a machine is usually as complicated as putting it together. Each part must be carefully taken apart, categorized, and packaged for shipping.

Millwrights use a variety of handtools, such as hammers and levels, as well as equipment for welding, brazing, and cutting. They also use measuring tools, such as micrometers, levels, measuring tapes, lasers, and other precision-measuring devices. On large projects, they commonly use cranes and trucks. When millwrights and managers determine the best place for a machine, millwrights bring the parts to the desired location using forklifts, hoists, winches, cranes, and other equipment.

Work Environment

Millwrights held about 36,500 jobs in 2010. Most worked at factories, power plants, and constructions sites. Many millwrights belong to a union.

The industries that employed the most millwrights in 2010 were as follows:

Building equipment contractors	29%
Nonresidential building construction	11
Pulp, paper, and paperboard mills	6
Motor vehicle parts manufacturing	5
Sawmills and wood preservation	3

Injuries

In production facilities, millwrights are subject to common shop injuries, such as cuts, bruises, and strains. In a construction setting, workers must be careful of heavy equipment. They also may work in awkward positions, including on top of ladders, or in cramped conditions under large machinery, both of which add to their risk of injury. To avoid injuries, workers must follow safety precautions and use protective equipment, such as hardhats, safety glasses, steel-toed shoes, and earplugs.

Work Schedules

Millwrights typically are employed on a contract basis and may spend only a few days or weeks at a single site. As a result, workers often have variable schedules and may experience downtime between jobs.

How to Become a Millwright

Millwrights typically go through a formal apprenticeship program that lasts about 4 years. Programs are usually a combination of technical instruction and on-the-job training. Others learn their trade through a 2-year associate's degree program in industrial maintenance. A high school diploma or equivalent is the typical education needed to become a millwright.

Training

Most millwrights learn their trade through a 3- or 4-year apprenticeship. For each year of the program, apprentices must have at least 144 hours of related technical instruction and 2,000 hours of paid on-the-job training. On the job, apprentices learn to set up, clean, lubricate, repair, and start machinery. During technical instruction, they are taught mathematics, how to read blueprints, welding, electronics, and pneumatics (using air pressure). Many also receive computer training.

After completing an apprenticeship program, millwrights are considered fully qualified and can usually perform tasks with less guidance.

Apprenticeship programs are often sponsored by employers, local unions, contractor associations, and the state labor department. The basic qualifications for entering an apprenticeship program are as follows:

- Minimum age of 18
- High school diploma or equivalent
- Physically able to do the work

Millwrights typically receive on-the-job training lasting a few months to 1 year. During training, they perform routine tasks such as setting up, cleaning, lubricating, and starting machinery. This training may be offered by experienced workers, professional trainers, or representatives of equipment manufacturers.

Education

A high school diploma is the typical education needed to become a millwright. However, several 2-year associate's degree programs in industrial maintenance also provide good preparation for prospective millwrights. Some employers offer onsite classroom training or send workers to local technical schools while they get on-the-job training. Classroom instruction focuses on subjects such as shop mathematics, how to read blueprints, welding, electronics, and computer training.

Important Qualities

Mechanical aptitude. Millwrights must be able to use a variety of tools, such as blowtorches and hydraulic torque wrenches, to assemble and take apart machines on a factory floor.

Physical strength. Millwrights must be strong enough to lift or move tools, heavy parts, and equipment.

Technical skills. Millwrights must be able to understand technical manuals for a wide range of machinery in order to disassemble and assemble them correctly.

Troubleshooting skills. Millwrights must be able to diagnose and solve problems. For example, if a moving part is not perfectly aligned, millwrights must find and repair the problem.

Pay

Millwrights
Median hourly wages, May 2010

Millwrights	$23.25
Other Installation, Maintenance, and Repair Occupations	$18.28
Total, All Occupations	$16.27

Note: All Occupations includes all occupations in the U.S. Economy.
Source: U.S. Bureau of Labor Statistics, Occupational Employment Statistics

The median hourly wage of millwrights was $23.25 in May 2010. The median wage is the wage at which half the workers in an occupation earned more than that amount and half earned less. The lowest 10 percent earned less than $14.96, and the top 10 percent earned more than $34.86. Wages often vary by industry and geographic region.

In May 2010, median hourly wages in industries employing the largest numbers of millwrights were as follows:

Motor vehicle parts manufacturing	$32.88
Pulp, paper, and paperboard mills	26.16
Nonresidential building construction	22.94
Building equipment contractors	22.04
Sawmills and wood preservation	19.68

Millwrights typically are employed on a contract basis and may spend only a few days or weeks at a single site. As a result, workers often have variable schedules and may experience downtime between jobs.

Job Outlook

Millwrights
Percent change in employment, projected 2010-20

Other Installation, Maintenance, and Repair Occupations	15%
Total, All Occupations	14%
Millwrights	-5%

Note: All Occupations includes all occupations in the U.S. Economy.
Source: U.S. Bureau of Labor Statistics, Employment Projections program

Employment of millwrights is expected to decline 5 percent from 2010 to 2020. Although the increased use of machinery in manufacturing will require millwrights to install this equipment, the demand for workers is driven largely by manufacturing businesses purchasing new equipment, and purchasing is expected to remain flat over the coming decade.

In addition, the greater reliability of many new computer-controlled machines should slow the growth of millwrights somewhat.

Job Prospects

Despite declining employment, applicants with broad skills in machine maintenance should have favorable job opportunities. The need to replace the many skilled workers who are expected to retire should be the reason for most job openings. Some employers have reported difficulty in recruiting young workers with the necessary skills.

Millwrights are not as affected by changes in production levels as are other manufacturing workers. They often stay during production downtime to overhaul major equipment and to keep expensive machinery in working order.

Employment projections data for millwrights, 2010-20

Occupational Title	SOC Code	Employment, 2010	Projected Employment, 2020	Change, 2010-20 Percent	Change, 2010-20 Numeric
Millwrights	49-9044	36,500	34,800	-5	-1,800

SOURCE: U.S. Bureau of Labor Statistics, Employment Projections program

Similar Occupations

This table shows a list of occupations with job duties that are similar to those of millwrights.

Occupation	Job Duties	Entry-Level Education	Median Annual Pay, May 2010
Electrical and Electronics Engineers	Electrical engineers design, develop, test, and supervise the manufacturing of electrical equipment such as electric motors, radar and navigation systems, communications systems, and power generation equipment.Electronics engineers design and develop electronic equipment, such as broadcast and communications systems—from portable music players to global positioning systems (GPS).	Bachelor's degree	$87,180
Electricians	Electricians install and maintain electrical systems in homes, businesses, and factories.	High school diploma or equivalent	$48,250
General Maintenance and Repair Workers	General maintenance and repair workers maintain and repair machines, mechanical equipment, and buildings. They work on plumbing, electrical, and air-conditioning and heating systems.	High school diploma or equivalent	$34,730
Machinists and Tool and Die Makers	Machinists and tool and die makers set up and operate a variety of computer-controlled or mechanically-controlled machine tools to produce precision metal parts, instruments, and tools.	High school diploma or equivalent	$39,910
Plumbers, Pipefitters, and Steamfitters	Plumbers, pipefitters, and steamfitters install and repair pipes that carry water, steam, air, or other liquids or gases to and in businesses, homes, and factories.	High school diploma or equivalent	$46,660
Welders, Cutters, Solderers, and Brazers	Welders, cutters, solderers, and brazers weld or join metal parts. They also fill holes, indentions, or seams of metal products, using hand-held welding equipment.	High school diploma or equivalent	$35,450

Contacts for More Information

For information about millwrights and the precision machined products industry, training, and apprenticeships, visit Precision Machined Products Association

For information about apprenticeships or job opportunities for millwrights, contact the local chapter of the United Brotherhood of Millwrights, a local joint union-management apprenticeship committee, or the nearest office of your state employment service or apprenticeship agency. Apprenticeship information is available from the U.S. Department of Labor's toll-free help line: 1 (877) 872-5627 or visit Employment and Training Administration .

Suggested citation:

Bureau of Labor Statistics, U.S. Department of Labor, Occupational Outlook Handbook, 2012-13 Edition, Millwrights, on the Internet at http://www.bls.gov/ooh/installation-maintenance-and-repair/millwrights.htm .

Small Engine Mechanics

Quick Facts: Small Engine Mechanics	
2010 Median Pay	$31,790 per year $15.29 per hour
Entry-Level Education	High school diploma or equivalent
Work Experience in a Related Occupation	None
On-the-job Training	See How to Become One
Number of Jobs, 2010	68,800
Job Outlook, 2010-20	21% (Faster than average)
Employment Change, 2010-20	14,300

What Small Engine Mechanics Do

Small engine mechanics inspect, service, and repair motorized power equipment. Mechanics often specialize in one type of equipment, such as motorcycles, motorboats, or outdoor power equipment.

Duties

Small engine mechanics typically do the following:

- Discuss equipment issues, maintenance plans, and work performed with customers
- Perform routine engine maintenance, such as lubricating parts and replacing spark plugs
- Test and inspect engines for malfunctioning parts
- Repair or replace worn, defective, or broken parts
- Reassemble and reinstall components and engines following repairs
- Keep records of inspections, test results, work performed, and parts used

Small engine mechanics regularly work on power equipment ranging from snowmobiles to chainsaws. When equipment breaks down, mechanics use many strategies to diagnose the source and the extent of the problem. Small engine mechanics determine mechanical, electrical, and fuel problems and make necessary repairs.

Mechanics' tasks vary in complexity and difficulty. Many jobs, such as maintenance inspections and repairs, involve minor

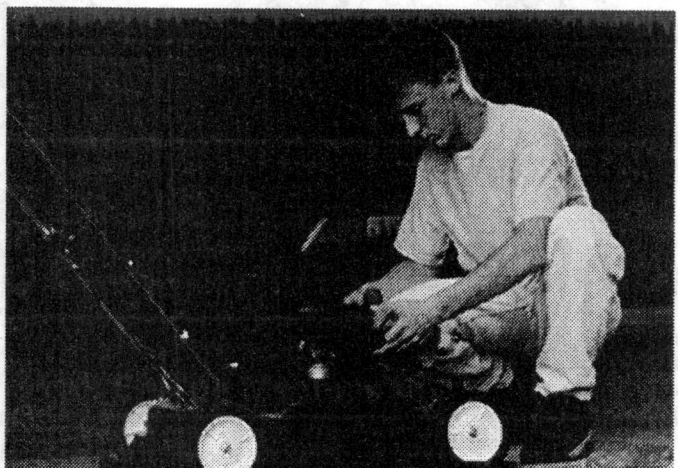

Small engine mechanics repair different types of motorized equipment, such as motorcycles and outdoor power equipment.

adjustments or the replacement of a single part. Others, including piston calibration and spark plug replacement, may require taking an engine apart completely. Some highly skilled mechanics use computerized equipment for tasks, such as customizing and tuning racing motorcycles and motorboats.

Mechanics use a variety of handtools, including screwdrivers, wrenches, and pliers, for many common tasks. Some mechanics also may regularly use compression gauges, ammeters, and voltmeters to test engine performance. For more complicated procedures, they commonly use pneumatic power tools, computerized engine analyzers, and other diagnostic equipment.

Although employers usually provide the more expensive tools and testing equipment, mechanics are often expected to buy their own handtools. Some mechanics have thousands of dollars invested in their tool collections.

The following are types of small engine mechanics:

Motorcycle mechanics specialize in working on motorcycles, scooters, mopeds, dirt bikes, and all-terrain vehicles. They service engines, transmissions, brakes, and ignition systems and make minor body repairs, among other tasks. Most work is for individual dealers, servicing and repairing specific makes and models.

Motorboat and marine equipment mechanics maintain and repair the mechanical and electrical components of boat engines. Most of their work, whether on small outboard engines or large diesel-powered inboard motors, is performed at docks and marinas where the repair shop is located. Motorboat mechanics also may work on propellers, steering mechanisms, marine plumbing, and other boat equipment.

Outdoor power equipment and other small engine mechanics service and repair outdoor power equipment, such as lawnmowers, edge trimmers, garden tractors, and portable generators. In certain parts of the country, mechanics may work on snowblowers and snowmobiles, but this work is both highly seasonal and regional.

For information about technicians and mechanics who work primarily on automobiles, see the profile on automotive service technicians and mechanics .

For information about technicians who work primarily on large trucks and buses, see the profile on diesel service technicians and mechanics .

For information on technicians and mechanics who work primarily on farm equipment, construction vehicles and rail cars, see the profile on heavy vehicle and mobile equipment service technicians .

Work Environment

Small engine mechanics held about 68,800 jobs in 2010. Although the majority worked for equipment dealers and repair shops, about 19 percent were self-employed.

Industries employing the most small engine mechanics in 2010 were as follows:

Other motor vehicle dealers	31%
Lawn and garden equipment and supplies stores	12
Other amusement and recreation industries	9
Personal and household goods repair and maintenance	9
Machinery, equipment, and supplies wholesalers	3

Small engine mechanics generally work in well-ventilated but noisy repair shops. They sometimes make onsite repair calls, which may require working in poor weather conditions. When repairing onboard engines, motorboat mechanics may work in cramped and uncomfortable positions.

Work Schedules

Most small engine mechanics work full time during regular business hours. However, seasonal work hours often fluctuate.Most mechanics are busiest during the spring and summer, when demand for work on equipment, such as lawnmowers and boats, is the highest. During the peak seasons, many mechanics work considerable overtime hours.

In contrast, some mechanics are not as busy during the winter, when demand for small engine work is low. Many employers, however, schedule major repair work to be performed during the off-season, to try to keep work consistent.

How to Become a Small Engine Mechanic A small engine mechanic repairs a go cart.

As motorized power equipment becomes more sophisticated, employers increasingly prefer to hire mechanics who have completed formal training programs. However, many mechanics learn their trade informally on the job.

Education and Training

A growing number of motorcycle and marine equipment mechanics complete formal postsecondary programs in small engine repair. Employers prefer to hire these workers because they usually require significantly less on-the-job training. Because of the limited number of postsecondary programs, however, employers often have difficulty finding qualified workers.

As a result, many mechanics begin work with a high school degree and learn on the job. Generally, employers look for candidates who have completed courses in small engine repair, automobile mechanics, and science. Some employers may hire applicants with less education if they have adequate reading, writing, and math skills.

Trainees work closely with experienced mechanics while learning basic tasks, such as replacing spark plugs or disassembling engine components. As they gain experience, trainees move on to more difficult tasks, such as advanced computerized diagnosis and engine overhauls. Achieving competency may take from several months to 3 years, depending on a mechanic's specialization and ability.

Because of the increased complexity of boat and motorcycle engines, motorcycle and marine equipment mechanics often need more on-the-job training than outdoor power equipment mechanics.

Employers frequently send mechanics to training courses run by motorcycle, motorboat, and outdoor power equipment manufacturers and dealers. Courses may last up to 2 weeks, teaching mechanics the most up-to-date technology and techniques. Often, these courses are a prerequisite for warranty and manufacturer-specific work.

Important Qualities

Customer-service skills. Mechanics must discuss equipment problems and repairs with their customers. They should be courteous, good listeners, and ready to answer customers' questions. In addition, self-employed workers frequently depend on repeat clients for business.

Detail oriented. Mechanical and electronic malfunctions often are due to misalignments or other easy-to-miss errors. Mechanics must, therefore, account for those problems when inspecting or repairing engines and components.

Dexterity. Many tasks, such as disassembling engine parts, connecting or attaching components, and using hand tools, require a steady hand and good hand–eye coordination.

Mechanical skills. Mechanics must be familiar with engine components and systems and know how they interact with each other. They must frequently disassemble major parts for repairs and be able to reassemble them properly.

Technical skills. Mechanics, especially marine equipment and motorcycle specialists, often use computerized diagnostic equipment on engines, systems, and components. They must be familiar with electronic control systems and the tools needed to fix and maintain them.

Troubleshooting skills. Mechanics must be able to identify and diagnose engine problems. They also should be able to repair increasingly complicated mechanical and electronic systems.

Pay

Small Engine Mechanics
Median annual wages, May 2010

Motorboat Mechanics and Service Technicians	$35,600
Total, All Occupations	$33,840
Motorcycle Mechanics	$31,980
Small Engine Mechanics	$31,790
Outdoor Power Equipment and Other Small Engine Mechanics	$29,580

Note: All Occupations includes all occupations in the U.S. Economy.
Source: U.S. Bureau of Labor Statistics, Occupational Employment Statistics

The median annual wage of small engine mechanics was $31,790 in May 2010. The median wage is the wage at which half the workers in an occupation earned more than that amount and half earned less. The lowest 10 percent earned less than $20,310, and the top 10 percent earned more than $49,680.

Median annual wages for specialty occupations in May 2010 were as follows:

- $35,600 for motorboat mechanics and service technicians
- $31,980 for motorcycle mechanics
- $29,580 for outdoor power equipment and other small engine mechanics

Most small engine mechanics work full time during regular business hours. However, seasonal work hours often fluctuate.

Most mechanics are busiest during the spring and summer, when demand for work on equipment from lawnmowers to boats is the highest. During the peak seasons, many mechanics work considerable overtime hours. In contrast, some mechanics are not busy during the winter, when demand for small engine work is low. As a result, during these months they work only part time.

Many employers, however, schedule major repair work to be performed during the off-season, to try to keep work consistent.

Mechanics employed in large shops often receive benefits, such as health insurance, sick leave, and paid vacation time. Conversely, those in small repair shops usually receive few benefits. Some employers pay for work-related training and help mechanics purchase new tools.

Job Outlook

Small Engine Mechanics

Percent change in employment, projected 2010-20

Motorcycle Mechanics	24%
Motorboat Mechanics and Service Technicians	21%
Small Engine Mechanics	21%
Outdoor Power Equipment and Other Small Engine Mechanics	19%
Total, All Occupations	14%

Note: All Occupations includes all occupations in the U.S. Economy.
Source: U.S. Bureau of Labor Statistics, Employment Projections program

Employment of small engine mechanics is expected to grow 21 percent from 2010 to 2020, faster than the average for all occupations. Employment growth will vary be specialty.

Employment of motorcycle mechanics is expected to grow 24 percent, faster than the average for all occupations. The number of registered motorcycles has increased steadily in recent years, leading to corresponding greater demand for motorcycle repair services. This trend is expected to continue, leading to new job opportunities for motorcycle mechanics. Most new jobs will continue to be in the motorcycle dealer industry, as service operations are an important aspect of business for many firms in this industry.

Employment of motorboat mechanics is expected to grow 21 percent, faster than the average for all occupations. Although the retail boat industry, the primary employer of motorboat mechanics, has consolidated in recent years, demand for repair services is expected to rise as boat engines become increasingly sophisticated.

Employment of outdoor power equipment mechanics is expected to grow 19 percent, about as fast as the average for all occupations. Demand for repair services is expected to rise as outdoor power equipment becomes more complex. Most new jobs are projected in the industries that are related to lawn and garden care, in which small engine equipment is frequently used and regular servicing of that equipment is required.

Job Prospects

Job opportunities are expected to be very good for candidates with formal training. Those without formal training can expect to face strong competition for jobs.

Employment projections data for small engine mechanics, 2010-20

Occupational Title	SOC Code	Employment, 2010	Projected Employment, 2020	Change, 2010-20	
				Percent	Numeric
Small Engine Mechanics	—	68,800	83,100	21	14,300
Motorboat Mechanics and Service Technicians	49-3051	20,800	25,000	21	4,300
Motorcycle Mechanics	49-3052	18,000	22,200	24	4,200
Outdoor Power Equipment and Other Small Engine Mechanics	49-3053	30,100	35,800	19	5,700
SOURCE: U.S. Bureau of Labor Statistics, Employment Projections program					

Similar Occupations

This table shows a list of occupations with job duties that are similar to those of small engine mechanics.

Occupation	Job Duties	Entry-Level Education	Median Annual Pay, May 2010
Automotive Service Technicians and Mechanics	Automotive service technicians and mechanics, often called service technicians or service techs, inspect, maintain, and repair cars and light trucks.	High school diploma or equivalent	$35,790
Diesel Service Technicians and Mechanics	Diesel service technicians and mechanics inspect, repair, or overhaul buses, trucks, and anything else with a diesel engine.	High school diploma or equivalent	$40,850
Heavy Vehicle and Mobile Equipment Service Technicians	Heavy vehicle and mobile equipment service technicians inspect, maintain, and repair vehicles and machinery used in construction, farming, rail transportation, and other industries.	High school diploma or equivalent	$42,630
Home Appliance Repairers	Home appliance repairers install and repair household appliances, such as refrigerators, microwaves, and washer and dryers.	High school diploma or equivalent	$34,730

Contacts for More Information

To learn about job opportunities, contact local motorcycle, motorboat, and lawn and garden equipment dealers; boatyards; and marinas. Local offices of the state employment service also may have information about employment and training opportunities.

Suggested citation:

Bureau of Labor Statistics, U.S. Department of Labor, Occupational Outlook Handbook, 2012-13 Edition, Small Engine Mechanics, on the Internet at http://www.bls.gov/ooh/installation-maintenance-and-repair/small-engine-mechanics.htm .

Telecommunications Equipment Installers and Repairers Except Line Installers

Quick Facts: Telecommunications Equipment Installers and Repairers Except Line Installers	
2010 Median Pay	$54,710 per year $26.30 per hour
Entry-Level Education	Postsecondary non-degree award
Work Experience in a Related Occupation	None
On-the-job Training	Moderate-term on-the-job training
Number of Jobs, 2010	194,900
Job Outlook, 2010-20	15% (About as fast as average)
Employment Change, 2010-20	28,400

What Telecommunications Equipment Installers and Repairers Except Line Installers Do

Telecommunications equipment installers and repairers, also known as telecom technicians, set up and maintain devices or equipment that carry communications signals, connect to telephone lines, or access the Internet.

Duties

Telecommunications equipment installers and repairers typically do the following:

- Install communications equipment in offices, private homes, and buildings that are under construction
- Set up, rearrange, or replace routing and dialing equipment
- Perform equipment maintenance, such as inspecting wiring and phone jacks
- Repair or replace faulty, damaged, or malfunctioning parts
- Test repaired, newly installed, or updated equipment to ensure that it works properly
- Adjust or modify equipment to improve its performance
- Demonstrate and explain the use of equipment to customers

Telephone, computer, and cable telecommunications systems rely on sophisticated equipment to process and transmit vast amounts of information. Telecommunications equipment installers and repairers—often called telecom technicians—install and service this

Telecommunication technicians install communications equipment in offices and homes.

equipment.

To inspect equipment and diagnose problems, telecom technicians use many different tools. For instance, to locate distortions in signals, they may use spectrum analyzers and polarity probes. They also commonly use handtools, including screwdrivers and pliers, to take equipment apart and repair it. In addition, telecom technicians frequently install and update software and programs for some devices.

Equipment installers who work mainly outdoors are classified as telecommunications line installers and repairers. For more information, see the profile on line installers and repairers .

Telecom technicians do many tasks, often depending on their specialization and where they work. The following are examples of the types of telecommunications equipment installers and repairers:

Central office technicians set up and maintain switches, routers, fiber-optic cables, and other equipment at switching hubs, called central offices. These hubs send, process, and amplify data from thousands of telephones, Internet connections, and other sources. Increasingly reliable, self-monitoring switches alert central office repairers to malfunctions, and might allow repairers to correct problems remotely.

Headend technicians do almost the same work as central office installers and repairers, but work at distribution centers for cable and television companies, called headends.

PBX installers and repairers set up and service private branch exchange—or PBX—switchboards. This equipment relays incoming, outgoing, and interoffice telephone calls at a single location. Some systems use voiceover Internet protocol—or VoIP—technology, which functions like PBX systems, but uses computers to run Internet access, network applications, and telephone communications.

PBX installers connect telecom equipment to communications cables. They install frames, supports, power systems, alarms, and telephone sets. They test the connections to ensure that adequate power is available and communication links work properly. Because switches and switchboards are now computerized, PBX installers often need to also install software or program the equipment to provide specific features.

Station installers and repairers—sometimes known as home installers and repairers—set up and repair telecommunications equipment in customers' homes and businesses. They install telephone, Internet, and cable television services, often setting up modems and other computer hardware and software.

When customers have problems, station repairers test the customer's lines to determine if the problem is inside or outside. If the problem is inside, they try to repair it. If the problem is outside, they refer the repair to line repairers.

Work Environment

Telecommunications equipment installers and repairers held about 194,900 jobs in 2010. The majority worked full time for private companies. Industries employing the largest numbers of telecommunications equipment installers and repairers in 2010 were as follows:

Wired telecommunications carriers	55%
Building equipment contractors	10
Other telecommunications	8
Cable and other subscription programming	5
Electronic and precision equipment repair and maintenance	3

Central Office technicians generally work in climate-controlled central offices or electronic service centers. PBX and station installers and repairers travel frequently to installation and repair sites, such as homes and offices. Installation may require climbing on rooftops and into attics, and climbing ladders and telephone poles.

Telecom technicians occasionally work in cramped, awkward positions where they must stoop, crouch, crawl, or reach high to do their work. Sometimes they must lift or move heavy equipment and parts. In some cases, they may be required to work on equipment while it is powered.

About 26 percent of all telecom technicians are members of unions. Union members who work for large telecommunications companies often have good benefits in addition to their pay, including health, dental, vision, and life insurance. They also usually have retirement benefits.

Injuries

Telecom technicians have a rate of injuries and illnesses that is higher than the average among all occupations. Although minor falls, burns, and electrical shocks are common, the work is generally not dangerous if safety precautions are taken.

Work Schedules

Most telecom technicians work full time, and overtime is common. Some employers offer 24-hour repair services. Telecom technicians who work for these firms work a variety of shifts, including evenings, holidays, and weekends. Some are on call around the clock in case of emergencies.

How to Become a Telecommunications Equipment Installer or Repairer Except Line Installer

Postsecondary education in electronics and computer technology is important for telecommunications equipment technicians. For more complex work, a 4-year degree may be the best preparation. Industry certification is required for some positions.

Education

To keep pace with rapidly expanding telecommunications technology, telecom technicians increasingly need advanced training. As a result, many employers prefer candidates with formal postsecondary education in electronics and a familiarity with computers.

Telecom technicians may get training through a certificate or 2-year associate's degree program in electronics repair, computer science, or related subjects. Equipment and software manufacturers also offer educational and training programs on specific products.

Central office technicians, headend technicians, and those working with commercial communications systems are increasingly expected to have a bachelor's degree. By contrast, educational requirements are generally lower for workers such as station installers and repairers.

Because technology in this field evolves quickly, telecom technicians must continue to educate themselves over the course of their careers. They may attend manufacturers' training classes, read equipment manuals, or get hands-on experience with the latest equipment.

Training

Most telecom technicians complete some on-the-job training. Generally, this training involves informal hands-on work with an experienced technician. Training may last several weeks to a few months. Workers who have completed postsecondary training often require less on-the-job instruction than those who have not.

Large companies also may send new employees to training sessions to learn about new equipment, procedures, and technology offered by equipment manufacturers or industry organizations.

Certification

Some technicians must be certified to do certain tasks or to work on specific equipment. Certification requirements vary by jurisdiction, employer and specialization.

Organizations such as the Society of Cable and Telecommunications Engineers and the Telecommunications Industry Association offer certifications for telecom technicians. Some manufacturers also provide certifications for working with specific equipment.

Advancement

Experienced repairers with advanced training may become specialists or troubleshooters who help other repairers diagnose difficult problems.

Because of their familiarity with equipment, repairers are particularly well qualified to become manufacturers' sales workers.

Home installers may advance to wiring computer networks or working as a central office installer and repairer.

Important Qualities

Bookkeeping skills. When working at clients' locations, telecom technicians must often track hours worked, parts used, and bills collected.

Color vision. Installers and repairers must be able to distinguish different colors because the wires they work with are color coded.

Customer-service skills. Many telecom technicians work in customers' homes and offices, so it is important that they be friendly and polite. Also, they often must explain how to maintain and operate complicated equipment to people who have little or no technical knowledge.

Manual dexterity. Many telecom technician tasks, such as repairing small devices, connecting or attaching components, and using handtools, require a steady hand and good hand–eye coordination.

Technical skills. Telecom technicians frequently work with computers, sophisticated diagnostic equipment, and specialized hardware. Therefore, they must be familiar with these devices, their internal parts, and the appropriate tools needed to use, install, or fix them.

Troubleshooting skills. As telecommunications equipment becomes more sophisticated, malfunctions become more difficult to identify. As a result, technicians must be able to devise solutions to complex problems that are not immediately apparent.

Pay

Telecommunications Equipment Installers and Repairers Except Line Installers

Median annual wages, May 2010

Telecommunications Equipment Installers and Repairers,

Except Line Installers	$54,710
Installation, Maintenance, and Repair Occupations	$40,120
Total, All Occupations	$33,840

Note: All Occupations includes all occupations in the U.S. Economy.
Source: U.S. Bureau of Labor Statistics, Occupational Employment Statistics

The median annual wage of telecommunications equipment installers and repairers was $54,710 in May 2010. The median wage is the wage at which half the workers in an occupation earned more than that amount and half earned less. The lowest 10 percent earned less than $31,170, and the top 10 percent earned more than $72,940.

In May 2010, median annual wages in industries employing the largest numbers of telecommunications equipment installers and repairers were as follows:

Other telecommunications	$62,090
Wired telecommunications carriers	55,820
Cable and other subscription programming	50,780
Building equipment contractors	43,340
Electronic and precision equipment repair and maintenance	37,150

Most telecom technicians work full time, overtime is common.

Some employers offer 24-hour repair services. Telecom technicians who work for these firms work a variety of shifts, including nights, holidays, and weekends. Some are on call around the clock in case of emergencies.

About 26 percent of all telecom technicians are members of unions. Union members who work for large telecommunications companies often have good benefits in addition to their pay, including health, dental, vision, and life insurance. They also usually have retirement benefits.

Employees of small independent companies and contractors may get fewer benefits.

Job Outlook

Telecommunications Equipment Installers and Repairers Except Line Installers

Percent change in employment, projected 2010-20

Telecommunications Equipment Installers and Repairers,

Except Line Installers	15%
Installation, Maintenance, and Repair Occupations	15%
Total, All Occupations	14%

Note: All Occupations includes all occupations in the U.S. Economy.
Source: U.S. Bureau of Labor Statistics, Employment Projections program

Employment of telecommunications equipment installers and repairers is expected to grow 15 percent from 2010 to 2020, about as fast as the average for all occupations.

Demand for telecommunications equipment will continue to grow as Internet connections become faster, hundreds of cable television stations are added, and emerging technologies become more popular. Although building, maintaining, and upgrading these networks should create some jobs, employment gains may be offset by a decline in maintenance work.

Modern equipment is more reliable, sturdier, easier to repair, and more resistant to damage from the elements, significantly limiting the need for new telecom technicians.

Job Prospects

Although job opportunities will vary by specialty, those with postsecondary electronics training and strong computer skills should have the best job prospects.

Popular technologies, such as video on demand and broadband Internet connections, require high data transfer rates in telecommunications systems. Central office, PBX installers, and headend technicians will be needed to service and upgrade switches and routers to handle increased traffic, resulting in very good job opportunities.

By contrast, station installers and repairers can expect strong competition for most positions. Prewired buildings, the reliability of existing telephone lines, and increasing wireless technology usage may reduce the need for general installation and maintenance work.

Employment projections data for telecommunications equipment installers and repairers except line installers, 2010-20

Occupational Title	SOC Code	Employment, 2010	Projected Employment, 2020	Change, 2010-20	
				Percent	Numeric
Telecommunications Equipment Installers and Repairers, Except Line Installers	49-2022	194,900	223,300	15	28,400
SOURCE: U.S. Bureau of Labor Statistics, Employment Projections program					

Similar Occupations

This table shows a list of occupations with job duties that are similar to those of telecommunications equipment installers and repairers except line installers.

Occupation	Job Duties	Entry-Level Education	Median Annual Pay, May 2010
Broadcast and Sound Engineering Technicians	Broadcast and sound engineering technicians set up, operate, and maintain the electrical equipment for radio and television broadcasts, concerts, sound recordings, and movies and in office and school buildings.	See How to Become One	$39,870
Computer, ATM, and Office Machine Repairers	Computer, ATM, and office machine repairers install, fix, and maintain many of the machines that businesses, households, and other consumers use.	Postsecondary non-degree award	$37,280

Home Entertainment Equipment Installers and Repairers	Home entertainment equipment installers and repairers set up and fix household audio and video equipment, such as televisions, stereo components, and home theater systems.	Postsecondary non-degree award	$32,940
Line Installers and Repairers	Line installers and repairers install or repair electrical power systems and telecommunications cables, including fiber optics.	High school diploma or equivalent	$54,290

Contacts for More Information

For information on career, training and certification opportunities, visit International Brotherhood of Electrical Workers , Communications Workers of America , National Coalition for Telecommunication Education and Learning , Society of Cable Telecommunications Engineers ,Telecommunications Industry Association

Suggested citation:

Bureau of Labor Statistics, U.S. Department of Labor, Occupational Outlook Handbook, 2012-13 Edition, Telecommunications Equipment Installers and Repairers Except Line Installers, on the Internet at http://www.bls.gov/ooh/installation-maintenance-and-repair/telecommunications-equipment-installers-and-repairers-except-line-installers.htm .

Legal Occupations

Court Reporters

Quick Facts: Court Reporters	
2010 Median Pay	$47,700 per year $22.93 per hour
Entry-Level Education	Postsecondary non-degree award
Work Experience in a Related Occupation	None
On-the-job Training	Short-term on-the-job training
Number of Jobs, 2010	22,000
Job Outlook, 2010-20	14% (About as fast as average)
Employment Change, 2010-20	3,100

What Court Reporters Do

Court reporters attend legal proceedings and public speaking events and create word-for-word transcriptions. Some court reporters provide captioning for television and at public events.

Duties

Court reporters typically do the following:

- Attend events that require written transcripts
- Record spoken dialogue with specialized equipment, such as covered microphones
- Report gestures and actions
- Review notes for names of speakers and technical terminology
- Prepare transcripts for the record
- Edit transcripts for typographical errors
- Provide copies of transcripts and recordings to the courts, counsels, and parties involved

Court reporters create word-for-word transcripts of speeches,

Court reporters attend legal proceedings to create word-for-word transcriptions.

conversations, legal proceedings, meetings, and other events. They play a critical role in legal proceedings and other meetings where it is important to have a record of exactly what was said. They are responsible for producing a complete, accurate, and secure legal record.

Court reporters who work in courts also help judges and trial attorneys by organizing the official record and searching for information in it.

Other court reporters do not work in courtrooms. They also transcribe speech to writing as the speech occurs. However, they primarily serve people who cannot hear the spoken word by providing captions for television programs (called closed captioning). They may also transcribe speech for deaf and hard-of-hearing people in meetings.

Court reporters who work with deaf and hard-of-hearing people turn speech into writing. For information on workers who help deaf and hard-of-hearing people through sign language, cued speech, and other spoken or gestural means, see the profile on interpreters and translators.

Court reporters often specialize in a specific method of recording, such as using stenotype machines, steno masks (covered microphones), or digital recording.

Stenotype machine. Court reporters use stenotype machines to record dialogue as it is spoken. Stenotype machines work like keyboards but create words through key combinations rather than single characters, allowing court reporters to keep up with fast-moving dialogue. Court reporters who use stenotype machines are known as stenographers.

As with a regular keyboard, the symbols are recorded in a computer program. The program uses computer-assisted transcription (CAT) to translate the key combinations into the words and phrases they represent, creating readable text. The court reporter then reviews the text for accuracy and corrects spelling and grammar errors.

Steno mask. Court reporters who use steno masks speak directly into a covered microphone, recording dialogue and reporting gestures and actions. Because the microphone is covered, others cannot hear what the reporter is saying. The recording is converted by computerized voice-recognition software into a transcript that the court reporter reviews for accuracy, spelling, and grammar.

For both stenotype machine recording and steno mask recording, court reporters must create and maintain the online dictionary that the computer uses to transcribe the key presses or voice recordings into text. For example, they may put in the names of people involved in the court case or specific words that are used in that type of meeting.

Digital recording. Digital recording creates an audio, rather than a written, transcript. Court reporters who use digital recorders operate and monitor the recording equipment. They also take notes to identify the speakers and provide context. In some cases, the reporter uses the audio recording to create a written transcript.

Court reporters who work with deaf and hard-of-hearing people use a technique called Communication Access Real-Time Translation (CART). They go with their clients to events, doctor's appointments, or wherever they are needed. These court reporters also caption high school and college classes and provide transcripts to students who are hard-of-hearing or learning English as a second language. They also sometimes work remotely because an Internet or phone connection allows them to hear and type without having to be in the room.

Work Environment

Court reporters held about 22,000 jobs in 2010. The following industries employed the most court reporters in 2010:

State government, excluding education and hospitals	31%
Business support services	27
Local government, excluding education and hospitals	25
Information	1

Most court reporters work for state and local governments, in courts and legislatures. Others work as freelance reporters for pretrial depositions and other events. Some captioners work remotely from their home, although others work from a central office.

Work Schedules

Court reporters generally work full time recording events and preparing transcripts. Freelance reporters have more flexibility in setting their schedules.

How to Become a Court Reporter

Many community colleges and technical institutes offer postsecondary certificate programs for court reporters. Many states require court reporters who work in legal settings to be licensed.

Education

Many court reporters receive formal training at community colleges or technical institutes. There are different programs for the different transcription methods. Programs in using steno masks and in digital recording typically last 6 months and lead to a certificate. Programs in stenography, in which students are taught to use stenotype machines, last about 2 to 4 years and often lead to an associate's degree.

Most programs include courses in English grammar and phonetics, legal procedures, and terminology. Students also practice preparing transcripts to improve speed and accuracy.

Licenses and Certification

Many states require court reporters who work in legal settings to be licensed. License requirements vary by method of court reporting.

The National Court Reporters Association (NCRA) offers certification for court reporters and broadcast captioners. Certification as a Registered Professional Reporter (RPR) includes a written test and a skills test, in which court reporters must type at least 225 words per minute.

Currently, 22 states currently accept or use the RPR in place of a state certification or licensing exam.

Digital and voice reporters also may obtain certification.

Training

After completing their formal program, court reporters must complete short-term on-the-job training.

To maintain their certification with the NCRA, court reporters must complete continuing education and online training.

Specific continuing education requirements to maintain state licensure can be found by going to the state association's website.

Important Qualities

Concentration skills. Court reporters must be able to concentrate for long periods. Even when there are distractions, they must remain focused on the dialogue they are recording.

Detail oriented. Court reporters create a transcript that serves as a legal record, so it must be mistake-free.

Listening skills. Court reporters must give their full attention to the speaker and capture every word that is said.

Writing skills. Court reporters need a good command of grammar, vocabulary, and punctuation.

Pay

Court Reporters
Median annual wages, May 2010

Legal Occupations	$74,580
Court Reporters	$47,700
Total, All Occupations	$33,840

Note: All Occupations includes all occupations in the U.S. Economy.
Source: U.S. Bureau of Labor Statistics, Occupational Employment Statistics

The median annual wage for court reporters was $47,700 in May 2010. The median wage is the wage at which half the workers in an occupation earned more than that amount and half earned less. The lowest 10 percent earned less than $25,710, and the top 10 percent earned more than $91,280.

Freelance court reporters are paid for their time but can also sell their transcripts per page for an additional profit.

Court reporters generally work full time recording events and preparing transcripts. Freelance reporters have more flexibility to set their schedule.

Job Outlook

Court Reporters
Percent change in employment, projected 2010-20

Total, All Occupations	14%
Court Reporters	14%
Legal Occupations	11%

Note: All Occupations includes all occupations in the U.S. Economy.
Source: U.S. Bureau of Labor Statistics, Employment Projections program

Employment of court reporters is expected to grow by 14 percent from 2010 to 2020, as fast as the average for all occupations. Demand for court reporter services will be influenced by new federal legislation requiring increased captioning for the Internet and other technologies.

Reporters will increasingly be needed for captioning outside of legal proceedings. All new television programming will continue to need closed captioning, while broadcasters are adding closed captioning to their online programming in order to comply with new federal regulations.

Growth of the elderly population will also increase demand for court reporters who provide Communication Access Real-Time Translation (CART) services and can accompany their clients to doctor's appointments, town hall meetings, and religious services. In addition, movie theaters and sports stadiums will provide closed captioning for disabled customers.

Employment growth may be negatively affected by the increased use of digital audio recording technology (DART). Some states have already replaced court reporters with this technology, while some others are currently assessing the reliability, accuracy, and costs associated with installing and maintaining recorders.

Even with the increased use of DART, however, court reporters will still be needed to verify, check, and supervise the production of the transcripts after the proceedings have been digitally recorded. Despite the cost-savings that may be associated with DART, some state and federal courts may still prefer the quality provided by highly-trained court reporters.

Job prospects

Job prospects for graduates of court reporting programs are expected to be very good. Many training programs report that nearly all graduates are able to find jobs. Those with experience and training in CART and real-time captioning will have the best job prospects.

Employment projections data for court reporters, 2010-20

Occupational Title	SOC Code	Employment, 2010	Projected Employment, 2020	Change, 2010-20	
				Percent	Numeric
Court Reporters	23-2091	22,000	25,100	14	3,100
SOURCE: U.S. Bureau of Labor Statistics, Employment Projections program					

Similar Occupations

This table shows a list of occupations with job duties that are similar to those of court reporters.

Occupation	Job Duties	Entry-Level Education	Median Annual Pay, May 2010
Interpreters and Translators	Interpreters and translators convert information from one language to another. Interpreters work in spoken or sign language, translators in written language.	Bachelor's degree	$43,300
Medical Transcriptionists	Medical transcriptionists listen to voice recordings that physicians and other health professionals make and convert them into written reports. They interpret medical terminology and abbreviations in preparing patients' medical histories, discharge summaries, and other documents.	Postsecondary non-degree award	$32,900

Contacts for More Information

For more information on becoming a court reporter, including training programs and certification as a Register Professional Reporters, visit National Court Reporters Association

For more information on certification and legal resources, as well as becoming an electronic/digital reporter, visit American Association of Electronic Reporters

For more information on voice writing and certification, visit National Verbatim Reporters Association

Suggested citation:

Bureau of Labor Statistics, U.S. Department of Labor, Occupational Outlook Handbook, 2012-13 Edition, Court Reporters, on the Internet at http://www.bls.gov/ooh/legal/court-reporters.htm .

Judges, Mediators, and Hearing Officers

Quick Facts: Judges, Mediators, and Hearing Officers	
2010 Median Pay	$91,880 per year $44.17 per hour
Entry-Level Education	See How to Become One
Work Experience in a Related Occupation	See How to Become One
On-the-job Training	See How to Become One
Number of Jobs, 2010	62,700
Job Outlook, 2010-20	7% (Slower than average)
Employment Change, 2010-20	4,600

What Judges, Mediators, and Hearing Officers Do

Judges, mediators, and hearing officers apply the law to court cases and oversee the legal process in courts. They also resolve administrative disputes and facilitate negotiations between opposing parties.

Duties

Judges, mediators, and hearing officers typically do the following:

- Research legal issues
- Read and evaluate information from documents such as motions, claim applications, or records
- Preside over hearings and listen to or read arguments by opposing parties
- Determine if the information presented supports the charge, claim, or dispute
- Decide if the procedure is being conducted according to the rules and law
- Analyze, research, and apply laws, regulations, or precedents to reach judgments, conclusions, or agreements
- Write opinions, decisions, or instructions regarding the case, claim, or dispute

Judges commonly preside over trials or hearings of cases regarding nearly every aspect of society, from individual traffic offenses to issues concerning the rights of large corporations. Judges listen to arguments and determine whether the evidence presented deserves a trial. In criminal cases, judges may decide that people charged with crimes should be held in jail until the trial, or they may set conditions for their release. They also approve search and arrest warrants.

Judges interpret the law to determine how a trial will proceed, which is particularly important when unusual circumstances arise for which standard procedures have not been established. They ensure that hearings and trials are conducted fairly and the legal rights of all involved parties are protected.

In trials in which juries are selected to decide the case, judges instruct jurors on applicable laws and direct them to consider the facts from the evidence. For other trials, judges decide the case. A judge who determines guilt in criminal cases may impose a sentence or penalty on the guilty party. In civil cases, the judge may award relief, such as compensation for damages, to the parties who win the lawsuit.

Some judges, such as appellate court judges, review decisions and records made by lower courts, and make decisions based on lawyers' written and oral arguments.

Judges use various forms of technology, such as electronic databases and software, to manage cases and prepare for trials. In some cases, a judge also may manage the court's administrative and clerical staff.

The following are examples of types of judges, mediators, and hearing officers:

Judges, magistrate judges, and magistrates preside over trials or hearings. They typically work in local, state, and federal courts.

In local and state court systems, they have a variety of titles, such as **municipal court judge, county court judge, magistrate**, and **justice of the peace**. Traffic violations, misdemeanors, small-claims cases, and pretrial hearings make up the bulk of these judges' work.

In federal and state court systems, **general trial court judges** have authority over any case in their system. **Appellate court judges** rule on a small number of cases by reviewing decisions of the lower courts and lawyers' written and oral arguments.

Hearing officers, also known as **administrative law judges** or **adjudicators,** usually work for government agencies. They decide many issues, such as if a person is eligible for workers' compensation benefits, or if employment discrimination occurred.

Arbitrators, mediators, or conciliators help opposing parties settle disputes outside of court. They hold private, confidential hearings, which are less formal than a court trial.

Arbitrators are usually attorneys or business people with expertise in a particular field. They hear and decide disputes between opposing parties as an impartial third party. When arbitration is required, if one side is not happy with the decision, they can still take the matter to court. Arbitration may also be voluntary, in which the opposing sides agree that whatever the arbitrator decides will be a final, binding decision.

Mediators are neutral parties who help people resolve their disputes. Mediators suggest solutions, but they do not make binding decisions. If the opposing sides cannot reach a settlement with the

Judges, mediators, and hearing officers apply the law to resolve disputes and facilitate negotiations between parties.

mediator's help, they are free to pursue other options.

Conciliators are similar to mediators. Their role is to help guide opposing sides to a settlement. The opposing sides must decide in advance if they will be bound by the conciliator's recommendations.

Work Environment

Judges, mediators, and hearing officers held about 62,700 jobs in 2010, and most were employed by local, state, and federal governments. Some arbitrators, mediators, and conciliators work for state and local governments. The following industries employed the most judges, mediators, and hearing officers in 2010:

State government, excluding education and hospitals	36%
Local government, excluding education and hospitals	28
Federal government, excluding postal service	7
Professional, scientific, and technical services	3

Judges, mediators, and hearing officers do most of their work in offices and courtrooms. Their jobs can be demanding because they must sit in the same position in the court or hearing room for long periods and give undivided attention to the process.

Arbitrators, mediators, and conciliators usually work in private offices or meeting rooms. They may travel to a neutral site chosen for negotiations.

Work Schedules

Most judges, mediators, and hearing officers work full time, but many often work longer hours to prepare for hearings. Some judges work part time and divide their time between their judicial responsibilities and other careers.

How to Become a Judge, Mediator, or Hearing Officer

Judges, magistrate judges, magistrates, and administrative law judges are often required to have a law degree and work experience as a lawyer. For more information on how to become a lawyer, see the profile on lawyers .

Additionally, most judges and magistrates must be either appointed or elected into judge positions, a procedure that often takes political support. Many local and state judges are appointed to serve fixed renewable terms, ranging from 4 years to 14 years. A few judges, such as appellate court judges, are appointed for life. Judicial nominating commissions screen candidates for judgeships in many states and for some federal judgeships. Some local and state judges are elected to a specific term, commonly 4 years, in an election process.

Arbitrators, mediators, and conciliators learn their skills through education, training, or work experience.

Education

For most jobs as a local, state, or federal judge, a law degree is necessary. Getting a law degree usually takes 7 years of full-time study after high school—4 years of undergraduate study, followed by 3 years of law school. Law degree programs include courses such as constitutional law, contracts, property law, civil procedure, and legal writing.

In some states, administrative law judges and other hearing officials do not have to be lawyers. However, federal administrative law judges must be lawyers and must pass a competitive exam from the U.S. Office of Personnel Management.

For mediators, arbitrators, and conciliators, education is one pathway. They can take a certificate program in conflict resolution at a college or university, a 2-year master's degree in dispute resolution or conflict management, or get a doctoral degree through a 4-year or 5-year program. Many mediators have a law degree, but master's

degrees in public policy, law, and related fields also provide good backgrounds.

Work Experience

Most judges, mediators, and hearing officers get their skills through years of experience as practicing lawyers. About 40 states allow those who are not lawyers to hold limited-jurisdiction judgeships, but opportunities are better for those with law experience.

Arbitrators, mediators, and conciliators are usually lawyers or business professionals with expertise in a particular field, such as construction or insurance. They need to have knowledge of that industry and be able to relate well to people from different cultures and backgrounds.

Training

All states have some type of orientation for newly elected or appointed judges. The Federal Judicial Center , American Bar Association , National Judicial College , and National Center for State Courts provide judicial education and training for judges and other judicial branch personnel.

More than half of all states, as well as Puerto Rico, require judges to take continuing education courses while serving on the bench. General and continuing education courses usually last from a few days to 3 weeks.

Training for arbitrators, mediators, and conciliators is available through independent mediation programs, national and local mediation membership organizations, and postsecondary schools. To practice in state-funded or court-funded mediation programs, mediators must usually meet specific training or experience standards, which vary by state and court. Most mediators complete a 40-hour basic course and a 20-hour advanced training course. Some people get training by volunteering at a community mediation center or by co-mediating cases with an experienced mediator.

Licenses

Judges who are lawyers already hold a license.

Federal administrative law judges must be licensed to practice law.

For mediators, arbitrators, and conciliators, no national license exists. State requirements vary widely. Some states require arbitrators to be experienced lawyers.

Advancement

Advancement for some judicial workers means moving to courts with a broader jurisdiction. Advancement for various hearing officers includes taking on more complex cases, starting businesses, practicing law, or becoming district court judges.

Important Qualities

Critical-reasoning skills. Judges, mediators, and hearing officers must apply rules of law. They cannot let their own personal assumptions interfere with the proceedings. For example, they must base their decisions on specific meanings of the law when evaluating and deciding whether a person is a threat to others and must be sent to jail.

Decision-making skills. Judges, mediators, and hearing officers must be able to weigh the facts, apply the law or rules, and make a decision relatively quickly.

Listening skills. Judges, mediators, and hearing officers must pay close attention to what is being said in order to evaluate information.

Reading comprehension. Judges, mediators, and hearing officers must be able to evaluate and distinguish the important facts from large amounts of complex information.

Writing skills. Judges, mediators, and hearing officers write recommendations or decisions on appeals or disputes. They must be able to write their decisions clearly so that all sides understand the decision.

Pay

Judges, Mediators, and Hearing Officers
Median annual wages, May 2010

Judges, Magistrate Judges, and Magistrates	$119,270
Judges, Mediators, and Hearing Officers	$91,880
Administrative Law Judges, Adjudicators, and Hearing Officers	$85,500
Arbitrators, Mediators, and Conciliators	$55,800
Total, All Occupations	$33,840

Note: All Occupations includes all occupations in the U.S. Economy.
Source: U.S. Bureau of Labor Statistics, Occupational Employment Statistics

The median annual wage of judges, mediators and hearing officers was $91,880 in May 2010. The median wage is the wage at which half the workers in an occupation earned more than that amount and half earned less. The lowest 10 percent earned less than $35,400, and the top 10 percent earned more than $164,510.

The median wages for judges, mediators, and hearing officer occupations in May 2010 were the following:

- $119,270 for judges, magistrate judges, and magistrates
- $85,500 for administrative law judges, adjudicators, and hearing officers
- $55,800 for arbitrators, mediators, and conciliators

According to the Administrative Office of the U.S. Courts, in the federal court system, the Chief Justice of the U.S. Supreme Court earned $223,500, and the Associate Justices averaged $213,900. Federal circuit judges earned an average of $184,500 a year. District court judges and judges in the Court of Federal Claims and the Court of International Trade had average salaries of $174,000.

Although federal judges' pay has not changed since January 2009, the average pay for state judges has increased.

According to a 2011 survey by the National Center for State Courts, the median annual wage of chief justices of the states' highest courts was $152,500 and ranged from $115,160 to $228,856. The median annual wage of associate justices of the states' highest courts was $146,917 and ranged from $112,530 to $218,237. The median annual wage of state intermediate appellate court judges was $140,732 and ranged from $105,050 to $204,599. The median annual wage of state judges of general jurisdiction trial courts was $132,500 and ranged from $104,170 to $178,835.

Most judges, mediators, and hearing officers work full time, and many often work longer hours to prepare for case hearings. Some judges work part time and divide their time between their judicial responsibilities and other careers.

Job Outlook

Judges, Mediators, and Hearing Officers
Percent change in employment, projected 2010-20

Arbitrators, Mediators, and Conciliators	15%
Total, All Occupations	14%
Judges, Magistrate Judges, and Magistrates	9%
Judges, Mediators, and Hearing Officers	7%
Administrative Law Judges, Adjudicators, and Hearing Officers	0%

Note: All Occupations includes all occupations in the U.S. Economy.
Source: U.S. Bureau of Labor Statistics, Employment Projections program

Employment of judges, mediators, and hearing officers is expected to grow by 7 percent from 2010 to 2020, slower than the average for all occupations. The number of federal and state judgeships is expected to experience little to no change because nearly every new position for a judge must be authorized and approved by legislature.

Budgetary constraints in federal, state, and local governments are expected to limit the employment growth of judges, magistrates, and administrative law judges, despite the continued need for these workers to settle disputes.

Arbitration and other alternatives to litigation are often faster and less expensive than trials. However, employment growth of arbitrators, mediators, and conciliators is expected to be moderate. This is primarily because conflicting parties often opt for court proceedings or try to resolve the problem on their own without a judge or mediator.

Job Prospects

The prestige associated with becoming a judge will ensure continued competition for these positions. Most job openings will arise as a result of judges, mediators, and hearing officers leaving the occupations because of retirement, teaching, or expiration of elected term.

As with judges, turnover is low for arbitrators, mediators, and conciliators, so opportunities may be limited. Those who specialize in one or more areas of arbitration, mediation, or conciliation should have the best job opportunities.

Employment projections data for judges, mediators, and hearing officers, 2010-20

Occupational Title	SOC Code	Employment, 2010	Projected Employment, 2020	Change, 2010-20 Percent	Change, 2010-20 Numeric
Judges, Mediators, and Hearing Officers	—	62,700	67,300	7	4,600
Administrative Law Judges, Adjudicators, and Hearing Officers	23-1021	19,200	19,200	0	0
Arbitrators, Mediators, and Conciliators	23-1022	9,400	10,900	15	1,500
Judges, Magistrate Judges, and Magistrates	23-1023	34,000	37,200	9	3,100
SOURCE: U.S. Bureau of Labor Statistics, Employment Projections program					

Similar Occupations

This table shows a list of occupations with job duties that are similar to those of judges, mediators, and hearing officers.

Occupation	Job Duties	Entry-Level Education	Median Annual Pay, May 2010
Lawyers	Lawyers advise and represent individuals, businesses, or government agencies on legal issues or disputes.	Doctoral or professional degree	$112,760

Paralegals and Legal Assistants	Paralegals and legal assistants do a variety of tasks to support lawyers, including maintaining and organizing files, conducting legal research, and drafting documents.	Associate's degree	$46,680
Private Detectives and Investigators	Private detectives and investigators find facts and analyze information about legal, financial, and personal matters. They offer many services, including verifying people's backgrounds, tracing missing persons, investigating computer crimes, and protecting celebrities.	Some college, no degree	$42,870

Contacts for More Information

For more information about state courts and judgeships, visit National Center for State Courts

For more information about federal judges, visit Administrative Office of the United States Courts

For more information about arbitrators, mediators, and conciliators, visit American Arbitration Association

For more information about judicial education and training for judges and other judicial branch personnel, visit Federal Judicial Center ,American Bar Association ,National Judicial College

Suggested citation:

Bureau of Labor Statistics, U.S. Department of Labor, Occupational Outlook Handbook, 2012-13 Edition, Judges, Mediators, and Hearing Officers, on the Internet at http://www.bls.gov/ooh/legal/judges-mediators-and-hearing-officers.htm .

Lawyers

Quick Facts: Lawyers	
2010 Median Pay	$112,760 per year $54.21 per hour
Entry-Level Education	Doctoral or professional degree
Work Experience in a Related Occupation	None
On-the-job Training	None
Number of Jobs, 2010	728,200
Job Outlook, 2010-20	10% (About as fast as average)
Employment Change, 2010-20	73,600

What Lawyers Do

Lawyers advise and represent individuals, businesses, or government agencies on legal issues or disputes.

Duties

Lawyers typically do the following:

- Advise and represent clients in courts, before government agencies, or in private legal matters
- Communicate with their clients and others
- Conduct research and analysis of legal problems
- Interpret laws, rulings, and regulations for individuals and businesses
- Present facts in writing or verbally to their clients or others and argue on their behalf
- Prepare and file legal documents, such as lawsuits, appeals, wills, contracts, and deeds

Lawyers, also called attorneys, act as both advocates and advisors.

As advocates, they represent one of the parties in criminal and civil trials by presenting evidence and arguing in court to support their client.

As advisors, lawyers counsel their clients about their legal rights and obligations and suggest courses of action in business and personal matters. All attorneys research the intent of laws and judicial decisions and apply the laws to the specific circumstances that their clients face.

To prepare for cases more efficiently, lawyers increasingly use the Internet, online legal databases, and virtual law libraries. Lawyers also often oversee the work of support staff, such as paralegals and legal assistants. For more information about legal support staff, see the profile on paralegals and legal assistants .

Lawyers may have different titles and different duties, depending on where they work.

Lawyers advise and represent individuals, businesses, or government agencies on legal issues or disputes.

Criminal law attorneys are also known as **prosecutors** or **defense attorneys**. **Prosecutors** work for the government to file a lawsuit, or charge, against an individual or corporation accused of violating the law.

Defense attorneys work for either individuals or the government (as public defenders) to represent, or defend, the accused.

Government counsels commonly work in government agencies. They write and interpret laws and regulations and set up procedures to enforce them. Government counsels also write legal reviews on agencies' decisions. They argue civil and criminal cases on behalf of the government.

Corporate counsels, also called **in-house counsels**, are lawyers who work for corporations. They advise a corporation's executives about legal issues related to the corporation's business activities. These issues might involve patents, government regulations, contracts with other companies, property interests, taxes, or collective-bargaining agreements with unions.

Legal aid lawyers work for private, nonprofit organizations for disadvantaged people. They generally handle civil cases, such as those about leases, job discrimination, and wage disputes, rather than criminal cases.

Lawyers often specialize in a particular area. The following are some examples of types of lawyers:

Environmental lawyers deal with issues and regulations that are related to the environment. They might represent advocacy groups, waste disposal companies, or government agencies to make sure they comply with the relevant laws.

Tax lawyers handle a variety of tax-related issues for individuals and corporations. Tax lawyers may help clients navigate complex tax regulations so that they pay the appropriate tax on income, profits, property, and so on. For example, they might advise a corporation on how much tax it needs to pay from profits made in different states to comply with the Internal Revenue Service's (IRS) rules.

Intellectual property lawyers deal with the laws related to inventions, patents, trademarks, and creative works such as music, books, and movies. An intellectual property lawyer might advise a client about whether it is okay to use published material in the client's forthcoming book.

Family lawyers handle a variety of legal issues that pertain to the family. They may advise clients regarding divorce, child custody, and adoption proceedings.

Securities lawyers work on legal issues arising from the buying and sell of stocks, ensuring that all disclosure requirements are met. They may advise corporations that are interested in listing in the stock exchange through an initial public offering (IPO) or buying shares in another corporation.

Litigation lawyers handle all lawsuits and disputes between parties. These could be contract disputes, personal injury disputes, or real estate and property disputes. Litigation lawyers may specialize in a certain area, such as personal injury law, or may be a general lawyer for all types of disputes and lawsuits.

Some attorneys become teachers in law schools. For more information on law school professors, see the profile on postsecondary teachers .

Work Environment

Lawyers held about 728,200 jobs in 2010. A majority of lawyers work in private or corporate legal offices. Some are employed in local, state and federal governments. About 22 percent of lawyers are self-employed.

The following industries employed the most lawyers in 2010:

Legal services	51%
Government	18
Finance and insurance	3
Management of companies and enterprises	2

Lawyers work mostly in offices. However, some travel to attend meetings with clients at various locations, such as homes, hospitals, or prisons. Some lawyers gather evidence; others appear before courts. Lawyers who represent clients in courts may face heavy pressure during trials.

Work Schedules

The majority of lawyers work full time, and many work long hours. Lawyers who are in private practice or those who work in large firms often work long hours conducting research and preparing or reviewing documents.

How to Become a Lawyer

Formal requirements to become a lawyer usually include a 4-year college degree, 3 years of law school, and passing a written bar examination. However, some requirements vary by state.

Education

Becoming a lawyer usually takes 7 years of full-time study after high school—4 years of undergraduate study followed by 3 years of law school. Most states and jurisdictions require future lawyers to complete a juris doctor (J.D.) degree from a law school accredited by the American Bar Association (ABA). ABA accreditation signifies that the law school—particularly its curricula and faculty—meets certain standards.

A bachelor's degree is required for entry into most law schools, and courses in English, public speaking, government, history, economics, and mathematics are useful.

Many law schools, particularly those approved by the ABA, also require applicants to take the Law School Admission Test (LSAT), a test that measures applicants' aptitude for the study of law.

As of August 2011, ABA had approved 200 law schools; others were approved by state authorities only. Admission to law schools—especially the most prestigious ones—is competitive because the number of applicants greatly exceeds the number that can be admitted each year.

A J.D. degree program includes courses such as constitutional law, contracts, property law, civil procedure, and legal writing. Law students may choose specialized courses in areas such as tax, labor, or corporate law.

Law students often gain practical experience by participating in school-sponsored legal clinics, in a school's moot court competitions, in practice trials under the supervision of experienced lawyers and judges, and through research and writing on legal issues for a school's law journals.

Part-time or summer jobs in law firms, government agencies, and corporate legal departments also provide valuable experience. These experiences can help law students decide what kind of legal work they want to focus on in their careers. These experiences may also lead directly to a job after graduation.

Licenses

Becoming licensed as a lawyer is called being "admitted to the bar" and licensing exams are called "bar exams."

To practice law in any state, a person must be admitted to its bar under rules established by the jurisdiction's highest court. The requirements vary by individual states and jurisdictions. For more details on individual state and jurisdiction requirements, visit the National Conference of Bar Examiners.

Most states require that applicants graduate from an ABA-accredited law school, pass one or more written bar exams, and be found by an admitting board to have the character to represent and advise others. Lawyers who want to practice in more than one state must often take separate bar exams in each state.

Training

After graduation, lawyers must keep informed about legal developments that affect their practices. In 2011, 45 states required lawyers to participate in continuing legal education either every year or every 3 years.

Many law schools and state and local bar associations provide continuing legal education courses that help lawyers stay current with recent developments. Courses vary by state and are generally related to the practice of law, such as legal ethics, taxes and tax fraud, and health care. Some states allow lawyers to take their continuing education credits through online courses.

Advancement

Newly hired attorneys usually start as associates and work with more experienced lawyers or judges. After several years, some lawyers may be admitted to partnership and become partial owners of the firm they work for. Some lawyers go into practice for themselves or move to the legal department of a large corporation.

A few experienced lawyers may be nominated or elected to judgeships. Other lawyers may become full-time law school faculty or administrators. For more information about judges and law school faculty, see the profile on judges, mediators, and hearing officers , and the profile on postsecondary teachers .

Important Qualities

Analytical skills. Lawyers help their clients resolve problems or issues. As a result, they must be able to analyze large amounts of information, determine relevant facts, and propose viable solutions.

Interpersonal skills. Lawyers must win the respect and confidence of their clients by building a trusting relationship so that clients feel comfortable and share personal information related to their case.

Problem-solving skills. Lawyers must separate their emotions and prejudice from their clients' problems and objectively evaluate the matter. Therefore, good problem-solving skills are important for lawyers to prepare the best defense or recommendation.

Research skills. Preparing legal advice or representation for a client commonly requires substantial research. All lawyers need to be able to find what applicable laws and regulations apply to a specific matter.

Speaking skills. Lawyers are hired by their clients to speak on their behalf. Lawyers must be able to clearly present and explain evidence to a judge and jury.

Writing skills. Lawyers need to be precise and specific when preparing documents, such as wills, trusts, and powers of attorney.

Pay

Lawyers
Median annual wages, May 2010

Lawyers	$112,760
Legal Occupations	$74,580
Total, All Occupations	$33,840

Note: All Occupations includes all occupations in the U.S. Economy.
Source: U.S. Bureau of Labor Statistics, Occupational Employment Statistics

The median annual wage of lawyers was $112,760 in May 2010. The median wage is the wage at which half the workers in an occupation earned more than that amount and half earned less. The lowest 10 percent earned less than $54,130, and the top 10 percent earned more than $166,400.

Salaries of experienced lawyers vary widely according to the type, size, and location of their employer. Lawyers who own their own practices usually earn less than those who are partners in law firms.

The majority of lawyers work full time and many work long hours. Lawyers who are in private practice or those who work in large firms often work long hours conducting research and preparing or reviewing documents.

Job Outlook

Lawyers
Percent change in employment, projected 2010-20

Total, All Occupations	14%
Legal Occupations	11%
Lawyers	10%

Note: All Occupations includes all occupations in the U.S. Economy.
Source: U.S. Bureau of Labor Statistics, Employment Projections program

Employment of lawyers is expected to grow by 10 percent from 2010 to 2020, about as fast as the average for all occupations. Demand for legal work will continue as individuals, businesses, and all levels of government will need legal services in many areas.

However, growth in demand for lawyers will be constrained as businesses increasingly use large accounting firms and paralegals to do some of the same tasks that lawyers do. For example, accounting firms may provide employee-benefit counseling, process documents, or handle various other services that law firms previously handled.

Lawyers will continue to be needed in the federal government to prosecute or defend civil cases on behalf of the United States, prosecute criminal cases brought by the federal government, and collect money owed to the federal government. However, budgetary constraints at all levels of government, including federal, will moderate employment growth.

Job Prospects

Competition should continue to be strong because more students are graduating from law school each year than there are jobs available. As in the past, some recent law school graduates who have been unable to find permanent positions are turning to the growing number of temporary staffing firms that place attorneys in short-term jobs. This service allows companies to hire lawyers "as-needed" and permits beginning lawyers to develop practical skills.

Job opportunities are typically affected by cyclical swings in the economy. During recessions, demand declines for some discretionary legal services, such as planning estates, drafting wills, and handling real estate transactions. Also, corporations are less likely to litigate cases when declining sales and profits restrict their budgets. Some corporations and law firms may even cut staff to contain costs until business improves.

Because of the strong competition, a law graduate's willingness to relocate and work experience are becoming more important. However, to be licensed in another state, a lawyer may have to take an additional state bar examination.

Employment projections data for lawyers, 2010-20

Occupational Title	SOC Code	Employment, 2010	Projected Employment, 2020	Change, 2010-20	
				Percent	Numeric
Lawyers	23-1011	728,200	801,800	10	73,600
SOURCE: U.S. Bureau of Labor Statistics, Employment Projections program					

Similar Occupations

This table shows a list of occupations with job duties that are similar to those of lawyers.

Occupation	Job Duties	Entry-Level Education	Median Annual Pay, May 2010
Judges, Mediators, and Hearing Officers	Judges, mediators, and hearing officers apply the law to court cases and oversee the legal process in courts. They also resolve administrative disputes and facilitate negotiations between opposing parties.	See How to Become One	$91,880
Paralegals and Legal Assistants	Paralegals and legal assistants do a variety of tasks to support lawyers, including maintaining and organizing files, conducting legal research, and drafting documents.	Associate's degree	$46,680
Postsecondary Teachers	Postsecondary teachers instruct students in a wide variety of academic and vocational subjects beyond the high school level. They also conduct research and publish scholarly papers and books.	Doctoral or professional degree	$62,050

Contacts for More Information

For more information about law schools and a career in law, visit American Bar Association ,National Association for Law Placement

For more information about the Law School Admission Test (LSAT) and the law school application process, visit Law School Admission Council

For a list of state and jurisdiction admission bar offices, visit National Conference of Bar Examiners

The requirements for admission to the bar in a particular state or other jurisdiction may be obtained at the state capital, from the clerk of the Supreme Court, or from the administrator of the State Board of Bar Examiners.

Suggested citation:

Bureau of Labor Statistics, U.S. Department of Labor, Occupational Outlook Handbook, 2012-13 Edition, Lawyers, on the Internet at http://www.bls.gov/ooh/legal/lawyers.htm .

Paralegals and Legal Assistants

Quick Facts: Paralegals and Legal Assistants	
2010 Median Pay	$46,680 per year $22.44 per hour
Entry-Level Education	Associate's degree
Work Experience in a Related Occupation	None
On-the-job Training	None
Number of Jobs, 2010	256,000
Job Outlook, 2010-20	18% (About as fast as average)
Employment Change, 2010-20	46,900

What Paralegals and Legal Assistants Do

Paralegals and legal assistants do a variety of tasks to support lawyers, including maintaining and organizing files, conducting legal research, and drafting documents.

Duties

Paralegals and legal assistants typically do the following:

- Investigate the facts of a case
- Conduct research on relevant laws, regulations, and legal articles
- Organize and present the information
- Keep information related to cases or transactions in computer databases
- Write reports to help lawyers prepare for trials
- Draft correspondence and other documents, such as contracts and mortgages
- Get affidavits and other formal statements that may be used as evidence in court
- Help lawyers during trials

Paralegals and legal assistants help lawyers prepare for hearings, trials, and corporate meetings. However, their specific duties may vary depending on the size of the firm or organization.

In smaller firms, paralegals duties tend to vary more. In addition to reviewing and organizing information, paralegals may prepare written reports that help lawyers determine how to handle their cases. If lawyers decide to file lawsuits on behalf of clients, paralegals may help prepare the legal arguments and draft documents to be filed with the court.

In larger organizations, paralegals work mostly on a particular phase of a case, rather than handling a case from beginning to end. For example, a litigation paralegal might only review legal material for internal use, maintain reference files, conduct research for lawyers, and collect and organize evidence for hearings. Litigation paralegals often do not attend trials, but might prepare trial documents or draft settlement agreements.

Law firms increasingly use technology and computer software for managing documents and preparing for trials. Paralegals use computer software to draft and index documents and prepare presentations. In addition, paralegals must be familiar with electronic database management and be up to date on the latest software used for electronic discovery. Electronic discovery refers to all electronic materials that are related to a trial, such as emails, data, documents, accounting databases, and websites.

Paralegals can assume more responsibilities by specializing in areas such as litigation, personal injury, corporate law, criminal law, employee benefits, intellectual property, bankruptcy, immigration, family law, and real estate. In addition, experienced paralegals may assume supervisory responsibilities, such as overseeing team projects or delegating work to other paralegals.

Paralegal tasks may differ depending on the type of department or the size of the law firm they work for.

The following are examples of types of paralegals:

Corporate paralegals often help lawyers prepare employee contracts, shareholder agreements, stock-option plans, and companies' annual financial reports. Corporate paralegals may monitor and review government regulations to ensure that the corporation is aware of new legal requirements.

Litigation paralegals maintain documents received from clients, conduct research for lawyers, and retrieve and organize evidence for use at depositions and trials.

Work Environment

Paralegals and legal assistants held about 256,000 jobs in May 2010. Paralegals are found in all types of organizations, but most work for law firms, corporate legal departments, and government agencies. The following industries employed the most paralegals and legal assistants in 2010:

Legal services	70%
State and local government, excluding education and hospitals	9
Federal government	6
Finance and insurance	4

Paralegals and legal assistants perform a variety of tasks to support their attorneys.

Paralegals do most of their work in offices and law libraries. Occasionally, they travel to gather information and do other tasks.

Work Schedules

Paralegals who work for law firms, corporations, and government agencies usually work full time. Although most paralegals work year round, some are temporarily employed during busy times of the year. Paralegals who work for law firms may work very long hours and overtime to meet deadlines.

How to Become a Paralegal or Legal Assistant

Most paralegals and legal assistants have an associate's degree in paralegal studies, or a bachelor's degree in another field and a certificate in paralegal studies. In some cases, employers may hire college graduates with a bachelor's degree but no legal experience or education and train them on the job.

Education

There are several paths to become a paralegal. Candidates can enroll in a community college paralegal program to earn an associate's degree. A small number of schools also offer bachelor's and master's degrees in paralegal studies. Those who already have a bachelor's degree in another subject can earn a certificate in paralegal studies. Finally, some employers hire entry-level paralegals without any experience or education in paralegal studies and train them on the job, though these jobs typically require a bachelor's degree.

Associate's and bachelor's degree programs in paralegal studies usually combine paralegal training, such as courses in legal research and the legal applications of computers, with other academic subjects. Most certificate programs provide this intensive paralegal training for people who already hold college degrees. Some certificate programs only take a few months to complete.

More than 1,000 colleges and universities offer formal paralegal training programs. However, only about 270 paralegal programs are approved by the American Bar Association (ABA).

Many paralegal training programs also offer an internship, in which students gain practical experience by working for several months in a private law firm, the office of a public defender or attorney general, a corporate legal department, a legal aid organization, or a government agency. Internship experience helps students improve their technical skills and can enhance their employment prospects.

Training

Employers sometimes hire college graduates with no legal experience or education and train them on the job. In these cases, the new employee often has experience in a technical field that is useful to law firms, such tax preparation or criminal justice.

Work Experience

In many cases, employers prefer candidates who have at least one year of experience in a law firm or other office setting. In addition, a technical understanding of a specific legal specialty can be helpful. For example, a personal-injury law firm may desire a paralegal with a background in nursing or health administration.

Work experience in a law firm or other office setting is particularly important for people who do not have formal paralegal training.

Certification

Although not required by most employers, earning voluntary certification may help applicants get a paralegal job. Many national and local paralegal organizations offer voluntary paralegal certifications to students able to pass an exam. Other organizations offer voluntary paralegal certifications for paralegals who meet certain experience and education criteria. For more information about paralegal certifications, see the Contacts for More Info section.

Advancement

Paralegals usually are given more responsibilities and require less supervision as they gain work experience. Experienced paralegals may supervise and delegate assignments to other paralegals and clerical staff.

Important Qualities

Computer skills. Paralegals need to be familiar with using computers for legal research and litigation support. They also use computer programs for organizing and maintaining important documents.

Interpersonal skills. Paralegals spend most of their time working with clients or other professionals and must be able to develop good relationships. They must make clients feel comfortable sharing personal information related to their cases.

Organizational skills. Paralegals may be responsible for many cases at one time. They must adapt quickly to changing deadlines.

Research skills. Paralegals need good research and investigative skills to conduct legal research.

Speaking and writing skills. Paralegals must be able to document and present their research and related information to their supervising attorney.

Pay

Paralegals and Legal Assistants
Median annual wages, May 2010

Legal Occupations	$74,580
Paralegals and Legal Assistants	$46,680
Total, All Occupations	$33,840

Note: All Occupations includes all occupations in the U.S. Economy.
Source: U.S. Bureau of Labor Statistics, Occupational Employment Statistics

The median annual wage of paralegals and legal assistants was $46,680 in May 2010. The median wage is the wage at which half the workers in an occupation earned more than that amount and half earned less. The lowest 10 percent earned less than $29,460, and the top 10 percent earned more than $74,870.

In general, paralegals that work for large law firms or in large cities earn more than those who work for smaller firms or in smaller cities.

Paralegals who work for law firms, corporations, and government agencies usually work full time. Although most paralegals work year round, some are temporarily employed during busy times of the year. Paralegals who work for law firms may work very long hours and overtime to meet deadlines.

Job Outlook

Paralegals and Legal Assistants
Percent change in employment, projected 2010-20

Paralegals and Legal Assistants	18%
Total, All Occupations	14%
Legal Occupations	11%

Note: All Occupations includes all occupations in the U.S. Economy.
Source: U.S. Bureau of Labor Statistics, Employment Projections program

Employment of paralegals and legal assistants is expected to grow by 18 percent from 2010 to 2020, about as fast as the average for all occupations.

As employers try to reduce costs and increase the efficiency of legal services, they are expected to hire more paralegals and legal assistants. Following the cutbacks experienced during the recent recession, some law firms are rebuilding their support staff by hiring paralegals. Paralegals can be a less costly alternative to lawyers and perform a wider variety of duties, including tasks once done by lawyers. This will cause an increase in demand for paralegals and legal assistants.

In addition, paralegals' work is less likely to be offshored than that of other legal workers. Paralegals routinely file and store important documents and work with lawyers to gather documents for important transactions, hearings, and depositions. They frequently handle documents and take statements, which must be done in person.

Law firms will continue to be the largest employers of paralegals, but many large corporations are increasing their in-house legal departments to cut costs. For many companies, the high cost of lawyers and their support staff makes it much more economical to have an in-house legal department rather than to retain outside counsel. This will lead to an increase in the demand of legal workers in a variety of settings, such as finance and insurance firms, consulting firms, and health care providers.

However, demand for paralegals could be limited by law firms' work loads. When work is slow, lawyers may increase the number of hours they can bill a client by doing tasks that were previously delegated to paralegals. This may make a firm less likely to keep some paralegals on staff or hire new ones until the work load increases.

Job Prospects

This occupation attracts many applicants, and competition for jobs will be strong. Experienced, formally trained paralegals should have the best job prospects. In addition, many firms will prefer paralegals with experience and specialization in high-demand practice areas.

Employment projections data for paralegals and legal assistants, 2010-20

Occupational Title	SOC Code	Employment, 2010	Projected Employment, 2020	Change, 2010-20	
				Percent	Numeric
Paralegals and Legal Assistants	23-2011	256,000	302,900	18	46,900
SOURCE: U.S. Bureau of Labor Statistics, Employment Projections program					

Similar Occupations

This table shows a list of occupations with job duties that are similar to those of paralegals and legal assistants.

Occupation	Job Duties	Entry-Level Education	Median Annual Pay, May 2010
Claims Adjusters, Appraisers, Examiners, and Investigators	Claims adjusters, appraisers, examiners, and investigators evaluate insurance claims. They decide whether an insurance company must pay a claim, and if so, how much.	See How to Become One	$58,460
Lawyers	Lawyers advise and represent individuals, businesses, or government agencies on legal issues or disputes.	Doctoral or professional degree	$112,760
Occupational Health and Safety Specialists	Occupational health and safety specialists analyze many types of work environments and work procedures. Specialists inspect workplaces for adherence to regulations on safety, health, and the environment. They also design programs to prevent disease or injury to workers and damage to the environment.	Bachelor's degree	$64,660
Occupational Health and Safety Technicians	Occupational health and safety technicians collect data on the safety and health conditions of the workplace. Technicians work with occupational health and safety specialists in conducting tests and measuring hazards to help prevent harm to workers, property, the environment, and the general public.	High school diploma or equivalent	$45,330
Secretaries and Administrative Assistants	Secretaries and administrative assistants perform routine clerical and organizational tasks. They organize files, draft messages, schedule appointments, and support other staff.	High school diploma or equivalent	$34,660

Contacts for More Information

For more information about paralegal careers, visit American Bar Association , International Paralegal Management Association , Standing Committee on Paralegals, American Bar Association , American Alliance of Paralegals

For more information on the Certified Legal Assistant certification, schools that offer training programs in a specific State, and standards and guidelines for paralegals, visit NALA – The Association for Legal Assistants/Paralegals

For information on the Professional Paralegal certification, visit NALS – The Association for Legal Professionals

For information on the Paralegal Advanced Competency Exam, paralegal careers, and paralegal training programs visit National Federation of Paralegal Associations

Suggested citation:

Bureau of Labor Statistics, U.S. Department of Labor, Occupational Outlook Handbook, 2012-13 Edition, Paralegals and Legal Assistants, on the Internet at http://www.bls.gov/ooh/legal/paralegals-and-legal-assistants.htm .

Life, Physical, and Social Science Occupations

Agricultural and Food Science Technicians

Quick Facts: Agricultural and Food Science Technicians	
2010 Median Pay	$32,760 per year $15.75 per hour
Entry-Level Education	Associate's degree
Work Experience in a Related Occupation	None
On-the-job Training	None
Number of Jobs, 2010	21,300
Job Outlook, 2010-20	7% (Slower than average)
Employment Change, 2010-20	1,500

What Agricultural and Food Science Technicians Do

Under the supervision of scientists, agricultural and food science technicians measure and analyze the quality of food and agricultural products.

Duties

Specific duties of these technicians vary, depending on their specialty.

Agricultural technicians typically do the following:

- Follow protocols to prepare, analyze, and store crop or animal samples properly
- Examine animals and other specimens to determine the presence of diseases or other problems
- Measure ingredients used in testing or animal feed and other purposes

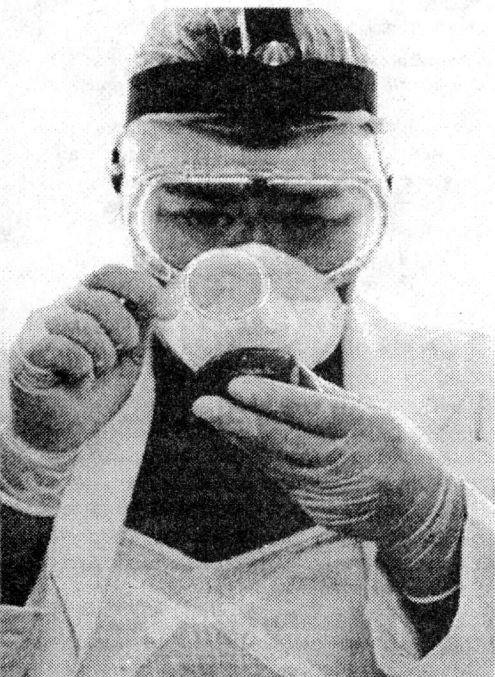

Agricultural and food science technicians measure and analyze the quality of food and agricultural products under the supervision of related scientists.

- Compile and analyze test results that go into charts, presentations, and reports
- Prepare and operate complex equipment to do laboratory tests

Food science technicians typically do the following:

- Prepare samples following established procedures
- Test food, food additives, and food containers to ensure they comply with established safety standards
- Help food scientists with food research, development, and quality control
- Analyze chemical properties of food to determine ingredients and formulas
- Compile and analyze test results that go into charts, presentations, and reports
- Keep a safe, sterile laboratory environment

Agricultural technicians who work in private industry focus on the condition of crops and animals, not on processed foods. These workers may prepare samples for analyses, ensure that samples meet proper safety standards, and test crops and animals for disease.

Food science technicians who work in private industry inspect food and crops, including processed food, to ensure the product is fit for distribution. A large portion of food science technicians' time is spent inspecting foodstuffs, chemicals, and additives to determine whether they are safe and have the proper combination of ingredients.

Agricultural and food science technicians who work for the federal government monitor regulatory compliance for the Food and Drug Administration (FDA), the Department of Agriculture , and other agencies. As a result of the recent passage of the FDA Food Safety Modernization Act, the frequency of food inspections has increased, along with improvements in performance standards.

Work Environment

Agricultural and food science technicians held about 21,300 jobs in 2010. The following industries employed the largest number of agricultural and food science technicians in 2010:

Colleges, universities, and professional schools; state, local, and private	27%
Support activities for agriculture and forestry	13
Scientific research and development services	8
Animal slaughtering and processing	7
Dairy product manufacturing	5

Technicians work in a variety of settings including offices, laboratories, and in processing plants. Technicians who work in processing plants may face unpleasant working conditions, such as noise from processing machinery.

How to Become an Agricultural or Food Science Technician

Agricultural and food science technicians typically need an associate's degree in animal science or a related field. Technicians who have only a high school diploma typically get more on-the-job training than do those with a college degree.

Education and Training

People interested in this occupation should take as many high school science and math classes as possible. A solid background in applied chemistry, physics, and math is vital.

Agricultural and food science technicians typically need an associate's degree in animal science or a related field from an accredited college or university. While in college, prospective technicians learn through a combination of classroom and hands-on learning, such as an internship.

A background in the biological sciences is important for food and agricultural technicians. Students should take courses in biology, chemistry, animal science, and agricultural engineering as part of their programs. Many schools offer internships, cooperative-education, and other experiential programs designed to enhance employment prospects.

Technicians with a high school diploma usually complete an extensive training program under the supervision of a more-experienced technician. These training programs can last a year or more.

Important Qualities

Analytical skills. Agricultural and food science technicians must conduct a variety of observations and on-site measurements, all of which require precision and accuracy.

Critical-thinking skills. Agricultural and food science technicians reach conclusions through sound reasoning and judgment. They determine how to improve food quality and must test products for a variety of safety standards.

Interpersonal skills. Agricultural and food science technicians need to work well with others. They may supervise agricultural and food science workers and receive instruction from scientists or specialists, so effective communication is critical.

Listening skills. Agricultural and food science technicians must follow instructions given to them by food scientists and agricultural engineers.

Speaking skills. Agricultural and food science technicians must give clear instructions to field and laboratory workers, who typically perform the tasks necessary for food quality testing.

Pay

Agricultural and Food Science Technicians
Median annual wages, May 2010

Life, Physical, and Social Science Technicians	$40,690
Total, All Occupations	$33,840
Agricultural and Food Science Technicians	$32,760

Note: All Occupations includes all occupations in the U.S. Economy.
Source: U.S. Bureau of Labor Statistics, Occupational Employment Statistics

The median annual wage of agricultural and food science technicians was $32,760 in May 2010. The median wage is the wage at which half the workers in an occupation earned more than that amount and half earned less. The lowest 10 percent earned less than $21,730, and the top 10 percent earned more than $52,600.

Median annual wages in the industries employing the largest number of agricultural and food science technicians in May 2010 were as follows:

Colleges, universities, and professional schools; state, local, and private	$35,020
Dairy product manufacturing	33,930
Scientific research and development services	33,220
Support activities for agriculture and forestry	29,190
Animal slaughtering and processing	26,500

Job Outlook

Agricultural and Food Science Technicians
Percent change in employment, projected 2010-20

Total, All Occupations	14%
Life, Physical, and Social Science Technicians	11%
Agricultural and Food Science Technicians	7%

Note: All Occupations includes all occupations in the U.S. Economy.
Source: U.S. Bureau of Labor Statistics, Employment Projections program

Employment of agricultural and food technicians is expected to grow by 7 percent from 2010 to 2020, slower than the average for all occupations. Increased awareness and enforcement of food safety regulations will increase inspection requirements and, therefore, demand for agricultural and food science technicians.

Most growth over the next 10 years is expected to be in federal food inspection jobs. Jobs in private industry will also grow, but at a more modest rate.

Employment projections data for agricultural and food science technicians, 2010-20

Occupational Title	SOC Code	Employment, 2010	Projected Employment, 2020	Change, 2010-20 Percent	Change, 2010-20 Numeric
Agricultural and Food Science Technicians	19-4011	21,300	22,800	7	1,500
SOURCE: U.S. Bureau of Labor Statistics, Employment Projections program					

Similar Occupations

This table shows a list of occupations with job duties that are similar to those of agricultural and food science technicians.

Occupation	Job Duties	Entry-Level Education	Median Annual Pay, May 2010
Agricultural and Food Scientists	Agricultural and food scientists work to ensure agricultural productivity and food safety.	See How to Become One	$58,450

Biological Technicians	Biological technicians help biological and medical scientists conduct laboratory tests and experiments.	Bachelor's degree	$39,020
Chemical Technicians	Chemical technicians use special instruments and techniques to help chemists and chemical engineers in researching, developing, and producing chemical products and processes.	Associate's degree	$42,040
Farmers, Ranchers, and Other Agricultural Managers	Farmers, ranchers, and other agricultural managers run establishments that produce crops, livestock, and dairy products.	High school diploma or equivalent	$60,750
Occupational Health and Safety Technicians	Occupational health and safety technicians collect data on the safety and health conditions of the workplace. Technicians work with occupational health and safety specialists in conducting tests and measuring hazards to help prevent harm to workers, property, the environment, and the general public.	High school diploma or equivalent	$45,330

Contacts for More Information

For more information about agricultural and soil science occupations, including certification, visit Soil Science Society of America

For more information about food and animal science occupations, including certifications, visit American Registry of Professional Animal Scientists

Suggested citation:

Bureau of Labor Statistics, U.S. Department of Labor, Occupational Outlook Handbook, 2012-13 Edition, Agricultural and Food Science Technicians, on the Internet at http://www.bls.gov/ooh/life-physical-and-social-science/agricultural-and-food-science-technicians.htm .

Agricultural and Food Scientists

Quick Facts: Agricultural and Food Scientists	
2010 Median Pay	$58,450 per year $28.10 per hour
Entry-Level Education	See How to Become One
Work Experience in a Related Occupation	None
On-the-job Training	None
Number of Jobs, 2010	33,500
Job Outlook, 2010-20	10% (About as fast as average)
Employment Change, 2010-20	3,500

What Agricultural and Food Scientists Do

Agricultural and food scientists work to ensure agricultural productivity and food safety.

Duties

Agricultural and food scientists typically do the following:

- Conduct research and experiments concerning animal nutrition and field crops
- Develop ways to improve the quantity and quality of field crops and farm animals
- Create new food products and develop new and better ways to process, package, and deliver them
- Study the composition of soil as it relates to plant growth
- Communicate research findings to the scientific community, food producers, and the public

Agricultural and food scientists play an important role in maintaining the nation's food supply. Many work in basic or applied research and development. Basic research seeks to understand the biological and chemical processes by which crops and livestock grow. Applied research uses this knowledge to discover ways to improve the quality, quantity, and safety of agricultural products.

Many agricultural and food scientists work with little supervision, forming their own hypotheses and developing research methods accordingly. In addition, they often lead teams of technicians or students who help in their research.

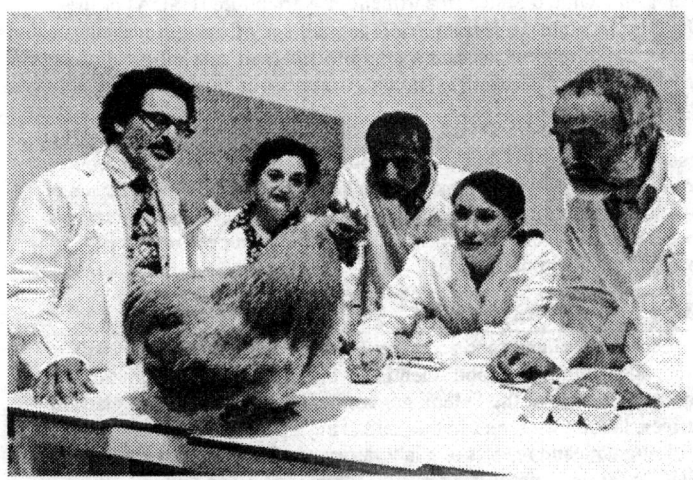

Agricultural and food scientists work to ensure agricultural productivity and food safety.

The following are types of agricultural and food scientists:

Animal scientists typically conduct research on domestic farm animals. With a focus on food production, they explore animal genetics, nutrition, reproduction, diseases, growth, and development. They work to develop efficient ways to produce and process meat, poultry, eggs, and milk. Animal scientists may crossbreed animals to get new combinations of desirable characteristics. They advise farmers on how to upgrade housing for animals, lower animal death rates, handle waste matter, and increase production.

Food scientists and technologists use chemistry and other sciences to study the underlying principles of food. They analyze nutritional content, discover new food sources, and research ways to make processed foods safe and healthy. Food technologists generally work in product development, applying findings from food science research to develop new or better ways of selecting, preserving, processing, packaging, and distributing food. Some food scientists use nanotechnology to develop sensors that can detect contaminants in food. Other food scientists enforce government regulations, inspecting food processing areas to ensure that they are sanitary and meet waste management standards.

Soil and plant scientists conduct research on soil, crops, and other agricultural products.

Soil scientists examine the scientific composition of soil as it relates to plant or crop growth, and investigate effects of alternative soil treatment practices on crop productivity. They develop methods of conserving and managing soil that farmers and forestry companies can use. Because soil science is closely related to environmental science, people trained in soil science also work to ensure environmental quality and effective land use.

Plant scientists work to improve crop yields and give advice to food and crop developers about techniques that could enhance production efforts. They develop ways to control pests and weeds safely and effectively.

Agricultural and food scientists in private industry commonly work for food production companies, farms, and processing plants. They typically improve inspection standards or overall food quality. They spend their time in a laboratory, where they do tests and experiments, or in the field, where they take samples or assess overall conditions. Other agricultural and food scientists work for pharmaceutical companies, where they use biotechnology processes to develop drugs or other medical products. Some look for ways to use agricultural products for fuels, such as ethanol produced from corn.

At universities, agricultural and food scientists do research and investigate new methods of improving animal or soil health, nutrition, and other facets of food quality. They also write grants to organizations such as the United States Department of Agriculture (USDA) or the National Institutes of Health (NIH) to get steady funding for their research. For more information on professors who teach agricultural and food science at universities, see the profile on postsecondary teachers .

In the federal government, agricultural and food scientists conduct research on animal safety and methods of improving food and crop production. They spend most of their time conducting clinical trials or developing experiments on animal and plant subjects. Agricultural and food scientists eventually present their findings in peer-reviewed journals or other publications.

Work Environment

Agricultural and food scientists held about 33,500 jobs in 2010. Most agricultural and food scientists work in research universities, private industry, or the federal government. Their work takes place in offices, laboratories, and in the field. They spend most of their time studying data and reports in a laboratory or office. Field work includes visits to farms or processing plants. When visiting an animal production facility, they must follow biosecurity measures, wear

suitable clothing, and tolerate animal waste and odor.

The largest numbers of animal scientists worked in the following industries in May 2010:

Colleges, universities, and professional schools; state, local, and private	46%
Professional, scientific, and technical services	13
State government, excluding education and hospitals	6

The largest numbers of food scientists and technologists worked in the following industries in May 2010:

Food manufacturing	35%
Scientific research and development services	13
Colleges, universities, and professional schools; state, local, and private	8

The largest numbers of soil and plant scientists worked in the following industries in May 2010:

Professional, scientific, and technical services	23%
Colleges, universities, and professional schools; state, local, and private	16
Scientific research and development services	14

How to Become an Agricultural or Food Scientist

Agricultural and food scientists need at least a bachelor's degree from an accredited postsecondary institution, although many obtain a doctoral degree. Food scientists and technologists and soil and plant scientists typically earn bachelor's degrees. Some scientists earn a Doctorate of Veterinary Medicine (DVM). Most animal scientists earn a Ph.D.

Education

Every state has a land-grant college that offers agricultural science degrees. Many other colleges and universities also offer agricultural science degrees or agricultural science courses. Degrees in related sciences, such as biology, chemistry, or physics, or in a related engineering specialty also may qualify people for many agricultural science jobs.

Undergraduate coursework for food scientists and technologists and for soil and plant scientists typically includes biology, chemistry, botany, and plant conservation. Students preparing to be food scientists take courses such as food chemistry, food analysis, food microbiology, food engineering, and food processing operations. Students preparing to be soil and plant scientists take courses in plant pathology, soil chemistry, entomology (the study of insects), plant physiology, and biochemistry.

Students typically gain a strong foundation in their field, with an emphasis on teamwork, internships, and research opportunities. In addition to science coursework, undergraduates sometimes take humanities courses, which help them develop good communication skills.

Many people with bachelor's degrees in agricultural sciences find work in related jobs rather than becoming an agricultural or food scientist. For example, a bachelor's degree in agricultural science is useful for managerial jobs in farm-related or ranch-related businesses, such as farming, ranching, agricultural inspection, farm credit institutions, or companies that make or sell feed, fertilizer, seed, and farm equipment.

Graduate study further develops an animal scientist's knowledge, and it typically takes students 6 years to complete their Ph.D. During graduate school, there is additional emphasis on lab work and original research, where prospective animal scientists have the opportunity to do experiments and sometimes supervise undergraduates.

Advanced research topics include genetics, animal reproduction, and biotechnology, among others. Advanced coursework also emphasizes statistical analysis and experiment design, which are important as Ph.D. candidates begin their research.

Some agricultural and food scientists receive a Doctor of Veterinary Medicine before they begin their animal science training. Like candidates for a Ph.D. in animal science, a prospective veterinarian must first have a bachelor's degree before getting into veterinary school. For more information, see the profile on veterinarians .

Important Qualities

Communication skills. Communication skills are critical for agricultural and food scientists. They must be able to explain their studies: what they were trying to learn, the methods they used, what they found, and what they think the implications are of their findings. They must also be able to communicate well when working with others, including technicians and student assistants.

Critical-thinking skills. Agricultural and food scientists must use their expertise to determine the best way to answer a specific research question.

Data-analysis skills. Agricultural and food scientists, like other researchers, collect data using a variety of methods, including quantitative surveys. They must then apply standard data analysis techniques to understand the data and get the answers to the questions they are studying.

Decision-making skills. Agricultural and food scientists must use their expertise and experience to determine whether their findings will have an impact on the food supply, farms, and other agricultural products.

Observation skills. Agricultural and food scientists conduct experiments that require precise observation of samples and other data. Any mistake could lead to inconclusive or inaccurate results.

Certification

Agricultural and food scientists can get certifications from organizations like the American Registry of Professional Animal Scientists (ARPAS), or the Soil Science Society of America (SSSA). These certifications recognize expertise in agricultural and food science and enhance the status of those who are certified.

According to the organizations, certification of professional expertise is broadly based on education, a comprehensive exam, and previous professional experience. Scientists must take continuing education courses every year to keep their certification, and they must follow the organization's code of ethics. Certification is not required, but the agricultural and food science community recognizes its importance. Some states require soil scientists to be licensed to practice. Licensing requirements vary by state, but generally include holding a bachelor's degree with a certain number of credit hours in soil science, a certain number of years working under a licensed scientist, and passage of an examination.

Pay

Agricultural and Food Scientists
  Median annual wages, May 2010

Food Scientists and Technologists	$60,180
Agricultural and Food Scientists	$58,450
Animal Scientists	$58,250
Soil and Plant Scientists	$57,340
Total, All Occupations	$33,840

Note: All Occupations includes all occupations in the U.S. Economy.
Source: U.S. Bureau of Labor Statistics, Occupational Employment Statistics

The median annual wage of agricultural and food scientists was $58,450 in May 2010. The median wage is the wage at which half the workers in an occupation earned more than that amount and half earned less. The lowest 10 percent earned less than $34,320, and the top 10 percent earned more than $105,040.

Median annual wages in selected industries for animal scientists in May 2010 were the following:

State government, excluding education and hospitals	$86,550
Professional, scientific, and technical services	76,790
Colleges, universities, and professional schools; state, local, and private	49,250

Median annual wages in selected industries for food scientists and technologists in May 2010 were the following:

Scientific research and development services	$69,470
Food manufacturing	55,690
Colleges, universities, and professional schools; state, local, and private	46,940

Median annual wages in selected industries for soil and plant scientists in May 2010 were the following:

Scientific research and development services	$62,210
Professional, scientific, and technical services	57,680
Colleges, universities, and professional schools; state, local, and private	46,630

Job Outlook

Agricultural and Food Scientists
  Percent change in employment, projected 2010-20

Total, All Occupations	14%
Animal Scientists	13%
Soil and Plant Scientists	12%
Agricultural and Food Scientists	10%
Food Scientists and Technologists	8%

Note: All Occupations includes all occupations in the U.S. Economy.
Source: U.S. Bureau of Labor Statistics, Employment Projections program

Employment of agricultural and food scientists is expected to increase by 10 percent from 2010 to 2020, about as fast as the average for all occupations.

Ongoing animal science research, as well as an increased reliance on food safety through biotechnology and nanotechnology, is expected to increase demand for agricultural and food scientists moderately. Agricultural scientists will also be needed to balance increased agricultural output with protecting and preserving soil, water, and ecosystems. They increasingly will help develop sustainable agricultural practices by creating and carrying out plans to manage pests, crops, soil fertility, erosion, and animal waste in ways that reduce the use of harmful chemicals and minimize damage to the natural environment. In addition, demand for biofuels—renewable energy sources from plants—is expected to increase.

Job growth for food scientists and technologists is expected to be driven by the demand for new food products and food safety measures. Food research is expected to increase because the public is more aware of nutrition, health, food safety, and the need to keep herd animals from getting infections.

Most growth over the next 10 years for agricultural and food scientists will be in private industry. Private industry has increased its demand for agricultural and food scientists because their expertise is necessary for developing food, crops, and drugs, along with ensuring quality and safety.

Furthermore, research in genomics and agricultural sustainability also is expected to increase the number of available agricultural science positions. Findings from these scientists' studies may improve crop yields or have an impact on other fields, such as biofuels.

Job Prospects

A number of job vacancies will arise as many scientists are expected to retire within the next 10 years.

Employment projections data for agricultural and food scientists, 2010-20

Occupational Title	SOC Code	Employment, 2010	Projected Employment, 2020	Change, 2010-20	
				Percent	Numeric
Agricultural and Food Scientists	19-1010	33,500	37,000	10	3,500
Animal Scientists	19-1011	3,300	3,800	13	400
Food Scientists and Technologists	19-1012	13,900	15,000	8	1,100
Soil and Plant Scientists	19-1013	16,300	18,300	12	2,000
SOURCE: U.S. Bureau of Labor Statistics, Employment Projections program					

Similar Occupations

This table shows a list of occupations with job duties that are similar to those of agricultural and food scientists.

Occupation	Job Duties	Entry-Level Education	Median Annual Pay, May 2010
Agricultural and Food Science Technicians	Under the supervision of scientists, agricultural and food science technicians measure and analyze the quality of food and agricultural products.	Associate's degree	$32,760
Biochemists and Biophysicists	Biochemists and biophysicists study the chemical and physical principles of living things and of biological processes such as cell development, growth, and heredity.	Doctoral or professional degree	$79,390
Biological Technicians	Biological technicians help biological and medical scientists conduct laboratory tests and experiments.	Bachelor's degree	$39,020
Chemical Technicians	Chemical technicians use special instruments and techniques to help chemists and chemical engineers in researching, developing, and producing chemical products and processes.	Associate's degree	$42,040
Conservation Scientists and Foresters	Conservation scientists and foresters manage overall land quality of forests, parks, rangelands, and other natural resources.	Bachelor's degree	$57,420
Environmental Scientists and Specialists	Environmental scientists and specialists use their knowledge of the natural sciences to protect the environment. They identify problems and find solutions that minimize hazards to the health of the environment and the population.	Bachelor's degree	$61,700
Farmers, Ranchers, and Other Agricultural Managers	Farmers, ranchers, and other agricultural managers run establishments that produce crops, livestock, and dairy products.	High school diploma or equivalent	$60,750
Microbiologists	Microbiologists study the growth, development, and other characteristics of microscopic organisms such as bacteria, algae, and fungi.	Bachelor's degree	$65,920
Veterinarians	Veterinarians care for the health of animals. They diagnose, treat, or research medical conditions and diseases of pets, livestock, and animals in zoos, racetracks, and laboratories.	Doctoral or professional degree	$82,040
Zoologists and Wildlife Biologists	Zoologists and wildlife biologists study the characteristics and habitats of animals and wildlife.	Bachelor's degree	$57,430

Contacts for More Information

For more information food and animal scientists, including certifications, visit American Registry of Professional Animal Scientists

For more information about agricultural and soil scientists, including certifications, visit Soil Science Society of America

Suggested citation:

Bureau of Labor Statistics, U.S. Department of Labor, Occupational Outlook Handbook, 2012-13 Edition, Agricultural and Food Scientists, on the Internet at http://www.bls.gov/ooh/life-physical-and-social-science/agricultural-and-food-scientists.htm .

Anthropologists and Archeologists

Quick Facts: Anthropologists and Archeologists	
2010 Median Pay	$54,230 per year $26.07 per hour
Entry-Level Education	Master's degree
Work Experience in a Related Occupation	None
On-the-job Training	None
Number of Jobs, 2010	6,100
Job Outlook, 2010-20	21% (Faster than average)
Employment Change, 2010-20	1,300

What Anthropologists and Archeologists Do

Anthropologists and archeologists study the origin, development, and behavior of human beings, past and present. They examine the cultures, languages, archeological remains, and physical characteristics of people in various parts of the world.

Duties

Anthropologists and archeologists typically do the following:

- Plan research projects to answer questions and test hypotheses about humans
- Develop data collection methods tailored to a particular specialty, project, or culture
- Collect information from observations, interviews, and documents
- Record and manage records of observations taken in the field
- Analyze data, laboratory samples, and other sources to uncover patterns about human life, culture, and origins
- Write reports and give presentations on research findings
- Advise organizations on the cultural impact of proposed plans, policies, and programs

Drawing and building on knowledge from the humanities and social, physical, and biological sciences, anthropologists and archeologists examine the ways of life, languages, archeological remains, and physical characteristics of people in various parts of the world. They also examine the customs, values, and social patterns of different cultures. Some anthropologists study the social and cultural consequences of current human issues, such as overpopulation, natural disasters, warfare, and poverty. Others study the prehistory and evolution of Homo sapiens.

Many anthropologists and archeologists use sophisticated tools and technologies in their work. Although tasks vary by specialty, materials often include excavating tools, laboratory equipment, statistical and database software, and geographic information systems (GIS).

Anthropologists typically specialize in one of the following occupations:

Archeologists examine, recover, and preserve evidence and artifacts from past human cultures. They analyze skeletal remains and artifacts, such as tools, pottery, cave paintings, and ruins of buildings. They connect artifacts with information about past environments to learn about the history, customs, and living habits of people in earlier civilizations.

Archeologists also manage and protect archeological sites. Some work in national parks or historical sites, where they protect known historical or archeological sites and educate the public. Others assess building sites to ensure that construction plans comply with federal regulations regarding preservation of these sites. Archeologists often specialize in a particular geographic area, time period, or subject matter, such as animal remains or underwater sites.

Biological anthropologists, also known as **physical anthropologists**, research the evolution of humans and their relatives. They look for early evidence of human life, analyze genetics, study primates, and examine the biological variations in humans. They analyze how culture and biology influence one another. Some may examine human remains found at archeological sites to understand population demographics and factors, such as nutrition and disease, which affected these populations. Others work as forensic anthropologists in medical or legal settings, identifying and analyzing skeletal remains and DNA.

Cultural anthropologists study the customs, cultures, and social lives of groups. They investigate the internal logic of societies in settings that range from unindustrialized villages to modern urban centers. Cultural anthropologists often spend time living in the societies they study and collect information through observations, interviews, and surveys.

Linguistic anthropologists study how humans communicate and how language shapes social life. They investigate nonverbal communication, the structure and development of languages, and differences among languages. They also examine the role of language in different cultures, how social and cultural factors affect language, and how language affects a person's experiences. Most linguistic anthropologists study non-European languages, which they learn directly from native speakers.

Work Environment

Anthropologists and archeologists held about 6,100 jobs in 2010. They worked for research organizations, colleges and universities,

Archeologists may assess the archeological significance of a potential construction site.

museums, consulting firms, private corporations, and in all levels of government.

The following industries employed the largest numbers of anthropologists and archeologists in 2010:

Scientific research and development services	29%
Federal government, excluding postal service	25
Management, scientific, and technical consulting services	11
Educational services; state, local, and private	7

The work of anthropologists varies widely, depending on the specific job. Although many work in a typical office setting, others analyze samples in laboratories or work in the field.

Archeologists often work for cultural resource management (CRM) firms. CRM firms identify, assess, and preserve archeological sites and ensure that organizations, such as developers and builders, comply with regulations regarding archeological sites. Archeologists also work in museums, at historic sites, and for government agencies, such as the U.S. Department of the Interior's National Park Service.

Anthropologists and archeologists sometimes do fieldwork, either in the United States or in foreign countries. This may involve learning foreign languages, living in remote villages, or examining and excavating archeological sites.

Fieldwork for anthropologists and archeologists usually requires travel for extended periods of time. This also may require travel to remote areas, where anthropologists must live with the people they study to learn about the culture. They may work under rugged conditions, and their work may involve strenuous physical exertion.

Work Schedules

Many anthropologists and archeologists in government, research and consulting firms, museums, and businesses work full-time schedules during regular business hours. When doing fieldwork, anthropologists and archeologists might be required to travel and work long hours.

How to Become an Anthropologist or Archeologist

Anthropologists and archeologists need a master's degree or Ph.D. for most positions. Experience doing anthropological fieldwork is also important.

Education

Anthropologists and archeologists may qualify for many positions with a master's degree. Most master's degree programs are 2 years in duration and include field research.

Although a master's degree is enough for many positions, jobs that require leadership roles and more technical experience may require a Ph.D. A Ph.D. takes several years of study beyond a master's degree and completion of a doctoral dissertation. Ph.D. students typically spend between 12 months and 30 months doing field research for their dissertation.

To direct projects outside the United States, anthropologists and archeologists typically need a Ph.D. to comply with the requirements of foreign governments.

Most graduates with a bachelor's degree in anthropology find jobs in other fields, although a limited number find jobs as field, laboratory, or research assistants.

Those with a bachelor's degree in archeology and work experience in an internship or field school can work as a field archeologist or do basic laboratory work. However, archeologists need a master's degree to advance beyond entry-level positions.

Many people with a Ph.D. in anthropology or archeology become professors or museum curators. For more information on these occupations, see the profiles on postsecondary teachers and curators and museum technicians .

Work Experience

To become an anthropologist or archeologist, graduates need related work experience. Many candidates fulfill this requirement through field experience or internships with museums, historical societies, or nonprofit organizations.

Anthropologists and archeologists typically spend part of their graduate program conducting field research. Many students also attend archeological field schools, which teach students how to excavate, record, and interpret historical and archeological sites.

Important Qualities

Analytical skills. Anthropologists and archeologists often use scientific methods and data analysis in their research.

Critical-thinking skills. Anthropologists and archeologists must draw logical conclusions from observations, laboratory experiments, and other methods of research.

Investigative skills. Anthropologists and archeologists must seek and explore all facts relevant to their research. They must combine pieces of information to try to solve problems and to answer research questions.

Writing skills. Anthropologists and archeologists need strong writing skills, because they often write reports detailing their research findings.

Pay

Anthropologists and Archeologists
Median annual wages, May 2010

Social Scientists and Related Workers	$67,090
Anthropologists and Archeologists	$54,230
Total, All Occupations	$33,840

Note: All Occupations includes all occupations in the U.S. Economy.
Source: U.S. Bureau of Labor Statistics, Occupational Employment Statistics

The median annual wage of anthropologists and archeologists was $54,230 in May 2010. The median wage is the wage at which half the workers in an occupation earned more than that amount and half earned less. The lowest 10 percent earned less than $31,310, and the top 10 percent earned more than $89,440.

Median annual wages in the industries employing the largest numbers of anthropologists and archeologists in May 2010 were as follows:

Federal executive branch	$70,800
Management, scientific, and technical consulting services	46,280
Scientific research and development services	45,370
Educational services; state, local, and private	44,280

Many anthropologists and archeologists in government, research and consulting firms, museums, and businesses work full-time schedules during regular business hours. When doing fieldwork, anthropologists and archeologists might be required to travel and work long hours.

Job Outlook

Anthropologists and Archeologists
Percent change in employment, projected 2010-20

Anthropologists and Archeologists	21%
Social Scientists and Related Workers	18%
Total, All Occupations	14%

Note: All Occupations includes all occupations in the U.S. Economy.
Source: U.S. Bureau of Labor Statistics, Employment Projections program

Employment of anthropologists and archeologists is expected to grow 21 percent from 2010 to 2020, faster than the average for all occupations. However, because it is a small occupation, the fast growth will result in only about 1,300 new jobs over the 10-year period. More anthropologists will be needed to research human life, history, and culture, and apply that knowledge to current issues.

In addition to traditional research areas, a growing number of corporations are increasingly relying on anthropological research. Specifically, corporations are expected to use anthropologists' analyses to understand increasingly diverse workforces and markets, allowing businesses to better serve their clients or to target new customers.

Because anthropological research is highly dependent on the amount of research funding, federal budgetary decisions will affect the rate of employment growth in research.

Outside of research, employment of archeologists will be largely influenced by the level of construction activity. As construction projects increase, more archeologists will be needed to ensure that builders comply with federal regulations regarding the preservation of archeological and historical artifacts.

Job Prospects

Overall job prospects for anthropologists and archeologists are expected to be competitive. Those with a Ph.D. and extensive experience doing anthropological or archeological fieldwork will have the best job opportunities.

Although job opportunities for anthropologists will expand in businesses, consulting firms, and other non-traditional settings, workers will face strong competition for jobs because of the small number of positions.

Archeologists should have the best job prospects in cultural resource management (CRM) firms. However, due to the large number of qualified graduates and relatively few positions available, jobseekers may face very strong competition.

Employment projections data for anthropologists and archeologists, 2010-20

Occupational Title	SOC Code	Employment, 2010	Projected Employment, 2020	Change, 2010-20	
				Percent	Numeric
Anthropologists and Archeologists	19-3091	6,100	7,400	21	1,300
SOURCE: U.S. Bureau of Labor Statistics, Employment Projections program					

Similar Occupations

This table shows a list of occupations with job duties that are similar to those of anthropologists and archeologists.

Occupation	Job Duties	Entry-Level Education	Median Annual Pay, May 2010
Economists	Economists study the production and distribution of resources, goods, and services.	Bachelor's degree	$89,450
Geographers	Geographers study the earth and its land, features, and inhabitants. They also examine phenomena such as political or cultural structures as they relate to geography. They study the physical or human geographic characteristics or both of a region, ranging in scale from local to global.	Bachelor's degree	$72,800
Geoscientists	Geoscientists study the physical aspects of the Earth, such as its composition, structure, and processes, to learn about its past, present, and future.	Bachelor's degree	$82,500
Historians	Historians research, analyze, interpret, and present the past by studying a variety of historical documents and sources.	Master's degree	$53,520
Psychologists	Psychologists study mental processes and human behavior by observing, interpreting, and recording how people and other animals relate to one another and the environment.	See How to Become One	$68,640
Sociologists	Sociologists study society and social behavior by examining the groups, cultures, organizations, social institutions, and processes that people develop.	Master's degree	$72,360
Survey Researchers	Survey researchers design or conduct surveys and analyze survey data. Many groups use surveys to collect factual data, such as employment and salary information, or to ask questions that help them understand people's opinions, attitudes, beliefs, or desires.	Bachelor's degree	$36,050
Archivists	Archivists appraise, edit, and maintain permanent records and historically valuable documents. Many perform research on archival material.	Bachelor's degree	$45,200
Curators, Museum Technicians, and Conservators	Curators oversee collections, such as artwork and historic items, and may conduct public service activities for an institution. Museum technicians and conservators prepare and restore objects and documents in museum collections and exhibits.	See How to Become One	$42,310
Postsecondary Teachers	Postsecondary teachers instruct students in a wide variety of academic and vocational subjects beyond the high school level. They also conduct research and publish scholarly papers and books.	Doctoral or professional degree	$62,050

Contacts for More Information

For more information about careers in anthropology and archeology, visit American Anthropological Association

For more information about careers in archeology, visit Archaeological Institute of America , Society for American Archaeology

For more information about physical anthropologists, visit: American Association of Physical Anthropologists

Suggested citation:

Bureau of Labor Statistics, U.S. Department of Labor, Occupational Outlook Handbook, 2012-13 Edition, Anthropologists and Archeologists, on the Internet at http://www.bls.gov/ooh/life-physical-and-social-science/anthropologists-and-archeologists.htm .

Atmospheric Scientists, Including Meteorologists

Quick Facts: Atmospheric Scientists, Including Meteorologists	
2010 Median Pay	$87,780 per year $42.20 per hour
Entry-Level Education	Bachelor's degree
Work Experience in a Related Occupation	None
On-the-job Training	None
Number of Jobs, 2010	9,500
Job Outlook, 2010-20	11% (About as fast as average)
Employment Change, 2010-20	1,000

What Atmospheric Scientists, Including Meteorologists Do

Atmospheric scientists study weather, climate, and other aspects of the atmosphere. They develop reports and forecasts from their analysis of weather and climate data.

Duties

Atmospheric scientists typically do the following:

- Measure temperature, air pressure, and other properties of the atmosphere
- Develop and use computer models that analyze data about the atmosphere (also called meteorological data)
- Produce weather maps and graphics
- Report current weather conditions
- Prepare long- and short-term weather forecasts using sophisticated computer and mathematical models, satellite and radar data
- Issue warnings to protect life and property during severe weather, such as hurricanes, tornadoes, and flash floods

Atmospheric scientists use highly developed instruments and computer programs to do their jobs. For example, they use weather balloons, radar systems, satellites, and sensors to monitor the weather and collect data. The data they collect and analyze are critical to understanding air pollution, drought, loss of the ozone layer, and other problems. Atmospheric scientists also use graphics software to illustrate their forecasts and reports.

Many atmospheric scientists work with scientists and professionals in other fields to help solve problems in areas such as commerce, energy, transportation, agriculture, and the environment. For example, some atmospheric scientists work on teams with other scientists and engineers to find the best locations for new wind farms, which are groups of wind turbines used to generate electricity. Others work closely with hydrologists to monitor the impact climate change has on water supplies and to manage water resources.

The following are examples of types of atmospheric scientists:

Broadcast meteorologists give forecasts to the general public through television, radio, and the Internet. They use graphics software to develop maps and charts that explain their forecasts.

Climate scientists study historical weather patterns to interpret and forecast long-term weather patterns or shifts in climate, such as expected precipitation levels years or decades in the future. Their studies are used to design buildings, plan heating and cooling systems, and aid in efficient land use and agricultural production. Global climate change is one of the largest areas of study for climatologists. Some climate scientists work with specialists in other areas, such as economists or urban and regional planners, to help those experts assess the meaning of projected climate changes.

Atmospheric scientists use computer software to develop weather forecasts.

Forensic meteorologists use historical weather data to reconstruct the weather conditions for a specific location and time. They investigate what role weather played in unusual events such as traffic accidents and fires. Forensic meteorologists may be called as experts to testify in court.

Research meteorologists develop new methods of data collection, observation, and forecasting. They also conduct studies to improve basic understandings of climate, weather, and other aspects of the atmosphere. For example, some research meteorologists study severe weather patterns, such as hurricanes and tornadoes, to understand why cyclones form and to develop better ways of predicting them. Others focus on environmental problems, such as air pollution. Research meteorologists often work with scientists in other fields. For example, they may work with computer scientists to develop new forecasting software or with oceanographers to study interactions between the ocean and the atmosphere.

Weather forecasters use computer and mathematical models to produce weather reports and short-term forecasts that can range from a few minutes to more than a week. They develop forecasts for the general public and for specific customers such as airports, farmers, utilities, and other businesses. For example, they provide forecasts to power suppliers so that the suppliers can plan for events, such as heat waves, that would cause an increase in electricity demand. They also develop warnings for severe weather such as blizzards and hurricanes. Some forecasters prepare long-range outlooks, predicting whether temperatures and precipitation levels will be above or below average in a particular month or season.

Some people with an atmospheric science background may become professors or teachers. For more information, see the profile on postsecondary teachers .

Work Environment

Atmospheric scientists, including meteorologists held about 9,500 jobs in 2010. The following industries employed the largest numbers of atmospheric scientists in 2010:

Federal government, excluding postal service	36%
Other professional, scientific, and technical services	15
Colleges, universities, and professional schools; state	15
Research and development in the physical, engineering, and life sciences	12
Radio and television broadcasting	7

In the federal government, most atmospheric scientists worked as weather forecasters with the National Weather Service of the National Oceanic and Atmospheric Administration (NOAA) in weather stations throughout the United States —at airports, in or near cities, and in isolated and remote areas. In smaller stations, they often work alone; in larger ones, they work as part of a team. The U.S. Department of Defense employed several hundred atmospheric scientists in 2010. In addition, hundreds of members of the Armed Forces are involved in atmospheric science.

Atmospheric scientists involved in research often work in offices and laboratories, but they may travel frequently to collect data in the field and to observe weather events, such as tornadoes, up close. They watch actual weather conditions from the ground or from an aircraft.

Atmospheric scientists who work in private industry may have to travel to meet with clients or to gather information in the field. For example, forensic meteorologists may need to collect information from the scene of an accident as part of their investigation.

Broadcast meteorologists give their reports to the general public from television and radio studios. They may also broadcast from outdoor locations to tell audiences about current weather conditions.

Work Schedules

Most atmospheric scientists work full time. Weather conditions can change at a moment's notice, so weather forecasters need to continuously monitor conditions. They work rotating shifts to cover all 24 hours in a day, and they work on nights, weekends, and holidays to provide the most current weather information. In addition, they work extended hours during severe weather, such as hurricanes. Other atmospheric scientists have a standard work week, although researchers may work nights and weekends on particular projects.

How to Become an Atmospheric Scientist

Atmospheric scientists need a bachelor's degree in meteorology or a closely related field for most positions. For research positions, atmospheric scientists usually need a master's degree at minimum, but preferably a Ph.D.

Education

Atmospheric scientists typically need a bachelor's degree, either in atmospheric science or a related scientific field. There were about 100 undergraduate and graduate programs in atmospheric, oceanic, hydrologic, and related sciences in the United States in 2010, according to the American Meteorological Society. However, many schools also offer atmospheric science courses through other departments, such as physics and geosciences.

When considering colleges, prospective students should make certain that the colleges offer those courses required by the federal government and other employers as one of their hiring requirements. Course requirements, in addition to courses in meteorology and atmospheric science, usually include advanced courses in physics and mathematics. Classes in computer programming are important because many atmospheric scientists have to write and edit the computer software programs that produce forecasts.

Students should also take courses in subjects that are relevant to their desired area of specialization. For example, those who wish to become broadcast meteorologists for radio or television stations should develop excellent speaking skills through courses in speech, journalism, and related fields.

Atmospheric scientists who work in research usually need a master's degree at minimum, and preferably a Ph.D. in atmospheric sciences or a related field. Most graduate programs do not require prospective students to have a bachelor's degree in atmospheric science; an undergraduate degree in mathematics, physics, or engineering provides excellent preparation for graduate study in atmospheric science. In addition to advanced meteorological coursework, graduate students take courses in other disciplines, such as oceanography and geophysics.

Although it is not necessary, a master's degree in atmospheric science can greatly enhance employment opportunities, pay, and advancement potential for meteorologists in government and private industry. A master's degree in business administration (MBA) may be useful for meteorologists interested in working in private industry as consultants who help firms make important business decisions on the basis of their forecasts.

Important Qualities

Critical-thinking skills. Atmospheric scientists need to be able to analyze the results of their computer models and determine the most likely outcome.

Math skills. Atmospheric scientists use calculus, statistics, and other advanced topics in mathematics to develop models used to forecast the weather. They also use mathematical calculations to analyze the relationship between properties of the atmosphere, such as how changes in air pressure may affect air temperature.

Speaking skills. Atmospheric scientists must be able to explain their forecasts and research to their audience. This skill is particularly relevant for broadcast meteorologists who must present their forecasts to the general public.

Writing skills. Atmospheric scientists prepare detailed reports of their forecasts and research.

Pay

Atmospheric Scientists, Including Meteorologists
Median annual wages, May 2010

Atmospheric and Space Scientists	$87,780
Life, Physical, and Social Science Occupations	$58,530
Total, All Occupations	$33,840

Note: All Occupations includes all occupations in the U.S. Economy.
Source: U.S. Bureau of Labor Statistics, Occupational Employment Statistics

The median annual wage of atmospheric scientists was $87,780 in May 2010. The median wage is the wage at which half the workers in an occupation earned more than that amount and half earned less. The lowest 10 percent earned less than $45,050, and the top 10 percent earned more than $132,130.

Median annual wages in industries employing the largest numbers of atmospheric scientists in 2010 were:

Federal government, excluding postal service	$95,460
Research and development in the physical, engineering, and life sciences	87,130
Colleges, universities, and professional schools; state	81,010
Radio and television broadcasting	80,250
Other professional, scientific, and technical services	57,860

Most atmospheric scientists work full time. Weather conditions can change at a moment's notice, so weather forecasters need to continuously monitor conditions. They work rotating shifts to cover all 24 hours in a day, and they work on nights, weekends, and holidays to provide the most current weather information. In addition, they work extended hours during severe weather, such as hurricanes. Other atmospheric scientists have a standard work week, although researchers may work nights and weekends on particular projects.

Job Outlook

Atmospheric Scientists, Including Meteorologists
Percent change in employment, projected 2010-20

Life, Physical, and Social Science Occupations	16%
Total, All Occupations	14%
Atmospheric and Space Scientists	11%

Note: All Occupations includes all occupations in the U.S. Economy.
Source: U.S. Bureau of Labor Statistics, Employment Projections program

Employment of atmospheric scientists is projected to grow by 11 percent from 2010 to 2020, about as fast as the average for all occupations. New computer models have vastly improved the accuracy of forecasts and allow atmospheric scientists to tailor forecasts to specific purposes. This should increase the need for atmospheric scientists working in private industry as businesses demand more specialized weather information.

Job Prospects

Prospective atmospheric scientists should expect competition because the number of graduates from meteorology programs is expected to exceed the number of job openings. Workers with a graduate degree should enjoy better prospects than those whose highest level of education is a bachelor's degree.

Competition may be strong for research positions at colleges and universities because of the limited number of positions available. Few opportunities are expected in federal government because atmospheric scientists will be hired only to replace workers who retire or leave for other reasons. Budget constraints are also expected to limit hiring by federal agencies such as the National Weather Service. The best job prospects for meteorologists will be in private industry.

Employment projections data for atmospheric scientists, including meteorologists, 2010-20

Occupational Title	SOC Code	Employment, 2010	Projected Employment, 2020	Change, 2010-20 Percent	Numeric
Atmospheric and Space Scientists	19-2021	9,500	10,400	11	1,000
SOURCE: U.S. Bureau of Labor Statistics, Employment Projections program					

Similar Occupations

This table shows a list of occupations with job duties that are similar to those of atmospheric scientists, including meteorologists.

Occupation	Job Duties	Entry-Level Education	Median Annual Pay, May 2010
Chemists and Materials Scientists	Chemists and materials scientists study the structures, compositions, reactions, and other properties of substances. They use their knowledge to develop new and improved products, processes, and materials.	Bachelor's degree	$69,790
Environmental Engineers	Environmental engineers use the principles of engineering, soil science, biology, and chemistry to develop solutions to environmental problems. They are involved in efforts to improve recycling, waste disposal, public health, and control of water and air pollution.	Bachelor's degree	$78,740
Environmental Scientists and Specialists	Environmental scientists and specialists use their knowledge of the natural sciences to protect the environment. They identify problems and find solutions that minimize hazards to the health of the environment and the population.	Bachelor's degree	$61,700
Geoscientists	Geoscientists study the physical aspects of the Earth, such as its composition, structure, and processes, to learn about its past, present, and future.	Bachelor's degree	$82,500

Hydrologists	Hydrologists study water and the water cycle. They use their expertise to solve problems in the areas of water quality or availability.	Master's degree	$75,690
Mathematicians	Mathematicians use high-level mathematics and technology to develop new mathematical principles, understand relationships between existing principles, and solve real-world problems.	Master's degree	$99,380
Physicists and Astronomers	Physicists and astronomers study the fundamental nature of the universe, ranging from the vastness of space to the smallest of subatomic particles. They develop new technologies, methods, and theories based on the results of their research that deepen our understanding of how things work and contribute to innovative, real-world applications.	Doctoral or professional degree	$105,430
Postsecondary Teachers	Postsecondary teachers instruct students in a wide variety of academic and vocational subjects beyond the high school level. They also conduct research and publish scholarly papers and books.	Doctoral or professional degree	$62,050

Contacts for More Information

For more information about atmospheric scientists, including a list of colleges and universities offering atmospheric science programs, visit American Meteorological Society

For information about atmospheric science careers in research, visit University Corporation for Atmospheric Research

For information on federal government education requirements for atmospheric science positions, visit U.S. Office of Personnel Management

For information about federal government atmospheric science careers in the National Weather Service and other agencies within the National Oceanic and Atmospheric Administration, visit National Oceanic and Atmospheric Administration

Suggested citation:

Bureau of Labor Statistics, U.S. Department of Labor, Occupational Outlook Handbook, 2012-13 Edition, Atmospheric Scientists, Including Meteorologists, on the Internet at http://www.bls.gov/ooh/life-physical-and-social-science/atmospheric-scientists-including-meteorologists.htm .

Biochemists and Biophysicists

Quick Facts: Biochemists and Biophysicists	
2010 Median Pay	$79,390 per year $38.17 per hour
Entry-Level Education	Doctoral or professional degree
Work Experience in a Related Occupation	None
On-the-job Training	None
Number of Jobs, 2010	25,100
Job Outlook, 2010-20	31% (Much faster than average)
Employment Change, 2010-20	7,700

What Biochemists and Biophysicists Do

Biochemists and biophysicists study the chemical and physical principles of living things and of biological processes such as cell development, growth, and heredity.

Duties

Biochemists and biophysicists typically do the following:

- Plan and conduct complex projects in basic and applied research
- Manage laboratory teams and monitor the quality of their work
- Isolate, analyze, and synthesize proteins, enzymes, DNA, and other molecules
- Research the effects of substances such as drugs, hormones, and food on tissues and biological processes
- Prepare technical reports, research papers, and recommendations based on their research
- Present research findings to scientists, engineers, and other colleagues

Biochemists and biophysicists also use electron microscopes, lasers, and other laboratory instruments and equipment to carry out

their research. Biochemists and biophysicists use advanced technologies to conduct scientific experiments and analysis. For example, they use computer modeling software to determine the three-dimensional structures of proteins and other molecules. Biochemists and biophysicists involved in biotechnology research use chemical enzymes to synthesize recombinant DNA.

Most biochemists and biophysicists work on teams. Research projects are often interdisciplinary, and biochemists and biophysicists frequently work with experts in other fields, such as physics, chemistry, computer science, and engineering.

Biochemists and biophysicists work in basic and applied research. Basic research is conducted without any immediately known application; the goal is simply to expand human knowledge. Applied research is directed toward solving a particular problem.

Biochemists involved in basic research may study the genetic mutations in organisms that lead to cancer and other diseases. Others may study the evolution of plants and animals to understand how genetic traits are carried through successive generations.

Biophysicists may conduct basic research to learn how nerve cells communicate or how proteins work. Biochemists and biophysicists who conduct basic research typically must submit written grant proposals to colleges and universities, private foundations, and the federal government to get the money they need for their research.

Biochemists and biophysicists who do applied research develop products and processes that improve our lives. For example, in medicine, biochemists and biophysicists develop tests used to detect diseases, genetic disorders, and other illnesses. They also develop new drugs and medications, such as those used to treat cancer or Alzheimer's disease.

Applied research in biochemistry and biophysics has many uses outside of medicine. In agriculture, biochemists and biophysicists develop genetically engineered crops that are more resistant to drought, disease, insects, and other afflictions. Biochemists and biophysicists also develop alternative fuels, such as biofuels—renewable energy sources from plants. In addition, they develop ways to protect the environment and clean up pollution.

Many people with a biochemistry background become professors and teachers. For more information, see the profile on <u>postsecondary teachers</u> .

Work Environment

Biochemists and biophysicists held about 25,100 jobs in 2010. The industries employing the largest numbers of biochemists and biophysicists in 2010 were as follows:

Research and development in the physical, engineering, and life sciences	44%
Pharmaceutical and medicine manufacturing	22
Colleges, universities, and professional schools; state, local, and private	14

Biochemists and biophysicists typically work in laboratories and offices to conduct experiments and analyze the results. Those who work with dangerous organisms or toxic substances in the laboratory must follow safety procedures to avoid contamination.

Most biochemists and biophysicists work full time and keep regular hours.

How to Become a Biochemist or Biophysicist

Biochemists and biophysicists need a Ph.D. to work in independent research and development positions. Most Ph.D. holders begin their careers in a temporary postdoctoral research position, which typically lasts 2 to 3 years. Bachelor's and master's degree holders are qualified for some entry-level positions in biochemistry and biophysics.

Education

Most Ph.D. holders in biochemistry and biophysics have bachelor's degrees in biochemistry or a related field, such as biology, chemistry, physics, or engineering. Many schools have bachelor's degree programs in biochemistry, but few schools have bachelor's degree programs in biophysics. In addition to completing required courses in biology and chemistry, students must typically take courses in mathematics, physics, and computer science. Courses in mathematics and computer science are important for biochemists and biophysicists, who must be able to do complex data analysis.

Most bachelor's degree programs include required laboratory coursework. Additional laboratory coursework is excellent preparation for graduate school or for getting an entry-level position in industry. Students also can gain valuable laboratory experience through internships with prospective employers such as pharmaceutical and medicine manufacturers.

Ph.D. programs typically include 2 years of advanced coursework in topics such as toxicology, genetics, and proteomics (the study of proteins). Graduate students also spend a lot of time conducting

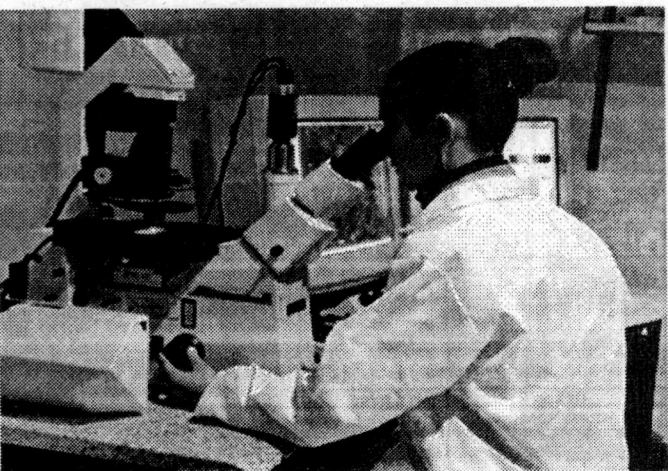

Biochemists and biophysicists use electron microscopes to study the chemical and physical properties of cells.

laboratory research. It typically takes 4 to 6 years to earn a doctoral degree in biochemistry or biophysics.

Training

Most biochemistry and biophysics Ph.D. holders begin their careers in a temporary postdoctoral research position, which typically lasts 2 to 3 years. During their postdoctoral appointment, they work with experienced scientists as they continue to learn about their specialties or develop a broader understanding of related areas of research.

Postdoctoral positions frequently offer the opportunity to publish research findings. A solid record of published research is essential to get a permanent position doing basic research, especially for those seeking a permanent college or university faculty position.

Important Qualities

Analytical skills. Biochemists and biophysicists must be able to conduct scientific experiments and analyses with accuracy and precision.

Critical-thinking skills. Biochemists and biophysicists draw conclusions from experimental results through sound reasoning and judgment.

Interpersonal skills. Biochemists and biophysicists typically work on research teams and need to be able to work well with others toward a common goal. Many also serve as team leaders and must be able to motivate and direct other team members.

Math skills. Biochemists and biophysicists regularly use complex equations and formulas in their work, and they need a broad understanding of mathematics, including calculus and statistics.

Perseverance. Scientific research involves substantial trial and error, and biochemists and biophysicists must not become discouraged in their work.

Problem-solving skills. Biochemists and biophysicists use scientific experiments and analysis to find solutions to complex scientific problems.

Speaking skills. Biochemists and biophysicists frequently give presentations and must be able to explain their research to others.

Writing skills. Biochemists and biophysicists write memos, reports, and research papers that explain their findings.

Advancement

Biochemists and biophysicists typically receive greater responsibility and independence in their work as they gain experience. They may lead research teams and have control over the direction and content of projects.

Some biochemists and biophysicists move into managerial positions—often as natural sciences managers. Those who pursue management careers spend much of their time on administrative tasks, such as preparing budgets and schedules. For more information, see the profile on natural sciences managers .

Pay

Biochemists and Biophysicists
Median annual wages, May 2010

Biochemists and Biophysicists	$79,390
Life, Physical, and Social Science Occupations	$58,530
Total, All Occupations	$33,840

Note: All Occupations includes all occupations in the U.S. Economy.
Source: U.S. Bureau of Labor Statistics, Occupational Employment Statistics

The median annual wage of biochemists and biophysicists was $79,390 in May 2010. The median wage is the wage at which half the workers in an occupation earned more than that amount and half earned less. The lowest 10 percent earned less than $43,050, and the top 10 percent earned more than $142,420.

Median annual wages in the industries employing the most biochemists and biophysicists in May 2010 were:

Pharmaceutical and medicine manufacturing	$84,970
Research and development in the physical, engineering, and life sciences	83,590
Colleges, universities, and professional schools; state, local, and private	50,760

Most biochemists and biophysicists work full time and keep regular hours.

Job Outlook

Biochemists and Biophysicists
Percent change in employment, projected 2010-20

Biochemists and Biophysicists	31%
Life, Physical, and Social Science Occupations	16%
Total, All Occupations	14%

Note: All Occupations includes all occupations in the U.S. Economy.
Source: U.S. Bureau of Labor Statistics, Employment Projections program

Employment of biochemists and biophysicists is projected to increase by 31 percent from 2010 to 2020, much faster than the average for all occupations. However, because it is a small occupation, the fast growth will result in only about 7,700 new jobs over the 10-year

period. More biochemists and biophysicists are expected to be needed to do basic research that increases scientific knowledge and to research and develop biological products and processes that improve our lives.

The aging of the baby-boom population and the demand for lifesaving new drugs and procedures to cure and prevent disease will likely drive demand for biochemists and biophysicists involved in biomedical research. For example, biochemists will be needed to conduct genetic research and to develop new medicines and treatments that are used to fight genetic disorders and diseases such as cancer. They will also be needed to develop new tests used to detect diseases and other illnesses.

Aside from improving our health, other areas of research and development in biotechnology are expected to provide employment growth for biochemists and biophysicists. Greater demand for clean energy should increase the need for biochemists who research and develop alternative energy sources, such as biofuels. A growing population and rising food prices are expected to fuel the development of genetically engineered crops that provide greater yields and require fewer resources to produce. Finally, efforts to discover new and improved ways to clean up and preserve the environment will increase demand for biochemists and biophysicists.

Job Prospects

Biochemists and biophysicists involved in basic research should expect strong competition for permanent research and faculty positions at colleges and universities. Biochemists and biophysicists with postdoctoral experience who have had research articles published in scientific journals should have the best prospects for these positions. Many biochemists and biophysicists work through multiple postdoctoral appointments before getting a permanent position in academia.

A large portion of basic research in biochemistry and biophysics is dependent on funding from the federal government through the National Institutes of Health and the National Science Foundation. Therefore, federal budgetary decisions will have a large impact on job prospects in basic research from year to year. Typically, there is strong competition among biochemists and biophysicists for research funding.

Most applied research projects that biochemists and biophysicists are involved in require the expertise of scientists in multiple fields such as microbiology, medicine, and chemistry. Biochemists and biophysicists who have a broad understanding of biochemistry and its relationship to other disciplines should have the best opportunities.

For entry-level biochemist positions, strong competition is expected because of the growing interest in biochemistry and other biological sciences at the undergraduate level. Applicants who have previous laboratory experience, either through coursework or prior work experience, should have the best opportunities.

Employment projections data for biochemists and biophysicists, 2010-20

Occupational Title	SOC Code	Employment, 2010	Projected Employment, 2020	Change, 2010-20	
				Percent	Numeric
Biochemists and Biophysicists	19-1021	25,100	32,900	31	7,700
SOURCE: U.S. Bureau of Labor Statistics, Employment Projections program					

Similar Occupations

This table shows a list of occupations with job duties that are similar to those of biochemists and biophysicists.

Occupation	Job Duties	Entry-Level Education	Median Annual Pay, May 2010
Agricultural and Food Scientists	Agricultural and food scientists work to ensure agricultural productivity and food safety.	See How to Become One	$58,450
Biological Technicians	Biological technicians help biological and medical scientists conduct laboratory tests and experiments.	Bachelor's degree	$39,020
Chemists and Materials Scientists	Chemists and materials scientists study the structures, compositions, reactions, and other properties of substances. They use their knowledge to develop new and improved products, processes, and materials.	Bachelor's degree	$69,790
Epidemiologists	Epidemiologists investigate the causes of disease and other public health problems to prevent them from spreading or from happening again. They report their findings to public policy officials and to the general public.	Master's degree	$63,010
Medical Scientists	Medical scientists conduct research aimed at improving overall human health. They often use clinical trials and other investigative methods to reach their findings.	Doctoral or professional degree	$76,700
Microbiologists	Microbiologists study the growth, development, and other characteristics of microscopic organisms such as bacteria, algae, and fungi.	Bachelor's degree	$65,920
Natural Sciences Managers	Natural sciences managers supervise the work of scientists, including chemists, physicists, and biologists. They direct research and development projects and coordinate activities such as testing, quality control, and production.	Bachelor's degree	$116,020
Physicians and Surgeons	Physicians and surgeons diagnose and treat injuries and illnesses in patients. Physicians examine patients, take medical histories, prescribe medications, and order, perform, and interpret diagnostic tests. Surgeons operate on patients to treat injuries, such as broken bones; diseases, such as cancerous tumors; and deformities, such as cleft palates.	Doctoral or professional degree	This wage is equal to or greater than $166,400 per year.
Physicists and Astronomers	Physicists and astronomers study the fundamental nature of the universe, ranging from the vastness of space to the smallest of subatomic particles. They develop new technologies, methods, and theories based on the results of their research that deepen our understanding of how things work and contribute to innovative, real-world applications.	Doctoral or professional degree	$105,430
Postsecondary Teachers	Postsecondary teachers instruct students in a wide variety of academic and vocational subjects beyond the high school level. They also conduct research and publish scholarly papers and books.	Doctoral or professional degree	$62,050
Zoologists and Wildlife Biologists	Zoologists and wildlife biologists study the characteristics and habitats of animals and wildlife.	Bachelor's degree	$57,430

Contacts for More Information

For more information about biochemists, visit American Chemical Society ,American Society for Biochemistry and Molecular Biology

For more information about biophysicists, visit Biophysical Society

For general information about careers in biological sciences, visit American Institute of Biological Sciences ,Federation of American Societies for Experimental Biology

Suggested citation:

Bureau of Labor Statistics, U.S. Department of Labor, Occupational Outlook Handbook, 2012-13 Edition, Biochemists and Biophysicists, on the Internet at http://www.bls.gov/ooh/life-physical-and-social-science/biochemists-and-biophysicists.htm.

Biological Technicians

Quick Facts: Biological Technicians	
2010 Median Pay	$39,020 per year $18.76 per hour
Entry-Level Education	Bachelor's degree
Work Experience in a Related Occupation	None
On-the-job Training	None
Number of Jobs, 2010	80,200
Job Outlook, 2010-20	14% (About as fast as average)
Employment Change, 2010-20	10,900

What Biological Technicians Do

Biological technicians help biological and medical scientists conduct laboratory tests and experiments.

Duties

Biological technicians typically do the following:

- Set up, maintain, and clean laboratory instruments and equipment, such as microscopes, scales, and test tubes
- Gather and prepare samples of substances, such as blood, food, or bacteria cultures, for laboratory analysis
- Conduct biological tests and experiments
- Document their work, including procedures, observations, and results
- Analyze experimental data and interpret results
- Write reports that summarize their findings

Most biological technicians work on teams. Typically, technicians are responsible for doing scientific tests, experiments, and analyses under the supervision of biologists or other scientists who direct and evaluate their work. Biological technicians use traditional laboratory instruments and advanced robotics and automated equipment to conduct experiments. They use specialized computer software to collect, analyze, and model experimental data.

Biological technicians work in many areas of research. They may assist with medical research by helping develop new medicines and treatments used to prevent, treat, or cure diseases.

Biological technicians who work in microbiology, sometimes referred to as laboratory assistants, studying living organisms and infectious agents.

Technicians working in biotechnology apply the knowledge and techniques they have gained from basic research to product development.

Work Environment

Biological technicians held about 80,200 jobs in 2010. The industries employing the largest numbers of biological technicians in 2010 were as follows:

Colleges, universities, and professional schools; state, local, and private	31%
Research and development in the physical, engineering, and life sciences	25
Federal government, excluding postal service	17
Pharmaceutical and medicine manufacturing	8
Health care	6

Biological technicians typically work in laboratories and offices, where they conduct experiments and analyze the results under the supervision of biological scientists and medical scientists.

Those who work with dangerous organisms or toxic substances in the laboratory must follow strict safety procedures to avoid contamination.

Most biological technicians work full time and keep regular hours.

How to Become a Biological Technician

Biological technicians typically need a bachelor's degree in biology or a closely related field. It is important for prospective biological technicians to gain laboratory experience while they are in school.

Biological technicians help biological and medical scientists conduct research.

Education

Biological technicians typically need a bachelor's degree in biology or a closely related field. Most colleges and universities offer bachelor's degree programs in biological science.

Biological science programs usually include courses in general biology, as well as in specific subfields such as ecology, microbiology, and molecular biology. In addition to taking courses in biology, students must study chemistry, mathematics, and physics. Computer science courses are helpful for modeling and simulating biological processes and for operating some laboratory equipment.

It is important for students to gain laboratory experience before entering the workforce. Students should take biology courses that emphasize laboratory work. They often can also gain laboratory experience through summer internships with prospective employers, such as pharmaceutical and medicine manufacturers.

Important Qualities

Analytical skills. Biological technicians need to able to conduct scientific experiments and analyses with accuracy and precision.

Critical-thinking skills. Biological technicians draw conclusions from experimental results through sound reasoning and judgment.

Listening skills. Biological technicians must carefully follow the instructions of biochemists, microbiologists, and other scientists when carrying out experiments and analyses.

Observation skills. Biological technicians must constantly monitor their experiments. They need to keep a complete, accurate record of their work, such as the conditions under which the experiment was carried out, the procedures they followed, and the results they obtained.

Teamwork. Biological technicians work together on teams under the direction of biologists or other scientists.

Technical skills. Biological technicians must be able to set up and operate sophisticated equipment and instruments. They also may need to adjust equipment to ensure that experiments are conducted properly.

Writing skills. Biological technicians must write reports that summarize their findings and results clearly.

Advancement

Biological technicians may be able to advance to scientist positions, such as microbiologist, after a few years of experience working as a technician or after earning a graduate degree.

Pay

Biological Technicians
Median annual wages, May 2010

Life, Physical, and Social Science Occupations	$58,530
Biological Technicians	$39,020
Total, All Occupations	$33,840

Note: All Occupations includes all occupations in the U.S. Economy.
Source: U.S. Bureau of Labor Statistics, Occupational Employment Statistics

The median annual wage of biological technicians was $39,020 in May 2010. The median wage is the wage at which half the workers in an occupation earned more than that amount and half earned less. The lowest 10 percent earned less than $24,930, and the top 10 percent earned more than $62,890.

Median annual wages in selected industries employing biological technicians in May 2010 were as follows:

Colleges, universities, and professional schools; private	$44,950
Pharmaceutical and medicine manufacturing	43,010
Research and development in the physical, engineering, and life sciences	42,280
Colleges, universities, and professional schools; state	38,480
Federal government, excluding postal service	32,350

Most biological technicians work full time and keep regular hours.

Job Outlook

Biological Technicians
Percent change in employment, projected 2010-20

Life, Physical, and Social Science Occupations	16%
Total, All Occupations	14%
Biological Technicians	14%

Note: All Occupations includes all occupations in the U.S. Economy.
Source: U.S. Bureau of Labor Statistics, Employment Projections program

Employment of biological technicians is projected to increase 14 percent from 2010 to 2020, as fast as the average for all occupations. Greater demand for biotechnology research is expected to increase the need for these workers.

Biotechnology research plays a key role in scientific advancements that improve our way of life. Biological technicians will be needed to help scientists develop new medicines and treatments for diseases such as cancer and Alzheimer's.

In agriculture, biotechnology research will be used to create genetically engineered crops that provide greater yields and require less pesticide and fertilizer. In addition, efforts to discover new and improved ways to clean and preserve the environment will continue to add to job growth. Finally, biological technicians will be needed to help develop alternative sources of energy, such as biofuels and biomass.

Job Prospects

Strong competition for jobs is expected. There have been large increases in the number of bachelor's degrees in biology and other life sciences awarded each year, and this trend is expected to continue. Applicants who have laboratory experience, either through coursework or previous work experience, should have the best opportunities.

Employment projections data for biological technicians, 2010-20

Occupational Title	SOC Code	Employment, 2010	Projected Employment, 2020	Change, 2010-20	
				Percent	Numeric
Biological Technicians	19-4021	80,200	91,100	14	10,900
SOURCE: U.S. Bureau of Labor Statistics, Employment Projections program					

Similar Occupations

This table shows a list of occupations with job duties that are similar to those of biological technicians.

Occupation	Job Duties	Entry-Level Education	Median Annual Pay, May 2010
Agricultural and Food Science Technicians	Under the supervision of scientists, agricultural and food science technicians measure and analyze the quality of food and agricultural products.	Associate's degree	$32,760
Biochemists and Biophysicists	Biochemists and biophysicists study the chemical and physical principles of living things and of biological processes such as cell development, growth, and heredity.	Doctoral or professional degree	$79,390
Chemical Technicians	Chemical technicians use special instruments and techniques to help chemists and chemical engineers in researching, developing, and producing chemical products and processes.	Associate's degree	$42,040
Epidemiologists	Epidemiologists investigate the causes of disease and other public health problems to prevent them from spreading or from happening again. They report their findings to public policy officials and to the general public.	Master's degree	$63,010
Medical and Clinical Laboratory Technologists and Technicians	Medical laboratory technologists (also known as medical laboratory scientists) and medical laboratory technicians collect samples and perform tests to analyze body fluids, tissue, and other substances.	See How to Become One	$46,680
Medical Scientists	Medical scientists conduct research aimed at improving overall human health. They often use clinical trials and other investigative methods to reach their findings.	Doctoral or professional degree	$76,700
Microbiologists	Microbiologists study the growth, development, and other characteristics of microscopic organisms such as bacteria, algae, and fungi.	Bachelor's degree	$65,920
Zoologists and Wildlife Biologists	Zoologists and wildlife biologists study the characteristics and habitats of animals and wildlife.	Bachelor's degree	$57,430

Contacts for More Information

For more information on career opportunities in the biological sciences, visit American Institute for Biological Sciences , American Society for Cell Biology , American Society for Microbiology , Federation of American Societies for Experimental Biology

For information on biological technician careers with the federal government, visit USAJOBS

Suggested citation:

Bureau of Labor Statistics, U.S. Department of Labor, Occupational Outlook Handbook, 2012-13 Edition, Biological Technicians, on the Internet at http://www.bls.gov/ooh/life-physical-and-social-science/biological-technicians.htm .

Chemical Technicians

Quick Facts: Chemical Technicians	
2010 Median Pay	$42,040 per year $20.21 per hour
Entry-Level Education	Associate's degree
Work Experience in a Related Occupation	None
On-the-job Training	Moderate-term on-the-job training
Number of Jobs, 2010	61,000
Job Outlook, 2010-20	7% (Slower than average)
Employment Change, 2010-20	4,100

What Chemical Technicians Do

Chemical technicians use special instruments and techniques to help scientists and engineers in researching, developing, and producing chemical products and processes.

Duties

Chemical technicians typically do the following:

- Monitor chemical processes and test the quality of products to make sure that they meet standards and specifications

- Set up and maintain laboratory instruments and equipment

- Prepare chemical solutions for use in their work

- Conduct chemical and physical experiments, tests, and analyses for a variety of purposes, including research and development

- Compile and interpret results of tests and analyses

- Prepare technical reports, graphs, and charts, and give presentations that summarize their results

Most chemical technicians work on teams. Typically, they are supervised by chemists or chemical engineers who direct their work and evaluate their results. For example, some chemical technicians help chemists and other scientists develop new medicines. Others help chemical engineers develop more efficient production processes.

Chemical technicians' duties and titles often depend on where they work. The following are the two main types of chemical technicians:

Laboratory technicians typically help scientists conduct experiments and analyses. For example, they prepare chemical solutions, test products for quality and performance, and analyze compounds produced through complex chemical processes. Other laboratory technicians analyze samples of air and water to monitor pollution levels. Laboratory technicians usually set up and maintain laboratory equipment and instruments.

Processing technicians monitor the quality of products and processes at chemical manufacturing facilities. For example, they adjust processing equipment to improve production efficiency and output. They collect samples from production batches, which then are tested for impurities and other defects. Processing technicians also test product packaging to make sure it is well designed, will hold up well, and will be good for the environment.

Work Environment

Chemical technicians held about 61,000 jobs in 2010. The industries employing the largest numbers of chemical technicians in 2010 were as follows:

Testing laboratories	19%
Research and development in the physical, engineering, and life sciences	11
Pharmaceutical and medicine manufacturing	10
Basic chemical manufacturing	8
Colleges, universities, and professional schools; state, local, and private	6

Chemical technicians typically work in laboratories or in industrial facilities such as chemical and pharmaceutical manufacturing plants. Some chemical technicians are exposed to health or safety hazards when handling certain chemicals, but there is little risk if they follow proper procedures.

Work Schedules

Most technicians work full time. Processing technicians often work longer and later shifts than research and development technicians because many manufacturing facilities operate around the clock.

How to Become a Chemical Technician

Chemical technicians need an associate's degree or 2 years of postsecondary training for most jobs. Most chemical technicians receive on-the-job training.

Education

For most jobs, chemical technicians need an associate's degree in applied science or chemical technology or 2 years of postsecondary training.

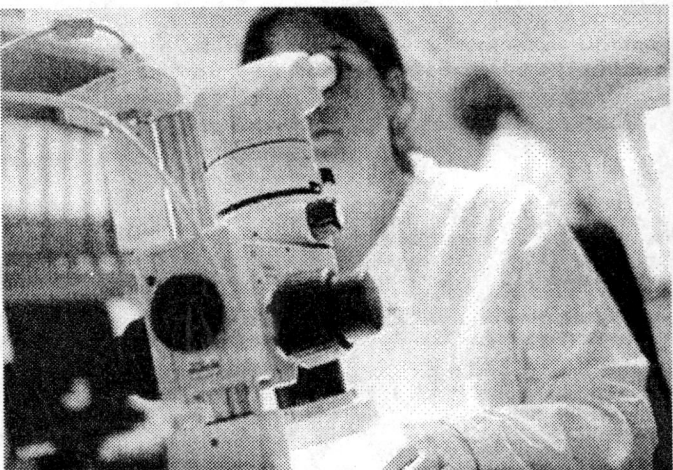

Chemical technicians often use laboratory equipment, such as microscopes, to do their work.

Many technical and community colleges offer programs in applied sciences or chemical technology. Students typically take classes in mathematics, physics, and biology in addition to chemistry courses. Coursework in statistics and computer science is also useful because technicians routinely do data analysis and modeling.

One of the most important aspects of any degree program is laboratory time. Laboratory coursework provides students with hands-on experience in conducting experiments and using various instruments and techniques properly. Many schools also offer internships and cooperative-education programs that help students gain employment experience while attending school. That experience can enhance students' job prospects.

Important Qualities

Analytical skills. Chemical technicians must be able to conduct scientific experiments with accuracy and precision.

Critical-thinking skills. Chemical technicians reach their conclusions through sound reasoning and judgment. They also must be able to evaluate the work of others.

Interpersonal skills. Chemical technicians must be able to work well with others as part of a team, because they often work with scientists, engineers, and other technicians.

Observation skills. Chemical technicians must carefully monitor chemical experiments and processes. They must keep complete records of their work, including conditions, procedures, and results.

Speaking skills. Chemical technicians must explain their work to scientists and engineers and to workers who may not have a technical background.

Technical skills. Chemical technicians must be able to set up and operate sophisticated equipment and instruments. They also may need to adjust the equipment to ensure that experiments and processes are running properly.

Time-management skills. Chemical technicians often work on multiple tasks and projects at the same time and must be able to prioritize their assignments.

Writing skills. Chemical technicians must write reports that summarize their findings and results.

Training

Most chemical technicians receive on-the-job training. Typically, experienced technicians teach new employees proper methods and procedures for conducting experiments and operating equipment. Length of training varies with the new employee's level of experience and education and the industry the worker is employed in.

Advancement

Technicians who have a bachelor's degree are often able to advance to positions as chemists and chemical engineers.

Pay

Chemical Technicians
Median annual wages, May 2010

Life, Physical, and Social Science Occupations	$58,530
Chemical Technicians	$42,040
Total, All Occupations	$33,840

Note: All Occupations includes all occupations in the U.S. Economy.
Source: U.S. Bureau of Labor Statistics, Occupational Employment Statistics

The median annual wage of chemical technicians was $42,040 in May 2010. The median wage is the wage at which half the workers in an occupation earned more than that amount and half earned less. The lowest 10 percent earned less than $26,030, and the top 10 percent earned more than $66,710.

Median annual wages in the industries employing the largest numbers of chemical technicians in May 2010 were as follows:

Basic chemical manufacturing	$48,440
Research and development in the physical, engineering, and life sciences	46,320
Pharmaceutical and medicine manufacturing	45,180
Colleges, universities, and professional schools; state, local, and private	41,050
Testing laboratories	32,930

Most technicians work full time. Processing technicians often work longer and later shifts than research and development technicians because many manufacturing facilities operate around the clock.

Job Outlook

Chemical Technicians
Percent change in employment, projected 2010-20

Life, Physical, and Social Science Occupations	16%
Total, All Occupations	14%
Chemical Technicians	7%

Note: All Occupations includes all occupations in the U.S. Economy.
Source: U.S. Bureau of Labor Statistics, Employment Projections program

Employment of chemical technicians is expected to increase by 7 percent from 2010 to 2020, slower than the average for all occupations. Chemical technicians will continue to be needed in scientific research and development (R&D) and to monitor the quality of chemical products and processes. Greater interest in environmental issues, such as pollution control, clean energy, and sustainability, are expected to increase the demand for chemistry research and development.

Declines are expected in chemical and pharmaceutical manufacturing. Many chemical and pharmaceutical manufacturers are expected to outsource their scientific R&D and testing operations to professional, scientific, and technical services firms that specialize in these services. In addition, many companies are expected to increase the amount of manufacturing done overseas, further limiting the demand for chemical technicians in those industries.

Job Prospects

As the instrumentation and techniques used in research, development, and production become more complex, employers will seek job candidates with highly developed technical skills. Job opportunities are expected to be best for graduates of applied science technology programs who are well trained on equipment used in laboratories or production facilities.

In addition to job openings created by growth, many openings should arise from the need to replace technicians who retire or leave the labor force for other reasons.

Employment projections data for chemical technicians, 2010-20

Occupational Title	SOC Code	Employment, 2010	Projected Employment, 2020	Change, 2010-20	
				Percent	Numeric
Chemical Technicians	19-4031	61,000	65,100	7	4,100
SOURCE: U.S. Bureau of Labor Statistics, Employment Projections program					

Similar Occupations

This table shows a list of occupations with job duties that are similar to those of chemical technicians.

Occupation	Job Duties	Entry-Level Education	Median Annual Pay, May 2010
Biological Technicians	Biological technicians help biological and medical scientists conduct laboratory tests and experiments.	Bachelor's degree	$39,020
Chemical Engineers	Chemical engineers apply the principles of chemistry, biology, and physics to solve problems. These problems involve the production or use of chemicals, fuel, drugs, food, and many other products. They design processes and equipment for large-scale safe and sustainable manufacturing, plan and test methods of manufacturing products and treating byproducts, and supervise production.	Bachelor's degree	$90,300
Chemists and Materials Scientists	Chemists and materials scientists study the structures, compositions, reactions, and other properties of substances. They use their knowledge to develop new and improved products, processes, and materials.	Bachelor's degree	$69,790
Environmental Science and Protection Technicians	Environmental science and protection technicians do laboratory and field tests to monitor the environment and investigate sources of pollution, including those affecting health. Many work under the supervision of environmental scientists and specialists, who direct their work and evaluate their results.	Associate's degree	$41,380
Forensic Science Technicians	Forensic science technicians help investigate crimes by collecting and analyzing physical evidence. Most technicians specialize in either crime scene investigation or laboratory analysis.	Bachelor's degree	$51,570
Geological and Petroleum Technicians	Geological and petroleum technicians provide support to scientists and engineers in exploring and extracting natural resources, such as minerals, oil, and natural gas.	Associate's degree	$54,020
Nuclear Technicians	Nuclear technicians assist physicists, engineers, and other professionals in nuclear research and nuclear production. They operate special equipment used in these activities and monitor the levels of radiation that are produced.	Associate's degree	$68,090

Contacts for More Information

For more information about chemical technicians, visit American Chemical Society

Suggested citation:

Bureau of Labor Statistics, U.S. Department of Labor, Occupational Outlook Handbook, 2012-13 Edition, Chemical Technicians, on the Internet at http://www.bls.gov/ooh/life-physical-and-social-science/chemical-technicians.htm.

Chemists and Materials Scientists

Quick Facts: Chemists and Materials Scientists	
2010 Median Pay	$69,790 per year $33.55 per hour
Entry-Level Education	Bachelor's degree
Work Experience in a Related Occupation	None
On-the-job Training	None
Number of Jobs, 2010	90,900
Job Outlook, 2010-20	4% (Slower than average)
Employment Change, 2010-20	4,000

What Chemists and Materials Scientists Do

Chemists and materials scientists study the structures, compositions, reactions, and other properties of substances. They use their knowledge to develop new and improved products, processes, and materials.

Duties

Chemists and materials scientists typically do the following:

- Plan and carry out complex research projects, such as the development of new products, processes, and testing methods
- Direct technicians and other workers in testing procedures to analyze components and physical properties of materials
- Instruct scientists and technicians on proper chemical processing and testing procedures, such as ingredients, mixing times, and operating temperatures
- Prepare test solutions, compounds, and reagents (such as acids) used in laboratory procedures
- Analyze substances to determine their chemical and physical properties, such as their structure and composition
- Conduct tests on materials and other substances to ensure that safety and quality standards are met
- Write technical reports that detail methods and findings
- Present research findings to scientists, engineers, and other colleagues

Many chemists and materials scientists work in basic and applied research. In basic research, chemists investigate the properties, composition, and structure of matter. They also experiment with the laws that govern the combination of elements and reactions of substances to each other.

In applied research, chemists create new products and processes or improve existing ones, often using knowledge gained from basic research. Chemistry research has led to the discovery and development of new and improved drugs, plastics, cleaners, and thousands of other products.

Almost all materials scientists work in applied research. They study the structures and chemical properties of various materials to develop new products or enhance existing ones. They also determine ways to strengthen or combine materials or develop new materials for use in a variety of products. Applications of materials science include superconducting materials, ceramics, and metallic alloys.

Chemists and materials scientists use computers and a wide variety of sophisticated laboratory instrumentation for modeling, simulation, and experimental analysis. For example, some chemists use three-dimensional (3D) computer modeling software to study the structure and other properties of complex molecules that they make.

Most chemists and materials scientists work as part of a team. An increasing number of scientific research projects involve multiple disciplines, and it is common for chemists and materials scientists to work on teams with other scientists, such as biologists and physicists, computer specialists, and engineers. For example, in pharmaceutical research, chemists may work with biologists to develop new drugs and with engineers to design ways to mass produce them. For more information, see the profiles on biochemists and biophysicists , microbiologists , zoologists and wildlife biologists , physicists and astronomers , computer and information technology occupations , and engineers .

Chemists often specialize in a particular branch of the field. The following are examples of some types of chemists:

Analytical chemists determine the structure, composition, and nature of substances by examining and identifying their various elements or compounds. They also study the relationships and interactions between the parts of compounds and develop new techniques for carrying out their work. Their research has a wide range of applications, including food safety, pharmaceuticals, and pollution control.

Inorganic chemists study the structure, properties, and reactions of molecules that do not contain carbon, such as metals. They work to understand the behavior and the characteristics of inorganic substances. Inorganic chemists figure out how these materials can be modified, separated, or used in products, such as ceramics and superconductors.

Medicinal chemists research and develop chemical compounds that can be used as pharmaceutical drugs. They work on teams with other scientists and engineers to create and test new drug products. They also help develop new and improved manufacturing processes to produce new drugs on a large scale effectively.

Organic chemists study the structure, properties, and reactions of

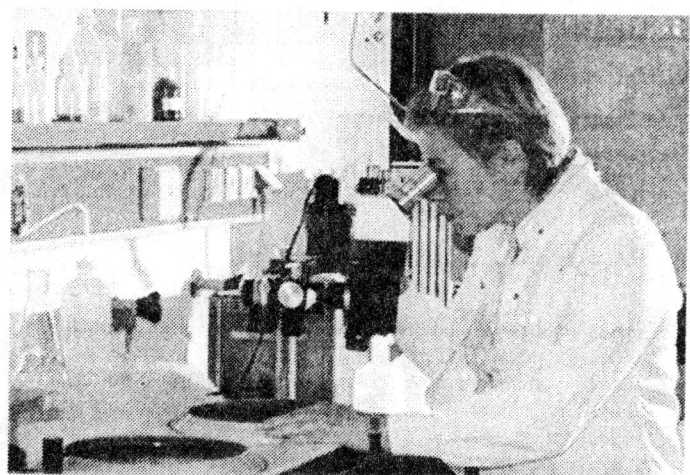

Chemists and materials scientists use powerful microscopes to examine the structures of substances.

molecules that contain carbon. They also design and make new organic substances that have unique properties and applications. These compounds have, in turn, been used to develop many commercial products, such as pharmaceutical drugs and plastics.

Physical chemists study the fundamental characteristics of how matter behaves on a molecular and atomic level and how chemical reactions occur. Based on their analyses, physical chemists may develop new theories, such as how complex structures are formed. Physical chemists often work closely with materials scientists to research and develop potential uses for new materials.

A growing numbers of chemists work in interdisciplinary fields, such as biochemistry and geochemistry.For more information, see the profiles on biochemists and biophysicists and geoscientists .

Many people with a chemistry background become professors or teachers. For more information, see the profiles on high school teachers and postsecondary teachers .

Work Environment

Chemists and material scientists held about 90,900 jobs in 2010. The industries employing the largest numbers of chemists in 2010 were the following:

Research and development in the physical, engineering, and life sciences	19%
Pharmaceutical and medicine manufacturing	18
Testing laboratories	11
Federal government, excluding postal service	8
Colleges, universities, and professional schools; state, local, and private	5

Most materials scientists work in manufacturing and scientific research and development.

Chemists and materials scientists typically work in laboratories and offices where they conduct experiments and analyze their results. In addition to laboratories, materials scientists work with engineers and processing specialists in industrial manufacturing facilities. Some chemists also work in these facilities and are usually responsible for monitoring the environmental conditions at the plant.

Chemists and materials scientists can be exposed to health or safety hazards when handling certain chemicals, but there is little risk if proper procedures are followed.

Most chemists and materials scientists work full time and regular hours, though longer hours are common.

How to Become a Chemist or Materials Scientist

Chemists and materials scientists need at least a bachelor's degree in chemistry or a related field. However, a master's degree or Ph.D. is needed for many research jobs.

Education

A bachelor's degree in chemistry or in a related field is needed for entry-level chemist jobs. Although some materials scientists hold a degree in materials science, these scientists commonly have a degree in chemistry, physics, or engineering. Many employers, particularly in the pharmaceutical industry, prefer to hire chemists and materials scientists with a Ph.D and postdoctoral experience to lead basic and applied research.

Many colleges and universities offer degree programs in chemistry. The number of colleges that offer degree programs in materials science is small but gradually increasing. Also, many engineering schools offer degrees in the joint field of materials science and engineering.

Undergraduate chemistry majors are typically required to take courses in analytical, organic, inorganic, and physical chemistry. In addition to chemistry coursework, they also take classes in

mathematics, biological sciences, and physics.Computer science courses are essential, because chemists and materials scientists need computer skills to perform modeling and simulation tasks and to operate computerized laboratory equipment.

Experience, either in a college or university laboratory, or through internships, fellowships, or work-study programs in industry, is also useful

Graduate students studying chemistry commonly specialize in a subfield, such as analytical chemistry or inorganic chemistry, depending on their interests and the kind of work they wish to do. For example, those interested in doing research in the pharmaceutical industry usually develop a strong background in medicinal or organic chemistry.

Important Qualities

Analytical skills. Chemists and materials scientists need to be able to carry out scientific experiments and studies. They must be precise and accurate in their analyses because any errors could invalidate their research.

Critical-thinking skills. Chemists and materials scientists carefully evaluate their own work and the work of others. They must determine if results and conclusions are based on sound science.

Mathematical skills. Chemists and materials scientists regularly use complex mathematical equations and formulas, and they need a broad understanding of mathematics, including calculus, algebra, and statistics.

Problem-solving skills. Chemists and materials scientists research and develop new and improved chemical products, processes, and materials. This work requires a great deal of trial and error on the part of chemists and materials scientists before a unique solution is found.

Speaking skills. Chemists and materials scientists frequently give presentations that describe their findings.

Teamwork. Chemists and materials scientists typically work on research teams. They need to be able to work well with others towards a common goal. Many serve in a leadership capacity and need to able to motivate and direct other team members.

Writing skills. Chemists and materials scientists often write memos, reports, and research papers that explain their findings.

Advancement

Chemists typically receive greater responsibility and independence in their work as they gain experience. Greater responsibility is also gained through further education. Ph.D. chemists usually lead research teams and have control over the direction and content of projects.

Some chemists and materials scientists move into managerial positions, often as natural sciences managers .

Pay

Chemists and Materials Scientists Median annual wages, May 2010	
Materials Scientists	$84,720
Chemists and Materials Scientists	$69,790
Chemists	$68,320
Total, All Occupations	$33,840

Note: All Occupations includes all occupations in the U.S. Economy.
Source: U.S. Bureau of Labor Statistics, Occupational Employment Statistics

The median annual wage of chemists was $68,320 in May 2010. The median wage is the wage at which half the workers in an occupation earned more than that amount and half earned less. The lowest 10 percent earned less than $39,250, and the top 10 percent more than $116,130.

Median annual wages in the industries employing the largest numbers of chemists in May 2010 were the following:

Federal government, excluding postal service	$100,910
Research and development in the physical, engineering, and life sciences	77,110
Pharmaceutical and medicine manufacturing	67,540
Testing laboratories	52,220
Colleges, universities, and professional schools; state, local, and private	49,430

The median annual wage for materials scientists was $84,720 in May 2010. The lowest 10 percent earned less than $45,810, and the top 10 percent more than $130,070.

Most chemists and materials scientists work full time and keep regular hours, though longer hours are not uncommon.

Job Outlook

Chemists and Materials Scientists

Percent change in employment, projected 2010-20

Total, All Occupations	14%
Materials Scientists	10%
Chemists and Materials Scientists	4%
Chemists	4%

Note: All Occupations includes all occupations in the U.S. Economy.
Source: U.S. Bureau of Labor Statistics, Employment Projections program

Employment of chemists and materials scientists is expected to increase by 4 percent from 2010 to 2020, which is slower than the average for all occupations.

Employment of chemists is expected to grow by 4 percent, as they will continue to be needed in scientific research and development and to monitor the quality of chemical products and processes.

Employment of materials scientists is expected to grow by 10 percent, owing to demand for cheaper, safer, and better quality materials for a variety of purposes, such as electronics, energy, and transportation.

Declines in employment of chemists is expected at chemical and drug manufacturers. To control costs and minimize risks, many of these companies are expected to partner with research universities and smaller scientific research and development (R&D) and testing services firms to perform work formerly done by in-house chemists. Additionally, companies in these industries are expected to conduct an increasing amount of manufacturing and R&D in other countries, further limiting domestic employment growth.

Environmental research will offer many new opportunities for chemists and materials scientists. For example, chemical manufacturing industries will continue to invest billions of dollars each year to develop technologies and processes that reduce pollution and improve energy efficiency at manufacturing facilities.

Also, the development of improved battery technologies and alternative energy sources should lead to greater demand for chemists and materials scientists. Chemists will continue to be needed to monitor pollution levels at manufacturing facilities and ensure compliance with local, state, and federal environmental regulations.

Job Prospects

In addition to job openings resulting from employment growth, some job openings will result from the need to replace chemists and materials scientists who retire or otherwise leave the occupation.

Chemists and materials scientists with advanced degrees, particularly those with a Ph.D., are expected to experience better opportunities. Large pharmaceutical and biotechnology firms provide openings for these workers at research laboratories, and many others work in colleges and universities. Furthermore, chemists with advanced degrees will continue to fill most senior research and upper management positions.

Employment projections data for chemists and materials scientists, 2010-20

Occupational Title	SOC Code	Employment, 2010	Projected Employment, 2020	Change, 2010-20	
				Percent	Numeric
Chemists and Materials Scientists	19-2030	90,900	94,900	4	4,000
Chemists	19-2031	82,200	85,400	4	3,200
Materials Scientists	19-2032	8,700	9,500	10	900
SOURCE: U.S. Bureau of Labor Statistics, Employment Projections program					

Similar Occupations

This table shows a list of occupations with job duties that are similar to those of chemists and materials scientists.

Occupation	Job Duties	Entry-Level Education	Median Annual Pay, May 2010
Agricultural and Food Scientists	Agricultural and food scientists work to ensure agricultural productivity and food safety.	See How to Become One	$58,450
Biochemists and Biophysicists	Biochemists and biophysicists study the chemical and physical principles of living things and of biological processes such as cell development, growth, and heredity.	Doctoral or professional degree	$79,390
Chemical Engineers	Chemical engineers apply the principles of chemistry, biology, and physics to solve problems. These problems involve the production or use of chemicals, fuel, drugs, food, and many other products. They design processes and equipment for large-scale safe and sustainable manufacturing, plan and test methods of manufacturing products and treating byproducts, and supervise production.	Bachelor's degree	$90,300
Environmental Scientists and Specialists	Environmental scientists and specialists use their knowledge of the natural sciences to protect the environment. They identify problems and find solutions that minimize hazards to the health of the environment and the population.	Bachelor's degree	$61,700

Geoscientists	Geoscientists study the physical aspects of the Earth, such as its composition, structure, and processes, to learn about its past, present, and future.	Bachelor's degree	$82,500
High School Teachers	High school teachers help prepare students for life after graduation. They teach academic lessons and various skills that students will need to attend college and to enter the job market.	Bachelor's degree	$53,230
Materials Engineers	Materials engineers develop, process, and test materials used to create a range of products, from computer chips and aircraft wings to golf clubs and snow skis. They also help select materials and develop new ways to use materials.	Bachelor's degree	$83,120
Natural Sciences Managers	Natural sciences managers supervise the work of scientists, including chemists, physicists, and biologists. They direct research and development projects and coordinate activities such as testing, quality control, and production.	Bachelor's degree	$116,020
Physicists and Astronomers	Physicists and astronomers study the fundamental nature of the universe, ranging from the vastness of space to the smallest of subatomic particles. They develop new technologies, methods, and theories based on the results of their research that deepen our understanding of how things work and contribute to innovative, real-world applications.	Doctoral or professional degree	$105,430
Postsecondary Teachers	Postsecondary teachers instruct students in a wide variety of academic and vocational subjects beyond the high school level. They also conduct research and publish scholarly papers and books.	Doctoral or professional degree	$62,050

Contacts for More Information

For information on career opportunities, earnings, and education for chemists and materials scientists, visit American Chemical Society

For information on obtaining a position as a chemist with the federal government, visit USAJOBS

Suggested citation:

Bureau of Labor Statistics, U.S. Department of Labor, Occupational Outlook Handbook, 2012-13 Edition, Chemists and Materials Scientists, on the Internet at http://www.bls.gov/ooh/life-physical-and-social-science/chemists-and-materials-scientists.htm .

Conservation Scientists and Foresters

Quick Facts: Conservation Scientists and Foresters	
2010 Median Pay	$57,420 per year $27.60 per hour
Entry-Level Education	Bachelor's degree
Work Experience in a Related Occupation	None
On-the-job Training	None
Number of Jobs, 2010	34,900
Job Outlook, 2010-20	5% (Slower than average)
Employment Change, 2010-20	1,700

What Conservation Scientists and Foresters Do

Conservation scientists and foresters manage overall land quality of forests, parks, rangelands, and other natural resources.

Duties

Conservation scientists and foresters typically do the following:

- Monitor forestry and conservation activities to assure compliance with government regulations
- Establish plans for managing forest lands and resources
- Supervise activities of other forestry and conservation workers
- Choose and prepare sites for new trees using controlled burning, bulldozers, or herbicides to clear land
- Negotiate terms and conditions for forest harvesting and land-use contracts
- Direct and participate in forest-fire suppression
- Determine ways to remove timber with minimum environmental damage
- Monitor forest-cleared lands to ensure that they are suitable for future use

Conservation scientists manage, improve, and protect the country's natural resources. They work with landowners and federal, state, and local governments to devise ways to use and improve the land while safeguarding the environment. Conservation scientists advise farmers, farm managers, and ranchers on how they can improve their land for agricultural purposes and control erosion.

Foresters have a wide range of duties, and their responsibilities vary depending on their employer. Some primary duties of foresters include drawing up plans to regenerate forested lands, monitoring the progress of those lands, and supervising tree harvests. They also come up with plans to keep forests free from disease, harmful insects, and damaging wildfires.

Foresters may choose and direct the preparation of sites on which trees will be planted. They advise on the type, number, and placement of trees to be planted. When the trees reach a certain size, foresters decide which trees should be harvested and sold to sawmills.

Many conservation scientists and foresters supervise forest and conservation workers and technicians, directing their work and evaluating their progress. For more information, see the profiles on forest and conservation workers and forest and conservation technicians .

Conservation scientists and foresters evaluate data on forest and soil quality, assessing damage to trees and forest lands caused by fires and logging activities. In addition, they lead activities such as fire suppression and planting seedlings. Fire suppression activities include measuring how quickly fires will spread and how successful the planned suppression activity turns out.

Scientists and foresters use their skills to determine a fire's impact on a region's environment. Communication with firefighters and other forest workers is an important component of fire suppression activities because the information that conservation scientists and foresters give can change how firefighters work.

Conservation scientists and foresters use a number of tools to perform their jobs. They use clinometers to measure the heights of trees, diameter tapes to measure a tree's circumference, and increment borers and bark gauges to measure the growth of trees so that timber volumes can be computed and growth rates estimated.

In addition, conservation scientists and foresters often use remote sensing (aerial photographs and other imagery taken from airplanes and satellites) and geographic information systems (GIS) data to map large forest or range areas and to detect widespread trends of forest and land use. They make extensive use of hand-held computers and global positioning systems (GPS) to study these maps.

The following are some types of conservation scientists and foresters:

Procurement foresters buy timber by contacting local forest owners and negotiating a sale. This activity typically involves taking inventory on the type, amount, and location of all standing timber on the property. Procurement foresters then appraise the timber's worth, negotiate its purchase, and draw up a contract. The forester then subcontracts with loggers or pulpwood cutters to remove the trees and to help lay out roads to get to the timber.

Other foresters, mostly in the federal government, study issues facing forests and related natural resources. They may study issues such as tree improvement and harvesting techniques, global climate change, improving wildlife habitats, and protecting forests from pests, diseases, and wildfires.

Urban foresters live and work in larger cities and manage urban trees. They are concerned with quality-of-life issues, including air quality, shade, and storm water runoff.

Conservation education foresters train teachers and students about issues facing forest lands.

Two of the most common types of conservation scientists are range managers and soil conservationists.

Range managers, also called range conservationists, protect rangelands to maximize their use without damaging the environment. Rangelands contain many natural resources and cover hundreds of millions of acres in the United States, mainly in the western states and Alaska.

Range managers may inventory soils, plants, and animals; develop resource management plans; help to restore degraded ecosystems; or help manage a ranch. They also maintain soil stability and vegetation for uses such as wildlife habitats and outdoor recreation. Like foresters, they work to prevent and reduce wildfires and invasive animal species.

Soil and water conservationists give technical help to people who are concerned with the conservation of soil, water, and related natural resources. For private landowners, they develop programs to make the most productive use of land without damaging it. They also help landowners with issues such as dealing with erosion. They help private landowners and governments by advising on water quality, preserving water supplies, preventing groundwater contamination, and conserving water.

Conservation scientists and foresters manage and monitor overall land quality of forests, parks, rangelands, and other natural resources.

Work Environment

Conservation scientists and foresters held about 34,900 jobs in 2010. The industries employing the largest numbers of conservation scientists in 2010 were as follows:

Federal government, excluding postal service	33%
State government, excluding education and hospitals	22
Local government, excluding education and hospitals	15
Social advocacy organizations	7
Management, scientific, and technical consulting services	3

The industries employing the largest numbers of foresters in 2010 were as follows:

State government, excluding education and hospitals	31%
Federal government, excluding postal service	16
Local government, excluding education and hospitals	13
Sawmills and wood preservation	6
Logging	4

Conservation scientists and foresters work for governments (federal, state, or local) or on privately owned lands. In the western and southwestern United States, they usually work for the federal government because of the number of national parks in that part of the country. In the eastern United States, they often work for private landowners.

Conservation scientists and foresters typically work in offices, in laboratories, and in the outdoors, sometimes doing fieldwork in remote locations. When visiting or working near logging operations or wood yards, they wear a hardhat.

The work can be physically demanding. Some conservation scientists and foresters work outdoors in all types of weather, occasionally in isolated areas. They may need to walk long distances through dense woods and underbrush to carry out their work.

In an isolated location, a forester or conservation scientist may work alone, measuring tree densities, regeneration, or other outdoor activities. Other foresters work closely with the public, educating them about the forest or the proper use of recreational sites.

Fire suppression activities are an important aspect of their duties, which involve prevention as well as emergency response. Therefore, their work has occasional risk.

Work Schedules

Most conservation scientists and foresters work full time and have a routine work schedule. Responding to emergencies or fires may require conservation scientists and foresters to work longer hours.

How to Become a Conservation Scientist or Forester

Conservation scientists and foresters typically need a bachelor's degree in forestry or a related field.Employers seek applicants who have degrees from programs that are accredited by the Society of American Foresters (SAF) and other organizations.

Education

Conservation scientists and foresters typically need a bachelor's degree in forestry or a related field, such as agricultural science, rangeland management, or environmental science. Although graduate work is not generally required, some conservation scientists and foresters get a master's degree or Ph.D.

Most forest and conservation technology programs are accredited by the Society of American Foresters , and there are accredited programs in every state.

Many colleges and universities offer degrees in forestry or a related field. Bachelor's degree programs are designed to prepare conservation scientists and foresters for their career or a graduate degree. Alongside practical skills, theory and education are important parts of these programs.

Courses for bachelor's and advanced degree programs in forestry and related fields typically include ecology, biology, and forest resource measurement. Scientists and foresters also typically have a background in a geographic information system (GIS) technology and other forms of computer modeling.

Licenses

Sixteen states sponsor some type of credentialing process for foresters. Alabama, California, Connecticut, Maine, Maryland, Massachusetts, and New Hampshire have licensing laws. Arkansas, Georgia, Mississippi, North Carolina, and South Carolina have laws requiring registration. Michigan, New Jersey, Oklahoma, and West Virginia have laws about voluntary registration.

Both licensing and registration requirements usually require a 4-year degree in forestry and several years of forestry work experience. Candidates who want a license also may be required to pass an exam.

Advancement

Many conservation scientists and foresters advance to take on managerial duties. They also may conduct research or work on policy issues, often after getting an advanced degree. Foresters in management usually leave fieldwork behind, spending more of their time in an office, working with teams to develop management plans and supervising others.

One option for advancement in these occupations is to become certified. The Society of American Foresters certifies foresters who have at least a bachelor's degree from one of the 50 forestry or natural resources degree programs accredited by the society or from a forestry program that is substantially equivalent. The candidate must also have 5 years of qualifying professional experience and pass an exam.

The Society for Range Management also offers a professional certification in rangeland management or range management consultant.

Soil conservationists usually begin working within one district and may advance to a state, regional, or national level. Also, soil conservationists can transfer to occupations such as farm or ranch management advisor or land appraiser.

Important Qualities

Analytical skills. Conservation scientists and foresters must evaluate the results of a variety of field tests and experiments, all of which require precision and accuracy.

Critical-thinking skills. Conservation scientists and foresters reach conclusions through sound reasoning and judgment. They determine how to improve forest conditions, and they must react appropriately to fires.

Decision-making skills. Conservation scientists and foresters must use their expertise and experience to determine whether their findings will have an impact on soil, forest lands, and the spread of fires.

Interpersonal skills. Conservation scientists and foresters need to work well with the forest and conservation workers and technicians they supervise, so effective communication is critical.

Physical stamina. Conservation scientists and foresters often walk long distances in steep and wooded areas. They work in all kinds of weather, including extreme heat and cold.

Speaking skills. Conservation scientists and foresters must give clear instructions to forest and conservation workers and technicians, who typically do the labor necessary for proper forest maintenance.

Pay

Conservation Scientists and Foresters
Median annual wages, May 2010

Conservation Scientists	$59,310
Conservation Scientists and Foresters	$57,420
Foresters	$54,540
Total, All Occupations	$33,840

Note: All Occupations includes all occupations in the U.S. Economy.
Source: U.S. Bureau of Labor Statistics, Occupational Employment Statistics

The median annual wage of conservation scientists was $59,310 in May 2010. The median wage is the wage at which half the workers in an occupation earned more than that amount and half earned less. The lowest 10 percent earned less than $36,050, and the top 10 percent earned more than $89,440.

The median annual wage of foresters was $54,540 in May 2010. The lowest 10 percent earned less than $35,670, and the top 10 percent earned more than $75,540.

Median annual wages in the industries employing the largest number of conservation scientists in May 2010 were as follows:

Federal government, excluding postal service	$71,100
Management, scientific, and technical consulting services	63,310
Social advocacy organizations	51,710
State government, excluding education and hospitals	51,270
Local government, excluding education and hospitals	49,860

Median annual wages in the industries employing the largest number of foresters in May 2010 were as follows:

Federal government, excluding postal service	$61,680
Logging	59,830
Sawmills and wood preservation	56,880
Local government, excluding education and hospitals	53,150
State government, excluding education and hospitals	49,710

Most conservation scientists and foresters work full time and have a routine work schedule. Responding to emergencies or fires may require conservation scientists and foresters to work longer hours.

Job Outlook

Conservation Scientists and Foresters
Percent change in employment, projected 2010-20

Total, All Occupations	14%
Conservation Scientists and Foresters	5%
Conservation Scientists	5%
Foresters	5%

Note: All Occupations includes all occupations in the U.S. Economy.
Source: U.S. Bureau of Labor Statistics, Employment Projections program

Employment of conservation scientists and foresters is expected to increase by 5 percent between 2010 and 2020, slower than the average for all occupations.

Heightened demand for American timber and wood pellets will help increase the overall job prospects for conservation scientists and foresters. Most growth from 2010 to 2020 for conservation scientists and foresters is expected to be in federally owned forest lands, particularly in the southwestern United States. Jobs in private forests will grow alongside demand for timber and pellets, but ongoing fiscal crises will likely lessen the number of available positions in state and local governments.

In recent years, preventing and suppressing wildfires has become the primary concern for government agencies managing forests and rangelands. The development of previously unused lands, in addition to changing weather conditions, has contributed to increasingly devastating and costly fires.

Increases in funding and new programs should create opportunities for foresters and range managers. Restoring lands affected by fires also will be a major task, particularly in the southwestern and western states, where such fires are most common.

Employment projections data for conservation scientists and foresters, 2010-20

Occupational Title	SOC Code	Employment, 2010	Projected Employment, 2020	Change, 2010-20 Percent	Change, 2010-20 Numeric
Conservation Scientists and Foresters	19-1030	34,900	36,600	5	1,700
Conservation Scientists	19-1031	23,400	24,600	5	1,200
Foresters	19-1032	11,500	12,000	5	500

SOURCE: U.S. Bureau of Labor Statistics, Employment Projections program

Similar Occupations

This table shows a list of occupations with job duties that are similar to those of conservation scientists and foresters.

Occupation	Job Duties	Entry-Level Education	Median Annual Pay, May 2010
Agricultural and Food Scientists	Agricultural and food scientists work to ensure agricultural productivity and food safety.	See How to Become One	$58,450
Environmental Science and Protection Technicians	Environmental science and protection technicians do laboratory and field tests to monitor the environment and investigate sources of pollution, including those affecting health. Many work under the supervision of environmental scientists and specialists, who direct their work and evaluate their results.	Associate's degree	$41,380
Firefighters	Firefighters protect the public by responding to fires and other emergencies. They are frequently the first emergency personnel on the scene of an accident.	Postsecondary non-degree award	$45,250
Forest and Conservation Technicians	Forest and conservation technicians measure and improve the quality of forests, rangeland, and other natural areas.	Associate's degree	$33,390
Forest and Conservation Workers	Forest and conservation workers measure and improve the quality of forests. Under the supervision of foresters and forest and conservation technicians, they help to develop, maintain, and protect forests.	High school diploma or equivalent	$23,900

Contacts for More Information

For more information about conservation scientists and foresters, including schools offering education in forestry, visit Society of American Foresters

For information about careers in forestry, particularly conservation forestry and land management, visit Forest Guild ,
Society for Range Management

Suggested citation:
Bureau of Labor Statistics, U.S. Department of Labor, Occupational Outlook Handbook, 2012-13 Edition, Conservation Scientists and Foresters, on the Internet at http://www.bls.gov/ooh/life-physical-and-social-science/conservation-scientists.htm .

Economists

Quick Facts: Economists	
2010 Median Pay	$89,450 per year $43.00 per hour
Entry-Level Education	Bachelor's degree
Work Experience in a Related Occupation	None
On-the-job Training	None
Number of Jobs, 2010	15,400
Job Outlook, 2010-20	6% (Slower than average)
Employment Change, 2010-20	900

What Economists Do

Economists study the production and distribution of resources, goods, and services.

Duties

Economists typically do the following:

- Research and analyze economic issues
- Conduct surveys and collect data
- Analyze data using mathematical models and statistical techniques
- Prepare reports, tables, and charts that present research results
- Interpret and forecast market trends
- Advise businesses, governments, and individuals on economic topics
- Design policies or make recommendations for solving economic problems
- Write articles for publication in newsletters and academic journals

Economists apply economic analysis to issues within a variety of fields, such as education, health, development, and the environment. Some economists study the cost of products, healthcare, or energy. Others examine employment levels, business cycles, or exchange rates. Still others analyze the effect of taxes, inflation, or interest rates.

Economists often study historical trends and use them to make forecasts. They research and analyze data using a variety of software programs, including spreadsheets, statistical analysis, and database management programs.

More than half of all economists work in federal, state, and local

Economists interpret and forecast market trends.

government. Federal government economists collect and analyze data about the U.S. economy. They also project spending needs and inform policy makers on the economic impact of laws and regulations.

Many economists work for corporations and help them understand how the economy will affect their business. Specifically, economists may analyze issues such as consumer demand and sales to help a company maximize its profits.

Economists also work for research firms and think tanks, where they study and analyze a variety of economic issues. Their analyses and forecasts are frequently published in newspapers and journal articles.

Some economists work abroad for companies with major international operations and for international organizations such as the World Bank, International Monetary Fund, and United Nations.

Many people with an economics background become professors or teachers. For more information, see the profile on postsecondary teachers .

The following are examples of common economist specialties:

Econometricians develop models and use mathematical analyses to test economic relationships. They use techniques such as calculus, game theory, and regression analysis to explain economic facts or trends in all areas of economics.

Financial economists analyze savings, investments, and risk. They also study financial markets and financial institutions.

Industrial organization economists study how companies within an industry are organized and how they compete. They also examine how antitrust laws, which regulate attempts by companies to restrict competition, affect markets.

International economists study international trade and the impact of globalization. They also examine global financial markets and exchange rates.

Labor economists study the supply of workers and the demand for labor by employers. Specifically, they research employment levels and how wages are set. They also analyze the effects of labor-related policies—such as minimum wage laws—and institutions, such as unions.

Macroeconomists and **monetary economists** examine the economy as a whole. They may research trends related to unemployment, inflation, and economic growth. They also study fiscal and monetary policies, which examine the effect of the money supply and interest rates on the economy.

Microeconomists study the supply and demand decisions of individuals and firms. For example, they may determine the quantity of products consumers will demand at a particular price.

Public finance economists study the role of the government in the economy. Specifically, they may analyze the effects of tax cuts, budget deficits, and welfare policies.

Work Environment

Economists held about 15,400 jobs in 2010, of which 52 percent were in government.

The following industries employed the most economists in 2010:

Federal government, excluding postal service	32%
State government, excluding education and hospitals	13
Management, scientific, and technical consulting services	13
Scientific research and development services	8
Local government, excluding education and hospitals	7

Economists often work independently in an office. However, many economists collaborate with other economists and statisticians, sometimes working on teams. Some economists work from home, and others may be required to travel as part of their job or to attend conferences.

Some economists combine a full-time job in universities or business with part-time consulting work.

Work schedules

Most economists work full time. Some work under pressure of deadlines and tight schedules that may require overtime.

How to Become an Economist

Most economist jobs require an advanced degree, but some entry-level jobs are available with a bachelor's degree.

Education

A master's degree or Ph.D. is required for most economist jobs. Positions in business, research, or international organizations often require a combination of advanced education and work experience.

Students can pursue an advanced degree in economics with a bachelor's degree in a number of fields, but a strong background in math is essential. A Ph.D. in economics requires several years of study after earning a bachelor's degree, including doing detailed research in a specialty field.

Candidates with a bachelor's degree qualify for some entry-level economist positions, including jobs with the federal government. An advanced degree is sometimes required for advancement to higher level positions.

Most who complete a bachelor's degree in economics find jobs outside the economics profession as research assistants, financial analysts, market analysts, and similar positions in business and finance.

Work Experience

Aspiring economists can gain valuable experience from internships that involve gathering and analyzing data, conducting interviews and surveys, and writing reports on their findings. In addition, related experience, such as working in business or finance, can be advantageous.

Important Qualities

Analytical skills. Economists must be able to review data, observe patterns, and draw logical conclusions. For example, some economists analyze historical employment trends to make future projections on jobs.

Critical-thinking skills. Economists must be able to use logic and reasoning to solve complex problems. For instance, they might identify how economic trends may affect an organization.

Detail oriented. Economists must pay attention to details. Precise data analysis is necessary to ensure accuracy in their findings.

Math skills. Economists use the principles of statistics, calculus, and other advanced topics in mathematics in their economic analyses.

Speaking skills. Economists must be able to explain their work to others. They may give presentations, explain reports, or advise clients on economic issues. They may collaborate with colleagues and sometimes must explain economic concepts to those without a background in economics.

Writing skills. Economists must be able to present their findings clearly. Many economists prepare reports for colleagues or clients; others write for publication in journals or for news media.

Pay

Economists

Median annual wages, May 2010

Economists	$89,450
Social Scientists and Related Workers	$67,090
Total, All Occupations	$33,840

Note: All Occupations includes all occupations in the U.S. Economy.
Source: U.S. Bureau of Labor Statistics, Occupational Employment Statistics

The median annual wage of economists was $89,450 in May 2010. The median wage is the wage at which half the workers in an occupation earned more than the amount and half earned less. The lowest 10 percent earned less than $48,250, and the top 10 percent earned more than $155,490.

Median annual wages in the industries employing the largest numbers of economists in May 2010 were as follows:

Scientific research and development services	$109,720
Federal executive branch	106,840
Management, scientific, and technical consulting services	93,250
Local government	69,950
State government	61,620

Most economists work full time. Some work under pressure of deadlines and tight schedules that may require overtime.

Job Outlook

Economists

Percent change in employment, projected 2010-20

Social Scientists and Related Workers	18%
Total, All Occupations	14%
Economists	6%

Note: All Occupations includes all occupations in the U.S. Economy.
Source: U.S. Bureau of Labor Statistics, Employment Projections program

Employment of economists is projected to grow 6 percent from 2010 to 2020, slower than the average for all occupations.

Businesses and organizations across many industries are increasingly relying on economic analysis and quantitative methods to analyze and forecast business, sales, and other economic trends. As a result, demand for economists should be best in private industry, especially in management, scientific, and professional consulting services.

However, employment in the federal government—the largest employer of economists—is expected to decline. As a result, demand for economists in the federal government is likely to be limited.

Job Prospects

Despite slower than average employment growth, job opportunities for individuals with a master's degree or Ph.D. are expected to be good. In particular, those with strong quantitative and analytical skills and related work experience should have the best job prospects.

As more companies contract out economics-related work, most job openings for economists will be in consulting services.

Applicants with a bachelor's degree are expected to face stiff competition for jobs. Although there will be greater demand for workers with knowledge of economics, many bachelor's degree holders will likely find jobs outside the economist occupation, working instead as research assistants, financial analysts, market analysts, and in similar positions in business and finance.

Employment opportunities in government are expected to be highly competitive.

Employment of economists is concentrated in large cities.

Employment projections data for economists, 2010-20

Occupational Title	SOC Code	Employment, 2010	Projected Employment, 2020	Change, 2010-20	
				Percent	Numeric
Economists	19-3011	15,400	16,400	6	900
SOURCE: U.S. Bureau of Labor Statistics, Employment Projections program					

Similar Occupations

This table shows a list of occupations with job duties that are similar to those of economists.

Occupation	Job Duties	Entry-Level Education	Median Annual Pay, May 2010
Budget Analysts	Budget analysts help public and private institutions organize their finances. They prepare budget reports and monitor institutional spending.	Bachelor's degree	$68,200
Financial Analysts	Financial analysts provide guidance to businesses and individuals making investment decisions. They assess the performance of stocks, bonds, and other types of investments.	Bachelor's degree	$74,350
Actuaries	Actuaries analyze the financial costs of risk and uncertainty. They use mathematics, statistics, and financial theory to assess the risk that an event will occur and to help businesses and clients develop policies that minimize the cost of that risk.	Bachelor's degree	$87,650
Mathematicians	Mathematicians use high-level mathematics and technology to develop new mathematical principles, understand relationships between existing principles, and solve real-world problems.	Master's degree	$99,380
Operations Research Analysts	Operations research analysts use advanced methods of analysis to help organizations solve problems and make better decisions.	Bachelor's degree	$70,960
Statisticians	Statisticians use mathematical techniques to analyze and interpret data and draw conclusions.	Master's degree	$72,830
Market Research Analysts	Market research analysts study market conditions in local, regional, or national areas to examine potential sales of a product or service. They help companies understand what products people want, who will buy them, and at what price.	Bachelor's degree	$60,570
Postsecondary Teachers	Postsecondary teachers instruct students in a wide variety of academic and vocational subjects beyond the high school level. They also conduct research and publish scholarly papers and books.	Doctoral or professional degree	$62,0.
Political Scientists	Political scientists study the origin, development, and operation of political systems. They research political ideas and analyze the structure and operation of governments, policies, political trends, and related issues.	Master's degree	$107,420
Survey Researchers	Survey researchers design or conduct surveys and analyze survey data. Many groups use surveys to collect factual data, such as employment and salary information, or to ask questions that help them understand people's opinions, attitudes, beliefs, or desires.	Bachelor's degree	$36,050

Contacts for More Information

For more information about economists, visit American Economic Association

For information about careers in business economics, visit National Association for Business Economics

For information about economist careers with the federal government, visit USAJOBS

Suggested citation:

Bureau of Labor Statistics, U.S. Department of Labor, Occupational Outlook Handbook, 2012-13 Edition, Economists, on the Internet at http://www.bls.gov/ooh/life-physical-and-social-science/economists.htm.

Environmental Science and Protection Technicians

Quick Facts: Environmental Science and Protection Technicians	
2010 Median Pay	$41,380 per year $19.90 per hour
Entry-Level Education	Associate's degree
Work Experience in a Related Occupation	None
On-the-job Training	Moderate-term on-the-job training
Number of Jobs, 2010	29,600
Job Outlook, 2010-20	24% (Faster than average)
Employment Change, 2010-20	7,000

What Environmental Science and Protection Technicians Do

Environmental science and protection technicians monitor the environment and investigate sources of pollution and contamination, including those affecting health.

Duties

Environmental science and protection technicians typically do the following:

- Inspect establishments, including public places and businesses, to ensure that there are no environmental, health, or safety hazards
- Set up and maintain equipment used to monitor pollution levels, such as remote sensors that measure emissions from smokestacks
- Collect samples of air, soil, water, and other materials for laboratory analysis
- Perform scientific tests to identify and measure levels of pollutants in samples
- Prepare charts and reports that summarize test results
- Discuss test results and analyses with clients

Many environmental science and protection technicians work under the supervision of environmental scientists and specialists, who direct their work and evaluate their results. In addition, they often work on teams with scientists, engineers, and technicians in other fields to solve complex problems related to environmental degradation and public health. For example, they may work on teams with geoscientists and hydrologists to manage the cleanup of contaminated soils and ground water.

Most environmental science and protection technicians work either for state or local government or for private consulting firms.

In **state and local governments**, environmental science and protection technicians enforce regulations that protect the environment and people's health. They spend a lot of time inspecting businesses and public places and investigating complaints related to air quality, water quality, and food safety. They may issue fines or close establishments that violate environmental or health regulations.

In **private consulting firms**, environmental science and protection technicians help clients monitor and manage the environment and comply with regulations. For example, they help businesses develop cleanup plans for contaminated sites, and they recommend ways to reduce, control, or eliminate pollution. Also, environmental science and protection technicians conduct feasibility studies for, and monitor the environmental impact of, new construction projects.

Work Environment

Environmental science and protection technicians held about 29,600 jobs in 2010. The industries employing the largest numbers of environmental science and protection technicians in 2010 were as follows:

Management, scientific, and technical consulting services	24%
Local government, excluding education and hospitals	23
Architectural, engineering, and related services	19
Testing laboratories	12
State government, excluding education and hospitals	12

Most environmental science and protection technicians work for professional, scientific, and technical services firms or for state or local government.

Environmental science and protection technicians work in laboratories, offices, and the field. Fieldwork offers a variety of settings; for example, a technician may investigate a chemical spill inside a manufacturing plant or spend time outdoors testing the water quality of lakes and rivers.

In the field, technicians spend most of their time on their feet, which can be physically demanding. Also, they may need to set up monitoring or testing equipment, which can involve some heavy lifting and frequent bending and crouching.

Many environmental science and protection technicians work outdoors measuring levels of pollution and collecting samples.

Work Schedules

Environmental science and protection technicians must often travel to meet with clients or perform fieldwork. This may occasionally require technicians to work long or irregular hours.

How to Become an Environmental Science or Protection Technician

Environmental science and protection technicians need an associate's degree or comparable postsecondary training for most jobs. New technicians are often trained on the job by more experienced environmental science and protection technicians.

Education

Most employers prefer applicants who have at least an associate's degree, or 2 years of postsecondary training, in a natural science or science-related technology. However, some entry-level positions require a high school diploma.

Many technical and community colleges offer programs in environmental studies or a related technology, such as remote sensing or geographic information systems (GIS). Associate's degree programs at community colleges are traditionally designed to provide easy transfer to bachelor's degree programs at colleges and universities because a bachelor's degree can be useful for future career advancement. Technical institutes usually offer technical training but provide less theory and general education than community colleges offer.

A well-rounded background in natural sciences is important for environmental science technicians, so students should take courses in chemistry, biology, geology, and physics. Coursework in mathematics, statistics, and computer science also is useful because technicians routinely do data analysis and modeling. Many schools offer internships and cooperative-education programs, which help students gain valuable experience while attending school. Internships and cooperative-education experience can enhance the students' employment prospects.

Important Qualities

Analytical skills. Environmental science and protection technicians must be able to carry out a wide range of laboratory and field tests, and their results must be accurate and precise.

Critical-thinking skills. Environmental science and protection technicians reach their conclusions through sound reasoning and judgment. They have to be able to determine the best way to address environmental hazards.

Interpersonal skills. Environmental science and protection technicians need to be able to work well with others as part of a team, because they often work together with scientists and other technicians.

Listening skills. Environmental science and protection technicians must carefully follow instructions given to them by environmental scientists and specialists, because any mistakes can invalidate the results of their experiments and investigations.

Speaking skills. Environmental science and protection technicians must be able to discuss their results with clients and colleagues.

Writing skills. Environmental science and protection technicians must document the results of their work in written reports.

Training

Most environm.ental science and protection technicians receive on-the-job training. The length of training varies with the new employee's level of experience and education.

Typically, experienced technicians teach new employees proper methods and procedures for conducting experiments, inspections, and other tasks. Technicians usually learn about relevant environmental and health regulations and standards as part of their training.

Licenses

In some states, environmental science and protection technicians need a license to do certain types of environmental and health inspections. For example, some states require licensing for technicians who test buildings for radon. Licensure requirements vary by state but typically include minimum levels of education and experience and a passing score on an exam.

Advancement

Technicians who have a bachelor's degree are often able to advance to environmental scientist positions. For more information, see the profile on environmental scientists and specialists.

Pay

Environmental Science and Protection Technicians
Median annual wages, May 2010

Environmental Science and Protection Technicians, Including Health	$41,380
Life, Physical, and Social Science Technicians	$40,690
Total, All Occupations	$33,840

Note: All Occupations includes all occupations in the U.S. Economy.
Source: U.S. Bureau of Labor Statistics, Occupational Employment Statistics

The median annual wage of environmental science and protection technicians was $41,380 in May 2010. The median wage is the wage at which half the workers in an occupation earned more than that amount and half earned less. The lowest 10 percent earned less than $26,590, and the top 10 percent earned more than $67,630.

Job Outlook

Environmental Science and Protection Technicians
Percent change in employment, projected 2010-20

Environmental Science and Protection Technicians, Including Health	24%
Total, All Occupations	14%
Life, Physical, and Social Science Technicians	11%

Note: All Occupations includes all occupations in the U.S. Economy.
Source: U.S. Bureau of Labor Statistics, Employment Projections program

Employment of environmental science and protection technicians is expected to grow by 24 percent from 2010 to 2020, faster than the average for all occupations. Heightened public interest in the hazards facing the environment, as well as the increasing demands placed on the environment by population growth, are expected to spur demand for environmental science and protection technicians. Further demand is expected as a result of new and increasingly complex environmental laws and regulations.

Most employment growth for environmental science and protection technicians is projected to be in private consulting firms. More businesses and governments are expected to use these firms in the future to help them monitor and manager the environment and comply with regulations.

Job Prospects

Environmental science and protection technicians should have good opportunities for employment. In addition to openings due to growth, many job openings are expected to be created by those who retire or leave the occupation for other reasons. Job candidates with an associate's degree or experience should have the best opportunities.

Job opportunities available in state and local governments will vary from year to year with the budgets of state and local environmental protection agencies.

Employment projections data for environmental science and protection technicians, 2010-20

Occupational Title	SOC Code	Employment, 2010	Projected Employment, 2020	Change, 2010-20 Percent	Numeric
Environmental Science and Protection Technicians, Including Health	19-4091	29,600	36,600	24	7,000
SOURCE: U.S. Bureau of Labor Statistics, Employment Projections program					

Similar Occupations

This table shows a list of occupations with job duties that are similar to those of environmental science and protection technicians.

Occupation	Job Duties	Entry-Level Education	Median Annual Pay, May 2010
Biological Technicians	Biological technicians help biological and medical scientists conduct laboratory tests and experiments.	Bachelor's degree	$39,020
Chemical Technicians	Chemical technicians use special instruments and techniques to help chemists and chemical engineers in researching, developing, and producing chemical products and processes.	Associate's degree	$42,040
Environmental Engineering Technicians	Environmental engineering technicians carry out the plans that environmental engineers develop. They test, operate, and, if necessary, modify equipment for preventing or cleaning up environmental pollution. They may collect samples for testing, or they may work to mitigate sources of environmental pollution.	Associate's degree	$43,390
Environmental Engineers	Environmental engineers use the principles of engineering, soil science, biology, and chemistry to develop solutions to environmental problems. They are involved in efforts to improve recycling, waste disposal, public health, and control of water and air pollution.	Bachelor's degree	$78,740
Environmental Scientists and Specialists	Environmental scientists and specialists use their knowledge of the natural sciences to protect the environment. They identify problems and find solutions that minimize hazards to the health of the environment and the population.	Bachelor's degree	$61,700
Geoscientists	Geoscientists study the physical aspects of the Earth, such as its composition, structure, and processes, to learn about its past, present, and future.	Bachelor's degree	$82,500
Hydrologists	Hydrologists study water and the water cycle. They use their expertise to solve problems in the areas of water quality or availability.	Master's degree	$75,690
Occupational Health and Safety Technicians	Occupational health and safety technicians collect data on the safety and health conditions of the workplace. Technicians work with occupational health and safety specialists in conducting tests and measuring hazards to help prevent harm to workers, property, the environment, and the general public.	High school diploma or equivalent	$45,330

Contacts for More Information

For information on careers as environmental science and protection technicians focusing on how environmental hazards affect human health, visit National Environmental Health Association

Suggested citation:

Bureau of Labor Statistics, U.S. Department of Labor, Occupational Outlook Handbook, 2012-13 Edition, Environmental Science and Protection Technicians, on the Internet at http://www.bls.gov/ooh/life-physical-and-social-science/environmental-science-and-protection-technicians.htm .

Environmental Scientists and Specialists

Quick Facts: Environmental Scientists and Specialists	
2010 Median Pay	$61,700 per year $29.66 per hour
Entry-Level Education	Bachelor's degree
Work Experience in a Related Occupation	None
On-the-job Training	None
Number of Jobs, 2010	89,400
Job Outlook, 2010-20	19% (About as fast as average)
Employment Change, 2010-20	16,700

What Environmental Scientists and Specialists Do

Environmental scientists and specialists use their knowledge of the natural sciences to protect the environment. They identify problems and find solutions that minimize hazards to the health of the environment and the population.

Duties

Environmental scientists and specialists typically do the following:

- Determine data collection methods for research projects, investigations, and surveys
- Collect environmental data, such as samples of air, soil, water, food, and other materials, for scientific analysis
- Analyze samples, surveys, and other information to identify and assess threats to the environment
- Develop plans to prevent, control, or fix environmental problems, such as pollution and harm to land or water
- Develop plans to restore polluted or contaminated land or water
- Provide information and guidance to government officials, businesses, and the general public on possible environmental hazards and health risks
- Prepare technical reports and presentations that explain their research and findings

Environmental scientists and specialists analyze environmental problems and develop solutions. For example, many environmental scientists and specialists work to reclaim lands and waters that have been contaminated by pollution. Others assess the risks new construction projects pose to the environment and make recommendations to governments and businesses on how to minimize the environmental impact of these projects. They also identify ways that human behavior can be changed to avoid problems such as the depletion of the ozone layer.

The federal government and many state and local governments have regulations to ensure that there is clean air to breathe, safe water to drink, and no hazardous materials in the soil. The regulations also place limits on development, particularly near sensitive parts of the ecosystem, such as wetlands. Many environmental scientists and specialists work for the government to ensure that these regulations are followed. Other environmental scientists work for consulting firms that help companies comply with regulations and policies.

Some environmental scientists and specialists focus on environmental regulations that are designed to protect people's health, while others focus on regulations designed to minimize society's impact on the ecosystem. The following are examples of types of specialists:

Environmental health specialists study how environmental factors impact human health. They investigate potential health risks, such as unsafe drinking water, disease, and food safety. They also educate the public about potential health risks present in the environment.

Environmental protection specialists monitor the effect human activity has on the environment. They investigate sources of pollution and develop prevention, control, and remediation plans.

Other environmental scientists do work and receive training that is similar to that of other physical or life scientists, but they focus on environmental issues. Environmental chemists are an example.

Environmental chemists study the effects that various chemicals have on ecosystems. For example, they look at how acids affect plants, animals, and people. Some areas in which they work include waste management and the remediation of contaminated soils, water, and air.

Many people with backgrounds in environmental science become professors and teachers. For more information, see the profile on postsecondary teachers .

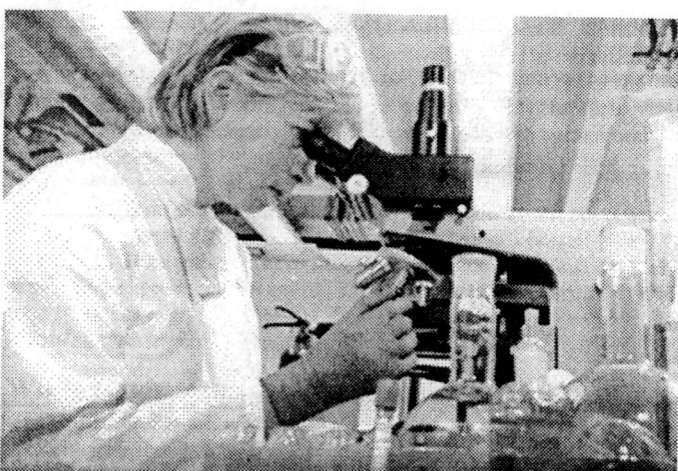

Environmental scientists and specialists analyze samples of air, water, and other substances to identify and assess threats to people and the environment.

Work Environment

Environmental scientists and specialists held about 89,400 jobs in 2010. Most environmental scientists and specialists work for private consulting firms or for federal, state, or local governments. The largest employers of environmental scientists and specialists in 2010 were the following:

State government, excluding education and hospitals	23%
Management, scientific, and technical consulting services	19
Architectural, engineering, and related services	13
Local government, excluding education and hospitals	13
Federal government, excluding postal service	7

Environmental scientists and specialists work in offices and laboratories. They also may spend time in the field gathering data and monitoring environmental conditions firsthand. Fieldwork can be physically demanding, and environmental scientists and specialists may work in all types of weather. Environmental scientists and specialists often have to travel to meet with clients.

Most consulting firms fall into one of two categories: large multidisciplinary engineering companies that employ thousands of workers, or small specialty firms that employ only a few workers. Larger firms are more likely to engage in large-scale, long-term projects in which environmental scientists work with scientists and engineers in other disciplines. In smaller specialty firms, environmental scientists work directly with small businesses and clients in government and the private sector.

Work Schedules

Most environmental scientists and specialists work full time. They may have to work long or irregular hours when working in the field.

How to Become an Environmental Scientist or Specialist

For most jobs, environmental scientists and specialists need at least a bachelor's degree in a natural science.

Education

For most entry-level jobs, environmental scientists and specialists must have a bachelor's degree in environmental science or another natural science, such as biology, chemistry, or geosciences. However, a master's degree may be needed for advancement. A doctoral degree is typically needed only for college teaching and some research positions.

A bachelor's degree in environmental science offers a broad approach to the natural sciences. Students typically take courses in biology, chemistry, geology, and physics. Students often take specialized courses in hydrology, waste management, and fluid mechanics as part of their degree as well. Classes in environmental policy and regulation are also beneficial.

Students should look for opportunities, such as through classes and internships, to work with computer modeling, data analysis, and geographic information systems. Students with experience in these programs will be the best prepared to enter the job market.

Important Qualities

Analytical skills. Environmental scientists and specialists base their conclusions on careful analysis of scientific data. They must consider all possible methods and solutions in their analyses.

Interpersonal skills. Environmental scientists and specialists typically work on teams with scientists, engineers, and technicians. Team members must be able to work together effectively to achieve their goals.

Problem-solving skills. Environmental scientists and specialists try to find the best possible solution to problems that affect the environment and people's health.

Speaking skills. Environmental scientists and specialists often give presentations that explain their findings, and they need to convince others to accept their recommendations.

Writing skills. Environmental scientists and specialists write technical reports that explain their methods, findings, and recommendations.

Advancement

Environmental scientists and specialists often begin their careers as field analysts, research assistants, or technicians in laboratories and offices. As they gain experience, they get more responsibilities and autonomy and may supervise the work of technicians or other scientists. Eventually, they may be promoted to project leader, program manager, or some other management or research position.

Other environmental scientists and specialists go on to work as researchers or faculty at colleges and universities.

Pay

Environmental Scientists and Specialists
Median annual wages, May 2010

Environmental Scientists and Specialists, Including Health	$61,700
Life, Physical, and Social Science Occupations	$58,530
Total, All Occupations	$33,840

Note: All Occupations includes all occupations in the U.S. Economy.
Source: U.S. Bureau of Labor Statistics, Occupational Employment Statistics

The median annual wage of environmental scientists and specialists was $61,700 in May 2011. The median wage is the wage at which half the workers in an occupation earned more than that amount and half earned less. The lowest 10 percent earned less than $37,850, and the top 10 percent earned more than $107,990.

Most environmental scientists and specialists work full time. They may have to work long or irregular hours when working in the field.

Job Outlook

Environmental Scientists and Specialists
Percent change in employment, projected 2010-20

Environmental Scientists and Specialists, Including Health	19%
Life, Physical, and Social Science Occupations	16%
Total, All Occupations	14%

Note: All Occupations includes all occupations in the U.S. Economy.
Source: U.S. Bureau of Labor Statistics, Employment Projections program

Employment of environmental scientists and specialists is expected to grow by 19 percent from 2010 to 2020, about as fast as the average for all occupations. Heightened public interest in the hazards facing the environment, as well as the increasing demands placed on the environment by population growth, is projected to spur demand for environmental scientists and specialists. Further demand is also expected as a result of new and increasingly complex environmental laws and regulations.

Most employment growth for environmental scientists and specialists is projected to be in private consulting firms that help clients monitor and manage environmental concerns and comply with regulations.

More businesses are expected to consult with environmental scientists in the future to help them minimize the impact their operations have on the environment. For example, environmental consultants help businesses develop practices that minimize waste, prevent pollution, and conserve resources. Other environmental scientists are expected to be needed to help planners develop and construct buildings, utilities, and transportation systems that protect natural resources and limit damage to the land.

Job Prospects

Environmental scientists and specialists should have good job opportunities. In addition to growth, many job openings will be created by scientists who retire, advance to management positions, or change careers.

Employment projections data for environmental scientists and specialists, 2010-20

Occupational Title	SOC Code	Employment, 2010	Projected Employment, 2020	Change, 2010-20	
				Percent	Numeric
Environmental Scientists and Specialists, Including Health	19-2041	89,400	106,100	19	16,700
SOURCE: U.S. Bureau of Labor Statistics, Employment Projections program					

Similar Occupations

This table shows a list of occupations with job duties that are similar to those of environmental scientists and specialists.

Occupation	Job Duties	Entry-Level Education	Median Annual Pay, May 2010
Chemists and Materials Scientists	Chemists and materials scientists study the structures, compositions, reactions, and other properties of substances. They use their knowledge to develop new and improved products, processes, and materials.	Bachelor's degree	$69,790
Environmental Engineers	Environmental engineers use the principles of engineering, soil science, biology, and chemistry to develop solutions to environmental problems. They are involved in efforts to improve recycling, waste disposal, public health, and control of water and air pollution.	Bachelor's degree	$78,740
Environmental Science and Protection Technicians	Environmental science and protection technicians do laboratory and field tests to monitor the environment and investigate sources of pollution, including those affecting health. Many work under the supervision of environmental scientists and specialists, who direct their work and evaluate their results.	Associate's degree	$41,380
Epidemiologists	Epidemiologists investigate the causes of disease and other public health problems to prevent them from spreading or from happening again. They report their findings to public policy officials and to the general public.	Master's degree	$63,010
Geoscientists	Geoscientists study the physical aspects of the Earth, such as its composition, structure, and processes, to learn about its past, present, and future.	Bachelor's degree	$82,500
Hydrologists	Hydrologists study water and the water cycle. They use their expertise to solve problems in the areas of water quality or availability.	Master's degree	$75,690
Microbiologists	Microbiologists study the growth, development, and other characteristics of microscopic organisms such as bacteria, algae, and fungi.	Bachelor's degree	$65,920
Natural Sciences Managers	Natural sciences managers supervise the work of scientists, including chemists, physicists, and biologists. They direct research and development projects and coordinate activities such as testing, quality control, and production.	Bachelor's degree	$116,020
Occupational Health and Safety Specialists	Occupational health and safety specialists analyze many types of work environments and work procedures. Specialists inspect workplaces for adherence to regulations on safety, health, and the environment. They also design programs to prevent disease or injury to workers and damage to the environment.	Bachelor's degree	$64,660
Postsecondary Teachers	Postsecondary teachers instruct students in a wide variety of academic and vocational subjects beyond the high school level. They also conduct research and publish scholarly papers and books.	Doctoral or professional degree	$62,050

Contacts for More Information

For more information about environmental scientists and specialists, including training, visit American Geosciences Institute

For information about careers and training as an environmental health specialist, visit National Environmental Health Association

For information about getting a job as an environmental scientist and specialist with the federal government, visit USAJOBS

Suggested citation:

Bureau of Labor Statistics, U.S. Department of Labor, Occupational Outlook Handbook, 2012-13 Edition, Environmental Scientists and Specialists, on the Internet at http://www.bls.gov/ooh/life-physical-and-social-science/environmental-scientists-and-specialists.htm .

Epidemiologists

Quick Facts: Epidemiologists	
2010 Median Pay	$63,010 per year $30.29 per hour
Entry-Level Education	Master's degree
Work Experience in a Related Occupation	None
On-the-job Training	None
Number of Jobs, 2010	5,000
Job Outlook, 2010-20	24% (Faster than average)
Employment Change, 2010-20	1,200

What Epidemiologists Do

Epidemiologists investigate the causes of disease and other public health problems to prevent them from spreading or from happening again. They report their findings to public policy officials and to the general public.

Duties

Epidemiologists typically do the following:

- Plan and direct studies of public health problems to find ways to prevent and to treat the problems
- Collect and analyze data—including using observations, interviews, surveys, and samples of blood or other bodily fluids—to find the causes of diseases or other health problems
- Communicate their findings to health practitioners, policymakers, and the public
- Manage public health programs by planning programs, monitoring progress, analyzing data, and seeking ways to improve them, among other activities
- Supervise professional, technical, and clerical personnel

Epidemiologists collect and analyze data to investigate health issues. For example, an epidemiologist might collect and analyze demographic data to determine who is at the highest risk for a particular disease.

Research epidemiologists typically work for universities. Applied epidemiologists work with governments, addressing health crises directly. The most common problem both types of epidemiologists work on is infectious diseases, but they examine other public health issues, as well.

Epidemiologists who work in private industry commonly work for health insurance companies or pharmaceutical companies. Those in non-profit companies often do public advocacy work.

According to a 2009 national survey by the Council of State and Territorial Epidemiologists , local government epidemiologists study one or more of the following public health areas:

- Infectious diseases
- Bioterrorism/emergency response
- Maternal and child health
- Chronic diseases
- Environmental health
- Injury
- Occupational health
- Substance abuse
- Oral health

Work Environment

Epidemiologists held about 5,000 jobs in 2010. They work in health departments, offices, universities, laboratories, or in the field.

They spend most of their time studying data and reports in a safe lab or office setting. Epidemiologists have minimal risk when they work in laboratories or in the field, because they take extensive precautions before interacting with samples or patients.

In 2010, 54 percent of epidemiologists worked for federal, state, and local governments. Other epidemiologists worked for pharmaceutical companies, hospitals, colleges, or in life science research and development. As shown in the following tabulation, 13 percent of epidemiologists were employed by hospitals in 2010:

Federal, state, and local government	54%
Hospitals; state, local, and private	13
Colleges, universities, and professional schools	9
Scientific research and development services	7
Pharmaceutical and medicine manufacturing	5

Work Schedules

Most epidemiologists work full time and have a routine work schedule. Fieldwork or public health emergencies occasionally may cause epidemiologists to work irregular hours.

How to Become an Epidemiologist

Epidemiologists need at least a master's degree from an accredited postsecondary institution. Most have a master's degree in epidemiology or a related field. Some epidemiologists have a Ph.D.

Epidemiologists investigate the causes of disease and other public health problems in an effort to prevent them from spreading.

Education

Epidemiologists need at least a master's degree from an accredited postsecondary institution. Most have a master's degree in public health, with an emphasis in epidemiology or a related field. Advanced epidemiologists—including those in colleges and universities—have a Ph.D. in their chosen field.

Coursework in epidemiology includes public health, biology, and biostatistics. Classes emphasize statistical methods, causal analysis, and survey design. Advanced courses emphasize multiple regression, medical informatics, review of previous biomedical research, and practical applications of data.

A number of epidemiologists have a professional background (for example, a medical degree) with a dual degree in epidemiology. In medical school, students spend most of the first 2 years in laboratories and classrooms, taking courses such as anatomy, biochemistry, physiology, pharmacology, psychology, microbiology, pathology, medical ethics, and laws governing medicine. They also learn to take medical histories, examine patients, and diagnose illnesses.

Important Qualities

Communication skills. Epidemiologists must use their expertise and experience to determine how they can disseminate their findings to the public properly.

Critical-thinking skills. Epidemiologists analyze their findings to determine how best to respond to a public health problem or a more grave health-related emergency.

Detail oriented. Epidemiologists must be precise and accurate in moving from observation and interview to conclusions.

Math and statistical skills. Epidemiologists work with both qualitative methods (observations and interviews) and quantitative methods (surveys and analysis of biological data) in their work.

Speaking skills. Epidemiologists must communicate complex findings so that public policy officials and the public can understand the magnitude of a health problem.

Writing skills. Written communication is critical for helping decision makers and the public understand the conclusions and recommendations that epidemiologists make.

Pay

Epidemiologists
Median annual wages, May 2010

Life Scientists	$67,400
Epidemiologists	$63,010
Total, All Occupations	$33,840

Note: All Occupations includes all occupations in the U.S. Economy.
Source: U.S. Bureau of Labor Statistics, Occupational Employment Statistics

The median annual wage of epidemiologists was $63,010 in May 2010. The median wage is the wage at which half the workers in an occupation earned more than that amount and half earned less. The lowest 10 percent earned less than $42,360, and the top 10 percent earned more than $98,380.

Median annual wages in the industries employing the largest numbers of epidemiologists in May 2010 were:

Pharmaceutical and medicine manufacturing	$92,920
Hospitals; state, local, and private	72,990
Scientific research and development services	67,160
Colleges, universities, and professional schools	61,870
Federal, state, and local government	57,390

Most epidemiologists work full time and have a routine work schedule. Fieldwork or public health emergencies occasionally may cause epidemiologists to work irregular hours.

Job Outlook

Epidemiologists
Percent change in employment, projected 2010-20

Epidemiologists	24%
Life Scientists	20%
Total, All Occupations	14%

Note: All Occupations includes all occupations in the U.S. Economy.
Source: U.S. Bureau of Labor Statistics, Employment Projections program

Employment of epidemiologists is expected to increase by 24 percent from 2010 to 2020, faster than the average for all occupations. Ongoing public health awareness, as well as an increased reliance on medical records for public health analysis, will maintain demand for epidemiologists. New legislation that will improve medical record-keeping is expected to create more opportunities for epidemiologists to track infection and demographic data.

Employment growth over the next 10 years for epidemiologists is expected to be strong in state and local governments. Governments have increased their demand for epidemiologists because the analyses that epidemiologists do are important to preventive healthcare, as well as to emergency responses.

Job Prospects

Epidemiologists generally should have favorable opportunities. Many states report shortages of qualified workers for applied epidemiology positions.

Employment projections data for epidemiologists, 2010-20

Occupational Title	SOC Code	Employment, 2010	Projected Employment, 2020	Change, 2010-20 Percent	Numeric
Epidemiologists	19-1041	5,000	6,100	24	1,200
SOURCE: U.S. Bureau of Labor Statistics, Employment Projections program					

Similar Occupations

This table shows a list of occupations with job duties that are similar to those of epidemiologists.

Occupation	Job Duties	Entry-Level Education	Median Annual Pay, May 2010
Health Educators	Health educators teach people about behaviors that promote wellness. They develop programs and materials to encourage people to make healthy decisions.	Bachelor's degree	$45,830

Medical Scientists	Medical scientists conduct research aimed at improving overall human health. They often use clinical trials and other investigative methods to reach their findings.	Doctoral or professional degree	$76,700
Microbiologists	Microbiologists study the growth, development, and other characteristics of microscopic organisms such as bacteria, algae, and fungi.	Bachelor's degree	$65,920
Physicians and Surgeons	Physicians and surgeons diagnose and treat injuries and illnesses in patients. Physicians examine patients, take medical histories, prescribe medications, and order, perform, and interpret diagnostic tests. Surgeons operate on patients to treat injuries, such as broken bones; diseases, such as cancerous tumors; and deformities, such as cleft palates.	Doctoral or professional degree	This wage is equal to or greater than $166,400 per year.

Contacts for More Information

For more information about epidemiologists, including schools offering education in epidemiology, visit Council of State and Territorial Epidemiologists

For more information about epidemiology careers in the federal government, visit Centers for Disease Control and Prevention

Suggested citation:

Bureau of Labor Statistics, U.S. Department of Labor, Occupational Outlook Handbook, 2012-13 Edition, Epidemiologists, on the Internet at http://www.bls.gov/ooh/life-physical-and-social-science/epidemiologists.htm .

Forensic Science Technicians

Quick Facts: Forensic Science Technicians	
2010 Median Pay	$51,570 per year $24.79 per hour
Entry-Level Education	Bachelor's degree
Work Experience in a Related Occupation	None
On-the-job Training	Moderate-term on-the-job training
Number of Jobs, 2010	13,000
Job Outlook, 2010-20	19% (About as fast as average)
Employment Change, 2010-20	2,400

What Forensic Science Technicians Do

Forensic science technicians help investigate crimes by collecting and analyzing physical evidence. Most technicians specialize in either crime scene investigation or laboratory analysis.

Duties

At **crime scenes**, forensic science technicians, also known as crime scene investigators, typically do the following:

- Walk through the scene to determine what and how evidence should be collected
- Take photographs of the crime scene and evidence
- Make sketches of the crime scene
- Keep written notes of their observations and findings, such as the location and position of evidence as it is found
- Collect all relevant physical evidence, including weapons, fingerprints, and bodily fluids
- Catalog and preserve evidence before transferring it to a crime lab

Crime scene investigators may use tweezers, black lights, and specialized kits to identify and collect evidence. In addition to processing crime scenes, they may also attend autopsies.

In **laboratories**, forensic science technicians typically do the following:

- Identify and classify crime scene evidence through scientific analysis
- Explore possible links between suspects and criminal activity using the results of chemical and physical analyses

- Consult with experts in related or specialized fields, such as toxicology, about the evidence and their findings
- Reconstruct crime scenes based on scientific findings

Forensic science technicians reconstruct crime scenes by carefully studying information gathered by investigators and conducting scientific tests on physical evidence. For example, lab technicians may look at photographs of blood splatter patterns and conduct ballistics tests on bullets found at the crime scene to determine the direction

Forensic scientists and crime scene investigators help solve crimes by collecting and analyzing evidence.

from which a shot was fired.

Forensic science technicians who work in laboratories use chemicals and laboratory equipment such as microscopes when analyzing evidence. They also use computer databases to examine fingerprints, DNA, and other evidence collected at crime scenes in order to match them to people and things that have already been identified. Most forensic science technicians who perform laboratory analysis specialize in a specific type of evidence analysis, such as DNA or ballistics.

All forensic science technicians prepare written reports that detail their findings and investigative methods. They must be able to explain their reports to lawyers, detectives, and other law enforcement officials. In addition, forensic science technicians may be called to testify in court about their findings and methods.

Work Environment

Forensic science technicians held about 13,000 jobs in 2010. About 9 in 10 forensic science technicians work in state and local government in the following workplaces:

- Police departments
- Crime laboratories
- Morgues
- Medical examiner/coroner offices

Crime scene investigators must travel to different locations around a city or region because crimes can occur anywhere. Crime scene investigation can be distressing and unpleasant because investigators see many disturbing sights.

Work Schedules

Crime scene investigators work staggered day, evening, or night shifts and may have to work overtime because they must always be available to collect evidence. Technicians working in laboratories usually work a standard work week, although they may have to be on call outside of normal business hours if they are needed to work immediately on a crime scene.

How to Become a Forensic Science Technician

The educational requirements for crime scene investigators vary by employer. Forensic science technicians need a bachelor's degree to work in crime labs. Extensive amounts of on-the-job training are required for both those who investigate crime scenes and those who work in labs.

Education

Many crime scene investigators are sworn police officers and have met educational requirements necessary for admittance to the police academy. Applicants for non-uniform crime scene investigator jobs at larger law enforcement agencies should have a bachelor's degree in either forensic science or a natural science, but many rural agencies hire applicants with a high school diploma. For more information on police officers, see the profile on police and detectives .

Technicians who work in crime laboratories typically need a bachelor's degree in either forensic science or a natural science such as biology or chemistry. Students who major in forensic science should ensure that their program includes extensive course work in mathematics, chemistry, and biology. A list of schools that offer degrees in forensic science is available from the American Academy of Forensic Sciences .

Important Qualities

Composure. Crime scenes can be gruesome, but technicians have to maintain their professionalism.

Critical-thinking skills. Forensic science technicians use their best judgment when matching physical evidence, such as fingerprints and DNA, to suspects.

Detail oriented. Forensic science technicians cannot afford to make mistakes when they collect and analyze evidence.

Problem-solving skills. Forensic science technicians use scientific tests and methods to help law enforcement officials solve crimes.

Speaking skills. Forensic science technicians frequently present their findings to police and other law enforcement workers. They may be called upon to provide expert testimony in a court of law.

Writing skills. Forensic science technicians prepare written reports that must stand up to legal scrutiny.

Training

Forensic science technicians need extensive on-the-job training before they are ready to work on cases independently.

Newly hired crime scene investigators serve as apprentices to more experienced investigators. During their apprenticeship, investigators learn proper procedures and methods for collecting and documenting evidence.

Forensic science technicians learn laboratory specialties on the job. The length of this training varies by specialty. Most DNA-analysis training programs last 6 to 12 months, but firearms-analysis training may last up to 3 years. Technicians need to pass a proficiency exam before they may perform independent casework or testify in court.

Throughout their careers, forensic science technicians need to keep abreast of advances in technology and science that improve the collection or analysis of evidence.

Pay

Forensic Science Technicians
Median annual wages, May 2010

Forensic Science Technicians	$51,570
Life, Physical, and Social Science Technicians	$40,690
Total, All Occupations	$33,840

Note: All Occupations includes all occupations in the U.S. Economy.
Source: U.S. Bureau of Labor Statistics, Occupational Employment Statistics

The median annual wage of forensic science technicians was $51,570 in May 2010. The median wage is the wage at which half the workers in an occupation earned more than that amount and half earned less. The lowest 10 percent earned less than $32,900, and the top 10 percent earned more than $82,990.

Crime scene investigators work staggered day, evening, or night shifts and may have to work overtime because they must always be available to collect evidence. Technicians working in laboratories usually work a standard workweek, although they may have to be on call outside of normal business hours if they are needed to work immediately on a crime scene.

Job Outlook

Forensic Science Technicians
Percent change in employment, projected 2010-20

Forensic Science Technicians	19%
Total, All Occupations	14%
Life, Physical, and Social Science Technicians	11%

Note: All Occupations includes all occupations in the U.S. Economy.
Source: U.S. Bureau of Labor Statistics, Employment Projections program

Employment of forensic science technicians is projected to grow by 19 percent from 2010 to 2020, about as fast as the average for all occupations. Technological advances and the growing awareness of forensic evidence among potential jurors are expected to increase the use of forensic evidence in criminal proceedings. More forensic science technicians will be needed to provide timely forensics information to law enforcement agencies and courts.

Job Prospects

Competition for jobs should be stiff because of the substantial interest in forensic science and crime scene investigation spurred by its portrayal in popular media. Applicants with experience or a bachelor's degree in forensic science or a related field should have the best opportunities.

Year to year, the number of job openings available will vary based on federal, state, and local law enforcement budgets.

Employment projections data for forensic science technicians, 2010-20

Occupational Title	SOC Code	Employment, 2010	Projected Employment, 2020	Change, 2010-20	
				Percent	Numeric
Forensic Science Technicians	19-4092	13,000	15,400	19	2,400
SOURCE: U.S. Bureau of Labor Statistics, Employment Projections program					

Similar Occupations

This table shows a list of occupations with job duties that are similar to those of forensic science technicians.

Occupation	Job Duties	Entry-Level Education	Median Annual Pay, May 2010
Biochemists and Biophysicists	Biochemists and biophysicists study the chemical and physical principles of living things and of biological processes such as cell development, growth, and heredity.	Doctoral or professional degree	$79,390
Chemists and Materials Scientists	Chemists and materials scientists study the structures, compositions, reactions, and other properties of substances. They use their knowledge to develop new and improved products, processes, and materials.	Bachelor's degree	$69,790
Medical Scientists	Medical scientists conduct research aimed at improving overall human health. They often use clinical trials and other investigative methods to reach their findings.	Doctoral or professional degree	$76,700
Police and Detectives	Police officers protect lives and property. Detectives and criminal investigators, who sometimes are called agents or special agents, gather facts and collect evidence of possible crimes. Law enforcement officers' duties depend on the size and type of their organizations.	High school diploma or equivalent	$55,010
Private Detectives and Investigators	Private detectives and investigators find facts and analyze information about legal, financial, and personal matters. They offer many services, including verifying people's backgrounds, tracing missing persons, investigating computer crimes, and protecting celebrities.	Some college, no degree	$42,870

Contacts for More Information

For more information about forensic science technicians and for a list of schools that offer degrees in forensic science, visit American Academy of Forensic Sciences

Suggested citation:

Bureau of Labor Statistics, U.S. Department of Labor, Occupational Outlook Handbook, 2012-13 Edition, Forensic Science Technicians, on the Internet at http://www.bls.gov/ooh/life-physical-and-social-science/forensic-science-technicians.htm .

Forest and Conservation Technicians

Quick Facts: Forest and Conservation Technicians	
2010 Median Pay	$33,390 per year $16.05 per hour
Entry-Level Education	Associate's degree
Work Experience in a Related Occupation	None
On-the-job Training	None
Number of Jobs, 2010	36,500
Job Outlook, 2010-20	-1% (Little or no change)
Employment Change, 2010-20	-400

What Forest and Conservation Technicians Do

Forest and conservation technicians measure and improve the quality of forests, rangeland, and other natural areas.

Duties

Forest and conservation technicians typically do the following:

- Gather data on water and soil quality, disease, and insect damage to trees and other plants, and conditions that may pose a fire hazard
- Locate property lines and evaluate forested areas to determine the species, quality, and amount of standing timber
- Select and mark trees to be cut
- Track where wildlife goes, help build roads, and maintain trails, campsites, and other recreational facilities
- Train and lead seasonal workers who plant seedlings
- Monitor the activities of loggers and others who remove trees for timber sales or for other reasons
- Patrol forest areas and enforce environmental protection regulations
- Communicate with foresters, scientists, and sometimes the public about ongoing forestry and conservation activities
- Suppress forest fires with fire control activities, including training other forestry workers and coordinating detection programs

Forest and conservation technicians generally work under the supervision of foresters or conservation scientists. For more information, see the profile on conservation scientists and foresters .

Increasing numbers of forest and conservation technicians work in

Forest and conservation technicians measure and improve the quality of forests, which includes fire suppression activities.

urban forestry—the study and management of trees and associated plants, individually or in groups within cities, suburbs and towns—and other nontraditional specialties, rather than in forests or rural areas.

Work Environment

Forest and conservation technicians held 36,500 jobs in 2010. The industries employing the largest numbers of forest and conservation technicians in 2010 were as follows:

Federal government, excluding postal service	78%
State government, excluding education and hospitals	10
Local government, excluding education and hospitals	7

Forest and conservation workers work for governments (federal, state, or local) or on privately owned forest lands. Most government technicians are employed by the federal government. Technicians in the eastern United States usually work for private forests. Because many national parks are in the West and Southwest, most technicians in these areas work for the federal government.

Forest and conservation technicians typically work outdoors, sometimes in remote locations and in all types of weather. The work can be physically difficult. They must walk long distances, sometimes on steep slopes and in heavily forested areas or wetlands.

When working near logging operations or in wood yards, technicians must wear a hardhat.

Other technicians work closely with the public, educating them about forest conservation or proper use of recreational sites.

Work Schedules

Most forest and conservation technicians work full time and have a routine work schedule. Seasonal employees may work longer hours and at night. In addition, technicians may need to work longer hours to respond during emergencies.

How to Become a Forest and Conservation Technician

Forest and conservation technicians typically need an associate's degree in forestry or a related field. Employers look for technicians who have a degree that is accredited by the Society of American Foresters (SAF).

Education

Forestry and conservation technicians typically need an associate's degree in a forestry technology or technician program or in a related field. Most forestry and conservation technology programs are accredited by SAF, and every state has accredited programs.

Many technical and community colleges offer programs in forestry technology or a related field. Associate's degree programs at community colleges are designed to provide easy transfer to bachelor's degree programs at colleges and universities. Training at technical institutes usually includes less theory and education than that in community colleges.

Coursework for an associate's degree in forestry technology or a related field includes ecology, biology, and forest resource measurement. Some technicians also have a background in a Geographic Information System (GIS) technology and other forms of computer modeling.

Important Qualities

Analytical skills. Forest and conservation technicians conduct a variety of field tests and onsite measurements, all of which require precision and accuracy.

Critical-thinking skills. Forest and conservation technicians reach conclusions through sound reasoning and judgment. They determine how to improve forest conditions and must react appropriately to fires.

Interpersonal skills. Forest and conservation technicians need to work well with others. They supervise forest and conservation workers and also receive instruction from scientists and specialists, so effective communication is critical.

Listening skills. To avoid making dangerous mistakes, forest and conservation technicians must follow instructions given to them by foresters and conservation scientists.

Physical stamina. Forest and conservation technicians often walk long distances in steep and wooded areas. They work in all kinds of weather, including extreme heat and cold.

Speaking skills. Forest and conservation technicians must clearly instruct forest and conservation workers, who typically do the labor necessary to take care of the forest.

Pay

Forest and Conservation Technicians
Median annual wages, May 2010

Life, Physical, and Social Science Technicians	$40,690
Total, All Occupations	$33,840
Forest and Conservation Technicians	$33,390

Note: All Occupations includes all occupations in the U.S. Economy.
Source: U.S. Bureau of Labor Statistics, Occupational Employment Statistics

The median annual wage of forest and conservation technicians was $33,390 in May 2010. The median wage is the wage at which half the workers in an occupation earned more than that amount and half earned less. The lowest 10 percent earned less than $24,930, and the top 10 percent earned more than $53,780.

Median annual wages in the industries employing the largest number of forestry and conservation technicians in May 2010 were as follows:

State government, excluding education and hospitals	$36,930
Local government, excluding education and hospitals	34,010
Federal government, excluding postal service	31,330

Most forest and conservation technicians work full time and have a routine work schedule. Seasonal employees may work longer hours and at night. In addition, technicians may need to work longer hours to respond during emergencies.

Job Outlook

Forest and Conservation Technicians
Percent change in employment, projected 2010-20

Total, All Occupations	14%
Life, Physical, and Social Science Technicians	11%
Forest and Conservation Technicians	-1%

Note: All Occupations includes all occupations in the U.S. Economy.
Source: U.S. Bureau of Labor Statistics, Employment Projections program

Employment of forest and conservation technicians is expected to experience little or no change from 2010 to 2020.

Heightened demand for American timber and wood pellets will help increase overall job prospects for forest and conservation technicians. Most growth in employment over the next 10 years for forest and conservation technicians is expected to be in federally owned forest lands. Jobs in private forests should grow alongside the demand for timber and pellets, but ongoing fiscal crises will likely lessen the number of available positions in state and local governments.

Employment projections data for forest and conservation technicians, 2010-20

Occupational Title	SOC Code	Employment, 2010	Projected Employment, 2020	Change, 2010-20	
				Percent	Numeric
Forest and Conservation Technicians	19-4093	36,500	36,100	-1	-400
SOURCE: U.S. Bureau of Labor Statistics, Employment Projections program					

Similar Occupations

This table shows a list of occupations with job duties that are similar to those of forest and conservation technicians.

Occupation	Job Duties	Entry-Level Education	Median Annual Pay, May 2010
Agricultural and Food Science Technicians	Under the supervision of scientists, agricultural and food science technicians measure and analyze the quality of food and agricultural products.	Associate's degree	$32,760
Biological Technicians	Biological technicians help biological and medical scientists conduct laboratory tests and experiments.	Bachelor's degree	$39,020
Conservation Scientists and Foresters	Conservation scientists and foresters manage overall land quality of forests, parks, rangelands, and other natural resources.	Bachelor's degree	$57,420

Environmental Science and Protection Technicians	Environmental science and protection technicians do laboratory and field tests to monitor the environment and investigate sources of pollution, including those affecting health. Many work under the supervision of environmental scientists and specialists, who direct their work and evaluate their results.	Associate's degree	$41,380
Firefighters	Firefighters protect the public by responding to fires and other emergencies. They are frequently the first emergency personnel on the scene of an accident.	Postsecondary non-degree award	$45,250
Forest and Conservation Workers	Forest and conservation workers measure and improve the quality of forests. Under the supervision of foresters and forest and conservation technicians, they help to develop, maintain, and protect forests.	High school diploma or equivalent	$23,900

Contacts for More Information

For more information about forest and conservation technicians, visit Forest Guild

For more information about forestry careers and schools offering education in forestry, visit Society of American Foresters

Suggested citation:

Bureau of Labor Statistics, U.S. Department of Labor, Occupational Outlook Handbook, 2012-13 Edition, Forest and Conservation Technicians, on the Internet at http://www.bls.gov/ooh/life-physical-and-social-science/forest-and-conservation-technicians.htm .

Geographers

Quick Facts: Geographers	
2010 Median Pay	$72,800 per year $35.00 per hour
Entry-Level Education	Bachelor's degree
Work Experience in a Related Occupation	None
On-the-job Training	None
Number of Jobs, 2010	1,600
Job Outlook, 2010-20	35% (Much faster than average)
Employment Change, 2010-20	600

What Geographers Do

Geographers study the earth and its land, features, and inhabitants. They also examine phenomena such as political or cultural structures as they relate to geography. They study the physical or human geographic characteristics or both of a region, ranging in scale from local to global.

Duties

Geographers typically do the following:

- Gather geographic data through field observations, maps, photographs, satellite imagery, and censuses
- Use surveys, interviews, focus groups, and other qualitative methods in their research
- Use quantitative methods, such as statistical analysis, in their research
- Create and modify maps, graphs, diagrams, or other visual representations of geographic data
- Analyze the geographic distribution of physical and cultural characteristics and occurrences
- Use geographic information system (GIS) technology to collect, analyze, and display data
- Write reports and present research findings
- Assist, advise, or lead others in using GIS and geographic data
- Combine geographic data with data about a particular specialty, such as economics, the environment, health, or politics

Geographers use several technologies in their work, such as GIS, remote sensing, and global positioning systems (GPS). Geographers use GIS to find relationships and trends in geographic data. GIS allows them to present data visually as maps, reports, and charts. For example, a geographer can overlay aerial or satellite images with GIS data, such as population density in a given region, and create computerized maps. They then use the results to advise governments, businesses, and the general public on a variety of issues, such as marketing strategies; planning homes, roads, and landfills; or disaster responses.

In addition, many people who study geography and who work with GIS technology work in other occupations. For more information on these related occupations, see the profiles on surveyors , cartographers and photogrammetrists , surveying and mapping technicians , urban

Geographers study the earth and its land, features, and inhabitants.

and regional planners , and geoscientists .

The following are examples of common geographer specialties:

Physical geographers examine the physical aspects of a region. They study features of the natural environment such as land forms, climates, soils, vegetation, water, plants, and animals. For example, they may map where a natural resource occurs in a country and analyze its implications.

Human geographers, also known as **cultural geographers,** analyze the organization of human activity and its relationships with the physical environment. Human geographers often combine issues from other disciplines into their research, which may include economic, social, or political topics. In their research, some rely primarily on statistical techniques, while others rely on nonstatistical sources, such as field observations and interviews.

Many human geographers are further classified by their area of specialty:

- **Economic geographers** study economic activities and the distribution of resources. They may research subjects such as regional employment or the location of industries.
- **Environmental geographers** research the impact humans have on the environment and how human activities affect natural processes. Environmental geographers combine aspects of both physical and human geography and commonly study issues such as climate change, desertification, and deforestation.
- **Medical geographers** investigate the distribution of health issues, health care, and disease; for example, a medical geographer may examine the incidence of disease in a certain region.
- **Political geographers** study the relationship between geography and political structures and processes.
- **Regional geographers** focus on the geographic factors in a particular region, ranging in size from a neighborhood or congressional district to an entire continent.
- **Urban geographers** study cities and metropolitan areas. For example, they may examine how certain geographic factors, such as climate, affect population density in cities.

Some people with a geography background become professors and teachers. For more information, see the profile on postsecondary teachers .

Work Environment

Geographers held about 1,600 jobs in 2010, the majority of which were in the federal government. Most others were employed in professional, scientific, and technical services; colleges, universities, and professional schools; and state and local government.

Many geographers work full time during regular business hours, and some must travel to do fieldwork. They often travel to the region they are studying, which sometimes includes foreign countries and remote locations, to gather information and data.

How to Become a Geographer

Geographers need a master's degree for most positions. Those with a bachelor's degree may qualify for some entry-level jobs, but these often require previous geography experience or training in using geographic information system (GIS) technology.

Education

Most geographers need a master's degree in geography. Students usually choose to concentrate their courses in physical, human, or regional geography. Most programs include courses in both physical and human geography, statistics or mathematics, remote sensing, and GIS. In addition, courses in business, economics, or real estate are increasingly important as more geographers are employed in private industry.

Those with a bachelor's degree may qualify for some jobs in government, businesses, or nonprofits; some mid-level positions allow candidates to substitute experience or GIS proficiency for an advanced degree. Top research positions usually require a Ph.D. or a master's degree and several years of relevant work experience.

Positions for geography professors require a Ph.D. For more information, see the profile on postsecondary teachers .

Certification

Most positions require geographers to be proficient in GIS technology. Geographers can become certified as a GIS professional (GISP) through the GIS Certification Institute . Although certification is not mandatory, it can demonstrate a level of professional expertise. Candidates may qualify for certification through a combination of education, professional experience, and contributions to the profession, such as publications or conference participation. GISP certification can often help those without a master's degree or Ph.D. qualify for jobs.

Important Qualities

Analytical skills. Geographers commonly analyze information and spatial data from a variety of sources, such as maps, photographs, and censuses. They must then be able to draw conclusions from sets of data.

Computer skills. Geographers who use GIS technology need strong computer skills. They must be proficient in GIS programming and database management and should be comfortable creating and manipulating digital images. Most geographers benefit from having some familiarity with GIS to enable them to collaborate and communicate effectively with technical staff.

Critical-thinking skills. Geographers need critical thinking skills when doing research, as they must choose the appropriate data, methods, and scale of analysis for projects. For example, after reviewing a set of population data, they may determine the implications of a particular development plan.

Presentation skills. Geographers often present their research, typically using visual representations of data. They must describe their findings and explain how the findings are represented.

Writing skills. Writing skills are important for geographers, who often write reports or articles detailing their research findings, communicating with diverse stakeholders, and justifying proposed projects. Some geographers also must write proposals for funding.

Pay

Geographers

Median annual wages, May 2010

Geographers	$72,800
Social Scientists and Related Workers	$67,090
Total, All Occupations	$33,840

Note: All Occupations includes all occupations in the U.S. Economy.
Source: U.S. Bureau of Labor Statistics, Occupational Employment Statistics

The median annual wage of geographers was $72,800 in May 2010. The median wage is the wage at which half the workers in an occupation earned more than that amount and half earned less. The lowest 10 percent earned less than $42,450, and the top 10 percent earned more than $102,440.

Median annual wages in the industries employing the largest numbers of geographers in May 2010 were:

Federal executive branch (OES designation)	$75,820
Professional, scientific, and technical services	69,700
Colleges, universities, and professional schools	49,800

Many geographers work full time during regular business hours. Some do fieldwork that may include travel to foreign countries or remote locations.

Job Outlook

Geographers

Percent change in employment, projected 2010-20

Geographers	35%
Social Scientists and Related Workers	18%
Total, All Occupations	14%

Note: All Occupations includes all occupations in the U.S. Economy.
Source: U.S. Bureau of Labor Statistics, Employment Projections program

Employment of geographers is expected to grow 35 percent from 2010 to 2020, much faster than the average for all occupations. However, because it is a small occupation, the fast growth will result in only about 600 new jobs over the 10-year period.

More widespread use of geographic information system (GIS) technology allows firms to use geographic data to make better business and planning decisions. Job growth is expected to be fastest in the professional, scientific, and technical services industry, as businesses and developers need geographers to analyze information and advise on topics such as land use, building or infrastructure location, or environmental impact.

Due to an increasing focus on environmental and sustainable practices, geographers are increasingly needed to understand human impacts on the environment. Geographic analysis will be used to inform developers and policy makers of sustainable business practices and ensure adherence to increased regulations.

Job Prospects

Despite faster than average employment growth, a limited number of positions means applicants are expected to face strong competition for jobs. Those with advanced degrees, knowledge of business concepts, and experience working with GIS should have the best job prospects.

Job opportunities in the federal government should be limited as this sector is expected to decline. Additionally, some of the work previously done by government agencies is expected to be contracted to consulting firms in the future.

Employment projections data for geographers, 2010-20

Occupational Title	SOC Code	Employment, 2010	Projected Employment, 2020	Change, 2010-20 Percent	Change, 2010-20 Numeric
Geographers	19-3092	1,600	2,200	35	600

SOURCE: U.S. Bureau of Labor Statistics, Employment Projections program

Similar Occupations

This table shows a list of occupations with job duties that are similar to those of geographers.

Occupation	Job Duties	Entry-Level Education	Median Annual Pay, May 2010
Anthropologists and Archeologists	Anthropologists and archeologists study the origin, development, and behavior of human beings, past and present. They examine the cultures, languages, archeological remains, and physical characteristics of people in various parts of the world.	Master's degree	$54,230
Economists	Economists study the production and distribution of resources, goods, and services.	Bachelor's degree	$89,450
Geoscientists	Geoscientists study the physical aspects of the Earth, such as its composition, structure, and processes, to learn about its past, present, and future.	Bachelor's degree	$82,500
Political Scientists	Political scientists study the origin, development, and operation of political systems. They research political ideas and analyze the structure and operation of governments, policies, political trends, and related issues.	Master's degree	$107,420
Sociologists	Sociologists study society and social behavior by examining the groups, cultures, organizations, social institutions, and processes that people develop.	Master's degree	$72,360
Urban and Regional Planners	Urban and regional planners develop plans and programs for the use of land. They use planning to create communities, accommodate growth, or revitalize physical facilities in towns, cities, counties, and metropolitan areas.	Master's degree	$63,040
Cartographers and Photogrammetrists	Cartographers and photogrammetrists measure, analyze, and interpret geographic information to create maps and charts for political, cultural, educational, and other purposes. Cartographers are general mapmakers, and photogrammetrists are specialized mapmakers who use aerial photographs to create maps.	Bachelor's degree	$54,510
Surveying and Mapping Technicians	Surveying and mapping technicians assist surveyors and cartographers in collecting data and making maps of the earth's surface. Surveying technicians visit sites to take measurements of the land. Mapping technicians use geographic data to create maps.	High school diploma or equivalent	$37,900
Surveyors	Surveyors establish official land, airspace, and water boundaries. Surveyors work with civil engineers, landscape architects, and urban and regional planners to develop comprehensive design documents.	Bachelor's degree	$54,880
Postsecondary Teachers	Postsecondary teachers instruct students in a wide variety of academic and vocational subjects beyond the high school level. They also conduct research and publish scholarly papers and books.	Doctoral or professional degree	$62,050

Contacts for More Information

For more information about geographers, visit Association of American Geographers

Suggested citation:

Bureau of Labor Statistics, U.S. Department of Labor, Occupational Outlook Handbook, 2012-13 Edition, Geographers, on the Internet at http://www.bls.gov/ooh/life-physical-and-social-science/geographers.htm .

Geological and Petroleum Technicians

Quick Facts: Geological and Petroleum Technicians	
2010 Median Pay	$54,020 per year $25.97 per hour
Entry-Level Education	Associate's degree
Work Experience in a Related Occupation	None
On-the-job Training	Moderate-term on-the-job training
Number of Jobs, 2010	14,400
Job Outlook, 2010-20	15% (About as fast as average)
Employment Change, 2010-20	2,100

What Geological and Petroleum Technicians Do

Geological and petroleum technicians provide support to scientists and engineers in exploring and extracting natural resources, such as minerals, oil, and natural gas.

Duties

Geological and petroleum technicians typically do the following:

- Compile information from reports, computer databases, and other sources for use in looking for natural resources (geological prospecting)
- Install and maintain laboratory and field equipment
- Gather geological data and samples such as rocks and soils in the field and prepare samples for laboratory analysis
- Conduct scientific tests on samples to determine their content and characteristics
- Prepare notes, sketches, and maps to display geological characteristics of the land
- Monitor well exploration and drilling activities
- Prepare reports and presentations that document their investigation and findings

In the field, geological and petroleum technicians use sophisticated equipment such as seismic instruments and gravity-measuring devices to gather geological data. They also use handtools to collect samples of rocks and other materials for scientific analysis.

Geological and petroleum technicians use computers and laboratory equipment to analyze data and samples collected in the field. They also use mapping software and geographic information systems (GIS) to catalog and plot data. With the results of their analysis, they can evaluate a site to gauge its potential for further exploration and development or they can monitor quality at an existing production site.

Geological and petroleum technicians often work on geological prospecting and surveying teams under the supervision of scientists and engineers who evaluate their work for accuracy and determine whether the site should be further explored. In addition, they might work with scientists and technicians in other fields. For example, geological and petroleum technicians might work with environmental scientists and technicians to monitor the environmental impact of drilling and other activities.

Work Environment

Geological and petroleum technicians held about 14,400 jobs in 2010. Industries employing the largest numbers of geological and petroleum technicians in 2010 were as follows:

Oil and gas extraction	27%
Support activities for mining	27
Architectural, engineering, and related services	17
Petroleum and coal products manufacturing	6

About 41 percent of all technicians were employed in Texas, because of its prominence in the oil and gas industry.

Geological and petroleum technicians spend most of their time collecting data in the field or analyzing data at offices and laboratories.

Geological and petroleum technicians often work outdoors gathering data and collecting samples of rocks, soils, and other materials for further testing.

Fieldwork requires technicians to work outdoors, sometimes in remote locations, where they are exposed to all types of weather. In addition, technicians may need to stay on location in the field for days or weeks to collect data and monitor equipment.

Work Schedules

Most geological and petroleum technicians work full time. Technicians generally work a routine schedule in laboratories and offices, but hours spent in the field may be long and irregular.

How to Become a Geological or Petroleum Technician

Most employers prefer applicants who have at least an associate's degree or 2 years of postsecondary training in applied science or science-related technology. Geological and petroleum technicians also receive on-the-job training.

Education

Postsecondary training is needed for most geological and petroleum technician jobs, although some entry-level positions require a high school diploma. However, most employers prefer applicants who have at least an associate's degree or 2 years of postsecondary training in applied science or a science-related technology.

Many community colleges and technical institutes offer programs in geosciences, petroleum, mining, or a related technology such as geographic information systems (GIS). Community colleges offer associate's degree programs designed to provide an easy transition to bachelor's degree programs at colleges and universities; such programs can be useful for future career advancement.

Technical institutes typically offer 1-year certificate programs and 2-year associate's degree programs. Technical institutes usually offer technical training, but they provide less theory and fewer general education courses than community colleges offer.

Regardless of the degree program, most students take classes in geology, mathematics, computer science, chemistry, and physics. Many schools also offer internships and cooperative-education programs that help students gain experience while attending school. With this experience, it may be easier to get a job.

Important Qualities

Analytical skills. Geological and petroleum technicians examine data, using a variety of complex techniques, including laboratory experimentation and computer modeling.

Critical-thinking skills. Geological and petroleum technicians must use their best judgment when interpreting scientific data and determining what is relevant to their work.

Interpersonal skills. Geological and petroleum technicians need to be able to work well with others and as part of a team.

Stamina. To do fieldwork, geological and petroleum technicians need to be in good physical shape to hike to remote locations while carrying testing and sampling equipment.

Speaking skills. Technicians need to be able to explain their methods and findings to others.

Writing skills. Technicians document their work in reports that scientists, engineers, and other technicians use, so they need to write their methods and results clearly.

Training

Most geological and petroleum technicians receive on-the-job training under the supervision of technicians who have more experience. During training, new technicians gain hands-on experience using field and laboratory equipment, as well as computer programs such as modeling and mapping software. The length of training varies with the technician's previous experience and education. Most training programs last from a few months to 2 years.

Pay

Geological and Petroleum Technicians
Median annual wages, May 2010

Geological and Petroleum Technicians	$54,020
Life, Physical, and Social Science Technicians	$40,690
Total, All Occupations	$33,840

Note: All Occupations includes all occupations in the U.S. Economy.
Source: U.S. Bureau of Labor Statistics, Occupational Employment Statistics

The median annual wage of geological and petroleum technicians was $54,020 in May 2010. The median wage is the wage at which half the workers in an occupation earned more than that amount and half earned less. The lowest 10 percent earned less than $29,950, and the top 10 percent earned more than $99,860.

The median annual wages in the industries employing the largest numbers of technicians in May 2010 were as follows:

Petroleum and coal products manufacturing	$88,860
Oil and gas extraction	61,340
Support activities for mining	46,640
Architectural, engineering, and related services	41,560

Most geological and petroleum technicians work full time. Technicians generally work a routine schedule while in laboratories and offices, but hours spent in the field may be long or irregular.

Job Outlook

Geological and Petroleum Technicians
Percent change in employment, projected 2010-20

Geological and Petroleum Technicians	15%
Total, All Occupations	14%
Life, Physical, and Social Science Technicians	11%

Note: All Occupations includes all occupations in the U.S. Economy.
Source: U.S. Bureau of Labor Statistics, Employment Projections program

Employment of geological and petroleum technicians is expected to grow by 15 percent from 2010 to 2020, about as fast as the average for all occupations. High prices and growing demand for natural resources—especially oil and natural gas—are expected to increase demand for geological exploration and extraction in the future. Historically, when oil and natural gas prices are low, companies limit exploration and hire fewer technicians. When prices are high, however, companies explore and extract more. If oil prices remain high over the long run, the demand for geological and petroleum technicians will remain high as well.

Employment projections data for geological and petroleum technicians, 2010-20

Occupational Title	SOC Code	Employment, 2010	Projected Employment, 2020	Change, 2010-20	
				Percent	Numeric
Geological and Petroleum Technicians	19-4041	14,400	16,500	15	2,100
SOURCE: U.S. Bureau of Labor Statistics, Employment Projections program					

Similar Occupations

This table shows a list of occupations with job duties that are similar to those of geological and petroleum technicians.

Occupation	Job Duties	Entry-Level Education	Median Annual Pay, May 2010
Civil Engineering Technicians	Civil engineering technicians help civil engineers plan and design the construction of highways, bridges, utilities, and other major infrastructure projects. They also help with commercial, residential, and land development. Civil engineering technicians work under the direction of a licensed civil engineer.	Associate's degree	$46,290
Civil Engineers	Civil engineers design and supervise large construction projects, including roads, buildings, airports, tunnels, dams, bridges, and systems for water supply and sewage treatment.	Bachelor's degree	$77,560
Geoscientists	Geoscientists study the physical aspects of the Earth, such as its composition, structure, and processes, to learn about its past, present, and future.	Bachelor's degree	$82,500
Hydrologists	Hydrologists study water and the water cycle. They use their expertise to solve problems in the areas of water quality or availability.	Master's degree	$75,690
Petroleum Engineers	Petroleum engineers design and develop methods for extracting oil and gas from deposits below the earth's surface. Petroleum engineers also find new ways to extract oil and gas from older wells.	Bachelor's degree	$114,080
Surveying and Mapping Technicians	Surveying and mapping technicians assist surveyors and cartographers in collecting data and making maps of the earth's surface. Surveying technicians visit sites to take measurements of the land. Mapping technicians use geographic data to create maps.	High school diploma or equivalent	$37,900

Contacts for More Information

For more information about careers in geology, visit American Geological Institute

For more information about careers in oil and gas exploration, visit American Association of Petroleum Geologists , Society of Petroleum Engineers

Suggested citation:

Bureau of Labor Statistics, U.S. Department of Labor, Occupational Outlook Handbook, 2012-13 Edition, Geological and Petroleum Technicians, on the Internet at http://www.bls.gov/ooh/life-physical-and-social-science/geological-and-petroleum-technicians.htm .

Geoscientists

Quick Facts: Geoscientists	
2010 Median Pay	$82,500 per year $39.66 per hour
Entry-Level Education	Bachelor's degree
Work Experience in a Related Occupation	None
On-the-job Training	None
Number of Jobs, 2010	33,800
Job Outlook, 2010-20	21% (Faster than average)
Employment Change, 2010-20	7,100

What Geoscientists Do

Geoscientists study the physical aspects of the Earth, such as its composition, structure, and processes, to learn about its past, present, and future.

Duties

Geoscientists typically do the following:

- Plan and conduct field studies, in which they visit locations to collect samples and conduct surveys
- Analyze aerial photographs, well logs (detailed records of geologic formations found during drilling), and other data to locate natural resource deposits and estimate their size
- Conduct laboratory tests on samples collected in the field
- Produce geologic maps and charts
- Prepare written scientific reports
- Present their findings to clients, colleagues, and other interested parties
- Review reports and research done by other scientists

Geoscientists use a wide variety of tools, both simple and complex. In a day in the field, they may use a hammer and chisel to collect rock samples and then use sophisticated radar equipment to search for oil underground. In laboratories, they may use x rays and electron microscopes to determine the chemical and physical composition of rock samples. They also use remote sensing equipment to collect data and advanced geographic information systems (GIS) and modeling software to analyze data.

Geoscientists often supervise the work of technicians, both in the field and in the lab. They also usually work as part of a team with other scientists and engineers. For example, they work closely with petroleum engineers to find and develop new sources of oil and natural gas.

Many geoscientists are involved in the search for and development of natural resources and minerals such as petroleum. Others work in environmental protection and preservation and are involved in projects to clean up and reclaim land. Some specialize in a particular aspect of the Earth, such as its oceans.

The following are examples of types of geoscientists:

Engineering geologists apply geologic principles to civil and environmental engineering. They offer advice on major construction projects and help in other projects, such as environmental cleanup and reducing natural hazards.

Geologists study the materials, processes, and history of the Earth. They investigate how rocks were formed and what has happened to them since their formation.

Geochemists use physical and organic chemistry to study the composition of elements found in groundwater, such as water from wells or aquifers, and earth materials, such as rocks and sediment.

Geophysicists use the principles of physics to learn about the Earth's surface and interior. They also study the properties of Earth's magnetic, electric, and gravitational fields.

Oceanographers study the motion and circulation of ocean waters; the physical and chemical properties of the oceans; and how these properties affect coastal areas, climate, and weather.

Paleontologists study fossils found in geological formations to trace the evolution of plant and animal life and the geologic history of the Earth.

Petroleum geologists explore the Earth for oil and gas deposits. They analyze geological information to identify sites that should be explored. They collect rock and sediment samples from sites through drilling and other methods and test them for the presence of oil and gas. They also estimate the size of oil and gas deposits and work to develop sites to extract oil and gas.

Seismologists study earthquakes and related phenomena like tsunamis. They use seismographs and other instruments to collect data on these events.

For a more extensive list of geoscientist specialties, visit the American Geological Institute .

People with a geosciences background may become professors or teachers. For more information, see the profile on postsecondary teachers .

Geoscientists study the Earth by examining rocks, soils, and other materials.

Work Environment

Geoscientists held about 33,800 jobs in 2010. Industries employing the largest numbers of geoscientists in 2010 were as follows:

Architectural, engineering, and related services	22%
Oil and gas extraction	19
Management, scientific, and technical consulting services	14
State government, excluding education and hospitals	9
Federal government, excluding postal service	8

About 3 out of 10 geoscientists were employed in Texas, because of the prominence of the oil and gas industry in that state.

Most geoscientists split their time between working in the field, in laboratories, and in offices. Fieldwork can take geoscientists to remote locations all over the world and can be physically demanding. For example, oceanographers may spend months at sea on a research ship.

The search for natural resources often takes geoscientists involved in exploration to remote areas and foreign countries. When in the field, geoscientists may work in both warm and cold climates, in all types of weather. They may have to travel by helicopter or 4-wheel-drive vehicles and cover large areas on foot.

Work Schedules

Most geoscientists work full time. They may work long or irregular hours when doing fieldwork. Geoscientists travel frequently to meet with clients and to conduct fieldwork.

How to Become a Geoscientist

Most geoscientist jobs require at least a bachelor's degree. In several states, geoscientists may need a license to offer their services to the public.

Education

Geoscientists need at least a bachelor's degree for entry-level positions. A Ph.D. is necessary for most high-level research and college teaching positions.

A degree in geosciences is preferred, although degrees in physics, chemistry, biology, mathematics, engineering, or computer science are usually accepted if they include coursework in geology.

Most geosciences programs include geology courses in mineralogy, petrology, and structural geology, which are important for all geoscientists. In addition to classes in geology, most programs require students to take courses in other physical sciences, mathematics, engineering, and computer science.

Computer knowledge is essential for geoscientists. Students who have experience with computer modeling, data analysis, and digital mapping will be the most prepared to enter the job market.

Many employers seek applicants who have gained field and laboratory experience while pursuing a degree. Summer field camp programs offer students the opportunity to work closely with professors and to apply their classroom knowledge in the field. Students can gain valuable experience in data collection and geologic mapping.

Important Qualities

Critical-thinking skills. Geoscientists base their findings on sound observation and careful evaluation of data.

Interpersonal skills. Most geoscientists work as part of a team with engineers, technicians, and other scientists.

Problem-solving skills. Geoscientists work on complex projects filled with challenges.

Speaking skills. Geoscientists must be able to explain their findings to clients or professionals who do not have a background in geosciences.

Stamina. Geoscientists may need to hike to remote locations while carrying testing and sampling equipment when they conduct fieldwork.

Writing skills. Geoscientists write reports and research papers that explain their findings.

Licenses

Geoscientists need a license to practice in some states. Requirements vary by state but typically include minimum education and experience requirements and a passing score on an exam.

Pay

Geoscientists

Median annual wages, May 2010

Geoscientists, Except Hydrologists and Geographers	$82,500
Life, Physical, and Social Science Occupations	$58,530
Total, All Occupations	$33,840

Note: All Occupations includes all occupations in the U.S. Economy.
Source: U.S. Bureau of Labor Statistics, Occupational Employment Statistics

The median annual wage of geoscientists was $82,500 in May 2010. The median wage is the wage at which half the workers in an occupation earned more than that amount and half earned less. The lowest 10 percent earned less than $43,820, and the top 10 percent more than $160,910.

Median annual wages in the industries employing the largest numbers of geoscientists in May 2010 were as follows:

Oil and gas extraction	$125,350
Federal government, excluding postal service	93,300
Architectural, engineering, and related services	68,790
Management, scientific, and technical consulting services	67,840
State government, excluding education and hospitals	59,820

Most geoscientists work full time and may work long or irregular hours when doing fieldwork. Geoscientists travel frequently to meet with clients and to conduct fieldwork.

Job Outlook

Geoscientists

Percent change in employment, projected 2010-20

Geoscientists, Except Hydrologists and Geographers	21%
Life, Physical, and Social Science Occupations	16%
Total, All Occupations	14%

Note: All Occupations includes all occupations in the U.S. Economy.
Source: U.S. Bureau of Labor Statistics, Employment Projections program

Employment of geoscientists is projected to grow by 21 percent from 2010 to 2020, faster than the average for all occupations. The need for energy, environmental protection, and responsible land and resource management will spur demand for geoscientists in the future. Most new jobs will be in management, scientific, and technical consulting services as more geoscientists are hired as consultants.

Job Prospects

Job opportunities should be excellent for geoscientists who graduate with a master's degree. In addition to job growth, many geoscientists are approaching retirement age and a large number of openings are expected as those geoscientists leave the workforce.

Geoscientists with a doctoral degree will likely face competition for positions in academia and research.

Many openings are expected in consulting firms and the oil and gas industry. Historically, when oil and natural gas prices are low, companies limit exploration and hire fewer geoscientists. When prices are high, however, companies explore and extract more. If oil prices remain high over the long run, the demand for geoscientists will remain high as well.

Fewer opportunities are expected in state and federal government than in the past. Budget constraints are expected to limit hiring by state governments and federal agencies such as the U.S. Geological Survey. Further, more of the work traditionally done by government agencies is expected to be contracted out to consulting firms in the future.

Employment projections data for geoscientists, 2010-20

Occupational Title	SOC Code	Employment, 2010	Projected Employment, 2020	Change, 2010-20 Percent	Change, 2010-20 Numeric
Geoscientists, Except Hydrologists and Geographers	19-2042	33,800	40,900	21	7,100
SOURCE: U.S. Bureau of Labor Statistics, Employment Projections program					

Similar Occupations

This table shows a list of occupations with job duties that are similar to those of geoscientists.

Occupation	Job Duties	Entry-Level Education	Median Annual Pay, May 2010
Agricultural and Food Scientists	Agricultural and food scientists work to ensure agricultural productivity and food safety.	See How to Become One	$58,450
Atmospheric Scientists, Including Meteorologists	Atmospheric scientists study weather, climate, and other aspects of the atmosphere. They develop reports and forecasts from their analysis of weather and climate data.	Bachelor's degree	$87,780
Civil Engineers	Civil engineers design and supervise large construction projects, including roads, buildings, airports, tunnels, dams, bridges, and systems for water supply and sewage treatment.	Bachelor's degree	$77,560
Environmental Engineers	Environmental engineers use the principles of engineering, soil science, biology, and chemistry to develop solutions to environmental problems. They are involved in efforts to improve recycling, waste disposal, public health, and control of water and air pollution.	Bachelor's degree	$78,740
Environmental Scientists and Specialists	Environmental scientists and specialists use their knowledge of the natural sciences to protect the environment. They identify problems and find solutions that minimize hazards to the health of the environment and the population.	Bachelor's degree	$61,700
Geological and Petroleum Technicians	Geological and petroleum technicians provide support to scientists and engineers in exploring and extracting natural resources, such as minerals, oil, and natural gas.	Associate's degree	$54,020
Hydrologists	Hydrologists study water and the water cycle. They use their expertise to solve problems in the areas of water quality or availability.	Master's degree	$75,690
Petroleum Engineers	Petroleum engineers design and develop methods for extracting oil and gas from deposits below the earth's surface. Petroleum engineers also find new ways to extract oil and gas from older wells.	Bachelor's degree	$114,080
Postsecondary Teachers	Postsecondary teachers instruct students in a wide variety of academic and vocational subjects beyond the high school level. They also conduct research and publish scholarly papers and books.	Doctoral or professional degree	$62,050

Contacts for More Information

For more information about geoscientists, visit American Geological Institute

For information about petroleum geologists, visit American Association of Petroleum Geologists

For information about getting a position as a geologist, geophysicist, or oceanographer with the federal government, visit USAJOBS

Suggested citation:

Bureau of Labor Statistics, U.S. Department of Labor, Occupational Outlook Handbook, 2012-13 Edition, Geoscientists, on the Internet at http://www.bls.gov/ooh/life-physical-and-social-science/geoscientists.htm .

Historians

Quick Facts: Historians	
2010 Median Pay	$53,520 per year $25.73 per hour
Entry-Level Education	Master's degree
Work Experience in a Related Occupation	None
On-the-job Training	None
Number of Jobs, 2010	4,000
Job Outlook, 2010-20	18% (About as fast as average)
Employment Change, 2010-20	700

What Historians Do

Historians research, analyze, interpret, and present the past by studying a variety of historical documents and sources.

Duties

Historians typically do the following:

- Gather historical data from sources that include archives, books, and artifacts
- Analyze and interpret historical information to determine its authenticity and significance
- Trace historical developments in a particular field
- Engage with, educate, and make presentations to the public
- Archive or preserve materials and artifacts in museums, visitor centers, and historic sites
- Provide advice or guidance on historical topics and preservation issues
- Write reports, articles, and books on findings and theories

Historians conduct research and analysis for governments,

Historians consult a variety of sources in their work.

businesses, nonprofits, historical associations, and other organizations. They use a variety of sources in their work, including government and institutional records, newspapers, photographs, interviews, films, and unpublished manuscripts such as personal diaries and letters. They also may process, catalog, and archive these documents and artifacts.

Most historians present and interpret history for the public. They often trace and build a historical profile of a particular person, area, idea, organization, or event. Once their research is complete, they present their findings through articles, books, reports, exhibits, websites, and educational programs.

In government, some historians do research to provide historical context for current policy issues. For example, they may research the history of Social Security as background for a new bill or upcoming funding debate. Others write about the history of a particular government activity or program, such as a military operation or the space program.

In historical associations, historians preserve artifacts and explain the historical significance of a wide variety of subjects, such as historic buildings, religious groups, and battlegrounds.

Historians who work for businesses may examine historical evidence for legal cases and regulatory matters.

Many people with a background in history become professors and teachers. For more information on those who teach at colleges and universities, see the profile on postsecondary teachers . For more information on those who work as high school history teachers, see the profile on high school teachers .

Work Environment

Historians held about 4,000 jobs in 2010, 57 percent of which were in government. Historians also work in museums, archives, historical societies, research organizations, and nonprofits. Some provide consulting work for these organizations while employed by consulting firms or as independent consultants.

The following industries employed the most historians in 2010:

Local government, excluding education and hospitals	25%
Federal government, excluding postal service	22
Professional, scientific, and technical services	14
State government, excluding education and hospitals	11

Work Schedules

Most historians work full time. Some, including those who are self-employed, work independently and are able to set their own schedules. Some travel to do fieldwork, which may involve collecting artifacts, going to sources, conducting interviews, or visiting an area to better understand its culture and environment.

How to Become a Historian

Although most historian positions require a master's degree, some research positions require a Ph.D. Candidates with a bachelor's degree may qualify for a limited number of positions, but most will not work in traditional historian jobs.

Education

Historians need a master's degree or Ph.D. for most positions. Many historians have a master's degree in history or public history, which takes 2 years to complete. Others complete degrees in related fields, such as museum studies, historical preservation, or archival management. Many programs require an internship or other onsite work experience as a part of the degree program.

Some research positions require a Ph.D. Students in history Ph.D. programs usually concentrate in a specific area of history. Possible specializations include a particular country or region, period, or field, such as social, political, or cultural history.

Candidates with a bachelor's degree in history usually work outside of traditional historian jobs. Often, their liberal arts background and writing and researching skills are suitable for jobs in education, communications, law, business, publishing, or journalism.

Many people with a background in history become professors and teachers. For more information on those who teach at colleges and universities, see the profile on postsecondary teachers . For more information on those who work as high school history teachers, see the profile on high school teachers .

Work Experience

Many historians benefit from internships or field experience when they look for positions outside of colleges and universities. Most master's programs in public history and similar fields require an internship as part of the curriculum. Internships offer an opportunity for students to learn practical skills, such as handling and preserving artifacts and creating exhibits. They also allow students to apply their academic knowledge in a hands-on setting.

Those without internship experience can benefit from volunteering or working in an entry-level position to gain similar practical, onsite experience. Positions are often available at local museums, historical societies, government agencies, or nonprofit and other organizations.

Important Qualities

Analytical skills. Historians must be able to examine the information and data in historical sources and draw logical conclusions from them, whether the sources are written documents, visual images, or material artifacts.

Communication skills. Communication skills are important for historians because many interpret history for the public through presentations. Historians also need communication skills when they interview people to collect oral histories, consult with clients, or collaborate with colleagues in the workplace.

Problem-solving skills. Historians try to answer questions about the past. They may investigate something unknown about a past idea, event, or person; decipher historical information; or identify how the past has affected the present.

Reading-comprehension skills. Historians must be able to read through and digest information from a large number of historical documents, texts, and other sources.

Writing skills. Writing skills are essential for historians, who present their research conclusions in reports, articles, and books.

Pay

Historians

Median annual wages, May 2010

Social Scientists and Related Workers	$67,090
Historians	$53,520
Total, All Occupations	$33,840

Note: All Occupations includes all occupations in the U.S. Economy.
Source: U.S. Bureau of Labor Statistics, Occupational Employment Statistics

The median annual wage of historians was $53,520 in May 2010. The median wage is the wage at which half the workers in an occupation earned more than that amount and half earned less. The lowest 10 percent earned less than $26,370, and the top 10 percent earned more than $95,690.

Median annual wages in the industries employing the largest numbers of historians in May 2010 were as follows:

Federal executive branch	$84,860
Professional, scientific, and technical services	55,410
State government	49,990
Local government	30,950

Most historians work full time. Some work independently and are able to set their own schedules. Some travel to do fieldwork.

Job Outlook

Historians

Percent change in employment, projected 2010-20

Social Scientists and Related Workers	18%
Historians	18%
Total, All Occupations	14%

Note: All Occupations includes all occupations in the U.S. Economy.
Source: U.S. Bureau of Labor Statistics, Employment Projections program

Employment of historians is expected to grow 18 percent from 2010 to 2020, about as fast as the average for all occupations.

Federal, state, and local governments, which employ 57 percent of all historians, are expected to experience slower-than-average employment growth, which will lead to a limited number of new historian positions. Historians will experience more employment growth outside of government, in historical societies, research organizations, and historical consulting firms. However, many types of organizations that employ historians depend on donations or public funding, so employment growth from 2010 to 2020 will depend largely on the amount of funding available.

Job Prospects

Historians will face strong competition for most jobs. Because of the popularity of history degree programs, applicants are expected to outnumber positions available. Those with practical skills or hands-on work experience should have the best job prospects.

Many workers with a background in history will likely work in a closely related field. Because historians have broad training and education in writing, analytical research, and critical thinking, they can apply their skills to many different occupations. Many find work as researchers, writers, educators, or policy analysts.

Employment projections data for historians, 2010-20

Occupational Title	SOC Code	Employment, 2010	Projected Employment, 2020	Change, 2010-20	
				Percent	Numeric
Historians	19-3093	4,000	4,700	18	700
SOURCE: U.S. Bureau of Labor Statistics, Employment Projections program					

Similar Occupations

This table shows a list of occupations with job duties that are similar to those of historians.

Occupation	Job Duties	Entry-Level Education	Median Annual Pay, May 2010
Anthropologists and Archeologists	Anthropologists and archeologists study the origin, development, and behavior of human beings, past and present. They examine the cultures, languages, archeological remains, and physical characteristics of people in various parts of the world.	Master's degree	$54,230
Economists	Economists study the production and distribution of resources, goods, and services.	Bachelor's degree	$89,450
Geographers	Geographers study the earth and its land, features, and inhabitants. They also examine phenomena such as political or cultural structures as they relate to geography. They study the physical or human geographic characteristics or both of a region, ranging in scale from local to global.	Bachelor's degree	$72,800
Political Scientists	Political scientists study the origin, development, and operation of political systems. They research political ideas and analyze the structure and operation of governments, policies, political trends, and related issues.	Master's degree	$107,420
Sociologists	Sociologists study society and social behavior by examining the groups, cultures, organizations, social institutions, and processes that people develop.	Master's degree	$72,360
Archivists	Archivists appraise, edit, and maintain permanent records and historically valuable documents. Many perform research on archival material.	Bachelor's degree	$45,200
Curators, Museum Technicians, and Conservators	Curators oversee collections, such as artwork and historic items, and may conduct public service activities for an institution. Museum technicians and conservators prepare and restore objects and documents in museum collections and exhibits.	See How to Become One	$42,310
High School Teachers	High school teachers help prepare students for life after graduation. They teach academic lessons and various skills that students will need to attend college and to enter the job market.	Bachelor's degree	$53,230
Postsecondary Teachers	Postsecondary teachers instruct students in a wide variety of academic and vocational subjects beyond the high school level. They also conduct research and publish scholarly papers and books.	Doctoral or professional degree	$62,050
Editors	Editors plan, review, and revise content for publication.	Bachelor's degree	$51,470

Contacts for More Information

For more information about historians, visit American Historical Association , National Council on Public History

Suggested citation:

Bureau of Labor Statistics, U.S. Department of Labor, Occupational Outlook Handbook, 2012-13 Edition, Historians, on the Internet at http://www.bls.gov/ooh/life-physical-and-social-science/historians.htm .

Hydrologists

Quick Facts: Hydrologists	
2010 Median Pay	$75,690 per year $36.39 per hour
Entry-Level Education	Master's degree
Work Experience in a Related Occupation	None
On-the-job Training	None
Number of Jobs, 2010	7,600
Job Outlook, 2010-20	18% (About as fast as average)
Employment Change, 2010-20	1,400

What Hydrologists Do

Hydrologists study water and the water cycle. They study the movement, distribution, and other properties of water, and they analyze how these influence the surrounding environment. They use their expertise to solve problems concerning water quality and availability, for example.

Duties

Hydrologists typically do the following:

- Measure the properties of bodies of water, such as volume and stream flow
- Collect water and soil samples to test for certain properties, such as levels of pollution
- Apply research findings to help minimize the environmental impacts of pollution, erosion, and other problems
- Research ways to improve water conservation and preservation
- Use computer models to forecast future water supplies, the spread of pollution, and other events
- Evaluate the feasibility of water-related projects, such as hydroelectric power plants, irrigation systems, and waste treatment facilities
- Prepare written reports and presentations of their findings

Hydrologists use remote sensing equipment to collect data. They or technicians whom they supervise usually install and maintain this equipment.

They also use sophisticated computer programs to analyze and model data. They use sophisticated laboratory equipment to analyze chemical samples collected in the field.

Hydrologists work closely with engineers, scientists, and public officials to study and manage the water supply. For example, they work with policy makers to develop water conservation plans and with biologists to monitor marine wildlife.

Most hydrologists specialize in a specific water source or a certain aspect of the water cycle, such as the evaporation of water from lakes and streams. Some of the most common specialties are:

Groundwater hydrologists study the water below the Earth's surface. They decide the best locations for wells and the amount of water that should be pumped. They are often consulted about the best places to build waste disposal sites to ensure that the waste does not contaminate the groundwater.

Hydrometeorologists study the relationship between surface waters and water in the atmosphere. For example, to predict and prepare for droughts, they study how much rain or snow a particular area gets and how that evaporates.

Surface water hydrologists study water from above ground sources such as streams, lakes, and snow packs. They may predict future water levels and usage to help reservoir managers decide when to release or store water. They also produce flood forecasts and help develop flood management plans.

Some people with a hydrology background become professors or teachers. For more information, see the profile on postsecondary teachers .

Work Environment

Hydrologists held about 7,600 jobs in 2010. Industries employing the largest numbers of hydrologists in 2010 were as follows:

Federal government, excluding postal service	30%
Architectural, engineering, and related services	22
Management, scientific, and technical consulting services	19
State government, excluding education and hospitals	14
Local government, excluding education and hospitals	6

Hydrologists work in the field and in offices and laboratories. In the field, hydrologists may have to wade into lakes and streams to collect samples or inspect monitoring equipment. In the office, hydrologists spend most their time using computers to analyze data and model their findings.

Work Schedules

Most hydrologists work full time. However, the length of daily shifts may vary when hydrologists are doing field work.

Hydrologists often need to collect samples in the field.

How to Become a Hydrologist

For most jobs, hydrologists need a master's degree with a focus in the natural sciences. Hydrologists may need a license in some states.

Education

Most hydrologists need a master's degree, but a bachelor's degree is adequate for some entry-level positions. Applicants for advanced research and university faculty positions typically need a Ph.D.

Few universities offer degrees in hydrology; instead, most universities offer hydrology concentrations in their geosciences, environmental science, or engineering programs. Students interested in becoming a hydrologist need extensive coursework in math, statistics, and physical, computer, and life sciences.

Students who have experience with computer modeling, data analysis, and digital mapping will be the most prepared to enter the job market. Also, hydrologists use geographic information systems (GIS), remote sensing, and global positioning system (GPS) equipment to do their jobs.

Important Qualities

Analytical skills. Hydrologists need to analyze data collected in the field and then examine the results of laboratory testing in their research.

Critical-thinking skills. Hydrologists assess risks posed to the water supply by pollution, floods, and other threats. They develop water management plans to handle these threats.

Interpersonal skills. Most hydrologists work as part of a diverse team with engineers, technicians, and other scientists.

Speaking skills. Hydrologists often have to present their findings in an understandable way to people who do not have a technical background, such as government officials or the general public.

Stamina. When they are in the field, hydrologists may need to hike to remote locations while carrying testing and sampling equipment.

Writing skills. Hydrologists prepare detailed reports documenting their research methods and findings.

Licenses

In some states, hydrologists need a license to practice. Requirements vary by state, but they typically include minimum education and experience requirements and passing an exam.

Pay

Hydrologists
Median annual wages, May 2010

Hydrologists	$75,690
Life, Physical, and Social Science Occupations	$58,530
Total, All Occupations	$33,840

Note: All Occupations includes all occupations in the U.S. Economy.
Source: U.S. Bureau of Labor Statistics, Occupational Employment Statistics

The median annual wage of hydrologists was $75,690 in May 2010. The median wage is the wage at which half the workers in an occupation earned more than that amount and half earned less. The lowest 10 percent earned less than $48,280, and the top 10 percent more than $112,490.

Median annual wages in the industries employing the largest numbers of hydrologists in May 2010 were as follows:

Federal government, excluding postal service	$84,540
Management, scientific, and technical consulting services	77,850
Architectural, engineering, and related services	77,750
Local government, excluding education and hospitals	68,600
State government, excluding education and hospitals	61,830

Most hydrologists work full time. However, the length of daily shifts may vary when hydrologists are doing field work.

Job Outlook

Hydrologists
Percent change in employment, projected 2010-20

Hydrologists	18%
Life, Physical, and Social Science Occupations	16%
Total, All Occupations	14%

Note: All Occupations includes all occupations in the U.S. Economy.
Source: U.S. Bureau of Labor Statistics, Employment Projections program

Employment of hydrologists is expected to grow by 18 percent from 2010 to 2020, about as fast as the average for all occupations. Population growth and environmental concerns, especially global climate change, are expected to increase demand for hydrologists in the future.

As the population grows, a greater strain will be placed on the nation's water resources. More hydrologists will be needed to help develop plans to meet increased demand while preserving water supplies for future generations. For example, as the population expands into places that were not previously inhabited, hydrologists will be needed to examine the risk of flooding and to assess the availability of water for new communities.

More hydrologists will be needed to assess the threats that global climate change poses to local, state, and national water supplies. For example, changes in climate affect the severity and frequency of droughts and floods. Hydrologists will be needed to develop comprehensive water management plans that address these and other problems linked to global climate change.

Job Prospects

Hydrologists with computer modeling experience are expected to have the best opportunities in the future.

Employment projections data for hydrologists, 2010-20

Occupational Title	SOC Code	Employment, 2010	Projected Employment, 2020	Change, 2010-20 Percent	Change, 2010-20 Numeric
Hydrologists	19-2043	7,600	9,000	18	1,400
SOURCE: U.S. Bureau of Labor Statistics, Employment Projections program					

Similar Occupations

This table shows a list of occupations with job duties that are similar to those of hydrologists.

Occupation	Job Duties	Entry-Level Education	Median Annual Pay, May 2010
Atmospheric Scientists, Including Meteorologists	Atmospheric scientists study weather, climate, and other aspects of the atmosphere. They develop reports and forecasts from their analysis of weather and climate data.	Bachelor's degree	$87,780
Civil Engineers	Civil engineers design and supervise large construction projects, including roads, buildings, airports, tunnels, dams, bridges, and systems for water supply and sewage treatment.	Bachelor's degree	$77,560
Environmental Engineers	Environmental engineers use the principles of engineering, soil science, biology, and chemistry to develop solutions to environmental problems. They are involved in efforts to improve recycling, waste disposal, public health, and control of water and air pollution.	Bachelor's degree	$78,740
Environmental Science and Protection Technicians	Environmental science and protection technicians do laboratory and field tests to monitor the environment and investigate sources of pollution, including those affecting health. Many work under the supervision of environmental scientists and specialists, who direct their work and evaluate their results.	Associate's degree	$41,380
Environmental Scientists and Specialists	Environmental scientists and specialists use their knowledge of the natural sciences to protect the environment. They identify problems and find solutions that minimize hazards to the health of the environment and the population.	Bachelor's degree	$61,700
Geoscientists	Geoscientists study the physical aspects of the Earth, such as its composition, structure, and processes, to learn about its past, present, and future.	Bachelor's degree	$82,500
Postsecondary Teachers	Postsecondary teachers instruct students in a wide variety of academic and vocational subjects beyond the high school level. They also conduct research and publish scholarly papers and books.	Doctoral or professional degree	$62,050

Contacts for More Information

For more information about hydrology and the work of hydrologists in the federal government, visit United States Geological Survey

For more information about careers in hydrology, visit American Geological Institute , American Institute of Hydrology

Suggested citation:

Bureau of Labor Statistics, U.S. Department of Labor, Occupational Outlook Handbook, 2012-13 Edition, Hydrologists, on the Internet at http://www.bls.gov/ooh/life-physical-and-social-science/hydrologists.htm .

Medical Scientists

Quick Facts: Medical Scientists	
2010 Median Pay	$76,700 per year $36.87 per hour
Entry-Level Education	Doctoral or professional degree
Work Experience in a Related Occupation	None
On-the-job Training	None
Number of Jobs, 2010	100,000
Job Outlook, 2010-20	36% (Much faster than average)
Employment Change, 2010-20	36,400

What Medical Scientists Do

Medical scientists conduct research aimed at improving overall human health. They often use clinical trials and other investigative methods to reach their findings.

Duties

Medical scientists typically do the following:

- Plan and direct studies to investigate human diseases, preventive methods, and the treatment of disease
- Develop methods, instruments, and procedures for medical applications and data analysis
- Prepare and analyze medical samples to identify toxicity, bacteria, or microorganisms or to study cell structure
- Standardize drug doses and immunization methods for manufacturing drugs and other medicinal compounds
- Work with health departments, industry personnel, and physicians to develop programs that improve health safety standards

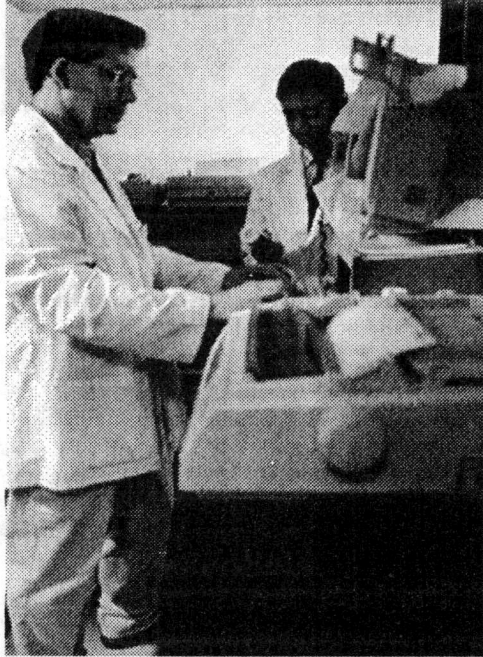

Medical scientists conduct research with the goal of improving overall human health.

- Prepare research grant proposals to get funding from government agencies
- Follow safety procedures to avoid contamination

Many medical scientists, especially in universities, work with little supervision, forming their own hypotheses and developing experiments accordingly. In addition, they often lead teams, technicians, and, sometimes, students who do support tasks. For example, a medical scientist working in a university laboratory may have undergraduate assistants take measurements and observations for the scientist's research.

Medical scientists study biological systems to understand the causes of diseases and other health problems. For example, medical scientists who do cancer research might put together a combination of drugs that could slow the progress of the disease. They would then study that combination in a clinical trial. Physicians may work with the medical scientists to try the new combination with patients who are willing to participate in the study.

In a clinical trial, patients agree to help find out if a particular drug, or combination of drugs, or other medical intervention works. Without knowing which group they are in, patients in a drug-related clinical trial either receive the trial drug or receive a placebo, a drug that looks like the trial drug but does not have the special ingredients.

Medical scientists analyze the data from all the patients in the clinical trial to see if the trial drug did better than the placebo, for whom it worked better, and to answer other research questions. They then write up and report their findings.

Medical scientists do research both to develop new treatments and to try to prevent health problems. For example, they may study the link between smoking and lung cancer or between alcoholism and liver disease.

Medical scientists who work in private industry usually have less freedom to choose their research topics. Although they may not have the pressure of writing grant proposals to get money for their research, they may have to explain their research plans to nonscientist managers or executives.

Many medical scientists work in the federal government, in research universities, or in private industry.

In the federal government, medical scientists conduct research on human diseases and on exploratory methods of solving medical problems. They spend most of their time carrying out clinical trials or developing experiments on nonhuman subjects. Medical scientists eventually present their findings in medical journals or other publications.

In universities, medical scientists do research and investigate new medicinal methods of improving health. They also write grants, to organizations such as the National Institutes of Health (NIH) and the National Science Foundation (NSF), to secure steady funding for their research.

In addition to doing research, medical scientists in universities and in government who are also medical doctors may see patients, particularly those participating in clinical trials.

In private industry, medical scientists focus on the development of products such as pharmaceutical drugs and medical instruments. Companies place strong emphasis on the development of products, a process that they hope will culminate with approval from a government agency, often the <u>Food and Drug Administration</u> (FDA). The approval process can take several years and be very costly, so private companies typically emphasize development over research.

Work Environment

Medical scientists held about 100,000 jobs in 2010. The industries employing the largest numbers of medical scientists in 2010 were as follows:

Scientific research and development services	35%
Colleges, universities, and professional schools; state, local, and private	24
Pharmaceutical and medicine manufacturing	12
General medical and surgical hospitals; state, local, and private	11
Drugs and druggists' sundries merchant wholesalers	2

Medical scientists usually work in offices and laboratories. They spend most of their time studying data and reports in an office or laboratory. Medical scientists sometimes work with inherently unsafe samples, but they take appropriate precautions to ensure that their environment is safe, stable, and sterile.

Most medical scientists work full time.

How to Become a Medical Scientist

Medical scientists typically need a Ph.D., usually in biology or a related life science, from an accredited postsecondary institution. Some medical scientists get a medical degree instead of a Ph.D. but prefer doing research to practicing as a physician. It is helpful for medical scientists to have both a Ph.D. and a medical degree.

Education

Students planning careers as medical scientists should pursue a bachelor's degree in a biological science. Undergraduate programs typically include courses in life sciences, as well as chemistry, physics, and mathematics. Humanities courses also are beneficial for developing writing and communication skills, which are necessary for drafting grant proposals and publishing research results.

After students have completed undergraduate studies, there are two main degree paths for prospective medical scientists: either a Ph.D. or a joint M.D.-Ph.D. Students can enroll in a university Ph.D. program in the biological sciences, which typically take about 6 years of study. Ph.D. students specialize in one particular field, such as genetics, pathology, or bioinformatics. For a joint M.D.-Ph.D. program, students enroll at a medical college that typically takes 7 to 8 years of study. Students learn both the clinical skills needed to be a physician and the research skills needed to be a scientist.

Graduate programs place additional emphasis on laboratory work and original research. These programs offer prospective medical scientists the opportunity to develop their experiments and, sometimes, to supervise undergraduates. A Ph.D. culminates in a thesis, which the candidate presents before a committee of professors.

Those who go to medical school spend most of the first 2 years in labs and classrooms, taking courses such as anatomy, biochemistry, physiology, pharmacology, psychology, microbiology, pathology,

medical ethics, and medical law. They also learn to take medical histories, examine patients, and diagnose illnesses. For more information, see the profile on <u>physicians and surgeons</u> .

Medical scientists often continue their education with postdoctoral work at universities or with federal agencies, such as the National Institutes of Health. Postdoctoral work provides valuable lab experience, including in specific processes and techniques such as gene splicing, which is transferable to other research projects. In some institutions, the postdoctoral position leads to a permanent job.

Licenses

Medical scientists who administer drug or gene therapy to human patients, or who otherwise interact medically with patients—drawing blood, excising tissue, or performing other invasive procedures—must be licensed physicians. To be licensed, physicians must graduate from an accredited medical school, pass a licensing examination, and complete 1 to 7 years of graduate medical education.

Important Qualities

Communication skills. Communication is critical because medical scientists must be able to explain their conclusions. Also, communication skills are important when medical scientists write grant proposals, which are often required to continue their research.

Critical-thinking skills. Medical scientists must use their expertise to determine the best method for solving a specific research question.

Data-analysis skills. Medical scientists use statistical techniques so that they can properly quantify and analyze health research questions.

Decision-making skills. Medical scientists must use their expertise and experience to determine what research questions to ask, how best to investigate the questions, and what data to will best answer the questions.

Observation skills. Medical scientists conduct experiments that require precise observation of samples and other health data. Any mistake could lead to inconclusive results.

Pay

Medical Scientists
Median annual wages, May 2010

Medical Scientists, Except Epidemiologists	$76,700
Life Scientists	$67,400
Total, All Occupations	~~3~~3,840

Note: All Occupations includes all occupations in the U.S. Economy.
Source: U.S. Bureau of Labor Statistics, Occupational Employment Statistics

The median annual wage of medical scientists was $76,700 in May 2010. The median wage is the wage at which half the workers in an occupation earned that amount and half earned less. The lowest 10 percent earned less than $41,560, and the top 10 percent earned more than $142,800.

Median annual wages in the industries employing the largest numbers of medical scientists in May 2010 were as follows:

Pharmaceutical and medicine manufacturing	$95,530
Drugs and druggists' sundries merchant wholesalers	89,730
Scientific research and development services	82,140
General medical and surgical hospitals; state, local, and private	74,570
Colleges, universities, and professional schools; state, local, and private	53,470

Most medical scientists work full time.

Job Outlook

Medical Scientists
Percent change in employment, projected 2010-20

Medical Scientists, Except Epidemiologists	36%
Life Scientists	20%
Total, All Occupations	14%

Note: All Occupations includes all occupations in the U.S. Economy.
Source: U.S. Bureau of Labor Statistics, Employment Projections program

Employment of medical scientists is expected to increase by 36 percent between 2010 and 2020, much faster than the average for all occupations.

Ongoing medical research, as well as an increased reliance on pharmaceuticals, will likely maintain current levels of demand for medical scientists. A growing and aging population also is expected to increase demand for these scientists.

Most employment growth for medical scientists over the next 10 years will likely be in private industry. Demand has increased because medical scientists' expertise is needed in developing prescription drugs and other biomedical tools. Pharmaceutical companies and other firms whose work is not just in biotechnology have adopted biotechnology techniques in their other work, thus creating employment for medical scientists.

Employment also should grow as a result of an expected expansion in research related to illnesses such as AIDS, Alzheimer's disease, and cancer. Treatment problems, such as antibiotic resistance, also should spur growth. Moreover, environmental conditions, such as overcrowding and the increasing frequency of international travel, will spread existing diseases and give rise to new ones. Medical scientists will continue to be needed because they contribute to the development of treatments and medicines that improve human health.

The federal government is a major source of funding for medical research. Large budget increases at the National Institutes of Health in the early part of the decade led to increases in federal basic research and development spending, with research grants growing both in number and dollar amount. However, the increase in spending slowed substantially in recent years. Going forward, the level of federal funding will continue to impact competition for winning and renewing research grants.

Employment projections data for medical scientists, 2010-20

Occupational Title	SOC Code	Employment, 2010	Projected Employment, 2020	Change, 2010-20 Percent	Numeric
Medical Scientists, Except Epidemiologists	19-1042	100,000	136,500	36	36,400

SOURCE: U.S. Bureau of Labor Statistics, Employment Projections program

Similar Occupations

This table shows a list of occupations with job duties that are similar to those of medical scientists.

Occupation	Job Duties	Entry-Level Education	Median Annual Pay, May 2010
Biochemists and Biophysicists	Biochemists and biophysicists study the chemical and physical principles of living things and of biological processes such as cell development, growth, and heredity.	Doctoral or professional degree	$79,390
Epidemiologists	Epidemiologists investigate the causes of disease and other public health problems to prevent them from spreading or from happening again. They report their findings to public policy officials and to the general public.	Master's degree	$63,010
Health Educators	Health educators teach people about behaviors that promote wellness. They develop programs and materials to encourage people to make healthy decisions.	Bachelor's degree	$45,830
Physicians and Surgeons	Physicians and surgeons diagnose and treat injuries and illnesses in patients. Physicians examine patients, take medical histories, prescribe medications, and order, perform, and interpret diagnostic tests. Surgeons operate on patients to treat injuries, such as broken bones; diseases, such as cancerous tumors; and deformities, such as cleft palates.	Doctoral or professional degree	This wage is equal to or greater than $166,400 per year.
Postsecondary Teachers	Postsecondary teachers instruct students in a wide variety of academic and vocational subjects beyond the high school level. They also conduct research and publish scholarly papers and books.	Doctoral or professional degree	$62,050

Contacts for More Information

For more information about medical scientists, including careers and schools offering education in medical science, visit American Society for Biochemistry and Molecular Biology

For more information about medical science career requirements in the federal government and for information about the grant application process, visit National Institutes of Health

Suggested citation:

Bureau of Labor Statistics, U.S. Department of Labor, Occupational Outlook Handbook, 2012-13 Edition, Medical Scientists, on the Internet at http://www.bls.gov/ooh/life-physical-and-social-science/medical-scientists.htm .

Microbiologists

Quick Facts: Microbiologists	
2010 Median Pay	$65,920 per year $31.69 per hour
Entry-Level Education	Bachelor's degree
Work Experience in a Related Occupation	None
On-the-job Training	None
Number of Jobs, 2010	20,300
Job Outlook, 2010-20	13% (About as fast as average)
Employment Change, 2010-20	2,700

What Microbiologists Do

Microbiologists study the growth, development, and other characteristics of microscopic organisms such as bacteria, algae, and fungi.

Duties

Microbiologists typically do the following:

- Plan and conduct complex research projects, such as developing new drugs to combat infectious diseases
- Supervise the work of biological technicians and other workers and evaluate the accuracy of their results
- Isolate and maintain cultures of bacteria or other microorganisms for future study
- Identify and classify microorganisms found in specimens collected from humans, water, food, and other sources
- Monitor the effect of microorganisms on plants, animals, and other microorganisms and on the environment
- Keep up with findings from other research groups by reading research reports and attending conferences
- Prepare technical reports, research papers, and recommendations based on their research findings
- Present research findings to scientists, non-scientist executives, engineers, other colleagues, and the public

Most microbiologists work in research and development. Many conduct basic research with the aim of increasing scientific knowledge. Others conduct applied research, using knowledge from basic research to develop new products or solve particular problems. For example, microbiologists help to develop genetically engineered crops, biofuels, and ways to protect the environment.

Microbiologists use computers and a wide variety of sophisticated laboratory instruments to do their experiments and analyze the results. For example, microbiologists use powerful electron microscopes to study bacteria. They use advanced computer software to analyze the growth of microorganisms found in samples.

Most microbiologists work as part of a team. An increasing number of scientific research projects involve multiple disciplines, and it is common for microbiologists to work on teams with technicians and scientists in other fields.

For example, microbiologists researching new drugs may work with medical scientists and biochemists to develop new medicines such as antibiotics and vaccines. As another example, microbiologists in medical diagnostic laboratories work alongside physicians, nurses, medical laboratory technologists and technicians and other health professionals to help prevent, treat, and cure diseases.

The following are examples of types of microbiologists:

Bacteriologists study the growth, development, and other properties of bacteria, including the positive and negative effects bacteria have on plants, animals, and humans.

Clinical microbiologists study microorganisms that can cause, cure, or be used to treat diseases in humans.

Immunologists study how organisms' immune systems react to and defend against microorganisms.

Mycologists study the properties of fungi such as yeast and mold, as well as the ways fungi can be used (for example, in food and medicine) to benefit society.

Virologists study the structure, development, and other properties of viruses and any effects they would have on organisms they infect.

Many people with a microbiology background become high school teachers or professors. For more information, see the profiles on high school and postsecondary teachers .

Work Environment

Microbiologists held about 20,300 jobs in 2010. They typically work in laboratories and offices, where they conduct experiments and analyze the results. Microbiologists who work with dangerous organisms must follow strict safety procedures to avoid contamination. Most microbiologists work full time and keep regular hours.

Basic researchers usually choose the focus of their research. Applied researchers who work for companies spend more time working on products that the company can sell.Basic researchers are often under pressure to meet deadlines and follow specifications for grants to fund their research. They may face competition for research grants.

Microbiologists use laboratory equipment such as microscopes to study microorganisms.

The industries employing the largest numbers of microbiologists in 2010 were as follows:

Research and development in the physical, engineering, and life sciences	25%
Pharmaceutical and medicine manufacturing	23
Federal government, excluding postal service	14
Colleges, universities, and professional schools; state	7
State government, excluding education and hospitals	7

Work Schedules

Most microbiologists work full time and keep regular hours.

How to Become a Microbiologist

A bachelor's degree in microbiology or a closely related field is needed for entry-level microbiologist jobs. A Ph.D. is needed to carry out independent research and to work in colleges and universities.

Education

Microbiologists need at least a bachelor's degree in microbiology or a closely related field such as biochemistry or cell biology. Many colleges and universities offer degree programs in biological sciences, including microbiology.

Most microbiology majors take introductory courses in microbial genetics and microbial physiology before taking classes in more advanced topics such as environmental microbiology and virology. Students also must take classes in other sciences, such as biochemistry, chemistry, and physics, because it is important for microbiologists to have a broad understanding of the sciences. Courses in statistics, mathematics, and computer science are important for microbiologists because they must be able to do complex data analysis.

It is important for prospective microbiologists to have laboratory experience before entering the workforce. Most undergraduate microbiology programs include a mandatory laboratory requirement, but additional laboratory coursework is recommended. Students also can gain valuable laboratory experience through internships with prospective employers such as drug manufacturers.

Microbiologists typically need a Ph.D. to carry out independent research and work in colleges and universities. Graduate students studying microbiology commonly specialize in a subfield such as bacteriology or virology. Ph.D. programs usually include class work, laboratory research, and completing a thesis or dissertation. It typically takes 4 to 6 years to complete a doctoral degree program in microbiology.

Training

Many microbiology Ph.D. holders begin their careers in a temporary postdoctoral research position, which typically lasts 2 to 3 years. During their postdoctoral appointment, they work with experienced scientists as they continue to learn about their specialties or develop a broader understanding of related areas of research.

Postdoctoral positions typically offer the opportunity to publish research findings. A solid record of published research is essential to get a permanent position in basic research, especially a permanent faculty position in a college or university.

Important Qualities

Analytical skills. Microbiologists must be able to conduct scientific experiments and analyses with accuracy and precision.

Critical-thinking skills. Microbiologists draw conclusions from experimental results through sound reasoning and judgment.

Interpersonal skills. Microbiologists typically work on research teams and thus must work well with others toward a common goal. Many also lead research teams and must be able to motivate and direct other team members.

Mathematical skills. Microbiologists regularly use complex mathematical equations and formulas in their work. Therefore, they need a broad understanding of mathematics, including calculus and statistics.

Observation skills. Microbiologists must constantly monitor their experiments. They need to keep a complete, accurate record of their work such as conditions, procedures, and results.

Perseverance. Microbiological research involves substantial trial and error, and microbiologists must not become discouraged in their work.

Problem-solving skills. Microbiologists use scientific experiments and analysis to find solutions to complex scientific problems.

Speaking skills. Microbiologists frequently give presentations and must be able to explain their research to others.

Writing skills. Microbiologists write memos, reports, and research papers that explain their findings.

Advancement

Microbiologists typically receive greater responsibility and independence in their work as they gain experience. They also gain greater responsibility through more education. Ph.D. microbiologists usually lead research teams and control the direction and content of projects.

Some microbiologists move into managerial positions, often as natural sciences managers. Those who pursue management careers spend much of their time on administrative tasks such as preparing budgets and schedules. For more information, see the profile on natural sciences managers .

Pay

Microbiologists
Median annual wages, May 2010

Microbiologists	$65,920
Life, Physical, and Social Science Occupations	$58,530
Total, All Occupations	$33,840

Note: All Occupations includes all occupations in the U.S. Economy.
Source: U.S. Bureau of Labor Statistics, Occupational Employment Statistics

The median annual wage of microbiologists was $65,920 in May 2010. The median wage is the wage at which half the workers in an occupation earned more than that amount and half earned less. The lowest 10 percent earned less than $39,180, and the top 10 percent earned more than $115,720.

Median annual wages in the industries employing the largest numbers of microbiologists in May 2010 were as follows:

Federal government, excluding postal service	$94,960
Research and development in the physical, engineering, and life sciences	68,040
State government, excluding education and hospitals	63,950
Pharmaceutical and medicine manufacturing	62,350
Colleges, universities, and professional schools; state	49,360

Most microbiologists work full time and keep regular hours.

Job Outlook

Microbiologists

Percent change in employment, projected 2010-20

Life, Physical, and Social Science Occupations	16%
Total, All Occupations	14%
Microbiologists	13%

Note: All Occupations includes all occupations in the U.S. Economy.
Source: U.S. Bureau of Labor Statistics, Employment Projections program

Employment of microbiologists is projected to increase by 13 percent from 2010 to 2020, about as fast as the average for all occupations. More microbiologists will be needed to apply knowledge from basic research to develop biological products and processes that improve our lives.

The development of new medicines and treatments is expected to increase the demand for microbiologists in pharmaceutical and biotechnology research. Microbiologists will be needed to research and develop new medicines and treatments, such as vaccines and antibiotics that are used to fight infectious diseases. In addition, microbiologists will be needed to help pharmaceutical and biotechnology companies develop biological drugs that are produced with the aid of microorganisms.

Aside from improving our health, other areas of research and development in biotechnology are expected to provide employment growth for microbiologists. Greater demand for clean energy should increase the need for microbiologists who research and develop alternative energy sources such as biofuels and biomass. In agriculture, more microbiologists will be needed to help develop genetically engineered crops that provide greater yields and require less pesticide and fertilizer. Finally, efforts to discover new and improved ways to clean up and preserve the environment also will increase demand for microbiologists.

Job Prospects

Most of the applied research projects that microbiologists are involved in require the expertise of scientists in multiple fields such as biochemistry, chemistry, and medicine. Microbiologists who have a broad understanding of microbiology and its relationship to other disciplines should have the best opportunities.

A large portion of basic research in microbiology depends on funding from the federal government through the National Institutes of Health and the National Science Foundation. Therefore, federal budgetary decisions will affect job prospects in basic research from year to year. Typically, there is strong competition among microbiologists for research funding.

Employment projections data for microbiologists, 2010-20

Occupational Title	SOC Code	Employment, 2010	Projected Employment, 2020	Change, 2010-20 Percent	Change, 2010-20 Numeric
Microbiologists	19-1022	20,300	22,900	13	2,700
SOURCE: U.S. Bureau of Labor Statistics, Employment Projections program					

Similar Occupations

This table shows a list of occupations with job duties that are similar to those of microbiologists.

Occupation	Job Duties	Entry-Level Education	Median Annual Pay, May 2010
Agricultural and Food Scientists	Agricultural and food scientists work to ensure agricultural productivity and food safety.	See How to Become One	$58,450
Biochemists and Biophysicists	Biochemists and biophysicists study the chemical and physical principles of living things and of biological processes such as cell development, growth, and heredity.	Doctoral or professional degree	$79,390
Epidemiologists	Epidemiologists investigate the causes of disease and other public health problems to prevent them from spreading or from happening again. They report their findings to public policy officials and to the general public.	Master's degree	$63,010
Medical and Clinical Laboratory Technologists and Technicians	Medical laboratory technologists (also known as medical laboratory scientists) and medical laboratory technicians collect samples and perform tests to analyze body fluids, tissue, and other substances.	See How to Become One	$46,680
Medical Scientists	Medical scientists conduct research aimed at improving overall human health. They often use clinical trials and other investigative methods to reach their findings.	Doctoral or professional degree	$76,700
Natural Sciences Managers	Natural sciences managers supervise the work of scientists, including chemists, physicists, and biologists. They direct research and development projects and coordinate activities such as testing, quality control, and production.	Bachelor's degree	$116,020
Physicians and Surgeons	Physicians and surgeons diagnose and treat injuries and illnesses in patients. Physicians examine patients, take medical histories, prescribe medications, and order, perform, and interpret diagnostic tests. Surgeons operate on patients to treat injuries, such as broken bones; diseases, such as cancerous tumors; and deformities, such as cleft palates.	Doctoral or professional degree	This wage is equal to or greater than $166,400 per year.

Postsecondary Teachers	Postsecondary teachers instruct students in a wide variety of academic and vocational subjects beyond the high school level. They also conduct research and publish scholarly papers and books.	Doctoral or professional degree	$62,050
Zoologists and Wildlife Biologists	Zoologists and wildlife biologists study the characteristics and habitats of animals and wildlife.	Bachelor's degree	$57,430

Contacts for More Information

For more information about microbiologists, visit American Society for Microbiology

For information about microbiologist careers with the federal government, visit USAJOBS

For general information about careers in biological sciences, visit American Institute of Biological Sciences , Federation of American Societies for Experimental Biology

Suggested citation:

Bureau of Labor Statistics, U.S. Department of Labor, Occupational Outlook Handbook, 2012-13 Edition, Microbiologists, on the Internet at http://www.bls.gov/ooh/life-physical-and-social-science/microbiologists.htm .

Nuclear Technicians

Quick Facts: Nuclear Technicians	
2010 Median Pay	$68,090 per year $32.73 per hour
Entry-Level Education	Associate's degree
Work Experience in a Related Occupation	None
On-the-job Training	Moderate-term on-the-job training
Number of Jobs, 2010	7,100
Job Outlook, 2010-20	14% (About as fast as average)
Employment Change, 2010-20	1,000

What Nuclear Technicians Do

Nuclear technicians assist physicists, engineers, and other professionals in nuclear research and nuclear production. They operate special equipment used in these activities and monitor the levels of radiation that are produced.

Duties

Nuclear technicians typically do the following:

- Monitor the performance of equipment used in nuclear experiments and power generation
- Measure the levels and types of radiation produced by nuclear experiments, power generation, and other activities
- Collect and test samples of air, water, and other substances for levels of radioactive contamination
- Instruct personnel on radiation safety procedures and warn them when conditions are hazardous
- Maintain radiation monitoring and operating equipment

Job duties and titles of nuclear technicians often depend on where they work and what purpose the facility serves. Most nuclear technicians work in nuclear power plants, where they ensure that reactors and other equipment are operated safely and efficiently. Two examples of technicians who work in nuclear power plants are operating technicians and radiation protection technicians.

Operating technicians use computers, gauges, and other instruments to monitor the performance of nuclear power plants under the supervision of nuclear reactor operators and engineers. They base calculations on factors such as temperature, pressure, and radiation intensity to determine whether equipment is functioning properly.

Operating technicians must make adjustments to improve the performance of reactors and other equipment, such as opening and closing valves and electrical breakers.

Radiation protection technicians monitor radiation levels at nuclear power plants to protect personnel, facilities, and the surrounding environment from contamination. They use radiation detectors to measure levels in the environment and dosimeters to measure the levels present in people and objects. Radiation protection technicians also are responsible for setting up and testing instruments that monitor radiation levels remotely. They use the data collected by these instruments to map radiation levels throughout the plant and the surrounding environment. From their findings, they recommend radioactive decontamination plans and safety procedures for personnel.

Nuclear technicians also work in waste management and treatment facilities, where they monitor the disposal, recycling, and storage of nuclear waste. They perform duties similar to those of radiation protection technicians at nuclear power plants.

Other nuclear technicians work in laboratories. They help nuclear physicists, nuclear engineers, and other scientists conduct research and develop new types of nuclear reactors, fuels, medicines, and other technologies. They use equipment such as radiation detectors, spectrometers (used to measure gamma ray and x-ray radiation), and particle accelerators to conduct experiments and gather data. They also may use remote-controlled equipment to manipulate radioactive materials or materials exposed to radiation.

Work Environment

Nuclear technicians held about 7,100 jobs in 2010. The industries employing the largest number of nuclear technicians in 2010 were as follows:

Utilities	45%
Professional, scientific, and technical services	30
Administrative and support and waste management and remediation services	12

In nuclear power plants, nuclear technicians typically work in offices and control rooms where they use computers and other equipment to monitor and help operate nuclear reactors. Nuclear technicians also need to measure radiation levels onsite, requiring them to travel to several plant locations throughout the workday. Nuclear technicians who conduct scientific tests for scientists and engineers typically work in laboratories.

Nuclear technicians must take precautions when working with or around nuclear materials. They often have to wear protective clothing and film badges that indicate if they have been exposed to radiation. Many technicians also wear respirators as a safety precaution.

Work Schedules

Most nuclear technicians work full time. In power plants, which operate 24 hours a day, technicians may work nights, holidays, and weekends. In laboratories, technicians typically work during normal business hours.

How to Become a Nuclear Technician

Most employers prefer applicants who have at least an associate's degree in nuclear science or a nuclear-related technology. Nuclear technicians also go through extensive on-the-job training.

Education

Although many jobs typically require a high school diploma, most employers prefer applicants who have at least an associate's degree. Many community colleges and technical institutes offer associate's degree programs in nuclear science, nuclear technology, or related fields. Students study nuclear energy, radiation, and the equipment and components used in nuclear power plants and laboratories. Other

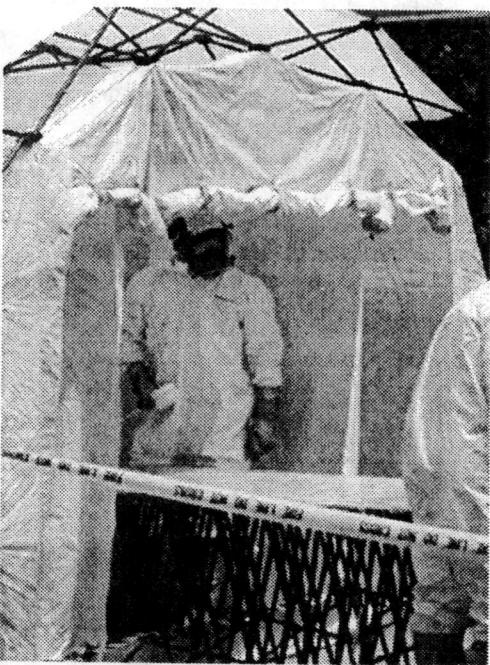

Nuclear technicians must take safety precautions when working with or around nuclear materials.

coursework includes mathematics, physics, and chemistry.

Training

In nuclear power plants, nuclear technicians start out as trainees under the supervision of more experienced technicians. During their training, they are taught the proper ways to use operating and monitoring equipment. They are also instructed on safety procedures, regulations, and plant policies.

Training varies with the technician's previous experience and education. Most training programs last between 6 months and 2 years. Throughout their careers, nuclear technicians take additional training and education to keep up with advances in nuclear science and technology.

Important Qualities

Critical-thinking skills. Nuclear technicians must carefully evaluate all available information before deciding on a course of action. For example, radiation protection technicians must evaluate data from radiation detectors to determine if an area is unsafe and then must develop a decontamination plan to handle the situation.

Listening skills. Nuclear technicians receive complex instructions from scientists and engineers that they must follow exactly. They have to be able to ask questions to clarify anything they do not understand.

Math skills. Nuclear technicians use scientific and mathematical formulas to analyze experimental and production data such as reaction rates and radiation exposures.

Monitoring skills. Nuclear technicians must be able to assess data from sensors, gauges, and other instruments to make sure that equipment and experiments are functioning properly and that radiation levels are controlled.

Speaking skills. Nuclear technicians must be able to explain their work to scientists, engineers, and reactor operators. They also must instruct others on safety procedures and warn them when conditions are hazardous.

Licenses

Although nuclear technicians do not need to be licensed, they may need to obtain security clearances for positions at nuclear power plants and nuclear research facilities that involve doing work related to nuclear weapons and national defense.

Advancement

With additional training and experience, technicians may become nuclear power reactor operators at nuclear power plants. Technicians can become nuclear engineers by earning a bachelor's degree in nuclear engineering. Nuclear physicists need a Ph.D. in physics. For more information, see the profiles on power plant operators, distributors, and dispatchers ; nuclear engineers ; and physicists and astronomers.

Pay

Nuclear Technicians
Median annual wages, May 2010

Nuclear Technicians	$68,090
Life, Physical, and Social Science Technicians	$40,690
Total, All Occupations	$33,840

Note: All Occupations includes all occupations in the U.S. Economy.
Source: U.S. Bureau of Labor Statistics, Occupational Employment Statistics

The median annual wage of nuclear technicians was $68,090 in May 2010. The median wage is the wage at which half the workers in an occupation earned more than that amount and half earned less. The lowest 10 percent earned less than $40,570, and the top 10 percent earned more than $93,890.

Most nuclear technicians work full time. In power plants, which operate 24 hours a day, technicians may work nights, holidays, and weekends. In laboratories, technicians typically work during normal business hours.

Job Outlook

Nuclear Technicians

Percent change in employment, projected 2010-20

Total, All Occupations	14%
Nuclear Technicians	14%
Life, Physical, and Social Science Technicians	11%

Note: All Occupations includes all occupations in the U.S. Economy.
Source: U.S. Bureau of Labor Statistics, Employment Projections program

Employment of nuclear technicians is expected to grow by 14 percent from 2010 to 2020, as fast as the average for all occupations. Most growth will be due to higher demand for nuclear energy, stemming from overall growth in energy demand and greater interest in energy sources that do not emit greenhouse gases.

Demand for technicians should grow because of higher levels of production at existing nuclear power plants, as well as new nuclear power plant operations.

Greater interest in nuclear energy also is expected to increase demand for research in nuclear physics and nuclear engineering. Technicians will be needed to help scientists and engineers develop smaller and more efficient reactors, as well as fuels that are safer, last longer, and produce less waste.

Technicians are also expected to be in demand to develop nuclear medical technology, enforce waste management safety standards, and work in defense-related areas such as nuclear security.

Job Prospects

Nuclear technicians should have good job opportunities over the next decade. In the nuclear power industry, many openings should arise from technicians who retire or leave the occupation for other reasons.

Employment projections data for nuclear technicians, 2010-20

Occupational Title	SOC Code	Employment, 2010	Projected Employment, 2020	Change, 2010-20	
				Percent	Numeric
Nuclear Technicians	19-4051	7,100	8,000	14	1,000
SOURCE: U.S. Bureau of Labor Statistics, Employment Projections program					

Similar Occupations

This table shows a list of occupations with job duties that are similar to those of nuclear technicians.

Occupation	Job Duties	Entry-Level Education	Median Annual Pay, May 2010
Chemical Technicians	Chemical technicians use special instruments and techniques to help chemists and chemical engineers in researching, developing, and producing chemical products and processes.	Associate's degree	$42,040
Hazardous Materials Removal Workers	Hazardous materials (hazmat) removal workers identify and dispose of asbestos, radioactive and nuclear waste, arsenic, lead, and other hazardous materials. They also clean up materials that are flammable, corrosive, reactive, or toxic.	High school diploma or equivalent	$37,600
Mechanical Engineering Technicians	Mechanical engineering technicians help mechanical engineers design, develop, test, and manufacture industrial machinery, consumer products, and other equipment. They may make sketches and rough layouts, record and analyze data, make calculations and estimates, and report their findings.	Associate's degree	$50,110
Nuclear Engineers	Nuclear engineers research and develop the processes, instruments, and systems used to get benefits from nuclear energy and radiation. Many of these engineers find industrial and medical uses for radioactive materials—for example, in equipment used in medical diagnosis and treatment.	Bachelor's degree	$99,920
Nuclear Medicine Technologists	Nuclear medicine technologists use a scanner to create images of various areas of a patient's body. They prepare radioactive drugs and administer them to patients undergoing the scans. The radioactive drugs cause abnormal areas of the body to appear different from normal areas in the images.	Associate's degree	$68,560
Occupational Health and Safety Technicians	Occupational health and safety technicians collect data on the safety and health conditions of the workplace. Technicians work with occupational health and safety specialists in conducting tests and measuring hazards to help prevent harm to workers, property, the environment, and the general public.	High school diploma or equivalent	$45,330
Physicists and Astronomers	Physicists and astronomers study the fundamental nature of the universe, ranging from the vastness of space to the smallest of subatomic particles. They develop new technologies, methods, and theories based on the results of their research that deepen our understanding of how things work and contribute to innovative, real-world applications.	Doctoral or professional degree	$105,430

Power Plant Operators, Distributors, and Dispatchers	Power plant operators, distributors, and dispatchers control the systems that generate and distribute electric power.	High school diploma or equivalent	$65,360

Contacts for More Information

For more information about nuclear technicians, visit Nuclear Energy Institute

Suggested citation:

Bureau of Labor Statistics, U.S. Department of Labor, Occupational Outlook Handbook, 2012-13 Edition, Nuclear Technicians, on the Internet at http://www.bls.gov/ooh/life-physical-and-social-science/nuclear-technicians.htm .

Physicists and Astronomers

Quick Facts: Physicists and Astronomers	
2010 Median Pay	$105,430 per year $50.69 per hour
Entry-Level Education	Doctoral or professional degree
Work Experience in a Related Occupation	None
On-the-job Training	None
Number of Jobs, 2010	20,600
Job Outlook, 2010-20	14% (About as fast as average)
Employment Change, 2010-20	2,800

What Physicists and Astronomers Do

Physicists and astronomers study the fundamental nature of the universe, ranging from the vastness of space to the smallest of subatomic particles. They develop new technologies, methods, and theories based on the results of their research to deepen our understanding of how things work and contribute to innovative, real-world applications.

Duties

Physicists and astronomers typically do the following:
- Develop scientific theories and models to explain the properties of the natural world, such as atom formation
- Plan and conduct scientific experiments and studies to test theories and discover properties of matter and energy
- Write proposals and apply for research grants
- Do complex mathematical calculations to analyze physical and astronomical data, such as finding new planets in distant solar systems
- Design scientific equipment, such as telescopes and lasers
- Develop computer software to analyze and model data
- Write scientific papers that may be published in scholarly journals
- Present research findings at scientific conferences and lectures

Physicists explore the fundamental properties and laws that govern space, time, energy, and matter. Some physicists study theoretical areas, such as the fundamental nature of atoms and molecules and the evolution of the universe. Others design and perform experiments with sophisticated equipment such as particle accelerators, electron microscopes, and lasers. On the basis of their observations and analysis, they try to discover and formulate laws that explain the forces of nature, such as gravity, electromagnetism, and nuclear interactions. Others apply their knowledge of physics to practical areas, such as the development of advanced materials and medical equipment.

Astronomers study the motions, compositions, origins, and other properties of planets, stars, galaxies and other celestial bodies. They use ground-based equipment, such as radio and optical telescopes, and space-based equipment, such as the Hubble Space Telescope, to make observations and collect data. Some astronomers focus their research on objects in our own solar system, such as the sun or planets, while others study distant stars, galaxies, and phenomena such as neutron stars and black holes.

Many physicists and astronomers do basic research with the aim of increasing scientific knowledge. For example, they may develop theories to better explain what gravity is or how the universe was formed.

Others do applied research, using knowledge gained from basic research to develop new devices, processes, and other practical applications. Their work may lead to advances in areas such as energy, electronics, communications, navigation, and medical technology. For example, lasers are now used in surgery and microwave technology is now in most kitchens.

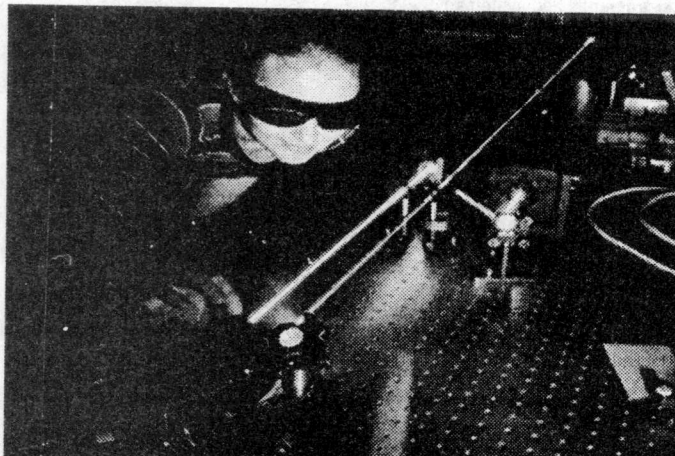

Physicists and astronomers conduct scientific research with specialized equipment such as lasers.

Astronomers and physicists typically work on research teams with engineers, technicians, and other scientists. Some senior astronomers and physicists may be responsible for assigning tasks to other team members and monitoring their progress.

While all physics involves the same fundamental principles, physicists generally specialize in one of many subfields. The following are examples of how physicists may specialize:

Condensed matter physicists study the physical properties of condensed phases of matter, such as liquids and solids. They study phenomena ranging from superconductivity to liquid crystals.

Astrophysicists study the physical properties of the universe, such as its physical expansion. The work of astrophysicists is closely related to that of astronomers. Astrophysics is often classified as a subfield of both astronomy and physics.

Particle and nuclear physicists study the properties of atomic and subatomic particles, such as quarks, electrons, and nuclei, and the forces that cause their interactions.

Medical physicists work in healthcare and use their knowledge of physics to develop new medical technologies and radiation-based treatments. For example, some develop better and safer radiation therapies for cancer patients. Others may develop more accurate imaging technologies that use radiation, such as magnetic resonance imaging (MRI) and ultrasound imaging.

Atomic, molecular, and optical physicists study atoms, simple molecules, electrons, and light and their interactions. Some look for ways to control the states of individual atoms, which might allow further miniaturization and new materials and computer technology.

Plasma physicists study plasmas, which are considered a distinct state of matter and occur naturally in stars and interplanetary space and artificially in neon signs and plasma screen televisions. Many plasma physicists study ways to create possible fusion reactors that might be a future source of energy.

Growing numbers of physicists work in interdisciplinary fields, such as biophysics, chemical physics, and geophysics. For more information, see the profiles on biochemists and biophysicists and geoscientists .

Many people with a physics or astronomy background become professors or teachers. For more information, see the profile on postsecondary teachers .

Work Environment

Physicists held about 18,300 jobs and astronomers held about 2,200 jobs in May 2010. Industries employing the largest numbers of physicists in 2010 were as follows:

Research and development in the physical, engineering, and life sciences	32%
Federal government, excluding postal service	20
Colleges, universities, and professional schools; state, local, and private	16
Health care	7
Management, scientific, and technical consulting services	6

Industries employing the largest numbers of astronomers in 2010 were as follows:

Colleges, universities, and professional schools; state, local, and private	53%
Federal government, excluding postal service	23
Research and development in the physical, engineering, and life sciences	22

The National Aeronautics and Space Administration (NASA) and the U.S. Department of Defense are two of the largest employers of physicists and astronomers in the federal government. The scientific research-and-development industry includes both private and federally funded national laboratories, such as the Fermi National Accelerator Laboratory in Illinois.

Physics research is usually done in small- or medium-sized laboratories. However, experiments in some areas of physics, such as nuclear and high-energy physics, require extremely large and expensive equipment, such as particle accelerators and nuclear reactors. Although physics research may require extensive experimentation in laboratories, physicists still spend much of their time in offices, planning, analyzing, and reporting on research.

Most astronomers work in offices, but they also may spend many hours working in observatories. At observatories, they use ground-based telescopes to gather data and make observations. Increasingly, observations are done remotely via the Internet without the need for travel to an observatory.

Some physicists and astronomers temporarily work away from home at national or international facilities that have unique equipment, such as particle accelerators and gamma ray telescopes. They also frequently travel to meetings to present research results, discuss ideas with colleagues, and learn more about new developments in their field.

Work Schedules

Most physicists and astronomers work full time. Astronomers may need to work at odd hours, especially at night, to observe celestial events, such as eclipses.

How to Become a Physicist or Astronomer

Physicists and astronomers need a Ph.D. for most jobs. After receiving a Ph.D. in physics or astronomy, many begin their careers in a temporary postdoctoral research position, which typically lasts 2 to 3 years.

Education

A Ph.D. in physics, astronomy, or a related field is needed for most jobs, especially those in basic research or in independent research in industry.

A typical Ph.D. program takes about 5 to 7 years to complete.

Approximately 190 universities have doctoral programs in physics; about 40 schools have doctoral programs in astronomy. Graduate students usually concentrate in a subfield of physics or astronomy, such as condensed matter physics or optics. In addition to taking courses in physics or astronomy, Ph.D. students need to take courses in mathematics, such as calculus, linear algebra, and statistics. Computer science classes are also essential, because physicists and astronomers often develop specialized computer programs that are used to gather, analyze, and model data.

Those with a master's degree in physics may qualify for jobs in applied research and development for manufacturing and healthcare companies. Many master's degree programs specialize in preparing students for physics-related research-and-development positions that do not require a Ph.D.

Most physics and astronomy graduate students have bachelor's degrees in physics or a related field. Because astronomers need a strong background in physics, a bachelor's degree in physics is often considered the best preparation for Ph.D. programs in astronomy. Undergraduate physics programs provide a broad background in the natural sciences and mathematics. Typical courses are classical and quantum mechanics, thermodynamics, optics, and electromagnetism.

Those with only a bachelor's degree in physics or astronomy typically are not qualified to fill research positions. However, they may be qualified to work as technicians and research assistants in related fields, such as engineering and computer science.

Some master's degree and bachelor's degree holders may become science teachers in middle schools and high schools. For more information, see the profiles on <u>middle</u> and <u>high school teachers</u> .

Training

Many physics and astronomy Ph.D. holders begin their careers in a temporary postdoctoral research position, which typically lasts 2 to 3 years. During their postdoctoral appointment, they work with experienced scientists as they continue to learn about their specialties or develop a broader understanding of related areas of research. Their initial work may be carefully supervised by senior scientists, but as they gain experience, they do more complex tasks and have greater independence in their work.

Important Qualities

Advanced mathematical skills. Physicists and astronomers perform complex calculations involving calculus, geometry, algebra, and other areas of mathematics. They must be able to express their research in mathematical terms.

Analytical skills. Physicists and astronomers need to be able to carry out scientific experiments and studies. They must be precise and accurate in their analysis because errors could invalidate their research.

Critical-thinking skills. Physicists and astronomers must carefully evaluate their own work and the work of others. They must determine whether results and conclusions are based on sound science.

Interpersonal skills. Physicists and astronomers must collaborate extensively with others—in both academic and industrial research contexts. They need to be able to work well with others towards a common goal.

Problem-solving skills. Physicists and astronomers use scientific observation and analysis to solve complex scientific questions.

Speaking skills. Physicists and astronomers present their research at scientific conferences, to the public, or to company management and other employees.

Writing skills. Physicists and astronomers write reports that may be published in scientific journals. They also write proposals for research funding.

Certification

Some positions with the federal government, such as those involving nuclear energy and other sensitive research areas, may require applicants to be U.S. citizens and hold a security clearance.

Advancement

With experience, physicists and astronomers may gain greater independence in their work, larger research budgets, or tenure in university positions. Some physicists and astronomers move into managerial positions, typically as a natural science manager, and spend a large part of their time preparing budgets and schedules. Physicists and astronomers need a Ph.D. for most management positions. For more information, see the profile on <u>natural sciences managers</u> .

Pay

Physicists and Astronomers
Median annual wages, May 2010

Physicists	$106,370
Physicists and Astronomers	$105,430
Astronomers	$87,260
Total, All Occupations	$33,840

Note: All Occupations includes all occupations in the U.S. Economy.
Source: U.S. Bureau of Labor Statistics, Occupational Employment Statistics

The median annual wage of physicists was $106,370 in May 2010. The median wage is the wage at which half the workers in an occupation earned more than that amount and half earned less. The lowest 10 percent earned less than $58,850, and the top 10 percent

earned at least $166,400.

Median annual wages in the industries employing the largest numbers of physicists in May 2010 were as follows:

Health care and social assistance	$151,970
Management, scientific, and technical consulting services	132,040
Federal government, excluding postal service	112,220
Research and development in the physical, engineering, and life sciences	102,420
Colleges, universities, and professional schools	80,130

The median annual wage for astronomers was $87,260 in May 2010. The lowest 10 percent earned less than $48,710, and the top 10 percent earned more than $155,480.

Median annual wages in the industries employing the largest numbers of astronomers in May 2010 were as follows:

Federal government, excluding postal service	$137,420
Research and development in the physical, engineering, and life sciences	92,040
Colleges, universities, and professional schools; state, local, and private	64,070

Most physicists and astronomers work full time. Astronomers may need to work at odd hours, especially at night, to observe celestial events, such as eclipses.

Job Outlook

Physicists and Astronomers
Percent change in employment, projected 2010-20

Total, All Occupations	14%
Physicists and Astronomers	14%
Physicists	14%
Astronomers	11%

Note: All Occupations includes all occupations in the U.S. Economy.
Source: U.S. Bureau of Labor Statistics, Employment Projections program

Employment of physicists and astronomers is expected to increase by 14 percent from 2010 to 2020, as fast as the average for all occupations.

Expected growth in federal government spending for physics and astronomy research should increase the need for physicists and astronomers, especially at colleges and universities and national laboratories.

Federal spending is the primary source of physics- and astronomy-related research funds, especially for basic research. Additional federal funding for energy and for advanced manufacturing research is expected to increase the need for physicists. Funding growth for astronomy research is expected to be smaller because of the limited applications of work in astronomy.

Declines in basic research are expected to be offset by growth in applied research in private industry. People with a physics background will continue to be in demand in medicine, information technology, communications technology, semiconductor technology, and other applied research-and-development fields.

Job Prospects

Competition for permanent research appointments, such as those at colleges and universities, is expected to be strong. Increasingly, those with a Ph.D. need to work through multiple postdoctoral appointments before finding a permanent position. In addition, the number of research proposals submitted for funding has been growing faster than the amount of funds available, causing more competition for research grants.

Despite competition for traditional research jobs, prospects should be good for physicists in applied research, development, and related technical fields. Graduates with any academic degree in physics or astronomy, from bachelor's degree to doctorate, will find their knowledge of science and mathematics useful for entry into many other occupations.

A large part of physics and astronomy research depends on federal funds, so federal budgets have a large impact on job prospects from year to year. This is especially true for astronomers, who are more likely than physicists to depend on federal funding for their work.

Employment projections data for physicists and astronomers, 2010-20

Occupational Title	SOC Code	Employment, 2010	Projected Employment, 2020	Change, 2010-20	
				Percent	Numeric
Astronomers and Physicists	19-2010	20,600	23,400	14	2,800
Astronomers	19-2011	2,200	2,500	11	200
Physicists	19-2012	18,300	20,900	14	2,600
SOURCE: U.S. Bureau of Labor Statistics, Employment Projections program					

Similar Occupations

This table shows a list of occupations with job duties that are similar to those of physicists and astronomers.

Occupation	Job Duties	Entry-Level Education	Median Annual Pay, May 2010
Biochemists and Biophysicists	Biochemists and biophysicists study the chemical and physical principles of living things and of biological processes such as cell development, growth, and heredity.	Doctoral or professional degree	$79,390
Chemists and Materials Scientists	Chemists and materials scientists study the structures, compositions, reactions, and other properties of substances. They use their knowledge to develop new and improved products, processes, and materials.	Bachelor's degree	$69,790
Civil Engineers	Civil engineers design and supervise large construction projects, including roads, buildings, airports, tunnels, dams, bridges, and systems for water supply and sewage treatment.	Bachelor's degree	$77,560
Computer and Information Research Scientists	Computer and information research scientists invent and design new technology and find new uses for existing technology. They study and solve complex problems in computing for business, science, medicine, and other uses.	Doctoral or professional degree	$100,660
Computer Hardware Engineers	Computer hardware engineers research, design, develop, and test computer equipment such as chips, circuit boards, or routers. By solving complex problems in computer hardware, these engineers create rapid advances in computer technology.	Bachelor's degree	$98,810
Electrical and Electronics Engineers	Electrical engineers design, develop, test, and supervise the manufacturing of electrical equipment such as electric motors, radar and navigation systems, communications systems, and power generation equipment.Electronics engineers design and develop. electronic equipment, such as broadcast and communications systems—from portable music players to global positioning systems (GPS).	Bachelor's degree	$87,180
Geoscientists	Geoscientists study the physical aspects of the Earth, such as its composition, structure, and processes, to learn about its past, present, and future.	Bachelor's degree	$82,500
Mathematicians	Mathematicians use high-level mathematics and technology to develop new mathematical principles, understand relationships between existing principles, and solve real-world problems.	Master's degree	$99,380
Nuclear Engineers	Nuclear engineers research and develop the processes, instruments, and systems used to get benefits from nuclear energy and radiation. Many of these engineers find industrial and medical uses for radioactive materials—for example, in equipment used in medical diagnosis and treatment.	Bachelor's degree	$99,920
Postsecondary Teachers	Postsecondary teachers instruct students in a wide variety of academic and vocational subjects beyond the high school level. They also conduct research and publish scholarly papers and books.	Doctoral or professional degree	$62,050

Contacts for More Information

For more information about astronomy careers and for a listing of colleges and universities offering astronomy programs, visit American Astronomical Society

For more information about physics careers and education, visit American Institute of Physics , American Physics Society

For more information about federal government astronomy and physics careers, visit USAJOBS

Suggested citation:

Bureau of Labor Statistics, U.S. Department of Labor, Occupational Outlook Handbook, 2012-13 Edition, Physicists and Astronomers, on the Internet at http://www.bls.gov/ooh/life-physical-and-social-science/physicists-and-astronomers.htm .

Political Scientists

Quick Facts: Political Scientists	
2010 Median Pay	$107,420 per year $51.65 per hour
Entry-Level Education	Master's degree
Work Experience in a Related Occupation	None
On-the-job Training	None
Number of Jobs, 2010	5,600
Job Outlook, 2010-20	8% (Slower than average)
Employment Change, 2010-20	400

What Political Scientists Do

Political scientists study the origin, development, and operation of political systems. They research political ideas and analyze the structure and operation of governments, policies, political trends, and related issues.

Duties

Political scientists typically do the following:

- Research political subjects, such as the U.S. political system, relations between the United States and foreign countries, and political ideologies
- Collect and analyze data from sources such as public opinion surveys and election results
- Use qualitative sources, such as historical documents, to develop theories
- Use quantitative methods, such as statistical analysis, to test theories
- Evaluate the effects of policies and laws on government, businesses, and people
- Identify new political issues to study
- Monitor current events, recent policy decisions, and other issues relevant to their work
- Forecast political, economic, and social trends
- Present research results by writing reports, giving presentations, and publishing in academic journals

Political scientists usually conduct research within one of four primary subfields: American politics, comparative politics, international relations, or political theory.

Often, political scientists use qualitative methods, gathering information from numerous sources. For example, they may use historical documents to analyze the effects of past government structures and policies. They may evaluate current policies and events using public opinion surveys, economic data, and election results. From these sources, they may learn the expected impact of new policies.

Political scientists also rely heavily on quantitative methods to develop and research theories. For example, they may analyze data to see whether a relationship exists between a certain political system and a particular outcome. In so doing, they may study topics such as U.S. political parties, how political structures differ among countries, globalization, and the history of political thought.

Political scientists also work as policy analysts. In this position, they may work for a variety of organizations that have a stake in policy, such as government, labor, and political organizations. They provide information and analysis that help in planning, developing, or carrying out policies. Alternatively, political scientists may assess existing policies and study their impact on different groups.

Many people with a political science background become professors and teachers. For more information, see the profile on postsecondary teachers.

Work Environment

Political scientists held about 5,600 jobs in 2010. Most political scientists—about 53 percent—work for the federal government. Others work for think tanks, nonprofit organizations, colleges and universities, political lobbying groups, and labor organizations.

Work Schedules

Political scientists work in offices. They generally work full time, although some may work overtime to finish reports and meet deadlines

How to Become a Political Scientist

Political scientists need a master's degree or Ph.D. in political science, public administration, or a related field.

Jobseekers with a bachelor's degree in political science usually qualify for entry-level positions in many related fields. Some qualify for entry-level positions as research assistants, others as policy analysts for research organizations, political campaigns, nonprofit organizations, or government agencies. Many go into fields outside of politics and policy, such as business or law.

Education

Political scientists can complete either a master's or Ph.D. program. To be admitted to a graduate program, applicants should

Political scientists use a variety of resources to research political issues and test theories.

complete undergraduate courses in political science, writing, and statistics. Applicants also benefit from having related work or internship experience. For example, working in an internship on a congressional staff or for a research organization helps applicants gain experience writing and researching, analyzing data, or working with policy issues.

Political scientists often complete a Master of Public Administration (MPA), Master of Public Policy (MPP), or Master of Public Affairs degree. These programs usually combine several disciplines, and students can choose to concentrate in a specific area of interest. Most offer core courses in research methods, policy formation, program evaluation, and statistics. Some colleges and universities also offer master's degrees in political science, international relations, or other applied political science specialties.

Political scientists can also complete a Ph.D. program, which requires several years of coursework followed by independent research for a dissertation. Most Ph.D. candidates choose to specialize in one of four primary subfields of political science: American politics, comparative politics, international relations, or political theory. A Ph.D. in political science is primarily a research degree.

Political scientists who teach at colleges and universities need a Ph.D. Graduates with a master's degree in political science may qualify for teaching positions in community colleges. For more information, see the profile on postsecondary teachers .

Important Qualities

Analytical skills. Political scientists often use mathematical and statistical research methods. They rely on their analytical skills when they collect, evaluate, and interpret data.

Critical-thinking skills. Political scientists need critical-thinking skills when conducting research and analyzing issues. They must be able to examine and process available information and draw logical conclusions.

Intellectual curiosity. Political scientists must continually explore new ideas and information to produce original papers and research. They must stay current on political subjects and come up with new ways to think about and address issues.

Writing skills. Writing skills are essential for political scientists, who often write papers on political issues and must be able to convey their research results clearly.

Pay

Political Scientists
Median annual wages, May 2010

Political Scientists	$107,420
Social Scientists and Related Workers	$67,090
Total, All Occupations	$33,840

Note: All Occupations includes all occupations in the U.S. Economy.
Source: U.S. Bureau of Labor Statistics, Occupational Employment Statistics

The median annual wage of political scientists was $107,420 in May 2010. The median wage is the wage at which half the workers in an occupation earned more than that amount and half earned less. The lowest 10 percent earned less than $48,720, and the top 10 percent earned more than $155,490.

Median annual wages in the industries employing the largest numbers of political scientists in May 2010 were:

Federal government, excluding postal service	$119,130
Scientific research and development services	95,640
Colleges, universities, and professional schools	47,810

Political scientists work in offices.They generally work full time, although some may work overtime to finish reports and meet deadlines.

Job Outlook

Political Scientists
Percent change in employment, projected 2010-20

Social Scientists and Related Workers	18%
Total, All Occupations	14%
Political Scientists	8%

Note: All Occupations includes all occupations in the U.S. Economy.
Source: U.S. Bureau of Labor Statistics, Employment Projections program

Employment of political scientists is expected to grow 8 percent from 2010 to 2010, slower than the average for all occupations. Employment will increase in response to a growing interest in public policy and political issues. There will be demand for those with extensive knowledge of political systems, institutions, and policies.

Political organizations, lobbying firms, and many nonprofit, labor, and social organizations will rely on the knowledge of political scientists to manage increasingly complicated legal and regulatory issues and policies. Some political scientists will be needed at think tanks to focus specifically on politics and political theory. Organizations that research or advocate for specific causes, such as immigration, health care, or the environment, will also need political scientists to analyze policies relating to their field.

Because the federal government employs more than half of all political scientists, employment growth will be tempered as overall employment in the federal government declines. However, political scientists will still be needed to assess the impact of government policies, such as the efficiencies of public services, effects of departmental cuts, and advantages of proposed improvements.

Job Prospects

Political scientists should face strong competition for most jobs. The small number of positions, combined with the popularity of political science programs in colleges and universities, means that there will likely be many qualified candidates for relatively few positions. Candidates with a graduate degree, strong writing and analytical skills, and experience researching or performing policy analysis should have the best job prospects. Candidates who have specialized knowledge or experience in their field of interest will also have better opportunities.

Some of those with a bachelor's degree in political science may find entry-level jobs as research assistants or analysts. Many will also find positions outside of politics and policy in fields such as business and law.

Employment projections data for political scientists, 2010-20

Occupational Title	SOC Code	Employment, 2010	Projected Employment, 2020	Change, 2010-20 Percent	Numeric
Political Scientists	19-3094	5,600	6,000	8	400
SOURCE: U.S. Bureau of Labor Statistics, Employment Projections program					

Similar Occupations

This table shows a list of occupations with job duties that are similar to those of political scientists.

Occupation	Job Duties	Entry-Level Education	Median Annual Pay, May 2010
Postsecondary Teachers	Postsecondary teachers instruct students in a wide variety of academic and vocational subjects beyond the high school level. They also conduct research and publish scholarly papers and books.	Doctoral or professional degree	$62,050
Anthropologists and Archeologists	Anthropologists and archeologists study the origin, development, and behavior of human beings, past and present. They examine the cultures, languages, archeological remains, and physical characteristics of people in various parts of the world.	Master's degree	$54,230
Economists	Economists study the production and distribution of resources, goods, and services.	Bachelor's degree	$89,450
Sociologists	Sociologists study society and social behavior by examining the groups, cultures, organizations, social institutions, and processes that people develop.	Master's degree	$72,360
Survey Researchers	Survey researchers design or conduct surveys and analyze survey data. Many groups use surveys to collect factual data, such as employment and salary information, or to ask questions that help them understand people's opinions, attitudes, beliefs, or desires.	Bachelor's degree	$36,050
Urban and Regional Planners	Urban and regional planners develop plans and programs for the use of land. They use planning to create communities, accommodate growth, or revitalize physical facilities in towns, cities, counties, and metropolitan areas.	Master's degree	$63,040
Market Research Analysts	Market research analysts study market conditions in local, regional, or national areas to examine potential sales of a product or service. They help companies understand what products people want, who will buy them, and at what price.	Bachelor's degree	$60,570
Legislators	Legislators are elected officials who develop laws for the federal government, or for local or state governments.	Bachelor's degree	$19,260
Historians	Historians research, analyze, interpret, and present the past by studying a variety of historical documents and sources.	Master's degree	$53,520

Contacts for More Information

For more information about political scientists, visit American Political Science Association

For information about college programs in public affairs and administration, visit National Association of Schools of Public Affairs and Administration

Suggested citation:

Bureau of Labor Statistics, U.S. Department of Labor, Occupational Outlook Handbook, 2012-13 Edition, Political Scientists, on the Internet at http://www.bls.gov/ooh/life-physical-and-social-science/political-scientists.htm .

Psychologists

Quick Facts: Psychologists	
2010 Median Pay	$68,640 per year $33.00 per hour
Entry-Level Education	See How to Become One
Work Experience in a Related Occupation	None
On-the-job Training	Internship/residency
Number of Jobs, 2010	174,000
Job Outlook, 2010-20	22% (Faster than average)
Employment Change, 2010-20	37,700

What Psychologists Do

Psychologists study mental processes and human behavior by observing, interpreting, and recording how people and other animals relate to one another and the environment.

Duties

Psychologists typically do the following:

- Conduct scientific studies to study behavior and brain function
- Collect information through observations, interviews, surveys, tests, and other methods
- Find patterns that will help them understand and predict behavior
- Use their knowledge to increase understanding among individuals and groups
- Develop programs that improve schools and workplaces by addressing psychological issues
- Work with individuals, couples, and families to help them make desired changes to behaviors
- Identify and diagnose mental, behavioral, or emotional disorders
- Develop and carry out treatment plans
- Collaborate with physicians or social workers to help treat patients

Psychology seeks to understand and explain thoughts, emotions, feelings, and behavior. Depending on the topic of study, psychologists use techniques such as observation, assessment, and experimentation to develop theories about the beliefs and feelings that influence a person's actions.

Psychologists often gather information and evaluate behavior through controlled laboratory experiments, psychoanalysis, or psychotherapy. They also may administer personality, performance, aptitude, or intelligence tests. They look for patterns of behavior or cause-and-effect relationships between events, and use this information when testing theories in their research or treating patients.

The following are common occupational specialties:

Clinical psychologists assess, diagnose, and treat mental, emotional, and behavioral disorders. Clinical psychologists help people deal with problems ranging from short-term personal issues to severe, chronic conditions.

Clinical psychologists are trained to use a variety of approaches to help individuals. Although strategies generally differ by specialty, psychologists often interview patients, give diagnostic tests, and provide individual, family, or group psychotherapy. They also design behavior modification programs and help patients implement their particular program.

Some clinical psychologists focus on certain populations, such as children or the elderly, or certain specialties, such as the following:

- **Health psychologists** study how psychological factors affect health and illness. They educate both patients and medical staff about psychological issues, and promote healthy-living strategies. They also investigate health issues, such as substance abuse or

teenage pregnancy, and develop programs to address the problems.
- **Neuropsychologists** study the relation between the brain and behavior. They typically work with patients who have sustained a brain injury.

Clinical psychologists often consult with other medical personnel regarding the best treatment for patients, especially treatment that includes medication. Two states, Louisiana and New Mexico, currently allow clinical psychologists to prescribe medication to patients. In most states, however, only psychiatrists and medical doctors may prescribe medication for treatment. For more information, see the profile on physicians and surgeons .

Counseling psychologists advise people on how to deal with their problems. They help patients understand their problems, including issues in the home, workplace, or community. Through counseling, they work with patients to identify the strengths or resources they can use to manage problems. For information on similar workers, see the profiles on mental health counselors and marriage and family therapists , substance abuse and behavioral disorder counselors , and social workers .

Developmental psychologists study the psychological progress and development that takes place throughout life. Many focus on children and adolescents. Development psychologists also increasingly study aging and problems faced by the elderly.

Forensic psychologists use psychological principles in the legal and criminal justice system to help judges, attorneys, and other legal specialists understand the psychological findings of a particular case. They often appear in court as expert witnesses. They typically specialize in family court, civil court, or criminal court.

Psychologists diagnose and evaluate mental and emotional disorders.

Industrial-organizational psychologists apply psychology to the workplace by using psychological principles and research methods to solve problems and improve the quality of work life. They study issues such as workplace productivity, management or employee working styles, and morale. They also work with management on matters such as policy planning, employee screening or training, and organizational development.

School psychologists apply psychological principles and techniques to education-related issues. For example, they may address students' learning and behavioral problems, evaluate students' performances, and counsel students and families. They also may consult with other school-based professionals to suggest improvements to teaching, learning, and administrative strategies.

Social psychologists study how people's mindsets and behavior are shaped by social interactions. They examine both individual and group interactions and may investigate ways to improve negative interactions.

Some psychologists become professors or combine research with teaching. For more information, see the profiles on postsecondary teachers and high school teachers .

Work Environment

Psychologists held about 174,000 jobs in 2010. About 34 percent of psychologists were self-employed, 29 percent worked in educational services, and 20 percent worked in healthcare settings.

Some psychologists work alone, which may include independent research or individually counseling patients. Others work as part of a healthcare team, collaborating with physicians, social workers, and others to treat illness and promote overall wellness.

Many clinical and counseling psychologists in private practice have their own offices and can set their own schedules. Other typical workplaces include clinics, hospitals, rehabilitation facilities, and community and mental health centers.

Most research psychologists work in colleges and universities, government agencies, or private research organizations.

Most school psychologists work in public schools, ranging in level from nursery school through college. They also work in private schools, universities, hospitals and clinics, community treatment centers, and independent practice.

Work Schedules

Psychologists in private practice can often set their own hours, and many work part time as independent consultants. However, they often offer evening or weekend hours to accommodate clients. Those employed in hospitals, nursing homes, or other healthcare facilities also may have evening or weekend shifts. Most psychologists working in clinics, government, industry, or schools work full-time schedules during regular business hours.

How to Become a Psychologist

Psychologists need a master's, specialist, or doctoral degree in psychology. Practicing psychologists also need a license or certification.

Education

Most clinical, counseling, and research psychologists need a doctoral degree. Psychologists can complete a Ph.D. in psychology or a Doctor of Psychology (Psy.D.) degree. A Ph.D. in psychology is a research degree that culminates in a comprehensive exam and a dissertation based on original research. In clinical, counseling, school, or health service settings, students usually complete a 1-year internship as part of the doctoral program. The Psy.D. is a clinical degree and is often based on practical work and examinations rather than a dissertation.

School psychologists need a master's, specialist (Ed. S. degree,

which requires a minimum of 60 graduate semester hours), or doctoral degree in school psychology. Because their work addresses education and mental health components of students' development, school psychologists' training includes coursework in both education and psychology.

Graduates with a master's degree in psychology can work as industrial-organizational psychologists. When working under the supervision of a doctoral psychologist, master's graduates also can work as psychological assistants in clinical, counseling, or research settings. Master's degree programs typically include courses in industrial-organizational psychology, statistics, and research design.

Entry into psychology graduate programs is competitive. Most master's degree programs do not require an undergraduate major in psychology, but do require coursework in introductory psychology, experimental psychology, and statistics. Some doctoral degree programs require applicants to have a master's degree in psychology, while others will accept applicants with a bachelor's degree and a major in psychology.

Most graduates with a bachelor's degree in psychology find work in other fields such as business administration, sales, or education.

Licenses and Certification

In most states, practicing psychology or using the title of "psychologist" requires licensure or certification.

In all states and the District of Columbia, psychologists who practice independently must be licensed. Licensing laws vary by state and type of position. Most clinical and counseling psychologists need a doctorate in psychology, an internship, at least 1 to 2 years of professional experience, and to pass the Examination for Professional Practice in Psychology. Information on specific requirements by state can be found from the Association of State and Provincial Licensing Boards . In many states, licensed psychologists must complete continuing education courses to keep their licenses.

School psychologists must be licensed or certified to practice in schools. This credential varies by state and is usually obtained through the state's department of education. Information on specific requirements by state can be found from the National Association of School Psychologists (NASP).

In addition, NASP awards the Nationally Certified School Psychologist (NCSP) designation, which is a nationally recognized certification. Currently, 30 states accept the NCSP as a route to licensing or certification. To become nationally certified, candidates need a minimum of 60 graduate semester hours in a school psychology program, a 1,200-hour supervised internship, and to pass the National School Psychology Examination.

The American Board of Professional Psychology awards specialty certification in 13 areas of psychology, such as clinical health, couple and family, psychoanalysis, or rehabilitation. Although board certification is not required for most psychologists, it can demonstrate professional expertise in a specialty area. Some hospitals and clinics do require certification. In those cases, candidates must have a doctoral degree in psychology, state license or certification, and any additional criteria of the specialty field.

Training

Psychologists typically need previous related work experience. To become licensed, for example, psychologists must have completed one or more of the following: predoctoral or postdoctoral supervised experience, an internship, or a residency program. School psychologists also must complete a yearlong supervised internship program to become licensed or certified.

Important Qualities

Analytical skills. Analytical skills are important when performing psychological research. Psychologists must be able to examine the information they collect and draw logical conclusions from them.

Communication skills. Psychologists must have strong communications skills because they spend much of their time listening to and speaking with patients.

Observational skills. Psychologists study attitude and behavior. They must be able to watch people and understand the possible meanings of people's facial expressions, body positions, actions, and interactions.

Patience. Because research or treatment of patients may take a long time, psychologists must be able to demonstrate patience. They also must be patient when dealing with people who have mental or behavioral disorders.

People skills. Psychologists study people and help people. They must be able to work well with their clients, patients, and other medical professionals.

Problem-solving skills. Psychologists need problem solving skills to find treatments or solutions for mental and behavioral problems.

Trustworthiness. Patients must be able to trust their psychologists. Psychologists also must keep patients' problems in confidence, and patients must be able to trust psychologists' expertise in treating sensitive problems.

Pay

Psychologists

Median annual wages, May 2010

Psychologists, All Other	$89,900
Industrial-Organizational Psychologists	$87,330
Psychologists	$68,640
Clinical, Counseling, and School Psychologists	$66,810
Total, All Occupations	$33,840

Note: All Occupations includes all occupations in the U.S. Economy.
Source: U.S. Bureau of Labor Statistics, Occupational Employment Statistics

The median annual wage of psychologists was $68,640 in May 2010. The median wage is the wage at which half of the workers in an occupation earned more than that amount and half earned less. The lowest 10 percent earned less than $39,200, and the top 10 percent earned more than $111,810.

The median annual wages of psychologist occupations in May 2010 were the following:
* $87,330 for industrial-organizational psychologists
* $66,810 for clinical, counseling, and school psychologists
* $89,900 for psychologists, all other

Psychologists in private practice can often set their own hours, and many work part time as independent consultants. However, they often offer evening or weekend hours to accommodate clients. Those employed in hospitals, nursing homes, or other healthcare facilities may also have evening or weekend shifts. Most psychologists working in clinics, government, industry, or schools work full-time schedules during regular business hours.

Job Outlook

Psychologists

Percent change in employment, projected 2010-20

Industrial-Organizational Psychologists	35%
Clinical, Counseling, and School Psychologists	22%
Psychologists	22%
Psychologists, All Other	18%
Total, All Occupations	14%

Note: All Occupations includes all occupations in the U.S. Economy.
Source: U.S. Bureau of Labor Statistics, Employment Projections program

Overall employment of psychologists is expected to grow 22 percent from 2010 to 2020, faster than the average for all occupations. Employment growth will vary by specialty.

Employment of clinical, counseling, and school psychologists is expected to grow 22 percent, faster than the average for all occupations. Greater demand for psychological services in schools, hospitals, mental health centers, and social services agencies should drive employment growth.

Demand for clinical and counseling psychologists will increase as people continue to turn to psychologists to help solve or manage their problems. More psychologists will be needed to help people deal with issues such as depression and other mental disorders, marriage and family problems, job stress, and addiction. Psychologists also will be needed to provide services to an aging population, helping people deal with the mental and physical changes that happen as they grow older. Through both research and practice, psychologists are also helping other special groups, such as veterans suffering from war trauma, other trauma survivors, and individuals with autism.

Demand for psychologists in the health care industry is also expected to increase, because their work on teams with doctors, social workers, and other healthcare professionals provides patients with comprehensive, interdisciplinary treatments. In addition to treating mental and behavioral health issues, psychologists work on teams to develop or administer prevention or wellness programs.

As the overall number of students grows, more school psychologists will be needed to work with students, particularly those with special needs, learning disabilities, and behavioral issues. Schools also rely on school psychologists to assess and counsel students. Additionally, school psychologists will be needed to study how both in-school and out-of-school factors affect learning, which teachers and administrators can use to improve education.

Employment of industrial-organizational psychologists is expected to grow 35 percent, much faster than the average for all occupations, as organizations use these psychologists to help select and keep employees, increase productivity, and identify potential workplace improvements. However, because it is a small occupation, the fast employment growth will result in only about 800 new jobs over the 10-year period.

Job Prospects

Job prospects should be best for those who have a doctoral degree in an applied specialty and those with a specialist or doctoral degree in school psychology. Because admission to psychology graduate programs is so selective, job opportunities for doctoral graduates are expected to be fair.

Employment of school psychologists will grow to accommodate the increasing number of children in schools, and many will also be needed to replace workers who retire. Because of the limited number of graduates in this specialty, school psychologists are expected to have good job opportunities.

Candidates with a master's degree will face competition for positions, and many master's degree holders will find jobs in a related field outside of psychology. Even industrial-organizational psychologists, despite much faster than average employment growth, are expected to face competition for positions due to the large number of qualified graduates. Industrial-organizational psychologists with extensive training in quantitative research methods and computer science may have a competitive edge.

Employment projections data for psychologists, 2010-20

Occupational Title	SOC Code	Employment, 2010	Projected Employment, 2020	Change, 2010-20	
				Percent	Numeric
Psychologists	19-3030	174,000	211,600	22	37,700
Clinical, Counseling, and School Psychologists	19-3031	154,300	188,000	22	33,700
Industrial-Organizational Psychologists	19-3032	2,200	3,000	35	800
Psychologists, All Other	19-3039	17,500	20,600	18	3,200
SOURCE: U.S. Bureau of Labor Statistics, Employment Projections program					

Similar Occupations

This table shows a list of occupations with job duties that are similar to those of psychologists.

Occupation	Job Duties	Entry-Level Education	Median Annual Pay, May 2010
Anthropologists and Archeologists	Anthropologists and archeologists study the origin, development, and behavior of human beings, past and present. They examine the cultures, languages, archeological remains, and physical characteristics of people in various parts of the world.	Master's degree	$54,230
Sociologists	Sociologists study society and social behavior by examining the groups, cultures, organizations, social institutions, and processes that people develop.	Master's degree	$72,360
Mental Health Counselors and Marriage and Family Therapists	Mental health counselors and marriage and family therapists help people manage or overcome mental and emotional disorders and problems with their family and relationships. They listen to clients and ask questions to help the clients understand their problems and develop strategies to improve their lives.	Master's degree	$39,710
School and Career Counselors	School counselors help students develop social skills and succeed in school. Career counselors assist people with the process of making career decisions by helping them choose a career or educational program.	Master's degree	$53,380
Social Workers	There are two main types of social workers: direct-service social workers, who help people solve and cope with problems in their everyday lives, and clinical social workers, who diagnose and treat mental, behavioral, and emotional issues.	See How to Become One	$42,480
Substance Abuse and Behavioral Disorder Counselors	Substance abuse and behavioral disorder counselors advise people who have alcoholism or other types of addiction, eating disorders, or other behavioral problems. They provide treatment and support to help the client recover from addiction or modify problem behaviors.	High school diploma or equivalent	$38,120
Physicians and Surgeons	Physicians and surgeons diagnose and treat injuries and illnesses in patients. Physicians examine patients, take medical histories, prescribe medications, and order, perform, and interpret diagnostic tests. Surgeons operate on patients to treat injuries, such as broken bones; diseases, such as cancerous tumors; and deformities, such as cleft palates.	Doctoral or professional degree	This wage is equal to or greater than $166,400 per year.
Postsecondary Teachers	Postsecondary teachers instruct students in a wide variety of academic and vocational subjects beyond the high school level. They also conduct research and publish scholarly papers and books.	Doctoral or professional degree	$62,050
Special Education Teachers	Special education teachers work with students who have a wide range of learning, mental, emotional and physical disabilities. With students who have mild or moderate disabilities, they ensure that lessons and teaching strategies are modified to meet the students' needs. With students who have severe disabilities, they teach the students independent living skills and basic literacy, communication, and math.	Bachelor's degree	$53,220
Survey Researchers	Survey researchers design or conduct surveys and analyze survey data. Many groups use surveys to collect factual data, such as employment and salary information, or to ask questions that help them understand people's opinions, attitudes, beliefs, or desires.	Bachelor's degree	$36,050
Market Research Analysts	Market research analysts study market conditions in local, regional, or national areas to examine potential sales of a product or service. They help companies understand what products people want, who will buy them, and at what price.	Bachelor's degree	$60,570

Contacts for More Information

For more information on careers in all fields in psychology, visit American Psychological Association

For more information on careers for school psychologists, visit National Association of School Psychologists

For more information on state licensing requirements, visit Association of State and Provincial Psychology Boards

For more information about psychology specialty certifications, visit American Board of Professional Psychology

For more information about industrial-organizational psychologists, visit Society for Industrial and Organizational Psychology

Suggested citation:

Bureau of Labor Statistics, U.S. Department of Labor, Occupational Outlook Handbook, 2012-13 Edition, Psychologists, on the Internet at http://www.bls.gov/ooh/life-physical-and-social-science/psychologists.htm.

Sociologists

Quick Facts: Sociologists	
2010 Median Pay	$72,360 per year $34.79 per hour
Entry-Level Education	Master's degree
Work Experience in a Related Occupation	None
On-the-job Training	None
Number of Jobs, 2010	4,000
Job Outlook, 2010-20	18% (About as fast as average)
Employment Change, 2010-20	700

What Sociologists Do

Sociologists study society and social behavior by examining the groups, cultures, organizations, social institutions, and processes that people develop.

Duties

Sociologists typically do the following:
- Design research projects to test theories about social issues
- Collect data through surveys, observations, interviews, and other sources
- Analyze and draw conclusions from data
- Prepare reports, articles, or presentations detailing their research findings
- Collaborate with other sociologists or social scientists
- Consult with and advise clients, policymakers, or other groups on research findings and sociological issues

Sociologists study human social lives, activities, interactions, processes, and organizations within the context of larger social, political, and economic forces. They examine how social influences affect different individuals and groups, and the ways organizations and institutions affect people's lives.

They study the behavior of, and interaction among, groups, organizations, institutions, and nations. They look at activities in social, religious, political, economic, and business organizations. They also trace the origin and growth of these groups and interactions.

Educators, lawmakers, administrators, and social workers use sociological research to solve social problems and formulate public policy. Sociologists specialize in a wide range of social topics, including the following:
- Health
- Crime
- Education
- Racial and ethnic relations
- Families
- Population
- Gender
- Poverty
- Aging

Many people with a sociology background become professors and teachers. Others often find work in related jobs outside the sociologist profession as survey researchers, statisticians, policy analysts, and demographers. For more information, see the profiles on postsecondary teachers , survey researchers , and statisticians .

Work Environment

Sociologists held about 4,000 jobs in 2010, most of which were in research organizations and colleges and universities.

The following industries employed the largest numbers of sociologists in 2010:

Research and development in the social sciences and humanities	36%
Colleges, universities, and professional schools; state, local, and private	30
Research and development in the physical, engineering, and life sciences	7
Local government, excluding education and hospitals	6

Sociologists typically work behind a desk, researching and writing reports. They may occasionally work outside the office to meet with colleagues, conduct field research though interviews or observations, or present research results.

Work Schedules

Most sociologists work full time during regular business hours.

How to Become a Sociologist

Most sociology jobs require a master's degree or Ph.D.

Education

Sociologists typically need a master's degree or Ph.D. There are two types of sociology master's degree programs: traditional programs and applied, clinical, and professional programs. Traditional programs prepare students to enter a Ph.D. program. Applied, clinical, and professional programs prepare students to enter the professional

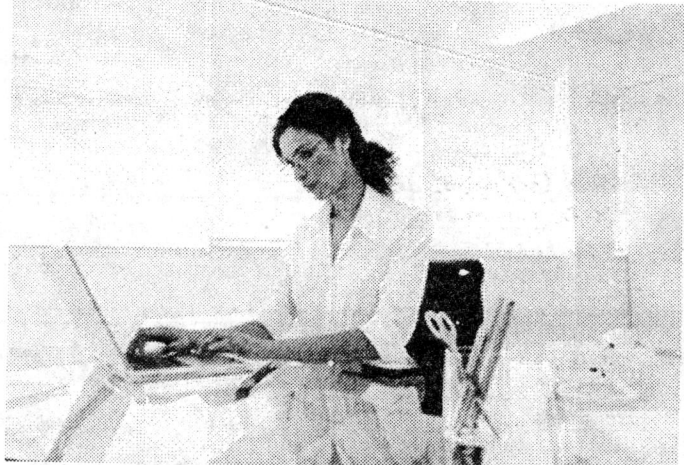

Sociologists often perform independent research on human society and social behavior.

workplace, teaching them the necessary analytical skills to perform sociological research in a professional setting.

Most students who complete a Ph.D. in sociology become professors or teachers. For more information, see the profile on postsecondary teachers . However, an increasing number of Ph.D. graduates are becoming research sociologists for nonprofits, businesses, and governments.

Courses in research methods and statistics are important for both master's and Ph.D. candidates. Many programs also offer opportunities to get experience through internships or by preparing reports for clients.

Although some graduates with a bachelor's degree find work as sociology research assistants, most find positions in other fields, such as social services, administration, management, or sales and marketing.

Important Qualities

Analytical skills. Sociologists must be able to carefully analyze data and other information, often utilizing statistical processes to test their theories.

Communication skills. Sociologists need strong communication skills when they conduct interviews, collaborate with colleagues, and present research results.

Critical-thinking skills. Sociologists must be able to think critically when doing research. They must design research projects and collect, process, and analyze information in order to draw logical conclusions about society and the groups it comprises.

Problem-solving skills. Sociologists' research is typically focused on identifying, studying, and solving sociological problems.

Writing skills. Sociologists frequently write reports detailing their findings.

Pay

Sociologists
Median annual wages, May 2010

Sociologists	$72,360
Social Scientists and Related Workers	$67,090
Total, All Occupations	$33,840

Note: All Occupations includes all occupations in the U.S. Economy.
Source: U.S. Bureau of Labor Statistics, Occupational Employment Statistics

The median annual wage of sociologists was $72,360 in May 2010. The median wage is the wage at which half the workers in an occupation earned more than that amount and half earned less. The lowest 10 percent earned less than $44,000, and the top 10 percent earned more than $129,870.

Most sociologists work full time during regular business hours.

Job Outlook

Sociologists
Percent change in employment, projected 2010-20

Social Scientists and Related Workers	18%
Sociologists	18%
Total, All Occupations	14%

Note: All Occupations includes all occupations in the U.S. Economy.
Source: U.S. Bureau of Labor Statistics, Employment Projections program

Employment of sociologists is expected to grow 18 percent from 2010 to 2020, about as fast as the average for all occupations.

Employment gains will be driven by a growing interest in using sociological research to further understand society and human social interactions. Specifically, social, political, and business organizations will need sociologists to research, evaluate, and address many different social issues, programs, and problems.

In addition, sociologists will be needed to apply sociological principles and research to other disciplines. For example, sociologists may collaborate with researchers in other fields to study how social structures or groups influence policy decisions about health, education, politics, business, or economics.

Job Prospects

Jobseekers can expect to face competition for most sociologist research positions. Sociology is a popular field of study, with a relatively small number of research positions.

Instead, many bachelor's and master's degree holders will find positions in related fields, such as social services, education, public policy, or other areas. Although these fields require the skills and concepts that sociologists learn as part of their education, workers should face less competition for positions not specifically labeled as "sociologists."

Candidates with an advanced degree, strong statistical and research skills, and a background in applied sociology will have the best job prospects.

Employment projections data for sociologists, 2010-20

Occupational Title	SOC Code	Employment, 2010	Projected Employment, 2020	Change, 2010-20	
				Percent	Numeric
Sociologists	19-3041	4,000	4,800	18	700
SOURCE: U.S. Bureau of Labor Statistics, Employment Projections program					

Similar Occupations

This table shows a list of occupations with job duties that are similar to those of sociologists.

Occupation	Job Duties	Entry-Level Education	Median Annual Pay, May 2010
Anthropologists and Archeologists	Anthropologists and archeologists study the origin, development, and behavior of human beings, past and present. They examine the cultures, languages, archeological remains, and physical characteristics of people in various parts of the world.	Master's degree	$54,230
Economists	Economists study the production and distribution of resources, goods, and services.	Bachelor's degree	$89,450
Historians	Historians research, analyze, interpret, and present the past by studying a variety of historical documents and sources.	Master's degree	$55,520

Political Scientists	Political scientists study the origin, development, and operation of political systems. They research political ideas and analyze the structure and operation of governments, policies, political trends, and related issues.	Master's degree	$107,420
Psychologists	Psychologists study mental processes and human behavior by observing, interpreting, and recording how people and other animals relate to one another and the environment.	See How to Become One	$68,640
Social Workers	There are two main types of social workers: direct-service social workers, who help people solve and cope with problems in their everyday lives, and clinical social workers, who diagnose and treat mental, behavioral, and emotional issues.	See How to Become One	$42,480
Postsecondary Teachers	Postsecondary teachers instruct students in a wide variety of academic and vocational subjects beyond the high school level. They also conduct research and publish scholarly papers and books.	Doctoral or professional degree	$62,050
Statisticians	Statisticians use mathematical techniques to analyze and interpret data and draw conclusions.	Master's degree	$72,830
Survey Researchers	Survey researchers design or conduct surveys and analyze survey data. Many groups use surveys to collect factual data, such as employment and salary information, or to ask questions that help them understand people's opinions, attitudes, beliefs, or desires.	Bachelor's degree	$36,050
Urban and Regional Planners	Urban and regional planners develop plans and programs for the use of land. They use planning to create communities, accommodate growth, or revitalize physical facilities in towns, cities, counties, and metropolitan areas.	Master's degree	$63,040

Contacts for More Information

For more information about careers in sociology, visit American Sociological Association

Suggested citation:

Bureau of Labor Statistics, U.S. Department of Labor, Occupational Outlook Handbook, 2012-13 Edition, Sociologists, on the Internet at http://www.bls.gov/ooh/life-physical-and-social-science/sociologists.htm.

Survey Researchers

Quick Facts: Survey Researchers	
2010 Median Pay	$36,050 per year $17.33 per hour
Entry-Level Education	Bachelor's degree
Work Experience in a Related Occupation	None
On-the-job Training	None
Number of Jobs, 2010	19,600
Job Outlook, 2010-20	24% (Faster than average)
Employment Change, 2010-20	4,700

What Survey Researchers Do

Survey researchers design or conduct surveys and analyze survey data. Many groups use surveys to collect factual data, such as employment and salary information, or to ask questions that help them understand people's opinions, attitudes, beliefs, or desires.

Duties

Survey researchers typically do the following:

- Conduct background research on survey topics
- Plan and design surveys and develop appropriate survey methods
- Test their surveys to make sure that people will understand the questions
- Conduct surveys and collect data
- Account for and solve problems caused by non-respondents or other sampling issues
- Analyze data using statistical software and techniques
- Summarize survey data using tables, graphs, and fact sheets
- Evaluate surveys, methods, and performance to improve future surveys

Survey researchers design and conduct surveys for scientific, public opinion, and marketing research purposes. Surveys for scientific research cover various fields, including government, health, social sciences, and education. A survey researcher may, for example, try to accurately capture information such as prevalence of drug use or disease.

Some survey researchers design public opinion surveys, which are intended to gather information about the attitudes and opinions of a certain group. Surveys cover a wide variety of topics, including political issues, social issues, culture, the economy, or health.

Other survey researchers design marketing surveys that examine products or services consumers want, need, or prefer. Researchers who both collect and analyze market research data are known as market research analysts. For more information, see the profile on market research analysts .

Survey researchers design and may conduct surveys in many different formats, such as interviews, questionnaires, and focus groups

Survey researchers develop surveys for research, marketing, and other purposes.

(in-person, small group sessions with a facilitator). They use different mediums to conduct surveys, including the Internet, mail, and telephone and in-person interviews.

Some surveys solicit the opinion of the entire population and others target a smaller group, such as residents of a particular state, a specific demographic group, or members of a political party. Researchers survey a sample of the population and use statistics to make sure the sample accurately represents the target population group. Researchers use a variety of statistical techniques and analytical software to plan surveys and analyze the results.

Survey researchers sometimes supervise interviewers who collect the survey data though in-person or telephone interviews.

Work Environment

Survey researchers held about 19,600 jobs in 2010. They work in research firms, polling organizations, nonprofits, corporations, colleges and universities, and government agencies.

The following industries employed the largest numbers of survey researchers in 2010:

Other professional, scientific, and technical services (includes market research and public opinion polling)	41%
Scientific research and development services	15
Management, scientific, and technical consulting services	14
Educational services; state, local, and private	9

Survey researchers who conduct interviews have frequent contact with the public. Some occasionally work outside the office, traveling to conduct in-person interviews and focus group sessions. When designing surveys and analyzing data, they usually work alone in a typical office setting, though some work on teams with other researchers. Most survey researchers work full time during regular business hours.

How to Become a Survey Researcher

Although some survey researchers have a bachelor's degree, many technical research positions require a graduate degree. Employers generally prefer candidates who have previous work experience using statistics, analyzing data, or conducting interviews or surveys.

Education

Survey researchers can have a bachelor's degree in a variety of fields, including business, psychology, and political science. Students should take courses in research methods, survey methodology, and statistics. Many also may benefit from taking business courses, such as marketing and consumer behavior, and social science courses, such as psychology, sociology, and economics.

Most technical or advanced research positions require a master's degree or Ph.D. Some survey researchers take degree programs in survey research, survey methodology, or marketing research. Others complete a Master of Business Administration (MBA) or concentrate in social sciences or statistics.

Prospective survey researchers can gain valuable experience through internships. Several research and marketing firms offer internships for college students or recent graduates who want to work in market and survey research.

Certification

The Marketing Research Association offers the Professional Researcher Certification (PRC) for survey researchers. Although not mandatory, certification can show a level of professional competency. Candidates qualify based on experience and knowledge, including at least 3 years working in opinion and marketing research, passing an exam, and membership in a professional organization. To keep their certification valid, researchers must take continuing education courses and apply for renewal every 2 years.

Important Qualities

Analytical skills. Survey researchers must be able to apply statistical techniques to large amounts of data and interpret the analysis correctly.

Communication skills. Survey researchers need strong communication skills when conducting surveys and interpreting and presenting results to clients.

Critical-thinking skills. Survey researchers must design or choose a survey and survey method that best captures the information needed. They must also be able to look at the data and analyses and understand what can be learned from the survey.

Detail oriented. Survey researchers must pay attention to details as they work because survey results depend on collecting, analyzing, and reporting the data accurately.

People skills. Depending on their technique, survey researchers may talk with people in face-to-face or during telephone interviews or in focus group sessions. Survey researchers must be able to make people comfortable enough to give meaningful responses and reveal their opinions.

Pay

Survey Researchers
Median annual wages, May 2010

Social Scientists and Related Workers	$67,090
Survey Researchers	$36,050
Total, All Occupations	$33,840

Note: All Occupations includes all occupations in the U.S. Economy.
Source: U.S. Bureau of Labor Statistics, Occupational Employment Statistics

The median annual wage of survey researchers was $36,050 in May 2010. The median wage is the wage at which half the workers in an occupation earned more than that amount and half earned less. The lowest 10 percent earned less than $18,660, and the top 10 percent earned more than $78,030.

Median annual wages in the industries employing the largest numbers of sociologists in May 2010 were as follows:

Scientific research and development services	$61,140
Educational services	41,540
Management, scientific, and technical consulting services	34,100
Other professional, scientific, and technical services (includes market research and public opinion polling)	28,910

Most survey researchers work full time during regular business hours.

Job Outlook

Survey Researchers

Percent change in employment, projected 2010-20

Survey Researchers	24%
Social Scientists and Related Workers	18%
Total, All Occupations	14%

Note: All Occupations includes all occupations in the U.S. Economy.
Source: U.S. Bureau of Labor Statistics, Employment Projections program

Employment of survey researchers is expected to grow 24 percent from 2010 to 2020, faster than the average for all occupations. However, because it is a small occupation, the fast growth will result in only about 4,700 new jobs over the 10-year period. Companies throughout all industries are increasingly using research, and survey researchers play an important role in the research process.

The market research and public opinion polling industry will continue to employ the largest number of survey researchers. Governments and organizations will continue to use public opinion research to help make decisions on transit systems, social programs, and numerous other issues.

Survey researchers also will be needed to design surveys for businesses and organizations. In an increasingly competitive economy, firms will continue to use market and consumer research surveys to help make business decisions and compete in the market. Many of these researcher jobs will be in consulting firms.

However, employment growth will be tempered by changing research methods. Research is an evolving field and companies occasionally adopt new research methods or adapt to new data sources. For example, collecting information from social media sites and data mining—finding trends in large sets of existing data—are expected to reduce the need for some surveys.

Job Prospects

Job prospects are expected to be good for those with an advanced degree in survey methodology, survey research, or statistics. Qualified candidates should find job opportunities in market research, public opinion polling, and consulting firms.

Although survey researchers also may qualify with a background in a variety of other fields, those with strong statistical and analytical skills and experience working in a research firm will have more job opportunities. Due to the relatively small number of survey researcher positions, bachelor's degree holders will likely face competition from more qualified candidates.

Employment projections data for survey researchers, 2010-20

Occupational Title	SOC Code	Employment, 2010	Projected Employment, 2020	Change, 2010-20	
				Percent	Numeric
Survey Researchers	19-3022	19,600	24,300	24	4,700
SOURCE: U.S. Bureau of Labor Statistics, Employment Projections program					

Similar Occupations

This table shows a list of occupations with job duties that are similar to those of survey researchers.

Occupation	Job Duties	Entry-Level Education	Median Annual Pay, May 2010
Advertising, Promotions, and Marketing Managers	Advertising, promotions, and marketing managers plan programs to generate interest in a product or service. They work with art directors, sales agents, and financial staff members.	Bachelor's degree	$108,260
Public Relations Managers and Specialists	Public relations managers and specialists create and maintain a favorable public image for their employer or client. They write material for media releases, plan and direct public relations programs, and raise funds for their organizations.	Bachelor's degree	$57,550
Operations Research Analysts	Operations research analysts use advanced methods of analysis to help organizations solve problems and make better decisions.	Bachelor's degree	$70,960
Statisticians	Statisticians use mathematical techniques to analyze and interpret data and draw conclusions.	Master's degree	$72,830
Economists	Economists study the production and distribution of resources, goods, and services.	Bachelor's degree	$89,450
Political Scientists	Political scientists study the origin, development, and operation of political systems. They research political ideas and analyze the structure and operation of governments, policies, political trends, and related issues.	Master's degree	$107,420

Psychologists	Psychologists study mental processes and human behavior by observing, interpreting, and recording how people and other animals relate to one another and the environment.	See How to Become One	$68,640
Sociologists	Sociologists study society and social behavior by examining the groups, cultures, organizations, social institutions, and processes that people develop.	Master's degree	$72,360
Market Research Analysts	Market research analysts study market conditions in local, regional, or national areas to examine potential sales of a product or service. They help companies understand what products people want, who will buy them, and at what price.	Bachelor's degree	$60,570

Contacts for More Information

For information about careers in survey research, visit American Association for Public Opinion Research , Council of American Survey Research Organizations

Suggested citation:

Bureau of Labor Statistics, U.S. Department of Labor, Occupational Outlook Handbook, 2012-13 Edition, Survey Researchers, on the Internet at http://www.bls.gov/ooh/life-physical-and-social-science/survey-researchers.htm .

Urban and Regional Planners

Quick Facts: Urban and Regional Planners	
2010 Median Pay	$63,040 per year $30.31 per hour
Entry-Level Education	Master's degree
Work Experience in a Related Occupation	None
On-the-job Training	None
Number of Jobs, 2010	40,300
Job Outlook, 2010-20	16% (About as fast as average)
Employment Change, 2010-20	6,500

What Urban and Regional Planners Do

Urban and regional planners develop plans and programs for the use of land. They use planning to create communities, accommodate growth, or revitalize physical facilities in towns, cities, counties, and metropolitan areas.

Duties

Urban and regional planners typically do the following:

Urban and regional planners often collaborate with community officials and developers.

- Meet with public officials, developers, and the public regarding development plans and land use
- Gather and analyze economic and environmental studies, censuses, and market research data
- Conduct field investigations to analyze factors affecting land use
- Review site plans submitted by developers
- Assess the feasibility of proposals and identify needed changes
- Recommend whether proposals should be approved or denied
- Present projects to planning officials and planning commissions
- Stay current on zoning or building codes, environmental regulations, and other legal issues

Urban and regional planners identify community needs and develop short- and long-term plans to create, grow, or revitalize a community or area. For example, planners may examine plans for proposed facilities, such as schools, to ensure that these facilities will meet the needs of a changing population.

As an area grows or changes, planners help communities manage the related economic, social, and environmental issues, such as planning a new park, sheltering the homeless, or making the region more attractive to businesses.

Some planners work on broad, community-wide plans, while others focus on specific issues. Ultimately, all planners promote the best use of a community's land and resources for residential, commercial, or recreational purposes.

When beginning a project, planners work with public officials, community members, and other groups to identify community issues or goals. Using research, data analysis, and collaboration with interest groups, planners formulate strategies to address issues or meet goals.

They also may help carry out community plans, oversee projects, and organize the work of the groups involved. Projects may range from a policy recommendation for a specific initiative to a long-term, comprehensive area plan.

Planners use a variety of tools and technology in their work, including geographic information systems (GIS) tools that analyze and manipulate data. GIS is used to integrate the data with electronic maps. For example, planners may use GIS to overlay a land map with population density indicators. They also use statistical software, visualization and presentation programs, financial spreadsheets, and other database and software programs.

Many planners specialize. The following are common types of urban and regional planners:

Land use and code enforcement planners are concerned with the way land is used and whether development plans comply with codes, which are the standards and laws of a jurisdiction. These planners work to carry out effective planning and zoning policies and ordinances. For example, a planner may develop a policy to encourage development in an underutilized location and discourage development in an environmentally sensitive area.

Transportation planners develop transportation plans and programs for an area. They identify transportation needs or issues, assess the impact of services or systems, and attempt to predict future transportation patterns. For example, as growth outside the city creates more jobs, the need for public transportation to get workers to those jobs increases. Transportation planners develop and model possible solutions and explain the possibilities to planning boards and the public.

Environmental and natural resources planners attempt to mitigate the harmful effects of development on the environment. They may focus on conserving resources, preventing destruction of ecosystems, or cleaning polluted areas.

Economic development planners focus on the economic activities of an area. They may work to expand or diversify commercial activity, attract businesses, create jobs, or build housing.

Urban design planners strive to make building architecture and public spaces look and function in accordance with an area's development and design goals. They combine planning with aspects of architecture and landscape architecture. Urban design planners focus on issues such as city layout, street design, and building and landscape patterns.

Work Environment

Urban and regional planners held about 40,300 jobs in 2010, a majority of which—about 64 percent—were in local government.

Most other planners worked for state and federal government, real estate developers, nonprofits, and planning consulting firms. Planners work throughout the country in all sizes of municipality, but most work in large metropolitan areas.

The following industries employed the largest numbers of urban and regional planners in 2010:

Local government, excluding education and hospitals	64%
Architectural, engineering, and related services	14
State government, excluding education and hospitals	10
Management, scientific, and technical consulting services	6

Most planners spend much of their time working with others. They often collaborate with public officials, engineers, architects, and developers, and must give presentations, attend meetings, and manage projects.

Because planners must balance conflicting interests and negotiate deals, the work can be stressful. Planners face pressure from politicians, developers, and the public to design or recommend specific plans. They also sometimes work against tight deadlines.

Urban and regional planners often travel to sites to inspect the features of the land. Those involved in inspecting development sites may spend much of their time in the field.

Work Schedules

Most planners work during normal business hours, but many also work evenings or weekends to attend meetings with planning commissions or neighborhood groups.

How to Become an Urban or Regional Planner

Urban and regional planners usually need a master's degree from an accredited planning program to qualify for professional positions. These jobs often require several years of related work experience.

Education

Most urban and regional planners have a master's degree from an accredited urban or regional planning program. In 2012, 73 colleges and universities offered an accredited master's degree program in planning.

Many programs accept students with a wide range of undergraduate backgrounds. Many people who enter master's degree programs have a bachelor's degree in economics, geography, political science, or environmental design.

Although most master's programs have a similar core curriculum, they often differ in the courses they offer and the issues on which they focus. For example, programs located in agricultural states may focus on rural planning and programs located in an area with high population density may focus on urban revitalization.

Most master's programs include considerable time in seminars, workshops, and laboratory courses, in which students learn to analyze and solve planning problems.

Some planners have a background in a related field, such as public administration, architecture, or landscape architecture.

Aspiring planners with a bachelor's degree but not a master's degree can qualify for a small number of jobs as assistant or junior planners. There are currently 15 accredited bachelor's degree programs in planning. Candidates with a bachelor's degree typically need work experience in planning, public policy, or a related field.

Work Experience

Entry-level planners typically need 1 to 2 years of work experience in a related field, such as architecture, public policy, or economic development. Many students get experience through real-world planning projects or part-time internships while enrolled in a planning program. They often complete summer internships during their master's program.

Others enroll in full-time internships after completing their degree.

Mid- and senior-level planner positions usually require several years of work experience in planning or in a specific planning specialty.

Licenses

As of 2011, New Jersey was the only state that required planners to be licensed, although Michigan required registration to use the title "community planner." More information can be requested from the regulatory boards of New Jersey and Michigan .

Certification

The American Institute of Certified Planners (AICP) offers the professional AICP Certification for planners. To become certified, candidates must meet certain education and experience requirements and pass an exam. Although not required, certification can show a level of professional expertise in the field. Some organizations prefer to hire certified planners.

Important Qualities

Analytical skills. Planners analyze information and data from a variety of sources, such as market research studies, censuses, and environmental impact studies. They use statistical techniques and technologies, such as geographic information systems (GIS), in their analyses to determine the significance of the data.

Collaboration skills. In making planning decisions, urban and regional planners must collaborate with a wide range of people. They often work with or receive input from public officials, engineers, architects, and interest groups. Some may act as mediators when these groups have conflicting opinions.

Decision-making skills. Planners must weigh all possible planning options and combine analysis, creativity, and realism to choose the appropriate action or plan.

Management skills. Planners must be able to manage projects, which may include overseeing tasks, planning assignments, and making decisions.

Speaking skills. Urban and regional planners must be able to communicate clearly and effectively because they often give presentations and meet with a wide variety of audiences, including public officials, interest groups, and community members.

Writing skills. Urban and regional planners need strong writing skills because they often prepare research reports, write grant proposals, and correspond with colleagues and stakeholders.

Pay

Urban and Regional Planners
Median annual wages, May 2010

Social Scientists and Related Workers	$67,090
Urban and Regional Planners	$63,040
Total, All Occupations	$33,840

Note: All Occupations includes all occupations in the U.S. Economy.
Source: U.S. Bureau of Labor Statistics, Occupational Employment Statistics

The median annual wage of urban and regional planners was $63,040 in May 2010. The median wage is the wage at which half the workers in an occupation earned more than that amount and half earned less. The lowest 10 percent earned less than $40,410, and the top 10 percent earned more than $96,420.

Median annual wages in the industries employing the largest numbers of urban and regional planners in May 2010 were:

Architectural, engineering, and related services	$68,240
Management, scientific, and technical consulting services	66,280
State government	63,480
Local government	61,050

Most planners work during normal business hours, but many also work evenings or weekends to attend meetings with planning commissions or neighborhood groups.

Job Outlook

Urban and Regional Planners
Percent change in employment, projected 2010-20

Social Scientists and Related Workers	18%
Urban and Regional Planners	16%
Total, All Occupations	14%

Note: All Occupations includes all occupations in the U.S. Economy.
Source: U.S. Bureau of Labor Statistics, Employment Projections program

Employment of urban and regional planners is expected to grow 16 percent from 2010 to 2020, about as fast as the average for all occupations. Population growth and environmental concerns will drive employment growth for planners in cities, suburbs, and other areas.

Urban areas will need planners to accommodate an expected influx of people into metropolitan areas. Within cities, urban planners will be needed to develop revitalization projects and address problems associated with population growth.

Suburbs are the fastest-growing communities in most metropolitan areas. As suburban areas become more heavily populated, municipalities will need planners to address changing housing needs and to improve transportation systems.

Planners also will be important as new communities will require extensive development and infrastructure, including housing, roads, sewer systems, schools.

An increased focus on sustainable and environmentally-conscious development also will increase demand for planners. Issues such as storm water management, permits, environmental regulation, and historic preservation should drive employment growth.

Employment growth should be fastest in private engineering, architectural, and consulting services. Engineering and architecture firms are increasingly using planners for land use, development, and building. In addition, many real estate developers and governments will continue to contract out various planning services to these consulting firms, further driving employment growth.

Employment of planners in local or state government may suffer because many projects are canceled or deferred when municipalities have too little money for development. Expected tight budgets over the coming decade should slow planners' employment growth in government.

Job Prospects

Job opportunities for planners often depend on economic conditions. When municipalities and developers have funds for development projects, planners are in higher demand. However, planners may face strong competition for jobs in an economic downturn, when there is less funding for development work.

Although government funding issues will affect employment of planners in the short term, job prospects should improve over the 2010–20 decade. Planners will be needed to help plan, oversee, and carry out development projects that were deferred because of poor economic conditions. Combined with the increasing demands of a growing population, long-term prospects for qualified planners should be good.

Job prospects will be best for those with a master's degree from an accredited planning program and relevant work experience. Planners who are willing to relocate for work also will have more job opportunities.

Employment projections data for urban and regional planners, 2010-20

Occupational Title	SOC Code	Employment, 2010	Projected Employment, 2020	Change, 2010-20	
				Percent	Numeric
Urban and Regional Planners	19-3051	40,300	46,800	16	6,500
SOURCE: U.S. Bureau of Labor Statistics, Employment Projections program					

Similar Occupations

This table shows a list of occupations with job duties that are similar to those of urban and regional planners.

Occupation	Job Duties	Entry-Level Education	Median Annual Pay, May 2010
Architects	Architects plan and design buildings and other structures.	Bachelor's degree	$72,550
Cartographers and Photogrammetrists	Cartographers and photogrammetrists measure, analyze, and interpret geographic information to create maps and charts for political, cultural, educational, and other purposes. Cartographers are general mapmakers, and photogrammetrists are specialized mapmakers who use aerial photographs to create maps.	Bachelor's degree	$54,510
Civil Engineers	Civil engineers design and supervise large construction projects, including roads, buildings, airports, tunnels, dams, bridges, and systems for water supply and sewage treatment.	Bachelor's degree	$77,560
Landscape Architects	Landscape architects plan and design land areas for parks, recreational facilities, highways, airports, and other properties. Projects include subdivisions and commercial, industrial, and residential sites.	Bachelor's degree	$62,090
Surveyors	Surveyors establish official land, airspace, and water boundaries. Surveyors work with civil engineers, landscape architects, and urban and regional planners to develop comprehensive design documents.	Bachelor's degree	$54,880
Market Research Analysts	Market research analysts study market conditions in local, regional, or national areas to examine potential sales of a product or service. They help companies understand what products people want, who will buy them, and at what price.	Bachelor's degree	$60,570
Economists	Economists study the production and distribution of resources, goods, and services.	Bachelor's degree	$89,450
Geographers	Geographers study the earth and its land, features, and inhabitants. They also examine phenomena such as political or cultural structures as they relate to geography. They study the physical or human geographic characteristics or both of a region, ranging in scale from local to global.	Bachelor's degree	$72,800
Survey Researchers	Survey researchers design or conduct surveys and analyze survey data. Many groups use surveys to collect factual data, such as employment and salary information, or to ask questions that help them understand people's opinions, attitudes, beliefs, or desires.	Bachelor's degree	$36,050
Environmental Engineers	Environmental engineers use the principles of engineering, soil science, biology, and chemistry to develop solutions to environmental problems. They are involved in efforts to improve recycling, waste disposal, public health, and control of water and air pollution.	Bachelor's degree	$78,740

Contacts for More Information

For more information on careers and certification in urban and regional planning, visit American Planning Association

For information on accredited urban and regional planning programs, visit Association of Collegiate Schools of Planning

Suggested citation:

Bureau of Labor Statistics, U.S. Department of Labor, Occupational Outlook Handbook, 2012-13 Edition, Urban and Regional Planners, on the Internet at http://www.bls.gov/ooh/life-physical-and-social-science/urban-and-regional-planners.htm .

Zoologists and Wildlife Biologists

Quick Facts: Zoologists and Wildlife Biologists	
2010 Median Pay	$57,430 per year $27.61 per hour
Entry-Level Education	Bachelor's degree
Work Experience in a Related Occupation	None
On-the-job Training	None
Number of Jobs, 2010	19,800
Job Outlook, 2010-20	7% (Slower than average)
Employment Change, 2010-20	1,500

What Zoologists and Wildlife Biologists Do

Zoologists and wildlife biologists study the characteristics and habitats of animals and wildlife.

Duties

Zoologists and wildlife biologists typically do the following:

- Develop and conduct experimental studies with animals in controlled or natural surroundings
- Collect biological data and specimens for further analysis
- Study the characteristics of animals, such as their interactions with other species, reproduction, diseases, and movement patterns
- Analyze the influence that human activity has on wildlife and their natural habitats
- Estimate wildlife populations
- Write research papers, reports, and scholarly articles that explain their findings
- Give presentations on research findings
- Make recommendations to policymakers and the general public on wildlife conservation and management issues

Zoologists and wildlife biologists perform a variety of scientific tests and experiments. For example, they take blood samples from animals to assess their levels of nutrition.

Zoologists and wildlife biologists use geographic information systems, modeling software, and other computer programs to estimate populations and track the behavior patterns of animals. They also use these programs to forecast the spread of invasive species, diseases, and

Zoologists and wildlife biologists often work outdoors in the field gathering data and studying animals in their natural habitats.

other potential threats to wildlife.

Zoologists and wildlife biologists conduct research for a variety of purposes. For example, many zoologists and wildlife biologists work to increase knowledge and understanding of wildlife species. They also work closely with public officials to develop wildlife management and conservation plans to ensure species are protected from threats and animal populations remain at sustainable levels.

Most zoologists and wildlife biologists work on research teams with other scientists and technicians. For example, zoologists and wildlife biologists may work with environmental scientists and hydrologists to monitor the effects of water pollution on fish populations.

Many zoologists and wildlife biologists are identified by the types of species they study. The following are examples of those who specialize by species:

- **Entomologists** study insects.
- **Herpetologists** study reptiles and amphibians, such as snakes and frogs.
- **Ichthyologists** study fish.
- **Mammalogists** study mammals, such as monkeys and bears.
- **Ornithologists** study birds.

Some wildlife biologists study animals by where they live. The following are examples of those who specialize by habitat:

- **Marine biologists** study organisms that live in saltwater.
- **Limnologists** study organisms that live in freshwater.

Other zoologists and wildlife biologists are identified by the aspects of zoology and wildlife biology they study, such as evolution and animal behavior. The following are some examples:

- **Ecologists** study the ecosystem, which is the relationship between organisms and with the surrounding environment.
- **Evolutionary biologists** study the origins of species and the changes in their inherited characteristics over generations.

Many people with a zoology and wildlife biology background become high school teachers or professors. For more information, see the profiles on high school teachers and postsecondary teachers.

Work Environment

Zoologists and wildlife biologists held about 19,800 jobs in 2010. They work in offices, laboratories, or outdoors. Depending on their position, they may spend considerable time in the field gathering data and studying animals in their natural habitats.

Fieldwork can require zoologists and wildlife biologists to travel to remote locations all over the world. For example, marine biologists may spend months at sea on a research ship. Fieldwork can be physically demanding, and zoologists and wildlife biologists work in both warm and cold climates and in all types of weather.

Industries employing the largest numbers of zoologists and wildlife biologists in 2010 were as follows:

State government, excluding education and hospitals	34%
Federal government, excluding postal service	26
Management, scientific, and technical consulting services	7
Research and development in the physical, engineering, and life sciences	7
Self-employed workers	5

Work Schedules

Most zoologists and wildlife biologists work full time. They may work long or irregular hours when doing fieldwork.

How to Become a Zoologist or Wildlife Biologist

Zoologists and wildlife biologists need a bachelor's degree for entry-level positions, but a master's degree is often needed for advancement. A Ph.D. is necessary for independent research and for college teaching positions.

Education

Zoologists and wildlife biologists need at least a bachelor's degree. Many schools offer bachelor's degree programs in zoology and wildlife biology or a closely related field such as ecology. An undergraduate degree in biology with coursework in zoology and wildlife biology is also good preparation for a career as a zoologist or wildlife biologist. Zoologists and wildlife biologists typically need at least a master's degree for higher-level positions. A Ph.D. is necessary for most independent research and for college teaching positions.

Students typically take zoology and wildlife biology courses in ecology, anatomy, wildlife management, and cellular biology. They also take courses that focus on a particular group of animals, such as ichthyology (fish) or ornithology (birds). Courses in botany, chemistry, and physics are important because zoologists and wildlife biologists must have a well-rounded scientific background. Students should also take courses in mathematics and statistics because zoologists and wildlife biologists must be able to do complex data analysis.

Knowledge of computer science is important because zoologists and wildlife biologists frequently use advanced computer software, such as geographic information systems and modeling software, to do their work.

Important Qualities

Critical-thinking skills. Zoologists and wildlife biologists need sound reasoning and judgment to draw conclusions from experimental results and scientific observations.

Interpersonal skills. Zoologists and wildlife biologists typically work on teams. They must be able to work effectively with others to achieve their goals.

Observation skills. Zoologists and wildlife biologists must be able to notice slight changes in an animal's characteristics, such as their behavior or appearance.

Problem-solving skills. Zoologists and wildlife biologists try to find the best possible solutions to threats that affect wildlife, such as disease and habitat loss.

Speaking skills. Zoologists and wildlife biologists often give presentations to colleagues, managers, policymakers, and the general public. They need to be able to educate others on wildlife conservation and management issues.

Writing skills. Zoologists and wildlife biologists write scientific papers, reports, and articles that explain their findings.

Advancement

Zoologists and wildlife biologists typically receive greater responsibility and independence in their work as they gain experience. More education can also lead to greater responsibility. Zoologists and

wildlife biologists with a Ph.D. usually lead research teams and control the direction and content of projects.

Pay

Zoologists and Wildlife Biologists
Median annual wages, May 2010

Life, Physical, and Social Science Occupations	$58,530
Zoologists and Wildlife Biologists	$57,430
Total, All Occupations	$33,840

Note: All Occupations includes all occupations in the U.S. Economy.
Source: U.S. Bureau of Labor Statistics, Occupational Employment Statistics

The median annual wage of zoologists and wildlife biologists was $57,430 in May 2010. The median wage is the wage at which half the workers in an occupation earned more than that amount and half earned less. The lowest 10 percent earned less than $35,660, and the top 10 percent earned more than $93,450.

Median annual wages in the industries employing the largest numbers of zoologists and wildlife biologists in May 2010 were:

Federal government, excluding postal service	$71,110
Research and development in the physical, engineering, and life sciences	63,740
State government, excluding education and hospitals	52,360
Management, scientific, and technical consulting services	50,040

Most zoologists and wildlife biologists work full time. They may work long or irregular hours when doing fieldwork.

Job Outlook

Zoologists and Wildlife Biologists
Percent change in employment, projected 2010-20

Life, Physical, and Social Science Occupations	16%
Total, All Occupations	14%
Zoologists and Wildlife Biologists	7%

Note: All Occupations includes all occupations in the U.S. Economy.
Source: U.S. Bureau of Labor Statistics, Employment Projections program

Employment of zoologists and wildlife biologists is projected to grow by 7 percent from 2010 to 2020, slower than the average for all occupations. More zoologists and wildlife biologists will be needed to study the impact of population growth and development on wildlife and their habitats. However, demand for zoologists and wildlife biologists in local, state, and federal government agencies, such as the United States Fish and Wildlife Service, will vary based on the budgets for these agencies.

As the population grows and expands into new areas it will expose wildlife to threats such as disease, invasive species, and habitat loss. Increased human activity causes problems, such as pollution and climate change, that endanger wildlife. For example, changes in climate patterns can be detrimental to the migration habits of animals, and increased sea levels can destroy wetlands. Zoologists and wildlife biologists will be needed to research, develop, and carry out wildlife management and conservation plans that combat these threats and protect our biological resources.

Job Prospects

Zoologists and wildlife biologists should have good job opportunities. In addition to job growth, many job openings will be created by zoologists and wildlife biologists who retire, advance to management positions, or change careers.

Year to year, the number of job openings available in local, state, and federal government agencies, such as the United States Fish and Wildlife Service, will vary based on the budgets for these agencies.

Employment projections data for zoologists and wildlife biologists, 2010-20

Occupational Title	SOC Code	Employment, 2010	Projected Employment, 2020	Change, 2010-20	
				Percent	Numeric
Zoologists and Wildlife Biologists	19-1023	19,800	21,300	7	1,500
SOURCE: U.S. Bureau of Labor Statistics, Employment Projections program					

Similar Occupations

This table shows a list of occupations with job duties that are similar to those of zoologists and wildlife biologists.

Occupation	Job Duties	Entry-Level Education	Median Annual Pay, May 2010
Agricultural and Food Scientists	Agricultural and food scientists work to ensure agricultural productivity and food safety.	See How to Become One	$58,450
Biochemists and Biophysicists	Biochemists and biophysicists study the chemical and physical principles of living things and of biological processes such as cell development, growth, and heredity.	Doctoral or professional degree	$79,390
Biological Technicians	Biological technicians help biological and medical scientists conduct laboratory tests and experiments.	Bachelor's degree	$39,020
Conservation Scientists and Foresters	Conservation scientists and foresters manage overall land quality of forests, parks, rangelands, and other natural resources.	Bachelor's degree	$57,420
Environmental Scientists and Specialists	Environmental scientists and specialists use their knowledge of the natural sciences to protect the environment. They identify problems and find solutions that minimize hazards to the health of the environment and the population.	Bachelor's degree	$61,700
Microbiologists	Microbiologists study the growth, development, and other characteristics of microscopic organisms such as bacteria, algae, and fungi.	Bachelor's degree	$65,920
Postsecondary Teachers	Postsecondary teachers instruct students in a wide variety of academic and vocational subjects beyond the high school level. They also conduct research and publish scholarly papers and books.	Doctoral or professional degree	$62,050
Veterinarians	Veterinarians care for the health of animals. They diagnose, treat, or research medical conditions and diseases of pets, livestock, and animals in zoos, racetracks, and laboratories.	Doctoral or professional degree	$82,040

Contacts for More Information

For more information about zoologists and wildlife biologists, visit The Wildlife Society

For information about careers in zoology and wildlife biology with the federal government, visit USAJOBS

Suggested citation:

Bureau of Labor Statistics, U.S. Department of Labor, Occupational Outlook Handbook, 2012-13 Edition, Zoologists and Wildlife Biologists, on the Internet at http://www.bls.gov/ooh/life-physical-and-social-science/zoologists-and-wildlife-biologists.htm .

Management Occupations

Administrative Services Managers

Quick Facts: Administrative Services Managers	
2010 Median Pay	$77,890 per year $37.45 per hour
Entry-Level Education	High school diploma or equivalent
Work Experience in a Related Occupation	1 to 5 years
On-the-job Training	None
Number of Jobs, 2010	254,300
Job Outlook, 2010-20	15% (About as fast as average)
Employment Change, 2010-20	36,900

What Administrative Services Managers Do

Administrative services managers plan, direct, and coordinate supportive services of an organization. Their specific responsibilities vary by the type of organization and may include keeping records, distributing mail, and planning and maintaining facilities. In a small organization, they may direct all support services and may be called the business office manager. Large organizations may have several layers of administrative managers who specialize in different areas.

Duties

Administrative services managers typically do the following:

- Buy, store, and distribute supplies
- Supervise clerical and administrative personnel
- Recommend changes to policies or procedures to improve operations, such as changing what supplies the organization keeps and improving how the organization handles records
- Plan budgets for contracts, equipment, and supplies
- Monitor the facility to ensure that it remains safe, secure, and well maintained
- Oversee the maintenance and repair of machinery, equipment, and electrical and mechanical systems
- Ensure that facilities meet environmental, health, and security standards and comply with government regulations

Administrative services managers plan, coordinate, and direct a broad range of services that allow organizations to operate efficiently.

Administrative services managers supervise clerical and administrative personnel.

An organization may have several managers who oversee activities that meet the needs of multiple departments, such as mail, printing and copying, recordkeeping, security, building maintenance, and recycling.

The work of administrative services managers can make a difference in employees' productivity and satisfaction. For example, an administrative services manager might be responsible for making sure the organization has the supplies and services it needs. Also, an administrative services manager who is responsible for coordinating space allocation might take into account employee morale and available funds when determining the best way to arrange a given physical space.

Administrative services managers also ensure that the organization honors its contracts and follows government regulations and safety standards.

Administrative services managers may examine energy consumption patterns, technology usage, and office equipment. For example, managers may recommend buying new or different equipment or supplies to lower energy costs or improve indoor air quality.

They also plan for maintenance and the future replacement of equipment, such as computers. A timely replacement of equipment can help save money for the organization, because eventually the cost of upgrading and maintaining equipment becomes higher than the cost of buying new equipment.

The following are examples of types of administrative service managers:

Contract administrators handle buying, storing, and distributing equipment and supplies. They also oversee getting rid of surplus or unclaimed property.

Facility managers oversee buildings, grounds, equipment, and supplies. Their duties fall into several categories, including overseeing operations and maintenance, planning and managing projects, and dealing with environmental factors.

Facility managers may oversee renovation projects to improve efficiency or ensure that facilities meet government regulations and environmental, health, and security standards. For example, they may influence building renovation projects by recommending energy-saving alternatives or efficiencies that reduce waste. In addition, facility managers continually monitor the facility to ensure that it remains safe, secure, and well maintained. Facility managers also are responsible for directing staff, including maintenance, grounds, and custodial workers.

Work Environment

Administrative services managers held about 254,300 jobs in 2010.

Administrative services managers spend much of their day in an office. They sometimes make site visits around the building, go outdoors to supervise groundskeeping activities, or inspect other facilities under their management.

The following industries employed the most administrative services managers in 2010:

Educational services; state, local, and private	15%
Health care	13
State and local government, excluding education and hospitals	13
Professional, scientific, and technical services	8
Finance and insurance	8

Work Schedules

Most administrative services managers worked full time in 2010. However, about 1 in 4 worked 50 or more hours per week. Facility managers often are on call to address a variety of problems that can arise in a facility during nonworking hours.

How to Become an Administrative Services Manager

Educational requirements vary by the type of organization and the work they do. They must have related work experience.

Education

A high school diploma or a General Educational Development (GED) diploma is typically required for someone to become an administrative services manager. However, some administrative services managers need at least a bachelor's degree. Those with a bachelor's degree typically study business, engineering, or facility management.

Certification

The International Facility Management Association offers a competency-based professional certification program for administrative services managers. Completing this program may give prospective job candidates an advantage. The program has two levels: the Facilities Management Professional (FMP) certification and the Certified Facility Manager (CFM) certification. People entering the profession can get the FMP as a steppingstone to the CFM. For the CFM, applicants must meet certain educational and experience requirements.

Work Experience

Administrative services managers must have related work experience reflecting managerial and leadership abilities. For example, contract administrators need experience in purchasing and sales, as well as knowledge of the variety of supplies, machinery, and equipment that the organization uses. Managers who are concerned with supply, inventory, and distribution should be experienced in receiving, warehousing, packaging, shipping, transportation, and related operations.

Advancement

Advancement of facility managers is based on the practices and size of individual organizations. Some facility managers transfer among departments within an organization or work their way up from technical positions. Others advance through a progression of facility management positions that offer additional responsibilities. Advancement is easier in large organizations that employ several levels and types of administrative services managers.

A master's degree in business administration or a related field can enhance a manager's opportunities to advance to higher level positions, such as director of administrative services. Some experienced managers may join or establish a management consulting firm to provide administrative management services to other organizations on a contract basis.

Important Qualities

Analytical skills. Administrative services managers must be able to review an organization's procedures and find ways to improve efficiency.

Communication skills. Much of an administrative services manager's time is spent working with other people. Therefore, communication is a key quality.

Detail oriented. Administrative services managers must pay attention to details. This quality is necessary across a range of tasks, from ensuring that the organization complies with building codes to managing the process of buying equipment.

Leadership skills. In managing workers and coordinating administrative duties, administrative services managers must be able to motivate employees and deal with issues that may arise.

Pay

Administrative Services Managers
Median annual wages, May 2010

Management Occupations	$91,440
Administrative Services Managers	$77,890
Total, All Occupations	$33,840

Note: All Occupations includes all occupations in the U.S. Economy.
Source: U.S. Bureau of Labor Statistics, Occupational Employment Statistics

The median annual wage of administrative services managers was $77,890 in May 2010. The median wage is the wage at which half the workers in an occupation earned more than that amount and half earned less. The lowest 10 percent earned less than $41,420 and the top 10 percent earned more than $135,300.

Most administrative services managers worked full time in 2010. However, about 1 in 4 worked 50 or more hours per week. Facility managers often are on call to address a variety of problems that can arise in a facility during nonworking hours.

Job Outlook

Administrative Services Managers
Percent change in employment, projected 2010-20

Administrative Services Managers	15%
Total, All Occupations	14%
Management Occupations	7%

Note: All Occupations includes all occupations in the U.S. Economy.
Source: U.S. Bureau of Labor Statistics, Employment Projections program

Employment of administrative services managers is expected to grow 15 percent from 2010 to 2020, about as fast as the average for all occupations.

Tasks such as managing facilities and being prepared for emergencies will remain important in a wide range of industries. Facility managers will be needed to plan for natural disasters, ensuring that any damage to a building will be minimal and that the organization can get back to work quickly.

Employment growth is also expected as organizations increasingly realize the importance of operating their facilities efficiently.

In addition, facility managers will be in demand because there will be a greater focus on the environmental impact and energy efficiency of the buildings they manage. Improving energy efficiency can reduce costs and is often required by regulation. For example, building codes typically ensure that buildings meet environmental standards. Facility managers will be needed to oversee these improvements, in areas from heating and air systems to roofing.

Contract administrators are also expected to be in demand as organizations contract out many services, such as food services, janitorial services, grounds maintenance, and repair.

Job Prospects

Applicants will likely face strong competition for the limited number of higher level administrative services management jobs.

Competition should be less severe for lower level management jobs. Job prospects also are expected to be better for those who can manage a wide range of responsibilities than for those who specialize in particular functions.

In addition to the new administrative services management jobs expected to arise through growth in the occupation, many job openings will stem from the need to replace workers who transfer to other jobs, retire, or leave the occupation for other reasons.

Job opportunities may vary from year to year because the strength of the economy affects demand for administrative services managers. Industries least likely to be affected by economic fluctuations are usually the most stable places for employment.

Employment projections data for administrative services managers, 2010-20

Occupational Title	SOC Code	Employment, 2010	Projected Employment, 2020	Change, 2010-20 Percent	Numeric
Administrative Services Managers	11-3011	254,300	291,200	15	36,900
SOURCE: U.S. Bureau of Labor Statistics, Employment Projections program					

Similar Occupations

This table shows a list of occupations with job duties that are similar to those of administrative services managers.

Occupation	Job Duties	Entry-Level Education	Median Annual Pay, May 2010
Cost Estimators	Cost estimators collect and analyze data to estimate the time, money, resources, and labor required for product manufacturing, construction projects, or services. Some specialize in a particular industry or product type.	Bachelor's degree	$57,860
Property, Real Estate, and Community Association Managers	Property, real estate, and community association managers take care of the many aspects of residential, commercial, or industrial properties. They make sure the property looks nice, operates smoothly, and preserves its resale value.	High school diploma or equivalent	$51,480
Purchasing Managers, Buyers, and Purchasing Agents	Purchasing managers, buyers, and purchasing agents buy products for organizations to use or resell. They evaluate suppliers, negotiate contracts, and review product quality.	See How to Become One	$58,360
Top Executives	Top executives devise strategies and policies to ensure that an organization meets its goals. They plan, direct, and coordinate operational activities of companies and public or private-sector organizations.	See How to Become One	$101,250

Contacts for More Information

For more information about administrative services management, as well as the Certified Facility Manager designation, visit International Facility Management Association

Suggested citation:

Bureau of Labor Statistics, U.S. Department of Labor, Occupational Outlook Handbook, 2012-13 Edition, Administrative Services Managers, on the Internet at http://www.bls.gov/ooh/management/administrative-services-managers.htm

Advertising, Promotions, and Marketing Managers

Quick Facts: Advertising, Promotions, and Marketing Managers	
2010 Median Pay	$108,260 per year $52.05 per hour
Entry-Level Education	Bachelor's degree
Work Experience in a Related Occupation	1 to 5 years
On-the-job Training	None
Number of Jobs, 2010	216,800
Job Outlook, 2010-20	14% (About as fast as average)
Employment Change, 2010-20	29,400

What Advertising, Promotions, and Marketing Managers Do

Advertising, promotions, and marketing managers plan programs to generate interest in a product or service. They work with art directors, sales agents, and financial staff members.

Duties

Advertising, promotions, and marketing managers typically do the following:

- Work with department heads or staff to discuss topics such as contracts, selection of advertising media, or products to be advertised
- Gather and organize information to plan advertising campaigns
- Plan the advertising, including which media to advertise in, such as radio, television, print, online, and billboards
- Negotiate advertising contracts
- Inspect layouts, which are sketches or plans for an advertisement
- Initiate market research studies and analyze their findings
- Develop pricing strategies for products to be marketed, balancing the goals of a firm with customer satisfaction
- Meet with clients to provide marketing or technical advice
- Direct the hiring of advertising, promotions, and marketing staff and oversee their daily activities

Advertising, promotions, and marketing managers work with art directors, sales agents, and financial staff members.

Advertising managers create interest among potential buyers of a product or service for a department, for an entire organization, or on a project basis (account). They work in advertising agencies that put together advertising campaigns for clients, in media firms that sell advertising space or time, and in organizations that advertise heavily.

Advertising managers work with sales staff and others to generate ideas for an advertising campaign. They oversee the staff that develops the advertising. They work with the finance department to prepare a budget and cost estimates for the advertising campaign.

Often, advertising managers serve as liaisons between the client requiring the advertising and an advertising or promotion agency that develops and places the ads. In larger organizations with an extensive advertising department, different advertising managers may oversee in-house accounts and creative and media services departments.

In addition, some advertising managers specialize in a particular field or type of advertising. For example, media directors determine the way in which an advertising campaign reaches customers. They can use any or all of various media, including radio, television, newspapers, magazines, the Internet, and outdoor signs.

Advertising managers known as account executives manage clients' accounts, but they don't develop or supervise the creation or presentation of the advertising. That becomes the work of the creative services department.

Promotions managers direct programs that combine advertising with purchasing incentives to increase sales. Often, the programs use direct mail, inserts in newspapers, Internet advertisements, in-store displays, product endorsements, or special events to target customers. Purchasing incentives may include discounts, samples, gifts, rebates, coupons, sweepstakes, and contests.

Marketing managers estimate the demand for products and services that an organization and its competitors offer. They identify potential markets for the organization's products.

Marketing managers also develop pricing strategies to help organizations maximize profits and market share while ensuring that the organizations' customers are satisfied. They work with sales, public relations, and product development staff.

For example, a marketing manager may monitor trends that indicate the need for new products and services. Then they oversee the development of that new product. For more information on sales or public relations, see the profiles on sales managers , public relations managers and specialists , and market research analysts .

Work Environment

Advertising and promotions managers held about 38,700 jobs in 2010. The following industries employed the most advertising and promotions managers in 2010:

Advertising, public relations, and related services	22%
Information	12
Religious, grantmaking, civic, professional, and similar organizations	10
Management of companies and enterprises	8
Wholesale trade	7

Marketing managers held about 178,200 jobs in 2010. The following industries employed the most marketing managers in 2010:

Professional, scientific, and technical services	18%
Manufacturing	14
Management of companies and enterprises	13
Finance and insurance	12
Information	9

Advertising, promotions, and marketing managers typically work in offices close to those of top executives. The jobs of advertising, promotions, and marketing managers are usually stressful, particularly near deadlines. They may travel to meet with clients or representatives of communications media.

Work Schedules

Most advertising, promotions, and marketing managers work full time. In 2010, 19 percent of advertising and promotions managers worked 50 or more hours per week.

How to Become an Advertising, Promotions, or Marketing Manager

A bachelor's degree is required for most advertising, promotions, and marketing management positions. These managers typically have work experience in advertising, marketing, promotions, or sales.

Education

A bachelor's degree is required for most advertising, promotions, and marketing management positions. For advertising management positions, some employers prefer a bachelor's degree in advertising or journalism. A relevant course of study might include classes in marketing, consumer behavior, market research, sales, communication methods and technology, visual arts, art history, and photography.

Most marketing managers have a bachelor's degree. Courses in business law, management, economics, accounting, finance, mathematics, and statistics are advantageous. In addition, completing an internship while in school is highly recommended.

Work Experience

Advertising, promotional, and marketing managers typically have work experience in advertising, marketing, promotions, or sales. For example, many managers are former sales representatives; purchasing agents; buyers; or product, advertising, promotions, or public relations specialists.

Important Qualities

Analytical skills. As the advertising industry changes with the rise of digital media, advertising, promotions, and marketing managers must be able to analyze industry trends to determine the most promising strategies for their organization.

Creativity. Advertising, promotions, and marketing managers must

be able to generate new and imaginative ideas.

Decision-making skills. Managers often must choose between competing advertising and marketing strategies put forward by staff.

Interpersonal skills. These managers must deal with a range of people in different roles, both inside and outside the organization.

Management skills. Advertising, promotions, and marketing managers must manage their time and budget efficiently while directing and motivating staff members.

Pay

Advertising, Promotions, and Marketing Managers
Median annual wages, May 2010

Marketing Managers	$112,800
Advertising, Promotions, and Marketing Managers	$108,260
Advertising and Promotions Managers	$83,890
Total, All Occupations	$33,840

Note: All Occupations includes all occupations in the U.S. Economy.
Source: U.S. Bureau of Labor Statistics, Occupational Employment Statistics

The median annual wage of advertising and promotions managers was $83,890 in May 2010. The median wage is the wage at which half the workers in an occupation earned more than that amount and half earned less. The lowest 10 percent earned less than $41,480, and the top 10 percent earned more than $166,400.

The median annual wage for marketing managers was $112,800 in May 2010. The lowest 10 percent earned less than $57,750, and the top 10 percent earned more than $166,400.

Most advertising, promotions, and marketing managers work full time. In 2010, 19 percent of advertising and promotions managers worked 50 or more hours per week.

Job Outlook

Advertising, Promotions, and Marketing Managers
Percent change in employment, projected 2010-20

Total, All Occupations	14%
Marketing Managers	14%
Advertising, Promotions, and Marketing Managers	14%
Advertising and Promotions Managers	13%

Note: All Occupations includes all occupations in the U.S. Economy.
Source: U.S. Bureau of Labor Statistics, Employment Projections program

Employment of advertising and promotions managers is expected to grow 13 percent from 2010 to 2020, about as fast as the average for all occupations.

Employment of marketing managers is expected to grow 14 percent from 2010 to 2020, as fast as the average for all occupations.

Advertising, promotions, and marketing will continue to be essential for organizations as they look to maintain and expand their share of the market.

Advertising and promotions managers will be needed to plan, direct, and coordinate advertising and promotion campaigns, as well as to introduce new products to the marketplace. They will also be needed to manage digital media campaigns, which often target customers through the use of websites, social media, and live chats.

Newspaper publishers, one of the top-employing industries of advertising and promotions managers, are expected to decline 22 percent from 2010 to 2020. The continued rise of electronic media will result in decreasing demand for print newspapers. However, advertising and promotions managers are expected to see employment growth in other areas, as they will be needed to plan the digital advertisements that replace print ads.

Because marketing managers and their departments are important to an organization's revenue, marketing managers are less likely to be let go than other types of managers. Marketing managers will continue to be in demand as organizations seek to market their products to specific customers and localities.

Job Prospects

Advertising, promotions, and marketing manager positions are highly desirable and are often sought by other managers and experienced professionals. As a result, strong competition is expected. With Internet-based advertising becoming more important, advertising managers who can navigate the digital world should have the best prospects.

Employment projections data for advertising, promotions, and marketing managers, 2010-20

Occupational Title	SOC Code	Employment, 2010	Projected Employment, 2020	Change, 2010-20 Percent	Change, 2010-20 Numeric
Advertising, Promotions, and Marketing Managers	—	216,800	246,200	14	29,400
Advertising and Promotions Managers	11-2011	38,700	43,800	13	5,200
Marketing Managers	11-2021	178,200	202,400	14	24,200

SOURCE: U.S. Bureau of Labor Statistics, Employment Projections program

Similar Occupations

This table shows a list of occupations with job duties that are similar to those of advertising, promotions, and marketing managers.

Occupation	Job Duties	Entry-Level Education	Median Annual Pay, May 2010
Advertising Sales Agents	Advertising sales agents sell advertising space to businesses and individuals. They contact potential clients, make sales presentations, and maintain client accounts.	High school diploma or equivalent	$45,350
Art Directors	Art directors are responsible for the visual style and images in magazines, newspapers, product packaging, and movie and television productions. They create the overall design and direct others who develop artwork or layouts.	Bachelor's degree	$80,630
Demonstrators and Product Promoters	Demonstrators and product promoters create public interest in products, such as cosmetics, housewares, and food. They encourage people and stores to buy their products by showing the products to prospective customers and answering questions.	High school diploma or equivalent	$23,110
Editors	Editors plan, review, and revise content for publication.	Bachelor's degree	$51,470
Graphic Designers	Graphic designers create visual concepts, by hand or using computer software, to communicate ideas that inspire, inform, or captivate consumers. They help to make an organization recognizable by selecting color, images, or logo designs that represent a particular idea or identity to be used in advertising and promotions.	Bachelor's degree	$43,500
Market Research Analysts	Market research analysts study market conditions in local, regional, or national areas to examine potential sales of a product or service. They help companies understand what products people want, who will buy them, and at what price.	Bachelor's degree	$60,570
Public Relations Managers and Specialists	Public relations managers and specialists create and maintain a favorable public image for their employer or client. They write material for media releases, plan and direct public relations programs, and raise funds for their organizations.	Bachelor's degree	$57,550
Sales Managers	Sales managers direct organizations' sales teams. They set sales goals, analyze data, and develop training programs for the organization's sales representatives.	Bachelor's degree	$98,530
Technical Writers	Technical writers, also called technical communicators, produce instruction manuals and other supporting documents to communicate complex and technical information more easily. They also develop, gather, and disseminate technical information among customers, designers, and manufacturers.	Bachelor's degree	$63,280
Writers and Authors	Writers and authors develop original written content for advertisements, books, magazines, movie and television scripts, songs, and online publications.	Bachelor's degree	$55,420

Contacts for More Information

For more information about advertising managers, visit American Association of Advertising Agencies

Suggested citation:

Bureau of Labor Statistics, U.S. Department of Labor, Occupational Outlook Handbook, 2012-13 Edition, Advertising, Promotions, and Marketing Managers, on the Internet at http://www.bls.gov/ooh/management/advertising-promotions-and-marketing-managers.htm .

Architectural and Engineering Managers

Quick Facts: Architectural and Engineering Managers	
2010 Median Pay	$119,260 per year $57.34 per hour
Entry-Level Education	Bachelor's degree
Work Experience in a Related Occupation	More than 5 years
On-the-job Training	None
Number of Jobs, 2010	176,800
Job Outlook, 2010-20	9% (Slower than average)
Employment Change, 2010-20	15,200

What Architectural and Engineering Managers Do

Architectural and engineering managers plan, coordinate, and direct activities in architecture and engineering, including research and development in these fields.

Duties

Architectural and engineering managers typically do the following:

- Make detailed plans to reach technical goals, such as development of new products and designs
- Manage research and development teams that produce new products, processes, or designs, or improve existing ones
- Check the technical accuracy of the work and soundness of the methods their staff uses
- Direct and coordinate the design of equipment and machinery
- Confer with other levels of management on architectural and engineering activities
- Propose budgets for projects and programs and determine staff, training, and equipment needs
- Hire, assign, and supervise staff

Architectural and engineering managers use their knowledge in architecture or engineering to oversee a variety of activities. They determine technical goals, such as improving manufacturing or building processes, or developing new products or designs, and then they make detailed plans to accomplish these goals.

They may direct and coordinate production, operations, quality assurance, testing, or maintenance in industrial plants. They may develop the overall concepts of a new product or identify technical problems preventing the completion of a project.

Architectural and engineering managers must know how to budget, hire, and supervise. They propose budgets for projects and programs and determine staff, training, and equipment needs. Architectural and engineering managers hire and assign people to carry out specific parts of each project. They supervise the work of these employees and set administrative procedures, policies, or standards, such as environmental standards.

Architectural and engineering managers spend a great deal of time coordinating the activities of their unit with the activities of other units or organizations. They confer with other managers, including financial, production, and marketing managers, and with contractors and equipment and materials suppliers.

Work Environment

Architectural and engineering managers held about 176,800 jobs in 2010. They spend most of their time working in offices. Some may also work in laboratories and industrial production plants or at construction sites.

As shown below, 21 percent of architectural and engineering managers worked for architectural and engineering services firms in 2010:

Architectural, engineering, and related services	21%
Semiconductor and other electronic component manufacturing	5
Navigational, measuring, electromedical, and control instruments manufacturing	5
Research and development in the physical, engineering, and life sciences	5
Management of companies and enterprises	4

Work Schedules

Architectural and engineering managers may need to work long hours to meet production deadlines. Most worked full time. In 2010, 47 percent worked more than 40 hours a week. They may also experience considerable pressure to meet technical goals on a short deadline or within a tight budget.

How to Become an Architectural or Engineering Manager

Architectural and engineering managers usually advance to management positions after years of employment in their fields. Nearly

Architectural and engineering managers need to review plans when they oversee projects.

all architectural and engineering managers, therefore, have at least a bachelor's degree in some specialty of engineering or a professional degree in architecture.

Education

Nearly all architectural and engineering managers have at least a bachelor's degree in an engineering specialty or a professional degree in architecture. Many also gain business management skills by completing a master's degree in engineering management (MEM) or technology management (MSTM), or a master's in business administration (MBA), either before or after advancing to management positions. Employers often pay for such training. Typically, those who prefer to manage in technical areas pursue an MEM or MSTM, and those interested in more general management skills earn an MBA.

Engineering management programs typically include classes in accounting, engineering economy, financial management, industrial and human resources management, industrial psychology, and quality control. Technology management programs usually provide instruction in production and operations management, project management, computer applications, quality control, safety and health issues, statistics, and general management principles.

Important Qualities

Analytical skills. Architectural and engineering managers should be able to evaluate information and solve complex problems.

Communication skills. Architectural and engineering managers oversee staff and confer with other levels of management. They must be able to communicate well to lead teams in meeting goals.

Detail oriented. Architectural and engineering managers must pay attention to detail. Their duties require an understanding of complex systems, and a minor error can cause major problems.

Math skills. Architectural and engineering managers use calculus and other advanced mathematics to develop new products and processes.

Organizational skills. Architectural and engineering managers keep track of many workers, schedules, and budgets all at once.

Technical skills. Managers in these fields must thoroughly understand the specific area (architecture or a specific type of engineering) that they are managing.

Licenses

Architectural and engineering managers are typically experienced architects or engineers, and many states license these occupations. For more information, see the profiles on architects and engineering occupations .

Work Experience

Architectural and engineering managers advance to their positions after years of employment in their fields. Managers typically have experience working on increasingly difficult projects, developing designs, solving problems, and making decisions. Before moving up to a management position, they also typically have experience leading engineering teams.

Pay

Architectural and Engineering Managers
Median annual wages, May 2010

Architectural and Engineering Managers	$119,260
Management Occupations	$91,440
Total, All Occupations	$33,840

Note: All Occupations includes all occupations in the U.S. Economy.
Source: U.S. Bureau of Labor Statistics, Occupational Employment Statistics

The median annual wage of architectural and engineering managers was $119,260 in May 2010. The median wage is the wage at which half of the workers in an occupation earned more than that amount and half earned less. The lowest 10 percent earned less than $77,440, and the top 10 percent earned more than $166,400.

Median annual wages in selected industries employing architectural and engineering managers in 2010 were as follows:

Research and development in the physical, engineering, and life sciences	$138,590
Semiconductor and other electronic component manufacturing	132,720
Navigational, measuring, electromedical, and control instruments manufacturing	132,380
Management of companies and enterprises	122,480
Architectural, engineering, and related services	119,830

In addition, architectural and engineering managers, especially those at higher levels, often receive more benefits—such as expense accounts, stock-option plans, and bonuses—than do workers who are not managers in their organizations.

Architectural and engineering managers may need to work long hours to meet production deadlines. In 2010, 47 percent worked more than 40 hours a week. They may also experience considerable pressure to meet technical goals on a short deadline or within a tight budget.

Job Outlook

Architectural and Engineering Managers
Percent change in employment, projected 2010-20

Total, All Occupations	14%
Architectural and Engineering Managers	9%
Management Occupations	7%

Note: All Occupations includes all occupations in the U.S. Economy.
Source: U.S. Bureau of Labor Statistics, Employment Projections program

Employment of architectural and engineering managers is projected to grow 9 percent from 2010 to 2020, slower than average for all occupations. Employment growth should be affected by many of the same factors that affect the growth of the staff that these managers supervise. However, job growth for managers is expected to be somewhat slower than for architects and engineers because companies are increasingly outsourcing research and development to specialized engineering services firms, leading to some consolidation of management.

Job Prospects

Job opportunities should be better in rapidly growing disciplines, such as environmental and biomedical engineering, than in more slowly growing areas, such as electrical and mechanical engineering. Those with advanced technical knowledge and strong communication skills will likely be in the best position to become managers.

Because architectural and engineering managers are involved in the financial, production, and marketing activities of their firm, business management skills are a plus for those seeking management positions. In addition to the openings resulting from employment growth, job openings will result from the need to replace managers who retire or move into other occupations.

Employment projections data for architectural and engineering managers, 2010-20

Occupational Title	SOC Code	Employment, 2010	Projected Employment, 2020	Change, 2010-20 Percent	Numeric
Architectural and Engineering Managers	11-9041	176,800	192,000	9	15,200

SOURCE: U.S. Bureau of Labor Statistics, Employment Projections program

Similar Occupations

This table shows a list of occupations with job duties that are similar to those of architectural and engineering managers.

Occupation	Job Duties	Entry-Level Education	Median Annual Pay, May 2010
Architects	Architects plan and design buildings and other structures.	Bachelor's degree	$72,550
Construction Managers	Construction managers plan, coordinate, budget, and supervise construction projects from early development to completion.	Associate's degree	$83,860
Industrial Production Managers	Industrial production managers oversee the daily operations of manufacturing and related plants. They coordinate, plan, and direct the activities used to create a wide range of goods, such as cars, computer equipment, or paper products.	Bachelor's degree	$87,160
Natural Sciences Managers	Natural sciences managers supervise the work of scientists, including chemists, physicists, and biologists. They direct research and development projects and coordinate activities such as testing, quality control, and production.	Bachelor's degree	$116,020

Contacts for More Information

For information on architecture and engineering management programs, visit The American Institute of Architects , ABET , The Association of Technology, Management, and Applied Engineering

Suggested citation:

Bureau of Labor Statistics, U.S. Department of Labor, Occupational Outlook Handbook, 2012-13 Edition, Architectural and Engineering Managers, on the Internet at http://www.bls.gov/ooh/management/architectural-and-engineering-managers.htm.

Compensation and Benefits Managers

Quick Facts: Compensation and Benefits Managers	
2010 Median Pay	$89,270 per year $42.92 per hour
Entry-Level Education	Bachelor's degree
Work Experience in a Related Occupation	1 to 5 years
On-the-job Training	None
Number of Jobs, 2010	31,800
Job Outlook, 2010-20	3% (Slower than average)
Employment Change, 2010-20	900

What Compensation and Benefits Managers Do

Compensation managers plan, direct, and coordinate how and how much an organization pays its employees. Benefits managers do the same for retirement plans, health insurance, and other benefits an organization offers its employees.

Duties

Compensation and benefits managers typically do the following:
- Set the organization's pay structure and benefits offerings so the organization can compete for employees
- Participate in or buy salary surveys to see how their organization's pay compares with that in other organizations
- Determine competitive wage rates and develop or modify compensation plans

- Evaluate employee benefits policies to assess whether they are current, competitive, and legal
- Coordinate and supervise the work activities of specialists and support staff
- Oversee the distribution of pay and benefits information to the organization's employees
- Ensure that pay and benefits plans comply with federal and state regulations
- Collaborate with outside partners such as benefits vendors and investment managers
- Prepare a program budget and keep operations within budget

Although some managers administer both the compensation and benefits programs in an organization, other managers—particularly at large organizations—often specialize and oversee one or the other. All managers, however, routinely meet with senior staff, managers of other

Compensation and benefits managers often give presentations on different benefit plans.

human resources departments, and the financial officers of their organization.

In addition to their administrative responsibilities, compensation and benefits managers also have several technical and analytical duties. For example, they may do complex data analysis to determine the best pay and benefits plans for an organization. They also must monitor trends affecting pay and benefits and assess how their organization can improve its practices or policies. Using a variety of analytical, database, and presentation software, managers frequently identify and present their findings to other managers in the organization.

Compensation managers are responsible for managing an organization's pay structure. They monitor market conditions and government regulations to ensure their pay rates are current and competitive. They may collect and analyze data on wages and salaries, and they evaluate how their organization's pay structure compares with other companies. Compensation managers then use this information to maintain or develop pay scales for an organization. Some also design pay-for-performance plans, which include guidelines for bonuses and incentive pay. They may help to determine commission rates and other incentives for sales staff.

Benefits managers administer a company's employee benefits program, which includes retirement plans and insurance policies such as health, life, and disability. They work closely with benefits vendors and manage the enrollment, renewal, and distribution processes for an organization's employees. They must frequently monitor government regulations and the costs of other plans to ensure that their programs are current and competitive.

Work Environment

Compensation and benefits managers held about 31,800 jobs in 2010 and were employed throughout the economy. About 16 percent were employed in the management of companies and enterprises industry.

They typically work in offices. Most compensation and benefits managers work full time and may work long hours.

How to Become a Compensation or Benefits Manager

Candidates need a combination of education and related work experience to become a compensation and benefits manager.

Education

Compensation and benefits managers need at least a bachelor's degree for most positions, although some jobs require a master's

degree. Because not all undergraduate programs offer a degree in human resources, managers often have a bachelor's degree in business administration, business management, finance, or a related field.

Many employers prefer to hire managers who have a master's degree, particularly one with a concentration in human resources management, finance, or business administration (MBA).

Work Experience

Related work experience is essential for compensation and benefits managers.

Compensation managers usually need experience in compensation or another job where they performed complex financial analysis.

In addition to experience working with benefits plans, most benefits managers must have strong knowledge of benefits practices and government regulations. Work experience in other human resource fields, finance, or management is also helpful for getting a job as a benefits manager.

Certification

Many professional associations for human resources professionals offer classes to enhance the skills of their members. Some associations, including the International Foundation of Employee Benefit Plans and WorldatWork , specialize in compensation and benefits and offer certification programs.

Although not required, certification can show professional expertise and credibility. In fact, many employers prefer to hire certified candidates, and some positions may require certification. Certification programs for management positions often require several years of related work experience to qualify for the credential.

Important Qualities

Analytical skills. Analytical skills are essential for compensation and benefits managers. In addition to analyzing data on salaries and the cost of benefits, they must assess and devise programs that best fit an organization and its employees.

Decision-making skills. Compensation and benefits managers need strong decision-making skills. They must weigh the strengths and weaknesses of different pay structures and benefits plans and choose the best options for an organization.

Managerial skills. Compensation and benefits managers must coordinate the work activities of their staff and properly administer compensation and benefits programs.

Speaking skills. Compensation and benefits managers rely on speaking skills when directing their staff and giving presentations. For example, they may present the advantages of a certain pay scale to management or inform employees of their benefits plan options.

Writing skills. Compensation and benefits managers need strong writing skills to prepare informational materials on compensation and benefits plans for an organization's employees. They also must clearly convey recommendations in written reports.

Pay

Compensation and Benefits Managers
Median annual wages, May 2010

Management Occupations	$91,440
Compensation and Benefits Managers	$89,270
Total, All Occupations	$33,840

Note: All Occupations includes all occupations in the U.S. Economy.
Source: U.S. Bureau of Labor Statistics, Occupational Employment Statistics

The median annual wage of compensation and benefits managers was $89,270 in May 2010. The median wage is the wage at which half the workers in an occupation earned more than that amount and half earned less. The lowest 10 percent earned less than $52,150, and the top 10 percent earned more than $151,090.

Most compensation and benefits managers work full time and may work long hours.

Job Outlook

Compensation and Benefits Managers

Percent change in employment, projected 2010-20

Total, All Occupations	14%
Management Occupations	7%
Compensation and Benefits Managers	3%

Note: All Occupations includes all occupations in the U.S. Economy.
Source: U.S. Bureau of Labor Statistics, Employment Projections program

Employment of compensation and benefits managers is expected to grow 3 percent from 2010 to 2020, slower than the average for all occupations.

Many organizations contract out a portion of their compensation and benefits functions to human resources consulting firms to reduce costs and gain access to technical expertise. For example, to reduce administrative costs, organizations commonly use an outside vendor for processing payroll and insurance claims.

Similarly, as benefits packages grow more complicated, employers increasingly contract out their benefits work to human resources organizations that have expertise in complex benefits programs and knowledge of federal and state regulations. These consulting firms are able to automate tasks and operate overseas call centers, reducing the need for managers.

Therefore, even as healthcare costs rise and healthcare coverage options expand, employment of compensation and benefits managers is not expected to experience comparable growth.

Job Prospects

Candidates are expected to face competition for jobs. Those who have a master's degree, certification, or experience working with compensation or benefits plans should have the best job prospects.

Employment projections data for compensation and benefits managers, 2010-20

Occupational Title	SOC Code	Employment, 2010	Projected Employment, 2020	Change, 2010-20 Percent	Change, 2010-20 Numeric
Compensation and Benefits Managers	11-3111	31,800	32,700	3	900
SOURCE: U.S. Bureau of Labor Statistics, Employment Projections program					

Similar Occupations

This table shows a list of occupations with job duties that are similar to those of compensation and benefits managers.

Occupation	Job Duties	Entry-Level Education	Median Annual Pay, May 2010
Administrative Services Managers	Administrative services managers plan, direct, and coordinate supportive services of an organization. Their specific responsibilities vary by the type of organization and may include keeping records, distributing mail, and planning and maintaining facilities.	High school diploma or equivalent	$77,890
Financial Managers	Financial managers are responsible for the financial health of an organization. They produce financial reports, direct investment activities, and develop strategies and plans for the long-term financial goals of their organization.	Bachelor's degree	$103,910
Human Resources Managers	Human resources managers plan, direct, and coordinate the administrative functions of an organization. They oversee the recruiting, interviewing, and hiring of new staff; consult with top executives on strategic planning; and serve as a link between an organization's management and its employees.	Bachelor's degree	$99,180
Top Executives	Top executives devise strategies and policies to ensure that an organization meets its goals. They plan, direct, and coordinate operational activities of companies and public or private-sector organizations.	See How to Become One	$101,250
Training and Development Managers	Training and development managers plan, direct, and coordinate programs to enhance the knowledge and skills of an organization's employees. They also oversee a staff of training and development specialists.	Bachelor's degree	$89,170
Purchasing Managers, Buyers, and Purchasing Agents	Purchasing managers, buyers, and purchasing agents buy products for organizations to use or resell. They evaluate suppliers, negotiate contracts, and review product quality.	See How to Become One	$58,360
Human Resources Specialists	Human resources specialists recruit, screen, interview, and place workers. They also may handle human resources work in a variety of other areas, such as employee relations, payroll and benefits, and training.	Bachelor's degree	$52,690

Contacts for More Information

For more information about compensation and benefits managers, including certification, visit International Foundation of Employee Benefit Plans , WorldatWork

For information about human resources management careers and certification, visit Society for Human Resource Management

Suggested citation:

Bureau of Labor Statistics, U.S. Department of Labor, Occupational Outlook Handbook, 2012-13 Edition, Compensation and Benefits Managers, on the Internet at http://www.bls.gov/ooh/management/compensation-and-benefits-managers.htm .

Computer and Information Systems Managers

Quick Facts: Computer and Information Systems Managers	
2010 Median Pay	$115,780 per year $55.67 per hour
Entry-Level Education	Bachelor's degree
Work Experience in a Related Occupation	More than 5 years
On-the-job Training	None
Number of Jobs, 2010	307,900
Job Outlook, 2010-20	18% (About as fast as average)
Employment Change, 2010-20	55,800

What Computer and Information Systems Managers Do

Computer and information systems managers, often called information technology managers (IT managers or IT project managers), plan, coordinate, and direct computer-related activities in an organization. They help determine the information technology goals of an organization and are responsible for implementing computer systems to meet those goals.

Duties

Computer and information systems managers typically do the following:

- Analyze their organization's computer needs and recommend possible upgrades to top executives
- Plan and direct installing and upgrading computer hardware and software
- Ensure the security of an organization's network and electronic documents
- Assess the costs and benefits of a new project to justify spending to top executives
- Learn about new technology and look for ways to upgrade their organization's computer systems
- Determine short- and long-term personnel needs for their department
- Plan and direct the work of other IT professionals, including computer systems analysts, software developers, information security analysts, and computer support specialists
- Negotiate with technology vendors to get the highest level of service for their organization

Few managers do all of these duties. There are various types of computer and information systems managers, and the specific duties of each are determined by the size and structure of the firm. Smaller firms may not employ every type of manager.

The following are types of computer and information systems managers:

Chief information officers (CIOs) are responsible for the overall technology strategy of their organizations. They help determine the technology or information goals of an organization and then oversee planning to implement technology to meet those goals.

They may focus on a specific area such as electronic data processing or information systems, but they differ from chief technology officers (CTOs; see next) in that the CIO is more focused on long-term, or "big picture," issues. CIOs who do not have technical expertise and focus solely on the business aspects of creating an overall company vision are included in a separate profile on top executives. For more information, see the profile on top executives .

Chief technology officers (CTOs) evaluate new technology and how it can help their organization. When both CIOs and CTOs are present, the CTO usually has more technical expertise.

The CTO is responsible for designing and recommending the appropriate technology solutions to support the policies and directives issued by the CIO. CTOs also work with different departments to implement the organization's technology plans.

The CTO usually reports directly to the CIO and also may be responsible for overseeing the development of new technologies or other research and development activities. When a company does not have a CIO, the CTO determines the overall technology strategy for the firm and presents it to top executives.

IT directors, including management information systems (MIS) directors, are in charge of their organizations' information technology (IT) departments, and they directly supervise other employees. They help to determine the business requirements for IT systems and they implement the policies that have been chosen by top executives. It is the IT director's job to ensure the availability of data and network services by coordinating IT activities. IT directors also oversee the financial aspects of their department, such as budgeting.

IT security managers oversee their organizations' network and data security. They work with top executives to plan security policies and training for employees. These managers must keep up to date on IT security measures. They also supervise investigations if there is a security violation.

Work Environment

Computer and information systems managers held about 307,900 jobs in 2010.

The largest percentage of computer and information systems

Computer and information systems managers oversee the work of an IT department.

managers works for computer systems design and related services firms. They are employed by both small and large organizations. A smaller, but still considerable, percentage works for financial firms, manufacturing firms, and for federal, state, or local governments.

The following industries employed the most computer and information systems managers in 2010:

Computer systems design and related services	17%
Finance and insurance	14
Manufacturing	9
Management of companies and enterprises	8
Government	7

As network speeds increase, telecommuting is becoming more common. Although few managers can work remotely, many have to supervise employees who work from home.

Work Schedules

More than 90 percent of computer and information systems managers work full time. Many of them must work overtime to solve problems. In 2010, about 24 percent worked more than 50 hours per week.

How to Become a Computer and Information Systems Manager

A bachelor's degree in computer or information science plus related work experience is typically required. Many computer and information systems managers also have a graduate degree.

Education

Computer and information systems managers normally must have a bachelor's degree in a computer- or information science-related field. This usually takes 4 years to complete and includes courses in computer programming, software development, and mathematics. Management information systems (MIS) programs usually include business classes as well as computer-related ones.

Many organizations require their computer and information systems managers to have a graduate degree as well. A Master of Business Administration (MBA) is common and takes 2 years beyond the undergraduate level to complete. Many people pursuing an MBA take classes while working, an option that can increase the time required to complete it.

Work Experience

Most jobs for computer and information systems managers require several years of experience in a related information technology (IT) job. Lower level management positions may require only a few years of experience. Directors are more likely to need 5 to 10 years of related work experience. A chief technology officer (CTO), who oversees the technology plan for an organization, may need more than 15 years of experience in the IT field before being considered for a job.

The number of years of experience required varies by organization. Generally, smaller companies do not require as much experience as larger, more established ones.

Computer systems are used throughout the economy, and IT employees may gain experience in a variety of industries. However, an applicant's work experience should be related to the industry the applicant plans to manage. For example, an IT security manager should have previously worked in information security. A hospital IT director should have experience in the healthcare field.

Advancement

Most computer and information systems managers start out as lower level managers and advance to higher positions within the IT department. IT directors or project managers can advance to become chief technology officers (CTOs). A CTO or other manager who is especially business-minded can advance to become a chief information officer (CIO), who is in charge of all IT-related decisions in an organization.

Important Qualities

Analytical skills. IT managers must be able to analyze a problem, consider ways to solve the problem, and select the best one.

Communication skills. IT managers must be able to explain their work to top executives and give clear instructions to their subordinates.

Decision-making skills. Some IT managers must make important decisions about how to allocate their organizations' resources in order to reach their goals.

Leadership skills. IT managers must be able to lead and motivate IT teams or departments so workers are efficient and effective.

Organizational skills. Some IT managers must coordinate the work of several different IT departments to make the organization run efficiently.

Pay

Computer and Information Systems Managers
Median annual wages, May 2010

Computer and Information Systems Managers	$115,780
Management Occupations	$91,440
Total, All Occupations	$33,840

Note: All Occupations includes all occupations in the U.S. Economy.
Source: U.S. Bureau of Labor Statistics, Occupational Employment Statistics

The median annual wage of computer and information systems managers was $115,780 in May 2010. The median wage is the wage at which half the workers in an occupation earned more than that amount and half earned less. The lowest 10 percent earned less than $71,420, and the top 10 percent earned more than $166,400.

As the following table shows, the median annual wage varies by industry:

Computer systems design and related services	$123,570
Finance and insurance	118,010
Manufacturing	117,050
Government	110,030
Health care and social assistance	101,840

More than 90 percent of computer and information systems managers work full time. Many of them must work overtime to solve problems. In 2010, about 24 percent worked more than 50 hours per week.

Job Outlook

Computer and Information Systems Managers
Percent change in employment, projected 2010-20

Computer and Information Systems Managers	18%
Total, All Occupations	14%
Management Occupations	7%

Note: All Occupations includes all occupations in the U.S. Economy.
Source: U.S. Bureau of Labor Statistics, Employment Projections program

Employment of computer and information systems managers is projected grow 18 percent from 2010 to 2020, about as fast as the average for all occupations.

Growth will be driven by organizations upgrading their information technology (IT) systems and switching to newer, faster, and more mobile networks. Consequently, more employees at all management levels will be needed to help in the transition.

Additional growth will likely result from the need to increase security in IT departments. More attention is being directed at cyber threats, a trend that is expected to increase over the next decade.

A number of jobs in this occupation is expected to be created in the healthcare industry, which is far behind in its use of information technology. This industry is expected to greatly increase IT use, resulting in job growth.

An increase in cloud computing may shift some IT services to computer systems design and related services firms, concentrating jobs in that industry.

A number of IT jobs are at risk of being sent to other countries with lower wages, dampening some employment growth. However, this risk may be reduced by a recent trend of firms moving jobs to lower cost regions of the United States instead of to other countries.

Job Prospects

Prospects should be favorable for this occupation. Many companies note that it is difficult to find qualified applicants for positions.

Because innovation is fast paced in IT, opportunities should be best for those who have knowledge of the newest technology.

Employment projecions data for computer and information systems managers, 2010-20

Occupational Title	SOC Code	Employment, 2010	Projected Employment, 2020	Change, 2010-20	
				Percent	Numeric
Computer and Information Systems Managers	11-3021	307,900	363,700	18	55,800
SOURCE: U.S. Bureau of Labor Statistics, Employment Projections program					

Similar Occupations

This table shows a list of occupations with job duties that are similar to those of computer and information systems managers.

Occupation	Job Duties	Entry-Level Education	Median Annual Pay, May 2010
Computer Hardware Engineers	Computer hardware engineers research, design, develop, and test computer equipment such as chips, circuit boards, or routers. By solving complex problems in computer hardware, these engineers create rapid advances in computer technology.	Bachelor's degree	$98,810
Computer Programmers	Computer programmers write code to create software programs. They turn the program designs created by software developers and engineers into instructions that a computer can follow.	Bachelor's degree	$71,380
Computer Systems Analysts	Computer systems analysts study an organization's current computer systems and procedures and make recommendations to management to help the organization operate more efficiently and effectively. They bring business and information technology (IT) together by understanding the needs and limitations of both.	Bachelor's degree	$77,740
Database Administrators	Database administrators use software to store and organize data, such as financial information and customer shipping records. They make sure that data are available to users and are secure from unauthorized access.	Bachelor's degree	$73,490
Information Security Analysts, Web Developers, and Computer Network Architects	Information security analysts, web developers, and computer network architects all use information technology (IT) to advance their organization's goals. Security analysts ensure a firm's information stays safe from cyberattacks. Web developers create websites to help firms have a public face. Computer network architects create the internal networks all workers within organizations use.	Bachelor's degree	$75,660
Network and Computer Systems Administrators	Network and computer systems administrators are responsible for the day-to-day operation of an organization's computer networks. They organize, install, and support an organization's computer systems, including local area networks (LANs), wide area networks (WANs), network segments, intranets, and other data communication systems.	Bachelor's degree	$69,160
Software Developers	Software developers are the creative minds behind computer programs. Some develop the applications that allow people to do specific tasks on a computer or other device. Others develop the underlying systems that run the devices or control networks.	Bachelor's degree	$90,530
Top Executives	Top executives devise strategies and policies to ensure that an organization meets its goals. They plan, direct, and coordinate operational activities of companies and public or private-sector organizations.	See How to Become One	$101,250

Contacts for More Information

For more information about computer careers, visit Association for Computing Machinery , Institute of Electrical and Electronics Engineers Computer Society , Computing Research Association

For more information about an education in information technology, visit National Workforce Center for Emerging Technologies

For more information about opportunities for women pursuing information technology careers, visit National Center for Women and Information Technology

Suggested citation:

Bureau of Labor Statistics, U.S. Department of Labor, Occupational Outlook Handbook, 2012-13 Edition, Computer and Information Systems Managers, on the Internet at http://www.bls.gov/ooh/management/computer-and-information-systems-managers.htm .

Construction Managers

Quick Facts: Construction Managers	
2010 Median Pay	$83,860 per year $40.32 per hour
Entry-Level Education	Associate's degree
Work Experience in a Related Occupation	More than 5 years
On-the-job Training	None
Number of Jobs, 2010	523,100
Job Outlook, 2010-20	17% (About as fast as average)
Employment Change, 2010-20	86,600

What Construction Managers Do

Construction managers plan, coordinate, budget, and supervise construction projects from early development to completion.

Duties

Construction managers typically do the following:

- Prepare and negotiate cost estimates, budgets, and work timetables
- Select appropriate construction methods and strategies
- Interpret and explain contracts and technical information to workers and other professionals
- Report on work progress and budget matters to clients
- Collaborate with architects, engineers, and other construction and building specialists
- Instruct and supervise construction personnel and activities onsite
- Respond to work delays and other problems and emergencies
- Select, hire, and instruct laborers and subcontractors
- Comply with legal requirements, building and safety codes, and other regulations

Construction managers, often called general contractors or project managers, coordinate and supervise a wide variety of projects, including the building of all types of residential, commercial, and industrial structures, roads, bridges, powerplants, schools, and hospitals. They oversee specialized contractors and other personnel. Construction managers schedule and coordinate all design and construction processes to ensure a productive and safe work environment. They also make sure jobs are completed on time and on budget with the right amount of tools, equipment, and materials. Many managers also are responsible for obtaining necessary permits and licenses. They are often responsible for multiple projects at a time.

Construction managers work closely with other building specialists, such as architects, engineers, and a variety of trade workers, such as stonemasons, electricians, and carpenters. Projects may require specialists in everything from structural metalworking and painting, to landscaping, building roads, installing carpets, and excavating sites. Depending on the project, construction managers also may interact with lawyers and local government officials. For example, when working on city-owned property or municipal buildings, managers sometimes confer with city council members to ensure that all regulations are met.

For projects too large to be managed by one person, such as office buildings and industrial complexes, a construction manager would only be in charge of one part of the project. Each construction manager would oversee a specific construction phase and choose subcontractors to complete it. Construction managers may need to collaborate and coordinate with other construction managers who are responsible for different aspects of the project.

To maximize efficiency and productivity, construction managers often use specialized cost-estimating and planning software to effectively budget the time and money required to complete specific projects. Many managers also use software to determine the best way to get materials to the building site. For more information, see the profile on cost estimators .

Work Environment

Construction managers held about 523,100 jobs in 2010. The industries that employed the most construction managers in 2010 were as follows:

Nonresidential building construction	9%
Residential building construction	5
Building equipment contractors	5
Heavy and civil engineering construction	4
Architectural, engineering, and related services	2

Many construction managers work from a main office, but most work out of a field office at the construction site where they monitor the project and make daily decisions about construction activities. For those who manage multiple projects, frequent travel may be common.

Construction managers supervise a project from start to finish.

Work Schedules

Most construction managers work full time. However, the need to meet deadlines and to respond to delays and emergencies often requires longer hours. Construction managers also can be on call 24 hours a day for projects that continue around the clock.

How to Become a Construction Manager

Employers increasingly prefer candidates with both work experience and a bachelor's degree in a construction-related field. However, some construction managers may qualify with a high school diploma and by working many years in a construction trade. Certification, although not required, is becoming increasingly important.

Education

It is increasingly important for construction managers to have a bachelor's degree in construction science, construction management, architecture or engineering. As construction processes become increasingly complex, employers are placing more importance on specialized education.

More than 100 colleges and universities offer bachelor's degree programs in construction science, building science, or construction engineering. These programs include courses in project control and management, design, construction methods and materials, cost estimation, building codes and standards, and contract administration. Courses in mathematics and statistics are also relevant.

An associate's degree combined with work experience may be enough for some positions. A number of 2-year colleges offer construction management or construction technology programs.

In addition, those with a high school diploma and years of relevant work experience will be able to work as construction managers, though they will do so primarily as self-employed general contractors.

Work Experience

Practical construction experience is important when entering the occupation because it reduces the need for initial on-the-job training. Internships, cooperative education programs, and long-term jobs in the industry provide that experience. Some construction managers become qualified solely through extensive construction experience, spending many years in carpentry, masonry, or general subcontracting.

Training

New construction managers are generally hired as assistants to experienced managers before beginning independent work. Work as an assistant can last from several weeks to several months, depending on the firm.

Certification

Certification is becoming increasingly important for construction managers. Although not required, certification can be valuable because it can demonstrate knowledge and experience.

The Construction Management Association of America awards the Certified Construction Manager (CCM) designation to workers who have the required experience and who pass a technical exam. Applicants for this certification must also complete a self-study course that covers the professional role of a construction manager, legal issues, the allocation of risk, and other topics related to construction management.

The American Institute of Constructors awards the Associate Constructor (AC) and Certified Professional Constructor (CPC) designations to candidates who meet its requirements and pass the appropriate construction exams.

Important Qualities

Analytical skills. Most managers plan a project strategy and must identify and solve unexpected issues and delays.

Decision-making skills. Construction managers choose personnel and subcontractors for specific tasks. Often, these decisions must be made quickly to meet deadlines.

Initiative. Self-employed construction managers generate their own business opportunities and must be proactive to find new clients. They often market their services, bid on jobs, and learn how to work on a wide variety of projects.

Managerial skills. Construction managers address budget matters and coordinate and supervise workers. Choosing competent staff and employees, as well as establishing good working relationships with them, is critical. Managers also must delegate tasks to workers, subcontractors, and other lower level managers effectively.

Speaking skills. Managers must give clear orders, explain complex information to workers and clients, and discuss technical details with other building specialists. Self-employed construction managers must get their own projects, so the need to sell their services to potential clients is critical.

Technical skills. Managers must know construction methods and technologies, and be able to interpret contracts and technical drawings.

Time-management skills. Construction managers must meet deadlines. They ensure that construction phases are completed on time so that the next phase can begin. For instance, constructing a building foundation cannot begin until the land excavation is completed.

Writing skills. Construction managers must write proposals, plans, and budgets clearly for clients and others involved in the building process.

Pay

Construction Managers
Median annual wages, May 2010

Management Occupations	$91,440
Construction Managers	$83,860
Total, All Occupations	$33,840

Note: All Occupations includes all occupations in the U.S. Economy.
Source: U.S. Bureau of Labor Statistics, Occupational Employment Statistics

The median annual wage of construction managers was $83,860 in May 2010. The median wage is the wage at which half the workers in an occupation earned more than that amount and half earned less. The lowest 10 percent earned less than $50,240, and the highest 10 percent earned more than $150,250.

Salaried construction managers also may earn bonuses and overtime pay. About two-thirds of construction managers are self-employed. Their earnings are highly dependent on the amount of business they generate.

Most construction managers work full time. However, the need to meet deadlines and to respond to delays and emergencies often requires longer hours. Construction managers also can be on call 24 hours a day for projects that continue around the clock.

Job Outlook

Construction Managers
Percent change in employment, projected 2010-20

Construction Managers	17%
Total, All Occupations	14%
Management Occupations	7%

Note: All Occupations includes all occupations in the U.S. Economy.
Source: U.S. Bureau of Labor Statistics, Employment Projections program

Employment of construction managers is expected to grow 17

percent from 2010 to 2020, about as fast as the average for all occupations.

Construction managers will be needed as the level and variety of construction projects expands. Population and business growth will result in new construction of residential dwellings, office buildings, retail outlets, hospitals, schools, restaurants, and other structures.

In addition to new construction projects, a growing emphasis on retrofitting buildings to make them more energy efficient should create additional jobs for construction managers. The need to address portions of the national infrastructure will also spur employment growth, as roads, bridges, and sewer pipe systems are upgraded or replaced.

As building construction companies' budgets remain tight, firms increasingly will focus on hiring specialized construction managers to ensure that projects are completed on time and within budget. In addition, construction processes and building technology are becoming more complex, requiring greater oversight and spurring demand for specialized management personnel. Sophisticated technology, worker safety, environmental protection, and new laws setting standards for

building and construction material also will drive employment growth.

Job Prospects

Job opportunities for qualified jobseekers are expected to be good. Those with a bachelor's degree in construction science, construction management, or civil engineering, coupled with construction experience, will have the best job prospects.

Employment growth will provide many new job openings. A substantial number of construction managers are expected to retire over the next decade, resulting in additional job opportunities.

Employment of construction managers, like that of many other construction workers, is sensitive to fluctuations in the economy. On the one hand, workers in these trades may experience periods of unemployment when the overall level of construction falls. On the other hand, peak periods of building activity may produce abundant job opportunities for construction managers.

Employment projections data for construction managers, 2010-20

Occupational Title	SOC Code	Employment, 2010	Projected Employment, 2020	Change, 2010-20	
				Percent	Numeric
Construction Managers	11-9021	523,100	609,600	17	86,600
SOURCE: U.S. Bureau of Labor Statistics, Employment Projections program					

Similar Occupations

This table shows a list of occupations with job duties that are similar to those of construction managers.

Occupation	Job Duties	Entry-Level Education	Median Annual Pay, May 2010
Architects	Architects plan and design buildings and other structures.	Bachelor's degree	$72,550
Architectural and Engineering Managers	Architectural and engineering managers plan, coordinate, and direct activities in architecture and engineering, including research and development in these fields.	Bachelor's degree	$119,260
Civil Engineers	Civil engineers design and supervise large construction projects, including roads, buildings, airports, tunnels, dams, bridges, and systems for water supply and sewage treatment.	Bachelor's degree	$77,560
Cost Estimators	Cost estimators collect and analyze data to estimate the time, money, resources, and labor required for product manufacturing, construction projects, or services. Some specialize in a particular industry or product type.	Bachelor's degree	$57,860
Landscape Architects	Landscape architects plan and design land areas for parks, recreational facilities, highways, airports, and other properties. Projects include subdivisions and commercial, industrial, and residential sites.	Bachelor's degree	$62,090

Contacts for More Information

For information about construction manager certification, visit American Institute of Constructors

For information about construction management and construction manager certification, visit Construction Management Association of America

For information on accredited construction science and management educational programs, visit American Council for Construction Education ,

National Center for Construction Education and Research

Suggested citation:

Bureau of Labor Statistics, U.S. Department of Labor, Occupational Outlook Handbook, 2012-13 Edition, Construction Managers, on the Internet at http://www.bls.gov/ooh/management/construction-managers.htm .

Elementary, Middle, and High School Principals

Quick Facts: Elementary, Middle, and High School Principals	
2010 Median Pay	$86,970 per year
Entry-Level Education	Master's degree
Work Experience in a Related Occupation	1 to 5 years
On-the-job Training	None
Number of Jobs, 2010	236,100
Job Outlook, 2010-20	10% (About as fast as average)
Employment Change, 2010-20	23,200

What Elementary, Middle, and High School Principals Do

Elementary, middle, and high school principals lead teachers and other members of school staff. They manage the day-to-day operations of elementary, middle, and high schools. They set goals and objectives and evaluate the school's progress toward meeting them.

Duties

Elementary, middle, and high school principals typically do the following:

- Supervise teachers and other school staff, such as counselors and librarians
- Observe and monitor teachers to evaluate their effectiveness
- Help teachers improve their teaching skills by arranging professional development programs and mentorships
- Ensure that staff have the tools and resources they need to do their jobs effectively
- Discipline students and help teachers manage students' behavior
- Meet with parents and teachers to discuss students' progress and behavior
- Review test scores and other data to assess the school's progress toward local, state, and federal standards
- Manage the school's budget and finances
- Ensure school facilities are safe for students and staff
- Advocate on behalf of the school to ensure it has the necessary financial support

Elementary, middle, and high school principals provide leadership to teachers and other members of school staff and manage the day-to-day operations of schools.

Elementary, middle, and high school principals manage the overall operation of schools, including building maintenance and cafeteria services. In addition, they set and oversee academic standards and ensure that teachers have the tools and resources, such as training, necessary to meet these standards. Principals establish the school as a resource to students and their families, by ensuring schools have strong counseling, a special education program, and before- and after-school child care programs.

Principals serve as the public face of their school. They meet with superintendents, legislators, and members of the community to ensure the school has the resources it needs to serve its students. They are also responsible for responding to the concerns of parents and members of the community.

The job duties of principals vary by the size of the school and the school district. In larger schools and districts, principals have more resources and staff to help them achieve goals and meet standards. For example, large school districts may have instructional coordinators who help with data analysis and with teachers' professional development. However, principals in large districts may have less flexibility and may need to follow rules and guidelines set at the district level. Those in small school districts need to do all of these duties themselves and may have more flexibility to try new ideas.

Many schools have assistant principals that help principals with school administration. Assistant principals often take the lead on student safety and discipline. They may interact with the students more than the principal does. In addition, assistant principals may administer student activities, help coordinate buses, and supervise building and grounds maintenance. Larger schools may have several assistant principals.

Work Environment

Elementary, middle, and high school principals held about 236,100 jobs in 2010.

Elementary, middle, and high school principals are employed in public and private schools. Some work in public magnet and charter schools. Others work in private religious and secular schools.

Elementary, middle, and high school principals hold leadership positions with significant responsibility. Most find working with students extremely rewarding. Coordinating and interacting with faculty, parents, students, community members, and state and local policymakers can be fast paced and stimulating, but demanding. Principals are held accountable for their schools meeting state and federal guidelines for student performance and teacher qualifications, which can be stressful.

Work Schedules

Generally, principals work full time. However, they also sometimes work in the evening to meet parents and other members of the community and to attend school functions, such as concerts and athletic events.

Many principals work year-round and do not have summers off, even if students are not in school. During the summer, principals prepare for the upcoming school year.

How to Become an Elementary, Middle, or High School Principal

Most schools require elementary, middle, and high school principals to have a master's degree in education administration or leadership. Most principals also have experience as teachers.

Education

In public schools, principals often must have a master's degree in education leadership or education administration. These programs prepare future principals to lead teachers and other instructional staff, prepare and manage budgets, set goals and carry out plans to meet them, and work with parents and the community.

Education leadership or administration programs require candidates to have a bachelor's degree in education, school counseling, or a related field to enter the program.

Work Experience

Principals often gain experience in education by working as a teacher before entering a master's program or applying for a job as a school principal. For information about how to become a teacher, see the profiles on kindergarten and elementary school teachers , middle school teachers , and high school teachers .

Licenses

Most states require public school principals to be licensed as school administrators. Licensure requirements vary from state to state, but most require a master's degree or some other training. Some require candidates to pass a test and take continuing education classes to keep their license. Working with a mentor may be required, as well. Some states have alternative programs for job candidates who do not have a degree in education administration or leadership but have experience in another field.

Principals in private schools do not have to be licensed as school administrators.

Advancement

An assistant principal can advance to become a principal. Some principals advance to become superintendents. Others become instructional coordinators. For more information, see the profile on instructional coordinators .

Important Qualities

Communication skills. Principals need good communication skills to explain the goals and vision of the school. They also need to be able to advocate on behalf of the school to their community.

Critical-thinking skills. Principals need to analyze data from students' tests and evaluate trends in the data to determine how best to meet students' needs and where the school needs to improve.

Decision-making skills. Principals are responsible for students, staff members, and matters that affect the school community. They make decisions often, sometimes quickly, and must be able to consider many factors.

Leadership skills. Principals set educational goals and establish policies and procedures for the school. They need to be able to motivate and inspire teachers and other staff members to improve their skills and do their best work.

People skills. Principals work with many different members of the community, as well as teachers, students, and parents. They need to be able to develop good working relationships with all groups.

Problem-solving skills. Teachers, students, and other staff members bring problems to the attention of the principal. Principals need to be able to think creatively to develop solutions.

Pay

Elementary, Middle, and High School Principals
Median annual wages, May 2010

Management Occupations	$91,440
Elementary, Middle, and High School Principals	$86,970
Total, All Occupations	$33,840

Note: All Occupations includes all occupations in the U.S. Economy.
Source: U.S. Bureau of Labor Statistics, Occupational Employment Statistics

The median annual wage for elementary, middle, and high school principals was $86,970 in May 2010. The median wage is the wage at which half the workers in an occupation earned more than that amount and half earned less. The lowest 10 percent earned less than $58,300, and the top 10 percent earned more than $129,480.

Generally, principals work full time. However, they also sometimes work in the evening to meet parents and other members of the community and to attend school functions, such as concerts and athletic events.

Many principals work year-round and do not have summers off, even if students are not in school. During the summer, principals prepare for the upcoming school year.

Job Outlook

Elementary, Middle, and High School Principals
Percent change in employment, projected 2010-20

Total, All Occupations	14%
Elementary, Middle, and High School Principals	10%
Management Occupations	7%

Note: All Occupations includes all occupations in the U.S. Economy.
Source: U.S. Bureau of Labor Statistics, Employment Projections program

Employment of elementary, middle, and high school principals is projected to grow by 10 percent from 2010 to 2020, about as fast as the average for all occupations. Growth is expected due to increases in enrollment. However, employment growth will vary by region.

From 2010 to 2020, the number of students is projected to increase. As student enrollment grows, the number of schools and principals needed to accommodate these students will rise. As a result, demand for principals is expected to grow.

Although overall student enrollment is expected to grow, there will be variation by region. Enrollment is projected to grow fastest in the South and West. In the Midwest, enrollment is expected to hold steady, and the Northeast is projected to have declines in enrollment. As a result, employment growth for principals is expected to be faster in the South and West than in the Midwest and Northeast.

However, despite expected increases in enrollment, employment growth for public school principals will depend on state and local government budgets. When state and local governments have budget deficits, they may lay off employees, including principals. As a result, employment growth of principals may be somewhat slowed by state and local government budget deficits.

Employment projections data for elementary, middle, and high school principals, 2010-20

Occupational Title	SOC Code	Employment, 2010	Projected Employment, 2020	Change, 2010-20 Percent	Numeric
Education Administrators, Elementary and Secondary School	11-9032	236,100	259,300	10	23,200
SOURCE: U.S. Bureau of Labor Statistics, Employment Projections program					

Similar Occupations

This table shows a list of occupations with job duties that are similar to those of elementary, middle, and high school principals.

Occupation	Job Duties	Entry-Level Education	Median Annual Pay, May 2010
Career and Technical Education Teachers	Career and technical education teachers help students in middle school and high school develop career-related and technical skills. They help students explore or prepare to enter a particular occupation, such as one in auto repair, healthcare, business, or the culinary arts.	Bachelor's degree	$53,920
High School Teachers	High school teachers help prepare students for life after graduation. They teach academic lessons and various skills that students will need to attend college and to enter the job market.	Bachelor's degree	$53,230
Instructional Coordinators	Instructional coordinators oversee school districts' curriculums and teaching standards. They work with teachers and school administrators to implement new teaching techniques to improve the quality of education.	Master's degree	$58,830
Kindergarten and Elementary School Teachers	Kindergarten and elementary school teachers prepare younger students for future schooling by teaching them the basics of subjects such as math and reading.	Bachelor's degree	$51,380
Librarians	Librarians help people find information from many sources. They maintain library collections and do other work as needed to keep the library running.	Master's degree	$54,500
Middle School Teachers	Middle school teachers educate students, most of whom are in sixth through eighth grades. They help students build on the fundamentals they learned in elementary school and prepare them for the more difficult lessons they will learn in high school.	Bachelor's degree	$51,960
Preschool Teachers	Preschool teachers educate and care for children, usually ages 3 to 5, who have not yet entered kindergarten. They explain reading, writing, science, and other subjects in a way that young children can understand.	Associate's degree	$25,700
School and Career Counselors	School counselors help students develop social skills and succeed in school. Career counselors assist people with the process of making career decisions by helping them choose a career or educational program.	Master's degree	$53,380
Social Workers	There are two main types of social workers: direct-service social workers, who help people solve and cope with problems in their everyday lives, and clinical social workers, who diagnose and treat mental, behavioral, and emotional issues.	See How to Become One	$42,480
Special Education Teachers	Special education teachers work with students who have a wide range of learning, mental, emotional and physical disabilities. With students who have mild or moderate disabilities, they ensure that lessons and teaching strategies are modified to meet the students' needs. With students who have severe disabilities, they teach the students independent living skills and basic literacy, communication, and math.	Bachelor's degree	$53,220
Teacher Assistants	Teacher assistants work under a teacher's supervision to give students additional attention and instruction.	High school diploma or equivalent	$23,220

Contacts for More Information

For more information on elementary, middle, and high school principals, visit National Association of Elementary School Principals , National Association of Secondary School Principals

Suggested citation:

Bureau of Labor Statistics, U.S. Department of Labor, Occupational Outlook Handbook, 2012-13 Edition, Elementary, Middle, and High School Principals, on the Internet at http://www.bls.gov/ooh/management/elementary-middle-and-high-school-principals.htm .

Farmers, Ranchers, and Other Agricultural Managers

Quick Facts: Farmers, Ranchers, and Other Agricultural Managers	
2010 Median Pay	$60,750 per year $29.21 per hour
Entry-Level Education	High school diploma or equivalent
Work Experience in a Related Occupation	More than 5 years
On-the-job Training	None
Number of Jobs, 2010	1,202,500
Job Outlook, 2010-20	-8% (Decline moderately)
Employment Change, 2010-20	-96,100

What Farmers, Ranchers, and Other Agricultural Managers Do

Farmers, ranchers, and other agricultural managers run establishments that produce crops, livestock, and dairy products.

Duties

Farmers, ranchers, and other agricultural managers typically do the following:

- Supervise all steps of the crop production and ranging process, including planting, fertilizing, harvesting, and herding
- Determine how to raise crops or livestock according to factors such as market conditions, federal program availability, and soil conditions
- Select and purchase supplies, such as seed, fertilizers, and farm machinery
- Operate and repair farm machinery so it cultivates, harvests, and hauls crops
- Adapt what they do as needed for weather and where the crop is in its growing cycle
- Maintain farm facilities, including its water pipes, hoses, fences, and animal shelters
- Serve as the sales agent for livestock and crops
- Keep financial, tax, production, and employee records

American farmers, ranchers, and other agricultural managers

Farmers, ranchers, and other agricultural managers operate establishments that produce crops, livestock, and dairy products.

produce enough food and fiber to meet the needs of the United States and for export. However, farm output and income are strongly influenced by weather, disease, fluctuations in prices, and federal farm programs.

Farmers, ranchers, and other agricultural managers monitor the constantly changing prices for their product. They use different strategies to protect themselves from unpredictable changes in the markets.

Many farmers carefully plan the combination of crops that they grow, so if the price of one crop drops, they will have enough income from another crop to make up the loss. When farmers and ranchers plan ahead, they may be able to store their crops or keep their livestock to take advantage of higher prices later in the year.

Most farm output goes to food-processing companies. However, some farmers now choose to sell their goods directly to consumers through farmer's markets or use cooperatives to reduce their financial risk and gain a larger share of the final price of their goods. In community-supported agriculture, cooperatives sell shares of a harvest to consumers before the planting season to ensure a market for the farm's produce.

Farmers, ranchers, and other agricultural managers also negotiate with banks and other credit lenders to get financing because they must buy seed, livestock, and equipment before they have products to sell.

Farmers and ranchers own and operate mainly family-owned farms. They also may lease land from a landowner and operate it as a working farm.

The size of the farm or range determines which tasks farmers and ranchers handle. Those who operate small farms or ranges usually do all tasks. In addition to growing crops and raising animals, they keep records, service machinery, and maintain buildings.

Those who operate large farms, however, have employees—including agricultural workers — who help with physical work. Some employees of large farms are in nonfarm occupations, working as truck drivers, sales representatives, bookkeepers, and IT specialists.

Both farmers and ranchers operate machinery and maintain their equipment and facilities. They track technological improvements in animal breeding and seeds, choosing new products that might improve output.

Agricultural managers take care of the day-to-day operation of one or more farms, ranches, nurseries, timber tracts, greenhouses, or other agricultural establishments for corporations, farmers, or owners who do not live and work on their farm or ranch.

Agricultural managers usually do not do production activities themselves. Instead, they hire and supervise farm and livestock workers to do most daily production tasks.

Managers may determine budgets. They may decide how to store and transport the crops. They oversee proper maintenance of equipment and property.

The following are some types of farmers, ranchers, and other agricultural managers:

Crop farmers and managers—those who grow grain, fruits and vegetables, and other crops—are responsible for all steps of plant growth. After a harvest, they make sure that the crops are properly packaged and stored.

Livestock, dairy, and poultry farmers, ranchers, and managers feed and care for animals. They keep livestock in barns, pens, and other well-maintained farm buildings. These workers also oversee breeding and marketing.

Horticultural specialty farmers and managers oversee the production of fruits, vegetables, flowers, and plants (including turf) used for landscaping. They also grow grapes, berries, and nuts used in making wine.

Aquaculture farmers and managers raise fish and shellfish in ponds, floating net pens, raceways, or recirculating systems. They stock, feed, protect, and maintain aquatic life used for food and for recreational fishing.

Work Environment

Farmers, ranchers, and other agricultural managers held about 1.2 million jobs in 2010. Nearly 80 percent were self-employed farmers and ranchers. The rest were wage and salary agricultural managers.

Farmers, ranchers, and other agricultural managers typically work outdoors and may spend some time in offices. They sometimes do strenuous physical work.

Some farmers work primarily with crops and vegetables. Other farmers and ranchers handle livestock.

During the planting and harvesting seasons, those who work on crop farms may work from sunrise to sunset. During the rest of the year, they plan next season's crops, market their output, and repair machinery.

On livestock-producing farms and ranches, work is ongoing. Animals, unless they are grazing, must be fed and given fresh water every day, and dairy cows milked two to three times a day. Many livestock and dairy farmers monitor and attend to the health of their herds, which may include assisting in births. These farmers and ranchers rarely get the chance to get away unless they hire an assistant or arrange for a substitute.

On very large farms, farmers, ranchers, and other agricultural mangers may spend a lot of time meeting with farm supervisors. Professional agricultural managers overseeing several farms may divide their time between traveling to meet farmers and planning operations in their offices. More farmers and managers are using computers in managing their businesses.

The work environment for farmers, ranchers, and other agricultural managers can be hazardous. Tractors and other farm machinery can cause serious injury, so workers must be alert on the job. They must operate equipment and handle chemicals properly to avoid accidents and safeguard the surrounding environment.

Work Schedules

Most farmers, ranchers, and other agricultural managers work full time. Farmers and farm managers on crop farms usually work from sunrise to sunset during the planting and harvesting seasons. The rest of the year, they plan next season's crops, market their output, and repair machinery.

On livestock-producing farms and ranches, work goes on throughout the year. Animals require care every day.

On very large farms, farmers and farm managers spend time meeting farm supervisors. Managers who oversee several farms may divide their time between traveling to meet farmers or landowners and planning the farm operations in their offices.

How to Become a Farmer, Rancher, or Other Agricultural Manager

Farmers, ranchers, and other agricultural managers typically gain skills through hands-on training and usually have at least a high school diploma. Traditionally, experience growing up on or working on a family farm or ranch was the most common way farmers and ranchers learn their trade.

However, as farm and land management has grown more complex, more farmers, ranchers, and other agricultural managers now have a bachelor's degree in agriculture or a related field. In addition, a number of government programs help new farmers get training.

Education

Most farmers, ranchers, and other agricultural managers have a high school diploma. Completing a degree at a college of agriculture is becoming important for workers who want to make a living from this occupation.

All state university systems have at least one land-grant college or university with a school of agriculture. Common programs of study include business with a concentration in agriculture, farm management, agronomy, dairy science, and agricultural economics.

At an agricultural college, students learn about crops, growing conditions, and plant diseases.

Prospective ranchers and dairy farmers, on the other hand, learn basics of veterinary science, including how pesticides can affect livestock.

Training

Prospective farmers, ranchers, and agricultural managers typically train and gain experience under more experienced farmers. Universities and forms of government assistance give prospective farmers alternatives to the traditional training method of being raised on a family farm.

Those without postsecondary education take a longer time to learn the more complex aspects of farming. A small number of farms offer formal apprenticeships to help young people learn the practical skills of farming and ranching. With government projects, such as Beginner Farmer and Rancher Competitive Grants Program , even those without any farm training can be paired with experienced farmers, learning through internships or apprentice programs.

Certification

To show competency in farm management, agricultural managers may choose to become certified. The American Society of Farm Managers and Rural Appraisers (ASFMR) offers a farm manager accreditation to ASFMR members who have 4 years of work experience and a bachelor's degree. A complete list of requirements, including consultant course work and exams, is available from ASFMR.

Important Qualities

Analytical skills. Farmers, ranchers, and other agricultural managers must monitor and assess the quality of their land or livestock. These tasks require precision and accuracy.

Critical-thinking skills. Farmers, ranchers, and other agricultural managers make tough decisions through sound reasoning and judgment. They determine how to improve their harvest and must react appropriately to weather conditions.

Interpersonal skills. Farmers, ranchers, and other agricultural managers supervise laborers and other workers, so effective communication is critical.

Machine-operation skills. Farmers, ranchers, and other agricultural managers—particularly those working on smaller farms—must be able to operate complex machinery and occasionally do routine maintenance.

Pay

Farmers, Ranchers, and Other Agricultural Managers
Median annual wages, May 2010

Other Management Occupations	$79,590
Farmers, Ranchers, and Other Agricultural Managers	$60,750
Total, All Occupations	$33,840

Note: All Occupations includes all occupations in the U.S. Economy.
Source: U.S. Bureau of Labor Statistics, Occupational Employment Statistics

The median annual wage of farmers, ranchers, and other agricultural managers was $60,750 in May 2010. The median wage is the wage at which half the workers in an occupation earned more than that amount and half earned less. The lowest 10 percent earned less than $29,280 and the top 10 percent earned more than $106,980.

Incomes of farmers and ranchers vary from year to year because prices of farm products fluctuate with weather conditions and other factors. In addition to income from their farm business, farmers often get government subsidies or other payments that add to their income and reduce some of the risk of farming.

More and more farmers, especially operators of small farms, also rely on off-farm sources of income. Most farmers, ranchers, and agricultural managers work full time.

Job Outlook

Farmers, Ranchers, and Other Agricultural Managers
Percent change in employment, projected 2010-20

Total, All Occupations	14%
Other Management Occupations	6%
Farmers, Ranchers, and Other Agricultural Managers	-8%

Note: All Occupations includes all occupations in the U.S. Economy.
Source: U.S. Bureau of Labor Statistics, Employment Projections program

Employment of farmers, ranchers, and other agricultural managers is expected to decline moderately by eight percent from 2010 to 2020. The continuing ability of the agricultural sector to produce more with fewer workers will cause some farmers to go out of business.

As land, machinery, seed, and chemicals become more expensive, only well-capitalized farmers and corporations will be able to buy many of the farms that become available. These larger, more productive farms are better able to withstand the adverse effects of climate and price fluctuations on farm output and income.

Still, several new programs in the Farm Bill, ones designed to help beginning farmers and ranchers acquire land and operating capital, may offset these market pressures.

In contrast, agricultural managers should have more opportunities. Owners of large tracts of land, who often do not live on the property they own, increasingly will seek the expertise of agricultural managers to run their farms and ranches as businesses.

Despite the expected continued consolidation of farmland and the projected decline in overall employment of this occupation, an increasing number of small-scale farmers have developed successful market niches that involve personalized, direct contact with their customers. Many are finding opportunities in horticulture and organic food production, which are among the fastest growing segments of agriculture. Others use farmer's markets that cater directly to urban and suburban consumers, allowing the farmers to capture a greater share of consumers' food dollars.

Some small-scale farmers belong to collectively owned marketing cooperatives that process and sell their products. Other farmers participate in community-supported agriculture cooperatives that allow consumers to buy a share of the farmer's harvest directly.

Employment projections data for farmers, ranchers, and other agricultural managers, 2010-20

Occupational Title	SOC Code	Employment, 2010	Projected Employment, 2020	Change, 2010-20	
				Percent	Numeric
Farmers, Ranchers, and Other Agricultural Managers	11-9013	1,202,500	1,106,400	-8	-96,100
SOURCE: U.S. Bureau of Labor Statistics, Employment Projections program					

Similar Occupations

This table shows a list of occupations with job duties that are similar to those of farmers, ranchers, and other agricultural managers.

Occupation	Job Duties	Entry-Level Education	Median Annual Pay, May 2010
Agricultural and Food Science Technicians	Under the supervision of scientists, agricultural and food science technicians measure and analyze the quality of food and agricultural products.	Associate's degree	$32,760
Agricultural and Food Scientists	Agricultural and food scientists work to ensure agricultural productivity and food safety.	See How to Become One	$58,450
Agricultural Workers	Agricultural workers maintain the quality of farms, crops, and livestock by operating machinery and doing physical labor under the supervision of agricultural managers.	See How to Become One	$18,970
Purchasing Managers, Buyers, and Purchasing Agents	Purchasing managers, buyers, and purchasing agents buy products for organizations to use or resell. They evaluate suppliers, negotiate contracts, and review product quality.	See How to Become One	$58,360

Contacts for More Information

For more information about agriculture policy and farm advocacy, visit Center for Rural Affairs

For more information about the Beginner Farmer and Rancher Competitive Grants Program, visit National Institute of Food and Agriculture

For more general information about farming in the United States, visit Farm Service Agency

For more information on farm manager certification, visit American Society of Farm Managers and Rural Appraisers

Financial Managers

Quick Facts: Financial Managers	
2010 Median Pay	$103,910 per year $49.96 per hour
Entry-Level Education	Bachelor's degree
Work Experience in a Related Occupation	More than 5 years
On-the-job Training	None
Number of Jobs, 2010	527,100
Job Outlook, 2010-20	9% (Slower than average)
Employment Change, 2010-20	46,300

What Financial Managers Do

Financial managers are responsible for the financial health of an organization. They produce financial reports, direct investment activities, and develop strategies and plans for the long-term financial goals of their organization.

Duties

Financial managers typically do the following:
- Prepare financial statements, business activity reports, and forecasts
- Monitor financial details to ensure that legal requirements are met
- Supervise employees who do financial reporting and budgeting
- Review company financial reports and seek ways to reduce costs
- Analyze market trends to find opportunities for expansion or for acquiring other companies

Financial managers prepare financial statements, business activity reports, and forecasts.

- Help management make financial decisions

The role of the financial manager, particularly in business, is changing in response to technological advances that have significantly reduced the amount of time it takes to produce financial reports. Financial managers' main responsibility used to be monitoring a company's finances, but they now do more data analysis and advise senior managers on ideas to maximize profits. They often work on teams, acting as business advisors to top executives.

Financial managers also do tasks that are specific to their organization or industry. For example, government financial managers must be experts on government appropriations and budgeting processes, and healthcare financial managers must know about issues in healthcare finance. Moreover, financial managers must be aware of special tax laws and regulations that affect their industry. For more information on chief financial officers, see the profile on top executives

The following are examples of types of financial managers:

Controllers direct the preparation of financial reports that summarize and forecast the organization's financial position, such as income statements, balance sheets, and analyses of future earnings or expenses. Controllers also are in charge of preparing special reports required by governmental agencies that regulate businesses. Often, controllers oversee the accounting, audit, and budget departments.

Treasurers and **finance officers** direct their organization's budgets to meet its financial goals. They oversee the investment of funds. They carry out strategies to raise capital (such as issuing stocks or bonds) to support the firm's expansion. They also develop financial plans for mergers (two companies joining together) and acquisitions (one company buying another).

Credit managers oversee the firm's credit business. They set credit-rating criteria, determine credit ceilings, and monitor the collections of past-due accounts.

Cash managers monitor and control the flow of cash that comes in and goes out of the company to meet the company's business and investment needs. For example, they must project cash flow (amounts coming in and going out) to determine whether the company will not have enough cash and will need a loan or will have more cash than needed and so can invest some of its money.

Risk managers control financial risk by using hedging and other strategies to limit or offset the probability of a financial loss or a company's exposure to financial uncertainty. Among the risks they try to limit are those due to currency or commodity price changes.

Insurance managers decide how best to limit a company's losses by obtaining insurance against risks such as the need to make disability payments for an employee who gets hurt on the job and costs imposed by a lawsuit against the company.

Work Environment

Financial managers held about 527,100 jobs in 2010. They work in many places, including banks and insurance companies. They work closely with top executives and with departments that develop the data that financial managers need.

The following industries employed the most financial managers in 2010:

Finance and insurance	29%
Management of companies and enterprises	9
Professional, scientific, and technical services	9
Manufacturing	8
Government	8

Work Schedules

Most financial managers work full time, and many work long hours.

How to Become a Financial Manager

Financial managers must usually have a bachelor's degree and more than 5 years of experience in another business or financial occupation, such as loan officer, accountant, auditor, securities sales agent, or financial analyst.

Education

A bachelor's degree in finance, accounting, economics, or business administration is often the minimum education needed for financial managers. However, many employers now seek candidates with a master's degree, preferably in business administration, finance, or economics. These academic programs help students develop analytical skills and learn financial analysis methods and software.

Certification

Professional certification is not required, but some financial managers still get it. The CFA Institute confers the Chartered Financial Analyst (CFA) certification to investment professionals who have at least a bachelor's degree, have 4 years of work experience, and pass three exams. The Association for Financial Professionals confers the Certified Treasury Professional credential to those who pass a computer-based exam and have a minimum of 2 years of relevant experience.

Work Experience

Financial managers usually have experience in another business or financial occupation, such as loan officer, accountant or auditor, securities sales agent, or financial analyst.

In some cases, companies provide formal management training programs to help prepare highly motivated and skilled financial workers to become financial managers.

Advancement

Because financial management is so important in keeping business

operations efficient, experienced financial managers who display a strong grasp of the operations of various departments within their organization may be promoted to management positions. Some financial managers transfer to closely related positions in other industries. Those with extensive experience may start their own consulting firms.

Important Qualities

Analytical skills. Financial managers increasingly assist executives in making decisions that affect the organization, a task for which they need analytical ability.

Communication skills. Excellent communication skills are essential because financial managers must explain and justify complex financial transactions.

Detail oriented. In preparing and analyzing reports such as balance sheets and income statements, financial managers must pay attention to detail.

Math skills. Financial managers must be skilled in math, including algebra. An understanding of international finance and complex financial documents also is important.

Organizational skills. Financial managers deal with a range of information and documents. They must stay organized to their jobs effectively.

Pay

Financial Managers
Median annual wages, May 2010

Financial Managers	$103,910
Management Occupations	$91,440
Total, All Occupations	$33,840

Note: All Occupations includes all occupations in the U.S. Economy.
Source: U.S. Bureau of Labor Statistics, Occupational Employment Statistics

The median annual wage of financial managers was $103,910 in 2010. The median wage is the wage at which half the workers in an occupation earned more than that amount and half earned less. The lowest 10 percent earned less than $56,120, and the top 10 percent earned more than $166,400.

Financial managers work in many places, including banks and insurance companies. Most financial managers work full time, and many work long hours.

Job Outlook

Financial Managers
Percent change in employment, projected 2010-20

Total, All Occupations	14%
Financial Managers	9%
Management Occupations	7%

Note: All Occupations includes all occupations in the U.S. Economy.
Source: U.S. Bureau of Labor Statistics, Employment Projections program

Employment among financial managers is expected to grow 9 percent from 2010 to 2020, slower than the average for all occupations. However, growth will vary by industry.

Services provided by financial managers, such as planning, directing, and coordinating investments, will continue to be in demand as the economy grows. The United States remains an international financial center, meaning that the economic growth of countries around the world will likely contribute to employment growth in the U.S. financial industry.

Employment of financial managers in management of companies and enterprises is expected to grow by 3 percent from 2010 to 2020, slower than the average for all occupations. However, employment of self-employed financial managers is expected to grow at 20 percent from 2010 to 2020, faster than the average for all occupations.

Overall growth of employment for financial managers will be limited by expected employment declines in depository credit intermediation. This industry includes commercial banking and savings institutions, and employs the largest percent of these managers. From 2010 to 2020, employment of financial managers is expected to decline 14 percent in the depository credit intermediation industry.

Job Prospects

As with other managerial occupations, jobseekers are likely to face competition because the number of job openings is expected to be fewer than the number of applicants. Candidates with expertise in accounting and finance—particularly those with a master's degree or certification—should enjoy the best job prospects. An understanding of international finance and complex financial documents is important.

Employment projections data for financial managers, 2010-20

Occupational Title	SOC Code	Employment, 2010	Projected Employment, 2020	Change, 2010-20	
				Percent	Numeric
Financial Managers	11-3031	527,100	573,400	9	46,300
SOURCE: U.S. Bureau of Labor Statistics, Employment Projections program					

Similar Occupations

This table shows a list of occupations with job duties that are similar to those of financial managers.

Occupation	Job Duties	Entry-Level Education	Median Annual Pay, May 2010
Accountants and Auditors	Accountants and auditors prepare and examine financial records. They ensure that financial records are accurate and that taxes are paid properly and on time. Accountants and auditors assess financial operations and work to help ensure that organizations run efficiently.	Bachelor's degree	$61,690
Budget Analysts	Budget analysts help public and private institutions organize their finances. They prepare budget reports and monitor institutional spending.	Bachelor's degree	$68,200
Financial Analysts	Financial analysts provide guidance to businesses and individuals making investment decisions. They assess the performance of stocks, bonds, and other types of investments.	Bachelor's degree	$74,350
Insurance Sales Agents	Insurance sales agents help insurance companies generate new business by contacting potential customers and selling one or more types of insurance. An agent explains various insurance policies and helps clients choose plans that suit them.	High school diploma or equivalent	$46,770
Insurance Underwriters	Insurance underwriters decide whether to provide insurance and under what terms. They evaluate insurance applications and determine coverage amounts and premiums.	Bachelor's degree	$59,290
Loan Officers	Loan officers evaluate, authorize, or recommend approval of loan applications for people and businesses.	High school diploma or equivalent	$56,490
Personal Financial Advisors	Personal financial advisors give financial advice to people. They help with investments, taxes, and insurance decisions.	Bachelor's degree	$64,750
Real Estate Brokers and Sales Agents	Real estate brokers and sales agents help clients buy, sell, and rent properties. Brokers and agents do the same type of work, but brokers are licensed to manage their own real estate businesses. Sales agents must work with a broker.	High school diploma or equivalent	$42,680
Securities, Commodities, and Financial Services Sales Agents	Securities, commodities, and financial services sales agents connect buyers and sellers in financial markets. They sell securities to individuals, advise companies in search of investors, and conduct trades.	Bachelor's degree	$70,190
Top Executives	Top executives devise strategies and policies to ensure that an organization meets its goals. They plan, direct, and coordinate operational activities of companies and public or private-sector organizations.	See How to Become One	$101,250

Contacts for More Information

For more information about financial managers, including certification, visit Financial Management Association International

For information about careers in financial and treasury management and the Certified Treasury Professional program, visit Association for Financial Professionals

For information about the Chartered Financial Analyst program, visit CFA Institute

Suggested citation:

Bureau of Labor Statistics, U.S. Department of Labor, Occupational Outlook Handbook, 2012-13 Edition, Financial Managers, on the Internet at http://www.bls.gov/ooh/management/financial-managers.htm .

Food Service Managers

Quick Facts: Food Service Managers	
2010 Median Pay	$48,130 per year $23.14 per hour
Entry-Level Education	High school diploma or equivalent
Work Experience in a Related Occupation	1 to 5 years
On-the-job Training	None
Number of Jobs, 2010	320,600
Job Outlook, 2010-20	-3% (Decline moderately)
Employment Change, 2010-20	-10,600

What Food Service Managers Do

Food service managers are responsible for the daily operations of restaurants and other establishments that prepare and serve food and beverages to customers. Managers ensure that customers are satisfied with their dining experience.

Duties

Food service managers typically do the following:

- Interview, hire, train, oversee, and sometimes fire employees
- Oversee the inventory and ordering of food and beverage, equipment, and supplies
- Monitor food preparation methods, portion sizes, and the overall presentation of food
- Comply with health and food safety standards and regulations
- Monitor the actions of employees and patrons to ensure everyone's personal safety
- Investigate and resolve complaints regarding food quality or service
- Schedule staff hours and assign duties
- Keep budgets and payroll records and review financial transactions
- Establish standards for personnel performance and customer service

Besides coordinating activities among the kitchen and dining room staff, managers must ensure that customers are served properly and in a timely manner. They monitor orders in the kitchen and, if needed, they work with the chef to remedy any delays in service.

Food service managers are generally responsible for all functions of the business related to people. For example, most managers interview, hire, train, and, when necessary, fire employees. Finding and keeping good employees is a challenge for food service managers. Managers schedule work hours, making sure that enough workers are present to cover each shift—or managers may have to fill in themselves.

Food service managers plan and arrange for clean tablecloths and napkins, for heavy cleaning when the dining room and kitchen are not in use, for trash removal, and for pest control when needed.

In addition, managers do many administrative tasks, such as keeping employee records, preparing the payroll, and completing paperwork to comply with licensing, tax and wage, unemployment compensation, and Social Security laws. While they may give some of these tasks to an assistant manager or bookkeeper, most general managers are responsible for the accuracy of business records. Managers also keep records of supply and equipment purchases and ensure that suppliers are paid.

Many full-service restaurants have a management team that includes a general manager, one or more assistant managers, and an executive chef. Managers add up the cash and charge slips and secure them in a safe place. Many managers also lock up the establishment; check that ovens, grills, and lights are off; and switch on the alarm system.

Work Environment

Food service managers held about 320,600 jobs in 2010.

The following industries employed the most food service managers in 2010:

Limited-service eating places	20%
Full-service restaurants	20
Special food services	4
Traveler accommodation	2
Elementary and secondary schools	2

Some food service managers work in the kitchens, dining rooms, and cafeterias at a variety of establishments, such as schools, hospitals, factories, or offices. Many others work in fine-dining restaurants and fast-food chains and franchises. About 42 percent of food service managers were self-employed.

Many food service managers work long hours, and the job is often hectic. Dealing with unhappy customers can sometimes be stressful.

Work Schedules

Most food service managers work full time. Managers at fine-dining and fast-food restaurants that operate extended hours often work longer hours—12 to 15 per day, 50 or more per week—and sometimes 7 days a week. Managers of institutional food service

Food service managers ensure that customers are satisfied with their dining experience.

facilities in schools, factories, or office buildings tend to work more regular hours. Those who oversee multiple locations of a chain or franchise may be called in on short notice, including on nights and weekends.

How to Become a Food Service Manager

Experience in the food services industry—as a cook , waiter or waitress , or counter attendant—is the most common training for food service managers. Many jobs, particularly for managers of self-service and fast-food restaurants, are filled by promoting experienced food service workers. However, a growing number of manager positions require postsecondary education in a hospitality or food service management program.

Education

Although most food service managers have less than a bachelor's degree, some postsecondary education is increasingly preferred for many manager positions. Many food service management companies and national or regional restaurant chains recruit management trainees from college hospitality or food service management programs, which require internships and real-life experience to graduate.

Almost 1,000 colleges and universities offer bachelor's degree programs in restaurant and hospitality management or institutional food service management. For those not interested in a bachelor's degree, community and junior colleges, technical institutes, and other institutions offer programs in the field leading to an associate's degree or other formal certification.

Both degree and certification programs provide instruction in subjects such as nutrition, sanitation, and food planning and preparation, as well as accounting, business law and management, and computer science. Some programs combine classroom and laboratory study with internships and thus provide on-the-job training and experience. In addition, many educational institutions offer programs in food preparation.

Training

Most restaurant chains and food service management companies have rigorous training programs for management positions. Through a combination of classroom and on-the-job training, trainees get instruction and work experience in all aspects of how to run a restaurant or institutional food service facility, including food preparation, nutrition, sanitation, security, company policies and procedures, personnel management, recordkeeping, and report preparation. Training on the use of the restaurant's computer system is increasingly important as well.

Certification

The Foodservice Management Professional (FMP) designation is a measure of professional achievement for food service managers. Although not required, voluntary certification shows professional competence, particularly for managers who learned their skills on the job. The National Restaurant Association Educational Foundation awards the FMP designation to managers who meet several criteria, including passing a written exam, completing coursework, and meeting experience requirements.

Important Qualities

Customer-service skills. Food service managers must have good customer service skills when dealing with patrons. Satisfying customers and exceeding their needs is critical for success and ensures customer loyalty.

Detail oriented. Managers must deal with many different types of activities at the same time. They deal with workers, customers, making sure there's enough food, taking care of records, making sure the place is in good condition, and more.

Leadership skills. All managers must establish good working relationships to ensure a productive work environment. This may involve motivating workers, resolving conflicts, or actively listening to complaints or criticism from customers.

Managerial skills. Food service managers may deal with budget matters; they also coordinate and supervise workers. Choosing the best people for a job is important, as is the need to guide and motivate employees.

Organizational skills. Food service managers keep track of many different schedules, budgets, and people at once. This becomes more complex as the size of the restaurant or food service facility increases.

Problem-solving skills. The ability to resolve personnel issues and customer-related problems is imperative to the work of managers. As a result, they must be creative and practical when solving problems.

Speaking skills. Food service managers must give clear orders to staff and be able to explain information to employees and customers.

Stamina. Especially for owners of small establishments, food service managers may spend a lot of time on their feet, often working long hours. They need stamina to handle the physical and other stresses of the job.

Pay

Food Service Managers
Median annual wages, May 2010

Management Occupations	$91,440
Food Service Managers	$48,130
Total, All Occupations	$33,840

Note: All Occupations includes all occupations in the U.S. Economy.
Source: U.S. Bureau of Labor Statistics, Occupational Employment Statistics

The median annual wage of food service managers was $48,130 in May 2010. The median wage is the wage at which half the workers in an occupation earned more than that amount and half earned less. The lowest 10 percent earned less than $30,480, and the top 10 percent earned more than $80,410.

In May 2010, the median annual wages in industries employing the largest numbers of food service managers were as follows:

Traveler accommodation	$55,010
Special food services	52,890
Full-service restaurants	51,210
Elementary and secondary schools	46,810
Limited-service eating places	43,080

Most food service managers work full time. Managers at fine-dining and fast-food restaurants that operate extended hours often work longer hours—12 to 15 per day, 50 or more per week—and sometimes 7 days a week. Managers of institutional food service facilities in schools, factories, or office buildings tend to work more regular hours. Those who oversee multiple locations of a chain or franchise may be called in on short notice, including on nights and weekends.

Job Outlook

Food Service Managers
Percent change in employment, projected 2010-20

Total, All Occupations	14%
Management Occupations	7%
Food Service Managers	-3%

Note: All Occupations includes all occupations in the U.S. Economy.
Source: U.S. Bureau of Labor Statistics, Employment Projections program

Employment of food service managers is expected to decline 3 percent from 2010 to 2020, as the number of eating and drinking establishments opening is expected to decline from the previous decade. Despite these reductions, new employment opportunities for food service managers will emerge in grocery stores and other retail and recreation industries to meet the growing demand for quick food in a variety of settings.

Job Prospects

Job opportunities for food service managers are expected to be highly competitive. Most openings will result from the need to replace managers who retire or transfer to other occupations.

Although practical experience is an integral part of becoming a food service manager, applicants with a degree in hospitality or restaurant or institutional food service management should have an edge when competing for jobs at upscale restaurants.

Employment projections data for food service managers, 2010-20

Occupational Title	SOC Code	Employment, 2010	Projected Employment, 2020	Change, 2010-20 Percent	Change, 2010-20 Numeric
Food Service Managers	11-9051	320,600	310,000	-3	-10,600
SOURCE: U.S. Bureau of Labor Statistics, Employment Projections program					

Similar Occupations

This table shows a list of occupations with job duties that are similar to those of food service managers.

Occupation	Job Duties	Entry-Level Education	Median Annual Pay, May 2010
Bartenders	Bartenders mix and serve drinks to customers directly or through wait staff.	Less than high school	$18,680
Chefs and Head Cooks	Chefs and head cooks oversee the daily food preparation at restaurants or other places where food is served. They direct kitchen staff and handle any food-related concerns.	High school diploma or equivalent	$40,630
Cooks	Cooks prepare, season, and cook a wide range of foods, such as soups, salads, entrees, and desserts.	See How to Become One	$20,260
Lodging Managers	Lodging managers make sure that guests on vacation or business travel have a pleasant experience, while also ensuring that an establishment is run efficiently and profitably.	High school diploma or equivalent	$46,880
Sales Managers	Sales managers direct organizations' sales teams. They set sales goals, analyze data, and develop training programs for the organization's sales representatives.	Bachelor's degree	$98,530
Waiters and Waitresses	Waiters and waitresses take orders and serve food and beverages to customers in dining establishments.	Less than high school	$18,330

Contacts for More Information

For more information about food service managers, including a directory of college programs in food service, visit National Restaurant Association

For more information about food service managers and certification as a Foodservice Management Professional, visit National Restaurant Association Educational Foundation

For general information about food service managers, visit Society for Foodservice Management

Suggested citation:

Bureau of Labor Statistics, U.S. Department of Labor, Occupational Outlook Handbook, 2012-13 Edition, Food Service Managers, on the Internet at http://www.bls.gov/ooh/management/food-service-managers.htm .

Human Resources Managers

Quick Facts: Human Resources Managers	
2010 Median Pay	$99,180 per year $47.68 per hour
Entry-Level Education	Bachelor's degree
Work Experience in a Related Occupation	1 to 5 years
On-the-job Training	None
Number of Jobs, 2010	71,800
Job Outlook, 2010-20	13% (About as fast as average)
Employment Change, 2010-20	9,300

What Human Resources Managers Do

Human resources managers plan, direct, and coordinate the administrative functions of an organization. They oversee the recruiting, interviewing, and hiring of new staff; consult with top executives on strategic planning; and serve as a link between an organization's management and its employees.

Duties

Human resources managers typically do the following:

- Plan and coordinate an organization's workforce to best use employees' talents
- Link an organization's management with its employees by handling questions, administering employee services, and resolving work-related problems
- Advise managers on organizational policies, such as equal employment opportunity and sexual harassment
- Coordinate and supervise the work of specialists and support staff
- Oversee an organization's recruitment, interview, selection, and hiring processes
- Handle staffing issues, such as mediating disputes, firing employees, and directing disciplinary procedures

Every organization wants to attract, motivate, and keep qualified employees and match them to jobs for which they are well suited. Human resources managers accomplish this by directing the administrative functions of an organization. Their work involves overseeing employee relations, regulatory compliance, and

Human resources managers deal with workplace complaints and may referee disputes.

employee-related services such as payroll, training, and benefits. They supervise the department's specialists and support staff and ensure that tasks are completed accurately and on time.

Human resources managers also consult with top executives on the organization's strategic planning. They identify ways to maximize the value of the organization's employees and ensure that they are used as efficiently as possible. For example, they might assess worker productivity and recommend changes to the organization's structure to help it meet budgetary goals.

Some human resources managers oversee all aspects of an organization's human resources department, including the compensation and benefits or training and development programs. In many larger organizations, these programs are directed by specialized managers. For more information, see the profiles on compensation and benefits managers and training and development managers .

The following are types of human resources managers:

Labor relations managers, also called **employee relations managers**, oversee employment policies in union and non-union settings. They draw up, negotiate, and administer labor contracts that cover issues such as grievances, wages, benefits, and union and management practices. They also handle labor complaints between employees and management and coordinate grievance procedures.

Payroll managers supervise the operations of an organization's payroll department. They ensure that all aspects of payroll are processed correctly and on time. They administer payroll procedures, prepare reports for the accounting department, and resolve any payroll problems or discrepancies.

Recruiting managers, sometimes called **staffing managers**, oversee the recruiting and hiring responsibilities of the human resources department. They often supervise a team of recruiters, and some take on recruiting duties when trying to fill high-level positions. They must develop a recruiting strategy that helps them meet the staffing needs of their organization and effectively compete for the best employees.

Work Environment

Human resources managers held about 71,800 jobs in 2010 and were employed throughout the economy.

The following industries employed the most human resources managers in 2010:

Government	14%
Management of companies and enterprises	14
Manufacturing	13
Professional, scientific, and technical services	9
Health care and social assistance	9

Human resources managers work in offices, and most work full time.

Some managers, especially those working for organizations that have offices nationwide, must travel to visit other branches as well as to attend professional meetings or to recruit employees.

How to Become a Human Resources Manager

Candidates need a combination of education and related work experience to become a human resources manager.

Education

Human resources managers usually need a bachelor's degree in human resources or business administration. Alternatively, as not all undergraduate programs offer a degree in human resources, candidates can get a bachelor's degree in another field and take courses in human resources subjects, such as labor or industrial relations, organizational development, or industrial psychology. Some positions are also filled by experienced individuals with other backgrounds, including finance, business management, education, and information technology.

Some higher-level jobs require a master's degree in human resources, labor relations, or a Master of Business Administration (MBA) degree.

Work Experience

To demonstrate an ability to organize, manage, and lead others, related work experience is essential for human resources managers. Some positions accept management experience in a variety of fields, but many positions require experience working with human resources programs, such as compensation and benefits plans or with a Human Resources Information System (HRIS), and require solid understanding of federal, state, and local employment laws.

Certification

Although certification is voluntary, it can show professional expertise and credibility and may enhance advancement opportunities. Many employers prefer to hire certified candidates, and some positions may require certification. The Society for Human Resource Management is among many professional associations that offer a variety of certification programs.

Important Qualities

Decision-making skills. Human resources managers must be able to balance the strengths and weaknesses of different options and decide the best course of action. Many of their decisions have a significant impact on workers or operations, such as deciding whether to fire an employee.

Interpersonal skills. Human resources managers need strong interpersonal skills because they regularly interact with people. They often collaborate on teams and must develop positive working relationships with their colleagues.

Managerial skills. Human resources managers must be able to direct a staff and oversee the operations of their department. They must coordinate work activities and ensure that workers in the department complete their duties and fulfill their responsibilities.

Organizational skills. Organizational skills are essential for human resources managers. They must be able to manage several projects at once and prioritize tasks.

Speaking skills. Human resources managers rely on speaking skills to give presentations and direct their staff. They must clearly communicate information and instructions to their staff and other employees.

Pay

Human Resources Managers
Median annual wages, May 2010

Human Resources Managers	$99,180
Management Occupations	$91,440
Total, All Occupations	$33,840

Note: All Occupations includes all occupations in the U.S. Economy.
Source: U.S. Bureau of Labor Statistics, Occupational Employment Statistics

The median annual wage of human resources managers was $99,180 in 2010. The median wage is the wage at which half the workers in an occupation earned more than that amount and half earned less. The lowest 10 percent earned less than $61,560, and the top 10 percent earned more than $166,400.

Most human resources managers work full time, and some are required to travel to visit other branches, attend professional meetings, or recruit employees.

Job Outlook

Human Resources Managers
Percent change in employment, projected 2010-20

Total, All Occupations	14%
Human Resources Managers	13%
Management Occupations	7%

Note: All Occupations includes all occupations in the U.S. Economy.
Source: U.S. Bureau of Labor Statistics, Employment Projections program

Employment of human resources managers is expected to grow 13 percent from 2010 to 2020, about as fast as the average for all occupations.

Employment growth for human resources managers largely depends on the performance and growth of individual companies. As new companies form and organizations expand their operations, they will need more human resources staff to oversee and administer their programs.

Managers will be needed to ensure that firms adhere to changing, complex employment laws regarding occupational safety and health, equal employment opportunity, healthcare, wages, and retirement plans.

Job growth is expected to be tempered, however, by the use of computerized human resources information systems, which allow companies to handle many administrative processes more productively and with fewer workers.

Job Prospects

Job opportunities are expected to vary, depending on the staffing needs of individual companies. Job opportunities should be best in the professional, scientific, and technical consulting industry as organizations continue to contract with outside consulting firms for some of their human resources functions.

Candidates with certification or a master's degree—particularly those with a concentration in human resources management or an MBA—should have the best job prospects. Those with a solid background in human resources programs, policies, and employment law should also have better job opportunities.

Employment projections data for human resources managers, 2010-20

Occupational Title	SOC Code	Employment, 2010	Projected Employment, 2020	Change, 2010-20 Percent	Numeric
Human Resources Managers	11-3121	71,800	81,000	13	9,300
SOURCE: U.S. Bureau of Labor Statistics, Employment Projections program					

Similar Occupations

This table shows a list of occupations with job duties that are similar to those of human resources managers.

Occupation	Job Duties	Entry-Level Education	Median Annual Pay, May 2010
Judges, Mediators, and Hearing Officers	Judges, mediators, and hearing officers apply the law to court cases and oversee the legal process in courts. They also resolve administrative disputes and facilitate negotiations between opposing parties.	See How to Become One	$91,880
Administrative Services Managers	Administrative services managers plan, direct, and coordinate supportive services of an organization. Their specific responsibilities vary by the type of organization and may include keeping records, distributing mail, and planning and maintaining facilities.	High school diploma or equivalent	$77,890
Compensation and Benefits Managers	Compensation managers plan, direct, and coordinate how and how much an organization pays its employees. Benefits managers do the same for retirement plans, health insurance, and other benefits an organization offers its employees.	Bachelor's degree	$89,270
Medical and Health Services Managers	Medical and health services managers, also called healthcare executives or healthcare administrators, plan, direct, and coordinate medical and health services. They might manage an entire facility, specialize in managing a specific clinical area or department, or manage a medical practice for a group of physicians.	Bachelor's degree	$84,270
Top Executives	Top executives devise strategies and policies to ensure that an organization meets its goals. They plan, direct, and coordinate operational activities of companies and public or private-sector organizations.	See How to Become One	$101,250
Training and Development Managers	Training and development managers plan, direct, and coordinate programs to enhance the knowledge and skills of an organization's employees. They also oversee a staff of training and development specialists.	Bachelor's degree	$89,170
Human Resources Specialists	Human resources specialists recruit, screen, interview, and place workers. They also may handle human resources work in a variety of other areas, such as employee relations, payroll and benefits, and training.	Bachelor's degree	$52,690

Contacts for More Information

For more information about human resources managers, including certification, visit Society for Human Resource Management

For information about careers and certification in employee compensation and benefits, visit International Foundation of Employee Benefit Plans

WorldatWork

For information about careers in employee training and development and certification, visit American Society for Training and Development

International Society for Performance Improvement

Suggested citation:

Industrial Production Managers

Quick Facts: Industrial Production Managers	
2010 Median Pay	$87,160 per year $41.91 per hour
Entry-Level Education	Bachelor's degree
Work Experience in a Related Occupation	1 to 5 years
On-the-job Training	None
Number of Jobs, 2010	150,300
Job Outlook, 2010-20	9% (Slower than average)
Employment Change, 2010-20	13,700

What Industrial Production Managers Do

Industrial production managers oversee the daily operations of manufacturing and related plants. They coordinate, plan, and direct the activities used to create a wide range of goods, such as cars, computer equipment, or paper products.

Duties

Industrial production managers typically do the following:

- Decide how best to use a plant's workers and equipment to meet production goals
- Ensure that production stays on schedule and within budget
- Hire, train, and evaluate workers
- Analyze production data
- Write routine production reports
- Monitor a plant's workers to ensure they meet performance and safety requirements
- Create ways to make the production process more efficient
- Determine whether new machines are needed, or whether overtime work is necessary
- Fix any production problems that may arise

Depending on the size of the manufacturing plant, industrial production managers may oversee the entire plant or just one area of it.

Industrial production managers are responsible for carrying out quality control programs to make sure the finished product meets a prescribed level of quality. They generally choose from a number of programs that are standard in manufacturing industries, such as ISO 9000 or Six Sigma. These programs help a manager identify defects in

products, identify the cause of the defect, and solve the problem creating it. For example, a manager may determine that a defect is being caused by parts from an outside supplier. The manager can then work with the supplier to improve the quality of the parts.

Industrial production managers work closely with managers from other departments. For example, the procurement (buying) department orders the supplies that the production department uses. A breakdown in communication between these two departments can cause production slowdowns. Just-in-time production techniques mean that companies keep inventory low, so communication among managers in each department and suppliers is important.

They also communicate with other departments, such as sales, warehousing, and research and design, to assure the company's success.

Work Environment

Industrial production managers split their time between the production area and a nearby office. When they are working in the production area, they may have to wear protective equipment such as a helmet or safety goggles.

Industrial production managers held about 150,300 jobs in 2010. Almost 80 percent of industrial production managers work in various manufacturing industries. The manufacturing industries employing the most industrial production managers in 2010 are as follows:

Fabricated metal product manufacturing	10%
Transportation equipment manufacturing	9
Chemical manufacturing	8
Computer and electronic product manufacturing	7

Work Schedules

Most industrial production managers work full time, and many work long hours. In some facilities, managers work night or weekend shifts and must be on call to deal with emergencies at any time of day.

How to Become an Industrial Production Manager

Most employers require production managers to have a bachelor's degree and 2 to 5 years of related work experience.

Education

Most industrial production managers have a bachelor's degree in business administration or industrial engineering. Sometimes, production workers with many years of experience take management classes and become a production manager. At large plants, where

Industrial production managers supervise employees at manufacturing plants.

managers have more oversight responsibilities, employers may look for managers who have a Master of Business Administration (MBA) or a graduate degree in industrial management.

Training

Some managers begin working at a company directly after college or graduate school. They spend their first few months in training programs, becoming familiar with the production process, company policies, and safety regulations. In large companies, many also spend short periods of time working in other departments, such as purchasing or accounting, to learn more about the company.

Work Experience

Some industrial production managers begin as production workers and move up through the ranks. They first advance to a first-line supervisory position before eventually being selected for management. Most get a college degree in business management or take company-sponsored classes to increase their chances of a promotion.

Production managers who join a firm immediately after graduating from college sometimes work as first-line supervisors before beginning their jobs as production managers.

Certification

Industrial production managers can earn optional certificates that show a higher level of competency in quality or management systems. The Association for Operations Management offers a Certified in Production and Inventory Management (CPIM) credential. The American Society for Quality offers credentials in quality control.

Important Qualities

Interpersonal skills. Industrial production must have excellent communication skills so they can work with managers from other departments, as well as with the company's senior-level management.

Leadership skills. To keep the production process running smoothly, industrial production managers must motivate and direct the employees they manage.

Problem-solving skills. Production managers must be able to identify problems immediately and solve them. For example, if a product has a defect, the manger determines whether it is a onetime problem or the result of the production process.

Time-management skills. To meet production deadlines, managers must carefully manage their employees' time as well as their own.

Pay

Industrial Production Managers
Median annual wages, May 2010

Management Occupations	$91,440
Industrial Production Managers	$87,160
Total, All Occupations	$33,840

Note: All Occupations includes all occupations in the U.S. Economy.
Source: U.S. Bureau of Labor Statistics, Occupational Employment Statistics

The median annual wage of industrial production managers was $87,160 in May 2010. The median wage is the wage at which half the workers in the occupation earned more than the amount and half earned less. The lowest 10 percent earned less than $52,640, and the top 10 percent earned more than $148,020.

The table below lists the May 2010 median annual wages of industrial production managers in the manufacturing industries where they are most commonly employed.

Computer and electronic product manufacturing	$98,470
Chemical manufacturing	95,240
Transportation equipment manufacturing	91,460
Fabricated metal product manufacturing	80,970

Most industrial production managers work full time, and many work long hours. In some facilities, managers work night or weekend shifts and must be on call to deal with emergencies at any time of day.

Job Outlook

Industrial Production Managers
Percent change in employment, projected 2010-20

Total, All Occupations	14%
Industrial Production Managers	9%
Management Occupations	7%

Note: All Occupations includes all occupations in the U.S. Economy.
Source: U.S. Bureau of Labor Statistics, Employment Projections program

Employment of industrial production managers is projected to grow 9 percent from 2010 to 2020, slower than the average for all occupations. Most of these managers are employed in various manufacturing industries, which are expected to decline as manufacturing continues to experience foreign competition. In addition, the manufacturing process is becoming more automated, which is expected to cause job declines in the field. However, because managers coordinate the work of both workers and machines, their employment is not expected to decline as fast as overall manufacturing employment. Projected employment growth of industrial production managers from 2010 to 2020 in the four manufacturing industries that employ the most industrial production managers is as follows:

Fabricated metal product manufacturing	19%
Transportation equipment manufacturing	7
Chemical manufacturing	1
Computer and electronic product manufacturing	-6

Job Prospects

Despite the projected decline in employment, job openings are expected, due to the need to replace workers who retire. Applicants who have a bachelor's degree in industrial management or business administration should have the best prospects.

Employment projections data for industrial production managers, 2010-20

Occupational Title	SOC Code	Employment, 2010	Projected Employment, 2020	Change, 2010-20	
				Percent	Numeric
Industrial Production Managers	11-3051	150,300	164,000	9	13,700
SOURCE: U.S. Bureau of Labor Statistics, Employment Projections program					

Similar Occupations

This table shows a list of occupations with job duties that are similar to those of industrial production managers.

Occupation	Job Duties	Entry-Level Education	Median Annual Pay, May 2010
Advertising, Promotions, and Marketing Managers	Advertising, promotions, and marketing managers plan programs to generate interest in a product or service. They work with art directors, sales agents, and financial staff members.	Bachelor's degree	$108,260
Construction Managers	Construction managers plan, coordinate, budget, and supervise construction projects from early development to completion.	Associate's degree	$83,860
Health and Safety Engineers	Health and safety engineers develop procedures and design systems to keep people from getting sick or injured and to keep property from being damaged. They combine knowledge of health or safety and of systems engineering to make sure that chemicals, machinery, software, furniture, and other products are not going to cause harm to people or buildings.	Bachelor's degree	$75,430
Industrial Engineers	Industrial engineers find ways to eliminate wastefulness in production processes. They devise efficient ways to use workers, machines, materials, information, and energy to make a product or provide a service.	Bachelor's degree	$76,100
Management Analysts	Management analysts, often called management consultants, propose ways to improve an organization's efficiency. They advise managers on how to make organizations more profitable through reduced costs and increased revenues.	Bachelor's degree	$78,160
Mechanical Engineers	Mechanical engineering is one of the broadest engineering disciplines. Mechanical engineers design, develop, build, and test mechanical devices, including tools, engines, and machines.	Bachelor's degree	$78,160
Operations Research Analysts	Operations research analysts use advanced methods of analysis to help organizations solve problems and make better decisions.	Bachelor's degree	$70,960
Sales Managers	Sales managers direct organizations' sales teams. They set sales goals, analyze data, and develop training programs for the organization's sales representatives.	Bachelor's degree	$98,530
Top Executives	Top executives devise strategies and policies to ensure that an organization meets its goals. They plan, direct, and coordinate operational activities of companies and public or private-sector organizations.	See How to Become One	$101,250

Contacts for More Information

For more information about careers in production management and certification, visit: Association for Operations Management (APICS)

For more information about quality management and certification, visit: American Society for Quality

Suggested citation:

Bureau of Labor Statistics, U.S. Department of Labor, Occupational Outlook Handbook, 2012-13 Edition, Industrial Production Managers, on the Internet at http://www.bls.gov/ooh/management/industrial-production-managers.htm .

Legislators

Quick Facts: Legislators	
2010 Median Pay	$19,260 per year
Entry-Level Education	Bachelor's degree
Work Experience in a Related Occupation	1 to 5 years
On-the-job Training	None
Number of Jobs, 2010	67,700
Job Outlook, 2010-20	0% (Little or no change)
Employment Change, 2010-20	200

What Legislators Do

Legislators are elected officials who develop laws for the federal government, or for local or state governments.

Duties

Legislators typically do the following:

- Develop bills—drafts of laws that they want their fellow legislators to approve
- Draft or approve policies, regulations, budgets, and programs
- Debate and analyze the impact of proposed laws
- Vote on bills and on motions to enact them into law
- Collaborate and negotiate with other legislators to resolve differences and reach agreements
- Seek funding for projects and programs in their district
- Appoint nominees to leadership posts or approve appointments by the chief executive
- Serve on committees, panels, and study groups for special policy issues
- Listen to and address the concerns of people they represent
- Invite and listen to testimony from people who are concerned about an issue or likely to be affected by a law if it is passed

Legislators are members of the legislative branch of government, which is responsible for making new laws and changing existing laws. Legislators include members of the U.S. Congress; state senators and representatives; and city, county, and township commissioners and council members. For more information about government officials in the executive branch, including the President of the United States, state governors, and mayors, see the profile on top executives .

Legislators govern by proposing bills, holding votes, and passing laws. Most legislators serve on committees that oversee different areas of government policy. Legislators are expected to develop expertise in those areas, as well as keep up with current local, national, and international events. Most bills are proposed and developed in committees. To make informed decisions, legislators also hear testimonies from private citizens, political leaders, and interest groups.

The work of legislators relies on meeting with, listening to, and forming relationships with others. Legislators confer with and debate colleagues about the merits of proposed laws and determine their colleagues' level of support. In doing so, legislators must negotiate a compromise among different interest groups and review and respond to the concerns of the people they represent or the general public.

Frequent public appearances at community and social events are customary for legislators.

Legislators work in each level of government:

Federal legislators are members of the U.S. Senate and House of Representatives. There are 541 U.S. Senators and Representatives. U.S. legislators work to represent the interests of the people in their districts, such as encouraging investment and economic development in their jurisdiction, while also considering the needs of the entire nation.

State legislators are senators and representatives in state governments. According to the National Conference of State Legislatures, there are 7,382 state legislators, ranging from 49 in Nebraska to 424 in New Hampshire.

Local legislators include city, county, town, and township commissioners and council members. About 9 out of 10 legislators work in local government. Many small communities have legislators who are volunteers and receive no salary. These workers are not included in the employment or salary numbers in this profile.

Work Environment

The working conditions of legislators vary by position and level of government. Although some legislators work only a few hours a week, others work long hours and have stressful schedules. State and federal legislators travel often and may need to live away from home while the legislature is in session. Many legislators spend a considerable amount of time meeting with people they represent and attending social functions in addition to their scheduled work hours.

Work Schedules

The work schedules of legislators vary with the size and budget of the governmental unit. Time spent at work ranges from meeting once a month for a local council member to full time with long hours for a U.S. Senator. U.S. Senators and Representatives and legislators in large local jurisdictions usually work full time, year round, as do county and city managers.

Members of Congress frequently travel between Washington, D.C., and their home districts. When Congress is not in session, legislators

Legislators often give speeches.

are expected to spend much of their time meeting with the people they represent.

According to the National Conference of State Legislatures, legislators in 10 state governments hold full-time positions. Most part-time legislators work full time while the legislature is in session and part time when not in session. Some continue to work part time in the occupation they held before they were elected. State legislators often have to live away from home while the legislature is in session to be present in the state capitol.

How to Become a Legislator

Although most legislative positions have minimum age, residency, and citizenship requirements, there is no established education or training requirement to become a legislator. For most positions, however, candidates need a bachelor's degree or higher to be competitive in elections. Successful candidates come from a variety of occupations, but many have experience in politics or management positions.

Because legislators are elected, most candidates must campaign for a position. While candidates in some local elections may run unopposed, campaigning for positions in federal, state, and large local governments often requires long hours, persistence, and a significant amount of money. Candidates must, therefore, raise funds, make frequent public appearances, and meet with local voters.

Education

Although there is no educational requirement to become a legislator, most candidates hold a bachelor's degree or higher. Graduate degrees in law and business are also common, particularly in federal and state offices.

A master's degree in public administration, including courses such as public financial management and legal issues in public administration, can be helpful.

Work Experience

Work experience is important for legislators. Candidates for legislative office often must demonstrate that they can make good decisions and lead effectively. Many candidates have experience or a strong record of accomplishment working in law, management, business, education, or politics. Some have experience as members of community boards or commissions. Others become well-known for their work with charities, political action groups, political campaigns, or with religious or social organizations.

Many people enter politics on a local level and gain experience there before seeking state office. Many people serve in state legislatures before running for Congress.

Important Qualities

Decision-making skills. Legislators must consider the implications of legislation and decide which positions to support. They must weigh the needs of private citizens, government, and society, and determine which bills to pass.

Interpersonal skills. Legislators use interpersonal skills both to be elected to their position and to be effective at their job. It is important for legislators to build relationships with colleagues, public officials, organization leaders, and the people they represent. They often meet new people and must be able to communicate effectively with others.

Leadership skills. Legislators make the laws that govern our society. Legislators need leadership skills to organize people effectively and enlist others—both colleagues and the people they represent—in support of policies.

Negotiating skills. Legislators often work with people with opposing viewpoints and must find ways to negotiate compromises to accomplish tasks. For example, they may have to be flexible on one issue to gain the support of their colleagues on another issue.

Problem-solving skills. Legislators must assess issues and draft legislation that addresses the needs and problems of the people they represent, government, and society.

Speaking skills. Speaking skills are essential for legislators. They must be able to explain their views when speaking with colleagues and the people they represent. Legislators often give speeches, debate ideas, and attempt to persuade others.

Pay

Legislators
Median annual wages, May 2010

Management Occupations	$91,440
Total, All Occupations	$33,840
Legislators	$19,260

Note: All Occupations includes all occupations in the U.S. Economy.
Source: U.S. Bureau of Labor Statistics, Occupational Employment Statistics

The median annual wage of legislators was $19,260 in May 2010. The median wage is the wage at which half the workers in an occupation earned more than that amount and half earned less. The lowest 10 percent earned less than $15,790, and the top 10 percent earned more than $84,320.

Salaries vary based on position, level of government, and full- or part-time status. Salaries range from very little for part-time positions to $174,000 a year for most members of the U.S. Congress. A few members earn more, including the Speaker of the U.S. House of Representatives, who earns $223,500 per year.

For members of state legislatures, salaries range from $100 per year to more than $100,000 per year. According to the National Council of State Legislators, legislators who worked full time earned an average of $68,599, and those who worked part time earned an average of $15,984.

The work schedules of legislators vary with the size and budget of the governmental unit. Time spent at work ranges from meeting once a month for a local council member to full time with long hours for a U.S. Senator. U.S. Senators and Representatives and legislators in large local jurisdictions usually work full time, year round, as do many county and city managers.

Job Outlook

Legislators
Percent change in employment, projected 2010-20

Total, All Occupations	14%
Management Occupations	7%
Legislators	0%

Note: All Occupations includes all occupations in the U.S. Economy.
Source: U.S. Bureau of Labor Statistics, Employment Projections program

Employment of legislators will experience little or no change from 2010 to 2020. The number of legislators in current governments rarely changes, and few new governments are likely to form. Most positions are competitive and require candidates to campaign for the job.

Job Prospects

Because legislators are elected, many opportunities exist for newcomers to enter the occupation. The level of competition varies by place and size of government.

Positions at the federal and state level, as well as in some large municipalities, are very competitive.

There will be more opportunities for potential legislators in lower paying jobs in small governments. Part-time positions are usually less competitive. Turnover can be high, and many positions have term limits; however, in some positions without term limits, it can difficult to unseat an incumbent (the person who has the job).

Employment projections data for legislators, 2010-20

Occupational Title	SOC Code	Employment, 2010	Projected Employment, 2020	Change, 2010-20	
				Percent	Numeric
Legislators	11-1031	67,700	67,900	0	200
SOURCE: U.S. Bureau of Labor Statistics, Employment Projections program					

Similar Occupations

This table shows a list of occupations with job duties that are similar to those of legislators.

Occupation	Job Duties	Entry-Level Education	Median Annual Pay, May 2010
Top Executives	Top executives devise strategies and policies to ensure that an organization meets its goals. They plan, direct, and coordinate operational activities of companies and public or private-sector organizations.	See How to Become One	$101,250
Judges, Mediators, and Hearing Officers	Judges, mediators, and hearing officers apply the law to court cases and oversee the legal process in courts. They also resolve administrative disputes and facilitate negotiations between opposing parties.	See How to Become One	$91,880
Lawyers	Lawyers advise and represent individuals, businesses, or government agencies on legal issues or disputes.	Doctoral or professional degree	$112,760
Political Scientists	Political scientists study the origin, development, and operation of political systems. They research political ideas and analyze the structure and operation of governments, policies, political trends, and related issues.	Master's degree	$107,420

Contacts for More Information

For more information about the U.S. Congress, visit U.S. Senate , U.S. House of Representatives

For more information about state legislatures, visit National Conference of State Legislatures

Suggested citation:

Bureau of Labor Statistics, U.S. Department of Labor, Occupational Outlook Handbook, 2012-13 Edition, Legislators, on the Internet at http://www.bls.gov/ooh/management/legislators.htm .

Lodging Managers

Quick Facts: Lodging Managers	
2010 Median Pay	$46,880 per year $22.54 per hour
Entry-Level Education	High school diploma or equivalent
Work Experience in a Related Occupation	1 to 5 years
On-the-job Training	None
Number of Jobs, 2010	51,400
Job Outlook, 2010-20	8% (Slower than average)
Employment Change, 2010-20	4,300

What Lodging Managers Do

Lodging managers make sure that guests on vacation or business travel have a pleasant experience, while also ensuring that an establishment is run efficiently and profitably.

Duties

Lodging managers typically do the following:

- Inspect guest rooms, public areas, and grounds for cleanliness and appearance
- Greet and register guests
- Ensure that standards for guest service, dÃ©cor, housekeeping, and food quality are met
- Answer questions from guests about hotel policies and services
- Keep track of how much money the hotel or lodging facility is making
- Interview, hire, train, and sometimes fire staff members
- Monitor staff performance to ensure that guests are happy and the hotel is well run
- Coordinate front-office activities of hotels or motels and resolve problems
- Set room rates and budgets, approve expenditures, and allocate funds to various departments

A comfortable room, good food, and a helpful staff can make being away from home an enjoyable experience for guests on vacation or business travel. Lodging managers make sure that guests have that good experience.

Lodging establishments vary in size from independently owned bed and breakfast inns and motels with just a few rooms to hotels that can have more than 1,000 guests. Services can vary from offering a room to having a swimming pool; from free breakfast to having a full-service restaurant; from having a lobby to also operating a casino and hosting conventions.

The following are types of lodging managers:

General managers oversee all lodging operations at a property. At larger hotels with several departments and multiple layers of management, the general manager and several assistant managers coordinate the activities of separate departments. These departments may include housekeeping, personnel, office administration, marketing and sales, purchasing, security, maintenance, recreational facilities, and other activities. For more information, see the profiles on human resources managers ; public relations managers and specialists ; financial managers ; advertising, promotions, and marketing managers ; and food service managers .

Revenue managers work in financial management, monitoring room sales and reservations, overseeing accounting and cash-flow matters at the hotel, projecting occupancy levels, and deciding which rooms to discount and when to offer special rates.

Front-office managers coordinate reservations and room assignments and train and direct the hotel's front-desk staff. They ensure that guests are treated courteously, complaints and problems are resolved, and requests for special services are carried out. Most front-office managers also are responsible for handling adjustment to bills.

Convention service managers coordinate the activities of various departments to accommodate meetings, conventions, and special events. They meet with representatives of groups to plan the number of conference rooms to be reserved, design the configuration of the meeting space, and determine what other services the group will need, such as catering or audiovisual requirements. During the meeting or event, they resolve unexpected problems and ensure that hotel operations meet the group's expectations.

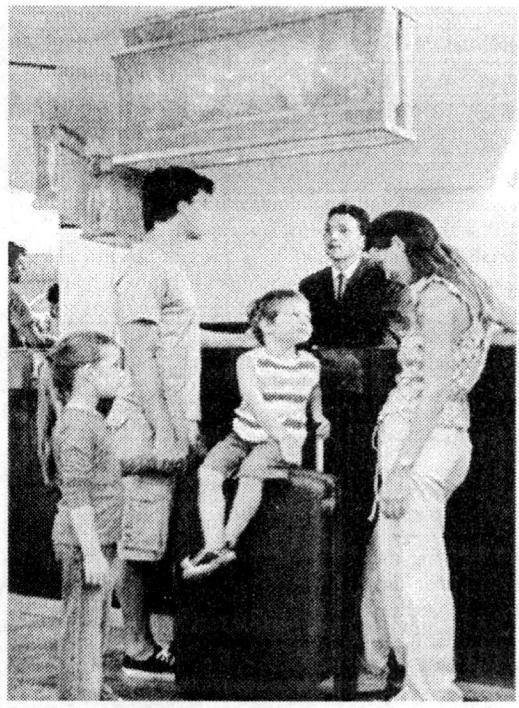

Lodging managers ensure that vacationing families have a pleasurable experience.

Work Environment

Lodging managers held about 51,400 jobs in 2010. More than half were employed in the traveler accommodation industry, which includes hotels and motels.

Most of the remainder work in other lodging establishments such as recreational vehicle (RV) and recreational camps, youth hostels, inns, boardinghouses, bed-and-breakfasts, and resorts. About 40 percent are self-employed.

The pressures of coordinating a wide range of activities, turning a profit for investors, and dealing with angry guests can sometimes be stressful.

Work Schedules

Most lodging managers work full time. Because hotels are open around the clock, evening and weekend work is common. Some managers must be on call 24 hours a day.

How to Become a Lodging Manager

Most large, full-service hotels require applicants to have a bachelor's degree. Smaller hotels generally seek applicants who have an associate's degree or certificate in hotel management or operations. Some applicants may qualify with long-term experience working at a hotel.

Education

More than 500 educational facilities across the United States provide academic training for prospective lodging managers.

Most full-service hotel chains hire people with a bachelor's degree in hospitality or hotel management. Hotel management programs typically include instruction in hotel administration, accounting, economics, marketing, housekeeping, food service management and catering, and hotel maintenance and engineering. Computer training is also an integral part of many degree programs, because hotels use hospitality-specific software in reservations, billing, and housekeeping management.

The Accreditation Commission for Programs in Hospitality Administration accredits about 100 hospitality management programs.

At hotels that provide fewer services, candidates with an associate's degree or certificate in hotel, restaurant, or hospitality management may qualify for a job as a lodging manager.

Many technical institutes and vocational and trade schools also offer courses leading to formal recognition in hospitality management.

About 245 high schools in 45 states offer the Lodging Management Program created by the American Hotel and Lodging Educational Institute. This 2-year program for high school juniors and seniors teaches management principles and leads to a professional certification called the Certified Rooms Division Supervisor.

Work Experience

Many hotel employees who do not have hospitality management training, but who show leadership potential and have several years of experience, may qualify for assistant manager positions.

Advancement

Large hotel chains may offer better opportunities than small, independently owned hotels for advancing from assistant manager to manager or from managing one hotel to being a regional manager. However, these opportunities also usually involve relocating to a different city or state.

Important Qualities

Customer-service skills. Lodging managers must have good customer-service skills when dealing with guests. Satisfying guests' needs is critical to a hotel's success and ensures customer loyalty.

Interpersonal skills. Lodging managers need strong interpersonal skills because they interact regularly with many different types of people. They must be effective communicators and must have positive interactions with guests and hotel staff, even in stressful situations.

Leadership skills. All lodging managers must establish good

working relationships to ensure a productive work environment. This objective may involve motivating personnel, resolving conflicts, or listening to complaints or criticism from guests.

Listening skills. All lodging managers should have excellent listening skills. Listening to the needs of guests allows managers to take the appropriate course of action, ensuring guests' satisfaction. Listening to the needs of workers helps them keep good working relationships with the staff.

Managerial skills. Lodging managers address budget matters and coordinate and supervise workers. Operating a profitable hotel is important, as is the need to motivate and direct the work of employees.

Organizational skills. Lodging managers keep track of many different schedules, budgets, and people at once. This task becomes more complex as the size of the hotel increases.

Problem-solving skills. The ability to resolve personnel issues and guest-related dissatisfaction is critical to the work of lodging managers. As a result, they must be creative and practical when solving problems.

Pay

Lodging Managers
Median annual wages, May 2010

Management Occupations	$91,440
Lodging Managers	$46,880
Total, All Occupations	$33,840

Note: All Occupations includes all occupations in the U.S. Economy.
Source: U.S. Bureau of Labor Statistics, Occupational Employment Statistics

The median annual wage of lodging managers was $46,880 in May 2010. The median wage is the wage at which half the workers in an occupation earned more than that amount and half earned less. The lowest 10 percent earned less than $29,460, and the top 10 percent earned more than $87,920.

In May 2010, the median annual wages in industries employing the largest numbers of lodging managers were as follows:

Management of companies and enterprises	$64,640
Activities related to real estate	56,080
Full-service restaurants	46,840
Traveler accommodation	46,550
RV (recreational vehicle) parks and recreational camps	42,070

Most lodging managers work full time. Because hotels are open around the clock, evening and weekend work is common. Some managers must be on call 24 hours a day.

Job Outlook

Lodging Managers
Percent change in employment, projected 2010-20

Total, All Occupations	14%
Lodging Managers	8%
Management Occupations	7%

Note: All Occupations includes all occupations in the U.S. Economy.
Source: U.S. Bureau of Labor Statistics, Employment Projections program

Employment of lodging managers is expected to grow 8 percent from 2010 to 2010, slower than the average for all occupations. Despite expected growth in tourism and travel, fewer managers will be needed as the lodging industry shifts to building more limited-service hotels and fewer full-service properties that have separate departments to manage.

In addition, some lodging places are streamlining operations to cut expenses by either eliminating some managers or scaling back the total number. Chain hotels, for instance, are increasingly assigning a single manager to oversee multiple properties within a region. Still, some larger full-service hotels, including casinos, resorts, and convention hotels that provide a wider range of services to a larger customer base, will continue to generate job openings for experienced managers.

are expected to face strong competition as these jobs are highly sought after by people trained in hospitality management or administration. Job opportunities at smaller hotels should be better. Those with a college degree in hotel or hospitality management are expected to have the best job opportunities, particularly at upscale and luxury hotels.

Job Prospects

Those seeking jobs at hotels with the highest level of guest services

Employment projections data for lodging managers, 2010-20

Occupational Title	SOC Code	Employment, 2010	Projected Employment, 2020	Change, 2010-20	
				Percent	Numeric
Lodging Managers	11-9081	51,400	55,700	8	4,300
SOURCE: U.S. Bureau of Labor Statistics, Employment Projections program					

Similar Occupations

This table shows a list of occupations with job duties that are similar to those of lodging managers.

Occupation	Job Duties	Entry-Level Education	Median Annual Pay, May 2010
Food Service Managers	Food service managers are responsible for the daily operations of restaurants and other establishments that prepare and serve food and beverages to customers. Managers ensure that customers are satisfied with their dining experience.	High school diploma or equivalent	$48,130
Gaming Services Occupations	Gaming services workers serve customers in gambling establishments, such as casinos or racetracks. Some workers tend slot machines or deal cards. Others take bets or pay out winnings. Still others supervise gaming workers and operations.	See How to Become One	$20,260
Human Resources Managers	Human resources managers plan, direct, and coordinate the administrative functions of an organization. They oversee the recruiting, interviewing, and hiring of new staff; consult with top executives on strategic planning; and serve as a link between an organization's management and its employees.	Bachelor's degree	$99,180
Property, Real Estate, and Community Association Managers	Property, real estate, and community association managers take care of the many aspects of residential, commercial, or industrial properties. They make sure the property looks nice, operates smoothly, and preserves its resale value.	High school diploma or equivalent	$51,480
Public Relations Managers and Specialists	Public relations managers and specialists create and maintain a favorable public image for their employer or client. They write material for media releases, plan and direct public relations programs, and raise funds for their organizations.	Bachelor's degree	$57,550
Sales Managers	Sales managers direct organizations' sales teams. They set sales goals, analyze data, and develop training programs for the organization's sales representatives.	Bachelor's degree	$98,530

Contacts for More Information

For information about careers in the lodging industry and professional development and training programs, visit American Hotel and Lodging Educational Institute

For information about educational programs in hotel and restaurant management, including correspondence courses, visit International Council on Hotel, Restaurant, and Institutional Education

For information about accreditation standards and for a list of accredited educational programs in hospitality administration, visit Accreditation Commission for Programs in Hospitality Administration

Suggested citation:

Bureau of Labor Statistics, U.S. Department of Labor, Occupational Outlook Handbook, 2012-13 Edition, Lodging Managers, on the Internet at http://www.bls.gov/ooh/management/lodging-managers.htm .

Medical and Health Services Managers

Quick Facts: Medical and Health Services Managers	
2010 Median Pay	$84,270 per year $40.52 per hour
Entry-Level Education	Bachelor's degree
Work Experience in a Related Occupation	None
On-the-job Training	None
Number of Jobs, 2010	303,000
Job Outlook, 2010-20	22% (Faster than average)
Employment Change, 2010-20	68,000

What Medical and Health Services Managers Do

Medical and health services managers, also called healthcare executives or healthcare administrators, plan, direct, and coordinate medical and health services. They might manage an entire facility or specialize in managing a specific clinical area or department, or manage a medical practice for a group of physicians. As healthcare changes, medical and health services managers must be able to adapt to changes in laws, regulations, and technology.

Duties

Medical and health services managers typically do the following:

* Work to improve efficiency and quality in delivering healthcare services
* Keep up to date on new laws and regulations so the facility complies with them
* Supervise assistant administrators in facilities that are large enough to need them
* Manage finances of the facility, such as patient fees and billing
* Create work schedules
* Represent the facility at investor meetings or on governing boards
* Keep and organize records of the facility's services, such as the number of inpatient beds used
* Communicate with members of the medical staff and department heads

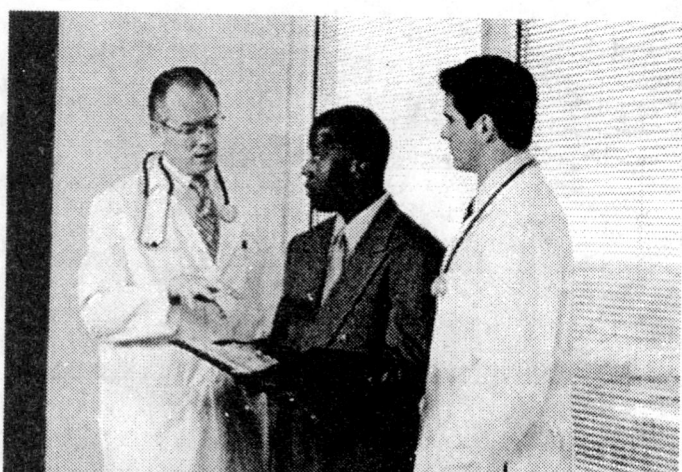

Medical and health services managers often work closely with medical staff to plan, direct, and coordinate the delivery of healthcare.

In group medical practices, managers work closely with physicians, nurses, laboratory technicians, and other healthcare employees. For more information, see the profiles on physicians and surgeons , registered nurses , and medical and clinical laboratory technologists and technicians .

Medical and health services managers' titles depend on the facility or area of expertise in which they work. The following are some examples of types of medical and health services managers:

Nursing home administrators manage staff, admissions, finances, and care of the building, as well as care of the residents in nursing homes. All states require them to be licensed; licensing requirements vary by state.

Clinical managers manage a specific department, such as nursing, surgery, or physical therapy and have responsibilities based on that specialty. Clinical managers set and carry out policies, goals, and procedures for their departments; evaluate the quality of the staff's work; and develop reports and budgets.

Health information managers are responsible for the maintenance and security of all patient records. They must stay up to date with evolving information technology and current or proposed laws about health information systems. Health information managers must ensure that databases are complete, accurate, and accessible only to authorized personnel.

Assistant administrators work under the top administrator in larger facilities and often handle daily decisions. Assistants might direct activities in clinical areas, such as nursing, surgery, therapy, medical records, or health information.

Work Environment

Medical and health services managers held about 303,000 jobs in 2010. Most medical and health services managers work in offices in healthcare facilities, including hospitals and nursing homes, and group medical practices.

The following industries were the largest employers of medical and health services managers in 2010:

Hospitals; state, local, and private	39%
Offices of physicians	9
Nursing care facilities	7
Home health care services	6
Outpatient care centers	5

Work Schedules

Most medical and health services managers work full time. Because their services are sometimes needed in emergencies or at facilities that are always open, some work may be required during evenings, on weekends, or overnight.

How to Become a Medical or Health Services Manager

Most medical and health services managers have at least a bachelor's degree before entering the field; however, master's degrees also are common. Requirements vary by facility.

Education

Medical and health services managers typically need at least a bachelor's degree to enter the occupation. However, master's degrees in health services, long-term care administration, public health, public administration, or business administration also are common.

Prospective medical and health services managers have a bachelor's degree in health administration. These programs prepare students for higher level management jobs than programs that graduate students with other degrees. Courses needed for a degree in health administration often include hospital organization and management, accounting and budgeting, human resources administration, strategic planning, law and ethics, health economics, and health information systems. Some programs allow students to specialize in a particular type of facility, such as a hospital, a nursing care home, a mental health facility, or a group medical practice. Graduate programs often last between 2 and 3 years and may include up to 1 year of supervised administrative experience.

Work Experience

Although bachelor's and master's degrees are the most common educational pathways to work in this field, some facilities may hire those with on-the-job experience instead of formal education. For example, managers of physical therapy may be experienced physical therapists who have administrative experience. For more information, see the profile on physical therapists .

Important Qualities

Analytical skills. Medical and health services managers must be able to understand and follow current regulations and be able to adapt to new laws.

Communication skills. These managers must be able to communicate effectively with other health professionals.

Detail oriented. Medical and health services managers must pay attention to detail. They might be required to organize and maintain scheduling and billing information for very large facilities, such as hospitals.

Interpersonal skills. Medical and health services managers need to be able to discuss staffing problems and patient information with other professionals, such as physicians and health insurance representatives. They must be able to motivate and lead staff.

Problem-solving skills. These managers are often responsible for finding creative solutions to staffing or other administrative problems.

Technical skills. Medical and health services managers must be able to follow advances in health care technology. For example, they may need to use coding and classification software and electronic health record (EHR) systems as their facility adopts these technologies.

Advancement

Medical and health services managers advance by moving into more responsible and higher paying positions. In large hospitals, graduates of health administration programs usually begin as administrative assistants or assistant department heads. In small hospitals or nursing care facilities, they may begin as department heads or assistant administrators. Some experienced managers also may become consultants or professors of healthcare management. The level of the starting position varies with the experience of the applicant and the size of the organization.

For those already in a different healthcare occupation, a master's degree in health services administration or a related field might be required to advance. For example, nursing service administrators usually are supervisory registered nurses with administrative experience and graduate degrees in nursing or health administration. For more information, see the profile on registered nurses .

Licenses

All states require nursing care facility administrators to be licensed; requirements vary by state. In most states, these administrators must have a bachelor's degree, pass a licensing exam, and complete a state-approved training program. Some states also require administrators in assisted-living facilities to be licensed. A license is not required in other areas of medical and health services management.

Pay

Medical and Health Services Managers
Median annual wages, May 2010

Management Occupations	$91,440
Medical and Health Services Managers	$84,270
Total, All Occupations	$33,840

Note: All Occupations includes all occupations in the U.S. Economy.
Source: U.S. Bureau of Labor Statistics, Occupational Employment Statistics

The median annual wage of medical and health services managers was $84,270 in May 2010. The median wage is the wage at which half the workers in an occupation earned more than that amount and half earned less. The lowest 10 percent earned less than $51,280, and the top 10 percent earned more than $144,880.

Earnings of medical and health services managers vary by type and size of the facility and by level of responsibility. For example, the Medical Group Management Association reported that, in 2010, median compensation for administrators was $86,459 in practices with six or fewer physicians; $115,000 in practices with seven to 25 physicians; and $150,756 in practices with 26 or more physicians.

Most medical and health services managers work full time. Because their services are sometimes needed in emergencies or at facilities that are always open, some work may be required during evenings, on weekends, or overnight.

Job Outlook

Medical and Health Services Managers
Percent change in employment, projected 2010-20

Medical and Health Services Managers	22%
Total, All Occupations	14%
Management Occupations	7%

Note: All Occupations includes all occupations in the U.S. Economy.
Source: U.S. Bureau of Labor Statistics, Employment Projections program

Employment of medical and health services managers is expected to grow by 22 percent from 2010 to 2020, faster than the average for all occupations. As the large baby-boom population ages and people remain active later in life, the healthcare industry as a whole will see an increase in the demand for medical services. This increase will in turn result in an increase in the number of physicians, patients, and procedures, as well as in the number of facilities. Managers will be needed to organize and manage medical information and staffs in the healthcare industry. There will likely be increased demand for nursing care facility administrators as well as baby boomers age.

Employment is expected to grow in offices of health practitioners. Many services previously provided in hospitals will shift to these settings, especially as medical technologies improve. Demand in medical group practice management is expected to grow as medical group practices become larger and more complex.

Employment projections data for medical and health services managers, 2010-20

Occupational Title	SOC Code	Employment, 2010	Projected Employment, 2020	Change, 2010-20	
				Percent	Numeric
Medical and Health Services Managers	11-9111	303,000	371,000	22	68,000
SOURCE: U.S. Bureau of Labor Statistics, Employment Projections program					

Similar Occupations

This table shows a list of occupations with job duties that are similar to those of medical and health services managers.

Occupation	Job Duties	Entry-Level Education	Median Annual Pay, May 2010
Human Resources Managers	Human resources managers plan, direct, and coordinate the administrative functions of an organization. They oversee the recruiting, interviewing, and hiring of new staff; consult with top executives on strategic planning; and serve as a link between an organization's management and its employees.	Bachelor's degree	$99,180
Insurance Underwriters	Insurance underwriters decide whether to provide insurance and under what terms. They evaluate insurance applications and determine coverage amounts and premiums.	Bachelor's degree	$59,290
Social and Community Service Managers	Social and community service managers coordinate and supervise social service programs and community organizations. They direct and lead staff who provide services to the public.	Bachelor's degree	$57,950

Contacts for More Information

For information about medical and healthcare office managers, visit Professional Association of Health Care Office Management , American Health Information Management Association , American College of Health Care Administrators

For more information about academic programs in this field, visit Association of University Programs in Health Administration , Commission on Accreditation of Healthcare Management Education

For information about career opportunities in healthcare management, visit American College of Healthcare Executives

For information about career opportunities in medical group practices and ambulatory care management, visit Medical Group Management Association

Suggested citation:

Bureau of Labor Statistics, U.S. Department of Labor, Occupational Outlook Handbook, 2012-13 Edition, Medical and Health Services Managers, on the Internet at http://www.bls.gov/ooh/management/medical-and-health-services-managers.htm .

Natural Sciences Managers

Quick Facts: Natural Sciences Managers	
2010 Median Pay	$116,020 per year $55.78 per hour
Entry-Level Education	Bachelor's degree
Work Experience in a Related Occupation	More than 5 years
On-the-job Training	None
Number of Jobs, 2010	49,300
Job Outlook, 2010-20	8% (Slower than average)
Employment Change, 2010-20	3,800

What Natural Sciences Managers Do

Natural sciences managers supervise the work of scientists, including chemists, physicists, and biologists. They plan and direct research and development projects and coordinate activities such as testing, quality control, and production.

Duties

Natural sciences managers typically do the following:

- Work with top executives to determine scientific and technical goals of research and development and make detailed plans to accomplish these goals
- Prepare budgets for projects and programs and determine staff, training, and equipment needs
- Hire, supervise, and evaluate scientists, engineers, technicians, and other staff

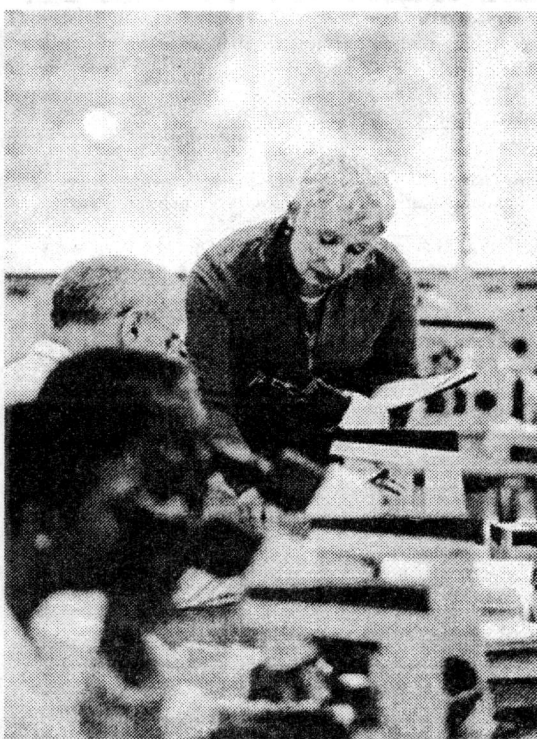

Natural sciences managers hire, supervise, and evaluate scientists, technicians, and other staff.

- Review the accuracy of their staff's work and the soundness of the methods the staff uses
- Monitor the progress of projects and prepare and review research, testing, and operational reports
- Provide technical assistance to scientists, technicians, and support staff
- Establish administrative procedures, policies, or standards—such as environmental standards
- Communicate with clients and top management to explain proposals, present research findings, establish specifications, or discuss the status of a project

Natural sciences managers direct scientific research and development projects and coordinate activities such as testing, quality control, and production. Research projects can have many aims, including improving manufacturing processes, advancing scientific research, and developing new products. Most natural sciences managers are former scientists, and after becoming managers, many continue to conduct their own research in addition to overseeing the work of others.

During all stages of a project, natural sciences managers spend a lot of time coordinating the activities of their unit with those of other units or organizations. They confer with higher levels of management; with financial, production, marketing, and other managers; with contractors; and with equipment and materials suppliers.

Work Environment

Natural sciences managers held about 49,300 jobs in 2010. They spend most of their time in offices, but they also may spend time in laboratories. Natural sciences managers can be exposed to health or safety hazards in laboratories, but there is little risk if proper procedures are followed.

Industries employing the largest numbers of natural sciences managers in 2010 were as follows:

Research and development in the physical, engineering, and life sciences	22%
Federal government, excluding postal service	22
Pharmaceutical and medicine manufacturing	12
State government, excluding education and hospitals	8

Work Schedules

Almost all natural sciences managers work full time. Managers often work long hours to meet project deadlines. They also may experience considerable pressure to meet technical or scientific goals on a short deadline or within a tight budget.

How to Become a Natural Sciences Manager

Natural sciences managers usually advance to management positions after years of employment as scientists. Natural sciences managers typically have a bachelor's, master's, or Ph.D. degree in a scientific discipline or a related field such as engineering.

Work Experience

Natural sciences managers usually advance to management positions after years of employment as scientists. While employed as scientists, they are typically given more responsibility and independence in their work as they gain experience. Eventually, they may lead research teams and have control over the direction and content of projects before being promoted to an executive position.

Education

Because natural sciences managers typically begin their careers as scientists, most have a bachelor's, master's, or Ph.D. degree in a scientific discipline or a closely related field such as engineering. Strong scientific and technical knowledge is essential for managers because they must be able to understand the work of their subordinates and provide technical assistance when needed.

Natural sciences managers interested in management that is more technical may earn a traditional master's or Ph.D. degree in a natural science or a master's degree in a science that incorporates business management skills. Those interested in management that is more general may pursue a Master of Business Administration (MBA).

Given the rapid pace of scientific developments, science managers must continually upgrade their knowledge.

Important Qualities

Critical-thinking skills. Natural sciences managers must carefully evaluate the work of others. They must determine if methods and results are based on sound science.

Interpersonal skills. Natural sciences managers lead research teams and need to be able to work well with others toward a common goal.

Leadership skills. Natural sciences managers must be able to organize, direct, and motivate others. They need to identify the strengths and weaknesses of their workers and put the workers in a position to succeed.

Problem-solving skills. Natural sciences managers use scientific observation and analysis to find solutions to complex scientific and technical questions.

Speaking skills. Natural sciences managers must be able to discuss their research projects with clients, top managers, and others who do not have a technical background.

Time-management skills. Natural sciences managers must be able to do multiple administrative, supervisory, and technical tasks while ensuring that projects remain on schedule.

Writing skills. Natural sciences managers write project proposals and reports that detail their research goals and findings.

Pay

Natural Sciences Managers
Median annual wages, May 2010

Natural Sciences Managers	$116,020
Management Occupations	$91,440
Total, All Occupations	$33,840

Note: All Occupations includes all occupations in the U.S. Economy.
Source: U.S. Bureau of Labor Statistics, Occupational Employment Statistics

The median annual wage of natural sciences managers was $116,020 in May 2010. The median wage is the wage at which half the workers in an occupation earned more than that amount and half earned less. The lowest 10 percent earned less than $67,290, and the top 10 percent earned more than $166,400.

Median annual wages in the industries employing the largest numbers of natural sciences managers in May 2010 were as follows:

Research and development in the physical, engineering, and life sciences	$145,160
Pharmaceutical and medicine manufacturing	143,120
Federal government, excluding postal service	107,590
State government, excluding education and hospitals	72,900

Almost all natural sciences managers work full time. Managers often work long hours to meet project deadlines. They also may experience considerable pressure to meet technical or scientific goals on a short deadline or within a tight budget.

Job Outlook

Natural Sciences Managers
Percent change in employment, projected 2010-20

Total, All Occupations	14%
Natural Sciences Managers	8%
Management Occupations	7%

Note: All Occupations includes all occupations in the U.S. Economy.
Source: U.S. Bureau of Labor Statistics, Employment Projections program

Employment of natural sciences managers is projected to grow by 8 percent from 2010 to 2020, slower than the average for all occupations. Employment growth should be affected by many of the same factors that affect employment growth for scientists whom these managers supervise. However, job growth for managers is expected to be somewhat slower than that for scientists, because research and development activities are increasingly being outsourced to specialized scientific research services firms. This outsourcing will lead to some consolidation of management.

Job Prospects

In addition to job openings resulting from employment growth, openings will result from the need to replace managers who retire or move into other occupations. Competition for job openings will likely be strong because of the high salaries that natural sciences managers command and the greater resources and control over projects that scientists can gain from becoming managers.

Employment projections data for natural sciences managers, 2010-20

Occupational Title	SOC Code	Employment, 2010	Projected Employment, 2020	Change, 2010-20 Percent	Change, 2010-20 Numeric
Natural Sciences Managers	11-9121	49,300	53,100	8	3,800

SOURCE: U.S. Bureau of Labor Statistics, Employment Projections program

Similar Occupations

This table shows a list of occupations with job duties that are similar to those of natural sciences managers.

Occupation	Job Duties	Entry-Level Education	Median Annual Pay, May 2010
Architectural and Engineering Managers	Architectural and engineering managers plan, coordinate, and direct activities in architecture and engineering, including research and development in these fields.	Bachelor's degree	$119,260
Biochemists and Biophysicists	Biochemists and biophysicists study the chemical and physical principles of living things and of biological processes such as cell development, growth, and heredity.	Doctoral or professional degree	$79,390
Chemists and Materials Scientists	Chemists and materials scientists study the structures, compositions, reactions, and other properties of substances. They use their knowledge to develop new and improved products, processes, and materials.	Bachelor's degree	$69,790
Environmental Scientists and Specialists	Environmental scientists and specialists use their knowledge of the natural sciences to protect the environment. They identify problems and find solutions that minimize hazards to the health of the environment and the population.	Bachelor's degree	$61,700
Geoscientists	Geoscientists study the physical aspects of the Earth, such as its composition, structure, and processes, to learn about its past, present, and future.	Bachelor's degree	$82,500
Medical Scientists	Medical scientists conduct research aimed at improving overall human health. They often use clinical trials and other investigative methods to reach their findings.	Doctoral or professional degree	$76,700
Physicists and Astronomers	Physicists and astronomers study the fundamental nature of the universe, ranging from the vastness of space to the smallest of subatomic particles. They develop new technologies, methods, and theories based on the results of their research that deepen our understanding of how things work and contribute to innovative, real-world applications.	Doctoral or professional degree	$105,430
Postsecondary Teachers	Postsecondary teachers instruct students in a wide variety of academic and vocational subjects beyond the high school level. They also conduct research and publish scholarly papers and books.	Doctoral or professional degree	$62,050
Top Executives	Top executives devise strategies and policies to ensure that an organization meets its goals. They plan, direct, and coordinate operational activities of companies and public or private-sector organizations.	See How to Become One	$101,250

Contacts for More Information

For information about science careers with the federal government, visit USAJOBS

Suggested citation:

Bureau of Labor Statistics, U.S. Department of Labor, Occupational Outlook Handbook, 2012-13 Edition, Natural Sciences Managers, on the Internet at http://www.bls.gov/ooh/management/natural-sciences-managers.htm .

Postsecondary Education Administrators

Quick Facts: Postsecondary Education Administrators	
2010 Median Pay	$83,710 per year $40.24 per hour
Entry-Level Education	Master's degree
Work Experience in a Related Occupation	1 to 5 years
On-the-job Training	None
Number of Jobs, 2010	146,200
Job Outlook, 2010-20	19% (About as fast as average)
Employment Change, 2010-20	27,800

What Postsecondary Education Administrators Do

Postsecondary education administrators oversee student services, academics, and research at colleges and universities. Their job duties vary depending on the area of the college they manage, such as admissions, the office of the registrar, or student affairs.

Duties

Postsecondary education administrators who work in **admissions** decide whether potential students should be admitted to the school. They typically do the following:

- Determine how many students to admit to fill the available spaces
- Prepare promotional materials, such as brochures and videos, about the school
- Meet with prospective students to discuss the school and encourage them to apply
- Review applications to determine if each potential student should be admitted
- Analyze data about applicants and admitted students

Many admissions counselors are assigned a region of the country and travel to that region to speak to high school counselors and students.

In addition, they often work with the financial aid department,

Postsecondary education administrators oversee student services, academics, and research at colleges and universities.

which helps students determine if they are able to afford tuition.

Postsecondary education administrators who work in the **registrar's office** maintain student and course records. They typically do the following:

- Schedule and register students for classes
- Ensure that students meet graduation requirements
- Plan commencement ceremonies
- Prepare transcripts and diplomas for students
- Produce data about students and classes

How registrars spend their time varies depending on the time of year. Before students register for classes, registrars must prepare schedules and course offerings. Then during registration and for the first few weeks of the semester, they help students sign up for, drop, and add courses. Toward the end of the semester, they plan graduation and ensure that students meet the requirements to graduate. Many of them need advanced computer skills to create and maintain databases.

Postsecondary education administrators who work in **student affairs** are responsible for a variety of nonacademic school functions, such as student athletics and activities. They typically do the following:

- Advise students on topics such as housing issues, personal problems, or academics
- Communicate with parents and families
- Create and maintain student records
- Create, support, and assess nonacademic programs for students
- Schedule programs and services, such as athletic events or recreational activities

Postsecondary education administrators in student affairs can specialize in student activities, housing and residential life, or multicultural affairs. In student activities, education administrators plan events and advise student clubs and organizations. In housing and residential life, education administrators assign students rooms and roommates, ensure that residential facilities are well maintained, and train student staff, such as residential advisers. Education administrators who specialize in multicultural affairs plan events to celebrate different cultures and diverse backgrounds. Sometimes, they manage multicultural centers on campus.

Other **postsecondary education administrators** are **provosts** or **academic deans**. Provosts, also sometimes called chief academic officers, help college presidents develop academic policies, participate in making faculty appointments and tenure decisions, and manage budgets. Academic deans direct and coordinate the activities of the individual colleges or schools. For example, in a large university, there may be a dean who oversees the law school.

Education administrators have varying duties depending on the size of their college or university. Small schools often have smaller staffs who take on many different responsibilities, but larger schools may have different offices for each of these functions. For example, at a small college, the Office of Student Life may oversee student athletics and other activities, whereas a large university may have an Athletics Department.

Work Environment

Postsecondary education administrators held about 146,200 jobs in 2010.

Postsecondary education administrators work in colleges, universities, community colleges, and technical and trade schools. Some work for public schools, and others work for private schools.

In 2010, 73 percent of postsecondary education administrators worked for colleges, universities and professional schools and 17 percent worked for junior colleges.

Work Schedules

Postsecondary education administrators generally work full time. Most work year-round, but some schools may reduce their hours during the summer.

How to Become a Postsecondary Education Administrator

Although a bachelor's degree may be acceptable for some entry-level positions, a master's or higher degree is often required. Employers often require candidates for some positions, particularly for registrars and academic deans to have some experience.

Education

Educational requirements vary for different positions. For entry-level positions, a bachelor's degree may be sufficient. Degrees can be in a variety of disciplines, such as social work, accounting, or marketing.

For higher level positions, a master's degree or doctorate is generally required. Provosts and deans often must have a Ph.D. Some provosts and deans begin their career as professors and later move into administration. These administrators have doctorates in the field in which they taught, such as English or chemistry. Other provosts and deans have a Ph.D. in higher education or a related field.

Work Experience

Employers often require candidates for some positions, particularly for registrars and academic deans, to have some experience.For other positions, such as those in admissions and student affairs, experience may or may not be necessary depending on the position.

Advancement

Education administrators with advanced degrees can be promoted to higher level positions within their department or the college. Some become college presidents. For more information about college presidents, see the profile on top executives.

Important Qualities

Computer skills. Registrars often need to be adept at working with computers so they can create and maintain databases and computer programs to manage student and school records.

Organizational skills. Regardless of their field, administrators need to be organized so they can manage records, prioritize tasks, and coordinate the activities of their staff.

People skills. Postsecondary education administrators need to build good relationships with colleagues, students, and parents. Those in

admissions and student affairs need to be outgoing so they can encourage students to apply to the school or participate in co-curricular activities.

Problem-solving skills. Administrators often need to respond to difficult situations, develop creative solutions to problems, and react calmly when problems arise.

Pay

Postsecondary Education Administrators
Median annual wages, May 2010

Management Occupations	$91,440
Education Administrators, Postsecondary	$83,710
Total, All Occupations	$33,840

Note: All Occupations includes all occupations in the U.S. Economy.
Source: U.S. Bureau of Labor Statistics, Occupational Employment Statistics

The median annual wage for postsecondary education administrators was $83,710 in May 2010. The median wage is the wage at which half the workers in an occupation earned more than that amount and half earned less. The lowest 10 percent earned less than $47,130, and the top 10 percent earned more than $164,540.

Postsecondary education administrators generally work full time. Most work year-round, but some schools may reduce their hours during the summer.

Job Outlook

Postsecondary Education Administrators
Percent change in employment, projected 2010-20

Education Administrators, Postsecondary	19%
Total, All Occupations	14%
Management Occupations	7%

Note: All Occupations includes all occupations in the U.S. Economy.
Source: U.S. Bureau of Labor Statistics, Employment Projections program

Employment of postsecondary education administrators is expected to grow by 19 percent from 2010 to 2020, about as fast as the average. Expected growth is due to increases in enrollments.

The number of people attending postsecondary school will increase as people seek additional education and skills to meet their career goals. As more people enter colleges and universities, more postsecondary education administrators will be needed to serve the needs of these additional students.

Additional admissions officers will be needed to process students' applications. More registrars will be needed to register students for classes and ensure that they meet graduation requirements. More student affairs workers will be needed to make housing assignments and plan events for students.

In particular, significant increases in enrollment are expected in online colleges and universities. As a result, there will more demand for postsecondary education administrators in these types of schools.

However, despite expected increases in enrollment, employment growth in public colleges and universities will depend on state and local government budgets. When state and local governments have budget deficits, they may lay off employees, including administrators. As a result, employment growth may be somewhat slowed by state and local government budget deficits.

Job Prospects

Between 2010 and 2020, a large number of postsecondary education administrators are expected to retire. This should open opportunities for new workers entering the field due to the occupation's need to replace workers who are leaving.

Employment projections data for postsecondary education administrators, 2010-20

Occupational Title	SOC Code	Employment, 2010	Projected Employment, 2020	Change, 2010-20	
				Percent	Numeric
Education Administrators, Postsecondary	11-9033	146,200	174,000	19	27,800
SOURCE: U.S. Bureau of Labor Statistics, Employment Projections program					

Similar Occupations

This table shows a list of occupations with job duties that are similar to those of postsecondary education administrators.

Occupation	Job Duties	Entry-Level Education	Median Annual Pay, May 2010
Administrative Services Managers	Administrative services managers plan, direct, and coordinate supportive services of an organization. Their specific responsibilities vary by the type of organization and may include keeping records, distributing mail, and planning and maintaining facilities.	High school diploma or equivalent	$77,890
Human Resources Managers	Human resources managers plan, direct, and coordinate the administrative functions of an organization. They oversee the recruiting, interviewing, and hiring of new staff; consult with top executives on strategic planning; and serve as a link between an organization's management and its employees.	Bachelor's degree	$99,180
Postsecondary Teachers	Postsecondary teachers instruct students in a wide variety of academic and vocational subjects beyond the high school level. They also conduct research and publish scholarly papers and books.	Doctoral or professional degree	$62,050
Public Relations Managers and Specialists	Public relations managers and specialists create and maintain a favorable public image for their employer or client. They write material for media releases, plan and direct public relations programs, and raise funds for their organizations.	Bachelor's degree	$57,550
School and Career Counselors	School counselors help students develop social skills and succeed in school. Career counselors assist people with the process of making career decisions by helping them choose a career or educational program.	Master's degree	$53,380
Training and Development Managers	Training and development managers plan, direct, and coordinate programs to enhance the knowledge and skills of an organization's employees. They also oversee a staff of training and development specialists.	Bachelor's degree	$89,170
Top Executives	Top executives devise strategies and policies to ensure that an organization meets its goals. They plan, direct, and coordinate operational activities of companies and public or private-sector organizations.	See How to Become One	$101,250

Contacts for More Information

For more information on registrars or admissions counselors, visit American Association of Collegiate Registrars and Admissions Officers

For more information about education administrators specializing in student affairs, visit NASPA: Student Affairs Administrators in Higher Education

Preschool and Childcare Center Directors

Quick Facts: Preschool and Childcare Center Directors	
2010 Median Pay	$42,960 per year $20.65 per hour
Entry-Level Education	Bachelor's degree
Work Experience in a Related Occupation	1 to 5 years
On-the-job Training	None
Number of Jobs, 2010	63,600
Job Outlook, 2010-20	25% (Faster than average)
Employment Change, 2010-20	15,800

What Preschool and Childcare Center Directors Do

Preschool and childcare center directors are responsible for all aspects of their program. They direct and lead staff, oversee daily activities, and prepare plans and budgets.

Duties

Preschool and childcare center directors typically do the following:

- Supervise preschool teachers and childcare workers
- Establish policies and communicate them to staff and parents
- Provide training and professional development opportunities for staff
- Assist staff in resolving conflicts between children and communicating with parents
- Meet with parents and staff to discuss students' progress
- Establish budgets and set fees for programs
- Ensure facilities are maintained and cleaned according to state regulations
- Hire and train new staff members
- Develop educational programs and set educational standards

Some preschools and childcare centers are independently owned and operated. In these facilities, directors must follow the instructions and guidelines of the owner. Sometimes, directors own the facilities, so they decide how to operate the facilities.

Other preschools and childcare centers are part of a national chain or franchise. The director of a chain or franchise must also ensure that the facility meets its parent organization's standards and regulations.

In addition, some preschools and childcare centers, such as Head Start programs, receive state and federal funding. Directors of these schools and centers must ensure that their programs, staff, and facilities meet state and federal guidelines. For example, they must ensure that the staff meets the educational requirements set by the Department of Health and Human Services .

Work Environment

Preschool and childcare center directors held about 63,600 jobs in 2010. Most work for child day care services. However, some work for religious or charitable organizations and for elementary and secondary schools that have preschool and childcare programs.

The following industries employed the most preschool and childcare center directors in 2010:

Child day care services	55%
Religious, grantmaking, civic, professional, and similar organizations	16
Elementary and secondary schools; state, local, and private	14
Individual and family services	5

Many preschool and child care center directors find working in an early childhood educational environment rewarding, but they also have significant responsibilities. Coordinating and interacting with staff, parents, and children can be fast paced and stimulating, but also stressful.

Work Schedules

Preschool and childcare center directors generally work full time. Some work more than 40 hours per week.

How to Become a Preschool or Childcare Center Director

Education and training requirements vary by state. Requirements range from a high school diploma to a college degree.

Education

Most states require preschool and childcare center directors to have at least a high school diploma, but some require an associate's or

Preschool and childcare center directors provide direction and leadership to the staff who teach preschool classes and care for children.

bachelor's degree in early childhood education. These degree programs teach students about child development, strategies to teach young children, and how to observe and document children's progress. Employers may prefer candidates who have a degree in early childhood education or at least some postsecondary education in early childhood education.

Work Experience

Some states require preschool and childcare center directors to have experience in early childhood education. The amount of necessary experience varies by state.

Certification

Some states and employers require preschool and childcare center directors to have nationally recognized certification. Most states require the Child Development Associate (CDA) certification offered by the Council for Professional Recognition . Requirements to earn the CDA include a high school diploma, experience in the field, and coursework.

Some states recognize the Child Care Professional (CCP) designation offered by the National Child Care Association . Requirements to earn the CCP include a high school diploma, experience in the field, and continuing education courses.

Licenses

Many states require childcare facilities to be licensed. To meet licensure requirements, the facility's staff, including the director, must meet certain requirements: they must pass a background check, have the right immunizations, and meet a minimum training requirement.

Important Qualities

Communication skills. Preschool and childcare center directors need to inform parents and colleagues about the progress of the children. They need good writing and speaking skills to convey this information effectively.

Leadership skills. Preschool and childcare center directors supervise staff, so they need good leadership skills to inspire staff to work diligently. They also must enforce rules and regulations.

People skills. Preschool and childcare center directors must be able to develop good relationships with parents, children, and colleagues.

Pay

Preschool and Childcare Center Directors
Median annual wages, May 2010

Management Occupations	$91,440
Preschool and Childcare Center Directors	$42,960
Total, All Occupations	$33,840

Note: All Occupations includes all occupations in the U.S. Economy.
Source: U.S. Bureau of Labor Statistics, Occupational Employment Statistics

The median annual wage of preschool and childcare center directors was $42,960 in May 2010. The median wage is the wage at which half the workers in an occupation earned more than that amount and half earned less. The lowest 10 percent earned less than $27,210,

and the top 10 percent earned more than $85,110.

In May 2010, the median annual wages of preschool and childcare center directors in the top employing industries were as follows:

Elementary and secondary schools; state, local, and private	$70,670
Individual and family services	46,000
Religious, grantmaking, civic, professional, and similar organizations	42,810
Child day care services	39,200

Preschool and childcare center directors generally work full time. Some work more than 40 hours per week.

Job Outlook

Preschool and Childcare Center Directors
Percent change in employment, projected 2010-20

Preschool and Childcare Center Directors	25%
Total, All Occupations	14%
Management Occupations	7%

Note: All Occupations includes all occupations in the U.S. Economy.
Source: U.S. Bureau of Labor Statistics, Employment Projections program

Employment of preschool and childcare center directors is expected to grow by 25 percent from 2010 to 2020, faster than the average for all occupation. Working parents will continue to need help caring for children. The number of children who are of preschool age is increasing, leading to a greater need for child care and increasing the demand for preschool and childcare center directors.

Additionally, there is a continued focus on the importance of early childhood education, specifically preschool. Early childhood education is widely recognized as important for a child's intellectual and emotional development. As the number of preschool programs grows, the need for preschool and childcare center directors will increase as well.

From 2010 to 2020, employment growth of preschool and childcare center directors in the top employing industries is projected to be as follows:

Individual and family services	51%
Child day care services	30
Religious, grantmaking, civic, professional, and similar organizations	16
Elementary and secondary schools; state, local, and private	12

Job Prospects

Workers with formal postsecondary education, such as an associate's or bachelor's degree, should have better job prospects than those with a high school diploma. Those with a bachelor's degree should have the best prospects.

Employment projections data for preschool and childcare center directors, 2010-20

Occupational Title	SOC Code	Employment, 2010	Projected Employment, 2020	Change, 2010-20	
				Percent	Numeric
Education Administrators, Preschool and Childcare Center/Program	11-9031	63,600	79,500	25	15,800

SOURCE: U.S. Bureau of Labor Statistics, Employment Projections program

Similar Occupations

This table shows a list of occupations with job duties that are similar to those of preschool and childcare center directors.

Occupation	Job Duties	Entry-Level Education	Median Annual Pay, May 2010
Childcare Workers	Childcare workers care for children when parents and other family members are unavailable. They care for children's basic needs, such as bathing and feeding. In addition, some help children prepare for kindergarten, and many help older children with homework.	High school diploma or equivalent	$19,300
High School Teachers	High school teachers help prepare students for life after graduation. They teach academic lessons and various skills that students will need to attend college and to enter the job market.	Bachelor's degree	$53,230
Kindergarten and Elementary School Teachers	Kindergarten and elementary school teachers prepare younger students for future schooling by teaching them the basics of subjects such as math and reading.	Bachelor's degree	$51,380
Middle School Teachers	Middle school teachers educate students, most of whom are in sixth through eighth grades. They help students build on the fundamentals they learned in elementary school and prepare them for the more difficult lessons they will learn in high school.	Bachelor's degree	$51,960
Preschool Teachers	Preschool teachers educate and care for children, usually ages 3 to 5, who have not yet entered kindergarten. They explain reading, writing, science, and other subjects in a way that young children can understand.	Associate's degree	$25,700
Special Education Teachers	Special education teachers work with students who have a wide range of learning, mental, emotional and physical disabilities. With students who have mild or moderate disabilities, they ensure that lessons and teaching strategies are modified to meet the students' needs. With students who have severe disabilities, they teach the students independent living skills and basic literacy, communication, and math.	Bachelor's degree	$53,220
Teacher Assistants	Teacher assistants work under a teacher's supervision to give students additional attention and instruction.	High school diploma or equivalent	$23,220

Contacts for More Information

For information about early childhood education, visit National Association for the Education of Young Children

For more information about professional credentials, visit Council for Professional Recognition

National Child Care Association

Suggested citation:

Bureau of Labor Statistics, U.S. Department of Labor, Occupational Outlook Handbook, 2012-13 Edition, Preschool and Childcare Center Directors, on the Internet at http://www.bls.gov/ooh/management/preschool-and-childcare-center-directors.htm.

Property, Real Estate, and Community Association Managers

Quick Facts: Property, Real Estate, and Community Association Managers	
2010 Median Pay	$51,480 per year $24.75 per hour
Entry-Level Education	High school diploma or equivalent
Work Experience in a Related Occupation	1 to 5 years
On-the-job Training	None
Number of Jobs, 2010	303,900
Job Outlook, 2010-20	6% (Slower than average)
Employment Change, 2010-20	18,400

What Property, Real Estate, and Community Association Managers Do

Property, real estate, and community association managers take care of the many aspects of residential, commercial, or industrial properties. They make sure the property looks nice, operates smoothly, and preserves its resale value.

Duties

Property, real estate, and community association managers typically do the following:

- Meet with, and show properties to, prospective renters
- Discuss the lease and explain the terms of occupancy
- Collect monthly fees from tenants
- Inspect all building facilities, including the grounds and equipment
- Arrange for new equipment or repairs as needed to keep up the property
- Pay or delegate paying of bills, such as mortgage, taxes, insurance, payroll, and cleaning
- Contract for trash removal, swimming pool maintenance, landscaping, security, and other services
- Investigate and settle complaints, disturbances, and violations
- Keep records of rental activity
- Prepare budgets and financial reports
- Know and comply with relevant laws such as the Americans with Disabilities Act, the Federal Fair Housing Amendment Act, and local fair housing laws; not discriminate when renting or

Property association managers show properties to potential renters.

advertising

When owners of homes, apartments, office buildings, or retail or industrial properties lack the time or expertise needed for the day-to-day management of their real estate properties, they often hire a property or real estate manager or a community association manager. Managers are employed either directly by the owner or indirectly through a contract with a property management firm.

The following are examples of occupational specialties:

Property and real estate managers oversee the operation of income-producing commercial or residential properties and ensure that real estate investments achieve their expected revenues. They handle the financial operations of the property, making certain that rent is collected and that mortgages, taxes, insurance premiums, payroll, and maintenance bills are paid on time. They may oversee financial statements, and periodically report to the owners on the status of the property, occupancy rates, expiration dates of leases, and other matters. When vacancies occur, property managers may advertise the property or hire a leasing agent to find a tenant. They also may suggest to the owners what rent to charge.

Community association managers manage the communal property and services of condominiums, cooperatives, and planned communities through their homeowner or community associations. Like property managers, community association managers collect monthly fees, prepare financial statements and budgets, negotiate with contractors, and help to resolve complaints. Usually hired by a volunteer board of directors of the association, they manage the daily affairs and supervise the maintenance of property and facilities that the homeowners use jointly through the association. Community association managers also help the board and owners comply with association and government rules and regulations.

Onsite property managers are responsible for the day-to-day operation of a single property, such as an apartment complex, an office building, or a shopping center. To ensure that the property is safe and properly maintained, onsite managers routinely inspect the grounds, facilities, and equipment to determine whether maintenance or repairs are needed. They meet with current tenants as needed to handle requests for repairs or to resolve complaints. They also meet with prospective tenants to show vacant apartments or office space. In addition, onsite managers enforce the terms of rental or lease contracts. They make sure that tenants pay their rent on time, follow restrictions on parking or pets, and follow procedures when the lease is up. Other important duties of onsite managers include keeping accurate, up-to-date records of income and expenditures from property operations and submitting regular expense reports to the senior-level property manager or the owner(s).

Real estate asset managers plan and direct the purchase, sale, and development of real estate properties on behalf of businesses and investors. They focus on long-term strategic financial planning, rather than on the day-to-day operations of the property. In deciding to acquire property, real estate asset managers consider several factors, such as property values, taxes, zoning, population growth, transportation, and traffic volume and patterns. Once a site is selected, they negotiate contracts to buy or lease the property on the most favorable terms. Real estate asset managers review their company's real estate holdings periodically and identify properties that are no longer financially profitable. They then negotiate the sale of or end the lease on those properties.

Work Environment

Property, real estate, and community association managers held about 303,900 jobs in 2010. About half were self-employed.

The following industries employed the most property, real estate, and community association managers in 2010:

Activities related to real estate	19%
Lessors of real estate	14
Offices of real estate agents and brokers	3
Local government, excluding education and hospitals	3
Business, professional, labor, political, and similar organization	2

Nearly all property, real estate, and community association managers work out of an office. However, many managers spend much of their time away from their desks. Onsite managers, in particular, may spend a large part of their workday visiting the building engineer, showing apartments, checking on the janitorial and maintenance staff, or investigating problems reported by residents. Real estate asset managers may spend time away from home while traveling to company real estate holdings or searching for properties to buy.

Work Schedules

Property, real estate, and community association managers often must attend evening meetings with residents, property owners, community association boards of directors, or civic groups. As a result, long hours are common. Some apartment managers are required to live in the apartment complexes where they work, so that they are available to handle emergencies, even when they are off duty.

Most property, real estate, and community association managers work full time.

How to Become a Property, Real Estate, or Community Association Manager

Although many employers prefer to hire college graduates, a high school diploma or equivalent is enough for some jobs. Some property, real estate, and community association managers have vocational training. Knowledge of property management is required.

Education

Many employers prefer to hire college graduates for property management positions, particularly for offsite positions dealing with a property's finances or contract management. Employers also prefer to hire college graduates to manage commercial properties. A bachelor's or master's degree in business administration, accounting, finance, real estate, or public administration is preferred for these positions. Managers of commercial properties and those dealing with a property's finances and contract management increasingly are finding that they need a bachelor's or master's degree in business administration,

accounting, finance, or real estate management, especially if they do not have much practical experience.

Work Experience

Experience in real estate sales is a good background for onsite managers because real estate sales people also show properties to prospective tenants or buyers.

Licenses

Real estate managers who buy or sell property must be licensed by the state in which they practice. In a few states, property association managers must be licensed. Managers of public housing subsidized by the federal government must hold certifications.

Certification

Many property, real estate, and community association managers get professional certification showing competence and professionalism. Oftentimes, employers require managers to attend formal training programs from various professional and trade real estate associations. Employers send managers to these programs to develop their management skills and expand their knowledge of specialized fields, such as how to run and maintain mechanical systems in buildings, how to improve property values, insurance and risk management, personnel management, business and real estate law, community association risks and liabilities, tenant relations, communications, accounting and financial concepts, and reserve funding. Managers also participate in these programs to prepare themselves for positions of greater responsibility in property management. With related job experience, completing these programs and receiving a satisfactory score on a written exam can lead to certification or the formal award of a professional designation by the sponsoring association.

Obtaining these certifications also can help in getting a job.

Advancement

Many people begin property management careers as assistants, working closely with a property manager. In time, many assistants advance to property manager positions.

Some people start as onsite managers of apartment buildings, office complexes, or community associations. As they gain experience, they may advance to positions of greater responsibility. Those who excel as onsite managers often transfer to assistant offsite property manager positions, in which they can gain experience handling a broad range of property management responsibilities.

The responsibilities and pay of property, real estate, and community association managers increase as these workers manage more and larger properties. Property managers are responsible for several properties at a time. As their careers advance, they gradually are entrusted with larger properties that are more complex to manage. Some experienced managers open their own property management firms.

Important Qualities

Customer-service skills. Property, real estate, and community association managers must provide excellent customer service to keep existing clients and expand their business with new ones.

Interpersonal skills. Because property, real estate, and community association managers interact with people every day, they must have excellent interpersonal skills.

Negotiating skills. Real estate asset managers must be adept at persuading and working with people and good at analyzing data to assess the value of potential future value of a property.

Organizational skills. Property, real estate, and community association managers must be able to plan, coordinate, and direct multiple contractors at the same time, often for multiple properties.

Speaking skills. Property, real estate, and community association managers must understand leasing or renting contracts and must be able to clearly explain and answer any questions a tenant may have.

Tact. Property, real estate, and community association managers must be able to mediate disputes or legal issues between residents, homeowners, or board members.

Pay

Property, Real Estate, and Community Association Managers
Median annual wages, May 2010

Other Management Occupations	$79,590
Property, Real Estate, and Community Association Managers	$51,480
Total, All Occupations	$33,840

Note: All Occupations includes all occupations in the U.S. Economy.
Source: U.S. Bureau of Labor Statistics, Occupational Employment Statistics

The median annual wage of property, real estate, and community association managers was $51,480 in May 2010. The median wage is the wage at which half the workers in an occupation earned more than that amount and half earned less. The lowest 10 percent earned less than $26,180, and the top 10 percent earned more than $111,320.

In May 2010, the median annual wages in industries employing the largest numbers of property, real estate, and community association managers were as follows:

Local government	$58,670
Offices of real estate agents and brokers	51,330
Activities related to real estate	51,050
Business, professional, labor, political, and similar organizations	48,040
Lessors of real estate	44,790

Property, real estate, and community association managers often must attend evening meetings with residents, property owners,

community association boards of directors, or civic groups. As a result, long hours are common. Some apartment managers are required to live in the apartment complexes where they work, so that they are available to handle emergencies, even when they are off duty. Most property, real estate, and community association managers work full time. Many apartment managers get time off during the week so that they can work on weekends to show apartments to prospective renters.

Job Outlook

Property, Real Estate, and Community Association Managers
Percent change in employment, projected 2010-20

Total, All Occupations	14%
Other Management Occupations	6%
Property, Real Estate, and Community Association Managers	6%

Note: All Occupations includes all occupations in the U.S. Economy.
Source: U.S. Bureau of Labor Statistics, Employment Projections program

Employment of property, real estate, and community association managers is expected to grow 6 percent from 2010 to 2020, slower than the average for all occupations.

Employment will grow because more people will live in apartment buildings, condominiums, homeowner communities, and senior housing that property management companies manage. New developments are increasingly being organized with community or homeowner associations that provide community services and oversee jointly owned common areas requiring professional management.

Property owners are becoming increasingly aware that property management firms help make properties more profitable and improve the resale value of homes and commercial property.

Job Prospects

Job opportunities should be best for those with a college degree in business administration, real estate, or a related field and for those who get a professional certification. Because of the projected increase in the elderly population, particularly good job opportunities are expected for those with experience managing housing for older people and with experience managing healthcare facilities.

Employment projections data for property, real estte, and community association managers, 2010-20

Occupational Title	SOC Code	Employment, 2010	Projected Employment, 2020	Change, 2010-20 Percent	Numeric
Property, Real Estate, and Community Association Managers	11-9141	303,900	322,200	6	18,400
SOURCE: U.S. Bureau of Labor Statistics, Employment Projections program					

Similar Occupations

This table shows a list of occupations with job duties that are similar to those of property, real estate, and community association managers.

Occupation	Job Duties	Entry-Level Education	Median Annual Pay, May 2010
Administrative Services Managers	Administrative services managers plan, direct, and coordinate supportive services of an organization. Their specific responsibilities vary by the type of organization and may include keeping records, distributing mail, and planning and maintaining facilities.	High school diploma or equivalent	$77,890
Food Service Managers	Food service managers are responsible for the daily operations of restaurants and other establishments that prepare and serve food and beverages to customers. Managers ensure that customers are satisfied with their dining experience.	High school diploma or equivalent	$48,130

Lodging Managers	Lodging managers make sure that guests on vacation or business travel have a pleasant experience, while also ensuring that an establishment is run efficiently and profitably.	High school diploma or equivalent	$46,880
Medical and Health Services Managers	Medical and health services managers, also called healthcare executives or healthcare administrators, plan, direct, and coordinate medical and health services. They might manage an entire facility, specialize in managing a specific clinical area or department, or manage a medical practice for a group of physicians.	Bachelor's degree	$84,270
Real Estate Brokers and Sales Agents	Real estate brokers and sales agents help clients buy, sell, and rent properties. Brokers and agents do the same type of work, but brokers are licensed to manage their own real estate businesses. Sales agents must work with a broker.	High school diploma or equivalent	$42,680
Urban and Regional Planners	Urban and regional planners develop plans and programs for the use of land. They use planning to create communities, accommodate growth, or revitalize physical facilities in towns, cities, counties, and metropolitan areas.	Master's degree	$63,040

Contacts for More Information

For information about professional designation and certification programs for property, real estate, and community association managers, visit BOMI International , Community Associations Institute , Institute of Real Estate Management , National Association of Residential Property Managers National Board of Certification for Community Association Managers

Suggested citation:

Bureau of Labor Statistics, U.S. Department of Labor, Occupational Outlook Handbook, 2012-13 Edition, Property, Real Estate, and Community Association Managers, on the Internet at http://www.bls.gov/ooh/management/property-real-estate-and-community-association-managers.htm .

Public Relations Managers and Specialists

Quick Facts: Public Relations Managers and Specialists	
2010 Median Pay	$57,550 per year $27.67 per hour
Entry-Level Education	Bachelor's degree
Work Experience in a Related Occupation	See How to Become One
On-the-job Training	See How to Become One
Number of Jobs, 2010	320,000
Job Outlook, 2010-20	21% (Faster than average)
Employment Change, 2010-20	68,300

What Public Relations Managers and Specialists Do

Public relations managers and specialists create and maintain a favorable public image for their employer or client. They write material for media releases, plan and direct public relations programs, and raise funds for their organizations.

Duties

Public relations managers and specialists typically do the following:

- Write press releases and prepare information for the media
- Identify main client groups and audiences and determine the best way to reach them
- Respond to requests for information from the media or designate an appropriate spokesperson or information source
- Help clients communicate effectively with the public
- Develop and maintain their organization's corporate image and identity, using logos and signs
- Draft speeches and arrange interviews for an organization's top executives
- Evaluate advertising and promotion programs to determine whether they are compatible with their organization's public relations efforts
- Develop and carry out fundraising strategies for an organization by identifying and contacting potential donors and applying for grants

Public relations specialists, also called communications specialists and media specialists, handle an organization's communication with the public, including consumers, investors, reporters, and other media specialists. In government, public relations specialists may be called press secretaries. They keep the public informed about the activities of government officials and agencies.

Public relations specialists must understand the attitudes and concerns of the groups they interact with to maintain cooperative relationships with them.

Public relations specialists draft press releases and contact people in the media who might print or broadcast their material. Many radio or television special reports, newspaper stories, and magazine articles start at the desks of public relations specialists. For example, a press release might describe a public issue, such as health, energy, or the environment, and what an organization does to advance that issue. In addition to publication through traditional media outlets, releases are increasingly being sent through the Web and social media.

Public relations managers review and sometimes write press releases. They also sponsor corporate events to help maintain and improve the image and identity of their organization or client.

In addition, they help to clarify their organization's point of view to its main audience through media releases and interviews. Public relations managers observe social, economic, and political trends that might ultimately affect the organization, and they recommend ways to enhance the firm's image based on those trends. For example, in response to a growing concern about the environment, an oil company may create a public relations campaign to publicize its efforts to develop cleaner fuels.

In large organizations, public relations managers may supervise a staff of public relations specialists. They also work with advertising and marketing staffs to make sure that advertising campaigns are compatible with the image the company or client is trying to portray. For example, if the firm has decided to emphasize its appeal to a certain group, such as younger people, the public relations manager ensures that current advertisements will be well received by that group.

In addition, public relations managers may handle internal communications, such as company newsletters, and may help financial managers produce an organization's reports. They may help the organization's top executives by drafting speeches, arranging interviews, and maintaining other forms of public contact. Public relations managers must be able to work well with many types of specialists to accurately report the facts. In some cases, the information they write has legal consequences. They must work with the company's or client's lawyers to be sure that the information they release is both legally accurate and clear to the public.

Work Environment

Public relations specialists held about 258,100 jobs in 2010. Public relations managers held about 61,900 jobs in 2010.

Employment of public relations managers and specialists was concentrated in the following industries in 2010:

Religious, grantmaking, civic, professional, and similar organizations	22%
Professional, scientific, and technical services	17
Educational services; state, local, and private	13
Health care and social assistance	9
Government	8

Public relations managers and specialists usually work in offices, but they also deliver speeches, attend meetings and community activities, and travel. They work in fairly high-stress environments, often managing and organizing several events at the same time.

Work Schedules

Most public relations managers and specialists work full time, which often includes long hours. In 2010, almost one-third of public relations managers and specialists worked more than 40 hours per week.

How to Become a Public Relations Manager or Specialist

Public relations managers and specialists typically need a bachelor's degree. Public relations managers also need related work experience.

Education

Public relations specialists typically need a bachelor's degree. Employers usually want candidates who have studied public relations, journalism, communications, English, or business.

For public relations management positions, a bachelor's degree in public relations, communication, or journalism is generally required. Courses in advertising, business administration, public affairs, public speaking, political science, and creative and technical writing are helpful. In addition, some employers prefer a master's degree in public

relations or journalism. In 2010, one-fourth of public relations managers held a master's degree.

Training

Public relations specialists typically are trained on the job, either in a formal program or by working closely under more experienced staff members. Entry-level workers often maintain files of material about an organization's activities, skim newspapers and magazines for appropriate articles to clip, and assemble information for speeches and pamphlets. Training typically lasts between 1 month and 1 year. After gaining experience, public relations specialists write news releases, speeches, and articles for publication or plan and carry out public relations programs.

Certification

The Public Relations Society of America offers a certification program for public relations managers that is based on years of experience and on passing an exam. The Accredited Business Communicator credential is also available from the International Association of Business Communicators.

Work Experience

Public relations managers must have several years of experience in a related public relations position. Lower level management positions may require only a few years of experience, whereas directors are more likely to need 5 to 10 years of related work experience.

Important Qualities

Interpersonal skills. Public relations managers and specialists deal with the public regularly; therefore, they must be open and friendly to build rapport and get good cooperation from their media contacts.

Organizational skills. Public relations managers and specialists are often in charge of managing several events at the same time, requiring superior organizational skills.

Problem-solving skills. Public relations managers and specialists sometimes must explain how the company or client is handling sensitive issues. They must use good judgment in what they report and how they report it.

Research skills. Public relations managers and specialists must often do research, including interviewing executives or other experts, to get the information they need.

Speaking skills. Public relations managers and specialists regularly speak on behalf of their organization. When doing so, they must be able to explain the organization's position clearly.

Writing skills. Public relations managers and specialists must be able to write well-organized and clear press releases and speeches. They must be able to grasp the key messages they want to get across and write them in a short, succinct way to get the attention of busy readers or listeners.

Pay

Public Relations Managers and Specialists
Median annual wages, May 2010

Public Relations and Fundraising Managers	$91,810
Public Relations Managers and Specialists	$57,550
Public Relations Specialists	$52,090
Total, All Occupations	$33,840

Note: All Occupations includes all occupations in the U.S. Economy.
Source: U.S. Bureau of Labor Statistics, Occupational Employment Statistics

The median annual wage of public relations managers was $91,810 in May 2010. The median wage is the point at which half the workers in an occupation earned more than that amount and half earned less. The lowest 10 percent earned less than $49,720, and the top 10 percent earned more than $166,400.

The median annual wage of public relations specialists was $52,090 in May 2010. The lowest 10 percent earned less than $30,560, and the top 10 percent earned more than$ 95,200.

Most public relations managers and specialists work full time, and some work additional hours. In 2010, almost one-third of public relations managers and specialists worked more than 40 hours per week.

Job Outlook

Public Relations Managers and Specialists
Percent change in employment, projected 2010-20

Public Relations Specialists	23%
Public Relations Managers and Specialists	21%
Public Relations and Fundraising Managers	16%
Total, All Occupations	14%

Note: All Occupations includes all occupations in the U.S. Economy.
Source: U.S. Bureau of Labor Statistics, Employment Projections program

Employment of public relations managers and specialists is expected to grow 21 percent from 2010 to 2020, faster than the average for all occupations. Employment of public relations specialists is expected to grow 23 percent during the same period, faster than the average for all occupations. Employment of public relations managers

is expected to grow 16 percent from 2010 to 2020, about as fast as the average for all occupations. The trends affecting public relations specialists will also affect managers, as the increasing importance of public relations will require more managers to plan and direct public relations departments.

Organizations are increasingly emphasizing community outreach and customer relations as a way to enhance their reputation and visibility. Public opinion can change quickly, particularly because both good and bad news spreads rapidly through the Internet. Consequently, public relations specialists are expected to be needed to respond to news developments and maintain their organization's reputation.

Increased use of social media also is expected to increase employment growth for public relations specialists. These new media outlets will create more work for public relations workers, increasing the number and kinds of avenues of communication between organizations and the public. Public relations specialists will be needed to help their clients use these new types of media effectively.

Employment is likely to grow in public relations firms as organizations contract out public relations services rather than support more full-time staff when additional work is needed.

Job Prospects

In addition to job growth for other reasons, opportunities should come from the need to replace public relations managers and specialists who retire or leave the occupation.

Competition for entry-level jobs will likely be strong.

Employment projections data for public relations managers and specialists, 2010-20

Occupational Title	SOC Code	Employment, 2010	Projected Employment, 2020	Change, 2010-20	
				Percent	Numeric
Public Relations Managers and Specialists	—	320,000	388,300	21	68,300
Public Relations and Fundraising Managers	11-2031	61,900	72,100	16	10,200
Public Relations Specialists	27-3031	258,100	316,200	23	58,200
SOURCE: U.S. Bureau of Labor Statistics, Employment Projections program					

Similar Occupations

This table shows a list of occupations with job duties that are similar to those of public relations managers and specialists.

Occupation	Job Duties	Entry-Level Education	Median Annual Pay, May 2010
Advertising, Promotions, and Marketing Managers	Advertising, promotions, and marketing managers plan programs to generate interest in a product or service. They work with art directors, sales agents, and financial staff members.	Bachelor's degree	$108,260
Advertising Sales Agents	Advertising sales agents sell advertising space to businesses and individuals. They contact potential clients, make sales presentations, and maintain client accounts.	High school diploma or equivalent	$45,350
Demonstrators and Product Promoters	Demonstrators and product promoters create public interest in products, such as cosmetics, housewares, and food. They encourage people and stores to buy their products by showing the products to prospective customers and answering questions.	High school diploma or equivalent	$23,110
Editors	Editors plan, review, and revise content for publication.	Bachelor's degree	$51,470
Market Research Analysts	Market research analysts study market conditions in local, regional, or national areas to examine potential sales of a product or service. They help companies understand what products people want, who will buy them, and at what price.	Bachelor's degree	$60,570
Multimedia Artists and Animators	Multimedia artists and animators create animation and visual effects for television, movies, video games, and other media. They create two- and three-dimensional models and animation.	Bachelor's degree	$58,510
Producers and Directors	Producers and directors are in charge of creating motion pictures, television shows, live theater, and other performing arts productions. They interpret a writer's script to entertain or inform an audience.	Bachelor's degree	$68,440

| Wholesale and Manufacturing Sales Representatives | Wholesale and manufacturing sales representatives sell goods for wholesalers or manufacturers to businesses, government agencies, and other organizations. They contact customers, explain product features, answer any questions that their customers may have, and negotiate prices. | See How to Become One | $56,620 |
| Writers and Authors | Writers and authors develop original written content for advertisements, books, magazines, movie and television scripts, songs, and online publications. | Bachelor's degree | $55,420 |

Contacts for More Information

For more information about public relations managers, including professional certification in public relations, visit Public Relations Society of America , International Association of Business Communicators

Suggested citation:

Bureau of Labor Statistics, U.S. Department of Labor, Occupational Outlook Handbook, 2012-13 Edition, Public Relations Managers and Specialists, on the Internet at http://www.bls.gov/ooh/management/public-relations-managers-and-specialists.htm .

Sales Managers

Quick Facts: Sales Managers	
2010 Median Pay	$98,530 per year $47.37 per hour
Entry-Level Education	Bachelor's degree
Work Experience in a Related Occupation	1 to 5 years
On-the-job Training	None
Number of Jobs, 2010	342,100
Job Outlook, 2010-20	12% (About as fast as average)
Employment Change, 2010-20	40,100

What Sales Managers Do

Sales managers direct organizations' sales teams. They set sales goals, analyze data, and develop training programs for the organization's sales representatives.

Duties

Sales managers typically do the following:
- Oversee regional and local sales managers and their staffs
- Resolve customer complaints regarding sales and service
- Prepare budgets and approve budget expenditures
- Monitor customer preferences to determine the focus of sales efforts
- Analyze sales statistics
- Project sales and determine the profitability of products and services
- Determine discount rates or special pricing plans
- Plan and coordinate training programs for sales staff

Sales managers' responsibilities vary with the size of the organization they work for. However, most sales managers direct the distribution of goods and services by assigning sales territories, setting sales goals, and establishing training programs for the organization's sales representatives.

In some cases, they recruit, hire, and train new members of the sales staff. For more information about sales workers, see the profiles on retail sales workers and wholesale and manufacturing sales representatives .

Sales managers advise sales representatives on ways to improve their sales performance. In large multiproduct organizations, they oversee regional and local sales managers and their staffs.

Sales managers also stay in contact with dealers and distributors. They analyze sales statistics that their staff gathers, both to determine the sales potential and inventory requirements of products and stores and to monitor customers' preferences.

Sales managers work closely with managers from other departments. For example, the marketing department identifies new customers that the sales department can target. The relationship between these two departments is critical to helping an organization expand its client base. Because sales managers monitor customers' preferences and stores' and organizations' inventory needs, they work closely with research and design departments and warehousing departments.

Work Environment

Sales managers set sales goals, analyze data, and develop training programs for the organization's sales representatives.

Sales managers held about 342,100 jobs in 2010.

Sales managers have a lot of responsibility, and the position can be stressful. Many sales managers travel to national, regional, and local offices and to dealers' and distributors' offices.

Sales managers were concentrated in the following industries in 2010:

Retail trade	20%
Wholesale trade	18
Manufacturing	12
Finance and insurance	10
Management of companies and enterprises	7

Work Schedules

Most sales managers work full time. Long hours, including evenings and weekends, are common.

How to Become a Sales Manager

Most sales managers have a bachelor's degree and work experience as a sales representative.

Education

Most sales managers have a bachelor's degree, although some have a master's degree. Educational requirements are less strict for job candidates who have significant experience as a sales representative. Courses in business law, management, economics, accounting, finance, mathematics, marketing, and statistics are advantageous.

Work Experience

Work experience is typically required for someone to become a sales manager. The preferred duration varies, but employers usually seek candidates who have at least 1 to 5 years of experience.

Sales managers typically enter the occupation from other sales and related occupations, such as sales representatives or purchasing agents. In small organizations, the number of sales manager positions is often limited, so advancement for sales workers usually comes slowly. In large organizations, promotion may occur more quickly.

Important Qualities

Analytical skills. Sales managers must collect and interpret complex data to target the most promising areas and determine the most effective sales strategies.

Communication skills. Sales managers need to work with people in other departments and with customers, so they must be able to communicate clearly.

Customer-service skills. When helping to make a sale, sales managers must listen and respond to the customer's needs.

Managerial skills. Sales managers must be able to evaluate how sales staff perform and develop ways for struggling members to improve.

Pay

Sales Managers

Median annual wages, May 2010

Sales Managers	$98,530
Management Occupations	$91,440
Total, All Occupations	$33,840

Note: All Occupations includes all occupations in the U.S. Economy.
Source: U.S. Bureau of Labor Statistics, Occupational Employment Statistics

The median annual wage of sales managers was $98,530 in May 2010. The median wage is the wage at which half the workers in an occupation earned more than that amount and half earned less. The lowest 10 percent earned less than $49,960, and the top 10 percent earned more than $166,400.

Compensation methods for sales managers vary significantly with the type of organization and the product sold. Most employers use a combination of salary and commissions or salary plus bonuses. Commissions usually are based on the value of sales, whereas bonuses may depend on individual performance, on the performance of all sales workers in the group or district, or on the organization's performance.

Most sales managers work full time. Long hours, including evenings and weekends, are common.

Job Outlook

Sales Managers

Percent change in employment, projected 2010-20

Total, All Occupations	14%
Sales Managers	12%
Management Occupations	7%

Note: All Occupations includes all occupations in the U.S. Economy.
Source: U.S. Bureau of Labor Statistics, Employment Projections program

Employment of sales managers is expected to grow 12 percent from 2010 to 2020, about as fast as the average for all occupations.

An effective sales team remains crucial for profitability. As the economy grows, organizations will focus on generating new sales and will look to their sales strategy as a way to increase competitiveness.

Growth is expected to be stronger for sales managers involved in business-to-business sales, rather than business-to-consumer sales, because the rise of online shopping will reduce the need for sales calls to individual consumers.

Sales managers and their departments are some of the most important personnel in an organization. Therefore, they are less likely to be let go or to have their jobs contracted out than are other types of managers, except in the case of organizations that are merging and consolidating.

Employment of these managers, therefore, is expected to vary primarily on the basis of growth or contraction in the industries that employ them.

Job Prospects

Strong competition is expected for jobs because other managers and highly experienced professionals often seek these jobs.

Employment projections data for sales managers, 2010-20

Occupational Title	SOC Code	Employment, 2010	Projected Employment, 2020	Change, 2010-20	
				Percent	Numeric
Sales Managers	11-2022	342,100	382,300	12	40,100
SOURCE: U.S. Bureau of Labor Statistics, Employment Projections program					

Similar Occupations

This table shows a list of occupations with job duties that are similar to those of sales managers.

Occupation	Job Duties	Entry-Level Education	Median Annual Pay, May 2010
Advertising, Promotions, and Marketing Managers	Advertising, promotions, and marketing managers plan programs to generate interest in a product or service. They work with art directors, sales agents, and financial staff members.	Bachelor's degree	$108,260
Advertising Sales Agents	Advertising sales agents sell advertising space to businesses and individuals. They contact potential clients, make sales presentations, and maintain client accounts.	High school diploma or equivalent	$45,350
Demonstrators and Product Promoters	Demonstrators and product promoters create public interest in products, such as cosmetics, housewares, and food. They encourage people and stores to buy their products by showing the products to prospective customers and answering questions.	High school diploma or equivalent	$23,110
Market Research Analysts	Market research analysts study market conditions in local, regional, or national areas to examine potential sales of a product or service. They help companies understand what products people want, who will buy them, and at what price.	Bachelor's degree	$60,570
Public Relations Managers and Specialists	Public relations managers and specialists create and maintain a favorable public image for their employer or client. They write material for media releases, plan and direct public relations programs, and raise funds for their organizations.	Bachelor's degree	$57,550
Retail Sales Workers	Retail sales workers include both those who sell retail merchandise, such as clothing, furniture, and automobiles, (called retail salespersons) and those who sell spare and replacement parts and equipment, especiallycar parts, (called parts salespersons). Both groups help customers find the products they want and process customers' payments.	Less than high school	$20,990
Sales Engineers	Sales engineers sell complex scientific and technological products or services to businesses. They must have extensive knowledge of the products' parts and functions and must understand the scientific processes that make these products work.	Bachelor's degree	$87,390
Wholesale and Manufacturing Sales Representatives	Wholesale and manufacturing sales representatives sell goods for wholesalers or manufacturers to businesses, government agencies, and other organizations. They contact customers, explain product features, answer any questions that their customers may have, and negotiate prices.	See How to Become One	$56,620

Contacts for More Information

For more information about sales managers, visit Sales Management Association

Suggested citation:

Bureau of Labor Statistics, U.S. Department of Labor, Occupational Outlook Handbook, 2012-13 Edition, Sales Managers, on the Internet at http://www.bls.gov/ooh/management/sales-managers.htm

Social and Community Service Managers

Quick Facts: Social and Community Service Managers	
2010 Median Pay	$57,950 per year $27.86 per hour
Entry-Level Education	Bachelor's degree
Work Experience in a Related Occupation	1 to 5 years
On-the-job Training	None
Number of Jobs, 2010	134,100
Job Outlook, 2010-20	27% (Faster than average)
Employment Change, 2010-20	35,800

What Social and Community Service Managers Do

Social and community service managers coordinate and supervise social service programs and community organizations. They direct and lead staff who provide social services to the public.

Duties

Social and community service managers typically do the following:
- Discuss with members of the community what types of programs and services are needed
- Design and oversee programs to meet the needs of the target audience or community
- Create methods to gather information, such as statistics, about the impact of their programs
- Supervise staff, such as social workers, who provide services to clients
- Analyze data to determine the effectiveness of programs
- Suggest and carry out improvements to programs and services
- Develop and manage budgets for programs and organizations
- Get funding for programs though the agency's budget process or fundraising

Social and community service managers work for a variety of social and human service organizations. The organizations may focus on working with a particular population, such as children, homeless people, or veterans. Other organizations may focus on helping people with particular challenges, such as hunger or joblessness.

Social and community service managers provide direction and leadership to staff who provide a range of services to the public.

Social and community service managers are often expected to show that their programs and services are effective. To do so, they collect statistics and other information to evaluate the impact that programs have in their community or on their target audience. They may be required to report this information to administrators or funders. They may also use evaluations to identify areas that need improvement for the program to be more effective.

Many social and community service managers have supervisory responsibilities. They may recruit, hire, and train new members of staff.

The job duties of social and community service managers vary based on the size of the organization they work for.

In large agencies, managers have more specialized duties. They may be responsible for running only one program in an organization that includes many programs. Social and community service managers report to the agency's administration or upper management. They usually have less freedom to design programs. Instead, they supervise and carry out programs set up by administrators, elected officials, or other stakeholders.

In small organizations, social and community managers often fill many roles. They represent the organization to the public through speaking engagements or in community-wide committees. They design, carry out, and oversee programs. In small organizations, they may spend a lot of time on administrative tasks, such as managing budgets. They may also spend time raising funds and meeting with potential donors.

Work Environment

Social and community service managers held 134,100 jobs in 2010. They work for nonprofit organizations, private for-profit social service companies, and government agencies. Social and community service managers work in a variety of settings, including offices, clinics, hospitals, and shelters.

Some social and community service managers focus on working with a particular population, such as children, homeless people, or veterans; others focus on helping people with particular challenges, such as hunger or joblessness. In 2010, the industries employing the most social and community service managers were as follows:

Individual and family services	22%
State and local government, excluding education and hospitals	19
Religious, grantmaking, civic, professional, and similar organizations	18
Nursing and residential care facilities	11
Community and vocational rehabilitation services	11

Some aspects of the work, such as fundraising or balancing budgets, may be stressful, particularly during economic downturns.

Work Schedules

Social and community service managers typically work full time.

How to Become a Social and Community Service Manager

Social and community service managers need at least a bachelor's degree and some work experience. However, many employers prefer candidates who have a master's degree.

Education

A bachelor's degree in social work, urban studies, public administration, or a related field is the minimum requirement. Most employers require those whose highest level of education is a bachelor's degree to have some work experience as well.

Many employers prefer workers with a master's degree in social work, public or business administration, public health, or a related field. Coursework in statistics, program management, and policy analysis is helpful.

Work Experience

Work experience is often needed to become a social and community service manager and is essential for those wishing to enter the occupation with a bachelor's degree. Workers must demonstrate an ability to lead other workers and manage services and programs. They can get this experience by working as a social worker or in a similar occupation. For more information, see the profile on social workers . Lower level management positions may require only a few years of experience; directors typically have more experience.

Important Qualities

Analytical skills. Managers need to understand and evaluate data and information from a variety of sources.

Communication skills. Working with the community and employees requires effective communication. Managers need to be able to speak and write clearly so others understand them. Public speaking experience is also helpful.

Leadership skills. Social and community service managers must motivate and lead their employees to inspire workers and set the direction of the program.

Managerial skills. Social and community service managers spend much of their time administering budgets and dealing with personnel issues.

People skills. Managers need to foster good relationships with members of the community and their employees.

Pay

Social and Community Service Managers
Median annual wages, May 2010

Management Occupations	$91,440
Social and Community Service Managers	$57,950
Total, All Occupations	$33,840

Note: All Occupations includes all occupations in the U.S. Economy.
Source: U.S. Bureau of Labor Statistics, Occupational Employment Statistics

The median annual wage of social and community service managers was $57,950 in May 2010. The median wage is the wage at which half the workers in an occupation earned more than that amount and half earned less. The lowest 10 percent earned less than $34,330, and the top 10 percent earned more than $96,920.

In May 2010, the wages of social and community service managers in the industries employing most of the occupation were as follows:

Local government, excluding education and hospitals	$69,670
State government, excluding education and hospitals	64,220
Individual and family services	54,060
Vocational rehabilitation services	52,510
Nursing and residential care facilities	50,160

Social and community service managers typically work full time.

Job Outlook

Social and Community Service Managers
Percent change in employment, projected 2010-20

Social and Community Service Managers	27%
Total, All Occupations	14%
Management Occupations	7%

Note: All Occupations includes all occupations in the U.S. Economy.
Source: U.S. Bureau of Labor Statistics, Employment Projections program

Employment of social and community service managers is expected to grow by 27 percent from 2010 to 2020, faster than the average for all occupations.

Growth is due to the needs of an aging population. An increase in the number of older adults will result in growth in demand for social services. Elderly people often need services, such as adult day care and meal delivery. Social and community service managers, who administer programs that provide these services, will likely be needed to meet this increased demand. As a result, employment of social and community service managers is expected to grow fastest in industries serving the elderly, such as home health care services and services for the elderly and persons with disabilities.Services for the elderly and persons with disabilities are included in the individual and family services industry.

In addition, employment growth is expected as more people seek treatment for their addictions and as drug offenders are increasingly being sent to treatment programs rather than to jail. As a result, an increase is expected in demand for social and community service managers who direct treatment programs.

General increases in the population are expected to increase demand for all types of social services—resulting in increased demand for social and community service managers.

Although this occupation is expected to experience growth, it could be limited by budget cuts in state and local governments. Social and human services rely heavily on government funding, and if funding decreases, services may not grow fast enough to meet demand.

From 2010 to 2020, employment growth of social and community service managers in the industries employing most of the occupation is expected to be as follows:

Individual and family services	53%
Community and vocational rehabilitation services	31
Nursing and residential care facilities	22
Religious, grantmaking, civic, professional, and similar organizations	20
State and local government, excluding education and hospitals	7

Employment projections data for social and community service managers, 2010-20

Occupational Title	SOC Code	Employment, 2010	Projected Employment, 2020	Change, 2010-20	
				Percent	Numeric
Social and Community Service Managers	11-9151	134,100	169,900	27	35,800
SOURCE: U.S. Bureau of Labor Statistics, Employment Projections program					

Similar Occupations

This table shows a list of occupations with job duties that are similar to those of social and community service managers.

Occupation	Job Duties	Entry-Level Education	Median Annual Pay, May 2010
Health Educators	Health educators teach people about behaviors that promote wellness. They develop programs and materials to encourage people to make healthy decisions.	Bachelor's degree	$45,830
Mental Health Counselors and Marriage and Family Therapists	Mental health counselors and marriage and family therapists help people manage or overcome mental and emotional disorders and problems with their family and relationships. They listen to clients and ask questions to help the clients understand their problems and develop strategies to improve their lives.	Master's degree	$39,710
Probation Officers and Correctional Treatment Specialists	Probation officers and correctional treatment specialists work with and monitor offenders to prevent them from committing new crimes.	Bachelor's degree	$47,200
Rehabilitation Counselors	Rehabilitation counselors help people with emotional and physical disabilities live independently. They help their clients overcome personal, social, and professional effects of disabilities as they relate to employment or independent living.	Master's degree	$32,350
School and Career Counselors	School counselors help students develop social skills and succeed in school. Career counselors assist people with the process of making career decisions by helping them choose a career or educational program.	Master's degree	$53,380
Social and Human Service Assistants	Social and human service assistants help people get through difficult times or get additional support. They help other workers, such as social workers, and they help clients find benefits or community services.	High school diploma or equivalent	$28,200
Social Workers	There are two main types of social workers: direct-service social workers, who help people solve and cope with problems in their everyday lives, and clinical social workers, who diagnose and treat mental, behavioral, and emotional issues.	See How to Become One	$42,480
Substance Abuse and Behavioral Disorder Counselors	Substance abuse and behavioral disorder counselors advise people who have alcoholism or other types of addiction, eating disorders, or other behavioral problems. They provide treatment and support to help the client recover from addiction or modify problem behaviors.	High school diploma or equivalent	$38,120

Contacts for More Information

For more information about social and community service managers, visit National Association of Social Workers , National Network for Social Work Managers

Suggested citation:

Bureau of Labor Statistics, U.S. Department of Labor, Occupational Outlook Handbook, 2012-13 Edition, Social and Community Service Managers, on the Internet at http://www.bls.gov/ooh/management/social-and-community-service-managers.htm .

Top Executives

Quick Facts: Top Executives	
2010 Median Pay	$101,250 per year $48.68 per hour
Entry-Level Education	See How to Become One
Work Experience in a Related Occupation	See How to Become One
On-the-job Training	None
Number of Jobs, 2010	2,136,900
Job Outlook, 2010-20	5% (Slower than average)
Employment Change, 2010-20	97,000

What Top Executives Do

Top executives devise strategies and policies to ensure that an organization meets its goals. They plan, direct, and coordinate operational activities of companies and public or private-sector organizations.

Duties

Top executives typically do the following:

- Establish and carry out departmental or organizational goals, policies, and procedures
- Direct and oversee an organization's financial and budgetary activities
- Manage general activities related to making products and providing services
- Consult with other executives, staff, and board members about general operations
- Negotiate or approve contracts and agreements
- Appoint department heads and managers
- Analyze financial statements, sales reports, and other performance indicators
- Identify places to cut costs and to improve performance, policies, and programs

The responsibilities of top executives largely depend on an organization's size. For example, an owner or manager of a small organization, such as an independent retail store, often is responsible for purchasing, hiring, training, quality control, and day-to-day supervisory duties. In large organizations, on the other hand, top executives typically focus more on formulating policies and strategic planning, while general and operations managers direct day-to-day operations.

The following are examples of common types of top executives:

Chief executive officers (CEOs), who are also known by titles such as **executive director**, **president**, and **vice president**, provide overall direction for companies and organizations. CEOs manage company operations, formulate policies, and ensure goals are met. They collaborate with and direct the work of other top executives and typically report to a board of directors.

Companies may also have chief officers who lead various departments or focus on specific areas of work:

- **Chief financial officers** are accountable for the accuracy of a company's or organization's financial reporting, especially among publicly traded companies. They direct the organization's financial goals, objectives, and budgets. For example, they may oversee the investment of funds and manage associated risks.
- **Chief information officers** are responsible for the overall technological direction of an organization, which includes managing the information technology and computer systems. They organize and supervise information-technology-related workers, projects, and policies.
- **Chief operating officers** oversee other executives who direct the activities of various departments, such as human resources and sales. They also carry out the organization's guidelines on a day-to-day basis.
- **Chief sustainability officers** address sustainability issues by enacting or overseeing a corporate sustainability strategy. For instance, they may manage programs and policies relating to environmental issues and ensure that the organization complies with environmental or other government regulations.

Mayors, along with **governors**, **city managers**, and **county administrators**, are chief executive officers of governments. They typically oversee budgets, programs, and uses of resources. Mayors and governors must be elected to office, and managers and administrators typically are appointed.

School superintendents and **college or university presidents** are chief executive officers of school districts and postsecondary schools. In addition to overseeing operations, they also manage issues, such as student achievement, budgets and resources, and relations with government agencies and other stakeholders.

General and operations managers oversee operations that are too diverse and general to be classified into one area of management or administration. Responsibilities may include formulating policies, managing daily operations, and planning the use of materials and

Top executives are the highest-level management in a firm.

human resources. They make staff schedules, assign work, and ensure projects are completed. In some organizations, the tasks of chief executive officers may overlap with those of general and operations managers.

Work Environment

Top executives held about 2.1 million jobs in 2010. About 83 percent of those jobs belonged to general and operations managers and 17 percent belonged to chief executives. Top executives work in nearly every industry. They work for both large and small businesses, ranging from one-person businesses to firms with thousands of employees.

Top executives of large organizations typically have large offices and numerous support staff. However, the work of top executives is often stressful, because these workers are under intense pressure to succeed. Executives in charge of poorly performing organizations or departments may find their jobs in jeopardy.

Top executives may travel a lot to attend meetings and conferences or to visit their company's local, regional, national, and international offices. In large organizations, executives may occasionally transfer jobs, moving between local offices or subsidiaries.

Work Schedules

Long hours, including evenings and weekends, are standard for most executives and general managers. However, some have the ability to set their own schedules.

How to Become a Top Executive

Although education and training vary widely by position and industry, many top executives have at least a bachelor's degree and a considerable amount of work experience.

Education

Many top executives have a bachelor's or master's degree in business administration or in an area related to their field of work. College presidents and school superintendents typically have a doctoral degree in the field in which they originally taught or in education administration. Top executives in the public sector often have a degree in business administration, public administration, law, or the liberal arts. Top executives of large corporations often have a Master of Business Administration (MBA).

Top executives who are promoted from lower level managerial or supervisory positions within their own firm often can substitute experience for education. In industries such as retail trade or transportation, for example, people without a college degree may work their way up to higher levels within the company and become executives or general managers.

Work Experience

Top executives must have related work experience. Top executives in some companies are promoted from within their organization. However, other companies may prefer to hire from outside the organization.

Chief executives typically need extensive managerial experience. Executives also are expected to have experience in the organization's area of specialty. Most general and operations managers hired from outside an organization need lower level supervisory or management experience in a related field.

Advancement

Some general managers advance to higher level managerial or executive positions. Company training programs, executive development programs, and certification can often benefit managers or executives hoping to advance. Chief executive officers often become a

member of the board of directors.

Many top executives advance within their own firm, moving up from lower level managerial or supervisory positions.

Certification

Top executives may complete a certification program through the Institute of Certified Professional Managers to earn the Certified Manager (CM) credential. To become a CM, candidates must meet education and experience requirements and pass three exams. Although not mandatory, certification can show management competency and potential leadership skills. Certification also can help those seeking advancement or can give jobseekers a competitive edge.

Important Qualities

Communication skills. Top executives must be able to communicate clearly and persuasively. They must effectively discuss issues and negotiate with others, direct subordinates, and explain their policies and decisions to those within and outside the organization.

Decision-making skills. Top executives need decision-making skills when setting policies and managing an organization. They must assess different options and choose the best course of action, often daily.

Leadership skills. Top executives must be able to lead a successful organization by coordinating policies, people, and resources.

Management skills. Top executives must organize and direct the operations of an organization. For example, they must manage business plans, employees, and budgets.

Problem-solving skills. Top executives need problem-solving skills after identifying issues within an organization. They must be able to recognize shortcomings and effectively carry out solutions.

Time-management skills. Top executives must be able to do many tasks at the same time, typically under their own direction, to ensure that their work gets done and that they meet their goals.

Pay

Top Executives Median annual wages, May 2010	
Chief Executives	$165,080
Top Executives	$101,250
General and Operations Managers	$94,400
Total, All Occupations	$33,840

Note: All Occupations includes all occupations in the U.S. Economy.
Source: U.S. Bureau of Labor Statistics, Occupational Employment Statistics

Top executives are among the highest paid workers in the United States. However, salary levels vary substantially, depending on executives' responsibilities and lengths of service and the types, sizes, and locations of the firms, organizations, or government agencies for which they work. For example, a top manager in a large corporation can earn significantly more than the mayor of a small town.

The median annual wage for chief executives was $165,080 in May 2010. The median wage is the wage at which half the workers in an occupation earned more than that amount and half earned less. The lowest 10 percent earned less than $75,160, and the top 10 percent earned more than $166,400.

The median annual wage for general and operations managers was $94,400 in May 2010. The lowest 10 percent earned less than $47,280, and the top 10 percent earned more than $166,400. Because the responsibilities of general and operations managers vary significantly among industries, earnings also tend to vary considerably.

Median annual wages in the industries employing the largest numbers of general and operations managers were as follows:

Professional, scientific, and technical services	$129,520
Manufacturing	107,600
Wholesale trade	104,110
Administrative and support and waste management and remediation services	82,550
Retail trade	73,620

In addition to salaries, total compensation for corporate executives often includes stock options and other performance bonuses. Workers also may enjoy benefits, such as access to expense allowances, use of company-owned aircraft and cars, club memberships, and company-paid insurance premiums. Nonprofit and government executives usually receive fewer benefits.

Working long hours, including evenings and weekends, is standard for most executives and general managers. However, some have the ability to set their own schedules.

Job Outlook

Top Executives

Percent change in employment, projected 2010-20

Total, All Occupations	14%
Top Executives	5%

Note: All Occupations includes all occupations in the U.S. Economy.
Source: U.S. Bureau of Labor Statistics, Employment Projections program

Employment of top executives is expected to grow 5 percent from 2010 to 2020, slower than the average for all occupations. Employment growth will vary widely by industry and is largely dependent on the rate of industry growth.

Top executives are essential for running companies and organizations. Their work—formulating strategies and policies—is central to the success of a company. However, as a business grows, the number of top executives does not grow as quickly as the number of employees. Therefore, top executives are not expected to experience as much employment growth as the employees they oversee.

Employment growth will be driven by the formation of new organizations and expansion of existing ones, which will require more managers and executives. However, employment will be negatively affected by mergers. When companies consolidate, management jobs often are lost.

Job Prospects

Top executives should face very strong competition for jobs. High pay and the prestige associated with the positions attract a substantial number of qualified applicants. For chief executives, those with an advanced degree and extensive managerial experience will have the best job prospects. For general and operations managers, educational requirements vary by industry, but candidates who can demonstrate strong leadership abilities and experience getting positive results will have better job opportunities.

Employment projections data for top executives, 2010-20

Occupational Title	SOC Code	Employment, 2010	Projected Employment, 2020	Change, 2010-20	
				Percent	Numeric
Top Executives	—	2,136,900	2,233,900	5	97,000
Chief Executives	11-1011	369,900	385,300	4	15,400
General and Operations Managers	11-1021	1,767,100	1,848,600	5	81,600
SOURCE: U.S. Bureau of Labor Statistics, Employment Projections program					

Similar Occupations

This table shows a list of occupations with job duties that are similar to those of top executives.

Occupation	Job Duties	Entry-Level Education	Median Annual Pay, May 2010
Administrative Services Managers	Administrative services managers plan, direct, and coordinate supportive services of an organization. Their specific responsibilities vary by the type of organization and may include keeping records, distributing mail, and planning and maintaining facilities.	High school diploma or equivalent	$77,890
Advertising, Promotions, and Marketing Managers	Advertising, promotions, and marketing managers plan programs to generate interest in a product or service. They work with art directors, sales agents, and financial staff members.	Bachelor's degree	$108,260
Architectural and Engineering Managers	Architectural and engineering managers plan, coordinate, and direct activities in architecture and engineering, including research and development in these fields.	Bachelor's degree	$119,260
Computer and Information Systems Managers	Computer and information systems managers, often called information technology managers (IT managers or IT project managers), plan, coordinate, and direct computer-related activities in an organization. They help determine the information technology goals of an organization and are responsible for implementing the appropriate computer systems to meet those goals.	Bachelor's degree	$115,780
Construction Managers	Construction managers plan, coordinate, budget, and supervise construction projects from early development to completion.	Associate's degree	$83,860
Financial Managers	Financial managers are responsible for the financial health of an organization. They produce financial reports, direct investment activities, and develop strategies and plans for the long-term financial goals of their organization.	Bachelor's degree	$103,910
Human Resources Managers	Human resources managers plan, direct, and coordinate the administrative functions of an organization. They oversee the recruiting, interviewing, and hiring of new staff; consult with top executives on strategic planning; and serve as a link between an organization's management and its employees.	Bachelor's degree	$99,180

Industrial Production Managers	Industrial production managers oversee the daily operations of manufacturing and related plants. They coordinate, plan, and direct the activities used to create a wide range of goods, such as cars, computer equipment, or paper products.	Bachelor's degree	$87,160
Medical and Health Services Managers	Medical and health services managers, also called healthcare executives or healthcare administrators, plan, direct, and coordinate medical and health services. They might manage an entire facility, specialize in managing a specific clinical area or department, or manage a medical practice for a group of physicians.	Bachelor's degree	$84,270
Sales Managers	Sales managers direct organizations' sales teams. They set sales goals, analyze data, and develop training programs for the organization's sales representatives.	Bachelor's degree	$98,530

Contacts for More Information

For more information on top executives, including educational programs, visit American Management Association , National Management Association (NMA)

For more information on executive financial management careers, visit Financial Executives International , Financial Management Association International

For information about management skills development, including the Certified Manager (CM) credential, visit Institute for Certified Professional Managers

Suggested citation:

Bureau of Labor Statistics, U.S. Department of Labor, Occupational Outlook Handbook, 2012-13 Edition, Top Executives, on the Internet at http://www.bls.gov/ooh/management/top-executives.htm .

Training and Development Managers

Quick Facts: Training and Development Managers	
2010 Median Pay	$89,170 per year $42.87 per hour
Entry-Level Education	Bachelor's degree
Work Experience in a Related Occupation	1 to 5 years
On-the-job Training	None
Number of Jobs, 2010	29,800
Job Outlook, 2010-20	15% (About as fast as average)
Employment Change, 2010-20	4,300

What Training and Development Managers Do

Training and development managers plan, direct, and coordinate programs to enhance the knowledge and skills of an organization's employees. They also oversee a staff of training and development specialists.

Duties

Training and development managers typically do the following:
- Assess employees' needs for training
- Align training with the organization's strategic goals
- Create a training budget and keep operations within budget
- Develop or update training programs to ensure that they are current and make the best use of available resources
- Oversee the creation of training manuals, online learning modules, and other educational materials for employees
- Review training materials from a variety of vendors and select materials with appropriate content
- Teach training methods and skills to instructors and supervisors
- Evaluate the effectiveness of training programs and instructors

Executives increasingly realize that developing the skills of their organization's workforce is essential to staying competitive in business. Providing opportunity for development is a selling point for recruiting high-quality employees, and it helps in retaining employees who can contribute to business growth. Training and development managers work to align training and development with an organization's goals.

Training and development managers oversee training programs, staff, and budgets. They are responsible for organizing training programs, including creating or selecting course content and materials. Most training takes place in a classroom, computer laboratory, or training facility. But some training is in the form of a video, Web-based program, or self-guided instructional manual. Regardless of how it is conducted, managers must ensure that training content, software, systems, and equipment are appropriate and meaningful.

Training and development managers typically supervise a staff of training and development specialists, such as instructional designers, program developers, and instructors. Managers teach training methods

Training and development managers direct the work of training and development specialists.

to specialists who, in turn, instruct the organization's employees, both new and experienced. Managers direct the daily activities of specialists and evaluate their effectiveness. Although most managers primarily oversee specialists and training and development program operations, some—particularly those in smaller companies—also may direct training courses.

To enhance employees' skills and an organization's overall quality of work, training and development managers often confer with managers of each department to identify its training needs. They may work with top executives and financial officers to identify and match training priorities with overall business goals. They also prepare training budgets and ensure that expenses stay within budget.

Work Environment

Training and development managers held about 29,800 jobs in 2010 and are employed throughout the economy.

In 2010, the industries employing the largest numbers of training and development managers were as follows:

Management of companies and enterprises	15%
Finance and insurance	15
Professional, scientific, and technical services	10
Health care and social assistance	9
Administrative and support services	9

Training and development managers typically work in offices. Some travel between a main office and regional offices or training facilities. They spend much of their time working with people, giving presentations, and leading training activities. Most work full time.

How to Become a Training and Development Manager

Candidates need a combination of education and related work experience to become a training and development manager.

Education

Although a bachelor's degree is sufficient for many positions, some jobs for training and development managers require a master's degree. Managers can come from a variety of educational backgrounds but often have a bachelor's degree in human resources, business administration, or a related field.

Some employers prefer or require that managers have a master's degree, usually with a concentration in training and development, human resources management, organizational development, or business administration.

Training and development managers also may benefit from studying instructional design, behavioral psychology, or educational psychology. In addition, as technology continues to play a larger role in training and development, a growing number of organizations seek candidates who have a background in information technology.

Work Experience

Related work experience is essential for training and development managers. Many positions require work experience in training and development or another human resources field, management, or teaching. Some employers also prefer experience in the industry in which the company operates. Increasingly, employers look for workers with experience in information technology as organizations introduce more e-learning.

Certification

Although not required, certification can show professional expertise and credibility. In fact, many employers prefer to hire certified candidates, and some positions may require certification. The American Society for Training and Development and International Society for Performance Improvement offer certification programs in the training and development field.

Important Qualities

Critical-thinking skills. Training and development managers use critical-thinking skills when assessing classes, materials, and programs. They must identify the training needs of an organization and recognize where changes and improvements can be made.

Decision-making skills. Training and development managers must decide the best training programs to meet the needs of the organization. For example, they must review available training methods and materials and choose those that best fit each program.

Interpersonal skills. Training and development managers need strong interpersonal skills because delivering training programs requires collaborating with staff, trainees, subject matter experts, and the organization's leaders. They also accomplish much of their work through teams.

Managerial skills. Managerial skills are important for these managers, who are often in charge of a staff and are responsible for many programs. Training and development managers must be able to organize, motivate, and instruct those working under them.

Speaking skills. Speaking skills are essential for training and development managers, who often give presentations. They must be able to communicate information clearly and facilitate learning by diverse audiences. They also must be able to effectively convey instructions to their staff.

Pay

Training and Development Managers
Median annual wages, May 2010

Management Occupations	$91,440
Training and Development Managers	$89,170
Total, All Occupations	$33,840

Note: All Occupations includes all occupations in the U.S. Economy.
Source: U.S. Bureau of Labor Statistics, Occupational Employment Statistics

The median annual wage of training and development managers was $89,170 in May 2010. The median wage is the wage at which half the workers in an occupation earned more than that amount and half earned less. The lowest 10 percent earned less than $50,470, and the top 10 percent earned more than $148,950.

Most training and development managers work full time, and some must travel for work.

Job Outlook

Training and Development Managers
Percent change in employment, projected 2010-20

Training and Development Managers	15%
Total, All Occupations	14%
Management Occupations	7%

Note: All Occupations includes all occupations in the U.S. Economy.
Source: U.S. Bureau of Labor Statistics, Employment Projections program

Employment of training and development managers is expected to grow 15 percent from 2010 to 2020, about as fast as the average for all occupations.

As baby boomers reach retirement age and begin to leave the workforce, organizations will need capable training and development staff to train their replacements. The need to replace a large workforce of highly skilled and knowledgeable employees should result in organizations increasing their training staff, or contracting out services, to sustain a workforce of high quality employees and maintain a competitive edge.

In many fields, the increasing complexity of jobs and the rapid pace of change require employees to take continuing education and skill development courses throughout their careers. In addition, innovations in training methods and learning technology should continue throughout the next decade. For example, organizations increasingly use social media, visual simulations, mobile learning, and social networks in their training programs. Training and development managers will need to modify their programs to fit a new generation of workers for whom technology is a part of daily life and work.

Job Prospects

Across most industries, employment of training and development managers is expected to grow as companies develop and introduce new media and technology into their training programs. Job prospects will vary by organization, but opportunities for training and development managers should be best in the management, scientific, and technical consulting services industry. Training and development contracting firms are often better equipped with the technology and technical expertise to produce new training initiatives, so some organizations will likely contract out portions of their training or program development work to these companies.

Those who have a master's degree, certification, or work experience in training and development, another human resource field, management, or teaching should have the best job prospects.

Employment projections data for training and development managers, 2010-20

Occupational Title	SOC Code	Employment, 2010	Projected Employment, 2020	Change, 2010-20	
				Percent	Numeric
Training and Development Managers	11-3131	29,800	34,100	15	4,300
SOURCE: U.S. Bureau of Labor Statistics, Employment Projections program					

Similar Occupations

This table shows a list of occupations with job duties that are similar to those of training and development managers.

Occupation	Job Duties	Entry-Level Education	Median Annual Pay, May 2010
Human Resources Specialists	Human resources specialists recruit, screen, interview, and place workers. They also may handle human resources work in a variety of other areas, such as employee relations, payroll and benefits, and training.	Bachelor's degree	$52,690
Human Resources Managers	Human resources managers plan, direct, and coordinate the administrative functions of an organization. They oversee the recruiting, interviewing, and hiring of new staff; consult with top executives on strategic planning; and serve as a link between an organization's management and its employees.	Bachelor's degree	$99,180
Compensation and Benefits Managers	Compensation managers plan, direct, and coordinate how and how much an organization pays its employees. Benefits managers do the same for retirement plans, health insurance, and other benefits an organization offers its employees.	Bachelor's degree	$89,270
Postsecondary Education Administrators	Postsecondary education administrators oversee student services, academics, and research at colleges and universities. Their job duties vary depending on the area of the college they manage, such as admissions, student life, or the office of the registrar.	Master's degree	$83,710
Top Executives	Top executives devise strategies and policies to ensure that an organization meets its goals. They plan, direct, and coordinate operational activities of companies and public or private-sector organizations.	See How to Become One	$101,250
Instructional Coordinators	Instructional coordinators oversee school districts' curriculums and teaching standards. They work with teachers and school administrators to implement new teaching techniques to improve the quality of education.	Master's degree	$58,830
School and Career Counselors	School counselors help students develop social skills and succeed in school. Career counselors assist people with the process of making career decisions by helping them choose a career or educational program.	Master's degree	$53,380
Psychologists	Psychologists study mental processes and human behavior by observing, interpreting, and recording how people and other animals relate to one another and the environment.	See How to Become One	$68,640

Contacts for More Information

For more information about training and development managers, including certification, visit American Society for Training and Development , International Society for Performance Improvement

For information about human resources management careers and certification, visit Society for Human Resource Management

Suggested citation:

Bureau of Labor Statistics, U.S. Department of Labor, Occupational Outlook Handbook, 2012-13 Edition, Training and Development Managers, on the Internet at http://www.bls.gov/ooh/management/training-and-development-managers.htm .

Math Occupations

Actuaries

Quick Facts: Actuaries	
2010 Median Pay	$87,650 per year $42.14 per hour
Entry-Level Education	Bachelor's degree
Work Experience in a Related Occupation	None
On-the-job Training	Long-term on-the-job training
Number of Jobs, 2010	21,700
Job Outlook, 2010-20	27% (Faster than average)
Employment Change, 2010-20	5,800

What Actuaries Do

Actuaries analyze the financial costs of risk and uncertainty. They use mathematics, statistics, and financial theory to assess the risk that an event will occur and help businesses and clients develop policies that minimize the cost of that risk. Actuaries' work is essential to the insurance industry.

Duties

Actuaries typically do the following:

- Compile statistical data and other pertinent information for further analysis
- Estimate the probability and likely economic cost of an event such as death, sickness, an accident, or a natural disaster
- Design, test, and administer insurance policies, investments, pension plans, and other business strategies to minimize risk and maximize profitability
- Produce charts, tables, and reports that explain their calculations and proposals
- Explain their findings and proposals to company executives, government officials, shareholders, and clients

Most actuarial work is done with computers. Actuaries use database software to compile information. They use advanced statistics and modeling software to forecast the cost and probability of an event.

Actuaries typically work on teams that often include managers and professionals in other fields, such as accounting, underwriting, and finance. For example, some actuaries work with accountants and financial analysts to set the price for security offerings or with market research analysts to forecast demand for new products.

With experience, actuaries are often given supervisory roles. They are responsible for delegating tasks and providing advice to senior management. They also may be called on to testify before public agencies on proposed laws that affect their business, such as a law placing caps on auto insurance prices by states.

Most actuaries work at insurance companies, where they help design policies and determine the premiums that should be charged for each policy. They must ensure that the premiums are profitable, yet competitive with other insurance companies. Actuaries in the insurance industry typically specialize in a specific field of insurance, such as one of the following:

- **Health insurance.** Actuaries specializing in this field help develop long-term care and health insurance policies by predicting expected costs of providing care under the terms of an insurance contract. Their predictions are based on numerous factors, including family history, geographic location, and occupation.
- **Life insurance.** Actuaries in this field help develop annuity and life insurance policies for individuals and groups by estimating, on the basis of risk factors such as age, gender, and tobacco use, how long someone is expected to live.
- **Property and casualty insurance.** Actuaries in this field help develop insurance policies that insure policyholders against property loss and liability resulting from accidents, natural disasters, fires, and other events. They calculate the expected number of claims resulting from automobile accidents, which varies depending on the insured person's age, sex, driving history, type of car, and other factors.

Some actuaries apply their expertise to financial matters outside of insurance. For example, they develop investment strategies that manage risks and maximize returns for companies or individuals. Some actuaries help companies develop broad policies and strategies that assess risks across all areas of business, a practice known as enterprise risk management.

Pension and retirement benefits actuaries design, test, and evaluate company pension plans to determine if the expected funds available in the future will be enough to ensure payment of future benefits. They must report the results of their evaluations to the federal government. Pension actuaries also help businesses develop other types of retirement plans, such as 401Ks, and healthcare plans for retirees. In addition, they provide retirement planning advice to individuals.

Consulting actuaries provide advice to clients on a contract basis. Many consulting actuaries audit the work of internal actuaries at insurance companies or handle actuarial duties for insurance companies that are not large enough to keep their own actuaries on staff. Other consulting actuaries work for employee benefits firms. These firms

Actuaries use database software to compile information and advanced statistics and modeling software to forecast the cost and probability of an event.

design, analyze, and manage employee benefit programs such as employer-sponsored healthcare and retirement plans for companies.

Some people with an actuarial science background may become professors and teachers. For more information, see the profile on postsecondary teachers.

Work Environment

Actuaries held about 21,700 jobs in 2010. The following table lists the largest employers of actuaries in 2010:

Agencies, brokerages, and other insurance related activities	13%
Management, scientific, and technical consulting services	13
Direct insurance (except life, health, and medical) carriers	12
Management of companies and enterprises	6

About 6 percent of actuaries were self employed in 2010.

Actuaries typically work in an office setting. Actuaries who work for consulting firms frequently need to travel to meet with clients. Their work is similar to that of actuaries in other industries.

Work Schedules

Most actuaries work full time. Actuaries who work for consulting firms often work longer hours than actuaries who are employed by insurance companies.

How to Become an Actuary

Actuaries need a bachelor's degree and must pass a series of exams to become certified professionals. Students must complete coursework in economics, applied statistics, and corporate finance, all which are required for professional certification.

Education

Actuaries must have a strong background in mathematics, statistics, and business. Typically, an actuary has an undergraduate degree in mathematics, statistics, business, or actuarial science.

To become certified professionals, students must complete coursework in economics, applied statistics, and corporate finance. Coursework in calculus and business, such as accounting and management, are essential for students as well.

Students should also take classes outside of mathematics and business to prepare them for a career as an actuary. Coursework in computer science, especially programming languages and the ability to use and develop spreadsheets, databases, and statistical analysis tools, is valuable. Classes in writing and public speaking will improve students' ability to communicate in the business world.

Many students take internships, which are a valuable way to gain experience outside of the classroom while they are still in school. Many employers offer their interns permanent jobs after they graduate.

An increasing number of employers expect students to have passed at least one of the initial actuary exams needed for professional certification (as described in the certification section) before graduation.

Certification

Two professional societies—the Casualty Actuarial Society (CAS) and the Society of Actuaries (SOA) —sponsor programs leading to full professional status. The CAS and SOA offer two levels of certification: associate and fellowship.

The CAS certifies actuaries who work in the property and casualty field, which includes automobile, homeowners', medical malpractice, and workers' compensation insurance.

The SOA certifies actuaries who work in life insurance, health insurance, retirement benefits, investments, and finance. Most actuaries in the United States are certified by the SOA.

The main requirement for associate certification in each society is the successful completion of exams. The SOA requires that candidates pass five exams for associate (ASA) certification. The CAS requires that candidates pass seven exams for associate (ACAS) certification. In addition, both CAS and SOA require that candidates take seminars on professionalism. Both societies have mandatory e-learning courses for candidates.

It typically takes 4 to 6 years for an actuary to get an ACAS or an ASA certification because each exam requires hundreds of hours of study and months of preparation.

After becoming associates, it typically takes actuaries another 2 to 3 years to earn fellowship status.

The SOA offers fellowship certification in five separate tracks: life and annuities, group and health benefits, retirement benefits, investments, and finance/enterprise risk management. Unlike the SOA, the CAS does not offer specialized study tracks for fellowship certification.

Both the CAS and the SOA have continuing education requirements. Most actuaries meet this requirement by attending training seminars that are sponsored by their employers or the societies.

Important Qualities

Analytical skills. Actuaries use analytical skills to identify patterns and trends in complex sets of data to determine the factors that have an effect on certain types of events.

Computer skills. Actuaries must know programming languages and be able to use and develop spreadsheets, databases, and statistical analysis tools.

Interpersonal skills. Actuaries serve as leaders and members of teams, so they must be able to listen to other people's opinions and suggestions before reaching a conclusion.

Math skills. Actuaries quantify risk by using the principles of calculus, statistics, and probability.

Problem-solving skills. Actuaries identify risks and develop ways for businesses to manage those risks.

Speaking skills. Actuaries must be able to explain complex technical matters to those who lack an actuarial background in a way that helps them understand the subject.

Writing skills. Actuaries must be able to communicate clearly through the reports and memos that describe their work and recommendations.

Training

Most entry-level actuaries start out as trainees. They are typically on teams with more experienced actuaries who serve as mentors. At first they perform basic tasks such as compiling data, but as they gain more experience, they may conduct research and write reports. Beginning actuaries may spend time working in other departments, such as marketing, underwriting, and product development, to learn all aspects of the company's work and how actuarial work applies to them.

Most employers support their actuaries throughout the certification process. For example, employers typically pay the cost of exams and study materials. Many firms provide paid time to study and encourage their employees to set up study groups. Employees usually receive raises or bonuses for each exam that they pass.

Licenses

Pension actuaries must be enrolled by the U.S. Department of Labor and U.S. Department of the Treasury's Joint Board for the Enrollment of Actuaries. Applicants must meet certain experience requirements and pass two exams administered through the SOA to qualify for enrollment.

Advancement

Advancement depends largely on job performance and the number of actuarial exams passed. For example, actuaries who achieve fellowship status often supervise the work of other actuaries and provide advice to senior management. Actuaries with a broad knowledge of risk management and how it applies to business can rise to executive positions in their companies, such as chief risk officer or chief financial officer.

Pay

Actuaries

Median annual wages, May 2010

Actuaries	$87,650
Computer and Mathematical Occupations	$73,720
Total, All Occupations	$33,840

Note: All Occupations includes all occupations in the U.S. Economy.
Source: U.S. Bureau of Labor Statistics, Occupational Employment Statistics

The median annual wage of actuaries was $87,650 in May 2010. The median wage is the wage at which half the workers in an occupation earned more than that amount and half earned less. The lowest 10 percent earned less than $53,100, and the top 10 percent earned more than $160,000.

Median annual wages in the industries employing the largest numbers of actuaries in May 2010 were the following:

Agencies, brokerages, and other insurance related activities	$91,080
Direct insurance (except life, health, and medical) carriers	89,320
Management, scientific, and technical consulting services	87,410
Management of companies and enterprises	82,140

Most actuaries work full time. Actuaries who work for consulting firms tend to work longer hours than actuaries employed in insurance companies.

Job Outlook

Actuaries

Percent change in employment, projected 2010-20

Actuaries	27%
Computer and Mathematical Occupations	22%
Total, All Occupations	14%

Note: All Occupations includes all occupations in the U.S. Economy.
Source: U.S. Bureau of Labor Statistics, Employment Projections program

Employment of actuaries is expected to increase by 27 percent from 2010 to 2020, faster than the average for all occupations. The largest employment growth for actuaries is expected in consulting services.

Employment of actuaries in the insurance industry is expected to grow by 25 percent because actuaries will be needed to develop, price, and evaluate a variety of insurance products and calculate the costs of new risks. In health insurance, more actuaries will be needed to evaluate the effects that new healthcare laws, such as changes in coverage and expansion of customer pools, pose to insurance companies and to develop new products in response. Changes in healthcare laws will also boost demand for consulting actuaries who evaluate healthcare plans for companies.

More actuaries will be needed in property and casualty insurance to evaluate the risks posed to property by the effects of climate change.

Demand is not expected to be as strong for actuaries who specialize in life insurance. Consolidation in the industry is expected to limit the number of new jobs.

Rapid employment growth of 58 percent is expected in consulting services from a continuing need to evaluate and manage employee benefit plans for employers and to do contract work for insurers. In addition, more industries are expected to use consulting actuaries to assess risks across all areas of business, a practice known as enterprise risk management.

Job Prospects

Actuaries should expect strong competition for most jobs. Actuaries are a small field, and the relatively high pay and comfortable working conditions make being an actuary a desirable career. Students who have passed at least one actuarial exam and have had an internship while in college should have the best job prospects for entry-level positions.

Employment projections data for actuaries, 2010-20

Occupational Title	SOC Code	Employment, 2010	Projected Employment, 2020	Change, 2010-20 Percent	Numeric
Actuaries	15-2011	21,700	27,500	27	5,800
SOURCE: U.S. Bureau of Labor Statistics, Employment Projections program					

Similar Occupations

This table shows a list of occupations with job duties that are similar to those of actuaries.

Occupation	Job Duties	Entry-Level Education	Median Annual Pay, May 2010
Accountants and Auditors	Accountants and auditors prepare and examine financial records. They ensure that financial records are accurate and that taxes are paid properly and on time. Accountants and auditors assess financial operations and work to help ensure that organizations run efficiently.	Bachelor's degree	$61,690
Budget Analysts	Budget analysts help public and private institutions organize their finances. They prepare budget reports and monitor institutional spending.	Bachelor's degree	$68,200

Cost Estimators	Cost estimators collect and analyze data to estimate the time, money, resources, and labor required for product manufacturing, construction projects, or services. Some specialize in a particular industry or product type.	Bachelor's degree	$57,860
Economists	Economists study the production and distribution of resources, goods, and services.	Bachelor's degree	$89,450
Financial Analysts	Financial analysts provide guidance to businesses and individuals making investment decisions. They assess the performance of stocks, bonds, and other types of investments.	Bachelor's degree	$74,350
Insurance Underwriters	Insurance underwriters decide whether to provide insurance and under what terms. They evaluate insurance applications and determine coverage amounts and premiums.	Bachelor's degree	$59,290
Mathematicians	Mathematicians use high-level mathematics and technology to develop new mathematical principles, understand relationships between existing principles, and solve real-world problems.	Master's degree	$99,380
Personal Financial Advisors	Personal financial advisors give financial advice to people. They help with investments, taxes, and insurance decisions.	Bachelor's degree	$64,750
Postsecondary Teachers	Postsecondary teachers instruct students in a wide variety of academic and vocational subjects beyond the high school level. They also conduct research and publish scholarly papers and books.	Doctoral or professional degree	$62,050
Statisticians	Statisticians use mathematical techniques to analyze and interpret data and draw conclusions.	Master's degree	$72,830

Contacts for More Information

For more information about actuaries, visit American Academy of Actuaries

For more information about actuaries in property and casualty insurance, visit Casualty Actuarial Society

For more information about actuaries in life and health insurance, retirement benefits, investments, and finance/enterprise risk management, visit Society of Actuaries

For more information about how to become an actuary, visit Be an Actuary , a site sponsored by the Society of Actuaries and the Casualty Actuarial Society

For more information about pension actuaries, visit American Society of Pension Professionals and Actuaries

Mathematicians

Quick Facts: Mathematicians	
2010 Median Pay	$99,380 per year $47.78 per hour
Entry-Level Education	Master's degree
Work Experience in a Related Occupation	None
On-the-job Training	None
Number of Jobs, 2010	3,100
Job Outlook, 2010-20	16% (About as fast as average)
Employment Change, 2010-20	500

What Mathematicians Do

Mathematicians use high-level mathematics and technology to develop new mathematical principles, understand relationships between existing principles, and solve real-world problems.

Duties

Mathematicians typically do the following:

- Expand mathematical knowledge by developing new principles
- Recognize previously unknown relationships between known mathematical principles
- Create models to resolve practical problems in fields such as business, government, engineering, and the sciences
- Develop computational methods and computer codes
- Compare inferences derived from models with observations or experiments

The following are examples of types of mathematicians:

Applied mathematicians use theories and techniques, such as mathematical modeling, to solve practical problems. For example, they may analyze the effectiveness of new drugs or the aerodynamic characteristics of new automobiles.

Mathematicians create models to solve practical problems in fields such as business, government, engineering, and the sciences.

Theoretical mathematicians identify unexplained issues and seek to resolve them. Although they often strive to increase basic knowledge without considering its practical use, the knowledge they develop has been an important part of many scientific and engineering achievements.

Workers other than formal mathematicians use mathematical techniques. For example, engineers, computer scientists, physicists, and economists use mathematics extensively. Some workers, such as statisticians, actuaries, and operations research analysts, are specialists in a particular branch of mathematics. For more information, see the profiles on engineers , computer and information scientists , physicists and astronomers , economists , statisticians , actuaries , and operations research analysts .

Some people with a mathematics background become math teachers. For more information, see the profiles on middle school , high school , and postsecondary teachers .

Work Environment

Mathematicians held about 3,100 jobs in 2010. They worked primarily in the following industries:

Federal government, excluding postal service	37%
Scientific research and development services	26
Colleges, universities, and professional schools; state, local, and private	16
Management, scientific, and technical consulting services	8
Architectural, engineering, and related services	6

Mathematicians work in the federal government and in private science and engineering research companies. They work on teams with engineers, scientists, and other professionals and therefore must often work around others' schedules.

Mathematicians who work in postsecondary education usually have a mix of teaching and research responsibilities. Many academic mathematicians do research by themselves or in collaboration with other mathematicians. Collaborators work together at the same institution or from different locations, communicating electronically. Mathematicians in academia often have help from graduate students.

How to Become a Mathematician

A graduate degree in mathematics is the most common educational requirement for mathematicians. However, there are positions for those whose highest level of education is a bachelor's degree.

Education

Students who are interested in mathematics should take as many math courses as possible in high school.

For jobs as a mathematician with the federal government,

candidates need at least a bachelor's degree with a major in mathematics or significant coursework in mathematics. Also, holders of bachelor's degrees who meet state certification requirements may become middle or high school mathematics teachers.

Most colleges and universities offer a bachelor's degree in mathematics. Courses usually include calculus, differential equations, and linear and abstract algebra. Many colleges and universities advise or require mathematics students to take courses in a related field, such as computer science, engineering, or physical science. Candidates who have a double major in mathematics and a related discipline are particularly desirable to many employers.

In private industry, mathematicians typically need an advanced degree, either a master's degree or a doctorate. Many universities offer master's and doctoral degrees in theoretical or applied mathematics.

A master's degree generally takes 2 years beyond the bachelor's degree. That is often enough for many positions in applied mathematics. However, most people with a master's degree in mathematics do not work as mathematicians. Instead, they work in related fields, including computer science, where they have titles such as computer programmer, systems analyst, and systems engineer, and statistics, where they are called statisticians.

For a position as a professor of mathematics in a college or university, a doctorate is usually required. A doctoral degree usually takes at least 5 years of study beyond the bachelor's degree.

Important Qualities

Communication skills. Mathematicians must interact with and propose solutions to people who do not have extensive knowledge of mathematics.

Critical-thinking skills. Mathematicians need to identify, analyze, and apply basic principles.

Problem-solving skills. Mathematicians must devise new solutions to problems encountered by scientists or engineers.

Pay

Mathematicians

Median annual wages, May 2010

Mathematicians	$99,380
Mathematical Science Occupations	$74,040
Total, All Occupations	$33,840

Note: All Occupations includes all occupations in the U.S. Economy.
Source: U.S. Bureau of Labor Statistics, Occupational Employment Statistics

The median annual wage of mathematicians was $99,380 in May 2010. The median wage is the point at which half the workers in an occupation earned more than that amount and half earned less. The lowest 10 percent earned less than $52,850, and the top 10 percent

earned more than $153,620.

Median annual wages in industries employing the largest numbers of mathematicians in May 2010 were as follows:

Scientific research and development services	$108,230
Federal government, excluding postal service	106,370
Management, scientific, and technical consulting services	100,890
Architectural, engineering, and related services	76,350
Colleges, universities, and professional schools; state, local, and private	62,010

Job Outlook

Mathematicians

Percent change in employment, projected 2010-20

Mathematical Science Occupations	17%
Mathematicians	16%
Total, All Occupations	14%

Note: All Occupations includes all occupations in the U.S. Economy.
Source: U.S. Bureau of Labor Statistics, Employment Projections program

Employment of mathematicians is expected to increase by 16 percent from 2010 to 2020, about as fast as the average for all occupations. Advancements in technology that allow for better collection and processing of data will lead to an expanding need for mathematicians to analyze the data.

Job Prospects

Competition for jobs is expected because there are relatively few mathematician positions.

The number of Ph.D. degrees awarded in mathematics continues to exceed the number of available university positions. Therefore, many graduates will need to find jobs in industry or government. Those with a Ph.D. and a strong background in a related discipline—such as engineering, computer science, physics, or operations research—should have the best job prospects in related occupations, because they can best apply mathematical theory to real-world problems.

Those with a master's degree should have opportunities in applied mathematics. One use for applied mathematics will be in the growing field of cloud computing, in which companies and governments buy access to data storage and computing power over the Internet. Increasing migration to cloud computing is creating many new sources of data that have to be mined and analyzed. Mathematicians who have a master's degree will likely find opportunities in private industry.

Employment projections data for mathematicians, 2010-20

Occupational Title	SOC Code	Employment, 2010	Projected Employment, 2020	Change, 2010-20	
				Percent	Numeric
Mathematicians	15-2021	3,100	3,600	16	500
SOURCE: U.S. Bureau of Labor Statistics, Employment Projections program					

Similar Occupations

This table shows a list of occupations with job duties that are similar to those of mathematicians.

Occupation	Job Duties	Entry-Level Education	Median Annual Pay, May 2010
Actuaries	Actuaries analyze the financial costs of risk and uncertainty. They use mathematics, statistics, and financial theory to assess the risk that an event will occur and to help businesses and clients develop policies that minimize the cost of that risk.	Bachelor's degree	$87,650

Computer Programmers	Computer programmers write code to create software programs. They turn the program designs created by software developers and engineers into instructions that a computer can follow.	Bachelor's degree	$71,380
Computer Systems Analysts	Computer systems analysts study an organization's current computer systems and procedures and make recommendations to management to help the organization operate more efficiently and effectively. They bring business and information technology (IT) together by understanding the needs and limitations of both.	Bachelor's degree	$77,740
Database Administrators	Database administrators use software to store and organize data, such as financial information and customer shipping records. They make sure that data are available to users and are secure from unauthorized access.	Bachelor's degree	$73,490
Financial Analysts	Financial analysts provide guidance to businesses and individuals making investment decisions. They assess the performance of stocks, bonds, and other types of investments.	Bachelor's degree	$74,350
Market Research Analysts	Market research analysts study market conditions in local, regional, or national areas to examine potential sales of a product or service. They help companies understand what products people want, who will buy them, and at what price.	Bachelor's degree	$60,570
Nuclear Engineers	Nuclear engineers research and develop the processes, instruments, and systems used to get benefits from nuclear energy and radiation. Many of these engineers find industrial and medical uses for radioactive materials—for example, in equipment used in medical diagnosis and treatment.	Bachelor's degree	$99,920
Operations Research Analysts	Operations research analysts use advanced methods of analysis to help organizations solve problems and make better decisions.	Bachelor's degree	$70,960
Postsecondary Teachers	Postsecondary teachers instruct students in a wide variety of academic and vocational subjects beyond the high school level. They also conduct research and publish scholarly papers and books.	Doctoral or professional degree	$62,050
Physicists and Astronomers	Physicists and astronomers study the fundamental nature of the universe, ranging from the vastness of space to the smallest of subatomic particles. They develop new technologies, methods, and theories based on the results of their research that deepen our understanding of how things work and contribute to innovative, real-world applications.	Doctoral or professional degree	$105,430
Statisticians	Statisticians use mathematical techniques to analyze and interpret data and draw conclusions.	Master's degree	$72,830
Survey Researchers	Survey researchers design or conduct surveys and analyze survey data. Many groups use surveys to collect factual data, such as employment and salary information, or to ask questions that help them understand people's opinions, attitudes, beliefs, or desires.	Bachelor's degree	$36,050

Contacts for More Information

For more information about mathematicians, including training, especially for doctoral-level employment, visit American Mathematical Society

For specific information on careers in applied mathematics, visit Society for Industrial and Applied Mathematics

For information on job openings as a mathematician with the federal government, visit Office of Personnel Management

Suggested citation:

Bureau of Labor Statistics, U.S. Department of Labor, Occupational Outlook Handbook, 2012-13 Edition, Mathematicians, on the Internet at http://www.bls.gov/ooh/math/mathematicians.htm .

Operations Research Analysts

Quick Facts: Operations Research Analysts	
2010 Median Pay	$70,960 per year $34.12 per hour
Entry-Level Education	Bachelor's degree
Work Experience in a Related Occupation	None
On-the-job Training	None
Number of Jobs, 2010	64,600
Job Outlook, 2010-20	15% (About as fast as average)
Employment Change, 2010-20	9,400

What Operations Research Analysts Do

Operations research analysts use advanced methods of analysis to help organizations solve problems and make better decisions.

Duties

Operations research analysts typically do the following:
- Identify and define business problems, such as those in production, logistics, or sales
- Collect and organize information from a variety of sources, such as computer databases
- Gather input from workers involved in all aspects of the problem or from others who have specialized knowledge that can help solve the problem
- Examine information to figure out what is relevant to the problem and what methods should be used to analyze it

Operations research analysts use sophisticated computer software, such as databases and statistical and modeling packages, to analyze and solve problems.

- Use statistical analysis, simulation, and optimization (minimizing or maximizing a function based on a set of variables) to analyze information and develop practical solutions to business problems
- Based on their findings, advise managers and other decision makers on the appropriate course of action to take to solve a problem
- Write memos, reports, and other documents outlining their findings and recommendations for managers, executives, and other officials

Operations research analysts are involved in all aspects of an organization. For example, they help allocate resources, develop production schedules, manage the supply chain, and set prices.

Operations research analysts use sophisticated computer software, such as databases and statistical and modeling packages, to analyze and solve problems. For example, they help decide how to organize products in supermarkets and help companies figure out the most effective way to ship and distribute products. Analysts break down problems into their various parts and analyze the effect that different changes and circumstances would have on each of these parts. For example, to help an airline schedule flights and decide what to charge for tickets, analysts might take into account the cities that have to be connected, the amount of fuel required to fly those routes, the expected number of passengers, pilots' schedules, maintenance costs, and fuel prices.

There is no one way to solve a problem, and analysts must weigh the costs and benefits of alternative solutions or approaches in their recommendations to managers.

Because problems are complex and often require expertise from many disciplines, most analysts work on teams. Once a manager reaches a final decision, these teams may work with others in the organization to ensure that the plan is successful.

Work Environment

Operations research analysts held about 64,600 jobs in 2010. The industries employing the largest numbers of analysts in 2010 were as follows:

Professional, scientific, and technical services	23%
Finance and insurance	21
Government	17
Manufacturing	8
Information	8

Most operations research analysts in the federal government work for the Department of Defense, which also employs a large number of analysts through private consulting firms.

Operations research analysts spend most of their time in offices. Many also spend some time in the field, gathering information and analyzing processes through direct observation.

Work Schedules

Almost all operations research analysts work full time. Analysts often travel to work with clients and company executives and to attend conferences. Because they work on projects that are of immediate interest to top managers, operations research analysts often are under pressure to meet deadlines.

How to Become an Operations Research Analyst

Applicants need a master's degree for most operations research positions, but a bachelor's degree is enough for many entry-level positions. Many schools offer bachelor's and advanced degree programs in operations research, but it is common for analysts to have degrees in related fields.

Education

Most employers prefer to hire applicants with a master's degree, but many entry-level positions are available for those with a bachelor's degree. Many schools offer bachelor's and advanced degree programs in operations research, management science, or a related field. Many operations research analysts have degrees in other technical fields, such as engineering, computer science, mathematics, and physics.

Because operations research is based on quantitative analysis, students need extensive coursework in mathematics. Courses include statistics, calculus, and linear algebra. Coursework in computer science is important because analysts rely on advanced statistical and database software to analyze and model data. Courses in other areas, such as engineering, economics, and political science, are useful because operations research is a multidisciplinary field with a wide variety of applications.

Continuing education is important for operations research analysts. Keeping up with advances in technology, software tools, and improved analytical methods is vital.

Important Qualities

Analytical skills. Operations research analysts use a wide range of methods, such as forecasting, data mining, and statistical analysis, to examine and interpret data.

Critical-thinking skills. Operations research analysts must be able to figure out what information is relevant to their work. They also must be able to evaluate the costs and benefits of alternative solutions before making a recommendation.

Ingenuity. Solutions to operations problems are not usually obvious, and analysts need to be able to think creatively to solve problems.

Interpersonal skills. Operations research analysts typically work on teams. They also need to be able to convince managers and top executives to accept their recommendations.

Mathematical skills. The models and methods used by operations research analysts are rooted in statistics, calculus, linear algebra, and other advanced mathematical disciplines.

Problem-solving skills. Operations research analysts need to be able to diagnose problems on the basis of information given to them by others. They then analyze relevant information to solve the problems.

Communication skills. Operations research analysts need to be able to gather information, which includes interviewing people and listening carefully to the answers. They also need to communicate technical information to people who do not have a technical background.

Writing skills. Operations research analysts write memos, reports, and other documents outlining their findings and recommendations for managers, executives, and other officials.

Work Experience

Many operations research analysts who work with the military are veterans of the U.S. Armed Forces.

Pay

Operations Research Analysts
Median annual wages, May 2010

Computer and Mathematical Occupations	$73,720
Operations Research Analysts	$70,960
Total, All Occupations	$33,840

Note: All Occupations includes all occupations in the U.S. Economy.
Source: U.S. Bureau of Labor Statistics, Occupational Employment Statistics

The median annual wage of operations research analysts was $70,960 in May 2010. The median wage is the wage at which half of the workers in an occupation earned more than that amount and half earned less. The lowest 10 percent earned less than $39,920, and the top 10 percent earned more than $122,750.

Almost all operations research analysts work full time. Analysts often travel to work with clients and company executives and to attend conferences.

Job Outlook

Operations Research Analysts
Percent change in employment, projected 2010-20

Computer and Mathematical Occupations	22%
Operations Research Analysts	15%
Total, All Occupations	14%

Note: All Occupations includes all occupations in the U.S. Economy.
Source: U.S. Bureau of Labor Statistics, Employment Projections program

Employment of operations research analysts is expected to grow by 15 percent from 2010 to 2020, about as fast as the average for all occupations. As technology advances and companies further emphasize efficiency and cost savings, demand for operations research analysis should continue to grow. Operations research analysts will continue to be needed to provide support for our nation's military and to assist in the development and implementation of policies and programs in other areas of government.

Technological advances have made it faster and easier for organizations to get data. In addition, improvements in analytical software have made operations research more applicable to a wider range of areas and more affordable to the people who work in them. More companies are expected to use operations research analysts to help them turn data into valuable information that managers can use to make better decisions in all aspects of their business. For example, operations research analysts will be needed to help businesses improve their manufacturing operations and logistics.

Job Prospects

Analysts who are able to communicate their recommendations to managers and to workers outside of operations research should have the best job prospects.

Opportunities should be better for those who have a master's or Ph.D. degree in operations research, management science, or a related field.

Employment projections data for operations research analysts, 2010-20

Occupational Title	SOC Code	Employment, 2010	Projected Employment, 2020	Change, 2010-20	
				Percent	Numeric
Operations Research Analysts	15-2031	64,600	74,000	15	9,400

SOURCE: U.S. Bureau of Labor Statistics, Employment Projections program

Similar Occupations

This table shows a list of occupations with job duties that are similar to those of operations research analysts.

Occupation	Job Duties	Entry-Level Education	Median Annual Pay, May 2010
Economists	Economists study the production and distribution of resources, goods, and services.	Bachelor's degree	$89,450
Industrial Engineers	Industrial engineers find ways to eliminate wastefulness in production processes. They devise efficient ways to use workers, machines, materials, information, and energy to make a product or provide a service.	Bachelor's degree	$76,100
Management Analysts	Management analysts, often called management consultants, propose ways to improve an organization's efficiency. They advise managers on how to make organizations more profitable through reduced costs and increased revenues.	Bachelor's degree	$78,160
Market Research Analysts	Market research analysts study market conditions in local, regional, or national areas to examine potential sales of a product or service. They help companies understand what products people want, who will buy them, and at what price.	Bachelor's degree	$60,570
Mathematicians	Mathematicians use high-level mathematics and technology to develop new mathematical principles, understand relationships between existing principles, and solve real-world problems.	Master's degree	$99,380
Software Developers	Software developers are the creative minds behind computer programs. Some develop the applications that allow people to do specific tasks on a computer or other device. Others develop the underlying systems that run the devices or control networks.	Bachelor's degree	$90,530
Statisticians	Statisticians use mathematical techniques to analyze and interpret data and draw conclusions.	Master's degree	$72,830

Contacts for More Information

For more information about operations research analysts, visit
Institute for Operations Research and the Management Sciences
,Military Operations Research Society

Suggested citation:

Bureau of Labor Statistics, U.S. Department of Labor, Occupational Outlook Handbook, 2012-13 Edition, Operations Research Analysts, on the Internet at
http://www.bls.gov/ooh/math/operations-research-analysts.htm

Statisticians

Quick Facts: Statisticians	
2010 Median Pay	$72,830 per year $35.02 per hour
Entry-Level Education	Master's degree
Work Experience in a Related Occupation	None
On-the-job Training	None
Number of Jobs, 2010	25,100
Job Outlook, 2010-20	14% (About as fast as average)
Employment Change, 2010-20	3,500

What Statisticians Do

Statisticians use mathematical techniques to analyze and interpret data and draw conclusions. Many economic, social, political, and military decisions rely on the work of statisticians.

Duties

Statisticians typically do the following:

- Determine the questions or problems to be addressed
- Decide what data are needed to answer the questions or problems
- Determine methods for finding or collecting data
- Design surveys or experiments or opinion polls to collect data
- Collect data or train others to do so
- Analyze and interpret data
- Report conclusions from their analyses

Statisticians design surveys, experiments, and opinion polls to

Statisticians design surveys, experiments, and opinion polls to collect data.

collect data. Some surveys, such as the U.S. census, include data from nearly everyone. For most surveys and opinion polls, however, statisticians use sampling to collect data from some people in a particular group. Statisticians determine the type and size of the sample to be surveyed or polled.

Statisticians develop survey questionnaires or reporting forms for collecting the data they need. They also often write instructions for workers who collect and tabulate the data. Surveys may be mailed, conducted over the phone, or collected online or through some other means. Statisticians analyze the data that are collected. In their analyses, statisticians calculate averages, reliability, and other specifics of the data. They also choose and conduct tests to find out the data's reliability and validity.

Statisticians explain the limitations of the data to prevent inaccurate conclusions from being drawn, and they identify trends and relationships. Statisticians use computers with specialized statistical software to analyze data. Some statisticians help to create new statistical software packages to analyze data more accurately and efficiently.

Statisticians write reports to explain their findings and the data's limitations. They may present their reports to other team members and to clients with tables, charts, and graphs. Statisticians also recommend how to improve the design of future surveys or experiments.

Statisticians work in many fields, such as education, marketing, psychology, and sports: any field that requires collection and analysis of large amounts of data. In particular, government, health, and manufacturing employ many statisticians:

Government. Nearly every agency in the federal government employs statisticians. Some government statisticians develop and analyze surveys that measure unemployment, wages, and other estimates of jobs and workers. Other statisticians help to figure out the average level of pesticides in drinking water, the number of endangered species living in a particular area, or the number of people who have a certain disease, for example. At national defense agencies, statisticians use computer programs to test the likely outcomes of different defense strategies.

Health. Statisticians known as biostatisticians or biometricians work in pharmaceutical companies, public health, and medicine. They design studies that test whether drugs successfully treat diseases or conditions. They also work for hospitals and public health agencies, where they help identify the sources of outbreaks of illnesses in humans and animals.

Manufacturing. Statisticians design experiments for product testing and development. For instance, they help to design experiments to see how car engines perform when exposed to extreme weather conditions. Statisticians also contribute to the design of marketing strategies and prices for final goods.

Work Environment

Statisticians held about 25,100 jobs in 2010. About a third of statisticians work for government, mostly at the federal level. Most federal statisticians are employed at the Bureau of the Census, the Bureau of Economic Analysis, the National Agricultural Statistical Service, or the Bureau of Labor Statistics. Many statisticians hired by the federal government are known as mathematical statisticians. These workers develop advanced statistical models for several purposes, such as filling in gaps from nonresponses to surveys.

Many statisticians work for private businesses, such as pharmaceutical and insurance companies, and often work in teams with other professionals. For example, in pharmaceutical companies, statisticians may work with scientists to test drugs for government approval. In insurance companies, they may work with actuaries to calculate the risks of insuring different situations. Because statisticians in business provide advice on research projects or oversee the gathering of data, they travel occasionally for face-to-face meetings with team members.

The following tabulation includes selected industries which employed statisticians in 2010:

Federal government, excluding postal service	20%
Scientific research and development services	12
Colleges, universities, and professional schools; state, local, and private	9
State government, excluding education and hospitals	8
Insurance carriers	7

Work Schedules

Statisticians generally work full time. Overtime may be needed to meet deadlines.

How to Become a Statistician

A bachelor's degree in statistics is sufficient for many entry-level jobs. However, most statisticians pursue further education and earn a master's degree in statistics, mathematics, or survey methodology. Research and academic jobs generally require a Ph.D.

Education

Many colleges and universities offer undergraduate and graduate degree programs in statistics. A bachelor's degree in statistics is not needed to enter a graduate program, although significant training in mathematics is essential. Required subjects for a bachelor's degree in statistics include differential and integral calculus, statistical methods, mathematical modeling, and probability theory.

Because statisticians use and write computer programs for many calculations, a strong background in computer science is helpful. Training in engineering or physical science is useful for statisticians working in manufacturing on quality control or productivity improvement. A background in biology, chemistry, or health sciences is useful for work involving testing pharmaceutical or agricultural products.

Important Qualities

Critical-thinking skills. Statisticians use logic and reasoning to identify the strengths and weaknesses of alternative solutions, conclusions, or approaches to problems.

Problem-solving skills. Statisticians must develop techniques to overcome problems in data collection and analysis, such as high nonresponse rates, so that they can draw meaningful conclusions.

Speaking skills. Because statisticians often work in teams, they must be able to orally communicate statistical information and ideas so that others will understand.

Writing skills. Good writing skills are important for statisticians because they need to explain technical matters to persons without their level of statistical expertise.

Advancement

Opportunities for promotion are greater for people with master's degrees or Ph.D.s. Statisticians with a master's degree or a Ph.D. usually can design their own work. They may develop new statistical methods. They may become independent consultants.

Pay

Statisticians
Median annual wages, May 2010

Computer and Mathematical Occupations	$73,720
Statisticians	$72,830
Total, All Occupations	$33,840

Note: All Occupations includes all occupations in the U.S. Economy.
Source: U.S. Bureau of Labor Statistics, Occupational Employment Statistics

The median annual wage of statisticians was $72,830 in May 2010. The median wage is the wage at which half the workers in an occupation earned more than that amount and half earned less. The lowest 10 percent earned less than $39,090 and the top 10 percent earned more than $119,100.

In March 2011, the average annual salary in the federal government was $95,695 for statisticians and $108,868 for mathematical statisticians.

As shown in the tabulation below, statisticians working for the federal government had the highest median annual wage in May 2010:

Federal government, excluding postal service	$94,970
Scientific research and development services	83,140
Insurance carriers	66,050
Colleges, universities, and professional schools; state, local, and private	65,020
State government, excluding education and hospitals	45,370

Statisticians generally work full time. Overtime may be needed to meet deadlines.

Job Outlook

Statisticians
Percent change in employment, projected 2010-20

Computer and Mathematical Occupations	22%
Total, All Occupations	14%
Statisticians	14%

Note: All Occupations includes all occupations in the U.S. Economy.
Source: U.S. Bureau of Labor Statistics, Employment Projections program

Employment of statisticians is projected to grow 14 percent from 2010 to 2020, about as fast as the average for all occupations. Growth will result from more widespread use of statistical analysis to make informed decisions. In addition, the large increase in available data from the Internet will open up new areas for analysis.

Government agencies will employ more statisticians to improve the quality of the data available for policy analysis. This occupation will also see growth in research and development in the physical, engineering, and life sciences, where statisticians' skills in designing tests and assessing results prove highly useful.

Statisticians will continue to be needed in the pharmaceutical industry. As pharmaceutical companies develop new treatments and medical technologies, biostatisticians will be needed to do research and conduct clinical trials. Research and testing are necessary to help companies obtain approval for their products from the Food and Drug Administration.

A large amount of data is generated from Internet searching. Businesses will need statisticians to organize, analyze, and sort through the data for commercial reasons.

Job Prospects

Job prospects for statisticians will be very good. Graduates with a master's degree in statistics and with a strong background in an allied related field, such as finance, biology, engineering, or computer science, should have the best prospects of finding jobs related to their field of study.

Employment projections data for statisticians, 2010-20

Occupational Title	SOC Code	Employment, 2010	Projected Employment, 2020	Change, 2010-20 Percent	Change, 2010-20 Numeric
Statisticians	15-2041	25,100	28,600	14	3,500
SOURCE: U.S. Bureau of Labor Statistics, Employment Projections program					

Similar Occupations

This table shows a list of occupations with job duties that are similar to those of statisticians.

Occupation	Job Duties	Entry-Level Education	Median Annual Pay, May 2010
Actuaries	Actuaries analyze the financial costs of risk and uncertainty. They use mathematics, statistics, and financial theory to assess the risk that an event will occur and to help businesses and clients develop policies that minimize the cost of that risk.	Bachelor's degree	$87,650
Computer Systems Analysts	Computer systems analysts study an organization's current computer systems and procedures and make recommendations to management to help the organization operate more efficiently and effectively. They bring business and information technology (IT) together by understanding the needs and limitations of both.	Bachelor's degree	$77,740
Economists	Economists study the production and distribution of resources, goods, and services.	Bachelor's degree	$89,450
Financial Analysts	Financial analysts provide guidance to businesses and individuals making investment decisions. They assess the performance of stocks, bonds, and other types of investments.	Bachelor's degree	$74,350
Market Research Analysts	Market research analysts study market conditions in local, regional, or national areas to examine potential sales of a product or service. They help companies understand what products people want, who will buy them, and at what price.	Bachelor's degree	$60,570
Mathematicians	Mathematicians use high-level mathematics and technology to develop new mathematical principles, understand relationships between existing principles, and solve real-world problems.	Master's degree	$99,380
Operations Research Analysts	Operations research analysts use advanced methods of analysis to help organizations solve problems and make better decisions.	Bachelor's degree	$70,960
Postsecondary Teachers	Postsecondary teachers instruct students in a wide variety of academic and vocational subjects beyond the high school level. They also conduct research and publish scholarly papers and books.	Doctoral or professional degree	$62,050
Survey Researchers	Survey researchers design or conduct surveys and analyze survey data. Many groups use surveys to collect factual data, such as employment and salary information, or to ask questions that help them understand people's opinions, attitudes, beliefs, or desires.	Bachelor's degree	$36,050

Contacts for More Information

For more information about statisticians, visit American Statistical Association

For more information on doctoral-level careers and training in mathematics, a field closely related to statistics, visit American Mathematical Society

For information on job openings for statisticians or mathematical statisticians in the federal government, visit Office of Personnel Management

Suggested citation:

Bureau of Labor Statistics, U.S. Department of Labor, Occupational Outlook Handbook, 2012-13 Edition, Statisticians, on the Internet at http://www.bls.gov/ooh/math/statisticians.htm .

Media and Communication Occupations

Announcers

Quick Facts: Announcers	
2010 Median Pay	$27,010 per year $12.99 per hour
Entry-Level Education	See How to Become One
Work Experience in a Related Occupation	None
On-the-job Training	See How to Become One
Number of Jobs, 2010	61,900
Job Outlook, 2010-20	7% (Slower than average)
Employment Change, 2010-20	4,100

What Announcers Do

Announcers present music, news, and sports and may provide commentary or interview guests about these topics or other important events. Some act as a master of ceremonies (emcee) or disc jockey (DJ) at weddings, parties, or clubs.

Duties

Radio and television announcers typically do the following:

- Present music, news, sports, the weather, the time, and commercials
- Interview guests and moderate panels or discussions on their shows
- Announce station programming information, such as program schedules and station breaks for commercials, or public-service information
- Research topics for comment and discussion during shows
- Read prepared scripts on radio or television shows
- Comment on important news stories
- Provide commentary for the audience during sporting events, at parades, and on other occasions
- Select program content
- Make promotional appearances at public or private events

Radio and television announcers present music or the news and comment on important current events. Announcers are expected to be up to date on current events or a specific field, such as politics or sports, so that they comment on these issues during their programs. They may research and prepare information on these topics before appearing on-air. In addition, announcers schedule guests on their shows and work with producers to develop other creative content for their programs.

Radio and television announcers also may be responsible for other aspects of television or radio. They may operate studio equipment, sell commercial time to advertisers, and produce advertisements and other recorded material. At many radio stations, announcers do much of the work that editors and broadcast technicians used to do, such as broadcasting programming, commercials, and public-service announcements.

Many radio and television announcers increasingly maintain a presence on social media networking sites. Establishing a presence allows them to promote their stations and better engage with their audiences through listener feedback, music requests, or program contests.

Many radio stations now require DJs to update their station's website with show schedules, interviews, or photos.

Public address system and other announcers typically do the following:

- Meet with the event director to review the schedule and obtain other event details
- Present information or announcements, such as train schedules or security precautions
- Introduce up-coming acts and guide the audience through the entertainment
- Provide commentary for a live audience during sporting events
- Make promotional appearances at public or private events

The work of public address system announcers varies greatly depending on where they are working. For example, a ringmaster at a circus directs the audience's attention to the appropriate act. Their role is to enhance the performance and entertain and inform the audience. They may prepare their own scripts or improvise lines in their speeches.

Train announcers are responsible for reading prepared scripts containing details and data related to train schedules and safety procedures. Their work is not entertainment, but informational.

Public address announcers for a sports team may have to give starting lineups—an official list of players who will participate in the event—read advertisements, and announce the players as they enter and exit the game.

The following are examples of types of announcers:

DJs broadcast music for radio stations, typically specializing in one kind of music genre and announcing selections as they air them. While on-air, DJs comment on the music, weather, and traffic. They may take requests from listeners, interview guests, and manage listener contests.

Talk show hosts may work in radio or television and specialize in a certain area of interest, such as politics, personal finance, sports, or health. They contribute to the preparation of the program's content,

Announcers present music, sports, and news to audiences.

interview guests, and discuss issues with viewers, listeners, or the studio or radio audience.

Public address system announcers provide information to the audience at sporting, performing arts, and other events.

Party DJs are hired to provide music and commentary at an event, such as a wedding, birthday party, or corporate party. Many DJs use digital files or portable media devices.

Emcees host planned events. They introduce speakers or performers to the audience. They may tell jokes or provide commentary to transition from one speaker to the next.

Work Environment

Radio and television announcers held about 50,200 jobs in 2010. Approximately 60 percent were employed in the radio and television broadcasting industry, and 35 percent were self-employed. These self-employed workers can record their shows at home and sell them to networks and stations, advertising agencies, or other independent producers.

Public address system and other announcers held about 11,700 jobs in 2010. Approximately 35 percent were self-employed, while 26 percent work in the arts, entertainment, and recreation industry. The radio and television broadcasting industry employs approximately 5 percent of these workers.

Radio and television announcers usually work in well-lit, air-conditioned, soundproof studios.

The tight schedules that announcers work on can be stressful.

Work Schedules

Although most announcers work full time, many work part time.

Many radio and television stations are on-air 24 hours a day. Some announcers present early-morning shows, when most people are getting ready for work or commuting. Others do late-night programs.

The shifts, however, are not as varied as in the past. Technology has allowed stations to eliminate most of the overnight hours, because shows that air during the night can now be recorded earlier in the day.

How to Become an Announcer

Educational requirements for announcers vary. Radio and television announcers typically have a bachelor's degree in journalism, broadcasting, or communications, along with work experience gained from working at their college radio or television station. Public address announcers typically need a high school diploma, along with short-term on-the-job training.

Education

Although public address announcers do not require any formal education beyond a high school diploma, radio announcers should have a bachelor's degree to be competitive for entry-level positions. Television announcers typically need a bachelor's degree in programs such as communications, broadcasting, or journalism.

College broadcasting programs offer courses, such as voice and diction, to help students improve their vocal qualities. In addition, these programs prepare students to work with the computer equipment and software that they would work with at radio and television studios.

Training

Public address systems and other announcers typically need short-term on-the-job training upon being hired. This training allows these announcers to become familiar with the equipment they will be using during sporting and entertainment events. For sports public address announcers, training may also go over basic rules and information for the sports they are covering.

Advancement

Because smaller market stations have smaller staff, advancement within the same radio or television station is unlikely. Rather, many

radio and television announcers advance by relocating to a station in a larger market.

Announcers typically require a few years at a smaller market to work out the "kinks" of their on-air personalities. They learn to sound more comfortable and credible as an on-air talent and become more conversational with audiences and guests. Therefore, time and experience allows applicants to advance to larger markets with higher pay and more responsibility and challenges.

When making hiring decisions, large market stations rely on announcers' personalities. Radio and television announcers need to have proven that they can attract, engage, and keep a sizeable audience. Therefore, ratings for an announcer's show in the smaller market are important in increasing advancement opportunities.

Larger stations also rely on radio and television announcers to do other tasks that the station needs. Therefore, an applicant needs to have demonstrated versatility and flexibility at the smaller market in duties such as creating and updating a social media presence on social networking sites, making promotional appearances on behalf of the station, or even selling commercial time to advertisers.

Important Qualities

Appearance. Television announcers need a neat, pleasing appearance.

Computer skills. Announcers, especially those seeking radio careers, should have good computer skills and be able to use computers, editing equipment, and other broadcast-related devices.

People skills. Radio and television announcers may interview guests and answer phone calls on air. Party DJs and emcees work with clients to plan entertainment options.

Persistence. Entry into this occupation is very competitive, and many auditions may be needed for an opportunity to work on the air. Many entry-level announcers must work for a small station and be flexible to move to a small market to secure their first job.

Research skills. Announcers must research the important topics of the day in order to be knowledgeable enough to comment on them during their program.

Speaking skills. Announcers must have a pleasant and well-controlled voice, good timing, and excellent pronunciation.

Writing skills. Announcers need strong writing skills because they normally write their own material.

Pay

Announcers	
Median annual wages, May 2010	
Total, All Occupations	$33,840
Public Address System and Other Announcers	$27,910
Announcers	$27,010
Radio and Television Announcers	$26,850

Note: All Occupations includes all occupations in the U.S. Economy.
Source: U.S. Bureau of Labor Statistics, Occupational Employment Statistics

The median annual wage of radio and television announcers was $26,850 in May 2010. The median wage is the wage at which half the workers in an occupation earned more than that amount and half earned less. The lowest 10 percent earned less than $16,590, and the top 10 percent earned more than $72,500.

The median annual wage of public address and other system announcers was $27,910 in May 2010. The lowest 10 percent earned less than $16,940, and the top 10 percent earned more than $70,120.

In general, announcers who work in larger markets earn more than those working in smaller markets.

Although most announcers work full time, many work part time.

Many radio and television stations are on-air 24 hours a day. Some announcers present early-morning shows, when most people are getting ready for work or commuting. Others do late-night programs.

The shifts, however, are not as varied as in the past. Technology has allowed stations to eliminate most of the overnight hours, because shows that air during the night can now be recorded earlier in the day.

Job Outlook

Announcers

Percent change in employment, projected 2010-20

Total, All Occupations	14%
Announcers	7%
Radio and Television Announcers	7%
Public Address System and Other Announcers	5%

Note: All Occupations includes all occupations in the U.S. Economy.
Source: U.S. Bureau of Labor Statistics, Employment Projections program

Employment of radio and television announcers is projected to grow by 7 percent from 2010 to 2020, slower than the average for all occupations.

Employment of public address system and other announcers is projected to grow by 5 percent from 2010 to 2020, slower than the average for all occupations.

Improving technology and consolidation of radio and television stations will limit the growth in this field. Many stations are able to do more tasks with less staff. Technology continues to increase the productivity of radio and television announcers and reduce the time required to edit material or do other off-air technical and production work.

For example, radio stations use voice-tracking or "cyber jockeying," which allows radio announcers to prerecord their segments rather than air them live. A radio announcer can record many segments for use at a later date or even on another radio station.

This technique lets the station use fewer employees while still appearing to have live shows. This technology has eliminated most late-night shifts and allowed multiple stations to use material from the same announcer.

Consolidation among broadcasting companies may also contribute to increasing use of syndicated programming and programs originating outside a station's viewing or listening area.

Despite these negatives, the increase of national news and satellite stations may increase the demand for more local radio and television stations. Listeners want localized programs with news and information more relevant to their communities. Therefore, to distinguish themselves from other stations or other media formats, stations are adding a local element to their broadcasts.

In addition, Internet radio may positively influence occupation growth. Start-up costs for internet radio stations are relatively lower than for land-based radio. These stations can cheaply target a specific demographic or listening audience and create new opportunities for announcers.

Demand for public address announcers will remain stable. Public address announcers will continue to inform customers of important information or provide entertainment for special events.

Job Prospects

Strong competition is expected for jobs as a radio or television announcer. Many of the openings will be due to people leaving jobs and the need to replace workers who move out of smaller markets or out of the radio or television field entirely.

Consolidation of stations has decreased the jobs for radio and television announcers and pushed experienced announcers into medium and smaller market stations. Therefore, an entry-level announcer may be competing with an on-air announcer who already has years of experience.

Applicants need to be persistent and flexible because many entry-level positions will require moving to a smaller market city. Small radio and television stations are more inclined to hire beginners, but the pay is low.

Those with a formal education in journalism, broadcasting, or mass communications and with hands-on work experience at a radio or television network will have the best job prospects.

Employment projections data for announcers, 2010-20

Occupational Title	SOC Code	Employment, 2010	Projected Employment, 2020	Change, 2010-20 Percent	Numeric
Announcers	27-3010	61,900	65,900	7	4,100
Radio and Television Announcers	27-3011	50,200	53,600	7	3,500
Public Address System and Other Announcers	27-3012	11,700	12,300	5	600
SOURCE: U.S. Bureau of Labor Statistics, Employment Projections program					

Similar Occupations

This table shows a list of occupations with job duties that are similar to those of announcers.

Occupation	Job Duties	Entry-Level Education	Median Annual Pay, May 2010
Actors	Actors express ideas and portray characters in theater, film, television, and other performing arts media. They also work at theme parks or for other live events. They interpret a writer's script to entertain or inform an audience.	Some college, no degree	The annual wage is not available.
Broadcast and Sound Engineering Technicians	Broadcast and sound engineering technicians set up, operate, and maintain the electrical equipment for radio and television broadcasts, concerts, sound recordings, and movies and in office and school buildings.	See How to Become One	$39,870
Musicians and Singers	Musicians and singers play instruments or sing for live audiences and in recording studios. They perform in a variety of styles, such as classical, jazz, opera, rap, or rock.	High school diploma or equivalent	The annual wage is not available.

Producers and Directors	Producers and directors are in charge of creating motion pictures, television shows, live theater, and other performing arts productions. They interpret a writer's script to entertain or inform an audience.	Bachelor's degree	$68,440
Reporters, Correspondents, and Broadcast News Analysts	Reporters, correspondents, and broadcast news analysts inform the public about news and events happening internationally, nationally, and locally. They report the news for newspapers, magazines, websites, television, and radio.	Bachelor's degree	$36,000
Writers and Authors	Writers and authors develop original written content for advertisements, books, magazines, movie and television scripts, songs, and online publications.	Bachelor's degree	$55,420

Contacts for More Information

For more information about the broadcasting industry, in which many announcers are employed, visit National Association of Broadcasters

Suggested citation:

Bureau of Labor Statistics, U.S. Department of Labor, Occupational Outlook Handbook, 2012-13 Edition, Announcers, on the Internet at http://www.bls.gov/ooh/media-and-communication/announcers.htm .

Broadcast and Sound Engineering Technicians

Quick Facts: Broadcast and Sound Engineering Technicians	
2010 Median Pay	$39,870 per year $19.17 per hour
Entry-Level Education	See How to Become One
Work Experience in a Related Occupation	None
On-the-job Training	See How to Become One
Number of Jobs, 2010	116,900
Job Outlook, 2010-20	10% (About as fast as average)
Employment Change, 2010-20	11,600

What Broadcast and Sound Engineering Technicians Do

Broadcast and sound engineering technicians set up, operate, and maintain the electrical equipment for radio and television broadcasts, concerts, sound recordings, and movies and in office and school buildings.

Duties

Broadcast and sound engineering technicians typically do the following:

- Operate, monitor, and adjust audio and video equipment to regulate the volume and ensure quality in radio and television broadcasts, concerts, and other performances
- Set up and tear down equipment for events and live performances
- Record speech, music, and other sounds on recording equipment
- Synchronize sounds and dialogue with action taking place on television or in movie productions
- Convert video and audio records to digital formats for editing
- Install audio, video, and sometimes lighting equipment in hotels, offices, and schools
- Report and repair equipment problems
- Keep records of recordings and equipment used

These workers may be called broadcast or sound engineering technicians or operators or engineers. At smaller radio and television stations, broadcast and sound technicians may do many jobs. At larger stations, they are likely to specialize more, although even their job assignments may change from day to day. They set up and operate audio and video equipment, although the kind of equipment they use may depend on the particular type of technician or industry.

Although some of the duties of broadcast and sound engineering technicians are similar, there are some differences.

Audio and video equipment technicians set up and operate audio and video equipment. They also connect wires and cables and set up and operate sound and mixing boards and related electronic equipment.

Audio and video equipment technicians work with microphones, speakers, video screens, projectors, video monitors, and recording equipment. The equipment they operate is used for meetings, concerts, sports events, conventions, news conferences, as well as lectures, conferences, and presentations in businesses and universities.

Audio and video equipment technicians may also set up and operate custom lighting systems. They frequently work directly with clients and must listen to, understand, and provide solutions to problems in a simple and clear manner. In addition, many audio and video equipment technicians are self-employed and must spend time marketing their practice to prospective clients.

Broadcast technicians set up, operate, and maintain equipment that regulates the signal strength, the clarity, and the ranges of sounds and colors of radio or television broadcasts. They operate transmitters to broadcast radio or television programs and use computers to program the equipment and to edit audio and video recordings.

Sound engineering technicians operate machines and equipment that record, synchronize, mix, or reproduce music, voices, or sound effects in recording studios, sporting arenas, theater productions, or movie and video productions. They record audio performances or events and may combine tracks that were recorded separately to create a multilayered final product. Sound engineering technicians operate transmitters to broadcast radio or television programs and use computers both to program the equipment and to edit audio recordings.

Broadcast and sound engineering technicians operate controls to ensure quality audio and video recordings for radio and television broadcasts.

(Information on foley artists , a type of sound engineering technician, can be accessed from the Occupational Outlook Quarterly.)

The following are examples of types of broadcast technicians and sound engineering technicians:

Recording engineers operate and maintain video and sound recording equipment. They may operate equipment designed to produce special effects for radio, television, or movies.

Sound mixers, or **rerecording mixers**, produce soundtracks for movies or television programs. After filming or recording is complete, these workers may use a process called dubbing to insert sounds.

Field technicians set up and operate portable equipment outside the studio—for example, for television news coverage. This coverage requires so much electronic equipment, and the technology is changing so rapidly, that many stations assign some of their technicians exclusively to news.

Chief engineers, transmission engineers, and **broadcast field supervisors** oversee other technicians and maintain broadcasting equipment.

Work Environment

Broadcast and sound engineering technicians held about 116,900 jobs in 2010. Their employment was distributed among the detailed occupations as follows:

Audio and video equipment technicians	61,200
Broadcast technicians	36,700
Sound engineering technicians	19,000

Broadcast and sound engineering technicians typically work indoors in radio, television, movie, or recording studios. However, some work outdoors in all types of conditions to broadcast news and other programs. Audio and video technicians also set up audiovisual systems in offices, schools, government agencies, hospitals, and homes. The following table shows the industries employing the most broadcast and sound engineering technicians in 2010:

Radio and television broadcasting	23%
Motion picture and video industries	10
Performing arts, spectator sports, and related industries	10
Educational services; state, local, and private	9

Technicians doing maintenance may climb poles or antenna towers, and those setting up equipment do heavy lifting.

Work Schedules

Technicians typically work full time. Some may occasionally work overtime to meet broadcast deadlines or set up for live events. Evening, weekend, and holiday work is common because most stations are on the air 24 hours a day.

Technicians who work on motion pictures may be on a tight schedule and may work long hours to meet contract deadlines with movie studios.

How to Become a Broadcast or Sound Engineering Technician

Most broadcast and sound engineering technicians have an associate's degree or vocational certification, although some are hired with only a high school diploma. Some formal training, gained through either work experience or education, is often required.

Education

Audio and video equipment technicians need to have at least a high school diploma or a General Educational Development (GED) certificate to be eligible for entry-level positions. However, many also have an associate's degree or vocational certificate.

Technical training for audio and video equipment technicians may take several months to a year to complete. In this training, they get hands-on experience with the equipment they will use in many entry-level positions. Coursework and practical experience from a high school or college audiovisual club can prepare a student to be an audio and video equipment technician.

Similarly, broadcast technicians need at least a high school diploma or a GED, although many also have some college education or a vocational training certificate in a related field. Because of the competitiveness of the industry, an associate's or bachelor's degree in broadcast technology, electronics, computer networking, or a related field can help a technician's career.

Sound engineering technicians usually complete a vocational program, which may take up to a year. Many technicians have an associate's degree.

Prospective broadcast and sound engineering technicians should complete high school courses in math, physics, and electronics and need to have excellent computer skills to be successful in this field.

Training

Technicians who have work experience and formal training in their field will have the best opportunities for a job. Because technology is constantly improving, technicians often enroll in continuing education and receive on-the-job training to become skilled in new equipment and systems. On-the-job training may include topics such as setting up cables, testing electrical equipment, learning the codes and standards of the industry, and following safety procedures.

Training for new hires can be accomplished in a variety of ways, depending on the types of products and services the employer provides. Although some formal apprenticeship programs do exist, more frequently a new technician will accompany a more senior level technician to get the training and skills necessary for advancement.

Certification

Although not required by most employers, earning voluntary certification may offer advantages in getting a job as a broadcast or sound engineering technician. Certification allows employers to be sure that the technician meets certain industry standards and has kept up to date with new technologies.

For example, the Society of Broadcast Engineers offers eight broadcast engineering certifications, two operator certifications, and a broadcast networking certification, each of which requires passing an exam. Similarly, InfoComm International offers an audiovisual Certified Technology Specialist credential.

Advancement

Although many broadcast and sound engineering technicians work first in small markets or with small stations in big markets, after they gain the necessary experience and skills they often transfer to larger, better paying radio or television stations. Large stations almost never hire someone without previous experience, and they value more specialized skills.

Experienced workers with strong technical skills can become supervisory technicians or chief engineers. A college degree in engineering is typically needed to become chief engineer at large television stations.

Important Qualities

Communication skills. Technicians need to communicate with supervisors and coworkers to ensure that clients' needs are met and that equipment is set up properly before broadcasts, live performances, and presentations.

Computer skills. Technicians use computer systems to program the equipment and edit audio and video recordings.

Manual dexterity. Technicians set up audio and visual equipment and cables which requires a steady hand and good hand-eye coordination. Others adjust small knobs, dials, and sliders during radio and television broadcasts and live performances.

Problem-solving skills. Technicians need to recognize problems with the equipment and propose possible solutions to them. Employers typically desire applicants with a variety of skills who are able to set up equipment, maintain the equipment, and troubleshoot and solve any problems.

Technical skills. Technicians work with and repair a variety of electrical, electronic, and mechanical systems and equipment.

Pay

Broadcast and Sound Engineering Technicians
Median annual wages, May 2010

Sound Engineering Technicians	$47,080
Audio and Video Equipment Technicians	$40,540
Broadcast and Sound Engineering Technicians	$39,870
Broadcast Technicians	$35,120
Total, All Occupations	$33,840

Note: All Occupations includes all occupations in the U.S. Economy.
Source: U.S. Bureau of Labor Statistics, Occupational Employment Statistics

The median annual wage for broadcast and sound engineering technicians was $39,870 in May 2010. The median wage is the wage at which half the workers in an occupation earned more than that amount and half earned less.

The median annual wages for broadcast and sound engineering technician occupations in May 2010 were the following:
- $47,080 for sound engineering technicians
- $40,540 for audio and video equipment technicians
- $35,120 for broadcast technicians

Technicians working in major cities typically earn more than those working in smaller locations.

Technicians usually work full time. Some may occasionally work overtime to meet broadcast deadlines or set up for live events. Evening, weekend, and holiday work is common because most radio and television stations are on the air 24 hours a day.

Technicians who work on motion pictures may be on a tight schedule and may work long hours to meet contract deadlines with the movie studio.

Job Outlook

Broadcast and Sound Engineering Technicians
Percent change in employment, projected 2010-20

Total, All Occupations	14%
Audio and Video Equipment Technicians	13%
Broadcast and Sound Engineering Technicians	10%
Broadcast Technicians	9%
Sound Engineering Technicians	1%

Note: All Occupations includes all occupations in the U.S. Economy.
Source: U.S. Bureau of Labor Statistics, Employment Projections program

Employment of broadcast and sound engineering technicians is expected to grow 10 percent from 2010 to 2020, about as fast as the average for all occupations. Growth is expected as businesses, schools, and radio and television stations demand new equipment to improve their audio and video capabilities.

As a result, employment of audio and visual equipment technicians is expected to grow 13 percent from 2010 to 2020. Audio and video equipment is in demand in many buildings, where technicians set up new equipment or work to upgrade and maintain old systems. More companies are increasing their video budgets, including increasing the use of video conferencing to reduce travel costs and communicate worldwide with other offices and clients.

An increase in the use of digital signage for schools, hospitals, and hotels also will lead to higher demand for audio and video equipment technicians.

Schools and universities are seeking to improve their audio and video capabilities to attract and keep the best students. They are building classrooms with interactive whiteboards and video equipment that allow teachers to give more interactive multimedia presentations and to record lectures.

Employment of broadcast technicians is expected to grow 9 percent from 2010 to 2020, while employment of sound engineering technicians is expected to grow 1 percent. The television and motion picture industry will continue to need technicians to improve the picture quality of shows and movies. The industry is installing the latest technologies, such as digital or 3D screens, in movie and home theaters and is converting existing theaters to new formats.

However, growth will be slowed by consolidation of radio and television stations and by technological improvements that will increase the productivity of technicians. Laborsaving advances, such as computer-controlled programming, may result in fewer broadcasting positions needed to produce the same number of programs.

Job Prospects

Competition for jobs will be strong. This occupation attracts many applicants who are interested in working with the latest technology and electronic equipment. Many applicants also are attracted to working in the radio and television industry.

Those looking for work in this industry will have the most job opportunities in smaller markets or stations. Those with hands-on experience with electronics or with work experience at a radio or television station will have the best job prospects. In addition, technicians are expected to be versatile and contribute to the set up, operation, and maintenance of equipment, whereas previously technicians typically specialized in one area.

Employment projections data for broadcast and sound engineering technicians, 2010-20

Occupational Title	SOC Code	Employment, 2010	Projected Employment, 2020	Change, 2010-20	
				Percent	Numeric
Broadcast and Sound Engineering Technicians	—	116,900	128,600	10	11,600
Audio and Video Equipment Technicians	27-4011	61,200	69,400	13	8,200
Broadcast Technicians	27-4012	36,700	40,000	9	3,300
Sound Engineering Technicians	27-4014	19,000	19,100	1	100
SOURCE: U.S. Bureau of Labor Statistics, Employment Projections program					

Similar Occupations

This table shows a list of occupations with job duties that are similar to those of broadcast and sound engineering technicians.

Occupation	Job Duties	Entry-Level Education	Median Annual Pay, May 2010
Computer Support Specialists	Computer support specialists provide help and advice to people and organizations using computer software or equipment. Some, called technical support specialists, support information technology (IT) employees within their organization. Others, called help-desk technicians, assist non-IT users who are having computer problems.	Some college, no degree	$46,260
Electrical and Electronic Engineering Technicians	Electrical and electronic engineering technicians help engineers design and develop computers, communications equipment, medical monitoring devices, navigational equipment, and other electrical and electronic equipment. They often work in product evaluation and testing, using measuring and diagnostic devices to adjust, test, and repair equipment.	Associate's degree	$56,040
Electrical and Electronics Installers and Repairers	Electrical and electronics installers and repairers install, repair, or replace a variety of electrical equipment in telecommunications, transportation, utilities, and other industries.	Postsecondary non-degree award	$49,170
Film and Video Editors and Camera Operators	Film and video editors and camera operators record images that entertain or inform an audience. Camera operators capture a wide range of material for TV shows, motion pictures, music videos, documentaries, or news and sporting events. Editors construct the final productions from the many different images camera operators capture. They collaborate with producers and directors to create the final production.	Bachelor's degree	$45,490

Contacts for More Information

For more career information and links to employment resources, visit National Association of Broadcasters

For more information on certification and links to employment information, visit Society of Broadcast Engineers

For more information on certification and career information for audio and video equipment technicians, visit InfoComm International ,National Systems Contractors Association

Suggested citation:

Bureau of Labor Statistics, U.S. Department of Labor, Occupational Outlook Handbook, 2012-13 Edition, Broadcast and Sound Engineering Technicians, on the Internet at http://www.bls.gov/ooh/media-and-communication/broadcast-and-sound-engineering-technicians.htm .

Editors

Quick Facts: Editors	
2010 Median Pay	$51,470 per year $24.75 per hour
Entry-Level Education	Bachelor's degree
Work Experience in a Related Occupation	1 to 5 years
On-the-job Training	None
Number of Jobs, 2010	127,200
Job Outlook, 2010-20	1% (Little or no change)
Employment Change, 2010-20	800

What Editors Do

Editors plan, review, and revise content for publication. An editor's responsibilities vary with the employer and the type and level of editorial position.

Duties

Editors typically do the following:

- Read content and correct for errors in spelling, punctuation, and grammar
- Rewrite copy to make it easier for people to understand
- Verify facts, using standard reference sources
- Evaluate submissions from writers to decide what to publish
- Work with writers to help their ideas and stories succeed
- Plan the content of publications according to the publication's style and editorial policy
- Develop story and content ideas while being mindful of the audience
- Allocate space for the text, photos, and illustrations that make up a story
- Approve final versions submitted by staff

Editors plan, coordinate, and revise material for publication.

Editors plan, coordinate, and revise material for publication in books, newspapers, magazines, or websites. Editors review story ideas and decide what material will appeal most to readers. They also review and edit drafts of books and articles, offer comments to improve the product, and suggest titles and headlines. In smaller organizations, a single editor may perform all of the editorial duties or share them with only a few other people.

The following are examples of types of editors:

Copy editors review copy for errors in grammar, punctuation, and spelling and check the copy for readability, style, and agreement with editorial policy. They suggest revisions, such as changing words and rearranging sentences and paragraphs to improve clarity or accuracy. They also may carry out research, confirm sources for writers, and verify facts, dates, and statistics. In addition, they may arrange page layouts of articles, photographs, and advertising.

Publication assistants who work for book-publishing houses may read and evaluate manuscripts submitted by freelance writers, proofread uncorrected proofs, and answer questions about published material. Assistants on small newspapers or in smaller media markets may compile articles available from wire services or the Internet, answer phones, and proofread articles.

Executive editors oversee assistant editors and generally have the final say about what stories are published and how they are covered. Executive editors typically hire writers, reporters, and other employees. They also plan budgets and negotiate contracts with freelance writers, sometimes called "stringers" in the news industry. Although many executive editors work for newspaper publishers, some work for television broadcasters, magazines, or advertising and public relations firms.

Assistant editors have responsibility for a particular subject, such as local news, international news, feature stories, or sports. Most assistant editors work for newspaper publishers, television broadcasters, magazines, book publishers, or advertising and public relations firms.

Managing editors typically work for magazines, newspaper publishers, and television broadcasters, and are responsible for the daily operation of a news department.

Work Environment

Editors held about 127,200 jobs in 2010. The industries that employed the most editors in 2010 were:

Newspaper, periodical, book, and directory publishers	45%
Religious, grantmaking, civic, professional, and similar organizations	9
Professional, scientific, and technical services	6
Colleges, universities, and professional schools; state, local, and private	4

Editors work mainly in offices, but advances in technology allow some editors to work wherever they have a computer. They often use desktop or electronic publishing software, scanners, and other electronic communications equipment to produce their material.

Jobs are somewhat concentrated in major media and entertainment markets—Boston, Chicago, Los Angeles, New York, and Washington, DC—but improved communications and Internet capabilities now allow editors to work from a greater variety of locations.

Work Schedules

Editors' schedules generally are determined by the production schedule and the type of editorial position. Most salaried editors work in busy offices much of the time and have to deal with production deadline pressures and the stresses of ensuring that the information they publish is accurate. As a result, editors often work long hours, especially at those times leading up to a publication deadline, which can be daily or even more frequently when an editor is editing material for the Internet or for a live broadcast.

Overseeing and coordinating multiple writing projects simultaneously is common among editors and may lead to stress, fatigue, or other chronic problems. Freelance editors face the added pressures of finding work on an ongoing basis and continually adjusting to new work environments.

Most editors work full time.

How to Become an Editor

A college degree is typically required for someone to be an editor. Proficiency with computers and communications equipment also is necessary.

Education and Training

Employers generally prefer candidates with a bachelor's degree in communications, journalism, or English. Those with other backgrounds who can show strong writing skills also may find jobs as editors. Editors who deal with specific subject matter may need experience related to that field. Fashion editors, for example, may need expertise in fashion that they get through formal training or work experience.

The ability to use computers and communications equipment is necessary for editors to stay in touch with writers and other editors and to work on the increasingly important online side of a publication. Familiarity with electronic publishing, graphics, Web design, and multimedia production is important as well, because more and more material is being read online.

Work Experience

Editors can gain experience by working on their high school and college newspapers, or for magazines, radio and television stations, advertising and publishing companies, or not-for-profit organizations. Magazines and newspapers also have internships for students. Interns may write stories, conduct research and interviews, and gain general publishing experience.

Many editors start off as writers or reporters. For more information, see the profiles on writers and authors and reporters, correspondents, and broadcast news analysts . Those who are particularly skilled at identifying good stories, recognizing writing talent, and interacting with writers may be interested in editing jobs.

Advancement

Except for copy editors, most editors hold management positions and must make decisions related to running a business. For them, advancement generally means moving up the corporate ladder or to publications with larger circulation or greater prestige. Copy editors may move into original writing or substantive editing positions or become freelancers.

Important Qualities

Creativity. Editors must be creative, be curious, and have knowledge in a broad range of topics. Some editors must regularly come up with interesting story ideas and attention-grabbing headlines.

Decision-making skills. Editors must decide if certain stories are ethical or if there is enough evidence to report them.

Detail oriented. One of an editor's main tasks is to make sure that material is free of error and matches the style of a publication.

Interpersonal skills. In working with writers, editors must have tact and the ability to guide and encourage them in their work.

Language skills. Editors must ensure that all written content has correct grammar, punctuation, and syntax. As a result, strong language skills are essential for an editor.

Writing skills. Editors should enjoy writing and must be excellent writers overall. They must have good knowledge of grammar and punctuation rules and be able to express ideas clearly and logically.

Pay

Editors
Median annual wages, May 2010

Editors	$51,470
Media and Communication Workers	$49,060
Total, All Occupations	$33,840

Note: All Occupations includes all occupations in the U.S. Economy.
Source: U.S. Bureau of Labor Statistics, Occupational Employment Statistics

The median annual wage of editors was $51,470 in May 2010. The median wage is the wage at which half the workers in an occupation earned more than that amount and half earned less. The lowest 10 percent earned less than $28,880, and the highest 10 percent earned more than $96,800.

Editors' schedules generally are determined by the production schedule and the type of editorial position. Most salaried editors work in busy offices much of the time and have to deal with production deadline pressures and the stresses of ensuring that the information they publish is accurate. As a result, editors often work long hours, especially at those times leading up to a publication deadline, which can be daily or even more frequently when an editor is editing material for the Internet or for a live broadcast.

Overseeing and coordinating multiple writing projects simultaneously is common among editors and may lead to stress, fatigue, or other chronic problems. Freelance editors face the added pressures of finding work on an ongoing basis and continually adjusting to new work environments.

Most editors work full time.

Job Outlook

Editors
Percent change in employment, projected 2010-20

Total, All Occupations	14%
Media and Communication Workers	13%
Editors	1%

Note: All Occupations includes all occupations in the U.S. Economy.
Source: U.S. Bureau of Labor Statistics, Employment Projections program

Employment of editors is expected to experience little or no change from 2010 to 2020 as print media continue to face strong pressure from online publications. Despite some job growth for editors in online media, the number of traditional editing jobs in print newspapers and magazines is declining and will temper overall employment growth.

Job Prospects

Competition for jobs with established newspapers and magazines will be particularly strong because the publishing industry is projected to decline in employment. Editors who have adapted to online media and are comfortable writing for and working with a variety of electronic and digital tools should have an advantage in finding work.

Some job openings will arise as workers retire, transfer to other occupations, or leave the labor force. Although the way in which people consume media is changing, editors will continue to add value by reviewing and revising drafts and keeping the style and voice of a publication consistent.

Employment projections data for editors, 2010-20

Occupational Title	SOC Code	Employment, 2010	Projected Employment, 2020	Change, 2010-20 Percent	Change, 2010-20 Numeric
Editors	27-3041	127,200	128,000	1	800
SOURCE: U.S. Bureau of Labor Statistics, Employment Projections program					

Similar Occupations

This table shows a list of occupations with job duties that are similar to those of editors.

Occupation	Job Duties	Entry-Level Education	Median Annual Pay, May 2010
Announcers	Announcers present music, news, and sports and may provide commentary or interview guests about these topics or other important events. Some act as a master of ceremonies (emcee) or disc jockey (DJ) at weddings, parties, or clubs.	See How to Become One	$27,010
Reporters, Correspondents, and Broadcast News Analysts	Reporters, correspondents, and broadcast news analysts inform the public about news and events happening internationally, nationally, and locally. They report the news for newspapers, magazines, websites, television, and radio.	Bachelor's degree	$36,000
Technical Writers	Technical writers, also called technical communicators, produce instruction manuals and other supporting documents to communicate complex and technical information more easily. They also develop, gather, and disseminate technical information among customers, designers, and manufacturers.	Bachelor's degree	$63,280
Writers and Authors	Writers and authors develop original written content for advertisements, books, magazines, movie and television scripts, songs, and online publications.	Bachelor's degree	$55,420

Contacts for More Information

For more information about editors, visit American Copy Editors Society

Suggested citation:

Bureau of Labor Statistics, U.S. Department of Labor, Occupational Outlook Handbook, 2012-13 Edition, Editors, on the Internet at http://www.bls.gov/ooh/media-and-communication/editors.htm .

Film and Video Editors and Camera Operators

Quick Facts: Film and Video Editors and Camera Operators	
2010 Median Pay	$45,490 per year $21.87 per hour
Entry-Level Education	Bachelor's degree
Work Experience in a Related Occupation	See How to Become One
On-the-job Training	See How to Become One
Number of Jobs, 2010	58,300
Job Outlook, 2010-20	4% (Slower than average)
Employment Change, 2010-20	2,200

What Film and Video Editors and Camera Operators Do

Film and video editors and camera operators record images that entertain or inform an audience. Camera operators capture a wide range of material for TV shows, motion pictures, music videos, documentaries, or news and sporting events. Editors construct the final productions from the many different images that camera operators capture. They collaborate with producers and directors to create the final production.

Duties

Camera operators and film and video editors typically do the following:

- Choose and present interesting material for an audience
- Work with a director to determine the overall vision of the production
- Discuss filming and editing techniques with a director to improve a scene
- Select the appropriate equipment, from type of camera to software for editing
- Shoot or edit a scene based on the director's vision

Most camera operators have one or more assistants working under their supervision. The assistants set up the camera equipment and may be responsible for storing it and caring for it. They also help the operator determine the best shooting angle and make sure that the camera stays in focus.

Likewise, editors usually have a few assistants. The assistant

Editors and camera operators sometimes work on location.

supports the editor by keeping track of each shot in a database. Assistants may do some editing themselves.

The increased use of digital filming has changed the work of many camera operators and editors. Many camera operators prefer using digital cameras, because these instruments give the operator more angles to shoot from. Digital cameras have also changed the job of some camera assistants: instead of loading film or choosing lenses, they download digital images or choose a type of software program to use with the camera.

Nearly all editing work is done on a computer, and editors often are trained in a specific type of editing software.

The following are examples of types of camera operators.

Studio camera operators work in a broadcast studio and videotape their subjects from a fixed position. There may be one or several cameras in use at a time. Operators normally follow directions that give the order of the shots. They often have time to practice camera movements before shooting begins. If they are shooting a live event, they must be able to make adjustments at a moment's notice and follow the instructions of the show's director.

Electronic news gathering (ENG) operators work on location as part of a reporting team. ENG operators follow events as they unfold and often record live events or breaking news. To capture these events, operators must anticipate the action and act quickly to shoot it. They sometimes edit their own footage in the field and then send it back to a studio to be broadcast.

Cinematographers film motion pictures. They usually have a team of camera operators and assistants working under them. They determine the best angles and types of cameras to capture a shot.

They may use stationary cameras that shoot whatever passes in front of them or use a camera mounted on a track and move around the action. Some operators sit on cranes and follow the action. Others carry the camera on their shoulder while they move around the action.

Some cinematographers specialize in filming cartoons or special effects.

Videographers film or videotape private ceremonies or special events, such as weddings. They also may work with companies and make corporate documentaries on a variety of topics. Some videographers post short videos on websites for businesses. Most videographers edit their own material.

Many videographers run their own business or do freelance work. They may submit bids, write contracts, and get permission to shoot on locations that may not be open to the public. They also get copyright protection for their work and keep financial records.

Work Environment

Camera operators held about 26,800 jobs in 2010. About 24 percent work in television broadcasting and another 21 percent work in motion picture and video industries. About 34 percent of camera operators are self-employed.

Film and video editors held about 31,600 jobs in 2010. About 42 percent are employed by motion picture and video industries and 9 percent work in television broadcasting. About 35 percent of editors are self-employed.

Electronic news gathering (ENG) operators usually travel locally and may have to stay overnight to cover a major event. Cinematographers and operators who film movies or TV shows may film on location and be away from home for months at a time. Operators who travel usually carry heavy equipment.

Some camera operators work in uncomfortable or even dangerous conditions, such as severe weather, military conflicts, and natural disasters. They may have to stand for long periods waiting for an event to take place. They may carry heavy equipment.

Work Schedules

Work hours vary with the type of operator or editor, though most work full time. Those who work in broadcasting might have to work long hours to meet a deadline. Those who work in the motion picture industry may have long, irregular hours while filming but go through a period of unemployment after their work on the film is complete and before they are hired for their next job.

How to Become a Film and Video Editor or Camera Operator

Camera operators typically need a bachelor's degree and some on-the-job training. Most film editors have a bachelor's degree and several years of experience as an assistant to a film editor.

Education

Most camera operator and editor positions require a bachelor's degree in a field related to film or broadcasting. Many colleges offer courses in camera operation or video editing software.

Camera operators must have an understanding of digital cameras and computer technology, because both are now used on film sets. Most editing is now done digitally, so film and video editors should have experience with different types of video editing software. Most editors eventually specialize in one type of software, but beginners should be familiar with as many as possible.

Training

On movie sets, many camera operators start out as a production assistant for the camera department to learn how film production works. Production assistants typically run errands or do simple tasks for operators. With some moderate on-the-job training production assistants can become camera assistants and, eventually, operators.

In broadcasting, operators also begin as an assistant and work their way up to operator. Operators typically start out working for a small TV station or on a small movie set. As they become more experienced, they move on to larger productions.

Work Experience

Most film editors have had several years of experience in related jobs before they are given an opportunity as an editor. They normally start out as an edit room assistant, taking notes or doing other simple tasks for an editor, before becoming an assistant editor. After several years of learning about editing as an assistant, they may be given an opportunity as an editor.

Like camera operators, editors typically start out on small productions and move on to bigger and more expensive ones as they gain experience.

Advancement

Some camera operators or editors become producers or directors. For more information, see the profile on producers and directors .

Important Qualities

Creativity. Camera operators and editors should be able to imagine what the result of their filming or editing will look like to an audience.

Detail oriented. Editors look at every frame of film and decide what should be kept and what should be cut to make the best production.

Hand–eye coordination. In the field, camera operators need to be able to move about the action while holding a camera steady.

Technical skills. Camera operators must understand the high-end cameras they use. Editors must know how to use many features of sophisticated editing software.

Visual skills. Camera operators must be able to see clearly what they are filming.

Pay

Film and Video Editors and Camera Operators
Median annual wages, May 2010

Film and Video Editors	$50,930
Film and Video Editors and Camera Operators	$45,490
Camera Operators, Television, Video, and Motion Picture	$40,390
Total, All Occupations	$33,840

Note: All Occupations includes all occupations in the U.S. Economy.
Source: U.S. Bureau of Labor Statistics, Occupational Employment Statistics

The median annual wage of camera operators was $40,390 in May 2010. The median wage is the wage at which half the workers in an occupation earned more than that amount and half earned less. The lowest 10 percent earned less than $20,300, and the top 10 percent earned more than $81,270.

The median annual wage of film and video editors was $50,930 in May 2010. The lowest 10 percent earned less than $25,960, and the top 10 percent earned more than $111,860.

Work hours vary with the type of operator or editor, though most work full time. Those who work in broadcasting might have to work long hours to meet a deadline. Those who work in the motion picture industry may have long, irregular hours while filming but endure a period of unemployment after their work on the film is complete and before they are hired for their next job.

Job Outlook

Film and Video Editors and Camera Operators
Percent change in employment, projected 2010-20

Total, All Occupations	14%
Film and Video Editors	5%
Film and Video Editors and Camera Operators	4%
Camera Operators, Television, Video, and Motion Picture	2%

Note: All Occupations includes all occupations in the U.S. Economy.
Source: U.S. Bureau of Labor Statistics, Employment Projections program

Employment of camera operators is projected to experience little or no change, growing 2 percent from 2010 to 2020.

In broadcasting, job growth is expected to be slow because automatic camera systems reduce the need for camera operators at many TV stations. Despite the public's continued strong demand for new movies and TV shows, companies won't hire as many people as might be expected as the motion picture industry becomes more productive. They will be able to produce more movies without hiring many more workers.

Production companies are experimenting with new content delivery methods, such as mobile and online TV, which may lead to more work for operators in the future. However, these delivery methods are still in their early stages, and it remains to be seen how successful they will be.

Employment of film and video editors is projected to grow 5 percent from 2010 to 2020, slower than the average for all occupations.

In broadcasting, the consolidation of roles, such as field reporters who edit their own work, may lead to fewer of jobs for editors at TV stations. However, more editors are expected to be needed in the motion picture industry because of an increase in special effects, which are complicated and require more planning.

Job Prospects

There will be some job openings due to workers leaving the occupation, however, camera operators and film and video editors will still face strong competition for jobs. The broadcasting and motion picture industries attract many more applicants than there are jobs available. Those with more experience at a TV station or on a film set should have the best job prospects.

Employment projections data for film and video editors and camea operators, 2010-20

Occupational Title	SOC Code	Employment, 2010	Projected Employment, 2020	Change, 2010-20	
				Percent	Numeric
Television, Video, and Motion Picture Camera Operators and Editors	27-4030	58,300	60,500	4	2,200
Camera Operators, Television, Video, and Motion Picture	27-4031	26,800	27,300	2	600
Film and Video Editors	27-4032	31,600	33,200	5	1,600
SOURCE: U.S. Bureau of Labor Statistics, Employment Projections program					

Similar Occupations

This table shows a list of occupations with job duties that are similar to those of film and video editors and camera operators.

Occupation	Job Duties	Entry-Level Education	Median Annual Pay, May 2010
Actors	Actors express ideas and portray characters in theater, film, television, and other performing arts media. They also work at theme parks or for other live events. They interpret a writer's script to entertain or inform an audience.	Some college, no degree	The annual wage is not available.
Broadcast and Sound Engineering Technicians	Broadcast and sound engineering technicians set up, operate, and maintain the electrical equipment for radio and television broadcasts, concerts, sound recordings, and movies and in office and school buildings.	See How to Become One	$39,870
Editors	Editors plan, review, and revise content for publication.	Bachelor's degree	$51,470
Multimedia Artists and Animators	Multimedia artists and animators create animation and visual effects for television, movies, video games, and other media. They create two- and three-dimensional models and animation.	Bachelor's degree	$58,510
Photographers	Photographers use their technical expertise, creativity, and composition skills to produce and preserve images that visually tell a story or record an event.	High school diploma or equivalent	$29,130
Producers and Directors	Producers and directors are in charge of creating motion pictures, television shows, live theater, and other performing arts productions. They interpret a writer's script to entertain or inform an audience.	Bachelor's degree	$68,440
Announcers	Announcers present music, news, and sports and may provide commentary or interview guests about these topics or other important events. Some act as a master of ceremonies (emcee) or disc jockey (DJ) at weddings, parties, or clubs.	See How to Become One	$27,010
Reporters, Correspondents, and Broadcast News Analysts	Reporters, correspondents, and broadcast news analysts inform the public about news and events happening internationally, nationally, and locally. They report the news for newspapers, magazines, websites, television, and radio.	Bachelor's degree	$36,000

Contacts for More Information

For more information about camera operators and film and video editors, visit International Cinematographers Guild

Suggested citation:

Bureau of Labor Statistics, U.S. Department of Labor, Occupational Outlook Handbook, 2012-13 Edition, Film and Video Editors and Camera Operators, on the Internet at http://www.bls.gov/ooh/media-and-communication/film-and-video-editors-and-camera-operators.htm .

Interpreters and Translators

Quick Facts: Interpreters and Translators	
2010 Median Pay	$43,300 per year $20.82 per hour
Entry-Level Education	Bachelor's degree
Work Experience in a Related Occupation	None
On-the-job Training	Long-term on-the-job training
Number of Jobs, 2010	58,400
Job Outlook, 2010-20	42% (Much faster than average)
Employment Change, 2010-20	24,600

What Interpreters and Translators Do

Interpreters and translators convert information from one language to another. Interpreters work in spoken or sign language, translators in written language.

Duties

Interpreters and translators typically do the following:

- Convert concepts in the source language to equivalent concepts in the target language
- Speak, read, and write fluently in at least two languages, including English and one or more others
- Relay style and tone
- Manage work schedules to meet deadlines
- Render spoken ideas accurately, quickly, and clearly

Interpreters and translators aid communication by converting information from one language into another. Although some people do both, interpreting and translating are different professions: interpreters deal with spoken words, translators with written words.

Interpreters convert information from one spoken language into another—or, in the case of sign language interpreters, between spoken language and sign language. Interpreters must usually be fluent speakers or signers of both languages because they communicate back and forth among the people who do not share each other's language.

There are two modes of interpreting: simultaneous and consecutive.

Interpreters work in spoken or sign language, while translators work in written language.

Simultaneous interpreting requires interpreters to listen or watch and speak or sign at the same time someone is speaking or signing. Simultaneous interpreting requires a high level of concentration. For that reason, simultaneous interpreters usually work in pairs, each interpreting for about 20 to 30 minutes and then resting while the other interprets. Simultaneous interpreters are often familiar with the subject matter so they can anticipate the end of a speaker's sentences.

In contrast, consecutive interpreting begins only after the speaker has said or signed a group of words or sentences. Consecutive interpreters often take notes while listening to or watching the speakers, so they must develop some type of notetaking or shorthand system.

Translators convert written materials from one language into another. The goal of a translator is to have people read the translation as if it were the original. To do that, the translator must be able to write sentences that flow as well as the original did while keeping the ideas and facts of the original accurate. Translators must consider any cultural references, including slang, and other expressions that do not translate literally.

Translators must read the original language fluently but may not need to speak it fluently. They usually translate only into their native language.

Nearly all translation work is done on a computer, and translators receive and submit most assignments electronically. Translations often go through several revisions before becoming final.

Interpreters' and translators' services are needed in a number of subject areas. Although these workers often do not specialize in any particular field or industry, many focus on one area of expertise.

The following are examples of occupational specialties:

Health or medical interpreters and translators typically work in healthcare settings and help patients communicate with doctors, nurses, and other medical staff. Both interpreters and translators must have a strong grasp of medical terminology and the common words for those medical terms in both languages.

Health or medical interpreters must also have sensitivity to participate in patients' personal situations with healthcare providers.

Health or medical translators don't usually have the same level of personal interaction with patients and providers that interpreters do. They primarily convert information brochures, materials that patients must read and sign, and website information from one language to another.

Legal or judiciary interpreters and translators typically work in courts and other legal settings. At hearings, arraignments, depositions, and trials, they help people who have limited English proficiency. They must understand legal terminology. Many court interpreters must sometimes read documents aloud in a language other than that in which they were written, a task known as sight translation.

Literary translators rewrite journal articles, books, poetry, and short stories from one language into another language. They strive to keep the author's tone and style as well as meaning. Whenever possible, literary translators work closely with authors to capture their intended meaning and literary characteristics.

Localization translators adapt text for a product or service from one language into another. Localization specialists strive to make it appear as though the product originated in the country where it will be sold. They must know not only both languages, but they must also understand the technical information they are working with and must understand the culture of the people who will be using the product or service.

Localization may include adapting Internet sites, marketing materials, instruction manuals, and other publications. Usually, these are related to products and services in manufacturing and other business sectors.

Localization may be helped by computer-assisted translation, where a computer program develops an early draft of a translation for the localization translator to work with. Also, translators may use computers to compare previous translations with current assignments.

Sign language interpreters help people who are deaf or hard of hearing and people who can hear communicate with each other. Sign language interpreters must be fluent in English and in American Sign Language (ASL), which combines signing, finger spelling, and specific body language. ASL is a separate language from English with its own grammar.

Some interpreters specialize in other forms of interpreting for people who are deaf or hard of hearing.

Some people who are deaf or hard of hearing lip-read English instead of signing in ASL. Interpreters who work with these people do "oral interpretation," mouthing speech silently and very carefully so their lips can be read easily. They may also use facial expressions and gestures to help the lip-reader understand.

Other specialties include using cued speech, which uses hand shapes placed near the mouth to give lip-readers more information; signing exact English; and tactile signing, which is interpreting for people who are blind as well as deaf by making hand signs into the deaf-blind person's hand.

Guide or escort interpreters accompany either U.S. visitors abroad or foreign visitors in the United States to ensure that they are able to communicate during their stay. These specialists interpret informally and on a professional level. Frequent travel for these workers is common.

Conference interpreters work at conferences that have non-English-speaking attendees. The work is often in the field of international business or diplomacy, although conference interpreters can interpret for any organization that works with speakers of foreign languages. Employers prefer high-level interpreters who have the ability to translate from at least two languages into one native language—for example, the ability to interpret from Spanish and French into English. For some positions, such as those with the United Nations, this qualification is required.

Conference interpreters often do simultaneous interpreting. People at the conference who do not understand the language of the speaker wear earphones tuned to the interpreter who speaks the language they want to hear. The interpreter listens to a bit of the speaker's talk and then translates that bit. Simultaneous interpreters must be able to listen to the next bit the speaker is saying while translating the previous bit of what the speaker said.

Work Environment

Interpreters and translators held about 58,400 jobs in 2010. About 23 percent were self-employed.

The industries that employed the most interpreters and translators in 2010 were:

Professional, scientific, and technical services	26%
Educational services; state, local, and private	25
Health care and social assistance	13
Government	7

Interpreters work in settings such as schools, hospitals, courtrooms, and conference centers. They must sometimes travel to conferences. Simultaneous interpreting can be stressful, as the interpreter must keep up with the speaker, who may not know to slow down when an interpreter is present.

Translators typically work from home. They receive and submit their work electronically. They must sometimes deal with the pressure of deadlines and tight schedules.

Work Schedules

Because many interpreters and translators are self-employed, their schedules often vary, with alternating periods of limited work and periods of long, irregular hours. Still, most work full time during regular business hours.

How to Become an Interpreter or Translator

Although interpreters and translators typically need a bachelor's degree, the most important requirement is that they be fluent in English and at least one other language. Many complete job-specific training programs. It is not necessary for interpreters and translators to have been raised in two languages to succeed in these jobs, but many grew up communicating in both languages in which they work.

Education

The educational backgrounds of interpreters and translators vary, but it is essential that they be fluent in English and at least one other language.

High school students interested in becoming an interpreter or translator should take a broad range of courses that includes English writing and comprehension, foreign languages, and computer proficiency. Other helpful pursuits for prospective foreign-language interpreters and translators include spending time abroad, engaging in direct contact with foreign cultures, and reading extensively on a variety of subjects in English and at least one other language. Through community organizations, students interested in sign language interpreting may take introductory classes in ASL and seek out volunteer opportunities to work with people who are deaf or hard of hearing.

Beyond high school, people interested in becoming an interpreter or translator have many educational options. Although a bachelor's degree is often required for jobs, majoring in a language is not always necessary. An educational background in a particular field of study can provide a natural area of subject-matter expertise.

However, interpreters and translators generally need specialized training on how to do the work. Formal programs in interpreting and translating are available at colleges and universities nationwide and through nonuniversity training programs, conferences, and courses.

Many people who work as conference interpreters or in more technical areas—such as localization, engineering, or finance—have a master's degree. Those working in the community as court or medical interpreters or translators are more likely to complete job-specific training programs.

Certification

There is currently no universal certification required of interpreters and translators. However, workers can take a variety of tests that show proficiency. For example, the American Translators Association provides certification for its members in 24 language combinations involving English.

Federal courts provide certification for Spanish, Navajo, and Haitian Creole interpreters, and many state and municipal courts offer their own forms of certification. The National Association of Judiciary Interpreters and Translators also offers certification for court interpreting.

The National Association of the Deaf and the Registry of Interpreters for the Deaf (RID) jointly offer certification for general sign language interpreters. In addition, the registry offers specialty tests in legal interpreting, speech reading, and deaf-to-deaf interpreting—which includes interpreting among deaf speakers with different native languages and from ASL to tactile signing.

The U.S. Department of State has a three-test series for prospective interpreters—one test in simple consecutive interpreting (for escort work), another in simultaneous interpreting (for court or seminary work), and a third in conference-level interpreting (for international conferences)—as well as a test for prospective translators. These tests are not considered a credential, but their completion indicates that a person has significant skill in the occupation.

The International Association of Conference Interpreters offers certification for conference interpreters.

Advancement

After interpreters and translators have enough experience, they may move up to more difficult or prestigious assignments, seek certification, get editorial responsibility, or manage or start their own business.

Many self-employed interpreters and translators start a business by establishing themselves in their field. They may submit resumes and samples to many different translation and interpreting agencies and work for agencies that match their skills with a job. Many then get work based on their reputation or through referrals from existing clients.

Work Experience

Work experience is essential. In fact, some agencies hire only interpreters or translators who have related work experience.

A good way for translators to learn firsthand about the occupation is to start working in-house for a translation company. Doing informal or volunteer work is an excellent way for people seeking to get interpreter or translator jobs to get experience.

Volunteer opportunities for interpreters are available through community organizations, hospitals, and sporting events, such as marathons, that involve international competitors. The American Translators Association works with the Red Cross to provide volunteer interpreters during crises.

Paid or unpaid internships are other ways that interpreters and translators can get experience. Escort interpreting may offer an opportunity for inexperienced candidates to "shadow," or work alongside, a more experienced interpreter. Interpreters also might find it easier to break into areas with particularly high demand for language services, such as court or medical interpreting.

To show experience in translation, any translation—even translation done as practice—can be used as a sample for potential clients.

Whatever path of entry they pursue, new interpreters and translators should develop relationships with mentors to build their skills, confidence, and professional network. Mentoring may be formal, such as that through a professional association, or informal, such as with a coworker or an acquaintance who has experience as an interpreter or translator. Both the American Translators Association and the Registry of Interpreters for the Deaf offer formal mentoring programs.

Important Qualities

Business skills. Self-employed and freelance interpreters and translators need general business skills to manage their finances and careers successfully. They must set prices for their work, bill customers, keep records, and market their services to attract new business and build their client base.

Concentration. The ability to concentrate while others are speaking or moving around them is critical for interpreters and translators.

Cultural sensitivity. Interpreters and translators must be sensitive to cultural differences and expectations among the people whom they are helping to communicate. Successful interpreting and translating is not only a matter of knowing the words in different languages but also of understanding people's cultures.

Dexterity. Sign language interpreters must have quick and coordinated hands, fingers, and arm movements when interpreting sign language for a targeted audience.

Listening skills. Interpreters and translators must listen carefully when interpreting for audiences to ensure that they interpret or translate correctly.

Speaking skills. Interpreters and translators must speak clearly in the languages they are translating.

Writing skills. Interpreters and translators must be able to write clearly and effectively in the languages they are talking in or translating.

Pay

Interpreters and Translators
Median annual wages, May 2010

Media and Communication Workers	$49,060
Interpreters and Translators	$43,300
Total, All Occupations	$33,840

Note: All Occupations includes all occupations in the U.S. Economy.
Source: U.S. Bureau of Labor Statistics, Occupational Employment Statistics

The median annual wage of interpreters and translators was $43,300 in May 2010. The median wage is the wage at which half the workers in an occupation earned more than the amount and half earned less. The lowest 10 percent earned less than $22,950, and the top 10 percent earned more than $86,410.

The median annual wages in industries that employed the most interpreters and translators in 2010 were as follows:

Other professional, scientific, and technical services	$51,650
Junior colleges	43,980
General medical and surgical hospitals	41,720
Local government	41,040
Elementary and secondary schools	37,300

Wages depend on the language, subject matter, skill, experience, education, certification, and type of employer. Wages of interpreters and translators vary widely. Interpreters and translators who know languages for which there is a greater demand or that relatively few people can translate often earn higher wages, as do those who perform services requiring a high level of skill, such as conference interpreters.

For those who are not salaried, earnings typically fluctuate, depending on the availability of work. Self-employed interpreters usually charge an hourly rate. Self-employed translators typically charge a rate per word or per hour.

Because many interpreters and translators are self-employed, their schedules may vary, with alternating periods of limited work and periods of long, irregular hours. Still, most work full time during regular business hours.

Job Outlook

Interpreters and Translators

Percent change in employment, projected 2010-20

Interpreters and Translators	42%
Total, All Occupations	14%
Media and Communication Workers	13%

Note: All Occupations includes all occupations in the U.S. Economy.
Source: U.S. Bureau of Labor Statistics, Employment Projections program

Employment of interpreters and translators is expected to grow 42 percent from 2010 to 2020, much faster than the average for all occupations. Employment growth reflects an increasingly diverse U.S. population, which is expected to require more interpreters and translators.

Demand will likely remain strong for translators of frequently translated languages, such as French, German, Italian, Portuguese, and Spanish. Demand also should be strong for translators of Arabic and other Middle Eastern languages and for the principal East Asian languages: Chinese, Japanese, and Korean.

Demand for American Sign Language interpreters is expected to grow rapidly, driven by the increasing use of video relay services, which allow people to conduct online video calls and use a sign language interpreter.

In addition, growing international trade and broadening global ties should require more interpreters and translators. The need to interpret and translate languages in the military should result in more jobs as well.

Computers have made the work of translators and localization specialists easier. However, these jobs cannot be entirely automated. Computers cannot yet produce work comparable to the work that human translators do.

Job Prospects

Job opportunities should be best for those who have professional certification. In addition, urban areas—especially Washington, DC, New York, and Los Angeles—should continue to provide the largest numbers of employment possibilities, especially for interpreters

Job prospects for interpreters and translators should also vary by specialty and language. For example, interpreters and translators of Spanish should have good job opportunities because of expected increases in the population of Hispanics in the United States. In particular, job opportunities should be plentiful for interpreters and translators specializing in healthcare and law, because of the critical need for all parties to fully understand that information.

In addition, there should be many job opportunities for specialists in localization, driven by the globalization of business and the expansion of the Internet.

Interpreters for the deaf will continue to have favorable employment prospects because there is a shortage of people with the needed skill levels.

Conference interpreters and literary translators will likely face competition because of the small number of job opportunities in these specialties.

Employment projections data for interpreters and translators, 2010-20

Occupational Title	SOC Code	Employment, 2010	Projected Employment, 2020	Change, 2010-20 Percent	Change, 2010-20 Numeric
Interpreters and Translators	27-3091	58,400	83,100	42	24,600
SOURCE: U.S. Bureau of Labor Statistics, Employment Projections program					

Similar Occupations

This table shows a list of occupations with job duties that are similar to those of interpreters and translators.

Occupation	Job Duties	Entry-Level Education	Median Annual Pay, May 2010
Adult Literacy and GED Teachers	Adult literacy and General Education Development (GED) teachers instruct adults and youths who are out of school in basic skills, such as reading, writing, and speaking English. They also help students earn their GED or high school diploma.	Bachelor's degree	$46,530
Career and Technical Education Teachers	Career and technical education teachers help students in middle school and high school develop career-related and technical skills. They help students explore or prepare to enter a particular occupation, such as one in auto repair, healthcare, business, or the culinary arts.	Bachelor's degree	$53,920
Court Reporters	Court reporters attend legal proceedings and public speaking events to create word-for-word transcriptions. Some court reporters provide captioning for television and at public events.	Postsecondary non-degree award	$47,700
High School Teachers	High school teachers help prepare students for life after graduation. They teach academic lessons and various skills that students will need to attend college and to enter the job market.	Bachelor's degree	$53,230
Kindergarten and Elementary School Teachers	Kindergarten and elementary school teachers prepare younger students for future schooling by teaching them the basics of subjects such as math and reading.	Bachelor's degree	$51,380
Medical Transcriptionists	Medical transcriptionists listen to voice recordings that physicians and other health professionals make and convert them into written reports. They interpret medical terminology and abbreviations in preparing patients' medical histories, discharge summaries, and other documents.	Postsecondary non-degree award	$32,900

Middle School Teachers	Middle school teachers educate students, most of whom are in sixth through eighth grades. They help students build on the fundamentals they learned in elementary school and prepare them for the more difficult lessons they will learn in high school.	Bachelor's degree	$51,960
Postsecondary Teachers	Postsecondary teachers instruct students in a wide variety of academic and vocational subjects beyond the high school level. They also conduct research and publish scholarly papers and books.	Doctoral or professional degree	$62,050
Self-enrichment Teachers	Self-enrichment teachers instruct in a variety of subjects that students take for fun or self-improvement, such as music and foreign languages. These classes generally do not lead to a degree or certification, and students take them voluntarily to learn new skills or gain understanding of a subject.	High school diploma or equivalent	$36,340
Special Education Teachers	Special education teachers work with students who have a wide range of learning, mental, emotional and physical disabilities. With students who have mild or moderate disabilities, they ensure that lessons and teaching strategies are modified to meet the students' needs. With students who have severe disabilities, they teach the students independent living skills and basic literacy, communication, and math.	Bachelor's degree	$53,220
Technical Writers	Technical writers, also called technical communicators, produce instruction manuals and other supporting documents to communicate complex and technical information more easily. They also develop, gather, and disseminate technical information among customers, designers, and manufacturers.	Bachelor's degree	$63,280
Writers and Authors	Writers and authors develop original written content for advertisements, books, magazines, movie and television scripts, songs, and online publications.	Bachelor's degree	$55,420

Contacts for More Information

For more information about interpreters, visit Discover Interpreting

For more information about translators, including professional certification, visit American Translators Association

For more information about interpreter and translator specialties, including professional certification, visit American Literary Translators Association , Certification Commission for Healthcare Interpreters , National Association of Judiciary Interpreters and Translators Registry of Interpreters for the Deaf

For more information about testing to become a federal contract interpreter or translator, visit U.S. State Department

Suggested citation:

Bureau of Labor Statistics, U.S. Department of Labor, Occupational Outlook Handbook, 2012-13 Edition, Interpreters and Translators, on the Internet at http://www.bls.gov/ooh/media-and-communication/interpreters-and-translators.htm .

Photographers

Quick Facts: Photographers	
2010 Median Pay	$29,130 per year $14.00 per hour
Entry-Level Education	High school diploma or equivalent
Work Experience in a Related Occupation	None
On-the-job Training	Long-term on-the-job training
Number of Jobs, 2010	139,500
Job Outlook, 2010-20	13% (About as fast as average)
Employment Change, 2010-20	17,500

What Photographers Do

Photographers use their technical expertise, creativity, and composition skills to produce and preserve images that visually tell a story or record an event.

Duties

Photographers typically do the following:

- Market and advertise services to attract clients
- Analyze and decide how to compose a subject
- Use various photographic techniques and equipment
- Capture subjects in commercial-quality photographs
- Enhance the subject's appearance with natural or artificial light
- Maintain a digital portfolio, often a website, to demonstrate work

Today, most photographers use digital cameras instead of the traditional silver-halide film cameras. Digital cameras capture images electronically, so the photographer can edit the image on a computer. Images can be stored on portable memory devices, such as compact disks, memory cards, and flash drives. Once the raw image has been transferred to a computer, photographers can use processing software to crop or modify the image and enhance it through color correction and other specialized effects. Photographers who edit their own pictures use computers, high-quality printers, and editing software. For information on workers who specialize in developing and processing photographic images from film or digital media, see photographic process workers and processing machine operators included in occupations not covered in detail .

Photographers who work for commercial clients will often present finalized photographs in a digital format to the client. However, wedding and portrait photographers, who primarily serve noncommercial clients, often also provide framing services and present the photographs they capture in albums.

Many wedding and portrait photographers are self-employed. Photographers who own and operate their own business have additional responsibilities. They must advertise, schedule appointments, set and adjust equipment, purchase supplies, keep records, bill customers, pay bills, and—if they have employees—hire, train, and direct their workers.

In addition, some photographers teach photography classes or conduct workshops in schools or in their own studios. For more information on workers who teach photography classes, see the profile on self-enrichment teachers .

The following are examples of types of photographers:

Portrait photographers take pictures of individuals or groups of people and usually work in their own studios. Photographers who specialize in weddings, religious ceremonies, or school photographs may work on location.

Commercial and industrial photographers take pictures of various subjects, such as buildings, models, merchandise, artifacts, and landscapes. These photographs are used for a variety of purposes, including magazine covers and images to supplement analysis of engineering projects. These photographs are frequently taken on location.

Aerial photographers use planes or helicopters to capture photographs of buildings and landscapes. They often use gyrostabilizers to counteract the movement of the aircraft and ensure high-quality images.

Scientific photographers focus on the accurate visual representation of subjects and limit the use of image manipulation software for clarifying an image. Scientific photographs record scientific or medical data or phenomena. Scientific photographers typically use microscopes to photograph subjects.

News photographers, also called photojournalists, photograph people, places, and events for newspapers, journals, magazines, or television. In addition to taking still photos, photojournalists often work with digital video.

Fine arts photographers sell their photographs as artwork. In addition to technical knowledge, such as lighting and use of lenses, fine arts photographers need artistic talent and creativity. Most use traditional silver-halide film instead of digital cameras.

University photographers serve as general photographers for academic institutions. They may be required to take portraits, document an event, or take photographs for press releases. University photographers are found primarily in larger academic institutions, because smaller institutions often contract with freelancers to do their photography work.

Some photographers travel for photo shoots, others work in their own studios.

Work Environment

Photographers held about 139,500 jobs in May 2010. Employers for these workers can vary. The following industries employed the most photographers in May 2010:

Photographic services	24%
Newspaper, periodical, book, and directory publishers	3
Television broadcasting	3
Retail trade	1
Colleges, universities, and professional schools; state, local, and private	1

In 2010, 63 percent of photographers were self-employed.

The work environment for photographers can vary considerably, depending on their specialty.

Portrait photographers work in studios where they can take photographs, but they also often travel to take photographs at a client's location, such as a school, a company office, or a private home.

News and commercial photographers may travel locally or internationally. News photographers often work long, irregular hours in uncomfortable or even dangerous surroundings and must be available to work on short notice. For example, a news photographer may be sent to a war zone to capture images for a newspaper.

Aerial photographers often work in planes or helicopters.

Most photographers stand or walk for long periods while carrying heavy equipment.

Work Schedules

Many photographers work part time. Hours often are flexible so they can meet with current and potential clients or visit the sites where they will work. Demand for certain types of photographers may fluctuate with the season. For example, the demand for wedding photographers typically increases in the spring and summer.

How to Become a Photographer

Formal education is not required for portrait photographers. Photojournalists and industrial and scientific photographers often need a bachelor's degree. Employers usually seek applicants with a "good eye" and creativity, as well as a good technical understanding of photography.

Education

Although formal education is not required for most photographers, many take classes or earn a bachelor's degree in a related field, which can improve their skills and employment prospects.

Many universities, community and junior colleges, vocational–technical institutes, and private trade and technical schools offer classes in photography. Basic courses in photography cover equipment, processes, and techniques. Art schools may offer useful training in photographic design and composition.

Entry-level positions in photojournalism or in industrial or scientific photography generally require a college degree in photography or in a field related to the industry in which the photographer seeks employment. For example, classes in biology, medicine, or chemistry may be useful for scientific photographers.

Business, marketing, and accounting classes can be helpful for self-employed photographers.

Training

Photographers often start working as an assistant to a professional photographer. This work provides an opportunity to gain experience, build their portfolio, and gain exposure to prospective clients.

For many artists, including photographers, developing a portfolio—a collection of an artist's work that demonstrates his or her styles and abilities—is essential. This portfolio is necessary because art directors, clients, and others look at an artist's portfolio when deciding whether to hire or contract with the photographer.

Important Qualities

Artistic ability. Photographers capture their subjects in images, and they must be able to evaluate the artistic quality of a photograph. Photographers need "a good eye"—the ability to use colors, shadows, shades, light, and distance to compose good photographs.

Business skills. Photographers must be able to plan marketing strategies, reach out to prospective clients, and anticipate seasonal employment.

Computer skills. Most photographers do their own postproduction work and must be familiar with photo editing software. They also use computers to keep a digital portfolio and to communicate with clients.

Customer service skills. Photographers must be able to understand the needs of their clients and propose solutions.

Detail-oriented skills. Photographers who do their own postproduction work must be careful not to overlook details and must be thorough when editing photographs. In addition, photographers accumulate many photographs and must maintain them in an orderly fashion.

Interpersonal skills. Photographers often photograph people. They must communicate effectively to achieve a certain composition in a photograph.

Pay

Photographers
Median hourly wages, May 2010

Arts, Design, Entertainment, Sports, and Media Occupations	$20.61
Total, All Occupations	$16.27
Photographers	$14.00

Note: All Occupations includes all occupations in the U.S. Economy.
Source: U.S. Bureau of Labor Statistics, Occupational Employment Statistics

The median hourly wage of photographers was $14.00 in May 2010. The median wage is the wage at which half the workers in an occupation earned more than that amount and half earned less. The lowest 10 percent earned less than $8.34, and the top 10 percent earned more than $30.48.

Photographers in the District of Columbia earned the highest hourly median wage, earning $23.57 in May 2010.

Many photographers work part time. Hours often are flexible so they can meet with current and potential clients or visit the sites where they will work. Demand for certain types of photographers may fluctuate with the season. For example, the demand for wedding photographers typically increases in the spring and summer.

Job Outlook

Photographers
Percent change in employment, projected 2010-20

Total, All Occupations	14%
Arts, Design, Entertainment, Sports, and Media Occupations	13%
Photographers	13%

Note: All Occupations includes all occupations in the U.S. Economy.
Source: U.S. Bureau of Labor Statistics, Employment Projections program

Employment of photographers is projected to grow by 13 percent from 2010 to 2020, about as fast as the average for all occupations. Overall growth will be limited because of the decreasing cost of digital cameras and the increasing number of amateur photographers and hobbyists. Improvements in digital technology reduce barriers of entry into this profession and allow more individual consumers and businesses to produce, store, and access photographic images on their own.

Employment of self-employed photographers is expected to grow by 15 percent from 2010 to 2020. Demand for wedding and portrait photographers will continue as people continue to get married and need new portraits. In addition, corporations will continue to require the services of commercial photographers to develop compelling advertisements to sell products.

Declines in the newspaper industry will reduce demand for news photographers to provide still images for print. Employment of news photographers in newspaper publishing is expected to decline by 30 percent from 2010 to 2020.

Job Prospects

Photographers will face strong competition for most jobs. Because of reduced barriers to entry, there will be many qualified candidates for relatively few positions.

In addition, salaried jobs may be more difficult to obtain as companies increasingly contract with freelancers rather than hire their own photographers. Job prospects will be best for candidates who are multitalented and possess related skills such as picture editing and capturing digital video.

Employment projections data for photographers, 2010-20

Occupational Title	SOC Code	Employment, 2010	Projected Employment, 2020	Change, 2010-20 Percent	Numeric
Photographers	27-4021	139,500	156,900	13	17,500

SOURCE: U.S. Bureau of Labor Statistics, Employment Projections program

Similar Occupations

This table shows a list of occupations with job duties that are similar to those of photographers.

Occupation	Job Duties	Entry-Level Education	Median Annual Pay, May 2010
Architects	Architects plan and design buildings and other structures.	Bachelor's degree	$72,550
Craft and Fine Artists	Craft and fine artists use a variety of materials and techniques to create art for sale and exhibition. Craft artists create handmade objects, such as pottery, glassware, textiles, or other objects that are designed to be functional. Fine artists, including painters, sculptors, and illustrators, create original works of art for their aesthetic value, rather than a functional one.	High school diploma or equivalent	$43,470
Desktop Publishers	Desktop publishers use computer software to design page layouts for newspapers, books, brochures, and other items that will be printed or put online. They collect the text, graphics, and other materials they will need and then format them into a finished product.	Associate's degree	$36,610
Fashion Designers	Fashion designers create original clothing, accessories, and footwear. They sketch designs, select fabrics and patterns, and give instructions on how to make the products they designed.	High school diploma or equivalent	$64,530
Film and Video Editors and Camera Operators	Film and video editors and camera operators record images that entertain or inform an audience. Camera operators capture a wide range of material for TV shows, motion pictures, music videos, documentaries, or news and sporting events. Editors construct the final productions from the many different images camera operators capture. They collaborate with producers and directors to create the final production.	Bachelor's degree	$45,490
Graphic Designers	Graphic designers create visual concepts, by hand or using computer software, to communicate ideas that inspire, inform, or captivate consumers. They help to make an organization recognizable by selecting color, images, or logo designs that represent a particular idea or identity to be used in advertising and promotions.	Bachelor's degree	$43,500
Industrial Designers	Industrial designers develop the concepts for manufactured products, such as cars, home appliances, and toys. They combine art, business, and engineering to make products that people use every day.	Bachelor's degree	$58,230
Printing Workers	Printing workers produce print material in three stages: prepress, press, and binding and finishing. They review specifications, identify and fix problems with printing equipment, and assemble pages.	See How to Become One	$33,150
Reporters, Correspondents, and Broadcast News Analysts	Reporters, correspondents, and broadcast news analysts inform the public about news and events happening internationally, nationally, and locally. They report the news for newspapers, magazines, websites, television, and radio.	Bachelor's degree	$36,000
Self-enrichment Teachers	Self-enrichment teachers instruct in a variety of subjects that students take for fun or self-improvement, such as music and foreign languages. These classes generally do not lead to a degree or certification, and students take them voluntarily to learn new skills or gain understanding of a subject.	High school diploma or equivalent	$36,340

Contacts for More Information

For more information about careers in photography, visit American Society of Media Photographers

For more information about university photographers, visit University Photographers' Association of America

Suggested citation:

Bureau of Labor Statistics, U.S. Department of Labor, Occupational Outlook Handbook, 2012-13 Edition, Photographers, on the Internet at http://www.bls.gov/ooh/media-and-communication/photographers.htm .

Reporters, Correspondents, and Broadcast News Analysts

Quick Facts: Reporters, Correspondents, and Broadcast News Analysts	
2010 Median Pay	$36,000 per year $17.31 per hour
Entry-Level Education	Bachelor's degree
Work Experience in a Related Occupation	None
On-the-job Training	None
Number of Jobs, 2010	58,500
Job Outlook, 2010-20	-6% (Decline moderately)
Employment Change, 2010-20	-3,200

What Reporters, Correspondents, and Broadcast News Analysts Do

Reporters, correspondents, and broadcast news analysts inform the public about news and events happening internationally, nationally, and locally. They report the news for newspapers, magazines, websites, television, and radio.

Duties

Reporters, correspondents, and broadcast news analysts typically do the following:

- Research topics and stories that an editor or news director has assigned to them
- Interview people who have information, analysis, or opinions relating to a story or article
- Write articles for newspapers, blogs, and magazines and write scripts to be read on television or radio
- Review articles to ensure their accuracy and their use of proper style and grammar
- Develop relationships with experts and contacts who provide tips and leads on stories
- Analyze and interpret information to increase their audiences' understanding of the news
- Update stories as new information becomes available

Reporters and correspondents, also called **journalists**, often work for a particular type of media organization, such as a television or radio station, or a newspaper. Those who work in television and radio set up and conduct interviews, which can be broadcast live or recorded for future broadcasts.

These workers are often responsible for editing interviews and other recordings into a cohesive story and for writing and recording voiceovers that provide the audience with the facts of the story. They may create multiple versions of the same story for different broadcasts.

Most television and radio shows have hosts, also called anchors, who report the news and introduce stories from reporters.

Journalists for print media write articles to be used in newspapers, magazines, and online publications. Most newspapers and magazines have both print and online versions, so reporters must produce content for both versions. Often, doing so requires staying up to date on new developments of a story so that the online editions can be updated with the most current information.

Some journalists convey stories through both broadcast and print media. For example, television stations often also have a website, and a reporter may produce a blog post or article for the website. In addition, those working for newspapers or magazines may create videos or podcasts that people access online.

Some journalists cover a particular topic, such as sports, medicine, or politics. Others cover a wide range of issues.

Journalists in large cities or working for large news organizations are more likely to specialize. Journalists who work in small cities, towns, or organizations may need to cover a wider range of subjects.

Some reporters live in other countries and cover international news. Some journalists, called **commentators** or **columnists**, interpret the news or offer opinions to readers, viewers, or listeners.

Although some broadcast news analysts present weather reports, broadcast meteorologists are a type of atmospheric scientist. For more information about workers who create and provide weather reports and short-term forecasts, see the profile on atmospheric scientists, including meteorologists .

Some reporters—particularly those who work for print news—are self-employed and take freelance assignments from news

Reporters, correspondents, and broadcast news analysts inform the public about news and events happening internationally, nationally, and locally.

organizations. Freelance assignments are given to writers on an as-needed basis. Because these reporters are paid for the individual story, they work with many organizations and often spend some of their time marketing their stories and looking for their next assignment.

Some people with a background as a reporter, correspondent, or broadcast news analyst teach journalism or communications at colleges and universities. For information on workers who teach at colleges and universities, see the profile on postsecondary teachers .

Work Environment

Reporters, correspondents, and broadcast news analysts held about 58,500 jobs in 2010. In 2010, the following industries employed the most reporters, correspondents and broadcast news analysts:

Newspaper publishers	46%
Television broadcasting	20
Radio broadcasting	6

Reporters, correspondents, and broadcast news analysts spend a lot of time in the field, conducting interviews and investigating stories. Many reporters spend little to no time in an office. They travel to be on location for events or to meet contacts and file stories remotely.

Reporters, correspondents, and broadcast news analysts covering international news often live in other countries. Stories such as natural disasters and wars can put reporters in dangerous situations.

Work Schedules

Most reporters, correspondents, and broadcast news analysts work full time. The work of journalists is often fast paced, with constant demands to meet deadlines and be the first reporter to publish a news story on a subject. When news is breaking, reporters may need to work long hours or change their work schedule to follow the story. Because news can happen any time of the day, journalists may need to work nights and weekends.

How to Become a Reporter, Correspondent, or Broadcast News Analyst

Employers generally prefer workers who have a bachelor's degree in journalism or communications and have experience from an internship or from working on a college newspaper.

Education

Most employers prefer workers who have a bachelor's degree in journalism or communications. However, some employers hire applicants who have a degree in a related subject, such as English or political science, if they have relevant work experience.

Bachelor's degree programs in journalism and communications include classes in journalistic ethics and how to research stories and conduct interviews. Many programs require students to take liberal arts classes, such as English, history, economics, and political science, so that they are prepared to cover stories on a wide range of subjects.

Some schools offer graduate programs in journalism and communications. These programs prepare students who have a bachelor's degree in another field to become journalists.

Employers generally require workers to have experience from internships or from working on school newspapers. While attending college, many students seek multiple internships with different news organizations.

Advancement

With experience, reporters and correspondents can advance from news organizations in small cities or towns to news organizations in large cities. Alternatively, they may become editors or news directors.

Important Qualities

Communication skills. Journalists need to be able to report the news both verbally and in writing. Strong writing skills are particularly important for journalists in all kinds of media.

Objectivity. Journalists need to report the facts of the news impartially and without inserting their opinion or bias into the story.

People skills. To develop contacts and conduct interviews, reporters need to build good relationships with many people. They also need to work well with other journalists, editors, and news directors.

Persistence. Sometimes, getting the facts of a story is difficult, particularly when those involved refuse to be interviewed or provide comment. Journalists need to be persistent in their pursuit of the story.

Stamina. The work of journalists is often fast paced, and the hours can be long and exhausting. Reporters need to be able to keep up with the long hours.

Pay

Reporters, Correspondents, and Broadcast News Analysts
Median annual wages, May 2010

Broadcast News Analysts	$54,140
Reporters, Correspondents, and Broadcast News Analysts	$36,000
Reporters and Correspondents	$34,530
Total, All Occupations	$33,840

Note: All Occupations includes all occupations in the U.S. Economy.
Source: U.S. Bureau of Labor Statistics, Occupational Employment Statistics

The median annual wage of broadcast news analysts was $54,140 in May 2010. The median wage is the wage at which half the workers in an occupation earned more than that amount and half earned less. The lowest 10 percent earned less than $27,560, and the top 10 percent earned more than $146,230.

The median annual wage of reporters and correspondents was $34,530 in May 2010. The lowest 10 percent earned less than $19,970, and the top 10 percent earned more than $75,230.

Most reporters, correspondents, and broadcast news analysts work full time. The work of journalists is often fast paced, with constant demands to meet deadlines and be the first reporter to publish a news story on subject. When news is breaking, reporters may need to work long hours or change their work schedule to follow the story. Because news can happen any time of the day, journalists may need to work nights and weekends.

Job Outlook

Reporters, Correspondents, and Broadcast News Analysts
Percent change in employment, projected 2010-20

Total, All Occupations	14%
Broadcast News Analysts	10%
Reporters, Correspondents, and Broadcast News Analysts	-6%
Reporters and Correspondents	-8%

Note: All Occupations includes all occupations in the U.S. Economy.
Source: U.S. Bureau of Labor Statistics, Employment Projections program

Employment of reporters and correspondents is expected to moderately decline by 8 percent from 2010 to 2020. Declines are expected because of the consolidation of news organizations, decreases in the readership of newspapers, and declines in viewership for many news television shows.

Employment of broadcast news analysts is expected to grow by 10 percent from 2010 to 2020, about as fast as the average for all occupations. Growth is expected as news agencies prefer news analysts over traditional reporters to provide insight and commentary about the news.

In recent years, news organizations have begun to merge and

consolidate, meaning that larger organizations acquire smaller organizations. Often, after a merger, the news agency reduces the number of reporters and correspondents on staff. As a result, the demand for journalists has decreased.

In addition, readership of newspapers and the viewing audience for many news television shows have been declining. As a result, news organizations may have more difficulty selling advertising, which is often their primary source of revenue.

To make up for decreased revenue, news organizations may need to downsize and employ fewer journalists. However, an increase in demand for online news and podcasts (audio or video digital media files that can often be downloaded from a website) may offset some of the downsizing.

Job Prospects

Opportunities are expected to be limited because of both the number of workers who are interested in entering this field and declines in the number of positions. Prospects should be best for those with experience in the field, often gained through internships or by working on school papers.

In addition, opportunities will likely be better in small local newspapers or television and radio stations.

Competition will be particularly strong in large metropolitan areas, at national newspapers with higher circulation figures, and at network television stations.

Employment projections data for reporters, correspondents, and broadcast news analysts, 2010-20

Occupational Title	SOC Code	Employment, 2010	Projected Employment, 2020	Change, 2010-20 Percent	Change, 2010-20 Numeric
News Analysts, Reporters and Correspondents	27-3020	58,500	55,300	-6	-3,200
Broadcast News Analysts	27-3021	6,600	7,200	10	700
Reporters and Correspondents	27-3022	51,900	48,000	-8	-3,900
SOURCE: U.S. Bureau of Labor Statistics, Employment Projections program					

Similar Occupations

This table shows a list of occupations with job duties that are similar to those of reporters, correspondents, and broadcast news analysts.

Occupation	Job Duties	Entry-Level Education	Median Annual Pay, May 2010
Atmospheric Scientists, Including Meteorologists	Atmospheric scientists study weather, climate, and other aspects of the atmosphere. They develop reports and forecasts from their analysis of weather and climate data.	Bachelor's degree	$87,780
Broadcast and Sound Engineering Technicians	Broadcast and sound engineering technicians set up, operate, and maintain the electrical equipment for radio and television broadcasts, concerts, sound recordings, and movies and in office and school buildings.	See How to Become One	$39,870
Editors	Editors plan, review, and revise content for publication.	Bachelor's degree	$51,470
Photographers	Photographers use their technical expertise, creativity, and composition skills to produce and preserve images that visually tell a story or record an event.	High school diploma or equivalent	$29,130
Postsecondary Teachers	Postsecondary teachers instruct students in a wide variety of academic and vocational subjects beyond the high school level. They also conduct research and publish scholarly papers and books.	Doctoral or professional degree	$62,050
Announcers	Announcers present music, news, and sports and may provide commentary or interview guests about these topics or other important events. Some act as a master of ceremonies (emcee) or disc jockey (DJ) at weddings, parties, or clubs.	See How to Become One	$27,010
Public Relations Managers and Specialists	Public relations managers and specialists create and maintain a favorable public image for their employer or client. They write material for media releases, plan and direct public relations programs, and raise funds for their organizations.	Bachelor's degree	$57,550
Technical Writers	Technical writers, also called technical communicators, produce instruction manuals and other supporting documents to communicate complex and technical information more easily. They also develop, gather, and disseminate technical information among customers, designers, and manufacturers.	Bachelor's degree	$63,280
Writers and Authors	Writers and authors develop original written content for advertisements, books, magazines, movie and television scripts, songs, and online publications.	Bachelor's degree	$55,420

Contacts for More Information

For more information about broadcast news analysts, visit National Association of Broadcasters

For more information about careers in journalism and about internships, visit Dow Jones News Fund

For more information about accredited programs in journalism and mass communications, visit Accrediting Council on Education in Journalism and Mass Communications

Suggested citation:

Bureau of Labor Statistics, U.S. Department of Labor, Occupational Outlook Handbook, 2012-13 Edition, Reporters, Correspondents, and Broadcast News Analysts, on the Internet at http://www.bls.gov/ooh/media-and-communication/reporters-correspondents-and-broadcast-news-analysts.htm .

Technical Writers

Quick Facts: Technical Writers	
2010 Median Pay	$63,280 per year $30.42 per hour
Entry-Level Education	Bachelor's degree
Work Experience in a Related Occupation	1 to 5 years
On-the-job Training	Short-term on-the-job training
Number of Jobs, 2010	49,500
Job Outlook, 2010-20	17% (About as fast as average)
Employment Change, 2010-20	8,500

What Technical Writers Do

Technical writers, also called technical communicators, produce instruction manuals and other supporting documents to communicate complex and technical information more easily. They also develop, gather, and disseminate technical information among customers, designers, and manufacturers.

Duties

Technical writers typically do the following:

- Determine the needs of end users of technical documentation
- Study product samples and talk with product designers and developers
- Work with technical staff to make products easier to use, and thus need fewer instructions
- Organize and write supporting documents for products
- Select photographs, drawings, diagrams, and charts that increase users' understanding
- Get usability feedback from customers, designers, and manufacturers
- Revise documents as new issues arise

Technical writers create operating instructions, how-to manuals, assembly instructions, and "frequently asked questions" pages to help technical support staff, consumers, and other users within a company or an industry. After a product is released, technical writers also may work with product liability specialists and customer service managers to improve the end-user experience through product design changes.

Technical writers often work with engineers, scientists, computer specialists, and software developers to manage the flow of information among project workgroups during development and testing. Therefore, technical writers must be able to understand complex information and communicate the information to people with diverse professional backgrounds.

Applying their knowledge of the user of the product, technical writers may serve as part of a team conducting usability studies to help improve the design of a product that is in the prototype stage. Technical writers may conduct research on their topics through personal observation, library and Internet research, and discussions with technical specialists.

Increasingly, technical information is being delivered online, and technical writers are using the interactive technologies of the Web to blend text, graphics, multidimensional images, sound, and video.

Work Environment

Technical writers held about 49,500 jobs in 2010. The following industries employed the most technical writers in 2010:

Computer systems design and related services	17%
Architectural, engineering, and related services	7
Management, scientific, and technical consulting services	7
Software publishers	5
Scientific research and development services	4

Most technical writers work in offices. They routinely work with engineers and other technology professionals to manage the flow of information throughout an organization. Although most technical writers are employed directly by the companies that use their services, some work on a freelance basis and get paid per assignment. Either they are self-employed, or they work for a technical consulting firm and are given specific short-term or recurring assignments, such as writing about a new product or coordinating the work and communication among different offices to keep a project on track. Technical writing jobs are usually concentrated in locations with information technology or scientific and technical research companies, such as California and Texas.

Work Schedules

Technical writers may be expected to work evenings and weekends to coordinate with those in other time zones or to meet deadlines. Most work full time.

How to Become a Technical Writer

A college degree is usually required for a position as a technical writer. In addition, experience with a technical subject, such as computer science, Web design, or engineering, is important.

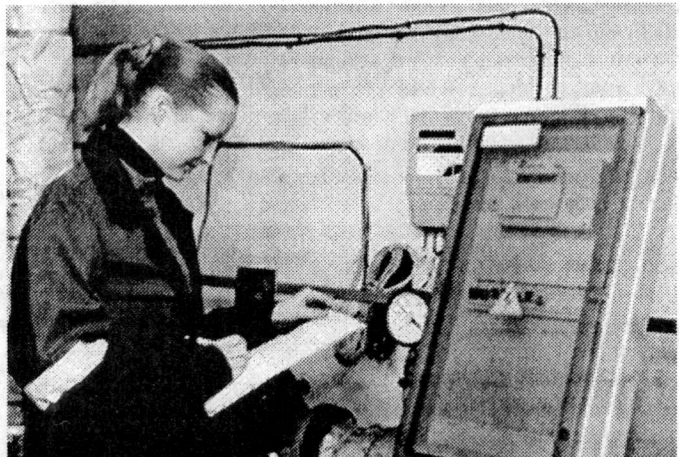

Technical writers communicate technical information through charts and manuals.

Education

Employers generally prefer candidates with a bachelor's degree in journalism, English, or communications. Many technical writing jobs require both a degree and knowledge in a specialized field, such as engineering, computer science, or medicine. Web design experience also is helpful because of the growing use of online technical documentation.

Work Experience

Some technical writers begin their careers not as writers, but as specialists or research assistants in a technical field. By developing technical communication skills, they eventually assume primary responsibilities for technical writing. In small firms, beginning technical writers may work on projects right away; in larger companies with more standard procedures, beginners may observe experienced technical writers and interact with specialists before being assigned projects.

Prospects for advancement generally include working on more complex projects, leading or training junior staff, and getting enough work to succeed as a freelancer.

Important Qualities

Communication skills. Technical writers must be able to take complex, technical information and translate it for colleagues and consumers who have nontechnical backgrounds.

Detail oriented. Technical writers create detailed instructions for others to follow. As a result, they must be detailed and precise at every step for the instructions to be useful.

Imagination. Technical writers must be able to think about a procedure or product in the way that a person without technical experience would think about it.

Teamwork. Technical writers must be able to work well with others. They are almost always part of a team: with other writers; with designers, editors, and illustrators; and with the technical people whose information they are explaining.

Technical skills. Technical writers must be able to understand and then explain highly technical information. Many technical writers need a background in engineering or computer science in order to do this.

Writing skills. Technical communicators must have excellent writing skills to be able to explain technical information clearly.

Pay

Technical Writers
 Median annual wages, May 2010

Technical Writers	$63,280
Media and Communication Workers	$49,060
Total, All Occupations	$33,840

Note: All Occupations includes all occupations in the U.S. Economy.
Source: U.S. Bureau of Labor Statistics, Occupational Employment Statistics

The median annual wage of technical writers was $63,280 in May 2010. The median wage is the wage at which half the workers in an occupation earned more than that amount and half earned less. The lowest 10 percent earned less than $37,160, and the highest 10 percent earned more than $100,910.

Median annual wages in the industries employing the largest numbers of technical writers in May 2010 were:

Software publishers	$76,410
Computer systems design and related services	66,860
Scientific research and development services	64,890
Architectural, engineering, and related services	62,350
Management, scientific, and technical consulting services	62,290

Technical writers may be expected to work evenings and weekends to coordinate with those in other time zones or to meet deadlines. Most work full time.

Job Outlook

Technical Writers
 Percent change in employment, projected 2010-20

Technical Writers	17%
Total, All Occupations	14%
Media and Communication Workers	13%

Note: All Occupations includes all occupations in the U.S. Economy.
Source: U.S. Bureau of Labor Statistics, Employment Projections program

Employment of technical writers is expected to grow 17 percent from 2010 to 2020, about as fast as the average for all occupations. Employment growth will be driven by the continuing expansion of scientific and technical products and by growth in Web-based product support. Growth and change in the high-technology and electronics industries will result in a greater need for those who can write instruction manuals and communicate information clearly to users.

Professional, scientific, and technical services firms will continue to grow rapidly and should be a good source of new jobs even as the occupation finds acceptance in a broader range of industries, including data processing, hosting, and related services.

Job Prospects

Job opportunities, especially for applicants with technical skills, are expected to be good. The growing reliance on technologically sophisticated products in the home and the workplace and the increasing complexity of medical and scientific information needed for daily living will create many new job opportunities for technical writers. In addition to job openings stemming from employment growth, some openings will arise as experienced workers retire, transfer to other occupations, or leave the labor force. However, there will be competition among freelance technical writers.

Employment projections data for technical writers, 2010-20

Occupational Title	SOC Code	Employment, 2010	Projected Employment, 2020	Change, 2010-20 Percent	Numeric
Technical Writers	27-3042	49,500	58,000	17	8,500
SOURCE: U.S. Bureau of Labor Statistics, Employment Projections program					

Similar Occupations

This table shows a list of occupations with job duties that are similar to those of technical writers.

Occupation	Job Duties	Entry-Level Education	Median Annual Pay, May 2010
Computer Hardware Engineers	Computer hardware engineers research, design, develop, and test computer equipment such as chips, circuit boards, or routers. By solving complex problems in computer hardware, these engineers create rapid advances in computer technology.	Bachelor's degree	$98,810
Computer Programmers	Computer programmers write code to create software programs. They turn the program designs created by software developers and engineers into instructions that a computer can follow.	Bachelor's degree	$71,380
Editors	Editors plan, review, and revise content for publication.	Bachelor's degree	$51,470
Interpreters and Translators	Interpreters and translators convert information from one language to another. Interpreters work in spoken or sign language, translators in written language.	Bachelor's degree	$43,300
Public Relations Managers and Specialists	Public relations managers and specialists create and maintain a favorable public image for their employer or client. They write material for media releases, plan and direct public relations programs, and raise funds for their organizations.	Bachelor's degree	$57,550
Writers and Authors	Writers and authors develop original written content for advertisements, books, magazines, movie and television scripts, songs, and online publications.	Bachelor's degree	$55,420

Contacts for More Information

For more information about technical writers, visit Society for Technical Communication

Suggested citation:

Bureau of Labor Statistics, U.S. Department of Labor, Occupational Outlook Handbook, 2012-13 Edition, Technical Writers, on the Internet at http://www.bls.gov/ooh/media-and-communication/technical-writers.htm .

Writers and Authors

Quick Facts: Writers and Authors	
2010 Median Pay	$55,420 per year $26.64 per hour
Entry-Level Education	Bachelor's degree
Work Experience in a Related Occupation	None
On-the-job Training	Long-term on-the-job training
Number of Jobs, 2010	145,900
Job Outlook, 2010-20	6% (Slower than average)
Employment Change, 2010-20	9,500

What Writers and Authors Do

Writers and authors develop original written content for advertisements, books, magazines, movie and television scripts, songs, and online publications.

Duties

Writers and authors typically do the following:

- Choose subject matter that interests readers
- Write fiction or nonfiction through scripts, novels, and biographies
- Conduct research to get factual information and authentic detail
- Write advertising copy for use by newspapers, magazines, broadcasts, and the Internet
- Present drafts to editors and clients for feedback
- Work with editors and clients to shape the material so it can be published

Writers and authors develop original written material, namely, stories and advertisements, for books, magazines, and online publications.

Writers must establish their credibility with editors and readers through strong research and the use of appropriate sources and citations. Writers and authors select the material they want to use and then convey the information to readers. With help from editors, they may revise or rewrite sections, searching for the best organization and the most appropriate phrasing. For more information, see the profile on editors .

An increasing number of writers are freelance writers—that is, they are self-employed and make their living by selling their written content to book and magazine publishers; news organizations; advertising agencies; and movie, theater, and television producers. Many freelance writers are hired to complete specific short-term or recurring assignments, such as writing a newspaper column, contributing to a series of articles in a magazine, or producing an organization's newsletter.

Writers and authors develop original written material.

An increasing number of writers are producing material that is published directly online in videos and on blogs.

The following are types of writers and authors:

Copywriters prepare advertisements to promote the sale of a good or service. They often work with a client to produce advertising themes, jingles, and slogans.

Biographers write a thorough account of a person's life. They gather information from interviews and research about the person to accurately portray important events in that person's life.

Novelists write books of fiction, creating characters and plots that may be imaginary or may be based on real events.

Songwriters compose music and lyrics for songs. They may write and perform their own songs or sell their work to a music publisher. They sometimes work with a client to produce advertising themes, jingles, and slogans and may be involved in marketing the product or service.

Playwrights write scripts for theatrical productions. They produce lines for actors to say, stage direction for actors to follow, and ideas for theatrical set design.

Screenwriters create scripts for movies and television. They may produce original stories, characters, and dialogue or turn a book into a movie or television script. Some may produce content for radio broadcasts and other types of performance.

Work Environment

Writers and authors held about 145,900 jobs in 2010. About 68 percent were self-employed.

The industries that employed the most writers and authors in 2010 were:

Religious, grantmaking, civic, professional, and similar organizations	6%
Newspaper, periodical, book, and directory publishers	5
Advertising, public relations, and related services	4
Motion picture and video industries	2
Radio and television broadcasting	2

Writers and authors work in an office, at home, or wherever else they have access to a computer.

Jobs are somewhat concentrated in major media and entertainment markets—Boston, Chicago, Los Angeles, New York, and Washington, DC—but improved communications and Internet capabilities allow writers and authors to work from almost anywhere. Many prefer to work outside these cities and travel regularly to meet with publishers and clients and to do research or conduct in-person interviews.

Work Schedules

About 26 percent of writers and authors work part time. Some writers keep regular office hours, either to stay in contact with sources and editors or to set up a writing routine, but many writers set their own hours. Freelance writers are paid per assignment; therefore, they work any number of hours necessary to meet a deadline. As a result, writers must be willing to work nights and weekends to produce something acceptable to an editor or client. Although many freelance writers enjoy running their own businesses and the advantages of working flexible hours, most routinely face the pressures of juggling multiple projects or continually looking for new work.

How to Become a Writer or Author

A college degree is generally required for a salaried position as a writer or author. Proficiency with computers and communications equipment is necessary for staying in touch with sources, editors, and other writers while working on assignments.

Education

A bachelor's degree is typically needed for a salaried job as a writer. Because writing skills are essential in this occupation, many employers like to hire people who have a degree in English, journalism, or communications.

Those with other backgrounds who demonstrate strong writing skills also may find jobs as writers. Writers who want to write about a particular topic may need formal training or experience related to that topic.

Because many writers today prepare material directly for the Internet, they should be knowledgeable about graphic design, page layout, and multimedia software.

Work Experience

Writers can get job experience by working for high school and college newspapers, magazines, radio and television stations, advertising and publishing companies, or not-for-profit organizations. College theater and music programs offer playwrights and songwriters an opportunity to have their work performed. Many magazines and newspapers also have internships for students. Interns may write stories, conduct research and interviews, and gain general publishing experience.

In addition, Internet blogs can provide writing experience to anyone with access to the Internet. Some of this writing may lead to paid assignments regardless of education, because the quality of writing, the unique perspective, and the size of the potential audience are the greatest determinants of success for a piece of writing. Online publications require knowledge of computer software and editing tools that are used to combine text with graphics, audio, video, and animation.

Advancement

Writers and authors generally advance by building a reputation, taking on more complex writing assignments, and getting published in more prestigious markets and publications. Having previously published work that was well received and maintaining a track record of meeting deadlines are important for advancement. Writing for smaller businesses, local newspapers, advertising agencies, and not-for-profit organizations allows beginning writers and authors to start taking credit for their work immediately. However, opportunities for advancement within these organizations may be limited because they either do not have enough regular work or do not need more advanced writing.

Many editors begin work as writers. Those who are particularly skilled at identifying stories, correcting writing style, and interacting with writers may be interested in editing jobs.

Important Qualities

Creativity. Writers and authors must be able to develop new and interesting plots, characters, or ideas so they can come up with new stories.

Determination. Writers and authors sometimes work on projects that take years to complete. Freelance writers who are paid per assignment must demonstrate persistence and personal drive.

Persuasion. Writers, especially those in advertising, must be able to persuade others to feel a certain way about a good or service.

Social perceptiveness. Writers and authors must understand how readers react to certain ideas in order to connect with their audience.

Writing skills. Writers and authors must be able to write effectively in order to convey feeling and emotion and communicate with readers.

Pay

Writers and Authors
Median annual wages, May 2010

Writers and Authors	$55,420
Media and Communication Workers	$49,060
Total, All Occupations	$33,840

Note: All Occupations includes all occupations in the U.S. Economy.
Source: U.S. Bureau of Labor Statistics, Occupational Employment Statistics

The median annual wage of writers and authors was $55,420 in May 2010. The median wage is the wage at which half the workers in an occupation earned more than that amount and half earned less. The lowest 10 percent earned less than $28,610, and the top 10 percent earned more than $109,440.

Median annual wages in the industries employing the largest numbers of writers and authors in May 2010 were:

Advertising, public relations, and related services	$62,260
Motion picture and video industries	62,000
Radio and television broadcasting	53,400
Religious, grantmaking, civic, professional, and similar organizations	52,750
Newspaper, periodical, book, and directory publishers	47,230

Freelance writers earn income from their articles, books, and, less commonly, television and movie scripts. Although most freelance writers work on an individual project basis for multiple publishers, many support themselves with income derived from other sources. Freelancers generally have to provide for their own health insurance and pension, unless they receive coverage from another job.

About 26 percent of writers and authors work part time. Some writers keep regular office hours, either to stay in contact with sources and editors or to set up a writing routine, but many writers set their own hours. Freelance writers are paid per assignment; therefore, they work any number of hours necessary to meet a deadline. As a result, writers must be willing to work nights and weekends to produce something that is acceptable to an editor or client. Although many freelance writers enjoy running their own businesses and the advantages of working flexible hours, most routinely face the pressures of juggling multiple projects or continually looking for new work.

Job Outlook

Writers and Authors
Percent change in employment, projected 2010-20

Total, All Occupations	14%
Media and Communication Workers	13%
Writers and Authors	6%

Note: All Occupations includes all occupations in the U.S. Economy.
Source: U.S. Bureau of Labor Statistics, Employment Projections program

Employment of writers and authors is projected to grow 6 percent from 2010 to 2020, slower than the average for all occupations. Despite slower-than-average employment growth, online publications and services are growing in number and sophistication, spurring demand for writers and authors with Web and multimedia experience. Some experienced writers should find work in the public relations departments of corporations and nonprofit organizations. Others will likely find freelance work for newspaper, magazine, or journal publishers, and some will write books.

Job Prospects

Strong competition is expected, given that many people are attracted to this occupation. Competition for jobs with established newspapers and magazines will be particularly strong because the publishing industry is projected to become smaller. Writers and authors who have adapted to online media and are comfortable writing for and working with a variety of electronic and digital tools should have an advantage in finding work. The declining costs of self-publishing, the growing popularity of electronic books, and the increasing number of readers of electronic books will allow many freelancer writers to get their work published. Some job openings will arise as experienced workers retire, transfer to other occupations, or leave the labor force.

Employment projections data for writers and authors, 2010-20

Occupational Title	SOC Code	Employment, 2010	Projected Employment, 2020	Change, 2010-20	
				Percent	Numeric
Writers and Authors	27-3043	145,900	155,400	6	9,500
SOURCE: U.S. Bureau of Labor Statistics, Employment Projections program					

Similar Occupations

This table shows a list of occupations with job duties that are similar to those of writers and authors.

Occupation	Job Duties	Entry-Level Education	Median Annual Pay, May 2010
Editors	Editors plan, review, and revise content for publication.	Bachelor's degree	$51,470
Reporters, Correspondents, and Broadcast News Analysts	Reporters, correspondents, and broadcast news analysts inform the public about news and events happening internationally, nationally, and locally. They report the news for newspapers, magazines, websites, television, and radio.	Bachelor's degree	$36,000
Public Relations Managers and Specialists	Public relations managers and specialists create and maintain a favorable public image for their employer or client. They write material for media releases, plan and direct public relations programs, and raise funds for their organizations.	Bachelor's degree	$57,550
Announcers	Announcers present music, news, and sports and may provide commentary or interview guests about these topics or other important events. Some act as a master of ceremonies (emcee) or disc jockey (DJ) at weddings, parties, or clubs.	See How to Become One	$27,010
Technical Writers	Technical writers, also called technical communicators, produce instruction manuals and other supporting documents to communicate complex and technical information more easily. They also develop, gather, and disseminate technical information among customers, designers, and manufacturers.	Bachelor's degree	$63,280

Contacts for More Information

For more information about writers and authors, visit American Society of Journalists and Authors , Association of Writers and Writing Programs

Suggested citation:

Bureau of Labor Statistics, U.S. Department of Labor, Occupational Outlook Handbook, 2012-13 Edition, Writers and Authors, on the Internet at http://www.bls.gov/ooh/media-and-communication/writers-and-authors. htm .

Bill and Account Collectors

Quick Facts: Bill and Account Collectors	
2010 Median Pay	$31,310 per year $15.05 per hour
Entry-Level Education	High school diploma or equivalent
Work Experience in a Related Occupation	None
On-the-job Training	Moderate-term on-the-job training
Number of Jobs, 2010	401,700
Job Outlook, 2010-20	14% (About as fast as average)
Employment Change, 2010-20	57,200

What Bill and Account Collectors Do

Bill and account collectors, sometimes called collectors, try to recover payment on overdue bills. They negotiate repayment plans with debtors and help them find solutions to make paying their overdue bills easier.

Duties

Bill and account collectors typically do the following:

- Find consumers and businesses who have overdue bills
- Track down consumers who have an out-of-date address by using the Internet, post office, credit bureaus, or neighbors, a process called "skip tracing"
- Inform debtors that they have an overdue bill and try to negotiate a payment
- Go over the terms of sale or contract with the debtor, when necessary
- Learn the reasons for the overdue bills, which can help with the negotiations
- Offer credit advice or refer a consumer to a debt counselor, when appropriate

Bill and account collectors generally contact debtors by phone, although sometimes they do so by mail. They use computer systems to update contact information and record past collection attempts with a particular debtor. Keeping these records can help collectors with future negotiations.

The main job of bill and account collectors is finding a solution that is acceptable to the debtor and maximizes payment to the creditor.

Bill and account collectors try to recover payment on overdue bills.

Listening to the debtor and paying attention to his or her concerns can help the collector negotiate a solution.

After the collector and debtor agree on a repayment plan, the collector continually checks to ensure that the debtor pays on time. If the debtor does not pay, the collector submits a statement to the creditor, who can take legal action. In extreme cases, this legal action may include taking back goods or disconnecting service.

Collectors must follow federal and state laws that govern debt collection. These laws require that a collector make sure they are talking with the debtor before announcing that the purpose of the call is to collect a debt. A collector also must give a statement, called "mini-Miranda," which informs the account holder that they are speaking with a bill or debt collector.

Although many collectors work for third-party collection agencies, some work in-house for the original creditor, such as a credit-card company or a health care provider. The day-to-day activities of in-house collectors are generally the same as those of other collectors.

Collectors usually have goals they are expected to meet. Typically, these include calls per hour and success rates.

Work Environment

Bill and account collectors held about 401,700 jobs in 2010. Many work in a call center for a third-party collection agency rather than the original creditor. The following table shows the industries that employ the largest number of collectors in 2010:

Business support services	26%
Credit intermediation and related activities	20
Offices of physicians	8
Wholesale trade	5

Whichever industry the collectors work in, most of their time is spent on the phone tracking down or negotiating with debtors. They also spend time on the computer, updating information and recording the results of their calls.

Collectors' work can be stressful because many people become angry and confrontational when pressed about their debts. Collectors often face resistance while trying to do their job tasks. Successful collectors must face regular rejection and still be ready to make the next call in a polite and positive voice. Fortunately, some consumers appreciate help in resolving their outstanding debts and can be quite grateful.

Work Schedules

Most bill and account collectors work full time. Some collectors work flexible schedules, often calling people on weekends or during the evenings as they learn the best times to call.

797

How to Become a Bill and Account Collector

Collectors must usually have a high school diploma and experience in a call center. A few months of on-the-job training is common.

Education

Most bill and account collectors are required to have a high school diploma, although some employers prefer applicants who have taken some college courses. Communication, accounting, and basic computer courses are examples of classes that are helpful for entering this occupation.

Training

Collectors usually get 1 to 3 months of on-the-job training after being hired. Training includes learning the company's policies and computer software and learning the laws for debt collection in the Fair Debt Collection Practices Act, as well as their state's debt collection regulations. If they do not have experience, they may also be trained in how to negotiate.

Work Experience

Some employers prefer applicants who have experience in call centers. At least 6 months to 1 year is common. However, some agencies want a collector to have several years of experience.

Important Qualities

Listening skills. When trying to negotiate a repayment plan, collectors must pay attention to what debtors say. Learning the particular situation of the debtors and how they fell into debt can help collectors suggest solutions.

Negotiating skills. Reconciling the differences between two parties (the debtor and the creditor) and offering a solution that is acceptable to both parties are the main aspects of a collector's job.

Speaking skills. Collectors must be able to speak to debtors to explain their choices and ensure that they fully understand what is being said.

Pay

Bill and Account Collectors
Median annual wages, May 2010

Total, All Occupations	$33,840
Bill and Account Collectors	$31,310
Office and Administrative Support Occupations	$30,710

Note: All Occupations includes all occupations in the U.S. Economy.
Source: U.S. Bureau of Labor Statistics, Occupational Employment Statistics

The median annual wage of bill and account collectors was $31,310 in May 2010. The median wage is the wage at which half the workers in an occupation earned more than that amount and half earned less. The lowest 10 percent earned less than $21,320, and the top 10 percent earned more than $47,180. These wage data include money earned from commissions. They earn more when their collection rate is high.

As shown in the table below, the median annual wage for bill and account collectors working in the wholesale trade industry was $34,950, the highest among those industries employing much of the occupation.

Wholesale trade	$34,950
Offices of physicians	32,580
Credit intermediation and related activities	31,860
Business support services	27,310

Most bill and account collectors work full time. Some collectors work flexible schedules, often calling people on weekends or during the evenings as they learn the best times to call.

Job Outlook

Bill and Account Collectors
Percent change in employment, projected 2010-20

Total, All Occupations	14%
Bill and Account Collectors	14%
Office and Administrative Support Occupations	10%

Note: All Occupations includes all occupations in the U.S. Economy.
Source: U.S. Bureau of Labor Statistics, Employment Projections program

Employment of bill and account collectors is projected to grow 14 percent from 2010 to 2020, as fast as the average for all occupations.

The increasing efficiency of collectors is expected to slow employment growth for this occupation. New software and automated calling systems should increase productivity and allow collectors to handle more accounts.

In addition, some collection jobs will likely be sent to other countries where wages are lower. Nevertheless, creditors will continue to hire collectors in the United States because workers in this country tend to have greater success in negotiating with debtors.

Collectors in medical industries should see more job growth. As the cost of health care increases, the amount of medical debt that people incur is likely to rise as well. In addition, credit card companies are more commonly selling their debts to third-party agencies, likely also increasing job growth in the collections industry.

The following table shows the projected growth rates for bill and account collectors in the industries they are most commonly employed in:

Offices of physicians	44%
Business support services	30
Credit intermediation and related activities	1
Wholesale trade	0

Job Prospects

Job prospects should be excellent for this occupation. Workers frequently leave the occupation, which leads to numerous job openings. Prospects should be best for applicants who have worked in a call center before because some companies prefer to hire collectors with this kind of experience.

Unlike many other occupations, collections jobs usually remain stable during economic downturns. When the economy weakens, many consumers and businesses fall behind on their financial obligations, increasing the amount of debt to be collected. However, the success rate of collectors decreases because fewer people can afford to pay their debts.

Employment projections data for bill and account collectors, 2010-20

Occupational Title	SOC Code	Employment, 2010	Projected Employment, 2020	Change, 2010-20	
				Percent	Numeric
Bill and Account Collectors	43-3011	401,700	458,900	14	57,200

SOURCE: U.S. Bureau of Labor Statistics, Employment Projections program

Similar Occupations

This table shows a list of occupations with job duties that are similar to those of bill and account collectors.

Occupation	Job Duties	Entry-Level Education	Median Annual Pay, May 2010
Bookkeeping, Accounting, and Auditing Clerks	Bookkeeping, accounting, and auditing clerks produce financial records for organizations. They record financial transactions, update statements, and check financial records for accuracy.	High school diploma or equivalent	$34,030
Customer Service Representatives	Customer service representatives interact with customers on behalf of an organization. They provide information about products and services and respond to customer complaints. Some also take orders and process returns.	High school diploma or equivalent	$30,460
Financial Clerks	Financial clerks do administrative work for banking, insurance, and other companies. They keep records, help customers, and carry out financial transactions.	High school diploma or equivalent	$33,710
Information Clerks	Information clerks provide administrative and clerical support in a variety of settings. They help maintain records, collect data and information, and respond to customers' questions or concerns.	See How to Become One	$29,990
Loan Officers	Loan officers evaluate, authorize, or recommend approval of loan applications for people and businesses.	High school diploma or equivalent	$56,490

Contacts for More Information

For more information about bill and account collectors, visit ACA International, The Association of Credit and Collections Professionals

Suggested citation:

Bureau of Labor Statistics, U.S. Department of Labor, Occupational Outlook Handbook, 2012-13 Edition, Bill and Account Collectors, on the Internet at http://www.bls.gov/ooh/office-and-administrative-support/bill-and-account-collectors.htm .

Bookkeeping, Accounting, and Auditing Clerks

Quick Facts: Bookkeeping, Accounting, and Auditing Clerks	
2010 Median Pay	$34,030 per year $16.36 per hour
Entry-Level Education	High school diploma or equivalent
Work Experience in a Related Occupation	None
On-the-job Training	Moderate-term on-the-job training
Number of Jobs, 2010	1,898,300
Job Outlook, 2010-20	14% (About as fast as average)
Employment Change, 2010-20	259,000

What Bookkeeping, Accounting, and Auditing Clerks Do

Bookkeeping, accounting, and auditing clerks produce financial records for organizations. They record financial transactions, update statements, and check financial records for accuracy.

Duties

Bookkeeping, accounting, and auditing clerks typically do the following:

- Use bookkeeping software as well as online spreadsheets and databases
- Enter (post) financial transactions into the appropriate computer software
- Receive and record cash, checks, and vouchers
- Put costs (debits) as well as income (credits) into the software, assigning each to an appropriate account

- Produce reports, such as balance sheets (costs compared to income), income statements, and totals by account
- Check figures, postings, and reports for accuracy
- Reconcile or note and report any differences they find in the records

The records that bookkeeping, accounting, and auditing clerks work with include expenditures (money spent), receipts (money that comes in), accounts payable (bills to be paid), accounts receivable (invoices, or what other people owe the organization), and profit and loss (a report that shows the organization's financial health).

Workers in this occupation have a wide range of tasks. Some in this occupation are full-charge bookkeeping clerks who maintain an entire organization's books. Others are accounting clerks who handle specific tasks.

These clerks use basic mathematics (adding, subtracting) throughout the day.

As organizations continue to computerize their financial records, many bookkeeping, accounting, and auditing clerks use specialized accounting software, spreadsheets, and databases. Most clerks now enter information from receipts or bills into computers, and the information is then stored electronically. They must be comfortable using computers to record and calculate data.

The widespread use of computers also has enabled bookkeeping, accounting, and auditing clerks to take on additional responsibilities, such as payroll, billing, purchasing (buying), and keeping track of overdue bills. Many of these functions require clerks to communicate with clients.

Bookkeeping clerks, also known as **bookkeepers**, often are responsible for some or all of an organization's accounts, known as the general ledger. They record all transactions and post debits (costs) and credits (income).

They also produce financial statements and other reports for supervisors and managers. Bookkeepers prepare bank deposits by compiling data from cashiers, verifying receipts, and sending cash, checks, or other forms of payment to the bank.

In addition, they may handle payroll, make purchases, prepare invoices, and keep track of overdue accounts.

Accounting clerks typically work for larger companies and have more specialized tasks. Their titles, such as accounts payable clerk or accounts receivable clerk, often reflect the type of accounting they do.

Often, their responsibilities vary by level of experience. Entry-level accounting clerks may enter (post) details of transactions (including date, type, and amount), add up accounts, and determine interest charges. They also may monitor loans and accounts to ensure that payments are up to date.

More advanced accounting clerks may add up and balance billing vouchers, ensure that account data is complete and accurate, and code documents according to an organization's procedures.

Auditing clerks check figures, postings, and documents to ensure that they are mathematically accurate and properly coded. They also correct or note errors for accountants or other workers to fix.

Work Environment

Bookkeeping, accounting, and auditing clerks held about 1.9 million jobs in 2010.

They following industries employed the most bookkeeping, accounting, and auditing clerks in 2010:

Professional, scientific, and technical services	11%
Retail trade	9
Finance and insurance	7
Wholesale trade	7
Health care and social assistance	7

Bookkeeping, accounting, and auditing clerks work in offices.

Work Schedules

Many bookkeeping, accounting, and auditing clerks work full time. About 1 of 4 clerks worked part time in 2010. They may work longer hours to meet deadlines at the end of the fiscal year, during tax time, or when monthly or yearly accounting audits are done. Those who work in hotels, restaurants, and stores may put in overtime during peak holiday and vacation seasons.

How to Become a Bookkeeping, Accounting, or Auditing Clerk

Most bookkeeping, accounting, and auditing clerks need a high school diploma, and they usually learn some of their skills on the job. They must have basic math and computer skills, including knowledge of spreadsheets and bookkeeping software.

Bookkeeping, accounting, and auditing clerks record financial transactions, update statements, and check them for accuracy.

Education

Most bookkeeping, accounting, and auditing clerks need a high school diploma. However, some employers prefer candidates who have some postsecondary education, particularly coursework in accounting. In 2009, 25 percent of these workers had an associate's or higher degree.

Training

Bookkeeping, accounting, and auditing clerks usually get on-the-job training. Under the guidance of a supervisor or another experienced employee, new clerks learn how to do their tasks, including double-entry bookkeeping. (Double-entry bookkeeping means that each transaction is entered twice, once as a debit (cost) and once as a credit (income) to ensure that all accounts are balanced.)

Some formal classroom training also may be necessary, such as training in specialized computer software. This on-the-job training typically takes around 6 months.

Certification

Some bookkeeping, accounting, and auditing clerks become certified. The Certified Bookkeeper (CB) designation, awarded by the American Institute of Professional Bookkeepers , shows that people have the skills and knowledge needed to carry out all bookkeeping tasks, including overseeing payroll and balancing accounts, according to accepted accounting procedures.

For certification, candidates must have at least 2 years of bookkeeping experience, pass a four-part exam, and adhere to a code of ethics.

Several colleges and universities offer a preparatory course for certification. Some offer courses online. In addition, certified bookkeepers are required to meet a continuing education requirement every 3 years to keep their certification.

The National Bookkeepers Association also offers certification. The Uniform Bookkeeper Certification Examination is an online test with 50 multiple-choice questions. Test takers must answer 80 percent of the questions correctly to pass the exam.

Advancement

With appropriate experience and education, some bookkeeping, accounting, and auditing clerks may become accountants or auditors.

Important Qualities

Detail oriented. These clerks are responsible for producing accurate financial records. They must pay attention to detail to avoid making errors and to recognize errors that others have made.

Math skills. Bookkeeping, accounting, and auditing clerks should be comfortable with basic arithmetic because they deal with numbers daily.

Computer skills. Bookkeeping, accounting, and auditing clerks need basic computer skills. They should be comfortable using spreadsheets and bookkeeping software.

Also, these workers have control of an organization's financial documentation, which they must use properly and keep confidential. It is vital that they keep records transparent and guard against misappropriating an organization's funds.

Pay

Bookkeeping, Accounting, and Auditing Clerks
Median annual wages, May 2010

Bookkeeping, Accounting, and Auditing Clerks	$34,030
Total, All Occupations	$33,840
Office and Administrative Support Occupations	$30,710

Note: All Occupations includes all occupations in the U.S. Economy.
Source: U.S. Bureau of Labor Statistics, Occupational Employment Statistics

The median annual wage of bookkeeping, accounting, and auditing clerks was $34,030 in May 2010. The median wage is the wage at which half the workers in an occupation earned more than that amount and half earned less. The lowest 10 percent earned less than $21,270 and the top 10 percent earned more than $51,470.

Many bookkeeping, accounting, and auditing clerks work full time. About 1 of 4 clerks worked part time in 2010. They may work longer hours to meet deadlines at the end of the fiscal year, during tax time, or when monthly or yearly accounting audits are performed. Those who work in hotels, restaurants, and stores may put in overtime during peak holiday and vacation seasons.

Job Outlook

Bookkeeping, Accounting, and Auditing Clerks
Percent change in employment, projected 2010-20

Total, All Occupations	14%
Bookkeeping, Accounting, and Auditing Clerks	14%
Office and Administrative Support Occupations	10%

Note: All Occupations includes all occupations in the U.S. Economy.
Source: U.S. Bureau of Labor Statistics, Employment Projections program

Employment of bookkeeping, accounting, and auditing clerks is expected to grow 14 percent from 2010 to 2020, as fast as the average for all occupations.

Job growth for these workers is largely driven by overall economic growth. As the number of organizations increases, more bookkeepers will be needed to keep these organizations' books. In addition, in response to the recent financial crisis, investors will pay increased attention to the accuracy of corporate books. Stricter regulation in the financial sector will create demand for accounting services, creating opportunities for accounting clerks.

Some tasks that these clerks do have been affected by technological changes. For example, electronic banking and bookkeeping software has reduced the need for bookkeepers and clerks to send and receive checks. However, when checks are sent or received, these workers are still needed to update statements and check for accuracy. These changes are therefore expected to help bookkeeping, accounting, and auditing clerks do their jobs, rather than reduce the need for these workers.

Job Prospects

Because this is a large occupation, there will be a large number of job openings from workers leaving the occupation. This means that opportunities to enter the occupation should be plentiful.

Employment projections data for bookkeeping, accounting, and auditing clerks, 2010-20

Occupational Title	SOC Code	Employment, 2010	Projected Employment, 2020	Change, 2010-20 Percent	Change, 2010-20 Numeric
Bookkeeping, Accounting, and Auditing Clerks	43-3031	1,898,300	2,157,400	14	259,000
SOURCE: U.S. Bureau of Labor Statistics, Employment Projections program					

Similar Occupations

This table shows a list of occupations with job duties that are similar to those of bookkeeping, accounting, and auditing clerks.

Occupation	Job Duties	Entry-Level Education	Median Annual Pay, May 2010
Accountants and Auditors	Accountants and auditors prepare and examine financial records. They ensure that financial records are accurate and that taxes are paid properly and on time. Accountants and auditors assess financial operations and work to help ensure that organizations run efficiently.	Bachelor's degree	$61,690
Budget Analysts	Budget analysts help public and private institutions organize their finances. They prepare budget reports and monitor institutional spending.	Bachelor's degree	$68,200
Cost Estimators	Cost estimators collect and analyze data to estimate the time, money, resources, and labor required for product manufacturing, construction projects, or services. Some specialize in a particular industry or product type.	Bachelor's degree	$57,860
Financial Clerks	Financial clerks do administrative work for banking, insurance, and other companies. They keep records, help customers, and carry out financial transactions.	High school diploma or equivalent	$33,710
Loan Officers	Loan officers evaluate, authorize, or recommend approval of loan applications for people and businesses.	High school diploma or equivalent	$56,490

Tax Examiners and Collectors, and Revenue Agents	Tax examiners and collectors, and revenue agents ensure that governments get their tax money from businesses and citizens. They review tax returns, conduct audits, identify taxes owed, and collect overdue tax payments.	Bachelor's degree	$49,360

Contacts for More Information

For more information about bookkeepers, visit American Institute of Professional Bookkeepers , National Bookkeepers Association

Suggested citation:

Bureau of Labor Statistics, U.S. Department of Labor, Occupational Outlook Handbook, 2012-13 Edition, Bookkeeping, Accounting, and Auditing Clerks, on the Internet at http://www.bls.gov/ooh/office-and-administrative-support/bookkeeping-accounting-and-auditing-clerks.htm .

Cargo and Freight Agents

Quick Facts: Cargo and Freight Agents	
2010 Median Pay	$37,150 per year $17.86 per hour
Entry-Level Education	High school diploma or equivalent
Work Experience in a Related Occupation	None
On-the-job Training	Short-term on-the-job training
Number of Jobs, 2010	82,200
Job Outlook, 2010-20	29% (Much faster than average)
Employment Change, 2010-20	24,100

What Cargo and Freight Agents Do

Cargo and freight agents coordinate and facilitate incoming and outgoing shipments for transportation companies and other businesses.

Duties

Cargo and freight agents typically do the following:

- Determine shipping methods and routes from pick-up location to final destination
- Advise clients on transportation and payment options
- Coordinate transportation and logistics details with shipping and freight companies
- Estimate, negotiate, and determine postal rates, shipment costs, and other charges
- Notify clients of cargo shipments, status en route, and time of delivery
- Prepare bills of lading, invoices, and other required shipping documents
- Record information such as cargo amount, weight, dimensions, and time of shipment
- Trace lost shipments as necessary

Cargo and freight agents facilitate shipments of goods through airline, train, and trucking terminals and shipping docks. Agents ensure that shipments are picked up and delivered on time, paperwork is completed, and fees are collected. For international shipments, agents prepare and verify customs and tariff forms.

Agents typically manage shipments for multiple clients at once. They often arrange their clients' cargo and freight by destination, and send out many clients' shipments simultaneously.

Most cargo and freight agents store and use records on computers. They use bar codes and the Internet to track shipments and use spreadsheets to manage inventories.

Although cargo and freight agents sometimes pack items for shipping and take them to a loading dock or station, that is not their primary role. For more information on workers who specialize in that type of delivery work, see the profile on couriers and messengers .

Work Environment

Cargo and freight agents held about 82,200 jobs in 2010. Industries that employed the most cargo and freight agents in 2010 were as follows:

Freight transportation arrangement	45%
Scheduled air transportation	15
Couriers and express delivery services	9

Cargo and freight agents typically work in warehouses, stockrooms, or shipping and receiving stations. Often, these worksites are not temperature-controlled. As a result, some agents spend time working in cold storage facilities or may be exposed to all types of weather on outdoor loading platforms.

Cargo and freight agents coordinate transportation with shipping companies.

Cargo and freight agents' work can by physically demanding. Agents spend considerable time standing, walking, bending, and stretching. Additionally, agents may lift and carry small items around the worksite although equipment, such as a forklift, is often used for moving heavy cargo.

Injuries

Cargo and freight agents have a rate of injuries and illnesses that is higher than the average for all occupations. Injuries are usually minor and may include muscle strains, cuts, and bruises. The work is generally not dangerous as long as agents are careful and follow basic safety procedures.

Work Schedules

Most cargo and freight agents work full time. Some may work overtime when managing large shipments or short deadlines.

How to Become a Cargo or Freight Agent

High school graduates usually qualify for cargo and freight agent positions. Workers typically train informally on the job.

Education and Training

Employers prefer to hire cargo and freight agents who have a high school diploma or GED.

Cargo and freight agents normally start their careers working under an experienced agent and helping with basic tasks, such as weighing packages, organizing stockrooms, and double-checking addresses. As trainees gain experience, they gradually take on more responsibility. Over time, they begin working more independently and on more complicated tasks, such as tracking shipments en route and notifying clients of cargo pick-up or delivery.

Cargo and freight agents often use computer databases and spreadsheets for large portions of their work, and must be familiar with the necessary software. This may involve taking short-term training programs over the course of their careers.

Important Qualities

Bookkeeping skills. Accurate record keeping is essential for tracking shipment updates, inventories, client and payment records, and other information.

Computer skills. Agents use computer programs to store records, track inventory, and communicate with clients. They must be familiar with and feel comfortable using various software and programs.

Customer-service skills. Cargo and freight agents interact frequently with clients, logistics companies, and others in the shipping industry. They must be able to courteously and promptly provide shipment updates, price quotes, and other information upon request.

Organizational skills. Cargo and freight agents must make sure that cargo arrives or is picked up at its destination on time. Agents must be able to plan shipments to ensure prompt delivery.

Pay

Cargo and Freight Agents
Median annual wages, May 2010

Cargo and Freight Agents	$37,150
Total, All Occupations	$33,840
Material Recording, Scheduling, Dispatching, and Distributing Workers	$27,590

Note: All Occupations includes all occupations in the U.S. Economy.
Source: U.S. Bureau of Labor Statistics, Occupational Employment Statistics

The median annual wage of cargo and freight agents was $37,150 in May 2010. The median wage is the wage at which half the workers in an occupation earned more than that amount and half earned less. The lowest 10 percent earned less than $22,110, and the top 10 percent earned more than $58,400.

Most cargo and freight agents work full time. Some may work overtime when managing large shipments or short deadlines.

Job Outlook

Cargo and Freight Agents
Percent change in employment, projected 2010-20

Cargo and Freight Agents	29%
Total, All Occupations	14%
Material Recording, Scheduling, Dispatching, and Distributing Workers	0%

Note: All Occupations includes all occupations in the U.S. Economy.
Source: U.S. Bureau of Labor Statistics, Employment Projections program

Employment of cargo and freight agents is projected to grow 29 percent from 2010 to 2020, much faster than the average for all occupations.

As the economy grows, the volume of cargo traffic will also increase. More cargo and freight agents will be needed to coordinate and manage these additional shipments, which increasingly involve multiple modes of transportation. In particular, the growing popularity of online shopping is likely to result in more goods being shipped across the country from central shipment centers and warehouses.

Large numbers of companies have begun outsourcing their shipping and logistics work to third-party firms, many of which employ large numbers of cargo and freight agents. This trend will likely increase demand for agents, resulting in further employment growth.

Job Prospects

Job prospects should be best for those with strong computer and customer-service skills. Some employers report difficulty finding workers who have these abilities.

Although job opportunities are expected to be good, employment of cargo and freight agents is sensitive to fluctuations in the economy. Workers may experience higher levels of unemployment when the overall level of economic activity falls.

Employment projections data for cargo and freight agents, 2010-20

Occupational Title	SOC Code	Employment, 2010	Projected Employment, 2020	Change, 2010-20 Percent	Change, 2010-20 Numeric
Cargo and Freight Agents	43-5011	82,200	106,300	29	24,100
SOURCE: U.S. Bureau of Labor Statistics, Employment Projections program					

Similar Occupations

This table shows a list of occupations with job duties that are similar to those of cargo and freight agents.

Occupation	Job Duties	Entry-Level Education	Median Annual Pay, May 2010
Couriers and Messengers	Couriers and messengers transport documents and packages for individuals, businesses, institutions, and government agencies.	High school diploma or equivalent	$24,080
Postal Service Workers	Postal Service workers sell postal products and collect, sort, and deliver mail.	High school diploma or equivalent	$53,090

Contacts for More Information

For information about the freight and cargo industry, including training opportunities, visit Transportation Intermediaries Association

Suggested citation:

Bureau of Labor Statistics, U.S. Department of Labor, Occupational Outlook Handbook, 2012-13 Edition, Cargo and Freight Agents, on the Internet at http://www.bls.gov/ooh/office-and-administrative-support/cargo-and-freight-agents.htm .

Couriers and Messengers

Quick Facts: Couriers and Messengers	
2010 Median Pay	$24,080 per year $11.58 per hour
Entry-Level Education	High school diploma or equivalent
Work Experience in a Related Occupation	None
On-the-job Training	Short-term on-the-job training
Number of Jobs, 2010	116,200
Job Outlook, 2010-20	13% (About as fast as average)
Employment Change, 2010-20	14,600

What Couriers and Messengers Do

Couriers and messengers transport documents and packages for individuals, businesses, institutions, and government agencies.

Duties

Couriers and messengers typically do the following:

- Pick up and deliver items to their final destinations

Couriers and messengers transport documents and packages for individuals and organizations.

- Verify delivery information, such as names, addresses, and telephone numbers
- Load items onto delivery vehicles
- Plan and follow the most efficient routes for delivery
- Collect necessary payments and signatures from clients
- Record delivery information, such as time of delivery and recipient's name

Couriers and messengers provide door-to-door delivery service for a variety of clients, including law offices, banks, and hospitals. Most workers specialize in local deliveries, often in large urban areas. They offer same-day or 1-hour delivery services. Packages delivered may include important legal or financial documents, passports, and medical samples that senders are unwilling to entrust to other means of delivery.

Couriers and messengers receive their instructions either in person or by cell phone or two-way radio. With this information, they plan the most efficient route and delivery schedule.

Some couriers and messengers carry items only for specific clients, such as law firms, financial institutions, or medical laboratories.

Work Environment

Couriers and messengers held about 116,200 jobs in 2010. About one-fifth worked for courier and delivery service businesses; about one-quarter were self-employed.

Industries employing the largest numbers of couriers and messengers in 2010 were as follows:

Couriers and messengers	20%
Ambulatory health care services	14
Professional, scientific and technical services	11
Hospitals	5
Credit intermediation and related activities	4

Couriers and messengers spend most of their time making deliveries and are not closely supervised. The expectation to make multiple deliveries in a safe and timely manner can make the job stressful. Those who deliver by bicycle must be physically fit and able to cope with all weather conditions and the hazards of heavy traffic. Car, van, and truck couriers often have to deal with traffic jams, road construction, and difficult parking situations.

Nearly 19 percent of couriers and messengers are members of a union. These workers may enjoy higher earnings, better benefits, and more job stability.

Most independent contractors do not get benefits, but they may get higher pay.

Work Schedules

While most couriers and messengers work full time during regular business hours, evening and weekend hours are common.

Injuries

The rate of injuries and illnesses for couriers and messengers is higher than the average for all occupations. Car, van, and truck couriers must sometimes carry heavy loads, either manually or with a hand truck. As a result, workers may suffer minor work-related injuries, such as muscle strains or bruises. Still, if workers follow basic safety precautions, the work is not dangerous.

How to Become a Courier or Messenger

Although there is no educational requirement for entering the occupation, employers generally prefer to hire high school graduates. Most couriers and messengers train informally on the job. Almost all couriers and messengers are required to have a valid state driver's license and a good driving record.

Education

Most courier and messenger jobs do not have strict education requirements. However, a high school diploma or its equivalent can be helpful in finding a job. Some employers will only hire candidates who have a high school diploma or GED.

Training

Couriers and messengers typically train informally on the job. They usually work alongside an experienced courier or messenger for 1 to 2 weeks and help with tasks such as loading and unloading packages and collecting signatures or payments. Once trainees understand the collection and delivery process, they are generally expected to work on their own.

Many courier and delivery contractors specialize in delivering sensitive items, such as medical specimens or donated organs. In these cases, employers generally provide specific training that may last from several hours to a few days, depending on the item.

Important Qualities

Bookkeeping skills. Accurate record keeping is necessary for tracking deliveries, payments, signatures, and other important information. This is especially true for self-employed couriers and messengers.

Customer-service skills. Because couriers and messengers frequently interact with clients, they must be courteous, polite, and ready to answer customers' questions regarding deliveries, payments, and other issues.

Directional skills. Couriers and messengers spend a considerable amount of time traveling to make deliveries. Therefore, they must be familiar with delivery routes and areas and have a good sense of direction.

Time-management skills. Couriers and messengers must often make deliveries on tight time schedules. As a result, they must be able to plan their day and make deliveries efficiently so items do not arrive late.

Pay

Couriers and Messengers
Median annual wages, May 2010

Total, All Occupations	$33,840
Office and Administrative Support Occupations	$30,710
Couriers and Messengers	$24,080

Note: All Occupations includes all occupations in the U.S. Economy.
Source: U.S. Bureau of Labor Statistics, Occupational Employment Statistics

The median annual wage of couriers and messengers was $24,080 in May 2010. The median wage is the wage at which half the workers in an occupation earned more than that amount and half earned less. The lowest 10 percent earned less than $17,170, and the top 10 percent earned more than $37,830.

In May 2010, median annual wages in industries employing the largest numbers of couriers and messengers were as follows:

Hospitals	$25,730
Ambulatory health care services	25,660
Credit intermediation and related activities	23,480
Professional, scientific and technical services	23,380
Couriers and messengers	22,440

While most couriers and messengers work full time during regular business hours, evening and weekend hours are common.

Nearly 19 percent of couriers and messengers are members of a union. These workers may enjoy higher earnings, better benefits, and more job stability.

Most independent contractors do not get benefits, but they may get higher pay.

Job Outlook

Couriers and Messengers
Percent change in employment, projected 2010-20

Total, All Occupations	14%
Couriers and Messengers	13%
Office and Administrative Support Occupations	10%

Note: All Occupations includes all occupations in the U.S. Economy.
Source: U.S. Bureau of Labor Statistics, Employment Projections program

Employment of couriers and messengers is expected to grow 13 percent from 2010 to 2020, about as fast as the average for all occupations.

Although many documents are now transferred digitally, the need to deliver items that cannot be sent electronically, including blueprints and passports, will require couriers and messengers. As the population continues to grow and age, couriers will also be required by medical and dental laboratories to send a growing number of medical samples and specimens.

Job Prospects

Job opportunities are expected to be best for those who deliver sensitive items, particularly medical samples and specimens that cannot be sent electronically. Those who specialize in document delivery, however, will face limited job opportunities.

Applicants with strong customer service skills are likely to have better job opportunities.

Employment projections data for couriers and messengers, 2010-20

Occupational Title	SOC Code	Employment, 2010	Projected Employment, 2020	Change, 2010-20	
				Percent	Numeric
Couriers and Messengers	43-5021	116,200	130,800	13	14,600
SOURCE: U.S. Bureau of Labor Statistics, Employment Projections program					

Similar Occupations

This table shows a list of occupations with job duties that are similar to those of couriers and messengers.

Occupation	Job Duties	Entry-Level Education	Median Annual Pay, May 2010
Cargo and Freight Agents	Cargo and freight agents coordinate and facilitate incoming and outgoing shipments for transportation companies and other businesses.	High school diploma or equivalent	$37,150
Delivery Truck Drivers and Driver/Sales Workers	Delivery truck drivers and driver/sales workers pick up, transport, and drop off packages within a small region or urban area. Most of the time, they transport merchandise from a distribution center to businesses and households.	High school diploma or equivalent	$27,050
Postal Service Workers	Postal Service workers sell postal products and collect, sort, and deliver mail.	High school diploma or equivalent	$53,090

Contacts for More Information

For information about jobs, contact local courier and messenger services. Local offices of the state employment service may be able to provide additional information about job opportunities.

For general information on careers as couriers and messengers, visit Messenger Courier Association of America

Suggested citation:

Bureau of Labor Statistics, U.S. Department of Labor, Occupational Outlook Handbook, 2012-13 Edition, Couriers and Messengers, on the Internet at http://www.bls.gov/ooh/office-and-administrative-support/couriers-and-messengers.htm .

Customer Service Representatives

Quick Facts: Customer Service Representatives	
2010 Median Pay	$30,460 per year $14.64 per hour
Entry-Level Education	High school diploma or equivalent
Work Experience in a Related Occupation	None
On-the-job Training	Short-term on-the-job training
Number of Jobs, 2010	2,187,300
Job Outlook, 2010-20	15% (About as fast as average)
Employment Change, 2010-20	338,400

What Customer Service Representatives Do

Customer service representatives interact with customers on behalf of an organization. They provide information about the organization's products and services and respond to customer complaints. Some also take orders and process returns.

Duties

Customer service representatives typically do the following:

- Listen and respond to customers' needs and concerns
- Provide information about products and services
- Take orders, determine charges, and oversee billing or payments
- Review or make changes to customer accounts
- Handle returns or complaints
- Record details of customer contacts and actions taken
- Research answers or solutions as needed
- Refer customers to supervisors, managers, or others who can help

Customer service representatives answer questions and resolve problems. When the customer has an account with the company, a representative will usually open the customer's file in the company's computer system. Representatives use this information to solve problems and may make changes to customer accounts, such as to update an address on file or cancel an order.

They also have access to responses for the most commonly asked questions and to specific guidelines for dealing with requests or complaints. In the event that the representative does not know the answer to a question or is unable to solve a specific problem, a supervisor or other experienced worker may help.

Many customer service representatives answer incoming calls in telephone call centers, which are increasingly called customer contact centers. Others interact with customers face to face or by email, live chat, or other methods.

Some workers specialize in a particular mode of communication, such as voice, email, or chat, but others communicate with customers through more than one contact channel. For example, voice agents, who primarily deal with customers over the phone, may respond to email questions when there is downtime between calls.

Customer service representatives work in almost every industry, and their job tasks can vary depending on where they work. For instance, representatives who work in banks may answer customers' questions about their accounts, whereas representatives who work for utility and communication companies may help customers with service problems, such as outages. Representatives who work in retail stores often handle returns and help customers find items in their stores. Some representatives may help to generate sales leads, sometimes making outbound calls in addition to answering inbound ones, although selling is not their main job.

Work Environment

Customer service representatives held about 2,187,300 jobs in 2010. Many customer service representatives work in telephone call or customer contact centers. Others work in insurance agencies, banks, stores, or other organizations that interact with customers.

Some work from home. Although the number of at-home agents is still relatively small, their numbers are growing.

The following industries employed the most customer service representatives in 2010:

Administrative and support services	15%
Retail trade	11
Credit intermediation and related activities	9
Wholesale trade	8
Insurance carriers	7

Customer contact center workers usually sit at a workstation with a telephone, headset, and computer. These centers may be crowded and noisy, and the work can be repetitive or stressful, with little time between calls.

Customer service representatives who work in retail stores may interact in person with customers.

Whether they interact by phone, chat, or in-person, customer service representatives may have to deal with difficult or angry customers, which can be challenging.

Customer service representatives provide information to customers and respond to questions and complaints.

Companies usually keep statistics on customer service representatives to make sure they are working efficiently. This helps them keep up with their call volume and ensure that customers do not have to wait on hold for a long time. However, this also may put pressure on customer service representatives to handle each call quickly. Supervisors may listen in on or tape calls to ensure that customers are getting quality service.

Work Schedules

Most customer service representatives work full time. About 1 in 5 worked part time or variable schedules in 2010.

Because many call or customer contact centers are open extended hours or are staffed around the clock, these positions may require workers to take on early morning, evening, or late night shifts. Weekend or holiday work is also common.

In retail stores, customer service representatives may have to work evenings and weekends as these are peak times for customer traffic in stores.

Because of the part-time possibilities, this occupation is well suited to people who want or need a flexible work schedule. Also, many companies hire additional employees at certain times of the year when higher call volumes are expected.

How to Become a Customer Service Representative

Customer service representatives typically have at least a high school diploma and are usually trained on the job. They must be good at communicating and interacting with people. They also need basic computer and phone skills.

Training

Customer service representatives are typically trained on the job. Training usually lasts about 2 to 3 weeks, although it can last as long as several months. This training generally focuses on the company and its products, customers' most commonly asked questions, and the computer and telephone systems the representatives will be using. New workers may handle easier questions or complaints and receive extra supervision and support. An increasing number of customer service representatives receive training in a classroom setting and also through shadowing another customer service representative.

Some customer service representatives are expected to update their training regularly. This is particularly true of workers in industries, such as banking, in which regulations and products are continually changing.

Education

Customer service representatives typically have at least a high school diploma. Some workers may need some college education or an associate's or bachelor's degree, as employers increasingly demand a more skilled workforce.

Licenses

Customer service representatives who answer questions about insurance or financial services often need a state license. Licensure requirements vary, but usually include passing a written exam. Some employers may provide training for these exams.

Important Qualities

Communication skills. Customer service representatives need strong listening and speaking skills to clearly and accurately respond to customer inquiries and concerns. They must listen carefully to customers to understand their needs and concerns to be able to resolve the call as efficiently and effectively as possible. Workers who interact with customers by email, live chat, or other non-voice contact channels must write well, using correct grammar, spelling, and punctuation.

Customer service skills. Customer service representatives must respond to questions and complaints in a friendly and professional manner.

Interpersonal skills. Customer service representatives interact with many different people. Creating and maintaining positive relationships is an essential part of a customer service representative's job.

Patience. Workers must be patient and polite, especially when dealing with difficult or angry customers.

Problem-solving skills. When addressing customer issues, customer service representatives need to analyze situations, investigate problems, and determine solutions.

Pay

Customer Service Representatives
Median hourly wages, May 2010

Total, All Occupations	$16.27
Office and Administrative Support Occupations	$14.77
Customer Service Representatives	$14.64

Note: All Occupations includes all occupations in the U.S. Economy.
Source: U.S. Bureau of Labor Statistics, Occupational Employment Statistics

The median hourly wage of customer service representatives was $14.64 in May 2010. The median wage is the wage at which half the workers in an occupation earned more than that amount and half earned less. The lowest 10 percent earned less than $9.40, and the top 10 percent earned more than $23.71.

The median hourly wages of customer service representatives in the industries employing the largest number of workers were as follows:

Wholesale trade	$16.48
Insurance carriers	16.41
Credit intermediation and related activities	14.53
Administrative and support services	12.66
Retail trade	11.49

Most customer service representatives work full time. About 1 in 5 worked part time or had variable schedules in 2010. Because many call or customer contact centers are open extended hours or are staffed around the clock, these positions may require workers to take on early morning, evening, or late night shifts. Weekend or holiday work is also common.

Job Outlook

Customer Service Representatives
Percent change in employment, projected 2010-20

Customer Service Representatives	15%
Total, All Occupations	14%
Office and Administrative Support Occupations	10%

Note: All Occupations includes all occupations in the U.S. Economy.
Source: U.S. Bureau of Labor Statistics, Employment Projections program

Employment of customer service representatives is projected to grow by 15 percent from 2010 to 2020, about as fast as the average for all occupations.

Providing quality customer service is important to nearly every company. In addition, because companies are expected to begin placing greater emphasis on customer relationships as a way to differentiate themselves from competitors, the need for customer service representatives is projected to increase.

Employment also will increase as consumers continue to demand products and services that require customer support. When a new product is introduced in the marketplace, additional customer service representatives will be needed to answer questions and resolve problems related to its use.

Technology has tempered growth of this occupation to some degree. For example, some technologies, such as Internet self-service or interactive voice-response systems, help customers get the assistance they need without having to interact with a representative. Routing of calls or emails to those representatives who are best able to respond to a specific inquiry will also help make workers more productive, thereby reducing the need for customer service representatives.

However, technology also creates new opportunities for job growth. For example, online banking might reduce the need for in-branch customer service representatives to handle banking tasks for account holders, but it also might increase the need for customer service representatives to help those account holders with using the web site.

The number of contacts with customers is expected to continue increasing, especially with the greater use of social media, live chat, or other means of communication. These increased communications will help spur demand for workers who interact with customers through these channels.

Customer service representatives are projected to grow 46 percent in telephone call centers, much faster than the average. This growth is due in part to industry growth, as many firms continue to hire call center firms that specialize in handling customer contacts.

Outsourcing, the practice in which companies shift call centers and customer service representatives to other countries, will also continue. However, new jobs will be created in the United States as well, as some companies recognize consumers' preferences for U.S.-based customer support.

Job Prospects

Job prospects for customer service representatives are expected to be good. Many job openings will arise from the need to replace workers who leave the occupation.

There will be greater competition for in-house customer service jobs—which often have higher pay and greater advancement potential—than for those jobs in the call center industry.

Employment projections data for customer service representatives, 2010-20

Occupational Title	SOC Code	Employment, 2010	Projected Employment, 2020	Change, 2010-20	
				Percent	Numeric
Customer Service Representatives	43-4051	2,187,300	2,525,600	15	338,400
SOURCE: U.S. Bureau of Labor Statistics, Employment Projections program					

Similar Occupations

This table shows a list of occupations with job duties that are similar to those of customer service representatives.

Occupation	Job Duties	Entry-Level Education	Median Annual Pay, May 2010
Bill and Account Collectors	Bill and account collectors, sometimes called collectors, try to recover payment on overdue bills. They negotiate repayment plans with debtors and help them find solutions to make paying their overdue bills easier.	High school diploma or equivalent	$31,310
Cashiers	Cashiers handle payments from customers purchasing goods and services.	Less than high school	$18,500
Computer Support Specialists	Computer support specialists provide help and advice to people and organizations using computer software or equipment. Some, called technical support specialists, support information technology (IT) employees within their organization. Others, called help-desk technicians, assist non-IT users who are having computer problems.	Some college, no degree	$46,260
Financial Clerks	Financial clerks do administrative work for banking, insurance, and other companies. They keep records, help customers, and carry out financial transactions.	High school diploma or equivalent	$33,710
Information Clerks	Information clerks provide administrative and clerical support in a variety of settings. They help maintain records, collect data and information, and respond to customers' questions or concerns.	See How to Become One	$29,990
Insurance Sales Agents	Insurance sales agents help insurance companies generate new business by contacting potential customers and selling one or more types of insurance. An agent explains various insurance policies and helps clients choose plans that suit them.	High school diploma or equivalent	$46,770
Retail Sales Workers	Retail sales workers include both those who sell retail merchandise, such as clothing, furniture, and automobiles, (called retail salespersons) and those who sell spare and replacement parts and equipment, especiallycar parts, (called parts salespersons). Both groups help customers find the products they want and process customers' payments.	Less than high school	$20,990
Securities, Commodities, and Financial Services Sales Agents	Securities, commodities, and financial services sales agents connect buyers and sellers in financial markets. They sell securities to individuals, advise companies in search of investors, and conduct trades.	Bachelor's degree	$70,190
Tellers	Tellers are responsible for accurately processing routine transactions at a bank. These transactions include cashing checks, depositing money, and collecting loan payments.	High school diploma or equivalent	$24,100

Wholesale and Manufacturing Sales Representatives	Wholesale and manufacturing sales representatives sell goods for wholesalers or manufacturers to businesses, government agencies, and other organizations. They contact customers, explain product features, answer any questions that their customers may have, and negotiate prices.	See How to Become One	$56,620

Contacts for More Information

The Handbook does not have Contacts for More Info for this occupation.

Suggested citation:

Bureau of Labor Statistics, U.S. Department of Labor, Occupational Outlook Handbook, 2012-13 Edition, Customer Service Representatives, on the Internet at http://www.bls.gov/ooh/office-and-administrative-support/customer-service-representatives.htm .

Desktop Publishers

Quick Facts: Desktop Publishers	
2010 Median Pay	$36,610 per year $17.60 per hour
Entry-Level Education	Associate's degree
Work Experience in a Related Occupation	None
On-the-job Training	Short-term on-the-job training
Number of Jobs, 2010	22,600
Job Outlook, 2010-20	-15% (Decline rapidly)
Employment Change, 2010-20	-3,300

What Desktop Publishers Do

Desktop publishers use computer software to design page layouts for newspapers, books, brochures, and other items to be printed or put online. They collect the text, graphics, and other materials they will need and format them into a finished product.

Duties

Desktop publishers typically do the following:

- Gather existing materials or work with designers and writers to create new artwork or text
- Find and edit graphics, such as photographs or illustrations
- Use scanners to turn drawings and other materials into digital images
- Import text and graphics into desktop publishing software programs
- Position artwork and text on the page layout
- Select formatting properties, such as text size, column width, and spacing
- Check proofs, or preliminary layouts, for errors and make corrections
- Convert files for printing or websites
- Send final files to a commercial printer or print the documents on a high-resolution printer

Desktop publishers use publishing software to create page layouts for print or web publication. Some desktop publishers may help to create web pages using Hypertext Markup Language (HTML), although this is usually the job of web designers. For more information on workers who design, create, and modify websites, see the profile on information security analysts, web developers, and computer network architects .

Desktop publishers work with other design and media professionals, such as writers, editors and graphic designers. For example, desktop publishers work with graphic designers to come up with images that complement the text and fit the available space.

In addition to designing pages, desktop publishers may edit or write text. Some desktop publishers might be responsible for correcting spelling, punctuation, and grammar or for writing original content themselves.

Desktop publishers' responsibilities may vary widely from project to project and employer to employer. Smaller firms typically use desktop publishers to perform a wide range of tasks, while desktop publishers at larger firms may specialize in one part of the publishing process.

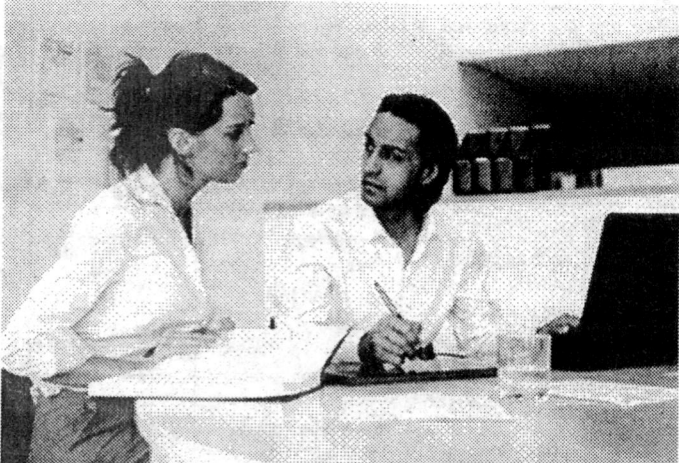

Desktop publishers use computer software to design layouts for books, newspapers, and other published items.

Work Environment

Desktop publishers held about 22,600 jobs in 2010. About half of them worked in the publishing and printing industries. Most of the rest worked for companies in other industries that produce their own printed materials, including advertising and public relations industries which are included in professional, scientific, and technical services.

The following industries employed the most desktop publishers in 2010:

Publishing industries (except Internet)	32%
Printing and related support activities	15
Administrative and support services	8
Professional, scientific, and technical services	8
Educational services; state, local, and private	4

Some desktop publishers are self-employed and work on a contract basis.

Work Schedules

Many desktop publishers work part time. They may need to work long hours to meet publication deadlines.

How to Become a Desktop Publisher

Desktop publishers have a variety of educational backgrounds, but most complete some form of postsecondary education, such as an associate's degree. Workers also usually learn some of their skills on the job. Computer skills, including knowledge of desktop publishing software, are important.

Education

Desktop publishers can prepare for the occupation in several ways. Many workers earn an associate's degree. Others earn a bachelor's degree. Still others qualify with a postsecondary non-degree award. Experience can sometimes substitute for education.

Those who earn a degree usually study a field such as graphic design, graphic arts, or graphic communications. Community colleges and trade and technical schools also may offer desktop publishing courses. These classes teach students about desktop publishing software used to format pages and how to import text and graphics into electronic page layouts.

Training

Desktop publishers often learn many of their skills on the job. They learn by observing more experienced workers or by taking classes that teach them how to use desktop publishing software. Ongoing training is often necessary, as technologies and desktop publishing software change.

Work Experience

Many employers prefer to hire workers who have experience in preparing layouts. This experience can sometimes substitute for formal education, such as a degree in graphic design.

Important Qualities

Artistic ability. Desktop publishers must have a good eye for how graphics and text will look to create pages that are visually appealing, legible, and easy to use.

Communication skills. Desktop publishers talk through different concepts for a page layout with writers, editors, and graphic designers. They listen to others' ideas and explain their own.

Computer skills. Desktop publishers use computer software extensively when creating page layouts and formatting text and graphics.

Detail oriented. When designing and reviewing page layouts, desktop publishers must pay careful attention to details such as

margins, font sizes, and the overall appearance and accuracy of their work.

Organizational skills. Desktop publishers often work under strict deadlines and must be good at scheduling and prioritizing tasks in order to have a document ready on time for publication.

Pay

Desktop Publishers
Median hourly wages, May 2010

Desktop Publishers	$17.60
Total, All Occupations	$16.27
Other Office and Administrative Support Workers	$13.35

Note: All Occupations includes all occupations in the U.S. Economy.
Source: U.S. Bureau of Labor Statistics, Occupational Employment Statistics

The median hourly wage of desktop publishers was $17.60 in May 2010. The median wage is the wage at which half the workers in an occupation earned more than that amount and half earned less. The lowest 10 percent earned less than $10.46, and the top 10 percent earned more than $28.52.

Many desktop publishers work part time. They may need to work long hours to meet publication deadlines.

Job Outlook

Desktop Publishers
Percent change in employment, projected 2010-20

Total, All Occupations	14%
Other Office and Administrative Support Workers	12%
Desktop Publishers	-15%

Note: All Occupations includes all occupations in the U.S. Economy.
Source: U.S. Bureau of Labor Statistics, Employment Projections program

Employment of desktop publishers is projected to decline by 15 percent from 2010 to 2020. Companies are expected to hire fewer desktop publishers as other types of workers—such as graphic designers, Web designers, and copy editors—increasingly take on desktop publishing tasks.

Desktop publishing is commonly used to design printed materials, such as advertisements, brochures, newsletters, and forms. However, increased computer-processing capacity and the widespread availability of more elaborate desktop publishing software will make it easier and more affordable for nonprinting professionals to create their own materials. As a result, there will be less need for people to specialize in desktop publishing.

Some of the tasks that desktop publishers do, such as creating initial page layouts or converting pages to PDF files, can now be automated, further reducing employment. And as companies increasingly look to save on costs, sending desktop publishing tasks to workers in other countries may increase.

Overall declines in the printing and publishing industries—those most likely to employ desktop publishers—will also restrict growth. As organizations increasingly publish their materials on the Internet instead of in print form, to save on printing and distribution costs, employment of desktop publishers may decline further.

Job Prospects

Prospects will be better for those with a degree in graphic design or a related field, or for those with experience in desktop publishing. Electronic and Web-publishing expertise are increasingly in demand. Workers with a diverse range of skills, such as in graphic design, Web design, writing, and editing may have better prospects.

Employment projections data for desktop publishers, 2010-20

Occupational Title	SOC Code	Employment, 2010	Projected Employment, 2020	Change, 2010-20	
				Percent	Numeric
Desktop Publishers	43-9031	22,600	19,200	-15	-3,300
SOURCE: U.S. Bureau of Labor Statistics, Employment Projections program					

Similar Occupations

This table shows a list of occupations with job duties that are similar to those of desktop publishers.

Occupation	Job Duties	Entry-Level Education	Median Annual Pay, May 2010
Editors	Editors plan, review, and revise content for publication.	Bachelor's degree	$51,470
Film and Video Editors and Camera Operators	Film and video editors and camera operators record images that entertain or inform an audience. Camera operators capture a wide range of material for TV shows, motion pictures, music videos, documentaries, or news and sporting events. Editors construct the final productions from the many different images camera operators capture. They collaborate with producers and directors to create the final production.	Bachelor's degree	$45,490
Graphic Designers	Graphic designers create visual concepts, by hand or using computer software, to communicate ideas that inspire, inform, or captivate consumers. They help to make an organization recognizable by selecting color, images, or logo designs that represent a particular idea or identity to be used in advertising and promotions.	Bachelor's degree	$43,500
Information Security Analysts, Web Developers, and Computer Network Architects	Information security analysts, web developers, and computer network architects all use information technology (IT) to advance their organization's goals. Security analysts ensure a firm's information stays safe from cyberattacks. Web developers create websites to help firms have a public face. Computer network architects create the internal networks all workers within organizations use.	Bachelor's degree	$75,660
Multimedia Artists and Animators	Multimedia artists and animators create animation and visual effects for television, movies, video games, and other media. They create two- and three-dimensional models and animation.	Bachelor's degree	$58,510
Printing Workers	Printing workers produce print material in three stages: prepress, press, and binding and finishing. They review specifications, identify and fix problems with printing equipment, and assemble pages.	See How to Become One	$33,150
Technical Writers	Technical writers, also called technical communicators, produce instruction manuals and other supporting documents to communicate complex and technical information more easily. They also develop, gather, and disseminate technical information among customers, designers, and manufacturers.	Bachelor's degree	$63,280

Contacts for More Information

For more information about the printing industry, visit Printing Industries of America , Society for Technical Communication

Suggested citation:

Bureau of Labor Statistics, U.S. Department of Labor, Occupational Outlook Handbook, 2012-13 Edition, Desktop Publishers, on the Internet at http://www.bls.gov/ooh/office-and-administrative-support/desktop-publishers.htm .

Financial Clerks

Quick Facts: Financial Clerks	
2010 Median Pay	$33,710 per year $16.21 per hour
Entry-Level Education	High school diploma or equivalent
Work Experience in a Related Occupation	None
On-the-job Training	See How to Become One
Number of Jobs, 2010	1,395,500
Job Outlook, 2010-20	11% (About as fast as average)
Employment Change, 2010-20	152,600

What Financial Clerks Do

Financial clerks do administrative work for banking, insurance, and other companies. They keep records, help customers, and carry out financial transactions.

Duties

Financial clerks typically do the following:

- Keep and update financial records
- Compute bills and charges
- Offer customer assistance
- Carry out financial transactions

Financial clerks give administrative and clerical support in financial settings. Their specific job duties vary by specialty and by setting.

Billing and posting clerks calculate charges, develop bills, and prepare them to be mailed to customers. They review documents such as purchase orders, sales tickets, charge slips, and hospital records to compute fees or charges due. They also contact customers to get or give account information.

Gaming cage workers work in casinos and other gaming establishments. The "cage" in which they work is the central depository for money and gaming chips. Gaming cage workers sell gambling chips, tokens, or tickets to patrons. They count funds and reconcile daily summaries of transactions to balance books.

Payroll and timekeeping clerks compile and post employee time and payroll data. They verify and record attendance, hours worked, and pay adjustments. They ensure that employees are paid on time and that their paychecks are accurate.

Procurement clerks compile requests for materials, prepare purchase orders, keep track of purchases and supplies, and handle questions about orders. They respond to questions from customers and suppliers about the status of orders. They handle requests to change or cancel orders. They make sure that purchases arrive on schedule and that they meet the purchaser's specifications.

Brokerage clerks help with tasks about securities such as stocks, bonds, commodities, and other kinds of investments. Their duties include writing orders for stock purchases and sales, computing transfer taxes, verifying stock transactions, accepting and delivering securities, distributing dividends, and keeping records of daily transactions and holdings.

Credit authorizers, checkers, and clerks review the credit history and get the information needed to determine the creditworthiness of individuals or businesses applying for credit. Credit authorizers evaluate customers' computerized credit records and payment histories to decide, based on predetermined standards, whether to approve new credit. Credit checkers call or write credit departments of business and service establishments to get information about applicants' credit standing.

Loan interviewers, also called loan processors or loan clerks, interview applicants and others to get and verify personal and financial information needed to complete loan applications. They also prepare the documents that go to the appraiser and are issued at the closing of a loan.

New accounts clerks interview people who want to open accounts in financial institutions. They explain the account services available to prospective customers and help them fill out applications. They also investigate and correct errors in accounts.

Insurance claims and policy processing clerks process applications for insurance policies. They also handle customers' requests to change or cancel their existing policies. Their duties include interviewing clients and reviewing insurance applications to ensure that all questions have been answered. They also notify insurance agents and accounting departments of policy cancellations or changes.

Work Environment

Financial clerks held about 1.4 million jobs in 2010.

Financial clerks work in a variety of office settings, including bank branches, medical offices, and government agencies. Financial clerks were employed primarily in the following industries in 2010:

Financial clerks provide customer service and maintain financial records.

Credit intermediation and related activities	18%
Insurance carriers and related activities	18
Ambulatory health care services	11
Professional, scientific, and technical services	7

Work Schedules

Most financial clerks work full time. However, about 16 percent of billing and posting clerks worked part time in 2010.

How to Become a Financial Clerk

A high school diploma is enough for most jobs as a financial clerk. These workers usually learn their duties through on-the-job training.

Education

Financial clerks typically need a high school diploma to enter the occupation. Employers of brokerage clerks may prefer candidates with a 2- or 4-year college degree in business or economics.

Training

Most financial clerks learn how to do their job duties through on-the-job training. The length of this training varies, but typically lasts less than 1 month. Under the guidance of a supervisor or another senior worker, new employees learn company procedures. Some formal technical training also may be necessary; for example, gaming cage workers may need training in specific gaming regulations and procedures.

Important Qualities

Basic math skills. The job duties of financial clerks, including calculating charges and checking credit scores, require basic math skills.

Communication skills. Financial clerks should have good communication skills so that they can explain policies and procedures to colleagues and customers.

Organizational skills. Strong organizational skills are important for financial clerks because they must be able to find files quickly and efficiently.

Pay

Financial Clerks
Median annual wages, May 2010

Total, All Occupations	$33,840
Financial Clerks	$33,710
Office and Administrative Support Occupations	$30,710

Note: All Occupations includes all occupations in the U.S. Economy.
Source: U.S. Bureau of Labor Statistics, Occupational Employment Statistics

The median annual wage of financial clerks was $33,710 in May 2010. The median wage is the wage at which half the workers in an occupation earned more than that amount and half earned less. The lowest 10 percent earned less than $22,920, and the top 10 percent earned more than $49,500.

The median annual wages for financial clerk occupations in May 2010 were as follows:

- $40,160 for brokerage clerks
- $36,790 for procurement clerks
- $36,330 for payroll and timekeeping clerks
- $34,760 for insurance claims- and policy-processing clerks

- $33,970 for loan interviewers and clerks
- $32,490 for credit authorizers, checkers, and clerks
- $32,170 for billing and posting clerks
- $30,440 for new-accounts clerks
- $25,690 for gaming cage workers

Most financial clerks work full time. However, about 16 percent of billing and posting clerks worked part time in 2010.

Job Outlook

Financial Clerks
Percent change in employment, projected 2010-20

Total, All Occupations	14%
Financial Clerks	11%
Office and Administrative Support Occupations	10%

Note: All Occupations includes all occupations in the U.S. Economy.
Source: U.S. Bureau of Labor Statistics, Employment Projections program

Overall, employment of financial clerks is expected to grow by 11 percent from 2010 to 2010, about as fast as the average for all occupations. Projected employment change will vary by specialty as follows:

- Employment of billing and posting clerks is projected to grow 20 percent. Job growth will be particularly strong for those in medical billing because increased demand for healthcare services will require more of these workers.
- Employment of payroll and timekeeping clerks is projected to grow 15 percent. Although payroll and timekeeping functions continue to be important for companies, the automation of this work and the use of computer software that allows employees to update and record their own payroll and timekeeping information will limit the growth of this occupation.
- Employment of insurance claims- and policy-processing clerks is projected to grow 9 percent. These workers are heavily concentrated in the insurance industry; therefore, their job growth will be determined mainly by the performance of the insurance industry as a whole.
- Employment of procurement clerks is projected to grow 6 percent. The need for procurement clerks will be limited as a result of the increasing use of computers to place orders over the Internet.
- Employment of brokerage clerks is projected to grow 6 percent. The automation of securities transactions will lead to slower growth for these workers.
- Employment of credit authorizers, checkers, and clerks is projected to grow 5 percent. The availability of online credit reports will reduce the need for these workers, leading to slower growth.
- Employment of new accounts clerks is projected to grow 2 percent. Although some of these workers' duties have been automated, the workers will still be needed to perform customer service.
- Employment of loan interviewers and clerks is projected to decline 3 percent. The use of online loan applications will reduce the need for these workers to conduct in-person interviews.
- Employment of gaming cage workers is projected to decline 13 percent. Fewer of these workers will be needed in casinos and other gaming establishments because transactions are becoming increasingly self-service.

Job Prospects

Job prospects for financial clerks should be favorable, because many workers are expected to leave this occupation. Employers will need to hire new workers to replace those leaving the occupation.

Employment projections data for financial clerks, 2010-20

Occupational Title	SOC Code	Employment, 2010	Projected Employment, 2020	Change, 2010-20	
				Percent	Numeric
Financial Clerks	—	1,395,500	1,548,100	11	152,600
Billing and Posting Clerks	43-3021	504,800	604,400	20	99,600
Gaming Cage Workers	43-3041	15,900	13,900	-13	-2,000
Payroll and Timekeeping Clerks	43-3051	187,000	214,300	15	27,300
Procurement Clerks	43-3061	76,900	81,300	6	4,400
Brokerage Clerks	43-4011	58,000	61,400	6	3,400
Credit Authorizers, Checkers, and Clerks	43-4041	54,300	56,900	5	2,600
Loan Interviewers and Clerks	43-4131	182,500	176,800	-3	-5,700
New Accounts Clerks	43-4141	68,000	69,400	2	1,400
Insurance Claims and Policy Processing Clerks	43-9041	248,100	269,700	9	21,600

SOURCE: U.S. Bureau of Labor Statistics, Employment Projections program

Similar Occupations

This table shows a list of occupations with job duties that are similar to those of financial clerks.

Occupation	Job Duties	Entry-Level Education	Median Annual Pay, May 2010
Bill and Account Collectors	Bill and account collectors, sometimes called collectors, try to recover payment on overdue bills. They negotiate repayment plans with debtors and help them find solutions to make paying their overdue bills easier.	High school diploma or equivalent	$31,310
Bookkeeping, Accounting, and Auditing Clerks	Bookkeeping, accounting, and auditing clerks produce financial records for organizations. They record financial transactions, update statements, and check financial records for accuracy.	High school diploma or equivalent	$34,030
Gaming Services Occupations	Gaming services workers serve customers in gambling establishments, such as casinos or racetracks. Some workers tend slot machines or deal cards. Others take bets or pay out winnings. Still others supervise gaming workers and operations.	See How to Become One	$20,260
Information Clerks	Information clerks provide administrative and clerical support in a variety of settings. They help maintain records, collect data and information, and respond to customers' questions or concerns.	See How to Become One	$29,990
Tellers	Tellers are responsible for accurately processing routine transactions at a bank. These transactions include cashing checks, depositing money, and collecting loan payments.	High school diploma or equivalent	$24,100

Contacts for More Information

For more information about financial clerks, visit American Bankers Association , Insurance Information Institute , Mortgage Bankers Association

Suggested citation:

Bureau of Labor Statistics, U.S. Department of Labor, Occupational Outlook Handbook, 2012-13 Edition, Financial Clerks, on the Internet at http://www.bls.gov/ooh/ office-and-administrative-support/financial-clerks.htm .

General Office Clerks

Quick Facts: General Office Clerks	
2010 Median Pay	$26,610 per year $12.79 per hour
Entry-Level Education	High school diploma or equivalent
Work Experience in a Related Occupation	None
On-the-job Training	Short-term on-the-job training
Number of Jobs, 2010	2,950,700
Job Outlook, 2010-20	17% (About as fast as average)
Employment Change, 2010-20	489,500

What General Office Clerks Do

General office clerks do a broad range of administrative tasks, including answering telephones, typing or word processing, and filing. However, tasks vary widely in different jobs.

Duties

General office clerks typically do the following:

- Use office equipment, such as fax machines and photocopiers
- Answer telephones
- Update and maintain office filing, inventory, mailing, and database systems
- Respond to questions and provide information
- Type, format, proofread, and edit correspondence and other documents
- Handle incoming and outgoing mail
- Manage schedules and calendars and arrange appointments
- Run errands
- Order materials, supplies, and services
- Keep records of business transactions and other office activities

Rather than doing a single specialized task, general office clerks have responsibilities that often change daily with the needs of the specific job and the employer. Some clerks spend their time filing or answering the phone. Others enter data into computers. They also operate photocopiers, fax machines, and other office equipment; prepare mailings; proofread documents; and deliver messages. Some may sort checks, keep payroll records, and take inventory.

The specific duties assigned to clerks can vary significantly, depending on the type of office in which they work. For example, a general office clerk at a college or university might process application materials or answer questions from prospective students. A clerk at a hospital might file and retrieve medical records.

Clerks' duties also vary by level of experience. Inexperienced employees may make photocopies, stuff envelopes, and take phone messages. Experienced clerks usually get additional responsibilities. For example, they may maintain financial records, set up spreadsheets, make sure statistical reports are accurate, handle customer complaints, arrange purchases with vendors, make travel arrangements, take inventory of equipment and supplies, answer questions on departmental services and functions, and help prepare invoices or budgets.

Senior office clerks also may be expected to monitor and direct the work of lower level clerks.

Work Environment

General office clerks held about 3 million jobs in 2010.

General office clerks work in many places. Some of the largest employers are schools, healthcare facilities, and federal, state, and local governments.

The table below shows the industries employing the most general office clerks in 2010.

Educational services; state, local, and private	13%
Health care and social assistance	13
Government	10
Administrative and support services	8

General office clerks usually work in comfortable office settings.

Work Schedules

Most general office clerks work full time, although 1 in 4 clerks worked part time in 2010. Many clerks also work in temporary positions.

How to Become a General Office Clerk

General office clerks usually need a high school diploma or General Educational Development (GED) credential. Workers often learn their skills on the job.

Education

Most general office clerks have a high school diploma or GED.

Business education programs offered in high schools, community and junior colleges, and postsecondary vocational schools can help people prepare for an entry-level job as a general office clerk. Courses in office practices, word processing, and other computer applications are particularly helpful.

General office clerks perform a variety of administrative tasks, like photocopying.

Training

General office clerks often learn their skills on the job. On-the-job training typically lasts up to 1 month and may include guidance on how to use office systems or equipment.

Advancement

After gaining some work experience or specialized skills, many workers transfer to jobs with higher pay or greater advancement potential. Some may move into other administrative jobs, such as receptionists and secretaries and administrative assistants. For more information, see the profiles on receptionists and secretaries and administrative assistants .

General office clerks who exhibit strong communication, interpersonal, and analytical skills may be promoted to supervisory positions. However, advancement to professional occupations within an organization often requires additional formal education, such as a college degree.

Important Qualities

Communication skills. General office clerks must understand and communicate information effectively when interacting with others in person, by phone, or in writing.

Computer skills. Word processing and other basic computer skills help office clerks do many of their tasks. Because organizations frequently keep files and records on computers, some office clerks also use and maintain computer databases.

Customer service skills. Office clerks respond to questions and provide information to a wide variety of people, ranging from coworkers to the public.

Detail oriented. Many administrative tasks, such a proofreading documents and arranging schedules, require excellent attention to detail.

Interpersonal skills. Good people skills are important because office clerks often work closely with others in their office, as well as with people from outside the office.

Organizational skills. Being organized helps office clerks find files and other important information quickly and efficiently. General office clerks should be able to decide which tasks are most important and manage their time efficiently.

Pay

General Office Clerks
Median hourly wages, May 2010

Total, All Occupations	$16.27
Other Office and Administrative Support Workers	$13.35
General Office Clerks	$12.79

Note: All Occupations includes all occupations in the U.S. Economy.
Source: U.S. Bureau of Labor Statistics, Occupational Employment Statistics

The median hourly wage of general office clerks was $12.79 in May 2010. The median wage is the wage at which half the workers in an occupation earned more than that amount and half earned less. The lowest 10 percent earned less than $8.31, and the top 10 percent earned more than $20.12.

The median hourly wages of general office clerks in the industries employing the most of this occupation were as follows:

Government	$14.82
Health care and social assistance	12.80
Educational services; state, local, and private	12.75
Administrative and support services	12.06

Most general office clerks work full time, although 1 in 4 clerks worked part time in 2010. Many clerks also work in temporary positions.

Job Outlook

General Office Clerks
Percent change in employment, projected 2010-20

General Office Clerks	17%
Total, All Occupations	14%
Other Office and Administrative Support Workers	12%

Note: All Occupations includes all occupations in the U.S. Economy.
Source: U.S. Bureau of Labor Statistics, Employment Projections program

Employment of general office clerks is projected to grow by 17 percent from 2010 to 2020, about as fast as the average for all occupations.

Employment will grow as organizations increasingly hire administrative support workers who can do a variety of tasks rather than a single, specialized task.

However, growth will be moderated as technology makes these workers more productive and reduces the need for general office clerks. For example, some organizations are going paperless or using automated phone systems, which can decrease demand for general office clerks who file papers or answer phones.

In addition, other support workers may increasingly do tasks that general office clerks used to do, further reducing growth in this occupation.

Employment growth of general office clerks will vary by industry. Healthcare, for example, is expected to add many new jobs, and as it does, jobs for general office clerks will increase. The federal government, on the other hand, is projected to have employment declines.

The job outlook for general office clerks also may depend on the state of the economy. Employers who are reducing their staff often cut general office clerk jobs. But, as organizations cut back on administrative staff, they may increase employment of general office clerks because these workers can cover several administrative support functions.

Job Prospects

Job prospects are expected to be good in this large occupation. Workers will be needed to fill new jobs and replace those who leave the occupation. General office clerks who can learn new skills and adapt to changing technologies will have the best prospects.

Employment projections data for general office clerks, 2010-20

Occupational Title	SOC Code	Employment, 2010	Projected Employment, 2020	Change, 2010-20 Percent	Numeric
Office Clerks, General	43-9061	2,950,700	3,440,200	17	489,500
SOURCE: U.S. Bureau of Labor Statistics, Employment Projections program					

Similar Occupations

This table shows a list of occupations with job duties that are similar to those of general office clerks.

Occupation	Job Duties	Entry-Level Education	Median Annual Pay, May 2010
Bookkeeping, Accounting, and Auditing Clerks	Bookkeeping, accounting, and auditing clerks produce financial records for organizations. They record financial transactions, update statements, and check financial records for accuracy.	High school diploma or equivalent	$34,030
Customer Service Representatives	Customer service representatives interact with customers on behalf of an organization. They provide information about products and services and respond to customer complaints. Some also take orders and process returns.	High school diploma or equivalent	$30,460
Information Clerks	Information clerks provide administrative and clerical support in a variety of settings. They help maintain records, collect data and information, and respond to customers' questions or concerns.	See How to Become One	$29,990
Material Recording Clerks	Material recording clerks keep track of information to keep businesses and supply chains on schedule. They ensure proper scheduling, recordkeeping, and inventory control.	See How to Become One	$24,100
Receptionists	Receptionists perform various administrative tasks, including answering telephones and giving information to the public and customers.	High school diploma or equivalent	$25,240
Secretaries and Administrative Assistants	Secretaries and administrative assistants perform routine clerical and organizational tasks. They organize files, draft messages, schedule appointments, and support other staff.	High school diploma or equivalent	$34,660
Tellers	Tellers are responsible for accurately processing routine transactions at a bank. These transactions include cashing checks, depositing money, and collecting loan payments.	High school diploma or equivalent	$24,100

Contacts for More Information

For more information about administrative occupations, visit
International Association of Administrative Professionals

Suggested citation:

Bureau of Labor Statistics, U.S. Department of Labor, Occupational Outlook Handbook, 2012-13 Edition, General Office Clerks, on the Internet at http://www.bls.gov/ooh/office-and-administrative-support/general-office-clerks.htm .

Information Clerks

Quick Facts: Information Clerks	
2010 Median Pay	$29,990 per year $14.42 per hour
Entry-Level Education	See How to Become One
Work Experience in a Related Occupation	None
On-the-job Training	See How to Become One
Number of Jobs, 2010	1,605,300
Job Outlook, 2010-20	7% (Slower than average)
Employment Change, 2010-20	108,900

What Information Clerks Do

Information clerks provide administrative and clerical support in a variety of settings. They help maintain records, collect data and information, and respond to customers' questions or concerns.

Duties

Information clerks typically do the following:

- Keep records and information
- Help colleagues and customers with routine administrative work
- Prepare and locate records and information that colleagues and customers need
- Ensure that colleagues and customers follow proper procedures

Information clerks generally manage a particular kind of information or record. Some clerks work in a particular setting.

Correspondence clerks review and respond to inquiries from the public, other businesses, or other departments. They gather information and data so that they can give accurate answers to questions and requests. Correspondence clerks write letters or email in reply to requests for merchandise, damage claims, credit and other information, delinquent accounts, incorrect billings, or unsatisfactory services. They may have to gather data before replying.

Court clerks organize and maintain the records of the court for which they work. They prepare the calendar of cases, also known as a docket, and tell attorneys and witnesses when they need to appear in court. Court clerks put together materials for court proceedings and prepare, file, and forward case files. They also keep records of, and answer inquiries about, court proceedings.

Eligibility interviewers do interviews both in person and over the phone to determine if applicants qualify for government assistance and resources. They answer applicants' questions about benefits and programs and refer them to other agencies or programs when their own agency cannot help.

File clerks keep companies' and organizations' paper or electronic records. They enter data into, organize, and retrieve files. In organizations with electronic filing systems, file clerks scan and upload documents.

Hotel, motel, and resort desk clerks provide customer service to guests, often at the facility's front desk. They check guests in and out, assign rooms, and verify guests' method of payment. They also keep records about which rooms are occupied and take reservations. These clerks answer guests' questions and respond to their concerns. For example, they may give guests directions or send housekeeping staff to their room if it is not clean.

Human resources assistants provide administrative support to human resource departments. They keep personnel records, collecting information about employees, such as their addresses, employment history, and performance evaluations. They post information about job openings and review the resumes and applications of candidates for employment to ensure that they are eligible for the positions for which they have applied.

Interviewers do interviews over the phone, in person, through the mail, or electronically. They use the information they get to complete forms, applications, or questionnaires for market research surveys, Census forms, and medical histories. Interviewers are usually given specific instructions about what questions to ask and what information to collect. They compile and record information from their interviews.

License clerks help the public with applications for licenses and permits. They process applications and collect application fees. They determine if applicants are qualified to receive the particular license or permit. They keep records of applications received and licenses issued. License clerks keep applicants informed about the status of their application and notify them if they need to provide additional

Information clerks assist with maintaining records, collecting data and information, and responding to customers' questions or concerns.

information.

Municipal clerks provide administrative support to town and city governments. They keep minutes of town and city council meetings and then distribute the minutes to local officials and staff. Municipal clerks help prepare for elections by creating ballots and training election officials. They respond to requests for information from the public, local and state officials, and state and federal legislators. Municipal clerks also maintain town and city records.

Order clerks receive orders from customers and enter the information into their company's order entry system. They also answer customers' questions about prices and shipping. Order clerks collect information about customers, such as their address and method of payment, to put into the order entry system.

Reservation and transportation ticket agents and travel clerks take and confirm passengers' reservations for hotels and transportation. They also sell and issue tickets and answer questions about itineraries, rates, and package tours. These clerks prepare invoices outlining rates and fees and accept payment from passengers. They may check baggage and assign boarding passes to passengers.

Work Environment

Information clerks held about 1.6 million jobs in 2010.
Information clerks are employed throughout the economy. Some of the places they work include medical offices, government agencies, law offices, and private businesses.

Work Schedules

Most information clerks work full time. However, part-time work is common for hotel, motel, and resort clerks, for file clerks, and for interviewers.

How to Become an Information Clerk

A high school diploma is enough for most positions, but some employers prefer workers who have some education beyond high school.

Education

A high school diploma is generally enough for most positions as an information clerk. However, some employers prefer to hire candidates who have some college education or an associate's or higher degree.

Training

Most information clerks are trained on the job in the policies and procedures of the business or government agency that employs them. Some types of information clerks, such as those who work for government agencies, may have to go through longer periods of training.

Important Qualities

Communication skills. Information clerks must be able to explain policies and procedures clearly to colleagues and customers.

Computer skills. Many organizations maintain files and records on computers. Therefore, information clerks must be comfortable working with computer databases.

Discretion. Information clerks, particularly human resources assistants, have access to confidential information, and they need to be able to keep this information private.

Organizational skills. Information clerks manage files, applications, and correspondences, so they need to have good organizational skills to find files quickly and efficiently.

People skills. Many information clerks interact with others regularly in person or on the phone. They must be able to work effectively with others to get the information they need and to understand and satisfy the needs of others.

Pay

Information Clerks
Median annual wages, May 2010

Total, All Occupations	$33,840
Office and Administrative Support Occupations	$30,710
Information Clerks	$29,990

Note: All Occupations includes all occupations in the U.S. Economy.
Source: U.S. Bureau of Labor Statistics, Occupational Employment Statistics

The median annual wage of information clerks was $29,990 in May 2010. The median wage is the wage at which half the workers in an occupation earned more than that amount and half earned less. The lowest 10 percent earned less than $18,210, and the top 10 percent earned more than $47,700.

The median wages for information clerks in May 2010 were the following:
- $39,960 for eligibility clerks
- $36,800 for human resources assistants
- $34,390 for court, municipal, and license clerks
- $33,410 for correspondence clerks
- $31,740 for reservation and transportation ticket agents and travel clerks
- $28,820 for interviewers
- $28,710 for order clerks
- $25,090 for file clerks
- $19,930 for hotel, motel, and resort desk clerks
- $37,010 for all other information and record clerks

Most information clerks work full time. However, part-time work is common for hotel, motel, and resort clerks, for file clerks, and for interviewers.

Job Outlook

Information Clerks
Percent change in employment, projected 2010-20

Total, All Occupations	14%
Office and Administrative Support Occupations	10%
Information Clerks	7%

Note: All Occupations includes all occupations in the U.S. Economy.
Source: U.S. Bureau of Labor Statistics, Employment Projections program

Employment of information clerks is expected to grow by 7 percent from 2010 to 2020, slower than the average for all occupations. However, employment growth will vary by specialty. Projected employment change for specific types of information clerks from 2010 to 2020 is as follows:
- Employment of interviewers is projected to grow by 17 percent. Rapid growth in the healthcare and market research industries that employ most of these workers will generate jobs for interviewers. However, the expanding use of online surveys and questionnaires for market research, as well as the increasing use of digital health records, is expected to limit growth.
- Employment of human resources assistants is expected to grow by 11 percent. Because more offices are moving toward electronic methods of recordkeeping, demand for these workers, who help maintain personnel records, will decrease.
- Employment of hotel, motel, and resort desk clerks: is projected to grow by 11 percent. As developers open new hotels, the number of jobs for hotel, motel, and resort desk clerks should increase. In addition, jobs should be created through demand from consumers who begin traveling again as the economy recovers from the 2007-09 recession.
- Employment of court, municipal, and license clerks is expected grow by 8 percent. Growth is expected because of increases in demand for government and court services. As more citizens seek

licenses and other municipal records, towns, cities, and courts will need to hire more clerks to handle their requests.

- Employment of order clerks is projected to grow by 7 percent. Improvements to technology have decreased the need for these workers. As more consumers buy online, demand for order clerks will continue to decline.
- Employment of reservation and transportation ticket agents and travel clerks is expected to grow by 6 percent. Increased use of online reservations systems and self-service ticketing machines will reduce the number of people needed to provide the services these workers offer.
- Employment of eligibility interviewers is projected to grow by 3 percent. The increase in the number of baby boomers retiring and becoming eligible for Social Security and other government entitlement programs will be the main cause of growth in this

occupation. However, automation should reduce employment growth for some eligibility interviewers as more government programs allow people to apply for assistance online.
- Employment of file clerks is expected to decline by 5 percent. Declines are expected as businesses, including doctors' offices, increasingly convert to electronic recordkeeping systems. As a result, fewer file clerks will be needed to maintain and organize files. In addition, duties that file clerks used to do will increasingly be done by other workers.
- Employment of correspondence clerks is projected to decline by 12 percent. As duties previously handled by correspondence clerks are increasingly given to other workers, such as administrative assistants, fewer jobs will be available for correspondence clerks.
- Employment of all other information and recordkeeping clerks is expected to grow by 1 percent.

Employment projections data for information clerks, 2010-20

Occupational Title	SOC Code	Employment, 2010	Projected Employment, 2020	Change, 2010-20 Percent	Change, 2010-20 Numeric
Information Clerks	—	1,605,300	1,714,300	7	108,900
Correspondence Clerks	43-4021	10,200	9,000	-12	-1,200
Court, Municipal, and License Clerks	43-4031	129,500	139,900	8	10,400
Eligibility Interviewers, Government Programs	43-4061	125,700	129,600	3	3,900
File Clerks	43-4071	185,000	176,200	-5	-8,800
Hotel, Motel, and Resort Desk Clerks	43-4081	227,500	252,700	11	25,200
Interviewers, Except Eligibility and Loan	43-4111	213,500	250,400	17	36,900
Order Clerks	43-4151	212,100	227,900	7	15,700
Human Resources Assistants, Except Payroll and Timekeeping	43-4161	156,900	174,500	11	17,600
Reservation and Transportation Ticket Agents and Travel Clerks	43-4181	124,300	131,500	6	7,200
Information and Record Clerks, All Other	43-4199	220,600	222,700	1	2,100

SOURCE: U.S. Bureau of Labor Statistics, Employment Projections program

Similar Occupations

This table shows a list of occupations with job duties that are similar to those of information clerks.

Occupation	Job Duties	Entry-Level Education	Median Annual Pay, May 2010
Bookkeeping, Accounting, and Auditing Clerks	Bookkeeping, accounting, and auditing clerks produce financial records for organizations. They record financial transactions, update statements, and check financial records for accuracy.	High school diploma or equivalent	$34,030
Compensation and Benefits Managers	Compensation managers plan, direct, and coordinate how and how much an organization pays its employees. Benefits managers do the same for retirement plans, health insurance, and other benefits an organization offers its employees.	Bachelor's degree	$89,270
Financial Clerks	Financial clerks do administrative work for banking, insurance, and other companies. They keep records, help customers, and carry out financial transactions.	High school diploma or equivalent	$33,710
General Office Clerks	General office clerks do a broad range of administrative tasks, including answering telephones, typing or word processing, and filing. However, tasks vary widely in different jobs.	High school diploma or equivalent	$26,610
Human Resources Managers	Human resources managers plan, direct, and coordinate the administrative functions of an organization. They oversee the recruiting, interviewing, and hiring of new staff; consult with top executives on strategic planning; and serve as a link between an organization's management and its employees.	Bachelor's degree	$99,180
Human Resources Specialists	Human resources specialists recruit, screen, interview, and place workers. They also may handle human resources work in a variety of other areas, such as employee relations, payroll and benefits, and training.	Bachelor's degree	$52,690

Lodging Managers	Lodging managers make sure that guests on vacation or business travel have a pleasant experience, while also ensuring that an establishment is run efficiently and profitably.	High school diploma or equivalent	$46,880
Material Recording Clerks	Material recording clerks keep track of information to keep businesses and supply chains on schedule. They ensure proper scheduling, recordkeeping, and inventory control.	See How to Become One	$24,100
Receptionists	Receptionists perform various administrative tasks, including answering telephones and giving information to the public and customers.	High school diploma or equivalent	$25,240
Training and Development Managers	Training and development managers plan, direct, and coordinate programs to enhance the knowledge and skills of an organization's employees. They also oversee a staff of training and development specialists.	Bachelor's degree	$89,170

Contacts for More Information

For more information about hotel, motel and resort desk clerks, visit American Hotel & Lodging Association

For more information about human resources assistants, visit Society for Human Resource Management

Suggested citation:

Bureau of Labor Statistics, U.S. Department of Labor, Occupational Outlook Handbook, 2012-13 Edition, Information Clerks, on the Internet at http://www.bls.gov/ooh/office-and-administrative-support/information-clerks.htm .

Material Recording Clerks

Quick Facts: Material Recording Clerks	
2010 Median Pay	$24,100 per year $11.59 per hour
Entry-Level Education	See How to Become One
Work Experience in a Related Occupation	None
On-the-Job Training	See How to Become One
Number of Jobs, 2010	2,812,900
Job Outlook, 2010-20	2% (Little or no change)
Employment Change, 2010-20	48,700

What Material Recording Clerks Do

Material recording clerks keep track of information to keep businesses and supply chains on schedule. They ensure proper scheduling, recordkeeping, and inventory control.

Duties

Material recording clerks typically do the following:

- Keep records of items shipped, received, or transferred to another location
- Compile reports on various aspects of changes in production or inventory
- Find, sort, or move goods between different parts of the business
- Check records for accuracy

As warehouses increase their use of automation and computers, clerks will become more adept at using technology. Many clerks use tablets or hand-held computers to keep track of inventory. New sensors and tags enable these computers to automatically detect when and where products are moved, making clerks' jobs more efficient.

Production, planning, and expediting clerks ease the flow of information, work, and materials within or among offices in a business. They compile reports on the progress of work and on any production problems that arise. These clerks set workers' schedules, estimate costs, keep track of materials, and write special orders for new materials. Expediting clerks are in contact with vendors to ensure that supplies and equipment are shipped on time. They also may inspect the quality of products.

Shipping, receiving, and traffic clerks keep track of and record

all outgoing and incoming shipments and ensure that they have been filled correctly. Many of these clerks scan barcodes with hand-held devices or use radiofrequency identification (RFID) scanners to keep track of inventory. They also compute freight costs and prepare invoices for other parts of the organization. Some of these clerks move goods from the warehouse to the loading dock.

Stock clerks and order fillers receive, unpack, and track merchandise. They retrieve customer orders and transport products from a warehouse to shelves in stores. They keep a record of all items that enter or leave the stockroom and inspect for damaged goods. These clerks also use hand-held scanners to keep track of merchandise.

Material and product inspectors weigh, measure, check sample, and keep accurate records on materials, supplies, and other equipment that enters a warehouse. They verify the quantity and quality of items they are assigned, checking for defects and recording what they find. To gather information, they use scales, counting devices, and calculators. Some clerks also prepare reports on warehouse inventory levels.

Work Environment

Most material recording clerks spend significant time in warehouses.

Shipping, receiving, and traffic clerks; production, planning, and expediting clerks; and material inspectors usually work in an office inside a warehouse or manufacturing plant.

Production clerks spend more of their time in their office on the computer or phone, setting up schedules or writing production reports.

Although shipping clerks and material inspectors prepare reports in an office, too, they also spend time in the warehouse, where they

Some clerks take inventory by counting items in a store.

sometimes handle packages or automatic equipment such as conveyor systems.

Stock clerks and order fillers usually work in retail settings and sometimes help customers. They move items from the back room to the store's shelves, a job that can involve frequent bending and lifting. However, automated devices usually transport heavy items.

Production, planning, and expediting clerks held about 271,000 jobs in 2010, most commonly in the following industries:

Manufacturing	37%
Wholesale trade	9
Transportation and warehousing	6

Shipping, receiving, and traffic clerks held about 687,600 jobs in 2010, most commonly in the following industries:

Manufacturing	26%
Wholesale trade	22
Retail trade	22
Transportation and warehousing	14

Stock clerks and order fillers held about 1.8 million jobs in 2010, most commonly in the following industries:

Grocery stores	23%
Department stores	18
Other general merchandise stores	12

Material and product inspectors held about 66,900 jobs in 2010, most commonly in the following industries:

Administrative and support services	20%
Manufacturing	20
Wholesale trade	18

Work Schedules

Production, planning, and expediting clerks; shipping, receiving, and traffic clerks; and material inspectors usually work full time. Many have standard Monday-through-Friday shifts, although some work nights and weekends or holidays when large shipments arrive.

About one-third of stock clerks and order fillers are part-time employees. Evening and weekend work is common because these clerks work when retail stores are open. They sometimes work overnight shifts when large shipments arrive or it is time to take inventory.

How to Become a Material Recording Clerk

Most workers are trained on the job in 1 to 6 months and must usually have a high school diploma.

Education

Most material recording clerks must have a high school diploma or equivalent. Production, planning, and expediting clerks need to have some basic computer skills. Candidates who have taken some business classes may be given preference over those who haven't.

Stock clerks and order fillers generally are not required to have a high school diploma.

Training

Material recording clerks usually learn their work on the job. Training for stock clerks and material inspectors may last less than a month. For shipping and production clerks, it can take up to 6 months. The more complex automatic equipment and sensors that are used in warehouses, the longer on-the-job training can take.

Typically, a supervisor or more experienced worker trains new clerks.

Clerks first learn to count stock and mark inventory and then move onto more difficult tasks, such as recordkeeping. Production clerks need to learn how their company operates before they can write production and work schedules.

Advancement

With additional training or education, material recording clerks can advance to other similar positions within their firm, such as purchasing agent. For more information, see the profile on purchasing managers, buyers, and purchasing agents .

Important Qualities

Clerical skills. Typing, filing, and recordkeeping are common tasks for most material recording clerks.

Communication skills. Production, planning, and expediting clerks are often in contact with suppliers, vendors, and production managers and need to be able to communicate the firm's scheduling needs effectively.

Customer-service skills. Stock clerks sometimes interact with customers in retail stores. They may have to get the item the customer is looking for from the storeroom.

Detail oriented. Material inspectors check items for defects, some of which are small and difficult to spot.

Pay

Material Recording Clerks
Median annual wages, May 2010

Total, All Occupations	$33,840
Office and Administrative Support Occupations	$30,710
Material Recording Clerks	$24,100

Note: All Occupations includes all occupations in the U.S. Economy.
Source: U.S. Bureau of Labor Statistics, Occupational Employment Statistics

The median annual wage for material recording clerks was $24,100 in May 2010. The median wage is the wage at which half the workers in an occupation earned more than that amount and half earned less. The lowest 10 percent earned less than $16,860 and the top 10 percent earned more than $43,340.

The median wages for material recording clerk occupations in May 2010 were the following:

- $42,220 for production, planning, and expediting clerks
- $28,370 for shipping, receiving, and traffic clerks
- $27,170 for material and product inspectors
- $21,290 for stock clerks and order fillers

Production, planning, and expediting clerks; shipping, receiving, and traffic clerks; and material inspectors usually work full time. Many have standard Monday-through-Friday shifts, although some work nights and weekends or holidays when large shipments arrive or inventory is taken.

About one-third of stock clerks and order fillers are part-time employees. Evening and weekend work is common because these clerks work when retail stores are open. They sometimes work overnight shifts when large shipments arrive or it is time to take inventory.

Job Outlook

Material Recording Clerks

Percent change in employment, projected 2010-20

Total, All Occupations	14%
Office and Administrative Support Occupations	10%
Material Recording Clerks	2%

Note: All Occupations includes all occupations in the U.S. Economy.
Source: U.S. Bureau of Labor Statistics, Employment Projections program

Employment of shipping, receiving, and traffic clerks is projected to grow 0 percent from 2010 to 2020, and employment of stock clerks and order fillers is projected to grow 1 percent during the same period, both experiencing little or no change.

An expected increase in the use of radiofrequency identification (RFID) tags will enhance the productivity of these two occupations. RFID tags allow stock clerks to locate an item or count inventory much faster than they previously could. In warehouses, shipping, receiving, and traffic clerks will be affected by RFID tags as well as increased automation, because both devices should make it easier to keep track of material. The productivity increases resulting from these technologies will allow fewer clerks to do the same amount of work that previously required more workers.

Employment of material and product inspectors is projected to grow 12 percent from 2010 to 2020, about as fast as the average for all occupations. RFID tags are expected to increase accuracy in shipping, reducing the number of times a product needs to be weighed, checked, or measured, and in turn reducing the demand for material inspectors. In addition, certain types of automation may do some of the job functions of these clerks.

Employment of production, planning, and expediting clerks is projected to grow 7 percent from 2010 to 2020, slower than the average for all occupations. These clerks are less likely to be affected by RFID or automation because they spend more time doing office work than shipping or stock clerks do. However, production clerks are employed mostly by slow-growing or declining manufacturing industries, which will limit their growth.

Job Prospects

There should be favorable job opportunities for material recording clerks because of the need to replace workers who leave the occupation. The increase in RFID and other sensors will enable clerks who are more comfortable with computers to have better job prospects.

Employment projections data for material recording clerks, 2010-20

Occupational Title	SOC Code	Employment, 2010	Projected Employment, 2020	Change, 2010-20 Percent	Change, 2010-20 Numeric
Material Recording Clerks	—	2,812,900	2,861,600	2	48,700
Production, Planning, and Expediting Clerks	43-5061	271,000	288,900	7	17,800
Shipping, Receiving, and Traffic Clerks	43-5071	687,600	689,500	0	2,000
Stock Clerks and Order Fillers	43-5081	1,787,400	1,808,300	1	20,900
Weighers, Measurers, Checkers, and Samplers, Recordkeeping	43-5111	66,900	74,900	12	8,000
SOURCE: U.S. Bureau of Labor Statistics, Employment Projections program					

Similar Occupations

This table shows a list of occupations with job duties that are similar to those of material recording clerks.

Occupation	Job Duties	Entry-Level Education	Median Annual Pay, May 2010
Delivery Truck Drivers and Driver/Sales Workers	Delivery truck drivers and driver/sales workers pick up, transport, and drop off packages within a small region or urban area. Most of the time, they transport merchandise from a distribution center to businesses and households.	High school diploma or equivalent	$27,050
General Office Clerks	General office clerks do a broad range of administrative tasks, including answering telephones, typing or word processing, and filing. However, tasks vary widely in different jobs.	High school diploma or equivalent	$26,610
Heavy and Tractor-trailer Truck Drivers	Heavy and tractor-trailer truck drivers transport goods from one location to another. Most tractor-trailer drivers are long-haul drivers and operate trucks with a capacity of at least 26,001 pounds per gross vehicle weight (GVW). They deliver goods over intercity routes, sometimes spanning several states.	High school diploma or equivalent	$37,770

Information Clerks	Information clerks provide administrative and clerical support in a variety of settings. They help maintain records, collect data and information, and respond to customers' questions or concerns.	See How to Become One	$29,990
Hand Laborers and Material Movers	Hand laborers and material movers transport objects without using machines. Some workers move freight, stock, or other materials around storage facilities; others clean vehicles; some pick up unwanted household goods; and still others pack materials for moving.	Less than high school	$22,560
Material Moving Machine Operators	Material moving machine operators use machinery to transport various objects. Some operators move construction materials around building sites or earth around a mine. Others move goods around a warehouse or onto and off of container ships.	Less than high school	$30,800

Contacts for More Information

For more information about material recording clerks, visit Material Handling Industry of America , The Warehousing Education and Research Council

Suggested citation:

Bureau of Labor Statistics, U.S. Department of Labor, Occupational Outlook Handbook, 2012-13 Edition, Material Recording Clerks, on the Internet at http://www.bls.gov/ooh/office-and-administrative-support/material-recording-clerks.htm .

Police, Fire, and Ambulance Dispatchers

Quick Facts: Police, Fire, and Ambulance Dispatchers	
2010 Median Pay	$35,370 per year $17.00 per hour
Entry-Level Education	High school diploma or equivalent
Work Experience in a Related Occupation	None
On-the-job Training	Moderate-term on-the-job training
Number of Jobs, 2010	100,100
Job Outlook, 2010-20	12% (About as fast as average)
Employment Change, 2010-20	11,700

What Police, Fire, and Ambulance Dispatchers Do

Police, fire, and ambulance dispatchers, also called 9-1-1 operators or public safety telecommunicators, answer emergency and non-emergency calls. They take information from the caller and send the appropriate type and number of units.

Duties

Police, fire and ambulance dispatchers typically do the following:

- Answer 9-1-1 telephone calls
- Determine, from the caller, the type of emergency and its location
- Decide the appropriate emergency response based on agency policies and procedures
- Relay information to the appropriate emergency or non-emergency service agency or agencies
- Coordinate sending emergency response personnel
- Give over-the-phone medical help and other instructions before emergency personnel get to the scene
- Monitor and track the status of police, fire, and ambulance units on assignment
- Synchronize responses with other area communication centers
- Keep detailed records about calls

Dispatchers answer calls for service when someone needs help from police, fire fighters, emergency services, or a combination of the three. They take both emergency and non-emergency calls.

Dispatchers must stay calm while collecting vital information from callers to determine the severity of a situation. They then give the appropriate first responder agencies information about the call.

Some dispatchers only take calls. Others only use radios to send appropriate personnel. Many dispatchers do both tasks.

Dispatchers keep detailed records about the calls that they take. They may use a computer system to log important facts, such as the name and location of the caller.

They may also use crime databases, maps, and weather reports, when helping emergency response teams. Dispatchers may monitor alarm systems, alerting law enforcement or fire personnel when a crime

Dispatchers receive calls for emergency and non-emergency assistance.

or fire occurs. In some situations, dispatchers must work with people in other jurisdictions to share information or to transfer calls.

Dispatchers must often give instructions on what to do before responders arrive. Some dispatchers are trained to give medical help over the phone, For example, they might help someone give first aid until emergency medical services get to the scene.

Work Environment

Police, fire, and ambulance dispatchers held about 100,100 jobs in 2010.

They work in a communication center, often called a Public Safety Answering Point (PSAP).

Most dispatchers work for local governments, but some work for state governments or for private companies. They are largely employed by law enforcement agencies and fire departments.

Most dispatchers work 8- to 12-hour shifts, but some agencies choose to use 24-hour shifts.

Dispatchers often have to work weekends, holidays, and overtime, as emergency calls can come in at any time.

Work as a dispatcher can be stressful. Dispatchers may have to work long hours, take many calls, and deal with troubling situations. Some calls may be distressing, and the pressure to respond to emergency situations quickly can be demanding.

How to Become a Police, Fire, or Ambulance Dispatcher

Most police, fire, and ambulance dispatchers have a high school diploma or GED. Additional requirements vary. Many states require dispatchers to become certified.

Important Qualities

Ability to multitask. Responding to an emergency over the phone can be stressful. Dispatchers must stay calm to simultaneously answer calls, collect vital information, coordinate responders, and assist callers.

Empathy. People who call 9-1-1 are often in distress. Dispatchers must be willing and able to help callers with a wide variety of needs. They must be calm, polite, and sympathetic, while also quickly getting information.

Leadership skills. Dispatchers work with law enforcement, emergency response teams, and civilians in emergency situations. They must be able to efficiently communicate the nature of the emergency and coordinate the appropriate response.

Listening skills. When answering an emergency call or handling radio communications, a dispatcher must listen carefully. Some callers might have trouble speaking because of anxiety or stress. Dispatchers must be able to record the call accurately.

Problem-solving skills. Dispatchers must be able to choose wisely between tasks that are competing for their attention. They must be able to quickly determine the appropriate action when people call for help.

Education and Training

The typical entry-level education is a high school diploma or a GED. However, some employers may not specify any educational requirements. Others prefer to hire dispatchers who have a related 2- or 4-year degree in a subject such as criminal justice, computer science, or communications.

Most dispatcher jobs require an applicant to complete an interview as well as to pass a written exam and a typing test. In addition, applicants may need to pass a background check, lie detector and drug tests, as well as tests for hearing and vision.

Most states require a dispatcher to be a U.S. citizen, and some jobs require a driver's license. Both computer skills and customer service skills can be helpful, as is the ability to speak a second language.

Training requirements vary by state. Some states require dispatchers to be certified.

Several states require 40 hours or more of initial training. Some require continuing education every 2 to 3 years. Other states do not mandate any specific training, leaving individual agencies to conduct their own courses.

Some agencies have their own programs for certifying dispatchers; others use training from a professional association. The Association of Public-Safety Communications Officials (APCO), the National Emergency Number Association (NENA), and the National Academies of Emergency Dispatch (NAED) have established a number of recommended standards and best practices that agencies may use as a guideline for their own training programs.

Training is usually conducted in both a classroom setting and on the job, and is often followed by a probationary period of about 1 year. However, this may vary by agency as there is no national standard of how training is conducted or the length of probation.

Training covers a wide variety of topics, such as local geography, agency protocols, and standard procedures. Dispatchers are also taught how to use specialized equipment, such as a 2-way radio and computer-aided dispatch (CAD) software. They receive training to prepare for specific types of incidents, such as a child abduction or a suicidal caller. Some dispatchers receive emergency medical dispatcher (EMD) training, which enables them to give medical assistance over the phone.

Certification

Dispatchers may choose to pursue additional certifications, such as NENA's emergency number professional (ENP) or APCO's Registered Public-Safety Leader (RPL) to prove their leadership skills and knowledge of the profession.

Advancement

Dispatchers can become senior dispatchers or supervisors before going on to administrative positions, in which they may focus on a specific area, such as training or policy and procedures. Additional education and related work experience may be helpful in advancing to management level positions. Technology skills also may be helpful in becoming a supervisor.

Pay

| Police, Fire, and Ambulance Dispatchers | |
Median annual wages, May 2010	
Police, Fire, and Ambulance Dispatchers	$35,370
Total, All Occupations	$33,840
Office and Administrative Support Occupations	$30,710

Note: All Occupations includes all occupations in the U.S. Economy.
Source: U.S. Bureau of Labor Statistics, Occupational Employment Statistics

The median annual wage of police, fire, and ambulance dispatchers was $35,370 in May 2010. The median wage is the wage at which half the workers in an occupation earned more than that amount, and half earned less. The lowest 10 percent earned $22,310, and the top 10 percent earned more than $54,350.

Most dispatchers work 8- to 12-hour shifts, but some agencies choose to use 24-hour shifts.

Dispatchers often have to work weekends, holidays, and overtime, as emergency calls can come in at any time.

Job Outlook

Police, Fire, and Ambulance Dispatchers
Percent change in employment, projected 2010-20

Total, All Occupations	14%
Police, Fire, and Ambulance Dispatchers	12%
Office and Administrative Support Occupations	10%

Note: All Occupations includes all occupations in the U.S. Economy.
Source: U.S. Bureau of Labor Statistics, Employment Projections program

Employment of police, fire, and ambulance dispatchers is expected to grow by 12 percent from 2010 to 2020, about as fast as average for all occupations. A larger and older population is likely to mean more emergency calls; and, therefore, a need for more dispatchers.

The prevalence of cellular phones has increased the number of calls that dispatchers receive. This trend is likely to continue in the future, as new technologies, such as text messages and videos, will be used to communicate with dispatchers.

Job Prospects

Favorable opportunities are expected, largely due to job openings arising from the need to replace workers who transfer to other occupations or who leave the occupation.

The technology and equipment dispatchers use continues to evolve, creating a demand for workers with related technical skills. Job prospects will be best for those with customer service and computer skills.

Employment projections data for police, fire, and ambulance dispatchers, 2010-20

Occupational Title	SOC Code	Employment, 2010	Projected Employment, 2020	Change, 2010-20	
				Percent	Numeric
Police, Fire, and Ambulance Dispatchers	43-5031	100,100	111,800	12	11,700
SOURCE: U.S. Bureau of Labor Statistics, Employment Projections program					

Similar Occupations

This table shows a list of occupations with job duties that are similar to those of police, fire, and ambulance dispatchers.

Occupation	Job Duties	Entry-Level Education	Median Annual Pay, May 2010
Air Traffic Controllers	Air traffic controllers coordinate the movement of air traffic to ensure that planes stay safe distances apart.	Associate's degree	$108,040
EMTs and Paramedics	Emergency medical technicians (EMTs) and paramedics care for the sick or injured in emergency medical settings. People's lives often depend on their quick reaction and competent care. EMTs and paramedics respond to emergency calls, performing medical services and transporting patients to medical facilities.	Postsecondary non-degree award	$30,360
Customer Service Representatives	Customer service representatives interact with customers on behalf of an organization. They provide information about products and services and respond to customer complaints. Some also take orders and process returns.	High school diploma or equivalent	$30,460

Contacts for More Information

For more information about police, fire, and ambulance dispatcher training and certification, visit The Association of Public-Safety Communications Officials , National Emergency Number Association , National Academies of Emergency Dispatch

For professional information, including grants, and useful links, visit U.S. Department of Transportation's National 911 Program

Suggested citation:

Bureau of Labor Statistics, U.S. Department of Labor, Occupational Outlook Handbook, 2012-13 Edition, Police, Fire, and Ambulance Dispatchers, on the Internet at http://www.bls.gov/ooh/office-and-administrative-support/police-fire-and-ambulance-dispatchers.htm .

Postal Service Workers

Quick Facts: Postal Service Workers	
2010 Median Pay	$53,090 per year $25.52 per hour
Entry-Level Education	High school diploma or equivalent
Work Experience in a Related Occupation	None
On-the-job Training	Short-term on-the-job training
Number of Jobs, 2010	524,200
Job Outlook, 2010-20	-26% (Decline rapidly)
Employment Change, 2010-20	-138,600

What Postal Service Workers Do

Postal Service workers sell postal products and collect, sort, and deliver mail.

Duties

Postal Service workers typically do the following:
- Collect letters and parcels
- Sort incoming letters and parcels
- Sell stamps and other postal products to customers
- Get customer signatures for registered, certified, and insured mail
- Operate various types of postal equipment
- Distribute incoming mail from postal trucks

Postal Service workers receive and process mail for delivery to homes, businesses, and post office boxes. Workers are classified based on the type of work they perform.

Postal Service mail carriers deliver mail to homes and businesses in cities, towns, and rural areas. Most travel established routes, delivering and collecting mail. Mail carriers cover their routes on foot, by vehicle, or by a combination of both. Some mail carriers collect money for postage due and COD (cash-on-delivery). Others, particularly in rural areas, sell postal products such as stamps and money orders. All carriers, however, must be able to answer customers' questions about postal regulations and services and, upon request, provide change-of-address cards and other postal forms.

Postal Service clerks sell stamps, money orders, postal stationary, mailing envelopes, and boxes in post offices throughout the country. These workers register, certify, and insure mail, calculate and collect postage, and answer questions about other postal matters.

Postal Service mail sorters, processors, and processing machine operators prepare incoming and outgoing mail for distribution at post offices and mail processing centers. They load and unload postal trucks and move mail around mail processing centers. They also operate, and occasionally adjust and repair, mail processing, sorting, and canceling machinery.

Work Environment

Postal Service workers held about 524,200 jobs in 2010. Nearly all worked in the federal government. Employment in the detailed occupations that make up Postal Service workers was distributed as follows:

Postal Service mail carriers	316,700
Postal Service mail sorters, processors, and processing machine operators	142,000
Postal Service clerks	65,600

Postal Service clerks and mail sorters, processors, and processing machine operators work indoors, typically in a post office. Mail carriers mostly work outdoors, delivering mail in all kinds of weather. Although carriers face many natural hazards, such as extreme temperatures and wet and icy roads and sidewalks, the work is not especially dangerous. However, repetitive stress injuries from lifting and bending are common.

Work Schedules

Most career Postal Service workers work full time. However, overtime may be required for workers, particularly during the holiday season. Because mail is delivered 6 days a week, many Postal Service workers must work on Saturdays.

How to Become a Postal Service Worker

Although there is no specific education requirement to become a Postal Service worker, all applicants for these jobs must take an exam.

Postal Service workers perform many tasks in a post office such as collecting and delivering mail.

Education and Training

Although there are no specific education requirements to become a Postal Service worker, all applicants must have a good command of English. Workers typically receive additional training on the job.

Postal Service mail carriers must be at least 18 years old. They must be U.S. citizens or have permanent resident-alien status. Males must have registered with the Selective Service when they reached age 18.

All applicants must pass a written exam that measures speed and accuracy at checking names and numbers and the ability to memorize mail distribution procedures. Jobseekers should contact the post office or mail processing center where they want to work to find out when an exam will be given.

When accepted, applicants must undergo a criminal-history check and pass a physical exam and a drug test. Applicants also may be asked to show that they can lift and handle mail sacks weighing 50 pounds. Mail carriers who drive at work must have a safe driving record, and applicants must get a passing grade on a road test.

Important Qualities

Customer-service skills. Postal Service workers, particularly clerks, interact with customers regularly. They must be courteous and tactful and provide service and help to customers.

Stamina. Postal Service workers must be able to stand or walk for long periods.

Physical strength. Postal Service workers must be able to lift heavy mail bags and parcels without injuring themselves.

Pay

Postal Service Workers
Median annual wages, May 2010

Postal Service Workers	$53,090
Total, All Occupations	$33,840
Material Recording, Scheduling, Dispatching, and Distributing Workers	$27,590

Note: All Occupations includes all occupations in the U.S. Economy.
Source: U.S. Bureau of Labor Statistics, Occupational Employment Statistics

The median annual wage of Postal Service workers was $53,090 in May 2010. The median wage is the wage at which half the workers in an occupation earned more than that amount and half earned less. The lowest 10 percent earned less than $38,490, and the top 10 percent earned more than $54,620.

Median annual wages for Postal Service occupations in May 2010 were the following:

- $53,100 for Postal Service clerks
- $53,860 for Postal Service mail carriers

- $53,080 for Postal Service mail sorters, processors, and processing machine operators

Most career Postal Service workers work full time. However, overtime may be required for workers, particularly during the holiday season. Because mail is delivered 6 days a week, many Postal Service workers must work on Saturdays.

Job Outlook

Postal Service Workers
Percent change in employment, projected 2010-20

Total, All Occupations	14%
Material Recording, Scheduling, Dispatching, and Distributing Workers	0%
Postal Service Workers	-26%

Note: All Occupations includes all occupations in the U.S. Economy.
Source: U.S. Bureau of Labor Statistics, Employment Projections program

Overall employment of Postal Service workers is expected to decline 26 percent from 2010 to 2020. Employment declines, however, will vary by specialty.

Employment of Postal Service clerks is projected to decline by 48 percent from 2010 to 2020. Employment will be adversely affected by the decline in first-class mail volume because of the increasing use of automated bill pay and email.

Employment of Postal Service mail carriers is projected to decline by 12 percent from 2010 to 2020. Employment will be adversely affected by the use of automated "delivery point sequencing" systems that sort letter mail and flat mail directly. This reduces the amount of time that carriers spend sorting their mail, allowing them to spend more time on the streets delivering mail.

The amount of time carriers save on sorting letter mail and flat mail will allow them to increase the size of their routes, which should reduce the need to hire more carriers. In addition, the Postal Service is moving toward more centralized mail delivery, such as the use of cluster mailboxes, to cut down on the number of door-to-door deliveries.

Employment of Postal Service mail sorters, processors, and processing machine operators is projected to decline by 49 percent from 2010 to 2020. Employment will be adversely affected by new mail sorting technology that will read text and automatically sort, forward, and process mail, reducing the need for workers. The greater use of online services to pay bills and the increased use of email should further reduce the need for sorting and processing workers.

Job Prospects

Very strong competition is expected for all jobs, as the number of applicants typically is greater than the number of available positions.

Employment projections data for postal service workers, 2010-20

Occupational Title	SOC Code	Employment, 2010	Projected Employment, 2020	Change, 2010-20 Percent	Numeric
Postal Service Workers	—	524,200	385,600	-26	-138,600
Postal Service Clerks	43-5051	65,600	34,000	-48	-31,600
Postal Service Mail Carriers	43-5052	316,700	278,500	-12	-38,100
Postal Service Mail Sorters, Processors, and Processing Machine Operators	43-5053	142,000	73,000	-49	-68,900

SOURCE: U.S. Bureau of Labor Statistics, Employment Projections program

Similar Occupations

This table shows a list of occupations with job duties that are similar to those of postal service workers.

Occupation	Job Duties	Entry-Level Education	Median Annual Pay, May 2010
Couriers and Messengers	Couriers and messengers transport documents and packages for individuals, businesses, institutions, and government agencies.	High school diploma or equivalent	$24,080
Retail Sales Workers	Retail sales workers include both those who sell retail merchandise, such as clothing, furniture, and automobiles, (called retail salespersons) and those who sell spare and replacement parts and equipment, especiallycar parts, (called parts salespersons). Both groups help customers find the products they want and process customers' payments.	Less than high school	$20,990
Delivery Truck Drivers and Driver/Sales Workers	Delivery truck drivers and driver/sales workers pick up, transport, and drop off packages within a small region or urban area. Most of the time, they transport merchandise from a distribution center to businesses and households.	High school diploma or equivalent	$27,050

Contacts for More Information

For more information about Postal Service workers, including job requirements, entrance examinations, and employment opportunities, visit United States Postal Service , U.S. Postal Regulatory Commission , National Association of Letter Carriers

For information about national Postal Service unions, visit American Postal Workers Union , National Postal Mail Handlers Union

Suggested citation:

Bureau of Labor Statistics, U.S. Department of Labor, Occupational Outlook Handbook, 2012-13 Edition, Postal Service Workers, on the Internet at http://www.bls.gov/ooh/office-and-administrative-support/postal-service-workers.htm .

Receptionists

Quick Facts: Receptionists	
2010 Median Pay	$25,240 per year $12.14 per hour
Entry-Level Education	High school diploma or equivalent
Work Experience in a Related Occupation	None
On-the-job Training	Short-term on-the-job training
Number of Jobs, 2010	1,048,500
Job Outlook, 2010-20	24% (Faster than average)
Employment Change, 2010-20	248,500

What Receptionists Do

Receptionists perform various administrative duties, including answering telephones and giving information to the public and customers.

Duties

Receptionists typically do the following:

- Answer, screen, and forward telephone calls
- Greet walk-in customers and other visitors and escort them to specific destinations
- Contribute to the security of the office by helping to monitor visitors' access
- Obtain or send information or documents using a computer, mail, or a fax machine
- Perform other administrative support tasks, such as keeping appointment calendars
- Copy, file, and maintain documents and records
- Collect, sort, distribute, and prepare mail and courier deliveries
- Process and prepare travel vouchers or other documents

Receptionists are often the first employee that the public or customer has contact with. They are responsible for making a good first impression for the organization, which can affect the organization's success.

Although some tasks are common to most receptionists, their specific responsibilities vary depending on their work establishment. For example, receptionists in hospitals and in doctors' offices may gather patients' personal and insurance information and direct patients to the proper waiting room. In corporate headquarters, they may greet visitors and manage the scheduling of the board room or common conference area.

In beauty or hair salons, they arrange appointments, direct clients to the hairstylist, and may serve as cashiers. In factories, large corporations, and government offices, receptionists may provide identification cards for visitors and arrange for escorts to take visitors to the proper office. Those working for bus and train companies respond to passengers' inquiries about departures, arrivals, stops, and other related matters.

Receptionists use the telephone, computers, and other electronic devices. Despite the widespread use of voice mail or other automated systems, many receptionists still take messages and inform other employees of the public's or customers' arrivals or cancellations of appointments. When they are not busy with callers, most workers are expected to help other administrative employees by doing a variety of other office tasks.

Work Environment

Receptionists held about 1 million jobs in 2010.

Industries that employed the most receptionists in 2010 were as follows:

Offices of physicians	17%
Offices of dentists	6
Administrative and support services	6
Educational services; state, local, and private	5
Personal care services	5

Although receptionists work in almost every industry, many are concentrated in healthcare and social assistance, including physicians' offices, hospitals, and nursing homes.

Receptionists who greet customers and visitors usually work in areas that are highly visible, clean, well-lit, and relatively quiet. The work that some receptionists do may be tiring, repetitious, and stressful as they may spend all day answering continually ringing telephones and sometimes encounter difficult or irate callers.

Work Schedules

Although most receptionists work full time, about 30 percent worked part time in 2010. Some receptionists, including those who work in hospitals and nursing homes, may have to work evenings and weekends.

How to Become a Receptionist

Although hiring requirements vary by industry and employer, most receptionists need a high school diploma.

Education and Training

Receptionists generally need a high school diploma or its equivalent.

Most receptionists receive their training on the job. They learn how to operate the telephone system and computers and learn the proper procedures for greeting visitors. While many of these skills can be learned quickly, those who give information to the public or customers may need several weeks to learn details about the organization.

Employers often look for applicants who know spreadsheets, word processing software, or other industry specific software applications. Some employers may prefer applicants who have some formal office education or training.

Advancement

Receptionists typically advance by transferring to an occupation with more responsibility or by being promoted to a supervisory position. Receptionists with especially strong computer skills, some postsecondary education, and several years of experience may advance to a better paying job as a secretary or an administrative assistant.

Important Qualities

Computer skills. Receptionists need a working knowledge of different software packages or industry-specific software applications.

Customer service skills. Receptionists represent an organization. As a result, they must be courteous, professional, and helpful toward the public and customers.

Listening skills. Receptionists must be good listeners. They must listen patiently to the points being made, wait to speak until others have finished, and ask appropriate questions when necessary.

Speaking skills. The ability to communicate clearly is essential for receptionists because much of their job involves conveying information over the phone or in person.

Receptionists provide information to the general public, customers, and visitors.

Pay

Receptionists

Median hourly wages, May 2010

Total, All Occupations	$16.27
Office and Administrative Support Occupations	$14.77
Receptionists and Information Clerks	$12.14

Note: All Occupations includes all occupations in the U.S. Economy.
Source: U.S. Bureau of Labor Statistics, Occupational Employment Statistics

The median hourly wage of receptionists was $12.14 in May 2010. The median wage is the wage at which half the workers in an occupation earned more than that amount and half earned less. The lowest 10 percent earned less than $8.44, and the top 10 percent earned more than $17.75.

Median hourly wages in the industries employing the largest numbers of receptionists in May 2010 were as follows:

Offices of dentists	$13.91
Offices of physicians	12.64
Educational services; state, local, and private	12.59
Administrative and support services	12.08
Personal care services	9.40

Although most receptionists work full time, about 30 percent worked part time in 2010. Some receptionists, including those who work in hospitals and nursing homes, may have to work evenings and weekends.

Job Outlook

Receptionists

Percent change in employment, projected 2010-20

Receptionists and Information Clerks	24%
Total, All Occupations	14%
Office and Administrative Support Occupations	10%

Note: All Occupations includes all occupations in the U.S. Economy.
Source: U.S. Bureau of Labor Statistics, Employment Projections program

Employment of receptionists is projected to grow 24 percent from 2010 to 2020, faster than the average for all occupations.

Receptionists perform a wide variety of clerical tasks, so they should continue to be in demand. Furthermore, because they interact with people, their tasks are not easily automated, ensuring continued demand for their services in a variety of industries.

Employment growth is expected to result primarily from growth in the healthcare industry. Specifically, physicians' offices, dentists' offices, and community care facilities for the elderly are expected to add the most jobs.

Technology will have conflicting effects on employment growth. The increasing use of voice mail and other telephone automation reduces the need for receptionists because one receptionist can now do the work that previously required several. At the same time, however, the increasing use of other technology has caused a consolidation of clerical responsibilities and growing demand for workers with diverse clerical and technical skills.

Job Prospects

Job opportunities are expected to be very good. Many job openings will arise from the need to replace those who transfer to other occupations. Those with related work experience and good computer skills should have the best job opportunities.

Employment projections data for receptionists, 2010-20

Occupational Title	SOC Code	Employment, 2010	Projected Employment, 2020	Change, 2010-20	
				Percent	Numeric
Receptionists and Information Clerks	43-4171	1,048,500	1,297,000	24	248,500
SOURCE: U.S. Bureau of Labor Statistics, Employment Projections program					

Similar Occupations

This table shows a list of occupations with job duties that are similar to those of receptionists.

Occupation	Job Duties	Entry-Level Education	Median Annual Pay, May 2010
Customer Service Representatives	Customer service representatives interact with customers on behalf of an organization. They provide information about products and services and respond to customer complaints. Some also take orders and process returns.	High school diploma or equivalent	$30,460
General Office Clerks	General office clerks do a broad range of administrative tasks, including answering telephones, typing or word processing, and filing. However, tasks vary widely in different jobs.	High school diploma or equivalent	$26,610
Secretaries and Administrative Assistants	Secretaries and administrative assistants perform routine clerical and organizational tasks. They organize files, draft messages, schedule appointments, and support other staff.	High school diploma or equivalent	$34,660

Contacts for More Information

For information about administrative professionals, including training and certification, visit American Society of Administrative Professionals

Association of Executive and Administrative Professionals , International Association of Administrative Professionals

Suggested citation:

Bureau of Labor Statistics, U.S. Department of Labor, Occupational Outlook Handbook, 2012-13 Edition, Receptionists, on the Internet at http://www.bls.gov/ooh/office-and-administrative-support/receptionists.htm .

Secretaries and Administrative Assistants

Quick Facts: Secretaries and Administrative Assistants	
2010 Median Pay	$34,660 per year $16.66 per hour
Entry-Level Education	High school diploma or equivalent
Work Experience in a Related Occupation	See How to Become One
On-the-job Training	See How to Become One
Number of Jobs, 2010	4,010,200
Job Outlook, 2010-20	12% (About as fast as average)
Employment Change, 2010-20	492,900

What Secretaries and Administrative Assistants Do

Secretaries and administrative assistants perform routine clerical and organizational tasks. They organize files, draft messages, schedule appointments, and support other staff.

Duties

Secretaries and administrative assistants typically do the following:

- Maintain paper and electronic filing systems for records and messages
- Route and distribute incoming mail and email
- Answer routine letters and email
- Reply and attach files to incoming messages
- Correct spelling and grammar to ensure accuracy
- Operate fax machines, videoconferencing and phone systems, and other office equipment
- Use computers for spreadsheet, word processing, database management, and other applications
- Complete forms in accordance with company procedures

Secretaries and administrative assistants perform a variety of clerical and organizational tasks that are necessary to run an organization efficiently. They use computer software to create spreadsheets, compose messages, manage databases, and produce presentations, reports, and documents. They also may negotiate with vendors, buy supplies, manage stockrooms or corporate libraries, and get data from various sources. Specific job duties vary by experience, job title, and specialty.

Secretaries and administrative assistants support an office by performing clerical functions.

The following are types of secretaries and administrative assistants:

Executive secretaries and executive administrative assistants provide high-level administrative support for an office and for top executives of an organization. They often handle more complex responsibilities, such as reviewing incoming documents, conducting research, preparing reports, and arranging meetings. They may supervise clerical staff.

Legal secretaries do specialized work requiring knowledge of legal terminology and procedures. Legal secretaries prepare messages and legal papers, such as summonses, complaints, motions, responses, and subpoenas under the supervision of an attorney or a paralegal. They also may review legal journals and help with legal research—for example, by verifying quotes and citations in legal briefs.

Medical secretaries transcribe dictation, prepare messages, and help physicians or medical scientists with reports, speeches, articles, and conference proceedings. They also take simple medical histories, arrange for patients to be hospitalized, and order supplies. Medical secretaries need to be familiar with medical terminology, insurance rules, billing practices, medical records, and hospital or laboratory procedures.

Secretaries and administrative assistants, except legal, medical, and executive is the largest subcategory of secretaries and administrative assistants. They handle an office's administrative activities in almost every sector of the economy, including schools, government agencies, and private corporations. Secretaries in schools are often responsible for handling most of the communications among parents, the community, teachers, and school administrators. They schedule appointments, keep track of students' records, and handle matters that do not require the principal's attention.

Virtual assistants work from a home office. They use the Internet, email, and fax machines to communicate with clients. Although their assignments often vary from short term to long term, their typical duties are similar to those of other secretaries and administrative assistants. Working from a remote location allows virtual assistants to support multiple clients in different industries at the same time.

Work Environment

Secretaries and administrative assistants held about 4 million jobs in 2010. The industries that employed the most secretaries and administrative assistants in 2010 were:

Educational services; state, local, and private	14%
Offices of health practitioners	11
Government	9
Legal services	7

Although secretaries and administrative assistants work in nearly every industry, many are concentrated in schools, hospitals, government agencies, and legal and medical offices. Most work full time in comfortable office settings. Virtual assistants typically work from a home office.

How to Become a Secretary or Administrative Assistant

High school graduates who have basic office and computer skills usually qualify for entry-level secretarial and administrative assistant positions.

Education and Training

High school graduates can get basic office, computer, and English grammar skills in various ways: through high school vocational education programs, vocational–technical schools, or community colleges. Many temporary placement agencies also provide formal training in computer and office skills.

Employers of more specialized positions, including medical and legal secretaries, often require applicants to have some knowledge of industry-specific terminology and practices. Community colleges and vocational-technical schools usually offer instruction in these areas.

Certification

Though not required, certification can demonstrate competency to employers. Legal secretaries have a few certification options. For example, those with 1 year of experience in the legal field, or who have concluded an approved training course and who want to be certified as a legal support professional, can acquire the Accredited Legal Secretary (ALS) designation through a testing process administered by NALS . NALS offers two additional designations: Professional Legal Secretary (PLS), considered an advanced certification for legal support professionals, and a designation for proficiency as a paralegal.

Legal Secretaries International confers the Certified Legal Secretary Specialist (CLSS) designation in areas such as intellectual property, criminal law, civil litigation, probate, and business law to those who have 5 years of legal experience and pass an examination. In some instances, certain requirements may be waived.

Advancement

Secretaries and administrative assistants generally advance through promotion to other administrative positions with more responsibilities. Qualified administrative assistants who broaden their knowledge of a company's operations and enhance their skills may be promoted to senior or executive secretary or administrative assistant, clerical supervisor, or office manager. With additional training, many legal secretaries become paralegals. For more information, see the profile on paralegals and legal assistants . Once hired, most secretaries and administrative assistants tend to get more advanced skills through on-the-job instruction.

Important Qualities

Computer skills. Secretaries and administrative assistants use computers for email, word processing, spreadsheets, and database management. Therefore, having good computer skills is very important.

Interpersonal skills. Secretaries and administrative assistants work with many different individuals each day. Being pleasant and attentive contributes to a positive work environment and client experience.

Organizational skills. Whether filing papers or filling out forms, secretaries and administrative assistants must make sure that files, folders, and schedules are in proper order so an office can run efficiently.

Writing skills. Secretaries frequently write memos and email when communicating with managers, employees, and customers. Therefore,

they must have good grammar, ensure accuracy, and maintain a professional tone.

Pay

Secretaries and Administrative Assistants
Median annual wages, May 2010

Secretaries and Administrative Assistants	$34,660
Total, All Occupations	$33,840
Office and Administrative Support Occupations	$30,710

Note: All Occupations includes all occupations in the U.S. Economy.
Source: U.S. Bureau of Labor Statistics, Occupational Employment Statistics

The median annual wage for secretaries and administrative assistants was $34,660 in May 2010. The median wage is the wage at which half the workers in an occupation earned more than that amount and half earned less. The lowest 10 percent earned less than $21,730, and the top 10 percent earned more than $55,960.

The median annual wages fordifferent types of secretaries and administrative assistants in May2010 were the following:

- $43,520 for executive secretaries
- $41,500 for legal secretaries
- $30,530 for medical secretaries
- $30,830 for secretaries, except legal, medical, and executive

Although secretaries and administrative assistants work in nearly every industry, many are concentrated in schools, hospitals, government agencies, and legal and medical offices. Most work full time in comfortable office settings.

Job Outlook

Secretaries and Administrative Assistants
Percent change in employment, projected 2010-20

Total, All Occupations	14%
Secretaries and Administrative Assistants	12%
Office and Administrative Support Occupations	10%

Note: All Occupations includes all occupations in the U.S. Economy.
Source: U.S. Bureau of Labor Statistics, Employment Projections program

Overall employment of secretaries and administrative assistants is expected to grow 12 percent from 2010 to 2020, about as fast as the average for all occupations. Employment growth, however, will differ by occupational specialty.

Employment of executive secretaries and administrative assistants is projected to grow 13 percent from 2010 to 2020, about as fast as the average for all occupations, as these workers continue to provide high-level support for executives.

Employment of medical secretaries is projected to grow 41 percent from 2010 to 2020, much faster than the average for all occupations. Employment growth will be driven by rapid growth of the healthcare and social assistance industries. An anticipated increase in the use of medical services by an aging population will require many additional medical secretaries.

Employment of legal secretaries is expected to grow 4 percent from 2010 to 2020, slower than the average for all occupations. This slow employment growth is due primarily to the slower-than-average growth of the legal industry overall.

Employment of secretaries, except legal, medical, and executive, is expected to grow 6 percent from 2010 to 2020, slower than the average for all occupations. Although developments in office technology are certain to continue, many secretarial and administrative duties are of a personal, interactive nature and are not easily automated. Responsibilities such as planning meetings, working with clients, and instructing staff require tact and communication skills. Because technology cannot currently substitute for these interpersonal skills, secretaries and administrative assistants will continue to play a key role in most organizations.

Job Prospects

In addition to jobs coming from employment growth, numerous job openings will arise from the need to replace secretaries and administrative assistants who transfer to other occupations or retire. Job opportunities should be best for applicants with extensive knowledge of computer software applications. Applicants with a bachelor's degree are expected to be in great demand and will act as managerial assistants who perform more complex tasks.

Employment projections data for secretaries and administrative assistants, 2010-20

Occupational Title	SOC Code	Employment, 2010	Projected Employment, 2020	Change, 2010-20 Percent	Change, 2010-20 Numeric
Secretaries and Administrative Assistants	43-6000	4,010,200	4,503,100	12	492,900
Executive Secretaries and Executive Administrative Assistants	43-6011	1,236,100	1,392,100	13	156,000
Legal Secretaries	43-6012	233,200	241,400	4	8,200
Medical Secretaries	43-6013	508,700	718,900	41	210,200
Secretaries and Administrative Assistants, Except Legal, Medical, and Executive	43-6014	2,032,200	2,150,800	6	118,500
SOURCE: U.S. Bureau of Labor Statistics, Employment Projections program					

Similar Occupations

This table shows a list of occupations with job duties that are similar to those of secretaries and administrative assistants.

Occupation	Job Duties	Entry-Level Education	Median Annual Pay, May 2010
Bookkeeping, Accounting, and Auditing Clerks	Bookkeeping, accounting, and auditing clerks produce financial records for organizations. They record financial transactions, update statements, and check financial records for accuracy.	High school diploma or equivalent	$34,030
Court Reporters	Court reporters attend legal proceedings and public speaking events to create word-for-word transcriptions. Some court reporters provide captioning for television and at public events.	Postsecondary non-degree award	$47,700
General Office Clerks	General office clerks do a broad range of administrative tasks, including answering telephones, typing or word processing, and filing. However, tasks vary widely in different jobs.	High school diploma or equivalent	$26,610
Information Clerks	Information clerks provide administrative and clerical support in a variety of settings. They help maintain records, collect data and information, and respond to customers' questions or concerns.	See How to Become One	$29,990
Medical Records and Health Information Technicians	Medical records and health information technicians organize and manage health information data by ensuring its quality, accuracy, accessibility, and security in both paper and electronic systems. They use various classification systems to code and categorize patient information for reimbursement purposes, for databases and registries, and to maintain patients' medical and treatment histories.	Postsecondary non-degree award	$32,350
Paralegals and Legal Assistants	Paralegals and legal assistants do a variety of tasks to support lawyers, including maintaining and organizing files, conducting legal research, and drafting documents.	Associate's degree	$46,680
Receptionists	Receptionists perform various administrative tasks, including answering telephones and giving information to the public and customers.	High school diploma or equivalent	$25,240

Contacts for More Information

For more information on careers in secretarial and administrative work, visit Association of Executive and Administrative Professionals , International Association of Administrative Professionals

For more information on legal secretaries and administrative assistants, visit Legal Secretaries International Inc , NALS

For more information on virtual assistants, visit International Virtual Assistants Association

Suggested citation:

Bureau of Labor Statistics, U.S. Department of Labor, Occupational Outlook Handbook, 2012-13 Edition, Secretaries and Administrative Assistants, on the Internet at http://www.bls.gov/ooh/office-and-administrative-support/secretaries-and-administrative-assistants.htm .

Tellers

Quick Facts: Tellers	
2010 Median Pay	$24,100 per year $11.59 per hour
Entry-Level Education	High school diploma or equivalent
Work Experience in a Related Occupation	None
On-the-job Training	Short-term on-the-job training
Number of Jobs, 2010	560,000
Job Outlook, 2010-20	1% (Little or no change)
Employment Change, 2010-20	7,300

What Tellers Do

Tellers are responsible for accurately processing routine transactions at a bank. These transactions include cashing checks, depositing money, and collecting loan payments.

Duties

Tellers typically do the following:
- Count the cash in their drawer at the start of their shift
- Accept checks, cash, and other forms of payment from customers
- Answers questions from customers about their accounts
- Prepare specialized types of funds, such as traveler's checks, savings bonds, and money orders
- Exchange dollars for foreign currency
- Order bank cards and checks for customers
- Record all transactions electronically throughout their shift
- Count the cash in their drawer at the end of their shift and make sure the amounts balance

Tellers are responsible for the safe and accurate handling of the money they process. When cashing a check, they must verify the customer's identity and make sure that the account has enough money to cover the transaction. When counting cash, a teller must be careful not to make errors.

Tellers also seek out customers who might want to buy more financial products or services from the bank, such as certificates of deposits (CDs) and loans. When they think a customer is interested, tellers explain the products and services the bank offers and refer the customer to the appropriate sales personnel.

In most banks, tellers record account changes by using computer terminals that give them easy access to the customer's financial information. Tellers also can use this information when recommending a new product or service.

Head tellers manage teller operations. They do the same tasks as other tellers as well as some managerial tasks, such as setting work schedules or helping less experienced tellers. Because of their experience, head tellers may deal with difficult customer problems, such as a customer questioning an error with an account. Head tellers also go to the vault (where larger amounts of money are kept) and ensure that the rest of the tellers have enough cash to cover their shift.

Work Environment

Tellers held about 560,000 jobs in 2010.

Most tellers work in bank branches. They sit at a computer station and interact with customers from behind a glass partition. Some banks are experimenting with new formats that allow the teller to more closely interact with a customer by changing the place of the teller station or removing the glass barrier.

Work Schedules

Most tellers work full time, Monday-through-Friday work schedules. Some tellers work on Saturdays. About 27 percent work part time, which is more than the average for other administrative and support occupations.

How to Become a Teller

Most tellers have a high school diploma and get about 1 month of on-the-job training. Some banks do background checks before hiring a new teller.

Education

Tellers usually must have a high school diploma or equivalent. A few tellers have some college experience, but a degree is rarely needed for a job applicant to be hired.

Tellers work in bank branches and assist customers with simple financial transactions.

Training

Tellers usually have a brief period of on-the-job training, typically lasting about 1 month. Normally, a head teller or another experienced teller trains them. A new teller may also need to learn the computer software that their bank uses and the financial products and services the bank offers.

Advancement

Experienced tellers can advance within their bank. They can become a head teller or move into another supervisory position. Some tellers can advance to other occupations, such as loan officer. They can also move to sales positions. For more information, see the profile on loan officers .

Important Qualities

Basic math skills. Because they count and handle large amounts of money, tellers must be good at arithmetic.

Customer-service skills. Tellers spend their day interacting with bank customers. They must be friendly, helpful, and patient. They must be able to understand what customers are looking for and explain the customers' options.

Detail oriented. Tellers must be sure not to make errors when dealing with customers' money.

Pay

Tellers

Median annual wages, May 2010

Total, All Occupations	$33,840
Office and Administrative Support Occupations	$30,710
Tellers	$24,100

Note: All Occupations includes all occupations in the U.S. Economy.
Source: U.S. Bureau of Labor Statistics, Occupational Employment Statistics

The median annual wage of tellers was $24,100 in May 2010. The median wage is the wage at which half the workers in an occupation earned more than that amount and half earned less. The lowest 10 percent earned less than $18,730, and the top 10 percent earned more than $32,650.

Most tellers work full time, Monday-through-Friday work schedules. Some tellers work on Saturdays. About 27 percent work part time, which is more than the average for other administrative and support occupations.

Job Outlook

Tellers

Percent change in employment, projected 2010-20

Total, All Occupations	14%
Office and Administrative Support Occupations	10%
Tellers	1%

Note: All Occupations includes all occupations in the U.S. Economy.
Source: U.S. Bureau of Labor Statistics, Employment Projections program

Employment of tellers is projected to experience little or no change, growing 1 percent from 2010 to 2020.

Past job growth for tellers was driven by a rapid expansion of bank branches, where most tellers work. However, the growth of bank branches is expected to slow because of both changes to the industry and the fact that certain areas now have an abundance of banks.

Additionally, online and mobile banking allows customers to handle many of the same transactions as tellers do. As more people use online banking, fewer bank customers will visit the teller window. This will result in decreased demand for tellers.

Job Prospects

Job prospects for tellers should be excellent because many workers leave this occupation.

Employment projections data for tellers, 2010-20

Occupational Title	SOC Code	Employment, 2010	Projected Employment, 2020	Change, 2010-20	
				Percent	Numeric
Tellers	43-3071	560,000	567,300	1	7,300
SOURCE: U.S. Bureau of Labor Statistics, Employment Projections program					

Similar Occupations

This table shows a list of occupations with job duties that are similar to those of tellers.

Occupation	Job Duties	Entry-Level Education	Median Annual Pay, May 2010
Bookkeeping, Accounting, and Auditing Clerks	Bookkeeping, accounting, and auditing clerks produce financial records for organizations. They record financial transactions, update statements, and check financial records for accuracy.	High school diploma or equivalent	$34,030
Cashiers	Cashiers handle payments from customers purchasing goods and services.	Less than high school	$18,500
Customer Service Representatives	Customer service representatives interact with customers on behalf of an organization. They provide information about products and services and respond to customer complaints. Some also take orders and process returns.	High school diploma or equivalent	$30,460
Information Clerks	Information clerks provide administrative and clerical support in a variety of settings. They help maintain records, collect data and information, and respond to customers' questions or concerns.	See How to Become One	$29,990

| Loan Officers | Loan officers evaluate, authorize, or recommend approval of loan applications for people and businesses. | High school diploma or equivalent | $56,490 |
| Receptionists | Receptionists perform various administrative tasks, including answering telephones and giving information to the public and customers. | High school diploma or equivalent | $25,240 |

Contacts for More Information

For general information on the banking industry, visit American Banking Association

Suggested citation:

Bureau of Labor Statistics, U.S. Department of Labor, Occupational Outlook Handbook, 2012-13 Edition, Tellers, on the Internet at http://www.bls.gov/ooh/office-and-administrative-support/tellers.htm .

Personal Care and Service Occupations

Animal Care and Service Workers

Quick Facts: Animal Care and Service Workers	
2010 Median Pay	$19,780 per year $9.51 per hour
Entry-Level Education	See How to Become One
Work Experience in a Related Occupation	None
On-the-job Training	See How to Become One
Number of Jobs, 2010	234,900
Job Outlook, 2010-20	23% (Faster than average)
Employment Change, 2010-20	54,000

What Animal Care and Service Workers Do

Animal care and service workers care for the needs of animals. They feed, water, groom, bathe, and exercise pets and other nonfarm animals. Job tasks vary by position and place of work.

Duties

Animal care and service workers typically do the following:
- Feed and give water to animals
- Clean equipment and the living spaces of animals
- Monitor animals and record information such as their diet, physical condition, and behavior
- Examine animals for signs of illness or injury
- Exercise animals
- Bathe animals, trim nails, clip hair, and attend to other grooming needs
- Train animals to obey or to do specific behaviors

Animal care and service workers train, feed, groom, and exercise animals. They also clean, disinfect, and repair the animals' cages. They play with the animals, provide companionship, and observe behavioral changes that could indicate illness or injury.

Boarding kennels, pet stores, animal shelters, rescue leagues, veterinary hospitals and clinics, stables, laboratories, aquariums and natural aquatic habitats, and zoological parks all house animals and employ animal care and service workers.

Nonfarm animal caretakers typically work with cats and dogs in animal shelters or rescue leagues. All caretakers attend to the basic needs of animals, but experienced caretakers may have more responsibilities, such as helping to vaccinate or euthanize animals under the direction of a veterinarian. Caretakers also may have administrative duties, such as keeping records on the animals, answering questions from the public, educating visitors about pet health, or screening people who want to adopt an animal.

Animal trainers train animals for riding, security, performance, obedience, or assisting people with disabilities. They familiarize animals with human voices and contact, and they teach animals to respond to commands. Most animal trainers work with dogs and horses, but some work with marine mammals, such as dolphins. Trainers teach a variety of skills. For example, some may train dogs to guide people with disabilities; others teach animals to cooperate with veterinarians or train animals for a competition or show.

The following are examples of types of animal care and service workers:

Groomers specialize in maintaining a pet's appearance. Groomers may operate their own business, work in a grooming salon, or, increasingly, run their own mobile grooming service that travels to clients' homes. Demand for mobile grooming services is growing because these services are convenient for pet owners, allowing the pet to stay in its familiar environment.

Some groomers are employed by kennels, veterinary clinics, or pet supply stores, where they groom mostly dogs, but some cats, too. In addition to cutting, trimming, and styling the pet's fur, groomers clip nails, clean ears, and bathe pets. Some groomers also schedule appointments, sell products to pet owners, and identify problems that may require veterinary attention.

Grooms care for horses. Grooms work at stables and are responsible for feeding, grooming, and exercising these animals. They saddle and unsaddle horses, give them rubdowns, and cool them off after a ride. In addition, they clean out stalls, polish saddles, and organize the tack room where they keep harnesses, saddles, and bridles. They take care of food and supplies for the horses. Experienced grooms also may help train horses.

Keepers are animal care and service workers who work in zoos. They plan the animals' diets, feed them, and monitor their eating patterns. They also clean the animals' enclosures, monitor their behavior, and watch for signs of illness or injury. Depending on the size of the zoo, they may work with either a broad or a limited group of animals. They may help raise young animals, and they often spend time answering questions from the public.

Kennel attendants care for pets while their owners are working or are traveling. Basic attendant duties include cleaning cages and dog runs, and feeding, exercising, and playing with animals. Experienced attendants also may provide basic healthcare, bathe animals, and attend to other basic grooming needs.

Pet sitters look after animals while the owner is away. They go to the pet owner's home, allowing the pet to stay in its familiar

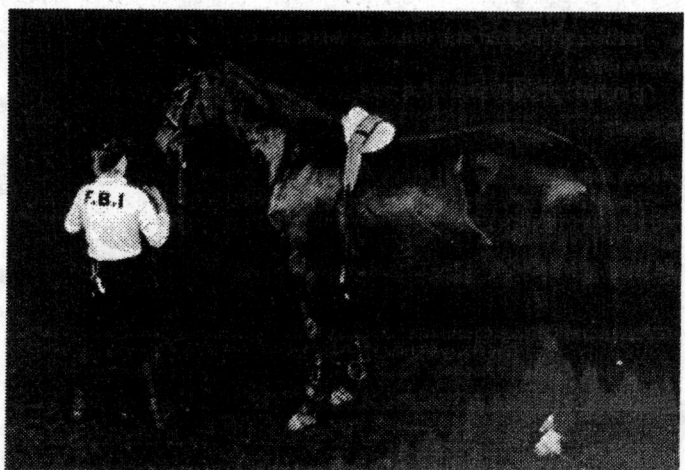

While most animal trainers train dogs, others work with horses or marine mammals.

surroundings and follow its routine. Most pet sitters feed, walk, and play with pets daily. More experienced pet sitters also may bathe, groom, or train pets. Most watch over dogs, but a few take care of cats.

Work Environment

Animal care and service workers held about 234,900 jobs in 2010. About 81 percent of these workers were nonfarm animal caretakers, and 19 percent were animal trainers.

Animal care and service workers work in a variety of settings. Although many work in kennels, others work in zoos, stables, animal shelters, pet stores, veterinary clinics, and aquariums. Mobile groomers and pet sitters typically travel to customers' homes. Caretakers of show and sports animals travel to competitions.

The work of animal care and service workers may be unpleasant and emotionally distressing. For example, those who work in shelters may see abused, injured, or sick animals. Some caretakers may have to help euthanize seriously injured or unwanted animals. Depending on their work setting, animal caretakers may work outdoors in all kinds of weather. Some facilities can be noisy.

Injuries

Animal care and service workers experience a work-related injury and illness rate that is much higher than that of most occupations. When working with scared or aggressive animals, caretakers may be bitten, scratched, or kicked. Also, injuries may happen while the caretaker is holding, cleaning, or restraining an animal. In addition, most animal care and service work involves many physical tasks, such as moving and cleaning cages, lifting bags of food, and exercising animals.

Work Schedules

Animals need care around the clock; many facilities, such as kennels, zoos, animal shelters, and stables, must be staffed 24 hours a day. Therefore, animal caretakers often work irregular hours and night, weekend, and holiday shifts. About 35 percent of nonfarm animal caretakers work part time.

About 28 percent of animal care and service workers are self-employed, and many of them can set their own schedule.

How to Become an Animal Care and Service Worker

Most animal care and service workers learn on the job. Still, many employers prefer to hire people who have experience with animals. Zookeeper and marine mammal trainer positions require formal education.

Education

Most animal care and service worker positions do not require formal education, but many animal care facilities require at least a high school diploma or the equivalent.

Although pet groomers typically learn by working under the guidance of an experienced groomer, they can also attend one of 50 state-licensed grooming schools. The length of each program varies with the school and the number of advanced skills taught.

Most zoos require keepers to have a bachelor's degree in biology, animal science, or a related field.

Animal trainers usually need a high school diploma or the equivalent, although some positions may require a bachelor's degree. For example, marine mammal trainers usually need a bachelor's degree in marine biology, animal science, biology, or a related field.

Dog trainers and horse trainers typically qualify by taking courses at community colleges or vocational and private training schools.

Training

Most animal care and service workers learn through short-term on-the-job training. They begin by doing basic tasks and work up to positions that require more responsibility and experience.

Some animal care and service workers may receive training before they enter their position. For example, caretakers in shelters can attend training programs through the Humane Society of the United States and the American Humane Association . Pet groomers often learn their trade by completing an informal apprenticeship, usually lasting 12 to 20 weeks, under the guidance of an experienced groomer.

Certification

Although not required, certifications available in many of these occupations may help workers establish their credentials and enhance their skills. For example, several professional associations and hundreds of private vocational and state-approved trade schools offer certification for dog trainers. The National Dog Groomers Association of America offers certification for master status as a groomer. Both the National Association of Professional Pet Sitters and Pet Sitters International offer a home-study certification program for pet sitters. Marine mammal trainers should be certified in SCUBA.

Work Experience

For many caretaker positions, it helps to have experience working with animals. Nearly all animal trainer and zookeeper positions require candidates to have experience with animals.

Important Qualities

Compassion. All workers must be compassionate when dealing with animals and their owners. They should like animals and must treat them with kindness.

Customer-service skills. Animal care and service workers should understand pet owners' needs so they can provide services that leave the owners satisfied. Some animal care and service workers may need to deal with distraught pet owners; for example, caretakers working in animal shelters may need to reassure owners looking for a lost pet.

Detail oriented. Workers must be detail oriented because they are often responsible for keeping animals on a strict diet, maintaining records, and monitoring changes in animals' behavior.

Patience. Many animal caretakers and all animal trainers need to be patient when teaching or dealing with animals that do not respond to commands.

Problem-solving skills. Animal trainers must have problem-solving skills when teaching an animal obedience and other behaviors. They must assess whether the animals are responding to the trainer's teaching methods and identify which methods are most successful.

Stamina. Stamina is important for animal care and service workers because their work often involves kneeling, crawling, bending, and, occasionally, lifting heavy supplies, such as bags of food.

Pay

Animal Care and Service Workers
Median annual wages, May 2010

Total, All Occupations	$33,840
Animal Trainers	$26,580
Animal Care and Service Workers	$19,780
Nonfarm Animal Caretakers	$19,550

Note: All Occupations includes all occupations in the U.S. Economy.
Source: U.S. Bureau of Labor Statistics, Occupational Employment Statistics

The median annual wage of nonfarm animal caretakers was $19,550 in May 2010. The median wage is the wage at which half the workers in an occupation earned more than that amount and half earned less. The lowest 10 percent earned less than $16,050, and the top 10 percent earned more than $31,880.

The median annual wage of animal trainers was $26,580 in May 2010. The lowest 10 percent earned less than $17,240, and the top 10 percent earned more than $53,580.

Animals need care around the clock; many facilities, such as kennels, animal shelters, and stables, must be staffed 24 hours a day. Therefore, animal caretakers often work irregular hours and night, weekend, and holiday shifts. About 35 percent of nonfarm animal caretakers work part time.

About 28 percent of animal care and service workers are self-employed, and many of them can set their own schedule.

Job Outlook

Animal Care and Service Workers
Percent change in employment, projected 2010-20

Nonfarm Animal Caretakers	28%
Animal Care and Service Workers	23%
Total, All Occupations	14%
Animal Trainers	3%

Note: All Occupations includes all occupations in the U.S. Economy.
Source: U.S. Bureau of Labor Statistics, Employment Projections program

Overall employment of animal care and service workers is expected to grow 23 percent from 2010 to 2020, faster than the average for all occupations. However, employment growth will vary by specialty: for example, employment of nonfarm animal caretakers is expected to grow 28 percent, while employment of animal trainers is expected to grow 3 percent.

Animal care and service workers will be needed to keep up with a growing pet population. In addition, many people consider their pets to be a part of their family and are willing to pay more for pet care than owners have in the past. Employment in kennels, grooming shops, pet stores, and veterinary clinics and hospitals is projected to increase to keep up with the growing demand for animal services.

Demand for zookeepers, marine mammal trainers, and horse trainers is projected to grow more slowly.Many work at zoos, shows, and amusement and recreation establishments, none of which is expected to add as many positions as other traditional pet care facilities. Furthermore, the cost of owning and riding horses is still too high for many people, so employment of horse trainers is not expected to grow as fast as employment of those who work with companion pets, such as dogs and cats.

Job Prospects

Job opportunities should be excellent for most positions. Employment growth and high turnover are expected to lead to many openings for dog trainers, groomers, pet sitters, kennel attendants, and caretakers in shelters and rescue leagues. As the companion animal population grows and the number of pet services increase, more workers will be needed. In addition, entry requirements are low for most animal care occupations, so positions should continue to be available for workers looking to enter the field.

However, candidates will face strong competition for positions as marine mammal trainers, horse trainers, and zookeepers. The relatively few positions and the popularity of the occupations should result in far more applicants than available positions.

Employment projections data for animal care and service workers, 2010-20

Occupational Title	SOC Code	Employment, 2010	Projected Employment, 2020	Change, 2010-20	
				Percent	Numeric
Animal Care and Service Workers	—	234,900	288,900	23	54,000
Animal Trainers	39-2011	45,800	47,300	3	1,500
Nonfarm Animal Caretakers	39-2021	189,100	241,500	28	52,500
SOURCE: U.S. Bureau of Labor Statistics, Employment Projections program					

Similar Occupations

This table shows a list of occupations with job duties that are similar to those of animal care and service workers.

Occupation	Job Duties	Entry-Level Education	Median Annual Pay, May 2010
Agricultural Workers	Agricultural workers maintain the quality of farms, crops, and livestock by operating machinery and doing physical labor under the supervision of agricultural managers.	See How to Become One	$18,970
Farmers, Ranchers, and Other Agricultural Managers	Farmers, ranchers, and other agricultural managers run establishments that produce crops, livestock, and dairy products.	High school diploma or equivalent	$60,750
Veterinarians	Veterinarians care for the health of animals. They diagnose, treat, or research medical conditions and diseases of pets, livestock, and animals in zoos, racetracks, and laboratories.	Doctoral or professional degree	$82,040
Veterinary Assistants and Laboratory Animal Caretakers	Veterinary assistants and laboratory animal caretakers look after nonfarm animals in laboratories, animal hospitals, and clinics. They care for the well-being of animals by doing routine tasks under the supervision of veterinarians, scientists, or veterinary technologists or technicians.	High school diploma or equivalent	$22,040
Veterinary Technologists and Technicians	Veterinary technologists and technicians perform medical tests under the supervision of a licensed veterinarian to treat or to help veterinarians diagnose the illnesses and injuries of animals.	Associate's degree	$29,710

Contacts for More Information

For more information about pet groomers, visit National Dog Groomers Association of America , Petgroomer.com

For more information about pet sitters, including certification information, visit National Association of Professional Pet Sitters

For more information about marine mammal trainers, visit International Marine Animal Trainers' Association

Barbers, Hairdressers, and Cosmetologists

Quick Facts: Barbers, Hairdressers, and Cosmetologists	
2010 Median Pay	$22,500 per year $10.82 per hour
Entry-Level Education	See How to Become One
Work Experience in a Related Occupation	None
On-the-job Training	See How to Become One
Number of Jobs, 2010	712,200
Job Outlook, 2010-20	14% (About as fast as average)
Employment Change, 2010-20	100,900

What Barbers, Hairdressers, and Cosmetologists Do

Barbers, hairdressers, and cosmetologists provide hair styling and beauty services.

Duties

Barbers, hairdressers, and cosmetologists typically do the following:

- Inspect hair, face, and scalp, to recommend treatment
- Discuss hairstyle options
- Wash, color, and condition hair
- Cut or trim, dry, and style hair
- Receive payments from clients
- Clean and sanitize all tools and work areas

Barbers, hairdressers, and cosmetologists focus on providing hair and beauty services to enhance clients' appearance. Those who operate their own barbershops or salons have managerial duties that may

Barbers, hairdressers, and cosmetologists provide hair styling and beauty services.

include hiring, supervising, and firing workers, as well as keeping business and inventory records, ordering supplies, and arranging for advertising.

Barbers cut, trim, shampoo, and style hair, mostly for male clients. They also may fit hairpieces and offer facial shaving. In every state, barbers are licensed to color, bleach, and highlight hair and to offer permanent-wave services. Common tools include combs, scissors, and clippers.

Hairdressers, or **hairstylists**, offer a wide range of hair services, such as shampooing, cutting, coloring, and styling. They often advise clients, both male and female, on how to care for their hair at home. They also keep records of products and services provided to clients, such as hair color, shampoo, conditioner, and hair treatment used. Tools include hairbrushes, scissors, blow dryers, and curling irons.

Cosmetologists provide scalp and facial treatments and makeup analysis. Some also clean and style wigs and hairpieces. A growing number actively sell skin care products.

Shampooers wash and rinse customers' hair so a hairstylist can cut and style it.

Work Environment

Barbers, hairdressers, and cosmetologists held about 712,200 jobs in 2010. Nearly half were self-employed.

Employment in the detailed occupations that make up barbers, hairdressers, and cosmetologists was distributed as follows:

Hairdressers, hairstylists, and cosmetologists	627,700
Barbers	62,200
Shampooers	22,300

Barbers, hairdressers, and cosmetologists work mostly in a barbershop or salon, although some work in a spa, hotel, or resort. Some lease booth space in other people's salons. Some manage salons or open their own after several years of experience.

Barbers, hairdressers, and cosmetologists usually work in pleasant surroundings with good lighting. Physical stamina is important, because they are on their feet for most of their shift. Prolonged exposure to some chemicals may cause irritation, so they might wear protective clothing, such as disposable gloves or aprons.

Work Schedules

Many barbers, hairdressers, and cosmetologists work part time. However, some self-employed workers may have long hours. Work schedules often include evenings and weekends€•the times when barbershops and beauty salons are busiest. Those who are self-employed usually determine their own schedules.

How to Become a Barber, Hairdresser, or Cosmetologist

All states require barbers, hairdressers, and cosmetologists to be licensed. To qualify for a license, candidates are required to graduate from a state-approved cosmetology program. Shampooers do not need a license.

Education and Training

A high school diploma or equivalent is required for some positions. In addition, every state requires that barbers, hairdressers, and cosmetologists complete a program in a state-licensed barber or cosmetology school. Programs in hairstyling, skin care, and other personal appearance services are available both in high schools and in public or private postsecondary vocational schools.

Full-time programs in barbering and cosmetology usually last at least 9 months and may lead to an associate's degree. Most of these workers take advanced courses in hairstyling or in other personal appearance services to keep up with the latest trends. Those who want to open their own business also may take courses in sales and marketing.

Shampooers do not need formal training. Some short-term on-the-job training under the supervision of a hairstylist or a more experienced shampooer is sufficient.

Licenses

All states require barbers, hairdressers, and cosmetologists to be licensed. Qualifications for a license vary by state; but generally, a person must have a high school diploma or equivalent, be at least 16 years old, and have graduated from a state-licensed barber or cosmetology school. After graduating from a state-approved training program, students take a state licensing exam. The exam includes a written test and, in some cases, a practical test of styling skills or an oral exam.

In many states, cosmetology training may be credited toward a barbering license, and vice versa, and a few states combine the two licenses. A fee is usually required to apply for a license, and periodic license renewals may be necessary.

Some states have reciprocity agreements that allow licensed barbers and cosmetologists to get a license in another state without needing additional formal training, but such agreements are uncommon. Consequently, people who want to work in a particular state should review the laws of that state before entering a training program.

Important Qualities

Creativity. Barbers, hairdressers, and cosmetologists must keep up with the latest trends and be able to try new hairstyles for their clients.

Customer-service skills. To help retain clients, barbers, hairdressers, and cosmetologists must be pleasant, friendly, and able to interact with customers.

Listening skills. Barbers, hairdressers, and cosmetologists should be good listeners. They must listen carefully to what the client wants to make sure the client is happy with the result.

Stamina. Barbers, hairdressers, and cosmetologists must be able to stand on their feet for long periods of time.

Time-management skills. Time management skills are important when scheduling appointments and providing services. For example, routine haircuts and trims do not require the precise timing of some other services, such as applying neutralizer after a permanent wave. Clients who receive timely hair care service are more likely to return.

In addition, barbers, hairdressers, and cosmetologists must keep a neat personal appearance and must keep their work area clean and sanitary. This is necessary for the health and safety of their clients, as well as to make clients comfortable enough to want to return.

Pay

Barbers, Hairdressers, and Cosmetologists Median hourly wages, May 2010	
Total, All Occupations	$16.27
Barbers	$11.45
Hairdressers, Hairstylists, and Cosmetologists	$10.94
Barbers, Hairdressers, and Cosmetologists	$10.82
Shampooers	$8.78

Note: All Occupations includes all occupations in the U.S. Economy.
Source: U.S. Bureau of Labor Statistics, Occupational Employment Statistics

The median hourly wage of barbers, hairdressers, and cosmetologists was $10.82 in May 2010. The median wage is the wage at which half the workers in an occupation earned more than that amount and half earned less.

Median hourly wages for occupational specialties in May 2010 were as follows:

- $11.45 for barbers
- $10.94 for hairdressers, hairstylists, and cosmetologists
- $8.78 for shampooers

Many barbers, hairdressers, and cosmetologists work part time. However, some self-employed workers have long hours. Work schedules often include evenings and weekends€•the times when beauty salons and barbershops are busiest. Those who are self-employed usually determine their own schedules.

Job Outlook

Barbers, Hairdressers, and Cosmetologists Percent change in employment, projected 2010-20	
Hairdressers, Hairstylists, and Cosmetologists	16%
Total, All Occupations	14%
Barbers, Hairdressers, and Cosmetologists	14%
Barbers	7%
Shampooers	-9%

Note: All Occupations includes all occupations in the U.S. Economy.
Source: U.S. Bureau of Labor Statistics, Employment Projections program

Overall employment of barbers, hairdressers, cosmetologists, and shampooers is expected to grow 14 percent from 2010 to 2020, as fast as the average for all occupations. Growth rates will vary by specialty.

Employment of barbers is projected to grow 7 percent, slower than the average for all occupations. The need for barbers will stem primarily from an increasing population, which will lead to greater demand for basic hair-care services.

Employment of hairdressers, hairstylists, and cosmetologists is projected to grow 16 percent, about as fast as the average for all occupations. Demand for hair coloring, hair straightening, and other advanced hair treatments has increased in recent years, a trend that is expected to continue over the coming decade.

Employment of shampooers is projected to decline 9 percent as more barbers, hairdressers, and hairstylists perform shampooing services themselves.

Job Prospects

Overall job opportunities for barbers, hairdressers, and cosmetologists are expected to be good. A large number of job openings will stem from the need to replace workers who transfer to other occupations, retire, or leave the occupations for other reasons.

However, workers should expect stiff competition for jobs and clients at higher paying salons, of which there are relatively few and for which applicants must compete with a large pool of experienced hairdressers and cosmetologists.

Because employment of shampooers is expected to decline, job opportunities should be somewhat limited, available only from the need to replace those who leave the occupation.

Employment projections data for barbers, hairdressers, and cosmetologists, 2010-20

Occupational Title	SOC Code	Employment, 2010	Projected Employment, 2020	Change, 2010-20	
				Percent	Numeric
Barbers, Hairdressers, and Cosmetologists	—	712,200	813,000	14	100,900
Barbers	39-5011	62,200	66,700	7	4,500
Hairdressers, Hairstylists, and Cosmetologists	39-5012	627,700	726,100	16	98,400
Shampooers	39-5093	22,300	20,300	-9	-2,000
SOURCE: U.S. Bureau of Labor Statistics, Employment Projections program					

Similar Occupations

This table shows a list of occupations with job duties that are similar to those of barbers, hairdressers, and cosmetologists.

Occupation	Job Duties	Entry-Level Education	Median Annual Pay, May 2010
Manicurists and Pedicurists	Manicurists and pedicurists clean, shape, and beautify fingernails and toenails.	Postsecondary non-degree award	$19,650
Skincare Specialists	Skincare specialists cleanse and beautify the face and body to enhance a person's appearance.	Postsecondary non-degree award	$28,920

Contacts for More Information

For more information about barbers, hairdressers, and cosmetologists, including training, visit American Association of Cosmetology Schools , Professional Beauty Association , National Association of Barber Boards of America

Suggested citation:

Bureau of Labor Statistics, U.S. Department of Labor, Occupational Outlook Handbook, 2012-13 Edition, Barbers, Hairdressers, and Cosmetologists, on the Internet at http://www.bls.gov/ooh/personal-care-and-service/barbers-hairdressers-and-cosmetologists.htm .

Childcare Workers

Quick Facts: Childcare Workers	
2010 Median Pay	$19,300 per year $9.28 per hour
Entry-Level Education	High school diploma or equivalent
Work Experience in a Related Occupation	None
On-the-job Training	Short-term on-the-job training
Number of Jobs, 2010	1,282,300
Job Outlook, 2010-20	20% (Faster than average)
Employment Change, 2010-20	262,000

What Childcare Workers Do

Childcare workers care for children when parents and other family members are unavailable. They care for children's basic needs, such as bathing and feeding. In addition, some help children prepare for kindergarten, and many help older children with homework.

Duties

Childcare workers typically do the following:

- Supervise and monitor the safety of children in their care
- Prepare meals and organize mealtimes and snacks for children
- Help children keep good hygiene
- Change the diapers of infants and toddlers
- Organize activities so that children can learn about the world and explore interests
- Develop schedules and routines to ensure that children have enough physical activity, rest, and playtime
- Watch for signs of emotional or developmental problems in children and bring the problems to the attention of parents
- Keep records of children's progress, routines, and interest

Childcare workers care for the basic needs of infants and toddlers, changing their diapers and preparing their meals. They also maintain the children's schedules, such as play, nap, and meal times.

They introduce babies and toddlers to basic concepts by reading to them and playing with them. For example, they teach young children how to share and take turns by playing games with other children.

Childcare workers often help preschool-aged children prepare for kindergarten. Young children learn from playing, solving problems, questioning, and experimenting. Childcare workers use children's play to improve the children's language—for example, through storytelling and acting games—and their social skills—for example, through having them build something together in the sandbox. They may involve the children in creative activities, such as art, dance, and music.

Childcare workers often watch school-aged children before and after school. They help these children with homework and ensure that they attend afterschool activities, such as athletic practices and club meetings.

During the summer, when children are out of school, childcare workers may watch older children as well as younger ones for the entire day while the parents are at work.

The following are examples of types of childcare workers:

Childcare center workers work in teams in formal childcare centers, including Head Start and Early Head Start programs. They often work with preschool teachers and teacher assistants to teach children through a structured curriculum. They prepare daily and long-term schedules of activities to stimulate and educate the children in their care. They also monitor and keep records of children's progress. For more information, see the profiles on preschool teachers and teacher assistants .

Family childcare providers care for children in the provider's own home during traditional working hours. They need to ensure that their homes and all staff they employ meet the regulations for family childcare centers.

After the children go home, the providers often have more responsibilities, such as shopping for food or supplies, doing accounting, keeping records, and cleaning. In addition, family childcare providers frequently must spend some of their time marketing their services to prospective families.

Nannies work in the homes of the children they care for and the parents that employ them. Most often, they work full time for one family. They may be responsible for driving children to school, appointments, or afterschool activities. Some live in the homes of the families of that employ them.

Babysitters, like nannies, work in the homes of the children in their care. However, they work for many families instead of just one. In addition, they generally do not work full time, but rather take care of the children on occasional nights and weekends when parents have other obligations.

Work Environment

Childcare workers spend much of their day moving around the room to work with the children in their care. Carrying children, bending to lift children, and kneeling to be at eye level with children can be physically exhausting.

Childcare workers held about 1.3 million jobs in 2010. They are employed in childcare centers, preschools, public schools, and private

Childcare workers watch children when parents and other family members are unavailable.

homes.

Family childcare workers work in their own homes. They may convert a portion of their living space into a dedicated space for the children. About 30 percent of childcare workers are self-employed.

Nannies and babysitters usually work in their employers' homes. Some live in the home of their employer and generally are provided with their own room and bath.

The industries employing the most childcare workers in 2010 were as follows:

Child day care services	22%
Private households	15
Elementary and secondary schools	11
Religious, grantmaking, civic, professional, and similar organizations	8

Many states limit the number of children that each staff member is responsible for by regulating the ratio of staff to children. The ratios vary with the age of the children. With babies and toddlers, staff are responsible for relatively few children. As the children get older, staff can be responsible for more.

Work Schedules

Although many childcare workers work full time, a large portion, about 39 percent, work part time.

Childcare workers' schedules vary widely. Childcare centers usually are open year round, with long hours so that parents can drop off and pick up their children before and after work. Some centers employ full-time and part-time staff with staggered shifts to cover the entire day.

Family childcare providers usually have daily routines, but they may work long or unusual hours to fit parents' work schedules.

Live-in nannies usually work longer hours than do childcare workers who live in their own homes. However, although nannies may work evenings or weekends, they usually get other time off.

How to Become a Childcare Worker

Education and training requirements vary with settings, state regulations, and employer preferences. They range from less than a high school diploma to early childhood education certification.

Education

Childcare workers must meet education and training requirements, which vary with state regulations. Some states require these workers to have a high school diploma, but many states do not have any education requirements.

However, employers often prefer to hire workers with at least a high school diploma and, in some cases, some postsecondary education in early childhood education.

Beginning in 2013, workers in Head Start programs must at least be enrolled in a program in which they will earn an associate's degree in early childhood education or a child development credential.

Many states require providers to complete some training before beginning work. Often, these requirements can be satisfied by having some college credits or by earning a degree in early childhood education.

States do not regulate educational requirements for nannies and babysitters. However, some employers may prefer to hire workers with at least some formal instruction in education or a related field, particularly when they will be hired as full-time nannies.

Certification

Some states and employers require childcare workers to have a nationally recognized certification. Most often, states require the Child

Development Associate (CDA) certification offered by the Council for Professional Recognition. CDA certification includes coursework, experience in the field, and a high school diploma.

Some states recognize the Child Care Professional (CCP) designation offered by the National Child Care Association. Candidates for the CCP must have a high school diploma, experience in the field, and continuing education.

Some employers may require certifications in CPR and first aid.

Licenses

Many states require childcare centers, including those in private homes, to be licensed. To qualify for licensure, staff must pass a background check, have a complete record of immunizations, and meet a minimum training requirement.

Important Qualities

Communication skills. Childcare workers must be able to talk with parents and colleagues about the progress of the children in their care. They need both good writing and speaking skills to provide this information effectively.

Instructional skills. Childcare workers need to be able to explain things in terms young children can understand.

Patience. Working with children can be frustrating, so childcare workers need to be able to respond to overwhelming and difficult situations calmly.

People skills. Childcare workers need to work well with people to develop good relationships with parents, children, and colleagues.

Physical stamina. Working with children can be physically taxing, so childcare workers should have a lot of energy.

Pay

Childcare Workers
Median hourly wages, May 2010

Total, All Occupations	$16.27
Personal Care and Service Occupations	$9.92
Childcare Workers	$9.28

Note: All Occupations includes all occupations in the U.S. Economy.
Source: U.S. Bureau of Labor Statistics, Occupational Employment Statistics

The median hourly wage of childcare workers was $9.28 in May 2010. The median wage is the wage at which half the workers in an occupation earned more than that amount and half earned less. The lowest 10 percent earned less than $7.65, and the top 10 percent earned more than $14.08.

Pay varies with the worker's education and work setting. Those in formal childcare settings and those with more education usually earn higher wages. Pay for self-employed workers is based on the number of hours they work and the numbers and ages of the children in their care.

Although many childcare workers work full time, a large portion, about 39 percent, work part time.

The following table shows the median hourly wages of childcare workers in the industries employing the most childcare workers in May 2010:

Elementary and secondary schools	$10.75
Religious, grantmaking, civic, professional, and similar organizations	9.00
Child day care services	8.82

Childcare workers' schedules vary widely. Childcare centers usually are open year round, with long hours so that parents can drop off and pick up their children before and after work. Some centers employ full-time and part-time staff with staggered shifts to cover the entire day.

Family childcare providers usually have daily routines, but they may work long or unusual hours to fit parents' work schedules.

Live-in nannies usually work longer hours than do childcare workers who live in their own homes. However, although nannies may work evenings or weekends, they usually get other time off.

Job Outlook

Childcare Workers

Percent change in employment, projected 2010-20

Personal Care and Service Occupations	27%
Childcare Workers	20%
Total, All Occupations	14%

Note: All Occupations includes all occupations in the U.S. Economy.
Source: U.S. Bureau of Labor Statistics, Employment Projections program

Employment of childcare workers is expected to grow by 20 percent from 2010 to 2020, faster than the average for all occupations.

Parents will continue to need assistance during working hours to care for their children. Because the number of children requiring childcare is expected to grow, demand for childcare workers is expected to grow as well.

In the past decade, early childhood education has become widely recognized as important for children's development. Childcare workers often work alongside preschool teachers as assistants. This continued focus on the importance of early childhood education, in addition to increases in the number of children in this age group, will spur demand for preschool programs and thus for childcare workers as well.

Job Prospects

Workers with formal education should have the best job prospects. However, even those without formal education who are interested in the occupation should have little trouble finding employment because of the need to replace workers who leave the occupation.

Employment projections data for childcare workers, 2010-20

Occupational Title	SOC Code	Employment, 2010	Projected Employment, 2020	Change, 2010-20 Percent	Numeric
Childcare Workers	39-9011	1,282,300	1,544,300	20	262,000
SOURCE: U.S. Bureau of Labor Statistics, Employment Projections program					

Similar Occupations

This table shows a list of occupations with job duties that are similar to those of childcare workers.

Occupation	Job Duties	Entry-Level Education	Median Annual Pay, May 2010
Kindergarten and Elementary School Teachers	Kindergarten and elementary school teachers prepare younger students for future schooling by teaching them the basics of subjects such as math and reading.	Bachelor's degree	$51,380
Preschool and Childcare Center Directors	Preschool and childcare center directors are responsible for all aspects of their program. They direct and lead staff, oversee daily activities, and prepare plans and budgets.	Bachelor's degree	$42,960
Preschool Teachers	Preschool teachers educate and care for children, usually ages 3 to 5, who have not yet entered kindergarten. They explain reading, writing, science, and other subjects in a way that young children can understand.	Associate's degree	$25,700
Special Education Teachers	Special education teachers work with students who have a wide range of learning, mental, emotional and physical disabilities. With students who have mild or moderate disabilities, they ensure that lessons and teaching strategies are modified to meet the students' needs. With students who have severe disabilities, they teach the students independent living skills and basic literacy, communication, and math.	Bachelor's degree	$53,220
Teacher Assistants	Teacher assistants work under a teacher's supervision to give students additional attention and instruction.	High school diploma or equivalent	$23,220

Contacts for More Information

For more information about becoming a childcare provider, visit National Child Care Information Center

For more information about working as a nanny, visit International Nanny Association

For more information about early childhood education, visit National Association for the Education of Young Children

For more information about professional credentials, visit Council for Professional Recognition , National Child Care Association

Suggested citation:

Bureau of Labor Statistics, U.S. Department of Labor, Occupational Outlook Handbook, 2012-13 Edition, Childcare Workers, on the Internet at http://www.bls.gov/ooh/personal-care-and-service/childcare-workers.htm .

Fitness Trainers and Instructors

Quick Facts: Fitness Trainers and Instructors	
2010 Median Pay	$31,090 per year $14.95 per hour
Entry-Level Education	High school diploma or equivalent
Work Experience in a Related Occupation	None
On-the-job Training	Short-term on-the-job training
Number of Jobs, 2010	251,400
Job Outlook, 2010-20	24% (Faster than average)
Employment Change, 2010-20	60,400

What Fitness Trainers and Instructors Do

Fitness trainers and instructors lead, instruct, and motivate individuals or groups in exercise activities, including cardiovascular exercise (exercises for the heart and blood system), strength training, and stretching. They work with people of all ages and skill levels.

Duties

Fitness trainers and instructors typically do the following:

- Demonstrate how to carry out various exercises and routines
- Watch clients do exercises and show or tell them correct techniques to minimize injury and improve fitness
- Give alternative exercises during workouts or classes for different levels of fitness and skill
- Monitor clients' progress and adapt programs as needed
- Explain and enforce safety rules and regulations on sports, recreational activities, and the use of exercise equipment
- Give clients information or resources about nutrition, weight control, and lifestyle issues
- Give emergency first aid if needed

Both group and specialized fitness instructors often plan or choreograph their own classes. They choose music that is appropriate for their exercise class and create a routine or a set of moves for a class to follow. Some may teach pre-choreographed routines that were originally created by fitness companies or other organizations.

Fitness trainers and instructors lead, instruct, and motivate individuals or groups in exercise activities.

Personal fitness trainers design and carry out workout routines specific to the needs of their clients. In larger facilities, personal trainers must often sell their training sessions to members. They start by evaluating their clients' current fitness level, personal goals, and skills. Then, they develop personalized training programs for their clients to follow, and they monitor the clients' progress.

Fitness trainers and instructors in smaller facilities often do a variety of tasks in addition to their fitness duties, such as tending the front desk, signing up new members, giving tours of the fitness center, writing newsletter articles, creating posters and flyers, and supervising the weight-training and cardiovascular equipment areas.

In some facilities, a single trainer or instructor may provide individual sessions and teach group classes.

Gyms and other types of health clubs offer many different activities for clients. However, trainers and instructors often specialize in only a few areas. The following are some types of fitness trainers and instructors:

Personal fitness trainers work with a single client or a small group. They may train in a gym or in the clients' homes. Personal fitness trainers assess the clients' level of physical fitness and help them set and reach their fitness goals.

Group fitness instructors organize and lead group exercise sessions, which can include aerobic exercise, stretching, muscle conditioning, or meditation. Some classes are set to music. In these classes, instructors may select the music and choreograph an exercise sequence.

Specialized fitness instructors teach popular conditioning methods such as Pilates or yoga. In these classes, instructors show the different moves and positions of the particular method. They also watch students and correct those who are doing the exercises improperly.

Fitness directors oversee the fitness-related aspects of a gym or other type of health club. They often handle administrative duties, such as scheduling personal training sessions for clients or creating workout incentive programs. They often select and order fitness equipment for their facility.

Work Environment

Fitness trainers and instructors held about 251,400 jobs in 2010.

Fitness trainers and instructors work in health clubs, fitness or recreation centers, gyms, country clubs, hospitals, universities, yoga and Pilates studios, resorts, and clients' homes. Some fitness trainers and instructors also work in offices, where they organize and direct health and fitness programs for employees.

As shown in the below tabulation, most fitness trainers and instructors worked for fitness and recreational sports centers in 2010:

Fitness and recreational sports centers	61%
Civic and social organizations	13
Self-employed workers	8
Other educational services; state, local, and private	4
Hospitals; state, local, and private	2

Work Schedules

Some group fitness instructors and personal fitness trainers work other full-time jobs and teach fitness classes or offer personal training sessions during the week or on the weekend. Fitness trainers and instructors may work nights, weekends, or holidays. Some travel to different gyms or to clients' homes to teach classes or offer personal training sessions.

How to Become a Fitness Trainer or Instructor

The education and training required for fitness trainers and instructors vary by type of specialty, and employers often hire those with certification. Personal fitness trainers, group fitness instructors, and specialized fitness instructors each need different preparation. Requirements vary by facility.

Personal fitness trainers often start out by taking classes to become certified. Then they work alongside an experienced trainer before being allowed to train clients alone.

Many group fitness instructors often take training and become certified, and then they must audition for instructor positions. If they succeed at the audition, they may begin teaching classes.

Training for specialized fitness instructors can vary greatly. For example, the duration of programs for yoga instructors can range from a few days to more than 2 years. The Yoga Alliance has training standards requiring at least 200 hours with a specified number of hours in techniques, teaching methods, anatomy, physiology, philosophy, and other areas.

Certification

Employers prefer to hire certified fitness trainers and instructors. Personal trainers are often required to be certified to begin working with clients or with members of a gym or other type of health club. Group fitness instructors may be allowed to begin without certification, but employers often encourage or require them to become certified.

Most trainers or instructors need certification in cardiopulmonary resuscitation (CPR) before applying for certification in physical fitness.

Many organizations offer certification. The National Commission for Certifying Agencies (NCCA), part of the Institute for Credentialing Excellence , lists certifying organizations that are accredited.

All certification exams have a written part, and some also have a practical part. The exams measure the candidate's knowledge of human physiology, understanding of proper exercise techniques, assessment of clients' fitness levels, and development of appropriate exercise programs.

No specific education or training is required for certification. Many certifying organizations offer study materials, including books, CDs, other audio and visual materials, and exam preparation workshops and seminars.

Advanced certification requires an associate's or bachelor's degree in an exercise-related subject that presents more specialized instruction, such as training athletes, working with people who are injured or ill, or advising clients on general health.

Education

Almost all trainers and instructors have at least a high school diploma before entering the occupation. An increasing number of employers require fitness workers to have an associate's or bachelor's degree related to a health or fitness field, such as exercise science, kinesiology, or physical education. Programs often include courses in nutrition, exercise techniques, and group fitness.

Important Qualities

Customer service skills. Many fitness trainers and instructors must sell their services, motivating clients to hire them as personal trainers or to sign up for the classes they lead. Therefore, fitness trainers and instructors must be polite, friendly, and encouraging to get and keep their clients.

Listening skills. Fitness trainers and instructors must be able to listen carefully to what clients tell them to determine the client's fitness levels and desired fitness goals.

Motivational skills. Getting fit and staying fit takes a lot of work for many clients. To keep clients coming back for more classes or to continue personal training, fitness trainers and instructors must be able to keep their clients motivated.

Physical fitness. Fitness trainers and instructors need to be physically fit because their job requires a considerable amount of exercise. Group instructors often participate in classes, and personal trainers often need to show exercises to their clients.

Problem-solving skills. Fitness trainers and instructors must evaluate each client's level of fitness and create an appropriate fitness plan to meet the client's individual needs.

Speaking skills. Fitness trainers and instructors must be able to communicate well because they need to be able to explain exercises and movements to clients, as well as motivate them verbally during exercises.

Advancement

Fitness trainers and instructors who are interested in management positions should get a bachelor's degree in exercise science, physical education, kinesiology, or a related area. Experience is often required to advance to management positions in a health club or fitness center. Some organizations require a master's degree.

Personal trainers may eventually advance to a head trainer position and become responsible for hiring and overseeing the personal training staff or for bringing in new personal training clients. Some fitness trainers and instructors go into business for themselves and open their own fitness centers. Group fitness instructors may be promoted to group exercise director, a position responsible for hiring instructors and coordinating exercise classes. Trainers and instructors may eventually become a fitness director or general manager.

Pay

Fitness Trainers and Instructors
Median annual wages, May 2010

Total, All Occupations	$33,840
Fitness Trainers and Instructors	$31,090
Personal Care and Service Occupations	$20,640

Note: All Occupations includes all occupations in the U.S. Economy.
Source: U.S. Bureau of Labor Statistics, Occupational Employment Statistics

The median annual wage of fitness trainers and instructors was $31,090 in May 2010. The median wage is the wage at which half the workers in an occupation earned more than that amount and half earned less. The lowest 10 percent earned less than $17,070, and the top 10 percent earned more than $63,400.

Some group fitness instructors and personal fitness trainers work other full-time jobs and teach fitness classes or offer personal training sessions during the week or on the weekend. Fitness trainers and instructors may work nights, weekends, or holidays. Some travel to different gyms or to clients' homes to teach classes or offer personal training sessions.

Job Outlook

Fitness Trainers and Instructors

Percent change in employment, projected 2010-20

Personal Care and Service Occupations	27%
Fitness Trainers and Instructors	24%
Total, All Occupations	14%

Note: All Occupations includes all occupations in the U.S. Economy.
Source: U.S. Bureau of Labor Statistics, Employment Projections program

Employment of fitness trainers and instructors is expected to grow by 24 percent from 2010 to 2020, faster than the average for all occupations.

As businesses and insurance organizations continue to recognize the benefits of health and fitness programs for their employees, incentives to join gyms or other types of health clubs is expected to increase the need for fitness trainers and instructors. Some businesses may even decide to open their own onsite facility to decrease the need for their employees to travel for exercise.

As baby boomers age, they will be encouraged to remain active to help prevent injuries and illnesses associated with aging. With the increasing number of older residents in nursing homes or residential care facilities and communities, jobs for fitness trainers and instructors are expected to arise from the need for workers in the fitness centers in these locations.

Other employment growth is likely to come from the continuing emphasis on exercise for young people to combat obesity and encourage healthy lifestyles. More young people and families are likely to join fitness institutions or commit to personal training programs.

Participation in yoga and Pilates is expected to continue to increase, driven partly by older adults who want low-impact forms of exercise and relief from arthritis and other ailments.

Job Prospects

Job prospects should be best for workers with professional certification or increased levels of formal education in health or fitness.

Employment projections data for fitness trainers and instructors, 2010-20

Occupational Title	SOC Code	Employment, 2010	Projected Employment, 2020	Change, 2010-20 Percent	Change, 2010-20 Numeric
Fitness Trainers and Aerobics Instructors	39-9031	251,400	311,800	24	60,400
SOURCE: U.S. Bureau of Labor Statistics, Employment Projections program					

Similar Occupations

This table shows a list of occupations with job duties that are similar to those of fitness trainers and instructors.

Occupation	Job Duties	Entry-Level Education	Median Annual Pay, May 2010
Athletic Trainers	Athletic trainers specialize in preventing, diagnosing, and treating muscle and bone injuries and illnesses. They work with people of all ages and all skill levels, from young children to soldiers and professional athletes.	Bachelor's degree	$41,600
Physical Therapists	Physical therapists help people who have injuries or illnesses improve their movement and manage their pain. They are often an important part of rehabilitation and treatment of patients with chronic conditions or injuries.	Doctoral or professional degree	$76,310
Physical Therapist Assistants and Aides	Physical therapist assistants and physical therapist aides work under the direction of physical therapists. They help patients who are recovering from injuries, illnesses, and surgeries regain movement and manage pain.	See How to Become One	$37,710
Recreation Workers	Recreation workers design and lead leisure activities for groups in volunteer agencies or recreation facilities, such as playgrounds, parks, camps and senior centers. They may lead activities in areas such as arts and crafts, sports, games, music, and camping.	Bachelor's degree	$22,260
Recreational Therapists	Recreational therapists plan, direct, and coordinate recreation programs for people with disabilities or illnesses. They use a variety of techniques, including arts and crafts, drama, music, dance, sports, games, and field trips. These programs help maintain or improve a client's physical and emotional well-being.	Bachelor's degree	$39,410

Contacts for More Information

For more information about fitness careers and about health and fitness programs in universities and other institutions, visit American College of Sports Medicine , National Strength and Conditioning Association

For information about certifications for personal trainers and group fitness instructors, visit American Council on Exercise , National Academy of Sports Medicine , Institute for Credentialing Excellence , National Federation of Professional Trainers

For information about health clubs and sports clubs, visit International Health, Racquet, & Sportsclub Association

For information about yoga teacher certification and a list of registered schools, visit Yoga Alliance

Suggested citation:

Bureau of Labor Statistics, U.S. Department of Labor, Occupational Outlook Handbook, 2012-13 Edition, Fitness Trainers and Instructors, on the Internet at http://www.bls.gov/ooh/personal-care-and-service/fitness-trainers-and-instructors.htm .

Funeral Directors

Quick Facts: Funeral Directors	
2010 Median Pay	$54,330 per year $26.12 per hour
Entry-Level Education	Associate's degree
Work Experience in a Related Occupation	None
On-the-job Training	Apprenticeship
Number of Jobs, 2010	29,300
Job Outlook, 2010-20	18% (About as fast as average)
Employment Change, 2010-20	5,300

What Funeral Directors Do

Funeral directors, also called morticians and undertakers, manage funeral homes and arrange the details of a funeral.

Duties

Funeral directors typically do the following:

- Arrange transportation of the deceased
- Prepare the remains (body)
- Submit paperwork and legal documents
- Consult with the deceased's family
- Help plan funerals
- Train junior staff
- Discuss and plan funerals with people who wish to arrange their own service in advance

Most funeral directors arrange the details and handle the logistics of funerals. Together with the family, funeral directors establish the locations, dates, and times of wakes, memorial services, and burials. They handle other details as well, such as determining whether the body should be buried, entombed, or cremated. This decision is critical because funeral practices vary among cultures and religions.

Although family members or others may handle some details, funeral directors must be able to assist family members in preparing obituary notices and arranging for pallbearers (people who carry the coffin) and clergy. They may decorate and prepare the sites of services,

arrange for flowers, and provide transportation for the deceased and mourners.

Most funeral directors handle paperwork involved with the person's death, including submitting papers to state officials to get a formal death certificate. Some help resolve insurance claims or apply for veterans' funeral benefits on behalf of the family. They also may notify the Social Security Administration of the death.

In many settings, funeral directors embalm the deceased. Embalming is a sanitary and cosmetic process through which the body is prepared for burial, usually in a casket.

Funeral services may take place in a home, house of worship, or funeral home or at the gravesite or crematory.

A growing number of funeral directors work with clients who wish to plan their own funerals in advance to ensure that their needs are met.

Many funeral directors also help prepare and ship bodies if the person dies in one place and is to be buried or cremated elsewhere.

Work Environment

Funeral directors held about 29,300 jobs in 2010. About 92 percent worked in the funeral services industry.

Funeral directors work mostly in funeral homes and crematories. The mood can be quiet and somber, and the work is often stressful. Funeral directors have to arrange the many details of a funeral within 24 to 72 hours of death. Funeral directors also may be responsible for multiple funerals on the same day.

Although funeral directors handle corpses, the health risk is minimal. Still, funeral directors must follow safety and health regulations.

Work Schedules

Most funeral directors work full time. They are often on call and work long hours, including nights and weekends.

How to Become a Funeral Director

High school students can prepare for a job as a funeral director by taking courses in biology and chemistry and by participating in public speaking. Part-time or summer jobs in funeral homes also are good experience.

An associate's degree in mortuary science is the minimum educational requirement. All funeral directors must be licensed by the state in which they work.

Education and Training

Funeral directors must have at least an associate's degree in mortuary science. A growing number of employers, however, prefer applicants to have a bachelor's degree.

Together with the family, funeral directors handle details of the memorial services.

The American Board of Funeral Service Education (ABFSE) accredits 57 mortuary science programs, most of which are 2-year associate's degree programs offered at community colleges. About 9 programs give a bachelor's degree.

In all mortuary science programs, students take courses in ethics, grief counseling, funeral service, and business law. All AFSBE-accredited programs also include embalming and restorative techniques courses.

Funeral directors must complete hands-on training under the direction of a licensed funeral director, usually lasting 1 to 3 years. The apprenticeship may be completed before, during, or after completing a mortuary program.

Licenses

All states require funeral directors to be licensed. Licensing laws vary by state, but most applicants should

- Be 21 years old
- Complete 2 years in an AFSBE mortuary science program
- Serve an apprenticeship lasting 1 to 3 years

Applicants must then pass a qualifying exam. Working in multiple states may require multiple licenses. For specific requirements, applicants should contact their state licensing board.

Most states require funeral directors to receive continuing education credits to keep their licenses.

Important Qualities

Compassion. Death is a delicate and emotional matter. Funeral directors must be able to treat clients with care and sympathy in their time of loss.

Interpersonal skills. Funeral directors should have good interpersonal skills. When speaking with families, for instance, they must be tactful and able to explain and discuss all matters about services that are needed or expected.

Time-management skills. Funeral directors must be able to handle numerous tasks for multiple customers, often in a short period.

Pay

Funeral Directors
Median annual wages, May 2010

Funeral Directors	$54,330
Total, All Occupations	$33,840
Funeral Service Workers	$33,600

Note: All Occupations includes all occupations in the U.S. Economy.
Source: U.S. Bureau of Labor Statistics, Occupational Employment Statistics

The median annual wage of funeral directors was $54,140 in May 2010. The median wage is the wage at which half the workers in an occupation earned more than that amount and half earned less. The lowest 10 percent earned less than $29,890, and the top 10 percent earned more than $98,340.

Most funeral directors work full time. They are frequently on call and work nights and weekends. Long hours are common.

Job Outlook

Funeral Directors
Percent change in employment, projected 2010-20

Funeral Directors	18%
Total, All Occupations	14%
Funeral Service Workers	11%

Note: All Occupations includes all occupations in the U.S. Economy.
Source: U.S. Bureau of Labor Statistics, Employment Projections program

Employment of funeral directors is expected to increase 18 percent from 2010 to 2020, about as fast as the average for all occupations.

Employment growth reflects an increase in the number of expected deaths among the largest segment of the population: aging baby boomers. Also, a growing number of older people are expected to prearrange their end-of-life services, increasing the need for funeral directors. This service gives family and friends a stress-free understanding that their final wishes will be met.

Job prospects

Job prospects for funeral directors are expected to be good overall, and more favorable for those who embalm and are willing to relocate. Some job openings should result from the need to replace workers who leave the occupation.

Employment projections data for funeral directors, 2010-20

Occupational Title	SOC Code	Employment, 2010	Projected Employment, 2020	Change, 2010-20 Percent	Numeric
Funeral Service Managers, Directors, Morticians, and Undertakers	39-4831	29,300	34,600	18	5,300
SOURCE: U.S. Bureau of Labor Statistics, Employment Projections program					

Similar Occupations

This table shows a list of occupations with job duties that are similar to those of funeral directors.

Occupation	Job Duties	Entry-Level Education	Median Annual Pay, May 2010
Physicians and Surgeons	Physicians and surgeons diagnose and treat injuries and illnesses in patients. Physicians examine patients, take medical histories, prescribe medications, and order, perform, and interpret diagnostic tests. Surgeons operate on patients to treat injuries, such as broken bones; diseases, such as cancerous tumors; and deformities, such as cleft palates.	Doctoral or professional degree	This wage is equal to or greater than $166,400 per year.

Psychologists	Psychologists study mental processes and human behavior by observing, interpreting, and recording how people and other animals relate to one another and the environment.	See How to Become One	$68,640
Social Workers	There are two main types of social workers: direct-service social workers, who help people solve and cope with problems in their everyday lives, and clinical social workers, who diagnose and treat mental, behavioral, and emotional issues.	See How to Become One	$42,480

Contacts for More Information

For more information about funeral directors, including accredited mortuary science programs, visit National Funeral Directors Association

For scholarships and educational programs in funeral service and mortuary science, visit American Board of Funeral Service Education

For information about crematories, visit Cremation Association of North America , International Cemetery, Cremation and Funeral Association

Candidates should contact their state board for specific licensing requirements.

Suggested citation:

Bureau of Labor Statistics, U.S. Department of Labor, Occupational Outlook Handbook, 2012-13 Edition, Funeral Directors, on the Internet at
http://www.bls.gov/ooh/personal-care-and-service/funeral-directors.htm

Gaming Services Occupations

Quick Facts: Gaming Services Occupations	
2010 Median Pay	$20,260 per year $9.74 per hour
Entry-Level Education	See How to Become One
Work Experience in a Related Occupation	See How to Become One
On-the-job Training	See How to Become One
Number of Jobs, 2010	177,100
Job Outlook, 2010-20	13% (About as fast as average)
Employment Change, 2010-20	22,900

What Gaming Services Occupations Do

Gaming services workers serve customers in gambling establishments, such as casinos or racetracks. Some workers tend slot machines or deal cards. Others take bets or pay out winnings. Still others supervise gaming workers and operations.

Duties

Gaming services workers typically do the following:

- Interact with customers and ensure that they have a pleasant experience
- Monitor customers for suspicious behavior
- Inform their supervisor or a security employee of any irregularities they observe
- Enforce safety rules and report hazards

Gaming managers and supervisors direct and oversee the gaming operations and personnel in their assigned area. Supervisors circulate among the tables to make sure that everything is running smoothly and that all areas are properly staffed. Gaming managers and supervisors typically do the following:

- Keep an eye on customers and employees to make sure that all rules are followed
- Address customers' complaints about service
- Explain house operating rules, such as betting limits, if customers do not understand them
- Schedule when and where employees in their section will work
- Interview, hire, and train new employees

Slot supervisors oversee the activities of the slot department. The job duties of this occupation have changed significantly, as slot machines have become more automated. Because most casinos use video slot machines that give out tickets instead of cash and thus require very little oversight, workers in this occupation spend most of their time providing customer service to slot players. Slot supervisors typically do the following:

- Watch over the slot section and ensure that players are satisfied with the games
- Provide input when new slot machines are purchased
- Determine if unpopular machines should be replaced
- Decide on where to put machines to maximize the number of customers playing at a time
- Refill machines with tickets or money when they run out
- Reset cash slot machines after a payout

Gaming dealers operate table games such as craps, blackjack, and roulette. They stand or sit behind tables while serving customers. Dealers control the pace and action of the game. They announce each player's move to the rest of the table and let players know when it is their turn. Most dealers can work with at least two games, usually blackjack or craps. Gaming dealers typically do the following:

- Give out cards and provide dice or other equipment to customers
- Determine winners, calculate and pay off winning bets, and collect on losing bets
- Continually inspect cards or dice
- Inform players of the rules of the game
- Keep track of the amount of money that customers have already bet
- Exchange paper money for gaming chips

Many gaming services workers are employed by casinos.

Gaming and sports book writers and runners handle bets on sporting events and take and record bets for customers. Sports book writers and runners also verify tickets and pay out winning tickets. In addition, they help run games such as bingo and keno. Some gaming runners collect winning tickets from customers in a casino. Gaming and sports book writers and runners typically do the following:

● Scan tickets and calculate winnings
● Operate the equipment that randomly selects bingo or keno numbers
● Announce bingo or keno numbers when they are selected
● Are responsible for the cash that comes in (on bets) and goes out (on winnings) during their shift

Work Environment

Some gaming services occupations are physically demanding. Gaming dealers spend most of their shift standing behind a table. Managers and supervisors are constantly walking up and down the casino floor. A casino atmosphere exposes workers to hazards such as secondhand smoke from cigarettes, cigars, and pipes. Noise from slot machines, gaming tables, and loud customers may be distracting to some, although workers wear protective headgear in areas where machinery is used to count money.

Workers in gaming services occupations held about 177,100 jobs in 2010. Many of the jobs were in commercial casinos, riverboat casinos, casino hotels, Native American casinos, and racetracks with casinos. However, these establishments are not legal in every state.

Workers in gaming services occupations are most often employed in the following industries:

Casino hotels	30%
Local government, excluding education and hospitals	26
Gambling industries	21

Work Schedules

Most casinos are open 24 hours a day, 7 days a week. Employees work nights, weekends, and holidays. Most managers and supervisors have full-time work schedules. However, many gaming dealers and sports book writers work part time.

How to Become a Gaming Services Worker

Most gaming jobs require a high school diploma or a GED. However, the most important quality in a gaming worker is customer service skills.

Education

Gaming dealers, supervisors, sports book writers and runners, and slot supervisors typically need a high school diploma or a GED. Gaming managers typically take formal management classes, although many of them do not need a postsecondary degree. Those who choose to pursue a degree may study hotel management or gaming management programs that lead to certificates or degrees that some colleges offer.

Training

Individual casinos or other gaming establishments have their own training requirements. Usually, new gaming dealers are sent to gaming school for 4 to 8 weeks to learn a casino game, such as blackjack or craps. These schools teach the rules and procedures of the game, as well as state and local laws and regulations related to the game. Gaming school is not just for new employees: dealers who have been employed for many years have to go to gaming school if they want to be trained in a new casino game. Completing gaming school before being hired may increase a prospective dealer's chances of being hired, but it does not guarantee a job. Casinos usually audition prospective dealers for open positions to assess their personal qualities.

Gaming and sports book writers and runners usually do not have to go to gaming school. They can be trained by the casino in less than 1 month. The casino teaches them state and local laws and regulations related to the game, as well the particulars of their job, such as keno calling.

Licenses

Gaming services workers must be licensed by a state regulatory agency, such as a state casino control board or gaming commission. Applicants for a license must provide photo identification and pay a fee. They must also pass a background check and drug test. Age requirements vary by state.

Work Experience

Gaming and slot supervisors usually have several years of experience working in a casino. Gaming supervisors often spend time as a dealer or in the customer outreach arm of the casino. Slot supervisors also usually begin in low-level marketing jobs or customer service. They may have experience as a gaming dealer or slot technician.

Gaming managers are often promoted from positions as slot or gaming supervisors. They may also be moved from a management job in another portion of the resort, such as hospitality, after learning about casino operations.

Advancement

Gaming dealers can advance to gaming supervisors and eventually managers. A slot supervisor can also advance to gaming manager.

Important Qualities

Customer-service skills. All gaming jobs involve a lot of interaction with customers. The success or failure of a casino depends on how customers view the casino, making customer service important for all gaming services occupations.

Leadership skills. Gaming managers and supervisors oversee other gaming services workers and must be able to guide them in doing their jobs.

Math skills. Because they deal with large amounts of money, many casino workers must be good at math.

Organizational skills. Gaming managers and supervisors must be well organized to handle administrative and other tasks required in overseeing gaming services workers.

Patience. All gaming workers have to be able to keep their composure when they handle a customer who becomes upset or breaks a rule.

Speaking skills. Dealers and gaming writers and runners must be able to explain the rules of the game to customers and answer any questions they have. Simple misunderstandings can cost a customer a lot of money and damage the reputation of the casino.

Pay

Gaming Services Occupations
Median annual wages, May 2010

Total, All Occupations	$33,840
Gaming Services Occupations	$20,260

Note: All Occupations includes all occupations in the U.S. Economy.
Source: U.S. Bureau of Labor Statistics, Occupational Employment Statistics

The median annual wage of workers in gaming services occupations was $20,260 in May 2010. The median wage is the wage at which half the workers in an occupation earned more than that amount and half earned less. The lowest 10 percent earned less than $15,940, and the top 10 percent earned more than $53,150.

The median wages for gaming service occupations in May 2010 were the following:

- $66,960 for gaming managers
- $48,530 for gaming supervisors
- $26,630 for slot supervisors
- $23,940 for all other gaming service workers
- $20,850 for gaming and sports book writers and runners
- $18,090 for gaming dealers

Most casinos are open 24 hours a day, 7 days a week. Employees work nights, weekends, and holidays. Most managers and supervisors have full-time work schedules. However, many gaming dealers and sports book writers work part time.

Job Outlook

Gaming Services Occupations
Percent change in employment, projected 2010-20

Total, All Occupations	14%
Gaming Services Occupations	13%

Note: All Occupations includes all occupations in the U.S. Economy.
Source: U.S. Bureau of Labor Statistics, Employment Projections program

Employment in gaming services occupations is projected to grow 13 percent from 2010 to 2020, about as fast as the average for all occupations. Employment growth of gaming managers and supervisors is projected to be 11 and 7 percent, respectively. Employment of gaming and sports book writers and runners is projected to grow 12 percent.

These occupations will be driven by the increasing popularity of gambling establishments such as Native American casinos and "racinos," racetracks that also offer slots or table games. Because some states benefit from casinos in the form of tax revenues or by favorable agreements with Native American tribes, additional states are considering expanding the number of gambling establishments over the next decade.

An increased demand for table games will drive growth for gaming dealers, whose employment is projected to grow 17 percent from 2010 to 2020. Many jurisdictions that currently allow only slot machines are expected to begin allowing table games for the additional money they bring. However, new electronic table games, which eliminate the need for a dealer, may moderate growth.

Employment of slot supervisors is projected to grow 6 percent from 2010 to 2020. Growth is expected to be slower than that of other gaming services occupations because of advancements in slot machine technology. Machines that don't take coins, known as "ticket-in, ticket-out machines," reduce the need for workers to pay out jackpots, fill hoppers, and reset machines. In addition, slot machines linked to a network can be adjusted from a central computer rather than one at a time on the floor.

Job Prospects

Although job openings will occur due to workers leaving the occupation, strong competition is expected for jobs at casinos. Those with work experience in customer service at a hotel or resort should have better job prospects because of the importance of customer service in casinos.

Employment projections data for gaming services occupations, 2010-20

Occupational Title	SOC Code	Employment, 2010	Projected Employment, 2020	Change, 2010-20 Percent	Change, 2010-20 Numeric
Gaming Services Occupations	—	177,100	200,000	13	22,900
Gaming Managers	11-9071	3,300	3,600	11	400
Gaming Supervisors	39-1011	36,100	38,600	7	2,500
Slot Supervisors	39-1012	18,900	20,000	6	1,100
Gaming Dealers	39-3011	91,000	106,600	17	15,500
Gaming and Sports Book Writers and Runners	39-3012	15,300	17,200	12	1,900
Gaming Service Workers, All Other	39-3019	12,400	14,000	13	1,600

SOURCE: U.S. Bureau of Labor Statistics, Employment Projections program

Similar Occupations

This table shows a list of occupations with job duties that are similar to those of gaming services occupations.

Occupation	Job Duties	Entry-Level Education	Median Annual Pay, May 2010
Customer Service Representatives	Customer service representatives interact with customers on behalf of an organization. They provide information about products and services and respond to customer complaints. Some also take orders and process returns.	High school diploma or equivalent	$30,460
Lodging Managers	Lodging managers make sure that guests on vacation or business travel have a pleasant experience, while also ensuring that an establishment is run efficiently and profitably.	High school diploma or equivalent	$46,880
Public Relations Managers and Specialists	Public relations managers and specialists create and maintain a favorable public image for their employer or client. They write material for media releases, plan and direct public relations programs, and raise funds for their organizations.	Bachelor's degree	$57,550
Retail Sales Workers	Retail sales workers include both those who sell retail merchandise, such as clothing, furniture, and automobiles, (called retail salespersons) and those who sell spare and replacement parts and equipment, especiallycar parts, (called parts salespersons). Both groups help customers find the products they want and process customers' payments.	Less than high school	$20,990
Sales Managers	Sales managers direct organizations' sales teams. They set sales goals, analyze data, and develop training programs for the organization's sales representatives.	Bachelor's degree	$98,530
Security Guards and Gaming Surveillance Officers	Security guards and gaming surveillance officers patrol and inspect property against fire, theft, vandalism, terrorism, and illegal activity. They monitor people and buildings in an effort to prevent crime.	High school diploma or equivalent	$24,380

Contacts for More Information

For more information about gaming services occupations, visit
American Gaming Association, Casino Careers

Suggested citation:

Bureau of Labor Statistics, U.S. Department of Labor, Occupational Outlook Handbook, 2012-13 Edition, Gaming Services Occupations, on the Internet at http://www.bls.gov/ooh/personal-care-and-service/gaming-services-occupations.htm .

Manicurists and Pedicurists

Quick Facts: Manicurists and Pedicurists	
2010 Median Pay	$19,650 per year $9.45 per hour
Entry-Level Education	Postsecondary non-degree award
Work Experience in a Related Occupation	None
On-the-job Training	None
Number of Jobs, 2010	81,700
Job Outlook, 2010-20	17% (About as fast as average)
Employment Change, 2010-20	13,600

What Manicurists and Pedicurists Do

Manicurists and pedicurists clean, shape, and beautify fingernails and toenails.

Duties

Manicurists and pedicurists typically do the following:

- Discuss nail treatments and services available
- Remove nail polish and rough skin
- Clean, trim, and file nails
- Massage and moisturize hands (for manicure) and feet (for pedicure)
- Polish or buff nails
- Advise clients about nail care
- Promote and sell nail care products
- Clean and disinfect their work area and tools

Manicurists and pedicurists work exclusively on the hands and feet, providing treatments to groom fingernails and toenails. A typical treatment involves soaking the clients' hands or feet to soften the skin to remove dead skin-cells. Manicurists and pedicurists also apply lotion or oil to hands and feet to moisturize the skin. They may also apply, shape, and apply polish to artificial fingernails.

Manicurists and pedicurists use a variety of tools, including nail clippers, nail files, and specialized cuticle tools. They must be focused while they perform their duties because most of the tools they use are sharp. They must also keep their work area and tools clean and sanitary.

Some manicurists and pedicurists operate their own businesses, typically at salons. They manage the daily decision-making tasks, such as keeping inventory records and ordering supplies. They also hire and supervise workers and sell nail care products, such as nail polish and hand or foot cream, to clients. A small but growing number of workers make house calls. These mobile manicure and pedicure services are popular because of their convenience.

Work Environment

Manicurists and pedicurists held about 81,700 jobs in 2010, of which 60 percent worked in the personal care services industry. About 37 percent were self-employed, many running their own nail salon business.

Manicurists and pedicurists usually work in a spa or nail salon. The job involves a lot of sitting. Those who own a mobile grooming company must travel to their clients' homes.

Manicurists and pedicurists sometimes use chemicals when working on fingernails and toenails, so they often wear latex gloves, masks, and protective clothing.

Work Schedules

Although most manicurists and pedicurists work full time, many have variable schedules and work part time. Their schedules are often determined by the type of establishment they work for. For example, a full service salon may require manicurists and pedicurists to work an eight-hour day. A boutique hair salon, however, may require shorter work hours on a part-time basis. Longer hours are not unusual for self-employed workers. Weekends and evenings tend to be the busiest times for manicurists and pedicurists.

How to Become a Manicurist or Pedicurist

Manicurists and pedicurists must complete a state-approved cosmetology program. After they finish the program, they must pass a state exam for licensure, which all states except Connecticut require.

Education and Training

Manicurists and pedicurists must complete a state-approved cosmetology program. Currently, there are 474 programs nationwide. Some high schools offer this training.

Licenses

State licensing requirements vary. However, applicants need to be at least 16 years old and have a high school diploma or equivalent. After completing a state-approved cosmetology program, manicurists and pedicurists must take a written and practical exam to get a license through their state board.

Manicurists and pedicurists clean, shape, and beautify fingernails and toenails.

Important Qualities

Creativity. The ability to neatly finish small, intricate designs is important, as is the ability to suggest and match nail designs for individual tastes.

Customer-service skills. Good listening and interpersonal skills are important when working with clients. Also, meeting the needs of clients, including interacting with them while doing a manicure or pedicure, helps to encourage repeat business.

Dexterity. A steady hand is essential in achieving a creative and precise nail design. Because manicurists and pedicurists often use sharp tools, they must also be well coordinated.

Pay

Manicurists and Pedicurists
Median hourly wages, May 2010

Total, All Occupations	$16.27
Personal Appearance Workers	$10.77
Manicurists and Pedicurists	$9.45

Note: All Occupations includes all occupations in the U.S. Economy.
Source: U.S. Bureau of Labor Statistics, Occupational Employment Statistics

The median hourly wage of manicurists and pedicurists was $9.45 in May 2010. The median wage is the wage at which half the workers in an occupation earned more than that amount and half earned less. The lowest 10 percent earned less than $7.85, and the top 10 percent earned more than $14.71.

Although most manicurists and pedicurists work full time, many have variable schedules and work part time. Their schedules are often determined by the type of establishment they work for. For example, a full service salon may require manicurists and pedicurists to work an eight-hour day. A boutique hair salon, however, may require shorter work hours on a part-time basis. Longer hours are not unusual for self-employed workers. Weekends and evenings tend to be the busiest times for manicurists and pedicurists.

Job Outlook

Manicurists and Pedicurists
Percent change in employment, projected 2010-20

Manicurists and Pedicurists	17%
Personal Appearance Workers	15%
Total, All Occupations	14%

Note: All Occupations includes all occupations in the U.S. Economy.
Source: U.S. Bureau of Labor Statistics, Employment Projections program

Employment of manicurists and pedicurists is expected to grow 17 percent from 2010 to 2020, about as fast as the average for all occupations.

The increase in employment reflects demand for new nail services being offered, such as mini sessions (quick manicures at a low cost) and mobile manicures and pedicures (house calls). The desire among young women and a growing number of men to lead a more healthful lifestyle through better grooming and wellness should also result in higher employment.

Considered a low-cost luxury service, manicures and pedicures will continue to be in demand by individuals at all income levels.

Job Prospects

Job opportunities should be very good overall. The growing number of nail salons and the need to replace workers who transfer to other occupations will result in many job openings.

Employment projections data for manicurists and pedicurists, 2010-20

Occupational Title	SOC Code	Employment, 2010	Projected Employment, 2020	Change, 2010-20 Percent	Change, 2010-20 Numeric
Manicurists and Pedicurists	39-5092	81,700	95,300	17	13,600

SOURCE: U.S. Bureau of Labor Statistics, Employment Projections program

Similar Occupations

This table shows a list of occupations with job duties that are similar to those of manicurists and pedicurists.

Occupation	Job Duties	Entry-Level Education	Median Annual Pay, May 2010
Barbers, Hairdressers, and Cosmetologists	Barbers, hairdressers, and cosmetologists provide hair styling and beauty services.	See How to Become One	$22,500
Skincare Specialists	Skincare specialists cleanse and beautify the face and body to enhance a person's appearance.	Postsecondary non-degree award	$28,920

Contacts for More Information

For information about training and cosmetology schools, visit American Association of Cosmetology Schools International Pedicure Association , Professional Beauty Association

Suggested citation:

Bureau of Labor Statistics, U.S. Department of Labor, Occupational Outlook Handbook, 2012-13 Edition, Manicurists and Pedicurists, on the Internet at http://www.bls.gov/ooh/personal-care-and-service/manicurists-and-pedicurists.htm .

Recreation Workers

Quick Facts: Recreation Workers	
2010 Median Pay	$22,260 per year $10.70 per hour
Entry-Level Education	Bachelor's degree
Work Experience in a Related Occupation	None
On-the-job Training	None
Number of Jobs, 2010	339,100
Job Outlook, 2010-20	19% (About as fast as average)
Employment Change, 2010-20	64,300

What Recreation Workers Do

Recreation workers design and lead leisure activities for groups in volunteer agencies or recreation facilities, such as playgrounds, parks, camps and senior centers. They may lead activities in areas such as arts and crafts, sports, games, music, and camping.

Duties

Recreation workers typically do the following:

- Plan and organize activities for groups or recreation centers
- Explain the rules of the activities and instruct participants
- Enforce safety rules to prevent injury
- Administer first aid if needed
- Modify activities to suit the needs of specific groups, such as seniors
- Keep the equipment used in activities organized

The specific responsibilities of recreation workers vary greatly with their job title, their level of training, or the state they work in. The following are examples of types of recreation workers:

Camp counselors work directly with children in residential (overnight) or day camps. They often lead and instruct children and teenagers in a variety of outdoor activities, such as swimming, hiking, horseback riding, or camping. In residential camps, counselors also provide guidance and supervise daily living and socialization. Some counselors may teach campers special subjects, such as archery, boating, music, drama, or gymnastics.

Camp directors typically supervise camp counselors, plan camp activities or programs, and do the administrative tasks that keep the camp running.

Activity specialists provide instruction and coaching primarily in one activity, such as art, music, drama, swimming, or tennis. These workers may work in camps or anywhere else where there is interest in a single activity.

Recreation leaders are responsible for a recreation program's daily operation. They primarily organize and direct participants, schedule the use of facilities, keep records of equipment use, and ensure that recreation facilities and equipment are used properly. They may lead classes and provide instruction in a recreational activity, such as tennis.

Recreation supervisors oversee recreation leaders. They often serve as a point of contact between the director of a park or recreation center and the recreation leaders. Some supervisors also may direct special activities or events or oversee a major activity, such as aquatics, gymnastics, or one or more performing arts.

Directors of recreation and parks develop and manage comprehensive recreation programs in parks, playgrounds, and other settings. Directors usually serve as technical advisors to state and local recreation and park commissions and may be responsible for recreation and park budgets.

Work Environment

Recreation workers held about 339,100 jobs in 2010. They are employed in a variety of settings, including summer camps, recreation centers, parks, and cruise ships. Many workers spend much of their time outdoors.

Recreation directors and supervisors, however, typically spend most of their time in an office, planning programs and special events. All recreation workers may risk suffering injuries while participating in physical activities.

The following industries employed the largest number of recreation workers in 2010:

Local government, excluding education and hospitals	31%
Nursing and residential care facilities	16
Civic and social organizations	10
Arts, entertainment, and recreation	9
Fitness and recreational sports centers	4

Work Schedules

Some recreation workers, such as camp counselors, may work weekends or irregular hours or may be seasonally employed.

How to Become a Recreation Worker

The education and training requirements for recreation workers vary with the type of job but many workers have a bachelor's degree.

Many recreation workers spend most of their time outdoors in various weather conditions.

Education and Training

Although a degree can be helpful, for many part-time recreation workers, such as camp counselors and activity specialists, other qualities are more important. These qualities include a worker's maturity level, experience leading activities, ability to work well with children or the elderly, and ability to ensure safety of participants.

Most seasonal and part-time workers learn through on-the-job training. Specialized training or experience in a particular field, such as art, music, drama, or athletics, may help in obtaining a job.

Most recreation workers who work full time need at least a bachelor's degree. Recreation workers who work full time include those working in administrative positions or for large organizations.

Degrees in parks and recreation or in leisure studies may prepare a student better than a liberal arts degree. However, either type of degree may be enough for some jobs.

Associate's and bachelor's degree programs in parks and recreation, leisure studies, or related fields are available at colleges and universities. Master's or doctoral degree programs also may be available, but are less common.

All programs include courses in management, community organization, supervision, administration, and development of programs for populations with specific needs, such as the elderly or disabled. Students may specialize in areas such as therapeutic recreation, park management, outdoor recreation, industrial or commercial recreation, and camp management.

Employers hiring recreation workers in supervisory or administrative positions often prefer applicants with work experience and at least a master's degree in parks and recreation, business administration, or public administration. Most require at least an associate's degree in recreation studies or a related field.

Important Qualities

Communication skills. Recreation workers must be able to communicate well to work with large groups of people while maintaining order and safety. They also must be able to motivate people to be active and to learn or improve skills.

Leadership skills. Recreation workers should be able to lead both large and small groups. They often lead activities for people of all ages and abilities.

Physical strength. Recreation workers need to be physically fit. Their job requires a considerable amount of movement because they often demonstrate activities while explaining them.

Problem-solving skills. Recreation workers need strong problem-solving skills. They must be able to create and reinvent activities and programs for all types of participants.

Speaking skills. Recreation workers must be able to communicate well. They often work with large groups of people and need to maintain order and safety.

Certification

The National Recreation and Park Administration (NRPA) provides certification for recreation workers. To qualify for the certification exam, individuals must follow one of four pathways:

- Earn a bachelor's degree in a major such as recreation, park resources, or leisure services from a program accredited by the NRPA

- Earn a bachelor's degree in a related major from any institution and, if the program is not accredited, have at least 1 year of experience

- Earn any other bachelor's degree and have at least 3 years of relevant full-time work experience

- Have at least 5 years of full-time experience in the field.

Some recreation jobs require certification. For example, a lifesaving certificate is required for teaching or coaching water-related activities. These certifications are available from organizations such as the YMCA or Red Cross. Specific requirements vary by job and employer.

Advancement

As workers gain experience, they may get promoted to positions with greater responsibilities. Recreation workers with experience and managerial skills may advance to supervisory or managerial positions. Eventually, they may become directors of a recreation department.

Pay

Recreation Workers
Median annual wages, May 2010

Total, All Occupations	$33,840
Recreation Workers	$22,260
Personal Care and Service Occupations	$20,640

Note: All Occupations includes all occupations in the U.S. Economy.
Source: U.S. Bureau of Labor Statistics, Occupational Employment Statistics

The median annual wage of recreation workers was $22,260 in May 2010. The median wage is the wage at which half the workers in an occupation earned more than that amount and half earned less. The lowest 10 percent earned less than $16,470, and the top 10 percent earned more than $38,460.

Job Outlook

Recreation Workers
Percent change in employment, projected 2010-20

Personal Care and Service Occupations	27%
Recreation Workers	19%
Total, All Occupations	14%

Note: All Occupations includes all occupations in the U.S. Economy.
Source: U.S. Bureau of Labor Statistics, Employment Projections program

Employment of recreation workers is expected to grow by 19 percent from 2010 to 2020, about as fast as the average for all occupations. The growth of fitness centers, sports centers, and camps specializing in younger participants is expected to increase demand for recreation workers, as more emphasis is placed on youth exercise to combat obesity. However, budget restrictions in state and local government might limit the number of jobs added to this occupation.

As baby boomers age and retire, they are encouraged to remain active to help combat injuries and illnesses associated with aging. Many of the new jobs for recreation workers will be in social assistance organizations and in nursing and residential care facilities.

Job Prospects

Job prospects will be best for those seeking part-time, seasonal, or temporary recreation jobs. Because workers in these jobs tend to be students or young people, they must be replaced when they leave for school or jobs in other occupations, thus creating many job openings.

Workers with higher levels of formal education related to recreation should have better prospects at getting full-time positions. Volunteer experience, part-time work during school, and a summer job also are viewed favorably for both full- and part-time positions.

Employment projections data for recreation workers, 2010-20

Occupational Title	SOC Code	Employment, 2010	Projected Employment, 2020	Change, 2010-20	
				Percent	Numeric
Recreation Workers	39-9032	339,100	403,400	19	64,300
SOURCE: U.S. Bureau of Labor Statistics, Employment Projections program					

Similar Occupations

This table shows a list of occupations with job duties that are similar to those of recreation workers.

Occupation	Job Duties	Entry-Level Education	Median Annual Pay, May 2010
Athletic Trainers	Athletic trainers specialize in preventing, diagnosing, and treating muscle and bone injuries and illnesses. They work with people of all ages and all skill levels, from young children to soldiers and professional athletes.	Bachelor's degree	$41,600
Fitness Trainers and Instructors	Fitness trainers and instructors lead, instruct, and motivate individuals or groups in exercise activities, including cardiovascular exercise (exercises for the heart and blood system), strength training, and stretching. They work with people of all ages and skill levels.	High school diploma or equivalent	$31,090
Probation Officers and Correctional Treatment Specialists	Probation officers and correctional treatment specialists work with and monitor offenders to prevent them from committing new crimes.	Bachelor's degree	$47,200
Psychologists	Psychologists study mental processes and human behavior by observing, interpreting, and recording how people and other animals relate to one another and the environment.	See How to Become One	$68,640
Recreational Therapists	Recreational therapists plan, direct, and coordinate recreation programs for people with disabilities or illnesses. They use a variety of techniques, including arts and crafts, drama, music, dance, sports, games, and field trips. These programs help maintain or improve a client's physical and emotional well-being.	Bachelor's degree	$39,410
Rehabilitation Counselors	Rehabilitation counselors help people with emotional and physical disabilities live independently. They help their clients overcome personal, social, and professional effects of disabilities as they relate to employment or independent living.	Master's degree	$32,350
School and Career Counselors	School counselors help students develop social skills and succeed in school. Career counselors assist people with the process of making career decisions by helping them choose a career or educational program.	Master's degree	$53,380
Social Workers	There are two main types of social workers: direct-service social workers, who help people solve and cope with problems in their everyday lives, and clinical social workers, who diagnose and treat mental, behavioral, and emotional issues.	See How to Become One	$42,480

Contacts for More Information

For information on careers, certification, and academic programs in parks and recreation, visit National Recreation and Park Association

For information about a career as a camp counselor, visit American Camp Association

Suggested citation:

Bureau of Labor Statistics, U.S. Department of Labor, Occupational Outlook Handbook, 2012-13 Edition, Recreation Workers, on the Internet at http://www.bls.gov/ooh/personal-care-and-service/recreation-workers.htm .

Skincare Specialists

Quick Facts: Skincare Specialists	
2010 Median Pay	$28,920 per year $13.90 per hour
Entry-Level Education	Postsecondary non-degree award
Work Experience in a Related Occupation	None
On-the-job Training	None
Number of Jobs, 2010	47,600
Job Outlook, 2010-20	25% (Faster than average)
Employment Change, 2010-20	11,700

What Skincare Specialists Do

Skincare specialists cleanse and beautify the face and body to enhance a person's appearance.

Duties

Skincare specialists typically do the following:

- Evaluate clients' skin condition and appearance
- Discuss available treatments and determine which products will improve clients' skin quality
- Remove unwanted hair using wax or laser treatment
- Clean the skin before applying makeup
- Recommend skincare products, such as cleansers, lotions, or creams
- Teach and advise clients on how to apply makeup and how to take care of their skin
- Refer clients to other skincare specialists, such as a dermatologist, for serious skin problems
- Sterilize equipment and clean work areas

Skincare specialists give facials, full-body treatments, and head and neck massages to improve the health and appearance of the skin. Some may provide other skincare treatments, such as peels, masks, or scrubs, to remove dead or dry skin.

In addition to working with clients, skincare specialists also keep records of skincare regimens that their regular clients use. A growing number of specialists actively sell skincare products, such as cleansers, lotions, and creams.

Those who operate their own salons have managerial duties that may include hiring, supervising, and firing workers, as well as keeping business and inventory records, ordering supplies, and arranging for advertising.

Work Environment

Skincare specialists held about 47,600 jobs in 2010, of which 47 percent worked in the personal care services industry. About 37 percent were self-employed.

Skincare specialists usually work in salons, health and beauty spas or, less frequently, in medical offices. The job may involve a lot of standing.

Because skincare specialists must evaluate the skins' condition, good lighting and clean surroundings are important. Protective clothing and good ventilation also may be necessary because skincare specialists often use chemicals on the face and body.

Work Schedules

Skincare specialists typically work full time, with many working nights and weekends. Long hours are common, especially for self-employed workers.

How to Become a Skincare Specialist

Skincare specialists must complete a state-approved cosmetology program. After completing the program, they must pass a state exam for licensure, which all states except Connecticut require.

Education and Training

Skincare specialists usually take a state-approved cosmetology program. Some high schools offer vocational training. Most people, however, receive their training from a postsecondary vocational school.

Newly hired specialists often receive one or two years of on-the-job training working alongside an experienced skincare specialist. Skincare specialists working in a medical environment often receive additional training.

Licenses

After completing an approved cosmetology program, skincare specialists take a written and practical exam to get a state license. Licensing requirements vary by state, so those interested should contact their state board.

Many states offer continuing education seminars and programs designed to keep skincare specialists current on new techniques and products.

Important Qualities

Customer-service skills. Skincare specialists should be friendly and courteous when dealing with clients. Repeat business is important, particularly for self-employed workers.

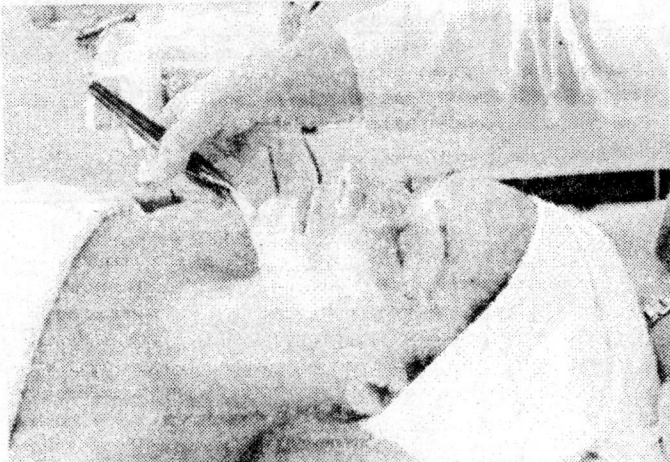

Skincare specialists cleanse and beautify a client's face and body.

Stamina. Skincare specialists must be able to spend most of their day standing and massaging clients' face and body.

Pay

Skincare Specialists
Median hourly wages, May 2010

Total, All Occupations	$16.27
Skincare Specialists	$13.90
Personal Appearance Workers	$10.77

Note: All Occupations includes all occupations in the U.S. Economy.
Source: U.S. Bureau of Labor Statistics, Occupational Employment Statistics

The median hourly wage of skincare specialists was $13.90 in May 2010. The median wage is the wage at which half the workers in an occupation earned more than that amount and half earned less. The lowest 10 percent of skincare specialists earned less than $8.22, and the top 10 percent earned more than $24.47.

In May 2010, median annual wages in industries employing the largest numbers of skincare specialists were as follows:

Offices of physicians	$18.45
Other amusement and recreation industries	17.37
Personal care services	12.98
Health and personal care stores	11.89
Traveler accommodation	11.80

Skincare specialists typically work full time, with many working nights and weekends. Long hours are common, especially for self-employed workers.

Job Outlook

Skincare Specialists
Percent change in employment, projected 2010-20

Skincare Specialists	25%
Personal Appearance Workers	15%
Total, All Occupations	14%

Note: All Occupations includes all occupations in the U.S. Economy.
Source: U.S. Bureau of Labor Statistics, Employment Projections program

Employment of skincare specialists is expected to grow 25 percent from 2010 to 2020, faster than the average for all occupations.

The increase in employment reflects demand for new services being offered, such as mini sessions (quick facials at a lower cost) and mobile facials (making house calls). In addition, the desire among women and a growing number of men to reduce the effects of aging and to lead a healthier lifestyle through better grooming should result in employment growth, including skin treatments for relaxation and well-being.

Job Prospects

Job opportunities should be good due to the growing number of beauty salons and spas. Those with experience are expected to have the best job prospects.

Employment projections data for skincare specialists, 2010-20

Occupational Title	SOC Code	Employment, 2010	Projected Employment, 2020	Change, 2010-20	
				Percent	Numeric
Skincare Specialists	39-5094	47,600	59,300	25	11,700
SOURCE: U.S. Bureau of Labor Statistics, Employment Projections program					

Similar Occupations

This table shows a list of occupations with job duties that are similar to those of skincare specialists.

Occupation	Job Duties	Entry-Level Education	Median Annual Pay, May 2010
Barbers, Hairdressers, and Cosmetologists	Barbers, hairdressers, and cosmetologists provide hair styling and beauty services.	See How to Become One	$22,500
Manicurists and Pedicurists	Manicurists and pedicurists clean, shape, and beautify fingernails and toenails.	Postsecondary non-degree award	$19,650
Massage Therapists	Massage therapists treat clients by using touch to manipulate the soft-tissue muscles of the body. With their touch, therapists relieve pain, rehabilitate injuries, reduce stress, increase relaxation, and aid in the general wellness of clients.	Postsecondary non-degree award	$34,900

Contacts for More Information

For more information about skincare specialists, visit Aesthetics International Association

For information about cosmetology schools, visit American Association of Cosmetology Schools

For information about the professional beauty industry, visit Professional Beauty Association

For information about the spa industry, visit International Spa Association

Suggested citation:

Bureau of Labor Statistics, U.S. Department of Labor, Occupational Outlook Handbook, 2012-13 Edition, Skincare Specialists, on the Internet at http://www.bls.gov/ooh/personal-care-and-service/skincare-specialists.htm .

Production Occupations

Assemblers and Fabricators

Quick Facts: Assemblers and Fabricators	
2010 Median Pay	$28,360 per year $13.63 per hour
Entry-Level Education	High school diploma or equivalent
Work Experience in a Related Occupation	None
On-the-job Training	See How to Become One
Number of Jobs, 2010	1,626,500
Job Outlook, 2010-20	5% (Slower than average)
Employment Change, 2010-20	88,000

What Assemblers and Fabricators Do

Assemblers and fabricators assemble both finished products and the parts that go into them. They use tools, machines, and their hands to make engines, computers, aircraft, toys, electronic devices, and more.

Duties

Assemblers and fabricators typically do the following:
- Read and understand detailed schematics and blueprints
- Use hand tools or machines to assemble parts
- Conduct quality control checks
- Work closely with designers and engineers in product development

Assemblers and fabricators have an important role in the manufacturing process. They assemble both finished products and the pieces that go into them. The products encompass a full range of manufactured products, including aircraft, toys, household appliances, automobiles, computers, and electronic devices.

Changes in technology have transformed the manufacturing and assembly process. Modern manufacturing systems use robots, computers, programmable motion-control devices, and various sensing technologies. These systems change the way in which goods are made and affect the jobs of those who make them. Advanced assemblers must be able to work with these new technologies and use them to produce goods.

The job of an assembler or fabricator ranges from very easy to very complicated, requiring a range of knowledge and skills. Skilled assemblers putting together complex machines, for example, read detailed schematics or blueprints that show how to assemble the machine. After determining how parts should connect, they use hand or power tools to trim, shim, cut, and make other adjustments to fit components together and align them properly. Once the parts are properly aligned, they connect them with bolts and screws or weld or solder pieces together.

Quality control is important throughout the assembly process, so assemblers look for faulty components and mistakes in the assembly process. They help to fix problems before defective products are made.

Manufacturing techniques are moving away from traditional assembly line systems toward lean manufacturing systems, which use teams of workers to produce entire products or components. Lean manufacturing has changed the nature of the assemblers' duties.

It has become more common to involve assemblers and fabricators in product development. Designers and engineers consult manufacturing workers during the design stage to improve product reliability and manufacturing efficiency. Some experienced assemblers work with designers and engineers to build prototypes or test products.

Although most assemblers and fabricators are classified as team assemblers, others specialize in producing one type of product or do the same or similar tasks throughout the assembly process.

The following are types of assemblers and fabricators:

Aircraft structure, surfaces, rigging, and systems assemblers fit, fasten, and install parts of airplanes, space vehicles, or missiles, such as wings, fuselage, landing gear, rigging and control equipment, or heating and ventilating systems.

Coil winders, tapers, and finishers wind wire coils of electrical components used in a variety of electric and electronic products, including resistors, transformers, generators, and electric motors.

Electrical and electronic equipment assemblers build products such as electric motors, computers, electronic control devices, and sensing equipment. Automated systems have been put in place because many small electronic parts are too small or fragile for human assembly. Much of the remaining work of electrical and electronic assemblers is done by hand during the small-scale production of electronic devices used in all types of aircraft, military systems, and medical equipment. Production by hand requires these workers to use devices such as soldering irons.

Electromechanical equipment assemblers assemble and modify

Assemblers and fabricators assemble both finished products and the pieces that go into them.

865

electromechanical devices such as household appliances, computer tomography scanners, or vending machines. The workers use a variety of tools, such as rulers, rivet guns, and soldering irons.

Engine and machine assemblers construct, assemble, or rebuild engines, turbines, and machines used in automobiles, construction and mining equipment, and power generators.

Structural metal fabricators and fitters cut, align, and fit together structural metal parts and may help weld or rivet the parts together.

Fiberglass laminators and fabricators laminate layers of fiberglass on molds to form boat decks and hulls, bodies for golf carts, automobiles, or other products.

Team assemblers work on an assembly line, but they rotate through different tasks, rather than specializing in a single task. The team may decide how the work is assigned and how different tasks are done. Some aspects of lean production, such as rotating tasks and seeking worker input on improving the assembly process, are common to all assembly and fabrication occupations.

Timing device assemblers, adjusters, and calibrators do precision assembling or adjusting of timing devices within very narrow tolerances.

Work Environment

Assemblers and fabricators held about 1.6 million jobs in 2010, most of which worked in manufacturing industries.

Employment in the detailed occupations that make up assemblers and fabricators was distributed as follows:

Team assemblers	952,600
Electrical and electronic equipment assemblers	182,900
Structural metal fabricators and fitters	80,900
Electromechanical equipment assemblers	49,400
Aircraft structure, surfaces, rigging, and systems assemblers	36,300
Engine and other machine assemblers	33,700
Fiberglass laminators and fabricators	19,400
Coil winders, tapers, and finishers	15,100
Timing device assemblers and adjusters	1,600
Assemblers and fabricators, all other	254,500

Most assemblers and fabricators work in manufacturing plants, and working conditions vary by plant and by industry. Many physically difficult tasks have been automated or made easier through the use of power tools, such as tightening massive bolts or moving heavy parts into position. Assembly work, however, may still involve long periods of standing or sitting.

Injuries

Some assemblers may come into contact with potentially harmful chemicals or fumes, but ventilation systems normally minimize any harmful effects. Other assemblers may come in contact with oil and grease, and their work areas may be noisy. Fiberglass laminators and fabricators are exposed to fiberglass, which may irritate the skin. Therefore, fiberglass workers must wear gloves and long sleeves and must use respirators for safety.

Work Schedules

Most assemblers and fabricators are employed full time, sometimes working evenings and weekends.

How to Become an Assembler or Fabricator

The education level and qualifications needed to enter these jobs vary depending on the industry and employer. Although a high school

diploma is enough for most jobs, experience and extra training is needed for more advanced assembly work.

Education and Training

Most employers require a high school diploma or equivalent for assembler positions. Workers usually receive on-the-job training, sometimes including employer-sponsored technical instruction.

Some employers may require specialized training or an associate's degree for the most skilled assembly jobs. For example, jobs with electrical, electronic, and aircraft and motor vehicle products manufacturers typically require more formal education through technical schools.

Certification

The Fabricators & Manufacturers Association International (FMA) offers the Precision Sheet Metal Operator (PSMO) Certification . Although not required, becoming certified can demonstrate competence and professionalism. It also may help a candidate advance in the profession.

In addition, many employers that hire electrical and electronic assembly workers, especially those in the aerospace and defense industries, require certifications in soldering, such as those offered by the Association Connecting Electronics Industries .

Important Qualities

Color vision. Assemblers and fabricators who make electrical and electronic products must be able to distinguish different colors because the wires they work with often are color coded.

Dexterity. Assemblers and fabricators must grasp, manipulate, or assemble parts and components that are often very small. As a result, they should have a steady hand and good hand-eye coordination.

Math skills. As the manufacturing process continues to advance technologically, assemblers and fabricators must know basic math and must be able to use computers.

Mechanical skills. Modern production systems require assemblers and fabricators to be able to use programmable motion control devices, computers, and robots on the factory floor.

Physical strength. Assemblers and fabricators must be strong enough to lift heavy components or pieces of machinery. Some assemblers, such as those in the aerospace industry, must frequently bend or climb ladders when assembling parts.

Stamina. Assemblers and fabricators must be able to stand for long periods and perform repetitious work.

Technical skills. Assemblers and fabricators must be able to understand technical manuals and schematics for a wide range of products and machines to properly manufacture the final product.

Pay

Assemblers and Fabricators
Median annual wages, May 2010

Total, All Occupations	$33,840
Production Occupations	$30,330
Assemblers and Fabricators	$28,360

Note: All Occupations includes all occupations in the U.S. Economy.
Source: U.S. Bureau of Labor Statistics, Occupational Employment Statistics

Wages vary by industry, geographic region, skill, educational level, and complexity of the machinery operated.

The median annual wage of assemblers and fabricators was $28,360 in May 2010. The median wage is the wage at which half the workers in an occupation earned more than that amount, and half earned less. The lowest 10 percent earned less than $18,290, and the top 10 percent earned more than $47,960.

In May 2010, median annual wages for assemblers and fabricators were as follows:

- $44,820 for aircraft structure, surfaces, rigging, and systems assemblers
- $36,310 for engine and other machine assemblers
- $34,530 for structural metal fabricators and fitters
- $31,640 for electromechanical equipment assemblers
- $31,250 for timing device assemblers and adjusters
- $29,100 for electrical and electronic equipment assemblers
- $28,650 for coil winders, tapers, and finishers
- $28,600 for fiberglass laminators and fabricators
- $27,180 for team assemblers
- $27,040 for assemblers and fabricators, all other

Some assemblers and fabricators are members of labor unions. These unions include the International Association of Machinists and Aerospace Workers ; the United Automobile, Aerospace and Agricultural Implement Workers of America ; the International Brotherhood of Electrical Workers ; and the United Steelworkers of America .

Most assemblers and fabricators are employed full time, sometimes working evenings and weekends.

Job Outlook

Assemblers and Fabricators

Percent change in employment, projected 2010-20

Total, All Occupations	14%
Assemblers and Fabricators	5%
Production Occupations	4%

Note: All Occupations includes all occupations in the U.S. Economy.
Source: U.S. Bureau of Labor Statistics, Employment Projections program

Employment of assemblers and fabricators is expected to grow 5 percent from 2010 to 2020, slower than the average for all occupations. Within the manufacturing sector, employment of assemblers and fabricators will be determined largely by the growth or decline in the production of certain manufactured goods. In general, overall employment is not expected to grow as fast as all other occupations because many manufacturing sectors are expected to become more efficient and able to produce more with fewer workers.

However, some individual industries are projected to have more jobs than others. The aircraft products and parts manufacturing industry is projected to gain jobs over the decade as demand for new commercial planes grows significantly. Thus, the need for assemblers for aircraft structures, surfaces, rigging, and systems is expected to grow.

In most other manufacturing industries, improved processes, tools, and, in some cases, automation will reduce job growth. Automation will replace workers in operations with a large volume of simple, repetitive work.

However, automation is not expected to have a large effect on the assembly of products that are low in volume or very complicated. Intricate products and complicated techniques often cannot be automated.

The use of team production techniques has been one factor in the continuing success of the manufacturing sector, boosting productivity and improving the quality of goods. Thus, while the number of assemblers overall is expected to decline in manufacturing, the number of team assemblers should grow as more manufacturing plants convert to team production techniques.

Some manufacturers have sent their assembly functions to countries where labor costs are lower. Decisions by U.S. corporations to move manufacturing to other nations may limit employment growth for assemblers in some industries.

The largest increase in the number of assemblers and fabricators is projected to be in the employment services industry, which supplies temporary workers to various industries. Temporary workers are gaining in importance in the manufacturing sector and other sectors, as companies facing cost pressures strive for a more flexible workforce to meet fluctuations in the market.

Job Prospects

Qualified applicants, including those with technical vocational training and certification, should have the best job opportunities in the manufacturing sector, particularly in growing, high-technology industries, such as aerospace and electromedical devices.

Some employers report difficulty finding qualified applicants looking for manufacturing employment. Many job openings should result from the need to replace workers leaving or retiring from this large occupation.

Employment projections data for assemblers and fabricators, 2010-20

Occupational Title	SOC Code	Employment, 2010	Projected Employment, 2020	Change, 2010-20	
				Percent	Numeric
Assemblers and Fabricators	—	1,626,500	1,714,500	5	88,000
Aircraft Structure, Surfaces, Rigging, and Systems Assemblers	51-2011	36,300	41,500	14	5,200
Coil Winders, Tapers, and Finishers	51-2021	15,100	12,700	-16	-2,400
Electrical and Electronic Equipment Assemblers	51-2022	182,900	172,400	-6	-10,400
Electromechanical Equipment Assemblers	51-2023	49,400	49,800	1	400
Engine and Other Machine Assemblers	51-2031	33,700	35,500	5	1,800
Structural Metal Fabricators and Fitters	51-2041	80,900	93,700	16	12,700
Fiberglass Laminators and Fabricators	51-2091	19,400	19,100	-2	-300
Team Assemblers	51-2092	952,600	1,004,900	5	52,300
Timing Device Assemblers and Adjusters	51-2093	1,600	1,600	1	0
Assemblers and Fabricators, All Other	51-2099	254,500	283,200	11	28,700

SOURCE: U.S. Bureau of Labor Statistics, Employment Projections program

Similar Occupations

This table shows a list of occupations with job duties that are similar to those of assemblers and fabricators.

Occupation	Job Duties	Entry-Level Education	Median Annual Pay, May 2010
Industrial Machinery Mechanics and Maintenance Workers	Industrial machinery mechanics and maintenance workers maintain and repair factory equipment and other industrial machinery, such as conveying systems, production machinery, and packaging equipment.	High school diploma or equivalent	$44,160
Metal and Plastic Machine Workers	Metal and plastic machine workers set up and operate machines that cut, shape, and form metal and plastic materials or pieces.	High school diploma or equivalent	$31,910
Millwrights	Millwrights install, dismantle, repair, reassemble, and move machinery in factories, power plants, and construction sites.	High school diploma or equivalent	$48,360
Welders, Cutters, Solderers, and Brazers	Welders, cutters, solderers, and brazers weld or join metal parts. They also fill holes, indentions, or seams of metal products, using hand-held welding equipment.	High school diploma or equivalent	$35,450

Contacts for More Information

For more information about assemblers and fabricators, including certification, training, and professional development, visit Fabricators & Manufacturers Association International

For information about careers in manufacturing, visit Nuts, Bolts and Thingamajigs

For information about unions, visit International Association of Machinists and Aerospace Workers , International Brotherhood of Electrical Workers , United Automobile, Aerospace and Agricultural Implement Workers of America , United Steelworkers of America

For information about certifications in electronics soldering, visit Association Connecting Electronics Industries

Bakers

Quick Facts: Bakers	
2010 Median Pay	$23,450 per year $11.27 per hour
Entry-Level Education	Less than high school
Work Experience in a Related Occupation	None
On-the-job Training	Long-term on-the-job training
Number of Jobs, 2010	149,800
Job Outlook, 2010-20	2% (Little or no change)
Employment Change, 2010-20	3,500

What Bakers Do

Bakers mix and bake ingredients according to recipes to make a variety of breads, pastries, and other baked goods.

Duties

Bakers typically do the following:

- Check the quality of ingredients
- Prepare equipment for baking
- Measure and weigh flour and other ingredients
- Combine measured ingredients in mixers or blenders
- Knead, roll, cut, and shape dough
- Place dough in pans, molds, or on sheets
- Set oven temperatures
- Place and bake items in hot ovens or on grills
- Observe color and state of products being baked
- Apply glazes, icings, or other toppings using spatulas or brushes

Bakers produce various types and quantities of breads, pastries, and other baked goods sold by grocers, wholesalers, restaurants, and institutional food services.

The following are types of bakers:

Commercial bakers are commonly employed in manufacturing facilities that produce breads and pastries. In these manufacturing facilities, bakers use high-volume mixing machines, ovens, and other equipment to mass produce standardized baked goods. Commercial bakers often operate large, automated machines, such as commercial mixers, ovens, and conveyors. They follow daily instructions for production schedules and recipes, and also may develop new recipes.

Bakers produce various types and quantities of breads.

Retail bakers work primarily in grocery stores and specialty shops, including bakeries. In these settings, they produce smaller quantities of baked goods for people to eat in the shop or for sale as specialty baked goods. Retail bakers may take orders from customers, prepare baked goods to order, and serve customers. Although the quantities prepared and sold in these stores are often small, they often come in a wide variety of flavors and sizes.

Some retail bakers own bakery shops or other types of businesses where they make and sell breads, pastries, pies, and other baked goods. In addition to preparing the baked goods and overseeing the entire baking process, these workers are also responsible for hiring, training, and supervising their staff. They must also budget for supplies, set prices, and know how much to produce each day.

Work Environment

Bakers held about 149,800 jobs in 2010. The majority worked full time for private companies, and about 28 percent worked part time.

Industries employing the largest numbers of bakers in 2010 were as follows:

Bakeries and tortilla manufacturing	31%
Grocery stories	27
Limited-service eating places	12
Other general merchandise stores	8
Full-service restaurants	4

Most bakers work in bakeries, grocery stores, and restaurants. Some, however, work in manufacturing facilities that distribute breads and pastries through established wholesale and retail outlets, mail order, or manufacturer's outlets.

Bakeries are often hot and noisy. The work can be stressful because bakers often work under strict deadlines and critical, time-sensitive baking requirements.

Work Schedules

Although most bakers work full time, about 28 percent work part time.

Grocery stores and restaurants, which employ more than half of all bakers, often schedule bakers to work early mornings, late evenings, weekends, and holidays. Because these establishments sell freshly baked goods throughout the day, bakers often are required to work in shifts.

Bakers who work in commercial bakeries that bake continuously may have to work late evenings and weekends.

Injuries

The rate of injuries and illnesses for bakers is higher than the average for all occupations. Although their work is generally safe, bakers occasionally suffer from back strains caused by repetitive lifting or moving heavy bags of flour or other packages. Other hazards include cuts, scrapes, and burns from hot ovens.

How to Become a Baker

Although long-term on-the-job training is the most common path, some bakers start their careers through an apprenticeship program or by attending a technical or culinary school. No formal education is required.

Education and Training

Bakers often start as apprentices in craft bakeries or trainees in store bakeries and learn the basics of baking, icing, and decorating. Most apprentices and trainees study topics such as nutrition, safe food handling, and basic baking. Many apprentice bakers participate in correspondence study and may work toward a certificate in baking.

In manufacturing facilities, commercial bakers must learn how to operate and maintain the industrial mixing and blending machines used to produce baked goods.

Bakers need to learn how to combine ingredients and how ingredients are affected by heat. They also need to learn how to operate various types of equipment used in the production process.

If running a small business, bakers need to know how to operate a business.

All bakers must follow government sanitation and health regulations.

Work Experience

Some bakers learn their skills through work experience related to baking. For example, they may start as a baker's assistant and progress into a full-fledged baker as they learn baking techniques.

Certification

Bakers have the option of getting certification through the Retail Bakers of America . Although not required, certification can show that a baker has the skills and knowledge to work at a retail baking establishment.

The Retail Bakers of America offers certification in four levels of competence, with a focus on several specialties, including baking sanitation, management, retail sales, and staff training. Those who wish to become certified must satisfy a combination of education and experience requirements before taking an exam.

The education and experience requirements vary by the level of certification desired. For example, a certified journey baker requires no formal education but must have at least 1 year of work experience. A certified baker must have 4 years of work experience, and a certified master baker must have 8 years of work experience, 30 hours of sanitation course work, and 30 hours of professional development training.

Important Qualities

Arithmetic skills. All bakers should have basic knowledge of arithmetic, especially fractions, to precisely mix formulas, weigh ingredients, or make adjustments to the mixes.

Communication skills. Bakers must often consult with other workers involved in the baking process, such as dough mixers, so they can adjust baking temperatures accordingly.

Detail oriented. Bakers must closely watch their products in the oven to keep from burning or overbaking the goods. They also should have an eye for detail because many pastries and cakes require intricate decorations.

Stamina. Most bakers must be able to work on their feet for long periods while kneading dough and lifting heavy items.

Pay

Bakers
Median annual wages, May 2010

Total, All Occupations	$33,840
Production Occupations	$30,330
Bakers	$23,450

Note: All Occupations includes all occupations in the U.S. Economy.
Source: U.S. Bureau of Labor Statistics, Occupational Employment Statistics

The median annual wage of bakers was $23,450 in May 2010. The median wage is the wage at which half the workers in an occupation earned more than that amount and half earned less. The lowest 10 percent earned less than $16,910, and the top 10 percent earned more than $37,320.

In May 2010, median annual wages in industries employing the largest numbers of bakers were as follows:

Bakeries and tortilla manufacturing	$24,580
Grocery stories	24,180
Full-service restaurants	22,620
Other general merchandise stores	22,300
Limited-service eating places	20,290

Although most bakers work full time, about 28 percent work time. Grocery stores and restaurants, which employ more than half of all bakers, often schedule bakers to work early mornings, late evenings, weekends, and holidays. Because these establishments sell freshly baked goods throughout the day, bakers often work in shifts.

Bakers who work in commercial bakeries where baking is done on continuous basis may have to work late evenings and weekends.

Job Outlook

Bakers
Percent change in employment, projected 2010-20

Total, All Occupations	14%
Production Occupations	4%
Bakers	2%

Note: All Occupations includes all occupations in the U.S. Economy.
Source: U.S. Bureau of Labor Statistics, Employment Projections program

Employment of bakers is expected to experience little or no change from 2010 to 2020. As the nation's population grows, people will continue to demand more baked goods to eat at home or to eat at grocery stores, bakeries, and restaurants.

However, manufacturing facilities are increasingly using more automated and computerized production processes, which reduce the need for bakers. As a result, employment growth of bakers is expected to be limited.

Job Prospects

Highly skilled, experienced bakers should have the best job opportunities because of the growing demand for specialty products that require years of baking experience.

Employment projections data for bakers, 2010-20

Occupational Title	SOC Code	Employment, 2010	Projected Employment, 2020	Change, 2010-20	
				Percent	Numeric
Bakers	51-3011	149,800	153,300	2	3,500
SOURCE: U.S. Bureau of Labor Statistics, Employment Projections program					

Similar Occupations

This table shows a list of occupations with job duties that are similar to those of bakers.

Occupation	Job Duties	Entry-Level Education	Median Annual Pay, May 2010
Chefs and Head Cooks	Chefs and head cooks oversee the daily food preparation at restaurants or other places where food is served. They direct kitchen staff and handle any food-related concerns.	High school diploma or equivalent	$40,630
Cooks	Cooks prepare, season, and cook a wide range of foods, such as soups, salads, entrees, and desserts.	See How to Become One	$20,260
Food Preparation Workers	Food preparation workers perform many routine tasks under the guidance of cooks or food supervisors. They prepare cold foods, slice meat, peel and cut vegetables, brew coffee or tea, and do many other tasks.	Less than high school	$19,100

Contacts for More Information

For information about job opportunities, contact local employers and local offices of the state employment service.

For information on certification programs, visit Retail Bakers of America

Suggested citation:
Bureau of Labor Statistics, U.S. Department of Labor, Occupational Outlook Handbook, 2012-13 Edition, Bakers, on the Internet at http://www.bls.gov/ooh/production/bakers.htm .

Dental Laboratory Technicians

Quick Facts: Dental Laboratory Technicians	
2010 Median Pay	$35,140 per year $16.90 per hour
Entry-Level Education	High school diploma or equivalent
Work Experience in a Related Occupation	None
On-the-job Training	Moderate-term on-the-job training
Number of Jobs, 2010	40,900
Job Outlook, 2010-20	1% (Little or no change)
Employment Change, 2010-20	300

What Dental Laboratory Technicians Do

Dental laboratory technicians use impressions, or molds, of a patient's teeth to create crowns, bridges, dentures and other dental appliances. They work closely with dentists but have limited contact with patients.

Duties

Dental laboratory technicians typically do the following:

- Follow detailed work orders and prescriptions from a dentist, to create a dental appliance
- Mix plaster and other pastes to fill molds from impressions taken by a dentist
- Cover molds and frameworks with mixtures and allow them to set
- Place the dental appliance on an apparatus that mimics the patient's bite and jaw movement
- Examine the appliance, noting the size and shape of adjacent teeth and gaps in the gumline
- Sculpt or carve parts of an appliance, such as individual teeth
- Adjust prosthetics to allow for a more natural look or to improve function
- Repair dental appliances that may be cracked or damaged, such as dentures and crowns

Dental laboratory technicians work with small handtools, such as files and polishers. They work with many different materials to make prosthetic appliances, including wax, plastic, and porcelain. In some

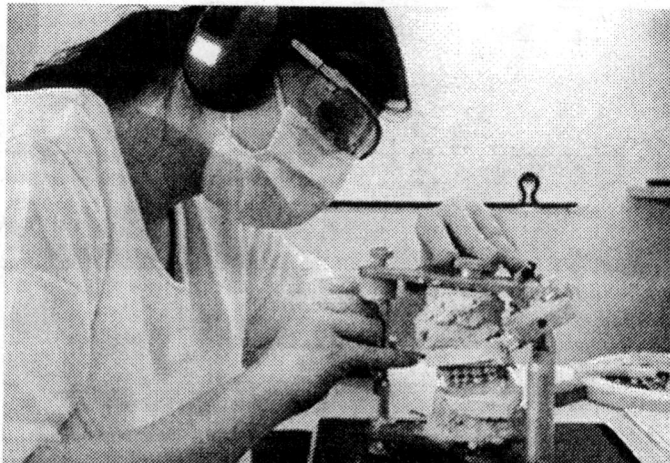

Dental laboratory technicians create crowns, bridges, dentures, and other dental prosthetics.

cases, technicians work with computer programs to create appliances or to get impressions sent from a dentist's office.

In small laboratories, technicians do all stages of the work. In large laboratories, technicians may work on only one step of the process, such as waxing or polishing appliances.

Dental laboratory technicians can specialize in one of six areas: orthodontic appliances, crowns and bridges, complete dentures, partial dentures, implants, and ceramics. Technicians may have different job titles, depending on their specialty. For example, technicians who make porcelain and acrylic restorations, such as veneers and bridges, are called dental ceramists.

Dental laboratory technicians are part of a larger dental team. They work closely with dentists and other technicians. For more information, see the profile on dentists .

Work Environment

Dental laboratory technicians held about 40,900 jobs in 2010.

Dental laboratory technicians work in clean, well-lit, and well-ventilated laboratories. They usually have limited contact with the public.

Most dental laboratories are small and employ only a few workers. Some dental laboratories, however, have as many as several hundred employees.

Technicians may wear goggles to protect their eyes, gloves to handle hot objects, and masks to avoid inhaling dust.

How to Become a Dental Laboratory Technician

There are no formal education or training requirements to be a dental laboratory technician, but most have at least a high school diploma. Technicians usually learn their skills on the job.

Training

Most dental laboratory technicians learn through on-the-job training. They usually begin as helpers in a laboratory and learn more advanced skills as they gain experience. For example, technicians may begin by pouring plaster into an impression to make a model. As they become more experienced, they may progress to more complex tasks, such as making porcelain crowns and bridges. Because all laboratories are different, the length of training varies.

Education

A high school diploma is the standard requirement for getting a job as a dental laboratory technician. High school students interested in becoming dental laboratory technicians should take courses in science, mathematics, computer programming, and art.

Formal education programs are available for dental laboratory technicians through vocational schools, community colleges, and universities. Most programs take 2 years to complete, though there are a few 4-year programs available. All programs have courses in dental anatomy, dental ceramics, dentures, and partial dentures. As laboratories continue to manufacture parts for dental appliances using advanced computer programs, it may be helpful for technicians to take courses in computer skills and programming.

Important Qualities

Detail oriented. Dental laboratory technicians must pay attention to details. To create realistic prosthetics for each patient's mouth, they must notice slight differences in color and shape.

Dexterity. Dental laboratory technicians must work well with their hands because they use precise laboratory instruments.

Technical skills. Dental laboratory technicians must understand how to operate complex machinery. Some procedures are automated, so technicians must know how to operate and change the programs that run the machinery.

Certification

The National Board for Certification in Dental Laboratory Technology (NBCCERT) offers certification as a Certified Dental Technician (CDT). Certification is available in six specialty areas: orthodontic appliances, crowns and bridges, complete dentures, partial dentures, implants, and ceramics.

To qualify for the CDT, technicians must have at least 5 years of on-the-job training or experience in dental technology, or have graduated from an accredited dental laboratory technician program. They must also pass three exams.

The NBCCERT also provides a modularization program that leads to a Certificate of Competency. Dental technicians can also get at Certificate of Competency in each specific skill through a written and practical exam on that skill.

Advancement

In large laboratories, dental laboratory technicians may work their way up to a supervisory level and may train new technicians. Some may go on to own their own laboratory.

Pay

Dental Laboratory Technicians
Median annual wages, May 2010

Dental Laboratory Technicians	$35,140
Total, All Occupations	$33,840
Production Occupations	$30,330

Note: All Occupations includes all occupations in the U.S. Economy.
Source: U.S. Bureau of Labor Statistics, Occupational Employment Statistics

The median annual wage of dental laboratory technicians was $35,140 in May 2010. The median wage is the wage at which half the workers in an occupation earned more than that amount and half earned less. The lowest 10 percent earned more than $20,940, and the top 10 percent earned more than $58,560.

Job Outlook

Dental Laboratory Technicians
Percent change in employment, projected 2010-20

Total, All Occupations	14%
Production Occupations	4%
Dental Laboratory Technicians	1%

Note: All Occupations includes all occupations in the U.S. Economy.
Source: U.S. Bureau of Labor Statistics, Employment Projections program

Employment of dental laboratory technicians is expected to experience little or no change from 2010 to 2020.

As cosmetic prosthetics, such as veneers and crowns, become less expensive, there should be an increase in demand for these appliances. Accidents and poor oral health, which can cause damage and loss of teeth, will continue to create a need for dental laboratory technician services. Dental technician services will be in demand, as dentists work to improve the aesthetics and function of patients' teeth.

On the other hand, baby boomers and their children are more likely to retain their teeth than previous generations. This is due to increased visits to dentists, increased use of fluoride, and more dental health education. These factors will likely lead to a decrease in the number of full and partial dentures and other prosthetics used to replace missing teeth and will temper demand for the technicians that make them.

Employment projections data for dental laboratory technicians, 2010-20

Occupational Title	SOC Code	Employment, 2010	Projected Employment, 2020	Change, 2010-20 Percent	Numeric
Dental Laboratory Technicians	51-9081	40,900	41,200	1	300
SOURCE: U.S. Bureau of Labor Statistics, Employment Projections program					

Similar Occupations

This table shows a list of occupations with job duties that are similar to those of dental laboratory technicians.

Occupation	Job Duties	Entry-Level Education	Median Annual Pay, May 2010
Dentists	Dentists diagnose and treat problems with a patient's teeth, gums, and other parts of the mouth. They provide advice and instruction on taking care of teeth and gums and on diet choices that affect oral health.	Doctoral or professional degree	$146,920
Medical Appliance Technicians	Medical appliance technicians construct, fit, and repair medical supportive devices, including prosthetic limbs, arch supports, facial parts, and foot and leg braces.	High school diploma or equivalent	$35,670
Ophthalmic Laboratory Technicians	Ophthalmic laboratory technicians make prescription eyeglasses and contact lenses. They are also commonly known as manufacturing opticians, optical mechanics, or optical goods workers.	High school diploma or equivalent	$27,970

| Optometrists | Optometrists perform eye exams to check for vision problems and diseases. They prescribe eyeglasses or contact lenses as needed. | Doctoral or professional degree | $94,990 |
| Orthotists and Prosthetists | Orthotists and prosthetists, also called O&P professionals, design medical support devices and measure and fit patients for them. These devices include artificial limbs (arms, hands, legs, and feet), braces, and other medical or surgical devices. | Master's degree | $65,060 |

Contacts for More Information

For a list of accredited programs in dental laboratory technology, visit Commission on Dental Accreditation, American Dental Association

For information on requirements for certification of dental laboratory technicians, visit National Board for Certification in Dental Laboratory Technology

For information on career opportunities in commercial dental laboratories, visit National Association of Dental Laboratories

Suggested citation:

Bureau of Labor Statistics, U.S. Department of Labor, Occupational Outlook Handbook, 2012-13 Edition, Dental Laboratory Technicians, on the Internet at http://www.bls.gov/ooh/production/dental-laboratory-technicians.htm .

Food Processing Occupations

Quick Facts: Food Processing Occupations	
2010 Median Pay	$23,950 per year $11.51 per hour
Entry-Level Education	Less than high school
Work Experience in a Related Occupation	None
On-the-job Training	See How to Become One
Number of Jobs, 2010	311,300
Job Outlook, 2010-20	12% (About as fast as average)
Employment Change, 2010-20	37,400

What Food Processing Occupations Do

Food processing occupations include butchers and meat cutters; meat, poultry, and fish cutters and trimmers; and operators and tenders of roasting, baking, and drying machinery. These workers cut, trim, or otherwise process food items, such as meat, or nonfood items, such as tobacco, for retail sale.

Duties

Butchers and meat cutters typically do the following:
- Cut steaks and chops and shape and tie roasts
- Grind meats for sale as chopped meats or sausage
- Maintain inventory quantities and track the freshness of products
- Sharpen knives and take care of equipment
- Clean all knives, equipment, and workspaces to meet health guidelines
- Prepare and package meats for display cases
- Create attractive displays to promote the sale of products
- Help customers with special orders

Meat, poultry, and fish cutters and trimmers typically do the following:
- Perform a cut in the production of a meat, poultry, or fish product
- Clean, trim, and cut carcasses to prepare them for further processing
- Lift carcasses onto conveyors
- Inspect products for defects and irregularities
- Operate handtools, such as hand vacuums, knives, and saws
- Sharpen knives and take care of equipment
- Label or identify goods to make transporting and using them easy

Roasting, baking, and drying machinery operators and tenders typically do the following:

- Control the temperature, humidity, and pressure of machinery using thermostats and valves
- Ensure that gauges and sensors work properly by touching, seeing, and smelling the products they measure
- Watch the flow of products through machinery and listen for malfunctions
- Fill work orders, weigh, and otherwise check products to ensure accuracy

Butchers and meat cutters cut and trim meat from larger, wholesale portions into steaks, chops, roasts, and other cuts that shoppers want.

Meat, poultry, and fish cutters and trimmers produce ready-to-eat, partially cooked, easy-to-prepare, and display-ready packages of meat, poultry, and fish products at processing plants, ultimately for sale in grocery and specialty food stores. This often involves filleting meat, poultry or fish; cutting it into bite-sized pieces; and adding vegetables, sauces, flavorings, or breading.

Fish cutters and trimmers remove non-edible parts and then cut the fish into steaks or fillets. In retail stores, these workers also may wait on customers and clean fish to order. Some processing is done aboard ships, where fish are caught, processed, and flash frozen to preserve freshness.

Roasting, baking, and drying machinery operators and tenders work primarily in animal processing plants but also roast, bake, or dry other food and nonfood products, such as tortillas, fruits and vegetables, dairy products, coffee beans, and tobacco products. They use equipment such as hearth ovens, kiln driers, roasters, char kilns, and vacuum dryers in their work.

The following are examples of types of food processing occupations:

Meat carvers have special skills that enhance the final presentation of meats.

Poultry eviscerators clean birds so that they can be made into

Butchers may need to lift large cuts of meat.

various products.

Fish filleters use sharp knives and precise movements to separate fillets of fish from the bones.

Oyster shuckers and **shrimp pickers** separate the flesh of oysters and shrimp from the shells or exoskeleton for packaging and wholesale or retail sale.

Meat roasters, dryers, and fish smokers operate large commercial roasters, dryers, or smokers to prepare fish and other meats for packaging and sale in wholesale or retail outlets.

Commercial bakers and tortilla makers operate large mixing and baking machines to produce large quantities of baked goods, such as bread or tortillas.

Coffee roasters follow or create recipes to produce standard or specialty coffees.

Tobacco roasters cure tobacco for wholesale distribution to cigarette manufacturers and other makers of tobacco products.

Dryers of fruits and vegetables operate machines that produce raisins or other dehydrated foods.

Work Environment

There were about 311,300 food processing jobs in 2010. Most butchers and meat cutters work in retail stores, such as grocery stores. Most meat, poultry, and fish cutters and trimmers work in food manufacturing plants.

Both environments require employees to stand for most, if not all, of their shift. Heavy lifting may be required, and working in cold rooms (below 40 degrees Fahrenheit) for extended periods is likely.

Retail grocery butchers often interact with customers and fill special orders. However, some butchers work in specialty shops that provide meat to restaurants; these butchers, therefore, have little contact with the general public. About 9 percent of butchers and meat cutters worked in animal slaughtering and processing plants in 2010.

Meat trimmers and cutters in the food processing industry may have a more limited range of activities and duties than do butchers and meat cutters. Because they are usually working on an assembly line, meat processing workers usually do one specific function (that is, one

cut) during their shift. Workers often rotate between stations each shift. The retail food and beverage stores accounted for 18 percent of employment for meat, poultry, and fish cutters and trimmers in 2010.

Operators of roasting, baking, and drying machinery may be exposed to high temperatures for long periods. Also, the environment may be loud. Heavy lifting is likely.

All of these occupations typically require the use of dangerous tools and machinery, such as knives, saws, and ovens. Workers may have to wear protective safety equipment or sanitary garments to prevent food from becoming contaminated.

Most workers in food processing occupations work full time.

Injuries

Workers in food processing occupations have a higher rate of injuries and illnesses than other manufacturing workers because of their constant exposure to sharp cutting tools. Rates have been improving over the past few decades and are expected to continue to improve.

How to Become a Food Processing Worker

There are no formal education requirements for workers in food processing occupations; workers receive on-the-job training. Butchers typically need previous work experience.

Food preparation workers may need to be certified by the appropriate governmental agency to ensure conformity with health standards. Education and training for certification will most likely be carried out on the job.

Training

Butchers and meat, poultry, and fish cutters and trimmers receive on-the-job training. The length of training varies considerably. Simple cutting operations require a few days to learn. More complicated cutting tasks generally require several months of training. The training period for butchers at the retail level may be 1 or 2 years. Apprentice butchers can spend several years learning the skills and building the strength they need to become fully qualified butchers.

Generally, trainees begin by doing less difficult jobs, such as making simple cuts or removing bones. Under the guidance of experienced workers, trainees learn the proper use and care of tools and equipment while also learning how to prepare various cuts of meat. After demonstrating skill with various meat cutting tools, trainees learn to divide wholesale cuts into retail and individual portions.

Trainees also may learn to roll and tie roasts, prepare sausage, and cure meat. Those employed in retail food establishments often are taught to perform basic business operations, such as inventory control, meat buying, and recordkeeping. In addition, growing concern about foodborne pathogens in meats has led employers to offer numerous seminars and extensive training in food safety to employees.

On-the-job training is common among food and tobacco roasting, baking, and drying machine operators and tenders. These workers learn to run the different types of equipment by watching and helping other workers. Training can last anywhere from a month to a year, depending on the complexity of the tasks and the number of products involved.

Certification

Food handlers may need to be certified by an appropriate government agency. Specialized workers, including butchers who follow religious guidelines for food preparation, may be required to undergo a lengthy apprenticeship, certification process, or both before becoming completely qualified and endorsed by an organization to perform their duties.

Work Experience

Butchers usually enter the occupation after getting experience in a related occupation. Butchers gain experience by starting at a position that requires less experience, such as a meat cutter at a grocery store or a line worker in a meat processing facility. They sometimes gain this experience through an apprenticeship, although formal apprenticeship programs are rare.

Education

There are no formal education requirements for workers in food processing occupations. A degree in an appropriate area—dairy science for those working in dairy product operations, for example—can be helpful for advancing to a lead worker or supervisory role.

A bachelor's or associate's degree may allow a prospective butcher or manager to enter his or her occupation of choice more easily. There are programs that offer hands-on training cutting meat. There are also degree programs, such as meat merchandising and meat marketing, that are designed specifically for training butchers and meat sellers.

Important Qualities

Concentration. Workers in food processing occupations must be able to pay close attention to what they are doing so that they avoid injury and waste of product.

Coordination. Hand–eye coordination is needed to prepare products safely and in a timely manner.

Customer-service skills. Those who work in retail stores should be able to identify and meet the needs of customers while making them feel comfortable and happy about their purchases.

Listening skills. Workers must pay close attention to directions so they avoid costly mistakes.

Stamina. Workers in this occupation must be physically active for long periods.

Teamwork. Food processing occupations usually require high levels of teamwork, and workers are often closely supported by managerial staff.

Pay

Food Processing Occupations
Median annual wages, May 2010

Total, All Occupations	$33,840
Butchers and Meat Cutters	$28,600
Food and Tobacco Roasting, Baking, and Drying Machine Operators and Tenders	$27,140
Food Processing Occupations	$23,950
Meat, Poultry, and Fish Cutters and Trimmers	$22,330

Note: All Occupations includes all occupations in the U.S. Economy.
Source: U.S. Bureau of Labor Statistics, Occupational Employment Statistics

The median annual wage of food processing occupations was $23,950 in May 2010. The median wage is the wage at which half the workers in an occupation earned more than that amount and half earned less. The lowest 10 percent earned less than $17,600, and the top 10 percent earned more than $40,350.

Median wages for food processing occupations in May 2010 were as follows:

- $28,600 for butchers and meat cutters
- $27,140 for food and tobacco roasting, baking, and drying machine operators and tenders
- $22,330 for meat, poultry, and fish cutters and trimmers

Most workers in food processing occupations work full time. Like many workers in manufacturing, those in food processing occupations may work a shift that requires either early mornings or nights and evenings.

Job Outlook

Food Processing Occupations
Percent change in employment, projected 2010-20

Meat, Poultry, and Fish Cutters and Trimmers	16%
Total, All Occupations	14%
Food Processing Occupations	12%
Butchers and Meat Cutters	8%
Food and Tobacco Roasting, Baking, and Drying Machine Operators and Tenders	8%

Note: All Occupations includes all occupations in the U.S. Economy.
Source: U.S. Bureau of Labor Statistics, Employment Projections program

Employment of food processing occupations is expected to grow by 12 percent from 2010 to 2020, about as fast as the average for all occupations. More people around the world are demanding prepared and pre-cut food. Also, more people are buying partially prepared and easy-to-cook products. Both of these trends are expected to drive demand for food processing workers. These trends will create growth in the occupation even as new machines make the work more productive.

As the food processing industry becomes more consolidated, production processes become more streamlined. Therefore, the ability of processing facilities to employ meat cutters and trimmers should remain strong because of reduced costs in other areas of the industry.

A growing global population and increasing wealth among developing countries should cause demand for meat to increase worldwide. This is especially true for U.S.-made food products because they are produced to comparatively high food safety standards. Increased demand and steady turnover create good prospects for those wanting to enter food processing occupations.

Employment projections data for food processing occupations, 2010-20

Occupational Title	SOC Code	Employment, 2010	Projected Employment, 2020	Change, 2010-20	
				Percent	Numeric
Food Processing Occupations	—	311,300	348,700	12	37,400
Butchers and Meat Cutters	51-3021	126,800	136,800	8	10,100
Meat, Poultry, and Fish Cutters and Trimmers	51-3022	166,100	192,000	16	25,800
Food and Tobacco Roasting, Baking, and Drying Machine Operators and Tenders	51-3091	18,400	19,900	8	1,500
SOURCE: U.S. Bureau of Labor Statistics, Employment Projections program					

Similar Occupations

This table shows a list of occupations with job duties that are similar to those of food processing occupations.

Occupation	Job Duties	Entry-Level Education	Median Annual Pay, May 2010
Bakers	Bakers mix and bake ingredients according to recipes to make a variety of breads, pastries, and other baked goods.	Less than high school	$23,450
Chefs and Head Cooks	Chefs and head cooks oversee the daily food preparation at restaurants or other places where food is served. They direct kitchen staff and handle any food-related concerns.	High school diploma or equivalent	$40,630
Fishers and Related Fishing Workers	Fishers and related fishing workers catch and trap various types of marine life. The fish they catch are for human food, animal feed, bait, and other uses.	Less than high school	$25,590
Food Processing Operators	Food processing operators include food batchmakers and food cooking machine operators and tenders. These workers may set up, operate, and tend cooking equipment that mixes, blends, cooks, or otherwise processes ingredients used to manufacture food products.	High school diploma or equivalent	$24,250
Slaughterers and Meat Packers	Slaughterers and meat packers kill and clean animals, divide carcasses into manageable sections, and grind or otherwise prepare and pack products, such as boxed beef, for shipping to distribution centers.	Less than high school	$23,380

Contacts for More Information

For information about the meat processing industry and related trends, visit American Meat Institute

Suggested citation:

Bureau of Labor Statistics, U.S. Department of Labor, Occupational Outlook Handbook, 2012-13 Edition, Food Processing Occupations, on the Internet at http://www.bls.gov/ooh/production/food-processing-occupations.htm .

Food Processing Operators

Quick Facts: Food Processing Operators	
2010 Median Pay	$24,250 per year $11.66 per hour
Entry-Level Education	High school diploma or equivalent
Work Experience in a Related Occupation	Less than 1 year
On-the-job Training	Short-term on-the-job training
Number of Jobs, 2010	131,000
Job Outlook, 2010-20	2% (Little or no change)
Employment Change, 2010-20	2,300

What Food Processing Operators Do

Food processing operators include food batchmakers and food cooking machine operators and tenders. These workers may set up, operate, and tend cooking equipment that mixes, blends, cooks, or otherwise processes ingredients used to manufacture food products.

Duties

Food processing operators typically do the following:

- Set up and calibrate equipment for daily use
- Weigh ingredients
- Make mixtures
- Control temperatures, oil or water flow rates, humidity, and pressures of cooking machinery with thermostats and valves
- Operate mixers and manage ingredients to meet product quality and uniformity standards
- Monitor products by watching, tasting, or listening to machinery
- Comply with food safety regulations
- Report equipment malfunctions to team leaders, supervisors, or maintenance staff in a timely manner
- Maintain clean workspaces and equipment to meet health and safety standards
- Fill work orders and weigh and otherwise check products to ensure accuracy and quality
- Dismantle, clean, and store equipment for future use

Although workers in food processing operations share many similar duties, there are differences depending on the work being done. The following are types of food processing operators:

Food batchmakers are more likely to work in facilities producing baked goods, pasta, and tortillas. They mix ingredients to make dough, load and unload ovens, operate noodle extruders, and do tasks specific to large-scale commercial baking.

Food cooking machine operators and tenders operate or tend cooking equipment to prepare food products. For example, workers

Food processing operators use machines to make large batches of foodstuffs.

who preserve and can fruits and vegetables usually operate equipment that boils water to cook and preserve their products.

Potato and corn chip manufacturers employ workers who operate frying machines and work around hot oil. Sugar and confectionary manufacturers have an enormous assortment of equipment that stretches, blends, heats, coats, decorates, and cools candies, chocolates, doughnuts, or other sweets.

Other workers may operate equipment that mixes spices for meat products, mills grains, or extracts oil from seeds. Almost all of these machines require skilled operators to report malfunctions or make adjustments.

Work Environment

Food processing operators held about 131,000 jobs in 2010.

Food processing operators typically work in food processing facilities, although they also work in many other industries. Besides being employed in the following industries, some food batchmakers were self-employed or worked in retail grocery-type environments in 2010:

Bakeries and tortilla manufacturing	21%
Fruit and vegetable preserving and specialty food manufacturing	12
Dairy product manufacturing	11
Sugar and confectionery product manufacturing	8
Animal slaughtering and processing	7

In 2010, the largest numbers of food cooking machine operators and tenders were employed in the following industries:

Fruit and vegetable preserving and specialty food manufacturing	20%
Animal slaughtering and processing	14
Bakeries and tortilla manufacturing	12
Grocery stores	7
Sugar and confectionery product manufacturing	5

As with other manufacturing and food processing occupations, work tends to be in large, loud facilities. Food processing operators also are frequently exposed to high temperatures when working around

cooking machinery. Workers also may work in cold environments for long periods if the goods being produced need to be refrigerated.

Food processing operators typically stand for the majority of their shifts. Their equipment is often large, and loading, unloading, cleaning, and prepping it for use may require heavy lifting, bending, kneeling, and reaching.

Food processing operators typically work on assembly lines, and workers must be able to keep up with the line speed while maintaining product quality. They wear protective clothing to keep both themselves and the food safe.

Injuries

Working around hot liquids or machinery that cuts or presses can be dangerous. Food processing operators, like many other production occupations, have a rate of injuries and illnesses that is higher than the average for all other occupations.

Work Schedules

Most food processing operators work full time. About one-quarter of food batchmakers worked part time in 2010.

How to Become a Food Processing Operator

Most food processing operators have at least a high school degree. Because of the increasing complexity of the equipment, math and English skills may be required. Physical stamina is required, and some previous experience in manufacturing is preferred.

Work Experience

Employers may prefer or require some manufacturing experience. If a worker does not have experience in manufacturing, employers favor experience in some other physically demanding occupation such as construction.

A work record showing reliability, trustworthiness, and the ability to work well on a team is important. The more technical jobs in this category require workers to set up and calibrate machinery, and prospective workers need previous relevant experience and training if they do not hold an appropriate postsecondary qualification.

Education

Math and reading skills are important because workers may be required to take measurements for tracking and quality control. A high school education is preferred by most employers and required by many. However, almost a quarter of all workers in this occupation have less than a high school diploma or its equivalent.

General production workers, also called line workers, who do not calibrate or maintain equipment are not expected to have job-specific knowledge. They are trained on the job.

Workers who set up and calibrate equipment may need a degree or special training and experience. A small number of jobs in this occupation require a bachelor's degree in science or engineering and may require an understanding of thermodynamics or engineering principles.

Training

Most food processing operators learn on the job and are not expected to know what to do before they start. On-the-job training may last only a few days or as long as 1 month. They also usually get periodic health and safety training to update their knowledge of rules or procedures.

Experienced workers show trainees how to properly use and care for tools and equipment.

Companies also usually train their employees for more advanced technical work because they tend to promote from within rather than hire new employees for advanced positions.

Advancement

Interested and achievement-oriented workers may be able to advance to positions that formulate new products or production techniques. This type of work would probably require a degree in engineering or a science, such as chemistry or biology. Workers may also advance to jobs in quality assurance or management.

Important Qualities

Concentration. Food processing operators should be able to focus on what they are doing so that they may avoid injury and wasted products.

Coordination. Food processing operators need good hand-eye coordination to prepare products safely and keep up with the assembly line.

Detail oriented. Food processing operators must be able to detect small changes in quality or quantity and closely follow health and safety standards. They carefully watch gauges, dials, or other indicators to ensure a machine is working properly.

Mechanical skills. Food processing operators need some knowledge of machines and tools to understand how they work, how to use them, and how to maintain and repair them.

Speed. Food processing operators must be able to keep up with the flow of the assembly line.

Stamina. Food processing operators must be able to stay on their feet and be physically active for long periods.

Teamwork. Food processing operators work with others to keep the assembly line running smoothly. They are often closely supported by technical and managerial staff.

Pay

Food Processing Operators
Median annual wages, May 2010

Total, All Occupations	$33,840
Food Batchmakers	$24,640
Food Processing Operators	$24,250
Food Cooking Machine Operators and Tenders	$23,380

Note: All Occupations includes all occupations in the U.S. Economy.
Source: U.S. Bureau of Labor Statistics, Occupational Employment Statistics

The median annual wage of food batchmakers was $24,640 in May 2010. The median wage is the wage at which half the workers in an occupation earned more than that amount and half earned less. The lowest 10 percent earned less than $17,220, and the top 10 percent earned more than $40,760.

The median annual wage of food cooking machine operators and tenders was $23,380 in May 2010. The lowest 10 percent earned less than $16,890, and the top 10 percent earned more than $37,270.

Most food processing operators work full time and have regular hours. About one-quarter of food batchmakers worked part time in 2010.

Job Outlook

Food Processing Operators
Percent change in employment, projected 2010-20

Total, All Occupations	14%
Food Cooking Machine Operators and Tenders	5%
Food Processing Operators	2%
Food Batchmakers	1%

Note: All Occupations includes all occupations in the U.S. Economy.
Source: U.S. Bureau of Labor Statistics, Employment Projections program

Employment of food batchmakers is expected to experience little or no change, growing 1 percent from 2010 to 2020.

Employment of food cooking machine operators and tenders is expected to grow by 5 percent from 2010 to 2020, slower than the average for all occupations

Food processing operators are employed in many industries but are concentrated in food manufacturing industries, such as bakeries and tortilla manufacturing, dairy products, and fruit and vegetable manufacturing. These industries are always seeking ways to increase productivity, usually through automation, which decreases the need for workers.

Population growth, international trade, and consumer preference for convenience foods will maintain demand for these workers.

However, manufacturing industries can be volatile, and employment of food processing workers is likely to differ by industry and type of food being processed. Although employment for this occupation is projected to increase across all industries, some industries may shrink by 2020, which will generally reduce employment of food processing operators in those industries. These occupations have higher-than-average job turnover and may provide good opportunities despite slow employment growth.

Job Prospects

Food processing industries are becoming more and more consolidated. Job prospects should be best in rural areas or near smaller cities where the large processing facilities are located.

The need to replace food processing operators who retire or leave the occupation for other reasons will create many job openings.

Employment projections data for food processing operators, 2010-20

Occupational Title	SOC Code	Employment, 2010	Projected Employment, 2020	Change, 2010-20	
				Percent	Numeric
Food Processing Operators	—	131,000	133,400	2	2,300
Food Batchmakers	51-3092	98,700	99,400	1	700
Food Cooking Machine Operators and Tenders	51-3093	32,300	34,000	5	1,600
SOURCE: U.S. Bureau of Labor Statistics, Employment Projections program					

Similar Occupations

This table shows a list of occupations with job duties that are similar to those of food processing operators.

Occupation	Job Duties	Entry-Level Education	Median Annual Pay, May 2010
Bakers	Bakers mix and bake ingredients according to recipes to make a variety of breads, pastries, and other baked goods.	Less than high school	$23,450
Chefs and Head Cooks	Chefs and head cooks oversee the daily food preparation at restaurants or other places where food is served. They direct kitchen staff and handle any food-related concerns.	High school diploma or equivalent	$40,630
Construction Equipment Operators	Construction equipment operators drive, maneuver, or control the heavy machinery used to construct roads, bridges, buildings, and other structures.	High school diploma or equivalent	$39,460
Construction Laborers and Helpers	Construction laborers and helpers do many basic tasks that require physical labor on construction sites.	See How to Become One	$28,410
Food Processing Occupations	Food processing occupations include butchers and meat cutters; meat, poultry, and fish cutters and trimmers; and operators and tenders of roasting, baking, and drying machinery. These workers cut, trim, or otherwise process food items, such as meat, or nonfood items, such as tobacco, for retail sale.	Less than high school	$23,950
Slaughterers and Meat Packers	Slaughterers and meat packers kill and clean animals, divide carcasses into manageable sections, and grind or otherwise prepare and pack products, such as boxed beef, for shipping to distribution centers.	Less than high school	$23,380
Sewers and Tailors	Sewers and tailors sew, join, reinforce, or finish clothing or other items. They may create new pieces of clothing from patterns and designs or alter existing garments to fit customers better.	Less than high school	$25,850
Stationary Engineers and Boiler Operators	Stationary engineers and boiler operators control stationary engines, boilers, or other mechanical equipment to provide utilities for buildings or for industrial purposes.	High school diploma or equivalent	$52,140
Upholsterers	Upholsterers make, replace, and repair coverings on furniture and in vehicles.	High school diploma or equivalent	$29,960

Contacts for More Information

For more training information about line workers and food safety, visit U.S. Department of Agriculture Food Safety and Inspection Service

Suggested citation:

Bureau of Labor Statistics, U.S. Department of Labor, Occupational Outlook Handbook, 2012-13 Edition, Food Processing Operators, on the Internet at http://www.bls.gov/ooh/production/food-processing-operators.htm .

Jewelers and Precious Stone and Metal Workers

Quick Facts: Jewelers and Precious Stone and Metal Workers	
2010 Median Pay	$35,170 per year $16.91 per hour
Entry-Level Education	High school diploma or equivalent
Work Experience in a Related Occupation	None
On-the-job Training	Long-term on-the-job training
Number of Jobs, 2010	39,200
Job Outlook, 2010-20	-5% (Decline moderately)
Employment Change, 2010-20	-2,000

What Jewelers and Precious Stone and Metal Workers Do

Jewelers and precious stone and metal workers design, manufacture, and sell jewelry. They also adjust, repair, and appraise gems and jewelry.

Duties

Jewelers and precious stone and metal workers typically do the following:

- Examine and grade diamonds and other gems
- Create jewelry from gold, silver, and precious gemstones
- Shape metal to hold the gems when making individual pieces
- Make a model with carved wax (a mold) or with computers, and then make (cast) pieces with the model
- Solder pieces together and insert stones

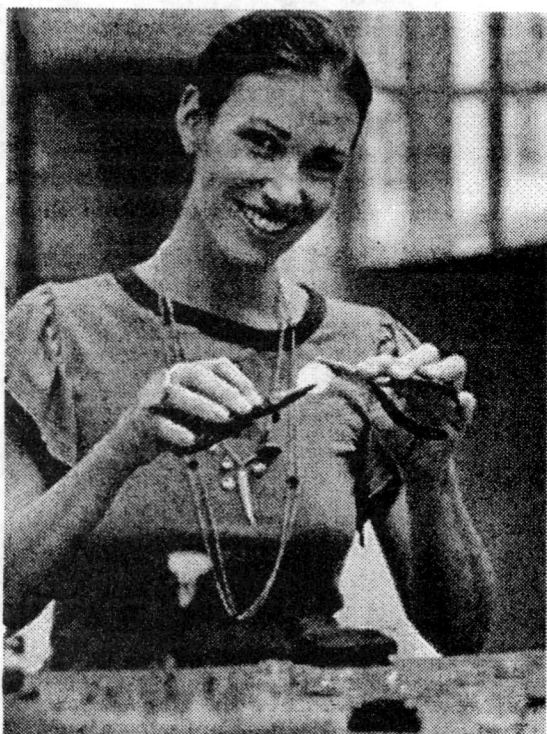

Jewelers and precious stone and metal workers typically work at a jeweler's bench.

- Smooth joints and rough spots and polish smoothed areas
- Inspect finished products to ensure proper gem spacing and metal shine
- Repair jewelry by replacing broken clasps, enlarging or reducing ring sizes, resetting stones, or soldering pieces together

New technology is helping to produce high-quality jewelry at a reduced cost and in less time. For example, lasers are often used for cutting and improving the quality of stones, for intricate engraving or design work, and for inscribing personal messages or identification on jewelry. Jewelers also use lasers to weld metals together with no seams or blemishes, improving the quality and appearance of jewelry.

Some manufacturing firms use computer-aided design and manufacturing (CAD/CAM) to make product design easier and to automate some steps. With CAD, jewelers can create a model of a piece of jewelry on the computer and then see the effect of changing different aspects—the design, the stone, the setting—before cutting a stone or taking other costly steps. With CAM, they then create a mold of the piece, which makes producing many copies easy.

Individual jewelers also use CAD software to design custom jewelry. They let the customer review the design on the computer and see the effect of changes so the customer is satisfied before committing to the expense of a customized piece of jewelry.

Jewelers and precious stone and metal workers usually specialize:

Precious metal workers expertly manipulate gold, silver, and other metals.

Gemologists analyze, describe, and certify the quality and characteristics of gem stones. After using microscopes, computerized tools, and other grading instruments to examine gem stones or finished pieces of jewelry, they write reports certifying that the items are of a particular quality.

Jewelry appraisers carefully examine jewelry to determine its value and then write appraisal documents. They determine value by researching the jewelry market and by using reference books, auction catalogs, price lists, and the Internet. They may work for jewelry stores, appraisal firms, auction houses, pawnbrokers, or insurance companies. Many gemologists also become appraisers.

Bench jewelers usually work for jewelry retailers, doing tasks from simple jewelry cleaning and repair to making molds and pieces from scratch.

Work Environment

Jewelers and precious stone and metal workers held about 39,200 jobs in 2010. Almost half were self-employed, and many work from home and sell their products at trade and craft shows on weekends.

Most wage and salary workers in this occupation are employed in jewelry stores, repair shops, and manufacturing plants.

The industries that employed the most workers in 2010 were:

Jewelry, luggage, and leather goods stores	23%
Jewelry and silverware manufacturing	18
Miscellaneous durable goods merchant wholesalers	6
Personal and household goods repair and maintenance	2

Jewelers and precious stone and metal workers spend much of their time at a workbench, using different tools and chemicals. Computers are also becoming an increasingly important tool in the jewelry industry as computer-aided design (CAD) can save workers time and resources. Many tools, such as jeweler's torches and lasers, must be handled carefully to avoid injury. Sharp or pointed tools also may pose hazards.

In repair shops, jewelers usually work alone with little supervision. In retail stores, they may talk with customers about repairs, do custom design work, and even do some selling. Because many of their materials are valuable, jewelers must follow security procedures, including making use of burglar alarms and, in larger jewelry stores, working in the presence of security guards.

Work Schedules

Jewelers and precious stone and metal workers have varied work schedules. Self-employed workers often decide their own hours; many work weekends, showing and selling their products at trade and craft shows. Retail store workers might also work nonstandard hours because they must be available when consumers are not working, such as on holidays and weekends.

How to Become a Jeweler or Precious Stone and Metal Worker

Jewelers have traditionally learned their trade through long-term on-the-job training. This method is still common, particularly in jewelry manufacturing, but a growing number of workers now learn their skills at trade schools.

Education

Many trade schools offer training for jewelers. Course topics can include introduction to gems and metals, resizing, repair, and computer-aided design (CAD). Programs vary from 6 months to 1 year, and many teach students how to design, cast, set, and polish jewelry and gems, as well as how to use and care for a jeweler's tools and equipment. Graduates of these programs may be more attractive to employers because they require less on-the-job training.

Some students earn a bachelor's degree in fine arts or a master's degree in jewelry design.

Work Experience

Some workers gain their skills through related work experience. This may include previous experience as a sales person in retail jewelry stores.

Training

In jewelry manufacturing plants, workers develop their skills through informal apprenticeships and on-the-job training. The apprenticeship or training lasts up to 1 year, depending on the difficulty of the specialty. Training usually focuses on casting, setting stones, making models, or engraving.

Advancement

Advancement opportunities are limited and depend on an individual's skill and initiative. In manufacturing, some jewelers advance to supervisory jobs, such as master jeweler or head jeweler.

Jewelers who work in jewelry stores or repair shops may become managers; some open their own business.

Jewelers and precious stone and metal workers who want to open their own store should first establish themselves and build a reputation for their work within the jewelry trade. After they get sufficient sales, they can acquire the necessary inventory for a store from a jewelry wholesaler. Also, because the jewelry business is highly competitive, jewelers who plan to open their own store should have sales experience and knowledge of marketing and business management.

Important Qualities

Artistic ability. Jewelers must have the ability to create designs that are unique and beautiful.

Detail oriented. Creating designs requires concentration and patience. Jewelers and precious stone and metal workers must be detail oriented to stay focused on their tasks.

Fashion sense. Jewelry designers must know what is stylish and attractive because that is what people are likely to buy.

Finger dexterity. Jewelers and precious stone and metal workers must precisely move their fingers in order to grasp, manipulate, and assemble very small objects.

Interpersonal skills. Whether selling products in stores or at craft shows, jewelers and precious stone and metal workers interact with customers.

Visualization skills. Jewelers and precious stone and metal workers must imagine how something might look after its shape is altered or when its parts are rearranged.

Pay

Jewelers and Precious Stone and Metal Workers
Median annual wages, May 2010

Jewelers and Precious Stone and Metal Workers	$35,170
Total, All Occupations	$33,840
Other Production Occupations	$28,740

Note: All Occupations includes all occupations in the U.S. Economy.
Source: U.S. Bureau of Labor Statistics, Occupational Employment Statistics

The median annual wage for jewelers and precious stone and metal workers was $35,170 in May 2010. The median wage is the wage at which half the workers in an occupation earned more than that amount and half earned less. The lowest 10 percent earned less than $19,460, and the highest 10 percent earned more than $61,380.

Jewelers and precious stone and metal workers have varied work schedules. Self-employed workers often decide their own hours; many work weekends, showing and selling their products at trade and craft shows. Retail store workers might also work nonstandard hours because they must be available when consumers are not working, such as on holidays and weekends. Jewelers who work in retail stores may earn a commission for jewelry sold.

Job Outlook

Jewelers and Precious Stone and Metal Workers
Percent change in employment, projected 2010-20

Total, All Occupations	14%
Other Production Occupations	4%
Jewelers and Precious Stone and Metal Workers	-5%

Note: All Occupations includes all occupations in the U.S. Economy.
Source: U.S. Bureau of Labor Statistics, Employment Projections program

Employment of jewelers and precious stone and metal workers is expected to decline 5 percent from 2010 to 2020. Low-skilled workers will likely face limited opportunities because most jewelry manufacturing is now done outside of the country.

Traditional jewelry stores may continue to lose some of their customers to nontraditional sellers, such as department stores, but they will still maintain a large customer base. In addition, new jewelry sold by nontraditional retailers should create some demand for skilled jewelers who can size, clean, and repair jewelry.

Job Prospects

Despite declining employment, job opportunities should be available for bench jewelers who are skilled at design or repair. New jewelers will be needed to replace those who retire or who leave the occupation for other reasons. As master jewelers retire, shops lose expertise and knowledge that is difficult and costly to replace. Job opportunities in jewelry stores and repair shops should be best for those who have graduated from a training program and have related work experience.

Strong competition is expected for lower skilled manufacturing jobs that are susceptible to automation. Jewelry designers who wish to create their own jewelry lines should expect intense competition. Although demand for customized and boutique jewelry is strong, it is difficult for independent designers to establish themselves. Experience with computer-aided design (CAD) makes creating custom pieces of jewelry easier.

During economic downturns, demand for jewelry products and for jewelers usually decreases. However, demand for repair workers should remain strong even during economic slowdowns because maintaining and repairing jewelry is cheaper than buying new jewelry.

Employment projections data for jewelers and precious stone and metal workers, 2010-20

Occupational Title	SOC Code	Employment, 2010	Projected Employment, 2020	Change, 2010-20	
				Percent	Numeric
Jewelers and Precious Stone and Metal Workers	51-9071	39,200	37,100	-5	-2,000
SOURCE: U.S. Bureau of Labor Statistics, Employment Projections program					

Similar Occupations

This table shows a list of occupations with job duties that are similar to those of jewelers and precious stone and metal workers.

Occupation	Job Duties	Entry-Level Education	Median Annual Pay, May 2010
Craft and Fine Artists	Craft and fine artists use a variety of materials and techniques to create art for sale and exhibition. Craft artists create handmade objects, such as pottery, glassware, textiles, or other objects that are designed to be functional. Fine artists, including painters, sculptors, and illustrators, create original works of art for their aesthetic value, rather than a functional one.	High school diploma or equivalent	$43,470
Fashion Designers	Fashion designers create original clothing, accessories, and footwear. They sketch designs, select fabrics and patterns, and give instructions on how to make the products they designed.	High school diploma or equivalent	$64,530
Industrial Designers	Industrial designers develop the concepts for manufactured products, such as cars, home appliances, and toys. They combine art, business, and engineering to make products that people use every day.	Bachelor's degree	$58,230
Retail Sales Workers	Retail sales workers include both those who sell retail merchandise, such as clothing, furniture, and automobiles, (called retail salespersons) and those who sell spare and replacement parts and equipment, especiallycar parts, (called parts salespersons). Both groups help customers find the products they want and process customers' payments.	Less than high school	$20,990
Welders, Cutters, Solderers, and Brazers	Welders, cutters, solderers, and brazers weld or join metal parts. They also fill holes, indentions, or seams of metal products, using hand-held welding equipment.	High school diploma or equivalent	$35,450
Wholesale and Manufacturing Sales Representatives	Wholesale and manufacturing sales representatives sell goods for wholesalers or manufacturers to businesses, government agencies, and other organizations. They contact customers, explain product features, answer any questions that their customers may have, and negotiate prices.	See How to Become One	$56,620
Woodworkers	Woodworkers build a variety of products, such as cabinets and furniture, using wood.	High school diploma or equivalent	$28,010

Contacts for More Information

For more information about jewelers and gemologists, including job opportunities and training programs, visit Gemological Institute of America ,Manufacturing Jewelers and Suppliers of America

Suggested citation:

Bureau of Labor Statistics, U.S. Department of Labor, Occupational Outlook Handbook, 2012-13 Edition, Jewelers and Precious Stone and Metal Workers, on the Internet at http://www.bls.gov/ooh/production/jewelers-and-precious-stone-and-metal-workers.htm .

Laundry and Dry-cleaning Workers

Quick Facts: Laundry and Dry-cleaning Workers	
2010 Median Pay	$19,540 per year $9.40 per hour
Entry-Level Education	Less than high school
Work Experience in a Related Occupation	None
On-the-job Training	Short-term on-the-job training
Number of Jobs, 2010	225,200
Job Outlook, 2010-20	1% (Little or no change)
Employment Change, 2010-20	1,600

What Laundry and Dry-cleaning Workers Do

Laundry and dry-cleaning workers clean clothing, linens, drapes, and other articles, using washing, drying, and dry-cleaning machines. They also may clean leather, suede, furs, and rugs.

Duties

Laundry and dry-cleaning workers typically do the following:
- Receive items from customers and mark them with codes or names
- Inspect articles for stains and fabrics that require special care
- Sort articles to be cleaned by fabric type, color, and cleaning technique
- Load clothing into laundry and dry-cleaning machines
- Add detergent, bleach, and other chemicals to laundry and dry-cleaning machines
- Remove, sort, and hang clothing and other articles after they are removed from the machines
- Clean and maintain laundry and dry-cleaning machines

Laundry and dry-cleaning workers ensure proper cleaning of clothing, linens, and other articles. They adjust machine settings for a given fabric or article, as determined by the cleaning instructions on each item of clothing.

When necessary, workers treat spots and stains on articles before washing or dry-cleaning. They monitor machines during the cleaning process and ensure that items are not lost or placed with items of another customer.

Sometimes, laundry and dry-cleaning workers interact with customers. They take the receipts, find the customer's clothing, take payment, make change, and do the cash register work that retail sales people do.

Some dry-cleaners offer alteration services. Often, sewers and tailors do these tasks, but some laundry and dry-cleaning workers do them as well. For more information, see the profile on sewers and tailors .

Work Environment

Laundry and dry-cleaning workers held about 225,200 jobs in 2010.

As shown in the following table, in 2010 most laundry and dry-cleaning staff worked for laundry and dry-cleaning services, healthcare facilities, or hotels and motels.

Drycleaning and laundry services	46%
Nursing care facilities	14
Traveler accommodation, including hotels and motels	13
Hospitals; state, local, and private	6

Laundry and dry-cleaning machines can make the work environment warm and noisy. Workers may also be exposed to harsh chemicals, although newer environmentally friendly and less-toxic cleaning solvents are improving their work environment.

In addition, laundry and dry-cleaning workers spend many hours standing.

Work Schedules

Most workers are employed full time. However, about 23 percent work part time. Workers may need to begin work early in the day to have customers' cleaning done on time.

How to Become a Laundry or Dry-cleaning Worker

There are no formal education or training requirements to become a laundry or dry-cleaning worker. Most workers are trained on the job.

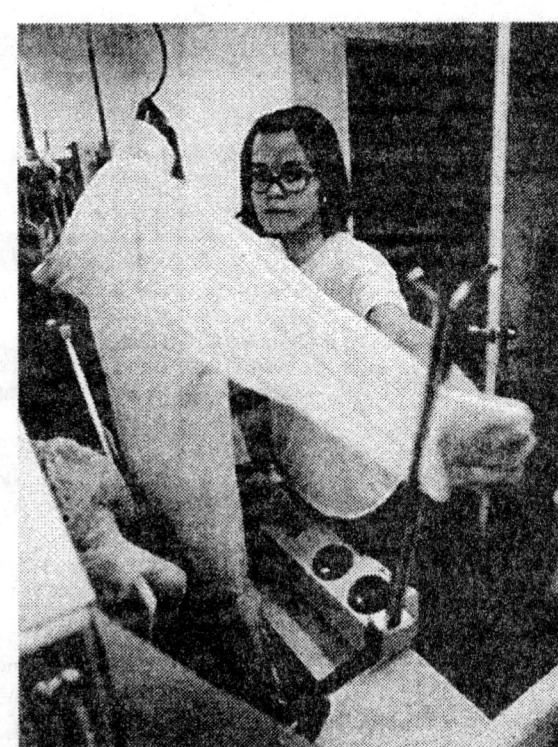

Laundry and dry-cleaning workers clean clothing, linens, drapes, and other articles using washing and dry-cleaning machines.

Education

There are no formal education requirements. Most laundry and dry-cleaning workers have a high school diploma or less. Some take classes in cleaning techniques or sewing, but most employers do not require this.

Training

Workers generally receive short-term on-the-job training. This training includes proper cleaning techniques, how to clean different fabrics, and how to treat stains.

Important Qualities

Customer-service skills. Laundry and dry-cleaning workers interact with customers who drop off and pick up their clothes. Workers may need to respond to customers who are unsatisfied with the quality of the cleaning.

Detail oriented. Many fabrics are delicate and require special care in cleaning. In addition to looking for spots and stains, laundry and dry-cleaning workers must pay attention to the type of fabric to ensure that the item is cleaned properly.

Stamina. Laundry and dry-cleaning workers often spend many hours standing in a warm environment.

Pay

Laundry and Dry-cleaning Workers
Median hourly wages, May 2010

Total, All Occupations	$16.27
Production Occupations	$14.58
Laundry and Dry-Cleaning Workers	$9.40

Note: All Occupations includes all occupations in the U.S. Economy.
Source: U.S. Bureau of Labor Statistics, Occupational Employment Statistics

The median hourly wage of laundry and dry-cleaning workers was $9.40 in May 2010. The median wage is the wage at which half the workers in an occupation earned more than that amount and half earned less. The lowest 10 percent earned less than $7.71, and the top 10 percent earned more than $14.07.

Most workers are employed full time. However, about 23 percent work part time. Workers may need to begin work early in the day to have customers' cleaning done on time.

Job Outlook

Laundry and Dry-cleaning Workers
Percent change in employment, projected 2010-20

Total, All Occupations	14%
Production Occupations	4%
Laundry and Dry-Cleaning Workers	1%

Note: All Occupations includes all occupations in the U.S. Economy.
Source: U.S. Bureau of Labor Statistics, Employment Projections program

Employment of laundry and dry-cleaning workers is expected to experience little or no change, growing 1 percent from 2010 to 2020.

A growing population will continue to demand laundry and dry-cleaning services, particularly the dry-cleaning of professional attire. This should translate into demand for laundry and dry-cleaning workers.

However, employment growth may be slowed as consumers continue to choose clothing and other articles that can be cleaned at home. Many clothing manufacturers produce more casual clothing that does not need to be dry-cleaned.

Employment projections data for laundry and dry-cleaning workers, 2010-20

Occupational Title	SOC Code	Employment, 2010	Projected Employment, 2020	Change, 2010-20	
				Percent	Numeric
Laundry and Dry-Cleaning Workers	51-6011	225,200	226,800	1	1,600
SOURCE: U.S. Bureau of Labor Statistics, Employment Projections program					

Similar Occupations

This table shows a list of occupations with job duties that are similar to those of laundry and dry-cleaning workers.

Occupation	Job Duties	Entry-Level Education	Median Annual Pay, May 2010
Fashion Designers	Fashion designers create original clothing, accessories, and footwear. They sketch designs, select fabrics and patterns, and give instructions on how to make the products they designed.	High school diploma or equivalent	$64,530
Interior Designers	Interior designers make interior spaces functional, safe, and beautiful for almost every type of building: offices, homes, airport terminals, shopping malls, and restaurants. They select and specify colors, finishes, fabrics, furniture, flooring and wallcoverings, lighting, and other materials to create useful and stylish interiors for buildings.	Bachelor's degree	$46,280
Sewers and Tailors	Sewers and tailors sew, join, reinforce, or finish clothing or other items. They may create new pieces of clothing from patterns and designs or alter existing garments to fit customers better.	Less than high school	$25,850
Upholsterers	Upholsterers make, replace, and repair coverings on furniture and in vehicles.	High school diploma or equivalent	$29,960

Contacts for More Information

For more information about laundry and dry-cleaning workers, visit
The Drycleaning and Laundry Institute

Suggested citation:

Bureau of Labor Statistics, U.S. Department of Labor, Occupational Outlook Handbook, 2012-13 Edition, Laundry and Dry-cleaning Workers, on the Internet at
http://www.bls.gov/ooh/production/laundry-and-dry-cleaning-workers.htm .

Machinists and Tool and Die Makers

Quick Facts: Machinists and Tool and Die Makers	
2010 Median Pay	$39,910 per year $19.19 per hour
Entry-Level Education	High school diploma or equivalent
Work Experience in a Related Occupation	None
On-the-job Training	Long-term on-the-job training
Number of Jobs, 2010	438,100
Job Outlook, 2010-20	7% (Slower than average)
Employment Change, 2010-20	29,900

What Machinists and Tool and Die Makers Do

Machinists and tools and die makers set up and operate a variety of computer-controlled or mechanically-controlled machine tools to produce precision metal parts, instruments, and tools.

Duties

Machinists typically do the following:
- Work from blueprints, sketches, or computer-aided design (CAD) or computer-aided manufacturing (CAM) files
- Set up, operate, and tear down manual, automatic, or computer numeric controlled (CNC) machine tools
- Calculate dimensions using measuring instruments
- Install, align, secure, and adjust cutting tools and workpieces
- Monitor the feed and speed of machines
- Turn, mill, drill, shape, and grind machine parts to specifications
- Measure, examine, and test completed products for defects
- Deburr all surfaces of parts or products to ensure that they conform to specifications

Tool and die makers typically do the following:
- Study blueprints, sketches, specifications, or CAD or CAM files for making tools and dies
- Compute and verify dimensions, sizes, shapes, and tolerances of workpieces
- Set up, operate, and tear down conventional, manual, or computer numeric controlled (CNC) machine tools
- File, grind, and adjust parts so that they fit together properly
- Test completed tools or dies to ensure that they meet specifications
- Inspect for proper dimensions and defects
- Smooth and polish surfaces of tools and dies

Machinists use machine tools that are either conventionally controlled or computer numerically controlled, such as lathes, milling machines, and grinders, to produce precision metal parts. Although they may produce large quantities of one part, precision machinists often produce small batches or one-of-a-kind items. The parts that machinists make range from simple bolts of steel or brass to titanium bone screws for orthopedic implants. Hydraulic parts, anti-lock brakes and automobile pistons are other widely known products that machinists make.

Machinists may further be classified by specialty:
- **Production machinists** produce large quantities of one part, especially parts requiring the use of complex operations and great precision. Many modern machine tools are computer numerically controlled (CNC). CNC machines control the cutting tool speed and do all necessary cuts to create a part. The machinist determines the cutting path, the speed of the cut, and the feed rate by programming instructions into the CNC machine. Many machinists must be able to use both manual and computer-controlled machinery in their job.

- **Maintenance machinists** repair or make new parts for existing machinery. After an industrial machinery mechanic discovers the broken part of a machine, the machinist gets the broken part. For more information, see the profile on industrial machinery mechanics and maintenance workers . To replace or remanufacture broken parts, maintenance machinists refer to blueprints and do the same machining operations that were needed to create the original part.

Although production machinists are concentrated in a few industries, maintenance machinists work in many manufacturing industries.

Because the technology of machining is changing rapidly, machinists must learn to operate a wide range of machines. Some newer manufacturing processes use lasers, water jets, electrical discharge machines (EDM), or electrified wires to cut the workpiece. Although some of the computer controls are similar to those of other machine tools, machinists must understand the unique capabilities of these different machines. As engineers create new types of machine tools, machinists must constantly learn new machining properties and techniques.

Toolmakers craft precision tools and toolholders that are used to cut, shape, and form metal and other materials. They also produce jigs and fixtures—devices that hold metal while it is bored, stamped, or drilled—and gauges and other measuring devices.

Die makers construct metal forms, called dies, that are used to shape metal in stamping and forging operations. They also make metal molds for diecasting and for molding plastics, ceramics, and composite materials.

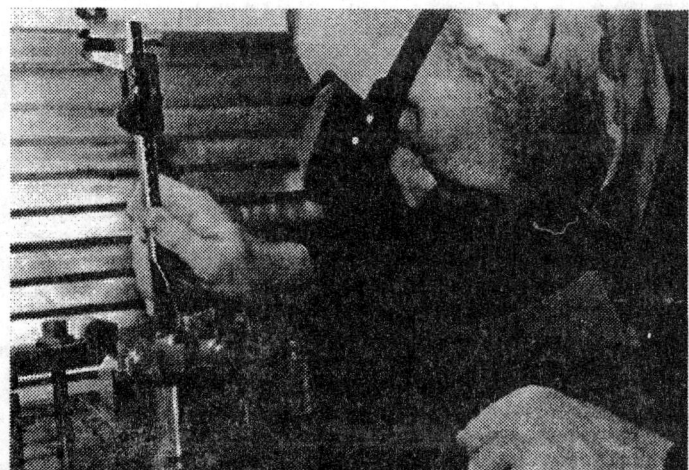

Machinists and tool and die makers set up and operate many different machines.

Many tool and die makers use computer-aided design (CAD) to develop products and parts. Specifications entered into computer programs can be used to electronically develop blueprints for the required tools and dies. Computer numeric control programmers use CAD and computer-aided manufacturing (CAM) programs to convert electronic drawings into CAM-based computer programs that contain instructions for a sequence of cutting tool operations. Once these programs are developed, CNC machines follow the set of instructions contained in the program to produce the part. Machinists normally operate CNC machines, but tool and die makers are often trained to both operate CNC machines and write CNC programs, and they may do either task.

Work Environment

Machinists and tool and die makers held about 438,100 jobs in 2010. The vast majority worked in manufacturing.

Machinists and tool and die makers work in machine shops and toolrooms and on factory floors, where work areas are well lit and ventilated.

Injuries

Although the work of machinists and tool and die makers generally is not dangerous, working around machine tools presents certain hazards, and workers must follow precautions. For example, workers must wear protective equipment, such as safety glasses to shield against bits of flying metal and earplugs to dampen the noise produced by machinery.

Work Schedules

Most machinists and tool and die makers work full time during regular business hours. However, overtime is common. Because many manufacturers run the machinery for long hours, evening and weekend work is also common.

How to Become a Machinist or Tool and Die Maker

Machinists train in apprenticeship programs, vocational schools, or community or technical colleges, or informally on the job. To become a fully trained tool and die maker takes 4 or 5 years of technical instruction and on-the-job training. Good math, problem-solving, and computer skills are important.

Education

There are many different ways to become a skilled machinist or tool and die maker. In high school, students should take math courses, especially trigonometry and geometry. They should also take courses in blueprint reading, metalworking, and drafting, if available.

Some advanced positions, such as those in the aircraft manufacturing industry, require the use of advanced applied calculus and physics. The increasing use of computer controlled machinery requires machinists and tool and die makers to have basic computer skills before entering a training program.

Training

Formal apprenticeship programs, typically sponsored by a union or manufacturer, are an excellent way to become a machinist or tool and die maker, but they are often hard to get into. Apprentices usually must have a high school diploma or equivalent, and most have taken algebra and trigonometry classes.

Apprenticeship programs consist of paid shop training and related technical instruction lasting between 4 and 5 years. Apprenticeship classes are often taught in cooperation with local community colleges or vocational-technical schools.

Although apprenticeship programs may be the best way to learn the job, a growing number of machinists and tool and die makers receive their formal technical training from community and technical colleges. These employees often learn while employed by a manufacturer that supports the employee's training goals and gives the needed on-the-job training less formally.

Apprentices usually work 40 hours per week and get technical instruction at night. Trainees often begin as machine operators and gradually take on more difficult assignments. Machinists and tool and die makers must have good computer skills to work with CAD/CAM technology, CNC machine tools, and computerized measuring machines. Many machinists become tool and die makers.

Even after completing a formal training program, tool and die makers still need years of experience to become highly skilled.

Certification

To boost the skill level of machinists and tool and die makers and to create a more uniform standard of competency, a number of training facilities, state apprenticeship boards, and colleges offer certification programs.

Completing a recognized certification program provides machinists and tool and die makers with better job opportunities and helps employers judge the abilities of new hires. Journey-level certification is available from state apprenticeship boards after completing an apprenticeship. Many employers recognize this certification, and it often leads to better job opportunities.

Important Qualities

Analytical skills. Machinists and tool and die makers must understand highly technical electronic or written blueprints, models, and specifications so they can craft precision tools and metal parts.

Detail oriented. The work of machinists and tool and die makers must be highly accurate. For example, tolerances may reach 50/1,000,000ths of an inch, which requires workers' precision, concentration, and attention to detail.

Math and computer skills. These workers must have good math and computer skills to work with CAD/CAM technology, CNC machine tools, and computerized measuring machines.

Mechanical skills. Machinists and tool and die makers must be mechanically inclined. They operate milling machines, lathes, grinders, laser and water cutting machines, wire electrical discharge machines, and other machine tools. They also may use a variety of hand tools and power tools.

Stamina. The ability to endure long periods of standing and doing repetitive movements is important for machinists and tool and die makers.

Technical skills. Machinists and tool and die makers must understand computerized measuring machines and metalworking processes, such as stock removal, chip control, and heat treating and plating.

Pay

Machinists and Tool and Die Makers
Median hourly wages, May 2010

Tool and Die Makers	$22.56
Machinists	$18.52
Total, All Occupations	$16.27
Production Occupations	$14.58

Note: All Occupations includes all occupations in the U.S. Economy.
Source: U.S. Bureau of Labor Statistics, Occupational Employment Statistics

Wages of machinists and tool and die makers vary with their skill and with the industry and establishment in which they work.

The median hourly wage of machinists was $18.52 in May 2010.

The median wage is the wage at which half the workers in an occupation earned more than that amount and half earned less. The lowest 10 percent earned less than $11.59, and the top 10 percent earned more than $27.91.

The median hourly wage of tool and die makers was $22.56 in May 2010. The lowest 10 percent earned less than $15.34, and the top 10 percent earned more than $33.57.

The pay of apprentices is tied to their skill level. As they gain more skills and reach specific levels of performance and experience, their pay increases.

In 2010, about 17 percent of machinists and 26 percent of tool and die makers were members of a union.

Most machinists and tool and die makers work full time during regular business hours. However, overtime is common. Also, many manufacturers run the machinery for long hours, so they have shifts with evening and weekend work.

Job Outlook

Machinists and Tool and Die Makers
Percent change in employment, projected 2010-20

Total, All Occupations	14%
Machinists	8%
Production Occupations	4%
Tool and Die Makers	-2%

Note: All Occupations includes all occupations in the U.S. Economy.
Source: U.S. Bureau of Labor Statistics, Employment Projections program

Overall employment of machinists and tool and die makers is expected to grow 7 percent from 2010 to 2020, slower than the average for all occupations. Employment growth will vary by specialty.

Employment of machinists is projected to grow 8 percent from 2010 to 2020, slower than the average for all occupations.

Despite improvements in technologies such as CNC machine tools, autoloaders, high-speed machining, and lights-out manufacturing, machinists will still be required to set up, monitor, and maintain these automated systems.

In addition, employers are expected to continue needing machinists who have a wide range of skills and are capable of performing modern production techniques and almost any task in a machine shop. As manufacturers will continue to rely heavily on skilled machinists as they invest in new equipment, modify production techniques, and implement product design changes more rapidly.

Employment of tool and die makers is projected to experience little or no change from 2010 to 2020. Foreign competition in manufacturing and advances in automation, including CNC machine tools and computer-aided design, should improve worker productivity, requiring fewer workers.

Job Prospects

Job opportunities for machinists and tool and die makers should be excellent as employers continue to value the wide-ranging skills of these workers. Also, many young people with the educational and personal qualifications needed to become machinists or tool and die makers prefer to attend college or may not wish to enter production occupations.

In fact, employers in certain parts of the country report difficulty attracting skilled workers and apprenticeship candidates with the abilities necessary to fill job openings.

Therefore, the number of workers learning to be machinists or tool and die makers is expected to be smaller than the number of job openings arising each year from the need to replace experienced machinists who retire or leave the occupation for other reasons.

Employment projections data for machinists and tool and die makers, 2010-20

Occupational Title	SOC Code	Employment, 2010	Projected Employment, 2020	Change, 2010-20	
				Percent	Numeric
Machinists and Tool and Die Makers	—	438,100	468,000	7	29,900
Machinists	51-4041	370,400	401,900	8	31,500
Tool and Die Makers	51-4111	67,700	66,100	-2	-1,500
SOURCE: U.S. Bureau of Labor Statistics, Employment Projections program					

Similar Occupations

This table shows a list of occupations with job duties that are similar to those of machinists and tool and die makers.

Occupation	Job Duties	Entry-Level Education	Median Annual Pay, May 2010
Industrial Machinery Mechanics and Maintenance Workers	Industrial machinery mechanics and maintenance workers maintain and repair factory equipment and other industrial machinery, such as conveying systems, production machinery, and packaging equipment.	High school diploma or equivalent	$44,160
Metal and Plastic Machine Workers	Metal and plastic machine workers set up and operate machines that cut, shape, and form metal and plastic materials or pieces.	High school diploma or equivalent	$31,910
Millwrights	Millwrights install, dismantle, repair, reassemble, and move machinery in factories, power plants, and construction sites.	High school diploma or equivalent	$48,360
Welders, Cutters, Solderers, and Brazers	Welders, cutters, solderers, and brazers weld or join metal parts. They also fill holes, indentions, or seams of metal products, using hand-held welding equipment.	High school diploma or equivalent	$35,450

Contacts for More Information

For more information about machinists and tool and die makers, including training and certification, visit Fabricators & Manufacturers Association International , National Institute for Metalworking Skills (NIMS)

For general information about manufacturing careers, including machinery and tool and die makers, visit American Mold Builders Association (AMBA) ,Association for Manufacturing Technology (AMT) ,National Tooling and Machining Association (NTMA) ,Precision Machined Products Association (PMPA)

Suggested citation:

Bureau of Labor Statistics, U.S. Department of Labor, Occupational Outlook Handbook, 2012-13 Edition, Machinists and Tool and Die Makers, on the Internet at http://www.bls.gov/ooh/production/machinists -and-tool-and-die-makers.htm .

Medical Appliance Technicians

Quick Facts: Medical Appliance Technicians	
2010 Median Pay	$35,670 per year $17.15 per hour
Entry-Level Education	High school diploma or equivalent
Work Experience in a Related Occupation	None
On-the-job Training	Long-term on-the-job training
Number of Jobs, 2010	14,200
Job Outlook, 2010-20	4% (Slower than average)
Employment Change, 2010-20	500

What Medical Appliance Technicians Do

Medical appliance technicians construct, fit, and repair medical supportive devices, including prosthetic limbs, arch supports, facial parts, and foot and leg braces.

Duties

Medical appliance technicians typically do the following:

- Read work orders or specifications from a podiatrist, orthotist, prosthetist, or other healthcare professional
- Decide which materials and tools will be needed
- Create a pattern for the unmolded or unshaped plastic and metal
- Bend, form, and shape fabric or material
- Use hand or power tools to polish and shape the devices

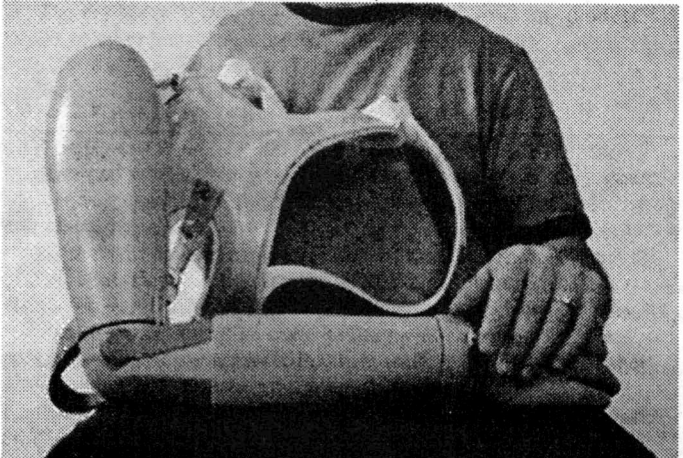

Medical appliance technicians construct, fit, maintain, and repair braces, artificial limbs, arch supports, and other medical and surgical appliances.

- Repair or change medical supportive devices as directed by a healthcare professional

Medical appliance technicians use many different types of materials, such as metal, plastic, and leather, to create a variety of medical devices for patients who need them because of a birth defect, an accident, disease, amputation, or the effects of aging. For example, some medical appliance technicians make hearing aids.

Orthotic and prosthetic technicians are medical appliance technicians who create orthoses (braces, supports, and other devices) and prostheses (replacement limbs and facial parts).

Work Environment

Medical appliance technicians held about 14,200 jobs in 2010.

In 2010, most medical appliance technicians worked in manufacturing laboratories. Others worked in health and personal care stores. Technicians may be exposed to health and safety hazards when they handle certain materials, but there is little risk if they follow proper procedures, such as wearing goggles, gloves, or masks.

How to Become a Medical Appliance Technician

There are no formal educational requirements for becoming an entry-level medical appliance technician.Many technicians learn through on-the-job training.

Training

Most medical appliance technicians learn their duties through on-the-job training. Experienced technicians teach new employees how to create and repair orthotic and prosthetic devices or equipment. The amount of training varies. For example, a new technician may be trained for up to a year before independently creating an orthotic or prosthetic device.

Education

There are no formal education or training requirements for

becoming a medical laboratory technician. Most technicians have at least a high school diploma. Some community colleges and technical or vocational schools have formal education programs, but such programs are not common.

High school students interested becoming a technician should take courses in mathematics, science, metal and wood shop, and computers.

Important Qualities

Analytical skills. Because medical appliance technicians must construct medical appliances with accuracy and precision, they need to have an in-depth knowledge of how different tools and materials work.

Interpersonal skills. Medical appliance technicians need to be able to get along with others because they may be part of a team of technicians working on a single project. In addition, they need good communication to ensure safety when they work with hazardous materials.

Technical skills. When creating medical devices, medical appliance technicians set up and operate sophisticated equipment and instruments. They also may need to make adjustments to equipment.

Certification

Medical appliance technicians are not required to be certified. However, employers prefer to hire certified technicians. The American Board for Certification in Orthotics, Prosthetics and Pedorthics (ABC) offers certification for technicians after they pass an exam. Technicians are eligible for the exam after completing an accredited program or if they have 2 years of experience as a technician under the direct supervision of a certified technician.

Advancement

Medical appliance technicians can advance to become orthotists or prosthetists after completing additional formal education. These practitioners work with patients who need braces, prostheses, or related devices. For more information, see the profile on orthotists and prosthetists .

Pay

Medical Appliance Technicians
Median annual wages, May 2010

Medical Appliance Technicians	$35,670
Total, All Occupations	$33,840
Other Production Occupations	$28,740

Note: All Occupations includes all occupations in the U.S. Economy.
Source: U.S. Bureau of Labor Statistics, Occupational Employment Statistics

The median annual wage of medical appliance technicians was $35,670 in May 2010. The median wage is the wage at which half the workers in an occupation earned more than that amount and half earned less. The lowest 10 percent earned less than $23,450, and the top 10 percent earned more than $58,060.

Job Outlook

Medical Appliance Technicians
Percent change in employment, projected 2010-20

Total, All Occupations	14%
Medical Appliance Technicians	4%
Other Production Occupations	4%

Note: All Occupations includes all occupations in the U.S. Economy.
Source: U.S. Bureau of Labor Statistics, Employment Projections program

Employment is expected to grow 4 percent from 2010 to 2020, slower than the average for all occupations.

An aging baby-boomer population will create a need for technicians because diabetes and cardiovascular disease, the two leading causes of loss of limbs, are more likely to occur in older people. The demand for orthotic devices, such as braces and orthopedic footwear, will increase because older people tend to need these supportive devices.

Although advances in technology may spur demand for prostheses that allow for more natural movement, increased productivity in manufacturing due to automation will slow growth for technicians.

Employment projections data for medical appliance technicians, 2010-20

Occupational Title	SOC Code	Employment, 2010	Projected Employment, 2020	Change, 2010-20	
				Percent	Numeric
Medical Appliance Technicians	51-9082	14,200	14,700	4	500
SOURCE: U.S. Bureau of Labor Statistics, Employment Projections program					

Similar Occupations

This table shows a list of occupations with job duties that are similar to those of medical appliance technicians.

Occupation	Job Duties	Entry-Level Education	Median Annual Pay, May 2010
Orthotists and Prosthetists	Orthotists and prosthetists, also called O&P professionals, design medical support devices and measure and fit patients for them. These devices include artificial limbs (arms, hands, legs, and feet), braces, and other medical or surgical devices.	Master's degree	$65,060
Dental Laboratory Technicians	Dental laboratory technicians use impressions, or molds, of a patient's teeth to create crowns, bridges, dentures, and other dental appliances. They work closely with dentists but have limited contact with patients.	High school diploma or equivalent	$35,140
Ophthalmic Laboratory Technicians	Ophthalmic laboratory technicians make prescription eyeglasses and contact lenses. They are also commonly known as manufacturing opticians, optical mechanics, or optical goods workers.	High school diploma or equivalent	$27,970
Medical Equipment Repairers	Medical equipment repairers install, maintain, and repair patient care equipment.	Associate's degree	$44,490

Contacts for More Information

For a list of accredited programs for orthotic and prosthetic technicians, visit American Academy of Orthotists & Prosthetists , National Commission on Orthotic & Prosthetic Education

For information on requirements for certification of orthotic and prosthetic technicians, visit American Board for Certification in Orthotics, Prosthetics and Pedorthics

Suggested citation:

Bureau of Labor Statistics, U.S. Department of Labor, Occupational Outlook Handbook, 2012-13 Edition, Medical Appliance Technicians, on the Internet at http://www.bls.gov/ooh/production/medical-appliance-technicians.htm .

Metal and Plastic Machine Workers

Quick Facts: Metal and Plastic Machine Workers	
2010 Median Pay	$31,910 per year $15.34 per hour
Entry-Level Education	High school diploma or equivalent
Work Experience in a Related Occupation	None
On-the-job Training	See How to Become One
Number of Jobs, 2010	939,700
Job Outlook, 2010-20	6% (Slower than average)
Employment Change, 2010-20	56,100

What Metal and Plastic Machine Workers Do

Metal and plastic machine workers set up and operate machines that cut, shape, and form metal and plastic materials or pieces.

Duties

Metal and plastic machine workers typically do the following:

- Set up machines and monitor them for unusual sound or vibration
- Lift material onto machines, manually or with a hoist
- Operate metal or plastic molding, casting, or coremaking machines
- Adjust the machines' speed and other settings
- Adjust cutting machine settings to account for irregularities
- Stop machines and remove finished products
- Test and measure finished products
- Remove and replace dull cutting tools
- Document production numbers in a computer database

Consumer products are made with many metal and plastic parts.

Metal and plastic machine workers set up and operate automated and computer-controlled machinery.

These parts are produced by machines that are operated by metal and plastic machine workers. In general, these workers are separated into two groups: those who set up machines for operation and those who operate machines during production.

Although many workers both set up and operate the machines, some specialize in one of the following job types:

Machine setters, or setup workers, prepare the machines before production, perform test runs, and, if necessary, adjust and make minor repairs to the machinery before and during operation.

If, for example, the cutting tool inside a machine becomes dull after extended use, it is common for a setter to remove the tool, use a grinder or file to sharpen it, and place it back into the machine.

New tools are produced by tool and die makers. For more information, see the profile on machinists and tool and die makers .

After installing the tools into a machine, setup workers often produce the initial batch of goods, inspect the products, and turn the machine over to an operator.

Machine operators and tenders monitor the machinery during operation.

After a setter prepares a machine for production, an operator observes the machine and the products it produces. Operators may have to load the machine with materials for production or adjust the machine's speeds during production. They must periodically inspect the parts a machine produces. If they detect a minor problem, operators may fix it themselves. If the repair is more serious, they may have an industrial machinery mechanic fix it. For more information, see the profile on industrial machinery mechanics and maintenance workers .

Setters, operators, and tenders usually are identified by the type of machine they work with. Job duties usually vary with the size of the manufacturer and the type of machine being operated. Although some workers specialize in one or two types of machinery, many are trained to set up or operate a variety of machines. Increasing automation allows machine setters to operate multiple machines at the same time.

In addition, newer production techniques, such as team-oriented "lean" manufacturing, require machine operators to rotate between different machines. Rotating assignments results in more varied work but also requires workers to have a wider range of skills.

The following are types of metal and plastic machine workers:

Computer-controlled machine tool operators, metal and plastic operate computer-controlled machines or robots to perform functions on metal or plastic workpieces.

Computer numerically controlled machine tool programmers, metal and plastic develop programs to control the machining or processing of metal or plastic parts by automatic machine tools, equipment, or systems.

Extruding and drawing machine setters, operators, and tenders, metal and plastic set up or operate machines to extrude (pull out) or draw thermoplastic or metal materials into tubes, rods, hoses, wire, bars, or structural shapes.

Forging machine setters, operators, and tenders, metal and plastic set up or operate machines that taper, shape, or form metal or plastic parts.

Rolling machine setters, operators, and tenders, metal and plastic set up or operate machines to roll steel or plastic or to flatten, temper, or reduce the thickness of material.

Cutting, punching, and press machine setters, operators, and tenders, metal and plastic set up or operate machines to saw, cut, shear, notch, bend, or straighten metal or plastic material.

Drilling and boring machine tool setters, operators, and tenders, metal and plastic set up or operate drilling machines to drill, bore, mill, or countersink metal or plastic workpieces.

Grinding, lapping, polishing, and buffing machine tool setters, operators, and tenders, metal and plastic set up or operate grinding and related tools that remove excess material from surfaces, sharpen edges or corners, or buff or polish metal or plastic workpieces.

Lathe and turning machine tool setters, operators, and tenders, metal and plastic set up or operate lathe and turning machines to turn, bore, thread, form, or face metal or plastic materials, such as wire or rod.

Milling and planing machine setters, operators, and tenders, metal and plastic set up or operate milling or planing machines to shape, groove, or profile metal or plastic workpieces.

Metal-refining furnace operators and tenders operate or tend furnaces, such as gas, oil, coal, electric-arc or electric induction, open-hearth or oxygen furnaces to melt and refine metal before casting or to produce specified types of steel.

Pourers and casters, metal operate hand-controlled mechanisms to pour and regulate the flow of molten metal into molds to produce castings or ingots.

Model makers, metal and plastic set up and operate machines, such as milling and engraving machines and jig borers, to make working models of metal or plastic objects.

Patternmakers, metal and plastic lay out, machine, fit, and assemble castings and parts to metal or plastic foundry patterns, coreboxes, or match plates.

Foundry mold and coremakers make or form wax or sand cores or molds used in the production of metal castings in foundries.

Molding, coremaking, and casting machine setters, operators, and tenders, metal and plastic set up or operate metal or plastic molding, casting, or coremaking machines to mold or cast metal or thermoplastic parts or products.

Multiple machine tool setters, operators, and tenders, metal and plastic set up or operate more than one type of cutting or forming machine tool or robot.

Welding, soldering, and brazing machine setters, operators, and tenders (including workers who operate laser cutters or laser-beam machines) set up or operate welding, soldering, or brazing machines or robots that weld, braze, solder, or heat treat metal products, components, or assemblies.

Heat treating equipment setters, operators, and tenders, metal and plastic set up or operate heating equipment, such as heat treating furnaces, flame-hardening machines, induction machines, soaking pits, or vacuum equipment, to temper, harden, anneal, or heat treat metal or plastic objects.

Plating and coating machine setters, operators, and tenders,

metal and plastic set up or operate plating or coating machines to coat metal or plastic products with zinc, copper, nickel, or some other metal to protect or decorate surfaces (includes electrolytic processes).

Work Environment

Metal and plastic machine workers held about 939,700 jobs in 2010. Nearly all worked in manufacturing industries.

Employment in the detailed occupations that make up this group was distributed as follows:

Cutting, punching, and press machine setters, operators, and tenders, metal and plastic	183,900
Computer-controlled machine tool operators, metal and plastic	125,100
Molding, coremaking, and casting machine setters, operators, and tenders, metal and plastic	115,200
Extruding and drawing machine setters, operators, and tenders, metal and plastic	76,500
Grinding, lapping, polishing, and buffing machine tool setters, operators, and tenders, metal and plastic	72,600
Multiple machine tool setters, operators, and tenders, metal and plastic	70,400
Lathe and turning machine tool setters, operators, and tenders, metal and plastic	41,900
Welding, soldering, and brazing machine setters, operators, and tenders	41,500
Rolling machine setters, operators, and tenders, metal and plastic	32,200
Plating and coating machine setters, operators, and tenders, metal and plastic	31,200
Drilling and boring machine tool setters, operators, and tenders, metal and plastic	22,700
Forging machine setters, operators, and tenders, metal and plastic	22,500
Milling and planing machine setters, operators, and tenders, metal and plastic	20,800
Heat treating equipment setters, operators, and tenders, metal and plastic	18,600
Computer numerically controlled machine tool programmers, metal and plastic	16,600
Metal-refining furnace operators and tenders	15,600
Pourers and casters, metal	11,500
Foundry mold and coremakers	10,200
Model makers, metal and plastic	6,200
Patternmakers, metal and plastic	4,500

Metal and plastic machine workers are employed mainly in factories. Although the work is generally not dangerous, hazards exist and workers must adhere to safety standards. Most work in areas that are clean, well lit, and well ventilated.

Injuries

These workers operate powerful, high-speed machines that can be dangerous, so they must observe safety rules. Operators usually wear protective equipment, such as safety glasses, to protect them from flying particles of metal or plastic, earplugs to guard against noise from the machines, and steel-toed boots, to shield their feet from heavy objects that are dropped.

Many modern machines are enclosed, minimizing the exposure of workers to noise, dust, and lubricants used during machining.

Other required safety equipment varies by work setting and

machine. For example, respirators are common for those in the plastics industry who work near materials that emit dangerous fumes or dust.

Work Schedules

Most metal and plastic machine workers are employed full time during regular business hours. Overtime is common, and because many manufacturers run the machinery long hours, evening and weekend work also is common.

How to Become a Metal or Plastic Machine Worker

A few weeks of on-the-job training are enough for most workers to learn basic machine operations, but 1 year or more is required to become highly skilled. Although a high school diploma is not required, employers prefer to hire workers who have one.

Education

For jobs as machine setters, operators, and tenders, employers generally prefer workers who have a high school diploma. Those interested in this occupation can improve their employment opportunities by completing high school courses in shop and blueprint reading and by gaining a working knowledge of the properties of metals and plastics. A solid math background, including courses in algebra, geometry, trigonometry, and basic statistics, also is useful, along with experience working with computers.

Some community colleges and other schools offer courses and certificate programs in operating metal and plastics machines.

Training

Machine operator trainees usually begin by watching and helping experienced workers on the job, often through informal apprenticeships. Under supervision, they may start by supplying materials, starting and stopping the machines, or removing finished products from it. Then they advance to more difficult tasks that operators perform, such as adjusting feed speeds, changing cutting tools, or inspecting a finished product for defects. Eventually, some develop the skills and experience to set up machines and help newer operators.

It is largely the complexity of the equipment that determines the time required to become an operator. Most operators learn the basic machine operations and functions in a few weeks, but they may need a year or more to become skilled operators or to advance to the more highly skilled job of setter.

In addition to providing on-the-job training, employers may pay for some machine operators to attend classes. Other employers prefer to hire workers who have completed or are enrolled in a training program.

As the manufacturing process continues to advance with computerized machinery, knowledge of computer-aided design (CAD), computer-aided manufacturing (CAM), and computer numerically controlled (CNC) machines also can be helpful.

Certification

Although certification is not required, a growing number of employers prefer that applicants become certified. Certification can show competence and professionalism and can be helpful for advancement. The National Institute for Metalworking Skills (NIMS) has developed skills standards in 24 operational areas and offers 52 skills certifications.

The Fabricators & Manufacturers Association International also has developed a Precision Sheet Metal Operator (PSMO) certification program.

Advancement

Advancement usually includes higher pay and a wider range of responsibilities. With experience and expertise, workers can become trainees for more highly skilled positions. For example, it is common for machine operators to move into setup or machinery maintenance positions. Setup workers may move into maintenance, machinist, or tool and die maker roles. For more information, see the profiles on industrial machinery mechanics and maintenance workers , millwrights , and machinists and tool and die makers .

Skilled workers with good communication and analytical skills may move into supervisory positions.

Important Qualities

Computer skills. Modern technology systems require that metal and plastic machine workers be able to use programmable devices, computers, and robots on the factory floor.

Mechanical skills. Although modern technology has brought a lot of computer-based systems to this occupation, metal and plastic machine workers still set up and operate machinery. They must be comfortable working with machines and have a good understanding of how the machines and all their parts work.

Physical strength. Although most material handling is done using automated systems or is mechanically aided, some metal and plastic machine workers must be strong enough to guide and load heavy and bulky parts and materials into machines.

Stamina. Metal and plastic machine workers must be able to stand for long periods and perform repetitive work.

Pay

Metal and Plastic Machine Workers
Median hourly wages, May 2010

Total, All Occupations	$16.27
Metal and Plastic Machine Workers	$15.34
Production Occupations	$14.58

Note: All Occupations includes all occupations in the U.S. Economy.
Source: U.S. Bureau of Labor Statistics, Occupational Employment Statistics

The median hourly wage of metal and plastic machine workers was $15.34 in May 2010. The median wage is the wage at which half the workers in an occupation earned more than that amount and half earned less. The lowest 10 percent earned less than $9.96, and the top 10 percent earned more than $23.57.

Wages for metal and plastic machine workers vary by size of the company, union status, industry, and skill level and experience of the operator.

In May 2010, median hourly wages for metal and plastic machine workers were as follows:
- $22.07 for computer numerically controlled machine tool programmers, metal and plastic
- $20.55 for model makers, metal and plastic
- $18.49 for metal-refining furnace operators and tenders
- $17.88 for patternmakers, metal and plastic
- $17.63 for rolling machine setters, operators, and tenders, metal and plastic
- $17.47 for milling and planing machine setters, operators, and tenders, metal and plastic
- $16.70 for computer-controlled machine tool operators, metal and plastic
- $16.66 for lathe and turning machine tool setters, operators, and tenders, metal and plastic
- $16.36 for pourers and casters, metal
- $16.26 for welding, soldering, and brazing machine setters, operators, and tenders
- $16.13 for forging machine setters, operators, and tenders, metal and plastic
- $15.86 for heat treating equipment setters, operators, and tenders,

metal and plastic
- $15.56 for drilling and boring machine tool setters, operators, and tenders, metal and plastic
- $15.30 for multiple machine tool setters, operators, and tenders, metal and plastic
- $15.26 for extruding and drawing machine setters, operators, and tenders, metal and plastic
- $14.74 for grinding, lapping, polishing, and buffing machine tool setters, operators, and tenders, metal and plastic
- $14.66 for foundry mold and coremakers
- $14.12 for cutting, punching, and press machine setters, operators, and tenders, metal and plastic
- $13.93 for plating and coating machine setters, operators, and tenders, metal and plastic
- $13.54 for molding, coremaking, and casting machine setters, operators, and tenders, metal and plastic

Most metal and plastic machine workers are employed full time during regular business hours. Overtime is common, and because many manufacturers run the machinery long hours, evening and weekend work also is common.

Job Outlook

Metal and Plastic Machine Workers
Percent change in employment, projected 2010-20

Total, All Occupations	14%
Metal and Plastic Machine Workers	6%
Production Occupations	4%

Note: All Occupations includes all occupations in the U.S. Economy.
Source: U.S. Bureau of Labor Statistics, Employment Projections program

Employment of metal and plastic machine workers is projected to grow 6 percent from 2010 to 2020, slower than the average for all occupations. Employment will be affected by advances in technology, changing demand for the goods these workers produce, foreign competition, and the reorganization of production processes.

One of the most important factors influencing employment growth in these occupations is the use of labor-saving machinery. Many firms are adopting new technologies, such as computer-controlled machine tools and robots, to improve quality, lower production costs, and remain competitive. The switch to computer-controlled machinery requires computer programmers instead of machine setters, operators, and tenders. The lower-skilled manual machine tool operator and tender jobs are more likely to be eliminated by these new technologies because the computer-controlled machinery does the work more effectively.

The demand for metal and plastic machine workers also is affected by the demand for the parts they produce. Both the plastic and metal manufacturing industries face stiff foreign competition that is limiting the orders for parts produced in this country. Some U.S. manufacturers have recently sent their production to foreign countries, limiting jobs for machine setters and operators.

Job Prospects

Despite slower than average employment growth, a number of these jobs are expected to become available for highly skilled workers because of an expected increase in retirements, primarily of baby boomers, in the coming years.

In addition, workers who have a thorough background in machine operations, certifications from industry associations, and a good working knowledge of the properties of metals and plastics should have the best job opportunities.

Employment projections data for metal and plastic machine workers, 2010-20

Occupational Title	SOC Code	Employment, 2010	Projected Employment, 2020	Change, 2010-20	
				Percent	Numeric
Metal and Plastic Machine Workers	—	939,700	995,800	6	56,100
Computer-Controlled Machine Tool Operators, Metal and Plastic	51-4011	125,100	149,000	19	24,000
Computer Numerically Controlled Machine Tool Programmers, Metal and Plastic	51-4012	16,600	18,300	11	1,800
Extruding and Drawing Machine Setters, Operators, and Tenders, Metal and Plastic	51-4021	76,500	82,900	8	6,400
Forging Machine Setters, Operators, and Tenders, Metal and Plastic	51-4022	22,500	23,200	3	700
Rolling Machine Setters, Operators, and Tenders, Metal and Plastic	51-4023	32,200	34,800	8	2,600
Cutting, Punching, and Press Machine Setters, Operators, and Tenders, Metal and Plastic	51-4031	183,900	188,500	2	4,500
Drilling and Boring Machine Tool Setters, Operators, and Tenders, Metal and Plastic	51-4032	22,700	21,100	-7	-1,600
Grinding, Lapping, Polishing, and Buffing Machine Tool Setters, Operators, and Tenders, Metal and Plastic	51-4033	72,600	73,600	1	1,000
Lathe and Turning Machine Tool Setters, Operators, and Tenders, Metal and Plastic	51-4034	41,900	39,900	-5	-2,000
Milling and Planing Machine Setters, Operators, and Tenders, Metal and Plastic	51-4035	20,800	21,600	4	700
Metal-Refining Furnace Operators and Tenders	51-4051	15,600	18,200	16	2,500
Pourers and Casters, Metal	51-4052	11,500	12,000	4	500
Model Makers, Metal and Plastic	51-4061	6,200	5,700	-8	-500
Patternmakers, Metal and Plastic	51-4062	4,500	4,400	-2	-100

Occupational Title	SOC Code	Employment, 2010	Projected Employment, 2020	Change, 2010-20	
				Percent	Numeric
Foundry Mold and Coremakers	51-4071	10,200	11,300	12	1,200
Molding, Coremaking, and Casting Machine Setters, Operators, and Tenders, Metal and Plastic	51-4072	115,200	121,000	5	5,800
Multiple Machine Tool Setters, Operators, and Tenders, Metal and Plastic	51-4081	70,400	73,000	4	2,700
Welding, Soldering, and Brazing Machine Setters, Operators, and Tenders	51-4122	41,500	44,200	7	2,700
Heat Treating Equipment Setters, Operators, and Tenders, Metal and Plastic	51-4191	18,600	18,800	1	100
Plating and Coating Machine Setters, Operators, and Tenders, Metal and Plastic	51-4193	31,200	34,100	9	2,900

SOURCE: U.S. Bureau of Labor Statistics, Employment Projections program

Similar Occupations

This table shows a list of occupations with job duties that are similar to those of metal and plastic machine workers.

Occupation	Job Duties	Entry-Level Education	Median Annual Pay, May 2010
Assemblers and Fabricators	Assemblers and fabricators assemble both finished products and the parts that go into them. They use tools, machines, and their hands to make engines, computers, aircraft, toys, electronic devices, and more.	High school diploma or equivalent	$28,360
Industrial Machinery Mechanics and Maintenance Workers	Industrial machinery mechanics and maintenance workers maintain and repair factory equipment and other industrial machinery, such as conveying systems, production machinery, and packaging equipment.	High school diploma or equivalent	$44,160
Machinists and Tool and Die Makers	Machinists and tool and die makers set up and operate a variety of computer-controlled or mechanically-controlled machine tools to produce precision metal parts, instruments, and tools.	High school diploma or equivalent	$39,910
Millwrights	Millwrights install, dismantle, repair, reassemble, and move machinery in factories, power plants, and construction sites.	High school diploma or equivalent	$48,360
Painting and Coating Workers	Painting and coating workers paint and coat a wide range of products, including cars, jewelry, lacquer, and candy.	High school diploma or equivalent	$31,170
Computer Programmers	Computer programmers write code to create software programs. They turn the program designs created by software developers and engineers into instructions that a computer can follow.	Bachelor's degree	$71,380

Contacts for More Information

For more information about metal and plastic machine workers, including training and certification, visit Fabricators & Manufacturers Association International (FMA) , National Institute for Metalworking Skills (NIMS)

For general information about manufacturing careers, machinery, and equipment, visit Association for Manufacturing Technology (AMT) , National Tooling and Machining Association (NTMA) , Precision Machined Products Association (PMPA) ,Precision Metalforming Association (PMA)

Suggested citation:

Bureau of Labor Statistics, U.S. Department of Labor, Occupational Outlook Handbook, 2012-13 Edition, Metal and Plastic Machine Workers, on the Internet at
http://www.bls.gov/ooh/production/metal-and-plastic-machine-workers.htm

Ophthalmic Laboratory Technicians

Quick Facts: Ophthalmic Laboratory Technicians	
2010 Median Pay	$27,970 per year $13.45 per hour
Entry-Level Education	High school diploma or equivalent
Work Experience in a Related Occupation	None
On-the-job Training	Moderate-term on-the-job training
Number of Jobs, 2010	29,800
Job Outlook, 2010-20	13% (About as fast as average)
Employment Change, 2010-20	3,800

What Ophthalmic Laboratory Technicians Do

Ophthalmic laboratory technicians make prescription eyeglasses and contact lenses. They are also commonly known as manufacturing opticians, optical mechanics, or optical goods workers.

Duties

Ophthalmic laboratory technicians typically do the following:

- Cut lenses to the appropriate prescription that they get from ophthalmologists, dispensing opticians, or optometrists
- Shape lenses so that they fit into frames
- Dip lenses into dyes or coatings if the prescription requires the lenses to be tinted
- Polish lenses either by hand or mechanically
- Assemble lenses and frames together to create prescription glasses
- Inspect the final product for quality and accuracy

Although they make some lenses by hand, ophthalmic laboratory technicians often use automated equipment. Some technicians manufacture lenses for other optical instruments, such as telescopes and binoculars.

In small laboratories, technicians may handle every phase of production. In larger ones, technicians may be responsible for only one phase of production, such as polishing.

Ophthalmic laboratory technicians should not be confused with workers in other vision care occupations, such as ophthalmologists, optometrists, and dispensing opticians. For more information, see the profiles on physicians and surgeons (including ophthalmologists), optometrists , and opticians, dispensing .

Work Environment

Ophthalmic laboratory technicians held about 29,800 jobs in 2010. Ophthalmic laboratory technicians work in medical equipment and supplies manufacturing laboratories, health and personal care stores, and offices of ophthalmologists and optometrists.

The following industries employed the largest numbers of ophthalmic laboratory technicians in 2010:

Health and personal care stores	27%
Medical equipment and supplies manufacturing	26
Offices of optometrists	13
Offices of physicians	10
Commercial and service industry machinery manufacturing	6

Ophthalmic laboratory technicians often have limited contact with the public. To avoid injuries, technicians may wear goggles, gloves, or masks while working. They may spend a great deal of time standing or bending.

How to Become an Ophthalmic Laboratory Technician

There are no formal education or training requirements for becoming an ophthalmic laboratory technician, but most technicians have at least a high school diploma. Technicians usually learn their skills on the job.

Training

Most ophthalmic laboratory technicians learn through on-the-job training. They usually begin by marking or blocking lenses for grinding in a laboratory and learn more advanced skills such as grinding, cutting, and edging lenses as they gain experience. The length of the training varies from one laboratory to another.

Important Qualities

Detail oriented. Ophthalmic laboratory technicians must be able to notice slight imperfections to create lenses.

Dexterity. Ophthalmic laboratory technicians must work well with their hands. They work closely with precise laboratory instruments in small work areas.

Technical skills. Ophthalmic laboratory technicians must understand how to operate complex machinery. Some procedures are automated, and technicians must know how to operate or change the programs that run the machinery.

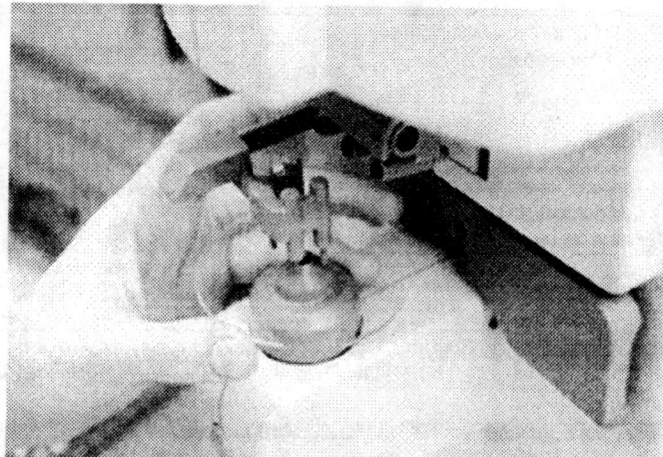

Although some lenses are produced by hand, technicians often use automated equipment to make lenses.

Education

Most ophthalmic laboratory technicians are hired with a high school diploma and then learn their tasks through on-the-job training. They usually begin as helpers and gradually learn new skills as they gain experience. High school students interested in entering the occupation should take classes in design, computer technology, and industrial arts.

Advancement

In large laboratories, ophthalmic laboratory technicians may work their way up to a supervisory level and may train new technicians. Some may go on to own and operate a laboratory.

Pay

Ophthalmic Laboratory Technicians
Median annual wages, May 2010

Total, All Occupations	$33,840
Production Occupations	$30,330
Ophthalmic Laboratory Technicians	$27,970

Note: All Occupations includes all occupations in the U.S. Economy.
Source: U.S. Bureau of Labor Statistics, Occupational Employment Statistics

The median annual wage of ophthalmic laboratory technicians was $27,970 in May 2010. The median wage is the wage at which half the workers in an occupation earned more than that amount and half earned less. The lowest 10 percent earned more than $18,480, and the top 10 percent earned more than $43,220.

Job Outlook

Ophthalmic Laboratory Technicians
Percent change in employment, projected 2010-20

Total, All Occupations	14%
Ophthalmic Laboratory Technicians	13%
Production Occupations	4%

Note: All Occupations includes all occupations in the U.S. Economy.
Source: U.S. Bureau of Labor Statistics, Employment Projections program

Employment is expected to grow by 13 percent from 2010 to 2020, about as fast as the average for all occupations.

Most people need vision correction at some point in their lives. As the total population continues to grow, people will need more vision aids, such as glasses and contacts.

Middle age is a time when many people use corrective lenses for the first time, and the need for vision care continues to increase with age. As the large baby-boom generation and their children get older, the need for vision correction will create a demand for ophthalmic laboratory services.

As laser vision correction becomes less expensive, there will be an increase in the demand for that service and a decrease in the demand for eyeglasses. However, even with laser correction, almost all adults need reading glasses or corrective eyewear later in their lives. The cause is retinal hardening, which happens naturally as people age, making it harder for the eye to focus.

Employment projections data for ophthalmic laboratory technicians, 2010-20

Occupational Title	SOC Code	Employment, 2010	Projected Employment, 2020	Change, 2010-20 Percent	Numeric
Ophthalmic Laboratory Technicians	51-9083	29,800	33,600	13	3,800
SOURCE: U.S. Bureau of Labor Statistics, Employment Projections program					

Similar Occupations

This table shows a list of occupations with job duties that are similar to those of ophthalmic laboratory technicians.

Occupation	Job Duties	Entry-Level Education	Median Annual Pay, May 2010
Opticians, Dispensing	Dispensing opticians help fit eyeglasses and contact lenses, following prescriptions from ophthalmologists and optometrists. They also help customers decide which eyeglass frames or type of contact lenses to buy.	High school diploma or equivalent	$32,940
Optometrists	Optometrists perform eye exams to check for vision problems and diseases. They prescribe eyeglasses or contact lenses as needed.	Doctoral or professional degree	$94,990
Medical Equipment Repairers	Medical equipment repairers install, maintain, and repair patient care equipment.	Associate's degree	$44,490

Contacts for More Information

For more information about ophthalmic laboratory technicians, visit Optical Laboratories Association

Suggested citation:

Bureau of Labor Statistics, U.S. Department of Labor, Occupational Outlook Handbook, 2012-13 Edition, Ophthalmic Laboratory Technicians, on the Internet at http://www.bls.gov/ooh/production/ophthalmic-laboratory-technicians.htm .

Painting and Coating Workers

Quick Facts: Painting and Coating Workers	
2010 Median Pay	$31,170 per year $14.99 per hour
Entry-Level Education	High school diploma or equivalent
Work Experience in a Related Occupation	None
On-the-job Training	Moderate-term on-the-job training
Number of Jobs, 2010	155,200
Job Outlook, 2010-20	9% (Slower than average)
Employment Change, 2010-20	13,800

What Painting and Coating Workers Do

Painting and coating workers paint and coat a wide range of products, including cars, jewelry, lacquer, and candy.

Duties

Painting and coating workers typically do the following:

* Set up and operate machines that paint or coat products
* Select the paint or coating needed for the job
* Clean and prepare products to be painted or coated
* Determine the required flow of paint and the quality of the coating
* Clean and maintain tools and equipment

Millions of items ranging from cars to candy are covered by paint, plastic, varnish, chocolate, or some other type of coating. Painting or coating is used to make a product more attractive or protect it from the elements. The paint finish on an automobile, for example, makes the vehicle more attractive and provides protection from corrosion.

Before workers begin to apply the paint or other coating, they often need to prepare the surface by sanding or cleaning it carefully to prevent dust from becoming trapped under the paint. Sometimes, masking is required, which involves carefully covering portions of the product with tape and paper.

After the product is prepared, workers may use a number of techniques to apply the paint or coating. Perhaps the most straightforward technique is dipping an item in a large vat of paint or some other coating. Spraying products with a solution of paint or another coating is also common. Some factories use automated painting systems.

Painters use spray guns to apply paint to a bumper.

The following are types of painting and coating workers:

Dippers use power hoists to immerse products in vats of paint, liquid plastic, or other solutions. This technique is commonly used for small parts in electronic equipment, such as cell phones.

Spray machine operators use spray guns to coat metal, wood, ceramic, fabric, paper, and food products with paint and other coating solutions.

Coating, painting, and spraying machine setters, operators, and tenders position the spray guns, set the nozzles, and synchronize the action of the guns with the speed of the conveyor carrying products through the machine and through drying ovens. During the operation of the painting machines, these workers tend the equipment, watch gauges on the control panel, and check products to ensure that they are being painted evenly. The operator may use a manual spray gun to "touch up" flaws.

Painting, coating, and decorating workers paint, coat, or decorate products such as furniture, glass, pottery, toys, cakes, and books. Some workers coat confectionery, bakery, and other food products with melted chocolate, cheese, oils, sugar, or other substances. Paper is often coated to give it its gloss. Silver, tin, and copper solutions are frequently sprayed on glass to make mirrors.

Transportation equipment painters are the best known group of painting and coating workers. There are three major specialties:

Transportation equipment workers who refinish old or damaged cars, trucks, and buses in automotive body repair and paint shops normally apply paint by hand with a controlled spray gun. Those who work in repair shops are among the most highly skilled manual spray operators: They perform intricate, detailed work and mix paints to match the original color, a task that is especially difficult if the color has faded. Preparing an old car is similar to painting other metal objects.

Transportation equipment painters who work on new cars oversee several automated steps. A modern car is first dipped in an anticorrosion bath, coated with colored paint, and then painted in several coats of clear paint to prevent damage to the colored paint.

Other transportation equipment painters either paint equipment too large to paint automatically—such as ships or giant construction equipment—or do touchup work to fix flaws in the paint caused by damage either during assembly or during the automated painting process.

Work Environment

Painting and coating workers held about 155,200 jobs in 2010. Employment in the detailed occupations that make up painting and coating worker was distributed as follows:

Coating, painting, and spraying machine setters, operators, and tenders	83,600
Painters, transportation equipment	46,200
Painting, coating, and decorating workers	25,300

Painting, coating, and decorating are usually done in special ventilated areas. Workers typically wear masks or respirators that cover their nose and mouth.

They often stand for long periods. When using a spray gun, they may have to bend, stoop, or crouch in uncomfortable positions to reach different parts of the products.

Injuries

Painting, coating, and decorating workers have one of the highest rates of injuries and illnesses compared to all others occupations. Workers risk muscle strains and exposure to toxic materials. More sophisticated paint booths and fresh-air systems are increasingly being used to provide a safer work environment.

Work Schedules

Most painting and coating workers work full time. Automotive painters in repair shops often work more than 50 hours a week, depending on the number of vehicles that need repainting.

How to Become a Painting and Coating Worker

Most painting and coating workers need a high school diploma or equivalent. Although training for new workers usually lasts from a few days to several months, those who paint automobiles generally need 1 to 2 years of training and experience.

Education

Painting and coating workers in the manufacturing sector usually must have a high school diploma or equivalent. Employers in other sectors may be willing to hire workers without a high school diploma.

Automobile repair painters often get training in technical school to learn the intricacies of mixing and applying different types of paint.

Training

Training for beginning painting and coating machine setters, operators, and tenders and for painting, coating, and decorating workers may last from a few days to a few months. Workers who modify the operation of computer-controlled equipment may require additional training in computer operations and programming.

Transportation equipment painters typically learn their skills on the job or through postsecondary education in painting.

Certification

Voluntary certification by the National Institute for Automotive Service Excellence (ASE) is recognized as the standard of achievement for automotive painters. To obtain certification, painters must pass a written exam and have at least 2 years of experience in the field.

High school, trade or vocational school, or community college training in automotive refinishing that meets ASE standards may substitute for up to 1 year of experience. To keep the certification, painters must retake the exam at least every 5 years.

Few painting and coating workers other than automobile painters obtain certification.

Important Qualities

Artistic ability. Some workers make elaborate or decorative designs. For example, some automotive painters specialize in making custom designs for vehicles.

Color vision. Workers must be able to properly blend new paint colors to perfectly match existing colors on a surface.

Mechanical skills. Because workers must operate and maintain sprayers that apply paints and coatings, they should have good mechanical skills.

Pay

Painting and Coating Workers
Median annual wages, May 2010

Painters, Transportation Equipment	$39,040
Total, All Occupations	$33,840
Painting Workers	$31,170
Coating, Painting, and Spraying Machine Setters, Operators, and Tenders	$29,710
Painting, Coating, and Decorating Workers	$24,400

Note: All Occupations includes all occupations in the U.S. Economy.
Source: U.S. Bureau of Labor Statistics, Occupational Employment Statistics

The median annual wage of painting and coating workers was $31,170 in May 2010. The median wage is the wage at which half the workers in an occupation earned more than that amount and half earned less.

In May 2010, median annual wages for painting and coating occupations were as follows:

- $39,040 for transportation equipment painters
- $29,710 for coating, painting, and spraying machine setters, operators, and tenders
- $24,400 for painting, coating, and decorating workers

Many automotive painters who work for motor vehicle dealers and independent automotive repair shops get a commission. Employers frequently guarantee commissioned painters a minimum weekly salary.

Helpers and trainees usually get an hourly rate until they become skilled enough to work on commission.

Trucking companies, bus lines, and other organizations that repair and refinish their own vehicles generally pay by the hour.

Most painting and coating workers work full time. Automotive painters in repair shops often work overtime, depending on the number of vehicles that need repainting.

Some painting and coating machine operators belong to unions, including the United Auto Workers and the International Brotherhood of Teamsters. Most union operators work for manufacturers and large motor vehicle dealers.

Job Outlook

Painting and Coating Workers
Percent change in employment, projected 2010-20

Painting, Coating, and Decorating Workers	17%
Total, All Occupations	14%
Painters, Transportation Equipment	9%
Painting Workers	9%
Coating, Painting, and Spraying Machine Setters, Operators, and Tenders	6%

Note: All Occupations includes all occupations in the U.S. Economy.
Source: U.S. Bureau of Labor Statistics, Employment Projections program

Overall employment of painting and coating workers is projected to grow 9 percent from 2010 to 2020, slower than the average for all occupations. Employment growth will vary by specialty and industry.

Employment of coating, painting, and spraying machine setters, operators, and tenders is projected to grow 6 percent, slower than the average for all occupations. Employment growth will be driven by the overall growth of the economy. The many consumer, commercial, and industrial products that require painting or coating will require these workers. However, productivity gains are expected to moderate employment growth.

Employment of transportation equipment painters is projected to grow 9 percent, slower than the average for all occupations. Nearly all employment growth will be driven by the need for painters in auto repair shops.

Employment of painting, coating, and decorating workers is projected to grow 17 percent, about as fast as the average for all occupations. Employment growth will be driven by the need to decorate made-to-order cakes in grocery stores.

Job Prospects

As with many skilled manufacturing jobs, employers often report difficulty finding qualified workers. Therefore, job opportunities should be very good for those with painting experience.

Job openings also should result from the need to replace workers who leave the occupation and from increased specialization in manufacturing. Although higher educational requirements would normally reduce competition for automotive painters in repair shops, the large number of people who enjoy working on cars should offset that reduction.

Employment projections data for painting and coating workers, 2010-20

Occupational Title	SOC Code	Employment, 2010	Projected Employment, 2020	Change, 2010-20	
				Percent	Numeric
Painting and Coating Workers	—	155,200	169,000	9	13,800
Coating, Painting, and Spraying Machine Setters, Operators, and Tenders	51-9121	83,600	88,700	6	5,100
Painters, Transportation Equipment	51-9122	46,200	50,600	9	4,400
Painting, Coating, and Decorating Workers	51-9123	25,300	29,700	17	4,400
SOURCE: U.S. Bureau of Labor Statistics, Employment Projections program					

Similar Occupations

This table shows a list of occupations with job duties that are similar to those of painting and coating workers.

Occupation	Job Duties	Entry-Level Education	Median Annual Pay, May 2010
Automotive Body and Glass Repairers	Automotive body and glass repairers restore, refinish, and replace vehicle bodies and frames, windshields, and window glass.	High school diploma or equivalent	$37,580
Painters, Construction and Maintenance	Painters apply paint, stain, and coatings to walls, buildings, bridges, and other structures.	Less than high school	$34,280

Contacts for More Information

For more information about job opportunities for painting and coating workers, visit

- Local manufacturers
- Automotive body repair shops
- Motor vehicle dealers
- Vocational schools
- Local unions representing painting and coating workers
- Local offices of state employment services

For a directory of certified automotive painting programs, visit National Automotive Technician Education Foundation , National Institute for Automotive Service Excellence

Suggested citation:

Bureau of Labor Statistics, U.S. Department of Labor, Occupational Outlook Handbook, 2012-13 Edition, Painting and Coating Workers, on the Internet at http://www.bls.gov/ooh/production/painting-and-coating-workers.htm .

Power Plant Operators, Distributors, and Dispatchers

Quick Facts: Power Plant Operators, Distributors, and Dispatchers	
2010 Median Pay	$65,360 per year $31.42 per hour
Entry-Level Education	High school diploma or equivalent
Work Experience in a Related Occupation	None
On-the-job Training	Long-term on-the-job training
Number of Jobs, 2010	55,900
Job Outlook, 2010-20	-2% (Little or no change)
Employment Change, 2010-20	-1,100

What Power Plant Operators, Distributors, and Dispatchers Do

Power plant operators, dispatchers, and distributors control the systems that generate and distribute electric power.

Duties

Power plant operators, distributors, and dispatchers typically do the following:

- Control power-generating equipment, such as boilers, turbines, generators, and reactors
- Read charts, meters, and gauges to monitor voltage and electricity flows
- Check equipment and indicators to detect evidence of operating problems
- Adjust controls to regulate the flow of power
- Start or stop generators, turbines, and other equipment as necessary

Electricity is one of our nation's most vital resources. Power plant operators, distributors, and dispatchers control power plants and the flow of electricity from plants to substations, which distribute electricity to businesses, homes, and factories. Electricity is generated from many sources, including coal, gas, nuclear energy, hydroelectric energy (from water sources), and wind and solar power.

The following are types of power plant operators, distributors, and dispatchers:

Nuclear power reactor operators control nuclear reactors. They adjust control rods, which affect how much electricity a reactor generates. They monitor reactors, turbines, generators, and cooling systems, adjusting controls as necessary. Operators also start and stop equipment and record the data. They may need to respond to abnormalities, determine the cause, and take corrective action.

Power distributors and dispatchers, also known as **systems operators**, control the flow of electricity as it travels from generating stations to substations and users over a network of transmission and distribution lines. They prepare and issue switching orders to route electrical currents around areas that need maintenance or repair. Distributors and dispatchers also monitor and operate current converters, voltage transformers, and circuit breakers. They must detect and respond to emergencies, such as transformer or transmission line failures.

Power plant operators control, operate, and maintain machinery to generate electric power. They use control boards to distribute power among generators and regulate the output from several generators. They regulate the flow of power between generating stations and substations, and they monitor instruments to maintain voltage and electricity flows from the plant.

Work Environment

Power plant operators, distributors, and dispatchers held about 55,900 jobs in 2010. About 72 percent were power plant operators, 18 percent were power distributors and dispatchers, and 9 percent were nuclear power reactor operators.

About 72 percent of power plant operators, distributors, and dispatchers worked in the electric power generation, transmission, and distribution industry. Government employed 16 percent, most of which worked in local government.

Operators, distributors, and dispatchers who work in control rooms generally sit or stand at a control station. The work is not physically strenuous, but it does require constant attention. Workers also may do rounds, checking equipment and doing other work outside the control room.

Because power transmission is both vitally important and sensitive to attack, security is a major concern for utility companies. Nuclear power plants and transmission stations have especially high security, and workers should be prepared to work in secured environments.

When operators are on rounds or doing other work outside the control room, they may be exposed to danger from electric shock, falls, and burns. Still, workers in these jobs experience rates of injuries and illnesses that are lower than the average for all occupations.

Work Schedules

Because electricity is provided around the clock, operators, distributors, and dispatchers usually work rotating 8- or 12-hour shifts. As a result, all operators share the less desirable shifts. Work on

Power plant operators do rounds to check that equipment is working properly.

rotating shifts can be stressful and tiring because of the constant changes in living and sleeping patterns.

How to Become a Power Plant Operator, Distributor, or Dispatcher

Power plant operators, dispatchers, and distributors need a combination of education and extensive on-the-job training. Nuclear power reactor operators also need a license. Many jobs require a background check, and workers are subject to drug and alcohol screenings.

Many companies require potential workers to take the Power Plant Maintenance (MASS) and Plant Operator (POSS) exams from the Edison Electrical Institute to see if they have the right aptitudes for this work. These tests measure reading comprehension, understanding of mechanical concepts, spatial ability, and mathematical ability.

Training

Power plant operators and dispatchers undergo rigorous, long-term on-the-job training and technical instruction. Several years of onsite training and experience are necessary to become fully qualified. Even fully qualified operators and dispatchers must take regular training courses to keep their skills current.

Nuclear power reactor operators usually start working as equipment operators or auxiliary operators, helping more experienced workers operate and maintain the equipment while learning the basics of how to operate the power plant.

Along with this extensive on-the-job training, nuclear power plant operators typically receive formal technical training to prepare for the license exam from the U.S. Nuclear Regulatory Commission (NRC). Once licensed, operators are authorized to control equipment that affects the power of the reactor in a nuclear power plant. Operators continue frequent onsite training.

Licenses and Certification

Nuclear power reactor operators must be licensed through the NRC. To become licensed, operators must meet training and experience requirements, pass a medical exam, and pass the NRC licensing exam. To keep their license, operators must pass a plant-operating exam each year, pass a medical exam every 2 years, and apply for license renewal every 6 years. Licenses cannot be transferred between plants, so an operator must get a new license to operate in another facility.

Power plant operators who do not work at a nuclear power reactor may be licensed as engineers or fire fighters by state licensing boards. Requirements vary by state and depend on the specific job functions that the operator performs.

Power distributors and dispatchers who are in positions in which they could affect the power grid must be certified through the North American Energy Reliability Corporation 's (NERC) System Operator Certification Program. NERC offers four types of certification, and each qualifies a worker to handle a different job function. A dispatcher's certification is valid for 3 years, and a worker must fulfill continuing education requirements to renew the credential.

Education

Power plant operators, distributors, and dispatchers need at least a high school diploma. However, employers may prefer workers with college or vocational school degrees.

Employers generally look for people with strong math and science backgrounds for these highly technical jobs. Understanding electricity and math, especially algebra and trigonometry, is important.

Work Experience

Previous related work experience can be helpful. Many employers prefer experience in electricity generation, transmission, and distribution, or in other occupations in the utilities industry, such as line worker or helper, or laborer in a power plant.

Some nuclear power reactor operators gain experience working with nuclear reactors in the Navy.

Advancement

After finishing work in the classroom, most entry-level workers start as helpers or laborers and advance to more responsible positions as they become comfortable in the plant. Workers are generally classified into levels on the basis of their experience. For each level, there are training requirements, mandatory waiting times, and exams. With sufficient training and experience, workers can become shift supervisors, trainers, or consultants.

Nuclear power plant operators begin working in nuclear power plants, typically as non-licensed operators. After in-plant training and passing the NRC licensing exam, they become licensed reactor operators. Licensed operators can advance to senior reactor operators, who supervise the operation of all controls in the control room. Senior reactor operators may also become plant managers or licensed operator instructors.

Important Qualities

Detail oriented. Power plant operators, distributors, and dispatchers must monitor complex controls and intricate machinery to ensure that everything is operating properly.

Diligence. Power plant operators, distributors, and dispatchers must be careful, attentive, and persistent.

Mechanical skills. Power plant operators, distributors, and dispatchers must know how to work with machines and use tools. They must be familiar with how to operate, repair, and maintain equipment.

Problem-solving skills. Power plant operators, distributors, and dispatchers must find and quickly solve problems that arise with equipment or controls.

Pay

Power Plant Operators, Distributors, and Dispatchers
Median annual wages, May 2010

Nuclear Power Reactor Operators	$75,650
Power Distributors and Dispatchers	$68,900
Power Plant Operators, Distributors, and Dispatchers	$65,360
Power Plant Operators	$63,080
Total, All Occupations	$33,840

Note: All Occupations includes all occupations in the U.S. Economy.
Source: U.S. Bureau of Labor Statistics, Occupational Employment Statistics

The median annual wage of power plant operators, distributors, and dispatchers was $65,360 in May 2010. The median wage is the wage at which half the workers in an occupation earned more than that amount and half earned less. The lowest 10 percent earned less than $42,550, and the top 10 percent earned more than $88,330.

Median annual wages for power plant operator, distributor, and dispatcher occupations in May 2010 were as follows:
- $75,650 for nuclear power reactor operators
- $68,900 for power distributors and dispatchers
- $63,080 for power plant operators

Many power plant operators, distributors, and dispatchers are members of a union.

Because electricity is provided around the clock, operators, distributors, and dispatchers usually work rotating 8- or 12-hour shifts. As a result, all operators share the less desirable shifts. Work on rotating shifts can be stressful and tiring because of the constant changes in living and sleeping patterns.

Job Outlook

Power Plant Operators, Distributors, and Dispatchers
Percent change in employment, projected 2010-20

Total, All Occupations	14%
Nuclear Power Reactor Operators	4%
Power Plant Operators, Distributors, and Dispatchers	-2%
Power Plant Operators	-3%
Power Distributors and Dispatchers	-3%

Note: All Occupations includes all occupations in the U.S. Economy.
Source: U.S. Bureau of Labor Statistics, Employment Projections program

Employment of power plant operators, distributors, and dispatchers is expected to experience little or no change from 2010 to 2020. Although electricity usage is expected to grow, advances in technology and increased energy efficiency are projected to result in a 2 percent decline in employment for the occupation. Employment growth will vary by specialty.

Employment of power plant operators in nonnuclear power plants is expected to decline 3 percent from 2010 to 2020. Energy companies are increasingly promoting energy efficiency to cut costs and comply with environmental regulations. Consequently, the demand for electricity is expected to grow much more slowly than in the past, resulting in fewer new job opportunities for workers.

In addition, as old power plants close, they will be replaced with new plants that produce electricity more efficiently and, in many cases, have higher capacities. New plants are also built with more digital controls, which require fewer operators. As a result, fewer workers will be needed to produce the same amount of energy.

Employment of power distributors and dispatchers is expected to decline 3 percent from 2010 to 2020. Although some distributors and dispatchers will be needed to manage an increasingly complex electrical grid, employment growth will be tempered by advances in technology and smart grid projects that automate some of the work of dispatchers.

Employment of nuclear power reactor operators is expected to grow 4 percent from 2010 to 2020 as a result of new plant construction. Although no new plants have opened since the 1990s, new sites have applied for construction and operating licenses, and they will need to be staffed before the end of the decade.

Job Prospects

Job prospects should be good for those with related training and good mechanical skills. As many power plant operators, distributors, and dispatchers near retirement age, companies will need workers to replace operators and dispatchers who retire. Many individuals may show interest in these high-paying jobs, and job prospects will be best for those with strong technical and mechanical skills.

Employment projections data for power plant operators, distributors, and dispatchers, 2010-20

Occupational Title	SOC Code	Employment, 2010	Projected Employment, 2020	Change, 2010-20	
				Percent	Numeric
Power Plant Operators, Distributors, and Dispatchers	51-8010	55,900	54,800	-2	-1,100
Nuclear Power Reactor Operators	51-8011	5,200	5,300	4	200
Power Distributors and Dispatchers	51-8012	10,300	10,000	-3	-300
Power Plant Operators	51-8013	40,500	39,500	-3	-1,000
SOURCE: U.S. Bureau of Labor Statistics, Employment Projections program					

Similar Occupations

This table shows a list of occupations with job duties that are similar to those of power plant operators, distributors, and dispatchers.

Occupation	Job Duties	Entry-Level Education	Median Annual Pay, May 2010
Water and Wastewater Treatment Plant and System Operators	Water and wastewater treatment plant and system operators manage a system of machines, often through the use of control boards, to transfer or treat water or wastewater.	High school diploma or equivalent	$40,770
Stationary Engineers and Boiler Operators	Stationary engineers and boiler operators control stationary engines, boilers, or other mechanical equipment to provide utilities for buildings or for industrial purposes.	High school diploma or equivalent	$52,140
Construction Equipment Operators	Construction equipment operators drive, maneuver, or control the heavy machinery used to construct roads, bridges, buildings, and other structures.	High school diploma or equivalent	$39,460
Electricians	Electricians install and maintain electrical systems in homes, businesses, and factories.	High school diploma or equivalent	$48,250
Electrical and Electronics Installers and Repairers	Electrical and electronics installers and repairers install, repair, or replace a variety of electrical equipment in telecommunications, transportation, utilities, and other industries.	Postsecondary non-degree award	$49,170
Line Installers and Repairers	Line installers and repairers install or repair electrical power systems and telecommunications cables, including fiber optics.	High school diploma or equivalent	$54,290

Contacts for More Information

For general information about power plant operators, nuclear power reactor operators, and power plant distributors and dispatchers, visit American Public Power Association , Center for Energy Workforce Development , International Brotherhood of Electrical Workers

For information on nuclear power reactor operators including licensing, visit U.S. Nuclear Regulatory Commission , Nuclear Energy Institute

For information on certification for power distributors and dispatchers, visit North American Electric Reliability Corporation

Suggested citation:

Bureau of Labor Statistics, U.S. Department of Labor, Occupational Outlook Handbook, 2012-13 Edition, Power Plant Operators, Distributors, and Dispatchers, on the Internet at http://www.bls.gov/ooh/production/power-plant-operators-distributors-and-dispatchers.htm .

Printing Workers

Quick Facts: Printing Workers	
2010 Median Pay	$33,150 per year $15.94 per hour
Entry-Level Education	See How to Become One
Work Experience in a Related Occupation	None
On-the-job Training	See How to Become One
Number of Jobs, 2010	304,600
Job Outlook, 2010-20	-4% (Decline moderately)
Employment Change, 2010-20	-12,600

What Printing Workers Do

Printing workers produce print material in three stages: prepress, press, and binding and finishing. They review specifications, identify and fix problems with printing equipment, and assemble pages.

Duties

Printing workers typically do the following:
- Arrange pages so that materials can be printed
- Operate laser plate-making equipment that converts electronic data to plates
- Review job orders to determine quantities to be printed, paper specifications, colors, and special printing instructions
- Feed paper through press cylinders and adjust equipment controls

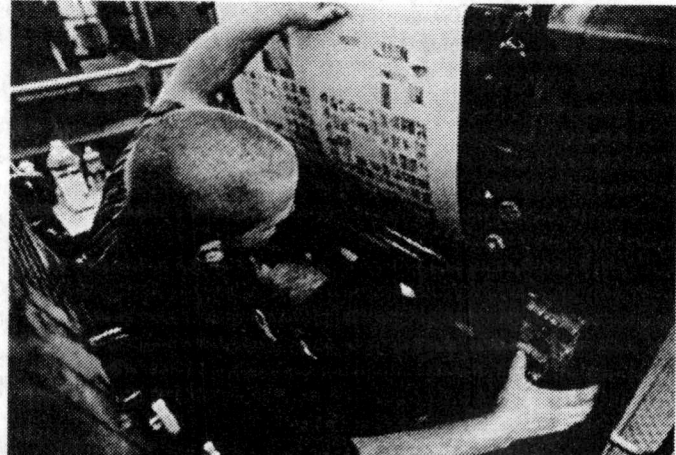

Printing workers review specifications, identify and fix problems with printing equipment, and assemble pages.

- Collect and inspect random samples during print runs to identify any needed adjustments
- Bind new books, using hand tools such as bone folders, knives, hammers, or brass binding tools
- Cut material to specified dimensions, fitting and gluing material to binder boards by hand or machine
- Compress sewed or glued sets of pages, called "signatures," using hand presses or smashing machines

The printing process has three stages: prepress, press, and binding or finishing. In small print shops, the same person may take care of all three stages. However, in most print shops, the following workers specialize in one of the three stages:

Prepress technicians and workers prepare print jobs. They do a variety of tasks to help turn text and pictures into finished pages and prepare the pages for print. Some prepress technicians, known as "preflight technicians," take images from graphic designers or customers and check them for completeness. They review job specifications and designs from submitted sketches or clients' electronic files to ensure that everything is correct and all files and photos are included.

Some prepress workers use a photographic process to make offset printing plates (sheets of metal that carry the final image to be printed). This is a complex process involving ultraviolet light and chemical exposure through which the text and images of a print job harden on a metal plate and become water repellent. These hard, water-repellent portions of the metal plate are in the form of the text and images that will be printed.

More recently, however, the printing industry has moved to technology known as "direct-to-plate." Many prepress technicians now send the data directly to a plating system, bypassing the need for the photographic technique. The direct-to-plate technique is an example of how digital imaging technology has largely replaced cold-type print technology.

Printing press operators prepare, run, and maintain printing presses. Their duties vary according to the type of press they operate. Traditional printing methods, such as offset lithography, gravure, flexography, and letterpress, use a plate or roller that carries the final image that is to be printed and then copies the image to paper.

In addition to the traditional printing processes, plateless or nonimpact processes are becoming more common. Plateless processes—including digital, electrostatic, and ink-jet printing—are used for copying, duplicating, and document and specialty printing, usually in quick-printing shops and smaller printing shops.

Commercial printers are increasingly using digital presses with longer-run capabilities for short-run or customized printing jobs. Digital presses also allow printers to transfer files, blend colors, and proof images electronically, thus avoiding the costly and time-consuming steps of making printing plates that are common in offset printing.

Print binding and finishing workers combine printed sheets into a finished product, such as a book, magazine, or catalog. Their duties depend on what they are binding. Some types of binding and finishing jobs take only one step. Preparing leaflets or newspaper inserts, for example, requires only folding and trimming.

Binding books and magazines, however, takes several steps. Bindery workers first assemble the books and magazines from large, flat, printed sheets of paper. They then operate machines that fold printed sheets into "signatures," which are groups of pages arranged sequentially. They assemble the signatures in the right order and join them by saddle stitching (stapling them through the middle of the binding) or perfect binding (using glue, not stitches or staples).

Some bookbinders repair rare books by sewing, stitching, or gluing the covers or the pages.

Work Environment

Printing workers held about 304,600 jobs in 2010. Prepress technicians usually work in quiet areas. Printing press operators and print binding and finishing workers work in noisy settings. Press operators' jobs may require considerable lifting, standing, and carrying. Binding often resembles an assembly line on which workers do tedious, repetitive tasks, such as folding and trimming leaflets or newspaper inserts.

The following industries employed the most printing workers in 2010:

Printing and related support activities	59%
Converted paper product manufacturing	6
Newspaper publishers	6
Advertising, public relations, and related services	3
Plastics product manufacturing	2

Work Schedules

Most printing workers work full time. Weekend and holiday hours may be necessary to meet production schedules. For example, newspaper printing may need to take place at night.

How to Become a Printing Worker

Prepress technicians typically need an associate's degree or postsecondary vocational award. Printing press operators and print binding and finishing workers need a high school diploma and on-the-job training.

Education

Most prepress technicians receive some formal postsecondary classroom instruction before entering the occupation. They typically get either a postsecondary non-degree award or an associate's degree from a technical school, junior college, or community college. Workers with experience in other printing techniques can take a few

college-level graphic communications or prepress-related courses to upgrade their skills and qualify for prepress jobs.

For printing press operators and print binding and finishing workers, a high school diploma is sufficient to enter the occupation. Postsecondary coursework is offered through community colleges and vocational schools, although most workers learn the required skills through on-the-job training.

There are also 4-year bachelor's degree programs in graphic design aimed primarily at students who plan to move into management positions in printing or design.

Training

Beginning press operators load, unload, and clean presses. With time and training, they become fully qualified to operate a particular type of press. Operators can gain experience on more than one kind of printing press during the course of their career.

Experienced operators periodically get retraining to update their skills. For example, printing plants that change from sheet-fed offset presses to digital presses have to retrain the entire press crew because skill requirements for the two types of presses are different.

Most bookbinders and bindery workers learn through on-the-job training. Inexperienced workers may start out as helpers and do simple tasks, such as moving paper from cutting machines to folding machines, or catching stock as it comes off machines.

They learn basic binding skills, including the characteristics of paper and how to cut large sheets of paper into different sizes with the least amount of waste. Usually, it takes 1 to 3 months to learn to operate simpler machines, but it can take up to 1 year to become completely familiar with more complex equipment, such as computerized binding machines.

As workers gain experience, they learn to operate more types of equipment. To keep pace with changing technology, retraining is increasingly important for bindery workers.

Important Qualities

Basic math skills. Printing workers use basic math when computing percentages, weights, and measures and when calculating the amount of ink and paper needed to do a job.

Communication skills. Prepress workers in particular need good communication skills because they must confer with clients about the details of a printing order.

Computer skills. The printing process is computer-based, requiring printing workers to have basic computer skills.

Detail oriented. Printing workers must pay attention to detail to identify and fix problems with print jobs.

Mechanical skills. Printing press operators must be comfortable with printing equipment and be prepared to make adjustments if a printing error occurs. Mechanical aptitude is also important for print binding and finishing workers, who use automated binding machines.

Pay

Printing Workers
Median annual wages, May 2010

Prepress Technicians and Workers	$36,280
Total, All Occupations	$33,840
Printing Press Operators	$33,680
Printing Workers	$33,150
Print Binding and Finishing Workers	$28,920

Note: All Occupations includes all occupations in the U.S. Economy.
Source: U.S. Bureau of Labor Statistics, Occupational Employment Statistics

The median annual wage of printing workers was $33,150 in May 2010. The median wage is the wage at which half the workers in an occupation earned more than that amount and half earned less. The lowest 10 percent earned less than $20,060, and the top 10 percent earned more than $52,950.

The median wages of printing occupations in May 2010 were the following:

- $36,280 for prepress technicians and workers
- $33,680 for printing press operators
- $28,920 for print binding and finishing workers

Most printing workers work full time. Weekend and holiday hours may be necessary to meet production schedules. For example, newspaper printing may need to take place at night.

Job Outlook

Printing Workers
Percent change in employment, projected 2010-20

Total, All Occupations	14%
Printing Press Operators	-1%
Print Binding and Finishing Workers	-3%
Printing Workers	-4%
Prepress Technicians and Workers	-16%

Note: All Occupations includes all occupations in the U.S. Economy.
Source: U.S. Bureau of Labor Statistics, Employment Projections program

Employment of printing workers is expected to decline 4 percent from 2010 to 2020. Newspapers and magazines have seen substantial declines in print volume in recent years, as these media have increasingly moved to online formats. With a declining volume of printed material in these areas, demand for print workers has decreased.

This trend is expected to continue, which is expected to result in further employment declines in the printing industry. Employment declines for printing workers should be moderated by other segments of the industry that will likely experience steady demand, including print logistics (labels, wrappers, and packaging) and print marketing (catalogs and direct mail).

Employment of prepress technicians and workers is expected to decline 16 percent from 2010 to 2020. Computer software now allows office workers to specify text typeface and style and to format pages. This development shifts traditional prepress functions away from printing plants and toward advertising and public relations agencies, graphic design firms, and large corporations. In addition, new technologies are increasing the amount of automation in printing companies, so that it takes fewer prepress workers to accomplish the same amount of work.

The employment of printing press operators is expected to decline 1 percent from 2010 to 2020, driven by trends in the printing industry. Their employment is not expected to decline as rapidly as that of prepress technicians, however, because printing press operators are less susceptible to automation.

Employment of print binding and finishing workers is expected to decline 3 percent from 2010 to 2020. The growth of electronic books should reduce demand for print books, which will limit employment of these workers. Demand for quick turnaround for commercial printing, however, will provide some employment opportunities.

Employment projections data for printing workers, 2010-20

Occupational Title	SOC Code	Employment, 2010	Projected Employment, 2020	Change, 2010-20	
				Percent	Numeric
Printing Workers	51-5100	304,600	292,000	-4	-12,600
Prepress Technicians and Workers	51-5111	50,800	42,800	-16	-8,100
Printing Press Operators	51-5112	200,100	197,200	-1	-2,900
Print Binding and Finishing Workers	51-5113	53,700	52,000	-3	-1,700
SOURCE: U.S. Bureau of Labor Statistics, Employment Projections program					

Similar Occupations

This table shows a list of occupations with job duties that are similar to those of printing workers.

Occupation	Job Duties	Entry-Level Education	Median Annual Pay, May 2010
Graphic Designers	Graphic designers create visual concepts, by hand or using computer software, to communicate ideas that inspire, inform, or captivate consumers. They help to make an organization recognizable by selecting color, images, or logo designs that represent a particular idea or identity to be used in advertising and promotions.	Bachelor's degree	$43,500
Multimedia Artists and Animators	Multimedia artists and animators create animation and visual effects for television, movies, video games, and other media. They create two- and three-dimensional models and animation.	Bachelor's degree	$58,510
Metal and Plastic Machine Workers	Metal and plastic machine workers set up and operate machines that cut, shape, and form metal and plastic materials or pieces.	High school diploma or equivalent	$31,910
Desktop Publishers	Desktop publishers use computer software to design page layouts for newspapers, books, brochures, and other items that will be printed or put online. They collect the text, graphics, and other materials they will need and then format them into a finished product.	Associate's degree	$36,610

Contacts for More Information

For more information about printing workers, visit Graphic Arts Education and Research Foundation , Printing Industries of America ,National Association for Printing Leadership (NAPL) ,The Association for Suppliers of Printing, Publishing and Converting Technologies (NPES)

Suggested citation:

Bureau of Labor Statistics, U.S. Department of Labor, Occupational Outlook Handbook, 2012-13 Edition, Printing Workers, on the Internet at http://www.bls.gov/ooh/production/printing-workers.htm .

Quality Control Inspectors

Quick Facts: Quality Control Inspectors	
2010 Median Pay	$33,030 per year $15.88 per hour
Entry-Level Education	High school diploma or equivalent
Work Experience in a Related Occupation	None
On-the-job Training	Moderate-term on-the-job training
Number of Jobs, 2010	416,100
Job Outlook, 2010-20	8% (Slower than average)
Employment Change, 2010-20	33,300

What Quality Control Inspectors Do

Quality control inspectors examine products and materials for defects or deviations from manufacturers' or industry specifications.

Duties

Quality control inspectors typically do the following:

- Read and understand blueprints and specifications
- Monitor or observe operations to ensure that they meet production standards
- Recommend adjustments to the process or assembly
- Inspect, test, or measure materials or products being produced
- Measure products with rulers, calipers, gauges, or micrometers
- Accept or reject finished items
- Remove all products and materials that fail to meet specifications
- Discuss inspection results with those responsible for products
- Report inspection and test data

Quality control inspectors ensure that your food will not make you sick, that your car will run properly, and that your pants will not split

Quality control inspectors monitor production operations, ensuring that specifications are met.

the first time you wear them. These workers monitor quality standards for nearly all manufactured products, including foods, textiles, clothing, glassware, motor vehicles, electronic components, computers, and structural steel. Specific job duties vary across the wide range of industries in which these inspectors work.

Quality control workers rely on a number of tools to do their jobs. Although some still use hand-held measurement devices, such as calipers and alignment gauges, they more commonly operate electronic inspection equipment, such as coordinate-measuring machines (CMMs). Inspectors testing electrical devices may use voltmeters, ammeters, and ohmmeters to test potential difference, current flow, and resistance, respectively.

Quality control workers record the results of their inspections and prepare test reports. When they find defects, inspectors notify supervisors and help to analyze and correct the production problems.

In some firms, the inspection process is completely automated, with advanced vision inspection systems installed at one or several points in the production process. Inspectors in these firms monitor the equipment, review output, and do random product checks.

The following are types of quality control inspectors:

Inspectors mark, tag, or note problems. They may reject defective items outright, send them for repair, or fix minor problems themselves. If the product is acceptable, the inspector certifies it. Inspectors may further specialize:

- **Materials inspectors** check products by sight, sound, or feel to locate imperfections such as cuts, scratches, missing pieces, or crooked seams.
- **Mechanical inspectors** generally verify that parts fit, move correctly, and are properly lubricated. They may check the pressure of gases and the level of liquids, test the flow of electricity, and do test runs to ensure that machines run properly.

Testers repeatedly test existing products or prototypes under real-world conditions. Through these tests, manufacturers determine how long a product will last, what parts will break down first, and how to improve durability.

Sorters separate goods according to length, size, fabric type, or color.

Samplers test or inspect a sample for malfunctions or defects during a batch or production run.

Weighers weigh quantities of materials for use in production.

Work Environment

Quality control inspectors held about 416,100 jobs in 2010. Most worked in manufacturing industries.

Work environments vary by industry and establishment size. As a result, some inspectors examine similar products for an entire shift. Others examine a variety of items.

In manufacturing, it is common for most inspectors to stay at one workstation. Inspectors in some industries may be on their feet all day and may have to lift heavy objects. In other industries, workers may sit during their shift and read electronic printouts of data.

Workers in heavy-manufacturing plants may be exposed to the noise and grime of machinery. In other plants, inspectors work in clean, air-conditioned environments suitable for testing products.

Injuries

Although the work is generally not dangerous, some workers may be exposed to airborne particles, which may irritate the eyes and skin. As a result, workers typically wear protective eyewear, ear plugs, and appropriate clothing.

Work Schedules

Although most quality control inspectors work full time during regular business hours, some inspectors work evenings or weekends. Shift assignments generally are based on seniority. Overtime may be required to meet production deadlines.

How to Become a Quality Control Inspector

Although a high school diploma is enough for the basic testing of products, complex precision-inspecting positions are filled by experienced workers.

Education and Training

Prospective quality control inspectors improve their chances of finding work by studying industrial trades, including computer-aided design (CAD), in high school or in a postsecondary vocational program. Laboratory work in the natural or biological sciences also may improve analytical skills and increase the chances of finding work in medical or pharmaceutical labs, where many of these workers are employed.

Education and training requirements vary with the responsibilities of the quality-control worker. For inspectors who do simple pass/fail tests of products, a high school diploma and some in-house training are generally enough.

Training for new inspectors may cover the use of special meters, gauges, computers, and other instruments; quality-control techniques; blueprint reading; safety; and reporting requirements. Some postsecondary training programs exist, but many employers prefer to train inspectors on the job.

As manufacturers use more automated inspection techniques that need less inspection by hand, workers in this occupation will have to learn to operate and program more sophisticated equipment and software applications. Because these operations require additional skills, higher education may be necessary. To address this need, some colleges are offering associate's degrees in fields such as quality control management.

Certification

The American Society for Quality (ASQ) offers many different certifications for workers in quality control. These certifications may help workers advance in the occupation. They generally require a certain number of years of experience in the field and passing an exam.

Important Qualities

Dexterity. Quality control inspectors should be able to quickly remove sample parts or products during the manufacturing process.

Math skills. Knowledge of basic math and computer skills are important because measuring, calibrating, and calculating specifications is a major part of quality control testing.

Mechanical skills. Quality control inspectors must be able to use specialized tools and machinery when testing products.

Physical strength. Because workers sometimes lift heavy objects, inspectors should be in good physical condition.

Stamina. Quality control inspectors must be able to stand for long periods on the job.

Technical skills. Quality control inspectors must understand blueprints, technical documents, and manuals, ensuring that products and parts fully meet quality standards.

Pay

Quality Control Inspectors
Median hourly wages, May 2010

Total, All Occupations	$16.27
Inspectors, Testers, Sorters, Samplers, and Weighers	$15.88
Other Production Occupations	$13.82

Note: All Occupations includes all occupations in the U.S. Economy.
Source: U.S. Bureau of Labor Statistics, Occupational Employment Statistics

The median hourly wage of quality control inspectors was $15.88 in May 2010. The median wage is the wage at which half the workers in an occupation earned more than that amount and half earned less. The lowest 10 percent earned less than $9.68, and the top 10 percent earned more than $26.72.

Although most quality control inspectors work full time during regular business hours, some inspectors work evenings or weekends. The most desirable shifts are generally given to workers who have seniority. Overtime may be required to meet production deadlines.

Job Outlook

Quality Control Inspectors
Percent change in employment, projected 2010-20

Total, All Occupations	14%
Inspectors, Testers, Sorters, Samplers, and Weighers	8%
Other Production Occupations	4%

Note: All Occupations includes all occupations in the U.S. Economy.
Source: U.S. Bureau of Labor Statistics, Employment Projections program

Employment of quality control inspectors is expected to grow 8 percent from 2010 to 2020, slower than the average for all occupations. Projected employment growth reflects the continuing need to have quality assurance testing in a variety of manufacturing industries, particularly in pharmaceuticals and medical equipment.

Despite technological advances in quality control in many industries, automation is not always a substitute for inspecting by hand. Automation will likely become more important for inspecting elements related to size, such as length, width, or thickness. But inspections will continue to be done by workers for products that require tests of taste, smell, texture, appearance, complexity of fabric, or performance of the product.

Nonetheless, many manufacturers have invested in automated inspection equipment to improve quality and productivity. Continued improvements in technology allow manufacturers to automate inspection tasks, increasing workers' productivity and reducing the demand for inspectors.

Manufacturers increasingly are integrating quality control into the production process. Many inspection duties are being reassigned from specialized inspectors to fabrication and assembly workers, who monitor quality at every stage of production. In addition, the growing use of statistical process control results in smarter inspections. Using this system, manufacturers survey the sources and incidence of defects so that they can focus their efforts on reducing the number of defective products. These factors are expected to result in less demand for quality control inspectors.

Job Prospects

Numerous jobs in the manufacturing industry are expected to arise over the coming decade as workers retire or leave the occupation for other reasons. Those with advanced skills and experience should qualify for many of these positions.

The best job opportunities are expected to be in the employment services industry and in plastic product manufacturing.

Employment projections data for quality control inspectors, 2010-20

Occupational Title	SOC Code	Employment, 2010	Projected Employment, 2020	Change, 2010-20	
				Percent	Numeric
Inspectors, Testers, Sorters, Samplers, and Weighers	51-9061	416,100	449,400	8	33,300
SOURCE: U.S. Bureau of Labor Statistics, Employment Projections program					

Similar Occupations

This table shows a list of occupations with job duties that are similar to those of quality control inspectors.

Occupation	Job Duties	Entry-Level Education	Median Annual Pay, May 2010
Construction and Building Inspectors	Construction and building inspectors ensure that new construction, changes, or repairs comply with local and national building codes and ordinances, zoning regulations, and contract specifications.	High school diploma or equivalent	$52,360
Fire Inspectors and Investigators	Fire inspectors visit and inspect buildings and other structures, such as sports arenas and shopping malls, to search for fire hazards and to ensure that federal, state, and local fire codes are met. They also test and inspect fire protection and fire extinguishing equipment to ensure that it works. Fire investigators determine the origin and cause of fires by searching the surrounding scene and collecting evidence.	High school diploma or equivalent	$52,230

Contacts for More Information

For more information about quality control inspectors, including certification, visit American Society for Quality (ASQ)

For more information about quality control training, visit Quality Assurance Association , The International Society of Automation (ISA)

Suggested citation:

Bureau of Labor Statistics, U.S. Department of Labor, Occupational Outlook Handbook, 2012-13 Edition, Quality Control Inspectors, on the Internet at http://www.bls.gov/ooh/production/quality-control-inspectors.htm .

Semiconductor Processors

Quick Facts: Semiconductor Processors	
2010 Median Pay	$33,130 per year $15.93 per hour
Entry-Level Education	Associate's degree
Work Experience in a Related Occupation	None
On-the-job Training	Moderate-term on-the-job training
Number of Jobs, 2010	21,100
Job Outlook, 2010-20	-18% (Decline rapidly)
Employment Change, 2010-20	-3,800

What Semiconductor Processors Do

Semiconductor processors oversee the manufacturing of electronic semiconductors, which are commonly known as integrated circuits or microchips. These microchips are found in all electronic devices—including cell phones, cars, and laptops—and are an important part of modern life.

Duties

Semiconductor processors typically do the following:

- Look over work orders, instructions, and processing charts to determine a work schedule
- Monitor machines that slice silicon crystals into wafers for processing
- Use robots to clean and polish the silicon wafers
- Load wafers into the equipment that creates patterns and forms the electronic circuitry
- Set and adjust controls to regulate the manufacturing equipment's power level, temperature, and other process parameters
- Adjust the process equipment and repair as needed during the manufacturing process
- Test completed microchips to ensure they work properly
- Review the manufacturing process and suggest improvements

Semiconductor processors, also known as process technicians, are largely responsible for quality control in the manufacturing process. They check equipment regularly for problems and test completed chips to make sure they work properly. If a problem with a chip does arise, they determine if it is due to contamination of that particular wafer or if it was caused by a flaw in the manufacturing process.

Work Environment

Semiconductor processors held 21,100 jobs in 2010. About 90 percent worked in the semiconductor and other electronic component manufacturing industry.

Microchips must be kept completely clean and free of impurities. To ensure this, semiconductor processors work in clean rooms that are kept free of contamination.

They wear special lightweight garments, called "bunny suits," over their clothes to keep lint or other particles from contaminating the clean room. Managers closely monitor workers going in and out of the clean, and workers must put on a new bunny suit each time they go in.

The work pace in clean rooms is deliberately slow. Because the machinery sets the operators' rate of work, workers keep a relaxed pace. Limiting movement in the clean room is important to keep the air as dust-free as possible.

The temperature in the clean rooms is generally comfortable for workers. Although bunny suits cover almost the entire body, the lightweight fabric keeps the temperature inside fairly comfortable.

Work Schedules

Most employees work full time, but some have variable schedules. Because semiconductor factories, also known as fabricating plants, run around the clock, night and weekend work is common for these workers. Although some plants schedule workers for a standard 40-hour week (8-hour shifts, 5 days a week), others schedule workers in 12-hour shifts to minimize disrupting the clean room.

How to Become a Semiconductor Processor

Many employers prefer that semiconductor processors have an associate's degree, although sometimes completing a 1-year certificate program is enough.

Education

Many semiconductor processors have an associate's degree in a field such as advanced manufacturing or microelectronics. Some employers accept candidates who have completed a 1-year certificate program in a similar field. These programs are usually offered at community colleges.

There is an emerging trend of employers preferring semiconductor processors to have a bachelor's degree in engineering or a physical science because of the increasing complexity of the manufacturing plants.

Training

New semiconductor processors need on-the-job training from 1 month to 1 year. During this training, a processor learns how to operate

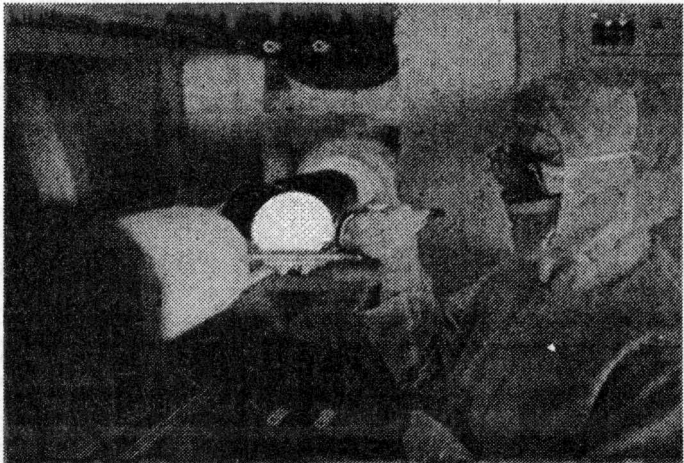

Semiconductor processors preside over the microchip manufacturing.

equipment and test new chips. Manufacturing microchips is a complex process, and it takes months of supervised work to become fully proficient.

Workers with more education may have learned some techniques in school and need less on-the-job training. Because the technology used in manufacturing microchips is always evolving, processors must continue to be trained on new techniques and methods throughout their careers.

Important Qualities

Critical-thinking skills. Semiconductor processors use logic and reasoning to uncover problems and determine solutions during the manufacturing process.

Detail oriented. Because a minor error or impurity can ruin a chip, processors must be able to spot tiny imperfections.

Dexterity. Semiconductor processors must be able to use tools and operate equipment to make precise cuts and measurements.

Science skills. Processors must understand the chemical composition and properties of certain substances that they may use in manufacturing semiconductors.

Technical ability. Because of the complex nature of manufacturing microchips, semiconductor processors need to know a lot about electronics and about the manufacturing process.

Pay

Semiconductor Processors
    Median annual wages, May 2010

Total, All Occupations	$33,840
Semiconductor Processors	$33,130
Production Occupations	$30,330

Note: All Occupations includes all occupations in the U.S. Economy.
Source: U.S. Bureau of Labor Statistics, Occupational Employment Statistics

The median annual wage of semiconductor processors was $33,130 in May 2010. The median wage is the wage at which half the workers in an occupation earned more than that amount and half earned less. The lowest 10 percent of semiconductor processors earned less than $23,300, and the top 10 percent earned more than $48,260.

Processors employed in the semiconductor and other electronic component manufacturing industry earned $32,880 in May 2010.

Most employees work full time, but some have variable schedules. Because semiconductor factories, also known as fabricating plants, run around the clock, night and weekend work is common for these workers. Although some plants schedule workers for the standard 40-hour week (8-hour shifts, 5 days a week), others schedule workers in 12-hour shifts to minimize disrupting the clean room.

Job Outlook

Semiconductor Processors
    Percent change in employment, projected 2010-20

Total, All Occupations	14%
Production Occupations	4%
Semiconductor Processors	-18%

Note: All Occupations includes all occupations in the U.S. Economy.
Source: U.S. Bureau of Labor Statistics, Employment Projections program

Employment of semiconductor processors is projected to decline rapidly, by 18 percent from 2010 to 2020. Although there is a strong demand for semiconductors in many products, automation at fabricating plants is expected to grow, meaning the plants will hire fewer workers. Because the rooms have to be kept so clean, it is more effective to use robots to do many of the simple tasks that processors once did. In addition, the increasing complexity of chips, combined with their reduced size, makes it difficult for people to work on them.

The semiconductor manufacturing industry, where most processors work, is also expected to decline, leading to more job losses. Operating a plant in the United States is more expensive than operating one in another country where manufacturing costs are often lower. This leads to companies sending the manufacturing of chips abroad, even though designing the chips will continue to take place in the United States.

Job Prospects

Competition for semiconductor processor jobs is expected to be tough because of the decline in employment. Prospects should be best for those who have a bachelor's degree or experience in other high-tech manufacturing jobs.

Employment projections data for semiconductor processors, 2010-20

Occupational Title	SOC Code	Employment, 2010	Projected Employment, 2020	Change, 2010-20	
				Percent	Numeric
Semiconductor Processors	51-9141	21,100	17,300	-18	-3,800
SOURCE: U.S. Bureau of Labor Statistics, Employment Projections program					

Similar Occupations

This table shows a list of occupations with job duties that are similar to those of semiconductor processors.

Occupation	Job Duties	Entry-Level Education	Median Annual Pay, May 2010
Assemblers and Fabricators	Assemblers and fabricators assemble both finished products and the parts that go into them. They use tools, machines, and their hands to make engines, computers, aircraft, toys, electronic devices, and more.	High school diploma or equivalent	$28,360
Chemical Engineers	Chemical engineers apply the principles of chemistry, biology, and physics to solve problems. These problems involve the production or use of chemicals, fuel, drugs, food, and many other products. They design processes and equipment for large-scale safe and sustainable manufacturing, plan and test methods of manufacturing products and treating byproducts, and supervise production.	Bachelor's degree	$90,300
Computer Hardware Engineers	Computer hardware engineers research, design, develop, and test computer equipment such as chips, circuit boards, or routers. By solving complex problems in computer hardware, these engineers create rapid advances in computer technology.	Bachelor's degree	$98,810

Electrical and Electronic Engineering Technicians	Electrical and electronic engineering technicians help engineers design and develop computers, communications equipment, medical monitoring devices, navigational equipment, and other electrical and electronic equipment. They often work in product evaluation and testing, using measuring and diagnostic devices to adjust, test, and repair equipment.	Associate's degree	$56,040
Electrical and Electronics Engineers	Electrical engineers design, develop, test, and supervise the manufacturing of electrical equipment such as electric motors, radar and navigation systems, communications systems, and power generation equipment.Electronics engineers design and develop electronic equipment, such as broadcast and communications systems—from portable music players to global positioning systems (GPS).	Bachelor's degree	$87,180
Machinists and Tool and Die Makers	Machinists and tool and die makers set up and operate a variety of computer-controlled or mechanically-controlled machine tools to produce precision metal parts, instruments, and tools.	High school diploma or equivalent	$39,910
Quality Control Inspectors	Quality control inspectors examine products and materials for defects or deviations from manufacturers' or industry specifications.	High school diploma or equivalent	$33,030

Contacts for More Information

For more information about semiconductor processors, visit Maricopa Advanced Technology Education Center , SEMI , Semiconductor Industry Association

Suggested citation:

Bureau of Labor Statistics, U.S. Department of Labor, Occupational Outlook Handbook, 2012-13 Edition, Semiconductor Processors, on the Internet at http://www.bls.gov/ooh/production/semiconductor-processors.htm .

Sewers and Tailors

Quick Facts: Sewers and Tailors	
2010 Median Pay	$25,850 per year $12.43 per hour
Entry-Level Education	Less than high school
Work Experience in a Related Occupation	None
On-the-job Training	Moderate-term on-the-job training
Number of Jobs, 2010	57,500
Job Outlook, 2010-20	1% (Little or no change)
Employment Change, 2010-20	400

What Sewers and Tailors Do

Sewers and tailors sew, join, reinforce, or finish clothing or other items. They may create new pieces of clothing from patterns and designs or alter existing garments to fit customers better.

Duties

Sewers and tailors typically do the following:

- Measure clients to ensure that clothing will fit properly
- Cut and measure fabric according to the pattern or design
- Mark garments to note where alterations are necessary
- Open seams to hem garments and to make other alterations
- Sew clothing by hand, using a needle and thread or with sewing machines
- Fit clothing on customers to determine if additional alterations are necessary

Sewers and tailors can specialize in alterations or in sewing custom garments.

Those who do alterations ensure that clothes fit customers properly. They make changes to garments, such as hemming pants to make them shorter or taking in seams to make clothing smaller.

Some specialize in a certain type of garment, such as bridal gowns. Others specialize in a particular type of material, such as fur. Fur tailors may restyle older clothing, add a fur collar to a coat or a dress, or sew the inner lining of a garment to the inside of fur skin by hand.

Some dressmakers and custom sewers work with designers or customers to create new garments. They take orders from customers and help them select fabric and colors. When working with a designer, tailors help translate designs into finished pieces of clothing. For example, a couture dressmaker may work with a fashion designer to create exclusive custom-fitted clothing.

In addition to working with clothing, sewers may produce other items, such as textiles and quilts. Hand weavers produce custom-made textiles, such as placemats, napkins, and pillowcases. Hand quilters produce a bed cover or display item, traditionally composed of two layers of fabric.

Some sewers and tailors own their business. In these cases, they may do management and administrative tasks, such as managing the business's finances and taking orders.

Work Environment

Sewers and tailors held about 57,500 jobs in 2010.

Sewers and tailors work for textile and apparel manufacturers, department stores, and drycleaners. About 44 percent are self-employed.

Work Schedules

Most sewers and tailors work full time. Some work nights and weekends to accommodate customers' schedules. Self-employed workers may need to work longer hours to run their business and complete customer orders.

Sewers and tailors may create new pieces of clothing from patterns and designs or alter existing garments to better fit a customer.

How to Become a Sewer or Tailor

There are no formal education requirements for someone to work as a sewer or tailor. Most workers are trained informally on the job or through apprenticeship programs. Some take classes to learn how to sew and alter clothing.

Education

Generally, employers do not have any formal education requirements for positions as a sewer or tailor. Some sewers and tailors take classes to learn how to sew and alter clothing, but there are few formal programs to teach students how to become a tailor.

Training

Those interested in becoming a sewer or tailor are often trained while working in a tailor shop. Some are trained through apprenticeships, in which they are hired by a tailor and receive training to help them develop the skills necessary to work as a tailor. However, formal apprenticeships are difficult to find. Most of those interested in becoming sewers or tailors find employment working with a tailor and are trained informally on the job.

Important Qualities

Customer-service skills. Sewers and tailors need to meet customers' and designers' requirements while managing their expectations. If fulfilling a customer's request is not possible, the sewer or tailor must be able to explain to the customer why that is so.

Detail oriented. Sewers and tailors must be precise. They need to take careful measurements and follow patterns. Paying attention to detail is essential to their work.

Sensitivity. Sewers and tailors often need to get physically close to customers to take measurements, and in doing so, they must be sensitive to the customers' needs and personal space.

Pay

Sewers and Tailors	
Median hourly wages, May 2010	
Total, All Occupations	$16.27
Tailors, Dressmakers, and Custom Sewers	$12.77
Sewers and Tailors	$12.43
Sewers, Hand	$11.13

Note: All Occupations includes all occupations in the U.S. Economy.
Source: U.S. Bureau of Labor Statistics, Occupational Employment Statistics

The median hourly wage of hand sewers was $11.13 in May 2010. The median wage is the wage at which half the workers in an occupation earned more than that amount and half earned less. The lowest 10 percent earned less than $8.31, and the top 10 percent earned more than $17.57.

The median annual wage of tailors, dressmakers, and custom sewers was $12.77 in May 2010. The lowest 10 percent earned less than $8.48, and the top 10 percent earned more than $20.21.

Most sewers and tailors work full time. Some work nights and weekends to accommodate customers' schedules. Self-employed workers may need to work longer hours to run their business and complete customer orders.

Job Outlook

Sewers and Tailors	
Percent change in employment, projected 2010-20	
Total, All Occupations	14%
Tailors, Dressmakers, and Custom Sewers	2%
Sewers and Tailors	1%
Sewers, Hand	-5%

Note: All Occupations includes all occupations in the U.S. Economy.
Source: U.S. Bureau of Labor Statistics, Employment Projections program

Employment of sewers and tailors is expected to experience little or no change, growing 1 percent from 2010 to 2020. Growth will be limited as clothing continues to be made in other countries and the demand for custom clothing keeps declining.

Employment of hand sewers is expected to decline moderately by 5 percent as the production of clothing continues to move abroad. Fierce competition in the market for clothing should keep domestic clothing and textile firms under intense pressure to cut costs and produce more with fewer workers.

Although the industry is already highly automated, business is expected to continue increasing worker productivity by using laborsaving machinery. As a result, there will be decreased demand for sewers who specialize in working by hand.

Employment of tailors, dressmakers, and custom sewers is expected to experience little or no change, growing 2 percent from 2010 to 2020. Many of these workers are self-employed or work in clothing stores.

Although custom home furnishings and clothing face strong competition from the cheaper off-the-rack products, there will always be some demand from upscale stores and certain clients. Made-to-order apparel and other handmade goods appeal to people looking for one-of-a-kind items, and tailors will continue to be needed to alter ready-to-wear clothing for a better fit.

Job Prospects

Job prospects should be best for highly skilled workers who have experience.

Employment projections data for sewers and tailors, 2010-20

Occupational Title	SOC Code	Employment, 2010	Projected Employment, 2020	Change, 2010-20	
				Percent	Numeric
Tailors, Dressmakers, and Sewers	51-6050	57,500	57,900	1	400
Sewers, Hand	51-6051	10,400	9,800	-5	-600
Tailors, Dressmakers, and Custom Sewers	51-6052	47,200	48,100	2	900
SOURCE: U.S. Bureau of Labor Statistics, Employment Projections program					

Similar Occupations

This table shows a list of occupations with job duties that are similar to those of sewers and tailors.

Occupation	Job Duties	Entry-Level Education	Median Annual Pay, May 2010
Craft and Fine Artists	Craft and fine artists use a variety of materials and techniques to create art for sale and exhibition. Craft artists create handmade objects, such as pottery, glassware, textiles, or other objects that are designed to be functional. Fine artists, including painters, sculptors, and illustrators, create original works of art for their aesthetic value, rather than a functional one.	High school diploma or equivalent	$43,470
Fashion Designers	Fashion designers create original clothing, accessories, and footwear. They sketch designs, select fabrics and patterns, and give instructions on how to make the products they designed.	High school diploma or equivalent	$64,530
Interior Designers	Interior designers make interior spaces functional, safe, and beautiful for almost every type of building: offices, homes, airport terminals, shopping malls, and restaurants. They select and specify colors, finishes, fabrics, furniture, flooring and wallcoverings, lighting, and other materials to create useful and stylish interiors for buildings.	Bachelor's degree	$46,280
Laundry and Dry-cleaning Workers	Laundry and dry-cleaning workers clean clothing, linens, drapes, and other articles, using washing, drying, and dry-cleaning machines. They also may clean leather, suede, furs, and rugs.	Less than high school	$19,540
Upholsterers	Upholsterers make, replace, and repair coverings on furniture and in vehicles.	High school diploma or equivalent	$29,960

Contacts for More Information

For more information about tailors, visit Custom Tailors and Designers Association

Suggested citation:

Bureau of Labor Statistics, U.S. Department of Labor, Occupational Outlook Handbook, 2012-13 Edition, Sewers and Tailors, on the Internet at http://www.bls.gov/ooh/production/sewers-and-tailors.htm .

Slaughterers and Meat Packers

Quick Facts: Slaughterers and Meat Packers	
2010 Median Pay	$23,380 per year $11.24 per hour
Entry-Level Education	Less than high school
Work Experience in a Related Occupation	None
On-the-job Training	Moderate-term on-the-job training
Number of Jobs, 2010	89,100
Job Outlook, 2010-20	8% (Slower than average)
Employment Change, 2010-20	7,400

What Slaughterers and Meat Packers Do

Slaughterers and meat packers kill and clean animals, divide carcasses into manageable sections, and grind or otherwise prepare and pack products, such as boxed beef, for shipping to distribution centers.

Duties

Slaughterers and meat packers typically do the following:

- Slaughter animals and cut meat into smaller portions
- Operate machinery, such as motorized saws, conveyors, or electrical stunning equipment
- Grind, chop, or cut meat into retail sizes and package it for shipping
- Comply with industry health standards

Slaughterers and meat packers may use large, suspended power saws for quartering beef carcasses, knives for boning, or wrapping machines and forklifts for packing and shipping the meat. Most food-manufacturing plants require slaughterers and meat packers to clean, salt, and cut beef quarters and large portions into tenders and chucks to prepare them for retail sale.

Slaughterers and meat packers typically work in either slaughtering yards or processing facilities. They may be rotated through stations, doing different tasks each shift.

Some types of slaughterers follow religious specifications. For example, **halal and kosher slaughterers** follow strict guidelines during the slaughtering process to make sure that the product can qualify for religious specifications of what is permissible to eat.

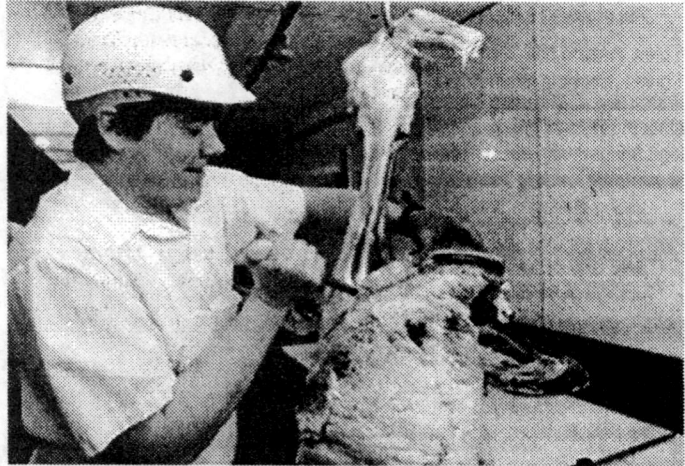

Many beef processing workers remove the bones from large sections of beef.

Work Environment

Slaughterers and meat packers held about 89,100 jobs in 2010.

The slaughtering floors of most processing facilities are rarely climate controlled and may become very hot during the summer and very cold during the winter. Slaughterers and meat packers have to stand for the majority, if not all, of their shift.

Because they typically work on an assembly line, slaughterers and meat packers tend to do one specific function (one cut) during their shift. However, they may change stations each shift. Thus, in some plants, slaughterers and meat packers are as likely to be trimming meat as they are to be hygienically packing products in boxes for shipping.

Work Schedules

Most workers in this occupation work full time. Most workers will work shift assignments based on seniority. Like many workers in manufacturing, those in food processing occupations may work a shift that requires either early mornings or nights and evenings.

Injuries

Injury rates have improved greatly over the past decades, but injury and illness rates for slaughterers and meat packers are still significantly higher than those of most other manufacturing occupations. However, slaughterers and meat packers have the lowest illness and injury rates of all of the production workers in the food manufacturing industry. They work near dangerous equipment, such as knives and saws, perform strenuous activities, walk on slippery floors, and are exposed to animal waste.

How to Become a Slaughterer or Meat Packer

Slaughterers and meat packers do not need formal education. They get on-the-job training. Some positions require previous work experience.

Training

Slaughterers and meat packers get on-the-job training. They are not expected to know the job before they start.

On-the-job training may last a few days or a few months, but slaughterers and meat packers often get more training every year. Generally, trainees begin by doing less difficult jobs, such as making simple cuts or removing bones. Trainees learn how to properly use and care for tools and equipment under the guidance of experienced workers.

Work Experience

Slaughterers and meat packers typically enter the occupation after gaining experience in a related occupation. They start in positions that generally do not require any experience at the entry level. Employers may prefer to hire slaughterers and meat packers who have experience in construction trades or other physically demanding occupations.

Education

Formal education is not required for slaughterers and meat packers. However, education may help them advance into managerial and other positions with more responsibility. Slaughterers and meat packers must have basic reading and math skills because they use, calibrate, and manipulate machinery.

Important Qualities

Concentration. Slaughterers and meat packers must pay close attention to what they are doing to avoid injuring themselves and wasting products.

Coordination. Hand–eye coordination is needed for the timely and safe preparation of products.

Good eyesight. Slaughterers and meat packers must be able to see small portions of fat, bone, or cartilage to remove them.

Physical stamina. Slaughterers and meat packers must be able to stand and work on the production line for 8 or more hours during a shift.

Physical strength. Slaughterers and meat packers must be able to lift and move large portions of meat while working in the slaughtering yard or processing facility.

Teamwork. Slaughterers and meat packers must work as a team both in the yard and on the line to ensure that the operation runs smoothly. They are often closely supported by managerial staff.

Certification

Slaughterers and meat packers may be certified by an appropriate government agency to show that they know how to process meat hygienically.

Specialized workers, including butchers who follow religious guidelines for food preparation, may be required to go through a lengthy apprenticeship or certification process or both before becoming completely qualified and endorsed by their organization to do their duties.

Pay

Slaughterers and Meat Packers
Median annual wages, May 2010

Total, All Occupations	$33,840
Production Occupations	$30,330
Slaughterers and Meat Packers	$23,380

Note: All Occupations includes all occupations in the U.S. Economy.
Source: U.S. Bureau of Labor Statistics, Occupational Employment Statistics

The median annual wage of slaughterers and meat packers was $23,380 in May 2010. The median wage is the wage at which half the workers in an occupation earned more than that amount and half earned less. The lowest 10 percent earned less than $17,310, and the top 10 percent earned more than $31,790.

Most slaughterers and meat packers work full time. Most workers will work shift assignments based on seniority. Like many workers in manufacturing, slaughterers and meat packers may work a shift that requires either early mornings or nights and evenings.

Job Outlook

Slaughterers and Meat Packers
Percent change in employment, projected 2010-20

Total, All Occupations	14%
Slaughterers and Meat Packers	8%
Production Occupations	4%

Note: All Occupations includes all occupations in the U.S. Economy.
Source: U.S. Bureau of Labor Statistics, Employment Projections program

Employment of slaughterers and meat packers is expected to grow by 8 percent from 2010 to 2020, slower than the average for all occupations. An expanding population and international trade will create demand for meat and related products.

As the meat-processing industry becomes more integrated, production processes are becoming more streamlined. The ability of processing facilities to employ slaughterers and meat packers should remain strong because of reduced costs in other areas of the industry.

Most food-manufacturing plants require slaughterers and meat packers to clean, salt, and cut beef quarters and large portions into tenders and chucks to prepare them for retail sale.

Retailers and grocers increasingly prefer prepackaged meat products because they can be easily displayed and sold without the need of a butcher.

A growing global population and increasing wealth among developing countries should cause demand for meat to increase worldwide. Compared to food products from other countries, U.S.-made food products are produced under very high quality and safety standards. As a result, exports of U.S. meat products face few extra quality and safety regulations when imported by other countries.

Job Prospects

The animal slaughtering and processing industry is continuing to consolidate. Most jobs are in areas where there are large processing facilities. The majority of large meat-packing plants are located in the Midwestern and High Plains regions of the country. The five states with the largest number of slaughterers and meat packers are Texas, North Carolina, Minnesota, Nebraska, and Iowa. Processing facilities tend to be in rural areas or near smaller cities.

Employment projections data for slaughterers and meat packers, 2010-20

Occupational Title	SOC Code	Employment, 2010	Projected Employment, 2020	Change, 2010-20 Percent	Numeric
Slaughterers and Meat Packers	51-3023	89,100	96,500	8	7,400

SOURCE: U.S. Bureau of Labor Statistics, Employment Projections program

Similar Occupations

This table shows a list of occupations with job duties that are similar to those of slaughterers and meat packers.

Occupation	Job Duties	Entry-Level Education	Median Annual Pay, May 2010
Bakers	Bakers mix and bake ingredients according to recipes to make a variety of breads, pastries, and other baked goods.	Less than high school	$23,450
Chefs and Head Cooks	Chefs and head cooks oversee the daily food preparation at restaurants or other places where food is served. They direct kitchen staff and handle any food-related concerns.	High school diploma or equivalent	$40,630
Fishers and Related Fishing Workers	Fishers and related fishing workers catch and trap various types of marine life. The fish they catch are for human food, animal feed, bait, and other uses.	Less than high school	$25,590
Food Processing Occupations	Food processing occupations include butchers and meat cutters; meat, poultry, and fish cutters and trimmers; and operators and tenders of roasting, baking, and drying machinery. These workers cut, trim, or otherwise process food items, such as meat, or nonfood items, such as tobacco, for retail sale.	Less than high school	$23,950
Food Processing Operators	Food processing operators include food batchmakers and food cooking machine operators and tenders. These workers may set up, operate, and tend cooking equipment that mixes, blends, cooks, or otherwise processes ingredients used to manufacture food products.	High school diploma or equivalent	$24,250

Contacts for More Information

For training information regarding line workers and food safely, visit U.S. Department of Agriculture Food Safety and Inspection Service

For information about the meat-processing industry and related trends, visit American Meat Institute

Suggested citation:

Bureau of Labor Statistics, U.S. Department of Labor, Occupational Outlook Handbook, 2012-13 Edition, Slaughterers and Meat Packers, on the Internet at http://www.bls.gov/ooh/production/slaughterers-and-meat-packers.htm .

Stationary Engineers and Boiler Operators

Quick Facts: Stationary Engineers and Boiler Operators	
2010 Median Pay	$52,140 per year $25.07 per hour
Entry-Level Education	High school diploma or equivalent
Work Experience in a Related Occupation	None
On-the-job Training	Long-term on-the-job training
Number of Jobs, 2010	37,600
Job Outlook, 2010-20	6% (Slower than average)
Employment Change, 2010-20	2,300

What Stationary Engineers and Boiler Operators Do

Stationary engineers and boiler operators control stationary engines, boilers, or other mechanical equipment to provide utilities for buildings or for industrial purposes.

Duties

Stationary engineers and boiler operators typically do the following:

- Operate engines, boilers, and auxiliary equipment
- Read gauges, meters, and charts to track boiler operations
- Monitor boiler water, chemical, and fuel levels
- Activate valves to change the amount of water, air, and fuel in boilers
- Fire coal furnaces or feed boilers, using gas feeds or oil pumps
- Inspect equipment to ensure that it is operating efficiently
- Check safety devices routinely
- Record data and keep logs of operation, maintenance, and safety activity

Most large office buildings, malls, warehouses, and other commercial facilities have extensive heating, ventilation, and air-conditioning systems that maintain comfortable temperatures all year long. Industrial plants often have additional facilities to provide electrical power, steam, or other services. Stationary engineers and boiler operators control and maintain these systems, which include boilers, air-conditioning and refrigeration equipment, turbines, generators, pumps, and compressors.

Workers manage utility or industrial equipment such as boilers, stationary engines, and generators.

Stationary engineers and boiler operators start up, regulate, repair, and shut down equipment. They monitor meters, gauges, and computerized controls to ensure that equipment operates safely and within established limits. They use sophisticated electrical and electronic test equipment when servicing, troubleshooting, repairing, and monitoring heating, cooling, and ventilation systems.

Stationary engineers and boiler operators also regularly perform routine maintenance. They may do a complete overhaul or replace defective valves, gaskets, or bearings. In addition, stationary engineers and boiler operators lubricate moving parts, replace filters, and remove soot and corrosion that can make a boiler less efficient.

Work Environment

Stationary engineers and boiler operators held about 37,600 jobs in 2010.

They were employed in a variety of industries. Because most stationary engineers and boiler operators work in large commercial or industrial buildings, the majority of jobs were in manufacturing, government, educational services, and hospitals.

The industries employing the largest numbers of stationary engineers and boiler operators in 2010 were as follows:

Manufacturing	22%
Hospitals; state, local, and private	16
Colleges, universities, and professional schools; state, local, and private	14
Local government, excluding education and hospitals	10
State government, excluding education and hospitals	8

In a large building or industrial plant, a senior stationary engineer or boiler operator may be in charge of all mechanical systems in the building and may supervise a team of assistant stationary engineers, assistant boiler tenders, and other operators or mechanics.

In small buildings, there may be only one stationary engineer or boiler operator who operates and maintains all of the systems.

Injuries

Some stationary engineers and boiler operators are exposed to high temperatures, dust, dirt, and loud noise from the equipment. Maintenance duties also may require contact with oil, grease, and smoke.

Workers spend much of their time on their feet. They also may have to crawl inside boilers and work while crouched or kneel to inspect, clean, or repair equipment.

Stationary engineers and boiler operators have a much-higher-than-average rate of occupational injuries and illnesses. Because they work around hazardous machinery, they must follow procedures to guard against burns, electric shock, noise, dangerous moving parts, and exposure to hazardous materials.

Work Schedules

Most stationary engineers and boiler operators work full time during regular business hours. In facilities that operate around the clock, engineers and operators usually work one of three 8-hour shifts on a rotating basis. Because buildings are open 365 days a year, many must work weekends and holidays.

How to Become a Stationary Engineer or Boiler Operator

Stationary engineers and boiler operators need at least a high school diploma. They typically begin their careers in mechanic or helper positions and are trained on the job by more experienced engineers.

Training

Stationary engineers and boiler operators typically learn their work through long-term on-the-job training. They learn their trade by working as helpers, mechanics, or technicians under the supervision of an experienced engineer. After training and gaining experience, they are eligible to advance to operator and engineer positions within that facility.

Some stationary engineers and boiler operators complete apprenticeship programs sponsored by the International Union of Operating Engineers . Apprenticeships usually last 4 years, include 8,000 hours of on-the-job training, and require 600 hours of technical instruction. Apprentices learn about the operation and maintenance of equipment; controls and balancing of heating, ventilation, and air conditioning (HVAC) systems; safety; electricity; and air quality.

Many employers encourage and pay for skill improvement training for their employees. Experienced stationary engineers and boiler operators update their skills regularly through training, especially when new equipment is introduced or when regulations change.

Licenses

Some state and local governments require licensure for stationary engineers and boiler operators. These governments typically have several classes of stationary engineer and boiler operator licenses. Each class specifies the type and size of equipment the engineer is permitted to operate without supervision.

A top-level engineer or operator is qualified to run a large facility, supervise others, and operate equipment of all types and capacities. Engineers and operators with licenses below this level are limited in the types or capacities of equipment they may operate without supervision.

Applicants for licensure usually must be at least 18 years of age, meet experience requirements, and pass a written exam. Many job openings require that workers be licensed before starting the job, although some jobs may offer apprenticeships. A stationary engineer or boiler operator who moves from one state or city to another may have to pass an examination for a new license because of regional differences in licensing requirements.

Education

Stationary engineers and boiler operators need at least a high school diploma. Students should take courses in math, science, and mechanical and technical subjects.

With the growing complexity of the work, vocational school or college courses may benefit workers trying to advance in the occupation.

Work Experience

Stationary engineers and boiler operators who do not complete a formal apprenticeship or vocational program usually need several years of work experience. Many gain experience working as maintenance helpers, mechanics, or technicians.

Advancement

Generally, stationary engineers and boiler operators advance as they obtain higher class licenses, which allow them to work with larger, more powerful, and more varied equipment. In jurisdictions where licenses are not required, workers usually advance by taking company-administered exams. Due to the growing complexity of the work, continuing education, such as taking vocational school or college courses, can benefit workers who want to advance in the occupation.

Important Qualities

Detail oriented. Stationary engineers and boiler operators monitor intricate machinery, gauges, and meters to ensure that everything is operating properly.

Manual dexterity. Stationary engineers and boiler operators must use precise motions to control or repair machines. They grasp tools and use their hands to perform many tasks.

Mechanical skills. Stationary engineers and boiler operators must know how to use tools and work with machines. They must be able to repair, maintain, and operate equipment.

Problem-solving skills. Stationary engineers and boiler operators must figure out how things work and quickly solve problems that arise with equipment or controls.

Technical skills. Stationary engineers and boiler operators must be able to understand and operate machines and electronic and computer controls.

Pay

Stationary Engineers and Boiler Operators
   Median annual wages, May 2010

Plant and System Operators	$52,230
Stationary Engineers and Boiler Operators	$52,140
Total, All Occupations	$33,840

Note: All Occupations includes all occupations in the U.S. Economy.
Source: U.S. Bureau of Labor Statistics, Occupational Employment Statistics

The median annual wage of stationary engineers and boiler operators was $52,140 in May 2010. The median wage is the wage at which half the workers in an occupation earned more than that amount and half earned less. The lowest 10 percent earned less than $32,640, and the top 10 percent earned more than $73,580.

Starting pay for apprentice stationary engineers and boiler operators is typically 45 percent to 60 percent of that of a fully trained worker.

Many stationary engineers and boiler operators are members of a union.

Most stationary engineers and boiler operators work full time during regular business hours. In facilities that operate around the clock, engineers and operators usually work one of three 8-hour shifts on a rotating basis. Because buildings are open 365 days a year, many must work weekends and holidays.

Job Outlook

Stationary Engineers and Boiler Operators
   Percent change in employment, projected 2010-20

Total, All Occupations	14%
Stationary Engineers and Boiler Operators	6%
Plant and System Operators	1%

Note: All Occupations includes all occupations in the U.S. Economy.
Source: U.S. Bureau of Labor Statistics, Employment Projections program

Employment of stationary engineers and boiler operators is projected to grow 6 percent from 2010 to 2020, slower than the average for all occupations.

Employment growth will be driven by continuing commercial and industrial development. New development and construction will increase the number of buildings with stationary engines and boiler systems that will need to be operated and maintained.

Although employment is spread across many industries, it is concentrated in those that require large commercial and industrial buildings. As a result, most employment gains will come from growth in these industries.

Faster employment growth is expected in educational services and hospitals as more buildings are built to accommodate a growing population in need of such services. Stationary engineers and boiler operators are especially important in buildings that operate around the clock and need precise temperature control, such as hospitals.

Fewer jobs will be added in manufacturing and government as employment slows or declines in these sectors.

Job Prospects

Job opportunities should be best for those with apprenticeship training. Stationary engineer and boiler operator positions are relatively high paying, and engineering staffs are typically small.

Although apprenticeship programs have a competitive application process, they are the most reliable path into the occupation. In addition, workers who are licensed before they look for work will have better job opportunities.

Employment projections data for stationary engineers and boiler operators, 2010-20

Occupational Title	SOC Code	Employment, 2010	Projected Employment, 2020	Change, 2010-20	
				Percent	Numeric
Stationary Engineers and Boiler Operators	51-8021	37,600	40,000	6	2,300
SOURCE: U.S. Bureau of Labor Statistics, Employment Projections program					

Similar Occupations

This table shows a list of occupations with job duties that are similar to those of stationary engineers and boiler operators.

Occupation	Job Duties	Entry-Level Education	Median Annual Pay, May 2010
General Maintenance and Repair Workers	General maintenance and repair workers maintain and repair machines, mechanical equipment, and buildings. They work on plumbing, electrical, and air-conditioning and heating systems.	High school diploma or equivalent	$34,730
Heating, Air Conditioning, and Refrigeration Mechanics and Installers	Heating, air conditioning, and refrigeration mechanics and installers—often referred to as HVACR technicians—work on heating, ventilation, cooling, and refrigeration systems that control the air quality in many types of buildings.	Postsecondary non-degree award	$42,530
Industrial Machinery Mechanics and Maintenance Workers	Industrial machinery mechanics and maintenance workers maintain and repair factory equipment and other industrial machinery, such as conveying systems, production machinery, and packaging equipment.	High school diploma or equivalent	$44,160
Millwrights	Millwrights install, dismantle, repair, reassemble, and move machinery in factories, power plants, and construction sites.	High school diploma or equivalent	$48,360
Power Plant Operators, Distributors, and Dispatchers	Power plant operators, distributors, and dispatchers control the systems that generate and distribute electric power.	High school diploma or equivalent	$65,360
Water and Wastewater Treatment Plant and System Operators	Water and wastewater treatment plant and system operators manage a system of machines, often through the use of control boards, to transfer or treat water or wastewater.	High school diploma or equivalent	$40,770
Boilermakers	Boilermakers assemble, install, and repair boilers, closed vats, and other large vessels or containers that hold liquids and gases.	High school diploma or equivalent	$54,640

Contacts for More Information

For information about apprenticeships, vocational training, and job opportunities, contact

- State employment service offices
- Local chapters of the International Union of Operating Engineers
- Vocational schools
- State and local licensing agencies

Information about apprenticeships is also available from the U.S. Department of Labor's toll-free help line: (877) 872-5627 or the Employment and Training Administration .

For more information about training or becoming a stationary engineer or boiler operator, visit National Association of Power Engineers

Suggested citation:

Bureau of Labor Statistics, U.S. Department of Labor, Occupational Outlook Handbook, 2012-13 Edition, Stationary Engineers and Boiler Operators, on the Internet at http://www.bls.gov/ooh/production/stationary-engineers-and-boiler-operators.htm .

Upholsterers

Quick Facts: Upholsterers	
2010 Median Pay	$29,960 per year $14.40 per hour
Entry-Level Education	High school diploma or equivalent
Work Experience in a Related Occupation	None
On-the-job Training	Moderate-term on-the-job training
Number of Jobs, 2010	46,900
Job Outlook, 2010-20	4% (Slower than average)
Employment Change, 2010-20	2,000

What Upholsterers Do

Upholsterers make, replace, and repair coverings on furniture and in vehicles.

Duties

Upholsterers typically do the following:
- Consult with clients to discuss alterations to the furniture and to help customers choose fabric
- Estimate costs for the project, including approximate fabric and labor costs
- Inspect furniture to find needed repairs in the frame, upholstery, and springs
- Remove and replace old and worn padding, filling, and broken springs
- Measure, cut, and sew fabric, and attach it to the furniture frame with tacks, staples and glue

Upholsterers replace and repair the coverings on furniture or in vehicles and upholster new pieces of furniture.

Upholsterers put on covering and cushions to create new furniture and update old furniture and vehicle interiors. Although some upholsterers specialize in either working with old furniture or creating new furniture, most do both.

Upholsterers need to stay current with trends in furniture design and styles. They help choose fabrics that meet their customer's lifestyle, preferences, and needs. For example, upholsterers may help a client who has young children choose a long-lasting and durable fabric for a family room sofa that matches other furniture.

Sometimes they have to choose fabrics that meet building codes—such as being fire resistant—or fabrics that reflect the style of the building. They also may work with interior designers and architects who need furniture for a new building. For more information, see the profiles on interior designers and architects .

Upholsterers may specialize in working on cars and other vehicles. These workers create and replace upholstery for the interiors of cars and other vehicles. They upholster seats, carpet floors, and cover door panels. To replace interiors with another fabric or other material, such as leather, these workers first remove the seats from the vehicle before replacing the upholstery.

Some upholsterers own their business. In these cases, they may do management and administrative tasks, such as managing the finances of their business and taking orders.

Work Environment

Upholsterers held about 46,900 jobs in 2010.

Most upholsterers work for household and institutional furniture manufacturers, upholstery shops, and automotive interior repair shops. About 36 percent of workers are self-employed. Some self-employed upholsterers work out of their home.

In 2010, the following industries employed the most upholsterers:

Household and institutional furniture manufacturing	26%
Personal and household goods repair and maintenance	15
Transportation equipment manufacturing	6
Automotive body, paint, interior, and glass repair	5

Injuries

Full-time upholsterers experience a rate of work-related injury and illness that is higher than the average among all occupations. Upholsterers usually wear protective gloves and clothing when using sharp tools and lifting and hanging furniture or springs.

During most of the workday, upholsterers stand and may do a lot of bending and heavy lifting. They also may work in awkward positions for short periods.

Work Schedules

Most upholsterers work full time. Some work nights and weekends to accommodate customers' schedules.

How to Become an Upholsterer

There are no formal education requirements to work as an upholsterer. Most workers have a high school diploma and are trained informally on the job. Some take classes to learn how to sew and upholster furniture.

Education

Generally, employers do not have any formal education requirements for upholsterers. Some upholsterers take classes to learn how to sew and upholsterer furniture, but there are few formal programs to teach someone how to become an upholsterer.

Training

Those interested in becoming an upholsterer are often trained while working in an upholstery shop. Some are trained through apprenticeships, where they are hired by an upholsterer and get training to develop their skills. However, formal apprenticeships are difficult to find.

Most who are interested in becoming an upholsterer find employment working with an upholsterer and are trained informally on the job. Others teach themselves by taking furniture apart to learn how it is made and what appears to be needed to replace the fabric, padding, and broken springs.

Important Qualities

Creativity. Upholsterers should be able to help customers choose and use fabrics to match the design style they are trying to achieve with their furniture. Upholsterers must have a good eye for color and pattern to help customers fit the newly upholstered furniture with the rest of their dÃ©cor.

Customer-service skills. Upholsterers need to meet customers' requirements while managing customer expectations.

Detail oriented. Upholsterers need to take careful measurements to avoid wasting fabric and to do a neat and accurate job. Paying attention to details is essential to their work.

Problem-solving skills. Every piece of furniture and every upholstery job is different. Upholsterers need to use creativity to solve problems and to determine the best way to approach each job.

Pay

Upholsterers

Median annual wages, May 2010

Total, All Occupations	$33,840
Production Occupations	$30,330
Upholsterers	$29,960

Note: All Occupations includes all occupations in the U.S. Economy.
Source: U.S. Bureau of Labor Statistics, Occupational Employment Statistics

The median annual wage of upholsterers was $29,960 in May 2010. The median wage is the wage at which half the workers in an occupation earned more than that amount and half earned less. The lowest 10 percent earned less than $19,540, and the top 10 percent earned more than $46,350.

Most upholsterers work full time. Some work nights and weekends to accommodate customers' schedules.

Job Outlook

Upholsterers

Percent change in employment, projected 2010-20

Total, All Occupations	14%
Upholsterers	4%
Production Occupations	4%

Note: All Occupations includes all occupations in the U.S. Economy.
Source: U.S. Bureau of Labor Statistics, Employment Projections program

Employment of upholsterers is expected to grow by 4 percent from 2010 to 2020, slower than the average for all occupations. Growth is expected because demand is projected to increase for reupholstering work on used and antique furniture.

People are increasingly interested in refurbishing furniture that they find in antique and second-hand stores and at flea markets. In addition, people often want to repair their furniture—especially if it is high quality—rather than replace it. As a result, there has been an increased demand for the services of upholsterers.

However, growth will be slowed, as customers continue to demand relatively inexpensive furniture. As this furniture becomes worn or broken, it is more likely to be replaced than repaired. This could decrease the demand for upholstery services.

Although overall employment of upholsters is expected to increase by 4 percent, employment of upholsterers in manufacturing industries is expected to decline by 3 percent from 2010 to 2020. Much furniture manufacturing has been sent to countries where labor is less expensive, limiting the demand for upholsterers.

Employment projections data for upholsterers, 2010-20

Occupational Title	SOC Code	Employment, 2010	Projected Employment, 2020	Change, 2010-20 Percent	Numeric
Upholsterers	51-6093	46,900	48,900	4	2,000

SOURCE: U.S. Bureau of Labor Statistics, Employment Projections program

Similar Occupations

This table shows a list of occupations with job duties that are similar to those of upholsterers.

Occupation	Job Duties	Entry-Level Education	Median Annual Pay, May 2010
Craft and Fine Artists	Craft and fine artists use a variety of materials and techniques to create art for sale and exhibition. Craft artists create handmade objects, such as pottery, glassware, textiles, or other objects that are designed to be functional. Fine artists, including painters, sculptors, and illustrators, create original works of art for their aesthetic value, rather than a functional one.	High school diploma or equivalent	$43,470

Fashion Designers	Fashion designers create original clothing, accessories, and footwear. They sketch designs, select fabrics and patterns, and give instructions on how to make the products they designed.	High school diploma or equivalent	$64,530
Interior Designers	Interior designers make interior spaces functional, safe, and beautiful for almost every type of building: offices, homes, airport terminals, shopping malls, and restaurants. They select and specify colors, finishes, fabrics, furniture, flooring and wallcoverings, lighting, and other materials to create useful and stylish interiors for buildings.	Bachelor's degree	$46,280
Laundry and Dry-cleaning Workers	Laundry and dry-cleaning workers clean clothing, linens, drapes, and other articles, using washing, drying, and dry-cleaning machines. They also may clean leather, suede, furs, and rugs.	Less than high school	$19,540
Sewers and Tailors	Sewers and tailors sew, join, reinforce, or finish clothing or other items. They may create new pieces of clothing from patterns and designs or alter existing garments to fit customers better.	Less than high school	$25,850

Contacts for More Information

The Handbook does not have contacts for more information for this occupation.

Water and Wastewater Treatment Plant and System Operators

Quick Facts: Water and Wastewater Treatment Plant and System Operators	
2010 Median Pay	$40,770 per year $19.60 per hour
Entry-Level Education	High school diploma or equivalent
Work Experience in a Related Occupation	None
On-the-job Training	Long-term on-the-job training
Number of Jobs, 2010	110,700
Job Outlook, 2010-20	12% (About as fast as average)
Employment Change, 2010-20	12,900

What Water and Wastewater Treatment Plant and System Operators Do

Water and wastewater treatment plant and system operators manage a system of machines, often through the use of control boards, to transfer or treat water or wastewater.

Operators add chemicals to disinfect water and wastewater.

Duties

Water and wastewater treatment plant and system operators typically do the following:

- Add chemicals, such as ammonia, chlorine, or lime, to disinfect water or other liquids
- Inspect equipment on a regular basis
- Monitor operating conditions, meters, and gauges
- Collect and test water and sewage samples
- Record meter and gauge readings and operational data
- Operate equipment to purify and clarify water or to process or dispose of sewage
- Clean and maintain equipment, tanks, filter beds, and other work areas
- Stay current on U.S. Environmental Protection Agency regulations
- Ensure safety standards are met

It takes a lot of work to get water from natural sources—reservoirs, streams, and groundwater—into our taps. Similarly, it is a complicated process to convert the wastewater in our drains and sewers into a form that is safe to release into the environment.

The specific duties of plant operators depend on the type and size of the plant. In a small plant, one operator may be responsible for maintaining all of the systems. In large plants, multiple operators work the same shifts and are more specialized in their duties, often relying on computerized systems to help them monitor plant processes.

Occasionally, operators must work during emergencies. For example, weather conditions may cause large amounts of storm water or wastewater to flow into sewers, exceeding a plant's capacity. Emergencies also may be caused by malfunctions within a plant, such as chemical leaks or oxygen deficiencies. Operators are trained in emergency management procedures and use safety equipment to protect their health, as well as that of the public.

Water treatment plant and system operators work in water treatment plants. Fresh water is pumped from wells, rivers, streams, and reservoirs to water treatment plants, where it is treated and distributed to customers. Water treatment plant and system operators run the equipment, control the processes, and monitor the plants that treat water to make it safe to drink.

Wastewater treatment plant and system operators do similar work to remove pollutants from domestic and industrial waste. Used water, also known as wastewater, travels through sewage pipes to treatment plants where it is treated and either returned to streams, rivers, and oceans, or used for irrigation.

Work Environment

Water and wastewater treatment plant and system operators held about 110,700 jobs in 2010, of which 78 percent were in local government. Many others worked for water, sewage, and other systems utilities and for waste treatment and disposal services.

Injuries

Water and wastewater treatment plant and system operators work both indoors and outdoors. They may be exposed to noise from machinery and are often exposed to unpleasant odors. Operators' work is physically demanding and usually is performed in locations that are unclean or difficult to access.

They must pay close attention to safety procedures because of hazardous conditions, such as slippery walkways, dangerous gases, and malfunctioning equipment. As a result, workers experience an occupational injury and illness rate that is much higher than the average for all occupations.

Work Schedules

Plants operate 24 hours a day, 7 days a week. In small plants, operators are likely to work during the day and be on call nights and weekends. In medium- and large-size plants that require constant monitoring, operators work in shifts to control the plant at all hours. Operators may have to work overtime, weekends, or holidays.

How to Become a Water or Wastewater Treatment Plant and System Operator

Water and wastewater treatment plant and system operators typically need a high school diploma and are trained on the job.

Training

Water and wastewater treatment plant and system operators need long-term on-the-job training to become fully qualified. Trainees usually start as attendants or operators-in-training and learn their skills on the job under the direction of an experienced operator. The trainees learn by observing and doing routine tasks, such as recording meter readings, taking samples of wastewater and sludge, and doing simple maintenance and repair work on plant equipment.

Larger treatment plants generally combine this on-the-job training with formal classroom or self-paced study programs. As plants get larger and more complicated, operators need more skills before they are allowed to work without supervision.

Licenses

Water and wastewater treatment plant and system operators must be licensed by the state in which they work. Requirements and standards vary widely depending on the state.

States licenses typically have four levels, which depend on the operator's experience and training. Although some states will honor

licenses from other states, operators who move from one state to another may need to take a new set of exams to become licensed in their new state.

Education

Water and wastewater treatment plant and system operators need a high school diploma or equivalent to become operators. Employers may prefer applicants who have completed a certificate or an associate's degree program in water quality management or wastewater treatment technology, because the education minimizes the training a worker will need. Community colleges, technical schools, and trade associations offer these certificate or associate's degree programs.

Work Experience

Water and wastewater treatment plant and system operators typically need related work experience to become operators. They often gain experience working as trainees or in other lower level positions in the plant.

Advancement

Most states have four levels of licenses for water and wastewater treatment plant and system operators. Each increase in license level allows the operator to control a larger plant and more complicated processes without supervision.

At the largest plants, operators who have the highest license level work as shift supervisors and may be in charge of large teams of operators.

Important Qualities

Analytical skills. Water and wastewater treatment plant and system operators must conduct tests and inspections on water or wastewater and evaluate the results.

Detail oriented. Water and wastewater treatment plant and system operators must monitor machinery, gauges, dials, and controls to ensure everything is operating properly. Because tap water and wastewater are highly regulated by the U.S. Environmental Protection Agency, operators must be careful and thorough in completing these tasks.

Math skills. Water and wastewater treatment plant and system operators must have the ability to apply data to formulas that determine treatment requirements, flow levels, and concentration levels.

Mechanical skills. Water and wastewater treatment plant and system operators must know how to work with machines and use tools. They must be familiar with how to operate, repair, and maintain equipment.

Pay

Water and Wastewater Treatment Plant and System Operators
Median annual wages, May 2010

Plant and System Operators	$52,230
Water and Wastewater Treatment Plant and System Operators	$40,770
Total, All Occupations	$33,840

Note: All Occupations includes all occupations in the U.S. Economy.
Source: U.S. Bureau of Labor Statistics, Occupational Employment Statistics

The median annual wage of water and wastewater treatment plant and system operators was $40,770 in May 2010. The median wage is the wage at which half the workers in an occupation earned more than that amount and half earned less. The lowest 10 percent earned less than $24,860, and the top 10 percent earned more than $63,680.

In 2010, about 40 percent of water and wastewater treatment plant and system operators were members of a union.

Plants operate 24 hours a day, 7 days a week. In small plants, operators are likely to work during the day and be on call nights and weekends. In medium- and large-size plants that require constant monitoring, operators work in shifts to control the plant at all hours. Operators may be required to work overtime, weekends, or holidays.

Job Outlook

Water and Wastewater Treatment Plant and System Operators

Percent change in employment, projected 2010-20

Total, All Occupations	14%
Water and Wastewater Treatment Plant and System Operators	12%
Plant and System Operators	1%

Note: All Occupations includes all occupations in the U.S. Economy.
Source: U.S. Bureau of Labor Statistics, Employment Projections program

Employment of water and wastewater treatment plant and system operators is projected to grow 12 percent from 2010 to 2020, about as fast as the average for all occupations.

A growing population and increased demand for water and wastewater-treatment services will drive employment growth. Population growth, particularly in suburban areas, will require new plants or increased capacity at current plants. As existing plants expand and new plants are built to meet this demand, new operator jobs will be created.

Plants will also need more operators to ensure compliance with increased environmental and safety regulations. New regulations often require that plants install new systems or features that operators need to control. Further, while some work can be automated, plants will need skilled workers to operate increasingly complex controls and water and wastewater systems.

Job Prospects

Job prospects for water and wastewater treatment plant and system operators should be excellent. New jobs will be created when existing plants expand and new plants are built. Applicants will also have many job opportunities because many current operators are expected to retire.

In addition, the number of applicants for these positions is normally low, primarily because of the physically demanding and unappealing nature of some of the work. Job prospects will be best for those with training or education in water or wastewater systems and good mechanical skills.

Employment projections data for water and wastewater treatment plant and system operators, 2010-20

Occupational Title	SOC Code	Employment, 2010	Projected Employment, 2020	Change, 2010-20 Percent	Change, 2010-20 Numeric
Water and Wastewater Treatment Plant and System Operators	51-8031	110,700	123,600	12	12,900
SOURCE: U.S. Bureau of Labor Statistics, Employment Projections program					

Similar Occupations

This table shows a list of occupations with job duties that are similar to those of water and wastewater treatment plant and system operators.

Occupation	Job Duties	Entry-Level Education	Median Annual Pay, May 2010
Construction Equipment Operators	Construction equipment operators drive, maneuver, or control the heavy machinery used to construct roads, bridges, buildings, and other structures.	High school diploma or equivalent	$39,460
General Maintenance and Repair Workers	General maintenance and repair workers maintain and repair machines, mechanical equipment, and buildings. They work on plumbing, electrical, and air-conditioning and heating systems.	High school diploma or equivalent	$34,730
Power Plant Operators, Distributors, and Dispatchers	Power plant operators, distributors, and dispatchers control the systems that generate and distribute electric power.	High school diploma or equivalent	$65,360
Stationary Engineers and Boiler Operators	Stationary engineers and boiler operators control stationary engines, boilers, or other mechanical equipment to provide utilities for buildings or for industrial purposes.	High school diploma or equivalent	$52,140

Contacts for More Information

For information on employment opportunities, contact state or local water pollution control agencies, state water and wastewater operator associations, state environmental training centers, or local offices of the state employment service.

For educational information related to a career as a water or wastewater treatment plant and system operator, visit American Water Works Association , The National Rural Water Association , Water Environment Federation, Work for Water

Suggested citation:

Bureau of Labor Statistics, U.S. Department of Labor, Occupational Outlook Handbook, 2012-13 Edition, Water and Wastewater Treatment Plant and System Operators, on the Internet at http://www.bls.gov/ooh/production/water-and-wastewater-treatment-plant-and-system-operators.htm .

Welders, Cutters, Solderers, and Brazers

Quick Facts: Welders, Cutters, Solderers, and Brazers	
2010 Median Pay	$35,450 per year $17.04 per hour
Entry-Level Education	High school diploma or equivalent
Work Experience in a Related Occupation	Less than 1 year
On-the-job Training	Moderate-term on-the-job training
Number of Jobs, 2010	337,300
Job Outlook, 2010-20	15% (About as fast as average)
Employment Change, 2010-20	50,700

What Welders, Cutters, Solderers, and Brazers Do

Welders, cutters, solderers, and brazers weld or join metal parts. They also fill holes, indentions, or seams of metal products, using hand-held welding equipment.

Duties

Welders, cutters, solderers, and brazers typically do the following:
- Study blueprints, sketches, or specifications
- Calculate dimensions to be welded
- Inspect structures or materials to be welded
- Ignite torches or start power supplies
- Monitor the welding process to avoid overheating
- Smooth and polish all surfaces
- Maintain equipment and machinery

Welding is the most common way of permanently joining metal parts. In this process, heat is applied to metal pieces, melting and fusing them to form a permanent bond. Because of its strength, welding is used in shipbuilding, automobile manufacturing and repair, aerospace applications, and thousands of other manufacturing activities. Welding also is used to join beams in the construction of buildings, bridges, and other structures and to join pipes in pipelines, power plants, and refineries.

Welders work in a wide variety of industries, from car racing to manufacturing. The work that welders do and the equipment they use vary, depending on the industry. The most common and simplest type of welding today, arc welding, uses electrical currents to create heat and bond metals together—but there are more than 100 different processes that a welder can use. The type of weld is normally determined by the types of metals being joined and the conditions under which the welding is to take place.

Cutters use heat to cut and trim metal objects to specific dimensions. The work of **arc, plasma,** and **oxy-gas cutters** is closely related to that of welders. However, instead of joining metals, cutters use the heat from an electric arc, a stream of ionized gas called plasma, or burning gases to cut and trim metal objects to specific dimensions. Cutters also dismantle large objects, such as ships, railroad cars, automobiles, buildings, or aircraft. Some operate and monitor cutting machines similar to those used by welding machine operators.

Solderers and **brazers** also use heat to join two or more metal items together. Soldering and brazing are similar, except the temperature used to melt the filler metal is lower in soldering. Soldering uses metals with a melting point below 840 degrees Fahrenheit. Brazing uses metals with a higher melting point.

Soldering and brazing workers use molten metal to join two pieces of metal. However, the metal added during the soldering and brazing process has a melting point lower than that of the piece, so only the added metal is melted, not the piece. Therefore, these processes normally do not create the distortions or weaknesses in the pieces that can occur with welding.

Soldering commonly is used to make electrical and electronic circuit boards, such as computer chips. Soldering workers tend to work with small pieces that must be precisely positioned.

Brazing often is used to connect copper plumbing pipes and thinner metals that the higher temperatures of welding would warp. Brazing also can be used to apply coatings to parts to reduce wear and protect against corrosion.

Work Environment

Welders, cutters, solderers, and brazers held about 337,300 jobs in 2010. Industries employing the most welders, cutters, solderers, and brazers in 2010 were as follows:

Manufacturing	61%
Construction	11
Wholesale trade	5
Repair and maintenance	5

Welders and cutters may work outdoors, often in inclement weather, or indoors, sometimes in a confined area designed to contain sparks and glare. When working outdoors, they may work on a scaffold or platform high off the ground. In addition, they may have to lift heavy objects and work in awkward positions while bending, stooping, or standing to work overhead.

Welders, cutters, solderers, and brazers join metals using hand-held welding, flame-cutting, and soldering tools.

Injuries

Welders, cutters, solderers, and brazers often are exposed to a number of hazards, including very hot materials and the intense light created by the arc. They wear safety shoes, goggles, masks with protective lenses, and other equipment to prevent burns and eye injuries and to protect them from falling objects.

The Occupational Safety and Health Administration (OSHA) requires that welders work in safely ventilated areas to avoid danger from inhaling gases and fine particles that can result from welding processes. Because of these hazards, welding, cutting, soldering, and brazing workers have a rate of work-related injuries and illnesses that is higher than most other occupations, but they can minimize injuries if they follow safety procedures.

Work Schedules

Most welders, cutters, solderers, and brazers work full time, and overtime is common. Many manufacturing firms have two or three shifts each day, ranging from 8 to 12 hours, which allow the firm to continue production around the clock if needed. Therefore, welders, cutters, solderers, and brazers may work evenings and weekends.

How to Become a Welder, Cutter, Solderer, or Brazer

Training for welding, cutting, soldering, and brazing workers ranges from a few weeks of school or on-the-job training for low-skilled positions to several years of combined school and on-the-job training for highly skilled jobs.

Education and Training

Formal training is available in high school technical education courses and in postsecondary institutions, such as vocational-technical institutes, community colleges, and private welding, soldering, and brazing schools. The U.S. Armed Forces also operate welding and soldering schools.

Some employers are willing to hire inexperienced entry-level workers and train them on the job, but many prefer to hire workers who have been through formal training programs. Courses in blueprint reading, shop mathematics, mechanical drawing, physics, chemistry, and metallurgy are helpful.

An understanding of electricity also is helpful, and knowledge of computers is gaining importance as welding, soldering, and brazing machine operators become more responsible for programming robots and other computer-controlled machines.

Because understanding the welding process and inspecting welds is important for both welders and welding machine operators, companies hiring machine operators prefer workers with a background in welding.

Certification

Some welding positions require general certification in welding or certification in specific skills, such as inspection or robotic welding. The American Welding Society certification courses are offered at many welding schools. Some employers pay training and testing costs for employees.

The Institute for Printed Circuits offers certification and training in soldering. In industries such as aerospace and defense, which need highly-skilled workers, many employers require these certifications. Certification can show mastery of lead-free soldering techniques, which are important to many employers.

Important Qualities

Detail oriented. Welders, cutters, solderers, and brazers must do precision work, often with straight edges and minimal flaws. Therefore, workers should have a keen eye for detail.

Dexterity. Welders, cutters, solderers, and brazers must have a steady hand to hold a torch in one place. Workers must also have good hand-eye coordination.

Physical strength. Welders, cutters, solderers, and brazers must be in good physical condition. They often must lift heavy pieces of metal and sometimes bend, stoop, or reach while working.

Stamina. The ability to endure long periods of standing or repetitive movements is important for welders, cutters, solderers, and brazers.

Technical skills. Welders, cutters, solderers, and brazers must be able to operate manual or semiautomatic welding equipment to fuse metal segments.

Troubleshooting skills. Welders, cutters, solderers, and brazers must have the ability to detect cracked pieces of metal and be able to repair them.

Visual acuity. The ability to see details and characteristics of the joint and detect changes in molten metal flows requires good eyesight.

Pay

Welders, Cutters, Solderers, and Brazers
Median annual wages, May 2010

Welders, Cutters, Solderers, and Brazers	$35,450
Total, All Occupations	$33,840
Production Occupations	$30,330

Note: All Occupations includes all occupations in the U.S. Economy.
Source: U.S. Bureau of Labor Statistics, Occupational Employment Statistics

The median annual wage of welders, cutters, solderers and brazers was $35,450 in May 2010. The median wage is the wage at which half the workers in an occupation earned more than that amount and half earned less. The lowest 10 percent earned less than $23,940, and the top 10 percent earned more than $53,690.

Wages for welders, cutters, solderers, and brazers vary based on experience, skill level, industry, and company size.

About 17 percent of welders belong to a union.

Although most welders, solderers, cutters, and brazers work full time, overtime is common in this occupation. Many manufacturing firms have two or three shifts each day, ranging from 8 to 12 hours, which allow the firm to continue production around the clock if needed. Therefore, welders, cutters, solderers, and brazers may work evenings and weekends.

Job Outlook

Welders, Cutters, Solderers, and Brazers
Percent change in employment, projected 2010-20

Welders, Cutters, Solderers, and Brazers	15%
Total, All Occupations	14%
Production Occupations	4%

Note: All Occupations includes all occupations in the U.S. Economy.
Source: U.S. Bureau of Labor Statistics, Employment Projections program

Employment of welders, cutters, solderers, and brazers is expected to grow 15 percent from 2010 to 2020, about as fast as the average for all occupations.

Employment growth reflects the need for welders in manufacturing because of the importance and versatility of welding as a manufacturing process. The basic skills of welding are the same across industries, so welders can easily shift from one industry to another, depending on where they are needed most. For example, welders laid off in the automotive manufacturing industry may be able to find work in the oil and gas industry.

Growth of the defense industry, including the manufacturing of aircrafts and missiles, is expected to contribute to employment growth. In addition, the nation's aging infrastructure will require the expertise of many welders, cutters, solderers, and brazers to rebuild bridges, highways, and buildings, resulting in some new jobs.

Job Prospects

Overall job prospects will vary by skill level. Job prospects should be good for welders trained in the latest technologies. Welding schools report that graduates have little difficulty finding work, and many welding employers report difficulty finding properly skilled welders. However, welders who do not have up-to-date training may face competition for jobs.

For all welders, job prospects should be better for those willing to relocate.

Employment projections data for welders, cutters, solderers, and brazers, 2010-20

Occupational Title	SOC Code	Employment, 2010	Projected Employment, 2020	Change, 2010-20	
				Percent	Numeric
Welders, Cutters, Solderers, and Brazers	51-4121	337,300	388,000	15	50,700
SOURCE: U.S. Bureau of Labor Statistics, Employment Projections program					

Similar Occupations

This table shows a list of occupations with job duties that are similar to those of welders, cutters, solderers, and brazers.

Occupation	Job Duties	Entry-Level Education	Median Annual Pay, May 2010
Assemblers and Fabricators	Assemblers and fabricators assemble both finished products and the parts that go into them. They use tools, machines, and their hands to make engines, computers, aircraft, toys, electronic devices, and more.	High school diploma or equivalent	$28,360
Boilermakers	Boilermakers assemble, install, and repair boilers, closed vats, and other large vessels or containers that hold liquids and gases.	High school diploma or equivalent	$54,640
Jewelers and Precious Stone and Metal Workers	Jewelers and precious stone and metal workers design, manufacture, and sell jewelry. They also adjust, repair, and appraise gems and jewelry.	High school diploma or equivalent	$35,170
Machinists and Tool and Die Makers	Machinists and tool and die makers set up and operate a variety of computer-controlled or mechanically-controlled machine tools to produce precision metal parts, instruments, and tools.	High school diploma or equivalent	$39,910
Metal and Plastic Machine Workers	Metal and plastic machine workers set up and operate machines that cut, shape, and form metal and plastic materials or pieces.	High school diploma or equivalent	$31,910
Plumbers, Pipefitters, and Steamfitters	Plumbers, pipefitters, and steamfitters install and repair pipes that carry water, steam, air, or other liquids or gases to and in businesses, homes, and factories.	High school diploma or equivalent	$46,660
Sheet Metal Workers	Sheet metal workers fabricate or install products that are made from thin metal sheets, such as ducts used for heating and air-conditioning.	High school diploma or equivalent	$41,710

Contacts for More Information

For more information about welders, cutters, solderers, and brazers, visit American Welding Society, Fabricators & Manufacturers Association International, Institute for Printed Circuits, Precision Machined Products Association

Suggested citation:

Bureau of Labor Statistics, U.S. Department of Labor, Occupational Outlook Handbook, 2012-13 Edition, Welders, Cutters, Solderers, and Brazers, on the Internet at http://www.bls.gov/ooh/production/welders-cutters-solderers-and-brazers.htm .

Woodworkers

Quick Facts: Woodworkers	
2010 Median Pay	$28,010 per year $13.47 per hour
Entry-Level Education	High school diploma or equivalent
Work Experience in a Related Occupation	None
On-the-job Training	See How to Become One
Number of Jobs, 2010	217,200
Job Outlook, 2010-20	18% (About as fast as average)
Employment Change, 2010-20	39,300

What Woodworkers Do

Woodworkers build a variety of products, such as cabinets and furniture, using wood.

Duties

Woodworkers typically do the following:
- Read detailed schematics and blueprints
- Prepare and set up equipment
- Lift wood pieces onto machines, either by hand or with hoists
- Operate wood-making and cutting machines
- Listen for unusual sounds or detect excessive vibration
- Ensure that products meet specifications, making adjustments as necessary
- Use hand tools to trim pieces or assemble products
- Remove and replace dull saw blades

Despite the abundance of plastics, metals, and other materials, wood products continue to be an important part of our daily lives.

Woodworkers build or carve products using wood.

Woodworkers make wood products, using lumber and synthetic wood materials. Many of these products are mass produced, including most furniture, kitchen cabinets, and musical instruments. Other products are custom made with specialized tools in small shops.

Although the term "woodworker" may evoke the image of a craftsman who builds ornate furniture using hand tools, the modern woodworking trade is highly technical and relies on advanced equipment and highly skilled operators. Workers use automated machinery, such as computerized numerical control (CNC) machines, to do much of the work.

Even specialized artisans generally use a variety of power tools in their work. Much of the work is done in a high-production assembly line facility, but there is also some work that is customized and does not lend itself to being made in an assembly line. Woodworkers are employed in every part of the secondary wood products industry, from sawmill to finished product, and their activities vary.

Woodworkers set up, operate, and tend all types of woodworking machines, such as drill presses, lathes, shapers, routers, sanders, planers, and wood-nailing machines. Operators set up the equipment, cut and shape wooden parts, and verify dimensions, using a template, caliper, and rule. After wood parts are made, woodworkers add fasteners and adhesives and connect the pieces to form a complete unit. They then sand, stain, and, if necessary, coat the wood product with a sealer, such as a lacquer or varnish.

Many of these tasks are handled by different workers with specialized training.

The following are types of woodworkers:

Cabinetmakers and **bench carpenters** cut, shape, assemble, and make parts for wood products. They often design and create sets of cabinets that are customized for particular spaces. In some cases, their duties begin with designing a set of cabinets to specifications and end with installing them.

Furniture finishers shape, finish, and refinish damaged and worn furniture. They often work with antiques and must judge how to best preserve and repair them. They also do the staining and sealing at the end of the process of making wooden products.

Wood sawing machine setters, operators, and tenders specialize in operating specific pieces of woodworking machinery. They often operate computerized numerical control (CNC) machines.

Woodworking machine setters, operators, and tenders, except sawing, operate woodworking machines, such as drill presses, lathes, routers, sanders, and planers.

Work Environment

Woodworkers held about 217,200 jobs in 2010, a majority of which worked in manufacturing industries.

Employment in the detailed occupations that make up woodworkers was distributed as follows:

Cabinetmakers and bench carpenters	97,000
Woodworking machine setters, operators, and tenders, except sawing	60,600
Sawing machine setters, operators, and tenders, wood	39,000
Furniture finishers	20,600

Working conditions vary, depending on specific job duties. Often, workers have to handle heavy, bulky materials, and they encounter a lot of noise and dust. Workers must often wear earplugs, gloves, and goggles to protect themselves. Most work full time during regular business hours.

Injuries

Woodworkers are exposed to several hazards in their work environments. When making wood products or finishing wood surfaces, woodworkers may come into contact with potentially harmful dust, chemicals, or fumes. However, advances in ventilation systems and other safety precautions minimize harmful effects. Other woodworkers work in noisy areas. Often, workers must wear earplugs, gloves, and goggles.

Woodworkers have rates of injuries and illnesses that are higher than the national average. In particular, sawing machine operators experience a work-related injury and illness rate that is much higher than the average for all occupations.

Most injuries for these workers, however, involve sprains, back soreness, carpal tunnel syndrome, hernia, and connective tissue diseases and disorders. These injuries or illnesses come from excessive awkward bending, reaching, twisting, and overexertion or repetition.

How to Become a Woodworker

Although some entry-level jobs can be learned in less than 1 year, becoming a fully trained woodworker requires many skills and generally takes at least 3 years of on-the-job training. Skill with computers and computer-controlled machinery is increasingly important.

Education and Training

Many employers seek applicants who have a high school diploma or the equivalent, because of the growing sophistication of machinery and the constant need for retraining. People seeking woodworking jobs can enhance their employment and advancement prospects by completing high school and getting training in computer applications and math.

Some woodworkers obtain their skills by taking courses at technical schools or community colleges. Others attend universities that offer training in wood technology, furniture manufacturing, wood engineering, and production management. These programs prepare students for jobs in production, supervision, engineering, and management and are increasingly important as woodworking technology advances.

Education is helpful, but woodworkers are primarily trained on the job, where they learn skills from experienced workers. Beginning workers are given basic tasks, such as putting a piece of wood through a machine and catching the wood at the end of the process.

As they gain experience, new woodworkers do more complex tasks with less supervision. In about 1 year, they can learn basic machine operations and job tasks. Becoming a skilled woodworker often takes 3 or more years. Skilled workers can read blueprints, set up machines, and plan work sequences.

Important Qualities

Detail oriented. Woodworkers must pay attention to details to be certain that the products meet specifications and to keep themselves safe.

Dexterity. Woodworkers must make precise cuts with a variety of saws, so they need a steady hand and good hand-eye coordination.

Math skills. Knowledge of basic math and computer skills are important, particularly for those who work in manufacturing, where technology continues to advance. Woodworkers need to understand geometry to visualize how the wood pieces will fit together to make a 3-dimensional object, such as a cabinet or piece of furniture.

Mechanical skills. Modern technology systems require woodworkers be able to use programmable devices, computers, and robots on the factory floor.

Physical strength. Woodworkers must be strong enough to lift bulky and heavy sheets of wood, such as plywood.

Stamina. The ability to endure long periods of standing and repetitive movements is crucial for woodworkers, as they often stand for extended periods when manufacturing parts and products.

Technical skills. Woodworkers must be able to understand blueprints and technical manuals for a range of products and machines.

Troubleshooting skills. To avoid unnecessary and costly waste, woodworkers must recognize mistakes during the manufacturing or finishing process.

Pay

Woodworkers
Median hourly wages, May 2010

Total, All Occupations	$16.27
Production Occupations	$14.58
Woodworkers	$13.47

Note: All Occupations includes all occupations in the U.S. Economy.
Source: U.S. Bureau of Labor Statistics, Occupational Employment Statistics

The median hourly wage of woodworkers was $13.47 in May 2010. The median wage is the wage at which half the workers in an occupation earned more than that amount and half earned less. The lowest 10 percent earned less than $8.94, and the highest 10 percent earned more than $20.56.

Median hourly wages for woodworker occupations in May 2010 were the following:
- $14.48 for cabinetmakers and bench carpenter
- $13.37 for furniture finishers
- $12.75 for woodworking machine setters, operators, and tenders, except sawing
- $12.59 for sawing machine setters, operators, and tenders, wood
- $11.79 for all other woodworkers

Job Outlook

Woodworkers
Percent change in employment, projected 2010-20

Woodworkers	18%
Total, All Occupations	14%
Production Occupations	4%

Note: All Occupations includes all occupations in the U.S. Economy.
Source: U.S. Bureau of Labor Statistics, Employment Projections program

Employment of woodworkers is projected to grow 18 percent from 2010 to 2020, about as fast as the average for all occupations.

Employment growth will stem from growing demand for domestic wood products. In addition, increases in population, personal income, and business spending and the continuing need for repair and renovation of residential and commercial properties will likely require more woodworkers.

Employment growth should be good for woodworkers who specialize in items used in renovation, such as moldings, cabinets, stairs, and windows. Firms that focus on custom woodwork should be able to compete against imports without the need to outsource jobs to other countries.

Increasing use of automated systems is expected to require more workers to operate and maintain the newer equipment in manufacturing establishments.

Job Prospects

Those with advanced skills, including advanced math and the ability to read blueprints, should have the best job opportunities in manufacturing industries. Woodworkers who know how to create and carry out custom designs on a computer will likely be in strong demand. Some job openings will result from the need to replace those who retire or leave the occupation for other reasons.

However, employment in all woodworking specialties is highly sensitive to economic cycles. During economic downturns, workers are subject to layoffs or reductions in hours.

Employment projections data for woodworkers, 2010-20

Occupational Title	SOC Code	Employment, 2010	Projected Employment, 2020	Change, 2010-20 Percent	Change, 2010-20 Numeric
Woodworkers	—	217,200	256,500	18	39,300
Cabinetmakers and Bench Carpenters	51-7011	97,000	113,300	17	16,300
Furniture Finishers	51-7021	20,600	21,800	6	1,100
Sawing Machine Setters, Operators, and Tenders, Wood	51-7041	39,000	48,600	25	9,600
Woodworking Machine Setters, Operators, and Tenders, Except Sawing	51-7042	60,600	72,900	20	12,200
SOURCE: U.S. Bureau of Labor Statistics, Employment Projections program					

Similar Occupations

This table shows a list of occupations with job duties that are similar to those of woodworkers.

Occupation	Job Duties	Entry-Level Education	Median Annual Pay, May 2010
Carpenters	Carpenters construct and repair building frameworks and structures—such as stairways, doorframes, partitions, and rafters—made from wood and other materials. They also may install kitchen cabinets, siding, and drywall.	High school diploma or equivalent	$39,530
Computer Programmers	Computer programmers write code to create software programs. They turn the program designs created by software developers and engineers into instructions that a computer can follow.	Bachelor's degree	$71,380
Machinists and Tool and Die Makers	Machinists and tool and die makers set up and operate a variety of computer-controlled or mechanically-controlled machine tools to produce precision metal parts, instruments, and tools.	High school diploma or equivalent	$39,910
Sheet Metal Workers	Sheet metal workers fabricate or install products that are made from thin metal sheets, such as ducts used for heating and air-conditioning.	High school diploma or equivalent	$41,710
Structural Iron and Steel Workers	Structural iron and steel workers install iron or steel beams, girders, and columns to form buildings, bridges, and other structures. They are often referred to as ironworkers.	High school diploma or equivalent	$44,540

Contacts for More Information

For more information about woodworkers, visit Architectural Woodwork Institute, The Association for Manufacturing Technology, Fabricators & Manufacturers Association International, National Tooling and Machining Association, WoodLINKS, Wood Machinery Manufacturers of America, Woodworking Machinery Industry Association

Suggested citation:

Bureau of Labor Statistics, U.S. Department of Labor, Occupational Outlook Handbook, 2012-13 Edition, Woodworkers, on the Internet at http://www.bls.gov/ooh/production/woodworkers.htm .

Protective Service Occupations

Correctional Officers

Quick Facts: Correctional Officers	
2010 Median Pay	$39,020 per year $18.76 per hour
Entry-Level Education	High school diploma or equivalent
Work Experience in a Related Occupation	None
On-the-job Training	Moderate-term on-the-job training
Number of Jobs, 2010	493,100
Job Outlook, 2010-20	5% (Slower than average)
Employment Change, 2010-20	26,000

What Correctional Officers Do

Correctional officers are responsible for overseeing individuals who have been arrested and are awaiting trial or who have been sentenced to serve time in a jail, reformatory, or prison. Typically, offenders serving time at county jails are sentenced to a year or less. Those serving a year or more are usually in state or federal prisons.

Duties

Correctional officers typically do the following:

- Enforce rules and keep order within jails or prisons
- Supervise activities of inmates
- Aid in rehabilitation and counseling of offenders
- Inspect conditions within facilities to ensure that they meet established standards
- Search inmates for contraband items
- Report on inmate conduct

Inside the prison or jail, correctional officers enforce rules and regulations. They maintain security by preventing any disturbances, assaults, or escapes. Correctional officers supervise the daily activities of inmates, ensuring that inmates obey the rules and finish their work. Correctional officers also ensure that they know where all inmates are.

Officers must search inmates for contraband such as weapons or drugs, settle disputes between inmates, and enforce discipline. The officers enforce regulations through effective communication and the use of progressive sanctions, which involve punishments such as loss of privileges. Sanctions are progressive in that they start out small for a lesser or single offense but become more severe for more serious offenses or when repeat offenses occur. In addition, officers may aid inmates in their rehabilitation by scheduling work assignments, counseling, and educational opportunities.

Correctional officers periodically inspect facilities. They check cells and other areas for unsanitary conditions, contraband, signs of a security breach such as any tampering with window bars or doors, and any other evidence of violations of the rules. Officers also inspect mail and visitors for prohibited items. They write reports or fill out daily logs detailing inmate behavior and anything of note that occurred during their shift.

Correctional officers may have to restrain inmates in handcuffs and leg irons to escort them safely to and from cells and other areas and to see authorized visitors. Officers also escort prisoners between the institution and courtrooms, medical facilities, and other destinations.

Correctional officers cannot show favoritism and must report any inmate who violates the rules. If a crime is committed within their institution or an inmate escapes, they help the responsible law enforcement authorities investigate or search for the escapee.

Correctional officers have no responsibilities for law enforcement outside of their place of work. For information on other law enforcement occupations, see the profile on police and detectives . For information on counseling offenders outside of prisons, see the profile on probation officers and correctional treatment specialists .

Bailiffs, also known as marshals or court officers, are law enforcement officers who maintain safety and order in courtrooms. Their duties, which vary by location, include enforcing courtroom rules, assisting judges, guarding juries from outside contact, delivering court documents, and providing general security for courthouses.

Work Environment

Correctional officers held about 493,100 jobs in 2010. Ninety-five percent of correctional officers worked for federal, state, and local governments in May 2010. Most of the remainder were employed by private companies that provide correctional services to prisons and jails.

Working in a correctional institution can be stressful and dangerous. Every year, correctional officers are injured in confrontations with inmates. Correctional officers have one of the highest rates of nonfatal on-the-job injuries. Correctional officers may work indoors or outdoors. Some correctional institutions are well

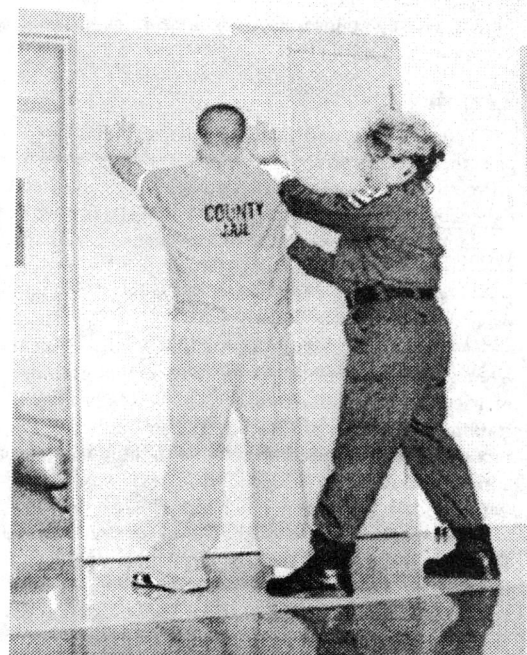

Correctional officers may need to search inmates for prohibited items.

931

lighted, temperature controlled, and ventilated, but others are old, overcrowded, hot, and noisy.

Because offenders typically stay longer in state and federal prisons than in county jails, correctional officers in prisons come to know the people with whom they are dealing. They know what they need in terms of security and being taken care of. Therefore, state and federal prisons tend to be safer places to work than county jails.

Injuries

Correctional officers have a higher rate of injury and illness than the national average. They may face physical injury when conflicts with inmates occur. They may also be exposed to contagious diseases at work, although precautions are taken to avoid this possibility. The job demands that officers be alert and ready to react throughout their entire shift. The work can be stressful, and some officers experience anxiety.

Work Schedules

Correctional officers usually work 8 hours per day, 5 days per week, on rotating shifts. Some correctional facilities have longer shifts and more days off between scheduled workweeks. Because jail and prison security must be provided around the clock, officers work all hours of the day and night, weekends, and holidays. In addition, officers may be required to work paid overtime.

How to Become a Correctional Officer

Correctional officers go through a training academy and then are assigned to a facility for on-the-job training. Qualifications vary by agency, but all agencies require a high school diploma or equivalent. Some also require some college education or work experience.

Education

Correctional officers must have at least a high school diploma or equivalent. Some state and local corrections agencies require some college credits, but law enforcement or military experience may be substituted for this requirement. For employment in federal prisons, the Federal Bureau of Prisons requires entry-level correctional officers to have at least a bachelor's degree; 3 years of full-time experience in a field providing counseling, assistance, or supervision to individuals; or a combination of the two.

Training

Federal, state, and some local departments of corrections, as well as some private corrections companies, provide training for correctional officers based on guidelines established by the American Correctional Association (ACA). Some states have regional training academies that are available to local agencies. Academy trainees receive instruction in a number of subjects, including institutional policies, regulations, and operations, as well as custody and security procedures.

After formal academy instruction, state and local correctional agencies provide on-the-job training, including training on legal restrictions and interpersonal relations. Many systems also provide training in firearms proficiency and self-defense. Trainees typically receive several weeks or months of training in a job under the supervision of an experienced officer. However, on-the-job training varies widely from agency to agency.

New federal correctional officers must undergo 200 hours of formal training within the first year of employment, including 120 hours of specialized training at the U.S. Federal Bureau of Prisons residential training center. Experienced officers receive annual in-service training to keep up on new developments and procedures.

Correctional officers who are members of prison tactical response teams are trained to respond to disturbances, riots, hostage situations, and other potentially dangerous confrontations. Team members practice disarming prisoners, wielding weapons, and using other tactics to maintain the safety of inmates and officers alike.

Certification

Officers may complete a variety of certifications that provide additional resources for their daily work. These certifications also are a means to further the officers' careers because they may lead to promotions.

Advancement

Qualified officers may advance to the position of correctional sergeant, who is responsible for maintaining security and directing the activities of other officers. Qualified officers also can be promoted to supervisory or administrative positions, including warden. Officers sometimes transfer to related jobs, such as probation officer, parole officer, or correctional treatment specialist. For more information, see the profile on probation officers and correctional treatment specialists .

Important Qualities

Critical-thinking skills. Correctional officers must determine the best practical approach to solving a problem.

Good judgment. Officers must use both their training and common sense to quickly determine the best course of action and to take necessary steps to achieve a desired outcome.

Interpersonal skills. Correctional officers must be able to interact and effectively communicate with inmates and others to maintain order in correctional facilities and courtrooms.

Negotiation skills. Officers must be able to assist others in resolving differences to avoid conflict.

Physical strength. Correctional officers must have the strength to physically move or subdue inmates.

Self discipline. Correctional officers must control their emotions when confronted with hostile situations.

Writing skills. Officers must be able to understand and learn training materials and write reports regularly.

Correctional officers usually must be at least 18 to 21 years of age, must be a U.S. citizen or permanent resident, and must have no felony convictions. New applicants for federal corrections positions must be appointed before they are 37 years old.

Pay

Correctional Officers
Median annual wages, May 2010

Law Enforcement Workers	$48,720
Correctional Officers and Jailers	$39,040
Bailiffs	$38,570
Total, All Occupations	$33,840

Note: All Occupations includes all occupations in the U.S. Economy.
Source: U.S. Bureau of Labor Statistics, Occupational Employment Statistics

The median annual wage of correctional officers and jailers was $39,040 in May 2010. The median wage is the wage at which half the workers in an occupation earned more than that amount and half earned less. The lowest 10 percent earned less than $26,040, and the top 10 percent earned more than $67,250.

The median annual wage in the public sector was $54,310 in the federal government, $38,690 in state government, and $38,980 in local government in May 2010. In the facilities support services industry, in which a relatively small number of officers employed by privately operated prisons is classified, the median annual wage was $30,460.

The median annual wage of bailiffs was $38,570 in May 2010. The lowest 10 percent earned less than $18,980, and the top 10 percent earned more than $66,400. The median annual wage of bailiffs employed by local governments was $34,490.

In addition to receiving typical benefits, correctional officers employed in the public sector usually are provided with uniforms or with a clothing allowance to buy their own uniforms. Many departments offer retirement benefits, although benefits vary. Unionized correctional officers often have slightly higher wages and benefits.

Correctional officers usually work 8 hours per day, 5 days per week, on rotating shifts. Some correctional facilities have longer shifts and more days off between scheduled workweeks. Because prison and jail security must be provided around the clock, officers work all hours of the day and night, weekends, and holidays. In addition, officers may be required to work paid overtime.

Job Outlook

Correctional Officers
Percent change in employment, projected 2010-20

Total, All Occupations	14%
Bailiffs	8%
Law Enforcement Workers	7%
Correctional Officers and Jailers	5%

Note: All Occupations includes all occupations in the U.S. Economy.
Source: U.S. Bureau of Labor Statistics, Employment Projections program

Employment of correctional officers is expected to grow by 5 percent from 2010 to 2020, slower than the average for all occupations.

Demand for correctional officers will come from population growth. However, because of budgetary constraints and a general downward trend in crime rates in recent years, demand will likely grow at a slower rate. Faced with growing costs for keeping people in prison, many state governments have moved toward laws requiring shorter prison terms and alternatives to prison. Community-based programs designed to rehabilitate offenders and limit their risk of repeated offenses while keeping the public safe may reduce prison rates.

Job Prospects

Some local and state corrections agencies experience high job turnover because of low salaries and shift work, as well as the stress that many correctional officers feel. The need to replace correctional officers who transfer to other occupations, retire, or leave the labor force, coupled with rising employment demand, should generate job openings.

Some employment opportunities also will come in the private sector as public authorities contract with private companies to provide and staff corrections facilities. Some state and federal corrections agencies use private prison services.

Employment projections data for correctional officers, 2010-20

Occupational Title	SOC Code	Employment, 2010	Projected Employment, 2020	Change, 2010-20 Percent	Numeric
Bailiffs, Correctional Officers, and Jailers	33-3010	493,100	519,000	5	26,000
Bailiffs	33-3011	17,800	19,200	8	1,400
Correctional Officers and Jailers	33-3012	475,300	499,800	5	24,500
SOURCE: U.S. Bureau of Labor Statistics, Employment Projections program					

Similar Occupations

This table shows a list of occupations with job duties that are similar to those of correctional officers.

Occupation	Job Duties	Entry-Level Education	Median Annual Pay, May 2010
Police and Detectives	Police officers protect lives and property. Detectives and criminal investigators, who sometimes are called agents or special agents, gather facts and collect evidence of possible crimes. Law enforcement officers' duties depend on the size and type of their organizations.	High school diploma or equivalent	$55,010
Security Guards and Gaming Surveillance Officers	Security guards and gaming surveillance officers patrol and inspect property against fire, theft, vandalism, terrorism, and illegal activity. They monitor people and buildings in an effort to prevent crime.	High school diploma or equivalent	$24,380
Probation Officers and Correctional Treatment Specialists	Probation officers and correctional treatment specialists work with and monitor offenders to prevent them from committing new crimes.	Bachelor's degree	$47,200

Contacts for More Information

For more information about correctional officers, visit American Correctional Association , American Jail Association

For information about career opportunities for correctional officers at the federal level, visit Federal Bureau of Prisons

Information on obtaining a position as a correctional officer with the federal government is available from the Office of Personnel Management through USAJOBS , the federal government's official employment information system.

Suggested citation:

Bureau of Labor Statistics, U.S. Department of Labor, Occupational Outlook Handbook, 2012-13 Edition, Correctional Officers, on the Internet at http://www.bls.gov/ooh/protective-service/correctional-officers.htm .

Fire Inspectors and Investigators

Quick Facts: Fire Inspectors and Investigators	
2010 Median Pay	$52,230 per year $25.11 per hour
Entry-Level Education	High school diploma or equivalent
Work Experience in a Related Occupation	More than 5 years
On-the-job Training	Moderate-term on-the-job training
Number of Jobs, 2010	13,600
Job Outlook, 2010-20	9% (Slower than average)
Employment Change, 2010-20	1,200

What Fire Inspectors and Investigators Do

Fire inspectors visit and inspect buildings and other structures, such as sports arenas and shopping malls, to search for fire hazards and to ensure that federal, state, and local fire codes are met. They also test and inspect fire protection and fire extinguishing equipment to ensure that it works. Fire investigators determine the origin and cause of fires by searching the surrounding scene and collecting evidence.

Duties

Fire inspectors typically do the following:
- Search for fire hazards
- Ensure that buildings comply with fire codes
- Test fire alarms, sprinklers, and other fire protection and extinguishing equipment
- Inspect equipment such as gasoline storage tanks and air compressors
- Review emergency evacuation plans

Fire investigators take photographs and collect evidence at the scene of a fire.

- Conduct follow-up visits when an infraction is found
- Confer with developers and planners to review plans for residential and commercial buildings
- Conduct fire and life safety education programs
- Keep detailed records that can be used in a court of law
Fire investigators typically do the following:
- Collect and analyze evidence
- Interview witnesses
- Determine the origin and cause of a fire
- Process and document evidence, such as photographs and diagrams
- Reconstruct the scene of a fire or arson
- Confer with other specialists, such as chemists, engineers, and attorneys, to analyze information
- Send evidence to laboratories to be tested for fingerprints or an accelerant
- Keep detailed records that can be used in a court of law
- Testify in civil and criminal legal proceedings
Unlike fire inspectors, many fire investigators have police powers and carry a weapon.

Forest fire inspectors and prevention specialists assess fire hazards in both public and residential areas. They look for issues that pose a wildfire risk and recommend ways to reduce the fire hazard. During patrols, they ensure that the public is following fire regulations and report fire conditions to central command.

Work Environment

Fire inspectors and investigators held about 13,600 jobs in 2010.

Most fire inspectors and investigators work for state and local fire departments and law enforcement agencies, although some work for private companies and organizations, such as insurance companies or an attorney's office. Some investigators work for the Bureau of Alcohol, Tobacco, Firearms and Explosives (ATF).

The following table shows the industries that employed the most fire inspectors and investigators in 2010:

Local government, excluding education and hospitals	73%
State government, excluding education and hospitals	18
Insurance carriers and related activities	2
Self-employed workers	1

Fire inspectors and investigators work both in offices and in the field. In the field, inspectors examine public buildings and multi-family residential buildings. They may also visit and inspect other structures, such as arenas and industrial plants. Investigators often visit the scene where a fire has occurred.

Inspectors and investigators must usually wear a uniform. They may also need to wear protective clothing, such as boots, gloves, and a helmet, when working in the field.

Work Schedules

Most fire inspectors and investigators work in shifts. Although the length of the shift may vary, 24 hour shifts are common. Inspectors and investigators often work evenings, weekends, and holidays.

How to Become a Fire Inspector or Investigator

Most fire inspectors and investigators have a high school diploma and experience working in either a fire or police department. They attend training academies and receive on-the-job training in inspection or investigation.

Fire inspectors and investigators usually must pass a background check, which may include a drug test. Most positions also require inspectors to be U.S. citizens and have a valid driver's license.

Education

Most fire inspectors and investigators jobs require a high school diploma. However, some employers prefer candidates with a 2- or 4-year degree in related disciplines, such as fire science, engineering, or chemistry.

Work Experience

Most fire inspectors and investigators are required to have work experience in a related occupation. Some fire departments or law enforcement agencies require investigators to have a certain number of years within the organization or to be a certain rank, such as lieutenant or captain, before they are eligible for promotion to an inspector or investigator position.

Training

Training requirements vary by state, but programs usually include instruction both in a classroom setting and on the job.

Classroom training often takes place at a fire or police academy over the course of several months. A variety of topics are covered, such as guidelines for conducting an inspection or investigation, legal codes, courtroom procedures, hazardous materials and bomb protocols, and the proper use of equipment.

In most agencies, after inspectors and investigators have finished their classroom training, they must also go through on-the-job training or a probationary period, during which they work with a more experienced officer.

After completing training, applicants may need to pass an exam to become certified in their state. Tests often cover information on standards established by the National Fire Protection Association (NFPA). Many agencies require some additional annual training for an inspector or investigator to remain certified.

Most states also require fire investigators who work for private companies to have a private investigation license.

Important Qualities

Communication skills. Inspectors must explain codes clearly, and investigators must carefully interview witnesses.

Critical-thinking skills. Inspectors must be able to recognize code violations and recommend a way to fix the problem. Investigators must be able to analyze evidence and determine a reasonable conclusion.

Detail oriented. Fire inspectors and investigators must notice details when inspecting a site for code violations or investigating the cause of a fire.

Integrity. Inspectors must be consistent in the methods they use to enforce fire codes. Investigators must be unbiased when conducting their research and when testifying as an expert witness in court.

Certification

For fire inspectors, the National Fire Protection Association offers several certifications. Some jobs in the private sector require that job candidates already have these certifications.

Fire investigators may also choose to pursue certification from a nationally recognized professional association, such as the International Association of Arson Investigators (IAAI) - Certified Fire Investigator (CFI) or the National Association of Fire Investigators (NAFI) - Certified Fire and Explosion Investigator (CFEI). The Bureau of Alcohol, Tobacco, Firearms and Explosives (ATF) also offers a CFI certification. However, this program is available only to ATF employees.

Pay

Fire Inspectors and Investigators
Median annual wages, May 2010

Fire Inspectors and Investigators	$52,230
Protective Service Occupations	$36,660
Total, All Occupations	$33,840

Note: All Occupations includes all occupations in the U.S. Economy.
Source: U.S. Bureau of Labor Statistics, Occupational Employment Statistics

The median annual wage of fire inspectors and investigators was $52,230 in May 2010. The median wage is the wage at which half the workers in an occupation earned more than that amount and half earned less. The lowest 10 percent earned less than $34,210, and the top 10 percent earned more than $85,260.

Most fire inspectors and investigators work in shifts. Although the length of the shift may vary, 24 hour shifts are common. Inspectors and investigators often work evenings, weekends, and holidays.

Job Outlook

Fire Inspectors and Investigators
Percent change in employment, projected 2010-20

Total, All Occupations	14%
Protective Service Occupations	11%
Fire Inspectors and Investigators	9%

Note: All Occupations includes all occupations in the U.S. Economy.
Source: U.S. Bureau of Labor Statistics, Employment Projections program

Employment of fire inspectors and investigators is expected to grow 9 percent from 2010 to 2020, slower than average for all occupations.

As cities and other areas grow, there are more buildings to inspect and fires to investigate. Employment of fire inspectors and investigators should grow as the population grows.

Public demand for new and revised codes to make buildings safer will continue. For example working sprinklers will become more commonplace in residential buildings. However, while building codes are always evolving, the demand for inspectors and investigators won't necessarily increase.

Job Prospects

Jobseekers should expect limited opportunities due to competition for limited positions. Those who have experience in fire suppression, have completed some fire suppression education at a community college, or have experience and training related to criminal investigation should have an advantage.

Employment projections data for fire inspectors and investigators, 2010-20

Occupational Title	SOC Code	Employment, 2010	Projected Employment, 2020	Change, 2010-20	
				Percent	Numeric
Fire Inspectors and Investigators	33-2021	13,600	14,800	9	1,200

SOURCE: U.S. Bureau of Labor Statistics, Employment Projections program

Similar Occupations

This table shows a list of occupations with job duties that are similar to those of fire inspectors and investigators.

Occupation	Job Duties	Entry-Level Education	Median Annual Pay, May 2010
Firefighters	Firefighters protect the public by responding to fires and other emergencies. They are frequently the first emergency personnel on the scene of an accident.	Postsecondary non-degree award	$45,250
Private Detectives and Investigators	Private detectives and investigators find facts and analyze information about legal, financial, and personal matters. They offer many services, including verifying people's backgrounds, tracing missing persons, investigating computer crimes, and protecting celebrities.	Some college, no degree	$42,870
Police and Detectives	Police officers protect lives and property. Detectives and criminal investigators, who sometimes are called agents or special agents, gather facts and collect evidence of possible crimes. Law enforcement officers' duties depend on the size and type of their organizations.	High school diploma or equivalent	$55,010

Contacts for More Information

For more information about federal fire investigator jobs, visit Bureau of Alcohol, Tobacco, Firearms and Explosives

For more information about fire inspectors and investigators training, visit National Fire Academy

For information about standards for fire inspectors and investigators, visit National Fire Protection Association

For information about certifications, visit International Association of Arson Investigators , National Association of Fire Investigators

Suggested citation:

Bureau of Labor Statistics, U.S. Department of Labor, Occupational Outlook Handbook, 2012-13 Edition, Fire Inspectors and Investigators, on the Internet at http://www.bls.gov/ooh/protective-service/fire-inspectors-and-investigators.htm .

Firefighters

Quick Facts: Firefighters	
2010 Median Pay	$45,250 per year $21.76 per hour
Entry-Level Education	Postsecondary non-degree award
Work Experience in a Related Occupation	None
On-the-job Training	Long-term on-the-job training
Number of Jobs, 2010	310,400
Job Outlook, 2010-20	9% (Slower than average)
Employment Change, 2010-20	26,600

What Firefighters Do

Firefighters protect the public by responding to fires and other emergencies. They are frequently the first emergency personnel on the scene of an accident.

Duties

Firefighters typically do the following:

- Drive fire trucks and other emergency vehicles to emergencies
- Put out fires using hoses and pumps
- Find and rescue victims in burning buildings or in other emergency conditions
- Treat victims' injuries with emergency medical services
- Prepare written reports on fire or emergency incidents
- Clean and maintain equipment
- Conduct drills and training in fire fighting techniques
- Provide public education on fire safety

When responding to an emergency, firefighters do tasks assigned by a superior officer. They might be responsible for connecting hoses to hydrants, operating pumps to power the hoses, climbing ladders, or using tools to break through debris. Other firefighters might be responsible for providing medical attention.

Most calls firefighters respond to are medical, not fire, emergencies.

Firefighters' duties may change several times while they are at the scene of an emergency. In some cases, they might remain at disaster scenes for days, rescuing trapped survivors and assisting with medical treatment.

Firefighters may specialize in responding to forest fires or hazardous materials incidents.

Forest firefighters use heavy equipment and water hoses to control forest fires. They also frequently create fire lines—a swathe of cut-down trees and dug-up grass in the path of a fire—to deprive a fire of fuel. Some elite forest firefighters, known as smoke jumpers, parachute from airplanes to reach otherwise inaccessible areas.

Some firefighters work in hazardous materials units and are specially trained to control, prevent, and clean up hazardous materials, such as oil spills and chemical accidents. For more information, see the profile on hazardous materials removal workers.

Work Environment

Firefighters held about 310,400 jobs in 2010.

About 91 percent of paid firefighters worked for local governments in 2010. Most of the remainder worked for federal or state governments. Firefighters also work at airports, chemical plants, and other industrial sites. They work in both cities and rural areas.

These employment numbers include only paid career fire fighters. They do not cover volunteer fire fighters.

Volunteer firefighters have the same duties as paid firefighters and account for the majority of firefighters in many areas. According to the National Fire Protection Association, about 70 percent of fire departments were staffed entirely by volunteer firefighters in 2008.

When not on the scene of an emergency, firefighters work at fire stations, where they sleep, eat, and remain on call. When an alarm sounds, firefighters respond, regardless of the weather or the hour.

Injuries

Firefighters generally have a higher rate of injury and illness than the national average. They often encounter dangerous situations, including collapsing floors and walls, traffic accidents, and overexposure to flames and smoke. Firefighters wear protective gear to help lower these risks. The protective gear can be very heavy and hot.

Work Schedules

Firefighters typically work long and varied hours, often about 50 hours a week. Most firefighters work 24-hour shifts on duty and are off the following 48 or 72 hours. Others work 10-hour day shifts for 3 to 4 days, followed by 14-hour night shifts for 3 to 4 nights before receiving 3 to 4 days off. Additional hours may be required when responding to a fire or medical emergency.

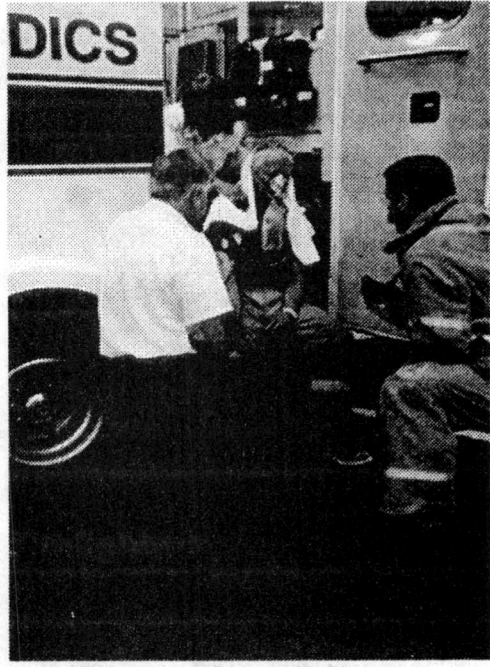

Fire fighting can be a hazardous occupation.

How to Become a Firefighter

Firefighters usually must have at least a high school diploma, but some have a postsecondary degree in fire science or a related discipline. Most firefighters must pass written and physical tests, complete a series of interviews, and hold an emergency medical technician (EMT) certification. All firefighters receive extensive training after being hired.

Applicants for firefighter jobs typically must be at least 18 years old and have a valid driver's license. They must also pass a medical exam and drug screening to be hired. After being hired, firefighters may be monitored on a random basis for drug use.

Education

Most firefighters must have a high school diploma. However, an increasing number of firefighters also have postsecondary education. Some colleges offer certificate programs or degrees in fire engineering or fire science.

Training

Entry-level firefighters receive several weeks of training at fire academies run by the department or by the state. Through classroom instruction and practical training, recruits study fire-fighting and fire-prevention techniques, local building codes, and emergency medical procedures. They also learn how to fight fires with standard equipment, including axes, chain saws, fire extinguishers, and ladders.

Some fire departments have accredited apprenticeship programs that last up to 4 years. These programs combine formal instruction with on-the-job-training under the supervision of experienced firefighters.

In addition to participating in training programs conducted by local or state fire departments and agencies, some firefighters attend federal training sessions sponsored by the National Fire Academy . These training sessions cover topics including executive development, antiarson techniques, disaster preparedness, hazardous materials control, and public fire safety and education.

Important Qualities

Analytical skills. Firefighters need to quickly evaluate emergency scenes and decide what to do.

Communication skills. Firefighters must be able to communicate conditions at an emergency scene to other firefighters and to emergency-response crews.

Courage. Firefighters must enter dangerous situations to do their jobs.

Physical stamina. Firefighters may have to stay at disaster scenes for long periods of time to rescue and to treat victims. They may be called to respond to emergencies at any hour of the day.

Physical strength. Firefighters must be strong enough to move equipment and debris at an emergency site. They also need to be able to carry victims who cannot walk.

Teamwork. When working at dangerous emergency sites, firefighters must work as well-trained teams to react quickly and to minimize injuries.

Certification

Firefighters must usually be certified as emergency medical technicians at the EMT-Basic level. Some fire departments require firefighters to be certified as paramedics.

In some departments, it is possible to earn these certifications after being hired. For more information, see the profile on emergency medical technicians and paramedics.

Some states have mandatory or voluntary firefighter training and certification programs.

Advancement

Fire fighters can be promoted to engineer, then lieutenant, captain, battalion chief, assistant chief, deputy chief, and finally, chief. For promotion to positions beyond battalion chief, many fire departments now require a bachelor's degree, preferably in fire science, public administration, or a related field. The National Fire Academy also offers a certification as executive fire officer. Fire fighters need at least an associate's degree to be eligible for that certification.

Pay

Firefighters

Median annual wages, May 2010

Firefighters	$45,250
Protective Service Occupations	$36,660
Total, All Occupations	$33,840

Note: All Occupations includes all occupations in the U.S. Economy.
Source: U.S. Bureau of Labor Statistics, Occupational Employment Statistics

The median annual wage of firefighters was $45,250 in May 2010. The median wage is the wage at which half the workers in an occupation earned more than that amount and half earned less. The lowest 10 percent earned less than $23,050, and the top 10 percent earned more than $75,390.

In 2010, 67 percent of firefighters were union members or covered by a union contract.

Firefighters typically work long and varied hours. Many work about 50 hours a week. Some firefighters work 24-hour shifts on duty and are off the following 48 or 72 hours. Others work 10-hour day shifts for 3 to 4 days, followed by 14-hour night shifts for 3 to 4 nights before receiving 3 to 4 days off. Additional hours may be required when responding to a fire or medical emergency.

Job Outlook

Firefighters

Percent change in employment, projected 2010-20

Total, All Occupations	14%
Protective Service Occupations	11%
Firefighters	9%

Note: All Occupations includes all occupations in the U.S. Economy.
Source: U.S. Bureau of Labor Statistics, Employment Projections program

Employment of firefighters is expected to grow 9 percent, slower than the average for all occupations.

Continued population growth will increase the number of emergency calls requiring firefighter responses. The majority of situations that firefighters respond to are medical—rather than fire—emergencies, and the aging of the population will lead to an increased demand for emergency responders.

In addition, jobs will be created as volunteer firefighters are converted to paid positions in areas where population growth creates the need for a full-time workforce. An increase in urban populations, where full-time firefighters are more common, also is expected to increase the demand for firefighters.

Job Prospects

Prospective firefighters will face tough competition for positions. Many people are attracted to the job's challenge, opportunity for public service, relatively low formal educational requirements, and pensions that are usually guaranteed after 25 years of service. As a result, a department often receives hundreds or thousands of applicants for a single position. Physically-fit applicants with high test scores, some post-secondary firefighter education, and paramedic training have the best prospects.

Employment projections data for firefighters, 2010-20

Occupational Title	SOC Code	Employment, 2010	Projected Employment, 2020	Change, 2010-20 Percent	Numeric
Firefighters	33-2011	310,400	336,900	9	26,600
SOURCE: U.S. Bureau of Labor Statistics, Employment Projections program					

Similar Occupations

This table shows a list of occupations with job duties that are similar to those of firefighters.

Occupation	Job Duties	Entry-Level Education	Median Annual Pay, May 2010
Correctional Officers	Correctional officers are responsible for overseeing individuals who have been arrested and are awaiting trial or who have been sentenced to serve time in a jail, reformatory, or prison.	High school diploma or equivalent	$39,020
Fire Inspectors and Investigators	Fire inspectors visit and inspect buildings and other structures, such as sports arenas and shopping malls, to search for fire hazards and to ensure that federal, state, and local fire codes are met. They also test and inspect fire protection and fire extinguishing equipment to ensure that it works. Fire investigators determine the origin and cause of fires by searching the surrounding scene and collecting evidence.	High school diploma or equivalent	$52,230
Police and Detectives	Police officers protect lives and property. Detectives and criminal investigators, who sometimes are called agents or special agents, gather facts and collect evidence of possible crimes. Law enforcement officers' duties depend on the size and type of their organizations.	High school diploma or equivalent	$55,010
Security Guards and Gaming Surveillance Officers	Security guards and gaming surveillance officers patrol and inspect property against fire, theft, vandalism, terrorism, and illegal activity. They monitor people and buildings in an effort to prevent crime.	High school diploma or equivalent	$24,380
EMTs and Paramedics	Emergency medical technicians (EMTs) and paramedics care for the sick or injured in emergency medical settings. People's lives often depend on their quick reaction and competent care. EMTs and paramedics respond to emergency calls, performing medical services and transporting patients to medical facilities.	Postsecondary non-degree award	$30,360

Contacts for More Information

For information about a career as a firefighter, contact your local fire department or visit International Association of Fire Fighters , International Association of Women in Fire & Emergency Services , U.S. Fire Administration

For information about professional qualifications and a list of colleges and universities offering 2-year or 4-year degree programs in fire science or fire prevention, visit National Fire Academy

Suggested citation:

Bureau of Labor Statistics, U.S. Department of Labor, Occupational Outlook Handbook, 2012-13 Edition, Firefighters, on the Internet at http://www.bls.gov/ooh/protective-service/firefighters.htm .

Police and Detectives

Quick Facts: Police and Detectives	
2010 Median Pay	$55,010 per year $26.45 per hour
Entry-Level Education	High school diploma or equivalent
Work Experience in a Related Occupation	See How to Become One
On-the-job Training	See How to Become One
Number of Jobs, 2010	794,300
Job Outlook, 2010-20	7% (Slower than average)
Employment Change, 2010-20	58,700

What Police and Detectives Do

Police officers protect lives and property. Detectives and criminal investigators, who sometimes are called agents or special agents, gather facts and collect evidence of possible crimes. Law enforcement officers' duties depend on the size and type of their organizations.

Duties

Uniformed police officers typically do the following:

- Enforce laws
- Respond to calls for service
- Patrol assigned areas
- Conduct traffic stops and issue citations
- Arrest suspects
- Write detailed reports and fill out forms
- Prepare cases and testify in court

Detectives and criminal investigators typically do the following:

- Investigate crimes
- Collect evidence of crimes
- Conduct interviews with suspects and witnesses
- Observe the activities of suspects
- Arrest suspects
- Write detailed reports and fill out forms
- Prepare cases and testify in court

Police officers enforce laws to protect people and their property.

Police officers pursue and apprehend people who break the law and then warn them, cite them, or arrest them. Most police officers patrol their jurisdictions and investigate any suspicious activity they notice. They also respond to calls, issue traffic tickets, investigate domestic issues, and give first aid to accident victims.

Detectives perform investigative duties such as gathering facts and collecting evidence.

The daily activities of police and detectives vary with their occupational specialty and whether they are working for a local, state, or federal agency. Duties also differ among federal agencies, which enforce different aspects of the law. Regardless of job duties or location, police officers and detectives at all levels must write reports and keep detailed records that will be needed if they testify in court.

The following are examples of types of police and detectives who work in state and local law enforcement and in federal law enforcement:

STATE AND LOCAL LAW ENFORCEMENT

Uniformed police officers have general law enforcement duties. They wear uniforms that allow the public to easily recognize them as police officers. They have regular patrols and also respond to calls for service.

Police agencies are usually organized into geographic districts, with uniformed officers assigned to patrol a specific area. Officers in large agencies often patrol with a partner. During patrols, officers look for any signs of criminal activity and may conduct searches or arrest suspected criminals. They may also respond to emergency calls, investigate complaints, and enforce traffic laws.

Some police officers work only on a specific type of crime, such as narcotics. Officers, especially those working in large departments, may also work in special units, such as horseback, motorcycle, and canine corps or special weapons and tactics (SWAT) teams. Typically, officers must work as patrol officers for a certain number of years before they may be appointed to one of these units.

Many city police agencies are involved in community policing, a philosophy of bringing police and members of the community together to prevent crime. A neighborhood watch program is one type of community policing.

Some agencies have special geographic and enforcement responsibilities. Examples include public college and university police forces, public school district police, and transit police. Most law enforcement workers in special agencies are uniformed officers.

State police officers, sometimes called **state troopers** or **highway patrol officers**, have many of the same duties as other police officers, but they may spend more time enforcing traffic laws and issuing traffic citations. State police officers have authority to work anywhere in the state and are frequently called on to help other law enforcement agencies, especially those in rural areas or small towns. State highway patrols operate in every state except Hawaii.

Transit and railroad police patrol railroad yards and transit stations. They protect property, employees, and passengers from crimes such as thefts and robberies. They remove trespassers from railroad and transit properties and check the IDs of people who try to enter secure areas.

Sheriffs and deputy sheriffs enforce the law on the county level. Sheriffs' departments tend to be relatively small. Sheriffs usually are elected by the public and do the same work as a local or county police chief. Some sheriffs' departments do the same work as officers in urban police departments. Others mainly operate the county jails and provide services in the local courts. Police and sheriffs' deputies who provide security in city and county courts are sometimes called bailiffs.

Detectives and criminal investigators are plainclothes investigators who gather facts and collect evidence for criminal cases. They conduct interviews, examine records, observe the activities of suspects, and participate in raids or arrests. Detectives usually specialize in investigating one type of crime, such as homicide or fraud. Detectives are typically assigned cases on a rotating basis and work on them until an arrest and conviction is made or until the case is dropped.

Fish and game wardens enforce fishing, hunting, and boating laws. They patrol hunting and fishing areas, conduct search and rescue operations, investigate complaints and accidents, and educate the public about laws pertaining to their environment.

FEDERAL LAW ENFORCEMENT
Federal law enforcement officials carry out many of the same duties that other police officers do; however, they have jurisdiction over the entire country. Many federal agents are highly specialized. The following are examples of federal agencies in which officers and agents enforce particular types of laws.

- **Federal Bureau of Investigation (FBI) agents** are the federal government's principal investigators, responsible for enforcing more than 300 federal statutes and conducting sensitive national security investigations.
- **U.S. Drug Enforcement Administration (DEA) agents** enforce laws and regulations relating to illegal drugs.
- **U.S. Secret Service uniformed officers** protect the President, the Vice President, their immediate families, and other public officials.
- **Federal Air Marshals** provide air security by guarding against attacks targeting U.S. aircraft, passengers, and crews.
- **U.S. Border patrol agents** protect international land and water boundaries.

See the Contacts for More Information section for more information about federal law enforcement agencies.

Work Environment
Police and detectives held about 794,300 jobs in 2010.

Police and detective work can be physically demanding, stressful, and dangerous. Police officers have one of the highest rates of on-the-job injuries and fatalities.

In addition to confrontations with criminals, police officers and detectives need to be constantly alert and ready to deal appropriately with a number of other threatening scenarios. Officers regularly work at crime or accident scenes and other traumatic events as well as deal with the death and suffering that they encounter. Although a career in law enforcement may take a toll on their private lives, many officers find it rewarding to help members of their communities.

The jobs of some federal agents, such as U.S. Secret Service and DEA special agents, require extensive travel, often on short notice. These agents may relocate a number of times over the course of their careers. Some special agents, such as those in the U.S. Border Patrol, may work outdoors in rugged terrain and in all kinds of weather.

Injuries
Police and detectives have a higher rate of injuries and illness than the national average. They may face physical injury when conflicts with criminals occur, during motor-vehicle pursuits, when exposure to communicable diseases occurs, or through many other high-risk situations. Police work can be both physically and mentally demanding as officers must be alert and ready to react throughout their entire shift. Police and detectives may minimize these risks by following proper procedures.

Work Schedules
Uniformed officers, detectives, agents, and inspectors usually are scheduled to work full time. Paid overtime is common. Shift work is necessary because protection must be provided around the clock. Because more experienced employees typically receive preference, junior officers frequently work weekends, holidays, and nights. Some police officers chose to work off duty as security for restaurants, retail stores, and other establishments.

How to Become a Police Officer or Detective
Education requirements range from a high school diploma to a college or higher degree. Most police and detectives must graduate from their agency's training academy before completing a period of on-the-job training. Candidates must be U.S. citizens, usually at least 21 years old, and meet rigorous physical and personal qualifications.

Important Qualities
Ability to multi-task. Officers and detectives may find that the demands of their job vary from day to day. But multiple tasks and extensive paperwork must be completed on time.

Communication skills. Police and detectives must be able to speak with people when gathering facts about a crime and to then express details about a given incident in writing.

Empathetic personality. Police officers need to understand the perspectives of a wide variety of people in their jurisdiction and have a willingness to help the public.

Good judgment. Police and detectives must be able to determine the best way to solve a wide array of problems quickly.

Leadership skills. Police officers must be comfortable with being a highly visible member of their community, as the public looks to them for assistance in emergency situations.

Perceptiveness. Officers must be able to anticipate another person's reactions and understand why people act a certain way.

Strength and stamina. Officers and detectives must be in good physical shape both to pass required tests for entry into the field and to keep up with the daily rigors of the job.

Education and Training
Police and detective applicants usually must have at least a high school education or GED and be a graduate of their agency's training academy. Many agencies require some college coursework or a college degree. Knowledge of a foreign language is an asset in many federal agencies and urban departments.

Candidates must be U.S. citizens, must usually be at least 21 years old, have a driver's license, and must meet specific physical qualifications. Applicants may have to pass physical exams of vision, hearing, strength, and agility as well as competitive written exams. Previous work or military experience is often seen as a plus. Candidates typically go through a series of interviews and may be asked to take lie detector and drug tests. A felony conviction may disqualify a candidate.

Applicants usually have recruit training before becoming an officer. In state and large local police departments, recruits get training in their agency's police academy. In small agencies, recruits often attend a regional or state academy. Training includes classroom instruction in constitutional law, civil rights, state laws and local ordinances, and police ethics. Recruits also receive training and supervised experience in areas such as patrol, traffic control, use of firearms, self-defense, first aid, and emergency response.

Some police departments have cadet programs for people interested in a career in law enforcement who do not yet meet age requirements for becoming an officer. These cadets do clerical work and attend classes until they reach the minimum age requirement and can apply for a position with the regular force.

Detectives normally begin their career as police officers before being promoted to detective.

State and local agencies encourage applicants to continue their education after high school by taking courses or training related to law enforcement. Many applicants for entry-level police jobs have taken some college classes, and a significant number are college graduates. Many junior colleges, colleges, and universities offer programs in law enforcement or criminal justice. Many agencies offer financial assistance to officers who pursue these or related degrees.

Fish and game wardens also must meet specific requirements; however, these vary. Candidates applying for federal jobs with the U.S. Fish and Wildlife Service typically need a college degree and those applying to work for state departments often need a high school diploma or some college study in a related field such as biology or natural resources management. Military or police experience may be considered an advantage. Once hired, fish and game wardens attend a training academy and sometimes get additional training in the field.

Although similar to state and local requirements, the requirements for federal law enforcement agencies, such as with the FBI or Secret Service, are generally stricter. Federal agencies require a bachelor's degree, related work experience, or a combination of the two. For example, FBI special agent applicants typically must be college graduates with at least 3 years of professional work experience. There are lie detector tests as well as interviews with references. Jobs that require security clearances have additional requirements.

Federal law enforcement agents undergo extensive training, usually at the U.S. Marine Corps base in Quantico, Virginia, or the Federal Law Enforcement Training Center in Glynco, Georgia. Furthermore, some federal positions have a maximum age for applicants. The specific educational requirements, qualifications, and training information for a particular federal agency are available on its website. (See the Contacts for More Info section for links to various federal agencies.)

Advancement

Police officers usually become eligible for promotion after a probationary period. Promotions to corporal, sergeant, lieutenant, and captain usually are made according to a candidate's position on a promotion list, as determined by scores on a written examination and on-the-job performance. In large departments, promotion may enable an officer to become a detective or to specialize in one type of police work, such as working with juveniles.

Federal agents often are on the General Services (GS) pay scale. Most begin at the GS-5 or GS-7 level. As agents meet time-in-grade and knowledge and skills requirements, they move up the GS scale. Jobs at and above GS-13 are often managerial positions. Many agencies hire internally for these supervisory positions. A few agents may be able to enter the Senior Executive Service ranks of upper management.

Pay

Police and Detectives

Median annual wages, May 2010

Police and Detectives	$55,010
Protective Service Occupations	$36,660
Total, All Occupations	$33,840

Note: All Occupations includes all occupations in the U.S. Economy.
Source: U.S. Bureau of Labor Statistics, Occupational Employment Statistics

The median annual wage of police and detectives was $55,010 in May 2010. The median wage is the wage at which half the workers in an occupation earned more than that amount and half earned less. The lowest 10 percent earned less than $32,440, and the top-10 percent earned more than $88,870.

The median wages for police and detectives occupations in May 2010 were as follows:
- $68,820 for detectives and criminal investigators
- $54,330 for transit and railroad police
- $53,540 for police and sheriff's patrol officers
- $49,730 for fish and game wardens

Uniformed officers, detectives, agents, and inspectors usually are scheduled to work full time. Paid overtime is common. Shift work is necessary because protection must be provided around the clock. Because more experienced employees typically receive preference, junior officers frequently work weekends, holidays, and nights.

Many agencies provide officers with an allowance for uniforms as well as extensive benefits and the option to retire at an age that is younger than a more typical retirement age.

Job Outlook

Police and Detectives

Percent change in employment, projected 2010-20

Total, All Occupations	14%
Protective Service Occupations	11%
Police and Detectives	7%

Note: All Occupations includes all occupations in the U.S. Economy.
Source: U.S. Bureau of Labor Statistics, Employment Projections program

Employment of police and detectives is expected to grow by 7 percent from 2010 to 2020, slower than the average for all occupations. Continued demand for public safety will lead to new openings for officers in local departments; however, both state and federal jobs may be more competitive.

Because they typically offer low salaries, many local departments face high turnover rates, making opportunities more plentiful for qualified applicants. However, some smaller departments may have fewer opportunities as budgets limit the ability to hire additional officers.

Jobs in state and federal agencies will remain more competitive as they often offer high pay and more opportunities for both promotions and inter-agency transfers. Bilingual applicants with a bachelor's degree and law enforcement or military experience, especially investigative experience, should have the best opportunities in federal agencies.

The level of government spending determines the level of employment for police and detectives. The number of job opportunities, therefore, can vary from year to year and from place to place. Layoffs are rare because retirements enable most staffing cuts to be handled through attrition. Trained law enforcement officers who lose their jobs because of budget cuts usually have little difficulty finding jobs with other agencies.

Employment projections data for police and detectives, 2010-20

Occupational Title	SOC Code	Employment, 2010	Projected Employment, 2020	Change, 2010-20 Percent	Numeric
Police and Detectives	—	794,300	853,100	7	58,700
Detectives and Criminal Investigators	33-3021	119,400	122,900	3	3,500
Fish and Game Wardens	33-3031	7,600	7,900	5	400
Police and Sheriff's Patrol Officers	33-3051	663,900	718,500	8	54,600
Transit and Railroad Police	33-3052	3,600	3,800	6	200
SOURCE: U.S. Bureau of Labor Statistics, Employment Projections program					

Similar Occupations

This table shows a list of occupations with job duties that are similar to those of police and detectives.

Occupation	Job Duties	Entry-Level Education	Median Annual Pay, May 2010
Correctional Officers	Correctional officers are responsible for overseeing individuals who have been arrested and are awaiting trial or who have been sentenced to serve time in a jail, reformatory, or prison.	High school diploma or equivalent	$39,020
EMTs and Paramedics	Emergency medical technicians (EMTs) and paramedics care for the sick or injured in emergency medical settings. People's lives often depend on their quick reaction and competent care. EMTs and paramedics respond to emergency calls, performing medical services and transporting patients to medical facilities.	Postsecondary non-degree award	$30,360
Firefighters	Firefighters protect the public by responding to fires and other emergencies. They are frequently the first emergency personnel on the scene of an accident.	Postsecondary non-degree award	$45,250
Private Detectives and Investigators	Private detectives and investigators find facts and analyze information about legal, financial, and personal matters. They offer many services, including verifying people's backgrounds, tracing missing persons, investigating computer crimes, and protecting celebrities.	Some college, no degree	$42,870
Probation Officers and Correctional Treatment Specialists	Probation officers and correctional treatment specialists work with and monitor offenders to prevent them from committing new crimes.	Bachelor's degree	$47,200
Security Guards and Gaming Surveillance Officers	Security guards and gaming surveillance officers patrol and inspect property against fire, theft, vandalism, terrorism, and illegal activity. They monitor people and buildings in an effort to prevent crime.	High school diploma or equivalent	$24,380

Contacts for More Information

For general information about sheriffs, visit National Sheriffs' Association

For information about chiefs of police, visit International Association of Chiefs of Police

For more information about careers in state and local law enforcement, visit The IACP and Bureau of Justice Assistance's career website

For more information about federal law enforcement, visit Federal Bureau of Investigation , U.S. Secret Service , Drug Enforcement Administration , U.S. Marshals Service , U.S. Bureau of Alcohol, Tobacco, Firearms, and Explosives , U.S. Customs and Border Protection , U.S. Department of Homeland Security

Suggested citation:

Bureau of Labor Statistics, U.S. Department of Labor, Occupational Outlook Handbook, 2012-13 Edition, Police and Detectives, on the Internet at http://www.bls.gov/ooh/protective-service/police-and-detectives.htm .

Private Detectives and Investigators

Quick Facts: Private Detectives and Investigators	
2010 Median Pay	$42,870 per year $20.61 per hour
Entry-Level Education	Some college, no degree
Work Experience in a Related Occupation	1 to 5 years
On-the-job Training	Moderate-term on-the-job training
Number of Jobs, 2010	34,700
Job Outlook, 2010-20	21% (Faster than average)
Employment Change, 2010-20	7,100

What Private Detectives and Investigators Do

Private detectives and investigators find facts and analyze information about legal, financial, and personal matters. They offer many services, including verifying people's backgrounds, tracing missing persons, investigating computer crimes, and protecting celebrities.

Duties

Private detectives and investigators typically do the following:

- Interview people to gather information
- Do various types of searches, using a computer or non-computerized records
- Conduct surveillance (looking for, following, or watching a person without that person noticing)
- Collect evidence to present in court
- Verify employment, income, and facts on a person's background
- Investigate computer crimes, such as identity theft and illegal downloads
- Help in cases of criminal and civil liability, missing-persons cases, and insurance claims and fraud

Private detectives and investigators typically work for individuals, attorneys, and businesses. Some have their own investigative agency.

Private detectives and investigators offer many services, based on clients' needs. They may perform pre-employment background checks

Private detectives and investigators perform computer searches when researching a crime or conducting a background check.

or look into a charge that someone has been stealing money from a company. They might be hired to prove or disprove infidelity in a divorce case.

Private detectives and investigators use a variety of tools when researching the facts in a case. Much of their work is done with a computer, which allows them to quickly get information, such as records of a person's prior arrests, telephone numbers, social networking-site details, and emails.

They make phone calls to verify facts, such as a person's income and place of employment. They also interview people when conducting a background investigation.

Investigators may go undercover, pretending to be someone else to go unnoticed, to get information, or to observe a suspect.

Detectives also conduct surveillance when investigating a case. They may watch a site, such as the person's home or office, often from an inconspicuous location or a vehicle. Using photographic and video cameras, binoculars, and global positioning systems (GPS), detectives gather information on persons of interest. Surveillance can be time consuming.

Detectives and investigators must be mindful of the law when conducting investigations. They must have a good understanding of federal, state, and local laws, such as privacy laws, and other legal issues affecting their work.

However, as the legality of certain methods may be unclear, investigators and detectives must make use good judgment when deciding how to pursue a case. They must collect evidence properly, so that it can be used legally in court.

The following are examples of types of private detectives and investigators:

Computer forensic investigators specialize in recovering, analyzing, and presenting data from computers for use in investigations or as evidence. They may be able to recover deleted emails and documents.

Legal investigators help prepare criminal defenses, verify facts in civil law suits, locate witnesses, and serve legal documents. They often work for lawyers and law firms.

Corporate investigators conduct internal and external investigations for corporations. Internally, they may investigate drug use in the workplace or ensure that expense accounts are not abused. Externally, they may try to thwart criminal schemes, such as fraudulent billing by a supplier.

Financial investigators may be hired to develop confidential financial profiles of individuals and companies that are prospective parties to large financial transactions. These investigators often are certified public accountants (CPAs), who work closely with investment bankers and other accountants. For more information, see the profile on accountants and auditors . Investigators also might search for assets to recover damages awarded by a court in fraud and theft cases.

Store detectives, also known as **loss prevention agents**, catch people who try to steal merchandise or destroy store property.

Hotel detectives protect guests from theft of their belongings and preserve order in hotel restaurants and bars. They also may keep undesirable individuals, such as known thieves, off the premises.

Work Environment

Private detectives and investigators held about 34,700 jobs in 2010.

Private detectives and investigators work in a wide variety of environments, depending on the case that they are working on. Some spend more time in their offices conducting computer searches and making phone calls. Others spend more time in the field, conducting interviews or doing surveillance.

Investigators generally work alone, but they may work with others while conducting surveillance or following a subject.

Some of the work involves confrontation, so the job can be stressful and dangerous. Some situations, such as certain bodyguard assignments for corporate or celebrity clients, call for the investigator to be armed. In most cases, however, a weapon is not necessary because private detectives and investigators' purpose is information gathering and not law enforcement or criminal apprehension.

Owners of investigative agencies have the added stress of having to deal with demanding and, sometimes, distraught clients.

Private detectives and investigators often work irregular hours because they need to conduct surveillance and to contact people outside of normal work hours. They may work early mornings, evenings, weekends, and holidays. In addition, they may have to work outdoors, or from a vehicle, in all kinds of weather.

How to Become a Private Detective or Investigator

Private detectives and investigators usually have some college education. However, many jobs do not have formal education requirements and private detectives and investigators learn on the job. Previous experience in investigative work can be beneficial. Private detectives and investigators need a license in most states.

Important Qualities

Communication skills. Detectives and investigators must be able to listen carefully and ask appropriate questions when interviewing a person of interest.

Honesty. Detectives and investigators must tell the truth to gain the trust of their clients and people they interview, as well as to establish credibility in a court of law.

Inquisitiveness. Private detectives and investigators must want to ask questions and to search for the truth.

Problem-solving skills. Detectives and investigators must be able to think on their feet and make quick decisions based on the information that they have at a given time.

Resourcefulness. Detectives and investigators must work persistently with whatever leads they have, no matter how limited, to determine the next step toward their goal. They sometimes need to figure out what a person of interest will do next.

Education and Training

Most private detectives and investigators learn on the job.

Although new investigators must learn how to gather information, additional training depends on the type of firm that hires them. For instance, at an insurance company, a new investigator will learn to recognize insurance fraud. Learning by doing, in which new investigators are put on cases and gain skills as they go, is a common approach. Corporate investigators hired by large companies, however, may receive formal training in business practices, management structure, and various finance-related topics.

Private detectives and investigators usually have some college education. Although some investigation jobs may not have specific education requirements, others require candidates to have a high school diploma.

Some jobs may require an associate's or bachelor's degree. Postsecondary courses in criminal justice and political science are helpful to aspiring private detectives and investigators.

Although previous work experience is generally required, some people enter the occupation directly after graduating from college with an associate's degree or bachelor's degree in criminal justice or police science.

Corporate investigators typically need a bachelor's degree. Coursework in finance, accounting, and business is often preferred. Because many financial investigators have an accountant's background, they typically have a bachelor's degree in accounting or a related field.

Many computer forensics investigators need a bachelor's degree in a related field, such as computer science or criminal justice. Many colleges and universities now offer certificate programs in computer forensics, and others offer a bachelor's or a master's degree. Because computer forensics specialists need both computer skills and investigative skills, extensive training may be required.

Many computer forensic investigators learn their trade while working for a law enforcement agency, where they are taught how to gather evidence and to spot computer-related crimes. Many people enter law enforcement to get this training and to establish a reputation before moving on to the private sector.

Because they work with changing technologies, computer forensic investigators never stop training. They must learn the latest methods of fraud detection and new software programs and operating systems by attending conferences and courses offered by software vendors and professional associations.

Work Experience

Private detectives and investigators typically have previous work experience. Some have worked for insurance or collections companies, as paralegals, in finance, or in accounting. Many investigators enter the field after serving in law enforcement, the military, or federal intelligence jobs. These people, who frequently are able to retire after 25 years of service, often become private detectives or investigators as a second career.

Licenses

Most states license private detectives and investigators. However, requirements vary by state. Some states have few requirements, and many others have stringent regulations.

In most states, detectives and investigators who carry handguns must meet additional requirements. Some states require an additional license to work as a bodyguard.

Because laws change, jobseekers should verify the licensing laws related to private investigators with the state and locality in which they want to work.

There are no licenses specifically for computer forensic investigators, but some states require them to be licensed private investigators. Even in states or localities where licensure is not required, having a private investigator license is useful, because it allows computer forensic investigators to do follow-up and related investigative work.

Certification

Some private detectives and investigators can get certification from a professional organization to demonstrate competency, which may help them to advance their careers. For investigators who specialize in negligence or criminal defense investigation, the National Association of Legal Investigators offers the Certified Legal Investigator certification. For investigators who specialize in security, ASIS International offers the Professional Certified Investigator certification.

Advancement

Most private detective agencies are small, with little room for advancement. Usually, there are no defined ranks or steps, so advancement takes the form of increases in salary and better assignments. Many detectives and investigators start their own firms after gaining a few years of experience. Corporate and legal investigators may rise to supervisor or manager of the security or investigations department.

Pay

Private Detectives and Investigators
Median annual wages, May 2010

Private Detectives and Investigators	$42,870
Protective Service Occupations	$36,660
Total, All Occupations	$33,840

Note: All Occupations includes all occupations in the U.S. Economy.
Source: U.S. Bureau of Labor Statistics, Occupational Employment Statistics

The median annual wage of private detectives and investigators was $42,870 in May 2010. The median wage is the wage at which half the workers in an occupation earned more than that amount and half earned less. The lowest 10 percent earned less than $25,760, and the top 10 percent earned more than $74,970.

Private detectives and investigators often work irregular hours because they need to conduct surveillance and to contact people outside of normal work hours. They may work early mornings, evenings, weekends, and holidays. In addition, they may have to work outdoors, or from a vehicle, in all kinds of weather.

Job Outlook

Private Detectives and Investigators
Percent change in employment, projected 2010-20

Private Detectives and Investigators	21%
Total, All Occupations	14%
Protective Service Occupations	11%

Note: All Occupations includes all occupations in the U.S. Economy.
Source: U.S. Bureau of Labor Statistics, Employment Projections program

Employment of private detectives and investigators is expected to grow 21 percent from 2010 to 2020, faster than the average for all occupations. Increased demand for private detectives and investigators will stem from heightened security concerns and the need to protect property and confidential information.

Technological advances have led to an increase in cyber crimes, such as identity theft and spamming. Internet scams, as well as various other types of financial and insurance fraud, create demand for investigative services.

Background checks will continue to be a source of work for many investigators, as both employers and personal contacts want to verify that people are credible. More individuals are investigating care facilities, such as childcare providers and hospitals.

Job Prospects

Competition is expected for most jobs, because private detective and investigator careers attract many qualified people, including relatively young retirees from law enforcement or military careers.

The best opportunities for jobseekers will be in entry-level jobs in detective agencies. People with related work experience, as well as those with interviewing and computer skills, may find more opportunities.

Employment projections data for private detectives and investigators, 2010-20

Occupational Title	SOC Code	Employment, 2010	Projected Employment, 2020	Change, 2010-20	
				Percent	Numeric
Private Detectives and Investigators	33-9021	34,700	41,900	21	7,100

SOURCE: U.S. Bureau of Labor Statistics, Employment Projections program

Similar Occupations

This table shows a list of occupations with job duties that are similar to those of private detectives and investigators.

Occupation	Job Duties	Entry-Level Education	Median Annual Pay, May 2010
Bill and Account Collectors	Bill and account collectors, sometimes called collectors, try to recover payment on overdue bills. They negotiate repayment plans with debtors and help them find solutions to make paying their overdue bills easier.	High school diploma or equivalent	$31,310
Accountants and Auditors	Accountants and auditors prepare and examine financial records. They ensure that financial records are accurate and that taxes are paid properly and on time. Accountants and auditors assess financial operations and work to help ensure that organizations run efficiently.	Bachelor's degree	$61,690
Claims Adjusters, Appraisers, Examiners, and Investigators	Claims adjusters, appraisers, examiners, and investigators evaluate insurance claims. They decide whether an insurance company must pay a claim, and if so, how much.	See How to Become One	$58,460
Financial Analysts	Financial analysts provide guidance to businesses and individuals making investment decisions. They assess the performance of stocks, bonds, and other types of investments.	Bachelor's degree	$74,350

Personal Financial Advisors	Personal financial advisors give financial advice to people. They help with investments, taxes, and insurance decisions.	Bachelor's degree	$64,750
Police and Detectives	Police officers protect lives and property. Detectives and criminal investigators, who sometimes are called agents or special agents, gather facts and collect evidence of possible crimes. Law enforcement officers' duties depend on the size and type of their organizations.	High school diploma or equivalent	$55,010
Security Guards and Gaming Surveillance Officers	Security guards and gaming surveillance officers patrol and inspect property against fire, theft, vandalism, terrorism, and illegal activity. They monitor people and buildings in an effort to prevent crime.	High school diploma or equivalent	$24,380

Contacts for More Information

For more information about private detectives and investigators, including certification information and a list of colleges and universities that offer security-related courses, visit National Association of Legal Investigators, ASIS International

Suggested citation:

Bureau of Labor Statistics, U.S. Department of Labor, Occupational Outlook Handbook, 2012-13 Edition, Private Detectives and Investigators, on the Internet at http://www.bls.gov/ooh/protective-service/private-detectives-and-investigators.htm .

Security Guards and Gaming Surveillance Officers

Quick Facts: Security Guards and Gaming Surveillance Officers	
2010 Median Pay	$24,380 per year $11.72 per hour
Entry-Level Education	High school diploma or equivalent
Work Experience in a Related Occupation	None
On-the-job Training	See How to Become One
Number of Jobs, 2010	1,090,600
Job Outlook, 2010-20	18% (About as fast as average)
Employment Change, 2010-20	200,200

What Security Guards and Gaming Surveillance Officers Do

Security guards and gaming surveillance officers patrol and inspect property against fire, theft, vandalism, terrorism, and illegal activity. They monitor people and buildings in an effort to prevent crime.

Duties

Security guards and gaming surveillance officers typically do the following:

- Protect and enforce laws on an employer's property
- Monitor alarms and closed-circuit TV cameras
- Control access for employees, visitors, and outside contractors
- Conduct security checks over a specified area
- Write comprehensive reports outlining what they observed while on patrol
- Interview witnesses for later court testimony
- Detain criminal violators

Guards must remain alert, looking for anything out of the ordinary throughout their shift. In an emergency, guards may call for assistance from police, fire, or ambulance services. Some security guards may be armed.

A security guard's job responsibilities vary from one employer to another. In retail stores, guards protect people, records, merchandise, money, and equipment. They may work with undercover store detectives to prevent theft by customers or employees, detain shoplifting suspects until the police arrive, or patrol parking lots.

In office buildings, banks, hotels, and hospitals, guards maintain order and protect the organization's customers, staff, and property. Guards who work in museums or art galleries protect paintings and exhibits by watching people and inspecting packages entering and leaving the building. In factories, government buildings, and military bases, security guards protect information and products and check the credentials of people and vehicles entering and leaving the premises.

Guards working at universities, in parks, and at sports stadiums do crowd control, supervise parking and seating, and direct traffic. Security guards stationed at the entrance to bars and nightclubs keep under-age people from entering, collect cover charges at the door, and maintain order among customers.

Guards who work as transportation security screeners protect people, transportation equipment, and freight at airports, train stations, and other transportation facilities.

The following are examples of types of security guards and gaming surveillance officers:

Security guards, also called **security officers,** protect property, enforce laws on the property, deter criminal activity, and deal with other problems. Some guards are assigned a stationary position from which they may monitor alarms or surveillance cameras. Other guards may be assigned a patrol area where they conduct security checks.

Transportation security screeners, many of whom are Transportation Security Administration (TSA) officers, work at air, sea, and rail terminals and other transportation facilities, protecting people, freight, property, and equipment. They use metal detectors, x-ray machines, and other equipment to screen passengers and visitors for weapons and explosives, ensure that nothing is stolen while a vehicle is being loaded or unloaded, and watch for fires and criminals. Some officers work with dogs, which alert them to the presence of

Security guards monitor closed-circuit TV cameras, looking for any indication of criminal activity.

dangerous materials, such as bombs.

Armored car guards protect money and valuables during transit. They pick up money or other valuables from businesses and transport them to another location. These guards usually wear bulletproof vests and carry firearms, because transporting money between the truck and the business can be extremely hazardous.

Gaming surveillance officers, also known as **surveillance agents** and **gaming investigators**, act as security agents for casino employees, managers, and patrons. Using audio and video equipment in an observation room, they watch casino operations for irregular activities, such as cheating or theft, and monitor compliance with rules, regulations, and laws. They maintain and organize recordings from security cameras, which are sometimes used as evidence in police investigations. In addition, surveillance agents occasionally leave the observation room and walk the casino floor.

Work Environment

Security guards and gaming surveillance officers held about 1.1 million jobs in 2010. Security guards work in a wide variety of environments, including public buildings, retail stores, and office buildings. Guards who serve as transportation security screeners work in air, sea, and rail terminals and other transportation facilities. Gaming surveillance officers do most of their work in casino observation rooms, using audio and video equipment.

The following industries employed the most security guards and gaming surveillance officers in 2010:

Investigation and security services	53%
Government	9
Educational services; state, local, and private	6
Accommodation and food services	5
Hospitals; state, local, and private	4

In 2010, most gaming surveillance officers worked in gaming industries, casino hotels, and local governments. They are employed only in those states, and on those Indian reservations, where gambling is legal.

Transportation security screeners are employed by the federal government.

Most security guards and gaming surveillance officers spend considerable time on their feet, either assigned to a specific post or patrolling buildings and grounds. Some may sit for long hours behind a counter or in a guardhouse at the entrance to a gated facility or community.

Guards who work during the day may have a great deal of contact with other employees and the public.

Although the work can be routine, it can also be hazardous, particularly when an altercation occurs.

Injuries

Gaming surveillance officers have one of the highest rates of injury and illness of any occupation and security guards have a higher rate than the national average. The work usually is routine, but these jobs can be hazardous. Guards must be constantly alert for threats to themselves and the property they are protecting.

Work Schedules

Security guards and gaming surveillance officers provide surveillance around the clock by working shifts of 8 hours or longer with rotating schedules. Some security guards choose to work part time while others may take on a second job.

How to Become a Security Guard or Gaming Surveillance Officer

Most security guard jobs require an applicant to have a high school diploma or GED. Gaming surveillance officers sometimes need additional coursework beyond a high school diploma. Most states require guards to be licensed.

Important Qualities

Communication skills. Security guards must be able to speak with members of the public, suspected offenders, and law enforcement officers.

Decision-making skills. Guards must be able to quickly determine the best course of action when a dangerous situation arises.

Honesty. Guards must be honest because they are trusted to protect confidential information or expensive equipment.

Observation skills. Guards must be alert and aware of their surroundings, able to quickly recognize anything out of the ordinary.

Physical strength. Guards must be strong enough to deal with offenders and to handle emergency situations.

Education and Training

Unarmed guards generally need to have a high school diploma or GED, although some jobs may not have any specific educational requirement. For armed guards, employers usually prefer people who are high school graduates or who have some coursework in criminal justice.

Some employers prefer to hire security guards with some higher education, such as a police science or criminal justice degree. Programs and courses that focus specifically on security guards also are available at some postsecondary schools.

Many employers give newly hired guards instruction before they start the job and provide on-the-job training. The amount of training guards receive varies. Training covers numerous topics, such as emergency procedures, detention of suspected criminals, and communication skills.

ASIS International has written voluntary guidelines that recommend minimum criteria for selecting and training private security officers. The guidelines recommend that security guards receive preassignment training in accordance with all applicable legal requirements, 8–16 hours of on-the-job training, and 8 hours of annual training. This may include training in protection, public relations, report writing, deterring crises, first aid, and specialized training related to the guard's assignment. The guidelines also recommend that security guards be required to pass one or more written or performance exams.

In addition, the guidelines recommend annual firearms training for armed officers as required by the state in which they work. Training is more rigorous for armed guards because their employers are legally responsible for any use of force. Armed guards may be periodically tested in the use of firearms.

Transportation security screeners who work for the TSA must have a high school diploma, a GED, or 1 year of related work experience. They must be at least 18 years old and a U.S. citizen. TSA screeners must pass a background check, drug testing, and a physical exam. Candidates who meet these requirements must complete both classroom and on-the-job training before passing a certification exam. Ongoing training is usually required.

Gaming surveillance officers and investigators usually need some training beyond high school, but not necessarily a bachelor's degree. Several educational institutions offer certification programs. Classroom training generally is conducted in a casino like atmosphere and includes the use of surveillance camera equipment. Employers may prefer individuals with casino experience or investigation experience. Technical skills and experience with computers also is a plus.

Licenses

Most states require that guards be licensed. To be licensed as a guard, individuals must usually be at least 18 years old, pass a background check, and complete classroom training. However, licensing requirements vary from state to state.

Drug testing is often required and may be ongoing and random. Many jobs also require a driver's license. An increasing number of states are making ongoing training a legal requirement for keeping a license.

Guards who carry weapons must be licensed by the appropriate government authority. Armed guard positions also have more stringent background checks and entry requirements than those of unarmed guards. Rigorous hiring and screening programs, including background, criminal record, and fingerprint checks, are typical for armed guards.

Certification

In addition to being licensed, some security guards may choose to become certified. ASIS International offers the Certified Protection Professional certification for security workers who want a transferable validation of their knowledge and skills.

Advancement

Because many people do not stay long in this occupation, opportunities for advancement are good for those who make a career in security.

Some guards may advance to positions of supervisor or security manager. Guards with postsecondary education or with related certifications may be preferred. Armed security guards have a greater potential for advancement and enjoy higher earnings.

Guards with management skills may open their own contract security guard agencies. Guards also can move to an organization that needs higher levels of security, which may result in more prestige or higher pay.

Pay

Security Guards and Gaming Surveillance Officers
Median annual wages, May 2010

Transportation Security Screeners (Federal Only)	$37,070
Total, All Occupations	$33,840
Gaming Surveillance Officers and Gaming Investigators	$30,680
Security Guards and Gaming Surveillance Officers	$24,380
Security Guards	$23,920

Note: All Occupations includes all occupations in the U.S. Economy.
Source: U.S. Bureau of Labor Statistics, Occupational Employment Statistics

The median annual wage of security guards and gaming surveillance officers was $24,380 in May 2010. The median wage is the wage at which half the workers in an occupation earned more than that amount and half earned less. The lowest 10 percent earned $17,210, and the top 10 percent earned more than $41,680.

The median annual wages for security guard and gaming surveillance officer occupations in May 2010 were as follows:
- $37,070 for transportation security screeners
- $30,680 for gaming surveillance officers and gaming investigators
- $23,920 for security guards

Security guards and gaming surveillance officers provide surveillance around the clock by working shifts of 8 hours or longer with rotating schedules. Some security guards choose to work part time while others may take on a second job.

Job Outlook

Security Guards and Gaming Surveillance Officers
Percent change in employment, projected 2010-20

Security Guards	19%
Security Guards and Gaming Surveillance Officers	18%
Total, All Occupations	14%
Transportation Security Screeners (Federal Only)	10%
Gaming Surveillance Officers and Gaming Investigators	9%

Note: All Occupations includes all occupations in the U.S. Economy.
Source: U.S. Bureau of Labor Statistics, Employment Projections program

Employment of security guards is expected to grow by 19 percent from 2010 to 2020, about as fast as the average for all occupations.

Security guards will be needed to protect both people and property. This occupation is expected to add 195,000, a large number of jobs, over the 2010–2020 decade. Concern about crime, vandalism, and terrorism continue to increase the need for security. Demand should be strong in the private sector as private security firms take over some of the work police officers used to do.

Employment of transportation security screeners is expected to grow by 10 percent, about as fast as the average for all occupations. Demand for TSA screeners, who work for the federal government, will stem from transportation security concerns.

Employment of gaming surveillance officers is expected to grow by 9 percent, slower than the average for all occupations. As gambling continues to be legalized in more states and casinos grow in number, gaming surveillance officers will see additional job openings.

Technological advances will continue to create demand for casino security guards who have knowledge of computers and video surveillance equipment.

Job Prospects

Job opportunities for security guards will stem from growing demand for various forms of security.

Additional opportunities will be due to turnover. Although many people are attracted to part time positions because of the limited training requirements, there will be more competition for higher paying positions that require more training.

Those with related work experience, such as a background in law enforcement, and those with computer and technology skills should find the best job prospects.

Employment projections data for security guards and gaming surveillance officers, 2010-20

Occupational Title	SOC Code	Employment, 2010	Projected Employment, 2020	Change, 2010-20 Percent	Numeric
Security Guards and Gaming Surveillance Officers	—	1,090,600	1,290,800	18	200,200
Gaming Surveillance Officers and Gaming Investigators	33-9031	6,800	7,400	9	600
Security Guards	33-9032	1,035,700	1,230,700	19	195,000
Transportation Security Screeners (Federal Only)	33-9093	48,100	52,700	10	4,600
SOURCE: U.S. Bureau of Labor Statistics, Employment Projections program					

Similar Occupations

This table shows a list of occupations with job duties that are similar to those of security guards and gaming surveillance officers.

Occupation	Job Duties	Entry-Level Education	Median Annual Pay, May 2010
Correctional Officers	Correctional officers are responsible for overseeing individuals who have been arrested and are awaiting trial or who have been sentenced to serve time in a jail, reformatory, or prison.	High school diploma or equivalent	$39,020
Police and Detectives	Police officers protect lives and property. Detectives and criminal investigators, who sometimes are called agents or special agents, gather facts and collect evidence of possible crimes. Law enforcement officers' duties depend on the size and type of their organizations.	High school diploma or equivalent	$55,010
Private Detectives and Investigators	Private detectives and investigators find facts and analyze information about legal, financial, and personal matters. They offer many services, including verifying people's backgrounds, tracing missing persons, investigating computer crimes, and protecting celebrities.	Some college, no degree	$42,870
Gaming Services Occupations	Gaming services workers serve customers in gambling establishments, such as casinos or racetracks. Some workers tend slot machines or deal cards. Others take bets or pay out winnings. Still others supervise gaming workers and operations.	See How to Become One	$20,260

Contacts for More Information

For more information on security careers and training, visit ASIS International

Suggested citation:

Bureau of Labor Statistics, U.S. Department of Labor, Occupational Outlook Handbook, 2012-13 Edition, Security Guards and Gaming Surveillance Officers, on the Internet at http://www.bls.gov/ooh/protective-service/security-guards.htm .

Sales Occupations

Advertising Sales Agents

Quick Facts: Advertising Sales Agents	
2010 Median Pay	$45,350 per year $21.80 per hour
Entry-Level Education	High school diploma or equivalent
Work Experience in a Related Occupation	None
On-the-job Training	Moderate-term on-the-job training
Number of Jobs, 2010	160,400
Job Outlook, 2010-20	13% (About as fast as average)
Employment Change, 2010-20	20,900

What Advertising Sales Agents Do

Advertising sales agents, also called account executives and advertising sales representatives, sell advertising space to businesses and individuals. They contact potential clients, make sales presentations, and maintain client accounts.

Duties

Advertising sales agents typically do the following:

- Locate and contact potential clients to offer advertising services
- Explain to clients how specific types of advertising will help promote their products or services in the most effective way possible
- Provide clients with estimates of the costs of advertising products or services
- Process all correspondence and paperwork related to accounts
- Prepare and deliver sales presentations to new and existing clients
- Inform clients of available options for advertising art, formats, or features and provide samples
- Deliver advertising or illustration proofs to clients for approval
- Prepare promotional plans, sales literature, media kits, and sales contracts
- Recommend appropriate sizes and formats for advertising

Advertising sales agents contact potential clients, make sales presentations, and maintain customer accounts.

Most advertising sales agents work outside the office occasionally, calling on clients and prospective clients at their places of business. Some may make telephone sales calls as well—calling prospects, attempting to sell the media firm's advertising space or time, and arranging follow-up appointments with interested prospects.

A critical part of building relationships with clients is learning about their needs. Before the first meeting with a client, a sales agent gathers background information on the client's products, current clients, prospective clients, and the geographic area of the target market.

The sales agent then meets with the client to explain how specific types of advertising will help promote the client's products or services most effectively. If a client wishes to proceed, the advertising sales agent prepares an advertising proposal to present to the client. The proposal may include an overview of the advertising medium to be used, sample advertisements, and cost estimates for the project.

Because of consolidation among media industries, agents increasingly sell several types of ads in one package.

In addition to maintaining sales and overseeing clients' accounts, advertising sales agents' other duties include analyzing sales statistics and preparing reports about clients' accounts. They keep up to date on industry trends by reading about new and existing products, and they monitor the sales, prices, and products of their competitors.

In many firms, the advertising sales agent drafts contracts, which specify the cost and the advertising work to be done. Agents may also continue to help the client, answering questions or addressing problems the client may have with the proposal.

Sales agents also are responsible for developing sales tools, promotional plans, and media kits, which they use to help make a sale.

Work Environment

Advertising sales agents held about 160,400 jobs in 2010.

Selling can be stressful because income and job security depend directly on agents' ability to keep and expand their client base. Companies generally set monthly sales quotas and place considerable pressure on advertising sales agents to meet those quotas.

Getting new accounts is an important part of the job, and agents may spend much of their time traveling to and visiting prospective advertisers and maintaining relationships with current clients. Sales agents also may work in their employer's offices and handle sales for walk-in clients or for those who telephone the firm to ask about advertising.

The following industries employed the most advertising sales agents in 2010:

951

Advertising, public relations, and related services	32%
Publishing industries (except Internet)	29
Broadcasting (except Internet)	17

Work Schedules

Most advertising sales agents work full time. Many advertising sales agents work more than 40 hours a week; frequently involving irregular hours and work on weekends and holidays. Nine percent of advertising sales agents were employed part time in 2010.

How to Become an Advertising Sales Agent

Although a high school diploma is typically enough for an entry-level advertising sales position, some employers prefer applicants with a bachelor's degree. Proven sales success and communication ability are essential. Most training for advertising sales agents takes place informally on the job.

Education

Although a high school diploma is typically enough for an entry-level advertising sales position, some employers prefer applicants with a college degree. Courses in marketing, communications, business, and advertising are helpful. For those who have a proven record of successfully selling other products, educational requirements are not likely to be strict.

Training

Most training takes place on the job and can be either formal or informal. In most cases, an experienced sales manager instructs a newly hired advertising sales agent who lacks sales experience. In this one-on-one environment, supervisors typically coach new hires and observe them as they make sales calls and contact clients. Supervisors then advise the new hires on ways to improve their interaction with clients. Employers may bring in consultants to lead formal training sessions when agents sell to a specialized market segment, such as automotive dealers or real estate professionals.

Advancement

Agents with proven leadership ability and a strong sales record may advance to supervisory and managerial positions, such as sales supervisor, sales manager, or vice president of sales. Successful advertising sales agents also may advance to positions in other industries, such as corporate sales.

Important Qualities

Communication skills. Advertising sales agents must be persuasive during sales calls. In addition, they should listen to the client's desires and concerns, and recommend an appropriate advertising package.

Initiative. Advertising sales agents must actively seek new clients and keep in touch with current clients to meet sales quotas.

Organization skills. Agents work with many clients, each of whom may be at a different stage in the sales process. Agents must be well-organized to keep track of their clients or potential clients.

Persistence. Advertising sales agents must continue making sales calls even if rejected at first, because potential clients are often unwilling to commit on a first call.

Self-confidence. Advertising sales agents should be confident when calling potential clients (cold calls) and when following up with potential and existing clients.

Pay

Advertising Sales Agents
Median annual wages, May 2010

Advertising Sales Agents	$45,350
Total, All Occupations	$33,840
Sales and Related Occupations	$24,370

Note: All Occupations includes all occupations in the U.S. Economy.
Source: U.S. Bureau of Labor Statistics, Occupational Employment Statistics

The median annual wage for advertising sales agents was $45,350 in May 2010. The median wage is the wage at which half the workers in an occupation earned more than that amount and half earned less. The lowest 10 percent earned less than $22,780 and the top 10 percent earned more than $96,040.

Performance-based pay, including bonuses and commissions, can make up a large portion of an advertising sales agent's earnings. Most employers pay some combination of salaries, commissions, and bonuses. Commissions are usually based on individual sales numbers. Bonuses may depend on individual performance, the performance of all sales workers in a group, or the performance of the entire firm.

Most advertising sales agents work full time. Many advertising sales agents work more than 40 hours a week; frequently involving irregular hours and work on weekends and holidays. Nine percent of advertising sales agents were employed part time in 2010.

Job Outlook

Advertising Sales Agents
Percent change in employment, projected 2010-20

Total, All Occupations	14%
Advertising Sales Agents	13%
Sales and Related Occupations	13%

Note: All Occupations includes all occupations in the U.S. Economy.
Source: U.S. Bureau of Labor Statistics, Employment Projections program

Employment of advertising sales agents is expected to increase 13 percent from 2010 to 2020, about as fast as the average for all occupations.

Media companies will continue to rely on advertising revenue for profitability, driving growth in the advertising industry as a whole. Growth in the occupation will largely follow these broader industry trends.

From 2010 to 2020, an increasing amount of advertising is expected to be concentrated in digital media, including digital ads made to be seen on cell phones, tablet-style computers, and online radio stations. This will drive increases in employment of advertising sales agents in Internet publishing.

Digital advertising allows companies to directly target potential consumers because websites usually are associated with the types of products individuals would like to buy. Targeting clients through digital advertising is labor-intensive; therefore, the role of the sales agent will not be automated. This, combined with the broader range of media outlets, will lead to a greater need for advertising sales agents.

Although newspaper print advertising is expected to decline, much of this decline will be offset as newspapers sell online ad space. Growth in traditional media outlets—such as television and radio—should remain strong.

Job Prospects

Competition is expected to be strong for advertising sales agents. Applicants with experience in sales or a bachelor's degree should have the best opportunities.

Employment projections data for advertising sales agents, 2010-20

Occupational Title	SOC Code	Employment, 2010	Projected Employment, 2020	Change, 2010-20 Percent	Change, 2010-20 Numeric
Advertising Sales Agents	41-3011	160,400	181,300	13	20,900
SOURCE: U.S. Bureau of Labor Statistics, Employment Projections program					

Similar Occupations

This table shows a list of occupations with job duties that are similar to those of advertising sales agents.

Occupation	Job Duties	Entry-Level Education	Median Annual Pay, May 2010
Advertising, Promotions, and Marketing Managers	Advertising, promotions, and marketing managers plan programs to generate interest in a product or service. They work with art directors, sales agents, and financial staff members.	Bachelor's degree	$108,260
Insurance Sales Agents	Insurance sales agents help insurance companies generate new business by contacting potential customers and selling one or more types of insurance. An agent explains various insurance policies and helps clients choose plans that suit them.	High school diploma or equivalent	$46,770
Sales Managers	Sales managers direct organizations' sales teams. They set sales goals, analyze data, and develop training programs for the organization's sales representatives.	Bachelor's degree	$98,530
Wholesale and Manufacturing Sales Representatives	Wholesale and manufacturing sales representatives sell goods for wholesalers or manufacturers to businesses, government agencies, and other organizations. They contact customers, explain product features, answer any questions that their customers may have, and negotiate prices.	See How to Become One	$56,620

Contacts for More Information

For information about advertising sales in the newspaper industry, visit Newspaper Association of America

For information about the radio advertising industry, visit Radio Advertising Bureau

Suggested citation:

Bureau of Labor Statistics, U.S. Department of Labor, Occupational Outlook Handbook, 2012-13 Edition, Advertising Sales Agents, on the Internet at http://www.bls.gov/ooh/sales/advertising-sales-agents.htm.

Cashiers

Quick Facts: Cashiers	
2010 Median Pay	$18,500 per year $8.89 per hour
Entry-Level Education	Less than high school
Work Experience in a Related Occupation	None
On-the-job Training	Short-term on-the-job training
Number of Jobs, 2010	3,362,600
Job Outlook, 2010-20	7% (Slower than average)
Employment Change, 2010-20	250,200

What Cashiers Do

Cashiers handle payments from customers purchasing goods and services.

Duties

Cashiers typically do the following:
- Greet customers
- Use scanners, cash registers, and calculators to ring up items that customers buy
- Accept payments from customers and give change and receipts
- Bag or wrap customers' purchases
- Handle returns and exchanges of merchandise, including seeing if the items are in good condition and using the right procedure for cash, credit cards, or other types of payment
- Answer customers' questions and give information about the store's procedures and policies
- Help customers to sign up for store rewards programs and to apply for store credit cards
- Count how much money is in their register at the beginning and end of their shift

In some establishments, cashiers may have to check customers' age when selling age-restricted products, such as alcohol and tobacco. Some cashiers may have duties not directly related to sales and customer service, such as mopping floors, taking out the trash, and doing other custodial tasks. Others may stock shelves or mark prices on items.

Work Environment

Cashiers held about 3,362,600 jobs in 2010. Most cashiers work indoors, usually in retail establishments such as supermarkets, department stores, movie theaters, and restaurants.

Grocery stores are the largest employers of cashiers.

As shown in the following tabulation, 25 percent of cashiers worked in grocery stores in 2010:

Grocery stores	25%
Gasoline stations	13
Department stores	6
Limited-service eating places	6
Pharmacies and drug stores	5

The work is often repetitive, and cashiers spend most of their time standing behind counters or checkout stands.

The work can sometimes be dangerous; the risk from robberies and homicides is higher for cashiers than for most other workers. However, more safety precautions, such as installing safes and security cameras, are being taken to help deter criminals.

Work Schedules

Work hours vary by employer, but cashiers typically must work nights, weekends, and holidays. Employers may restrict the use of vacation time from Thanksgiving through early January, because that is the busiest time of year for most retailers.

How to Become a Cashier

Cashiers are usually trained on the job. There are usually no formal educational requirements.

Education

Many jobs for cashiers have no specific educational requirements, although some employers prefer applicants with at least a high school diploma. Cashiers should have a basic knowledge of mathematics, because they need to be able to make change and count the money in their registers.

Important Qualities

Customer service skills. Cashiers need to be courteous and friendly when helping customers.

Dexterity. Cashiers constantly use their hands to operate registers and scan purchases.

Listening skills. Cashiers must pay attention to their customers'

questions, instructions, and complaints.

Patience. Cashiers frequently interact with customers who are upset or angry, and the cashiers must be able to remain calm.

Stamina. Cashiers must be able to stand for long periods.

Training

Cashiers go through a brief training period when they are hired. In small firms, an experienced worker typically trains beginners. In larger businesses, trainees spend time in training classes before being placed at cash registers. During training, new cashiers are taught store policies and procedures and how to operate equipment such as cash registers.

Advancement

Working as a cashier is often a steppingstone to other careers in retail. For example, with experience, cashiers may become customer service representatives, retail salespersons, or supervisors. Cashiers with at least a high school diploma typically have the best chances for promotion. For more information, see the profiles on customer service representatives and retail sales workers .

Pay

Cashiers
Median hourly wages, May 2010

Total, All Occupations	$16.27
Retail Sales Workers	$9.33
Cashiers	$8.89

Note: All Occupations includes all occupations in the U.S. Economy.
Source: U.S. Bureau of Labor Statistics, Occupational Employment Statistics

The median hourly wage of cashiers was $8.89 in May 2010. The median wage is the wage at which half the workers in an occupation earned more than that amount and half earned less. The lowest 10 percent earned less than $7.56, and the top 10 percent earned more than $12.40.

Many cashiers start at the federal minimum wage, which is $7.25 an hour. Some states set the minimum wage above $7.25 an hour.

Work hours vary by employer, but cashiers typically must work nights, weekends, and holidays. Employers may restrict the use of vacation time from Thanksgiving through early January, because that is the busiest time of year for most retailers.

Job Outlook

Cashiers
Percent change in employment, projected 2010-20

Total, All Occupations	14%
Retail Sales Workers	13%
Cashiers	7%

Note: All Occupations includes all occupations in the U.S. Economy.
Source: U.S. Bureau of Labor Statistics, Employment Projections program

Employment of cashiers is expected to grow by 7 percent from 2010 to 2020, slower than the average for all occupations. Retail sales are expected to grow, leading to increased need for cashiers over the projections decade. However, employment growth will be limited by advances in technology, such as a rise in the number of self-service checkout stands in retail stores and increasing online sales that may decrease the need for cashiers.

Job Prospects

Job opportunities should be good because of the need to replace the large number of workers who leave the occupation for a variety of reasons each year.

Historically, workers under the age of 25 have filled many of the openings for cashiers. In 2010, about 46 percent of all cashiers were 24 years old or younger.

Employment projections data for cashiers, 2010-20

Occupational Title	SOC Code	Employment, 2010	Projected Employment, 2020	Change, 2010-20	
				Percent	Numeric
Cashiers	41-2011	3,362,600	3,612,800	7	250,200
SOURCE: U.S. Bureau of Labor Statistics, Employment Projections program					

Similar Occupations

This table shows a list of occupations with job duties that are similar to those of cashiers.

Occupation	Job Duties	Entry-Level Education	Median Annual Pay, May 2010
Customer Service Representatives	Customer service representatives interact with customers on behalf of an organization. They provide information about products and services and respond to customer complaints. Some also take orders and process returns.	High school diploma or equivalent	$30,460
Retail Sales Workers	Retail sales workers include both those who sell retail merchandise, such as clothing, furniture, and automobiles, (called retail salespersons) and those who sell spare and replacement parts and equipment, especiallycar parts, (called parts salespersons). Both groups help customers find the products they want and process customers' payments.	Less than high school	$20,990
Tellers	Tellers are responsible for accurately processing routine transactions at a bank. These transactions include cashing checks, depositing money, and collecting loan payments.	High school diploma or equivalent	$24,100
Waiters and Waitresses	Waiters and waitresses take orders and serve food and beverages to customers in dining establishments.	Less than high school	$18,330

Contacts for More Information

The Handbook does not have contacts for more information for this occupation.

Suggested citation:

Bureau of Labor Statistics, U.S. Department of Labor, Occupational Outlook Handbook, 2012-13 Edition, Cashiers, on the Internet at http://www.bls.gov/ooh/sales/cashiers.htm .

Demonstrators and Product Promoters

Quick Facts: Demonstrators and Product Promoters	
2010 Median Pay	$23,110 per year $11.11 per hour
Entry-Level Education	High school diploma or equivalent
Work Experience in a Related Occupation	None
On-the-job Training	Short-term on-the-job training
Number of Jobs, 2010	90,100
Job Outlook, 2010-20	18% (About as fast as average)
Employment Change, 2010-20	15,800

What Demonstrators and Product Promoters Do

Demonstrators and product promoters create public interest in products, such as cosmetics, housewares, and food. They encourage people and stores to buy their products by showing the products to prospective customers and answering questions.

Duties

Demonstrators and product promoters typically do the following:

- Research the product they are selling to learn about competitors and the interests of the target audience
- Design an exhibit and customize it for a particular audience
- Identify people who may be interested in the product
- Greet customers and try to get their attention
- Show and sometimes sell the product
- Distribute information, such as brochures and order forms
- Gather the names and contact information of potential customers to contact later

Demonstrators and product promoters sell both sophisticated and simple products, ranging from computer software to household cleaners. They attract potential customers by offering samples, holding contests, or distributing prizes.

Their presentation may include models, testimonials, or surveys. The equipment they use varies by product. For example, a food demonstrator might use cooking utensils; a software demonstrator may use a computer.

Some demonstrations are intended to generate immediate sales through impulse buying. Others are intended to create future sales by increasing brand awareness.

Demonstrations and product promotions are conducted in retail stores, at trade shows, or at outdoor fairs. Locations are selected according to the product being offered and its target audience. For example, many food demonstrations are conducted in supermarkets or wholesale clubs.

Demonstrators and product promoters encourage people to buy their products.

At large events, a team of demonstrators may be needed to handle the crowds.

Some demonstrators promote products on TV in infomercials or home shopping programs.

Work Environment

Demonstrators and product promoters held about 90,100 jobs in 2010. They work long hours while standing or walking, with little time for rest. They also often work at crowded trade shows or fairs, which can be hectic.

In 2010, the following industries employed the most demonstrators and product promoters:

Advertising, public relations, and related services	22%
Retail trade	20
Wholesale trade	13
Employment services	11

Work Schedules

Many demonstrators and product promoters work part time and have variable work schedules. Some work long hours and travel frequently. Night and weekend work is common. Some jobs are brief and may only last for a few hours to a week.

How to Become a Demonstrator or Product Promoter

Demonstrators and product promoters need customer service skills and are usually trained on the job.

Education

Most employers prefer demonstrators and product promoters who have a high school diploma or equivalent.

Training

Demonstrators and product promoters usually receive on-the-job training. The amount of time it takes to be trained varies, depending on the product they are promoting. For example, it may take only a couple hours to train someone who is handing out material on an upcoming movie. However, someone demonstrating a new cell phone may need several days to be fully trained.

Training often focuses on the product and is usually given by the company the product promoter is representing. The demonstrator learns about the product and the philosophy of the company that sells it. Some product promoters interact with the media and receive special training on how to speak with them.

Work Experience

Some companies prefer to hire demonstrators or product promoters who have customer service or sales experience.

Important Qualities

Customer service skills. Demonstrators must be able to determine what a customer's needs are and how their product or brand can meet those needs.

People skills. Demonstrators are constantly interacting with the public and require an energetic and cheerful personality.

Public speaking skills. Many demonstrators give speeches to large crowds when promoting a product.

Responsibility. When promoting a product at an event, demonstrators often work without supervision, so a company must be able to trust them with their products.

Pay

Demonstrators and Product Promoters
Median annual wages, May 2010

Total, All Occupations	$33,840
Sales and Related Occupations	$24,370
Demonstrators and Product Promoters	$23,110

Note: All Occupations includes all occupations in the U.S. Economy.
Source: U.S. Bureau of Labor Statistics, Occupational Employment Statistics

The median annual wage of demonstrators and product promoters was $23,110 in May 2010. The median wage is the wage at which half the workers in an occupation earned more than that amount and half earned less. The lowest 10 percent earned less than $17,230 and the top 10 percent earned more than $44,070 in May 2010.

Many demonstrators and product promoters work part time and have variable work schedules. Some work long hours and travel frequently. Night and weekend work is common. Some jobs are brief and may only last for a few hours to a week.

Job Outlook

Demonstrators and Product Promoters
Percent change in employment, projected 2010-20

Demonstrators and Product Promoters	18%
Total, All Occupations	14%
Sales and Related Occupations	13%

Note: All Occupations includes all occupations in the U.S. Economy.
Source: U.S. Bureau of Labor Statistics, Employment Projections program

Employment of demonstrators and product promoters is projected to grow 18 percent from 2010 to 2020, about as fast as the average for all occupations.

An increase in hands-on and interactive marketing is expected to lead to growth for this occupation. Many companies have found that promoting their products directly to the public creates a more positive impression of their brand than more traditional marketing methods.

Demonstrators and product promoters are important to the success of this strategy because they are the ones showcasing the product.

In addition, many demonstrators and product promoters work in supercenters and warehouse clubs, a subset of the general merchandise store industry, which is projected to grow very rapidly from 2010 to 2020. Growth in that industry will contribute to new jobs for this occupation.

Job Prospects

Job prospects for demonstrators and product promoters should be favorable. Many people enter this occupation and then leave to take jobs in other occupations, creating openings for new workers. Employers look for candidates who are energetic and outgoing. Some employers prefer applicants with customer service experience.

Employment projections data for demonstrators and product promoters, 2010-20

Occupational Title	SOC Code	Employment, 2010	Projected Employment, 2020	Change, 2010-20 Percent	Change, 2010-20 Numeric
Demonstrators and Product Promoters	41-9011	90,100	105,800	18	15,800
SOURCE: U.S. Bureau of Labor Statistics, Employment Projections program					

Similar Occupations

This table shows a list of occupations with job duties that are similar to those of demonstrators and product promoters.

Occupation	Job Duties	Entry-Level Education	Median Annual Pay, May 2010
Advertising Sales Agents	Advertising sales agents sell advertising space to businesses and individuals. They contact potential clients, make sales presentations, and maintain client accounts.	High school diploma or equivalent	$45,350
Customer Service Representatives	Customer service representatives interact with customers on behalf of an organization. They provide information about products and services and respond to customer complaints. Some also take orders and process returns.	High school diploma or equivalent	$30,460
Meeting, Convention, and Event Planners	Meeting, convention, and event planners coordinate all aspects of professional meetings and events. They choose meeting locations, arrange transportation, and coordinate other details.	Bachelor's degree	$45,260
Public Relations Managers and Specialists	Public relations managers and specialists create and maintain a favorable public image for their employer or client. They write material for media releases, plan and direct public relations programs, and raise funds for their organizations.	Bachelor's degree	$57,550
Retail Sales Workers	Retail sales workers include both those who sell retail merchandise, such as clothing, furniture, and automobiles, (called retail salespersons) and those who sell spare and replacement parts and equipment, especiallycar parts, (called parts salespersons). Both groups help customers find the products they want and process customers' payments.	Less than high school	$20,990

Contacts for More Information

For more information about product promoters and demonstrators, visit Promotion Marketing Association , Promotional Products Association International

Suggested citation:

Bureau of Labor Statistics, U.S. Department of Labor, Occupational Outlook Handbook, 2012-13 Edition, Demonstrators and Product Promoters, on the Internet at http://www.bls.gov/ooh/sales/demonstrators-and-product-promoters.htm

Insurance Sales Agents

Quick Facts: Insurance Sales Agents	
2010 Median Pay	$46,770 per year $22.48 per hour
Entry-Level Education	High school diploma or equivalent
Work Experience in a Related Occupation	None
On-the-job Training	Moderate-term on-the-job training
Number of Jobs, 2010	411,500
Job Outlook, 2010-20	22% (Faster than average)
Employment Change, 2010-20	90,200

What Insurance Sales Agents Do

Insurance sales agents help insurance companies generate new business by contacting potential customers and selling one or more types of insurance. An agent explains various insurance policies and helps clients choose plans that suit them.

Duties

Insurance sales agents typically do the following:

- Call potential clients to expand their customer base
- Interview prospective clients to get data about their financial resources and discuss existing coverage
- Explain the features of various policies
- Analyze clients' current insurance policies and suggest additions or changes
- Customize insurance programs to suit individual clients
- Do administrative tasks, such as keeping records and handling policy renewals
- Help policyholders settle claims

Insurance sales agents commonly sell one or more types of insurance, such as property and casualty, life, and health and long-term care.

Property and casualty insurance agents sell policies that protect people and businesses from financial loss resulting from automobile accidents, fire, theft, and other events that can damage property. For

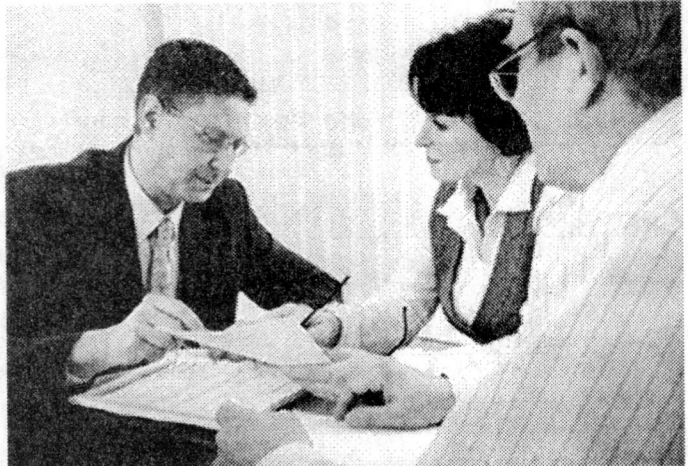

Insurance sales agents interview prospective clients to obtain data about their financial resources and discuss existing coverage.

businesses, property and casualty insurance also covers injured workers' compensation, product liability claims, or medical malpractice claims.

Life insurance agents specialize in selling policies that pay beneficiaries when a policyholder dies. Life insurance agents also sell annuities that promise a retirement income.

Health and long-term care insurance agents sell policies that cover the costs of medical care and assisted living services in old age. They may also sell dental insurance and short-term and long-term disability insurance.

Agents may specialize in any one of these products or function as generalists providing multiple products.

An increasing number of insurance sales agents offer their clients comprehensive financial planning services, especially for clients approaching retirement. These services include retirement planning, estate planning, and help in setting up pension plans for businesses. In addition to offering insurance, these agents may become licensed to sell mutual funds, variable annuities, and other securities. This practice is most common with life insurance agents who already sell annuities, but many property and casualty agents also sell financial products. For more information, see the profile on securities, commodities, and financial services sales agents .

Many agents spend a lot of time marketing their services and creating their own base of clients. They do this in a variety of ways, including by making "cold" sales calls to people who are not current clients.

Clients often learn about policies themselves on their own, by doing comparison shopping online and getting information from the insurance companies. Then they contact the company directly to buy a policy, so the client comes to the agent ready to buy.

Insurance agents also find new clients through referrals by current clients. Keeping clients happy so they recommend the agent to others is a key to success for insurance sales agents.

The following are types of insurance sales agents:

Captive agents are insurance sales agents who work exclusively for one insurance company. They can only sell policies provided by the company that employs them.

Independent insurance agents work for insurance brokerages, selling the policies of several companies. They match insurance policies for their clients with the company that offers the best rate and coverage.

Work Environment

Insurance sales agents held about 411,500 jobs in 2010. In 2010, more than 3 out of 4 insurance sales agents worked in the insurance industry. Although most insurance sales agents, 56 percent, worked for insurance brokerages selling the policies of several companies, some worked directly for a single insurance carrier.

Most insurance sales agents work in offices, although some may spend much of their time traveling to meet with clients. Their work environment may vary depending on the type of company that employs them. Since some agencies are small, agents may work alone or with only a few others.

Work Schedules

Insurance sales agents usually determine their own hours of work and often schedule evening and weekend appointments for the convenience of clients. Some sales agents meet with clients during business hours and then spend evenings doing paperwork and preparing presentations to prospective clients. Most agents work full time and some work more than 40 hours per week.

How to Become an Insurance Sales Agent

Most employers require agents to have a high school diploma; however, more than one-third of insurance sales agents have a bachelor's degree. Agents must be licensed in the states where they work.

Education

A high school diploma is the typical requirement for insurance sales agents, although more than one-third of insurance sales agents have a bachelor's degree. Public speaking classes can be useful in improving sales techniques, and often agents will have taken courses in business, finance, or economics. Business knowledge is also helpful for sales agents hoping to advance to a managerial position.

Training

Insurance sales agents learn many of their job duties on the job from other agents. Many employers have new agents shadow an experienced agent. This allows the new agent to learn how to conduct the company's business and how the agency interacts with clients.

Employers also are increasingly placing greater emphasis on continuing professional education as the variety of financial products sold by insurance sales agents increases. Changes in tax laws, government benefits programs, and other state and federal regulations can affect the insurance needs of clients and the way in which agents conduct business. Agents can enhance their selling skills and broaden their knowledge of insurance and other financial services by taking courses at colleges and universities or by attending conferences and seminars sponsored by insurance organizations.

Licenses

Insurance sales agents must have a license in each of the states where they work. Separate licenses are required for agents to sell life and health insurance and property and casualty insurance. In most states, licenses are issued only to applicants who complete specified courses and who pass state exams covering insurance fundamentals and state insurance laws. Most state licensing authorities also require agents to take continuing education courses every 2 years, focusing on insurance laws, consumer protection, ethics, and the technical details of various insurance policies.

As the demand for financial products and financial planning services increases, many agents also choose to get licensed and certified to sell securities and other financial products. Doing so, however, requires substantial study and passing an additional exam—either the Series 6 or Series 7 licensing exam, both of which are administered by the National Association of Securities Dealers (NASD). The Series 6 exam is for people who want to sell only mutual funds and variable annuities. The Series 7 exam is the main NASD series license that qualifies agents as general securities sales representatives.

Certification

A number of organizations offer certifications that show an agent's expertise in insurance specialties. These certifications are not required for employment, but they can give job candidates an advantage over other applicants. Certifications can also be a source of continuing education credit. For details on specific designations, contact The American Institute for Chartered Property and Casualty Underwriters and The American College .

Important Qualities

Analytical skills. Insurance sales agents must evaluate the characteristics of each client to determine the appropriate insurance policy.

Customer-service skills. Insurance sales agents must be able to communicate effectively with customers by listening to their requests and suggesting suitable policies.

Initiative. Insurance sales agents need to actively seek out new customers to maintain a flow of commissions.

Self-confidence. Insurance sales agents should be confident when making "cold" calls (calls to prospective customers who have not been contacted before). They must speak clearly and persuasively and maintain their composure if rejected.

Pay

Insurance Sales Agents
Median annual wages, May 2010

Insurance Sales Agents	$46,770
Total, All Occupations	$33,840
Sales and Related Occupations	$24,370

Note: All Occupations includes all occupations in the U.S. Economy.
Source: U.S. Bureau of Labor Statistics, Occupational Employment Statistics

The median annual wage of insurance sales agents was $46,770 in May 2010. The median wage is the wage at which half the workers in an occupation earned more than that amount and half earned less. The lowest 10 percent earned less than $25,940, and the top 10 percent earned more than $115,340.

Many independent agents are paid by commission only. Sales workers who are employees of an agency or an insurance carrier may be paid in one of three ways: salary only, salary plus commission, or salary plus bonus.

In general, commissions are the most common form of compensation, especially for experienced agents. The amount of the commission depends on the type and amount of insurance sold and on whether the transaction is a new policy or a renewal. When agents meet their sales goals or when an agency meets its profit goals, agents usually get bonuses. Some agents involved with financial planning receive a fee for their services, rather than a commission.

Insurance sales agents usually determine their own hours of work and often schedule evening and weekend appointments for the convenience of their clients. Some sales agents meet with clients during business hours and then spend evenings doing paperwork and preparing presentations to prospective clients. Most agents work full time and some work more than 40 hours per week.

Job Outlook

Insurance Sales Agents
Percent change in employment, projected 2010-20

Insurance Sales Agents	22%
Total, All Occupations	14%
Sales and Related Occupations	13%

Note: All Occupations includes all occupations in the U.S. Economy.
Source: U.S. Bureau of Labor Statistics, Employment Projections program

Employment of insurance sales agents is projected to grow 22 percent from 2010 to 2020, faster than the average for all occupations.

The insurance industry generally grows with the economy as a whole. Overall economic growth will continue to create demand for insurance policies. Direct online purchases of insurance are not expected to negatively affect employment of traditional sales agents, because they will continue to have a critical role in the insurance industry. Because the profitability of insurance companies depends on a steady stream of new customers, the demand for insurance sales agents is expected to continue. Employment growth should be strongest for independent sales agents, as insurance companies will rely more on brokerages and less on captive agents as a way to control costs.

Many clients do their own Internet research and get quotes from insurance companies online. Agents are still needed to interact with clients, however, and many people lack the time or expertise to study the different types of insurance to decide what they need. These clients will continue to rely on the advice from insurance sales agents.

Employment growth should be stronger for agents selling health and long-term care insurance. As the population ages over the next decade, demand will likely increase for packages that cover long-term care. In addition, federal regulation of health insurance is expected to bring many new customers into the market. Insurance companies will rely on sales agents to enroll people from this new customer base.

Job Prospects

College graduates who have sales ability, excellent customer-service skills, and expertise in a range of insurance and financial services products should enjoy the best prospects. Multilingual agents should have an advantage, because they can serve a wider customer base. Additionally, insurance language is often technical, so agents who have a firm understanding of the relevant technical and legal terms should also be desirable to employers.

Many beginning agents fail to earn enough from commissions to meet their income goals and eventually transfer to other careers. Many job openings are likely to result from the need to replace agents who leave the occupation or retire.

Agents may face some competition from traditional securities brokers and bankers, who also sell insurance policies. Insurance sales agents will need to expand the products and services they offer as consolidation increases among insurance companies, banks, and brokerage firms and as demand increases from clients for more comprehensive financial planning.

Employment projections data for insurance sales agents, 2010-20

Occupational Title	SOC Code	Employment, 2010	Projected Employment, 2020	Change, 2010-20	
				Percent	Numeric
Insurance Sales Agents	41-3021	411,500	501,700	22	90,200
SOURCE: U.S. Bureau of Labor Statistics, Employment Projections program					

Similar Occupations

This table shows a list of occupations with job duties that are similar to those of insurance sales agents.

Occupation	Job Duties	Entry-Level Education	Median Annual Pay, May 2010
Wholesale and Manufacturing Sales Representatives	Wholesale and manufacturing sales representatives sell goods for wholesalers or manufacturers to businesses, government agencies, and other organizations. They contact customers, explain product features, answer any questions that their customers may have, and negotiate prices.	See How to Become One	$56,620
Advertising Sales Agents	Advertising sales agents sell advertising space to businesses and individuals. They contact potential clients, make sales presentations, and maintain client accounts.	High school diploma or equivalent	$45,350
Real Estate Brokers and Sales Agents	Real estate brokers and sales agents help clients buy, sell, and rent properties. Brokers and agents do the same type of work, but brokers are licensed to manage their own real estate businesses. Sales agents must work with a broker.	High school diploma or equivalent	$42,680
Securities, Commodities, and Financial Services Sales Agents	Securities, commodities, and financial services sales agents connect buyers and sellers in financial markets. They sell securities to individuals, advise companies in search of investors, and conduct trades.	Bachelor's degree	$70,190
Sales Managers	Sales managers direct organizations' sales teams. They set sales goals, analyze data, and develop training programs for the organization's sales representatives.	Bachelor's degree	$98,530
Insurance Underwriters	Insurance underwriters decide whether to provide insurance and under what terms. They evaluate insurance applications and determine coverage amounts and premiums.	Bachelor's degree	$59,290
Personal Financial Advisors	Personal financial advisors give financial advice to people. They help with investments, taxes, and insurance decisions.	Bachelor's degree	$64,750

Contacts for More Information

For more information about insurance sales agents, visit National Association of Professional Insurance Agents , Insurance Information Institute

For information about insurance sales agents in the healthcare industry, visit National Association of Health Underwriters

For more information about certifications, visit The American Institute for Chartered Property and Casualty Underwriters , The American College

Suggested citation:

Bureau of Labor Statistics, U.S. Department of Labor, Occupational Outlook Handbook, 2012-13 Edition, Insurance Sales Agents, on the Internet at http://www.bls.gov/ooh/sales/insurance-sales-agents.htm .

Models

Quick Facts: Models	
2010 Median Pay	$32,920 per year $15.83 per hour
Entry-Level Education	Less than high school
Work Experience in a Related Occupation	None
On-the-job Training	None
Number of Jobs, 2010	1,400
Job Outlook, 2010-20	14% (About as fast as average)
Employment Change, 2010-20	200

What Models Do

Models pose for artists, photographers, or customers in order to help advertise a variety of products, including clothing, cosmetics, food, and appliances.

Duties

Models typically do the following:

- Pose for workers taking photos or creating paintings or sculptures
- Promote products in commercials
- Display clothing, such as dresses, coats, underclothing, swimwear, and suits, for a variety of audiences and in various media
- Model accessories, such as handbags, shoes, and jewelry, and promote beauty products, including fragrances and cosmetics
- Work closely with photographers, hair and clothing stylists, makeup artists, and clients to produce a desired look
- Wear designers' clothing for runway fashion shows
- Create and maintain a portfolio of their work
- Travel to meet and interview with potential clients
- Conduct research on the product being promoted—for example, the designer or type of fabric of a particular article of clothing

Many modeling jobs are for printed publications, such as magazine covers and articles or magazine, newspaper, catalogue, billboard, and online advertisements. Print models participate in photo shoots, in which they pose for photographers to show off the features of clothing and other products. Models change their posture and facial expressions to capture the look the client wants. The photographer usually takes many pictures of the model in different poses and expressions during the photo shoot.

Models also pose live in a variety of locations. At fashion shows, models stand, turn, and walk to show off clothing to an audience of photographers, journalists, designers, and garment buyers. In retail establishments and department stores, models display clothing directly for shoppers and may be required to describe the features and prices of the clothing. Other models pose for sketch artists, painters, and sculptors.

Almost all models work with agents, who provide a link between the models and clients. Clients prefer to work with agents, which makes it very difficult for a model to pursue a freelance career. Agents look for "fresh faces," advise and train models, and promote them to clients in return for a portion of the model's earnings.

Models may also work with hair stylists and makeup artists to prepare for photo shoots or fashion shows. The stylist and makeup artist may touch up the model's hair and makeup and change the model's look throughout the event. Models might sometimes be responsible for applying their own makeup and bringing their own clothing.

Models spend a considerable amount of time promoting themselves by putting together and maintaining portfolios, printing composite cards, and traveling to meet potential clients. A portfolio is a collection of a model's previous work and is carried to all client meetings and bookings. A composite card contains the best photographs from a model's portfolio, along with his or her measurements.

Because advertisers often need to target specific segments of the population, models may specialize in a certain area. For example, petite and plus-size fashions are modeled by women whose size is, respectively, smaller and larger than that worn by the typical model. Models who are disabled may be used to model fashions or products for consumers with disabilities. "Parts" models have a body part, such as a hand or foot, particularly well suited to model products such as fingernail polish or shoes.

Work Environment

Models held about 1,400 jobs in May 2010. Most models work for educational services, including modeling schools; however, others work for retail trade establishments or for employment placement services, such as casting and modeling agencies.

Models work in a variety of conditions, from comfortable studios and runway fashion shows to outdoors in all weather conditions. Schedules can be demanding and stressful, although some models may enjoy the frequent travel to meet clients in different cities.

Work Schedules

Many models work part time, often with unpredictable work schedules. They must be ready at a moment's notice to attend photo shoots or shows. Most models have periods of unemployment.

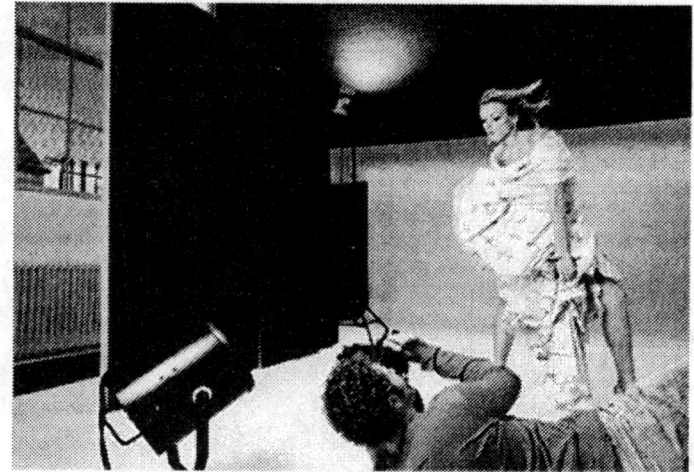

Models pose for artists and photographers.

How to Become a Model

No formal education is required and training is limited. Specific requirements depend on the client, but most models must be within certain ranges for height, weight, and clothing size to meet the needs of fashion designers, photographers, and advertisers.

Education

Some aspiring models attend modeling schools that provide training in posing, walking, applying makeup, and other basic tasks. Attending such schools, however, does not necessarily lead to job opportunities. Some models are discovered when agents scout for "fresh faces" at modeling schools, but most agencies have "open calls" and allow applicants to email photos directly to the agency. Models who are well liked are then invited to be interviewed and seen in person by an agent. Some agencies sponsor modeling contests and searches.

Advancement

Because models' advancement depends on their previous work, maintaining a good portfolio of high–quality, up-to-date photographs is important to getting assignments.

Models advance by working more regularly and being selected for assignments that have higher pay. They may appear in magazines, print campaigns, commercials, or runway shows with higher profiles. They may work with clients who will provide them with more widespread exposure.

A model's selection of an agency is an important factor for advancement in the occupation: the better the reputation and skill of the agency, the more assignments a model is likely to get.

Important Qualities

Specific requirements depend on the client, but most models must be within certain ranges for height, weight, and clothing size to meet the needs of fashion designers, photographers, and advertisers. Requirements may change slightly from time to time, along with common public perceptions of physical beauty.

Courteous. Models must interact with a large number of people, so it is important to be polite, professional, prompt, and respectful.

Discipline. A model's career depends on the preservation of his or her physical characteristics, so models must control their diet, exercise regularly, and get enough sleep to stay healthy and photogenic. Haircuts, pedicures, and manicures are necessary work-related expenses.

Organized. Models must be able to manage their portfolios and their work and travel schedules.

Persistence. Competition for jobs is strong and clients' needs are specific, so patience and persistence are essential.

Photogenic. Models spend most of their time being photographed. They must be comfortable in front of a camera for photographers to capture the desired look.

Style. Models must have a basic knowledge of hair styling, makeup, and clothing. For photographic and runway work, models must be able to move gracefully and confidently.

Pay

Models

Median hourly wages, May 2010

Total, All Occupations	$16.27
Models	$15.83
Other Sales and Related Workers	$14.21

Note: All Occupations includes all occupations in the U.S. Economy.
Source: U.S. Bureau of Labor Statistics, Occupational Employment Statistics

The median hourly wage of models was $15.83 in May 2010. The median wage is the wage at which half the workers in an occupation earned more than that amount and half earned less. The lowest 10 percent earned less than $9.53 per hour, and the top 10 percent earned more than $28.86 per hour.

Many models work part time, often with unpredictable work schedules. They must be ready at a moment's notice to attend photo shoots or shows. Most models have periods of unemployment.

Job Outlook

Models

Percent change in employment, projected 2010-20

Total, All Occupations	14%
Models	14%
Other Sales and Related Workers	9%

Note: All Occupations includes all occupations in the U.S. Economy.
Source: U.S. Bureau of Labor Statistics, Employment Projections program

Employment of models is expected to grow by 14 percent from 2010 to 2020, as fast as the average for all occupations. However, because it is a small occupation, the growth will result in only about 200 new jobs over the 10-year period.

Growth in the occupation will be driven primarily by the use of models in advertisements, in both print and digital formats. Advertisers will continue to use models in fashion shows, catalogs, and print campaigns as a way to increase awareness of their product. Models also will be needed for online publications as spending on digital advertisements grows in response to the continuing increase in online sales. However, businesses may cut back on their advertising budgets during economic downturns, making them less likely to develop new advertising campaigns or hire models.

As the U.S. population becomes increasingly diverse and businesses become more globalized, demand for racially and ethnically diverse models may increase.

Job Prospects

Many people are drawn to this occupation because of its glamour and potential for fame. Some enjoy traveling and modeling for famous designers. In addition, there are no education or training requirements for entering this occupation. Therefore, many applicants will be competing for very few job openings.

Modeling careers are typically short, and many agencies and clients look for "fresh faces." Therefore, younger models with a solid portfolio will have the best opportunities for jobs.

Job opportunities are expected to be best for those willing to relocate to large metropolitan cities. Although small cities also need models for local businesses and shows, these job opportunities are limited. The largest number of job opportunities will be in large cities, such as New York and Los Angeles.

Employment projections data for models, 2010-20

Occupational Title	SOC Code	Employment, 2010	Projected Employment, 2020	Change, 2010-20 Percent	Numeric
Models	41-9012	1,400	1,600	14	200

SOURCE: U.S. Bureau of Labor Statistics, Employment Projections program

Similar Occupations

This table shows a list of occupations with job duties that are similar to those of models.

Occupation	Job Duties	Entry-Level Education	Median Annual Pay, May 2010
Actors	Actors express ideas and portray characters in theater, film, television, and other performing arts media. They also work at theme parks or for other live events. They interpret a writer's script to entertain or inform an audience.	Some college, no degree	The annual wage is not available.
Barbers, Hairdressers, and Cosmetologists	Barbers, hairdressers, and cosmetologists provide hair styling and beauty services.	See How to Become One	$22,500
Demonstrators and Product Promoters	Demonstrators and product promoters create public interest in products, such as cosmetics, housewares, and food. They encourage people and stores to buy their products by showing the products to prospective customers and answering questions.	High school diploma or equivalent	$23,110
Fashion Designers	Fashion designers create original clothing, accessories, and footwear. They sketch designs, select fabrics and patterns, and give instructions on how to make the products they designed.	High school diploma or equivalent	$64,530
Photographers	Photographers use their technical expertise, creativity, and composition skills to produce and preserve images that visually tell a story or record an event.	High school diploma or equivalent	$29,130

Contacts for More Information

For information about modeling schools and agencies in your area, contact a local consumer affairs organization, such as the Better Business Bureau .

Suggested citation:

Bureau of Labor Statistics, U.S. Department of Labor, Occupational Outlook Handbook, 2012-13 Edition, Models, on the Internet at http://www.bls.gov/ooh/sales/models.htm .

Real Estate Brokers and Sales Agents

Quick Facts: Real Estate Brokers and Sales Agents	
2010 Median Pay	$42,680 per year $20.52 per hour
Entry-Level Education	High school diploma or equivalent
Work Experience in a Related Occupation	See How to Become One
On-the-job Training	See How to Become One
Number of Jobs, 2010	466,100
Job Outlook, 2010-20	11% (About as fast as average)
Employment Change, 2010-20	52,500

What Real Estate Brokers and Sales Agents Do

Real estate brokers and sales agents help clients buy, sell, and rent properties. Brokers and agents do the same type of work, but brokers are licensed to manage their own real estate businesses. Sales agents must work with a broker.

Duties

Real estate brokers and sales agents typically do the following:

- Solicit potential clients to buy, sell, and rent properties
- Advise clients on prices, mortgages, market conditions, and other related information
- Compare properties to determine a competitive market price
- Generate lists of properties for sale, including details such as location and features
- Promote properties through advertisements, open houses, and listing services
- Take prospective buyers or renters to see properties
- Present purchase offers to sellers for consideration
- Mediate negotiations between the buyer and seller
- Ensure all terms of purchase contracts are met
- Prepare documents such as loyalty contracts, purchase agreements, and deeds

Because of the complexity of buying or selling a home or commercial property, people often seek help from real estate brokers and sales agents. Although most real estate brokers and sales agents sell residential property, others sell commercial property, and a small number sell industrial, agricultural, or other types of real estate.

Brokers and agents can represent either the buyer or the seller in a transaction. Buyers' brokers and agents meet with clients to understand what they are looking for and how much they can afford. Sellers' brokers and agents meet with clients to help them decide how much to ask for and to convince them that the agent or broker can find them a qualified buyer.

Real estate brokers and sales agents must be knowledgeable about the real estate market in their area. To match properties to clients' needs, they should be familiar with local communities, including knowledge of the crime rate and the proximity to schools and shopping. Brokers and agents also must stay current on financing options; government programs; types of available mortgages; and real estate, zoning, and fair housing laws.

Real estate brokers are licensed to manage their own businesses. Brokers, as independent businesspeople, often sell real estate owned by others. In addition to helping clients buy and sell properties, they may help rent or manage properties for a fee. Many operate a real estate office, handling business details and overseeing the work of sales agents.

Real estate sales agents must work with a broker. Sales agents often work for brokers on a contract basis, earning a portion of the commission from each property they sell.

Work Environment

Real estate brokers and sales agents held about 466,100 jobs in 2010. About 57 percent were self-employed.

Most of the remainder worked in the real estate industry in brokerage offices, leasing offices, and other real estate establishments. Workplace size can range from a one-person business to a large firm with numerous branch offices. Many brokers have franchise agreements with national or regional real estate companies. Under this arrangement, the broker pays a fee to be affiliated with a widely known real estate organization.

While some real estate brokers and sales agents work in a typical office environment, others are able to telecommute and work out of their homes. In both cases, however, workers spend much of their time away from their desks—showing properties to customers, traveling to see properties for sale, and meeting with prospective clients.

Work Schedules

Many real estate brokers and sales agents work more than a standard 40-hour workweek. They often work evenings and weekends to accommodate clients' schedules. Additionally, beginners, in particular, may spend a significant amount of time networking and

Real estate brokers and sales agents help clients buy or sell real estate.

attending community events to meet potential clients. Although they frequently work long or irregular hours, many can set their own schedules.

Some brokers and sales agents work part time, often combining their real estate activities with other careers.

How to Become a Real Estate Broker or Sales Agent

Real estate brokers and sales agents need at least a high school diploma. Both brokers and sales agents must be licensed. To become licensed, candidates complete a particular number of hours of real estate courses.

Licenses

In all states and the District of Columbia, real estate brokers and sales agents must be licensed. Licensing requirements vary by state, but most have similar basic requirements:

- Candidates must be 18 years old
- Pass an exam
- Complete a number of hours of real estate courses

Some states have additional requirements, such as passing a background check. In many cases, licenses are not transferrable among states, but some states have reciprocity agreements and will accept licenses issued by other states.

To obtain a broker's license, individuals need a specific amount of experience as a licensed sales agent, usually 1 to 3 years. They must also take additional formal classroom training. In some states, a bachelor's degree may be substituted in place of some experience or training requirements.

State licenses typically must be renewed every 2 to 4 years. In most states, brokers and agents must complete continuing education courses to renew their license. To verify exact licensing requirements, prospective brokers and agents should contact the real estate licensing commission of the state in which they wish to work.

Education

Real estate brokers and sales agents must have at least a high school diploma or equivalent. To become licensed, brokers and agents must take state-accredited pre-licensing courses. Some states may waive pre-licensing course requirements if the candidate has taken college courses in real estate.

As the real estate market becomes more competitive and complex, some employers prefer to hire candidates with college courses or a college degree. Some community colleges, colleges, and universities offer courses in real estate. Some offer associate's and bachelor's degree programs in real estate, and many others offer certificate programs. Courses in finance, business administration, economics, and law also can be useful. Brokers intending to open their own company often take business courses, such as marketing and accounting.

In addition to offering pre-licensing courses, many real estate associations have courses and professional development programs for both beginners and experienced agents. These courses cover a variety of topics, such as real estate fundamentals, real estate law, and mortgage financing.

Work Experience

To get a broker's license in most states, real estate brokers must have experience working as a licensed sales agent. Requirements vary by state, but most require 1 to 3 years of experience.

Advancement

In larger firms, experienced agents can advance to sales manager or general manager. Sales agents who earn their broker's license may open their own offices.

Important Qualities

Independence. Real estate brokers and sales agents must be able to work independently, managing their own time and organizing, planning, and prioritizing their work. Some brokers manage a one-person business in which they must handle every aspect of the business.

Interpersonal skills. Strong interpersonal skills are essential for real estate brokers and sales agents, because they spend much of their time interacting with clients and customers. As a result, they must be pleasant, enthusiastic, and trustworthy to attract clients.

Persuasion skills. Real estate brokers and sales agents need to be persuasive to convince potential clients of their ability to sell real estate and to persuade customers to buy available properties.

Problem-solving skills. Real estate brokers and sales agents need problem-solving skills to address, often immediately, any concerns clients or potential customers may have with a property. They also mediate negotiations between the seller and buyer.

Pay

Real Estate Brokers and Sales Agents
Median annual wages, May 2010

Real Estate Brokers	$54,910
Real Estate Brokers and Sales Agents	$42,680
Real Estate Sales Agents	$40,030
Total, All Occupations	$33,840

Note: All Occupations includes all occupations in the U.S. Economy.
Source: U.S. Bureau of Labor Statistics, Occupational Employment Statistics

The median annual wage of real estate brokers was $54,910 in May 2010. The median wage is the wage at which half the workers in an occupation earned more than that amount and half earned less. The lowest 10 percent earned less than $25,550, and the top 10 percent earned more than $161,820.

The median annual wage of real estate sales agents was $40,030 in May 2010. The lowest 10 percent earned less than $20,460, and the top 10 percent earned more than $95,220.

Brokers and sales agents earn most of their income from commissions on sales. The commission varies by the type of property and its value. Commissions are often divided among the buying and selling agents, brokers, and firms.

An agent's income often depends on economic conditions, the agent's individual motivation, and the types of property available. Income usually increases as agents become better and more experienced at sales. Earnings can be irregular, especially for beginners, as agents sometimes go weeks or months without a sale. Some agents become active in community organizations and local real estate organizations to broaden their contacts and increase their sales.

Many real estate brokers and sales agents work more than a standard 40-hour workweek. They often work evenings and weekends to accommodate clients' schedules. Additionally, beginners, in particular, may spend a significant amount of time networking and attending community events to meet potential clients. Although they frequently work long or irregular hours, many can set their own schedules.

Some brokers and sales agents work part time, often combining their real estate activities with other careers.

Job Outlook

Real Estate Brokers and Sales Agents
Percent change in employment, projected 2010-20

Total, All Occupations	14%
Real Estate Sales Agents	12%
Real Estate Brokers and Sales Agents	11%
Real Estate Brokers	8%

Note: All Occupations includes all occupations in the U.S. Economy.
Source: U.S. Bureau of Labor Statistics, Employment Projections program

Employment of real estate brokers and sales agents is expected to grow 11 percent from 2010 to 2020, about as fast as the average for all occupations.

Employment of real estate brokers and agents will grow as the real estate market rebounds from the recent economic recession. Both financial and non-financial factors spur demand for home sales. Real estate is perceived as a good long-term investment, and many people want to own their homes.

Population growth and mobility also will continue to stimulate the need for new brokers and agents. In addition to first-time home buyers, people will need brokers and agents when looking for a larger home, relocating for a new job, and other reasons.

The real estate market is sensitive to fluctuations in the economy, and employment of real estate brokers and agents will vary accordingly. In periods of economic growth or stability, employment will grow to accommodate families and individuals looking to buy homes. Alternatively, the amount of work for brokers and agents will slow and employment may decline during periods of declining economic activity or rising interest rates.

Job Prospects

Although the real estate market depends on economic conditions, it is relatively easy to enter the occupation. In times of economic growth, brokers and sales agents will have good job opportunities. In an economic downturn, there tend to be fewer job opportunities, and brokers and agents often have a lower income due to fewer sales and purchases.

Beginning agents will face competition from well-established, more experienced brokers and agents. Because income is dependent on sales, beginners may have trouble sustaining themselves in the occupation during periods of slower activity.

Brokers should fare better because they generally have a large client base from years of experience as sales agents. Those with strong sales ability and extensive social and business connections in their communities should have the best chances for success.

Employment projections data for real estate brokers and sales agents, 2010-20

Occupational Title	SOC Code	Employment, 2010	Projected Employment, 2020	Change, 2010-20	
				Percent	Numeric
Real Estate Brokers and Sales Agents	41-9020	466,100	518,600	11	52,500
Real Estate Brokers	41-9021	98,600	106,200	8	7,500
Real Estate Sales Agents	41-9022	367,500	412,500	12	45,000

SOURCE: U.S. Bureau of Labor Statistics, Employment Projections program

Similar Occupations

This table shows a list of occupations with job duties that are similar to those of real estate brokers and sales agents.

Occupation	Job Duties	Entry-Level Education	Median Annual Pay, May 2010
Appraisers and Assessors of Real Estate	Appraisers and assessors of real estate estimate the value of real property—land and the buildings on that land— before it is sold, mortgaged, taxed, insured, or developed.	High school diploma or equivalent	$48,500
Loan Officers	Loan officers evaluate, authorize, or recommend approval of loan applications for people and businesses.	High school diploma or equivalent	$56,490
Advertising Sales Agents	Advertising sales agents sell advertising space to businesses and individuals. They contact potential clients, make sales presentations, and maintain client accounts.	High school diploma or equivalent	$45,350
Insurance Sales Agents	Insurance sales agents help insurance companies generate new business by contacting potential customers and selling one or more types of insurance. An agent explains various insurance policies and helps clients choose plans that suit them.	High school diploma or equivalent	$46,770
Wholesale and Manufacturing Sales Representatives	Wholesale and manufacturing sales representatives sell goods for wholesalers or manufacturers to businesses, government agencies, and other organizations. They contact customers, explain product features, answer any questions that their customers may have, and negotiate prices.	See How to Become One	$56,620
Securities, Commodities, and Financial Services Sales Agents	Securities, commodities, and financial services sales agents connect buyers and sellers in financial markets. They sell securities to individuals, advise companies in search of investors, and conduct trades.	Bachelor's degree	$70,190
Property, Real Estate, and Community Association Managers	Property, real estate, and community association managers take care of the many aspects of residential, commercial, or industrial properties. They make sure the property looks nice, operates smoothly, and preserves its resale value.	High school diploma or equivalent	$51,480

Contacts for More Information

Information on licensing requirements for real estate brokers and sales agents is available from most local real estate organizations and from the state real estate commission or board.

For more information about opportunities in real estate, visit National Association of Realtors

Suggested citation:

Bureau of Labor Statistics, U.S. Department of Labor, Occupational Outlook Handbook, 2012-13 Edition, Real Estate Brokers and Sales Agents, on the Internet at http://www.bls.gov/ooh/sales/real-estate-brokers-and-sales-agents.htm .

Retail Sales Workers

Quick Facts: Retail Sales Workers	
2010 Median Pay	$20,990 per year $10.09 per hour
Entry-Level Education	Less than high school
Work Experience in a Related Occupation	None
On-the-job Training	See How to Become One
Number of Jobs, 2010	4,465,500
Job Outlook, 2010-20	17% (About as fast as average)
Employment Change, 2010-20	739,400

What Retail Sales Workers Do

Retail sales workers include both those who sell retail merchandise, such as clothing, furniture, and cars, (called retail salespersons) and those who sell spare and replacement parts and equipment, especiallycar parts, (called parts salespersons). Both groups help customers find the products they want and process customers' payments.

Duties

Retail sales workers generally do the following:

- Greet customers and determine what each customer wants or needs
- Recommend merchandise based on customers' wants and needs
- Explain the use and benefit of merchandise to customers
- Answer customers' questions
- Show how merchandise works, if applicable
- Add up customers' total purchases and accept payment
- Know about current sales and promotions, policies about payments and exchanges, and security practices

Retail sales workers assist customers in finding the products they want and process payments.

The following are the types of retail sales workers

Retail salespersons work in stores where they sell goods, such as books, cars, clothing, cosmetics, electronics, furniture, lumber, plants, shoes, and many other types of merchandise.

In addition to helping customers find and select items to buy, many retail salespersons process the payment for the sale. This involves operating cash registers.

After taking payment for the purchases, retail salespersons may bag or package the purchases.

Depending on the hours they work, retail salespersons may have to open or close cash registers. This includes counting the money in the register and separating charge slips, coupons, and exchange vouchers. They may also make deposits at a cash office.

For information about other workers who receive and disburse money, see the profile on cashiers .

In addition, retail salespersons may help stock shelves or racks, arrange for mailing or delivery of purchases, mark price tags, take inventory, and prepare displays.

For some retail sales jobs, particularly those involving expensive and complex items, retail sales workers need special knowledge or skills. For example, those who sell cars must be able to explain the features of various models, the manufacturers' specifications, the types of options on the car and financing available, and the details of associated warranties.

In addition, retail sales workers must recognize security risks and thefts and understand their organization's procedures for handling thefts—procedures that may include notifying security guards or calling police.

Parts salespersons sell spare and replacement parts and equipment. Most deal with car parts, by working in either automotive parts stores or automobile dealerships. They take customers' orders, inform customers of part availability and price, and take inventory.

Work Environment

Retail salespersons held about 4.3 million jobs in 2010.

The following industries employed the most retail salespersons in 2010:

Clothing and clothing accessories stores	22%
General merchandise stores	19
Building material and garden equipment and supplies dealers	10
Motor vehicle and parts dealers	8
Sporting goods, hobby, book, and music stores	8

Parts salespersons held about 203,900 jobs in 2010.

The following industries employed the most parts salespersons in 2010:

Automotive parts, accessories, and tire stores	34%
Wholesale trade	25
Automobile dealers	24

Most retail sales workers work in clean, comfortable, well-lit stores. However, they often stand for long periods and may need permission from a supervisor to leave the sales floor. If they sell items such as cars, plants, or lumberyard materials, they may work outdoors.

Work Schedules

Many sales workers work evenings and weekends, particularly during holidays and other peak sales periods. Because the end-of-year holiday season is often the busiest time, many employers limit retail sales workers' use of vacation time between November and the beginning of January

About 37 percent of retail salespersons worked part time in 2010.

How to Become a Retail Sales Worker

Typically, retail sales workers do not need a formal education. However, some employers prefer applicants who have a high school diploma or its equivalent.

Education

Although retail or parts sales positions usually have no formal education requirements, some employers prefer applicants who have a high school diploma or equivalent, especially those who sell technical products or "big-ticket" items, such as electronics or cars.

Training

Most retail sales workers receive on-the-job training, which usually lasts a few days to a few months. In small stores, newly hired workers often are trained by an experienced employee. In large stores, training programs are more formal and generally are conducted over several days.

Topics often include customer service, security, the store's policies and procedures, and how to operate the cash register.

Depending on the type of product they are selling, employees may be given additional specialized training. For example, salespersons working in cosmetics get instruction on the types of products the store offers and for whom the cosmetics would be most beneficial. Likewise, those who sell computers may be instructed on the technical differences between computer products.

Because providing exceptional service to customers is a priority for many employers, employees often get periodic training to update and refine their skills.

Advancement

Retail sales workers typically have opportunities to advance to managerial positions. Some employers want candidates for managerial positions to have a college degree.

As sales workers gain experience and seniority, they often move into positions that have greater responsibility and may be given their choice of departments in which to work. This opportunity often means moving to positions with higher potential earnings and commissions. The highest earnings potential usually lies in selling "big-ticket" items—such as cars, jewelry, furniture, and electronics. These positions often require workers with extensive knowledge of the product and an excellent talent for persuasion.

Important Qualities

Customer-service skills. Retail sales workers must be responsive to the wants and needs of customers. They should explain the product options available to customers and make appropriate recommendations.

People skills. A friendly and outgoing personality is important for these workers because the job requires almost constant interaction with people.

Persistence. A large number of attempted sales may not be successful, so sales workers should not be discouraged easily. They must start each new sales attempt with a positive attitude.

Selling skills. Retail sales workers must be persuasive when interacting with customers. They must clearly and effectively explain the benefits of merchandise.

Pay

Retail Sales Workers
Median hourly wages, May 2010

Total, All Occupations	$16.27
Parts Salespersons	$13.88
Retail Sales Workers	$10.09
Retail Salespersons	$9.94

Note: All Occupations includes all occupations in the U.S. Economy.
Source: U.S. Bureau of Labor Statistics, Occupational Employment Statistics

The median hourly wage of retail salespersons was $9.94 in May 2010. The median wage is the wage at which half of the workers in an occupation earned more than that amount and half earned less. The lowest 10 percent earned less than $7.75, and the top 10 percent earned more than $18.54.

The median hourly wage of parts salespersons was $13.88 in May 2010. The lowest 10 percent earned less than $8.77, and the top 10 percent earned more than $23.12.

Compensation systems vary by type of establishment and merchandise sold. Retail sales workers get hourly wages, commissions, or a combination of the two. Under a commission system, they get a percentage of the sales they make. This system offers sales workers the opportunity to increase their earnings considerably, but they may find that their earnings depend strongly on their ability to sell their product and on the ups and downs of the economy.

Many retail sales workers work evenings and weekends, particularly during holidays and other peak sales periods. Because the end-of-year holiday season is often the busiest time, many employers limit sales workers' use of vacation time between November and the beginning of January. About 37 percent of retail salespersons worked part time in 2010.

Job Outlook

Retail Sales Workers
Percent change in employment, projected 2010-20

Retail Sales Workers	17%
Retail Salespersons	17%
Parts Salespersons	16%
Total, All Occupations	14%

Note: All Occupations includes all occupations in the U.S. Economy.
Source: U.S. Bureau of Labor Statistics, Employment Projections program

Employment of retail salespersons is expected to grow 17 percent from 2010 to 2020, about as fast as the average for all occupations.

Employment of retail salespersons has traditionally grown with the overall economy, and this trend is expected to continue. Population growth will increase retail sales and demand for these workers.

Although consumers are increasing their online retail shopping, they will continue to do most of their retail shopping in stores. Retail salespersons will be needed in stores to help customers and complete sales.

Among the various retail industries, other general merchandise stores, which include warehouse clubs and supercenters, are expected to see strong job growth. These large stores sell a wide range of goods from a single location. Thus, employment in the warehouse clubs and supercenters industry is expected to grow 51 percent during the next decade.

However, employment in department stores has declined in recent years and will likely continue to be weak.

Employment of parts salespersons is expected to grow 16 percent from 2010 to 2020, about as fast as the average for all occupations. People are keeping their cars longer and are buying new cars less often.

Older cars need to be serviced more frequently, creating demand for car parts and parts salespersons.

Job Prospects

Many workers leave this occupation, which means there will be a large number of job openings. This large number of job openings combined with the large size of the occupation should result in many employment opportunities.

Employment projections data for retail sales workers, 2010-20

Occupational Title	SOC Code	Employment, 2010	Projected Employment, 2020	Change, 2010-20	
				Percent	Numeric
Retail Sales Workers	—	4,465,500	5,204,900	17	739,400
Parts Salespersons	41-2022	203,900	236,500	16	32,600
Retail Salespersons	41-2031	4,261,600	4,968,400	17	706,800
SOURCE: U.S. Bureau of Labor Statistics, Employment Projections program					

Similar Occupations

This table shows a list of occupations with job duties that are similar to those of retail sales workers.

Occupation	Job Duties	Entry-Level Education	Median Annual Pay, May 2010
Cashiers	Cashiers handle payments from customers purchasing goods and services.	Less than high school	$18,500
Customer Service Representatives	Customer service representatives interact with customers on behalf of an organization. They provide information about products and services and respond to customer complaints. Some also take orders and process returns.	High school diploma or equivalent	$30,460
Information Clerks	Information clerks provide administrative and clerical support in a variety of settings. They help maintain records, collect data and information, and respond to customers' questions or concerns.	See How to Become One	$29,990
Insurance Sales Agents	Insurance sales agents help insurance companies generate new business by contacting potential customers and selling one or more types of insurance. An agent explains various insurance policies and helps clients choose plans that suit them.	High school diploma or equivalent	$46,770
Real Estate Brokers and Sales Agents	Real estate brokers and sales agents help clients buy, sell, and rent properties. Brokers and agents do the same type of work, but brokers are licensed to manage their own real estate businesses. Sales agents must work with a broker.	High school diploma or equivalent	$42,680
Sales Engineers	Sales engineers sell complex scientific and technological products or services to businesses. They must have extensive knowledge of the products' parts and functions and must understand the scientific processes that make these products work.	Bachelor's degree	$87,390
Securities, Commodities, and Financial Services Sales Agents	Securities, commodities, and financial services sales agents connect buyers and sellers in financial markets. They sell securities to individuals, advise companies in search of investors, and conduct trades.	Bachelor's degree	$70,190
Wholesale and Manufacturing Sales Representatives	Wholesale and manufacturing sales representatives sell goods for wholesalers or manufacturers to businesses, government agencies, and other organizations. They contact customers, explain product features, answer any questions that their customers may have, and negotiate prices.	See How to Become One	$56,620

Contacts for More Information

For information about training for a career in automobile sales, visit National Automobile Dealers Association

Suggested citation:

Bureau of Labor Statistics, U.S. Department of Labor, Occupational Outlook Handbook, 2012-13 Edition, Retail Sales Workers, on the Internet at http://www.bls.gov/ooh/sales/retail-sales-workers.htm .

Sales Engineers

Quick Facts: Sales Engineers	
2010 Median Pay	$87,390 per year $42.01 per hour
Entry-Level Education	Bachelor's degree
Work Experience in a Related Occupation	None
On-the-job Training	Moderate-term on-the-job training
Number of Jobs, 2010	66,400
Job Outlook, 2010-20	14% (About as fast as average)
Employment Change, 2010-20	9,500

What Sales Engineers Do

Sales engineers sell complex scientific and technological products or services to businesses. They must have extensive knowledge of the products' parts and functions and must understand the scientific processes that make these products work.

Duties

Sales engineers typically do the following:

- Prepare and deliver technical presentations that explain products or services to customers and prospective customers
- Confer with customers and engineers to assess equipment needs and to determine system requirements
- Collaborate with sales teams to understand customer requirements and provide sales support
- Secure and renew orders and arrange delivery
- Plan and modify products to meet customer needs

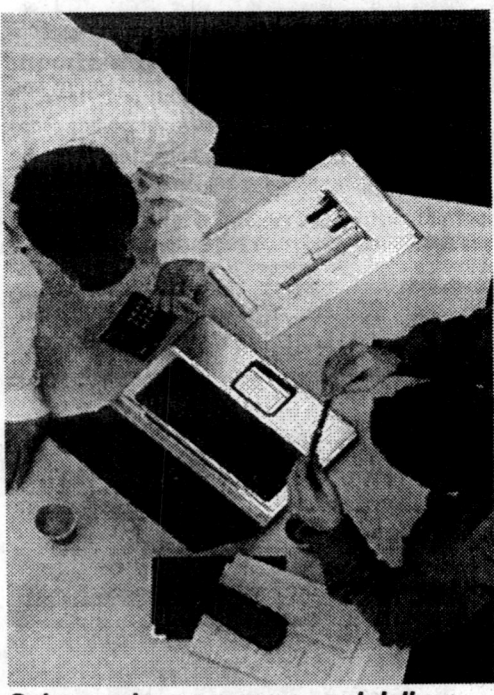

Sales engineers prepare and deliver technical presentations that explain products or services to customers and prospective customers.

- Help clients solve problems with installed equipment
- Recommend improved materials or machinery to customers, showing how changes will lower costs or increase production
- Help in researching and developing new products

Sales engineers specialize in technologically and scientifically advanced products. They use their technical skills to explain the benefits of their products or services to potential customers and to show how their products or services are better than their competitors' products. Some sales engineers work for the companies that design and build technical products. Others work for independent sales firms.

Many of the duties of sales engineers are similar to those of other salespersons. They must interest the client in buying their products or services, negotiate a price, and complete the sale. To do this, sales engineers give technical presentations during which they explain the technical aspects of the product and how it will solve a specific customer problem.

Some sales engineers, however, team with salespersons who concentrate on marketing and selling the product, which lets the sales engineer concentrate on the technical aspects of the job. By working as part of a sales team, each member is able to focus on his or her strengths and expertise. For more information on other sales occupations, see the profile on wholesale and manufacturing sales representatives .

In addition to giving technical presentations, sales engineers are increasingly doing other tasks related to sales, such as market research. They also may ask for technical requirements from customers and modify and adjust products to meet customers' specific needs. Some sales engineers work with research and development (R&D) departments to help identify and develop new products.

Work Environment

Sales engineers held about 66,400 jobs in 2010. Sales engineers encounter stress because their income and job security often depend directly on their success in sales and customer service. Some sales engineers have large territories and travel extensively. Because sales regions may cover several states, sales engineers may be away from home for several days or even weeks at a time. Other sales engineers cover a smaller region and spend only a few nights away from home. International travel to secure contracts with foreign clients is becoming more common.

The following industries employed the most sales engineers in 2010:

Wholesale trade	34%
Professional, scientific, and technical services	23
Computer and electronic product manufacturing	10
Telecommunications	9

Work Schedules

Some sales engineers may work long and irregular hours to meet sales goals and client needs. However, many sales engineers can decide their own schedules.

How to Become a Sales Engineer

A bachelor's degree is typically required for a sales engineer. Successful sales engineers combine technical knowledge of the products or services they are selling with strong interpersonal skills.

Education

Sales engineers typically need a bachelor's degree in engineering or a related field. However, workers without a degree but with previous sales experience as well as technical experience or training sometimes hold the title of sales engineer. Also, workers who have a degree in a science, such as chemistry, or in business with little or no previous sales experience may be called sales engineers.

University engineering programs generally require 4 years of study. They vary in content, but all programs include courses in math and the physical sciences. In addition, most require developing strong computer skills.

Some programs offer a general engineering curriculum; students then specialize on the job or in graduate school. Most programs, however, require students to choose an area of specialization. The most common majors are electrical, mechanical, or civil engineering, but some programs offer additional majors, such as chemical, biomedical, or computer hardware engineering.

Training

New graduates with engineering degrees may need sales experience and training before they can work independently as sales engineers. Training may involve teaming with a sales mentor who is familiar with the employer's business practices, customers, procedures, and company culture. After the training period, sales engineers may continue to partner with someone who lacks technical skills yet excels in the art of sales.

It is important for sales engineers to continue their engineering and sales education throughout their careers. Much of their value to their employers depends on their knowledge of, and ability to sell, the latest technologies. Sales engineers in high-technology fields, such as information technology and advanced electronics, may find that their technical knowledge rapidly becomes obsolete, requiring frequent retraining.

Advancement

Promotion may include a higher commission rate, a larger sales territory, or elevation to the position of supervisor or marketing manager.

Important Qualities

Complex problem-solving skills. Sales engineers must be able to listen to the customer's desires and concerns and then recommend solutions, possibly including customizing a product.

Interpersonal skills. Strong interpersonal skills are a valuable characteristic for sales engineers, both for building relationships with clients and effectively communicating with other members of the sales team.

Self-confidence. Sales engineers should be confident and persuasive when making sales presentations.

Technological skills. Sales engineers must have extensive knowledge of the technologically sophisticated products they sell in order to explain their advantages and answer questions.

Pay

Sales Engineers
Median annual wages, May 2010

Sales Engineers	$87,390
Total, All Occupations	$33,840
Sales and Related Occupations	$24,370

Note: All Occupations includes all occupations in the U.S. Economy.
Source: U.S. Bureau of Labor Statistics, Occupational Employment Statistics

The median annual wage of sales engineers was $87,390 in May 2010. The median wage is the wage at which half the workers in an occupation earned more than that amount and half earned less. The lowest 10 percent earned less than $51,940 and the top 10 percent earned more than $146,580.

How much a sales engineer earns varies significantly by the type of firm and the product sold. Most employers offer a combination of salary and commission payments or salary plus a bonus. Some sales engineers who work for independent sales companies earn only commissions. Commissions usually are based on the value of sales. Bonuses may depend on individual performance, on the performance of all workers in the group or district, or on the company's performance. Earnings from commissions and bonuses may vary from year to year depending on sales ability, the demand for the company's products or services, and the overall economy.

In addition to their earnings, sales engineers who work for manufacturers usually are reimbursed for expenses such as transportation, meals, hotels, and customer entertainment. Besides receiving typical benefits, sales engineers may get personal use of a company car and frequent-flyer miles. Some companies offer incentives such as free vacation trips or gifts for outstanding performance. Sales engineers who work in independent firms may have higher, but less stable earnings and, often, relatively few benefits. For example, most independent sales engineers do not get paid vacations, a common benefit for many other workers.

Some sales engineers may work long and irregular hours to meet sales goals and client needs. However, many sales engineers can decide their own schedules.

Job Outlook

Sales Engineers
Percent change in employment, projected 2010-20

Total, All Occupations	14%
Sales Engineers	14%
Sales and Related Occupations	13%

Note: All Occupations includes all occupations in the U.S. Economy.
Source: U.S. Bureau of Labor Statistics, Employment Projections program

Employment of sales engineers is expected to grow by 14 percent from 2010 to 2020, as fast as the average for all occupations. As a wider range of technologically sophisticated products comes on the market, sales engineers will be in demand to help sell products or services related to these products. Employment is expected to be strongest in independent sales agencies, as manufacturing companies outsource their sales staff as a way to control costs. Growth is also likely to be strong for sales engineers selling computer software and hardware. Employment of sales engineers in computer systems design and related services is expected to grow by 43 percent from 2010 to 2020.

Job Prospects

Successful sales engineers must have strong technical knowledge of the products they are selling, in addition to having interpersonal skills and the ability to persuade. Job prospects should be good for candidates with these abilities.

Employment projections data for sales engineers, 2010-20

Occupational Title	SOC Code	Employment, 2010	Projected Employment, 2020	Change, 2010-20 Percent	Change, 2010-20 Numeric
Sales Engineers	41-9031	66,400	75,900	14	9,500
SOURCE: U.S. Bureau of Labor Statistics, Employment Projections program					

Similar Occupations

This table shows a list of occupations with job duties that are similar to those of sales engineers.

Occupation	Job Duties	Entry-Level Education	Median Annual Pay, May 2010
Aerospace Engineers	Aerospace engineers design aircraft, spacecraft, satellites, and missiles. In addition, they test prototypes to make sure that they function according to design.	Bachelor's degree	$97,480
Computer Hardware Engineers	Computer hardware engineers research, design, develop, and test computer equipment such as chips, circuit boards, or routers. By solving complex problems in computer hardware, these engineers create rapid advances in computer technology.	Bachelor's degree	$98,810
Electrical and Electronics Engineers	Electrical engineers design, develop, test, and supervise the manufacturing of electrical equipment such as electric motors, radar and navigation systems, communications systems, and power generation equipment.Electronics engineers design and develop electronic equipment, such as broadcast and communications systems—from portable music players to global positioning systems (GPS).	Bachelor's degree	$87,180
Industrial Engineers	Industrial engineers find ways to eliminate wastefulness in production processes. They devise efficient ways to use workers, machines, materials, information, and energy to make a product or provide a service.	Bachelor's degree	$76,100
Insurance Sales Agents	Insurance sales agents help insurance companies generate new business by contacting potential customers and selling one or more types of insurance. An agent explains various insurance policies and helps clients choose plans that suit them.	High school diploma or equivalent	$46,770
Mechanical Engineers	Mechanical engineering is one of the broadest engineering disciplines. Mechanical engineers design, develop, build, and test mechanical devices, including tools, engines, and machines.	Bachelor's degree	$78,160
Purchasing Managers, Buyers, and Purchasing Agents	Purchasing managers, buyers, and purchasing agents buy products for organizations to use or resell. They evaluate suppliers, negotiate contracts, and review product quality.	See How to Become One	$58,360
Securities, Commodities, and Financial Services Sales Agents	Securities, commodities, and financial services sales agents connect buyers and sellers in financial markets. They sell securities to individuals, advise companies in search of investors, and conduct trades.	Bachelor's degree	$70,190
Wholesale and Manufacturing Sales Representatives	Wholesale and manufacturing sales representatives sell goods for wholesalers or manufacturers to businesses, government agencies, and other organizations. They contact customers, explain product features, answer any questions that their customers may have, and negotiate prices.	See How to Become One	$56,620

Contacts for More Information

For more information about careers in sales occupations, visit Manufacturers' Agents National Association , Manufacturers' Representatives Educational Research Foundation

Suggested citation:

Bureau of Labor Statistics, U.S. Department of Labor, Occupational Outlook Handbook, 2012-13 Edition, Sales Engineers, on the Internet at http://www.bls.gov/ooh/sales/sales-engineers.htm .

Securities, Commodities, and Financial Services Sales Agents

Quick Facts: Securities, Commodities, and Financial Services Sales Agents	
2010 Median Pay	$70,190 per year $33.75 per hour
Entry-Level Education	Bachelor's degree
Work Experience in a Related Occupation	None
On-the-job Training	Moderate-term on-the-job training
Number of Jobs, 2010	312,200
Job Outlook, 2010-20	15% (About as fast as average)
Employment Change, 2010-20	47,500

What Securities, Commodities, and Financial Services Sales Agents Do

Securities, commodities, and financial services sales agents connect buyers and sellers in financial markets. They sell securities to individuals, advise companies in search of investors, and conduct trades.

Duties

Securities, commodities, and financial services sales agents typically do the following:

- Contact prospective clients to present information and explain available services
- Offer advice on the purchase or sale of particular securities
- Buy and sell securities, such as stocks and bonds
- Buy and sell commodities, such as corn, oil, and gold
- Monitor financial markets and the performance of individual securities
- Analyze company finances to provide recommendations for public offerings, mergers, and acquisitions
- Evaluate cost and revenue of agreements

Securities, commodities, and financial services sales agents deal with a wide range of products and clients. Agents spend much of the day interacting with people, whether selling stock to an individual or discussing the status of a merger deal with a company executive. The work is usually stressful because agents deal with large amounts of money and have time constraints.

A security or commodity can be traded in two ways: electronically or in an auction-style setting on the floor of an exchange market. Markets such as the National Association of Securities Dealers Automated Quotation system (NASDAQ) use vast computer networks rather than human traders to match buyers and sellers. Others, such as the New York Stock Exchange (NYSE), rely on floor brokers to complete transactions.

The following are some types of securities, commodities, and financial services sales agents:

Brokers sell securities and commodities directly to individual clients. They advise people on appropriate investments based on the client's needs and financial ability. The people they advise may have very different levels of expertise in financial matters.

Finding clients is a large part of a broker's job. They must create their own client base by calling from a list of potential clients. Some agents network by joining social groups, and others may rely on referrals from satisfied clients.

Investment bankers connect businesses that need money to finance their operations or expansion plans with investors who are interested in providing that funding. This process is called underwriting, and it is the main function of investment banks. The banks first sell their advisory services to help companies issue new stocks or bonds, and then the banks sell the issued securities to investors.

Some of the most important services that investment bankers provide are initial public offerings (IPOs) and mergers and acquisitions.

An IPO is the process by which a company becomes open for public investment by issuing its first stock. Investment bankers must estimate how much the company is worth and ensure that it meets the legal requirements to become publicly traded.

Investment bankers connect companies in mergers (when two companies join together) and acquisitions (when one company buys another). Investment bankers provide advice throughout the process to ensure that the transaction goes smoothly.

Investment banking sales agents and traders carry out buy-and-sell orders for stocks, bonds, and commodities from clients and make trades on behalf of the firm itself. These workers are primarily employed by investment banks, although some work for commercial banks, hedge funds, and private equity groups. Because

Securities, commodities, and financial services sales agents sell securities to individuals, advise companies in search of investors, and carry out trades.

markets fluctuate so much, trading is a split-second decision-making process. Slight changes in the price of a trade can greatly affect its profitability, making the trader's decision extremely important.

Floor brokers work directly on the floor—a large room where trading is done—of a securities or commodities exchange. After a trader places an order for a security, floor brokers negotiate the price, make the sale, and forward the purchase price to the trader.

Financial services sales agents consult on a wide variety of banking, securities, insurance, and related services to individuals and businesses, often catering the services to meet the client's financial needs. They contact potential clients to explain their services, which may include checking accounts, loans, certificates of deposit, individual retirement accounts, credit cards, and estate and retirement planning.

Work Environment

Securities, commodities, and financial services sales agents held about 312,200 jobs in 2010.

The following industries employed the most securities, commodities, and financial services sales agents in 2010:

Securities and commodity contracts intermediation and brokerage	40%
Depository credit intermediation	23
Other financial investment activities	10

Most securities, commodities, and financial services sales agents work long hours under stressful conditions. The pace of work is fast, and managers are usually demanding of their workers, because both commissions and advancements are tied to sales.

Investment bankers travel extensively because they frequently work with companies in other countries.

Because computers can conduct trades more quickly than people, electronic trading is quickly replacing verbal auction-style trades on exchange floors. The environment of the stock exchange is changing as a result, with more traders carrying out orders behind a desk and fewer working on the exchange floor.

A growing number of securities sales agents, employed mostly by discount or online brokerage firms, work in call-center environments. In these centers, hundreds of agents spend much of the day on the telephone taking orders from clients or offering help and information on their accounts.

Most of the major investment banks are located in New York City, making employment in the occupation of securities, commodities, and financial services sales agents concentrated in this metropolitan area.

The following metropolitan areas had the highest employment level of securities, commodities, and financial services sales agents in 2010:

New York-White Plains-Wayne, NY-NJ Metropolitan Division	40,790
Chicago-Naperville-Joliet, IL Metropolitan Division	16,830
Houston-Sugar Land-Baytown, TX	7,970
Los Angeles-Long Beach-Glendale, CA Metropolitan Division	7,920
Dallas-Plano-Irving, TX Metropolitan Division	7,430

Work Schedules

Securities, commodities, and financial services sales agents usually work full time and many work more than 40 hours per week. In addition, they may work evenings and weekends because many of their clients work during the day. Call centers often operate 24 hours a day, requiring agents to work in shifts.

How to Become a Securities, Commodities, or Financial Services Sales Agent

A bachelor's degree is required for entry-level jobs, and a Master of Business Administration (MBA) is useful for advancement.

Education

Securities, commodities, and financial services sales agents generally must have a bachelor's degree to get an entry-level job. Studies in business, finance, accounting, or economics are important, especially for larger firms. Many firms hire summer interns before their last year of college, and those who are most successful are offered full-time jobs after they graduate.

Numerous agents eventually get a Master of Business Administration (MBA), which is often a requirement for high-level positions in the securities industry. Because the MBA exposes students to real-world business practices, it can be a major asset for jobseekers. Employers often reward MBA holders with higher-level positions, better compensation, and large signing bonuses.

Training

Most employers provide intensive on-the-job training, teaching employees the specifics of the firm, such as the products and services offered. Trainees in large firms may receive technical instruction in securities analysis and selling strategies. Firms often rotate their trainees among various departments to give them a broad understanding of the securities business.

Securities and commodities sales agents must keep up with new products and services and other developments. They regularly attend conferences and training seminars.

Licenses

Brokers and investment bankers must register as representatives of their firm with the Financial Industry Regulatory Authority (FINRA). To obtain the license, potential agents must pass a series of exams.

Many other licenses are available, each of which gives the holder the right to sell different investment products and services. Traders and some other sales representatives also need licenses, although these vary by firm and specialization. Financial services sales agents may need to be licensed, especially if they sell securities or insurance. Most firms offer training to help their employees pass the licensing exams.

Agents who are registered with FINRA must attend continuing education classes to keep their licenses. Courses consist of computer-based training on legal requirements or new financial products or services.

Certification

Although not always required, certification enhances professional standing and is recommended by employers. Brokers, investment bankers, and financial services sales agents can earn the Chartered Financial Analyst (CFA) certification, sponsored by the CFA Institute. To qualify for this certification, applicants need a bachelor's degree and 4 years of related work experience and must pass three exams, which require several hundred hours of self-study. Exams cover subjects in accounting, economics, securities analysis, financial markets and instruments, corporate finance, asset valuation, and portfolio management. Applicants can take the exams while they are getting the required work experience.

Advancement

Securities, commodities, and financial services sales agents usually advance to senior positions in a firm by accumulating a greater number of accounts. Although beginners often service the accounts of individual investors, they may eventually service large institutional accounts, such as those of banks and retirement funds.

After taking a series of tests, some brokers become portfolio managers and have greater authority to make investment decisions regarding an account. For more information on portfolio managers, see the profile on financial analysts .

Some experienced sales agents become branch office managers and supervise other sales agents while continuing to provide services for their own clients. A few agents advance to top management positions or become partners in their firms.

Many investment banks use an "up or out" policy, in which entry-level investment bankers are either promoted or terminated after 2 or 3 years. Investment banks use this policy to ensure that entry-level positions are not occupied long term, allowing the bank to steadily bring in new workers.

Important Qualities

Customer-service skills. Securities, commodities, and financial services sales agents must be persuasive and make clients feel comfortable with the agent's recommendations.

Decision-making skills. Investment banking traders must make split-second decisions with large sums of money at stake.

Detail oriented. Investment bankers must pay close attention to the details of initial public offerings and mergers and acquisitions because small changes can have large consequences.

Initiative. Securities, commodities, and financial services sales agents must create their own client base by making "cold" sales calls to people to whom they have not been referred and to people not expecting the call.

Math skills. To judge the profitability of potential deals, financial services sales agents must have strong math skills.

Pay

Securities, Commodities, and Financial Services Sales Agents
  Median annual wages, May 2010

Securities, Commodities, and Financial Services Sales Agents	$70,190
Total, All Occupations	$33,840
Sales and Related Occupations	$24,370

Note: All Occupations includes all occupations in the U.S. Economy.
Source: U.S. Bureau of Labor Statistics, Occupational Employment Statistics

The median annual wage of securities, commodities, and financial services sales agents was $70,190 in May 2010. The median wage is the wage at which half the workers in an occupation earned more than that amount and half earned less. The lowest 10 percent earned less than $31,330, and the top 10 percent earned more than $166,400.

Many securities and commodities brokers earn a commission based on the monetary value of the products they sell. Most firms pay brokers a minimum salary in addition to commissions.

Trainee brokers usually earn a salary until they develop a client base. The salary gradually decreases in favor of commissions as the broker gains clients.

Investment bankers in corporate finance and mergers and acquisitions generally earn a base salary with the opportunity to earn a substantial bonus. At higher levels, bonuses far exceed base salary.

Securities, commodities, and financial services sales agents usually work full time and many work more than 40 hours per week. In addition, they may work evenings and weekends because many of their clients work during the day. Call centers often operate 24 hours a day, requiring agents to work in shifts.

Job Outlook

Securities, Commodities, and Financial Services Sales Agents
  Percent change in employment, projected 2010-20

Securities, Commodities, and Financial Services Sales Agents	15%
Total, All Occupations	14%
Sales and Related Occupations	13%

Note: All Occupations includes all occupations in the U.S. Economy.
Source: U.S. Bureau of Labor Statistics, Employment Projections program

Employment of securities, commodities, and financial services sales agents is expected to grow 15 percent from 2010 to 2020, about as fast as the average for all occupations.

The financial services industry experienced some consolidation because of the recent financial crisis, but the industry has resumed growth. Overall, employment in the finance and insurance industry is expected to grow by 14 percent from 2010 to 2020.

Financial regulation, including restrictions on proprietary trading, may create a shift of employment among traders from investment banks to hedge funds, however, overall employment growth for the occupation should not be affected.

Services that investment bankers provide, such as helping with initial public offerings and mergers and acquisitions, will continue to be in demand as the economy grows. The United States remains an international financial center, meaning that the economic growth of countries around the world will contribute to employment growth in the American financial industry.

In addition, employment growth should be particularly strong for commodities brokers and traders. Trading in commodities markets has increased substantially in recent years, driven by large group investors, such as retirement funds, entering the market. As the number of transactions increases in commodities trading, such as oil futures, employment of commodities sales agents will increase to meet this demand.

Although employment growth for securities, commodities, and financial services sales agents as a whole is expected to be strong, the use of online stock trading sites will restrict growth for stock brokers. As clients themselves conduct transactions online, the need for stock brokers will diminish.

Job Prospects

The high pay associated with securities, commodities, and financial services sales agents draws many more applicants than there are openings. Therefore, competition for jobs is intense.

Certification and a graduate degree, such as a Chartered Financial Analyst (CFA) certification and a master's degree in business or finance, can significantly improve an applicant's prospects. For entry-level jobs, having an excellent grade-point average (GPA) in college is important.

Employment projections data for securities, commodities, and financial services sales agents, 2010-20

Occupational Title	SOC Code	Employment, 2010	Projected Employment, 2020	Change, 2010-20	
				Percent	Numeric
Securities, Commodities, and Financial Services Sales Agents	41-3031	312,200	359,700	15	47,500
SOURCE: U.S. Bureau of Labor Statistics, Employment Projections program					

Similar Occupations

This table shows a list of occupations with job duties that are similar to those of securities, commodities, and financial services sales agents.

Occupation	Job Duties	Entry-Level Education	Median Annual Pay, May 2010
Financial Analysts	Financial analysts provide guidance to businesses and individuals making investment decisions. They assess the performance of stocks, bonds, and other types of investments.	Bachelor's degree	$74,350
Financial Managers	Financial managers are responsible for the financial health of an organization. They produce financial reports, direct investment activities, and develop strategies and plans for the long-term financial goals of their organization.	Bachelor's degree	$103,910
Insurance Sales Agents	Insurance sales agents help insurance companies generate new business by contacting potential customers and selling one or more types of insurance. An agent explains various insurance policies and helps clients choose plans that suit them.	High school diploma or equivalent	$46.770
Personal Financial Advisors	Personal financial advisors give financial advice to people. They help with investments, taxes, and insurance decisions.	Bachelor's degree	$64,750
Real Estate Brokers and Sales Agents	Real estate brokers and sales agents help clients buy, sell, and rent properties. Brokers and agents do the same type of work, but brokers are licensed to manage their own real estate businesses. Sales agents must work with a broker.	High school diploma or equivalent	$42,680

Contacts for More Information

For more information about securities, commodities, and financial services sales agents, visit American Academy of Financial Management

Securities Industry and Financial Markets Association

For more information about licensing of securities, commodities, and financial services sales agents, visit Financial Industry Regulatory Authority (FINRA)

For more information about certification for securities, commodities, and financial services sales agents, visit CFA Institute

Suggested citation:

Bureau of Labor Statistics, U.S. Department of Labor, Occupational Outlook Handbook, 2012-13 Edition, Securities, Commodities, and Financial Services Sales Agents, on the Internet at http://www.bls.gov/ooh/sales/securities-commodities-and-financial-services-sales-agents.htm .

Travel Agents

Quick Facts: Travel Agents	
2010 Median Pay	$31,870 per year $15.32 per hour
Entry-Level Education	High school diploma or equivalent
Work Experience in a Related Occupation	None
On-the-job Training	Moderate-term on-the-job training
Number of Jobs, 2010	82,800
Job Outlook, 2010-20	10% (About as fast as average)
Employment Change, 2010-20	8,300

What Travel Agents Do

Travel agents sell transportation, lodging, and admission to entertainment activities to individuals and groups who are planning trips. They offer advice on destinations, plan trip itineraries, and make travel arrangements for clients.

Duties

Travel agents typically do the following:

- Arrange travel for business and vacation customers
- Determine customers' needs and preferences, such as schedules and costs
- Plan and arrange tour packages, excursions, and day trips
- Find fare and schedule information
- Calculate total travel costs
- Book reservations for travel, hotels, rental cars, and special events, such as tours and excursions
- Tell clients about their trip, including details on required documents, such as passports or visas
- Give advice about local weather conditions, customs, and attractions
- Make alternate booking arrangements if changes arise before or during the trip

Travel agents help travelers by sorting through vast amounts of information to find the best possible travel arrangements. In addition, resorts and specialty travel groups use travel agents to promote travel packages to their clients.

Travel agents may also visit destinations to get first-hand experience so they can make recommendations to clients or colleagues. They may visit hotels, resorts, and restaurants to evaluate the comfort,

Travel agents sell transportation, lodging, and admission to activities to those planning trips.

cleanliness, and quality of the establishment. However, most of their time is spent talking with clients, promoting tours, and contacting airlines and hotels to make travel arrangements.

A growing number of travel agents focus on a specific type of travel, such as adventure tours. Some may cater to a specific group of people, such as senior citizens or single people. Other travel agents primarily make corporate travel arrangements for employee business travel. Some work for tour operators and are responsible for selling the company's tours and services.

Work Environment

Travel agents held about 82,800 jobs in 2010. Travel agents work in offices, where they spend much of their time on the phone and on the computer. In some cases, busy offices or call centers may be noisy and crowded. Agents may face stress during travel emergencies or unanticipated schedule changes.

In 2010, 79 percent of all travel agents worked for the travel arrangement and reservation services industry, this includes those who work for travel agencies. Additionally, 14 percent of travel agents were self-employed.

Work Schedules

Most travel agents work full time. Some work longer hours during peak travel times or when they must accommodate customers' schedule changes and last-minute needs.

How to Become a Travel Agent

A high school diploma is typically required for entry. However, many employers prefer formal training. Good communication and computer skills are essential for travel agents.

Education

Employers may prefer candidates who have taken classes related to the travel industry. Many community colleges, vocational schools, and industry associations offer technical training or continuing education classes in professional travel planning. Classes usually focus on reservations systems, regulations regarding international travel, and marketing. In addition, a few colleges offer degrees in travel and tourism. In all cases, employers will provide some on-the-job training related to the company's specific travel systems. For example, a travel agent could be trained to use a particular airline's reservation system.

Certification

Some associations offer certification that may help travel agents once they are on the job. The Travel Institute and the International Airline Transport Association's Training and Development Institute , for example, provide training and professional development opportunities for experienced travel agents. Examinations for different levels of certification are offered depending on a travel agent's experience.

Licenses

Some states require agents to have a business license to sell travel services. Requirements among states vary greatly. Contact individual state licensing agencies for more information.

Important Qualities

Adventurousness. Travel agencies that specialize in exotic destinations or particular types of travel, such as adventure travel or ecotourism, may prefer to hire travel agents who share these interests.

Communication skills. Travel agents must listen to customers, understand their travel needs, and offer appropriate travel advice and information.

Detail oriented. Travel agents must pay attention to details to ensure that the reservations they make match travelers' needs. They must make reservations at the correct dates, times, and locations to meet travelers' schedules.

Organizational skills. Travel agents should have strong organizational skills because they often work on itineraries for many customers at once. Keeping client information in order and ensuring that bills and receipts are processed in a timely manner is essential.

Sales skills. Travel agents must be able to persuade clients to buy transportation, lodging, or tours. Sometimes they might need to persuade tour operators, airline staff, or others to take care of their clients' special needs. Earnings for many travel agents depend on commissions and service fees.

Pay

Travel Agents
Median annual wages, May 2010

Total, All Occupations	$33,840
Travel Agents	$31,870
Sales and Related Occupations	$24,370

Note: All Occupations includes all occupations in the U.S. Economy.
Source: U.S. Bureau of Labor Statistics, Occupational Employment Statistics

The median annual wage of travel agents was $31,870 in May 2010. The median wage is the wage at which half the workers in an occupation earned more than that amount and half earned less. The lowest 10 percent earned less than $19,610, and the top 10 percent earned more than $50,620. These wage data include money earned from commissions.

Most travel agents work full time. Some work longer hours during peak travel times or when they must accommodate customers' schedule changes and last-minute needs.

Job Outlook

Travel Agents
Percent change in employment, projected 2010-20

Total, All Occupations	14%
Sales and Related Occupations	13%
Travel Agents	10%

Note: All Occupations includes all occupations in the U.S. Economy.
Source: U.S. Bureau of Labor Statistics, Employment Projections program

Employment of travel agents is projected to grow by 10 percent from 2010 to 2020, about as fast as the average for all occupations.

Clients who want customized travel experiences, such as adventure tours, will continue to require the expertise of agents. However, the ability of travelers to research vacations and book their own trips using the Internet is expected to continue to suppress demand for travel agents.

Job prospects

Job prospects should be best for travel agents who specialize in specific destinations or particular types of travelers, such as groups with a special interest or corporate travelers.

Employment projections data for travel agents, 2010-20

Occupational Title	SOC Code	Employment, 2010	Projected Employment, 2020	Change, 2010-20 Percent	Change, 2010-20 Numeric
Travel Agents	41-3041	82,800	91,100	10	8,300

SOURCE: U.S. Bureau of Labor Statistics, Employment Projections program

Similar Occupations

This table shows a list of occupations with job duties that are similar to those of travel agents.

Occupation	Job Duties	Entry-Level Education	Median Annual Pay, May 2010
Information Clerks	Information clerks provide administrative and clerical support in a variety of settings. They help maintain records, collect data and information, and respond to customers' questions or concerns.	See How to Become One	$29,990
Meeting, Convention, and Event Planners	Meeting, convention, and event planners coordinate all aspects of professional meetings and events. They choose meeting locations, arrange transportation, and coordinate other details.	Bachelor's degree	$45,260
Secretaries and Administrative Assistants	Secretaries and administrative assistants perform routine clerical and organizational tasks. They organize files, draft messages, schedule appointments, and support other staff.	High school diploma or equivalent	$34,660

Contacts for More Information

For more information about training opportunities, visit American Society of Travel Agents

For more information about voluntary certification opportunities, visit The Travel Institute

Suggested citation:

Bureau of Labor Statistics, U.S. Department of Labor, Occupational Outlook Handbook, 2012-13 Edition, Travel Agents, on the Internet at http://www.bls.gov/ooh/sales/travel-agents.htm .

Wholesale and Manufacturing Sales Representatives

Quick Facts: Wholesale and Manufacturing Sales Representatives	
2010 Median Pay	$56,620 per year $27.22 per hour
Entry-Level Education	See How to Become One
Work Experience in a Related Occupation	None
On-the-job Training	Moderate-term on-the-job training
Number of Jobs, 2010	1,830,000
Job Outlook, 2010-20	16% (About as fast as average)
Employment Change, 2010-20	288,900

What Wholesale and Manufacturing Sales Representatives Do

Wholesale and manufacturing sales representatives sell goods for wholesalers or manufacturers to businesses, government agencies, and other organizations. They contact customers, explain product features, answer any questions that their customers may have, and negotiate prices.

Duties

Wholesale and manufacturing sales representatives typically do the following:

- Identify prospective customers by using business directories, following leads from existing clients, and attending trade shows and conferences
- Contact new and existing customers to discuss their needs and to explain how specific products and services can meet these needs
- Help customers select products based on the customers' needs, product specifications, and regulations
- Emphasize product features based on analyses of customers' needs and on technical knowledge of product capabilities and limitations

Wholesale and manufacturing sales representatives contact customers, explain product features, answer any questions that their customers may have, and negotiate prices.

- Answer customers' questions about prices, availability, and product uses
- Negotiate prices and terms of sales and service agreements
- Prepare sales contracts and submit orders for processing
- Collaborate with colleagues to exchange information, such as selling strategies and marketing information
- Follow up with customers to make sure they are satisfied with their purchases and to answer any questions or concerns
- Stay up-to-date on new products and changes to products that they sell

Wholesale and manufacturing sales representatives—sometimes called manufacturers' representatives or manufacturers' agents—generally work for manufacturers, wholesalers, or technical companies. Some work for a single organization, while others represent several companies and sell a range of products.

Rather than selling goods directly to consumers, wholesale and manufacturing sales representatives deal with businesses, government agencies, and other organizations. For more information about people who sell directly to consumers, see the profile on retail sales workers . For more information about people who specialize in sales of technical products and services, see the profile for sales engineers .

Some wholesale and manufacturing sales representatives specialize in technical and scientific products, ranging from agricultural and mechanical equipment to computer and pharmaceutical goods. Other representatives deal with nonscientific products such as food, office supplies, and clothing.

Wholesale and manufacturing sales representatives who lack expertise about a given product frequently team with a technical expert. In this arrangement, the technical expert—sometimes a sales engineer—attends the sales presentation to explain the product and answer questions or concerns. The sales representative makes the initial contact with customers, introduces the company's product, and obtains final agreement from the potential buyer.

By working with a technical expert, the representative is able to spend more time maintaining and soliciting accounts and less time gaining technical knowledge.

After the sale, representatives may make follow-up visits to ensure that equipment is functioning properly and may even help train customers' employees to operate and maintain new equipment.

Those selling consumer goods often suggest how and where merchandise should be displayed. When working with retailers, they may help arrange promotional programs, store displays, and advertising.

In addition to selling products, wholesale and manufacturing sales representatives analyze sales statistics, prepare reports, and handle administrative duties such as filing expense accounts, scheduling appointments, and making travel plans.

Staying up-to-date on new products and the changing needs of their customers is important. Sales representatives accomplish this in a variety of ways, including attending trade shows at which new products and technologies are showcased. They attend conferences and conventions to meet other sales representatives and clients and discuss new product developments. They also read about new and existing products and monitor the sales, prices, and products of their competitors.

There are two main types of wholesale and manufacturing sales representatives: inside and outside.

Inside sales representatives work mostly in offices while making sales. Frequently, they are responsible for getting new clients by "cold calling" various organizations—calling potential customers to establish an initial contact. They also take incoming calls from customers who are interested in their product and process paperwork to complete the sale.

Outside sales representatives spend much of their time traveling to, and visiting with, current clients and prospective buyers. During a sales call, they discuss the client's needs and suggest how their merchandise or services can meet those needs. They may show samples or catalogs that describe items their company provides, and they may inform customers about prices, availability, and ways in which their products can save money and boost productivity. Because many sales representatives sell several complementary products made by different manufacturers, they may take a broad approach to their customers' businesses. For example, sales representatives may help install new equipment and train employees in its use.

Work Environment

The following industries employed the most wholesale and manufacturing sales representatives in 2010.

Wholesale and manufacturing sales representatives were employed in the following industries in 2010:

Merchant wholesalers, durable goods	28%
Merchant wholesalers, nondurable goods	18
Wholesale electronic markets and agents and brokers	16
Manufacturing	14
Professional, scientific, and technical services	4

Some wholesale and manufacturing sales representatives have large territories and travel considerably. Because a sales region may cover several states, representatives may be away from home for several days or weeks at a time. Others cover a smaller region, spending few nights away from home.

Inside wholesale and manufacturing sales representatives spend a lot of their time on the phone, selling goods, taking orders, and resolving problems or complaints about the merchandise. They also use web technology, including chat,
e-mail, and video conferencing, to contact clients.

Workers in this occupation can under considerable stress because their income and job security often depend directly on the amount of merchandise they sell, and their companies usually set goals or quotas that they are expected to meet.

Work Schedules

Most wholesale and manufacturing sales representatives work full time, and almost a quarter worked 50 or more hours per week. Since sales calls take place during regular working hours, many do much of the planning and paperwork involved with sales in the evening and on weekends. Although the hours are often irregular, many sales representatives may determine their own schedules.

How to Become a Wholesale or Manufacturing Sales Representative

Educational requirements vary, depending on the type of product sold. If the products are not scientific or technical, a high school diploma is generally enough for entry into the occupation. If the products are scientific or technical, sales representatives typically need at least a bachelor's degree.

Education

A high school diploma is sufficient for many positions, primarily for selling nontechnical or scientific products. However, those selling scientific and technical products typically must have a bachelor's degree. Scientific and technical products include pharmaceuticals, medical instruments, and industrial equipment. A degree in a field related to the product sold, such as chemistry, biology, or engineering, is often required.

Many sales representatives attend seminars in sales techniques or take courses in marketing, economics, communication, or even a foreign language to improve their ability to make sales.

Training

Many companies have formal training programs for beginning wholesale and manufacturing sales representatives that last up to 1 year. In some programs, trainees rotate among jobs in plants and offices to learn all phases of producing, installing, and distributing the product. In others, trainees take formal technical instruction at the plant, followed by on-the-job training under the supervision of a field sales manager.

Regardless of where they work, new employees may be trained by going along with experienced workers on their sales calls. As they gain familiarity with the firm's products and clients, the new workers gain more responsibility until they eventually get their own territory.

Certification

Many in this occupation have either the Certified Professional Manufacturers' Representative (CPMR) certification or the Certified Sales Professional (CSP) certification, both offered by the Manufacturers' Representatives Education Research Foundation . Certification typically involves completing formal technical training and passing an exam.

Work Experience

Sales experience is helpful for being hired as a sales representative, particularly nontechnical positions.

Advancement

Frequently, promotion takes the form of an assignment to a larger account or territory, where commissions are likely to be greater. Those who have good sales records and leadership ability may advance to higher level positions, such as sales supervisor, district manager, or vice president of sales.

Important Qualities

Customer-service skills. Sales representatives must be able to listen to the customer's needs and concerns before and after the sale.

Interpersonal skills. Sales representatives must be able to work well with many types of people. They must be able to build good relationships with clients and with other members of the sales team.

Self-confidence. Sales representatives must be confident and persuasive when making sales presentations. In addition, making a call to a potential customer who is not expecting to be contacted, or "cold calling," requires confidence and composure.

Stamina. Sales representatives are often on their feet for long periods of time and may carry heavy sample products.

Pay

Wholesale and Manufacturing Sales Representatives
Median annual wages, May 2010

Sales Representatives, Wholesale and Manufacturing, Technical and Scientific Products	$73,710
Wholesale and Manufacturing Sales Representatives	$56,620
Sales Representatives, Wholesale and Manufacturing, Except Technical and Scientific Products	$52,440
Total, All Occupations	$33,840

Note: All Occupations includes all occupations in the U.S. Economy.
Source: U.S. Bureau of Labor Statistics, Occupational Employment Statistics

The median annual wage of wholesale and manufacturing sales representatives, technical and scientific products was $73,710 in May 2010. The median wage is the wage at which half of the workers in an occupation earned more than that amount and half earned less. The lowest 10 percent earned less than $36,740, and the top 10 percent earned more than $144,420.

The median annual wage of wholesale and manufacturing sales representatives, except technical and scientific products was $52,440 in May 2010. The lowest 10 percent earned less than $26,970, and the top 10 percent earned more than $108,750.

Compensation methods for representatives vary significantly by the type of firm and the product sold. Most employers use a combination of salary and commissions or salary plus bonuses. Commissions usually are based on the value of sales. Bonuses may depend on individual performance, on the performance of all sales workers in the group or district, or on the company's performance.

Most wholesale and manufacturing sales representatives work full time. In 2010, about a quarter of sales representatives worked more than 50 hours per week.

Job Outlook

Wholesale and Manufacturing Sales Representatives
Percent change in employment, projected 2010-20

Sales Representatives, Wholesale and Manufacturing, Technical and Scientific Products	16%
Wholesale and Manufacturing Sales Representatives	16%
Sales Representatives, Wholesale and Manufacturing, Except Technical and Scientific Products	16%
Total, All Occupations	14%

Note: All Occupations includes all occupations in the U.S. Economy.
Source: U.S. Bureau of Labor Statistics, Employment Projections program

Employment of wholesale and manufacturing sales representatives is expected to grow by 16 percent from 2010 to 2020, about as fast as the average for all occupations.

Employment growth for wholesale and manufacturing sales representatives will largely follow growth of the overall economy.

In addition to the total volume of sales, a wider range of products and technologies will lead to increased demand for sales representatives

Because this work requires a lot of face-to-face interaction with potential buyers, the work of wholesale goods sales representatives is not likely to be sent to other countries.

Employment growth is expected to be strongest for sales representatives working at independent sales agencies. Companies are increasingly giving their sales activities to independent companies as a way to cut costs and boost revenue. These independent companies do not buy and hold the products they are selling. Instead, they operate on a fee or commission basis in representing the product manufacturer. Employment of sales representatives in this industry—wholesale electronic markets and agents and brokers—is expected to grow by 51 percent from 2010 to 2020.

Job Prospects

Job candidates should see very good opportunities. Because workers frequently leave this occupation, there are usually a relatively large number of openings.

Employment projections data for wholesale and manufacturing sales representatives, 2010-20

Occupational Title	SOC Code	Employment, 2010	Projected Employment, 2020	Change, 2010-20 Percent	Change, 2010-20 Numeric
Sales Representatives, Wholesale and Manufacturing	41-4000	1,830,000	2,118,900	16	288,900
Sales Representatives, Wholesale and Manufacturing, Technical and Scientific Products	41-4011	400,000	465,500	16	65,500
Sales Representatives, Wholesale and Manufacturing, Except Technical and Scientific Products	41-4012	1,430,000	1,653,400	16	223,400
SOURCE: U.S. Bureau of Labor Statistics, Employment Projections program					

Similar Occupations

This table shows a list of occupations with job duties that are similar to those of wholesale and manufacturing sales representatives.

Occupation	Job Duties	Entry-Level Education	Median Annual Pay, May 2010
Advertising Sales Agents	Advertising sales agents sell advertising space to businesses and individuals. They contact potential clients, make sales presentations, and maintain client accounts.	High school diploma or equivalent	$45,350
Insurance Sales Agents	Insurance sales agents help insurance companies generate new business by contacting potential customers and selling one or more types of insurance. An agent explains various insurance policies and helps clients choose plans that suit them.	High school diploma or equivalent	$46,770

Purchasing Managers, Buyers, and Purchasing Agents	Purchasing managers, buyers, and purchasing agents buy products for organizations to use or resell. They evaluate suppliers, negotiate contracts, and review product quality.	See How to Become One	$58,360
Real Estate Brokers and Sales Agents	Real estate brokers and sales agents help clients buy, sell, and rent properties. Brokers and agents do the same type of work, but brokers are licensed to manage their own real estate businesses. Sales agents must work with a broker.	High school diploma or equivalent	$42,680
Retail Sales Workers	Retail sales workers include both those who sell retail merchandise, such as clothing, furniture, and automobiles, (called retail salespersons) and those who sell spare and replacement parts and equipment, especiallycar parts, (called parts salespersons). Both groups help customers find the products they want and process customers' payments.	Less than high school	$20,990
Sales Engineers	Sales engineers sell complex scientific and technological products or services to businesses. They must have extensive knowledge of the products' parts and functions and must understand the scientific processes that make these products work.	Bachelor's degree	$87,390
Securities, Commodities, and Financial Services Sales Agents	Securities, commodities, and financial services sales agents connect buyers and sellers in financial markets. They sell securities to individuals, advise companies in search of investors, and conduct trades.	Bachelor's degree	$70,190

Contacts for More Information

For more information about wholesale sales representatives, visit Manufacturers' Agents National Association

For more information about certification, visit Manufacturers' Representatives Educational Research Foundation

Suggested citation:

Bureau of Labor Statistics, U.S. Department of Labor, Occupational Outlook Handbook, 2012-13 Edition, Wholesale and Manufacturing Sales Representatives, on the Internet at http://www.bls.gov/ooh/sales/wholesale-and-manufacturing-sales-representatives.htm.

Transportation and Material Moving Occupations

Airline and Commercial Pilots

Quick Facts: Airline and Commercial Pilots	
2010 Median Pay	$92,060 per year
Entry-Level Education	See How to Become One
Work Experience in a Related Occupation	See How to Become One
On-the-job Training	See How to Become One
Number of Jobs, 2010	103,500
Job Outlook, 2010-20	11% (About as fast as average)
Employment Change, 2010-20	11,500

What Airline and Commercial Pilots Do

Airline and commercial pilots fly and navigate airplanes or helicopters. Airline pilots fly for airlines that transport people and cargo on a fixed schedule. Commercial pilots fly aircraft for other reasons, such as charter flights, rescue operations, firefighting, aerial photography, and crop dusting.

Duties

Pilots typically do the following:
- Follow a checklist of preflight checks on engines, hydraulics, and other systems
- Ensure that all cargo has been loaded and that the aircraft weight is properly balanced
- Check fuel, weather conditions, and flight schedules
- Contact the control tower for takeoff and arrival instructions
- Start engines, operate controls, and steer aircraft along planned routes
- Monitor engines, fuel consumption, and other aircraft systems during flight
- Navigate the aircraft, using cockpit instruments
- Ensure a smooth takeoff and landing

For all but small aircraft, two pilots usually make up the cockpit crew. Generally, the most experienced pilot, the captain, is in command and supervises all other crew members. The copilot, often called the first officer, shares flight duties with the captain.

These duties include communicating with air traffic controllers, monitoring instruments, and steering the plane.

Some older planes require a third pilot known as a flight engineer. This person helps the other pilots by monitoring instruments and operating controls. New technology has automated many of these tasks, and most new planes do not require a flight engineer.

Before departure, pilots plan their flights carefully, checking various systems on the aircraft and making sure that baggage and cargo have been loaded correctly. They also confer with air traffic controllers to learn about weather conditions and to confirm the flight route.

Takeoffs and landings are the most difficult parts of the flight and require close coordination between the pilot and copilot. Once in the air, the captain and first officer usually alternate flying each leg of the flight. After landing, pilots must fill out records that document their flight and the maintenance status of the plane.

Some airline pilots may have to help handle customer complaints.

With proper training, airline pilots may also be deputized as federal law enforcement officers and be issued firearms to protect the cockpit.

Commercial pilots employed by charter companies usually have many more nonflight duties. For example, they may schedule flights, arrange for maintenance of the plane, and load luggage to ensure a balanced weight.

Pilots who fly helicopters must constantly look out for trees, bridges, power lines, transmission towers, and other dangerous obstacles.

Regardless of the type of aircraft, all pilots must monitor warning devices that detect sudden shifts in wind patterns.

The following are occupational specialties:

Airline pilots work for airline companies that transport passengers and cargo according to fixed schedules.

Commercial pilots are involved in other flight activities, such as crop dusting, charter flights, and aerial photography.

Flight instructors use simulators and dual-controlled aircraft to teach students how to fly.

Work Environment

Pilots held about 103,500 civilian jobs in 2010. About 68 percent worked as airline pilots and 32 percent worked as commercial pilots.

In 2010, most airline pilots—about 85 percent—worked for airline companies; the remainder worked for the federal government or express delivery companies.

Commercial pilots are typically employed by charter companies, private businesses, flight schools, and hospitals. About 9 percent of these pilots were self-employed in 2010. In 2010, the following industries employed the largest numbers of commercial pilots:

Nonscheduled air transportation	31%
Technical and trade schools	13
Support activities for air transportation (including airports)	8
Other ambulatory health care services	6
Aerospace product and parts manufacturing	3

The pilot and co-pilot prepare for takeoff.

Pilots are located throughout the country, and many are based near large airports.

About 62 percent of all pilots are members of a union. The figure is even higher for the airline industry, in which 95 percent of airline pilots are members of a union, including the Air Line Pilots Association, International , and the Coalition of Airline Pilots Associations .

Pilots must learn to cope with several work-related hazards. For example, airline pilots assigned to international routes may experience jetlag. To guard against fatigue, the Federal Aviation Administration (FAA) requires airline companies to allow pilots at least 8 hours of uninterrupted rest between shifts.

Commercial pilots face other types of job hazards. Crop dusters, for example, may be exposed to toxic chemicals and seldom have the benefit of a regular landing strip. Helicopter pilots involved in rescue operations may be required to navigate dangerous airspace. All pilots face the risk of hearing loss due to prolonged exposure to engine noise.

Although flying does not involve much physical effort, the mental stress of being responsible for the safety of passengers can be fatiguing. Pilots must be alert and quick to react if something goes wrong, particularly during takeoff and landing. As a result, federal law requires pilots to retire at age 65.

Work Schedules

Airline pilots fly an average of 75 hours per month and work an additional 150 hours per month doing nonflight duties. Pilots also have variable work schedules, according to which they work several days in a row followed by several days off. Flight shifts also are variable, because airline companies operate flights throughout the day. Flight assignments are based on seniority. In general, that means that pilots who have worked at the company for a long time get preferred routes.

Pilots spend a considerable amount of time away from home because flight assignments often involve overnight layovers—sometimes up to 3 nights a week. When pilots are away from home, the airlines provide hotel accommodations, transportation to the airport, and an allowance for meals and other expenses.

Commercial pilots also have irregular schedules, typically flying between 30 hours and 90 hours each month. Because commercial pilots frequently have many nonflight responsibilities, they have much less free time than airline pilots. Although most commercial pilots remain near their home overnight, they may still work odd hours. Pilots for a corporate fleet may fly regular schedules.

How to Become an Airline or Commercial Pilot

Many pilots learn to fly in the military, but a growing number now earn an associate's or bachelor's degree from a civilian flying school. All pilots who are paid to transport passengers or cargo must have a commercial pilot's license and an instrument rating. To qualify for a commercial pilot's license, applicants must be at least 18 years old and have at least 250 hours of flight experience.

Education and Training

Military veterans have always been an important source of experienced pilots because of the extensive training and flight time that the military provides. However, an increasing number of people are becoming pilots by attending flight school or taking lessons from a Federal Aviation Administration (FAA) certified instructor. The FAA certifies hundreds of civilian flight schools, including some colleges and universities that offer pilot training as part of an aviation degree.

In addition, most airline companies require at least 2 years of college and prefer to hire college graduates. In fact, most pilots today have a bachelor's degree. Because the number of college-educated applicants continues to increase, many employers are making a college degree an entry-level requirement. Preferred courses for airline pilots

include English, math, physics, and aeronautical engineering.

Because pilots must be able to make quick decisions and react appropriately under pressure, airline companies will often reject applicants who do not pass psychological and aptitude tests.

Once hired by an airline, new pilots undergo additional company training that usually includes 6-8 weeks of ground school and 25 hours of additional flight time. After they finish this training, airline pilots must keep their certification by attending training once or twice a year.

Licenses

Commercial pilot's license. All pilots who are paid to transport passengers or cargo must have a commercial pilot's license. To qualify for this license, applicants must be at least 18 years old and have at least 250 hours of flight experience.

Applicants must also pass a strict physical exam to make sure that they are in good health, must have vision that is correctable to 20/20, and must have no physical handicaps that could impair their performance.

In addition, they must pass a written test that includes questions about safety procedures, navigation techniques, and FAA regulations. Finally, they must demonstrate their flying ability to an FAA-designated examiner.

Instrument rating. To fly during periods of low visibility, pilots must be rated to fly by instruments. They may qualify for this rating by having at least 40 hours of instrument flight experience. Pilots also must pass a written exam and show an examiner their ability to fly by instruments.

Airline certifications. Currently, airline captains must have an airline transport pilot certificate. In 2013, new regulations will require first officers to have this certificate as well. Applicants must be at least 23 years old, have a minimum of 1,500 hours of flight time, and pass written and flight exams. Furthermore, airline pilots usually maintain one or more advanced ratings, depending on the requirements of their particular aircraft.

All licenses are valid as long as a pilot can pass periodic physical, eye, and flight examinations.

Advancement

Many civilian pilots start as flight instructors, building up their flight hours while they earn money teaching. As they become more experienced, these instructors can move into jobs as commercial pilots.

Commercial pilots may begin their careers flying charter planes, helicopters, or crop dusters. These positions typically require less experience than airline jobs require. Some commercial pilots may advance to flying corporate planes.

In nonairline jobs, a first officer may advance to captain and, in large companies, to chief pilot or director of aviation. However, many pilots use their commercial experience as a steppingstone to becoming an airline pilot.

Airline pilots may begin as flight engineers or first officers for regional airline companies. Newly hired pilots at regional airline companies typically have about 2,000 hours of flight experience.

Over time, experience gained at these jobs may lead to higher paying jobs with major airline companies. Newly hired pilots at major airline companies typically have about 4,000 hours of flight experience.

For airline pilots, advancement depends on a system of seniority outlined in union contracts. Typically, after 1 to 5 years, flight engineers may advance to first officer and, after 5 to 15 years, to captain.

Important Qualities

Communication skills. Pilots must speak clearly when conveying information to air traffic controllers. They must also listen carefully for instructions.

Depth perception. Pilots must be able to see clearly and judge the distance between objects.

Detail oriented. Pilots must watch many systems at the same time. Even small changes can have significant effects, so they must constantly pay close attention to many details.

Monitoring skills. Pilots must regularly watch over gauges and dials to make sure that all systems are in working order.

Problem-solving skills. Pilots must be able to identify complex problems and figure out appropriate solutions. When a plane encounters turbulence, for example, pilots assess the weather conditions, select a calmer airspace, and request a route change from air traffic control.

Quick reaction time. Because warning signals can appear with no notice, pilots must be able to respond quickly to any impending danger.

Teamwork. Pilots work closely with air traffic controllers and flight dispatchers. As a result, they need to be able to coordinate actions on the basis of the feedback they receive.

Pay

Airline and Commercial Pilots
Median annual wages, May 2010

Airline Pilots, Copilots, and Flight Engineers	$103,210
Airline and Commercial Pilots	$92,060
Commercial Pilots	$67,500
Total, All Occupations	$33,840

Note: All Occupations includes all occupations in the U.S. Economy.
Source: U.S. Bureau of Labor Statistics, Occupational Employment Statistics

The median annual wage of airline pilots, copilots, and flight engineers was $103,210 in May 2010. The median wage is the wage at which half the workers in an occupation earned more than that amount and half earned less. Among airline pilots, the lowest 10 percent earned less than $54,980 and the top 10 percent earned more than $166,400.

The median annual wage of commercial pilots was $67,500 in May 2010. Among commercial pilots, the lowest 10 percent earned less than $34,860 and the top 10 percent earned more than $119,650.

According to the Air Line Pilots Association, International, most airline pilots begin their careers at about $20,000 per year. Wages increase each year until the pilot accumulates the experience and seniority needed to become a captain. The average captain at a regional airline company earns about $55,000 per year, while the average captain at a major airline company earns about $135,000 per year.

In addition, airline pilots receive an expense allowance, or "per diem," for every hour they are away from home, and they may earn extra pay for international flights. Airline pilots also are eligible for health insurance and retirement benefits, and their immediate families usually are entitled to free or reduced-fare flights.

About 62 percent of all pilots are members of a union. The figure is even higher for the airline industry, in which 95 percent of airline pilots are members of a union, including the Air Line Pilots Association and the Coalition of Airline Pilots Associations .

In May 2010, average annual wages in industries employing the largest numbers of commercial pilots were as follows:

Aerospace product and parts manufacturing	$98,640
Nonscheduled air transportation	68,720
Other ambulatory health care services	64,130
Support activities for air transportation (including airports)	57,550
Technical and trade schools	57,080

Airline pilots fly an average of 75 hours per month and work an additional 150 hours per month doing nonflight duties. Pilots also have variable work schedules, according to which they work several days in a row followed by several days off. Flight shifts also are variable, because airline companies operate flights throughout the day. Flight assignments are based on seniority, so more experienced pilots get preferred routes.

Pilots spend a considerable amount of time away from home because flight assignments often involve overnight layovers—sometimes up to 3 nights a week. When pilots are away from home, the airlines provide hotel accommodations, transportation to the airport, and an allowance for meals and other expenses.

Commercial pilots also have irregular schedules, typically flying between 30 hours and 90 hours each month. Because commercial pilots frequently have many nonflight responsibilities, they have much less free time than airline pilots. Although most commercial pilots remain near their home overnight, they may still work odd hours. Pilots for a corporate fleet may fly regular schedules.

Job Outlook

Airline and Commercial Pilots
Percent change in employment, projected 2010-20

Commercial Pilots	21%
Total, All Occupations	14%
Airline and Commercial Pilots	11%
Airline Pilots, Copilots, and Flight Engineers	6%

Note: All Occupations includes all occupations in the U.S. Economy.
Source: U.S. Bureau of Labor Statistics, Employment Projections program

Employment of airline and commercial pilots is projected to grow 11 percent from 2010 to 2020, about as fast as the average for all occupations. Modest employment growth is expected as air travel gradually increases over the decade and as more travel takes place between Asia and the United States.

Job opportunities will be spread among both passenger and cargo airline companies.

However, employment growth may be tempered if airline companies raise prices to pay for higher taxes and fuel costs.

Job Prospects

Most job opportunities will arise from the need to replace pilots who leave the workforce. Between 2010 and 2020, many pilots are expected to retire as they reach the required retirement age of 65. As older pilots retire and younger pilots advance, entry-level positions may open up. And the demand for flight instructors may increase as they are needed to train a greater number of student pilots.

Job prospects should be best with regional airlines, on low-cost carriers, or in general aviation, because these segments are anticipated to grow faster than the major airlines. In addition, entry-level requirements are lower for regional and commercial jobs.

However, pilots with less than 500 flight hours will probably need to accumulate hours as flight instructors or commercial pilots before qualifying for regional airline jobs.

Pilots seeking jobs at the major airlines will face strong competition because those firms tend to attract many more applicants than the number of job openings. Applicants also will have to compete with furloughed pilots for available jobs.

Pilots with the greatest number of flight and instrument hours usually have the best prospects. For this reason, military and experienced pilots will have an advantage over entry-level applicants.

Employment projections data for airline and commercial pilots, 2010-20

Occupational Title	SOC Code	Employment, 2010	Projected Employment, 2020	Change, 2010-20 Percent	Numeric
Airline and Commercial Pilots	P311	103,500	114,900	11	11,500
Airline Pilots, Copilots, and Flight Engineers	53-2011	70,800	75,300	6	4,500
Commercial Pilots	53-2012	32,700	39,700	21	6,900

SOURCE: U.S. Bureau of Labor Statistics, Employment Projections program

Similar Occupations

This table shows a list of occupations with job duties that are similar to those of airline and commercial pilots.

Occupation	Job Duties	Entry-Level Education	Median Annual Pay, May 2010
Air Traffic Controllers	Air traffic controllers coordinate the movement of air traffic to ensure that planes stay safe distances apart.	Associate's degree	$108,040

Contacts for More Information

For more information about pilots, visit Federal Aviation Administration , Air Line Pilots Association, International , Coalition of Airline Pilots Associations ,Helicopter Association International

For additional career information about pilots, see the Occupational Outlook Quarterly article " Sky-high careers: jobs related to airlines ."

For more information about job opportunities, contact an airline company personnel manager, browse the classified section of aviation trade magazines, or contact companies that operate aircraft at local airports.

Suggested citation:

Bureau of Labor Statistics, U.S. Department of Labor, Occupational Outlook Handbook, 2012-13 Edition, Airline and Commercial Pilots, on the Internet at http://www.bls.gov/ooh/transportation-and-material-moving/airline-and-commercial-pilots.htm .

Air Traffic Controllers

Quick Facts: Air Traffic Controllers	
2010 Median Pay	$108,040 per year $51.94 per hour
Entry-Level Education	Associate's degree
Work Experience in a Related Occupation	None
On-the-job Training	Long-term on-the-job training
Number of Jobs, 2010	27,000
Job Outlook, 2010-20	-3% (Decline moderately)
Employment Change, 2010-20	-800

What Air Traffic Controllers Do

Air traffic controllers coordinate the movement of air traffic to ensure that planes stay safe distances apart.

Duties

Air traffic controllers typically do the following:

- Coordinate the arrival and departure of airplanes
- Issue landing and takeoff instructions to pilots
- Monitor and direct the movement of aircraft, using radar equipment
- Authorize flight path changes
- Provide weather updates to pilots
- Alert airport response staff in the event of an aircraft emergency

Air traffic controllers' immediate concern is safety, but they also must direct planes efficiently to minimize delays. They manage the flow of airplanes in and out of the airport, guide pilots during takeoff and landing, and monitor airplanes as they travel through the skies.

Controllers usually manage multiple airplanes at the same time and often must make quick decisions about completely different activities. For example, a controller might direct one plane on its landing approach while providing another plane with weather information.

The following are types of air traffic controllers:

Tower controllers direct the movement of planes on the runway. They check flight plans, give pilots clearance for takeoff or landing, and direct the movement of planes on the runways and other parts of the airport. Most work from air traffic control towers.

Radar approach/departure controllers ensure that planes traveling within an airport's airspace keep a minimum safe distance apart. This airspace is normally a 40 mile radius around the main airport.

These controllers' primary responsibility is to manage the flow of airplanes coming in and out of the airport. They sequence the arrival and departure of airplanes, guide pilots during takeoff and landing, and

Air traffic controllers give pilots clearance for takeoff and landing.

use radar equipment to monitor flight paths. They also provide pilots with information on weather conditions.

These controllers work in buildings known as terminal radar approach control centers (TRACONs).

En route controllers monitor airplanes once they leave an airport's airspace. They work at any of the 21 air route traffic control centers located throughout the country.

Each center is assigned an airspace based on the geography and altitude of the area in which it is located. As an airplane approaches a center's airspace, en route controllers guide the airplane along its route. For example, if two airplanes enter a center's airspace at the same time, an en route controller may arrange for one plane to change altitude to avoid the other plane.

As an airplane goes along its route, en route controllers hand the plane off to the next center along the path. About 150 miles from the airport, en route controllers begin monitoring the plane's descent path. When the airplane is about 50 miles from the airport, en route controllers turn the plane over to the airport's radar approach controllers.

Some air traffic controllers work at the Air Traffic Control Systems Command Center. These controllers look for traffic patterns that could create bottlenecks in the system. When they find one, they provide instructions to prevent traffic jams. Their objective is to keep traffic levels manageable for the airport and for en route controllers.

Work Environment

Air traffic controllers held about 27,000 jobs in 2010. The vast majority of controllers—about 94 percent—worked for the Federal Aviation Administration (FAA).

Air traffic controllers work in control towers, approach control facilities, or route centers. Many tower and radar controllers work near large airports. En route controllers work in secure office buildings located across the country.

Radar controllers often work in semidark rooms. The airplanes they control appear on their radar as blips moving across the screen.

During busy times, controllers must work rapidly and efficiently while maintaining total concentration. Oftentimes, the mental stress of being responsible for the safety of airplanes and their passengers can be exhausting. As a result, controllers tend to retire earlier than most workers: those with 20 years of experience are eligible to retire at age 50. In addition, controllers are required to retire at age 56.

According to the National Air Traffic Controllers Association, about 90 percent of air traffic controllers are union members.

Work Schedules

Most air traffic controllers work full time, and some must work additional hours. Because most control towers and route centers operate around the clock, controllers rotate shifts between day, evening, and night. Controllers also work weekend and holiday shifts.

How to Become an Air Traffic Controller

To become an air traffic controller, a person must be a U.S. citizen, complete an air traffic management degree from a Federal Aviation Administration (FAA) certified school, achieve a qualifying score on the FAA preemployment test, and complete a training course at the FAA Academy. Controllers with previous air traffic control experience, such as from the military, may not need to complete the FAA education requirements. Those without previous air traffic control experience must be younger than 31 to become an air traffic controller.

Controllers also must pass a physical exam each year and a job performance exam twice a year. In addition, they must pass periodic drug screenings.

Education and Training

There are two main pathways to becoming an air traffic controller:

Previous controller experience. Candidates with previous experience with the FAA or the U.S. Armed Forces are automatically eligible to apply for air traffic controller positions. They do not need to take the FAA preemployment test.

AT-CTI degree. Those without previous experience must obtain an air traffic management degree through the FAA Air Traffic-Collegiate Training Initiative (AT-CTI). AT-CTI schools offer 2- or 4-year degrees that teach courses in aviation and air traffic management.

Candidates who complete an AT-CTI program of study are automatically eligible to take the FAA preemployment test. Applicants who pass the test can then become eligible to enroll in a 2-month training course at the FAA Academy. The invitation to attend the training course is dependent on the number of available job openings.

After graduating from the Academy, trainees are assigned to an air traffic control facility as developmental controllers until they complete all requirements for becoming a certified air traffic controller.

Advancement

New air traffic controllers, referred to as developmental controllers, begin their careers by supplying pilots with basic flight data and airport information. They then advance to different positions within the control room.

As the developmental controllers master various duties, they earn increases in pay and advance in their training. Generally, it takes new controllers 2 to 4 years to complete the on-the-job training that leads to full certification. Those with previous controller experience may take less time to become fully certified.

Trainees who fail to complete the Academy or their on-the-job training are usually dismissed.

There are limited opportunities for a controller to switch from an en route position to an airport position. However, within these categories, controllers can transfer to jobs at different locations or advance to supervisory positions.

Important Qualities

Communication skills. When pilots contact the control tower for instructions, air traffic controllers must listen carefully to their requests and respond by speaking clearly.

Concentration skills. Controllers must be able to concentrate in a room where multiple conversations occur at once. For example, in a large airport tower, several controllers may be speaking with several pilots at the same time.

Decision-making skills. Controllers must make quick decisions. For example, when a pilot requests a change of altitude, a controller must respond quickly so that the plane can avoid unnecessary turbulence.

Multitasking skills. Controllers must be able to coordinate the actions of multiple flights. For example, a controller may be required to guide several pilots through turbulent weather at the same time.

Problem-solving skills. Controllers must be able to understand complex situations, such as the impact of changing weather patterns on a plane's flight path. Controllers must be able to review important information and provide pilots with an appropriate solution.

Pay

Air Traffic Controllers

Median annual wages, May 2010

Air Traffic Controllers	$108,040
Total, All Occupations	$33,840
Transportation and Material Moving Occupations	$28,400

Note: All Occupations includes all occupations in the U.S. Economy.
Source: U.S. Bureau of Labor Statistics, Occupational Employment Statistics

The median annual wage of air traffic controllers was $108,040 in May 2010. The median wage is the wage at which half the workers in an occupation earned more than that amount and half earned less. The lowest 10 percent earned less than $54,480, and the top 10 percent earned more than $165,660.

According to the Federal Aviation Administration (FAA), the starting salary for new controllers was $37,070 in 2010. Controllers' salaries increase as they complete each new training phase. According to the FAA, controllers who have already completed on-the-job training had an average annual salary of $118,000 in 2010. For all air traffic controllers, including trainees, the average annual salary was $104,000 in 2010.

Most air traffic controllers work full time, and some must work additional hours. Because most control towers and route centers operate around the clock, controllers rotate shifts between day, evening, and night. Controllers also work weekend and holiday shifts.

Job Outlook

Air Traffic Controllers

Percent change in employment, projected 2010-20

Transportation and Material Moving Occupations	15%
Total, All Occupations	14%
Air Traffic Controllers	-3%

Note: All Occupations includes all occupations in the U.S. Economy.
Source: U.S. Bureau of Labor Statistics, Employment Projections program

Employment of air traffic controllers is projected to decline by 3 percent from 2010 to 2020. Most employment opportunities will result from the need to replace workers who retire.

Despite an expected increase in air traffic, employment growth will not keep pace because the Federal Aviation Administration (FAA) already hired many new controllers over the last several years. In addition, federal budget constraints should limit the hiring of new controllers, and the NextGen satellite based system is expected to allow individual controllers to handle more air traffic.

Job Prospects

Most new jobs will result as the majority of today's air traffic control workforce retires over the next decade. Despite the increasing number of job openings, competition to get into the FAA Academy will remain high because there are generally more test applicants than job openings. Job opportunities will be best for individuals in their early 20s who obtain an air traffic management degree from a FAA certified school.

Employment projections data for air traffic controllers, 2010-20

Occupational Title	SOC Code	Employment, 2010	Projected Employment, 2020	Change, 2010-20 Percent	Numeric
Air Traffic Controllers	53-2021	27,000	26,200	-3	-800

SOURCE: U.S. Bureau of Labor Statistics, Employment Projections program

Similar Occupations

This table shows a list of occupations with job duties that are similar to those of air traffic controllers.

Occupation	Job Duties	Entry-Level Education	Median Annual Pay, May 2010
Airline and Commercial Pilots	Airline and commercial pilots fly and navigate airplanes or helicopters. Airline pilots fly for airlines that transport people and cargo on a fixed schedule. Commercial pilots fly aircraft for other reasons, such as charter flights, rescue operations, firefighting, aerial photography, and crop dusting.	See How to Become One	$92,060

Contacts for More Information

For more information about air traffic controllers, visit Federal Aviation Administration , National Air Traffic Controllers Association

For additional career information about air traffic controllers, see the Occupational Outlook Quarterly article " Sky-high careers: jobs related to airlines ."

Suggested citation:

Bureau of Labor Statistics, U.S. Department of Labor, Occupational Outlook Handbook, 2012-13 Edition, Air Traffic Controllers, on the Internet at http://www.bls.gov/ooh/transportation-and-material-moving/air-traffic-controllers.htm .

Bus Drivers

Quick Facts: Bus Drivers	
2010 Median Pay	$29,160 per year $14.02 per hour
Entry-Level Education	High school diploma or equivalent
Work Experience in a Related Occupation	None
On-the-job Training	Moderate-term on-the-job training
Number of Jobs, 2010	647,200
Job Outlook, 2010-20	13% (About as fast as average)
Employment Change, 2010-20	83,000

What Bus Drivers Do

Bus drivers transport people between a variety of places including, work, school, shopping and across state borders. Some drive regular routes, and others transport passengers on chartered trips or sightseeing tours. They drive a range of vehicles, from 15-passenger buses to 60-foot articulated buses (with two connected sections) that can carry more than 100 passengers.

Duties

Bus drivers typically do the following:
- Check the bus tires, lights, and oil and do other basic maintenance
- Pick up and drop off passengers at designated locations
- Follow a planned route on a time schedule
- Help disabled passengers get on and off the bus
- Follow traffic laws and state and federal transit regulations
- Follow safety procedures to make sure they and all passengers are safe
- Keep passengers informed of possible delays

Most bus drivers are school bus drivers.

The following are examples of types of bus drivers.

Local transit bus drivers follow a daily schedule while transporting people on regular routes along the same city or suburban streets. They usually stop frequently, often only a few blocks apart and when a passenger requests a stop. Local transit drivers typically do the following:
- Collect bus fares, sometimes making change for passengers
- Answer questions about schedules, routes, and transfer points
- Report accidents or other traffic disruptions to a central dispatcher, and follow directions when using an alternate route

Intercity bus drivers transport passengers between cities or towns, sometimes crossing state lines. They may travel between distant cities or between towns only a few miles apart. They usually pick up and drop off passengers at bus stations, where passengers buy tickets. Increasingly, intercity buses are using curbside locations in downtown urban areas instead of stations. Intercity drivers typically do the following:
- Ensure all passengers have a valid ticket to ride the bus
- May sell tickets to passengers when there are unsold seats available
- Follow a central dispatcher's instruction when taking an alternate route
- Help passengers load or unload baggage

Motor coach drivers transport passengers on charted trips or sightseeing tours. Their schedule and route are generally arranged by a trip planner for the convenience of the passengers, who often are on vacation. Motor coach drivers are usually away for long periods of time because they usually stay with vacationers for the length of the trip. Motor coach drivers typically do the following:
- Listen to and sometimes address passenger complaints
- Ensure the tour stays on schedule
- Sometimes act as tour guides for passengers
- Help passengers load or unload baggage
- Account for all passengers before leaving a location

School bus drivers transport students to and from school and other activities. On school days, drivers pick up students in the morning and return them home or to the designated bus stop in the afternoon. School bus drivers also drive students to field trips, sporting events, and other activities. Some drivers work at school in other occupations, such as janitors, cafeteria workers, or mechanics, between morning and afternoon trips. School bus drivers typically do the following:
- Watch traffic and people carefully to ensure the safety of children getting on and off the bus
- Take care of the needs of children with disabilities
- Keep order and safety on the school bus
- Understand and enforce the school system's rules regarding student conduct
- Report disciplinary problems to the school district or parents

Work Environment

Driving through heavy traffic or bad weather and dealing with unruly passengers can be stressful for bus drivers. Bus drivers held 647,200 jobs in 2010, and of those, about 70 percent were school or special client bus drivers.

As the following table shows, most transit or intercity bus drivers worked for local governments or urban transit systems, which are private companies that contract with a city or town to provide bus service. Most motor coach drivers worked in the charter bus industry.

Local government, excluding education and hospitals	50%
Urban transit systems	14
Charter bus industry	9
Other transit and ground passenger transportation	8

School or special client bus drivers are usually employed by a school district or private transportation company that contracts with a district to provide bus service. As the following table shows, some school bus service is provided by a local government.

Elementary and secondary schools	48%
School and employee bus transportation	32
Local government, excluding education and hospitals	10
Social assistance	4

Injuries

Bus drivers, especially transit and intercity drivers, had a higher rate of work related injury and illness in 2010 than the national average. Most injuries to bus drivers are due to highway accidents.

Work Schedules

About 54 percent of all bus drivers worked full time in 2010, and 39 percent worked part time. The rest had variable schedules. School bus drivers work only when school is in session. Some make multiple runs if different schools in their district open and close at different times. Others make only two runs, one in the morning and one in the afternoon, limiting their hours.

Transit drivers may work weekends, late nights, and early mornings. Some intercity bus drivers have long-distant routes, so they spend some nights away. Other intercity bus drivers make a round trip and go home at the end of each shift.

Motor coach drivers travel with their vacationing passengers. Their hours are dictated by a tour schedule, and they may work all hours of the day, including weekends and holidays.

How to Become a Bus Driver

Bus drivers must have a commercial driver's license (CDL) and complete a short training. A driver must also meet hearing and vision requirements. In addition, they often need a high school diploma or the equivalent.

Training

Bus drivers typically go through 1 to 3 months of training. Part of the training is spent on a driving course, where drivers practice various maneuvers with a bus. They then begin to drive in light traffic and eventually make practice runs on the type of route that they expect to drive. New drivers make regularly scheduled trips with passengers, accompanied by an experienced driver who gives helpful tips, answers questions, and evaluates the new driver's performance.

Some drivers' training is also spent in the classroom. They learn their company's rules and regulations, state and municipal traffic laws, and safe driving practices. Drivers also learn about schedules and bus routes, fares, and how to interact with passengers.

Licenses

All bus drivers must have a commercial driver's license (CDL). The qualifications for getting one vary by state but generally include passing both knowledge and driving tests. States have the right not to issue a license to someone who has had a CDL suspended by another state.

Drivers can get endorsements to a CDL, which reflect their ability to drive a special type of vehicle. All bus drivers must have a passenger (P) endorsement, and school bus drivers must also have a school bus (S) endorsement. Getting the P and S endorsements requires additional knowledge and driving tests administered by a certified examiner.

Many states require all bus drivers to be 18 years of age or older and those who cross state lines to be at least 21 years old.

Federal regulations require testing bus drivers for drug or alcohol abuse and random testing while on duty. In addition, bus drivers can have their CDL suspended if they are convicted of a felony involving the use of a motor vehicle or driving under the influence of alcohol or drugs. Other actions also can result in a suspension after multiple violations. A list of violations is available from the U.S. Federal Motor Carrier Safety Administration .

Education

Some employers prefer drivers to have a high school diploma or equivalent.

Advancement

Opportunities for promotion are generally limited, but experienced drivers may become supervisors or dispatchers. Some veteran bus drivers become instructors of new bus drivers.

Important Qualities

Customer-service skills. Bus drivers regularly interact with passengers and must be courteous and helpful.

Hand-eye coordination. Driving a bus requires the controlled use of multiple limbs based on what a person observes. Federal regulations require drivers to have normal use of their arms and legs.

Hearing ability. Bus drivers need good hearing. Federal regulations require the ability to hear a forced whisper in one ear at five feet (with or without the use of a hearing aid).

Patience. Due to possible traffic congestion and sometimes unruly passengers, bus drivers are put in stressful situations and must be able to continue to calmly operate their bus.

Physical health. Federal regulations do not allow people to become bus drivers if they have a medical condition that may interfere with their operation of a bus, such as high blood pressure or epilepsy. A full list of medical reasons that keep someone from becoming a licensed bus driver is available from the U.S. Federal Motor Carrier Safety Administration .

Visual ability. Bus drivers must be able to pass vision tests. Federal regulations require at least 20/40 vision with a 70 degree field of vision in each eye and the ability to distinguish colors on a traffic light.

Pay

Bus Drivers
Median annual wages, May 2010

Bus Drivers, Transit and Intercity	$35,520
Total, All Occupations	$33,840
Bus Drivers	$29,160
Bus Drivers, School or Special Client	$27,580

Note: All Occupations includes all occupations in the U.S. Economy.
Source: U.S. Bureau of Labor Statistics, Occupational Employment Statistics

The median annual wage of transit and intercity bus drivers, which includes motor coach drivers, was $35,520 in May 2010. The median wage is the wage at which half the workers in an occupation earned more than that amount and half earned less. The lowest 10 percent earned less than $21,020, and the top 10 percent earned more than $56,500. The median annual wage of school or special client bus drivers was $27,580 in May 2010. The lowest 10 percent earned less than $16,930, and the top 10 percent earned more than $42,690.

Earnings for transit and intercity bus drivers vary by industry. The median annual wages for transit and intercity bus drivers in the top-employing industries are as follows:

Local government, excluding education and hospitals	$43,860
Urban transit systems	30,620
Other transit and ground passenger transportation	27,780
Charter bus industry	27,310

The median annual wages for school or special client bus drivers in the top-employing industries are as follows:

Local government, excluding education and hospitals	$30,720
School and employee bus transportation	28,930
Elementary and secondary schools	26,800
Social assistance	20,820

About 54 percent of all bus drivers worked full time in 2010, and 39 percent worked part time. The rest had variable schedules. School bus drivers work only when school is in session. Some make multiple runs if different schools in their district open and close at different times. Others make only two runs, one in the morning and one in the afternoon, limiting their hours.

Transit drivers may work weekends, late nights, and early mornings. Some intercity bus drivers have long-distant routes, so they spend some nights away. Other intercity bus drivers make a round trip and go home at the end of each shift.

Motor coach drivers travel with their vacationing passengers. Their hours are dictated by a tour schedule, and they may work all hours of the day, including weekends and holidays.

Job Outlook

Bus Drivers

Percent change in employment, projected 2010-20

Bus Drivers, Transit and Intercity	15%
Total, All Occupations	14%
Bus Drivers	13%
Bus Drivers, School or Special Client	12%

Note: All Occupations includes all occupations in the U.S. Economy.
Source: U.S. Bureau of Labor Statistics, Employment Projections program

Employment of bus drivers is projected to grow 13 percent from 2010 to 2020, about as fast as the average for all occupations.

Employment of transit and intercity drivers (including motor coach) is expected to grow 15 percent. Demand for buses is expected to remain relatively flat over the next decade. An increase in gas prices could lead more people to choose the bus; however, trains are often preferred when available. Employment in the charter bus industry is expected to continue to decline, limiting opportunities for motor coach drivers.

Recently, intercity bus travel has grown rapidly. Although it is expected to continue to grow, intercity bus service is still a relatively small part of bus travel and is unlikely to create many new jobs.

For local transit, a new type of bus service has gotten a lot of attention lately: bus rapid transit (BRT). BRT creates routes in cities where buses can travel quickly with only a few stops. Because it is less expensive than light rail, some cities are considering BRT lines instead of rail lines, which would create more jobs for bus drivers.

Employment of school or special client bus drivers is expected to grow 12 percent, largely due to an increase in the number of school age children. However, growth will be tempered as budget limitations lead school districts to focus on increasing efficiency. They do this by using computer programs to determine more efficient bus routes, allowing some routes (and drivers) to be cut.

Job Prospects

Job opportunities for bus drivers should be favorable, especially for school bus drivers, as many drivers leave the occupation. Those willing to work part time or irregular shifts should have the best prospects. Prospects for motor coach drivers will depend on tourism, which fluctuates with the economy.

Employment projections data for bus drivers, 2010-20

Occupational Title	SOC Code	Employment, 2010	Projected Employment, 2020	Change, 2010-20	
				Percent	Numeric
Bus Drivers	53-3020	647,200	730,200	13	83,000
Bus Drivers, Transit and Intercity	53-3021	186,300	213,800	15	27,500
Bus Drivers, School or Special Client	53-3022	460,900	516,400	12	55,500
SOURCE: U.S. Bureau of Labor Statistics, Employment Projections program					

Similar Occupations

This table shows a list of occupations with job duties that are similar to those of bus drivers.

Occupation	Job Duties	Entry-Level Education	Median Annual Pay, May 2010
Delivery Truck Drivers and Driver/Sales Workers	Delivery truck drivers and driver/sales workers pick up, transport, and drop off packages within a small region or urban area. Most of the time, they transport merchandise from a distribution center to businesses and households.	High school diploma or equivalent	$27,050
Heavy and Tractor-trailer Truck Drivers	Heavy and tractor-trailer truck drivers transport goods from one location to another. Most tractor-trailer drivers are long-haul drivers and operate trucks with a capacity of at least 26,001 pounds per gross vehicle weight (GVW). They deliver goods over intercity routes, sometimes spanning several states.	High school diploma or equivalent	$37,770

Railroad Conductors and Yardmasters	Conductors and yardmasters coordinate the daily activities of both freight and passenger train crews. Conductors work on the train. Yardmasters work in the rail yard.	High school diploma or equivalent	$49,770
Subway and Streetcar Operators	Subway and streetcar operators transport passengers in urban and suburban areas. The vehicles they drive travel underground, on above-ground and elevated tracks, on streets, or on separate tracks.	High school diploma or equivalent	$56,880
Taxi Drivers and Chauffeurs	Taxi drivers and chauffeurs drive people to and from the places they need to go, such as homes, workplaces, airports, and shopping centers. They must know their way around a city to take both residents and visitors to their destinations.	Less than high school	$22,440
Train Engineers and Operators	Train engineers and train operators ensure that freight trains and passenger trains stay on time and travel safely. Train engineers drive trains. Train operators work the brakes, signals, or switches.	High school diploma or equivalent	$46,100
Water Transportation Occupations	Workers in water transportation occupations operate and maintain ships that take cargo and people over water. These ships travel to and from foreign ports across the ocean, to domestic ports along the coasts, across the Great Lakes, and along the country's many inland waterways.	See How to Become One	$46,610

Contacts for More Information

For more information about school bus drivers, visit National School Transportation Association , National Association of State Directors of Pupil Transportation Services

For more information about transit bus drivers, visit American Public Transportation Association

For more information about motor coach drivers, visit United Motor Coach Association

For more information on federal regulations for commercial vehicle drivers, visit Federal Motor Carrier Safety Administration

Suggested citation:

Bureau of Labor Statistics, U.S. Department of Labor, Occupational Outlook Handbook, 2012-13 Edition, Bus Drivers, on the Internet at http://www.bls.gov/ooh/transportation-and-material-moving/bus-drivers.htm.

Delivery Truck Drivers and Driver/Sales Workers

Quick Facts: Delivery Truck Drivers and Driver/Sales Workers	
2010 Median Pay	$27,050 per year $13.00 per hour
Entry-Level Education	High school diploma or equivalent
Work Experience in a Related Occupation	None
On-the-job Training	Short-term on-the-job training
Number of Jobs, 2010	1,262,600
Job Outlook, 2010-20	13% (About as fast as average)
Employment Change, 2010-20	167,500

What Delivery Truck Drivers and Driver/Sales Workers Do

Delivery truck drivers and driver/sales workers pick up, transport, and drop off packages within a small region or urban area. They drive trucks with a capacity of 26,000 pounds gross vehicle weight (GVW) or less. Most of the time, they transport merchandise from a distribution center to businesses and households.

Duties

Delivery truck drivers and driver/sales workers typically do the following:

- Load and unload their cargo
- Report any incidents they encounter on the road to a dispatcher
- Follow all applicable traffic laws
- Report serious mechanical problems to the appropriate personnel
- Keep their truck and associated equipment clean and in good working order

- May accept payments for the shipment
- Handle paperwork, such as receipts or delivery confirmation notices

Most drivers plan their routes. Some have a regular daily or weekly schedule. Others have different routes each day.

These drivers generally receive instructions to go to a delivery location at a particular time, and it is up to them to find a way there. They must have a thorough understanding of an area's street grid and know which roads allow trucks and which do not.

Light truck drivers, often called pick-up and deliver or P&D drivers, are the most common type of delivery driver. They drive small trucks or vans from distribution centers to delivery locations. Drivers make deliveries based on a set schedule. Some drivers stop only at the distribution center once, in the morning, and make many stops throughout the day. Others make multiple trips between the distribution center and delivery locations.

Driver/sales workers are delivery drivers with added sales responsibility. They recommend new products to businesses and solicit new customers. For example, they may make regular deliveries to a hardware store and encourage the store's manager to offer a new type

Delivery drivers and driver/sales workers transport goods around an urban area or small region.

of product. Driver/sales workers also deliver goods, such as take-out food to consumers, and accept payment for those goods.

Work Environment

Light truck drivers or delivery services drivers held about 856,000 jobs in 2010 and are mostly employed in the following industries:

Retail trade	20%
Wholesale trade	18
Couriers and messengers	17

Driver/sales workers held about 406,600 jobs in 2010 and are mostly employed in the following industries:

Food services and drinking places	35%
Grocery and related product wholesalers	17
Retail trade	13

Delivery truck drivers and driver/sales workers have a physically demanding job. Driving a truck for long periods of time can be tiring. When loading and unloading cargo, drivers do a lot of lifting, carrying, and walking.

Injuries

Given the nature of their job, these workers are at risk of being involved in motor vehicle accidents and have a higher risk of injury than workers in most other occupations.

Work Schedules

Most drivers work full time, and many work additional hours.

Those who work on regular routes sometimes must begin work very early in the morning or late at night. For example, a driver who delivers bread to a deli every day must be there before the deli opens. Drivers often work weekends and holidays.

How to Become a Delivery Truck Driver or Driver/Sales Worker

Delivery truck drivers and driver/sales workers generally have a high school diploma and go through a few months of on-the-job training. They must have a driver's license for the state in which they work.

Education

Some companies prefer a delivery truck driver or driver/sales worker to have a high school diploma or equivalent, although it is not required.

Training

Companies train new delivery truck drivers and driver/sales workers on the job, usually in 2 to 3 months. This may include driving training with a driver-mentor who rides along with a new employee to ensure that a new driver is able to operate a truck on crowded streets.

New drivers also have classroom training to learn company policies about package drop offs, returns, taking payment, and what to do with damaged goods.

Driver/sales workers must learn detailed information about the products they offer.

Licenses

All delivery drivers need a driver's license issued by the state in which they live.

Important Qualities

Math skills. Because delivery truck drivers and driver/sales workers sometimes take payment, they have to be able to count cash and to make change quickly.

Customer service skills. When completing deliveries, drivers often interact with customers and should make a good impression to ensure repeat business.

Hand-eye coordination. When driving, delivery drivers have to observe their surroundings while operating a complex machine.

Patience. When driving through heavy traffic congestion, delivery drivers must be calm and composed.

Sales skills. Driver/sales workers are expected to convince customers to purchase new or different products from them.

Speaking ability. Drivers have to be able to speak English well enough to read road signs, prepare reports, and communicate with the pubic and law enforcement officials.

Visual ability. To have a driver's license, delivery truck drivers and driver/sales workers must be able to pass a state vision test.

Pay

Delivery Truck Drivers and Driver/Sales Workers
Median annual wages, May 2010

Total, All Occupations	$33,840
Light Truck or Delivery Services Drivers	$28,630
Delivery Truck Drivers and Driver/Sales Workers	$27,050
Driver/Sales Workers	$22,540

Note: All Occupations includes all occupations in the U.S. Economy.
Source: U.S. Bureau of Labor Statistics, Occupational Employment Statistics

The median annual wage of driver/sales workers was $22,540 in May 2010. The median wage is the wage at which half the workers in an occupation earned more than that amount and half earned less. The lowest 10 percent earned less than $16,000 and the top 10 percent earned more than $45,340.

The median annual wage of light truck or delivery services drivers was $28,630 in May 2010. The lowest 10 percent earned less than $17,770 and the top 10 percent earned more than $54,850.

Most drivers work full time, and many work additional hours. Those who work on regular routes sometimes must begin work very early in the morning or late at night. For example, a driver who delivers bread to a deli every day must be there before the deli opens. Drivers often work weekends and holidays.

Job Outlook

Delivery Truck Drivers and Driver/Sales Workers

Percent change in employment, projected 2010-20

Motor Vehicle Operators	17%
Light Truck or Delivery Services Drivers	15%
Total, All Occupations	14%
Driver/Sales Workers	10%

Note: All Occupations includes all occupations in the U.S. Economy.
Source: U.S. Bureau of Labor Statistics, Employment Projections program

Employment of light truck or delivery services drivers is projected to increase 15 percent from 2010 to 2020, about as fast as the average for all occupations.

Employment of driver/sales workers is projected to grow 10 percent over the same period, about as fast as the average for all occupations.

Improved routing through GPS technology can make truck drivers more productive, which may limit the need for more drivers. With improved routing, drivers can be more efficient, navigating better in traffic and spending less time idling at each stop.

Additionally, higher diesel prices could cause companies to limit their hiring of new drivers and increase their focus on technological solutions. This will be especially true for drivers at large shipping companies.

However, as the economy grows, the need for more deliveries is expected to increase. From the distribution of goods from warehouses to the package delivery to households, nearly all goods are brought to their final destination by delivery drivers.

Job Prospects

Delivery truck driver and driver/sales worker jobs are expected to be competitive. Because these drivers do not have to spend long periods away from home, these local jobs are more desirable than long-haul trucking jobs. Those with experience, or who work for the company in another occupation, should have the best job prospects.

Employment projections data for delivery truck drivers and driver/sales workers, 2010-20

Occupational Title	SOC Code	Employment, 2010	Projected Employment, 2020	Change, 2010-20	
				Percent	Numeric
Delivery Truck Drivers and Driver/Sales Workers	—	1,262,600	1,430,200	13	167,500
Driver/Sales Workers	53-3031	406,600	448,500	10	42,000
Light Truck or Delivery Services Drivers	53-3033	856,000	981,600	15	125,600
SOURCE: U.S. Bureau of Labor Statistics, Employment Projections program					

Similar Occupations

This table shows a list of occupations with job duties that are similar to those of delivery truck drivers and driver/sales workers.

Occupation	Job Duties	Entry-Level Education	Median Annual Pay, May 2010
Couriers and Messengers	Couriers and messengers transport documents and packages for individuals, businesses, institutions, and government agencies.	High school diploma or equivalent	$24,080
Bus Drivers	Bus drivers transport people between a variety of places including work, school, shopping, and across state borders. Some drive regular routes, and others transport passengers on chartered trips or sightseeing tours.	High school diploma or equivalent	$29,160
Heavy and Tractor-trailer Truck Drivers	Heavy and tractor-trailer truck drivers transport goods from one location to another. Most tractor-trailer drivers are long-haul drivers and operate trucks with a capacity of at least 26,001 pounds per gross vehicle weight (GVW). They deliver goods over intercity routes, sometimes spanning several states.	High school diploma or equivalent	$37,770
Hand Laborers and Material Movers	Hand laborers and material movers transport objects without using machines. Some workers move freight, stock, or other materials around storage facilities; others clean vehicles; some pick up unwanted household goods; and still others pack materials for moving.	Less than high school	$22,560
Material Recording Clerks	Material recording clerks keep track of information to keep businesses and supply chains on schedule. They ensure proper scheduling, recordkeeping, and inventory control.	See How to Become One	$24,100
Postal Service Workers	Postal Service workers sell postal products and collect, sort, and deliver mail.	High school diploma or equivalent	$53,090

Railroad Conductors and Yardmasters	Conductors and yardmasters coordinate the daily activities of both freight and passenger train crews. Conductors work on the train. Yardmasters work in the rail yard.	High school diploma or equivalent	$49,770
Subway and Streetcar Operators	Subway and streetcar operators transport passengers in urban and suburban areas. The vehicles they drive travel underground, on above-ground and elevated tracks, on streets, or on separate tracks.	High school diploma or equivalent	$56,880
Taxi Drivers and Chauffeurs	Taxi drivers and chauffeurs drive people to and from the places they need to go, such as homes, workplaces, airports, and shopping centers. They must know their way around a city to take both residents and visitors to their destinations.	Less than high school	$22,440
Water Transportation Occupations	Workers in water transportation occupations operate and maintain ships that take cargo and people over water. These ships travel to and from foreign ports across the ocean, to domestic ports along the coasts, across the Great Lakes, and along the country's many inland waterways.	See How to Become One	$46,610

Contacts for More Information

For more information about truck drivers, including delivery truck drivers and driver/sales workers, visit American Trucking Association , Professional Truck Driver Institute , The International Brotherhood of Teamsters

Suggested citation:

Bureau of Labor Statistics, U.S. Department of Labor, Occupational Outlook Handbook, 2012-13 Edition, Delivery Truck Drivers and Driver/Sales Workers, on the Internet at http://www.bls.gov/ooh/transportation-and-material-moving/delivery-truck-drivers-and-driver-sales-workers.htm .

Flight Attendants

Quick Facts: Flight Attendants	
2010 Median Pay	$37,740 per year
Entry-Level Education	High school diploma or equivalent
Work Experience in a Related Occupation	None
On-the-job Training	Moderate-term on-the-job training
Number of Jobs, 2010	90,500
Job Outlook, 2010-20	0% (Little or no change)
Employment Change, 2010-20	-200

What Flight Attendants Do

Flight attendants provide personal services to ensure the safety and comfort of airline passengers.

Duties

Flight attendants typically do the following:
- Attend preflight briefings on details of the flight
- Ensure that adequate supplies of refreshments and emergency equipment are on board
- Demonstrate the use of emergency equipment
- Ensure that all passengers fasten their seatbelts
- Serve, and sometimes sell, beverages, meals, or snacks
- Take care of passengers' needs
- Assist passengers with special needs
- Reassure passengers during flight, such as when the aircraft hits turbulence
- Administer first aid to passengers, when needed
- Direct passengers in case of emergency

Airline companies are required by law to provide flight attendants for the safety and security of passengers. The primary job of flight attendants is to keep passengers safe and to ensure that everyone follows security regulations. Flight attendants also try to make flights comfortable and enjoyable for passengers.

At least 1 hour before takeoff, the captain (pilot) informs attendants about evacuation procedures, the length of the flight, and weather conditions. Flight attendants must ensure that emergency equipment is working, the cabin is clean, and there is an adequate supply of food and beverages on board. As passengers board the plane, flight attendants greet them and direct them to their seats.

Before the plane takes off, flight attendants instruct all passengers on the use of safety equipment, either by playing a video recording or demonstrating its use in person. They also ensure that seatbelts are fastened, seats are in the upright position, and all carry-on items are properly stowed.

A flight attendant's most important responsibility, however, is to help passengers in the event of an emergency. This responsibility ranges from reassuring nervous passengers to performing first aid and evacuating passengers. Flight attendants also answer questions about the flight, attend to passengers with special needs, and help anyone else needing assistance.

Before the plane lands, flight attendants once again ensure that seatbelts are fastened, seats are in the upright position, and all carry-on items are properly stowed.

Before they leave the plane, flight attendants take inventory of headsets, alcoholic beverages, and payments. They also submit reports to the airline company on the condition of the cabin, as well as on any medical problems that may have occurred during the flight.

Work Environment

Flight attendants work primarily in the cabin of an airplane. Although they enjoy much free time and many travel benefits, flight attendants' work can be strenuous. Flight attendants stand during much of the flight and must remain pleasant, regardless of passenger

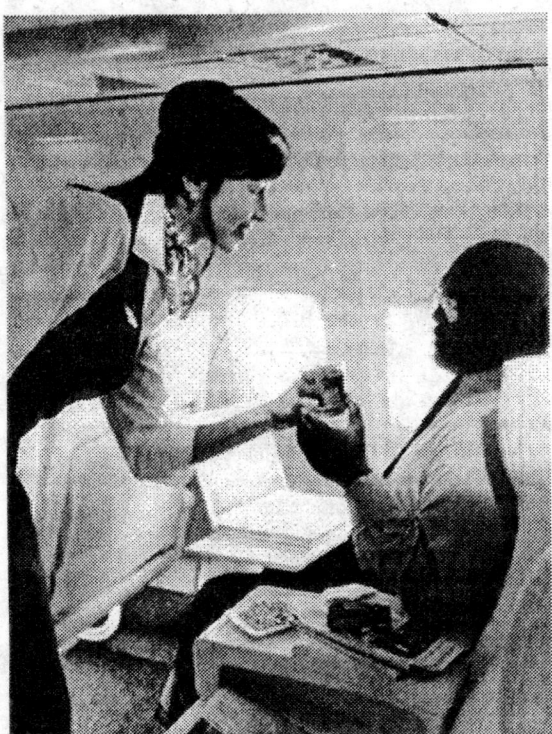

Serving beverages is a common task for flight attendants.

demands or their own fatigue. Occasionally, flight attendants must deal with turbulence, which can make service more difficult and causes anxiety in some passengers.

Flight attendants held about 90,500 jobs in 2010. Although most worked for major airline companies, a small number worked for corporations or chartered flight companies.

Many flight attendants are members of a union.

Injuries

Working in a moving aircraft can be somewhat dangerous. Injuries may occur when opening overhead compartments or while pushing carts. In addition, medical problems can arise from irregular sleep patterns, stress, and working in a pressurized cabin during flight. As a result, flight attendants experience a higher-than-average rate of work-related injuries and illnesses.

Work Schedules

Most flight attendants have a variable schedule. Because airline companies operate around the clock, flight attendants often work nights, weekends, and holidays. In most cases, a contract between the airline company and flight attendant union determines the total daily and monthly worktime. A typical on-duty shift is usually about 12 to 14 hours per day. However, duty time can be increased for international flights. The Federal Aviation Administration (FAA) requires that flight attendants receive nine consecutive hours of rest following any duty period.

Attendants usually fly 75 to 90 hours a month and generally spend another 50 hours a month on the ground, preparing flights, writing reports, and waiting for planes to arrive. On average, they spend about two to three nights a week away from home. During this time, their employer provides them with hotel accommodations and a meal allowance.

Because an attendant's assignments of home base and route are based on seniority, new flight attendants must be flexible with their schedule and location. Almost all flight attendants start out working on call, otherwise known as reserve status. Flight attendants on reserve usually live near their home airport, because they have to report to work on short notice.

As their seniority improves, attendants gain more control over their schedule. For example, some senior flight attendants may choose to live outside their home base and commute to work. Others may choose to work only on regional flights. On small corporate airlines, flight attendants often work on an as-needed basis and must be able to adapt to various schedules and personalities.

How to Become a Flight Attendant

Education and Training

A high school diploma or GED is the minimum educational requirement for becoming a flight attendant. However, airlines increasingly prefer to hire applicants who have a college degree. Applicants with a degree in hospitality, tourism, public relations, or communications may have an advantage over others. Most airlines also require 1 to 2 years of customer service experience. Those who work on international flights may have to speak a foreign language fluently in addition to English.

Applicants must be at least 18 years old and eligible to work in the United States. Applicants also should have a valid passport and are required to pass a background check.

Airlines also have physical requirements. For example, flight attendants must be a certain height to reach overhead bins, and most airlines prefer candidates with weight proportionate to height. Flight attendants must be in excellent health, and a medical evaluation is required.

Once a flight attendant is hired, airline companies provide the worker with initial training, ranging from 3 to 6 weeks. The training usually takes place at the airline's flight training center and is required for Federal Aviation Administration (FAA) certification.

Trainees learn emergency procedures such as evacuating an airplane, operating emergency equipment, and administering first aid. They also receive specific instruction on flight regulations, company operations, and job duties.

Toward the end of the training, students go on practice flights. They must successfully complete the training to keep a job with the airline. Once they have passed initial training, new flight attendants receive the FAA Certificate of Demonstrated Proficiency. To maintain their certification, flight attendants must take periodic retraining throughout their career.

Certification

All flight attendants must be certified by the FAA. To become certified, flight attendants must complete their employer's initial training program and pass a proficiency check. Because flight attendants are certified for a specific type of aircraft, they must take new training for each type of aircraft on which they are to work to maintain their certification.

Advancement

After completing initial training, new flight attendants are placed on call, also known as reserve status. While on reserve, attendants must be able to report to the airport on short notice because they are often called on to staff extra flights and fill in for other crewmembers.

New attendants usually remain on reserve for at least 1 year, but in some cities attendants may be on reserve for several years. After a few years, flight attendants gain enough experience to bid on monthly assignments. Because assignments are based on seniority, the most preferred routes go to the most experienced attendants.

Career advancement is based on seniority. Senior flight attendants exercise the most control over route assignments; therefore, they can often choose how much time to spend away from home. On international flights, senior attendants often oversee the work of other attendants. Senior attendants may be promoted to management positions in which they are responsible for recruiting, instructing, and scheduling.

Important Qualities

Attentiveness. Flight attendants must be aware of passengers' needs to ensure a pleasant travel experience.

Communication skills. Flight attendants should speak clearly and interact comfortably with passengers.

Customer-service skills. Flight attendants should have poise, tact, and resourcefulness to handle stressful situations and meet passengers' needs.

Listening skills. To fully meet passengers' needs, attendants must be able to give their full attention to the passengers, ask appropriate questions of them, and answer their questions politely.

Neat appearance. Because airlines usually have appearance requirements, applicants should not have visible tattoos, body piercings, or unusual hairstyle or makeup.

Proper vision. Flight attendants must have vision that is correctable to at least 20/40.

Pay

Flight Attendants
Median annual wages, May 2010

Flight Attendants	$37,740
Total, All Occupations	$33,840
Transportation and Material Moving Occupations	$28,400

Note: All Occupations includes all occupations in the U.S. Economy.
Source: U.S. Bureau of Labor Statistics, Occupational Employment Statistics

The median annual wage of flight attendants was $37,740 in May 2010. The median wage is the wage at which half the workers in an occupation earned more than that amount and half earned less. The lowest 10 percent earned less than $24,930, and the top 10 percent earned more than $63,990.

According to data from the Association of Flight Attendants, the average annual wage for an entry-level position was $16,597 in 2011.

Attendants typically receive health and retirement benefits as part of their compensation package. Some airlines also offer incentive pay

for working holidays, nights, and weekends. While working away from home, attendants also receive an allowance for meals and accommodations. Flight attendants are required to purchase their initial set of uniforms and luggage, but the airline companies usually pay for replacements.

Attendants typically fly 75 to 90 hours a month and generally spend another 50 hours a month on the ground, preparing flights, writing reports, and waiting for planes to arrive. On average, they spend about two to three nights a week away from home. Most work variable schedules.

Many flight attendants are members of a union.

Job Outlook

Flight Attendants
Percent change in employment, projected 2010-20

Transportation and Material Moving Occupations	15%
Total, All Occupations	14%
Flight Attendants	0%

Note: All Occupations includes all occupations in the U.S. Economy.
Source: U.S. Bureau of Labor Statistics, Employment Projections program

Employment of flight attendants is projected to experience little or no change from 2010 to 2020. Despite modest growth in air travel, higher fuel prices and union contracts may prevent airline companies from hiring new flight attendants.

Job Prospects

Competition for jobs will remain strong because the occupation is expected to attract more applicants than there are job openings. When entry-level positions do become available, job prospects should be best for applicants with a college degree and 1 to 2 years of customer service experience. Job opportunities may be slightly better at regional or low-cost airliners.

Some job opportunities may arise from the need to replace attendants who leave the workforce. Over the next decade, a number of flight attendants are expected to retire. However, if airline companies decide to slim down their workforce or hire back furloughed attendants, the number of job openings for entry-level candidates may be reduced.

Employment projections data for flight attendants, 2010-20

Occupational Title	SOC Code	Employment, 2010	Projected Employment, 2020	Change, 2010-20	
				Percent	Numeric
Flight Attendants	53-2031	90,500	90,300	0	-200
SOURCE: U.S. Bureau of Labor Statistics, Employment Projections program					

Similar Occupations

This table shows a list of occupations with job duties that are similar to those of flight attendants.

Occupation	Job Duties	Entry-Level Education	Median Annual Pay, May 2010
Bartenders	Bartenders mix and serve drinks to customers directly or through wait staff.	Less than high school	$18,680
EMTs and Paramedics	Emergency medical technicians (EMTs) and paramedics care for the sick or injured in emergency medical settings. People's lives often depend on their quick reaction and competent care. EMTs and paramedics respond to emergency calls, performing medical services and transporting patients to medical facilities.	Postsecondary non-degree award	$30,360

Food and Beverage Serving and Related Workers	Food and beverage serving and related workers perform a variety of customer service, food preparation, and cleaning duties in full-service restaurants, casual dining eateries, and other eating and drinking places.	Less than high school	$18,130

Contacts for More Information

For more information about flight attendants, visit the career webpage of any airline company, contact its personnel department, or visit Association of Flight Attendants—CWA

Suggested citation:

Bureau of Labor Statistics, U.S. Department of Labor, Occupational Outlook Handbook, 2012-13 Edition, Flight Attendants, on the Internet at http://www.bls.gov/ooh/transportation-and-material-moving/flight-attendants.htm.

Hand Laborers and Material Movers

Quick Facts: Hand Laborers and Material Movers	
2010 Median Pay	$22,560 per year $10.85 per hour
Entry-Level Education	Less than high school
Work Experience in a Related Occupation	None
On-the-job Training	Short-term on-the-job training
Number of Jobs, 2010	3,315,400
Job Outlook, 2010-20	14% (About as fast as average)
Employment Change, 2010-20	465,500

What Hand Laborers and Material Movers Do

Hand laborers and material movers transport objects without using machines. Some workers move freight, stock, or other materials around storage facilities; others clean vehicles; some pick up unwanted household goods; and still others pack materials for moving.

Duties

Hand laborers and material movers typically do the following:

- Manually move material from one place to another
- Pack or wrap material by hand
- Keep a record of the material they move
- Use signals to assist machine operators who are moving larger pieces of material, when necessary

In warehouses and wholesale and retail operations, hand material movers work closely with material-moving machine operators and material recording clerks. Automatic sensors and tags are increasingly being used to track items that allow these employees to work faster. Some workers are employed in manufacturing industries in which they load material onto conveyor belts or other machines.

The following are some examples of hand laborers and material movers:

Laborers and hand freight, stock, and material movers move materials to and from storage and production areas, loading docks, delivery trucks, ships, and containers. Most of these movers work in warehouses, although their specific duties vary. Some workers, called pickers, find products in storage and transport them to the loading area. Other workers load and unload cargo from a truck. Sometimes they open containers and sort the material.

Hand packers and packagers package a variety of materials by hand. They may label cartons, inspect items for defects, and record items packed. Some of these workers pack materials for shipment and transport them to a loading dock. Others work in retail as gift wrappers. Many hand packers are employed by grocery stores, where they bag groceries for customers at checkout.

Machine feeders and offbearers process materials by feeding them into equipment or by removing materials from equipment. This equipment is generally operated by other workers, such as material-moving machine operators. Machine feeders and offbearers might help the operator if the machine becomes jammed or needs minor repairs. Machine feeders track the amount of material they process during a shift.

Cleaners of vehicles and equipment clean automobiles and other vehicles, as well as storage tanks, pipelines, and related machinery. They use cleaning products, vacuums, hoses, and brushes. Most of these workers clean cars at a carwash, automobile dealership, or rental agency. Some clean industrial equipment at manufacturing firms.

Some laborers help move goods from ships into storage facilities.

Refuse and recyclable material collectors gather garbage and recyclables from homes and businesses to transport to a dump, landfill, or recycling center. Many collectors lift garbage cans by hand and empty them into their truck. Some collectors drive the garbage or recycling truck along a scheduled route. When collecting materials from a dumpster, drivers use a hydraulic lift to empty contents of the dumpster into their truck.

Work Environment

The work of hand laborers and material movers is usually repetitive and physically demanding. Workers may lift and carry heavy objects. They bend, kneel, crouch, or crawl in awkward positions.

Hand laborers and material movers held 3,315,400 jobs in 2010. They work in a variety of industries.

Laborers and hand, freight, stock, and material movers work in the following industries:

Transportation and warehousing	21%
Wholesale trade	17
Retail trade	16
Employment services	15
Manufacturing	13

Hand packers and packagers work in the following industries:

Grocery stores	24%
Employment services	17
Food manufacturing	9

Machine feeders and offbearers work in the following industries:

Food manufacturing	12%
Wood product manufacturing	10
Paper manufacturing	8
Plastics and rubber products manufacturing	7

Cleaners of vehicles and equipment work in the following industries:

Automotive repair and maintenance	37%
Automobile dealers	21
Automotive equipment rental and leasing	5

Refuse and recyclable material collectors work in the following industries:

Waste collection	37%
Local government, excluding education and hospitals	35
Waste treatment and disposal	13

Injuries

Some material moving jobs can be dangerous. Hand laborers and freight, stock, and material movers, as well as refuse and recyclable material collectors, have some of the highest rates of injury and illness of all occupations. When hand laborers and freight, stock and material movers move heavy objects around a warehouse or onto trucks, accidents can happen, which could cause injury. Because refuse and recyclable material collectors drive so much to complete their rounds, they are vulnerable to traffic accidents.

Some vehicle and equipment cleaners work with heavy machinery, which also can lead to injury. However, these jobs have become less dangerous as safety equipment and regulations have improved. For protection, many workers wear safety equipment, such as gloves or hard hats.

Work Schedules

Most hand laborers and material movers work full time. In addition, most work 8-hour shifts, although longer shifts and overtime are common. Because materials are shipped around the clock, some workers, especially those in warehousing, work overnight shifts.

How to Become a Hand Laborer or Material Mover

Generally, hand laborers and material movers need no work experience or minimum level of education. Employers require only that applicants be physically able to do the work.

Education

Some employers may prefer to hire workers who have a high school diploma, although it is generally not required for these jobs.

Training

Most of these positions require less than 1 month of on-the-job training. Some workers need only a few days of training. Certain hand freight, stock, and material movers and refuse and recyclable material collectors have up to 3 months of training. Most training is done by a supervisor or a more experienced worker who decides when trainees are ready to work on their own.

Workers learn a safety rules as part of their training. Many of these rules are standardized through the Occupational Safety and Health Administration (OSHA). Workers who handle hazardous materials receive additional training.

Licenses

Depending on the size of the truck, refuse and recyclable material collectors who drive the truck may have to have a commercial driver's license (CDL). Getting a CDL requires passing written, skills, and vision tests.

Advancement

Many of these workers advance to other jobs. Some become material-moving machine operators; others become construction laborers or production workers. In warehousing or retail, experienced workers can move to other parts of the company, such as sales.

Important Qualities

Customer service skills. Laborers and material handlers who work with the public, such as grocery baggers or carwash attendants, must be pleasant and courteous to customers.

Listening skills. Laborers and material movers often need to follow instructions that a supervisor gives them.

Physical strength. Some workers must be able to lift heavy objects throughout the day.

Pay

Hand Laborers and Material Movers
Median annual wages, May 2010

Total, All Occupations	$33,840
Transportation and Material Moving Occupations	$28,400
Hand Laborers and Material Movers	$22,560

Note: All Occupations includes all occupations in the U.S. Economy.
Source: U.S. Bureau of Labor Statistics, Occupational Employment Statistics

The median annual wage of hand laborers and material movers was $22,560 in May 2010. The median wage is the wage at which half the workers in an occupation earned more than that amount and half earned less. The lowest 10 percent earned less than $16,600, and the top 10 percent earned more than $37,700 in May 2010.

The median wages of hand laborers and material moving occupations in May 2010 were the following:
- $32,640 for refuse and recyclable material collectors
- $27,000 for machine feeders and offbearers
- $23,460 for laborers and hand freight, stock, and material movers
- $19,680 for cleaners of vehicles and equipment
- $19,630 for hand packers and packagers

Most hand laborers and material movers work full time. In addition, most work 8-hour shifts, although longer shifts and overtime are common. Because materials are shipped around the clock, some workers, especially those in warehousing, work overnight shifts.

Job Outlook

Hand Laborers and Material Movers

Percent change in employment, projected 2010-20

Transportation and Material Moving Occupations	15%
Total, All Occupations	14%
Hand Laborers and Material Movers	14%

Note: All Occupations includes all occupations in the U.S. Economy.
Source: U.S. Bureau of Labor Statistics, Employment Projections program

Overall employment of hand laborers and material movers is projected to grow 14 percent from 2010 to 2020, as fast as the average of all occupations.

Projected employment change for specific groups of workers within this occupation is as follows:
- Employment of refuse and recyclable material collectors is expected to grow 20 percent from 2010 to 2020. Trash collection will continue to grow as population and income grow, and collectors will be needed to remove trash. An increase in recycling collection is expected to drive the rapid growth of this occupation.

- Employment of cleaners of vehicles and equipment is projected to increase 19 percent from 2010 to 2020. Faster than average growth in automobile dealers, where many of these workers are employed is expected to drive employment growth for this occupation. However, a decline in the use of full-service carwashes in favor of automatic conveyors may to limit their job growth somewhat.
- Employment of laborers and hand, freight, stock, and material movers is projected to increase by15 percent from 2010 to 2020. The need for warehouses is expected to grow as consumer spending increases. However, greater automation will increase the efficiency of hand material movers. Most warehouses are installing equipment, such as high-speed conveyors and sorting systems and robotic pickers, that decreases the number of workers needed.
- Employment of hand packers and packagers is projected to grow 9 percent from 2010 to 2020. A decline in the use of baggers in grocery stores, where many workers are employed, is expected to dampen growth in this occupation. An increase in the use of self-service technology, such as self-checkout, and the growing number of cashiers who also bag groceries are contributing to the decline in baggers. However, those employed in warehouses are expected to see some employment growth.
- Employment of machine feeders and offbearers is expected to experience little or no change from 2010 to 2020. They are heavily employed in declining manufacturing industries in which automation is further decreasing the need for these workers. Additionally, other workers who operate the machines are increasingly doing the tasks of these workers.

Job Prospects

Job prospects for hand laborers and material movers should be favorable. Despite slower growth in these occupations, the need to replace workers who leave the occupations should create a large number of job openings. As automation increases, the technology used by workers in some of these occupations will become more complex. Employers will likely prefer workers who are comfortable using technology such as tablet computers and handheld scanners.

Employment projections data for hand laborers and material movers, 2010-20

Occupational Title	SOC Code	Employment, 2010	Projected Employment, 2020	Change, 2010-20 Percent	Change, 2010-20 Numeric
Hand Laborers and Material Movers	—	3,315,400	3,780,900	14	465,500
Cleaners of Vehicles and Equipment	53-7061	310,600	370,800	19	60,100
Laborers and Freight, Stock, and Material Movers, Hand	53-7062	2,068,200	2,387,300	15	319,100
Machine Feeders and Offbearers	53-7063	119,400	119,600	0	100
Packers and Packagers, Hand	53-7064	677,300	735,200	9	57,900
Refuse and Recyclable Material Collectors	53-7081	139,900	168,100	20	28,200
SOURCE: U.S. Bureau of Labor Statistics, Employment Projections program					

Similar Occupations

This table shows a list of occupations with job duties that are similar to those of hand laborers and material movers.

Occupation	Job Duties	Entry-Level Education	Median Annual Pay, May 2010
Construction Laborers and Helpers	Construction laborers and helpers do many basic tasks that require physical labor on construction sites.	See How to Become One	$28,410
Delivery Truck Drivers and Driver/Sales Workers	Delivery truck drivers and driver/sales workers pick up, transport, and drop off packages within a small region or urban area. Most of the time, they transport merchandise from a distribution center to businesses and households.	High school diploma or equivalent	$27,050

Heavy and Tractor-trailer Truck Drivers	Heavy and tractor-trailer truck drivers transport goods from one location to another. Most tractor-trailer drivers are long-haul drivers and operate trucks with a capacity of at least 26,001 pounds per gross vehicle weight (GVW). They deliver goods over intercity routes, sometimes spanning several states.	High school diploma or equivalent	$37,770
Material Moving Machine Operators	Material moving machine operators use machinery to transport various objects. Some operators move construction materials around building sites or earth around a mine. Others move goods around a warehouse or onto and off of container ships.	Less than high school	$30,800
Material Recording Clerks	Material recording clerks keep track of information to keep businesses and supply chains on schedule. They ensure proper scheduling, recordkeeping, and inventory control.	See How to Become One	$24,100
Water Transportation Occupations	Workers in water transportation occupations operate and maintain ships that take cargo and people over water. These ships travel to and from foreign ports across the ocean, to domestic ports along the coasts, across the Great Lakes, and along the country's many inland waterways.	See How to Become One	$46,610

Contacts for More Information

For more information about hand laborers and material movers, visit Material Handling Industry of America , The Warehousing Education and Research Council

Suggested citation:

Bureau of Labor Statistics, U.S. Department of Labor, Occupational Outlook Handbook, 2012-13 Edition, Hand Laborers and Material Movers, on the Internet at http://www.bls.gov/ooh/transportation-and-material-moving/hand-laborers-and-material-movers.htm.

Heavy and Tractor-trailer Truck Drivers

Quick Facts: Heavy and Tractor-trailer Truck Drivers	
2010 Median Pay	$37,770 per year $18.16 per hour
Entry-Level Education	High school diploma or equivalent
Work Experience in a Related Occupation	1 to 5 years
On-the-job Training	Short-term on-the-job training
Number of Jobs, 2010	1,604,800
Job Outlook, 2010-20	21% (Faster than average)
Employment Change, 2010-20	330,100

What Heavy and Tractor-trailer Truck Drivers Do

Heavy and tractor-trailer truck drivers transport goods from one location to another. Most tractor-trailer drivers are long-haul drivers and operate trucks with a capacity of at least 26,001 pounds per gross vehicle weight (GVW). They deliver goods over intercity routes, sometimes spanning several states.

Duties

Heavy and tractor-trailer truck drivers typically do the following:

- Load and unload cargo
- Drive long distances
- Report to a dispatcher any incidents encountered on the road
- Follow all applicable traffic laws
- Inspect their trailer before and after the trip, and record any defects they find
- Keep a log of their activities
- Report serious mechanical problems to the appropriate personnel
- Keep their truck, and associated equipment, clean and in good working order

Most heavy and tractor-trailer truck drivers plan their own routes. They may use satellite tracking to help them plan.

Before leaving, a driver usually is told a delivery location and time; but it is up to the driver to find a way to get the cargo there.

A driver has to know which roads allow trucks and which do not. Drivers also must plan legally required rest periods into their trip. Some have one or two routes that they drive regularly and others drivers take many different routes throughout the country. Some also drive to Mexico or Canada.

Companies sometimes use two drivers on long runs to minimize downtime. On these "sleeper" runs, one driver sleeps in a berth behind the cab while the other drives.

Some heavy truck drivers transport hazardous materials, such as chemical waste, and so have to take special precautions when driving. Also, these drivers normally carry specialized safety equipment in case of an accident. Other specialized drivers, such as those carrying liquids, oversized loads, or cars, have to follow rules that apply specifically to them.

Some long-haul truck drivers, called owner-operators, buy or lease trucks and go into business for themselves. They then have business tasks, including finding and keeping clients and doing business work such as accounting, in addition to their driving tasks.

Work Environment

Heavy and tractor-trailer truck drivers held about 1.6 million jobs in 2010.

Many heavy and tractor-trailer truck drivers are employed in general freight trucking. The following table lists the industries that

Truck drivers transport goods around the country.

employed the most truck drivers in 2010.

General freight trucking	33%
Specialized freight trucking	12
Wholesale trade	12
Manufacturing	8

Working as a long-haul truck driver is a major lifestyle choice, because these drivers can be away from home for days or weeks at a time. They spend much of this time alone. Truck driving can be a physically demanding job as well. Driving for many hours in a row can be tiring, and drivers must load and unload cargo.

Injuries

Due to the risk of traffic accidents, heavy and tractor-trailer truck drivers have a higher risk of injury than most other occupations.

Work Schedules

The Federal Motor Carrier Safety Administration regulates the hours that a long-haul truck driver may work. Drivers may not work more than 14 straight hours, 11 of which can be spent driving and the remaining time spent doing other work, such as unloading cargo. Between working periods drivers must have at least 10 hours off duty. Drivers are also limited to driving no more than 60 hours within 7 days or 70 hours within 8 days. They must take 34 hours off before starting another 7 or 8 day run. They must record their hours in a logbook. Truck drivers often work nights, weekends, and holidays.

How to Become a Heavy or Tractor-trailer Truck Driver

Heavy and tractor-trailer truck drivers usually have a high school diploma and 2 years of related work experience. They must have a Commercial Driver's License (CDL).

Education

Some companies require their truck drivers to have a high school diploma or equivalent.

Licenses

All long-haul truck drivers must have a Commercial Driver's License (CDL). Qualifications for obtaining a CDL vary by state but generally include passing both a knowledge and driving test. States have the right to refuse to issue a CDL to anyone who has had a CDL

suspended by another state.

Drivers can get endorsements to their CDL that show their ability to drive a specialized type of vehicle. Truck drivers transporting hazardous materials (HAZMAT) must have a hazardous materials endorsement (H). Getting this endorsement requires an additional knowledge test and a background check.

Federal regulations require testing truck drivers for drug or alcohol abuse with random testing while on duty. In addition, truck drivers can have their CDL suspended if they are convicted of a felony involving the use of a motor vehicle or while driving under the influence of alcohol or drugs.

Other actions can result in a suspension after multiple violations. The Federal Motor Carrier Safety Administration website has a list of these violations. Additionally, some companies have higher standards than what federal regulations require.

Work Experience

Most trucking companies prefer their drivers to have at least 2 years of related experience. Many heavy and tractor-trailer truck drivers work as delivery drivers or as motor coach drivers before joining this occupation. For more information, see the profiles on delivery truck drivers and driver/sales workers and bus drivers .

Training

Some drivers attend professional driving schools, where they take training courses to learn how to maneuver large vehicles on highways or through crowded streets. During these classes, drivers also learn the federal laws and regulations governing interstate truck driving.

In the near future, the U.S. Department of Transportation may require all interstate truck drivers to take a truck-driving course.

The Professional Truck Driver Institute (PTDI) certifies a small percentage of driver-training courses at truck driver training schools that meet industry standards and the U.S. Department of Transportation guidelines for training tractor-trailer drivers.

Important Qualities

Hand-eye coordination. Drivers of heavy trucks and tractor-trailers must be able to coordinate their legs, hands, and eyes together well to always be aware of the situation around them and to drive such a heavy vehicle safely.

Hearing ability. Truck drivers need good hearing. Federal regulations require that a driver be able to hear a forced whisper in one ear at five feet (with or without the use of a hearing aid).

Physical health. Federal regulations do not allow people to become truck drivers if they have a medical condition, such as high blood pressure or epilepsy, that may interfere with their ability to operate a truck. The Federal Motor Carrier Safety Administration website has a full list of medical conditions that disqualify someone from driving a long-haul truck.

Visual ability. Truck drivers must be able to pass vision tests. Federal regulations require a driver to have at least 20/40 vision with a 70-degree field of vision in each eye and the ability to distinguish the colors on a traffic light.

Pay

Heavy and Tractor-trailer Truck Drivers
Median annual wages, May 2010

Heavy and Tractor-Trailer Truck Drivers	$37,770
Total, All Occupations	$33,840
Motor Vehicle Operators	$31,950

Note: All Occupations includes all occupations in the U.S. Economy.
Source: U.S. Bureau of Labor Statistics, Occupational Employment Statistics

The median annual wage of heavy and tractor-trailer truck drivers was $37,770 in May 2010. The median wage is the wage at which half the workers in an occupation earned more than the amount and half earned less. The lowest 10 percent earned less than $24,730, and the top 10 percent earned more than $57,480.

Drivers of heavy trucks and tractor-trailers are usually paid by how many miles they have driven, plus bonuses. The per-mile rate varies from employer to employer and may depend on the type of cargo. Some long-distance drivers, especially owner-operators, are paid a share of the revenue from shipping.

The Federal Motor Carrier Safety Administration regulates the hours that a long-haul truck driver may work. Drivers may not work more than 14 straight hours, 11 of which can be spent driving and the remaining time spent doing other work, such as unloading cargo. Between working periods, drivers must have at least 10 hours off duty. Also, drivers are limited to driving no more than 60 hours within 7 days or 70 hours within 8 days. They must take 34 hours off before starting another 7 or 8 day run. They must record their hours in a logbook. Truck drivers often work nights, weekends, and holidays.

Job Outlook

Heavy and Tractor-trailer Truck Drivers

Percent change in employment, projected 2010-20

Heavy and Tractor-Trailer Truck Drivers	21%
Motor Vehicle Operators	17%
Total, All Occupations	14%

Note: All Occupations includes all occupations in the U.S. Economy.
Source: U.S. Bureau of Labor Statistics, Employment Projections program

Employment of heavy and tractor-trailer truck drivers is projected to grow 21 percent from 2010 to 2020, faster than the average of all occupations.

As the economy grows, the demand for goods will increase, and more truck drivers will be needed to keep supply chains moving. Trucks transport most of the freight in the United States, so as households and businesses increase their spending, the trucking industry will grow.

Global positioning system (GPS) technology and better routing can make trucks more productive, limiting the need for more drivers. Also, as fuel prices rise, some companies may switch their shipping to rail to lower costs.

However, rail is unlikely to take much market share away from trucks, because even with high diesel prices, trucks are more efficient for short distances. Additionally, many products need to be delivered within the short time frame that only trucks can handle.

Job Prospects

Job prospects for heavy and tractor-trailer truck drivers are expected to be favorable. Due to the somewhat difficult lifestyle and time spent away from home, many companies have trouble finding qualified long-haul drivers. Those who have the necessary experience and other qualifications should be able to find jobs.

Employment projections data for heavy and tractor-trailer truck drivers, 2010-20

Occupational Title	SOC Code	Employment, 2010	Projected Employment, 2020	Change, 2010-20	
				Percent	Numeric
Heavy and Tractor-Trailer Truck Drivers	53-3032	1,604,800	1,934,900	21	330,100
SOURCE: U.S. Bureau of Labor Statistics, Employment Projections program					

Similar Occupations

This table shows a list of occupations with job duties that are similar to those of heavy and tractor-trailer truck drivers.

Occupation	Job Duties	Entry-Level Education	Median Annual Pay, May 2010
Bus Drivers	Bus drivers transport people between a variety of places including work, school, shopping, and across state borders. Some drive regular routes, and others transport passengers on chartered trips or sightseeing tours.	High school diploma or equivalent	$29,160
Delivery Truck Drivers and Driver/Sales Workers	Delivery truck drivers and driver/sales workers pick up, transport, and drop off packages within a small region or urban area. Most of the time, they transport merchandise from a distribution center to businesses and households.	High school diploma or equivalent	$27,050
Hand Laborers and Material Movers	Hand laborers and material movers transport objects without using machines. Some workers move freight, stock, or other materials around storage facilities; others clean vehicles; some pick up unwanted household goods; and still others pack materials for moving.	Less than high school	$22,560
Material Recording Clerks	Material recording clerks keep track of information to keep businesses and supply chains on schedule. They ensure proper scheduling, recordkeeping, and inventory control.	See How to Become One	$24,100
Railroad Conductors and Yardmasters	Conductors and yardmasters coordinate the daily activities of both freight and passenger train crews. Conductors work on the train. Yardmasters work in the rail yard.	High school diploma or equivalent	$49,770
Subway and Streetcar Operators	Subway and streetcar operators transport passengers in urban and suburban areas. The vehicles they drive travel underground, on above-ground and elevated tracks, on streets, or on separate tracks.	High school diploma or equivalent	$56,880

Taxi Drivers and Chauffeurs	Taxi drivers and chauffeurs drive people to and from the places they need to go, such as homes, workplaces, airports, and shopping centers. They must know their way around a city to take both residents and visitors to their destinations.	Less than high school	$22,440
Train Engineers and Operators	Train engineers and train operators ensure that freight trains and passenger trains stay on time and travel safely. Train engineers drive trains. Train operators work the brakes, signals, or switches.	High school diploma or equivalent	$46,100
Water Transportation Occupations	Workers in water transportation occupations operate and maintain ships that take cargo and people over water. These ships travel to and from foreign ports across the ocean, to domestic ports along the coasts, across the Great Lakes, and along the country's many inland waterways.	See How to Become One	$46,610

Contacts for More Information

For more information about truck drivers, visit Professional Truck Driver Institute , The International Brotherhood of Teamsters , Federal Motor Carrier Safety Administration

Suggested citation:

Bureau of Labor Statistics, U.S. Department of Labor, Occupational Outlook Handbook, 2012-13 Edition, Heavy and Tractor-trailer Truck Drivers, on the Internet at http://www.bls.gov/ooh/transportation-and-material-moving/heavy-and-tractor-trailer-truck-drivers.htm.

Material Moving Machine Operators

Quick Facts: Material Moving Machine Operators	
2010 Median Pay	$30,800 per year $14.81 per hour
Entry-Level Education	Less than high school
Work Experience in a Related Occupation	See How to Become One
On-the-Job Training	See How to Become One
Number of Jobs, 2010	669,000
Job Outlook, 2010-20	12% (About as fast as average)
Employment Change, 2010-20	83,000

What Material Moving Machine Operators Do

Duties

Material moving machine operators typically do the following:
- Control equipment with levers, wheels, or foot pedals
- Move material according to a plan or schedule they receive from their superiors
- Set up and inspect material moving equipment

Many excavating machine operators are employed in construction.

- Make minor repairs to their equipment
- Record the material they have moved and where they moved it from and to

In warehouse environments, most material moving machine operators use forklifts and conveyor belts. Automated sensors and tags are increasingly used to keep track of merchandise, allowing operators to work faster.

In warehouses, operators usually work closely with hand material movers. For more information, see the profile on hand laborers and material movers .

Many operators work for underground and surface mining companies. They help to dig or expose the mine, remove the earth and rock, and extract the ore and other mined materials.

In construction, material movers remove earth to clear space for buildings. Some work on a building site for the entire length of the construction project. For example, material moving machine operators often help to construct high-rise buildings by transporting materials to workers far above ground level.

The following are types of material moving machine operators:

Industrial truck and tractor operators drive trucks and tractors that move materials around warehouses, storage yards, or worksites. These trucks, often called forklifts, have a lifting mechanism and forks, which makes them useful for moving heavy and large objects. Some industrial truck and tractor operators drive tractors that pull trailers loaded with material around factories or storage areas.

Excavating and loading machine and dragline operators use machines equipped with scoops or shovels. They dig sand, earth, or other materials and load them onto conveyors for transport elsewhere. Most of these operators work in construction or mining industries.

Dredge operators excavate waterways. They remove sand, gravel, or rock from harbors or lakes to help prevent erosion and improve trade. Removing these materials helps maintain navigable waterways and allows larger ships to use more ports. Dredging is also used to help restore wetlands and maintain beaches.

Underground mining loading machine operators load coal, ore, and other rocks onto shuttles, mine cars, or conveyors for transport from a mine to the surface. These workers generally work underground in mines. They may use power shovels, hoisting engines equipped with scrapers or scoops, and automatic gathering arms that move materials onto a conveyor.

Crane and tower operators use tower and cable equipment to lift and move materials, machinery, or other heavy objects. Operators extend and retract horizontal arms and lower and raise hooks attached to cables at the end of their crane or tower. Operators are usually guided by other workers on the ground using hand signals or a radio. Most crane and tower operators work at construction sites or major ports, where they load and unload cargo. Some also work in iron and steel mills.

Hoist and winch operators, also called **derrick operators** or **hydraulic boom operators**, control the movement of platforms, cables, and cages that transport workers or materials for industrial operations, such as constructing a high-rise building. Many of these operators raise platforms up far above the ground. Most work in manufacturing or construction industries. For more information about rig derrick equipment workers, see the profile on oil and gas workers .

Conveyor operators and tenders control conveyor systems that move materials on an automatic belt. They move materials to and from places such as building sites, storage areas, and vehicles.

Work Environment

Material moving machine operators work in a variety of industries. The tables that follow show the distribution of the different kinds of material moving machine operators across the industries listed.

Industrial truck and tractor operators held about 522,200 jobs in 2010, most commonly in the following industries:

Manufacturing	34%
Transportation and warehousing	22
Wholesale trade	18
Retail trade	11

Excavating and loading machine and dragline operators held about 61,500 jobs in 2010, most commonly in the following industries:

Specialty trade contractors	22%
Mining (except oil and gas)	16
Heavy and civil engineering construction	14

Dredge operators held about 2,100 jobs in 2010, most commonly in the following industries:

Nonmetallic mineral mining and quarrying	47%
Heavy and civil engineering construction	18
Government	6

Underground mining loading machine operators held about 3,900 jobs in 2010, most commonly in the following industries:

Coal mining	55%
Nonmetallic mineral mining and quarrying	11
Metal ore mining	9

Crane and tower operators held about 40,100 jobs in 2010, most commonly in the following industries:

Specialty trade contractors	22%
Primary metal manufacturing	14
Support activities for water transportation	8

Hoist and winch operators held about 2,800 jobs in 2010, most commonly in the following industries:

Manufacturing	33%
Support activities for water transportation	11
Support activities for mining	11

Conveyor operators and tenders held about 36,300 jobs in 2010, most commonly in the following industries:

Couriers and express delivery services	22%
Farm product raw material merchant wholesalers	15
Food manufacturing	12
Warehousing and storage	7

Injuries

Some material moving machine operator jobs can be dangerous. For example, crane operators and hoist and winch operators work outdoors at great heights in all types of weather.

Operators in some industries might be exposed to harmful chemicals or dangerous machinery. However, these jobs have become far less dangerous as safety equipment and regulations have improved. Many workers wear gloves, hardhats, or respirators.

Work Schedules

Most material movers work full time and have 8-hour shifts, although longer shifts and overtime are common. Because materials are shipped around the clock, some operators—especially those in warehousing—work overnight shifts.

How to Become a Material Moving Machine Operator

There are generally no formal education requirements. Some employers require previous work experience.

Education

Although it is usually not required, some companies prefer material movers with a high school degree.

Training

Most material moving machine operators are trained on the job in less than a month. Some machines are more complex than others, so the amount of time spent in training will vary with the type of machine the operator is using. Training time also can vary by industry. Most workers are trained by a supervisor or another experienced employee, who decides when the workers are ready to work on their own.

The International Union of Operating Engineers offers apprenticeship programs for heavy equipment operators, such as excavating machine operators or crane operators. Apprenticeships combine paid on-the-job training with technical instruction.

During their training, machine operators learn a number of safety rules, many of which are standardized through the Occupational Safety and Health Administration (OSHA) and the Mine Safety and Health Administration (MSHA). Employers must certify that each operator has received the proper training. Operators who work with hazardous materials receive further specialized training.

Licenses

Several states and many cities require crane operators to be licensed. To get a license, operators typically must complete a skills test in which they show that they can control a crane. They also usually must pass a written exam that tests their knowledge of safety rules and procedures.

Work Experience

Forklift operators usually have a few years of experience in a related occupation, such as hand mover or conveyor operator. For more information see the profile on hand laborers and material movers .

Crane operators and excavating machine operators usually have several years of experience in related occupations. They may start as construction laborers and work as construction equipment operators or hoist and winch operators. For more information, see the profiles on construction laborers and helpers and construction equipment operators

Advancement

Some material moving machine operators become construction equipment operators. Others find work as a production or mining worker. In warehousing or retail environments, experienced workers can move to other parts of the company, such as the sales department.

Important Qualities

Alertness. Machine operators must stay aware of their surroundings while operating machinery.

Manual dexterity. Operators sometimes have to maneuver their machines through tight spaces, around large objects, and on uneven surfaces.

Mechanical ability. Operators make minor adjustments to their machines when necessary.

Visual ability. When operating their machines, operators must be able to see clearly where they are driving or what they are moving. They also must watch for nearby workers, who may unknowingly get in their path.

Pay

Material Moving Machine Operators
Median annual wages, May 2010

Total, All Occupations	$33,840
Material Moving Machine Operators	$30,800
Transportation and Material Moving Occupations	$28,400

Note: All Occupations includes all occupations in the U.S. Economy.
Source: U.S. Bureau of Labor Statistics, Occupational Employment Statistics

The median annual wage of material moving machine operators was $30,800 in May 2010. The median wage is the wage at which half the workers in an occupation earned more than that amount and half earned less. The lowest 10 percent earned less than $20,780, and the top 10 percent earned more than $49,100.

The median wages for material moving machine operator occupations in May 2010 were the following:
- $46,230 for crane and tower operators
- $45,910 for underground mining loading machine operators
- $37,670 for hoist and winch operators
- $36,920 for excavating and loading machine and dragline operators
- $33,690 for dredge operators
- $29,780 for industrial truck and tractor operators
- $29,270 for conveyor operators and tenders

Many material moving machine operators are members of a union.

Most material movers work full time and have 8-hour shifts, although longer shifts and overtime are common. Because materials are shipped around the clock, some operators—especially those in warehousing—work overnight shifts.

Job Outlook

Material Moving Machine Operators
Percent change in employment, projected 2010-20

Transportation and Material Moving Occupations	15%
Total, All Occupations	14%
Material Moving Machine Operators	12%

Note: All Occupations includes all occupations in the U.S. Economy.
Source: U.S. Bureau of Labor Statistics, Employment Projections program

Employment of material moving machine operators is projected to grow 12 percent from 2010 to 2020, about as fast as the average for all occupations.

Employment of both conveyor operators and tenders and industrial truck and tractor operators is expected to grow 12 percent. Both of these occupations are heavily concentrated in warehouse environments. The need for warehouses will grow as consumer spending increases.

However, employment growth will be limited as automation becomes more commonplace. Most warehouses are installing equipment such as high-speed conveyors, high-speed sorting systems, and robotic pickers. This equipment increases the efficiency of material movers, allowing warehouses to trim the numbers of workers they employ.

Employment of crane and tower operators is projected to grow 16 percent. As global shipping increases, more of these operators will be needed at ports to load and unload large cargo ships. Employment growth also will be driven by the recovery of the construction industry, in which many of these workers are employed. Employment of crane operators is projected to grow 31 percent in construction and 26 percent in support activities for water transportation.

Employment of hoist and winch operators is projected to grow 6 percent. Like crane and tower operators they will be needed at ports to help load and unload cargo. Employment of hoist and winch operators is projected to grow 14 percent in support activities for water transportation. However, they are also heavily concentrated in declining manufacturing industries, which will contribute to slower growth.

Employment of excavating and loading machine and dragline operators is projected to grow 17 percent. Many of these operators work in the construction industry, whose projected fast growth will drive job growth in this occupation.

Employment of dredge operators is projected to grow 15 percent as the need for more dredging in the Great Lakes and in other large ports increases. However, environmental concerns are expected to hold up some dredging projects, limiting the growth of this occupation.

Employment of underground mining loading machine operators is projected to decline by 2 percent, largely due to an expected decline in coal mining, where many of these workers are employed. This will be caused by technology gains that boost worker productivity. Employment of these operators is projected to decline 7 percent in coal mining.

Job Prospects

Job prospects should be favorable. A high number of job openings should be created by the need to replace workers who leave these occupations.

As automation increases, the technology used by these occupations will become more complex. Employers will prefer workers who are comfortable using technology such as tablet computers and hand-held scanners.

Employment projections data for material moving machine operators, 2010-20

Occupational Title	SOC Code	Employment, 2010	Projected Employment, 2020	Change, 2010-20 Percent	Numeric
Material Moving Machine Operators	—	669,000	752,100	12	83,000
Conveyor Operators and Tenders	53-7011	36,300	40,500	12	4,200
Crane and Tower Operators	53-7021	40,100	46,400	16	6,300
Dredge Operators	53-7031	2,100	2,400	15	300
Excavating and Loading Machine and Dragline Operators	53-7032	61,500	72,200	17	10,700
Loading Machine Operators, Underground Mining	53-7033	3,900	3,800	-2	-100
Hoist and Winch Operators	53-7041	2,800	3,000	6	200
Industrial Truck and Tractor Operators	53-7051	522,200	583,800	12	61,500
SOURCE: U.S. Bureau of Labor Statistics, Employment Projections program					

Similar Occupations

This table shows a list of occupations with job duties that are similar to those of material moving machine operators.

Occupation	Job Duties	Entry-Level Education	Median Annual Pay, May 2010
Construction Equipment Operators	Construction equipment operators drive, maneuver, or control the heavy machinery used to construct roads, bridges, buildings, and other structures.	High school diploma or equivalent	$39,460
Delivery Truck Drivers and Driver/Sales Workers	Delivery truck drivers and driver/sales workers pick up, transport, and drop off packages within a small region or urban area. Most of the time, they transport merchandise from a distribution center to businesses and households.	High school diploma or equivalent	$27,050
Heavy and Tractor-trailer Truck Drivers	Heavy and tractor-trailer truck drivers transport goods from one location to another. Most tractor-trailer drivers are long-haul drivers and operate trucks with a capacity of at least 26,001 pounds per gross vehicle weight (GVW). They deliver goods over intercity routes, sometimes spanning several states.	High school diploma or equivalent	$37,770
Hand Laborers and Material Movers	Hand laborers and material movers transport objects without using machines. Some workers move freight, stock, or other materials around storage facilities; others clean vehicles; some pick up unwanted household goods; and still others pack materials for moving.	Less than high school	$22,560
Material Recording Clerks	Material recording clerks keep track of information to keep businesses and supply chains on schedule. They ensure proper scheduling, recordkeeping, and inventory control.	See How to Become One	$24,100
Water Transportation Occupations	Workers in water transportation occupations operate and maintain ships that take cargo and people over water. These ships travel to and from foreign ports across the ocean, to domestic ports along the coasts, across the Great Lakes, and along the country's many inland waterways.	See How to Become One	$46,610

Contacts for More Information

For more information about careers as a material moving machine operator, visit Material Handling Industry of America , The Warehousing Education and Research Council , International Union of Operating Engineers, National Commission for the Certification of Crane Operators

Suggested citation:

Bureau of Labor Statistics, U.S. Department of Labor, Occupational Outlook Handbook, 2012-13 Edition, Material Moving Machine Operators, on the Internet at http://www.bls.gov/ooh/transportation-and-material-moving/material-moving-machine-operators.htm .

Railroad Conductors and Yardmasters

Quick Facts: Railroad Conductors and Yardmasters	
2010 Median Pay	$49,770 per year $23.93 per hour
Entry-Level Education	High school diploma or equivalent
Work Experience in a Related Occupation	None
On-the-job Training	Moderate-term on-the-job training
Number of Jobs, 2010	40,800
Job Outlook, 2010-20	5% (Slower than average)
Employment Change, 2010-20	1,900

What Railroad Conductors and Yardmasters Do

Conductors and yardmasters coordinate the daily activities of both freight and passenger train crews. Conductors work on the train. Yardmasters work in the rail yard.

Duties

Conductors typically do the following:

- Check passengers' tickets
- Take payments from passengers who did not buy tickets in advance
- Announce stations and give other announcements as needed
- Help passengers to safety when needed
- Deal with unruly passengers when needed
- Oversee loading and unloading of cargo

Conductors travel on both freight and passenger trains. They coordinate activities of the train crew. On passenger trains, they ensure safety and comfort and make announcements to keep passengers informed. On freight trains, they oversee, and are ultimately responsible for, the loading and unloading of cargo.

Yardmasters typically do the following:

- Review schedules, switching orders, and shipping records of freight trains
- Operate freight cars within rail yards that use remote locomotive technology
- Arrange for defective cars to be removed from a train for repairs
- Switch train traffic to a certain section of the line to allow other inbound and outbound trains to get around

Conductors help passengers board a train.

- Break up or put together train cars according to a schedule

Yardmasters do work similar to that of conductors, except that they do not travel on trains. They oversee and coordinate the activities of workers in the rail yard. They tell yard engineers where to move cars to fit the planned configuration or to load freight. Yardmasters ensure that trains are carrying the correct material before leaving the yard. Not all rail yards use yardmasters. In rail yards that do not have yardmasters, a conductor performs the duties of a yardmaster.

Freight trains move billions of tons of goods around the country and to ports where the goods are shipped around the world. Passenger trains move millions of passengers and commuters to destinations around the country.

Before a train leaves, the conductor or yardmaster discusses the train's route, timetable, and cargo with the locomotive engineer. Conductors are in constant contact with engineers while en route, and they keep each other informed of any changes in the condition of the train. Conductors also receive information from dispatchers about delays and other trains' locations.

Work Environment

Conductors and yardmasters held about 40,800 jobs in 2010.

Almost 90 percent of conductors and yardmasters work in the rail transportation industry.

Conductors on passenger trains generally work in cleaner, more comfortable conditions than conductors on freight trains. However, conductors on passenger trains sometimes must respond to upset or unruly passengers when a train is delayed.

Work Schedules

Most conductors and yardmasters have full-time schedules, although they do not necessarily work a standard 9-to-5 workweek. Because trains run 24 hours a day, 7 days a week, many conductors and yardmasters work weekends, nights, and holidays.

Conductors who work on long freight routes may be away from home for long periods. Conductors on shorter passenger routes and yardmasters have more predictable schedules.

How to Become a Railroad Conductor or Yardmaster

Employers of conductors and yardmasters generally require a high school diploma and several months of on-the-job training.

Education

Most conductors and yardmasters have at least a high school diploma or equivalent. Some take training courses at a community college.

Training

Most railroad companies have 1 to 3 months of on-the-job training for conductors and yardmasters. Amtrak (the passenger train company) and some of the larger freight railroad companies operate their own training programs. Smaller and regional railroads may send conductors to a central training facility or a community college.

Yardmasters may be sent to training programs or may be trained by an experienced yardmaster. They learn how to operate remote locomotive technology and how to manage railcars in the yard.

Conductors and yardmasters also learn the proper procedures for loading and unloading different types of cargo.

Work Experience

Some conductors and yardmasters are promoted from within the railroad company. They may have worked as signal, switch, or brake operators. For more information, see the profile on train engineers and operators.

Certification

Recent legislation will soon require conductors who operate on national, regional, or commuter railroads to become certified. New conductors will have to pass a test that has been designed and administered by the railroad and approved by the Federal Railroad Administration. Existing conductors will be granted automatic certification. The new rule is expected to go into effect in late 2012.

Advancement

Some conductors or yardmasters advance to become locomotive engineers.

Important Qualities

Communication skills. Conductors and yardmasters constantly speak with locomotive engineers and dispatchers to prevent accidents and ensure that the train stays on schedule. Conductors and yardmasters must be easily understood.

Customer-service skills. Conductors on passenger trains ensure customers' comfort, make announcements, and answer any questions a passenger has. They must be courteous and patient. They may have to deal with unruly or upset passengers.

Leadership skills. On some trains, a conductor directs a crew. Yardmasters oversee other rail yard workers.

Speaking skills. Conductors on passenger trains announce stations and make other announcements. They must be able to speak clearly so passengers understand what they are saying.

Pay

Railroad Conductors and Yardmasters
Median annual wages, May 2010

Railroad Conductors and Yardmasters	$49,770
Rail Transportation Workers	$47,620
Total, All Occupations	$33,840

Note: All Occupations includes all occupations in the U.S. Economy.
Source: U.S. Bureau of Labor Statistics, Occupational Employment Statistics

The median annual wage of conductors and yardmasters was $49,770 in May 2010. The median wage is the wage at which half the workers in an occupation earned more than that amount and half earned less. The lowest 10 percent earned less than $33,510 and the top 10 percent earned more than $76,270.

The median annual wage of conductors and yardmasters in the rail transportation industry, where most are employed, was $48,580 in May 2010.

Most conductors and yardmasters are members of one of the two major unions representing rail workers.

Most conductors and yardmasters have full-time schedules, although they do not necessarily work a standard 9-to-5 workweek. Because trains run 24 hours a day, 7 days a week, many conductors and yardmasters work weekends, nights, and holidays.

Conductors who work on long freight routes may be away from home for long periods. Conductors on shorter passenger routes and yardmasters have more predictable schedules.

Job Outlook

Railroad Conductors and Yardmasters
Percent change in employment, projected 2010-20

Total, All Occupations	14%
Railroad Conductors and Yardmasters	5%
Rail Transportation Workers	3%

Note: All Occupations includes all occupations in the U.S. Economy.
Source: U.S. Bureau of Labor Statistics, Employment Projections program

Employment of railroad conductors and yardmasters is projected to grow 5 percent from 2010 to 2020, slower than the average for all occupations.

This occupation's growth will depend on demand for rail transportation. Demand for rail is being driven by population growth and an increase in global trade. In addition, rising gas prices may send some travelers to passenger rail and some shipping to freight rail. An increase in intermodal freight—the shipment of goods through multiple transportation modes—may shift some goods from trucks to freight rail.

Although the increase in rail traffic will likely increase demand for these workers, not many new tracks are expected to be built, which may hold back some rail growth. Because building new tracks is expensive, freight companies have found other ways to increase capacity, such as double-stacking (stacking one rail car on top of another) or running longer trains. With both of these approaches, passenger rail can add more cars to existing trains to increase capacity without increasing either the number of locomotives or the number of conductors on these trains.

Job Prospects

Job opportunities should be favorable for this occupation. Although workers typically stay in railroad conductor and yardmaster jobs longer than workers in many other occupations, more conductors and yardmasters are nearing retirement than are workers in most occupations. When these workers begin to retire, many jobs should open up.

Employment projections data for railroad conductors and yardmasters, 2010-20

Occupational Title	SOC Code	Employment, 2010	Projected Employment, 2020	Change, 2010-20	
				Percent	Numeric
Railroad Conductors and Yardmasters	53-4031	40,800	42,700	5	1,900
SOURCE: U.S. Bureau of Labor Statistics, Employment Projections program					

Similar Occupations

This table shows a list of occupations with job duties that are similar to those of railroad conductors and yardmasters.

Occupation	Job Duties	Entry-Level Education	Median Annual Pay, May 2010
Bus Drivers	Bus drivers transport people between a variety of places including work, school, shopping, and across state borders. Some drive regular routes, and others transport passengers on chartered trips or sightseeing tours.	High school diploma or equivalent	$29,160
Delivery Truck Drivers and Driver/Sales Workers	Delivery truck drivers and driver/sales workers pick up, transport, and drop off packages within a small region or urban area. Most of the time, they transport merchandise from a distribution center to businesses and households.	High school diploma or equivalent	$27,050
Flight Attendants	Flight attendants provide personal services to ensure the safety and comfort of airline passengers.	High school diploma or equivalent	$37,740
Heavy and Tractor-trailer Truck Drivers	Heavy and tractor-trailer truck drivers transport goods from one location to another. Most tractor-trailer drivers are long-haul drivers and operate trucks with a capacity of at least 26,001 pounds per gross vehicle weight (GVW). They deliver goods over intercity routes, sometimes spanning several states.	High school diploma or equivalent	$37,770
Subway and Streetcar Operators	Subway and streetcar operators transport passengers in urban and suburban areas. The vehicles they drive travel underground, on above-ground and elevated tracks, on streets, or on separate tracks.	High school diploma or equivalent	$56,880
Taxi Drivers and Chauffeurs	Taxi drivers and chauffeurs drive people to and from the places they need to go, such as homes, workplaces, airports, and shopping centers. They must know their way around a city to take both residents and visitors to their destinations.	Less than high school	$22,440
Train Engineers and Operators	Train engineers and train operators ensure that freight trains and passenger trains stay on time and travel safely. Train engineers drive trains. Train operators work the brakes, signals, or switches.	High school diploma or equivalent	$46,100
Water Transportation Occupations	Workers in water transportation occupations operate and maintain ships that take cargo and people over water. These ships travel to and from foreign ports across the ocean, to domestic ports along the coasts, across the Great Lakes, and along the country's many inland waterways.	See How to Become One	$46,610

Contacts for More Information

For more information about conductors and yardmasters, visit United Transportation Union

For more information about commuter rail, visit American Public Transportation Association

For more information about conductors and yardmasters who work on freight rail, visit Association of American Railroads

For more information about opportunities in passenger rail, visit National Railroad Passenger Corporation (Amtrak)

Suggested citation:

Bureau of Labor Statistics, U.S. Department of Labor, Occupational Outlook Handbook, 2012-13 Edition, Railroad Conductors and Yardmasters, on the Internet at http://www.bls.gov/ooh/transportation-and-material-moving/railroad-conductors-and-yardmasters.htm .

Subway and Streetcar Operators

Quick Facts: Subway and Streetcar Operators	
2010 Median Pay	$56,880 per year $27.35 per hour
Entry-Level Education	High school diploma or equivalent
Work Experience in a Related Occupation	None
On-the-job Training	Moderate-term on-the-job training
Number of Jobs, 2010	6,500
Job Outlook, 2010-20	10% (About as fast as average)
Employment Change, 2010-20	600

What Subway and Streetcar Operators Do

Subway and streetcar operators transport passengers in urban and suburban areas. Subway operators drive trains that run on separate tracks that may be underground or above ground. Streetcar operators drive electric-powered streetcars, trolleys, and light-rail vehicles that run on streets or on separate tracks above ground.

Duties

Subway and streetcar operators typically do the following:

- Observe signals on the track that indicate when they are supposed to start, stop, or slow down
- Make announcements, such as the stop, final destination, or delays
- Control the vehicle's speed based on regulations for the section of track on which they are operating
- Open and close vehicle doors at scheduled stops
- Watch to make sure all passengers get on and off the vehicle safely
- Communicate with dispatchers to report or be informed of delays or other problems
- Ensure the safe evacuation of passengers during a breakdown or emergency situation
- Test vehicles during non-operating hours and report problems to management

Subway trains and streetcars are normally electric powered, with no separate locomotive pulling the rest of the vehicle. Trains with a separate locomotive travel much further, often through several states or across the country, while subways and streetcars operate within a single metropolitan area.

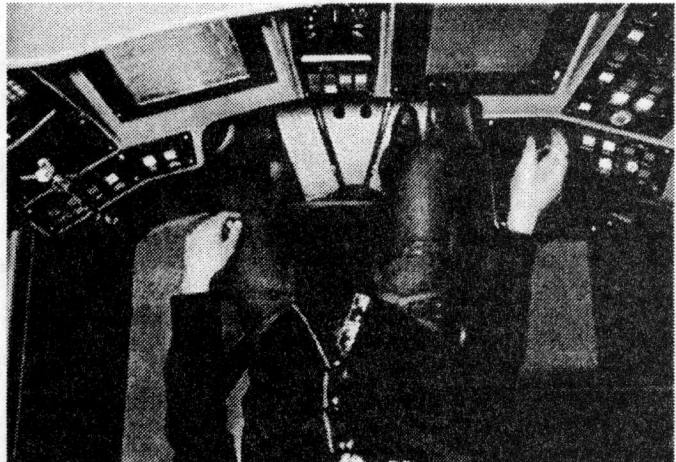

Operators use a variety of controls to drive their vehicle.

Operators work a variety of controls. Although some subways are driven by a computer while in route, most operators control when to start and stop a train. On manually driven subways and on streetcars, operators monitor the speed of the vehicle. Most also control the vehicle doors, helping to ensure that passengers get off and on safely.

Subway operators drive heavy-rail trains that travel on their own right-of-way on underground, above-ground, or elevated tracks. The train's speed often is controlled by a computer, not the operator. However, drivers must be able to take over and drive the train manually in case of an emergency.

Streetcar operators drive electric streetcars, trolleys, and other light-rail vehicles in an urban area. Some streetcar tracks are built in the street, and operators must drive in regular traffic and obey all traffic laws. Operators start, stop, and slow down so that passengers can get on and off. Some operators collect fares and make change. Answering questions about fares, schedules, and routes, streetcar operators interact more with passengers than subway operators do.

Work Environment

Subway and streetcar operators held 6,500 jobs in 2010. About 95 percent of subway and streetcar operators work for local governments that run transit systems within their jurisdiction. Usually, these governments also run bus systems. Some transit agencies use subway and streetcar operators as bus drivers as well, switching workers between modes, depending on the agencies' needs.

Work Schedules

Most subway and streetcar operators work full time. Schedules may vary, based on the transit system's schedule. Operators transport passengers whenever transit systems are open, including weekends, holidays, late nights, early mornings, and, sometimes, around the clock.

How to Become a Subway or Streetcar Operator

Operators need a high school diploma or equivalent and several months of on-the-job training to enter the occupation.

Education

Subway and streetcar operators typically need to have a high school diploma or equivalent.

Training

Operators generally get 1 to 3 months of on-the-job training before they drive their own route. The transit agency provides this training. Following the training, operators must pass a test to ensure that they understand the applicable rules and regulations.

Work Experience

Some transit agencies prefer to hire subway and streetcar operators who have had at least 1 year of experience as a bus driver. For more information, see the profile on bus drivers .

Important Qualities

Communication skills. Operators have to be able to communicate effectively with each other to avoid accidents and to keep the trains on schedule.

Customer-service skills. Streetcar drivers regularly interact with passengers and must be courteous and helpful.

Hand-eye coordination. These workers have to operate various controls while staying aware of their surroundings.

Hearing ability. Good hearing is important for operators. They must be able to hear automated warning signals. If they are operating a streetcar in mixed traffic, they must be able to hear other drivers.

Visual ability. Excellent vision is required to drive safely. Operators must watch for signal changes and obstructions.

Pay

Subway and Streetcar Operators
  Median annual wages, May 2010

Subway and Streetcar Operators	$56,880
Rail Transportation Workers	$47,620
Total, All Occupations	$33,840

Note: All Occupations includes all occupations in the U.S. Economy.
Source: U.S. Bureau of Labor Statistics, Occupational Employment Statistics

The median annual wage of subway and streetcar operators was $56,880 in May 2010. The median wage is the wage at which half the workers in an occupation earned more than the amount and half earned less. The lowest 10 percent earned less than $36,180, and the top 10 percent earned more than $66,570.

The median annual wage of subway and streetcar operators in local government, where most are employed, was $57,310 in May 2010.

Most subway and streetcar operators work full time. Schedules may vary, based on the transit system's schedule. Operators transport passengers whenever transit systems are open, including weekends, holidays, late nights, early mornings, and, sometimes, around the clock.

Job Outlook

Subway and Streetcar Operators
  Percent change in employment, projected 2010-20

Total, All Occupations	14%
Subway and Streetcar Operators	10%
Rail Transportation Workers	3%

Note: All Occupations includes all occupations in the U.S. Economy.
Source: U.S. Bureau of Labor Statistics, Employment Projections program

Employment of subway and streetcar operators is projected to grow 10 percent from 2010 to 2020, about as fast as the average for all occupations. Growth is expected because several cities have proposed building new subway or streetcar systems or expanding existing systems.

Demand for new rail systems is driven by population growth in cities. In addition, an expected increase in gas prices will likely cause some drivers to switch to rail for their commutes.

However, despite expected increases in demand for rail systems, employment growth for subway and streetcar operators depends on state and local government budgets. Building rail systems is expensive, and, during economic downturns, the costs might cause some cities to scale back or cancel their plans for new systems.

Cities could also look to replace some planned lines with buses, which are cheaper to operate and still may satisfy commuters' demand for public transit. As a result, employment growth of subway and streetcar operators may be lower than expected if state and local governments have budget shortfalls.

Job Prospects

Job opportunities for subway and streetcar operators should be good in cities where new rail systems are being built. There is likely to be more competition for jobs in cities with existing systems. Opportunities should be best for applicants with experience driving public transportation vehicles, such as buses. For more information, see the profile on bus drivers.

Employment projections data for subway and streetcar operators, 2010-20

Occupational Title	SOC Code	Employment, 2010	Projected Employment, 2020	Change, 2010-20 Percent	Numeric
Subway and Streetcar Operators	53-4041	6,500	7,100	10	600
SOURCE: U.S. Bureau of Labor Statistics, Employment Projections program					

Similar Occupations

This table shows a list of occupations with job duties that are similar to those of subway and streetcar operators.

Occupation	Job Duties	Entry-Level Education	Median Annual Pay, May 2010
Bus Drivers	Bus drivers transport people between a variety of places including work, school, shopping, and across state borders. Some drive regular routes, and others transport passengers on chartered trips or sightseeing tours.	High school diploma or equivalent	$29,160
Delivery Truck Drivers and Driver/Sales Workers	Delivery truck drivers and driver/sales workers pick up, transport, and drop off packages within a small region or urban area. Most of the time, they transport merchandise from a distribution center to businesses and households.	High school diploma or equivalent	$27,050
Heavy and Tractor-trailer Truck Drivers	Heavy and tractor-trailer truck drivers transport goods from one location to another. Most tractor-trailer drivers are long-haul drivers and operate trucks with a capacity of at least 26,001 pounds per gross vehicle weight (GVW). They deliver goods over intercity routes, sometimes spanning several states.	High school diploma or equivalent	$37,770

Material Moving Machine Operators	Material moving machine operators use machinery to transport various objects. Some operators move construction materials around building sites or earth around a mine. Others move goods around a warehouse or onto and off of container ships.	Less than high school	$30,800
Railroad Conductors and Yardmasters	Conductors and yardmasters coordinate the daily activities of both freight and passenger train crews. Conductors work on the train. Yardmasters work in the rail yard.	High school diploma or equivalent	$49,770
Taxi Drivers and Chauffeurs	Taxi drivers and chauffeurs drive people to and from the places they need to go, such as homes, workplaces, airports, and shopping centers. They must know their way around a city to take both residents and visitors to their destinations.	Less than high school	$22,440
Train Engineers and Operators	Train engineers and train operators ensure that freight trains and passenger trains stay on time and travel safely. Train engineers drive trains. Train operators work the brakes, signals, or switches.	High school diploma or equivalent	$46,100
Water Transportation Occupations	Workers in water transportation occupations operate and maintain ships that take cargo and people over water. These ships travel to and from foreign ports across the ocean, to domestic ports along the coasts, across the Great Lakes, and along the country's many inland waterways.	See How to Become One	$46,610

Contacts for More Information

For more transportation statistics and career information, visit American Public Transit Association

Suggested citation:

Bureau of Labor Statistics, U.S. Department of Labor, Occupational Outlook Handbook, 2012-13 Edition, Subway and Streetcar Operators, on the Internet at http://www.bls.gov/ooh/transportation-and-material-moving/subway-and-streetcar-operators.htm .

Taxi Drivers and Chauffeurs

Quick Facts: Taxi Drivers and Chauffeurs	
2010 Median Pay	$22,440 per year $10.79 per hour
Entry-Level Education	Less than high school
Work Experience in a Related Occupation	None
On-the-job Training	Short-term on-the-job training
Number of Jobs, 2010	239,900
Job Outlook, 2010-20	20% (Faster than average)
Employment Change, 2010-20	47,000

What Taxi Drivers and Chauffeurs Do

Taxi drivers and chauffeurs drive people to and from the places they need to go, such as homes, workplaces, airports, and shopping centers. They must know their way around a city to take both residents and visitors to their destinations.

Duties

Taxi drivers and chauffeurs typically do the following:

- Check their car for problems and do basic maintenance
- Keep both the inside and outside of their car clean
- Refuel their car when necessary
- Pick up passengers and listen to where they want to go
- Operate wheelchair lifts when needed
- Help passengers when loading and unloading their luggage
- Drive to the passengers' destination
- Follow all traffic laws
- Collect fares, including allowed extra charges
- Give a receipt if the passenger wants one
- Keep a record of miles traveled

Taxi drivers and chauffeurs must stay alert and monitor the conditions of the road. They have to take precautions to ensure their passengers safety, especially in heavy traffic or bad weather. They must also follow all vehicle-for-hire or livery regulations, such as where they can pick up passengers and how much they can charge.

Good drivers are familiar with the streets in the areas they serve. They choose the most efficient routes, considering the traffic at that time of day. They know where the most frequently requested destinations are, such as airports, train stations, convention centers, hotels, and other points of interest. They also know where to find fire and police stations and hospitals in case of an emergency.

Taxi drivers, also called cabbies, generally use a meter to determine the fare when a passenger requests a destination. There are three ways cab drivers typically find passengers. The most common is that a customer calls a central dispatcher to request a cab, and the central dispatcher then tells the taxi driver where to go to pick up the customer. Some drivers pick up passengers waiting in lines at cabstands or in the taxi line at airports, train stations, and hotels. In some large cities, cabbies drive around the streets looking for passengers, although this is not legal in all places.

Chauffeurs take passengers on prearranged trips. They operate limousines, vans, or private cars. They may work for hire for single trips or they may work for a private business or citizen or for a government agency. Customer service is important for chauffeurs, especially luxury car drivers. Some do the duties of executive

Taxi drivers and chauffeurs transport passengers to various destinations.

assistants, acting as driver, secretary, and itinerary planner. Other chauffeurs drive large vans between airports or train stations and hotels.

Paratransit drivers transport people with special needs, such as the elderly or those with disabilities. They operate specially equipped vehicles designed to help people with a variety of needs in nonemergency situations. For example, their vehicles may be equipped with wheelchair lifts, and the driver helps a passenger with boarding.

Work Environment

Driving for long periods of time, especially in heavy traffic, can be stressful for taxi drivers and chauffeurs. In addition, they often have to pick up heavy luggage and packages.

Taxi drivers and chauffeurs held 239,900 jobs in 2010. About 31 percent of taxi drivers and chauffeurs were self-employed. Self-employed drivers usually own their own car and contract with a company. The company refers passengers and allows the driver to use their facilities for a fee. Drivers keep all their fares and pay their own expenses.

Other taxi drivers and chauffeurs are directly employed by a company that provides them with a car. They are commonly employed in the following industries:

Taxi and limousine service	18%
Other transit and ground passenger transportation	10
Nursing and residential care facilities	5
Individual, family, community, and vocational rehabilitation services	5

Injuries

In 2010, this occupation had a higher rate of work-related injuries than the national average. This is due to car accidents and robbery or assaults from a violent passenger. Taxi drivers are at risk for robbery because they work alone and often carry large amounts of cash.

Work Schedules

Work hours for taxi drivers and chauffeurs vary. About 16 percent worked part time in 2010 and another 14 percent had variable schedules. Evening and weekend work is common. Some drivers work very late at night or early in the morning.

Taxi drivers work with little supervision, and their work schedules are flexible. They can break for a meal or rest whenever they do not have a passenger.

Chauffeurs' work schedules are much more structured. The hours they work are based on the needs of their clients. Some chauffeurs are on call while they are not at work.

How to Become a Taxi Driver or Chauffeur

Most taxi drivers and chauffeurs go through a brief training. Many states require them to get a taxi or limousine license. Although a high school diploma is not required, many taxi drivers and chauffeurs have one.

Training

Most taxi and limousine companies provide their new drivers with a short period of on-the-job training. This training usually takes from 1 day to 2 weeks, depending on the company and the location. Some municipalities require training by law.

Training typically covers local traffic laws, driver safety, and the local street layout. Taxi drivers also get training in operating the taximeter and communications equipment. Taxi drivers are trained in accordance with local regulations; in contrast, limousine chauffeurs usually are trained by their company, and customer service is emphasized. Paratransit drivers receive special training in how to handle wheelchair lifts and other mechanical devices.

Licenses

All taxi drivers and chauffeurs must have a regular automobile driverâ's license. States set other requirements; many require drivers to get a taxi or chauffeur's license, commonly referred to as a â"hackâ" license.

The Federal Motor Carrier Safety Administration requires that limousine drivers who transport at least 16 passengers at a time (including the driver) have a commercial driverâ's license (CDL) with a passenger (P) endorsement. To get these, a driver has to pass knowledge and driving skills tests.

Education

Many drivers have a high school diploma; but, generally, it is not required.

Advancement

Taxi drivers and chauffeurs have limited advancement opportunities. Some take dispatching and managerial positions.

Important Qualities

Basic math skills. Taxi drivers count cash when a customer pays a fare and have to be able to make change quickly.

Customer-service skills. Taxi drivers and chauffeurs regularly interact with their customers and have to represent their company positively and make sure passengers are satisfied with their ride.

Dependability. Customers rely on taxi drivers and chauffeurs to pick them up at the agreed-upon time so they get to their destinations when they need to be there.

Hand-eye coordination. Taxi drivers and chauffeurs have to be able to observe their surroundings while operating a vehicle.

Map reading skills. Although many cabs and limousines have GPS systems, it is still important for taxi drivers and chauffeurs to be able to understand directions and read maps.

Patience. When driving through heavy traffic congestion or dealing with rude passengers, drivers must be calm and composed.

Visual ability. To hold a drivers license, taxi drivers and chauffeurs must be able to pass a state-issued vision test.

Taxi drivers and chauffeurs usually work without supervision, so they must be self-motivated and able to take initiative to earn a living.

Pay

Taxi Drivers and Chauffeurs
   Median annual wages, May 2010

Total, All Occupations	$33,840
Motor Vehicle Operators	$31,950
Taxi Drivers and Chauffeurs	$22,440

Note: All Occupations includes all occupations in the U.S. Economy.
Source: U.S. Bureau of Labor Statistics, Occupational Employment Statistics

The median annual wage of taxi drivers and chauffeurs was $22,440 in May 2010. The median wage is the point at which half the workers in an occupation earned more than that amount and half earned less. The lowest 10 percent earned less than $16,480, and the top 10 percent earned more than $36,450. These wage data include money earned from tips. The better the service taxi drivers and chauffeurs provide their customers, the more likely they are to make a good tip on each fare.

Taxi drivers and chauffeurs who lease their car from a company may pay a fee for the use of the car. This fee covers storage, insurance, and maintenance costs. Drivers who own their cars can contract with a company that allows the drivers to use their facilities for a fee. In addition, drivers usually pay their own fuel costs, so those who use hybrid taxis will have lower expenses.

Work hours for taxi drivers and chauffeurs vary. About 16 percent worked part time in 2010 and another 14 percent had variable schedules. Evening and weekend work is common. Some drivers work very late at night or early in the morning.

Taxi drivers work with little supervision, and their work schedules are flexible. They can break for a meal or rest whenever they do not have a passenger.

Chauffeursâ' work schedules are more structured. The hours they work are based on the needs of their clients. Some chauffeurs are on call while they are not at work.

Job Outlook

Taxi Drivers and Chauffeurs
   Percent change in employment, projected 2010-20

Taxi Drivers and Chauffeurs	20%
Motor Vehicle Operators	17%
Total, All Occupations	14%

Note: All Occupations includes all occupations in the U.S. Economy.
Source: U.S. Bureau of Labor Statistics, Employment Projections program

Employment of taxi drivers and chauffeurs is projected to grow 20 percent from 2010 to 2020, faster than the average for all occupations.

Job growth is expected to be driven by an increase in demand for taxi drivers. Taxis generally complement public transit systems well, because people who regularly take a train or bus are more likely to use a taxi than would people who drive their own car. Therefore, as public transport systems grow, the demand for taxis should grow.

Paratransit is expected to grow rapidly. The growing number of elderly people who wish to remain independent should increase use of these types of services to get around. Some growth will also come from federal legislation that requires transit agencies to offer paratransit services for the elderly and people with disabilities.

On the other hand, the employment growth for chauffeurs is expected to be held back by reductions in corporate travel.

Job Prospects

Job prospects for taxi drivers and chauffeurs should be excellent. The occupation has low barriers to entry and a lot of turnover. Applicants with a clean driving record and flexible schedules should have the best chance of being hired. Most taxi drivers and chauffeurs work in metropolitan areas, and those areas that are experiencing fast economic growth should offer the most job opportunities.

Employment projections data for taxi drivrs and chauffeurs, 2010-20

Occupational Title	SOC Code	Employment, 2010	Projected Employment, 2020	Change, 2010-20	
				Percent	Numeric
Taxi Drivers and Chauffeurs	53-3041	239,900	286,900	20	47,000
SOURCE: U.S. Bureau of Labor Statistics, Employment Projections program					

Similar Occupations

This table shows a list of occupations with job duties that are similar to those of taxi drivers and chauffeurs.

Occupation	Job Duties	Entry-Level Education	Median Annual Pay, May 2010
Bus Drivers	Bus drivers transport people between a variety of places including work, school, shopping, and across state borders. Some drive regular routes, and others transport passengers on chartered trips or sightseeing tours.	High school diploma or equivalent	$29,160
Delivery Truck Drivers and Driver/Sales Workers	Delivery truck drivers and driver/sales workers pick up, transport, and drop off packages within a small region or urban area. Most of the time, they transport merchandise from a distribution center to businesses and households.	High school diploma or equivalent	$27,050
Heavy and Tractor-trailer Truck Drivers	Heavy and tractor-trailer truck drivers transport goods from one location to another. Most tractor-trailer drivers are long-haul drivers and operate trucks with a capacity of at least 26,001 pounds per gross vehicle weight (GVW). They deliver goods over intercity routes, sometimes spanning several states.	High school diploma or equivalent	$37,770
Railroad Conductors and Yardmasters	Conductors and yardmasters coordinate the daily activities of both freight and passenger train crews. Conductors work on the train. Yardmasters work in the rail yard.	High school diploma or equivalent	$49,770
Subway and Streetcar Operators	Subway and streetcar operators transport passengers in urban and suburban areas. The vehicles they drive travel underground, on above-ground and elevated tracks, on	High school diploma or equivalent	$56,880

	streets, or on separate tracks.		
Train Engineers and Operators	Train engineers and train operators ensure that freight trains and passenger trains stay on time and travel safely. Train engineers drive trains. Train operators work the brakes, signals, or switches.	High school diploma or equivalent	$46,100
Water Transportation Occupations	Workers in water transportation occupations operate and maintain ships that take cargo and people over water. These ships travel to and from foreign ports across the ocean, to domestic ports along the coasts, across the Great Lakes, and along the country's many inland waterways.	See How to Become One	$46,610

Contacts for More Information

For more information about taxi drivers, chauffeurs, and paratransit drivers, visit Taxicab, Limousine and Paratransit Association

For more information about limousine drivers, visit National Limousine Association

Suggested citation:

Bureau of Labor Statistics, U.S. Department of Labor, Occupational Outlook Handbook, 2012-13 Edition, Taxi Drivers and Chauffeurs, on the Internet at http://www.bls.gov/ooh/transportation-and-material-moving/taxi-drivers-and-chauffeurs.htm.

Train Engineers and Operators

Quick Facts: Train Engineers and Operators	
2010 Median Pay	$46,100 per year $22.17 per hour
Entry-Level Education	High school diploma or equivalent
Work Experience in a Related Occupation	See How to Become One
On-the-job Training	See How to Become One
Number of Jobs, 2010	67,100
Job Outlook, 2010-20	1% (Little or no change)
Employment Change, 2010-20	500

What Train Engineers and Operators Do

Train engineers and train operators ensure that freight trains and passenger trains stay on time and travel safely. Train engineers drive trains. Train operators work the brakes, signals, or switches.

Duties

Train engineers and operators typically do the following:
- Check the mechanical condition of locomotives and make adjustments when necessary
- Document issues with a train that require further inspection
- Operate locomotive engines within or between stations

These workers operate both freight and passenger trains.

Freight trains move billions of tons of goods around the country to ports where they are shipped around the world. Passenger trains transport millions of passengers and commuters to destinations around the country. Train engineers and operators are essential to keeping freight and passenger trains running properly.

All railroad occupations work together closely. Locomotive engineers travel with conductors and, sometimes, brake operators. Locomotive engineers and conductors are in constant contact and keep each other informed of any changes in the condition of the train. For more information, see the profile on railroad conductors and yardmasters .

Signal and switch operators communicate with both locomotive and rail yard engineers to make sure that trains end up where they are supposed to. All occupations are in contact with dispatchers, who give them directions on where to go and what to do.

The following are types of train engineers and operators:

Locomotive engineers drive freight or passenger trains between stations. They drive long-distance trains and commuter trains, but not subway trains. For more information on those who drive subway trains, see the profile on subway and streetcar operators .

Most locomotive engineers drive diesel-electric engines, although some drive locomotives powered by battery or electricity.

Engineers must be aware of the goods their train is carrying because different types of freight require different types of driving, based on the conditions of the rails. For example, a train carrying hazardous material though a snowstorm is driven differently than a train carrying coal though a mountain region.

Locomotive engineers typically do the following:
- Monitor speed, air pressure, battery use, and other instruments to ensure that the locomotive runs smoothly
- Use a variety of controls, such as throttles and airbrakes, to operate the train

- Communicate with dispatchers over radios to get information about delays or changes in the schedule

Rail yard engineers operate train engines within the rail yard. They move locomotives between tracks to keep the trains organized and on schedule. Some operate small locomotives called dinkeys. Sometimes, rail yard engineers are called hostlers and drive small locomotives to and from maintenance shops.

Locomotive firers are part of a train crew and typically monitor tracks and train instruments. They look for equipment that is dragging, obstacles on the tracks, and other potential safety problems.

Firers also monitor oil, temperature, and pressure gauges on train dashboards to determine if engines are operating safely and efficiently. Firers relay traffic signals from yard workers to engineers in a railroad yard.

Few trains still use firers, because their work has been automated or is now done by a locomotive engineer or conductor.

Railroad brake, signal, or switch operators control equipment that keeps the trains running safely.

Brake operators help couple and decouple train cars. Some travel with the train as part of the crew.

Signal operators install and maintain the signals along tracks and in the rail yard. Signals are important in preventing accidents because they allow increased communication between trains and yards.

Switch operators control the track switches in rail yards. These switches allow trains to move between tracks.

Work Environment

Train engineers and operators held about 67,100 jobs in 2010.

Nearly all locomotive engineers and brake, signal, and switch operators work in the rail transportation industry. Rail yard engineers work in both rail transportation and support activities for rail.

Rail yard engineers spend most of their time working outside, regardless of weather conditions.

Most train engineers and operators are members of one of the two major unions for railroad workers.

Injuries

Rail yard engineers have higher rates of work-related injuries than most occupations have. They must move heavy equipment around and climb up and down equipment, which can be dangerous.

Work Schedules

Trains are scheduled to operate 24 hours a day, 7 days a week, meaning that many train engineers and operators sometimes work nights, weekends, and holidays. Most rail employees work full time. In 2010, nearly one-third worked at least 50 hours a week, although federal regulations require a minimum number of rest hours for operators.

Locomotive engineers whose trains travel long routes can be away from home for long spans of time. Those who work on passenger trains with short routes generally have a more predictable schedule. Workers on some freight trains have irregular schedules.

For engineers, seniority (number of years on the job) usually dictates who receives the most desired shifts. Some engineers are hired on a temporary basis, called "extra board," and get an assignment only when a railroad needs substitutes for workers who are absent.

How to Become a Train Engineer or Operator

Many rail companies require locomotive engineers to have a high school diploma or equivalent, although some companies do not have education requirements for rail yard workers. Train engineers and operators are trained on the job through company training programs.

Education

Some rail companies require a high school diploma or equivalent, especially for locomotive engineers. Other positions sometimes do not have education requirements.

Training

Locomotive engineers generally receive 2 to 3 months of on-the-job training before they can operate a train on their own. Typically, this training involves riding with an experienced engineer who teaches them the nuances of that particular train route.

During training, an engineer learns the track length, where the switches are, or any unusual features of the track. An experienced engineer who switches to a new route also has to spend a few months in training to learn the route with an engineer who is familiar with it.

In addition, railroad companies provide continuing education so that engineers can maintain their skills.

Rail yard engineers and signal and switch operators also receive on the job training, generally through a company training program. This program may last a few weeks to a few months, depending on the company and the complexity of the job.

Licenses

Some rail yard engineers drive large vehicles around the yard and must have a Commercial Driver's License (CDL). The qualifications for obtaining a CDL vary by state but generally include passing both a knowledge and a driving test. For more information about getting a CDL, contact the Federal Motor Carrier Safety Association .

Certification

Locomotive engineers must be certified by the Federal Railroad Administration (FRA). The certification, conducted by the railroad that employs them, involves a written knowledge test, a skills test, and a supervisor determining that the engineer understands all physical aspects of the particular route on which he or she will be operating.

An experienced engineer who changes routes must be recertified for the new route. Even engineers who do not switch routes must be recertified every few years.

At the end of the certification process, the engineer must pass a vision and hearing test.

Work Experience

Most locomotive engineers first work as conductors for several years. For more information, see the profile on conductors and yardmasters .

Advancement

Switch and signal operators can advance to become conductors or yardmasters.

Important Qualities

Communication skills. All rail employees have to be able to communicate effectively with each other to avoid accidents and keep the trains on schedule.

Decision making skills. When operating a locomotive, engineers must be able to make fast decisions to avoid accidents.

Hand-eye coordination. Locomotive engineers have to operate various controls while staying aware of their surroundings.

Hearing ability. To show that they can hear warning signals and communicate with other employees, locomotive engineers have to pass a hearing test conducted by their rail company.

Mechanical skills. All rail employees work with complex

machines. Most have to be able to adjust equipment when it does not work properly. Some rail yard engineers spend most of their time fixing broken equipment.

Physical strength. Some rail yard engineers have to lift heavy equipment.

Visual ability. To drive a train, locomotive engineers have to pass a vision test conducted by their rail company. Eyesight, peripheral vision, and color vision may be tested.

In addition, locomotive operators must be at least 21 years of age and pass a background test. They also must pass random drug and alcohol screenings over the course of their employment.

Pay

Train Engineers and Operators
Median annual wages, May 2010

Rail Transportation Workers	$47,620
Train Engineers and Operators	$46,100
Total, All Occupations	$33,840

Note: All Occupations includes all occupations in the U.S. Economy.
Source: U.S. Bureau of Labor Statistics, Occupational Employment Statistics

The median annual wage of train engineers and operators was $46,100 in May 2010. The median wage is the wage at which half the workers in an occupation earned more than that amount and half earned less. The lowest 10 percent earned less than $31,000 and the top 10 percent earned more than $71,350.

Median wages for train engineer and operator occupations in May 2010 were as follows:

- $47,670 for brake, signal, and switch operators
- $46,630 for locomotive engineers
- $43,510 for locomotive firers
- $35,480 for rail yard engineers, dinkey operators, and hostlers

Trains are scheduled to operate 24 hours a day, 7 days a week, meaning that many train engineers and operators sometimes work nights, weekends, and holidays. Most rail employees work full time. In 2010, nearly one-third worked at least 50 hours a week, although federal regulations require a minimum number of rest hours for operators.

Locomotive engineers whose trains travel long routes can be away from home for long spans of time. Those who work on passenger trains with short routes generally have a more predictable schedule. Workers on some freight trains have irregular schedules.

For engineers, seniority (number of years on the job) usually dictates who receives the most desired shifts. Some engineers are hired on a temporary basis, called "extra board," and get an assignment only when a railroad needs substitutes for workers who are absent.

Job Outlook

Train Engineers and Operators
Percent change in employment, projected 2010-20

Total, All Occupations	14%
Rail Transportation Workers	3%
Train Engineers and Operators	1%

Note: All Occupations includes all occupations in the U.S. Economy.
Source: U.S. Bureau of Labor Statistics, Employment Projections program

Employment of train engineers and operators is projected to experience little or no change, growing 1 percent from 2010 to 2020.

Employment of locomotive engineers is projected to grow 4 percent from 2010 to 2020, slower than the average for all occupations.

Employment of brake, signal, and switch operators is expected to decline 4 percent over the same period.

Although demand for rail transportation is expected to rise because of population growth and an increase in global trade, a lack of new track capacity will hold back growth. Building new tracks is expensive, so freight companies have found other ways to increase capacity, such as double-stacking (stacking one train car on top of another) or running longer trains.

Passenger rail can add more cars to existing train sets to increase capacity without increasing the number of locomotives. These types of measures can meet the growing demand for rail without significant increases in employment.

Employment of rail yard engineers, dinkey operators, and hostlers is projected to decline 4 from 2010 to 2020, while that of locomotive firers is projected to decline 5 percent.

Although demand for rail transportation is expected to grow, these occupations will be more affected by increases in productivity. Increased use of remote-control locomotive technology allows engines to be moved around rail yards remotely and is replacing some of these workers.

Job Prospects

Job opportunities should be favorable for these occupations. Although many workers stay in these occupations for a long time, currently more workers are nearing retirement than is the case in most occupations. When these workers begin to retire, many jobs should become available.

Employment projections data for train engineers and operators, 2010-20

Occupational Title	SOC Code	Employment, 2010	Projected Employment, 2020	Change, 2010-20	
				Percent	Numeric
Train Engineers and Operators	—	67,100	67,600	1	500
Locomotive Engineers	53-4011	38,700	40,400	4	1,700
Locomotive Firers	53-4012	1,100	1,000	-5	-100
Rail Yard Engineers, Dinkey Operators, and Hostlers	53-4013	5,600	5,400	-4	-200
Railroad Brake, Signal, and Switch Operators	53-4021	21,700	20,800	-4	-900
SOURCE: U.S. Bureau of Labor Statistics, Employment Projections program					

Similar Occupations

This table shows a list of occupations with job duties that are similar to those of train engineers and operators.

Occupation	Job Duties	Entry-Level Education	Median Annual Pay, May 2010
Bus Drivers	Bus drivers transport people between a variety of places including work, school, shopping, and across state borders. Some drive regular routes, and others transport passengers on chartered trips or sightseeing tours.	High school diploma or equivalent	$29,160
Delivery Truck Drivers and Driver/Sales Workers	Delivery truck drivers and driver/sales workers pick up, transport, and drop off packages within a small region or urban area. Most of the time, they transport merchandise from a distribution center to businesses and households.	High school diploma or equivalent	$27,050
Heavy and Tractor-trailer Truck Drivers	Heavy and tractor-trailer truck drivers transport goods from one location to another. Most tractor-trailer drivers are long-haul drivers and operate trucks with a capacity of at least 26,001 pounds per gross vehicle weight (GVW). They deliver goods over intercity routes, sometimes spanning several states.	High school diploma or equivalent	$37,770
Material Moving Machine Operators	Material moving machine operators use machinery to transport various objects. Some operators move construction materials around building sites or earth around a mine. Others move goods around a warehouse or onto and off of container ships.	Less than high school	$30,800
Railroad Conductors and Yardmasters	Conductors and yardmasters coordinate the daily activities of both freight and passenger train crews. Conductors work on the train. Yardmasters work in the rail yard.	High school diploma or equivalent	$49,770
Subway and Streetcar Operators	Subway and streetcar operators transport passengers in urban and suburban areas. The vehicles they drive travel underground, on above-ground and elevated tracks, on streets, or on separate tracks.	High school diploma or equivalent	$56,880
Water Transportation Occupations	Workers in water transportation occupations operate and maintain ships that take cargo and people over water. These ships travel to and from foreign ports across the ocean, to domestic ports along the coasts, across the Great Lakes, and along the country's many inland waterways.	See How to Become One	$46,610

Contacts for More Information

For more information about commuter rail, visit American Public Transportation Association

For more information about training programs and job opportunities in passenger rail, visit National Railroad Passenger Corporation (Amtrak)

For general information about career opportunities for train engineers and operators, visit Brotherhood of Locomotive Engineers and Trainmen, United Transportation Union

Suggested citation:

Water Transportation Occupations

Quick Facts: Water Transportation Occupations	
2010 Median Pay	$46,610 per year $22.41 per hour
Entry-Level Education	See How to Become One
Work Experience in a Related Occupation	None
On-the-job Training	See How to Become One
Number of Jobs, 2010	82,600
Job Outlook, 2010-20	20% (Faster than average)
Employment Change, 2010-20	16,700

What Water Transportation Occupations Do

Workers in water transportation occupations operate and maintain ships that take cargo and people over water. These ships travel to and from foreign ports across the ocean, to domestic ports along the coasts, across the Great Lakes, and along the country's many inland waterways.

Duties

Water transportation workers typically do the following:

- Operate and maintain private ships
- Follow their ship's strict chain of command
- Ensure the safety of all people and cargo on board

These workers, sometimes called merchant mariners, work on a variety of ships.

Some operate large deep-sea container ships to transport manufactured goods around the world.

Others work on bulk carriers that move heavy commodities, such as coal or steel across the oceans and over the Great Lakes.

Still others work on both large and small tankers that carry oil and other liquid products around the country and the world. Others work on supply ships that transport equipment and supplies to offshore oil and gas platforms.

Workers on tugboats help barges and other boats maneuver in small harbors and at sea.

Salvage vessels that offer emergency services also employ merchant mariners.

Water transportation workers work on many different types of boats, such as barges.

Cruise ships employ a large number of water transportation workers, and some merchant mariners work on ferries to transport passengers along shorter distances.

A typical deep sea merchant ship, large coastal ship, or Great Lakes merchant ship employs a captain and chief engineer, along with three mates, three assistant engineers, and a number of sailors and marine oilers. Smaller vessels that operate in harbors or rivers may have a smaller crew, with a captain, sometimes a mate, and one to a few sailors.

Also, there are other workers on ships, such as cooks, electricians, and mechanics, who do not need a merchant marine license. For more information, see the profiles on cooks , electricians , and general maintenance and repair workers .

The following are some types of water transportation occupations:

Captains, sometimes called **masters**, have overall command of a ship. They have the final responsibility for the safety of the crew, cargo, and passengers. Captains typically do the following:

- Supervise the work of other officers and the crew
- Ensure that proper safety procedures are followed
- Assess their crew's abilities and determine if more workers are needed
- Prepare a maintenance and repair budget
- Oversee the loading and unloading of cargo or passengers
- Keep logs and other records that track the ship's movements and activities
- Interact with passengers on cruise ships

Mates, or **deck officers**, direct the operation of a ship while the captain is off duty. Large ships have three officers, called first, second, and third mates. The first mate has the highest authority and takes command of the ship if the captain is incapacitated. Usually, the first mate is in charge of the cargo and/or passengers, the second mate is in charge of navigation, and the third mate is in charge of safety. On smaller vessels, there may be only one mate. Deck officers typically do the following:

- Alternate watches with the captain and other officers
- Supervise and coordinate the activates of the deck crew
- Directly oversee docking the ship
- Monitor the ship's position, using charts and other navigational aides
- Determine the speed and direction of the vessel
- Inspect the cargo hold during loading, to ensure that the cargo is stowed according to specifications
- Make announcements to passengers, when needed

Pilots guide ships in harbors, on rivers, and on other confined waterways. They work in places where a high degree of familiarity with local tides, currents, and hazards is needed. Many pilots are independent contractors and go aboard a ship to guide it through a particular waterway. Some, called **harbor pilots**, work for ports and help many ships coming into the harbor during the day.

Sailors, or **deckhands**, operate and maintain the vessel and deck equipment. They make up the deck crew and keep all parts of a ship, other than areas related to the engine and motor, in good working order. New deckhands are called **ordinary seamen** and do the least-complicated tasks. Experienced deckhands are called **able seamen** and usually make up most of a crew. Some large ships have a **boatswain**, who is the chief of the deck crew. Sailors typically do the following:

- Stand watch, looking for other vessels or obstructions in their ship's path, as well as looking for navigational aids, such as buoys and lighthouses
- Steer the ship and measure water depth in shallow water
- Do routine maintenance, such as painting the deck and chipping away rust
- Keep the inside of the ship clean
- Handle lines when docking or departing
- Tie barges together when they are being towed
- Load and unload cargo
- Help passengers, when needed

Ship engineers operate and maintain a vessel's propulsion system. This includes the engine, boilers, generators, pumps and other machinery. Large vessels usually carry a **chief engineer**, who has command of the engine room and its crew, and a first, second, and third assistant engineer. The engineer's alternate oversees the engine and related machinery. Engineers typically do the following:

- Maintain the electrical, refrigeration, and ventilation systems of a ship
- Start the engine and regulate the vessel's speed, based on the captain's orders
- Record information in an engineering log
- Keep an inventory of mechanical parts and supplies
- Do routine maintenance checks throughout the day
- Calculate refueling requirements

Marine oilers work in the engine room, helping the engineers keep the propulsion system in working order. They are the engine room equivalent of sailors. New oilers are usually called **wipers** or **pumpmen** on vessels handling liquid cargo. With experience, an oiler can become a Qualified Member of the Engine Department (QMED). Marine oilers typically do the following:

- Lubricate gears, shafts, bearings, and other parts of the engine or motor
- Read pressure and temperature gauges and record data
- Help engineers with repairs to machinery
- Connect hoses, operate pumps, and clean tanks

Motorboat operators run small, motor-driven boats that carry six or fewer passengers. They work for a variety of services, such as fishing charters, tours, and harbor patrols.

Work Environment

Workers in water transportation occupations held about 82,600 jobs in 2010.

Most water transportation workers are employed in the following industries:

Inland water transportation	21%
Support activities for water transportation	21
Deep sea, coastal, and great lakes water transportation	20
Government	10
Scenic and sightseeing transportation, water	7

Workers in water transportation occupations usually work for long periods on small and cramped ships, which can be uncomfortable. Many people decide life at sea is not for them because of difficult conditions onboard ships and long periods away from home.

However, companies have worked hard to improve living conditions on their ships. Most ships are now air-conditioned and include comfortable living quarters. Many ships also include entertainment systems with satellite TV and Internet connections. Large ships usually have a full-time cook, as well.

Injuries

Water transportation jobs, especially for sailors and marine oilers, are more dangerous than most jobs. Crew members work outside in storms and other bad weather, which increases the risk of injury.

Workers can also be hurt working with certain machinery, heavy equipment, and cargo. However, modern safety procedures and communication systems have greatly improved safety for mariners.

Work Schedules

Workers on deep sea ships can spend months at a time away from home.

Workers on supply ships have shorter trips, usually lasting for a few hours to a week.

Tugboats and barges travel along the coasts and on inland waterways and are usually away for 2 to 3 weeks at a time.

Those who work on the Great Lakes have longer trips, around 2 months, but often do not work in the winter when the lakes freeze.

Crews often work long hours, 7 days a week, while aboard a ship.

Ferry workers and motorboat operators usually are away only for a few hours at a time and return home each night. Many ferry and motorboat operators service ships for vacation destinations and have seasonal schedules.

How to Become a Water Transportation Worker

Education and training requirements vary by the type of job. Officers and engineers usually must have a bachelor's degree. Most water transportation jobs require the Transportation Worker Identification Credential (TWIC) from the U.S. Department of Homeland Security and a Merchant Marine Credential (MMC).

Education

Most deck officers, engineers, and pilots have a bachelor's degree from a merchant marine academy. The programs offer a bachelor's degree and a Merchant Marine Credential (MMC) with an endorsement as a third mate or third assistant engineer. Graduates of these programs can also choose to receive a commission as an ensign in the U.S. Naval Reserve, Merchant Marine Reserve, or U.S. Coast Guard Reserve.

Non-officers, such as sailors or marine oilers, usually do not have to have a degree.

Training

Ordinary seamen, wipers, and other entry-level mariners get on-the-job training for several months to a year. Length of training depends on the size and type of ship and waterway they work on. For example, workers on deep sea vessels need more complex training than those whose ships travel on a river.

Licenses

All mariners working on ships with U.S. flags must have a Transportation Worker Identification Credential (TWIC) from the U.S. Department of Homeland Security. This credential states that a person is a U.S. citizen or permanent resident and has passed a security screening.

Most mariners must also have a Merchant Marine Credential (MMC). They can apply for an MMC at a U.S. Coast Guard regional examination center. Entry-level employees, such as ordinary seamen or wipers, do not have to pass a written exam. However, they do have to pass physical, hearing, and vision tests, as well as a drug screening, to get their MMC.

Crew members can apply for endorsements to their MMC that allow them to move into more-advanced positions.

Wipers can get an endorsement to become a Qualified Member of the Engine Department (QMED) after 6 months of experience by passing a written test.

Ordinary seamen can get an able seamen endorsement after 6 months to 3 years of experience, depending on the type of ship they work on, by passing a written test.

Able seamen can complete a number of training and testing requirements, after at least 3 years of experience in the deck department, to get an endorsement as a third mate. Experience and testing requirements increase with the size and complexity of the ship.

Officers who graduate from a maritime academy receive an MMC with a third mate or third assistant engineer endorsement, depending on which department they are trained in.

To move up each step of the occupation ladder from third mate/third assistant engineer to second to first and then to captain or chief engineer requires 365 days of experience at the previous level. A second mate or second assistant engineer who wants to move to first mate/first assistant engineer must also complete a 12-week training course and pass an exam.

Pilots are licensed by the state in which they work. The U.S. Coast Guard licenses pilots on the Great Lakes. The requirements for these licenses vary, depending on where a pilot works.

More information on MMCs and endorsements is available from the U.S. Coast Guard National Maritime Center .

Work Experience

Instead of attending a maritime academy, captains and mates can attain their position after at least 3 to 4 years of experience as a member of a deck crew. This experience must be on a ship similar to the type they hope to serve on as an officer. They must also take several training courses and pass written and on-board exams. The difficulty of these requirements increases with the complexity and size of the vessel. Most officers who take this career path work on inland waterways, rather than on deep-sea ships.

Although there are no license requirements for motorboat operators, most employers prefer applicants who have several years of boating experience.

Important Qualities

Customer-service skills. Many motorboat operators interact with passengers and must ensure that passengers have a pleasant experience.

Hand-eye coordination. Officers and pilots who steer ships have to operate various controls while staying aware of their surroundings.

Hearing ability. Mariners must pass a hearing test to get an MMC.

Manual-dexterity. Crew members need good balance to maneuver through tight spaces and on wet or uneven surfaces.

Mechanical ability. Members of the engine department keep complex machines working properly.

Physical strength. Sailors on freight ships load and unload cargo. While away at sea, most workers likely have to do some heavy lifting.

Visual ability. Mariners must pass a vision test to get an MMC.

Pay

Water Transportation Occupations
Median annual wages, May 2010

Water Transportation Workers	$46,610
Total, All Occupations	$33,840
Transportation and Material Moving Occupations	$28,400

Note: All Occupations includes all occupations in the U.S. Economy.
Source: U.S. Bureau of Labor Statistics, Occupational Employment Statistics

The median annual wage of water transportation occupations was $46,610 in May 2010. The median wage is the wage at which half the workers in an occupation earned more than that amount and half earned less. The lowest 10 percent earned less than $24,890, and the top 10 percent earned more than $99,690.

Median annual wages for water transportation occupations in May 2010 were as follows:

- $65,880 for ship engineers
- $64,180 for captains, mates, and pilots of water vessels
- $38,510 for motorboat operators
- $36,260 for of sailors and marine oilers

Workers on deep-sea ships can spend months at a time away from home.

Workers on supply ships have shorter trips, usually lasting for a few hours to a week.

Tugboats and barges travel along the coasts and on inland waterways and are usually away for 2 to 3 weeks at a time.

Those who work on the Great Lakes have longer trips, around 2 months, but often do not work in the winter when the lakes freeze.

Crews often work long hours, 7 days a week, while aboard a ship.

Ferry workers and motorboat operators usually are away only for a few hours at a time and return home each night. Many ferry and motorboat operators service ships for vacation destinations and have seasonal schedules.

Job Outlook

Water Transportation Occupations
Percent change in employment, projected 2010-20

Water Transportation Workers	20%
Transportation and Material Moving Occupations	15%
Total, All Occupations	14%

Note: All Occupations includes all occupations in the U.S. Economy.
Source: U.S. Bureau of Labor Statistics, Employment Projections program

Overall employment of water transportation occupations is projected to grow 20 percent from 2010 to 2020, faster than the average for all occupations.

Employment of captains, mates, and pilots is projected to grow 20 percent. Employment of ship engineers is projected to grow 18 percent. Employment of sailors and marine oilers is projected to grow 21 percent.

As the economy recovers, the demand for waterway freight shipping will grow, increasing the need for these workers. Job growth is likely to be concentrated on inland rivers, the Great Lakes, and along the coasts. This will be driven by the demand for commodities such as coal, grain, and petroleum. In addition, the need to supply offshore oil platforms will drive growth of supply ships.

However, growth in domestic waterways freight may be limited by an increase in intermodal shipping. Intermodal shipping means that shippers use more than one method to transport a good. An increase in intermodal shipping may send some freight from barges to trains. For some products, rail is a more direct route from the Midwest to a coastal port, saving time and money.

Jobs in deep-sea shipping will likely continue to decline, as more companies use foreign vessels to transport goods internationally. However, there is a limit to the decline because federal laws and subsidies ensure that there will always be a fleet of merchant ships with U.S. flags. Keeping a fleet of merchant ships is considered important for the nation's defense.

The popularity of cruises as a type of vacation is growing. However, most cruises go to international destinations; and these ships generally do not employ U.S. workers. Nonetheless, because vessels operating between U.S. ports are legally required to be U.S. flagged, a growing interest in cruises to Alaska and Hawaii should lead to more opportunities for domestic workers on cruise ships.

Employment of motorboat operators is projected to grow 15 percent from 2010 to 2020, about as fast as the average for all occupations. Demand for these workers will be driven by growth in tourism and recreational activities, where they are primarily employed.

Job Prospects

Job prospects should be favorable for most water transportation occupations. Many workers leave these occupations, especially sailors and marine oilers, because recently hired workers often decide they do not enjoy spending a lot of time away at sea.

In addition, a number of officers and engineers are approaching retirement, creating job openings. The number of applicants for all types of jobs may be limited by high regulatory and security requirements.

Employment projections data for water transportation occupations, 2010-20

Occupational Title	SOC Code	Employment, 2010	Projected Employment, 2020	Change, 2010-20	
				Percent	Numeric
Water Transportation Occupations	—	82,600	99,300	20	16,700
Sailors and Marine Oilers	53-5011	33,400	40,500	21	7,100
Captains, Mates, and Pilots of Water Vessels	53-5021	36,100	43,400	20	7,300
Motorboat Operators	53-5022	3,100	3,500	15	500
Ship Engineers	53-5031	10,100	11,900	18	1,800
SOURCE: U.S. Bureau of Labor Statistics, Employment Projections program					

Similar Occupations

This table shows a list of occupations with job duties that are similar to those of water transportation occupations.

Occupation	Job Duties	Entry-Level Education	Median Annual Pay, May 2010
Fishers and Related Fishing Workers	Fishers and related fishing workers catch and trap various types of marine life. The fish they catch are for human food, animal feed, bait, and other uses.	Less than high school	$25,590
Electrical and Electronics Installers and Repairers	Electrical and electronics installers and repairers install, repair, or replace a variety of electrical equipment in telecommunications, transportation, utilities, and other industries.	Postsecondary non-degree award	$49,170
Heavy and Tractor-trailer Truck Drivers	Heavy and tractor-trailer truck drivers transport goods from one location to another. Most tractor-trailer drivers are long-haul drivers and operate trucks with a capacity of at least 26,001 pounds per gross vehicle weight (GVW). They deliver goods over intercity routes, sometimes spanning several states.	High school diploma or equivalent	$37,770
Heavy Vehicle and Mobile Equipment Service Technicians	Heavy vehicle and mobile equipment service technicians inspect, maintain, and repair vehicles and machinery used in construction, farming, rail transportation, and other industries.	High school diploma or equivalent	$42,630
Material Moving Machine Operators	Material moving machine operators use machinery to transport various objects. Some operators move construction materials around building sites or earth around a mine. Others move goods around a warehouse or onto and off of container ships.	Less than high school	$30,800
Plumbers, Pipefitters, and Steamfitters	Plumbers, pipefitters, and steamfitters install and repair pipes that carry water, steam, air, or other liquids or gases to and in businesses, homes, and factories.	High school diploma or equivalent	$46,660
Railroad Conductors and Yardmasters	Conductors and yardmasters coordinate the daily activities of both freight and passenger train crews. Conductors work on the train. Yardmasters work in the rail yard.	High school diploma or equivalent	$49,770
Stationary Engineers and Boiler Operators	Stationary engineers and boiler operators control stationary engines, boilers, or other mechanical equipment to provide utilities for buildings or for industrial purposes.	High school diploma or equivalent	$52,140
Train Engineers and Operators	Train engineers and train operators ensure that freight trains and passenger trains stay on time and travel safely. Train engineers drive trains. Train operators work the brakes, signals, or switches.	High school diploma or equivalent	$46,100

Contacts for More Information

For more information about water transportation occupations, including employment and training information, visit Maritime Administration, U.S. Department of Transportation

For more information about licensing requirements, visit The U.S. Coast Guard National Maritime Center

For information about jobs on inland and coastal waterways on barges, tugboats, and towboats, visit The American Waterways Operators

Suggested citation:

Bureau of Labor Statistics, U.S. Department of Labor, Occupational Outlook Handbook, 2012-13 Edition, Water Transportation Occupations, on the Internet at http://www.bls.gov/ooh/transportation-and-material-moving/water-transportation-occupations.htm .

MILITARY CAREERS

What They Do

The U.S. Military provides training and work experience in a variety of military careers. Members of the Armed Forces work in almost all occupations that are available to civilians in addition to occupations that are specific to the military. Service men and women serve on active duty in the <u>Army</u> , <u>Navy</u> , <u>Air Force</u> , and <u>Marine Corps</u> , or in the Reserve components of these branches, and the <u>Air National Guard</u> and <u>Army National Guard</u> . (The <u>Coast Guard</u> , which is included in this profile, is part of the <u>Department of Homeland Security</u>.)

Duties

The military distinguishes between enlisted and officer careers. Enlisted personnel make up about 83 percent of the Armed Forces and carry out the fundamental operations of the military. Officers make up the remaining 17 percent and are leaders of the military, supervising and managing activities in every occupational specialty in the military.

Enlisted personnel typically do the following:

- Participate in combat operations
- Operate, maintain, and repair equipment
- Serve as technicians and specialists in a variety of fields
- Serve as front-line supervisors of junior enlisted personnel

Officers typically do the following:

- Lead troops in ground combat operations
- Serve as supervisors and managers of enlisted personnel
- Operate and control aircraft, ships, or armored vehicles
- Serve as professionals for the military in medical, legal, engineering, and other fields

Types of Enlisted Personnel

The following are examples of types of occupations for enlisted personnel:

Administrative personnel work in a variety of jobs. The military must keep accurate information for planning and managing its operations. Both paper and electronic records are kept on personnel and on equipment, funds, and all other aspects of the military. Administrative personnel record information, prepare reports, and maintain files. They may work in a specialized area, such as finance, accounting, legal affairs, maintenance, supply, or transportation.

Combat specialty personnel work in specialty occupations, such as infantry, artillery, and Special Forces. People in these occupations normally specialize by type of weapon system or combat operation. Examples include infantry specialists who conduct ground combat operations, tank crews who operate battle tanks, or seamanship specialists who are responsible for operating and maintaining ships. Combat specialty personnel may maneuver against enemy forces and positions and fire artillery, guns, mortars, or missiles to destroy enemy positions. They may also operate various types of combat vehicles, such as amphibious assault vehicles, tanks, or small boats, in combat missions. Especially difficult or specialized missions are performed by elite Special Operations teams, who are constantly ready to respond anywhere in the world on a moment's notice.

Construction personnel in the military build or repair buildings, airfields, bridges, and other structures. They may also operate heavy equipment, such as bulldozers, tractors, or cranes. They work with engineers and other building specialists as part of military construction teams. Some personnel specialize in areas such as plumbing, electrical wiring, or water purification.

Electronic and electrical equipment repair personnel maintain and repair electronic equipment used in the military. Repairers

normally specialize by general area, such as aircraft electrical systems, computers, optical equipment, communications, or weapons systems. For example, weapons electronic maintenance technicians maintain and repair electronic components and systems that help locate targets and help aim and fire weapons.

Engineering, science, and technical personnel in the military use specialized knowledge to perform a variety of tasks. They operate technical equipment, solve complex problems, or provide and interpret information. They typically specialize in one area, such as information technology, environmental health and safety, or intelligence.

- Information technology specialists develop software programs and operate computer systems.
- Environmental health and safety specialists inspect military facilities and food supplies to ensure that they are safe for use.
- Intelligence specialists gather and study information needed by the military and prepare reports on this information.

Healthcare personnel help medical professionals provide medical services for men and women in the military. They may work as part of a patient-service team in close contact with doctors, nurses, or other healthcare professionals. Some specialize in providing emergency medical treatment in combat or remote areas where medical care is unavailable. Others specialize in laboratory testing of tissue and blood samples; maintaining pharmacy supplies or patients' records; assisting with dental procedures; operating diagnostic tools, such as x-ray and ultrasound machines; or other healthcare tasks.

Human resources development personnel recruit qualified people into the military, place them in suitable occupations, and provide training programs. These specialists usually focus on a particular duty.

- Recruiting specialists provide information about military careers to young people, parents, schools, and local communities, and explain the Armed Services' employment and training opportunities, pay and benefits, and service life.
- Personnel specialists collect and store information about military personnel, including information on their previous and current training, job assignments, promotions, and health.
- Training specialists and instructors teach classes and instruct military personnel on how to perform their jobs.

Machine operator and production personnel operate industrial equipment and machinery to fabricate and repair parts for a variety of items and structures. They may operate engines, nuclear reactors, or water pumps. Often, they specialize by the type of work performed. Welders and metalworkers, for example, work with various types of metals to repair or form the structural parts of ships, buildings, or other equipment. Survival equipment specialists inspect, maintain, and repair survival equipment, such as parachutes and aircraft life support equipment.

Media and public affairs personnel help present military information and events to the public. They take photographs, make video programs, present news and music programs, or produce artwork and other visual displays. Other public affairs specialists act as interpreters and translators to convert foreign languages into English or other languages.

Protective service personnel enforce military laws and regulations and provide emergency responses to disasters.

- Military police responsibilities include controlling traffic, preventing crime, and responding to emergencies.
- Other law enforcement and security specialists investigate crimes committed on military property and guard inmates in military correctional facilities.
- Firefighters extinguish and prevent fires in buildings, on aircraft, and aboard ships.

Support service personnel provide subsistence services and support the morale and well-being of military personnel and their families. Food service specialists prepare all types of food in dining halls, hospitals, and ships. Religious program specialists assist chaplains with religious services, religious education programs, and related administrative duties.

Transportation and material-handling personnel ensure the safe transport of people and cargo. Most personnel within this occupational group are classified according to mode of transportation, such as aircraft, motor vehicle, or ship.

- Aircrew members operate equipment on aircraft.
- Vehicle drivers operate all types of heavy military vehicles, including fuel or water tank trucks, and passenger buses.
- Quartermasters and boat operators navigate and pilot many types of small watercraft, including tugboats, gunboats, and barges.
- Cargo specialists load and unload military supplies using equipment such as forklifts and cranes.

Vehicle and machinery mechanical personnel conduct preventive and corrective maintenance on aircraft, automotive and heavy equipment, and powerhouse station equipment. These workers typically specialize by the type of equipment that they maintain.

- Aircraft mechanics inspect and service various types of aircraft.
- Automotive and heavy equipment mechanics maintain and repair vehicles, such as Humvees, trucks, tanks, and other combat vehicles. They also repair bulldozers and other construction equipment.
- Heating and cooling mechanics install and repair air-conditioning, refrigeration, and heating equipment.
- Marine engine mechanics repair and maintain engines on ships, boats, and other watercraft. They also repair shipboard mechanical and electrical equipment.
- Powerhouse mechanics install, maintain, and repair electrical and mechanical equipment in power-generating stations.

Table 1 shows the number of military enlisted personnel by branch and broad occupational category in August 2011.

Types of Officers

The following are examples of types of officers:

Combat specialty officers are leaders of combat units. They plan and direct military operations, oversee combat activities, and serve as combat leaders. This category includes officers in charge of tanks and other armored assault vehicles, artillery systems, Special Operations, and infantry. Combat specialty officers normally specialize by the type of unit they lead. This group also includes naval surface warfare and submarine warfare officers, combat pilots, and aircrews.

Engineering, science, and technical officers have a range of responsibilities, depending on their area of expertise. These officers work in many of the scientific and professional fields outside of the Armed Forces, which include occupations such as atmospheric scientists, meteorologists, physical scientists, biological scientists,

Table 1. Active Duty Enlisted personnel by broad occupational group and branch of military, and Coast Guard, August 2011

Enlisted	Army	Air Force	Coast Guard	Marine Corps	Navy	Total enlisted personnel in each occupation group
OCCUPATIONAL GROUP						
Administrative occupations	6,661	15,302	2,274	11,669	19,585	55,491
Combat Specialty occupations	129,684	639	616	32,706	7,854	192,499
Construction occupations	20,499	5,185	–	5,067	5,206	35,957
Electronic and Electrical Equipment Repair occupations	40,214	31,048	4,475	14,098	48,118	137,953
Engineering, Science, and Technical occupations	45,684	47,436	1,288	25,297	40,436	160,141
Health Care occupations	31,317	15,935	693	–	24,068	72,013
Human Resource Development occupations	18,974	12,532	–	8,407	4,108	44,021
Machine Operator and Production occupations	5,398	6,234	1,946	2,532	9,599	25,709
Media and Public Affairs occupations	8,209	6,848	122	2,381	3,854	21,414
Protective Service occupations	27,380	34,738	2,837	9,534	11,959	86,448
Support Service occupations	13,109	1,483	1,218	2,119	8,032	25,961
Transportation and Material Handling occupations	63,566	31,279	10,900	23,154	38,148	167,047
Vehicle and Machinery Mechanic occupations	52,974	42,032	5,554	18,586	47,022	166,168
Non-occupation or unspecified coded personnel	3,441	13,117	1,663	1,926	606	20,753
Total enlisted personnel for each military branch and Coast Guard	467,110	263,808	33,586	178,476	268,595	1,211,575

SOURCE: U.S. Department of Defense, Defense Manpower Data Center

social scientists, and attorneys. For example, meteorologists in the military may study the weather to determine flight paths for aircraft. Physical scientists may develop and launch spacecraft.

Executive, administrative, and managerial officers are responsible for administrative functions of the Armed Forces. This includes human resources management, training, personnel, information, police, public information, and inspectors. This category also includes officers who oversee the various Armed Forces bands and those who manage recreation or other special services.

Healthcare officers provide health services at military facilities on the basis of their area of specialization. Officers who examine, diagnose, and treat patients include physicians, physician assistants, nurses, and dentists. Other healthcare officers provide therapy, rehabilitative treatment, and additional healthcare for patients.

- Physicians, surgeons, and physician assistants provide the majority of medical services to the military and their families.
- Dentists treat diseases, disorders, and injuries of the mouth.
- Physical and occupational therapists plan and administer therapy to help patients adjust to disabilities, regain independence, and return to work.
- Pharmacists manage the purchase, storage, and dispensing of drugs and medicines.
- Optometrists treat vision problems by prescribing eyeglasses or contact lenses.
- Psychologists provide mental healthcare and also conduct research on behavior and emotions.

For more information, see the profiles on physicians and surgeons , dentists , physical therapists , occupational therapists , pharmacists , optometrists , and psychologists .

Human resource development officers manage recruitment, placement, and training programs in the military.

- Recruiting managers direct recruiting efforts and provide information about military careers to young people, parents, schools, and local communities.
- Personnel managers direct military personnel functions, such as job assignments, staff promotions, and career counseling.
- Training and education directors identify training needs and develop and manage educational programs designed to keep military personnel current in the skills they need.

Media and public affairs officers oversee the development, production, and presentation of information or events for the public. These officers may produce and direct videos, and television and radio broadcasts that are used for training, news, and entertainment. Some plan, develop, and direct the activities of military bands. Public information officers respond to inquiries about military activities and prepare news releases and reports to keep the public informed.

Protective service officers are responsible for the safety and protection of individuals and property on military bases and vessels. Emergency management officers plan and prepare for all types of disasters by developing warning and evacuation procedures to be used in the event of a disaster. Law enforcement and security officers enforce all applicable laws on military bases and investigate crimes when the law has been broken.

Support services officers oversee and direct military activities in key functional areas, such as logistics, transportation, and supply. They may oversee the transportation and distribution of materials by ground vehicles, aircraft, or ships. They also direct food service facilities and other support activities. Purchasing and contracting managers negotiate and monitor contracts for the purchase of the billions of dollars worth of equipment, supplies, and services that the military buys from private industry each year.

Transportation officers manage and perform activities related to the safe transport of military personnel and material by air and water. These officers normally specialize by mode of transportation or area of expertise because they must meet licensing and certification requirements in many cases.

- Pilots in the military fly various types of specialized airplanes and helicopters to carry troops and equipment.
- Navigators use radar, radio, and other navigation equipment to determine their position and plan their route of travel.
- Officers on ships and submarines work as a team to manage the various departments aboard their vessels.
- Ships' engineers direct engineering departments aboard ships and submarines, including engine operations, maintenance, and power generation.

Table 2 shows the number of military officers by branch and broad occupational category in August 2011.

Table 2. Active Duty Officer personnel by broad occupational group and branch of military, and Coast Guard, August 2011

Officer	Army	Air Force	Coast Guard	Marine Corps	Navy	Total officer personnel in each occupational group
OCCUPATIONAL GROUP						
Combat Specialty occupations	19,029	3,986	–	4,039	6,036	33,090
Engineering, Science, and Technical occupations	21,573	14,841	3	3,922	9,556	49,895
Executive, Administrative, and Managerial occupations	12,422	7,760	61	2,620	7,082	29,945
Health Care occupations	11,092	8,917	–	–	5,896	25,905
Human Resource Development occupations	2,890	2,989	19	284	3,032	9,214
Media and Public Affairs occupations	340	297	7	170	270	1,084
Protective Service occupations	3,074	1,015	1	358	1,003	5,451
Support Service occupations	1,866	685	7	39	928	3,525
Transportation occupations	13,535	18,158	1	6,349	11,374	49,417
Non-occupation or unspecified coded personnel	12,168	7,088	8,381	4,296	8,375	40,308
Total officer personnel for each military branch and Coast Guard	97,989	65,736	8,480	22,077	53,552	247,834

SOURCE: U.S. Department of Defense, Defense Manpower Data Center

Work Environment

In August 2011, more than 2.3 million people served in the Armed Forces. More than 1.4 million were on active duty, including about 565,000 in the Army, 322,000 in the Navy, 330,000 in the Air Force, and 201,000 in the Marines. In addition, about 846,000 people served in the Reserve components of the branches and in the Air National Guard and Army National Guard, and about 42,000 people served in the Coast Guard, which is part of the Department of Homeland Security. Table 3 shows the officers, warrant officers, and enlisted ranks by service in April 2011.

Table 3. Military rank and employment for Active Duty Personnel, April 2011

Grade	Army	Navy	Air Force	Marine Corps	Coast Guard	Active Duty Personnel (excluding Coast Guard)
COMMISSIONED OFFICERS:						
O-10	General	Admiral	General	General	Admiral	39
O-9	Lieutenant General	Vice Admiral	Lieutenant General	Lieutenant General	Vice Admiral	155
O-8	Major General	Rear Admiral (Upper Half)	Major General	Major General	Rear Admiral (Upper Half)	313
O-7	Brigadier General	Rear Admiral (Lower Half)	Brigadier General	Brigadier General	Rear Admiral (Lower Half)	457
O-6	Colonel	Captain	Colonel	Colonel	Captain	12,265
O-5	Lieutenant Colonel	Commander	Lieutenant Colonel	Lieutenant Colonel	Commander	28,838
O-4	Major	Lieutenant Commander	Major	Major	Lieutenant Commander	45,759
O-3	Captain	Lieutenant	Captain	Captain	Lieutenant	73,092
O-2	1st Lieutenant	Lieutenant Junior Grade	1st Lieutenant	1st Lieutenant	Lieutenant Junior Grade	28,729
O-1	2nd Lieutenant	Ensign	2nd Lieutenant	2nd Lieutenant	Ensign	25,502
WARRANT OFFICERS:						
W-5	Chief Warrant Officer 5	Chief Warrant Officer 5		Chief Warrant Officer 5		807
W-4	Chief Warrant Officer 4	Chief Warrant Officer 4		Chief Warrant Officer 4	Chief Warrant Officer 4	3,483
W-3	Chief Warrant Officer 3	Chief Warrant Officer 3		Chief Warrant Officer 3	Chief Warrant Officer 3	4,766
W-2	Chief Warrant Officer 2	Chief Warrant Officer 2		Chief Warrant Officer 2	Chief Warrant Officer 2	7,561
W-1	Warrant Officer 1			Warrant Officer 1		2,894
ENLISTED PERSONNEL:						
E-9	Sergeant Major	Master Chief Petty Officer	Chief Master Sergeant	Sergeant Major/Master Gunnery Sergeant	Master Chief Petty Officer	10,128
E-8	First Sergeant/Master Sergeant	Senior Chief Petty Officer	Senior Master Sergeant	First Sergeant/Master Sergeant	Senior Chief Petty Officer	26,955
E-7	Sergeant First Class	Chief Petty Officer	Master Sergeant	Gunnery Sergeant	Chief Petty Officer	94,794
E-6	Staff Sergeant	Petty Officer First Class	Technical Sergeant	Staff Sergeant	Petty Officer First Class	171,083
E-5	Sergeant	Petty Officer Second Class	Staff Sergeant	Sergeant	Petty Officer Second Class	247,012
E-4	Corporal/Specialist	Petty Officer Third Class	Senior Airman	Corporal	Petty Officer Third Class	286,706
E-3	Private First Class	Seaman	Airman First Class	Lance Corporal	Seaman	233,263
E-2	Private	Seaman Apprentice	Airman	Private First Class	Seaman Apprentice	73,178
E-1	Private	Seaman Recruit	Airman Basic	Private	Seaman Recruit	41,381

SOURCE: U.S. Department of Defense, Defense Manpower Data Center

The specific work environments and conditions for military occupations depend on occupational specialty, unit, branch of service, and other factors. Most active-duty military personnel live and work on or near military bases and facilities throughout the United States and the world. These bases and facilities usually offer comfortable housing and amenities, such as stores and recreation centers. Service members move regularly for training or job assignments, with most rotations lasting 2 to 4 years. Some are deployed internationally to defend national interests.

Military members must be physically fit, mentally stable, and ready to participate in or support combat missions that may be difficult and dangerous and involve long periods of time away from family; however, some personnel are rarely deployed near combat areas.

Injuries

Members of the military are often placed in dangerous situations with the risk of serious injury or death. Members deployed to combat zones or those who work in dangerous areas, such as the flight deck of an aircraft carrier, face a higher rate of injury and death.

Work Schedules

In many circumstances, military personnel work standard full time. However, hours vary significantly, depending on occupational specialty, rank, branch of service, and the needs of the military. In all cases, personnel must be prepared to work long hours to fulfill missions.

How to Become a Member of the Armed Forces

To join the military, applicants must meet age, educational, aptitude, physical, and character requirements. These requirements vary by branch of service and between officers and enlisted members. Members are assigned an occupational specialty based on their aptitude, former training, and the needs of their branch of service. All service members must sign a contract and commit to a minimum term of service.

Those considering enlisting in the military should learn as much as they can about military life before making a decision. Potential applicants should speak to friends and relatives with military experience and weigh the pros and cons of a career in the military.

The next step is talking to a recruiter, who can determine whether the applicant qualifies for enlistment, explain the various enlistment options, and tell which military occupational specialties currently have openings. Applicants should bear in mind that a recruiter's job is to recruit promising applicants into his or her branch of service, so they are likely to stress the positive aspects of military life in the branch in which he or she serves.

The military uses a placement exam called the Armed Forces Vocational Aptitude Battery (ASVAB) to determine an applicant's suitability for various occupational specialties, and test scores largely determine an individual's chances of being accepted into a particular training program. Selection for a certain type of training depends on the needs of the service and the applicant's general and technical aptitudes and personal preferences.

Because all prospective recruits are required to take the ASVAB, those who do so before committing themselves to enlisting know in advance whether they stand a good chance of being accepted for training in a particular specialty. The recruiter can schedule applicants to take the ASVAB without any obligation to join. Many high schools offer the exam as an easy way for students to explore the possibility of

a military career, and the test also lets students see which careers they show aptitude and interest in.

The ASVAB is not part of the process of joining the military as an officer.

If an applicant decides to join the military, the next step is to pass the physical examination and sign an enlistment contract. Negotiating the contract involves choosing, qualifying for, and agreeing on a number of enlistment options, such as the length of active-duty time, which may vary according to the option. Most active-duty programs have first-term enlistments of 4 years, although there are some 2-year, 3-year, and 6-year programs. The contract also will state the date of enlistment and other options–for example, bonuses and the types of training the recruit will receive. If the service is unable to fulfill any of its obligations under the contract, such as providing a certain kind of training, the contract may become null and void.

All branches of the Armed Services offer a delayed entry program by which a person can delay entry into active duty for up to 1 year after enlisting. High school students can enlist during their senior year and enter service after graduation. Others choose this program because the job training they desire is not currently available but will be within the coming year, or because they need time to arrange their personal affairs.

Education

All branches of the Armed Forces require their members to be high school graduates or have equivalent credentials, such as a GED. In 2011, more than 99 percent of recruits were high school graduates. Officers usually need a bachelor's or graduate degree. Training varies for enlisted and officer personnel and varies by occupational specialty.

Those who want to become an officer have several routes, including the Federal service academies (Military, Naval, Air Force, and Coast Guard); the Reserve Officer Training Corps (ROTC) program offered at many colleges and universities; Officer Candidate School (OCS); and other programs.

Important Qualities

Mental preparedness. Armed Forces members must be mentally stable and able to withstand stressful situations that can occur during military operations.

Physical fitness. Military members must be physically fit to participate in or support combat missions that may be difficult or dangerous.

Readiness. Members of the Armed Forces must be ready and able to report for military assignments on short notice.

Entry requirements for each service vary, but certain qualifications for enlistment are common to all branches. The following are typical enlistment requirements:

- At least 17 years of age
- U.S. citizenship or permanent resident status
- Never convicted of a felony
- Able to pass a drug test

Applicants who are 17 years old must have the consent of a parent or legal guardian before entering the service. For active service in the Army, the maximum age is 42; for the Navy, 34; for the Marine Corps, 29; and for the Air Force and Coast Guard, 27. All applicants must meet certain minimum physical standards for height, weight, vision, and overall health. Officers must meet different age and physical standards, depending on their branch of service.

Women are eligible to enter most military specialties; for example, they may become mechanics, missile maintenance technicians, heavy equipment operators, and fighter pilots, or they may enter into medical care, administrative support, and intelligence specialties. Generally, only occupations involving direct exposure to combat are excluded to women.

Training

Enlisted personnel training. Following enlistment, new members of the Armed Forces undergo initial-entry training, better known as basic training or boot camp. Through courses in military skills and protocol, basic training provides an 8- to 13-week introduction to military life. Days and nights are carefully structured and include rigorous physical exercise designed to improve strength and endurance and build each unit's cohesion.

Following basic training, most recruits take additional training at technical schools that prepare them for a particular military occupational specialty. The formal training period generally lasts from 10 to 20 weeks, although training for certain occupations–nuclear power plant operator, for example–may take as long as a year. Recruits not assigned to classroom instruction receive on-the-job training at their first duty assignment.

Many service people get college credit for the technical training they receive on duty. Combined with off-duty courses, such training can lead to an associate's degree through programs in community colleges, such as the Community College of the Air Force. In addition to receiving on-duty training, military personnel may choose from a variety of educational programs. Most military installations have tuition assistance programs for people who want to take courses during off-duty hours. The courses may be correspondence courses or courses in degree programs offered by local colleges or universities. Tuition assistance pays up to 100 percent of college costs, but there is usually an annual credit-hour limit. Each branch of the service provides opportunities for full-time study to a limited number of exceptional applicants. Military personnel accepted into these highly competitive programs receive full pay, allowances, tuition, and related fees. In return, they must agree to serve an additional amount of time in the service. Other highly selective programs enable enlisted personnel to qualify as commissioned officers through additional military training.

Warrant officer training. Warrant officers are technical and tactical leaders who specialize in a specific technical area; for example, Army aviators make up one group of warrant officers. About 1 percent of the total personnel in the military are warrant officers. Although the number is small in size, the level of responsibility is high. Warrant officers receive extended career opportunities, worldwide leadership assignments, and increased pay and retirement benefits. Selection to attend Warrant Officer Candidate School is highly competitive and restricted to those who meet rank and length-of-service requirements. The only exception is the selection process for Army aviator warrant officer, which has no requirement of prior military service.

Officer training. Officer training in the Armed Forces is provided through the federal service academies (Military, Naval, Air Force, and Coast Guard); the Reserve Officers' Training Corps (ROTC) program offered at many colleges and universities; Officer Candidate School (OCS) or Officer Training School (OTS); the National Guard (State Officer Candidate School programs); the Uniformed Services University of Health Sciences; and other programs. All are highly selective and are good options for those who want to make the military a career. Some personnel are directly appointed to attend one of these academies or programs. People interested in getting training through the federal service academies must be unmarried and without dependents to enter and graduate, while those seeking training through OCS, OTS, or ROTC may be married.

Federal service academies provide a 4-year college program leading to a Bachelor of Science (B.S.) degree. Midshipmen or cadets receive free room and board, tuition, medical and dental care, and a monthly allowance. Graduates receive regular or reserve commissions and have a 5-year active-duty obligation, or more if they are entering flight training.

To become a candidate for appointment as a cadet or midshipman in one of the service academies, applicants must be nominated by an authorized source, usually a member of Congress. Candidates do not need to personally know a member of Congress to request a nomination. Nominees must have an academic record of the requisite quality, college aptitude test scores above an established minimum, and recommendations from teachers or school officials; they also must pass a medical examination. Appointments are made from the list of eligible nominees. Appointments to the Coast Guard Academy, however, are based strictly on merit and do not require a nomination.

Participants in ROTC programs take regular college courses along with 3 to 5 hours of military instruction per week. After graduation, they may serve as officers on active duty for a specific period. Some may serve their obligation in the Reserves or National Guard. In the last 2 years of an ROTC program, students typically receive a monthly allowance while attending school, as well as additional pay for summer training. ROTC scholarships for 2, 3, and 4 years of school are available on a competitive basis. All scholarships pay for tuition and have allowances for textbooks, supplies, and other costs.

College graduates can earn a commission in the Armed Forces through OCS or OTS programs in the Army, Navy, Air Force, Marine Corps, Coast Guard, and National Guard. These programs consist of several weeks of intensive academic, physical, and leadership training. Those who graduate as officers generally must serve their obligation on active duty.

Personnel with training in certain health professions may qualify for direct appointment as officers. In the case of people studying for the health professions, financial assistance and internship opportunities are available from the military in return for specified periods of military service. Prospective medical students can apply to the Uniformed Services University of Health Sciences, which offers a salary and free tuition in a program leading to a Doctor of Medicine (M.D.) degree. In return, graduates must serve for 7 years in either the military or the Public Health Service. Direct appointments also are available for those qualified to serve in other specialty areas, such as the U.S. Navy Judge Advocate General's (JAG) Corps for those in the legal field or the Chaplain Corps for those in religious ministry. Flight training is available to commissioned officers in each branch of the Armed Forces. In addition, the Army has a direct enlistment option to become a warrant officer aviator.

Licenses

Certain occupational specialties require licensure, such as physicians, dentists, nurses, and many of the other medical specialties. For more information, see the profiles on physicians and surgeons, dentists, and registered nurses.

Certification

Depending on the occupational specialty, members of the military may be eligible for civilian certifications. Some of these include air traffic controllers, dental assistants, medical laboratory technicians, and many others. Currently, the U.S. military is working with several different certifying bodies to ensure that members who separate from the Armed Forces receive formal recognition in the private sector for their military-based technical training. In addition, the military is now required to provide job transition assistance when members separate, to help veterans match their military training with civilian employment.

Advancement

Each service has different criteria to determine the promotion of personnel. Generally, the first few promotions for both enlisted personnel and officers come easily; subsequent promotions are much more competitive. Criteria for promotion may include time in service and in grade, job performance, a fitness report, and passing scores on written exams. People planning to apply the skills they gained through military training to a civilian career should first determine how good the prospects are for civilian employment in jobs related to the military specialty that interests them. Second, they should know the prerequisites for the related civilian job. Because many civilian occupations require a license, certification, or minimum level of education, it is important to determine whether military training is enough to enter the civilian equivalent occupation or whether additional training will be needed. School counselors often have additional information.

Pay

Basic pay is based on rank and time in service. The pay structure for military personnel is shown in table 4. Pay bands are the same for all branches of service. Members of the Armed Forces receive additional pay for foreign duty, hazardous duty, submarine duty, flight duty, and for being medical officers. Retirement pay is generally available after 20 years of service.

Table 4. Monthly Pay by Military Rank, January 2011

Pay Grade	Years of Service										
	2 or less	Over 2	Over 3	Over 4	Over 6	Over 8	Over 10	Over 12	Over 14	Over 16	Over 20
O-10											$15,401
O-9											13,470
O-8	$9,531	$9,843	$10,050	$10,108	$10,367	$10,798	$10,899	$11,309	$11,426	$11,780	12,762
O-7	7,919	8,287	8,457	8,593	8,838	9,080	9,360	9,639	9,919	10,798	11,541
O-6	5,870	6,449	6,872	6,872	6,898	7,193	7,232	7,232	7,643	8,370	9,223
O-5	4,893	5,512	5,894	5,966	6,204	6,346	6,659	6,889	7,186	7,641	8,070
O-4	4,222	4,887	5,213	5,286	5,589	5,913	6,317	6,632	6,851	6,977	7,049
O-3	3,712	4,208	4,542	4,952	5,189	5,449	5,618	5,895	6,039	6,039	6,039
O-2	3,207	3,653	4,207	4,349	4,439	4,439	4,439	4,439	4,439	4,439	4,439
O-1	2,784	2,897	3,503	3,503	3,503	3,503	3,503	3,503	3,503	3,503	3,503
W-5											6,821
W-4	3,836	4,127	4,245	4,361	4,562	4,761	4,961	5,264	5,530	5,782	6,190
W-3	3,503	3,649	3,799	3,848	4,005	4,314	4,635	4,786	4,961	5,142	5,685
W-2	3,100	3,393	3,483	3,545	3,746	4,059	4,214	4,366	4,553	4,698	4,988
W-1	2,721	3,014	3,092	3,259	3,456	3,746	3,881	4,070	4,257	4,403	4,702
E-9							4,635	4,740	4,872	5,028	5,185
E-8						3,794	3,962	4,066	4,190	4,325	4,568
E-7	2,637	2,879	2,989	3,135	3,249	3,445	3,555	3,751	3,914	4,025	4,189
E-6	2,281	2,510	2,621	2,729	2,841	3,094	3,192	3,383	3,441	3,484	3,533
E-5	2,090	2,230	2,338	2,448	2,620	2,801	2,948	2,966	2,966	2,966	2,966
E-4	1,916	2,014	2,123	2,231	2,326	2,326	2,326	2,326	2,326	2,326	2,326
E-3	1,730	1,839	1,950	1,950	1,950	1,950	1,950	1,950	1,950	1,950	1,950
E-2	1,645	1,645	1,645	1,645	1,645	1,645	1,645	1,645	1,645	1,645	1,645
E-1	1,468										

SOURCE: U.S. Department of Defense, Defense Manpower Data Center

In addition to basic pay, members of the military are housed free of charge on base or receive allowances for housing, with higher allowances for those with dependents.

The military and Department of Veterans Affairs offer many entitlements to those who serve. This includes the Montgomery GI Bill, which will pay for a portion of educational costs at accredited institutions; medical care at military or VA hospitals; and guaranteed home loans.

Job Outlook

Opportunities should be excellent for qualified individuals in all branches of the Armed Forces.

The United States spends a significant portion of its overall budget on national defense. The number of active-duty personnel is expected to remain roughly constant through 2020. However, the drawdown from recent conflicts may lead to a decrease in the number of active-duty personnel. This should be balanced by the need to fill entry-level positions as members of the Armed Forces move up through the ranks, leave the service, or retire. The current goal of the Armed Forces is to maintain a force sufficient to fight and win two major regional conflicts at the same time. Political events, however, could lead to a significant restructuring.

Job Prospects

Opportunities should be excellent for qualified individuals in all branches of the Armed Forces through 2020. Many military personnel retire with a pension after 20 years of service, while they still are young enough to start a new career.

About 165,000 personnel must be recruited each year to replace those who complete their commitment or retire. Since the end of the draft in 1973, the military has met its personnel requirements with volunteers.

When the economy is thriving and civilian employment opportunities generally are more favorable, it is more difficult for all the services to meet their recruitment quotas. It is also more difficult to meet these goals during times of war, when recruitment goals typically rise. When there are economic downturns, recruits may face more competition for various occupational specialties.

Educational requirements will continue to rise as military jobs become more technical and complex. High school graduates and applicants with a college background will be sought to fill the ranks of enlisted personnel, while nearly all officers will likely need at least a bachelor's degree and, in some cases, a graduate degree as well.

Similar Occupations

The military employs people in many different occupational specialties, many of which are similar to civilian occupations. To match military occupations with similar civilian occupations, O*Net OnLine offers the Military Crosswalk Search tool.

Contacts for More Information

Each of the military services publishes handbooks, fact sheets, and pamphlets describing its entrance requirements, its training opportunities, and other aspects of military careers. These publications are available at all recruiting stations, at most state employment service offices, and in high schools, colleges, and public libraries.

For more information on the individual services, visit U.S. Air Force, Air National Guard, U.S. Army, Army National Guard, U.S. Coast Guard, U.S. Marine Corps, U.S. Navy

In addition, the Defense Manpower Data Center, an agency of the Department of Defense , publishes Military Career Guide Online, a comprehensive guide to military occupational training, and career information designed for use by students and jobseekers.

To see the guide, visit Today's Military

Data for Occupations Not Covered in Detail

Employment for the hundreds of occupations covered in detail in the Handbook accounts for more than 121 million, or 85 percent of all, jobs in the economy. This page presents summary data on 163 additional occupations for which employment projections are prepared but detailed occupational information is not developed. These occupations account for about 11 percent of all jobs. For each occupation, the Occupational Information Network (O*NET) code, the occupational definition, 2010 employment, the May 2010 median annual wage, the projected employment change and growth rate from 2010 to 2020, and education and training categories are presented. For guidelines on interpreting the descriptions of projected employment change, refer to the section titled "Occupational Information Included in the OOH."

Approximately 5 percent of all employment is not covered either in the detailed occupational profiles or in the summary data given here. The 5 percent includes categories such as "all other managers," for which little meaningful information could be developed.

Management Occupations

Transportation, Storage, and Distribution Managers
(O*NET 11-3071.00 , 11-3071.01 , 11-3071.02 , and 11-3071.03)
Plan, direct, or coordinate transportation, storage, or distribution activities in accordance with organizational policies and applicable government laws or regulations. Includes logistics managers.
- 2010 employment: **98,600**
- May 2010 median annual wage: **$80,210**
- Projected employment change, 2010-20:
  - Number of new jobs: **9,900**
  - Growth rate: **10 percent (about as fast as average)**
- Education and training:
  - Typical entry-level education: **High school diploma or equivalent**
  - Work experience in a related occupation: **More than 5 years**
  - Typical on-the-job-training: **None**

Postmasters and Mail Superintendants
(O*NET 11-9131.00)
Plan, direct, or coordinate operational, administrative, management, and supportive services of a U.S. post office. Also coordinate activities of workers engaged in postal and related work in assigned post office.
- 2010 employment: **24,500**
- May 2010 median annual wage: **$60,300**
- Projected employment change, 2010-20:
  - Number of new jobs: **–6,800**
  - Growth rate: **–28 percent (decline rapidly)**
- Education and training:
  - Typical entry-level education: **High school diploma or equivalent**
  - Work experience in a related occupation: **1 to 5 years**
  - Typical on-the-job-training: **Moderate-term on-the-job training**

Emergency Management Directors
(O*NET 11-9161.00)
Plan and direct disaster response or crisis management activities, provide disaster preparedness training, and prepare emergency plans and procedures for natural (e.g., hurricanes, floods, earthquakes), wartime, or technological (e.g., nuclear power plant emergencies or hazardous materials spills) disasters or hostage situations.
- 2010 employment: **12,100**
- May 2010 median annual wage: **$55,360**
- Projected employment change, 2010-20:
  - Number of new jobs: **1,600**
  - Growth rate: **13 percent (about as fast as average)**
- Education and training:
  - Typical entry-level education: **Bachelor's degree**
  - Work experience in a related occupation: **1 to 5 years**
  - Typical on-the-job-training: **Long-term on-the-job training**

Business and Financial Occupations

Agents and Business Managers of Artists, Performers, and Athletes
(O*NET 13-1011.00)
Represent and promote artists, performers, and athletes in dealings with current or prospective employers. May handle contract negotiations and other business matters for clients.
- 2010 employment: **24,100**
- May 2010 median annual wage: **$63,130**
- Projected employment change, 2010-20:
  - Number of new jobs: **3,400**
  - Growth rate: **14 percent (as fast as average)**
- Education and training:
  - Typical entry-level education: **Bachelor's degree**
  - Work experience in a related occupation: **1 to 5 years**
  - Typical on-the-job-training: **None**

Compliance Officers
(O*NET 13-1041.00 , 13-1041.01 , 13-1041.02 , 13-1041.03 , 13-1041.04 , 13-1041.06 , and 13-1041.07)
Examine, evaluate, and investigate eligibility for or conformity with laws and regulations governing contract compliance of licenses and permits. Perform other compliance and enforcement inspection and analysis activities not classified elsewhere. Excludes "Financial Examiners" (13-2061), "Tax Examiners and Collectors, and Revenue Agents" (13-2081), "Occupational Health and Safety Specialists" (29-9011), "Occupational Health and Safety Technicians" (29-9012), "Transportation Security Screeners" (33-9093), "Agricultural Inspectors" (45-2011), "Construction and Building Inspectors" (47-4011), and "Transportation Inspectors" (53-6051).
- 2010 employment: **216,600**
- May 2010 median annual wage: **$58,720**
- Projected employment change, 2010-20:
  - Number of new jobs: **32,400**
  - Growth rate: **15 percent (about as fast as average)**
- Education and training:
  - Typical entry-level education: **Bachelor's degree**
  - Work experience in a related occupation: **None**
  - Typical on-the-job-training: **Moderate-term on-the-job training**

Farm Labor Contractors
(O*NET 13-1074.00)Recruit and hire seasonal or temporary agricultural laborers. May transport, house, and provide meals for workers.
- 2010 employment: **300**
- May 2010 median annual wage: **$29,990**

- Projected employment change, 2010-20:
  - Number of new jobs: **0**
  - Growth rate: **−1 percent (little or no change)**
- Education and training:
  - Typical entry-level education: **Less than high school**
  - Work experience in a related occupation: **Less than 1 year**
  - Typical on-the-job-training: **Short-term on-the-job training**

Compensation, Benefits, and Job Analysis Specialists

(O*NET 13-1141.00)Conduct programs of compensation, benefits, and job analysis. May specialize in specific areas, such as position classification and pension programs.
- 2010 employment: **109,500**
- May 2010 median annual wage: **$57,000**
- Projected employment change, 2010-20:
  - Number of new jobs: **5,500**
  - Growth rate: **5 percent (slower than average)**
- Education and training:
  - Typical entry-level education: **Bachelor's degree**
  - Work experience in a related occupation: **None**
  - Typical on-the-job-training: **None**

Training and Development Specialists

(O*NET 13-1151.00)Design and conduct training and development programs to improve individual and organizational performance. May analyze training needs.
- 2010 employment: **217,700**
- May 2010 median annual wage: **$54,160**
- Projected employment change, 2010-20:
  - Number of new jobs: **61,600**
  - Growth rate: **28 percent (faster than average)**
- Education and training:
  - Typical entry-level education: **Bachelor's degree**
  - Work experience in a related occupation: **None**
  - Typical on-the-job-training: **None**

Credit Analysts

(O*NET 13-2041.00)Analyze credit data and financial statements of individuals or firms to determine the degree of risk involved in extending credit or lending money. Prepare reports with credit information for use in decision making.
- 2010 employment: **63,300**
- May 2010 median annual wage: **$58,850**
- Projected employment change, 2010-20:
  - Number of new jobs: **12,500**
  - Growth rate: **20 percent (faster than average)**
- Education and training:
  - Typical entry-level education: **Bachelor's degree**
  - Work experience in a related occupation: **None**
  - Typical on-the-job-training: **None**

Credit Counselors

(O*NET 13-2071.00 and 13-2071.01)Advise and educate individuals or organizations on acquiring and managing debt. May provide guidance in determining the best type of loan and may explain loan requirements or restrictions. May help develop debt management plans, advise on credit issues, or provide budget, mortgage, and bankruptcy counseling.
- 2010 employment: **33,100**
- May 2010 median annual wage: **$38,140**
- Projected employment change, 2010-20:
  - Number of new jobs: **6,700**
  - Growth rate: **20 percent (faster than average)**
- Education and training:
  - Typical entry-level education: **Bachelor's degree**

- Work experience in a related occupation: **None**
- Typical on-the-job-training: **Moderate-term on-the-job training**

Tax Preparers

(O*NET 13-2082.00)Prepare tax returns for individuals or small businesses. Excludes "Accountants and Auditors" (13-2011).
- 2010 employment: **81,500**
- May 2010 median annual wage: **$30,990**
- Projected employment change, 2010-20:
  - Number of new jobs: **8,000**
  - Growth rate: **10 percent (about as fast as average)**
- Education and training:
  - Typical entry-level education: **High school diploma or equivalent**
  - Work experience in a related occupation: **None**
  - Typical on-the-job-training: **Moderate-term on-the-job training**

Math Occupations

Mathematical Technicians

(O*NET 15-2091.00)Apply standardized mathematical formulas, principles, and methodology to technological problems in engineering and physical sciences to improve industrial processes, equipment, and products.
- 2010 employment: **1,100**
- May 2010 median annual wage: **$44,880**
- Projected employment change, 2010-20:
  - Number of new jobs: **100**
  - Growth rate: **6 percent (slower than average)**
- Education and training:
  - Typical entry-level education: **Bachelor's degree**
  - Work experience in a related occupation: **None**
  - Typical on-the-job-training: **None**

Life, Physical, and Social Science Occupations

Social Science Research Assistants

(O*NET 19-4061.00 and 19-4061.01)Assist social scientists in laboratory, survey, and other research. May help prepare findings for publication and assist in laboratory analysis, quality control, or data management. Excludes "Graduate Teaching Assistants" (25-1191).
- 2010 employment: **29,700**
- May 2010 median annual wage: **$37,230**
- Projected employment change, 2010-20:
  - Number of new jobs: **4,400**
  - Growth rate: **15 percent (about as fast as average)**
- Education and training:
  - Typical entry-level education: **Associate's degree**
  - Work experience in a related occupation: **None**
  - Typical on-the-job-training: **None**

Community and Social Service Occupations

Clergy

(O*NET 21-2011.00)Conduct religious worship and perform other spiritual functions associated with beliefs and practices of religious faith or denomination. Provide spiritual and moral guidance.
- 2010 employment: **230,800**
- May 2010 median annual wage: **$43,970**
- Projected employment change, 2010-20:
  - Number of new jobs: **40,500**

- ○ Growth rate: **18 percent (about as fast as average)**
- Education and training:
  - ○ Typical entry-level education: **Bachelor's degree**
  - ○ Work experience in a related occupation: **None**
  - ○ Typical on-the-job-training: **Moderate-term on-the-job training**

Directors, Religious Activities and Education

(O*NET 21-2021.00)Plan, direct, or coordinate programs designed to promote the religious education or activities of a denominational group. May provide counseling and guidance for marital, health, financial, and religious problems.

- 2010 employment: **126,000**
- May 2010 median annual wage: **$36,170**
- Projected employment change, 2010-20:
  - ○ Number of new jobs: **21,200**
  - ○ Growth rate: **17 percent (about as fast as average)**
- Education and training:
  - ○ Typical entry-level education: **Bachelor's degree**
  - ○ Work experience in a related occupation: **1 to 5 years**
  - ○ Typical on-the-job-training: **None**

Legal Occupations

Judicial Law Clerks

(O*NET 23-1012.00)Assist judges in court, by conducting research, or by preparing legal documents. Excludes "Lawyers" (23-1011) and "Paralegals and Legal Assistants" (23-2011).

- 2010 employment: **29,800**
- May 2010 median annual wage: **$39,780**
- Projected employment change, 2010-20:
  - ○ Number of new jobs: **2,300**
  - ○ Growth rate: **8 percent (slower than average)**
- Education and training:
  - ○ Typical entry-level education: **Doctoral or professional degree**
  - ○ Work experience in a related occupation: **None**
  - ○ Typical on-the-job-training: **None**

Title Examiners, Abstractors, and Searchers

(O*NET 23-2093.00)Search real estate records, examine titles, or summarize pertinent legal or insurance documents. May compile lists of mortgages, contracts, and other instruments pertaining to titles by searching public and private records for law firms, real estate agencies, or title insurance companies.

- 2010 employment: **59,000**
- May 2010 median annual wage: **$38,990**
- Projected employment change, 2010-20:
  - ○ Number of new jobs: **–800**
  - ○ Growth rate: **–1 percent (little or no change)**
- Education and training:
  - ○ Typical entry-level education: **High school diploma or equivalent**
  - ○ Work experience in a related occupation: **None**
  - ○ Typical on-the-job-training: **Short-term on-the-job training**

Education, Library, and Training Occupations

Audio-Visual and Multimedia Collections Specialists

(O*NET 25-9011.00)Prepare, plan, and operate multimedia teaching aids for use in education. May record, catalogue, and file materials.

- 2010 employment: **8,400**
- May 2010 median annual wage: **$42,710**
- Projected employment change, 2010-20:

- ○ Number of new jobs: **1,100**
- ○ Growth rate: **13 percent (about as fast as average)**
- Education and training:
  - ○ Typical entry-level education: **Bachelor's degree**
  - ○ Work experience in a related occupation: **1 to 5 years**
  - ○ Typical on-the-job-training: **None**

Farm and Home Management Advisors

(O*NET 25-9021.00)Advise, instruct, and assist individuals and families engaged in agriculture, agricultural-related processes, or home economics activities. Demonstrate procedures and apply research findings to solve problems; and instruct and train in product development, sales, and the use of machinery and equipment to promote general welfare. Includes county agricultural agents, feed and farm management advisors, home economists, and extension service advisors.

- 2010 employment: **13,000**
- May 2010 median annual wage: **$45,520**
- Projected employment change, 2010-20:
  - ○ Number of new jobs: **2,200**
  - ○ Growth rate: **17 percent (about as fast as average)**
- Education and training:
  - ○ Typical entry-level education: **Master's degree**
  - ○ Work experience in a related occupation: **None**
  - ○ Typical on-the-job-training: **None**

Arts and Design Occupations

Merchandise Displayers and Window Trimmers

(O*NET 27-1026.00)Plan and erect commercial displays, such as those in windows and interiors of retail stores and at trade exhibitions.

- 2010 employment: **91,200**
- May 2010 median annual wage: **$25,960**
- Projected employment change, 2010-20:
  - ○ Number of new jobs: **11,700**
  - ○ Growth rate: **13 percent (about as fast as average)**
- Education and training:
  - ○ Typical entry-level education: **High school diploma or equivalent**
  - ○ Work experience in a related occupation: **None**
  - ○ Typical on-the-job-training: **Moderate-term on-the-job training**

Media and Communication Occupations

Radio Operators

(O*NET 27-4013.00)Receive and transmit communications, using radiotelephone equipment in accordance with government regulations. May repair equipment. Excludes "Radio, Cellular, and Tower Equipment Installers and Repairers" (49-2021).

- 2010 employment: **1,200**
- May 2010 median annual wage: **$44,630**
- Projected employment change, 2010-20:
  - ○ Number of new jobs: **100**
  - ○ Growth rate: **7 percent (slower than average)**
- Education and training:
  - ○ Typical entry-level education: **High school diploma or equivalent**
  - ○ Work experience in a related occupation: **None**
  - ○ Typical on-the-job-training: **Short-term on-the-job training**

Healthcare Occupations

Dietetic Technicians

(O*NET 29-2051.00)Assist in the provision of food service and nutritional programs under the supervision of a dietitian. May plan and produce meals based on established guidelines, teach principles of food and nutrition, or counsel individuals.

- 2010 employment: **24,200**
- May 2010 median annual wage: **$27,060**
- Projected employment change, 2010-20:
  - Number of new jobs: **3,900**
  - Growth rate: **16 percent (about as fast as average)**
- Education and training:
  - Typical entry-level education: **High school diploma or equivalent**
  - Work experience in a related occupation: **None**
  - Typical on-the-job-training: **Moderate-term on-the-job training**

Respiratory Therapy Technicians

(O*NET 29-2054.00)Provide respiratory care under the direction of respiratory therapists and physicians.

- 2010 employment: **13,800**
- May 2010 median annual wage: **$45,210**
- Projected employment change, 2010-20:
  - Number of new jobs: **600**
  - Growth rate: **4 percent (slower than average)**
- Education and training:
  - Typical entry-level education: **Associate's degree**
  - Work experience in a related occupation: **None**
  - Typical on-the-job-training: **Moderate-term on-the-job training**

Medical Equipment Preparers

(O*NET 31-9093.00)Prepare, sterilize, install, or clean laboratory or healthcare equipment. May perform routine laboratory tasks and operate or inspect equipment.

- 2010 employment: **49,200**
- May 2010 median annual wage: **$29,490**
- Projected employment change, 2010-20:
  - Number of new jobs: **8,600**
  - Growth rate: **17 percent (about as fast as average)**
- Education and training:
  - Typical entry-level education: **High school diploma or equivalent**
  - Work experience in a related occupation: **None**
  - Typical on-the-job-training: **Moderate-term on-the-job training**

Pharmacy Aides

(O*NET 31-9095.00)Record drugs delivered to the pharmacy, store incoming merchandise, and inform the supervisor of stock needs. May operate cash register and accept prescriptions for filling.

- 2010 employment: **50,800**
- May 2010 median annual wage: **$21,430**
- Projected employment change, 2010-20:
  - Number of new jobs: **14,500**
  - Growth rate: **29 percent (much faster than average)**
- Education and training:
  - Typical entry-level education: **High school diploma or equivalent**
  - Work experience in a related occupation: **None**
  - Typical on-the-job-training: **Short-term on-the-job training**

Protective Service Occupations

First-Line Supervisors of Correctional Officers

(O*NET 33-1011.00)Directly supervise and coordinate activities of correctional officers and jailers.

- 2010 employment: **41,500**
- May 2010 median annual wage: **$55,910**
- Projected employment change, 2010-20:
  - Number of new jobs: **2,300**
  - Growth rate: **6 percent (slower than average)**
- Education and training:
  - Typical entry-level education: **High school diploma or equivalent**
  - Work experience in a related occupation: **1 to 5 years**
  - Typical on-the-job-training: **Moderate-term on-the-job training**

First-Line Supervisors of Police and Detectives

(O*NET 33-1012.00)Directly supervise and coordinate activities of members of police force.

- 2010 employment: **106,100**
- May 2010 median annual wage: **$78,260**
- Projected employment change, 2010-20:
  - Number of new jobs: **2,300**
  - Growth rate: **2 percent (little or no change)**
- Education and training:
  - Typical entry-level education: **High school diploma or equivalent**
  - Work experience in a related occupation: **1 to 5 years**
  - Typical on-the-job-training: **Moderate-term on-the-job training**

First-Line Supervisors of Fire Fighting and Prevention Workers

(O*NET 33-1021.00 , 33-1021.01 , and 33-1021.02)Directly supervise and coordinate activities of workers engaged in fire fighting and fire prevention and control.

- 2010 employment: **60,100**
- May 2010 median annual wage: **$68,240**
- Projected employment change, 2010-20:
  - Number of new jobs: **4,900**
  - Growth rate: **8 percent (slower than average)**
- Education and training:
  - Typical entry-level education: **Postsecondary non-degree award**
  - Work experience in a related occupation: **1 to 5 years**
  - Typical on-the-job-training: **None**

Forest Fire Inspectors and Prevention Specialists

(O*NET 33-2022.00)Enforce fire regulations, inspect forests for fire hazards, and recommend forest fire prevention or control measures. May report forest fires and weather conditions.

- 2010 employment: **1,600**
- May 2010 median annual wage: **$34,910**
- Projected employment change, 2010-20:
  - Number of new jobs: **100**
  - Growth rate: **6 percent (slower than average)**
- Education and training:
  - Typical entry-level education: **High school diploma or equivalent**
  - Work experience in a related occupation: **More than 5 years**
  - Typical on-the-job-training: **Moderate-term on-the-job training**

Parking Enforcement Workers

(O*NET 33-3041.00)Patrol assigned area, such as public parking lot or city streets to issue tickets to overtime parking violators and illegally parked vehicles.

- 2010 employment: **9,800**

- May 2010 median annual wage: **$35,390**
- Projected employment change, 2010-20:
  - Number of new jobs: **900**
  - Growth rate: **10 percent (about as fast as average)**
- Education and training:
  - Typical entry-level education: **High school diploma or equivalent**
  - Work experience in a related occupation: **None**
  - Typical on-the-job-training: **Short-term on-the-job training**

Animal Control Workers

(O*NET 33-9011.00)Handle animals to investigate possible mistreatment; control abandoned, dangerous, or unattended animals.
- 2010 employment: **15,500**
- May 2010 median annual wage: **$32,050**
- Projected employment change, 2010-20:
  - Number of new jobs: **1,800**
  - Growth rate: **12 percent (about as fast as average)**
- Education and training:
  - Typical entry-level education: **High school diploma or equivalent**
  - Work experience in a related occupation: **None**
  - Typical on-the-job-training: **Moderate-term on-the-job training**

Crossing Guards

(O*NET 33-9091.00)Guide or control vehicular or pedestrian traffic at places such as streets, schools, railroad crossings, or construction sites.
- 2010 employment: **69,300**
- May 2010 median annual wage: **$23,610**
- Projected employment change, 2010-20:
  - Number of new jobs: **700**
  - Growth rate: **1 percent (little or no change)**
- Education and training:
  - Typical entry-level education: **High school diploma or equivalent**
  - Work experience in a related occupation: **None**
  - Typical on-the-job-training: **Short-term on-the-job training**

Lifeguards, Ski Patrol, and Other Recreational Protective Service Workers

(O*NET 33-9092.00)Monitor recreational areas, such as pools, beaches, or ski slopes, to provide assistance and protection to participants.
- 2010 employment: **121,500**
- May 2010 median annual wage: **$18,840**
- Projected employment change, 2010-20:
  - Number of new jobs: **14,900**
  - Growth rate: **12 percent (about as fast as average)**
- Education and training:
  - Typical entry-level education: **High school diploma or equivalent**
  - Work experience in a related occupation: **None**
  - Typical on-the-job-training: **Short-term on-the-job training**

Food Preparation and Serving Occupations

First-Line Supervisors of Food Preparation and Serving Workers

(O*NET 35-1012.00)Directly supervise and coordinate activities of workers who prepare and serve food.
- 2010 employment: **801,100**
- May 2010 median annual wage: **$29,560**

- Projected employment change, 2010-20:
  - Number of new jobs: **78,500**
  - Growth rate: **10 percent (about as fast as average)**
- Education and training:
  - Typical entry-level education: **High school diploma or equivalent**
  - Work experience in a related occupation: **1 to 5 years**
  - Typical on-the-job-training: **None**

Dishwashers

(O*NET 35-9021.00)Clean dishes, utensils, kitchens, and food preparation equipment.
- 2010 employment: **510,200**
- May 2010 median annual wage: **$18,150**
- Projected employment change, 2010-20:
  - Number of new jobs: **35,900**
  - Growth rate: **7 percent (slower than average)**
- Education and training:
  - Typical entry-level education: **Less than high school**
  - Work experience in a related occupation: **None**
  - Typical on-the-job-training: **Short-term on-the-job training**

Building and Grounds Cleaning Occupations

First-Line Supervisors of Housekeeping and Janitorial Workers

(O*NET 37-1011.00)Directly supervise and coordinate work activities of cleaning personnel in hotels, hospitals, offices, and other establishments.
- 2010 employment: **226,700**
- May 2010 median annual wage: **$35,090**
- Projected employment change, 2010-20:
  - Number of new jobs: **1,900**
  - Growth rate: **1 percent (little or no change)**
- Education and training:
  - Typical entry-level education: **High school diploma or equivalent**
  - Work experience in a related occupation: **1 to 5 years**
  - Typical on-the-job-training: **None**

First-Line Supervisors of Landscaping, Lawn Service, and Groundskeeping Workers

(O*NET 37-1012.00)Directly supervise and coordinate activities of workers engaged in landscaping or groundskeeping activities. Work may involve reviewing contracts to determine service, machine, and workforce requirements; answering inquiries from potential customers regarding methods, materials, and price ranges; and preparing estimates according to labor, material, and machine costs.
- 2010 employment: **202,900**
- May 2010 median annual wage: **$41,860**
- Projected employment change, 2010-20:
  - Number of new jobs: **30,700**
  - Growth rate: **15 percent (about as fast as average)**

- Education and training:
  - Typical entry-level education: **High school diploma or equivalent**
  - Work experience in a related occupation: **1 to 5 years**
  - Typical on-the-job-training: **None**

Personal Care and Service Occupations

First-Line Supervisors of Personal Service Workers

(O*NET <u>39-1021.00</u> and <u>39-1021.01</u>)Directly supervise and coordinate activities of personal service workers, such as flight attendants, hairdressers, or caddies.
- 2010 employment: **218,900**
- May 2010 median annual wage: **$35,290**
- Projected employment change, 2010-20:
  - Number of new jobs: **29,600**
  - Growth rate: **14 percent (as fast as average)**
- Education and training:
  - Typical entry-level education: **High school diploma or equivalent**
  - Work experience in a related occupation: **1 to 5 years**
  - Typical on-the-job-training: **None**

Motion Picture Projectionists

(O*NET <u>39-3021.00</u>)Set up and operate motion picture projection and related sound reproduction equipment.
- 2010 employment: **10,400**
- May 2010 median annual wage: **$20,370**
- Projected employment change, 2010-20:
  - Number of new jobs: **–1,100**
  - Growth rate: **–11 percent (decline rapidly)**
- Education and training:
  - Typical entry-level education: **Less than high school**
  - Work experience in a related occupation: **None**
  - Typical on-the-job-training: **Short-term on-the-job training**

Ushers, Lobby Attendants, and Ticket Takers

(O*NET <u>39-3031.00</u>)Assist patrons at entertainment events by collecting admission tickets and passes from patrons, assisting in finding seats, searching for lost articles, and locating rest rooms and telephones.
- 2010 employment: **109,100**
- May 2010 median annual wage: **$18,560**
- Projected employment change, 2010-20:
  - Number of new jobs: **11,100**
  - Growth rate: **10 percent (about as fast as average)**
- Education and training:
  - Typical entry-level education: **Less than high school**
  - Work experience in a related occupation: **None**
  - Typical on-the-job-training: **Short-term on-the-job training**

Amusement and Recreation Attendants

(O*NET <u>39-3091.00</u>)Perform a variety of duties at amusement or recreation facilities. May schedule the use of recreation facilities, maintain and provide equipment to participants of sporting events or recreational pursuits, or operate amusement concessions and rides.
- 2010 employment: **261,300**
- May 2010 median annual wage: **$18,450**
- Projected employment change, 2010-20:
  - Number of new jobs: **37,200**
  - Growth rate: **14 percent (as fast as average)**
- Education and training:
  - Typical entry-level education: **Less than high school**
  - Work experience in a related occupation: **None**
  - Typical on-the-job-training: **Short-term on-the-job training**

Costume Attendants

(O*NET <u>39-3092.00</u>)Select, fit, and take care of costumes for cast members, and aid entertainers. May assist with multiple costume changes during performances.
- 2010 employment: **5,500**
- May 2010 median annual wage: **$29,150**
- Projected employment change, 2010-20:
  - Number of new jobs: **500**

- Growth rate: **10 percent (about as fast as average)**
- Education and training:
  - Typical entry-level education: **High school diploma or equivalent**
  - Work experience in a related occupation: **None**
  - Typical on-the-job-training: **Short-term on-the-job training**

Locker Room, Coatroom, and Dressing Room Attendants

(O*NET <u>39-3093.00</u>)Provide personal items to patrons or customers in locker rooms, dressing rooms, or coatrooms.
- 2010 employment: **17,600**
- May 2010 median annual wage: **$19,450**
- Projected employment change, 2010-20:
  - Number of new jobs: **2,600**
  - Growth rate: **15 percent (about as fast as average)**
- Education and training:
  - Typical entry-level education: **High school diploma or equivalent**
  - Work experience in a related occupation: **None**
  - Typical on-the-job-training: **Short-term on-the-job training**

Embalmers

(O*NET <u>39-4011.00</u>)Prepare bodies for interment in conformity with legal requirements.
- 2010 employment: **7,100**
- May 2010 median annual wage: **$43,480**
- Projected employment change, 2010-20:
  - Number of new jobs: **400**
  - Growth rate: **5 percent (slower than average)**
- Education and training:
  - Typical entry-level education: **Postsecondary non-degree award**
  - Work experience in a related occupation: **None**
  - Typical on-the-job-training: **Short-term on-the-job training**

Funeral Attendants

(O*NET <u>39-4021.00</u>)Perform a variety of tasks during funerals, such as placing caskets in the parlor or chapel prior to services, arranging floral offerings or lights around caskets, directing or escorting mourners, closing caskets, and issuing and storing funeral equipment.
- 2010 employment: **31,000**
- May 2010 median annual wage: **$22,990**
- Projected employment change, 2010-20:
  - Number of new jobs: **1,600**
  - Growth rate: **5 percent (slower than average)**
- Education and training:
  - Typical entry-level education: **High school diploma or equivalent**
  - Work experience in a related occupation: **None**
  - Typical on-the-job-training: **Short-term on-the-job training**

Makeup Artists, Theatrical and Performance

(O*NET <u>39-5091.00</u>)Apply makeup to performers to reflect the period, setting, and situation of their roles.
- 2010 employment: **3,500**
- May 2010 median annual wage: **$38,130**
- Projected employment change, 2010-20:
  - Number of new jobs: **100**
  - Growth rate: **3 percent (slower than average)**
- Education and training:
  - Typical entry-level education: **Postsecondary non-degree award**
  - Work experience in a related occupation: **None**
  - Typical on-the-job-training: **None**

Baggage Porters and Bellhops

(O*NET 39-6011.00)Handle baggage for travelers at transportation terminals or for guests at hotels or similar establishments.

- 2010 employment: **46,000**
- May 2010 median annual wage: **$20,270**
- Projected employment change, 2010-20:
  - Number of new jobs: **5,700**
  - Growth rate: **12 percent (about as fast as average)**
- Education and training:
  - Typical entry-level education: **High school diploma or equivalent**
  - Work experience in a related occupation: **None**
  - Typical on-the-job-training: **Short-term on-the-job training**

Concierges

(O*NET 39-6012.00)Assist patrons at hotels, apartments, or office buildings with personal services. May take messages; arrange or give advice on transportation, business services, or entertainment; or monitor guests' requests for housekeeping and maintenance.

- 2010 employment: **20,300**
- May 2010 median annual wage: **$27,860sa**
- Projected employment change, 2010-20:
  - Number of new jobs: **2,400**
  - Growth rate: **12 percent (about as fast as average)**
- Education and training:
  - Typical entry-level education: **High school diploma or equivalent**
  - Work experience in a related occupation: **None**
  - Typical on-the-job-training: **Moderate-term on-the-job training**

Tour Guides and Escorts

(O*NET 39-7011.00)Escort individuals or groups on sightseeing tours or through places of interest, such as industrial establishments, public buildings, and art galleries.

- 2010 employment: **34,900**
- May 2010 median annual wage: **$23,290**
- Projected employment change, 2010-20:
  - Number of new jobs: **6,300**
  - Growth rate: **18 percent (about as fast as average)**
- Education and training:
  - Typical entry-level education: **High school diploma or equivalent**
  - Work experience in a related occupation: **None**
  - Typical on-the-job-training: **Moderate-term on-the-job training**

Travel Guides

(O*NET 39-7012.00)Plan, organize, and conduct long distance travel, tours, and expeditions for individuals and groups.

- 2010 employment: **4,200**
- May 2010 median annual wage: **$29,780**
- Projected employment change, 2010-20:
  - Number of new jobs: **1,000**
  - Growth rate: **24 percent (faster than average)**
- Education and training:
  - Typical entry-level education: **High school diploma or equivalent**
  - Work experience in a related occupation: **None**
  - Typical on-the-job-training: **Moderate-term on-the-job training**

Residential Advisors

(O*NET 39-9041.00)Coordinate activities in residential facilities in secondary school and college dormitories, group homes, or similar establishments. Order supplies and determine necessary maintenance, repairs, and furnishings. May maintain household records and assign rooms. May help residents solve problems or refer residents to counseling resources.

- 2010 employment: **72,600**
- May 2010 median annual wage: **$24,440**
- Projected employment change, 2010-20:
  - Number of new jobs: **18,100**
  - Growth rate: **25 percent (faster than average)**
- Education and training:
  - Typical entry-level education: **Some college, no degree**
  - Work experience in a related occupation: **Less than 1 year**
  - Typical on-the-job-training: **Short-term on-the-job training**

Sales Occupations

First-Line Supervisors of Retail Sales Workers

(O*NET 41-1011.00)Directly supervise and coordinate activities of retail sales workers in an establishment or a department. Duties also may include management functions, such as purchasing, budgeting, accounting, and personnel work.

- 2010 employment: **1,619,500**
- May 2010 median annual wage: **$35,820**
- Projected employment change, 2010-20:
  - Number of new jobs: **136,00**
  - Growth rate: **8 percent (slower than average)**
- Education and training:
  - Typical entry-level education: **High school diploma or equivalent**
  - Work experience in a related occupation: **1 to 5 years**
  - Typical on-the-job-training: **None**

First-Line Supervisors of Non-Retail Sales Workers

(O*NET 41-1012.00)Directly supervise and coordinate activities of sales workers other than retail sales workers. Duties also may include budgeting, accounting, and personnel work.

- 2010 employment: **422,900**
- May 2010 median annual wage: **$68,880**
- Projected employment change, 2010-20:
  - Number of new jobs: **17,100**
  - Growth rate: **4 percent (slower than average)**
- Education and training:
  - **Typical entry-level education: High school diploma or equivalent**
  - Work experience in a related occupation: **More than 5 years**
  - Typical on-the-job-training: **None**

Gaming Change Persons and Booth Cashiers

(O*NET 41-2012.00)Exchange coins, tokens, and chips for patrons' money. May issue payoffs and obtain customer's signature on receipt. May operate a booth in the slot machine area and furnish change persons with money bank at the start of the shift, or count and audit money in drawers. Excludes "Cashiers" (41-2011).

- 2010 employment: **20,100**
- May 2010 median annual wage: **$23,170**
- Projected employment change, 2010-20:
  - Number of new jobs: **–2,400**
  - Growth rate: **–12 percent (decline rapidly)**
- Education and training:
  - Typical entry-level education: **High school diploma or equivalent**
  - Work experience in a related occupation: **None**

o Typical on-the-job-training: **Short-term on-the-job training**

Counter and Rental Clerks

(O*NET 41-2021.00)Receive orders, generally in person, for repairs, rentals, and services. May describe available options, compute costs, and accept payment. Excludes "Counter Attendants, Cafeteria, Food Concession, and Coffee Shop" (35-3022), "Hotel, Motel, and Resort Desk Clerks" (43-4081), "Order Clerks" (43-4151), and "Reservation and Transportation Ticket Agents and Travel Clerks" (43-4181).

- 2010 employment: **419,500**
- May 2010 median annual wage: **$22,100**
- Projected employment change, 2010-20:
  - Number of new jobs: **51,100**
  - Growth rate: **12 percent (about as fast as average)**
- Education and training:
  - Typical entry-level education: **Less than high school**
  - Work experience in a related occupation: **None**
  - Typical on-the-job-training: **Short-term on-the-job training**

Telemarketers

(O*NET 41-9041.00)Solicit donations or orders for goods or services over the telephone.

- 2010 employment: **290,700**
- May 2010 median annual wage: **$22,310**
- Projected employment change, 2010-20:
  - Number of new jobs: **21,500**
  - Growth rate: **7 percent (slower than average)**
- Education and training:
  - Typical entry-level education: **Less than high school**
  - Work experience in a related occupation: **None**
  - Typical on-the-job-training: **Short-term on-the-job training**

Door-to-Door Sales workers, News and Street Vendors, and Related Workers

(O*NET 41-9091.00)Sell goods or services door-to-door or on the street.

- 2010 employment: **153,800**
- May 2010 median annual wage: **$22,190**
- Projected employment change, 2010-20:
  - Number of new jobs: **-11,500**
  - Growth rate: **-7 percent (decline moderately)**
- Education and training:
  - Typical entry-level education: **High school diploma or equivalent**
  - Work experience in a related occupation: **None**
  - Typical on-the-job-training: **Short-term on-the-job training**

Office and Administrative Support Occupations

First-Line Supervisors of Office and Administrative Support Workers

(O*NET 43-1011.00)Directly supervise and coordinate the activities of clerical and administrative support workers.

- 2010 employment: **1,424,400**
- May 2010 median annual wage: **$47,460**
- Projected employment change, 2010-20:
  - Number of new jobs: **203,400**
  - Growth rate: **14 percent (as fast as average)**
- Education and training:
  - Typical entry-level education: **High school diploma or equivalent**
  - Work experience in a related occupation: **1 to 5 years**
  - Typical on-the-job-training: **None**

Switchboard Operators, Including Answering Service

(O*NET 43-2011.00)Operate telephone business systems equipment or switchboards to relay incoming, outgoing, and interoffice calls. May supply information to callers and record messages.

- 2010 employment: **142,500**
- May 2010 median annual wage: **$24,920**
- Projected employment change, 2010-20:
  - Number of new jobs: **-33,200**
  - Growth rate: **-23 percent (decline rapidly)**
- Education and training:
  - Typical entry-level education: **High school diploma or equivalent**
  - Work experience in a related occupation: **None**
  - Typical on-the-job-training: **Short-term on-the-job training**

Telephone Operators

(O*NET 43-2021.00)Provide information by accessing alphabetical, geographical, or other directories. Assist customers with special billing requests, such as charges to a third party and credits or refunds for incorrectly dialed numbers or bad connections. May handle emergency calls and assist children or people with physical disabilities with making telephone calls.

- 2010 employment: **18,500**
- May 2010 median annual wage: **$31,970**
- Projected employment change, 2010-20:
  - Number of new jobs: **-3,100**
  - Growth rate: **-17 percent (decline rapidly)**
- Education and training:
  - Typical entry-level education: **High school diploma or equivalent**
  - Work experience in a related occupation: **None**
  - Typical on-the-job-training: **Short-term on-the-job training**

Dispatchers, Except Police, Fire, and Ambulance

(O*NET 43-5032.00)Schedule and dispatch workers, work crews, equipment, or service vehicles for conveyance of materials, freight, or passengers or for normal installation, service, or emergency repairs rendered outside the place of business. Duties may include using a radio, telephone, or computer to transmit assignments and compiling statistics and reports on work progress.

- 2010 employment: **185,200**
- May 2010 median annual wage: **$34,560**
- Projected employment change, 2010-20:
  - Number of new jobs: **34,400**
  - Growth rate: **19 percent (about as fast as average)**
- Education and training:
  - Typical entry-level education: **High school diploma or equivalent**
  - Work experience in a related occupation: **None**
  - Typical on-the-job-training: **Moderate-term on-the-job training**

Meter Readers, Utilities

(O*NET 43-5041.00)Read meters and record the consumption of electricity, gas, water, or steam.

- 2010 employment: **40,500**
- May 2010 median annual wage: **$34,820**
- Projected employment change, 2010-20:
  - Number of new jobs: **500**
  - Growth rate: **1 percent (little or no change)**
- Education and training:
  - Typical entry-level education: **High school diploma or equivalent**
  - Work experience in a related occupation: **None**
  - Typical on-the-job-training: **Short-term on-the-job training**

Computer Operators

(O*NET 43-9011.00)Monitor and control electronic computer and peripheral electronic data processing equipment to process business, scientific, engineering, and other data according to operating instructions. Monitor and respond to operating and error messages. May enter commands at a computer terminal and set controls on computer and peripheral devices. Excludes "Computer Occupations" (15-1100) and "Data Entry Keyers" (43-9021).

- 2010 employment: **86,400**
- May 2010 median annual wage: **$36,930**
- Projected employment change, 2010-20:
  - Number of new jobs: **–7,400**
  - Growth rate: **–9 percent (decline moderately)**
- Education and training:
  - Typical entry-level education: **High school diploma or equivalent**
  - Work experience in a related occupation: **None**
  - Typical on-the-job-training: **Moderate-term on-the-job training**

Data Entry Keyers

(O*NET 43-9021.00)Operate a data entry device, such as a keyboard or photo composing perforator. Duties may include verifying data and preparing materials for printing. Excludes "Word Processors and Typists" (43-9022).

- 2010 employment: **234,700**
- May 2010 median annual wage: **$27,450**
- Projected employment change, 2010-20:
  - Number of new jobs: **–15,900**
  - Growth rate: **–7 percent (decline moderately)**
- Education and training:
  - Typical entry-level education: **High school diploma or equivalent**
  - Work experience in a related occupation: **None**
  - Typical on-the-job-training: **Moderate-term on-the-job training**

Word Processors and Typists

(O*NET 43-9022.00)Use a word processor, computer, or typewriter to type letters, reports, forms, or other material from rough draft, corrected copy, or voice recordings. May perform other clerical duties as assigned. Excludes "Data Entry Keyers" (43-9021), "Secretaries and Administrative Assistants" (43-6011 through 43-6014), "Court Reporters" (23-2091), and "Medical Transcriptionists" (31-9094).

- 2010 employment: **115,300**
- May 2010 median annual wage: **$33,400**
- Projected employment change, 2010-20:
  - Number of new jobs: **–13,200**
  - Growth rate: **–11 (decline rapidly)**
- Education and training:
  - Typical entry-level education: **High school diploma or equivalent**
  - Work experience in a related occupation: **None**
  - Typical on-the-job-training: **Short-term on-the-job training**

Mail Clerks and Mail Machine Operators, Except Postal Service

(O*NET 43-9051.00)Prepare incoming and outgoing mail for distribution. Use hand or mail handling machines to time stamp, open, read, sort, and route incoming mail; address, seal, stamp, fold, stuff, and affix postage to outgoing mail or packages. Duties also may include keeping necessary records and completed forms.

- 2010 employment: **126,300**
- May 2010 median annual wage: **$26,090**

- Projected employment change, 2010-20:
  - Number of new jobs: **15,200**
  - Growth rate: **12 percent (about as fast as average)**
- Education and training:
  - Typical entry-level education: **High school diploma or equivalent**
  - Work experience in a related occupation: **None**
  - Typical on-the-job-training: **Short-term on-the-job training**

Office Machine Operators, Except Computer

(O*NET 43-9071.00)Operate one or more of a variety of office machines, such as photocopying, photographic, and duplicating machines. Excludes "Computer Operators" (43-9011), "Mail Clerks and Mail Machine Operators, Except Postal Service" (43-9051), and "Billing and Posting Clerks" (43-3021).

- 2010 employment: **69,800**
- May 2010 median annual wage: **$27,080**
- Projected employment change, 2010-20:
  - Number of new jobs: **–6,800**
  - Growth rate: **–10 percent (decline rapidly)**
- Education and training:
  - Typical entry-level education: **High school diploma or equivalent**
  - Work experience in a related occupation: **None**
  - Typical on-the-job-training: **Short-term on-the-job training**

Proofreaders and Copy Markers

(O*NET 43-9081.00)Read transcripts or proof type to detect and correct any grammatical, typographical, or compositional errors. Excludes workers whose primary duty is editing copy. Includes proofreaders of Braille.

- 2010 employment: **14,000**
- May 2010 median annual wage: **$31,360**
- Projected employment change, 2010-20:
  - Number of new jobs: **700**
  - Growth rate: **5 percent (slower than average)**
- Education and training:
  - Typical entry-level education: **Bachelor's degree**
  - Work experience in a related occupation: **None**
  - Typical on-the-job-training: **Moderate-term on-the-job training**

Statistical Assistants

(O*NET 43-9111.00 and 43-9111.01)Compile and compute data according to statistical formulas for use in statistical studies. May perform actuarial computations and compile charts and graphs for actuaries. Includes actuarial clerks.

- 2010 employment: **16,600**
- May 2010 median annual wage: **$34,530**
- Projected employment change, 2010-20:
  - Number of new jobs: **1,000**
  - Growth rate: **6 percent (slower than average)**
- Education and training:
  - Typical entry-level education: **Bachelor's degree**
  - Work experience in a related occupation: **None**
  - Typical on-the-job-training: **None**

Farming, Fishing, and Forestry Occupations

First-Line Supervisors of Farming, Fishing, and Forestry Workers

(O*NET 45-1011.00 , 45-1011.05 , 45-1011.06 , 45-1011.07 , and 45-1011.08)Directly supervise and coordinate the activities of agricultural, forestry, aquacultural, and related workers. Excludes "First-Line Supervisors of Landscaping, Lawn Service, and Groundskeeping Workers" (37-1012).

- 2010 employment: **47,000**
- May 2010 median annual wage: **$41,800**
- Projected employment change, 2010-20:
  - Number of new jobs: **–700**
  - Growth rate: **–1 percent (little or no change)**
- Education and training:
  - Typical entry-level education: **High school diploma or equivalent**
  - Work experience in a related occupation: **1 to 5 years**
  - Typical on-the-job-training: **None**

Agricultural Inspectors

(O*NET 45-2011.00)Inspect agricultural commodities, processing equipment and facilities, and fish and logging operations, to ensure compliance with regulations and laws governing health, quality, and safety.

- 2010 employment: **19,300**
- May 2010 median annual wage: **$41,670**
- Projected employment change, 2010-20:
  - Number of new jobs: **300**
  - Growth rate: **1 percent (little or no change)**
- Education and training:
  - Typical entry-level education: **Bachelor's degree**
  - Work experience in a related occupation: **None**
  - Typical on-the-job-training: **Moderate-term on-the-job training**

Graders and Sorters, Agricultural Products

(O*NET 45-2041.00)Grade, sort, or classify unprocessed food and other agricultural products by size, weight, color, or condition. Excludes "Agricultural Inspectors" (45-2011).

- 2010 employment: **48,200**
- May 2010 median annual wage: **$19,180**
- Projected employment change, 2010-20:
  - Number of new jobs: **600**
  - Growth rate: **1 percent (little or no change)**
- Education and training:
  - Typical entry-level education: **Less than high school**
  - Work experience in a related occupation: **None**
  - Typical on-the-job-training: **Short-term on-the-job training**

Construction and Extraction Occupations

First-Line Supervisors of Construction Trades and Extraction Workers

(O*NET 47-1011.00 and 47-1011.03)Directly supervise and coordinate activities of construction or extraction workers.

- 2010 employment: **558,500**
- May 2010 median annual wage: **$58,680**
- Projected employment change, 2010-20:
  - Number of new jobs: **131,000**
  - Growth rate: **23 percent (faster than average)**
- Education and training:
  - Typical entry-level education: **High school diploma or equivalent**
  - Work experience in a related occupation: **More than 5 years**
  - Typical on-the-job-training: **None**

Floor Layers, Except Carpet, Wood, and Hard Tiles

(O*NET 47-2042.00)Apply blocks, strips, or sheets of shock-absorbing, sound-deadening, or decorative coverings to floors.

- 2010 employment: **17,600**

- May 2010 median annual wage: **$36,100**
- Projected employment change, 2010-20:
  - Number of new jobs: **1,200**
  - Growth rate: **7 percent (slower than average)**
- Education and training:
  - Typical entry-level education: **High school diploma or equivalent**
  - Work experience in a related occupation: **None**
  - Typical on-the-job-training: **Moderate-term on-the-job training**

Floor Sanders and Finishers

(O*NET 47-2043.00)Scrape and sand wooden floors to smooth surfaces using floor scrapers and floor sanding machines. May also apply coats of finish.

- 2010 employment: **10,700**
- May 2010 median annual wage: **$31,340**
- Projected employment change, 2010-20:
  - Number of new jobs: **1,900**
  - Growth rate: **18 percent (about as fast as average)**
- Education and training:
  - Typical entry-level education: **High school diploma or equivalent**
  - Work experience in a related occupation: **None**
  - Typical on-the-job-training: **Moderate-term on-the-job training**

Paperhangers

(O*NET 47-2142.00)Cover interior walls or ceilings of rooms with decorative wallpaper or fabric, or attach advertising posters on surfaces such as walls and billboards. May remove old materials or prepare surfaces to be papered.

- 2010 employment: **9,100**
- May 2010 median annual wage: **$37,600**
- Projected employment change, 2010-20:
  - Number of new jobs: **900**
  - Growth rate: **10 percent about (as fast as average)**
- Education and training:
  - Typical entry-level education: **High school diploma or equivalent**
  - Work experience in a related occupation: **None**
  - Typical on-the-job-training: **Moderate-term on-the-job training**

Pipelayers

(O*NET 47-2151.00)Lay pipe for storm or sanitation sewers, drains, and water mains. Perform any combination of the following tasks: grade trenches or culverts, position pipes, or seal joints. Excludes "Welders, Cutters, Solderers, and Brazers" (51-4121).

- 2010 employment: **53,100**
- May 2010 median annual wage: **$34,800**
- Projected employment change, 2010-20:
  - Number of new jobs: **13,400**
  - Growth rate: **25 percent (faster than average)**
- Education and training:
  - Typical entry-level education: **High school diploma or equivalent**
  - Work experience in a related occupation: **None**
  - Typical on-the-job-training: **Short-term on-the-job training**

Fence Erectors

(O*NET 47-4031.00)Erect and repair fences, including gates, using hand and power tools.

- 2010 employment: **32,100**

- May 2010 median annual wage: **$28,970**
- Projected employment change, 2010-20:
  - Number of new jobs: **7,600**
  - Growth rate: **24 percent (faster than average)**
- Education and training:
  - Typical entry-level education: **High school diploma or equivalent**
  - Work experience in a related occupation: **None**
  - Typical on-the-job-training: **Moderate-term on-the-job training**

Highway Maintenance Workers

(O*NET 47-4051.00)Maintain highways, municipal and rural roads, airport runways, and rights-of-way. Duties include patching broken or eroded pavement and repairing guard rails, highway markers, and snow fences. Also may mow or clear brush from along roads or plow snow from roadways. Excludes "Tree Trimmers and Pruners" (37-3013).

- 2010 employment: **148,500**
- May 2010 median annual wage: **$34,780**
- Projected employment change, 2010-20:
  - Number of new jobs: **12,200**
  - Growth rate: **8 percent (slower than average)**
- Education and training:
  - Typical entry-level education: **High school diploma or equivalent**
  - Work experience in a related occupation: **None**
  - Typical on-the-job-training: **Moderate-term on-the-job training**

Rail-Track Laying and Maintenance Equipment Operators

(O*NET 47-4061.00)Lay, repair, and maintain track for standard or narrow-gauge railroad equipment used in regular railroad service or in plant yards, quarries, sand and gravel pits, and mines. Includes ballast cleaning machine operators and railroad bed tamping machine operators.

- 2010 employment: **15,000**
- May 2010 median annual wage: **$45,970**
- Projected employment change, 2010-20:
  - Number of new jobs: **300**
  - Growth rate: **2 percent (little or no change)**
- Education and training:
  - Typical entry-level education: **High school diploma or equivalent**
  - Work experience in a related occupation: **None**
  - Typical on-the-job-training: **Moderate-term on-the-job training**

Septic Tank Servicers and Sewer Pipe Cleaners

(O*NET 47-4071.00)Clean and repair septic tanks, sewer lines, or drains. May patch walls and partitions of tanks, replace damaged drain tiles, or repair breaks in underground piping.

- 2010 employment: **25,300**
- May 2010 median annual wage: **$33,570**
- Projected employment change, 2010-20:
  - Number of new jobs: **5,200**
  - Growth rate: **21 percent (faster than average)**
- Education and training:
  - Typical entry-level education: **Less than high school**
  - Work experience in a related occupation: **None**
  - Typical on-the-job-training: **Moderate-term on-the-job training**

Segmental Pavers

(O*NET 47-4091.00)Lay out, cut, and place segmental paving units. Includes installers of bedding and restraining materials for the paving units.

- 2010 employment: **1,300**
- May 2010 median annual wage: **$30,430**
- Projected employment change, 2010-20:
  - Number of new jobs: **400**
  - Growth rate: **33 percent (much faster than average)**
- Education and training:
  - Typical entry-level education: **High school diploma or equivalent**
  - Work experience in a related occupation: **None**
  - Typical on-the-job-training: **Moderate-term on-the-job training**

Earth Drillers, Except Oil and Gas

(O*NET 47-5021.00)Operate a variety of drills, such as rotary, churn, and pneumatic drills, to tap subsurface water and salt deposits, to remove core samples during mineral exploration or soil testing, and to facilitate the use of explosives in mining or construction. May use explosives. Includes horizontal and earth boring machine operators.

- 2010 employment: **17,800**
- May 2010 median annual wage: **$39,350**
- Projected employment change, 2010-20:
  - Number of new jobs: **2,500**
  - Growth rate: **14 percent (as fast as average)**
- Education and training:
  - Typical entry-level education: **High school diploma or equivalent**
  - Work experience in a related occupation: **None**
  - Typical on-the-job-training: **Moderate-term on-the-job training**

Explosives Workers, Ordnance Handling Experts, and Blasters

(O*NET 47-5031.00)Place and detonate explosives to demolish structures or to loosen, remove, or displace earth, rock, or other materials. May perform specialized handling, storage, and accounting procedures. Includes seismograph shooters. Excludes "Earth Drillers, Except Oil and Gas" (47-5021) who also may work with explosives.

- 2010 employment: **6,800**
- May 2010 median annual wage: **$43,730**
- Projected employment change, 2010-20:
  - Number of new jobs: **0**
  - Growth rate: **0 percent (little or no change)**
- Education and training:
  - Typical entry-level education: **High school diploma or equivalent**
  - Work experience in a related occupation: **None**
  - Typical on-the-job-training: **Moderate-term on-the-job training**

Continuous Mining Machine Operators

(O*NET 47-5041.00)Operate self-propelled mining machines that rip coal, metal and nonmetal ores, rock, stone, or sand from the mine face and load it onto conveyors or into shuttle cars in a continuous operation.

- 2010 employment: **13,900**
- May 2010 median annual wage: **$48,750**
- Projected employment change, 2010-20:
  - Number of new jobs: **100**
  - Growth rate: **0 percent (little or no change)**
- Education and training:
  - Typical entry-level education: **High school diploma or equivalent**
  - Work experience in a related occupation: **None**
  - Typical on-the-job-training: **Moderate-term on-the-job training**

Mine Cutting and Channeling Machine Operators

(O*NET 47-5042.00)Operate machinery such as longwall shears, plows, and cutting machines to cut or channel along the faces or seams of coal mines, stone quarries, or other mining surfaces in order to facilitate blasting, separating, or removing minerals or materials from mines or the Earth's surface. Includes shale planers.

- 2010 employment: **7,000**
- May 2010 median annual wage: **$44,950**
- Projected employment change, 2010-20:
  - Number of new jobs: **100**
  - Growth rate: **2 percent (little or no change)**
- Education and training:
  - Typical entry-level education: **High school diploma or equivalent**
  - Work experience in a related occupation: **None**
  - Typical on-the-job-training: **Moderate-term on-the-job training**

Rock Splitters, Quarry

(O*NET 47-5051.00)Separate blocks of rough-dimension stone from quarry mass, using a jackhammer and wedges.

- 2010 employment: **3,500**
- May 2010 median annual wage: **$30,120**
- Projected employment change, 2010-20:
  - Number of new jobs: **400**
  - Growth rate: **12 percent (about as fast as average)**
- Education and training:
  - Typical entry-level education: **High school diploma or equivalent**
  - Work experience in a related occupation: **None**
  - Typical on-the-job-training: **Moderate-term on-the-job training**

Roof Bolters, Mining

(O*NET 47-5061.00)Operate machinery to install roof support bolts in underground mines.

- 2010 employment: **5,700**
- May 2010 median annual wage: **$49,850**
- Projected employment change, 2010-20:
  - Number of new jobs: **100**
  - Growth rate: **2 percent (little or no change)**
- Education and training:
  - Typical entry-level education: **High school diploma or equivalent**
  - Work experience in a related occupation: **None**
  - Typical on-the-job-training: **Moderate-term on-the-job training**

Helpers—Extraction Workers

(O*NET 47-5081.00)Help extraction craft workers, such as earth drillers, blasters and explosives workers, derrick operators, and mining machine operators, by performing duties requiring less skill. Duties include supplying equipment or cleaning work areas. Apprentices are classified with the appropriate skilled construction trade occupation (47-2011 through 47-2231).

- 2010 employment: **24,600**
- May 2010 median annual wage: **$34,170**
- Projected employment change, 2010-20:
  - Number of new jobs: **1,400**
  - Growth rate: **5 percent (slower than average)**
- Education and training:
  - Typical entry-level education: **High school diploma or equivalent**
  - Work experience in a related occupation: **None**
  - Typical on-the-job-training: **Short-term on-the-job training**

Installation, Maintenance and Repair Occupations

First-Line Supervisors of Mechanics, Installers, and Repairers

(O*NET 49-1011.00)Directly supervise and coordinate the activities of mechanics, installers, and repairers. Excludes team or work leaders.

- 2010 employment: **431,200**
- May 2010 median annual wage: **$59,150**
- Projected employment change, 2010-20:
  - Number of new jobs: **51,400**
  - Growth rate: **12 percent (about as fast as average)**
- Education and training:
  - Typical entry-level education: **High school diploma or equivalent**
  - Work experience in a related occupation: **1 to 5 years**
  - Typical on-the-job-training: **None**

Radio, Cellular, and Tower Equipment Installers and Repairers

(O*NET 49-2021.00 and 49-2021.01)Repair, install, or maintain mobile or stationary radio transmitting, broadcasting, and receiving equipment; two-way radio communications systems used in cellular telecommunications, mobile broadband, ship-to-shore, and aircraft-to-ground communications; and radio equipment in service and emergency vehicles. May test and analyze network coverage.

- 2010 employment: **9,900**
- May 2010 median annual wage: **$39,740**
- Projected employment change, 2010-20:
  - Number of new jobs: **2,900**
  - Growth rate: **29 percent (much faster than average)**
- Education and training:
  - Typical entry-level education: **Associate's degree**
  - Work experience in a related occupation: **None**
  - Typical on-the-job-training: **Moderate-term on-the-job training**

Security and Fire Alarm Systems Installers

(O*NET 49-2098.00)Install, program, maintain, and repair security and fire alarm wiring and equipment. Ensure that work is in accordance with relevant codes. Excludes "Electricians" (47-2111) who do a broad range of electrical wiring.

- 2010 employment: **63,800**
- May 2010 median annual wage: **$38,500**
- Projected employment change, 2010-20:
  - Number of new jobs: **21,000**
  - Growth rate: **33 percent (much faster than average)**
- Education and training:
  - Typical entry-level education: **High school diploma or equivalent**
  - Work experience in a related occupation: **None**
  - Typical on-the-job-training: **Moderate-term on-the-job training**

Bicycle Repairers

(O*NET 49-3091.00)Repair and service bicycles.

- 2010 employment: **9,900**
- May 2010 median annual wage: **$23,660**
- Projected employment change, 2010-20:

○ Number of new jobs: **3,700**
○ Growth rate: **38 percent (much faster than average)**
● Education and training:
  ○ Typical entry-level education: **High school diploma or equivalent**
  ○ Work experience in a related occupation: **None**
  ○ Typical on-the-job-training: **Moderate-term on-the-job training**

Recreational Vehicle Service Technicians

(O*NET 49-3092.00)Diagnose, inspect, adjust, repair, or overhaul recreational vehicles, including travel trailers. May specialize in maintaining gas, electrical, hydraulic, plumbing, or chassis/towing systems, as well as in repairing generators, appliances, and interior components. Includes workers who perform customized van conversions. Excludes "Automotive Service Technicians and Mechanics" (49-3023) and "Bus and Truck Mechanics and Diesel Engine Specialists" (49-3031), who also work on recreation vehicles.
● 2010 employment: **9,900**
● May 2010 median annual wage: **$32,570**
● Projected employment change, 2010-20:
  ○ Number of new jobs: **2,200**
  ○ Growth rate: **22 percent (faster than average)**
● Education and training:
  ○ Typical entry-level education: **High school diploma or equivalent**
  ○ Work experience in a related occupation: **None**
  ○ Typical on-the-job-training: **Long-term on-the-job training**

Tire Repairers and Changers

(O*NET 49-3093.00)Repair and replace tires.
● 2010 employment: **99,000**
● May 2010 median annual wage: **$23,170**
● Projected employment change, 2010-20:
  ○ Number of new jobs: **18,300**
  ○ Growth rate: **19 percent (about as fast as average)**
● Education and training:
  ○ Typical entry-level education: **High school diploma or equivalent**
  ○ Work experience in a related occupation: **None**
  ○ Typical on-the-job-training: **Moderate-term on-the-job training**

Mechanical Door Repairers

(O*NET 49-9011.00)Install, service, or repair automatic door mechanisms and hydraulic doors. Includes garage door mechanics.
● 2010 employment: **12,800**
● May 2010 median annual wage: **$35,780**
● Projected employment change, 2010-20:
  ○ Number of new jobs: **3,100**
  ○ Growth rate: **25 percent (faster than average)**
● Education and training:
  ○ Typical entry-level education: **High school diploma or equivalent**
  ○ Work experience in a related occupation: **None**
  ○ Typical on-the-job-training: **Moderate-term on-the-job training**

Control and Valve Installers and Repairers, Except Mechanical Door

(O*NET 49-9012.00)Install, repair, and maintain mechanical regulating and controlling devices, such as electric meters, gas regulators, thermostats, safety and flow valves, and other mechanical governors.

● 2010 employment: **43,800**
● May 2010 median annual wage: **$48,430**
● Projected employment change, 2010-20:
  ○ Number of new jobs: **0**
  ○ Growth rate: **0 percent (little or no change)**
● Education and training:
  ○ Typical entry-level education: **High school diploma or equivalent**
  ○ Work experience in a related occupation: **None**
  ○ Typical on-the-job-training: **Moderate-term on-the-job training**

Refractory Materials Repairers, Except Brickmasons

(O*NET 49-9045.00)Build or repair equipment, such as furnaces, kilns, cupolas, boilers, converters, ladles, soaking pits, and ovens, using refractory materials.
● 2010 employment: **2,100**
● May 2010 median annual wage: **$42,350**
● Projected employment change, 2010-20:
  ○ Number of new jobs: **200**
  ○ Growth rate: **9 percent (slower than average)**
● Education and training:
  ○ Typical entry-level education: **Postsecondary non-degree award**
  ○ Work experience in a related occupation: **None**
  ○ Typical on-the-job-training: **Moderate-term on-the-job training**

Camera and Photographic Equipment Repairers

(O*NET 49-9061.00)Repair and adjust cameras and photographic equipment, including commercial video and motion picture camera equipment.
● 2010 employment: **3,300**
● May 2010 median annual wage: **$37,180**
● Projected employment change, 2010-20:
  ○ Number of new jobs: **300**
  ○ Growth rate: **10 percent (about as fast as average)**
● Education and training:
  ○ Typical entry-level education: **Associate's degree**
  ○ Work experience in a related occupation: **None**
  ○ Typical on-the-job-training: **Long-term on-the-job training**

Musical Instrument Repairers and Tuners

(O*NET 49-9063.00)Repair percussion, stringed, reed, or wind instruments. May specialize in one area, such as piano tuning. Excludes "Electronic Home Entertainment Equipment Installers and Repairers" (49-2097), who repair electrical and electronic musical instruments.
● 2010 employment: **6,300**
● May 2010 median annual wage: **$31,760**
● Projected employment change, 2010-20:
  ○ Number of new jobs: **100**
  ○ Growth rate: **2 percent (little or no change)**
● Education and training:
  ○ Typical entry-level education: **Postsecondary non-degree award**
  ○ Work experience in a related occupation: **None**
  ○ Typical on-the-job-training: **Long-term on-the-job training**

Watch Repairers

(O*NET 49-9064.00)Repair, clean, and adjust mechanisms of timing instruments, such as watches and clocks. Includes watchmakers, watch technicians, and mechanical timepiece repairers.
● 2010 employment: **2,500**
● May 2010 median annual wage: **$37,180**
● Projected employment change, 2010-20:

○ Number of new jobs: **200**
○ Growth rate: **6 percent (slower than average)**
● Education and training:
○ Typical entry-level education: **High school diploma or equivalent**
○ Work experience in a related occupation: **None**
○ Typical on-the-job-training: **Long-term on-the-job training**

Coin, Vending, and Amusement Machine Servicers and Repairers

(O*NET 49-9091.00)Install, service, adjust, or repair coin, vending, or amusement machines, including video games, jukeboxes, pinball machines, or slot machines.
● 2010 employment: **39,100**
● May 2010 median annual wage: **$30,490**
● Projected employment change, 2010-20:
○ Number of new jobs: **8,600**
○ Growth rate: **22 percent (faster than average)**
● Education and training:
○ Typical entry-level education: **High school diploma or equivalent**
○ Work experience in a related occupation: **None**
○ Typical on-the-job-training: **Short-term on-the-job training**

Commercial Divers

(O*NET 49-9092.00)Work below the surface of waters, using scuba gear to inspect, repair, remove, or install equipment and structures. May use a variety of power and hand tools, such as drills, sledge hammers, torches, and welding equipment. May conduct tests or experiments, rig explosives, or photograph structures or marine life. Excludes "Fishers and Related Fishing Workers" (45-3011), "Athletes and Sports Competitors" (27-2021), and "Police and Sheriff's Patrol Officers" (33-3051).
● 2010 employment: **3,800**
● May 2010 median annual wage: **$51,360**
● Projected employment change, 2010-20:
○ Number of new jobs: **600**
○ Growth rate: **16 percent (about as fast as average)**
● Education and training:
○ Typical entry-level education: **Postsecondary non-degree award**
○ Work experience in a related occupation: **None**
○ Typical on-the-job-training: **Moderate-term on-the-job training**

Fabric Menders, Except Garment

(O*NET 49-9093.00)Repair tears, holes, and other defects in fabrics, such as draperies, linens, parachutes, and tents.
● 2010 employment: **800**
● May 2010 median annual wage: **$26,380**
● Projected employment change, 2010-20:
○ Number of new jobs: **–100**
○ Growth rate: **–6 percent (decline moderately)**
● Education and training:
○ Typical entry-level education: **Less than high school**
○ Work experience in a related occupation: **None**
○ Typical on-the-job-training: **Long-term on-the-job training**

Locksmiths and Safe Repairers

(O*NET 49-9094.00)Repair and open locks, make keys, change locks and safe combinations, and install and repair safes.
● 2010 employment: **25,700**
● May 2010 median annual wage: **$35,550**
● Projected employment change, 2010-20:
○ Number of new jobs: **4,600**
○ Growth rate: **18 percent (about as fast as average)**

● Education and training:
○ Typical entry-level education: **High school diploma or equivalent**
○ Work experience in a related occupation: **None**
○ Typical on-the-job-training: **Long-term on-the-job training**

Manufactured Building and Mobile Home Installers

(O*NET 49-9095.00)Move or install mobile homes or prefabricated buildings.
● 2010 employment: **7,800**
● May 2010 median annual wage: **$28,760**
● Projected employment change, 2010-20:
○ Number of new jobs: **1,100**
○ Growth rate: **14 percent (as fast as average)**
● Education and training:
○ Typical entry-level education: **High school diploma or equivalent**
○ Work experience in a related occupation: **None**
○ Typical on-the-job-training: **Moderate-term on-the-job training**

Riggers

(O*NET 49-9096.00)Set up or repair rigging for construction projects, manufacturing plants, logging yards, ships and shipyards, or the entertainment industry.
● 2010 employment: **15,200**
● May 2010 median annual wage: **$42,780**
● Projected employment change, 2010-20:
○ Number of new jobs: **1,600**
○ Growth rate: **11 percent (about as fast as average)**
● Education and training:
○ Typical entry-level education: **High school diploma or equivalent**
○ Work experience in a related occupation: **None**
○ Typical on-the-job-training: **Short-term on-the-job training**

Signal and Track Switch Repairers

(O*NET 49-9097.00)Install, inspect, test, maintain, or repair electric gate crossings, signals, signal equipment, track switches, section lines, or intercommunications systems within a railroad system.
● 2010 employment: **7,100**
● May 2010 median annual wage: **$53,230**
● Projected employment change, 2010-20:
○ Number of new jobs: **-100**
○ Growth rate: **-2 percent (little or no change)**
● Education and training:
○ Typical entry-level education: **Postsecondary non-degree award**
○ Work experience in a related occupation: **None**
○ Typical on-the-job-training: **Moderate-term on-the-job training**

Helpers—Installation, Maintenance, and Repair Workers

(O*NET 49-9098.00)Help installation, maintenance, and repair workers replace parts and maintain and repair vehicles, industrial machinery, and electrical and electronic equipment. Perform duties such as furnishing tools, materials, and supplies to other workers; cleaning work areas, machines, and tools; and holding materials or tools for other workers.
● 2010 employment: **125,000**
● May 2010 median annual wage: **$24,260**
● Projected employment change, 2010-20:
○ Number of new jobs: **23,000**
○ Growth rate: **18 percent (about as fast as average)**

- Education and training:
  - Typical entry-level education: **High school diploma or equivalent**
  - Work experience in a related occupation: **None**
  - Typical on-the-job-training: **Moderate-term on-the-job training**

Production Occupations

First-Line Supervisors of Production and Operating Workers

(O*NET 51-1011.00)Directly supervise and coordinate the activities of production and operating workers, such as inspectors, precision workers, machine setters and operators, assemblers, fabricators, and plant and system operators. Excludes team or work leaders.
- 2010 employment: **588,500**
- May 2010 median annual wage: **$53,090**
- Projected employment change, 2010-20:
  - Number of new jobs: **10,900**
  - Growth rate: **2 percent (little or no change)**
- Education and training:
  - Typical entry-level education: **Postsecondary non-degree award**
  - Work experience in a related occupation: **1 to 5 years**
  - Typical on-the-job-training: **None**

Layout Workers, Metal and Plastic

(O*NET 51-4192.00)Lay out reference points and dimensions on metal or plastic stock or workpieces, such as sheets, plates, tubes, structural shapes, castings, or machine parts, for further processing. Includes shipfitters.
- 2010 employment: **8,900**
- May 2010 median annual wage: **$39,830**
- Projected employment change, 2010-20:
  - Number of new jobs: **1,200**
  - Growth rate: **14 percent (as fast as average)**
- Education and training:
  - Typical entry-level education: **High school diploma or equivalent**
  - Work experience in a related occupation: **None**
  - Typical on-the-job-training: **Moderate-term on-the-job training**

Tool Grinders, Filers, and Sharpeners

(O*NET 51-4194.00)Perform precision smoothing, sharpening, polishing, or grinding of metal objects.
- 2010 employment: **13,100**
- May 2010 median annual wage: **$34,440**
- Projected employment change, 2010-20:
  - Number of new jobs: **900**
  - Growth rate: **7 percent (slower than average)**
- Education and training:
  - Typical entry-level education: **High school diploma or equivalent**
  - Work experience in a related occupation: **None**
  - Typical on-the-job-training: **Moderate-term on-the-job training**

Pressers, Textile, Garment, and Related Materials

(O*NET 51-6021.00)Press or shape articles by hand or machine.
- 2010 employment: **57,800**
- May 2010 median annual wage: **$19,400**
- Projected employment change, 2010-20:
  - Number of new jobs: **-6,800**

  - Growth rate: **-12 percent (decline rapidly)**
- Education and training:
  - Typical entry-level education: **Less than high school**
  - Work experience in a related occupation: **None**
  - Typical on-the-job-training: **Short-term on-the-job training**

Sewing Machine Operators

(O*NET 51-6031.00)Operate or tend sewing machines to join, reinforce, decorate, or perform related sewing operations in the manufacture of garments or nongarment products.
- 2010 employment: **163,200**
- May 2010 median annual wage: **$20,600**
- Projected employment change, 2010-20:
  - Number of new jobs: **-42,100**
  - Growth rate: **-26 percent (decline rapidly)**
- Education and training:
  - Typical entry-level education: **Less than high school**
  - Work experience in a related occupation: **None**
  - Typical on-the-job-training: **Short-term on-the-job training**

Shoe and Leather Workers and Repairers

(O*NET 51-6041.00)Construct, decorate, or repair leather and leather-like products, such as luggage, shoes, and saddles.
- 2010 employment: **10,200**
- May 2010 median annual wage: **$23,000**
- Projected employment change, 2010-20:
  - Number of new jobs: **-1,400**
  - Growth rate: **-14 percent (decline rapidly)**
- Education and training:
  - Typical entry-level education: **High school diploma or equivalent**
  - Work experience in a related occupation: **None**
  - Typical on-the-job-training: **Moderate-term on-the-job training**

Shoe Machine Operators and Tenders

(O*NET 51-6042.00)Operate or tend a variety of machines to join, decorate, reinforce, or finish shoes and shoe parts.
- 2010 employment: **3,200**
- May 2010 median annual wage: **$26,280**
- Projected employment change, 2010-20:
  - Number of new jobs: **-1,700**
  - Growth rate: **-53 percent (decline rapidly)**
- Education and training:
  - Typical entry-level education: **High school diploma or equivalent**
  - Work experience in a related occupation: **None**
  - Typical on-the-job-training: **Short-term on-the-job training**

Textile Bleaching and Dyeing Machine Operators and Tenders

(O*NET 51-6061.00)Operate or tend machines that bleach, shrink, wash, dye, or finish textiles or synthetic or glass fibers.
- 2010 employment: **13,900**
- May 2010 median annual wage: **$22,970**
- Projected employment change, 2010-20:
  - Number of new jobs: **-2,100**
  - Growth rate: **-15 percent (decline rapidly)**
- Education and training:
  - Typical entry-level education: **High school diploma or equivalent**
  - Work experience in a related occupation: **None**
  - Typical on-the-job-training: **Short-term on-the-job training**

Textile Cutting Machine Setters, Operators, and Tenders

(O*NET 51-6062.00)Set up, operate, or tend machines that cut textiles.

- 2010 employment: **14,900**
- May 2010 median annual wage: **$23,490**
- Projected employment change, 2010-20:
  - Number of new jobs: **−3,300**
  - Growth rate: **−22 percent (decline rapidly)**
- Education and training:
  - Typical entry-level education: **High school diploma or equivalent**
  - Work experience in a related occupation: **None**
  - Typical on-the-job-training: **Moderate-term on-the-job training**

Textile Knitting and Weaving Machine Setters, Operators, and Tenders

(O*NET 51-6063.00)Set up, operate, or tend machines that knit, loop, weave, or draw in textiles. Excludes "Sewing Machine Operators" (51-6031).

- 2010 employment: **22,500**
- May 2010 median annual wage: **$25,870**
- Projected employment change, 2010-20:
  - Number of new jobs: **−4,100**
  - Growth rate: **−18 percent (decline rapidly)**
- Education and training:
  - Typical entry-level education: **High school diploma or equivalent**
  - Work experience in a related occupation: **None**
  - Typical on-the-job-training: **Moderate-term on-the-job training**

Extruding and Forming Machine Setters, Operators, and Tenders, Synthetic and Glass Fibers

(O*NET 51-6091.00)Set up, operate, or tend machines that extrude and form continuous filaments from synthetic materials, such as liquid polymer, rayon, and fiberglass.

- 2010 employment: **14,700**
- May 2010 median annual wage: **$32,400**
- Projected employment change, 2010-20:
  - Number of new jobs: **−200**
  - Growth rate: **−2 percent (little or no change)**
- Education and training:
  - Typical entry-level education: **High school diploma or equivalent**
  - Work experience in a related occupation: **None**
  - Typical on-the-job-training: **Moderate-term on-the-job training**

Fabric and Apparel Patternmakers

(O*NET 51-6092.00)Draw and construct sets of precision master fabric patterns or layouts. Also may mark and cut fabrics and apparel.

- 2010 employment: **6,000**
- May 2010 median annual wage: **$38,970**
- Projected employment change, 2010-20:
  - Number of new jobs: **−2,100**
  - Growth rate: **−36 percent (decline rapidly)**
- Education and training:
  - Typical entry-level education: **High school diploma or equivalent**
  - Work experience in a related occupation: **None**
  - Typical on-the-job-training: **Moderate-term on-the-job training**

Model Makers, Wood

(O*NET 51-7031.00)Construct full-size and scale wooden precision models of products. Includes wood jig builders and loft workers.

- 2010 employment: **1,600**
- May 2010 median annual wage: **$29,370**
- Projected employment change, 2010-20:
  - Number of new jobs: **200**
  - Growth rate: **11 percent (about as fast as average)**
- Education and training:
  - Typical entry-level education: **High school diploma or equivalent**
  - Work experience in a related occupation: **None**
  - Typical on-the-job-training: **Moderate-term on-the-job training**

Patternmakers, Wood

(O*NET 51-7032.00)Plan, lay out, and construct wooden unit or sectional patterns used in forming sand molds for castings.

- 2010 employment: **1,200**
- May 2010 median annual wage: **$34,640**
- Projected employment change, 2010-20:
  - Number of new jobs: **100**
  - Growth rate: **4 percent (slower than average)**
- Education and training:
  - Typical entry-level education: **High school diploma or equivalent**
  - Work experience in a related occupation: **None**
  - Typical on-the-job-training: **Moderate-term on-the-job training**

Chemical Plant and System Operators

(O*NET 51-8091.00)Control or operate entire chemical processes or systems through the use of machines.

- 2010 employment: **43,300**
- May 2010 median annual wage: **$55,490**
- Projected employment change, 2010-20:
  - Number of new jobs: **−5,300**
  - Growth rate: **−12 percent (decline rapidly)**
- Education and training:
  - Typical entry-level education: **High school diploma or equivalent**
  - Work experience in a related occupation: **None**
  - Typical on-the-job-training: **Long-term on-the-job training**

Gas Plant Operators

(O*NET 51-8092.00)Distribute or process gas for utility companies and others by controlling compressors to maintain specified pressures on main pipelines.

- 2010 employment: **13,700**
- May 2010 median annual wage: **$57,200**
- Projected employment change, 2010-20:
  - Number of new jobs: **−900**
  - Growth rate: **−6 percent (decline moderately)**
- Education and training:
  - Typical entry-level education: **High school diploma or equivalent**
  - Work experience in a related occupation: **None**
  - Typical on-the-job-training: **Long-term on-the-job training**

Petroleum Pump System Operators, Refinery Operators, and Gaugers

(O*NET 51-8093.00)Operate or control petroleum-refining or petroleum-processing units. May specialize in controlling manifold and pumping systems, gauging or testing oil in storage tanks, or regulating the flow of oil into pipelines.

- 2010 employment: **44,200**
- May 2010 median annual wage: **$60,040**
- Projected employment change, 2010-20:
  - Number of new jobs: **-6,200**
  - Growth rate: **-14 percent (decline rapidly)**
- Education and training:
  - Typical entry-level education: **High school diploma or equivalent**
  - Work experience in a related occupation: **None**
  - Typical on-the-job-training: **Long-term on-the-job training**

Chemical Equipment Operators and Tenders

(O*NET 51-9011.00)Operate or tend equipment that controls chemical changes or reactions in the processing of industrial or consumer products. Equipment used includes devulcanizers, steam-jacketed kettles, and reactor vessels. Excludes "Chemical Plant and System Operators" (51-8091).

- 2010 employment: **47,400**
- May 2010 median annual wage: **$45,150**
- Projected employment change, 2010-20:
  - Number of new jobs: **-3,500**
  - Growth rate: **-7 percent (decline moderately)**
- Education and training:
  - Typical entry-level education: **High school diploma or equivalent**
  - Work experience in a related occupation: **None**
  - Typical on-the-job-training: **Moderate-term on-the-job training**

Separating, Filtering, Clarifying, Precipitating, and Still Machine Setters, Operators, and Tenders

(O*NET 51-9012.00)Set up, operate, or tend continuous-flow or vat-type equipment; filter presses; shaker screens; centrifuges; condenser tubes; precipitating, fermenting, or evaporating tanks; scrubbing towers; or batch stills. These machines extract, sort, or separate liquids, gases, or solids from other materials in order to recover a refined product. Includes dairy processing equipment operators. Excludes "Chemical Equipment Operators and Tenders" (51-9011).

- 2010 employment: **38,400**
- May 2010 median annual wage: **$37,840**
- Projected employment change, 2010-20:
  - Number of new jobs: **2,000**
  - Growth rate: **5 percent (slower than average)**
- Education and training:
  - Typical entry-level education: **High school diploma or equivalent**
  - Work experience in a related occupation: **None**
  - Typical on-the-job-training: **Moderate-term on-the-job training**

Crushing, Grinding, and Polishing Machine Setters, Operators, and Tenders

(O*NET 51-9021.00)Set up, operate, or tend machines to crush, grind, or polish materials, such as coal, glass, grain, stone, food, or rubber.

- 2010 employment: **33,400**
- May 2010 median annual wage: **$32,440**
- Projected employment change, 2010-20:
  - Number of new jobs: **1,700**
  - Growth rate: **5 percent (slower than average)**
- Education and training:
  - Typical entry-level education: **High school diploma or equivalent**

- Work experience in a related occupation: **None**
- Typical on-the-job-training: **Moderate-term on-the-job training**

Grinding and Polishing Workers, Hand

(O*NET 51-9022.00)Grind, sand, or polish, using hand tools or hand-held power tools, a variety of metal, wood, stone, clay, plastic, or glass objects. Includes chippers, buffers, and finishers.

- 2010 employment: **27,900**
- May 2010 median annual wage: **$27,370**
- Projected employment change, 2010-20:
  - Number of new jobs: **2,100**
  - Growth rate: **8 percent (slower than average)**
- Education and training:
  - Typical entry-level education: **Less than high school**
  - Work experience in a related occupation: **None**
  - Typical on-the-job-training: **Moderate-term on-the-job training**

Mixing and Blending Machine Setters, Operators, and Tenders

(O*NET 51-9023.00)Set up, operate, or tend machines that mix or blend materials, such as chemicals, tobacco, liquids, color pigments, or explosive ingredients. Excludes "Food Batchmakers" (51-3092).

- 2010 employment: **124,600**
- May 2010 median annual wage: **$32,870**
- Projected employment change, 2010-20:
  - Number of new jobs: **-2,700**
  - Growth rate: **-2 percent (little or no change)**
- Education and training:
  - Typical entry-level education: **High school diploma or equivalent**
  - Work experience in a related occupation: **None**
  - Typical on-the-job-training: **Moderate-term on-the-job training**

Cutters and Trimmers, Hand

(O*NET 51-9031.00)Use hand tools or hand-held power tools to cut and trim a variety of manufactured items, such as carpet, fabric, stone, glass, or rubber.

- 2010 employment: **17,400**
- May 2010 median annual wage: **$24,410**
- Projected employment change, 2010-20:
  - Number of new jobs: **-1,000**
  - Growth rate: **-6 percent (decline moderately)**
- Education and training:
  - Typical entry-level education: **Less than high school**
  - Work experience in a related occupation: **None**
  - Typical on-the-job-training: **Short-term on-the-job training**

Cutting and Slicing Machine Setters, Operators, and Tenders

(O*NET 51-9032.00)Set up, operate, or tend machines that cut or slice materials, such as glass, stone, cork, rubber, tobacco, food, paper, or insulating material. Excludes "Woodworking Machine Setters, Operators, and Tenders" (51-7040), "Cutting, Punching, and Press Machine Setters, Operators, and Tenders, Metal and Plastic" (51-4031), and "Textile Cutting Machine Setters, Operators, and Tenders" (51-6062).

- 2010 employment: **61,400**
- May 2010 median annual wage: **$30,000**
- Projected employment change, 2010-20:
  - Number of new jobs: **-100**

o Growth rate: **0 percent (little or no change)**
- Education and training:
  o Typical entry-level education: **High school diploma or equivalent**
  o Work experience in a related occupation: **None**
  o Typical on-the-job-training: **Short-term on-the-job training**

Extruding, Forming, Pressing, and Compacting Machine Setters, Operators, and Tenders

(O*NET 51-9041.00)Set up, operate, or tend machines, such as glass-forming machines, plodder machines, and tuber machines, to shape and form products, such as glassware, food, rubber, soap, brick, tile, clay, wax, tobacco, or cosmetics. Excludes "Paper Goods Machine Setters, Operators, and Tenders" (51-9196) and "Shoe Machine Operators and Tenders" (51-6042).
- 2010 employment: **65,400**
- May 2010 median annual wage: **$31,210**
- Projected employment change, 2010-20:
  o Number of new jobs: **1,200**
  o Growth rate: **2 percent (little or no change)**
- Education and training:
  o Typical entry-level education: **High school diploma or equivalent**
  o Work experience in a related occupation: **None**
  o Typical on-the-job-training: **Moderate-term on-the-job training**

Furnace, Kiln, Oven, Drier, and Kettle Operators and Tenders

(O*NET 51-9051.00)Operate or tend heating equipment other than basic metal-, plastic-, or food-processing equipment. Includes activities such as annealing glass, drying lumber, curing rubber, removing moisture from materials, and boiling soap.
- 2010 employment: **20,400**
- May 2010 median annual wage: **$34,400**
- Projected employment change, 2010-20:
  o Number of new jobs: **200**
  o Growth rate: **1 percent (little or no change)**
- Education and training:
  o Typical entry-level education: **High school diploma or equivalent**
  o Work experience in a related occupation: **None**
  o Typical on-the-job-training: **Moderate-term on-the-job training**

Packaging and Filling Machine Operators and Tenders

(O*NET 51-9111.00)Operate or tend machines that prepare industrial or consumer products for storage or shipment. Includes cannery workers who pack food products.
- 2010 employment: **337,200**
- May 2010 median annual wage: **$25,270**
- Projected employment change, 2010-20:
  o Number of new jobs: **12,800**
  o Growth rate: **4 percent (slower than average)**
- Education and training:
  o Typical entry-level education: **High school diploma or equivalent**
  o Work experience in a related occupation: **None**
  o Typical on-the-job-training: **Moderate-term on-the-job training**

Photographic Process Workers and Processing Machine Operators

(O*NET 51-9151.00)Perform work to develop and process photographic images from film or from digital media. May perform precision tasks, such as editing photographic negatives and prints.
- 2010 employment: **58,700**
- May 2010 median annual wage: **$22,010**
- Projected employment change, 2010-20:
  o Number of new jobs: **–4,500**
  o Growth rate: **–8 percent (decline moderately)**
- Education and training:
  o Typical entry-level education: **High school diploma or equivalent**
  o Work experience in a related occupation: **None**
  o Typical on-the-job-training: **Short-term on-the-job training**

Adhesive Bonding Machine Operators and Tenders

(O*NET 51-9191.00)Operate or tend bonding machines that use adhesives to join items for further processing or to form a completed product. Processes include joining veneer sheets into plywood; gluing paper; and joining rubber and rubberized fabric parts, plastic, simulated leather, or other materials. Excludes "Shoe Machine Operators and Tenders" (51-6042).
- 2010 employment: **15,100**
- May 2010 median annual wage: **$29,310**
- Projected employment change, 2010-20:
  o Number of new jobs: **700**
  o Growth rate: **5 percent (slower than average)**
- Education and training:
  o Typical entry-level education: **High school diploma or equivalent**
  o Work experience in a related occupation: **None**
  o Typical on-the-job-training: **Moderate-term on-the-job training**

Cleaning, Washing, and Metal Pickling Equipment Operators and Tenders

(O*NET 51-9192.00)Operate or tend machines that wash or clean products, such as barrels or kegs, glass items, tin plates, food, pulp, coal, plastic, or rubber, to remove impurities.
- 2010 employment: **17,700**
- May 2010 median annual wage: **$25,660**
- Projected employment change, 2010-20:
  o Number of new jobs: **200**
  o Growth rate: **1 percent (little or no change)**
- Education and training:
  o Typical entry-level education: **Less than high school**
  o Work experience in a related occupation: **None**
  o Typical on-the-job-training: **Moderate-term on-the-job training**

Cooling and Freezing Equipment Operators and Tenders

(O*NET 51-9193.00)Operate or tend equipment, such as cooling and freezing units, refrigerators, batch freezers, and freezing tunnels that cools or freezes products, food, blood plasma, and chemicals.
- 2010 employment: **8,900**
- May 2010 median annual wage: **$29,320**
- Projected employment change, 2010-20:
  o Number of new jobs: **100**
  o Growth rate: **1 percent (little or no change)**
- Education and training:
  o Typical entry-level education: **High school diploma or equivalent**
  o Work experience in a related occupation: **None**
  o Typical on-the-job-training: **Moderate-term on-the-job training**

Etchers and Engravers

(O*NET 51-9194.00)Engrave or etch metal, wood, rubber, or other materials. Includes such workers as etcher-circuit processors, pantograph engravers, and silk-screen etchers. Photoengravers are included in "Prepress Technicians and Workers" (51-5111).

- 2010 employment: **10,900**
- May 2010 median annual wage: **$28,180**
- Projected employment change, 2010-20:
  - Number of new jobs: **−300**
  - Growth rate: **−3 percent (decline moderately)**
- Education and training:
  - Typical entry-level education: **High school diploma or equivalent**
  - Work experience in a related occupation: **None**
  - Typical on-the-job-training: **Moderate-term on-the-job training**

Molders, Shapers, and Casters, except Metal and Plastic

(O*NET 51-9195.00 , 51-9195.03 , 51-9195.04 , 51-9195.05 , and 51-9195.07)Mold, shape, form, cast, or carve products, such as food products, figurines, tile, pipes, and candles, consisting of clay, glass, plaster, concrete, stone, or combinations of materials.

- 2010 employment: **43,400**
- May 2010 median annual wage: **$28,830**
- Projected employment change, 2010-20:
  - Number of new jobs: **3,500**
  - Growth rate: **8 percent (slower than average)**
- Education and training:
  - Typical entry-level education: **High school diploma or equivalent**
  - Work experience in a related occupation: **None**
  - Typical on-the-job-training: **Long-term on-the-job training**

Paper Goods Machine Setters, Operators, and Tenders

(O*NET 51-9196.00)Set up, operate, or tend paper goods machines that perform a variety of functions, such as converting, sawing, corrugating, banding, wrapping, boxing, stitching, forming, or sealing paper or paperboard sheets into products.

- 2010 employment: **90,900**
- May 2010 median annual wage: **$34,130**
- Projected employment change, 2010-20:
  - Number of new jobs: **−5,500**
  - Growth rate: **−6 percent (decline moderately)**
- Education and training:
  - Typical entry-level education: **High school diploma or equivalent**
  - Work experience in a related occupation: **None**
  - Typical on-the-job-training: **Moderate-term on-the-job training**

Tire Builders

(O*NET 51-9197.00)Operate machines that build tires.

- 2010 employment: **15,500**
- May 2010 median annual wage: **$39,250**
- Projected employment change, 2010-20:
  - Number of new jobs: **−900**
  - Growth rate: **−6 percent (decline moderately)**
- Education and training:
  - Typical entry-level education: **High school diploma or equivalent**
  - Work experience in a related occupation: **None**
  - Typical on-the-job-training: **Moderate-term on-the-job training**

Helpers—Production Workers

(O*NET 51-9198.00)Help production workers by performing duties requiring less skill. Duties include supplying or holding

materials or tools and cleaning work areas and equipment. Apprentices are classified in the appropriate production occupations (51-0000).

- 2010 employment: **395,100**
- May 2010 median annual wage: **$22,450**
- Projected employment change, 2010-20:
  - Number of new jobs: **34,400**
  - Growth rate: **9 percent (slower than average)**
- Education and training:
  - Typical entry-level education: **Less than high school**
  - Work experience in a related occupation: **None**
  - Typical on-the-job-training: **Short-term on-the-job training**

Transportation and Material Moving Occupations

Aircraft Cargo-Handling Supervisors

(O*NET 53-1011.00)Supervise and coordinate the activities of ground crews in the loading, unloading, securing, and staging of aircraft cargo or baggage. May determine the quantity and orientation of cargo and compute aircraft center of gravity. May accompany flight crew in aircraft, monitor and handle cargo in flight, and assist and brief passengers on safety and emergency procedures. Includes loadmasters.

- 2010 employment: **6,300**
- May 2010 median annual wage: **$49,190**
- Projected employment change, 2010-20:
  - Number of new jobs: **1,300**
  - Growth rate: **20 percent (faster than average)**
- Education and training:
  - Typical entry-level education: **High school diploma or equivalent**
  - Work experience in a related occupation: **1 to 5 years**
  - Typical on-the-job-training: **None**

First-Line Supervisors of Helpers, Laborers, and Material Movers, Hand

(O*NET 53-1021.00 and 53-1021.01)Directly supervise and coordinate the activities of helpers, laborers, or material movers.

- 2010 employment: **167,400**
- May 2010 median annual wage: **$43,800**
- Projected employment change, 2010-20:
  - Number of new jobs: **45,500**
  - Growth rate: **27 percent (faster than average)**
- Education and training:
  - Typical entry-level education: **High school diploma or equivalent**
  - Work experience in a related occupation: **1 to 5 years**
  - Typical on-the-job-training: **None**

First-Line Supervisors of Transportation and Material-Moving Machine and Vehicle Operators

(O*NET 53-1031.00)Directly supervise and coordinate activities of transportation and material-moving machine and vehicle operators and helpers.

- 2010 employment: **198,700**
- May 2010 median annual wage: **$52,720**
- Projected employment change, 2010-20:
  - Number of new jobs: **28,400**
  - Growth rate: **14 percent (as fast as average)**
- Education and training:
  - Typical entry-level education: **High school diploma or equivalent**

○ Work experience in a related occupation: **1 to 5 years**
○ Typical on-the-job-training: **None**

Airfield Operations Specialists

(O*NET 53-2022.00)Ensure the safe takeoff and landing of commercial and military aircraft. Duties include coordinating between air-traffic control and maintenance personnel, dispatching, using airfield landing and navigational aids, implementing airfield safety procedures, monitoring and maintaining flight records, and applying knowledge of weather information.

● 2010 employment: **6,900**
● May 2010 median annual wage: **$45,080**
● Projected employment change, 2010-20:
  ○ Number of new jobs: **600**
  ○ Growth rate: **8 percent (slower than average)**
● Education and training:
  ○ Typical entry-level education: **High school diploma or equivalent**
  ○ Work experience in a related occupation: **None**
  ○ Typical on-the-job-training: **Long-term on-the-job training**

Ambulance Drivers and Attendants, Except Emergency Medical Technicians

(O*NET 53-3011.00)Drive ambulance or assist ambulance driver in transporting sick, injured, or convalescent persons. Assist in lifting patients.

● 2010 employment: **19,600**
● May 2010 median annual wage: **$22,940**
● Projected employment change, 2010-20:
  ○ Number of new jobs: **6,300**
  ○ Growth rate: **32 percent (much faster than average)**
● Education and training:
  ○ Typical entry-level education: **High school diploma or equivalent**
  ○ Work experience in a related occupation: **None**
  ○ Typical on-the-job-training: **Moderate-term on-the-job training**

Bridge and Lock Tenders

(O*NET 53-6011.00)Operate and tend bridges, canal locks, and lighthouses to permit marine passage on inland waterways, near shores, and at danger points in waterway passages. May supervise such operations. Includes drawbridge operators, lock operators, and slip bridge operators.

● 2010 employment: **3,500**
● May 2010 median annual wage: **$45,930**
● Projected employment change, 2010-20:
  ○ Number of new jobs: **0**
  ○ Growth rate: **–1 percent (little or no change)**
● Education and training:
  ○ Typical entry-level education: **Less than high school**
  ○ Work experience in a related occupation: **None**
  ○ Typical on-the-job-training: **Short-term on-the-job training**

Parking Lot Attendants

(O*NET 53-6021.00)Park vehicles or issue tickets for customers in a parking lot or garage. May collect fee.
● 2010 employment: **125,100**
● May 2010 median annual wage: **$19,530**
● Projected employment change, 2010-20:
  ○ Number of new jobs: **–2,200**
  ○ Growth rate: **–2 percent (little or no change)**
● Education and training:

○ Typical entry-level education: **Less than high school**
○ Work experience in a related occupation: **None**
○ Typical on-the-job-training: **Short-term on-the-job training**

Automotive and Watercraft Service Attendants

(O*NET 53-6031.00)Service automobiles, buses, trucks, boats, and other automotive or marine vehicles with fuel, lubricants, and accessories. Collect payment for services and supplies. May lubricate vehicle, change motor oil, install antifreeze, or replace lights or other accessories, such as windshield wiper blades or fan belts. May repair or replace tires.

● 2010 employment: **86,300**
● May 2010 median annual wage: **$19,540**
● Projected employment change, 2010-20:
  ○ Number of new jobs: **19,200**
  ○ Growth rate: **22 percent (faster than average)**
● Education and training:
  ○ Typical entry-level education: **Less than high school**
  ○ Work experience in a related occupation: **None**
  ○ Typical on-the-job-training: **Short-term on-the-job training**

Traffic Technicians

(O*NET 53-6041.00)Work under the direction of a traffic engineer to conduct field studies determining volume and speed of traffic, effectiveness of signals, adequacy of lighting, and other factors that influence traffic conditions.

● 2010 employment: **6,900**
● May 2010 median annual wage: **$41,130**
● Projected employment change, 2010-20:
  ○ Number of new jobs: **800**
  ○ Growth rate: **11 percent (about as fast as average)**
● Education and training:
  ○ Typical entry-level education: **Less than high school**
  ○ Work experience in a related occupation: **None**
  ○ Typical on-the-job-training: **Short-term on-the-job training**

Transportation Inspectors

(O*NET 53-6051.00 , 53-6051.01 , 53-6051.07 , and 53-6051.08)Inspect equipment or goods in connection with the safe transport of cargo or people. Includes rail transportation inspectors, such as freight inspectors; rail inspectors; and other inspectors of transportation vehicles, not elsewhere classified. Excludes "Transportation Security Screeners" (33-9093).

● 2010 employment: **27,400**
● May 2010 median annual wage: **$57,640**
● Projected employment change, 2010-20:
  ○ Number of new jobs: **4,000**
  ○ Growth rate: **14 percent (as fast as average)**
● Education and training:
  ○ Typical entry-level education: **Some college, no degree**
  ○ Work experience in a related occupation: **None**
  ○ Typical on-the-job-training: **Short-term on-the-job training**

Transportation Attendants, Except Flight Attendants

(O*NET 53-6061.00)Provide services to ensure the safety and comfort of passengers aboard ships, buses, and trains or within the station or terminal. Perform duties such as greeting passengers, explaining the use of safety equipment, serving meals or beverages, and answering questions related to travel. Excludes "Baggage Porters and Bellhops" (39-6011).

● 2010 employment: **24,800**
● May 2010 median annual wage: **$20,930**
● Projected employment change, 2010-20:
  ○ Number of new jobs: **2,800**
  ○ Growth rate: **11 percent (about as fast as average)**
● Education and training:

- Typical entry-level education: **High school diploma or equivalent**
- Work experience in a related occupation: **None**
- Typical on-the-job-training: **Short-term on-the-job training**

Gas Compressor and Gas Pumping Station Operators

(O*NET 53-7071.00)Operate steam, gas, electric motor, or internal combustion engine–driven compressors. Transmit, compress, or recover gases, such as butane, nitrogen, hydrogen, and natural gas.

- 2010 employment: **4,500**
- May 2010 median annual wage: **$50,590**
- Projected employment change, 2010-20:
  - Number of new jobs: **−500**
  - Growth rate: **−10 percent (decline rapidly)**
- Education and training:
  - Typical entry-level education: **Less than high school**
  - Work experience in a related occupation: **None**
  - Typical on-the-job-training: **Moderate-term on-the-job training**

Pump Operators, Except Wellhead Pumpers

(O*NET 53-7072.00)Tend, control, or operate power-driven, stationary, or portable pumps and manifold systems to transfer gases, oil, other liquids, slurries, or powdered materials to and from various vessels and processes.

- 2010 employment: **10,800**
- May 2010 median annual wage: **$43,740**
- Projected employment change, 2010-20:
  - Number of new jobs: **400**
  - Growth rate: **4 percent (slower than average)**
- Education and training:
  - Typical entry-level education: **Less than high school**
  - Work experience in a related occupation: **None**
  - Typical on-the-job-training: **Moderate-term on-the-job training**

Wellhead Pumpers

(O*NET 53-7073.00)Operate power pumps and auxiliary equipment to produce and maintain the flow of oil or gas from wells in oil fields.

- 2010 employment: **15,100**
- May 2010 median annual wage: **$40,640**
- Projected employment change, 2010-20:

- Number of new jobs: **700**
- Growth rate: **5 percent (slower than average)**
- Education and training:
  - Typical entry-level education: **Less than high school**
  - Work experience in a related occupation: **Less than 1 year**
  - Typical on-the-job-training: **Moderate-term on-the-job training**

Mine Shuttle Car Operators

(O*NET 53-7111.00)Operate diesel or electric-powered shuttle cars in underground mines to transport materials from the working face to mine cars or conveyors.

- 2010 employment: **3,100**
- May 2010 median annual wage: **$48,110**
- Projected employment change, 2010-20:
  - Number of new jobs: **−200**
  - Growth rate: **−6 percent (decline moderately)**
- Education and training:
  - Typical entry-level education: **Less than high school**
  - Work experience in a related occupation: **None**
  - Typical on-the-job-training: **Short-term on-the-job training**

Tank Car, Truck, and Ship Loaders

(O*NET 53-7121.00)Use material-moving equipment to load and unload chemicals and bulk solids, such as coal, sand, and grain, into or from tank cars, trucks, or ships. May perform a variety of other tasks relating to the shipment of products. May gauge or sample shipping tanks and test them for leaks.

- 2010 employment: **10,400**
- May 2010 median annual wage: **$42,780**
- Projected employment change, 2010-20:
  - Number of new jobs: **200**
  - Growth rate: **2 percent (little or no change)**
- Education and training:
  - Typical entry-level education: **Less than high school**
  - Work experience in a related occupation: **None**
  - Typical on-the-job-training: **Short-term on-the-job training**

Glossary

A

Annual: recurring, done, or performed every year; yearly

Applicant: a person who formally applies for a job

Apprenticeship: a formal relationship between the worker and sponsor that consists of a combination of on-the-job training and related occupation-specific instruction. Apprenticeship programs usually provide at least 144 hours of occupation-specific technical instruction and 2,000 hours of on-the-job training per year over a 3- to 5-year period. Apprenticeships are associated mostly with the trades. Examples of occupations that utilize apprenticeships are electricians and structural iron and steel workers; see On-the-job training

Associate's degree: degree awarded usually for at least 2 years of full-time academic study beyond high school; see Education

Average: the quantity calculated by adding a set of numbers and dividing the resulting sum by the quantity of numbers summed; see Mean

B

Bachelor's degree: degree awarded usually for at least 4 years of full-time academic study beyond high school; see Education

Base year: year used as a reference point for comparison with later years. For example, 2010 is the base year for the 2010–2020 employment projections. Employment in the base year is actual 2010 data, whereas employment in the target, or projection, year is projected

Business cycle: The periods of growth and decline in an economy. There are four stages in the cycle: expansion, when the economy grows; peak, the high point of an expansion; contraction, when the economy slows down; and trough, the low point of a contraction

Baby-boom generation: individuals born between 1946 and 1964

C

Certification: award for demonstrating competency in a skill or set of skills, typically through the passage of an examination, work experience, training, or some combination thereof. Certification is always voluntary. Some certification programs may require a certain level of educational achievement for eligibility.

Consolidation: the merger of two or more commercial interests or corporations

Current Population Survey (CPS): a national survey that samples 60,000 households on a monthly basis and collects information on labor force characteristics of the U.S. civilian noninstitutional population; the CPS is conducted by the Census Bureau for the Bureau of Labor Statistics

D

Demand for workers: total job openings resulting from employment growth and the need to replace workers who leave jobs

Doctoral or professional degree: degree awarded usually for at least 3 years of full-time academic work beyond a bachelor's degree; for example, some science and other occupations need a doctoral degree, and all lawyers, physicians, and dentists need a professional degree for employment; see Education

Domestic sourcing: moving jobs to lower cost regions of the United States instead of to other countries

Duties: the major tasks or activities that employees in an occupation usually perform

E

Earnings: Pay or wages of a worker or group of workers for services performed during a specific period—for example, hourly, daily, weekly, or annually. Also see Pay, Wages

Education: levels of education typically needed for entry into an occupation are classified as follows:

  Doctoral or professional degree: degree awarded usually for at least 3 years of full-time academic work beyond a bachelor's degree; e.g., lawyers, physicians and surgeons, and dentists

  Master's degree: degree awarded usually for 1 or 2 years of full-time academic study beyond a bachelor's degree

  Bachelor's degree: degree awarded usually for at least 4 years of full-time academic study beyond high school

  Associate's degree: degree awarded usually for at least 2 years of full-time academic study beyond high school

  Postsecondary nondegree award: usually a certificate or other award that is not a degree. Certifications issued by professional organizations or certifying bodies are not included in this category. Programs may last only a few weeks to 2 years. e.g., nursing aides, EMTs and paramedics, and hairstylists

  Some college, no degree: a high school diploma or the equivalent, plus the completion of one or more postsecondary courses that did not result in any degree or award

  High school diploma or equivalent: the completion of high school or the equivalent resulting in the award of a high school diploma or the equivalent, such as the General Education Development (GED) credential

  Less than high school: the completion of any level of primary or secondary education that did not result in the awarding of a high school diploma or the equivalent

Employment growth/shrinkage: increase or decrease in the number of jobs

Entry level: the starting level for workers who are new to an occupation; different occupations may require different levels of education, training, or experience upon entry

Employed: the situation of a person who has an agreement with an employer to work full time, part time, or on a contractual basis for that employer

Employment: the number of jobs in an occupation, including full-time, part-time, and self-employed. For example, employment of accountants and auditors was 1,216,900 in 2010

F

Fieldwork: an investigation or search for material, data, etc., made in the field as opposed to the classroom, the laboratory, or official headquarters. For example, archeologists working at a dig site in the desert; historians or curators finding or collecting artifacts for museums; and environmental technicians collecting water samples from a pond, a stream, or an ocean

Fixed work schedules: schedules of employees who work the same hours on an ongoing basis—for example, 9 a.m.–5p.m.; see Work schedules

Flexible work schedules: schedules of employees who set their own hours within specified guidelines and with a fixed number of total hours; see Work schedules

Full time: 35 hours or more per week, according to the Current Population Survey; see Work schedules

G

GDP (gross domestic product): the market value of all final goods and services produced within a country in a given period; the most commonly used measure of the size of the overall economy. The Bureau of Economic Analysis (BEA) produces estimates of GDP.

GED (General Educational Development): a credential signifying the completion of a program that is equivalent to a high school curriculum; see Education

Greater than full time: more than 40 hours per week; see Work schedules

Growth rate: the percent change in the number of jobs added or lost in a U.S. occupation or industry over a given projection period; see "Information Found in the Occupational Outlook Handbook"; growth rate adjectives used in the OOH are defined by the following percent changes for the 2010–20 employment projections:

- much faster than the average: 29 percent or more
- faster than the average: 20 percent to 28 percent
- as fast as the average: 10 percent to 19 percent
- more slowly than the average: 3 percent to 9 percent
- little or no change: –2 percent to 2 percent
- decline moderately: –3 percent to –9 percent
- decline rapidly: –10 percent or less

H

High school diploma or equivalent: award or credential that is equivalent to a high school diploma, such as a high school diploma itself or the General Educational Development (GED) credential; see Education

Household: all persons who occupy a housing unit

I

Important qualities: characteristics and personality traits that are likely needed for workers to be successful in given occupations

Industry: a group of establishments that produce similar products or provide similar services; see NAICS

Internship: training under supervision in a professional setting. This category does not include internships that are suggested for advancement; see On-the-job training

Injury and illness rate: ratio expressing the number of workers sustaining a wound, strain, or infection due to an incident or exposure at the workplace per 100 workers; the Occupational Safety and Health Administration (OSHA) considers an injury or illness to be work related if an event or exposure in the work environment either caused or contributed to the resulting condition or significantly aggravated a preexisting condition; in general, a Handbook profile will cite an injury and illness rate only if it is particularly high compared with the rate for all other occupations

J

Job openings: job openings occur when occupations grow, creating new jobs, and when workers leave an occupation permanently, resulting in the need to replace them

Job: a specific instance of employment; a position of employment to be filled at an establishment; see Employment

Job outlook: a statement that conveys the projected rate of growth or decline in employment in an occupation over the next 10 years; also compares the projected growth rate with that projected for all other occupations; Also see growth rate

Job prospects: a qualitative measure of the competition for jobs that takes into consideration factors such as the growth or decline in numbers of jobs, the expected number of qualified workers, and/or the expected number of applicants; a comparison of the number of jobs with the number of potential workers and jobseekers

K

No entries

L

Labor force: the sum of all persons 16 years and older in the civilian noninstitutional population who are either employed, or unemployed but available for work and actively looking for work

Less than high school: the completion of any level of primary or secondary education that did not result in the awarding of a high school diploma or the equivalent; see Education

Less than 1 year (of work experience in a related occupation): the level of experience in another occupation typically needed for entry into a given occupation; see Required training for entry; also Work experience in a related occupation

Long-term on-the-job training: more than 12 months of on-the-job training or programs not including apprenticeships; see On-the-job training

Licenses: permission granted by government agencies or other accrediting bodies that allows for the selling of certain goods or services

M

Master's degree: degree awarded usually for 1 or 2 years of full-time academic study beyond a bachelor's degree; see Education

Mean: the mathematical average of a set of numbers, calculated by adding the numbers and dividing the total by the number of numbers summed; see Average

Median: the middle number in an ordered list of numbers

Moderate-term on-the-job training: 1 to 12 months of on-the-job training or programs, not including apprenticeships; see On-the-job training

More than 5 years (of work experience in a related occupation): the number of years of experience in a related occupation typically needed for entry into a given occupation; see Required training for entry; also Work experience in a related occupation

N

North American Industry Classification System (NAICS): Industry classification system used by federal statistical agencies in classifying business establishments for the purpose of collecting, analyzing, and publishing statistical data related to the U.S. economy

New job: an addition of a position to an establishment's payroll, usually as a result of economic expansion

Nonfixed work schedules: schedules of employees who work different hours on one job; often used to accommodate particular traits of individual workers or because the work required by the employers varies for each individual; see Work schedules

None (on-the-job training): the situation when no additional occupation-specific training or preparation is typically required to attain competency in an occupation; see On-the-job training

None (required training for entry): the situation when no work experience in a related occupation is typically required to enter a given occupation; see Required training for entry; also Work experience in a related occupation

Number of jobs: number of actual instances of employment according to the BLS National Employment Matrix; see the projection methods page for more information about the Matrix

Numeric change in employment: a projected change in the number of jobs in an occupation or industry

O

On-the-job training: training or preparation that is typically needed, once employed in an occupation, to attain competency in the occupation. Training is occupation specific rather than job specific; skills learned can be transferred to another job in the same occupation

Internship/Residency: training under supervision in a professional setting. This category does not include internships that are suggested for advancement.

Apprenticeship: a formal relationship between a worker and his or her sponsor that consists of a combination of on-the-job training and related occupation-specific instruction. Apprenticeship programs usually provide at least 144 hours of occupation-specific technical instruction and 2,000 hours of on-the-job training per year over a 3-to-5-year period. Apprenticeships are associated mostly with the trades. Examples of occupations that utilize apprenticeships include electricians and structural iron and steel workers.

Long-term on-the-job training: more than 12 months of on-the-job training or programs, not including apprenticeships.

Moderate-term on-the-job training: 1 to 12 months of combined on-the-job experience and informal training

Short-term on-the-job training: 1 month or less of combined on-the-job experience and informal training

None: no additional occupation-specific training or preparation

Occupation: a craft, trade, profession, or other means of earning a living. Also, a set of activities or tasks that employees are paid to perform and that together go by a certain name. Employees who are in the same occupation perform essentially the same tasks, whether or not they work in the same industry

P

Pay: Earnings or wages of a worker or a group of workers for services performed during a specific period—for example, hourly, daily, weekly, or annually. Also see Earnings, Wages

Part time: less than 35 hours of work per week, according to the Current Population Survey; see Work schedules

Percent: one part in a hundred. For example, 62 percent (also written 62%) means 62 parts out of 100

Percentile wage estimate: the value of a wage below which a certain percentage of workers fall

Percent change in employment: growth rates expressed as percentages

Personal consumption: total goods and services purchased by individuals in the U.S. economy; the amount of goods and services used or purchased by individuals or households in the U.S. economy; a key statistic in measuring or calculating overall GDP

Population: The total number of inhabitants of the United States

Postsecondary nondegree award: a certificate or other credential that is awarded by an educational institution upon completion of formal postsecondary schooling. (The postsecondary nondegree certificate is different from certifications issued by professional organizations or certifying bodies.) Postsecondary nondegree award programs may last from just a few weeks to 2 years. Examples of those who need postsecondary nondegree awards are nursing aides, emergency medical technicians, and hairstylists ; see Education

Q

Qualifications: personality traits, education, training, work experience, or other qualities workers need to enter an occupation

Important qualities: characteristics and personality traits that are likely needed for workers to be successful in given occupations

R

Related occupations: occupations that have similar job duties; see Similar occupations

Replacement rate: the rate at which workers permanently leave the occupations in which they are employed; large occupations that have high replacement rates need many workers to fill jobs that are vacated.

Replacement needs: the number of projected openings expected to result from workers who retire or permanently leave an occupation; replacement needs are calculated from monthly CPS data

Residency: training under supervision in a professional setting. This category does not include internships that are suggested for advancement; see On-the-job training

Rotating work schedules: schedules that have a fixed number of hours and time off over a period of more than 1 week, but not a set weekly schedule, according to data from the 2010 Current Population Survey; see Work schedules

S

Salary: earnings of a worker or a group of workers for services performed during a specific period—for example, an hourly straight-time wage rate or, for workers not paid on an hourly basis, straight-time earnings divided by hours worked

Seasonal employment: employment that is not expected to last a full year, but that may reoccur; for example, many retail sales associates are hired only for the busy holiday season, and forest firefighters are more likely to be employed during the summer months, when vegetation is dryer

Short-term on-the-job training: 1 month or less of on-the-job experience and informal training; see On-the-job training

Similar occupations: occupations that tend to share common daily tasks or require similar skill sets, rather than similar wages or education

Self-employed: those who work for profit or fees in their own business, profession, trade, or farm; only the unincorporated self-employed are included in the self-employed category

SOC code: the Standard Occupational Classification (SOC) system, which is used by all federal statistical agencies to classify workers into occupational categories for the purpose of collecting, calculating, or disseminating data

Some college, no degree: a high school diploma or equivalent, plus the completion of one or more postsecondary courses that did not result in a degree or award; see Education

Supply of workers: the number of people in the labor force; for most occupations, the supply of workers is smaller than the total number in the labor force because the supply is limited to those with particular education or training requirements

T

Training: see On-the-job training; or Required training for entry; or Work experience in a related occupation

U

Undergraduate degree: Bachelor's degree; see Education

Union membership: the group of workers who join labor unions, hold union memberships, and enjoy benefits of the organized, coordinated efforts of the union to improve the work environment

V

Vocational school: a secondary school that teaches vocational trades, such as construction trades; vocational schools may or may not award degrees; see Education

W

Wage: earnings or pay of a worker or a group of workers for services performed during a specific period—for example, hourly, daily, weekly, or annually. Also see Earnings, Pay

Work schedules: the number of daily hours, weekly hours, and annual weeks that employees in an occupation are scheduled to, and do, work. Short-term fluctuations and one-time events are not considered unless the change becomes permanent; for more details, visit Work Schedules in the National Compensation Survey

  Fixed work schedules: schedules under which employees who work those schedules do so on an ongoing basis; e.g., 9 a.m.–5 p.m.

Flexible work schedules: schedules under which employees set their own hours within guidelines and with a fixed number of total hours

Rotating work schedules: schedules that have a fixed number of hours and time off over a period of more than 1 week, but not a set weekly schedule

Nonfixed work schedules: schedules of employees who work different hours on one job; often utilized to accommodate particular traits of individual workers or because the work required varies by individual

Greater than full time: more than 40 hours per week

Full time: between 35 and 40 hours of work per week

Part time: Less than 35 hours of work per week

Work experience in a related occupation: the level of work experience in an occupation related to a given occupation; may be a typical method of entry into the given occupation

X, Y, Z

No entries

Index

D

H

J

Manufacturing industries, 6, 18, 28, 35, 44, 49, 61, 63, 96, 713–14, 866–67, 878, 885, 891, 907–8; declining, 824, 1000, 1006

Manufacturing of electrical equipment, 6, 26, 29–30, 36, 58, 69, 216, 238, 556, 560, 566, 661, 911, 972

Manufacturing sales representatives, 165, 740, 742, 810, 882, 953, 960, 966, 969–70, 972, 979–82

Manufacturing sectors, 32, 867, 898

Manufacturing workers, 555, 565, 865, 874

Manufacturing, 18, 28–31, 47–49, 60–61, 132–33, 148–49, 163–64, 282–83, 763–64, 823, 867–68, 877, 886–87, 925–26, 980–81; chemical, 17, 445, 713–14; computer-aided, 885–86, 892; tortilla, 869–70, 877–78

Map makers, see: Cartographers and Photogrammetrists

Mappers, see: Cartographers and Photogrammetrists

Mapping technicians, 14, 16, 22, 28, 30, 52, 73–77, 238, 634, 636, 639

Mapping technicians, see: Surveying and Mapping Technicians

Marble installers, see: Tile and Marble Setters

Marble setters, 226, 229, 232, 234, 242, 244, 248, 257, 272, 281, 288–90

Marble setters, see: Tile and Marble Setters

Marble, 224, 226, 229, 232, 234, 248, 255, 257, 272, 281, 288–89

Margin clerks, see: Financial Clerks

Marine architects, see: Marine Engineers and Naval Architects

Marine biologists, see: Biochemists and Biophysicists

Marine biologists, see: Microbiologists

Marine biologists, see: Zoologists and Wildlife Biologists

Marine diesel technicians, see: Diesel Service Technicians and Mechanics

Marine drafters, see: Drafters

Marine engineering professors, see: Postsecondary Teachers

Marine Engineers and Naval Architects, 53–55

Marine engineers, 53–55

Marine equipment engineers, see: Marine Engineers and Naval Architects

Marine equipment mechanics, see: Small Engine Mechanics

Marine firefighters, see: Firefighters

Marine fisheries technicians, see: Biological Technicians

Marine mammal trainers, see: Animal Care and Service Workers

Marine photographers, see: Photographers

Marine propulsion technicians, see: Small Engine Mechanics

Marine structural designers, see: Marine Engineers and Naval Architects

Marine technicians, see: Small Engine Mechanics

Market news reporters, see: Reporters, Correspondents, and Broadcast News Analysts

Market research analysts, 153–55, 208, 671, 684, 753

Market research interviewers, see: Information Clerks

Market research managers, see: Advertising, Promotions, and Marketing Managers

Market research specialists, see: Market Research Analysts

Marketing administrators, see: Advertising, Promotions, and Marketing Managers

Marketing agents, see: Advertising, Promotions, and Marketing Managers

Marketing analysts, see: Market Research Analysts

Marketing consultants, see: Market Research Analysts

Marketing directors, see: Advertising, Promotions, and Marketing Managers

Marketing instructors, see: Postsecondary Teachers

Marketing managers, 94, 155, 164, 673, 684–87, 715, 719, 739, 742, 748, 953, 971

Marketing managers, see: Advertising, Promotions, and Marketing Managers

Marketing professors, see: Postsecondary Teachers

Marketing representatives, see: Advertising, Promotions, and Marketing Managers

Marketing specialists, see: Market Research Analysts

Marking and identification printing machine operators, see: Printing Workers

Marriage counselors, see: Mental Health Counselors and Marriage and Family Therapists

Marriage therapists, see: Mental Health Counselors and Marriage and Family Therapists

Marriage, 171–75, 180, 183, 187, 191, 194, 665, 667–68, 745

Martial arts instructors, see: Self-enrichment Teachers

Masonry instructors, see: Postsecondary Teachers

Masons, see: Brickmasons, Blockmasons, and Stonemasons

Massage therapists, see: Massage Therapists

Massage therapy instructors, see: Postsecondary Teachers

Masseurs, see: Massage Therapists

Masseuse, see: Massage Therapists

Massotherapists, see: Massage Therapists

Master of Business Administration. See MBA

Master of ceremonies, see: Announcers

Master of Fine Arts (MFA), 80, 360

Master of Landscape Architecture (MLA), 51

Master of Physical Therapy (MPT), 474

Master's degree holders, 602, 667, 670

Master's degree, 153–55, 173–74, 179–80, 182–83, 193–94, 292–93, 295–96, 298–303, 305–7, 325–27, 596–97, 625–28, 635–36, 661–64, 666–76

Material control clerk, see: Material Recording Clerks

Material expeditors, see: Material Recording Clerks

Material handlers, see: Hand Laborers and Material Movers

Material inspectors, 822–24

Material movers work, 998–1000, 1005–6

Material movers, 825, 994, 998–1001, 1003–7

Material Moving Machine Operators, 241, 245, 825, 1001, 1004–7, 1013, 1019, 1023

Material Moving Occupations, 983, 985, 987–89, 991, 993, 995, 997, 999–1001, 1003, 1005–7, 1009, 1011, 1013, 1015, 1021–23

Material Recording Clerks Material recording clerks, 818, 822, 994, 1001, 1003, 1007

Material recording clerks, 822–25, 998

Materials Engineers Materials, 6, 50, 63, 72, 614

Materials engineers work, 56–58

Materials science, 56–57, 611–12

W